The
International Directory of Little Magazines & Small Presses
46th Edition, 2010-2011

Len Fulton, Editor

● Dustbooks ●

CONTENTS

If you have a press or magazine you would like to list in the Dustbooks directories, simply go to our website at www.dustbooks.com, click on the Directory Listing Forms button and follow the instructions.

PAPER: $37.95/copy ISBN 978-1-935742-00-5
         $135.00/4-year subscription

CLOTH: $55.00/copy ISBN 978-1-935742-21-0
         $145.00/4-year subscription

e-mail: info@dustbooks.com

website: www.dustbooks.com

Published annually by Dustbooks, PO Box 100, Paradise, CA 95967, also publishers of the *Directory of Editors, Directory of Poetry Publishers* and *Small Press Review/Small Magazine Review* (bimonthly). Systems design, typesetting format and computer programming by Neil McIntyre, 3135 Prince Henry Drive, Sacramento, CA 95833.

THE GREAT AMERICAN POETRY SHOW

www.tgaps.net

NINE MUSES BOOKS
NINE MUSES MYSTERY THEATRE

books written out of the soul's own need,
designed to meet the eye with a hint of what's inside,
and performances to the same purpose.

margareta waterman, publisher
mw9muses@teleport.com

what is the work of artists? to invoke deities.
it takes a deity to fight a demon. it is how our artists are made.
– eliot pattison

books & recordings by

Carol Barth	Gretchan Mattila
Charlie Burks	Chris Piuma
Fire & Jorje Cruxent	Tom Prince
Gary David	dan raphael
Louise Dovell	Robbo
Stephen Fandrich	Judith Roche
Jean Ferner	Donna Sandstrom
Martina Goodin	Robin Schultz
Larry Griffin	Bill Shively
Glenda J. Guilmet	Wally Shoup
Michael Hureaux-Perez	Willie Smith
Michelle Inouchi	Douglas Spangle
Joseph F. Keppler	Roberto Valenza
Josef Knoepfler	margareta waterman
Marion Kimes	David Lloyd Whited
Maryrose Larkin	Carletta Wilson
Ezra Mark	Don Wilsun

language is like shot silk; so much depends on the angle at which it is held.
—john fowles

complete catalog at dustbooks.com

THE POETRY CENTER
AT
PASSAIC COUNTY COMMUNITY COLLEGE

Allen Ginsberg Poetry Awards 2011
Honoring

Allen Ginsberg's Contribution to American Literature
Sponsored by

The Poetry Center at Passaic County Community College

First Prize:	$1,000
Second Prize:	$200
Third Prize:	$100

Winners will be asked to participate in a reading to take place in the Paterson Historic District.

Please note: The entry fee of **$18.00** for the Allen Ginsberg Poetry Awards covers the cost of a subscription to The Paterson Literary Review. The winning poems and all Honorable Mention winners as well as Editor's Choice poems, will be published in The Paterson Literary Review.

Deadline: April 1, 2011 (postmark)

For Contest Rules, call
the Poetry Center at (973) 684-6555 or
visit our website at www.pccc.edu/poetry

Send poems to: Maria Mazziotti Gillan, Executive Director,
Poetry Center
Passaic County Community College
One College Boulevard
Paterson, NJ 07505-1179

OFF THE GRID PRESS

Off the Grid Press was founded in the fall of 2005 to provide a forum for older, previously published poets who have been overlooked by the current marketplace. OTG offers an alternative publishing model that combines valuable features of traditional publishing and publishing cooperatives. So far, we have published books of poems by Henry Braun, Lee Sharkey, Terry Adams, and Janet Winans. Our website is http://www.offthegridpress.net.

Manuscripts are evaluated and selected by our editors, Tam Lin Neville and Bert Stern, whose editorial vision and expertise assure the quality and distinct identity of the OTG imprint. There are no contests, reading fees, or prescreening by non-editors. We plan to publish one or two books per year.

Rather than finance the press through contest fees, we ask the writer to bear the cost of book design, printing, and distribution. The money the poet might spend covering the bases of book contests goes instead directly to the production of the book. All proceeds from book sales go to the author.

Once a manuscript is chosen, the editors work closely with the author in editing it for publication. Authors work directly with the designer in creating a book that embodies the spirit of the text. The press provides administrative assistance with publication, and promotes and sells the book on our website and in other venues.

Those submitting manuscripts should be over sixty years old and have already published at least one book of poems or five or more poems in three or more nationally distributed literary magazines. If your poetry, however innovative, honors the work of Keats, Yeats, Stevens, Dickinson, Whitman, Williams, and Reznikoff as well as Szymborska, Neruda, Rilke, and Akhmatova, we invite your submission. See our submissions guidelines on our website for more detailed information.

Tam Lin Neville and Bert Stern

Off The Grid Press
24 Quincy Street
Somerville, MA 02143

Key to Directory Listings

Listings are of two basic kinds: Those for **magazines** (periodicals, printed in all caps), and those for **presses** (book publishers).

A complete **magazine** listing would include, in following order: name of magazine, name of press (if any), name(s) of editors, address, phone number(s), fax number, email address, website address, founding year, type of material used, additional comments by editors including recent contributors, circulation, frequency of publication, number of issues published in 2009, expected in 2010 and 2011, one-year subscription price, single copy price, sample copy price, back issue price, discount schedules, average number of pages, length of reporting time on manuscripts, policy on simultaneous submissions, percentage of submissions published, payment rates, rights purchased and/or copyright arrangements, number of reviews published in 2009, areas of interest for review materials and advertising rates.

A complete **press** listing would include, in the following order: names of press, name of magazine published by that press, if any, name(s) of editor(s), address, phone number(s), fax, email and website information, founding year, type of material used, additional comments by editors including recent contributors, average press run, number of titles published in 2009, expected in 2010 and 2011, discount schedules, average number of pages, length of reporting time on manuscripts, policy on simultaneous submissions, percentage of submissions published, payment or royalty arrangements, rights purchased and/or copyright arrangements.

New Feature – Subject indexing in main listings: Each publisher is listed in the Subject Index under those subjects that publisher has indicated. In addition, the subjects are listed at the end of each publisher's main listing. This should further help to characterize each publishing program.

A listing preceded by a bullet (•) is a new listing to this edition. A listing preceded by a double-dagger (‡) means that the publisher has not reported to us for some time – though we have reason to believe the press is still operating.

For those who wish to list a press or magazine in future editions of *The International Directory of Little Magazines & Small Presses* or the companion *Directory of Poetry Publishers*, special forms are available on the Dustbooks website www.dustbooks.com. Once you have registered, logged into the listing and filled out the data, a request for update is sent 1-3 months before the next editions go to press in July. New editions are published on September 15th every year.

--**Len Fulton**
Fall, 2010

A

A & U AMERICA'S AIDS MAGAZINE, David Waggoner, Editor-in-Chief & Publisher, 25 Monroe Street, Suite 205, Albany, NY 12210-2729, 518-426-9010, Fax 518-436-5354, mailbox@aumag.org. 1991. Poetry, fiction, articles, art, photos, cartoons, interviews, satire, criticism, reviews, music, letters, parts-of-novels, long-poems, collages, plays, news items, non-fiction. "Recent contributors: John Ashbery, Gwendolyn Brooks, Michael Lassell, Mark Doty, Mark O'Donnell, Edward Field, Eve Ensler, David Bergman, Walter Holland, Leslea Newman, Paula Martinac, Diamanda Galas, William Parker, Assoto Saint, etc." circ. 180M. 12/yr. Pub'd 12 issues 2009; expects 12 issues 2010, 12 issues 2011. sub. price $24.95, $80.00 Library; per copy $3.95; sample $5. Back issues: $10 for all back issues, except 1991 fall premiere $30.00. 40pp. Reporting time: 6 months to 1 year. Simultaneous submissions accepted: yes. Publishes 5% of manuscripts submitted. Payment: 5 complimentary copies and negotiable honorariums. Copyrighted, reverts to author. Pub's reviews: 60 in 2009. §Anything AIDS-related, especially the arts and AIDS. Ads: Back cover $32,010/full page $22,488/1/2 page $15,291, all rates for color. Subjects: AIDS, Arts, Avant-Garde, Experimental Art, Literature (General), Theatre, Visual Arts.

A Cappela Publishing, Patrika Vaughn, P.O. Box 3691, Sarasota, FL 34230-3691, 941-351-4735, 941-351-2050, acappub@aol.com, www.acappela.com. 1996. Fiction, art, criticism, non-fiction. "Our mission is to help new voices achieve publication. To achieve this, we work with them from conception through successful publication, offering marketing and public relations services as well." Pub'd 8 titles 2009; expects 12 titles 2010, 12 titles 2011. 26 titles listed in the *Small Press Record of Books in Print* (36th Edition, 2010-11). Discounts: 4-10 = 10% 10-49 = 25% 50-99 = 35% 100+ =50%. 350pp. Reporting time: 5-10 working days. Simultaneous submissions accepted: No. Payment: varies. Copyrights for author. Subjects: Autobiography, Business & Economics, Creative Non-fiction, Experimental, Fiction, Juvenile Fiction, Literature (General), Memoirs, Motivation, Success, Mystery, New Age, Non-Fiction, Novels, Picture Books, Trade.

A Midsummer Night's Press, Lawrence Schimel, 16 West 36th Street, 2nd Floor, New York, NY 10018, www.amidsummernightspress.com. 2007. Poetry, long-poems. "A Midsummer Night's Press publishes perfect bound books in three imprints: Fabula Rasa: devoted to works inspired by mythology, folklore, and fairy tales. The first titles from this imprint are FAIRY TALES FOR WRITERS by Lawrence Schimel and FORTUNE'S LOVER: A BOOK OF TAROT POEMS by Rachel Pollack. Funny Bones: devoted to works of humor and light verse. The first title from this imprint is THE GOOD-NEIGHBOR POLICY, a murder mystery told in double dactyls by Edgar Award-winner Charles Ardai, editor of the Hard Case Crime imprint. Body Language: devoted to texts exploring questions of gender and sexual identity. The first titles from this imprint are THIS IS WHAT HAPPENED IN OUR OTHER LIFE, a collection of poems by Lambda Literary Award-winner Achy Obejas; BANALITIES by Brane Mozetic, translated from the Slovene by Elizabeta Zargi; HANDMATE LOVE by Julie R. enszer; and MUTE by Raymond Luczak." avg. press run 1000. Expects 3 titles 2010, 6 titles 2011. 7 titles listed in the *Small Press Record of Books in Print* (36th Edition, 2010-11). Discounts: Bookstores: 40% discount for orders with minimum 5 copies. 32-64pp. Reporting time: The press is not currently open to submissions as our lists for the next few years is currently full. Simultaneous submissions accepted: No. Copyrights for author. Subjects: Anthology, Bilingual, Bisexual, Cuba, Fantasy, Gay, Holocaust, Humor, Latino, Lesbianism, Mystery, Myth, Mythology, Poetry, Sex, Sexuality, Translation.

•A2Z Publications LLC, Adrian Krieg Dr., POB 101163, Bradenton, FL 34211, 941-322-2739. 2000. Non-fiction. "Better old history than new lies!" avg. press run 4000. Expects 1 title 2010. 8 titles listed in the *Small Press Record of Books in Print* (36th Edition, 2010-11). Discounts: 15% one book 30% 3 books 40% over 10 books 50% per case. 350pp. Reporting time: one day. Simultaneous submissions accepted: No. Payment: standard. Copyrights for author. Subjects: Engineering, German, History, Immigration, Libertarian, Political Science, Politics, Presidents, Public Affairs, Race, Science.

AAIMS Publishers, Edward Torrey, 11000 Wilshire Boulevard, PO Box 241777, Los Angeles, CA 90024-0777, 480-243-9022, 888-490-2276, fax 213-931-7217, email aaims1@aol.com. 1969. avg. press run 4M. Pub'd 1 title 2009; expects 1 title 2010, 2 titles 2011. 10 titles listed in the *Small Press Record of Books in Print* (36th Edition, 2010-11). Discounts: 1 copy 30%, 2 35%, 3 40%, 4 41%, 15 45%, 30 47%, 45 49%, 200+ 50%. 250pp. Reporting time: 3 weeks. Copyrights for author. Subjects: African Literature, Africa, African Studies, Black, Family, Military, Veterans, Religion, Women.

Aardvark Enterprises (Sole Proprietorship of J. Alvin Speers), J. Alvin Speers, 204 Millbank Drive S.W.,

1

Calgary, Alberta T2Y 2H9, Canada, 403-256-4639. 1977. Poetry, fiction, articles, photos, cartoons, interviews, reviews, letters, news items, non-fiction. "Open to proposals." avg. press run varies. Pub'd 6 titles 2009; expects 6 titles 2010, 6 titles 2011. 77 titles listed in the *Small Press Record of Books in Print* (36th Edition, 2010-11). Discounts: inquiries invited - quantity discounts only. 100pp. Reporting time: fast, return mail usually. Publishes 50% of manuscripts submitted. Payment: by arrangement on individual project. Copyrights for author. Subjects: Canada, Ethics, Family, History, Politics, Religion, Storytelling.

AARO Publishing,Inc., Carolyn White, Post Office Box 1281, Palisade, CO 81526, 970 314 7690, 970 985 4018, 1 877 766 9333, carolynwhite@snowff.com, www.snowff.com. avg. press run 3000. 2 titles listed in the *Small Press Record of Books in Print* (36th Edition, 2010-11). Discounts: Wholesalers - 55% Bookstores - 40% Institutions - 20% Classrooms - 20%. 60pp. Subject: Education.

Aaron Communications III, Aaron Johnson, P.O. Box 63270, Colorado Springs, CO 80962-3270, 719-487-0342. 2005. Fiction, art, plays, non-fiction. "Aaron Communications III is purposeful in its mission of communicating to youth and young adults around the world a message of hope, Gods love, and divine purpose in life through faith and personal relationship with Jesus Christ. Our mission is accomplished by publishing contemporary books/subjects/topics and state of the art publications that are relevant to todays youth and young adults in light of current youth culture without compromising or deviating from sound scripture, the Holy Bible." avg. press run 1500. Expects 4 titles 2010, 8 titles 2011. No titles listed in the *Small Press Record of Books in Print* (36th Edition, 2010-11). Discounts: industry standards. 200pp. Reporting time: Six weeks minimum. Will immediately acknowledge receipt. Simultaneous submissions accepted: Yes. Publishes 10% of manuscripts submitted. Payment: t.b.d. Copyrights for author. Subjects: Arts, Autobiography, Biography, Children, Youth, Christianity, Fiction, Guidance, Inspirational, Juvenile Fiction, Motivation, Success, Non-Fiction, Non-Violence, Performing Arts, Prison, U.S. Hispanic.

AAS HISTORY SERIES, Univelt, Inc., Donald C. Elder, Series Editor, PO Box 28130, San Diego, CA 92198, 760-746-4005, Fax 760-746-3139, sales@univelt.com, www.univelt.com. 1977. Non-fiction. "History of Science (esp. Space Science and Technology). Science Fiction and Space Futures. An irregular serial. Standing orders accepted. Vols 1-26 published." circ. 400. Irregular. Pub'd 3 issues 2009; expects 2 issues 2010, 2 issues 2011. sub. price varies. Back issues: no. Discounts: 20% and more by arrangement; reduced prices for classroom use. 200-500pp. Reporting time: 90 days. Payment: 10% (if the volume author). Copyrighted, authors may republish material with appropriate credits given and authorization from publishers. Ads: none. Subjects: History, Science, Science Fiction, Space.

AB, c¢o Lisa Ahne, PO Box 181, Alsea, OR 97324-0181. 2003. Articles, interviews, criticism, reviews, letters, news items, non-fiction. "*Ab* is a reader-written zine discussing how and where to live better and longer; including, how to steer clearer of increasingly-berserk political/economic/social/religious systems. *Ab* is an ab-apa: I prefer concise, *compact*, single-spaced, one-sided, two *full* pages ready to copy, text 6x10 inches (153x254mm). Disposable copies preferred. Authors may include small ads on their pages. Reviews should be mostly quotes or paraphrases of the most useful info in the book or article, not merely a description." circ. 400. 1/yr. Pub'd 1 issue 2009; expects 1 issue 2010, 1 issue 2011. sub. price $2; per copy $2; sample $2. Back issues: 6 for $10. 16pp. Reporting time: 1 month. Simultaneous submissions accepted: yes. Publishes 50% of manuscripts submitted. Payment: subscription/back issues or token cash. Not copyrighted. Pub's reviews: 2 in 2009. Subjects: Anthropology, Archaelogy, Aviation, Bicycling, Botany, Clothing, Health, How-To, Human Rights, Immigration, Lifestyles, Nutrition, Safety, Science, Technology, Transportation, Travel.

Abaton Book Company, Lauri Bortz, 100 Gifford Avenue, Jersey City, NJ 07304-1704, web: www.abatonbookcompany.com. 1997. Art, photos, music, plays. "Unique limited edition projects." Pub'd 4 titles 2009; expects 4 titles 2010, 4 titles 2011. 1 title listed in the *Small Press Record of Books in Print* (36th Edition, 2010-11).

ABBEY, White Urp Press, David Greisman, 5360 Fallriver Row Court, Columbia, MD 21044-1910, e-mail at greisman@aol.com. 1970. Poetry, articles, art, interviews, criticism, reviews, letters. "*Abbey* recently was named the 341st best informalzine in America and still claims to be the Molson's Ale of Small Press rags. We published our 100th issue in March of 2004, continuing a standard for excellent poetry and artwork mixed with production values that the Amercian Association of Informalzines noted has remained embarassingly mediocre during the entirety of the rag's 40 year publication history. Recent contributors: Taylor Graham, Spiel, David Chorlton, Carol Hamilton, D.E. Steward, Luis Cuauhtemoc Berriozabal,Edmund Conti, Richard Peabody, Harry Calhoun, Kate Duvall, Cheryl Townsend, Ruth Moon Kempher, Wayne Hogan, Joan Payne Kincaid, and Joel Poudrier." circ. 200. 3-4/yr. Pub'd 4 issues 2009; expects 4 issues 2010, 4 issues 2011. sub. price per copy 50¢; sample 50¢. Back issues: 50¢ for regular issues, $2 for Abbey #100 (while supplies last). 28pp. Reporting time: 2 minutes-2 years. Simultaneous submissions accepted: Not cool. Hold Abbey to a response deadline if you must, but show some respect, will ya? Payment: nothing. Copyrighted, reverts to author. Pub's reviews: None in 2009. §Poetry, baseball. Ads: $10/$5. Subject: Poetry.

Abbey Press, Northern Ireland, Adrian Rice, Courtenay Hill, Newry, Country Down BT34 2ED, United Kingdom, 01693-63142, Fax 01693-62514, Molly71Freeman@aol.com, www.geocities.com/abbeypress/. 1997. Poetry, fiction, interviews, satire, criticism, reviews, letters, long-poems, plays, non-fiction. "Recent publication - *A Conversation Piece: Poetry & Art*, edited by Adrian Rice and Angela Reid. 50 poets on 50 artworks from the collections of the National Museums and Galleries of Northern Ireland. Some poets include: Seamus Heaney, Michael Longley, Brendan Kennelly, Paul Muldoon, Tom Paulin, Medbh McGuckian, Ruth Padel, Paula Meehan, and John Montague." avg. press run 1000. Pub'd 4 titles 2009; expects 4 titles 2010, 4 titles 2011. No titles listed in the *Small Press Record of Books in Print* (36th Edition, 2010-11). 64pp. Simultaneous submissions accepted: yes. Copyrights for author. Subject: Poetry.

Abecedarian books, Inc., Alan C Reese, 2817 Forest Glen Drive, Baldwin, MD 21013, 410-692-6777, fax 410-692-9175, toll free 877-782-2221, books@abeced.com, www.abeced.com. 2005. Poetry, fiction, photos, plays, non-fiction. avg. press run 1000. Expects 12 titles 2010, 25 titles 2011. 5 titles listed in the *Small Press Record of Books in Print* (36th Edition, 2010-11). 156pp. Reporting time: 2-3 weeks. Simultaneous submissions accepted: Yes. Copyrights for author. Subjects: Erotica, Fantasy, Fiction, Health, Humor, Mystery, Non-Fiction, Poetry, Science Fiction, Short Stories, T'ai Chi, Vegetarianism, Women, Young Adult, Zen.

Abernathy House Publishing, Sandra S. Walling Publisher, John W. Walling Editor, PO Box 1109, Yarmouth, ME 04096-1109, 207-838-6170, info@abernathyhousepub.com, www.abernathyhousepub.com. 2002. avg. press run 5000. Pub'd 2 titles 2009; expects 2 titles 2010, 3 titles 2011. No titles listed in the *Small Press Record of Books in Print* (36th Edition, 2010-11). Discounts: 40 to 55%. 36pp. Reporting time: 6 Weeks. Simultaneous submissions accepted: yes. Publishes 30% of manuscripts submitted. Payment: Royalty paid or flat fee. Author and Illustrator. Subjects: African-American, Aging, AIDS, Animals, Children, Youth, Family, Marine Life, Native American, Non-Violence, Reading, Relationships, Young Adult.

Abigon Press, Jack Avery, 12135 Valley Spring Lane, Studio City, CA 91604, ascap@pacbell.net. 1991. Non-fiction. "Will review health related books and general non-fiction for publication, but prefer a synopsis or treatment form first." avg. press run 5,000-10,000. 2 titles listed in the *Small Press Record of Books in Print* (36th Edition, 2010-11). 385pp. Subjects: Health, Medicine, Nutrition.

ABLAZE Publishing, 2800 122nd Place NE, Bellevue, WA 98005-1520, 877-624-0230, Fax 509-275-5817, welcome@familypearls.org www.familypearls.org. 2003. avg. press run 3M. Pub'd 1 title 2009; expects 1 title 2010. 3 titles listed in the *Small Press Record of Books in Print* (36th Edition, 2010-11). Discounts: 10 or more books, 40% discount. 6-9 books, 30% discount, 3-5 books, 20% discount, 1-2 books, no discount but free shipping to resellers. 120pp. Simultaneous submissions accepted: no. Publishes 1% of manuscripts submitted. Payment: determined on individual basis. Copyrights for author. Subjects: Audio/Video, Cartoons, Christianity, Classical Studies, Cooking, Handicapped, Health, Mental Health.

ABLE MUSE, Alex Pepple, Editor, 467 Saratoga Avenue #602, San Jose, CA 95129, www.ablemuse.com, editor@ablemuse.com. Poetry, fiction, art, photos, interviews, criticism, reviews, long-poems, concrete art, non-fiction. Pub's reviews. §Poetry Books, Poets.

ABOL TABOL, Sasabindu Chaudhuri, 7/1 d Kalicharan Ghosh Road, Kolkata, W. Bengal, India, 033-25571767, babychowin@yahoo.co.in. Poetry. "Translated 35 comedy poetry of a famous poet *Sukumar Roy* in German." 1/yr. Copyrighted, reverts to author. Pub's reviews. §Poetry and classical based songs.

ABRAMELIN: a Journal of Poetry and Magick, Vanessa Kittle, Box 337, Brookhaven, NY 11719, 631 803-2211. 2006. Poetry, fiction, articles, art, photos, interviews, reviews, long-poems, non-fiction. "www.abramelin.net. What we want...Essays on Magick and Thelema. By magick I mean with a K if you know what I mean.Poetry that shows rather than tells. Poems that make me jealous of the writer. Poems that are inspired with wonderful language and imagery. In short literature.Poetry submissions needn't be about magick at all. I feel that real poetry is magick. In fact, poetry that is literally magickal in theme has to be twice as good. Please note that I hate rhyming poems. Very short fiction. But beware, I learned from the best. Thelemic artwork. How we want it. Words should be pasted into an email. Art should be attached to an email (please query first!). I will not open attachments from unknown senders. My address is: Nessaralindaran@aol.com. Please include a subject line (for example, poetry submission). Please send only 1 story or essay, and up to 3 poems. Feel free to include a bio if it is your will. Abramelin takes one-time rights. All other rights revert to author after publication. By submitting, author certifies it is her work, and holds Abramelin and me harmless from any legal concerns. Issues will be published when I feel a sense of completion. I expect this will be somewhere between 2 and 4 times a year." 3/yr. Expects 2 issues 2010. 1 title listed in the *Small Press Record of Books in Print* (36th Edition, 2010-11). 93pp. Reporting time: A few days to a couple weeks. Simultaneous submissions accepted: No. Publishes 5% of manuscripts submitted. Pub's reviews. §Poetry books and books concerning magick. Subjects: Anarchist, Astrology, Astronomy, Avant-Garde, Experimental Art, Beat, Buddhism, Counter-Culture, Alternatives, Communes, Erotica, Human Rights, Literary Review, Magic, Philosophy, Poetry, Spiritual, Women.

3

ABRAXAS, Ingrid Swanberg, Editor-in-Chief; Warren Woessner, Senior Editor, PO Box 260113, Madison, WI 53726-0113, 608-238-0175, abraxaspress@hotmail.com. 1968. Poetry, articles, art, photos, criticism, letters, collages, concrete art. "Address for exchanges and large packages: 2518 Gregory Street, Madison, WI 53711. *Abraxas* is no longer considering unsolicited poetry except for special projects. We will announce submission policies as projects arise (inquire with SASE). We are particularly interested in lyric poetry and contemporary poetry in translation. *Abraxas Press* has published an anthology of jazz poetry, *Bright Moments* ($15.00), and a translation of Cesar Vallejo's *Trilce*, based on the only authorized edition ($25). The most recent issue, #47, continues our new format, presenting larger selections of the work of fewer writers every issue. Inquiries should be sent to Ingrid Swanberg at the above address (include SASE). We have recently published Tom Kryss, Jeanne Bryan, Grace Butcher, Lee Ballentine, Roselyn Elliott, Andrea Moorhead, prospero saiz." circ. 500+. Irregular. Expects 1 issue 2010, 2 issues 2011. 4 titles listed in the *Small Press Record of Books in Print* (36th Edition, 2010-11). sub. price $16/4 issues, $36/4 issues foreign; per copy $4; sample $4 (please add $1.50 shipping for first copy, $1 for each additional copy; $9 foreign). Back issues: catalog on request, SASE please. Discounts: 20% 1-4 copies; 40% 5-9 copies; 50% on orders of more than 10 copies. 60-88pp, 120-144pp double issues. Reporting time: 1 month to 2 years or longer. We currently have a *very* great backlog of unsolicited mss. Simultaneous submissions accepted: Yes; please inform us of acceptance elsewhere. Publishes 2% of manuscripts submitted. Payment: copies; 40% author's discount on additional copies. Copyrighted, reverts to author. Pub's reviews. Ads: none. Subjects: Avant-Garde, Experimental Art, Native American, Poetry, Satire, Translation.

Absey & Co., 23011 Northcrest Drive, Spring, TX 77389, 888-412-2739, Fax 281-251-4676, abseyland@aol.com. 1992. Poetry, fiction, photos, non-fiction. avg. press run 10000. Pub'd 4 titles 2009; expects 4 titles 2010, 12 titles 2011. 28 titles listed in the *Small Press Record of Books in Print* (36th Edition, 2010-11). Discounts from 10% to 50% with agreements. Reporting time: 6 to 12 months. Simultaneous submissions accepted: NO. Publishes 5% of manuscripts submitted. Payment: royalty of 10% of net sales. Generally do not pay advances. Payment schedule in late March early April. Copyrights for author. Subjects: Bibliography, Children, Youth, Creativity, Education, English, Holocaust, How-To, Juvenile Fiction, Language, Literature (General), Mystery, Non-Fiction, Novels, Picture Books, Young Adult.

ABSINTHE: New European Writing, Dwayne D. Hayes, P.O. Box 2297, Farmington Hills, MI 48333-2297, www.absinthenew.com, dhayes@absinthenew.com, http://absinthenew.blogspot.com/. 2003. Poetry, fiction, art, interviews, reviews, letters, parts-of-novels, plays, non-fiction. "Absinthe: New European Writing presents work (poetry and prose) by European writers who have not appeared widely in English. Recent contributors include Yuri Andrukhovych, Christa Wolf, Sandor Kanyadi, Saviana Stanescu, Juan Jose Millas, and Sophia Nikolaidou." circ. 500. 2/yr. Pub'd 2 issues 2009; expects 2 issues 2010, 2 issues 2011. sub. price $12; per copy $10; sample $10. Back issues: $10. 120pp. Reporting time: 12-15 weeks. Simultaneous submissions accepted: No. Payment: 2 copies and a subscription. Copyrighted, reverts to author. Pub's reviews: 10 in 2009. §Books by European writers in translation. Subjects: Danish, Europe, France, French, German, Greek, Ireland, Italy, Poland, Russia, Scandinavia, Scotland, Spain, Translation, U.S.S.R., Wales.

ABZ A Magazine of Poetry, ABZ Poetry Press, John McKernan, John McKernan, Editor Marshall University, One John Marshall Drive, Huntington, WV 25755-2646. 2006. circ. 500. 1/yr. Expects 1 issue 2010, 1 issue 2011. price per copy $8.00; sample $8.00. Back issues: Please inquire. Discounts: 40%. 48pp. Reporting time: Submisions read only September 1 to December 31. 3-4 months. Simultaneous submissions accepted: Yes. Payment: Small amount per poem. Copyrighted, reverts to author. Pub's reviews: none in 2009. Ads: None. Subject: Poetry.

ABZ Poetry Press (see also ABZ A Magazine of Poetry), John McKernan, PO Box 2746, Huntington, WV 25727-2746, www.abzpress.com, editorial@abzpress.com. 2006. Poetry. "See our web page for INFO about our annual first-book poetry contest." avg. press run 800. Pub'd 1 title 2009; expects 1 title 2010, 1 title 2011. 3 titles listed in the *Small Press Record of Books in Print* (36th Edition, 2010-11). Discounts: 40%. 48-72pp. Reporting time: Magazine Submissions September 1-December 1 Yearly: Book Contest Submissions must have May 2007 postmark for 2007 Contest. Write for complete Guidelines and Official Entry Blank. Simultaneous submissions accepted: Yes. Payment: Standard Book Contract. Copyrights for author. Subject: Poetry.

Academic Innovations, Mindy Bingham, 929 West Sunset Boulevard, St. George, UT 84770-4865, 800-967-8016, 800-967-4027. 1990. avg. press run 10000. Expects 1 title 2010. No titles listed in the *Small Press Record of Books in Print* (36th Edition, 2010-11). Subjects: Education, Family.

Academy Press of America, 19700 Fairchild Road, Suite 300, Irvine, CA 92612-2512, telephone: 1-949-720-3860, toll free: 1-800-935-6020, Email address: orders@academypressofamerica.com, web site: www.academypressofamerica.com. 1994. Pub'd 3 titles 2009; expects 1 title 2010, 1 title 2011. 1 title listed in the *Small Press Record of Books in Print* (36th Edition, 2010-11). 350pp. Reporting time: 30 days. Simultaneous submissions accepted: yes. Payment: 55%/45%. Does not copyright for author. Subjects: Autobiography, Family, Global Affairs, Government, Guidance, History, How-To, Middle East, Peace,

Philosophy, Political Science, Presidents, Reading, Writers/Writing.

Accendo Publishing, Tammy McClure, 4211 Rickeys Way Unit G, Palo Alto, CA 94306, 408-406-6697 phone. 2005. Fiction, art, photos, non-fiction. avg. press run 500. Expects 1 title 2010, 3 titles 2011. 1 title listed in the *Small Press Record of Books in Print* (36th Edition, 2010-11). 300pp. Subjects: Alternative Medicine, Anthology, Autobiography, Energy, Erotica, Fiction, Global Affairs, Memoirs, Motivation, Success, Mystery, Non-Fiction, Picture Books, Relationships, Water, Women.

Accent On Music, LLC, Mark Hanson, PMB 252, 19363 Willamette Drive, West Linn, OR 97068, (503)699-1814, (503)699-1813(FAX), (800)313-4406, info@accentonmusic.com. Music. "Please email request to submit before submitting any material for possible publication. Outside material rarely accepted." Pub'd 1 title 2009; expects 1 title 2010, 1 title 2011. 11 titles listed in the *Small Press Record of Books in Print* (36th Edition, 2010-11). Reporting time: 4 weeks. Simultaneous submissions accepted: No. Publishes 1% of manuscripts submitted. Payment: Negotiable. Copyrights for author.

Accent Press Ltd, Hazel Cushion, The Old School, Upper High Street, Bedlinog CF46 6SA, United Kingdom, info@accentpress.co.uk www.accentpress.co.uk. 2003. Fiction, non-fiction. "Accent Press is a vibrant independent publishing company. Founded by Hazel Cushion in 2003, Accent is based in the beautiful green valleys of Southern Wales. Accent can already claim some important achievements; Hazel was even invited to meet the Queen in 2007 at a reception for Women in Business! Never content to sit still, Accent launched erotic imprint Xcite Books which produces a series of spicy stories aimed primarily at female readers. In 2008 Accent Press set its sights on the North American market, and not by half-measures either, weve opened up a marketing office to oversee the operation, working hand-in-hand with our new distributor National Book Network." avg. press run 3000. Expects 6 titles 2010, 12 titles 2011. No titles listed in the *Small Press Record of Books in Print* (36th Edition, 2010-11). 240-400pp.

ACME Press, PO Box 1702, Westminster, MD 21158, 410-848-7577. 1991. Fiction, satire. "Our basic requirement is that a work be funny. We prefer comic novels (60K-90K words)." Pub'd 1 title 2009; expects 1 title 2010, 1 title 2011. 6 titles listed in the *Small Press Record of Books in Print* (36th Edition, 2010-11). Discounts: standard. 250pp. Reporting time: 4 weeks. Simultaneous submissions accepted: yes. Publishes less than 1% of manuscripts submitted. Payment: varies. Copyrights for author. Subjects: Fiction, Humor, Novels, Satire.

Act on Wisdom, Victor Shamas Ph.D., PO Box 12484, Tucson, AZ 85732-2484, 520-326-4674(voice), 773-661-7447 (fax). 2006. Music, non-fiction. "We publish materials on health and consciousness, with a specific emphasis on spiritual healing, chanting, shamanism, and creative inspiration." avg. press run 5000. Pub'd 2 titles 2009; expects 5-10 titles 2010, 10-20 titles 2011. 2 titles listed in the *Small Press Record of Books in Print* (36th Edition, 2010-11). Discounts: National distributors 67%, wholesalers 60%, retailers 40%, college bookstores 25%, online bookstores 40-55%. Discount schedule- 1: none, 2-4: 20%, 5-9: 30%, 10-24: 40%, 25-49: 42%, 50-74: 44%, 100-199: 48%, 200: 50%. 250-350pp. Reporting time: 4-6 weeks. Simultaneous submissions accepted: No. Publishes 20% of manuscripts submitted. Payment: 10% of net receipts. Does not copyright for author. Subjects: Alternative Medicine, Counter-Culture, Alternatives, Communes, Creativity, Environment, Health, Hypnosis, Mental Health, Music, New Age, Non-Violence, Peace, Psychology, Religion, Self-Help, Spiritual.

ACUMEN, Patricia Oxley, General Editor, 6 The Mount, Higher Furzeham, Brixham, South Devon TQ5 8QY, United Kingdom. 1985. "*Acumen* places an emphasis on publishing a wide range of poetry both in style and in its poets. Work is considered from both established and talented newcomers, on an equal basis. It publishes around 50 poems per issue (out of around 3,000 submitted in each four-month period) as well as reviews, poetry comment, and reader feedback. *Acumen* is published three times a year (January, May and September), A5 perfect bound, with at least 120pp per issue." sub. price £12.50 / $45/50 surface/air; per copy £4.50 / $10. Back issues: £2.50 / $5. Reporting time: 1 week or up to four months from time of receipt of TSS. Publishes 1% of manuscripts submitted. Pub's reviews: 60 in 2009. §Collections of poetry. Ads: see website: www.acumen-poetry.co.uk.

•**Adamantine Publishing House,** ET Renna, Publisher, PO Box 6338, Burbank, CA 91510-6338, 818-843-3427. Fiction. "Adamantine Publishing House specialized in Science Fiction and Fantasy exclusively. To submit a manuscript for consideration, send a cover letter and the first ten pages of your work to the Editor include a SASE with your address for our response. Full unsolicited manuscripts will not be reviewed or acknowledged. We do not accept submissions by email. Our breakout new talent this year is Christina Moss, author of the INTWINE series." 1 title listed in the *Small Press Record of Books in Print* (36th Edition, 2010-11). 320pp. Reporting time: About 3 weeks after receiving cover letter/10 pages. Simultaneous submissions accepted: No. Copyrights for author. Subjects: Fantasy, Science Fiction.

Adams-Blake Publishing, Paul Raymond, 8041 Sierra Street, Fair Oaks, CA 95628, 916-962-9296. 1992. Non-fiction. "We look for technology or management titles that we can sell direct to business and government for very high margins. For example, if we had a book titles "Quality Control in the Semiconductor Manufacturing Environment" we could sell about 800 a year for a few years... at $125 each. We do modified Print on Demand (we keep a low inventory) and only look for books that we can get top-dollar for... thus we are not trade publishers... so if you have a trade book (i.e. one sold via Borders or B&N) we are NOT for you. But if you have niche-market science or techology titles, do contact us." avg. press run 5M. Expects 7 titles 2010, 10 titles 2011. 4 titles listed in the *Small Press Record of Books in Print* (36th Edition, 2010-11). Discounts: 40-50% industry standard. 300pp. Reporting time: 3-4 weeks. Simultaneous submissions accepted: yes. Publishes 5% of manuscripts submitted. Payment: 10% net. Copyrights for author. Subjects: Business & Economics, Computers, Calculators, Consulting, Energy, Engineering, Management, Marketing, Medicine, Nursing, Physics, Real Estate, Technology, Textbooks.

Adastra Press, Gary Metras, 16 Reservation Rd., Easthampton, MA 01027-1227. 1978. Poetry. "All chapbooks and some books are hand-set letterpress printed and hand-sewn with flat spine paper wrapper. Each book is individually designed with the poetry in mind. I pay attention to the craft and art of printing and expect poets to pay attention to their art. Interested authors may query first but it is not necessary to do so. The poetry should have some bite to it and be grounded in experience. Poem cycles, thematic groups and long poems are always nice to produce in chapbook format. Accepted authors can expect to help with publicity. Payment is copies. *Adastra Press* is a one man operation, paying for itself as it goes without grants of any kind, and I am always overworked and booked in advance. Some titles to date are: *Home Test* by Gregory Dunne. *A Clock with No Hands* by Tom Sexton. *Season of Mangos* by Clarence Wolfshohl *Falling off the Bicycle Forever* by Micahel Rattee, and *Voyager* by Dawnell Harrison. Send $8 for a sample chapbook." avg. press run 200. Pub'd 4 titles 2009; expects 4 titles 2010, 3 titles 2011. 40 titles listed in the *Small Press Record of Books in Print* (36th Edition, 2010-11). Discounts: bookstores 30%, distributors 40%, more than 1 copy, 20% on cl/signed editions. 18pp. Reporting time: up to 3 months. Simultaneous submissions accepted: yes. Publishes less than 1% of manuscripts submitted. Payment: usually percent of print run, but each arrangement made individually. Does not copyright for author. Subject: Poetry.

Addicus Books, Inc., Rod Colvin, Publisher; Jack Kusler, Associate Publisher, PO Box 45327, Omaha, NE 68145, 402-330-7493. 1994. "We publish high-quality non-fiction books with a focus on consumer health, self-help, business, and true crime." avg. press run 5, 000 to 10,000. Pub'd 7 titles 2009; expects 7 titles 2010, 10 titles 2011. 62 titles listed in the *Small Press Record of Books in Print* (36th Edition, 2010-11). Discounts: retailers 40%, wholesalers, distributors 55%. STOP 40%, plus shipping. 170pp. Reporting time: 1 month. Simultaneous submissions accepted: yes. Publishes 2-3% of manuscripts submitted. Payment: royalty contract based on percentage of net revenues. Copyrights for author. Subjects: Business & Economics, Crime, Drugs, Health, How-To.

ADIRONDAC, Adirondack Mountain Club, Inc., Neal S. Burdick, Editor, 814 Goggins Road, Lake George, NY 12845-4117, 518-668-4447, e-mail ADKinfo@adk.org. 1922. Poetry, articles, art, photos, interviews, reviews, letters, news items, non-fiction. "Avg. length: 1000-3000 words, with conservation, education, and recreation focus, representing different stances on issues of concern to the Adirondack and Catskill constitutionally-protected Forest Preserves. Contributors include ADK members, state authorities, Forest Preserve historians, outdoor recreationists, etc." circ. 20M. 6/yr. Pub'd 7 issues 2009; expects 6 issues 2010, 6 issues 2011. sub. price $20; per copy $2.95; sample $2.95. Back issues: $4.95. Discounts: retailers 40% (min. 10 copies); libraries $15/yr. 32pp. Reporting time: 3 months. Payment: none. Copyrighted, does not revert to author. Pub's reviews: approx. 24 in 2009. §Natural history, conservation, "muscle-powered" recreation, Adirondack or Catskill history and lore. Ads: Full page: $660; 1/2 page $345; 1/4 page $200. Classifieds $5.00 per line. Subjects: Adirondacks, Conservation, Earth, Natural History, Ecology, Foods, Environment, Sports, Outdoors.

Adirondack Mountain Club, Inc. (see also ADIRONDAC), Andrea Masters, Publications Editor; Neal Burdick, Editor of Adirondac; John Kettlewell, Publications and Marketing Director, 814 Goggins Road, Lake George, NY 12845-4117, 518-668-4447, FAX 518-668-3746, e-mail pubs@adk.org. 1922. Articles, non-fiction. "We publish guidebooks—hiking, canoeing, climbing, skiing, and biking guides—as well as natural and cultural histories about the Forest Preserve of New York State (which comprises the Adirondack and Catskill parks). We also publish a history of the Adirondack Park for young people (ages 10+), trail maps, and an annual calendar of Adirondack nature photography." avg. press run 3M. Pub'd 2 titles 2009; expects 3 titles 2010, 3 titles 2011. 26 titles listed in the *Small Press Record of Books in Print* (36th Edition, 2010-11). Discounts: retail 1-5 20%, 6-99 40%, 100+ 42%, STOP 40%; schools & libraries 25%; wholesalers, 10-49 40%, 50-99 46%, 100+ 50%, and free freight. 200pp. Reporting time: 3 weeks to 3 months (decided by Committee). We accept simultaneous submissions (must be disclosed). Publishes 1% of manuscripts submitted. Payment: typical is 7-1/2% royalty on gross. Copyrights for author. Subjects: Adirondacks, Children, Youth, Conservation, Earth, Natural History, Education, Nature, New York, Sports, Outdoors, Travel.

THE ADIRONDACK REVIEW, Angela Leroux-Lindsey, New York, NY 10003, editors@theadirondackreview.com. 2000. Poetry, fiction, articles, art, photos, cartoons, interviews, criticism, reviews, long-poems, non-fiction. "TAR publishes an eclectic mix of fresh voices in literature, as well as interviews, art, photography, and French and German translations. Poets whose work has appeared in the Review include: Denise Duhamel, Walt McDonald, Timothy Liu, D.C. Berry, Lee Upton, R.T. Smith, Bob Hicok, Lola Haskins, James Reidel, Ilya Kaminsky, as well as many newcomers." circ. 6000. Quarterly. Pub'd 3 issues 2009; expects 4 issues 2010, 4 issues 2011. sub. price free; per copy free; sample free. Back issues: free. Discounts: N/A (on-line). 50pp. Reporting time: same day to one year (depending on backlog and editorial load), but we try to respond within 2 months. Simultaneous submissions accepted: Yes. Publishes 3% of manuscripts submitted. Payment: none. Copyrighted, reverts to author. Pub's reviews: approx. 12 in 2009. §Literary fiction, poetry, and non-fiction. Ads: see website for current ad specs. Subjects: Adirondacks, Arts, Book Reviewing, Fiction, France, French, German, Literary Review, Literature (General), Poetry, Short Stories, Translation.

Adonis Designs Press, Anita Stienstra, P.O. Box 202, Chatham, IL 62629, info@adonisdesignspress.com, www.adonisdesignspress.com. 2008. Poetry, non-fiction. avg. press run 500. Pub'd 1 title 2009; expects 3 titles 2010, 3 titles 2011. 1 title listed in the *Small Press Record of Books in Print* (36th Edition, 2010-11). 100pp. Reporting time: We acknowledge receipt of submissions to NTM and JAM immediately. Wait time for acceptance varies. Simultaneous submissions accepted: No. Does not copyright for author.

AD/VANCE, Vance Philip Hedderel, Editor-in-Chief, 1593 Colonial Terrace #206, Arlington, VA 22209-1430. 1992. Articles, interviews, music, letters, news items. 250. 3/yr. Pub'd 3 issues 2009; expects 3 issues 2010, 3 issues 2011. sub. price $5; per copy $2; sample $1. Back issues: negotiable, however back issues are not generally available. Discounts: none. 8pp. Reporting time: usually within 3 weeks. Simultaneous submissions accepted: no. Publishes less than 10% of manuscripts submitted. Payment: 2 sample issues. Not copyrighted. Pub's reviews: 4 in 2009. §Art, Brontes, Dada, surrealism, film, gays, poetry, music, lesbianism, London, Post Modernism, tapes and records. Ads: none. Subjects: Advertising, Self-Promotion, Avant-Garde, Experimental Art, Dada, Electronics, Gay, Music, Post Modern.

Advanced Learning Press, Anne Fenske Mrs., 317 Inverness Way South, Suite 150, Englewood, CO 80112, 303-504-9312, 303-504-9417, 800-844-6599. 1992. Non-fiction. "Professional development for educators in the areas of standards, assessment, accountability, and leadership. Douglas B. Reeves, Ph.D. Larry Ainsworth." avg. press run 4000. Pub'd 2 titles 2009; expects 2 titles 2010, 6 titles 2011. 31 titles listed in the *Small Press Record of Books in Print* (36th Edition, 2010-11). Discounts: 40% for quantities of 1-49, 50% for quantities of 50 or more. 200pp. Reporting time: 2 weeks. Simultaneous submissions accepted: No. Publishes 80% of manuscripts submitted. Payment: 1-1,000 7.5%, 1001-3,000 10%, 3001+ 15%. Copyrights for author. Subjects: Education, Leadership.

ADVANCES IN THANATOLOGY, Center for Thanatology Research & Education, Inc., Austin H. Kutscher, Editor; Roberta Halporn, Executive Editor, 391 Atlantic Ave., Brooklyn, NY 11217-1708, 718-858-3026, 718-852-1846, no 800, rhalporn@pipeline.com, thanatology.org. 1970. Non-fiction. "Death & Dying, Grief and Recovery from Grief, Medical Education in Thanatology." circ. 500. 4/yr. Pub'd 3 issues 2009; expects 4 issues 2010, 4 issues 2011. sub. price $72; per copy $20.; sample Free. Back issues: $2-. Discounts: 20% none to institutions or classrooms, unless multiple copies of same issue. 120pp. Simultaneous submissions accepted: No. Copyrighted, does not revert to author. Pub's reviews. Ads: Fill page:$125.00Half page:$65.00. Subjects: Euthanasia, Death, Family.

ADVANCES IN THE ASTRONAUTICAL SCIENCES, Univelt, Inc., R.H. Jacobs, Series Editor, PO Box 28130, San Diego, CA 92198, 760-746-4005, Fax 760-746-3139, sales@univelt.com, www.univelt.com. 1957. "Space and related fields. An irregular serial. Publishers for the American Atronautical Society. Vols. 1-122 published. Standing orders accepted." circ. 400. Irregular. Pub'd 2 issues 2009; expects 4 issues 2010, 5 issues 2011. sub. price varies. Back issues: no. Discounts: normally 20% but more by arrangement; discounts for classroom use. 400-700pp. Reporting time: 60 days. Payment: none. Copyrighted, authors may republish material with appropriate credits given and authorization from publishers. Ads: none. Subjects: Engineering, Science, Space.

Adventure Books Inc., Dina J. Daniel, PO Box 5196, Fresno, CA 93755, 559-294-8781, adventure-books@juno.com. 2000. Poetry, fiction, long-poems, non-fiction. avg. press run 1M. Pub'd 1 title 2009; expects 3 titles 2010, 12 titles 2011. 4 titles listed in the *Small Press Record of Books in Print* (36th Edition, 2010-11). Discounts: 60% offered on bulk orders. 150pp. Reporting time: 1-2 months. Simultaneous submissions accepted: yes. Publishes 10% of manuscripts submitted. Payment: yes. Copyrights for author. Subjects: Fantasy, Fiction, Mystery, Non-Fiction, Poetry.

ADVENTURES, Pamela Smits, Editor, 6401 The Paseo, Kansas City, MO 64131, 816-333-7000. 1969. Fiction, articles, non-fiction. "Inspirational and character building for 6 to 8-year-old children focusing on learning features with Bible lesson." circ. 42M. 52/yr. Pub'd 52 issues 2009. sub. price $7.95; sample free with SASE. 4pp. Reporting time: 8-12 weeks. Simultaneous submissions accepted: no. Publishes 30% of

7

manuscripts submitted. Payment: $25 per story (100-150 words). Copyrighted, we retain all rights. Subjects: Children, Youth, Religion.

Aegean Publishing Company, PO Box 6790, Santa Barbara, CA 93160, 805-964-6669. 1993. Non-fiction. "Technology-oriented popular books." avg. press run 5M. Expects 1 title 2010, 1 title 2011. 3 titles listed in the *Small Press Record of Books in Print* (36th Edition, 2010-11). Discounts: schedules available on request. 256pp. Reporting time: contact publisher. Payment: contact publisher. Copyrights for author. Subjects: Design, Engineering, Technology.

AERIAL, Rod Smith, PO Box 25642, Washington, DC 20007, 202-362-6418, aerialedge@aol.com. 1984. Poetry, fiction, articles, art, photos, cartoons, interviews, satire, criticism, reviews, music, letters, parts-of-novels, long-poems, collages, plays, concrete art, news items, non-fiction. "*Aerial* #9, just published, is a special issue on the work of Bruce Andrews." circ. 1M. Irregular. sub. price $25/2 issues; per copy varies; sample $15.00. Back issues: #6/7 is $15, #5 is $7.50. Discounts: 40% to retailers. 200pp. Reporting time: 1 week-6 months. Payment: contributors copies. Copyrighted, reverts to author. Pub's reviews. §Lit. mags, poetry, fiction, criticism, art. Ads: $100/$60/will consider exchanges. Subjects: Arts, Culture, Essays, Language, Literature (General), Poetry.

AESTHETICA MAGAZINE, Cherie Federico, PO Box 371, York, United Kingdom, +441904 527560. 2002. Articles, art, interviews, criticism, reviews, parts-of-novels. "We have 2 publications, the Aesthetica Annual, which shows original fiction, poetry and artwork from the finalists of the Aesthetica Creative Works Competition, and Aesthetica Magazine, a bi-monthly publication profiling current events in the areas of art, literature, film, theatre and music.Aesthetica Magazine does not publish submissions but shows reviews, interviews and features on upcoming events in the worlds of visual art, literature, theatre, film and music." circ. 45000. 6/yr. Pub'd 6 issues 2009; expects 6 issues 2010, 6 issues 2011. sub. price $42; per copy 3.90; sample 3.90. Back issues: 3.90 subject to availability. Discounts: 20% discount on the cover price for all subscriptions + free P&P for students. 66pp. Reporting time: 2 weeks. Simultaneous submissions accepted: Yes. Publishes 4% of manuscripts submitted. Payment: contact for details. Copyrighted, does not revert to author. Pub's reviews: approx 36 in 2009. §Newly published fiction and art books. Ads: Full Page: 875 (approx $1320)Half Page: 495 (approx $750)Classified: 75 (approx $110).

AETHLON, Joyce Duncan, Editor in Chief, Sport Literature Association, Box 70270 ETSU, Johnson City, TN 37614. "*Aethlon* is a print journal designed to celebrate the intersection of literature with the world of play, games, and sport. Aethlon publishes works about sport and sport literature, including original fiction and poetry, juried scholarly and critical essays, and book reviews. All submissions must relate to sports."

Affinity Publishers Services, A. Doyle, Founder, c/o Continuous, PO Box 416, Denver, CO 80201-0416, 303-575-5676, email: emailstreet@gmail.com. 1981. avg. press run 55. Expects 2 titles 2011. 1 title listed in the *Small Press Record of Books in Print* (36th Edition, 2010-11). Discounts: standard. 70pp. Subjects: Biography, Business & Economics, Consumer, Crafts, Hobbies, Gardening, Homemaking, How-To, How-To, Newsletter, Reference, Tapes & Records, Vegetarianism.

Affluent Publishing Corp., Charity Heller Hogge, Senior Editor, 1040 Ave. of the Americas, 24th floor, New York, NY 10018, Phone: (888) 488-9517, Fax: (888) 861-3175, Email: info@Affluent-Publishing.com, Website: http://wwww.Affluent-Publishing.com. 2008. Fiction. No titles listed in the *Small Press Record of Books in Print* (36th Edition, 2010-11). Reporting time: 3 to 6 months. Simultaneous submissions accepted: Yes. Subjects: African-American, Family, Fiction, Literature (General), Mystery, Novels, Romance, Science Fiction.

African American Images, Jawanza Kunjufu, 1909 West 95th Street, Chicago, IL 60643-1105, 773-445-0322, Fax 773-445-9844. 1980. Non-fiction. avg. press run 5M. Pub'd 10 titles 2009. 67 titles listed in the *Small Press Record of Books in Print* (36th Edition, 2010-11). Discounts: 5-100 40%, 101-199 46%, 200+ 50%. 125pp. Reporting time: 2 months. Publishes 10% of manuscripts submitted. Payment: 10% net. Copyrights for author. Subjects: Black, Education, Family, Sociology.

AFRICAN AMERICAN REVIEW, Nathan Grant Ph.D., Editor; Aileen Keenan, Managing Editor; Yoshinobu Hakutani Ph.D., Book Review Editor, Saint Louis University, Adorjan Hall 317, 3800 Lindell Boulevard, St. Louis, MO 63108-3414, 314-977-3688, FAX 314-977-1514, ngrant2@slu.edu, keenan-am@slu.edu, http://aar.slu.edu. 1967. Poetry, fiction, articles, art, photos, interviews, criticism, reviews, long-poems, collages, non-fiction. "As the official publication of the Division on Black American Literature and Culture of the Modern Language Association, the quarterly journal *African American Review* promotes a lively exchange among writers and scholars in the arts, humanities, and social sciences who hold diverse perspectives on African American literature and culture." 4/yr. Pub'd 4 issues 2009; expects 4 issues 2010, 4 issues 2011. sub. price $40 individuals, $80 institutions (foreign add $15); per copy $12, $24 institutions (no foreign single issues); sample $12. Back issues: $12. 200pp. Reporting time: 3 months. Simultaneous submissions accepted: no. Publishes 10% of manuscripts submitted. Payment: 1 copy and 5 offprints;

honorarium. AAR holds copyright on entire issue, author on individual article or poem. Pub's reviews: 36 in 2009. §African American literary criticism, essays, poetry. Ads: $200/$120. Subjects: African Literature, Africa, African Studies, Black, Book Reviewing, Community, Criticism, Dance, Education, Fiction, History, Literary Review, Men, Music, Poetry, Theatre, Women.

THE AFRICAN HERALD, Good Hope Enterprises, Inc., Dr. Richard O. Nwachukwu, PO Box 132394, Dallas, TX 75313-2394. 1989. Articles, photos, interviews, news items, non-fiction. "Additional address: 4300 N. Central Expressway, Suite 201, Dallas, TX 75206." circ. 15M. 12/yr. Pub'd 12 issues 2009; expects 12 issues 2010, 12 issues 2011. sub. price $15 corps, libraries; $12 individuals; per copy $1; sample free. Back issues: $1.50. Discounts: 30% to 40%. 32pp. Publishes 95% of manuscripts submitted. Payment: none. Copyrighted, does not revert to author. Pub's reviews: 6 in 2009. §African/African-American Books. Ads: $1365/$725/$475/$295/$155 business card size.

AFRO-HISPANIC REVIEW, William Luis, Editor, The Bishop Joseph Johnson Black Cultural Center, Vanderbilt University, VU Station B #351666, Nashville, TN 37235-1666. 1982. Poetry, fiction, articles, interviews, criticism, reviews, letters, news items. "We also publish creative writing and translations." circ. 500. 2/yr. Pub'd 2 issues 2009; expects 2 issues 2010, 2 issues 2011. sub. price $30 indiv. ($35 international), $70 instit. ($75 international).; per copy Individuals, $20.00 + $2.00 shipping, institutions, $40.00 + 2.00 (USA) or $5.00 (international).; sample $20.00. Back issues: $20.00. Discounts: 0%. 250pp. Reporting time: 60 days. Simultaneous submissions accepted: no. Publishes 30% of manuscripts submitted. Payment: 1 copy of issue containing contribution. Copyrighted, does not revert to author. Pub's reviews: 10 in 2009. §Afro-Hispanic history, literature, politics, and sociology. Ads: $100/$50/50¢. Subjects: Black, Latin America.

AFTERIMAGE, Visual Studies Workshop, Karen vanMeenen, 31 Prince Street, Rochester, NY 14607, 585/442.8676, fax 585.442.1992, afterimage@vsw.org, www.vsw.org/afterimage/. 1972. Articles, art, photos, interviews, criticism, reviews, concrete art, news items. "Afterimage features critical articles about the visual arts, photography, independent film and video, alternative publishing, and multimedia, also covering important issues and debates within art history and sociology, cultural studies, communication studies, and related fields." 6/yr. Pub'd 6 issues 2009; expects 5 issues 2010, 6 issues 2011. sub. price $33; per copy $5.50; sample free. Back issues: $5 + SH. Discounts: distributors & bookstores 50% discount.Afterimage in the classroom 50% discount. 60pp. Reporting time: 4-6 weeks. Simultaneous submissions accepted: No. Publishes 15% of manuscripts submitted. Payment: 5 cents per word after publication. Pub's reviews. Ads: $750 front cover inside (full color)/$700 back cover inside (full color)/ $800 back cover (full color)/$500 full page/ $300 1/2 page/$200 1/4 page/ $125 bottom runner/$25 highlighted notice. Subjects: Arts, Audio/Video, Avant-Garde, Experimental Art, Book Arts, Criticism, Culture, Photography, Visual Arts.

AFTERTOUCH: New Music Discoveries & Gifts For Your Creative Imagination, Ronald A. Wallace, 1024 West Willcox Avenue, Peoria, IL 61604-2675, 309-685-4843. 1984. Articles, art, interviews, music. circ. 10,000. 2/yr. Pub'd 1 issue 2009; expects 1 issue 2010, 2 issues 2011. No subscriptions; price per copy $2.50; sample $2.50. Discounts: none. 36pp. Publishes 0% of manuscripts submitted. §Music. Ads: Yes. Subject: Music.

Agathon Books, Allen A. Huemer, PO Box 630, Lander, WY 82520-0630, 307-332-5252, Fax 307-332-5888, agathon@rmisp.com, www.rmisp.com/agathon/. 1998. "Issues in philosophy and related areas, using a clearly-reasoned, good-spirited approach." avg. press run 3M. Expects 3 titles 2010, 4+ titles 2011. 1 title listed in the *Small Press Record of Books in Print* (36th Edition, 2010-11). Discounts: trade 40%, colleges and libraries 25%, bulk and jobber 60% max. 300pp. Reporting time: 6 months. Simultaneous submissions accepted: yes. Publishes 25% of manuscripts submitted. Payment: arranged individually. Copyrights for author. Subjects: Myth, Mythology, Philosophy, Poetry.

Ageless Press, Iris Forrest, 3759 Collins St., Sarasota, FL 34232-3201, 941-365-1367, irishope@comcast.net. 1992. Fiction, articles, non-fiction. "First book is an anthology of experiences of dealing with computers. Fiction & nonfiction." avg. press run 5M. Expects 1 title 2010, 1 title 2011. 4 titles listed in the *Small Press Record of Books in Print* (36th Edition, 2010-11). 160pp. Reporting time: 2 weeks. Simultaneous submissions accepted: Yes. Payment: negotiable. Does not copyright for author. Subjects: Artificial Intelligence, Computers, Calculators, Fiction, Health, Humor, Mystery, Non-Fiction, Short Stories.

Agityne Corp, PO Box 690, Upton, MA 01568, 508-529-4135, www.agityne.com/. 2002. Non-fiction. Expects 2 titles 2010, 3 titles 2011. No titles listed in the *Small Press Record of Books in Print* (36th Edition, 2010-11). 200pp. Simultaneous submissions accepted: No. Copyrights for author.

AGNI, Sven Birkerts, Editor; William Pierce, Senior Editor, Boston University, 236 Bay State Road, Boston, MA 02215, 617-353-7135, agni@bu.edu. 1972. Poetry, fiction, non-fiction. "We look for the honest voice, the idiosyncratic signature, experimental where necessary but not willfully so. Writing that grows from a vision, a perspective, and a passion will interest us, regardless of structure or approach. Recent contributors include William T. Vollmann, Alexandra Chasin, Vivek Narayanan, Kim Addonizio, Rick Moody, Edith Pearlman,

Magdalena Tulli, Peter LaSalle, and Lia Purpura. We strongly encourage you to buy a sample copy before submitting your work.'' circ. 3,000. 2/yr. Pub'd 2 issues 2009; expects 2 issues 2010, 2 issues 2011. sub. price $20, $25 institutions; per copy $11.95; sample $9.95 for issue 57 to issue 65 (spring 2007). Back issues: see https://www.bu.edu/agni/back-issues.html. Discounts: $38 for 2 years and free back issue, $53 for 3 years and 2 back issues (for individuals only). 200-270pp. Reporting time: 2-4 months. Reading period is September 1st to May 31st only (check www.bu.edu/agni/submit.html for changes). Simultaneous submissions encouraged. Publishes ~1% of manuscripts submitted. Payment: $10/page for prose, $20/page for poetry, up to $150 maximum. Copyrighted, reverts to author. Ads: $500/$350. Subjects: Essays, Fiction, Memoirs, Poetry, Translation.

AGRICULTURAL HISTORY, University of California Press, Claire Strom, Editor, University of California Press, 2000 Center Street, Suite 303, Berkeley, CA 94704-1223, 510-643-7154. 1926. Articles, reviews, non-fiction. ''Editorial address: Department of History, Minard Hall, North Dakota State University, Fargo, ND 58105-5075. Copyrighted by Agricultural History Society.'' circ. 957. 4/yr. Pub'd 4 issues 2009; expects 4 issues 2010, 4 issues 2011. sub. price $47 indiv., $158 instit., $22 students; per copy $12 indiv.; $42 instit., $12 students. Back issues: $12 indiv.; $42 instit., $12 students. Discounts: foreign subs. agent 10%, one-time orders 10+ 30%. 128pp. Reporting time: 2-3 weeks. Payment: varies. Copyrighted, does not revert to author. Pub's reviews: 100 in 2009. §Agricultural history and economics. Ads: $295/$220. Subject: Agriculture.

THE AGUILAR EXPRESSION, Xavier F. Aguilar, 1329 Gilmore Avenue, Donora, PA 15033, 724-379-8019, www.wordrunner.com/xfaguilar. 1986. Poetry, fiction, art, reviews, letters. circ. 150. 1/yr. Pub'd 2 issues 2009; expects 2 issues 2010, 2 issues 2011. 2 titles listed in the *Small Press Record of Books in Print* (36th Edition, 2010-11). sub. price $10; per copy $10; sample $10. 8-16pp. Reporting time: 2 months. Simultaneous submissions accepted: no. Publishes 10% of manuscripts submitted. Payment: 2 free copies, byline. Not copyrighted. Pub's reviews: 2 in 2009. §Poetry books and short story collections. Ads: by request. Subjects: Fiction, Poetry.

Ahsahta Press, Janet Holmes, Director, Boise State University, 1910 University Drive, Boise, ID 83725-1525, 208-426-3134, ahsahta@boisestate.edu, http://ahsahtapress.boisestate.edu. 1975. Poetry. ''We run the Sawtooth Poetry Prize competition annually.'' avg. press run 1000. Pub'd 6 titles 2009; expects 7 titles 2010, 7 titles 2011. 92 titles listed in the *Small Press Record of Books in Print* (36th Edition, 2010-11). Discounts: 40% to trade, bulk, jobber, classroom; distributed by Small Press Distribution. 100pp. Reporting time: Currently we do not have a reading period. Simultaneous submissions accepted: yes. Publishes 1% of manuscripts submitted. Payment: 25 copies of book; 8% for first 1,000 sold, 10% for next 1,000 sold, 12% thereafter. Copyrights for author. Subject: Poetry.

AIM MAGAZINE, Ruth Apilado, Editor; Myron Apilado, Managing Editor, PO Box 390, Milton, WA 98354-0390. 1973. ''*AIM* is a national magazine that uses the written word to help purge racism from the human bloodstream. A consistent theme that winds its way through the prose poetry of the magazine is one that depicts how people from one ethnic group, usually through some personal experience, come to realize the common humanity of all ethnic groups. We're looking for compelling, well-written pieces with lasting social significance. The story should not moralize. Maximum length is 4,000 words.'' circ. 7M. 4/yr. Pub'd 4 issues 2009; expects 4 issues 2010, 4 issues 2011. sub. price $12; per copy $4; sample $5. Back issues: $6. Discounts: 30%. 48pp. Reporting time: 2 months. Simultaneous submissions accepted: yes. Publishes 70% of manuscripts submitted. Payment: $15-$25 articles and stories. Not copyrighted. Pub's reviews: 2 in 2009. §Black and Hispanic life. Ads: $250/$150/$90 1/4 page. Subjects: African Literature, Africa, African Studies, Black, Book Reviewing, Fiction, Socialist, Sociology.

Aircraft Owners Group (see also CESSNA OWNER MAGAZINE; PIPERS MAGAZINE), Joe Jones, Publisher, PO Box 5000, Iola, WI 54945-5000, 800-331-0038, e-mail cessna@aircraftownergroup.com or piper@aircraftownergroup.com. 1974. Articles, photos, interviews, reviews, letters. avg. press run 5M-6M. No titles listed in the *Small Press Record of Books in Print* (36th Edition, 2010-11).

Airlie Press, Anita Sullivan, Carter McKenzie, Jessica Lamb, Donna Henderson, Cecelia Hagen, Chris Anderson, PO Box 434, Monmouth, OR 97361, 541-344-7403, www.airliepress.org. 2007. Poetry. ''We are a nonprofit publishing collective dedicated to cultivating and sustaining fine contemporary poetry. Our mission is to offer writers working in the Willamette Valley region of Oregon a local, shared-work publishing alternative.'' avg. press run 1000. Pub'd 2 titles 2009; expects 2 titles 2010, 2 titles 2011. 2 titles listed in the *Small Press Record of Books in Print* (36th Edition, 2010-11). Discount to subscribers 9%. 55-75pp. Reporting time: 1 month. Simultaneous submissions accepted: No. Publishes 25% of manuscripts submitted. Payment: All funds from book sales return to the Press for creation of new books of poetry. Copyrights for author.

AIS Publications (see also GENRE: WRITER AND WRITINGS), Alexis James, PO Box 42603, Indianapolis, IN 46242-0603, Office: (317) 856-8942, Cell: (317) 292-2615. 1996. Poetry, photos, parts-of-novels, non-fiction. ''To publish biographies, reporting as near as factual as possible and to offer opportunities to up and coming writers in varoius genre. Recently we have T. Chandler, A. Skriloff, N. Yelton, M. Kondritz and R.Ciras who have contributed works in their individual genre." Expects 2 titles 2010, 3 titles 2011. 1 title listed in the *Small Press Record of Books in Print* (36th Edition, 2010-11). Reporting time: 3 months. Simultaneous submissions accepted: Yes. Publishes 10% of manuscripts submitted. Payment: No advances at this time. Payment in copies of author's works. Copyrights for author. Subjects: Autobiography, Biography, Business & Economics, Civil Rights, Haiku, Holocaust, Human Rights, Humanism, Indigenous Cultures, Mental Health, Native American, Non-Fiction, Poetry, Prison, Quotations.

AK Press, Ramsey Kanaan, 674-A 23rd Street, Oakland, CA 94612, 415-864-0892, FAX 415-864-0893, akpress@org.org. 1994. Fiction, art, criticism, long-poems, non-fiction. "Most of what we publish is solicited. However we have published the occasional unsolicited work. We largely publish non-fiction of a radical nature, in the fields of anarchism, art & culture." avg. press run 2M-10M. Pub'd 15 titles 2009; expects 18 titles 2010, 25 titles 2011. 82 titles listed in the *Small Press Record of Books in Print* (36th Edition, 2010-11). Normal discounts to trade, depending on whether it's to a retailer, distributor, library, etc. 100-400pp. Reporting time: a couple of months. Publishes 2% of manuscripts submitted. Payment: usually 10% of net sales, no advance. Subjects: Anarchist, Arts, Biography, Dada, Entertainment, Environment, Feminism, Fiction, History, Literature (General), Non-Fiction, Philosophy, Political Science, Sex, Sexuality, Surrealism.

Akashic Books, Johnny Temple, Publisher; Johanna Ingalls, Managing Editor, PO Box 1456, New York, NY 10009, 212-433-1875, 212-414-3199, Akashic7@aol.com, www.akashicbooks.com. 1997. "Dedicated to publishing urban literary fiction and political nonfiction by authors who are either ignored by the mainstream or who have no interest in working within the ever-consolidating ranks of the major corporate publishers." No titles listed in the *Small Press Record of Books in Print* (36th Edition, 2010-11).

ALABAMA HERITAGE, University of Alabama Press, Donna Cox, Box 870342, 500 Margaret Drive, Tuscaloosa, AL 35487-0342, 205-348-7434, www.AlabamaHeritage.com.

‡ALABAMA LITERARY REVIEW, Theron E. Montgomery III, Editor; James G. Davis, Fiction Editor; Ed Hicks, Poetry Editor; Steve Cooper, Prose Editor, Smith 253, Troy State University, Troy, AL 36082, 334-670-3971, Fax 334-670-3519. 1987. Poetry, fiction, articles, art, photos, cartoons, interviews, criticism, reviews, parts-of-novels, long-poems, plays. "No bias against style or length of poetry, fiction or drama. First issue included Eve Shelnutt and Elise Sanguinetti." circ. 800+. 1/yr. Pub'd 1 issue 2009; expects 1 issue 2010, 1 issue 2011. sub. price $10; per copy $10; sample $5. 100pp. Reporting time: 2-3 months. Publishes 5-10% of manuscripts submitted. Payment: copies and honorarium when available; $5-10 per printed page. Copyrighted, reverts to author. Pub's reviews: 5 in 2009. §All kinds, particularly poetry and fiction by new authors and/or smaller presses. Ads: $25. Subjects: Book Reviewing, Criticism, Fiction, Photography, Poetry.

Alamo Square Press, Bert Herrman, 103 FR 321, Tajique, NM 87016, 505-384-9766, alamosquare@earth-link.net. 1988. Non-fiction. "Book length, gay, non-pornographic, social or spiritual importance only." avg. press run 5M. Pub'd 1 title 2009. 14 titles listed in the *Small Press Record of Books in Print* (36th Edition, 2010-11). Discounts: 40% retail, 55% distributor. 144pp. Reporting time: 2 weeks. Simultaneous submissions accepted: no. Payment: negotiable. Copyrights for author. Subjects: Gay, Lesbianism, Occult, Psychology, San Francisco, Spiritual, Zen.

Alan Wofsy Fine Arts, Milton J. Goldbaum, Zeke Greenberg, Adios Butler, PO Box 2210, San Francisco, CA 94126, 415-292-6500, www.art-books.com, order@art-books.com. 1969. Art, cartoons. "Art reference books only." avg. press run 500. Pub'd 4 titles 2009; expects 4 titles 2010, 5+ titles 2011. 32 titles listed in the *Small Press Record of Books in Print* (36th Edition, 2010-11). Discounts: 20-40. 300pp. Payment: varies. Copyrights for author. Subjects: Arts, Comics, Reference, Reprints.

ALARM CLOCK, Allen Salyer, PO Box 1551, Royal Oak, MI 48068, 248-442-8634. 1990. Music. "Women in Music." circ. 200. 4/yr. Pub'd 5 issues 2009; expects 4 issues 2010, 4 issues 2011. sample price $2. 32pp. Payment: contributor's copy. Copyrighted, reverts to author. Pub's reviews: 10-15 per issue in 2009. §Music, science fiction, fashion, women's issues. Subject: Music.

Alaska Native Language Center, Tom Alton, University of Alaska, PO Box 757680, Fairbanks, AK 99775-7680, 907-474-7874, Fax 907-474-6586. 1972. Non-fiction. "We publish materials in or about Alaska Native languages only." avg. press run 500-1M. Pub'd 2 titles 2009; expects 5 titles 2010, 6 titles 2011. 47 titles listed in the *Small Press Record of Books in Print* (36th Edition, 2010-11). Discounts: wholesalers 40% on 5 each or more; 20% on fewer than 5 each. 300pp. Sometimes copyrights for author—joint copyright or ANLC alone. Subjects: Alaska, Autobiography, Bilingual, Culture, Education, Folklore, Genealogy, How-To, Indians, Language, Memoirs, Native American, Non-Fiction, Storytelling, Women.

ALASKA QUARTERLY REVIEW, Ronald Spatz, Fiction Editor, Executive Editor, University of Alaska-Anchorage, 3211 Providence Drive, Anchorage, AK 99508, 907-786-6916. 1981. Poetry, fiction, parts-of-novels, long-poems, plays, non-fiction. "We are looking for high quality traditional and unconventional fiction, poetry, short plays, and literary nonfiction. Unsolicited manuscripts welcome between August 15 and May 15.'' circ. 2.2M. 2/yr. Pub'd 2 issues 2009; expects 2 issues 2010, 2 issues 2011. 2 titles listed in the *Small Press Record of Books in Print* (36th Edition, 2010-11). sub. price $18; per copy $6.95; sample $6. Back issues: $6 and up. 250pp. Reporting time: 6-16 weeks. Publishes less than 1% of manuscripts submitted. Payment: 1 contributor's copy and a one-year subscription; additional payment depends on terms of grants. Copyrighted, reverts to author. Subjects: Drama, Essays, Fiction, Literary Review, Literature (General), Memoirs, Non-Fiction, Novels, Poetry, Prose, Short Stories, Writers/Writing.

ALBERTA HISTORY, Historical Society of Alberta, Hugh A. Dempsey, 95 Holmwood Ave NW, Calgary Alberta T2K 2G7, Canada, 403-289-8149. 1953. Articles, reviews, non-fiction. ''3.5M to 5M word articles on Western Canadian History.'' circ. 1.6M. 4/yr. Pub'd 4 issues 2009; expects 4 issues 2010, 4 issues 2011. sub. price $25; per copy $5.50; sample free. Back issues: $5.50. Discounts: 33%. 28pp. Reporting time: 2 months. Simultaneous submissions accepted: no. Publishes 50% of manuscripts submitted. Payment: nil. Copyrighted. Pub's reviews: 12 in 2009. §In our field-Western Canadian History. No ads. Subjects: History, Native American.

Alcatraz Editions, Gary Young, 3965 Bonny Doon Road, Santa Cruz, CA 95060. 1978. Poetry, fiction, articles, art, photos, cartoons, satire, criticism, reviews, music, long-poems, collages. ''See *Alcatraz 3* for current biases. No new books until further notice.'' avg. press run 500. Pub'd 1 title 2009. 4 titles listed in the *Small Press Record of Books in Print* (36th Edition, 2010-11). Discounts: 40% to trade on orders of 3 or more. 80-120pp. Subject: Translation.

ALCHEMY, Student Editors, Portland Community College P.O Box 19000, Portland, OR 97280-0990, (503) 977-4793. 1973. Poetry, fiction, art, photos, satire, parts-of-novels, long-poems, plays, non-fiction. ''Alchemy is a student-produced and student-edited magazine that is interested in publishing the strongest work it can find. Favors image-based, metaphorically rich poetry and fiction with serious concerns and a discernible narrative line.'' circ. 350. 1/yr. Pub'd 1 issue 2009; expects 1 issue 2010, 1 issue 2011. price per copy $5; sample $5. Back issues: $2/ Recent issues available. 80pp. Reporting time: 3-6 months. Simultaneous submissions accepted: Yes. Publishes 10% of manuscripts submitted. Payment: 2 complimentary copies. Copyrighted, reverts to author. Subject: Literary Review.

ALEHOUSE, Jay Rubin, Editor, PO Box 31655, San Francisco, CA 94131. ''*Alehouse* is happy to consider queries for both essays and book reviews. Our essay topics focus on the current state of poetry, the work of particular authors, the personal experience of poets, plus other appropriate areas of interest. For our 2009 issue, we are especially interested in essays on African-American poets and poetry. Query us with an idea. In general, unsolicited poetry is considered through the Alehouse Happy Hour Poetry Awards. For details on how to enter our subscription contest, please visit our contest page. Poets preferring not to enter our contest may query the editor regarding submissions. Our book reviews focus on work published since 2007, but also include older, under-appreciated work that reviewers may want to promote to our readers. Our essays run approximately 500-2000 words, our book reviews run approximately 500-1000 words per title. Please contact us for our book review guidelines.''

•**THE ALEMBIC,** English Department, Providence College, Providence, RI 02918. ''The Alembic is an international literary journal featuring the work of both established and student writers. It is published each April by Providence College in Providence, Rhode Island. We encourage potential contributors tobecome familiar with the journal. The subscription rate in the United States is $15 for two years and sample copies are available for $7. Submissions are read from August 1st through November 15th only. Please include a sentence or two for "Contributor's Notes." No manuscripts or artwork can be returned, nor any query answered, unless accompanied by a self-addressed, stamped envelope. The Alembic accepts no responsibility for unsolicited submissions and will not enter into correspondence about their loss or delay. Materials published in The Alembic may not be reprinted, in whole or in part, without written permission from the editors.'' No titles listed in the *Small Press Record of Books in Print* (36th Edition, 2010-11).

The Alembic Press, Claire M. Bolton, Editor, Hyde Farm House, Marcham, Abingdon, Oxford, Oxford OX13 6NX, United Kingdom. ''A Fine Press creating and printing limited edition books by traditional letterpress.'' No titles listed in the *Small Press Record of Books in Print* (36th Edition, 2010-11).

Al-Galaxy Publishing Corporation, Martin Mathias, PO Box 2591, Wichita, KS 67201, 316-651-0464, Fax 316-651-0461, email: sales@algalaxypress.com. 1994. Reviews, non-fiction. avg. press run 100M. Pub'd 1 title 2009; expects 3 titles 2010, 5 titles 2011. 1 title listed in the *Small Press Record of Books in Print* (36th Edition, 2010-11). Discounts: 2-4 books 20%, 5-9 30%, 10-24 40%, 25-49 42%, 50-74 44%, 75-99 46%, 100-199 48%, 20-499 50%, 500+ 52%. 180pp. Reporting time: 60 days. Simultaneous submissions accepted: yes. Publishes 10% of manuscripts submitted. Payment: 8-10% of net (agreed fraction paid in advance). Copyrights for author unless he/she requests otherwise. Subjects: New Age, Physics, Religion, Self-Help, Sex, Sexuality.

Alice James Books, April Ossmann, Executive Director, University of Maine at Farmington, 238 Main Street,

Farmington, ME 04938-1911, 207-778-7071 phone/Fax, ajb@umf.maine.edu. 1973. Poetry. "Alice James Books is a nonprofit cooperative poetry press. Named after Alice James—the sister of novelist Henry James and philosopher William James—whose fine journal and gift for writing were unrecognized within her lifetime, the press seeks out and publishes the best contemporary poetry by both established and beginning poets, with particular emphasis on involving poets in the publishing process. Since 1994, the press has been affiliated with the University of Maine at Farmington. The cooperative selects manuscripts for publication through both regional and national competitions: the Kinereth Gensler Awards, and the Beatrice Hawley Award. Winners of regional awards become active cooperative members, judging future contests and participating in editorial and executive decisions. National awards do not carry a cooperative work commitment. Known for its commitment to emerging and early career poets, AJB has published books by Jane Kenyon, Jean Valentine, B.H. Fairchild, Forrest Hamer, Richard McCann, Matthea Harvey, Donald Revell, Brian Turner, Sarah Manguso, and Larissa Szporluk." avg. press run 1.5M. Pub'd 6 titles 2009; expects 5 titles 2010, 6 titles 2011. 99 titles listed in the *Small Press Record of Books in Print* (36th Edition, 2010-11). 80pp. Reporting time: 2-4 months. We accept simultaneous submissions if notified. Publishes 1% of manuscripts submitted. Payment: no royalties; author receives cash award as part of cooperative's contract with author. Copyrights for author. Subjects: Poetry, Women.

ALIMENTUM - The Literature of Food, Paulette Licitra, Publisher-Editor; Peter Selgin, Editor; Cortney Davis, Poetry Editor, P. O. Box 776, New York, NY 10163, info@alimentumjournal.com www.alimentumjournal.com. 2005. Poetry, fiction, art, interviews, parts-of-novels, long-poems, non-fiction. "We publish original ficiton, poetry, and creative nonfiction all relating to a food theme. Recent contributors have included Oliver Sacks, Mark Kurlansky, Cortney Davis, Carly Sachs, Esther Cohen, Clifford A. Wright, Janna MaMahan." 2/yr. Expects 2 issues 2010, 2 issues 2011. sub. price $18; per copy $10; sample $10. Back issues: $10. Discounts: 20-55%. 128pp. Reporting time: 3 months. Simultaneous submissions accepted: Yes. Payment: contributor copies. Copyrighted, reverts to author. Subjects: Cooking, Food, Eating.

All Nations Press, Catherine McCormick, P.O. Box 601, White Marsh, VA 23183, 757-581-4063, www.allnationspress.com. 2002. Poetry, non-fiction. "All Nations Press publishes quality poetry and non-fiction from new and established writers. We pride ourselves in the top quality of the writing and the presentation of the book." avg. press run 1000. Pub'd 4 titles 2009; expects 5 titles 2010, 5 titles 2011. 12 titles listed in the *Small Press Record of Books in Print* (36th Edition, 2010-11). Discounts: 50% discount to all distributors and bookstores, etc.. 150pp. Reporting time: one month. Simultaneous submissions accepted: Yes. Publishes 10% of manuscripts submitted. Payment: varies. Copyrights for author. Subjects: Absurdist, African-American, Memoirs, Non-Fiction, Poetry, Post Modern, Russia, Travel.

•**All That Productions,Inc.,** Randy Elum, Brian Elum, Debra Starr, P.O. Box 1594, Humble, TX 77347, 281-878-2062. 1996. Poetry, fiction, articles, long-poems, plays. "Providing moral based material to inspire readers." avg. press run 1000. Pub'd 10 titles 2009; expects 12 titles 2010, 15 titles 2011. No titles listed in the *Small Press Record of Books in Print* (36th Edition, 2010-11). Discounts: Discounted Price for 2 or more copies. 120pp. Reporting time: 6-10 weeks. No unsolicited manuscripts accepted. No mss though agents. Simultaneous submissions accepted: Yes. Publishes 90% of manuscripts submitted. Payment: Royalty based on profits; no advance. Copyrights for author. Subjects: Christianity, Family, Fiction, Humor, Poetry, Women.

Allbook Books, Walter (Mankh) Harris III, P.O. Box 562, Selden, NY 11784, (631)716-1385, www.allbook-books.com. 2002. Poetry, fiction, articles, interviews, long-poems, news items, non-fiction. "Allbook Books publishes poetry and other writings that encourage one-world consciousnessand respect for various cultures, lifestyles and spiritual traditions. Recent contributors: Gertrude Halstead, Barbara Southard, Robert Savino." avg. press run 250. Pub'd 4 titles 2009; expects 4 titles 2010, 5 titles 2011. 14 titles listed in the *Small Press Record of Books in Print* (36th Edition, 2010-11). Discounts: E-mail for details.Individauls check website for additional book discounts. 90pp. Reporting time: 1 to 6 months. Simultaneous submissions accepted: Yes. Publishes 20% of manuscripts submitted. Payment: contact for details. copyright page lists (c) with author's name unless anthology where all rights revert to individual authors. Subjects: The Americas, Anthology, Counter-Culture, Alternatives, Communes, Creativity, Essays, Gay, Haiku, Indigenous Cultures, Metaphysics, Multicultural, Myth, Mythology, Native American, Poetry, Social Movements, Zen.

THE ALLEGHENY REVIEW, Beata Gomulak, Senior Editor, Box 32, Allegheny College, Meadville, PA 16335, 814-332-6553. 1983. Poetry, fiction, art, photos, criticism, long-poems, plays, non-fiction. "Editorial staff changes yearly. Publish work by undergraduate college students only, from across the country. *The Allegheny Review* has been used as a classroom text. National edition founded 1983; a local version under similar names has been published since 1983." circ. 100+. 1/yr. Pub'd 1 issue 2009; expects 1 issue 2010, 1 issue 2011. sub. price $4; per copy $4; sample $4. Back issues: $3. Discounts: 25 copies, $2 each for use in classroom. 100pp. Reporting time: 4 months after deadline. Simultaneous submissions accepted: no. Publishes 5% of manuscripts submitted. Payment: 1 copy, $150 to contest winners (best submission each genre; poetry, fiction, nonfiction, art). Copyrighted, rights revert to author upon request. Ads: none. Subjects: Drama, Fiction,

Literary Review, Photography, Poetry.

Glen Allen Press, Craig Biddle, Sarah Peyton, 4036-D Cox Road, Glen Allen, VA 23060, 804-747-1776, Fax 804-273-0500, mail@glenallenpress.com, www.glenallenpress.com. 2002. Art, non-fiction. "We publish non-fiction books aimed at helping customers to pursue, protect, and enjoy their life-serving values. Philosophically, we stand for rational self-interest, individual rights, and laissez-faire capitalism. In a word, we advocate Objectivism, the philosophy of Ayn Rand, and we are dedicated to publishing titles that demonstrate or apply the principles of this philosophy." avg. press run 3M. Pub'd 1 title 2009; expects 1 title 2010, 2 titles 2011. 1 title listed in the *Small Press Record of Books in Print* (36th Edition, 2010-11). 160pp. Reporting time: 8 weeks. Simultaneous submissions accepted: yes. Payment: varies. Copyrights for author. Subjects: Arts, Ethics, Non-Fiction, Parenting, Philosophy, Politics.

•**Allium Press of Chicago,** Emily Victorson, 1530 Elgin Avenue, Forest Park, IL 60130, emvic@allium-press.com. 2009. Fiction, non-fiction. "We publish books in the areas of history and historical fiction, especially those with a Chicago connection. We publish only books with writing of the highest quality, and produce them to meet exceptional design standards." Pub'd 2 titles 2009; expects 4 titles 2010, 6 titles 2011. 2 titles listed in the *Small Press Record of Books in Print* (36th Edition, 2010-11). Subjects: Anthology, Chicago, Fiction, Great Lakes, History, Illinois, Literature (General), Midwest, Mystery.

Allworth Press, Tad Crawford, Publisher, Nicole Potter, 10 East 23rd Street, Suite 510, New York, NY 10010, 212-777-8395, Fax 212-777-8261, Pub@allworth.com, www.allworth.com. 1989. Art, photos, criticism, music, non-fiction. "Allworth Press publishes business, legal, career guidance, and self-help books for creative individuals in the visual, performing, writing and fine arts as well as collections of criticism in aesthetics and graphic design. Allworth also publishes books for the general public on business, law and personal finance. Helios Press, an imprint of Allworth's parent company, Allworth Communications, Inc., features new and re-issued works in psychology, spirituality, and current affairs." avg. press run 5M. Pub'd 30 titles 2009; expects 30 titles 2010, 30 titles 2011. 246 titles listed in the *Small Press Record of Books in Print* (36th Edition, 2010-11). 225pp. Reporting time: varies. Simultaneous submissions accepted: yes. Publishes 2% of manuscripts submitted. Copyrights for author. Subjects: Arts, Cartoons, Comics, Communication, Journalism, Crafts, Hobbies, Design, Desktop Publishing, Graphic Design, How-To, Law, Music, New Age, Photography, Visual Arts, Writers/Writing.

•**Allwrite Advertising and Publishing,** Annette Johnson, P.O. Box 1071, Atlanta, GA 30301, 678-691-9005. 2003. Fiction, non-fiction. avg. press run 200. Pub'd 3 titles 2009; expects 4 titles 2010, 5 titles 2011. No titles listed in the *Small Press Record of Books in Print* (36th Edition, 2010-11). Discounts: 55% distributors40% wholesalers15% librabries and schools. 200pp. Reporting time: 6-8 weeks. Simultaneous submissions accepted: Yes. Payment: 20%. Copyrights for author. Subjects: Biography, Children, Youth, Christianity, Family, Fiction, Health, History, Motivation, Success, Novels, Nutrition, Relationships, Religion, Self-Help, Spiritual, Textbooks.

Ally Press, Paul Feroe, 524 Orleans St., St. Paul, MN 55107, 651-291-2652, pferoe@comcast.net. 1973. Poetry. "The Ally Press is a publisher and distributor of books and tapes by Robert Bly. It will seek to maintain a blacklist of all Bly material in print through its mail-order service. In addition it publishes a quarterly newsletter detailing Bly's current reading schedule. Those desiring these free mailings can write care of the press. Ally Press is not accepting any manuscripts at this time." avg. press run 1.5M. Expects 2 titles 2011. 16 titles listed in the *Small Press Record of Books in Print* (36th Edition, 2010-11). Discounts: 1-4 20%, 4-49 40%. 60pp. Payment: in copies. Copyrights for author. Subject: Poetry.

ALMOST NORMAL COMICS and Other Oddities, W. E. Elliott, Almost Normal Comics, PO Box 12822, Ft. Huachuca, AZ 85670, info@almostnormalcomics.com, http://almostnormalcomics.com. 2001. Fiction, art, cartoons, interviews, letters. "Almost Normal Comics and Other Oddities is an anthology of alternative comics and weird stories showcasing the talents of artists and writers working in the small press." circ. 2000. Periodically. Pub'd 1 issue 2009; expects 1 issue 2010, 1 issue 2011. price per copy $3.50; sample $3.50. Back issues: $3.50. Discounts: 5 copies 50%. 88pp. Reporting time: 3 to 4 weeks. Simultaneous submissions accepted: Yes. Publishes 80% of manuscripts submitted. Payment: Complimentary copies of the issue work appears in. Copyrighted, reverts to author. No ads. Subjects: Arts, Avant-Garde, Experimental Art, Beat, William Blake, Charles Bukowski, Comics, Counter-Culture, Alternatives, Communes, Horror, H.P. Lovecraft, Movies, Music, Occult, Science Fiction, Tapes & Records, Zines.

Alms House Press, Alana Sherman, Lorraine S. DeGennaro, PO Box 218, Woodbourne, NY 12788-0218. 1985. Poetry. "16-24 pages of poetry that works as a collection. We seek variety and excellence in many styles. Each year we publish one or two chapbooks. Costs: $9 handling/reading fee. Chapbook sent to each contributor. Recent winners include Lenore Balliro, and William Vernon." avg. press run 200. Pub'd 4 titles 2009; expects 3-4 titles 2010, 3-4 titles 2011. 11 titles listed in the *Small Press Record of Books in Print* (36th Edition, 2010-11). Discounts: 50% bookstores; $10 set of five. 20pp. Reporting time: 4 months. We do not accept simultaneous submissions. Payment: 15 copies to the author. Copyrights for author. Subject: Poetry.

Alpine Guild, Inc., PO Box 4848, Dillon, CO 80435, Fax 970-262-9378, information@alpineguild.com. 1977. Non-fiction. "Publish books only, aimed at specific identifiable, reachable audiences. The book must provide information of value to the audience." Pub'd 3 titles 2009; expects 5 titles 2010, 3 titles 2011. 4 titles listed in the *Small Press Record of Books in Print* (36th Edition, 2010-11). Discounts: standard. Reporting time: within 30 days. Payment: depends on book, audience, etc. Copyrights for author. Subjects: Disabled, Education, Handicapped, Health, Leadership, Management, Medicine, Psychology, Publishing.

Alpine Press, S.F. Achenbach, PO Box 1930, Mills, WY 82644, 307-234-1990. 1985. Non-fiction. "*How To Be Your Own Veterinarian (Sometimes)*, by Ruth B. James, D.V.M. We do not read unsolicited manuscripts." avg. press run 15M. Pub'd 2 titles 2009; expects 1 title 2010, 2 titles 2011. 3 titles listed in the *Small Press Record of Books in Print* (36th Edition, 2010-11). Discounts: 1-2 copies 20%, 3-9 25%, 10+ 30%, freight paid with prepaid orders. 300pp. Reporting time: long. Payment: negotiated individually on merits of book. Copyrights for author. Subject: Agriculture.

Alpine Publications, Inc., Betty McKinney, Managing Editor, 38262 Linman Road, Crawford, CO 81415-9326, 970-921-5005, Fax 970-921-5081, alpinepubl@aol.com, www.alpinepub.com. 1975. Non-fiction. "We publish nonfiction hardback & trade paperback how-to books for the dog, horse, and pet markets. About half of our sales are by mail order. Our books are high quality, in-depth, thorough coverage of a specific subject or breed. Authors must know their field and be able to provide useful, how-to information with illustrations." avg. press run 2M. Pub'd 7 titles 2009; expects 10 titles 2010, 10 titles 2011. 89 titles listed in the *Small Press Record of Books in Print* (36th Edition, 2010-11). Discounts: 1-4 20%, 5-24 40%, 25+ 45%. 200pp. Reporting time: 8-12 weeks. Simultaneous submissions accepted: okay if notified as such. Payment: royalty. Copyrights for author. Subjects: Animals, Earth, Natural History, Pets.

Altair Publications, Edmond Wollmann, PO Box 221000, San Diego, CA 92192-1000, 858-453-2342, e-mail altair@astroconsulting.com. 1995. Art, photos, interviews. "Mostly academically oriented texts." avg. press run 5M. Pub'd 1 title 2009; expects 2 titles 2010, 3 titles 2011. 2 titles listed in the *Small Press Record of Books in Print* (36th Edition, 2010-11). Discounts: 40%. 300pp. Reporting time: 6-8 weeks. Simultaneous submissions accepted: no. Payment: negotiated. Copyrights for author. Subjects: Astrology, Metaphysics, Psychology, Spiritual, Theosophical.

AltaMira Press, Mitchell Allen, Publisher, 1630 N. Main Street #367, Walnut Creek, CA 94596, 301-459-3366, Fax 925-933-9720. 1995. Non-fiction. "AltaMira Press, a division of Rowman & Littlefield Publishers Inc., entered into a publishing agreement with the American Association for State and Local History Press in September, 1995. Under this agreement, AltaMira has assumed marketing, publishing, distributing, and selling of all book titles previously published by American Association for State and Local History Press." avg. press run 2M. Pub'd 40 titles 2009; expects 50 titles 2010, 60 titles 2011. 22 titles listed in the *Small Press Record of Books in Print* (36th Edition, 2010-11). Discounts: AASLH members 20%; trade 20%-40%. 200-300pp. Reporting time: 3-4 months. Payment: every 12 months. Copyrights for author. Subjects: Education, History.

ALTERNATIVE EDUCATION RESOURCE ORGANIZATION, Jerry Mintz, 417 Roslyn Road, Roslyn Heights, NY 11577, 516-621-2195, Fax 516-625-3257, jerryaero@aol.com. 1989. Articles, photos, interviews, satire, reviews, letters, news items, non-fiction. "Covers the latest developments and news in alternative education." circ. 700. 4/yr. Pub'd 3 issues 2009; expects 3 issues 2010, 4 issues 2011. sub. price $18.50; per copy $4.50. Back issues: $4.50. 24pp. Payment: none. Pub's reviews: 12 in 2009. §Only alternative education. Ads: subscription. Subject: Education.

ALTERNATIVE PRESS INDEX, Mary Burford, Co-Editor; Charles D'Adamo, Co-Editor; Kevin Jones, Co-Editor; Graham Stephenson, Co-Editor, Alternative Press Center, Inc., PO Box 47739, Chicago, IL 60647, 312-451-8133, altpress-AT-altpress.org. 1969. "The *Alternative Press Index* is a quarterly subject index to over 300 newspapers, magazines, and journals from around the world that focus on social theory and movements." circ. 700. biannual in print, quarterly online. Pub'd 4 issues 2009; expects 4 issues 2010, 4 issues 2011. sub. price $450 libraries (print), $75 individuals (print); sample free. Back issues: 50% discount if 3 or more print back volumes are purchased. Discounts: $75 individuals, high schools, movement groups. 700+pp. Copyrighted, reverts to author. No ads accepted. Subjects: Abstracts, Anarchist, Communism, Marxism, Leninism, Environment, Feminism, Gay, Global Affairs, Indexes & Abstracts, Indigenous Cultures, Political Science, Politics, Social Movements, Socialist, Sociology, Third World, Minorities.

ALTERNATIVE PRESS REVIEW, Jason McQuinn, Allan Antliff, Thomas Wheeler, PO Box 6245, Arlington, VA 22206. 1993. Articles, art, photos, cartoons, interviews, satire, criticism, reviews, music, letters, collages, news items, non-fiction. "Reprints from alternative press magazines, tabloids, newsletter & zines, plus original material covering the entire alternative press/alternative media scene, with an emphasis on periodical reviews & other media reviews." circ. 8M. 4/yr. Pub'd 2 issues 2009; expects 4 issues 2010, 4 issues 2011. sub.

price $16; per copy $4.95; sample $6. Discounts: wholesale 5-19 copies 20%, 20-59 40%, 60-99 45%, 100-249 50%, 250+ 55%. 68pp. Reporting time: 2-3 months. Simultaneous submissions accepted: yes. Publishes 5% of manuscripts submitted. Payment: 5¢/word for original contributions, or 2.5¢/word for reprints. Not copyrighted. Pub's reviews: 200 in 2009. §Alternative press, alternative media, alternative social issues & movements, critiques of mainstream media. Ads: $300/$187.50/$135 1/4 page/$120 1/6 page. Subjects: Communication, Journalism, Counter-Culture, Alternatives, Communes, Magazines, Reprints, Reviews.

Amadeus Press, Carol Flannery, Editorial Director, 19 West 21st Street, Suite 201, New York, NY 10010, 212-575-9265, fax 212-575-9270, www.amadeuspress.com. 1987. avg. press run 3000. Pub'd 10 titles 2009; expects 22 titles 2010, 22 titles 2011. No titles listed in the *Small Press Record of Books in Print* (36th Edition, 2010-11). 300pp. Reporting time: 4-6 weeks. We do not usually accept simultaneous submissions. Does not copyright for author. Subject: Music.

AMARILLO BAY, Jerry Craven, Editor-in-Chief, On-line journal, Jerry.Craven@amarillobay.org. *"Amarillo Bay* continues the tradition of literary magazines in the new medium of the Web. The Web eliminates the cost of printing, the major expense of most literary magazines. We seek the highest quality fiction, poetry, and creative nonfiction written in English anywhere in the world. Our editors will consider submissions from both unpublished and established writers. All submissions should be previously unpublished. Send all submissions as text files only. We will not read submissions that come to us as attached files. To send your work as a text file, copy and paste it into your e-mail. In your submission please include your post office address so that we can contact you if your e-mail address does not work. Send submissions to Jerry Craven. We normally respond to submissions within two months. Our funds are provided by donations and we solicit your contributions."

•THE AMBASSADOR POETRY PROJECT [online], www.ambassadorpoetry.com, info@ambassador-poetry.com. "The Ambassador Poetry Project aims to showcase poetic voices rooted in the MI & ON regions, regardless of author location. Emerging and established poets demonstrate the many themes and experiences relevant to the two regions whilst presenting individual tastes, styles, and voices. Please share the link with others and bookmark www.AmbassadorPoetry.com for future visits. If you have not yet submitted your poetry for consideration, please review the submission guidelines and consider sending in your work. Submissions are accepted year-round. The online periodical is published quarterly, in September, December, March, and June of each year. If you wish to be notified of news including web updates, event notifications, and special features, send an email to request the newsletter. Your email will not be shared with outside parties."

AMBIT, Martin Bax, 17 Priory Gardens, London, N6 5QY, England, 0181-340-3566. 1959. Poetry, fiction, art, photos, reviews, long-poems. "Always looking for material which excites and interests. Suggest contributors read the magazine before they submit." circ. 3M. 4/yr. Pub'd 4 issues 2009; expects 4 issues 2010, 4 issues 2011. sub. price £24 UK, £26 ($52) USA and overseas; per copy £6 UK, £8 overseas; sample £6 UK, £8 overseas. Back issues: recent back nos. £6 UK, £8 overseas; Archival issues £10. Discounts: bookstores 1-11 25%, 12+ 33%. 96pp. Reporting time: 4 months. Publishes less than 5% of manuscripts submitted. Payment: by arrangement. Copyrighted, reverts to author. Pub's reviews: 30+ in 2009. §Poetry. Ads: b&w: £325/£190/£115 1/4 page;colour £500/£280; serial ad discount 20% for 4 issues. Subjects: Fiction, Poetry.

AMERICA, 106 West 56th Street, New York, NY 10019, 212-581-4640. 1909. Poetry, articles, cartoons, interviews, reviews, letters, non-fiction. *"America* is a journal of opinion that publishes about 10 poems a year selected from over 1,000 submissions." circ. 40M. 41/yr. Pub'd 41 issues 2009; expects 41 issues 2010, 41 issues 2011. sub. price $43; per copy $2.25; sample $2.25. Back issues: $2.25. Discounts: call for details. 32pp. Reporting time: 3 weeks. Simultaneous submissions accepted: no. Payment: yes. Copyrighted, shared rights. Pub's reviews: 200+ in 2009. §General interest. Ads: call for ad brochure or ads@americapress.org.

America West Publishers, George Green, PO Box 2208, Carson City, NV 89702, 800-729-4131. 1985. Non-fiction. "New Age, new science & technology, new spirituality, metaphysics. Some recent contributors: Dr. Taki Anagoston, Dr. Eva Snead, and John Coleman, PhD." avg. press run 5M. Pub'd 14 titles 2009; expects 10 titles 2010. 15 titles listed in the *Small Press Record of Books in Print* (36th Edition, 2010-11). Discounts: bookstores 40%, distributors 50-60%, bulk (over 500) 50%, libraries 20%. 250pp. Reporting time: 4-6 weeks. Publishes 1% of manuscripts submitted. Payment: twice yearly—10% of wholesale net, 5% of retail price. Copyrights for author. Subjects: Earth, Natural History, Geology, Medicine, Politics, Psychology, Religion, Spiritual.

American Book Publishing, PMB 146, 5442 South 900 East, Salt Lake City, UT 84117-7204, info@american-book.com, http://www.american-book.com. Fiction, non-fiction. "Please submit electronically only, you can obtain our submission information at our website." Pub'd 70 titles 2009; expects 75 titles 2010, 75 titles 2011. No titles listed in the *Small Press Record of Books in Print* (36th Edition, 2010-11). 250pp. Reporting time: 30 days. Copyrights for author.

AMERICAN BOOK REVIEW, Jeffrey Di Leo, Publisher; Charles Alcorn, Managing Editor; David Felts, Associate Editor; Susie Albert, Senior Secretary, University of Houston-Victoria, School of Arts & Science,

Victoria, TX 77901, 361-570-4101, Fax. 1977. Reviews. "Length: ideally, 750-1.5M words. Reviewers should be primarily writers. Contributors: Marjorie Perloff, Michael Joyce, Steve Tomasula, Alicia Ostriker, Lance Olsen, Brian Evenson, etc." circ. 5M. 6/yr. Pub'd 6 issues 2009; expects 6 issues 2010, 6 issues 2011. sub. price $30 libraries & institutions, $35 foreign, $24 individuals, $40/2 years individuals; per copy $4; sample $4. Back issues: $4 (check w/office). 33pp. Reporting time: 1-2 months. Payment: $50 honorarium per review, or subscription. Copyrighted. Pub's reviews: 205 in 2009. §Literary or closely allied fields. Ads: check w/advertising manager. Subject: Literary Review.

American Canadian Publishers, Inc., Arthur Goodson, Editorial Director; Herman Zaage, Art Director, PO Box 4595, Santa Fe, NM 87502-4595, 505-983-8484, Fax 505-983-8484. 1972. Poetry, fiction, articles, art, photos, interviews, satire, criticism, reviews, music, letters, parts-of-novels, long-poems, collages, plays, concrete art, news items, non-fiction. "We are categorically against realism in the novel simply because it is by now a bankrupt form. We reject orthodox "story" because it generally tortures the truth to fit the formula. We support the novel that investigates "inner consciousness," that is multi-dimensional and open-structured in language and thought. Interested? Send SASE for free Catalog full of new examples. *No unsolicited manuscripts.* Thanks!" avg. press run 1.5M-3M. Pub'd 2 titles 2009; expects 2 titles 2010, 6 titles 2011. 11 titles listed in the *Small Press Record of Books in Print* (36th Edition, 2010-11). Discounts: 40% to dealers; 50% bulk-class adoptions: rates negotiable. 200pp. Payment: negotiable. Copyrights for author. Subjects: Arts, Criticism, Dada.

American Carriage House Publishing (see also LIFETIME MAGAZINE), Amie Weaver, Managing Editor; Joan Oas, Editor, P.O. Box 1130, Nevada City, California, CA 95959, phone 530.432.8860, fax 530.432.7379. 2003. Articles, news items, non-fiction. "Our mission is to educate the public on adoption, family and children's issues. Recent contributors include: Mardie Caldwell, Heather Featheston, Briana Caldwell, Heidi Zimmerman, and Amie Weaver. l." avg. press run 3500. Pub'd 1 title 2009; expects 4 titles 2010, 5 titles 2011. 15 titles listed in the *Small Press Record of Books in Print* (36th Edition, 2010-11). Discounts: Family, children, self-help, adoption. 390pp. Reporting time: 6 months. Simultaneous submissions accepted: No. Publishes 6% of manuscripts submitted. Payment: We are not accepting new submissions at this time. Copyrights for author. Subjects: Adoption, Children, Youth, Family.

THE AMERICAN DISSIDENT, G. Tod Slone, 1837 Main Street, Concord, MA 01742-3811, todslone@yahoo.com. 1998. Poetry, articles, art, cartoons, satire, criticism, reviews, non-fiction. "One page max. for poems, 750 words max. for essays. Material should be WRITTEN ON THE EDGE WITH A DASH OF RISK AND PERSONAL EXPERIENCE AND INVOLVEMENT. Suggested areas of critique include, though not exclusively, corruption in academe, poet laureates paid for by the Library of Congress, sell-out beatniks and hippies, artistes non-engags, politically-controlled state and national cultural councils, media whores, Medicare-bilking doctors, boards of wealthy used-car-salesperson trustees of public institutions, justice-indifferent lawyers, autocratic judges, thug cops, other dubious careerists, the happy-face culture of extreme denial and aberrant rationalization, the democratic sham masking the oligarchic plutocracy and, more generally, the human veil of charade placed upon the universe. If you are a professor, for example, send something critical of your college, not the President of the USA. Submissions should be negative, controversial, and confrontational with a strong dose of visceral indignation." circ. 200. 2/yr. Pub'd 2 issues 2009; expects 2 issues 2010, 2 issues 2011. 2 titles listed in the *Small Press Record of Books in Print* (36th Edition, 2010-11). sub. price $16; per copy $8; sample $8. Back issues: $8. Discounts: 10 copies for $70. 64pp. Reporting time: 1 week - 2 months. Simultaneous submissions accepted: yes. Publishes 4% of manuscripts submitted. Payment: 1 copy. Copyrighted, reverts to author. Pub's reviews: 2 in 2009. §Criticism, parrhesia, dissidence, poetry. Ads: $40/$20. Subjects: Absurdist, Anarchist, Arts, Beat, Bilingual, Cartoons, Counter-Culture, Alternatives, Communes, Education, Essays, Ethics, Literary Review, Literature (General), Magazines, Poetry, H.D. Thoreau.

THE AMERICAN DRIVEL REVIEW, Tara Blaine, 3561 SE Cora Drive, Portland, OR 97202, 503-236-6377 info@americandrivelreview.com www.americandrivelreview.com. 2004. Poetry, fiction, articles, art, photos, cartoons, interviews, satire, criticism, reviews, letters, parts-of-novels, long-poems, collages, plays, concrete art, news items, non-fiction. "The American Drivel Review: A Unified Field Theory of Wit. The American Drivel Review is a quarterly-published independent journal of literary humor founded in 2004. The editors put forth that humor holds, at best, an unexamined place in the literary world or, at worst, that the place of humor is one of an emaciated, flesh-eating cousin, locked in the attic to subsist solely on the occasional stray bat. Featuring works of humor ranging from the intellectual to the intestinal, ADR aims within its pages to liberate the elements of the comedic impulse from the pedestrian, observational trenches of culture and thereby fashion a true Unified Field Theory of Wit. Please view complete submission guidelines at http://www.americandrivelreview.com/submit.php." circ. 150. 4/yr. Pub'd 4 issues 2009; expects 4 issues 2010, 4 issues 2011. sub. price $20; per copy $3.50 + $1.50 shipping; sample $3.50 + $1.50 shipping. Back issues: $3.50 + $1.50 shipping. Discounts: 7-10 copies 50%. 100pp. Reporting time: 1-6 months. Simultaneous submissions accepted: No. Publishes 35% of manuscripts submitted. Payment: 2 contributor copies.

Copyrighted, reverts to author. Pub's reviews: none in 2009. §Humor, scientific studies, abstract concepts. Subjects: Absurdist, Anarchist, Arts, Cartoons, Comics, Dada, Entertainment, Experimental, Humor, Literature (General), Non-Fiction, Poetry, Prose, Reviews, Short Stories.

AMERICAN FORESTS, Michelle Robbins, Editor, PO Box 2000, Washington, DC 20013, 202-737-1944. 1895. Articles, art, photos, interviews, reviews, news items, non-fiction. "We are looking for factual articles that are well written, well illustrated, and will inform, entertain, and perhaps inspire. *We do not accept fiction and rarely accept poetry.* We welcome informative news stories on issues of interest to American Forests readers—look for topics that touch on projects or issues in which we have been involved. Articles should be neither too elementary nor too technical. A written or e-mailed query is required; we cannot accept phone queries. Include SASE with submissions." circ. 20M. 4/yr. Pub'd 4 issues 2009; expects 4 issues 2010, 4 issues 2011. sub. price $25 membership; per copy $3; sample $2 postage w/SASE. 48pp. Reporting time: 12-16 weeks. Simultaneous submissions accepted: yes. Payment: full length feature articles, *with photo or other illustrative support* ranges from $300 to $1,800; cover photos $500. Copyrighted, reverts to author. Ads: available on request. Subjects: Children, Youth, Conservation, Earth, Natural History, Environment, Folklore, History, Interviews, Nature, Photography, Sports, Outdoors.

AMERICAN HIKER, American Hiking Society, Gwyn Hicks, 1422 Fenwick Lane, Silver Spring, MD 20910-2160, 301-565-6704. 1977. Articles, photos, cartoons, interviews, reviews, news items. circ. 10M. 6/yr. Pub'd 6 issues 2009; expects 6 issues 2010, 6 issues 2011. sub. price $25; sample $2. Back issues: $4 if available. 32pp. Reporting time: 6 weeks. Publishes 5-10% of manuscripts submitted. Payment: $25-$50 for briefs, $75-$125 for lectures. Pub's reviews: 20 in 2009. §Books on the outdoors. Subjects: Cities, Conservation, Earth, Natural History, Environment, Sports, Outdoors.

American Hiking Society (see also AMERICAN HIKER), Darren Schwartz, 1422 Fenwick Lane, Silver Spring, MD 20910-2160, 301-565-6704. 1977. Articles, photos, interviews, reviews, news items. avg. press run 10M. Pub'd 6 titles 2009; expects 6 titles 2010, 6 titles 2011. 2 titles listed in the *Small Press Record of Books in Print* (36th Edition, 2010-11). Discounts: please inquire. 28pp. Reporting time: 6 weeks. Publishes 5% of manuscripts submitted. Payment: none. Does not copyright for author. Subjects: Conservation, Earth, Natural History, Environment, Sports, Outdoors.

American Homeowners Foundation Press, Bruce Hahn, 6776 Little Falls Road, Arlington, VA 22213, 703-536-7776, www.americanhomeowners.org. 1984. Non-fiction. "Booklets through books." avg. press run 3-10M. Pub'd 2 titles 2009; expects 3 titles 2010, 3 titles 2011. 3 titles listed in the *Small Press Record of Books in Print* (36th Edition, 2010-11). Discounts: standard. 160pp. Reporting time: varies. Payment: varies. We can copyright for author.

AMERICAN INDIAN CULTURE AND RESEARCH JOURNAL, American Indian Studies Center, Duane Champagne, UCLA, 3220 Campbell Hall, Los Angeles, CA 90095-1548, 310-825-7315, Fax 310-206-7060, www.sscnet.ucla.edu/esp/aisc/index.html. 1972. Poetry, fiction, articles, criticism, reviews. "*AICRJ* is a multidisciplinary journal that focuses on historical and contemporary issues as they pertain to American Indians. Some poetry and fiction are also published." circ. 1.2M. 4/yr. Pub'd 4 issues 2009; expects 4 issues 2010, 4 issues 2011. sub. price $25 individuals, $60 institutions; per copy $12. Back issues: $7 (varies by year). Discounts: bookstores and jobbers 20%, 40% if 10+. 300pp. Reporting time: 4 months (articles are refereed). Simultaneous submissions accepted: no. Publishes 10% of manuscripts submitted. Payment: none. Copyrighted, rights don't revert to author, but authors have permission to reprint free. Pub's reviews: 80 in 2009. Ads: $150/$75. Subjects: Essays, Native American, Poetry.

American Indian Studies Center (see also AMERICAN INDIAN CULTURE AND RESEARCH JOURNAL), Duane Champagne, 3220 Campbell Hall, Box 951458, UCLA, Los Angeles, CA 90095-1548, 310-825-7315, Fax 310-206-7060, www.sscnet.ucla.edu/esp/aisc/index.html. 1969. Poetry, fiction, articles, non-fiction. "AISC publishes books of interest to scholars and the general public that address contemporary and historical issues as they pertain to American Indians in addition to the quarterly *American Indian Culture and Research Journal.*" avg. press run 1M-2M. Pub'd 1 title 2009; expects 4 titles 2010, 2-3 titles 2011. 5 titles listed in the *Small Press Record of Books in Print* (36th Edition, 2010-11). Discounts: bookstores and jobbers 20%, 10+ 40%. 300pp. Reporting time: 6 months. Simultaneous submissions accepted: no. Publishes 5% of manuscripts submitted. Payment: varies per project. Does not copyright for author. Subjects: Essays, Fiction, Native American, Poetry.

AMERICAN JONES BUILDING & MAINTENANCE, Missing Spoke Press, Von G. Binuia, Editor, P.O. Box 4014, Concord, NH 03302, Tel:603-708-0093; Email: von@spokepress.com. 1997. Poetry, fiction, art, photos, interviews, satire, parts-of-novels, long-poems, non-fiction. "No line limits. No word limits. Send query with or regarding works of 9,000 or more words. Poetry, short fiction, essays, and interviews that address the interests and concerns of the working class in *American Jones Building & Maintenance.*" circ. 200. sub. price $12; per copy $6; sample $3. Back issues: $6. 128pp. Reporting time: 3-4 months. Simultaneous submissions accepted: yes. Publishes 2% of manuscripts submitted. Payment: various and 2 copies. Copyrighted, reverts to author. Pub's reviews: none in 2009. §Poetry. Subjects: Americana, Charles Bukowski, Community, Conservation, Bob Dylan, Essays, Fiction, Human Rights, Labor, New England, New Hampshire, Poetry, Short Stories, Washington (state), Worker.

AMERICAN JUROR (formerly FIJACTIVIST, 1989-2007), Iloilo Marguerite Jones, PO Box 5570, Helena, MT 59604-5570, 406-442-7800. 1989. Articles, art, photos, cartoons, interviews, reviews, letters, news items, non-fiction. "Mostly in-house, but we have arranged to publish relevant articles." circ. 3M. 4/yr. Pub'd 4 issues 2009; expects 4 issues 2010, 4 issues 2011. sub. price $35; per copy $10.; sample free info. package; sample FIJActivist $3. Discounts: ea/$10; 20 + $5 each. 12pp. Payment: none. Not copyrighted. Pub's reviews: 2 in 2009. §Law, juries, justice, court decisions, human rights, civil rights, individual rights, jurors, the jury. Ads: none. Subject: Law.

American Legacy Media, William Wood D., 1544 W 1620 N STE 1-G, Clearfield, UT 84015-8243, 801-774-5472, 1-866-233-8165, info@americanlegacymedia.com, http://americanlegacymedia.com. 2004. Non-fiction. "American Legacy Media specializes in publishing biographies, autobiographies, historic and military compilations; and essays focusing on historic review. Titles include "The Quiet Hero" Gary W. Toyn, Foreword by Bob Dole, Intro. by Orrin Hatch; "Kamikaze" by Yasuo Kuwahara and Gordon T. Allred; "Skinny Boy" by Gary A. Grahl. Unsolicited work is welcomed, but must comply with our submission guidelines found at AmericanLegacyMedia.com." avg. press run 3000. Pub'd 6 titles 2009; expects 8 titles 2010, 10 titles 2011. 7 titles listed in the *Small Press Record of Books in Print* (36th Edition, 2010-11). Exclusive Distributor: IPG (Independent Publishers Group. Standard discount rates apply. 300pp. Reporting time: 2-3 weeks. Simultaneous submissions accepted: Yes. Publishes 25% of manuscripts submitted. Payment: Standard royalty arrangments apply. Copyrights for author. Subjects: Autobiography, Biography, History, Memoirs, Mental Health, Military, Veterans, Mormon, Non-Fiction, Utah, War, World War II.

AMERICAN LETTERS & COMMENTARY, David Ray Vance, Co-editor; Catherine Kasper, Co-Editor, Dept. of English, Univ. of Texas at San Antonio, One UTSA Circle, San Antonio, TX 78249, amerletters@satx.rr.com, www.amletters.org. 1988. Poetry, fiction, articles, art, criticism, reviews, long-poems, non-fiction. "*AL&C* is an eclectic literary magazine featuring innovative and challenging writing in all forms. Past contributors include Barbara Guest, Paul Hoover, Christine Hume, Amy England, Ann Lauterbach, Donald Revell, C.D. Wright, Clauda Rankine and Susan Wheeler. Particularly interested in hybrid-genre works and experimental poetics. Open to new and lively voices in all genres." circ. 1.5M. 1/yr. Pub'd 1 issue 2009; expects 1 issue 2010, 1 issue 2011. sub. price $12/issue includes shipping to US; per copy $10 (+$2.00 s&h); sample $12 (includes US shipping). Back issues: $12 (includes US shipping). 200pp. Reporting time: Response for accepted work only. We accept simultaneous submissions if advised. Payment: one copy. Copyrighted, reverts to author. Pub's reviews: approx. 3 in 2009. §Poetry, literary fiction and nonfiction. Ads: $100/$50/exchange ads. Subjects: Essays, Experimental, Fiction, Literary Review, Poetry, Prose, Short Stories.

American Literary Press, Joe Cooney, Managing Editor, 8019 Belair Road #10, Baltimore, MD 21236, 410-882-7700, 800-873-2003, Fax 410-882-7703, amerlit@americanliterarypress.com, www.americanliterary-press.com. 1991. Poetry, fiction, long-poems, non-fiction. avg. press run 500-1M. Pub'd 50 titles 2009; expects 60 titles 2010, 70 titles 2011. 129 titles listed in the *Small Press Record of Books in Print* (36th Edition, 2010-11). Discounts: 1-5 40%, 6-25 43%, 26-50 46%. 200pp. Reporting time: 3-4 weeks. Simultaneous submissions accepted: yes. Publishes 20% of manuscripts submitted. Payment: 40%-50%. Copyrights for author. Subjects: African-American, Autobiography, Christianity, Fantasy, Feminism, Fiction, How-To, Humor, Inspirational, New Age, Novels, Peace, Poetry, Women.

AMERICAN LITERARY REVIEW, John Tait, Editor; C. L. Elerson, Managing Editor, PO Box 311307, University of North Texas, Denton, TX 76203-1307, 940-565-2755. 1990. Poetry, fiction. "Recent contributors: Nancy Eimers, Nance Van Winckel, Eric Pankey, Kathleen Peirce, William Olseon, Jesse Lee Kercheval, Andrew Feld, G.C. Waldrep, Michael Czyzniejewski, Dulcie Leimbach, Danit Brown, George Rabosa, William Pierce, Sandra Jacobs, Kurt Rheinheimer, Neela Vaswani." circ. 900. 2/yr. Pub'd 2 issues 2009; expects 2 issues 2010, 2 issues 2011. sub. price $14 individual, $25 institution; per copy $7 + $1 for shipping and handling; sample $7 + $1 for shipping and handling. Back issues: $6, if available. Discounts: standard. 128pp. Reporting time: 8-12 weeks. We accept simultaneous submissions if indicated. Publishes 5% of manuscripts submitted. Payment: 2 copies. Copyrighted, reverts to author. Pub's reviews: 2 in 2009. §Contemporary poetry, short story collections, creative nonfiction essays and memoirs. Ads: $150/$75/$50 must be camera ready. Subjects: Essays, Poetry, Short Stories.

AMERICAN LITERATURE, Duke University Press, Cathy N. Davidson, Editor; Michael Moon, Associate Editor, Box 90660, Duke University, Durham, NC 27708-0660, 919-684-3948. 1929. Articles, criticism, reviews. "American literature *only*. This journal of literary history, criticism, and bibliography reaches academics worldwide in literature, history, and American studies. Send review copies to Carol Rigsby, 304E Allen Building, Box 90020, Duke University, Durham, NC 27708-0020." circ. 5.5M. 4/yr. Pub'd 4 issues 2009;

expects 4 issues 2010, 4 issues 2011. sub. price $34 individuals, $80 institutions, $17 students with photocopy of current ID, foreign add $12 postage; per copy $18. Back issues: single $18; volume $72. 250pp. Reporting time: 3 months. Simultaneous submissions accepted: no. Publishes 7% of manuscripts submitted. Payment: 50 reprints. Copyrighted, rights optional with author. Pub's reviews: 175 in 2009. §American literary criticism, scholarship, bibliography. Ads: $325/$225. Subjects: Bibliography, Criticism.

American Poet, Dan Brady, Managing Editor, The Academy of American Poets, 584 Broadway, Suite 604, New York, NY 10012, 212-274-0343, fax 212-274-9427, www.poets.org. *"American Poet* is the journal of the Academy of American Poets." No titles listed in the *Small Press Record of Books in Print* (36th Edition, 2010-11).

THE AMERICAN POETRY JOURNAL, J.P. Dancing Bear, PO Box 2080, Aptos, CA 95001-2080, editor@americanpoetryjournal.com, www.americanpoetryjournal.com. 2003. Poetry, articles, criticism, reviews. *"The APJ* seeks to publish work using poetic device, favoring image, metaphor and good sound. We like alliteration, extended metaphors, image, movement and poems that can pass the 'so what' test. *The APJ* has in mind the reader who delights in discovering what a poem can do to the tongue and what the poem paints on the cave of the mind. *The APJ* wants to provide the poems published within its pages the best possible focus and seeks to further promote them through reviewers and literary websites as well as by nominating works to the Pushcart Prize. *The APJ* also offers the American Poet Prize. We now accept email submissions—number of poems and guidelines apply to electronic submisions, email to: apjsubmission@yahoo.com. Please send submissions of no more than five poems either in the body of the message or as a DOC or RTF file. A cover letter is a nice way to break the ice but not necessary, however, be sure to include contact information such as: name, address, phone, and email address for response. Subscribers may submit work throughout the year. Submission period is Feb 1 through May 31, with responses by June 30." 1/yr. Pub'd 1 issue 2009; expects 1 issue 2010, 1 issue 2011. sub. price $12; per copy $12. 100pp. Simultaneous submissions accepted: yes. Publishes 1% of manuscripts submitted. Payment: 1 copy. Copyrighted, reverts to author. Pub's reviews. §Poetry. Subject: Poetry.

AMERICAN POETRY REVIEW, Stephen Berg, David Bonanno, Elizabeth Scanlon, 1700 Sansom St., Suite 800, Philadelphia, PA 19103-5214, 215-496-0439. 1972. Poetry, fiction, articles, art, photos, cartoons, interviews, satire, criticism, reviews, music, letters, parts-of-novels, long-poems, collages, plays, concrete art, news items, non-fiction. circ. 16,000. 6/yr. Pub'd 6 issues 2009; expects 6 issues 2010. sub. price $22; per copy $4.25; sample $4.25. Back issues: $5. Discounts: through Ingram for stores and newsstands. 56pp. Reporting time: 10 weeks. Simultaneous submissions accepted: no. Publishes less than 1% of manuscripts submitted. Payment: $1/line for poetry; $60/tabloid page for prose. Copyrighted, reverts to author. Pub's reviews: 30 in 2009. §Literary. Ads: $950/$575. Subject: Poetry.

AMERICAN ROAD, Mock Turtle Press, Thomas Repp MFA, Executive Editor, PO Box 46519, Mont Clemens, MI 48046, Orders 1-877-285-5434 x1. General information 586-468-7483, fax 877-285-5434, sales@americanroadmagazine.com, www.americanroadmagazine.com, General Manager Becky Repp 206-369-5782. 2003. "Writers should request a copy of our guidelines and become familiar with American Road magazine prior to submitting queries. E-mail queries preferred. Be sure to include information on photographic support." circ. 10M. 4/yr. Pub'd 4 issues 2009; expects 4 issues 2010, 4 issues 2011. sub. price $16.95 (US), Canadian orders add $13/yr s/h, foreign orders add $24/yr s/h; per copy $4.95; sample $5 (includes s/h) for authors. Back issues: $4.95 + $2.50 s/h or $5.00 s&h for 2-4 issues. $10.00 s&h for 5-15 issues. Discounts: 2-4 copies 30%, 5+ 40%; also distributed by Prestige. 68pp. Reporting time: 6 months average. Simultaneous submissions accepted: no. Publishes 1% of manuscripts submitted. Payment: 13¢/published word. Pub's reviews: 6 in 2009. §Historic highways. Ads: Full $2463, half $1479. Subjects: Americana, History, Non-Fiction, Transportation, Travel.

American Short Fiction, Stacey Swann, Editor; Jill Meyers, Managing Editor; Rebecca Bengal, Contributing Editor, PO Box 301209, Austin, TX 78703, 512.538.1305 (voice), 512.538.1306 (fax), web: americanshortfiction.org, email: editors@americanshortfiction.org, subscriptions@americanshortfiction.org. 1991-1998; Relaunched in 2006. "American Short Fiction is a quarterly magazine of new fiction and, occasionally essays and artwork that re-launched in Winter 2006. During its first run from 1991 to 1998, the magazine was a a two-time finalist for the National Magazine Award in Fiction. American Short Fiction has published some of the finest writers working in the form, including Joy Williams, Desmond Hogan, Reynolds Price, Gina Berriault, Louise Erdrich, Dagoberto Gilb, Andrea Barrett, Antonya Nelson, Joyce Carol Oates, Charles Baxter, Ursula K. Le Guin, and Dan Chaon, among many others. Four times a year, the magazine's editors select and publish short stories and novel excerpts by established and new writers. It is our goal to discover and publish new fiction in which transformations of language, narrative, and character occur swiftly, deftly, and unexpectedly. Authors wishing to submit short stories to American Short Fiction should read an issue of the magazine, which is available in bookstores and at http://www.americanshortfiction.org. Complete submission guidelines are also available on our Web site. Please note that we do not accept submissions by email, and we only read unsolicited fictionmeaning, we do not accept unsolicited submissions of essays or artwork." avg. press run 3000. Expects 4 titles 2010, 4 titles 2011. No titles listed in the *Small Press Record of Books in Print* (36th Edition, 2010-11). Simultaneous submissions are fine as long as they are clearly marked as such, and the author notifies the editors immediately if the submission is accepted elsewhere. Payment is competitive but varies.

AMERICAN TANKA, Tim Younce, 57 Fawn Drive, Fairfield, OH 45014, americantanka@earthlink.net, www.americantanka.com. 1996. Poetry. "This journal is dedicated exclusively to English-language tanka poetry." circ. 150. Annual. Pub'd 1 issue 2009; expects 1 issue 2010, 1 issue 2011. sub. price $20; per copy $12; sample $12. Back issues: 3 for $20. 96pp. Reporting time: 12-16 weeks. Simultaneous submissions accepted: no. Publishes 10% of manuscripts submitted. Copyrighted, reverts to author. Ads: none. Subject: Poetry.

AMERICAN VEGAN, Freya Dinshah, 56 Dinshah Lane, PO Box 369, Malaga, NJ 08328-0908, 856/694-2887, www.americanvegan.org. 1960. Articles, cartoons, interviews, reviews, letters, news items. "Our mission is to inform the general public about vegan living, amd to encourage and inspire people to adopt this compassiionate lifestyle." 4/yr. sub. price $20 or $10; per copy $3; sample $2. Back issues: $3. Discounts: 50%. 32pp. Reporting time: up to one month. Simultaneous submissions accepted: No. Payment: 1 year subscription. Copyrighted, reverts to author. Pub's reviews: approx 20 in 2009. §vegan lifestyle issues. Subjects: Environment, Ethics, Fashion, Food, Eating, Gardening, Health.

AMERICAN WRITER, Craig Withers, 509 Woodlake Ln, Pontiac, MI 48340, 810-625-6221 witherscraig@gmail.com. 2009. Fiction. "We are a publication that seeks to recognize new, talented American writers. We are looking for short stories of 2,000-20,000 words, in any genre. For each issue we will run a contest with monetary prizes." circ. 100. 4/yr. Expects 2 issues 2010, 4 issues 2011. sub. price $32; per copy $10; sample $10. Back issues: inquire. Discounts: 2 or more copies 25%. 50pp. Reporting time: 4-6 weeks. Simultaneous submissions accepted: Yes. Publishes 10% of manuscripts submitted. Payment: $25-$150 per published article; pays on publication. Not copyrighted. §Original short stories from American writers. Ads: $100/$50/$25.

The American Zen Association (see also HERE AND NOW), 748 Camp St, New Orleans, LA 70130, Phone 504-525-3533, Fax 504-565-4690, info@nozt.org, www.nozt.org. 5 titles listed in the *Small Press Record of Books in Print* (36th Edition, 2010-11).

Amherst Writers & Artists Press, Inc. (see also PEREGRINE), Pat Schneider, Editor; Nancy Rose, Assistant Editor, PO Box 1076, Amherst, MA 01004, 413-253-7764 phone/Fax, awapress@aol.com, www.amherstwriters.com. 1981. Poetry, fiction, reviews. avg. press run 800-1M. Pub'd 3 titles 2009; expects 3 titles 2010, 3 titles 2011. 17 titles listed in the *Small Press Record of Books in Print* (36th Edition, 2010-11). 100+pp. Simultaneous submissions accepted: yes. Copyrights for author. Subjects: Children, Youth, Dance.

Ammons Communications; Imprint: Catch the Spirit of Appalachia, Amy Garza Ammons, 29 Regal Ave, Amy, Sylva, NC 28779-2877, v.ammons@mchsi.com. 1985. Poetry, fiction, art, photos, plays, non-fiction. "Ammons Communications believes everyone has a story they could tell. Our mission is to give the writer a voice and suggestions as how to to best market his/her work. Much of what we publish is based on heritage or is something the author feels strongly about and has first hand knowledge that will benefit the reader. We are a cooperative publishing house. We take a manuscript and do all the work necessary for the author to have a book in his/her hand, and charge for our preparatory work only one time, giving the author full rights for his/her book. We find the most economical printer, and author pays for the printing. Free Estimates. Recent: Memories of Merritt Island by Gail Briggs Nolen, White Feather by Nancy M. Pafford." avg. press run 1000. Pub'd 5 titles 2009; expects 4 titles 2010. 37 titles listed in the *Small Press Record of Books in Print* (36th Edition, 2010-11). Discounts: 2-10 30%. 250pp. Reporting time: Upon receipt, we send a letter stating our terms. Publishing is in the hands of the writer. Simultaneous submissions accepted: Yes. Publishes 90% of manuscripts submitted. Payment: We are co-operative publishers. Authors have full rights for their work. Copyrights for author. Subjects: Americana, Appalachia, Arts, Family, Fiction, Folklore, History, Inspirational, North Carolina, Novels, Performing Arts, Photography, Picture Books, Poetry, Storytelling.

Amsterdam University Press, Saskia de Vries, Prinsengracht 747-751, 1017 JX, Amsterdam, The Netherlands, T 0031 (0)20 4200050, F 0031 (0)20 4203412, www.aup.nl. No titles listed in the *Small Press Record of Books in Print* (36th Edition, 2010-11).

Anacus Press, An Imprint of Finney Company (see also Finney Company, Inc.), Alan Krysan, President, 8075 215th Street West, Lakeville, MN 55044, (952) 469-6699, Fax: (952) 469-1968, (800) 326-9272, Fax: (800) 330-6232 feedback@finneyco.com, www.anacus.com. 1995. Non-fiction. "This imprint of Finney Company offers bicycling guides and bicycling narratives for hard-core bike riding enthusiasts and leisure riders. We have a Ride Guide Series and a Bed, Breakfast and Bike Series." avg. press run 5000. Expects 1 title 2010, 1-3 titles 2011. No titles listed in the *Small Press Record of Books in Print* (36th Edition, 2010-11). Discounts: 1-9 copies 20%; 10-24 copies 40%; 25-49 copies 45%; 50 or more copies 50%. 112-400pp.

Reporting time: 8-10 weeks. Simultaneous submissions accepted: Yes. Payment: varies. Subjects: Bicycling, Great Lakes, Leisure/Recreation, Non-Fiction, Pacific Northwest, Transportation, Travel.

Anagnosis, Aris Karey, Deliyianni 3, Maroussi 15122, Greece, +302106254654, Fax:+302106254089, www.anagnosis.gr. 2002. Non-fiction. "Anagnosis is a publishing house based in Athens, Greece. We publish and sell books in the English and Greek languages. We specialize in books on: Greek Life, History and Culture; and Educational Books (including texts for the International Baccalaureate)." Pub'd 4 titles 2009; expects 4 titles 2010, 5 titles 2011. No titles listed in the *Small Press Record of Books in Print* (36th Edition, 2010-11). Discounts: 35% to bookstores, retailers, to schools depending upon size of order. Reporting time: 1 month. Payment: to be discussed. Copyrights for author. Subjects: Anthropology, Archaelogy, Folklore, Greek, History, Philosophy, Travel.

Anancybooks, Beresford McLean, PO Box 28677, San Jose, CA 95159-8677, 408-286-0726, Fax 408-947-0668, info@anancybooks.com, www.anancybooks.com. Expects 1 title 2010. 2 titles listed in the *Small Press Record of Books in Print* (36th Edition, 2010-11). 503pp. Publishes 100% of manuscripts submitted. Copyrights for author.

ANARCHY: A Journal of Desire Armed, Lawrence Jararch, PO Box 3448, Berkeley, CA 94703, editor@anarchymag.org. 1980. Poetry, fiction, articles, art, photos, cartoons, satire, criticism, reviews, letters, collages, news items, non-fiction. "Features: 1,000 to 4,500 words. Reviews: 200-750 words (unless previously queried-up to 1,500 words)." circ. 7M. 2/yr. Pub'd 2 issues 2009; expects 2 issues 2010, 2 issues 2011. sub. price $8 media mail; per copy $8.00; sample $10 postpaid. Back issues: $6 for 1st, $4 each for additional back issues. Discounts: 10-19 copies 40%, 20-59 50%, 60-99 55%, 100-249 40%. 84pp. Reporting time: 6 months. Simultaneous submissions accepted: yes. Publishes 5-10% of manuscripts submitted. Payment: $28/4 issues in US; $50/4 issues outside US. Not copyrighted. Pub's reviews: 20 Books, 60 Magazines in 2009. §Anarchist, libertarian/anti-authoritarian books, sexual liberation, feminism, ecology, radical history, atheism. No ads. Subjects: Anarchist, Libertarian.

Anchor Cove Publishing, Inc., Thomas McEwen, PO Box 270588, Littleton, CO 80128, Tel 303-972-0099, Fax 303-265-9119. 2005. Non-fiction. "Primary focus is books on recreational boating." avg. press run 5000. Expects 1 title 2010. 1 title listed in the *Small Press Record of Books in Print* (36th Edition, 2010-11). Discounts: Bookstores and retailers 40%, Distributors 55%. 800pp. Reporting time: 2 to 3 weeks. Simultaneous submissions accepted: Yes. Publishes 5% of manuscripts submitted. Does not copyright for author. Subjects: Leisure/Recreation, Sports, Outdoors.

ANCIENT PATHS, Skylar Hamilton Burris, PO Box 7505, Fairfax Station, VA 22039, ssburris@cox.net http://www.editorskylar.com. 1998. Poetry, fiction, art, reviews, parts-of-novels. "The submission period for Issue 16 closes in June of 2010. Issue 16 will be published in January of 2011. Check the website for ordering information. Issue 16 will be the last issue of Ancient Paths literary magazine. However, Ancient Paths Publications will begin publishing chapbooks in 2012. See the website beginning in February of 2011 for submission guidelines." circ. 100-200. biennial (January of odd years). Pub'd 1 issue 2009; expects 1 issue 2011. 2 titles listed in the *Small Press Record of Books in Print* (36th Edition, 2010-11). sub. price $12; per copy $12; sample $8 (discounted price for Issue 14 or 15). Back issues: $8. Discounts: N/A. 80pp. Reporting time: initial response in 4-5 weeks. We accept simultaneous submissions and some reprints (entire ms. cannot be a reprint, but up to 30% may be). Publishes 8% of manuscripts submitted. Payment: 1 free copy and $50 total will go to each featured poet and writer. Artists are paid $10 per work. Not copyrighted. Ads: $35 one-half page. Subjects: Christianity, Fiction, Literature (General), Poetry, Prose, Religion, Short Stories.

ANDERBO.COM, Rick Rofihe, Editor, 270 Lafayette St., Suite 1412, New York, NY 10012, editors@anderbo.com. 2005. Poetry, fiction, photos, non-fiction. "On-line periodical. Send submissions to editors@anderbo.com. A submission may be sent in the body of an e-mail and/or as an attachment in any common file format such as doc or rtf. Mac users, please be sure that your doc files are readable by PCs. Poets, we prefer your poems to be in the e-mail, or together as a single attachment." circ. 500 unique visitors (3000 hits) daily. Continuous. Reporting time: Usually within 1 to 3 days. Simultaneous submissions accepted: OK. Publishes 1% of manuscripts submitted. Copyrighted, reverts to author.

Anderson Publishing; also RC Anderson Books (see also Redgreene Press), R.C. Anderson, Editor, Publisher, PO Box 22322, Pittsburgh, PA 15222, 412-231-0436. 1995. Poetry, fiction, articles, art, photos, interviews, satire, criticism, music, letters, collages, plays, non-fiction. "Query by letter with SASE or call during business hours; do NOT send unsolicited work, please - we must communicate first. I pride myself on quality editing and design as well as openness to the author's ideas. Usually the author pays all expenses." 2 titles listed in the *Small Press Record of Books in Print* (36th Edition, 2010-11). Payment: 15% royalties once I sell 300 copies, paid annually. Willing to copyright for author or to advise. Subjects: Alternative Medicine, Biography, Education, Erotica, Family, Feminism, How-To, Human Rights, Indexes & Abstracts, Inspirational, Metaphysics, New Age, Poetry, Science, Women.

Androgyne Books, Ken Weichel, 930 Shields, San Francisco, CA 94132, 415-586-2697. 1971. Poetry, fiction, articles, art, photos, criticism, collages, plays. "Please contact press before sending mss.See our website at: www.androgynebooks.org." avg. press run 500. Pub'd 2 titles 2009; expects 4 titles 2010. 27 titles listed in the *Small Press Record of Books in Print* (36th Edition, 2010-11). Discounts: 40% bookstores, 50% wholesalers. 200pp. Reporting time: 3 weeks. Payment: 10% of press run. Copyrights for author. Subjects: Avant-Garde, Experimental Art, Beat, Biography, California, Dada, Fiction, Literature (General), Poetry, Prose, Reviews, San Francisco, Short Stories, Surrealism.

Andros Books, Susanne L. Bain, Kevin R. Bain, P. O. Box 2887, Mesa, AZ 85204, androsbks@aol.com. 1999. Fiction, non-fiction. "Nonfiction relating to home school. Gentle women's fiction with a positive attitude. Printed length approximating 200 pages (ms. 300 pages). We are a new publisher and are looking for fresh, positive works. Nothing erotic or violent. We can only return ms. mailed with SASE (w/adequate postage)." avg. press run 1K. Pub'd 1 title 2009; expects 2 titles 2010, 3-4 titles 2011. 1 title listed in the *Small Press Record of Books in Print* (36th Edition, 2010-11). 200pp. Reporting time: 30-60 days. We accept simultaneous submissions, but notify us of status. Payment: 7%, no advance. Does not copyright for author. Subjects: Education, Parenting, Women.

ANHEDONIA, Brian Anderson, 4227 Elderwood Drive, Seabrook, TX 77586. 2006. Poetry, fiction, art, photos, plays, non-fiction. "*Anhedonia* is a psychological term meaning the inability to feel pleasure. Hence, our editorial tastes tend to run toward the dark side of the spectrum. The magazine is edited by college students but is not officially affiliated with a college. We welcome outside submissions, but since the magazine is only published once a year in conjunction with a class, submissions are only accepted Dec.-March of each year." circ. 100. 1/yr. Pub'd 1 issue 2009; expects 1 issue 2010, 1 issue 2011. price per copy $7; sample free online. Back issues: $7. Discounts: Free issues distributed to college students and surrounding community. 40pp. Reporting time: 1 month. Simultaneous submissions accepted: Yes. Payment: 1 contributor copy. Not copyrighted. Subjects: Adolescence, Death & Dying, Feminism, Mental Health, Sex, Sexuality.

Anhinga Press, Rick Campbell, Director; Lynne Knight, President, PO Box 10595, Tallahassee, FL 32302, 850-442-1408, Fax 850-442-6323, info@anhinga.org, www.anhinga.org. 1973. Poetry. "The Anhinga Prize is open to all poets writing in English who have not yet published a second full-length book of poetry, carries an award of $2000 plus publication, requires an entry fee of $20US, and is judged anonymously. See our web site or send SASE for complete details. Aside from the contest, we publish three or four additional manuscripts per year." avg. press run 1200. Pub'd 5 titles 2009; expects 5 titles 2010, 6 titles 2011. 26 titles listed in the *Small Press Record of Books in Print* (36th Edition, 2010-11). Discounts: 40%. 96pp. Reporting time: varies greatly, contest submissions 10 months. Simultaneous submissions accepted: yes. Publishes 1% of manuscripts submitted. Payment: varies. Copyrights for author. Subjects: Literature (General), Poetry.

ANIMAL PEOPLE, Merritt Clifton, Editor; Kim Bartlett, President & Administrator, PO Box 960, Clinton, WA 98236-0960. 1992. News items, non-fiction. "*Animal People*, published for people who care about animals enough to try to help them, is the leading independent newspaper and electronic information service covering animal protection worldwide. We emphasize original investigative reporting, both from the field and in hot pursuit of paper trails, on topics ranging from animal care-and-control in your own home town to zoological conservation in the middle of nowhere. We document problems and spotlight effective responses, with verifiable statistics; cut through the hyperbole of fundraising appeals to show who is really doing what with the money; and take seriously the late humane advocate William Randolph Hearst's maxim that the purpose of news media should be to 'Comfort the afflicted, afflict the comfortable, print the news and raise hell.' We have no alignment or affiliation with any other entity. Our policy is simply, 'Be kind to animals'; our interest is in all the many ways that may be done." circ. 15M. 9/yr. Pub'd 9 issues 2009; expects 9 issues 2010, 9 issues 2011. sub. price $24; per copy $3; sample send free sample on request. Back issues: $3. 24pp. Reporting time: 1 week maximum. Simultaneous submissions accepted: no. Payment: none for opinion pieces; 15¢ a word for features. Copyrighted, reverts to author. Pub's reviews: 36 in 2009. §Animals. Ads: $1785/$1.00 per word classified. Subject: Animals.

THE ANNALS OF IOWA, Marvin Bergman, 402 Iowa Avenue, Iowa City, IA 52240, 319-335-3931, fax 319-335-3935, e-mail marvin-bergman@uiowa.edu. 1863. Articles, reviews. circ. 1M. 4/yr. Pub'd 4 issues 2009; expects 4 issues 2010, 4 issues 2011. sub. price $20; per copy $7; sample none. Discounts: 20% for resale. 120pp. Reporting time: 90 days. Simultaneous submissions accepted: no. Publishes 25% of manuscripts submitted. Payment: none. Copyrighted, does not revert to author. Pub's reviews: c. 80 in 2009. §History of Iowa and the Midwest; other relevant state and local history. Subjects: Biography, Book Reviewing, History, Iowa, Midwest.

Annedawn Publishing, Don Langevin, PO Box 247, Norton, MA 02766-0247, 508-222-9069. 1992. Non-fiction. "I now accept unsolicited manuscripts, both of a horticultural and birdwatching nature, from writers in search of publishers." avg. press run 10M. Pub'd 1 title 2009; expects 1 title 2010, 1 title 2011. 8 titles listed in the *Small Press Record of Books in Print* (36th Edition, 2010-11). Discounts: Vary. 192pp.

23

Reporting time: 1 month. Publishes 10% of manuscripts submitted. Payment: credit card. Copyrights for author. Subjects: Birds, Gardening, How-To.

Annick Press Ltd., Rick Wilks, Colleen MacMillan, 15 Patricia Avenue, Toronto, ON M2M 1H9, Canada, 416-221-4802, Fax 416-221-8400, annickpress@annickpress.com. 1975. Fiction, non-fiction. "We cannot accept unsolicited manuscripts any longer." avg. press run 10M. Pub'd 23 titles 2009; expects 26 titles 2010, 30 titles 2011. 319 titles listed in the *Small Press Record of Books in Print* (36th Edition, 2010-11). Discounts: order from Firefly Books Ltd., 66 Leek Cr, Richmond Hill,Ont. L4B 1H1, or your favorite supplier. 24-400pp. Reporting time: 3 months. Payment: twice a year. Copyrights for author. Subjects: Children, Youth, Young Adult.

Anomaly Press, Selma Miriam, Betsey Beaven, Noel Furie, 85 Ferris Street, Bridgeport, CT 06605, 203-576-9168. 1980. "We publish cookbooks and material of interest to feminists." avg. press run 5M. Pub'd 1 title 2009; expects 1 title 2011. 4 titles listed in the *Small Press Record of Books in Print* (36th Edition, 2010-11). Discounts: 40% for 5 or more copies; single copies, net. 348pp. Payment: 10% royalty fees. Copyrights for author. Subjects: Ecology, Foods, Feminism, Health, Lesbianism, Women.

ANOTHER CHICAGO MAGAZINE(ACM), Barry Silesky, Senior Editor, 3709 North Kenmore, Chicago, IL 60613, 312-248-7665, www.anotherchicagomag.com. 1976. Poetry, fiction, articles, art, photos, cartoons, interviews, satire, criticism, reviews, long-poems. "Recent contributors have included Albert Goldbarth, Diane Wakoski, Wanda Coleman, Alan Cheuse, Perry Glasser, Sterling Plumpp, Stuart Dybek, and Nin Andrews. Send work from February 1st to August 31st." circ. 2.5M. 2/yr. Pub'd 2 issues 2009; expects 2 issues 2010, 2 issues 2011. sub. price $14.95; per copy $8; sample $8. Back issues: $8. Discounts: 10% on 10 or more. 220pp. Reporting time: 10 weeks. Simultaneous submissions accepted: yes. Publishes 2% of manuscripts submitted. Payment: copy + 1 year subscription, token honorarium when possible. Copyrighted, reverts to author. Pub's reviews: 20 in 2009. §Small press poetry, fiction, literary reviews or criticism. Ads: $250/$125. Subjects: Fiction, Photography, Poetry, Politics, Reviews.

ANQ: A Quarterly Journal of Short Articles, Notes, and Reviews, Elizabeth Foxwell, Managing Editor, 1319 18th Street NW, Washington, DC 20036, 202-296-6267 x275, Fax 202-293-6130, www.heldref.org. 1988. Articles, criticism, reviews. "*ANQ*, formerly titled *American Notes and Queries*, is a medium of exchange for bibliographers, biographers, editors, lexicographers, and textual scholars. From sources and analogues to the identification of allusions, from variant manuscript readings to previously neglected archives, from Old English word studies to *OED* supplements, from textual emendations to corrections of bibliographies and other scholarly reference works, *ANQ* provides a needed outlet for short factual research concerning the language and literature of the English-speaking world. We publish signed reviews of critical studies, new editions, and recently published bibliographies. Manuscripts offering only explication de textes are not appropriate. Manuscript length should not exceed 1,600 words in length; must be accompanied by loose stamps and a self-addressed envelope for the return mailings; and must follow the MLA documentation style that includes parenthetical citations in the text and an alphabetized list of Works Cited as described in *The MLA Style Manual*. Authors are responsible for reading and correcting proofs." circ. 500. 4/yr. Pub'd 4 issues 2009; expects 4 issues 2010, 4 issues 2011. sub. price $52 individual, $96 institution; per copy $24; sample same. Back issues: contact publisher for back issue prices. 64pp. Reporting time: 1 month. Simultaneous submissions accepted: no. Payment: 2 copies of the issue in which the author's contribution appears. Copyrighted, rights revert to author only upon request. Pub's reviews: 18 in 2009. §Bibliographies, new scholarly editions of the major poets, novelists, essayists, and men-of-letters of the English-speaking world, critical studies. Ads: $155. Subjects: Bibliography, Biography, Book Reviewing, Drama, English, Fiction, Literary Review, Literature (General), Theatre.

ANTHILLS, Centennial Press, Charles Nevsimal, Editor, PO Box 170322, Milwaukee, WI 53217-8026, www.centennialpress.com, chuck@centennialpress.com. 2000. Poetry. "Firm in our resolve to provide only the best poesy available in this (or any) hemisphere, Centennial Press is prepared to elicit a new era of quality in what we have christened: the language of the heart. Past issues have included words by A.D. Winans, William Taylor Jr., Antler, Gunther C. Fogle, John Sweet, Matt Cook, Susan Firer, justin.barrett, Hugh Fox, Alex Carlson, Glenn W. Cooper, and other substantial small press poets and underdog writers." Simultaneous submissions accepted: Yes. Payment: One (1) copy per contributor. Copyrighted, reverts to author.

Anthony Publishing Company, Carol K. Anthony, Hanna Moog, 206 Gleasondale Road, Stow, MA 01775-1356, 978-897-7191. 1980. "Certain work on the subject of I Ching only." avg. press run 5M. Pub'd 7 titles 2009. 8 titles listed in the *Small Press Record of Books in Print* (36th Edition, 2010-11). Discounts: 1-4 30%, 5+ 40%. 250pp. Reporting time: 1 week. Simultaneous submissions accepted: no. Publishes 1% of manuscripts submitted. Payment: yearly. Copyrights for author. Subjects: Asia, Indochina, Philosophy, Psychology.

Anti-Aging Press (see also SO YOUNG!), Julia Busch, Box 142174, Coral Gables, FL 33114, 305-662-3928, juliabusch@att.net. 1992. Poetry, articles, cartoons, reviews, non-fiction. "Additional address: 4185 Pamona Avenue, Coconut Grove, FL 33133. Committed to erasing wrinkles on all levels—mental, emotional, physical via books, cassettes, newsletters. Imprint Kosmic Kuprints for spiritual, metaphysical, New Age titles." avg. press run 3M-5M. Pub'd 1 title 2009; expects 2 titles 2010, 2 titles 2011. 9 titles listed in the *Small Press Record of Books in Print* (36th Edition, 2010-11). Discounts: 1-2 copies 20%, 3-4 30%, 5-199 40%, 200+ 50%; payment with order; returns. 128-256pp. Payment: royalty on wholesale, or outright buy. We copyright for author, but depends on individual arrangement. Subjects: Acupuncture, Aging, Book Reviewing, Health, How-To, Newsletter, Non-Fiction, Poetry, Self-Help.

THE ANTIGONISH REVIEW, Jeanette Lynes, Co-Editor; Gerald Trites, Co-Editor, St Francis Xavier University, PO Box 5000, Antigonish, Nova Scotia B2G 2W5, Canada, Phone: 902-867-3962; Email: TAR@stfx.ca; Website: www.antigonishreview.com. 1970. Poetry, fiction, articles, art, interviews, criticism, reviews. "All submissions from U.S. must be accompanied by Postal Reply Coupons; submissions accompanied by U.S. postage will not be returned." circ. 1000. 4/yr. Pub'd 4 issues 2009; expects 4 issues 2010, 4 issues 2011. sub. price $24 in Canada; $30 in US; $40.00 International; per copy $10; sample $7 accompanied by postage. Back issues: $7. plus postage. Discounts: 20%. 144pp. Reporting time: 4-6 months. Simultaneous submissions accepted: no. Publishes 20% of manuscripts submitted. Payment: $30.00/page for poetry; $100 for fiction; $50 reviews; $100 for articles and essays plus 2 copies of issue. Copyrighted. Pub's reviews: 26 in 2009. §Literary, biographies and autobiographies of poets, writers, artists. Ads: query to TAR@stfx.ca. Subjects: Book Reviewing, Criticism, Fiction, Literary Review, Poetry.

THE ANTIOCH REVIEW, Robert Fogarty, Editor; Judith Hall, Poetry Editor, PO Box 148, Yellow Springs, OH 45387, 937-769-1365. 1941. Poetry, fiction, articles, criticism, long-poems, non-fiction. "We do not accept submissions between June 1 and September 1.Recent contributors: Peter LaSalle, Nathan Oates, Rick DeMarinis, Edith Pearlman, Barbara Sjoholm. No unsolicited reviews accepted." circ. 4M. 4/yr. Pub'd 4 issues 2009; expects 4 issues 2010, 4 issues 2011. sub. price $40 ($52 Canada)($76 other foreign), $80 institutional ($96 Canada) ($116 other foreign); per copy $10.00; sample $7. Back issues: $7. Discounts: 5% to agents. 200pp. Reporting time: fiction 4 6 months, poetry 2 3 months. We do not read fiction from June 1 to September 1. We do not read poetry from May 1 to September 1. Simultaneous submissions accepted: no. Publishes 2% of manuscripts submitted. Payment: $20 per page (approx. 425 words). Copyrighted. Pub's reviews: 50 in 2009. §No unsolicited reviews considered. Ads: $250/$150. Subjects: Fiction, Poetry, Public Affairs.

•**Antrim House,** PO Box 111, Tariffville, CT 06081, 860-217-0023 [phone]. "Antrim House publishes emerging and established poets, with a special interest in those from New England. We look for poetry that is both clear and resonant, visceral and archetypal; you are invited to sample it on our website (www.AntrimHouseBooks.com) and learn about its makers. You may also be interested in our seminar section containing reviews, notes, new poems and more. Submissions to·Antrim House from anywhere in the country are welcome, especially those that combine clarity with resonance. For details and submission guidelines, see the About Us section of our website." No titles listed in the *Small Press Record of Books in Print* (36th Edition, 2010-11).

Anvil Press (see also SUB-TERRAIN), Brian Kaufman, Publisher, 278 East First Avenue, Vancouver, B.C. V5T 1A6, Canada, 604-876-8710, info@anvilpress.com, www.anvilpress.com. 1988. Fiction, photos, criticism, plays, non-fiction. "We publish literary trade titles in all genres, plus occasional broadsheets and pamphlets. Submissions should be accompanied by a sample chapter and outline with query letter. Canadian authors *only*." avg. press run 1M. Pub'd 9 titles 2009; expects 10 titles 2010, 10 titles 2011. 30 titles listed in the *Small Press Record of Books in Print* (36th Edition, 2010-11). Discounts: bookstores 40% on orders of 4+ books; 20% to libraries/institutions. 100-200pp. Publishes 2% of manuscripts submitted. Payment: Advance, plus 15% royalty on sales. Copyrights for author.

Anvil Publishers, Inc., Lee Xavier, Editor, PO Box 2694, Tucker, GA 30085-2694, 770-938-0289, Fax 770-493-7232, anvilpress@aol.com, www.anvilpub.com. 2001. Non-fiction. "History, biography, how-to." avg. press run 2M. Expects 3 titles 2010, 3 titles 2011. 3 titles listed in the *Small Press Record of Books in Print* (36th Edition, 2010-11). Discounts: retailers 1-2 books 0%, 3-4 20%, 5-24 30%, 25-99 40%, 100+ 45%, libraries and schools 1-24 20%, 25+ 25%. 300pp. Reporting time: 2 months. Simultaneous submissions accepted: yes. Payment: 5% first 1,000, 10% thereafter. Copyrights for author. Subjects: Americana, History, South.

APALACHEE REVIEW, Michael Trammell, Editor; Mary Jane Ryals, Fiction Editor; Dominika Wrozynski, Poetry Editor; Delores Bryant, Managing Editor; Kathleen Laufenberg, Nonfiction Editor, PO Box 10469, Tallahassee, FL 32302. 1973. "Unsolicited manuscripts are welcome. However, we are unable to enter into correspondence with writers about their manuscripts. We publish about two times a year. As soon as we have enough good material we publish an issue. We try to send a reply in 4 months, but sometimes we get bogged down. Your manuscript is one of hundreds, and we try to read every one. All our editors are volunteers; so if you don't hear from us, feel free to ask about the status of your manuscript, but be polite. We are interested in all genres (poetry, fiction, drama, creative nonfiction) for publication and reviewing. If you're a writer living outside of the U.S., please see special guidelines at our website (apalacheereview.org)." Lately, we've only had funds for one issue per year. sub. price $15.00/2 issues; per copy $8.00. Back issues: $5.00. 100-120pp. Reporting time: 3-11 months. Simultaneous submissions accepted: Yes! Publishes 3-5% of manuscripts submitted. Payment: 2 copies of the journal. Pub's reviews: 6 in 2009.

•**Apex Book Company,** Jason Sizemore, P.O. Box 24323, Lexington, KY 40524, (859) 312-3974. 2004. Fiction. "Publishes the leading edge of dark science fiction, dark fantasy, and horror, in the form of novellas, novels, short fiction collections, and anthologies. Previous contributors and Apex authors have included Maurice Broaddus, Wrath James White, Mary Robinette Kowal, Jennifer Pelland, Lavie Tidhar, Ekaterina Sedia, B.J. Burrow, Sara M. Harvey, and many more!" Pub'd 10 titles 2009; expects 10 titles 2010. No titles listed in the *Small Press Record of Books in Print* (36th Edition, 2010-11). 200-400pp. Reporting time: 1 Month. Simultaneous submissions accepted: No. Subjects: Fantasy, Fiction, Horror, Science Fiction.

APEX Magazine, Jason Sizemore, PO Box 24323, Lexington, KY 40524, 859-312-3974, http://www.apexbookcompany.com, apex.submission@gmail.com. 2004. Fiction, articles, art, interviews, non-fiction. "Offers up an international collection of science horror from the dark corners of the world. A flashy e-zine presentation, genre articles, and interviews add leavening to the brew, but make no mistake: Apex Magazine straddles the genre world with one foot in blood and the other in Strontium." circ. 3500 unique visitors per month. 12/yr. Pub'd 12 issues 2009; expects 12 issues 2010, 12 issues 2011. 2 titles listed in the *Small Press Record of Books in Print* (36th Edition, 2010-11). sub. price Free ezine; per copy Free ezine; sample Free ezine. Back issues: $5. Discounts: 2-10 copies 10% 11 copies 15%. 64pp. Reporting time: 30 days. Simultaneous submissions accepted: No. Publishes 5% of manuscripts submitted. Payment: 5 cents per word. Copyrighted, reverts to author. Ads: $40 1/2 Page - $75 Full interior page - $90 Inside Front Cover Right Flap - $90 Inside back cover left flap - $120 Inside Front Cover Left Flap (Full Color) - $120 Inside back cover right flap (Full Color) - $200 Back cover (full color). Subjects: Fiction, Horror, Science Fiction.

Apogee Press, 2308 Sixth Street, Berkeley, CA 94710, Email: editors@ApogeePress.com. 1998. "Apogee Press publishes the work of innovative and experimental poets. Culturally and formally diverse, our poets share an original use of language. Apogee Press does not read unsolicited manuscripts. Please query us via e-mail before submitting work." 11 titles listed in the *Small Press Record of Books in Print* (36th Edition, 2010-11).

The Apostolic Press, Terri Neimann, Associate Editor, 547 NW Coast Street, Newport, OR 97365, 541 264-0452. 1992. Non-fiction. "We are seeking material for either books or a quarterly newsletter consisting of Biblical Greek subject matter only." avg. press run 2M. Pub'd 1 title 2009; expects 1 title 2010, 1 title 2011. 1 title listed in the *Small Press Record of Books in Print* (36th Edition, 2010-11). 2240pp. Publishes 0% of manuscripts submitted. Copyrights for author. Subject: Religion.

APOSTROPHE: USCB Journal of the Arts, Sheila Tombe, Managing and Poetry Editor; Ellen Malphrus, Fiction Editor, 801 Carteret Street, Beaufort, SC 29902, 843-521-4158, sjtombe@gwm.sc.edu. 1996. Poetry, fiction, art, interviews, criticism, reviews, letters, parts-of-novels, plays. "'Eclectic excellence required.' Recent contributors: James Dickey, Lyn Lifshin, and Virgil Suarez. If books are submitted for review, we might review them." circ. 700. 1/yr. Pub'd 1 issue 2009; expects 1 issue 2010, 1 issue 2011. sub. price $10; per copy $10; sample $3. Back issues: $5. Discounts: student $5 per copy. 70pp. Reporting time: no deadlines; replies (as soon as) when can. Simultaneous submissions accepted: yes. Publishes 10% of manuscripts submitted. Payment: 2 copies. Rights revert to author. Pub's reviews: none in 2009. §Outstanding fiction, criticism, or poetry. Subjects: Arts, Classical Studies, Design, Drama, English, Fiction, Literary Review, Literature (General), Poetry, Shakespeare.

Appalachian Consortium Press, A 14-member publications committee acts as editorial board, University Hall, Appalachian State University, Boone, NC 28608, 704-262-2064, fax 704-262-6564. 1971. Poetry, fiction, articles, art, photos, interviews, criticism, music, non-fiction. "We publish occasional works of poetry but, most often, *non-fiction* relating to the Appalachian region." avg. press run 2M. Pub'd 3 titles 2009; expects 5 titles 2010, 4 titles 2011. 21 titles listed in the *Small Press Record of Books in Print* (36th Edition, 2010-11). Discounts: on purchases for resale, 1-3 books 0%, 4+ 20%. 150pp. Reporting time: at least 6 months. Payment: a negotiable 5-10% of sales. Copyrights for author. Subjects: Appalachia, Bibliography, Biography, History, Literature (General), Photography, Reference, Sociology, South.

APPALACHIAN HERITAGE, George Brosi, CPO 2166, Berea, KY 40404-3699, 859-985-3699, 859-985-3903, george_brosi@berea.edu, www.berea.edu/appalachianheritage. 1973. Poetry, fiction, articles, art, photos, interviews, non-fiction. "Usually under 1,500 words. Material must have Southern Appalachian author or focus." circ. 600. 4/yr. Pub'd 4 issues 2009; expects 4 issues 2010, 4 issues 2011. sub. price $25; per copy $8; sample $8. Back issues: $8. 120pp. Reporting time: 4-6 weeks. Simultaneous submissions accepted: no. Publishes 10% of manuscripts submitted. Payment: 3 copies. Copyrighted, reverts to author. Pub's reviews: 28 in 2009. §Appalachian subjects. Ads: none. Subject: Appalachia.

Appalachian House, Jeff Schmidt, P.O. Box 627, Boiling Springs, PA 17007, (717) 609-6234, apphouse@pa.net. 1999. Fiction, non-fiction. "fiction - middle-reader "educational-fiction"non-fiction - outdoor recreational activities (hiking, walking, bicycling, canoeing, orienteering, etc.—no hunting, fishing, trapping)regional topics acceptable (north-eastern US)." avg. press run 3000. Expects 1 title 2010, 1 title 2011. 1 title listed in the *Small Press Record of Books in Print* (36th Edition, 2010-11). Discounts: 1-10 copies 20%11- copies 40%. 288pp. Reporting time: 3 months. Simultaneous submissions accepted: Yes. Payment: to be determined. will copyright if needed. Subjects: Adirondacks, Appalachia, Bicycling, History, Non-Fiction, Outdoor Adventure, Sports, Outdoors.

APPLE VALLEY REVIEW: A Journal of Contemporary Literature, Leah Browning, Editor, http://www.applevalleyreview.com/. 2005. Poetry, fiction, non-fiction. "Each issue features a collection of beautifully crafted poetry, short fiction, and essays. We prefer work that has both mainstream and literary appeal. Prose submissions may range from 100 to 3000 words. Shorter pieces stand a better chance of being published, but you may query the editor if you have an exceptional longer piece. Preference is given to short (under two pages), non-rhyming poetry. We accept submissions only via e-mail and do not accept simultaneous submissions. All work must be original, previously unpublished, and in English. Translations are welcome if permission has been granted. Please do not send us genre fiction (e.g., horror, science fiction, mysteries); work that is scholarly or critical, inspirational, or intended for children; erotica or work containing explicit language; or anything that is extremely violent or depressing. Please note that these are purely editorial preferences. Work that is not a good fit here may be perfect for another market. Recent contributors include Kathy Anderson, Vince Corvaia, Pat Daneman, Anna Evans, Matthew Grice, Rob Hardy, Barry Jay Kaplan, Keetje Kuipers, Tai Dong Huai, and Lydia Williams." 2/yr. Expects 2 issues 2010, 2 issues 2011. price per copy $0; sample free. Back issues: $0/in archive. 50pp. Reporting time: 1 week to 2 mos. Simultaneous submissions accepted: No. Publishes less than 1% of manuscripts submitted. Copyrighted, reverts to author. Subjects: Appalachia, Essays, Family, Gender Issues, Marriage, Memoirs, Multicultural, Parenting, Poetry, Relationships, Short Stories, South, Southwest, Surrealism, Women.

APPLESEEDS, Cobblestone Publishing Company, Susan Buckley, Editor, 30 Grove Street, Suite C, Peterborough, NH 03458, 603-924-7209, Fax 603-924-7380, custsvc@cobblestone.mv.com. 1998. 9/yr. Pub'd 9 issues 2009; expects 9 issues 2010, 9 issues 2011. sub. price $29.95 (USA); per copy $6.95; sample $6.95. Back issues: $6.95. 36pp. Simultaneous submissions accepted: yes. Copyrighted, *APPLESEEDS* buys all rights. Ads: none.

Applied Probability Trust (see also MATHEMATICAL SPECTRUM), D. W. Sharpe, School of Mathematics and Statistics, University of Sheffield, Sheffield S3 7RH, England, tel: +44 (0)114 222-3920; fax: +44 (0)114 272-9782; email: apt@sheffield.ac.uk; web: http://www.appliedprobability.org. 1968. Articles, reviews, letters. 2 titles listed in the *Small Press Record of Books in Print* (36th Edition, 2010-11). Subjects: Education, Mathematics.

THE APUTAMKON REVIEW, The WordShed, LLC, Les Simon, Post Office Box 190, Jonesboro, ME 04648-0190, 207/434-5661, thewordshed@tds.net. 2006. Poetry, fiction, articles, art, photos, cartoons, interviews, satire, criticism, letters, parts-of-novels, collages, plays, concrete art, news items, non-fiction. "Only publishes those living in Downeast Maine or the Canadian Maritimes, or thereabouts. Publishes very Short Fiction, Tall Tales, Creative non-Fiction, Essays, Poetry, Haiku, Black & White Visual Arts, Lyrics, Games, Recipes, Quips, Quirks, Quotes That Should e Famous, Cartoons, Jokes, Witticisms, Follies, Riddles, Puzzles, Comic Strips.... Practically anything goes." circ. 500. 1-2/yr. Pub'd 1 issue 2009; expects 1 issue 2010, 1 issue 2011. sub. price Not available; per copy $13.95 plus S&H; sample $13.95 plus S&H. Back issues: $13.95 plus S&H. Discounts: $8.00 plus S&H. 180pp. Reporting time: One week to two months. Simultaneous submissions acceptced: Yes. ***SUBMISSIONS ACCEPTED FROM OCTOBER 1 TO JANUARY 31.***. Publishes 90% of manuscripts submitted. Payment: First North American Serial Rights. Copyrighted, reverts to author.

AQUARIUS, Eddie S. Linden, Flat 4, Room B, 116 Sutherland Avenue, Maida-Vale, London W9, England. 1968. Poetry, fiction, articles, reviews. "Special all Irish issue forthcoming with Seamus Heaney. 1992 *Aquarius* will publish in late summer a special issue on women and women writers. It will contain poetry, fictional prose, essays, interviews and reviews. Hilary Davies is the guest editor and we are seeking contributions that will reflect the best of women's writing today. They may be sent to Hilary Davies, 70 Wargrave Avenue, Stanford Hill, London N15-6UB, England. Postage cost must be sent to cover the return of material. Special issue in celebration of the 80th birthday of John Heath-Stubbs - *Aquarius* 23/24 English lost 5 pounds. Published - 1998 - also published Heath-Stubbs - collected 'literary essay' 1998 - Carcanet Press - Manchester, England." circ. 1.5M. 2/yr. sub. price $40; per copy $6; sample £5 - $12. Back issues: $5. Discounts: 33% trade. 120pp. Payment: special issues only. Pub's reviews: 40 in 2009. §Poetry, biography. Ads: £80/£40. Subject: Poetry.

•Aquarius Press (see also REVERIE: MIDWEST AFRICAN AMERICAN LITERATURE), Heather Buchanan, PO Box 23096, Detroit, MI 48223, 877-979-3639, aquariuspress@gmail.com, www.aquariuspressbookseller.net. 1999. Poetry, fiction, interviews, criticism, reviews, parts-of-novels, long-poems, plays, non-fiction. "The mission of Aquarius Press is to publish talented writers whose works have a universal message, but are typically overlooked in traditional markets." Pub'd 5 titles 2009; expects 6 titles 2010, 7 titles 2011. 6 titles listed in the *Small Press Record of Books in Print* (36th Edition, 2010-11). Reporting time: 3 months. Simultaneous submissions accepted: Yes. Subjects: African-American, Autobiography, Biography, Black, Children, Youth, Fiction, Literature (General), Midwest, Multicultural, Non-Fiction, Novels, Poetry, Reviews, Textbooks, Writers/Writing.

AQUATERRA, METAECOLOGY & CULTURE, Jacqueline Froelich, 5473 Highway 23N, Eureka Springs, AR 72631. 1986. Poetry, articles, art, cartoons, letters, news items. "Water-related information particularly compost toilet information and innovative conservation." circ. 3M. 1/yr. price per copy $9.95; sample $9.95. Back issues: $9.95. Discounts: inquire. 140pp. Reporting time: varies. Simultaneous submissions accepted: yes. Publishes 50% of manuscripts submitted. Payment: none. Copyrighted, reverts to author. Pub's reviews: 1 in 2009. §Submissions related to technical and/or spiritual experiences with water articles, research, interviews, ceremonies, prose, poetry, artwork, summaries of water organizations. Ads: inquire. Subjects: Conservation, Earth, Natural History, Ecology, Foods, Education, Energy, Engineering, Networking, Newsletter, Water.

Aquila Ink Publishing, Patricia Roland-James, P.O. Box 160, Rio Nido, CA 95471, 707-799-5981. 1999. Fiction, non-fiction. "Spiritual fiction and non-fiction, mystery and detective fiction, children's fictionPatricia Roland-James and Robert James, Something Wicked in the Land of Picatrix, children's fiction,Robert B. Tanner, Two Horns of the Devil, spiritual autobiography." avg. press run 200. Pub'd 1 title 2009; expects 3 titles 2010, 2 titles 2011. No titles listed in the *Small Press Record of Books in Print* (36th Edition, 2010-11). Discounts: 40%. 292pp. Reporting time: 3 months. Simultaneous submissions accepted: Yes. Publishes 5% of manuscripts submitted. Payment: 10%. Copyrights for author. Subjects: Astrology, Fantasy, Fiction, Juvenile Fiction, Metaphysics, Mystery, New Age, Novels, Occult, Political Science, Science Fiction, Spiritual, Tarot, Young Adult.

Ara Pacis Publishers, PO Box 1202, Des Plaines, IL 60017-1202. 1998. Poetry, fiction, non-fiction. Expects 3 titles 2010, 3 titles 2011. 1 title listed in the *Small Press Record of Books in Print* (36th Edition, 2010-11).

ARARAT, Leo Hamalian, 55 E 59th Street, New York, NY 10022-1112. 1960. Poetry, fiction, articles, art, criticism, reviews, parts-of-novels. "We prefer material in some way pertinent to Armenian life and culture." circ. 2.2M. 4/yr. Pub'd 4 issues 2009; expects 4 issues 2010, 4 issues 2011. sub. price $24; per copy $7; sample $4. Back issues: $4. Discounts: 15%. 74pp. Reporting time: 4 months. Payment: $10 a printed page (roughly). Copyrighted, reverts to author. Pub's reviews: 30 in 2009. §Ethnic Armenian. Ads: $250/$125. Subject: Armenian.

Arbutus Press, Susan Bays, 2364 Pinehurst Trail, Traverse City, MI 49686, phone 231-946-7240, FAX 231-946-4196, editor@arbutuspress.com, www.Arbutuspress. 1998. Fiction, non-fiction. avg. press run 3000. Pub'd 2 titles 2009; expects 5 titles 2010, 6 titles 2011. No titles listed in the *Small Press Record of Books in Print* (36th Edition, 2010-11). 200pp. Subjects: Great Lakes, Travel.

ARC, Ed Codish, Co-Editor, Issue 21; Jerome Mandel, Co-Editor, Issue 21, PO Box 39385, Tel Aviv 61393, Israel, iawe_mailbox@yahoo.com. 1982. Poetry, fiction, interviews, satire, criticism, parts-of-novels, non-fiction. "*Arc* prints works by Israeli residents who write in English, prints translations from Israelis who write in other languages, and occasionally prints works by Israeli writers who reside elsewhere. *Arc* is the showcase of the Israel Association of Writers in English." circ. 500. 1/yr. Pub'd 1 issue 2009; expects 1 issue 2010, 1 issue 2011. 1 title listed in the *Small Press Record of Books in Print* (36th Edition, 2010-11). 64pp. Reporting time: up to 1 year. Payment: none. Copyrighted, reverts to author. Subjects: Anthology, Arts, Avant-Garde, Experimental Art, Culture, Judaism, Literary Review, Literature (General), Middle East, Poetry, Prose.

ARCATA ARTS, Gordon Inkeles, P.O.B. 800, Bayside, CA 95524, 707 822 5839, 707 826 2002 fax, 888 687 8962, pub@arcata-arts.com, http://arcata-arts.com. 1998. Photos, music, non-fiction. "We publish massage books and videos by Gordon Inkeles." Pub'd 1 title 2009; expects 2 titles 2010, 1 title 2011. 4 titles listed in the *Small Press Record of Books in Print* (36th Edition, 2010-11). Discounts: 1—case quantities 45%, Contact us for case quantity discounts. 172pp. Simultaneous submissions accepted: No. Publishes 0% of manuscripts submitted. All our published material is copyrighted. Subjects: Health, Massage.

Archer Books, John Taylor-Convery, Rosemary Tribulato, PO Box 1254, Santa Maria, CA 93456, 805-878-8279 phone, email: jtc@archer-books.com, web site: www.archer-books.com. 1998. Poetry, non-fiction. "Non-fiction and poetry. Also provide editing, typesetting and book design services for other trade publishers and self-publishers." avg. press run 3000. Pub'd 4 titles 2009; expects 4 titles 2010, 6 titles 2011. 10 titles listed in the *Small Press Record of Books in Print* (36th Edition, 2010-11). Discounts: Titles available from Midpoint Trade Books, Ingram, Baker & Taylor, SPD, et al. Quantity discounts to 55%, STOP orders accepted. 250pp. Simultaneous submissions accepted: yes. Publishes 5% of manuscripts submitted. Payment:

percentage of net sales receipts. Copyrights for author. Subjects: Biography, Culture, Current Affairs, Human Rights, Latino, Memoirs, Non-Fiction, Political Science, Politics, Public Affairs, U.S. Hispanic.

Archipelago Books, 232 3rd St., #A111, Brooklyn, NY 11215. No titles listed in the *Small Press Record of Books in Print* (36th Edition, 2010-11).

Arctos Press, CB Follett, Editor, PO Box 401, Sausalito, CA 94966-0401, 415-331-2503, Fax 415-331-3092, runes@aol.com, http://members.aol.com/runes. 1996. Poetry. "Anthologies, theme oriented, send only in response to call for submissions. Looking for quality poems. Recent contributors: Lucille Clifton, Li Young Lee, David St. John, Richard Wilbur, Jane Hirshfield, Shirley Kaufman, Philip Levine, W. S. Merwin." avg. press run 1200. Pub'd 2 titles 2009; expects 2 titles 2010, 1 title 2011. 17 titles listed in the *Small Press Record of Books in Print* (36th Edition, 2010-11). Discounts: usual. 120pp. Reporting time: 4 months. We accept simultaneous submissions if notified. Publishes 1% of manuscripts submitted. Payment: in copies. Copyrights for author. Subject: Poetry.

Arden Press, Inc., Susan Conley, Editor, PO Box 418, Denver, CO 80201, 303-697-6766. 1980. Non-fiction. "We are actively pursuing women's topics of either historical or contemporary significance, reference works, nonfiction works including practical guides in all subject areas. No autobiographical works or memoirs are considered." avg. press run 3M. Pub'd 3 titles 2009; expects 4 titles 2010, 5 titles 2011. 14 titles listed in the *Small Press Record of Books in Print* (36th Edition, 2010-11). Discounts: 1-4 copies 20%, 5-49 40%, 50+ 50%, to trade. 250pp. Reporting time: 1 month. Simultaneous submissions accepted: yes. Payment: 8-15% according to number of copies sold; annual payments. Copyrights for author. Subjects: Bibliography, Biography, History, How-To, Motivation, Success, Non-Fiction, Politics, Reference, Self-Help, Women, Writers/Writing.

Argo Press (see also CHARLTON SPOTLIGHT), Michael E. Ambrose, PO Box 4201, Austin, TX 78765-4201, charspot01@austin.rr.com. 1972. Fiction, art. "All submissions are by solicitation only." avg. press run 500. Expects 1 title 2010. 6 titles listed in the *Small Press Record of Books in Print* (36th Edition, 2010-11). Discounts: 10 or more 40%. 200pp. Reporting time: varies. Simultaneous submissions accepted: no. Publishes a variable % of manuscripts submitted. Payment: individual terms. Copyrights for author. Subjects: Comics, Fantasy, Science Fiction.

Arias Press, Theresa Pugh, Vancouver, Canada V6T 2H2, Canada, www.ariaspress.com. 2009. "Body, Mind and Spirit Books only." avg. press run 2500. Expects 3 titles 2010, 3 titles 2011. 1 title listed in the *Small Press Record of Books in Print* (36th Edition, 2010-11). Discounts: 2 - 10 copies 25%. 200pp. Reporting time: 3 - 4 weeks. Subjects: Buddhism, Channelling, Metaphysics, Occult.

ARIEL, A Review of International English Literature, University of Calgary Press, Pamela McCallum, The University of Calgary, 2500 University Drive NW, Calgary, Alberta T2N 1N4, Canada, 403-220-4657, Fax 403-289-1123, ariel@ucalgary.ca, www.english.ucalgary.ca/ariel/. 1970. Articles, reviews. "*Ariel* is a refereed journal devoted to the critical and scholarly study of the new and the established literatures in English around the world. It welcomes particularly articles on the relationships among the new literatures and between the new and the established literatures. It publishes a limited number of original poems in each issue." circ. 950. 4/yr. Pub'd 4 issues 2009; expects 4 issues 2010, 4 issues 2011. sub. price $60 institution, $28 individual (orders outside Canada to be paid in US funds, Visa or Mastercard); per copy $15; sample G.S.T. Canada. Back issues: $35 indiv., $50 instit., payable in Cdn. funds, add G.S.T. in Canada; discount on 5 or more volumes. Discounts: $1 for agents, claim period is 6 months ($2 on p/h claims). 150pp. Reporting time: 3 months. Simultaneous submissions accepted: no. Payment: none. Copyrighted, contact editor regarding rights reverting to author. Pub's reviews: 12-14 in 2009. §English literature. Ads: write for info. Subjects: Literary Review, Literature (General).

Ariko Publications, Jonathan Musere, 8513 Venice Blvd #201, Los Angeles, CA 90034. 1998. Articles, non-fiction. "We primarily deal with translation, oral, literary and field research work associated with personal names and proverbs from the central, Southern and Eastern African region." Pub'd 3 titles 2009; expects 2 titles 2010, 3 titles 2011. 4 titles listed in the *Small Press Record of Books in Print* (36th Edition, 2010-11). Discounts: 60%. 200pp. Reporting time: 1 month. Simultaneous submissions accepted: yes. Payment: 10% on retail price copies. Copyrights for author. Subjects: African Literature, Africa, African Studies, Black, Culture, Folklore, Language, Non-Fiction, Reference, Textbooks, Translation.

Aristata Publishing, Craig Elliott, 16429 Lost Canyon Rd., Santa Clarita, CA 91387, Ph (661) 600-5011, Fx (661) 299-9478, general@aristatapublishing.com, www.aristatapublishing.com. 2003. Art. "Aristata creates projects that enable artists to bring their artwork to the public in a creative an innovative way." avg. press run 5000. Pub'd 1 title 2009; expects 3 titles 2010, 2 titles 2011. No titles listed in the *Small Press Record of Books in Print* (36th Edition, 2010-11). Discounts: 50%. 150pp. Reporting time: One Month. Simultaneous submissions accepted: Yes. Publishes 1% of manuscripts submitted. Payment: On Per Book Basis. Does not copyright for author. Subject: Arts.

Arizona Master Gardener Press, Cathy L. Cromell, 4341 E. Broadway Road, Phoenix, AZ 85040-8807, 602-470-8086 ext. 312, Fax 602-470-8092. 1996. Non-fiction. "We publish books that educate the public about appropriate plants and maintenance for arid, low-desert gardening. Non-fiction, any length." avg. press run 3M. Pub'd 1 title 2009; expects 1 title 2010, 1 title 2011. 4 titles listed in the *Small Press Record of Books in Print* (36th Edition, 2010-11). 150pp. Subjects: Gardening, Horticulture.

Arjuna Library Press (see also JOURNAL OF REGIONAL CRITICISM), Count Prof. Joseph A. Uphoff Jr., Executive Director, 1025 Garner St., D, Space 18, Colorado Springs, CO 80905-1774, Email address pfuphoff@earthlink.net Website address http://home.earthlink.net/~pfuphoff/. 1983. Fiction, art, photos, long-poems, non-fiction. "The current debate is regarding the use of meaning versus deliberate meaningless images. The language poets draw pictures without meaningful implication. They work with fragments and irrational splicing, Surrealist Fragmentation. The metaphorical poets use words as other meanings versus using words in other contexts. The message poets determine literal comprehension. Thus, there are three kinds of logic, rhetorical, cryptic, and definitive. There are two kinds of irony, dramatic and journalistic. There are two kinds of reality, fictional and factual. We are looking for examples of these including those in visual poetics. The universe we employ is complex with a fictional context in virtual reality and a factual context in forensics (Forensic Surrealism). The Surrealist Collage in Virtual Space, including the Internet, is being used to orchestrate online galleries where Visual Poetics can be supplemented by the presentation of literary frames. The Mail Art movement includes the opportunity for cost effective use of color illustration and large collections. There are now Joint Picture Group sites that can display poetry pages and anything that can be put in a jpg format." 34 titles listed in the *Small Press Record of Books in Print* (36th Edition, 2010-11). 30pp. Reporting time: indefinite. Payment: dependent on market, profit sharing. Does not copyright for author. Subjects: Anthropology, Archaelogy, Arts, Avant-Garde, Experimental Art, Communication, Journalism, Criticism, Dada, Drama, Martial Arts, Mathematics, Metaphysics, Myth, Mythology, Photography, Poetry, Surrealism.

The Ark, Geoffrey Gardner, 51 Pleasant Street, Marlborough, NH 03455-2532, 603-876-4160, anarkiss@mindspring.com. 1970. Poetry, long-poems. "This is a highly selective press. Publication is now primarily by invitation and occasional as economies allow. We will consider poetry of any form or style. Depth, power and excellence are what we want. We are especially interested in new translation of poetry from all languages and periods. Query before submission. Stringent finances have made it very unlikely that we will be able to take on any new publishing ventures over the next several years. We will continue to read all that comes to us. It is less likely than ever we will accept any new, unsolicited work for publication." avg. press run 1.5M+. Pub'd 1 title 2009; expects 1 title 2010, 2 titles 2011. 2 titles listed in the *Small Press Record of Books in Print* (36th Edition, 2010-11). Discounts: 40% to bookstores only. 116pp. Reporting time: at once to 3 months. Payment: unique to each project and by arrangement with each author. Copyrights for author. Subjects: Poetry, Translation.

ARKANSAS REVIEW, Tom Williams, Editor, Arkansas State University, PO Box 1890, State University, AR 72467, phone numbers: 870-972-3043, fax: 870-972-3045, email address: delta@astate.edu, www: www.clt.astate.edu/arkreview. Poetry, fiction, articles, interviews, criticism, reviews, parts-of-novels, non-fiction. "*Arkansas Review* is a journal of Delta Studies. All materials we print—academic and creative—must respond to or evoke the natural and/or cultural experience of the seven-state Mississippi River Delta region (IL, MO, KY, AR, TN, MS, LA). We read year round and welcome submissions from all manner of writers. As is best with any journal, reading at least one issue will reveal our interests and likes." circ. 1500 annually. 3/yr. sub. price $20.00; per copy $7.50. Back issues: $5.00. 72pp. Reporting time: 4 mos. Simultaneous submissions accepted: Yes, but only for creative work: poetry, fiction, creative nonfiction. Publishes 10% of manuscripts submitted. Payment: One year subscription. Pub's reviews: approx 45 in 2009. §Books written by Delta writers and about Delta writers.

Armadillo Publishing Corporation, Lawrence Simpson, PO Box 2052, Georgetown, TX 78627-2052, 512-863-8660. 1997. Poetry, fiction, art, non-fiction. "Publishing, co-publishing, and self-publishing production services for authors on all topics. We produce 70-400 page paperback books in runs of 25-200; archive electronic files for future runs. Over 50 titles, including Don Snell/art & poetry, Larry Simpson/fiction, Lucas Adams/nonfiction, and George Neuvirth/nonfiction, history, Ned Snead/commentary & analysis." avg. press run +/- 100. Pub'd 7 titles 2009; expects 8 titles 2010, 12 titles 2011. 54 titles listed in the *Small Press Record of Books in Print* (36th Edition, 2010-11). Discounts: 1-10 books 25%, 10+ 40%. 175pp. Reporting time: 1 week. Simultaneous submissions accepted: no. Publishes 75% of manuscripts submitted. Payment: co-publishing 10%. Does not copyright for author.

•**ARROYO LITERARY REVIEW,** Dept/English MB 2579, CSU-East Bay, 25800 Carlos Bee Blvd., Hayward, CA 94542. "*Arroyo Literary Review* is a print-based publication produced annually by the department of English at California State University, East Bay. Each issue remains as diverse as the staff that creates it, with material that ranges from prose and poetry, to personal essays, to interviews with distinguished writers." No titles listed in the *Small Press Record of Books in Print* (36th Edition, 2010-11).

ARSENIC LOBSTER MAGAZINE, Susan Yount, Managing Editor & Publisher; Lissa Kiernan, Poetry Editor; Katherine Blackbird, Associate Editor; Clarissa Jakobsons, Associate Editor, lobster@magere.com. Est.2000. Poetry, art, photos, criticism, reviews. *"Arsenic Lobster* seeks eloquent emotion, articulate experiment; the charlie-horse hearted, heavily quirked, the harrowing. Honed lyricism, stripped narrative... Be compelled, *compulsed, MOVED,* to write. INCLUDE ALL SUBMISSIONS IN BODY OF EMAIL (no attachments please). 3-5 POEMS, ANY LENGTH. (Lobster art/photos by PDF attachment only). PLEASE WRITE FIRST INITIAL, LAST NAME, DATE & SUBMISSION CATEGORY IN SUBJECT LINE (Example: D. Carson 3/6/07 Poetry). Address checks/other correspondence to: S. Yount, 1830 W 18th St, Chicago, IL 60608." Print circ at 300 & over 1,000 email subscribers. Online 3 times a year. Prints a Best Of issue annually. price per copy $10; sample $7. Back issues: Best of 2006, 2007, 2008. 70pp. Reporting time: about 4 months. Simultaneous submissions accepted: Yes. Publishes .5% of manuscripts submitted. Payment: 1 copy. Pub's reviews: 3 in 2009. §We publish reviews *online only* of poetry books or chapbooks. Ads: none. Subject: Poetry.

ART BUREAU, Bert Benson, 3321 SW Kelly Ave, Portland, OR 97239, 415-759-1788, www.artbureau.org. 2002. Articles, art, photos, cartoons, interviews, criticism, reviews, collages, concrete art. "Art Bureau is an art publication fostering a grassroots approach in promoting artists, artistic collaborations and the art community. The format is simple: 36 pages of artwork, by no more than four artists, with interviews and articles about networking and art organizations. Artists we have published include: Kelsey Brookes, Linzie Hunter, Daria Tessler and Bubi Au Yeung." circ. 500. 3/yr. Pub'd 3 issues 2009; expects 3 issues 2010, 3 issues 2011. 2 titles listed in the *Small Press Record of Books in Print* (36th Edition, 2010-11). sub. price $9; per copy $3; sample $3. Back issues: $3. 36pp. Reporting time: two-three weeks. Simultaneous submissions accepted: Yes. Publishes 25% of manuscripts submitted. Payment: 10-15 comp. copies. Copyrighted, reverts to author. Pub's reviews: 5 in 2009. §art-related magazines, zines or art books. Ads: Display ads: $25 (full)/$15 (1/2), $10 (1/4). Subjects: Arts, Avant-Garde, Experimental Art, Book Arts, Cartoons, Comics, Design, Graphic Design, Graphics, Printing, Publishing, Visual Arts, Zines.

THE ART OF ABUNDANCE, Pellingham Casper Communications, Paula Langguth Ryan, 1121 Annapolis Road, Suite 120, Odenton, MD 21113, 800-507-9244; 208-545-8164 (fax), www.ArtOfAbundance.com. 1999. Articles, reviews. "Our mission is to help people heal their relationship with money and create the life they truly desire. Recent contributors include Paula Langguth Ryan, William Deitrich, Catherine Ponder, Steve Rhode, Anita Law, Janet Hall, Alan Cohen." circ. 3336. 12/yr. Pub'd 12 issues 2009; expects 12 issues 2010, 12 issues 2011. sub. price $0; per copy $0; sample $0. Back issues: $0. Discounts: magazine is delivered electronically only at this time. 10pp. Reporting time: 3-6 months, send electronically, with article in body of email, will not accept attachments. Simultaneous submissions accepted: Yes. Publishes 10% of manuscripts submitted. No payment made. We provide links to your website, and contact info if readers wish to contribute directly to author of article. Copyrighted, reverts to author. Pub's reviews: approx 10 in 2009. §personal finance, self-help, inspirational, metaphysical, new age. Ads: do not currently accept advertising. Subjects: Aromatherapy, Careers, Finances, Guidance, Inspirational, Mentoring/Coaching, Metaphysics, Philosophy, Physics, Psychology, Reading, Relationships, Sociology, Spiritual.

•**Art of Living, PrimaMedia,Inc,** Michele Di Lisio, 1250 Bethlehem Pike, Suite #241, Hatfield, PA 19440, 215-660-5045; Fax: 734-448-4125; 1-800-581-9020; primamedia4@yahoo.com. 2006. Fiction, articles, photos, collages, non-fiction. "Books related to home, garden, cooking, Italian cooking ,Italian art, architecture ,travel, recipe novels, wine." avg. press run 5000. Pub'd 3 titles 2009; expects 4 titles 2010, 5 titles 2011. 4 titles listed in the *Small Press Record of Books in Print* (36th Edition, 2010-11). Discounts: Wholesalers: 55% retailers: 40% bookstores: 40% agents, jobbers, classrooms, institutions—email for discount info. 200-300pp. Reporting time: 6-8weeks. Simultaneous submissions accepted: Yes. Payment: TBD. Does not copyright for author. Subjects: Agriculture, Architecture, Autobiography, Consumer, Cooking, Design, Ecology, Foods, Environment, Europe, Family, Italian-American, Italy, Travel, Vegetarianism, Weddings.

ART TIMES, Raymond J. Steiner, PO Box 730, Mount Marion, NY 12456-0730, 845-246-6944, info@arttimesjournal.com, www.arttimesjournal.com. 1984. "Other address: 16 Fite Road, Saugerties, NY 12477. *Art Times* is a monthly journal and resource for all of the arts. Although the bulk is written by Staff members, we solicit poetry and short stories from free-lancers around the world (we are listed in *Writer's Market, Literary Market, Poet's Market,* etc). Fiction: short stories up to 1,500 words. No excessive sex, violence or racist themes. High literary quality sought. Poetry: up to 20 lines. All topics; all forms. High literary quality sought. Readers of *Art Times* are generally over 40, affluent and art conscious. Articles in *Art Times* are general pieces on the arts written by staff *and are not solicited.* General tone of paper governed by literary essays on arts—no journalistic writing, press releases. *Always include SASE.* Guidelines: business size envelope, 1 first-class stamp." circ. 28M. 10/yr. Pub'd 10 issues 2009; expects 10 issues 2010, 10 issues 2011. 1 title listed in the *Small Press Record of Books in Print* (36th Edition, 2010-11). sub. price $18, $30 foreign;

sample SASE + 3 first class stamps. Back issues: same. Discounts: bundles (25-100 copies) sent free to preforming art centers, galleries, museums and similar distribution points. 20pp. Reporting time: 6 months (24-48 months for publication). Simultaneous submissions accepted: yes. Publishes .01% of manuscripts submitted. Payment: poetry 6 free issues + 1 yr. sub.; short stories $25 + 1 yr. sub. Copyrighted, reverts to author. Pub's reviews: 75-100 in 2009. §We only review art books. Ads: $1514 full/$779 half /$420 1/4 page/ $218 1/8/ Classified $33 for 1st 15 words, 50¢ each additional word for classifieds. Subject: Arts.

ART:MAG, Peter Magliocco, Editor, PO Box 70896, Las Vegas, NV 89170, 702-734-8121. 1984. Poetry, fiction, art, photos, cartoons, interviews, satire, parts-of-novels, long-poems. "Subscribers receive chapbooks & 'surprises' now and then." circ. 100+. 2/yr. Pub'd 2 issues 2009; expects 1 issue 2010, 1 issue 2011. 5 titles listed in the *Small Press Record of Books in Print* (36th Edition, 2010-11). sub. price $8; per copy $5; sample $3. Back issues: query. Discounts: none. 35-90pp. Reporting time: 1-3 months. Simultaneous submissions accepted: yes. Publishes 25% of manuscripts submitted. Payment: 1 copy of magazine. Not copyrighted. Pub's reviews: 1-2 in 2009. §Poetry, fiction. Ads: exchange only. Subjects: Arts, Essays, Fiction, Poetry, Satire, Short Stories.

Artamo Press, Elvira Monika Laskowski-Caujolle, 11 W. Anapamu Street, Santa Barbara, CA 93101, phone(805) 568-1400, fax (805) 568-1400, contact@artamopress.com, www.artamopress.com. 2006. Poetry, fiction, plays. "ARTAMOPRESS is a new independent publisher of literary fiction, non-fiction, essays, and contemporary poetry." avg. press run 2500. Expects 3 titles 2010, 3-5 titles 2011. 6 titles listed in the *Small Press Record of Books in Print* (36th Edition, 2010-11). 64-400pp. Reporting time: 3 to 4 months. Copyrights for author. Subjects: Drama, Essays, Experimental, Fiction, Non-Fiction, Novels, Poetry, Post Modern, Prose, Writers/Writing.

Arte Publico Press, Nicolas Kanellos, Publisher, University of Houston, 452 Cullen Performance Hall, Houston, TX 77204-2004, 713-743-2999, fax 713-743-2847, www.artepublicopress.com. 1980. Poetry, fiction, art, photos. "Arte Pblico Press is the nation's largest and most established publisher of contemporary and recovered literature by U.S. Hispanic authors. Its imprint for children and young adults, Piata Books, is dedicated to the realistic and authentic portrayal of the themes, languages, characters, and customs of Hispanic culture in the United States. Based at the University of Houston, Arte Pblico Press, Piata Books and the Recovering the U.S. Hispanic Literary Heritage project provide the most widely recognized and extensive showcase for Hispanic literary arts, history, and politics. Arte Pblico Press, affiliated with the University of Houston, specializes in publishing contemporary novels, short stories, poetry, and drama based on U.S. Hispanic, Cuban American, Mexican American, Puerto Rican, and other themes and cultural issues. Arte Pblico also is interested in reference works, non-fiction studies, especially of Hispanic civil rights, womens issues and history. Manuscripts, queries, synopses, outlines, proposals, introductory chapters, etc. are accepted in either English or Spanish; the majority of our publications are in English. All submissions must be typed, double-spaced, and include a self-addressed, stamped envelope (SASE) to return those not selected for publication. Address all submissions to:." avg. press run 3M. Pub'd 22 titles 2009; expects 20 titles 2010, 20 titles 2011. 121 titles listed in the *Small Press Record of Books in Print* (36th Edition, 2010-11). Discounts: 40% trade. 120pp. Reporting time: 4 months. Payment: varies per type of book. Copyrights for author. Subjects: Chicano/a, Drama, Fiction, Poetry.

ARTELLA: the waltz of words and art, Marney Makridakis, P.O. Box 44418, Kamuela, HI 96743, www.ArtellaWordsandArt.com. Poetry, fiction, articles, art, photos, parts-of-novels, long-poems, collages, non-fiction. "UPDATED INFO: At this time, only submissions by email are accepted. See http://www.artellawordsandart.com/submit.html for details. Artella focuses on publishing works that combine words and art, with a heavy emphasis on fostering collaborations among writers and artists. The magazine often includes a multimedia component, such as CDs with music and audio interviews. Artella magazine alternates between full-color print issues and PDF e-issues that are distributed to subscribers online. The latter also includes resources and articles relevant to writers and artists, in addition to the creative pairings of writing and art. Artella also publishes The Artella Daily Muse, an online daily creativity newspaper." circ. 3500. 6/yr. Pub'd 6 issues 2009; expects 6 issues 2010, 6 issues 2011. sub. price $39; per copy $15; sample free electronic copy. Back issues: $15. Discounts: over 10 copies - 50% discount. 40pp. Reporting time: 30 days. Simultaneous submissions accepted: Yes. Publishes 40% of manuscripts submitted. Payment: pays in complimentary copies. Authors/artists retain copyright of their original work. Pub's reviews: approx 10 in 2009. §materials relevant to the creative life. Subjects: Abstracts, Arts, Avant-Garde, Experimental Art, Book Arts, Community, Crafts, Hobbies, Creativity, Experimental, Fiction, Poetry, Prose, Storytelling, Visual Arts, Writers/Writing, Zines.

ARTFUL DODGE, Daniel Bourne, Editor; David Wiesenberg, Managing Editor; Philip Metres, Poetry Editor; Nin Andrews, Associate Poetry Editor; Karin Lin-Greenberg, Fiction Editor; Carolyne Wright, Translations Editor; Leonard Kress, Creative Non-Fiction Editor, Department of English, College of Wooster, Wooster, OH 44691, 330 263-2577, artfuldodge@wooster.edu, www3.wooster.edu/artfuldodge. 1979. Poetry, fiction, art, photos, cartoons, interviews, satire, criticism, reviews, parts-of-novels, long-poems, collages, plays, non-fiction.

"Contributors of fiction include Dan Chaon, Bob Shacochis, Mark Axelrod, Lynne Sharon Schwartz, Joan Connor, Robert Mooney, William S. Burroughs, Sarah Willis. Poets include Gary Gildner, Julia Kasdorf, Charles Simic, Gregory Orr, Alfred Corn, Madeline DeFrees, Beth Ann Fennelly, Diane Glancy, Cynthia Hogue, William Pitt Root, John Kinsella, E. Ethelbert Miller, Lynn Powell, Daniel Tobin, Roger Weingarten, Denise Duhamel, Mong-Lan, H. L. Hix, Nin Andrews, Margaret Gibson, Venus Khoury-Ghata (translated by Marilyn Hacker), Horace (translated by William Matthews), Tim Seibles, Yannis Ritsos, Maj Ragain, Christopher Howell, Kate Fetherston, Stuart Dybek, John Haines. According to *Library Journal*, our interviews (Borges, Sarraute, Milosz, Merwin, Michael Dorris, Lee Smith, William Matthews, Stanislaw Baranczak, Tim O'Brien, Vaclav Havel, Charles Simic, William Least Heat-Moon, Tess Gallagher, William Heyen, Terry Tempest Williams, Rita Dove, Gregory Orr, James Laughlin, John Haines, Jim Daniels, Gwendolyn Brooks) are 'much more perceptive and informative than most.' Translations are heartily encouraged; we like to print special sections of contemporary writing beyond America's extensive, though not infinite, linguistic/cultural borders. We also do a 'poet as translator' series, featuring the original poetry and translations of such prominent and emerging practitioners as William Stafford, Tess Gallagher, Carolyne Wright, Pablo Medina, Khaled Mattawa, Nicholas Kolumban, Len Roberts, Mary Crow, Karen Kovacik, Orlando Ricardo Menes, etc." circ. 1M. 1 double issue/yr. Pub'd 1 issue 2009; expects 1 issue 2010, 1 issue 2011. sub. price indiv. $7, instit. $10; Current issues $7. Back issues $5. Discounts: at least 20%—please query. 180pp. Reporting time: 6 months or longer. Also, please note that we do not accept unsolicited submissions postmarked between May 1 and August 31 of each year. All work sent to us during that time will be returned unread. We accept simultaneous submissions, as long as we we are immediately notified of publication elsewhere. Publishes less than 1% of manuscripts submitted. Payment: Currently, we are able to pay only in contributors copies. Copyrighted, reverts to author. Pub's reviews. §Poetry, fiction, translation, creative nonfiction (especially work centered on place). Ads: $100/$60. Subjects: Fiction, Poetry, Translation.

Artifact, 2921B Folsom St., San Francisco, CA 94110, 415-647-7689.

•**ARTIFICE MAGAZINE,** James Tadd Adcox, Editor in Chief; Rebekah Silverman, Managing Editor, Chicago, IL, http://www.artificemag.com or email editors@artificemag.com. 2009. Poetry, fiction. "*Artifice Magazine* is devoted to fiction and poetry aware of its own artifice. Artifice Magazine is a print literary journal (5"x7" perfect bound) appearing in February and September. Please note that we have switched to email submissions. We are no longer accepting submissions through our old Submissions Manager. If you submitted work before we switched to email submissions, don't worry - we still have your piece, and are in the process of reviewing it. 1. Submissions should be sent to submissions AT artificemag DOT com. The subject line of your email should contain your name and the name of the piece or pieces you are submitting. 2. Please include a cover letter as the body of your email. Your cover letter should include your name, address, and email address, as well as the title of the piece(s) you are submitting, a short bio, previous publications, etc. 3. Attach your submission as a single file containing 3-5 poems or flash pieces, or one short story or other prose work. Files must be .doc, .rtf, or .pdf only; other file formats will be deleted unread. We cannot accept .docx files at this time. 4. Only one submission at a time, please. If you have not yet heard back from us about a previous submission, please do not send us another. 5. Simultaneous submissions are OK - make sure you send us an email (to editors AT artificemag DOT com) letting us know ASAP if something is accepted elsewhere." 2/yr. Expects 2 issues 2011. sub. price $10.00 + S&H; per copy $5.00. Back issues: $5.00. 112pp. Reporting time: 3-4 months. Simultaneous submissions accepted: Yes. Payment: 2 Contributors Copies. Copyrighted, reverts to author.

ARTISTIC RAMBLINGS, Red Tiger Press, A.D. Beache, P.O. Box 2907, Thomasville, NC 27361, PH: 832-634-7012, Fax: 530-323-8251, email: ArtisticRamblings@gmail.com. 2005. Poetry, fiction, articles, art, photos, interviews, music, letters, long-poems, non-fiction. 4/yr. Expects 4 issues 2011. sub. price $22; per copy $5.95; sample $5.95. Back issues: inquire. Discounts: 3-10 copies 25%. 48pp. Reporting time: 2-6 weeks. Simultaneous submissions accepted: Yes. Payment: 1 contributor's copies of the magazine. Copyrighted, reverts to author. Pub's reviews: none in 2009. §Fiction, poetry, essays, creative non-fiction, etc. Subjects: Book Arts, Creativity, Fantasy, Fiction, Futurism, Horror, Humor, Interviews, Occult, Photography, Poetry, Prose, Quotations, Science Fiction, Short Stories.

ARTS & LETTERS: Journal of Contemporary Culture, Martin Lammon, Georgia College & State University, Campus Box 89, Milledgeville, GA 31061-0490, 478-445-1289, al@gcsu.edu, http://al.gcsu.edu. 1998. Poetry, fiction, interviews, reviews, plays, non-fiction. "*Arts & Letters* strives to publish a range of literary works that express the vital force of contemporary culture as opposed to popular culture. We represent a wide variety of voices and genres: poetry, fiction, drama, creative nonfiction, translations, and book reviews. Recent contributors include Margaret Gibson, Ernest Gaines, Maxine Kumin, W.S. Merwin, Michael Waters, Dinty W. Moore, Brad Barkley, Jean Valentine, Donald Hall, Judith Ortiz Cofer, Bret Lott, Debra Marquart, Virgil Suarez, Janice Eidus, Laurie Lamon, and Daniel Wallace. Regular submission period is September 1 to March 1. *Arts & Letters* also sponsors a poetry, fiction, creative nonfiction, and drama competition every spring. Prizes are publication and $1,000 for each genre. Postmark deadline for the contest is usually mid-March (see web site for specific date each year). A $15 entry fee includes a year's subscription. Visit our web site or send SASE or email for guidelines." circ. 1.5M. 2/yr. Pub'd 2 issues 2009; expects 2 issues 2010, 2 issues 2011. sub. price $15; per copy $8; sample $5. Back issues: $25 for Issue #1, $5 for others. Discounts: 25% off cover price for bookstores ($6 per copy). 184pp. Reporting time: 4-8 weeks. Simultaneous submissions accepted: Yes, if we are notified immediately that the work has been accepted elsewhere. Publishes less than .5% of manuscripts submitted. Payment: $10 per published page, $50 minimum. Copyrighted, reverts to author. Pub's reviews: 4 in 2009. §Reviews are assigned only. Ads: $100 full page trade. Subjects: Arts, Culture, Drama, Essays, Fiction, Literature (General), Multicultural, Non-Fiction, Poetry, Translation.

Arts End Books (see also NOSTOC MAGAZINE), Marshall Brooks, Editor, PO Box 441, West Dover, VT 05356-0441, www.artsendbooks.com. 1979. Poetry, fiction, music, parts-of-novels, long-poems, non-fiction. "Send a SASE for our catalog describing our subscription package program. No submissions please; queries okay." avg. press run varies. Pub'd 2 titles 2009; expects 2 titles 2010, 2 titles 2011. 15 titles listed in the *Small Press Record of Books in Print* (36th Edition, 2010-11). Discounts: on request. Pages vary. Reporting time: a few weeks. Simultaneous submissions accepted: no. Publishes 1-5% of manuscripts submitted. Payment: worked out on an individual basis with each author, for each project. Copyrights for author. Subjects: Bibliography, Book Reviewing, Poetry.

Arx Publishing LLC (see also Evolution Publishing; THE TARPEIAN ROCK), Claudio R. Salvucci, PO Box 1333, Merchantville, NJ 08109, 856-486-1310, Fax 856-665-0170, info@arxpub.com, www.arxpub.com. 2001. Fiction. "Fantasy, sci-fi, action/adventure, allegorical and satirical novels. Preference for historical fiction focusing on ancient, classical Greco-Roman, Medieval, Church, Renaissance or Early American history." avg. press run 1M-1.5M. Pub'd 1 title 2009; expects 2 titles 2010, 2 titles 2011. No titles listed in the *Small Press Record of Books in Print* (36th Edition, 2010-11). Discounts: trade 40%. 250pp. Reporting time: 6-8 weeks. Simultaneous submissions accepted: yes. Publishes less than 1% of manuscripts submitted. Payment: varies by contract. Copyrights for author. Subjects: Fantasy, Fiction, Novels, Science Fiction.

ASCENT, W. Scott Olsen, Department of English, Concordia College, Moorhead, MN 56562, E-mail Ascent@cord.edu. 1975. Poetry, fiction, letters, parts-of-novels, long-poems, non-fiction. circ. 500. 3/yr. Pub'd 3 issues 2009; expects 3 issues 2010, 3 issues 2011. sub. price $12; per copy $5; sample $5. Back issues: $5. 100pp. Reporting time: 1 week to 3 months. Simultaneous submissions accepted: yes. We accept 60 manuscripts out of 2,600 submitted each year. Payment: none. Copyrighted, reverts to author. Subject: Literature (General).

ASCENT, Timeless Books, Clea McDougall, PO Box 9, Kootenay Bay BC V0B 1X0, Canada, 250-227-9224, Fax 514-499-3904, info@ascentmagazine.com, www.ascentmagazine.com. 1999. Articles, art, photos, interviews, reviews, music, letters, concrete art, non-fiction. circ. 7000. 4/yr. Pub'd 4 issues 2009; expects 4 issues 2010, 4 issues 2011. sub. price $15.95; per copy $4.95; sample $7.00. Back issues: $7.00. Discounts: contact distributors or magazine. 72pp. Simultaneous submissions accepted: no. Payment: 20¢ per published word. Copyrighted, reverts to author. Pub's reviews: 24 in 2009. §Spirituality, social action, yoga, Buddhism, environment. Subjects: Arts, Book Reviewing, Canada, Counter-Culture, Alternatives, Communes, Humanism, India, Inspirational, Interviews, Philosophy, Photography, Religion, Spiritual, Vegetarianism, Visual Arts, Zen.

Ash Lad Press, Bill Romey, PO Box 294, East Orleans, MA 02643, 508-255-2301 phone/Fax. 1975. Non-fiction. "No unsolicited submissions accepted." avg. press run 1.5M. Pub'd 1 title 2009; expects 2 titles 2010. 9 titles listed in the *Small Press Record of Books in Print* (36th Edition, 2010-11). Discounts: trade 40% for orders of over 5, 20% for 1-4, texts 20%, libraries 25%. 150pp. Payment: cooperative sharing of costs and income. Copyrights for author. Subjects: Education, Psychology, Travel.

Ash Tree Publishing, Susun Weed, PO Box 64, Woodstock, NY 12498, 845-246-8081. 1986. Non-fiction. "Women's health, women's spirituality." avg. press run 15M. Pub'd 1 title 2009; expects 2 titles 2010, 2 titles 2011. 9 titles listed in the *Small Press Record of Books in Print* (36th Edition, 2010-11). Discounts: 20% 1-2 copies, 30% 3-9, 40% 10-51, 40% S.T.O.P. orders, 45% 1 case, 50% 2-4 cases, 55% 5 cases. 240pp. Reporting time: 2-6 months. Publishes 1% of manuscripts submitted. Payment: standard. Copyrights for author. Subjects: Ecology, Foods, Health, Spiritual, Translation, Women.

The Ashland Poetry Press, Stephen Haven, Director; Deborah Fleming, Editor; Sarah Wells, Managing Editor, 401 College Avenue, Ashland, OH 44805, 419-289-5957, app@ashland.edu, www.ashland.edu/aupoetry. 1969. Poetry. "The Ashland Poetry Press runs two series - the McGovern Prize and the Snyder Prize. The McGovern Prize honors the memory of Robert McGovern, professor at Ashland University and co-founder of the Ashland Poetry Press. The McGovern Prize is given to poets over 40 who have published no more than one book and is by nomination only. The Snyder Prize honors the memory of Richard Snyder, long-time professor at Ashland University and co-editor of the Ashland Poetry Press. The Snyder Prize is an open competition and generally receives 350 manuscripts each year." avg. press run 1000. Pub'd 3 titles 2009; expects 3 titles 2010, 3 titles 2011. 11 titles listed in the *Small Press Record of Books in Print* (36th Edition, 2010-11). 80pp. Reporting time:

3 to 6 months. Simultaneous submissions accepted: Yes. Publishes 1% of manuscripts submitted. Payment: Snyder Prize Winners receive $1000, a print-run of 1000 copies, and 50 copies of their book in lieu of royalties. Subject: Poetry.

•**The Asian American Writers' Workshop,** 110-112 West 27th Street, Sixth Floor, New York, NY 10001, p) 212.494.0061, (f) 212.494.0062. "Mission Statement: The Asian American Writers' Workshop is a national not-for-profit arts organization devoted to the creating, publishing, developing and disseminating of creative writing by Asian Americans. Operating out of our 6,000 square-foot loft, we sponsor readings, book parties and panel discussions, and offer creative writing workshops. Each winter we present The Annual Asian American Literary Awards Ceremony to recognize outstanding literary works by Americans of Asian descent. Throughout the year, we offer various youth arts programs. In our space we operate a reading room of Asian American literature through the decades." No titles listed in the *Small Press Record of Books in Print* (36th Edition, 2010-11).

THE ASIAN PACIFIC AMERICAN JOURNAL, Hanya Yanagihara, 16 West 32nd Street, Suite 10A, New York, NY 10001-3814, 212-494-0061. 1992. Poetry, fiction, art, photos, parts-of-novels, long-poems, plays, non-fiction. circ. 2M. 2/yr. Pub'd 2 issues 2009; expects 2 issues 2010, 2 issues 2011. sub. price $45, includes membership to the Asian American Writers' Workshop; per copy $10; sample $12. Back issues: $12. Discounts: call for special prices. 200pp. Reporting time: 3 months. We accept simultaneous submissions but please let us know. Publishes 20% of manuscripts submitted. Payment: 2 free copies. Copyrighted, reverts to author. §Asian or Asian American. Ads: $250/$120/quarter page $60. Subject: Asian-American.

ASIAN SURVEY, University of California Press, Lowell Dittmer, Editor; David Fraser, Managing Editor; Bonnie Dehler, Assistant Editor, University of California Press, 2000 Center Street, Suite 303, Berkeley, CA 94704-1223, 510-643-7154. 1960. Non-fiction. "Editorial address: Institute of East Asian Studies, 6701 San Pablo Avenue, Room 408, Marchant Bldg., Oakland, CA 94608." circ. 2031. 6/yr. Pub'd 6 issues 2009; expects 6 issues 2010, 6 issues 2011. sub. price $75 indiv., $230 instit., $45 students ($20 air freight); per copy $16 indiv., $42 instit., $16 student; sample free. Back issues: $16 indiv., $42 instit., $16 student. Discounts: 10% foreign agents, 30% 10+ one time orders, standing orders (bookstores): 1-99 40%, 100+ 50%. 196pp. Reporting time: 1-2 months. Payment: varies. Copyrighted, does not revert to author. Ads: $295/$220. Subject: Asia, Indochina.

ASKEW REVIEWS, Bone Print Press, Denis Sheehan, P.O. Box 684, Hanover, MA 02339. 1997. Poetry, fiction, articles, art, cartoons, interviews, criticism, reviews, music, long-poems, non-fiction. "www.askewreviews.com. Prefer submissions be emailed. denis@askewreviews.com." circ. 5000. 1-2/yr. Pub'd 1 issue 2009; expects 1 issue 2010, 2 issues 2011. price per copy $3; sample free. Back issues: $3.00. 48pp. Pub's reviews: 20 in 2009.

Aspen Mountain Publishing, Thomas Smith J, 5885 Cumming Highway Suite 108, PMB 254, Sugar Hill, GA 30518, www.aspenmtnpublishing.com, www.whiteelkpress.com. 2006. Fiction, non-fiction. Expects 2 titles 2010, 2 titles 2011. 3 titles listed in the *Small Press Record of Books in Print* (36th Edition, 2010-11). Discounts: Wholesalers and Bookstores 40%. 204pp. Reporting time: 30 days. Simultaneous submissions accepted: Yes. Publishes 5% of manuscripts submitted. Payment: No advances, increasing % to authors over three years, quarterly payments. Does not copyright for author. Subjects: Americana, Business & Economics, Careers, Employment, Humor.

Aspermont Press, Roger Scott, 1249 Hayes Street, San Francisco, CA 94117, 415-863-2847. 3 titles listed in the *Small Press Record of Books in Print* (36th Edition, 2010-11).

•**Asphodel Press,** 12 Simonds Hill Road, Hubbardston, MA 01452, 978-928-4198. "Asphodel Press is a Pagan author cooperative organized by the First Kingdom Church of Asphodel. We specialize in Pagan religious books on unusual and controversial subjects. As Pagan religious practices grow, so does the need for specialized small-market books. Financial pressure prevents many Pagan/Occult publishers from printing books which do not have very broad market appeal. As a small volunteer-based organization, Asphodel Press is able to offer high-quality books targeted to very specific audiences. Our Devotionals are collections of essays, prayers, stories and poems dedicated to a specific deity or a small group of deities. Our line of Specialty Books address various aspects in Pagan religious belief and practice. Our Prayer Books are collections of short rituals and prayers. The Northern Tradition Shamanism Series covers methods, tools, and lore relevant to modern practitioners of Norse/Germanic/Anglo-Saxon shamanic techniques." No titles listed in the *Small Press Record of Books in Print* (36th Edition, 2010-11).

Aspicomm Media, Renee Flagler, Susan Herriott, PO Box 1212, Baldwin, NY 11510, Phone (516) 642-5976, Fax (516) 489-1199, www.aspicomm.com. 2001. Fiction, non-fiction. "Aspicomm Books missioin is to provide readers with exceptional quality and substance and create boundless opportunities for talented aspiring writers of all literary styles." Expects 2 titles 2010, 3 titles 2011. 3 titles listed in the *Small Press Record of Books in Print* (36th Edition, 2010-11). Discounts: 2-50 copies 25%50-100 Copies 40%over 100 copies 55%. 240pp.

Reporting time: 3 months. Simultaneous submissions accepted: Yes. Does not copyright for author. Subjects: African-American, Black, Caribbean, Family, Fiction, Mystery, Relationships, Singles.

Assilem 9 Publications, Melissa Currie-White S, 23838 Mark Twain, Moreno Valley, CA 92557, 310-412-1266. 2009. Poetry, fiction, long-poems, non-fiction. "Children's books are also in the process of being published through this company." 1 title listed in the *Small Press Record of Books in Print* (36th Edition, 2010-11). Reporting time: Not accepting manuscripts at this time. Simultaneous submissions accepted: No. Not at this time. Subjects: Alcohol, Alcoholism, Autobiography, Bisexual, Black, Communication, Journalism, Fiction, Gay, Genealogy, How-To, Lesbianism, Publishing, Sex, Sexuality, Sexual Abuse, Short Stories, Society.

Association For Research On Mothering / Demeter Press (see also JOURNAL OF THE ASSOCIATION FOR RESEARCH ON MOTHERING (JARM)), Andrea O'Reilly Ph.D, Rm 726, Atkinson College, York University, 4700 Keele Street, Toronto, Ontario M3J 1P3, Canada, 416-736-2100 x 60366; fax 416-736-5766; http://www.yorku.ca/arm. 1998. avg. press run 1000. Pub'd 2 titles 2009; expects 2 titles 2010, 2 titles 2011. 7 titles listed in the *Small Press Record of Books in Print* (36th Edition, 2010-11). Discounts: 20% - wholesalers, institutions, classrooms / 40% - bookstores, retailers. 250pp.

The Association of Freelance Writers (see also FREELANCE MARKET NEWS), A Cox, Sevendale House, 7 Dale Street, Manchester, M1 1JB, England, 0161-228-2362, Fax 0161-236-9440. 1968. "We use articles of interest to freelance writers." Pub'd 11 titles 2009; expects 11 titles 2010, 11 titles 2011. No titles listed in the *Small Press Record of Books in Print* (36th Edition, 2010-11). 16pp. Reporting time: 1 month. Simultaneous submissions accepted: no. Publishes 50% of manuscripts submitted. Payment: £50 per 1000 words. Does not copyright for author.

Asteroid Publishing, Inc., Maria Philip, P.O. Box 3, Richmond Hill, Ontario, Canada L4X 4X9, Canada, 416-319-5911, 416-352-1561. 2008. Fiction, non-fiction. avg. press run 1000. Expects 4 titles 2010, 6 titles 2011. 3 titles listed in the *Small Press Record of Books in Print* (36th Edition, 2010-11). Discounts: 2-10 copies 45%11-40 copies 55%41-100 copies 55%101 and more - 55%. 250pp. Reporting time: It usually takes up to one month to respond to submissions. Simultaneous submissions accepted: Yes. Payment: We pay 10% royalties, but no advance payments. Copyrights for author. Subjects: Fiction, Non-Fiction, Novels.

Asylum Arts (see also Leaping Dog Press), Jordan Jones, Editor and Publisher, c/o Leaping Dog Press, PO Box 90437, Raleigh, NC 27675-0473, Phone/fax: (877) 570-6873 E-mail: editor@leapingdogpress.com, Web: www.leapingdogpress.com, Chapbooks and ephemera: www.cafepress.com/ldp/. 1990. Poetry, fiction, art, photos, criticism, letters, long-poems, collages, plays, non-fiction. "Manuscripts by invitation only, and only during the months of May-July. Asylum Arts publishes high-quality literary titles—fiction, plays, translations, essays, and poetry—in attractive trade paperback format. Recent books by Gerard de Nerval, Robert Peters, Charles Baudelaire, Kenneth Bernard, Geoffrey Clark, Cynthia Hendershot, Eric Basso, Richard Martin, and Samuel Appelbaum." avg. press run 1000. Pub'd 10 titles 2009; expects 4 titles 2010, 3 titles 2011. 41 titles listed in the *Small Press Record of Books in Print* (36th Edition, 2010-11). Distributed to the book trade by AtlasBooks Distribution, 30 Amberwood Parkway, Ashland, OH 44805. Phone: (800) BookLog, Fax: (419) 281-6883. 128pp. Reporting time: 3-6 months. Simultaneous submissions accepted: no. Payment: varies from book to book. Copyrights for author. Subjects: Arts, Avant-Garde, Experimental Art, Dada, Drama, Dreams, Erotica, Essays, Fiction, Literature (General), Novels, Post Modern, Prose, Short Stories, Surrealism, Translation.

AT THE LAKE MAGAZINE, Barb Krause, Publisher; Jamie Rhodes, Managing Editor, 93 West Geneva St., P.O. Box 1080, Williams Bay, WI 53191, phone 262-245-1000; fax 262-245-2000; toll free 800-386-3228; e-mail jrhodes@ntmediagroup.com; web www.ntmediagroup.com. 1997. Articles, photos, non-fiction. "Regional magazine focusing on Southeastern Wisconsin." circ. 30M. 4/yr. Pub'd 4 issues 2009; expects 4 issues 2010, 4 issues 2011. sub. price $16.95; per copy $4. Back issues: $4. 84pp. Reporting time: 6 weeks. Simultaneous submissions accepted: yes. Publishes 10% of manuscripts submitted. Payment: $0.25/word. Not copyrighted. Ads: $1700 FP color. Subject: Wisconsin.

Atelier Press, Scott Reynolds, 1112 Montana Ave., #270, Santa Monica, CA 90403, info@atelierpress.com, www.atelierpress.com. Fiction. "Our focus is on literary fiction, historical fiction, fantasy, young adult and fiction with musical themes. Please see our website for more information about submissions and our philosophy." Expects 1-2 titles 2010, 3-4 titles 2011. No titles listed in the *Small Press Record of Books in Print* (36th Edition, 2010-11). Reporting time: 2 - 3 months. Simultaneous submissions accepted: Yes. Subjects: Fantasy, Fiction, History, Literature (General), Music, Novels, Prose, Publishing, Young Adult.

Athanata Arts, Ltd., Peter Arcese, P.O. Box 321, Garden City, NY 11530-0321. 2001. Poetry. "Publishers of the NYQ Poetry Series." avg. press run 1500. Pub'd 1 title 2009; expects 3 titles 2010, 5 titles 2011. 1 title listed in the *Small Press Record of Books in Print* (36th Edition, 2010-11). Discounts: 55% wholesale, 40% retail, 20% STOP. 92pp. Reporting time: Does not accept unsolicited manuscripts. Simultaneous submissions accepted: No. Payment: Advance & royalty negotiated on individual basis. Copyrights for author. Subjects: Arts, Drama, Fiction, Immigration, Literature (General), Novels, Performing Arts, Poetry.

Athanor Books, Bruce Schaffenberger, P.O.Box 22309, Sacramento, CA 95820-0309, 916-424-4355. 1993. Non-fiction. "We publish exclusively from in-house writers. We specialize in non-fiction books on spiritual and mystical topics such as sacred sites and truelife stories of otherworldly encounters. The formats we publish are handbooks, directories, course manuals, and ebooks." avg. press run 5M. Pub'd 1 title 2009; expects 3 titles 2010, 4 titles 2011. 2 titles listed in the *Small Press Record of Books in Print* (36th Edition, 2010-11). Discounts: 2-4 copies 20%, 5-99 40%, 100+ 50%. 300pp. Reporting time: 4-6 weeks. Simultaneous submissions accepted: yes. Publishes 2% of manuscripts submitted. Payment: 8% to 500 copies; 10% over. Copyrights for author. Subjects: Bibliography, New Age, Occult, Spiritual.

AT-HOME DAD, Peter Baylies, 61 Brightwood Avenue, North Andover, MA 01845, athomedad@aol.com, www.athomedad.com. 1994. Articles, satire, letters, news items, non-fiction. "First-hand experiences of being an at-home dad preferred; plus experiences of running a home business while caring for children. The At-Home Dad Newsletter is now a free online publication." circ. 100,000 hits per year on website. Weekly/ bi weekly as posted. sub. price Free; per copy free. Simultaneous submissions accepted: yes. Publishes 20% of manuscripts submitted. Payment: plus media exposure website is read by most all national news/parent media. Copyrighted, reverts to author. Pub's reviews: 10 in 2009. §Any on fatherhood, parenting, recipes, kid publications or products, home business. Ads: Advertising Accepted. Subjects: Birth, Birth Control, Population, Book Reviewing, Business & Economics, Children, Youth, Family, Humor, Men, Metaphysics, Parenting.

ATLANTA REVIEW, Dan Veach, PO Box 8248, Atlanta, GA 31106. 1994. Poetry, art, interviews. "Quality poetry of genuine human appeal, interviews with poets. Does not publish fiction, reviews or criticism. *Atlanta Review* has published Seamus Heaney, Derek Walcott, Billy Collins, Maxine Kumin, Charles Simic, Naomi Shibab Nye, Stephen Dunn, Rachel Hadas, and Charles Wright. Each spring issue features a new country or region: Asia, Africa, Ireland, England, Australia, the Caribbean, Greece, Spain, Turkey, etc. Art in black and white." circ. 3M. 2/yr. Pub'd 2 issues 2009; expects 2 issues 2010, 2 issues 2011. sub. price $12; per copy $6; sample $5. Back issues: $5. Discounts: negotiable. 128pp. Reporting time: 1 month. Simultaneous submissions accepted: yes. Publishes 1% of manuscripts submitted. Payment: 2 free copies. Copyrighted, reverts to author. Subject: Poetry.

ATLANTIC PACIFIC PRESS, The WhaleInn Publishing House (1998), Christine Walen, Editor; Luke Walen, Photography Editor, 279 Gulf Rd., South Dartmouth, MA 02748-1580, 508-994-7869. Established in 2008. Poetry, fiction, art, photos, parts-of-novels, plays. "*Atlantic and Pacific Press* is a quarterly literary journal of creative writing, art and photography. Publishes fiction, non-ficion, science fiction, children's stories, poetry, lyrics, prose poetry, flash fiction, drama, veterans/military, mystery, horror, romance, fantasy, art and photography. Recent contributors include Florence Appleseed, Robert Ludlow, Deborah Valianti, John Brantingham, Marjorie Bixler, M. Seamus Briscoe, Suzanne Del Sarto, Ray Greenblatt, Mediha F. Saliba, Eugene Carrington, Lynn Veach Sadler, Doug Bolling, Kendra E.S. Adams, Randall Brock, Mary Kipps, Simon Perchik, Laura A. Steeb, Brian C. Felder, Cathy Porter, D. Davis Philips, Claudia Barnett, David Radavich, Jason Wilkinson, Michael Foster, Michael Ceraolo, Jon Wesick, James Fowler, J.W. Major, J.P. Andreason, T. Anders Carson, Mark D. Cohen, Ron Koppelberger, Dena Mallory, John Marvin, Diane Webster, Greg Moglia, James Hoggard, Robert Cooperman, George Gott, John Grey, George W. Hayden, Lewis Horton, Mark Katrinak, Pamela L. Laskin, Sheryl L. Nelms, Charles Rammelkamp, Samantha R. Reiser, Ted Richer, Art Schwartz, Laurence Snydal, Vincent Tomeo, A.D. Winans, Yoseph Leibowitz-Shultz 1st and Arthur Winfield Knight. Artists include Jenna Walen (sculpture), Dennis Dreher, Guy R. Beining, Eric Walen, and Mary P. Leimbach. Photographers include Luke Walen, Crystal Walen, Max Buckley and U.S. Navy (1940's). Lois Shapley Bassen's The End of Shakespeare & Co. won the 2009 ATLANTIC PACIFIC PRESS DRAMA PRIZE. Ms. Bassen's play was published as a special edition of ATLANTIC PACIFIC PRESS. Query for copies. 2010 Drama Prize was cancelled. 2011 Drama prize submission deadline: January 30th. George W. Hayden will judge. Snail mail with a SASE for guidelines. Email queries to: lyrics_songs@yahoo.com." circ. 40. 4/yr. Pub'd 5 issues 2009; expects 4 issues 2010, 5 issues 2011. 1 title listed in the *Small Press Record of Books in Print* (36th Edition, 2010-11). sub. price $30; per copy $8 newstand; sample $10 postpaid. Back issues: $10 postpaid. Discounts: 2-10 copies 25%. 100pp. Reporting time: 1-3 months. Simultaneous submissions accepted: No. Publishes 80% of manuscripts submitted. Payment: Free contributor copy, publishes author bio with acknowledgements, contributors posted on web page. Copyright and international copyright notices are published on title pages for all contributors. Buy first North American and World serial rights. Rights revert to author upon publication. Ads: $35/180 character, $250 bus card, $500 half page, $1000 full page. Subjects: Arts, Avant-Garde, Experimental Art, Creative Non-fiction, Drama, Fantasy, Fiction, Humor, Military, Veterans, Mystery, Non-Fiction, Photography, Poetry, Vietnam, War, World War II.

Atlantic Path Publishing, 17 Hammond St., Gloucester, MA 01930, 978-283-1531, Fax 866-640-1412, contactus@atlanticpathpublishing.com, www.atlanticpathpublishing.com. 2002. Non-fiction. "Our titles include *Writing and Developing Your College Textbook, Second Edition: A Comprehensive Guide to Textbook Authorship and Higher Education Publishing* (2008), *Self-Publishing Textbooks and Instructional Materials* (2004), and *Writing and Developing College Textbook Supplements* (2005). Atlantic Path publishing specializes in books on writing and publishing for scholars, academics, instructors, teachers, textbook writers, educational content providers, publishers and editors." 3 titles listed in the *Small Press Record of Books in Print* (36th Edition, 2010-11).

Atlantic Publishing Group, Inc., 1210 SW 23rd Place, Ocala, FL 34474-7014, 800-814-1132, Fax 352-622-1875, sales@atlantic-pub.com, www.atlantic-pub.com. 1986. Non-fiction. "Your complete resource for small business, management, finance, hospitality online, and real estate books." avg. press run 4M. Pub'd 17 titles 2009; expects 20 titles 2010, 25 titles 2011. No titles listed in the *Small Press Record of Books in Print* (36th Edition, 2010-11). 288pp. Copyrights for author. Subjects: Advertising, Self-Promotion, Conservation, Education, Employment, Food, Eating, Fundraising, Gardening, How-To, Internet, Law, Non-Fiction, Parenting, Real Estate, Relationships, Wine, Wineries.

ATLANTIS: A Women's Studies Journal/Revue d'etudes sur les femmes, Katherine Side, Editor; Linda Kealey, Editor; Annalee Lepp, Editor, Institute for the Study of Women, Mt. Saint Vincent University, Halifax, N.S. B3M 2J6, Canada, 902-457-6319, Fax 902-443-1352, atlantis@msvu.ca, www.msvu.ca/atlantis. 1975. Articles, art, criticism, reviews. circ. 1M. 2/yr. Pub'd 2 issues 2009; expects 2 issues 2010, 2 issues 2011. sub. price individual $35Can, $40US, $45US overseas; institution $60Can, $65US, $70US overseas;; per copy $20 + p/h; sample same. Back issues: same. 200pp. Reporting time: 6-8 months. Simultaneous submissions accepted: no. Publishes 35-40% of manuscripts submitted. Payment: 1 complimentary issue. Copyrighted, does not revert to author. Pub's reviews: 15 in 2009. §Women's studies, feminism, interdisciplinary research, creative work on the topic of women. Ads: $250/$125. Subjects: Education, English, Feminism, Gender Issues, History, Humanism, Labor, Lesbianism, Liberal Arts, Literary Review, Political Science, Research, Science, Social Movements, Women.

AUFGABE, Litmus Press, Tracy Grinnell, Editor, PO Box 25526, Brooklyn, NY 11202-5526. 2001. Poetry, art, interviews, criticism, reviews, letters. "New experimental poetry, prose, and translations by established and emerging writers." circ. POD. Annual. 5 titles listed in the *Small Press Record of Books in Print* (36th Edition, 2010-11). sub. price $25 for 2 issues; per copy $15. 300pp. Simultaneous submissions accepted: Yes. Payment: 2 copies. Copyrighted, reverts to author. Pub's reviews: 4 in 2009. §Poetry. Ads: No.

August Press LLC, Wayne Dawkins, President; Rob King, Art Director, 108 Terrell Road, P.O. Box 6693, Newport News, VA 23606, wdawkins4bj@aol.com, www.augustpress.net. 1992. Pub'd 1 title 2009; expects 1 title 2010, 1 title 2011. No titles listed in the *Small Press Record of Books in Print* (36th Edition, 2010-11). Discounts: distributors 50-55 percent, wholesalers 50 percent, retailers 40 percent. Special discounts for institutions, classrooms and remainder buyers. 203pp.

Aunt Lute Books, Joan Pinkvoss, Senior Editor; Shay Brawn, Managing Editor, PO Box 410687, San Francisco, CA 94141, 415-826-1300; FAX 415-826-8300. 1978. Fiction, criticism, plays, non-fiction. "We publish multicultural, women's literature. Recent authors: Audre Lorde, Gloria Anzaldua, Melanie Kaye-Kantrowitz, Cherry Muhanji. Aunt Lute Books is part of the Aunt Lute Foundation, which is the non-profit entity that grew out of the work of Spinsters/Aunt Lute Book Co." avg. press run 3M-5M. Pub'd 2 titles 2009; expects 3 titles 2010, 5 titles 2011. 29 titles listed in the *Small Press Record of Books in Print* (36th Edition, 2010-11). Discounts: bookstores 20% on 1+ books, distributors 45-55%, no rate for single orders (unless bought at selected conferences). Reporting time: 3 months. Copyrights for author. Subjects: Feminism, Lesbianism, Third World, Minorities, Women.

AURA LITERARY ARTS REVIEW, Christopher Giganti, Editor-in-Chief; Daniel Robbins, Assistant Editor-in-Chief; Russell Helms, Editor, David Good, Steven Smith, HUC 135, 1530 3rd Avenue South, Birmingham, AL 35294, 205-934-3216. 1974. Poetry, fiction, articles, art, photos, interviews, reviews, plays. circ. 500. 2/yr. Pub'd 2 issues 2009; expects 2 issues 2010, 2 issues 2011. sub. price $12; per copy $6; sample none. Back issues: none. 140pp. Reporting time: asap, within 2 months usually. Simultaneous submissions accepted: no. Publishes 5-10% of manuscripts submitted. Payment: 2 copies. Copyrighted, reverts to author. Pub's reviews: none in 2009. §Fiction, poetry. Ads: $100/$50. Subjects: Literary Review, Literature (General), Poetry.

Aura Productions, LLC, Gennifer Marconette, 106 West 17th St, Hays, KS 67601, 785.259.6962. 2006. Criticism, news items, non-fiction. Pub'd 1 title 2009; expects 1 title 2010, 1 title 2011. 2 titles listed in the *Small Press Record of Books in Print* (36th Edition, 2010-11). 170pp. Publishes 90% of manuscripts submitted. Copyrights for author. Subjects: Christianity, Creative Non-fiction, Food, Eating, History, Non-Fiction, Research, Spiritual.

Auromere Books and Imports, 2621 W. US Highway 12, Lodi, CA 95242-9200, 800-735-4691, 209-339-3710, Fax 209-339-3715, books@auromere.com, www.auromere.com. 1974. "Sri Aurobindo Books, classical Indian Spiritual Texts, Children's Books, and Health books, including Ayurveda. We also have a few horticultural books. Also carry a number of side lines including imported bookmarks and incense. We are the exclusive U.S. representative of a number of publishers from India and their titles are significantly more in number. Including: Ganesh & Co.; National Book Trust of India; Hemkunt Books; All India Press; Children's Book Trust of India. In addition we also represent Sri Aurobindo Books Distribution Agency and here in the U.S., list has over titles. We do not accept submissions, as we publish existent classical texts. A free catalog of our books is available on request.'' avg. press run 5M-10M. Pub'd 1 title 2009; expects 3 titles 2010, 5 titles 2011. 28 titles listed in the *Small Press Record of Books in Print* (36th Edition, 2010-11). Discounts: trade 40%, $50 minimum order after discount; jobbers, distributors by arrangement. 200pp. Payment: variable. Does not copyright for author. Subjects: Children, Youth, Occult, Philosophy, Spiritual.

THE AUROREAN, Cynthia Brackett-Vincent, PO Box 187, Farmington, ME 04938, 207-778-0467. 1995. Poetry. "http://www.encirclepub.com. Biannual (Spring/Summer and Fall/Winter). One of 12 'Insider Reports' in 1999 *Poet's Market*, recommended by *Small Press Review*. Request guidelines or sample! Approx. 36 lines max. Always send proofs; always acknowledge receipt of manuscript. 1-2 Featured Poets each issue receive 10 copies, 100 word bio. and 1 year subscription. No e-mail submissions. Please do not fold poems individually. Also publishes *The Unrorean* twice yearly - editor's alter ego. You may submit solely to *Unrorean* or, unless otherwise requested, poems will be considered for both. *Unrorean* is 11x17, laser printed; $2 each; pays 1 copy per poem. Independent judge picks 'Best Poem' for each *Aurorean*; winner receives $30. Also, send quotes for 'Poetic Quote of the Season' - 4 lines max. from not too obscure poet; cannot be acknowledged or returned; winner receives 2 free issues of *Aurorean*. Editor picks one chapbook to recommend each issue; send recently published chaps; cannot be returned or acknowledged. (We do not publish reviews.) New: Creative Writing Student Outstanding Haiku Contest, see website for guidelines.'' circ. 500. 2/yr. Pub'd 2 issues 2009; expects 2 issues 2010, 2 issues 2011. sub. price $21, $23 international (two issues); per copy $11, $12 international: current 2 issues. Back issues: random previous quarterly format from our available stock: $3 each (U.S. only); biannuals over one year old $7 each (U.S. only). Reporting time: 3 months maximum. Simultaneous submissions accepted if noted up front; I discourage them as we always reply in stated time. Publishes 15% of manuscripts submitted. Payment: 2 copies per poem, up to 5 total copies per issue. Copyrighted, reverts to author. Ads: will do ad and subscription exchanges with other journals; send a sample with request. Subjects: Haiku, Inspirational, New England, Self-Help.

Authentic Publishing LLC, Julius Williams III, PO Box 8486, Philadelphia, PA 19101, 215-495-7300, www.AuthenticPublishingLLC.com, ContactUs@AuthenticPublishingLLC.com. Poetry, fiction, articles, letters, non-fiction. 1 title listed in the *Small Press Record of Books in Print* (36th Edition, 2010-11). Subjects: Children, Youth, Cities, Creative Non-fiction, Criticism, Education, Fiction, Juvenile Fiction, Non-Fiction, Picture Books, Poetry, Race, Social Work, Society, Sports, Outdoors, Young Adult.

Authorlink.com, Doris Booth, Editor-in-Chief, PO Box 140278, Irving, TX 75014-0278, http://www.authorlink.com, (972) 402-0101 /Fax 1-866-381-1587. "Authorlink is the award-winning online news, information, and marketing service for editors, agents, producers, writers, and readers. We serve more than one million unique visitors per year. Established in March 1996, we are among the longest-running and largest publishing and writing communities on the Internet.'' No titles listed in the *Small Press Record of Books in Print* (36th Edition, 2010-11).

Autumn House Press, Michael Simms, Editor in Chief, Poetry Editor; Sharon Dilworth, Fiction Editor, P.O. Box 60100, Pittsburgh, PA 15211, 412-381-4261, www.autumnhouse.org. 1998. Poetry, fiction. "Autumn House authors include Gerald Stern, Chana Bloch, George Bilgere, Samuel Ligon, Andrea Hollander Budy, Ed Ochester, Derek Green, Julie Suk, Jo McDougall, Sue Ellen Thompson, Samuel Hazo, Rita Dove, Jane Hirshfield, Naomi Shihab Nye, and others. Submissions come through one of our annual contests. Deadline June 30 for full-length collections of poetry and fiction: see guidelines www.autumnhouse.org. Deadline November 1 for poetry chapbooks: see guidelines www.coalhillreview.com.'' avg. press run 1500. Pub'd 8 titles 2009; expects 8 titles 2010, 9 titles 2011. No titles listed in the *Small Press Record of Books in Print* (36th Edition, 2010-11). Discounts: Trade: 40%, College Bookstores: 20%. 64-432pp. Reporting time: Contest deadline June 30 each year. Winner announced in September. See website for guidelines. www.autumnhouse.org. Simultaneous submissions accepted: Yes. Publishes 1% of manuscripts submitted. Payment: $2,500 for Prize winner and 7% royalty. Copyrights for author. Subjects: Fiction, Poetry.

Avari Press, Anthony Verrecchia, President and Publisher, P.O. Box 285, Smoketown, PA 17576, editorial@avaripress.com, http://www.avaripress.com. Fiction, non-fiction. "Avari Press is a publishing company devoted to fantasy literature, medieval studies, and nonfiction.'' avg. press run 5000. Pub'd 3 titles 2009; expects 5 titles 2010, 6 titles 2011. 3 titles listed in the *Small Press Record of Books in Print* (36th Edition, 2010-11). 250-350pp. Reporting time: One month or less. Simultaneous submissions accepted: Yes. Payment: Varies, but usually 7% of retail. Copyrights for author. Subjects: Fantasy, Fiction, Gay, History, Medieval, Mystery, Non-Fiction, Novels, Renaissance, J.R.R. Tolkien, Young Adult.

•**The Avery Anthology,** 3657 Broadway, Apt. 1E, New York, NY 10031. "Avery is an anthology of fiction fiction, because, in a world made meaningful by storytelling of all kinds, it's still what moves us most. Perhaps you've noticed that Avery also does something an anthology of fiction isnt supposed to do: it publishes stories that haven't been published anywhere else. Our stories are here, now, to be read, now. We Avery's readers, writers, and contributors are deciding whats worthwhile and whats necessary. You needn't wait for the Best Best Best of the Year we've got it for you in every issue. So what is worthwhile? What kind of stories do we read? Donald Barthelme once said the only criteria on which to judge a story is: Does it knock your socks off? We like that, but we dont think its entirely accurate. We like stories that knock our socks off, but we also like stories that slip our socks off gently, or rip our socks off unexpectedly, or tug and tug at our socks until theyre lying on the floor beside the bed. The important thing is that by the end of the story our feet are bare. We plan publish two anthologies per year. We hope that writers will find their way to us, so that readers can find their way to them." No titles listed in the *Small Press Record of Books in Print* (36th Edition, 2010-11).

Avery Color Studios, Wells Chapin, 511 D Avenue, Gwinn, MI 49841, 800-722-9925. 1956. Fiction, photos, non-fiction. "History, folklore, shipwrecks, pictorials. Contributors: Frederick Stonehouse, Joan Bestwick, Neil Moran, Cully Gage, Wes Oleszewski." avg. press run 5M. Pub'd 2 titles 2009; expects 4 titles 2010, 2 titles 2011. 38 titles listed in the *Small Press Record of Books in Print* (36th Edition, 2010-11). Discounts: 40% trade. 185pp. Reporting time: 30 days. Payment: negotiable. Copyrights for author. Subjects: Americana, Animals, Cooking, Fiction, Folklore, History, Michigan, Midwest, Native American, Non-Fiction, Photography, Reprints, Sports, Outdoors, Sports, Outdoors.

Avisson Press, Inc., M.L. Hester, 3007 Taliaferro Road, Greensboro, NC 27408, 336-288-6989 phone/FAX. 1995. Non-fiction. "Book-length only; history, serious nonfiction. Looking too for experts in cuting edge nutrition or supplements. Also young adult (age 12-18) biographies of famous people or historical period. PLEASE DO NOT SEND YOUR OWN LIFE STORY OR INSPIRATIONAL HOW-I-OVERCAME MY MISERABLE CHILDHOOD, ETC. type manuscripts.Additional address: PO Box 38816, Greensboro, NC 27438." avg. press run 1M-3M. Pub'd 7 titles 2009; expects 6 titles 2010, 7 titles 2011. No titles listed in the *Small Press Record of Books in Print* (36th Edition, 2010-11). Discounts: 20-40%. 144pp. Reporting time: 2-4 weeks. Simultaneous submissions accepted: yes. Publishes 3% of manuscripts submitted. Payment: standard royalty (6-10%). Copyrights for author. Subjects: Biography, Young Adult.

Avocet Press Inc., Melanie Kershaw, Cynthia Webb, 19 Paul Court, Pearl River, NY 10965, 212-754-6300, oopc@interport.net, www.avocetpress.com. 1997. Poetry, fiction. "Publishers of Renee Ashley's second book of poetry *The Various Reasons of Light*." avg. press run 3M. Pub'd 1 title 2009; expects 3 titles 2010, 6 titles 2011. 13 titles listed in the *Small Press Record of Books in Print* (36th Edition, 2010-11). Reporting time: 6 months. Simultaneous submissions accepted: yes. Publishes 1% of manuscripts submitted. Copyrights for author. Subjects: Fiction, Mystery, Poetry.

AWAREing Press, James Beach, 551 W. Cordova Rd., #369, Santa Fe, NM 87505. 2007. Poetry, fiction, non-fiction. "AWAREing Press strives to entertain, educate, enlighten. Our titles reflect a new awareness of the composition of life, beyond the biological and tangible aspects that are evident to most every body. We are a very small press; the esoteric nature of our work currently demands this. New titles out every year, in theory." avg. press run 1000. Pub'd 1 title 2009; expects 1-2 titles 2010, 1-2 titles 2011. 3 titles listed in the *Small Press Record of Books in Print* (36th Edition, 2010-11). Discounts: 1 copy 25%, 2 or more copies 40%. 300pp. Simultaneous submissions accepted: No. Copyrights for author.

AXE FACTORY REVIEW, Cynic Press, Joseph Farley, PO Box 40691, Philadelphia, PA 19107. 1986. Poetry, fiction, articles, art, photos, cartoons, interviews, satire, criticism, reviews, music, letters, parts-of-novels, long-poems, collages, plays, concrete art, news items, non-fiction. "Poetry, black and white art, and book reviews have the best shot. Also read short stories. Recent contributors include normal, Louis McKee, Taylor Graham, John Sweet, A.D. Winans, Xu Juan, Don Winter. Indexed in *Humanities International Complete*. It is recommended that writers read an issue or two before submitting. Samples back issues available for $8. All checks to "Cynic Press." Note: After a 24 year run, we are hanging up our guns." circ. 300. 2-3/yr. Pub'd 2 issues 2009; expects 1 issue 2010. sub. price $15/2 issues (all checks to Cynic Press); per copy $9; sample $8. Back issues: $8. Discounts: none. Pages vary. Reporting time: immediately. Simultaneous submissions accepted: yes. Publishes 10% of manuscripts submitted. Payment: 1 copy; more for featured poet. Copyrighted, reverts to author. Pub's reviews: 35 in 2009. §Poetry, sci-fi, martial arts, Asian literature and history, fiction, short stories, American history, Medeival history, sex, art history. Ads: $50/$25/trade. Subjects: Asia, Indochina, Book Reviewing, Cartoons, Erotica, Essays, Fantasy, Fiction, Horror, Interviews, Non-Fiction, Poetry, Satire, Science Fiction.

AXES & ALLEYS, Scott Birdseye, Jeremy Rosen, 25-26 44th Street #A1, Astoria, NY 11103, 718-204-0313, jeremy@danielbester.com. 2003. Fiction, articles, art, photos, cartoons, interviews, satire, criticism, reviews, music, letters, news items, non-fiction. circ. 40,000. 12/yr. Pub'd 12 issues 2009; expects 12 issues 2010, 12 issues 2011. sub. price free. 30pp. Reporting time: 3. Simultaneous submissions accepted: no. Copyrighted, reverts to author. Pub's reviews: 1 in 2009. §music, fiction. Subject: Experimental.

Axios Newletter, Inc., Daniel John Gorham, Joseph T. Magnin, 16 Maxi Street, PO Box 90, Santa Elena, Cayo, Belize, Belize, 501-824-2382 Daxgor@Yahoo.com. 1981. Articles, art, photos, cartoons, interviews, satire, criticism, reviews, letters, parts-of-novels, news items, non-fiction. "We publish Orthodox Christian books, art and pamphlets, also philosophy and historical books. Republish old out-of-print books, in some cases—would like to see some religious history of Russia, Greece, Albania, Bulgaria, Finland, Rumania, and also America, if it pertains to the Orthodox Christian." avg. press run varies. Pub'd 3 titles 2009; expects 5 titles 2010. 2 titles listed in the *Small Press Record of Books in Print* (36th Edition, 2010-11). Discounts: 40% trade. 355pp. Reporting time: 2-4 weeks. Payment: negotiated. Copyrights for author. Subjects: History, Libertarian, Religion.

Azro Press, PMB 342, 1704 Llano Street B, Santa Fe, NM 87505, gae@nets.com, www.azropress.com. 1997. avg. press run 1K-2.5K. Pub'd 2 titles 2009; expects 8 titles 2010, 5 titles 2011. 1 title listed in the *Small Press Record of Books in Print* (36th Edition, 2010-11). Discounts: 40% to 55%. 32pp. Reporting time: 6 months. Simultaneous submissions accepted: yes. Publishes 10% of manuscripts submitted. Payment: 5-10%. Copyrights for author. Subject: Children, Youth.

AZTLAN: A Journal of Chicano Studies, UCLA Chicano Studies Research Center Press, Chon A. Noriega, Editor; Wendy Belcher, Managing Editor, University of California-Los Angeles, 193 Haines Hall, Los Angeles, CA 90095-1544, 310-825-2642, press@chicano.ucla.edu, www.chicano.ucla.edu. 1970. Articles, criticism, reviews, news items. "*Aztlan* is the oldest continuously published journal focusing on the Chicano experience in the U.S. and Mexico. It is the journal of record in the field." circ. 1M. 2/yr. Pub'd 2 issues 2009; expects 2 issues 2010, 2 issues 2011. sub. price $30 individuals, $195 libraries & institutions. Back issues: $15.00 indiv., $95 instit. Discounts: classroom use. 300pp. Reporting time: 3 months. Simultaneous submissions accepted: no. Publishes 25% of manuscripts submitted. Payment: books in quantity. Copyrighted, does not revert to author. Pub's reviews: 9 in 2009. §Chicano studies. Ads: $225/$125. Subjects: Chicano/a, Society.

Azul Editions, Richard Schaaf, 2013 Park Rd., NW, Washington, DC 20010, 703.861.1298, info@azuleditions.com, www.azuleditions.com. 1986. Poetry, fiction, articles, interviews, criticism, long-poems. "We are looking for poetry, prose, art and literary theory that is socially and politically engaged. We produce fine books in limited editions, with the commitment to keep our titles in print always. Thus far our list of titles includes both important archival work as well as contemporary work." avg. press run 100-200. Pub'd 7 titles 2009; expects 6 titles 2010, 8 titles 2011. No titles listed in the *Small Press Record of Books in Print* (36th Edition, 2010-11). Discounts: bookstores 40% libraries 20%. 32-125pp. Reporting time: authors are requested to email samples of submission—1wk-4wk response time. Simultaneous submissions accepted: Yes. Payment: 10% of cover price royalty. Copyrights for author.

AzurAlive, Florence Chatzigianis, 751 Laurel Street, Suite 808, San Carlos, CA 94070, 650-276-0448, http://azuralive.com. 2007. Non-fiction. "AzurAlive publishes travel guides for engaged visitors who long to discover and learn about the natural side of their destination." avg. press run 1500. Expects 1 title 2010, 2 titles 2011. 1 title listed in the *Small Press Record of Books in Print* (36th Edition, 2010-11). 128pp. Subjects: Earth, Natural History, Ecology, Foods, Environment, Europe, France, French, Nature, Non-Fiction, Outdoor Adventure, Reviews, Sports, Outdoors, Travel.

B

The B & R Samizdat Express, Barbara Hartley Seltzer, Partner; Richard Seltzer, Partner; Robert Richard Seltzer, Vice-President; Heather Katherine Seltzer, Vice-President; Michael Richard Seltzer, Vice-President; Timothy Seltzer, Vice-President, 33 Gould Street, West Roxbury, MA 02132, 617-469-2269, seltzer@samizdat.com, main content site http://www.samizdat.com online store http://store.yahoo.com/samizdat. 1974. "We publish electronic books in collections on CD and DVD (to be read on a computer)—plain text books, organized for ease of use. We have about 200 offerings, including our "Complete Book DVD" with the full text of over 20,000 classic books. We also publish books for the Amazon Kindle, the Sony Reader, the Barnes and Noble Nook, and other devices that read the .epub format. We do not solicit manuscripts. You can see the tables of contents of all our CDs and DVDs at our Yahoo store http://store.yahoo.com/samizdat." Pub'd 40 titles 2009; expects 40 titles 2010, 60 titles 2011. 4 titles listed in the *Small Press Record of Books in Print* (36th Edition, 2010-11). Our books are in electronic form, hence they have no "pages".pp. Reporting time: We do not read manuscripts. We publish public domain books. Subjects: African Literature, Africa, African Studies,

Anthropology, Archaelogy, Children, Youth, Classical Studies, Drama, Fiction, History, Humor, Native American, Occult, Philosophy, Poetry, Political Science, Psychology, Religion.

BABYSUE, BABYSUE MUSIC REVIEW, Don W. Seven, PO Box 15749, Chattanooga, TN 37415. 1985. Poetry, cartoons, interviews, satire, reviews, music. "We mainly feature bizarre adult cartoons, although we feature poetry, interviews, and reviews as well." circ. 5M. 2/yr. Pub'd 2 issues 2009; expects 2 issues 2010, 2 issues 2011. No subscriptions; price per copy $5 (cash, check or money order payable to "Fievet"); sample $5 (cash, check or money order payable to "Fievet"). Back issues: $5 (cash, check or money order payable to "Fievet"). 32pp. Reporting time: 1 month. Simultaneous submissions accepted: yes. Publishes 5% of manuscripts submitted. Payment: 1 free copy of magazine in which work appears. Copyrighted, reverts to author. Pub's reviews: 500 in 2009. §Cartoons, music magazines, cassettes, CDs and vinyl. We do not accept advertisements. Subjects: Comics, Humor, Magazines, Music, Poetry, Satire.

BABYSUE MUSIC REVIEW, BABYSUE, Don W. Seven, S. Fievet, PO Box 15749, Chattanooga, TN 37415. 1985. Photos, cartoons, interviews, music, news items. "*Babysue Music Review* consists mostly of music reviews. We review all types of music on all formats (vinyl, CD, cassette)." circ. 5M. 4/yr. Pub'd 4 issues 2009; expects 4 issues 2010, 4 issues 2011. price per copy $5 (cash, check or money order payable to "Fievet"); sample $5 (cash, check or money order payable to "Fievet"). Back issues: $5 (cash, check or money order payable to "Fievet"). Discounts: varies. 32pp. Reporting time: 3 months. Payment: each contributor recieves 1 copy of the issue in which their contribution appears. Copyrighted, reverts to author. Pub's reviews: 500 in 2009. §Anything related to music. We do not accept advertisements. Subjects: Arts, Comics, Music.

The Bacchae Press, Robert Brown, c/o The Brown Financial Group, 10 Sixth Street, Suite 215, Astoria, OR 97103-5315, 503-325-7972; FAX 503-325-7959; 800-207-4358; E-mail brown@pacifier.com. 1992. Poetry, fiction. "We publish mostly poetry. In 1993, we published 5 books of poetry: 2 anthologies of local poets, 1 full-length collection of poetry, and two chapbooks. All of our books are professionally printed on high-quality paper. Chapbook contest deadline is April 15." avg. press run 500. Pub'd 3 titles 2009; expects 4 titles 2010, 4 titles 2011. 4 titles listed in the *Small Press Record of Books in Print* (36th Edition, 2010-11). Discounts: 40%. 70pp. Reporting time: 3 months. Simultaneous submissions accepted: yes. Publishes less than 1% of manuscripts submitted. Payment: 10%. Copyrights for author. Subjects: Fiction, Ohio, Poetry.

Back House Books (see also CAFE NOIR REVIEW), Philip Henderson, 1703 Lebanon Street, Adelphi, MD 20783. 1999. Poetry, fiction, articles, photos, cartoons, interviews, satire, criticism, reviews, letters, parts-of-novels, long-poems, plays, non-fiction. "We are looking for well-written, quality material. No neo-conservatives/far-rightists, please." avg. press run 300. Pub'd 1 title 2009; expects 1-2 titles 2010, 2-3 titles 2011. No titles listed in the *Small Press Record of Books in Print* (36th Edition, 2010-11). Pages vary. Reporting time: 1-3 months. Simultaneous submissions accepted: no. Publishes 1-2% of manuscripts submitted. Payment: 10% of sales on books. Copyrights for author. Subjects: African Literature, Africa, African Studies, Arts, Asian-American, Black, Chicano/a, Communism, Marxism, Leninism, Gay, Lesbianism, Literary Review, Poetry, Race, Society, Third World, Minorities, Women, Worker.

Backcountry Publishing, Michelle Riley, Editor; Matt Richards, Editor, 3303 Dick George Road, Cave Junction, OR 97523-9623, 541-955-5650. 1997. Non-fiction. "Books and booklets (40-600 pages); Only interested in authors who want to take strong role in publicizing, publishing their own books. We are a publishing co-op that supports, shares and directs authors through collective publishing. Topics limited to primitive skills, wilderness living, and simple living. Backcountry Publishing is distributed by Partners Publishers Group." avg. press run 5K. Pub'd 1 title 2009; expects 3 titles 2010. 1 title listed in the *Small Press Record of Books in Print* (36th Edition, 2010-11). Discounts: 3-20 40%, 20-199 40% + free shipping, 200-499 50%, 500+ 55%. 180pp. Reporting time: 4-6 weeks. Simultaneous submissions accepted: yes. Payment: individual basis. Does not copyright for author. Subjects: Crafts, Hobbies, How-To, Native American, Sports, Outdoors.

The Backwaters Press, Greg Kosmicki, Editor; Rich Wyatt, Editor, 3502 N 52nd St, Omaha, NE 68104-3506, 402-451-4052e-mail: gkosmicki@cox.net..comWebsite: www.thebackwaterspress.homestead.com. 1997. Poetry. "The Backwaters Press no longer offers any contests. We read year-round for Open Submissions; poets should note in the cover letter and on the mailing address "Open Submissions" when submitting. Send SASE for open submission details, or e-mail to gkosmicki@cox.net with the subject line "Open Submissions Guidelines;" or go to the website at www.thebackwaterspress.homestead.com. No deadlines; we read all year." avg. press run 200-300. Pub'd 8 titles 2009; expects 12 titles 2010, 12 titles 2011. 51 titles listed in the *Small Press Record of Books in Print* (36th Edition, 2010-11). Discounts: libraries and bookstores, please query, newest titles available through Ingram,all titles at Amazon.com. 80pp. Reporting time: Reports in one to two months for open submissions. Simultaneous submission OK, please note in cover letter. Publishes less than 1% of manuscripts submitted. Payment: Poets published under open submissions will receive 10% of the press run as payment, as well as generous discounts on their titles. Copyrights for author. Subject: Poetry.

Bad Noise Productions (see also GRAMMAR CRISIS), Saburo Taiso, 25 Kingsland Ave. #3L, Brooklyn, NY 11211-1530, www.badnoiseproductions.com, saburo@badnoiseproductions.com. 2006. Poetry, fiction, articles, art, photos, interviews, criticism, music, letters, long-poems, collages, concrete art, non-fiction. "Would you like to want Bad Noise Productions? Yeah! check da website (www.badnoiseproductions.com). The harder has come who is the noise blown-out super star." Expects 3-5 titles 2010. No titles listed in the *Small Press Record of Books in Print* (36th Edition, 2010-11). Discounts: Most publications available FREE in digital formats on-line at www.badnoiseproductions.com. 50-100pp. Simultaneous submissions accepted: Yes. Bad Noise Productions believes firmly in Creative Commons licensing for its creative output. Subjects: Anarchist, Cartoons, Dada, Death & Dying, Drugs, Erotica, Experimental, Fiction, Hunger, Language, Music, Occult, Poetry, Post Modern, Prose.

BAD PRESS SERIALS, Bad Press, Jow Lindsay Mr, 21 Portland Rise, Finsbury Park, London, United Kingdom, Email: badpress@gmail.com Web: http://badpress.infinology.net. Pub's reviews.

BAGAZINE, X-Ray Book Co., Johnny Brewton, Po Box 2234, Pasadena, CA 91102. 2005. Poetry, art, photos, satire, reviews, music, letters, parts-of-novels, collages, plays, concrete art. "Bagazine is an assemblage magazine in a bag. Contributors are asked to submit 126 pieces per guidelines for assembly. We do not print your stuff. Silkscreen, Gocco, Letterpress, Xerox, Potato Prints, Photography, rubberstamp, chapbooks, comics, poems, CDs etc... www.bagazine for guidelines and more information." circ. 126. 6/yr. Expects 2 issues 2010, 6 issues 2011. price per copy $55. Back issues: inquire. Discounts: inquire. 40pp. Reporting time: 10 Days. Simultaneous submissions accepted: No. Publishes 35% of manuscripts submitted. Payment: (1) copy. Copyright reverts to Artist or Author with permission to reprint in collected works book. §Jazz, Assemblage, D.I.Y., Novels, CDs and LPs, Film. Ads: Inquire. Subjects: Abstracts, Avant-Garde, Experimental Art, Book Arts, Crafts, Hobbies, Experimental, Futurism, Music, Photography, Poetry, Postcards, Zines.

Balanced Books Publishing, Robin Mastro, PO Box 14957, Seattle, WA 98144, 206-328-3995, fax 206-328-1339, toll free 877-838-4858, info@balancedbookspub.com, www.balancedbookspub.com. 2003. Non-fiction. "Balanced Books is a small press nestled in the heart of the Pacific Northwest. We chose the pristine beauty of this corner of the world to establish our business because it inspires us to seek balance between the outer world of activity and the inner world of peace. We at Balanced Books support ideas, concepts, and philosophies that encourage personal growth, inspire creative change, and bring joy into people's lives. The mission of Balanced Books is to inform, uplift, and support personal and planetary growth by offering beneficial techniques and philosophies through books that promote health, prosperity, positive relationships, and happiness. We are not accepting submissions at this time." avg. press run 5000. Expects 1 title 2010, 2 titles 2011. 2 titles listed in the *Small Press Record of Books in Print* (36th Edition, 2010-11). Discounts: Please check website - www.balancedbookspub.com. 200pp. Reporting time: We are not accepting submissions at this time. Subjects: Health, New Age, Non-Fiction, Self-Help, Spiritual.

Balcony Media, Inc. (see also FORM: pioneering design), Alexi Drosu, Editor in Chief, 512 E. Wilson Avenue, Suite 213, Glendale, CA 91206, 818-956-5313(T), web: www.balconypress.com, email: alexi@formmag.net. 1994. Art, non-fiction. "Prefer art and architecture submissions with a focus on cultural importance as opposed to analytical or reference material. Authors must be able to provide all images and illustrations with permissions." avg. press run 5M. Pub'd 4 titles 2009; expects 4 titles 2010, 5 titles 2011. 18 titles listed in the *Small Press Record of Books in Print* (36th Edition, 2010-11). Discounts: varies depending on quantity. 150pp. Reporting time: 1 month. Simultaneous submissions accepted: No. Publishes 10% of manuscripts submitted. Payment: 10% net, paid annually. Copyrights for author. Subjects: Architecture, Arts, Culture, Design, Los Angeles, Southwest.

BALLOT ACCESS NEWS, Richard Winger, PO Box 470296, San Francisco, CA 94147, 415-922-9779, fax 415-441-4268, e-Mail ban@igc.apc.org, www.ballot-access.org. 1985. News items. "Bias in favor of voter's right to vote for the party of his or her choice. Bias against laws which interfere with this right." circ. 1M. 12/yr. Pub'd 12 issues 2009; expects 12 issues 2010, 12 issues 2011. sub. price $13; per copy free; sample free. Back issues: $1 per issue. 6.25pp. Publishes 25% of manuscripts submitted. Payment: none. Not copyrighted. Pub's reviews: 3 in 2009. §Political parties. Ads: none. Subjects: Civil Rights, Political Science, Politics.

THE BALTIMORE REVIEW, Susan Muaddi Darraj, PO Box 36418, Towson, MD 21286, www.BaltimoreReview.org. 1996. Poetry, fiction, interviews, reviews, parts-of-novels, long-poems, non-fiction. "WE ACCEPT SUBMISSIONS VIA OUR WEBSITE ONLY. GO TO WWW.BALTIMOREREVIEW.ORG. Also see our website for information regarding our annual Fiction, Poetry, and Creative Nonfiction Competitions." 2/yr. Pub'd 2 issues 2009; expects 2 issues 2010, 2 issues 2011. sub. price $15; per copy $8; sample $10. Back issues: $10. Discounts: distributors 55% retailers 50%. 144pp. Reporting time: 4-6 months. Simultaneous submissions accepted: Yes. Publishes 10% of manuscripts submitted. Payment: 2 contributor copies. Copyrighted, reverts to author. Pub's reviews: 10 in 2009. §Fiction, poetry, and nonfiction by small, independent, or university presses. Ads: Full page only $150 per issue (discounts with more than one issue). Discount for non-profits or arts organizations. Subjects: Arts, Book Reviewing, Essays, Fiction, Interviews,

Literary Review, Non-Fiction, Novels, Poetry, Prose, Reviews, Short Stories.

Bamboo Ridge Press (see also BAMBOO RIDGE, Journal of Hawai'i Literature and Arts), Eric Chock, Darrell H.Y. Lum, PO Box 61781, Honolulu, HI 96839-1781, 808-626-1481 phone/Fax, brinfo@bamboor-idge.com. 1978. Poetry, fiction, plays. "Particular interest in island writers and writing which reflects the multi-ethnic culture of Hawaii." avg. press run 1M. Pub'd 2 titles 2009; expects 2 titles 2010, 2 titles 2011. 34 titles listed in the *Small Press Record of Books in Print* (36th Edition, 2010-11). Discounts: 40%. 125-200pp. Reporting time: 6 months. Simultaneous submissions accepted: no. Copyrights for author. Subjects: Asian-American, Hawaii, Literature (General).

BAMBOO RIDGE, Journal of Hawai'i Literature and Arts, Bamboo Ridge Press, Eric Chock, Darrell H.Y. Lum, PO Box 61781, Honolulu, HI 96839-1781. 1978. Poetry, fiction, articles, plays, non-fiction. "Particular interest in literature reflecting the multi-ethnic culture of the Hawaiian islands." circ. 600-1M. 2/yr. Pub'd 2 issues 2009; expects 2 issues 2010, 2 issues 2011. sub. price $20 individual, $25 institutions; per copy $8-18; sample $10. Back issues: varies. Discounts: 40%. 125-200pp. Reporting time: 6 months. Simultaneous submissions accepted: no. Payment: usually $10/poem, $20/prose piece. Copyrighted, reverts to author. Ads: $100/$60. Subjects: Asian-American, Hawaii, Literature (General).

Banana Productions (see also BANANA RAG; INTERNATIONAL ART POST), Anna Banana, 3747 Highway 101, Roberts Creek, BC V0N 2W2, Canada, 604-885-7156, no fax #. 1988. Art, photos. "Internatioinal Art Post (IAP) is a cooperatively published periodical. Contributors pay and get 1/2 the edition." avg. press run 1M. Pub'd 1 title 2009; expects 1 title 2010, 1 title 2011. 2 titles listed in the *Small Press Record of Books in Print* (36th Edition, 2010-11). Discounts: not applicable. IAP-1 page, Banana Rag 6-8 pages. Reporting time: acknowledgement within 1 week of receipt of deposit (50% up front). Simultaneous submissions accepted: yes. IAP- publish 100% of art or photos submitted, Banana Rag, 25-35%. Payment: they receive 500 copies of the stamp(s). Copyrights for author. Subjects: Advertising, Self-Promotion, Arts, Design, Graphics, Philately, Photography.

BANANA RAG, Banana Productions, Anna Banana, 3747 Highway 101, Roberts Creek, B.C. V0N 2W2, Canada, 604-885-7156. 1971. Articles, art, photos, cartoons, letters, collages, news items. "The Banana Rag is a long-time "zine" reflecting my connection with the International Mail-art Network (IMAN), and publishes material sent in by the network correspondents, along with an update on what's happening in my art life. The current issue (No. 38, Sept '08) has 2 pages of Banana News, 4 pages of reviews of mail-art catalogues, zines and books, all with several illustrations; a page of artistamps and postcards, and the usual single page letter from the editor. Subscriptions are $15/2 issues whenever they come out; $40 for deluxe edition accompanied by a signed and numbered limited color print by editor A. Banana. ISSN 1715-1341. Summer 2009 edition will report on the results of the upcoming European research tour/project, But is it Art? Where do you draw the line? conducted by Doktor Anna Freud Banana of the Specific Research Institute, Canada, in Rome, Cararra, Zierikzee, Gent, Minden, Berlin, Budapest, Bremen and Aalborg. Published 2 issues in '07 and '08, expects 1 in '09, '10." circ. 200. 1/yr. Pub'd 1 issue 2009; expects 1 issue 2010, 1 issue 2011. 1 title listed in the *Small Press Record of Books in Print* (36th Edition, 2010-11). sub. price $15/2 issues; $40 for deluxe edition that includes signed and numbered ltd. edition color print by A. Banana.; per copy $15/2 issues; $40 for deluxe edition that includes a signed and numbered, limited edition color print by editor, A. Banana.; sample $5. Back issues: many, please inquire. Discounts: nada. 4-8pp. Reporting time: usually within a year! Simultaneous submissions accepted: No. No payments given. Not copyrighted. Pub's reviews: 14 in 2009. §MAIL-ART ZINES, exhibition catalogues and related publications such as artist stamps; BANANA RELATED art, advertisements, postcards, information, articles, jokes, music, news-stories, products, photos, "slanguage," etc. etc. No ads. Subjects: Absurdist, Agriculture, Arts, Avant-Garde, Experimental Art, Botany, Cartoons, Conservation, Cooking, Dada, Entertainment, Experimental, Food, Eating, History, Humor, Postcards.

Bancroft Press, Bruce Bortz, Publisher, PO Box 65360, Baltimore, MD 21209-9945, 410-358-0658, Fax 410-764-1967. 1991. Fiction, non-fiction. "We are a general interest trade publisher specializing in books by journalists. However, submissions are welcome from all serious writers." avg. press run 3,000. Pub'd 4 titles 2009; expects 5 titles 2010, 4-6 titles 2011. 10 titles listed in the *Small Press Record of Books in Print* (36th Edition, 2010-11). Discounts: standard discounts apply. 300pp. Reporting time: varies. Simultaneous submissions accepted: yes. Publishes 1-5% of manuscripts submitted. Payment: yes. Copyrights for author. Subjects: African-American, Anthology, Arts, Biography, Book Reviewing, Current Affairs, Electronics, Essays, Fiction, Finances, Humor, Literary Review, Memoirs, Non-Fiction, Parenting.

Bandanna Books, Sasha "Birdie" Newborn, 1212 Punta Gorda Street #13, Santa Barbara, CA 93103-3568, Phone 805-899-2145, Fax 805-899-2145, bandanna@cox.net, www.bandannabooks.com. 1975. Fiction, art, parts-of-novels, plays, non-fiction. "Bandanna Books serves the college market with humanities classics and college prep materials. On request, BBooks can design and produce books for self-publishers. Also, the Book Doctor is in, for manuscripts in need of help." avg. press run Print on demand. Expects 2 titles 2010, 2 titles 2011. 14 titles listed in the *Small Press Record of Books in Print* (36th Edition, 2010-11). College bookstore discount 20% for 5+ copies. Credit for returned resaleable copies is good for 2 years. Shipping: $5+ $0.50 per book. No express shipping. Order by fax or on the Web at www.bbooks.info. 80pp. Reporting time: 2 months. Simultaneous submissions accepted: yes. Publishes 5% of manuscripts submitted. Payment: by agreement. Copyrights for author. Subjects: Atheism, Charles Bukowski, Creative Non-fiction, English, Erotica, Fiction, Gender Issues, Liberal Arts, Literature (General), Prose, Shakespeare, Short Stories, Textbooks, Writers/Writing, Young Adult.

Banks Channel Books, 2435 East North St. #245, Greenville, SC 29615, Order phone 215-589-5032; E-mail bankschan@aol.com. 1993. Fiction, art, photos, non-fiction. ''We publish Carolina authors only.'' avg. press run 1M-5M. Expects 2 titles 2010. 12 titles listed in the *Small Press Record of Books in Print* (36th Edition, 2010-11). Discounts: retailers 1-2 copies 20%, 3 or more 40%, 10+ prepaid, nonreturnable 45%. 200pp. Simultaneous submissions accepted: no. Payment: 10% of gross receipts. Copyrights for author. Subjects: Adolescence, Fiction, North Carolina, Novels, Religion, Social Movements, Women, Young Adult.

Banta & Pool Literary Properties, Gary Pool, Executive Editor; Frank Banta, Publisher, 1020 Greenwood Avenue, Bloomington, IN 47401, writerpool@aol.com. 1995. Poetry, fiction, non-fiction. avg. press run 2500 copies. No titles listed in the *Small Press Record of Books in Print* (36th Edition, 2010-11). Discounts: 40% discount to the trade, 20% to libraries. Payment: 2% 10, net 30 days. Copyrights for author. Subjects: Biography, Cooking, Gay, Immigration, Indiana, Literature (General), Poetry, Politics, U.S. Hispanic.

Bard Press (see also WATERWAYS: Poetry in the Mainstream), Richard Spiegel, Editor, 393 St. Pauls Avenue, Staten Island, NY 10304-2127, 718-442-7429. 1974. Poetry, art, long-poems. ''Chapbooks containing the work of one poet, most recently Enid Dame, Donald Lev, Gertrude Morris, Ronald Singer, Ida Fasel and Joy Hewitt Mann. Most poets come to us through our magazine *Waterways*. Publication by invitation only.'' avg. press run 300. Pub'd 2 titles 2009; expects 2 titles 2010, 2 titles 2011. 10 titles listed in the *Small Press Record of Books in Print* (36th Edition, 2010-11). Discounts: 40% to booksellers. 32pp. Reporting time: 2 months. Simultaneous submissions accepted: no. Payment: in copies. Copyrights for author. Subject: Poetry.

Bardsong Press, Ann Gilpin, PO Box 775396, Steamboat Springs, CO 80477, 970-819-9728, Fax 970-879-2657, bard@bardsongpress.com, www.bardsongpress.com. 1997. Fiction. ''Specializes in historical fiction, especially Celtic/Medieval/Britain. Currently not accepting submissions.'' avg. press run 2M. Pub'd 1 title 2009. 6 titles listed in the *Small Press Record of Books in Print* (36th Edition, 2010-11). Discounts: 40% to stores, 55% to wholesalers. 400pp. Reporting time: 4 months. Simultaneous submissions accepted: yes. Publishes 1% of manuscripts submitted. Payment: varies. Copyrights for author. Subjects: Celtic, Fiction, Novels.

Barefoot Press, Kent Bailey, Director, 1012 Danny Drive, Sarasota, FL 34243-4409, 941-751-3200, fax 941-751-3244. 1987. Fiction, art, photos, cartoons. ''We are concerned with publishing high quality, *lasting* graphics (posters and cards) and children's books. As such, we print on acid free paper wherever possible (as in our *California Girls* poster). Sorry, we do not accept submissions of any kind.'' avg. press run 5M. No titles listed in the *Small Press Record of Books in Print* (36th Edition, 2010-11). Subjects: Graphics, Photography, Picture Books, Postcards.

Barney Press, Donna Litherland, 2550 Honolulu Avenue Ste. 104, Montrose, CA 91020-1859, 805-871-9118. 1982. ''How to books on speed reading, imaging, Jungian psychology, changing human energy patterns, development of women's consciousness. Books designed to help students with study habits.'' avg. press run 500. Pub'd 1 title 2009; expects 1 title 2010, 1 title 2011. 7 titles listed in the *Small Press Record of Books in Print* (36th Edition, 2010-11). Discounts: 40/60, $5 for examination copy to schools. 128pp. Reporting time: 6 weeks. Simultaneous submissions accepted: yes. Publishes 5% of manuscripts submitted. Payment: 40%. Copyrights for author. Subjects: Cities, How-To, Novels, Spiritual.

•**BARNSTORM,** Matt Thompson, Editor-in-Chief, www.barnstorm.unh.edu. ''An online literary magazine sponsored by the UNH Creative Writing Program. Poetry, fiction, non-fiction. VWe only take online submissions. Please submit only once in a genre for each issue, and limit prose to 10,000 words and poetry to five poems. Simultaneous submissions are accepted; just let us know as soon as your work gets accepted elsewhere.''

BARNWOOD, The Barnwood Press, Tom Koontz, 4604 47th Ave., South, Seattle, WA 98118. 1975. Poetry. ''Online only, since 2002; poems added as accepted; submissions read only September 15 through May 31; no snail mail submissions please, email only, see editorial statement at barnwoodpress.org.'' Back issues: $10. Reporting time: 1 month. Simultaneous submissions accepted: yes. Publishes 2% of manuscripts submitted. Payment: $25/poem. Copyrighted, reverts to author. Subject: Poetry.

The Barnwood Press (see also BARNWOOD), Tom Koontz, 4604 47th Ave., South, Seattle, WA 98118. 1975. Poetry. ''Our organization is a nonprofit cooperative in support of contemporary poetry. Criterion is artistic excellence. Web site at *barnwoodpress.org*. Recent authors include: Bly, Carter, Collins, Davis, Friman,

Goedicke, Herz, Robinson, Ronnow, Watts.'' avg. press run 1M. Pub'd 2 titles 2009. 48 titles listed in the *Small Press Record of Books in Print* (36th Edition, 2010-11). Discounts: 50% to indie bookstores, 40% to other stores, 50% to members and for desk copies. 80pp. Reporting time: not currently reviewing manuscripts. Publishes 1% of manuscripts submitted. Payment: 10% of run, additional copies available at cost. Copyrights for author. Subject: Poetry.

BARROW STREET, Barrow Street Press, Patricia Carlin, Peter Covino, Lois Hirshkowitz, Melissa Hotchkiss, PO Box 1831, Murray Hill Stn., New York, NY 10156, 212-937-1970, www.barrowstreet.org. 1999. Poetry. circ. 1.5M. 2/yr. Pub'd 2 issues 2009; expects 2 issues 2010, 2 issues 2011. sub. price $15; per copy $8; sample $8. Discounts: trade and bulk 40%. 110pp. Reporting time: 6 months. Simultaneous submissions accepted: yes. Publishes 2% of manuscripts submitted. Payment: 2 copies. Copyrighted, reverts to author. Pub's reviews: 3 in 2009. §Poetry. Ads: none. Subject: Poetry.

Barrow Street Press (see also BARROW STREET), Patricia Carlin, Peter Covino, Lois Hirshkowitz, Melissa Hotchkiss, PO Box 1831, Murray Hill Stn., New York, NY 10156, 212-937-1970, info@barrowstreet.org, www.barrowstreet.org. 1999. Poetry. avg. press run 1250. Pub'd 3 titles 2009; expects 2 titles 2010, 2 titles 2011. No titles listed in the *Small Press Record of Books in Print* (36th Edition, 2010-11). Discounts: trade 40%. 80pp. Reporting time: 6 months. Simultaneous submissions accepted: yes. Publishes 2% of manuscripts submitted. Payment: as per contract. Copyrights for author. Subject: Poetry.

Barrytown/Station Hill Press, Kate Schapira, Managing Editor, 124 Station Hill Road, Barrytown, NY 12507, 845-340-4300, fax: 845-339-0780, web: www.stationhill.org, email: publisher@stationhill.org. 1978. Poetry, fiction, art, photos, satire, criticism, music, letters, long-poems, collages, plays, concrete art, non-fiction. "Publisher of international literature & visual and performing arts, emphasizing the contemporary & innovative, yet excluding neither the ancient nor the traditional, presented with a commitment to excellence in book design and production. Prose fiction by Maurice Blanchot, Rosemarie Waldrop, Franz Kamin, Lydia Davis, Spencer Holst; poetry by John Cage, Jackson Mac Low, Kenneth Irby, Robert Kelly, Paul Auster, Armand Schwerner, Charles Bernstein, Norman Weinstein, etc.; discourse by James Hillman, Ed Sanders, Blanchot, Porphyry, etc; visual arts by Russian avant-garde, Wolf Kahn, Thomas Dugan, etc. Other imprints and series include: *Artext, Contemporary Artist Series, Open Book,* and *P-U-L-S-E Books.*" avg. press run 1.5M-3M. Pub'd 12 titles 2009; expects 20 titles 2010, 20 titles 2011. 75 titles listed in the *Small Press Record of Books in Print* (36th Edition, 2010-11). Discounts: 50% distributor, 20% on single orders, escalating with qty. 64-200pp. Reporting time: no guarantee except by written arrangement. Payment: usually 10% of edition in copies or 10% of gross. Copyrights for author. Subjects: Arts, Classical Studies, Criticism, Fiction, France, French, James Joyce, Literature (General), Music, Occult, Philosophy, Photography, Poetry, Psychology, Spiritual, Tapes & Records.

BASALT, Jodi Varon, David Axelrod, School of Arts and Sciences, Eastern Oregon University, La Grande, OR 97850, 541-962-3633. 1981. Poetry, art, photos, interviews, reviews, long-poems, non-fiction. "Although we are open to all "schools" and persuasions, we prefer content and imagination uninhibited by experience. Basalt is especially interested in literary forms that cross genre boundaries and mix media, as well as contemporary translations from any language. If you send translations, please include originals and permissions to translate from the author. We also read queries, via e-mail, about proposed work, which should be briefly summarized and should include a complete word count. Recent contributors include Madeline DeFrees, Laurie Blauner, Laurie Lamon, Rich Ives, Michael McGriff, David Romvedt, Heather Dubrow,Dorianne Laux, James Crews, Christopher Howell, Joseph Millar, Michael McGriff. Artwork by Minor White, Tim Ely, Enrique Chagoya, James Lavadour, Marie Watt, and Mary Farrell." circ. 1M. 1/yr. Pub'd 1 issue 2009; expects 1 issue 2010, 1 issue 2011. sub. price $10; per copy $10; sample $5. Back issues: $5. 32pp. Reporting time: 1-3 months (longer if being seriously considered). Simultaneous submissions accepted: Yes, if noted in cover letter. Publishes 10% of manuscripts submitted. Payment: copies. Copyrighted, reverts to author. Pub's reviews: 1 in 2009. §Contemporary Poetry books and chapbooks, especially from writers and presses in the Pacific Northwest. Query first. Ads: gratis ads. Subjects: Literature (General), Poetry, Translation.

BAT CITY REVIEW, Sebastian Langdell, Editor, Dept. of English, The University of Texas at Austin, 1 University Station B5000, Austin, TX 78712. "*Bat City Review* is published annually. We try to give timely responses to submitted work. We also pride ourselves on being a green publication. We will consider manuscripts submitted in hard copy, but please help us reduce our reliance on paper by submitting your work electronically. We read submissions from June 1 to November 15, with responses sent primarily in late fall. Work which is submitted after this reading period will be held for consideration in the next year's publication. Fiction: fiction.batcityreview@gmail.com. Poetry: poetry.batcityreview@gmail.com. Art: art.batcityreview@gmail.com.''

BATEAU, Bateau Press, James Grinwis, Editor; Ashley Schaffer, Managing Editor, PO Box 1584, Northampton, MA 01061-1584, www.bateaupress.org. 2006. Poetry, fiction, art, cartoons, reviews, long-poems, plays. "Bateau subscribes to no trend but serves to represent as wide a cross-section of contemporary writing as

46

possible. For this reason, readers will most likely love and hate at least something in each issue. We consider this a good thing. To us, it means Bateau is eclectic, open-ended and not mired in a particular strain.Our standard is excellence. Work in Bateau succeeds because of its individual strengths and ability to move a wide-ranging readership. Craftsmanship and quality are delivered through the contents and its package, reflected in our letterpressed covers. Each issue works out of a mutual gifting and strives to be a kind of art piece." 2/yr. Pub'd 1 issue 2009; expects 2 issues 2010, 2 issues 2011. sub. price $22 includes postage; per copy $12 includes postage; sample $12 includes postage. Back issues: $12 includes postage. 80pp. Reporting time: 1-6 months. Simultaneous submissions accepted: Yes. Payment: payment in copies. Copyrighted, reverts to author. §creative reviews of any creative medium. No advertising.

Bateau Press (see also BATEAU), James Grinwis, PO Box 1584, Northampton, MA 01061-1584, www.bateaupress.org. 2006. Poetry. "We publish one chapbook annual via our Boom Chapbook Contest. The 06-07 winner was Allison Titus' Instructions from the Narwhal." avg. press run 300. Pub'd 1 title 2009; expects 1 title 2010, 1 title 2011. No titles listed in the *Small Press Record of Books in Print* (36th Edition, 2010-11). 25pp. Reporting time: 4-5 months. Simultaneous submissions accepted: Yes. Payment: $500. prize plus chapbooks. Copyrights for author.

BATHTUB GIN, Pathwise Press, Christopher Harter, 2311 Broadway Street, New Orleans, LA 70125-4127, pathwisepress@hotmail.com. 1997. Poetry, fiction, art, photos, interviews, satire, criticism, reviews, letters, parts-of-novels, collages, plays. "No strict length limits, prose around 2,500 words preferred. Looking for work that has the kick of bathtub gin (could be strong imagery, feeling within the work, or attitude). No trite rhymes. Recent issues featured Todd Moore, G. Tod Slone, Mark Terrill, Kell Robertson and Lindsay Wilson. Submission time: June1 to September 15. NOTE: Currently on hiatus until 2010." circ. 250-300. 2/yr. Pub'd 1 issue 2009. sub. price $8; per copy $5; sample $5. Back issues: $3.50. Discounts: sliding scale. 60pp. Reporting time: 1-2 months. Simultaneous submissions accepted: yes. Publishes 5% of manuscripts submitted. Payment: 2 contributer's copies, plus discount on extra copies. Copyrighted, reverts to author. Pub's reviews: 6 in 2009. §Poetry chapbooks and broadsides, works from small presses. Ads: 2.5 x 4 inches $15/issue or $25/year; 2.5 X 2 $10/issue or $17/year; 2.25 X 1 $7/issue or $12/year. Subjects: Absurdist, Avant-Garde, Experimental Art, Drama, Essays, Literature (General), Photography, Poetry.

Bauhan Publishing, LLC, Sarah Bauhan, 7 Main Street, 2nd Floor, Peterborough, NH 03458, 603-567-4430. 1959. Poetry, art, letters, non-fiction. "Specialize in New England regional books, plus arts and Americana." avg. press run 1.5M-2.5M. Pub'd 6 titles 2009; expects 8 titles 2010, 8 titles 2011. 56 titles listed in the *Small Press Record of Books in Print* (36th Edition, 2010-11). Discounts: 40% off on 5 or more copies, flat 20% off on textbooks, ltd. editions. 150pp. Reporting time: a month or so. Payment: 15% of net sales; less on poetry & small editions. Copyrights for author. Subjects: Americana, Architecture, Arts, Biography, History, Maine, Memoirs, New England, New Hampshire, Poetry, Wood Engraving/Woodworking, World War II.

Bauu Press, Peter Jones, PO Box 4445, Boulder, CO 80306, http://www.bauuinstitute.com, 303-827-6365. 1998. Fiction, articles, criticism, non-fiction. avg. press run 2000. Pub'd 3 titles 2009; expects 4 titles 2010. No titles listed in the *Small Press Record of Books in Print* (36th Edition, 2010-11). Discounts: 1-20 copies 40% 21-50 copies 45% 50+ copies 50%. 250-350pp. Reporting time: 1-2 months. Simultaneous submissions accepted: Yes. Payment: 10% of retail price on all sales. Does not copyright for author. Subjects: Anthropology, Archaelogy, Environment, Human Rights, Indians, Indigenous Cultures, Native American, Philosophy, Psychology, Science, Sociology.

Bay Area Poets Coalition (see also POETALK), Maggie Morley, POETALK, PO Box 11435, Berkeley, CA 94712-2435, poetalk@aol.com, www.bayareapoetscoalition.org. 1974. Poetry. "Poetry - under 35 lines preferred." avg. press run 400. Pub'd 1 title 2009; expects 2 titles 2010, 2 titles 2011. No titles listed in the *Small Press Record of Books in Print* (36th Edition, 2010-11). 36pp. Reporting time: 2-6 months (sometimes longer). Simultaneous submissions accepted: yes. Publishes 20-30% of manuscripts submitted. Payment: copy. Rights revert to authors. Subject: Poetry.

Bay Press, Sally Brunsman, 1411 4th Avenue, Suite 830, Seattle, WA 98101-2225, 206-284-5913. 1981. Criticism. "Contemporary cultural criticism." avg. press run 7M. 18 titles listed in the *Small Press Record of Books in Print* (36th Edition, 2010-11). Discounts: trade 20-50%. 192pp. Reporting time: 6 weeks. Simultaneous submissions accepted: yes. Publishes 1% of manuscripts submitted. Payment: net receipts, payable bi-annually. Copyrights for author. Subjects: AIDS, Architecture, Arts, Criticism, Culture, Gay, Media, Non-Fiction, Photography, Politics.

Bay Tree Publishing, David Cole, 32 Harbor View Drive, Richmond, CA 94804-6400, telephone 510-526-2916, fax 510-525-0842. 2002. Non-fiction. "Bay Tree publishes nonfiction in the areas of current affairs, business and psychology." avg. press run 4000. Expects 2 titles 2010, 2 titles 2011. No titles listed in the *Small Press Record of Books in Print* (36th Edition, 2010-11). Discounts: 1-4 copies 20%, 5+ copies 45%. 300pp. Reporting time: 1 month. Simultaneous submissions accepted: Yes. Publishes 5% of manuscripts submitted. Payment: Occasionally offer an advance up to $1500. Graduated royalties 10-12% of net sales. Copyrights for author. Subjects: Advertising, Self-Promotion, Aging, Business & Economics, Communication, Journalism, Community, Consumer, Environment, Finances, Immigration, Insurance, Marketing, Multicultural, Politics, Psychology, Public Affairs.

BAY WINDOWS, Rudy Kikel, Poetry Editor, 46 Plympton Street Suite 5, Boston, MA 02118-4201, 617-266-6670, X211. 1983. Poetry. "We're looking for short poems (1-36 lines) on themes of interest to gay men or lesbians." circ. 60M. 51/yr. Pub'd 51 issues 2009; expects 51 issues 2010, 51 issues 2011. sub. price $50; per copy 50¢; sample $3 (includes p/h). Back issues: not available. 80pp. Reporting time: 2-3 months. We accept simultaneous submissions if so advised. Publishes 10% of manuscripts submitted. Payment: copies. Copyrighted, reverts to author. Pub's reviews: 51+ in 2009. §Gay or lesbian—fiction, non-fiction, poetry. Ads: $716.10/$346.50/$173.25 1/4 page/$92.40 1/8 page. Subjects: Gay, Lesbianism.

Bayhampton Publications, Kelly Smith, Director of Marketing and Sales, 54 Mozart Crescent, Brampton, ON L6Y 2W7, Canada, 905-455-7331, Fax 905-455-0207, www.bayhampton.com. 1995. Fiction, non-fiction. avg. press run 5M. Expects 1 title 2010, 1 title 2011. 1 title listed in the *Small Press Record of Books in Print* (36th Edition, 2010-11). Discounts: available on request; bookstores, 40%; libraries, 20%. 250pp. Copyrights for author. Subjects: Education, Non-Fiction, Novels, Parenting, Psychology, Self-Help.

BAYOU, Laurie O'Brien, Editor, The University of West Florida/English Dept., 11000 University Parkway, Pensacola, FL 32514-5751, 904-474-2923. 1976. Poetry, fiction. "*The Panhandler* is a magazine of contemporary poetry and fiction. We want poetry and stories rooted in real experience of real people in language with a strong colloquial flavor. Works that are engaging and readable stand a better chance with us than works that are self-consciously literary. Recent contributors: Walter McDonald, Malcolm Glass, Enid Shomer, David Kirby, Joan Colby, Victor Gischler." circ. 500. 2/yr plus chapbook. Pub'd 3 issues 2009; expects 3 issues 2010, 3 issues 2011. sub. price $10 includes yearly chapbook; per copy $5; sample $5. Back issues: $4.50. Discounts: 10 or more 40%. 70pp. Reporting time: 4-6 months. Please inform us of simultaneous submissions and acceptance elsewhere. Publishes 5% of manuscripts submitted. Payment: copies. Copyrighted, reverts to author. Ads: $50/$25. Subjects: Fiction, Poetry.

BEACHCOMBER MAGAZINE, Autelitano Media Group (AMG), Phil Autelitano Jr., PO Box 2255, Delray Beach, FL 33445, 561-734-5428, Fax 561-276-0931, Autelitano@aol.com, www.AuteliMedia.com. 1985. Poetry, fiction, articles, art, photos, cartoons, interviews, reviews, letters, news items, non-fiction. "We prefer anything with a South Florida slant, primarily lifestyle-related. We also like anything 'beachy' - that is, poetry, fiction, nonfiction related in some way to the ocean, coastal living, etc." circ. 35M. 10/yr. Pub'd 10 issues 2009; expects 10 issues 2010, 10 issues 2011. sub. price $24.95; per copy $2.95; sample $2.95 w/full-color cover. Back issues: $2. 32pp. Reporting time: 2 weeks. Simultaneous submissions accepted: yes. Publishes 10% of manuscripts submitted. Payment: varies ($10 to $100). Copyrighted, reverts to author. Pub's reviews: 10 in 2009. §Small business, poetry, nonfiction, anything South Florida or coastal lifestyle/affluent related. Ads: $600/$330/$220. Subjects: Arts, Communication, Journalism, Entertainment, Florida, Leisure/Recreation.

BeachSide Press, Crystal Packard, 115 Doud Dr, Los Altos, CA 94022, 650-714-3069. 2006. Fiction. "Our most recent novel is *Moonlight at Monterey Bay*. This book is the first contemporary romance novel taking place in Carmel. The romance novel is a classy, charming book by Devin Pine. The cover photography is by local professional photographer Michael Santa Cruz. Will work to obtain celebrity/expert endorsements. Will submit to PW, NY Times Book Review, ... http://www.beachsidepress.com." avg. press run 30,000. Expects 4 titles 2010, 10 titles 2011. 1 title listed in the *Small Press Record of Books in Print* (36th Edition, 2010-11). Discounts: 1-30,000 copies 55% to bookstores nationwide. 250pp. Reporting time: 2 weeks. Simultaneous submissions accepted: Yes. Publishes 30% of manuscripts submitted. Payment: 30% royalties. Copyrights for author. Subjects: California, Children, Youth, Cities, Classical Studies, Consumer, Danish, England, Family, Fiction, Gardening, Health, Romance.

Beacon Press, 25 Beacon Street, Boston, MA 02108, 617-742-2110. 1854. Non-fiction. "No original fiction, poetry inspirational books, or memoirs accepted. We publish books on scholarly topics that have an interest for the general reader, and trade books with potential scholarly uses. Subjects: women's studies, environmental studies, religious studies, gay and lesbian studies, African-Americanm Asian-American, Jewish, Latino, and Native American studies, anthropology, politics and current affairs, legal studies, child and family issues, Irish studies, history, philosophy, education. Submit 2 sample chapters (typed double-spaced) with table of contents, synopsis, and curriculum vitae." avg. press run varies widely. Pub'd 60 titles 2009; expects 50 titles 2010, 60 titles 2011. No titles listed in the *Small Press Record of Books in Print* (36th Edition, 2010-11). Discounts: trade, nonreturnable and returnable special bulk, text...all different. Reporting time: 6-8 weeks. Simultaneous submissions accepted: yes. Publishes less than 1% of manuscripts submitted. Payment: negotiated separately. Copyrights for author. Subjects: Buddhism, Christianity, Civil Rights, Conservation, Earth, Natural History, Ecology, Foods, Ethics, Feminism, Gay, Human Rights, Ireland, Judaism, Lesbianism, Literature (General),

Men.

THE BEACON: Journal of Special Education Law & Practice, Harbor House Law Press, Inc., Pamela Wright, PO Box 480, Hartfield, VA 23071, 804-758-8400, Fax 202-318-3239, info@harborhouselaw.com, www.harborhouselaw.com. *"The Beacon* is a new electronic journal of special education law and practice. We publish articles and essays for attorneys and advocates who represent children with disabilities and others who are interested in special education legal topics." circ. 3.5M. 4/yr. Pub'd 2 issues 2009; expects 4 issues 2010, 4 issues 2011. sub. price free; sample free. Simultaneous submissions accepted: yes. Publishes 30% of manuscripts submitted. Not copyrighted. Subjects: Education, Law, Parenting.

Beagle Bay Books / Creative Minds Press, Jacqueline Simonds, Robin Simonds, 14120 Saddlebow Drive, Reno, NV 89511, 775-827-8654, Fax 775-827-8633, info@beaglebay.com, www.beaglebay.com. 1999. Non-fiction. "Personal development and travel (non-guidebook). Additionally, Beagle Bay, Inc. is a distributor of small press non-fiction titles." avg. press run 5k. Pub'd 3 titles 2009; expects 3 titles 2010, 3 titles 2011. 12 titles listed in the *Small Press Record of Books in Print* (36th Edition, 2010-11). Discounts: generous to trade, usual to wholesalers and distributors. 300pp. Reporting time: up to 6 months. Simultaneous submissions accepted: no. Publishes 1% of manuscripts submitted. Payment: industry standard. Copyrights for author. Subjects: Food, Eating, How-To, Humor, Indigenous Cultures, Native American, Self-Help, Travel.

Bear & Company, One Park Street, Rochester, VT 05767-0388, Tel: 802-767-3174, Toll Free: 1-800-246-8648, Fax: 802-767-3726, Email: info@innertraditions.com. 1981. Art, music, non-fiction. Pub'd 60 titles 2009; expects 60 titles 2010, 60 titles 2011. 69 titles listed in the *Small Press Record of Books in Print* (36th Edition, 2010-11). 300pp. Reporting time: 8 weeks SASE only. Publishes 1% of manuscripts submitted. Payment: 8%-10% of net. Copyrights for author. Subjects: Anthropology, Archaelogy, Astrology, Autobiography, Biography, Catholic, Community, Conservation, Counter-Culture, Alternatives, Communes, Ecology, Foods, Feminism, Health, Men, Metaphysics, Myth, Mythology.

THE BEAR DELUXE MAGAZINE, Thomas L. Webb, Editor, PO Box 10342, Portland, OR 97296, 503-242-1047, Fax 503-243-2645, bear@orlo.org. 1993. Poetry, fiction, articles, art, photos, cartoons, interviews, satire, criticism, reviews, music, letters, parts-of-novels, plays, news items, non-fiction. "Send most unique environmental story ideas in well-developed one-page query letter. Send clips and letter as initial contact. Follow-up with phone call and have patience. Non-fiction ideas are reviewed and assigned. Fiction, poetry and essay considered under open submission policy. Ideal word limit is 2,500 (up to 4,000 accepted)." circ. 44m. 4/yr. Pub'd 3 issues 2009; expects 3 issues 2010, 4 issues 2011. sub. price $20/4 issues; per copy $5; sample $5. Back issues: $8 if available. Discounts: possible trades. 48pp. Reporting time: 6 months. We accept simultaneous submissions, but must be noted. Publishes 5% of manuscripts submitted. Payment: $25-$400, copies; $40 photographs, subscription, contributor copies and invitations to events. Copyrighted, reverts to author. Pub's reviews: 16 in 2009. §Environmental, social justice, media, popular culture. Ads: $800/$500/$300 and up. Subjects: Arts, Book Reviewing, Conservation, Environment, Fiction, Literature (General), Non-Fiction, Poetry, Short Stories.

Bear House Publishing (see also LUCIDITY POETRY JOURNAL), Ted O. Badger, Editor, 14781 Memorial Drive #10, Houston, TX 77079-5210. 1985. Poetry, articles, criticism. "Contract Publication of chapbooks, write for prices and parameters." avg. press run 100-300. Pub'd 4 titles 2009; expects 6 titles 2010, 6 titles 2011. No titles listed in the *Small Press Record of Books in Print* (36th Edition, 2010-11). Discounts: negotiable. 30-50pp. Reporting time: 30 days or less. Publishes 90% of manuscripts submitted. Payment: primarily a press for self-publishing, but we do some promotion. Inserts copyright notice but does not register. Subjects: Poetry, Prose.

Bear Star Press, Beth Spencer, 185 Hollow Oak Drive, Cohasset, CA 95973, 530-891-0360, www.bearstarpress.com. 1996. Poetry. "Poets/poetry from Western and Pacific states with no restrictions as to form. Also occasional short fiction and chapbooks (infrequent—please query before sending). Annual poetry contest—rules change year to year. Not for profit!" avg. press run 500-1,000. Pub'd 3 titles 2009; expects 2 titles 2010, 2-3 titles 2011. 24 titles listed in the *Small Press Record of Books in Print* (36th Edition, 2010-11). Discounts: varies, stores usually take 40%. Chapbooks 35-40pp, other books 60-100pppp. Reporting time: 3-5 months. Simultaneous submissions accepted: yes. Payment: cash and copies to authors. We can copyright for author but usually do not. Subjects: Poetry, Short Stories.

The Bear Wallow Publishing Company, Jerry Gildemeister, 809 South 12th Street, La Grande, OR 97850, 541-962-7864, bearwallow@uwtc.net, www.bear-wallow.com. 1976. Art, photos, non-fiction. "Primarily, Bear Wallow is for in-house publishing projects; however, we work with authors wishing to self-publish; and consider special projects that fit our style. Specialize in one-of-a-kind, limited edition printing." avg. press run 1M-10M. Pub'd 1 title 2009; expects 1 title 2010, 1 title 2011. 5 titles listed in the *Small Press Record of Books in Print* (36th Edition, 2010-11). Discounts: school & library 20% - 50%; trade 40% from suggested retail. 96-208pp. Reporting time: promptly. Payment: 5-10%, quarterly. Copyrights for author. Subjects: Arts,

Aviation, History, Non-Fiction, Old West, Photography, The West, Wyoming.

BearManor Media, Ben Ohmart, PO Box 71426, Albany, GA 31708-1426, 580-252-3547, Fax: 814-690-1559, benohmart@gmail.com, www.bearmanormedia.com. 2001. Letters, non-fiction. "We are mostly interested in: Old time radio, voice actors, biographies and autobiographies of old movie stars, directors, writers, stage stars, composers; books on the golden age of entertainment (between 100 and 600 pages). No fiction or non-entertainment books, please. Our previous releases include biographies on Paul Frees (voice actor), The Great Gildersleeve (radio program), Alias Smith and Jones (TV biography), Agnes Moorehead, Guy Williams, John Holmes, Underdog, Jaws, Harold Lloyd, James Best (autobiography), 12 O'Clock High, Alan Reed (voice of Fred Flintstone), Judy Canova, 3 Stooges, The Bionic Man/Woman, Bob & Ray, Frank Tuttle (director), Jack Benny, Jack Mercer (voice of Popeye), Joyce Compton (autobiography), Quincy (TV biography), Shirley Booth, Twilight Zone scripts, Son of Harpo, Jean Seberg, and many more." Pub'd 70 titles 2009; expects 70 titles 2010, 70 titles 2011. 6 titles listed in the *Small Press Record of Books in Print* (36th Edition, 2010-11). Discounts: 40% to libraries, distributors, bulk resellers. 205pp. Reporting time: 1 month. Simultaneous submissions accepted: yes. Payment: 20%. Copyrights for author. Subjects: Arts, Autobiography, Biography, Broadcasting, Disney, Non-Fiction, North America, Radio.

BEATLICK NEWS, Joseph Speer, 1300 El Paseo Road, Suite G #308, Las Cruces, NM 88001, 505-496-8729. 1988. Poetry, fiction, articles, art, photos, cartoons, interviews, criticism, reviews, letters, parts-of-novels, non-fiction. "The mission of Beatlick News is to network with poets and writers around the world. We seek to serve the writing community by distributing news about chapbooks, events, talented writers, and literary opportunities. We publish the highest caliber of literature that we can find. Recent contributors: Gary Every, Barry Alfonso, James C. Floyd, Michael White, Stephanie Hiteshew, Jim Sullivan, Gary Brower, Antler..." circ. 200 copies per issue. 4/yr. Pub'd 4 issues 2009; expects 4 issues 2010, 4 issues 2011. sub. price $12.00; per copy $3.00; sample $1. Back issues: available. Discounts: No discounts. 16pp. Reporting time: two weeks. Simultaneous submissions accepted: Yes. Publishes 60% of manuscripts submitted. No payment, free copies. Copyrighted, reverts to author. Pub's reviews: approx 15 in 2009. §the books or our friends and books from the 1920's. Ads: We do not advertise. Subjects: Absurdist, African-American, Arts, Beat, Bilingual, Essays, Literary Review, Literature (General), New Mexico, Non-Fiction, Short Stories, Travel, Zines.

BEATLICK NEWS POETRY & ARTS NEWSLETTER, Joe Speer, 1300 El Paseo Road, Suite G #308, Las Cruces, NM 88001-2222, 575-621-9694. 1988. "We travel often and solicit material from writers we meet along the way." circ. 200 copies an issue. quarterly. sub. price $15.00 a year/4 issues; per copy free; sample $1.00. Back issues: not available. Discounts: none. 16pp. Reporting time: 3 months. Simultaneous submissions accepted: yes. Payment: one free copy. Pub's reviews: 12 in 2009. §poetry and fiction. Ads: we do not sell ads.

BEAUTY/TRUTH: A Journal of Ekphrastic Poetry, James Gapinski, Annabel Rauch, N8 W31309 Concord Lane, Delafield, WI 53018, http://www.BeautyTruthPoetry.com, JamesGapinski@BeautyTruthPoetry.com. 2006. Poetry, art, photos, long-poems. "Only publishes ekphrastic poetry (poetry written in response to visual art). Actively seeks poetry and cover art submissions year-round, casually reads short story and prose-poem submissions. Visit website or send SASE for complete submission guidelines. Sometimes comments on rejected materials. Recently published work by Kathleen Kirk, Phebe Davidson, Mary K. Lindberg, and Margo Berdeshevsky." 2/yr. Expects 1 issue 2010, 2 issues 2011. 1 title listed in the *Small Press Record of Books in Print* (36th Edition, 2010-11). sub. price $12; per copy $6; sample $6. Discounts: Please inquire regarding wholesale discounts. 40pp. Reporting time: 3 months. Simultaneous submissions accepted: No. Payment: 1 free contributor's copy and discounts on additional copies. All rights revert to author on publication. Subjects: Arts, Fiction, Literature (General), Photography, Poetry.

Beaver's Pond Press, Inc., 7104 Ohms Lane, Suite 216, Edina, MN 55439-2129, 952-829-8818, email: BeaversPondPress@integra.net, www.beaverspondpress.com. 1998. 1 title listed in the *Small Press Record of Books in Print* (36th Edition, 2010-11).

Beckham Publications Group, Barry Beckham, PO Box 4066, Silver Spring, MD 20914, phone: 301-384-7995; fax: 413-702-5632; editor@beckhamhouse.com, jv@beckhamhouse.com; www.beckham-house.com. 1996. Poetry, fiction, satire, plays, non-fiction. avg. press run 1,000. No titles listed in the *Small Press Record of Books in Print* (36th Edition, 2010-11).

Beekman Books, Inc., Michael Arthur, 300 Old All Angels Hill Road, Wappingers Falls, NY 12590, 845-297-2690. 1972. Art, music, non-fiction. "Beekman is a distributor of titles published in North America, England and other European countries. We do not accept unsolicited manuscripts. Beekman publishes a small number of non-fiction and gift books. We are known for our music, homoeopathic, business & finance, medical and other technical lines. No unsolicited mss." Pub'd 5 titles 2009; expects 5 titles 2010, 10 titles 2011. 20 titles listed in the *Small Press Record of Books in Print* (36th Edition, 2010-11). Discounts: 20%. 300pp. Reporting time: 6 months. Payment: 8-10%. Copyrights for author. Subjects: Agriculture, Architecture, Arts, Aviation, Biography, Business & Economics, Children, Youth, Communication, Journalism, Communism,

Marxism, Leninism, Ecology, Foods, Education, Health, History, Labor, Literature (General).

W.S. Beetle & Company, 732 County Street, New Bedford, MA 02740, 774-202-1285 phone, 774-202-1293 fax, info@wsbeetle.com, www.wsbeetle.com. 2006. Non-fiction. "Publisher of historical creative nonfiction." avg. press run 5000. Expects 1 title 2010, 2 titles 2011. 1 title listed in the *Small Press Record of Books in Print* (36th Edition, 2010-11). 250pp. Simultaneous submissions accepted: Yes. Copyrights for author. Subjects: Biography, Creative Non-fiction, History, Non-Fiction.

•**BEGGARS & CHEESEBURGERS,** Andrew Hilbert Jr, La Palma, CA 90623, submitbeggars@gmail.com. 2009. Poetry, articles, art, photos, cartoons, interviews. *"Beggars & Cheeseburgers* is an anarchic quarterly arts magazine that publishes poetry, art, and flash fiction. We are anarchic but tend to lean more toward the humorous, absurd, and the irreverent. Our first issue featured: Gerald Locklin, Joan Jobe Smith, Fred Voss, Catfish McDaris, Jim Valvis, G Murray Thomas, Edward Field and more." circ. 400. 4/yr. Expects 4 issues 2010, 4 issues 2011. sub. price $24; per copy $6; sample $5. Back issues: inquire. 30pp. Reporting time: 3-4 months. Simultaneous submissions accepted: No. Publishes 5% of manuscripts submitted. Payment: 1 free contributor's copy, extra copies at discounted rate. Copyrighted, reverts to author. Pub's reviews: approx. 10 in 2009. §Chapbook reviews, small press reviews, reading reviews. Ads: Full page: $50Half page: $25Quarter page: $10. Subjects: Absurdist, Arts, Avant-Garde, Experimental Art, Charles Bukowski, Cartoons, Comics, Creativity, Humor, Interviews, Literature (General), North America, Poetry, Zines.

•**BEGINNING MAGAZINE, Writers House Press,** Bro. John-Paul Ignatius Mary, 1111 S. Sheridan Ave., Ottumwa, IA 52501-5350, beginning.editor@writers-house-press.org. 1983. Poetry, fiction, articles, art, photos, interviews, letters, long-poems, non-fiction. "Manuscripts accepted only between January-April." circ. 100. Annual Journal. Expects 1 issue 2011. price per copy Electronic Edition cost is $10. Hard-copy Edition is $20. Generally back issues are available in the Electronic Edition. 64pp. Reporting time: one month. Simultaneous submissions accepted: Yes. Publishes 10% of manuscripts submitted. Payment: Free copies. Copyrighted, reverts to author. Subjects: The Americas, Arts, Christianity, Creative Non-fiction, Fiction, History, Humor, Iowa, Literature (General), Philosophy, Photography, Poetry, Prose, Psychology, Short Stories.

BEGINNINGS - A Magazine for the Novice Writer, Jenine Killoran, PO Box 214-R, Bayport, NY 11705-0214, 631-472-1143, jenineb@optonline.net, www.scbeginnings.com. 1998. Poetry, fiction, articles, cartoons, long-poems, non-fiction. "3,000 words max. for short stories. Children's section written or drawn by children. Need articles by published writers - how to get published, write better fiction, etc. Looking for poetry, 30 lines max. Serves as a showcase for beginning writers and poets only. Photos and artwork which accompany submissions may also be accepted. Send SASE for detailed guidelines. We also feature four contests per year with cash prizes for fiction and poetry. We also need writing related cartoons. Pays five dollar per cartoon." circ. 2,500. 3/yr. Pub'd 3 issues 2009; expects 3 issues 2010, 3 issues 2011. sub. price $14, $15 includes free back issue; per copy $6.00; sample $5. Back issues: $3. 54pp. Reporting time: 8-12 weeks. Simultaneous submissions accepted: yes. Publishes 30% of manuscripts submitted. Payment: copy in which work appears. Copyrighted, reverts to author. Ads: $200/$75/$25/ business card. Subjects: Fiction, Humor, Mystery, Poetry, Romance, Spiritual, Supernatural.

Behavioral Sciences Research Press, Inc., 12803 Demetra Drive, Ste. 100, Dallas, TX 75234, 972-243-8543, Fax 972-243-6349. 1979. Non-fiction. avg. press run 5K-25K. Pub'd 1 title 2009; expects 2 titles 2010, 4 titles 2011. 3 titles listed in the *Small Press Record of Books in Print* (36th Edition, 2010-11). 350pp. Reporting time: 60 days. Simultaneous submissions accepted: yes. Payment: by contract. Copyrights for author. Subjects: Business & Economics, Management, Motivation, Success, Psychology, Self-Help.

•**Bel Canto Press,** Sarah Kelly, 555 Westham Dr., Murrells Inlet, SC 29576-9160, 843-685-3711, 843-650-6267, editor@belcantopress.com, www.belcantopress.com. 2009. Fiction. "Bel Canto Press is dedicated to the publication of well-researched historical fiction, poetry, and creative non-fiction, with an emphasis on music and the arts. Our mission is to provide books that are entertaining, educational, and inspirational for readers of all ages." avg. press run 5000. Expects 3 titles 2010, 5 titles 2011. 1 title listed in the *Small Press Record of Books in Print* (36th Edition, 2010-11). 300pp. Reporting time: 1 month. Simultaneous submissions accepted: Yes. Publishes 10% of manuscripts submitted. Payment: no advance, royalties based on sales. Does not copyright for author. Subjects: Arts, Catholic, Creativity, Fiction, Juvenile Fiction, Liberal Arts, Literature (General), Music, Non-Fiction, Novels, Performing Arts, Poetry, Religion, Short Stories, Young Adult.

BELIEVERS EXCHANGE NEWSLETTER, VISIONHOPE NEWSLETTER, Annagail Lynes, 3540 East Amelia Avenue, Phoenix, AZ 85018, 206-350-2237, publisher@annagaillynes.net, www.annagaillynes.net. 1997. Articles, reviews, non-fiction. 6/yr. Pub'd 6 issues 2009; expects 6 issues 2010, 6 issues 2011. sub. price $15; per copy $3; sample $3. Back issues: $3. 12pp. Reporting time: 1 month. Simultaneous submissions accepted: yes. Publishes 50% of manuscripts submitted. Payment: complimentary copy, byline and free ad space. Copyrighted, reverts to author. Pub's reviews: 6 in 2009. §Christian books. Ads: Classified Ads - 1st 50 words - $1, .10/word for every word thereafter. Subjects: Christianity, Cooking, Family, Poetry, Religion.

•**Bellday Books,** P.O. Box 3687, Pittsburgh, PA 15230, 1-866-790-4041. "Founded in North Carolina, Bellday Books is a small press that specializes in publishing the finest in contemporary American poetry. Bellday Books celebrates Marc Jampole's debut in concert with our relatively new press. Please write to inquire about our other ventures. The press welcomes reader feedback and inquiries. For more information about Bellday Books, contact the publisher at office@belldaybooks.com. Annual Belday Poetry Prize: $2,000 prize to winning poet." No titles listed in the *Small Press Record of Books in Print* (36th Edition, 2010-11).

Bellevue Literary Press (see also BELLEVUE LITERARY REVIEW), Erika Goldman, Editorial Director; Jerome Lowenstein, Publisher, Dept. of Medicine, NYU School of Medicine, 550 First Avenue OBV 612, New York, NY 10016, 212-263-7802, FAX:212-263-7803, egoldman@BLReview.org. 2005. Fiction, non-fiction. "The Bellevue Literary Press will feature original authoritative and literary works, both fiction and nonfiction, in the sciences, social sciences and arts. It is the natural outgrowth of the *Bellevue Literary Review*, founded in 2000 as 'a journal of humanity and human experience...a well-regarded magazine featuring fiction, nonfiction and poetry by Bellevue's doctors and well-established writers.' (*Washington Post*) The *BLR* has published work by Rick Moody, Abraham Verghese, Julia Alvarez, Philip Levine, Rafael Campo, Sharon Olds, and David Lehman. As with the *Bellevue Literary Review*, the Press's authors will focus on relationships to the human body, illness, health and healing." avg. press run 2000. Pub'd 8 titles 2009; expects 7 titles 2010, 6 titles 2011. No titles listed in the *Small Press Record of Books in Print* (36th Edition, 2010-11). 200-500pp. Simultaneous submissions accepted: Yes. Copyrights for author. Subjects: Fiction, Medicine, Non-Fiction, Public Affairs, Science.

BELLEVUE LITERARY REVIEW, Bellevue Literary Press, Danielle Ofri, Editor-in-Chief; Jerome Lowenstein, Senior Nonfiction Editor; Ronna Wineberg, Senior Fiction Editor; Suzanne McConnell, Fiction Editor; Corie Feiner, Poetry Editor; Stacy Bodziak, Managing Editor, NYU School of Medicine, Dept. of Medicine, 550 First Avenue, OBV-A612, New York, NY 10016, www.BLReview.org, info@BLReview.org. 2000. Poetry, fiction, non-fiction. "The Editors invite submissions of previously unpublished works of fiction, nonfiction, and poetry about health, healing, illness, the body, and the mind. We encourage creative interpretation of these themes. Past contributors include Amy Hempel, David Wagoner, Martha Cooley, and Rachel Hadas. We are closed to submissions in July and August. The BLR's annual contest runs from February 1 through July 1, with a prize of $1000 in each category (fiction, nonfiction, poetry). See website for complete guidelines and to submit: www.BLReview.org." 2/yr. Pub'd 2 issues 2009; expects 2 issues 2010, 2 issues 2011. sub. price $15; per copy $9. Back issues: $7. Discounts: negotiable. 160pp. Reporting time: 3-5 months. Simultaneous submissions accepted: yes. Publishes 2-5% of manuscripts submitted. Payment: copies, one-year subscription + one-year gift subscription. Copyrighted, reverts to author. Ads: trades. Subjects: Disease, Fiction, Humanism, Literary Review, Medicine, Non-Fiction, Poetry, Prose.

BELLINGHAM REVIEW, Signpost Press Inc., Brenda Miller, Editor-in-Chief, Mail Stop 9053, WWU, Bellingham, WA 98225, 360-650-4863, bhreview@cc.wwu.edu. 1977. Poetry, fiction, non-fiction. "No prose over 9,000 words." circ. 2000. 2/yr. Pub'd 2 issues 2009; expects 1 issue 2010, 2 issues 2011. sub. price $14/2 issues, $27/4 issues, $40/6 issues; per copy $7; sample $7. Back issues: $7. 150pp. Reporting time: 1-4 months. Simultaneous submissions accepted: yes. Publishes 5% of manuscripts submitted. Payment: varies. Copyrighted, reverts to author. Ads: exchange with other non-profits. Subjects: Essays, Fiction, Literary Review, Non-Fiction, Poetry.

BELLOWING ARK, Bellowing Ark Press, Robert R. Ward, Editor, PO Box 55564, Shoreline, WA 98155, e-mail bellowingark@bellowingark.org. 1984. Poetry, fiction, art, photos, letters, parts-of-novels, long-poems, plays, non-fiction. "*Bellowing Ark* publishes high-quality literary works that affirm the fact that life has meaning. We are interested in poetry, fiction, essays and work in other forms that extends the philosophical ground established by the American Romantics and the transcendentalists. Our belief is that the techniques developed in the last 80 years (and particularly the last 30) are just that, technique; for us polish is a secondary consideration and work in the "modern" vein need not apply (i.e. stories should have a plot; poetry should contain a grain of universal truth). Our desire is to expand the philosophical and literary marketplace of ideas, not to be its arbiters—but we have very definite ideas about what our mission entails. Please write for a sample copy or subscription if you have any doubts. While form is generally not a consideration for selection we have one occasional feature, "Literal Lives", which presents well-developed memoirs. Other work particularly featured in the past have been serialized novels and poetry sequences; long and narrative poems; stories of childhood; and love, nature and erotic poetry. Our contributors over the past year have included Colleen Harris, Jerry Austin, Mary Jo Balistrieri, Robert King, Dolores Stewart, Mike Dillon, Tobi Cogswell, James Hobbs, Esther Cameron, Tom Cook. Each year the editors award three prizes of $100: The Lois and Marine Robert Warden Poetry Award, The Lucas Doolin Fiction Award and the Michael L. Newell Graphics Award." circ. 1M+. 6/yr. Pub'd 6 issues 2009; expects 6 issues 2010, 6 issues 2011. 2 titles listed in the *Small Press Record of Books in Print* (36th Edition, 2010-11). sub. price $20/year, $32/2year; per copy $4; sample $4. Back issues:

varies: Some back issues are now quite rare, quotes on request. Discounts: negotiable. 32pp. Reporting time: 6-10 weeks. Simultaneous submissions accepted: no. Publishes less than 1% of manuscripts submitted. Payment: in copy at present. Copyrighted, reverts to author on publication. Pub's reviews: 1 in 2009. §No unsolicited reviews. We review volumes of poetry that interest us. None. Subjects: Biography, Fiction, Poetry.

Bellowing Ark Press (see also BELLOWING ARK), Robert R. Ward, Editor-in-Chief, PO Box 55564, Shoreline, WA 98155, 206-440-0791. 1987. "As we are just beginning book publishing, we are not currently able to consider unsolicited manuscripts; however, we are interested in any work with a philosophical bent as described under the listing for the magazine we publish, *Bellowing Ark*. At this time the best approach would be to submit work to *Bellowing Ark* with a cover letter describing the complete project; also, *BA* has in the past published chapbook-length poetry manuscripts and has serialized complete book-length works." avg. press run 1M. Pub'd 4 titles 2009; expects 5 titles 2010, 5 titles 2011. 21 titles listed in the *Small Press Record of Books in Print* (36th Edition, 2010-11). Discounts: will negotiate. 48-192pp. Payment: negotiable (currently 10% of net). Copyrights for author. Subjects: Fiction, Poetry.

BELOIT POETRY JOURNAL, John Rosenwald, Editor; Lee Sharkey, Editor, P.O. Box 151, Farmington, ME 04938, (207) 778-0020, bpj@bpj.org, www.bpj.org. 1950. Poetry, reviews. "We have no biases as to length, form, subject, or school, but are looking for visions broader than the merely personal, fresh music, and language that makes us laugh, weep, recoil, resist-and pay attention. Occasional chapbooks on special themes, most recently the *Split This Rock Chapbook* of the poetry of witness and resistance. Some recent contributors: Lucille Clifton, Bei Dao, Carolyn Forche, Albert Goldbarth, Garth Greenwell, Lola Haskins, Galway Kinnell, Ben Lerner, Anne Marie Macari, Sonia Sanchez, Susan Tichy." circ. 1.3M. 4/yr. Pub'd 4 issues 2009; expects 4 issues 2010, 4 issues 2011. sub. price $18; per copy $5; sample $5. Back issues: $5 and up. Discounts: for classroom adoption. 48pp. Reporting time: Usually within 2-3 weeks; up to 4 months if the poem is under serious consideration. Simultaneous submissions accepted: no. Publishes .5% of manuscripts submitted. Payment: 3 copies. Copyrighted, reverts to author. Pub's reviews: 3 in 2009. §Poetry books, anthologies, and translations. No ads. Subjects: Poetry, Reviews.

THE BELTANE PAPERS: A Journal of Women's Mysteries, Lise Quinn, 11506 NE 113th Pl., Kirkland, WA 98033, 425-827-7004, editor@thebeltanepapers.net, www.thebeltanepapers.net. 1984. Poetry, fiction, articles, art, photos, cartoons, interviews, satire, criticism, reviews, letters, parts-of-novels, non-fiction. "We are a magazine focused on women's mysteries and Goddess spirituality but inclusive of all women's spiritual paths The Beltane Papers is womanspirit at work! This magazine is published by an all-volunteer, feminist, egalitarian group of women, working out of our homes from coast to coast in the USA. It is a conscious experiment in women working together for a common goal.personal experiences, your stories and journeys, dreams and inspirations, poetry and humor, Goddess and herb lore, recipes, rituals and reviews. We currently only accept submissions form women." circ. 500. 3/yr. Pub'd 3 issues 2009; expects 3 issues 2010, 3 issues 2011. sub. price $9.00; per copy 2.50; sample free. Back issues: 7.50 for 64 page versions, 2.50 for new 16 page B&W versions. 20pp. Reporting time: 2-3 months. Simultaneous submissions accepted: Yes. Publishes 75% of manuscripts submitted. Payment: We can't pay for content, but we can offer a free ad and copies of the magazine. Magazine is copyrighted, magazine reserves the right to use article/artwork in future conpendiums, advertising and marketing materials and fundraising merchandise. Artisits and writers are free to use their material as they pleaseas well. We both retain rights. Pub's reviews: 10 in 2009. §Goddess Spirituality, Femininst, Wiccan, Women's Health, Natual medicine, Metaphysics, Tarot, Astrology, Mythology. Ads: 1/6 page ad - $10.00 per issue. Subjects: Anthropology, Archaelogy, Astrology, Book Reviewing, Community, Dreams, Essays, Feminism, Food, Eating, Magic, Metaphysics, Multicultural, Myth, Mythology, Reviews, Spiritual, Women.

BELTWAY POETRY QUARTERLY, Kim Roberts, 626 Quebec Place NW, Washington, DC 20010-1609, http://www.beltwaypoetry.com. 2000. Poetry, articles. "*Beltway Poetry Quarterly* publishes authors who live or work in the greater Washington DC region. We strive to showcase the richness and diversity of Washington area authors in every issue, with poets from different backgrounds, races, ethnicities, ages, and sexual orientations represented. We have included Pulitzer Prize winners and those who have never previously published. We publish academic, spoken word, and experimental authors—and also those poets whose work defies categorization. We occasionally publish themed issues and issues of essays and interviews honoring and exploring the region's literary history.Beltway Poetry Quarterly also publishes a Poetry News section, updated monthly, with news on the regional literary community, including a listing of area readings and performances." 4/yr. Pub'd 4 issues 2009; expects 4 issues 2010, 4 issues 2011. Discounts: Available free online. 5-30pp. Reporting time: 2 months. Open submissions only accepted for annual themed issue. All other issues by invitation. Simultaneous submissions accepted: Yes. Publishes 25% of manuscripts submitted. Payment: Pays featured writers, but not contributors to themed issues. However, featured writers are selected from among those published earlier in theme issues. Pay usually $100 per author. Not copyrighted. §We publish poets from the greater Washington DC region. Publishers of geographically-appropriate writers invited to send books, for consideration for a feature on the writer. Subjects: Poetry, Washington, D.C.

Benchmark Publications Inc., Alice McElhone, Montclair, NJ 07042, 203-966-6653, Fax 973-718-4606 [secure], www.benchpress.com, BPIsmallpress@benchpress.com. 1995. Non-fiction. "Books and tools for business, education and the public interest." Pub'd 2 titles 2009; expects 3 titles 2010, 2 titles 2011. 8 titles listed in the *Small Press Record of Books in Print* (36th Edition, 2010-11). 275pp. Simultaneous submissions accepted: no. Rights are assigned to BPI for specific edition. Subjects: Business & Economics, Computers, Calculators, Government, How-To, Management, Non-Fiction, Politics.

R.J. Bender Publishing, R.J. Bender, J.R. Angolia, D. Littlejohn, H.P. Taylor, PO Box 23456, San Jose, CA 95153, 408-225-5777, Fax 408-225-4739, order@bender-publishing.com. 1967. Non-fiction. avg. press run 5M. Expects 4 titles 2010, 4 titles 2011. 14 titles listed in the *Small Press Record of Books in Print* (36th Edition, 2010-11). Discounts: 33%-55%. 400pp. Reporting time: 1-2 years. Payment: variable. Copyrights for author. Subjects: Airplanes, German, History, Military, Veterans, Non-Fiction, World War II.

Benecton Press, W. R. Klemm, 9001 Grassbur Road, Bryan, TX 77808, 979-589-2665. 2004. Non-fiction. avg. press run 1000. Expects 1 title 2010, 1 title 2011. 4 titles listed in the *Small Press Record of Books in Print* (36th Edition, 2010-11). Discounts: 30-45%, depending on other terms, such as shipping, consignment, etc. 312pp. Subjects: Non-Fiction, Research, Science.

Bereshith Publishing, Vincent Harper, Executive Editor, 7200 Danny Lane, Manassas, VA 20112-3658, 703-222-9387, Fax 707-922-0875, info@bereshith.com. 1998. Poetry, fiction, art. "Two imprints: ShadowLands Press and Final Frontier Books. Publishing schedule full until 2002." avg. press run 500-1.5M. Pub'd 2 titles 2009; expects 2 titles 2010, 3 titles 2011. 5 titles listed in the *Small Press Record of Books in Print* (36th Edition, 2010-11). 375pp. Reporting time: 2-3 months. Simultaneous submissions accepted: yes. Payment: advance and royalties for novels. Copyrights for author. Subjects: Fantasy, Science Fiction.

THE BERKELEY FICTION REVIEW, Jennifer Brown, Managing Editor, 10-B Eshleman Hall, University of California, Berkeley, CA 94720. 1983. Fiction, art, photos. "*The Berkeley Fiction Review* is a forum for short fiction, published annually. We invite submissions of previously unpublished short stories with these guidelines in mind:*Submissions should be typed, double-spaced, using a normal font size and type.*Please email submissions to bfictionreview@yahoo.com as PDF or Word attachments or mail submissions in a manila envelope (or something similar, approximately 9x12). Please do NOT send submissions in #10 (standard business-size) envelopes.*Max length is 8,500 words, not to exceed 25 pages.*Include your name, address, and phone number on the first page of the story.*Include a regular SASE for a reply or an envelope (9x12) with sufficient postage if you would like us to return your manuscript. We sometimes offer comments or suggestions on returned manuscripts, time permitting.*Cover letters should be brief; include your address, email address, phone number, and the title of the story. Please do not summarize the story. Let the work speak for itself.*Simultaneous submissions are welcome, but should be marked as such. Since our staff is composed solely of student volunteers, our response time can be as long as six months, but we are making every effort to decrease this time interval. While we accept story submissions year around, we only read them from September to early May, so if you submit during the summer, expect a longer response time. We hold a yearly Sudden Fiction Contest for flash fiction 1000 words or less. The winner gets $200 and the top three stories are published. For more details see our website: www.ocf.berkeley.edu/~bfr." circ. 300. 1/yr. price per copy $10; sample $10. Back issues: $8.50. Reporting time: 1-6 months, longer if you submit in the summer. Simultaneous submissions accepted: yes. Publishes 2% of manuscripts submitted. Payment: contributor's copy. Copyrighted.

THE BERKELEY REVIEW OF BOOKS, H.D. Moe, General Editor & Publisher; Paul Blake, Art Editor, 1731 10th Street, Apt. A, Berkeley, CA 94710. 1988. Poetry, fiction, articles, art, photos, interviews, satire, criticism, reviews, music, letters, parts-of-novels, long-poems, collages, plays, concrete art, non-fiction. "We want reviews (200-300 words) of what isn't reviewed; art, poems, fiction that couldn't have been possibly written or drawn. Open to any kind of books, very interested in experimental writing, art (*not* the language prose/poetry sponsored by the university presses—'Our American professors like their literature clear, cold and very dead'—Sinclair Lewis). Recent contributors: Jenifer Stone, Ivan Arguelles, Lisa Chang, D. McNaughton, Larry Eigner, Mary Rudge, Hadassal Haskale, David Meltzer, Denise du Roi, Norman Moser." circ. 500-1M. 1/yr. Pub'd 1 issue 2009; expects 1 issue 2010, 1 issue 2011. sub. price $35; per copy $35; sample $35. Back issues: $35 + $3 p/h. Discounts: 30%-70%. 400-450pp. Reporting time: 3-4 months. Simultaneous submissions accepted: yes. Publishes 10% of manuscripts submitted. Payment: none as of now. Copyrighted, reverts to author. Pub's reviews: 50 in 2009. §All subjects. Ads: $100/$60/$40 1/4 page/$25 1/8 page.

Berry Hill Press, Doris Bickford, Douglas Swarthout, 2349 State Route 12-B, Deansboro, NY 13328, 315-821-6188 phone/fax; dls@berryhillbookshop.com. 1995. "Subjects: gardening, history, cinema, women authors and artists." avg. press run 5M. Expects 1 title 2010, 1 title 2011. 4 titles listed in the *Small Press Record of Books in Print* (36th Edition, 2010-11). Copyrights for author.

The Bess Press, David DeLuca, 3565 Harding Avenue, Honolulu, HI 96816, 808-734-7159. 1979. Non-fiction. "The Bess Press is a regional, educational and trade publisher seeking manuscript materials for the el-hi, college and trade markets. We are actively seeking regional materials, including Asian/Pacific history texts, and cookbooks, humor, and children's books dealing with Hawaii." avg. press run 5M. Pub'd 8 titles 2009; expects 8 titles 2010, 8 titles 2011. 137 titles listed in the *Small Press Record of Books in Print* (36th Edition, 2010-11). Discounts: standard. 112pp. Reporting time: usually less than 4-6 weeks. Simultaneous submissions accepted: no. Publishes 3% of manuscripts submitted. Payment: standard 10%. Copyrights for author. Subjects: Asian-American, Cooking, Crafts, Hobbies, Dictionaries, Dining, Restaurants, Hawaii, How-To, Humor, Native American, Non-Fiction, Pacific Region, Elvis Presley, Reference, Travel, Young Adult.

Best Books Plus, Linda P. Morton, 2901 Skinner Heights, Greenwood, AR 72936, 479-650-5546, bestbooksplus@cox.net, www.bestbooksplus.com. 2000. Non-fiction. "Textbooks and other educational products." avg. press run 5K. Pub'd 1 title 2009; expects 1 title 2010, 1 title 2011. No titles listed in the *Small Press Record of Books in Print* (36th Edition, 2010-11). Discounts: 30% includes prepay and no returns for college bookstores. 300pp. Reporting time: 1 month. Simultaneous submissions accepted: no. Payment: 10% net sales. Copyrights for author. Subjects: Communication, Journalism, Graphic Design, Marketing, Public Relations/Publicity.

Best Life Media, Jiyoung Oh, 6560 Highway 179, Suite 114, Sedona, AZ 86351, 928.204.1106, http://www.bestlifemedia.com, moh@bestlifemedia.com. 2007. Music, non-fiction. "BEST Life Media produces energy healing and yoga books, CDs, DVDs, and other tools that are both educational and life-enhancing, and designed to support a lifestyle based on continuous personal growth and enrichment. Brain Education System Training (BEST), which serves to better the human condition through a variety of mind-body-spirit self-development techniques, serves as the underlying inspiration for many of our titles.As an independent publisher, our company is founded on the principle that the quality of information one consumes largely determines the quality of ones life. For this reason, we are dedicated to providing positive and supportive resources through which individuals can create happier, healthier, and more peaceful lives for themselves and their community. Many of our titles focus on the optimal development and use of the human brain.Our products offer inspiration and integrative body mind training methods that support holistic healing, healthy aging, brain fitness, chakra balancing, meditation, ki energy development, and other forms of healthy body mind spirit living. Through the work that we do, it is our hope and intention to create a more harmonious, mutually beneficial way of life on the planet. Our primary authors are South Korean-born brain educator and philosopher, Ilchi Lee, and Dahn Yoga Education." avg. press run 3,000. Pub'd 3 titles 2009; expects 5 titles 2010, 5 titles 2011. 11 titles listed in the *Small Press Record of Books in Print* (36th Edition, 2010-11). Discounts: 1-4 copies 20%, 5-19copies 30%, 20-99 copies 45%, 100-999 copies 50%. 120-300pp. Reporting time: We usually work with one author, so we do not have previous experience to comment about this. Simultaneous submissions accepted: No. Publishes 32% of manuscripts submitted. Copyrights for author. Subjects: Acupuncture, Alternative Medicine, Inspirational, Martial Arts, Massage, Metaphysics, Peace, Philosophy, Psychology, Self-Help, Spiritual, T'ai Chi, Tarot, Yoga, Zen.

Betelgeuse Books, David Pelly, Publisher; Glenna Munro, Associate Publisher, Suite 604, 71 Somerset West, Ottawa Ottawa K2P 2G2, Canada, betelgeuse@sympatico.ca, http://maxpages.com/betelgeuse. 1980. Fiction, non-fiction. "We are a small press specializing in 'northern wilderness literature.' No unsolicited manuscripts." avg. press run 3M. 6 titles listed in the *Small Press Record of Books in Print* (36th Edition, 2010-11). Discounts: 40% trade, 20% library. 192pp. Payment: varies. Subjects: Canada, History, The North.

Between The Lines, The Waywiser Press, Philip Hoy, Managing Editor, The Cottage, 14 Lyncroft Gardens, Ewell, Surrey KT17 1UR, United Kingdom, T/F: +44 (0)20 8393 7055, W: www.waywiser-press.com/imprints/. "*Between The Lines* was founded in 1998 and publishes unusually wide-ranging and unusually deep-going interviews with some of todays most accomplished poets. As well as the interview, each volume contains a sketch of the poets life and career as well as a bibliography. Some volumes also include a gathering of critical quotations and a gallery of photographs. It is hoped that the results will be of interest to the lay reader and specialist alike." 66 titles listed in the *Small Press Record of Books in Print* (36th Edition, 2010-11).

Beynch Press Publishing Company, Alyce P. Cornyn-Selby, 1928 S.E. Ladd Avenue, Portland, OR 97214, 503-232-0433. 1986. Non-fiction. avg. press run 5M. Pub'd 2 titles 2009; expects 4 titles 2010, 4-6 titles 2011. 13 titles listed in the *Small Press Record of Books in Print* (36th Edition, 2010-11). 100pp. Reporting time: 1 month. Simultaneous submissions accepted: no. Payment: each is different, money and number of copies. Copyrights for author. Subjects: How-To, Psychology.

Beyond Words Publishing, Inc., Cynthia Black, Editor, 20827 NW Cornell Road, Ste. 500, Hillsboro, OR 97124-9808, 503-531-8700, Fax 503-531-8773, www.beyondword.com. 1983. Non-fiction. "Hardcover and softcover titles 200 pages of text. Children's picture books approx. 30-50 words of text and illustrations. Children's authors must be willing to do school and other programs." avg. press run 7K. Pub'd 15 titles 2009; expects 15 titles 2010, 15 titles 2011. 64 titles listed in the *Small Press Record of Books in Print* (36th Edition, 2010-11). Discounts: bookstore standard 40%-high volume up to 45%. 200pp. Reporting time: 90 days. Simultaneous submissions accepted: yes. Publishes .5% of manuscripts submitted. Payment: 10% royalty and up. Copyrights for author if requested. Subjects: Children, Youth, Health, Inspirational, Metaphysics, Non-Fiction, Parenting, Psychology, Self-Help, Spiritual.

BIBLIOPHILOS, Dr. Gerald J. Bobango, 200 Security Building, Fairmont, WV 26554, 304-366-8107. 1982. Poetry, fiction, articles, art, photos, cartoons, satire, criticism, reviews, letters, non-fiction. "Query first - Unsolicited material not considered or answered. Scholarly nonfiction feature articles, 1500-3000 words, 750-1000 word book reviews; fiction, uses 7-8 per year, 1500-3000 words. Documentation Turabian/Chicago Style Manual only. Poetry submitted in batches of 5. We want nothing that Ann Landers or Erma Bombeck would publish. Recent contributors: G. James Patterson, Mardelle Fortier, and Patricia Fain Hutson." circ. 300-400. 6/yr. Pub'd 6 issues 2009; expects 6 issues 2010, 6 issues 2011. sub. price $18, $35/2 years; per copy $5.25; sample $5.25. Back issues: $5 + $1 p/h. 72pp. Reporting time: 30 days. Simultaneous submissions accepted: no. Publishes 20% of manuscripts submitted. Payment: $5-$25, complimentary issue. Copyrighted, we retain 1st N. American serial rights only. Pub's reviews: 25 in 2009. §History, literature, literary criticism, language and linguistics, art, music, book collecting. Ads: $35/$20/yearly rates available. Subjects: Americana, Appalachia, Autobiography, Bibliography, Book Arts, Book Collecting, Bookselling, Book Reviewing, Classical Studies, Emily Dickinson, Fiction, History, Italian-American, Literature (General), Medieval, Romanian Studies.

BIG BRIDGE: A Webzine of Poetry and Everything Else, Michael Rothenberg, Terri Carrion, 2000 Highway 1, Pacifica, CA 94044, www.bigbridge.org. 1997. Poetry, fiction, articles, art, photos, cartoons, interviews, satire, criticism, reviews, letters, parts-of-novels, long-poems, collages, plays, concrete art, non-fiction. "We think walls are good for keeping out the cold and rain. And for displaying some art. They're useless in the creation and propagation of art. We don't care if Language poetry appears next to sonnets, or haiku next to spoken word and workshop poetry beside agit-smut. Our tastes are catholiceven though we're Jews and pagans and Buddhists and libertines and run-of-the-mill Christians. We don't care how art is shapedround like moon, flat like roadkill, angular like love, twisted like political promises. We hear many voices (even when we're taking our meds) and are guided by whimsy and passion and urgency. We want more.Recent contributors include Philip Whalen, Joanne Kyger,David Meltzer,Ira Cohen, Jack Collom, Anselm Hollo. Louise Landes Levi, John Brandi, Anne Waldman, Bill Berkson, Lyn Hejinian, Renee Gregorio." 40,000 hits monthly. 1/yr. sub. price free online. Back issues: free archives online. 300 pages. Simultaneous submissions accepted: OK. Payment: none. Pub's reviews.

BIG HAMMER, Iniquity Press/Vendetta Books, David Roskos, Editor, PO Box 527, Point Pleasant, NJ 08742-0527, iniquitypress@hotmail.com (no email submissions). 1988. Poetry, fiction, art, photos, collages, concrete art. "Looking for poems & prose about working for a living, class antagonism, raising children, factories, gogo dancers, flea markets, kitchen sinks, 1960s mimeo magazines, meat poetry, concrete, record collecting, state-smashing, war-stopping, etc. Send poems about ANYTHING, if I can't use em, I'll mail em back; but, please,: no yuppies; no nambla poems; no mfa/workshop bullshit." circ. 250. 1/yr. Pub'd 1 issue 2009; expects 1 issue 2010, 1 issue 2011. sub. price $6; per copy same; sample $6. Back issues: same. Discounts: 60/40. 56-100pp. Reporting time: 1 day to one year. Simultaneous submissions accepted: yes. Publishes 30% of manuscripts submitted. Payment: 1 or 2 copies. Copyrighted, reverts to author. Pub's reviews: 5 in 2009. §Poetry, DIY publishing, zines. Ads: some, so far always in trade or free for folks / presses I like.

BIG MUDDY: Journal of the Mississippi River Valley, Southeast Missouri State University Press, Susan Swartwout, MS 2650, One University Plaza, Cape Girardeau, MO 63701, (573) 651-2044, fax (573)651-5188, upress@semo.edu, www6.semo.edu/universitypress. 2001. Poetry, fiction, articles, art, interviews, reviews, letters, non-fiction. "Contributors and authors have included Stephen Graham Jones, Virgil Suarez, Elaine Fowler Palencia, Philip Kolin, David Radavich, Colleen McElroy, Dixon Hearne, John Cantey Knight." circ. 300. 2/yr. Pub'd 2 issues 2009; expects 2 issues 2010, 2 issues 2011. sub. price $20; per copy $10; sample $6. Back issues: inquire. Discounts: bookstores 40%; classrooms 50%. 150pp. Reporting time: 8 - 12 weeks. Simultaneous submissions accepted: Yes. Publishes 10% of manuscripts submitted. Payment: 2 copies. Copyrighted, reverts to author. Pub's reviews: 30 in 2009. §particularly small press or general-interest university press books. Ads: $150 or approved exchange. Subjects: African-American, Americana, Conservation, Essays, Fiction, History, Interviews, Literary Review, Midwest, Native American, Non-Fiction, Novels, Poetry, Short Stories, South.

BIG SCREAM, Nada Press, David Cope, 2782 Dixie S.W., Grandville, MI 49418, 616-531-1442. 1974. Poetry, fiction, art. "We include 2-5 pages of each writer publ.- some longpoems tend to have imagist bias; prefer *personal* poems. Contributors: David Cope, Andy Clausen, Anne Waldman, Marcia Arrieta, Jim Cohn, Antler, Jeff Poniewaz. Poets and writers *must* include SASE with their submissions." circ. 100. 1/yr. Pub'd 1 issue 2009; expects 1 issue 2010, 1 issue 2011. sub. price $10; per copy $10; sample $10. Back issues: $10. 50pp. Reporting time: 1-3 months. Simultaneous submissions accepted: yes. Publishes 02% of manuscripts submitted. Payment: 1 copy, more if requested. Subjects: Fiction, Poetry.

BIG SKY JOURNAL, 1050 E. Main St., Suite 3, Bozeman, MT 59715. "*BIG SKY JOURNAL* is published 6 times per yearFebruary, April, June, August, October and December. February is a special Fly Fishing book, April (Spring Issue) is focused on ranch and the cowboy lifestyle, August is the Arts Issue, October (Fall) is Hunting and December (Winter) features fiction along with winter sports. All of our features, columns, poetry, fiction, and photography focus on the Northern Rocky Mountain landscape, culture, people, places and wildlife.''

Big Valley Press, Charlie Knower, S2104 Big Valley Road, La Farge, WI 54639, 608 489 3525. 2005. Non-fiction. avg. press run 3000. Expects 1 title 2010, 3 titles 2011. No titles listed in the *Small Press Record of Books in Print* (36th Edition, 2010-11). 100pp. Subjects: Adolescence, Family, Fiction, Inspirational, Libraries.

BIGFOOT TIMES, Daniel Perez, 10926 Milano Avenue, Norwalk, CA 90650, www.bigfoottimes.net. 1979. Articles. ''Manuscripts not accepted.'' circ. 550. 12/yr. Pub'd 12 issues 2009; expects 12 issues 2010, 12 issues 2011. sub. price $14/year. $15/year Canada. $17/year rest of world.; per copy $1.50; sample free. Back issues: $1.50/copy. 4pp. Simultaneous submissions accepted: yes. Publishes 0% of manuscripts submitted. Payment: check/paypal/money order. Copyrighted, reverts to author. Pub's reviews: 4 in 2009. §Bigfoot books. Ads: $50 full page.

BIGNEWS MAGAZINE, 484 West 43rd St., Apt. 24D, New York, NY 10036-6341, 212-679-4535, Fax 212-679-4573, bignewsmag@aol.com, www.mainchance.org. 2000. Fiction, articles, art, photos, cartoons, interviews, parts-of-novels, non-fiction. ''We generally represent the 'outcast' point of view.'' circ. 15M. 12/yr. Pub'd 9 issues 2009; expects 9 issues 2010, 12 issues 2011. sub. price $25; per copy $2; sample $2 (free on website). Back issues: When available, $2. Otherwise, back content on website. 16pp. Reporting time: 4 weeks. Simultaneous submissions accepted: yes. Publishes 2% of manuscripts submitted. Payment: $35-$65. Copyrighted, reverts to author. Pub's reviews: 8 in 2009. §The 'outcast' or 'outsider' point of view. Ads: Full Page $2,500 Half Page $1,500. Subjects: Arts, Literature (General).

Bilingual Review Press (see also BILINGUAL REVIEW/Revista Bilingue), Gary D. Keller, Publisher; Karen S. Van Hooft, Executive Editor, Hispanic Research Center, Arizona State Univ., Box 875303, Tempe, AZ 85287-5303. 1973. Poetry, fiction, articles, criticism, plays. ''We publish U.S. Hispanic creative literature (fiction, poetry, drama), art books, scholarship, and collections of articles in the following areas: U.S. Hispanic language and literature, Chicano and Puerto Rican studies, contemporary methods of literary analysis.'' avg. press run 1M cloth, 2M paper. Pub'd 4 titles 2009; expects 9 titles 2010, 9 titles 2011. 156 titles listed in the *Small Press Record of Books in Print* (36th Edition, 2010-11). Discounts: 20% for textbooks; trade—1-4 copies 20%, 5-24 42%, 25-99 43%, 100+ 44%. 256pp. Reporting time: 8-10 weeks. Payment: varies from author subsidy with repayment to author from royalties on copies sold, to standard 10% royalty with no subsidy, depending on commercial prospects of book. We copyright in our name. Subjects: Bilingual, Chicano/a, Criticism, Drama, Fiction, Language, Poetry.

BILINGUAL REVIEW/Revista Bilingue, Bilingual Review Press, Gary D. Keller, Editor; Karen S. Van Hooft, Managing Editor, Hispanic Research Center, Arizona State Univ., Box 875303, Tempe, AZ 85287-5303. 1974. Poetry, fiction, articles, interviews, criticism, reviews. ''Research and scholarly articles dealing with bilingualism, primarily but not exclusively Spanish-English; U.S.-Hispanic literature; English-Spanish contrastive linguistics; fiction, poetry, etc., concerning Hispanic life in the US.'' circ. 1M. 3/yr. Pub'd 3 issues 2009; expects 3 issues 2010, 3 issues 2011. sub. price $40 institutions, $25 individuals; per copy $14 institutions, $8 individuals; sample $14 institutions; $8 individuals. Back issues: depends on issue. Discounts: none. 96pp. Reporting time: 6-8 weeks. Payment: 2 complimentary copies of issue. Copyrighted, does not revert to author. Pub's reviews: 9 in 2009. §Books dealing with our primary areas of interest: bilingualism, U.S. Hispanic literature. Ads: $150/$90/2-pg spread $250, back cover $200, inside back cover $175. Subjects: Bilingual, Chicano/a, Education, Language, Latino, U.S. Hispanic.

Biographical Publishing Company, John R. Guevin, 95 Sycamore Drive, Prospect, CT 06712-1493, 203-758-3661, Fax 253-793-2618, biopub@aol.com. 1991. Poetry, non-fiction. avg. press run 100-1M. Pub'd 4 titles 2009; expects 6 titles 2010, 8 titles 2011. 54 titles listed in the *Small Press Record of Books in Print* (36th Edition, 2010-11). Discounts: wholesale 55%, stores 40%. 120pp. Reporting time: 2 weeks. Simultaneous submissions accepted: yes. Publishes 25% of manuscripts submitted. Payment: author gets all profits less printing, distribution, and shipping costs. Does not copyright for author. Subjects: AIDS, Animals, Autobiography, History, India, Inspirational, Non-Fiction, Pets, Poetry, Short Stories, Surrealism, Weddings, Women.

BIOLOGY DIGEST, Plexus Publishing, Inc., Mary Suzanne Hogan, 143 Old Marlton Pike, Medford, NJ 08055, 609-654-6500. 1977. Non-fiction. ''*Biology Digest* is an abstracting journal with subject and author indexes. Each issue also contains a full-length original feature article on some life science subject of particular timely interest. We also publish an annual cumulative index.'' circ. 2M. 9/yr. Pub'd 9 issues 2009; expects 9 issues 2010, 9 issues 2011. sub. price $149; per copy only sold by volume year. Back issues: same. Discounts: call for pricing. 170pp. Reporting time: 60 days. Payment: feature article varies. Copyrighted, reverts to author.

Pub's reviews: 4 books in 2009. §Biology, life sciences, medicine, health, ecology. Subject: Science.

Birch Brook Press, Tom Tolnay, PO Box 81, Delhi, NY 13753, phone/fax orders & sales inquiries: 607-746-7453, email: birchbrook@copper.net, website: www.birchbrookpress.info. 1982. Poetry, fiction, art. "Birch Brook Press prefers inquiries with samples from manuscript, SASE a must if writer wants a reply. BBP has its own complete letterpress print shop and uses monies from designing, printing, typesetting books for other publishers to do original, theme-oriented anthologies on a project-by-project basis, soliciting material for each. Because of our antique methods of production, BBP is not a good market for full-length novels. Among our most recent anthologies are *Tales for the Trail, The Suspense of Loneliness, Baseball & The Lyrical Life, Fateful Choices, Romance of the Book, Magic & Madness in the Library.* (These projects are now completed.) We sometimes bring out handcrafted books of unusual literary merit by individual writers under a cooperative book contract. While popular culture is an important interest at BBP, we publish two/three books of literary poetry/fiction each year. Recent titles include *The Sea-Crossing of St. Brendan* by Matthew Brennan; *The Bells of Moses Henry* by Peter Skinner; *Where Things Are When You Lose Them* by Martin Golan; *Woodstoves & Ravens* by Robert E. Farmer; *And This is What Happens Next* by Marcus Rome; *Tony's World* by Barry Wallenstein; *Seasons of Defiance* by Lance Lee; *Jack's Beans* by Tom Smith; *North of Easie* by Robert J. Romano, Jr.; *Synesthetics* by Harry Smith & Stanley Nelson. Some of our books arc crafted entirely by hand, are signed and numbered, and these are sold as Limited Editions." avg. press run 500-1.5M. Pub'd 4 titles 2009; expects 4 titles 2010, 4 titles 2011. 49 titles listed in the *Small Press Record of Books in Print* (36th Edition, 2010-11). Discounts: 1 copy 32%, 2-4 36%, 5-9 38%, 10-15 40%; these discounts do not apply to limited editions which are discounted to shops/wholesalers at 32% regardless of quantity. 56-150pp. Reporting time: 10-12 weeks. We accept simultaneous submissions if indicated. Payment: modest, varies. Copyrights for author. Subjects: Culture, Fiction, Literature (General), Poetry, Sports, Outdoors.

•**Bird Brain Press,** 37 Greenpoint Avenue, 4th Floor, Brooklyn, NY 11222. "This age of slick, offset, corporate-controlled publishing is also the age of photocopied zines, artist books, desktop publishing, and the small press. Booklyns mission is to encourage the proliferation and appreciation of people-made books as an antidote to industry-produced counterparts. Founded in 1999, Booklyn is an artist-run, nonprofit organization headquartered in Brooklyn, New York. Our mission is to promote artist books as an art form and educational resource; to provide educational institutions and the public with programming involving contemporary artist books; and to assist artists in exhibiting, distributing, and publishing innovative bookwork." No titles listed in the *Small Press Record of Books in Print* (36th Edition, 2010-11).

Birdsong Books, Nancy Carol Willis, 1322 Bayview Road, Middletown, DE 19709, birdsong@birdsong-books.com, www.birdsongbooks.com. 1998. Non-fiction. "Birdsong Books only publishes nonfiction and natural science educational trade books for children. Our focus is North American wildlife and habitats. Examples: Red Knot: A Shorebird's Incredible Journet, Nancy Carol Willis; The Animals' Winter Sleep, Lynda Graham-Barber." Expects 1 title 2011. No titles listed in the *Small Press Record of Books in Print* (36th Edition, 2010-11). Discounts: 10-19 copies 25%20-49 copies 45%50-199 copies 50%200+ copirs 55%. 32pp. Reporting time: 3 months. Simultaneous submissions accepted: Yes. Publishes 1% of manuscripts submitted. Payment: Varies based on the project and author or illustrator experience. The text and art in the book is copyrighted in author's/illustrator's names. Subjects: Animals, Birds, Botany, Children, Youth, Earth, Natural History, Marine Life, Nature, Non-Fiction, North America, Picture Books, Wildlife, Young Adult.

BIRMINGHAM POETRY REVIEW, Daniel Anderson, Co-Editor; Adam Vines, Co-Editor; Robert Collins, Editor Emeritus, English Department HB 205 UAB, 1530 3rd Ave. S., Birmingham, AL 35294, 205-934-8573. 1987. Poetry. circ. 600. 2/yr. Pub'd 2 issues 2009; expects 2 issues 2010, 2 issues 2011. sub. price $5; per copy $2; sample $2.50. Back issues: $2.50. 64pp. Reporting time: 1-6 months. Simultaneous submissions accepted: no. Publishes 0.5% of manuscripts submitted. Payment: 2 copies, plus a one year subscription. Copyrighted, reverts to author. Pub's reviews: 6 in 2009. §Contemporary poetry. Ads: none. Subject: Poetry.

Birth Day Publishing Company, PO Box 7722, San Diego, CA 92167. 1975. Poetry, articles, art, photos, interviews, reviews, letters, non-fiction. "We publish material dealing with spirituality in general and, in particular, the life and teachings of an Indian holy man named Sri Sathya Sai Baba. Published material has been book length, non-fiction. Recent contributors include Samuel H. Sandweiss, M.D., Dr. John S. Hislop, Ph.D, and Howard Murphet. Ms by invitation only." avg. press run 5M. Pub'd 2 titles 2009; expects 3 titles 2010, 3 titles 2011. 8 titles listed in the *Small Press Record of Books in Print* (36th Edition, 2010-11). Discounts: book trade 40%, bulk 50%, classroom/library 40%, jobber 50%. 225pp. Payment: usually none. Copyrights for author. Subjects: Psychology, Religion, Spiritual.

BITTER OLEANDER, Paul B. Roth, 4983 Tall Oaks Drive, Fayetteville, NY 13066-9776, Fax 315-637-5056, info@bitteroleander.com, www.bitteroleander.com. 1974. Poetry, fiction, interviews, long-poems. "We strive to preclude the conventional issues and sentiments on which mainstream poetry thrives, with a poetry not only rich in its imagination but one that treats words as sacred rather than vehicles to the same place over and over again. Some recent contributors are Duane Locke, Pierre-Albert Jourdan (France), Ana MInga (Ecuador),

Samanta Schweblin (Argentina), Manuel Xexakis (Greece) Shawn Fawson, Anthony Seidman, Christine Boyka Kluge, Silvia Scheibli, Rob Cook, Rich Ives and V. Ulea. We also welcome translations of living poets and short fiction (2500 word limit) from all writers helping to widen our imaginative base. We have been represented in the *Best American Poetry-1999* and Recognized as "Best Literary Journal for 2005" by Public Radio's *Excellence in Print Award.* Our annual *Frances Locke Memorial Poetry Award* offers a winning prize of $1000, publication in *The Bitter Oleander* and 5 copies of the Award issue for the most imaginative poem entered. Contact us for guidelines or click on our web-site." circ. 1000. 2/yr. Pub'd 2 issues 2009; expects 2 issues 2010, 2 issues 2011. 7 titles listed in the *Small Press Record of Books in Print* (36th Edition, 2010-11). sub. price $18; per copy $10; sample $10. Back issues: $10. We offer 15% discounts to Public and University libraries. 128pp. Reporting time: Within 1 month. Simultaneous submissions accepted: Yes. Publishes less than .10% of manuscripts submitted. Payment: 1 copy. Copyrighted, reverts to author. Ads: $225/$150. Subjects: Essays, Experimental, Fiction, Interviews, Poetry, Short Stories, Surrealism.

BkMk Press, Robert Stewart, Editor-in-Chief; Ben Furnish, Managing Editor, University of Missouri-Kansas City, 5101 Rockhill, University House, Kansas City, MO 64110, 816-235-2558, FAX 816-235-2611, bkmk@umkc.edu. 1971. Poetry, fiction, non-fiction. *"BkMk Press* ordinarily publishes non-commercial materials of high quality & cultural significance, poetry, fiction and essay collections. Check www.umkc.edu/bkmk for details on the annual John Ciardi Prize for Poetry and G. S. Sharat Chandra Prize for Short Fiction." avg. press run 750. Pub'd 5 titles 2009; expects 5 titles 2010, 4 titles 2011. 97 titles listed in the *Small Press Record of Books in Print* (36th Edition, 2010-11). Discounts: trade 40%. 75pp. Reporting time: 6 months. Simultaneous submissions accepted: yes. Payment: 10% royalty. Copyrights for author. Subjects: Essays, Fiction, Literature (General), Multicultural, Poetry, Prose, Short Stories.

Black Bear Publications (see also BLACK BEAR REVIEW), Ave Jeanne, 1916 Lincoln Street, Croydon, PA 19021-8026, bbreview@earthlink.net, www.blackbearreview.com. 1984. Poetry, articles, art, reviews. "Chapbook publications depends upon funding at present times. Usually no more than 3 per year. Manuscripts should reflect Black Bear image. Contributors should have a good knowledge of Black Bear and have worked with us before. Send complete manuscript. We have recently published *Tracers*, by Gerald Wheeler. We receive numerous chapbook submissions, so be prepared for competition. Follow guidelines. Samples available for $5 ppd. in the US and Canada. Illustrators receive cash payment on acceptance for illustrating our chapbooks. Query for current titles. Our main objective is to get more poets into print and off the streets. Enclose a $5 reading fee and SASE. Subsidy considered." avg. press run 500. Pub'd 3 titles 2009; expects 3 titles 2010, 3 titles 2011. 13 titles listed in the *Small Press Record of Books in Print* (36th Edition, 2010-11). 34pp. Reporting time: 2 weeks. Simultaneous submissions accepted: no. Publishes 5% of manuscripts submitted. Payment: in copies. Copyrights for author. Subject: Poetry.

BLACK BEAR REVIEW, Black Bear Publications, Ave Jeanne, Poetry & Art Editor, Black Bear Publications, 1916 Lincoln Street, Croydon, PA 19021, bbreview@earthlink.net, www.blackbearreview.com. 1984. Poetry, art, reviews, collages. "We like to see poetry that is pulssant, and explosive, reflecting social concern. Forms used are avant-garde, free verse and haiku. No line limit. We would like to see artwork in black & white, (4x6—no larger, signed by author. Cover illustrations, cash on publication. Poets published: John Elsberg, Sherman Alexic, Ivan Arguelles, Andrew Gettler, John Grey, Jon Daunt, A. D. Winans. Artists published: Nancy Glazer, Mark Z., Kathryn DiLego, Ruth Richards, Walt Phillips, Ristau. E-mail submissions only. No attached files please." circ. 500. 2/yr. Pub'd 2 issues 2009; expects 2 issues 2010, 2 issues 2011. sub. price $12; per copy $6; sample $6. Back issues: $5. Discounts: 40%. 64pp. Reporting time: 1 week. Simultaneous submissions accepted: no. Publishes 5% of manuscripts submitted. Payment: contributor copy. Copyrighted, reverts to author. Ads: $45/$25—barter. Subjects: Avant-Garde, Experimental Art, Haiku, Poetry.

BLACK BOOK PRESS: The Poetry Zine id, Kyle Van Heck, Editor in Chief; Chris Kulawik, Music Editor; Scott Tomes, Music Editor; Charleen Hamill, Assistant Editor, Black Book Press (id), 1608 Wilmette Ave., Wilmette, IL 60091, 847-302-9547. 2004. Poetry, articles, art, photos, cartoons, interviews, criticism, reviews, letters, collages, plays. "We try and publish the darker side of poetry. We are also moving into other areas: we publish art, photography, cd and concert reviews, mail art, and articles on zine making. Just added: Music review Section supported by two music editors. We like poetry that gets to the point and expresses darkness, evil, politics, war, greed, betrayal, Gothic ideas, or horror poetry, but will consider anything dark. Does not want: nature poetry, light verse, greeting card verse, religious verse, or anything sounding like Robert Frost. Must include SASE for response. Has published poetry by Gerald Zipper, David Stone, Lyn Lifshin, B.Z. Niditch, A.D. Winans, Alessio Zanelli, Anslem Brocki." circ. 60. 12/yr. Pub'd 12 issues 2009; expects 12 issues 2010, 12 issues 2011. sub. price $15; per copy $2; sample $2. Back issues: $2. 22pp. Reporting time: Responds in 2-3 months with publication or rejection note. (no acceptance notes). Simultaneous submissions accepted: Yes. Publishes 60% of manuscripts submitted. Not copyrighted. Pub's reviews: none in 2009. §Poetry Zines, Chap books, music. Ads: $10full/$8half. Subjects: Anarchist, Atheism, Counter-Culture, Alternatives, Communes, Cults, Culture, Diaries, Drugs, Illinois, Media, Photography, Poetry, Politics, Prose, Publishing.

Black Buzzard Press (see also VISIONS-INTERNATIONAL, The World Journal of Illustrated Poetry), Bradley R. Strahan, 3503 Ferguson Lane, Austin, TX 78754. 1979. Poetry, art. avg. press run 250-850. Expects 1 title 2010, 1 title 2011. 20 titles listed in the *Small Press Record of Books in Print* (36th Edition, 2010-11). Discounts: 20 or more 40%. 32pp. Reporting time: 2 weeks to 2 months. Simultaneous submissions accepted: no. Payment: by arrangement. Copyrights for author. Subject: Poetry.

BLACK CLOCK, Steve Erickson, Editor, Black Clock / CalArts, 24700 McBean Parkway, Valencia, CA 91355, info@blackclock.org, www.blackclock.org. 2003. Poetry, fiction, interviews, criticism, parts-of-novels, non-fiction. "Singular, idiosyncratic, and a little mysterious, *Black Clock* has become one of Americas leading literary journals since its inception three years ago, featuring such authors as Don DeLillo, David Foster Wallace, Richard Powers, Joanna Scott, Miranda July, Jonathan Lethem, Rick Moody, Samuel R. Delany, Carlos Ruiz Zafon, Aimee Bender, Greil Marcus along with a growing roster of striking new literary voices. Works appearing in Black Clock have been anthologized in best-of-the-year collections, nominated for O. Henry and Pushcart prizes, and two excerpted novels have gone on to win National Book Awards." circ. 3,000. Bi-annual. Pub'd 2 issues 2009; expects 2 issues 2010, 2 issues 2011. sub. price $20; per copy $13. Back issues: $13. Discounts: student, classrooms, wholesalers. 164pp. Reporting time: 6-9 months. Simultaneous submissions accepted: Yes. Copyrighted, reverts to author. Ads: Full-page $500, Half-page $300, Quarter-page $175, Web ad $50.

•Black Dolphin Publishing, PO Box 768931, Roswell, GA 30076. "Black Dolphin Publishing Company has been proud to publish books in the specialized field of love, dating and relationship since 2008. Browse through our titles, read descriptions of our books, and place your order through the online links to a couple of national bookstores today. We will even have a monthly book selection on sale for you!" No titles listed in the *Small Press Record of Books in Print* (36th Edition, 2010-11).

Black Dome Press Corp., 1011 Route 296, Hensonville, NY 12439, 518-734-6357, Fax 518-734-5802. 1990. Non-fiction. avg. press run 3M. Pub'd 5 titles 2009; expects 5 titles 2010, 6 titles 2011. 55 titles listed in the *Small Press Record of Books in Print* (36th Edition, 2010-11). Discounts: 40%. 200pp. Reporting time: 3 months. Simultaneous submissions accepted: yes. Publishes 5% of manuscripts submitted. Payment: varies per contract. Copyrights for author. Subjects: Adirondacks, Architecture, Arts, Biography, Earth, Natural History, Folklore, Geology, History, Native American, New York, Non-Fiction, Sports, Outdoors.

Black Dress Press (see also SPINNING JENNY), C.E. Harrison, P.O. Box 1067, New York, NY 10014, www.blackdresspress.com. 1994. Poetry, long-poems. avg. press run 1M. Pub'd 1 title 2009; expects 1 title 2010, 1 title 2011. No titles listed in the *Small Press Record of Books in Print* (36th Edition, 2010-11). Discounts: refer to DeBoer Distributors. 96pp. Reporting time: 1-4 months. Simultaneous submissions accepted: no. Publishes less than 5% of manuscripts submitted. Payment: complimentary copies. Copyrights for author. Subjects: Arts, Drama, Fiction, Literary Review, Literature (General), Music, Poetry.

Black Forest Press and The Tennessee Publishing House, Dahk Knox Ph.D., Publisher; Jan Knox Ph.D., Chief Financial Officer; Mary Inbody, Senior Editor; Kellie Warren-Underwood, Senior Cover Designer; Debra Luptak, Cover Designer; Rhoda Daniel, Editor; Linda Miles Ph.D., Editor; Young Elliott Ph.D., Editor, Belle Arden Run Estate, 496 Mountain View Drive, Mosheim, TN 37818-3524, 423-422-4711, ; E-mail: authorinfo@blackforestpress.net, web: www.blackforestpress.net. 1991. Poetry, fiction, satire, plays, non-fiction. "Kinder Books is an imprint for Childrens books. Black Forest Press is a small press which focuses on the publications of new authors who have difficulty obtaining large press publishers, but whose work has merit and is marketable. BFP also publishes books on Professional Growth and Career Development; Spiritual Religious books (Segen Books/imprint); Civil War (Southern Heritage Books) and World War II books (Abenteuer Books/imprint); Psychology and Educational books; Kinder Books/imprint for Childrens Books; Dichter Books/imprint for Ethnic and Poetry books and Abentenuer Books/imprint for Drama and Adventure books; Sonnenschein Books/imprint for Visionary and Contemporary books; Recht Books for Law and Political books." avg. press run POD books: 100-300; off-set printing: 2,000 to 5,000. Pub'd 101 titles 2009; expects 100+ titles 2010, 100+ titles 2011. 13 titles listed in the *Small Press Record of Books in Print* (36th Edition, 2010-11). Discounts: 20% on educational institutions who order quantities of 50 books/sets of books at a time; 15% on orders of 21-49; 10% on orders of 1-20; distributors/wholesalers regular discounts; 40% to bookstores. 200-250pp. Reporting time: 1-2 weeks. Simultaneous submissions are accepted, but no more than two by any one author at a time. Publishes 10% of manuscripts submitted. Payment: varies with promotion's agreement and terms. Copyrights for author. Subjects: Education, Employment, Fiction, Guidance, Networking, Newsletter, Non-Fiction, Poetry, Reference, Self-Help, Short Stories, Tapes & Records, Textbooks, Worker, World War II.

•Black Hawk Press, P.O. Box 10324, Charlotte, NC 28212, Website: www.blackhawkpress.com, Email: info@blackhawkpress.com. "Black Hawk Press is an independent publishing house that produces printed books, audio books, MP3 downloadable books, and e-books that are compatible with Amazons Kindle and other readers.The two primary genres represented by the company are adult counterterrorism thrillers and young adult fantasy adventures with positive messages." No titles listed in the *Small Press Record of Books in Print* (36th

Edition, 2010-11).

Black Heron Press, Jerry Gold, PO Box 13396, Mill Creek, WA 98082, 425-355-4929. 1984. Fiction. "May do something other than fiction, if it appeals to us." avg. press run 1.2M. Pub'd 4 titles 2009; expects 4 titles 2010, 4 titles 2011. 33 titles listed in the *Small Press Record of Books in Print* (36th Edition, 2010-11). Discounts: trade 45% with the right to return unsold copies, 50% nonreturnable. 200pp. Reporting time: 4-6 months. Simultaneous submissions accepted: yes. Publishes .003% of manuscripts submitted. Payment: 8% of retail price of book, payment semiannually. Copyrights for author. Subjects: Fiction, Literature (General), Novels, Short Stories.

BLACK LACE, BLK Publishing Company, Inc., Alycee J. Lane, PO Box 83912, Los Angeles, CA 90083-0912, 310-410-0808, fax 310-410-9250, e-mail newsroom@blk.com. 1991. Poetry, fiction, articles, art, photos, interviews, satire, criticism, reviews, letters, news items, non-fiction. circ. 9M. 4/yr. Expects 4 issues 2010, 4 issues 2011. sub. price $20; per copy $5.95; sample $7. Back issues: $7. Discounts: none. 48pp. Reporting time: 4 weeks. Simultaneous submissions accepted: yes. Publishes 10% of manuscripts submitted. Payment: varies. Copyrighted, rights reverting to author varies. Pub's reviews: 1 in 2009. §Black lesbian community. Ads: $420. Subjects: African-American, Black, Gay, Lesbianism, Sex, Sexuality.

Black Lawrence Press, Diane Goettel, 115 Center Ave, Aspinwall, PA 15215, www.blacklawrencepress.com. 2003. Poetry, fiction, non-fiction. "Black Lawrence Press is an independent press specializing in books of contemporary literature (poetry and fiction), politics, and modern culture and society. Black Lawrence will also publish the occasional translation." avg. press run 500. Pub'd 6 titles 2009; expects 14 titles 2010, 12 titles 2011. No titles listed in the *Small Press Record of Books in Print* (36th Edition, 2010-11). 80pp. Simultaneous submissions accepted: Yes. Publishes 2% of manuscripts submitted. Author's work is copyrighted. Subjects: Culture, Fiction, France, French, German, Literature (General), Memoirs, Non-Fiction, Novels, Poetry, Short Stories, Translation.

•**BLACK MAGNOLIAS LITERARY JOURNAL, Psychedelic Literature,** C. Liegh McInnis, 203 Lynn Lane, Clinton, MS 39056, (601) 383-0024, psychedeliclit@bellsouth.net, www.psychedelicliterature.com. 1996. Poetry, fiction, articles, interviews, satire, criticism, reviews, music, parts-of-novels, long-poems, plays, non-fiction. "The journal uses poetry, fiction, and essays to examine and celebrate the social, political, economic, and aesthetic accomplishments of African Americans with an emphasis on Afro-Mississippians and Afro-Southerners. Past contributors include Dr. Jerry Ward, Dr. Reginald Martin, Ahmos Zu-Bolton, Kalamu ya Salaam, Dr. Julius Thompson, Sterling Plump, Charlie Braxton, David Brian Williams, Jolivette Anderson, Kenneth Earl Stiggers, Sheree Renee Thomas, Dr. Howard Rambsy, Lenard D. Moore, Ronda Penrice, Marcus Uganda White, Waurene Roberson, Carlton Turner, and many others. We are seeking an equal amount of essays, poetry, and fiction. We welcome pieces on a variety of African American and Afro-Southern culture, including history, politics, education, incidents/events, social life, and literature. We also accept essays/critical analyses on literary works by white authors that have some significance or relevance to African American culture." 4/yr. Pub'd 4 issues 2009; expects 4 issues 2010, 4 issues 2011. sub. price $40; per copy $12; sample free. Back issues: $12. 75pp. Reporting time: Sixty Days. Simultaneous submissions accepted: Yes. Payment: One copy of the journal. Copyrighted, reverts to author. Pub's reviews: 4 in 2009. §Books, Music, Film, and Art by and about African Americans and Africans. Subjects: African Literature, Africa, African Studies, African-American, Black, Creative Non-fiction, Creativity, Criticism, Essays, Fiction, Interviews, Literary Review, Literature (General), Music, Non-Fiction, Poetry, Short Stories.

Black Mountain Press or Black Mountain College Museum + Arts Ctr, PO Box 18912, Asheville, NC 28814, Tel: 828-350-8484 email: bmcmac@bellsouth.net. 1994. Poetry, fiction, art, photos, interviews, criticism, music, long-poems, collages, plays, non-fiction. "We publish only works related to the former students and teachers of Black Mountain College, or related work." Pub'd 1 title 2009; expects 1 title 2010, 1 title 2011. 13 titles listed in the *Small Press Record of Books in Print* (36th Edition, 2010-11).

Black Oak Press, Tom Jennings, May Richards, PO Box 4663, University Place Stn., Lincoln, NE 68504, 402-467-4608. 1978. Poetry, fiction, art, parts-of-novels, long-poems, plays. "38 titles in print. Publish chapbooks besides hardcover and trade paperbacks. We solicit most of our material and prefer query letters to unsolicited manuscripts." avg. press run 1M. Pub'd 3 titles 2009; expects 3 titles 2010, 4 titles 2011. 10 titles listed in the *Small Press Record of Books in Print* (36th Edition, 2010-11). Discounts: negotiable. 64pp. Reporting time: 2 months for mss, 2 weeks for query letters. Simultaneous submissions accepted: yes. Publishes 1% of manuscripts submitted. Payment: negotiable. Copyrights for author. Subjects: Dada, Novels, Poetry, Satire.

•**Black Radish Books,** Lafayette, LA, blackradishbooks@gmail.com, blackradishbooks.org. 2010. "This independent press is the brainchild of Nicole Mauro and was created as a way to publish innovative and otherwise "unpublishable" poetry manuscripts. It began in May of 2009 and includes a diverse workforce of motivated poets. The consortium now has 16 members/ editors/ active participants." avg. press run 100-500.

Expects 7 titles 2010, 9 titles 2011. 3 titles listed in the *Small Press Record of Books in Print* (36th Edition, 2010-11). 100pp. Subjects: Avant-Garde, Experimental Art, Experimental, Poetry, Post Modern.

Black Rose Books Ltd., D. Roussopoulos, C.P. 1258, Succ. Place du Parc, Montreal, Quebec H2X 4A7, Canada, 514-844-4076, Fax 514-849-4797, blakrose@web.net, http://www.blackrosebooks.net. 1970. Non-fiction. "USA address: 2250 Military Road, Tonawanda, NY 14150, (716) 683-4547. Published over 250 books." avg. press run 3M. Pub'd 10 titles 2009; expects 10 titles 2010, 10 titles 2011. 176 titles listed in the *Small Press Record of Books in Print* (36th Edition, 2010-11). Discounts: regular trade. 200pp. Reporting time: 6 months. Simultaneous submissions accepted: yes. Publishes 10% of manuscripts submitted. Payment: 10% of list price. Copyrights for author. Subjects: Anarchist, Book Reviewing, Business & Economics, Canada, Cities, Community, Ecology, Foods, Feminism, Humanism, Labor, Philosophy, Sociology.

THE BLACK SCHOLAR: Journal of Black Studies and Research, Robert Chrisman, Editor; Robert L. Allen, Senior Editor, PO Box 2869, Oakland, CA 94609, 510-547-6633. 1969. Poetry, articles, art, photos, interviews, criticism, reviews, music. "Manuscripts for full-length articles may range in length from 2M to 5M words, include brief biographical statement, typewritten, double spaced. Articles may be historical and documented, they may be analytic and theoretical; they may be speculative. However, an article should not simply be a 'rap'; it should present a solid point of view convincingly and thoroughly argued. Recent Contributors: Jesse Jackson, Manning Marable, Jayne Cortez, Sonia Sanchez, Henry Louis Gates." circ. 10M. 4/yr. Pub'd 4 issues 2009; expects 4 issues 2010. sub. price $30 individual, $85 institution; per copy $6. Back issues: $6. Discounts: publishers 10% off above rates. 80pp. Reporting time: 1-2 months. Payment: in contributors copies of magazine and 1 year subscription. Rights become property of the *Black Scholar*. Pub's reviews: 22 in 2009. §The black experience or black related books. Ads: $1,200/$725/$550 1/4 page/classified $200 for 50 words or less, over 50 words add $22 per line per 7 words. Subjects: African Literature, Africa, African Studies, Black.

Black Thistle Press, Hollis Melton, 165 Wiswall Hill Road, Newfane, VT 05345-9548, 212-219-1898. 1990. Poetry, fiction. "We are no longer publishing new work, only selling books published." avg. press run 1M-5M. 2 titles listed in the *Small Press Record of Books in Print* (36th Edition, 2010-11). Discounts: 1-5 20%, 5+. 200pp. Payment: individual arrangements made. Copyrights for author. Subjects: Fiction, Non-Fiction, Poetry.

BLACK WARRIOR REVIEW, Jenny Gropp Hess, Editor; Farren Stanley, Managing Editor; Daniela Olszewska, Poetry Editor; Stephen Gropp-Hess, Fiction Editor; Katie Jean Shinkle, Nonfiction Editor, PO Box 862936, University of Alabama, Tuscaloosa, AL 35486-0027, 205-348-4518. 1974. Poetry, fiction, art, photos, cartoons, interviews, reviews, parts-of-novels, long-poems, non-fiction. "Publishes the freshest contemporary fiction, poetry, and nonfiction along with art and comics in each issue. Recent contributors include Sabrina Orah Mark, Peter Markus, James Grinwis, Andrew Zawacki, Joanna Klink, Aimee Bender, Jena Osman and Mary Caponegro. Holds annual fiction, poetry and nonfiction contests, each with a prize of $1000 and publication in the spring issue. The contest opens April 1, 2010 and closes September 1, 2010. Please send up to 3 poems or prose up to 7500 words per entry along with a $15 reading fee (which also gets you a 1-year subscription) and SASE." circ. 4800. 2/yr. Pub'd 2 issues 2009; expects 2 issues 2010, 2 issues 2011. sub. price $16; per copy $10; sample $10. Back issues: $8. Discounts: none at present. 180pp. Reporting time: 4 weeks to 5 months. Accepts simultaneous submissions; note on cover letter. Publishes 1% of manuscripts submitted. Payment: one-year subscription and honorarium. Copyrighted, reverts to author. Ads: $150/$90. Subjects: Arts, Cartoons, Essays, Fiction, Non-Fiction, Poetry.

•**Black Widow Press,** c/o Commonwealth Books, Inc, 9 Spring Lane, Boston, MA 02109. "Our goal as we progress with our publications is to become one of the best small poetry publishers: from the poets (and translators) we publish to the qualtiy of the books themselves (acid free paper, most titles put into sewn bindings). As an imprint of a bookstore we look first to what we would like to see available again, books (and authors) we would be excited about seeing on our shelves, and as important, books and authors we have enjoyed reading ourselves. For our first books we chose the best editions/translations of the legendary founder of Dada: Tristan Tzara, author of over 30 books of poetry, founder of the revolutionary Dada movement, and later on and off again collaborator of Andre Breton's Surrealist group." No titles listed in the *Small Press Record of Books in Print* (36th Edition, 2010-11).

BlackBerry Fields Press, Sandra Peoples, Publisher; Keisha Hawkins, Editor; Jashimbra Peoples, Assistant Editor, 2712 North Saginaw Street, Suite 103, Flint, MI 48505, Phone: (810) 275-8316, Fax (810)234-8593 web:www.bblit.info, www.myspace.com/bblit, email:bblit@hotmail.com. 2005. Poetry, fiction, articles, photos, cartoons, interviews, reviews, parts-of-novels, long-poems, plays, non-fiction. "Recently published titles: "Foolish", "Poetic Praise", "Beyond 141 Hinkle Street: The Sequel". Recently edited "A Trip to Hell in a Gasoline Jacket" by Monte Drake, and two series. Currently assisting with ten new author projects. The mission of BlackBerry Fields Press is to empower writers with the tools they need to become successful authors. We guide our authors through the entire self publishing process, from proofreading and editing to the actual printing. We currently do not purchase any manuscripts, and we do not collect a royalty. We simply help authors to see their dream work in print. Authors decide how many books they believe they can sell, and therefore determine their own initial print run. BlackBerry Fields Press will not consider assisting with pieces that deal with hate, pornography, or pieces that are poorly written.'' avg. press run 200. Pub'd 2 titles 2009; expects 10 titles 2010, 20 titles 2011. 2 titles listed in the *Small Press Record of Books in Print* (36th Edition, 2010-11). Discounts: 2-10 copies, 25%consider up to 55% for bookstores. 120pp. Reporting time: 2-4 weeks. Simultaneous submissions accepted: Yes. Publishes 90% of manuscripts submitted. Does not copyright for author. Subjects: Advertising, Self-Promotion, African-American, Family, Fiction, Finances, Food, Eating, Non-Fiction, Novels, Parenting, Picture Books, Poetry, Prison, Prose, Publishing, Religion.

BLACKBIRD, David Stone, PO Box 16235, Baltimore, MD 21210, e-mail chocozzz2@aol.com. 1997. Poetry, art, photos, cartoons, interviews, criticism, long-poems, collages, concrete art. ''Anthology of visual poetry, experimental poetry, art, photography, textual poetry and narrative that is theme related. Query by e-mail. Submit original for publication by mail with SASE. Recent contributors: Eric Basso, Guy Beining, Dave Chirot, Harry Burrus, Guido Vermeulen (Belgium). Experimental, Holocaust, visual poetry, political, blackbird art and myth, Paul Celan, international, new voices. Submission quantity: 1-10. Do not e-mail submissions.'' circ. 200. 1/yr. Pub'd 1 issue 2009; expects 1 issue 2010, 1 issue 2011. sub. price $30; per copy $26; sample $30w/postage US, $35 foreign (US dollars). Back issues: none. Discounts: none. 200pp. Reporting time: ASAP with SASE. We prefer exclusive submissions, not simultaneous submissions. Publishes 30% of manuscripts submitted. Payment: 1 copy. Copyrighted, reverts to author. Ads: none. Subjects: Avant-Garde, Experimental Art, Holocaust, Visual Arts.

BLACKFIRE, BLK Publishing Company, Inc., Alan Bell, PO Box 83912, Los Angeles, CA 90083-0912, 310-410-0808, fax 310-410-9250, e-mail newsroom@blk.com. 1992. Poetry, fiction, articles, art, photos, interviews, long-poems, non-fiction. circ. 12M. 6/yr. sub. price $30; per copy $5.95; sample $7.00. Back issues: $7.00. 48pp. Reporting time: 4 weeks. Simultaneous submissions accepted: yes. Payment: varies. Copyrighted, rights reverting to author varies. §Black gay male community. Ads: $1800. Subjects: African-American, Black, Gay, Interviews, Sex, Sexuality.

BLACKFLASH Magazine, John Shelling, Managing Editor, PO Box 7381 Station Main, Saskatoon, Saskatchewan S7K 4J3, Canada, 306-374-5115, editor@blackflash.ca. 1983. Articles, art, photos, interviews, criticism, reviews, letters. circ. 1,700. 3/yr. Pub'd 3 issues 2009; expects 3 issues 2010, 3 issues 2011. sub. price Individuals: $22 Canadian; $24 USD for American Subscribers; $32 USD for international; Institution: $32 Canadian; $36 USD for American institutions; $42 USD for international institutions; per copy $8; sample $5. Back issues: $5. Discounts: bulk. 64pp. Reporting time: 2 months. Simultaneous submissions accepted: no. Publishes 25% of manuscripts submitted. Copyrighted, reverts to author. Pub's reviews: 5 in 2009. §Contemporary visual arts, contemporary photography and critical writing on contemporary photography. Subjects: Arts, Photography.

Blackwater Publications, James P. Gannon, PO Box 595, Flint Hill, VA 22627-0595, 540/987-9536; www.blackwaterpublications.com. 2004. Criticism, non-fiction. ''Our mission is to publish quality non-fiction with emphasis on biography, autobiography, political commentary, journalism, local and regional history.'' avg. press run 500-1000. Expects 3 titles 2010, 3 titles 2011. 3 titles listed in the *Small Press Record of Books in Print* (36th Edition, 2010-11). Discounts: Bookstores: one copy, 20%; 2-4 copies, 35%; 5 or more copies, 40%; carton quantity, 50%.Wholesalers: 55%Classrooms: 25%. 140-200pp. Reporting time: 30 days. Simultaneous submissions accepted: Yes. Publishes 10% of manuscripts submitted. Payment: Negotiable. Does not copyright for author. Subjects: Americana, Biography, Book Collecting, Bookselling, Catholic, Celtic, Civil War, Communication, Journalism, History, Iowa, Ireland, Midwest, Minnesota, Politics, Presidents, Public Affairs.

BLADES, Francis Poole, Poporo Press, 335 Paper Mill Road, Newark, DE 19711-2254. 1977. Poetry, fiction, art, satire, letters, collages, news items. ''*Blades* is a tiny magazine, so send short poems (15 lines=one page). Occasionally we publish longer ones, 3 or 4 pages. We publish surrealism (drawings too), satire, humor, linguistically interesting work. Very short stories, dreams, and cultural documents also sought; prose should be short. We are interested in non-English poems, also. Editors like imagery and poems that examine the strange natural world.'' circ. 175. 2-3/yr. Pub'd 2 issues 2009; expects 2 issues 2010, 2 issues 2011. sub. price $5 or exchange of publications and SASE, libraries $35/year; per copy $1 with SASE; sample $1, or for exchange enclose SASE. Back issues: $2. 36pp. Reporting time: 2 months. Payment: copies. Copyrighted, reverts to author. Pub's reviews: none in 2009. §Poetry, film, art, music (rock, blues, jazz, world). Ads: exchange ads free. Subjects: Dada, Humor, Poetry, Transportation, Visual Arts.

Bladestar Publishing, Mary Jones, 1499 North 950 West, Orem, UT 84057, www.BladestarPublishing.com. 2005. Fiction. ''Fantasy / Science Fiction.'' avg. press run 2000. Expects 1 title 2010. No titles listed in the *Small Press Record of Books in Print* (36th Edition, 2010-11). Discounts: Libraries 20% Bookstores 40% Distributors & Wholesalers 55%. 528-624pp. Reporting time: Not accepting unsolicited manuscripts. Simultaneous submissions accepted: No. Publishes 10% of manuscripts submitted. Does not copyright for author. Subjects: Fantasy, Fiction, Novels, Science Fiction.

John F. Blair, Publisher, Carolyn Sakowski, 1406 Plaza Drive, Winston-Salem, NC 27103, 336-768-1374. 1954. Fiction, non-fiction. Pub'd 17 titles 2009; expects 20 titles 2010, 23 titles 2011. 61 titles listed in the *Small Press Record of Books in Print* (36th Edition, 2010-11). Discounts: wholesalers 50%, libraries and schools 50%, trade schedule is according to quantity of books ordered; non-returnable - 50% for retail, 55% wholesale. 100-300pp. Reporting time: 6-8 weeks. Simultaneous submissions accepted: yes. Publishes less than 1% of manuscripts submitted. Payment: % of net sales, bi-annual payments. Copyrights for author. Subjects: Civil War, Folklore, Non-Fiction, North Carolina, South, Sports, Outdoors, Transportation.

Blanket Fort Publishing, Sarah Phelan, 117 Lakeview Avenue, Lynn, MA 01904, 781-632-1824. 2005. Fiction. "To provide intelligent, realistic fiction for women." avg. press run 3000. Expects 1-3 titles 2010, 2-4 titles 2011. 1 title listed in the *Small Press Record of Books in Print* (36th Edition, 2010-11). Discounts: traditional 40%. 200-450pp. Reporting time: 1 month. Simultaneous submissions accepted: Yes. Publishes 5% of manuscripts submitted. Does not copyright for author. Subjects: Novels, Women.

BLAST poetry and critical writing, LK Holt, Editor, Publisher; Elizabeth Campbell, Reviews & Features Editor, 2008/22 Jane Bell Lane, Melbourne, VIC 3000, Australia, blastpoetry[at]gmail[dot]com, www.blast-poetry.com. 2005. Poetry, articles, interviews, criticism, reviews, letters, non-fiction. "BLAST is committed to publishing high quality poetry and other critical writing by Australian poets and writers. Only previously unpublished submissions considered; simultaneous submissions are not accepted. Deadlines are 31 January and 31 August. For guidelines and further information see www.blastpoetry.com." 2/yr. Pub'd 2 issues 2009; expects 2 issues 2010, 2 issues 2011. sub. price AU$20 pa; per copy AU$10; sample AU$10. 56pp. Reporting time: 1 to 5 months. Payment dependent on arts funding in a given year. Copyrighted, reverts to author.

Blink Chapbooks (see also BLINK: A little little magazine of little poems), Margaret Rabb, CB #3520, Greenlaw Hall, UNC, Chapel Hill, NC 27599-3520. No titles listed in the *Small Press Record of Books in Print* (36th Edition, 2010-11).

BLINK: A little little magazine of little poems, Blink Chapbooks, Margaret Rabb, English Department, Box 184, University of Central Oklahoma, 100 N. University Drive, Edmond, OK 73003. 2001. Poetry. "Dedicated to short forms, Blink publishes between four and six very brief poems in each issue." 4/yr. 1 title listed in the *Small Press Record of Books in Print* (36th Edition, 2010-11). sub. price $6; per copy $1; sample $1. 4pp. Reporting time: Varies. Simultaneous submissions accepted: Yes. Payment: Contributors' copies. Copyrighted, reverts to author.

BLITHE HOUSE QUARTERLY, www.blithe.com. "An online quarterly literary magazine for queer short fiction. Every issue features 6 to 10 short stories. We publish lesbian, gay, bisexual and transgendered fiction not as a genre or ghetto, but as a literature that can stand by any other in its quality and innovation."

BLK, BLK Publishing Company, Inc., Alan Bell, PO Box 83912, Los Angeles, CA 90083-0912, 310-410-0808, fax 310-410-9250, e-mail newsroom@blk.com. 1988. Articles, photos, cartoons, interviews, criticism, reviews, music, letters, news items, non-fiction. circ. 22M. 12/yr. Pub'd 12 issues 2009; expects 12 issues 2010, 12 issues 2011. sub. price $18; per copy $4; sample $2.95. Back issues: all $2.95 except #1 which is $10. Discounts: none. 60pp. Reporting time: 4 weeks. Simultaneous submissions accepted: yes. Payment: varies. Copyrighted, rights reverting to author varies. Pub's reviews: none in 2009. §Black lesbian and gay community. Ads: $1800/$1170/.40¢. Subjects: African-American, AIDS, Black, Book Reviewing, Cartoons, Civil Rights, Electronics, Entertainment, Fashion, Gay, Interviews, Lesbianism, Men, Race, Women.

BLK Publishing Company, Inc. (see also BLACK LACE; BLACKFIRE; BLK; KUUMBA), PO Box 83912, Los Angeles, CA 90083-0912, 310-410-0808, Fax 310-410-9250, newsroom@blk.com. 1988. No titles listed in the *Small Press Record of Books in Print* (36th Edition, 2010-11).

Bloated Toe Publishing, Lawrence P. Gooley, PO Box 324, Peru, NY 12972, (518)563-9469, info@bloatedtoe.com, www.bloatedtoe.com. 2004. Non-fiction. "*Winner, Best Non-Fiction, 2008 Adirondack Literary Awards.* At Bloated Toe, we have published seven books related to history, including one pictorial of more than 300 photographs. We are inclined to help the novice author or organization get their publications into print. We also feature a partnership program where we share the production costs with the author, and share in the profits. The partnership extends for the entire printing run, so we share an interest in the sale of every single book. In that way, the author is not alone in trying to sell books." avg. press run 1000. Pub'd 2 titles 2009; expects 5 titles 2010, 6 titles 2011. 11 titles listed in the *Small Press Record of Books in Print* (36th Edition, 2010-11). Discounts: 10 copies or more, any mix of titles, 20%. 250pp. Reporting time: 1-5 days. Simultaneous submissions accepted: No. Copyrights for author. Subjects: Animals, Biography, Diaries, History, Memoirs, Reprints.

BLOOD LOTUS JOURNAL, www.bloodlotus.org. 2006. "This an on-line publication. The editors of *Blood Lotus* are passionate writers and fierce critics. We know exactly what we want: to read - something we've never read before. We think there are so many engaging and enraging things in modern society to write about, and we refuse to believe that everything has already been written. Have we heard your viewpoint yet? Please, take risks. Write like words are beautiful, powerful, and dangerous—then send them to *Blood Lotus*.'' quarterly. Reporting time: within 3 mos. Simultaneous submissions accepted: yes.

•**Blood Moon Productions,** Danforth Prince, Publisher & CEO, 75 Saint Marks Place, Staten Island, NY 10301-1606, Tel. 718/556-9410, FAX 718/816-4092. ''Blood Moon Productions is a New York City publisher that salvages and documents the unrecorded oral histories of America's entertainment industry.'' No titles listed in the *Small Press Record of Books in Print* (36th Edition, 2010-11).

BLOODJET LITERARY MAGAZINE, New World Press, Noni Howard Ph.D, Edd, MD, Littd,, Publisher, 20 Driftwood Trail, Half Moon Bay, CA 94019-2349, 650-726-5939. 1974. Poetry, fiction, art, photos, letters, parts-of-novels, long-poems, collages. ''Length 100-200 pages, women preferred but will consider men, Jennifer Stone is a recent contributor. Persons able to write grants or obtain other funding especially considered. Please send nothing by mail without calling my phone number for a personal inquiry. Each is devoted to the work of one person.'' circ. 1.2M. varies each year. Pub'd none recently issues 2009. price per copy $10; sample $10. Back issues: $7.50. Discounts: 40% to bulk or educational institutions. 100pp. Reporting time: No submissions without phoning first. Simultaneous submissions accepted: No. Publishes less than 2% of manuscripts submitted. Payment: free copies. Copyrighted, reverts to author. Subjects: Literature (General), Poetry.

BLOOM: Queer Fiction, Art, Poetry and more, Charles Flowers, Editor, 5482 Wilshire Blvd, #1616, Los Angeles, CA 90036. 2004. ''*Bloom* is a publication of Arts in Bloom Project, Inc., a non-profit dedicated to queer artists, writers, and audiences.Mission: BLOOM was founded to support the work of lesbian, gay, bisexual, and transgendered writers and artists and to foster the appreciation of queer literature and creation. www.artsinbloom.com.'' 2/yr. sub. price $20/ 1 year, add $10 for Canada & Mexico, $15 for other countries; per copy $10. Back issues: Available. 200pp.

THE BLOOMSBURY REVIEW, Marilyn Auer, Publisher, Editor-in-Chief, 1553 Platte Street, Suite 206, Denver, CO 80202-1167, 303-455-3123, Fax 303-455-7039. 1980. Poetry, fiction, articles, art, photos, interviews, criticism, reviews, letters, long-poems, non-fiction. ''We do not publish original fiction at this time.'' circ. 35M. 6/yr. Pub'd 4 issues 2009; expects 4 issues 2010, 4 issues 2011. sub. price $20; per copy $3.50; sample $5. Back issues: $5. Discounts: inquiries about distribution are welcome. 28pp. Reporting time: 3 months. Simultaneous submissions accepted: No. Payment: $10 per review, $5 poetry, $20 features. Copyrighted. Ask for first-time rights and non-exclusive electronic rights. Pub's reviews: 900 in 2009. §Literature, history, biography, poetry, autobiography, politics-All subject areas. Ads: $4,590/$1,800/$50 first 25 words, $1.25 each additional word. Subjects: Agriculture, Anthropology, Archaelogy, Architecture, Arts, Biography, Book Reviewing, Chicano/a, Children, Youth, Conservation, Earth, Natural History, Ecology, Foods, Folklore, History, Labor, Latin America.

THE BLOTTER MAGAZINE, Inc., Garrison Somers, Editor-in-Chief, 1010 Hale St., Durham, NC 27705. 2003. Poetry, fiction, art, photos, cartoons, interviews, satire, parts-of-novels, long-poems, non-fiction. ''*The Blotter Magazine* exists to nurture underground, outsider literature and art and to provide it to a wide audience. We believe that the economic viability of good art and writing should not interfere with its life, liberty, or happiness; and we deliberately seek to avoid the pretension and overintellectualism for which the world of literature and art has become known. Our goal is to treat contributors, donors, and readers alike with dignity, friendship, and respec.'' circ. 7000 hard copies per month, distributed free in select cities, mirrored on website with 4000 downloads avg. per month. 12/yr. Pub'd 12 issues 2009; expects 12 issues 2010, 13 issues 2011. sub. price $25. Back issues: $1. 16 pages - 10 issues annually; 24 pages - 2 ''special issues'' annually.pp. Simultaneous submissions accepted: Yes. Publishes 10-15% of manuscripts submitted. Payment: Courtesy copies.

Blowtorch Press, Elizabeth Dearborn, 55 Lark Street, Buffalo, NY 14211, webmaster@blowtorchpress.com. 2005. Fiction, non-fiction. Expects 1 title 2010, 5 titles 2011. No titles listed in the *Small Press Record of Books in Print* (36th Edition, 2010-11). Discounts: Standard trade discount 55%. 644pp. Subjects: Fiction, Medicine, Non-Fiction, Reference.

Blue Brush Media, Kunle Oguneye, 851 Monroe Ave. NE, Renton, WA 98056, 425-818-8850, Fax: 425-228-6775, info@sikulu.com, www.sikulu.com. 2008. Fiction, cartoons. ''Blue Brush Media exists to expose children to the beauty of global cultures. Our initial focus is on introducing children to the beauty of Africa through books and related media.'' avg. press run 6000. Expects 1 title 2010, 3 titles 2011. 1 title listed in the *Small Press Record of Books in Print* (36th Edition, 2010-11). Standard discounts apply. 32pp. Reporting time: We are not accepting submissions at this time. Simultaneous submissions accepted: No. Payment: Negotiable. Does not copyright for author. Subjects: African Literature, Africa, African Studies, African-American, Black, Children, Youth.

BLUE COLLAR REVIEW, Partisan Press, Al Markowitz, Mary Franke, PO Box 11417, Norfolk, VA

23517, red-ink@earthlink.net. 1997. Poetry, fiction, art, photos, interviews, reviews, long-poems, non-fiction. "Poetry and writing of high quality with a progressive working class perspective. Abroad range of work, not polemic or screed. We have published work by Martin Espada, Robert Edwards, Tom McGrath, Sonia Sanchez. Please put name and address on every page, SASE for return of manuscript. For best results, see a sample issue." circ. 550. 4/yr. Pub'd 4 issues 2009; expects 4 issues 2010, 4 issues 2011. sub. price $15 - make checks to Partisan Press; per copy $5; sample $5. Discounts: $3 in quantity. 64pp. Reporting time: 3-8 weeks. Simultaneous submissions accepted: no. Publishes 10% of manuscripts submitted. Payment: copies. Copyrighted, reverts to author. Pub's reviews: 1 in 2009. §Working class issues or perspectives in fiction, novels, films...poetry. Ads: $60/$40. Subjects: Communism, Marxism, Leninism, Construction, Creative Non-fiction, Culture, Employment, Feminism, Homemaking, Human Rights, Labor, Multicultural, Peace, Race, Socialist, Society, Worker.

Blue Cubicle Press, LLC (see also THE FIRST LINE; WORKERS WRITE!), David LaBounty, P.O. Box 250382, Plano, TX 75025-0382, 9728240646. 2005. Poetry, fiction, cartoons, satire, reviews, parts-of-novels, plays, non-fiction. "Blue Cubicle Press is an independent publisher. We publish three literary journals, The First Line, Workers Write!, and Overtime, and books we enjoy reading. We are dedicated to giving voice to writers who realize their words may never pay the mortgage but who are too stubborn to stop trying. We're here to support the artists trapped in the daily grind." avg. press run 1000. Pub'd 1 title 2009; expects 2 titles 2010, 1 title 2011. No titles listed in the *Small Press Record of Books in Print* (36th Edition, 2010-11). 200pp. Reporting time: 1 month. Simultaneous submissions accepted: Yes. Payment: 15%, advances depending on book, royalty payment once a year. Copyrights for author. Subjects: Fiction, Labor, Literature (General), Prose, Reprints, Short Stories, Worker, Zines.

Blue Dolphin Publishing, Inc., Paul M. Clemens, PO Box 8, Nevada City, CA 95959, 530-477-1503. 1985. Non-fiction. "We publish books on comparative spiritual traditions, personal growth, self-help, and health. We offer high resolution computer output from our ECRM and accept both IBM and Macintosh. Call for price list. 10% discount to Dustbooks' users." avg. press run 3M-5M. Pub'd 20 titles 2009; expects 22 titles 2010, 24 titles 2011. 52 titles listed in the *Small Press Record of Books in Print* (36th Edition, 2010-11). Discounts: 40-55%. 200+pp. Reporting time: 3-6 months, bids 1 week. Simultaneous submissions accepted: yes. Publishes less than 1% of manuscripts submitted. Payment: 10%. Copyrights for author. Subjects: Aging, Anthropology, Archaelogy, Astrology, Christianity, Cooking, Danish, Ecology, Foods, Education, Energy, Feminism, Gardening, How-To, Humor, Italy, Marriage.

Blue Hull Press, Deborah Homsher, 225 Warren Place, Ithaca, NY 14850, 607 351 6615. 2007. Fiction. avg. press run 1000. Expects 1 title 2010, 1 title 2011. No titles listed in the *Small Press Record of Books in Print* (36th Edition, 2010-11). Discounts: Blue Hull Press books are distributed by AtlasBooks (BookMasters). Please contact AtlasBooks for discount information. 250pp. Reporting time: 3 months. Simultaneous submissions accepted: Yes. Publishes 5% of manuscripts submitted. Payment: Negotiable. Author pays production costs and reaps all income from sales through distributor. We provide support for a fee. Does not copyright for author. Subjects: Fiction, History, North America, Novels.

•**Blue Lion Books,** Peter Ganick, Editor, 45 Ravenwood Road, West Hartford, CT 06107-1539. "blue lion books publishes experimental poetry, visual poetry, and fiction. we specialize in books over 250 pages long,believing that an idea, if expressed, should be expressed in its fullest manner. Send manuscripts to our address or in electronic format (Word DOC or RTF-files, 250-550 pages formatted to 6x9 inches page size) to pganickz@gmail.com." No titles listed in the *Small Press Record of Books in Print* (36th Edition, 2010-11).

Blue Lupin Press, Dan Bessie, Partner; Jeanne Johnson, Partner, c/o Anita Thomas, 1919 Apache Avenue, South Lake Tahoe, CA 96150, (530) 573-1452. 2006. Fiction, non-fiction. "Open to any well written work of fiction or non-fiction. Commercial considerations are secondary to work that reflects individuality, and that serves (in a broadly defined manner) some socially relevant and humanistic purpose. Not interested in standard romance novels, sexist, racist, pornographic, or other material that in any way degrades our fellow human beings.We basically assist authors in getting published. We do not, however, finance publication ourselves. But we are also not a vaniety press." avg. press run 300. Pub'd 2 titles 2009; expects 4 titles 2010, 2 titles 2011. 4 titles listed in the *Small Press Record of Books in Print* (36th Edition, 2010-11). Discounts: bookstores - 40% on all copies. Others by inquiry. 200pp. Reporting time: 3 weeks. Simultaneous submissions accepted: Yes. Payment: Open to negotiation. Will assist authors in obtaining copyright. Subjects: Autobiography, Culture, Fiction, Folklore, Humanism, Humor, Liberal Arts, Literature (General), Movies, Non-Fiction, Performing Arts, Relationships, Self-Help, Short Stories, Visual Arts.

BLUE MESA REVIEW, Skye Pratt, Chris Wrenn, University of New Mexico, Creative Writing Program, MSC03-2170, Humanities 274, Albuquerque, NM 87131-0001, 505-277-6347. 1989. Poetry, fiction, interviews, reviews, parts-of-novels, non-fiction. "Distinguished by the multi-ethnic and diverse cultural heritage of its founders, its editors, and its contributors, Blue Mesa Review strives to combine personal vision and aesthetics with a high degree of intellectual curiosity.Blue Mesa publishes stories and poems along with essays, interviews, and book reviews that serve as a forum for thoughtful discussion on a broad range of issues, ideas, and literature. Past contributors include Arthur Sze, Joy Harjo, Paula Gunn Allen." circ. 1000. Yearly. Pub'd 1 issue 2009; expects 1 issue 2010, 2 issues 2011. sub. price $10; per copy $10; sample $10. Back issues: $8. Classroom Discounts Available. 200pp. Reporting time: 8-12 weeks. Simultaneous submissions accepted: Yes. Publishes 5% of manuscripts submitted. Payment: Two contributor's copies. Copyrighted, reverts to author. Pub's reviews: 4 in 2009. §fiction, poetry, nonfiction. Ads: Blue Mesa trades ads with other literary magazines. Subjects: Book Reviewing, Creative Non-fiction, Fiction, Poetry.

Blue Moose Press, Allison Willows, 1319 E Logan Street, Round Rock, TX 78664, 512-923-0475, 512-244-0140 fax, http://www.thebluemoosepress.com. 2007. Poetry, fiction, articles, art, photos, cartoons, satire, reviews. "Currently accepting material for our weekly newsletter." avg. press run 10000. Expects 1 title 2010, 2 titles 2011. 1 title listed in the *Small Press Record of Books in Print* (36th Edition, 2010-11). Discounts: 2-4(20% off), 5-9(30% off), 10-24(40% off), 25-49(42% off), 50-99 (44% off), 100-199(48% off), 200 or more(50% off);. 280pp. Reporting time: 1 week. Simultaneous submissions accepted: Yes. Publishes 80% of manuscripts submitted. Subjects: Celtic, Geoffrey Chaucer, Fantasy, Fiction, Medieval, Myth, Mythology, Renaissance, Shaker, Shakespeare, Vegetarianism, Young Adult.

BLUE MOUNTAIN, Christine Easwaran, PO Box 256, Tomales, CA 94971, 707-878-2369, 800-475-2369, Fax 707-878-2375, info@nilgiri.org, www.nilgiri.org. Articles, photos, interviews, reviews, letters, non-fiction. "We don't accept submissions." circ. 25M. 4/yr. Pub'd 4 issues 2009; expects 4 issues 2010, 4 issues 2011. sub. price free. Discounts: 16. Simultaneous submissions accepted: no. Copyrighted. Ads: none. Subjects: Aging, Audio/Video, Buddhism, Community, Education, Environment, Family, Health, Inspirational, Mental Health, Metaphysics, Non-Violence, Peace, Religion, Spiritual.

THE BLUE MOUSE, Swan Duckling Press, Mark Bruce, PO Box 8317, Eureka, CA 95502-8317. 1998. Poetry. "Poems about personal experience have the best chance." circ. 300. 4/yr. Pub'd 4 issues 2009; expects 4 issues 2010, 4 issues 2011. sub. price $6; per copy $2; sample $2. Back issues: $2. Discounts: none. 24pp. Reporting time: 6 months. Simultaneous submissions accepted: no. Publishes 20% of manuscripts submitted. Payment: 2 copies. Not copyrighted, author keeps copyright. Ads: $30/$15.

Blue Mouse Studio, Rex Schneider, Chris Buchman, 26829 37th Street, Gobles, MI 49055, 616-628-5160; fax 616-628-4970. 1980. Cartoons. "No unsolicited manuscripts." avg. press run 2M. Pub'd 1 title 2009; expects 1 title 2010, 1 title 2011. 1 title listed in the *Small Press Record of Books in Print* (36th Edition, 2010-11). Discounts: wholesalers 50%; retailers 40%. 80pp. Subjects: Americana, Children, Youth, Humor.

Blue Owl Press, Howard Bandy, 3700 S. Westport Ave, #1876, Sioux Falls, SD 57106, 5207051239, howard@blueowlpress.com, www.blueowlpress.com. 2007. Non-fiction. "We publish business, financial, investing, trading, stock market, futures market, mathematics, statistics, simulation. Two recent books are Introduction to AmiBroker and Quantitative Trading Systems. One or more books related to trading system development scheduled for 2009." avg. press run 2000. Pub'd 1 title 2009; expects 1 title 2010, 1-3 titles 2011. 2 titles listed in the *Small Press Record of Books in Print* (36th Edition, 2010-11). Discounts: full cartons (14 to 22) 30%. 500pp. Reporting time: 10 days. Simultaneous submissions accepted: Yes. Publishes 50% of manuscripts submitted. Payment: as negotiated. either. Subjects: Artificial Intelligence, Business & Economics, Finances, Mathematics, Non-Fiction.

Blue Planet Books Inc., Monique Johnson, 4619 W. McRae Way, Glendale, AZ 85308, Phone: 602-769-2066, Fax 623-780-0468, www.blueplanetbooksandsaudio.com. 2000. Fiction. "Submit only first chapter and synopsis - standard manuscript format. Only work ready for publication, 25 pages max., clean copy double-spaced. Anything less will not be considered. Professional presentation a must." avg. press run varies from 5M-50M. Pub'd 2 titles 2009; expects 2 titles 2010, 2 titles 2011. 4 titles listed in the *Small Press Record of Books in Print* (36th Edition, 2010-11). Discounts: 50% off cover price, add shipping and handling. 320pp. Reporting time: 1 month. Simultaneous submissions accepted: no. Publishes .1% of manuscripts submitted. Payment: standard contract, very small advance and royalty. Copyrights for author. Subjects: Fantasy, Medieval, Novels, Romance, Science Fiction.

Blue Raven Press, Barbara Gislason, 219 S.E. Main St., Suite 506, Minneapolis, MN 55414, 612-331-8039, 612-331-8115, www.blueravenpress.com. No titles listed in the *Small Press Record of Books in Print* (36th Edition, 2010-11).

Blue Scarab Press, Harald Wyndham, PO Box 4966, Pocatello, ID 83205-4966. 1984. Poetry, fiction. "Blue Scarab Press does not accept unsolicited manuscripts." avg. press run 350 to 500. Expects 1 title 2010, 1 title 2011. 19 titles listed in the *Small Press Record of Books in Print* (36th Edition, 2010-11). Discounts: 40% to booksellers or wholesalers, discounts for volume. 50-150pp. Publishes 100% of those we solicit% of manuscripts submitted. Payment: copies and royalty after recuperation of costs. Copyrights for author. Subject: Poetry.

Blue Tiger Press, Robert Kokan, 2016 Hwy 67, Dousman, WI 53118, 262-965-2751. 2005. Poetry. avg. press run 300. Expects 1 title 2010. No titles listed in the *Small Press Record of Books in Print* (36th Edition, 2010-11). Discounts: 15%. 85pp. Reporting time: 3 months. Simultaneous submissions accepted: Yes. Publishes 1% of manuscripts submitted. Payment: flexible. Copyrights for author. Subject: Poetry.

BLUE UNICORN, Ruth G. Iodice, John Hart, Fred Ostrander, 22 Avon Road, Kensington, CA 94707, 510-526-8439. 1977. Poetry, art. *"Blue Unicorn* is a journal looking for excellence of the individual voice, whether that voice comes through in a fixed form or an original variation or in freer lines. We publish poets who are established and those who are less known but deserve to be known better, and we are also proud to welcome new talent to our pages. We like poems which communicate in a memorable way whatever is deeply felt by the poet, and we believe in an audience that is delighted, like us, by a lasting image, a unique twist of thought, and a haunting music. We also use a limited number of expert translations. Among recent contributors to our tri-quarterly are: Rosalie Moore, Charles Edward Eaton, James Schevill, John Ditsky, Don Welch, Barbara A. Holland, Lawrence Spingarn, A.D. Winans, William Dickey, Adrianne Marcus, Stuart Silverman. Please send only unpublished poems." circ. 500. 3/yr. Pub'd 3 issues 2009; expects 3 issues 2010, 3 issues 2011. 1 title listed in the *Small Press Record of Books in Print* (36th Edition, 2010-11). sub. price $18; add $6 mailing for foreign subscriptions; per copy $7; add $2 mailing for copies sent abroad; sample $7; add $2 mailing for copies sent abroad. Back issues: $5. 40pp. Reporting time: 1-3 months. Simultaneous submissions accepted: no. We publish 5% or less of manuscripts submitted. Payment: 1 copy. Copyrighted, reverts to author. Ads: none. Subjects: Arts, Poetry.

Blue Unicorn Press, Inc., Wanda Z. Larson, Publisher, PO Box 40300, Portland, OR 97240-0300, 503-423-7781. 1990. Poetry, art, letters. avg. press run 200-1M. Pub'd 1 title 2009; expects 4 titles 2010, 2+ titles 2011. 5 titles listed in the *Small Press Record of Books in Print* (36th Edition, 2010-11). Discounts: 2-4 books 20%, 5-99 40%, 100+ 50%. 64-350pp. Reporting time: 1 month to 1 year. Simultaneous submissions accepted: yes. Publishes 5% of manuscripts submitted. Payment: to be worked out. Copyrights for author. Subjects: Anthropology, Archaelogy, Biography, History, Medieval, Minnesota, Poetry.

BLUELINE, Donald J McNutt, Editor, State University College, English Dept., Potsdam, NY 13676, 315-267-2043. 1979. Poetry, fiction, art, criticism, reviews, non-fiction. "We are interested in fiction and poetry that has some relationship to the Adirondack mountain region or similar areas. We also seek essays that interpret the literature and/or contemporary culture of the Adirondacks or surrounding areas, including New York State, New England, or eastern Canada. Short fiction and essays should be no more than 3.5M words, poems 75 lines or less. Recent contributors include Ginnah Howard, Joan Connor, Maggie Mitchell, M.J. Iuppa, Sandra L. Graff, Robert Schuler, Ken Fifer, Ginny Lowe Connors, and Richard Levine." circ. 600. 1/yr. Pub'd 1 issue 2009. 1 title listed in the *Small Press Record of Books in Print* (36th Edition, 2010-11). sub. price $12; per copy $12; sample $12. Back issues: $3. Discounts: $8 per copy to distributors. 180-200pp. Reporting time: By Mid-February. Simultaneous submissions accepted: no. Publishes 5% of manuscripts submitted. Payment: copies. Copyrighted, reverts to author. Pub's reviews: 10 in 2009. §Short fiction, novels, poetry, essays about the Adirondacks, and ecocriticism. No ads. Subjects: Adirondacks, Environment, Fiction, Literary Review, Memoirs, New England, Poetry, Short Stories.

BLUELINES, Lois Peterson, #202, 7027-134 Street, Surrey, BC V3W 4T1, Canada, 604-596-1601, lpwordsolutions@hotmail.com; www.lpwordsolutions.com. *"Bluelines* is a print newsletter 'exploring the relationship between writers and readers and the words that connect them.' Looking for articles, short columns, essays on a range of topics to do with reading and writing. Complete guidelines are available on our website." sub. price $15.

Bluestocking Press, Jane A. Williams, Kathryn Daniels, Ann Williams, PO Box 1014, Placerville, CA 95667-1014, 530-622-8586, Fax 530-642-9222, 1-800-959-8586 (orders only), website: www.bluestocking-press.com. 1987. Non-fiction. "UPS address: 3333 Gold Country Drive, El Dorado, CA 95623 Not accepting any new submissions. Unsolicited submissions will not be acknowledged or returned." avg. press run 5M. Expects 1 title 2010, 1 title 2011. 23 titles listed in the *Small Press Record of Books in Print* (36th Edition, 2010-11). Quantity discounts available to booksellers, wholesalers—query for schedule. 175pp. Simultaneous submissions accepted: no. Payment: by agreement. Does not copyright for author. Subjects: Business & Economics, Careers, Current Affairs, Finances, Government, History, Thomas Jefferson, Law, Middle East, Non-Fiction, Political Science, World War II.

BOA Editions, Ltd., Thom Ward, Editor; Peter Conners, Editor, 250 Goodman St, N., Suite 306, Rochester, NY 14607-1190, 585-546-3410, www.boaeditions.org. 1976. Poetry, fiction. "Authors include: W.D. Snodgrass, Anthony Piccione, Michael Waters, Dorianne Laux, Peter Makuck, Carolyn Kizer, Lucille Clifton, Li-Young Lee, Anne Hebert, Yannis Ritsos, David Ignatow, Ray Gonzalez, Laure-Anne Bosselaar, Debra Kang-Dean, and Russell Edson." avg. press run 500 cloth, 1,500 paper. Pub'd 12 titles 2009; expects 11 titles 2010, 11 titles 2011. 4 titles listed in the *Small Press Record of Books in Print* (36th Edition, 2010-11). 96pp. Reporting time: 3-4 months. Simultaneous submissions accepted: yes. Publishes 2% of manuscripts submitted.

Payment: royalty. Copyrights for author. Subjects: Fiction, Poetry, Translation.

Bob & Bob Publishing, Robert O. Owolabi, Bob & Bob Associates, Inc., P.O. Box 10246, Gaithersburg, MD 20898-0246, 301-518-9835, Fax 301-515-0962, bobandbobinc@comcast.net, www.bobandbob.com. 1995. 3 titles listed in the *Small Press Record of Books in Print* (36th Edition, 2010-11). Simultaneous submissions accepted: yes. Publishes 85% of manuscripts submitted. Copyrights for author.

Bogg Publications (see also BOGG: A Journal of Contemporary Writing), John Elsberg, 422 North Cleveland Street, Arlington, VA 22201. 1968. Poetry. "Only solicited mss considered from writers who have appeared in *Bogg* magazine." avg. press run 300. Pub'd 1 title 2009; expects 3 titles 2010, 2 titles 2011. 7 titles listed in the *Small Press Record of Books in Print* (36th Edition, 2010-11). 28pp. Reporting time: varies. Simultaneous submissions accepted: no. Payment: 25% of print run (in copies). All rights revert to author on publication. Subjects: Experimental, Haiku, Poetry.

BOGG: A Journal of Contemporary Writing, Bogg Publications, John Elsberg, Editor, 422 N Cleveland Street, Arlington, VA 22201-1424. 1968. Poetry, fiction, art, interviews, satire, reviews, letters, non-fiction. "Bogg is largely a poetry journal, to include prose poems, haiku/tanka, and visual poetry; we use some fiction, but only very short experimental/wry pieces. Some recent contributors include Ann Menebroker, Guy Beining, Hugh Fox, John M. Bennett, Miriam Sagan, Richard Peabody, Marcia Arrieta, Peter Bakowski, Kathy Ernst, Martin Galvin, Gerald England, J. Wesley Clark, Leroy Gorman, Ruth Moon Kempher, Robert Cooperman, David Chorlton, Carol Hamilton, Donald Lev, Louis McKee, Taylor Graham, and Steve Sneyd. The magazine puts out a series of free (for postage) pamphlets of poetry. Bogg has always included a leavening of British and Commonwealth work. ISSN 0882-648X." circ. 800. 2/yr. Expects 2 issues 2010, 2 issues 2011. 3 titles listed in the *Small Press Record of Books in Print* (36th Edition, 2010-11). sub. price $15/2 issues; per copy $8.00; sample $5.00. Back issues: negotiable. Discounts: 40% 10 copies or more, or additional copies bought by contributors. 56pp. Reporting time: 1 week. Simultaneous submissions accepted: no. Publishes 1% of manuscripts submitted. Payment: 2 copies of issue. Copyrighted, reverts to author. Pub's reviews. §Small press publications, particularly by writers who have appeared in Bogg; poetry, experimental poetry, haiku and tanka, prose poems, and short fiction. Subjects: Australia, Canada, Creative Non-fiction, Criticism, England, Essays, Experimental, Fiction, Haiku, Magazines, New Zealand, Poetry, Post Modern, Prose, Reviews.

The Bold Strummer Ltd., Nicholas Clarke, Publisher, 110-C Imperial Avenue, PO Box 2037, Westport, CT 06880-2037, 203-227-8588, toll free 866-518-9991 (orders only), Fax 203-227-8775, theboldstrummer@msn.com, www.boldstrummerltd.com. 1974. Cartoons, interviews, music. "The Bold Strummer publishes books on guitars and related instruments and equipment. Also importer and distributor of books of same. A leading publisher of boosk about flamenco." avg. press run 1M. Pub'd 6 titles 2009; expects 8 titles 2010, 4 titles 2011. 35 titles listed in the *Small Press Record of Books in Print* (36th Edition, 2010-11). Discounts: 20-50%. 130pp. Reporting time: approx. 6 months (if this means from contest to publication). Simultaneous submissions accepted: yes (20% as most are not our subject). Publishes 60% of manuscripts submitted. Payment: royalty 10% of retail. We copyright for author if required. Subject: Music.

BOMB MAGAZINE, Betsy Sussler, Editor-in-Chief; Monica de la Torre, Senior Editor; Sabine Russ, Managing Editor, 80 Hanson Place #703, Brooklyn, NY 11217-1505, 718-636-9100, email:generalinquiries@bombsite.com. 1981. Poetry, fiction, art, photos, interviews, parts-of-novels. circ. 60M. 4/yr. Pub'd 4 issues 2009; expects 4 issues 2010, 4 issues 2011. sub. price $22; per copy $7.95. Back issues: Range in prince from $10 to $500. Discounts: trade 40%, classroom 30%. 128pp. Reporting time: 3 months unsolicited. Simultaneous submissions accepted: yes. Publishes 5% of manuscripts submitted. Payment: yes. Copyrighted, reverts to author. Pub's reviews: 20 in 2009. §Art, literary fiction, poetry. Ads: $1,485/$795/$605 1/4 page. Subjects: Arts, Drama, Electronics, Fiction, Science Fiction, Theatre, Visual Arts.

BOMBAY GIN, Andrew Schelling, Editor-in-Chief; Amy Catanzano, Managing Editor, Naropa University, Writing & Poetics Dept., 2130 Arapahoe Avenue, Boulder, CO 80302. 1976. "Bombay Gin, the literary journal of The Jack Kerouac School of Disembodied Poetics at Naropa University, publishes poetry, prose, interviews, art, and more. Each issue features a transcript from the Naropa Audio Archive." circ. 1000. 2/yr. sub. price $20 (two issues); per copy $12. Back issues: $8. 200pp. Reporting time: 4 - 5 Months. Pub's reviews: approx. 8 in 2009. §fiction, poetry.

Bombshelter Press (see also ONTHEBUS), Jack Grapes, P.O Box 481266, Bicentennial Station, Los Angeles, CA 90048, 310-651-5488, jgrapes@bombshelterpress.com, http://www.bombshelterpress.com. 1975. Poetry. "We publish books of California poets, most specifically poets from the Los Angeles area. Poets should not send manuscripts without sending a query letter first. Recent books by Macdonald Carey, Doraine Poretz, Michael Andrews, John Oliver Simon, Lee Rossi, Ko Wan, Jack Grapes, Bill Mohr, James Krusoe, and an anthology of *New Los Angeles Poets. Onthebus* is a biannual literary magazine—open to submissions from anyone." avg. press run 800. Pub'd 3 titles 2009; expects 3 titles 2010, 3 titles 2011. 11 titles listed in the *Small Press Record of Books in Print* (36th Edition, 2010-11). Discounts: 40% consignment to bookstores, etc., 50%

to distributors. 72pp. Reporting time: 3-4 months. Simultaneous submissions accepted: no. Payment: free copies (usually 50) plus 10% of profits from sales. Copyrights for author. Subject: Poetry.

Bone Print Press (see also ASKEW REVIEWS), Denis Sheehan, P.O. Box 684, Hanover, MA 02339. 1997. Poetry, fiction, articles, art, interviews, criticism, reviews, music, letters, long-poems, non-fiction. avg. press run 1000. Expects 1 title 2010, 1 title 2011. No titles listed in the *Small Press Record of Books in Print* (36th Edition, 2010-11). 200pp.

Bonus Books, Inc., 1223 Wilshire Blvd., #597, Santa Monica, CA 90403-5400, www.bonusbooks.com. 1985. Non-fiction. avg. press run 5M-10M. Pub'd 25 titles 2009; expects 28 titles 2010, 30 titles 2011. 99 titles listed in the *Small Press Record of Books in Print* (36th Edition, 2010-11). Discounts: please inquire. 240pp. Reporting time: 2 months (send SASE). Simultaneous submissions accepted: yes. Publishes less than 5% of manuscripts submitted. Payment: standard scale. Copyrights for author. Subjects: Advertising, Self-Promotion, Aging, Autobiography, Biography, Broadcasting, Communication, Journalism, Current Affairs, Fundraising, Health, How-To, Non-Fiction, Nursing, Sports, Outdoors, Textbooks.

BOOK ARTS CLASSIFIED, Mary Tasillo, www.bookartsclassified.com. 1993. Subjects: Book Arts, Book Collecting, Bookselling, Calligraphy, Printing.

Book Coach Press, Blais Sabine Miss, 14 Moorside Private, Ottawa, Ontario K2C 3P4, Canada, (613) 226-4850, 1-877-GGR-RUNE, www.gentlegiantrunes.com, gentlegiantrunes@sympatico.ca. 2005. No titles listed in the *Small Press Record of Books in Print* (36th Edition, 2010-11). 216pp.

Book Garden Publishing,LLC, Jan Amenta, 147 A Roesch Avenue, Oreland, PA 19075, 215-576-5544. 2007. Fiction. "Writing and publishing childrens picture books." avg. press run 100. Expects 1 title 2010, 2 titles 2011. 2 titles listed in the *Small Press Record of Books in Print* (36th Edition, 2010-11). Discounts: 2-3 copies 25%. 24pp. Simultaneous submissions accepted: No. Copyrights for author. Subjects: Children, Youth, Picture Books.

Book Marketing Solutions, Thomas White, 10300 E. Leelanau Court, Traverse City, MI 49684, p. 231-939-1999, f. 231-929-1993, info@bookmarketingsolutions.com. 2003. Poetry, fiction, photos, non-fiction. Pub'd 6 titles 2009; expects 15 titles 2010, 20 titles 2011. 13 titles listed in the *Small Press Record of Books in Print* (36th Edition, 2010-11). 196pp. Reporting time: 7-14 days. Simultaneous submissions accepted: Yes. Copyrights for author. Subjects: Business & Economics, Children, Youth, Christianity, Consulting, Fiction, Holocaust, Indigenous Cultures, Leadership, Non-Fiction, Picture Books, Poetry, Self-Help, Speaking, Textbooks, Young Adult.

BOOK MARKETING UPDATE, Open Horizons Publishing Company, John Kremer, PO Box 205, Fairfield, IA 52556-0205, 641-472-6130, Fax 641-472-1560, e-mail johnkremer@bookmarket.com. 1986. Articles, art, photos, cartoons, interviews, reviews, letters, news items, non-fiction. "News, stories, and resources to help other publishers market their books more effectively." circ. 3M. 26/yr. Pub'd 26 issues 2009; expects 26 issues 2010, 26 issues 2011. sub. price $197; per copy $6; sample $6. 4-6pp. Reporting time: 1 week. Payment: none. Copyrighted, reverts to author. Pub's reviews: 3-4 in 2009. §Book publishing, marketing, direct mail, graphics, printing, publicity, directories. Ads: none. Subjects: Advertising, Self-Promotion, Book Arts, Book Collecting, Bookselling, Book Reviewing, Business & Economics, Graphics, Magazines, Media, Newspapers, Printing, Publishing, Radio, Reviews, Television, Writers/Writing.

BOOK/MARK QUARTERLY REVIEW, Mindy Kronenberg, PO Box 516, Miller Place, NY 11764-0516, 631-331-4118, cyberpoet@msn.com, www.writernetwork.com. 1994. Reviews, non-fiction. "Reviews run 600-1000 wds avg.. We look for objective assessments of books by writers who are empathetic with their material and connected to the genre of literature (poets, novelists, essayists, artists, serious hobbyists) or have experience/interest in the subject/field of the books reviewed. Recent contributors include Thomas Fink, Michael McIrvin, Jodee Stanley, Thaddeus Rutkowski, and Richard Kostelanetz." circ. 800. 4/yr. Pub'd 4 issues 2009; expects 4 issues 2010, 4 issues 2011. sub. price $12; per copy $3.50 ppd.; sample $3 ppd. Back issues: $2 ppd. 12pp. Reporting time: immediately, 3 weeks max. Simultaneous submissions accepted: yes. Publishes 60-80% of manuscripts submitted. Payment: copies/subscription, sometimes gratis ads. Copyrighted, reverts to author. Pub's reviews: 47-50 in 2009. §Poetry, fiction, the arts, sciences, popular culture, history—we're eclectic. Ads: $250/$135/$75 1/4 page; also on an exchange-basis. Subjects: Arts, Book Arts, Book Reviewing, Criticism, Culture, Current Affairs, Literary Review, Literature (General), Multicultural, Reviews, Writers/Writing.

Bookhaven Press, LLC, Erin Taylor, Victor Richards, Juran Robert, Dennis Damp, Duncan Linda, 249 Field Club Circle, McKees Rocks, PA 15136-1034, 412-494-6926, Fax 412-494-5749, bookhaven@aol.com, http://federaljobs.net. 1985. Articles, non-fiction. "Looking for new career and job search titles from computer literate authors." avg. press run 5M. Pub'd 2 titles 2009; expects 2 titles 2010, 2 titles 2011. 4 titles listed in the *Small Press Record of Books in Print* (36th Edition, 2010-11). Discounts: 1-4 20%, 5-9 30%, 10-24 40%, 25-49

42%, 50-74 44%, 75-99 46%, 100-199 48%, 200+ 50%; S.T.O.P. orders earn 40% discount CWO + $2 s/h. 288pp. Reporting time: 8 weeks. Simultaneous submissions accepted: yes. Publishes 1% of manuscripts submitted. Payment: negotiable. Copyrights for author. Subjects: Business & Economics, Careers, Employment, Environment, Government, How-To, Military, Veterans.

The Bookman Press, Barbara Wersba, PO Box 1892, Sag Harbor, NY 11963, 631-725-1115. 1994. Poetry, fiction, criticism, letters. "No unsolicited manuscripts. Work only with established authors and books in the public domain. Signed, limited editions aimed at collectors, universities, and special bookstores." avg. press run 300. Expects 1 title 2010, 3 titles 2011. No titles listed in the *Small Press Record of Books in Print* (36th Edition, 2010-11). Discounts: will sell through direct mail only. Copyrights for author.

Books for All Times, Inc. (see also EDUCATION IN FOCUS), Joe David, PO Box 202, Warrenton, VA 20188, 540-428-3175, staff@bfat.com. 1981. Fiction, non-fiction. "Currently seeking articles on important education issues for an upcoming book. Will only consider (always query) material of lasting quality (non-fiction). We have no fiction needs at this time. When we seek fiction, we want modern classics of mentally healthy and efficacious characters achieving. Example: *Dodsworth* by Sinclair Lewis." avg. press run 1M. Pub'd 3 titles 2009; expects 1 title 2010, 1 title 2011. 4 titles listed in the *Small Press Record of Books in Print* (36th Edition, 2010-11). Discounts: 20% libaries; 30% bookstores; 40% wholesalers and distributors; write publisher for details. 250pp. Reporting time: query always, 4 weeks at the most. Payment: to be negotiated. Copyrights for author. Subjects: Education, Fiction, Libertarian, Non-Fiction.

BOOKS FROM FINLAND: Online literature journal of writing from and about Finland, Soila Lehtonen, Editor-in-Chief; Hildi Hawkins, Editor (London), P.O.Box 259, FI-00171 Helsinki, Finland, 358 201 131345, www.booksfromfinland.fi, booksfromfinland@finlit.fi. 1967. Poetry, fiction, articles, photos, interviews, satire, criticism, reviews, parts-of-novels, plays, news items, non-fiction. Back issues: negotiable. Reporting time: 2 months. Payment: negotiable. All rights belong to authors/translators. Pub's reviews: more than 50 in 2009. §Fiction, history, politics, arts, nature, folklore. Ads: negotiable. Subjects: Book Reviewing, Fiction, Literary Review, Poetry, Prose.

BOOKS OF THE SOUTHWEST, Dr. Francine K. Ramsey Richter, Publisher; Rawlyn W. Richter, Editor, 2508 Garner Field Road, Uvalde, TX 78801-6250, e-mail richter@hilconet.com. 1957. Reviews. circ. 500. 4/yr. Pub'd 4 issues 2009; expects 4 issues 2010, 4 issucs 2011. sub. price $28 indiv., $36 instit., $60 foreign; per copy available on-line at www.geocities.com/booksofthesouthwest; sample available on-line. Back issues: ask for quote. Discounts: none. 30pp. Payment: none. Not copyrighted. Pub's reviews: 600 in 2009. §Anything Southwest Americana. Ads: none. Subject: Southwest.

BOOKS TO WATCH OUT FOR, Carol Seajay, PO Box 882554, San Francisco, CA 94188-2554, 415-642-9993, editor at BooksToWatchOutFor dot com, www.BooksToWatchOutFor.com. 2003. Interviews, reviews, news items. "Three subscription-based monthly book reviews - More Books for Women, The Lesbian Edition, The Gay Men's Edition - briefly review a wide range of 25-30 books in each issue, with news from the publishing world, occasional interviews and short features. The staff of Women & Children First bookstore compiles More Books for Women; Carol Seajay, former publisher of Feminist Bookstore News, compiles More Books for Women; and Richard Labonte compiles The Gay Men's Edition." circ. 5000. 10/yr. Pub'd 10 issues 2009; expects 10 issues 2010, 10 issues 2011. sub. price $30 via email; $42 via post; discounted combination packages available; per copy $5 print; sample $3 print. 16pp. Pub's reviews: 500 plus in 2009. §feminist, lesbian, gay, queer books. Ads: issue sponsorships available. Subjects: Bisexual, Feminism, Gay, Gender Issues, Lesbianism, Women.

Booksmart Publications, Harleen Jaggi, 19 Bolero, Mission Viejo, CA 92692, 949 462 0076. 2006. Fiction. "Booksmart Publications is a self publisher.Booksmart publications is dedicated to create books that entertain, motivate and inspire." avg. press run 500. Expects 1 title 2010, 1 title 2011. No titles listed in the *Small Press Record of Books in Print* (36th Edition, 2010-11). Discounts: 5-10 Copies 25%. 100-200pp. Reporting time: Not applicable. Copyrights for author. Subjects: Children, Youth, Family, Mystery.

THE BOOMERPHILE, Old Stage Publishing, Dan Culberson, Editor, Publisher, PO Box 17446, Boulder, CO 80308-0446, 303-444-3363, www.forums.delphiforums.com/boomer. 1992. Articles, interviews, satire, criticism, reviews, music, letters, news items, non-fiction. "Additional address: 6359 Old Stage Road, Boulder, CO 80302. *The BoomerPhile* is for and about Baby Boomers, to counteract all the negative publicity they have received all their lives, to talk about things that interest them today (health, old age, mortgages, kids in college, nostalgia, music, etc.), and to allow them to make fun of themselves, for a change." circ. 150. 12/yr. Pub'd 12 issues 2009; expects 12 issues 2010, 12 issues 2011. sub. price $20; per copy $2.50; sample $1. Back issues: $5. Discounts: standard rates. 8pp. Reporting time: 1-2 weeks. Simultaneous submissions accepted: yes. Publishes 25-50% of manuscripts submitted. Payment: 1 copy for items of interest; 2 copies for original work. Copyrighted, reverts to author. Pub's reviews: 1 in 2009. §Americana, arts, entertainment, humor, politics, sex, singles, society, baby boomers, history. Subjects: Americana, Business & Economics, Civil Rights,

Counter-Culture, Alternatives, Communes, Culture, Entertainment, Erotica, Family, Feminism, Health, History, Humor, Jack Kerouac, Politics, Elvis Presley.

Borden Publishing Co., Michele Reyes, 2244 S. Santa Fe Ave. Unit B-12, Vista, CA 92084, 760-594-0918, bordenpub@roadrunner.com, featured on www.amazon.com. 1939. Art, non-fiction. "Art, non-fiction, reference, occult, metaphysical, local histroy." avg. press run 2M-4M. 3 titles listed in the *Small Press Record of Books in Print* (36th Edition, 2010-11). Discounts: trade 1-4 books 25%, 5+ 40%. Payment: 10% royalty. Copyrights for author. Subjects: Arts, California, Collectibles, Hypnosis, Metaphysics, Occult.

BORDERLANDS: Texas Poetry Review, Guest editors, PO Box 33096, Austin, TX 78764, borderlandspoetry@sbcglobal.net, www.borderlands.org. 1992. Poetry, art, photos, interviews, reviews. "*Borderlands* provides a venue for contemporary American poetry that shows an awareness of the historical, social, political, ecological and spiritual. Past contributors include: Wendy Barker, Cyrus Cassells, Naomi Shihab Nye, Khaled Mattawa, Walter McDonald, William Stafford, Mario Susko, David Wevill, Larry D. Thomas, Scott Hightower and Abe Louise Young." 2/yr. Pub'd 2 issues 2009; expects 2 issues 2010, 2 issues 2011. sub. price $20 plus p/h; per copy $12 includes p/h or $10 retail; sample same as single copy ($12 plus p/h). Back issues: same. Discounts: varies with quantity. 145pp. Reporting time: varies up to 3 months. Simultaneous submissions accepted: No. Publishes 7% of manuscripts submitted. Payment: 1 copy. Copyrighted, reverts to author. Pub's reviews: 6 in 2009. §Poetry that addresses our general interests, outwardly-directed poetry, work that shows an awareness of connection: historical, social, political, and spiritual. Ads: exchange only. Subjects: Arts, Book Reviewing, Criticism, Essays, Journals, Literature (General), Poetry, Politics, Reviews, Society, Southwest, Texas, Third World, Minorities.

Bordighera, Inc., Anthony Julian Tamburri, Fred Gardophe, Paolo Giordano, PO Box 1374, Lafayette, IN 47902-1374, 818-205-1266, via1990@aol.com. 1990. Poetry, fiction, interviews, criticism, reviews, plays, non-fiction. avg. press run 500. Pub'd 3 titles 2009; expects 3 titles 2010, 3 titles 2011. 43 titles listed in the *Small Press Record of Books in Print* (36th Edition, 2010-11). Discounts: agents and jobbers 1-4 copies 30%, 5-9 35%, 10-25 40%, 26-50 45%, 51+ 50%. 35pp. Reporting time: 3 months. Accepts simultaneous submissions on occasion. Publishes 25% of manuscripts submitted. Payment: yes. Copyrights for author. Subjects: Americana, Communism, Marxism, Leninism, Essays, Feminism, Gay, Immigration, Italian-American, Italy, Lesbianism, Literature (General), Novels, Theatre, Third World, Minorities, Women, Writers/Writing.

Borealis Press Limited (see also JOURNAL OF CANADIAN POETRY), Frank Tierney, Glenn Clever, 110 Bloomingdale Street, Ottawa, Ont. K2C 4A4, Canada, 613-798-9299, Fax 379-897-4747. 1972. Poetry, fiction, criticism, plays, non-fiction. "With few exceptions, publish only material Canadian in authorship or orientation. Query first." avg. press run 1M. Pub'd 10 titles 2009; expects 10 titles 2010, 8 titles 2011. 47 titles listed in the *Small Press Record of Books in Print* (36th Edition, 2010-11). Discounts: 40% to retail; 20% to jobbers. 150pp. Reporting time: 6 months. Simultaneous submissions accepted: no. Publishes 2-3% of manuscripts submitted. Payment: 10% once yearly. Does not copyright for author. Subjects: Canada, Children, Youth, Criticism, Culture, Drama, English, Fiction, Folklore, Government, History, Literature (General), Native American, Poetry, Public Affairs, Society.

A. Borough Books, Evan Griffin, Editorial Director, 3901 Silver Bell Drive, Charlotte, NC 28211, 704-364-1788, 800-843-8490 (orders only), humorbooks@aol.com. 1994. Non-fiction. "Non-fiction book proposals only (no manuscripts), 200 pages or less. Topics: recent history, how-to, humor." avg. press run 1M-3M. Pub'd 2 titles 2009; expects 2 titles 2010, 2 titles 2011. 19 titles listed in the *Small Press Record of Books in Print* (36th Edition, 2010-11). Discounts: 20% library (2 or more), 20% academic (10 or more), 40% bookseller (5 or more), 55% jobber. 128pp. Reporting time: 2 months. Simultaneous submissions accepted: yes. Publishes 30% of manuscripts submitted. Payment: negotiable. Does not copyright for author. Subjects: History, How-To, Humor, World War II.

BOSTON REVIEW, Deborah Chasman, Editor; Josh Cohen, Editor, 35 Medford St., Suite 302, Someville, MA 02143, 617-591-0505, Fax 617-591-0440, website: bostonreview.net. 1975. Poetry, fiction, criticism, reviews, non-fiction. "Bi-monthly publication of politics, culture, and the arts." circ. 10,000. 6/yr. Pub'd 6 issues 2009; expects 6 issues 2010, 6 issues 2011. 2 titles listed in the *Small Press Record of Books in Print* (36th Edition, 2010-11). sub. price $25 individuals, $45 institutions; per copy $5; sample $5. Back issues: $5 and up. Discounts: varies. 60pp. Reporting time: up to 4 months. Payment: varies. Copyrighted, reverts to author. Pub's reviews: 40 in 2009. §Poetry, fiction, criticism, all the arts, politics, culture. Ads: full page $1,300 / junior $800 / half $680 / third $500 / quarter $375 / sixth $300 / eighth $225 / $200 twelfth. Subjects: Arts, Culture, Literary Review, Political Science.

BOTH SIDES NOW, Free People Press, Elihu Edelson, Editor, 10547 State Highway 110 North, Tyler, TX 75704-3731, 903-592-4263; web site: www.bothsidesnow.info. email: editor@bothsidesnow.info. 1969. Poetry, fiction, articles, art, cartoons, interviews, satire, criticism, reviews, music, letters, news items, non-fiction. "'A

Journal of Lightworking, Peacemaking, & Consciousness.' Articles on current events and thinkpieces with emphasis on alternatives which have implicit spiritual content. Unique spiritual/political synthesis related to such concepts as 'New Age politics' and 'the Aquarian conspiracy.' Editorial concerns include nonviolence, pacifism, decentralism, green politics, human rights, social justice, alternative lifestyles & institutions, healing, economics, appropriate technology, organic agriculture, philosophy, prophecy, psychic phenomena, the occult, metaphysics, and religion. Reprints of important material which deserves wider circulation." circ. 200. 4 double issues/year (quarterly). Pub'd 4 issues 2009; expects 4 issues 2010, 4 issues 2011. sub. price $9/10 issues, $6/6 issues; per copy $2 (double issue); sample $2 (double issue). Back issues: Listed on web site. Discounts: 30% on 10 or more copies. 22pp. Reporting time: ASAP. Simultaneous submissions accepted: yes. Publishes varies% of manuscripts submitted. Payment: subscription. Copyrighted, reverts to author. Pub's reviews: approx. 10 in 2009. §'New Age', spirituality, pacifism, anarchism, religion, the occult and metaphysics, radical and 'Green' politics, general alternatives. Ads: $50 (7-1/2 X 10)/smaller sizes pro-rated/classifieds 20¢/word. Subjects: Anarchist, Astrology, Counter-Culture, Alternatives, Communes, Metaphysics, New Age, Occult, Philosophy, Politics, Religion, Reprints, Spiritual.

BOTTLE, Bottle of Smoke Press, Bill R. Roberts, 902 Wilson Dr, Dover, DE 19904, bill@bospress.net, www.bospress.net. 2002. Poetry, fiction, art, long-poems, concrete art. "Charles Bukowski, Charles Plymell, Dan Fante, Henry Denander, David Barker, A.D. Winans, Gerald Locklin, Michael Madsen, Marc Snyder, S.A. Griffin, Gary Aposhian, Neeli Cherkovski, Ann Menebroker, and Bradley Mason Hamlin." circ. 226. 1/yr. Pub'd 1 issue 2009; expects 1 issue 2010, 1 issue 2011. price per copy $25; sample $25. Back issues: 3 - 5 are $25 each. Distributor discounts available. Please e-mail for discounts. 25pp. Reporting time: 2 months. Simultaneous submissions accepted: No. Payment: contributors copies. Copyrighted, reverts to author. Subjects: Charles Bukowski, Poetry.

Bottle of Smoke Press (see also BOTTLE), Bill R. Roberts, 902 Wilson Drive, Dover, DE 19904-2437, bill@bospress.net, www.bospress.net. 2002. Poetry, fiction, art, long-poems. "Limited edition, books by writers and poets including: Charles Bukowski, Gerald Locklin, A.D. Winans, t.l. kryss, Henry Denander, S.A. Griffin, David Barker, Adrian Manning, justin.barrett, Owen Roberts, Paul Krech, Kent Taylor, d.a. levy, Soheyl Dahi, Christopher Cunningham, & Marc Snyder." avg. press run 126. Pub'd 7 titles 2009; expects 10 titles 2010, 10 titles 2011. 39 titles listed in the *Small Press Record of Books in Print* (36th Edition, 2010-11). Discounts: bulk available, please inquire. 36-40pp. Reporting time: 2 months. Simultaneous submissions accepted: no. Payment: contributors copies only. Copyrights for author. Subjects: Beat, Bibliography, Book Collecting, Bookselling, Charles Bukowski, Fiction, Literature (General), Poetry, Printing.

BOTTLE ROCKETS: A collection of short verse, Stanford M. Forrester, Editor, PO Box 189, Windsor, CT 06095, e-mail address: bottlerockets_99@yahoo.com. 1998. "This is a magazine dedicated to haiku, senryu, and related poetry." twice a year/July & February. sub. price $20.00/yr.(USA) $22.00/yr.(Canada & Mexico) $24.00/yr.(Europe, Asia, and everywhere else); per copy $10(US), $11(Canada & Mexico) $12(Europe, Asia & everywhere else); sample same as single copy price. Back issues: Some back issues are available. Please e-mail Stanford M. Forrester for availability. Discounts: (Possibly for multiple copies. Please inquiry via e-mail.). 60-100pp. Reporting time: Submissions, on the average 3-4 weeks. Simultaneous submissions accepted: Absolutely no simultaneous, previously published or "appearing" material in any way or form considered. (No contests, newsletters, blogs, websites, e-zines, flyers, etc....). Payment: no contributor's payment. Copyrighted, reverts to author. Ads: Currently there are no ads, but would consider under the right circumstances.

Bottom Dog Press / Bird Dog Publishing, Larry Smith, PO Box 425, Huron, OH 44839, 419-433-5560, x20784 http://smithdocs.net. 1984. Poetry, fiction, parts-of-novels, long-poems. "We do books of poetry,fiction, personal essays and national anthologies on a theme. A book of poetry should be 65-100 poems with a unifying theme and form. We are particularly interested in the work of Midwest writers. Our Series include: Midwest Writers—Working Lives—Paul Laurence Dunbar—Harmony Series. We expect the writer to work with us on the book. Our slant is towards writing that is direct and human with clean, clear images and voice. We prefer the personal, but not the self-indulgent, simple but not simplistic, writing of value to us all. Our bias is towards sense of place writing—being who you are, where you are, and towards working-class writing. Authors we've published: d.a.levy, Robert Flanagan, Ed Sanders, Jim Ray Daniels, Ray McNiece, Daniel Thompson, Scott Sanders, David Shevin, Chris Llewellyn, Annabel Thomas, Kenneth Patchen, Todd Davis, Allen Frost. We also do some audio and CD books & DVD Exs. SONGS OF THE WOODCUTTER: ZEN POEMS OF WANG WEI AND TAIGU RYOKAN and D.A.LEVY AND THE MIMEOGRAPH REVOLUTION. Query first, $10 reading fee on POETRY manuscript submissions, $20 for a book of fiction; you'll get a full response. No e-mail submissions, though you might query on-line." avg. press run 650 poetry, 1M fiction. Pub'd 4 titles 2009; expects 5 titles 2010, 5 titles 2011. 40 titles listed in the *Small Press Record of Books in Print* (36th Edition, 2010-11). Discounts: 1-4 30%, 5-9 copies 35%, 40% 10+ copies. 160pp. Reporting time: 1-3 months, query by e-mail first. Simultaneous submissions accepted: We'll consider simultantious submissions as long as we are notified. Payment: through royalties and copies arrangement; books are contracted. Copyrights for author. Subjects: Community, Fiction, Poetry, Zen.

BOULDER HERETIC, Old Stage Publishing, Dan Culberson, PO Box 17446, Boulder, CO 80308-0446, 303-444-3363, danculberson@juno.com. 1999. Articles, interviews, satire, criticism, reviews, non-fiction. circ. 25-30. 12/yr. Pub'd 3 issues 2009; expects 5 issues 2010, 12 issues 2011. sub. price $20; per copy $1; sample $1. Back issues: $5. Discounts: $10/year. 6pp. Reporting time: 1 week. Simultaneous submissions accepted: yes. Publishes 33% of manuscripts submitted. Payment: 2 copies. Copyrighted, reverts to author. Pub's reviews: none in 2009. §Atheism, religion, philosophy, freethinking, Agnosticism, etc. Ads: none. Subjects: Atheism, Buddhism, Catholic, Christianity, Cults, Euthanasia, Death, Humanism, Judaism, Mormon, Myth, Mythology, Philosophy, Politics, Psychology, Religion, Mark Twain.

BOULEVARD, Richard Burgin, Editor, 6614 Clayton Road, PMB 325, Richmond Heights, MO 63117, 314-862-2643. 1985. Poetry, fiction, articles, art, photos, cartoons, interviews, criticism, music, parts-of-novels, long-poems, plays, non-fiction. "Contributors: John Barth, W.S. Merwin, John Updike, Tess Gallagher, Kenneth Koch, Tom Disch, Allen Ginsberg, Joyce Carol Oates, Alice Adams, David Mamet, Donald Hall, John Ashbery, Phillip Lopate. *Boulevard* is committed to publishing the best of contemporary fiction, poetry, and non-fiction." circ. 3.5M. 3/yr. Pub'd 3 issues 2009; expects 3 issues 2010, 3 issues 2011. sub. price $15 for three issues, $22 for six issues, $25 for nine issues.; per copy $8; sample $8 plus five first class stamps. Back issues: $10. Discounts: 50% agency. 200-225pp. Reporting time: 12 weeks; do not read during summer months. Simultaneous submissions accepted: yes. Publishes 1% of manuscripts submitted. Payment: $25-$300 (poetry), $50-$300 (fiction), plus one contributor's copy. Extra contributor's copies available at 50% discount. Copyrighted, reverts to author. §Fiction, poetry, lit. criticism, art/music criticism. We have a short fiction contest yearly with a $1500 prize and publication in Boulevard. Ads: $150/$500 for back cover. Subjects: Arts, Criticism, Fiction, Literature (General), Poetry.

•**BOUND OFF,** inquiry@boundoff.com. "Bound Off wants to read your best short stories out loud. We are seeking original literary fiction for our upcoming podcasts. Please send stories that are between 250 and 2500 words long. Although we are an audio publication, we will evaluate manuscripts the old-fashioned way. Our team of readers and podcast engineers will produce the audio version of your story. If you have the capability to create a high-quality MP3 file, then we could publish your story with you as the reader. (Although we aim to give authors the chance to read their own work, audio quality is a high priority, so the Bound Off editors reserve the right to make all final audio production decisions.) We are not considering the following types of writing: non-fiction or personal essays, poetry, stories for children. E-mail your submission to: submissions@bound-doff.com."

•**Bowery Poetry Books,** 310 Bowery, New York, NY 10012, www.bowerypoetry.com, 212-334-6414. "The Bowery Poetry Club's new publishing imprint, Bowery Poetry Books, has launched two books in its first six months of existence: Taylor Mead's A Simple Country Girl and The Bowery Bartenders Big Book of Poems." No titles listed in the *Small Press Record of Books in Print* (36th Edition, 2010-11).

Box Turtle Press (see also MUDFISH), Jill Hoffman, Poetry Editor, 184 Franklin Street, New York, NY 10013. 1983. avg. press run 1.2M. Pub'd 1 title 2009; expects 1 title 2010, 1 title 2011. 3 titles listed in the *Small Press Record of Books in Print* (36th Edition, 2010-11). Discounts: 1983. 200pp. Reporting time: immediately to 6 months. Simultaneous submissions accepted: no. Publishes 5% of manuscripts submitted. Payment: 1 copy.

Marion Boyars Publishers, Catheryn Kilgarriff, Director, 24 Lacy Road, London SW15 1NL, United Kingdom. "Marion Boyars Publishers started out in the sixties as the firm Calder and Boyars which was run jointly by John Calder and Marion Boyars. When the firm split in 1975, Marion Boyars Publishers was formed. When Marion Boyars died in 1999, her daughter Catheryn Kilgarriff took over and she is still the Managing Director. Renowned for publishing adventurous and occasionally controversial fiction and non-fiction, especially in translation, our best known authors include Ken Kesey, Hubert Selby Jr, Kenzaburo Oe, Ivan Illich and Georges Bataille. Today we strive to keep up these noble traditions and have had notable success in recent years introducing novelists such as Elif Shafak, Latife Tekin and Hong Ying as well the Iraqi blogger Riverbend, author of Baghdad Burning to an English speaking audience. Marion Boyars Publishers are pleased to receive submissions for non-fiction in the areas of contemporary culture, cookery, film and music. All submissions should be sent with an envelope and return postage. For fiction, submissions must be through a literary agent, and we would prefer a synopsis and sample chapter in the first instance. We are unable to read poetry submissions. We cannot accept email submissions in any category." No titles listed in the *Small Press Record of Books in Print* (36th Edition, 2010-11).

BR Anchor Publishing, Dalene Bickel, 4596 Capital Dome Drive, Jacksonville, FL 32246-7457, 904-641-1140. 1990. "International and domestic relocation books for adults, teens, preteens and young children." avg. press run 2000. Pub'd 5 titles 2009; expects 7-9 titles 2010, 8-10 titles 2011. No titles listed in the *Small Press Record of Books in Print* (36th Edition, 2010-11). Discounts: Single title order purchase is 55% plus shipping. Most books sold to large corporations. 128pp. Reporting time: 2-3 business days. Simultaneous submissions accepted: No. Payment: We work on a "Pay as you go" policy and authors reap all the benefits.

74

Copyrights for author.

BRADY MAGAZINE, Krissy Brady, 165 Old Muskoka Road, Suite 306, Gravenhurst, Ontario P1P 1N3, Canada, 705-687-3963 [phone], 705-687-8736 [fax], editor@bradymagazine.com [e-mail], http://www.brady-magazine.com [website]. 2003. Articles. "Brady Magazine is an online writer's trade directory that is updated on a daily basis. We accept article submissions from writers at any stage in their career, and working in any genre. Articles submitted must always be related to the writing field. Articles must be between 1,000 and 2,500 words. No typical article topics (such as How to Defeat Writer's Block) unless consisting of an interesting twist. No query is needed, just send us your work. Submissions must be sent to us using our online form, which can be found at http://www.bradymagazine.com/forms/subform.html. Any submissions sent to us not using our online form will be deleted immediately. We pay $20CDN for first electronic rights, and $10CDN for reprint rights. If sending us an article that has been previously published, please let us know where and when it was published. Payment is made upon acceptance. We no longer accept success stories, writing tips, or book reviews." Reporting time: 1-2 months. Simultaneous submissions accepted: Yes. Publishes 30% of manuscripts submitted. Payment: On acceptance. Copyrighted, reverts to author. Ads: Text Advertising- Website$30.00 weekly (7 days)$75.00 monthly (30 days)$135.00 bi-monthly (60 days)Text Advertising- Newsletters$10.00 per 4 (four)-line ad$30.00 per solo ad (unlimited lines). Subject: Writers/Writing.

•**Brain Injury Success Books,** Jessica Whitmore, 7025 NW 52nd Drive, Gainesville, FL 32653-7014, 352-672-6672, info@braininjurysuccess.org, www.braininjurysuccess.org. 2009. Non-fiction. "We focus on helping people with brain injuries and their families live full and rewarding lives." 1 title listed in the *Small Press Record of Books in Print* (36th Edition, 2010-11). Subjects: Creative Non-fiction, Disabled, Family, Handicapped, Health, How-To, Medicine, Memoirs, Non-Fiction, Self-Help.

Branden Books, Adolph Caso, PO Box 812094, Wellesley, MA 02482, 781-235-3634, Fax 781-790-1056, branden@brandenbooks.com, www.brandenbooks.com. 1909. Fiction, art, music, letters, long-poems, plays, non-fiction. "See our latest catalogue. No manuscripts accepted, only queries with SASE." avg. press run 5M. Pub'd 15 titles 2009; expects 10 titles 2010, 15 titles 2011. 61 titles listed in the *Small Press Record of Books in Print* (36th Edition, 2010-11). Discounts: from 1 copy 10% to 101+ copies 48%. 215pp. Reporting time: 1 week. Simultaneous submissions accepted: no. Publishes 1% of manuscripts submitted. Payment: 5%-10% net on monies from sales; 50% on monies from sales of rights. Copyrights for author. Subjects: Americana, Arts, Bilingual, Biography, Book Arts, Classical Studies, Drama, Education, Fiction, Health, History, Literature (General), Peace, Political Science, Religion.

Brandylane Publishers, Inc., R.H. Pruett, 5 S. 1st St., Richmond, VA 23219-3716, 804-644-3090, Fax 804-644-3092. 1985. Poetry, fiction, non-fiction. "We publish fiction, non-fiction, poetry and children's books. Especially interested in working with unpublished writers." avg. press run 1.5M. Pub'd 14 titles 2009; expects 12 titles 2010, 12 titles 2011. No titles listed in the *Small Press Record of Books in Print* (36th Edition, 2010-11). Discounts: standard 40%, 55% distributors, 30% STOP orders. 175pp. Reporting time: 12-16 weeks. Simultaneous submissions accepted: yes. Publishes 10% of manuscripts submitted. Payment: varies. Copyrights for author.

Brason-Sargar Publications, Sondra Anice Barnes, Publisher, PO Box 872, Reseda, CA 91337, 818-994-0089, Fax 305-832-2604, sonbar@bigfoot.com. 1978. Poetry, art. "We are primarily interested in gift books which express psychological truths. Must use as few words as possible. We publish thoughts, observations or statements expressing human truths written in a style which visually looks like poetry but is not poetry per se. If the poet reads our books *Life Is The Way It Is* or *We Are The Way We Are* and can write in this style, then we are interested and will negotiate payment." avg. press run 2M 1st printing, up to 20M subsequent printings. Pub'd 1 title 2009; expects 4 titles 2010, 6 titles 2011. 2 titles listed in the *Small Press Record of Books in Print* (36th Edition, 2010-11). Discounts: 40% bookstores, 50% distributers. 96pp. Reporting time: 30 days. Payment: to be negotiated. Copyrights for author. Subjects: New Age, Philosophy, Psychology, Quotations, Self-Help, Spiritual.

BRAVADO, Jenny Argante, Coordinating Editor; Sue Emms, Fiction Editor; Owen Bullock, Poetry Editor, PO Box 13-533, Grey Street, Tauranga 3001, New Zealand, 07 576 3040, fax:07 570 2446. "New magazine publishing poetry, fiction." 2/yr. sub. price $15; per copy $10.

Brave Ulysses Books, Cecil L. Bothwell III, POB 1877, Asheville, NC 28802, 828-713-8840, cecil@braveulysses.com, www.braveulysses.com. 1996. Satire, non-fiction. "Five titles in print, two collected essays, city guide *Finding your way in Asheville* (NC), child's picture book *Madeleine Claire and the Dinosaur*, critical biography *The Prince of War: Billy Graham's Crusade for a Wholly Christian Empire* We are a micro press and are unlikely to publish more than one title per year." avg. press run 2M. Pub'd 1 title 2009; expects 1 title 2010, 1-2 titles 2011. 4 titles listed in the *Small Press Record of Books in Print* (36th Edition, 2010-11). Discounts: 60% to all resellers. 110pp. Reporting time: 1 month, inquire first (1 week on inquiries). We accept simultaneous submissions, but inquire first. Publishes a small % of manuscripts submitted. Payment: negotiable.

Does not copyright for author. Subjects: Environment, Essays, Humor, Politics, Short Stories.

BRB Publications, Inc. (see also Facts on Demand Press), Michael Sankey, PO Box 27869, Tempe, AZ 85285-7869, 800-929-3811, Fax 800-929-4981, brb@brbpub.com, www.brbpub.com. 1989. Non-fiction. avg. press run 2.5 m. Pub'd 5 titles 2009; expects 7 titles 2010, 7 titles 2011. 5 titles listed in the *Small Press Record of Books in Print* (36th Edition, 2010-11).

Break Free Publishing, Jill Schmidt, PO Box 975, Routing 101, Chappaqua, NY 10514-0975, 914-773-4307, Jill.Schmidt@BreakFreePub.com, www.BreakFreePublishing.com. 2008. Non-fiction. Pub'd 1 title 2009; expects 2 titles 2010, 2 titles 2011. 1 title listed in the *Small Press Record of Books in Print* (36th Edition, 2010-11). 160pp. Reporting time: 2 weeks. Does not copyright for author. Subjects: Business & Economics, Education.

Brenner Information Group, Robert C. Brenner, Editor-in-Chief; Edythe Ade, Editor, PO Box 721000, San Diego, CA 92172-1000, 858-538-0093. 1988. Non-fiction. "50-300 pages published. How-to subjects (business)." avg. press run 1M. Pub'd 15 titles 2009; expects 8 titles 2010, 10 titles 2011. 7 titles listed in the *Small Press Record of Books in Print* (36th Edition, 2010-11). Discounts: 0-55%. 300pp. Reporting time: 4-6 weeks. Simultaneous submissions accepted: yes. Publishes 10% of manuscripts submitted. Payment: 10%-12%. Copyrights for author. Subjects: Business & Economics, Cartoons, Computers, Calculators, Desktop Publishing, Editing, Graphic Design, How-To, Internet, Marketing, Reference, Research, Self-Help, Solar, Technology.

Brentwood Christian Press, Jerry L. Luquire, 4000 Beallwood Avenue, Columbus, GA 31904. 1982. Fiction, articles, long-poems, non-fiction. "Also publishes religious and educational material." avg. press run 300-500. Pub'd 200 titles 2009; expects 200 titles 2010, 200 titles 2011. No titles listed in the *Small Press Record of Books in Print* (36th Edition, 2010-11). Discounts: 30%. 120pp. Reporting time: 2 days. Simultaneous submissions accepted: yes. Publishes 60% of manuscripts submitted. Copyrights for author. Subjects: Christianity, History, Poetry, Religion.

THE BRIAR CLIFF REVIEW, Tricia Currans-Sheehan, 3303 Rebecca St., Sioux City, IA 51104, 712-279-1651. 1988. Poetry, fiction, articles, art, photos, interviews, satire, criticism, reviews, concrete art, non-fiction. "The Briar Cliff Review is an eclectic literary and cultural magazine focusing on, but not limited to, Siouxland writers. We are looking for quality poetry, fiction, humor/satire, Siouxland history, thoughtful nonfiction, book reviews and art." circ. 1000. 1/yr. Pub'd 1 issue 2009; expects 1 issue 2010, 1 issue 2011. sub. price $15.; per copy $15.; sample $15. Back issues: $12. 120pp. Reporting time: 3-6 months. Simultaneous submissions accepted: Yes. Payment: one free copy. All rights return to the author, with acknowledgment to The Briar Cliff Review. Pub's reviews: 3 in 2009. §Poetry/short story collections novels and creative nonfiction. No advertising. Subjects: Arts, Fiction, History, Interviews, Iowa, Literary Review, Literature (General), Midwest, Minnesota, Native American, Nebraska, Non-Fiction, Photography, Poetry, Prose.

•**Brick Road Poetry Press,** Keith Badowski, P.O. Box 751, Columbus, GA 31902. 2009. Poetry. "We sponsor a $1000 Poetry Book Contest that runs from August 1 to November 1. Publication contract with Brick Road Poetry Press and $1000 prize, publication in both print and ebook formats, and 25 copies of the printed book. We may also offer publication contracts to the top finalists. We want to publish poets who are engaged in the writing community, including participating in poetry readings, workshops, and writers groups. The poets we are looking for are those who are avid readers (and purchasers) of contemporary poetry. We give preference to poets who are actively submitting their work to journals, magazines and contests, and who take part at writer's conferences/festivals-as an organizer, instructor or participant. Previous publications and/or recognitions can be an indicator of readiness for a book length collection. As a "small press," it's important that we publish poets who are putting themselves and their work out there. We have found that book-length poetry collections are most successful in reaching an appreciative audience when the poet takes an active role in marketing his/her book. All that said, we would never rule out an emerging poet who demonstrates ability and motivation to move in the direction we described above. /Preferences of the Editors/ /Qualities we admire:/ A coherent human voice,a sense of humor,words and language as springboard for playful exploration,narratives with surprise twists, persona poems that conjure a speaker from literature, art, or popular media, intense depiction of a scene, setting, or experience, philosophical or spiritual concepts explored through concrete image, illustration or drama /Characteristics we dislike:/ Overemphasis on rhyme, Intentional obscurity or riddling, highfalutin vocabulary, greeting card verse, overt religious statements of faith and/or praise, lack of recognizable theme or topic, abstractions apart from the concrete. /Recommended Poets:/ Kim Addonizio, Ken Babstock, Coleman Barks, Billy Collins, Morri Creech, Alice Friman, Beth A. Gylys, Jane Hirshfield, Jane Kenyon, Ted Kooser, Stanley Kunitz, Thomas Lux, Linda Pastan, Mark Strand, Natasha D. Trethewey." avg. press run 230. Pub'd 1 title 2009; expects 3 titles 2010, 4 titles 2011. No titles listed in the *Small Press Record of Books in Print* (36th Edition, 2010-11). Discounts: Negotiable. 75pp. Reporting time: 2-3 months. Simultaneous submissions accepted: Yes. Publishes 3% of manuscripts submitted. Payment: Authors are offered a percentage of profits after expenses. No advances. Copyrights for author. Subjects: Airplanes, Animals, Cartoons, Christianity,

Comics, Divorce, Food, Eating, History, Humor, Literature (General), Movies, Music, Reading, Relationships, Spiritual.

BRICK, A Literary Journal, Michael Redhill, Publisher, Editor; Michael Helm, Editor; Michael Ondaatje, Editor; Esta Spalding, Editor; Linda Spalding, Editor, Box 609, Station P, Toronto, ON M5S 2Y4, Canada, www.brickmag.com, info@brickmag.com, orders@brickmag.com. 1977. Articles, photos, interviews, non-fiction. "*Brick* does not accept unsolicited poetry or fiction submissions. Brick does not accept submissions by e-mail." 2/yr. Pub'd 2 issues 2009; expects 2 issues 2010, 2 issues 2011. sub. price US$41/2 years; per copy US$15 + shipping. Back issues: Please see website, www.brickmag.com. Discounts: institutions may subscribe for one year at a cost of US$30. 160pp. Copyrighted, reverts to author. Ads: Full page: US$800; half-page: US$475.

BrickHouse Books, Inc., Clarinda Harriss, Editor-in-Chief, 306 Suffolk Road, Baltimore, MD 21218, 410-235-7690, 410-704-2869. 1970. Poetry. "BrickHouse Books prints 250-1000 copies of about 4-6 books per year, poetry or prose. New Poets Series, formerly the corporate name as well as its premier imprint, is for first collections only. Poetry by authors with previous books, as well as fiction (55-90 pages), goes directly to BrickHouse Books. Stonewall is specifically for mss. with a gay/lesbian perspective." avg. press run 500. Pub'd 6 titles 2009; expects 6 titles 2010, 6 titles 2011. 66 titles listed in the *Small Press Record of Books in Print* (36th Edition, 2010-11). Discounts: 40% to bookstores; $10-15 retail depending on # of pages. 80pp. Reporting time: 3-12 mos. Simultaneous submissions accepted: yes. Publishes 5% of manuscripts submitted. Payment: all cash revenue from sales goes to publish the next issue; 25 copies free to author. Author holds own copyright. Subjects: Fiction, Graphics, Poetry.

BRIDGES: A Jewish Feminist Journal, Clare Kinberg, Editor, 4860 Washtenaw Ave., #I-165, Ann Arbor, MI 48108, E-mail clare@bridgesjournal.org. 1990. Poetry, fiction, articles, art, photos, cartoons, interviews, reviews, music, letters, parts-of-novels, long-poems, plays, news items, non-fiction. "*Bridges* seeks works of relevance to Jewish feminists which combines identity and social/political activism." 2/yr. Pub'd 2 issues 2009; expects 2 issues 2010, 2 issues 2011. 152pp. Reporting time: 6 months. Simultaneous submissions accepted: no. Payment: 1 copy. Poetry reverts to author, all else does not revert. Pub's reviews: 10 in 2009. §Feminism, multi-cultural alliances, Jewish identity. Subjects: Feminism, Judaism.

BRIDGES: An Interdisciplinary Journal of Theology, Philosophy, History, and Science, Robert S. Frey, Editor-Publisher, PO Box 3075, Oakton, VA 22124-3075, 703-281-4722, Fax 703-734-1976, E-mail Bridges23@aol.com. 1988. Articles, photos, reviews. "Each issue of "Bridges" provides a forum for interdisciplinary reflection on themes that share the common focus of values, humaneness, ethics, and meaning. Affiliated with Lebanon Valley College of Pennsylvania." circ. 650. 2/yr. Pub'd 2 issues 2009; expects 2 issues 2010, 2 issues 2011. sub. price $45 institutions, $30 individuals, $15 students; foreign: $50 instit., $35 indiv., $20 students; per copy $15 (US); sample $15 (US). Back issues: prices upon request. 175pp. Reporting time: 1 month. Simultaneous submissions accepted: no. Publishes 80% of manuscripts submitted. Payment: none, complimentary copies of particular issue. Copyrighted, does not revert to author. Pub's reviews: 40 in 2009. §Theology, philosophy, history, science, cultural criticism, Holocaust. Ads: $50/$25. Subjects: Book Reviewing, Culture, History, Holocaust, Philosophy, Religion, Science.

Briery Creek Press (see also THE DOS PASSOS REVIEW), Mary Carroll-Hackett, Editor, Department of English, Longwood University, Farmville, VA 23909, www.brierycreekpress.org. "Publisher of *The Dos Passos Review*. Also publishes the annual winner of the Liam Rector First Book Prize for poetry: 2010 winner - *hour of unfolding* by Candace Pearson." 1 title listed in the *Small Press Record of Books in Print* (36th Edition, 2010-11).

Bright Hill Press, Bertha Rogers, Editor, PO Box 193, Treadwell, NY 13846-0193, 607-829-5055, fax 607-829-5054, wordthur@stny.rr.com. web: www.brighthillpress.org. 1992. Poetry, fiction, art, photos, cartoons, criticism, parts-of-novels, long-poems, collages, plays, non-fiction. "We have 2 competitions per year: a chapbook (poetry) and a full-length poetry book competition - both national. Full-length poetry book competition judged by nationally-known poets. We also publish anthologies with a theme. We publish an anthology periodically and call for mss. periodically." avg. press run 500-1000. Pub'd 10 titles 2009; expects 10 titles 2010, 10 titles 2011. 7 titles listed in the *Small Press Record of Books in Print* (36th Edition, 2010-11). Discounts: trade 40%, bulk 40%, classroom 20-40%, agent 20%, jobber 40-55%. 70pp. Reporting time: 3-6 months. We accept simultaneous submissions, with notification if accepted elsewhere. Publishes 2% of manuscripts submitted. Payment: prize winnings and copies. Does not copyright for author. Subjects: Book Arts, Graphics, Native American, Poetry.

Bright Mountain Books, Cynthia Bright, 206 Riva Ridge Drive, Fairview, NC 28730-9764, booksbmb@charter.net. 1983. Non-fiction. "Length of material: booklength. Biases: regional, Southern Appalachians, Carolinas, nonfiction. Imprints: Historical Images, Ridgetop Books." avg. press run 1M. Pub'd 3 titles 2009; expects 4 titles 2010, 4 titles 2011. 33 titles listed in the *Small Press Record of Books in Print* (36th

Edition, 2010-11). Discounts: Distribution through John F. Blair (www.blairpub.com). 200pp. Reporting time: 3 months. Simultaneous submissions accepted: yes. Publishes 10% of manuscripts submitted. Payment: 10% of retail price on actual sales, paid quarterly. Copyrights for author. Subjects: Appalachia, Autobiography, Aviation, Civil War, Cooking, History, Horticulture, Humor, Memoirs, Myth, Mythology, Native American, Non-Fiction, North Carolina, South, Travel.

Bright Ring Publishing, Inc., MaryAnn F. Kohl, PO Box 31338, Bellingham, WA 98228-3338, 800-480-4278, www.brightring.com. 1985. Non-fiction. "We no longer accept unsolicited manuscripts. Our books are creative, independent, open-minded. First contribution, *Scribble Art And Other Independent Creative Art Experiences for Children*, 144 pages, black line drawings (120), 11 X 8-1/2, suitable for teachers, parents, children, and others who work with children ages 2-forever. We do not publish poetry, fiction, picture books, or books with fill-ins or coloring. Books mirror our format and design which can be viewed on our website. If someone has absolutely got our style, format, and philosophy down, we will look at the manuscript and offer advice and possibly a coauthoring position." avg. press run 5M. Pub'd 1 title 2009; expects 1 title 2010, 1 title 2011. No titles listed in the *Small Press Record of Books in Print* (36th Edition, 2010-11). Discounts: bulk. 150pp. Reporting time: 4 weeks. We are no longer accepting manuscripts. Payment: 4% of net, quarterly. We are no longer accepting manuscripts.

BRILLIANT CORNERS: A Journal of Jazz & Literature, Sascha Feinstein, Lycoming College, Williamsport, PA 17701, 570-321-4279. 1996. Poetry, fiction, art, photos, interviews, criticism, reviews, music, parts-of-novels, long-poems, collages, plays, non-fiction. "BRILLIANT CORNERS publishes jazz-related poetry, fiction, and nonfiction. It features a four-color cover and occasionally publishes art and photography within the issue (black-and-white reproduction only). Recent contributors include Yusef Komunyakaa, Sonia Sanchez, Amiri Baraka, Philip Levine, Hayden Carruth, and Gary Giddins." circ. 700. 2/yr. Pub'd 2 issues 2009; expects 2 issues 2010, 2 issues 2011. sub. price $12; per copy $7; sample $7. Back issues: $7. Discounts: Ingram Periodicals (distributor). 90pp. Reporting time: 2 to 4 months. Simultaneous submissions accepted: No. Publishes 4% of manuscripts submitted. Payment: 2 copies of the issue. Copyrighted, reverts to author. Pub's reviews: 2 in 2009. §Jazz-related literature. Ads: $125/full-page ad. Subjects: African-American, Arts, Essays, Fiction, Interviews, Memoirs, Music, Non-Fiction, Performing Arts, Poetry, Prose.

Brindle and Glass Publishing, Ruth Linka, Publisher, 6-356 Simcoe Street, Victoria, BC, V8V 1L1, Canada. "We are currently not accepting unsolicited manuscripts, in order to allow us to catch up with the volume of manuscripts and proposals we have received to date. If you have a manuscript you think we'd be particularly interested in you may send a short query to info@brindleandglass.com. Please check this page again for information on submissions; we will be opening the transom again in a short whle." No titles listed in the *Small Press Record of Books in Print* (36th Edition, 2010-11).

THE BROADKILL REVIEW: A Journal of Literature, James Brown, c/o John Milton and Company Quality Used Books, 104 Federal Street, Milton, DE 19968, (302) 684-3514, the_broadkill_review@earth-link.net. 2007. Poetry, fiction, articles, photos, interviews, criticism, reviews, letters, parts-of-novels, long-poems, news items, non-fiction. "PLEASE NOTE: WE ARE THE FIRST STATE-OF-THE-ART, ECO-FRIENDLY, PAPER-FREE LITERARY JOURNAL. THE BROADKILL REVIEW APPEARS SOLELY IN PDF-FORMAT AND NOTICE IS SENT WHEN EACH ISSUE IS PUBLISHED. SUBSCRIBERS DOWNLOAD TBR FROM A PASSWORD-PROTECTED SITE. THE PASSWORD IS SENT TO THE SUBSCRIBER. We are interested in publishing in our pages that which rises above the ordinary. We are not, on the other hand, interested in stories about your three-headed cat, zombies, flesh-eating bacteria, BEMs from outer-space, psychopathic axe murderers,.. in short, your stories and poems should not rely on the unusual circumstance IN PLACE OF actually having work which is finely crafted, insightful of the human condition, or which manages to make the reader continue to think about it after they have finished reading it. The best of language poetry does this, but so, too, does an expertly wrought sonnet which, though in an antique form, nonetheless shows us something new about life and ourselves and the contemporary world. We are open to almost everything which does what literature should do, which is to exact a price greater than the effort it takes to read it. The selection process is NOT AT ALL OBJECTIVE. Do not take a rejection from us as some sort of value judgement on your work. We are not representative of the whole world. We publish what moves US. If it doesn't, we don't use it." 6/yr. Expects 6 issues 2010, 6 issues 2011. sub. price $12.00; per copy $2.50; sample Free. Back issues: negotiable. Discounts: None $12 to Libraries Three year regular subscription for $20.00. 46pp. Reporting time: 3 months. Simultaneous submissions accepted: No. Publishes 40% of manuscripts submitted. Payment: a free copy of the issue—if a subscriber, we add an issue to your subscription. Copyrighted, reverts to author. Pub's reviews: none in 2009. §Poetry, fiction, lit- crit., biographies, anthologies, little magazines, essay collections, and so forth. Ads: $50.00 for an eighth of a page for all six issues, $20.00 for an eighth of a page in one issue; $95.00 for a quarter-page for six issues, $35.00 for a quarter page for one issue; $180.00 for a half-page for six issues, $60 for a half-page for one issue; $350.00 for a full-page ad for six issues, $110.00 for a full-page for one issue. Subjects: Arts, Classical Studies, Creative Non-fiction, Drama, Essays, Experimental, Fiction, Medieval, Non-Fiction, Poetry, Prose, Theatre,

Writers/Writing.

THE BROADSIDER: An Annual Magazine of Rescued Poems, Poor Souls Press/Scaramouche Books, Paul Fericano, Editor; Bruce Pryor, Associate Editor; Sue Hansen, Associate Edior; Vern Ferguson, Associate Editor, PO Box 236, Millbrae, CA 94030, website: www.thebroadsider.com. 2009. Poetry. "The Broadsider is an annual magazine that selects previously published poems only and produces limited editon broadsides (100 copies) that are numbered and signed by the poet. Each issue contains a minimum of 20 or a maximum of 30 series broadsides. The broadsides are 2 - 3 color on 65# acid free cover stock with an appropriate graphic to complement the text. Inclusion in the Broadsider is by invitation only. We peruse hundreds of poetry books, magazines, anthologies and online zines each year. Please do not send us your indvidual poems. You can send us your books of poems, magazines, etc., but there is absolutely no guarantee of selection. This is a labor of love project devoted to rescuing poems we love and giving them greater attention. We publish the individual broadsides from January to October and we release limited edition issues of the complete set in both a Numbered and Signed Issue and a Regular Issue in December. Poets included in Volume 1, Series 1-30 are: Paul Fericano, Angelica Jochim, Cielle Tewksbury, Klipschutz, Dan Gerber, Ann Menebroker, Barry Spacks, Ellen Bass, A.D. Winans, Joyce Odam, Edward Field, Robert Bly, Joyce La Mers, B.L. Kennedy, Wanda Coleman, Hugh Fox, leah angstman, Irene McKinney, Carol DeCanio, Roger Langton, Gerald Locklin, Laurel Speer, Ron Koertge, Lyn Lifshin, Penelope Rosemont, Perie Long, Ligi." 1/yr. Expects 1 issue 2010, 1 issue 2011. sub. price 2009. Volume 1, Series 1-30: Numbered and Signed Issue/ Limited to 20 Sealed Copies/$100/Complete Set; Volume 1, Series 1-30: Regular (Unsigned) Issue/Limited to 40 Sealed Copies/$40/Complete Set. 2010. Volume 2, Series 1-20: Numbered and Signed Issue/Limited to 30 Sealed Copies/$70/Complete Set.; per copy $5: Numbered and Signed Issue / each broadside; $3: Regular Issue / each broadside. Back issues: Not Available or Rare. Payment: Poets receive half the print run as payment (numbered and signed copies 1 - 50) + a regular issue PDF of their poem. In addition, each poet chosen for The Broadsider is nominated for a Bulitzer Prize in the category of Poetry Broadside. Copyrighted publication and broadsides. Previously published poems copyrighted by the poet, magazine and/or press and duly credited on the broadsides. Subject: Poetry.

Broken Jaw Press (see also NEW MUSE OF CONTEMPT), Joe Blades, PO Box 596 Stn A, Fredericton, NB E3B 5A6, Canada, ph/fax 506-454-5127, jblades@nbnet.nb.ca, www.brokenjaw.com. 1985. Poetry, fiction, cartoons, criticism, non-fiction. "Focus on Canadian, especially Canadian authors and/or subjects." avg. press run 700. Pub'd 12 titles 2009; expects 10 titles 2010, 12 titles 2011. 64 titles listed in the *Small Press Record of Books in Print* (36th Edition, 2010-11). Discounts: direct trade 40%, trade in U.S./Canada by General Distributions Services, e-book distribution by Publishing Online. 80pp. Reporting time: 4-6 months. Simultaneous submissions accepted: no. Publishes 1% of manuscripts submitted. Payment: 10% of list price. Copyrights for author. Subjects: Bisexual, Canada, Gay, Ernest Hemingway, History, Lesbianism, Literature (General), Poetry, Self-Help, Short Stories.

Broken Rifle Press, Gerald R. Gioglio, Publisher, 33 Morton Drive, Lavallette, NJ 08735-2826, 732-830-7014, grgioglio@verizon.net. 1987. Non-fiction. "Focus on peace, antiwar movements, non-violent resistance." avg. press run 3.5M. 2 titles listed in the *Small Press Record of Books in Print* (36th Edition, 2010-11). Discounts: 1-5 20%, 6-32 40%, 33-64 43%, 65-98 46%, 99+ 48%. Reporting time: Not Accepting Manuscripts at this time. Payment: standard. Copyrights for author. Subjects: History, Military, Veterans, Non-Fiction, Non-Violence, Peace, Sociology, Third World, Minorities.

Broken Shadow Publications, Gail Ford, 472 44th Street, Oakland, CA 94609-2136, 510 594-2200. 1993. Poetry, fiction, non-fiction. "Material we publish is honest, accessible, and deeply felt. Contributing authors place an emphasis on communication, and participate in regular peer reviews to ensure the clarity and power of their work. BSP does not accept unsolicited manuscripts." avg. press run 500. Expects 1 title 2010, 1 title 2011. 3 titles listed in the *Small Press Record of Books in Print* (36th Edition, 2010-11). 75pp. Simultaneous submissions accepted: no. Copyrights for author. Subjects: Essays, Poetry, Short Stories.

Bronx River Press, 3915 Dyre Ave. PMB #98, Bronx, NY 10466, info@bronxriverpress.com, http://www.bronxriverpress.com. 2006. Fiction. "A press based in the Bronx, New York, BXRP believes that readers of serious fiction are underserved by the current publishing climate. They seemingly have only two choices: (a) tired traditional narratives driven primarily by character psychology or (b) experimental work that abandons all notions of plot, character and setting in favor of lingual pyrotechnics. In the former type of book, nothing much happens, but you really become intimate (perhaps too intimate) with a character's inner desires. As for the latter, when have you truly enjoyed reading stream-of-consciousness spew (be honest)? We believe that there is a third way that rejects each style's dominant premise. We firmly believe: (a) it should be possible to read a well-told story containing intellectually satisfying subject matter; (b) there ought to be characters who engage the world rather than merely gaze at their navels; and (c) there can be formal invention without obscuring essential story elements. For those unfamiliar with our borough, the Bronx is a study in contrasts. On one hand, the Bronx is an industrial center that defines in many people's minds what the "inner city" looks like.

On the other hand, the Bronx contains more park land and green space than any other borough in New York City. BXRP aims to publish fiction that similarly contains multitudes (to paraphrase Walt Whitman, though he was based in Brooklyn). Authors who have called the Bronx home include Edgar Allen Poe, Mark Twain, Herman Wouk, E.L. Doctorow, Don Delillo and Richard Price, all of whom would have made ideal Bronx River Press authors." avg. press run 1000. Expects 1 title 2010, 1 title 2011. 2 titles listed in the *Small Press Record of Books in Print* (36th Edition, 2010-11). 196pp. Reporting time: 6-8 weeks. Only electronic queries submitted via email to the editors via the BXRP web site will be considered. Please do not send queries or manuscripts by mail. Simultaneous submissions accepted: Yes. Publishes 2% of manuscripts submitted. Payment: 20 author copies; 45% discount on additional copies; standard paperback royalty of 6%. Does not copyright for author. Subjects: Experimental, Fiction, Literature (General), New York, Novels, Prose, Satire.

Bronze Girl Productions, Inc., Christine Mitchell, Publisher, 1106 Sable Ridge Drive, Joliet, IL 60421-8853, fax 916-922-1989, bronzegirl.com. 2005. Poetry, fiction, non-fiction. "Query first. We accept poetry manuscripts, cookbooks, children fiction and non-fiction, self-help, and how-to's. No adult fiction. MS should be typed, double-spaced, clean, title of work on each page." avg. press run 2000. Expects 3 titles 2010, 6 titles 2011. No titles listed in the *Small Press Record of Books in Print* (36th Edition, 2010-11). Discounts: 1 copy 0%2-4 copies 25%5-99 copies 40%100+ copies 55%. 200pp. Reporting time: 2-4 months. Simultaneous submissions accepted: Yes. Publishes 10% of manuscripts submitted. Payment: Semi-annually payment of royalties. Royalties range from 7 1/2% to 15% based on sales. Copyrights for author. Subjects: African-American, Aging, Chicano/a, Children, Youth, Cooking, How-To, Juvenile Fiction, Motivation, Success, Non-Fiction, Parenting, Pets, Poetry, Relationships, Religion, Self-Help.

Brooding Heron Press, Samuel Green, Co-Publisher; Sally Green, Co-Publisher, Bookmonger Row, Waldron Island, WA 98294, 360-420-8181. 1984. Poetry. "No unsolicited manuscripts. Work by James Laughlin, Olav Hauge, Hayden Carruth, Donald Hall, Jane Hirshfield and Ted Kooser." avg. press run 300. Pub'd 1 title 2009; expects 1 title 2010, 1 title 2011. 14 titles listed in the *Small Press Record of Books in Print* (36th Edition, 2010-11). Discounts: 30% to bookstores for trade copies. 36-54pp. Reporting time: 1-2 weeks. Simultaneous submissions accepted: no. Publishes 1% of manuscripts submitted. Payment: copies, 10% of run. Copyrights for author. Subjects: Literary Review, Poetry.

Brook Farm Books, Jean Reed, PO Box 246, Bridgewater, ME 04735, 506-375-4680. 1981. Fiction, cartoons, satire, non-fiction. "Especially interested in home-school material. Canadian address: Box 101, Glassville, NB Canada E7L 4T4." avg. press run 3M. Pub'd 1 title 2009. 2 titles listed in the *Small Press Record of Books in Print* (36th Edition, 2010-11). Discounts: 1-9 40%, 10-49 45%, 50+ 50%, 40% STOP. 304pp. Reporting time: 2 months. Simultaneous submissions accepted: no. Payment: 10%, no advance. Copyrights for author. Subjects: Education, Humor.

Brooke-Richards Press, Brooke Sosa, Editor, 10713 Paradise Point Drive, Las Vegas, NV 89134, phone 702 982 6942; fax 702 254 8003. 1989. "Supplementary textbooks. Not accepting submissions at the present time." avg. press run varies. Pub'd 4 titles 2009. 4 titles listed in the *Small Press Record of Books in Print* (36th Edition, 2010-11). 96pp. Subjects: Biography, History.

Brookline Books, Milt Budoff, 34 University Rd, Brookline, MA 02445, 617-834-6772. 1978. Poetry, fiction. avg. press run 5000. Pub'd 6 titles 2009; expects 6 titles 2010, 6 titles 2011. 1 title listed in the *Small Press Record of Books in Print* (36th Edition, 2010-11). Discounts: bookstores 20%. 175pp. Reporting time: 2 months. Simultaneous submissions accepted: Yes. Publishes 1% of manuscripts submitted. Payment: varies. Copyrights for author. Subjects: AIDS, Alternative Medicine, Animals, Arts, Avant-Garde, Experimental Art, Disabled, Education, History, Interviews, Literature (General), Novels, Poetry, Psychiatry, Psychology, Textbooks.

Brooks Books (see also MAYFLY), Randy Brooks, 3720 N. Woodridge Drive, Decatur, IL 62526, (217) 877-2966. 1976. Poetry. "Brooks Books, formerly High/Coo Press, publishes English-language haiku books, chapbooks, online collections and Mayfly magazine. Founded in 1976 by Randy and Shirley Brooks, our goal is to feature the individual haiku as a literary event, and to celebrate excellence in the art through collections by the best contemporary writers practicing the art of haiku.Brooks Books is a private publisher of English-language haiku publications. Our publications include Mayfly, a small biannual magazine, clothbound books such as Almost Unseen: Selected Haiku of George Swede, dual-language trade paperback books of haiku by contemporary Japanese and English-language haiku writers, chapbooks, and haiga web collections. Brooks Books promotes the well-crafted haiku, with sensory images that evoke an immediate emotional response as well as a long-lasting, often spiritual, resonance in the imagination of the reader. Brooks Books exists to publish appreciated books and magazine issues of excellent haiku in English.Brooks Books is the sponsor of the English-language Haiku web site available online at:http://www.brooksbookshaiku.comThe web site features individual English-language haiku, haiku poets, online web collections of haiku, online collections of haiga, new books related to haiku, haiku magazines, a catalog of related books for sale and news about upcoming haiku events. We welcome submissions and encourage you to become a reader and writer of haiku." avg. press run 1000. Pub'd 2 titles 2009; expects 2 titles 2010, 2 titles 2011. 3 titles listed in the *Small Press Record of Books in Print* (36th Edition, 2010-11). Discounts: bookstores - 5 or more copies 40%distributors - 10 or more coies 50%. 128pp. Reporting time: 3-4 months. Simultaneous submissions accepted: No. Publishes 2% of manuscripts submitted. Payment: 10% of the press run OR equivalent wholesale value of 10% of the press run. For example, with a press run of 1000 the author may receive 100 copies or 50% of the retail price value for 100 copies. Copyright is returned to author who registers and owns copyright. Subjects: Haiku, Poetry, Zen.

Brookview Press, David Lee Drotar, 901 Western Road, Castleton-on-Hudson, NY 12033, 518-732-7093 phone/Fax, info@brookviewpress.com, www.brookviewpress.com. 2000. Non-fiction. "Brookview Press is a small independently owned publisher located in Castleton-on-Hudson, about 2 hours north of New York City. We publish unique, quality paperback books about nature and the environment." avg. press run 2.5M. Pub'd 1 title 2009; expects 1 title 2010, 2 titles 2011. 1 title listed in the *Small Press Record of Books in Print* (36th Edition, 2010-11). Discounts: trade 1-10 copies 40%, 10+ non-returnable 50%; bulk, classroom, wholesaler 10+ copies 50%. 300pp. Reporting time: 4 months. Simultaneous submissions accepted: yes. Publishes 1% of manuscripts submitted. Payment: royalties annually. Copyrights for author. Subjects: Environment, Essays, Leisure/Recreation, Literature (General), Nature, Non-Fiction.

•THE BROOME REVIEW, Andrei Guruianu, Editor, PO Box 900, Vestal, NY 13851. "We are now accepting submissions through the end of the year for Issue #4, Spring 2011: Poetry & Prose: Regular Mail Submissions Only. Include a brief cover letter, including a short bio, and a SASE with all submissions; submissions without a SASE will be recycled unread. Please do not send your original manuscript; due to the large number of submissions received all manuscripts will be recycled. Include a SASE for reply only. Do send only one genre per envelope to its appropriate section editor. Thank you for helping move your submissions quickly into the hands of our editors. Poetry: Submit 3-5 poems: no more than 10 pages. Poems - include name, address, phone number, and e-mail address on each page. Fiction/Creative Nonfiction: One prose piece of up to 8,000 words. Shorter work stands a better chance as we try to provide a space for as many voices as possible to be heard. Prose - include name, address, phone number, and e-mail address on first page, as well as word count."

Brown Books Publishing Group, Kathryn Grant, 16200 N. Dallas Parkway, Suite 170, Dallas, TX 75248-2616, 972-381-0009, fax: 972-248-4336, publishing@brownbooks.com, www.brownbooks.com. No titles listed in the *Small Press Record of Books in Print* (36th Edition, 2010-11).

Brown Fox Books, Mark Godfrey, 1090 Eugenia Place, Carpinteria, CA 93013, 805-684-5951, Fax 805-684-1628, Manager@Brownfoxbooks.com, www.Brownfoxbooks.com. 1985. Non-fiction. "We publish books of interest to automotive and motor sports enthusiasts." avg. press run 3M. Pub'd 1 title 2009; expects 2 titles 2010, 4 titles 2011. 2 titles listed in the *Small Press Record of Books in Print* (36th Edition, 2010-11). Discounts: 20-55% based on quantity. 288pp. Simultaneous submissions accepted: no. Copyrights for author. Subjects: Autos, Biography, Transportation.

BRYANT LITERARY REVIEW, Tom Chandler, Faculty Suite F, Bryant University, Smithfield, RI 02917, website http://bryant2.bryant.edu/~blr/. 2000. Poetry, fiction. "Contributors: Michael S. Harper, Denise Duhamel, and Baron Wormser." circ. 1M+. 1/yr. Pub'd 1 issue 2009; expects 1 issue 2010, 1 issue 2011. sub. price $8; per copy $8; sample $8. 120pp. Reporting time: approx. 3 months. Publishes 5% of manuscripts submitted. Payment: 2 copies. Copyrighted, reverts to author. Subjects: Fiction, Poetry.

BTW Press, LLC, Mary Jo Sherwood, PO Box 554, Chanhassen, MN 55317, 1-866-818-8029, www.btwpress.com. 2005. Non-fiction. avg. press run 5000. Pub'd 1 title 2009; expects 5 titles 2010, 10 titles 2011. No titles listed in the *Small Press Record of Books in Print* (36th Edition, 2010-11). Discounts: 2-5 copies 20%6-24 copies 40%25+ copies 45%. 200pp.

‡BUCKLE &, Bernhard Frank, PO Box 1653, Buffalo, NY 14205. 1998. Poetry. "No inspirational verse. Send 3-5 poems or poetry translations. No previously published poems, please." circ. 200. 2/yr. Pub'd 2 issues 2009; expects 2 issues 2010, 2 issues 2011. sub. price $9; per copy $5; sample $5. 56pp. Reporting time: 2 weeks for first submissions, 2 months for repeat submissions. Simultaneous submissions accepted: no. Publishes maybe 5% of manuscripts submitted. Payment: 1 year subscription. Copyrighted, reverts to author. Ads: none. Subjects: Poetry, Translation.

Buddhist Text Translation Society, Dharma Realm Buddhist Assn., 1777 Murchison Drive, Burlingame, CA 94010-4504, (707) 468-9112, e-mail EileenHu@drba.org. 1970. Poetry, articles, art, photos, interviews, non-fiction. "The Buddhist Text Translation Society (BTTS) began publishing in 1970 with the goal of making the principles of Buddhism available to an English-reading audience in a form that can be put directly into practice. BTTS translators are both scholars and practicing Buddhists. Translations are accompanied by contemporary commentary. To date, the following have been published, classics such as the *Shurangama Sutra,* the *Lotus Sutra,* and the *Vajra Sutra*; esoteric works such as the *Earth Store Bodhisattva Sutra* and the *Shurangama Mantra;* books on informal instruction in meditation; and books that have grown out of the

American Buddhist experience. Bilingual Chinese/English scriptures are also available including chapters from the *Avatamsaka Sutra*, *The Heart Sutra* and the *Brahma Net Sutra*. Extensive commentaries accompany each of these works in both languages. Limited material is available in Spanish, Vietnamese and French." avg. press run 2M. Pub'd 6 titles 2009; expects 8 titles 2010, 10 titles 2011. 114 titles listed in the *Small Press Record of Books in Print* (36th Edition, 2010-11). Discounts: retail stores 2-4 books 20%, 5-30 40%, Call for 31 plus books. Distributed by New Leaf Distributors. 200pp. Payment: none, Non-profit organization. Copyrights for author.

Buenos Books, Guy Bayard, 35 Avenue Ernest Reyer, 75014 PARIS, France, www.buenosbooks.fr. Non-fiction. "academic publishing: philosophy of law, international law, philosophy of scienceElectronic submissions only authors must hold a Ph. D in the field." No titles listed in the *Small Press Record of Books in Print* (36th Edition, 2010-11). Reporting time: one week. Simultaneous submissions accepted: Yes. Publishes 50% of manuscripts submitted. Does not copyright for author. Subjects: History, Law, Non-Fiction, Philosophy, Research, Science, U.S. Hispanic.

BUFFALO SPREE, Elizabeth Licata, 6215 Sheridan Drive, Buffalo, NY 14221-4837, 716-634-0820, fax 716-810-0075. 1967. Articles, photos, interviews, criticism, reviews, news items, non-fiction. "We have stopped publishing poetry and fiction, and are now a city/regional magazine. We normally assign articles and do not encourage unsolicited material, though we will review it." circ. 25M. 8/yr. sub. price $20; per copy $4.50; sample $4.50. Discounts: none. 225pp. Reporting time: 1 month. Simultaneous submissions accepted: no. Payment: varies, payment upon publication. Copyrighted, authors must request permission for rights to revert. Pub's reviews: 8 in 2009. §Biography, art, music, health, fitness, food. Subjects: Fiction, Non-Fiction, Short Stories.

Building Blocks Press, Jennifer Payne, 129 Bremmer St, Richland, WA 99352, (509) 374-7606, Fax: (815) 346-2486, Toll-free (877) 422-2386, jpayne@buildingblockspress.com, www.buildingblockspress.com. 2008. "Children's educational: pre-readers and kindergarten." avg. press run 5000. Expects 1 title 2010, 2 titles 2011. 1 title listed in the *Small Press Record of Books in Print* (36th Edition, 2010-11). Discounts: 15 copies 40%; 30 copies (1 case) 43%; 90 copies (3 cases) 45%; 150 copies (5 cases) 48%; 240 copies (1 gross) 55%; 720 copies (3 gross) 60%; 1200 copies (5 gross) call for pricing. 56pp. Reporting time: 6 weeks. Copyrights for author. Subjects: Education, Music.

‡**BULLETIN OF HISPANIC STUDIES, Liverpool University Press,** Dorothy Sherman Severin, Editor; Roger Wright, Associate Editor, The University of Liverpool, 18 Oxford St., Liverpool L69 7ZN, England, 051 794 2774/5. 1923. Articles, reviews. "Specialist articles on the languages and literatures of Spain, Portugal and Latin America, in English, Spanish, Portuguese and Catalan." circ. 1M. 4/yr. Pub'd 4 issues 2009; expects 4 issues 2010, 4 issues 2011. sub. price inland (European community) indiv. £29, instit. £75, overseas indiv. US $50, instit. US $155; per copy £20. Back issues: £40 per volume. 112pp. Reporting time: 3 months max. Payment: none. Not copyrighted. Pub's reviews: 200 in 2009. §Languages and literatures of Spain, Portugal and Latin America. Ads: £250/£150/£80 1/4 page. Subject: Language.

The Bunny & The Crocodile Press/Forest Woods Media Productions, Inc, Grace Cavalieri, President, Editor; Colleen Flynn, Vice Pres.; Cynthia Cavalieri, Senior Editor, Chief of Production; Kenneth Flynn, Treasurer, Editor, 1821 Glade Court, Annapolis, MD 21403-1945, 410-267-7432. 1976. Poetry. "Other address: Suite 1102, 4200 Cathedral Ave. NW. Manuscripts by invitation only, no unsolicited mss." avg. press run 500-1M. Pub'd 2 titles 2009; expects 10 titles 2010, 10 titles 2011. 38 titles listed in the *Small Press Record of Books in Print* (36th Edition, 2010-11). Discounts: 10% for orders of 12+. 77-100pp. Simultaneous submissions accepted: no. Payment: to date authors obtain grants to publish, get 80% of sales; publisher supplies 20% funding. Author owns copyright. Subject: Poetry.

Burd Street Press, Harold E. Collier, Acquisitions Editor, PO Box 708, 73 W. Burd Street, Shippensburg, PA 17257, 717-532-2237, Fax 717-532-6110. 1992. Fiction, non-fiction. "Burd Street Press brings military history to the novice reader." avg. press run 1M-2M. Pub'd 4 titles 2009; expects 10 titles 2010, 15 titles 2011. 117 titles listed in the *Small Press Record of Books in Print* (36th Edition, 2010-11). Discounts: available on request. 150-250pp. Reporting time: 30 days for proposals, 90 days for full manuscripts. Simultaneous submissions accepted: yes. Publishes 25% of manuscripts submitted. Payment: twice yearly. Copyrights for author. Subjects: Aviation, Biography, Civil War, Diaries, History, Non-Fiction, War, World War II.

Burning Books, Melody Sumner Carnahan, Michael Sumner, PO Box 2638, Santa Fe, NM 87504, Fax 505-820-6216, brnbx@nets.com, burningbooks.org. 1979. Poetry, fiction, art, interviews, music. "Burning Books has published books of and about contemporary music, literature, and art since 1979. We are artists and writers who publish books that extend possibilities in literature, music, art, and ideas. We use volunteer labor, donated professional services, income from previous publications and advance sales to create our books." avg. press run 1M-3M. Pub'd 1 title 2009; expects 2 titles 2010, 2 titles 2011. 13 titles listed in the *Small Press Record of Books in Print* (36th Edition, 2010-11). Discounts: 40/60. 84-450pp. Reporting time: 6 weeks.

Simultaneous submissions accepted: yes. Publishes 0% of manuscripts submitted. Payment: varies. We sometimes copyright for author. Subjects: Arts, Avant-Garde, Experimental Art, Fiction, Literature (General), Music, Philosophy, Short Stories, Visual Arts.

•**Burning Books Press,** PO Box 41053, Los Angeles, CA 90041-0053. "Burning Books Press of Los Angeles produces colorful, collectible artists books in limited editions in which each book is unique. Since its inception in Venice, California, in 1984, the look and feel of one-of-a-kind limited edition artists books from Burning Books Press is visual music. Artists books from Burning Books Press are a page-turning delight. Running color and narrative harmonies of graphics and text flow from page to rhythmically-linked page. In addition to a selection of one-of-a-kind collage books, original and classic Burning Books Press books are hand-cut and individually-assembled, using archival papers and archival-quality materials. The look and feel of each limited edition Burning Book is deliberately varied during production, making each Burning Books Press original and classic volume different and distinct. An affordable line of limited edition Edition Noir books features original designs on commercial papers. After assembly, works are numbered, signed, and dated by the artist. Each artist's book is shipped in a hand-made cardboard box to protect against damage in shipping, as well as light and excessive handling upon arrival." No titles listed in the *Small Press Record of Books in Print* (36th Edition, 2010-11).

Burning Deck Press, Keith Waldrop, Rosmarie Waldrop, 71 Elmgrove Avenue, Providence, RI 02906. 1962. Poetry. "Order from Small Press Distribution." avg. press run 500-1M. Pub'd 4 titles 2009; expects 4 titles 2010, 3 titles 2011. 132 titles listed in the *Small Press Record of Books in Print* (36th Edition, 2010-11). Discounts: see schedule of Small Press Distribution. 64-80pp. Reporting time: 2 months. Payment: 10% of edition (copies). Does not copyright for author. Subjects: Fiction, Poetry.

Burns Park Publishers, Anthony Putman, P.O. Box 4239, Ann Arbor, MI 48106, 734 663 5435, www.burnsparkpublishers.com. 1989. Non-fiction. "We publish "word-of-mouth" bestsellers: Books that make a significant, practical difference to their readers—who then tell their friends." avg. press run 2500. Pub'd 2 titles 2009; expects 1 title 2010, 2 titles 2011. 3 titles listed in the *Small Press Record of Books in Print* (36th Edition, 2010-11). Reporting time: Do not submit manuscripts—query only. Subjects: Business & Economics, Consulting, Inspirational, Leadership, Management, Marketing, Prison, Psychology, Relationships, Spiritual.

BURNSIDE REVIEW, Sid Miller, P.O. BOX 1782, Portland, OR 97207, sid@burnsidereview.org, www.burnsidereview.org. 2004. Poetry, fiction, art, photos, criticism, reviews, long-poems. "Published poetry, interviews and reviews. Reads poetry year round. Past contributors include Dorianne Laux, Virgil Suarez, Paul Guest and Robyn Art. We like the narrative, but would like to see more of a movement to the lyrical. See our website for complete guidelines, samples, and contest info." circ. 500. 2/yr. Expects 1 issue 2010, 2 issues 2011. 1 title listed in the *Small Press Record of Books in Print* (36th Edition, 2010-11). sub. price $14.00; per copy $8.00; sample $8.00. Back issues: $4.00. Discounts: n/a. 80pp. Reporting time: 2-4 months. Simultaneous submissions accepted: Yes. Publishes 5% of manuscripts submitted. Payment: one copy. Copyrighted, reverts to author. Pub's reviews: 2 in 2009. §poetry chapbooks and full poetry books. Ads: negotiable. Subjects: Arts, Liberal Arts, Oregon, Poetry.

Business Coach Press, Tom Leal, PO Box 301, Alamo, CA 94507-0301, 877-782-6226. 2006. Non-fiction. "Our titles focus on improving small businesses, particularly through coaching.We offer a team approach toward getting ideas into print and onto shelves—virtual and actual—more quickly.We prefer a query letter, followed by a conversation, rather than unsolicited manuscripts." avg. press run 200. Pub'd 1 title 2009; expects 2 titles 2010, 2 titles 2011. 1 title listed in the *Small Press Record of Books in Print* (36th Edition, 2010-11). 200pp. Simultaneous submissions accepted: Yes. Does not copyright for author. Subject: Business & Economics.

BUST DOWN THE DOOR AND EAT ALL THE CHICKENS: A Journal of Absurd and Surreal Fiction, Bradley Sands, http://www.absurdistjournal.com, bradleysands@comcast.net. Fiction, satire. "We are seeking stories of an absurdist or surrealist nature that are within the range of 2000 to 5000 words. They should not fit comfortably within any genre. We have peculiar tastes and recommend that you read an issue before sending in your work. Do not send more than one story at a time. Before submitting, please see website for more detailed guidelines and an online sample issue: www.absurdistjournal.comRecent contributors include Steve Aylett, D. Harlan Wilson, Kenji Siratori, John Edward Lawson, Kevin L. Donihe, Vincent W. Sakowski, and Alyssa Sturgill." circ. 200. 2/yr. Pub'd 2 issues 2009; expects 2 issues 2010, 2 issues 2011. price per copy $8.50. 80pp. Reporting time: Six weeks or less. Simultaneous submissions accepted: Yes. Publishes 4.35% of manuscripts submitted. Payment: $10 and one contributor's copy. Copyrighted, reverts to author. Pub's reviews: 4 in 2009. §Absurd and surreal fiction. Ads: trade. Subjects: Absurdist, Avant-Garde, Experimental Art, Dada, Fantasy, Fiction, Horror, Humor, Kafka, Literature (General), Prose, Satire, Science Fiction, Surrealism.

Butcher Shop Press, David Greenspan, Publisher Editor-in-Chief; H NGM N, Editor, 529 Beach 132nd St., Rockaway Park, NY 11694-1413. 1999. Poetry, fiction, articles, art, photos, interviews, criticism, reviews, long-poems, non-fiction. "*We consider ourselves to be everything that is right with poetry. We live through our art and our lives are our art. . .while some continue to Howl against the system we take it outside and beat it.*" Our Chapbooks usually run between 100-200 copies. The Butcher's Block runs anywhere above 500 copies. No titles listed in the *Small Press Record of Books in Print* (36th Edition, 2010-11). Payment: cash, checks money orders.

BUTTON, Sally Cragin, PO Box 77, Westminster, MA 01473, sally@moonsigns.net, www.moonsigns.net. 1993. Poetry, fiction, art, cartoons, music, parts-of-novels. "We like wit, brevity, the cleverly-conceived of essay/recipe, poetry that might have a rhyme scheme, but isn't a rhyme scheme that's abab or aabb or anything really obvious, true moments carefully preserved. We don't like whining, cheap sentimentality, egregious profanity, vampires, neuroses for neuroses' sake, most song lyrics passing as poetry, anything overlong, overdull or overreaching. Recent contributors include: Mary Campbell, Sven Birkerts, Stephen Sandys, They Might Be Giants, Brendan Galvin, Diana Der-Hovanessian. Sample material can be viewed on our website." circ. 1M. 1/yr. Pub'd 1 issue 2009; expects 1 issue 2010, 1 issue 2011. sub. price $10 for 6 issues; per copy $2.50; sample $2.50. Back issues: same. Discounts: none - our prices are low, low, low; stores are 60/40 split. 28pp. Reporting time: We only read between April 1 and September 30. MS. sent at other times will be discarded due to volume. Writers outside the U.S. may submit by email during those times. We return manuscripts only if we comment on them; otherwise, response only. Simultaneous submissions accepted: no. Publishes 5-10% of manuscripts submitted. Payment: subscriptions for writer + 1 friends + honorarium. Copyrighted, reverts to author. Pub's reviews: 1 in 2009. §Fiction, fashion, poetry, manuals. Ads: $100/$60/$25 minimum. Subjects: Cartoons, Crafts, Hobbies, Fiction, Music, Poetry.

Button Press, Debbie Campbell, 1518 W. Park Ave., Champaign, IL 61821, buttonpressbooks@gmail.com. 2008. Poetry, fiction, art, photos, interviews, letters, collages, non-fiction. "We publish limited run, hand-bound, special edition books. At this time, we can only publish solicited works." Expects 1 title 2010, 1 title 2011. 1 title listed in the *Small Press Record of Books in Print* (36th Edition, 2010-11). 40-100pp. Reporting time: one week. Simultaneous submissions accepted: No. Payment: by contract. Copyright is returned to author upon publication (author registers and owns copyright, unless stated otherwise in our contract).

BYLINE, Robbi Hess, Editor; Donna Marbach, Poetry Editor; Helen Nguyen, Fiction Editor, PO Box 111, Albion, NY 14411-0111, 585-355-8172. 1981. Poetry, fiction, articles, interviews, non-fiction. circ. 3M. 6/yr. Pub'd 11 issues 2009; expects 6 issues 2010, 6 issues 2011. sub. price $29; per copy $5; sample $5. Back issues: $5 (incl. p/h). 48pp. Reporting time: Four to five months. We accept simultaneous submissions except for poetry. Publishes 60% of manuscripts submitted. Payment: varies by department, approx. 5¢/word. Copyrighted, reverts to author. Pub's reviews. §How-to for writers relating to fiction, non-fiction, creative non-fiction and poetry—do not review fiction. Ads: $350/$200/$1 per word. Subjects: Fiction, How-To, Non-Fiction, Poetry, Writers/Writing.

C

C & M Online Media Inc., Nancy McAllister, 3905 Meadow Field Lane, Raleigh, NC 27606-4470, 919-233-8164, nancy@cmonline.com, www.bosonbooks.com. 1976. Fiction, plays, non-fiction. "We publish about 10 titles a year. Our imprint is Boson Books. (Not publishing at this time under the New South Company, but New South titles are still available.) We have ebook distribution primarily through Amazon, Apple, Sony, Mobipocket, Content Reserve, Powells, Ebooks, EbooksLib, Barnes and Noble, and NetLib. Selected titles are published as trade paperbacks. We publish over 120 books. You can find our list at bosonbooks.com." Pub'd 10 titles 2009; expects 10 titles 2010, 10 titles 2011. 35 titles listed in the *Small Press Record of Books in Print* (36th Edition, 2010-11). 300pp. Reporting time: 8-10 weeks. Simultaneous submissions accepted: no. Publishes 1% of manuscripts submitted. Payment: 25% Boson Books online, 25% Boson Books trade paper. Copyrights for author. Subjects: African-American, Drama, Fiction, Mystery, Non-Fiction, North Carolina, Numismatics, Old West, Poetry, Post Modern, Romance, Satire, Science Fiction, Trivia.

C & T Publishing, Gailen Runge, Managing Editor, 1651 Challenge Drive, Concord, CA 94520-5206, 925-677-0377. 1983. Non-fiction. "We publish how-to quilting books, most of which are softcover with an average of 112 pages. Most books are all color." avg. press run 15M. Pub'd 15 titles 2009; expects 18 titles 2010, 28 titles 2011. 105 titles listed in the *Small Press Record of Books in Print* (36th Edition, 2010-11). Discounts: Total retail amount: $50 or less 20%, $51-300 40%, $301-600 45%, $601+ 50%. 112pp. Reporting time: 8 weeks. Simultaneous submissions accepted: yes. Publishes 10% of manuscripts submitted. Copyrights for author. Subjects: Antiques, Arts, Collectibles, Crafts, Hobbies, How-To, Internet, Quilting, Sewing.

C&R Press, Chad Prevost Dr., Publisher-Founder-Editor; Ryan Van Cleave Dr., Publisher-Founder-Director, 1844 Knickerbocker Ave., Chattanooga, TN 37405-2216, www.crpress.org. 2007. Poetry, fiction, non-fiction. "C&R Press is committed to publishing books from new and emerging writers whose work might otherwise be ignored by commercial publishers. We are interested in supporting authors whose thoughtful and imaginative contribution to contemporary literature deserves recognition and support. In the near future, we hope to expand our commitment by offering Atlanta, Chattanooga, and Sarasota-area workshops on publishing, literary editing, and creative writing.We currently run two annual poetry book contests. The DeNovo Prize for a first book. $25 reading fee. Includes copy of winning book with a SASE to ship book. $500 prize plus book publication. 2008 Judge Denise Duhamel. 2007 Judge: Thomas Lux. Last year's winner: Michelle Bitting with GOOD FRIDAY KISS. Reading Period: August 1-September 30, 2008 [postmark deadline: please do not spend extra money shipping overnight].Fall Open Series open to all. $20 reading fee. Includes copy of winning book with a SASE to ship book. 2007 winner: Jon Veinberg's THE SPEED LIMIT OF CLOUDS. Reading Period: August 1-October 31, 2008.www.crpress.org for full guidelines and updates. Send hardcopy manuscripts with checks payable to C&R Press to:C&R Press, DEPT. W, BOX 4065, Chattanooga, TN 37405ORElectronic submissions welcome (and encouraged) with PayPal payment option through website. Email: crpress_org@yahoo.com." avg. press run 1000. Expects 3 titles 2010, 4 titles 2011. No titles listed in the *Small Press Record of Books in Print* (36th Edition, 2010-11). Discounts: Purchases made directly through us or 20 or more at 25% discount. 100pp. Reporting time: 2-4 months for full reply. Simultaneous submissions accepted: Yes. Payment: Varies. Copyrights for author. Subjects: Book Reviewing, Creative Non-fiction, Creativity, Editing, Fiction, Humor, Marketing, Memoirs, Non-Fiction, Novels, Poetry, Prose, Publishing, Spiritual, Writers/Writing.

•**CABINET,** 181 Wyckoff Street, Brooklyn, NY 11217. "Cabinet is an award-winning quarterly magazine of art and culture that confounds expectations of what is typically meant by the words "art," "culture," and sometimes even "magazine." Like the 17th-century cabinet of curiosities to which its name alludes, Cabinet is as interested in the margins of culture as its center. Presenting wide-ranging, multi-disciplinary content in each issue through the varied formats of regular columns, essays, interviews, and special artist projects, Cabinet's hybrid sensibility merges the popular appeal of an arts periodical, the visually engaging style of a design magazine, and the in-depth exploration of a scholarly journal."

Cable Publishing, Nan Wisherd, 14090 E Keinenen Rd, Brule, WI 54820, 715-372-8499, nan@cablepublishing.com. 2007. Fiction, non-fiction. "My focus is non-fiction, but all manuscript submissions are reviewed." avg. press run 2000. Pub'd 1 title 2009; expects 10 titles 2010, 8 titles 2011. 2 titles listed in the *Small Press Record of Books in Print* (36th Edition, 2010-11). Discounts: 2-5 copies 20%, 6-11 copies 30%, 12 or more 40%, distributor discount is 55%. 275pp. Reporting time: Approximately one month. Simultaneous submissions accepted: Yes. Publishes 25% of manuscripts submitted. Payment: 10-15% royalty, advances vary, quarterly payment schedule. Copyrights for author. Subjects: African-American, Airplanes, Aviation, Biography, Family, Fiction, Food, Eating, Great Lakes, Health, History, Medicine, Nature, North America, Novels, World War II.

Caddo Gap Press (see also EDUCATIONAL FOUNDATIONS; EDUCATIONAL LEADERSHIP & ADMINISTRATION; INTERNATIONAL JOURNAL OF EDUCATIONAL POLICY, RESEARCH, AND PRACTICE: RECONCEPTUALIZING CHILDHOOD STUDIES; ISSUES IN TEACHER EDUCATION; JOURNAL OF CURRICULUM THEORIZING; JOURNAL OF THOUGHT; MULTI-CULTURAL EDUCATION; NOTES AND ABSTRACTS IN AMERICAN AND INTERNATIONAL EDUCATION; SCHOLAR-PRACTITIONER QUARTERLY; SUMMER ACADEME: A Journal of Higher Education; TABOO: Journal of Education & Culture; TEACHER EDUCATION QUARTERLY; VITAE SCHOLASTICAE: The Journal of Educational Biography), Alan H. Jones, Publisher, 3145 Geary Boulevard, Suite 275, San Francisco, CA 94118, 415-666-3012 telephone, 415-666-3552 fax, caddogap@aol.com, www.caddogap.com. 1989. "Caddo Gap Press is primarily a publisher of educational books and journals, with particular interest in the fields of teacher education and the social foundations of education." avg. press run 2M. Pub'd 5 titles 2009; expects 5 titles 2010, 5 titles 2011. 45 titles listed in the *Small Press Record of Books in Print* (36th Edition, 2010-11). Discounts: 20% to educational institutions; 40% to bookstores; other discounts based on quantity. 150pp. Reporting time: 1 month. Simultaneous submissions accepted: yes. Publishes 10% of manuscripts submitted. Payment: to be arranged, usually 10%. Copyrights for author. Subject: Education.

Cadmus Editions, Jeffrey Miller, PO Box 126, Belvedere Tiburon, CA 94920-0126, 707-762-0510. 1979. Poetry, fiction, music, parts-of-novels. "Do not send unsolicited mss." avg. press run 1500. Pub'd 3 titles 2009; expects 3 titles 2010, 3 titles 2011. 33 titles listed in the *Small Press Record of Books in Print* (36th Edition, 2010-11). Discounts: Trade editions distributed by NBN, National Book Network, Lanham, Maryland. 250pp. Reporting time: 30 days. Simultaneous submissions accepted: no. Publishes .001% of manuscripts submitted. Payment: negotiable; paid annually. Copyrights for author. Subjects: Fiction, Poetry.

Caernarvon Press, Terry Hertzler, Publisher, 4435 Marlborough Ave. #3, San Diego, CA 92116, (619) 284-0411, terryh@cts.com. 1985. Poetry, fiction, long-poems, non-fiction. "Publishes poetry and short fiction, rarely unsolicited work. Poets published include Steve Kowit, LoVerne Brown, Brandon Cesmat and Karen Stromberg." avg. press run 300-2000. No titles listed in the *Small Press Record of Books in Print* (36th Edition, 2010-11). Discounts of up to 50%. Write for pricing list. 25-100pp. Subjects: Fantasy, Fiction, Poetry, Vietnam.

CAFE NOIR REVIEW, Back House Books, Philip Henderson, 1703 Lebanon Street, Adelphi, MD 20783. 1990. Poetry, fiction, articles, cartoons, interviews, satire, criticism, reviews, parts-of-novels, long-poems, plays. "Length of material: fiction, 2,500 words; poetry, no limits. Want good strong politically-oriented material. Will accept anything which is dangerous, erotic, even pornographic. We especially are looking for young black writers who are otherwise 'unpublishable.' We're just starting, but we intend to grow. Please, no trash. We demand *quality* poetry and fiction, nevertheless." circ. 250. Irregular. Pub'd 1 issue 2009; expects 1 issue 2010, 2-3 issues 2011. sub. price $16; per copy $4; sample $4. Back issues: $5. Discounts: 40%. 50pp. Reporting time: 3 weeks to 2 months. Payment: contributor copies. Copyrighted, reverts to author. Pub's reviews: 1 in 2009. §Fiction, race relations, music, general culture, world politics. Ads: $100/$50/$15 1/4 page/$7 1/8 page. Subjects: Anarchist, Black, Erotica, Fiction.

THE CAFE REVIEW, Steve Luttrell, Editor-in-Chief; Wayne Atherton, Editor; Alex Fisher, Editor, c/o Yes Books, 589 Congress Street, Portland, ME 04101, cafereviweditors@mailcity.com, www.thecafereview.com. 1989. Poetry, art, photos, interviews, criticism. "Send $1 handling fee per submission and SASE (very important)." circ. 300-500. 4/yr. Pub'd 4 issues 2009; expects 4 issues 2010, 4 issues 2011. sub. price $28; per copy $7.95 newsstand; sample $8 includes p/h. Back issues: $5 includes p/h. Discounts: none. 60-70pp. Reporting time: 2-4 months. Simultaneous submissions accepted: no. Publishes 10% of manuscripts submitted. Payment: 1 copy. Copyrighted, reverts to author. Pub's reviews: a few in 2009. §Small press poetry and visual art (photography). Subject: Beat.

CAIRN: The New St. Andrews Review, St. Andrews College Press, Caitlin Johnson, Managing Editor; Ron Bayes, Executive and Founding Editor; Thomas Heffernan, Consulting Editor; Ted Wojtasik, Consulting Editor; Kemp Gregory, Consulting Editor, St. Andrews Prebyterian College, 1700 Dogwood Mile, Laurinburg, NC 28352, 910-277-5310. 1970. Poetry, fiction, articles, criticism, reviews, non-fiction. "CAIRN: THE NEW ST. ANDREWS REVIEW, is especially interested in fiction and poetry by new writers. We have no editorial biases. We do not accept genre work or children's literature. Recent contributors include J.P. Dancing Bear, Theodore Enslin, Stephen Gyllenhaal, Tendai R. Mwanaka, and Lois Siegel. Submissions are read September through February. Please allow three months for response. We will read e-mail submissions but prefer typescript with SASE enclosed. Double space all prose, single space poetry." 1 issue per year. price per copy $8 + $2 S&H. 80 to 110pp. Reporting time: usually three months. Simultaneous submissions accepted: If informed of same & immediately advised if MS accepted elsewhere. Publishes o/a 5% of manuscripts submitted. Payment: contributor's copy. Copyrighted, reverts to author. Pub's reviews: 3 in 2009. §Fiction, poetry, and essays. Ads: Full page $300.00. Subjects: Absurdist, Arts, Asian-American, Experimental, Fiction, Human Rights, Non-Violence, Poetry, Short Stories.

CAKETRAIN, Caketrain Journal and Press, Amanda Raczkowski, Joseph Reed, PO Box 82588, Pittsburgh, PA 15218-1540, www.caketrain.org, caketrainjournal@hotmail.com. 2003. Poetry, fiction, non-fiction. "Caketrain is a literary journal and press based in Pittsburgh, Pennsylvania. Our interest is in bringing you, reader, the very best in contemporary creative writing, full stop. Our goals are for each issue of our journal to submerge you in a birthing tank for gelatinous language monsters, young masses of tentacular foci undulating as directed (in all, at once) by our eclectic stable of contributors; for each new book to seduce and ensnare you, sometimes intangibly, always undeniably; and for you, reader, to be able to draw at least one passage from our banks that prods your mind with a precision and power that feels as if it was written for your eyes alone." 2/yr. Pub'd 1 issue 2009; expects 1 issue 2010, 1 issue 2011. 5 titles listed in the *Small Press Record of Books in Print* (36th Edition, 2010-11). sub. price $16.00; per copy $8.00; sample $8. Back issues: $8. 300pp. Reporting time: Three months. Simultaneous submissions accepted: Yes. Publishes 1% of manuscripts submitted. Payment: One contributor copy. Copyrighted, reverts to author. Subjects: Experimental, Fiction, Non-Fiction, Poetry, Prose.

Caketrain Journal and Press (see also CAKETRAIN), Amanda Raczkowski, Editor; Joseph Reed, Editor, PO Box 82588, Pittsburgh, PA 15218, www.caketrain.org, caketrainjournal@hotmail.com. 2003. Poetry, fiction, art, photos, long-poems, non-fiction. "Amanda Raczkowski and Joseph Reed are the editors of Caketrain Journal and Press, a literary imprint co-founded in 2003 in Pittsburgh, Pennsylvania. Caketrain's primary efforts consist of an annual journal which, in its seven issues to date, has featured the fiction, poetry and nonfiction of over 200 new and established talents; and a press series that includes chapbooks from Lizzie Skurnick, Tina May Hall, Tom Whalen, Matt Bell, Kim Parko and Claire Hero. Caketrain's other ongoing projects include the free, digital reissue of back-catalog titles and an annual chapbook competition." Pub'd 3 titles 2009; expects 4 titles 2010, 4 titles 2011. No titles listed in the *Small Press Record of Books in Print* (36th Edition, 2010-11). Reporting time: Two weeks to six months. Simultaneous submissions accepted: Yes. Publishes 1% of manuscripts submitted. Payment: Payment is one copy of issue contributor appears in. Does not copyright for author. Subjects: Absurdist, Essays, Experimental, Fiction, Literature (General), Non-Fiction, Poetry.

Calaca Press, Cal A. Vera, Editor; Brent Beltran, Editor, Publisher, P.O. Box 2309, National City, CA 91951, (619) 434-9036, calacapress@cox.net, www.calacapress.com. 1997. Poetry, fiction, art, satire, music, plays, non-fiction. "Calaca Press is a Chicano family-owned small publishing house dedicated to publishing and producing unknown, emerging, and established progressive Chicano and Latino voices. With a commitment to social justice and human rights Calaca Press strives to bring about change through the literary arts. From poetry and the spoken word to fiction and creative non-fiction Calaca Press is determined to showcase authors from a community that has been marginalized and pushed to the side in literary circles, and in the real world, for far too long. Recognizing the need for more publishers of Chicano and Latino literature Calaca Press also actively encourages and assists individuals to self publish and/or start their own presses. Understanding the need for historical continuation Calaca Press is committed to continuing the tradition of the Chicano and Latino presses and publishing houses of the 1960's and 1970's that flourished due to community support and the need to have our stories told. Calacadelante!" avg. press run 1000. Pub'd 2 titles 2009; expects 3 titles 2010, 4 titles 2011. No titles listed in the *Small Press Record of Books in Print* (36th Edition, 2010-11). Simultaneous submissions accepted: No. Payment: In books. Does not copyright for author. Subjects: Bilingual, Chicano/a, Creative Non-fiction, Fiction, Human Rights, Immigration, Indigenous Cultures, Latino, Literature (General), Mexico, Multicultural, Native American, Poetry, Social Movements, U.S. Hispanic.

California Bill's Automotive Handbooks, Howard W. Fisher, Publisher, PO Box 91858, Tucson, AZ 85752-1858, 520-547-2462, Fax 888-511-1501, web: www.californiabills.com www.goodyearbooks.com www.nononsenseguides.com. 1987. Non-fiction. "Our focus is on automotive and outdoor recreation titles. Please do *not* send manuscripts; send letter of inquiry plus an outline. We require releases before reviewing manuscripts." avg. press run 3M first printing. Pub'd 1 title 2009; expects 3 titles 2010, 2 titles 2011. 18 titles listed in the *Small Press Record of Books in Print* (36th Edition, 2010-11). Discounts: retail, wholesale, mail order - upon request. 160pp. Reporting time: 1-2 months. Payment: upon request. Copyrights for author. Subject: Autos.

CALIFORNIA QUARTERLY (CQ), Kate Ozbirn, Editor, CSPS/CQ, PO Box 7126, Orange, CA 92863, 949-854-8024, jipalley@aol.com. 1973. Poetry. "For submissions and subscriptions send to: CSPS/CQ, PO Box 7126, Orange, CA 92863." circ. 400. 4/yr. Pub'd 4 issues 2009; expects 4 issues 2010, 4 issues 2011. sub. price $30.00; per copy $7.50; sample $7.50. Back issues: $2-3. Discounts: 50/50. 64pp. Reporting time: 6-8 months. Simultaneous submissions accepted: yes. Publishes 2-5% of manuscripts submitted. Payment: 1 copy of magazine. Copyrighted, reverts to author. Pub's reviews: 6 in 2009. §Books of poetry, in separate publication. Subject: Poetry.

CALLALOO, Charles Rowell, Editor, MS 4212 TAMU, Texas A&M University,, College Station, TX 77843-4212, Phone: 979-458-3108, Fax: 979-458-3275, Web: http://callaloo.tamu.edu, e-mail: callaloo@tamu.edu. Callaloo was founded in 1976 by its current editor, Charles Henry Rowell, when he was teaching at Southern University (Baton Rouge). Poetry, fiction, articles, art, photos, interviews, criticism, reviews, letters, parts-of-novels, long-poems, plays, concrete art, non-fiction. "*Callaloo,* the premier African Diaspora literary journal, publishes original works by, and critical studies of, black writers worldwide. The journal offers a rich mixture of fiction, poetry, plays, critical essays, cultural studies, interviews, and visual art. Frequent annotated bibliographies, special thematic issues, and original art and photography are some of the features of this highly acclaimed international showcase of arts and letters." 4/yr. sub. price http://callaloo.tamu.edu/subscription.html; per copy $15. 300pp. Simultaneous submissions accepted: No. Pub's reviews: Approx. 20 in 2009.

Callawind Publications / Custom Cookbooks / Children's Books, Marcy Claman, 3551 St. Charles Blvd., Suite 179, Kirkland, Quebec H9H 3C4, Canada, 514-685-9109, Fax 514-685-7952, info@callawind.com. 1995. Non-fiction. "Cookbook packager, children's book packager. We offer book production services—we are not a publisher." Pub'd 20 titles 2009; expects 20 titles 2010, 20 titles 2011. 10 titles listed in the *Small Press Record of Books in Print* (36th Edition, 2010-11). 125pp. Subjects: Children, Youth, Cooking, Dining, Restaurants, Lifestyles, Picture Books, Travel.

Calliope Press, Jo Curran, PO Box 2408, New York, NY 10108-2408, 212-564-5068. Fiction, non-fiction. avg. press run 2 M. 5 titles listed in the *Small Press Record of Books in Print* (36th Edition, 2010-11). Subject: Biography.

CALLIOPE: Exploring World History, Cobblestone Publishing Company, Rosalie F. Baker, Editor, 30 Grove Street, Suite C, Peterborough, NH 03458, 603-924-7209, Fax 603-924-7380, custsvc@cobblestone.mv.com. 1990. Poetry, articles, art, photos, reviews, non-fiction. "The magazine will accept freelance articles related to themes covered. Write for guidelines." circ. 10.5M. 9/yr. Pub'd 9 issues 2009; expects 9 issues 2010, 9 issues 2011. sub. price $29.95 + $8 foreign, Canadian subs add 7% GST; per copy $6.95; sample

$6.95. Back issues: $6.95. Discounts: 15% for sub. agencies, bulk rate 3+ $17.95/year sub. each. 52pp. Reporting time: queries sent well in advance of deadline may not be answered for several months. Go-aheads usually sent 5 months prior to publication date. Payment: after publication. Copyrighted, *Calliope* buys all rights. Pub's reviews: 39 in 2009. §Books pertaining to the issues' themes, and written for children ages 8-14. Ads: none. Subject: History.

Calyx Books (see also CALYX: A Journal of Art and Literature by Women), Margarita Donnelly, Director; Beverly McFarland, Senior Editor, PO Box B, Corvallis, OR 97330, 541-753-9384, Fax 541-753-0515, calyx@calyxpress.com, www.calyxpress.com. 1986. Poetry, fiction, non-fiction. "Until future notice, Calyx Books is not accepting book manuscripts at this time." avg. press run 3.5M. Pub'd 2 titles 2009; expects 1 title 2010, 2 titles 2011. 37 titles listed in the *Small Press Record of Books in Print* (36th Edition, 2010-11). Discounts: trade schedule as per Consortium Book Sales & Dist. Poetry 110pp; fiction & prose 200pp. Reporting time: 6-12 months. Simultaneous submissions accepted: yes. Publishes 1-2% of manuscripts submitted. Payment: individually contracted. Copyrights for author. Subjects: Fiction, Homelessness, Literature (General), Multicultural, Poetry, Women.

CALYX: A Journal of Art and Literature by Women, Calyx Books, Beverly McFarland, Senior Editor; Margarita Donnelly, Director, PO Box B, Corvallis, OR 97339, 541-753-9384, Fax 541-753-0515, info@calyxpress.org, www.calyxpress.org. 1976. Poetry, fiction, art, photos, reviews, parts-of-novels, non-fiction. "*Calyx* is the major West Coast publication of its kind. Recently reviewed as 'undoubtedly...one of the best literary mags in the U.S.'—New Pages Press. (128 pages). Manuscript queries and submissions must be accompanied by a SASE. The journal is no longer open to submissions all year round. Open reading dates for journal submissions are 10/1-12/31 annually. Reading period extended one month—to January 31, 2008. Be sure to include brief bio statement with all submissions. Since 2001 *Calyx Journal* has sponsored an annual poetry contest, The Lois Cranston Memorial Poetry Prize. Winner receives $300 and publication in *Calyx Journal*. Winning and runner-up poems are published on website. Submit up to 3 unpublished poems between March 1 and May 31 (inclusive) with a $15 reading fee. Please see *www.calyxpress.org* for guidelines." circ. 3.5M. 2/yr. Pub'd 2 issues 2009; expects 2 issues 2010, 2 issues 2011. sub. price $23 indiv., institutional & library $29 (subs are 3 issues but take 18 months to complete); International postage add $23 per volume, Canada/Mexico postage add $13 per volume.; per copy $10.; sample $10. + $4 p/h. Back issues: send for list. Discounts: trade 3 copies 30%, 4-5 35%, 6+ 40%. 128pp. Reporting time: 6-12 months. Simultaneous submissions accepted: yes. Publishes 4-5% of manuscripts submitted. Payment: in copies and subscriptions. Copyrighted, reverts to author. Pub's reviews: 15 in 2009. §Feminist criticism, reviews of books & films by women, autobiographies, literary or art books by woman. Ads: $550/$285/$150 1/4 page/75¢ classified. Subjects: Fiction, Literature (General), Poetry, Women.

Camel Press (see also DUST (From the Ego Trip)), James Hedges, Editor, Box 212, Needmore, PA 17238, 717-573-4526. 1984. Poetry, fiction, articles, non-fiction. "Autobiography, 1,000-2,500 words." avg. press run 700. Pub'd 1 title 2009; expects 1 title 2010, 1 title 2011. 11 titles listed in the *Small Press Record of Books in Print* (36th Edition, 2010-11). Discounts: on request. 20pp. Reporting time: 2 weeks. Simultaneous submissions accepted: yes. Publishes 5% of manuscripts submitted. Payment: 50 free copies, page charges may be requested from author. Copyrights for author. Subjects: Biography, History, Public Affairs.

Camino Bay Books, Ann Adams, 331 Old Blanco Road, Kendalia, TX 78027-1901, 830-336-3636, 800-463-8181. 1997. Non-fiction. avg. press run 5M. Expects 1-2 titles 2010, 1-2 titles 2011. 1 title listed in the *Small Press Record of Books in Print* (36th Edition, 2010-11). Discounts: 1-4 books 20%, 5-99 40%, 100+ 50%. 250pp. Reporting time: 6 weeks. Payment: negotiable. Does not copyright for author. Subjects: Animals, Earth, Natural History, Philosophy.

Camp Colton, Kathleen Lundstrom, 30000 S Camp Colton Dr., Colton, OR 97017, 503-824-2267. 1983. Art, concrete art, non-fiction. "So far only in house, will consider outside material; glass art subjects." avg. press run 15M. 3 titles listed in the *Small Press Record of Books in Print* (36th Edition, 2010-11). Discounts: 33% booksellers, 50% distributors. 140pp. Reporting time: 1-2 months. Payment: negotiable. Copyrights for author. Subjects: Arts, Avant-Garde, Experimental Art, Crafts, Hobbies, How-To.

Canadian Committee on Labour History (see also LABOUR/LE TRAVAIL), Bryan D. Palmer, Athabasca University Press, Peace Hills Trust Tower, 1200, 10011 - 109 Street, Edmonton, AB T5J 3S8, Canada, 709-737-2144. 1971. Non-fiction. "Recent contributors: Jeremy Milloy, Sean Tucker, Brian Thorn, Greg Patmore, Donica Belisle, Carmela Patrias, and Todd McCallum." avg. press run 750. Pub'd 1 title 2009; expects 1 title 2010, 1 title 2011. 12 titles listed in the *Small Press Record of Books in Print* (36th Edition, 2010-11). Discounts: 20% on orders over 5. 300-450pp. Reporting time: 6 months. Simultaneous submissions accepted: no. Publishes 25% of manuscripts submitted. Payment: variable. Copyrights for author. Subjects: History, Labor.

Canadian Educators' Press, S. Deonarine, 100 City Centre Drive, PO Box 2094, Mississauga, ON L5B 3C6,

Canada, 905-826-0578. 1995. Non-fiction. "E-mail: cepress@sympatico.ca." avg. press run 800. Pub'd 2 titles 2009; expects 5 titles 2010, 5 titles 2011. 9 titles listed in the *Small Press Record of Books in Print* (36th Edition, 2010-11). Discounts: depends on quantity. 250pp. Reporting time: 3 months. Simultaneous submissions accepted: no. Payment: 10% net sale. Copyrights for author. Subjects: Canada, Education, Management, Sociology, Textbooks, Textbooks.

CANADIAN JOURNAL OF COMMUNICATION, Kim Sawchuk, Editor; Richard K. Smith, Publisher, Canadian Centre for Studies in Publishing, Simon Fraser Univ., 515 West Hastings St., Vancouver BC V6B 5K3, Canada, (778) 782-5116. 1974. Articles, reviews. "3M words on communication and mass media." circ. 400 (plus online). 4/yr. Pub'd 4 issues 2009; expects 4 issues 2010. sub. price Individuals: print and online $60Can, $60US; online only $30Can, $30US; Institutions: print $140Can, $140US; online $100Can, $100US; print and online $160Can, $160US; per copy $30; sample $20. Back issues: $25. Discounts: none. 180pp. Reporting time: 3 months. Simultaneous submissions accepted: no. Publishes 35% of manuscripts submitted. Payment: none. Exclusive one-year licence to journal, perpetual non-exclusive all media licence. Pub's reviews: 40 in 2009. §All areas of communication. Ads: write for information. Subjects: Canada, Communication, Journalism.

CANADIAN JOURNAL OF COMMUNICATION, CCSP Press, Roberto Dosil, Simon Fraser University, 515 West Hastings Street, Vancouver, British Columbia V6B 5K3, Canada, T.778-782-5243, F.778-782-5239, ccsp-info@sfu.ca, www.ccsppress.com.

CANADIAN JOURNAL OF COUNSELLING, University of Calgary Press, Vivian Lalande, Editor, University of Calgary Press, 2500 University Drive NW, Calgary, AB T2N 1N4, Canada, 613-237-1099, toll-free 877-765-5565, Fax 613-237-9786, info@ccacc.ca, www.ccacc.ca/. 1967. Non-fiction. "*The Canadian Journal of Counselling* is a refereed, bilingual journal published quarterly for the Canadian Counselling Association. Published articles are of interest to counsellor educators as well as to practitioners working in private practice or in schools, community agencies, university and college counselling centres, and other institutions in which counselling psychology is practiced. Article topics include research reports, conceptual papers, innovative practices, professional issues commentaries, and critical summaries of research." circ. 2,350. 4/yr. Pub'd 4 issues 2009; expects 4 issues 2010, 4 issues 2011. sub. price $50 CAD individual Canadian nonmembers, $50 USD individual international nonmembers, $85 CAD Canadian institutions, $85 USD international institutions; per copy $15. 100pp. Pub's reviews. Ads: contact association for details.

CANADIAN JOURNAL OF LATIN AMERICAN AND CARIBBEAN STUDIES/Revue canadienne des etudes latino-americaines et caraibes, University of Calgary Press, V. Armony, Editor, CALACS, CCASLS SB-115, Concordia University, 1455 de Maisonneuve Ouest, Montreal, QC H3G 1M8, Canada, calacs@concordia.ca. 1976. Articles, reviews. "*The Canadian Journal of Latin American and Caribbean Studies* is published for the Canadian Assn. for Latin American and Caribbean Studies. *CJLACS* is a multidisciplinary, refereed journal. Articles are accepted in four languages - English, French, Spanish, and Portuguese." circ. 400. 2/yr. Pub'd 2 issues 2009; expects 2 issues 2010, 2 issues 2011. sub. price $40 individual, $23 student, $60 institutions. 150pp. Publishes 25% of manuscripts submitted. Payment: none. Copyrighted, does not revert to author. Pub's reviews: 9 in 2009. §All fields of scholarly Latin American and Caribbean studies. Ads: write for details. Subjects: Caribbean, Latin America.

CANADIAN JOURNAL OF PHILOSOPHY, University of Calgary Press, M. Stingl, Administrative Editor, University of Calgary Press, Univ. of Calgary, 2500 University Dr. N.W., Calgary, Alberta T2N 1N4, Canada, 403-220-3514, Fax 403-282-0085, ucpmail@ucalgary.ca. 1971. Articles, reviews. "Publishes philosophical work of high quality in any field of philosophy." circ. 900. 5/yr. Pub'd 5 issues 2009; expects 5 issues 2010, 5 issues 2011. sub. price $25 indiv., $50 instit., $15 student, add GST in Canada; outside Canada, prices in US dollars; per copy $9. Back issues: back volume of 4 issues $30. 150pp. Reporting time: 2 months. Payment: none. Copyrighted, does not revert to author. Pub's reviews: 4 in 2009. §Philosophy. Ads: write for info. Subject: Philosophy.

CANADIAN JOURNAL OF PROGRAM EVALUATION, University of Calgary Press, B. Cousins, Editor, Canadian Evaluation Society, 1485 Laperriere Avenue, Ottawa, ON K1Z 7S8, Canada, 613-725-2526, Fax 613-729-6206, ces@thewillowgroup.com. 1986. Articles, criticism, reviews. "Publishes all aspects of the theory and practice of evaluation including research and practice notes." circ. 1.8M. 2/yr plus occasional special issue. Pub'd 3 issues 2009; expects 2 issues 2010, 3 issues 2011. sub. price Indiv. $110 Canada; outside Canada price in U.S. dollars; libraries $145 Canada, outside Canada price in US dollars, $40 full time students, seniors (60+) $57.50; GST included; per copy $11 + G.S.T. Canada. 150pp. Reporting time: 2 months. Payment: none. Copyrighted, does not revert to author. Pub's reviews: 6 in 2009. §Evaluation of programs in all fields. Ads: write for info. Subject: Public Affairs.

Canadian Library Association (see also FELICITER), Judy Green, Editor, 1150 Morrison Drive, Suite 400, Ottawa, Ontario K2H 8S9, Canada, 613-232-9625 X322, fax: 613-563-9895, www.cla.ca. 1946. Non-fiction.

avg. press run 3200. Expects 2 titles 2010, 2 titles 2011. 7 titles listed in the *Small Press Record of Books in Print* (36th Edition, 2010-11). Discounts: bulk only. 56pp. Reporting time: 6 months. Simultaneous submissions accepted: no. Publishes 75% of manuscripts submitted. Payment: 10%. Copyright varies. Subject: Libraries.

CANADIAN LITERATURE, E.M. Kroller, University of British Columbia, Buchanan E158, 1866 Main Mall, Vancouver, B.C. V6T 1Z1, Canada, 604-822-2780, fax 604-822-5504. 1959. Poetry, criticism, reviews. "Criticism and reviews focus primarily on Canadian writers. All publication press releases can be sent to cl.reviews@ubc.ca." circ. 1.5M. 4/yr. Pub'd 3 issues 2009; expects 4 issues 2010, 4 issues 2011. sub. price indiv. $45, institution $60 plus $20 postage (outside Canada); per copy $15; sample $15-25. Back issues: may be obtained from Journal. Discounts: $2 for agencies. 192-208pp. Reporting time: 3 months. Publishes 10% of manuscripts submitted. Payment: none. Copyrighted, copyright remains with journal. Pub's reviews: 100-120 in 2009. §Canadian writers and writing. Ads: $300/$400/$250. Subjects: Canada, Criticism, Literary Review, Poetry.

CANADIAN MONEYSAVER, Dale L. Ennis, Box 370, 5540 Bath Road, Bath, Ontario K0H 1G0, Canada, www.canadianmoneysaver.ca, moneyinfo@canadianmoneysaver.ca. 1981. Articles, interviews, non-fiction. circ. 32.8M. 9/yr. Pub'd 10 issues 2009; expects 9 issues 2010, 9 issues 2011. sub. price Canada $24.95, Elsewhere $75, online $24.95; per copy $3.95; sample $3.95. Back issues: $3.95. Discounts: up to 50% off for large orders (100+). 44pp. Reporting time: 3 weeks. Publishes 95% of manuscripts submitted. Payment: negotiable. Copyrighted, reverts to author. Pub's reviews: 25-30 in 2009. §Finance, money management, investment, consumer savings, tax planning, financial and retirement planning. Ads: 6,000/4,000. Subjects: Business & Economics, Consumer, Finances, Real Estate, Self-Help, Taxes.

CANADIAN POETRY, D.M.R. Bentley, Editor, Department of English, University of Western Ontario, London, Ontario N6A 3K7, Canada, 519 661 2111 x85834. 1977. Articles, criticism, reviews. "*Canadian Poetry: Studies, Documents, Reviews* is a refereed journal devoted to the study of poetry from all periods in Canada. It is published twice yearly, in the Spring/Summer and Fall/Winter." circ. 400. Twice a year. Pub'd 2 issues 2009; expects 2 issues 2010, 2 issues 2011. sub. price $15 (individual), $18 (institutional); per copy $10; sample $10. Back issues: $10. 120pp. Reporting time: 4 to 6 weeks. Simultaneous submissions accepted: No. Publishes 30% of manuscripts submitted. Pub's reviews: 7 in 2009. §Scholarly and critical works about Canadian poetry. Ads: Exchange only. Subjects: Arts, Avant-Garde, Experimental Art, Bibliography, Canada, Editing, English, Gender Issues, Language, Nature, Poetry, Research, Writers/Writing.

Canadian Poetry Press, Department of English, University of Western Ontario, London, Ontario N6A 3K7, Canada. "The Canadian Poetry Press was founded in 1986 for the purposes of publishing scholarly editions of early Canadian long poems. Since then the Press has expanded its mandate to include editions of the work of the Confederation poets and critical studies of Canadian poetry. The Canadian Poetry Press series of Editions of Early Canadian Long Poems now runs to some twenty scholarly editions of poems that were originally published between 1789 and 1900. The Press has also published John Strachans Poetry, a scholarly edition based on a manuscript in the Ontario Archives, Early Long Poems on Canada, and an anthology of poems selected from the Early Canadian Long Poems series. In 1994, the Canadian Poetry Press initiated Post-Confederation Poetry: Texts and Contexts, a series of scholarly editions and critical studies of late nineteenth- and early twentieth-century Canadian poetry that now includes several volumes and has several more in preparation." No titles listed in the *Small Press Record of Books in Print* (36th Edition, 2010-11).

CANADIAN WOMAN STUDIES/les cahiers de la femme, Luciana Ricciutelli, Editor-In-Chief, 210 Founders College, York Univ., 4700 Keele Street, Toronto, Ontario M3J 1P3, Canada, 416-736-5356, fax 416-736-5765, e-mail cwscf@yorku.ca. 1978. Poetry, fiction, articles, art, photos, cartoons, interviews, reviews, non-fiction. "We do not publish sexist, racist, homophobic, or any other discriminatory material. Length of articles: 10 typed, double-spaced pages." circ. 3M. 3/yr. Pub'd 4 issues 2009; expects 3 issues 2010, 3 issues 2011. sub. price *All prices in Canadian dollars Print only* $38 individual, $75 institutional; outside Canada add $20 *Print & E-subscription* $50 indiv., $95 instit.; outside Canada add $20 *E-subscriptions only* $33 indiv., $75 instit.; per copy $15; sample $5. Back issues: usually $5 per issue unless out of print. 156pp. Reporting time: 6 months. Simultaneous submissions accepted: no. Publishes 10% of manuscripts submitted. Payment: complimentary copy of issue in which work appears. Copyrighted, reverts to author. Pub's reviews: 45 in 2009. §Women's studies, women's issues, feminism, literary works and criticism. Ads: contact for rates. Subjects: Feminism, Women.

CANDELABRUM POETRY MAGAZINE, Red Candle Press, M.L. McCarthy, 1 Chatsworth Court, Outram Rd., Southsea PO5 1RA, England, tel: 02392 753696, rcp@poetry7.fsnet.co.uk, www.members.tri-pod.com/redcandlepress. 1970. Poetry. "CPM is a formalist poetry magazine, but good quality free verse is not excluded. Authors keep the copyright. We send the usual British copyright copies." circ. 1M. 2/yr. Pub'd 2 issues 2009; expects 2 issues 2010, 2 issues 2011. Subscription to Volume 12 (2005-7) £15: Us $30. US subscription in bills only, to avoid the bank charge; price per copy £3, US$6 in bills. 40pp. Reporting time: 1-2 months. Simultaneous submissions accepted: no. Payment: 1 free copy, no cash payment. Copyrighted, reverts to author. Ads: £20/£10 (US $40/$20 in bills) for A5 flysheet insertion. Subject: Poetry.

Candlestick Publishing, David Alter, PO Box 39241, San Antonio, TX 78218-1241. 1988. Non-fiction. Pub'd 2 titles 2009; expects 2 titles 2010, 1 title 2011. 14 titles listed in the *Small Press Record of Books in Print* (36th Edition, 2010-11). Discounts: library editions 30%, paperbacks 50%. Simultaneous submissions accepted: yes. Publishes 10% of manuscripts submitted. Subjects: Christianity, History, Human Rights, Libertarian.

THE CANNON'S MOUTH, Greg Cox, 22 Margaret Grove, Harborne, Birmingham B17 9JH, United Kingdom, [+44] 121 449 3866. Poetry, articles, art, photos, interviews, criticism, reviews, long-poems. "The Cannon's Mouth is the quarterly journal of the Cannon Poets who meet monthly at the the Post Office Building, Alcester Road, Moseley, Birmimgham, UK. We publish poetry submitted by members and non members. We welcome original material that we think our readership will enjoy, find useful, amusing and/or of interest. Regular contributors include John Alcock and Don Barnard [Poet Laureate of Birmingham (UK) 2004/05]. We regret that we are not usually able to pay for material published." circ. 1200. 4/yr. Pub'd 4 issues 2009; expects 4 issues 2010, 4 issues 2011. sub. price £10.50; per copy £3.00; sample free. Back issues: £3.00. Discounts: over 10 copies £2.50 per copy plus plus cost of delivery. 56pp. Reporting time: up to 3 months. Publishes 25% of manuscripts submitted. Payment: Usually nil. Copyrighted, reverts to author. Pub's reviews: approx. 10 in 2009. §Anything related to poetry. Ads: quarter A5 5/Half A5 10/Full A5 15/Double A5 25/ Back Cover 30. Subjects: Creativity, Criticism, England, English, Haiku, Humor, Inspirational, Poetry, Writers/Writing.

Canonymous Press, Daniel Smith, PO Box 1328, Chapel Hill, NC 27514-1328, e-mail press@canon-ymous.com, www.canonymous.com. 1992. avg. press run 100-400. Pub'd 3 titles 2009. 5 titles listed in the *Small Press Record of Books in Print* (36th Edition, 2010-11).

Cantadora Press (see also COGNITIO: A Graduate Humanities Journal), Russell James, 5406 Persimmon Hollow Rd., Milton, FL 32583-6700. 2002. Articles, non-fiction. "Publisher of masters theses, local history books, genealogy books related to Florida, military history books, and peer-reviewed English-language hardcopy academic humanities journals." avg. press run 100. Expects 6 titles 2010, 10 titles 2011. No titles listed in the *Small Press Record of Books in Print* (36th Edition, 2010-11). Discounts: 10% discount to distributors, agents, jobbers, bookstores, wholesalers, retailers. 50pp. Reporting time: 1 day. Simultaneous submissions accepted: No. Publishes 90% of manuscripts submitted. Payment: 15%. Copyrights for author. Subjects: African-American, The Americas, Bibliography, Catholic, Civil Rights, Classical Studies, English, Ethics, Florida, Genealogy, Military, Veterans, Native American, Non-Fiction, Philosophy, Political Science.

Cantarabooks LLC, Cantara Christopher, New York, NY 10003, 917.674.7560, editor@cantarabooks.com, www.cantarabooks.com. 2005. Poetry, fiction, satire, criticism, letters, plays, non-fiction. "Cantarabooks: n, pl. Playful-serious works of fiction, nonfiction and poetry that explore the dark and light of human relationships. Our authors for 2006: John Edward Gill, Michael Matheny, Vicki Miller, Jason Shamai, Stephen Gyllenhaal." avg. press run 500. Expects 3 titles 2010, 7 titles 2011. No titles listed in the *Small Press Record of Books in Print* (36th Edition, 2010-11). Discounts: 30-50% "Reading Group" discount in lots of 10 on selected titles. Includes reading guide and author Q&A. For 2006-2007: Inquire for Quality Time by Michael Matheny and Claptrap by Stephen Gyllenhaal. Reporting time: 2 months. Simultaneous submissions accepted: Yes. Publishes 2% of manuscripts submitted. Payment: 40% of net after production/distribution costs on third-party sales; 40% of retail on direct website sales of ebooks. Does not copyright for author. Subjects: Cities, Counter-Culture, Alternatives, Communes, Essays, Fiction, Gender Issues, Global Affairs, Humanism, Memoirs, Movies, Novels, Relationships, Short Stories, Theatre.

Canvas Press (see also COLLECTION), James Gapinski, N8 W31309 Concord Lane, Delafield, WI 53018. 2007. Poetry, fiction, art, photos, long-poems. "As an imprint of Beauty/Truth Press, Canvas Press primarily publishes ekphrastic poems (poems written in response to visual art). Canvas Press was founded as an outlet for projects which the editors have a vested interest; it is more hands-on and often operates outside of the normal submission channels. For this reason, most publications come from recommendations or past contributors to Beauty/Truth Press projects. Visit http://www.BeautyTruthPoetry.com for more information. Please query for further details on current and upcoming publication opportunities." avg. press run 75-100. Expects 4 titles 2010, 3 titles 2011. 1 title listed in the *Small Press Record of Books in Print* (36th Edition, 2010-11). Discounts: Contact for wholesale discount information. 12-24pp. Reporting time: 2 months. Simultaneous submissions accepted: No. Payment: Payment varies with each project. Subjects: Arts, Avant-Garde, Experimental Art, Experimental, Fiction, Literature (General), Poetry.

Capalo Press, Carone Sturm, 3705 Arctic PMB 2571, Anchorage, AK 99503, 907-322-7105. Non-fiction. "The kind of work we publish is mainly alternative, evidence-based treatments dealing with substance abuse. The editorial mission is to get this crucial research out to the public, who unfortunately, are largely unaware of most of their options. Some of our recent contributors our Roberta Jewell, author of My Way Out, and Melanie Solomon, author of AA-Not the Only Way; Your One Stop Resource Guide to 12-Step Alternatives." No titles listed in the *Small Press Record of Books in Print* (36th Edition, 2010-11). Subjects: Alcohol, Alcoholism,

Alternative Medicine, Hypnosis, Self-Help.

CAPCAT, K. Slater, 8 Karen Drive, Guelph, Ontario N1G 2N9, Canada, 519-824-7423. 1978. "Currently accepting only Canadian plays (i.e. plays written by a resident of Canada, or by a Canadian living abroad, or with significant recognisable Canadian setting, content, etc.) for the CAPCAT series. CAPCAT (Canadian Amateur Playwrights' Catalogue) is a collective arrangement in which all members pay a fee (up to $200 per play, depending on the length of play submitted) for guaranteed publication if literary, etc., standards are met. Arrangements can be made for payment to be waived for high-quality plays in selected cases." Pub'd 5 titles 2009; expects 5 titles 2010, 6 titles 2011. 58 titles listed in the *Small Press Record of Books in Print* (36th Edition, 2010-11). Discounts: 20% for libraries and multiple orders. 70pp. Reporting time: 1 month. Simultaneous submissions accepted: yes. Publishes members 80%, non-members 20% of manuscripts submitted. Payment: 10% sales, 50% performance. Copyrights for author. Subjects: Drama, Environment, Fiction, History, Humor, Mystery, Short Stories, Theatre.

THE CAPE ROCK, Harvey Hecht, English Dept, Southeast Missouri State Univ., Cape Girardeau, MO 63701, 314-651-2500. 1964. Poetry, photos. "Our criterion for selection is the quality of the work, not the bibliography of the author. We consider poems of almost any style on almost any subject and favor poems under 75 lines. Each submission should have the author's name and complete address, preferably in the upper right hand corner. A self-addressed, stamped envelope (SASE) is required to guarantee return. We do not read submissions April through August. We feature the work of a single photographer in each issue; submit 20-25 thematically organized 5 x 7 B & W glossies. Submissions, subscriptions, and queries should be addressed to *The Cape Rock*, Harvey Hecht, Editor." circ. 600. 2/yr. Pub'd 2 issues 2009; expects 2 issues 2010. sub. price $10; per copy $6; sample $4. Back issues: $5. Discounts: 25% off on orders of 20 or more (our cost plus postage). 64pp. Reporting time: 2-4 months. Payment: $100 for photography in each issue; other payment in copies. Copyrighted, rights to contents released to authors and artists upon request, subject only to their giving credit to *The Cape Rock* whenever and wherever else the work is placed. *The Cape Rock* retains reprint rights. No ads. Subjects: Photography, Poetry.

THE CAPILANO REVIEW, Sharon Thesen, Editor; Carol Hamshaw, Managing Editor, 2055 Purcell Way, North Vancouver, B.C. V7J 3H5, Canada, 604-984-1712. 1972. Poetry, fiction, art, photos, interviews, criticism, parts-of-novels, long-poems, collages, plays, concrete art. circ. 1M. 3/yr. Pub'd 3 issues 2009; expects 3 issues 2010, 3 issues 2011. sub. price $25; per copy $9; sample $9. Back issues: $7 for regular back issues, $10-20 for special issues. Discounts: 25% to bookstores. 120pp. Reporting time: 4 months. Simultaneous submissions accepted: no. Publishes 3% of manuscripts submitted. Payment: $50-200 maximum. Copyrighted, reverts to author. Ads: $150/$75/$50 1/3 page. Subjects: Arts, Avant-Garde, Experimental Art, Canada, Experimental, Literary Review, Poetry, Post Modern, Race, Translation, Visual Arts, Writers/Writing.

Carapace Books, Carapace Publishing Group, 1450 West Horizon Ridge Parkway, Suite B304 #278, Henderson, NV 89012. No titles listed in the *Small Press Record of Books in Print* (36th Edition, 2010-11).

THE CARETAKER GAZETTE, Thea K. Dunn, 3 Estancia Lane, Boerne, TX 78006, 830-755-2300, www.caretaker.org. 1983. Articles, photos, cartoons, interviews, reviews, letters, news items, non-fiction. "Articles about property caretaking, homesteading, estate management, RV living, caretaker profiles." circ. 12M. 6/yr. Pub'd 6 issues 2009; expects 6 issues 2010, 6 issues 2011. sub. price $34.95; per copy $6; sample $6. Back issues: $6. Discounts: none. 16pp. Reporting time: 1 month. Simultaneous submissions accepted: yes. Publishes 40% of manuscripts submitted. Payment: no. Copyrighted, reverts to author. Pub's reviews: 6 in 2009. §Conservation, environment, property caretaking, house sitting, RV living. Ads: 65¢ per word classifieds. Subjects: Agriculture, Employment, Environment.

Caribbean Books-Panama, Warren White A, Publisher; Frankie White Ann, Editor, Apdo. 0301-01249, Colon, Republic of Panama, +507-433-0349, http://www.caribbeanbookspub.com, publisher@caribbeanbooks-pub.com. 2003. Fiction, non-fiction. "Caribbean Books is looking for well written books in most genre. The well crafted story or non fiction is more important than the genre." Pub'd 2 titles 2009; expects 12 titles 2010, 24 titles 2011. No titles listed in the *Small Press Record of Books in Print* (36th Edition, 2010-11). Discounts: 30%. 300-400pp. Reporting time: 1week-1 month. Simultaneous submissions accepted: Yes. Payment: negotiable. Copyrights negotiable. Subjects: Current Affairs, Earth, Natural History, Fantasy, Fiction, Indigenous Cultures, Mystery, Myth, Mythology, Non-Fiction, Novels, Political Science, Politics, Religion, Science Fiction, Shipwrecks, Storytelling.

THE CARIBBEAN WRITER, Marvin Williams, University of the Virgin Islands, RR 1, Box 10,000, Kingshill, St. Croix, VI 00850, Phone: 340-692-4152, Fax: 340-692-4026, e-mail: qmars@uvi.edu, submit@thecaribbeanwriter.org, orders@thecaribbeanwriter.org, website: www.TheCaribbeanWriter.org. 1987. Poetry, fiction, interviews, reviews, parts-of-novels, plays, non-fiction. "*The Caribbean Writer* is an international literary anthology with a Caribbean focus. The Caribbean should be central to the work or the work should reflect a Caribbean heritage, experience or perspective." circ. 1.2M. 1/yr. Pub'd 1 issue 2009;

expects 1 issue 2010, 1 issue 2011. sub. price $25 + p/h (2 Year Individual), $40 + p/h (2 Year Institutional); per copy $15 + $5 p/h; sample $7 + $5 p/h. Back issues: same. Call for discount information. 304pp. Reporting time: authors of accepted mss are notified within 3 months. Simultaneous submissions accepted: yes. Publishes 20% of manuscripts submitted. Payment: 2 copies. Copyrighted, reverts to author. Pub's reviews: 30 in 2009. §Caribbean fiction, poetry, or related reference materials. Ads: $250 (Full Page) / $150 (Half Page) / $100 1/4 page. Subject: Caribbean.

Don Carmichael, Don Carmichael, P.O. Box 1602, Woodbridge, VA 22193, 7035779051. 2008. Expects 1 title 2010, 1 title 2011. No titles listed in the *Small Press Record of Books in Print* (36th Edition, 2010-11). Discounts: 2-10 copies 25%11-20 copies 30%greater than 20 copies 50%. 256pp. Payment: Net 30. Warriors of Peace, Devotions for the Daily Battles of Life.

Carnegie Mellon University Press, Sharon Dilworth, Carnegie Mellon University, English Department, Pittsburgh, PA 15213, 412-268-6446. No titles listed in the *Small Press Record of Books in Print* (36th Edition, 2010-11).

Carolina Academic Press, Keith Sipe; Bob Conrow, Acquisitions Editor; Taylor Arnold, Acquisitions Editor, 700 Kent Street, Durham, NC 27701, 919-489-7486, fax:919-493-5668. 1976. "Legal, medical, and scholarly titles." avg. press run 1.5M. Pub'd 28 titles 2009; expects 30 titles 2010. No titles listed in the *Small Press Record of Books in Print* (36th Edition, 2010-11). Discounts: sliding scale for retailers. 450pp. Reporting time: 6 months. Payment: various. Copyrights for author. Subject: Medicine.

THE CAROLINA QUARTERLY, Evan Gurney, General Editor, CB# 3520 Greenlaw Hall, Univ of N. Carolina, Chapel Hill, NC 27599-3520, 919-962-0244, Fax 919-962-3520. 1948. Poetry, fiction, art, photos, reviews, long-poems. "Looking for well-crafted poems and stories. We do not read during May-July. Wood Award ($500) is given to author of best short story or poem *The Carolina Quarterly* publishes each year. Only writers without major publications are eligible for Award." circ. 900. 3/yr. Pub'd 3 issues 2009; expects 3 issues 2010, 3 issues 2011. sub. price $21 indiv., $25 instit.; per copy $7; sample $7 (postage paid). Back issues: $5. Discounts: 20% local stores, agent 10%. 88-100pp. Reporting time: 4-6 months. Simultaneous submissions accepted: no. Publishes 1% of manuscripts submitted. Payment: 3 copies. Copyrighted, reverts to author. Pub's reviews: 8 in 2009. §Fiction, poetry, non-fiction. Ads: $80/$40. Subjects: Fiction, Literature (General), Poetry.

Carolina Wren Press, Andrea Selch, President; Tanya Olson, Vice President; Lesley Landis, Art Director, 120 Morris Street, Durham, NC 27701, 919-560-2738; www.carolinawrenpress.org. 1976. Poetry, fiction, letters, non-fiction. "Our goal is to publish high-quality, non-stereotyping literature for adults and children that is both intellectually and artistically challenging. Our publishing priorities are: works which are written by women and/or minorities, works which deal with issues of concern to those same groups, works which are innovative. We publish very few books (2-3) per year, so please check the website guidelines to see if our pipeline is open before sending a 20-pp sample. In even years (Fall 2010, 2012, 2014, etc) we accept entries in our contest for a 1st or 2nd book of poetry. In odd years, we accept entries for the Doris Bakwin Award for writing by a Woman (Fall 2011, 2013, etc). Always include an SASE." avg. press run 1000 copies. Pub'd 1 title 2009; expects 2 titles 2010, 1 title 2011. 27 titles listed in the *Small Press Record of Books in Print* (36th Edition, 2010-11). Discounts: 40% to bookstores after 5 copies, (1-4 20%). 150pp. Reporting time: 6 months for regular submissions; longer for contests. Simultaneous submissions are accepted; please indicate status and let us know immediately if your work is accepted elsewhere. Publishes .1% of manuscripts submitted. Payment: 5% of printrun. Prize money, for contests. Copyright may stay with author. Subjects: Asian-American, Black, Chicano/a, Children, Youth, Disease, Fiction, Gay, Lesbianism, Mental Health, Multicultural, Native American, Poetry, Prose, U.S. Hispanic, Women.

THE CAROUSEL, The Writer's Center, Abdul Ali, Managing Editor, 4508 Walsh Street, Bethesda, MD 20815-6006, 301-654-8664. 1976. Articles, art, cartoons, interviews, reviews, letters, news items. "We are a writer's journal featuring articles and forums on the practice of writing and the writing trade, book reviews, literary journal reviews and a list of markets." circ. 6M. 4/yr. Pub'd 6 issues 2009; expects 6 issues 2010, 6 issues 2011. sub. price $40. 24pp. Reporting time: 30 days. Simultaneous submissions accepted: no. Payment: copies. Copyrighted. Pub's reviews: 24 in 2009. §Books about writing, new poetry, fiction and drama. Ads: write for rate sheet. Subjects: Book Reviewing, Communication, Journalism, Creativity, Editing, English, Interviews, Publishing.

Carousel Press, Carole T. Meyers, Editor & Publisher; Gene Meyers, Sales Manager, PO Box 6038, Berkeley, CA 94706-0038, 510-527-5849, carous4659@aol.com, www.carousel-press.com. 1976. Non-fiction. "We are interested in general round-up travel guides, 200-300 pages." avg. press run 5-10M. Pub'd 1 title 2009; expects 1 title 2010, 1 title 2011. 3 titles listed in the *Small Press Record of Books in Print* (36th Edition, 2010-11). Discounts: trade, bulk, jobber 40% 5-12 books; 41% 13-24; 42% 25-49; 43% 50-99; library 10% prepaid; STOP orders 20% disc. + $3.50 shipping prepaid. 350pp. Reporting time: 4 weeks, include return postage; or via e-mail. Simultaneous submissions accepted: no. Publishes 1% of manuscripts submitted. Payment: royalties.

Copyrights for author. Subjects: California, Cities, Europe, Family, Games, Reprints, San Francisco.

CARVE MAGAZINE, Matthew Limpede, Editor, P.O. Box 701510, Dallas, TX 75370. "Carve seeks to publish outstanding literary fiction and to strengthen its ties in the literary community. Though online-literary magazines are not the "norm," we at Carve believe that with time and consistent publishing of quality work, we can attain the same level of reputation enjoyed by print magazines. In addition, Carve takes special pride in the editorial process. While we cannot send a unique response to every submission, we certainly try. We offer suggestions and critiques for the stories that we feel are needing that "extra push" toward publication, and we will soon have an extensive list of resources for both beginner and experienced writers. The magazine is named in honor of Raymond Carver, short story pioneer and a master of the "minimalist" form (though his later works espoused a longer, more detailed form.)." 1 title listed in the *Small Press Record of Books in Print* (36th Edition, 2010-11).

Casperian Books LLC, Kimberley Bernhardt, PO Box 161026, Sacramento, CA 95816-1026. 2006. Fiction. "Most types of fiction, with particular interest in contemporary realism, family saga, historical fiction (especially stories set in the ancient world), satire, science fiction, dystopian fiction, alternate histories, edgy urban fiction, ethnic/multicultural fiction, gay/lesbian fiction, gen x/noir, and books that have strong race/class/politics/religion/sexuality/gender themes. Not interested in children's picture books. Check website at www.casperianbooks.com for full submission guidelines." Pub'd 7 titles 2009; expects 8 titles 2010, 8 titles 2011. 16 titles listed in the *Small Press Record of Books in Print* (36th Edition, 2010-11). Reporting time: 2 weeks. Simultaneous submissions accepted: No. Publishes less than 10% of manuscripts submitted. Payment: 66% of net receipts. Does not copyright for author. Subjects: Fantasy, Fiction, Gay, History, Literature (General), Multicultural, Novels, Post Modern, Prose, Romance, Satire, Science Fiction.

Cassandra Press, Inc., Fred Rubenfeld, President, PO Box 228, Boulder, CO 80306, 303 444 2590. 1985. Non-fiction. "We publish New Age and metaphysical and political tyranny and holistic health books. I like to see the full manuscript before making a final decision, although this isn't necessarily true with an established author. We are now actively looking for new titles to expand next year. We are not accepting novels or children's books." avg. press run 8M-12M. Pub'd 3 titles 2009. 22 titles listed in the *Small Press Record of Books in Print* (36th Edition, 2010-11). Discounts: 40% to stores, 1-3 copies 20%. 150-230pp. Reporting time: 1-2 months. Payment: varies. Copyrights for author if asked. Subjects: Astrology, Birth, Birth Control, Population, Counter-Culture, Alternatives, Communes, Ecology, Foods, Health, How-To, Occult, Politics, Spiritual.

CATAMARAN SAILOR, Ram Press, Rick White, Mary Wells, PO Box 2060, Key Largo, FL 33037, 05-451-3287, Fax 305-453-0255, rick@catsailor.comt, www.catsailor.com. 1995. Articles, photos, cartoons, interviews, satire, criticism, reviews, letters, news items, non-fiction. "40-60 pages - newsprint." circ. 20M. 10/yr. Pub'd 10 issues 2009; expects 10 issues 2010, 10 issues 2011. sub. price $10; per copy $1; sample free. Back issues: $1. Discounts: none. 60pp. Reporting time: 60 days. Simultaneous submissions accepted: yes. Publishes 90% of manuscripts submitted. Payment: none. Copyrighted, reverts to author. Pub's reviews: 3 in 2009. §Catamaran, multihull sailing. Ads: $150$90/$75 1/3 page/$60 1/4 page/$25 business card/$10 classified. Subject: Sports, Outdoors.

Cattpigg Press, Cal Beauregard, Joedi Johnson, PO Box 565, Billings, MT 59103, 406-248-4875, e-mail starbase@mcn.net, website www.mcn.net/~starbase/dawn. 1994. Photos, non-fiction. avg. press run 1-2M. Pub'd 1 title 2009; expects 2 titles 2010, 1 title 2011. 1 title listed in the *Small Press Record of Books in Print* (36th Edition, 2010-11). 100pp. Reporting time: 3-5 weeks. Publishes 10% of manuscripts submitted. Copyrights for author. Subjects: Antiques, Collectibles, Crafts, Hobbies.

CAUSE & EFFECT MAGAZINE, Poptritus Press, Ben J. Biesek, PO Box 15329, San Luis Obispo, CA 93406-5329, (805) 748-3521. 2007. Poetry, fiction, articles, art, photos, interviews, satire, criticism, reviews, music, letters, parts-of-novels, collages, non-fiction. "Cause & Effect is a journal of art, pop & words, practicing noosphere perzine hijinks since 2007. C&E was published monthly in 2008 (January - August), and will switch to quarterly status for 2009. Interested in words and images that address contemporary society, at a time when reality is indelibly changing." circ. 50. 6/yr. Pub'd 2 issues 2009; expects 8 issues 2010, 4 issues 2011. sub. price $20.00; per copy $7.50; sample $4.50. Back issues: Inquire. Discounts: Up to 10 copies at 33%. 64pp. Reporting time: 2-8 weeks. Simultaneous submissions accepted: Yes. Publishes 12% of manuscripts submitted. Payment: Ranges from Non-Paying to Token to Semi-Pro to Professional. Copyrighted, reverts to author. §Art and words that address the human condition. Fiction, non-fiction/essay/prose, art, poetry, criticism, reviews. Ads: $100 full/$65 half/$40 third/$30 quarter. Subjects: Arts, Criticism, Culture, Current Affairs, Drugs, Fashion, Fiction, Futurism, Humor, Peace, Philosophy, Poetry, Reviews, Sex, Sexuality, Short Stories.

Cave Hollow Press, Rose Marie Kinder, Editor; Georgia Nagel, Editor; James Taylor, Editor; Gail Crump, Editor, P. O. Drawer J, Warrensburg, MO 64093, 660-441-2500. 2001. Fiction. "Cave Hollow Press was established to promote and publish great writing by authors in Missouri and the surrounding Midwest. They publish literary, genre, anthologies, and young adult fiction. Contributing authors have included Lucy S. Lauer, Kevin Prufer, Carolyn Mulford, Donn Irving, and Emily Spreng Lowry.'' avg. press run 1000. Pub'd 1 title 2009; expects 1 title 2010, 1 title 2011. 6 titles listed in the *Small Press Record of Books in Print* (36th Edition, 2010-11). Discounts: Cave Hollow Press uses the standard discounts for booksellers, retailers, wholesalers, and distributors. 150-300pp. Reporting time: 4 weeks to 3 months. Simultaneous submissions accepted: Yes. Payment: Royalty contracts are negotiable with the individual authors. Copyrights for author. Subjects: Adolescence, Culture, Entertainment, Midwest, Missouri, Mystery, Young Adult.

•**CAVE WALL,** Rhett Iseman Trull, Editor, Cave Wall Press LLC, PO Box 29546, Greensboro, NC 27429-9546. "Cave Wall, published twice a year, is a national literary magazine dedicated to publishing the best in contemporary poetry. We are interested in poems of any length and style from both established and emerging poets. Each issue includes black & white art, as well. Cave Wall reads unsolicited poetry submissions twice a year. Our fall open reading period is from September 1- 30, 2010 (postmark deadline). We do not accept email submissions.''

The Caxton Press, 312 Main Street, Caldwell, ID 83605, 208-459-7421. 1895. Non-fiction. "Books around 40,000 words up, unless largely photo.'' avg. press run 3M. Pub'd 5 titles 2009; expects 6 titles 2010, 6 titles 2011. 65 titles listed in the *Small Press Record of Books in Print* (36th Edition, 2010-11). Discounts: 1-24 40% 25+ 45%. 236pp. Reporting time: 60-90 days. Simultaneous submissions accepted: yes. Payment: 10% of list. Copyrights for author. Subjects: Americana, Non-Fiction.

CC. Marimbo, Randy Fingland, Peggy Golden, PO Box 933, Berkeley, CA 94701-0933. 1996. Poetry. "CC. Marimbo currently publishes unique books, often hand-made, in limited editions. The object is to publish/promote underpublished writers in an accessible and artistic format.'' avg. press run 26-150. Pub'd 1 title 2009; expects 2 titles 2010, 2 titles 2011. 56 titles listed in the *Small Press Record of Books in Print* (36th Edition, 2010-11). Discounts: 1 copy, no discount; 2-5 copies, 30%; 6 or more copies, 40%. Wholesale terms available upon request. 40pp. Reporting time: 4-6 weeks. Simultaneous submissions accepted as long as it's up front. Publishes 5% of manuscripts submitted. Payment: yes, generally 10% of cover price. Copyrights for author. Subject: Poetry.

CCSP Press (see also CANADIAN JOURNAL OF COMMUNICATION), Roberto Dosil, Simon Fraser University, 515 West Hastings Street, Vancouver, British Columbia V6B 5K3, Canada, T.778-782-5243, F.778-782-5239, ccsp-info@sfu.ca, www.ccsppress.com. 2005. avg. press run 5000. Pub'd 1 title 2009; expects 1 title 2010, 2 titles 2011. 3 titles listed in the *Small Press Record of Books in Print* (36th Edition, 2010-11). Discounts: Varies. Contact publisher directly. 240pp.

•**Cedar Creek Publishing,** Linda M. Layne, Publisher, PO Box 115, Bremo Bluff, VA 23022. "Cedar Creek Publishing is a Virginia publisher of books with a Virginia setting or theme by exceptional and regional award-winning authors and artists. Up to four books are published each year to reach readers from toddlers to senior citizens and to build on an appreciation of Virginia's culture and history.'' No titles listed in the *Small Press Record of Books in Print* (36th Edition, 2010-11).

Cedars Press, LLC, Penniann Schumann, PO Box 581470, Salt Lake City, UT 84158, tel:(801)631-7811; fax(801)363-2945. 2008. Fiction, non-fiction. "Children's Books.'' avg. press run 1000. Expects 1 title 2010, 1 title 2011. 1 title listed in the *Small Press Record of Books in Print* (36th Edition, 2010-11). Discounts: Distributors 60% discount - Bookstores and retailers 50% discount - Schools and libraries 20% discount. 48pp. Reporting time: 60 days. Simultaneous submissions accepted: yes. Publishes 1% of manuscripts submitted. Payment: negotiable. Does not copyright for author.

CELEBRATION, Prospect Press, William Sullivan, 2707 Lawina Road, Baltimore, MD 21216-1608, (410) 542-8785, e-mail wjspoet@jhu.edu. 1975. Poetry. circ. 100. 1/yr. Expects 1 issue 2010, 1 issue 2011. price per copy $3.00; sample $3.00. Back issues: $3.00. 25pp. Reporting time: About 3 months. Simultaneous submissions accepted: No. Publishes 5% of manuscripts submitted. Payment: One copy of the issue in which your work appears. Copyrighted. Subject: Poetry.

Celebrity Profiles Publishing, Richard Grudens, Madeline Grudens, PO Box 344, Stonybrook, NY 11790, 631-862-8555, Fax 631-862-0139, celebpro4@aol.com, rgrudens1@aol.com. 1995. Interviews, music, non-fiction. avg. press run 5M. Pub'd 1 title 2009; expects 2 titles 2010, 2 titles 2011. 8 titles listed in the *Small Press Record of Books in Print* (36th Edition, 2010-11). Discounts: 55%. 300pp. Reporting time: 3 months. Simultaneous submissions accepted: yes. Publishes 30% of manuscripts submitted. Payment: by agreement. Copyrights for author. Subjects: Biography, Collectibles, Entertainment, Interviews, Music.

CELLAR, CONTEMPORARY GHAZALS, R.W. Watkins, PO Box 111, Moreton's Harbour, NL A0G 3H0, Canada. 2003. Poetry, articles, art, photos, cartoons, interviews, criticism, reviews, letters, news items. "*Cellar* publishes essays and reviews focusing on novelist/playwright/screenwriter Laird Koenig, the early and/or darker films of Jodie Foster, and the point at which these two themes intersect: Koenig's 1974 novel/Foster's 1976 film

The Little Girl Who Lives Down The Lane (the life and work of director Nicolas Gessner may receive future exploration as well). Each issue also features poetry (especially haiku, sijo, and other Eastern forms) connected in some way to Foster and/or Koenig, based on *Down The Lane*, or related to said tale in theme and/or mood. Contributors, recent and forthcoming, include Jena Von Brucker, Rynn Jacobs, Robin Tilley, G.B. Jones, and R.W. Watkins.'' circ. 100+. 2/yr. Expects 1 issue 2010, 1 issue 2011. 3 titles listed in the *Small Press Record of Books in Print* (36th Edition, 2010-11). sub. price $6US outside Canada; per copy $3US outside Canada; sample same. 24pp. Reporting time: shortly after receipt. Simultaneous submissions accepted: yes, provided you inform us. Publishes 75% of manuscripts submitted. Payment: free copy. Not copyrighted. Pub's reviews. §Anything regarding Laird Koenig, Jodie Foster, Nicolas Gessner (director), and their artistic output, related poetry or fiction, suspense, etc. Subjects: Disney, Electronics, Fantasy, Haiku, Movies, Mystery, Poetry.

Celo Valley Books, Diana M. Donovan, 160 Ohle Road, Burnsville, NC 28714, 828-675-5918. 1989. Poetry, fiction, non-fiction. avg. press run 25-3M. Pub'd 3 titles 2009; expects 5 titles 2010, 5 titles 2011. 24 titles listed in the *Small Press Record of Books in Print* (36th Edition, 2010-11). 176pp. Reporting time: 1 month. Payment: All our titles are paid for by the author. Copyrights for author. Subjects: Autobiography, Biography, Dictionaries, Fiction, Inspirational, Non-Fiction, Non-Violence, Novels, Poetry, Psychology, Religion.

Celtic Heritage Books, PO Box 770637, Woodside, NY 11377-0637, Tel/Fax: 718-478-8162; Toll Free 1-877-215-7861. 1985. Non-fiction. ''Desired works are approximately 150 pages.'' Expects 1 title 2010, 1 title 2011. 3 titles listed in the *Small Press Record of Books in Print* (36th Edition, 2010-11). Discounts: 30%. 90pp. Reporting time: 3 weeks. Payment: varies with each contributing author. Copyrights for author. Subjects: Anthropology, Archaelogy, Celtic, Folklore, Gaelic, History, Ireland, Religion, Scotland.

•**CENTAUR MAGAZINE: The Online Literary Journal of Equine Inspiration,** Becky Erpf, Johnson City, TN 37604, becky@centaurlit.com, www.centaurlit.com. 2009. Poetry, fiction, art, photos, criticism, reviews, non-fiction. ''*Centaur Magazine* is interested in all forms of art inspired by the world of horses and the relationships between people and horses. We are interested in any interpretation of this theme, as long as the inspiration of the equine is present in the work. Centaur Magazine will be updated weekly with new work online, and release bound complitation issues twice a year.'' Reporting time: 2-3 weeks. Simultaneous submissions accepted: Yes. Payment: non-paying. Pub's reviews. §We are interested in any review concerning equine themed literature or poetry.

Centennial Press (see also ANTHILLS), Charles Nevsimal, Editor, PO Box 170322, Milwaukee, WI 53217-8026. No titles listed in the *Small Press Record of Books in Print* (36th Edition, 2010-11).

Center for Japanese Studies, Bruce E. Willoughby, Executive Editor, The University of Michigan, 1007 E. Huron St., Ann Arbor, MI 48104-1690, 734-647-8885, Fax 734-647-8886. 1947. Poetry, fiction, criticism, non-fiction. ''We publish scholarly monographs, symposia, bibliographic and reference aids, language aids, literature in translation, and poetry on and about Japan.'' avg. press run 500-1M. Pub'd 3 titles 2009; expects 6 titles 2010, 5 titles 2011. 73 titles listed in the *Small Press Record of Books in Print* (36th Edition, 2010-11). 250pp. Reporting time: 2-6 months. Simultaneous submissions accepted: no. Payment: varies with series and book. We hold copyright. Subjects: Anthropology, Archaelogy, Bibliography, Buddhism, Business & Economics, Criticism, Fiction, History, Japan, Language, Poetry, Reference, Religion, Reprints, Theatre, Translation.

Center for Literary Publishing (see also COLORADO REVIEW), Stephanie G'Schwind, Director & Editor, Colorado Review / Dept of English, 9105 Campus Delivery / Colorado State University, Fort Collins, CO 80523-9105, 970-491-5449, creview@colostate.edu, http://coloradoreview.colostate.edu. 1992. Poetry, long-poems. ''The Center for Literary Publishing publishes the Colorado Prize for Poetry book series, an annual contest for a book-length manuscript of poems. Poets interested in submitting should obtain complete guidelines at our website.'' avg. press run 750 to 1,000. Pub'd 1 title 2009; expects 1 title 2010, 1 title 2011. 16 titles listed in the *Small Press Record of Books in Print* (36th Edition, 2010-11). Discounts: Book orders should be directed to University of Oklahoma Press, our distributor, at 800-627-7377. Subscriptions to and sample issues of Colorado Review should be directed to the Center for Literary Publishing. 64-128pp. Simultaneous submissions accepted: Yes. Publishes 1% of manuscripts submitted. Payment: The Colorado Prize offers $1,500 honorarium against royalties. Copyrights for author. Subject: Poetry.

Center For Self-Sufficiency, A.C. Doyle, Founder, PO Box 416, Denver, CO 80201-0416, 305-575-5676. 1982. ''www.centerforselfsufficiency.org.'' avg. press run 2M. 6 titles listed in the *Small Press Record of Books in Print* (36th Edition, 2010-11). Discounts: 25% to libraries & bookstores. 60pp. Subjects: Business & Economics, Consumer, Crafts, Hobbies, Gardening, Homemaking, How-To, Newsletter, Reference, Tapes & Records, Vegetarianism.

Center for Thanatology Research & Education, Inc. (see also ADVANCES IN THANATOLOGY), Roberta Halporn, 391 Atlantic Ave., Brooklyn, NY 11217-1708, 718-858-3026, 718-852-1846, no 800, rhalporn@pipeline.com, thanatology.org. 1980. Poetry, art, photos, non-fiction. ''We arc book publishers as well as journal publishers. We have two separate lines: 1 on straight death & dying and 1 on gravestone studies. Oddly enough most people think they have nothing to do with each other. Our customers are more concerned with treatment of the terminally ill and funerals. As a bookseller of all publishers relating to this subject, I can tell you it has become a hot item. I produce a separate list (from our own publications) listing the books available from all publishers that are relevant. The list has grown from 2 sides of an 81/2 x 11 sheet, to 3 sides of an 81/2 x 14 sheet." avg. press run 800. Pub'd 2 titles 2009; expects 5 titles 2010. No titles listed in the *Small Press Record of Books in Print* (36th Edition, 2010-11). Discounts: 1-4=20%, 5up=40,90up=52. 80-200pp. Reporting time: 1-2 months. Simultaneous submissions accepted: Yes. Does not copyright for author. Subjects: African-American, Arts, Asian-American, Children, Youth, Education, Euthanasia, Death, Feminism, Folklore, Grieving, History, Nursing, Poetry, Psychology, Self-Help, Visual Arts.

The Center Press, Susan Artof, PO Box 6936, Thousand Oaks, CA 91361, 818-889-7071, Fax 818-889-7072. 1991. "Looking for clear writing and good concept. Electronic query ok. Will consider IBM-PC 5-3/4" disk on MSWORD or WordPerfect." avg. press run 3M. Pub'd 2 titles 2009; expects 3 titles 2010, 5 titles 2011. 15 titles listed in the *Small Press Record of Books in Print* (36th Edition, 2010-11). Discounts: 2-19 books 38%, 20 books 40%, 21-100 42%, up to 55% if over 4 case orders; average distributors 55%, payment 60 days. 176-224pp. Reporting time: 4-6 weeks. Publishes 10% of manuscripts submitted. Payment: to be arranged. Copyrights for author. Subjects: Children, Youth, Humor, Psychology, Satire, Sports, Outdoors, Travel, Writers/Writing.

CENTER: A Journal of the Literary Arts, 107 Tate Hall, University of Missouri, Columbia, MO 65211-1500, Phone: (573) 882-4971. 2000. Poetry, fiction, parts-of-novels, long-poems, plays, non-fiction. "Center publishes poetry, fiction, creative non-fiction, and, on occasion, translations. We do not accept literary criticism, book reviews, or children's writing. We publish work from a broad range of aesthetic categories and privilege work that is deliberately crafted, engaging, and accessible." circ. 500. 1/yr. Pub'd 1 issue 2009; expects 1 issue 2010, 1 issue 2011. sub. price $7 (individual); $10 (institutional); per copy $7; sample $7 (current issue); $3.50 (back issue). Back issues: $3.50. 150pp. Reporting time: 3-5 months. Simultaneous submissions accepted: yes. Publishes 20% of manuscripts submitted. Payment: 2 copies. Copyrighted, reverts to author. Ads: 1-2. Subjects: Fiction, Literary Review, Non-Fiction, Poetry.

Central Avenue Press, John Oelfke, Editor; Scott Oelfke, Editor, PO Box 2132-A, #144, Albuquerque, NM 87106, (505) 323-9953 www.centralavepress.com. 2001. Poetry, non-fiction. "Central Avenue Press is a small, independent press that publishes fiction, poetry, literary nonfiction and writing/reference. We publish two or three manuscripts each year. Current year titles: *Growing Great Characters* (Writing/Reference) Martha Engber, November 2006 *20 Things You Must Know to Write a Great Screenplay* (Writing/Reference) Rick Reichman, November 2006." avg. press run 2000. Pub'd 1 title 2009; expects 2 titles 2010, 2 titles 2011. 7 titles listed in the *Small Press Record of Books in Print* (36th Edition, 2010-11). Discounts: All titles distributed to the trade by Biblio and Quality Books / Web site sales - 10 or more copies 10%. 200pp. Reporting time: six months. Simultaneous submissions accepted: Yes. Publishes 5% of manuscripts submitted. Payment: Advance on first 1000 copies. Standard trade paperback royalty of 7-10% of cover price, payable semi-annually. Copyrights for author. Subjects: Anthology, Catholic, Fantasy, Fiction, Literature (General), Mystery, Non-Fiction, Novels, Poetry, Science, Science Fiction, Short Stories, Travel, Writers/Writing, Young Adult.

Ceres Press, David Goldbeck, Nikki Goldbeck, PO Box 87, Woodstock, NY 12498, tel/fax: 845-679-5573, web: www.HealthyHighways.com. 1977. "Unsolicited mss. cannot be returned unless S.A.S.E." avg. press run 5M. Pub'd 1 title 2009; expects 1 title 2010. 11 titles listed in the *Small Press Record of Books in Print* (36th Edition, 2010-11). Discounts: normal trade. Reporting time: 2 months. Payment: as agreed. Subjects: Birth, Birth Control, Population, Design, Environment.

CERISE PRESS, Fiona Sze-Lorrain, Editor; Karen Rigby, Editor; Sally Molini, Editor, P O Box 241187, Omaha, NE 68124, editors@cerisepress.com. 2009. Poetry, fiction, art, photos, interviews, reviews, non-fiction. "*Cerise Press* is an online, international journal of literature, arts & culture published three times per year. Each issue features poetry, fiction, non-fiction, translations, reviews, artwork photography, and interviews. We accept simultaneous submissions. Our debut issue includes Tess Gallagher, Eleanor Wilner,Ray Gonzalez, Laura Kasischke, Robert Kelly, and others. Cerise Press is also based in France: *Cerise Press* c/o Fiona Sze-Lorrain, 6 rue Guillaume Bertrand, 75011 Paris FRANCE." 3/yr. Expects 2 issues 2010, 3 issues 2011. Reporting time: 2-3 months. Simultaneous submissions accepted: Yes. Copyrighted, reverts to author. Pub's reviews. Subjects: Arts, Essays, Fiction, Photography, Poetry, Reviews, Translation.

Cervena Barva Press, Gloria Mindock, P. O. Box 440357, West Somerville, MA 02144-3222, editor@cervenabarvapress.com, http://www.cervenabarvapress.com. 2005. Poetry, fiction, interviews, long-poems, plays. "I look for work that has a strong voice, is unique, and takes risks with writing. I usually only solicit but am willing to look at 5 poems in the body of an e-mail. I am open to queries from writers around the world and encourage writers from Central and Eastern Europe to query January 1st-February 10th. One open poetry and fiction chapbook contests are held each year. My website interviews writers monthly by invitation only. The website is updated regularly and has information about the press, contests, workshops, and readings. I have a newsletter that I send out monthly. This is open for anyone to sign up for. I have published books by Rane Arroyo, Catherine Sasanov, CL Bledsoe, Glenn Sheldon, UK playwright Michael Nash, Martin Burke, Denis Emorine, Nancy Mitchell, Doug Holder, Flavia Cosma, Gary Fincke, Andrey Gritsman, Mark Pawlak, Pamela L. Laskin, Roger Sedarat, Mary Bonina, Linda Nemec Foster, Ioan Tepelea, Grzegorz Wroblewski, Susan Tepper and others.'' avg. press run 300-500. Pub'd 20 titles 2009; expects 30 titles 2010, 22 titles 2011. 59 titles listed in the *Small Press Record of Books in Print* (36th Edition, 2010-11). 24-80pp. Simultaneous submissions accepted: No. Payment: Author gets 30% royalty on full-length books, 10 copies, and review copies. Chapbook authors receive 25 copies. Copyrights full-length books only. Subjects: Avant-Garde, Experimental Art, Fiction, Poetry, Prose, Short Stories, Theatre.

CESSNA OWNER MAGAZINE, Aircraft Owners Group, Joe Jones, Publisher, PO Box 5000, Iola, WI 54945-5000, 715-445-5000; E-mail cessna@aircraftownergroup.com. Articles, photos, interviews. ''Aimed at owners and pilots of Cessna aircraft.'' circ. 6.3M. 12/yr. Pub'd 12 issues 2009; expects 12 issues 2010, 12 issues 2011. sub. price $49.95, includes membership in Cessna Owner Organization. 64pp. Reporting time: varies. Payment: 5¢/word and up, on publication. Copyrighted. Pub's reviews: 6 in 2009. §Aviation, pilot's skills and experiences. Ads: call for media kit. Subjects: Airplanes, Aviation.

CESUM MAGAZINE, Adam Moore, 102 Clapp St, Iowa City, IA 52245-3306, 319-210-0951, cesiummagazine@gmail.com, www.cesium-online.com. 2005. Fiction, articles, art, photos, cartoons, interviews, reviews, music, letters, collages, non-fiction. ''Our editorial mission statement is simple: art. media. culture. politics. We publish works with a hip vantage point, that are edgy and relevant to intelligent, plugged-in readers from 18-30. We emphasize giving unrepresented authors exposure, and especially love essays and non-fiction exploring various cultures and ideas.'' circ. 300. 4/yr. Pub'd 1 issue 2009; expects 4 issues 2010, 4 issues 2011. sub. price $18; per copy $4.95; sample $4.95. Back issues: inquire. 40pp. Reporting time: less than two weeks. Simultaneous submissions accepted: Yes. Publishes 50% of manuscripts submitted. Payment: 1 contributor copy. Copyrighted, reverts to author. Pub's reviews: none in 2009. §movies, music, artists, bands,. Ads: please contact us or see the website. Subjects: Americana, Anarchist, Arts, Fashion, Gay, Gender Issues, Government, Human Rights, Politics, Post Modern, Presidents, Prose, Religion, Reviews, Sex, Sexuality.

Chandler & Sharp Publishers, Inc., E. J. Barrett, 11 Commercial Blvd.Suite A, Novato, CA 94949, 415-883-2353, FAX 415-440-5004, www.chandlersharp.com. 1972. ''College-level books in the social sciences with particular emphasis on anthropology, sociology and political science.'' avg. press run 3-5M. Pub'd 3 titles 2009; expects 4 titles 2010, 6 titles 2011. 33 titles listed in the *Small Press Record of Books in Print* (36th Edition, 2010-11). Discounts: textbooks 20%. 300pp. Reporting time: 6-8 weeks. Simultaneous submissions accepted: yes. Payment: royalties. Copyrights for author on request. Subjects: Anthropology, Archaelogy, Asian-American, Cities, Culture, Government, Indigenous Cultures, Political Science, Politics, Public Affairs, Sociology, Textbooks, Women.

Channel Lake, Inc., Dirk Vanderwilt, Executive Editor, P.O. Box 1771, New York, NY 10156, Phone #347.329.5576, e-mail:info@channellake.com. 2005. Non-fiction. ''We publish travel guidebooks for America's most popular vacation destinations.'' Pub'd 4 titles 2009; expects 10 titles 2010, 10 titles 2011. 4 titles listed in the *Small Press Record of Books in Print* (36th Edition, 2010-11). Discounts: We offer 55% discount to any distributor or wholesaler with 1 copy minimum per order. 200pp. Simultaneous submissions accepted: Yes. Subjects: Americana, Travel.

CHANTEH, the Iranian Cross-Cultural Quarterly, Saideh Pakravan, 7229 Vistas Lane, McLean, VA 22101, saideh_pakravan@yahoo.com, www.saideh-pakravan.com. 1992. Poetry, fiction, articles, art, photos, cartoons, interviews, satire, criticism, music, letters, non-fiction. ''Going online starting January 1, 2003. No longer hard copy. Open to writers of all nationalities interested in the multicultural experience, in exile and adaptation to new environments. Any and all writing, including political. The only criteria are relevance and excellence in writing.'' Reporting time: 4 weeks. We accept simultaneous submissions when notified. Payment: 2 copies. Copyrighted, reverts to author. Pub's reviews: 12 in 2009. §The exile and multicultural experience, culture shock, travel, politics in the Middle East. Ads: $350/$175. Subjects: Arts, Essays, Fiction, Poetry, Religion.

CHAPMAN, Dr Joy M Hendry, Editor, Chapman Publishing Ltd., 4 Broughton Place, Edinburgh EH1 3RX, Scotland, 0131-557-2207. 1970. Poetry, fiction, articles, art, interviews, criticism, reviews, long-poems. ''Literary material, philosophical orientation, Scottish bias, but *not* exclusive. High standards.'' circ. 2000. 2/yr. Pub'd 3 issues 2009; expects 3 issues 2010, 3 issues 2011. 50 titles listed in the *Small Press Record of Books in Print* (36th Edition, 2010-11). sub. price £24 (£29 overseas, US$55); per copy £7.50 ($12) + £1.00p ($4) postage; sample £5.00 ($10) + 70p ($4) postage. Back issues: list available. Discounts: variable. 144pp. Reporting time: 2 months. Simultaneous submissions accepted: no. Publishes 1% of manuscripts submitted. Payment: small fee and/or copies of magazine. Copyrighted. Pub's reviews: 70 in 2009. §Literature (general), politics, culture. Ads: £100/ £50. Subjects: Essays, Fiction, Literary Review, Magazines, Non-Fiction, Poetry.

Chapultepec Press, David Garza, 4222 Chambers, Cincinnati, Ohio 45223, OH 45223, chapultepecpress@hotmail.com http://www.tokyoroserecords.com. No titles listed in the *Small Press Record of Books in Print* (36th Edition, 2010-11).

THE CHARIOTEER, Pella Publishing Co., Carmen Capri-Karka, 337 West 36 Street, New York, NY 10018, 212-279-9586. 1960. Poetry, fiction, articles, art, criticism, reviews, letters, plays. "Purpose: to bring to English-speaking readers information on, appreciation of, and translations from modern Greek literature, with criticism and reproductions of modern Greek art and sculpture." circ. 1M. 1/yr. Pub'd 1 issue 2009; expects 1 issue 2010, 1 issue 2011. sub. price $15 US indiv., $20 foreign indiv., $20 US instit., $25 foreign instit.; per copy $15; sample free. Back issues: $9-single; $15-double. Discounts: jobbers 20%, bookstores 20%. 160pp. Reporting time: 1 year. Payment: 20 offprints. Copyrighted, rights revert to author if requested. Pub's reviews: none in 2009. §Modern Greek Literature & Poetry. Ads: $125/$75/Outside Back Cover-$250/Inside Covers-$200. Subjects: Culture, Greek.

CHARITON REVIEW, James DAgostino, Editor, Truman State University Press, 100 East Normal Avenue, Kirksville, MO 63501, 800-916-6802. 1975. Poetry, fiction, art, photos, reviews. "We try to keep open minds, but admit a bias to work that relies more on strong imagery than talkiness. We are very interested in translation, particularly translations of modern poets and especially those from languages other than French or Spanish though we have used numerous translations from those two languages. Recent contributors include Barry Targan, Steve Heller, David Ray, Grace Bauer, Mark Spencer, Natasha Partenheimer, Hugh Fox, Richard Robbins, Gladys Swan, John Wenke, Carol Cosman, Lance Larsen, Leslie Norris, Red Shuttleworth, Denise Low, Kimberly Johnson, Donald Levering, Wendy Baker, Daniel Lusk, Ian Caws, J. V. Brummels, D. E. Steward, and translations of Belli, Koteski, Huchel, Paulovski, Sabines, Aleixandre, Elytis, Nick. No xerox or carbons or dot matrix." circ. 650+. 2/yr. Pub'd 2 issues 2009; expects 2 issues 2010. sub. price $20 one year (2 issues), $35 two years (4 issues); per copy $10; sample $10. Back issues: Vol. 1 #1 $500, Vol. 1 #2 $100, Vol. 2 #1 $100; Vol. 2 #2 $100; others $10 when available. Discounts: request considered. 108pp. Reporting time: 1 month or less. Simultaneous submissions accepted: no. Publishes 1% of manuscripts submitted. Payment: $5/page up to $50 for fiction when funds are available and 1 copy. Copyrighted, reverts to author. Pub's reviews: 1 in 2009. §Modern poetry, fiction, translation, mags. Ads: $200/$100. Subjects: Fiction, Literary Review, Poetry, Translation.

Deborah Charles Publications, B.S. Jackson, 173 Mather Avenue, Liverpool L18 6JZ, United Kingdom, phone 44-151-724-2500 from outside UK. 1986. Non-fiction. "Mainly legal theory. Legal semiotics monographs. Jewish Law." avg. press run 300. 14 titles listed in the *Small Press Record of Books in Print* (36th Edition, 2010-11). Discounts: 5% subscription agents, 25% bookshops. 300pp.

CHARLTON SPOTLIGHT, Argo Press, Michael E. Ambrose, PO Box 4201, Austin, TX 78765-4201, charspot01@austin.rr.com. 2000. Articles, art, photos, cartoons, interviews, criticism, reviews, letters, news items, non-fiction. "The magazine focuses on the history and creators of the Charlton Comics Group. Potential contributors should have deep knowledge of Golden Age, Silver Age, and Bronze Age comic books and of particular comics creators, like Steve Ditko, Pat Boyette, Tom Sutton, Dick Giordano, et al. We specialize in an "oral history" approach to the Charlton Comics story, featuring in every issue personal memoirs by the writers, editors, and artists who were there, along with detailed checklists and analytical commentary." circ. 1,800. Annual. Expects 1 issue 2010. price per copy $7.95 & $2.00 postage (US), $3.00 postage (Can.), $10.00 postage (foreign); sample Same as single copy price. Back issues: inquire. Discounts: inquire. 76pp. Reporting time: varies. We don't consider simultaneous submissions; almost all submissions are by special arrangement/solicitation. Publishes a variable % of manuscripts submitted. Payment: varies. Copyrighted, reverts to author. Pub's reviews: 20 in 2009. §Charlton Comics or associated comics-related pubs. Ads: inquire. Subject: Comics.

Chase Publishing, Anne C. Chase, PO Box 1200, Glen, NH 03838-1200, 603-383-4166, achase@chasepublishing.com, www.chasepublishing.com. 1991. Poetry, fiction, non-fiction. "Publishers of *Moments*, *Undertones*, and *The Head of the Bull* by Philip E. Duffy (short story collections), the *Cafe Chimes Cookbook* by Kathleen Etter (vegetarian cookery), and *The Litter of Leaving: Collected Poems* by E.M. Beekman (2003 release)." avg. press run 1-2M. Expects 1 title 2011. 5 titles listed in the *Small Press Record of Books in Print* (36th Edition, 2010-11). Discounts: trade 1-4 copies 25%, 5-99 40%. 175pp. Reporting time: 4 weeks. Simultaneous submissions accepted: no. Payment: determined separately for each book. Copyrights for author. Subjects: Fiction, Non-Fiction, Poetry.

CHASQUI, David William Foster, School of International Languages and Cultures, Arizona State University, Tempe, AZ 85287-0202, 480-965-3752, fax: 480-965-0135, web: www.public.asu.edu/~atdwf. 1971. Articles, interviews, criticism, reviews. circ. 700. 2/yr. Pub'd 2 issues 2009; expects 2 issues 2010, 2 issues 2011. sub. price $25. Discounts: none. 180pp. Reporting time: 3 months. Simultaneous submissions accepted: no. Publishes 30% of manuscripts submitted. Payment: none. Copyrighted, reverts to author. Pub's reviews: 65 in 2009. §Brazilian and Spanish American literature, literary criticism, theory, film, photography. Ads: none. Subjects: Latin America, Literary Review.

Chatoyant, PO Box 832, Aptos, CA 95003, 831-662-3047 phone/Fax, books@chatoyant.com, www.chatoyant.com. 1997. Poetry, art. "Chatoyant publishes a small number of books per year. We cannot accept any unsolicited material at this time. Unsolicited materials will not be returned." avg. press run 1M. Pub'd 1 title 2009; expects 1 title 2010, 1 title 2011. 5 titles listed in the *Small Press Record of Books in Print* (36th Edition, 2010-11). Discounts: please contact us. 80pp. Simultaneous submissions accepted: no. Publishes 0% of manuscripts submitted. Copyrights for author. Subjects: Arts, Poetry.

THE CHATTAHOOCHEE REVIEW, Marc Fitten, Editor; Jo Ann Yeager Adkins, Managing Editor, Georgia Perimeter College, 2101 Womack Road, Dunwoody, GA 30338-4497, 770-274-5145. 1980. Poetry, fiction, articles, art, photos, interviews, reviews, parts-of-novels, non-fiction. "We publish a number of Southern writers, but *CR* is not by design a regional magazine. We prefer fiction marked by a distinctive voice and powered by innovative language, not gimmicks, which invites the reader's imagination to work along side of well-wrought characters. Recent contributors: William Gay, George Singleton, and Ignacio Padilla. In poetry we look for vivid imagery, unique point of view and voice, freshness of figurative language, and attention to craft. Recent contributors: Robert Dana, Ron Rash, Wendy Bishop, A.E. Stallings, and George Szirtes. All themes, forms, and styles are considered as long as they impact the whole person: heart, mind, intuition, and imagination." circ. 1200. 4/yr. Pub'd 4 issues 2009; expects 4 issues 2010, 4 issues 2011. sub. price $20/yr or $30/2 yrs; per copy $6; sample $6. Back issues: $6. Discounts: 50% to retailers, free ads. 120pp. Reporting time: 3-4 months. Simultaneous submissions accepted: yes, with notification. Publishes 1% of manuscripts submitted. Payment: See Website for guidelines and payment: www.chattahoochee-review.org. Copyrighted, reverts to author. Pub's reviews: 10 in 2009. §Poetry, fiction, plays, creative nonfiction. Ads: $250. Subject: Literary Review.

Chatterley Press International, 19 Dorothy Street, Port Jefferson Station, NY 11776, 631-928-9074 phone/Fax, info@chatterleypress.com. 2000. Fiction. "www.chatterleypress.com." avg. press run 150. Pub'd 7 titles 2009; expects 7 titles 2010, 7 titles 2011. 2 titles listed in the *Small Press Record of Books in Print* (36th Edition, 2010-11). Discounts: 55%. 200-250pp. Reporting time: 6 months. Simultaneous submissions accepted: yes. Publishes less than 1% of manuscripts submitted. Payment: Copies. Does not copyright for author. Subjects: Emily Dickinson, English, Fiction, Journals, D.H. Lawrence, Literature (General), Anais Nin, Renaissance, Women.

THE CHAUCER REVIEW: A Journal of Medieval Studies and Literary Criticism, Pennsylvania State University Press, Susanna Fein, Co-Editor; David Raybin, Co-Editor, 820 North University Drive, University Support Building 1, Suite C, University Park, PA 16802. "Founded in 1966, The Chaucer Review is the journal of Chaucerian research. The Chaucer Review publishes studies of language, sources, social and political contexts, aesthetics, and associated meanings of Chaucer's poetry, as well as articles on medieval literature, philosophy, theology, and mythography relevant to study of the poet and his contemporaries, predecessors, and audiences. It acts as a forum for the presentation and discussion of research and concepts about Chaucer and the literature of the Middle Ages."

Chax Press, Charles Alexander, 101 W. Sixth St., Tucson, AZ 85701-1000, 520-620-1626, http://chax.org. 1984. Poetry, fiction, art, long-poems. "Innovative writing, primarily poetry. Basis in inheritors of avant-garde writing tradition from Gertrude Stein, Objectivists, Black Mountain Poets, New York School, and Language poets. Recent books or chapbooks by Kathleen Fraser, Bruce Andrews, Nathaniel Mackey, Kass Fleisher, Joe Amato, Gil Ott, Linda Russo, Elizabeth Treadwell, Charles Bernstein. Also publish limited edition fine arts literary books, often in experimental structural formats." avg. press run 500. Pub'd 6 titles 2009; expects 14 titles 2010, 6 titles 2011. No titles listed in the *Small Press Record of Books in Print* (36th Edition, 2010-11). Discounts: 1-2 copies 10% 3-5 copies 2055 or more copies 40% distributors inquire please. 100pp. Reporting time: 2 months. Simultaneous submissions accepted: No. Publishes 5% of manuscripts submitted. Payment: 8-10% royalties, usually paid in copies of books. Other arrangements sometimes possible. Copyrights for author. Subjects: Arizona, Arts, Asian-American, Avant-Garde, Experimental Art, Book Arts, Cosmology, Culture, Dada, Experimental, Feminism, Language, Poetry, Post Modern, Printing, Writers/Writing.

CHEAP SHOTS: Poetry Series, Six Ft. Swells Press, Todd Cirillo, 417 Neal Street, Grass Valley, CA 95945, 530-271-0662, sixfootswells@yahoo.com, www.myspace.com/sixftswells.

Chelsea Editions, Alfredo de Palchi, Editor-Publisher, Box 125 Cooper Station, New York, NY 10276-0125, 212-989-3083, fax:212-989-3083, e:chelseaeditions@aol.com, web:www.chelseaeditionsbooks.org. 2003. "We publish modern and contemporary italian poets in translation. Quality paperbacks, 6 X9. Copyrights for author and translator." avg. press run 300. Pub'd 2 titles 2009; expects 5 titles 2010, 4 titles 2011. No titles listed in the *Small Press Record of Books in Print* (36th Edition, 2010-11). Discounts: 40% to libraries, bookstores, agents; 25% to individuals. 250pp. Reporting time: two months. Payment: a fixed amount for the translator. Copyrights for author.

Chelsea Green Publishing Company, Margo Baldwin, Publisher, PO Box 428, White River Junction, VT

05001-0428, 802-295-6300. 1984. Non-fiction. "Emphasis on non-fiction: politics and practice of sustainable living. Core areas include renewable energy, green building, eco-cuisine, organic gardening." avg. press run 10,000. Pub'd 25 titles 2009; expects 27 titles 2010, 29 titles 2011. 42 titles listed in the *Small Press Record of Books in Print* (36th Edition, 2010-11). Discounts: under 5 35% prepaid, 5+ 45% returnable, 10+ 50% non-returnable. 200pp. Reporting time: 2-3 months. Payment: varies. Copyrights for author. Subjects: Animals, Biography, Birds, Conservation, Earth, Natural History, Ecology, Foods, Essays, Gardening, History, How-To, New England, New York, Non-Fiction, Politics, Society.

Cheops Books, Gary Bennett, Vice-President; Kay Bognar, President, 8746 E. Wallen Ridge Drive, Tucson, AZ 85710-6235, (520)232-2152, occultus@cox.net, www.cheopsbooks.org. 2007. Fiction. "When Cheops Books was originally founded in 1990, its purpose was to publish the best in historical and historical/mythological fiction—the sort of thing the big publishers are NOT publishing. In those days it published To Follow the Goddess, the story of the Trojan War from the point-of-view of Helen. When it was re-founded in 2007, it expanded to provide not only historical fiction but suspense fiction with an historical or supernatural twist. In the future Cheops Books will promote not only adult fiction but young adult fiction as well. (Definition of young adult fiction: ages 10-14, mostly for middle school girls.) In May of 2008 we are bringing out *The Black Stone* by Linda Cargill. It is an adult thriller about how a key co-conspirator escapes the Twin Towers and is ready to strike again." avg. press run 3000. Expects 1 title 2011. No titles listed in the *Small Press Record of Books in Print* (36th Edition, 2010-11). Discounts: 1 copy No discount 2-4 copies 20% 5-9 copies 30% 10-24 copies 40% 25-49 copies 42% 50-100 copies 45% 100-199 copies 48% 200 or more copies 50%. 120-500pp. Reporting time: 1 month. Simultaneous submissions accepted: Yes. Publishes 2% of manuscripts submitted. Payment: Advance: $200.00. Royalty: 25/75 split between author and publisher or author/agent and publisher. Pays royalties in April and October. Copyrights for author. Subjects: Fiction, History, Horror, Supernatural, Young Adult.

Cherry Valley Editions, Elizabeth Plymell, PO Box 303, Cherry Valley, NY 13320, cveds@cherryvalley.com. 1974. avg. press run 200. No titles listed in the *Small Press Record of Books in Print* (36th Edition, 2010-11). Discounts: 1 copy 15%; 2-4 copies 20%; 5+ 40%. 100pp. Reporting time: 1 month. Simultaneous submissions accepted: No. Publishes 1% of manuscripts submitted. Payment: varies per author. Copyrights for author. Subjects: Fiction, Philosophy, Poetry.

THE CHESAPEAKE READER: An Online Literary Journal. "*The Chesapeake Reader* is dedicated to publishing poetry, fiction, and nonfiction of the highest quality by both emerging and established writers. We have a special interest in the work of writers living in the Chesapeake Bay region and in literature that reflects the area's unique inspirations. Our mission is to publish our area's finest new literature and to provide an online publication for both readers and writers.Our current submission period is May 1, 2008 to July 31, 2008.Please send submissions as email attachments in Microsoft Word (.doc) or Rich Text format (.rtf) to submissions@chesapeakereader.com. Please place the author's name only in the subject line of the email and a list of the poem titles or the title of the prose piece along with your name and contact information in the body of the email. Do not include cover pages or any identifying information in the actual file. No more than five poems will be reviewed per author per year. No more than one prose piece should be submitted at a time, and no more than two prose pieces should be submitted per author per year."

Cheshire House Books, Attn: Joanna Rees, PO Box 2484, New York, NY 10021, 212-861-5404 phone/Fax, publisher@samthecat.com/www.samthecat.com. 5 titles listed in the *Small Press Record of Books in Print* (36th Edition, 2010-11).

CHICAGO REVIEW, V. Joshua Adams, Editor; Michael Hansen, Poetry Editor; P. Genesius Durica, Fiction Editor, 5801 South Kenwood, Chicago, IL 60637. 1946. "please read the magazine (buy a copy or visit your library) to see what *CR* publishes." circ. 2900. 4/yr. Pub'd 3 issues 2009; expects 3 issues 2010, 3 issues 2011. sub. price $22 individuals, $42 institutions (plus overseas postage—see website); per copy $10; sample $8. Back issues: yes, on inquiry; see website. Discounts: agency 15% subscription. 144pp. Reporting time: Three to five months. Check website. Simultaneous submissions accepted: Very strongly discouraged. Publishes 1% of manuscripts submitted. Payment: Three free copies plus year subscription. Copyrighted, rights revert to author only on request. Pub's reviews: 35 in 2009. §Literature. Ads: $150/$75. Subjects: Arts, Literary Review.

Chicago Review Press, Gerilee Hundt, Managing Editor, 814 North Franklin Street, Chicago, IL 60610, 312-337-0747. 1973. Art, interviews, non-fiction. avg. press run 5M-7.5M. Pub'd 25 titles 2009. No titles listed in the *Small Press Record of Books in Print* (36th Edition, 2010-11). Discounts: distributed by Independent Publishers Group. 200pp. Reporting time: 1-2 months (if submission includes SASE). Simultaneous submissions accepted: yes. Publishes 5% of manuscripts submitted. Payment: royalty 7.5%-10% of retail price is our standard. Copyrights for author. Subjects: Adoption, Arts, Chicago, Children, Youth, Cooking, Crafts, Hobbies, Gardening, How-To, Illinois, Midwest, Politics, Science, Sports, Outdoors.

Chicago Spectrum Press, Dorothy Kavka, Senior Editor, 4824 Brownsboro Center, Louisville, KY

40207-2342, 502-899-1919; Fax 502-896-0246; editor@evanstonpublishing.com; www.evanstonpublishing.com. 1986. avg. press run 2M. Pub'd 35 titles 2009; expects 30 titles 2010, 30 titles 2011. 11 titles listed in the *Small Press Record of Books in Print* (36th Edition, 2010-11). Discounts: 2-10 20%, 11-49 40%, 50+ 50%. 224pp. Reporting time: 1 month. Simultaneous submissions accepted: no. Publishes 10% of manuscripts submitted. Payment: standard small press agreement. Copyrights for author. Subjects: African Literature, Africa, African Studies, Biography, Book Collecting, Bookselling, Civil War, Cooking, Desktop Publishing, How-To, Judaism, Kentucky, Literature (General), Non-Fiction, Poetry, Printing, Self-Help, Textbooks.

Chicken Soup Press, Inc., Margaret S. Campilonga, PO Box 164, Circleville, NY 10919-0164, 845-692-6320, Fax 845-692-7574, poet@hvc.rr.com. 1995. avg. press run 2.5M. Pub'd 3 titles 2009; expects 2 titles 2010, 2 titles 2011. 10 titles listed in the *Small Press Record of Books in Print* (36th Edition, 2010-11). Discounts: industry standard. Young adult 160pp, children's 32pp. Simultaneous submissions accepted: no. Payment: 10%. Copyrights for author. Subjects: Children, Youth, Young Adult.

Chicory Blue Press, Inc., 795 East Street North, Goshen, CT 06756, 860-491-2271, Fax 860-491-8619. 1987. Poetry, fiction, art, interviews, letters, parts-of-novels, non-fiction. "Chicory Blue Press specializes in writing by women, with a current focus on women poets past 65." avg. press run 500-1M. Pub'd 1 title 2009; expects 1 title 2010. 17 titles listed in the *Small Press Record of Books in Print* (36th Edition, 2010-11). Discounts: 3-199 40%, 200-499 50%, 500+ 55%. Reporting time: 3-5 months. Simultaneous submissions accepted: yes. Publishes 2-3% of manuscripts submitted. Payment: negotiable. Copyrights for author. Subjects: Communication, Journalism, Feminism, Fiction, Memoirs, Poetry, Women.

The Chicot Press, Randall P. Whatley, Box 53198, Atlanta, GA 30355, 770-640-9918, Fax 770-640-9819, info@cypressmedia.net. 1978. Non-fiction. avg. press run 2M. No titles listed in the *Small Press Record of Books in Print* (36th Edition, 2010-11). Discounts: 1-4 copies 20%, 5-9 30%, 10-99 40%, 100-499 45%, 500+ 50%. 100pp. Reporting time: 60 days. Payment: percentage of profits. Copyrights for author. Subjects: Agriculture, Bilingual, Business & Economics, France, French, Gardening, How-To, Language, Louisiana.

A Child Called Poor, Ayasha Banks, P O Box 5716, Albany, GA 31706, 229-291-7556, 229-435-8224, ACHILDCALLEDPOOR.COM. 2003. Poetry, fiction, art, photos, reviews, music, parts-of-novels, long-poems, plays, non-fiction. avg. press run 1000. Expects 1 title 2010, 2 titles 2011. No titles listed in the *Small Press Record of Books in Print* (36th Edition, 2010-11). Discounts: 5-15 copies 10%16-24 copies 25%. 224pp. Copyrights for author.

Children Of Mary (see also FIDELIS ET VERUS), Jack Law, PO Box 350333, Ft. Lauderdale, FL 33335-0333, 954-583-5108 phone/fax, mascmen8@bellsouth.net, www.catholicbook.com. 1981. Non-fiction. "Orthodox Roman Catholic views reflected in commentary apparitions of Jesus and Mary in Bayside, NY (1970-85) are completely recorded in two volumes *Roses* and also published in *Fidelis et Verus*, a Catholic quarterly newspaper, $10/yr." avg. press run 2M (newspaper) and 15K for books. Pub'd 3 titles 2009; expects 4 titles 2010, 4 titles 2011. 2 titles listed in the *Small Press Record of Books in Print* (36th Edition, 2010-11). Discounts: 40% trade, bulk, classroom, agent, jobber, etc. 300pp. Reporting time: 3 months. Payment: voluntary. Does not copyright for author. Subjects: Birth, Birth Control, Population, Book Collecting, Bookselling, Book Reviewing, Christianity, Communism, Marxism, Leninism, Electronics, Government, Newspapers, Non-Fiction, Philosophy, Politics, Religion, Socialist, Spiritual, Textbooks.

CHILDREN, CHURCHES AND DADDIES, A Non Religious, Non Familial Literary Magazine, Scars Publications, Janet Kuypers, Attn: Janet Kuypers, 829 Brian Court, Gurnee, IL 60031-3155, ccandd96@scars.tv, http://scars.tv. 1993. Poetry, fiction, art, photos, letters, long-poems, non-fiction. "cc&d is a magazine for contemporary poetry, short prose/prose/stories, art and even essays for our philosophy sections. I'm a computer artist, and a feminist specializing in acquaintance rape education. Anything about pertinent issues will be given attention (including anything astronomy related, or anything political in nature). We don't want rhyme. Try under 5 pp per poem, under 10 for prose, but since email submissions are what we prefer, you can always send us submissions, and we can consider anything reasonable in length. No racist/sexist/homophobic material. Include editor's name on address on emvelope. SASE necessary. I primarily accept work on disk (Mac Preferred, but email submissions are preferred. Submit as many pieces as you like, but no originals. Select accepted pieces go into annual collection books (both paperback and hardcover), so if we choose your work for an annual collection book, we will notify you. cc&d also ran book, chapbook, and calender contests, and currently runs contests to appear in books. Contact cc&d for more information. Issues available in print (paid only), electronic format, and on the internet for free at the above address. Email contact is preferred and any information about cc&d magazine is only a click away at http://scars.tv." circ. varies. monthly (with chapbook supplements). Pub'd 12 issues 2009; expects 12 issues 2010, 12 issues 2011. 32 titles listed in the *Small Press Record of Books in Print* (36th Edition, 2010-11). price per copy $11.95 for 2010 issues (which can be purchased on line through links at http://scars.tv/ccd.htm), $6.00 for 2008-2009 issues; sample $14.00 for a book, $11.95 for 2010 issues (which can be purchased on line through links at http://scars.tv/ccd.htm), $6.00 for 2008-2009 issues. Back issues: $14.00 for a book, $11.95 for 2010 issues (which can be purchased on line through links at http://scars.tv/ccd.htm), $6.00 for 2008-2009 issues. Issues are 84 pages as perfect-bound books with full color full bleed covers. In collection books, *Children, Churches and Daddies* appears with *Down in the Dirt* acceptances into a collection book, which on average is 200-400 pages. Reporting time: I'll get back to you within two weeks if there is a SASE; otherwise, you'll never hear from us. Email submissions (unless we are out of town, usually get a response in a day or two. Simultaneous submissions accepted: yes. Publishes 40% of manuscripts submitted. Payment: none. The magazine logo is copyrighted, but the individual work of each author is always theirs. Ads: contact CC&D. Subjects: Arts, Chicago, Counter-Culture, Alternatives, Communes, Culture, Dada, Feminism, Fiction, Graphics, Journals, Literature (General), Magazines, Midwest, Photography, Poetry, Women.

CHIMERA, Sean MacBeth, 921 N. Frederic Street, Burbank, CA 91505, 818 846 8700.

China Books & Periodicals, Inc., Greg Jones, Editor, 360 Swift Ave., Suite #48, South San Francisco, CA 94080-6220, 800-818-2017 [tel], 650-872-7808 [fax], email: orders@chinabooks.com, website: www.china-books.com. 1960. Fiction, photos, non-fiction. "China Books publishes only books relating to China, including history, language, culture, children, art, music, and other topics. We are less interested in Chinese American topics, but will consider the right books for our market. Recent authors include Peter Uhlmann, Jeannette Faurot, Stefan Verstappen, Tony Gallagher, and Elizabeth Chiu King. We also distribute books for other publishers to bookstores around the world, have an active web site, and retail bookstore." avg. press run 3M-5M. Pub'd 5 titles 2009; expects 6 titles 2010, 10 titles 2011. 3 titles listed in the *Small Press Record of Books in Print* (36th Edition, 2010-11). Discounts: trade 1-4 20%, 5-50 40%, 51-100 42%, 101-250 43%. 250pp. Reporting time: 1-3 months. Simultaneous submissions accepted: yes. Publishes 3% of manuscripts submitted. Payment: negotiable. Copyrights for author. Subjects: Acupuncture, Agriculture, Antiques, Architecture, Arts, Asia, Indochina, Asian-American, Autobiography, Bilingual, Biography, Birth, Birth Control, Population, Buddhism, Business & Economics, Calligraphy, China.

CHINA REVIEW INTERNATIONAL, Roger T. Ames, Executive Editor; Daniel Tschudi, Managing Editor, Center for Chinese Studies, Univ of Hawaii, 1890 East-West Road, Rm. 417, Honolulu, HI 96822-2318, 808-956-8891, Fax 808-956-2682. 1994. Reviews. "For subscriptions, contact: University of Hawaii Press Journals Department, 2840 Kolowalu Street, Honolulu, HI 96822, telephone (808) 956-8833. Reviews are commissioned, generally; however, unsolicited reviews are occasionally accepted." circ. 500. 2/yr. Pub'd 2 issues 2009; expects 2 issues 2010, 2 issues 2011. sub. price $30 individuals, $50 institutions, $18 students; per copy $20. Discounts: for one-time orders: 20% on 10-19 copies, and 30% on 20 or more. 300pp. Reporting time: 1 month. Simultaneous submissions accepted: no. Payment: complimentary copy of book that is reviewed to reviewers and tearsheets of published review. Copyrighted, does not revert to author. Pub's reviews: 125 in 2009. §Any field in Chinese studies. Ads: $200/$125. Subject: China.

‡**CHINESE LITERATURE, Chinese Literature Press,** He Jingzhi, 24 Baiwanzhuang Road, Beijing 100037, People's Republic of China, 892554. 1951. circ. 50M. 4/yr. Pub'd 4 issues 2009; expects 4 issues 2010, 4 issues 2011. sub. price $10.50. 200pp. Copyrighted. Pub's reviews: 4 in 2009. §Chinese literature and art areas.

‡**Chinese Literature Press (see also CHINESE LITERATURE),** Tang Jialong, 24 Baiwanzhuang Road, Beijing 100037, People's Republic of China. 1951. avg. press run 50M. Pub'd 4 titles 2009; expects 4 titles 2010, 4 titles 2011. 110 titles listed in the *Small Press Record of Books in Print* (36th Edition, 2010-11). 200pp. Payment: in Chinese and foreign currency. Copyrights for author. Subjects: Asia, Indochina, Literature (General).

CHIRON REVIEW, Michael Hathaway, Publisher and Editor; Gerald Locklin, Contributing Editor (Poetry); Ray Zepeda, Contributing Editor (Fiction); John Brantingham, Contributing Editor (Fiction), Zachary (Poetry) Locklin, 522 E South Ave, St. John, KS 67576-2212, 620-786-4955, editor@chironreview.com, chironreview.com. 1982. Poetry, fiction, reviews. "Postal submissions are welcome with SASE. Complete postal address must appear on every poem. E-mail submissions will be welcome, IF poems are sent in ONE MS Word attachment and complete postal address accompanies every submission, every time. Visit our website for guidelines. We do not consider simultaneous submissions, or previously published work." circ. 1,000. Quarterly. Expects 4 issues 2010, 4 issues 2011. 9 titles listed in the *Small Press Record of Books in Print* (36th Edition, 2010-11). sub. price Ind. & inst.: $20 year/4 issues. Foreign/overseas: $32.; per copy $7.00 ($14.00 US funds, foreign/overseas).; sample $7.00 ($14 US funds foreign/overseas). Back issues: $7.00 ($14 US funds foreign/overseas). Discounts: 20%. 48pp. Reporting time: 2-8 weeks. Simultaneous submissions accepted: no. Publishes 10% of manuscripts submitted. Payment: 1 copy, discounts on additional copies. Copyrighted, reverts to author. Pub's reviews: 80 in 2009. §Poetry, short fiction, anything of interest to the small press literary community. Ads: SASE for rates. Subjects: Fiction, Gay, Non-Fiction, Poetry, Reviews, Short Stories.

Chistell Publishing, Rhonda Campbell, Executive Director, 2500 Knights Road, Suite 19-01, Bensalem, PA 19020-3429. 1998. Pub'd 4 titles 2009. 4 titles listed in the *Small Press Record of Books in Print* (36th Edition, 2010-11). 250pp. Reporting time: 1 week. Simultaneous submissions accepted: yes. Publishes 15% of manuscripts submitted.

Choice Point Editions, Kathleen Bauer, 7883 N. Pershing Ave., Stockton, CA 95207, 209-952-7108, 866-952-7108, FAX 209-951-3216, choicepointeditions.com, info@choicepointeditions.com. 2006. avg. press run 500. Pub'd 3 titles 2009; expects 5 titles 2010, 15 titles 2011. No titles listed in the *Small Press Record of Books in Print* (36th Edition, 2010-11). Discounts: colleges 25% retail 40%. 350pp.

CHRISTIAN*NEW AGE QUARTERLY, Catherine Groves, PO Box 276, Clifton, NJ 07015-0276, www.christiannewage.com, info@christiannewage.com. 1989. Articles, art, cartoons, reviews, letters, non-fiction. *"Christian*New Age Quarterly* is a lively forum exploring the similarities and distinctions between Christianity and the New Age movement. Essentially a vehicle for communication—to draw the two ideological groups into genuine dialogue—articles must quickly cut through superficial divisions to explore the substance of our unity and differences. Pertinent controversy is fine. Garbage thinking (ie., 'I'm right - you're wrong') makes the editor frown. Submissions should sparkle with both insight and creativity. Article lengths vary from 400 to 1500 words (longer pieces accepted if excellent). Guidelines available, for more info see website. New for 2010: our *C*NAQ Plus* supplements are going strong! In addition to the 2 "full" issues we plan for 2010, we will be publishing 2 supplements, dubbed *C*NAQ Plus*. Still, a $12.50 (US) subscription continues to include 4 "full" issues. To learn more, please visit our website." 4/yr. Pub'd 4 issues 2009; expects 4 issues 2010, 4 issues 2011. sub. price $12.50 USA/$18.50 outside USA; per copy $3.50 USA/$5.00 outside USA; sample $3.50 USA/$5.00 outside USA. Back issues: $3.50 USA/$5.00 outside USA. Discounts: prepaid orders only; on 5 or more copies, 30%. Averages 20pp. Reporting time: 6 weeks (and we always respond, if SASE enclosed). Simultaneous submissions accepted: no. Publishes 20% of manuscripts submitted. Payment: in subscription or copies (depending on nature of article). Copyrighted, reverts to author. Pub's reviews: 2 in 2009. §Books which address both Christian and New Age issues. Before sending review copies, write for reviewer's address or see "A Message to Book Publishers" on website. Ads: $45/$35/$25 1/4 page/$15 1/6 page/cheap classifieds! Subjects: Christianity, New Age, Religion, Spiritual.

CHRYSALIS READER, Carol S. Lawson, Editor, Box 4510, Route 1, Dillwyn, VA 23936, 1-434-983-3021. 1985. Poetry, fiction, non-fiction. "The Chrysalis Reader is an annual anthology of original, never-before-published poetry, short stories, and essays based on a spiritual theme. Contact the editor for a list of upcoming themes: chrysalis@hovac.com." circ. 1,000 copies per year. Pub'd 1 issue 2009; expects 1 issue 2010, 1 issue 2011. 192pp. Publishes 20% of manuscripts submitted. Payment: $25 for poetry; $100—$150 for short story or essay. Copyright belongs to Chrysalis Reader.

CHRYSANTHEMUM, Goldfish Press, Koon Woon, 2012 18th Ave. South, Seattle, WA 98144-4324, 206-329-5566, nooknoow@aol.com. 1990. Poetry. *"Chrysanthemum* is a forum for all persuasions of the world community to communicate in a friendly manner through the art of poetry.We are not interested in academic exercises needing another publication credit. Rather, we are interested in poets who have mulled long and hard about things. We provide shelter to ordinary folks who also happen to love poetry,who are human first and "poet" second. We seek a multicultural mix and minorities of all types. Some recent contributors are Betty Priebe, Marjorie Pepper, Bob Holman, Norm Davis, Jim Cohn, Jack Foley, Mary-Marcia Casoly,changming(Michael) Yuan, and Cathy Ruiz." circ. 750. 2/yr. Pub'd 2 issues 2009; expects 2 issues 2010, 2 issues 2011. sub. price $20; per copy $10; sample $4, xerox. Back issues: none. Discounts: none. 120pp. Reporting time: 2 weeks. Simultaneous submissions accepted: no. Publishes 2% of manuscripts submitted. Payment: 1 copy. Copyrighted, reverts to author. Subject: Poetry.

Church Leadership Library (Canadian Office), Elizabeth McKitrick, 2 - 7201 72nd Street, Delta, British Columbia V4G 1M5, Canada, Phone: 604-952-0050, Fax: 604-952-4650, contact@outreach.ca, www.church-leadershiplibrary.org. 1990. Non-fiction. "Specializes in Christian ministry and church leadership training resources (books, manuals) and tools (videos, DVDs)." avg. press run 2500. Pub'd 3 titles 2009; expects 2 titles 2010, 2 titles 2011. 6 titles listed in the *Small Press Record of Books in Print* (36th Edition, 2010-11). Discounts: 5-10 copies 25%; 10+ copies 40%; bookstores, colleges 40%. 450pp. Reporting time: Manuscript responses: 2 weeks. Simultaneous submissions accepted: Yes. Does not copyright for author. Subjects: Christianity, Community, Inspirational, Leadership, Management, Mentoring/Coaching, Multicultural, Networking, Non-Fiction, Post Modern, Religion, Research, Spiritual, Textbooks.

Church Leadership Library (US Office), Elizabeth McKitrick, PO Box 1477, Point Roberts, WA 98281, 604-952-0050, 604-952-4650, admin@churchleadershiplibrary.org, www.churchleadershiplibrary.org. 1990. Non-fiction. "Specializes in Christian ministry and church leadership training resources (books, manuals) and tools (videos, DVDs). Publications - Nation Series: Reclaiming A Nation, Transforming Our Nation, Discipling Our Nation; Vision Renewal (manual); Starting Outward-Focused Churches (DVD Lecture Series); ChurchMap (CD-Rom Mapping Tool)." avg. press run 2500. Pub'd 3 titles 2009; expects 2 titles 2010, 2 titles 2011. 2 titles listed in the *Small Press Record of Books in Print* (36th Edition, 2010-11). Discounts: Bookstores, Colleges 40%; 5-10 Copies 30%; 10+ copies 40%. 400pp. Reporting time: 2 weeks. Simultaneous submissions accepted: Yes. Does not copyright for author. Subjects: Christianity, Community, Education, Guidance, How-To,

Leadership, Mentoring/Coaching, Multicultural, Non-Fiction, Post Modern, Relationships, Religion, Research, Spiritual, Textbooks.

•**Cider Press Review, A Journal of Contemporary Poetry,** 777 Braddock Lane, Halifax, PA 17032. *"Cider Press Review*, a journal of contemporary poetry, seeks to discover and publish the best of new poetry written in English. CPR actively seeks new original work and translations into English from both established and emerging poets. Our only criterion is excellence. Please review our complete submission guidelines before sending work. Authors are encouraged to use our online Submission Manger, ciderpressreview.com/submissions/." No titles listed in the *Small Press Record of Books in Print* (36th Edition, 2010-11).

CIMARRON REVIEW, E.P. Walkiewicz, Editor, 205 Morrill Hall, Oklahoma State University, Stillwater, OK 74078-4069, (405) 744-9476, cimarronreview@yahoo.com, http://cimarronreview.okstate.edu. 1967. Poetry, fiction, art, photos, interviews, reviews, parts-of-novels, long-poems, non-fiction. "Read an issue or two before submitting to get a feel for what we publish. Recent contributors include Nona Caspers, Catherine Brady, Boyer Rickel, Kim Addonizio, Gary Fincke, James Harms and Brian Henry. We read year round; no electronic submissions." circ. 600. 4/yr. Pub'd 4 issues 2009; expects 4 issues 2010, 4 issues 2011. sub. price $24 ($28 in Canada), $65/3 years ($72 Canada); per copy $7; sample $7. Back issues: $7. Discounts: Back issues more than one year old are $5. 96-128pp. Reporting time: One to six months. Simultaneous submissions accepted: Yes. Publishes 5% of manuscripts submitted. Payment: Two copies and a year's subscription. Copyrighted, reverts to author. Pub's reviews: 4 in 2009. §Poetry, fiction and non-fiction. Ads handled on individual basis. Subjects: Arts, English, Essays, Fiction, Literature (General), Non-Fiction, Photography, Poetry, Prose, Reviews, Short Stories, Writers/Writing.

THE CINCINNATI REVIEW, Nicola Mason, Dept. of English & Comparative Lit; University of Cincinnati, McMicken Hall, Room 369; PO Box 210069, Cincinnati, OH 45221-0069, (513) 556-3954. 2003. Poetry, fiction, art, interviews, reviews, non-fiction. "The Cincinnati Review is a semiannual literary journal published by the University of Cincinnati's Department of English and Comparative Literature. Each issue is filled with new fiction, poetry, essays, book reviews, a portfolio of full-color artwork from a local or national artist, and occasionally interviews. Within our pages, readers will find some of the finest creative and critical work from across the country. We strive to provide a venue for writers of any background, at any point in their literary careers, to showcase their best writing." 2/yr. Pub'd 2 issues 2009; expects 2 issues 2010, 2 issues 2011. sub. price $15; per copy $9.00; sample $9.00. Back issues: $7.00. 200pp. Reporting time: 6 weeks. Simultaneous submissions accepted: Yes. Copyrighted, reverts to author. Pub's reviews.

Cinco Puntos Press, 701 Texas, El Paso, TX 79901, Phone: (915) 838-1625, Fax: (915) 838-1635. "We don't always know what we're looking for until we actually see it, but the one thing that matters to us is that the writing is good, that it is work that comes from the heart and soul of the author and that it fits well with the concerns of our press. Because Cinco Puntos Press focuses on the U.S. / Mexico border region, the Southwest and Mexico, however, we've found that many writers assume that their work will be a good fit if it likewise focuses on this area. But that isn't always true. We like to range out, just like everybody else, explore different possibilities, experiment. It will help if you are familiar with what Cinco Puntos Press has already published, have even maybe bought some of our books." No titles listed in the *Small Press Record of Books in Print* (36th Edition, 2010-11).

CINEASTE MAGAZINE, Gary Crowdus, Editor-in-Chief; Dan Georgakas, Consulting Editor; Roy Grundmann, Contributing Editor; Cynthia Lucia, Editor; Richard Porton, Editor; Leonard Quart, Contributing Editor; Barbara Saltz, Advertising Rep., 243 Fifth Ave., #706, New York, NY 10016-8703, 212-366-5720. 1967. Articles, photos, interviews, satire, criticism, reviews, letters. "Offers a social & political perspective on the cinema—everything from the latest hollywood flicks & the American independent scene to political thrillers from Europe and revolutionary cinema from the Third World. Query before submitting." circ. 11M. 4/yr. Pub'd 4 issues 2009; expects 4 issues 2010, 4 issues 2011. sub. price $20 (institutions $40); per copy $6; sample $6. Back issues: $4 to subscribers/$5 to others. Discounts: 25%. 88pp. Reporting time: 2-3 weeks. Payment: reviews $50, articles $100 and up. Copyrighted. Pub's reviews: 60 in 2009. §Social, political perspective on all aspects of movies. Ads: $400/$300. Subjects: Criticism, Electronics, History, Politics, Sociology.

CIRCLE INC., THE MAGAZINE, Circle of Friends Books, Tommy W. Lee, PO Box 670096, Houston, TX 77267-0096, 281-580-8634. 2004. Fiction, articles, interviews, satire, reviews, non-fiction. "We publish all types of material that is geared towards uplifting the reader. Our literature should bring change, inspire positive development." Reporting time: 2 months. Simultaneous submissions accepted: yes. Subjects: African-American, Crime, Fiction, Spiritual.

Circle of Friends Books (see also CIRCLE INC., THE MAGAZINE), Tommy W. Lee, PO Box 670096, Houston, TX 77267-0096, 281-580-8634. 2004. Fiction, articles, interviews, satire, reviews, non-fiction. "We publish all types of material that is geared towards uplifting the reader. Our literature should bring change, inspire positive development." avg. press run 10M. Pub'd 1 title 2009; expects 3 titles 2010, 5 titles 2011. No titles listed in the *Small Press Record of Books in Print* (36th Edition, 2010-11). Discounts: bookstores 40%, distributors 50-55%, (all) qty: 2-4 20%, 5-99 40%, 100+ 50%. 280pp. Reporting time: 2 months. Simultaneous submissions accepted: yes. Publishes 25% of manuscripts submitted. Payment: $500-$1,500. Copyrights for author. Subjects: African-American, Crime, Fiction, Spiritual.

Citiria Publishing, Clive Warner, Paseo de los Sabinos 3701, Del Paseo, Monterrey, NL. 64920, Mexico, fiction1st@yahoo.co.uk, www.citiria.com. 2007. Fiction, non-fiction. "Nonfiction: We're interested at the moment in self-help books.Fiction: Interested in speculative fiction and fantasy, young adult, action adventure, historical, literary. No romance." Expects 5 titles 2010, 10 titles 2011. 3 titles listed in the *Small Press Record of Books in Print* (36th Edition, 2010-11). Discounts: 3-10 copies 30%. 300pp. Reporting time: 3 - 6 weeks. Simultaneous submissions accepted: Yes. Publishes 1% of manuscripts submitted. Payment: similar to Writers Guild contract. Copyrights for author. Subjects: Fantasy, Fiction, Medicine, Non-Fiction, Novels, Science Fiction, Self-Help, Surrealism, Textbooks, Young Adult.

City Life Books, LLC, Suzette Barclay, 21417 Providencia St, Woodland Hills, CA 91364. 2003. Poetry, fiction, non-fiction. "We publish books that fit our motto "Books About Life : Books For Life" that supports a positive outlook and uplifting message. As long as the subject matter is in this vein, we are open to various art and writing forms." avg. press run 3000. Pub'd 1 title 2009; expects 3 titles 2010, 5 titles 2011. No titles listed in the *Small Press Record of Books in Print* (36th Edition, 2010-11). Discounts: Wholesaled through Baker & Taylor, bulk discounts to retailers 1-5 copies 40%, 5 and up copies 50%. 150pp. Reporting time: 6-8 weeks. Simultaneous submissions accepted: Yes. Publishes 15% of manuscripts submitted. Payment: Each contract will be individually negotiated. Copyrights for author. Subjects: Animals, Christmas, Colorado, Family, Feminism, Fiction, Grieving, Inspirational, Motivation, Success, Novels, Pets, Poetry, Relationships, Women, Writers/Writing.

City Lights Books, Lawrence Ferlinghetti, Nancy J. Peters, Robert Sharrard, Elaine Katzenberger, Attn: Bob Sharrard, Editor, 261 Columbus Avenue, San Francisco, CA 94133, 415-362-8193. 1955. Poetry, fiction, articles, non-fiction. avg. press run 3M. Pub'd 5 titles 2009; expects 5 titles 2010. 73 titles listed in the *Small Press Record of Books in Print* (36th Edition, 2010-11). 100pp. Reporting time: 4 weeks. Payment: varies. Copyrights for author. Subjects: Anarchist, Ecology, Foods, Fiction, Libertarian, Literature (General), Poetry, Politics.

CKO UPDATE, Blueprint Books, Bette Daoust Ph.D., PO Box 10757, Pleasanton, CA 94588, 925-425-9513, Fax 1-800-605-2914, 1-800-605-2913, editor@blueprintbooks.com, blueprintbooks.com. 2005. Articles, interviews, reviews, non-fiction. 6/yr. Expects 5 issues 2010, 6 issues 2011. sub. price $19.95; per copy $3.95; sample free. Back issues: inquire. Discounts: 3 - 299: -40%300 - 499: -50%500 - up: -55%. 80pp. Reporting time: 5 - 10 business days. Simultaneous submissions accepted: Yes. Publishes 40% of manuscripts submitted. Payment upon acceptance. Copyrighted. Pub's reviews. §Business, Consulting, Business Self-Help. Subjects: Audio/Video, Book Reviewing, Business & Economics, Communication, Journalism, Consulting, Desktop Publishing, Finances, Government, Non-Fiction, Public Affairs, Public Relations/Publicity, Quotations.

CLACKAMAS LITERARY REVIEW, Amanda Coffey, Kate Gray, James Grabill, Andy Mingo, Trevor Dodge, 19600 South Molalla Avenue, Oregon City, OR 97045. 1996. Poetry, fiction, interviews, satire, reviews, non-fiction. "The *Clackamas Literary Review* is a nationally distributed magazine that publishes quality literature with a fresh voice. It is an annual magazine produced at Clackamas Community College under the direction of the English Department. *CLR* promotes the work of emerging writers and established writers of fiction, poetry, and creative nonfiction. Send poetry and prose separately. Submissions are limited to 6 poems, 1 story (7,000 words), or 1 essay per submission. Please include a SASE for response. We have previously published work by Ron Carlson, Naomi Shihab Nye, Denise Chavez, Pamela Uschuk, George Kalamaras, Christopher Howell, H. Lee Barnes, and Greg Sellers." circ. 1M. 1/yr. Pub'd 1 issue 2009; expects 1 issue 2010, 1 issue 2011. sub. price $10; per copy $10. Back issues: $5. 220pp. Reporting time: 30 weeks. Simultaneous submissions okay, please inform us if accepted elsewhere. Fiction and poetry contests ($15. entry fee) are held each spring. 2005 judges are Hannah Tinti and Elizabeth Woody. Prizes of $500 each. Publishes 4-5% of manuscripts submitted. Payment: copies. Pub's reviews: 2 in 2009. §Poetry, fiction, CNF. Ads: trade space.

Cladach Publishing, Catherine Lawton, PO Box 336144, Greeley, CO 80633, 970.371.9530, fax 970.351.8240, office@cladach.com, http://www.cladach.com. 1999. Fiction, non-fiction. "Authors with Christian worldview: novels, memoirs, relationships, health." avg. press run 1000. Pub'd 2 titles 2009; expects 3 titles 2010, 2 titles 2011. 2 titles listed in the *Small Press Record of Books in Print* (36th Edition, 2010-11). Discounts: Retailers prepaid 45%. 200pp. Reporting time: 3 to 6 months. Simultaneous submissions accepted: Yes. Publishes 1% of manuscripts submitted. Payment: 7 to 10 percent of net income. Copyrights for author. Subjects: Christianity, Fiction, Gardening, Health, Inspirational, Juvenile Fiction, Memoirs, Non-Fiction, Novels, Parenting, Relationships, Travel.

Claitor's Law Books & Publishing Division, Inc., Robert G. Claitor, 3165 S. Acadian, PO Box 261333, Baton Rouge, LA 70826-1333, 225-344-0476; FAX 225-344-0480; claitors@claitors.com; www.claitors.com. 1922. Non-fiction. "Unsolicited manuscripts not desired." avg. press run 1M. Pub'd 100 titles 2009; expects 110 titles 2010, 120 titles 2011. No titles listed in the *Small Press Record of Books in Print* (36th Edition, 2010-11). Discounts: trade 1 copy 20%, 2-4 33%, 5+ 40%. 500pp. Reporting time: 90 days. Simultaneous submissions accepted: no. Publishes 1% of manuscripts submitted. Payment: 6-10%. Copyrights for author. Subjects: Law, Louisiana, Taxes, Textbooks.

Clamp Down Press, Joshua Bodwell, PO Box 7270, Cape Porpoise, ME 04014-7270, 207-967-2605. 1997. Poetry, fiction, long-poems. "Recently published book of poems by Christopher Locke. The book was letterpress printed, silk-screened with original artwork and handbound in a paper and cloth edition. All Clamp Down Press books are handcrafted, limited editions, using different formats and binding techniques. Upcoming projects: back-to-back book by Fred Voss/Joan Jobe Smith,slaughter house poems by Dave Newman, a short poem seqeunce on death by David Mason Heminway.Almost all Clamp Down Press books and broadsides are illustrated. The broadside series includes work by Philip Levine, Billy Collins, Galway Kinnell, James Wright, Ed Ochester, David Mason Heminway and Tom Sexton." avg. press run 200-500. Pub'd 2 titles 2009; expects 4 titles 2010, 4 titles 2011. 2 titles listed in the *Small Press Record of Books in Print* (36th Edition, 2010-11). Discounts: Offer traditional trade discounts to dist., wholesalers, etc. 32 to 100pp. Reporting time: varies. Simultaneous submissions accepted: yes. Payment: No advances. Payment schedules vary with each author and project. Copyrighting for author varies. Subjects: Book Arts, Fiction, Literature (General), Miniature Books, Poetry, Wood Engraving/Woodworking.

Clamshell Press, D.L. Emblen, 160 California Avenue, Santa Rosa, CA 95405. 1973. "We do not read unsolicited book mss." avg. press run 250-500. Pub'd 1 title 2009; expects 2 titles 2010, 2 titles 2011. 19 titles listed in the *Small Press Record of Books in Print* (36th Edition, 2010-11). 48pp. Copyrights for author. Subjects: Arts, Criticism, Language, Poetry, Translation.

Clarity Press, Inc., Diana G. Collier, Editorial Director, 3277 Roswell Road NE, Suite 469, Atlanta, GA 30305, 877-613-1495; www.claritypress.com. 1984. Fiction, non-fiction. "Nonfiction human rights, foreign policy, social justice." avg. press run 3M. Pub'd 4 titles 2009; expects 4 titles 2010, 4 titles 2011. 35 titles listed in the *Small Press Record of Books in Print* (36th Edition, 2010-11). Discount schedule established by distributor, SCB Distributors, Gardena, California. 220pp. Reporting time: email query only claritypress@usa.net. Simultaneous submissions accepted: yes. Payment: negotiable. Copyrights for author. Subjects: African-American, Black, Civil Rights, Current Affairs, Human Rights, Middle East, Native American, Political Science, Socialist, Third World, Minorities.

Arthur H. Clark Co., Robert A. Clark, 2800 Venture Dr., Norman, OK 73069, 405-325-2000. 1902. "Documentary source material and non-fiction dealing with the history of the Western U.S." avg. press run 750-1.5M. Pub'd 8 titles 2009; expects 15 titles 2010, 15 titles 2011. 24 titles listed in the *Small Press Record of Books in Print* (36th Edition, 2010-11). 350pp. Reporting time: 2 months. Simultaneous submissions accepted: No. Publishes 30% of manuscripts submitted. Payment: 8% generally. Copyrights for author. Subjects: Arizona, Biography, California, Civil War, Diaries, History, Kansas, Montana, Old West, Oregon, Pacific Northwest, Texas, Utah, Washington (state), The West.

CLARK STREET REVIEW, Ray Foreman, PO Box 1377, Berthoud, CO 80513, clarkreview@earthlink.net, http://home.earthlink.net/~clarkreview/. 1990. Poetry, fiction. "Narrative poetry and (short shorts max. length 800 words) by previously published writers. Accepts previously published work. Recent contributors: Errol Miller, Ray Clark Dickson, Laurel Speer, and Lamar Thomas. Look for work that is clear, tuned to the mother tongue and above all, interesting to writer/readers." circ. 100. 8/yr. Pub'd 7 issues 2009; expects 8 issues 2010, 8 issues 2011. sub. price $10/10 issues; per copy $2; sample $2. Back issues: $2. Discounts: none. 20pp. Reporting time: 2 weeks. Simultaneous submissions accepted: yes. Publishes 20% of manuscripts submitted. Payment: 1 copy. Copyrighted, reverts to author. Subjects: Poetry, Prose.

Clark-Nova Books, Troy Cunningham, 2812 Bloor St.W Suite 2, Toronto, Ontario M8X 1A7, Canada, www.clarknovabooks.com. 2007. Fiction, criticism, music, non-fiction. "Clark-Nova Books publishes exclusively quality fiction and nonfiction by Canadian authors under thirty." avg. press run 725. Pub'd 2 titles 2009; expects 1 title 2010, 2 titles 2011. 3 titles listed in the *Small Press Record of Books in Print* (36th Edition, 2010-11). Discounts: Trade bookstores, Jobbers/Library Fulfillment, Schools/Universities: 40% of all orders of three or more books 20% off orders of one or two books 20% off all course orders Libraries: 20% off all ordersMail Orders:- 10% of all orders (non-returnable). 200pp. Reporting time: 6-8 weeks. Simultaneous submissions accepted: No. Payment: 10% of list price. Copyrights for author. Subjects: Creative Non-fiction, Criticism, English, Feminism, Fiction, History, Literature (General), Multicultural, Non-Fiction, Novels, Performing Arts, Short Stories, Trade, Young Adult.

CLASSICAL ANTIQUITY, University of California Press, Mark Griffith, Editor, Univ of California Press,

2000 Center Street, Suite 303, Berkeley, CA 94704-1223, 510-643-7154. 1981. Non-fiction. "Editorial address: Department of Classics, 7233 Dwinelle Hall 2520, Univ. of CA, Berkeley, CA 94720." circ. 592. 2/yr. Pub'd 2 issues 2009; expects 2 issues 2010, 2 issues 2011. sub. price $40 indiv.; $128 instit. (+ $15 air freight); $22 students; per copy $22 indiv.; $65 instit.; $22 students; sample free. Back issues: $22 indiv.; $65 instit.; $22 students. Discounts: 10% foreign subs., 30% one-time orders 10+, standing orders (bookstores): 1-99 40%, 100+ 50%. 176pp. Reporting time: 3 months. Payment: none. Copyrighted, does not revert to author. Ads: $295/$220. Subject: Classical Studies.

THE CLASSICAL OUTLOOK, Mary English C., Editor, Department of Classics and General Humanities, Dickson Hall, Montclair State University, Upper Montclair, NJ 07043. 1923. Poetry, articles, criticism, reviews. circ. 4M. 4/yr. Pub'd 4 issues 2009; expects 4 issues 2010, 4 issues 2011. sub. price $45 ($47 Canada, $50 overseas); per copy $10; sample $10. Back issues: same. 40pp. Reporting time: 6 months. Simultaneous submissions accepted: no. Publishes 19% of manuscripts submitted. Payment: 2 complimentary copies. Copyrighted, does not revert to author. Pub's reviews: 59 in 2009. §Latin, classical Greek, classical studies, pedagogy. Ads: $320/$250/$150 1/4 page. Subjects: Anthropology, Archaelogy, Book Reviewing, Classical Studies, Education, Language.

Cleanan Press, Inc., Lynn Daugherty, 106 North Washington Avenue, Roswell, NM 88201, 575-420-4064. 1983. Non-fiction. "A small independent eclectic publisher in the areas of Psychology (Child Sexual Abuse) and books of Regional Interest (Carolina Lowcountry, Santa Fe and the Southwest). We are not accepting manuscript submissions at this time." Pub'd 1 title 2009; expects 2 titles 2010, 5 titles 2011. 4 titles listed in the *Small Press Record of Books in Print* (36th Edition, 2010-11). Discounts: 35%. 100-200pp. Not accepting submissions at this time. Simultaneous submissions accepted: No. NA.

Clearbridge Publishing, PO Box 33772, Shoreline, WA 98133, 206-533-9357, Fax 206-546-9756, beckyw@clearbridge.com, www.clearbridge.com. 1999. 3 titles listed in the *Small Press Record of Books in Print* (36th Edition, 2010-11).

ClearPoint Press, Christiane Buchet, PO Box 170658, San Francisco, CA 94117, 415-386-5377 phone/Fax. 1991. Non-fiction. "We publish books on meditation and spiritual development. We do not accept unsolicited material." avg. press run 3M. Expects 1 title 2010, 1 title 2011. 10 titles listed in the *Small Press Record of Books in Print* (36th Edition, 2010-11). Discounts: standard industry. 136pp. Payment: 10%. Does not copyright for author. Subject: Buddhism.

Clearwater Publishing Co., PO Box 778, Broomfield, CO 80038-0778, 303-436-1982, fax 917-386-2769, e-mail wordguise@aol.com. 1990. "Readable, entertaining introductions to subjects taught in schools, like algebra and electronics. Primarily a vehicle for publishing books by Kenn Amdahl, who owns the company. Because we've been doing this for a while, we get submissions from hopeful authors which we have so far resisted. Our first title, There Are No Electrons: Electronics for Earthlings, was rejected 89 times before Kenn formed Clearwater. He did not intend to become a "publishing company," it just sort of happened. Self publishing was a good option for us, we suggest you investigate it as well. Sadly, Clearwater just isn't a very likely publisher for other authors. Growing would mean Kenn might have to actually work. More info on the company at www.clearwaterpublishing.com. And please turn our titles cover-out in book stores when you find them. It saves the manager time. Thanks." Pub'd 1 title 2009; expects 2 titles 2010, 1 title 2011. 7 titles listed in the *Small Press Record of Books in Print* (36th Edition, 2010-11). 260pp. Subjects: Business & Economics, Education, Fiction, Mathematics, Music, Physics, Science, Spiritual, Sports, Outdoors, Textbooks, Writers/Writing.

CLEMSON POETRY REVIEW, Adam Million, Executive Editor; Angelina Oberdan, Submissions Editor; Austin Grigg, Webmaster; Chase Hart, Associate Editor; Erin McCoy, Associate Editor; Gordon Saurer, Associate Editor; Katie Keith, Associate Editor, Clemson, SC 29630. 2006. Poetry, photos, criticism, reviews. "On-line journal. Our mission is to provide an accessible outlet for serious graduate and undergraduate poets. By publishing poets online, we hope to add previously unknown poets to the expansive body of poetry filling the internet and literary journals around the country." 2/yr. Pub'd 1 issue 2009; expects 2 issues 2010, 2 issues 2011. sub. price free; per copy free; sample free. Back issues: free. 50pp. Reporting time: 1-3 months. Simultaneous submissions accepted: Yes. Pub's reviews. §New books of poetry. Subject: Poetry.

•**Clemson University Digital Press,** 611 Strode Tower, Box 340522, Clemson University, Clemson, SC 29634-0522. No titles listed in the *Small Press Record of Books in Print* (36th Edition, 2010-11).

Cleveland State Univ. Poetry Center, Michael Dumanis, Director; Rita Grabowski, Manager, Cleveland State University, 2121 Euclid Avenue, Cleveland, OH 44115-2214, 216-687-3986; 888-278-6473 toll-free; Fax 216-687-6943; poetrycenter@csuohio.edu; www.csuohio.edu/poetrycenter. 1962. Poetry. "Awards $1,500 and publication for the best full-length volume of original poetry in English in two categories: First Book Award and Open Competition (which is for authors who have published at least one full-length collection of original poetry, 48+ pages, 500+ press run). Submit November 1, 2010 - February 15, 2011 (postmark deadline). 2011

First Book judge is Matthea Harvey. Guidelines at www.csuohio.edu/poetrycenter/contest1.html. Manuscripts accepted through the contests and by Director's invitation. Publisher of poetry collections: *You Don't Know What You Don't Know*, poems by John Bradley, winner of the 2009 CSUPC Open Competition; *Clamor*, poems by Elyse Fenton, the winner of the 2009 CSUPC First Book Award selected by D.A. Powell; *Horse Dance Underwater* by Helena Mesa; *Destruction Myth* by Mathias Svalina; *Sum of Every Lost Ship* by Allison Titus; *Trust* by Liz Waldner, and *Self-Portrait with Crayon* by Allison Benis White; and the novellas *Brazil* by Jesse Lee Kercheval; and *Snaketown* by Kathleen Wakefield. Forthcoming poetry publications (Fall 2010): *Rust or Go Missing* by Lily Brown; *Say So* by Dora Malech; and *Mule* by Shane McCrae.'' avg. press run 500 - 1M. Pub'd 5 titles 2009; expects 7 titles 2010, 5 titles 2011. 133 titles listed in the *Small Press Record of Books in Print* (36th Edition, 2010-11). Discounts: 40% to retail bookstores, 50% to wholesalers/jobbers. 80pp. Reporting time: 5-7 months. We accept simultaneous submissions, but ask to notified if manuscripts are accepted elsewhere. Publishes .5% of manuscripts submitted. Payment: Authors of all new titles will receive a standard royalties contract and/or cash award in lieu of, or as an advance against royalties. Authors receive a limited number of free copies of their book and the opportunity to purchase additional copies at a discount. Copyrights for author. Subjects: Essays, Fiction, Poetry, Writers/Writing.

THE CLIFFS "sounding", Miskwabik Press, Jikiwe, Editor, P.O. Box 7, 109 Fifth Street, Calumet, MI 49913-1608, 906-337-5970. 2005. Poetry, fiction, art, photos, interviews, satire, criticism, reviews, letters, parts-of-novels, long-poems, collages, plays, non-fiction. circ. 150. 4/yr. Expects 4 issues 2010, 4 issues 2011. sub. price $28; per copy $6; sample $7. Back issues: $7. Discounts: 20%. 40pp. Reporting time: within 4 weeks. Simultaneous submissions accepted: No. Payment: complimentary copy. Copyrighted, reverts to author. Pub's reviews. §Poetry.

Cloud 9 Publishing (see also MISSISSIPPI CROW), Nadia Giordana, PO Box 338, Champlin, MN 55316, mississippicrow@msn.com. 1992. Poetry, fiction, articles, non-fiction. "Publishes Mississippi Crow magazine. Email to MississippiCrow@msn.com. Other books: Published poetry books on occasion—inquire via email." Pub'd 1 title 2009; expects 2 titles 2010, 2 titles 2011. No titles listed in the *Small Press Record of Books in Print* (36th Edition, 2010-11). Reporting time: 2 weeks to 30 days. Publishes 55% of manuscripts submitted. Payment: ebook copy. Copyrights for author. Subjects: Avant-Garde, Experimental Art, Folklore, Haiku, Humor, Poetry, Prose, Short Stories.

•CLOUDBANK, Michael Malan, PO Box 610, Corvallis, OR 97339-0610, 541 752-0075, 877 762-6762, Fax 541 752-5475, michael@cloudbankbooks.com, www.cloudbankbooks.com. 2009. Poetry, fiction, reviews. "Cloudbank editors are are open to all types of quality writing. We welcome submissions of poetry, prose poems, reviews, essays on poetry, short fiction (500 words or less). Recent contributors are Vern Rutsala, Christopher Buckley, Penelope Schott, Tim Hunt, Karen Holmberg, George Drew. We sponsor a contest with a $200 prize. Submission information can be found at cloudbankbooks.com." circ. 350. 2/yr. Pub'd 1 issue 2009; expects 2 issues 2010, 2 issues 2011. sub. price $15; per copy $8; sample $8. Back issues: $8. Discounts: 2-10 copies 40%. 80pp. Reporting time: from 3 to 6 months. Simultaneous submissions accepted: Yes. Publishes 30% of manuscripts submitted. Payment: Contest winner receives $200 prize. Contributors receive 2 copies of the issue with their work. Copyrighted. Pub's reviews: 4 in 2009. §poetry books or books with flash fiction.

Cloudkeeper Press, Gloria Mindock, P.O. Box 440357, W. Somerville, MA 02144-3222, http://www.cloudkeeperpress.com, editor@cloudkeeperpress.com. 2007. Poetry, fiction. "Cloudkeeper Press is a Print-On-Demand Press. We publish for a fee, poetry and fiction books and chapbooks for writers. This is open for anyone who wants a published book. Visit our Webpage for more details or e-mail for more information. The press will also custom design a cover for your chapbook or book. We have published Barbara Thomas and Julia Carlson." POD. Pub'd 2 titles 2009. 2 titles listed in the *Small Press Record of Books in Print* (36th Edition, 2010-11). 32pp. Copyrights if writer pays for this. Subjects: Fiction, Poetry.

Cloudland Books, Diane McCarthy, Francis McCarthy, 585 Encina Drive, El Dorado Hills, CA 95762, www.cloudlandbooks.com. 2007. Poetry, fiction. Expects 1 title 2010, 2 titles 2011. No titles listed in the *Small Press Record of Books in Print* (36th Edition, 2010-11). Discount to wholesaler: 55%. Subject: Fiction.

Clover Park Press, Geraldine Kennedy, Publisher; Martha Grant, Acquisitions Editor, PO Box 5067, Santa Monica, CA 90409-5067, 310-452-7657, info@cloverparkpress.com, http://www.cloverparkpress.com. 1990. Non-fiction. "Non-fiction, send letter or email query first. Interested in science for non-scientists, literary travel, biography, California history, excellent writing that illuminates life's wonders and wanderings. Book length. All production details customized to individual book and market. See web site for guidelines and updated information. NO personal stories of abuse, addiction, mental illness, or incarceration." Expects 2 titles 2010, 5 titles 2011. 3 titles listed in the *Small Press Record of Books in Print* (36th Edition, 2010-11). Discounts: upon request. Reporting time: 4-6 weeks. Simultaneous submissions accepted: yes. Payment: as per contract. Copyrights for author. Subjects: African Literature, Africa, African Studies, Architecture, Biography, California, Cities, Earth, Natural History, Los Angeles, Nature, Science, Travel, The West, Women, Yosemite.

Clover Valley Press, LLC, Charlene J. Brown, 6286 Homestead Rd., Duluth, MN 55804-9621, 218-525-4552, charlene@clovervalleypress.com, http://clovervalleypress.com. 2007. Poetry, fiction, non-fiction. "Publishing quality books written by women of the Northland (primarily Minnesota, Wisconsin, and Michigan)." avg. press run 2000. Pub'd 3 titles 2009; expects 2 titles 2010, 2 titles 2011. 7 titles listed in the *Small Press Record of Books in Print* (36th Edition, 2010-11). Discounts: bookstores 40%, wholesalers 55%. 180pp. Copyrights for author. Subjects: Education, Essays, Family, Fiction, Lesbianism, Memoirs, Midwest, Minnesota, Mystery, The North, Novels, Parenting, Poetry, Wisconsin, Women.

Cloverfield Press, Matthew Greenfield, 1430 Cerro Gordo Street, Los Angeles, CA 90026-2010, submissions@cloverfieldpress.com, www.cloverfieldpress.com. 2004. Fiction. "Currently publishing only individual works of short fiction, with each short story as its own book. Each book has a hand-printed letterpress dust jacket and endpapers. We are not publishing collections of short stories or longer works of fiction or non-fiction. Recent authors and illustrators have included Haruki Murakami, Justus Ballard, Henry Baum, Miranda July, Mary Rechner, Laurence Dumortier, Carol Treadwell, Ann Faison, Michiko Yao, Elinor Nissley, Eric Ernest Johnson, Emma Hedditch, Nava Lubelski and Lecia Dole-Recio." Pub'd 2 titles 2009; expects 4 titles 2010, 4-6 titles 2011. No titles listed in the *Small Press Record of Books in Print* (36th Edition, 2010-11). Reporting time: Six months. Simultaneous submissions accepted: Yes.

CMP Publishing Group LLC, Edna Siniff, 27657 Highway 97, Okanogan, WA 98840, Web: www.cmppg.com; email: edna@cmppg.org. 1986. Non-fiction. "CMP Publishing, LLC publishes deep-hearted, quality books from a variety of genres, from children's books to contemporary women's fiction and young adult to adult fiction. Please submit a query letter first. See submissions guidelines on www.cmppg.com." avg. press run 1000. Pub'd 4 titles 2009; expects 5 titles 2010, 6 titles 2011. 13 titles listed in the *Small Press Record of Books in Print* (36th Edition, 2010-11). Discounts: Library 40%; Retailers 40%. 250pp. Reporting time: 2 months. We occasionally accept simultaneous submissions. Publishes 10% of manuscripts submitted. Payment: Bi-Annual Payments. Copyrights arranged with each author. Subjects: Adolescence, Children, Youth, Fantasy, Fiction, History, Midwest, Minnesota, Mystery, Non-Fiction, Novels, Pacific Northwest, Poetry, Washington (state), Women, Young Adult.

Coach House Books, Stan Bevington, Publisher; Alana Wilcox, Senior Editor; Christina Palassio, Managing Editor; Bill Kennedy, Web Editor, 401 Huron, on bpNichol Lane, Toronto, ON M5S 2G5, Canada, t: 800-367-6360, f: 416-977-1158, website: www.chbooks.com. "Located in a crumbling old coach house on bpNichol Lane, in the heart of Toronto's Annex neighborhood, Coach House has been publishing literary fiction, poetry, drama and artists' books for over forty years. Since its inception, the press has produced an impressive list of innovative and challenging literature by some of Canada's finest authors, including Margaret Atwood, Christian Bok, Nicole Brossard, Anne-Marie MacDonald, Anne Michaels and Michael Ondaatje." No titles listed in the *Small Press Record of Books in Print* (36th Edition, 2010-11).

COAL HILL REVIEW, www.coalhillreview.com, Michael Simms, 87 1/2 Westwood Street, Autumn House Press, Pittsburgh, PA 15211, 412-381-4261. 2007. Poetry. "Coal Hill Review is an online journal publishing poetry and a daily blog by a variety of writers. Recent poets who've published in CHR include Alicia Ostriker, William Heyen, and Chana Bloch. We ask that all poetry submissions come through our annual poetry chapbook contest. For guidelines, see our website: www.coalhillreview.com." 2/yr. Pub'd 2 issues 2009; expects 2 issues 2010, 2 issues 2011. sub. price Free. 15pp. Reporting time: less than 3 months. Simultaneous submissions accepted: Yes. Publishes 2% of manuscripts submitted. Payment: $1,000 prize to the chapbook winner. Copyrighted, reverts to author. Pub's reviews: 12 in 2009. §Poetry books, online literary journals.

COALITION FOR PRISONERS' RIGHTS NEWSLETTER, Mara Taub, PO Box 1911, Santa Fe, NM 87504, 505-982-9520. 1976. Articles, cartoons, interviews, letters, news items, non-fiction. "Length of material: 250+/- words. Politically progressive. Half of each issue is excerpts of letters from prisoners." circ. 7M+. 12/yr. Pub'd 12 issues 2009; expects 12 issues 2010, 12 issues 2011. sub. price $12 individuals, $25 to institutions, free to prisoners and their families; per copy free; sample free. Back issues: free if available. 8pp. Reporting time: 6 weeks. We accept simultaneous submissions from prisoners. Publishes (from prisoners) less than 20% of manuscripts submitted. Payment: none. Not copyrighted. Ads: none. Subjects: African-American, Civil Rights, Crime, Human Rights, Prison.

Coastal 181, Cary Stratton, 29 Water Street, Newburyport, MA 01950, 978-462-2436, 978 462-9198 (fax), 877-907-8181, www.coastal181.com. 2000. Non-fiction. "Focus on motorsports, particularly driver autobiographies, auto racing history." avg. press run 4000. Pub'd 2 titles 2009; expects 4 titles 2010, 6 titles 2011. 15 titles listed in the *Small Press Record of Books in Print* (36th Edition, 2010-11). Discounts: 40% wholesale. 272pp. Simultaneous submissions accepted: Yes. Publishes 20% of manuscripts submitted. Payment: Varies with author. Varies with book. Subjects: Autobiography, Autos, Biography, History, Sports, Outdoors, Transportation.

Cobblestone Publishing Company (see also APPLESEEDS; CALLIOPE: Exploring World History;

COBBLESTONE: Discover American History; DIG; FACES: People, Places, and Culture; ODYSSEY: Adventures in Science), Lou Waryncia, Managing Editor, 30 Grove Street, Suite C, Peterborough, NH 03458, 603-924-7209, Fax 603-924-7380, www.cricketmag.com (click on Customer Service). 1980. avg. press run 22M. Pub'd 55 titles 2009; expects 55 titles 2010, 50 titles 2011. 3 titles listed in the *Small Press Record of Books in Print* (36th Edition, 2010-11). 52pp. Reporting time: queries sent well in advance of deadline may not be answered for several months. Go-aheads usually sent 5 months prior to publication date. Simultaneous submissions accepted: yes. Publishes a variable % of manuscripts submitted. Payment: after publication. We own copyright.

COBBLESTONE: Discover American History, Cobblestone Publishing Company, Margaret E. Chorlian, Editor, 30 Grove Street, Suite C, Peterborough, NH 03458, 603-924-7209, Fax 603-924-7380, custsvc@cobblestone.mv.com. 1980. Fiction, articles, art, photos, interviews, reviews, music, plays, non-fiction. "Material must be written for children ages 8-14. Most articles do not exceed 1M words, write Editor for guidelines as we focus each issue on a particular theme." circ. 36M. 9/yr. Pub'd 9 issues 2009; expects 9 issues 2010, 9 issues 2011. sub. price $29.95 + $8/yr for foreign and Canada, Canadian subs add 7% GST; per copy $6.95; sample $6.95. Back issues: $6.95, annual set $48.95, includes slipcase and cumulative index. Discounts: 15% to agency, bulk rate 3 subs @ $17.95 each/year. 52pp. Reporting time: queries sent well in advance of deadline may not be answered for several months. Go-aheads usually sent 5 months prior to publication date. Payment: on publication. Copyrighted, *Cobblestone* buys all rights. Pub's reviews: 89 in 2009. §History books for children, ages 8-14, American history related only. No ads. Subjects: Children, Youth, History.

Cockeyed Press, PO Box 3669, Chapel Hill, NC 27515. No titles listed in the *Small Press Record of Books in Print* (36th Edition, 2010-11).

COCONUT, Coconut Books, Bruce Covey, submit@coconutpoetry.org; www.coconutpoetry.org. 2005. Poetry. "See the magazine, www.coconutpoetry.org, for the sort of work we publish. Please do not contact us by mail. Submissions are via email only. Please see our submission guidelines on our website." 4/yr. Pub'd 4 issues 2009; expects 4 issues 2010, 4 issues 2011. Reporting time: 4 months. Simultaneous submissions accepted: No. Publishes 1% of manuscripts submitted. Payment: none. Copyrighted, reverts to author. Subject: Poetry.

Coconut Books (see also COCONUT), Bruce Covey, submit@coconutpoetry.org; www.coconutpoetry.org. 2005. Poetry. "we publish books of experimental poetry. we do not accept unsolicited submissions to the press. all communications via email only." avg. press run 250. Expects 2 titles 2010, 4 titles 2011. No titles listed in the *Small Press Record of Books in Print* (36th Edition, 2010-11). 80pp. Reporting time: 6-9 months. Simultaneous submissions accepted: No. Publishes 1% of manuscripts submitted. Copyrights for author. Subject: Poetry.

COE REVIEW, Gordon Mennenga, 1220 1st Ave NE, Cedar Rapids, IA 52402. 1972. Poetry, fiction, art. "Poetry is read September-November and fiction is read January-March." circ. 500. 2/yr. Pub'd 2 issues 2009; expects 2 issues 2010, 2 issues 2011. sub. price $5; per copy $5; sample $5. Back issues: $5. 125pp. Simultaneous submissions accepted: No. Publishes 50% of manuscripts submitted. Payment: Free Copy. Copyrighted.

Coffee House Press, Allan Kornblum, Publisher; Christopher Fischbach, Associate Publisher, 79 13th Avenue NE Suite 110, Minneapolis, MN 55413-1073, 612-338-0125, Fax 612-338-4004, fish@coffeehousepress.org, www.coffeehousepress.org. 1984. Poetry, fiction, art, long-poems. "Books may be ordered directly from publisher." avg. press run 3M. Pub'd 12 titles 2009; expects 12 titles 2010, 12 titles 2011. 125 titles listed in the *Small Press Record of Books in Print* (36th Edition, 2010-11). Discounts: retail 1-4 copies 20%, 5-24 425, 25-99 43%, 100-249 44%, 250-499 45%, 500-750 46%, 750+ 47%; libraries, standing orders 10%. Reporting time: up to 6 months. Simultaneous submissions accepted: no. Publishes 1% of manuscripts submitted. Payment: 8% of list for trade books. Copyrights for author. Subjects: Essays, Fiction, Iowa, Literature (General), Novels, Poetry, Short Stories.

COFFEESPOONS, David Moore L, 1104 E. 38th Place, Tulsa, OK 74105, 918-712-9278. 2006. Monthly. Expects 3 issues 2010, 12 issues 2011. sub. price $20; per copy $3.25; sample $3. 60pp. Reporting time: 4-8 weeks. Simultaneous submissions accepted: Yes. Publishes 5% of manuscripts submitted. Payment: Two contributors copies. Copyrighted, reverts to author. Pub's reviews.

COGNITIO: A Graduate Humanities Journal, Cantadora Press, Russell James, 5406 Persimmon Hollow Rd., Milton, FL 32583-6700. 2002. Articles, non-fiction. circ. 100. 2/yr. Expects 1 issue 2010, 2 issues 2011. sub. price $10; per copy $10; sample $10. Back issues: $10. Discounts: 10%. 50pp. Reporting time: 1 day. Simultaneous submissions accepted: No. Publishes 90% of manuscripts submitted. Payment: 15% royalties on books payable every quarter, no compensation to journal authors. Copyrighted, reverts to author. Pub's reviews: none in 2009. §Humanities books. Ads: $10 per half-page, will trade for advertising space in other journals. Subjects: African-American, The Americas, Catholic, English, Ethics, Florida, Genealogy, History, Military,

Veterans, Non-Fiction, Political Science, Research, Reviews.

The Colbert House LLC, Jerry Jerman, Larry Colbert, PO Box 786, Mustang, OK 73064-0786, 405-329-7999, FAX 405-329-6977, 800-698-2644, customerservice@greatbargainbooks.com, www.greatbargainbooks.com. 1995. Fiction, non-fiction. avg. press run 3M. Expects 3 titles 2010, 5 titles 2011. 5 titles listed in the *Small Press Record of Books in Print* (36th Edition, 2010-11). Discounts: trade 2-4 books 20%, 5-24 40%, 25-49 45%, 50-99 46%, 100+ 50%. 192pp. Reporting time: 3 months. Simultaneous submissions accepted: no. Publishes less than 8% of manuscripts submitted. Payment: no royalties, profit division. Copyrights for author. Subjects: African-American, Children, Youth, Fiction, Religion.

Cold Tree Publishing, Rachel Fichter, 214 Overlook Court, Ste. 253, Brentwood, TN 37027, 615.309.4984, http://coldtreepublishing.com. Fiction, non-fiction. "Cold Tree Publishing consists of three imprints: Hooded Friar, Cold Tree, and Moorsgate, each separate and different in its own right. But each is dedicated to well-written works, the advancement of new authors, and the highest quality, both in design and content." No titles listed in the *Small Press Record of Books in Print* (36th Edition, 2010-11). Discounts: 55 percent discount to distributors and wholesalers40 percent discount to retailers. Reporting time: 1-3 Months. Simultaneous submissions accepted: Yes. Publishes 10% of manuscripts submitted. Payment: 10%, no advances, quarterly/biannually. Copyrights for author.

COLD-DRILL, Mitch Wieland, Faculty Editor, 1910 University Drive, Boise, ID 83725, 208-426-3862. 1970. Poetry, fiction, articles, art, photos, cartoons, parts-of-novels, plays, concrete art, non-fiction. "Submission deadline: December 1st for March 1 issue. Send xerox, SASE (we notify by Jan. 15 only if accepted). Open to literary and innovative forms of high quality." circ. 500. 1/yr. Pub'd 1 issue 2009; expects 1 issue 2010, 1 issue 2011. sub. price $15 (inc. p/h); per copy $15 (inc. p/h); sample $15 (inc. p/h). Back issues: same. Discounts: none. 150pp. Reporting time: by January 1 of each year. Payment: copy of magazine. Copyrighted, reverts to author. Subjects: Fiction, Idaho, Literature (General), Poetry, Short Stories.

Colerith Press, Jean Boggio, 175 Dickey Mill Rd., Belmont, ME 04952, 207-342-2619. 2007. "Colerith Press is dedicated to creating and producing quality nonfiction in the areas of memoir and family issues, as well as encouraging new authors." avg. press run 3000. Expects 1 title 2010, 2 titles 2011. 1 title listed in the *Small Press Record of Books in Print* (36th Edition, 2010-11). Discounts: Distributors 65% Wholesalers 55% Bookstores/Retailers 40% Libraries 25%. 250pp. Reporting time: 2 months. Simultaneous submissions accepted: No. Payment: in development. Copyrights for author. Subjects: Adoption, Aging, Alcohol, Alcoholism, Creative Non-fiction, Family, Genealogy, History, Lifestyles, Memoirs, Non-Fiction, Sexual Abuse.

Colgate Press, Jack Lohman, P.O.Box 597, Sussex, WI 53089, 414-477-8686. 2005. 1 title listed in the *Small Press Record of Books in Print* (36th Edition, 2010-11). Discounts: Retailers: 1 Book- 20% discount 2-3 Books- 30% 4 or more- 40% Wholesalers: 1-2 Books- 30% discount 3-4 Books- 40% 5 or more- 50% Quantity Stocking Orders- %55 Libraries, Universities, Companies, and Institutions: 1-2 Books- None 3-4 Books- 20% 5 or more- 30%. 272pp. Copyrights for author.

COLLECTION, Canvas Press, James Gapinski, N8 W31309 Concord Lane, Delafield, WI 53018. 2007. Poetry, art, photos, long-poems. "Rarely accepts unsolicited work. As is the case with most Canvas Press projects, the majority of published material is siphoned off of the Beauty/Truth Press publication channels. Please query regarding current and upcoming projects, and please visit http://www.BeautyTruthPoetry.com." 4/yr. Expects 4 issues 2010. price per copy $4.00; sample $4.00. Back issues: $4.00. Discounts: Contact for wholesale discount information. 12-24pp. Reporting time: 2 months. Simultaneous submissions accepted: No. Payment: Contributor's receive a large portion of the initial press run. Pub's reviews. Subjects: Arts, Avant-Garde, Experimental Art, Experimental, Literature (General), Poetry.

Collectors Press, Inc., Lisa Perry, Operations Manager; Jennifer Weaver-Neist, Editorial Manager, PO Box 230986, Portland, OR 97281, 503-684-3030, Fax 503-684-3777. 1992. Art, photos, non-fiction. "Collectors Press, Inc. is an award-winning pop culture publisher and is currently accepting manuscripts and proposals for books on the following topics: cooking, pop culture, fashion, art, crafts, hobbies, and advertising. Content should be visual in nature." avg. press run 7.5M. Pub'd 12 titles 2009; expects 13 titles 2010, 13 titles 2011. 42 titles listed in the *Small Press Record of Books in Print* (36th Edition, 2010-11). Trade discounts. 150pp. Reporting time: standard. Simultaneous submissions accepted: yes. Publishes 5% of manuscripts submitted. Payment: confidential. Copyrights for author.

COLLEGE LITERATURE, Kostas Myrsiades Ph.D., 210 East Rosedale Avenue, West Chester University, West Chester, PA 19383, 610-436-2901, fax 610-436-2275, collit@wcupa.edu, www.collegeliterature.org. 1975. Articles, reviews. circ. 500. 4/yr. Pub'd 4 issues 2009; expects 4 issues 2010, 4 issues 2011. sub. price $100.00; per copy $25.00; sample free. Back issues: inquire. Discounts: 10%. 212pp. Reporting time: usually 4 months. Simultaneous submissions accepted: No. Publishes 40% of manuscripts submitted. Payment: none. Copyrighted, does not revert to author. Pub's reviews: approx. 20 in 2009. §comparative literature and

112

pedagogy; teaching literature. Ads: $200 full page only, B/W. Subjects: African Literature, Africa, African Studies, Book Reviewing, Feminism, Gender Issues, Indexes & Abstracts, Indigenous Cultures, Language, Literature (General), Multicultural, Post Modern, Race, Reading, Reviews, Third World, Minorities.

COLORADO REVIEW, Center for Literary Publishing, Stephanie G'Schwind, Editor; Donald Revell, Poetry Editor; Sasha Steensen, Poetry Editor; Matthew Cooperman, Poetry Editor; Dan Beachy-Quick, Book Review Editor, Dept of English, Colorado State University, 9105 Campus Delivery, Fort Collins, CO 80523-9105, 970-491-5449, creview@colostate.edu, http://coloradoreview.colostate.edu. 1956. Poetry, fiction, reviews, parts-of-novels, long-poems, non-fiction. "Colorado Review publishes both new and established writers of contemporary short fiction, poetry, and creative nonfiction. Recent contributors include Charles Baxter, Lon Otto, Robin Black, Bill Capossere, Floyd Skloot, Robert Root, Margaret MacInnis, and Leslie Johnson." circ. 1100. 3/yr. Pub'd 3 issues 2009; expects 3 issues 2010, 3 issues 2011. sub. price $24; per copy $10.00; sample $10.00. Back issues: $10.00. Discounts: Discount to distributors is 50%. Bookstore discount is 30% on three or more copies. 200pp. Reporting time: Two months; do not read ms. in summer months. Simultaneous submissions accepted: Yes. Publishes 1% of manuscripts submitted. Payment: $5 per page plus two copies of the issue in which author is published. Copyrighted, reverts to author. Pub's reviews: 26 in 2009. §Poetry, literary fiction, and creative nonfiction. Book reviews are normally solicited, but writers may query. Ads: Full page is $150; half page is $75. Subjects: Essays, Fiction, Memoirs, Non-Fiction, Poetry.

COLORLINES, Daisy Hernandez, Managing Editor, PMB 319, 4096 Piedmont Ave, Oakland, CA 94609, 510-653-3415. 1997. Articles, photos, interviews, criticism, reviews, letters, news items, non-fiction. "We publish one issue a year of Fiction." 6/yr. Pub'd 6 issues 2009; expects 6 issues 2010, 6 issues 2011. sub. price $24.00; per copy 4.95; sample $7 includes postage. Back issues: 7.00 incl post. Discounts: 10+ 30%. 84pp. Reporting time: same week. Simultaneous submissions accepted: Yes. Payment: upon publication. Copyrighted. Colorlines retains reprint rights for academic and non profit reprints. All other rights revert to author. Pub's reviews: approx 36 in 2009. §racial justice. Ads: see:http://www.colorlines.com/advertise.php. Subjects: African-American, The Americas, Asian-American, Bigotry, Civil Rights, Feminism, Human Rights, Immigration, Indigenous Cultures, Multicultural, Native American, The North, Race, Third World, Minorities, U.S. Hispanic.

Columbia Alternative Library Press, Jason McQuinn, PO Box 1446, Columbia, MO 65205-1446, 573-442-4352 jmcquinn@calpress.org. 1989. avg. press run 2M. Expects 4 titles 2010, 4 titles 2011. 2 titles listed in the *Small Press Record of Books in Print* (36th Edition, 2010-11). Discounts: 10-19 copies 20%, 20-59 40%, 60-99 45%, 100-249 50%, 250+ 55%. 200pp. Reporting time: 2-3 months. Simultaneous submissions accepted: yes. Publishes 5-10% of manuscripts submitted. Payment: royalties = 5% of gross sales. Does not copyright for author. Subjects: Anarchist, Libertarian.

COLUMBIA POETRY REVIEW, Cora Jacobs, Managing Editor; David Trinidad, Faculty Advisor, English Department, Columbia College Chicago, 600 South Michigan Avenue, Chicago, IL 60605, 312/344-8212, 312/344-8001 (fax), columbiapoetryreview@colum.edu, http://english.colum.edu/cpr/. 1987. "Published annually by Columbias English Department, Columbia Poetry Review is a student-edited, nationally distributed literary journal. Recent issues contain the works of such reputable poets as Denise Duhamel, Kimiko Hahn, Matthea Harvey, Timothy Liu, Alice Notley, D.A. Powell, Ed Roberson, Rosemarie Waldrop and Rachel Zucker, as well as the best student writing and unsolicited work submitted to the review. Poems from CPR 16 an 18 were selected for inclusion in The Best American Poetry Review. Both undergraduate and graduate students edit the magazine, which was founded by Paul Hoover in 1988." 1/yr. sub. price $10; per copy $10. Back issues: Unavailable. 150pp. Reporting time: 2-4 months. Simultaneous submissions accepted: yes. Payment: Two contributors copies. Copyrighted, reverts to author.

COLUMBIA: A Journal of Literature & Art, Dawn Marie Knopf, Editor-in-Chief; Ryan Kearney, Managing Editor; Ramon Isao, Fiction Editor; Joseph Spece, Poetry Editor; Rachel Riederer, Nonfiction Editor, 415 Dodge Hall, Columbia University, 2960 Broadway, New York, NY 10027, www.columbiajournal.org (online submissions only!). 1977. Poetry, fiction, art, non-fiction. "Founded in 1977, *Columbia: A Journal of Literature and Art* is one of only a handful of national literary journals edited, designed, and produced, entirely by students. *Columbia* has published National Book Award-winners and Nobel laureates as well as Tom Perrotta's first short story, early poems by Alicia Ostriker, Suji Kwock Kim and others. From September 1-May 1, the journal accepts free unsolicited submissions of poetry, fiction, nonfiction, and visual art from across the country. We host a contest for each genre in our magazine in order to promote new voices. Online submissions only; www.columbiajournal.org." circ. 2000. 1/yr. sub. price $10; two years $17; per copy $10; sample $8. Back issues: Selected issues available for $10. 200pp. Simultaneous submissions accepted: Yes. Payment: 2 contributor copies.

COMICS REVUE, Manuscript Press, Rick Norwood, PO Box 336 -Manuscript Press, Mountain Home, TN 37684-0336, 432-926-7495. 1984. Cartoons. "We publish syndicated comic strips: Rick O'Shay, Buz Sawyer, Alley Oop, Tarzan, Krazy Kat, Little Orphan Annie, Steve Canyon, Modesty Blaise, The Phantom, Gasoline

Alley, and Flash Gordon. We are not interested in looking at submissions unless they are better than what is available from the syndicates. No submissions can be returned. Submissions are discouraged, but if you must submit a comic strip, send xerox copies only and include a SASE for a reply.'' circ. 1200. 12/yr. Pub'd 12 issues 2009; expects 12 issues 2010, 12 issues 2011. sub. price $45; per copy $9; sample same. Back issues: $9 for single copies, $45 for 12 copies, current or old. Discounts: 10-99 copies 40% off, 100-499 copies 50% off, 500+ copies 60% off. 64pp. Reporting time: indefinite. Simultaneous submissions accepted: no. Publishes 0% of manuscripts submitted. Payment: $5 per page. Copyrighted, reverts to author. Pub's reviews: 10-12 in 2009. §Comic strip reprints. Ads: $125/$70. Subject: Comics.

Command Performance Press, Contee Seely, 28 Hopkins Court, Berkeley, CA 94706-2512, 510-524-1191. 2005. Photos. ''Our first and only book is a book of photos of millinneum-era Berkeley, California, with historical and sociological commentary. The future is an open book.'' No titles listed in the *Small Press Record of Books in Print* (36th Edition, 2010-11). 216pp. Simultaneous submissions accepted: No. Copyrights to be determined. Subjects: Americana, California, History, Picture Books.

Common Boundaries, Debra J. Gawrych, Sherry Roberts, 2895 Luckie Road, Weston, FL 33331-3047, 954-385-8434, Fax 954-385-8652, www.commonboundaries.com, info@commonboundaries.com. 2001. Fiction, non-fiction. ''Published: *The Seven Aspects of Sisterhood: Empowering Women Through Self-Discovery* by Debra J. Gawrych. Next book: *The Art of Consulting* -.'' avg. press run 2M. Expects 1 title 2010, /1-2 titles 2011. No titles listed in the *Small Press Record of Books in Print* (36th Edition, 2010-11). Pages vary. Reporting time: 3-6 months. Simultaneous submissions accepted: yes. Publishes 10% of manuscripts submitted. Does not copyright for author. Subjects: Adolescence, Leadership, Psychology, Self-Help, Spiritual, Women.

Communication Creativity, Sue Collier, 4542 Melbourne Way, Highlands Ranch, CO 80130-6866, 720-344-4388, bookstore@CommunicationCreativity.com, www.communicationcreativity.com. 1977. Non-fiction. ''Communication Creativity books are designed to be both entertaining and informational. They deal primarily with subjects in the fields of business. Not soliciting submissions.'' avg. press run 5M. Pub'd 3 titles 2009; expects 3 titles 2010, 4 titles 2011. 9 titles listed in the *Small Press Record of Books in Print* (36th Edition, 2010-11). Discounts: from 20% to 50%. 224pp. Subjects: Advertising, Self-Promotion, Business & Economics, Communication, Journalism, Consumer, Fiction, Finances, History, How-To, Non-Fiction, Printing, Publishing, Real Estate, Self-Help, Women, Writers/Writing.

The Communication Press, Randall Harrison, PO Box 22541, San Francisco, CA 94122, 415-386-0178. 1977. Cartoons. ''Our focus is on humorous how-to, such as our *How To Cut Your Water Use—and Still Stay Sane and Sanitary*. We also are interested in art, psychology and communication. We're probably a poor market for freelancers as we already have as many projects as we can handle for the next few years; and we hope to stay small and quality oriented.'' avg. press run 5M. Pub'd 1-2 titles 2009. 11 titles listed in the *Small Press Record of Books in Print* (36th Edition, 2010-11). Discounts: 40% trade. 96-128pp. Reporting time: 6-8 weeks. Payment: variable. Copyrights for author. Subjects: How-To, Humor.

COMMUNITIES, Chris Roth, Editor, RR 1 Box 156, Rutledge, MO 63563-9720, 660-883-5545 (editorial), 828-669-0997 (advertising), editor AT(sub) ic.org (editorial), ads AT(sub) ic.org (advertising), www.ic.org, store.ic.org. 1972. Poetry, articles, art, photos, interviews, reviews, letters. ''Bias: limited to contributions relating to aspects of intentional communities, cooperative living, and creating community in one's life. Please see the most recent Call for Articles at http://communities.ic.org/submit.php before submitting an article proposal. We send Writers' Guidelines after receiving a proposal for an article that we think may find a place in Communities.'' circ. 4K. 4/yr. Pub'd 4 issues 2009; expects 4 issues 2010, 4 issues 2011. sub. price US $24/4 issues within USA, US$29/4 issues to Canada, US$31/4 issues to other countries; per copy $7 US / $8 Canada (newsstand), $9 postpaid US / $10 postpaid Canada / $15 postpaid elsewhere; sample $7 US / $8 Canada (newsstand), $9 postpaid US / $10 postpaid Canada / $15 postpaid elsewhere. Back issues: full available set (approx. 146), $420. Discounts: 3-4 copies 25%, 5-9 30%, 10-24 35%, 25-49 40%, 50+ 50%. 80pp. Reporting time: 60 days. Simultaneous submissions accepted: no. Payment: free copies, or 1 year subscription. Copyrighted, reverts to author. Pub's reviews: 8 in 2009. §Intentional communities, ecovillages, alternative culture, worker-owned co-ops, student co-ops, creating community. Ads: $275/$165/proportionals (additional discounts for multiple placements). Subjects: Community, Counter-Culture, Alternatives, Communes, Lifestyles.

Community Service, Inc. (see also NEW SOLUTIONS), PO Box 243, Yellow Springs, OH 45387-0243, 937-767-2161, www.smallcommunity.org. 1940. Articles, interviews, criticism, reviews, letters, news items, non-fiction. avg. press run 900. Pub'd 2 titles 2009; expects 1 title 2010, 1 title 2011. 27 titles listed in the *Small Press Record of Books in Print* (36th Edition, 2010-11). Discounts: write for schedule, 40% off for 10. 35pp. Reporting time: 4-6 weeks. Simultaneous submissions accepted: yes. Publishes 66% of manuscripts submitted. Payment: none. Does not copyright for author. Subjects: Biography, Business & Economics, Community, Education, Family, Newsletter, Philosophy, Society, Sociology.

Compact Clinicals, 40 Tall Pine Dr, Sudbury, MA 01776, 800-832-0034, 800-408-8830, Fax 978-443-8000. 1996. Non-fiction. "Psychology books - condensed reviews of assessment and treatment of mental disorders. A series produced for mental health professionals and educated lay public. Please contact before submitting." avg. press run 5M. Pub'd 2 titles 2009; expects 4 titles 2010, 6 titles 2011. 9 titles listed in the *Small Press Record of Books in Print* (36th Edition, 2010-11). Discounts: Retail: 1-3 0%; 4+ 20%; wholesalers/distrib. up to 24 books 35%, 25+ 50%. 96pp. Simultaneous submissions accepted: yes. Payment: 7% royalty. Does not copyright for author. Subjects: Mental Health, Psychiatry, Psychology.

A COMPANION IN ZEOR, Karen MacLeod, 1622-B Swallow Crest Drive, Sunrise Villas Apartments, Edgewood, MD 21040-1751, Fax 410-676-0164, Klitman323@aol.com, cz@simegen.com www.simegen.com/sgfandom/rimonslibrary/cz/. 1978. Poetry, fiction, art, cartoons, interviews, letters, news items. "Contributions based on the universes of Jacqueline Lichtenberg, and Jean Lorrah. Any and all universes they have created or worked in. Preferred, nothing obscene—no homosexuality unless relevant to story line. Science-fiction oriented. Limited only to creations based on Lichtenberg and Lorrah works. None other considered. Issues now produced for the website. Paper production is now secondary market, but available." circ. 100. Irregular. Expects 1 issue 2010, 2 issues 2011. price per copy issues are different prices, SASE for flyer, can negotiate for free issues on occasion; sample See price lists on line, with issue availability—http://www.simegen.com/marketplace/emporium/czordfor.html. Back issues: See website price list for available issues and costs—http://www.simegen.com/marketplace/emporium/czordfor.html. Discounts: willing to discuss and arrange. 60pp. Reporting time: 1 month. Payment: contributor copy, possibly more than one if arranged. Copyrighted, rights revert to author after 5 years to the contributor. Pub's reviews: 1 in 2009. §Almost anything but romance type, science fiction preferred for my own reading. Subject: Science Fiction.

COMPASS ROSE, Jennifer Monroe, Associate Editor, Chester College of New England, 40 Chester Street, Chester, NH 03036, 603-887-7432, compass.rose@chestercollege.edu, http://compassroseonline.wordpress.com. 1990. Poetry, fiction, long-poems, non-fiction. "We are looking for intelligent literary work with an attention to craft and quality, so please send us your best. Submit no more than five (5) poems, and fiction/non-fiction of 8,000 words or less. Our tastes range from the experimental to the traditional. Please see our website for complete submission guidelines." circ. 800. 1/yr. Pub'd 1 issue 2009; expects 1 issue 2010, 1 issue 2011. sub. price $10; per copy $10; sample $10. Back issues: $8. 100pp. Reporting time: 2-3 months. Simultaneous submissions accepted: Yes. Publishes 5% of manuscripts submitted. Payment: copies. Copyrighted, reverts to author. Subjects: Beat, Experimental, Fiction, Haiku, Literature (General), Non-Fiction, Poetry, Post Modern, Prose, Short Stories, Surrealism.

Comrades Press, Verian Thomas, Editor, 23 George Street, Stockton, Southam, Warwickshire CV47 8JS, England, editor@comrade.org.uk, www.comrade.org.uk/press. 2000. Poetry, fiction, photos, long-poems, non-fiction. "Comrades Press uses print on demand technology for hardback and paperback books and also publishes handmade chapbooks of poetry." avg. press run 50. Pub'd 3 titles 2009; expects 6 titles 2010, 6 titles 2011. No titles listed in the *Small Press Record of Books in Print* (36th Edition, 2010-11). 100pp. Reporting time: 3 months. Simultaneous submissions accepted: no. Publishes 3% of manuscripts submitted. Payment: 10 copies of chapbooks. Copyrights for author. Subjects: Experimental, Fiction, Non-Fiction, Poetry.

Comstock Bonanza Press, 18919 William Quirk Memorial Drive, Grass Valley, CA 95945-8611, 530-263-2906. 1979. Non-fiction. Pub'd 1 title 2009; expects 1 title 2010, 1 title 2011. 22 titles listed in the *Small Press Record of Books in Print* (36th Edition, 2010-11). Discounts: 40% trade and wholesale, 15% schools and libraries. 120-400pp. Reporting time: 45 days. Simultaneous submissions accepted: yes. Publishes 5% of manuscripts submitted. Payment: 10% to 15%. Copyrights for author. Subjects: Asian-American, Biography, California, Government, History, Memoirs, Native American, Non-Fiction, Politics, Race, Transportation, The West, Women.

THE COMSTOCK REVIEW, Georgia A. Popoff, Interim Managing Editor; Peggy Sperber Flanders, Assoc. Managing Editor, Comstock Writers' Group, Inc., 4956 St. John Drive, Syracuse, NY 13215, www.comstockreview.org. 1987. Poetry. "Formerly *Poetpourri*." circ. 500. 2/yr. Pub'd 2 issues 2009; expects 2 issues 2010, 2 issues 2011. 3 titles listed in the *Small Press Record of Books in Print* (36th Edition, 2010-11). sub. price $20/2 isssues; $36/4 issues; per copy $12 (2007 through current issues); sample $5 (issues prior to 2007). Back issues: $5 for Poetpourri. 108pp. Reporting time: approximately 3 months after end of reading period (presently January 1 to March 15 yearly). As of June 1, 2010, no simultaneous submissions accepted for publication. Publishes less than 10% of manuscripts submitted. Payment: contributor's copy only. Copyrighted, reverts to author. Pub's reviews: approx. 30 web only in 2009. §Poetry. Ads: none. Subjects: African-American, Appalachia, Chicano/a, Indigenous Cultures, Latino, Multicultural, Native American, Poetry, Third World, Minorities, Women, Writers/Writing.

•**COMSTOCK REVIEW,** 4956 St. John Drive, Syracuse, NY 13215. "Poetry@comstockreview.orgThis e-mail address is currently answered by Peggy Sperber Flanders, Associate Managing Editor as of Spring 2010. If you do not get an answer to a query within two weeks, we may not have been able to get her e-mail address past your block! We prefer few phone calls but if you need to call, use Peg's number at: 315-488-8077. If you need to talk to any other editor, she will help triage your query. WE DO NOT ACCEPT ANY SUBMISSIONS OF POETRY FOR READING PERIOD OR CONTEST OR CHAPBOOK BY E-MAIL. OTHER KINDS OF QUERIES ARE FINE. If you are looking for an order form, click here: http://www.comstockreview.org/orderform.html Submit Manuscripts only between August 1 & September 30 to: Chapbook Contest, 4956 St. John Drive, Syracuse, NY 13215.''

CONCEIT MAGAZINE, Perry Terrell, P. O. Box 884223, San Francisco, CA 94188-4223, http://www.myspace.com/conceitmagazine, conceitmagazine2007@yahoo.com. 2006. Poetry, fiction, articles, photos, interviews, satire, criticism, reviews, letters, long-poems, news items, non-fiction. ''CONCEIT MAGAZINE holds quite a few sponsored contests throughout each year. We read manuscripts all year - poetry, articles, essays and short stories. Contributors: Tamara Nahrstadt, Sheila B. Roark, D. Neil Simmers, Peggy Zuleika Lynch, Michael Levy, Michael Maiello, Dr. Mike Berger, Barbara Hantman, Linda Amos and Irene Ferraro-Sives.'' circ. 270. 12/yr. Expects 9 issues 2010, 12 issues 2011. sub. price $40; per copy $4.50; sample $3.00. Back issues: $3.00. Discounts: 2-10 copies 25%. 26pp. Acknowledgements: E-mail submissions - 1-20 days; snail mail submissions - 1 - 6 weeks; reading mss and scheduling - 6 months. Simultaneous submissions accepted: Yes. Publishes 99% of manuscripts submitted. Payment: Pays with one contributor's copy. Cash and subscriptions paid to winners of our contests. Copyrighted, reverts to author. Pub's reviews: 3 in 2009 in 2009. §poetry, short stories, articles, essays, websites, new books and magazine announcements. Ads: Small Press Publishers and Conceit Magazine writers - FREE. Businesses - $20.00 per issue. Subjects: Adolescence, African-American, Book Reviewing, Drama, Dreams, Family, Fiction, Mystery, Native American, Non-Fiction, Poetry, Prose, Romance, Short Stories, Spiritual.

CONCHO RIVER REVIEW, Mary Ellen Hartje Dr., General Editor; Jerry Bradley Dr., Poetry Editor; Terry Dalrymple Dr., Fiction Editor; Carol Reposa Ms., Nonfiction Editor; Nicole Madison Dr., Layout Editor, English Department, Angelo State University, San Angelo, TX 76909, 915-942-2269, me.hartje@angelo.edu. 1987. Poetry, fiction, articles, criticism, reviews, non-fiction. ''Fiction and non-fiction: 1500-5000 words; poetry open, book reviews. We read and consider all submissions. Circulation office: English Department, Angelo State University, Box 10894 ASU Station, San Angelo, TX 76909.'' circ. 300. 2/yr. Pub'd 2 issues 2009; expects 2 issues 2010, 2 issues 2011. sub. price $14; per copy $8; sample $5. Back issues: $5. Discounts: query. 115pp. Reporting time: 2-6 months. Simultaneous submissions accepted: yes. Publishes 10-15% of manuscripts submitted. Payment: copies. Copyrighted, reverts to author. Pub's reviews: 10 in 2009. §Fiction, poetry, nonfiction by writers of Texas and the Southwest or about Texas and the Southwest. Ads: query. Subjects: Southwest, Texas.

CONCRETE JUNGLE JOURNAL, Concrete Jungle Press, D. Wayne Dworsky, 163 Third Avenue #130, New York, NY 10003, 718-465-8573 URL: www.concretejunglepress.com. 2006. Poetry, fiction, articles, art, photos, cartoons, interviews, satire, reviews, parts-of-novels, long-poems, news items, non-fiction. ''The theme of Concrete Jungle Journal is nature in the city.'' circ. 100. 200/yr. Expects 200 issues 2010, 800 issues 2011. sub. price One year is $10/Two years is $18; per copy $3; sample $2. Back issues: $2. Discounts: 40% agents; 60%wholesalers, 40%retailers, 40%institutions, classrooms and bookstores. 16pp. Reporting time: within three months. Simultaneous submissions accepted: Yes. Payment: At the moment payment is in contributor copies. Copyrighted, reverts to author. Pub's reviews: §nature books, books for walks in the city, nature in the city. Ads: full page $50/half page $30/quarter page $20/text (20 words)$10. Subjects: Birds, Botany, Cities, Fiction, Haiku, Handicapped, Interviews, Maps, Nature, New York, Novels, Poetry, Reviews, Satire, H.D. Thoreau.

Concrete Jungle Press (see also CONCRETE JUNGLE JOURNAL), D. Wayne Dworsky, Editor; Lynette Perez, Editor; Stavreula Kristofkorski, Editor, 163 Third Avenue #130, New York, NY 10003, Tel: 718-465-8573, Fax: 718-468-3007, URL: www.concretejunglepress.com. 2004. Poetry, fiction, parts-of-novels, long-poems, non-fiction. avg. press run 1000. Pub'd 3 titles 2009; expects 1 title 2010, 1 title 2011. 1 title listed in the *Small Press Record of Books in Print* (36th Edition, 2010-11). Discounts: Wholsalers 60%/retailers, stores, schools, institutions 40%. 43-200pp. Reporting time: Reports in 3 months. Simultaneous submissions accepted: Yes. Copyrights for author. Subjects: Nature, New York, Novels, Poetry, Young Adult.

Concrete Wolf Press, Lana Ayers, PO Box 1808, Kingston, WA 98346-1808, ConcreteWolf@yahoo.com, http://concretewolf.com. 2001. Poetry, art, photos. ''Concrete Wolf is a chapbook-only press now via our annual contest. We have suspended publication of the quarterly journal.'' avg. press run 250-1000. Pub'd 2 titles 2009; expects 1 title 2010, 1 title 2011. 10 titles listed in the *Small Press Record of Books in Print* (36th Edition, 2010-11). Discounts: Author and school discounts. 40pp. Reporting time: 6-12 months. Simultaneous submissions accepted: yes. Publishes 0.5% of manuscripts submitted. Payment: Contest prize 100 perfect bound copies. Subject: Poetry.

CONDUIT, William D. Waltz, 788 Osceola Avenue, Saint Paul, MN 55105, www.conduit.org, info@conduit.org. 1993. Poetry, fiction, art, photos, cartoons, interviews, reviews, letters, non-fiction. ''Past contributors: John Ashbery, Mary Jo Bang, Gillian Conoley, Russell Edson, Alice Fulton, Bob Hicok, Noclle

Kocot, Geoffrey G. O'Brien, Tomaz Salamun, Cole Swensen, James Tate, Dean Young. Prose: 2,500-3,500 words maximum. Poetry: any length.'' circ. 1000. 2/yr. Pub'd 2 issues 2009; expects 2 issues 2010, 2 issues 2011. sub. price $18 individuals, $28 institutions; per copy $10; sample $8. Back issues: $8. Discounts: none. 96pp. Reporting time: 9 weeks-9 months. Simultaneous submissions accepted: no. Publishes 1% of manuscripts submitted. Payment: copies. Copyrighted, reverts to author. Ads: none. Subjects: Arts, Avant-Garde, Experimental Art, Literature (General), Philosophy, Poetry, Science.

CONFRONTATION, Martin Tucker, English Department, C.W. Post of Long Island Univ., Greenvale, NY 11548, 516-299-2720. 1968. Poetry, fiction, articles, interviews, parts-of-novels, long-poems, plays. circ. 2M. 2/yr. Expects 2 issues 2010. 24 titles listed in the *Small Press Record of Books in Print* (36th Edition, 2010-11). sub. price $15.00; per copy $12.00; sample $5.00. Back issues: $5 to $10 for special and rare editions. Discounts: 20% on orders of 10 or more copies. 325pp. Reporting time: 6-8 weeks. We accept simultaneous submissions, but not preferred. Publishes 10-15% of manuscripts submitted. Payment: $20-$150 stories, $10-$75 poetry. Copyrighted, reverts to author. Pub's reviews: 40 in 2009. §Fiction, poetry, criticism. Subjects: Literary Review, Magazines.

CONJUNCTIONS, Bradford Morrow, Editor, 21 East 10th Street #3E, New York, NY 10003-5924, Phone: 845-758-1539, fax: 845-758-2660, e-mail: conjunctions@bard.edu, URL: www.conjunctions.com. 1981. Poetry, fiction. "Contributing editors include: Walter Abish, Chinua Achebe, John Ashbery, Martine Bellen, Mei-mei Berssenbrugge, Mary Caponegro, William H. Gass, Peter Gizzi, Robert Kelly, Ann Lauterbach, Norman Manea, Rick Moody, Howard Norman, Joan Retallack, Joanna Scott, David Shields, Peter Straub, William Weaver, John Edgar Wideman. Among most recently published authors are: John Ashbery, David Shields, Mary Gaitskill, Joyce Carol Oates, Chimamanda Ngozi Adichie, Peter Orner, Can Xue, , Rikki Ducornet, Carole Maso, Jonathan Lethem, William H. Gass, Rae Armantrout, Brian Evenson, and H. G. Carrillo.'' circ. 7.5M. 2/yr. Pub'd 2 issues 2009; expects 2 issues 2010, 2 issues 2011. sub. price $18 indiv., $35 instit. and overseas; $32/2 yrs indiv., $70/2 yrs instit. and overseas; per copy $12; sample $12. Back issues: $12. Discounts: special rates to distributors. 380pp. Reporting time: solicited mss. immediately, unsolicited 4-6 weeks. Simultaneous submissions accepted: no. Publishes 3-5% of manuscripts submitted. Payment: $125 plus copies. Copyrighted, reverts to author. Ads: $350 full page. Subjects: Arts, Experimental, Fiction, Futurism, Humor, Interviews, Literature (General), Myth, Mythology, Non-Fiction, Poetry, Post Modern, Prose, Satire, Short Stories.

THE CONNECTICUT POET, Hanover Press, Faith Vicinanza, Editor; John Jeffrey, Editor, PO Box 596, Newtown, CT 06470-0596, 203-426-3388, Fax 203-426-3398, hanoverpress@faithvicinanza.com, www.poetz.com/connecticut. 1995. Poetry, articles, reviews. "This is an online poetry newsletter. Poetry, calls for submissions, calendar, websites, quotes are published monthly.'' circ. 1-100M. 12-24/yr. sub. price free. 20pp. Reporting time: 60 days. Simultaneous submissions accepted: yes. Publishes 1% of manuscripts submitted. Payment: none. Not copyrighted, rights revert to author on publication. Pub's reviews: 5 in 2009. §Poetry only. Ads: none. Subjects: Newsletter, Poetry.

CONNECTICUT REVIEW, Dr. Vivian Shipley, SCSU, 501 Crescent Street, New Haven, CT 06515, 203-392-6737, Fax 203-392-5748. 1967. Poetry, fiction, articles, art, photos, interviews, non-fiction. "SASE for reply only. We do not return ms. 2000-4000 words, put word count on work; 3-5 poems, black and white/color photograph and art work. Send 2 copies of typed work, send 1 copy of poems. Recent contributors: Maxine Kumin, Sherod Santos, Todd Jokl, Lawrence Ferlinghetti, John Searles, and Colette Inez.'' circ. 3M. 2/yr. Pub'd 2 issues 2009; expects 2 issues 2010, 2 issues 2011. sub. price $16; per copy $8; sample $8. 208pp. Reporting time: 2-4 months. Simultaneous submissions accepted: no. Publishes 10% of manuscripts submitted. Payment: 2 copies. Copyrighted, reverts to author. Ads: none. Subjects: Essays, Fiction, Poetry, Translation.

CONNEXIONS DIGEST, Connexions Information Services, Inc., Ulli Diemer, 489 College Street, Suite 305, Toronto, Ontario M6G 1A5, Canada, 416-964-1511, www.connexions.org. 1976. Articles, art, photos, cartoons, interviews, criticism, reviews, letters, news items. "A digest linking groups working for social justice—we are interested in materials that include reflection, analysis, report on action.'' circ. 1.2M. 4/yr. Pub'd 4 issues 2009; expects 4 issues 2010, 4 issues 2011. sub. price $15.50 Canada, $18 foreign; per copy $30 for directory issue; sample $1. Back issues: $1. Discounts: 40% for resale; other negotiable. 48pp. Reporting time: 3 months maximum. Payment: none. Not copyrighted. Pub's reviews: 200 in 2009. §Social justice struggles/analysis. Ads: $175/$100/25¢. Subjects: Canada, Indexes & Abstracts, Networking, Reference.

Connexions Information Services, Inc. (see also CONNEXIONS DIGEST), Ulli Diemer, Managing Editor, 489 College Street, Suite 305, Toronto, Ontario M6G 1A5, Canada, 416-964-1511, www.connexions.org. 1975. avg. press run 2M. Pub'd 1 title 2009; expects 2 titles 2010. 3 titles listed in the *Small Press Record of Books in Print* (36th Edition, 2010-11). 224pp. Subjects: Canada, Indexes & Abstracts, Networking, Reference.

CONSCIENCE: The Newsjournal of Catholic Opinion, David Nolan, Catholics for Choice, 1436 U Street NW #301, Washington, DC 20009-3997, 202-986-6093, Fax 202-332-7995, conscience@catholicsforchoice.org, www.conscience-magazine.org. 1980. Articles, interviews, reviews, letters, news items. "Conscience, the Newsjournal of Catholic Opinion published quarterly by Catholics for Choice, offers in-depth, cutting-edge coverage on many vital contemporary issues, including reproductive rights, sexuality and gender, feminism, the Religious Right, women's rights, the role of religion in formulating public policy, church/state issues and US politics." circ. 15,000. 4/yr. Pub'd 4 issues 2009; expects 4 issues 2010, 4 issues 2011. sub. price $15; per copy $5; sample free. Back issues: $6.50 depending on availability. Discounts: trade 33%, bulk by arrangement. 56pp. Reporting time: 1 month. Simultaneous submissions accepted: No. Publishes approx. 10% of manuscripts submitted. Payment: c. $200 for a 1,500 word article. Copyrighted, reverts to author. Pub's reviews: 10 in 2009. §Women's studies, Catholic church, abortion/family planning, sexuality, church/state issues. Ads: Rates on request. Subjects: AIDS, Biotechnology, Birth, Birth Control, Population, Catholic, Current Affairs, Feminism, Gender Issues, Politics, Public Affairs, Religion, Sex, Sexuality, Women.

Consumer Press, Joseph Pappas, 13326 SW 28th Street, Ste. 102, Fort Lauderdale, FL 33330-1102, 954-370-9153, info@consumerpress.com. 1989. Non-fiction. avg. press run 5M. Pub'd 2 titles 2009; expects 2 titles 2010, 3 titles 2011. 4 titles listed in the *Small Press Record of Books in Print* (36th Edition, 2010-11). Discounts: trade, bulk, jobber. 200pp. Reporting time: varies. Publishes 10% of manuscripts submitted. Payment: standard. Copyrights for author. Subjects: Construction, Consumer, Drugs, Health, How-To, Medicine, Mental Health, Non-Fiction, Nutrition, Parenting, Psychiatry, Psychology, Real Estate, Women.

CONTEMPORARY GHAZALS, CELLAR, R.W. Watkins, PO Box 111, Moreton's Harbour, NL A0G 3H0, Canada. 2003. Poetry, articles, art, interviews, criticism, reviews, letters. "The ghazal is a type of poetry featuring repetition and inner rhyme, and which finds its origin in 7th Century Arabia. *Contemporary Ghazals* publishes a) English-language ghazals, preferably written in the correct Persian style as introduced/popularized in the West by the late Agha Shahid Ali; b) English translations/adaptations (from the original Persian, Arabic, Urdu, etc.) of ancient ghazals; c) articles and book reviews focusing on ghazals, ghazal collections, and their authors; and d) related artwork or photographs. Contributors, as of recent or forthcoming, include Agha Shahid Ali, Denver Butson, Marcyn Del Clements, Teresa M. Pfeifer, Daniel Hales, Barbara Little, J.W. McMillan, I. H. Rizvi, R.W. Watkins, and Bill West." 2-3/yr. Expects 2 issues 2010, 2-3 issues 2011. 3 titles listed in the *Small Press Record of Books in Print* (36th Edition, 2010-11). sub. price $12US outside of Canada; per copy $4US outside of Canada; sample $4US outside of Canada. Back issues: same. 20pp. Reporting time: almost immediately. Simultaneous submissions accepted: yes. Publishes 80% of manuscripts submitted. Payment: free copy. Not copyrighted. Pub's reviews. §Ghazals, original or translated. Ads: $65/$40; other $55/$20. Subjects: Classical Studies, India, Medieval, Middle East, Poetry, Religion, Sufism.

CONTEMPORARY POETRY REVIEW, PO Box 5222, Arlington, VA 22205. "Call for Critics. *The Contemporary Poetry Review* is the largest online archive of poetry criticism in the world. The CPR has a regular staff of contributors. Though new positions may not be available, the editor invites interested critics to submit their work. Because of the volume of submissions, prospective contributors should understand that the process can take 1-3 months. Contributors are accepted on a permanent basis, and asked to contribute regularly. They are paid for each contribution, and are extended other courtesies."

CONTEMPORARY VERSE 2: the Canadian Journal of Poetry and Critical Writing, Clarise Foster, 207-100 Arthur Street, Winnipeg, Manitoba R3B 1H3, Canada, (204) 949-1365, cv2@mb.sympatico.ca, www.contemporaryverse2.ca. 1975. Poetry, articles, interviews. "Contemporary Verse 2 strives to bring the best poetry from around the world into the spotlight. Each issue features interviews with established and emerging poets, a selection of new poems, reviews and/or articles, and coming soon, a new section of French poetry." 4/yr. Pub'd 4 issues 2009; expects 4 issues 2010, 4 issues 2011. sub. price 25.00; per copy $7.00; sample $7.00. Back issues: $5.00 or inquire. 95pp. Simultaneous submissions accepted: No. Payment: Please visit our web site for details. Copyright remains with author. Pub's reviews: approx. 4 in 2009. §New collections of poetry. Ads: $150 (full page)/$100 (2/3 page)/$75 (half page)/$50 (1/3 page).

CONTEXTS: UNDERSTANDING PEOPLE IN THEIR SOCIAL WORLDS, University of California Press, Claude Fischer, Editor; Scott Savitt, Managing Editor, University of California Press, 2000 Center St., Suite 303, Berkeley, CA 94704-1223, 510-643-7154. 2002. Photos, reviews, non-fiction. "Editorial Office: Department of Sociology, University of California, Berkeley, CA 94720-1980. Copyrighted by the American Sociological Association." circ. 2858. 4/yr. Pub'd 4 issues 2009; expects 4 issues 2010, 4 issues 2011. sub. price $45 indiv., $139 inst.; per copy $12 indiv., $37 inst.; sample same as single copy. Discounts: foreign subs. agents 10%, 10+ one-time orders 30%, standing orders (bookstores): 1-99 40%, 100+ 50%. 72pp. Reporting time: varies. Copyrighted, does not revert to author. Pub's reviews: approx. 20 in 2009. §sociology and related fields. Ads: $295/$220. Subjects: Culture, Sociology.

Continuing Education Press, Alba Scholz, Portland State University, Continuing Education Press, PO Box 1394, Portland, OR 97207-1394, www.cep.pdx.edu. 1981. Non-fiction. avg. press run 10,000. Pub'd 1 title 2009; expects 1 title 2010, 1 title 2011. 9 titles listed in the *Small Press Record of Books in Print* (36th Edition, 2010-11). 100pp. Payment: contract terms by arrangement. Can copyright for author. Subjects: Education,

Handwriting/Written, Non-Fiction, Pacific Northwest, Public Affairs, Science.

CONTRARY, Jeff McMahon, Editor, 3133 S. Emerald Avenue, Chicago, IL 60616, (312) 264-0744, Accepts submissions online only: www.contrarymagazine.com. 2003. Poetry, fiction, reviews, non-fiction. "Founded at the University of Chicago, Contrary is a quarterly online journal that publishes commentary, fiction, poetry, and work that declines to conform to a single category. We favor writing that respects but surpasses traditional forms, and we blend established writers with fine new voices to foster a more open, more contrary literature." circ. 22,500. 4/yr. Pub'd 4 issues 2009; expects 4 issues 2010, 4 issues 2011. sample price free. Back issues: free. 40pp. Reporting time: 90 days. Simultaneous submissions accepted: Yes. Publishes 1% of manuscripts submitted. Payment: $20 per acceptance. $60 for featured work. Copyrighted. Most rights revert to author on publication, but Contrary retains archive and compilation rights. See submission guidelines at www.contrarymagazine.com/Contrary/Submissions.html. Pub's reviews: approx. 48 in 2009. §fiction, poetry, non-fiction, lost classics. Subjects: Cartoons, Essays, Fiction, Non-Fiction, Poetry.

CONTROLLED BURN, Carol Finke, Editor, Kirtland Community College, 10775 N. St. Helen Road, Roscommon, MI 48653, 989-275-5000, Fax 989-275-8219, cburn@kirtland.edu, http://www2.kirtland.edu/cburn/. 1994. Poetry, fiction, long-poems, non-fiction. "Reading period is May 1 through December 1—submittions sent outside that period are returned unread." circ. 350. 1/yr. Pub'd 1 issue 2009; expects 1 issue 2010, 1 issue 2011. sub. price 2 years (2 issues) for $9.00; per copy $5.00; sample $5. Back issues: $3.00. 100pp. Reporting time: 2 months. We prefer not to accept simultaneous submissions. Publishes 5% of manuscripts submitted. Payment: 2 copies. Copyrighted, reverts to author. Subject: Literary Review.

COOK PARTNERS, Kim Pettit, David C. Cook, 4050 Lee Vance View, Colorado Springs, CO 80918-7100, 719-536-0100, Fax 719-536-3266. 2007. Articles, interviews, letters, news items, non-fiction. "Trade journal for Christian publishers around the world." once every two months. Pub'd 8 issues 2009; expects 6 issues 2010, 6 issues 2011. sub. price free; per copy free; sample free. Back issues: free. 16pp. Reporting time: 1 month. Payment: varies. Copyrighted, does not revert to author. Subjects: Book Collecting, Bookselling, Communication, Journalism, Desktop Publishing, Editing, Publishing, Third World, Minorities, Translation, Writers/Writing.

Cookbook Resources, LLC, Sheryn Jones, 541 Doubletree Drive, Highland Village, TX 75077, 972-317-0245. 1995. "Cookbook Resources, LLC publishes family cookbooks with easy, everyday, family recipes. We believe that easy recipes encourage busy families to share meals at home. Universal concepts of family and strong values are at the center of CRs mission and it is committed to bringing family and friends to the table. The positioning statement is Bringing Family and Friends To The Table and it is part of the company logo.The personality of the cookbooks is down-home, friendly and good fun. Colors are bright, cheerful and friendly. Titles are simple and direct with positioning statements that clarify or define the titles. Quality is maintained through excellent recipe choices, design, copy preparation, materials used and manufacturing standards." avg. press run 10000. Pub'd 17 titles 2009; expects 15 titles 2010, 15 titles 2011. 37 titles listed in the *Small Press Record of Books in Print* (36th Edition, 2010-11). Discounts: wholesales- 55% discount; distributors- cost plus. 288pp. Simultaneous submissions accepted: No. Publishes 0% of manuscripts submitted. Payment: 4-10%. Does not copyright for author. Subjects: Cooking, Food, Eating, How-To, New England, Nutrition, Pacific Northwest, Vegetarianism.

Cooper Hill Press, Helen Knight, General Manager, 92 Naugatuck Ave., Milford, CT 06460, 203-387-7236 phone/Fax, editor@cooperhill.com, www.cooperhill.com. 1999. "Imprint: American Language Sourcebooks. We publish books by educators. Our latest publications are: The Cooper Hill Stylebook: a Guide to Writing and Revision, by Gregory Heyworth, PhD. The Cooper Hill College Application Essay Bible, edited by Rosette Liberman, EdD." avg. press run 2.5M. Pub'd 1 title 2009; expects 1 title 2010, 2 titles 2011. 2 titles listed in the *Small Press Record of Books in Print* (36th Edition, 2010-11). Discounts: wholesalers/distributors 55%, bookstores 40%, libraries 20%. 464pp. Reporting time: 8-10 weeks. Simultaneous submissions accepted: yes. Publishes no set % of manuscripts submitted. Payment: negotiable. Copyrights for author. Subjects: Editing, Education, English, Reference.

Cooperative Press, Shannon Okey, 13000 Athens Ave C288, Lakewood, OH 44107, 216-712-7667, http://www.cooperativepress.com, info@cooperativepress.com. 2007. Non-fiction. "Cooperative Press specializes in niche art and craft media, particularly in the field of knitting and other fiber arts. We are open to other nonfiction how-tos, such as cookbooks, if they have a strong specialization or are in an area of our expertise. We're DIY-friendly, and believe in promoting environmentally-friendly publishing practices as well as authors who share our values. Our owner has written books for multiple major publishers and believes strongly in a more author-centered publishing process." avg. press run 5000. Pub'd 1 title 2009; expects 3 titles 2010, 5 titles 2011. 1 title listed in the *Small Press Record of Books in Print* (36th Edition, 2010-11). Contact us for more information on discounts and for details on our digital publishing programs as well. 128pp. Reporting time: 1-2 weeks. Simultaneous submissions accepted: Yes. Publishes 5% of manuscripts submitted. Payment: We generally do not pay advances but provide instead a superlative royalty schedule compared to other houses.

Copyrights for author. Subjects: Acupuncture, Alternative Medicine, Clothing, Cooking, Crafts, Hobbies, Feminism, Internet, Quilting, Sewing, Textiles, Vegetarianism, Zines.

Copper Beech Press, M.K. Blasing, Director; Randy Blasing, Editor, P O Box 2578, English Department, Providence, RI 02906, 401-351-1253. 1973. Poetry, fiction, long-poems. avg. press run 1M. Pub'd 4 titles 2009; expects 3 titles 2010, 3 titles 2011. 18 titles listed in the *Small Press Record of Books in Print* (36th Edition, 2010-11). Discounts: bookstores, jobbers, etc. 1-5 20%; 6-9 33%; 10+ 40%. 64pp. Reporting time: ASAP, usually within 1 month. Payment: copies, 5%. Does not copyright for author. Subjects: Fiction, Poetry, Translation.

Copper Canyon Press, Michael Wiegers, Executive Editor; Joseph Bednarik, Marketing Director, PO Box 271, Port Townsend, WA 98368, poetry@coppercanyonpress.org, www.coppercanyonpress.org, 360-385 4925 (tel). 1972. Poetry. "Copper Canyon Press publishes poetry, poetry in translation, and letterpress broadsides. Authors include Ted Kooser, W.S. Merwin, Hayden Carruth, Carolyn Kizer, Pablo Neruda, C.D. Wright, Ruth Stone, Jim Harrison, Antonio Machado, Han Shan, James Galvin, Olga Broumas, Lucia Perillo, and translator Red Pine. The editors no longer consider unsolicited manuscripts; queries should include SASE. Copper Canyon books are distributed to the trade by Consortium, 34 Thirteenth Avenue NE, Suite 101 Minneapolis, MN 55413-1007, 800-283-3572." avg. press run 2.5M. Pub'd 18 titles 2009; expects 18 titles 2010, 18 titles 2011. 43 titles listed in the *Small Press Record of Books in Print* (36th Edition, 2010-11). Discounts: standard 40%, returnable, short 20% on cloth. 120pp. 4 months. No. Publishes less than 1% of manuscripts submitted. Payment: standard 7% royalty rate. Copyrights for author.

•**THE COPPER NICKEL,** Campus Box 175, PO Box 173364, Denver, CO 80217-3364. *"The Copper Nickel* accepts submissions of unpublished short fiction, poetry, essays, prose poems, and other written experiments. We are open to anything, but we highly recommend reading an issue of Copper Nickel before submitting. We are now accepting unsolicited submissions through our Submission Manager system ONLY. Please limit submissions to five poems or a single piece of prose. Submissions will not be accepted by snail mail or by email. And, please, please, please, indicate if yours is a simultaneous submission. We do consider simultaneous submissions, but we would be grateful for at least 6 weeks to make a proper review. Copper Nickel pays contributors in copies and in subscriptions and works to draw new readers to contributors' work, both within our pages and without."

Cornell Maritime Press/Tidewater Publishers, Jonna Jones, P.O. Box 456, Centreville, MD 21620, 1-800-638-7641, www.cmptp.com. 1938. avg. press run 2000. Pub'd 10 titles 2009; expects 10 titles 2010, 10 titles 2011. 12 titles listed in the *Small Press Record of Books in Print* (36th Edition, 2010-11). 32-250pp. Subjects: Children, Youth, Civil War, Cooking, Crafts, Hobbies, Environment, Mystery, Non-Fiction, Picture Books, Sports, Outdoors, Textbooks, Transportation, Water, The West, Wildlife, Wood Engraving/Woodworking.

CORNERSTONE, Jon Trott, Editor-in-Chief; Eric Pement, Senior Editor; Dawn Mortimer, Editorial Director; Chris Wiitala, Music Editor, 939 W. Wilson Avenue, Chicago, IL 60640, 773-561-2450 ext. 2080, Fax 773-989-2076. 1972. Poetry, fiction, articles, art, photos, cartoons, interviews, satire, criticism, reviews, music, letters, news items, non-fiction. "Call publication." circ. 38M. 3-4/yr. Pub'd 2 issues 2009; expects 3 issues 2010, 4 issues 2011. sub. price donation; per copy donation; sample SASE with 5 first class stamps. Back issues: call publication. Discounts: call for info. 64-72pp. Reporting time: 3-6 months, respond only if we wish to use work. Simultaneous submissions accepted: yes. Publishes 2% of manuscripts submitted. Payment: varies. Copyrighted, reverts to author. Pub's reviews: 14 in 2009. §Religious, social, political. Ads: $1,300/$840/50¢ classified. Subjects: Christianity, Religion.

Cornerstone Press, Anthony Summers, 1825 Bender Lane, Arnold, MO 63010-1269, (314)608-4175. 1974. Poetry, fiction, art, photos, satire, letters, plays, non-fiction. "The editorial mission is to keep publishing and promote good literature and give those who have the talent a chance to be heard. We are open to any type of submission, generally fiction, poetry, and plays. Recent contributors: Jack Crane, Al Montesi, Gharles Guenther, Jay Blumenfeld. Cornerstone Press has published 29 titles since its inception." avg. press run 500. Pub'd 1 title 2009; expects 3 titles 2010, 5 titles 2011. 30 titles listed in the *Small Press Record of Books in Print* (36th Edition, 2010-11). Discounts: Contact for discounts. 60-200pp. Reporting time: varies. Simultaneous submissions accepted: No. Publishes 3% of manuscripts submitted. Payment: Royalties and payment arrangements are arragned individually. Depends on the author. Subjects: Absurdist, Anthology, Creative Non-fiction, Experimental, Fantasy, Fiction, Memoirs, Mystery, Myth, Mythology, Non-Fiction, Novels, Performing Arts, Poetry, Prose, Translation.

Cornerstone Publishing, Inc., PO Box 707, New Albany, IN 47151, 267-975-7676, 770-842-8877, books@cornerstonepublishing.com, www.cornerstonepublishing.com. 1992. Poetry, non-fiction. "Our Vision: Cornerstone Publishing, our vision is "to take the message and the messenger to the masses." Our Mission: With a clarity of purpose and a focused vision, inspired authors from numerous walks of life have come together to join the Cornerstone family over the years with a united purpose: to inspire, motivate, educate and impact the lives of those who read their words.Has God called you to "write the vision"...?'' avg. press run 2000. Pub'd 10 titles 2009; expects 15 titles 2010, 25 titles 2011. 1 title listed in the *Small Press Record of Books in Print* (36th Edition, 2010-11). 150pp. Reporting time: 2-8 weeks. Simultaneous submissions accepted: Yes. Publishes 25% of manuscripts submitted. Payment: 50-50. Copyrights for author. Subjects: African-American, Children, Youth, Family, Multicultural, Non-Fiction, Parenting, Publishing, Relationships, Young Adult.

Cornucopia Press, Angela Harms, 1056 Green Acres Rd. #102-212, Eugene, OR 97408, www.Cornucopia-Press.com, query@cornucopiapress.com, 541-337-8088. 2008. Fiction. ''We are primarily looking for historical fiction and other fiction about real people and places. Please query first via email with a complete synopsis, or use the query page on our website: *cornucopiapress.com/query*. Unpublished authors are encouraged to query. Please be sure your manuscript is finished, edited and polished, and no longer than 120,000 words.'' Expects 3 titles 2010, 12 titles 2011. No titles listed in the *Small Press Record of Books in Print* (36th Edition, 2010-11). Reporting time: We will respond within two weeks if we would like to see your manuscript. Payment: Typical royalty: 15% of net. We are not able to offer advances at this time. Author owns the copyright to the material. Subjects: Americana, Fiction, History, Novels, Old West.

CORONA, Lynda Sexson, Co-Editor; Michael Sexson, Co-Editor; Sarah Merrill, Managing Editor, Dept. of Hist. & Phil., Montana State Univ., PO Box 172320, Bozeman, MT 59717-2320, 406-994-5200. 1980. Poetry, fiction, articles, art, photos, cartoons, satire, music, collages, plays, non-fiction. ''Journal of arts and ideas; imaginative treatment of cultural issues. Looking particularly for work that transcends categories. We are interested in everything from the speculative essay to recipes for the construction or revision of things; we publish art and ideas that surprise with their quality and content. Recent contributors: Frederick Turner, William Irwin Thompson, James Hillman, Rhoda Lerman, Philip Dacey, Ivan Doig, Donald Hall, A.B. Guthrie, Jr., Richard Hugo, William Matthews, Stephen Dixon, James Dickey, Rayna Green, Fritjof Capra, Wendy Battin, Charles Edward Eaton, Nick Johnson.'' circ. 2M. Occasional. Expects 1 issue 2011. sub. price $10; per copy $10; sample $10. Back issues: $10. Discounts: trade, classroom, 20% (orders of 10 or more). 130pp. Reporting time: 1 week to 6 months. Payment: nominal honorarium, 2 copies. Copyrighted. Pub's reviews: 10 in 2009. §All aspects of current thought, technology & the imagination, metaphor, art, religion. Ads: $150/$95/$65/back cover (inside) $200. Subjects: Arts, Culture.

CORRECTION(S): A Literary Journal for Inmate Writing, Correction(s), Editorial Board, PO Box 1326, Boone, NC 28607-1326. 2001. Poetry, fiction, art, parts-of-novels, long-poems. ''Please submit 4-6 poems or up to 8 pages (for fiction) of your work with a brief bio. *Correction(s)* is a biannual journal dedicated to the poetics and vision of incarcerated, American writers. Please proofread carefully before sending manuscript. Typed and handwritten manuscripts acceptable. Please print as neatly as possible. We do not accept previously published work. Also accepts artwork for front cover designs. Send SASE if you want your work returned. Acquires first rights.'' 2/yr. Expects 2 issues 2010, 2 issues 2011. sub. price $5 inmates, $15 everyone else; per copy $3 inmates, $8 everyone else. Discounts: for those that buy in bulk (20 or more): 10% (more if intended for use in a prison); please inquire. 30-40pp. Reporting time: 4-6 weeks. Simultaneous submissions accepted: yes. Payment: 1 copy. Not copyrighted. Subject: Prison.

CORRECTIONS TODAY, Susan Clayton, Managing Editor, American Correctional Association, 206 North Washington Street, Suite 200, Alexandria, VA 22314, 703-224-0000. 1938. Fiction, articles, art, photos, interviews, reviews, letters, news items, non-fiction. ''We accept manuscripts from members of the American Correctional Association on topics related to the field of corrections. Manuscripts should be submitted to the attention of Susan Clayton at the above address and should be no longer than 10 double-spaced, typed pages. We accept well-written pieces on new and informative programs and issues that would be of interest to our members.'' circ. 20M. 7/yr. Pub'd 7 issues 2009; expects 7 issues 2010, 7 issues 2011. sub. price free sub. with membership to the American Correctional Assn.; per copy $6.00; sample free. Back issues: $6.00 per issue. 200pp. Reporting time: 4-6 weeks. Payment: none, we are a non-profit organization. Copyrighted, does not revert to author. Pub's reviews: 25 in 2009. §Anything related to the corrections field of on criminal justice issues. Ads: b/w $1,233/b/w $960/2-color and 4-color fees apply, call for rates, frequency rates available. Subjects: Crime, Education, Employment, Fiction, Literary Review, Non-Fiction, Prison, Psychology, Reviews.

THE CORTLAND REVIEW, Guy Shahar, Founder & Editor Emeritus; Ginger Murchison, Editor; Greg Nicholl, Web Manager; Amy MacLennan, Managing Editor, 35 Grove Street, 5D, New York, NY 10014, http://www.cortlandreview.com, tcr@cortlandreview.com. 1997. Poetry, fiction, interviews, reviews, non-fiction. ''Online journal with audio component. Fiction, nonfiction, poetry. Query first for book reviews, interviews and essays.'' Quarterly Issues; Semi-annual Features. Pub'd 6 issues 2009; expects 6 issues 2010, 6 issues 2011. sub. price Free. Back issues: All Issues since Issue 3 archived on the site. Reporting time: About 6 months. Simultaneous submissions accepted: No. Publishes 20% of manuscripts submitted. Payment: None. Copyrighted, reverts to author. Pub's reviews: 6 in 2009. §Poetry and short fiction. Subjects: Fiction, Interviews, Non-Fiction, Poetry, Reviews.

Corvus Publishing Company, Dennis Padovan, 6021 South Shore Road, Anacortes, WA 98221-8915, 360-293-6068, DP@CorvusBooks.com, www.CorvusBooks.com. Non-fiction. "Publication of book length manuscripts dealing with wildlife health or disease." 1 title listed in the *Small Press Record of Books in Print* (36th Edition, 2010-11). Simultaneous submissions accepted: Yes. Subjects: Animals, Birds, Wildlife.

COSMOPSIS QUARTERLY, Jason Bulger, www.cosmopsis.com. 2005. Poetry, fiction, articles, interviews, satire, criticism, reviews, parts-of-novels, long-poems, plays, non-fiction. "With a love for modern and postmodern literature—the greats like Nabokov, Borges, Joyce—Cosmopsis Quarterly seeks to publish poetry and fiction from new and existing authors. We often receive more poetry than fiction, so short stories are always welcome, especially if they manage to balance humor and drama and have multiple layers within the text. Recent contributors include William Michaelian, Matthew David Brozik, Vanessa Kittle and Michael Fraley." circ. 200. 2/yr. Pub'd 2 issues 2009; expects 2 issues 2010, 2 issues 2011. sub. price $36 / 4 issues; per copy $10; sample $10. Back issues: $10. Discounts: 5 copies 12%; 10 copies 16%. 100pp. Reporting time: 2 weeks after the deadline. Simultaneous submissions accepted: Yes. Publishes 6% of manuscripts submitted. Payment: Complimentary copy of the book. Copyrighted, reverts to author. Ads: None. Subjects: Americana, Book Reviewing, Creative Non-fiction, Essays, Experimental, Fiction, Humanism, Humor, Literature (General), Novels, Poetry, Post Modern, Short Stories, Society, Storytelling.

Coteau Books, Geoffrey Ursell, Publisher; Edna Alford, Editor; Barbara Sapergia, Juvenile Fiction Editor; Robert Currie, Editor; Roberta Coulter, Editor, 2517 Victoria Ave., Regina, Sask. S4P 0T2, Canada, 306-777-0170, e-mail coteau@coteaubooks.com. 1975. Poetry, fiction, art, criticism, plays, non-fiction. "Coteau Books was established to publish prairie and Canadian writing: fiction, non-fiction, books for young readers, poetry. We do *not* consider manuscripts from non-Canadian writers. Coteau Books is committed to publishing the work of new as well as established writers." avg. press run 1.5M. Pub'd 16 titles 2009; expects 11 titles 2010, 10 titles 2011. 25 titles listed in the *Small Press Record of Books in Print* (36th Edition, 2010-11). Discounts: See Publishers Group Canada(our distributor in Canada) or Orca Book Publishers (our US distributor) for detailed discount schedule. 80-325pp. Reporting time: 2-6 months. Simultaneous submissions accepted: no. Publishes 4% of manuscripts submitted. Payment: normally 10% royalties. Subjects: Adolescence, Anthology, Arts, Autobiography, Biography, Canada, Children, Youth, Culture, Literature (General), Multicultural, Myth, Mythology, Native American, Nature, Poetry, Prose.

Cotsen Institute of Archaeology Publications, Shauna Mecartea, Executive Editor & Media Relations Officer, Univ. of California-Los Angeles, A210 Fowler, Los Angeles, CA 90095-1510, 310-825-7411. 1975. Non-fiction. avg. press run 500. Pub'd 4 titles 2009; expects 8 titles 2010, 4 titles 2011. 18 titles listed in the *Small Press Record of Books in Print* (36th Edition, 2010-11). Discounts: 20% to agencies. 200pp. Reporting time: Immediate follow-up; 60 day review period. Simultaneous submissions accepted: no. Payment: none. Does not copyright for author. Subjects: Anthropology, Archaelogy, History.

Cotton Tree Press, Elma Shaw, 2710 Ontario Road NW, Washington, DC 20009, 202-527-3991, 231 (6) 528 840, info@cottontreepress.com, www.cottontreepress.com. 2008. Poetry, fiction, non-fiction. "Cotton Tree Press was established to develop and publish the literary and non-fiction works of African writers. Recent Title: Redemption Road, by Elma Shaw. Forthcoming Titles: The Rainbow Song, by James Dwalu, Birds are Singing, by Wilton Sankawulo, and Kitchen Talk, by Hawa Knuckles." Expects 1 title 2010, 3 titles 2011. No titles listed in the *Small Press Record of Books in Print* (36th Edition, 2010-11). Discounts: Wholesalers 40%Retail Bookstores 40%College Bookstores 20%Other Stores 20%. 240pp. Reporting time: 6 weeks. Simultaneous submissions accepted: No. Publishes 25% of manuscripts submitted. Payment: 10-15% on net receipts. Authors own the copyright to their work. Subjects: African Literature, Africa, African Studies, Anthology, Creative Non-fiction, Culture, Essays, Fiction, Folklore, Memoirs, Non-Fiction, Novels, Picture Books, Poetry, Romance, Short Stories, Travel.

Cottontail Publications, Ellyn R. Kern, 9641 Drakes Ridge Rd, Bennington, IN 47011-1960, 812-427-3921, info@cottontailpublications.com. 1979. Articles, news items, non-fiction. avg. press run 1M. Pub'd 2 titles 2009; expects 1 title 2010, 1 title 2011. 3 titles listed in the *Small Press Record of Books in Print* (36th Edition, 2010-11). Discounts: 2-50 40%, short discount under $10 cover price. 90pp. Reporting time: 6 weeks or less. Payment: to be negotiated. Copyrights for author. Subjects: Americana, Collectibles, Crafts, Hobbies, Genealogy, History.

COTTONWOOD, Cottonwood Press, Tom Lorenz, Editor; Tom Lorenz, Fiction Editor; Philip Wedge, Poetry Editor; Denise Low, Review Editor, Room 400, Kansas Union, 1301 Jayhawk Blvd., University of Kansas, Lawrence, KS 66045, 785-864-2528 (Lorenz) 785-864-3777 (Wedge). 1965. Poetry, fiction, art, photos, interviews, reviews. "We publish a wide variety of styles of poetry, fiction, and nonfiction. Poetry submissions should be limited to the five best, fiction to one story. Past issues have included interviews with William Burroughs, Gwendolyn Brooks and Scott Heim. We have published recent work by Gerald Early, Wanda Coleman, Patricia Traxler, William Stafford, Jared Carter, Victor Contoski, Robert Day, W.S. Merwin, Antonya Nelson, Connie May Fowler, Oakley Hall, and Luci Tapahonso. We welcome submissions of photos, graphics, short fiction, poetry, and reviews from new as well as established writers." circ. 500-600. 1/yr. Pub'd 1 issue 2009; expects 2 issues 2010, 2 issues 2011. sub. price $15, $18 overseas; per copy $8.50; sample $5. Back issues: $4. Discounts: 30% trade, bulk negotiable. 112pp. Reporting time: 3-6 months. Simultaneous submissions accepted: Yes (fiction only). Publishes 1% of manuscripts submitted. Payment: 1 copy, eligibility for yearly Alice Carter Awards in poetry and fiction. Copyrighted. §national, midwest poetry or fiction chapbooks. Ads: none. Subjects: Arts, Biography, Black, Book Reviewing, Fiction, Kansas, Literary Review, Photography, Poetry, Translation.

Cottonwood Press (see also COTTONWOOD), Tom Lorenz, Editor, 400 Kansas Union, Box J, Univ. of Kansas, Lawrence, KS 66045, 785-864-2528. 1965. "We generally solicit material for the press." avg. press run 500-1M. Pub'd 1 title 2009; expects 1 title 2010, 1 title 2011. 16 titles listed in the *Small Press Record of Books in Print* (36th Edition, 2010-11). Discounts: 30% to bookstores. 80pp. Copyrights for author. Subjects: Arts, Biography, Black, Book Reviewing, Fiction, Kansas, Literary Review, Photography, Poetry, Translation.

Cottonwood Press, Inc., Cheryl Thurston, 109-B Cameron Drive, Fort Collins, CO 80525, 970-204-0715. 1986. Non-fiction. "We are interested primarily in practical books for language arts teachers, grades 5-12." avg. press run 2M. Pub'd 3 titles 2009; expects 3 titles 2010, 3-5 titles 2011. 43 titles listed in the *Small Press Record of Books in Print* (36th Edition, 2010-11). Discounts: available upon request. 100pp. Reporting time: 2-4 weeks. We accept simultaneous submissions only if notified. Payment: royalties of 10% of net sales. Copyrights for author. Subjects: Colorado, Drama, Education, English, History, How-To, Humor, Media, Poetry.

Michael E. Coughlin, Publisher (see also THE DANDELION), Michael E. Coughlin, PO Box 205, Cornucopia, WI 54827. 1978. avg. press run 600. Pub'd 2 titles 2009; expects 2 titles 2010, 1 title 2011. 16 titles listed in the *Small Press Record of Books in Print* (36th Edition, 2010-11). Discounts: 40% to bookstores ordering 3 or more copies. 200pp. Reporting time: 2 months. Payment: negotiated. Copyrights for author. Subjects: Anarchist, Libertarian.

Council For Indian Education, Hap Gilliland, President and Editor; Sue A. Clague, Assistant and Bus. Mgr., 1240 Burlington Avenue, Billings, MT 59102-4224, 406-248-3465 phone, 1-5 pm Mtn.time, FAX: (406)-248-1297 www.cie-mt.org., cie@cie-mt.org. 1963. Fiction, non-fiction. "Book ordering address: 1240 Burlington Avenue, Billings, MT 59102-4224. Books on themes related to authentic Native American life and culture, for all students, both fiction and non-fiction, also Indian crafts, and books on teaching Native American students." avg. press run 1M. Pub'd 4 titles 2009; expects 2 titles 2010, 2 titles 2011. 97 titles listed in the *Small Press Record of Books in Print* (36th Edition, 2010-11). Discounts: 1 20%, 2-9 30%, 10+ 40% to bookstores only. avg. 100pppp. Reporting time: 2-8 months. Simultaneous submissions accepted: yes. Publishes 3% of manuscripts submitted. Payment: 10% of wholesale price or 2¢ per word. We furnish author with copyright forms. Subjects: Alaska, Children, Youth, Crafts, Hobbies, Education, Folklore, Native American.

Counterpath Press (see also COUNTERPATH REVIEW), Tim Roberts, Copublisher; Julie Carr, Copublisher, P.O. Box 18351, Denver, CO 80218, www.counterpathpress.org. 2006. Poetry, fiction, articles, art, photos, cartoons, interviews, criticism, reviews, music, letters, parts-of-novels, long-poems, collages, plays, concrete art, non-fiction. avg. press run 750. Pub'd 7 titles 2009; expects 6 titles 2010, 10 titles 2011. 1 title listed in the *Small Press Record of Books in Print* (36th Edition, 2010-11). Discounts: all standard discounts. 100pp. Simultaneous submissions accepted: Yes. Copyrights for author. Subject: Experimental.

COUNTERPATH REVIEW, Counterpath Press, Tim Roberts, P.O. Box 18351, Denver, CO 80218, www.counterpathpress.org. 2008. Poetry, fiction, articles, art, photos, cartoons, interviews, criticism, reviews, music, letters, parts-of-novels, long-poems, collages, plays, concrete art, non-fiction. 1/yr. Expects 1 issue 2010, 1 issue 2011. sub. price $15; per copy $15; sample free. Back issues: inquire. Discounts: all standard discounts. 150pp. Reporting time: 6 months. Simultaneous submissions accepted: Yes. Copyrighted, reverts to author. Pub's reviews: none in 2009. §same as what is included in the magazine. Ads: $400/$300/$200. Subject: Experimental.

Counterpoint, Jack Shoemaker, Editorial Director, 2117 Fourth Street, Suite D, Berkeley, CA 94710. "The counterpoint list includes novels from Edgar Award-winning writer Eliot Pattison, and the PEN USA fiction winner Lydia Millet, as well as a clever novel from Graham Rawle. Counterpoint LLC is a new publishing venture created through the acquisition of three notable independent presses: Counterpoint, Shoemaker & Hoard, and Soft Skull Press. As of January 2008, the company has begun publishing under two imprints: Counterpoint and Soft Skull Press. Shoemaker & Hoard books will transition to being published as Counterpoint books. Also beginning in January, Counterpoint will publish books in association with Sierra Club Books. Counterpoint publishes fiction, literature, and poetry in addition to nonfiction, including history, memoir, biography, and nature. Soft Skull publishes contemporary fiction, as well as graphic novels, and nonfiction, including current affairs, counterculture, and politics. Sierra Club Books publishes books on environmental topics." No titles listed in the *Small Press Record of Books in Print* (36th Edition, 2010-11).

COUNTERPOISE: For Social Responsibilities, Liberty and Dissent, Charles Willett, Founding Editor, 1716 SW Williston Road, Gainesville, FL 32608-4049, 352-335-2200, editor@counterpoise.info, www.counterpoise.info. 1997. Articles, criticism, reviews, letters. "Review journal for alternative books, magazines and videos. Since 2004 *Counterpoise* incorporates *Librarians at Liberty*." circ. 200. 4/yr. Pub'd 4 issues 2009; expects 4 issues 2010, 4 issues 2011. sub. price $40 individual; $60 institution; per copy $12 + $5 S&H; sample free. Back issues: $12 + $5 S&H. Discounts: none. 67pp. Payment: none. Copyrighted, does not revert to author. Pub's reviews: 150 in 2009. §Alternative press. Ads: Full page $300; half-page $180. Subjects: Audio/Video, Bibliography, Book Reviewing, Counter-Culture, Alternatives, Communes, Criticism, Human Rights, Libraries, Magazines, Publishing, Reference, Reviews.

•**COURT GREEN,** Cora Jacobs, Managing Editor, Columbia College Chicago, English Dept., 600 South Michigan Ave., Chicago, IL 60605, 312/369-8212. "Each issue of Court Green features a dossier on a special topic or theme. For our eighth issue, we are seeking creative responses to the work, life, and legacy of Frank O'Hara. It has been over forty years since O'Hara's accident, and sudden death, on Fire Island. In the decades since, his influence has proven to be indelible. For this dossier, we would like to see fresh takes on and responses to O'Hara's life and work, however subtle or overt, in poetry and short lyric essays or prose. We imagine walk poems, "I do this, I do that" poems, celebrity elegies, fortune cookies, personal poems, odes and meditations, and a myriad of other homages. All styles are welcome. We are not looking for critical/academic works at this time. Submissions for dossier and regular sections of the magazine are welcome. If you would like to submit poems for either or both sections, our submission period is March 1-June 30 of each year. We do not accept more than one submission per poet during our submission/reading period. Please note that we do not accept more than five pages of poetry. We will respond by August 31."

Coyote's Journal, James Koller, PO Box 629, Brunswick, ME 04011, http://www.coyotesjournal.com. 1964. avg. press run 50-500. Expects 1 title 2010. 8 titles listed in the *Small Press Record of Books in Print* (36th Edition, 2010-11). Discounts: 40% to retail. 10-100pp. Copyright varies.

•**Cozy Cat Press,** Patricia Rockwell, 2452 Reflections Drive, Aurora, IL 60502, 630-820-1945. 2010. Fiction. "Publishes only "cozy" mysteries." avg. press run 100. Expects 2 titles 2010, 2 titles 2011. 2 titles listed in the *Small Press Record of Books in Print* (36th Edition, 2010-11). Discounts: 2-10 copies 25%. 200pp. Reporting time: a few days. Simultaneous submissions accepted: No. Payment: to be arranged individually with each author. Copyrights for author. Subjects: Fiction, Mystery, Novels.

CRAB CREEK REVIEW, Kelli Russell Agodon, Co-Editor; Annette Spaulding-Convy, Co-Editor; Lana Hechtman Ayers, Poetry Editor; Jen Betterley, Fiction Editor; Nancy Canyon, Fiction Editor; Star Rockers, Creative Non-Fiction Editor, PO Box 1524, Kingston, WA 98346, crabcreekreview@gmail.com, crabcreekeditors@gmail.com, www.crabcreekreview.org. 1983. Poetry, fiction, art, satire, non-fiction. "*CCR* is a perfect-bound print literary journal dedicated to publishing the best poetry, fiction, and creative non-fiction. We are interested in publishing both emerging and established poets and writers. Over the years we have published: Naomi Shihab Nye, David Guterson, Rebecca Wells, William Stafford, Madeline DeFrees, Dorianne Laux, Marvin Bell, Peter Pereira, Ilya Kaminsky, Denise Duhamel, Aimee Nezhukumatathil and other well-known poets and writers. Send up to 5 poems. Simultaneous submissions are accepted when clearly indicated in the cover letter, and must be withdrawn immediately if accepted elsewhere. *CCR* also seeks submissions of short fiction. We accept stories up to 4,000 words, with an admitted predilection for dynamic prose of distinct voice and strong images. Visit our website for more info: www.crabcreekreview.org Crab Creek Review, thanks to our subscribers, writers, readers, and donors for their ongoing support." circ. 1000. 2/yr. Pub'd 1 issue 2009; expects 2 issues 2010, 2 issues 2011. sub. price $15 (1 year)/ $28 (2 years) /$30 (libraries); per copy $8; sample $5; $3 for anniversary anthology (1994). Back issues: $6. 100pp. Reporting time: 3-5 months. Simultaneous submissions accepted: yes. Publishes 5% of manuscripts submitted. Payment: 2 copies. Copyrighted, rights revert to author but request mention of *Crab Creek Review* with subsequent printings. Pub's reviews: 10+ in 2009. §poetry, fiction, creative non-fiction/memoir. Subjects: Fiction, Literature (General), Poetry, Short Stories, Translation.

CRAB ORCHARD REVIEW, Jon Tribble, Managing Editor; Allison Joseph, Editor & Poetry Editor; Carolyn Alessio, Prose Editor, SIUC Dept. of English - Mail Code 4503, 1000 Faner Drive, Carbondale, IL 62901, 618-453-6833, www.siu.edu/~crborchd. 1995. Poetry, fiction, parts-of-novels, long-poems, non-fiction. "Journal of creative works publishing fiction, poetry, creative non-fiction, interviews, novel excerpts, and book reviews. Recent contributors include Donna Hemans, Lee Ann Roripaugh, Ned Balbo, A. Van Jordan, Jesse Lee Kercheval. Considers submissions for our Winter/Spring general issue from February through April. From August through October, we only consider submissions for our Summer/Fall special issue (theme announced on web site). Annual Poetry, Fiction, and Nonfiction contests held February 1 through April 1." circ. 3M. 2/yr. Pub'd 2 issues 2009; expects 2 issues 2010, 2 issues 2011. sub. price $20; per copy $12; sample $10. Back issues: $8. 220pp. Reporting time: 3 weeks to 7 months. We encourage simultaneous submissions, but do like to be informed. Publishes 2% of manuscripts submitted. Payment: $50 min. for poetry, $100 min. for prose, $20 per published page, plus a year's subscription and 2 copies. Copyrighted, reverts to author. Pub's reviews: 10 in 2009. §Small press and university press titles only (poetry, fiction, creative nonfiction); book reviews are done in-house by staff. Writers may send books for review to the Managing Editor. Ads: none. Subjects: Fiction, Interviews, Literary Review, Non-Fiction, Poetry, Short Stories.

Craftsman Book Company, Gary Moselle, Publisher; Laurence Jacobs, Editor, 6058 Corte Del Cedro, Carlsbad, CA 92011, 760-438-7828. 1952. Non-fiction. "Craftsman Book Company publishes *practical references for professional builders*. Craftsman books are loaded with step-by-step instructions, illustrations, charts, reference data, checklists, forms, samples, cost estimates, rules of thumb, and examples that solve actual problems in the builder's office or in the field. Every book covers a limited construction subject fully, becomes the builder's primary reference on that subject, has a high utility-to-cost ratio, and will help the builder make a better living in his profession. Length is variable but should be at least 500 manuscript pages including illustrations and charts. We seek queries and outlines and will consider material in nearly all construction areas and trades, including electrical, heating and air conditioning, lath and plaster, painting, prefab housing construction, heavy construction, estimating, and costing." avg. press run 5M. Pub'd 10 titles 2009; expects 12 titles 2010, 12 titles 2011. 27 titles listed in the *Small Press Record of Books in Print* (36th Edition, 2010-11). Discounts: trade 1-4 copies 33%, 5-49 copies 40%, 50+ copies 45%. 297pp. Reporting time: 3 weeks. Simultaneous submissions accepted: yes. Publishes 10% of manuscripts submitted. Payment: 12-1/2% of net of all books sold, 7-1/2% for discounts of 50% or more. Copyrights for author. Subjects: Architecture, Business & Economics.

Crandall, Dostie & Douglass Books, Inc., 245 West 4th Avenue, Roselle, NJ 07203-1135, Phone: 908.241.5439, Fax: 908.245.4972, Email: Publisher@CDDbooks.com, www.CDDbooks.com. 2002. "Crandall, Dostie & Douglass Books, Inc. invites authors to submit queries, proposals and manuscripts for our consideration regarding nonfiction works on topics of whiteness, white American culture, white anti-racism, white privilege, white supremacy, and the role of white Americans in a multiracial society.Contact us at the following: Crandall, Dostie & Douglass Books, Inc. 245 West 4th Avenue, Roselle, NJ 07203. Phone: 908.241.5439 Fax: 908.245.4972." Expects 1 title 2010, 1 title 2011. 3 titles listed in the *Small Press Record of Books in Print* (36th Edition, 2010-11). Subjects: Current Affairs, How-To, Human Rights, Multicultural, Non-Violence, Public Affairs, Race, Society.

Crane Press, Kurt DuNard, Suite #172, 3510 NE 3rd Avenue, Camas, WA 98607, 360-210-5982, fax 360-210-5983, 800-745-6273, Info@CranePress.com. Fiction, non-fiction. "Any fiction or non-fiction which will uplift and motivate the reader to live a better life." 1 title listed in the *Small Press Record of Books in Print* (36th Edition, 2010-11). Discounts: 4299: -40%300499: -50%500up: -55%. Reporting time: 30 days. Simultaneous submissions accepted: No. Payment: Industry standard. Does not copyright for author. Subjects: Autobiography, Bibliography, Business & Economics, Careers, Fiction, Futurism, How-To, Inspirational, Non-Fiction, Philosophy, Self-Help, Speaking, Tennessee.

CRANNOG, Tony O'Dwyer, Galway Language Center, Bridge Mills, Galway, Ireland, editor@crannogmaga-zine.com, www.crannogmagazine.com. 2002. Poetry, fiction, parts-of-novels, plays. "We publish quality material with strong, fresh imagery. We welcome submissions from all over the world and like to see international authors sit alongside local writers.Recent contributors have included Moya Cannon (former editor Poetry Ireland), Patricia Burke Brogan (Eclipsed), Rita Ann Higgins (Sunny Side Plucked), Joan McBreen (An Bhilleog Ban, The White Page), John Arden (British Playwright and poet now Galway resident)." circ. 200. 3/yr. Pub'd 3 issues 2009; expects 3 issues 2010, 3 issues 2011. sub. price 18; per copy 6; sample 6. Back issues: 3. Discounts: 20-25%. 64pp. Reporting time: 2-4 months. Simultaneous submissions accepted: Yes, but inform promptly of publication elsewhere. Publishes 40% of manuscripts submitted. Payment: copy of magazine and invitation to read at launch. Copyrighted, reverts to author. Subjects: Fiction, Literature (General), Poetry.

THE CRAPSHOOTER, Leaf Press, Larry Edell, Andrea Foote, PO Box 421440, San Diego, CA 92142, larryedell@aol.com. 1995. Articles, cartoons, non-fiction. "Gambling material *only*." circ. 2M. 4/yr. Pub'd 4 issues 2009; expects 4 issues 2010, 4 issues 2011. sub. price $25; per copy $7; sample $7. Back issues: 5 for $30 ppd. Discounts: 50% for subscription agents. 4pp. Reporting time: immediate. Simultaneous submissions accepted: yes. Publishes 50% of manuscripts submitted. Payment: varies. Copyrighted, reverts to author. Pub's reviews: 4 in 2009. §Gambling with emphasis on casino craps. Ads: none. Subject: Games.

Crazy Woman Creek Press, Harriett Gardner, 3073 Hanson, Cheyenne, WY 82001, 707-829-8568, www.jewsofwyoming.org. 1998. Photos, interviews. "Subject matter to be primarily photographic in nature and dealing with cultures in the American west." avg. press run 3M. Expects 1 title 2010. No titles listed in the *Small Press Record of Books in Print* (36th Edition, 2010-11). Discounts: trade 50%, no returns. 200pp. Reporting time: 2 months. Simultaneous submissions accepted: no. Payment: yes. Copyrights for author. Subjects: Americana, Genealogy, Photography, Picture Books, The West.

CRAZYHORSE, Garrett Doherty, Editor; Carol Ann Davis, Editor; Anthony Varallo, Fiction Editor, Dept. of English College of Charleston, 66 George Street, Charleston, SC 29424, crazyhorse@cofc.edu, http://www.crazyhorsejournal.org. 1960. Poetry, fiction, art, interviews, criticism, long-poems, non-fiction. circ. 2000. 2/yr. Pub'd 2 issues 2009; expects 2 issues 2010, 2 issues 2011. sub. price $16; per copy $9; sample $5. Back issues: $5. Discounts: please inquire. 160pp. Reporting time: 3-4 months. Simultaneous submissions accepted: Yes. Publishes 3% of manuscripts submitted. Payment: $20 per page for all. Copyrighted, reverts to author. Ads: $125 full page. Subjects: Fiction, Literature (General), Non-Fiction, Poetry, Prose.

THE CREAM CITY REVIEW, Jay Johnson, Editor-in-Chief; Drew Blanchard, Managing Editor, PO Box 413, English Dept, Curtin Hall, Univ. of Wisconsin, Milwaukee, WI 53201, 414-229-4708. 1975. Poetry, fiction, art, photos, interviews, criticism, reviews, parts-of-novels, long-poems, non-fiction. "We publish a variety of writers and writings, offering a range of perspectives, styles, and contents from new and well-known writers. We prefer prose of 25 pages or less, though we'll consider longer pieces. Please submit no more than one work of prose, or up to five poems. Short, small press book reviews and creative nonfiction are especially welcome, as are b/w camera-ready art and photos. Recent contributors: Marge Piercy, Maxine Kumin, Ted Kooser, Stuart Dybek, Amy Clampitt, Tess Gallagher, Lawrence Ferlinghetti, Denise Levertov, Alicia Ostriker, Cathy Song, Russell Edson, William Kittredge, Audre Lorde, Donald Hall, Albert Goldbarth, Adrienne Rich, Diane Glancy, Adrian C. Louis, Kate Braverman, William Stafford, and Gary Soto." circ. 2M. 2/yr. Pub'd 2 issues 2009; expects 2 issues 2010, 2 issues 2011. sub. price $22 for 1 year, $41 for 2 years; per copy $12; sample $7. Back issues: $7, double issues $12. Discounts: schools send SASE for rates. 200pp. Reporting time: 6-8 months, we read from Sept. 1st - April 1st only. Simultaneous submissions acceptable with notification. Publishes 5-7% of manuscripts submitted. Payment: 1 year subscription. Copyrighted, reverts to author. Pub's reviews: 5 in 2009. §Poetry, fiction, creative nonfiction, art. Ads: $100/$50/no classified word rate. Subjects: Chicano/a, Environment, Essays, Fiction, Gay, Interviews, Lesbianism, Literary Review, Memoirs, Native American, Non-Fiction, Poetry, Reviews, Short Stories, Translation.

Creative Arts Book Company, Paul Samuelson, George Samsa, Lissa Fox, 833 Bancroft Way, Berkeley, CA 94710, staff@creativeartsbooks.com. 1968. Poetry, fiction, criticism, music, letters, non-fiction. avg. press run 2.5M-5M. Pub'd 40 titles 2009; expects 70 titles 2010, 70 titles 2011. 2 titles listed in the *Small Press Record of Books in Print* (36th Edition, 2010-11). Reporting time: 6 weeks. Simultaneous submissions accepted: yes. Payment: yes. Copyrights for author. Subjects: Adoption, Autobiography, Black, California, Crime, Erotica, Fiction, Handicapped, Holocaust, Juvenile Fiction, Jack Kerouac, Literature (General), Memoirs, Music, Mystery.

The Creative Company, PO Box 227, Mankato, MN 56002. 1932. No titles listed in the *Small Press Record of Books in Print* (36th Edition, 2010-11).

•**Creative Creations Consulting Publishing Company (see also INSIDE LEADERSHIP NEWSLETTER),** DrTekemia Dorsey, P O Box 9671-4017, 617 Middle River Rd, Middle River, MD 21220, 410-391-3880 work; 443-413-5600 cell; 410-391-9036 fax; drdorsey@creativecreationsconsulting.com; www.creativecreationsconsulting.com. 2009. Fiction, articles, interviews, non-fiction. avg. press run 50. Expects 2 titles 2010, 5 titles 2011. No titles listed in the *Small Press Record of Books in Print* (36th Edition, 2010-11). Discounts: 2-25 copies (5%)26-50 copies (10%) 51-75 copies (15%) 76-100 copies (20%) 101-200 copies (25%). 250pp. Reporting time: 24-48 hours. Simultaneous submissions accepted: Yes. Payment: Discussed individually. Copyrights for author. Subjects: Advertising, Self-Promotion, Audio/Video, Autobiography, Awards, Foundations, Grants, Book Reviewing, Children, Youth, Creative Non-fiction, Education, Nutrition, Parenting, Reprints, Research, Self-Help, Textbooks.

CREATIVE NONFICTION, Lee Gutkind, 5501 Walnut Street #202, Pittsburgh, PA 15232-2329, 412-688-0304, fax 412-688-0262. 1993. Interviews, non-fiction. circ. 4500. 3/yr. Pub'd 3 issues 2009; expects 3 issues 2010, 3 issues 2011. sub. price $29.95/4 issues; per copy $10; sample $10. Back issues: $10. 164pp. Reporting time: 5 months. Simultaneous submissions accepted: yes. Publishes 1% of manuscripts submitted. Payment: varies. Copyrighted, does not revert to author. Ads: $275/$200. Subjects: English, Essays, Journals, Literature (General), Non-Fiction.

Creative Roots, Inc., Lloyd deMause, 140 Riverside Drive, New York, NY 10024, 212-799-2294. 1975. Non-fiction. "Book publishing." avg. press run 2M. Pub'd 1 title 2009; expects 2 titles 2010, 5 titles 2011. 2 titles listed in the *Small Press Record of Books in Print* (36th Edition, 2010-11). Discounts: 2 or more-20%. 350pp. Reporting time: 1 month. Payment: variable. Copyrights for author. Subjects: History, Psychology.

Creative With Words Publications (CWW) (see also THEECLECTICS), Brigitta Geltrich, Editor & Publisher; Bert Hower, Nature Editor, PO Box 223226, Carmel, CA 93922-3226, Fax: 831-655-8627; e-mail: cwwpub@usa.net; http://members.tripod.com/~creativewithwords. 1975. Poetry, fiction, cartoons, satire. "On any topic, written by all ages (poetry and prose)." Pub'd 12 titles 2009; expects 12-14 titles 2010, 12 titles 2011. 64 titles listed in the *Small Press Record of Books in Print* (36th Edition, 2010-11). Discounts: schools &

libraries 10%; authors receive 20% off on orders 1-9 copies; 30% off on orders 10-19 copies and 40% off on orders of 20 copies and more. There are no free copies. Pages vary (approx. 60+pp). Reporting time: 1 month for inquiries, SASE is always a must; if a seasonal anthology, reporting time is 2 months after set deadline. Simultaneous submissions accepted: no. Publishes 90% of manuscripts submitted. Payment: 20% reduction of regular cost to participants, no payment in copies; small fee for guest artists, readers, and guest editors. Copyrights for author. Subjects: Children, Youth, Folklore, Poetry, Senior Citizens.

Creative Writing and Publishing Company, Cheryl Britt, PO Box 511848, Milwaukee, WI 53203-0311, (414) 507-9677, (414) 447-7810 for Fax Machine. 1995. Non-fiction. "Creative Writing and Publishing contributes to exciting the imagination of young children. One of our missions is to put reading back in first place." avg. press run 250. Pub'd 1 title 2009; expects 2 titles 2010, 1 title 2011. 3 titles listed in the *Small Press Record of Books in Print* (36th Edition, 2010-11). Discounts: 3 to 12 copies 25%. 24pp. Reporting time: Right now not accepting any manuscripts. Simultaneous submissions accepted: No. Does not copyright for author. Subjects: African-American, Arts, Cartoons, Children, Youth, Family, Fantasy, Food, Eating, Health, Juvenile Fiction, Pets, Picture Books, Poetry, Publishing, Television, Theatre.

Crescent Moon (see also PAGAN AMERICA; PASSION), Jeremy Robinson, Cassidy Hughes, PO Box 393, Maidstone, Kent ME14 5XU, United Kingdom. 1988. Poetry, articles, art, photos, interviews, criticism, reviews, music, letters, parts-of-novels, news items. "We prefer a letter and sample first, not a whole manuscript. Return postage and envelope. We are open to many ideas for books." avg. press run 100-200. Pub'd 15 titles 2009; expects 15 titles 2010, 20 titles 2011. 4 titles listed in the *Small Press Record of Books in Print* (36th Edition, 2010-11). Discounts: Trade: single order 20%, 2+ 35%, add $1.50 postage. 120pp. Reporting time: 2 months. Simultaneous submissions accepted: yes. We publish 5% or less of manuscripts submitted. Payment: to be negotiated. Copyrights for author. Subjects: Arts, Biography, Book Reviewing, Creativity, Criticism, Culture, Emily Dickinson, Electronics, Feminism, Interviews, D.H. Lawrence, Literary Review, Literature (General), Magic, Media.

CRICKET, Marianne Carus, Editor-in-Chief; Alice Letvin, Editorial Director; Lonnie Plecha, Editor, 70 E. Lake St., Suite 300, Chicago, IL 60601, Phone: 312-701-1720. Fax: 312-701-1728. Website: www.cricket-mag.com. 1973. Poetry, fiction, articles, art, photos, interviews, music, plays, non-fiction. "Word limit for fiction: 2000 words; for non-fiction: 1500 words. SASE is required for response." circ. 74M. 12/yr. Pub'd 12 issues 2009; expects 12 issues 2010, 12 issues 2011. sub. price $35.97; per copy $5; sample $5. Back issues: $5. 48pp. Reporting time: up to 6 months. Please indicate that it's a simultaneous submission. Publishes 1% of manuscripts submitted. Payment: stories and articles up to 25¢ per word (2000 max), poems up to $3 per line. Copyrighted, does not revert to author. Pub's reviews: 60 one-paragraph in 2009. §Any good children's or young adult books: fiction or non-fiction. Subjects: Children, Youth, Literature (General), Magazines.

THE CRIER, Doree Shafrir, Associate Editor, 220 DeKalb Ave., Brooklyn, NY 11205. "The Crier is a new kind of magazinesmart, but not pretentious; timely and savvy, but not precious. Founded in summer 2006, its unconventional mix of art and culture, travel, science, and leisure make it a magazine youll want to read to the very last page. In the past, weve featured original reporting from New Yorks High Line project, the Texas-Mexico border and La Paz, Bolivia, where a group of female wrestlers struggle against an exploitative manager. Our critics and essayists have scratched their heads over Ray Kurzweil and his theory of the Singularity; forgotten southern sermons; artist Mark Leckey and New Age maestro Vangelis. Each of our issuesfour per yearbegins with The Quarterly Report, a collection of short items organized around a theme. No fiction or poetry."

CRITICAL INQUIRY, University of Chicago Press, W.J.T. Mitchell, University of Chicago, Wieboldt Hall 202, 1050 East 59th Street, Chicago, IL 60637, Telephone: (773) 702-8477; Fax: (773) 702-3397, http://www.journals.uchicago.edu/CI/home.html. 1974. "Founded 30 years ago, *Critical Inquiry* is an interdisciplinary journal devoted to publishing the best critical thought in the arts and humanities. Combining a commitment to rigorous scholarship with a vital concern for dialogue and debate, the journal presents articles by eminent and emerging critics, scholars, and artists on a wide variety of issues central to contemporary criticism and culture. In *CI* new ideas and reconsideration of those traditional in criticism and culture are granted a voice. The wide interdisciplinary focus creates surprising juxtapositions and linkages of concepts, offering new grounds for theoretical debate. In *CI,* authors entertain and challenge while illuminating such issues as improvisations, the life of things, Flaubert, and early modern women's writing. *CI* comes full circle with the electrically charged debates between contributors and their critics." 4/yr.

CRITICAL REVIEW, Jeffrey M. Friedman, Critical Review Foundation, P.O. Box 869, Helotes, TX 78023, edcritrev@gmail.com. 1987. Articles, reviews. "Uniquely, *Critical Review* offers its contributors the opportunity to explore problems in democratic decision making at length. In particular, the questions of public ignorance, irrationality, and demagoguery are treated in the journal with rigor but fearlessness. Inspired by, but not limited to, the "Austrian" economists' focus on economic ignorance, *Critical Review* is interested in comparisons of the cognitive problems faced by public- and private-sphere decision makers. Style guide online." circ. 3M. 4/yr. Pub'd 4 issues 2009; expects 4 issues 2010, 4 issues 2011. sub. price $58, libraries $330; per copy $18; sample $18. Back issues: $18 for single issues, $25 double issues, $35 triple issues. 160pp. Reporting time: 2 months. Payment: none. Copyrighted, rights revert to author if arranged. Pub's reviews: 14 in 2009. §Political science, political psychology, evolutionary psychology, cognitive psychology. Ads: $100 full page. Subjects: Philosophy, Political Science, Politics, Psychology, Society.

Crooked Hills Publishing, Eowyn Wood, PO Box 83066, Portland, OR 97283, www.crookedhills.com. 2005. Fiction. 1 title listed in the *Small Press Record of Books in Print* (36th Edition, 2010-11).

CROSS CURRENTS, Charles Henderson, Executive Director*; Carey Monserrate, Managing Editor, 475 Riverside Drive, Suite 1945, New York, NY 10115, 212-870-2544, Fax: 212-870-2539. 1950. Poetry, articles, interviews, reviews, letters, non-fiction. "Contributing Editors, Randi Rashkover, Scott Holland, Catherine Madsen and Stephanie Mitchem." circ. 4.5M. 4/yr. Pub'd 4 issues 2009; expects 4 issues 2010, 4 issues 2011. 1 title listed in the *Small Press Record of Books in Print* (36th Edition, 2010-11). sub. price $40, libraries $50, outside US $5 additional postage; per copy $7.50; sample $7.50. Back issues: $7.50. 144pp. Reporting time: 1 month. Payment: none. Copyrighted, reverts to author. Pub's reviews: 52 in 2009. §Theology, philosophy, world politics, literature, and arts. Ads: $400/$250/$150 1/4 pg. Subject: Religion.

Cross-Cultural Communications, Stanley H. Barkan, Publisher, 239 Wynsum Ave., Merrick, NY 11566-4725, Tel: 516-868-5635 Fax: 516-379-1901 E: cccpoetry@aol.com, www.cross-culturalcommunications.com. 1971. Poetry, fiction, art, photos, music, parts-of-novels, plays, non-fiction. "Focus: bilingual poetry from traditionally neglected languages and cultures. Recent contributors: Stanley Kunitz, Joan Alcover, John Amen, Kayvan Asgari, Fuad Attal, Sacha Beres, Bohdan Boychuk, Mia Barkan Clarke, Vince Clemente, Aleksey Dayen, Kristine Doll, Arthur Dobrin, John Dotson, Charles Fishman, John Gery, Isaac Goldemberg, Hafez, Theofil Halama, Joan Carole Hand, Mahmood Karimi-Hakak, Carolyn Mary Kleefeld, Danuta Kostewicz, Dariusz Tomasz Lebioda, Sung-Il Lee, Beverly Matherne, Bill Negron, Biljana D. Obradovic, Stanislao G. Pugliese, Clementine Rabassa, Kyung-nyun Kim Richards, Steffen F. Richards, Youngju Ryu, Nat Scammacca, Ignazio Silone, Gerald Stern, Lynn Strongin, Adam Szyper, Edward Tabachnik, Henry Taylor, Stoyan "Tchouki" Tchoukanov, Peter Thabit Jones, Aeronwy Thomas, Tino Villanueva, A. D. Winans, Bill Wolak, Yang Guija, Yun Humyong." avg. press run 1,000. Pub'd 15 titles 2009; expects 15 titles 2010, 15 titles 2011. 226 titles listed in the *Small Press Record of Books in Print* (36th Edition, 2010-11). Discounts: Wholesalers, Jobbers, Retailers: 40% Distributors: 50%/55%Authors: 40%. Copyrights for author. Subjects: Asia, Indochina, Bilingual, Eastern Europe, France, French, Holocaust, Italy, Judaism, Latin America, Multicultural, Native American, Poetry, Scandinavia, Dylan Thomas, Translation, Wales.

CROSSCURRENTS, Bob Fink, 516 Ave K South, Saskatoon, Sask. S7M 2E2, Canada, Fax 306-244-0795, green@webster.sk.ca—www.webster.sk.ca/greenwich/xc.htm. 1975—. Art, satire, criticism, music, non-fiction. "*Crosscurrents* is a musicolgy newsletter on issues of ancient music, origins, archaeology. It also deals (less often) with the arts, society, ecology and history. Under our imprint are new and recent books and essays as well: *On the Origin of Music—Readings and Essays* (http://www.webster.sk.ca/greenwich/readings.htm) ; Oldest known musical instrument: *Neanderthal Flute* (http://www.webster.sk.ca/greenwich/fl-compl.htm) and more. See our URL: http://www.webster.sk.ca/greenwich/fulllist.htm for the full list of our webpages." *Circ: 500-5M depending on subject and reprints.* Quarterly, irregular, includes reprints and *Extras.* Pub'd 4 issues 2009; expects 4 issues 2010, 4 issues 2011. Subscription $15 U.S.; price per copy $1.50 U.S.; sample $1.50 (postpaid). Back issues: *$5 for any 10, 1975 to present + $2 postage.* 4-8pp. Copyrighted. Pub's reviews: 1 in 2009. §Arts and musicology. Subjects: Anthropology, Archaelogy, Arts, Criticism, Environment, History, Human Rights, Music, Science.

•**CROSSING RIVERS INTO TWILIGHT,** Elizabeth Kate Switaj, Founder and General Editor, critjournal@gmail.com. "CRIT Journal [on-line] seeks to gather a set of artistic and literary works that reflect themes related to liminality, transition, border states, and the imperceptible. This could mean literally depicting dusk or fog, or it could mean something more metaphorical. Hybrid genres are especially desired for the purposes of this project.. Issues appear around the cross-quarter holidays. We currently have openings for section editors for visual art, vispo, music, and any other section you might wish to propose."

Crossway, Allan Fisher, Senior Vice President of the Book Division, 1300 Crescent Street, Wheaton, IL 60187, 630-682-4300. 1979. Non-fiction. "A publishing ministry of Good News Publishers. Publish books from an evangelical Christian perspective, including contemporary issues, theology, and the family." avg. press run 7M. Pub'd 85 titles 2009; expects 75 titles 2010, 70 titles 2011. No titles listed in the *Small Press Record of Books in Print* (36th Edition, 2010-11). Discounts: trade, jobber. 192pp. Reporting time: 6 months. Simultaneous submissions accepted: yes. Payment: based on net receipts. Copyrights for author. Subjects: Christianity, Non-Fiction.

R.L. Crow Publications, William S. Gainer, P.O. Box 262, Penn Valley, CA 95946, Fax and Message: (530) 432-8195, info@rlcrow.com. 2003. Poetry. "R.L. Crow Publications is a small publishing house, publishing from one to five books and several limited edition broadsides per year. We are currently focusing on contemporary poetry and prose. Though we are not limited to publishing one type or form of writing we do look for material that is written with a clarity of language, boldness of expression and uses an honesty of experience as its platform. We do lean toward the Meat and Street styles of writing. R.L. Crow believes that poetry is an expressive literary art form of which each poem is a stand-alone piece of art and that the best way to express this art is through the directness of the short poem. We appreciate an economy of language.R.L. Crow Publications' mission is to challenge contemporary poets and writers to work with a clarity of language and boldness of expression that leaves the reader with a new understanding of the familiar. It is R.L. Crow Publications' business to showcase and publish the best of these efforts.Please read our current back list: Roxy: Todd Cirillo, W. S Gainer, Will Staple; Leaning Against Time, Neeli Cherkovski; tiny teeth - the Woormwood Review poems, Ann Menebroker.'' avg. press run 1000+. Pub'd 2 titles 2009; expects 1 title 2010, 2 titles 2011. 4 titles listed in the *Small Press Record of Books in Print* (36th Edition, 2010-11). Discounts: We generally work though our distributors: Small Press Distribution or Baker and Taylor. We do sell direct to booksellers, with retail seller permits, at 45% discount with the buyer paying shipping for 20 units or less. 60-100pp. Reporting time: Please review our website (rlcrow.com) before submitting. Simultaneous submissions accepted: No. Publishes 1% of manuscripts submitted. Payment: Negotiated indiviually. Copyrights for author. Subject: Poetry.

CRUCIBLE, Terrence L. Grimes, Office of the Vice President for Academic Affairs, Barton College, Wilson, NC 27893, 252-399-6344. 1964. Poetry, fiction. ''Short stories should not exceed 8,000 words.'' circ. 300. 1/yr. Pub'd 1 issue 2009; expects 1 issue 2010, 1 issue 2011. sub. price $7; per copy $7; sample $7. Back issues: $7. Discounts: none. 70pp. Reporting time: 2-4 months. Simultaneous submissions accepted: no. Publishes 10% of manuscripts submitted. Payment: 2 complimentary copies of issue. Copyrighted, reverts to author. Subjects: Fiction, Literary Review, Literature (General), Poetry.

Crystal Dreams Publishing, Kevin Aguanno, Managing Editor; Sarah Schwersenska, Acquisitions Editor, Box 58043, Rosslynn RPO, Oshawa, Ontario, L1J 8L6, Canada, Phone: (905) 986-5848Toll-Free: 1-866-721-1540 (Canada and USA only)Fax: (905) 986-5777. 2000. Poetry, fiction, non-fiction. ''Fiction and general adult trade imprint of Multi-Media Publications Inc. Accepts email queries. Submission guidelines at http:/ /www.mmpubs.com.'' Pub'd 5 titles 2009; expects 20 titles 2010, 20 titles 2011. No titles listed in the *Small Press Record of Books in Print* (36th Edition, 2010-11). 30% discount to book trade, 20% discount to libraries. 200-400pp. Reporting time: 2-3 weeks. Simultaneous submissions accepted: Yes. Payment: Currently 20% royalties, paid quarterly. Does not copyright for author. Subjects: Erotica, Fantasy, Fiction, Horror, How-To, Humor, Non-Fiction, Novels, Occult, Romance, Science Fiction, Self-Help, Sex, Sexuality.

Crystal Press, John Baxter, 4212 E. Los Angeles Avenue # 42, Simi Valley, CA 93063-3308, 805-527-4369, Fax 805-527-3949, crystalpress@aol.com. 1992. Fiction, non-fiction. ''We publish books that give readers greater insight into business or education, and we wish to review Northwest fiction.'' avg. press run 1M. Pub'd 1 title 2009; expects 2 titles 2010, 2 titles 2011. No titles listed in the *Small Press Record of Books in Print* (36th Edition, 2010-11). 200pp. Reporting time: 60 days. Simultaneous submissions accepted: yes. Payment: by arrangement. Copyrights for author. Subjects: Business & Economics, Education, Futurism, New Hampshire.

Crystal Publishers, Inc., Frank Leanza, 3460 Lost Hills Drive, Las Vegas, NV 89122, 702-434-3037 phone/Fax. 1985. Music. avg. press run 5M. Pub'd 2 titles 2009; expects 2 titles 2010, 5 titles 2011. 30 titles listed in the *Small Press Record of Books in Print* (36th Edition, 2010-11). Discounts: 46-55% wholesaler. 224pp. Reporting time: 6-8 weeks. Payment: semi-annual. Copyrights for author. Subjects: Music, Textbooks.

CT Press (see also NIBBLE), Jeff Fleming, Oakland, CA, nibblepoems@gmail.com. 1995. Poetry. ''*Nibble* is a new magazine from CT Press looking for great short poetry.'' avg. press run 200. Pub'd 4 titles 2009; expects 8 titles 2010, 10 titles 2011. No titles listed in the *Small Press Record of Books in Print* (36th Edition, 2010-11). 32pp. Reporting time: 2 weeks. Simultaneous submissions accepted: No. Publishes 40% of manuscripts submitted. Payment: Free copies. Does not copyright for author.

Culturelink Press, Diane Asitimbay, P.O. Box 3538, San Diego, CA 92163, Tel. (619) 501-9873, www.culturelinkpress.com; Fax purchase and school orders: Tel(619) 501-1369. 2004. Criticism, news items, non-fiction. ''Culturelink Press is a small publishing house that is committed to publishing titles that inform readers of cultural differences among people within the United States as well as increase cultural awareness in the international community. *What's Up America?* is a cultural handbook for foreigners and Americans alike. It answers questions foreigners often ask Americans. Plans are underway to publish a collection of cultural essays, and a volume of short fiction on cultural themes for 2005-2006.'' avg. press run 1000. Expects 1 title 2010, 3 titles 2011. No titles listed in the *Small Press Record of Books in Print* (36th Edition, 2010-11). Discounts: Distributors - 25%Wholesalers - 55-65%Retailers - 40%Classrooms -Multiple orders discount. 200-300pp. Reporting time: Not accepting manuscript submissions at this time. Simultaneous submissions accepted: No. Does not accept manuscript submissions at this time. Subjects: Americana, The Americas, Culture, Current Affairs, Essays, Non-Fiction, Short Stories, Travel.

CUNE MAGAZINE, Cune Press, Scott C. Davis, PO Box 31024, Seattle, WA 98103, Fax (206) 782-1330; www.cunemagazines.com; www.cunepress.net; magazines@cunepress.com. 1995. Articles, art, photos, cartoons, interviews, satire, news items, non-fiction. "*Cune* (from "cuneiform") is devoted to publishing thoughtful nonfiction and literary fiction by talented new writers. Many of our authors are based in the Pacific Northwest or on the West Coast and are represented in our anthology, An Ear to the Ground (www.cunepress.net). Writers who wish to publish with us should study the writing in this volume (available in most libraries or we can provide the book to potential Cune Press contributors at half price: etg@cunepress.com) Equally important, we publish work across the East-West (Islamic-Western) divide." Payment: At this time submissions to Cune Magazines are pro bono.

Cune Press (see also CUNE MAGAZINE), Scott C. Davis, PO Box 31024, Seattle, WA 98103, Fax 206-774-0592, Tel 206-789-7055, www.cunepress.net, www.cunepress.com, www.cunemagazines.com, cunepress@gmail.com, cune@aol.com. 1994. Fiction, articles, art, cartoons, non-fiction. "Cune Press (from "cuneiform") is devoted to publishing thoughtful nonfiction and literary fiction by talented new writers. Many of our authors are based in the Pacific Northwest or on the West Coast and are represented in our anthology, *An Ear to the Ground* (www.cunepress.net). Writers who wish to publish with us should study the writing in this volume (available in most libraries or we can provide the book to potential Cune Press contributors at half price: etg@cunepress.com). Equally important, we publish work across the East-West (Islamic-Western) divide." avg. press run 2M. Pub'd 2 titles 2009; expects 4 titles 2010, 4 titles 2011. 17 titles listed in the *Small Press Record of Books in Print* (36th Edition, 2010-11). 256pp. Reporting time: 3 months. Simultaneous submissions accepted: We are not accepting book length manuscripts for publication at this time. Typically, we publish books by writers who have first gotten to know us by: 1) volunteering 2)publishing in our online magazines (blogs) 3)publishing in our anthology An Ear to the Ground. Publishes 2% of manuscripts submitted. Payment: 5% royalty on cover price. Copyrights for author.

Cuore Libre Publishing, Ralph DeAmicis, 19201 Sonoma Hwy #125, Sonoma, CA 95476, Tel: 707-320-4274 Fax: 707-320-0572. 2000. Non-fiction. "Books on travel, design, healing & business. We promote books that help people transform their lives for the better. We look for material that is innovative and goes beyond the conventional approaches, encompassing a global vision." avg. press run 1000. Pub'd 2 titles 2009; expects 3 titles 2010, 5 titles 2011. 9 titles listed in the *Small Press Record of Books in Print* (36th Edition, 2010-11). Discounts: 2 or more copies 40% consignment bookstores 5 copies minimum 50% net thirty days gift shops 25 copies minimum 45% distributors. 272pp. Reporting time: We don't accept unsolicited materials. Simultaneous submissions accepted: No. Payment: 10%. Copyrights for author. Subjects: Alternative Medicine, Aromatherapy, Astrology, California, Crystals, Design, Environment, Health, Marketing, Metaphysics, New Age, Nutrition, Wine, Wineries.

Curbstone Press, Alexander Taylor, 321 Jackson St., Willimantic, CT 06226. No titles listed in the *Small Press Record of Books in Print* (36th Edition, 2010-11).

CURRENTS: New Scholarship in the Human Services, University of Calgary Press, P. Miller, Editor; M. Rothery, Editor, Faculty of Social Work, Univ. of Calgary, 2500 University Drive NW, Calgary, AB T2N 1N4, Canada, 403-220-7550, Fax 403-282-7269, currents@ucalgary.ca, www.uofcpress.com/journals/currents. 2002. Articles, reviews. "*Currents* is a refereed electronic journal that publishes critical and research work by current graduate students in the Human Services as well as articles by guest scholars." Approx. 10 articles per volume year. Expects 1 issue 2010, 1 issue 2011. sub. price free access. Reporting time: 2 months or less. Publishes 50% of manuscripts submitted. Payment: none. Copyrighted, does not revert to author. Ads: email for information. Subjects: Adolescence, Adoption, Children, Youth, Family, Gender Issues, Mental Health, Sexual Abuse, Social Security, Social Work.

CUTBANK, Kate Rutledge Jaffe, Editor-in-Chief, English Department—LA 133, University of Montana, Missoula, MT 59812, cutbank@umontana.edu, www.cutbankonline.org. 1973. Poetry, fiction, art, interviews, parts-of-novels, long-poems, non-fiction. "CutBank publishes compelling poetry, fiction, and literary non-fiction by established writers and new voices alike. Our Montana roots are thick, and though we admit to a slight regional bias, CutBank is national in scope. Over our thirty-four year history, we've been pleased to feature work by Wendell Berry, Louise Erdrich, Seamus Heaney, Chris Offutt, Virgil Suarez, Aimee Bender, and a number of other writer's whose work we're fond of. That's the joy, we think, of both publishing and reading a publication like CutBank—discovering work one is fond of." circ. 1000. 2/yr. Pub'd 2 issues 2009; expects 2 issues 2010, 2 issues 2011. sub. price $12; per copy $10; sample $4. Back issues: $7. 125pp. Reporting time: Four months. Simultaneous submissions accepted: Yes. Publishes 5% of manuscripts submitted. Payment: Two contributors copies. Copyrighted, reverts to author. Ads: trade. Subjects: Fiction, Non-Fiction, Photography, Poetry, Prose.

CUTTHROAT, A JOURNAL OF THE ARTS, Pamela Uschuk, Editor-In-Chief; William Pitt Root, Poetry Editor; Beth Alvarado, Fiction Editor, P.O. Box 2414, Durango, CO 81302, 970-903-7914, www.cutthroat-mag.com, cutthroatmag@gmail.com. 2005. Poetry, fiction, reviews, long-poems. "Our editorial mission is to publish the best in well-crafted literary poetry and short fiction poetry in translation. We do not publish genre writing (i.e. no romance, sci-fi, mystery writing, horror, etc.). We have no regional, gender or racial biases. We offer two prizes—$1250 first/$250 second places each—The Joy Harjo Poetry Award and The Rick DeMarinis Short Fiction Award. 2009 judges are Dorianne Laux and Alan Cheuse. Reading fee is $15 and contest deadline is October 10, 2009. Our contributors have included Wendell Berry, Richard Jackson, Michael Waters, Fred Chappell, Dorianne Laux, Rebecca Seiferle, Joy Harjo, Rick DeMarinis, Marvin Bell, Naomi Shihab Nye, Karen Brennan, Kelly Cherry, BJ Buckley, Ann Fisher-Wirth and Naomi Benaron. Go to our website or email us for complete guidelines." 2/yr. Pub'd 1 issue 2009; expects 1 issue 2010, 1 issue 2011. sub. price 2 issues/$25; per copy $15; sample $10. Back issues: $10. Discounts: Trade discounts—5-10 copies 40%. 180pp. Reporting time: 2-6 months. Simultaneous submissions accepted: but authors must inform us of acceptances elsewhere. Payment is in contributors copies, except for the prize money distributions. Copyrighted, reverts to author. Pub's reviews: 10 in 2009. §Short story and poetry collections and poetry in translation. Ads: full page: $125/half page: $75/no classifieds. Subjects: The Americas, Environment, Experimental, Family, Fiction, Poetry, Politics, Short Stories.

CYBERFICT, Martin Kich, Editor, English Department, Wright State Univ - Lake Campus, 7600 State Routem 703, Celina, OH 45822, www.wright.edu/~martin.kich/. 2003. "*Cyberfict* is an online journal devoted to computer-related fiction of all kinds, including but not restricted to cyberpunk and other futuristic fiction, fiction published on the internet or on CD-ROM, the use or influence of hypertext in fiction, and fiction-related internet sites and software. We will consider any approach to this broad topic, including criticism of individual or multiple works, profiles of or interviews with authors, descriptions of pedagogical approches or issues, theoretical studies, interdisciplinary studies, bibliographical articles, notes, book reviews, and reports on related cultural phenomena. We are very open to submissions by graduate students, and, as a special feature, professors may submit groups of undergraduate essays/book reviews (500-700 words each). We welcome graphics with any submission. Submissions: 500-10,000 words; read year round. The journal is published when we receive enough creditable material for a new issue. Email submissions to martin.kich@wright.edu. Prefer submission to be attached as an rtf file, but Wordperfect, Word or html files accepted. SASE required for paper submissions. Inquiries welcome." Reporting time: within 90 days. Subject: Fiction.

Cyberwit.net (see also TAJ MAHAL REVIEW), Santosh Kumar, 4/2 B Lig, Govindpur Colony, Allahabad (UP) 211004, India, 91-9415091004. 2001. Poetry, fiction, articles, art, photos, criticism, reviews, concrete art, non-fiction. "Welcome to Cyberwit. Wonderful "must have" anthology of poems by poets all over the world. We specialize in the promotion of new poets, women poets, and also recognized authors. Devoted to the cause of poetry and literature so that our planet may be a better place to live in.Cyberwit publishes poems in English, some truly literary gems which might otherwise be unknown We publish Poetry Anthology and Literary Journal to enhance poetic sensibilities.Cyberwit is for poets who want to publish their poetry. Our published Anthologies and Journal Taj Mahal Review have poems that are sensuous, picturesque and impassioned. The poems reveal a fine combination of human elements of romance and the mystic & everyday realities." avg. press run 300. Pub'd 35 titles 2009; expects 40 titles 2010, 50 titles 2011. No titles listed in the *Small Press Record of Books in Print* (36th Edition, 2010-11). Discounts: 40 to 65 percent. Shipping charges will be ours. 500pp. Reporting time: Maximum 7 days. Simultaneous submissions accepted: Yes. Publishes 85% of manuscripts submitted. Payment: 11 to 15 percent. Copyrights for author. Subjects: African Literature, Africa, African Studies, Anthology, Christianity, Family, Fashion, Feminism, Fiction, Japan, Non-Fiction, North America, North Carolina, Novels, Poetry, Reviews, Short Stories.

Cycad Press, PO Box 10407, Panama City, FL 32404, 850-532-3106. No titles listed in the *Small Press Record of Books in Print* (36th Edition, 2010-11).

CYNIC BOOK REVIEW, Cynic Press, Joseph Farley, PO Box 40691, Philadelphia, PA 19107. 2001. Reviews. "Make checks out to Cynic Press for back issues. Ceased publication." 2/yr. Pub'd 1 issue 2009; expects 2 issues 2010, 2 issues 2011. sub. price $20/6 issues; per copy $4; sample $4. 20pp. Reporting time: 3 weeks. Simultaneous submissions accepted: yes. Publishes 15% of manuscripts submitted. Payment: 1 year subscription. Copyrighted for Cynic Press. Pub's reviews: 40 in 2009. §Poetry, short stories, novels, archeology, biography, Asia, prehistory, history. Ads: $20/$10. Subject: Reviews.

Cynic Press (see also AXE FACTORY REVIEW; CYNIC BOOK REVIEW; HOLY ROLLERS; LOW BUDGET ADVENTURE; LOW BUDGET SCIENCE FICTION), Joseph Farley, PO Box 40691, Philadelphia, PA 19107. 1996. Poetry, fiction, articles, art, photos, cartoons, interviews, satire, criticism, reviews, music, letters, parts-of-novels, long-poems, collages, plays, concrete art, news items. "Books are by invitation or contest. Unsolicited book manuscripts require a $15 reading fee, check made out to Cynic Press." avg. press run varies. Pub'd 1 title 2009; expects 1 title 2010, 1 title 2011. 11 titles listed in the *Small Press Record of Books in Print* (36th Edition, 2010-11). Pages vary. Reporting time: immediate to five weeks. Simultaneous submissions accepted: yes. Publishes 1% of manuscripts submitted. Payment: copies or special arrangement. Copyrights for author. Subjects: Asia, Indochina, Asian-American, China, Essays, Fiction,

Lapidary, Poetry, Religion, Sex, Sexuality, Tapes & Records, Translation.

Cypress Creek Publishing, David Messer, President; Doann Houghton-Alico, Editor; Stephanie Barko, Literary Publicist, P.O. Box 731, Florence, AL 35631, 256-767-9055. 2009. Poetry, fiction, art, photos, non-fiction. avg. press run 2000. Expects 5 titles 2010, 10 titles 2011. 1 title listed in the *Small Press Record of Books in Print* (36th Edition, 2010-11). 294pp. Reporting time: 2-4 weeks. Simultaneous submissions accepted: No. Publishes 90% of manuscripts submitted. Payment: Varies. Copyrights for author. Subjects: Advertising, Self-Promotion, Alaska, Arts, Biography, Children, Youth, Fiction, Graphic Design, Health, History, Military, Veterans, Non-Fiction, Pets, Photography, Picture Books, Poetry.

Cypress House, Joe Shaw, Editor, 155 Cypress Street, Fort Bragg, CA 95437, 707-964-9520, Fax 707-964-7531, publishing@cypresshouse.com. 1986. Fiction, art, non-fiction. ''Cypress House titles focus on biography, autobiography, self-help and how-to books. Our current list also includes quality fiction and poetry titles.'' avg. press run 2M. Pub'd 5 titles 2009; expects 5 titles 2010, 5 titles 2011. 20 titles listed in the *Small Press Record of Books in Print* (36th Edition, 2010-11). Discounts: 1-2 books 0%, 3-5 33%, 6+ 40%. 224pp. Reporting time: 3 months. Simultaneous submissions accepted: yes. Copyrights for author. Subjects: Biography, Fiction, Health, History, How-To, Literature (General), Memoirs, Self-Help, Women, World War II.

D

D.B.A. Books, Diane M. Bellavance, Editor, 291 Beacon Street #8, Boston, MA 02116, 617-262-0411. 1980. Non-fiction. avg. press run 5M. Pub'd 3 titles 2009; expects 4 titles 2010, 4 titles 2011. 4 titles listed in the *Small Press Record of Books in Print* (36th Edition, 2010-11). Discounts: 2-5 10%, 6-9 15%, 10+ 20%, also 10% for prepayment. 100pp. Reporting time: 2 weeks. Payment: by contract. Does not copyright for author. Subjects: Advertising, Self-Promotion, Broadcasting, Business & Economics, Communication, Journalism, Education, How-To, Marketing, Media, Public Relations/Publicity, Self-Help.

DAILY WORD, Unity House, Laura Harvey, Managing Editor, 1901 NW Blue Parkway, Unity Village, MO 64065, 816-524-3550, fax 816-251-3553. 1924. Poetry, articles, photos, non-fiction. ''Types of materials presented spiritual, Christian, motiviational. Daily affirmations and lessons. Not seeking submissions at this time.'' circ. 650K. 6/yr. Pub'd 12 issues 2009; expects 9 issues 2010, 6 issues 2011. sub. price $14.95; per copy $4.95; sample free. 80pp. Reporting time: 6 weeks. Simultaneous submissions accepted: no. Payment: upon acceptance. Copyrighted, reverts to author. Ads: none. Subjects: Health, History, Motivation, Success, Non-Fiction, Religion, Self-Help, Spiritual.

THE DALHOUSIE REVIEW, Ronald Huebert, Editor, Dalhousie University, Halifax, Nova Scotia B3H 3J5, Canada, 902-494-2541, fax 902-494-3561, email dalhousie.review@dal.ca. 1921. Poetry, fiction, articles, criticism, reviews. ''Authors change with each issue.'' circ. 500. 4/yr. Pub'd 4 issues 2009; expects 4 issues 2010, 4 issues 2011. sub. price institutional: $32.10 within Canada, outside $40 includes GST; individual: $22.50 within Canada, $28 outside; per copy $10 + mailing, handling (double issue $12); sample $10 + mailing and handling ($12 double issue). Back issues: vary from $10 to $25. Discounts: none. 144pp. Reporting time: 1-3 months. Simultaneous submissions accepted: yes. Publishes 10% of manuscripts submitted. Payment: 2 complimentary copies of issue and 10 offprints. Copyrighted, rights are held by both publisher and author. Pub's reviews: 30-40 in 2009. §All areas would be examined. Ads: $300/$150. Subjects: Anthropology, Archaelogy, Arts, Book Reviewing, Classical Studies, Criticism, Criticism, English, Fiction, History, Indexes & Abstracts, Literary Review, Philosophy, Poetry, Political Science, Theatre.

Dalkey Archive Press (see also THE REVIEW OF CONTEMPORARY FICTION), John O'Brien, University of Illinois, 1805 S. Wright Street, MC-011, Champaign, IL 61820, 217-244-5700. 1984. Fiction. ''No unsolicited manuscripts.'' avg. press run 6k. Pub'd 27 titles 2009; expects 25 titles 2010, 25 titles 2011. No titles listed in the *Small Press Record of Books in Print* (36th Edition, 2010-11). Discounts: 45% to bookstores with a minimum of 5 units. 200pp. Reporting time: 1 month. Payment: 10%. Copyrights for author. Subjects: Fiction, Literature (General).

Dancing Bridge Publishing, David Baker, 45 Green Street, Bath, ME 04530, 207 443-6084. 2006. Fiction, non-fiction. Expects 3 titles 2010, 5 titles 2011. 1 title listed in the *Small Press Record of Books in Print* (36th Edition, 2010-11). Discounts: 20-55 percent, depending on organization and number of copies. 200-350pp. Reporting time: 2-4 weeks. Simultaneous submissions accepted: Yes. Payment: 8-15 percent, depending on number of authors and copies sold. Copyrights for author. Subjects: Fiction, Management, Non-Fiction, Pets.

Dancing Lemur Press, L.L.C., Lesley Wolfe, P.O. Box 383, Pikeville, NC 27863-0383, 919-273-0939,

888-502-1117fax, www.dancinglemurpress.com, inquiries@dancinglemurpress.com. 2008. Fiction, non-fiction. "Our trademark is not just a logo the Dancing Lemur represents optimism, enthusiasm and belief.We strive to publish works that uplift and inspire, encouraging the reader to explore and discover while remaining morally grounded. At the heart of our YA fiction lies positive relationship dynamics, optimistic attitudes and non-salacious material. Our non-fiction offers insightful information, uplifting ideas and real-life opportunities. Our goal is to provide hope for the readers dreams and aspirations.Share the vision and come dance with us!" avg. press run 1500. Expects 5 titles 2010, 4 titles 2011. 7 titles listed in the *Small Press Record of Books in Print* (36th Edition, 2010-11). Discounts: Standard discount to wholesalers & distributors, Bookstores & retail - 40%, Libraries & schools - 20%. 300pp. Reporting time: Six to ten weeks. Simultaneous submissions accepted: Yes. Copyrights for author. Subjects: Christianity, Fiction, Inspirational, Juvenile Fiction, Leadership, Non-Fiction, Self-Help, Young Adult.

THE DANDELION, Michael E. Coughlin, Publisher, Michael E. Coughlin, PO Box 205, Cornucopia, WI 54827. 1977. Articles, cartoons, satire, criticism, reviews, letters. *"The Dandelion* is an occasional journal of philosophical anarchism which welcomes a wide variety of articles, cartoons, reviews, satire, criticism and news items. Prefers shorter articles, but will consider major pieces if appropriate. A sample copy is available for $2 to prospective authors." circ. about 400. 0/yr. Pub'd 1 issue 2009; expects 2 issues 2010, 1 issue 2011. sub. price $8/4 issues; per copy $2.00; sample $2.00. Back issues: $2.00. Discounts: 25% off listed price for bulk orders. 28pp. Reporting time: 1 month. Payment: copies of the magazine. Not copyrighted. Pub's reviews: none in 2009. §Anarchist/libertarian history, biographies, philosophy. Ads: none. Subjects: Anarchist, Libertarian.

DARK ANIMUS, James R. Cain, PO Box 750, Katoomba, NSW 2780, Australia, skullmnky@hotmail.com, www.darkanimus.com. 2002. Poetry, fiction, art. "Publishes dark pulp fiction, art and poetry, showcasing the work of emerging and established writers. Contributors include Mike Arnzen, Tim Curran, Graham Masterton, Hertzan Chimera, Paul Haines and Robert Hood." 4/yr. Expects 1 issue 2010, 4 issues 2011. sub. price $25; per copy $5; sample $5. Back issues: $5. Discounts: 40% for bulk orders. 80pp. Reporting time: 8 weeks. Simultaneous submissions accepted: no. Publishes 10% of manuscripts submitted. Payment: 1 contributor copy. Copyrighted, reverts to author. Pub's reviews: none in 2009. §f/sf/h books. Subjects: Fiction, Magazines, Poetry.

DARK GOTHIC RESURRECTED, Cinsearae Santiago, Accepts submissions via email., http://BloodTouch.webs.com/darkgothicmagazine.htm, GratistaVampires@yahoo.com. 2005. Poetry, fiction, art, photos, interviews, reviews, music. *"Dark Gothic Resurrected* is vampire/goth/creepy/paranormal themed. I do accept erotica, tastefully done of course, and stories with a good mix of erotica and horror as well. Not really into 'happily ever after' type stories, But a little, wicked justification for a wrongdoing is more my speed. More of a 'darker' happily-ever-after.Poetry—any length.Short Stories—up to 10,000 words.Artwork—use a .jpeg. gif. or bmp. format, but prefer the first two.ARTISTS!I am always seeking out talented artists for the 'zine. If you'd like to be considered, send me a link to where you showcase your art online, or just send them as attachments, but put "ART SUBMISSION" as your subject line and introduce yourself a bit!" circ. +100. 3/yr. Pub'd 3 issues 2009; expects 3 issues 2010, 3 issues 2011. 4 titles listed in the *Small Press Record of Books in Print* (36th Edition, 2010-11). sub. price (Magazine available 24-7 at www.lulu.com/gratistavampires); per copy Print: $10 (E-copy: $5.00); sample Print: $10 (E-copy: $5.00). Back issues: $10.00. 184pp. Reporting time: 4-6 weeks. Simultaneous submissions accepted: Yes. Publishes 70% of manuscripts submitted. Payment: contributor receives 1 e-copy of the magazine. Copyrighted, reverts to author. Pub's reviews: 4 in 2009. §Authors and artists of Goth, vampire, horror, paranormal romance, and erotica persuasion. Ads: full page, $25, half page, $10, 1/4 page, $5, weblink listing, $2 (this includes your website and three lines of descriptive info on your site. Subjects: Avant-Garde, Experimental Art, Book Reviewing, Erotica, Fantasy, Fiction, Gay, Horror, Interviews, Magic, Music, Occult, Poetry.

Dash-Hill, LLC, Andrew Stewart, Editor, 3540 W. Sahara Avenue #O94, Las Vegas, NV 89102-5816, 212-591-0384, www.dashhillpress.com. 2000. Non-fiction. "We publish only 2-3 titles per year. We do not want unsolicited manuscripts at this time. We have enough finished manuscripts for 2006-2007." avg. press run 3M. Pub'd 2 titles 2009; expects 2 titles 2010, 2 titles 2011. 2 titles listed in the *Small Press Record of Books in Print* (36th Edition, 2010-11). 246pp. Reporting time: 1-3 months. Publishes 8% of manuscripts submitted! Payment: royalty variable, payment quarterly. Copyrights for author. Subjects: Business & Economics, Crime, Health, How-To, Management, Marketing, Reference, Safety, Self-Help.

DATA DUMP, Hilltop Press, Steve Sneyd, 4 Nowell Place, Almondbury, Huddersfield, West Yorkshire HD5 8PB, England. 1991. "News, reviews, post-reviews in the genre poetry field." circ. 100. 12/yr. Pub'd 12 issues 2009; expects 12 issues 2010, 12 issues 2011. 4pp. Reporting time: usually within month. Simultaneous submissions accepted: will consider if informed of fact. Publishes a very small % of manuscripts submitted. copies deposited with UK copyright libraries.

Datamaster Publishing, LLC, John Baxter, Publisher, 1750 Orr Avenue, Simi Valley, CA 93065, Phone:805-527-4369 Fax:805-527-3949, www.CrystalPress.org. 1995. Non-fiction. "We publish books in the field of early childhood education for parents, daycare providers, therapists, and preschool teachers. We also publish books for writers as well as professional window cleaners." avg. press run 1M. Pub'd 2 titles 2009; expects 5 titles 2010, 5 titles 2011. 12 titles listed in the *Small Press Record of Books in Print* (36th Edition, 2010-11). Discounts: 20% for resale, larger for bulk orders. 120pp. Reporting time: 1 month. Simultaneous submissions accepted: yes. Publishes 30% of manuscripts submitted. Payment: yes. Copyrights for author. Subjects: Business & Economics, Family, Non-Fiction, Parenting.

Dawn Publications, Glenn Hovemann, Editor & Co-publisher; Muffy Weaver, Art Director & Co-publisher, 12402 Bitney Springs Rd., Nevada City, CA 95959, 530-274-7775, toll free 800-545-7475, fax 530-274-7778, nature@dawnpub.com. 1979. Fiction, non-fiction. avg. press run 10M. Pub'd 6 titles 2009; expects 6 titles 2010, 6 titles 2011. 83 titles listed in the *Small Press Record of Books in Print* (36th Edition, 2010-11). Discounts: 5-99 books returnable 45%, 5-99 books non-returnable 50%. 32pp. Reporting time: 2 months. Simultaneous submissions accepted: yes. Publishes less than 1/10% of manuscripts submitted. Payment: yes. Copyrights for author. Subjects: Animals, Children, Youth, Cosmology, Earth, Natural History, Education, Environment, Nature, Non-Fiction, Picture Books, Science.

Dawn Sign Press, Joe Dannis, 6130 Nancy Ridge Drive, San Diego, CA 92121-3223, 858-625-0600[v], 858-768-0478 [vp], www.dawnsign.com. 1983. Fiction, parts-of-novels, plays, non-fiction. "We are a specialty publisher of instructional sign language and educational deaf culture materials for both children and adults, deaf and hearing." avg. press run 5M-20M. Pub'd 5 titles 2009; expects 5 titles 2010, 5 titles 2011. 24 titles listed in the *Small Press Record of Books in Print* (36th Edition, 2010-11). Discounts: write for details. 100pp. Reporting time: 120 days. Payment: varies. Copyrights for author. Subjects: Arts, Bilingual, Children, Youth, Culture, Drama, Education, Games, Humor, Multicultural, Photography, Reference, Self-Help.

DayDream Publishing, Laney Dale, 808 Vincent ST, Redondo Beach, CA 90277, www.daydreampublishers.com. 2006. Poetry, fiction, photos, music, non-fiction. avg. press run 3000. Expects 15 titles 2010, 75 titles 2011. No titles listed in the *Small Press Record of Books in Print* (36th Edition, 2010-11). 250pp. Reporting time: 60 days. Simultaneous submissions accepted: Yes. Publishes 10% of manuscripts submitted. Copyrights for author.

dbS Productions, Bob Adams, PO Box 1894, University Station, Charlottesville, VA 22903-0594, 800-745-1581, Fax 434-293-5502, info@dbs-sar.com, www.dbs-sar.com. 1990. Non-fiction. "Outdoor skill related, first-aid, survival; biology skills; video production." avg. press run 10M. Pub'd 3 titles 2009; expects 4 titles 2010, 5 titles 2011. 7 titles listed in the *Small Press Record of Books in Print* (36th Edition, 2010-11). Discounts: 20% bulk, 40% retail. 250pp. Reporting time: 1 month. Payment: 10% biannual. Copyrights for author. Subjects: Biology, Electronics, Medicine, Scouting, Sports, Outdoors.

Russell Dean and Company, Bradd Hopkins, Executive Editor, Anne Schroeder, 141 Tesuque Village Road #12, Santa Fe, NM 87506-0023, 505-988-7153 phone and fax. Email: topdogrdc@peoplepc.com, www.RDandCo.com. 1997. Fiction, non-fiction. "2004 release: *Down to the Wire: The Lives of the Triple Crown Champions* by Robert Shoop (nonfiction). 2003 release: *Wolf's Rite* by Terry Person (fiction). 2002 releases: *Scent of Cedars*, edited by Anne Schroeder (anthology of emerging writers)." avg. press run 3M. Pub'd 2 titles 2009; expects 2 titles 2010, 2 titles 2011. No titles listed in the *Small Press Record of Books in Print* (36th Edition, 2010-11). Discounts: industry standard/as negotiated in bulk. 230pp. Reporting time: 3-6 months. Simultaneous submissions accepted: no. Publishes less than 1% of manuscripts submitted. Payment: industry standard with signing bonus. Copyrights for author. Subjects: Anthology, Fiction, Non-Fiction.

deep cleveland press, Mark S. Kuhar, PO Box 14248, Cleveland, OH 44114-0248, 216-706-3725, press@deepcleveland.com, www.deepcleveland.com. 2003. Poetry, fiction, art, photos, satire, parts-of-novels, long-poems, collages, plays, concrete art. avg. press run on-demand. Pub'd 1 title 2009; expects 5 titles 2010, 5-10 titles 2011. No titles listed in the *Small Press Record of Books in Print* (36th Edition, 2010-11). Discounts: bookstores 1-4 30%, 5-9 35%, 10+ 40%. 76pp. Reporting time: 1-6 months. Simultaneous submissions accepted: yes. Publishes 10% of manuscripts submitted. Payment: 10% after costs. Copyrights for author. Subject: Poetry.

DEEP SOUTH, Department of English, University of Otago, P.O. Box 56, Dunedin, New Zealand, email: deepsouthjournal@gmail.com. "Our submission period is now from the beginning of March to the end of May. You will be informed of our decision at the end of June. *Deep South* welcomes critical essays in the Humanities and Arts, extracts from work in progress, reviews, short stories, poems, and work by artists and photographers. We would encourage graduate students in particular to submit work to us, but submissions from anyone are welcome. Email submissions are encouraged, either in the body of an email or as an attachment. For attachments, Word files are preferred; *Deep South* is put together on a number of different computers, some of which find non-Word attachments very confusing." Annually.

Deep Well Publishing Company, Jim Martin, 1371 Peace Street SE #12, Salem, OR 97302-2572, 503-581-6339. 1992. Non-fiction. Expects 1 title 2011. No titles listed in the *Small Press Record of Books in*

Print (36th Edition, 2010-11). Discounts: 40% discount to retailers; 50% to wholesalers and educational institutions. 320pp. Subjects: Americana, Biography, Feminism, History, Literature (General), Native American, Newspapers, Old West, Oregon, Pacific Northwest, Poetry, San Francisco, Social Movements, The West, Women.

Deerbrook Editions, Jeffrey Haste, P.O. Box 542, Cumberland, ME 04021, phone & FAX: 207-829-5038, http://www.deerbrookeditions.com. 2002. Poetry, fiction, art, letters. "Deerbrook Editions honors authors with full length books who have published in reviews and journals and have been recognized by an award or contest. It is almost necessary to be active in the community. By acknowledging writers of some maturity in their craft, hope to encourage and enable emerging authors or overlooked authors to reach a larger audience. Deerbrook Editions has published 8 deserving poetry/authors in the New England region. Also one full color art children's book. Awarded authors: Joan I. Siegel, Mimi White (Jane Kenyon Award 2009), Dawn Potter, L.R. Berger (Jane Kenyon Award 2003), Martin Steingesser." avg. press run 500-1000. Pub'd 1 title 2009; expects 2 titles 2010, 2 titles 2011. 4 titles listed in the *Small Press Record of Books in Print* (36th Edition, 2010-11). Discounts: stores 40%. 82pp. Reporting time: One year or less. Possibly two years before decision. Publishes 4% of manuscripts submitted. Payment: 15% of sales, not list; special arrangement for fees apply. Copyrights for author. Subjects: Arts, Book Arts, Poetry, Short Stories.

THE DEFENDER - Rush Utah's Newsletter, Eborn Books, Rush Utah, Bret Brooks, Eborn Books, Box 559, Roy, UT 84067. 1993. Poetry, fiction, articles, art, photos, cartoons, satire, criticism, reviews, letters, news items, non-fiction. "Defends Mormonism against anti-Mormon claims." circ. 5M. 4/yr. Pub'd 4 issues 2009; expects 4 issues 2010, 4 issues 2011. sub. price $14.95; per copy $4.95; sample $4.95. 20pp. Payment: none. Not copyrighted. Pub's reviews: 8 in 2009. §Anti-Mormon. Ads: $100/$75. Subject: Mormon.

Defiant Times Press (see also Regent Press), Wendy-O Matik, 6020-A Adeline, Oakland, CA 94608, defianttimespress@lycos.com. 1/2/4. avg. press run 500. Pub'd 1 title 2009; expects 3 titles 2010, 3 titles 2011. 1 title listed in the *Small Press Record of Books in Print* (36th Edition, 2010-11). Discounts: standard. 100pp. Reporting time: 2 months. Simultaneous submissions accepted: yes. Payment: 10%. Does not copyright for author. Subject: Relationships.

Del Sol Press (see also THE DEL SOL REVIEW), Joan Houlihan, Editor, 2020 Pennsylvania Ave., Ste. 443, Washington, DC 20006. "Del Sol Press seeks to publish exceptional work by both new and recognized writers, as well as republish literary works that we consider extremely significant and that have gone out of print. Our approach is eclectic, but our emphasis is on original, unique, and accessible *work with an edge*. As such, we eschew noncommunicative forms (language poetry rip-offs, Finnegan's Wake imitations, and so forth) and genre fiction (unless exceptional)." No titles listed in the *Small Press Record of Books in Print* (36th Edition, 2010-11).

THE DEL SOL REVIEW, Del Sol Press, Michael Neff, Poetry Editor, 2020 Pennsylvania Ave., Ste. 443, Washington, DC 20006.

Delaney Day Press, Rhonda Oveson, 14014 North 64th Drive, Glendale, AZ 85306-3706, Tel:623-810-7590, Fax:623-486-8662, stoben1@cox.net. 2005. Fiction, non-fiction. "Currently we are publishing nonfiction inspirational and children's health books. Three children's fiction books are planned for fall/winter 2006." avg. press run 3000. Expects 3-4 titles 2011. No titles listed in the *Small Press Record of Books in Print* (36th Edition, 2010-11). Discounts: Trade 2-4 books 20%offdiscounts 5-9 books 30%off 10-24 books 40%off 25-199 books 46% 200 Or more books 50%offWholesale discount 50%Library discount 30%Nontradesales 45% nonreturnable. 200pp. Reporting time: 30-60 days. Simultaneous submissions accepted: Yes. Payment: Royalty rate for hardcover is 10% list price for first 5,000 sold, 12.5% for 5,000-10,000, 15% for over 10,000; Softcover is 7.5% list price. Copyrights for author. Subjects: Children, Youth, Christianity, Family, Health, Inspirational, Juvenile Fiction, Memoirs, Mental Health, Non-Fiction, Nursing, Nutrition, Parenting, Self-Help, Spiritual, Young Adult.

DELAWARE POETRY REVIEW, Dennis Forney, Cape Gazette, PO Box 213, Lewes, DE 19958, (302) 645-7700. 2007. Poetry. "*Delaware Poetry Review* is an online editorial collective which gathers contemporary poetry written by authors who live primarily in Delaware, Maryland, Washington D.C., and Virginia." 2/yr. Pub'd 1 issue 2009; expects 2 issues 2010, 2 issues 2011. Simultaneous submissions accepted: No. Subject: Poetry.

Demarche Publishing LLC, Paul Smith, Joy Cain, P.O. Box 36, Mohegan Lake, NY 10547, www.demarchepublishing.com, info@demarchepublishing.com. 2008. Fiction, non-fiction. "Demarche Publishing LLC was founded in 2008 to promote understanding and respect among peoples and cultures and impact the lives of readers. Reading is fun! It has the potential to spark imaginations, jump start discussions, and encourage new opinions." Expects 3 titles 2010, 6 titles 2011. 2 titles listed in the *Small Press Record of Books in Print* (36th Edition, 2010-11). 192pp. Reporting time: 3-4 months. Simultaneous submissions accepted: Yes. Payment: 10% royalty on net or retail price. Copyrights for author. Subjects: African-American, Caribbean,

Children, Youth, Civil Rights, Fantasy, Fiction, Health, Jamaica, Juvenile Fiction, Multicultural, Mystery, Novels, Religion, Romance, Science Fiction.

The Denali Press, Alan Edward Schorr, Editorial Director and Publisher, PO Box 21535, Juneau, AK 99802, 907-586-6014, Fax 907-463-6780, denalipress@alaska.com. 1986. Non-fiction. "Firm publishes only reference and scholarly publications oriented toward library (academic and public) market, with modest sales directly to stores and individuals. Principally interested in: directories, guides, handbooks, indexes/abstracts as well as scholarly academic works, principally in the area of cultural diversity, ethnic and minority groups as well as occasional titles on Alaskana. Emphasis on books about ethnic groups and refugees. Exclusive distributor in US for Hull University Press, Libris, and Meridian Books. Recent titles include national resource directories for Hispanics and refugees/immigrants, as well as books on Jewish refugee children, US policy in Micronesia, Southern social justice organizations." avg. press run 2M. Pub'd 3 titles 2009; expects 4 titles 2010, 3 titles 2011. 18 titles listed in the *Small Press Record of Books in Print* (36th Edition, 2010-11). Discounts: 20%. 320pp. Reporting time: 1 month. Simultaneous submissions accepted: yes. Publishes 1% of manuscripts submitted. Payment: 10%. Does not copyright for author. Subjects: Alaska, Anthropology, Archaelogy, Bibliography, Biology, Book Reviewing, Chicano/a, Counter-Culture, Alternatives, Communes, Geography, History, Indexes & Abstracts, Libraries, Native American, Public Affairs, Reference, Science.

DENVER QUARTERLY, Bin Ramke, Editor; Andrea Rexilius, Associate Editor, University of Denver, Denver, CO 80208, 303-871-2892. 1966. Poetry, fiction, articles, interviews, satire, criticism, reviews, parts-of-novels, long-poems, non-fiction. "Poems: John Ashbery, Christine Hume, James Tate, Benjamin Ivry, Jane Miller, Ann Lauterbach, Paul Hoover. Essays: John Felstiner, Daniel Tiffany, David Wojahn, Lee Upton, Malinda Markham. Fiction: Kass Fleisher, Charles Baxter, special fiction issues edited by Paul Maliszewski..." circ. 1,700. 4/yr. Pub'd 4 issues 2009; expects 4 issues 2010, 4 issues 2011. sub. price $24/institutions, $20/individuals; per copy $10; sample $10. Back issues: cost is based on rarity of the individual issue; usually $10. Discounts: individual: 1 yr $20, 2 yrs $37, 3 yrs $50. 136pp. Reporting time: 2-4 months. We accept simultaneous submissions if told. Publishes 5% of manuscripts submitted. Payment: $10 per page. Copyrighted, reverts to author. Pub's reviews: 6 in 2009. §Literature of last 100 years and contemporary fiction and poetry. Subjects: Arts, Poetry.

•**Dervla Publishing, LLC,** Linda Davis G, CEO; Oliver Woodburn, Editor, P.O. Box 1401, Alpharetta, GA 30009-1401, 678-521-4173, 678-521-4160-fax, info@dervlapublishing.com, dervlapublishing.com. 2009. Fiction, non-fiction. Expects 6 titles 2010, 10 titles 2011. No titles listed in the *Small Press Record of Books in Print* (36th Edition, 2010-11). Discounts: 2-10 copies 25% 11-50 copies 30% 51+ 40%. 340pp. Reporting time: 2-4 weeks immediate receipt email/script eval 2-4 weeks. Simultaneous submissions accepted: Yes. Payment: no advances, royalty payments monthly. Copyrights for author. Subjects: Creative Non-fiction, Folklore, Global Affairs, Myth, Mythology, Native American, Non-Fiction, Old West, Outdoor Adventure, Picture Books, Politics, Religion, Spiritual, The West, Women, Young Adult.

DESCANT, Dan Williams, Editor; Alex Lemon, Editor, English Department, TCU, Box 297270, Fort Worth, TX 76129. 1957. Poetry, fiction. "*Descant* does not publish poetry volumes or essays. We offer the Frank O'Connor Award, $500 for best story in an issue. Also the Gary Wilson Award for an outstanding story ($250), and the $500 Betsy Colquitt Poetry Award for the best poem in an issue, and the $250 Baskerville Publishers Award for an outstanding poem in an issue. There are no submission fees or entry forms, just submit your work with a SASE. Copyright is returned to authors upon request. We accept submissions from September 1 through April 1." circ. 500. 1 issue published each summer. Pub'd 1 issue 2009; expects 1 issue 2010, 1 issue 2011. sub. price $12, $18 foreign; per copy $12; sample $6. Back issues: $6. 150pp. Reporting time: 6 weeks. Simultaneous submissions accepted: yes. Publishes .5% of manuscripts submitted. Payment: in copies. We return copyright to author upon request. No ads. Subjects: Fiction, Poetry.

DESCANT, Karen Mulhallen, PO Box 314, Station P, M5S 2S8, Toronto, ON, Canada, phone: 416 593 2557, fax: 416 593 9362, email general: info@descant.on.ca, email subscriptions/back issues: circulation@descant.on.ca, web: www.descant.on.ca. 1970. Poetry, fiction, articles, art, photos, interviews, long-poems, plays, non-fiction. circ. 1M. 4/yr. Pub'd 4 issues 2009; expects 4 issues 2010, 4 issues 2011. sub. price individuals: $25/1 year, $40/2 years; institutions: $35/1 year, $70/2 years; add $6 per year outside Canada; per copy $15; sample $8.50. Back issues: $8.50 plus $2 postage in Canada and $4 shipping/handling outside Canada. 200pp. Reporting time: 9-12 months. Simultaneous submissions accepted: no. Publishes 2% of manuscripts submitted. Payment: $100. Copyrighted, reverts to author. Ads: Full Page Ad 21 x 14 cm / 9 x5 inches = $300.00, Half Page Ad 10.5 x 7 cm / 4.5x2.5 inches = $150.00, Quarter Page Ad 5 x 3.5 cm / 2x1 inches = $75.00. Ad exchanges considered also. Subjects: Arts, Canada, Criticism, Culture, Drama, Fiction, Literary Review, Literature (General), Photography, Poetry.

Desert Bloom Press, Newton Sanders, 7170 N. Harold Drive, Tucson, AZ 85743-8614, 520-572-1597 phone, 520-572-1597 fax, pub@desertbloompress.com. 1989. Fiction, non-fiction. "Not currently accepting submissions. Publishes young adult fiction, adult suspense, and literary criticism dealing with Italian culture."

avg. press run 500 (+ print-on-demand capability). Pub'd 2 titles 2009; expects 1 title 2010. 6 titles listed in the *Small Press Record of Books in Print* (36th Edition, 2010-11). Discounts: 1: 0%, 2-4: 20%, 5-9: 40%, 10-99: 50%, 100-up:55%, STOP orders: 40% discount plus $3.95 for priority mail. 250pp. Reporting time: 1 month. Simultaneous submissions accepted: no. Publishes 2% of manuscripts submitted. Payment: negotiable. Copyrights for author. Subjects: Fiction, Italy, Young Adult.

DESIRE, Eros Books, Mary Nicholaou, 463 Barlow Avenue, Staten Island, NY 10308, 718-317-7484, marynicholaou@aol.com, www.geocities.com/marynicholaou/classic_blue.html. 1999. Fiction, articles, art, cartoons, criticism, reviews, letters, parts-of-novels, non-fiction. "*Desire* is a postmodern magazine of literary fiction and nonfiction. We provide a forum for experiments in open forms that interrogate the canon and lead to transformation and redescription. Accepts any length and multiple submissions of literary merit." 4/yr. Pub'd 2 issues 2009; expects 4 issues 2010, 4 issues 2011. sub. price $20; per copy $5.00; sample $4. Back issues: $4. Discounts: 40%. 60pp. Reporting time: 8 weeks. Simultaneous submissions accepted: yes. Publishes 10% of manuscripts submitted. Payment: one year free subscription. Copyrighted, reverts to author. Pub's reviews: 1 in 2009. §Postmodern fiction (romance) and nonfiction. Ads: $10/$5. Subjects: Biography, Criticism, Culture, Education, Essays, Fiction, Gender Issues, Language, Lifestyles, Literary Review, Literature (General), Memoirs, Multicultural, Mystery, Myth, Mythology.

DESIRE STREET, Dr. Beau Boudreaux, Editor; Andrea S. Gereighty, President, New Orleans Poetry Forum, 257 Bonnabel Boulevard, Metairie, LA 70005-3738, 504-835-8472 (Andrea), 504-467-9034 (Jeanette), Fax 504-834-2005, ager80@worldnet.att.net, Fax 504-832-1116, neworleanspoetryforum@yahoo.com. 1984. Poetry. circ. 1.2M. 4/yr. Pub'd 4 issues 2009; expects 4 issues 2010, 4 issues 2011. 1 title listed in the *Small Press Record of Books in Print* (36th Edition, 2010-11). sub. price $30, also entitles subscribers to one free critique of one 1-page original poem and all 50 weekly Weds. night 3-hour workshops when/if in New Orleans, LA, or send poems to workshop and we'll critique and return to you; per copy $10; sample $5. Back issues: $5 + 66¢ p/h. 55pp. Reporting time: 6 months. Simultaneous submissions accepted: yes. Publishes 45% of manuscripts submitted. Payment: seeing their work in publication and 1 copy. Copyrighted, reverts to author. Pub's reviews. §Books of poetry. Ads: $100/$75. Subjects: Louisiana, Poetry.

Devenish Press, Jan Bachman, 1425 Blue Sage Court, Boulder, CO 80305, 303-926-0378 phone/fax, books@devenishpress.com, www.devenishpress.com. 1999. Art, photos, non-fiction. "Devenish Press has published books about Ireland by author and photographer Tom Quinn Kumpf. Topics have included The Troubles in Northern Ireland and Irish culture, including legends, myths, and the Otherworld. The latest book by Tom Quinn Kumpf, Two Sides: Haiku and Other Words, is photography in a Japanese sumi-e painting style with haiku poetry." avg. press run 3000. 7 titles listed in the *Small Press Record of Books in Print* (36th Edition, 2010-11). Discounts: Any amount 50%. 150pp. Reporting time: Two weeks. Simultaneous submissions accepted: No. Payment: Terms have varied according to author preference. Does not copyright for author. Subjects: Haiku, Ireland, Non-Fiction, Philosophy, Poetry.

Devi Press, Inc., Ethan Walker III, 126 W. Main, Norman, OK 73069, (405) 447-0364. 2003. Poetry, non-fiction. "Publisher of books about spirituality." avg. press run 5000. Pub'd 2 titles 2009; expects 1 title 2010, 1 title 2011. No titles listed in the *Small Press Record of Books in Print* (36th Edition, 2010-11). Discounts: 40%. 250pp. Reporting time: Not accepting submissions. Simultaneous submissions accepted: Yes. Publishes 1% of manuscripts submitted. Payment: Undetermined. Does not copyright for author. Subjects: Metaphysics, New Age, Spiritual.

Devil Mountain Books, Clark Sturges, PO Box 4115, Walnut Creek, CA 94596, 925-939-3415, Fax 925-937-4883, cbsturges@aol.com. 1984. Fiction, articles, non-fiction. "Go to www.devilmountainbooks.com for complete information." avg. press run 1,500. 4 titles listed in the *Small Press Record of Books in Print* (36th Edition, 2010-11). 100-300pp. Copyrights for author. Subjects: Alcohol, Alcoholism, Americana, Autobiography, Biography, California, Drugs, Essays, Medicine, San Francisco, Short Stories, The West.

•**DEVIL'S ADVOCATE,** Rebekah Luthye, 2123 S. Fulton Circle, Unit #202, Denver, CO 80247, 785-840-7348, rluthye@devilsad.net, http://www.devilsad.net.

Dharma Publishing, Elizabeth Cook, Editor; Rima Tamar, Publisher's Contact, 35788 Hauser Bridge Road, Cazadero, CA 95421, 707-847-3717, fax: 707-847-3380, web: www.dharmapublishing.com, email: dp@dharmapublishing.com. 1969. Articles, art, photos, interviews, reviews, news items. "91 titles currently in print; over 200 reproductions of Tibetan art in full color. Sepcializes in books on Buddhism. We have our own photo-typesetting and offset printing facilities." avg. press run 5M. Pub'd 4 titles 2009; expects 10 titles 2010, 10 titles 2011. 101 titles listed in the *Small Press Record of Books in Print* (36th Edition, 2010-11). Discounts: bookstores 2-4 20%, 5-25 40%, 26+ 45%; 40% maximum on returnable books; distributors by contract; libraries 20%; class adoptions 20%. 32-400pp. Reporting time: do not accept submissions. Publishes very small % of manuscripts submitted. Payment: subject to individual arrangement. Copyright is held by Dharma Publishing. Subjects: Buddhism, Children, Youth, Health, History, Humanism, Inspirational, Massage,

Metaphysics, New Age, Philosophy, Picture Books, Psychology, Religion, Spiritual, Yoga.

DIAGRAM, Ander Monson, Editor; Lauren Slaughter, Fiction Editor; Heidi Gotz, Poetry Editor, English Department, University of Arizona, ML 445, PO Box 210067, Tucson, AZ 85721. 1999. Poetry, fiction, reviews, long-poems, non-fiction. "*Diagram* is an electronic journal of text and art. As our name indicates, we're interested in representations. In naming. In indicating. In schematics. In the labelling and taxonomy of things. In poems that masquerade as stories; in stories that disguise themselves as indices or obituaries. Art, text, and schematic. Submission guidelines for *Diagram* are online (go to http://thediagram.com/subs.html). Read the magazine online too before sending." 6/yr. Pub'd 6 issues 2009; expects 6 issues 2010, 6 issues 2011. sub. price free—online. Reporting time: 1-2 months. Simultaneous submissions accepted: yes. Publishes 5% of manuscripts submitted. Payment: None. Pub's reviews: 12 in 2009. §fiction, poetry, essays, nonfiction, preferably small press books, first books especially; chapbooks too.

DIET SOAP, Douglas Lain, 1321 Monroe St, Oregon City, OR 97405. 2007. Poetry, fiction, articles, art, photos, cartoons, satire, criticism, parts-of-novels, collages, news items, non-fiction. "We are seeking fiction, essays, reportage, and art that documents and accelerates the deterioration of the late capitalist order rather than works that celebrate or reinforce the deterioration that is the late capitalist order.We want stories that defy genre distinctions because they seek to escape the confinement of ideology. We want essays that are personal and strange and full of passion without being sentimental, ahistorical, bourgeois or confessional. We want art that confronts rather than comforts.Some of our favorite fiction writers are Franz Kafka, Charlotte Perkins Gilman, Philip K. Dick. We like gonzo journalism and essayists who aren't afraid of philosophy and history.Some of our favorite artists are Max Ernst, George Seurat, Gee Vaucher, Cindy Sherman, and mental patients. We like collage work and black and white drawings. *Diet Soap* will take the form of quarterly themed issues. You can send us pieces of any length, in any format, but be advised that we probably won't print a 500,000 word screed or something written on a brick. Also, all submissions will be electronic, which means that it will be very hard to submit something written on a brick.We pay a flat $5 honorarium for everything.Send your work to douglain{at}dietsoap.org or mkhobson{at}dietsoap.org.Submission deadline for Issue #2 (Theme: Sex/Gender/ Commodity) is January 14th. Reprints welcome." circ. 250. 4/yr. Expects 1 issue 2010, 4 issues 2011. sub. price $20; per copy $5; sample $5. Back issues: inquire. Discounts: will trade Diet Soap for other 'zines. 40pp. Reporting time: from 2 days up to 90 days. Simultaneous submissions accepted: Yes. Publishes 10% of manuscripts submitted. Payment: $5 per story or 2 pieces of art, $10 for cover art. Copyrighted, reverts to author. §Anarchist works, Fiction, Art, Films, Music, Review Journals. Ads: None. Subjects: Absurdist, Anarchist, Arts, Dreams, Erotica, Experimental, Fantasy, Fiction, Futurism, Non-Fiction, Performing Arts, Science Fiction, Surrealism, Zines.

DIFFERENT KIND OF PARENTING, KotaPress, Kara L.C. Jones, PO Box 514, Vashon Island, WA 98070-0514. 2001. "This is a zine aimed at bereaved parents after the death of a child; those who have other living childen, those who do not, those who may someday have others. Focus is mainly grief, healing, and transformation in the parents lives after death of a child." 4/yr. 1 title listed in the *Small Press Record of Books in Print* (36th Edition, 2010-11). Back issues: Full archive of back issues soon to be available online at KotaPress.com for free as PDF files. Sometime in 2006. Simultaneous submissions accepted: yes. Payment: Free author copy with limited reproduction rights. Copyrighted, reverts to author. Pub's reviews: approx. 4 in 2009. §Anything with a grief and healing bent to it—based on real experiences with death of a child. Grief of this kind is hard enough, so we are not interested in materials that make up stories about it for entertainment.

DIG, Cobblestone Publishing Company, Rosalie F. Baker, 30 Grove Street, Suite C, Peterborough, NH 03458, 800-821-0115, digstuff@caruspub.com, www.digonsite.com. 1999. Articles, photos, interviews, letters, non-fiction. 9/yr. Pub'd 9 issues 2009; expects 9 issues 2010, 9 issues 2011. sub. price $29.95; per copy $6.95; sample $6.95. Back issues: $6.95. 32pp. Payment: payment after publication. Copyrighted, DIG buys all rights. Pub's reviews: 25 in 2009. §Books for young readers relating to the upcoming theme list. No advertising. Subject: Anthropology, Archaelogy.

Dignified Designs (see also OPEN RANGE MAGAZINE - The West's Premier Real Western Magazine), Amanda Smith, PO Box 1207, Glenrock, WY 82637, 307-436-5447, Editor@OpenRangeMagazine.com - www.OpenRangeMagazine.com. 1998. Articles, art, news items. "We publish The West's Premiere Real Western Magazine. Open Range Magazine is a unique and exciting new magazine catering to those who live in the West, and those who dream to experience the West... the real Western Way of life. It is a magazine covering the realities of living and working in the West. From Night Calving to Blacksmithing. Black rocking horse Oilfield Workers to the miners who run coal at night and herd cattle during the day. From hardcore ranching to the old style of law that keeps the West in check. Brand Inspectors to Sale Barn Auctioneers, this magazine covers it all...Touting the true spirit of the west, It isnt all glamour.... its real, and more and more people are turning back to the ways of the Open Range." Pub'd 2 titles 2009; expects 2 titles 2010, 3 titles 2011. No titles listed in the *Small Press Record of Books in Print* (36th Edition, 2010-11). Discounts: negotiable - please call. 40pp. Reporting time: Less than one day. Simultaneous submissions accepted: Yes. Publishes 75% of manuscripts submitted. Payment: Negotiable. Copyrights for author. Subjects: Agriculture, Fiction, Music, Non-Fiction, Old West, Outdoor Adventure, Photography, Poetry, The West, Women, Wyoming.

Paul Dilsaver, Publisher, 2802 Clydesdale Court, Fort Collins, CO 80526-1155. 1974. Poetry, fiction. "Have published limited edition chapbooks under the imprints of Blue Light Books, Rocky Mountain Creative Arts, Academic & Arts Press. Authors published include Pulitzer winner Yusef Komunyakaa, John Sweet, John Garmon, Clifton Snider, Elinor Meiskey, John Calderazzo, Howard McCord, Victoria McCabe, Bim Angst, Kirk Robertson, R.P. Dickey, Richard F. Fleck, and many others. Most current imprint: Scrooge's Ledger. New titles by Richard Houff, Joseph Shields, and Peter Magliocco. Submissions by open call for specific projects only." avg. press run 100-150. Pub'd 1 title 2009; expects 2 titles 2010, 2 titles 2011. No titles listed in the *Small Press Record of Books in Print* (36th Edition, 2010-11). Pages vary. Payment: copies. Does not copyright for author. Subjects: Fiction, Poetry.

DIODE POETRY JOURNAL, Patty Paine, Editor. 2007. Poetry. "What is electropositive poetry? Its poetry that excites and energizes. Its poetry that uses language that crackles and sparks. Were looking for poetry from all points on the arc, from formal to experimental (no light verse or erotic poetry, please). Simultaneous submissions are welcomed, but please notify us if they're accepted elsewhere. diode does not accept previously published work. Please submit 3-5 poems with a cover letter via email to: submit@diodepoetry.com Please attach poems in either Word (.doc) or Rich Text Format (.rtf). We read year round and will respond in 4-8 weeks." Three issues per year. Reporting time: 2-3 months. Simultaneous submissions accepted: Yes.

Dionysia Press Ltd. (see also UNDERSTANDING MAGAZINE), Denise Smith, Thom Nairn, 127 Milton Road West, 7, Duddingston House Courtyard, Edinburgh, EH15 1Jg, United Kingdom, 0131-6611153 [tel/fax, 0131 6614853 [tel]. 1989. Poetry, fiction, articles, criticism, reviews, plays. avg. press run 500. Pub'd 10-20 titles 2009; expects 10 titles 2010, 10 titles 2011. 16 titles listed in the *Small Press Record of Books in Print* (36th Edition, 2010-11). Discounts: 5 (poetry collections) £15 + postage. 150pp. Reporting time: 8 months. Simultaneous submissions accepted: no. Publishes 10% of manuscripts submitted. Payment: free copies. Does not copyright for author.

THE DIRTY GOAT, Host Publications, Inc., Elzbieta Szoka, Joe W. Bratcher III, 277 Broadway, Suite 210, New York, NY 10007, Phone: 212-905-2365, FAX: 212-905-2369, www.hostpublications.com, www.thedirty-goat.com, jbratcher@hostpublications.com. 1988. Poetry, fiction, art, photos, interviews, criticism, parts-of-novels, long-poems, plays. "Maximum length 20 pages. Strong focus on literature in translation, but will consider work originally written in English. All translated poetry appears along with the original. Two visual art sections in each issue. Recent contributors: Astrid Cabral, Jacques Rda, James Hoggard, Pascal Lain, Hai Zi." circ. 500. 2/yr. Pub'd 1 issue 2009; expects 2 issues 2010, 2 issues 2011. sub. price $20; per copy $10; sample $2. Back issues: none. Discounts: 1 copy 20%, 2-9 30%, 10-24 40%, 25-49 43%. 200pp. Reporting time: indeterminate. Payment: 2 free copies. Copyrighted, reverts to author. Ads: none. Subjects: African Literature, Africa, African Studies, The Americas, Arts, Avant-Garde, Experimental Art, Beat, Bilingual, Culture, Drama, Eastern Europe, English, Essays, Europe, Fiction, Literature (General), Translation.

DIRTY LINEN, Paul Hartman, Editor; Chip Eagle, Publisher, PO Box 66600, Baltimore, MD 21239-6600, 410-583-7973, Fax 410-337-6735. 1983. Articles, photos, interviews, reviews, music, news items, non-fiction. "Folk, world music. Record and concert reviews: preferably 200-300 words, max. 400 words. Feature articles and interviews: 1,000-2,000+ words depending on topic. No unsolicited manuscripts." circ. 11M. 6/yr. Pub'd 6 issues 2009; expects 6 issues 2010, 6 issues 2011. sub. price $25; per copy $5.99; sample $6. Back issues: $6 includes U.S. postage. Discounts: distributors 55%, retail stores 40%. 84pp. Simultaneous submissions accepted: no. Publishes 0% of manuscripts submitted. Copyrighted, rights revert to author upon request. Pub's reviews: approx. 60 in 2009. §Folk/World Music. Ads: b&w: $1015 full page; $565 1/2 page; $315 1/4 page; $430 1/3 page; $215 1/6 page; $110 business card; color: $1540 full page; $920 half page; $510 1/4 page; $700 1/3 page; $350 1/6 page. Frequency discounts available. Subjects: Celtic, Music, Tapes & Records.

THE DIRTY NAPKIN, Jeremy Ellis, Managing Director; Christopher Goodrich, Poetry Editor; Katie Schmid, Associate Poetry Editor; Tim Rhomberg, Associate Fiction Editor, Letters Editor, Philadelphia, PA, http://dirtynapkin.com/. 2007. Poetry, fiction, letters. "Our mission is to create an active community of exceptional writers via an online literary magazine. The Dirty Napkin acknowledges that writing cannot be separate from the voice, breath, and the personality of the author; that should a piece of writing be separated from this literal voice, much power will be lost. Therefore, the Dirty Napkin seeks to include voice by having each author read their work online. The Dirty Napkin also seeks to create a community of artists by creating a reading series and salons. Stay tuned." circ. 1000. 4/yr. Pub'd 1 issue 2009; expects 4 issues 2010, 4 issues 2011. sub. price $20. 30pp. Reporting time: less than one month. Simultaneous submissions accepted: Yes. Publishes 25% of manuscripts submitted.

DISCGOLFER, Rick Rothstein, Managing Editor; Joe Feidt, Senior Editor, 3828 Dogwood Lane, Appling, GA 30802-0312, 816.471.3472, email rickrothstein@pdga.com. 2009. Articles, photos, cartoons, interviews, reviews, letters, news items, non-fiction. circ. 12,000+. 4/yr. Expects 4 issues 2010, 4 issues 2011. sub. price $20 USA; $25 Canada; $35 Mexico; $50 Europe/Pacific Rim/Australia/Central and South America; per copy $5.00. Back issues: www.pdgastore.com. 64pp. Reporting time: 1-2 weeks. Simultaneous submissions are not usually accepted. Publishes 50-60% of manuscripts submitted. Payment: sometimes, in kind (merchandise). Copyrighted, reverts to author. Pub's reviews: none in 2009. §New sports and games, psychology of individual sports (especially golf), flying disc subjects. Ads: pdga.com/discgolfer-magazine or 706-261-6342. Subjects: Games, Sports, Outdoors.

Disclosure Research and Publishing, Samuel Clark, PO Box 262, Bartonsville, PA 18321-0262, 570-619-5271, www.disclosurepublishing.com. 2004. Non-fiction. "We are presently centering on true stories of police corruption and police whistle blowers." avg. press run 1000. Expects 2 titles 2010, 2 titles 2011. No titles listed in the *Small Press Record of Books in Print* (36th Edition, 2010-11). Discounts: 4-50 copies 30%. 250pp.

DISLOCATE, 207 Church Street, 207 Lind Hall, Minneapolis, MN 55455. "Dislocate, the newly reinvigorated literary journal published by the University of Minnesota's Creative Writing Program. Dislocate publishes the work of both established and emerging writers, and we are especially interested in unique voices and a wide range of styles. All submissions are blind. Attach submissions as Word documents to your email and send to submissions@dislocate.org. Attach also a separate document with your contact information (including name, address, phone, email, and title(s) of work(s) submitted). Please include this contact information in the text of your email, as well. The subject line of the email should specify both submission and genre (for example: Sub-mission Poetry). Poetry: 3-5 poems of no more than 10 pages total in length. Fiction and Nonfiction: up to 5000 words. Simultaneous submissions accepted provided we are notified immediately in the event of publication elsewhere. No previous publications accepted. Submissions which do not meet with our guidelines will not be considered."

•**Disparate Voices (see also VOICE(S)),** Stephanie Hicks, Los Angeles, CA 90028, editorial@disparate-voices.com, www.disparatevoices.com. 2009. Photos, non-fiction. "VOICE(S) is looking for literary nonfiction (personal essays/short, nonfiction stories) and black and white photography that celebrate the nuances of the world and the people in it. We'd like original pieces that haven't found a home in another publication.Current contributers include: Rafael Alvarez, James Cool, Jaquira Diaz, Luka Douridas, Don Durkee, Crystal Keli, Tiffany Lam, Noah Lederman, Kyle Moreno, and Robert Romano." avg. press run 50. Expects 1 title 2010, 2 titles 2011. No titles listed in the *Small Press Record of Books in Print* (36th Edition, 2010-11). Discounts: Not-for-profit, donations only. 35pp. Reporting time: Expect to hear back no sooner than a couple weeks to a month after the stated deadline. Simultaneous submissions accepted: No. Publishes 2% of manuscripts submitted. Payment: A complimentary copy will be sent to all selected contributers. Copyrights for author. Subjects: Death & Dying, Desktop Publishing, Diaries, Divorce, How-To, Humanism, Humor, Memoirs, Miniature Books, Non-Fiction, Photography, Third World, Minorities, U.S. Hispanic, Women, Writers/Writing.

DISSE: Directory of inmate shopping services and e-commerce, Vanessa Leschak, Publisher; George Kayer, Founding Editor, P.O. Box 91008, Tucson, AZ 85752, 1-877-884-7639, vanessa@disse.biz, www.disse.biz. 2008. Poetry, fiction, articles, art, reviews, long-poems, non-fiction. 4/yr. Expects 2 issues 2010, 4 issues 2011. sub. price 26; per copy 13.95; sample 13.95. Back issues: inquire. Discounts: 10 or more copies 25%. 116pp. Reporting time: 14 days. Simultaneous submissions accepted: No. Publishes 20% of manuscripts submitted. Payment: inquire. Copyrighted, reverts to author. Pub's reviews: none in 2009. §Prison focused businesses. Ads: Full Page $358. set up and $35 a month. $199. set up and $20 a month half page. Classifieds $20 for 6 lines for 3 months.

DIVIDE: Journal of Literature, Arts, and Ideas, Ginger Knowlton, Univ. of Colorado, Boulder / UCB 317, Boulder, CO 80309, www.colorado.edu/journals/divide. Poetry, fiction, art, photos, interviews, reviews, long-poems. 112pp. Simultaneous submissions accepted: okay. Payment: contributor's copies.

Dixon-Price Publishing, Kendall Hanson, PO Box 1360, Kingston, WA 98346-1360, 360-710-2936, Fax 360-297-8702, dixonpr@dixonprice.com, www.dixonprice.com. 1999. Fiction, non-fiction. "No longer accepting submissions." avg. press run 500. Pub'd 1 title 2009; expects 3 titles 2010, 3 titles 2011. 17 titles listed in the *Small Press Record of Books in Print* (36th Edition, 2010-11). Discounts: 2 or more copies, 20%. 220pp. Simultaneous submissions accepted: no. Publishes 1-5% of manuscripts submitted. Copyrights for author. Subjects: Animals, How-To, Marine Life, Reprints, Sports, Outdoors, Travel.

DLite Press, Paul Smith, P.O. Box 1644, New York, NY 10150, 718-379-0612. 2009. Poetry, fiction, non-fiction. "DLite Press lets you publish your work without going through a publisher, which means that you are taking charge of the distribution, selling and marketing of your book." Expects 2 titles 2010, 6 titles 2011. 1 title listed in the *Small Press Record of Books in Print* (36th Edition, 2010-11). Subjects: Caribbean, Fiction, Jamaica, Juvenile Fiction, Memoirs, Non-Fiction, Race, Romance, Science Fiction, Self-Help, Short Stories, Women, Young Adult.

140

THE DMQ REVIEW, Sally Ashton, Editor; Marjorie Manwaring, Assistant Editor; Jennifer K. Sweeney, Associate Editor; Arlene Kim, Associate Editor; Dean Rader, Associate Editor, editors@dmqreview.com, www.dmqreview.com. 1997. Poetry, art. "Please refer to online guidelines before submitting unpublished work." 3/yr. Pub'd 3 issues 2009; expects 3 issues 2010, 3 issues 2011. Reporting time: 3 months before querying. We accept simultaneous submissions with notification. Publishes less than 1% of manuscripts submitted. Copyrighted, rights revert to author, but we require first rights. Subjects: Arts, Poetry.

Dnar Kaker Basa (see also DNAR KAKER BASA), Pallab Chakraborty Mr., Akunji Bagan, 1ST Lane, Palpara, Chandannagore, Hoogly, West Bengal, India. Pin: 712136., India, 033-26851666. 2000. Poetry, fiction, articles, cartoons, interviews, satire, criticism, reviews, letters, parts-of-novels, long-poems, collages, non-fiction. "Published in Bengali language." avg. press run 1000. Pub'd 2 titles 2009; expects 3 titles 2010, 3 titles 2011. No titles listed in the *Small Press Record of Books in Print* (36th Edition, 2010-11). Discounts: Not any. 25-350pp. Reporting time: within one week from the day we receive the work. Simultaneous submissions accepted: No. Payment: We depend on free and volountery works for the magazine. Books are always negotiable. Copyrights for author. Subjects: Abstracts, Absurdist, Adolescence, Advertising, Self-Promotion, Anarchist, Cartoons, Creativity, Experimental, Fantasy, Feminism, Festivals, Fiction, Futurism, Post Modern, Zines.

DNAR KAKER BASA, Dnar Kaker Basa, Pallab Chakraborty Mr., Akunji Bagan, 1ST Lane, Palpara, Chandannagore, Hoogly, West Bengal, India. Pin: 712136., India, 033-26851666. 2000. Poetry, articles, cartoons, interviews, satire, criticism, reviews, letters, parts-of-novels, long-poems, collages, non-fiction. circ. 2500. 12/yr. Pub'd 12 issues 2009; expects 12 issues 2010, 12 issues 2011. sub. price $55; per copy $5; sample $5. Back issues: inquire. Discounts: standard rates in India apply. 25pp. Pub's reviews: 32 in 2009. §new little magazines published internationally. Ads: $150/full page$75/ half page$5/classifieds.

Doctor Jazz Press, A.J. Wright, 119 Pintail Drive, Pelham, AL 35124. 1979. Poetry, art. "DJ Press continues to issue poetry broadsides. No submissions, please; I am still overstocked. Until next time, this is Doctor Jazz signing off." avg. press run 100. Pub'd 2 titles 2009; expects 8 titles 2010. 10 titles listed in the *Small Press Record of Books in Print* (36th Edition, 2010-11). 1 page. Reporting time: less than a month. Payment: 25 copies. Copyrights for author. Subject: Poetry.

Dog's Eye View Media, Nola Kelsey, PO Box 888, Hot Springs, SD 57747, 605 745-4350. 2007. Art, satire, non-fiction. "Dog's Eye View Press publishes nonfiction titles only. We have a strong slant towards animals, nature, travel, humor and wicked satire. Our children's nonfiction series Let's Go Visit are primarily educational read alouds designed to teach children about nature and culture, leaning heavily towards zoology and domestic pets." Expects 5 titles 2010, 5 titles 2011. 6 titles listed in the *Small Press Record of Books in Print* (36th Edition, 2010-11). Discounts: 10-20 copies 40%, 20-50 copies 45%, 50 or more copies 50%. 200pp. Reporting time: One month. Simultaneous submissions accepted: Yes. Payment: No advances. Royalties are paid quarterly beginning four months after publication. Does not copyright for author. Subjects: Animals, Biology, Birds, How-To, Humor, Nature, Science, Society, Travel, Wildlife.

DOLLS UNITED INTERACTIVE MAGAZINE, Kathleen Chrisman, 6360 Camille Drive, Mechanicsville, VA 23111, http://www.dollsunited.com, 804-339-8579, editor@dollsunited.com. 2002. Articles, art, photos, interviews, reviews. "Dolls United Interactive Magazine is a multi-media magazine for cloth art doll makers, artists, and enthusiasts. We publish artcies about doll making in all mediums: beading, clay, sewing, designing, painting, sculpting, embossing, fabric manipulation, and more. We also like to publish articles that apply to doll making as a business: tax information, branding, web design, photo editing, and more. Issues often contain one-two interviews with doll makers, and conference coverage. Each issue follows a specific "theme" and we try to apply our articles and dolls to that theme. In the past we have done such themes as "Asian Influence", "Winter Romance", "Stage & Screen", "Mystical", and more." circ. 200. 4/yr. Pub'd 4 issues 2009; expects 4 issues 2010, 4 issues 2011. sub. price $24; per copy $7; sample free. Back issues: $7. 115pp. Reporting time: Within a week. Simultaneous submissions accepted: Yes. Pub's reviews: 2 in 2009. §Anything related to dollmaking. Ads: $100 - full page$50 - half page$30 - quarter page. Subjects: Arts, Avant-Garde, Experimental Art, Business & Economics, Color, Crafts, Hobbies, Creativity, Design, How-To, Internet, Interviews, Marketing, Photography, Quilting, Sewing, Textiles, Visual Arts.

Dominion Global Publishing, Michael Matthews, P.O. Box 630372, Houston, TX 77263, 281-277-6626, info@positiontoreceive.com. 2006. Non-fiction. "Our first book entitled Position To Receive is a Christian Inspirations/Business Motivation." avg. press run 5000. Expects 1 title 2010, 2 titles 2011. 1 title listed in the *Small Press Record of Books in Print* (36th Edition, 2010-11). Discounts: Contact our distributor Bookworld for discount information. 156pp. Reporting time: We respond within 2 weeks. Simultaneous submissions accepted: Yes. Payment: Varies from Author to Author, we also offer distribution and marketing services. Copyrights for author. Subjects: Advertising, Self-Promotion, African-American, Black, Business & Economics, Christianity, Creative Non-fiction, Family, Fiction, Finances, How-To, Marketing, Non-Fiction, Philosophy, Self-Help, Spiritual.

Doorjamb Press, P.O. Box 1296, Royal Oak, MI 48068-1296, Email: Editor@doorjambpress.org. "Doorjamb Press is a small press publisher in the Detroit Area, featuring works by national and local writers and artists, focusing on non-traditional poetry and prose. If you would like further information, have comments or are interested in submitting work, please contact us via email via email." No titles listed in the *Small Press Record of Books in Print* (36th Edition, 2010-11).

•**Dos Madres Press,** PO Box 294, Loveland, OH 45140. "Founded in 2004 by Robert J. Murphy, Dos Madres Press is dedicated to the belief that the small press is essential to the vitality of contemporary literature as a carrier of the new voice and new works by established poets, as well as the older, sometimes forgotten voices of the past. And in an ever more virtual world, to the creation of fine books pleasing to the eye and hand. Dos Madres is named in honor of Vera Murphy and Libbie Hughes, the Dos Madres whose contributions have made this press possible." No titles listed in the *Small Press Record of Books in Print* (36th Edition, 2010-11).

THE DOS PASSOS REVIEW, Briery Creek Press, Mary Carroll-Hackett, Editor, Department of English, Longwood University, Farmville, VA 23909. 2004. Poetry, fiction, non-fiction. "Originating from Longwood University's prestigious Dos Passos Prize for Fiction, *The Dos Passos Review* actively seeks the best American writing in the areas of literary fiction, creative nonfiction, and poetry. We are looking for writing that demonstrates characteristics found in the work of John Dos Passos, such as an intense and original exploration of specifically American themes; an innovative quality; and a range of literary forms, especially in the genres of fiction and creative non-fiction. We are not interested in genre fiction, or prose that is experiment for the sake of experiment. We are also not interested in nonfiction that is scholarly or critical in nature. Send us your best unpublished literary prose or poetry. Reading period: Feb 1- July 31. Complete guidelines at www.brierycreek-press.org." circ. 500. Twice a year: June, December. sub. price $18.00; per copy $8.00; sample $6.00. 110pp. Reporting time: No more than 120 days; avg reporting time 60 days. Simultaneous submissions accepted: With notification. Payment: Contributor copies.

DOUBLE ROOM: A Journal of Prose Poetry & Flash Fiction, Peter Conners, Founding Editor; Mark Tursi, Founding Editor; Cactus May, Associate Editor; Michael Neff, Publisher, double_room@hotmail.com, www.webdelsol.com/double_room. 2002. Poetry, fiction, art, photos, criticism, reviews. "In addition to publishing prose poetry and flash fiction, we ask each contributor to write roughly 250 words regarding one or both of the forms. Our goal is to not only present the best writing possible, but to advance the discussion regarding these forms. We have two open submission periods per year which are posted on our web site. Recent contributors include Rosmarie Waldrop, Cole Swenson, Daryl Scroggins, Ron Silliman, Holly Iglesias, Russell Edson, Bin Ramke, and Sean Thomas Dougherty." circ. online publication with unlimited circulation. 2/yr. Expects 2 issues 2010, 2 issues 2011. sub. price free; sample online. Back issues: free. 40pp. Reporting time: 1-4 months. Simultaneous submissions accepted: Yes. Payment: none. Copyrighted, reverts to author. Pub's reviews: 10 in 2009. §Books of prose poetry, flash fiction, or critical work regarding those forms. Ads: none.

DOWN IN THE DIRT LITERARY MAGAZINE, the prose & poetry magazine revealing all your dirty little secrets, Scars Publications, Alexandria Rand, Editor, Scars Publications, 829 Brian Court, Gurnee, IL 60031-3155, AlexRand@scars.tv, http://scars.tv. 1999. Poetry, fiction, art, photos, letters, long-poems, collages, non-fiction. "*down in the dirt* looks for new writers, so that new voices be heard. We publish print and internet issues of writings, preferring email submissions over letters (to avoid typing errors in reproduction), but select accepted writings, along with accepted writings from the literary magazine, *children, churches and daddies*, will appear in annual books (both paperback and hardcover), so if we choose your work for an annual collection book, we will notify you. Issues available in print (paid only), and on the internet for free at http://scars.tv. Email contact is preferred and any information about *down in the dirt* magazine is only a click away at http://scars.tv." circ. varies, usually always on internet, but can appear in collection books. monthly. 8 titles listed in the *Small Press Record of Books in Print* (36th Edition, 2010-11). price per copy around $14.00 for books, ~$11.95 for 2010 issues (which can be ordered on line through links at http://scars.tv/dirt.htm), $6.00 for 2008-2009 issues; sample around $14.00 for books, ~$11.95 for 2010 issues (which can be ordered on line through links at http://scars.tv/dirt.htm), $6.00 for 2008-2009 issues. Back issues: around $14.00 for books, ~$11.95 for 2010 issues (which can be ordered on line through links at http://scars.tv/dirt.htm), $6.00 for 2008-2009 issues. Issues are 84 pages as perfect-bound books with full color full bleed covers. In collection books, *Down in the Dirt* appears with *Children, Churches and Daddies* acceptances into a collection book, which on average is 200-400 pages. Reporting time: electronic requests receive responses within 3 days, you will hear from us within two weeks if you enclose a SASE, otherwise you will never hear from us. Simultaneous submissions accepted: Yes. Publishes 75% of manuscripts submitted. Payment: appearance of your work in text and e-books on the internet. Not copyrighted. Subjects: Arts, Chicago, Counter-Culture, Alternatives, Communes, Culture, Feminism, Fiction, Graphics, Language, Literary Review, Magazines, New Age, Photography, Poetry, Women.

Down The Shore Publishing, Ray Fisk, PO Box 100, West Creek, NJ 08092, 609-978-1233; fax 609-597-0422. 1984. Fiction, non-fiction. "We are primarily a regional publisher, producing trade and gift books for the NJ shore and mid-atlantic." avg. press run varies. Pub'd 3 titles 2009; expects 5 titles 2010, 5 titles 2011. 46 titles listed in the *Small Press Record of Books in Print* (36th Edition, 2010-11). Discounts: 1-2 books 0%, 3-5 20%, 6-11 40%, 12+ 42%. Pages vary. Reporting time: 1-3 months. Simultaneous submissions accepted: yes. Publishes 1% of manuscripts submitted. Payment: varies. We sometimes copyright for author. Subjects: Americana, Fiction, History, Literature (General), Nature.

Down There Press, Leigh Davidson, 938 Howard St., #101, San Francisco, CA 94103-4100, 415-974-8985 x 205, fax 415-974-8989, 800-289-8423, downtherepress@excite.com, www.goodvibes.com/dtp/dtp.html. 1975. Fiction, photos, non-fiction. "We publish sexual health books for children, women and men. Our books are sex-positive, innovative, lively, and practical, providing basic physiological information and realistic, non-judgmental techniques for strengthening sexual communication.We also publish award-winning erotica, both literary and photographic, for adults.Recent and best-selling titles include The Big Book of Masturbation, Photo Sex, Herotica 6, Anal Pleasure & Health, Exhibitionism for the Shy, A Kid's First Book About Sex." avg. press run 4000. Pub'd 4 titles 2009; expects 1 title 2011. No titles listed in the *Small Press Record of Books in Print* (36th Edition, 2010-11). Discounts: Distributed to the trade by SCB Distributors, Gardena CA, 800-729-6423. 200pp. Reporting time: 3 months. Simultaneous submissions accepted: Yes. Publishes 1% of manuscripts submitted. Payment: we pay small advances, and royalties based on net sales. Copyrights for author. Subjects: Counter-Culture, Alternatives, Communes, Culture, Fiction, Gay, Gender Issues, Health, Lesbianism, Photography, Psychology, Relationships, Self-Help, Senior Citizens, Singles, Visual Arts, Women.

Downeast Books, Karin Womer, Chris Cornell, PO Box 679, Camden, ME 04843, 207-594-9544, Fax 207-594-0147, books@downeast.com, www.downeastbooks.com, www.countrysportpress.com. 1967. Fiction, art, photos, non-fiction. "Maine or New England subject matter." avg. press run 3-5M. Pub'd 30 titles 2009; expects 30 titles 2010, 30 titles 2011. No titles listed in the *Small Press Record of Books in Print* (36th Edition, 2010-11). Discounts: trade 1-4 20%, 5-14 40%, 15-49 42%, 50-79 43%, 80-99 44%, 100+ 45%; call for cataloguer discounts. 165pp. Reporting time: 6-8 weeks. Simultaneous submissions accepted: yes. Publishes 2% of manuscripts submitted. Payment: varies. Copyrighting for author varies. Subjects: Antiques, Architecture, Arts, Biography, Children, Youth, Conservation, Crafts, Hobbies, Earth, Natural History, Fiction, Gardening, History, How-To, Humor, Literature (General), Newsletter.

DOWNSTATE STORY, Elaine Hopkins, 1825 Maple Ridge, Peoria, IL 61614, 309-688-1409, email ehopkins7@prodigy.net http://www.wiu.edu/users/mfgch/dss. 1992. Fiction, art. "2000 word maximum, mainstream fiction." 1/yr. Pub'd 1 issue 2009; expects 1 issue 2010, 1 issue 2011. price per copy $8; sample $8. Back issues: $5. Discounts: yes. 65pp. Reporting time: varies. Simultaneous submissions accepted: yes. Publishes 10% of manuscripts submitted. Payment: $50. Copyrighted, reverts to author. Ads: negotiable. Subject: Short Stories.

DOWNTOWN BROOKLYN: A Journal of Writing, Wayne Berninger, English Department; Long Island Univ., Brooklyn Campus, 1 University Plaza, Brooklyn, NY 11201. 1992. Poetry, fiction, art, photos, parts-of-novels, long-poems, plays, concrete art, non-fiction. "Submissions only accepted from current and former students, faculty, and staff of the Brooklyn Campus of Long Island University." circ. 2000 copies. 1/yr. Pub'd 1 issue 2009; expects 1 issue 2010, 1 issue 2011. sub. price free first come first served; per copy free first come first served; sample free first come first served. Back issues: available in LIU/Brooklyn library and at library at U of Wisconsin/Madison. 175pp. Reporting time: deadline first Monday in December; response in following April. Payment: none. Copyrighted, reverts to author.

DRAMA GARDEN, New Creature Press, Joseph Verrilli, PO Box 1158, Bridgeport, CT 06601-1158, 203-455-7285. 2006. Poetry, fiction, articles, art, photos, cartoons, satire, reviews, letters, collages, non-fiction. "Recent contributors: Marie Kazalia, Ana Christy, Laurel Speer, Lyn Lifshin, Colin Cross, D.J. Weston, Jonathan K. Rice, Laura Stamps, and Mark Sonnenfeld." circ. 50. 3/yr. Expects 3 issues 2010, 3 issues 2011. sub. price $10; per copy $4; sample $4. 21pp. Reporting time: 1 week. Simultaneous submissions accepted: yes. Publishes 95% of manuscripts submitted. Payment: contributor copy. Not copyrighted. Pub's reviews. §Poetry, prose on any subject, also art/collages. Subjects: Relationships, Religion, Society.

Dramaline Publications, Courtney Marsh, 36851 Palm View Road, Rancho Mirage, CA 92270-2417, 760-770-6076, FAX 760-770-4507, drama.line@verizon.net. 1983. Plays. "We publish scene-study books for actors. Monologues and scenes. The original monologues and scenes must be of no longer than a three minute duration, must embrace contemporary points of view, be written in modern language." avg. press run 2M. Pub'd 3 titles 2009; expects 4 titles 2010, 4 titles 2011. 47 titles listed in the *Small Press Record of Books in Print* (36th Edition, 2010-11). Discounts: Negotiable. 64pp. Reporting time: 1 month. Simultaneous submissions accepted: no. Publishes 5% of manuscripts submitted. Does not copyright for author. Subject: Drama.

THE DRAMATIST, Gregory Bossler, The Dramatists Guild of America Inc., 1501 Broadway Suite 701, New York, NY 10036. 1964. Articles, photos, interviews, letters, news items, non-fiction. circ. 7M. 6/yr. Pub'd 6 issues 2009; expects 6 issues 2010, 6 issues 2011. sub. price $25; per copy $5 (Canada $8). 48pp. Reporting time: 6 months. Simultaneous submissions accepted: Yes. Payment: $25 for under 250 words, $50 for 250-499, $75 for 500-999, $100 for 1,000-1,499, $150 for 1,500-2,499, $200 for 2,500 or more. Copyrighted, reverts to author. Ads: full page color $675, full page B&W $500, half page B&W $325, classified $40 for 40 words 75¢ each addional word. Subjects: Interviews, Theatre, Writers/Writing.

•**Dramatists Play Service,** 440 Park Ave. S, New York, NY 10016, (212) 683-8960[ph], 212) 213-1539[f]. Plays. "Dramatists Play Service, Inc. has grown steadily to become one of the premier play-licensing agencies in the English-speaking theatre. Offering an extensive list of titles, including a preponderance of the most significant American plays of the past half-century, Dramatists Play Service, Inc. works with thousands of theatres and supports the theatre's vital position in contemporary life." No titles listed in the *Small Press Record of Books in Print* (36th Edition, 2010-11).

Dream Catcher Publishing, Dwan Hightower, President, 3260 Keith Bridge Road #343, Cumming, GA 30041-4058, 770-887-7058, fax 888-771-2800, dcp@dreamcatcherpublishing.net, www.dreamcatcherpublishing.net. 2001. Poetry, fiction, non-fiction. avg. press run 5000. Pub'd 6 titles 2009; expects 8 titles 2010, 8 titles 2011. 14 titles listed in the *Small Press Record of Books in Print* (36th Edition, 2010-11). Discounts: 40%. 250pp. Simultaneous submissions accepted: no. Publishes 90% of manuscripts submitted. Copyrights for author. Subjects: Fantasy, Fiction, Native American, Non-Fiction, Picture Books, Poetry.

DREAM FANTASY INTERNATIONAL, Chuck Jones, Editor-in-Chief & Publisher, 411 14th Street #H1, Ramona, CA 92065-2769. 1980. Poetry, fiction, articles, art, cartoons, satire, non-fiction. "All prose to above address. All poetry submissions to Senior Poetry Editor Carmen M. Pursifull, 809 W. Maple, Champaign, IL 61820-2810. Length of prose material accepted: 1,000-2,000 words. *Not commonly accepted*: sexually explicit material or use of vulgar or 'four-letter' words. Basic type of subject accepted: anything relating to dreams; dream fragments, fiction, poetry, non-fiction, haiku, etc. Articles on precognition, astral projection, etc. Mss will not be returned unless so requested at time of submission. Also fantasy pieces, fiction, prose and poetry. Checks/money orders and overseas drafts must be made payable to Charles Jones rather than DIQ. Send prose to Editor-in-Chief, Chuck Jones." circ. 65-80. 1-2/yr. Pub'd 2 issues 2009. sub. price US $56 (domestic rate); per copy $14 ppd. (Domestic), guidelines $2 for LSASE with 2 1st class stamps; sample Outside US: $12. Consult US Editor for postage and handling costs. Back issues: $15 each. 99-111pp. Reporting time: 8-10 weeks. Simultaneous submissions accepted: yes. Publishes 40% of manuscripts submitted. Payment: in the form of complimentary copy upon receipt of $4.50 for s/h. Copyrighted, reverts to author. Ads: $57/$35/$10. Subjects: Dreams, Fantasy, Fiction, Haiku, Poetry, Prose, Psychology, Satire, Science Fiction, Short Stories, Spiritual.

Dream Horse Press, J.P. Dancing Bear, PO Box 2080, Aptos, CA 95001-2080, dreamhorsepress@yahoo.com, www.dreamhorsepress.com. 1997. Poetry. "DHP publishes two or more manuscripts a year: one from our American Poetry Journal Book Prize, deadline February 28; and The Orphic Poetry Book Prize, deadline August 31. See website for full and up-to-date details and guidelines. In addition we review all entrants for publication, 3 runner-ups from the 2008 Orphic Prize were selected for publication." avg. press run 500. Pub'd 3 titles 2009; expects 3 titles 2010, 3 titles 2011. 7 titles listed in the *Small Press Record of Books in Print* (36th Edition, 2010-11). Reporting time: 3 months. Simultaneous submissions accepted: yes. Publishes 1% of manuscripts submitted. Copyrights for author. Subject: Poetry.

DREAM NETWORK, Roberta Ossana, Editor & Publisher, PO Box 1026, Moab, UT 84532-3031, 435-259-5936; Publisher@DreamNetwork.net http:dreamnetwork.net http://DreamNetwork.com. 1982. Poetry, articles, art, photos, interviews, reviews, letters. "Articles: 1500-2000 words. Full color covers, reproducible black and white original art and high quality photos (can be submitted via email as .jpg scanned at 300dpi or .pdf files) are preferred. We receive articles from some of the finest Dreamworkers in the country, both lay and professional, such as Arnold Mindell, Stanley Krippner, Gayle Delaney, Montague Ullman, Deborah Hillman, David Feinstein, with emphahsis on people like you! Questions & experiential sharing of dream-related experience invited. Contributing artists include Deborah Koff-Chapin, Susan Boulet, Susan St. Thomas, etc. Spiritual, psychology, New Age. Exploration of the meaning of dreams and the evolution of relevant mythologies in our time." circ. 4M. 4/yr. Pub'd 4 issues 2009; expects 4 issues 2010, 4 issues 2011. sub. price $25 USA; $35 Canada, Mexico, libraries; $45 foreign airmail. Available Online in .pdf format an exact replica of the print publication. $16 Worldwide; per copy $7; sample $7. Back issues: $7. Discounts: 50% jobbers, agents, distributors, etc. 52pp. Reporting time: maximum 1-2 months. We accept simultanous submissions occassionally. Publishes 50-75% of manuscripts submitted. Payment: 10 copies of issue in which their work is published and 1-year subscription. Copyrighted, rights revert to author if requested. Pub's reviews: 20 in 2009. §Books on dreams, mythology, dream education—anything dream or myth related, vidoes, CD's, Cassette tapes. Ads: $700/$400/classified $10/20 words or $35 per year. Subjects: Anthropology, Archaelogy, Book Reviewing, Dreams, Education, Human Rights, Interviews, Journals, Magazines, Motivation, Success, Myth, Mythology, Native American, New Age, Poetry, Psychology, Reviews.

Dream Publishing Co., G. Robert Lyles III, 1304 Devonshire, Grosse Pointe Park, MI 48230, 313-882-6603, Fax 313-882-8280. 1999. Fiction. "A new media company that creates a children's picture book series on health that empowers kids to overcome adversity and live healthier lives. Acceptance, tolerance and diversity are key elements. Multicultural and fun characters show kids that they are not alone with these health issues. Approved by the Dept. of Education for California." avg. press run 1-3M. Pub'd 2 titles 2009; expects 2 titles 2010. 3 titles listed in the *Small Press Record of Books in Print* (36th Edition, 2010-11). Discounts: standard. 32pp. Simultaneous submissions accepted: no. Publishes 0% of manuscripts submitted. Copyrights for author. Subjects: African-American, Children, Youth, Education, Family, Health, Inspirational, Latino, Multicultural, Nursing, Nutrition, Picture Books.

Dreams Due Media Group, Inc., Meg Hamilton, P.O. Box 1018, Firestone, CO 80520, Phone 303.241.3155, Fax 303.682.2695, Toll Free 877.462.1710, info@dreamsdue.com, www.dreamsdue.com. 2006. Poetry, fiction. "Dreams Due Media Group is a publisher of children's books. *Why Are You My Mother?* is the first book in the company's line of adoption and foster care stories, which serve as a resource for foster and foster-to-adopt families who face situations unique to caring for a child from the child welfare system. The firm's poetry collections are written and illustrated for the enjoyment of children and adults alike. Many poems in the first collection, *Hammin' It Up, Volume I*, are inspired by everyday parenting challenges and humorous family moments. The Johnny and Millie stories, which follow the travel adventures of two children, are designed to encourage young people to learn about new places. Dreams Due Media Group also develops and markets its own merchandise, including bookmarks, ornaments and jewelry." Pub'd 1 title 2009; expects 4-6 titles 2010. 1 title listed in the *Small Press Record of Books in Print* (36th Edition, 2010-11). Discounts: Please call 877.462.1710 for volume pricing. 16-30pp. Subjects: Adoption, Birth, Birth Control, Population, Children, Youth, Family, Fiction, Humor, Inspirational, Parenting, Picture Books, Poetry, Relationships, Social Work, Travel.

dreamslaughter, dreamslaughter dreamslaughter, PO Box 571454, Tarzana, CA 91357, 8183216708, http://www.dreamslaughter.com. 2005. Non-fiction. "progressive politics." avg. press run 2000. Pub'd 1 title 2009; expects 2 titles 2010, 3 titles 2011. No titles listed in the *Small Press Record of Books in Print* (36th Edition, 2010-11). 200pp. Simultaneous submissions accepted: Yes. Publishes 100% of manuscripts submitted. Copyrights for author. Subjects: Education, Multicultural, Non-Fiction, Non-Violence, Philosophy, Political Science, Politics, Quotations, Reference, Self-Help, Sociology, Spiritual.

Drinian Press, Robert Smith, P.O. Box 63, Huron, OH 44839, www.DrinianPress.com, rob@smithwrite.net. 2006. Poetry, fiction, non-fiction. "Drinian Press is a small literary publishing house which supports emerging authors of quality fiction, creative non-fiction, and poetry. We also place an emphasis on cooperation with other small presses and artists in north central Ohio to promote literary arts. By taking advantage of technological advances in the printing industry, we are able to provide books for the online market as well as "brick and mortar" retail stores. Our authors play an active part in promoting their work through presentations and book signings.Query before making a submission." avg. press run 300. Pub'd 3 titles 2009; expects 4 titles 2010, 4 titles 2011. 15 titles listed in the *Small Press Record of Books in Print* (36th Edition, 2010-11). Standard discounts apply to books ordered through Ingram and Baker & Taylor. Books ordered through publisher are 45% discount for booksellers, 25% discount for schools and libraries. Books are returnable. 230pp. Simultaneous submissions accepted: yes. Does not copyright for author. Subjects: Fiction, Haiku, Literature (General), Memoirs, Ohio, Poetry.

DRT Press, Adrienne Bashista, PO Box 427, Pittsboro, NC 27312-0427, 1-919-542-1763 (phone/fax), editorial@drtpress.com, www.drtpress.com. 2004. Fiction, non-fiction. "DRT Press published books about adoption and families. Our focus is on books for children, but we will also consider manuscripts for adults as long as they are within our parameters. We are a very small press and very selective. We can only publish books that do not compete with other items in print. Please check our website (www.drtpress.com) to see if we are accepting unsolicited manuscripts at any given time." avg. press run 5000. Expects 1 title 2010, 2 titles 2011. No titles listed in the *Small Press Record of Books in Print* (36th Edition, 2010-11). Discounts: 5-20 copies, 40%; closed case (30 copies), 50%. We encourage adoption non-profits to contact us for use of our books as fundraising items. 38pp. Reporting time: 3 months. Simultaneous submissions accepted: Yes. Payment: Standard advance against royalties. Copyrights for author. Subjects: Adoption, Family.

DRUMVOICES REVUE, Eugene B. Redmond, Southern Illinois University, English Dept., Box 1431, Edwardsville, IL 62026-1431, 618-650-3991; Fax 618-650-3509; eredmon@siue.edu; www.siue/ENGLISH/ dvr/. 1990. Poetry, fiction, articles, art, photos, interviews, criticism, reviews, letters, non-fiction. "Prefer poems of no more than 3 pages. Multicultural-gender inclusive. Recent contributors: Maya Angelou, Gwendolyn Brooks, John Knoepfle, Carlos Cumpian, Rohan B. Preston, Derek Walcott, Amiri Baraka, Allison Funk, and Janice Mirikitani." circ. 1.5M. 1-2/yr. Pub'd 1-2 issues 2009; expects 2 issues 2010, 2 issues 2011. sub. price $10; per copy $10; sample $5. Back issues: twenty dollars, $20.00. Discounts: 40%. 132pp. Reporting time: seasonal. Simultaneous submissions accepted: yes. Publishes 50% of manuscripts submitted. Payment: 2 copies.

Copyrighted, reverts to author. Pub's reviews. §Anthologies, clusters of chapbooks or volumes of poetry, novels. Ads: $200/$100/others negotiable. Subjects: African Literature, Africa, African Studies, African-American, Literature (General), Midwest.

•**DRUNKEN BOAT Online Journal,** editor@drunkenboat.com. "Slant/Sex/: Decades after Womens Lib and Stonewall, in the time of queer theory, gurlesque and girls gone wild, there are still aspects of women and transgender peoples sexuality that are taboo or discounted (the sexuality of older women and women with disabilities, for example, or a joyful transgender sexual self). We are looking for poems, prose, and multimedia/interactive art that address these topics. This is a call for bold, honest investigations of the sexual female/trans self that polite society has yet to fully embrace. We particularly encourage submissions from women of color, older women, queer women, women with disabilities, and transgender/two-spirit/intersex/ gender nonconforming folks. # Poetry: No more than three poems per submission. No more than two submissions per year."

Dry Creek Press, Bill Bailey, 5753 Cada Circle, Carmichael, CA 95608, 916-531-1249, 916-218-6036, www.drycreekpress.com. 2003. Non-fiction. "Focus is on inspirational books. My first series scheduled for 2007 is called The Best of Us, and like chicken soup for the soul will feature inspiring stories of people from all walks of life.I also will be re-issuing my book, America's Good News Almanac (published in 1996 by Simon and Schuster) with new cover and new title, Good News About America." avg. press run 500. Expects 2 titles 2011. No titles listed in the *Small Press Record of Books in Print* (36th Edition, 2010-11). Discounts: 2-10 copies 30%10 up 50%. 180pp. Reporting time: 2 weeks. Simultaneous submissions accepted: Yes. Publishes 1% of manuscripts submitted. Payment: no advances, royalt of at least 20%. Copyrights for author. Subject: Creative Non-fiction.

Paul Dry Books, Paul Dry, 1616 Walnut St., Suite 808, Philadelphia, PA 19103, 215-231-9939, fax:215-231-9942, website: www.@pauldrybooks.com. "At Paul Dry Books, our aim is to publish lively books "to awaken, delight, and educate"and to spark conversation. We publish fiction, both novels and short stories, and nonfictionbiography, memoirs, history, and essays, covering subjects from Homer to Chekhov, bird watching to jazz music, New York City to shogunate Japan." No titles listed in the *Small Press Record of Books in Print* (36th Edition, 2010-11). Subjects: Biography, Essays, Fiction, History, Interviews, Philosophy, Poetry.

DTS Group, Inc., Trudy Smith Ms., P.O. Box 4217, Asheboro, NC 27204-4217, DTSgroupinc@aol.com, DTSGroupInc.com. 2006. Fiction, non-fiction. "Interest in publishing North Carolina based Non-fiction or fiction manuscripts. Query first before submission via email DTSgroupinc@aol.com." avg. press run 5000. Expects 2 titles 2010, 2 titles 2011. 1 title listed in the *Small Press Record of Books in Print* (36th Edition, 2010-11). Discounts: 2-10 copies 25% Email for volume sales. 200pp. Reporting time: 60 days. Simultaneous submissions accepted: No. Payment: negotiable. Does not copyright for author. Subjects: Aging, Animals, Antiques, Appalachia, Christmas, Civil War, Collectibles, Creative Non-fiction, Death & Dying, Indians, Inspirational, Jewelry, Gems, Mystery, Non-Fiction, Self-Help.

THE DUCKBURG TIMES, Dana Gabbard, Editor, 3010 Wilshire Blvd., #362, Los Angeles, CA 90010-1146, 213-388-2364. 1977. Articles, art, photos, cartoons, interviews, criticism, reviews, letters, news items, non-fiction. "Our sole criterion for the acceptance of material is that it in some way relate to the works of Walt Disney and associates. We run quite a lot on famed comic book artist Carl Barks, but are also interested in material on other Disney artists, the studio, Disney animation, the theme parks, etc. If in doubt, contact us first. Especially on the lookout for material from overseas fans. We have special guidelines to follow when running Disney copyrighted art available upon request. Always open to the unusual and critical." circ. 1.4M. 1/yr. sub. price $12; per copy inquire; sample $3. Back issues: inquire. 28pp. Reporting time: ASAP. Payment: copy of issue material appears in. Copyrighted, rights revert to author upon written request. Pub's reviews: none in 2009. §Walt Disney, animation, Carl Barks, comics, theme parks, and related. Classified free to subscriber if under 50 words, Disney-related. Subjects: Comics, Disney.

Dufour Editions Inc., Christopher May, President & Publisher; Brad Elliott, Creative Director, PO Box 7, Chester Springs, PA 19425-0007, 610-458-5005, Fax 610-458-7103. 1949. Poetry, fiction, articles, criticism, reviews, long-poems, plays, non-fiction. "Dufour Editions publishes, co-publishes, and exclusively distributes selected titles of British or Irish origin. We also publish some works of American origin." avg. press run 500-3000. Pub'd 4 titles 2009; expects 4 titles 2010, 4 titles 2011. 14 titles listed in the *Small Press Record of Books in Print* (36th Edition, 2010-11). Discounts: trade 1-4 20%, 5-14 40%, 15-24 41%, 25-49 42%, 50-99 43%, 100+ 44%; short discounted titles: 20% any quantity. SCOP & STOP 30%; libraries 10%. Pages vary. Reporting time: 1-6 months. Simultaneous submissions accepted: yes. Publishes 1% of manuscripts submitted. Payment: negotiated. Copyrights for author. Subjects: Celtic, Children, Youth, Classical Studies, Fiction, German, History, Humanism, Ireland, Literature (General), Non-Fiction, Philosophy, Poetry, Politics, Scotland, Socialist.

‡**Duke University Press (see also AMERICAN LITERATURE; POETICS TODAY: International Journal for Theory and Analysis of Literature and Communication)**, Box 90660, Durham, NC 27708-0660, 919-687-3600; Fax 919-688-4574, www.dukeupress.edu. "Street address: 905 W. Main Street, Durham, NC 27701. uke University Press publishes and distributes more than thirty periodicals that span a stimulating range of disciplines within the humanities and sciences—from East Asian cultural studies to French history, from lesbian and gay studies to mathematics and the history of economic thought, from feminism, culture and media studies to medieval and early modern studies." No titles listed in the *Small Press Record of Books in Print* (36th Edition, 2010-11). Subject: University Press.

Dumouriez Publishing, Tawan Chester, Torquemada Harrell, PO Box 12849, Jacksonville, FL 32209, 904.536.8910, http://www.dpublishing1.com, admin@dpublishing1.com, tocca@dpublishing1.com. 2005. Art, photos, letters, non-fiction. "Publish traditional and electronic books and reprints. Nonfiction: motvational,inspirational, self-help,religious/spiritual in nature Recent Titles: An Intimate Walk-The Ultimate Relationship, WOMEN(With Open Minds Eternally Nurtured), One Day of Overcoming-A Lifetime of Living." avg. press run 3000. Expects 3 titles 2010, 3 titles 2011. No titles listed in the *Small Press Record of Books in Print* (36th Edition, 2010-11). Discounts: STOP copy 20%, 2-10 copies 25%, 11-20 copies 35%, 21-30 copies 45%, 31+ copies 55%, 2+ Non returnable copies 65%(no FOB). 200pp. Reporting time: Responds 1 month after recieving query or proposal pkg with SASE. No phone calls accepted. Simultaneous submissions accepted: No. Publishes 2% of manuscripts submitted. Payment: Pays 5-10% royalty on net receipts. Prefer author to handle copyrighting but will consider it on a case by case basis. Subjects: Arts, Culture, Grieving, Hypnosis, Inspirational, Motivation, Success, Non-Fiction, Parenting, Publishing, Religion, Reprints, Spiritual, Travel, Women, Writers/Writing.

Dunamis House, Bette Filley, 19801 SE 123rd Street, Issaquah, WA 98027, 425-255-5274, fax 425-277-8780. 1991. Non-fiction. "Additional address: PO Box 321, Issaquah, WA 98027." avg. press run 3.5M. Pub'd 1 title 2009; expects 1 title 2010, 1-2 titles 2011. 5 titles listed in the *Small Press Record of Books in Print* (36th Edition, 2010-11). Discounts: 40% trade, 55% distributors. 264pp. Reporting time: 6 weeks. Payment: varies. Copyrights for author. Subjects: Aging, Christianity, How-To, Non-Fiction, Pacific Northwest, Religion, Senior Citizens, Sports, Outdoors, Washington (state).

•**DUNES REVIEW,** Denise Baker, Editor, Michigan Writers Inc., PO Box 1505, Traverse City, MI 49685. "The Dunes Review is Northern Michigans premicr literary journal. Founded in 1997 by Anne-Marie Oomen, the Dunes Review publishes the best of local, regional, and national writers. Submissions are accepted year-round for the June and December publications at dunes.review@yahoo.com. The Dunes Review also offers a yearly contest, The William J. Shaw Memorial Prize for Poetry."

DUST (From the Ego Trip), Camel Press, James Hedges, Editor, Box 212, Needmore, PA 17238, 717-573-4526. 1984. Poetry, fiction, articles, non-fiction. "Contributions of good literary quality are welcome; manuscripts should be between 1M and 2.5M words in length." circ. 700. Irregular. Expects 1 issue 2010, 1 issue 2011. sub. price $1-3 per issue on standing order; per copy $1-3; sample $1. Discounts: on request. 20pp. Reporting time: 2 weeks. Simultaneous submissions accepted: yes. Publishes 5% of manuscripts submitted. Payment: 50 free copies. Copyrighted, rights revert to author if requested. No ads. Subjects: Biography, History, Public Affairs.

Dustbooks (see also THE SMALL PRESS REVIEW/SMALL MAGAZINE REVIEW), Len Fulton, Editor-Publisher; Kathy Glanville, Webmaster; Neil McIntyre, Computer Programming; Richard Lauson, Associate Editor, PO Box 100, Paradise, CA 95967-0100, 530-877-6110, Fax 530-877-0222, email: publisher@dustbooks.com, Website: http://www.dustbooks.com/. 1963. "We have a small general trade list: poetry, novels, anthologies, non-fiction prose, how-to, etc. But our real expertise & commitment is small press/magazine information. We do three annuals in both print editions and CD-Rom editions: this Directory you're holding (now in its forty sixth annual edition); its companion volume, the *Directory of Small Press/Magazine Editors and Publishers* (forty first edition), and the *Directory of Poetry Publishers* (twenty sixth edition), which, by the way, contains our annual Sweepstakes—a listing of the dozen or so poets most popular with editors. We also publish annually the *Small Press Record of Books in Print* (36th edition) CD-ROM edition only. We publish an on-line bi-monthly magazine, the *Small Press Review/Small Magazine Review* (see separate listing). NOTE: To be listed in any of our reference titles go to our website at www.dustbooks.com and click on the Directory Listing Forms button and follow instructions." avg. press run 1M-2M. Pub'd 5 titles 2009; expects 5 titles 2010, 5 titles 2011. 27 titles listed in the *Small Press Record of Books in Print* (36th Edition, 2010-11). Discounts: Returns only after six months but before one year; returns are for credit ONLY. 300-1,000pp. Reporting time: 3-6 months. Simultaneous submissions accepted: yes. Publishes 1% of manuscripts submitted. Payment: royalty (15%). Copyrights for author. Subjects: Bibliography, Biography, How-To, Magazines, Publishing, Reference.

DWANG: Outsider poetry and prose, Tangerine Press, Michael Curran, 23 Khartoum Road, Tooting, London SW17 0JA, England, www.eatmytangerine.com. 2006. Poetry, fiction, art, cartoons, parts-of-novels.

"Handbound hardcover limited editions using acid-free boards and archival papers, conservation glue and hemp cord. Publishes neglected poets like William Wantling as well as the best of the current wave. Contributors include Dan Fante, Billy Childish, Jim Burns, Edward Lucie-Smith, Peter Finch, Tim Wells, Fred Voss, John Hartley Williams, Steve Richmond, Idris Caffrey, Salena Godden, Tony O'Neill. Graphics from Phil Corbett, Yasmin Ramli." circ. 126. 1/yr. Expects 1 issue 2011. sub. price £50; per copy £50; sample £50. Back issues: inquire. Discounts: please contact for details. 100pp. Reporting time: 2 weeks-2months. Simultaneous submissions accepted: No. Publishes 2% of manuscripts submitted. Payment: contributor copy. Copyrighted, reverts to author. §outsider poetry and prose. Also graphics. Ads: no advertising. Subjects: Avant-Garde, Experimental Art, Beat, Charles Bukowski, Cartoons, Counter-Culture, Alternatives, Communes, England, Fiction, Poetry, Prose.

Dwarf Lion Press, Jill D. Swenson Ph.D., Shirley Werner Ph.D., P.O. Box 436, Trumansburg, NY 14886, 607/387-9100, 607/387-9100, dwarflionpress@yahoo.com. 2007. Criticism, non-fiction. "Religious and theological books of intellectual merit; non-fiction primarily." avg. press run 500. Expects 1-3 titles 2010, 1-3 titles 2011. 1 title listed in the *Small Press Record of Books in Print* (36th Edition, 2010-11). 350pp. Reporting time: 4-6 weeks. Simultaneous submissions accepted: Yes. Publishes 10% of manuscripts submitted. Copyrights for author. Subjects: Atheism, Catholic, Christianity, Cults, Essays, Greek, History, Inspirational, Judaism, Non-Fiction, Occult, Philosophy, Religion, Theosophical.

DWELLING PORTABLY, Light Living Library, c/o Lisa Ahne, PO Box 181, Alsea, OR 97324-0181. 1980. Articles, reviews, letters. "Helpful suggestions about portable dwelling, long comfortable camping, low-cost light-weight living. How to save money, energy, weight, space, land, live and travel more imaginatively. Simultaneous, photocopy submission recommended." circ. 2M. 2/yr. Pub'd 2 issues 2009; expects 3 issues 2010, 3 issues 2011. 1 title listed in the *Small Press Record of Books in Print* (36th Edition, 2010-11). sub. price $3; per copy $1. Back issues: some tiny-type reprints, 5/$2. Discounts: 6/$5 (back issues). 12pp. Simultaneous submissions accepted: yes. Publishes 75% of manuscripts submitted. Payment: subscriptions or ads; token $5 if requested. Not copyrighted. Pub's reviews: 2 in 2009. Ads: 25¢ per word. Subjects: Bicycling, Conservation, Consumer, Counter-Culture, Alternatives, Communes, Crafts, Hobbies, Ecology, Foods, Energy, Environment, Food, Eating, How-To, Lifestyles, Miniature Books, Pacific Northwest, Sports, Outdoors, Transportation.

E

E & E Publishing, Eve Heidi Bine-Stock, 1001 Bridgeway, No. 227, Sausalito, CA 94965, Tel: 415-331-4025, Fax: 415-331-4023, www.EandEGroup.com/Publishing. 2001. Non-fiction. "We publish children's nonfiction picture books; nonfiction books for adults on how to write for children; and nonfiction books for children on how to write. For adults, our best-selling title is HOW TO WRITE A CHILDREN'S PICTURE BOOK. We welcome queries and submissions by email to EandEGroup@EandEGroup.com." Pub'd 3 titles 2009; expects 5 titles 2010, 5 titles 2011. No titles listed in the *Small Press Record of Books in Print* (36th Edition, 2010-11). Reporting time: 4-6 weeks. Simultaneous submissions accepted: Yes. Publishes 2% of manuscripts submitted. Payment: Author: 5% of Retail Cover Price; Illustrator: 5% of Retail Cover Price; No Advance; Pay Royalty from First Copy Sold. While we do not copyright for the author, we do provide two free copies of the book for the author to send to the Copyright Office. Subjects: Animals, Arts, Children, Youth, Picture Books, Writers/Writing.

Eagle's View Publishing, Monte Smith, Publisher-Editor; Denise Knight, Editor, 6756 North Fork Road, Liberty, UT 84310, 801-393-4555 (orders), editorial phone 801-745-0905. 1982. Non-fiction. "We also publish a line of frontier clothing patterns." avg. press run 10M. Pub'd 1 title 2009; expects 4 titles 2010, 4 titles 2011. 49 titles listed in the *Small Press Record of Books in Print* (36th Edition, 2010-11). Discounts: standard for trade and jobber. 112pp. Reporting time: 12 months. Simultaneous submissions accepted: yes. Publishes 10% of manuscripts submitted. Payment: varies. Copyrights for author. Subjects: Americana, Children, Youth, Clothing, Crafts, Hobbies, Great Plains, History, How-To, Humor, Indians, Jewelry, Gems, Native American, Old West, Quilting, Sewing, Reprints, The West.

Eakins Press, PO Box 21235, Waco, TX 76702-1235, www.eakinpress.com, sales@eakinpress.com, phone: 1-254-235-6161, Fax: 254-235-6230. No titles listed in the *Small Press Record of Books in Print* (36th Edition, 2010-11).

Earth Star Publications (see also THE STAR BEACON), Ann Ulrich Miller, Publisher, 216 Sundown Circle, Pagosa Springs, CO 81147, TEL 970-759-2983, starbeacon@gmail.com, www.earthstarpublica- tions.com. 1987. Fiction, non-fiction. "Open to any subject matter and length. Recent titles have included fiction, self-help, children's, and metaphysical and New Age subjects. New releases include *Night of the White Raven* (historical fiction) by Ethan Miller and *The Mystery at Hickory Hill* (young adult mystery) by Ann Carol Ulrich. In 2006, we published *All the Bad Stuff Comes in Threes*, a cozy mystery by Karen Weinant Gallob and *Zeti Child, Lost Upon a One Star World*, sequel to the autobiography by Commander Sanni Emyetti Ceto, who wrote *Stranded On Earth* which is in its fifth printing. Earth Star is a self-publishing service. Authors pay for the publishing of their work." avg. press run 500. Pub'd 5 titles 2009; expects 2 titles 2010, 3 titles 2011. 26 titles listed in the *Small Press Record of Books in Print* (36th Edition, 2010-11). Discounts: 40% to retailers. 180pp. Reporting time: 6 weeks. Simultaneous submissions accepted: yes. Payment: 100% to author; publisher collects one-time fee; open to other arrangements. Copyrights for author. Subjects: Biography, Fiction, Science Fiction, Spiritual.

EARTH'S DAUGHTERS: Feminist Arts Periodical, Kastle Brill, Co-Editor; Joan Ford, Co-Editor; Bonnie Johnson, Co-Editor; Robin Willoughby, Co-Editor; Ryki Zuckerman, Co-Editor; Joyce Kessel, Co-Editor; Pat Colvard, Co-Editor, PO Box 41, Central Park Station, Buffalo, NY 14215-0041, 716-627-9825, http://bfn.org/~edaught. 1971. Poetry, fiction, art, photos, satire, parts-of-novels, long-poems, collages, plays. "We are a feminist arts periodical. Format varies with preannounced themes. Most issues are flat-spined, digest-sized issues. Poetry can be up to 40 lines (rare exceptions for exceptional work), free form, experimental—we like unusual work. All must be strong, supportive of women in all their diversity. We like work by new writers. Rarely publish rhyme. Recent contributors: Diane DiPrima, Janine Pommy Vega, Lyn Lifshin, Joseph Bruchak, and Susan Fantl Spivack." circ. 1M. 2-3/yr. Pub'd 2 issues 2009; expects 2 issues 2010, 2-3 issues 2011. sub. price $18/3 issues, instit. $22/3 issues; per copy $6; sample $6. Back issues: collectors set (issues 1-53) $300. Discounts: libraries only. 60pp. Reporting time: 4-5 months. Simultaneous submissions accepted if notified immediately when published elsewhere. Publishes 30% of manuscripts submitted. Payment: 2 issues complimentary and reduced prices on further copies. Copyrighted, reverts to author. Ads: none. Subjects: Fiction, Literature (General), Poetry, Women.

Earthshaker Books, Bonnie Lenz, P.O. Box 300184, St. Louis, MO 63130-4602, (Tel)314-862-8177, earthshakerbooks.com. 2006. Fiction. "Our focus is on young adult fiction or general fiction that also appeals to youth." avg. press run 3000. Pub'd 1 title 2009; expects 1 title 2011. 2 titles listed in the *Small Press Record of Books in Print* (36th Edition, 2010-11). 150-200pp. Does not copyright for author. Subjects: Fiction, Juvenile Fiction, Literature (General), Young Adult.

EARTHSHINE, Sally Zaino, Poetry Editor; Julie Moffitt, Poetry Editor, P.O. Box 245, Hummelstown, PA 17036, 717.645.2908, poetry@ruminations.us, http://www.ruminations.us/esIndex.htm. 2007. Poetry, art. "Earthshine was begun in 2007. It is an on-line poetry and print journal. Volume I has now been printed and submissions are being reviewed for Volume II. Each Volume is available on-line until it closes, at which time it is printed. We seek poetry of high literary quality which offers illumination to our readers. Each poet has a voice; each poetry journal has a voice. The voice of Earthshine is one of reflection, depth, compassion,scientific understanding, humanity, reason and beauty." price per copy $8.00; sample $8.00. Discounts: Discounted for 10 or more copies. Reporting time: one month. Simultaneous submissions accepted: No. Publishes 3% of manuscripts submitted. Payment: Poets receive a copy of the journal and additional copies at discount. Copyrighted, reverts to author.

THE EAST HAWAII OBSERVER, Brandon Haleamau, P.O. Box 10247, Hilo, HI 96721, eho7148@hot-mail.com, http://easthawaiiobserver.blogspot.com. 2002. Poetry, fiction, articles, art, photos, cartoons, interviews, criticism, reviews, music, letters, long-poems, collages, news items, non-fiction. "The East Hawaii Observer is East Hawaii's premiere magazine of art and literature. In each issue is featured an area artist, whose work illustrates the magazine throughout. Our motto, "Casting light on the arts and artists of East Hawaii" sums it up. We publish fiction, poetry, nonfiction (travelogues have become a niche of ours), reviews of books, music, and movies, cartoons, photographs, and paintings. Work does not necessarily have to be about Hawaii, but Hawaii addressed in a fresh way also interests us. Contributors should feel free to write us and share ideas." circ. 70. 6/yr. Pub'd 1 issue 2009; expects 3 issues 2010, 6 issues 2011. sub. price $24; per copy $2; sample $2. Back issues: inquire. Discounts: None at this time. 20pp. Reporting time: Usually two to three weeks. Simultaneous submissions accepted: No. Publishes 70% of manuscripts submitted. Payment: We do not pay for content at this time. Copyrighted, reverts to author. Pub's reviews: 1 in 2009. §Poetry, fiction, and nonfiction. Material about the eastern part of the Big Islandespecially considered. Ads: $80/$40/$20. Call or write for details. Subjects: Arts, Creative Non-fiction, Culture, Experimental, Hawaii, Health, Pacific Region, Poetry, Prose, Travel, Visual Arts.

East West Discovery Press, Icy Smith, Editorial Director, PO Box 3585, Manhattan Beach, CA 90266, 310-545-3730, Fax 310-545-3731, info@eastwestdiscovery.com, web www.eastwestdiscovery.com. 2000. Photos, non-fiction. "East West Discovery Press is an independent publisher and distributor of multicultural and bilingual books in more than 30 different languages." Pub'd 4 titles 2009; expects 12 titles 2010, 4 titles 2011. 13 titles listed in the *Small Press Record of Books in Print* (36th Edition, 2010-11). Discounts: 40% to book trade. 200pp. Copyrights for author. Subjects: Asian-American, Bilingual, California, Children, Youth, Culture, Education, Games, History, Immigration, Los Angeles, Multicultural, Parenting, Photography, Trivia, Young Adult.

Eastern Washington University Press, Christopher Howell, Senior Editor; Pamela Holway, Managing Editor; Ivar Nelson, Director, Nonfiction Editor, 534 E. Spokane Falls Blvd. Suite 203, Spokane, WA 99202, Main line: 509-368-6574, Fax: 509-368-6596, 1-800-508-6596, Email: ewupress@mail.ewu.edu, Website: http://ewupress.ewu.edu. 1992. Poetry, fiction, criticism, long-poems, non-fiction. "The Eastern Washington University Press publishes innovative works that possess freshness in language and theme. A central aspect of our mission is the publication of works that address the history, culture, literature, and public policy of the Inland Northwest and Northern Rocky Mountain regions." avg. press run 1500. Pub'd 12 titles 2009; expects 15 titles 2010, 15-18 titles 2011. 1 title listed in the *Small Press Record of Books in Print* (36th Edition, 2010-11). Discounts: Bookstores, trade accounts & wholesalers. 80-250pp. Reporting time: 1-3 months. Simultaneous submissions accepted: Yes. Subjects: Asia, Indochina, Creative Non-fiction, Fiction, Idaho, Literature (General), Multicultural, Native American, Non-Fiction, Novels, Pacific Northwest, Poetry, Prose, Reprints, Translation, Washington (state).

EASTGATE QUARTERLY REVIEW OF HYPERTEXT, Eastgate Systems Inc., Diane Greco, 134 Main Street, Watertown, MA 02472, 617-924-9044, info@eastgate.com, www.eastgate.com. Poetry, fiction, articles, art, photos, interviews, satire, criticism, parts-of-novels, long-poems, collages, non-fiction. "Electronic submissions only; send disks, not paper. Please see our submission guidelines on our website. Works should be in some way 'hypertextual' (loosely construed). Recent contributors include Kathryn Cramer, Robert Kendall, Edward Falco, and Judith Kerman." Expects 1-2 issues 2010, 1-2 issues 2011. sub. price $49.95; per copy $19.95. Discounts: site licenses available, call for details. Reporting time: 6-8 weeks. Simultaneous submissions accepted: yes. Copyrighted, reverts to author. Subjects: Essays, Fantasy, Fiction, Literature (General), Science Fiction.

Eastgate Systems Inc. (see also EASTGATE QUARTERLY REVIEW OF HYPERTEXT), Diane Greco, 134 Main Street, Watertown, MA 02472, 617-924-9044, info@eastgate.com, www.eastgate.com. Poetry, fiction, articles, art, photos, satire, criticism, long-poems, non-fiction. "Electronic submissions only. Send disks or URLs, *not* paper. Works should be in some way 'hypertextual' (loosely construed). Please visit our website or view our catalogue before submitting; familiarity with our publications will give a good sense of what we're looking for. As a part of Eastgate Systems, the Reading Room is a showcase for World Wide Web-based work." avg. press run 1M-1.5M. Pub'd 2 titles 2009; expects 4 titles 2010, 4 titles 2011. 2 titles listed in the *Small Press Record of Books in Print* (36th Edition, 2010-11). Discounts: call for details. Reporting time: 6-8 weeks, longer submissions require more time. Simultaneous submissions accepted: yes. Publishes 1-2% of manuscripts submitted. Payment: varies, usually 15% of sales. Copyrights for author.

EbonyEnergy Publishing, Inc., Cheryl Katherine Wash, P.O. Box 43476, Chicago, IL 60643-0476, 773-445-4946; e-mail to: cheryl@ebonyenergy.com. 1999. Poetry, fiction, articles, art, photos, interviews, satire, criticism, reviews, music, letters, long-poems, plays, non-fiction. "EbonyEnergy Publishing, Inc. is a division of The EbonyEnergy Publishing Foundation. EbonyEnergy is a publishing house dedicated to publishing authors from diverse cultural and ethnic backgrounds speaking to the universality of our common humanity. EbonyEnergy Publishing, Inc. currently has 3 imprints: Highest Good Publications (self-help, inspirational, household), EbonyEnergy Books (general interest fiction, popular poetry, and general interest non-fiction), and Moonlight Halo Literary Press (literary fiction, literary poetry, and creative non-fiction). We reach our audience creatively via fiction, non-fiction, prose, poetry, plays, audio, and DVD/video. Our corporate keystone expression is, "Diverse Voices: One Humanity". While we evaluate work for its quality and freshness of expression, our companion consideration is its depth of humanity." avg. press run 1000. Pub'd 5 titles 2009; expects 10-15 titles 2010, 15-20 titles 2011. No titles listed in the *Small Press Record of Books in Print* (36th Edition, 2010-11). Discounts: Negotiable. Volume, trade, distributors, school. Discounts Available. pp varies by genrepp. Reporting time: 3 weeks to 3 months. Simultaneous submissions accepted: No. Publishes Highest Good Publications: 50%; EbonyEnergy Books: 50%;% of manuscripts submitted. Payment: Negotiable. We will copyright for author upon request. Subjects: African-American, Avant-Garde, Experimental Art, Chicago, Children, Youth, Creative Non-fiction, Culture, Inspirational, Literature (General), Non-Fiction, Poetry, Self-Help, Sex, Sexuality, Tapes & Records, Third World, Minorities, Visual Arts.

Eborn Books (see also THE DEFENDER - Rush Utah's Newsletter), Bret Eborn, Cynthia Eborn, 3601 S. 2700 W. B120, West Valley City, UT 84119, 801-965-9410, ebornbk@doitnow.com. 1988. Pub'd 10 titles 2009; expects 10 titles 2010, 10 titles 2011. 39 titles listed in the *Small Press Record of Books in Print* (36th Edition, 2010-11). 20pp. Subjects: Americana, Anthropology, Archaelogy, Arizona, Christianity, Mormon, Newsletter, Religion.

EcceNova Editions, Alex Allen, Assistant Editor, 308-640 Dallas Road, Victoria, BC V8V 1B6, Canada, Fax: 250-595-8401 email: info@eccenova.com URL: www.eccenova.com. 2003. Articles, non-fiction. "We accept

NON-FICTION submissions from credentialed (academic or professional)researchers in most fields of the PARANORMAL. Also accepting first-hand accounts of UFO encoutners, abductions, ghost sightings, etc. Recent works include a Fatima/UFO trilogy by Portuguese historians Dr. Joaquim Fernandes & Fina d'Armada. Tell us about your bacground in this field and provide some ideas on how you might help promote your work. Queries and proposals can be sent by email or post. Please supply a SASE, email address, or International Reply Coupon if not in Canada. Visit our website and read our up-to-date information on the "Submissions" page before sending your query." 12 titles listed in the *Small Press Record of Books in Print* (36th Edition, 2010-11). Reporting time: 1 month. Simultaneous submissions accepted: Not officially, but we understand that time issues are a concern for authors...if you must do this, just advise us. Payment: 15% on wholesale. Copyrights for author. Subjects: Ancient Astronauts, Astrology, Magic, Metaphysics, New Age, Non-Fiction, Occult, Space, Supernatural.

•**ECLECTICA MAGAZINE,** #102, 7575-140th Street, Surrey, BC V3W-5J9, Canada, Phone: (604) 543-1957 / (604) 590-2735. "We accept submissions on a wide variety of topics, and in a wide variety of forms. We ARE NOT particularly interested in politics, finances or sports - unless you happen to have a unique, interesting angle on them!The following is a guideline; if you have something that falls outside the guidelines, send it anyway! Who knows? We just might be interested. Fiction, poetry, humor, art/photography, non-fiction. Send submissions to jane@eclecticamagazine.ca or robynn@eclecticamagazine.ca."

Ecopress, An Imprint of Finney Company (see also Finney Company, Inc.), Alan Krysan, President, 8075 215th Street West, Lakeville, MN 55044, Phone: 952-469-6699 or (800) 846-7027, Fax: 952-469-1968 or (800) 330-6232, feedback@finneyco.com, www.ecopress.com. 1993. Non-fiction. avg. press run varies. Pub'd 1 title 2009; expects 2 titles 2010, 4 titles 2011. 8 titles listed in the *Small Press Record of Books in Print* (36th Edition, 2010-11). Discounts: 1-9 copies 20%; 10-24 copies 40%; 25-49 copies 45%; 50 or more copies 50%. Reporting time: 2-4 months. Simultaneous submissions accepted: yes. Publishes 5% of manuscripts submitted. Payment: negotiable. Copyrights for author. Subjects: Environment, Nature, Non-Fiction, Sports, Outdoors.

ECOTONE: Reimagining Place, David Gessner, UNCW Dept. of Creative Writing, 601 South College Road, Wilmington, NC 28403-3297, 910-962-3070. 2005. Poetry, fiction, art, photos, interviews, parts-of-novels, long-poems, non-fiction. "Ecotone is a literary journal of place that seeks to publish creative work about the environment and the natural world while avoiding the hushed tones and clichs of much of so-called nature writing. In the natural world an ecotone is a landscape where two separate ecosytems overlap, a place of danger and opportunity for animals. As we try to reimagine a new literature of place, our journal embraces literary ecotones, writing that breaks across genres and seeks out edges. These edgesbetween science and literature, the urban and rural, the personal and biologicalare places that are alive and electric, as well as new and dangerous." circ. 3000. 2/yr. Expects 1 issue 2010, 2 issues 2011. sub. price 1-Year: $16.95; per copy $9; sample $9. Back issues: $9. No discounts. 200pp + 8 page art insert. Reporting time: 5 months. Simultaneous submissions accepted: Yes. Publishes .5-2% of manuscripts submitted. Payment: 2 copies. Copyrighted, reverts to author. Ads: Free on exchange. Subjects: Appalachia, Conservation, Creativity, Culture, Environment, Essays, Fiction, Literature (General), Moving/Relocation, Nature, Poetry, Prose, Short Stories, Travel, Visual Arts.

Ecrivez!, Nancy McClary, Director; Alicia Williams, Local Ohio Author, Columbus, OH 43219-2002, 614-253-0773. 1996. Fiction, non-fiction. "n_boomer58@yahoo.com, Reading & Writing Book Camps (K-12), Self-Publishing Support." Pub'd 1 title 2009. 4 titles listed in the *Small Press Record of Books in Print* (36th Edition, 2010-11). Discounts: negotiable. 250pp. Does not copyright for author. Subjects: African-American, Bibliography, Children, Youth, Fiction, How-To, Juvenile Fiction, Men, Mystery, Non-Fiction, Race, Relationships, Reprints, Science Fiction, Self-Help, Short Stories.

Edenscape Publishing Company, Tim Tyler, P.O. Box 110650, Anchorage, AK 99511-0650, Phone:(907) 223-3624, Email:info@edenscapepublishing.com, Web Site:www.edenscapepublishing.com. 2007. Fiction, non-fiction. "Edenscape Publishing was established in 2007. We released our first book late 2008 and have two other books in progress. We believe that everyone has locked inside them the ability to live an extraordinary life. Our mission is to have a positive impact by helping you discover your full potential and to move from discovery to an abundant life. Our Approach: Create experiential learning, Discover the world through nontraditional eyes, Print books that inspire and challenge you to improve our world, See personal positive growth as a never-ending and unlimited journey, Examine ways to understand and break through barriers in our lives, Share our proven experiences, Unlock your passion for life." avg. press run 7000. Pub'd 2 titles 2009; expects 2 titles 2010, 3 titles 2011. 2 titles listed in the *Small Press Record of Books in Print* (36th Edition, 2010-11). Discounts: 1 to 9 books .. 0% off retail 10 to 24 books ... 40% off retail 25 to 49 books .. 45% off retail 50 to 99 book 50% off retail 100 to 999 books .. 55% off retail 1000 or more books .. 60% off retail. 256pp. Reporting time: 30 days. Simultaneous submissions accepted: Yes. Publishes 2% of manuscripts submitted. Copyrights for author. Subjects: Alaska, Business & Economics, Christianity, Creative Non-fiction, Creativity, Fiction, Leadership, Management, Motivation, Success, Non-Fiction, Novels, Numismatics, Outdoor Adventure, Self-Help, Short Stories.

EDGE Science Fiction and Fantasy Publishing, PO Box 1714, Calgary, AB T2P 2L7, Canada, 403-254-0160. 1996. Fiction. "We publish all types of science fiction and fantasy hardcover and trade paperback book-length literature from 70,000 to 100,000 words." avg. press run 2-3M. Pub'd 5 titles 2009; expects 6 titles 2010, 6 titles 2011. 19 titles listed in the *Small Press Record of Books in Print* (36th Edition, 2010-11). Discounts: trade 40%, bulk 42%, wholesale 50%, distribution 52% (minimums in effect). 350-375pp. Reporting time: 4-6 weeks. Simultaneous submissions accepted: no. Publishes 3-5% of manuscripts submitted. Payment: advance plus royalty. Copyrights for author. Subjects: Fantasy, Science Fiction.

Edgewise Press, Richard Milazzo, Howard B. Johnson Jr., Joy L. Glass, 24 Fifth Avenue #224, New York, NY 10011-8815, 212-982-4818, Fax 212-982-1364. 1995. Poetry, fiction, art, photos, interviews, criticism, letters. "Edgewise Press is dedicated to publishing quality paperback books of verse, essays, and other forms of writing." avg. press run 1M-2M. Pub'd 1 title 2009; expects 3 titles 2010, 4 titles 2011. 25 titles listed in the *Small Press Record of Books in Print* (36th Edition, 2010-11). Discounts: 60/40. 64pp. Publishes 0% of manuscripts submitted. Copyrights for author. Subjects: Arts, Criticism, Essays, Poetry, Visual Arts.

EDGZ, Blaine R. Hammond, Editor; Debra Brimacombe, Assistant Editor; Jack Turteltaub, Proof Editor, Edge Publications, PO Box 618, Scappoose, OR 97056. 2000. Poetry, art, photos, collages, concrete art. "Poetry and visual art only. Poetry must have some reference or application beyond the personal—struggling with issues of life and meaning. Want all sorts of voices and styles except disengaged, vague, abstract or dense language poetry. Also want cover and interior graphics. SASE for guidelines. I use recycled paper." circ. 200. 2/yr. Pub'd 2 issues 2009; expects 2 issues 2010, 2 issues 2011. sub. price $15; per copy $8; sample $4.00. Back issues: $4.00. Discounts: $4.00 to retail outlets. Pages vary. Reporting time: 1 week to 6 months or more. We accept simultaneous submissions if they promise not to withdraw anything once we've accepted it. Publishes 15% of manuscripts submitted. Payment: 1 copy, discount on extras. Copyrighted, reverts to author. Ads: $50/$30/$20 2-3", one free ad per year for subscribers. Subjects: Graphics, Poetry.

Edin Books, Inc., Linda S. Nathanson, Publisher and Editor, 102 Sunrise Drive, Gillette, NJ 07933-1944. 1994. Non-fiction. avg. press run 7.5M. Expects 1 title 2011. 5 titles listed in the *Small Press Record of Books in Print* (36th Edition, 2010-11). Discounts: 40%. 277pp. Simultaneous submissions accepted: no. Publishes 0% of manuscripts submitted. Copyrights for author. Subjects: Interviews, Metaphysics, New Age.

Edition Gemini, Gernot U. Gabel, Juelichstrasse 7, Huerth-Efferen D-50354, Germany, 02233/63550, Fax 02233/65866. 1979. Criticism, letters, non-fiction. avg. press run 150-300. Pub'd 3 titles 2009; expects 3 titles 2010. 3 titles listed in the *Small Press Record of Books in Print* (36th Edition, 2010-11). Discounts: trade 30%. 70pp. Reporting time: 1 month. Payment: yes. Copyrights for author. Subjects: Bibliography, History, Literature (General), Philosophy.

EDUCATION IN FOCUS, Books for All Times, Inc., Joe David, Editor, PO Box 2, Alexandria, VA 22313, 703-548-0457. "A semi-annual newsletter which provides an *in focus* look at education from a rational and humane viewpoint." 2/yr. Pub'd 2 issues 2009; expects 2 issues 2010, 2 issues 2011. price per copy $3. 6pp. Reporting time: 4 weeks. Payment: varies. Copyrighted, we buy rights to use in newsletter, book, and on Internet. Pub's reviews: none in 2009. §Education. Ads: $75 for 2-1/4 X 4-1/2/$25 for 2-1/4 X 1-1/2. Subject: Education.

EDUCATIONAL FOUNDATIONS, Caddo Gap Press, Darrell Cleveland, Editor, 3145 Geary Boulevard, Suite 275, San Francisco, CA 94118, 415-666-3012. 1986. Articles. "*Educational Foundations* seeks manuscripts of 20-25 double-spaced typewritten pages on issues, themes, research, and practice in the social foundations of education. Most contributors are scholars in the various social foundations disciplines." circ. 700. 4/yr. Pub'd 4 issues 2009; expects 4 issues 2010, 4 issues 2011. sub. price $50 individuals, $100 institutions; per copy $25. Discounts: agency 15%. 96pp. Reporting time: 1-2 months. Publishes 25% of manuscripts submitted. Payment: none. Copyrighted, rights revert to author if desired. Ads: $200 full page. Subject: Education.

EDUCATIONAL LEADERSHIP & ADMINISTRATION, Caddo Gap Press, Elizabeth O'Reilly, Editor, 3145 Geary Boulevard #275, San Francisco, CA 94118, 415-392-1911. 1988. Articles. "Annual journal of the California Association of Professors of Educational Administration." circ. 200. 1/yr. Pub'd 1 issue 2009; expects 1 issue 2010, 1 issue 2011. sub. price $50 individuals, $100 institutions; per copy $50. 96pp. Reporting time: 2 months. Publishes 25% of manuscripts submitted. Payment: none. Copyrighted, reverts to author. Ads: $200 per page. Subject: Education.

The Edwin Mellen Press (see also The Edwin Mellen Press), Herbert Richardson, PO Box 450, Lewiston, NY 14092, 716-754-2266. 1974. "United Kingdom Division: The Edwin Mellen Press, Ltd., Lampeter, Dyfed, Wales SA48 7DY. Canadian Division: The Edwin Mellen Press-Canada, PO Box 67, Queenston, Ontario L0S 1L0. We now have a poetry series (Mellen Poetry Press Series). These are small softcover/paper books including works by first published poets. The price range is $15-$30. By the way, we pay NO royalties at all on ANY books, but also require NO subsidies. We also require camera-ready copy to our specifications." avg.

press run 300. Pub'd 300 titles 2009; expects 300 titles 2010, 350 titles 2011. 371 titles listed in the *Small Press Record of Books in Print* (36th Edition, 2010-11). Discounts: 20% to resellers, special discounts for quantity orders, text prices for all books. 300pp. Reporting time: 2 months. Simultaneous submissions accepted: no. Payment: 5 free copies to the author/editor. We deposit 2 copies of the published book, copyrighted in the author's name, with the Copyright Office, and 1 copy with the Cataloging Division. Subjects: Black, Classical Studies, Counter-Culture, Alternatives, Communes, German, History, Judaism, Music, Philosophy, Poetry, Religion, Society, Translation, Women.

The Edwin Mellen Press (see also The Edwin Mellen Press), Herbert Richardson, Editor in Chief; John Rupnow, Director; Kelly Lang, Editor, PO Box 450, 415 Ridge Street, Lewiston, NY 14092-0450, 716-754-2266, Fax 716-754-4056, editor@mellenpress.com, www.mellenpress.com. 1974. Poetry, long-poems. "Send proposals to editor@mellenpress.com - Please Include: Abstract - CV - Table of Contents - 10-20 page sample." avg. press run 200. Pub'd 34 titles 2009; expects 40 titles 2010, 45 titles 2011. No titles listed in the *Small Press Record of Books in Print* (36th Edition, 2010-11). Discounts: bookstore 40% pre-publication on 10+ copies, 20% post-publication. 250 average *no page limit* pp. Reporting time: 2-4 months. We prefer not to accept simultaneous submissions. Publishes 20% of manuscripts submitted. Payment: 5 free copies to the author, no royalties. We deposit 2 copies of published book with copyright office; book is listed in C.P. with Library of Congress. Subjects: African Literature, Africa, African Studies, The Americas, Canada, Caribbean, Celtic, Classical Studies, Handicapped, History, Human Rights, Reference, Research, Sociology, Translation, University Press.

EEI Press, Janet Mullany, 66 Canal Center Plaza #200, Alexandria, VA 22314, 703-683-0683. 1972. Articles, interviews, reviews, news items. "We publish 7 titles for professional publications people." Expects 1 title 2010, 1 title 2011. 6 titles listed in the *Small Press Record of Books in Print* (36th Edition, 2010-11). Discounts: inquire. 100-300pppp. Reporting time: 1 month or less. Payment: inquire. EEI Press copyright. Subjects: Book Arts, Broadcasting, Communication, Journalism, Graphic Design, Internet, Language, Magazines, Newsletter, Paper, Photography, Publishing, Reading, Research, Reviews, Writers/Writing.

Wm.B. Eerdmans Publishing Co., Jon Pott, Editor-in-Chief, 2140 Oak Industrial Drive NE, Grand Rapids, MI 49505-6014, 616-459-4591. 1911. Photos, non-fiction. avg. press run 3M. Pub'd 106 titles 2009; expects 120 titles 2010, 130 titles 2011. No titles listed in the *Small Press Record of Books in Print* (36th Edition, 2010-11). Discounts: 40% trade. 250pp. Reporting time: 4-6 weeks. Simultaneous submissions accepted if so noted. Publishes 5% of manuscripts submitted. Payment: 7-10% of retail. Copyrights for author. Subjects: Children, Youth, Christianity, Ethics, Great Lakes, History, Michigan, Non-Fiction, Religion.

The Eighth Mountain Press, Ruth Gundle, 624 Southeast 29th Avenue, Portland, OR 97214, 503-233-3936, ruth@eighthmountain.com. 1985. Poetry, fiction, non-fiction. "We publish only women writers." avg. press run 4M. Pub'd 2 titles 2009; expects 2 titles 2010, 2 titles 2011. No titles listed in the *Small Press Record of Books in Print* (36th Edition, 2010-11). Discounts: books are distributed to the trade by Consortium & subject to their discount schedule. 200pp. Reporting time: 3 months. Simultaneous submissions not usually accepted; please notify if so. Publishes .01% of manuscripts submitted. Payment: 7% paper, 10% cloth usually. Copyrights for author. Subjects: Essays, Feminism, Fiction, Judaism, Lesbianism, Poetry, Prose, Travel, Women.

Eighth Sea Books, Lori Hall Steele, 223 West 7th Street, Traverse City, MI 49684-2426, 231-946-0678, info@8thSeaBooks.com, www.8thSeaBooks.com. 2003. Poetry, fiction, articles, photos, news items, non-fiction. avg. press run 5000. Expects 3 titles 2010, 5 titles 2011. No titles listed in the *Small Press Record of Books in Print* (36th Edition, 2010-11). Reporting time: 6 months. Simultaneous submissions accepted: yes. Copyrights for author.

88: A Journal of Contemporary American Poetry, Hollyridge Press, Ian Randall Wilson, Managing Editor, PO Box 2872, Venice, CA 90294, 310-712-1238, Fax 310-828-4860, t88ajournal@aol.com, guidelines at www.hollyridgepress.com. 2001. Poetry, criticism, reviews, long-poems. "88 IS ON HIATUS AND NOT CONSIDERING SUBMISSIONS AT THIS TIME." 1/yr. Pub'd 1 issue 2009; expects 1 issue 2010. price per copy $13.95. Available to bookstores through Ingram and Baker & Taylor at a short discount. 176pp. Reporting time: 3-6 months. Simultaneous submissions accepted: no. Publishes 2% of manuscripts submitted. Payment: contributor copies. Copyrighted, reverts to author. Pub's reviews: 4 in 2009. §Poetry and poetics. Ads: $300/$175/$100 1/4 page. Subjects: Criticism, Poetry, Reviews.

EKPHRASIS, Frith Press, Laverne Frith, Editor; Carol Frith, Editor, PO Box 161236, Sacramento, CA 95816-1236, www.ekphrasisjournal.com. 1997. Poetry. "A poetry journal focusing on the growing body of verse based on individual works from any artistic genre. Recent contributors: Peter Meinke, David Hamilton, William Greenway, Virgil Suarez, Linda Nemec Foster, Terry Blackhawk, Philip Dacey and Annie Finch. Visit our website for a link to guidelines for the Ekphrasis Prize." circ. 120+. 2/yr. Pub'd 2 issues 2009; expects 2 issues 2010, 2 issues 2011. sub. price $12; per copy $6; sample $6. Discounts: none. 36pp. Reporting time: 1

month - 6 months. Simultaneous submissions accepted: no. Publishes 5%-7% of manuscripts submitted. Payment: 1 copy. Copyrighted, reverts to author. Ads: none. Subjects: Arts, Poetry.

Elderberry Press, Inc., David W. St. John, 1393 Old Homestead Drive, Second Floor,, Oakland, OR 97462-9506, Tel: 541-459-6043, Email: editor@elderberrypress.com Site: elderberrypress.com. 1996. Poetry, fiction, articles, photos, cartoons, satire, letters, plays, non-fiction. "We are always looking for good politically incorrect fiction and nonfiction. All subjects considered excepting racist, hateful, ultra-violent or pornographic. Give me a call or drop me an email and let's discuss your MS. If I do ask for it in hard copy I'll get back to you by email as I read with my reactions—usually within 24-72 hours. I don't read queries, synopses, proposals or partially completed manuscripts. I read completed manuscripts, so send me the whole enchilada. No agents or agencies please. New writers welcome. Ring me and tell me what you've written and why you believe in it. I'll read it and see if I believe in it, too. If it's right for us I'll work with you personally throughout the process and for years afterward to find your book the readers it deserves." avg. press run 1M. Pub'd 12 titles 2009; expects 12 titles 2010, 12 titles 2011. 10 titles listed in the *Small Press Record of Books in Print* (36th Edition, 2010-11). Discounts: 40-55%. 250pp. Reporting time: 24-72 hours (Yes, really.). Simultaneous submissions accepted: yes. Publishes 20% of manuscripts submitted. Payment: 10-30% of retail. Copyrights for author. Subjects: Agriculture, Christianity, Current Affairs, Essays, Fiction, Libertarian, Memoirs, Military, Veterans, Non-Fiction, Philosophy, Politics, Religion, Science Fiction, War, Weather.

ELECTRONIC GREEN JOURNAL, Maria Anna Jankowska, Editor; Bill Johnson, Managing Editor, UCLA Charles E. Young Library, UCLA - Box 951575, Los Angeles, CA 90095-1575, e-mail majanko@uidaho.edu, http://repositories.cdlib.org/uclalib/egj/. 1994. Articles, reviews, non-fiction. "Contribution from authors on topics related to sources of information on environmental protection, conservation, management of natural resources, and ecologically balanced regional development. The international journal also seeks articles dealing with environmental issues specific to libraries, publishing industries, and information sciences. Our goal is to provide information in articles, essays, reports, annotated bibliographies and reviews that will be of interest to librarians, environmental educators, information consultants, publishers, booksellers, environmentalists, researchers, regional planners and students all over the world." circ. varies. 2/yr. Pub'd 2 issues 2009; expects 2 issues 2010, 2 issues 2011. sub. price free; per copy free; sample free. Back issues: free. 84pp. Reporting time: 6-8 weeks. Simultaneous submissions accepted: no. Publishes 60% of manuscripts submitted. Payment: none. Copyrighted, reverts to author. Pub's reviews: 25 in 2009. §Environmental protection, policy, science, nature/wildlife, global environment, conservation, environment information sources. Ads: $75/$50/$25 1/4 page. Subjects: Conservation, Environment.

ELEMENTS, Bernard Washington, PO Box 88086, Houston, TX 77288-0086, 713-252-5816, bWashington53@hotmail.com. 1979. Poetry, fiction, articles, art, photos, cartoons, interviews, satire, criticism, reviews, music, letters, news items, non-fiction. "We don't accept long stories or narratives." circ. 1K. 6/yr. Pub'd 6 issues 2009; expects 6 issues 2010, 6 issues 2011. sub. price $30; per copy $9.50; sample $9.50. Back issues: $9 each. Discounts: price varies on amount of order. 50pp. Reporting time: 1 week. Simultaneous submissions accepted: yes. Publishes 100% of manuscripts submitted. Payment: none. Copyrighted, reverts to author. Pub's reviews: 4 in 2009. §Music, politics, current events, movies, historic events, nonfiction. Ads: $75/$35/$20 (prices per year). Subjects: Advertising, Self-Promotion, African-American, Arts, Bibliography, Book Reviewing, Children, Youth, Communication, Journalism, Crystals, History, Interviews, Writers/Writing.

•**The Elevator Group,** PO Box 207, Paoli, PA 19301-0207. "The Elevator Group is dedicated to helping people rise above and lead an abundant life by developing books, broadcast media and motion pictures with meaning." No titles listed in the *Small Press Record of Books in Print* (36th Edition, 2010-11).

Elite Books, Dawson Church, PO Box 442, Fulton, CA 95439, 707-525-9292, Fax 800-330-9798, deb@authorspublishing.com, www.elitebooks.biz. 2002. Non-fiction. "Publishes primarily mind-body-spirit and health books." avg. press run 3-5K. Expects 10 titles 2011. 17 titles listed in the *Small Press Record of Books in Print* (36th Edition, 2010-11). Discounts: 40% retailers, 50% wholesalers, plus freight. 350pp. Reporting time: 8-12 weeks. Simultaneous submissions accepted: yes. Publishes 10% of manuscripts submitted. Payment: 10-20% biannually. Copyrights for author. Subjects: Alternative Medicine, Anthology, Motivation, Success, New Age, Self-Help.

ELIXIR, Elixir Press, Dana Curtis, PO Box 27029, Denver, CO 80227, www.elixirpress.com. 2000. Poetry, fiction. "Recent contributors: Donald Revell, Claudia Keelan, R.T. Smith, Sandra Kohler, Adrian Matejka. Reading period May 15 - Sept. 1. Interested in poetry and fiction." on hiatus. price per copy $5; sample $3. Back issues: $3. 120pp. Reporting time: 3-4 months. Simultaneous submissions accepted: yes. Publishes 1% of manuscripts submitted. Copyrighted, reverts to author. Subjects: Avant-Garde, Experimental Art, Experimental, Fiction, Poetry, Post Modern.

Elixir Press (see also ELIXIR), Dana Curtis, PO Box 27029, Denver, CO 80227-0029, www.elixirpress.com. 2000. Poetry, fiction. "Currently, we only consider unsolicited full-length and chapbook poetry and fiction

154

manuscripts through our contests. Recent contributors: Tracy Philpot, Michelle Mitchell-Foust,Jay Snodgrass, Sarah Kennedy, Jim McGarrah, Jane Satterfield, Duriel E. Harris, Samn Stockwell,and Jake Adam York.'' avg. press run 1M. Pub'd 3 titles 2009; expects 5 titles 2010, 5 titles 2011. 29 titles listed in the *Small Press Record of Books in Print* (36th Edition, 2010-11). 100pp. Reporting time: 6 months. Simultaneous submissions accepted: yes. Publishes 1% of manuscripts submitted. Copyrights for author. Subjects: Fiction, Poetry.

•**Ellechor Publishing House,** Al-Tajuan Petty, Acquisitions Editor; Olson Perry Sr., Acquisitions Director, P.O. Box 5693, Hillsboro, OR 97124, 559-744-ELLE, acquisitions@ellechor.org, http://www.ellechorpublishing.com. 2009. Poetry, fiction, non-fiction. ''Ellechor Publishing House, LLC focuses on Contemporary Christian fiction/non-fiction novels and inspirational anthologies. Our services include writers workshops, a free, professional critique of submitted manuscripts, and publishing/distribution to various sites and stores. We market all of our authors aggressively using websites, social media and author featured events to ensure they get maximum exposure to share their talent. We also host three major annual competitions with prizes.'' No titles listed in the *Small Press Record of Books in Print* (36th Edition, 2010-11). 200-350pp. Reporting time: 3-6 weeks. Simultaneous submissions accepted: Yes. Copyrights for author. Subjects: Book Reviewing, Children, Youth, Christianity, Creative Non-fiction, Fiction, Inspirational, Juvenile Fiction, Non-Fiction, Novels, Poetry, Publishing, Religion, Science Fiction, Textbooks, Writers/Writing.

•**ELLIPSIS,** Amanda Hobbs, Editor-in-Chief, Westminster College, 1840 South 1300 East, Salt Lake City, UT 84105. ''We invite you to join us! During August 1-November 1, send 3-5 poems, short fiction, or other prose under 6,000 words and visual art (preferably digital images). Include a stamped, self-addressed envelope for notification; unless you specifically ask that your submission be returned, well recycle it. Please include a brief contributors note in your cover letter, and make sure your cover letter and submissions have your phone numbers and email as well as name and address. We pay $10 per poem and piece of visual art, and $50 per prose piece, plus two copies of the issue.''

ELT Press (see also ENGLISH LITERATURE IN TRANSITION, 1880-1920), Robert Langenfeld, English Dept., Univ of N. Carolina, PO Box 26170, Greensboro, NC 27402-6170, 336-273-5507, Fax 336-334-3281, eltpress@gmail.com. 1988. Criticism, non-fiction. ''ELT Press publishes the 1880-1920 British Author Series. We print books which make available new critical, biographical, bibliographical and primary works on 1880-1920 British authors. Cloth-bound and original paperback books.'' avg. press run 500. Pub'd 2 titles 2009; expects 2 titles 2010, 2 titles 2011. 22 titles listed in the *Small Press Record of Books in Print* (36th Edition, 2010-11). Discounts: 20% to jobbers, agents. 300pp. Reporting time: 2-3 months. Simultaneous submissions accepted: no. Publishes 10% of manuscripts submitted. Payment: none. Copyrights for author. Subjects: Bibliography, Biography, Criticism, Fiction, Literature (General), Poetry.

•**The Emergency Response Unit,** Leigh Nash, Andrew Faulkner, 517 Runnymede Rd. Second Floor, Toronto, Ontario M6S 2Z8, Canada, http://theemergencyresponseunit.wordpress.com/. 2008. Poetry. ''The Emergency Response Unit was founded in 2008 by Leigh Nash and Andrew Faulkner and is a co-operatively edited chapbook press based in Toronto, Ontario.Our goal is to publish quality, affordable chapbooks that fill the space between one-off poems published in literary journals and full-length books. Were attracted to the idea of poems not necessarily as a sequence, but as a bundle, and believe the chapbook is ideal for this type of presentation. Also, we want to make pretty things.'' avg. press run 100. Pub'd 6 titles 2009; expects 5 titles 2010, 5 titles 2011. 11 titles listed in the *Small Press Record of Books in Print* (36th Edition, 2010-11). 24pp. Reporting time: 2 months. Simultaneous submissions accepted: Yes. Publishes 15% of manuscripts submitted. Payment: copies of book. Copyrights for author. Subject: Poetry.

EMERGING, LP Publications (Teleos Institute), Diane K. Pike, 7119 East Shea Blvd., Suite 109, PMB 418, Scottsdale, AZ 85254, 480-948-1800, Fax 480-948-1870, teleosinst@aol.com. 1972. Articles, photos, letters. circ. 100. 2/yr. Pub'd 2 issues 2009; expects 2 issues 2010, 2 issues 2011. 6 titles listed in the *Small Press Record of Books in Print* (36th Edition, 2010-11). sub. price $50; sample free. Discounts: none. 36pp. Payment: none. Not copyrighted. No ads. Subjects: Humanism, Metaphysics, Occult, Spiritual.

Empire Publishing Service, PO Box 1344, Studio City, CA 91614-0344. 1960. Fiction, music, plays, non-fiction. avg. press run 2M-10M. Pub'd 30 titles 2009; expects 20 titles 2010, 40 titles 2011. 202 titles listed in the *Small Press Record of Books in Print* (36th Edition, 2010-11). Discounts: 20%-45%. 150pp. Reporting time: 3-12 months. Simultaneous submissions accepted: no. Payment: varies. Copyrights for author. Subjects: Arts, Drama, Education, Entertainment, Shakespeare, Storytelling, Theatre.

Empyrean Hill Books, Inc., Elisabeth Scott, Editor, 1541 3rd Ave., Walnut Creek, CA 94597, submissions@empyreanhillbooks.com, www.empyreanhillbooks.com, 925-588-6083. 2008. Fiction. ''Empyrean Hill Books was established to publish high quality, imaginative fiction by previously unpublished authors, regardless of perceived commercial potential of their works. We chose books we find compelling and meaningful and are dedicated to the success of each of our titles and will nurture them to their full potential. Our publications, though specifically targeted at the young adult fantasy market, have universal appeal and the potential to become classics." avg. press run 2500. Expects 1 title 2010, 2-3 titles 2011. 1 title listed in the *Small Press Record of Books in Print* (36th Edition, 2010-11). Discounts: Standard trade discounts apply. Reporting time: 1 month. Simultaneous submissions accepted: Yes. Payment: Does not pay advance; royalty schedule based on number of books sold. Copyrights for author. Subjects: Fantasy, Fiction, Juvenile Fiction, Literature (General), Magic, Young Adult.

EMRYS JOURNAL, Emrys Press, L.B. Dishman, PO Box 8813, Greenville, SC 29601, www.emrys.org. 1983. "READING PERIOD IS FROM AUGUST 1 THROUGH NOVEMBER 1 ONLY. Submissions recieved at other times will be returned unread. This annual spring publication of poetry, short stories, and essays attracts hundreds of submissions from the United States and abroad. It is sponsored by the Emrys Foundation which promotes excellence in the arts, especially literary, visual, and musical works by women and minorities." circ. 200. 1/yr. Pub'd 1 issue 2009; expects 1 issue 2010, 1 issue 2011. sub. price $12; per copy $12; sample $12. Back issues: inquire. Discounts: 40% to wholesale and retail only. 120pp. Reporting time: 2 months. Simultaneous submissions accepted: NO. Publishes 10% of manuscripts submitted. Payment: 5 complimentary copies. Copyrighted, reverts to author. Subjects: Fiction, Non-Fiction, Poetry.

Emrys Press (see also EMRYS JOURNAL), L.B. Dishman, PO Box 8813, Greenville, SC 29601, www.emrys.org. 1983. Poetry, fiction, non-fiction. "We are looking for poetry, contemporary fiction and creative non fiction not to exceed 5000 words. Submit no more than 2 stories or essays and 5 poems per author. Please do not send any religious, romance, or science fiction. Also no gore, cliches, television dramas, or anything that would make our readers want to dump the entire work in the trash. READING PERIOD IS FROM AUGUST 1 through NOVEMBER 1 each year. We do not accept anything other than during that time." avg. press run 500. Pub'd 1 title 2009; expects 1 title 2010, 1 title 2011. No titles listed in the *Small Press Record of Books in Print* (36th Edition, 2010-11). Discounts: 40% to wholesale and retail only. 120pp. Reporting time: 2 months. Simultaneous submissions accepted: No. Publishes 10% of manuscripts submitted. Payment: Emrys has first rights, authors paid in contibutor's copies, no monetary payment at this time. Awards for best poetry, fiction and essay one per edition currently in the sum of $250. Does not copyright for author. Subjects: Dance, Essays, Fiction, Memoirs, Non-Fiction, Poetry.

Encore Publishing, Jon Wuebben, 124 S. Mercedes Rd, Fallbrook, CA 92028, (909) 437-7015, (760) 451-8670 fax. 2007. Non-fiction. avg. press run 3000. Expects 4 titles 2011. 1 title listed in the *Small Press Record of Books in Print* (36th Edition, 2010-11). Discounts: 2-4 20% 5-9 30%10-24 40%25-49 42%50-74 44%100-199 48%200 or more 50% off. 300pp. Reporting time: 30 days. Simultaneous submissions accepted: Yes. Payment: negotiable. Copyrights for author. Subjects: Business & Economics, Government, Health, Internet, Marketing, Politics, Writers/Writing.

Encounter Books, Peter Collier, 900 Broadway, Ste.400, New York, NY 10003-1239, 415-538-1460, Fax 415-538-1461, read@encounterbooks.com, www.encounterbooks.com. 1997. Non-fiction. "Quality non-fiction, serious books about history, culture, politics, religion, social criticism, public policy. Authors include William Kristol, Roger Kimball, Robert Spencer, Victor Davis Hanson, William McGowan." avg. press run 5M cl; 10M pa. Pub'd 12 titles 2009; expects 14 titles 2010, 14 titles 2011. No titles listed in the *Small Press Record of Books in Print* (36th Edition, 2010-11). Discounts: text 20%; trade 1-5 40%; 6-24 45%; 25-249 50%; 250 or more 55% and free freight. 240pp. Reporting time: 3 months. Simultaneous submissions accepted: yes. Publishes 2% of manuscripts submitted. Payment: 7% of list, advances vary. Copyrights for author. Subjects: Biography, Business & Economics, Criticism, Culture, Current Affairs, Politics, Religion.

Energy Psychology Press, Dawson Church, PO Box 442, Fulton, CA 95439, 707-525-9292, Fax 800-330-9798, dawson@authorspublishing.com, www.energypsychologypress.com. 2007. Non-fiction. "Publishes books and practical manuals on topics in the field of energy psychology and, sometimes, more generally, energy medicine." avg. press run 3-5K. Expects 5 titles 2010, 8 titles 2011. 15 titles listed in the *Small Press Record of Books in Print* (36th Edition, 2010-11). Discounts: 40% retailers, 50% wholesalers, plus freight. 300pp. Reporting time: 8-12 weeks. Simultaneous submissions accepted: yes. Publishes 10% of manuscripts submitted. Payment: 10-20% biannually. Copyrights for author. Subjects: Alternative Medicine, Psychology.

THE ENGLISH CLARION, SeaCrab Publishing, David Searle, Editor, 2 Nuffield Close, Shaw, Swindon SN5 5WT, England, seacrabart@googlemail.com. 2007. Poetry, articles, photos, interviews, reviews, letters, news items, non-fiction. "The English Clarion has one simple mission. To celebrate England and all things English. Particularly like historical articles about English Kings and Queens, seaside towns and anything with a friendly patriotic feel to it." circ. 100. 4/yr. Expects 1 issue 2010, 4 issues 2011. sub. price 19.99; per copy 4.99; sample 4.99. Back issues: 4.99. Discounts: 25 copies 10%. 32pp. Reporting time: 1 Month maximum, usually within a week. Simultaneous submissions accepted: Yes. Publishes 60% of manuscripts submitted. Payment: No money offered. But if we make any money, we'll share it fairly amongst all contributors. We always attribute copyright to the person who sends in the article, unless otherwise notified. Pub's reviews: none in 2009. §Any media which deals with English History & Culture, seaside towns, patriotic history, good photography of English subjects. Ads: Full page 80/half page 40/ Quarter page 20 per issue. Subjects:

Arthurian, William Blake, Culture, Charles Dickens, England, English, Festivals, Folklore, Food, Eating, Graphics, Sherlock Holmes, London, Photography, Shakespeare, World War II.

ENGLISH LITERATURE IN TRANSITION, 1880-1920, ELT Press, Robert Langenfeld, English Department/U of North Carolina, P.O. Box 26170, Greensboro, NC 27402-6170, 336-273-5507, Fax 336-334-3281; eltpress@gmail.com. 1957. Articles, criticism, reviews, letters, non-fiction. "ELT publishes essays on fiction, poetry, drama, or subjects of cultural interest in the 1880-1920 period of British literature. We do not print essays on Joyce, Conrad, Lawrence, Yeats, Virginia Woolf, or Henry James unless these authors are linked with minor figures in the period. 20-25 double-spaced pages is customary length for an essay." circ. 450 print/ 1600 online. 4/yr. Pub'd 4 issues 2009; expects 4 issues 2010, 4 issues 2011. sub. price US Online: $38; Print: $42; Print-Online: $58; Foreign Online: $38; Print: $50 + postage $30 = $80; Print & Online: $58 + postage $30 = $88; per copy $12 US; $14 + $15 postage $29 Foreign; sample free. Back issues: single-copy rate, discounts for run of 2 years or more. No discounts on regular issues. 128pp. Reporting time: 2-3 months. Simultaneous submissions accepted: no. Publishes 10% of manuscripts submitted. Payment: in advance. Copyrighted, does not revert to author. Pub's reviews: 60 in 2009. §Books related to the 1880-1920 period of British literature. Ads: $100 full-page; $150 for two ads. Subjects: Bibliography, Biography, Biography, Book Reviewing, Criticism, Drama, Sherlock Holmes, Rudyard Kipling, Literature (General), Reviews, G.B. Shaw.

Enigmatic Ink, Wayne Groen, 654 Grosvenor St, London, Ontario N5Y 3T4, Canada, www.enigmaticink.com. 2008. Poetry, fiction, art, cartoons, satire, long-poems, concrete art. Expects 21 titles 2010, 15 titles 2011. 10 titles listed in the *Small Press Record of Books in Print* (36th Edition, 2010-11). Reporting time: 2 months. Simultaneous submissions accepted: No. Publishes 1% of manuscripts submitted. Payment: 15% of gross revenue quarterly. Subjects: Abstracts, Absurdist, Arts, Avant-Garde, Experimental Art, Book Arts, Comics, Dada, Dreams, Experimental, Fantasy, Futurism, Post Modern, Supernatural, Surrealism, Zen.

Enlightened Living Publishing, LLC, Racina Stollings, P O Box 7291, Huntington, WV 25775-7291, telephone 304-486-9000, fax 304-486-5815, toll free 866-896-2665, e-mail: info@enlightenedlivingpublishing.com, www.enlightenedlivingpublishing.com. 2004. Non-fiction. "It is Enlightened Living Publishing, LLC's goal to publish authors that write, not from theory, but from extensive personal experience in the field addressed in their books." Expects 8 titles 2010, 12 titles 2011. No titles listed in the *Small Press Record of Books in Print* (36th Edition, 2010-11). Reporting time: 3 months. Simultaneous submissions accepted: Yes. Copyrights for author. Subjects: Business & Economics, Health, Sex, Sexuality.

EnlightenNext (see also WHAT IS ENLIGHTENMENT?), Andrew Cohen, PO Box 2360, Lenox, MA 01240-5360, 413-637-6000, Fax 415-637-6015, info@enlightennext.org. 1989. Photos, non-fiction. avg. press run 10K. Pub'd 1 title 2009; expects 1 title 2010, 1 title 2011. 9 titles listed in the *Small Press Record of Books in Print* (36th Edition, 2010-11). Discounts: 40%. 130pp. Payment: none. Copyrighting for author depends. Subjects: Religion, Spiritual.

J. M. Entrikin Publishing, James Entrikin, 351 Birch Bay Lynden Rd., Lynden, WA 98264, 360-201-8506, tianji@tianjishorserace.com. 2008. avg. press run 500. Expects 1 title 2010. No titles listed in the *Small Press Record of Books in Print* (36th Edition, 2010-11). Trade discounts range from 10 to 45 percent. 44pp.

ENVIRONMENTAL & ARCHITECTURAL PHENOMENOLOGY NEWSLETTER, David Seamon, 211 Seaton Hall, Architecture Dept., Kansas State University, Manhattan, KS 66506-2901, 913-532-1121. 1990. Poetry, articles, art, criticism, reviews, letters, news items, non-fiction. "Articles and other materials focusing on the nature of environmental and architectural experience. Also, the question of what places are, why they are important in peoples' lives, and architecture as place making." circ. 200. 3/yr. Pub'd 3 issues 2009. sub. price $10 US; $12 non-US payable in dollars; sample free. Back issues: $10/volume (1990-1999). 16pp. Reporting time: 2 months. Simultaneous submissions accepted: no. Publishes 25% of manuscripts submitted. Payment: none, we're entirely non profit. Not copyrighted. Pub's reviews: 15 in 2009. §Architecture as place making, environmental ethics, phenomenology, nature of place. Subjects: Architecture, Arts, Cities, Design, Ecology, Foods, Environment.

Ephemera Bound Publishing, Derek Dahlsad, 719 9th St N, Fargo, ND 58102, 701-306-6458. 2005. Fiction, articles, satire, non-fiction. "Our mix of books hopefully catches the works left behind by other publishers, either books that have fallen off the end of backlists or books from new or unproven authors. In earlier days, pulp magazines and novels were the domain of new and unproven authors, who developed their craft before expanding into so-called 'real' books. The cheaper nature of the pulps made them 'ephemera,' something that's used and discarded. Our goal is to redevelop the pulpy genre, bringing back the kind of books that were once dominated by writers missed by the big publishers." avg. press run 2000. Pub'd 4 titles 2009; expects 8 titles 2010, 18 titles 2011. 3 titles listed in the *Small Press Record of Books in Print* (36th Edition, 2010-11). Discounts: 40% off cover price for direct sales; also available through Ingram & Baker & Taylor at standard discounts. Rates subject to change; check our website for current information. 200pp. Reporting time: One To Two Weeks. Simultaneous submissions accepted: Yes. Publishes 20% of manuscripts submitted. Payment:

10%-15% of wholesale price. Does not copyright for author. Subjects: Erotica, Fantasy, Feminism, Fiction, Gender Issues, History, Horror, Lesbianism, Literature (General), Non-Fiction, Novels, Occult, Religion, Romance, Sex, Sexuality.

EPICENTER: A LITERARY MAGAZINE, Jeffery Green, Rowena Silver, Linfor Cali, PO Box 367, Riverside, CA 92502, www.epicentrermagazine.org. 1994. Poetry, fiction, articles, art, photos, cartoons, interviews, satire, criticism, reviews, long-poems, collages, concrete art, non-fiction. "Epicenter is a literary magazine. We publish poetry, short stories, creative non-fiction, and artwork. Our magazine is not clutered with adds, just literature. We have printed work by Stephen Pyle, Guy R Beining, Zdravka Evtimova, Virgil Suarez, Brad Maxfield, B.Z. Niditch, Egon H.E. Lass, and Elizabeth Hopp. We are open to a wide variety of styles and subjects and appreciate the non-depressing. Send us work with vivid imagery and fresh ideas. Any style is acceptable." circ. 500. 2/yr. Pub'd 2 issues 2009; expects 2 issues 2010, 2 issues 2011. sub. price $28.00; per copy $9.00; sample $1.00 PDF file. Back issues: $7.00. Discounts: More than 5 copies, $6.00. 128pp. Reporting time: one month. Simultaneous submissions accepted: Yes. Publishes 3% of manuscripts submitted. Payment: Copies of the magazine. Copyrighted, reverts to author. Pub's reviews: none in 2009. §Literary works. Ads: We do not print advertisments. Subjects: Absurdist, African Literature, Africa, African Studies, Anarchist, Arts, Essays, Experimental, Fiction, Literature (General), Non-Fiction, Philosophy, Poetry, Politics, Prose, Reviews, Satire.

EPIPHANY, A Literary Journal, Willard Cook, Editor, Jeffrey Gustavson, Elizabeth England, 71 Bedford Street, New York, NY 10014, 212-633-7987. 2003. Poetry, fiction, photos, interviews, parts-of-novels, non-fiction. "We love good writing, but it is hard to find. Good writing means a tale well told, but above all strong character that the reader believes is alive as the day is long. Good stories are like a fingerprint. Each one is unique but universal at the same time. We publish both established and beginning writers. Epiphany accepts submissions September through June. All work is considered for both the online and print issues. Before submitting, please familiarize yourself with the magazine. We will read everything. This takes time but we will respond to all submissions within five months. Please follow these instructions to expedite our reply: Submit one story or essay at a time. Submit no more than three poems at a time. Submit no more than two times per year. Submit artwork files in pdf and photographs in jpeg.Tell us if you're submitting simultaneously to other publications." circ. 1200. Two hard copy issues annually. sub. price $18 for 1 year$34 for 2 years; per copy $12; sample $12. Back issues: Yes. $10. Discounts: 10% for 10 copies 15% for 25 copies. 200pp. Reporting time: 3-4 months. Simultaneous submissions accepted: yes. Publishes 3% of manuscripts submitted. Payment: 2 copies. Copyrighted, reverts to author. Ads: $300 for full page $150 for 1/2 page $75 for 1/4 page. Ads for more than two issue are discounted. Subjects: Absurdist, African Literature, Africa, African Studies, Creative Non-fiction, Emily Dickinson, Fiction, Literature (General), Photography, Zen.

EPOCH MAGAZINE, Michael Koch, Editor, 251 Goldwin Smith Hall, Cornell University, Ithaca, NY 14853-3201, 607-255-3385, Fax 607-255-6661. 1947. Poetry, fiction, articles, art, cartoons, long-poems. "We are interested in the work of both new and established writers. Recent contributors include: Antonya Nelson, Jhumpa Lahiri, Yusef Komunyakaa, Heidi Jon Schmidt, Dan Chaon, Jim Daniels, Kevin Canty, many other fine writers, some of whom are not yet well known. Submissions received between April 15 and Sept. 21 will be returned unread." circ. 1M+. 3/yr. Pub'd 3 issues 2009; expects 3 issues 2010, 3 issues 2011. sub. price $11; per copy $6.50+; sample $5. Back issues: varies. 128pp. Reporting time: 4-6 weeks. Simultaneous submissions accepted: no. Payment: $5-$10 per printed magazine page, sometimes more, depending on our funding. Copyrighted, reverts to author. Ads: $180 (full cover); $160 (full page); $90 (half-page). Subjects: Fiction, Poetry.

EQUAL CONSTRUCTION RECORD, Toca Family Publishing, div. of Toca Family Communications Group, LLC, Heather Loveridge, 2483 Heritage Drive, Suite 16-184, Snellville, GA 30078, 404-348-4065, 404-348-4469, info@equalconstruction.com, www.equalconstruction.com. 2003. Articles, photos, interviews, news items, non-fiction. "We serve the commercial construction community in Georgia and the southeast with a focus on small to midsized contractors, civil engineers, architects, construction supply, and construction service providers.Recent contributors: Fergus Kennedy, Tiffany Wright, and Roxanne Smithers." circ. 5000. 12/yr. Pub'd 10 issues 2009; expects 12 issues 2010, 12 issues 2011. sub. price $24; per copy $3; sample free. Back issues: $3, if available. Discounts: 2-20 copies, 20% 21-50 copies, 35% 51-100 copies, 50% 100 copies, 60%. 24pp. Reporting time: 5-10 days. Simultaneous submissions accepted: Yes. Publishes 35% of manuscripts submitted. Payment: Payment upon publication, within 5 days of invoice. Copyrighted, reverts to author. Ads: B&W: 1732/1040/723/422 (display)4-Color: 2182/1309/873/546. Subjects: Business & Economics, Construction, Consulting, Finances, Internet, Interviews, Law, Management, Networking, Public Relations/Publicity, Real Estate, Technology.

EquiLibrium Press, Susan Goland, 10736 Jefferson Blvd. #680, Culver City, CA 90230. "** No longer accepting submissions.**." 5 titles listed in the *Small Press Record of Books in Print* (36th Edition, 2010-11).

Equine Graphics Publishing Group: New Concord Press, SmallHorse Press, SunDrop, Toni Leland, P.O.

158

Box 35, Nashport, OH 43830-9045, 740-828-2445, http://www.equinegraphicspublishing.com, writer-one@newconcordpress.com, http://www.newconcordpress.com. 1985. Poetry, fiction, non-fiction. avg. press run 2000. Pub'd 7 titles 2009; expects 7 titles 2010, 7 titles 2011. 50 titles listed in the *Small Press Record of Books in Print* (36th Edition, 2010-11). Discounts: wholesalers: 55%, returnsbookstores, retailers: 1-4 copies 20%, 5+ copies 40%. 250-450pp. Reporting time: queries: 1-2 weeks, manuscript: 1-2 months. Simultaneous submissions accepted: No. Publishes 2% of manuscripts submitted. Subjects: Animals, Anthology, Autobiography, Biography, Creative Non-fiction, Desktop Publishing, Fantasy, Fiction, Food, Eating, Gardening, History, Poetry, Romance, Self-Help, Senior Citizens.

ERASED, SIGH, SIGH, Via Dolorosa Press, Hyacinthe L. Raven, 701 East Schaaf Road, Cleveland, OH 44131-1227, ViaDolorosaPress@sbcglobal.net, www.angelfire.com/oh2/dolorosa/erased.html. 1994. Poetry, fiction, long-poems. "We do not accept submissions by phone, fax or e-mail. Send for submission guidelines or view them at www.angelfire.com/oh2/dolorosa/crusade.html We definitely recommend you read a couple issues prior to submitting; we have a particular style and tone of work that we print, and we ONLY print work that is about death, particularly suicide. Include SASE for response; we do not reply by email. Do not send disks." circ. 1M. 2/yr. Pub'd 2 issues 2009; expects 2 issues 2010, 2 issues 2011. sub. price $8 US, $10 foreign (checks/money orders drawn on a US bank made payable to Via Dolorosa Press); per copy $3.50 + postage; sample $4.25 (includes postage). Back issues: same as current issue prices. Discounts: rates available upon request for bookstores. 36pp. Reporting time: 2 months. Simultaneous submissions accepted: yes. Publishes 25% of manuscripts submitted. Payment: 1 copy. Not copyrighted. Ads: trades ad space with appropriate publications. Subjects: Euthanasia, Death, Grieving.

ERDC Publishing, Marko Mikulich, PO Box 1096, Drain, OR 97435, www.erdc.com. 1998. Non-fiction. "Educational materials How-to books." avg. press run 500. Expects 1 title 2010, 1-3 titles 2011. No titles listed in the *Small Press Record of Books in Print* (36th Edition, 2010-11). Discounts: 2-10 copies 25%11-24 copies 35%25-50 copies 40%51-100 copies 44%. 100-150pp. Reporting time: 6 mo- 1 year. Simultaneous submissions accepted: No. Publishes 1% of manuscripts submitted. Payment: Arranged. Does not copyright for author. Subjects: Graphic Design, Publishing.

Erespin Press, David L. Kent, Copy Editor, 6906 Colony Loop Drive, Austin, TX 78724-3749. 1980. Poetry, satire, non-fiction. "Particularly interested in historical translations." avg. press run 200. Pub'd 1 title 2009; expects 4 titles 2010, 4 titles 2011. 25 titles listed in the *Small Press Record of Books in Print* (36th Edition, 2010-11). 50pp. Reporting time: 1 week. Payment: by arrangement. Copyrights for author. Subjects: Classical Studies, History, Humanism, India, Medieval, Poetry, Satire, Translation.

Eros Books (see also DESIRE; PSYCHE), Mary Nicholaou, 463 Barlow Avenue, Staten Island, NY 10308, 718-317-7484. 1997. Fiction, articles, art, cartoons, interviews, criticism, reviews, letters, parts-of-novels, non-fiction. "We accept only postmodern, literary fiction and nonfiction. We expose the culture's effect on our soulful existence hoping to resurrect our psyche's true desire. Any length that has literary merit. Send SASE for reply." avg. press run 500. Pub'd 4 titles 2009; expects 4 titles 2010, 6 titles 2011. 9 titles listed in the *Small Press Record of Books in Print* (36th Edition, 2010-11). Discounts: 40%. 130pp. Reporting time: within 8 weeks. Simultaneous submissions accepted: yes. Publishes 50% of manuscripts submitted. Payment: 50% on net, negotiated. Copyrights for author. Subjects: Biography, Fiction, Gender Issues, Language, Literature (General), Memoirs, Non-Fiction, Novels, Philosophy, Post Modern, Research, Romance, Short Stories, Translation.

EROSHA, Artisan Studio Design, C.E. Laine, PO Box 185, Falls Church, VA 22040-0185, Fax 703-852-3906, editor@erosha.net, http://erosha.net. 2001. Poetry, fiction, articles, art, photos, interviews, satire, criticism, reviews, letters, long-poems, non-fiction. "*Erosha* looks for quality poetry of any length or style (except rhymed poetry). Prose submissions should be under 5,000 words. All material should in some way express human sexuality or romantic relations. Art and photography is also eligible for publication. Past contributors include Janet Buck, Lyn Lifshin, kris t kahn, Michael Meyerhofer, Dorothy Doyle Mienko, Rae Pater, Dan Sicoli, Debrah Kayla Sterling, Dan Tompsett and contributing editors Donna Hill and C.E. Laine. *Erosha* nominates for the Pushcart Prize." circ. electronic, POD. 8/8/8. price per copy free; sample $1. 20pp. Reporting time: 60 days. Simultaneous submissions accepted: yes. Publishes 5% of manuscripts submitted. Payment: none. Not copyrighted. Subjects: Avant-Garde, Experimental Art, Erotica, Essays, Experimental, Gender Issues, Photography, Poetry, Prose.

Eryon Press (see also TIFERET: A Journal of Spiritual Literature), Cynthia Brown, PO Box 309, Gladstone, NJ 07934, (908)246-8665. 2003. avg. press run 1000. Expects 2 titles 2010, 4 titles 2011. No titles listed in the *Small Press Record of Books in Print* (36th Edition, 2010-11). 350pp.

ESPERANTIC STUDIES, Jason M. Clark, Editor; Mark Fettes, Editor, 8888 University Drive, Faculty of Education, Burnaby, BC, V5A 1S6, Canada, Contact: jclark@esperantic.org, www.esperantic.org. 1991. Articles, reviews, non-fiction. "We publish Esperantic Studies in a print edition and also post it online at www.esperantic.org.'' circ. 12M. 2/yr. sub. price free. Back issues: free for SASE. 4pp. Payment: none. Not copyrighted. Pub's reviews: 1 in 2009. §Language problems (international, cross-cultural). Ads: none. Subjects: Communication, Journalism, Language, Sociology.

Espretto, Eyal Rosen, 10 Ehad Haam St., P.O. Box 11, Azur 58015, Israel, +972 3 550 9000 www.espretto.com. 2007. Non-fiction. "Coffee related." avg. press run 5000. Expects 1 title 2010. 1 title listed in the *Small Press Record of Books in Print* (36th Edition, 2010-11). Discounts: 2-4 copies 20% 5-9 copies 30% 10-24 copies 40% 25-49 copies 42% 50-74 copies 44% 100-199 copies 48% 200 or more copies 50%. 250pp. Reporting time: 2 weeks. Simultaneous submissions accepted: Yes. Publishes 1% of manuscripts submitted. Payment: TBD. Subjects: Cooking, Culture.

ETC Publications, James Berry, 1456 Rodeo Road, Palm Springs, CA 92262, 760-316-9695, fax 760-316-9681. 1972. "Considers timely topics in all non-fiction areas." avg. press run 2.5M. Pub'd 10 titles 2009; expects 12 titles 2010. 27 titles listed in the *Small Press Record of Books in Print* (36th Edition, 2010-11). Discounts: usual trade. 256pp. Reporting time: 4 weeks. Payment: standard book royalties. Copyrights for author. Subjects: Biography, Business & Economics, Crafts, Hobbies, Earth, Natural History, Ecology, Foods, Education, How-To, Native American, Psychology, Society, Sports, Outdoors.

Etched Press, Kevin Dublin, Box 3063, Wilmington, NC 28406, www.etchedpress.com, submit@etched-press.com. 2008. Poetry, long-poems, non-fiction. "We're interested mostly in well-written collections of poetry that aren't pretentious and have universal themes. Although primarily a poetry press, we will reply to interesting fiction and Creative-Non Fiction queries. The aim is to publish writing that remains in the minds of readers, years after the first consumption." avg. press run 100. Pub'd 1 title 2009; expects 3 titles 2010, 3 titles 2011. 2 titles listed in the *Small Press Record of Books in Print* (36th Edition, 2010-11). Discounts: 1-50 copies 25%50+ copies 40%. 24pp. Reporting time: 2-4 months. Simultaneous submissions accepted: Yes. Publishes 3% of manuscripts submitted. Payment: 20% paid quarterly. Copyrights for author. Subjects: Creative Non-fiction, Culture, Poetry.

Ethos Publishing, Harold Lewis Malt, 4224 Spanish Trail Place, Pensacola, FL 32504-8561. Fiction, art, non-fiction. avg. press run 3M. Expects 1 title 2010, 1 title 2011. 4 titles listed in the *Small Press Record of Books in Print* (36th Edition, 2010-11). Discounts: bookstores 40%, wholesalers 55%. 250pp. Reporting time: 1 month. We accept simultaneous submissions, but query first. Publishes 10% of manuscripts submitted. Payment: negotiated. Subjects: Aging, Arts, Fiction, How-To.

THE EUGENE O'NEILL REVIEW, Zander Brietzke, Editor; Ingrid Strange, Managing Editor, Department of English, Suffolk University, 41 Temple Street, Boston, MA 02114-4280, 617-573-8272. 1977. Articles, art, photos, cartoons, interviews, criticism, reviews, letters, plays, news items, non-fiction. "*The Review's* aim is to serve as a meeting ground for O'Neill enthusiasts of academe and those of the Theatre. So it tries to blend critical articles of a scholarly sort, with news and reviews of current productions and publications. Articles of all sizes—from pithy notes to lengthy analyses—are welcome. Over-long articles are serialized. ISSN 1040-9483." circ. 550. 1/yr. Pub'd 2 issues 2009; expects 2 issues 2010, 2 issues 2011. sub. price $35 for individuals in US + Canada, and all institutions; per copy $35; sample free. Back issues: $15 per copy. Discounts: none. 200pp. Reporting time: 2-6 months, frequently sooner. Simultaneous submissions accepted: yes. Publishes 60% of manuscripts submitted. Payment: none. Copyrighted, permissions to reprint (with acknowledgement) are never refused. Pub's reviews: 8 in 2009. §Any books or articles devoted to Eugene O'Neill (in whole or in part) or to 20th century drama and any film or stage performance of O'Neill's work. Ads: $200/$100. Subjects: Drama, Newsletter, Theatre.

•**EUPHONY,** Catherine Greim, Managing Editor; Laura Stiers, Poetry Editor, 5706 University Avenue, Room 001, Chicago, IL 60637. "Euphony welcomes submissions of unpublished poetry, fiction, essays, reviews, creative non-fiction, and plays. Nearly all our writing comes from outside our staff, and ranges from University of Chicago students as well as authors around the country (and internationally), professional to first-time writers and everything in between. Email submissions are strongly preferred over print. Manuscripts should be emailed to euphony@uchicago.edu and clearly state the genre of the work (poetry, fiction, etc.). Attach your submission in a file compatible with Microsoft Word or a basic text editornot in the body of the emailso the formatting of your work is preserved." 2/yr.

EVANSVILLE REVIEW, Preston Frasch, Editor-in-Chief; Jacob Roman, Editor-in-Chief, Univ. of Evansville, English Dept., 1800 Lincoln Avenue, Evansville, IN 47722, 812-488-1042. 1991. Poetry, fiction, interviews, satire, parts-of-novels, plays, non-fiction. "Nothing longer than 15 pages, please. We publish many undiscovered writers along with established writers. Please query with nonfiction and interviews. Recent contributors include Marge Piercy, David Ignatow, Lucian Stryk, John Updike, Felix Stefanile, Willis Barnstone, Charles Wright, and Tess Gallagher. All manuscripts are recycled, not returned. Please include SASE for reply. A brief bio or list of previous publications is appreciated as we print contributors notes." circ. 3M. 1/yr. Pub'd 1 issue 2009; expects 1 issue 2010, 1 issue 2011. price per copy $5; sample $5. Back issues: $5.

Discounts: negotiable. 200pp. Reporting time: Notification in December or early January. Reading period is from September 1 to December 1. We accept simultaneous submissions with notification. Publishes 3% of manuscripts submitted. Payment: 2 copies. Not copyrighted. Ads: none. Subjects: Creative Non-fiction, Drama, Essays, Fiction, Interviews, Literary Review, Literature (General), Non-Fiction, Poetry, Prose, Satire, Short Stories, Translation.

Evening Street Press (see also EVENING STREET REVIEW), Gordon Grigsby, 7652 Sawmill Road, #352, Dublin, OH 43016-9296, 614-847-1780, editor@eveningstreetpress.com, eveningstreetpress.com. 2007. Poetry, fiction, criticism, non-fiction. "Evening Street Press is centered on Elizabeth Cady Stanton's 1848 revision of the Declaration of Independence: "that all men—and women—are created equal," with equal rights to "life, liberty, and the pursuit of happiness." It focuses on the realities of experience, personal and historical, from the most gritty to the most dreamlike, including awareness of the personal and social forces that block or develop the possibilities of this new culture." avg. press run 250. Pub'd 4 titles 2009; expects 5 titles 2010, 5-8 titles 2011. 5 titles listed in the *Small Press Record of Books in Print* (36th Edition, 2010-11). 40-110pp. Reporting time: 1 month. Simultaneous submissions accepted: Yes. Publishes 8% of manuscripts submitted. Payment: No royalties; authors can purchase titles at half price. Does not copyright for author. Subjects: Creative Non-fiction, Essays, Feminism, Fiction, Non-Fiction, Poetry, Short Stories.

EVENING STREET REVIEW, Evening Street Press, Gordon Grigsby, 7652 Sawmill Road, #352, Dublin, OH 43016-9296, 614-847-1780, editor@eveningstreetpress.com, eveningstreetpress.com. 2007. Poetry, fiction, non-fiction. "Evening Street Press is centered on Elizabeth Cady Stanton's 1848 revision of the Declaration of Independence: "that all men—and women—are created equal," with equal rights to "life, liberty, and the pursuit of happiness." It focuses on the realities of experience, personal and historical, from the most gritty to the most dreamlike, including awareness of the personal and social forces that block or develop the possibilities of this new culture." circ. 250. 2/yr. Expects 1 issue 2010, 2 issues 2011. sub. price $24; per copy $15; sample $15. Back issues: $10. 110pp. Reporting time: 1 month. Simultaneous submissions accepted: Yes. Publishes 8% of manuscripts submitted. Payment: Copies of title, half price to buy additional copies. Copyrighted, reverts to author. Subjects: Creative Non-fiction, Essays, Fiction, Non-Fiction, Poetry.

EVENT, Rick Maddocks, Editor; Ian Cockfield, Managing Editor; Christine Dewar, Fiction Editor; Elizabeth Bachinsky, Poetry Editor; Susan Wasserman, Reviews Editor, Douglas College, PO Box 2503, New Westminster, B.C. V3L 5B2, Canada, 604-527-5293, Fax 604-527-5095, event@douglas.bc.ca, http://event.douglas.bc.ca. 1971. Poetry, fiction, reviews, long-poems, non-fiction. "From literary heavyweights to up-and-comers, EVENT has featured the very best in contemporary award-winning writing from North America and abroad for four decades, all topped off by stunning cover art. Previous contributors include Andre Alexis, Jen Sookfong Lee, Leon Rooke, Susan Musgrave, Sharon Thesen and David Zieroth. We do not accept e-mail submissions. EVENT also has a Reading Service for Writers and one of North America's longest-running annual Non-Fiction Contests. Visit our website for more information. Digital editions are also available." circ. 1,150. 3/yr. Pub'd 3 issues 2009; expects 3 issues 2010, 3 issues 2011. sub. price US$24.95, US$39.95/2 years, US$89.95/5 years; per copy US$12. Back issues: US$9. Discounts: subscription agencies 5-25%. 136pp. Reporting time: 1-6 months. Simultaneous submissions accepted: yes. Publishes 2% of manuscripts submitted. Payment: honorarium, $25-30/page upon publication. Copyrighted, reverts to author. Pub's reviews: 36 in 2009. §Poetry, short fiction, novels. Ads: $200/$100. Subjects: Fiction, Non-Fiction, Poetry, Prose, Reviews.

Everflowing Publications, Shonnese C.L. Coleman, PO Box 191536, Los Angeles, CA 90019, 323-993-8577, everflowing@nycmail.com. 2000. Poetry, art, long-poems. avg. press run 1M. Expects 1 title 2010, 1-2 titles 2011. 1 title listed in the *Small Press Record of Books in Print* (36th Edition, 2010-11). Discounts: 40% to bookstores, some bulk orders, agents, etc. 96pp. Reporting time: 3-6 months. Simultaneous submissions accepted: yes. Publishes 3% of manuscripts submitted. Payment: to be determined. Does not copyright for author. Subjects: African-American, Avant-Garde, Experimental Art, Black, Culture, Dance, Drama, Performing Arts, Poetry.

Evolution Publishing (see also Arx Publishing LLC), Claudio R. Salvucci, PO Box 13333, Merchantville, NJ 08109, 856-486-1310, Fax 856-665-0170, info@evolpub.com, www.evolpub.com. "An imprint of Arx Publishing. Monographs in Native American language, Native American history, Early Colonial history, North American dialectology, classical history, classical linguistics, philology, and archaeology." avg. press run 500-1M. Pub'd 5 titles 2009; expects 12 titles 2010, 15 titles 2011. No titles listed in the *Small Press Record of Books in Print* (36th Edition, 2010-11). Discounts: standard 20%. 150pp. Reporting time: 6-8 weeks. Simultaneous submissions accepted: yes. Publishes less than 10% of manuscripts submitted. Payment: varies by contract. Copyrights for author. Subjects: Classical Studies, History, Language, Native American, Non-Fiction.

EXCEPTIONALITY EDUCATION CANADA, Judy Lupart, Christina Rinaldi, Department of Educational Psychology, 6-102 Education North, University of Alberta, Edmonton, AB T6G 2G5, Canada, Telephone: (780) 492-2198/7471, Fax: (780) 492-1318, E-mail: eecj@ualberta.ca, judy.lupart@ualberta.ca, christina.rinaldi@ualberta.ca. 1991. Articles. "The journal is intended to provide a forum for scholarly exchange among Canadian professionals in education and related disciplines who work with students across the spectrum of exceptionality. The purpose is to present current research and theory and to identify emerging trends and visions for the education of students with exceptionalities." circ. 225. 3/yr. Pub'd 3 issues 2009; expects 3 issues 2010, 3 issues 2011. sub. price Inst. $60, Indiv. $40, Student $25; in Canada add GST, outside Canada price is in US dollars $55/2 years (indiv.); per copy $10 + GST in Canada; outside Canada in US dollars. 108pp. Reporting time: 2 months. Copyrighted, reverts to author. Pub's reviews: 1 in 2009. §Education of students with exceptionalities. Ads: none. Subjects: Children, Youth, Education.

EXIT 13 MAGAZINE, Tom Plante, Editor, PO Box 423, Fanwood, NJ 07023, Exit13magazine@yahoo.com (no attachments). 1987. Poetry, photos. "Previously published *Berkeley Works Magazine* (1981-1985). I seek manuscripts of poetry with a view of the terrain familiar to the writer. *Exit 13 Magazine* prefers a geographic bent and uses work from all over the U.S. and occasional contributions from outside these borders. Fresh faces and views are welcome. Back issues are available. Photos of Exit 13 road signs earn a free magazine. ISSN 1054-3937." circ. 500. 1/yr. Pub'd 1 issue 2009; expects 1 issue 2010, 1 issue 2011. price per copy $8; sample $8. Discounts: 40% for 5 or more copies of any one issue, prepaid. 76pp. Reporting time: 4 months. Simultaneous submissions accepted: yes. Publishes 10% of manuscripts submitted. Payment: copy of issue containing author's work. Copyrighted, rights revert to author but *Exit 13 Magazine* keeps anthology rights. Ads: $45 camera ready/$25/$13 1/4 page camera ready. Subjects: Americana, The Americas, Earth, Natural History, Folklore, Geography, Ireland, Poetry, Travel.

Expanded Media Editions, Pociao, Diezstr. 8, 53113 Bonn, Germany, 0228/22 95 83, FAX 0228/21 95 07. 1969. Poetry, fiction, art, photos, interviews, criticism, music, collages. "Recent contributors: W. S. Burroughs, Jurgen Ploog, Claude Pelieu-Washburn, Allen Ginsberg, Gerard Malanga, Paul Bowles." avg. press run 2M. Pub'd 3 titles 2009; expects 2 titles 2010, 4 titles 2011. 12 titles listed in the *Small Press Record of Books in Print* (36th Edition, 2010-11). Discounts: 1-5 copies 25%, 6-20 30%, 21-50 40%, 50+ 50%. 100pp. Payment: 10% per sold book. Copyrights for author. Subjects: Fiction, Poetry.

Explorer Press, Terry Collins, 1501 Edgewood Drive, Mount Airy, NC 27030-5215, 336-789-6005, Fax 336-789-6005, E-mail terryleecollins@hotmail.com. 1993. avg. press run 10M. Pub'd 2 titles 2009; expects 1 title 2010, 1 title 2011. 1 title listed in the *Small Press Record of Books in Print* (36th Edition, 2010-11). Discounts: inquire. 200pp. Reporting time: 3 months. Simultaneous submissions accepted: yes. Payment: inquire. Copyrights for author. Subjects: Biography, Comics, North Carolina, Television.

EXTRA INNINGS: The Writer's Home Encouragement, Marshall Cook, 4337 Felton Place, Madison, WI 53705, 608-238-4007, mcook@dcs.wisc.edu. 2009. Fiction, articles, interviews, reviews, letters. "We offer information, encouragement, and inspiration to writers. For 20 years we published as Creativity Connection, the last five years in print or pdf editions. Extra Innings will be offered in pdf format only." 12/yr. Pub'd 3 issues 2009; expects 12 issues 2010, 12 issues 2011. sub. price free. 16pp. Reporting time: Within a week. Simultaneous submissions accepted: Yes. Publishes 25% of manuscripts submitted. Payment: None. Copyrighted, reverts to author. Pub's reviews: none in 2009. §Novels, poetry, and craft books of interest to writers.

•**EZRA: An Online Journal of Translation,** Roger Williams University, Bristol, RI 02809. "*Ezra*—An Online Journal of Translation, is a forum for poetry and translation. We hope to stimulate the under-explored arts of reading in other tongues and translating for an English audience. We aim both for new knowledge of world writers and for the creation of beautiful new works. Ezra is interested in any form, style, tone or era. Please submit work via e-mail, as an attachment, to the addresses below. Submissions must be in Microsoft Word, 12 point Times New Roman. Be sure to specify the original title and author (with country and dates for the author, if not well known). Though only the translation to English will appear in Ezra, please include the original language version. All e-mails must have the following subject line (to elude our junk mail filter): yourlastname/ezratranslation. We prefer poetry and short prose(up to 1000 words) and it may be an excerpt from a work of any length. Ezra invites prose poems and scenes from plays. We accept work from any era."

F

Face to Face Press, Sheryl Koutsis, 3419 Fillmore St., Denver, CO 80205-4257, slevart@face2facepress.com, www.face2facepress.com. 1999. Poetry, fiction, articles, art, photos, interviews, satire, criticism, reviews, parts-of-novels, long-poems, collages, plays, news items, non-fiction. avg. press run 1.5M. Expects 1 title 2010, 2 titles 2011. No titles listed in the *Small Press Record of Books in Print* (36th Edition, 2010-11). Discounts: 40%. 120pp. Reporting time: 2 months. Simultaneous submissions accepted: yes. Payment: 10% net sales.

Copyrights for author. Subject: Multicultural.

FACES: People, Places, and Culture, Cobblestone Publishing Company, Elizabeth Crooker Carpentiere, Editor, 30 Grove Street, Suite C, Peterborough, NH 03458, 603-924-7209, Fax 603-924-7380, custsvc@cobblestone.mv.com. 1984. Articles, art, photos, reviews, non-fiction. *"Faces* is designed to expose young people to other peoples and cultures of the world; to help them realize that no country is any better than any other; to learn and understand how other people live and do things; to see the world in new ways and to help them reflect on how they assign importance to things, ideas and people in their own lives. Material must be written for children ages 8-14. Write for guidelines as we focus each issue on a particular theme." circ. 13.5M. 9/yr. Pub'd 9 issues 2009; expects 9 issues 2010, 9 issues 2011. sub. price $29.95; add $8 for foreign mail, Canadian subs add 7% GST; per copy $6.95; sample $6.95. Back issues: $6.95. Discounts: 15% for sub. agencies, bulk rate 3 or more $17.95/year sub. each. 52pp. Reporting time: queries sent well in advance of deadline may not be answered for several months. Go-aheads usually sent 5 months prior to publication date. Payment: on publication. Copyrighted, Cobblestone Publishing buys all rights. Pub's reviews: 81 in 2009. §Books for children, age 8-14, related to themes covered. No ads. Subjects: Anthropology, Archaelogy, Culture.

Facts on Demand Press (see also BRB Publications, Inc.), PO Box 27869, Tempe, AZ 85285-7869, 800-929-3811, Fax 800-929-4981, brb@brbpub.com, www.brbpub.com. 1996. avg. press run 5M. Pub'd 12 titles 2009; expects 10 titles 2010. 12 titles listed in the *Small Press Record of Books in Print* (36th Edition, 2010-11). Discounts: available through National Book Network.

Faded Banner Publications, Don Allison, PO Box 101, Bryan, OH 43506-0101, 419-636-3807, 419-636-3807 (fax), 888-799-3787, fadedbanner.com. 1997. Non-fiction. "We specialize in Civil War and local history titles." avg. press run 1150. Pub'd 1 title 2009; expects 1 title 2010, 2 titles 2011. No titles listed in the *Small Press Record of Books in Print* (36th Edition, 2010-11). Discounts: 5-99 copies 40%, 10 or more copies non-returnable 50%, 100 or more copies 50%. 290pp. Reporting time: 1 month. Simultaneous submissions accepted: Yes. Publishes 5% of manuscripts submitted. Payment: To be determined. Does not copyright for author. Subjects: Anthropology, Archaelogy, Civil War, Military, Veterans, Ohio, Wisconsin.

•**FAILBETTER.COM,** 2022 Grove Avenue, Richmond, VA 23220. *"failbetter.com* publishes original fiction, poetry, and visual art. We seek that which is at once original and personal. When choosing work to submit, be certain that what you have created could only have come from you. We do not consider work that has appeared elsewhere, either in print or on the Web. We accept simultaneous submissions.If you submit via email, expect to hear from us in eight to twelve weeks. If you submit via regular mail, expect to wait three to six months. Fiction writers and poets, submit your work by pasting it into the body of an email, then sending said email to "submissions AT failbetter DOT com." Do not send work to any other email address unless we specifically tell you to do so. Such submissions will be discarded. Do not send attachments. If you attach a file to your email, our server will delete it. If you insist, you may submit your work via regular mail."

Faith Builders Resource Group, Ernest Eby, PO Box 125, Guys Mills, PA 16327, 814-789-4769, 814-789-3396, 877-222-4769, clr@fbep.org, www.christianlearning.org. 2006. Non-fiction. "Mission Statement: Faith Builders Publishing serves the Christian community by producing quality books, curriculum, choral recordings, and audio-visual resources." avg. press run 4000. Expects 3 titles 2010, 4 titles 2011. 2 titles listed in the *Small Press Record of Books in Print* (36th Edition, 2010-11). Discounts: 1-4 copies 30% 5-99 copies 40% 100+ copies 50%. 100pp. Simultaneous submissions accepted: No. We publish books written by authors from our own institution. Subjects: Biography, Children, Youth, Christianity, Europe, Family, History, Music, Native American, Non-Fiction, North America, Philosophy, Storytelling, Young Adult.

Falcon Publishing, LTD, David L Fey Jr., P O Box 6099, Kingwood, TX 77345-6099, 713-417-7600, 281-360-8284, sales@falconpublishing.com, www.falconpublishing.com. 2004. Fiction. "The mission of Falcon Publishing, LTD is to assist new authors in the publication of their work. We provide complete pre-publication and publishing services that include, ISBN, LCCN, copyright, content editing, typesetting, cover design, illustrations, printing, marketing and sales through the Falcon Publishing web site and affiliates.Falcon Publishing does not publish pronographic material." avg. press run 2000. Expects 3 titles 2010, 1 title 2011. 6 titles listed in the *Small Press Record of Books in Print* (36th Edition, 2010-11). Discounts: 25-99 copies 20%100-499 copies 40%500-1000 copies 50%1000+ copies 60%. 300pp. Reporting time: Two weeks. Simultaneous submissions accepted: Yes. Payment: 40% for books sold by Falcon Publishing. $1.00 per book sent directly to author. Copyrights for author. Subjects: Children, Youth, Christianity, Fiction, Leadership, Mystery, Self-Help, Storytelling.

Falk Art Reference, Peter Hastings Falk, PO Box 833, Madison, CT 06443, 203-245-2246, peterfalk@comcast.net, www.falkart.com, www.illuminario.com. 1985. Art, non-fiction. "Publisher of the biographical dictionary, *Who Was Who In American Art,* and monographs on American artists in conjunction with museum or gallery exhibitions." avg. press run 2M. Pub'd 3 titles 2009; expects 3 titles 2010, 3 titles 2011. No titles listed in the *Small Press Record of Books in Print* (36th Edition, 2010-11). Discounts: varies by title. 250-1,750pp. Reporting time: 2 weeks. Simultaneous submissions accepted: yes. Payment: negotiable. Copyrights for author. Subjects: Arts, Reference.

Falls Media, David Smith, 1 Astor Place, PH K, New York, NY 10003, 917-667-2269, www.wouldyourather.com. 2004. "Humorous, pop-culture driven books & games." avg. press run 40000. Pub'd 2 titles 2009; expects 2 titles 2010, 3 titles 2011. 3 titles listed in the *Small Press Record of Books in Print* (36th Edition, 2010-11). Discounts: retailers, wholesalers - 40-60%. 120pp. Subjects: Absurdist, Culture, Games, Humor, Young Adult.

Famaco Publishers (Qalam Books), D.A. Miller, PO Box 440665, Jacksonville, FL 32244-0665, 904-434-5901, Fax 904-777-5901, famapub@aol.com. 1996. Non-fiction. "At least 50,000 words. Recent contributors: Mukhtar Muhammad and Dewayne E Moore." avg. press run 2.5M. Pub'd 2 titles 2009; expects 2 titles 2010. 1 title listed in the *Small Press Record of Books in Print* (36th Edition, 2010-11). Discounts: available on request. 500pp. Reporting time: variable. Simultaneous submissions accepted: yes. Publishes 20% of manuscripts submitted. Payment: specific arrangement. Copyrights for author. Subjects: How-To, Leadership, Management, Religion.

Fantail, PO Box 145, Johnson City, NY 13790-0145, http://www.fantail.com, liz@fantail.com. 1996. Art, photos, non-fiction. avg. press run 2.5M. Expects 1 title 2011. 3 titles listed in the *Small Press Record of Books in Print* (36th Edition, 2010-11). Discounts: 2-3 20%, 4-9 30%, 10-199 40%, 200+ 50%. 205pp. Simultaneous submissions accepted: yes. Copyrights for author. Subjects: African Literature, Africa, African Studies, Cooking, History, Transportation.

FAQs Press, Linda Resnik, Dee Brock, PO Box 130115, Tyler, TX 75713, 903-565-6653 phone/Fax, www.FAQsPress.com. 2000. Non-fiction. "FAQs Press publishes consumer reference books answering frequently asked questions about specific topics. We will accept written proposals for reference-type books on popular topics written for general audiences." Expects 4-6 titles 2011. 1 title listed in the *Small Press Record of Books in Print* (36th Edition, 2010-11).

Farcountry Press, Jessica Solberg, Senior Editor, PO Box 5630, Helena, MT 59604, 406-444-5111. 1980. Photos, non-fiction. Pub'd 13 titles 2009; expects 10 titles 2010, 20 titles 2011. No titles listed in the *Small Press Record of Books in Print* (36th Edition, 2010-11). Discounts: available upon request. Reporting time: 6 weeks. We accept simultaneous submissions if marked as such. Payment: varies. Does not copyright for author. Subjects: Children, Youth, Cooking, Great Lakes, Great Plains, History, Midwest, Photography, Travel, The West.

Farcountry Press, Jessica Soldberg, Kathy Springmeyer, PO Box 5630, Helena, MT 59604, 406-444-5128, 406-443-5480 fax, 800-821-3874. 1980. Photos. "Farcountry Press focuses on 4-color regional photography books, natural and local history, National Parks, and Lewis & Clark. Childresn's books include the Who Pooped in the Park? series and the Farcountry Explorer series." avg. press run 7500. Pub'd 50 titles 2009; expects 40 titles 2010, 40 titles 2011. No titles listed in the *Small Press Record of Books in Print* (36th Edition, 2010-11). Discounts: bookstores 5-10=40% 11-24=41% 25-49=42% 50-99=43% 100-249=44% 250-499=45% 500-999=46% 1000+ =47% Distribrots - call for terms. 100pp. Reporting time: 1 month. Simultaneous submissions accepted: Yes. Publishes 20% of manuscripts submitted. Payment: payments are made monthly. amount depends upon type of book. Subjects: Animals, Great Lakes, Great Plains, History, Idaho, Montana, New Mexico, Old West, Pacific Northwest, Photography, Utah, Virginia, Washington (state), Wildlife, Wyoming.

FAT TUESDAY, F.M. Cotolo, Editor-in-Chief; B. Lyle Tabor, Associate Editor-Emeritus; Thom Savion, Associate Editor; Lionel Stevroid, Associate Editor; Kristen Cotolo, Managing Editor, 560 Manada Gap Road, Grantville, PA 17028, 717-469-7159. 1981. Poetry, fiction, art, satire, parts-of-novels, collages. "As *Fat Tuesday* rolls through the new millennium, the publishing of small press editions becomes more difficult than ever. Money continues to be a major problem, mostly because small press seems to play to the very people who wish to be published in it. Sadly, the cast makes up the audience, and more people want to be in *Fat Tuesday* than want to buy it. Our audio-theater edition was a 40-plus-minute stereo cassette called *Fat Tuesday's Cool Noise*. It featured original music, poetry readings, sound collage and more by 20 artists. And next, Fat Tuesday released a few stereo-audio-cassette collections of original "musical poetry" by Frank Cotolo. "Fat" has also produced the ever-popular folk trio, Henry Morgan and The High Grass Boys' CDs. As far as what we want to publish when we receive financing to do so—send us shorter works. *Crystals of thought and emotion which reflect your individual experiences. As long as you dig into your guts and pull out pieces of yourself. Your work is your signature...Like time itself, it should emerge from the penetralia of your being and recede into the infinite region of the cosmos,* to coin a phrase. Certainly, perusing any of the issues we have published in the last decade will let you know what we admire in an author's work, an artist's stroke. However, all of those editions are now out of print. Also, join us at our website community, Fat Tuesday at YAHOO!. The club is free and features many writers and readers. You can post poetry, prose, editorials, etc. We often answer unsolicited submissions with personal comments, opinions, howdayados and the like. So, write to us, send us pieces of yourself, buy our products to keep our commercial-free policies intact (and keep this in mind for all other small presses, too), and please use SASEs and remember *Fat Tuesday* is mardi gras—so fill up before you fast. Bon soir.'' circ. 350-500. irreg. Expects 1 issue 2011. price per copy $5 (cassettes, zines and CDs), plus $1 postage; sample $5. Back issues: In-print issues are out of print. Cassette presentation and CDs available, but CDs are only for various artists. Inquire with a SASE about all product, old, new and projected. Discounts: inquire. 45pp. Reporting time: have patience, but we're usually quick! Simultaneous submissions accepted: no. Publishes 5% of manuscripts submitted. Payment: 1 complimentary copy in which work appears. Copyrighted, reverts to author. Ads: $100/$50/25¢ per classified word. Subjects: Comics, Dada, Fiction, Humor, Philosophy, Poetry, Satire, Zen.

Fathom Publishing Co., Constance Taylor, PO Box 200448, Anchorage, AK 99520-0448, 907-272-3305. 1978. Non-fiction. avg. press run 3M-5M. Pub'd 2 titles 2009; expects 2 titles 2010, 2 titles 2011. 16 titles listed in the *Small Press Record of Books in Print* (36th Edition, 2010-11). 500pp. Reporting time: 1 month. Simultaneous submissions accepted: yes. Publishes 1% of manuscripts submitted. Payment: varies. Copyrights for author. Subjects: Alaska, Law, Non-Fiction, Textbooks.

•**FAULTLINE,** 300 Boadway, Suite 28, San Francisco, CA 94133. ''Faultline's intent is to bring Californians accurate and compelling environmental news and information, on subjects ranging from environmental justice to wilderness protection. We want to foster a sense of awareness of California as a unique place with unique issues, to accentuate and promote the community of environmentally-aware Californians, and to encourage ways of living that are appropriate to the state's distinct environment and diverse cultures. Our goal is to launch and promote a green multimedia group consisting of this website, a mass-market print magazine and a series of production-quality audio broadcast features, all intended to bring California's environment to a broad section of the state's residents.''

•**FAULTLINE,** Department of English, University of California, Irvine, Irvine, CA 92697-2650, (949) 824-1573. ''Faultline is UCI's Pushcart prize-winning journal. We publish new poetry, fiction, translations, and artwork in an annual spring issue, and feature the work of emerging and established writers from the U.S. and abroad. Poetry: up to five poems. Fiction and Creative Nonfiction: up to twenty pages. Artwork: up to five 8 X 10 color or black and white prints (slides may be necessary if work is accepted for publication). V Submissions will be read between September 15 and February 15. Submissions received at any other time will not be read. Simultaneous submissions are acceptable, but please indicate if the manuscript is being considered elsewhere. Please include a cover letter with your name, mailing and email addresses, titles of work submitted, and an SASE with appropriate postage. (Be sure to include the original author's name if you are submitting a translation.) To assist anonymous judging, do not include name and address on manuscript. Send poetry separately from fiction and nonfiction.''

Featherproof Books, Zach Dodson, Co-Publisher; Jonathan Messinger, Co-Publisher, 2725 N Troy St 1, Chicago, IL 60647. 2005. ''Featherproof Books is a young indie publisher based in Chicago, dedicated to the small-press ideals of finding fresh, urban voices. We publish perfect-bound, full-length works of fiction and downloadable mini-books. Our novels are filled with the liveliest of fiction wrapped in the loveliest of designs. We're happy to read any story submissions, though we ask that you give us a bit* to get to it. (*OK, more than a bit, we're practically buried at the moment, and our turn-around time is super long. Patience is required.) Please send your tale to submissions [at] featherproof.com, pasted into the body of the email and attached as a word doc (or realtext, if you must). Were mostly interested in fiction. Especially if its fun. Theres no need to submit a query letter just go ahead and send us the first 50 pages or so, enough to give us a taste. Well let you know if we want more. Have patience, we read slowly, but we will get back to you.'' No titles listed in the *Small Press Record of Books in Print* (36th Edition, 2010-11).

FEDERAL SENTENCING REPORTER, University of California Press, Doug Berman, Editor, University of California Press, 2000 Center Street, Suite 303, Berkeley, CA 94704-1223, 510-643-7154. 1988. ''Editorial address: 233 Broadway, New York, NY 10279.'' circ. 2.5M. 5/yr. Pub'd 5 issues 2009; expects 5 issues 2010, 5 issues 2011. sub. price $225 indiv., $241 inst., add $20 air freight, $116 academics; per copy $50; sample free. Back issues: $50. 72pp. Ads: none.

FEILE-FESTA, Paradiso-Parthas Press, Frank Polizzi, Editor; Gil Fagiani, Assoc. Editor, Mediterranaean Celtic Cultural Association, PO Box 436, Prince Street Station, New York, NY 10012. 2006. ''*Feile-Festa* is a literary arts journal both in print and online versions. Please send 1-3 poems or 1 prose piece (microfiction - 500 words or less, an article - 1000 words or less) to MCCA, P.O Box 436, Prince Street Station, New York, NY 10012. Be sure to include a self-addressed stamped envelope for a response to your submission. No work will be returned, so make sure you keep a copy of everything. If you prefer, you may e-mail your writing to fpolizzi@medcelt.org. Please cut and paste your submission onto the e-mail or attach a PDF file of your submission. You will receive one copy of *Feile-Festa*, which will be your only payment. Please do not send any art work of any kind. One artist's work will be featured in each issue based on our own research and interest.

Though our preference is for creative work related to Irish and Italian/Sicilian themes, we are open to other Mediterranean and Celtic cultures, all of which can either relate to the respective country of origin or the diasporas to America, Argentina, Australia, Brazil, Canada and many other countries. We are also interested in writing that evokes life in New York City. *Feile-Festa* is an annual publication that comes out in the spring of each year. The reading period starts October 1st and ends January 1st. Please do not send submissions outside the time frame mentioned in the guidelines." Spring Annual. sub. price $17 / 2yrs; per copy $9. Back issues: $10. 68pp. Reporting time: 1-3 months. Payment: 1 copy. Copyrighted, reverts to author. Pub's reviews: 1 in 2009.

FELICITER, Canadian Library Association, Judy Green, Editor, 328 Frank Street, Ottawa, Ontario K2P 0X8, Canada, 613-232-9625, ext. 322. 1956. Articles, photos, cartoons, interviews, reviews, letters. circ. 3M. 6/yr. Pub'd 6 issues 2009; expects 6 issues 2010, 6 issues 2011. sub. price $95 Cdn.; per copy $20 Cdn.; sample free. 56pp. Reporting time: 3 months. Simultaneous submissions accepted: no. Publishes 75% of manuscripts submitted. Payment: none. Copyrighted, does not revert to author. Pub's reviews: 15 in 2009. §Library and information science, Canadian reference. Ads: $1600 Cdn./$1140 Cdn. Subject: Libraries.

FEMINIST COLLECTIONS: A QUARTERLY OF WOMEN'S STUDIES RESOURCES, Women's Studies Librarian, University of Wisconsin System, Phyllis Holman Weisbard, JoAnne Lehman, 430 Memorial Library, 728 State Street, Madison, WI 53706, 608-263-5754. 1980. Articles, interviews, criticism, reviews, non-fiction. "Publishes book and video reviews on a variety of topics, plus news of Internet, periodical, and other resources for feminist research and teaching. Contributors are drawn from the University of Wisconsin System and elsewhere. Submissions are solicited from women's studies scholars." circ. 1.1M. 4/yr. Pub'd 4 issues 2009; expects 4 issues 2010, 4 issues 2011. sub. price $35 individuals and women's programs, $65 institutions (includes subscriptions to *Feminist Collections, Feminist Periodicals,* and *New Books On Women, Gender & Feminism*) Please inquire about special rates in Wisconsin; per copy $10; sample $10. Back issues: $10. 40pp. Reporting time: 1-2 weeks. Simultaneous submissions accepted: no. Payment: we are unfortunately unable to pay contributors. Copyrighted. Pub's reviews: 100 in 2009. §Any feminist or women-related books or magazines are of interest and help us stay current; we particularly note feminist reference works. Subjects: Bibliography, Book Reviewing, Feminism, Lesbianism, Libraries, Printing, Wisconsin, Women.

FEMINIST PERIODICALS: A CURRENT LISTING OF CONTENTS, Women's Studies Librarian, University of Wisconsin System, Phyllis Holman Weisbard, Ingrid Markhardt, 430 Memorial Library, 728 State Street, Madison, WI 53706, 608-263-5754. 1981. "Designed to increase public awareness of feminist periodicals, this publication reproduces table of contents pages from over 120 periodicals on a quarterly basis. An introductory section provides bibliographic background on each periodical." circ. 1.1M. 4/yr. Pub'd 4 issues 2009; expects 4 issues 2010, 4 issues 2011. sub. price free online journal. Back issues: $10 (print issues available through v.27, n.4, Fall 2007). 160pp. Copyrighted. Subjects: Bibliography, Feminism, Indexes & Abstracts, Lesbianism, Libraries, Magazines, Women.

The Feminist Press at the City University of New York (see also WSQ (formerly WOMEN'S STUDIES QUARTERLY)), Florence Howe, Publisher; Anjoli Roy, Assistant Editor, The Graduate Center, 365 Fifth Avenue, Suite 5406, New York, NY 10016, 212-817-7915, Fax 212-817-1593, www.feministpress.org. 1970. Fiction, non-fiction. "We do not accept submissions. Queries may be sent to the publisher via e-mail." avg. press run 3000. Pub'd 11 titles 2009; expects 18 titles 2010, 18 titles 2011. No titles listed in the *Small Press Record of Books in Print* (36th Edition, 2010-11). Discounts: See Consortium, our distributor; or our catalog on line at www.feministpress.org. 300-400pp. Reporting time: If we request a manuscript, we are relatively quick responding; no more than a month. Simultaneous submissions accepted: Yes. Publishes 2% of manuscripts submitted. Payment: Normal professional contract. Copyrights for author. Subjects: African Literature, Africa, African Studies, African-American, Autobiography, Biography, Black, Chicano/a, Education, Feminism, History, Lesbianism, Literature (General), Non-Fiction, Reprints, Third World, Minorities, Women.

FEMINIST REVIEW, Feminist Review Collective, c/o Women's Studies, London North Campus, London Metropolitan University, 166-220 Holloway Road, London N7 8DB, United Kingdom. 1979. Fiction, articles, interviews, criticism, reviews. "A socialist *feminist* journal." circ. 4M. 3/yr. Pub'd 3 issues 2009; expects 3 issues 2010, 3 issues 2011. sub. price (institutions) £287 UK, (individuals) £45 U.K., £45 overseas, $78 U.S. Back issues: apply to publisher. 128pp. Reporting time: 16-20 weeks. Simultaneous submissions accepted: no. Publishes 5-10% of manuscripts submitted. Payment: none. Copyrighted, reverts to author. Pub's reviews: 4-8 per issue in 2009. §Women: theory, politics, fiction, research. Ads: £110/£70/£55 1/3 page/£45 1/4 page. Subjects: Politics, Women.

FEMINIST STUDIES, Claire G. Moses, Editorial Director, 0103 Taliaferro, University of Maryland, College Park, MD 20742-7726, 301-405-7415, Fax 301-405-8395, creative@feministstudies.org; www.feministstudies.org. 1972. Poetry, fiction, articles, art, photos, cartoons, interviews, criticism, reviews, parts-of-novels, long-poems. 6M. 3/yr. Pub'd 3 issues 2009; expects 3 issues 2010, 3 issues 2011. sub. price $250 institutions,

$35 individuals; per copy $83 inst., $15 indiv.; sample $83 inst., $15 indiv. Back issues: $83 inst., $15 indiv. Discounts: none. 200-235pp. Reporting time: 4 months. Simultaneous submissions accepted: no. Publishes 7% of manuscripts submitted. Payment: none. Copyrighted, does not revert to author. Pub's reviews: 4 in 2009. §All fields of women's studies, on feminism, on sexuality, on family, on human relations, on psychology, significant works by women authors. Ads: $360. Subjects: African Literature, Africa, African Studies, Bilingual, Criticism, Feminism, Global Affairs, History, Human Rights, Lesbianism, Multicultural, Poetry, Politics, Sex, Sexuality, Sociology, U.S. Hispanic, Women.

FENCE, Rebecca Wolff, Editor & Publisher; Lynne Tillman, Fiction Editor; Katy Lederer, Poetry Editor; Max Winter, Poetry Editor; Charles Valle, Poetry Editor; Jason Zuzga, Nonfiction Editor, New Library 320, University at Albany, Albany, NY 12222, www.fenceportal.org. 1998. "A biannual journal of poetry, fiction, art and criticism, *Fence* has a mission to publishing challenging writing and art distinguished by idiosyncrasy and intelligence rather than by allegiance with camps, schools or cliques. The Alberta Perize publication of a first or second book by a woman, as well as a $5000 cash prize. Our second prize series is the Fence Modern Poets Series open to either gender in any stage of their career." circ. 12,000. 2/yr. sub. price $17; per copy $10; sample $8. Back issues: $8. Reporting time: 4-9 mos. Simultaneous submissions accepted: yes. Publishes 2% of manuscripts submitted. Payment: 1 year sub. Ads: $750/$325.

FICTION, Mark Jay Mirsky, Editor; Nyshie Perkinson, Managing Editor, c/o Dept. of English, City College, 138th Street & Convent Ave., New York, NY 10031, 212-650-6319. 1972. Fiction, parts-of-novels. "We are a journal of new directions for the novel and short story. *Fiction* has brought the unknown and the famous together in handsome pages to an international and discriminating audience of readers for 20 years. We represent no particular school of fiction, except the innovative, and in that sense our pages have been a harbor for many writers often at odds with each other. As a result of our willingness to publish the difficult and experimental, to look at the unusual and obscure, while not excluding the well known, *Fiction* has won a unique reputation in the U.S. and abroad, including in recent years, O.Henry Award, Pushcart Prize, and Best of the South." circ. 3M. 2/yr. Pub'd 2 issues 2009; expects 2 issues 2010, 2 issues 2011. sub. price $38/4 issues; per copy $10; sample $5. Back issues: $8. 200pp. Reporting time: 3+ months. Simultaneous submissions accepted: yes. Publishes 1% of manuscripts submitted. Payment: $75 + copies. Copyrighted, reverts to author. Subjects: Fiction, Literature (General).

Fiction Collective Two (FC2), Carmen Edington, Managing Editor, Fiction Collective Two, 3007 N. Ben Wilson, Victoria, TX 77901-5731, 361-570-4118, Fax 361-580-5501. 1974. Fiction. "Novels and collections of short stories. Members are authors we have published or are about to publish. Distribution through University of Alabama Press, Chicago Distribution Center, 11030 South Langley Avenue, Chicago, IL 60628. Please read our submissions guidelines at http://fc2.org/queries.htm before submitting." avg. press run 2.2M. Pub'd 6 titles 2009; expects 7 titles 2010, 7 titles 2011. 182 titles listed in the *Small Press Record of Books in Print* (36th Edition, 2010-11). Discounts: 1-4 books 20%, 5-24 40%, 25-49 41%, 50-74 42%, 75-124 43%, 125-199 44%, 200-299 45%, 300+ 46%. 200pp. Reporting time: 6 months to 1 year. Reading period: Contest - August-November. Simultaneous submissions accepted: yes. Publishes 2% of manuscripts submitted. Payment: 10% royalties, 80% of subsidiary rights sales. Copyrights for author. Subjects: Avant-Garde, Experimental Art, Fiction, Literature (General).

The Fiction Works, Ray Hoy, 2070 SW Whiteside Drive, Corvallis, OR 97333, 541-730-2044, 541-738-2648, fictionworks@comcast.com, http://www.fictionworks.com. 1997. Fiction, non-fiction. "We are presently closed to all submissions due to a very long production queue." Pub'd 25 titles 2009; expects 20 titles 2010, 25 titles 2011. 88 titles listed in the *Small Press Record of Books in Print* (36th Edition, 2010-11). Discounts: Bookstores: 30% (no minimum order) Distributors: 50% (no minimum order) Libraries: 20% (no minimum order). 250pp. Reporting time: One week. Simultaneous submissions accepted: Yes. Publishes 5% of manuscripts submitted. Payment: We pay 10% (paperback titles) and 20% (eBook titles) of the cover price paid by the customer. Royalties are paid quarterly. Does not copyright for author. Subjects: Drama, Fantasy, Fiction, Horror, Internet, Mentoring/Coaching, Mystery, Non-Fiction, Old West, Reference, Romance, Science Fiction, Supernatural, Textbooks, Young Adult.

THE FIDDLEHEAD, Ross Leckie, Managing Editor; Lynn Davies, Poetry Editor; M.A. Jarman, Fiction Editor, Campus House, PO Box 4400, University of New Brunswick, Fredericton, NB E3B 5A3, Canada, 506-453-3501. 1945. Poetry, fiction, art, reviews, parts-of-novels, long-poems, plays. circ. 1.1M. 4/yr. Pub'd 4 issues 2009; expects 4 issues 2010, 4 issues 2011. sub. price $20 Canada, U.S. $20US + $6 postage; per copy $8 Can.; sample $8 + postage Can. and US. Back issues: $5-8. Discounts: 10% on purchases of 10 copies or more; bookstores 33-1/3%. 128-200pp. Reporting time: 10-30 weeks, include SASE with Canadian stamp, IRC, or cash. Simultaneous submissions accepted: no. Publishes 1% of manuscripts submitted. Payment: $10 printed page. Copyrighted. Pub's reviews: 30-40 in 2009. §Canadian literature. Ads: $100/$52. Subjects: Literary Review, Poetry.

FIDELIS ET VERUS, Children Of Mary, Jack Walsh, PO Box 350333, Ft. Lauderdale, FL 33335-0333,

Phone/fax 954-583-5108 E-mail: mascmen7@yahoo.com Website: http://www.catholicbook.com. 1985. News items. "Promotes Marian apparitions, traditional beliefs and practices, threats to Church by Masons,Non-Christians,Russia, China and Islam." circ. 1.2M. 4-6/yr. Pub'd 6 issues 2009; expects 6 issues 2010, 6 issues 2011. sub. price $10 for 10 issues; per copy $1; sample $1. Back issues: $1. Discounts: 10¢ per copy in bulk. 8-24pp. Reporting time: bi-monthly. Not copyrighted. Pub's reviews: none in 2009. §Only traditional Roman Catholic books/magazines. Ads: $100/$55/$10 per column inch (2 column page); columns 3-3/8 wide. Subjects: Birth, Birth Control, Population, Book Reviewing, Christianity, Communism, Marxism, Leninism, Electronics, Government, Magazines, Newsletter, Newspapers, Non-Fiction, Philosophy, Politics, Religion, Socialist, Textbooks.

FIELD: Contemporary Poetry and Poetics, Oberlin College Press, David Young, Co-editor; David Walker, Co-editor; Pamela Alexander, Associate Editor; Kazim Ali, Associate Editor; DeSales Harrison, Associate Editor; Martha Collins, Editor-at-Large, 50 N. Professor St., Oberlin, OH 44074-1091, 440-775-8408, Fax 440-775-8124, oc.press@oberlin.edu. 1969. Poetry. "Also essays on poetry and translations of poetry." circ. 1.5M. 2/yr. Pub'd 2 issues 2009; expects 2 issues 2010, 2 issues 2011. 7 titles listed in the *Small Press Record of Books in Print* (36th Edition, 2010-11). sub. price $16, $28/2 years; per copy $8 ppd.; sample $8 ppd. Back issues: $12, all backs, except most recent year. Discounts: 40% bookstores (minimum order 5 copies), 15% subscription agencies. 100pp. Reporting time: 6-8 weeks. Simultaneous submissions accepted: no. Publishes .25%-.50% of manuscripts submitted. Payment: $15 per page. Copyrighted, reverts to author. Pub's reviews: 7 in 2009. §new books of contemporary poetry and poetry in translation. Ads: none. Subjects: Poetry, Translation.

Nicolin Fields Publishing, Inc., Linda Chestney, 861 Lafayette Rd Unit 2A, Hampton, NH 03842-1232, 603-758-6363, Fax 603-758-6366, nfpi@comcast.net. 1994. Poetry, non-fiction. avg. press run 1.5-6M. Pub'd 5 titles 2009; expects 4 titles 2010, 3-4 titles 2011. 8 titles listed in the *Small Press Record of Books in Print* (36th Edition, 2010-11). Discounts: 40% retail stores (bike shops) and specialty stores, distributors 50-67%. 200pp. Reporting time: 1-2 months. Simultaneous submissions accepted: yes. Publishes 10% of manuscripts submitted. Payment: varies/standard. Copyrights for author. Subjects: Bicycling, Cooking, Health, Inspirational, New England, New Hampshire, Non-Fiction, Quotations, Self-Help, Sports, Outdoors.

Fieldstone Alliance, Tim Brostrom, Director of Product Innovation, 60 Plato Boulevard East, Suite 150, St. Paul, MN 55107, 800-274-6024, Fax 651-556-4517, books@fieldstonealliance.org, www.fieldstonealliance.org. 1990. Non-fiction. "Publishes practical, easy-to-use books for nonprofit organizations on topics such as nonprofit management, community building, and violence prevention." avg. press run 5M. Pub'd 5 titles 2009; expects 7 titles 2010, 4 titles 2011. No titles listed in the *Small Press Record of Books in Print* (36th Edition, 2010-11). 130pp. Payment: contact editor. Copyrights for author.

FIFTH ESTATE, Collective Staff, PO Box 201016, Ferndale, MI 48220-9016. 1965. Articles, photos, criticism, reviews, letters, non-fiction. "We don't encourage unsolicited mss." circ. 3,000. 3/yr. Pub'd 3 issues 2009; expects 3 issues 2010, 3 issues 2011. 1 title listed in the *Small Press Record of Books in Print* (36th Edition, 2010-11). sub. price $14 domestic, $20 Canada & Mexico; $24 foreign; $20 libraries & institutions; $500 police & government; per copy $4; sample free. Back issues: $5. Discounts: none. 48pp. Simultaneous submissions accepted: Please inform. Payment: none. Not copyrighted. Pub's reviews: 25 in 2009. §Ecology, politics, anarchism, feminism. Ads: not accepted. Subject: Politics.

5th Street Books, Patricia Turner, Manager, 1691 Norris landing Drive, Suite A, Snellville, GA 30039-0028, 678-413-9100, www.5thstreetbooks.com. 2005. Fiction. avg. press run 5000. Expects 3 titles 2010, 5 titles 2011. 5 titles listed in the *Small Press Record of Books in Print* (36th Edition, 2010-11). Discounts: undecided. 200pp. Simultaneous submissions accepted: Yes. Publishes 5% of manuscripts submitted. Copyrights for author.

•**FIFTH WEDNESDAY JOURNAL,** Vern Miller, Editor-Publisher, PO Box 4033, Lisle, IL 60532-9033. "*Fifth Wednesday Journal* is a literary print journal published twice a year by Fifth Wednesday Books in Lisle, Illinois. We seek to bring together readers and the best poets and storytellers we can find, both established writers and fresh new voices. We are committed to quality writing which is entertaining, intellectually stimulating, and emotionally meaningful for the reader. In short, we seek to publish work that we enjoy and can enthusiastically recommend to our readers. We welcome prose and poetry in any styletraditional, realistic, modern, and experimentalyou name it, as long as it meets our standards for high quality in content and form. We intend to offer a broad range of poems and stories with appeal for a wide range of quality readers. If you think we might like your work, but are in doubt, submit it and find out."

The Film Instruction Company of America, Henry C. Landa, 5928 W. Michigan Street, Wauwatosa, WI 53213-4248, 414-258-6492. 1960. Non-fiction. "We seek manuscripts and do not accept unsolicited works." avg. press run 800-3M. Pub'd 1 title 2009; expects 2 titles 2010, 2 titles 2011. 1 title listed in the *Small Press Record of Books in Print* (36th Edition, 2010-11). Discounts: 40% to retailers and brokers, 50% to true wholesalers. 150+pp. Simultaneous submissions accepted: no. Payment: 15%-25%. Copyrights for author.

Subjects: Airplanes, Aviation, Energy, Politics, Solar.

FILM QUARTERLY, University of California Press, Ann Martin, University of California Press, 2000 Center Street, Suite 303, Berkeley, CA 94704-1223, 510-643-7154. 1945. Interviews, criticism, reviews. circ. 4550. 4/yr. Pub'd 4 issues 2009; expects 4 issues 2010, 4 issues 2011. sub. price $30 indiv., $120 instit. (+ $20 air freight), $30 student; per copy $8 indiv., $35 instit., $8 student; sample free. Back issues: same as single copy price. Discounts: foreign subs. agents 10%, 10+ one-time orders 30%, standing orders (bookstores): 1-99 40%, 100+ 50%. 64pp. Reporting time: 2-3 weeks. Payment: 2¢ per word. Copyrighted, does not revert to author. Pub's reviews: about 100 in 2009. §Film. Ads: $430/$315.

FINANCIAL FOCUS, Jack W. Everett, 2140 Professional Drive Ste. 105, Roseville, CA 95661-3734, 916-791-1447, Fax 916-791-3444, jeverett@quiknet.com. 1980. Non-fiction. circ. 5M. 12/yr. Pub'd 12 issues 2009; expects 12 issues 2010, 12 issues 2011. sub. price $39.97; sample free. Discounts: call for info. 8pp. Reporting time: 1 month. Simultaneous submissions accepted: yes. Copyrighted, reverts to author. Pub's reviews: 1 in 2009. §Financial. Ads: none. Subject: Business & Economics.

FINE BOOKS & COLLECTIONS, Scott Brown, PO Box 106, Eureka, CA 95502, 707-443-9562, Fax 707-443-9572, scott@finebooksmagazine.com, www.finebooksmagazine.com. 2002. Articles, photos, cartoons, interviews, criticism, reviews, news items, non-fiction. "We publish articles and essays related to book collecting. Recent contributors include Larry McMurtry, Paul Collins, Dana Gioia, Amy Stewart, and Roy Parvin." circ. 2.5M. 6/yr. Pub'd 6 issues 2009; expects 6 issues 2010, 6 issues 2011. sub. price $25. Discounts: standard trade. 76pp. Reporting time: 6 weeks. Simultaneous submissions accepted: yes. Publishes 10% of manuscripts submitted. Payment: $200-$600, depending on length and difficulty. Copyrighted, reverts to author. Pub's reviews: 20 in 2009. §Books and magazines about books, book arts, collecting. Ads: $400/$200. Subjects: Book Arts, Book Collecting, Bookselling.

Fine Tooth Press, JJ Sargent, PO Box 11512, Waterbury, CT 06703, kolchak@snet.net, http://www.finetoothpress.com. 2004. Poetry, fiction, criticism, parts-of-novels, non-fiction. "Fine Tooth Press presents books by authors on the same page - perhaps at different corners and along the edges, but certainly off center! Our publications challenge genre specifications, erode boundaries and motivate readers to interact with texts that many times defy rational explanation or description. You wont find smarmy or meek prose here. These books are "in your face" and will stick with you for a very long time. We publish personal and intuitive poetry, bold speculative fiction with an edge, scholarly criticism with a hearty attitude, and more." avg. press run 500. Expects 8 titles 2010, 8 titles 2011. No titles listed in the *Small Press Record of Books in Print* (36th Edition, 2010-11). Retail discounts placed through publisher: 2-10 copies 20%, 11-24 copies 25%, 25+ copies 30%; Retail distribution via Ingram: 35-50%. 200pp. Reporting time: 3 months. Simultaneous submissions accepted: No. Publishes 25% of manuscripts submitted. Payment: 12-15%; no advance; annual dispersement. Does not copyright for author. Subjects: Anarchist, Anthropology, Archaelogy, Arts, Asian-American, Biography, Comics, Criticism, Ecology, Foods, English, Fiction, Humanism, Latin America, Lesbianism, Medieval, Men.

Finishing Line Press, CJ Morrison, Founding Editor; Leah Maines, Senior Editor; Kevin Murphy Maines, Production and Graphic Design Editor; Beth Dungan, Editorial Assistant; Elizabeth Cordell, Production Assistant, PO Box 1626, Georgetown, KY 40324, 859-514-8966, finishingbooks@aol.com, www.finishinglinepress.com. 1998. Poetry. "Some of our titles have won book awards and have been included in anthologies—including the San Diego Book Award for Poetry, and (anthology) Billy Collins' 180 MORE." avg. press run 500. Pub'd 80 titles 2009; expects 112 titles 2010, 112 titles 2011. 11 titles listed in the *Small Press Record of Books in Print* (36th Edition, 2010-11). Discounts: 40% to booksellers. 30pp. Reporting time: 3 months. Please don't call or email us every week to see what we have decided on your manuscript. We need 3 months to decide and then we will send you a letter with our decision. If you have not heard from us after 3 months, then please contact us via email or letter. Simultaneous submissions accepted: yes. Publishes 4% of manuscripts submitted. Payment: 10% of press run in copies. Copyrights for author. Subject: Poetry.

Finney Company, Inc. (see also Anacus Press, An Imprint of Finney Company; Ecopress, An Imprint of Finney Company; Hobar Publications, A Division of Finney Company; Windward Publishing, An Imprint of Finney Company), Alan Krysan, President, 8075 215th Street West, Lakeville, MN 55044, (952) 469-6699, Fax: (952) 469-1968, (800)846-7027, Fax: (800) 330-6232, feedback@finneyco.com, www.finneyco.com. 1958. Non-fiction. "Finney Company continues to expand, covering such areas as career development and exploration, school-to-work, tech prep, placement, and on the job. We publish the Occupational Guidance Series and our most recent release is Planning My Career." avg. press run 5000. Pub'd 1 title 2009; expects 2-3 titles 2010, 2-3 titles 2011. No titles listed in the *Small Press Record of Books in Print* (36th Edition, 2010-11). Discounts: 1-9 copies 20%; 10-24 copies 40%; 25-49 copies 45%; 50 or more copies 50%. Reporting time: 8-10 weeks. Simultaneous submissions accepted: Yes. Payment: varies. Subjects: Careers, Consulting, Education, Employment, Interviews, Leadership, Management, Mentoring/Coaching, Motivation, Success, Networking, Non-Fiction, Speaking, Worker, Young Adult.

The Fire!! Press, Thomas H. Wirth, 241 Hillside Road, Elizabeth, NJ 07208-1432, 908-289-3714 phone/Fax, tw@firepress.com, www.firepress.com. 1981. Poetry, fiction, art. "Not soliciting manuscripts at this time." avg. press run 2M. 3 titles listed in the *Small Press Record of Books in Print* (36th Edition, 2010-11). Discounts: 40%. Subjects: African-American, Black, Gay.

firefall editions, Robinson Joyce Jr., 4905 Tunlaw Street, Alexandria, VA 22312, 5105492461, www.firefallmedia.com. 1974. Art, photos, music, long-poems. "To create the visual novel, realistically imaged, without cartoons: to create a new american idiom: to be the penthouse of the imagination." avg. press run 5000. Pub'd 3 titles 2009; expects 5 titles 2010, 7 titles 2011. No titles listed in the *Small Press Record of Books in Print* (36th Edition, 2010-11). Discounts: distributors - 50%; educational - 25%. 200pp. Reporting time: 3 months or more. Simultaneous submissions accepted: No. Publishes 3% of manuscripts submitted. Payment: 50-50 split on net revenue. Copyrights for author. Subjects: Americana, Calligraphy, Cults, Medicine, New Mexico, Photography, Robotics, San Francisco, Science, U.S.S.R., Wyoming.

Firewheel Editions (see also SENTENCE, A Journal of Prose Poetics), Brian Clements, Box 7, WCSU, 181 White St., Danbury, CT 06810, http://firewheel-editions.org. 1999. Poetry. "Firewheel Editions publishes Sentence: a Journal of Prose Poetics, and many of our books follow in Sentence's commitment to prose poetry, hybrid poetry, and work that is hard to classify by genre. The Sentence Book Award is devoted to publishing a book of prose poems each year; the Firewheel Chapbook Competition is devoted to publishing work in any genre that might have difficulty finding publication elsewhere due to genre, content, typography, packaging, printing requirements, or other issues. For the foreseeable future, all books from Firewheel other than some titles in the chapbook series will be poetry. Outside the book awards, please query the editor before sending a manuscript." avg. press run 1000. Pub'd 2 titles 2009; expects 5 titles 2010, 5 titles 2011. 6 titles listed in the *Small Press Record of Books in Print* (36th Edition, 2010-11). Reporting time: 1-2 months. Simultaneous submissions accepted: Yes. Publishes 1% of manuscripts submitted. Payment: 10% Royalty contract, 25 copies. Will negotiate additional author copies in lieu of royalties, if the author prefers it. Past practice has been to copyright in the name of the press, but we are willing to copyright in the name of the author.

First Books (see also Inkwater Press), Jeremy Solomon, President, 6750 SW Franklin, # A, Portland, OR 97223-2542, 503-968-6777. 1988. Poetry, fiction, non-fiction. No titles listed in the *Small Press Record of Books in Print* (36th Edition, 2010-11). Discounts: 50%. Simultaneous submissions accepted: No. Subjects: Animals, Arts, Cooking, Fiction, Humor, Mathematics, Memoirs, Moving/Relocation, Non-Fiction, Novels, Parenting, Poetry, Real Estate, Weddings, Young Adult.

First Chance Publishing, Mary Holloman, 76 Cranbrook Road #232, Cockeysville, MD 21030, 443-912-8719. 2006. Fiction. Expects 2 titles 2010, 4 titles 2011. 2 titles listed in the *Small Press Record of Books in Print* (36th Edition, 2010-11). Discounts: 1-10 books 40% discount11-20 books 45% discount21 and up 50% discount. Simultaneous submissions accepted: yes. Does not copyright for author. Subjects: Children, Youth, Romance.

FIRST CLASS, Four-Sep Publications, Christopher M., PO Box 86, Friendship, IN 47021, christopherm@four-sep.com, www.four-sep.com. 1996. Poetry, fiction, photos, long-poems, plays. "Prefer short fiction. Cover letter preferred. Desires good, thought-provoking, graphic, uncommon pieces. Recent: John Bennett, Alan Catlin, Gary Every... check out web site for author listings and samples." circ. 150-300 depending on sub status. 2/yr. Pub'd 3 issues 2009; expects 3 issues 2010, 2 issues 2011. sub. price $11/2 issues; per copy $6 ppd.; sample $6 issue ppd. Back issues: inquire. Discounts: inquire, offer, selective trades, 60-40 for distributors. 44-48pp. Reporting time: 3-5 weeks initial response, 5 months accept./reject. Simultaneous submissions accepted: yes. Publishes 7-10% of manuscripts submitted. Payment: 1 copy. Copyrighted, reverts to author. §Short fiction and non-traditional poetics. Ads: inquire. Subjects: Absurdist, Counter-Culture, Alternatives, Communes, Literature (General), Poetry, Post Modern.

First Journey Publishing Company, Jeannie Barry-Sanders, Waianae, HI 96792, 808.548.5148 (office). 2006. Articles, non-fiction. "First Journey Publishing Company (FJPC) founded in 2006. FJPC is especially interested in publishing ebooks, ghostwriting, editing and proofreading. FJPC also writes grants for nonprofit organizations and churches. Organizations must be 501c3 status and established for at least one year." avg. press run 1000 (initial). Expects 5 titles 2011. No titles listed in the *Small Press Record of Books in Print* (36th Edition, 2010-11). Discounts: 10%. 300pp. Reporting time: 1-2 months. Simultaneous submissions accepted: No. Payment: 10% list price/hardcover and 7-12% softcovers for first 12,000 sold and 9% above 12,000. Prefer author to copyright but will provide this service. Subjects: African Literature, Africa, African Studies, African-American, Asian-American, Chicano/a, Children, Youth, Civil Rights, Education, Family, Fundraising, Multicultural, Native American, Non-Fiction, Non-Violence, Short Stories, Third World, Minorities.

THE FIRST LINE, Blue Cubicle Press, LLC, David LaBounty, PO Box 250382, Plano, TX 75025-0382, 972-824-0646, submission@thefirstline.com, www.thefirstline.com. 1999. Fiction, non-fiction. "Word Limit: 300-3,000. Fiction: General, but must begin with the first line provided on website. Nonfiction: Essays about books with interesting/memorable first lines." circ. 1,500. 4/yr. Pub'd 4 issues 2009; expects 4 issues 2010, 4 issues 2011. sub. price $12; per copy $3.50; sample $3.50. Back issues: $4. 60pp. Reporting time: 6 weeks. Simultaneous submissions accepted: no. Publishes 5% of manuscripts submitted. Payment: $20 for fiction, $10 for essay. Copyrighted, negotiable. Subject: Literature (General).

FISH DRUM MAGAZINE, Suzi Winson, www.fishdrum.com. 1988. Poetry, fiction, articles, art, photos, cartoons, interviews, criticism, reviews, music, letters, long-poems, collages, non-fiction. "*Fish Drum* prefers West Coast poetry, the exuberant 'continuous nerve movie' that follows the working of the mind and has a relationship to the world and the reader. Philip Whalen's work, for example, and much of *Calafia, The California Poetry,* edited by Ishmael Reed. Also magical-tribal-incantatory poems, exemplified by the future/primitive *Technicians of the Sacred,* ed. Rothenberg. *Fish Drum* has a soft spot for schmoozy, emotional, imagistic stuff. Literate, personal material that sings and surprises, OK? We've published poetry by Philip Whalen, Ira Cohen, Miriam Sagan, Leslie Scalapino, Alice Notley, John Brandi, Joanne Kyger and Leo Romero, all of whom have books around worth finding and reading. At this time, we are not accepting unsolicited submissions. *Fish Drum* is being produced in memory of and to honor Robert Winson (April 28, 1959 - October 20, 1995) the founder, editor and publisher." circ. 2M. 1-2/yr. Pub'd 2 issues 2009; expects 2 issues 2010, 2 issues 2011. sub. price $24/4 issues; sample $6. Discounts: 40%. 80pp. Reporting time: 2-6 months or longer. Simultaneous submissions accepted: no. Publishes 2-5% of manuscripts submitted. Payment: 2 or more copies. Copyrighted, reverts to author. Pub's reviews. §mostly Poetry, sometimes fiction, natural history, or Zen. Ads: exchange only. Subjects: Animals, Comics, Fiction, Literature (General), Poetry, Religion, Science Fiction, Southwest, Tapes & Records, Visual Arts, Zen.

Fisher King Press, Mel Mathews, P.O. Box 222321, Carmel, CA 93922-2321, 831-238-7799, 800-228-9316, queries@fisherkingpress.com, www.fisherkingpress.com. 2005. Fiction, non-fiction. "Fisher King Press publishes and distributes work concerning the study of Jungian theory dealing with depth psychology, myth, archetypal symbolism, and dreams. Occasionally we will consider Literary Fiction in the form of a novel, a non-fiction manuscript with a focus on Spirituality & Religion, and Poetry, which we publisher under our il piccolo editions imprint. Please note that we avoid anything that is steeped in fundamentalism, regardless of the particular religion or spiritual practice." avg. press run 5000. Pub'd 11 titles 2009; expects 10 titles 2010, 10 titles 2011. 23 titles listed in the *Small Press Record of Books in Print* (36th Edition, 2010-11). Discounts: Bookstores 40% retailers 40% Libraries 40%. 250pp. Payment: 10%, no advance, annually. Copyrights for author. Subjects: Arthurian, Buddhism, California, Europe, Fiction, Ireland, Italy, Literature (General), Henry Miller, Native American, Non-Fiction, North America, Novels, Psychology, Zen.

THE FIT CHRISTIAN A Christian Health & Fitness Magazine, His Work Christian Publishing, Angela Perez, P.O. Box 5732, Ketchikan, AK 99901, phone 206-274-8474, fax 614-388-0664, email editor@hiswork-pub.com, website http://www.hiswordpub.com. 2003. Articles, photos, cartoons, interviews, reviews, news items, non-fiction. "Promoting Health & Fitness and the Christian faith." 6/yr. Pub'd 6 issues 2009; expects 6 issues 2010, 6 issues 2011. 38pp. Reporting time: 2-6 weeks. Simultaneous submissions accepted: Yes. Publishes 10% of manuscripts submitted. Payment: pays $10-50.00. Copyrighted, reverts to author. Pub's reviews: 3 in 2009. §Health & Fitness titles, Christian fiction and non-fiction. Ads: Display Ads;1 block $75.00 2 block $140.00 3 block $200.00 4 block $265.00 6 block $350.00 8 block (1/2 page) $525.00 16 block (full page) $1000.00 32 block (2 page spread) $1850.00. Subjects: Cartoons, Children, Youth, Christianity, Family, Food, Eating, Interviews, Marriage, Non-Fiction, Nutrition, Parenting, Religion.

Fithian Press, John Daniel, Editor, PO Box 2790, McKinleyville, CA 95519-2790, 805-962-1780, Fax 805-962-8835, dandd@danielpublishing.com. 1985. Poetry, fiction, non-fiction. "We are open to anything but we specialize in memoir, fiction, poetry, and social issures. In addition to our general catalogue we issue annual catalogs in California and World War II books." avg. press run 1M. Pub'd 20 titles 2009; expects 20 titles 2010, 20 titles 2011. 3 titles listed in the *Small Press Record of Books in Print* (36th Edition, 2010-11). Discounts: trade 1-4 20%, 5+ 47%; wholesale 1-9 20%, 10+ 50%; library 20%. 160pp. Reporting time: 6-8 weeks. Simultaneous submissions accepted: yes. Publishes 5% of manuscripts submitted. Payment: author pays production costs and receives 60% net royalty. Copyrights for author. Subjects: Fiction, Literature (General), Memoirs, Novels, Poetry, Short Stories.

Fitness Press, Phyllis Rogers, 2112-A Montreat Lane, Birmingham, AL 35216, 205-637-7838; 205-999-5595, fitness9@mindspring.com. 2000. Non-fiction. "Mission is to publish health and fitness information for older adults." avg. press run 3000. Expects 1 title 2010, 1 title 2011. No titles listed in the *Small Press Record of Books in Print* (36th Edition, 2010-11). Discounts: 1-2 books no discount3-4—20% off5-9—30% off10-199—40% off200-499—50% off500+ - 55% off. 150pp. Reporting time: 30 days. Simultaneous submissions accepted: Yes. Publishes 1% of manuscripts submitted. Payment: TBD. Copyrights for author. Subjects: Aging, Alternative Medicine, Health, How-To, Senior Citizens.

5 AM, Ed Ochester, Co-editor; Judith Vollmer, Co-editor, Box 205, Spring Church, PA 15686. 1987. Poetry, criticism. "Open to all styles & content, except for religious propaganda. We're partial to well-made comic and political poems and, in general, other poems that are taboo at most academic quarterlies. Tabloid format.$20/2 years (4 issues). Sample $6. Authors: Denise Duhamel, Crystal Williams, Edward Field, Alicia Ostriker, Robin Becker, Michael Waters, Charles Harper Webb, Afaa Michael Weaver, Minnie Bruce Pratt, David Hernandez + many "new" poets." circ. 1100. 32pp. Reporting time: 6 weeks max. Simultaneous submissions accepted: no. Publishes 3% of manuscripts submitted. Payment: Copies. one-time use only. Subject: Poetry.

Five Bucks Press (see also RAGMAG DIGEST), J.D. Scheneman, PO Box 31, Stacyville, IA 50476-0031, 641-710-9953, fivebuckspress@omnitelcom.com, www.fivebuckspress.com. "See website for writer guidelines and deadlines for various publication opportunities or request details by snail mail, include #10 SASE for reply." No titles listed in the *Small Press Record of Books in Print* (36th Edition, 2010-11).

580 SPLIT, Erika Staiti, Mills College, P.O. Box 9982, Oakland, CA 94613-0982. 1999. Poetry, fiction, art, photos, cartoons, music, parts-of-novels, long-poems, collages, plays, non-fiction. "Not far from our office at Mills College in Oakland, California, the 580 Split is a risky jumble of ramps, overpasses, and interchanges, where highways cross, merge, intersect, and branch out in every direction. 580 Split, an annual journal of arts and literature, is both the convergence and divergence of many roads: a place of risk and possibility. We publish innovative prose and poetry and are open to well-crafted experimental approaches. Recent contributors have included Chris Abani, Will Alexander, Lisa Robertson. Featured interview with Yiyun Li. Please see our website for complete list of contributors, submission guidelines, contact information, and contest guidelines." circ. 650. 1/yr. Pub'd 1 issue 2009; expects 1 issue 2010, 1 issue 2011. sub. price 7.50; per copy 7.50; sample 7.50. Back issues: inquire. Discounts: Beginning in 2005, we will offer subscription rates to institutions, bookstores, and other retailers. Inquire via email. 120pp. Reporting time: 4-6 months. Simultaneous submissions accepted: Yes. Publishes 2% of manuscripts submitted. Payment: 2 contributor copies. Copyrighted, reverts to author. §Innovative and experimental prose, poetry, and art. We do not accept advertising for the journal; however, we are interested in link swaps for our website. Subjects: Arts, Experimental, Fiction, Journals, Photography, Poetry.

Five Fingers Press (see also FIVE FINGERS REVIEW), Jaime Robles, PO Box 4, San Leandro, CA 94577-0100. 1984. Fiction, interviews, non-fiction. avg. press run 1M. Pub'd 1 title 2009; expects 1 title 2010, 1 title 2011. 11 titles listed in the *Small Press Record of Books in Print* (36th Edition, 2010-11). Discounts: subs. $16/2 issues, 40% consignment; 50% outright sale. 200pp. Reporting time: 3-5 months. Payment: 2 copies of magazine, cash payment depends upon funding. Does not copyright for author. Subjects: Avant-Garde, Experimental Art, Culture, Essays, Fiction, Literary Review, Multicultural, Poetry, Short Stories, Translation.

FIVE FINGERS REVIEW, Five Fingers Press, Jaime Robles, PO Box 4, San Leandro, CA 94577-0100. 1984. Poetry, fiction, interviews, non-fiction. "*Five Fingers Review* seeks to publish fresh, innovative writing and artwork that is not necessarily defined by the currently 'correct' aesthetic or ideology. *Five Fingers Review* welcomes work that crosses or falls between genres. In addition to new fiction and poetry, *Five Fingers Review* presents essays, interviews, and translations. Past published writers include Norman Fischer, Peter Gizzi, Lyn Hejinian, Fanny Howe, Jaime Robles, Keith Waldrop, Rosmarie Waldrop. Each issue explores a theme; 2006 theme is: Foreign Lands and Alternate Universes. We have an annual contest as well. More information may be found at www.fivefingersreview.org." circ. 1M. 1/yr. Pub'd 1 issue 2009; expects 1 issue 2010, 1 issue 2011. 7 titles listed in the *Small Press Record of Books in Print* (36th Edition, 2010-11). sub. price $22/2 issues; sample $7.00. 224pp. Reporting time: We read from June 1 to August 30. Decisions are mailed in January. Submissions are returned outside of reading submission period. Annual contest deadline is June 1. Simultaneous submissions accepted: yes. Payment: 2 copies, cash payment depends upon funding. Copyrighted, reverts to author. Pub's reviews. Ads: $125 (4-1/2 X 7-1/2)/$75 (4-1/2 X 3-1/2)/$50 1/4 page (2 X 3). Subjects: Avant-Garde, Experimental Art, Culture, Essays, Fiction, Literary Review, Multicultural, Poetry, Short Stories, Translation.

FIVE POINTS, David Bottoms, Editor; Megan Sexton, Editor, P.O. Box 3999, Georgia State University, Atlanta, GA 30302-3999, 404.413.5812. 1996. Poetry, fiction, art, photos, interviews, parts-of-novels, long-poems, non-fiction. "Recent contributors:Ann Beattie, Philip Levine, Naomi Shihab Nye, Peter Davison, Phillip Booth, Rick Bass, and Tess Gallagher." circ. 6M. 3/yr. Pub'd 3 issues 2009; expects 3 issues 2010, 3 issues 2011. sub. price $21; per copy $10; sample $10. Back issues: $10. Discounts: classroom. 150pp. Reporting time: 4-6 months. Simultaneous submissions accepted: no. Payment: $50 per poem, $15 per prose page. Copyrighted, reverts to author. Ads: $200/$100/$50 1/4 page. Subjects: Arts, Fiction, Interviews, Non-Fiction, Poetry.

•Five Star Publications, Inc., Linda Radke, PO Box 6698, Chandler, AZ 85246-6698, 480-940-8182. 1985. Fiction, cartoons, plays, non-fiction. avg. press run 500. Pub'd 4 titles 2009; expects 6 titles 2010, 6 titles 2011. 1 title listed in the *Small Press Record of Books in Print* (36th Edition, 2010-11). Discounts: 5+ copies 45% non-returnable discount. 25% returnable discount. 200pp. Reporting time: 3 months. Simultaneous submissions accepted: Yes. Publishes 4% of manuscripts submitted. Payment: Per agreement. Does not copyright for author. Subjects: Arizona, Biography, Business & Economics, Children, Youth, Comics, Cooking, Fiction, Shakespeare.

172

FIVE WILLOWS MAGAZINE, Koon Woon, 202 6th Avenue South #1105, Seattle, WA 98104-2303, 202-682-3851. 2004. Poetry. circ. 300. 4/yr. Expects 2 issues 2010, 4 issues 2011. sub. price $20; per copy $5; sample $4. Back issues: none. Discounts: inquire. 44pp. Reporting time: 2 weeks. Simultaneous submissions accepted: no. Publishes 10% of manuscripts submitted. Payment: copy. Copyrighted, reverts to author. Ads: $100/$50. Subjects: Asian-American, Poetry.

Flapjack Press, Paul Neads, Andrew Myers, 6 Chiffon Way, Trinity Riverside, Gtr Manchester M3 6AB, England, +4407814570441, paul@mucusart.co.uk, www.mucusart.co.uk/press.htm. 2002. "Mucusart Publications aims to provide a voice and forum for stranded bards whilst not discriminating between the written and the spoken word. Mucusart explores the synergy between both through its performance poetry nights in the UK, its poetry magazine The Ugly Tree (three times a year), and its occasional single-poet pamphlet. 2006 sees the lauch of its twice yearly short fiction magazine, Ballista, featuring new writing on the supernatural." avg. press run 200. Pub'd 2 titles 2009; expects 4 titles 2010, 6 titles 2011. No titles listed in the *Small Press Record of Books in Print* (36th Edition, 2010-11). Discounts: 10-19 copies 10%, 20+ copies 15%. 48pp. Reporting time: 4-8 weeks. Simultaneous submissions accepted: No. Publishes 5% of manuscripts submitted. Payment: One off variable payment to authors for collected works; payment of GB5.00 + complimentary copy to authors featured in Ballista. Copyrights for author. Subjects: English, Fantasy, Horror, Myth, Mythology, Occult, Poetry, Science Fiction, Short Stories, Spiritual, Supernatural, Zines.

FLINT HILLS REVIEW, 1200 Commercial Street, 404 Plumb Hall Campus Box 4019, Emporia, KS 66801. "Flint Hills Review is an annual publication with a national circulation. We publish work with a particular interest in region, including regions of place, regions of ethnicity, regions of gender, and regions of memory. We welcome poetry, short fiction, nonfiction of literary quality, and art which can be successfully reproduced into black and white photography. The staff reads from January to mid-March each year. Manuscripts will not be returned unless accompanied by a SASE. Although we do accept simultaneous submissions, as a courtesy, please notify us at once if your work is accepted elsewhere."

Floating Bridge Press, Kathleen Flenniken, Editor; Devon Musgrave, Editor; Ron Starr, Editor; John Pierce, Editor; Joel Panchot, Editor; Jeff Crandall, Executive Director, PO Box 18814, Seattle, WA 98118, www.floatingbridgepress.org. E-mail: floatingbridgepress@yahoo.com. 1994. Poetry. "We publish at least 1 poetry chapbook and 1 poetry anthology per year from manuscripts submitted to our annual regional competition. We are committed to publishing high-quality books, printed on acid-free, archival-quality paper, with cardstock cover and engaging cover art. See website for guidelines; $10.00 ppd. for sample book. We have a variety of tastes, but tend to prefer manuscripts that hold together thematically as a collection." avg. press run 400 chapbook; 500-1000 anthology. Pub'd 2 titles 2009; expects 3 titles 2010, 2 titles 2011. 28 titles listed in the *Small Press Record of Books in Print* (36th Edition, 2010-11). Discounts: bookstores and libraries 40%. Chapbooks 40pp, anthologies 85-136pp. Reporting time: 3-6 months. Simultaneous submissions accepted: yes. Payment: honorarium plus copies. Copyrights for author. Subject: Poetry.

Floreant Press, Barbara Baer, 6195 Anderson Rd, Forestville, CA 95436, 7078877868. 1995. Poetry, fiction, non-fiction. "First two books were collections of regional women's writing from northern California of an environmental shade but not programmatic. Fiction, essays, poetry, artwork included. Third book, a volume of poetry by Fionna Perkins, also from the north coast of California. Fourth book, another collection with theme of tea, with color photographs. Fifth book this year: collection of travel essays by Maxine Rose Schur with illustrations. In 2006, Floreant published "Pomegranate Roads: A Soviet Botanist's Exile from Eden" by Dr. Gregory Levin." avg. press run 3000. Expects 1 title 2010, 1 title 2011. 1 title listed in the *Small Press Record of Books in Print* (36th Edition, 2010-11). Discounts: 2-10 copies 25%. 250pp. Reporting time: Does not accept unsolicited manuscripts. Publishes only when material or author intrigues the publisher. Simultaneous submissions accepted: No. Publishes 0% of manuscripts submitted. Payment: Varies—if it's a collection, a small honorarium; single authors receive more. Copyrights for author. Subjects: Fiction, Travel, The West, Women.

•Florentia Press, Kathleen Gehrt, 4616 25th Avenue NE #174, Seattle, WA 98105, 206-524-7084, kathy@discoverlavender.com, www.discoverlavender.com. Non-fiction. No titles listed in the *Small Press Record of Books in Print* (36th Edition, 2010-11). Subjects: Cooking, Food, Eating, Pacific Northwest.

Florida Academic Press, Alain Archambault, Managing Editor, PO Box 540, Gainesville, FL 32602-0540, 352-332-5104, Fax 352-331-6003, FAPress@gmail.com, web: www.FloridaAcademicPress.com. 1997. Fiction, non-fiction. "Non-fiction: scholarly. Fiction: serious fiction." avg. press run 2M. Pub'd 5 titles 2009; expects 6 titles 2010, 6 titles 2011. 3 titles listed in the *Small Press Record of Books in Print* (36th Edition, 2010-11). Discounts: 20% to distributers; bookstores up to 3, 20% on STOPS, 4+ 60% non-returnable/prepaid. Free shipping. 300pp. Reporting time: 2-3 months if submission is of interest; 3-4 weeks if it not for us. Simultaneous submissions accepted: no. Publishes 5% of manuscripts submitted. Payment: Within 90 days of the end of the year, 5-8% paperback/hardcover, or 10% if over 1,000 sales the preceding year. Copyrights for author. Subjects: African Literature, Africa, African Studies, Creative Non-fiction, Criticism, Culture, Current

Affairs, Eastern Europe, Fiction, Government, History, Judaism, Middle East, Non-Fiction, Philosophy, Political Science, Third World, Minorities.

THE FLORIDA REVIEW, Jocelyn Bartkevicius, Department of English, Univeristy of Central Florida, PO Box 161346, Orlando, FL 32816-1346, 407-823-2038, flreview@mail.ucf.edu, www.flreview.com. 1974. Poetry, fiction, photos, cartoons, interviews, reviews, non-fiction. "We look for the best new literary works—fresh voices and engaging characters—by new, emerging, and established writers of fiction, poetry, and literary nonfiction. Recent contributors include Denise Duhamel, Tony Hoagland, Alex Lemon, Baron Wormser, Terese Svoboda, Patricia Foster, Maureen Stanton, Karen Brown, and Marcia Aldrich." 2/yr. Pub'd 2 issues 2009; expects 2 issues 2010, 2 issues 2011. sub. price $15; per copy $8; sample $8. Back issues: Inquire. Discounts: 4-10 copies, 25%. 150pp. Reporting time: 4-6 months. Simultaneous submissions accepted: Yes. Publishes 1% of manuscripts submitted. Payment: Contributor copies for regular submissions. Annual Editors' Award winners receive $1,000. Copyrighted, reverts to author. Pub's reviews: approx. 5 in 2009. §reviews of literary fiction, memoir, personal essay collections, and poetry collections. Ads: Exchange advertising welcome. Otherwise, $500 for full-page ad. Subjects: Autobiography, Avant-Garde, Experimental Art, Book Reviewing, Comics, Experimental, Fiction, Literary Review, Memoirs, Poetry, Prose, Reading, Reviews, Short Stories, Translation, Visual Arts.

Flowerfield Enterprises, LLC, Nancy Essex, 10332 Shaver Road, Kalamazoo, MI 49024, 269-327-0108, www.wormwoman.com. 1976. "Flowerfield Enterprises continues to celebrate the energizing power of self-sufficiency by publishing books and videos which help people regain control over their own lives. Major focus is on composting organic wastes with earthworms (*Worms Eat My Garbage* has sold over 180,000 copies to date). *Worms Eat Our Garbage: Classroom Activities for a Better Environment* uses earthworms in a non-invasive manner to teach interested learners science, math, writing and other disciplines. *The Worm Cafe: Mid-Scale vermicomposting of Lunchroom Wastes* describes larger-scale recycling of food wastes in schools." avg. press run 10M. Pub'd 1 title 2009; expects 2 titles 2011. 9 titles listed in the *Small Press Record of Books in Print* (36th Edition, 2010-11). Discounts: 1-9 copies 20%, 10+ 40%. 150pp. Payment: royalties negotiated. Copyrights for author. Subjects: Animals, Audio/Video, Biology, Children, Youth, Disease, Earth, Natural History, Ecology, Foods, Education, Health, How-To, Medicine, Science, Young Adult.

•**FLOWERS & VORTEXES, CREATIVE MAGAZINE,** James Eric Watkins Sir, PO Box 11, Bedford, KY 40006, 502-663-1654 www.promiseoflight.com. 2006. Poetry, fiction, art, photos, letters, non-fiction. "Our intent is to publish high-quality poetry and prose, photographs and artwork. Pieces are selected by merit and not who you are and how many times you've been published and where. However these are things we would like to know. Read the guidlines completely before submitting, and it's not a bad (in fact it's a really good one) idea to sample or subscribe to the mgazine prior to submitting so that suitable works are submitted. We published dozens of writers. Some recent one include J.J. Steinfeld, Ben Nardolilli, Jill Koren, Ruth Naylor, Maude Lark, Joanne Faries, and many more." 2-4/yr. Pub'd 2 issues 2009; expects 4 issues 2010, 4 issues 2011. sub. price $34.00 for 4 issues; per copy $9.00; sample $5.00. Back issues: inquire. Discounts: 2-10 copies 25%. 24pp. Reporting time: 1-3 months. Simultaneous submissions accepted: Yes. Payment: Contributors recieve one free copy and a discount on others. Copyrighted, reverts to author. Ads: no ads.

FLUENT ASCENSION, Warren Norgaard, c/o FIERCE Concepts, PO Box 14581, Phoenix, AZ 85063-4581, submissions@fluentascension.com, www.fluentascension.com. 2002. Poetry, fiction, articles, art, photos, satire, criticism, reviews, music, letters, parts-of-novels, long-poems, collages, non-fiction. "We look for new innovative work in all genres from new, as well as established, writers, artists, poets, and photographers. If unsure about 'appropriateness' please query. Please note that while we do accept simultaneous submissions, we will not consider previously published material." 2/yr. Pub'd 2 issues 2009; expects 2 issues 2010, 2 issues 2011. 1 title listed in the *Small Press Record of Books in Print* (36th Edition, 2010-11). sub. price free. Back issues: Back Issues Available on CD-ROM for $5 each, which includes all back issues. Pages vary. Reporting time: 2-4 months. Simultaneous submissions accepted: yes. Payment: none. Copyrighted, reverts to author. Pub's reviews: 2 in 2009. §Poetry, innovative fiction, art, satire, essay, nonfiction. Ads: varies, please contact for information. Subjects: Arts, Avant-Garde, Experimental Art, Bilingual, Buddhism, Essays, Fiction, Gay, Journals, Non-Fiction, Poetry, Prose, Satire, Sex, Sexuality, Short Stories, Visual Arts.

Flume Press, Casey Huff, California State University, Chico, 400 W. First Street, Chico, CA 95929-0830, 530-898-5983. 1984. Poetry, fiction. "Flume Press at California State University, Chico will be closing down in September 2010. Funding cutbacks at the university have forced us to close our doors. To celebrate our 25-year span of publishing poetry and fiction chapbooks, we will publish one more book, an anthology of work from each of our chapbooks. Available in August. See our website for details: http://www.csuchico.edu/engl/flumepress/." avg. press run 500. Pub'd 1 title 2009; expects 1 title 2010, 1 title 2011. 21 titles listed in the *Small Press Record of Books in Print* (36th Edition, 2010-11). Discounts: 2-9 20%, 10-19 30%, 20+ 40%. 30-40pp. Reporting time: 16 weeks. Simultaneous submissions accepted: yes. Publishes 1% of manuscripts submitted. Payment: $500 + 25 copies. Does not copyright for author. Subjects: Fiction, Poetry, Short Stories.

Flying Pencil Publications, Madelynne Diness Sheehan, 33126 SW Callahan Road, Scappoose, OR 97056, 503-543-7171, fax: 503-543-7172. 1983. Non-fiction. "Fishing is our subject-specialty. New edition of *Fishing in Oregon* now out." avg. press run 5M. Pub'd 1 title 2009; expects 1 title 2010, 1 title 2011. 1 title listed in the *Small Press Record of Books in Print* (36th Edition, 2010-11). Discounts: 40% to retailers, 55% to distributors. 365pp. Reporting time: 30 days. Simultaneous submissions accepted: yes. Payment: variable. Copyrights for author. Subjects: Oregon, Pacific Northwest, Sports, Outdoors, The West.

FLYWAY: A Journal of Writing and Environment, Stephen Pett, 206 Ross Hall, Iowa State University, Ames, IA 50011, 515-294-8273, FAX 515-294-6814, flyway@iastate.edu. 1995. Poetry, fiction, non-fiction. "*Flyway* is interested in poetry, fiction, and nonfiction with an "environmental" sensibility or that is inextricably bound up in "place.". Recent contributors include Jane Smiley, Madison Smartt Bell, Ted Kooser, Neal Bowers, William Trowbridge, Ray A. Young Bear, Mary Swander, and Michael Martone. Reads submissions from September 15 to May 1." circ. 600. 2/yr. Pub'd 2 issues 2009; expects 2 issues 2010, 2 issues 2011. sub. price $24; per copy $8; sample $12. Back issues: $8. 120pp. Reporting time: 4 weeks to 2 months. Simultaneous submissions accepted: no. Publishes 1-2% of manuscripts submitted. Payment: 2 copies free, additional copies at cost. Copyrighted, reverts to author. Pub's reviews: 2 in 2009. §Poetry, fiction, literary non-fiction. Ads: exchange. Subjects: Fiction, Non-Fiction, Poetry.

FMA Publishing, Donna Ann Marshall, 1920 Pacific Ave, #16152, Long Beach, CA 90746, (T)310-438-3483, (F)310-438-3486, (E)info@fmapublishing.com, www.fmapublishing.com. 2002. Poetry, fiction, non-fiction. "Our Mission is to introduce books that promote positive change, self and educational awareness, compassion, effective discipline and a commitment to the betterment of self through the understanding that change starts with a solid foundation centered in God. Our Vision is to layout a foundation through our books for growth and development, inspiration and too discover that salvation comes from Jesus Christ and that walking daily in the power of God through the Holy Spirit will effectively change lives." avg. press run 2000. Pub'd 1 title 2009; expects 1 title 2010, 4 titles 2011. 1 title listed in the *Small Press Record of Books in Print* (36th Edition, 2010-11). Discounts: 1-100 copies 50%101-Above copies 55%. 192pp. Reporting time: 4-6 weeks. Simultaneous submissions accepted: No. Payment: Varies. Copyrights for author. Subjects: Crime, Fiction, Mystery, Non-Fiction, Self-Help, Women.

Focus Publishing/R. Pullins Co., Ron Pullins, PO Box 369, Newburyport, MA 01950, 800-848-7236, Fax 978-462-9035, pullins@pullins.com, www.pullins.com. 1987. Non-fiction. "Focus Publishing is a small, independent college and high school textbook publisher in the Classics, Philosophy, Political Science, Public Administration and Modern Languages. We accept proposals and finished manuscripts of any length in these areas of study by reputable scholars, professors and instructors." avg. press run 2M. Pub'd 12 titles 2009; expects 25 titles 2010, 25+ titles 2011. No titles listed in the *Small Press Record of Books in Print* (36th Edition, 2010-11). Discounts: textbook plan, library wholesaler and distributors plan, trade stores and agency plan, trade megastores, distributor and web giant plan. 200pp. Reporting time: 1 month. Simultaneous submissions accepted: yes. Publishes 20% of manuscripts submitted. Payment: negotiable. Copyrights for author. Subjects: Classical Studies, Greek, Horticulture, Language, Myth, Mythology, Non-Fiction, Philosophy, Political Science, Textbooks, Translation.

FOLIO: A Literary Journal of American University, Poetry and Prose Editors, Dept. of Literature, American University, Washington, DC 20016, folio.editors@gmail.com, www.american.edu/cas/literature/folio. 1984. Poetry, fiction, photos, interviews, parts-of-novels, non-fiction. "Recent contributors include: Bruce Weigl, E. Ethelbert Miller, Nathalie Handal, Henry Taylor, Maureen Seaton, Amy Bloom, as well as new writers. We look for quality fiction, nonfiction, poetry, and photography. Submit up to five poems or prose pieces up to 5,000 words. We read from August 1 to March 5." circ. 500. 2/yr. Pub'd 2 issues 2009; expects 2 issues 2010, 2 issues 2011. sub. price $12; per copy $6 (includes postage); sample $6. Back issues: $6. 64pp. Reporting time: 3-5 months. Publishes 4% of manuscripts submitted. Payment: 2 contributor copies. Copyrighted, reverts to author. Ads: Limited ad exchanges with other journals only. Subjects: Essays, Fiction, Interviews, Literature (General), Non-Fiction, Photography, Poetry, Prose, Short Stories, Translation, Visual Arts, Washington, D.C.

FOLK ART MESSENGER, Ann Oppenhimer, PO Box 17041, Richmond, VA 23226, 804-285-4532, 1-800-527-3655, fasa@folkart.org. 1987. Articles, art, photos, interviews, criticism, reviews, news items. "2,000 words or less. Subject: contemporary folk art. Rarely select unsolicited manuscripts. Contributors: Lynne Browne, Scott Rothstein, Randall Lott, Carol Millsom, Minhazz Majumdar, Bill Swislow, Carol Crown, Bud Goldstone, Tony Rajer, David Whaley, Jeffrey Hayes, Georgine Clarke, Betty-Carol Sellen." circ. 1.2M. 3/yr. Pub'd 3 issues 2009; expects 3 issues 2010, 3 issues 2011. sub. price $35; $60 overseas; per copy $15; sample $15. Back issues: $15. No discounts. 40pp. Reporting time: 30 days. Simultaneous submissions accepted: no. Payment: none. Copyrighted, rights revert to author after one year. Pub's reviews: 20 in 2009. §Folk art, contemporary self-taught art, Appalachia, outsider art. Ads: none. Subjects: Collectibles, Visual Arts.

Foodnsport Press, Gail Davis, 609 N Jade Drive, Key Largo, FL 33037, 541-688-8809, www.foodnsport.com.

2005. Non-fiction. avg. press run 3000. Pub'd 2 titles 2009; expects 2 titles 2010, 5 titles 2011. 4 titles listed in the *Small Press Record of Books in Print* (36th Edition, 2010-11). Discounts: STOP orders 40%. Subjects: Health, Nutrition.

Footsteps Media, Jillian Robinson, #621, 6929 N. Hayden Road, Suite C4, Scottsdale, AZ 85250, footstepsadventures@cox.net. No titles listed in the *Small Press Record of Books in Print* (36th Edition, 2010-11).

Fordham University Press, Tartar Helen, 2546 Belmont Avenue, University Box L, Bronx, NY 10458, 718-817-4781. 1907. Poetry, photos, letters, non-fiction. avg. press run 500. Pub'd 22 titles 2009; expects 24 titles 2010, 23 titles 2011. No titles listed in the *Small Press Record of Books in Print* (36th Edition, 2010-11). Discounts: Retail Trade Discount Titles (T)1 - 25%2-9 - 40%10-24 42%25-49 44%50+ - 46%Short discount titles (S)1 - 25%2-9 - 40%10+ - 20%Wholesale Trade discount titles (T)1-24 - 44%25-49 - 48%50+ - 50%Short discount titles (S)35% (any quantity). 250-300pp. Reporting time: 1 month. Simultaneous submissions accepted: Yes. Payment: Standard. Copyrights for author.

Foremost Press, Mary Holzrichter, 7067 Cedar Creek Rd., Cedarburg, WI 53012, 262.377.3180, mary@foremostpress.com, http://foremostpress.com. 2001. Fiction, non-fiction. ''Our objective is to build a fine library of books readers will enjoy. Both in hard copy and an electronic version. We are committed to great books of fiction and non-fiction. And above all else, to quality work that never lets you, the reader, down. While we prefer working with previously published authors, people who know the rules and what is expected of them, we will consider manuscripts from unpublished authors. But the work must be the equivalent of what a professional produces. By taking this position, we assure our readers quality books.'' Pub'd 6 titles 2009; expects 7 titles 2010, 8 titles 2011. No titles listed in the *Small Press Record of Books in Print* (36th Edition, 2010-11). 275pp. Reporting time: When your manuscript is received, we respond within 7-10 working days. Simultaneous submissions accepted: No. Publishes 10% of manuscripts submitted. Payment: 20% on hard copy sold through our website at retail. On wholesale, 50% of the net receipts from sales of book as collected by Publisher. On sales of electronic versions, we hold $0.97 as the transaction cost, then split the balance received with you, 50-50. Copyrights for author. Subjects: Biography, Fiction, Horror, How-To, Memoirs, Mystery, New Age, Non-Fiction, Novels, Romance, Science Fiction, Self-Help.

•**Forest Dale Publishing Company,** Kathleen Price, 2277 Windsor St., Salt Lake City, UT 84106, 801-883-9574, www.forestdalepublishing.com. 2009. Poetry, fiction, non-fiction. ''Forest Dale Publishing was formed to facilitate the publication of books written out of strong conviction by talented writers who might not otherwise be sought out in todays competitive and commercialized book publishing market. We seek writers with a fresh and vibrant skill who are willing to subsidize their project in order to maintain complete control of their work. We value an intense collaborative relationship and so are seeking only a few authors we will represent each year. We can provide a network of professionals who can assist in writing, editing, design, and promotion.'' Pub'd 1 title 2009; expects 2-3 titles 2010, 2-3 titles 2011. 1 title listed in the *Small Press Record of Books in Print* (36th Edition, 2010-11). Discounts: P.O.D. 55% trade discount. Reporting time: 3-4 weeks. Simultaneous submissions accepted: Yes. Does not copyright for author. Subjects: Adolescence, Aging, Creative Non-fiction, Family, Gender Issues, Grieving, Guidance, Handicapped, Health, History, Memoirs, Non-Fiction, Parenting, Race, Relationships.

•**FOREWORD,** Victoria Sutherland, Publisher; Whitney Hallberg, Managing Editor, 129 1/2 East Front Street, Traverse City, MI 49684, 231-933-3699. ''*ForeWord Reviews* is a print magazine and online review service for readers, booksellers, book buyers, publishing insiders, and librarians. ForeWord Reviews is published six times a year beginning with a January/February issue. We normally print 8,000 copies, with a few issues seeing 10,000+ when extra distribution is needed. Our magazine and review services affects the choices of booksellers and librarians across the country who tell millions what to read. Our typical print publication reaches an audience of 20,000; our Website receives a monthly average of 150,000 unique visitors.''

•**FORM: pioneering design, Balcony Media, Inc.,** Alexi Drosu, Editor in Chief, 512 E. Wilson Avenue, Suite 213, Glendale, CA 91206.

Fotofolio, Inc., Martin Bondell, Juliette Galant, Harold Wortsman, 561 Broadway, 2nd Floor, New York, NY 10012-3918, 212-226-0923. 1975. Art, photos, cartoons. ''Publishers of art and photography in poster, postcard, notecard, book and boxed gift formats. Recent contributors: Andre Kertesz, Edward Gorey, Gary Baseman, Robert Mapplethorpe, Duane Michals, Man Ray, Brassai, William Eggleston, Lauren Greenfield, Berenice Abbott, Herb Ritts, Georgia O'Keeffe, Helen Frankenthaler, The Quilts of Gee's Bend, William Wegman, Annie Leibovitz, Wolfgang Tillmans, David La Chapelle, Mark Rothko.'' avg. press run 5M. Pub'd 300 titles 2009. 17 titles listed in the *Small Press Record of Books in Print* (36th Edition, 2010-11). Subjects: African-American, Americana, Animals, Arts, Children, Youth, Comics, Entertainment, Fashion, History, Humor, Movies, New York, Non-Violence, Photography, Postcards.

FOTOTEQUE, Timson Edwards, Co., PO Box 55-0898, Jacksonville, FL 32255-0898, 904-705-6806, htpp://www.fototeque.com (must inquire prior to adding portfolios). 1995. Articles, photos, criticism, reviews. "We prefer work by new and emerging fine art photographers, particularly those using view cameras. Need exhibit reviews from all over the world, guidelines with SASE. Annual photo contest and free artist listings for directory section." 2/yr. Pub'd 4 issues 2009; expects 4 issues 2010, 2 issues 2011. sub. price $12.00 / $24.00 / $48.00 - a 9X12 version will soon be available. We only publish black and white work.; per copy $15 + p/h; sample same. Back issues: $20 + p/h. Discounts: request in writing on company letterhead, 40% off multiples of 10. 48pp. Reporting time: 12-18 weeks. Simultaneous submissions accepted: yes. 80% of the material we get, we publish. We only ask that it is presented in a professional manner. If you want your materials returned, please send enough postage and packing materials for their return. Payment: We publish portfolios and rarely pay cash for the photos we feature. We sometimes buy cover photos and the payment does vary widely. Normally though we pay with 4 copies for the artist and lots of exposure. We don't publish for a profit at this point in the magazine's life. Copyrighted, reverts to author. Pub's reviews: 4 in 2009. §Books and mags about photography only, fine art, commercial, anything, fine art and documentary; we only require that the review be well written. As if you were going for a Pulitzer. There is nothing more annoying than bad grammer and mispelled words. Send us a query first and make sure that photos are captioned. Do not send us a review of your own work, we usually know. Ads: We have an exchange program where we publish other service ads in exchange for ads in our magazine. Our rates range from $400/Full $225/Half $150/Quarter page. We also feature complimentary classified / directory ads. Subjects: Photography, Picture Books.

Fountain Publisher Limited, Jean-Christophe Clement, Flat 'C', 33/F, Block 10, Metro Harbour View, 8 Fuk Lee Stre, Tai Kok Tsui, Kowloon, Hong Kong, www.fountainpublisher.com. 2006. Fiction, non-fiction. "Fountain Publisher Ltd is a book publishing company based in Hong Kong, S.A.R, China.Our main mission is to find great authors from all over the world and publish them for the Asia-Pacific market.We also offer the services of international authors for the local Hong Kong supplementary school book publishers.We handle book distribution to the Hong Kong S.A.R. region and partner with distributors for other locales. While our main focus is on Asia-Pacific, selected titles are also distributed to North America and Europe.We take pride in our abilities to understand the needs and cultural realities of each of the locale we operate in. We hope that the books we publish will give its reader a novel view of his world. Recent contributors: Mark Fisher ('The Instant Millionaire', 'The Lazy Millionaire')Martin Bois, Sebastien Levesque ('Eloik')." avg. press run 4000. Pub'd 2 titles 2009; expects 9 titles 2010, 15 titles 2011. 1 title listed in the *Small Press Record of Books in Print* (36th Edition, 2010-11). Discounts: 10 copies 34%. 150pp. Reporting time: 2 days. Simultaneous submissions accepted: Yes. Publishes 10% of manuscripts submitted. Copyrights for author. Subjects: Business & Economics, Education, Fantasy, Fiction, Finances, Inspirational, Lifestyles, Non-Fiction, Novels, Real Estate, Textbooks.

Four Way Books, Martha Rhodes, PO Box 535, Village Station, New York, NY 10014, www.fourway-books.com editors@fourwaybooks.com. 1993. Poetry, fiction. "We seek to publish highest quality poetry and short fiction collections. We sponsor yearly poetry competitions. Past judges: Robert Pinsky, Stephen Dobyns, Gregory Orr, Heather McHugh. As well, we read poetry and fiction manuscripts in June of every year. We do charge a small reading fee for this service. Please go to our web site as deadlines and submissions guidelines may change." avg. press run 1500. Pub'd 8 titles 2009; expects 8 titles 2010, 8 titles 2011. 3 titles listed in the *Small Press Record of Books in Print* (36th Edition, 2010-11). Discounts: standard. Pages vary. Reporting time: ASAP. Simultaneous submissions accepted: Yes. Payment: standard. Copyrights for author. Subjects: Poetry, Short Stories.

4 Your Spirit Productions, Cheryl Bronson, P.O. Box 201718, Chicago, IL 60620-1718, 773.817.4161, 773.435.6335-Fax, cbronson@4yourspirit.com, www.4yourspirit.com. 2006. Fiction, reviews, plays. "Our mission is to publish Christian Literature that is based on the Word of God. Literature that is meaningful, insightful and inspirational with an enriching message. We focus on Plays, Poems, Comedy and Drama Fiction and prefer material which is of a non-condemning text, but causes one to look within oneself moreso than others." avg. press run 500. Expects 1 title 2010, 8 titles 2011. No titles listed in the *Small Press Record of Books in Print* (36th Edition, 2010-11). Discounts: 40% off all purchases in excess of 10 books. 288 pagespp. Reporting time: 7-21 days. Simultaneous submissions accepted: Yes. Payment: No Royalites or advances on manuscripts. Each material will be analyzed individually based on a scale. Optional. Subjects: Children, Youth, Christianity, Family, Fiction, Humor, Inspirational, Juvenile Fiction, Novels, Poetry, Prose, Relationships, Religion, Short Stories, Spiritual, Theatre.

4AllSeasons Publishing, S Goss M, P.O. Box 6473, Shreveport, LA 71136, 504-715-3094. 2001. Fiction. avg. press run 10000. Pub'd 1 title 2009; expects 1 title 2010, 1 title 2011. No titles listed in the *Small Press Record of Books in Print* (36th Edition, 2010-11). Discounts: Distributors standard 55 percent.Bookstores 40 percent. 275pp. Simultaneous submissions accepted: No. Publishes 1% of manuscripts submitted. Subjects: African-American, Romance, Women.

4AM POETRY REVIEW, Maria Thibodeau, 10631 Lindley Ave., Apt. 118, Northridge, CA 91326-3271, fourampoetryreview@gmail.com http://fourampoetryreview.i8.com. 2004. Poetry. "Conceived with the lofty belief that poetry is a form of condensed energy, that language holds power and, though it assumes different forms, one of its possibilities is to alter those who encounter it, *4AM* exists to give space to emerging and established poets who write because they cant not and to be the mere vessel through which carefully-wrought words are spread like a medicine against the eroding forces of cultural vacuity. *4AM* seeks poetry that is accessible without being shallow, rather, poems whose meaning isn't so oblique as to be irrelevant but whose language makes a visceral impact, leaves you shaken, your mind replaying the sounds over as you turn in sleep. We want: Imagery, language used in powerful and surprising ways, a careful interplay of sound and meaning. [Brand names we admire, among others: Neruda, Piercy, Atwood, Roethke, Hass, Rilke, Sexton, Hecht, Bedient, etc.] *4AM* 2005 included: matt robinson, Susan Case-Gray, Anthony Robinson, Sarah Blackman, Simon Perchik, Rebecca Loudon, Barbara Fletcher, Lyn Lifshin, Alex Stolis, Judson Simmons, Kimberley Fu, Juan Carlos Vargas, Michael Meyerhofer, Mark DeCarteret, Carine Topal, Arlene Ang, Gerry McFarland, Davide Trame, others.We do not want: first drafts, prose with line breaks, free-form gabble, obtrusive rhymes." circ. 200. 1/yr. Expects 1 issue 2010, 1 issue 2011. sub. price $5; per copy $5; sample $5. Back issues: $5. 50pp. Reporting time: 6 weeks. Simultaneous submissions accepted: Yes. Publishes 5% of manuscripts submitted. Payment: 2 copies. Copyrighted, reverts to author. No ads. Subject: Poetry.

Four-Sep Publications (see also FIRST CLASS), Christopher M., PO Box 86, Friendship, IN 47021, christopherm@four-sep.com, www.four-sep.com. 1996. Poetry, fiction, photos, long-poems, plays. "Prefer short fiction. Cover letter preferred. Desires good, thought-provoking, graphic, uncommon pieces." avg. press run 250-400. Pub'd 3 titles 2009; expects 3 titles 2010, 2 titles 2011. No titles listed in the *Small Press Record of Books in Print* (36th Edition, 2010-11). Discounts: inquire. 40-48pp. Reporting time: 4-6 week initial response. Simultaneous submissions accepted: yes. Publishes 7-10% of manuscripts submitted. Payment: Contributor Copy. Copyrights for author. Subjects: Absurdist, Counter-Culture, Alternatives, Communes, Literature (General), Poetry, Post Modern.

FOURTEEN HILLS: The SFSU Review, Creative Writing Dept., SFSU, 1600 Holloway Avenue, San Francisco, CA 94132, 415-338-3083, fax 415-338-0504, E-mail hills@sfsu.edu. 1994. Poetry, fiction, interviews, criticism, parts-of-novels, long-poems, plays, non-fiction. "*Fourteen Hills* is an entirely graduate-student run literary review dedicated to high-quality, innovative creative literary work. Submission guidelines:We accept the following unpublished unsolicited submissions:3 to 5 poems1 short story or novel excerpt (maximum around 25 pages)3 pieces of flash fiction (1 piece of creative nonfiction (note: we rarely publish nonfiction, so make sure it's of a very high quality)Up to 10 pages of experimental or cross-genre literature (including graphic stories)3 to 10 pieces of visual art, must be a series Writers may submit once per submission period. The submission periods are:September 1 to January 1 for inclusion in the spring issue (released in May)February 1 to July 1 for inclusion in the winter issue (released in December) Response times vary from four to nine months, depending on where your submission falls in the reading period, but we will usually respond within five months.Manuscripts and artwork should be mailed and addressed to the proper genre editor, and MUST be accompanied by a self-addressed, stamped envelope for notification, in addition to an e-mail and telephone contact. Due to the volume of submissions, manuscripts CANNOT BE RETURNED so please, do not send any originals. We accept simultaneous submissions; however, please be sure to notify us immediately by email (hills at sfsu.edu) should you need to withdraw submissions due to publication elsewhere. Please note that we do not accept electronic submissions at this time in the form of an email or otherwise. Please please please only send us your strongest unpublished work. Do not send us something you don't have full confidence in. We publish only the best work we receive. For examples, order a backissue or subscribe to the magazine. should include the writer's name, address, phone number and the name of the piece. Maximum word length: 5,000. Recent contributors:proseAndrew Palmer :: What She SaidSean Bernard :: The Houseguest Patricia Engel :: PalomaJoseph Martin :: The Comfort GameMarcus Practor :: Let MeRhea DeRose-Weiss :: The Neon ArtistTerese Svoboda :: Movie Business John Masterson :: WeaponsRandy F. Nelson :: For Women Are As RosesJames Carpenter :: Two Jews Walk into a Bar poetryAustin LaGrone :: Goosing the Muse :: PsalmChuck Carlise :: Katie Calls on an Evening I am Not Expecting Tom Bourguignon :: This is a Haiku Half in Sarah Cohen Powell :: The Tourist Gabrielle Myers :: The First Rain of Fall Susanna Rich :: Hush Jean-Paul Pecqueur :: Succession Myth MRB Chelko :: Definition:Gregory Mahrer :: Fable :: DriftKatie Cappello :: SignsRae Freudenberger :: Red Light, Green Light Kenneth Frost :: Stray Marc Stone :: Airport Shoeshine TransactionMary Hood :: They Call Me GirlCarolyn Hembree :: What is it that Breathes Fire into the Equation and Makes a Universe to Destroy? Steven D. Schroeder :: No Hope Except in ArmsMark Lamoureux :: [Fish Calendar6 days] Dan Pinkerton :: Scuffle at the Hermitage :: When TV Fails, There Are Always the Handicrafts." circ. 600. 2/yr. Pub'd 2 issues 2009; expects 2 issues 2010, 2 issues 2011. sub. price $17; per copy $9; sample $5-$7. 160pp. Reporting time: 2-4 months. Simultaneous submissions accepted: yes. Publishes 15% of manuscripts submitted. Payment: 2 contributor copies. Copyrighted, reverts to author. Ads: $120/$60/$30 business card/$500 cover 2/$400 cover 3, will trade. Subjects: Fiction, Literature (General), Poetry, Prose, Short Stories.

FOURTH GENRE: EXPLORATIONS IN NONFICTION, Michigan State University Press, David Cooper, Editor; Michael Steinberg, Editor, Dept. of Writing, Rhetoric, & American Cultures, 229 Bessey, Michigan State University, East Lansing, MI 48824, 517-432-2556; fax 517-353-5250; e-mail fourthgenre@cal.msu.edu. 1999. Non-fiction. "Seeking reflective personal essays, memoirs, literary journalism, and personal critical essays up to 8000 words, as well as interviews, book reviews, and photos. Reading periods March 15-June 15 and Sept. 15-Dec. 15 only. For submission guidelines and other information see our website at *www.msupress.msu.edu/FourthGenre* or email fourthgenre@cal.msu.edu. Recent contributors: Brent Lott, Floyd Skloot, Kim Barnes, Stuart Dybek, and Brenda Miller." circ. 300. 2/yr. Pub'd 2 issues 2009; expects 2 issues 2010, 2 issues 2011. sub. price $30; per copy $18; sample $18. Back issues: $18. Discounts: 5% agent discount. 200pp. Reporting time: 3-4 months. Simultaneous submissions accepted: yes. Publishes 5% of manuscripts submitted. Payment: none. Copyrighted, reverts to author. Pub's reviews: 20 in 2009. §All books of creative nonfiction. Ads: $250/$150. Subjects: Book Reviewing, Essays, Memoirs.

FOURTH WORLD REVIEW, John Papworth, 26 High Street, Purton, Wiltshire SN5 9AE, England, 01793-772214. 1966. Articles, interviews, criticism, reviews, letters, news items, non-fiction. "Any material bearing on human scale concepts—politics and economics." circ. 2M international. 5/yr. Pub'd 5 issues 2009; expects 5 issues 2010, 5 issues 2011. sub. price according to self-assessed income status; per copy £1; sample £1. Back issues: £2. Discounts: 50%. 32pp. Payment: none. Pub's reviews: 18 in 2009. §Economics, politics, ecology. Ads: on application. Subjects: Environment, Human Rights, Humanism, Political Science, Politics, Public Affairs, Society, Third World, Minorities.

Francis Asbury Press, Harold W. Burgess, Editor; Mark Royster, Director of Publications, PO Box 7, Wilmore, KY 40390, 859-858-4222, web: www.francisasburysociety.com. No titles listed in the *Small Press Record of Books in Print* (36th Edition, 2010-11).

FRANK: AN INTERNATIONAL JOURNAL OF CONTEMPORARY WRITING AND ART, David Applefield, Editor-Publisher, 32 rue Edouard Vaillant, 93100 Montreuil Sous Bois, France, (33) 1 48596658, e-mail david@paris-anglo.com. 1983. Poetry, fiction, art, photos, interviews, parts-of-novels, collages, plays. "All texts should be under 20 double-spaced typed pages—absolutely open to all styles, techniques, visions, genres, languages, but we are particularly interested in work with international and cross-cultural content. We also encourage literary work Recent contributors include: Jean Lamore, Billy Collins, Lewis Lapham, Gabriel Garcia Marquez, Aim Ccsaire, Leopold Senghor, President Jacques Chirac, George Plimpton, Octavio Paz, Jim Morrison, Vaclav Havel, W.S. Merwin, Gennadi Aigi, Maurice Girodias, Rita Dove, Frederick Barthelme, Samuel Beckett, Duo Duo, Stephen Dixon, A.I. Bezzerides, Dennis Hopper, John Sanford, Bukowski, Hubert Selby, Italo Calvino, Breyten Breytenbach, Paul Bowles, Derek Walcott, Tom Waits, John Berger, Edmond Jabes, E.M. Cioran, Robert Coover, Edmund White, Henry Miller, Nancy Huston, C.K. Williams, and special feature on English-language writing in Paris today! 40 Philippino protest poets, Congolese fiction, the best of Swiss writing, and unpublished Burroughs. And plenty of lesser known talent." circ. 4M. 2/yr. Pub'd 2 issues 2009; expects 2 issues 2010, 2 issues 2011. 2 titles listed in the *Small Press Record of Books in Print* (36th Edition, 2010-11). sub. price $38 (4 issues), $60 instit.; per copy $10; sample $9. Back issues: issues 1-5 pack for $70. Discounts: 40% for bookstores and orders over 6 copies. 224pp. Reporting time: 12 weeks. Simultaneous submissions accepted: yes. Publishes 5% of manuscripts submitted. Payment: 2 copies plus $5/printed page. Copyrighted, reverts to author. Pub's reviews. §Literature, poetry, politics, art, translation, interviews. Ads: $1,000/$500/$3500 back cover. Subjects: Arts, Avant-Garde, Experimental Art, Fiction, France, French, Jack Kerouac, Literary Review, Magazines, Poetry, Translation.

Free Books Inc., Ronnie Lane Sr., 1787 Rhoda, Lowell, MI 49331. 1973. Poetry, art, interviews, reviews, long-poems. avg. press run 1000. Pub'd 7 titles 2009; expects 5 titles 2010, 9 titles 2011. 3 titles listed in the *Small Press Record of Books in Print* (36th Edition, 2010-11). 24-48pp. Simultaneous submissions accepted: Yes. Publishes 50% of manuscripts submitted. Payment: copies: approx 25. Copyrights for author. Subjects: Photography, Poetry, Science Fiction, Tapes & Records, Visual Arts.

Free People Press (see also BOTH SIDES NOW), Elihu Edelson, 10547 State Hwy 110 N, Tyler, TX 75704-3731. 1974. "The main function of Free People Press is to publish *Both Sides Now*. It also publishes a few saddle-stitched booklets, both original and reprints." No titles listed in the *Small Press Record of Books in Print* (36th Edition, 2010-11). Reporting time: varies. Payment: copies. Author retains copyright. Subjects: Fiction, Metaphysics, New Age, Non-Violence, Occult, Peace, Philosophy, Politics, Religion, Reprints.

FREEDOM AND STRENGTH PRESS FORUM, Scars Publications, Gabriel Athens, Scars Publications, 829 Brian Court, Gurnee, IL 60031-3155, Editor@scars.tv, http://scars.tv to forum: http://www.quicktopic.com/5/H/xp9RaQTGMyH7EUeK5ZrQ. 1999. Poetry, fiction, art, photos, letters, long-poems, collages, non-fiction. "You can't be strong or free if you don't speak up. A lot of people have very good ideas and most do not feel as if their voice can be heard. We want to make sure you have your space and your opportunity to be heard. All postings to our boards are considered 'published'; if you are interested in having your essays or input published in print form you can e-mail, asking about your work being added on to Scars Publications' collection books (with *children, churches and daddies* and *down in the dirt* magazines as well). We want people to be heard when it feels like no one is there to listen, because no one should be stopped from thinking and expressing their ideas." circ. Internet only. Reporting time: work can be posted directly to the website, so response is immediate. Simultaneous submissions accepted: Yes. Publishes 100% of manuscripts submitted. Payment: appearance on the Internet. Not copyrighted. Subjects: Arts, Chicago, Counter-Culture, Alternatives, Communes, Culture, Feminism, Fiction, Graphics, Journals, Language, Magazines, Midwest, Photography, Poetry, Women.

THE FREEDONIA GAZETTE: The Magazine Devoted to the Marx Brothers, Paul G. Wesolowski, Editor-in-Chief, 335 Fieldstone Drive, New Hope, PA 18938-1224, 215-862-9734. 1978. Fiction, articles, photos, cartoons, interviews, satire, criticism, reviews, letters, plays, news items, non-fiction. "Articles range from 1 typewritten page (double-spaced) to 15 pages. We deal mainly with articles on the Marx Brothers and people associated with them, reviews of books on these topics, reviews of stage shows impersonating them, interviews with people who worked with the Marxes and with impersonators. We're especially in need of artwork, either drawings or caricatures of the Marxes. We have a strong reputation for well-researched articles which turn up facts not known to most fans and fanatics. U.K. subscriptions/submissions: Dr. Raymond D. White, 137 Easterly Road, Leeds LS8 2RY England." circ. 500. 2/yr. Pub'd 2 issues 2009; expects 2 issues 2010, 2 issues 2011. sub. price $10; per copy $5; sample $5. Back issues: $5 when available (#1-#4,#8 currently sold-out). Discounts: 10 or more of the same issue (current or back issues) $4.50 each; 50 or more (mix and match current and/or back issues) $4 each. 20pp. Reporting time: maximum 1 month. Simultaneous submissions accepted: yes. Publishes 75% of manuscripts submitted. Payment: sample copy of issue the work appears in. yes/no. Pub's reviews: 4 in 2009. §Marx Brothers, humor, classic film comedy. Subjects: Biography, Humor, Movies, Television, Theatre.

FREEFALL MAGAZINE, Micheline Maylor, Editor; Lynn C. Fraser, Managing Editor, 922 9th Ave. S.E., Calgary, Alberta T2G 0S4, Canada. "*FreeFall* is a literary magazine that is published twice a year in print. We publish poetry, fiction, creative non-fiction, visual arts (artwork and photography in high contrast black and white format), literary reviews, author interviews, author focus. Mission Is to encourage the voices of new, emerging, and experienced Canadian writers and provide a platform for their quality work. Although we accept work from all over the world we maintain a commitment to 85% Canadian content."

THE FREEFALL REVIEW, James Hannibal, Saratoga, CA 95070, http://www.freefallreview.t35.com. 1999. Poetry, fiction, articles, photos, non-fiction. 3/yr. Pub'd 3 issues 2009; expects 3 issues 2010, 3 issues 2011. sub. price $15; per copy $7.50; sample $7.50. Back issues: $7.50. 40pp. Reporting time: we only get back to people accepted for publication. Simultaneous submissions accepted: Yes. Publishes 50% of manuscripts submitted. Payment: One Contributor Copy. Copyrighted, reverts to author. §photography & creative fiction and non fiction writing. Ads: 1/4 page B&W - $25 1/2 page B&W - $50 Full Page B&W - $100 Full Page Back Cover Color - $200. Subjects: Creative Non-fiction, Current Affairs, Environment, Essays, Humanism, Humor, Indigenous Cultures, Leisure/Recreation, Lifestyles, Literature (General), Magazines, Nature, Newspapers, Non-Fiction, Photography.

FREELANCE MARKET NEWS, The Association of Freelance Writers, Angela Cox, Editor, Sevendale House, 7 Dale Street, Manchester, M1 1JB, England, 0161-228-2362, Fax 0161-228-3533. 1968. "Provides market information telling writers, poets and photographers where to sell. World-wide circulation." 11/yr. Pub'd 11 issues 2009; expects 11 issues 2010, 11 issues 2011. sub. price overseas £29; per copy £2.50; sample £2.50. 16pp. Reporting time: 1 month. Simultaneous submissions accepted: no. Publishes 50% of manuscripts submitted. Payment: £40 per 1000 words. Ads: classified: 35p per word.

FREELANCE WRITER'S REPORT, Dana K. Cassell, PO Box A, North Stratford, NH 03590, 603-922-8338, editor@writers-editors.com, www.writers-editors.com. 1977. Articles, interviews, news items, non-fiction. circ. 400. 12/yr. Pub'd 12 issues 2009; expects 12 issues 2010, 12 issues 2011. sub. price $39; per copy $4 current issue; sample free with 9X12 SASE with 1.00 p/h. 8pp. Reporting time: within a day or two, usually. Simultaneous submissions accepted: yes. Publishes 25% of manuscripts submitted. Payment: 10¢/word. Copyrighted, reverts to author. Pub's reviews: 25 in 2009. §Freelance writing and editing, home business. Ads: 50¢ per word with discount for multiple insertions. Subject: Communication, Journalism.

FREETHOUGHT HISTORY, Fred Whitehead, Box 5224, Kansas City, KS 66119, 913-588-1996. 1992. Poetry, articles, reviews, non-fiction. "A newsletter providing a center for exchange of information on research in the history of agnosticism, atheism, philosophical and religious controversy, also with attention to topics of freethought culture including poetry, art, music, etc. Features description and listing of work in progress, short biographies of freethinkers, notes and queries, reports on conferences and historic sites, and essays on the interpretation of intellectual history." circ. 200. 4/yr. Expects 4 issues 2010, 4 issues 2011. sub. price $10; per copy $3; sample $3. Discounts: none. 12pp. Reporting time: 1 week. Payment: in copies. Copyrighted, reverts to author. Pub's reviews. §Atheism, freethought, intellectual and philosophical history. Subjects: Philosophy, Religion.

French Bread Publications (see also PACIFIC COAST JOURNAL), Stillson Graham, P.O. Box 56, Carlsbad, CA 92018. 1992. Poetry, fiction. "Solely prints books authored by Stillson Graham. Does not accept manuscripts for book or chapbook publishing." avg. press run 300. Expects 1 title 2010, 1 title 2011. 1 title listed in the *Small Press Record of Books in Print* (36th Edition, 2010-11). No discounts. 320pp. Subjects: Fiction, Poetry.

FRESHWATER, Edwina Trentham, 170 Elm Street, Enfield, CT 06082-3873, 860-253-3105, freshwater@acc.commnet.edu, www.acc.commnet.edu/freshwater.htm. 2000. Poetry. "No length limit, but we are looking for originality and craft. We are unlikely to publish haiku unless it is exceptional. Submit up to five poems between August 15 and December 15 with name, address, and e-mail on each poem. Recent contributors include Margaret Gibson, Robert Cording, John Surowiecki, and Ellen Dore Watson. SASE for notification only." circ. 500. 1/yr. Pub'd 1 issue 2009; expects 1 issue 2010, 1 issue 2011. sub. price $6 + $1.00 postage and handling annually; per copy $6; sample $6 + $1.00 postage and handling. Back issues: $6.00 + $1.00 postage and handling for back issues. 70pp. Reporting time: 2-3 months. We accept simultaneous submissions if indicated and notified if accepted elsewhere. Publishes 5% of manuscripts submitted. Payment: 2 copies. Copyrighted, reverts to author. Ads: none. Subject: Poetry.

Friendly Oaks Publications, James D. Sutton, 227 Bunker Hill, PO Box 662, Pleasanton, TX 78064-0662, 830-569-3586, Fax 830-281-2617, E-mail friendly@docspeak.com. 1990. Non-fiction. avg. press run 5-7M. Pub'd 6 titles 2009; expects 3 titles 2010, 4 titles 2011. 3 titles listed in the *Small Press Record of Books in Print* (36th Edition, 2010-11). Discounts: bulk. 200pp. Reporting time: 6 weeks. Simultaneous submissions accepted: yes. Publishes 5-10% of manuscripts submitted. Payment: negotiable. Copyrights for author. Subjects: Consulting, Education, Family, Inspirational, Psychology.

FRIENDS OF PEACE PILGRIM, Bruce Nichols, Editor, PO Box 2207, Shelton, CT 06484. 1987. "Our newsletter focuses on the life of Peace Pilgrim and how her 28 year pilgrimage for peace and message continues to inspire people today. We are interested in current pilgrims and walkers who are traveling for peace and in stories and issues that enhance and inspire the lives of our readers to create more peace in their own lives, families, and communites. Friends of Peace Pilgrim is an all-volunteer non-profit organization. Our newsletter is distributed freely. We do not offer compensation for articles." circ. 6000. 3/yr. Pub'd 3 issues 2009; expects 3 issues 2010, 3 issues 2011. sub. price free; per copy free; sample free. Back issues: free. 8pp. Payment: none. Not copyrighted. Ads: none. Subjects: Community, Environment, Human Rights, Non-Violence, Peace, Spiritual.

•FRIGG: A Magazine of Fiction & Poetry, Ellen Parker, Publisher, Website: http://www.friggmagazine.com, webmaster@friggmagazine.com. "*FRiGG:* A Magazine of Fiction and Poetry, edited by Ellen Parker, has been publishing fiction and poetry for more than six years, since summer 2003. As of mid-2009, the tiny crew has put out twenty-five issues, with no end in sight. Over time it has become one of the premiere electronic literary journals. In an interview conducted by the writer Elizabeth Glixman, Ellen Parker once said, in an answer to the question, What kind of writing do you look for?: Above all, honest and daring. I would like writers to send FRiGG the stuff they wouldn't show their mother—and they certainly would not send to any self-respecting lit mag. So send it to us." No titles listed in the *Small Press Record of Books in Print* (36th Edition, 2010-11).

Frith Press (see also EKPHRASIS), Laverne Frith, Editor; Carol Frith, Editor, PO Box 161236, Sacramento, CA 95816-1236, www.ekphrasisjournal.com. 1995. Poetry. "After 2003, we are suspending our annual chapbook competition until further notice. We will continue to publish chapbooks from time to time by invitation only." avg. press run 200. 12 titles listed in the *Small Press Record of Books in Print* (36th Edition, 2010-11). 32pp. Does not copyright for author. Subject: Poetry.

FROGPOND: Journal of the Haiku Society of America, Haiku Society of America, George Swede, Editor; Anita Krumins, Assistant Editor, PO Box 279, Station P, Toronto, Ontario M5S 2S8, Canada, gswede@ryerson.ca. 1978. Poetry, articles, criticism, reviews. "Publishes Japanese short form poetry as well as articles and book reviews." circ. 1,000. 3/yr. Pub'd 3 issues 2009; expects 3 issues 2010, 3 issues 2011. sub. price $33 USA and Canada and $45 elsewhere; per copy $10 USA and Canada and $14 elsewhere; sample $10 USA and Canada and $14 elsewhere. Back issues: same. Discounts: none. 120pp. Reporting time: two weeks after the end of each submission period. Simultaneous submissions accepted: no. Publishes less than 10% of manuscripts submitted. Copyrighted, reverts to author. Pub's reviews: 54 in 2009. §Japanese short form poetry. Ads: none. Subject: Haiku.

From Here Press (see also XTRAS), William J. Higginson, Penny Harter, PO Box 1402, Summit, NJ 07902-1402. 1975. Poetry, criticism, long-poems, non-fiction. "Not reading unsolicited work. *XTRAS* is a series title." avg. press run 200-1M. Pub'd 1 title 2009; expects 1 title 2011. 22 titles listed in the *Small Press Record of Books in Print* (36th Edition, 2010-11). Discounts: 40% to trade (5 mixed titles). 40-120pp. Payment: varies. Copyrights for author. Subjects: Criticism, Haiku, Poetry.

Front Row Experience, Frank Alexander, 540 Discovery Bay Boulevard, Discovery Bay, CA 94514,

925-634-5710. 1974. Art, cartoons, non-fiction. "One page letter of inquiry first, submit manuscript only when requested. Submitted manuscripts should include self-addressed-stamped-return envelopes and should be typed double space of about 200 8-1/2 X 11 size pages. They should be lesson plans or guidebooks for *teachers* from preschool to 6th Grade. We are not interested in areas other than 'perceptual-motor development', 'movement education', 'special education.' Some recently published books are: *Funsical Fitness, School Based Home Developmental P.E. Program, Dimondball Games.*" avg. press run 500. 9 titles listed in the *Small Press Record of Books in Print* (36th Edition, 2010-11). Discounts: 1+ 20%, 5+ 45%, 100+ 50%. 100pp. Reporting time: 1 week for letter of inquiry, 1 month for manuscript (include SASE), and only send manuscript when requested to do so. Simultaneous submissions accepted: yes. Publishes 10% of manuscripts submitted. Payment: all authors 10% royalty. Copyrights for author. Subjects: Children, Youth, Education, Family, Games, Health, Non-Fiction, Sports, Outdoors, Textbooks.

THE FRONT STRIKER BULLETIN, Bill Retskin, The Retskin Report, PO Box 18481, Asheville, NC 28814-0481, 828-254-4487. 1986. Articles, photos, letters, news items, non-fiction. "The American Matchcover Collecting Club. Articles relating to matchcover collecting in America, and the matchbook industry in America, only." Back issues: $1 each plus S/H. (Minimum order 5). Payment: personal check or money order. Copyrighted, reverts to author. §Matchcover collecting-hobbies. Subject: Crafts, Hobbies.

Frontline Publications, Ernie Hernandez, PO Box 815, Lake Forest, CA 92609, 949-837-6258. 1982. Articles, non-fiction. "Books about lawyers, management, science, and computers. Am seeking manuscripts on computer technology—particularly 'how-to' guidebooks; also books about lawsuit abuse." avg. press run 5M. Expects 1 title 2010, 2 titles 2011. 5 titles listed in the *Small Press Record of Books in Print* (36th Edition, 2010-11). Discounts: trade-none, wholesaler-50%, college classrooms-10% (on verified orders: instructor desk copies-free). 279pp. Payment: 10-15% of net. Copyrights for author. Subjects: Business & Economics, Computers, Calculators, Internet, Law, Management, Politics, Research, Science, Society, Sociology, Technology.

FROZEN WAFFLES, Frozen Waffles Press/Shattered Sidewalks Press; 45th Century Chapbooks, Bro. Dimitrios, David Wade, Rick Fox, The Writer's Group, 329 West 1st St., Apt. 5, Bloomington, IN 47403-2474, 812-333-6304 c/o Rocky. 1976. Poetry, fiction, articles, art, interviews, reviews, collages, concrete art. "Additional address: c/o Rocky, Apt. #5, 329 W. 1st St., Bloomington, IN 47403-2474. Want poems using the magic of the banal, subreal, 'everyday' (cf Prevert, Zen poetry, D. Wade & Richard Gombar's poems in *Stoney Lonesomes* No. 4 & 5, Spike Jones writing about Stravinsky's shoes squeaking, etc.) or the magic of the 'meta-real' (cf Breton, Neruda, Bly, the school of Duane Locke at it's best, etc.) Frags from diaries (names changed to protect the guilty), anecdotes, weird observations, fresh interviews, art work (India ink only!) will also be appreciated. Ditto: book & mag reviews (short!). Would like black India ink sketches of poets accepted by us. Preferably self-portraits: or by fellow-artists of poets. We have been delayed until funding problems stabilize. *Zen Events, Banal Episodes* has been superseded by *Hungry Horse in a Blank Field* by Dimitrios/Wade. One copy of *Death of a Chinese Paratrooper* by David Wade may still be available at the rare (unsalable) price of $115. Three deaths in our family in a short time period, etc. But we continue to work toward publication. Plan to print special issues of a single poet, also. Actually, *Frozen Waffles* is the *anthology* of poetry and art work and short fiction, etc. which will appear irregularly until funding permits us to function on an annual basis. Are filled up totally! Will let you know in this directory when to submit again. Are re-organizing and will remain silent until finished! Please NO more unsolicited material until notified!" circ. 200-400. Irregular. sub. price will vary; per copy about $7.50 to rise to the occasion each year as inflation nibbles away; sample none. Back issues: $6 each (after 2 years: $10 each). Discounts: 10% off 5 or more. 36-80pp. Reporting time: 2 weeks-2 months; if no reply, you had no SASE, or material was lost in the mail. Payment: 1 copy. Copyrighted. Pub's reviews. §Poetry, poetics, bios of poets. No ads, not yet, anyway. Subjects: Asian-American, Book Reviewing, Dada, Fiction, Haiku, Native American, Photography, Poetry, Third World, Minorities, Translation, Zen.

Frozen Waffles Press/Shattered Sidewalks Press; 45th Century Chapbooks (see also FROZEN WAFFLES), David Wade, Bro. Dimitrios, Rick Fox, The Writer's Group, 329 West 1st Street #5, Bloomington, IN 47403-2474. 1980. Poetry, art, interviews, reviews, parts-of-novels, long-poems. "Address for packages: c/o Writer's Group, PO Box 1941, Bloomington, IN 47402. Poetry, prose poems; almost any kind of short work (plays, aphorisms, parables [modern], fantasy, Si Fi, futureworlds, etc.). Oral & visual qualities to be expressed in cassettes, post cards, poster poems, etc. Please NO more unsolicited material until notified in this directory! 'Poetry videos' in the future are a possibility! Would like *input* on this." avg. press run varies. 4 titles listed in the *Small Press Record of Books in Print* (36th Edition, 2010-11). Discounts: hope to give breaks to people over 40; mental institutions, prisons, etc. 22-45pp, 85-125pp. Reporting time: 5 seconds to 5 days; if you don't hear from us, we probably never got your material. Simultaneous submissions accepted: no. Percentage of manuscripts published depends on quality. Payment: at least one free copy of your work(s); money later, much money much later; inflation has bloated our poverty. Copyrights for author. Subjects: Beat, Buddhism, Dada, Fiction, Haiku, Indiana, Jack Kerouac, Native American, Poetry, Third World, Minorities, Translation, Zen.

Fruitbearer Publishing, LLC, Candy Abbott, P.O. Box 777, Georgetown, DE 19947, 302-856-6649, 302-856-7742 (fax), cfa@candyabbott.com, www.fruitbearer.com. 1999. Poetry, fiction, non-fiction. "We publish for the Christian audience. Our criteria is that the manuscript be family-friends, not necessarily religious. We also publish children's picture books, hardback and soft cover, full color interior pages; booklets; memoirs, etc. Fruitbearer Publishing, L.L.C. is an independent publishing house that offers services to authors who want to retain control over their creative ventures. Book publishing is a complex process that involves: cover design, typesetting, communication with editors and proofreaders, contracts, promotional materials, printer quotes, offset or POD, etc. Tiered services can be as limited as camera-ready printing or as complex as book packaging with a marketing strategy. Let us guide you through the process step-by-step, as simply and as economically as possible." Pub'd 6 titles 2009; expects 7-8 titles 2010, 7-10 titles 2011. No titles listed in the *Small Press Record of Books in Print* (36th Edition, 2010-11). Discounts: 40% retail2-10 copies 25% institutions. 200pp. Reporting time: Approx. 1 month. Simultaneous submissions accepted: Yes. Publishes 75% of manuscripts submitted. Payment: Our authors pay for Fruitbearer's services (ala carte) and for printing. They retain the books, and reprints are less costly because the design fee has already been paid. Distribution, warehousing, and marketing services are also available for a fee. Copyrights for author. Subjects: Children, Youth, Christianity, Divorce, Family, Fiction, Grieving, Inspirational, Marriage, Memoirs, Novels, Picture Books, Poetry, Quilting, Sewing, Religion, Singles.

FUGUE, Kendall Sand, Editor; Andrew Millar, Editor, Brink Hall, Room 200, Engl. Dept., University of Idaho, Moscow, ID 83844-1102, 208-885-6156. 1989. Poetry, fiction, art, photos, satire, criticism, long-poems, plays, non-fiction. circ. 550. 2/yr. Pub'd 2 issues 2009; expects 2 issues 2010, 2 issues 2011. sub. price $14; per copy $8; sample $8. Back issues: issue #13+ $5; others inquire. 100pp. Reporting time: 12 weeks. Simultaneous submissions accepted: yes. We publish 2% or less of manuscripts submitted. Payment: up to $50 for prose and $25 for poetry as funds allow. Copyrighted, reverts to author. Subjects: Criticism, Fiction, Non-Fiction, Poetry.

Fugue State Press, James Chapman, PO Box 80, Cooper Station, New York, NY 10276, 212-673-7922. 1990. Fiction. "We publish experimental novels, nothing else. We are looking for emotional, vulnerable experimental writing, not technically dazzling writing. By experimental we mean something so personal and idiosyncratic that it doesn't seem to belong in the world. Please don't send detective novels, science fiction, etc., nor ordinary literary fiction. Please query first, and please only contact by email (use the form at www.fuguestatepress.com). Please don't send mss. by regular mail...thanks." avg. press run 1M. Pub'd 3 titles 2009; expects 3 titles 2010, 3 titles 2011. 19 titles listed in the *Small Press Record of Books in Print* (36th Edition, 2010-11). Discounts: 40%. 200pp. Reporting time: Immediate response (often the same day) by email. By snail mail, it'll take months and months...don't use snail mail to query or submit to us! Simultaneous submissions accepted: but only submit by email after a query. Do not submit or query by snail mail. Publishes .3% (3/10ths of 1%) of manuscripts submitted. Payment: Minimal advance, sometimes paid in copies. The royalty rate is usually 10% of the cover price. Copyrights for author. Subject: Fiction.

Fulcrum, Inc., Robert C. Baron, Publisher, 16100 Table Mountain Pkwy #300, Golden, CO 80403-1672, 303-277-1623, website:www.fulcrumpoetry.com/reviews. 1984. Non-fiction. "Non-fiction only: gardening (including the Xeriscape Series and the Survival Guide Series,)outdoors and nature (including the Front Range Living Series and an extensive list of Colorado titles), travel and outdoor recreation, Native American culture (including the Keepers Series and Vine Deloria's God is Red), the American West (including Notable Westerners Series and Notable Western Women Series), western culture, American history, memoirs and literature, the environment, teacher resources and childrens literature." avg. press run 4-6M. Pub'd 40 titles 2009; expects 50 titles 2010, 50 titles 2011. No titles listed in the *Small Press Record of Books in Print* (36th Edition, 2010-11). Discounts: bookstore 42% for 5, 45% for 25; non returnable 50%, libraries 20%. 230pp. Reporting time: 6 weeks. Simultaneous submissions accepted: yes. Publishes 2% of manuscripts submitted. Payment: negotiable. Copyrights for author. Subjects: Asian-American, Biography, Children, Youth, Conservation, Earth, Natural History, Education, Folklore, Gardening, History, Humor, Native American, Public Affairs, Self-Help, Sports, Outdoors, Women.

FULLOSIA PRESS, Thomas Dean, RPPS, PO Box 280, Ronkonkoma, NY 11779, deanofrpps@aol.com, http://rpps_fullosia_press.tripod.com. 1971. Poetry, fiction, articles, art, photos, cartoons, interviews, satire, criticism, reviews, letters, parts-of-novels, plays, news items, non-fiction. "*FP* is right/conservative in orientation but accepts the other point of view. Likes Arthurian legend Keltic themes. Special issues for Christmas, St. Patrick's Day, Independence Day, Labor Day. Recently published Peter Vetrano & class, Dr. Kelley White, Geoff Jackson, Michael Ceraolo, John Grey, Dr Charles Fredrickson, Awesome David Lawrence. Short stories should be to the point, no more than 5 pages. *Submit by email*, text in message (no downloads); mail-ins must be accompanied by disk." circ. 500. 12/yr. Pub'd 14 issues 2009; expects 12 issues 2010, 12 issues 2011. sub. price $20; per copy $5; sample $5 e-publication. Back issues: $10. Discounts: free online. Reporting time: 1 week. Simultaneous submissions accepted: no. Publishes 30% of manuscripts submitted. Payment: none. Copyrighted, reverts to author. Pub's reviews: 15 in 2009. §Keltic issues, American Revolution. Ads: none. Subjects: Christianity, Civil War, Crime, Culture, English, H.L. Mencken, Military, Veterans,

Movies, Native American.

THE FUNNY TIMES, Ray Lesser, Susan Wolpert, PO Box 18530, Cleveland Heights, OH 44118, 216-371-8600, Fax 216-371-8696, www.funnytimes.com, ft@funnytimes.com. 1985. Fiction, cartoons, interviews, satire, reviews. "Prefer anything humorous, political (liberal), or satirical; mainly dealing with politics, relationships, animals, environment, and basic slice-of-life nonsense." circ. 74M. 12/yr. Pub'd 12 issues 2009; expects 12 issues 2010, 12 issues 2011. sub. price $25; per copy $2.95; sample $3. Back issues: $3 per issue. Discounts: available for newsstand distributors. 28pp. Reporting time: 6-8 weeks. Simultaneous submissions accepted: yes. Publishes 5% of manuscripts submitted. Payment: $160 per tabloid size (10 X 16") page, divided accordingly. Copyrighted, reverts to author. §Humor books, compilations of humor and/or political cartoons. Ads: none. Subjects: Humor, Politics, Short Stories.

THE FURNACE REVIEW, Ciara LaVelle, submissions@thefurnacereview.com, http://www.thefurnacereview.com. 2004. Poetry, fiction, photos. "Online-only. Accepts only previously unpublished work. Recent contributors: Sarah Lynn Knowles, Matt Alberhasky, Ben Berman, Jill Holtz, Jillian Foster Knight, Allison Landa, Kelly N. Patterson, Luivette Resto-Ometeotl. Contact editor@thefurnacereview.com with questions, and see us online at www.thefurnacereview.com." 4/yr. Pub'd 4 issues 2009; expects 4 issues 2010, 4 issues 2011. Reporting time: 6 months. Simultaneous submissions accepted: Yes. Publishes 5% of manuscripts submitted. Copyrighted, reverts to author. §poetry, prose, fiction and photography from emerging writers and artists. Ads: $50/link, no text; $75/banner ad.

Fuse Magazine, Izida Zorde, Editor, Artons Cultural Affairs Society, 454-401 Richmond Street West, Toronto, Ont., M5V 3A8, Canada. "*Fuse* is interested in writing that examines artworks and cultural events in terms of the relationship between political issues and contemporary culture. Articles to be considered for publication should provide a critical context for the work or event being addressed. Ideally, they should also provide some evaluation of the ways in which these works or events might encourage or facilitate social change. We are seeking writing in which strong opinions are developed through informed analysis. Keep in mind that *Fuse* is a magazine, not an academic journal. Our audience is typically well educated, but diverse, so knowledge of specialized academic jargon or concepts should not be presumed. We encourage writers to submit proposals. You can download submission guidelines in PDF format here: http://www.fusemagazine.org/downloads/FuseSubmissions.pdf."

Future Horizons, Inc., 721 West Abram Street, Arlington, TX 76013-6995, 817-277-0727, 1-800-4890727, Fax 817-277-2270, info@futurehorizons-autism.com. 1990. "Future Horizons specializes in autism/PDD information for families, employers, child care providers, and children. Although most our projects are first selected by our editor, we will accept outside proposals and manuscripts." avg. press run 5M. Pub'd 10 titles 2009; expects 5 titles 2010, 5 titles 2011. 37 titles listed in the *Small Press Record of Books in Print* (36th Edition, 2010-11). Discounts: 50-555. 256pp. Reporting time: 2 months. Publishes 2-3% of manuscripts submitted. Payment: 5-8%. Does not copyright for author. Subjects: Children, Youth, Disabled, Electronics, Family, Health, Medicine, Parenting, Safety, Self-Help.

FUTURECYCLE POETRY, FutureCycle Press, Robert S King, Director & Editor-in-Chief; Morton Rich, Associate Editor; Susanna Rich, Associate Editor; David Chorlton, Review Editor, 354 Dreadnaught Ct, Tallahassee, FL 32312, 850-559-1405, 1-800-755-7332, rsking@futurecycle.org, http://www.futurecycle.org. 2007. Poetry, art, photos, interviews, criticism, reviews, long-poems, news items. "What are our editorial tastes in poetry? We are eclectic but not easy. We want (but seldom find) poetry that achieves the "electric effect." We'll consider lower-voltage work, however, if it's otherwise well-written. We tend to like work relying on strong imagery and metaphor. Examples of things we've published in the past can be found in back issues of Gaia: A Journal of Literary and Environmental Arts (now defunct), which we published in the 1990s. See our Files section (Gaia) on our website to read or download those issues. One confession: We're not fond of haiku or any visual forms of poetry (e.g., "concrete" poetry). If you've got one such that will change our minds, though, feel free to send it. In general, we're not averse to rhyme and structure, as long as the work sounds fresh. Recent contributors include Greg Kosmicki, Donald M. Hassler, Lee Passarella, Mindy Kronenberg, Paula Brancato, Gary Fincke, Jennifer Lagier, Clarinda Harriss, Rustin Larson, Alexandra Oliver, William Doreski, and Joseph Hutchison. *Please note: We accept electronic submissions only (via email or our online form). Please see the guidelines on our website.*" circ. 300. 1/yr. Expects 4 issues 2010, 4 issues 2011. sub. price $16; per copy $16; sample $16. Back issues: $4.50. Discounts: 20%. 40pp. Reporting time: one to two months. Simultaneous submissions accepted: yes. Publishes 3% of manuscripts submitted. Payment: Pays in online publication and in one contributor's copy of the printed version of our magazine. Copyrighted, reverts to author. Pub's reviews: 6 in 2009. §Poetry Readings, Poetry Magazines, Poetry Books. Subjects: Interviews, Poetry, Reviews.

FutureCycle Press (see also FUTURECYCLE POETRY), Robert S. King, Director & Editor-in-Chief; Morton Rich, Associate Editor; Susanna Rich, Associate Editor; David Chorlton, Review Editor, P. O. Box 680695, Marietta, GA 30068, 404-805-6039, 1-800-755-7332 (FAX), rsking@futurecycle.org, http://

/www.futurecycle.org. 2007. Poetry, art, interviews, criticism, reviews, long-poems, news items. "We are open to any style, length, or subject (except hard-core pornography, spoken or visual). We eagerly look for new poets, but only those who have learned the craft. We are not interested in poets who consider themselves amateurs. For book or chapbook submission to our imprint, please submit the entire collection. There is no need to query. Complete submission guidelines are available on our website." avg. press run 300. Expects 6 titles 2010, 10 titles 2011. 4 titles listed in the *Small Press Record of Books in Print* (36th Edition, 2010-11). Discounts: 20%. 40pp. Reporting time: one to two months. Simultaneous submissions accepted: Yes. Publishes 3% of manuscripts submitted. Payment: For chapbooks authors receive 25 copies as payment. For full-length books, authors receive 25 copies plus 10% royalties. We also conduct an annual poetry competition, The FutureCycle Press Poetry Book Prize. The winner receives $1000, 25 copies, and 10% royalties. Contest begins January 1 of each year and ends March 31. Copyrights for author. Subjects: Interviews, Poetry, Reviews.

THE FUTURIST, Edward Cornish, Editor; Cynthia Wagner G., Managing Editor, World Future Society, 7910 Woodmont Avenue, Suite 450, Bethesda, MD 20814-3032, 301-656-8274. 1966. Articles, art, photos, interviews, reviews, letters, news items, non-fiction. "A journal of forecasts, trends, and ideas about the future. *The Futurist* does not normally encourage freelance writers. Most of our articles are written by experts in their field who are not writers by profession. Similarly, we do not publish books from outside our staff." circ. 20M. 6/yr. Pub'd 6 issues 2009; expects 6 issues 2010, 6 issues 2011. 4 titles listed in the *Small Press Record of Books in Print* (36th Edition, 2010-11). sub. price $59; per copy $5.95; sample $5.95 + $4.9 postage. 68pp. Reporting time: 8 weeks. Payment: author's copies (10). Copyrighted, does not revert to author. Pub's reviews: 35 in 2009. §Future studies. Ads: $1250/$750/$2. Subject: Futurism.

G

Gain Publications, Al Sheahen, Editor, PO Box 2204, Van Nuys, CA 91404, 818-981-1996. 1982. Non-fiction. avg. press run 5M. 4 titles listed in the *Small Press Record of Books in Print* (36th Edition, 2010-11). Discounts: 40%. 240pp. Subjects: Business & Economics, Politics, Public Affairs, Sociology.

Galaxy Press, Lance Banbury, 71 Recreation Street, Tweed Heads, N.S.W. 2485, Australia, (07) 5536-1997. 1979. Poetry, art, satire, criticism, long-poems, plays, non-fiction. "So far, only self-written (self aggrandizing? no) material, due to lack of real personal collaboration and ongoing contact in cases where material submitted was desirable. Traditional modes preferred with an emphasis on international contexts. Recent contributor: Sheila Williams." avg. press run 150. Pub'd 5 titles 2009; expects 5 titles 2010, 3 titles 2011. 31 titles listed in the *Small Press Record of Books in Print* (36th Edition, 2010-11). Discounts: 40%. 14pp. Reporting time: 2 weeks. Simultaneous submissions accepted: yes. Publishes 10% of manuscripts submitted. Payment: copies. Copyrights for author. Subjects: Australia, Christianity, Criticism, English, Poetry, Prose, Religion.

Galde Press, Inc., Phyllis Galde, PO Box 460, Lakeville, MN 55044, phone: 9528915991, email: galde@galdepress.com, web: www.galdepress.com. Poetry, fiction, articles, art, interviews, satire, long-poems, news items, non-fiction. avg. press run 1.5M. Pub'd 12 titles 2009; expects 12 titles 2010, 12 titles 2011. 26 titles listed in the *Small Press Record of Books in Print* (36th Edition, 2010-11). Discounts: 1-2 copies 20%, 3-4 30%, 5-99 43%, 100+ 50%. 200pp. Reporting time: 1-2 months. Simultaneous submissions accepted: yes. Publishes 20% of manuscripts submitted. Payment: 10% on collected monies. Copyrights for author. Subjects: Anthropology, Archaelogy, Biography, Children, Youth, Fiction, Folklore, Health, History, Metaphysics, Military, Veterans, Minnesota, Non-Fiction, Occult, Religion, Spiritual, Supernatural.

Galen Press, Ltd., M.L. Sherk, Jennifer Gilbert, PO Box 64400, Tucson, AZ 85728-4400, 520-577-8363, Fax 520-529-6459. 1993. Non-fiction. "We publish non-clinical, health related books directed towards both health professionals and the public. Current publication areas include biomedical ethics and guides for health profession students and educators. We concentrate on publishing books for which there is a defined need not currently being met." avg. press run 15M. Pub'd 3 titles 2009; expects 4 titles 2010, 4 titles 2011. 13 titles listed in the *Small Press Record of Books in Print* (36th Edition, 2010-11). Discounts: call. 448pp. Reporting time: 5 weeks. Simultaneous submissions accepted: no. Publishes 10% of manuscripts submitted. Payment: negotiable. Copyrights for author. Subjects: Careers, Civil War, Employment, Ethics, Euthanasia, Death, Forensic Science, Grieving, Health, Medicine, Non-Fiction, Nursing, Reference, Textbooks, Vietnam.

The Galileo Press Ltd., Julia Wendell, Editor-in-Chief, 3637 Black Rock Road, Upperco, MD 21155-9322. 1980. Poetry, fiction, long-poems, non-fiction. "Prints collections of poetry, short fiction, novellas, non-fiction and children's literature. It is best to query first before submitting." avg. press run 1M. Pub'd 3 titles 2009; expects 6 titles 2010, 5 titles 2011. 26 titles listed in the *Small Press Record of Books in Print* (36th Edition,

185

2010-11). Discounts: 40% to all bookstores; 40% to all classroom orders of 8 or more; 20%-55% wholesale; 10% courtesy library. 80pp. Reporting time: 3-6 months. Payment: 10% royalties plus author's copies. Copyrights for author. Subjects: Children, Youth, Fiction, Literature (General), Non-Fiction, Novels, Poetry, Short Stories.

Gallaudet University Press, David F. Armstrong, Director and Editor-in-Chief, 800 Florida Avenue NE, Washington, DC 20002-3695, 202-651-5488. 1980. Fiction, non-fiction. "Gallaudet University Press is a scholarly publisher specializing in work related to deafness, speech pathology, audiology, and related fields. The Press has a children's imprint called Kendall Green Publications that publishes children's texts and literature with a relation to hearing impairment, and an imprint called Clerc Books for instructional materials." avg. press run 3M-5M. Pub'd 12 titles 2009; expects 17 titles 2010, 13 titles 2011. 124 titles listed in the *Small Press Record of Books in Print* (36th Edition, 2010-11). Discounts: trade 40%, text 25%. 250pp. Reporting time: 2 months. Payment: 7.5% of net. Copyrights for author. Subjects: Autobiography, Biography, Children, Youth, Education, English, Fiction, History, Language, Mental Health, Non-Fiction, Parenting, Sociology, Textbooks, Trade, Young Adult.

Gallopade International, Michele Yother, President, 665 Highway 74 South #600, Peachtree City, GA 30269-3036, customerservice@gallopade.com. 1979. "We are not seeking submissions; do welcome inquiries about our writing/publishing books and workshops; as we begin developing CD-ROM titles, we will be looking for one freelance photographer in each state (video experience helpful); may hire one freelance writer in each state with Macintosh & who's willing to do work-for-hire following our guidelines. We also provide 3 month internships (non-paid) which include all aspects of our publishing company. Send resume and SASE for consideration." avg. press run based on demand. Pub'd 1200 titles 2009; expects 1000 titles 2010, 1000 titles 2011. 91 titles listed in the *Small Press Record of Books in Print* (36th Edition, 2010-11). Discounts: 1-9 20%, 10+ 50% non-returnable, all pre-paid; or returnable 1-4 20% FOB, 5-19 43% FOB, 20-49 45% FOB, 50+ 45% free freight. 36+pp. Subjects: Americana, Book Collecting, Bookselling, Business & Economics, Children, Youth, Cities, Communication, Journalism, Computers, Calculators, Drama, Education, English, Family, Fiction, Futurism, Games, Gardening.

Garden House Press (see also OUT OF LINE), Sam Longmire, P.O. Box 321 Trenton, Ohio 45067, Trenton, OH 45067, 513-988-7183. 2003. Poetry, fiction, articles, interviews, non-fiction. "GARDEN HOUSE PRESS (GHP) is interested in writing that promotes peace, social justice, tolerance, diversity, freedom, healthy relationships, environmental justice, creativity, and sprituality. GHP publishes OUT OF LINE, an annual anthology of writings with underlying themes of peace and justice. Recent contributors include Michael Casey, Maureen Tolman Flannery, CB Follett, Paula Friedman, Lyn Lifshin, Karen Malpede, and Liza Lowitz. GHP is also publishing the anthology, GARDENING AT A DEEPER LEVEL, a collection of writings about the significance of gardening for the individual and the community. GHP has a liberal and progressive perspective. No hate literature." avg. press run 750. Pub'd 1 title 2009; expects 2 titles 2010, 3 titles 2011. No titles listed in the *Small Press Record of Books in Print* (36th Edition, 2010-11). Discounts: 2-5 copies 5%. 200pp. Reporting time: Two months for reporting. Simultaneous submissions accepted: Yes. Payment: Contributors receive 2 free copies and the opportunity to purchase additional copies at a reduced cost. Copyrights for author. Subjects: Biography, Black, Community, Conservation, Ecology, Foods, Education, Fiction, Gardening, Gay, Health, History, Humanism, Latin America, Lesbianism, Libertarian.

GARGOYLE, Paycock Press, Richard Peabody, Co-Editor; Lucinda Ebersole, Co-Editor, 3819 North 13th Street, Arlington, VA 22201-4922, Phone/Fax 703-525-9296, hedgehog2@erols.com, gargoylemagazine@comcast.com, www.gargoylemagazine.com. 1976. Poetry, fiction, articles, art, photos, interviews, satire, reviews, music, parts-of-novels, collages, non-fiction. "We only read submissions during the summer months: June 1st-September 4th. Contributors: Kathy Acker, Gail Galloway Adams, Kwame Alexander, Roberta Allen, Nin Andrews, Naomi Ayala, Toby Barlow, Nicole Blackman, Victoria Bond, Kate Braverman, Kelly Cherry, Laura Chester, Jan Clausen, Quinn Dalton, Rikki Ducornet, John Dufresne, Thaisa Frank, Abby Frucht, Steve Gillis, Elizabeth Hand, Myronn Hardy, Lucy Honig, Nik Houser, Esther Iverem, Pagan Kennedy, Jesse Lee Kercheval, Doug Lawson, Nathan Leslie, Elise Levine, Norman Lock, Michael Martone, C. M. Mayo, Richard McCann, Pat MacEnulty, Mark Maxwell, Jean McGarry, Kat Meads, Thylias Moss, Daniel Mueller, Susan Smith Nash, Lance Olsen, Toby Olson, Mary Overton, Cheryl Pallant, Pedro Ponce, Shelagh Power-Chopra, Holly Prado, Kit Reed, Doug Rice, Steven Schutzman, Laurel Snyder, Marilyn Stablein, Megan Staffel, Patricia Storms, Elizabeth Swados, Todd Swift, Eileen Tabios, Eleanor Ross Taylor, Venus Thrash, Angel Threatt, Paul West, Elizabeth Swados, Lee Upton, and Lidia Yuknavitch." circ. 1.5M. 1/yr. Pub'd 2 issues 2009; expects 1 issue 2010, 1 issue 2011. 8 titles listed in the *Small Press Record of Books in Print* (36th Edition, 2010-11). sub. price $30 individuals (2 issues) $40 universities (2 Issues); per copy $18.95; sample $10. Back issues: inquire/limited. 350-500pp. Reporting time: 1-3 months. Simultaneous submissions accepted: yes. Publishes 10% of manuscripts submitted. Payment: 1 copy and 50% off on additional copies. Copyrighted, reverts to author. Ads: $100/$60. Subjects: Fiction, Poetry.

Garrett Publishing, Inc., Arnold S. Goldstein, 368 S. Military Trail, Deerfield Beach, FL 33442-6320, 561-953-1322, Fax 954-834-0295. 1990. Non-fiction. "Garrett Publishing, Inc. publishes mostly financially-based books, i.e. on asset protection and offshore financing, with the exception of *Dr. Amarnick's Mind Over Matter Pain Relief Program* and *Don't Put Me In A Nursing Home!*" avg. press run 5M. Pub'd 2 titles 2009; expects 5 titles 2010, 5 titles 2011. 3 titles listed in the *Small Press Record of Books in Print* (36th Edition, 2010-11). Discounts: U.S. book retailers, foreign accounts please inquire for schedule and terms. 300pp. Publishes 1% of manuscripts submitted. Payment: to be determined. Subject: Finances.

GASTRONOMICA: The Journal of Food and Culture, University of California Press, Darra Goldstein, 2000 Center Street, Suite 303, Journals Division, Berkeley, CA 94704-1223, 510-643-7154, Fax 510-642-9917, journals@ucpress.edu. 2001. Articles, art, photos, cartoons, reviews. "Send all editorial correspondence and submissions to Darra Goldstein, Editor, *Gastronomica*, Weston Hall, 995 Main Street, Williams College, Williamstown, MA 01267. *Gastronomica* is a vital forum for ideas, discussion, and thoughtful reflection on the history, literature, representation, and cultural impact of food. We welcome articles from any field touching on the history, production, uses, and depictions of food. Articles should generally not exceed 8,000 words. Each submission should be accompanied by a cover letter with the author's name, address, phone number and e-mail address, as well as a brief biographical statement, a 100-word abstract, and a word count. Since submissions are refereed anonymously, the author's name should appear only on the cover sheet. Send 3 copies. Manuscripts must be prepared according to the Chicago Manual of Style, with double-spaced notes at the end of the text. Artwork may be submitted as transparencies, JPEGS, or in clear photocopied form. Submissions will be returned only if accompanied by an SASE." circ. 10,332. 4/yr. Pub'd 4 issues 2009; expects 4 issues 2010, 4 issues 2011. sub. price $42 indiv., $175 inst., $30 student; per copy $10 indiv., $46 inst., $10 student. Back issues: $10 indiv., $46 inst., $10 student. Discounts: foreign subs. agents 10%, 10+ one-time orders 30%, standing orders (bookstores): 1-99 40%, 100+ 50%. 128pp. Reporting time: 4-6 weeks. Simultaneous submissions accepted: no. Payment: yes. Copyrighted, copyrights revert to author if requested. Pub's reviews. §Food studies, gastronomy, cookbooks, food and culture. Ads: $894/$600/$541 1/4 page. Subjects: Arts, Culture, Ecology, Foods.

Gateways Books And Tapes, Iven Lourie, Senior Editor; Tabatha Jones, Associate Editor; Matthias Schossig, Foreign Rights, Box 370, Nevada City, CA 95959-0370, 530-477-8101, fax 530-272-0184, orders 530-271-2239, info@gatewaysbooksandtapes.com, www.gatewaysbooksandtapes.com. 1972. "Length-varied, spiritual, metaphysical bias. E.J. Gold. Labyrinth trilogy. Publishers of Robert S. de Ropp (The Master Game), Reb Zalman Schachter-Shalomi (The Dream Assembly), Michael Hutchison (The Book of Floating), Dr. Claudio Naranjo (The Enneagram of Society), and others. We will read query letters and proposals, and we will let authors know if their books fit our list. Email via info@gatewaysbooksandtapes.com or write to our P.O. Box." avg. press run 1M-5M. Pub'd 5 titles 2009; expects 6 titles 2010, 6 titles 2011. 17 titles listed in the *Small Press Record of Books in Print* (36th Edition, 2010-11). Discounts: 25/40% trade, 50% wholesalers (negotiable). 200pp. Reporting time: 3 months maximum. Payment: negotiable. Subjects: Arts, Games, Humor, Metaphysics, Non-Fiction, Psychology, Science Fiction, Spiritual.

A GATHERING OF THE TRIBES, Amy Ouzoonian, Associate Editor; Cynthia Lowen, Associate Editor; Cynthia Kane, Associate Editor; Jack Tilton, Visual Editor; Steve Cannon, Editor-in-Chief; Renee McManus, Managing Editor, PO Box 20693, Tompkins Square, New York, NY 10009, 212-674-3778, Fax 212-674-5576, info@tribes.org, www.tribes.org. 1991. Poetry, fiction, articles, art, photos, cartoons, interviews, criticism, reviews, parts-of-novels, long-poems, collages. "*Tribes* is a multicultural literary magazine of the arts. Recent contributors are Ishmael Reed, Jessica Hagedorn, Quincy Troupe, Victor Hernandez Cruz, Jayne Cortez, Paul Beatty, Karen Yamashita, and David Hammons. We are interested in non-traditional, non-academic work only, accept few unsolicited contributions and will only return work with SASE." circ. 3M. 2/yr. Pub'd 1 issue 2009; expects 2 issues 2010, 2 issues 2011. 2 titles listed in the *Small Press Record of Books in Print* (36th Edition, 2010-11). sub. price $20; per copy $12.50; sample $12.50. Back issues: sold out except 1993. 96pp. Reporting time: 3 months. Simultaneous submissions accepted: yes. Publishes 10% of manuscripts submitted. Payment: copies of magazine. Copyrighted, reverts to author. Pub's reviews: 1 in 2009. §Art, literature, culture. Ads: $495/$395/$175 1/4 page/$100 business card. Subject: Multicultural.

GAYELLOW PAGES, Frances Green, Box 533 Village Station, New York, NY 10014-0533, 646-213-0263 http://gayellowpages.com, gypages@gmail.com. 1973. "Directory of organizations, businesses, publications, bars, AIDS resources, churches, etc., of interest to gay women and men in USA & Canada. No charge to be listed; self-addressed stamped #10 envelope for details." Print on demand, CD, online edition, mailing lists. Please see website for details. 1/yr. Pub'd 1 issue 2009; expects 1 issue 2010, 1 issue 2011. sub. price $25; per copy $25; sample $25 by mail. Discounts: 40% consigned, 50% prepaid. 554pp. §Gay-related topics, gay-supportive feminist. Ads: Contact for details. Subjects: Bisexual, Feminism, Gay, Lesbianism, Lifestyles, North America, Women.

Geekspeak Unique Press (see also PLOPLOP), John Clark, ploplopt@yahoo.com. 1991. Poetry, fiction, art, concrete art. "Recent books by Fielding Dawson, John Clark, Deb Sellers, J.T. Whitehead and Kit Andis. On-line submissions only to ploplopt@yahoo.com." avg. press run 100. Pub'd 2 titles 2009; expects 6 titles 2010, 6 titles 2011. 6 titles listed in the *Small Press Record of Books in Print* (36th Edition, 2010-11). Discounts: 20%. 25-30pp. Reporting time: 6-8 weeks. Simultaneous submissions accepted: yes. Publishes 5% of manuscripts submitted. Payment: negotiable. Sometimes copyrights for author. Subject: Poetry.

GEIST MAGAZINE, Mary Schendlinger, Senior Editor; Sarah Maitland, Managing Editor, 341 Water Street,#200, Vancouver, BC V6B 1B8, Canada, (604) 681-9161, 1-888-Geist-eh, Fax: (604) 669-8250. 1990. Poetry, fiction, articles, art, photos, cartoons, reviews, letters, long-poems, non-fiction. "Geist is a magazine of ideas and culture made in Canada with a strong literary focus and a sense of humour. The Geist tone is intelligent, plain-talking, inclusive and offbeat. Each issue reflects a convergence of fiction, non-fiction, photography, comix, reviews, little-known facts of interest, poetry, cartography and the legendary Geist crossword puzzle." circ. 10,000. 4/yr. sub. price $19.99; per copy 6.95; sample 8.00. 88pp. Pub's reviews.

GEM Literary Foundation Press, Cheryl Katherine Wash, P.O. Box 43476, Chicago, IL 60643-0476, 773-445-4946. 2002. Poetry, fiction, articles, art, photos, cartoons, interviews, satire, criticism, reviews, music, letters, parts-of-novels, long-poems, collages, plays, concrete art, news items, non-fiction. No titles listed in the *Small Press Record of Books in Print* (36th Edition, 2010-11). Copyrights for author. Subjects: Advertising, Self-Promotion, African Literature, Africa, African Studies, African-American, AIDS, Alcohol, Alcoholism, Festivals, Fiction, Novels, Picture Books, Poetry, Sex, Sexuality, Sexual Abuse.

Gemini Publishing Company, Don Diebel, 3102 West Bay Area Blvd., Suite 707, Friendswood, TX 77546, Phone: 281-316-4275, website: www.getgirls.com, email: getgirls@getgirls.com. 1978. Non-fiction. avg. press run 2M-3M. Expects 1 title 2011. 6 titles listed in the *Small Press Record of Books in Print* (36th Edition, 2010-11). Discounts: 1-24 50%, 25-49 55%, 50-99 60%, 100-199 65%, 200+ 70%. 200pp. Reporting time: 1 month. Simultaneous submissions accepted: yes. Payment: 5-10%. Copyrights for author. Subjects: Cities, How-To, Men, Women.

Gemstone House Publishing, Suzanne P. Thomas, PO Box 19948, Boulder, CO 80308, sthomas170@aol.com. 1998. Plays. "Focus on real estate books- NOT actively acquiring titles now due to slow sales (our sales mirror the country's real estate market!)." avg. press run 3-6M. 2 titles listed in the *Small Press Record of Books in Print* (36th Edition, 2010-11). Discounts: orders for 5+ books 40% if returnable, 50% if non-returnable. 304pp. Reporting time: 3 months max. Simultaneous submissions accepted: yes. Payment: varies-competitive. Copyrights for author. Subjects: Business & Economics, Finances, Publishing, Real Estate, Romance.

GenNext Publishing, Debra Clayton, 103 Elliott Circle, Anderson, SC 29621, 864-260-9818. 2006. Fiction. "Looking for women's fiction, chick lit, detective fiction." avg. press run 1000. Expects 3 titles 2011. 4 titles listed in the *Small Press Record of Books in Print* (36th Edition, 2010-11). 250pp. Reporting time: 3 months. Simultaneous submissions accepted: Yes. Copyrights for author. Subjects: African-American, Fiction, Mystery, Novels.

GENRE: WRITER AND WRITINGS, AIS Publications, Alexis James, PO Box 42603, Indianapolis, IN 46242-0603, Office: (317) 856-8942, Cell: (317) 292-2615. "To offer a venue for writers in their various genre. The work, eventualy, will vary. This is a start up publication, therefore we are looking for contributors. We intend to offer contests, where we will read the submitted works and also, where we do not read submitted works. We accept queries and proposals for articles, columns, i.e., various subject matter. Standaard query letters and proposals are accepted." 1 title listed in the *Small Press Record of Books in Print* (36th Edition, 2010-11). Reporting time: 2 months. Simultaneous submissions accepted: Yes, at this time we will accept simultaneous submissions, however, we would need to keep abreast of the status with your other submissions of the same manuscript. Publishes 10% of manuscripts submitted. Payment: Magazine copies with Author's article. in the process of copywriting publication. Pub's reviews: none in 2009. §We will review the reviews of books and magazines in most genres at this time. They must be clear, concise and contain no slander. Ads: Ads are accepted, however rates are in the works and soon to be published. Look for updates in the next 3 months. Subjects: Biography, Business & Economics, Euthanasia, Death, Finances, Forensic Science, Haiku, Holocaust, Human Rights, Humanism, Indigenous Cultures, Mental Health, Native American, Non-Fiction, Poetry.

GEORGETOWN REVIEW, Steve Carter, Editor, 400 East College St., Box 227, Georgetown, KY 40324, email: gtownreview@georgetowncollege.edu http://georgetownreview@georgetowncollege.edu. 1993. Poetry, fiction, parts-of-novels, long-poems, non-fiction. "*Georgetown Review* is an annual journal publishing the best fiction, poetry, and essays we can find. We read between September 1st and December 31st only. We do our best to respond within 3 months of your submission, though that is only a guideline. Work that comes in at other times will be returned unread.If your work is published, *Georgetown Review* acquires first North American rights, which means that after we publish the piece the rights to it revert back to you. There are no length guidelines on essays, short stories, or novel excerpts. However, please limit poetry submissions to 20 pages. In all cases, please do not submit new work until you hear from us.There are no particular guidelines on style, content, or form; we are looking for the best work we can find. Fiction and poetry manuscripts are not accepted via email. Annual contest. Check website for guidelines." circ. 1,000. 1/yr. Pub'd 1 issue 2009; expects 1 issue 2010, 1 issue 2011. sub. price $5; per copy $7; sample $7. Back issues: $7. 130pp. Reporting time: 1-4 months. Simultaneous submissions accepted: yes. Payment: 2 copies and free two-year subscription. Copyrighted, reverts to author.

THE GEORGIA REVIEW, Stephen Corey, Editor; David Ingle, Assistant Editor; Mindy Wilson, Managing Editor; Douglas Carlson, Assistant Editor, 285 S. Jackson St., Rm. 125, University of Georgia, Athens, GA 30602-9009, 706-542-3481. 1947. Poetry, fiction, art, photos, criticism, reviews, letters, non-fiction. "An international journal of arts and letters, past winner of the National Magazine Award in Fiction and in Essays. Contributors range from previously unpublished to the already famous. Nonfiction preferences: thesis-oriented essays, *not* scholarly articles. Fiction and poetry selections are especially competitive. Translations and novel excerpts are *not* desired. Between May 15 and August 15,unsolicited manuscripts are not considered (and will be returned unread)." circ. 4M. 4/yr. Pub'd 4 issues 2009; expects 4 issues 2010, 4 issues 2011. sub. price $35 in US, $50 outside US (foreign prices subject to change; please check GR web site); per copy $15; sample $10. Back issues: $15-$50 depending on availability. Discounts: agency sub. 10% ads 15%. 190pp. Reporting time: 2-3 months. Simultaneous submissions accepted: no. Publishes less than .5% of manuscripts submitted. Payment: $50 per page for prose; $4 per line for poetry; plus one copy and one-year subscription. Copyrighted, reverts to author. Pub's reviews: 61 in 2009. §General humanities and arts, poetry, fiction, essays, interdisciplinary studies, cultural criticism, biography. Ads: $425 inside front/back covers / $350 full page / $225 half page. Subjects: Criticism, Culture, Essays, Fiction, Literary Review, Non-Fiction, Poetry, Reviews, Short Stories.

GERMAN LIFE, Mark Slider, 1068 National Highway, LaVale, MD 21502-7501, 301-729-6190, Fax 301-729-1720, editor@germanlife.com. 1994. Articles, art, photos, interviews, reviews, letters, news items. "We publish articles from newsbriefs to feature length in size. For editorial guidelines and a sample of *German Life*, please send $4.95 to the attention of the Editor at above address." circ. 40M. 6/yr. Pub'd 6 issues 2009; expects 6 issues 2010, 6 issues 2011. sub. price $22.95; per copy $4.95; sample $4.95. Back issues: $5.95. Discounts: bulk 50%. 64pp. Reporting time: 8-10 weeks. Simultaneous submissions accepted: yes. Publishes 20% of manuscripts submitted. Payment: varies. Copyrighted. Pub's reviews: 15+ in 2009. §German culture, history, travel, German-Americana. Ads: $2575/$1675/$1110-1/3 page. Subjects: Europe, German, History, Travel.

GERTRUDE, Gertrude Press, Eric Delehoy, PO Box 83948, Portland, OR 97283, www.gertrudepress.org. 1997. Poetry, fiction, art, photos, parts-of-novels, concrete art, non-fiction. "Gertrude is the biannual literary publication of Gertrude Press. Gertrude Press is a non profit 501(c)3 (status pending) organization showcasing and developing the creative talents of lesbian, gay, bisexual, trans, queer-identified, and allied individuals." circ. 250. 2/yr. Pub'd 2 issues 2009; expects 2 issues 2010, 2 issues 2011. 64-96pp. Reporting time: 3-6 months depending on receipt. Simultaneous submissions accepted: Yes. Publishes 3% of manuscripts submitted. Payment: Contributor Copies. Not copyrighted. §Beginning in 2006 we will publish 1-2 per issue. Ads: No advertising. Subjects: AIDS, Avant-Garde, Experimental Art, Bisexual, Feminism, Fiction, Gay, Lesbianism, Multicultural, Non-Fiction, Poetry, Prose, Short Stories.

Gertrude Press (see also GERTRUDE), Eric Delehoy, PO Box 83948, Portland, OR 97283, www.gertrudepress.org. 1997. Poetry, fiction, art, photos, interviews, parts-of-novels, collages, concrete art, non-fiction. "Gertrude Press is a nonprofit 501(c)3 (status pending) organization showcasing and developing the creative talents of lesbian, gay, bisexual, trans, queer-identified, and allied individuals. We publish the biannual literary and arts journal, Gertrude, and limited edition poetry and fiction chapbooks." avg. press run 259. Pub'd 1 title 2009; expects 3 titles 2010, 4 titles 2011. No titles listed in the *Small Press Record of Books in Print* (36th Edition, 2010-11). 64pp. Reporting time: 3 months. Simultaneous submissions accepted: Yes. Payment: Literary Journal pays contributor copy, Chapbooks pay $50 plus 50 copies. Copyrights for chapbooks only; for journal, rights revert to author upon publication. Subjects: AIDS, Arts, Avant-Garde, Experimental Art, Bisexual, Experimental, Feminism, Fiction, Gay, Gender Issues, Interviews, Lesbianism, Multicultural, Non-Fiction, Poetry, Short Stories.

Gesture Press, Nicholas Power, 623 Christie St., #4, Toronto, Ontario M6G 3E6, Canada. 1983. Poetry, art, photos, long-poems, collages, concrete art. "We are currently *not* accepting submissions. (We're interested in expansive poems with new formal concepts or unique lexicons. The content will determine the form of publication, completing the gesture)." avg. press run 100-250. 7 titles listed in the *Small Press Record of Books in Print* (36th Edition, 2010-11). Discounts: trade-40%, short-30%, agents-10%, libraries-full price. 1-40pp. Reporting time: 3 months. Publishes 5% of manuscripts submitted. Payment: percentage of print run (usually 10%). Copyrights for author. Subjects: Fiction, Photography, Poetry, Postcards, Visual Arts.

THE GETTYSBURG REVIEW, Peter Stitt, Editor, Gettysburg College, Gettysburg, PA 17325, 717-337-6770. 1988. Poetry, fiction, articles, art, photos, satire, criticism, parts-of-novels, long-poems, collages, non-fiction. "Suggested length for essays and fiction: 3,000-7,000 words. Recent contributors include: Sidney Wade, Reginald Shepherd, Rebecca McClanahan, Robert Wrigley, Alice Friman, James Tate, Debora Greger, Linda Pastan, and Robert Bly. We publish essay-reviews that treat books in broader context. Reading period Sept-May. Include SASE for reply." circ. 4M. 4/yr. Pub'd 4 issues 2009; expects 4 issues 2010, 4 issues 2011. sub. price $28 U.S., $38 Canada & International; per copy $10; sample $10. Back issues: $8. Discounts: bookstores 40% with option to return unsold copies. 184pp. Reporting time: 1-6 months. Simultaneous submissions accepted: yes. Publishes approx. 2% of manuscripts submitted. Payment: $2.50 per line for poetry, $30 per page for prose. Copyrighted, reverts to author. Pub's reviews: 16 books reviewed in 2009. §all. Ads: $225. Subjects: Essays, Fiction, Literature (General), Poetry.

Ghost Pony Press, Ingrid Swanberg, Editor, PO Box 260113, Madison, WI 53726-0113, 608-238-0175, ghostponypress@hotmail.com, www.thing.net/~grist/l&d/dalevy/dalevy.htm, www.thing.net/~grist/ld/saiz/saiz.htm. 1980. Poetry, art, photos, interviews, long-poems, collages, concrete art. "We are interested in lyric poetry and prose-poems. Open to all forms. Considerable emphasis on the lyric mode. Books, chapbooks, pamphlets, broadsides. Past & upcoming contributors: Peter Wild, d.a.levy, Ivan Arguelles, Connie Fox, W.R. Rodriguez, Gerald Locklin, prospero saiz." avg. press run 500. Expects 2 titles 2011. 10 titles listed in the *Small Press Record of Books in Print* (36th Edition, 2010-11). Discounts: 20% 1-4 copies; 40% 5-9; 50% on orders of 10 and more copies. 120pp. Reporting time: 3 months or longer, we currently have a very great backlog of submissions (please send inquiries, not mss!). No email submissions. Simultaneous submissions accepted: yes. Publishes 2% of manuscripts submitted. Payment: copies. Copyrighting for author varies. Subjects: Avant-Garde, Experimental Art, Photography, Poetry.

GHOTI MAGAZINE, CL Bledsoe, editors@ghotimag.com, http://www.ghotimag.com. 2004. Poetry, fiction, articles, interviews, satire, reviews, parts-of-novels, plays, non-fiction. "We are an online-only literary journal." 4/yr. Pub'd 4 issues 2009; expects 4 issues 2010, 4 issues 2011. Reporting time: 2 months. Simultaneous submissions accepted: Yes. Publishes 5% of manuscripts submitted. Pub's reviews: approx. 20 in 2009. §Poetry collections, short story collections, chapbooks. Subjects: Absurdist, African Literature, Africa, African Studies, Arkansas, Atheism, Avant-Garde, Experimental Art, Creative Non-fiction, Experimental, Feminism, Fiction, Literary Review, Poetry, Post Modern, Prose, Reviews, Short Stories.

•Gihon River Review, Johnson State College, Johnson, VT 05656. "The Gihon River Review, published biannually, was founded in the fall of 2001 as a production of the BFA program at Johnson State College. Issues are $5 each. Submissions in poetry, fiction, and nonfiction are read from September to May. Poetry submissions may not exceed five poems; fiction and nonfiction may not exceed twenty-five pages. Send all correspondence to The Gihon River Review, Johnson State College, Johnson, Vermont 05656. Please enclose a SASE." No titles listed in the *Small Press Record of Books in Print* (36th Edition, 2010-11).

GIN BENDER POETRY REVIEW, T.A. Thompson, PO Box 150932, Lufkin, TX 75915-0932, ginbender@yahoo.com, www.ginbender.com. 2002. Poetry, fiction, photos, interviews, reviews. "*Gin Bender Poetry Review* is a literary webzine whose goal is not to replace the print journal, but supplement it. We look for writers who practice their craft. We have an annual poetry contest." 3/yr. Pub'd 1 issue 2009; expects 3 issues 2010, 3 issues 2011. sub. price free online. 20pp. Reporting time: 4-6 weeks. Simultaneous submissions accepted: no. Publishes 10% of manuscripts submitted. Payment: 1 copy of newsletter. Copyrighted, reverts to author. Pub's reviews. §Poetry books and chapbooks. Ads: none. Subjects: Fiction, Haiku, Nature, Poetry, Prose, Short Stories, Zines.

Gingerbread House, Maria Nicotra, 602 Montauk Highway, Westhampton Beach, NY 11978, 631-288-5119, Fax 631-288-5179, ghbooks@optonline.net, www.gingerbreadbooks.com. 1999. Fiction, non-fiction. "At this time we cannot accept unsolicited mss., and will return mss. unopened, or will destroy mss. that do not have SASE. We will put out calls through the usual industry venues when our submision policy changes." avg. press run 6M. Expects 1 title 2010, 3 titles 2011. 11 titles listed in the *Small Press Record of Books in Print* (36th Edition, 2010-11). Discounts: industry standards. 32pp. Simultaneous submissions accepted: no. Publishes 0% of manuscripts submitted. Payment: competitive with industry standard. Copyrights for author. Subjects: Catholic, Children, Youth, Christianity, Creative Non-fiction, Death & Dying, English, Family, Humor, Inspirational, Juvenile Fiction, Mathematics, Multicultural, Poetry, Writers/Writing, Young Adult.

GINGKO TREE REVIEW, Randall Fuller, Editor, Drury University, 900 North Benton Ave., Springfield, MO 65802. "*The Gingko Tree Review* is a national literary journal housed at Drury University. The journal, which publishes fiction, non-fiction, and poetry, has featured writers from around the world, including Mikhail Iossel, Michelle Herman, and Rick Moody."

GINOSKO LITERARY JOURNAL, Robert Paul Cesaretti, PO Box 246, Fairfax, CA 94978, www.GinoskoLiteraryJournal.com. 2003. Poetry, fiction, interviews, parts-of-novels, collages. "ghin-*oce*-ko: To perceive, understand, come to know; knowledge that has an inception, a progress, an attainment; recognition of truth by experience." circ. 4M. Semiannual. sub. price Free downloads; per copy Free downloads. Discounts:

none. 50-70pp. Reporting time: 1-2 months. Simultaneous submissions accepted: Yes. Payment: None. Copyrighted, reverts to author. Ads: $60/6 months; $90/12 months.

GIUSEPPE: A Magazine of Literature and Impersonation, Giuseppe Anello, Editor; Vern Ferguson, Associate Editor, PO Box 236, Millbrae, CA 94030, website: www.giuseppemagazine.com. 2009. Satire. "By solicitation and invitation only. Giuseppe Magazine is the annual online literary magazine and subsidiary of Yossarian Universal News Service, a professional parody news and disinformation syndicate. www. yunews.com." 1/yr. Expects 1 issue 2010, 1 issue 2011. Copyrighted. Subject: Satire.

Gival Press, Robert L. Giron, PO Box 3812, Arlington, VA 22203, 703-351-0079 phone, gival-press@yahoo.com, www.givalpress.com. 1998. Poetry, fiction, criticism, long-poems, plays, non-fiction. "An imprint of Gival Press, LLC. We publish in English, French, and Spanish." avg. press run 500. Pub'd 5 titles 2009; expects 6 titles 2010, 6 titles 2011. 40 titles listed in the *Small Press Record of Books in Print* (36th Edition, 2010-11). Discounts: varies. 100pp. Reporting time: 3-5 months. We accept simultaneous submissions only if told that it is. Publishes 20% of manuscripts submitted. Payment: varies. Copyrights for author. Subjects: Essays, Fiction, Gay, Non-Fiction, Poetry, Textbooks.

GLASS ART, Shawn Waggoner, PO Box 630377, Highlands Ranch, CO 80163-0377, 303-791-8998. 1985. Articles, art, photos, letters. circ. 7M. 6/yr. Pub'd 6 issues 2009; expects 6 issues 2010, 6 issues 2011. sub. price $30; per copy $7; sample $7. Back issues: $7. 48-88pp. Copyrighted. Pub's reviews.

•**Glass Tower Press,** Feliza Casano, 506 Ogden Ave., Toledo, OH 43609, Phone: (419)377-1361 E-mail: gtp.editor@gmail.com. 2010. Fiction, parts-of-novels, plays, non-fiction. "Glass Tower Press focuses on young adults (13-25) and publishes novels and nonfiction that would interest any person in that age. We prefer action/adventure, soft science fiction, and slice of life novels. We also accept urban fantasy, magical realism, speculative fiction, horror, graphic novels and religious fiction. Glass Tower Press is not currently accepting erotica, romantic fiction, chick lit, art books or photography books. We are currently accepting young adult novels, a limited number of adult novels, some adult poetry chapbooks, and nonfiction for all ages." avg. press run 500. Expects 1 title 2010, 2 titles 2011. 1 title listed in the *Small Press Record of Books in Print* (36th Edition, 2010-11). Discounts: 10 copies 25%10-50 copies 30%50-100 copies 40%100+ copies Please Contact. 200-400pp. Reporting time: 1-3 months reporting time. Simultaneous submissions accepted: Yes. Payment: Royalties arranged by author and project. Copyrights for author. Subjects: Fantasy, Fiction, Horror, Humor, Michigan, Midwest, Non-Fiction, Ohio, Science Fiction, Short Stories, Supernatural, Young Adult.

GLB Publishers, W.L Warner, Editor & Publisher, 1028 Howard Street #503, San Francisco, CA 94103-2868, 415-621-8307, www.GLBpubs.com. 1990. Poetry, fiction, long-poems. "GLB Publishers has not print-published a new book during 2008. I am trying to sell the company because of health problems, so we are only adding occasional e-books. A press for books of fiction, nonfiction and poetry by gay, lesbian, and bisexual authors. Both explicit and non-explicit. Also PO Box 78212, San Francisco, CA 94107. Large GLB Internet presence for print books and e-books (downloading). Also a separate Division (Personal Publishing) for publishing assistance to self-publishers (see http://www.perspublishing.com)." avg. press run 3M. Pub'd 4 titles 2009; expects 6 titles 2010, 6 titles 2011. 63 titles listed in the *Small Press Record of Books in Print* (36th Edition, 2010-11). Discounts: 55%. 200pp. Reporting time: 2 months. Simultaneous submissions accepted: no. Publishes 30% of manuscripts submitted. Payment: variable. Copyrights for author. Subjects: Bisexual, Erotica, Feminism, Fiction, Gay, Human Rights, Lesbianism, Men, Non-Fiction, Parenting, Poetry, Psychology, Sex, Sexuality, Society, Women.

Glenbridge Publishing Ltd., James A. Keene, Editor-in-Chief & Vice-President, 19923 E. Long Avenue, Centennial, CO 80016-1969, 720-870-8381, fax: 720-870-5598, website: www.glenbridgepublishing.com, email: glenbridge@qwest.net. 1986. Non-fiction. "Currently have 5 additional titles in process, all of which are appropriate for all types of libraries (university, historical, college, community college, public, reference, etc.), the trade market and use as auxiliary text/text material for college, university, and community college as well as for business (management, sales, etc.)." avg. press run 2.5-7.5M. Pub'd 6 titles 2009; expects 7 titles 2010, 7 titles 2011. 45 titles listed in the *Small Press Record of Books in Print* (36th Edition, 2010-11). Discounts: jobber 20%, trade: 1-2 books 20%, 3-9 30%, 10-49 40%, 50-99 42%, 100-299 44%, 300-499 46%, 500-999 48%, 1000 50%. 200-300pp. Reporting time: 6-8 weeks. Payment: hard cover, 10%, pay once yearly. Copyrights for author. Subjects: Americana, Anthropology, Archaelogy, Arts, Biography, Business & Economics, Health, How-To, Music, Philosophy, Political Science, Politics, Psychology.

The Glencannon Press, Walter Jaffee, Publisher; Bill Harris, Editor, PO Box 1428, El Cerrito, CA 94530-4428, 510-528-4216, fax 510-528-3194. 1993. Fiction, non-fiction. "All ms. must relate to maritime history or subjects. We will consider non-maritime fiction for our Palo Alto Books imprint." avg. press run 1.5M. Pub'd 4 titles 2009; expects 4 titles 2010, 4 titles 2011. 41 titles listed in the *Small Press Record of Books in Print* (36th Edition, 2010-11). Discounts: 40% to retailers. Cloth 500pp, paper 200+pp. Reporting time: 2 months. Simultaneous submissions accepted: yes. Publishes 10% of manuscripts submitted. Payment:

negotiable. Copyrights for author. Subjects: Fiction, History, Military, Veterans, Non-Fiction, Shipwrecks, Sports, Outdoors, Transportation, War, The West, World War II.

Glimmer Train Press, Inc. (see also **GLIMMER TRAIN STORIES**), Linda Swanson-Davies, Co-editor; Susan Burmeister-Brown, Co-editor, 1211 NW Glisan St., Suite 207, Portland, OR 97209, Ph: 503/221-0836 Web site address: www.glimmertrain.org. 1990. Fiction. "Literary short fiction. We look for work that is well written and emotionally significant. We offer quarterly Short Story Awards for New Writers." avg. press run 12000. Pub'd 4 titles 2009; expects 4 titles 2010, 4 titles 2011. No titles listed in the *Small Press Record of Books in Print* (36th Edition, 2010-11). Discounts: Distributors: 100+ copies, 50% discount. All others, prepaid and shipped to same address, 5+ copies, 40% discount. 250pp. Reporting time: Generally two months. See our writing guidelines at www.glimmertrain.org. Simultaneous submissions accepted: Yes. Publishes 1% of manuscripts submitted. Payment: Ranges by category from $700 - $2,000, payment on acceptance. We buy 1st-pub rights. When we print a story, we list author name, year, and copyright symbol. Subjects: Fiction, Literature (General).

GLIMMER TRAIN STORIES, Glimmer Train Press, Inc., Linda Swanson-Davies, 1211 NW Glisan St., Suite 207, Portland, OR 97209, Ph: 503/221-0836 Web site address: www.glimmertrain.org. 1990. Fiction. "We look for great writing with emotional significance. New authors are especially welcome. Please make all submissions online at www.glimmertrain.org." circ. 12000. 4/yr. Pub'd 4 issues 2009; expects 4 issues 2010, 4 issues 2011. sub. price $36; per copy $12; sample $12. Back issues: $12. Discounts: 100+ copies to distributors, 50% discount.All others, 5+ copies, prepaid, 40% discount. 250pp. Reporting time: Generally two months. See writing guidelines: www.glimmertrain.org. Simultaneous submissions accepted: Yes. Publishes 1% of manuscripts submitted. Payment: $700-$2000, depending on the category. Payment upon acceptance. Copyrighted, reverts to author. §Literary short stories. Subjects: Fiction, Literature (General).

Global Learning, Paul Ahrens-Gray, President; Kimberly Lewis, Editor, 1001 SE Water Avenue, Suite 310, Portland, OR 97214, www.1night1flight.com. Fiction, parts-of-novels. 1 title listed in the *Small Press Record of Books in Print* (36th Edition, 2010-11). Publishes 1% of manuscripts submitted. Subjects: Arts, Education, Global Affairs, History, Novels, Political Science, Writers/Writing.

GLOBAL ONE MAGAZINE, Knowledge Concepts Publishing, Ella Patterson, 136 South Laurel Springs Drive, DeSoto, TX 75115, 972-223-1558. 2003. Articles, photos, cartoons, interviews, reviews, letters, news items. "Mission: To disseminate information on auto, travel, cuisine, hotels, resorts." circ. 50,000. Pub'd 4 issues 2009; expects 4 issues 2010, 4 issues 2011. sub. price $12; per copy $1.00; sample $1.00. Back issues: inquire. Discounts: 2-10 copies 10%11-20 copies 15%20-above copis 20%. 32pp. Reporting time: 7 to 10 days. Simultaneous submissions accepted: No. Payment: 10 cents per word. Copyrighted, does not revert to author. Pub's reviews: 10 in 2009. §automotive, travel. hotels, resorts, cuisine. Ads: Full page 2000Half page 15001/4 page 10001/3 page 500. Subjects: Airplanes, Autos, Aviation, Careers, Family, Fashion, How-To, Humor, Insurance, Lifestyles, Nutrition, Performing Arts, Photography, Real Estate, Safety.

Global Options (see also **SOCIAL JUSTICE: A JOURNAL OF CRIME, CONFLICT, & WORLD ORDER**), Gregory Shank, PO Box 40601, San Francisco, CA 94140, 415-550-1703. 1974. Articles, interviews, reviews. "Send editorial material and ordering information: Social Justice, PO Box 40601, San Francisco, CA 94140." avg. press run 3M. Pub'd 4 titles 2009; expects 4 titles 2010, 4 titles 2011. 2 titles listed in the *Small Press Record of Books in Print* (36th Edition, 2010-11). Discounts: Distribution handled through DeBoer, Ingram, Ubiquity. 200pp. Reporting time: 1-3 months. Simultaneous submissions accepted: no. Publishes 40% of manuscripts submitted. Payment: varies. Copyrights for author. Subjects: Book Reviewing, Civil Rights, Community, Crime, Drugs, Human Rights, Labor, Law, Prison, Socialist, Society, Sociology, Tapes & Records, Third World, Minorities.

Global Sports Productions, Ltd., Edward Kobak Jr, 16810 Crystal Drive East, Enumclaw, WA 98022, 310-454-9480, www.sportsbooksempire.com, globalnw@earthlink.net, Fax (253) 874-1027. 1980. "Contact address from May 31 to October 30 each year-Global Sports Productions-PO Box 221, Clam Gulch, Alaska 99568, www.sportsbooksempire.com; globalnw@earthlink.net; tel: 907/260-6292.We do not read unsolicited work but will accept queries and proposals. Please contact us via telephone or email first. Do Not send manuscript until both parties agree. Thank you!" avg. press run 15M. Pub'd 5 titles 2009; expects 5 titles 2010, 6 titles 2011. 7 titles listed in the *Small Press Record of Books in Print* (36th Edition, 2010-11). Discounts: 20% to bookstores and distributors. 505pp. Simultaneous submissions accepted: no. Publishes 0% of manuscripts submitted. Copyrights for author. Subjects: Careers, Communication, Journalism, Crafts, Hobbies, Employment, Reference, Sports, Outdoors.

GLOBAL VEDANTA, Swami Bhaskarananda, Allen R. Freedman, Stafford Smith, 2716 Broadway Avenue East, Seattle, WA 98102-3909, 206-323-1228, Fax 206-329-1791, global@vedanta-seattle.org, www.vedanta-seattle.org. 1996. Poetry, fiction, articles, art, photos, cartoons, interviews, satire, reviews, letters, news items, non-fiction. "1,500 to 1,700 words. Recent contributors:Swami Adiswarananda, Swami Akhilananda, Swami

Asitananda, Russell Atkinson, Swami Atmajayananda, Elias Augustinho, Pravrajika Ajayaprana, Swami Ashokananda, Ila Basu, Swami Bhaktimayananda, Swami Bhaskarananda, Dr. Kidoor Bhat, Scott Cantrell, Arindam Chakrabarti, Dr. Malay Chakrabarti, Sujit Chakrabartty, Biswaranjan Chakraborty, Ramananda Chatterjee, Asim Chaudhuri, Swami Chetanananda, Sheldon Douglass, Richard Engstrom, Allen Freedman, Devra Freedman, Dr. Amit Goswami, Umesh Gulati, Terry Jang, John Kloeck, Dipak Lakhani, Dr. Peeyush K. Lala, Mrs. Angelica Landreani, Marion Lee, Pravrajika Madhavaprana, Swami Manishananda, Charles Mathias, Swami Medhasananda, Mrs. Runu Midy, Amita Modi, Luiz Antonio Souto Monteiro, Prabhat K Mukherjee, Swami Nikhilananda, Dr. Thillayvel Naidoo, Swami Nihsreyasananda, Henrique de Souza Nunes, Bahut Pagal, William Page, Vijai Pasricha, Joseph Peidle, Swami Prabhananda, Bhaskar Puri, Mrs. Charlene Ratcliffe, Carmen Lucia Reis, Dr. Bob Rice, Mithra Sankrithi, Swami Sarvatmananda,.Swami Satprakashananda, Swami Shraddhananda, Stafford Smith, Dr. Anil Sookdeo, Swami Sunirmalananda, Dr. Mohini Sindwani, Joao Trevisan, Pravrajika Varadaprana, Pravrajika Vidyaprana, Swami Vidyatmananda, Brahmachari Vimuktachaitanya, John Yale, Pr. Virajaprana.'' circ. 900. 4/yr. Pub'd 4 issues 2009; expects 4 issues 2010, 4 issues 2011. 1 title listed in the *Small Press Record of Books in Print* (36th Edition, 2010-11). sub. price $12, $14 Canada & Mexico, $18 all other countries; per copy $3.50; sample free. Back issues: $3.50. Discounts: none on subscriptions, otherwise 40% on individual copies for resale or bulk purchase. 16pp. Reporting time: a few days. Simultaneous submissions accepted: yes. Publishes 50% of manuscripts submitted. Payment: none. Copyrighted, reverts to author. Pub's reviews: 6 in 2009. §Broad-minded religious books of any tradition. Ads: none. Subject: Religion.

Gloger Family Books, Yehoshua Gloger, 2020 NW Northrup Street #311, Portland, OR 97209-1679. 1989. avg. press run 2M. Pub'd 1 title 2009; expects 1 title 2010, 1 title 2011. 6 titles listed in the *Small Press Record of Books in Print* (36th Edition, 2010-11). Discounts: 40%. 250pp. Reporting time: 1 month. Simultaneous submissions accepted: yes. Publishes 10% of manuscripts submitted. Payment: 50% net profit. Does not copyright for author. Subjects: Judaism, Religion, Spiritual.

Goblin Fern Press, Kira Henschel, 1288 Summit Ave, Suite 107, PMB 115, Oconomowoc, WI 53066, tel: 262-567-5915, fax 262-567-0091, www.goblinfernpress.com, info@goblinfernpress.com. 2002. Poetry, fiction, photos, criticism, long-poems, non-fiction. "Most of our work has been non-fiction, memoirs, family histories, with several successful forays into fiction. We will be focussing on non-fiction, self-help books in 2008 and beyond, with one or two historical fiction under our Lisque Books imprint." avg. press run 1000. Pub'd 7 titles 2009; expects 10 titles 2010, 10 titles 2011. No titles listed in the *Small Press Record of Books in Print* (36th Edition, 2010-11). Discounts: Distributors, wholesalers: 55% Bookstores, schools, institutions: 40% We haven't really dealt with quantity discounts. 320pp. Reporting time: We respond within 1 week to acknowledge receipt; length to respond re pub/not pub depends on length of manuscript, book proposal, etc. Simultaneous submissions accepted: Yes. Publishes 10% of manuscripts submitted. Payment: It depends on the project. We've gone from royalty publisher to custom publisher and are now returning to royalty. Does not copyright for author. Subjects: Consulting, Creative Non-fiction, How-To, Leadership, Management, Memoirs, Non-Fiction, Novels, Self-Help, Speaking, Spiritual, Translation, Water, Weather, Women.

•**GOLD DUST,** Omma Velada, 55 Elmdale Road, London E17 6PN, England. 2004. Poetry, fiction, articles, interviews, reviews, parts-of-novels, plays. "There are around 350 creative writing magazines in UK, but we believe ours is the very best, and here's why...We founded *Gold Dust* because we wanted to create something fresh and new by publishing off-beat, original pieces from all genres in one place - which is why you'll find a quirky film script alongside an avant-garde poem, followed by the funniest flash fiction - we put it all together and the result is pure Gold Dust!" circ. 2000. 2/yr. Pub'd 2 issues 2009; expects 2 issues 2010, 2 issues 2011. price per copy 1.99; sample 1.99. Back issues: inquire. 48pp. Reporting time: Within 12 weeks. Simultaneous submissions accepted: No. Publishes 10% of manuscripts submitted. Payment: No payment. Free PDF copy of magazine available to download. Copyrighted, reverts to author on publication, but we retain the right to re-publish in an anthology or future edition of the magazine. Pub's reviews: 6 in 2009. §Recently published novels, short story or poetry anthologies. Ads: full page 10half page 5. Subjects: Book Reviewing, Fiction, Literature (General), Novels, Poetry, Prose, Short Stories, Writers/Writing.

Golden Door Press, Keith Walker, 6450 Stone Bridge Road, Santa Rosa, CA 95409, (707) 538-5018. 1994. Fiction, non-fiction. Expects 1 title 2010. 1 title listed in the *Small Press Record of Books in Print* (36th Edition, 2010-11). Discounts: All copies 40%. 250pp. Copyrights for author.

Golden Quill Press, P.O. Box 83, Troutville, VA 24175-7130, 540 777 3700 thewritesource@pobox.com, goldenquillpress@mindspring.com, www.goldenquillpress.com. 1988. Poetry, fiction, non-fiction. "Only do cooperative publishing." avg. press run 1M. Pub'd 3 titles 2009; expects 5 titles 2010, 5 titles 2011. 4 titles listed in the *Small Press Record of Books in Print* (36th Edition, 2010-11). Discounts: 20-40%. 200pp. Simultaneous submissions accepted: no. Copyrights for author. Subjects: Fiction, History.

Golden West Books, Donald Duke, PO Box 80250, San Marino, CA 91118-8250, 626-458-8148. 1961. Photos. avg. press run 4M-5M. Expects 2 titles 2010, 2 titles 2011. No titles listed in the *Small Press Record of Books in*

Print (36th Edition, 2010-11). Discounts: 40%. 265pp. Reporting time: 3 weeks. Payment: 10% royalties. Copyrights for author. Subjects: Health, History, Transportation.

GoldenHouse Publishing Group, Greg Roadifer, 290 Energy Boulevard, Billings, MT 59102-6806, 406-655-1224, groadifer@msn.com. 1998. Non-fiction. "Very selective with self-help emphasis. Recent/ current project: The Golden Guru Book Series." avg. press run 5M. Pub'd 1 title 2009; expects 1 title 2011. 1 title listed in the *Small Press Record of Books in Print* (36th Edition, 2010-11). 144pp. Simultaneous submissions accepted: no. Publishes 1% of manuscripts submitted. Payment: variable. Does not copyright for author. Subjects: Health, Management, Marketing, Self-Help.

Goldfish Press (see also CHRYSANTHEMUM), Koon Woon, 2012 18th Ave. South, Seattle, WA 98144-4324, 206-329-5566, nooknoow@aol.com. 1989. Poetry, fiction, articles, satire, criticism, parts-of-novels, non-fiction. "Interested in works that combine literature with philosophy and socially-conscious." avg. press run 500. Expects 1 title 2010, 2 titles 2011. No titles listed in the *Small Press Record of Books in Print* (36th Edition, 2010-11). Discounts: negotiable. 200pp. Reporting time: 3 months. Payment: negotiable. Copyrights for author. Subjects: Asian-American, Black, Native American, Philosophy, Poetry, Third World, Minorities.

Good Book Publishing Company, Dick B., PO Box 837, Kihei, HI 96753-0837, 808-874-4876, dickb@dickb.com, www.dickb.com/index.shtml. 1991. Non-fiction. "Publishing company formed to enable books to be written and published and sold to members of Alcoholics Anonymous, Twelve Step programs, recovery centers and workers, the religious community, historians, archivists, and scholars. Titles should relate to the Biblical and spiritual roots of A.A. and to the history of the basic ideas A.A. derived from the Bible and Christian sources. Exclusive distributor of Paradise Research Publications, Inc." avg. press run 3M. Pub'd 3 titles 2009; expects 5 titles 2010, 6 titles 2011. No titles listed in the *Small Press Record of Books in Print* (36th Edition, 2010-11). Discounts: 20% individual, 40% volume. 400pp. Reporting time: 1 week. Simultaneous submissions accepted: yes. Payment: 10%, no advance. Does not copyright for author. Subjects: Alcohol, Alcoholism, Biography, Christianity, Health, History, Inspirational, Non-Fiction, Reference, Religion, Spiritual.

GOOD FOOT, Carmine Simmons, Co-Editor, 44 West Hamilton Place, Jersey City, NJ 07302. "Editorial Focus: *Good Foot*, a poetry magazine, publishes a provocative selection of today's freshest poetry. We consider a wide cross-section of work, formal and informal, experimental and traditional, original and in translation, from all styles and schools. Tips from the Editor: Please include SASE for response. Please be patient when waiting for a response, this takes time and focus. Please wait at least six months between submission, we try and review work from everyone, in order to publish a cross-section of authors."

GOOD GIRL, Nikko Snyder, Candis Steenbergen, 837 rue Gilford, Montreal, QB H2J 1P1, Canada, 514-288-5626, Fax 514-499-3904, info@goodgirl.ca, www.goodgirl.ca. 2002. Poetry, articles, art, photos, cartoons, interviews, satire, criticism, reviews, music, letters, collages, concrete art, news items, non-fiction. "See writers guidelines on our website." circ. 750. 3-4/yr. Pub'd 2 issues 2009; expects 3 issues 2010, 4 issues 2011. sub. price $19.95; per copy $5.50; sample $7. Back issues: $7. 32pp. Reporting time: 2-4 months. Simultaneous submissions accepted: no. Payment: none. Copyrighted, reverts to author. Pub's reviews: 15 in 2009. §Social justice, pop culture, environment, gender, race, feminism. Ads: $500/$200/$100. Subjects: African-American, AIDS, Alternative Medicine, Anarchist, Arts, Avant-Garde, Experimental Art, Birth, Birth Control, Population, Community, Feminism, Gay.

Good Hope Enterprises, Inc. (see also THE AFRICAN HERALD), Dr. Richard O. Nwachukwu, PO Box 132394, Dallas, TX 75313-2394, 214-823-7666, fax 214-823-7373. 1987. Non-fiction. "The company published *The Dark and Bright Continent: Africa in the Changing World*, *The Agony: The Untold Story of the Nigerian Society*." avg. press run 5M. Pub'd 1 title 2009; expects 2 titles 2010, 2 titles 2011. 2 titles listed in the *Small Press Record of Books in Print* (36th Edition, 2010-11). Discounts: 35% to 55%. 200pp. Reporting time: 3 months. Payment: based on sales. Copyrights for author. Subjects: African Literature, Africa, African Studies, Business & Economics, Politics.

Good Life Products, Martha Fernandez, PO Box 170070, Hialeah, FL 33017-0070, 305-362-6998, Fax 305-557-6123. 1986. Non-fiction. "We specialize in the field of Cosmetology. We publish books on haircutting, coloring and permanent waving. Also produce videotapes. We also publish in Spanish. Not accepting submissions at this time." avg. press run 5M. Pub'd 2 titles 2009; expects 2 titles 2010, 4 titles 2011. 7 titles listed in the *Small Press Record of Books in Print* (36th Edition, 2010-11). Discounts: 4-9 20%, 10-19 30%, 20-39 40%, 40+ 50%. 200pp. Copyrights for author. Subject: How-To.

Good Times Publishing Co., Dorothy Miller, #217 - 1027 Davie St., Vancouver, BC, V6E 4L2, Canada, 604-736-1045. 1989. Non-fiction. "Most recent publication is: *Food For Success*, by Dr. Barbarah Tinskamper. At present we limit ourselves to self-help books only. In particular, nutrition and psychology. The author should have a university education of a reputable institution and have several years of experience in the field that he/she is writing about. The book should be geared to the general public; the style and format should be easy and fun to read." avg. press run 5M. Pub'd 3 titles 2009; expects 1 title 2010, 2 titles 2011. No titles listed in the *Small Press Record of Books in Print* (36th Edition, 2010-11). Discounts: 55% wholesale, 40% bookstores. 140pp. Reporting time: 2 months. Payment: 2-4%. Copyrights for author. Subject: How-To.

GOODIE, Panther Books, Romy Ashby, Editor; Foxy Kidd, Publisher, 197 7th Avenue #4C, New York, NY 10011, www.goodie.org, romy@goodie.org, foxy@goodie.org. 1999. 4/yr. Pub'd 4 issues 2009; expects 4 issues 2010, 4 issues 2011. 3 titles listed in the *Small Press Record of Books in Print* (36th Edition, 2010-11). price per copy $5. Discounts: 30% for magazines; 40% for books. 20pp.

GoodSAMARitan Press (see also NEW MIRAGE QUARTERLY), Jerome Brooke, 95/31 Moo 10 Classic Village, T. Nongphure A. Banglamung, Chonburi 20150, Thailand, 66817177941. 1991. Poetry. avg. press run 9. Pub'd 7 titles 2009; expects 9 titles 2010, 16 titles 2011. No titles listed in the *Small Press Record of Books in Print* (36th Edition, 2010-11). Discounts: 50%. 12pp. Reporting time: 90 days. Simultaneous submissions accepted: Yes. Publishes 90% of manuscripts submitted. Payment: Copy payment. Does not copyright for author. Subjects: Anarchist, Ancient Astronauts, Family, Fantasy, Fiction, Novels, Occult, Poetry, Short Stories.

Goose River Press, Deborah J. Benner, 3400 Friendship Road, Waldoboro, ME 04572-6337, Telephone: 207-832-6665, e mail: gooseriverpress@roadrunner.com, web:www.gooseriverpress.com. 2000. Poetry, fiction, plays, non-fiction. avg. press run 500. Expects 5 titles 2010, 5 titles 2011. 131 titles listed in the *Small Press Record of Books in Print* (36th Edition, 2010-11). Discounts: to be negotiated. 100pp. Reporting time: 2 weeks. Simultaneous submissions accepted: no. Publishes 10% of manuscripts submitted. Payment: to be negotiated. Copyrights for author. Subjects: Adolescence, Children, Youth, Christianity, Cooking, Fiction, Inspirational, Non-Fiction, Poetry, Short Stories.

Gorilla Convict Publications, DK Schulte, Ben Osborne, 1019 Willott Road, St. Peters, MO 63376, www.gorillaconvict.com. 2004. Fiction, photos, non-fiction. "Gorilla Convict Publications was formed to give a voice to the convict. Its anthology series, "Prison Stories", is looking for the most real, violent, and bizarre stories from the belly of the beast. Seth M. Ferranti, the Gorilla Convict writer, penned the first Prison Stories title." avg. press run 10M. Expects 4 titles 2010, 5 titles 2011. 3 titles listed in the *Small Press Record of Books in Print* (36th Edition, 2010-11). Discounts: wholesale $7.50 for bulk to bookstores. 268pp. Reporting time: 3 months. Simultaneous submissions accepted: yes. Publishes 25% of manuscripts submitted. Payment: varies. Copyrights for author. Subjects: African-American, Black, Crime, Prison, Short Stories.

Gorilla Dreamz Publishing, Viktoriya Stinson, CEO, 3579 East Foothill Blvd., #593, Pasadena, CA 91107, Viki@GorillaDreamz.com, www.GorillaDreamz.com. "We focus on publishing urban titles. Our first title is *The Chicago Red Chronicles: Pimp Life* which came out in April of 2009." No titles listed in the *Small Press Record of Books in Print* (36th Edition, 2010-11).

Goss Press, Elisabeth Schleussner, 5353 Creekside Trail, Sarasota, FL 34243. 2000. Poetry, fiction, art, plays. "No unsolicited manuscripts accepted at this time." avg. press run 500. Expects 3 titles 2010, 2 titles 2011. 1 title listed in the *Small Press Record of Books in Print* (36th Edition, 2010-11). Discounts: 2-10 copies 25%. Subjects: Adirondacks, Anthology, Arts, Avant-Garde, Experimental Art, Book Arts, Fiction, Literature (General), New York, Novels, Poetry, Short Stories.

Gothic Press, Gary Crawford, 2272 Quail Oak, Baton Rouge, LA 70808-9023, 225-766-2906 www.gothicpress.com gothicpt12@aol.com. 1979. Poetry, fiction, criticism, long-poems. "Horror, Gothic, or dark fantasy." avg. press run 300. Pub'd 1 title 2009; expects 1 title 2010, 1 title 2011. 12 titles listed in the *Small Press Record of Books in Print* (36th Edition, 2010-11). Discounts: 40%. 50pp. Reporting time: 1 month. Simultaneous submissions accepted: No. Publishes 5% of manuscripts submitted. Payment: 10% royalty. Copyrights for author. Subjects: Criticism, Fantasy, Fiction, Horror.

Grace Acres Press, Anne Fenske, PO Box 22, Larkspur, CO 80118, (303)681-9995, (303) 681-9996, 888-700-GRACE (4722), Anne@GraceAcresPress.com, www.GraceAcresPress.com. 2006. Fiction, non-fiction. avg. press run 5000. Expects 8 titles 2010, 12 titles 2011. 12 titles listed in the *Small Press Record of Books in Print* (36th Edition, 2010-11). Discounts: 50% discount. 200pp. Reporting time: Acceptance or rejection, approx. 60-90 days. Simultaneous submissions accepted: Yes. Publishes 50% of manuscripts submitted. Payment: 10%-15%. No advances. Copyrights for author. Subjects: Christianity, Family, Parenting, Religion.

Grace Creek Press, Timothy McCutcheon, 3806 Bromley Drive, Fort Collins, CO 80525, telephone 970-282-0600 GraceCreekPress.books.officelive.com. 2008. Cartoons, non-fiction. "Our mission is to provide high quality entertaining, informative and inspirational titles to parents and other caregivers. Currently our flagship products are the humorous writings of stay at home dad T.J. McKenna." Expects 1 title 2010, 2 titles 2011. 1 title listed in the *Small Press Record of Books in Print* (36th Edition, 2010-11). All trade discounts are negotiable on a case by case basis depending upon volume. 100pp. Reporting time: 2-3 weeks. Simultaneous submissions accepted: Yes. Payment: No advances. Royalties are negotiable. Copyrights for author. Subjects:

Cooking, Family, Finances, How-To, Humor, Parenting, Relationships, Religion.

Grace House Publishing, Olivia McDonald, Grace House & Associates, LLC., P.O. Box 2265, Chesapeake, VA 23327, www.gracehousepublishing.com or www.cadipspress.com. Non-fiction. "The primary mission of Grace House Publishing as a division of Grace House & Associates, LLC, is to provide teaching materials and scholarly/devotional works for the purpose of enhancing quality of individual and family home life by providing a rewarding learning experience for adults and children consistent with the biblical worldview. Publications cover a wide array of themes associated with improved quality of life. Our publications include themes of social justice and personal faithfulness in response to the call for us to be *'Salt'* and *'Light'* in our homes, in our communities, and in our world. Each offering encourages God's love in action." Pub'd 3 titles 2009; expects 5-7 titles 2010, 8-10 titles 2011. 2 titles listed in the *Small Press Record of Books in Print* (36th Edition, 2010-11). 150-300pp. Reporting time: 6-8 weeks. Simultaneous submissions accepted: No. Payment: Royalty 5-8% on retail; some outright purchases. Complete manuscript; e-query OK. Subjects: Children, Youth, Christianity, Family, Non-Fiction, Public Affairs, Senior Citizens, Women, Young Adult.

GRAIN MAGAZINE, Saskatchewan Writers Guild, PO Box 67, Saskatoon, SK S7K 3K1, Canada, 306-244-2828, grainmag@sasktel.net. 1973. Poetry, fiction, art, long-poems, non-fiction. "Grain Magazine, published four times per year, is an internationally acclaimed literary journal that publishes engaging, surprising, eclectic, and challenging writing and art by Canadian and international writers and artists. If you are interested in submitting your work to Grain, take a look at the following Submission Guidelines. If possible, read back issues of our magazine before submitting. Sample issues of the latest issue of Grain are available for $13.00 (including GST and postage). If you'd like to order a copy, go to the Subscriptions section of our website. Grain has a nine-month reading period, September 1st to May 31st. Manuscripts postmarked and/or received between June 1st and August 31st will not be read. Please do not submit more than twice in one reading period (third and subsequent submissions will be returned, unread). If you have work currently under consideration by Grain, please do not submit again until you have received a response to that submission. Send typed, unpublished material only (we consider work published on-line to be previously published). Simultaneous submissions will not be considered. Please only submit work in one genre at one time. Poetry: Individual poems, sequences, or suites up to a maximum of 12 pages. Fiction: 1 or 2 stories, to a maximum of 5000 words each (stories at the longer end of the word count must be of exceptional quality). Literary non-fiction: To a maximum of 5000 words. The key here is "literary"—imaginative, inventive, culturally/critically relevant (no academic papers or reportage)....Surprise us. Other writing: Queries for submissions of work in other forms, less easy to categorize forms, cross-genre work, are welcome. Visual work: Mainly by invitation, though queries are welcome. All submissions will be read. Response time is typically from 3-6 months. In order to receive a response, submissions must include either a SASE (self-addressed stamped envelope) with sufficient CANADIAN postage or, for US and International submissions, IRCs (International Reply Coupons). If you'd like to save on postage and paper, we will reply by email if you provide an email address for that purpose only. Submissions must be typed in readable font (ideally 12 point, Times Roman or Courier), free of typos, printed on one side only. No staples. Your name and address MUST be on every page. Pieces of more than one page MUST be numbered. Include a cover letter with all contact information, title(s) and genre of work you are submitting. Brief bio is optional." circ. 1000. 4/yr. Pub'd 4 issues 2009; expects 4 issues 2010, 4 issues 2011. sub. price 1-Year $30.00; 2-Year $46.00. USA add $10.00 for p/h; Foreign add $20.00 (all CAD).; per copy $9.95; sample $13.00. Back issues: $6.50. 128pp. Simultaneous submissions accepted: no. Publishes 2% of manuscripts submitted. Payment: All contributors, regardless of genre, are paid $50/page to a maximum of $225, plus 2 copies of the issue in which their work appears. Visual work published inside the magazine (reproduced in black and white) is paid at the same page rate as text contributions. Cover images (full-colour) are paid at the current CAR/FAC rates. Grain purchases first Canadian serial rights only. Copyright remains with the writer or artist. Ads: Full page - $225 CAD.

GRAMMAR CRISIS, Bad Noise Productions, Saburo Taiso, 248 McKibbin St. #2T, Brooklyn, NY 11206-3577, www.badnoiseproductions.com, saburo@badnoiseproductions.com. 2006. Poetry, fiction, articles, art, photos, cartoons, interviews, criticism, music, letters, long-poems, collages, concrete art, non-fiction. "8-bit aesthetics, mollusks, crows, guns, Cabala, ruins, hentai, Fibonacci, Sri Yantra, noise, French eroticism, Catholic saints, Buddhist demons, Taoism, hip-hop, acephalia, remixed art, Upanishad cosmogony, sunflowers, recipes, alcohol, poetry, Dionysian fantasy, circuitry, grime, cartoons, sound-systems, and Japanese ghosts." Expects 1 issue 2010, 2-4 issues 2011. sub. price Free; per copy Free; sample Free. Back issues: Free. Discounts: GRAMMAR CRISIS is an occasional magazine published on-line in .PDF format at www.badnoiseproductions.com. 50pp. Simultaneous submissions accepted: Yes. GRAMMAR CRISIS operates under Creative Commons licensing. Subjects: Anarchist, Avant-Garde, Experimental Art, Dada, Death & Dying, Drugs, Erotica, Experimental, Games, Language, Music, Occult, Philosophy, Poetry, Post Modern, Prose.

GRAND LAKE REVIEW, Martin Kich, Wright State University-Lake Campus, 7600 State Route 703, Celina, OH 45822, 419-586-0374, Fax 419-586-0368, martin.kich@wright.edu, www.wright.edu/~martin.kich/. 1997. Poetry, fiction, art, photos, cartoons, interviews, long-poems, collages, plays. "Now published only online, the

Grand Lake Review was published for five years as an annual, paper publication, presenting the work of students and faculty at the Lake Campus, the work of writers in the communities the campus serves, and the invited work of selected writers from throughout the rest of Ohio. In 2006-2007, we published three online issues. Due to the volume of submissions that we have received, the Grand Lake Review will be published monthly beginning in September 2007. There are no geographical or any other kinds of restrictions on submissions. We are willing to consider all poetry, regardless of subject, form, or style (though we are not likely to publish work written mechanically in strict meter and rhyme schemes, work expressing greeting-card sentiments, or religious work that proselytizes). We are also very interested in receiving short stories, short plays, creative nonfiction, photos, and artwork. There is no submission fee and no payment. Published work will remain online." circ. online. 12/yr. Pub'd 2 issues 2009; expects 5 issues 2010, 12 issues 2011. Reporting time: 3-4 months. Simultaneous submissions accepted: yes. Payment: none. Copyright remains with author, although we do reserve the right to include work that we have published in future special collections. Subject: Literary Review.

Granite Publishing Group, Pamela Meyer, Brian Crissey, PO Box 1429, Columbus, NC 28722, 828-894-8444, Fax 828-894-8454, GraniteP@aol.com, www.5thworld.com. 1988. Articles, art, photos, interviews, music, letters, news items, non-fiction. avg. press run 3M. Pub'd 6 titles 2009; expects 6 titles 2010, 12 titles 2011. 5 titles listed in the *Small Press Record of Books in Print* (36th Edition, 2010-11). Discounts: trade 40%. 220pp. Reporting time: 6 weeks. Simultaneous submissions accepted: yes. Publishes 1% of manuscripts submitted. Payment: 10%. Copyrights for author. Subjects: Alternative Medicine, Ancient Astronauts, Astrology, Astronomy, Botany, Buddhism, Edgar Cayce, Channelling, Conservation, Cosmology, Counter-Culture, Alternatives, Communes, Creativity, Crystals, Ecology, Foods, Native American.

•**GRANTA,** Granta Publications, 12 Addison Avenue, London W11 4QR, United Kingdom, +44(0)20 7605 1360, www.granta.com. "Since 1979, the year of its rebirth, Granta has published many of the worlds finest writers tackling some of the worlds most important subjects, from intimate human experiences to the large public and political events that have shaped our lives. Its contributors have included Martin Amis, Julian Barnes, Saul Bellow, Peter Carey, Raymond Carver, Angela Carter, Bruce Chatwin, James Fenton, Richard Ford, Martha Gellhorn, Nadine Gordimer, Milan Kundera, Doris Lessing, Ian McEwan, Gabriel Garcia Marquez, Jayne Anne Phillips, Salman Rushdie, George Steiner, Graham Swift, Paul Theroux, Edmund White, Jeanette Winterson, Tobias Wolff. Every issue since 1979 is still in print. In the pages of Granta, readers met for the first time the narrative prose of writers such as Bill Bryson, Romesh Gunesekera, Blake Morrison, Arundhati Roy and Zadie Smith; and have encountered events and topics as diverse as the fall of Saigon, the mythology of the Titanic, adultery, psychotherapy and Chinese cricket fighting. Granta does not have a political or literary manifesto, but it does have a belief in the power and urgency of the story, both in fiction and non-fiction, and the story's supreme ability to describe, illuminate and make real. As theObserver wrote of Granta: In its blend of memoirs and photojournalism, and in its championing of contemporary realist fiction, Granta has its face pressed firmly against the window, determined to witness the world."

GRASSLANDS REVIEW, Department of English, Indiana State University, Terre Haute, IN 47809. 1989. Poetry, fiction, photos. "GLR is moving to Indiana State University (2007). New editors will be selected. In *FF5* #43 we are described as 'a litmag which consistently publishes an interesting mix of work, some good old-fashioned stories plus stuff from the more experimental (but still solid) edge.' Authors published include John E. White, Don Shockey, Jennifer Gomoll, Zan Gay, William Bedford Clark, J.E. McCarthy, Barry Brummett, Greg Jenkins, Brian Collier, Marlene Tilton, Christoph Meyer. Only material postmarked in October or March will be considered." circ. 300. 2/yr. Pub'd 2 issues 2009; expects 2 issues 2010, 2 issues 2011. sub. price $12 individual, $20 libraries; per copy $6 (recent); sample $5. Back issues: $4 pp. (published prior to 2007) contact the former editor: Editor, *Grasslands Review*, PO Box 626, Berea, OH 44018. Discounts: none. 80pp. Simultaneous submissions accepted: yes. Publishes 10% of manuscripts submitted. Payment: 1 copy with special rate for extra copies. Copyrighted, reverts to author. Subjects: Poetry, Short Stories.

GRASSLIMB, Valerie E. Polichar, P.O. Box 420816, San Diego, CA 92142-0816, editor@grasslimb.com, http://www.grasslimb.com. 2002. Poetry, fiction, art, cartoons. "Frequent contributors include Taylor Graham, Leonard Cirino, Simon Perchik, Susan Tepper. Although general topics are welcome, we're *less* likely to select work regarding romance, sex, the elderly, parents and children. Fiction in an experimental, avant-garde or surreal mode is often more interesting to us than a traditional story. Include word count in fiction; nothing over 2500 words can be read, prefer 1500. Okay to submit electronically (ASCII, RTF, Word, Pages, AppleWorks, HTML)." 2/yr. Pub'd 2 issues 2009; expects 2 issues 2010, 2 issues 2011. sub. price $6; per copy $3; sample $2.50. Back issues: $2.50. Discounts: wholesalers 65%. 8pp. Reporting time: 4 months. Simultaneous submissions accepted: yes. Payment: $10-$60 plus 2 copies. Copyrighted, reverts to author. Pub's reviews: 2 in 2009. Subjects: Crime, Experimental, Fiction, Literature (General), Poetry, Prose, Science Fiction, Short Stories, Surrealism.

GRASSROOTS FUNDRAISING JOURNAL, Stephanie Roth, Editor in Chief, 1904 Franklin St Ste 705,

Oakland, CA 94612, 510-452-4520, Fax 510-452-2122, info@grassrootsfundraising.org, www.grassrootsfundraising.org. 1981. Articles, non-fiction. "Grassroots fundraising for social justice causes. Contributors: Kim Klein, Stephanie Roth, and others." circ. 4M. 6/yr. Pub'd 6 issues 2009; expects 6 issues 2010, 6 issues 2011. sub. price $39 for organizations with budgets under $250,000; $48 for organizations with budgets between $250,000 and $1 million; $56 for organizations with budgets over $1 million; per copy $5; sample free. Back issues: $5. Discounts: 25% for 10+ subs ordered at one time, discounts for bulk back issues. 20pp. Reporting time: 2 months. Simultaneous submissions accepted: yes. Publishes 20% of manuscripts submitted. Payment: $100. Copyrighted, reverts to author. Pub's reviews: 2 in 2009. §Fundraising, economics, organizational development. Ads: full-page display $1150/half-page display $600/other sizes available/price varies by size and frequency. Subject: Fundraising.

Grateful Press, 11654 Plaza America Drive #123, Reston, VA 20190-4700, 877-588-7753, www.gratefulpress.com, info@gratefulpress.com. 2009. "Grateful Press is not accepting submissions at this time." Expects 1 title 2010, 1 title 2011. 1 title listed in the *Small Press Record of Books in Print* (36th Edition, 2010-11). Subjects: Euthanasia, Death, Spiritual.

GRAY AREAS, Netta Gilboa, PMB 624, 5838 West Olive Ave., STE C105, Glendale, AZ 85302-3155, www.grayarea.com. 1991. Articles, photos, cartoons, interviews, reviews, music, letters, news items, non-fiction. "*Gray Areas* is dedicated to examining the gray areas of life. We specialize in subject matter which is illegal, potentially illegal, immoral and/or controversial. Recent topics include: UFO's, adult films, drug testing, computer crimes, bootleg tapes, sampling, prank phone calls, etc. We also review books, movies, CDs, comics, concerts, magazines, catalogs, software, live video and audio tapes." circ. 10M. Irregular, 1-2/yr. Pub'd 1 issue 2009. sub. price $23, $32 1st class for 4 issues when published; per copy $6.95; sample $8. Back issues: $8 while available. Discounts: wholesaler and retail store available. 164pp. Reporting time: 1 month or less. Simultaneous submissions accepted if notified as such. Publishes 25% of manuscripts submitted. Payment: masthead listing, byline, copies. Copyrighted, rights reverting to author negotiable. Pub's reviews: 150+ per issue in 2009. §Virtually everything received—over 60 pages of reviews per issue. Ads: $600/$300/$150 1/4 page/$75 1/8 page $40. Subjects: Anarchist, Book Reviewing, Computers, Calculators, Counter-Culture, Alternatives, Communes, Crime, Drugs, Bob Dylan, Interviews, Law, Magazines, Music, Reviews, Sex, Sexuality, Sociology, Tapes & Records.

Gray Dog Press (see also SPOKEWRITE: The Spokane/Coeur d'Alene Journal of Art and Writing), Russel Davis, Andrew Corder, Merle Martin, 2727 S. Mt. Vernon #4, Spokane, WA 99223, P:509-534-0372, F:509-533-1897, editor@graydogpress.com, www.graydogpress.com. 2006. Poetry, fiction, non-fiction. "Fiction, Non-Fiction, Life-story, Memoir, Poetry." avg. press run 500. Pub'd 20 titles 2009; expects 12 titles 2010, 14 titles 2011. No titles listed in the *Small Press Record of Books in Print* (36th Edition, 2010-11). 250pp. Reporting time: 5-10 business days. Simultaneous submissions accepted: Yes. Publishes 35% of manuscripts submitted. Payment: 12.5% / Quarterly. Copyrights for author. Subjects: Christianity, Creative Non-fiction, Fiction, Folklore, Poetry, Prose, Religion, Romance, Science Fiction, Young Adult.

Grayson Books, Ginny Connors, Editor, PO Box 270549, W. Hartford, CT 06127, 860-523-1196 phone/Fax, GraysonBooks@aol.com, www.GraysonBooks.com. 1999. Poetry, non-fiction. "We are a small press publishing only a couple of titles each year. Focus on excellent contemporary poetry and issues related to family and education. Not actively seeking manuscripts at this time." Pub'd 2 titles 2009; expects 2 titles 2010, 2 titles 2011. 6 titles listed in the *Small Press Record of Books in Print* (36th Edition, 2010-11). Discounts: standard discounts given to wholesalers, retailers and institutions that order in bulk. Simultaneous submissions accepted: yes. Copyrights for author. Subjects: Family, Poetry.

Graywolf Press, Fiona McCrae, Director & Publisher, 2402 University Avenue #203, St. Paul, MN 55114. 1974. Poetry, fiction, criticism, non-fiction. Pub'd 25 titles 2009; expects 25 titles 2010, 25 titles 2011. 147 titles listed in the *Small Press Record of Books in Print* (36th Edition, 2010-11). 60-300pp. Reporting time: 12 weeks. Simultaneous submissions accepted: yes. Publishes less than 1% of manuscripts submitted. Payment: negotiable. Copyrights for author. Subjects: Criticism, Fiction, Literature (General), Non-Fiction, Poetry, Prose, Reading, Short Stories, Translation, Writers/Writing.

THE GREAT AMERICAN POETRY SHOW, A SERIAL POETRY ANTHOLOGY, The Muse Media, Larry Ziman, P.O. Box 69506, West Hollywood, CA 90069-0506, 1-323-656-6126. "See specifics under The Muse Media."

Great Little Books, LLC, Linda Jenkins, Barbara Worton, PMB 139, 233 Rock Road, Glen Rock, NJ 07452, www.greatlittlebooksllc.com. 2006. Poetry, fiction, non-fiction. "Also well-crafted children's books with a clear understanding of the target audience." avg. press run 3000. Expects 2 titles 2010, 3 titles 2011. 4 titles listed in the *Small Press Record of Books in Print* (36th Edition, 2010-11). Discounts: Contact Midpoint Trade Books for details. 200pp. Reporting time: 3 - 6 months. Simultaneous submissions accepted: Yes. Publishes 1% of manuscripts submitted. Payment: Case-by-case; no advances. Case-by-case.

Great Marsh Press (see also THE READING ROOM), Barbara Probst Solomon, Editor-in-Chief & Publisher, P.O. Box 2144, Lenox Hill Station, New York, NY 10021. "Great Marsh Press is a sponsored organization of The New York Foundation for the Arts." No titles listed in the *Small Press Record of Books in Print* (36th Edition, 2010-11).

The Great Rift Press, Katherine Daly, 1135 East Bonneville, Pocatello, ID 83201, Phone 208-232-6857, Fax 208-233-0410. 1987. Non-fiction. "We also sell publishing business software." avg. press run 3M. Pub'd 1 title 2009; expects 2 titles 2010, 2 titles 2011. 4 titles listed in the *Small Press Record of Books in Print* (36th Edition, 2010-11). Discounts: resalers 25%=1; 40%=2-10; 42%=11-20; additional 5% discount and FREE shipping on pre-paid orders of 2 or more. 288-352pp. Reporting time: 1 month. Simultaneous submissions accepted: yes. Payment: negotiable. Subjects: Bibliography, Biography, Idaho, Montana, Non-Fiction, Sports, Outdoors, Wyoming.

GREAT RIVER REVIEW, Robert Hedin, Richard Broderick, PO Box 406, Red Wing, MN 55066, 651-388-2009, info@andersoncenter.org, www.andersoncenter.org. 1977. Poetry, fiction, articles. "Poetry, fiction, essays, translations. Some authors recently published: Philip Levine, Maggie Anderson, Linda Pastan, Marvin Bell, Olga Broumas, and Ted Kooser." circ. 500. 2/yr. Pub'd 2 issues 2009; expects 2 issues 2010, 2 issues 2011. sub. price $14; per copy $6; sample $6. Back issues: $6. 120pp. Reporting time: 1-4 months. Publishes 5% of manuscripts submitted. Payment: copies. Copyrighted, reverts to author. Pub's reviews: 12 in 2009. §Poetry, fiction, non-fiction, translations. Ads: none. Subjects: Fiction, Poetry.

Great West Publishing, Hermelinda Vargas, P. O. Box 31631, Tucson, AZ 85751-1631, Tel: 520-396-1081, Fax: 520-514-9336, URL: www.sentrybooks.com. 2007. Fiction, non-fiction. "Sentry Books is an imprint of Great West Publishing, an independent press publishing young adult and children's literature since 2007. We are distributed to the trade by Biblio Distribution through which we offer quality fiction and non-fiction to our retail and bookstore customers. The publishers of Sentry Books believe that good story-telling fires the imagination, and that good books remain our best safeguard against ignorance, apathy, and social intolerance. Recent titles included *The Arborist* by M. S. Holm and *How Mohammed Saved Miss Liberty* by M. S. Holm." avg. press run 5000. Pub'd 2 titles 2009; expects 2 titles 2010, 2 titles 2011. 5 titles listed in the *Small Press Record of Books in Print* (36th Edition, 2010-11). Discounts: 2-10 copies: 30%10-50 copies: 40%51-100 copies: 50%100+ copies: 60%. 270pp. Reporting time: 45 days. Simultaneous submissions accepted: No. Payment: Advances: none. Royalty: 4 % wholesale. Does not copyright for author. Subjects: Children, Youth, Juvenile Fiction, Young Adult.

GREATCOAT, Scott Hartwich, Co-editor; Stephanie Walkenshaw, Co-editor; Elisabeth Whitehead, Co-editor, 3228 Peabody St., Bellingham, WA 98225, submissions@greatcoat.net, www.greatcoat.net. 2006. Poetry, photos, interviews, non-fiction. "Greatcoat is co-edited by three writers with vastly different aesthetics; we select work only by unanimous consent, and are not impressed by publication history or reputation. We'll consider any style, any length, any form. "Experimental" poetry and essays receive the same careful consideration as more "traditional" work. We steer clear of academic essays, poems about writing poems, and political diatribes. Recent contributors include David Wagoner, Michele Glazer, Lynn Strongin, G. C. Waldrep, Malena Morling, and Eric Baus. Please query about interviews. And please, please follow our guidelines carefully. They're available on our website." 2/yr. Expects 2 issues 2010, 2 issues 2011. sub. price $15.00; per copy $8.00; sample $8.00. Discounts: 40%. 80pp. Reporting time: 1 week to 1 year. Simultaneous submissions accepted: Yes. Publishes 3% of manuscripts submitted. Payment: We pay two copies. Copyrighted, reverts to author. Ads: Currently not accepting ads.

Greatland Graphics, Alissa Crandall, PO Box 141414, Anchorage, AK 99514, 907-337-1234, fax 907-337-4567, info@alaskacalendars.com, www.alaskacalendars.com. 1985. "Additional address: 2515 Wesleyan Drive, Anchorage, AK 99508." 8 titles listed in the *Small Press Record of Books in Print* (36th Edition, 2010-11). Subjects: Alaska, Nature, Photography, Wildlife.

GREEN ANARCHY, Volunteer Collective, PO Box 11331, Eugene, OR 97440, collective@greenanarchy.org, www.greenanarchy.org. 1999. Poetry, fiction, articles, art, interviews, criticism, reviews, letters, non-fiction. circ. 8000. 2/yr. Pub'd 3 issues 2009; expects 2 issues 2010, 2 issues 2011. sub. price Two year/4 issue subscription: US-$15, Canada-$19, Europe-$23 Elsewhere-$27 Free to prisoners; per copy $4; sample $4 or free review copies. Back issues: $4 for a single copy, $50 for a whole set. Discounts: inquiries welcome. 100pp. Simultaneous submissions accepted: yes. Publishes 40% of manuscripts submitted. Payment: none. Not copyrighted. Pub's reviews: 32 in 2009. §Politics, history, culture, technology. Ads: none. Subjects: Anarchist, Cities, Culture, Current Affairs, Earth, Natural History, Environment, Essays, Gender Issues, Non-Fiction, Politics, Prison, Reviews, Technology, War, Zines.

THE GREEN HILLS LITERARY LANTERN, Adam Brooke Davis, Managing Editor; Joe Benevento, Co-editor (poetry); Jack Smith, Co-editor (prose), Truman State University, Department of English, McClain Hall, Kirksville, MO 63501-4221, 660-785-4119, adavis@truman.edu, jksmith@grm.net, jbeneven@truman.edu, ll.truman.edu/ghllweb. 1990. Poetry, fiction, interviews, reviews, non-fiction. "GHLL shifted to electronic publication with #XVII (July 2006). Send mss to Green Hills Literary Lantern, Truman State University, McClain Hall, Kirksville, MO 63501. Please label and direct fiction and nonfiction mss to Adam Brooke Davis, poetry to Joe Benevento. GHLL strongly prefers snailmailed mss, but will accept e-submissions, particularly from writers living outside of North America. Fiction up to 7,000 words. No religious or genre fiction. No haiku, limericks, or poems over 2 pages. We're open to new writers. Recent contributors include DeWitt Henry, Karl Harshbarger, Gary Fincke, Doug Rennie, Grant Tracey, Walter Cummins, Ian MacMillan, Edmund de Chasca, Mark Wisniewski, Virgil Suarez, Jim Thomas, James Doyle, and Francine Marie Tolf." circ. infinite. 1/yr. Pub'd 1 issue 2009; expects 1 issue 2010, 1 issue 2011. sub. price n/a. 288pp in old print edition; digital magazine of similar proportionspp. Reporting time: 3 - 4 months. Simultaneous submissions accepted: Yes. Publishes 2-10% of manuscripts submitted. Payment: none. Copyrighted, reverts to author. Pub's reviews: 3 in 2009. §Novels, short story collections, poetry collections. Subjects: Interviews, Literary Review, Non-Fiction, Poetry, Reviews.

Green Hut Press, Janet Wullner-Faiss, 1015 Jardin Street East, Appleton, WI 54911, 920-734-9728, janwfcloak@uspower.net. 1972. Poetry, fiction, art, interviews, non-fiction. "We publish the writing and art work of the late German-American artist Fritz Faiss (1905-1981) *exclusively*. Limited editions. Mail order, except for a few selected bookstores. Library discount. Inquiries welcome. SASE please. Prices range between $9 and, for a hand-colored-by-artist edition, $200." avg. press run 200. 6 titles listed in the *Small Press Record of Books in Print* (36th Edition, 2010-11). Discounts: libraries 20% postpaid when accompanied by cash payment. 75pp. Subjects: Arts, Color, Creativity, German, Humanism, Non-Fiction, Poetry, Psychology, Textbooks, Visual Arts.

GREEN MOUNTAINS REVIEW, Neil Shepard, General Editor & Poetry Editor; Leslie Daniels, Fiction Editor, Johnson State College, Johnson, VT 05656, 802-635-1350. 1987. Poetry, fiction, articles, art, interviews, criticism, reviews, parts-of-novels, long-poems, non-fiction. circ. 1.7M. 2/yr. Pub'd 2 issues 2009; expects 2 issues 2010, 2 issues 2011. sub. price $15; per copy $9.50; sample $7. Back issues: $7. Discounts: 40% off for store buyers. 192pp. Reporting time: 3-6 months (we read Sept. 1-March 1). Simultaneous submissions accepted: yes. Publishes 2% of manuscripts submitted. Payment: 2 copies + 1 year subscription. Copyrighted, reverts to author. Pub's reviews: 2 in 2009. §Poetry, fiction, creative non-fiction, literary essays, interviews, book reviews. Ads: $150/$75. Subjects: Book Reviewing, Criticism, Culture, Fiction, Poetry.

GREEN PRINTS, "The Weeder's Digest", Pat Stone, PO Box 1355, Fairview, NC 28730, 828-628-1902, www.greenprints.com, patstone@atlantic.net. 1990. Poetry, fiction, articles, art, non-fiction. "Shares the human, *not* the how-to, side of gardening through fine stories and art. see writer's guidelines at website for lots of useful tips—please!" circ. 13M. 4/yr. Pub'd 4 issues 2009; expects 4 issues 2010, 4 issues 2011. sub. price $19.97; per copy $6.00; sample $6.00. Discounts: 1/2 price, min. order 6. 80pp. Reporting time: 1-3 months. Simultaneous submissions accepted: yes. Publishes 10% of manuscripts submitted. Payment: $50-200. Copyrighted, reverts to author. Ads: $400 1/2 page. Subject: Gardening.

Green River Press, Nancy A. Robinson, PO Box 6905, Santa Barbara, CA 93160, 805-964-4475, Fax 805-967-6208, narob@cox.net. 1999. Poetry, fiction, non-fiction. avg. press run 3.5M. Pub'd 1 title 2009; expects 1 title 2010, 1 title 2011. 1 title listed in the *Small Press Record of Books in Print* (36th Edition, 2010-11). Discounts: trade 55%. 350pp. Reporting time: 6 months. Simultaneous submissions accepted: yes. Publishes 60% of manuscripts submitted. Payment: copies and 40% discount. Copyright arrangements vary per book. Subjects: Adoption, Autobiography, Fiction, Non-Fiction, Parenting, Poetry.

Green River Writers, Inc./Grex Press, Mary E. O'Dell, 103 Logsdon Court, Louisville, KY 40243-1161, 502-245-4902. 1993. Poetry. "Solicited manuscripts only." avg. press run 1M. Expects 2 titles 2010, 1 title 2011. No titles listed in the *Small Press Record of Books in Print* (36th Edition, 2010-11). Discounts: 40% to booksellers. 60pp. Payment: on individual basis. Subject: Poetry.

Green Square Publishing, Valentina Sgro, 3718 Normandy Road, Cleveland, OH 44120, 216-283-2309, www.greensquarepublishing.com. 2007. Fiction, non-fiction. "Green Square Publishing - really organized books and recordings - publishes unique works about organizing and productivity. For example: GSP's inaugural title, Patience and the Porsche, is the first novel about a professional organizer, written by a professional organizer." avg. press run 1000. Expects 1 title 2010, 2 titles 2011. 2 titles listed in the *Small Press Record of Books in Print* (36th Edition, 2010-11). 200pp. Reporting time: two months. Simultaneous submissions accepted: Yes. Subjects: Creative Non-fiction, Fiction, How-To, Non-Fiction, Research, Self-Help.

GREENHOUSE REVIEW, Greenhouse Review Press, Gary Young, 3965 Bonny Doon Road, Santa Cruz, CA 95060.

Greenhouse Review Press (see also GREENHOUSE REVIEW), Gary Young, 3965 Bonny Doon Road, Santa Cruz, CA 95060-9706, 831-426-4355. 1975. Poetry, parts-of-novels, long-poems. "Greenhouse Review Press publishes a tradebook, chapbook and broadside series. Titles: *The Fugitive Vowels* by D.J. Waldie; *The*

Dreams of Mercurius by John Hall; *House Fires* by Peter Wild; *Thirteen Ways of Deranging An Angel* by Stephen Kessler; *Looking Up* by Christopher Budkley; *Any Minute* by Laurel Blossom; *Yes* by Timothy Sheehan; *By Me, By Any, Can and Can't Be Done* by Killarney Clary; *Begin, Distance* by Sherod Santos; *Jack the Ripper* by John Hall, *Unselected Poems* by Philip Levine." avg. press run varies. Pub'd 3 titles 2009; expects 4 titles 2010. 62 titles listed in the *Small Press Record of Books in Print* (36th Edition, 2010-11). Discounts: 30% to bookstores. Pages vary. Reporting time: 4 weeks. Payment: copies. Copyrights for author. Subject: Poetry.

THE GREENSBORO REVIEW, Jim Clark, Editor, Greensboro Review, MFA Program, 3302 MHRA, PO Box 26170, Univ. of North Carolina Greensboro, Greensboro, NC 27402-6170, 336-334-5459, Fax 336-256-1470, jlclark@uncg.edu, www.greensbororeview.org. 1966. Poetry, fiction. "We like to see the best being written regardless of subject, style, or theme. We publish new talent beside established writers, depending on quality. No restrictions on length of poetry; writers may submit 3-5 poems or short stories 7,500 words or less. Recent contributors include Peter Ho Davies, Stephen Dobyns, Claudia Emerson, Jack Gilbert, Linda Gregg, Thomas Lux, Jill McCorkle, Robert Morgan, Dale Ray Phillips, Stanley Plumly, George Singleton, Natasha Trethewey. Deadlines are September 15 and February 15 each year. SASE for Literary Awards guidelines. SASE with mss. Stories anthologized in editions of *The Best American Short Stories, Prize Stories: The O. Henry Awards, The Pushcart Prize*, and in *New Stories from the South*." circ. 1200. 2/yr. Pub'd 2 issues 2009; expects 2 issues 2010, 2 issues 2011. sub. price $14; per copy $8; sample $5. Back issues: $1.50-$5/according to price on cover. Discounts: none. 128pp. Reporting time: 3-6 months. Simultaneous submissions accepted: yes. Publishes 1.6% of manuscripts submitted. Payment: 3 copies. Copyrighted, reverts to author. Ads: Exchange. Subjects: Fiction, Poetry.

•**GREY SPARROW JOURNAL, Grey Sparrow Press,** Diane Smith, 812 Hilltop Road, Mendota Heights, MN 55118, 651-452-5066. "Grey Sparrow Journal offers a place for writers and artists to incubate new ideas, experiment with the written word and lay down fresh thoughts on international issues.We are a small, non-profit press that publishes an ezine and the 'best of the zine' once a year."

•**Grey Sparrow Press (see also GREY SPARROW JOURNAL),** Diane Smith, 812 Hilltop Road, Mendota Heights, MN 55118, 651-452-5066. 2009. Poetry, fiction, art, photos, long-poems. "Grey Sparrow offers a place for writers and artists to incubate new ideas, experiment with the written word and lay down fresh thoughts on international issues.We are a small, non-profit press that publishes an ezine and the 'best of the zine' once a year." Expects 1 title 2010, 1 title 2011. No titles listed in the *Small Press Record of Books in Print* (36th Edition, 2010-11). Discounts: 35%. 167pp. Reporting time: 52 days. Simultaneous submissions accepted: Yes. Payment in free copies of the book. Does not copyright for author. Subjects: Arts, Creativity, Culture, Experimental, Fiction, Indigenous Cultures, Inspirational, Literature (General), Minnesota, Multicultural, Photography, Poetry, Storytelling, Visual Arts, Zines.

Grip Publishing, Stacy Nelson, PO Box 091882, Milwaukee, WI 53209, 414-807-6403. 2004. Fiction. "Grip Publishing's mission is to provide literature to all genres of the reading populatation interested in urban fiction. Grip Publishing is interested in various forms of work. Work submitted for publishing should be sent at any time. Unsolicited work is acceptable. Queries and proposals are acceptable." avg. press run 2000. Expects 1 title 2010, 2 titles 2011. No titles listed in the *Small Press Record of Books in Print* (36th Edition, 2010-11). Discounts: 2-10 copies15%10-20 copies 20%20 or more copies 25%. 200pp. Reporting time: Two weeks. Simultaneous submissions accepted: Yes. Payment: Must be discussed. Copyrights for author. Subjects: African-American, Bisexual, Black, Fiction, Gay, Novels.

The Groundwater Press, Rosanne Wasserman, Eugene Richie, PO Box 704, Hudson, NY 12534, 516-767-8503. 1974. Poetry. "We're a nonprofit press, dependent upon grants. NO UNSOLICITED MS. Titles include: *Common Preludes* by Edward Barrett; *Double Time* by Star Black; *Every Question But One* by Pierre Martory, translated by John Ashbery; *Mecox Road* by Marc Cohen; *The History of Rain* by Tomoyuki Iino; *The Necessary Boat* by Susan Baran; *Calendar* by Michael Malinowitz; *Bee in the Sheets* by Beth Enson; *short history of the saxophone* by Tom Weatherly." avg. press run 500. Pub'd 2 titles 2009; expects 1-2 titles 2010, 1-2 titles 2011. 12 titles listed in the *Small Press Record of Books in Print* (36th Edition, 2010-11). Discounts: 60/40, 50/50 wholesalers. 32-80pp. Reporting time: 1 year. Simultaneous submissions accepted: no. Payment: varies according to grants and donations. Copyrights for author. Subject: Poetry.

GROUP Publishing (see also HOT FLASHES: Not a Menopause Thang), Robert Bell Jr, 93 Old York Road Suite 1-406, Jenkintown, PA 19046, 267 258-7967. 2006. Poetry, articles, parts-of-novels. "The magazine is designed to help couples enhance their relationships." avg. press run 12. Pub'd 1 title 2009; expects 2 titles 2010, 12 titles 2011. 1 title listed in the *Small Press Record of Books in Print* (36th Edition, 2010-11). 50pp. Reporting time: One Week. Simultaneous submissions accepted: Yes. Publishes 100% of manuscripts submitted. Payment: Self - Publishing contract. Copyrights for author. Subjects: Adolescence, Alcohol, Alcoholism, Bibliography, Bisexual, Black, Cartoons, Cities, Civil Rights, Clothing, Communication, Journalism, Community, Cooking, Creativity, Crime.

THE GROVE REVIEW, Matt Barry, 1631 NE Broadway, PMB #137, Portland, OR 97232, editor@thegrovereview.org, www.thegrovereview.org. 2004. Poetry, fiction, art, photos, interviews, letters, parts-of-novels, long-poems, plays. "The Grove Review offers a first-rate venue for unknown to renowned artists to publish their craft. We work to foster a vibrant artistic community. Recent contributors include author Ursula K. Le Guin and photographer Michael Kenna." 2/yr. Expects 1 issue 2010, 2 issues 2011. sub. price $20; per copy $11; sample $11. Back issues: inquire. Discounts: inquire. 160pp. Reporting time: Please allow 3 - 4 months prior to inquiring. Typically responds much sooner. Simultaneous submissions accepted: No. Publishes 1% of manuscripts submitted. Payment: $50 + 2 copies. Copyrighted, reverts to author. Ads: full page $500; half page $300; qtr. page $200.

THE GROWING EDGE MAGAZINE, New Moon Publishing, Inc., John Baur, Editor; Tom Alexander, Book Review Editor, PO Box 1027, Corvallis, OR 97339-1027, 514-757-8477. 1980. "Indoor and outdoor gardening for today's high-tech grower. Covers hydroponics, controlled environments, greenhouses, drip irrigation, organic and sustainable gardening, water conservation aquaponics, aquaculture and more." circ. 39,500. 6/yr. Pub'd 6 issues 2009; expects 6 issues 2010, 6 issues 2011. sub. price $37.95 1st class mail, $26.95 3rd class mail, $79.50 international; per copy $4.95 + $1.50 p/h; sample $4.95 + $1.50 p/h. Back issues: same. 96pp. Reporting time: 2 months. Simultaneous submissions accepted: yes. Publishes 50%-75% of manuscripts submitted. Payment: 20¢ per word/photos negotiable. Copyrighted, 1st and reprint rights to publisher then reverts back to author. Pub's reviews: 18 in 2009. §Hydroponic, greenhouse, and aquaculture. Ads: Full: b+w $1758, color $2563; half: b+w $1168, color $1975; marketplace ad $250, retailers club $50. Subjects: Agriculture, Counter-Culture, Alternatives, Communes, Gardening.

GROWING FOR MARKET, Lynn Byczynski, PO Box 3747, Lawrence, KS 66046, 785-748-0605, 800-307-8949, growing4market@earthlink.net, www.growingformarket.com. 1992. Articles. *"Growing for Market* is a practical, hands-on journal for farmers who direct-market produce and flowers. Therefore, writers must be knowledeable about growing on a commercial scale." circ. 4M. 12/yr. Pub'd 12 issues 2009; expects 12 issues 2010, 12 issues 2011. sub. price $33; per copy $5; sample $5. Back issues: $20/year. Discounts: none. 20pp. Reporting time: 6 months. Simultaneous submissions accepted: no. Publishes 75% of manuscripts submitted. Payment: $75/printed page, $200 maximum. Copyrighted, reverts to author. Pub's reviews: 12 in 2009. §Market gardening, small-scale farming, vegetables, fruits, cut flowers, herbs, food policy. Ads: $400/$240/$68 1/3 page/$120 1/4 page/$90 1/6 page. Subjects: Agriculture, Food, Eating, Gardening.

Gryphon Books (see also HARDBOILED; PAPERBACK PARADE), Gary Lovisi, PO Box 209, Brooklyn, NY 11228-0209. 1983. Fiction, articles, art, interviews, satire, criticism, reviews, parts-of-novels, non-fiction. "A small press publisher that (in addition to publishing the magazines *Hardboiled* and *Paperback Parade)* publish numerous books on a variety of subjects dealing with paperback collecting, pulp magazines, detective fiction, science fiction, and fantasy, Sherlock Holmes—in fiction and non-fiction. Please Note: *Do not send mss,* on anything over 3,000 words-*send only* query letter about the story/novel, *with SASE.* Material received without SASE will not be returned. Writers can send letter with SASE for guidelines. It is suggested you order a recent copy of our magazines or books to get an idea of what I am looking for." avg. press run 500-1M. Pub'd 5 titles 2009; expects 4 titles 2010, 5 titles 2011. 3 titles listed in the *Small Press Record of Books in Print* (36th Edition, 2010-11). Discounts: 40% on 5 or more of the same item/issue ordered. 50-200pp. Reporting time: 3-6 weeks. Simultaneous submissions accepted: no. Publishes 5% of manuscripts submitted. Payment: varies. Copyrights for author. Subjects: Bibliography, Book Arts, Book Collecting, Bookselling, Collectibles, Crime, Fantasy, Fiction, Sherlock Holmes, H.P. Lovecraft, Magazines, Mystery, Non-Fiction, Science Fiction, Writers/Writing, Zines.

Gryphon House, Inc., Kathy Charner, PO Box 207, Beltsville, MD 20704-0207, 800-638-0928. 1971. Non-fiction. "We publish books of activities for use by pre-school teachers and parents." Pub'd 13 titles 2009; expects 10 titles 2010, 11 titles 2011. 66 titles listed in the *Small Press Record of Books in Print* (36th Edition, 2010-11). Discounts: available upon request. 256pp. Reporting time: 3 weeks. Simultaneous submissions accepted: no. Publishes 5% of manuscripts submitted. Payment: 8-10-12.5% on net sales. Copyrights for author. Subjects: Children, Youth, Education.

Guarionex Press Ltd., William E. Zimmerman, Chief Editor & Publisher, 201 West 77th Street, New York, NY 10024, 212-724-5259. 1979. Non-fiction. "The goal of *Guarionex Press* is to publish books that help people articulate their thoughts and feelings. Our books affirm the power of the human spirit and imagination to overcome life's problems. Our first book is *How to Tape Instant Oral Biographies.* The book teaches youngsters and grownups how to interview family members and friends and use the tape or video recorder to capture their life stories, memories and traditions on tape. Great family, school and vacation activity. Its second book is a new form of diary/journal called *A Book of Questions to Keep Thoughts and Feelings*; it helps people keep a diary. The third book is *Make Beliefs,* a gift book to spark the imagination. A new activity book both for youngsters and adults. Our fourth is *Lifelines*; a book of hope to get you through the tough times of life." avg. press run 5M. Expects 1-2 titles 2010, 1-2 titles 2011. 4 titles listed in the *Small Press Record of Books in Print*

(36th Edition, 2010-11). Discounts: 10-50% depending on volume. 112pp. Reporting time: 3 months. Payment: fair arrangement negotiable. Copyrights for author. Subjects: Children, Youth, Communication, Journalism, Consumer, Crafts, Hobbies, Education, Family, Games, Genealogy, How-To, New Age, New Age, Senior Citizens, Spiritual.

GUD MAGAZINE (Greatest Uncommon Denominator), Julia Bernd, Editor; Sal Coraccio, Editor; Kaolin Fire, Editor; Sue Miller, Editor; Debbie Moorhouse, Editor; J. Dale Humphries, Editor; Michael Ellsworth, Consulting Editor, PO Box 1537, Laconia, NH 03247. 2007. Poetry, fiction, articles, art, photos, cartoons, interviews, satire, parts-of-novels, long-poems, collages, plays, concrete art, non-fiction. "Seeks material that extends or rejects the boundaries of its stereotype. We're looking for: genre fiction that literary folks can appreciate; literary fiction that genre folks can appreciate; and poetry that poets and non-poets alike can appreciate. We want strong writing, a solid understanding of the English language, characters to care about, and a compelling arc (be it character or plot—preferably both). *Submissions accepted via website only. See site for any current theme and guidelines. http://www.gudmagazine.com/.*" 2/yr. Pub'd 2 issues 2009; expects 2 issues 2010, 2 issues 2011. sub. price $22; per copy $3.50 PDF / $12 Print. Back issues: $3.50 PDF / $12 Print. 200pp. Reporting time: See http://www.gudmagazine.com/subs/stats.php; current average: 3 weeks. Simultaneous submissions accepted: yes. Publishes 2% of manuscripts submitted. Payment: 3c/word original; 1c/word reprint. Ads: website only. Subjects: Arts, Fantasy, Fiction, Folklore, Forensic Science, Horror, Non-Fiction, Photography, Poetry, Prose, Reprints, Research, Science Fiction, Short Stories, Visual Arts.

Guernica Editions, Inc., Antonio D'Alfonso, Editor & Publisher, 11 Mount Royal Avenue, Toronto, Ontario M6H 2S2, Canada, 416-658-9888, Fax 416-657-8885, guernicaeditions@cs.com. 1978. Poetry, fiction, photos, criticism, long-poems, plays, non-fiction. "Guernica Editions publish works of literature, criticism or culture. We specialize in translations and we focus on writing dealing with pluricultural realities. USA distributors: Paul and Company." avg. press run 1M. Pub'd 30 titles 2009; expects 39 titles 2010, 25 titles 2011. 355 titles listed in the *Small Press Record of Books in Print* (36th Edition, 2010-11). Discounts: 40% to bookstores, 40% to jobbers and wholesalers, 46% for 10+ library wholesalers. 50-400pp. Reporting time: 3-6 months; if we're definitely not interested, the answer is faster—within 2-4 weeks. We do not accept simultaneous submissions. Payment: authors receive about 10 copies and 10% royalty; copyright is shared by author and publisher for the duration of the edition. Does not copyright for author. Subjects: Literature (General), Politics.

GUERNICA: A Magazine of Art & Politics, Tara Jepson, Publisher; Liz Hartman, Publisher, 403 East 69th Street #3D, New York, NY 10021. "*Guernica*: A Magazine of Art and Politics is always looking to publish talented, insightful and creative new writers. Since the inception of *Guernica*, the steadily growing response from readers has been pleasing. This we largely attribute to the intelligent, thought-provoking and memorable writing of our contributors. Our nonfiction, fiction and poetry contributors, and interview subjects, come from all over the world, and we are always looking for more. Go to http://www.guernicamag.com/ for full description of the magazine and submission guidelines."

GULF COAST, Rebecca Wadlinger, Managing Editor; Ian Stansel, Editor, Dept. of English, University of Houston, Houston, TX 77204-3013. 1987. Poetry, fiction, art, photos, interviews, criticism, reviews, parts-of-novels, long-poems, non-fiction. "Reading period: 8/15-5/1. Contest held in March/April. Barthelme Prize for Short Fiction in August. See website for details. Electronic submissions. Recent contributors include: Terrance Hayes, Anne Carson, Dana Levin, Billy Collins, Linda Bierds, C, Dale Young, Sabrina Orah Mark, Joe Meno, G. C. Waldrep, Rick Barot, Robert Hass, Josip Novakovich, Michael Collier, Martha Ronk, Denise Duhamel, Matthea Harvey, Cate Marvin, Sarah Messer, Tomaz Salamun, R. T. Smith." circ. 2300. 2/yr. Pub'd 2 issues 2009; expects 2 issues 2010, 2 issues 2011. sub. price $14; per copy $8; sample $7. Back issues: Barthelme issue, $12; regular back issue, $7. 300pp. Reporting time: 4-6 months. Simultaneous submissions accepted: yes. Publishes 5% of manuscripts submitted. Payment: copies, $50 per poem, $100 per story. Copyrighted, reverts to author. Pub's reviews: 10 in 2009. §Poetry, fiction, nonfiction. Subjects: Fiction, Interviews, Literary Review, Literature (General), Non-Fiction, Poetry, Short Stories, Translation, Visual Arts.

GULF STREAM MAGAZINE, English Department FIU, Biscayne Bay Campus, 3000 NE 151 Street, North Miami, FL 33181-3000, http://www.gulfstreamlitmag.com. 1989. Poetry, fiction, non-fiction. "*Gulf Stream Magazine* has been publishing emerging and established writers of exceptional fiction, nonfiction and poetry since 1989. We also publish interviews, and book reviews. Past contributors include Sherman Alexie, David Kirby, Richard Blanco, Dennis Lehane, Ha Jin, Ann Hood, Susan Neville, Naomi Shihab Nye, and Virgil Suarez. You may submit your work electronically during our normal reading periods, which are September 15th -Decemeber 15th and January 15th - March 15th." circ. Online. Twice yearly. Reporting time: 2-3 months. Simultaneous submissions accepted: Yes. Ads: No.

Gurze Books, Lindsey Hall, Editor; Leigh Cohn, Publisher, PO Box 2238, Carlsbad, CA 92018, 800-756-7533; 760-434-7533; Fax 760-434-5476; email: info@gurze.net. 1980. Non-fiction. "Eating disorders; self-help, health/psychology." avg. press run 7.5M-10M. Pub'd 2 titles 2009; expects 3 titles 2010, 2 titles 2011. 32 titles listed in the *Small Press Record of Books in Print* (36th Edition, 2010-11). Discounts: trade distribution through

PGW, B&T, Ingram. 176pp. Reporting time: 2 months. Publishes 1% of manuscripts submitted. Payment: varies. Copyrights for author. Subjects: Health, Parenting, Psychology, Women.

The Gutenberg Press, Fred Foldvary, Editor in Chief, c/o Fred Foldvary, 1920 Cedar Street, Berkeley, CA 94709, 510-843-0248, e-mail gutenbergpress@pobox.com. 1980. Non-fiction. "Recent authors: Tertius Chandler, Fred Foldvary, John Hospers. Mostly publish books on social issues, social philosophy, and ancient history. Titles include: *The Soul of Liberty,* by Fred Foldvary. *The Tax We Need,* by Tertius Chandler. *Remote Kingdoms* and *Godly Kings and Early Ethics* by Tertius Chandler, *Anarchy or Limited Government?* by John Hospers. One art book also published." avg. press run 600. Pub'd 1 title 2009; expects 1 title 2010, 1 title 2011. 1 title listed in the *Small Press Record of Books in Print* (36th Edition, 2010-11). Discounts: 40% bookstores and 52% jobbers. 300pp. Reporting time: within 1 month. Simultaneous submissions accepted: ok. Publishes 10% of manuscripts submitted. Payment: after costs are met, profits are split 50/50. Copyrights for author. Subjects: History, Philosophy.

H

HAIGHT ASHBURY LITERARY JOURNAL, Indigo Hotchkiss, Editor; Alice E. Rogoff, Editor; Cesar Love, Editor; Taylor Landry, Editor, 558 Joost Avenue, San Francisco, CA 94127. 1980. Poetry, fiction, art, photos. "Recent contributors: Al Young, Clara Hsu, Diane Frank, Tony Vaughan, Jennifer Barone. Political and personal well-written poetry and fiction. Multi-cultural. Street life, poetry by prisoners,poems about nature, war,neighborhoods, love,occasionally uses poems in other languages than English with translation. Work submitted inbetween issues will be held to be considered for a later issue." circ. 2M. 1/yr. Pub'd 1 issue 2009; expects 1 issue 2010, 1 issue 2011. sub. price $40 lifetime, includes 6 back issues and future issues, $8 for 2 issues, $16 for 4 issues; per copy $4; sample $4(with postage). Back issues: This Far Together - anthology $15.00 with postage journals $4.00 with postage. Discounts: $13 for 10. 16pp. Reporting time: 3-6 months. Simultaneous submissions accepted: yes. Publishes 5% of manuscripts submitted. Payment: 3 copies if mailed, more copies per writer if picked up in person, "center" writers paid, some fiction paid. Copyrighted, reverts to author. Ads: $40 large/$30+/$20. Subjects: Literature (General), Poetry.

Haight-Ashbury Publications (see also JOURNAL OF PSYCHOACTIVE DRUGS), David E. Smith MD, Executive Editor; Terry Chambers, Managing Editor, 856 Stanyan Street, San Francisco, CA 94117, 415-752-7601, Fax 415-933-8674. 1967. Articles, art, photos, reviews, non-fiction. avg. press run 1000. Pub'd 1 title 2009; expects 1 title 2010, 1 title 2011. No titles listed in the *Small Press Record of Books in Print* (36th Edition, 2010-11). We provide quantity discounts for our books; price list available. 100pp. Reporting time: 60 days. Simultaneous submissions accepted: no. Publishes 33% of manuscripts submitted. Payment: none. Does not copyright for author. Subjects: Alcohol, Alcoholism, Drugs, Health, Mental Health, Sociology.

Haiku Society of America (see also FROGPOND: Journal of the Haiku Society of America), George Swede, Editor; Anita Krumins, Assistant Editor, PO Box 279, Station P, Toronto, Ontario M5S 2S8, Canada, gswede@ryerson.ca/http://www.hsa-haiku.org/frogpond.htm. 1978. Poetry. "Haiku and related material only." avg. press run 1M. No titles listed in the *Small Press Record of Books in Print* (36th Edition, 2010-11). 96pp. Reporting time: One month. Simultaneous submissions accepted: no. Publishes less than 1% of manuscripts submitted. Payment: None. Copyrights for author. Subject: Haiku.

Hallard Press, Bernard Gadd, 43 Landscape Rd, Papatoetoe, Auckland 1701, New Zealand, 64 09 2782731, 64 09 2782731. 1981. Poetry. "Mainly New Zealand poetry, ocassionally fiction, and usually of invited writers." avg. press run 100. Pub'd 1 title 2009; expects 3 titles 2010, 4 titles 2011. No titles listed in the *Small Press Record of Books in Print* (36th Edition, 2010-11). Discounts: 40%. 60-70pp. Reporting time: 1 week. Simultaneous submissions accepted: No. Payment: nil. Copyrights for author.

Halo Publishing International, Lisa Umina M, 5549 Canal Road, Valley View, OH 44125, 216-255-6756. 2002. Poetry, fiction, art, photos, cartoons, long-poems, non-fiction. "Halo Publishing International's We have blurred the lines and reduced the gap between traditional and subsidy publishers. Halo is a complete publishing service, and that includes marketing!HALO Helping Authors Launch Originals! We have professionals for every stage of your creation, from editorial to design to print to market to promotion." avg. press run 2000. Pub'd 5 titles 2009; expects 52 titles 2010, 100 titles 2011. 65 titles listed in the *Small Press Record of Books in Print* (36th Edition, 2010-11). Discounts: 45%. 32pp. Reporting time: 2 weeks. Simultaneous submissions accepted: Yes. Publishes 40% of manuscripts submitted. Payment: We retain 5% of Net Sales from the sale of any and all bound printed or electronic editions of the WORK. Copyrights for author. Subjects: Catholic, Children, Youth, Christianity, Christmas, Family, Fantasy, Fiction, Inspirational, Non-Fiction, Peace, Poetry,

Spiritual, Storytelling, Young Adult.

Hamilton Stone Editions (see also HAMILTON STONE REVIEW), PO Box 43, Maplewood, NJ 07040, web: www.hamiltonstone.org. 1997. No titles listed in the *Small Press Record of Books in Print* (36th Edition, 2010-11).

HAMILTON STONE REVIEW, Hamilton Stone Editions, P.O. Box 43, Maplewood, NJ 07040. "Submissions to *The Hamilton Stone Review* are open: We publish three times a year: in June, October, and February. Please send 1-7 poems in the body of your message and/or in ONE attachment; one story or up to three short shorts per message and/or attachment, please. Send bios with submissions. No snailmail submissions will be read. Poetry submissions should go directly to Halvard Johnson at halvard@earthlink.net. Send fiction to Lynda Schor at lyndaschor@earthlink.net."

HAMPTON ROADS HEALTH JOURNAL, Page Bishop, 4808 Courthouse Street, Suite 204, Williamsburg, VA 23188, 757-645-4475. 2007. Articles, photos, interviews, reviews, letters. circ. 76,400. 12/yr. Expects 12 issues 2010, 12 issues 2011. sub. price $24; sample Free. Back issues: $2.00. 40pp. Reporting time: 10 days. Simultaneous submissions accepted: No. Publishes 80% of manuscripts submitted. Payment: .15 per word paid upon publication. Not copyrighted. Pub's reviews: none in 2009. §books on health and fitness/well being. Subjects: Adolescence, Aging, Alcohol, Alcoholism, Alternative Medicine, Aromatherapy, Divorce, Health, Lifestyles, Mental Health, Nursing, Nutrition, Safety, Virginia, Women, Yoga.

Hamster Huey Press, Paul R Spadoni, 7627 84th Avenue Ct. NW, Gig Harbor, WA 98335-6237, Phone 253-851-7839 http://www.hamsterhueypress.com. 2004. Fiction. "We are not seeking additional manuscripts at this time." avg. press run 3000. Pub'd 1 title 2009; expects 1 title 2011. No titles listed in the *Small Press Record of Books in Print* (36th Edition, 2010-11). Discounts: Hamster Huey and the Gooey Kablooie1-2 copies: $6.95 for 3-99 copies: $4.50 for 100-199: $4.00 for 200-499: $3.50 for 500+: $3.15. 8pp. Simultaneous submissions accepted: No. Publishes 1% of manuscripts submitted. Copyrights for author.

HAND PAPERMAKING, Tom Bannister, Mina Takahashi, PO Box 1070, Beltsville, MD 20704-1070, 800-821-6604, Fax 301-220-2394, info@handpapermaking.org. 1986. Articles, interviews, criticism, reviews. "Dedicated to advancing traditional and contemporary ideas in the art of hand papermaking." circ. 1.5M. 2/yr. Pub'd 2 issues 2009; expects 2 issues 2010, 2 issues 2011. sub. price $55; per copy $22; sample $22. Back issues: $22. Discounts: none. 48pp. Reporting time: 2 months. Simultaneous submissions accepted: no. Publishes 25% of manuscripts submitted. Payment: $50-$150. Copyrighted, does not revert to author. Pub's reviews: 4 in 2009. §Paper and book arts. Ads: $300/$220/$1. Subjects: Book Arts, Visual Arts.

Handshake Editions, Jim Haynes, Atelier A2, 83 rue de la Tombe-Issoire, Paris 75014, France, 01-4327-1767, jim_haynes@wanadoo.fr, jim@jim-haynes.com, www.jim-haynes.com. 1971. Poetry, fiction, articles, photos, cartoons, parts-of-novels. "Only personal face-to-face submissions solicited. Handshake mainly publishes Paris-based writers. Small print-runs, but we attempt to keep everything in print (i.e., frequent re-prints). Libertarian bias. Writers recently published include Ted Joans, Sarah Bean, Michael Zwerin, Jim Haynes, Elaine J. Cohen, Ken Timmerman, Judith Malina, Lynne Tillman, Samuel Brecher, Suzanne Brogger, Jayne Cortez, Amanda P. Hoover, Echnaton, Yianna Katsoulos, William Levy, and Barry Gifford." avg. press run 1M. Pub'd 3 titles 2009; expects 12 titles 2010. 11 titles listed in the *Small Press Record of Books in Print* (36th Edition, 2010-11). Discounts: 1/3 prepaid; all cheques payable to Jim Haynes. Payment: copies of the book. Does not copyright for author. Subjects: Libertarian, Philosophy.

HANG GLIDING & PARAGLIDING, Nick Greece, U.S. Hang Gliding & Paragliding Assoc., Inc., PO Box 1330, Colorado Springs, CO 80901-1330, 719-632-8300, fax 719-632-6417. 1974. Articles, photos, cartoons, interviews, reviews, letters, news items. "Information pertaining to hang gliding, paragliding and soaring flight." circ. 9M. 12/yr. Pub'd 12 issues 2009; expects 12 issues 2010, 12 issues 2011. sub. price $52; per copy $6.95; sample same. Back issues: $6.95. Discounts: newsstand 50%. 80pp. Reporting time: 2 months. Simultaneous submissions accepted: no. Publishes 70% of manuscripts submitted. Payment: limited, cover photo $50, feature story. Copyrighted. Pub's reviews: 2 in 2009. §Aviation, outdoor recreation. Ads: $990 full page/$365 half page/25 words for $10 then $1 per word classified. Subjects: Aviation, Sports, Outdoors.

HANGING LOOSE, Hanging Loose Press, Robert Hershon, Dick Lourie, Mark Pawlak, Ron Schreiber (1934-2004); Donna Brook, Associate Editor; Marie Carter, Associate Editor, 231 Wyckoff Street, Brooklyn, NY 11217, www.hangingloosepress.com. 1966. Poetry, fiction. "Emphasis remains on the work of new writers—and when we find people we like, we stay with them. Among recent contributors: Kimiko Hahn, Paul Violi, Donna Brook, D. Nurkse, Sherman Alexie, Ron Overton, Gary Lenhart, Sharon Mesmer, Charles North. We welcome submissions to the magazine, but artwork & book mss. are by invitation only. We suggest strongly that people read the magazine before sending work." circ. 2M. 3/yr. Pub'd 3 issues 2009; expects 3 issues 2010. sub. price $22.00/3 issues (individuals); per copy $9.00; sample $11.00 (incl. postage). Back issues: prices on request, including complete sets. Discounts: 40% to bookstores, 20% to jobbers. 128pp. Reporting time: 2-3 months. Simultaneous submissions accepted: no. Payment: 2 copies + small check. Copyrighted, does not revert to author. §Poetry. No ads. Subjects: Fiction, Poetry.

Hanging Loose Press (see also HANGING LOOSE), Robert Hershon, Dick Lourie, Mark Pawlak, Ron Schreiber; Emmett Jarrett, Contributing Editor; Donna Brook, Contributing Editor; Marie Carter, Editorial Associate, 231 Wyckoff Street, Brooklyn, NY 11217, www.hangingloosepress.com. 1966. Poetry, fiction. "Book mss by invitation only." avg. press run 2M. Pub'd 6 titles 2009; expects 6 titles 2010, 6 titles 2011. 133 titles listed in the *Small Press Record of Books in Print* (36th Edition, 2010-11). Discounts: bookstores, 40% (more than 4 copies), 20%, 1-4 copies; STOP orders 30%. 96-120pp. Payment: yes. Copyrights for author. Subjects: Fiction, Poetry.

H-NGM-N, H_NGM_N B_ _KS, Nate Pritts, Natchitoches, LA 71457, nathanpritts@hotmail.com, www.h-ngm-n.com. 2000. Poetry, fiction, art, cartoons, interviews, criticism, reviews, long-poems, collages. "*H_ngm_n* is an online journal of poetry, poetics, &c." 2/yr. Expects 1 issue 2010, 2 issues 2011. Pages vary. Reporting time: quick, 1 month tops. Simultaneous submissions accepted: no. Payment: copies. Copyrighted, reverts to author. Ads: we'll do trade ads. Subject: Poetry.

H_NGM_N B_ _KS (see also H-NGM-N), Nate Pritts, EIC.; Matt Dube, Fiction Ed., NSU/Dept. of Language & Communication, Natchitoches, LA 71497, editor@h-ngm-n.com. 2000. Poetry, fiction, art, cartoons, criticism, non-fiction. "Online magazine, 2X year: http://www.h-ngm-n.com : Chapbooks - varies, see site for details." Pub'd 4 titles 2009; expects 4 titles 2010, ? titles 2011. 5 titles listed in the *Small Press Record of Books in Print* (36th Edition, 2010-11). 25-32pp. We accept simultaneous submissions, but let us know ASAP if something happens elsewhere. Payment: copies and huge support. Does not copyright for author.

Hannacroix Creek Books, Inc, Submissions Editor, 1127 High Ridge Road, #110, Stamford, CT 06905-1203, 203-321-8674, Fax 203-968-0193, hannacroix@aol.com. 1996. Poetry, fiction, non-fiction. "Not open to unsolicited manuscripts at this time." avg. press run 1M-3M; also POD (Print-on-Demand). Expects 4 titles 2010, 4-6 titles 2011. 3 titles listed in the *Small Press Record of Books in Print* (36th Edition, 2010-11). Pages vary. Payment: negotiable. Copyrights for author. Subjects: Children, Youth, Poetry, Self-Help.

HAPA NUI, Julianne Bonnet, East Palo Alto, CA 94303, www.hapanui.com. 2007. Poetry, fiction, art, photos, cartoons, satire, parts-of-novels, long-poems, collages, plays. "In Hawaiian "hapa nui" means majority or large part. The concept of the reader-driven lit mag is at the heart of what we see as a new movement in literature.One part on-line venue and one part print journal, Hapa Nui is a place where readers determine through a democratic voting process what they like and, ultimately, which work makes it into print.Work is pre-screened by our readers and those selections are placed online for a vote. We have posted work by Rob Carney, Sid Miller, Joyce Nower, among others." circ. 500. 1/yr. Expects 1 issue 2010, 1 issue 2011. sub. price $10.00; per copy $10.00; sample $5.00. Back issues: $5.00. Discounts: 2-10 copies 25%. 200pp. Reporting time: Four to eight weeks. Simultaneous submissions accepted: No. Publishes 5% of manuscripts submitted. Payment: Payment in copies. Copyrighted, reverts to author. Pub's reviews. Ads: Ad-swap. Subjects: Absurdist, Arts, Autobiography, Creative Non-fiction, Experimental, Fiction, Folklore, Graphics, Haiku, Memoirs, Novels, Poetry, Satire, Short Stories, Visual Arts.

HAPPENINGNOW!EVERYWHERE, Happening Writers' Collective, 22 Dell Street, Somerville, MA 02145, happeningmagazine@yahoo.com, www.happeningnoweverywhere.com. 2005. Poetry, fiction, articles, art, photos, cartoons, interviews, satire, criticism, reviews, music, letters, parts-of-novels, long-poems, collages, plays, concrete art, news items, non-fiction. "A magazine of general popular and cultural interest, written by writers age kid to 19. Readership includes kids, teens, teachers, parents, anyone intereted in young people and their unique perspectives. Peer edited. Writers under 20 years of age only, no minimum age. Original submissions are welcome for the editors' consideration. SASE must accompany mailed submissions. E-mailed submissions are OK." circ. 250. 4/yr. Expects 2 issues 2010, 4 issues 2011. 3 titles listed in the *Small Press Record of Books in Print* (36th Edition, 2010-11). sub. price $15.00; per copy $3.75; sample $3.00. Back issues: $3.00. Discounts: 30%. 24pp. Simultaneous submissions accepted: No. Publishes 40% of manuscripts submitted. Payment: 1 copy of magazine. Discount on purchase of more copies in which contributor appears. Copyrighted, reverts to author. Pub's reviews. §Anything of interest to young people under age 18. No ads. Subjects: Adolescence, Children, Youth, Fiction, Media, Movies, Music, Poetry, Prose, Reviews.

Happy About, Mitchell Levy, 20660 Stevens Creek Blvd, Suite 210, Cupertino, CA 95014, 408-257-3000, info@happyabout.info, http://www.happyabout.info. 1992. Satire, criticism, news items, non-fiction. "Our books contain wisdom. Looking for business related topics that contain war stories, test cases testimonials from people that have been there and done that. Our books are typically 80-130 pages and are published in tradebook, eBook and podbook formats." avg. press run varies. Pub'd 1 title 2009; expects 2 titles 2010, 3 titles 2011. 117 titles listed in the *Small Press Record of Books in Print* (36th Edition, 2010-11). Discounts: please inquire. 100-150pp, that said we have a number of 300-page books.pp. Payment: 25-33% of profit. Copyrights for author. Subjects: Advertising, Self-Promotion, Business & Economics, Computers, Calculators, Consulting, Consumer, Finances, Internet, Interviews, Libraries, Management, Marketing, Publishing, Quotations, Real

Estate, Research.

Harbor House, Peggy Cheney, Asst. Publisher; E. Randall Floyd, Founder; Nathan Elliott, Creative Director, 111 Tenth Street, Augusta, GA 30901, 706-738-0354(phone), 706-823-5999(fax), harborhouse@harborhouse-books.com, www.harborhousebooks.com. 1997. Fiction, non-fiction. "Founded in 1997, Harbor House seeks to publish the best in original adult fiction and non-fiction. Our current collection of titles includes contemporary non-fiction (social commentary, memoirs, biographies), thrillers, Civil War fiction and The Unexplained. BatWing Press is our new imprint which launched in 2005. BatWing is dedicated to publishing the finest in horror fiction.The Civil War Classics series premiers Civil War fiction inspired by true events.In June 2004, Harbor House began renovation of an 1879 cottage in the heart of downtown Augusta near the Savannah River. The cottage now serves as the corporate headquarters of Harbor House." Pub'd 15 titles 2009; expects 12 titles 2010, 15 titles 2011. 37 titles listed in the *Small Press Record of Books in Print* (36th Edition, 2010-11). Simultaneous submissions accepted: yes. Publishes 5% of manuscripts submitted. Payment: 7 percent to 10 percent royalty of net retail price. Royalty reports twice per year. Advances vary based on topic, exposure and experience. Copyrights for author. Subjects: Americana, Autobiography, Biography, Civil War, Folklore, Horror, Non-Fiction, Novels, Occult, Religion, South, Spiritual, Supernatural.

Harbor House Law Press, Inc. (see also THE BEACON: Journal of Special Education Law & Practice), PO Box 480, Hartfield, VA 23071, 804-758-8400, Fax 202-318-3239, info@harborhouselaw.com, www.harborhouselaw.com. 1999. Articles, non-fiction. "Our mission is to publish special education legal and advocacy information for parents, advocates, educators, and attorneys. Our goal is to ensure that children with disabilities have equality of opportunity, full participation, independent living, and economic self-sufficiency. We welcome inquiries from professionals who seek a publisher for their manuscripts." avg. press run 5M. Expects 1 title 2010, 1 title 2011. 3 titles listed in the *Small Press Record of Books in Print* (36th Edition, 2010-11). Discounts: bulk 50%, bookstore 40%. 390pp. Reporting time: 3-6 months. Publishes 10% of manuscripts submitted. Copyrights for author. Subjects: Education, Law, Parenting, Self-Help.

HARDBOILED, Gryphon Books, Gary Lovisi, PO Box 209, Brooklyn, NY 11228. 1988. Fiction, articles, interviews, letters, non-fiction. "Previously *Detective Story Magazine* and *Hardboiled Detective*. Publish the hardest, cutting-edge crime fiction, stories full of impact, action, violence. Also reviews, articles, interviews on hardboiled topics. Please Note: The best way to write for *Hardboiled* is to *read Hardboiled* and see *exactly* what we're after!" circ. 1M. 4/yr. Pub'd 4 issues 2009; expects 4 issues 2010, 4 issues 2011. sub. price $35/4 issues domestic, $55/4 issues outside USA; per copy $10 + postage; sample $10 + postage. Back issues: #1-9 $29, or $6 each, (only for the 9 early issues of *Detective Story Magazine*). Discounts: 40% on 5 or more of each issue. 100-110pp. Reporting time: 2-6 weeks. Simultaneous submissions accepted: no. Publishes 3% of manuscripts submitted. Payment: $5-$50 depending on quality and length, + 2 free copies on publication. Copyrighted, reverts to author. Pub's reviews: 18 in 2009. §Hardboiled, crime-fiction, mystery, suspense. Ads: $50/$25. Subjects: Crime, Mystery, Short Stories.

HARMONY: Voices for a Just Future, Sea Fog Press, Rose Evans, Managing Editor, PO Box 210056, San Francisco, CA 94121-0056, 415-221-8527. 1987. Poetry, articles, cartoons, interviews, criticism, reviews. "*Harmony Magazine* publishes articles on reverence for life—for animal rights, disabled rights, gay rights, peace, justice, ecology—against war, capital punishment, abortion, euthanasia, covert action, etc." circ. 1.4M. 6/yr. Pub'd 6 issues 2009; expects 6 issues 2010, 6 issues 2011. sub. price $12; per copy $2; sample $2. Back issues: $2. Discounts: 10+ copies 40%. 28pp. Reporting time: 3-8 weeks. Simultaneous submissions accepted: yes. Publishes .03% of manuscripts submitted. Payment: copies only. Copyrighted, reverts to author. Pub's reviews: 10 in 2009. §War & peace, social justice, hunger, abortion, death penalty. Ads: $100/$50/10¢ per word. Subjects: Non-Violence, Peace, Politics.

Harobed Publishing Creations, Deborah Tillman, P.O.Box 8195, Pittsburgh, PA 15217-0915, 412-243-9299 fax/phone(if beeps redial fax in use). 2004. Poetry, art, reviews, long-poems. "Harobed Publishing Creations publishes selected books of poetry. Prefers "personal" free verse, ryhtm or prose, regardless of style, form, and genre." We offer Poetry books (60-90 pages), slim volumes (44-55 pages)and chapbooks (20-30 pages),with full-color cover,perfect-binding,and ISBN. Press run 200-1000 copies. Send material for review consideration to Deborah Tillman, editor." Pub'd 1 title 2009; expects 3 titles 2010, 10 titles 2011. No titles listed in the *Small Press Record of Books in Print* (36th Edition, 2010-11). Reporting time: 30 days. Simultaneous submissions accepted: No. Does not copyright for author. Subjects: Book Collecting, Bookselling, Book Reviewing, Fashion, Literary Review, Literature (General), Newsletter, Performing Arts, Picture Books, Postcards, Printing, Prose, Visual Arts.

HARP-STRINGS, Madelyn Eastlund, Editor; Sybella Beyer Snyder, Associate Editor, PO Box 640387, Beverly Hills, FL 34464. 1989. Poetry. "Recent contributors: Robert Cooperman, Taylor Graham, Ruth F. Harrison, MIchael Keshigian, Amy Jo Schoonover, Howard F. Stein, Fredrick Zydek. No short poems (under 14 lines), maximum lines 80. Looking for *'poems to remember.'* Looking for narratives 'good story poems' ballads, patterned poetry. Annual contest: The Edna St. Vincent Millay Harp-Weaver Poetry Contest, *as well as* *three other quarterly contests—change each year.* Read only February, May, August, November. Each reading is to plan the following issue—no files are kept. Poems kept only for current issue." circ. 100. 4/yr. Pub'd 4 issues 2009; expects 4 issues 2010, 4 issues 2011. sub. price $14; per copy $4.50; sample $4.50. Back issues: a few for most recent years. 24-32pp. Reporting time: end of reading month. No simultaneous submissions read. Publishes 5% of manuscripts submitted. Payment: copy. Copyrighted, reverts to author. Subject: Poetry.

HARPUR PALATE, Holly Wendt, Editor; Devon Branca, Editor; Kim Vose, Editor, English Dept., PO Box 6000, Binghamton University, Binghamton, NY 13902-6000, http://harpurpalate.binghamton.edu. 2000. Poetry, fiction, art, photos, non-fiction. "Past contributors have included Ruth Stone, Lydia Davis, Lee K. Abbott, Marvin Bell, B. H. Fairchild, Jack Ridl, Sascha Feinstein, Jamie Wriston Colbert, Sean Thomas Dougherty, and Ryan G. Van Cleave. *Harpur Palate* has no restrictions on subject matter or form. Quite simply, send us your highest-quality fiction and poetry. We do not accept submissions via e-mail. Fiction: Length should be between 250 and 8,000 words; ONE submission per envelope. Poetry: Send 3-5 poems, no more than 10 pages total per author. Reading periods: We accept submissions all year around. The deadline for the Winter issue is October 15 and the deadline for the Summer issue is March 15. Mail us a copy of your manuscript, a cover letter, and SASE for our response. Manuscripts without SASEs will be discarded unread. Copies of manuscripts will NOT be returned. *Harpur Palate* also sponsors the Milton Kessler Memorial Prize for Poetry in the fall and the John Gardner Memorial Prize for Fiction in the spring. See website or send SASE for info." circ. 700. 2/yr. Pub'd 2 issues 2009; expects 2 issues 2010, 2 issues 2011. sub. price $16 (Institutions add $4; outside U.S. add $6). Send check or money order. Make sure the check is drawn on a U. S. bank and is made out to *Harpur Palate*; per copy $10. Back issues: $5. 180pp. Reporting time: 4 to 6 months. We accept simultaneous submissions if stated as such in cover letter. If your work is accepted elsewhere, please let us know immediately. Publishes 1% of manuscripts submitted. Payment: 2 contributor's copies per author. Copyrighted, reverts to author.

Hartley & Marks, Publishers, Rodger Reynolds, Managing Editor, PO Box 147, Point Roberts, WA 98281, (800) 277-5887. No titles listed in the *Small Press Record of Books in Print* (36th Edition, 2010-11).

THE HARVARD ADVOCATE, Greg Scruggs, President; Garrett Morgan, Publisher, 21 South Street, Cambridge, MA 02138, Fax 617-496-9740, contact@theharvardadvocate.com. 1866. Poetry, fiction, articles, art, photos, cartoons, interviews, criticism, reviews, long-poems, collages, plays, non-fiction. "*The Harvard Advocate* publishes work from Harvard undergraduates, affiliates, and alumni. We regret that we cannot read manuscripts from other sources." circ. 4M. 4/yr. Pub'd 4 issues 2009; expects 4 issues 2010, 4 issues 2011. sub. price $25 for 4 issues; per copy $8; sample $5. Back issues: price varies. Discounts: none. 60pp (16 color)pp. Reporting time: 4-6 weeks. Simultaneous submissions accepted: yes. Publishes 10% of manuscripts submitted. Payment: none. Copyrighted, does not revert to author. Pub's reviews: 12 in 2009. §fiction, poetry, features, film/animation, art,. Ads: $200-$1400. Subjects: Literary Review, Literature (General).

HARVARD JOURNAL OF LAW AND GENDER, Nora Flum, Editor-in-Chief; Cari Simon, Editor-in-Chief; Eleanor Simon, Managing Editor, Publications Center, Harvard Law School, Cambridge, MA 02138, 617-495-3726. 1978. Articles, reviews. "Founded in 1977 and currently working on its thirty-fourth volume, the Harvard Journal of Law and Gender (originally the Harvard Womens Law Journal) is the nations oldest continuously publishing feminist law journal. The JLG is devoted to the advancement of feminist jurisprudence and the study of law and gender. By combining political, economic, historical, sociological, and legal perspectives, we seek to clarify legal issues that have gendered aspects and implications, and to confront new challenges to full social equality. Our journal also explores the interconnections between race, class, sexuality, and gender in the law." circ. 900. 1/yr. Pub'd 1 issue 2009; expects 1 issue 2010, 1 issue 2011. sub. price $17 US, $20 foreign; per copy $17; sample not available. 350pp. Reporting time: varies. Copyrighted, does not revert to author. Pub's reviews: 7 in 2009. §Law related, legal histories and sociological literary perspectives on the law as it affects women and feminism. Ads: none. Subjects: Family, Feminism, Law, Sex, Sexuality, Women.

HARVARD REVIEW, Christina Thompson, Editor; Major Jackson, Poetry Editor; Nam Le, Fiction Editor, Lamont Library, Harvard University, Cambridge, MA 02138, 617-495-9775. 1992. Poetry, fiction, interviews, reviews, plays, non-fiction. "We publish writers at all stages of their careers, from the very well-known to the never-before-published. We are interested in most literary genres and styles (except sci-fi, horror, etc). Recent contributors include: Arthur Miller, Joyce Carol Oates, Jorie Graham, Jim Crace, Seamus Heaney, Alice Hoffman, Lyn Hejinian, Lan Samantha Chang, John Ashbery and Robert Creeley. We are pleased to announce the second issue of Harvard Review Online, a bi-monthly online literary journal designed to complement the print edition of Harvard Review." circ. 2500. 2/yr. Pub'd 2 issues 2009; expects 2 issues 2010, 2 issues 2011. sub. price $20; per copy $13; sample n/a. Back issues: $13 inquire for availability. 256pp. Reporting time: 6 months. Simultaneous submissions accepted: Yes. Payment: no payment. Copyrighted, reverts to author. Pub's reviews: approx. 50 in 2009. §fiction, poetry, essays, creative non-fiction. Ads: 1/2 page $350, full page $500. Subjects: Drama, Essays, Fiction, Literary Review, Poetry, Prose.

Harvest Shadows Publications, PO Box 378, Southborough, MA 01772-0378, Prefer contact by email.

dbharvest@harvestshadows.com, www.harvestshadows.com. 2003. Fiction, non-fiction. Pub'd 1 title 2009; expects 2 titles 2010, 2 titles 2011. No titles listed in the *Small Press Record of Books in Print* (36th Edition, 2010-11). Discounts: Discounts available. Contact for more info. 224-320pp. Copyrights for author. Subjects: Fiction, Horror, Supernatural, WICCA.

HAWAI'I REVIEW, Jay Hartwell, Advisor, 1755 Pope Road, Ka Leo Bldg. 31-D, Honolulu, HI 96822, 808-956-3030. 1973. Poetry, fiction, art, photos, cartoons, interviews, satire, music, parts-of-novels, long-poems, collages, plays, non-fiction. "Accept works of visual art, poetry, fiction, and non-fiction, including plays, short-short stories, essays, humor, cartoons. Publish all forms of literature including, but not limited to, works which focus on Hawai'i and the Pacific. Submissions *must* include SASE w/sufficient postage for return of material with reply." circ. 500. 2/yr. Pub'd 2 issues 2009; expects 2 issues 2010, 2 issues 2011. sub. price $20, $30/2 years; per copy $10; sample $10. Back issues: $10. 150-250pp. Reporting time: 3-5 months. Simultaneous submissions accepted: yes. Publishes 5% of manuscripts submitted. Payment: 4 copies. Copyrighted, reverts to author. Ads: call for prices. Subjects: Arts, Asian-American, Avant-Garde, Experimental Art, Biography, Essays, Fiction, Hawaii, Indigenous Cultures, Multicultural, Non-Fiction, Pacific Region, Poetry, Prose, Theatre, Translation.

HAWAI'I PACIFIC REVIEW, Patrice Wilson PhD, Editor, 1060 Bishop Street, Hawai'i Pacific University, Honolulu, HI 96813, 808-544-1108. 1987. Poetry, fiction, satire, reviews, parts-of-novels, long-poems, non-fiction. "The *Hawai'i Pacific Review* is looking for poetry, short fiction, and personal essays that speak with a powerful and unique voice. We encourage experimental narrative techniques and poetic styles. While we occasionally accept work from novice writers, we publish only work of the hightest quality. We will read one submission per contributor consisting of one prose piece of up to 5000 words or 5 poems. Please send as word or rtf attahment to email at hprsubmissions@hpu.edu after Sept. 1, 2010. Include a 5-line bio and names of works in the email. Experimental works, translations and long poetry (up to 100 lines) are all welcome. Our reading period is Sept. 1 to Dec. 31." circ. 500. 1/yr. Pub'd 1 issue 2009; expects 1 issue 2010, 1 issue 2011. sub. price $8.95; per copy $8.95; sample $5. Back issues: $7. Discounts: bulk $4 per copy. 100pp. Reporting time: 12-15 weeks. Simultaneous submissions accepted: No. Publishes 5% of manuscripts submitted. Payment: 2 copies. Copyrighted, reverts to author. Pub's reviews: 5 in 2009. §Poetry, fiction, essays. Ads: exchange. Subjects: Essays, Fiction, Poetry, Satire, Short Stories.

Hawk Publishing Group, Inc., William Bernhardt, Nita McPartland, 7107 S. Yale Avenue, PMB 345, Tulsa, OK 74136-6308, 918-492-3677, www.hawkpub.com. 1999. "Please read the submission guidelines on our website. We are only accepting queries by email and we are primarily interested in authors from the Southwest." Pub'd 15 titles 2009; expects 12 titles 2010, 12 titles 2011. No titles listed in the *Small Press Record of Books in Print* (36th Edition, 2010-11). Simultaneous submissions accepted: yes. Copyrights for author.

The Haworth Press, Zella Ondrey, Vice President of Publications, 325 Chestnut St., Philadelphia, PA 19106-1580, Tel.: (607)722-5857, Fax: (607)722-8465, Web: http://www.HaworthPress.com. 1978. Fiction, non-fiction. "The Haworth Press is an independent publisher of academic and professional books and journals on a wide range of subjects focusing on contemporary issues. For a list of all topics go to www.HaworthPress.com." avg. press run 1400. Pub'd 220 titles 2009; expects 250 titles 2010, 200 titles 2011. No titles listed in the *Small Press Record of Books in Print* (36th Edition, 2010-11). Discounts: Retail Bookstore Discount Schedule for Titles in the Haworth Trade Catalog: 1-4 books 25%, 5-49 books 42%, 50-99 books 44% 100+ books 46% Bookstores & Distributors; 33 1/3% on hardbound copies Discount Notes:1. Classroom adoption orders receive 20% discount; a. All orders identifiable as adoption orders. b. Orders for 5 copies or more 2. Wholesale discount: 20% on orders for less than 50 copies and 50% on orders for 50 copies or more. 350pp. Reporting time: Haworth will contact the author in eight to ten weeks after submission. Simultaneous submissions accepted: No. Publishes 30% of manuscripts submitted. Copyrights for author. Subjects: Aging, Agriculture, Children, Youth, Education, Family, Gender Issues, Journals, Libraries, Marketing, Medicine, Mental Health, Religion, Sex, Sexuality, Social Work, Textbooks.

HAYDEN'S FERRY REVIEW, Box 875002, Arizona State University, Tempe, AZ 85287-5002, 480-965-1337. 1986. Poetry, fiction, art, photos, interviews, non-fiction. "Accepts submissions online: http://submit.haydensferryreview.asu.edu. Publishes approximately 25 poems, 5 short stories. Past contributors: Raymond Carver, Rick Bass, Joy Williams, John Updike, T.C. Boyle, Rita Dove, Maura Stanton and Joseph Heller." circ. 1M. 2/yr. Pub'd 2 issues 2009; expects 2 issues 2010, 2 issues 2011. sub. price $14; per copy $6.00; sample $7.50. Back issues: $4.50. 180pp. Reporting time: 8-10 weeks after deadline. We accept simultaneous submissions with notification. Publishes less than 1% of manuscripts submitted. Payment: $50, 2 copies, 1-year subscription; $100 for cover art. Copyrighted, reverts to author. Subjects: Arts, Fiction, Photography, Poetry, Translation.

HAZMAT REVIEW, Norm Davis, Editor, PO Box 30507, Rochester, NY 14603. "*HazMat Review* is dedicated completely and uncompromisingly to literary freedom and artistic expression. All submissions should come in an envelope marked "Editor." All submissions remain the copyrighted material of the author or artist and are published in HazMat Review or on www.hazmatlitreview.org by assumed permission of the author. A self-addressed stamped envelope should accompany the material if the author wants the material returned.*HazMat Review* is currently seeking poetry, prose, and artwork which shows social or political awareness, but will consider all submissions which are of high quality. Fiction should be brief.''

HEAL Foundation Press, Stephan McLaughlin Jr., PO Box 241209, Memphis, TN 38002, www.healfoundation.org, info@healfoundation.org, (901) 320-9179. 1998. Non-fiction. "Writers include Stephan McLaughlin, Jr. and Victor La Cerva." avg. press run 5000. Expects 1 title 2010, 1 title 2011. 3 titles listed in the *Small Press Record of Books in Print* (36th Edition, 2010-11). 300pp. Subjects: New Age, Non-Violence, Relationships, Self-Help, Spiritual.

HEALMB Publishing, Lisa Bowles, P.O. Box 4005, Clovis, CA 93613-4005, 559-291-4387, 559-297-7077, comments@nailcareinfo.com, http://www.nailcareinfo.com. 2006. Non-fiction. Expects 1 title 2010, 1-3 titles 2011. No titles listed in the *Small Press Record of Books in Print* (36th Edition, 2010-11). Subjects: Christianity, Death & Dying, Divorce, Grieving, Health, Homelessness, Marriage, Nutrition, Safety, Senior Citizens, Women.

THE HEALTH JOURNALS, Page Bishop, 4808 Courthouse Street, Suite 204, Williamsburg, VA 23188, 757-645-4475. 2005. Articles, photos, interviews, reviews, letters, news items, non-fiction. "We hope to enlighten and entertain readers with honest and accurate information pertaining only to health and wellness. We are looking for family-friendly articles on a variety of topics in health and medicine. Physicians and other health care professionals, as well as free lance writers, submit articles on a conitnuing basis." circ. 76,400. 12/yr. Pub'd 12 issues 2009; expects 12 issues 2010, 12 issues 2011. sub. price $24; sample free. Back issues: $2.00. 40pp. Reporting time: 1 week. Simultaneous submissions accepted: No. Publishes 80% of manuscripts submitted. Payment: 15 cents per word paid upon publication. Not copyrighted. Pub's reviews: 5 in 2009. §Health and Wellness/Fitness books. Subjects: Acupuncture, Adolescence, Aging, Alcohol, Alcoholism, Alternative Medicine, Aromatherapy, Birth, Birth Control, Population, Disease, Divorce, Dreams, Education, Health, Nursing, Nutrition, Yoga.

Health Plus Publishers, Paula E. Clure, PO Box 1027, Sherwood, OR 97140, 503-625-0589, Fax 503-625-1525. 1965. Non-fiction. "We publish books on health, particularly holistic health, nutrition, and fitness. We are publishers of Dr. Paavo Airola's books, including *How to Get Well, Everywoman's Book,* and *Are You Confused?* Other publications include: *Change Your Mind/Change Your Weight,* by Dr. James McClernan, and *Exercise For Life,* by Mark L. Hendrickson and Gary J. Greene. Query first." avg. press run 7.5M-10M. Pub'd 1 title 2009; expects 2 titles 2010, 1 title 2011. 14 titles listed in the *Small Press Record of Books in Print* (36th Edition, 2010-11). Discounts: inquire. 250pp. Reporting time: 3-6 months. Payment: no advance, royalties negotiable. Copyrights for author. Subject: Health.

Health Press NA Inc., K. Frazier, PO Box 37470, Albuquerque, NM 87176-7470, goodbooks@healthpress.com. 1988. Non-fiction. "Books related to cutting-edge health topics, well-researched, geared to general public. Require outline with 3 chapters for submission—prefer complete manuscript. Authors must be credentialed (MD, PhD) or have credentialed professional write intro/preface. Controversial topics desired." avg. press run 5M. Pub'd 4 titles 2009; expects 4 titles 2010, 4 titles 2011. 9 titles listed in the *Small Press Record of Books in Print* (36th Edition, 2010-11). Discounts: bookstore 40%+, library 10%, (depending on quantity). 250pp. Reporting time: 8-10 weeks. Simultaneous submissions accepted: yes. Payment: standard royalty. Copyrights for author. Subjects: Drugs, Health, Medicine, Psychology, Self-Help.

HEALTHY WEIGHT JOURNAL, Frances M. Berg, Editor, 402 South 14th Street, Hettinger, ND 58639, 701-567-2646, Fax 701-567-2602, e-mail fmberg@healthyweight.net. 1986. "Publishing office: 4 Hughson Street South, Hamilton, ON Canada L8N 3K7, 800-568-7281, e-mail info@bcdecker.com." circ. 1.5M. 6/yr. Pub'd 6 issues 2009; expects 6 issues 2010, 6 issues 2011. sub. price US & Canada: $65 individuals, $95 institutions, $32.50 students; elsewhere: $85 individual, $125 institutions, $45 students (U.S. funds only); per copy $19 US & Canada, $25 elsewhere; sample free. Back issues: $19 US & Canada, $25 elsewhere. Discounts: agents 5%. 20pp. Payment: none. Copyrighted, does not revert to author. Pub's reviews: 12-16 in 2009. §Obesity, weight management, Nutrition, eating disorders. Ads: contact Bob Sutherland at Canadian address above. Subjects: Health, Medicine.

HEARING HEALTH, 641 Lexington Ave. 15th Floor, New York, NY 10022, 866-454-3924, TTY 888-435-6104. 1984. Articles, art, cartoons, interviews, reviews, news items, non-fiction. "Hearing Health is the ultimate consumer resource on hearing. We offer reviews of new research, technology, treatments and services in benefit of people of all ages with hearing loss, tinnitus and/or balance disorders. We print up to two human interest stories in each issue, up to two research articles (contributed by experts in the field) and the occasional book review. We often need personal experience essays to accompany articles on specific causes of hearing loss." 4/yr. Pub'd 4 issues 2009; expects 4 issues 2010, 4 issues 2011. sub. price free; per copy free;

sample free. Back issues: online archives free. 52pp. Reporting time: up to six months. Simultaneous submissions accepted: Yes. Publishes 20% of manuscripts submitted. Payment: small honorarium, $50. copyrighted, we retain rights, but rarely refuse permission to reprint an article with proper credit. Pub's reviews: 4 in 2009. §anything related to living with hearing loss, tinnitus, or balance disorders. Subjects: Consumer, Disabled, Handicapped, Health, Interviews, Medicine, Research.

HEARTLODGE: Honoring the House of the Poet, Andrea L. Watson, Editor and Publisher, P.O. Box 370627, Denver, CO 80237, email: heartlodgepoets@gmail.com web site: heartlodge.org. 2005. Poetry. "As three poets, editors, and publishers who founded HeartLodge, our mission was to welcome to our poetry journal both established and emerging writers, with an emphasis on poems containing unique voice, imagery, and sense of place. We value the writing of kindred spirits and receive high quality poems from all over the world. As of 2009, HeartLodge is closed as a poetry journal as the publisher decides to revamp its emphasis toward publication of chapbooks and books. HeartLodge is not accepting submissions until a date to be announced." 1/yr. Pub'd Closed issues 2009. 68pp. Reporting time: 3 months. Simultaneous submissions accepted: Yes, but notify editors if accepted elsewhere. Publishes 5% of manuscripts submitted. Payment: Contributor's copy upon publication. Copyrighted, reverts to author. Ads: None.

Heartsong Books, PO Box 370, Blue Hill, ME 04614-0370, publishers/authors phone: 207-266-7673, e-mail maggie@downeast.net, http://heartsongbooks.com. 1993. Fiction, non-fiction. "We are not accepting submissions at this time. The Heartsong vision is one of kinship. We trust that our books will help young people - all people - understand and respect the interconnectedness of all life and inspire them to act on that understanding in compassionate, powerful, and celebratory ways - for the good of Earth and for the good of generations to come. We at Heartsong express our kinship vision not only in the books we publish, but through gifts of money, outreach and opportunity." avg. press run 2M-4M. Pub'd 1 title 2009; expects 1 title 2011. 4 titles listed in the *Small Press Record of Books in Print* (36th Edition, 2010-11). Discounts: trade, bulk, classroom. Pages vary. Subjects: Children, Youth, Culture, Earth, Natural History, Education, Environment, Futurism, History, Inspirational, Metaphysics, Native American, Non-Fiction, Non-Violence, Occult, Peace, Spiritual.

Heat Press, Christopher Natale Peditto, Publisher & General Editor; Barbara Romain, Associate Editor; Teresa D'Ovido, Art Director; Harold Abramowitz, Associate Editor, PO Box 26218, Los Angeles, CA 90026, 213-482-8902, heatpresseditions@yahoo.com. 1993. Poetry, long-poems. "Heat Press's roots are in Philadelphia, PA. Current series of published poets, Open Mouth Poetry Series (originally the name of an open poetry series in Philly), features poets close to the Beat Generation in their coming out and oral word sensibilities. Allied interests include the culture of jazz, 'Black' and pan-African cultures, the 'road' and nomadic cross-cultural traditions (versewinds), street poets of the oral tradition, and miscegenated-polyglottal-mouth-music poetry texts. Currently not accepting unsolicited manuscripts, but inquires are welcomed. Recent authors include Eric Priestley (*Abracadabra*), Charles Bivins (*Music in Silence*), Elliott Levin (*does it swing?*) and Will Perkins (*!Scat*)." avg. press run 1.5M. Expects 1 title 2010, 1 title 2011. 4 titles listed in the *Small Press Record of Books in Print* (36th Edition, 2010-11). 100pp. Payment: negotiable. Copyrights for author. Subject: Poetry.

The Heather Foundation, Spencer H. MacCallum, 713 W. Spruce #48, Deming, NM 88030, 915-261-0502, sm@look.net. 1973. Non-fiction. "The Heather Foundation is dedicated to furthering understanding of society as an evolving, spontaneously ordered cooperation among free-acting individuals. Taxation and other institutionalized coercions are viewed as something to be outgrown. The Foundation sponsors research, lectures and publications. It also preserves and administers the intellectual estates of persons such as E.C. Riegel and Spencer Heath who contributed notably to the humane studies. Areas of interest include philosophy of science, the inspirational content of religion and the aesthetic arts, non-political money, and the multi-tenant income property as a model and forerunner of non-political communities. Interested persons are invited to request the Foundation's booklist, *'Creative Alternatives in Social Thought.'*" avg. press run 2M. Pub'd 1 title 2009; expects 1 title 2010, 1 title 2011. 4 titles listed in the *Small Press Record of Books in Print* (36th Edition, 2010-11). Discounts: 50% to bookstores, ppd. provided they supply name and address of customer. 175pp. Reporting time: 30 days. Simultaneous submissions accepted: yes. Copyrights for author. Subjects: Anarchist, Anthropology, Archaelogy, Business & Economics, Christianity, Community, Creativity, Inspirational, Libertarian, Peace, Philosophy, Political Science, Real Estate, Science, Society, Sociology.

HEAVEN BONE MAGAZINE, Heaven Bone Press, Steven Hirsch; Gordon Kirpal, Contributing Editor, 62 Woodcock Mt. Dr., Washingtonville, NY 10992-1828, 845-496-4109. 1986. Poetry, fiction, articles, art, photos, cartoons, interviews, satire, criticism, reviews, music, long-poems, collages, plays, concrete art. "Recent contributors: Anne Waldman, Kirpal Gordon, Diane D'Prima, Antler, Janine Pommy Vega, David Chorlton, Stephen-Paul Martin, Fielding Dawson, Jack Collom, Cynthia Hogue, Joseph Donahue. We like work that is deeply rooted in nature and image yet inspired by cosmic visions and spiritual practice. Current issues tending toward the surreal and eidetic. Editor loves work of Rilke. "Where are his followers?" Nothing turns us off more than artificially forced end-line rhyming; however, rhymed verse will be considered if obviously excellent and showing careful work. We would like to see more short stories and essays on various literary and esoteric topics. Reviews also being considered, but query first. SASE please.'' circ. 2.5M. 1/yr. Pub'd 1 issue 2009; expects 1 issue 2010, 1 issue 2011. sub. price $10; per copy $10; sample $10. Discounts: 40% to bookstores, 50% to distributors. 96-144pp. Reporting time: 3-36 weeks. Publishes 3% of manuscripts submitted. Payment: Free copy, 30% off additional copies. Copyrighted, reverts to author. Pub's reviews: 20 in 2009. §Literary, spiritual, experimental, metaphysical, music, spoken audio, spoken literature. Ads: $240/$130/$90 1/4 page. Subjects: Arts, Avant-Garde, Experimental Art, Book Reviewing, Buddhism, Essays, Fiction, Language, Metaphysics, New Age, Poetry, Spiritual.

Heaven Bone Press (see also HEAVEN BONE MAGAZINE), Steven Hirsch, 62 Woodcock Mtn. Dr., Washingtonville, NY 10992, 845-496-4109. 1986. Poetry, fiction, articles, art, photos, cartoons, interviews, satire, criticism, reviews, music, long-poems, collages, plays, concrete art. ''We publish a bi-annual poetry chapbook contest winner and 2-4 poetry and/or fiction titles. Recently published: *Things*, visual writing by Stephen-Paul Martin; *Walking the Dead*, poems by Lori Anderson; *Red Bracelets*, poems by Janine Pommy Vega; *Down With the Move*, by Kirpal Gordon; *Bright Garden at World's End*, by David Dahl; *Terra Lucida*, by Joseph Donahue; and *Fountains of Gold* by Wendy Vig and Jon Anderson.'' avg. press run 500. Pub'd 3 titles 2009; expects 2 titles 2010, 5 titles 2011. 7 titles listed in the *Small Press Record of Books in Print* (36th Edition, 2010-11). Discounts: 40% bookstores, 50% distributors. 40pp. Reporting time: 6-36 weeks. Payment: varies; set fee or individual percentage of sales. Copyrights for author. Subjects: Arts, Avant-Garde, Experimental Art, Book Reviewing, Buddhism, Essays, Fiction, Language, Metaphysics, New Age, Poetry, Spiritual.

HECATE, Hecate Press, Carole Ferrier, Editor, School of English, Media Studies & Art History, The University of Queensland, St. Lucia, Queensland 4072, Australia, phone: 07 336 53146, fax: 07 3365 2799, web: www.emsah.uq.edu.au/awrs, email: c.ferrier@mailbox.uq.edu.au. 1975. Poetry, fiction, articles, art, criticism, plays. ''Hecate's Australian Women's Book Reviewis now a separate publication at http://www.emsah,uq.edu.au/awsr/awbr. Hecate has articles on historical, sociological, literary, etc. topics. Aspects of women's oppression and resistance. Some interviews and reviews. Some creative writing. Please make all payments in equivalent in Australian currency if possible. We almost never run American poets.'' circ. 2M. 2/yr. Pub'd 3 issues 2009; expects 3 issues 2010, 3 issues 2011. sub. price A$35/yr (indiv), $154 (inst), please pay in Australian $; per copy $6 (Ind); $30 (Inst); sample $6 (ind); $10 (inst). Back issues: $8 volume (Ind); $100 (Inst); concession price *may* be negotiated for runs. Discounts: 33% for bookshops. 200pp. Reporting time: varies. Simultaneous submissions accepted: not welcomed. Publishes 6% of manuscripts submitted. Payment: $49 poem, $69 story, $99 article. Copyrighted. Pub's reviews: 30 in 2009. §Socialist, feminist. Ads: negotiable, exchange. Subject: Women.

Hecate Press (see also HECATE), Carole#Editor Ferrier, School of English, Media Studies and Art History, The University of Queensland, St. Lucia, Queensland 4072, Australia. 1975. Fiction, articles, cartoons, interviews, criticism, reviews, parts-of-novels, long-poems, non-fiction. No titles listed in the *Small Press Record of Books in Print* (36th Edition, 2010-11).

HEELTAP/Pariah Press, Pariah Press, Richard D. Houff, c/o Richard D. Houff, 3070 Shields Drive #106, Eagan, MN 55121. 1986. Poetry. ''Heeltap publishes poetry of merit. Poetry that rhymes is for the most part, very badly written. I would rather not look at it. We receive an overabundance of inappropriate material each year. The best advice for writers and poets, is to pick up samples of the magazine before submitting. Heeltap has a very loyal fan base.'' circ. 500. 2/yr. Pub'd 2 issues 2009; expects 2 issues 2010, 2 issues 2011. sub. price $18/4 issue sub.; per copy $5; sample $5. Back issues: $5. Discounts: none as yet. 48pp. Reporting time: 2 weeks to 1 month. Simultaneous submissions accepted: Send three to five poems. Short stories are usually of the flash variety, but I am open to longer works. Simultaneous submissions are fine as long as I'm notified. Publishes 5% of manuscripts submitted. Payment: copies. Copyrighted, reverts to author. Pub's reviews: Four in 2009. §poetry, novels, short story and essay collections. Ads: none as yet. Subjects: Anarchist, Avant-Garde, Experimental Art, Beat, Dada, Humor.

Heidelberg Graphics, Larry S. Jackson, 2 Stansbury Court, Chico, CA 95928-9410, 530-342-6582. 1972. ''Heidelberg Graphics publishes most manuscripts by invitation but welcomes queries. We offer complete services for authors and publishers. Stansbury Publishing and Memoir Books are imprints of Heidelberg Graphics. Recent books include *Sylvia's Book* (Linda Kathleen Peelle), *Annie Kennedy Bidwell: An Intimate History* (Lois H. McDonald), *The Chaining of the Dragon: A Commentary on the Book of Revelation* (Ralph Schreiber), *Around the World in 52 Words: Ritual Writing for this New Millennium* (Rob Burton), and *The Plains Beyond* (L D Clark). Visit www.HeidelbergGraphics.com for more information. We also invite unpublished publishable manuscripts for free posting in Forum on our Web site.'' avg. press run 600-6M. Pub'd 4 titles 2009; expects 5 titles 2010, 5 titles 2011. 30 titles listed in the *Small Press Record of Books in Print* (36th Edition, 2010-11). Discounts: write for prices or see ABA Book Buyers Handbook. 200pp. Reporting time: 4-16 weeks. Simultaneous submissions accepted: no. Publishes 30% of manuscripts submitted. Payment: negotiable. Copyrights for author. Subjects: Biography, Christianity, Fiction, History, How-To, Magazines, Native American, Newsletter, Non-Fiction, Poetry, Religion, Reprints, World War II.

Helicon Nine Editions, Gloria Vando Hickok, Editor-in-Chief, Box 22412, Kansas City, MO 64113, 816-753-1095, Fax 816-753-1016, helicon9@aol.com, www.heliconnine.com. 1977. Poetry, fiction. "We are publishing high quality volumes of fiction, poetry and/or essays. Please query before sending ms." avg. press run 1M-2.5M. Pub'd 2 titles 2009; expects 3 titles 2010, 2 titles 2011. 33 titles listed in the *Small Press Record of Books in Print* (36th Edition, 2010-11). Discounts: 40% bookstores, distributors. 55-512pp. Reporting time: varies. Payment: varies with individual writers. Copyrights for author. Subjects: Arts, Avant-Garde, Experimental Art, Bilingual, Essays, Fiction, Poetry, Short Stories, Visual Arts, Women.

HELIOTROPE, A JOURNAL OF POETRY, Susan Sindall, Co-Editor; Laurel Blossom, Co-Editor; Barbara Elovic, Co-Editor; Victoria Hallerman, Associate Editor, Website Editor, P.O Box 456, Shady, NY 12409, www.heliopoems.com. 2001. Poetry. "Founded by four women poets, Heliotrope agrees with Coleridge, that poems are, "...the best words in their best order." We publish an eclectic mix of style and form, and our poets are from all over the world. Recent contributors include: Billy Collins, Heather McHugh, Jean Valentine, D. Nurkse, Stephen Dunn, Carl Dennis, Rachel Hadas, among many others. Visit www.heliopoems.com to sample the magazine, subscribe, or access the guidelines for submission. We urge all poets to visit the guidelines before submitting, and, if possible, to purchase a sample copy of the magazine, which will give you a better sense of the kinds of poems we publish." circ. 450. 1/yr. Pub'd 1 issue 2009; expects 1 issue 2010, 1 issue 2011. sub. price $8.00; per copy $8.00; sample $6.00. Back issues: $8.00. 70pp. Reporting time: reporting time 1 year; *see website for reading period.* Simultaneous submissions accepted: Yes. Payment: 2 copies of the magazine; additional copies available at a discount. Copyrighted, reverts to author. Subject: Poetry.

Helm Publishing, Dianne Helm, Sr. Editor; Kristin Ginger, Editor, 3923 Seward Ave., Rockford, IL 61108-7658, work: 815-398-4660, dianne@publishersdrive.com, www.publishersdrive.com. 1995. Poetry, fiction, photos, interviews, reviews, parts-of-novels, news items, non-fiction. Pub'd 12 titles 2009; expects 15 titles 2010, 12 titles 2011. 28 titles listed in the *Small Press Record of Books in Print* (36th Edition, 2010-11). Discounts: 40% trade, 25% classroom, 15% agent, 10% jobber, 30% bulk. 200pp. Reporting time: varies. Simultaneous submissions accepted: yes. Copyrights for author. Subjects: Astrology, Biography, Book Reviewing, Business & Economics, Celtic, Children, Youth, Fantasy, Fiction, Medieval, Mystery, Non-Fiction, Novels, Publishing, Science Fiction, Writers/Writing.

HERE AND NOW, The American Zen Association, Temple Staff, 748 Camp St, New Orleans, LA 70130, info@nozt.org, www.nozt.org. 1991. Articles, photos, interviews, criticism, letters, news items, non-fiction. *"Here and Now* is the newsletter of the American Zen Association." circ. 200. 1/yr. 5 titles listed in the *Small Press Record of Books in Print* (36th Edition, 2010-11). sub. price $16. 8pp. Reporting time: 1 month. Payment: copies. Not copyrighted. Subject: Zen.

Heritage Books, Inc., Leslie Towle, 65 E. Main Street, Westminster, MD 21157-5026, 410-876-6101, Fax 410-871-2674, info@heritagebooks.com. 1978. Non-fiction. "Subject matter of interest includes local and regional histories pertaining to eastern U.S. and source records of interest to historians and genealogists." avg. press run 200-300. Pub'd 300 titles 2009; expects 450 titles 2010, 600 titles 2011. No titles listed in the *Small Press Record of Books in Print* (36th Edition, 2010-11). Discounts: 2-5 assorted titles 20%, 6+ assorted 40%. 250pp. Reporting time: 3 months. Simultaneous submissions accepted: yes. Publishes 25% of manuscripts submitted. Payment: 10% of sales, paid semi-annually. Does not copyright for author. Subjects: Abstracts, African-American, Americana, Genealogy, History, Immigration, Indexes & Abstracts, Newspapers, North America, Reprints.

Heritage Global Publishing, J.V. Goldbach, 908 Innergary Place, Valrico, FL 33594, 813-643-6029. 1998. Non-fiction. "Book released early 1999: *Help Your Child Avoid Multiple Sclerosis: A Parenting Decision."* avg. press run 3-5M. Expects 1 title 2010, 2-3 titles 2011. 1 title listed in the *Small Press Record of Books in Print* (36th Edition, 2010-11). Discounts: standard trade. 250pp. Simultaneous submissions accepted: yes. Publishes 2% of manuscripts submitted. Payment: flexible. Copyrights for author. Subjects: Health, Parenting, Religion.

Heritage House Publishers, PO Box 194242, San Francisco, CA 94119, 415-776-3156. 1990. Non-fiction. "Not currently accepting submissions. Heritage House Publishers specializes in regional/city guidebooks and in California history and biography. Our first title, published October 1991, is *Historic San Francisco: A Concise History and Guide* by Rand Richards. Heritage House Publishers is currently distributed to the trade by Great West Books, PO Box 1028, Lafayette, CA 94549." avg. press run 3K. Pub'd 1 title 2009; expects 1 title 2011. 2 titles listed in the *Small Press Record of Books in Print* (36th Edition, 2010-11). Discounts: 1-4 books 20% (prepaid), 5-24 42%, 25-49 44%, 50-99 46%, 100+ 48%. 400pp. Subjects: Biography, California, Cities, History, San Francisco, Transportation.

Heritage Library Press, Jayson Lee, 8772 Boysenberry Way, Elk Grove, CA 95624, 916-689-6806, Fax 916-689-6683, jaysonlee@frontiernet.net, www.heritagelibrarypress.com. 2006. Fiction. avg. press run 10K. Pub'd 1 title 2009; expects 1 title 2010, 2 titles 2011. No titles listed in the *Small Press Record of Books in Print* (36th Edition, 2010-11). Discounts: 55%. 450pp. Reporting time: 3 months. Simultaneous submissions accepted: yes. Publishes 5% of manuscripts submitted. Payment: 10%-15%. Copyrights for author. Subject: Fiction.

Hermes House Press (see also KAIROS, A Journal of Contemporary Thought and Criticism), Richard Mandell, Alan Mandell, 113 Summit Avenue, Brookline, MA 02446-2319, 617-566-2468. 1980. Poetry, fiction, parts-of-novels, long-poems, plays. "Unsolicited manuscripts currently not being read. Experimental works, translations and artwork are encouraged; copy price and number of pages vary. Recent work: *The Deadly Swarm,* short stories by LaVerne Harrell Clark; *The Bats,* a novel by Richard Mandell; *Three Stories,* by R.V. Cassill; *Going West,* poetry by Stanley Diamond; *Bella B.'s Fantasy,* short stories by Raymond Jean; *Crossings,* a novel by Marie Diamond; *O Loma! Constituting a Self* (1977-1984), writings by sociologist Kurt H. Wolff; *Thinking, Feeling, and Doing,* critical essays by Emil Oestereicher." avg. press run 1M. Pub'd 1 title 2009. 8 titles listed in the *Small Press Record of Books in Print* (36th Edition, 2010-11). Discounts: available upon request. Pages vary. Reporting time: 4-8 weeks. Payment: copies plus an agreed percentage after cost. Copyrights for author. Subjects: Fiction, Poetry.

THE HERON'S NEST, Christopher Herold, Founding Editor; John Stevenson, Managing Editor; Ferris Gilli, Associate Editor; Paul MacNeil, Associate Editor; Peggy Willis Lyles, Associate Editor; Alice Frampton, Associate Editor, 816 Taft Street, Port Townsend, WA 98368, www.theheronsnest.com. 1999. Poetry. "Quarterly Journal on-line with an annual print edition that includes the all issues of the previous year and the Readers' Choice Awards for that year. Over 100 Haiku in each quarterly issue, 1 quarterly award and 2 Editors' Choice Runners-Up. Commentary included with winning poem. Most of the best writers of English language haiku submit their works." Read regularly by thousands, including the vast majority of the English-speaking global haiku community. 4 quarterly issues and Readers' Choice Awards issue (on-line) ; 1 perfect-bound, annual paper edition. Pub'd 1 issue 2009; expects 1 issue 2010, 1 issue 2011. sub. price $17 US, $19 Canada and Mexico, $21 international. Back issues: Volumes I, II, and III: $1.25 in U.S.; $1.50 in Canada and Mexico; & $1.75 elsewhereVolumes IV, V, and VI: $1.50 in U.S.; $1.75 in Canada and Mexico; & $2.00 elsewhere. Volumes VII $15 in U.S.; $16 in Canada and Mexico; & $17 elsewhere. Volumes VIII and IX: $16 in U.S.; $18 in Canada and Mexico; & $20 elsewhere. Volume X: $17 in U.S.; $19 in Canada and Mexico; and $21 elsewhere. Discounts: none. Reporting time: less than 6 weeks. Simultaneous submissions accepted: no. Publishes 10% of manuscripts submitted. Payment: none. Copyrighted, reverts to author. Ads: none. Subject: Haiku.

Hexagon Blue, Mary Jesse, PO Box 1790, Issaquah, WA 98027-0073, 425-890-5351, www.hexagonblue.com. 2002. 2 titles listed in the *Small Press Record of Books in Print* (36th Edition, 2010-11).

Heyday Books (see also NEWS FROM NATIVE CALIFORNIA), Jeannine Gendar, Managing Editor; Malcolm Margolin, Publisher, PO Box 9145, Berkeley, CA 94709, 510-549-3564, Fax 510-549-1889. 1974. Poetry, art, photos, non-fiction. "Books on California history and literature, California Indians, women of California, natural history, and regional guidebooks, fiction and poetry." avg. press run 4M. Pub'd 14 titles 2009; expects 16 titles 2010, 20 titles 2011. 78 titles listed in the *Small Press Record of Books in Print* (36th Edition, 2010-11). Discounts: retail 1-4 copies 20%, 5-24 40%, 25-49 43%, 50-99 45%, 100+ 46%. 320pp. Reporting time: 6 weeks. Simultaneous submissions accepted: yes. Publishes 1% of manuscripts submitted. Payment: comparable to what's offered by major publishers, in fact modeled on their contracts. Copyrights for author. Subjects: Alaska, Bicycling, California, Earth, Natural History, Europe, History, Indians, Literature (General), Myth, Mythology, Native American, Politics, Sports, Outdoors, Third World, Minorities, Women.

The Heyeck Press, Robin R. Heyeck, 25 Patrol Court, Woodside, CA 94062, 650-851-7491, Fax 650-851-5039, heyeck@ix.netcom.com. 1976. Poetry, long-poems, non-fiction. "Books on paper marbling. All books are printed letterpress." avg. press run 500. Pub'd 1 title 2009; expects 2 titles 2010, 2 titles 2011. 15 titles listed in the *Small Press Record of Books in Print* (36th Edition, 2010-11). Discounts: fine editions, book dealers only 30%; letterpress paper wrappers (trade) 1-3 copies 20%, 4+ 40%. 80pp. Reporting time: 90 days. Simultaneous submissions accepted: no. Publishes 1-2% of manuscripts submitted. Payment: percentage of sales paid in cash. Copyrights for author. Subjects: Fiction, Literature (General), Poetry.

Hidden Valley Farm, Publisher (see also THE OTHER HERALD), T. F. Rice, P.O. Box 172, Perry, NY 14530, publisher.hiddenvalley@yahoo.com , theotherherald@yahoo.com , http://www.otherherald.com. 2002. Poetry, fiction, art, photos, cartoons, letters, collages, non-fiction. ""We believe everyone has a story to tell. However, we most often publish books with unique topics and ideas. We look at each submissions sort of as a 'unique creature', meaning that it should tell us it wants to be published, needs to be published, and we are the ones to do it."Query for more info by email or mail, with brief description of your ideas and sample page or two of your manuscript. We will respond whether we want to see more of it.In 2002, Hidden Valley published

214

"Seasonings For Life", a unique anthology of works by Wyoming County, NY writers, which also included writing exercises scattered throughout the book. Illustrations were by Mr. Scribbles, a local artist. The idea was to show that life is seasoned by one's experiences, and the experiences of others that one is exposed to. Here in Western NY, we are also able to experience the seasons of the year more fully, so the book was divided into four chapters, based on the four seasons. Initial publication of 50 copies were all hand-bound and tied, 176 pages. A second printing was done in a perfect binding, also with holes drilled and hand-tied accent binding. A lot of heart goes into each of our books, the efforts of the writer combined with that of the publisher.In 2007, Hidden Valley completed publication of "There are Monsters Coming Out of My Head", a special book because it is written and illustrated by a nine-year-old boy. The idea of this book was his creation: "Hi. My name is Gef. I love to draw monsters. When I draw them they come out of my head. If you draw your fears, then when the book is closed they are stuck there. Also, if you draw them, they don't look as scary as in your mind." This paperback, full of a selection of Gef's sketches from ages 7-9, includes his ideas expressed and extra pages for the reader to draw their own monsters. Helping children deal with real issues is important to us. The children truly are our future.Also in 2007, Hidden Valley published "The Wind Being", a children.'' avg. press run 100. Pub'd 3 titles 2009; expects 1-2 titles 2010, 2 titles 2011. 6 titles listed in the *Small Press Record of Books in Print* (36th Edition, 2010-11). Discounts: BOOKS: 5-9 copies 25%, 10+ copies 40%LIT NEWS: 10+ copies 50%. 60pp. Reporting time: Normally less than 3 months. Simultaneous submissions accepted: Yes. Publishes 5% of manuscripts submitted. Payment: Copies of the book given and/or payment of royalties on each book sold. Advances are unusual. Payment of royalties is typically made on a quarterly basis. Rights revert back to author after publication. One time publishing rights. Subjects: Adirondacks, Anthology, Arts, Avant-Garde, Experimental Art, Children, Youth, Comics, Crafts, Hobbies, Creativity, Essays, History, Poetry, Short Stories, Women, Writers/Writing, Zines.

Higganum Hill Books, Richard C. DeBold, Editor, PO Box 666, Higganum, CT 06441, rcdebold@connix.com. 1999. Poetry, non-fiction. avg. press run 500. Pub'd 1 title 2009; expects 2 titles 2010, 2 titles 2011. 1 title listed in the *Small Press Record of Books in Print* (36th Edition, 2010-11). Discounts: standard universal schedule. 72pp. Reporting time: 1 week. Simultaneous submissions accepted: yes. Publishes 10% of manuscripts submitted. Payment: standard. Does not copyright for author. Subjects: Counter-Culture, Alternatives, Communes, Education, Poetry.

HIGH COUNTRY NEWS, Paul Larmer, Publisher; Jonathan Thompson, Editor, PO Box 1090, 119 Grand Avenue, Paonia, CO 81428, 970-527-4898, editor@hcn.org. 1970. Articles, art, photos, cartoons, interviews, criticism, reviews, letters, news items. ''High Country News is an award-winning nonprofit newsmagazine. Since 1970, we've covered environmental, cultural, and social issues in the Western United States. HCN will consider well-researched stories on any natural resource or environmental topic, as long as it concerns the West. We define resources to include people, politics, culture and aesthetic values—not just coal, oil and timber. Send queries to editor at hcn dot org.'' circ. 25,000. 22/yr. Pub'd 23 issues 2009; expects 22 issues 2010, 22 issues 2011. sub. price $37 indiv., $47 instit.; per copy $4.00; sample free. Back issues: $4.00 (incl. p/h) single copy; bulk rates available on request. Discounts: sell in bulk to schools, libraries, organizations. 24 - 32pp. Reporting time: 4 weeks. Simultaneous submissions accepted: no. Payment: negotiable. Copyrighted, reverts to author. Pub's reviews: 50 short blurbs in 2009. §Conservation, natural resources, wildlife, energy, land use, growth, unions and the rural economy, and other western community issues. Ads: Visit www.hcn.org/advertising then select *Download Our Media Kit* for pricing, acceptable formats, issue dates/deadlines. Subjects: Conservation, Energy, Environment, Native American, The West.

HIGH DESERT JOURNAL, Elizabeth Quinn, Editor, P.O. BOX 7647, Bend, OR 97708. 2005. ''High Desert Journal strives for a deeper understanding of people and landscape in the interior West. "Just as I believe in an ecology of water, soil, air. I believe in an ecology of memory, story, and imagination. We accept poetry, fiction, creative nonfiction, memoirs, books reviews, essays on social issues and conditions of the region, interviews and visual arts. People not living in the interior West are encouraged to submit on themes of the region and those living in the region can submit on any theme.'' circ. 2,000. biannual. sub. price $16 for annual. $30 for two-year.; per copy $10. 54 with coverpp. Simultaneous submissions accepted: Yes. Pub's reviews: 2 in 2009. §all.

High Plains Press, Nancy Curtis, Box 123, 403 Cassa Road, Glendo, WY 82213, 307-735-4370, Fax 307-735-4590, 800-552-7819. 1984. Poetry, non-fiction. ''Specializes in Wyoming and the West.'' avg. press run 3M. Pub'd 3 titles 2009; expects 3 titles 2010, 4 titles 2011. 49 titles listed in the *Small Press Record of Books in Print* (36th Edition, 2010-11). Discounts: bookstores 1-4 20%, 5+ 40%, wholesales more. 200pp. Reporting time: 2 months. Simultaneous submissions accepted: yes. Publishes 3% of manuscripts submitted. Payment: based on material, usually 10% net sales. Copyrights for author. Subjects: History, Old West, Poetry, The West, Wyoming.

Highest Hurdle Press, Robert Pomerhn, 660 Cleveland Drive, Suite 3, Cheektowaga, NY 14225. 2006. Poetry, art, letters, collages, concrete art. avg. press run 500. Pub'd 1 title 2009; expects 1 title 2010, 2 titles 2011. No titles listed in the *Small Press Record of Books in Print* (36th Edition, 2010-11). 95pp. Reporting time: appx. one month. Simultaneous submissions accepted: Yes. Publishes 25% of manuscripts submitted. Payment: We pay neither advances nor royalties. Each contributor receives a complimentary copy of the issue in which his or her work appears. Contributors retain copyright. Subjects: Absurdist, Anarchist, Avant-Garde, Experimental Art, Dada, Essays, Experimental, Poetry, Post Modern, Surrealism, Visual Arts.

Hill Country Books, J.O. Walker, Editor, 1302 Desert Links, San Antonio, TX 78258, 830-980-5425. 1994. Non-fiction. "Prefer mss. under 400pp. Will consider any good non-fiction. Especially interested in Texas or Southwest material; also health and recovery subjects." avg. press run 5M. Pub'd 1 title 2009; expects 2 titles 2010, 3 titles 2011. 1 title listed in the *Small Press Record of Books in Print* (36th Edition, 2010-11). Discounts: averages 40%. 200pp. Reporting time: 2 weeks. Simultaneous submissions accepted: yes. Publishes 20% of manuscripts submitted. Payment: co-publishing arrangements. Copyrights for author. Subjects: Health, History, Southwest, Sports, Outdoors.

HILL COUNTRY SUN, Melissa Gilmere, 100 Commons Road, Suite 7, Number 319, Dripping Springs, TX 78620, 512-569-8212, melissa@hillcountrysun.com, www.hillcountrysun.com. 1990. Articles, photos, interviews, reviews, non-fiction. "Only material focused on the Central Texas hill country." circ. 42M. 11/yr. Pub'd 11 issues 2009; expects 11 issues 2010, 11 issues 2011. sub. price $18; per copy free; sample free. Back issues: $2 each. 32pp. Reporting time: return mail. Simultaneous submissions accepted: yes. Publishes 30% of manuscripts submitted. Payment: $60 per article. Copyrighted, reverts to author. Pub's reviews: 2 in 2009. §Texas travel. Ads: $800 full page. Subjects: Arts, Music, Texas, Travel.

Hill Song Press, Tom Mach, P.O. Box 486, Lawrence, KS 66044, (785) 749-3660. 5 titles listed in the *Small Press Record of Books in Print* (36th Edition, 2010-11).

Hilltop Press (see also DATA DUMP), Steve Sneyd, 4 Nowell Place, Almondbury, Huddersfield, West Yorkshire HD5 8PB, England. 1966. "Chapbooks: Science fiction in poetry, dark fantasy poetry. History of these genres." Pub'd 1 title 2009; expects 3 titles 2010, 3 titles 2011. 17 titles listed in the *Small Press Record of Books in Print* (36th Edition, 2010-11). Reporting time: usually within month. Simultaneous submissions accepted: will consider if informed of fact. Payment: 10 copies free to each chapbook author, additional copies at discount.

Himalayan Institute Press, Jon Janaka, 952 Bethany TPKE, Honesdale, PA 18341, 570-253-5551. 1976. Non-fiction. "Yoga, meditation, spirituality, health, wellness." Pub'd 2 titles 2009; expects 1 title 2011. No titles listed in the *Small Press Record of Books in Print* (36th Edition, 2010-11). Discounts: variable, please call for details. 150pp. Reporting time: 3 weeks. Simultaneous submissions accepted: Yes. Publishes 1% of manuscripts submitted. Payment: variable. Copyrights for author. Subjects: Alternative Medicine, Astrology, Buddhism, Cosmology, Death & Dying, Inspirational, Massage, Metaphysics, Multicultural, New Age, Religion, Self-Help, Spiritual, Vegetarianism, Yoga.

HIMALAYAN PATH, Yes International Publishers, Theresa King, 1317 Summit Ave., St. Paul, MN 55105, 651-645-6808, fax 651-645-7935, yes@yespublishers.com, www.yespublishers.com. "Authoritative, comprehensive, holistic, multilevel teachings in the Himalayan yoga tradition." 4/yr. sub. price $18/USA, $22/Canada, $25/Europe,India,Asia,So.Am.; per copy $5. Back issues: $5. 32pp.

•**Hip Pocket Press,** Charles Entrekin, Managing Editor; Gail Entrekin, Poetry Editor, 5 Del Mar Court, Orinda, CA 94563, 925-386-0611. 1998. Poetry, articles. "It is our belief that the arts are the embodiment of the soul of a culture, that the promotion of writers and artists is essential if our current culture, with its emphasis on television and provocative outcomes, is to have a chance to develop that inner voice and ear that expresses and listens to beauty. Toward that end, Hip Pocket Press will search out those undiscovered poets and writers whose voices can give us a clearer understanding of ourselves and of the culture which defines us." avg. press run Print on Demand. Pub'd 1 title 2009; expects 1 title 2010, 1 title 2011. 4 titles listed in the *Small Press Record of Books in Print* (36th Edition, 2010-11). Discounts: Book stores 60/40. 80pp. Simultaneous submissions accepted: Yes.

Hippopotamus Press (see also OUTPOSTS POETRY QUARTERLY), Roland John; B.A. Martin, Business Manager, Mansell Pargitter, 22 Whitewell Road, Frome, Somerset BA11 4EL, England, 0373-466653. 1974. Poetry, long-poems. "Size, number of pages, cost will vary with the material. Against: concrete, typewriter, neo-surrealism and experimental work. For: competent poetry in recognisable English, a knowledge of syntax and construction, finished work and not glimpses into the workshop, also translations. Recent books include G.S. Sharat Chandra (U.S.A.), Edward Lowbury (Canada), Stan Trevor (S. Africa) Shaun McCarthy, Peter Dale, William Bedford, Humphrey Chucas, Debjani Chatterjee, Peter Dent." avg. press run 750 paper, 250 cloth. Pub'd 2 titles 2009; expects 5 titles 2010. 32 titles listed in the *Small Press Record of Books in Print* (36th Edition, 2010-11). Discounts: 35% off singles, 45% off bulk orders. 80pp. Reporting time: 1 month. Payment: by arrangement/royalty. Standard UK copyright, remaining with author. Subjects: Criticism, Poetry.

HIRAM POETRY REVIEW, Willard Greenwood, Box 162, Hiram, OH 44234, 330-569-5331, Fax 330-569-5166, poetryreview@hiram.edu. 1967. Poetry, articles, art, photos, interviews, satire, criticism, reviews, letters, long-poems, collages, plays, concrete art. "We seek to discover the best new poets in America. Send 3-5 poems of your best work." circ. 500. 1/yr. Pub'd 1 issue 2009; expects 1 issue 2010, 1 issue 2011. sub. price $9, $23 for 3 years; per copy $9; sample $5. Back issues: No. 1 unavail.; others vary; send for info. Discounts: 60-40 to subscription agencies; 60-40 to retail bookstores. Reporting time: 1-3 months. Simultaneous submissions accepted: yes. Publishes 1-5% of manuscripts submitted. Payment: 2 copies. Copyrighted, rights revert to author by request. Pub's reviews: 2 in 2009. §Poetry, books, some little magazines. No ads. Subject: Poetry.

His Work Christian Publishing (see also THE FIT CHRISTIAN A Christian Health & Fitness Magazine), Angela Perez, P.O. Box 5732, Ketchikan, AK 99901, phone 206-274-8474, fax 614-388-0664, email editor@hisworkpub.com, website http://www.hisworkpub.com. 2006. Poetry, fiction, non-fiction. "The vision of His Work Christian Publishing is to bring the works that God has gifted to the minds of authors and illustrators, in to the hearts and homes of our world. We want to encourage, inspire and help new artists publish their work so it can touch your hearts, feed your brains, and provide you and your family with the entertainment and relaxation you can only get from jumping into a good book." avg. press run 1000. Pub'd 4 titles 2009; expects 7 titles 2010, 6 titles 2011. 5 titles listed in the *Small Press Record of Books in Print* (36th Edition, 2010-11). Discounts: Average discount is 40-50%. 32-200pp. Reporting time: 1-3 months. Simultaneous submissions accepted: Yes. Publishes 5% of manuscripts submitted. Payment: 10-20% royalties. Copyrights for author. Subjects: Alaska, Children, Youth, Christianity, Cooking, Family, Non-Fiction, Picture Books, Poetry, Writers/Writing.

Historical Resources Press, 2104 Post Oak Court, Corinth / Denton, TX 76210-1900, 940-321-1066, fax 940-497-1313, www.booksonhistory.com. 1994. Non-fiction. "The Mission of Historical Resources Press is: Seeking to find the truth about what really happened! We seek to publish the true story about HISTORY made YESTERDAY and TODAY as RESOURCES for TOMORROW! The truth is not always easy to find, but we believe, with much research, is possible, even these days after so much of real HISTORICAL importance has been, and is being, destroyed. We have published some of the truth, not all of it. We have published a history of photography during the Civil War, *Photographer .. Under Fire* by Jack C. Ramsay; history of a POW of WWII, *Patton's Ill-Fated Raid* by Harry Thompson; and an autobiography, *Angel Kisses And My Beating Heart, My Life and Near-Death Experiences* by Jack C. Ramsay. Last year we published a booklet of experiences and encouragement, *I Can Feel The Sunshine by One Suddenly Blind Patient, One Caregiver And One Little Dog.*" 4 titles listed in the *Small Press Record of Books in Print* (36th Edition, 2010-11). Simultaneous submissions accepted: no. Subjects: Autobiography, Biography, Civil War, History, Military, Veterans, Non-Fiction, Photography, Texas, World War II.

Historical Society of Alberta (see also ALBERTA HISTORY), Hugh A. Dempsey, 95 Holmwood Ave. NW, Calgary, Alberta T2K 2G7, Canada. 1907. Articles, reviews, non-fiction. "3,500 to 5,000 word articles on western Canadian history." avg. press run 1.6M. Pub'd 1 title 2009; expects 1 title 2010, 1 title 2011. 7 titles listed in the *Small Press Record of Books in Print* (36th Edition, 2010-11). Discounts: 33%. 28pp. Reporting time: 2 months. Simultaneous submissions accepted: no. Publishes 50% of manuscripts submitted. Payment: none. Does not copyright for author. Subjects: History, Native American.

HISTORICAL STUDIES IN THE PHYSICAL & BIOLOGICAL SCIENCES, University of California Press, J.L. Heilbron, Editor; Diana Wear, Managing Editor, University of California Press, 2000 Center Street, Suite 303, Berkeley, CA 94704-1223, 510-643-7154. 1970. Non-fiction. "Editorial address: Office for History of Science & Technology, 470 Stephens Hall, Univ. of CA, Berkeley, CA 94720." circ. 566. 2/yr. Pub'd 2 issues 2009; expects 2 issues 2010, 2 issues 2011. sub. price $32 indiv., $107 instit. (+ $15 air freight), $20 student; per copy $16 indiv., $55 instit., $16 student; sample free. Back issues: same as single copy price. Discounts: foreign subs. agent 10%, one-time orders 10+ 30%, standing orders (bookstores): 1-99 40%, 100+ 50%. 200pp. Reporting time: 1-2 months. Copyrighted, does not revert to author. Ads: $295/$220. Subject: History.

History Compass, LLC, Lisa Gianelly, Jeff Levinson, 25 Leslie Rd., Auburndale, MA 02466, www.historycompass.com, 617 332 2202 (O), 617 332 2210 (F). 2005. Plays, non-fiction. "Non-fiction. Primary source-based U.S. history materials for classrooms and historic site/museums. Publish books, plays, and teacher guides." 86 titles listed in the *Small Press Record of Books in Print* (36th Edition, 2010-11). Reporting time: 8 weeks, to queries only. Simultaneous submissions accepted: Only if notified. We occasionally copyright for author. Subjects: Biography, Black, Children, Youth, Education, History, Labor, Military, Veterans, Native American, Politics, Science, Transportation, Women.

HISTORY OF INTELLECTUAL CULTURE, L. Panayotidis, Editor; P. Stortz, Editor, Faculty of Education, EDT 722, Univ. of Calgary, 2500 Univ. Drive NW, Calgary, AB T2N 1N4, Canada, 403-220-6296, Fax 403-282-8479, elpanayo@ucalgary.ca, pjstortz@ucalgary.ca, www.ucalgary.ca/hic/. 2001. Articles, reviews.

1/yr. Pub'd 1 issue 2009; expects 1 issue 2010, 1 issue 2011. sub. price free access. Reporting time: 6 months. Simultaneous submissions accepted: no. Publishes 25% of manuscripts submitted. Payment: none. Copyrighted, both author and journal hold copyright. Pub's reviews: 5 in 2009. §Intellectual history and history in general. Ads: email for information. Subjects: Culture, History.

Ho Logos Press, William R Hougland, Managing Editor, 2311 G St, Washougal, WA 98671, 360-835-7838, 360-835-0785 (fax), hlpressmarketing@yahoo.com, hlpress@aol.com. 1999. Fiction, plays, non-fiction. "We call our publishing approach "New, Great Themes!", themes concerning the major issues the world faces, the West in particular. Issues such as terrorism, abortion, education, the military-industrial complex and more. The mission of the Press is to deconstruct these major issues to an origin where their essence can be presented to enlighten human life.Recent publications include "The Restoration" by David J. Bean and "Quote This!!!" by Vincent Fu. Our upcoming authors include Rene Cortes "USA 911: Terrorism: Terror Terrifies Terrorist" (part one of a 3 part essay)and Paul Stein "The Glass Forest" (fiction). We also represent author Robert Hougland (two plays - "Gold Rush" and "Who's Afraid of the Big Blair Witch" (on abortion)." avg. press run 4000. Pub'd 1 title 2009; expects 2 titles 2010, 2 titles 2011. 3 titles listed in the *Small Press Record of Books in Print* (36th Edition, 2010-11). Discounts: 50%, or upon agreement, higher. 300-400pp. Reporting time: 2-4 weeks. Simultaneous submissions accepted: Yes. Publishes 5% of manuscripts submitted. Subjects: Airplanes, Christianity, Current Affairs, Global Affairs, Government, History, Old West, Philosophy, Politics, Reference, Religion, Spiritual, Theosophical, War, World War II.

Hobar Publications, A Division of Finney Company (see also Finney Company, Inc.), Alan Krysan, President, 8075 215th Street West, Lakeville, MN 55044, (952) 469-6699, Fax:(952) 469-1968, (800)846-7027, Fax: (800) 330-6232, feedback@finney-hobar.com, www.finney-hobar.com. 1964. Non-fiction. "This division of Finney Company offers instructional material for career and technical educators. Recent titles include Horsemanship Handbook, Forest Management Digest and Concrete and Concrete Masonry." avg. press run 5000. Pub'd 2 titles 2009; expects 3-5 titles 2010, 3-5 titles 2011. No titles listed in the *Small Press Record of Books in Print* (36th Edition, 2010-11). Discounts: 1-9 copies 20%; 10-24 copies 40%; 25-49 copies 45%; 50 or more copies 50%. 128-500pp. Reporting time: 8-10 weeks. Simultaneous submissions accepted: Yes. Payment: varies. Subjects: Agriculture, Animals, Biology, Biotechnology, Birds, Business & Economics, Conservation, Construction, Co-ops, Crafts, Hobbies, Gardening, Nature, Non-Fiction, Technology, Wood Engraving/Woodworking.

HOBART, Aaron Burch, PO Box 1658, Ann Arbor, MI 48103, info@hobartpulp.com, submit@hobart-pulp.com, http://www.hobartpulp.com. 2001. Fiction. "Hobart is a literary journal featuring entertaining, inventive fiction with a particular fondness for stories involving truckers, vagabonding, entomology and mathematics. Current print issue, edited by Ryan Boudinot, features stories by Rick Moody, Aimee Bender, Stephen Elliott and Stephany Aulenback. Website updates monthly with short shorts. www.hobartpulp.com." circ. 700. 2/yr. Pub'd 2 issues 2009; expects 2 issues 2010, 2 issues 2011. sub. price $17; per copy $10; sample $6. Back issues: $7. 200pp. Reporting time: 1-3 months. Simultaneous submissions accepted: Yes. Publishes 10% of manuscripts submitted. Payment: 2 contributor copies, plus a 1 year (2 issue) subscription. Copyrighted, reverts to author. Subjects: Experimental, Fiction.

Hobblebush Books, Sidney Hall Jr., 17-A Old Milford Road, Brookline, NH 03033, Ph./Fax: 603-672-4317, E-mail: hobblebush@charter.net, Web: www.hobblebush.com. 1993. Poetry, criticism, non-fiction. "*Publishes literary and non-literary books that present a unique voice and make a difference. Book design services to authors and other publishers. See website.*" avg. press run 1M. Pub'd 4 titles 2009; expects 4 titles 2010, 5 titles 2011. 27 titles listed in the *Small Press Record of Books in Print* (36th Edition, 2010-11). 150pp. Reporting time: 4 weeks. Simultaneous submissions accepted: yes. Payment: Royalties on retail price. Copyrights for author. Subjects: Autobiography, Humor, Literature (General), Poetry.

Hochelaga Press, Raymond Beauchemin, Denise Roig, 8140 Ogilvie, LaSalle, QC H8P 3R4, Canada, 514-366-5655, Fax 514-364-5655, hochelaga@sympatico.ca. 1995. Poetry, fiction, non-fiction. avg. press run 500-1M. Pub'd 1 title 2009; expects 1 title 2011. 3 titles listed in the *Small Press Record of Books in Print* (36th Edition, 2010-11). Discounts: bookstore 40%, wholesale 50%. Reporting time: 4-6 months. Simultaneous submissions accepted: yes. Payment: yes. Copyrights for author.

Hohm Press, Dasya Zuccarello, General Manager, PO Box 2501, Prescott, AZ 86302, 928-778-9189, 800-381-2700, hppublisher@cableone.net. 1975. Non-fiction. "HOHM PRESS is committed to publishing books that provide readers with alternatives to the materialistic values of the current culture, and promote self-awareness, the recognition of interdependence, and compassion. Our subject areas include natural health, parenting, childrens health, religious studies, womens issues, the arts and poetry. We are proud to offer the acclaimed Family Health /World Health series for children and parents, covering such themes as nutrition, dental health, reading, and environmental education. Hohm Press presents the work of contemporary spiritual teachers, including Lee Lozowick, Arnaud Desjardins, Dr. Robert Frager, Philippe Coupcy and J. Krishnamurti, and books by authors distinguished in their fields: Georg Feuerstein (Yoga and Tantric Studies), Will Keepin

218

and Cynthia Brix (Gender Studies), Laurie Murphy and Nadir Baksh (Marriage and Family Counseling), Redhawk and Vraje Abramian (Poetry and Poetic Translations), and others.'' No titles listed in the *Small Press Record of Books in Print* (36th Edition, 2010-11). Simultaneous submissions accepted: YES. Subjects: Alternative Medicine, Biography, Buddhism, Nutrition, Parenting, Religion, Sufism.

Holbrook Street Press, PO Box 399, Cortaro, AZ 85652-0399, 520-616-7643, fax 520-616-7519, hsp@triconet.org, www.copshock.com www.writingpublishing.com. 1998. Non-fiction. avg. press run 5M. Expects 2 titles 2010, 2 titles 2011. 3 titles listed in the *Small Press Record of Books in Print* (36th Edition, 2010-11). Discounts: Varies. Call for discounts. 400pp. Reporting time: 4 weeks. Simultaneous submissions accepted: yes. Publishes 2% of manuscripts submitted. Subjects: Crime, Mental Health, Non-Fiction, Psychiatry, Psychology, Self-Help.

Hole Books, Dolly Sen, Editor, 2 Hailsham Avenue, London SW2 3AH, England, (0) 208 677 3121, fax (0) 208 677 3121, email holebooks@yahoo.co.uk, web www.holebooks.com. Established 2002. Poetry, fiction, non-fiction. ''Underground, alternative writings.'' Pub'd 3 titles 2009; expects 3 titles 2010, 3 titles 2011. No titles listed in the *Small Press Record of Books in Print* (36th Edition, 2010-11). Discounts: on request. 100pp. Reporting time: 6 weeks. Simultaneous submissions accepted: yes. Publishes 3% of manuscripts submitted. Copyrights for author. Subjects: African-American, Anarchist, Beat, Biography, Experimental, Fiction, Novels, Poetry, Psychiatry.

•Hole In The Head Press, Sam Stokes, P.O. Box 807, Bodega Bay, CA 94923-0807, 707-875-3928. 2002. Non-fiction. ''Hole In The Head Press creates original material and reworks public domain material focusing on Cold War weapon systems and the Atomic Age. We combine, edit, add new illustrations and photographs, update information and create new works from previously published public domain material relating to the Cold War and nuclear weapons.'' avg. press run 2000. Expects 2 titles 2011. 2 titles listed in the *Small Press Record of Books in Print* (36th Edition, 2010-11). 255pp. Reporting time: We respond withing days by e-mail. Simultaneous submissions accepted: No. Publishes 1% of manuscripts submitted. Payment: We have not paid any advances, and royalties vary from case to case. Depends on the circumstances. Subjects: History, Nuclear Energy, Weapons.

THE HOLLINS CRITIC, R.H.W. Dillard, Editor; Amanda Cockrell, Managing Editor, PO Box 9538, Hollins University, VA 24020. 1964. Poetry, criticism, reviews. ''Essay on particular work of one author; several poems. Essay approximately 5000 words, no footnotes. No unsolicited essay or review mss. Essays by prior commitment only. Short poems are published in every issue. We read poetry from September to December only. Other features are a cover picture of the author under discussion, a checklist of author's writing and a brief sketch of career, plus book reviews. Recent essayists: Lewis Turco, Henry Taylor, Howard Nelson, George Garrett.'' circ. 400. 5/yr. Pub'd 5 issues 2009; expects 5 issues 2010, 5 issues 2011. sub. price $10 U.S.; $15.00 elsewhere; per copy $4 U.S.; sample $3.00 U.S. Back issues: $4 U.S. ($5 elsewhere). 24pp. Reporting time: 2 months. Simultaneous submissions accepted with an SASE. Publishes 4% of manuscripts submitted. Payment: $25 for poems. Copyrighted, poetry rights revert to author. Pub's reviews: 15 in 2009. §Mainly current fiction and poetry and critical works. Subjects: Literary Review, Literature (General).

Hollyridge Press (see also 88: A Journal of Contemporary American Poetry), Ian Randall Wilson, Managing Editor, PO Box 2872, Venice, CA 90294, 310-712-1238, Fax 310-828-4860, hollyridge-press@aol.com, http://www.hollyridgepress.com. 2000. Poetry, fiction. ''Publishes literary fiction: novels, short story collections, novella collections. Also publishes poetry annual and chapbook series.'' Pub'd 2 titles 2009; expects 4 titles 2010, 4 titles 2011. 7 titles listed in the *Small Press Record of Books in Print* (36th Edition, 2010-11). Discounts: available through Ingram and Baker & Taylor. Payment: up to 15% hardcover. Copyrights for author. Subjects: Fiction, Literature (General).

Hollywood Creative Directory, Jeff Black, 5055 Wilshire Blvd., Los Angeles, CA 90036, 800-815-0503, 323-525-2369, Fax 323-525-2393, www.hcdonline.com. 1987. ''The many directories that make up the Hollywood Creative Directory catalogue, commonly known as "the phone books to Hollywood," offer the most comprehensive, up-to-date information available, listing the names, numbers, addresses and current titles of entertainment professionals from the film, television and music industries. For almost twenty years this "insider's guide to the insiders" has been a must-have for anyone working in the professional entertainment industry. The current catalogue includes the Hollywood Creative Directory, the Hollywood Representation Directory, the Hollywood Distributors Directory, and the Hollywood Music Industry Directory. All print directories are available in one searchable online database. The Hollywood Creative Directory is released three times a year in print. The company is also co-publishing The Hollywood Reporter Blu-Book Production Directory, the premier guide for below-the-line production services.'' avg. press run 5M. Pub'd 8 titles 2009; expects 8 titles 2010, 8 titles 2011. 28 titles listed in the *Small Press Record of Books in Print* (36th Edition, 2010-11). Discounts: 1-4 20%, 5-9 30%, 10-24 47%,. 400pp. Reporting time: 8 weeks. Copyrights for author. Subjects: Arts, Media, Music, Performing Arts, Reference, Television, Theatre, Visual Arts.

Holmes House, S.J. Holmes, 530 North 72nd Avenue, Omaha, NE 68114. 1999. Poetry. "We are committed to 4 poets but will look at other submissions. Always send for guidelines first." avg. press run 400. Pub'd 2 titles 2009; expects 2 titles 2010, 3-4 titles 2011. No titles listed in the *Small Press Record of Books in Print* (36th Edition, 2010-11). Discounts: 40% stores, 50% libraries. 40pp. Reporting time: 2 months. Simultaneous submissions accepted: no. Publishes 20% of manuscripts submitted. Payment: 25 copies to poet. Does not copyright for author. Subjects: Gay, Nebraska, Poetry, Spiritual.

Holy Cow! Press, Jim Perlman, PO Box 3170, Mount Royal Station, Duluth, MN 55803, 218-724-1653 phone/Fax. 1977. Poetry, fiction, articles, parts-of-novels, long-poems. "Holy Cow! Press is a Midwestern independent publisher that features new work by both well-known and younger writers. Besides single author collections, we try to tastefully assemble anthologies centered around important themes. We are supportive of first books by younger writers; PLEASE query before submitting manuscripts." avg. press run 1.5M. Pub'd 5 titles 2009; expects 4 titles 2010, 5 titles 2011. 36 titles listed in the *Small Press Record of Books in Print* (36th Edition, 2010-11). Discounts: 40% off to classrooms, bulk, institutions, bookstores. 96pp. Reporting time: 2-4 months. We accept simultaneous submissions if informed. Publishes 2% of manuscripts submitted. Payment: negotiable with each author. Copyrights for author. Subjects: Literature (General), Poetry.

Holy Macro! Books, Bill Jelen, 13386 Judy Avenue NW, PO Box 82, Uniontown, OH 44685-9310, 330-715-2875, Fax 707-220-4510, consult@MrExcel.com, www.HolyMacroBooks.com. 2002. Non-fiction. "Books, e-Books or CD-ROM's on Microsoft Office products." avg. press run 2M. Pub'd 5 titles 2009; expects 7 titles 2010, 7 titles 2011. 14 titles listed in the *Small Press Record of Books in Print* (36th Edition, 2010-11). Discounts: trade. 300pp. Reporting time: 4 weeks. Simultaneous submissions accepted: yes. Publishes 10% of manuscripts submitted. Payment: negotiable. Copyrights for author. Subject: Computers, Calculators.

HOLY ROLLERS, Cynic Press, PO Box 40691, Philadelphia, PA 19107. 2001. Poetry. "Checks made out to Cynic Press for back issues. Ceased publication." circ. 50. 2/yr. sub. price $20/6 issues; per copy $7; sample $5. Back issues: $5. 12pp. Reporting time: 3 weeks. Simultaneous submissions accepted: okay. Publishes 15% of manuscripts submitted. Payment: 2 copies. deceased. Ads: $20/$10. Subjects: Poetry, Religion, Spiritual.

Homa & Sekey Books, Shawn X. Ye, PO Box 103, Dumont, NJ 07628, 201-384-6692, Fax 201-384-6055, info@homabooks.com, www.homabooks.com. 1997. Fiction, art, non-fiction. "A member of PMA (Publishers Marketing Association) and AAS (Association for Asian Studies), Homa & Sekey Books is one of the few U.S. publishers of fine books on Asia, especially on China and Korea. Founded in 1997, Homa & Sekey Books was initially engaged in helping US and UK publishers sell translation rights to Asian publishing houses. The company soon grew into book publishing. Currently, our publishing focuses are fiction, art, business, biography, history and culture primarily on Asian topics. We will soon expand to include travel and juvenile books, among others. Journal publications are also on our drawing table. Under our English publishing program, we not only publish books translated from Asian languages, especially from Chinese and Korean, but also books written originally in English. We pride ourselves on this publishing endeavor aiming to help Western readers better understand and appreciate the East Asian cultures that are often too far away and somewhat mystified. We have a special program under which we publish, sometimes co-publish, highly selected titles in the Chinese language. Meanwhile, we serve as an international literary agency helping sell translation rights of American and British titles to Asian publishers. We also distribute, to the U.S. and Europe markets, books and journals published by Asian publishing houses." avg. press run 3M. Pub'd 6 titles 2009; expects 8 titles 2010, 10 titles 2011. 10 titles listed in the *Small Press Record of Books in Print* (36th Edition, 2010-11). Discounts: from 20% to 55%. 256pp. Reporting time: 2-6 weeks. Simultaneous submissions accepted: yes. Payment: yearly or by contract. Can copyright for author if necessary. Subjects: Arts, Asia, Indochina, Asian-American, Fiction, History, Literature (General), Romance, Short Stories.

HOME PLANET NEWS, Home Planet Publications, Donald Lev, Editor, PO Box 455, High Falls, NY 12440, 845-687-4084, homeplanetnews@yahoo.com. 1979. Poetry, fiction, articles, art, photos, cartoons, interviews, criticism, reviews, letters, parts-of-novels, long-poems, news items. "We like lively work of all types and schools. Poetry should run about a page. (Need shorter ones right now.) For articles, reviews, etc., please query first. Some recent contributors include: Richard Kostelanetz, Andrew Glaze, Tuli Kupferberg, Gerald Locklin, Lyn Lifshin, Frank Murphy, Hal Sirowitz, David Gershator, Barry Wallenstein, Bob Holman, Andy Clausen, A D. Winans, Linda Lerner, William Doreski, Enid Dame, Edward Sanders, Janine Pommy Vega, Peter Lamborn Wilson and Robert Kelly.." circ. 3M. 1-3/yr. Pub'd 2 issues 2009; expects 2 issues 2010, 2 issues 2011. sub. price $12; per copy $5; sample $5. Back issues: $5. Discounts: 40% consignment, 50% cash, 25% agents. 24pp. Reporting time: 3-6 months. Simultaneous submissions accepted: no. Publishes 5% of manuscripts submitted. Payment: copies & 1 year gift subscription. Copyrighted, reverts to author. Pub's reviews: 28 books,9 magazines in 2009. §Poetry, fiction. Ads: $150/$75. Subjects: Book Reviewing, Criticism, Fiction, Literary Review, Literature (General), Poetry, Theatre, Visual Arts.

Home Planet Publications (see also HOME PLANET NEWS), Donald Lev, PO Box 455, High Falls, NY 12440, 845-687-4084, homeplanetnews@yahoo.com. 1971. Poetry. "Home Planet Publications publishes occasional books of poetry, but does not consider unsolicited manuscripts and is presently inactive. For our magazine, *Home Planet News*, see listing above.'' avg. press run 400. No titles listed in the *Small Press Record of Books in Print* (36th Edition, 2010-11). Discounts: 50% cash to stores; 40% consignment; 25% agents. 60pp. Payment: negotiable. Copyrights for author. Subjects: Literary Review, Poetry.

Hood Press, Jason Sipe, 19130 SE Hwy 212, Damascus, OR 97089-8704. 2007. Fiction, cartoons, non-fiction. ''Hood Press is commited to providing quality Children and Adult contemporary fiction as well as informative educational books.'' avg. press run 1000. Expects 3 titles 2010, 5 titles 2011. No titles listed in the *Small Press Record of Books in Print* (36th Edition, 2010-11). Discounts: 1-10 copies 25% 10-50 copies 35%. 100pp. Reporting time: not accepting unsolicited manuscripts at present. Payment: to be determined per title. Subjects: Absurdist, Adolescence, African Literature, Africa, African Studies, Astrology, Children, Youth, Crafts, Hobbies, Family, Fantasy, Fiction, Folklore, Humor, New Age, Occult, Short Stories, Social Movements.

Hoover Institution Press, Jeff Bliss, Associate Director of Communications, Stanford University, Stanford, CA 94305-6010, 650-723-3373, e-mail bliss@hoover.stanford.edu. Non-fiction. ''Subjects usually published are: economics, political science, public policy, studies of nationalities in Central and Eastern Europe, Asian Studies, international studies.'' avg. press run 1M. Pub'd 8 titles 2009; expects 8 titles 2010, 6 titles 2011. 89 titles listed in the *Small Press Record of Books in Print* (36th Edition, 2010-11). Discounts: wholesale: 1-4 copies 20%, 5-24 42%, 25-49 45%, 50-99 48%, 100+ 50%; Retail 1-2 copies 20%, 3-24 40%, 25-49 42%, 50-249 44%, 250+ 46%. 200pp. Reporting time: varies, 2-4 months. Payment: individually arranged. Copyrights for author. Subjects: Asia, Indochina, Bibliography, Business & Economics, Communism, Marxism, Leninism, Education, History, Latin America, Middle East, Non-Fiction, Political Science, Politics, Public Affairs, U.S.S.R.

Hope Publishing House, Faith Annette Sand, Publisher, PO Box 60008, Pasadena, CA 91116, 626-792-6123; fax 626-792-2121. 1983. Criticism, non-fiction. ''We deal with religious and educational topics and like to facilitate getting women and minorities into print, although we publish men, too. We are a nonprofit publishing venture, a program unit of the So. Calif. Ecumenical Council and concentrate on subjects of import to the faith community like human rights and related issues for the Palestinians and Israelis. We are currently interested in concerns for the church and faith society, as well as ecology, health and justice issues.'' avg. press run 3M-5M. Pub'd 6 titles 2009; expects 6 titles 2010, 6 titles 2011. 47 titles listed in the *Small Press Record of Books in Print* (36th Edition, 2010-11). Discounts: as required to trade and bulk buyers. 228pp. Reporting time: 2 months. Payment: royalties are arranged, payments are made biannually. Copyrights for author. Subjects: Alcohol, Alcoholism, Biography, Christianity, Culture, Environment, Family, Feminism, Global Affairs, Health, Inspirational, Latin America, Non-Violence, Religion, South America, Spiritual.

Hopeace Press, Keith Moen, 188 Morley Ave, Winnepeg, MB R3L 0Y1, Canada, 250 335 0535, palesurface@hopeace.ca, www.palesurfaceofthings.com. 2006. Poetry, fiction. avg. press run 1000. Pub'd 1 title 2009; expects 2 titles 2010, 2 titles 2011. 1 title listed in the *Small Press Record of Books in Print* (36th Edition, 2010-11). Discounts: standard industry trade discounts. 300pp. Reporting time: not seeking submissions at this time. Simultaneous submissions accepted: No. Does not copyright for author. Subjects: Adolescence, Anthropology, Archaelogy, Architecture, British Columbia, Greek, Guidance, Mentoring/Coaching, Novels, Parenting.

The Hopkins review, John T. Irwin, Editor, The Johns Hopkins University Press, 2715 North Charles Street, Baltimore, MD 21218-4363. ''This new literary journal will publish fiction, poetry, memoirs, essays on literature, drama, film,the visual arts, music and dance. Contributors include Max Apple, J.M. Coetzee, James Salter, John Hollander, Richard Wilbur, Harold Bloom, Sir Frank Kermode, J. Hillis Miller, and Helen Vendler.''

Horned Owl Publishing, Rob Von Rudloff, J. Bryony Lake, 4605 Bearwood Court, Victoria, BC V8Y 3G1, Canada, fax 250-414-4987; e-mail hornowl@islandnet.com. 1992. Fiction, non-fiction. ''We publish scholarly books in the field of Pagan Studies and Pagan Children's Literature. We prefer submissions of at least 25,000 words for the former.'' avg. press run 4000. 5 titles listed in the *Small Press Record of Books in Print* (36th Edition, 2010-11). Discounts: trade 40%, distributor 55%. 200pp, children's literature 40pp. Reporting time: 2 months. Simultaneous submissions accepted only when identified as such. Publishes 2% of manuscripts submitted. Payment: advance based on anticipated production run; royalty 10% (less for foreign sales, etc.). Copyrights for author. Subjects: Anthropology, Archaelogy, Celtic, Children, Youth, Classical Studies, Greek, History, Magic, Metaphysics, Myth, Mythology, Religion, Scandinavia, WICCA.

HORTIDEAS, Greg Williams, Pat Williams, 750 Black Lick Road, Gravel Switch, KY 40328, 859-332-7606. 1984. Articles, reviews, news items, non-fiction. ''Short articles on vegetable, flower, and fruit growing, directed to amateur gardeners; including abstracts from the technical horticultural literature, new product reviews, and book reviews.'' circ. 1M. 6/yr. Pub'd 6 issues 2009; expects 6 issues 2010, 6 issues 2011. sub. price $25; per copy $5.00; sample $5. Back issues: $5.00. Discounts: none, mailorder only. 24pp. Reporting time: 1 month. Payment: free issue. Copyrighted, does not revert to author. Pub's reviews: 28 in 2009. §Gardening, horticulture, agriculture, botany, forestry. No ads. Subjects: Agriculture, Gardening, Indexes & Abstracts.

The Hosanna Press, Cathie Ruggie Saunders, 203 Keystone, River Forest, IL 60305, 708-771-8259. 1974. Poetry, fiction, art, concrete art. "Limited edition fine printings from foundry type on rag & unique handmade papers, w/ original graphics. Innovative concepts of book, paper, and print pursued." avg. press run 25-100. Expects 1 title 2010, 1 title 2011. 15 titles listed in the *Small Press Record of Books in Print* (36th Edition, 2010-11). Pages vary. Reporting time: 3-6 weeks. Payment: 10% of edition. Copyrights for author. Subjects: Arts, Book Arts, Graphics, Poetry, Visual Arts.

Host Publications, Inc. (see also THE DIRTY GOAT), Elzbieta Szoka, Joe W. Bratcher III, 1000 East 7th St., Suite 201, Austin, TX 78702-1953, Phone 212-905-2365; FAX 212-905-2369; jbratcher@hostpublications.com. 1988. Poetry, fiction, art, photos, interviews, criticism, parts-of-novels, long-poems, plays. "Host focuses on literature in translation. We publish poetry, novels, short stories and drama. Recent authors: Maria Rosa Lojo, Noni Benegas, Miguel Gonzalez-Gerth, Joao Almino. Prefer to publish books by authors with some reputation. Other material, by less established artists, considered for *The Dirty Goat.*" avg. press run 1M-1.5M. Pub'd 3 titles 2009; expects 3 titles 2010, 4 titles 2011. 31 titles listed in the *Small Press Record of Books in Print* (36th Edition, 2010-11). Discounts: 1 copy 20%, 2-9 40%, 10+ 55%. 150pp. Reporting time: indeterminate. Does not copyright for author. Subjects: African Literature, Africa, African Studies, The Americas, Arts, Avant-Garde, Experimental Art, Beat, Bilingual, Criticism, Culture, Dada, Drama, English, Erotica, Essays, Europe, Fiction.

Hot Box Press / Southern Roots Publishing, Joe Gaston, PO Box 161078, Mobile, AL 36616, 251-645-9018, info@hotboxpress.com. 2000. Non-fiction. "As a small company we look for titles that will cater to a specific or specialized market. The Hot Box Press side of the company deals specifically with books for the railroad enthusiast. The Southern Roots side is open to any topic with a specific niche in mind. We work closely with our authors in developing a marketing strategy that can be implemented by both parties. We prefer receiving queries as to unsolicited manuscripts. All queries should describe the subject matter and for non-railroad books, data on the specific market the book is targeting would be very helpful. All queries should be addressed to Joe Gaston." avg. press run 1000. Expects 1 title 2010, 2 titles 2011. 1 title listed in the *Small Press Record of Books in Print* (36th Edition, 2010-11). Discounts: 1-2 copies no discount3-199 copies 40%200-up 50%. 160pp. Simultaneous submissions accepted: yes. Payment: Negotiable. Copyrights for author. Subjects: Biography, History, Non-Fiction, Transportation.

HOT FLASHES: Not a Menopause Thang, GROUP Publishing, Robert Bell Jr, 93 Old York Road Suite 1-406, Jenkintown, PA 19046, 267 258-7967. 2006. Fiction, photos, letters, parts-of-novels. 12/yr. Expects 2 issues 2010, 12 issues 2011. sub. price $39.99; per copy $3.99; sample Free. Back issues: $3.99. 50pp. Reporting time: One week. Simultaneous submissions accepted: Yes. Publishes 100% of manuscripts submitted. assigned ISSN. Ads: 1/4 Page $200 In-Frt $10001/2/Page$400 Bk-In $9003/4Page$600 Bk $1200Full Page $800. Subjects: Bisexual, Fiction, Photography, Poetry, Sex, Sexuality, Storytelling.

Hot Pepper Press, Taylor Graham, Hatch Graham, 3541 Wildwood Lane, Placerville, CA 95667. 1991. Poetry. "Not currently reading for chapbooks." 5 titles listed in the *Small Press Record of Books in Print* (36th Edition, 2010-11).

HOTEL AMERIKA, David Lazar, Editor; Jean Cunningham, Managing Editor, Columbia College, English Department, 600 S. Michigan Ave., Chicago, IL 60605-1996, 740-597-1360, editors@hotelamerika.net, www.hotelamerika.net. 2002. Poetry, fiction, photos, satire, parts-of-novels, long-poems, non-fiction. "*Hotel Amerika* seeks to find and define a diverse constituency of writers and readers. Work we publish ranges from the utterly accessible writing that speaks to readers directly with subtle literary qualities whose effects may be profound to work that challenges the most sophisticated readers in our audience. Work we publish cuts across all genres, including poetry, fiction, essay, and translations. We have recently published John Ashbery, Maxine Kumin, Charles Wright, Leonard Kriegel, Guy Davenport. Work published in Hotel Amerika has been selected for Best American Poetry, Pushcart Prize, and named as notable in Best American Essays. Contest guidelines available on website." circ. 1200. 2/yr. Pub'd 1 issue 2009; expects 2 issues 2010, 2 issues 2011. sub. price $18; per copy $9; sample $9. Back issues: $5. 130pp. Reporting time: 2-4 months. Simultaneous submissions accepted: No. Copyrighted, reverts to author. Ads: Full page $150 one time; $100 two or more times.Half page $100 one time; $75 two or more times.Hotel Amerika participates in ad exchanges with interested publications.

Hotel des Bains Editions, Spec, 28, rue du Pont Perce, 27130, Verneuil sur Avre, France, 33-(0)2 32 32 46 15. 1995. "Please refer to: http://spec-speceditions.net/." 3 titles listed in the *Small Press Record of Books in Print* (36th Edition, 2010-11). Dpt lgal BNF. Subjects: Avant-Garde, Experimental Art, Bilingual, Book Arts, Essays, Visual Arts.

•The House of Worn (see also WORN FASHION JOURNAL), Serah-Marie McMahon, Editor-in-pants &

Publisher, 77 Maynard Ave., #3, Toronto, Ontario, Canada. No titles listed in the *Small Press Record of Books in Print* (36th Edition, 2010-11).

Emma Howard Books, Attn: Armando H. Luna, PO Box 385, Planetarium Stn., New York, NY 10024-0385, 212-996-2590 phone/Fax, emmahowardbooks@verizon.net, www.eelgrassgirls.com. 1994. Fiction. "Children's and Young Adult books." avg. press run 3M. Pub'd 1 title 2009; expects 2 titles 2010, 3 titles 2011. 7 titles listed in the *Small Press Record of Books in Print* (36th Edition, 2010-11). Discounts: 40%. 30pp. Reporting time: 1 month. Simultaneous submissions accepted: no. Publishes so far 50% of manuscripts submitted. Payment: individual arrangements. Copyrighting for author varies.

Howling Dog Press / Brave New World Order Books (see also OMEGA), Michael Annis, P.O. Box 853, Berthoud, CO 80513-0853, WritingDangerously@msn.com, www.howlingdogpress.com, www.howlingdogpress.com/OMEGA. 1981. Poetry, fiction, art, long-poems, non-fiction. "Recent and forthcoming contributors: Antler, Jim Corbett, Gregory Greyhawk, Will Inman, Heller Levinson, Oswald LeWinter, Mike Palecek, David Ray, Kenneth Rosen, Y St. Michel-Anon. We don't publish books for the hell of it; we don't slaughter trees for precious egos. Time is short, so don't waste yours sending us work that everyone else is doing. We are never convinced or persuaded by convention, by one's past, or what someone else may think of your work or your necktie. We care nothing about who you studied under or from what school, or if you shook hands with the poet laureate. Most of them will teach you the fine art of mediocrity. We notice crimes against criteria, cloning, and theft. Every manuscript must stand on its own in the present, regardless of all the accolades and votes of confidence you may have already received. Write as if it's the last opportunity you'll ever have to say something substantial and of actual importance, since it very well may be. If you have a statement you want to leave for posterity, come here. If you are interested in plug-and-play publishing, go somewhere else—far away. (And, absolutely NO right wing screed propaganda! NO Limbaughese, NO Dobson pontifications, NO save-me-from-myself-and-the-devil.) "Draw blood ... write a poem."." Pub'd 2 titles 2009; expects 5 titles 2010, 7 titles 2011. 1 title listed in the *Small Press Record of Books in Print* (36th Edition, 2010-11). Discounts: Bookstores, retailers: 1-4 copies = 30%, 5-9 copies = 40%, 10 or more = 45%. Classrooms: 30%. Howling Dog Press does NOT consign books, broadsides, tapes, or CDs. All books are on a purchase basis. Returns are allowed on merchandise in very good condition, preferably wrapped, if wrapped when shipped initially. Credit is given for future merchandise; $-refunds on wrapped merchandise only. Shipping and postage: Howling Dog Press pays for shipment of books to the outlet. It is expected that the outlet will pay any shipping charges for any items returned. Outlets are given wholesale prices. 208pp. Reporting time: Generally, we are not fooled. We respond as soon as we open it. Simultaneous submissions accepted: No. Publishes 5% of manuscripts submitted. Payment: There is not a "usual royalty." We craft contracts individually to fit the situation. Copyrights for author.

Howln Moon Press, Betty A. Mueller, 7222 State Highway 357, Franklin, NY 13775-3100, 607-829-2187 (office), 888-349-9438 (ordering), email: bmueller@hmpress.com. 1993. Art, photos, cartoons, non-fiction. "We publish books about dogs and dog training. Books with a 'new' point of view or fresh ideas get our attention. Query with outline or sample chapter first. No unsolicited manuscripts please." Pub'd 2 titles 2009; expects 2 titles 2010, 3-4 titles 2011. 24 titles listed in the *Small Press Record of Books in Print* (36th Edition, 2010-11). Discounts: 20% prepaid STOP orders, Small Retailers Program. Pages vary. Reporting time: one month. Simultaneous submissions accepted: no. Publishes 50% of manuscripts submitted. Payment: to be arranged. Does not copyright for author. Subjects: Animals, Health, How-To, Non-Fiction, Pets, Psychology, Reference.

HUBBUB, Lisa Steinman, Jim Shugrue, 5344 S.E. 38th Avenue, Portland, OR 97202, 503-775-0370. 1983. Poetry. "*Hubbub* publishes poetry reviews by invitation only, but accepts submissions of all kinds of poetry: excellence is our only criterion. Volume 26—to appear in 2010—will be a special issue dedicated to Vern Rutsala's poetry, including others' reviews, comments, anecdotes, and poems in tribute to (as well as a selection of poems by) Rutsala." circ. 350. 1/yr. Pub'd 1 issue 2009; expects 1 issue 2010, 1 issue 2011. sub. price $7; per copy $7 (volume 24 [2008] and following); sample $5. Back issues: $4.35 (full backlist flyer available). Discounts: 40%. 60pp. Reporting time: 1-3 months. Simultaneous submissions accepted: no. Publishes .05% of manuscripts submitted. Payment: 2 contributor copies. Copyrighted, reverts to author. Pub's reviews: none in 2009. §Poetry. Ads: $50/$25/will swap with other literary magazines in some cases. Subject: Poetry.

THE HUDSON REVIEW, Paula Deitz, Editor, 684 Park Avenue, New York, NY 10021, 212-650-0020, Fax 212-774-1911. 1948. Poetry, fiction, articles, criticism, reviews, parts-of-novels, long-poems, non-fiction. "Although we have developed a recognizable group of contributors who are identified with the magazine, we are always open to new writers and publish them in every issue. We have no university affiliation and are not committed to any narrow academic aim, nor to any particular political perspective. Unsolicited manuscripts will be read: Nonfiction - January 1 through March 31; Poetry - April 1 through June 30; Fiction - September 1 through November 30. Unsolicited manuscripts received at other times will be returned unread. Mss. submitted by subscribers who so identify themselves are read throughout the year." circ. 4.5M. 4/yr. Pub'd 4 issues 2009;

expects 4 issues 2010, 4 issues 2011. 5 titles listed in the *Small Press Record of Books in Print* (36th Edition, 2010-11). sub. price $32 domestic, $36 foreign; per copy $9; sample $9. Back issues: varies. Bulk rates and discount schedules on request. 176pp. Reporting time: 12 weeks maximum. Simultaneous submissions accepted: no. Payment: 2-1/2¢ per word for prose, 50¢ per line for poetry. Copyrighted, rights revert to author under l978 law on request. Pub's reviews: 80 in 2009. §Literature, fine and performing arts, sociology and cultural anthropology. Ads: $300/$200. Subjects: Arts, Literary Review.

A HUDSON VIEW POETRY DIGEST, Skyline Publications, Victoria Valentine, Publisher, Usa Editor; Amitabh Mitra, Editor, P.O. Box 295, Stormville, NY 12582-0295, http://www.hudsonview.us, email: hudsonviewpoetry@gmail.com. 2006. Poetry, fiction, non-fiction. "A Hudson View Poetry Digest publishes an attractive Quarterly print digest of 48 pages, color cover, containing poetry of International poets, including poet bios. Distributed in the USA and Internationally." 4/yr. Expects 1 issue 2010, 4 issues 2011. 1 title listed in the *Small Press Record of Books in Print* (36th Edition, 2010-11). price per copy 8.50; sample 8.50 if current. 6.50 if past issue. Back issues: Query: HudsonViewPoetry@gmail.com. Discounts: Universities, Schools, Libraries, 2-6 copies 10%. 48pp. Reporting time: 4 months. Simultaneous submissions accepted: Yes. Publishes 10% of manuscripts submitted. Payment: One free copy. Copyright notice of entire works, but not for each individual author. Author retains all rights and responsibilities for their personal copyright. Subjects: Fiction, Haiku, Inspirational, Interviews, Literature (General), Magazines, Multicultural, Myth, Mythology, Non-Fiction, Publishing, Romance, Short Stories, Spiritual, Storytelling, Zines.

Hug The Earth Publications (see also HUG THE EARTH, A Journal of Land and Life), Kenneth Lumpkin, 42 Greenwood Avenue, Pequannock, NJ 07440. 1980. Poetry, art, criticism, reviews, letters, long-poems. "We publish broadsides, chapbooks, calendars, and a one-time only journal on land & life." avg. press run 500-1M. Pub'd 2 titles 2009; expects 1 title 2010. 1 title listed in the *Small Press Record of Books in Print* (36th Edition, 2010-11). 40pp. Reporting time: 6-8 weeks. Copyrights for author.

HUG THE EARTH, A Journal of Land and Life, Hug The Earth Publications, Kenneth Lumpkin, 42 Greenwood Avenue, Pequannock, NJ 07440. "Features Charles Olson, Gary Snyder, Flavia Alaya, Ken Lumpkin, E. Durling Merrill, et al. Poems and prose on environment and place in literature." 24pp. Simultaneous submissions accepted: yes. Publishes 50% of manuscripts submitted. Copyrighted. §Myth, land, Magick.

Humanergy, Christi Barrett, 213 West Mansion Street, Marshall, MI 49068, www.humanergy.com. No titles listed in the *Small Press Record of Books in Print* (36th Edition, 2010-11).

HUMOR TIMES, James Israel, PO Box 162429, Sacramento, CA 95816-2429, 916-455-1217, www.humortimes.com, info@humortimes.com. 1991. Articles, cartoons, satire. "A humorous monthly 'review of the news' featuring editorial (and other) cartoons, columns and a 'fake news' section." circ. 5000. 12/yr. Pub'd 12 issues 2009; expects 12 issues 2010, 12 issues 2011. sub. price $18.95; per copy $3.00; sample $1.00. Back issues: $3.00. Discounts: 5+ copies 50%. 24pp. Reporting time: 30 days. Simultaneous submissions accepted: Yes. Publishes 5% of manuscripts submitted. Payment: Negotiable. Copyrighted, reverts to author. Ads: $699 full / $389 half / $199 qtr / $109 1/8 pg / $59 1/16 pg / $35 classified. Subjects: Cartoons, Comics, Humor, Politics, Satire.

HUNGER MOUNTAIN, The VCFA Journal of Arts, Miciah Bay Gault, Managing Editor, Vermont College of Fine Arts, 36 College Street, Montpelier, VT 05602, 802-828-8517, hungermtn@vermontcollege.edu, www.hungermtn.org. 2002. Poetry, fiction, art, photos, parts-of-novels, long-poems, plays, non-fiction. "*Hunger Mountain* is both a print and online journal for readers, writers, artists and art lovers. Our mission is to cultivate engagement with and conversation about the arts by publishing high-quality, innovative literary and visual art by both established and emerging artists, and by offering opportunities for interactivity and discourse. We hold four contests annually: the Howard Frank Mosher Short Fiction Prize (Deadline June 30th), the Ruth Stone Prize in Poetry (Deadline December 10th), the *Hunger Mountain* Creative Nonfiction Prize (Deadline September 10th), and the Katherine Paterson Prize for Young Adult and Children's Writing (Deadline June 30th). For guidelines, go to www.hungermtn.org.In general were looking for writing/art that shows vision, intent, craft, and an ability to transport the viewer/reader into the world of the artist. We believe in the arts as essential keeper and conveyer of culture and history, as well as the best vehicle for understanding, developing, and deepening our humanity. Past contributors to *Hunger Mountain* include Pinckney Benedict, Ron Carlson, Hayden Carruth, Matthew Dickman, Mark Doty, Rita Dove, Terrance Hayes, Alice Hoffman, Maxine Kumin, Dorianne Laux, Bret Lott, Michael Martone, Naomi Shihab Nye, Tomaz Salamun, Charles Simic, James Tate, and Jean Valentine.Please read our submission guidelines at www.hungermtn.org." circ. 1,000. 1/yr. Pub'd 2 issues 2009; expects 1 issue 2010, 1 issue 2011. sub. price One-year $12; Two-year $22; Four-year $40; per copy $12; sample $10. Back issues: $10. 200pp. Reporting time: 6 months. Simultaneous submissions accepted: yes. Publishes 5% of manuscripts submitted. Payment: Between $20 and $75 depending on length. Copyrighted, reverts to author. Ads: ncgotiable.

Hunter House Inc., Publishers, Kiran Rana, Publisher; Alexandra Mummery, Editor, PO Box 2914, Alameda, CA 94501, 510-865-5282, Fax 510-865-4295, info@hunterhouse.com, www.hunterhouse.com. 1978. Non-fiction. "We publish in the areas of health, women's health, fitness, sexuality and violence prevention." avg. press run 5M. Pub'd 17 titles 2009; expects 17 titles 2010, 18 titles 2011. 93 titles listed in the *Small Press Record of Books in Print* (36th Edition, 2010-11). Discounts: retailers/wholesalers: 1 10%, 2+ 20%, 6+ 40%, 100+ 45%; libraries: 2+ 10%, 6+ 20%. 288pp. Reporting time: 3-6 months. Simultaneous submissions accepted: yes. Payment: 12% of net up to 15% pa; 12% of net up to 15% on cl; report and pay twice a year. Copyrights for author. Subjects: Adolescence, Alternative Medicine, Children, Youth, Disease, Education, Games, Health, Mental Health, Non-Violence, Nutrition, Psychology, Relationships, Self-Help, Sex, Sexuality, Women.

Hunter Publishing Corporation, Victoria Hunter, 115 West California Boulevard, Suite 411, Pasadena, CA 91105, tel: 626 792 3316, fax: 626 792 7077, email: info@hpcwww.com, website: www.hpcwww.com. 2007. Art, non-fiction. "Hunter Publishing Corporation specializes in publishing fashion education materials. With an in-depth understanding of the fashion education process and experience in the fashion design and publishing industries, we provide both informative and inspirational one-stop solutions for educators, students and individuals. The company's mission is to publish materials that deliver the right information, at the right time and in the right format for success; AND to maximize an individual's unique creative ability." avg. press run 6000. Expects 1 title 2010, 4 titles 2011. 1 title listed in the *Small Press Record of Books in Print* (36th Edition, 2010-11). Discounts: For Educators & Educational Bookstores: 1-5 copies List Price, 6-50 copies 20%, 51-100 copies 25%, 101-250 copies 26%, 251-500 copies 27%, 501-1000 copies 29%, 1001+ copies 30%. For Book Trade: 1-4 copies 20%, 5-24 copies 40%, 25+ copies 42%. 300pp. Reporting time: 2-8 weeks. Payment: Assessed on an individual basis. Subjects: Arts, Clothing, Creativity, Design, Education, Fashion, How-To, Inspirational, Textbooks.

Huntington Library Press, Susan Green, 1151 Oxford Road, San Marino, CA 91108, 626-405-2172, Fax 626-585-0794, e-mail booksales@huntington.org. 1920. Non-fiction. avg. press run 1M. Pub'd 6 titles 2009; expects 6 titles 2010, 6 titles 2011. 66 titles listed in the *Small Press Record of Books in Print* (36th Edition, 2010-11). Discounts: 20% average. 200pp. Reporting time: varies. Simultaneous submissions accepted: no. Publishes 1% of manuscripts submitted. Payment: generally no royalties paid. Copyrights for author. Subjects: Americana, Arts, California, History, Horticulture, Literature (General).

HUNTINGTON LIBRARY QUARTERLY, University of California Press, Susan Green, Editor, University of California Press, 2000 Center St., Suite 303, Berkeley, CA 94704-1223, 626-405-2174. 1931. Non-fiction. "*The Huntington Library Quarterly* publishes articles that primarily relate to the Huntington Collections of 16th-18th century art, history and literature of Great Britain and America." circ. 740. 4/yr. Pub'd 4 issues 2009; expects 4 issues 2010, 4 issues 2011. sub. price $36 indiv., $127 inst.; per copy $10 indiv., $40 inst.; sample free to libraries. Back issues: same as single copy. Discounts: agents 20%. 150pp. Reporting time: varies. Simultaneous submissions accepted: no. Publishes 15% of manuscripts submitted. Payment: none. Copyrighted, does not revert to author. Pub's reviews: 12 in 2009. §Literary history, history, art history. Ads: $295/$220. Subjects: Arts, History, Literature (General).

Huntington Press, Anthony Curtis, Deke Castleman, 3665 S. Procyon Avenue, Las Vegas, NV 89103, 702-252-0655; Fax 702-252-0675; editor@huntingtonpress.com; http://www.huntingtonpress.com; http://www.lasvegasadvisor.com. 1983. Non-fiction. avg. press run 5M-10M. Pub'd 5 titles 2009; expects 6 titles 2010, 6 titles 2011. 5 titles listed in the *Small Press Record of Books in Print* (36th Edition, 2010-11). Discounts: trade 20%-50%. 218pp. Reporting time: 60 days. Simultaneous submissions accepted: yes. Payment: negotiable. Copyrights for author. Subjects: Games, Mathematics, Travel.

HYPATIA: A Journal of Feminist Philosophy, Hilde Lindemann, 503 South Kedzie Hall, Michigan State University, East Lansing, MI 48824. 1986. Articles, reviews, non-fiction. "Address business and subscription correspondence to: Journals Manager, Indiana University Press, 601 N.Morton Street, Bloomington, IN 47404." circ. 1.5M. 4/yr. Pub'd 4 issues 2009; expects 4 issues 2010, 4 issues 2011. sub. price $40 individual domestic (USA); $54 individual foreign; $110 institutional; per copy $15.00 individual; $30.00 institution. Back issues: $15. individual; $30 institution. Discounts: bulk 40% for 5 or more. 250pp. 4 months. Simultaneous submissions accepted: no. Publishes 15% of manuscripts submitted. Payment: none. Copyrighted, does not revert to author. Pub's reviews: 40 in 2009. §Feminist philosophy. Ads: $325 full page /$200 half page. Subjects: Ethics, Feminism, Gender Issues, Philosophy, Sex, Sexuality, Women.

I

IAMBS & TROCHEES, William F. Carlson, 6801 19th Avenue #5H, Brooklyn, NY 11204, 718-232-9268. 2001. Poetry, articles, reviews, long-poems. "Metrical verse only. Recent contributors: Dick Allen, X.J. Kennedy, Paul Lake, and Timothy Murphy." 2/yr. Expects 2 issues 2010, 2 issues 2011. sub. price $15; per copy $8; sample $8. Back issues: $8. 64-128pp. Reporting time: 2 months. Simultaneous submissions accepted: no. Payment: 1 copy. Copyrighted, reverts to author. Pub's reviews. §Metrical verse only. Ads: none. Subjects: Essays, Poetry, Reviews, Translation.

IBBETSON ST., Ibbetson St. Press, Doug Holder, Publisher Founder; Richard Wilhelm, Arts Editor; Dianne Robitaille, Consulting Editor; Robert K. Johnson, Consulting Editor; Linda Conte, Website Manager & Consulting Editor; Mary Rice, Poetry Editor; Dorian Brooks, Copy Editor; Harris Gardner, Poetry Editor, 25 School Street, Somerville, MA 02143, dougholder@post.harvard.edu. 1998. Poetry, articles, art, criticism, reviews. "Recent contributors: Dorian Brooks, Fred Marchant, Tim Gager, Steve Glines, Ed Galing, Richard Wilhelm, Sarah Hannah, Sam Cornish, Irene Koronas, Danielle Georges,John Flynn, Zvi Sesling, Linda Haviland Conte, Eric Greinke, A.D. Winans, Robert K. Johnson, Simon Perchik, Hugh Fox, etc..." circ. 200. 2/yr. Pub'd 2 issues 2009; expects 2 issues 2010, 2 issues 2011. 4 titles listed in the *Small Press Record of Books in Print* (36th Edition, 2010-11). sub. price $13; per copy $8; sample $8. 40-50pp. Reporting time: 3-6 months. Simultaneous submissions accepted: No. Publishes 10% of manuscripts submitted. Payment: 1 copy. Copyrighted, reverts to author. Pub's reviews. §Poetry reviewed by online Ibbetson Sreet Press Update. Ads: $40 full page. Subject: Poetry.

Ibbetson St. Press (see also IBBETSON ST.), Doug Holder, Dianne Robitaille, Dick Wilhelm, Robert K. Johnson, Dorian Brooks, Linda Conte, Glines Steve, Irene Koronas, 25 School Street, Somerville, MA 02143-1721, dougholder@post.harvard.edu. 1998. Poetry, articles, art, criticism, reviews. "Not accepting unsolicited manuscripts. Recent Contributors: Patricia Brodie, Molly Lynn Watt, Helen Bar Lev, michaelsimon." avg. press run 200. Pub'd 3 titles 2009; expects 3 titles 2010, 3 titles 2011. 21 titles listed in the *Small Press Record of Books in Print* (36th Edition, 2010-11). 50pp. Reporting time: 3-6 months. Simultaneous submissions accepted: no. Publishes 20% of manuscripts submitted. Does not copyright for author. Subject: Poetry.

Ibex Publishers, Inc., Farhad Shirzad, Publisher, PO Box 30087, Bethesda, MD 20824, toll free 888-718-8188, 301-718-8188, Fax 301-907-8707. 1979. Poetry, fiction, news items, non-fiction. "We publish books about Iran and in the Persian language." avg. press run 1M-2M. Pub'd 5 titles 2009; expects 9 titles 2010, 12 titles 2011. 13 titles listed in the *Small Press Record of Books in Print* (36th Edition, 2010-11). Discounts: 1-5 copy 20%, 5+ 40%. Copyrights for author. Subjects: Language, Middle East, Poetry, Sufism.

Ibexa Press, Dawn Devine, P.O. Box 611732, San Jose, CA 95161, www.ibexa.com, info@ibexa.com. 1997. Non-fiction. "Ibexa Press is devoted to publishing instructional guides for the design, history and construction of costumes. We currently specialize in the costume arts of Middle Eastern belly dance." avg. press run 3000. Pub'd 1 title 2009; expects 3 titles 2010, 3 titles 2011. No titles listed in the *Small Press Record of Books in Print* (36th Edition, 2010-11). Discounts: 25% discount on orders of 6-23. 50% discount on orders of 24 pieces. Titles can be mixed within an order. More detailed ordering information is available on our website. 200pp. Reporting time: 90 days. Simultaneous submissions accepted: No. Publishes 1% of manuscripts submitted. Payment: No advances, quarterly payment, royalties are calculated based on production costs and vary. Details are stipulated in each contract. Subjects: Clothing, Crafts, Hobbies, Dance, Design, Fashion, How-To, Multicultural, Non-Fiction.

•Ibis Editions, P.O. Box 8074, German Colony, Jerusalem 91080, Israel, Phone 972-2-627-7035, Fax 972-2-627-6058. "Ibis Editions is a small press and non-profit organization founded in Jerusalem in 1998 and dedicated to the publication of Levant-related books of poetry and belletristic prose. The press publishes translations from Hebrew, Arabic, Greek, French, and the other languages of the region. New writing is published, though special attention is paid to overlooked works from the recent and distant past. Ibis aims to make a modest contribution to the literature of this part of the world by drawing together a group of writers and translators whom both politics and market-forces would otherwise keep far apart, or out of print altogether. Ibis is motivated by the belief that literary work, especially when translated into a common language, can serve as an important vehicle for the promotion of understanding between individuals and peoples, and for the discovery of common ground." No titles listed in the *Small Press Record of Books in Print* (36th Edition, 2010-11).

Icarus Press, David Diorio, Non-fiction Editor, 1015 Kenilworth Drive, Baltimore, MD 21204, 410-821-7807, www.icaruspress.com. 1980. Poetry, non-fiction. avg. press run 1M. Pub'd 3 titles 2009; expects 3 titles 2010, 3 titles 2011. 12 titles listed in the *Small Press Record of Books in Print* (36th Edition, 2010-11). Discounts: 20-40%. 80pp. Payment: will vary depending on type. Subjects: Biography, History, Poetry.

Ice Cube Press, S.H. Semken, 205 North Front Street, North Liberty, IA 52317, 1-319-626-2055, fax 1-413-451-0223, steve@icecubepress.com, www.icecubepress.com. 1993. Fiction, non-fiction. "Publish an annual book on Midwest environment and spirituality. Midwest biographies, stories as well as being a book producer and designer for memoirs and family histories." avg. press run 500. Pub'd 6 titles 2009; expects 7 titles 2010, 8 titles 2011. 6 titles listed in the *Small Press Record of Books in Print* (36th Edition, 2010-11). Discounts: 45%, FF. 150pp. Reporting time: 1-6 months. Publishes 1% of manuscripts submitted. Payment: negotiable. Copyrights negotiable. Subjects: Americana, Community, Environment, Folklore, Memoirs, Nature, Psychology.

ICON, Dr. Michael Lynch, Advisor, Kent State University/ Trumbull campus, 4314 Mahoning Ave., Warren, OH 44483, 330-847-0571. 1966. Poetry, fiction, art, photos, non-fiction. "700 word limit on submissions. Limit of 6 prose, 6 poems, 6 artwork per issue. Typed or word processed only. Recent contributors: James Doyle, Barry Ballard, David Sapp, Richard Dinges, Jr. R.G. Cantalupo, Lyn Lifshin. Photos and art: color or black/white; will accept high quality reproductions; best size 5x7 inches. Deadlines: October 15, March 5. Press dates: early May and mid-December." 2/yr. Pub'd 2 issues 2009; expects 2 issues 2010, 2 issues 2011. sub. price $8; per copy $4. Back issues: some are available. Discounts: none. 48pp. Publishes 40% of manuscripts submitted. Payment: 1 copy. Not copyrighted, rights revert to author. Ads: none. Subjects: Essays, Fiction, Literature (General), Non-Fiction, Ohio, Photography, Poetry.

ICONOCLAST, Phil Wagner, 1675 Amazon Road, Mohegan Lake, NY 10547-1804. 1992. Poetry, fiction, articles, art, photos, cartoons, interviews, satire, criticism, reviews, letters, non-fiction. "Up to 3,500 words. Likes fiction literary and/or plotted, in the service of a noteworthy event or realization. Doesn't care for dreary, hopeless 'slice-of-life' stories or memoirs." circ. 700-3M. 4/yr. Pub'd 4 issues 2009; expects 4 issues 2010, 4 issues 2011. sub. price $20/8 issues; per copy $5; sample $5. Back issues: $5. Discounts: 5+/10%, 10+/20%, 15+/30%, 20+/40%. 64-80pp. Reporting time: 5-6 weeks. Simultaneous submission and publication is unacceptable. We desire first North American serial rights only. Publishes 2% of manuscripts submitted. Payment: 1-3 copies, 40% discount on additional copies, 1¢/word or $2-5/poem on publication for first N.A. serial rights (there is no cash payment for contributors with addresses outside the United States). Copyrighted, reverts to author. Pub's reviews: 75 in 2009. §Any work of intelligence and craft. Nearly all of our reviews cover small press publications or books ignored by the mass media. Ads: $100/$60/$35 1/4 page. Subjects: Book Reviewing, Creative Non-fiction, Essays, Fiction, Literary Review, Literature (General), Magazines, Poetry, Prose, Short Stories.

Iconoclast Press, Jack Haas, 3495 Cambie Street, Suite 144, Vancouver, BC V5Z 4R3, Canada, 604-682-3269 X8832, admin@iconoclastpress.com. 2002. Poetry, art, photos, non-fiction. "Query by email only please." Pub'd 3 titles 2009; expects 4 titles 2010, 4 titles 2011. 2 titles listed in the *Small Press Record of Books in Print* (36th Edition, 2010-11). 240pp. Reporting time: 2 months. Simultaneous submissions accepted: yes. Publishes 10% of manuscripts submitted. Payment: negotiable. Does not copyright for author. Subjects: Biography, California, Dreams, India, Libertarian, Occult, Pacific Northwest, Philosophy, Photography, Poetry, Religion, Spiritual, Sports, Outdoors, Women, Zen.

Idaho Center for the Book, 1910 University Drive, Boise, ID 83725-1525, 208-426-1999, Fax 208-426-4373, www.lili.org/icb. 1994. Non-fiction. "*James Castle: His Life & Art*, our most recent (2008) publication, Idaho Library Association "Book of the Year" award-winner, now in a second, revised/expanded edition with 50 new b&w and color illustrations and map." avg. press run 1K. Pub'd 1 title 2009; expects 1 title 2010, 1 title 2011. 2 titles listed in the *Small Press Record of Books in Print* (36th Edition, 2010-11). Discounts: 30-40%. 213pp. Reporting time: 1-3 months. Simultaneous submissions accepted: yes. Publishes 1% of manuscripts submitted. Payment: 10%/annual. Copyrights for author. Subjects: Book Arts, Idaho.

THE IDAHO REVIEW, Mitch Wieland, Boise State University, 1910 University Drive/English Dept., Boise, ID 83725, 208-426-1002, http://english.boisestate.edu/idahoreview/. 1998. Poetry, fiction, interviews, parts-of-novels, long-poems, non-fiction. "No word limit. Recent contributors: Richard Bausch, Ann Beattie, Rick Bass, Joy Williams, Madison Smartt Bell, and Ron Carlson. Work featured in *Best American Short Stories, O. Henry, Pushcart* and *New Stories From the South*." circ. 1M. 1/yr. Pub'd 1 issue 2009; expects 1 issue 2010, 1 issue 2011. sub. price $10.00 per year.; per copy $10.00; sample $5. Back issues: $6.95. 200pp. Reporting time: 3-5 months. Simultaneous submissions accepted: yes, if noted. Publishes 5% of manuscripts submitted. Payment: average $10 per page, $100 max. Copyrighted, reverts to author. Pub's reviews. §Fiction. Ads: $150/$75. Subjects: Fiction, Literary Review, Poetry.

Idylls Press, Debra Murphy, PO Box 3219, Ashland, OR 97520, phones: 541-905-1386, fax: 213-402-8967, idyllspress@gmail.com, www.idyllspress.com. 2004. Poetry, fiction, non-fiction. "We only take submissions by referrals." Pub'd 3 titles 2009; expects 5 titles 2010, 8 titles 2011. 7 titles listed in the *Small Press Record of Books in Print* (36th Edition, 2010-11). Discounts: etailers/bookstores who order directly from Idylls Press: 40%/returnable for paperbacks, 30%/returnable for hardcovers.Distributors/wholesalers: 25%/non-returnable for all books. 150-300pp. Reporting time: We are not taking new submissions at this time. Publishes 2 - 3% of manuscripts submitted. Payment: Advances: small or none. Royalties: 7.5% on paperbacks, 10% on hardcovers. Does not copyright for author. Subjects: Catholic, Fantasy, Fiction, Mystery, Non-Fiction, Novels, Pacific Northwest, Poetry, Science Fiction, Shakespeare, Writers/Writing.

Igneus Press, Peter Kidd, 310 N. Amherst Road, Bedford, NH 03110, 603-472-3466. 1990. Poetry. "Poetry books 50-150 pages. Recent authors: W.E. Butts, P.J. Laska, William Kemmett." avg. press run 500. Pub'd 1 title 2009; expects 4 titles 2010, 2-4 titles 2011. 9 titles listed in the *Small Press Record of Books in Print* (36th Edition, 2010-11). Discounts: 40%. 75pp. Reporting time: 1 month. Payment: 10% of run to author. Does not copyright for author. Subject: Poetry.

Ignite! Entertainment, Jeff Krell, P.O. Box 641131, Los Angeles, CA 90064-1980, 310-806-0325, jeffkrell@ignite-ent.com, www.ignite-ent.com. 1996. Cartoons. "Current biases: Gay-positive entertainment, cartoons, humor." avg. press run 2M. Pub'd 1 title 2009; expects 1 title 2010, 1 title 2011. 7 titles listed in the *Small Press Record of Books in Print* (36th Edition, 2010-11). Discounts: 50%. 96pp. Reporting time: 2 months. Simultaneous submissions accepted: yes. Payment: 5% cover price. Copyrights for author. Subjects: Cartoons, Comics, Gay, German, Humor.

Ika, LLC, Zachary Harris, 4630 Sansom Street, 1st Floor, Philadelphia, PA 19139-4630, 215-327-7341. 2005. Poetry, photos, satire, non-fiction. "The bulk of our focus are works that deal with any aspect of men in love and relationships. Anything from self-helf and psychology to satirical. Also, photo-essay works." avg. press run 3000. Pub'd 1 title 2009; expects 3 titles 2010. No titles listed in the *Small Press Record of Books in Print* (36th Edition, 2010-11). Discounts: 2-5 books - 25%, 6-10 books - 30%, 11-25 books - 40%, 26-49 books - 42%,50-74 books- 44%, 75-99 books 48%, 100+ books 50%. 200pp. Simultaneous submissions accepted: No. Publishes 1% of manuscripts submitted. Does not copyright for author. Subjects: Adolescence, African-American, Anthology, Culture, Food, Eating, Men, Multicultural, New Age, Non-Fiction, Non-Violence, Picture Books, Romance, Wine, Wineries, Women, Zen.

Ikon Inc., 151 First Ave. #46, New York, NY 10003. 1982. Poetry, fiction, non-fiction. "We are not accepting unsolicited manuscripts." avg. press run 1000. Pub'd 3 titles 2009; expects 4 titles 2010, 4 titles 2011. No titles listed in the *Small Press Record of Books in Print* (36th Edition, 2010-11). Discounts: 40%. Copyrights for author.

ILLOGICAL MUSE, Amber Rothrock, Editor, 115 Liberty St. Apt. 1, Buchanan, MI 49107, illogicalmuse@yahoo.com, http://geocities.com/illogicalmuse. 2004. Poetry, fiction, articles, art, photos, cartoons, reviews, parts-of-novels, non-fiction. "I have a huge backlog of poetry and art submissions and it may take longer than six months to respond. However fiction, essays, and book reviews stand a better chance." irregular. Pub'd 3 issues 2009; expects 3 issues 2010, 3 issues 2011. sub. price $20; per copy $5; sample $5. 20pp. Reporting time: 3-6 months. Simultaneous submissions accepted: yes. Publishes 75% of manuscripts submitted. Payment: 1 contributor's copy. Not copyrighted. Pub's reviews: 3 in 2009. §Will review anything pertaining to the arts. Please send a query letter and brief summary of what you'd like to have reviewed beforehand. Review material will not be returned. Subjects: Avant-Garde, Experimental Art, Cartoons, Creative Non-fiction, Creativity, Essays, Fiction, Handwriting/Written, Literature (General), Media, Photography, Poetry, Publishing, Reviews, Short Stories, Writers/Writing.

THE ILLUMINATA, Tyrannosaurus Press, Bret M. Funk, Garrie Keyman, Doug Roper, Terry Crotinger, PO Box 8337, New Orleans, LA 70182-8337, Illuminata@tyrannosauruspress.com, www.Tyrannosaurus-Press.com. 2002. Fiction, articles, interviews, satire, criticism, reviews, parts-of-novels, news items, non-fiction. "THE ILLUMINATA is the free speculative fiction (science fiction and fantasy) webzine of Tyrannosaurus Press. We publish SF-related articles, reviews, and original fiction. All submissions must be electronic. Visit our website for submission instructions." 12/yr. Pub'd 12 issues 2009; expects 12 issues 2010, 12 issues 2011. sub. price Free to download. Back issues: Available on website. 15pp. Simultaneous submissions accepted: yes. Payment: As a free publication, the Illuminata cannot compensate its contributors at this time. Interested parties must be content with gaining international exposure for their work. We require nonexclusive publication rights, but authors retain all rights to their articles/reviews/etc. and are free to seek placement for them elsewhere. Pub's reviews. §The Illuminata includes reviews of science fiction or fantasy related books, movies, comics, television, etc. Reviews should be approximately 500-750 words and should be honest and fair. Subjects: Fantasy, Science Fiction.

Illumination Arts, John Thompson, PO Box 1865, Bellevue, WA 98009, 425-644-7185. 1987. Fiction. "We publish inspiring/uplifting children's picture books with world-class artwork." Pub'd 2 titles 2009; expects 3 titles 2011. 2 titles listed in the *Small Press Record of Books in Print* (36th Edition, 2010-11). Discounts:

Normal trade discounts. 32pp. Reporting time: 6 months. Simultaneous submissions accepted: Yes. Payment: varies. Copyrights for author. Subjects: Children, Youth, Inspirational, Juvenile Fiction, Multicultural.

ILLUMINATIONS, Simon Lewis, English Dept., 66 George Street, College of Charleston, Charleston, SC 29424-0001, Tel: 843-953-1920, Fax: 843-953-1924, Web: www.cofc.edu/illuminations. 1982. Poetry, fiction, cartoons, interviews, letters, parts-of-novels, long-poems. *"Illuminations* is devoted to promoting the work of new writers by publishing their work within the context of the work of established figures. Bias: Serious writers; we mostly publish poetry—will consider short fiction or short extracts. Recent contributors: Carole Satyamurti, Dennis Brutus, Jeremy Cronin, Lam Thi My Da, Virgil Suarez, Sandor Kanyadi, Marcus Rediker, Geri Doran, Gabeba Baderoon; interviews with Tim O'Brien and Athol Fugard. Issues 9 and 10 were anthologies of East and South African writing. Issue 13 dedicated to Stephen Spender, Issue 14 to Southern African writing, Issue 16 to Vietnamese poetry, Issue 17 to Cuban and Latin-American poetry, Issue 20 to Dennis Brutus on his 80th birthday, Issue 22 to Haitian writing." circ. 400. 1/yr. Pub'd 1 issue 2009; expects 1 issue 2010, 1 issue 2011. sub. price $15/2 issues; per copy $10; sample $10. Back issues: negotiable. Discounts: 33-1/3 commission. 80pp. Reporting time: 2-3 months minimum. Simultaneous submissions accepted: no. Publishes 5% of manuscripts submitted. Payment: none. Copyrighted, reverts to author. Ads: $150/$75/$40 1/4 page. Subjects: Avant-Garde, Experimental Art, Fiction, Literature (General), Novels, Poetry, Reviews, Translation.

ILLUMINATIONS LITERARY JOURNAL, A.Michele Leslie, Editor, Illuminations Publications, P.O. Box 52049, Minneapolis, MN 55402. 1987. Poetry, fiction, cartoons, plays, non-fiction. "We are open to experimental as well as traditional submissions. Spiritually insightful work in a context of tolerance and encouragement is preferred. Recent contributors include: H.F. Noyes, Ruth Schuler, Najwa Brax, B. Z. Niditch, Swami Veda Bharati, Rod Farmer, Louis Cantoni." circ. 150+. Increasing from one or two times a year to three times a year (price for subscription always for three issues). Pub'd 1 issue 2009; expects 1 issue 2010, 3 issues 2011. sub. price $18 for three issues. $25 foreign; per copy $7; sample $3, EXCEPT JUNE 2009 ISSUE GIVING RULES FOR 2010 CONTESTS ($5.00). Back issues: $3 (when available). 40pp. Reporting time: 2-3 months. Include SASE. Simultaneous submissions accepted: yes. Publishes 15% of manuscripts submitted. Payment: due to increasing expenses, we are now asking that our contributors purchase a subscription or a copy of the issue they are in. Copyrighted, reverts to author. Pub's reviews: approx. 2 in 2009. §Publishes poetry, book and magazine reviews. Meditations, essays, interviews, welcome. Subjects: Alcohol, Alcoholism, Alternative Medicine, Cooking, Education, Fiction, Haiku, Nutrition, Pets, Poetry, Psychology, Spiritual, Theatre, Women, Writers/Writing, Yoga.

IMAGE: ART, FAITH, MYSTERY, Gregory Wolfe, 3307 Third Avenue West, Seattle, WA 98119-1940, phone 206-281-2988, fax 206-281-2979. 1989. Poetry, fiction, art, interviews, reviews, non-fiction. "IMAGE is a unique forum for the best writing and artwork that are informed by—or grapple with—Judeo-Christian religious faith. We have never been interested in art that merely regurgitates dogma or falls back on easy answers or didacticism. Instead, our focus has been on writing and visual artwork that embody a spiritual struggle, that seek to strike a balance between tradition and a profound openness to the world." circ. 4500. 4/yr. Pub'd 4 issues 2009; expects 4 issues 2010, 4 issues 2011. sub. price $39.95; per copy $12. Back issues: $12. 128pp. Reporting time: 12 to 15 weeks. Simultaneous submissions accepted: Yes. Publishes 2% of manuscripts submitted. Payment: $10/page (for prose) or $2/line (for poetry) plus four copies of the journal; payment is upon publication. Copyrighted, reverts to author. Pub's reviews: approx. 8 in 2009. §reviews poetry, fiction, memoir. Ads: $600 full page (b+w)/$360 half page (b+w)/$1,200 back cover (color). Subjects: Arts, Dance, Fiction, Memoirs, Movies, Music, Non-Fiction, Performing Arts, Photography, Poetry, Religion, Spiritual, Theatre, Visual Arts, Writers/Writing.

Images Unlimited and Snaptail Press, a Division of Images Unlimited Publishing, Ms. Lee Jackson, PO Box 305, Maryville, MO 64468, 660-582-4279, info@imagesunlimitedpub.com, www.imagesunlimited-pub.com. 1981. Non-fiction. "Publishes books for children, families, parenting professionals, cooks, and apple lovers." avg. press run 2M. Pub'd 1 title 2009; expects 1 title 2010, 1 title 2011. 7 titles listed in the *Small Press Record of Books in Print* (36th Edition, 2010-11). Discounts: 20% for 2-5, 40% for 6-99, 50% for 100+. 130pp. Reporting time: 2 months. Simultaneous submissions accepted: no. Publishes 1% of manuscripts submitted. Payment: to be arranged. Copyrights for author. Subjects: Children, Youth, Cooking, Family, Food, Eating, How-To, Juvenile Fiction, Parenting, Picture Books.

Imago Press, Leila Joiner, 3710 East Edison Street, Tucson, AZ 85716, 520-327-0540, ljoiner@dakotacom.net, www.ImagoBooks.com. 2002. Poetry, fiction, non-fiction. "Not accepting unsolicited manuscripts at this time. E-mail queries okay." Pub'd 7 titles 2009; expects 6 titles 2010, 6 titles 2011. 23 titles listed in the *Small Press Record of Books in Print* (36th Edition, 2010-11). Discounts: 20%-55%. 250pp. Reporting time: 1 month. Simultaneous submissions accepted: yes. Publishes 23% of manuscripts submitted. Copyrights for author. Subjects: African Literature, Africa, African Studies, Anthology, Essays, Fantasy, Fiction, Grieving, Memoirs, Mystery, Native American, New Age, Non-Fiction, Novels, Poetry, Science Fiction, Short Stories.

Immediate Direction Publications (see also MIDNIGHT STREET), Trevor Denyer, 7 Mountview, Church

Lane West, Aldershot, Hampshire GU11 3LN, England, tdenyer@ntlworld.com, www.midnightstreet.co.uk. 1998. Fiction, articles, art, interviews, reviews, non-fiction. "Publishes MIDNIGHT STREET magazine 3 times a year." Pub'd 3 titles 2009; expects 3 titles 2010, 3 titles 2011. No titles listed in the *Small Press Record of Books in Print* (36th Edition, 2010-11). 56pp. Reporting time: 3 months average. Simultaneous submissions accepted: No. Publishes 10% of manuscripts submitted. Payment: UK: £2.50 per 1,000 words for fiction and articles.A payment of £5.00 for interviews - to the interviewer. No financial payment to the interviewee, as this is a form of advertising.£2.50 per poem.£5.00 per internal illustration.£7.50 per colour cover illustration.In addition, one copy of the issue in which your work appears will be sent. Payment will be made upon publication.NON UK: By negotiation. First British Serial Rights only. Subjects: Book Reviewing, Essays, Fantasy, Fiction, Graphics, Horror, Interviews, Myth, Mythology, Non-Fiction, Poetry, Reviews, Science Fiction, Short Stories, Supernatural, Writers/Writing.

Immunizations for Public Health, Martin Myers, 301 University Blvd., Galveston, TX 77555-0350, 4097720199, 4097725208, nnii@i4ph.org, www.i4ph.org. 2005. Non-fiction. "We publish only books related to vaccines, immunizations, and infectious diseases." avg. press run 5000. Expects 1 title 2010, 1 title 2011. 1 title listed in the *Small Press Record of Books in Print* (36th Edition, 2010-11). Discounts: Bookstores 40%; Wholesalers 55%; Distributors 65%. 250-300pp. Reporting time: 8 weeks. Subjects: Health, Medicine, Science.

IMOCO Publishing, Paul Brodsky, President, PO Box 471721, Tulsa, OK 74147-1721, 918-814-4174, imoco@officefunnies.com, www.officefunnies.com. 1997. Fiction, cartoons, satire, non-fiction. avg. press run 4M. Pub'd 1 title 2009; expects 2 titles 2011. 2 titles listed in the *Small Press Record of Books in Print* (36th Edition, 2010-11). Discounts: Trade discounts available, contact for details. Less than 100pp. Copyrights for author. Subjects: Business & Economics, Humor, Self-Help.

Impact Publishers, Inc., Freeman Porter, Submissions Editor, PO Box 6016, Atascadero, CA 93423-6016, 805-466-5917, info@impactpublishers.com, www.impactpublishers.com. 1970. Non-fiction. "Self-help, popular psychology, personal development, divorce recovery, relationships, families, health, 'Little Imp' books for children.*Non-fiction only.*" avg. press run 3M-6M. Pub'd 5 titles 2009; expects 5 titles 2010, 5 titles 2011. 59 titles listed in the *Small Press Record of Books in Print* (36th Edition, 2010-11). Discounts: bookstores: up to 4 copies, 25% prepaid; 5-49 copies 40%; 50 plus copies, contact Impact re terms; libraries paper 10%; cloth 15%; wholesale distributors: contact Impact re terms. 200-300pp. Reporting time: 6-8 weeks minimum. Simultaneous submissions accepted: yes. Publishes less than 1% of manuscripts submitted. Payment: standard royalty contract. Copyrights for author. Subjects: Children, Youth, Divorce, Family, Grieving, Guidance, Health, Marriage, Non-Fiction, Parenting, Psychology, Relationships, Self-Help, Sex, Sexuality, Tapes & Records, Women.

Impassio Press, Olivia Dresher, Publisher & Editor, PO Box 31905, Seattle, WA 98103, 206-632-7675, Fax 775-254-4073, books@impassio.com, www.impassio.com. 2001. Fiction, letters, collages, non-fiction. "We publish fragmentary writing that's insightful, daring, and original, including: journals/diaries/notebooks; letters; philosophical essay-fragments; aphorisms; poetic prose fragments; vignettes; fiction in diary or letter form. NOTE: Currently our publication schedule is filled, but we are accepting submissions to our online magazine, FragLit. For information, visit www.fraglit.com." avg. press run 1M. 5 titles listed in the *Small Press Record of Books in Print* (36th Edition, 2010-11). Discounts: 40% bookstores. 150pp. Reporting time: 4-6 weeks. Simultaneous submissions accepted: yes. Publishes 2% of manuscripts submitted. Payment: 5%. Copyrights for author. Subjects: Autobiography, Diaries, Essays, Fiction, Journals, Literature (General), Memoirs, Non-Fiction, Philosophy, Prose, Writers/Writing.

IMPress, Madeleine Rose, 26 Oak Road, Withington, Manchester M2O 3DA, England, +44(0)161-2837636. 2000. Fiction, articles. "Titles include: Burning Worm by Carl Tighe, shortlisted for UK 2001 Whitbread First Novel Award and winner of Authors' Club Best First Novel. Pax:Variations by Carl Tighe. KssssS by Carl TIghe. We do not accept unsolicited manuscripts." Expects 1 title 2010, 1 title 2011. No titles listed in the *Small Press Record of Books in Print* (36th Edition, 2010-11). Trade orders from Gardners Wholesalers in UK. Subjects: Essays, Fiction, Novels, Science Fiction, Short Stories.

In Between Books, Karla Andersdatter, Ms., PO Box 790, Sausalito, CA 94966, 415 383-8447. 1972. Fiction. "Inquiries before sending MS. email*juno@inbetweenbooks.com.*" avg. press run up to 1200, but can vary. Pub'd 1 title 2009; expects 1 title 2010, 2 titles 2011. 29 titles listed in the *Small Press Record of Books in Print* (36th Edition, 2010-11). Discounts: 40% to stores, 20% to libraries. pp variespp. We prefer not to accept simultaneous submissions. Publishes a variable % of manuscripts submitted. Payment: varies. Copyrights for author. Subjects: Children, Youth, Diaries, Dreams, Experimental, Family, Fantasy, Literature (General), Myth, Mythology, Novels, Poetry, Relationships, Romance, Short Stories, The West, Writers/Writing.

IN OUR OWN WORDS, Amanda Majestie, P. O. Box 4658, Santa Rosa, CA 95402-4658, http://www.bbhooks.com. 2000. Poetry, fiction, articles, cartoons, satire, reviews, non-fiction. "Inspirational writing whose goal is to create a better, kinder world." 2/yr. Pub'd 1 issue 2009; expects 1 issue 2010, 1 issue

2011. Back issues: All are available on the site. Discounts: Online ezine only. 25pp. Reporting time: 9 months. Simultaneous submissions accepted: Yes. Payment: publication only. Copyrighted, reverts to author. Ads: Nonprofits & MA/MFA programs eligible to advertise at $50 for 125 words or 1/4 page. Half page: $100. Full page: $200. Subjects: African-American, Alternative Medicine, California, Chicano/a, Civil Rights, Current Affairs, Fiction, Florida, Gay, Health, Judaism, New York, Peace, Poetry, Women.

In Print Publishing, Tomi Keitlen, PO Box 6966, San Pedro, CA 90734-6966, 928-284-5298, Fax 928-284-5283. 1991. Fiction, non-fiction. "We are an eclectic publisher." avg. press run 3M-5M. Pub'd 1 title 2009; expects 3 titles 2010. 20 titles listed in the *Small Press Record of Books in Print* (36th Edition, 2010-11). Discounts: inquire. 200-350pp. Reporting time: 6-8 weeks. Simultaneous submissions accepted: yes. We publish 1 out of 50 books submitted. Payment: 6%-8% depending on book. Copyrights for author. Subjects: Anthology, Autobiography, Biography, How-To, Inspirational, Metaphysics, New Age, Religion, Spiritual, Tapes & Records.

INDEFINITE SPACE, Marcia Arrieta, PO Box 40101, Pasadena, CA 91114, www.indefinitespace.net. 1992. Poetry, art, photos. "Does not accept previously published poems. Open to modern, imagistic, abstract, philosophical, natural, surreal, and experimental creations." circ. 1M. 1/yr. Pub'd 1 issue 2009; expects 1 issue 2010, 1 issue 2011. sub. price $12/2 issues; per copy $7; sample $7. 40pp. Reporting time: 4 months or sooner. Payment: 1 copy. Subjects: Avant-Garde, Experimental Art, Photography, Poetry.

INDEPENDENT PUBLISHER ONLINE, Jim Barnes, Executive Editor, 1129 Woodmere Ave., Ste. B, Traverse City, MI 49686, 231-933-0445, Fax 231-933-0448, jimb@bookpublishing.com, www.independent-publisher.com. 1993. Poetry, fiction, articles, interviews, satire, criticism, reviews, letters, news items. "*Independent Publisher* reviews approx. 600 books from small presses each year." circ. 35M online subscribers. 11/yr. Pub'd 11 issues 2009; expects 11 issues 2010, 11 issues 2011. sub. price free; per copy free; sample free. 80pp. Simultaneous submissions accepted: no. Publishes 10% of manuscripts submitted. Payment: varies, $50-$150. Copyrighted, reverts to author. Pub's reviews: 500+ in 2009. §Books only - nonfiction. Ads: none. Subjects: Book Collecting, Bookselling, Book Reviewing, Libraries, Literary Review, Publishing, Reviews.

THE INDEPENDENT SHAVIAN, Dr. Richard Nickson, Douglas Laurie, Patrick Berry, The Bernard Shaw Society, PO Box 1159 Madison Square Stn., New York, NY 10159-1159, 212-982-9885. 1962. Poetry, articles, photos, cartoons, interviews, satire, criticism, reviews, letters, news items. "Publication deals with items concerning Bernard Shaw, his circle and his world: theatre, politics, music, etc." circ. 500 worldwide. 3/yr. Pub'd 3 issues 2009; expects 3 issues 2010, 3 issues 2011. sub. price $30 USA, $30 outside USA (airmail included); per copy $2; sample $2. Back issues: $2. Discounts: 13% for subscription agencies. single issues: 28pp; double issues: 48pp. Reporting time: none. Payment: none. Not copyrighted. Pub's reviews: 8 in 2009. §Anything pertaining to Bernard Shaw. Ads: none. Subject: G.B. Shaw.

INDEX TO FOREIGN LEGAL PERIODICALS, University of California Press, Thomas H. Reynolds, Editor; Kevin Durkin, Managing Editor, University of California Press, 2000 Center Street, Suite 303, Berkeley, CA 94704-1223, 510-643-7154. 1960. Non-fiction. "Editorial address: L250A Boalt Hall, Berkeley, CA 94720. Copyrighted by The American Association of Law Libraries." circ. 600. 3/yr. Pub'd 3 issues 2009; expects 3 issues 2010, 3 issues 2011. sub. price $746 (+ $25 air freight); per copy $746. Back issues: $746. 250pp. Copyrighted, does not revert to author. Ads: none accepted. Subject: Law.

INDIA CURRENTS, Vandana Kumar, Publisher; Ragini Srinivasan, Managing Editor, Box 21285, San Jose, CA 95151, 408-324-0488, Fax 408-324-0477, e-Mail editor@indiacurrents.com. 1987. Fiction, articles, art, photos, cartoons, interviews, satire, criticism, reviews, music, letters, parts-of-novels, collages, news items, non-fiction. "Between 500-1500 words. We look for insightful approach to India, its arts, culture, people. Recent contributors: Sandip Roy-Chowdhury, Rajeev Srinivasan, Ranjit Souri, Sarita Sarvate, Rupa Dev, Kalpana Mohan." circ. 33M. 11/yr. Pub'd 11 issues 2009; expects 11 issues 2010, 11 issues 2011. sub. price $19.95; per copy $1.95 + $1 s/h; sample same. Back issues: $3. 160pp. Reporting time: 3 months. Publishes 20% of manuscripts submitted. Payment: $50 for 1000 words. Copyrighted, reverts to author. Pub's reviews: 18 in 2009. §India and Indians, colonialism, immigration, multiculturalism, assimilation, racism. Ads: $840/$460/60¢. Subjects: Asia, Indochina, Asian-American, Buddhism, Sri Chinmoy, Immigration, India, Multicultural, Third World, Minorities, Vegetarianism, Yoga.

INDIANA REVIEW, Alessandra Simmons, Editor; Deborah Kim, Associate Editor, Ballantine Hall 465, Indiana University, 1020 E. Kirkwood Avenue, Bloomington, IN 47405-7103, 812-855-3439. 1976. Poetry, fiction, art, photos, interviews, reviews, parts-of-novels, long-poems, plays, non-fiction. "*Indiana Review* is a magazine of poetry, fiction, nonfiction, and book reviews. We prefer writing that shows both an awareness of language and of the world. We publish 6-8 stories and about 40-60 pages of poetry per issue. We like writers who take risks. Recent contributors have included Marilyn Hacker, Kwame Dawes, Bob Hicok, Marilyn Chin, Denise Duhamel, Roy Jacobstein, Dan Kaplan, Timothy Liu, Aimee Nezhukumatathil, Lucia Perillo, Terese

231

Svoboda, Maureen Seaton, Stuart Dybek, Rick Moody and Michael Martone. We also sponsor poetry, fiction, and short-short/prose-poem prizes judged by leading writers. Award $1,000 to each winner as well as publication. Deadlines in March (poetry), June (short-short/prose-poem) and October (fiction). Send SASE or visit our website (www.indianareview.org) for guidelines.'' circ. 2000. 2/yr. Pub'd 2 issues 2009; expects 2 issues 2010, 2 issues 2011. sub. price Individual $17, institutions $20, please add $12 for overseas ($7 for Canada); per copy $9; sample $9. Back issues: Based on availability. Discounts: trade 60/40% split; 50-50 to distributors. 180pp. Reporting time: 3 - 4 months. Please consult website for reading periods. Simultaneous submissions accepted: yes. Publishes less than 1% of manuscripts submitted. Payment: $5 per page poem, $5 per page story, $10 minimum. Copyrighted, reverts to author. §Recent collections of poetry or fiction; novels and poetry collections by new and established writers, especially from small presses; books of criticism or literary theory, both for literary works and the visual arts. Ads: $300/$150. Subjects: Comics, Fiction, Literary Review, Non-Fiction, Poetry, Prose, Reviews.

•**Indigo Ink Press, Inc.,** Jessica Bennett, 150 35th Street NW, Canton, OH 44709, 330-417-7715. 2009. Poetry, fiction, art, photos, parts-of-novels, long-poems, concrete art. "We are a small, nonprofit literary press that's just getting started. Currently, we accept submissions year-round in the areas of literary fiction, poetry and artistic non-fiction only (no straight genre fiction, please). We're especially interested in talented burgeoning storytellers, but we will consider submissions from both new and previously published authors. For more details, visit our submission page: www.indigoinkpress.org/submissions." Expects 1 title 2010, 2 titles 2011. No titles listed in the *Small Press Record of Books in Print* (36th Edition, 2010-11). Reporting time: 6 weeks. Simultaneous submissions accepted: Yes. Subjects: Anthology, Arts, Avant-Garde, Experimental Art, Literature (General), Novels, Poetry, Prose, Short Stories, Visual Arts.

INDUSTRY MINNE-ZINE, Tricia Heuring, 12 Vincent Avenue South, Minneapolis, MN 55405, 612.308.2467. 2003. Poetry, articles, art, photos, cartoons, interviews, satire, criticism, reviews, music, long-poems, collages, concrete art, news items, non-fiction. "A publication that focuses on music, art, fashion & culture in the Twin Cities and the Midwest." circ. 20000. 6/yr. Pub'd 6 issues 2009; expects 6 issues 2010, 12 issues 2011. sub. price 20; sample free. Back issues: inquire. 135pp. Reporting time: 2 days. Simultaneous submissions accepted: No. Publishes 0% of manuscripts submitted. Payment: 0-$150 per article. Not copyrighted. Ads: $1000. Subjects: Arts, Avant-Garde, Experimental Art, Cartoons, Clothing, Community, Creativity, Design, Fashion, Graphic Design, Graphics, Minnesota, Performing Arts, Photography, Poetry, Politics.

Infinite Love Publishing, 15127 N.E. 24th St., #341, Redmond, WA 98052. No titles listed in the *Small Press Record of Books in Print* (36th Edition, 2010-11).

The Infinity Group, Genie Lester, Publisher; Anne Nichandros, Editor, 22516 Charlene Way, Castro Valley, CA 94546, 510-581-8172; kenandgenie@yahoo.com. 1987. Poetry, fiction, articles, art, photos, cartoons, satire, parts-of-novels, long-poems, plays, non-fiction. "We are willing to look at submissions for our next anthology from people we previously published in our magazine, *Infinity Limited*." Pub'd 1 title 2009; expects 1 title 2010, 1 title 2011. 1 title listed in the *Small Press Record of Books in Print* (36th Edition, 2010-11). 256pp. Copyrights for author. Subjects: Anthology, Arts, Fiction, Literature (General), Memoirs, Poetry.

Infinity Publishing, 1094 New Dehaven St, Suite 100, West Conshohocken, PA 19428, info@infinitypublishing.com. 1997. Poetry, fiction, articles, art, photos, cartoons, interviews, satire, criticism, reviews, music, letters, parts-of-novels, long-poems, collages, plays, concrete art, news items, non-fiction. "We can publish any book in a matter of a few months. We have a bookstore return policy that stores love, and provide an easy way for authors to reach the masses. Our free publishing guide is also a sample of our printing quality." avg. press run print on demand. Pub'd 250 titles 2009; expects 400 titles 2010, 400 titles 2011. 1 title listed in the *Small Press Record of Books in Print* (36th Edition, 2010-11). Discounts: 40% provided on quantities of 5 or more (1-4, for retailers, get 20%). 237pp. Reporting time: indefinite. Simultaneous submissions accepted: yes. Publishes 95% of manuscripts submitted. Payment: 30% on retail sales. Does not copyright for author.

Info Net Publishing, Herb Wetenkamp, 21142 Canada Road Unit 1-C, Lake Forest, CA 92630-6714, 949-462-0224, Fax 949-462-9595, herb@infonetpublishing.com. 1986. Articles, art, photos, interviews, reviews, news items, non-fiction. "How to, business, retailing, specialty sports, women's issues, small business, home business, SoHo." avg. press run 10M-20M. Pub'd 2 titles 2009; expects 3 titles 2010, 6 titles 2011. 4 titles listed in the *Small Press Record of Books in Print* (36th Edition, 2010-11). Discounts: 55% distributor, 40% retailer. 200+pp. Reporting time: 1-2 months. Simultaneous submissions accepted: yes. Publishes 5% of manuscripts submitted. Payment: please inquire. Copyrights for author. Subjects: Advertising, Self-Promotion, Bicycling, Business & Economics, Cooking, History, How-To, Magazines, Marketing, Public Relations/Publicity, Sports, Outdoors, Women.

Iniquity Press/Vendetta Books (see also BIG HAMMER), David Roskos, PO Box 527, Point Pleasant, NJ 08742-0527, 732 664 3901 iniquitypress@hotmail.com. 1988. Poetry, fiction, criticism. "Chapbooks are done by solicitation only; can't read unsolicited chap-mss(no time/$; focusing on mag). Published 2 in 04, & 2 in 05. Writers published include Andrew Gettler, Harvey Pekar, rjs, Ken Greenley, Matt Borkowski, Joe Weil, Donald Lev, Hal Sirowitz, Ed Galing, Bob Rixen, Dwyer Jones, Loring Hughes, Chris Stroffolino, Lamont Steptoe, John Lunar Richey, Ed Galing, Boni Joi, Tom Obrzut, Anthony George, Mark Weber, Jeff Wright, Bertha Sanchez Bello & Michael Pingarron.'' avg. press run 300-1M. Pub'd 2 titles 2009; expects 2 titles 2010, 3 titles 2011. 43 titles listed in the *Small Press Record of Books in Print* (36th Edition, 2010-11). Discounts: 60/40. 40pp. Reporting time: 1 month. Payment: author gets 100-150 copies. Copyrights for author. Subjects: Absurdist, Anarchist, Beat, Charles Bukowski, Dreams, Drugs, Essays, Experimental, Homelessness, Labor, Music, Poetry, Resistance, Zines.

•**THE INK SLINGER REVIEW,** Donna Cooper, 3895 Esplanade Ave, Port Orange, FL 32129, 386-290-2435. 2009. Poetry, fiction, cartoons, satire, criticism, reviews, letters, parts-of-novels, long-poems, plays, non-fiction. ''Since my passion in life is equally split between reading and writing, I saw it only fitting to establish a literary review that will showcase both. The Ink Slinger Review will feature the literary works of Volusia and Flagler Counties most talented writers, poets, essayists and more.'' circ. 500. 4/yr. Expects 3 issues 2010, 4 issues 2011. sub. price $24; per copy $8.95; sample free. Back issues: inquire. Discounts: 10-20 copies 15%, 20-50 copies 25%. 45pp. Reporting time: 2-4 weeks. Simultaneous submissions accepted: Yes. Publishes 25% of manuscripts submitted. Not copyrighted. Pub's reviews: none in 2009. §fiction, non-fiction, poetry, essays. Ads: $150/$90/$75/$50/(display). Subjects: Creative Non-fiction, Fiction, Florida, Juvenile Fiction, Literary Review, Literature (General), Memoirs, Non-Fiction, Poetry, Prose, Short Stories.

Inkwater Press (see also First Books), Jeremy Solomon, 6750 SW Franklin Street, Suite A, Portland, OR 97223-2542, Phone: 503.968.6777; Fax: 503.968.6779; Web: www.inkwaterpress.com. 2002. Poetry, fiction, articles, art, photos, cartoons, interviews, satire, criticism, letters, parts-of-novels, long-poems, plays, concrete art, news items, non-fiction. Pub'd 44 titles 2009; expects 50 titles 2010, 55 titles 2011. No titles listed in the *Small Press Record of Books in Print* (36th Edition, 2010-11). Subjects: Adolescence, Employment, Fiction, Inspirational, Juvenile Fiction, Memoirs, Non-Fiction, Poetry, Prose, Science Fiction, Self-Help, Women, Young Adult.

INKWELL, Richard R. Binkele, Editor-in-Chief, Manhattanville College, 2900 Purchase Street, Purchase, NY 10577, www.inkwelljournal.org. 1995. Poetry, fiction, art, photos, interviews, parts-of-novels, non-fiction. ''Reading period is August 1st to November 15th. No submissions will be considered when postmarked outside the reading period.'' 2/yr. Pub'd 2 issues 2009. sub. price $18; per copy $10; sample $6. Back issues: $6. Discounts: 55% to distributors. 145pp. Reporting time: 4-6 months. Simultaneous submissions accepted: Yes. Publishes 3% of manuscripts submitted. Payment: $10/pg for essays, poetry and fiction. $25/art. $150/cover art. Copyrighted, reverts to author. §Short fiction (5,000 words or less), poetry, creative non-fiction, memoir. Ads: swap ads only. Subjects: Literature (General), Non-Fiction, Poetry, Prose.

INKY TRAIL NEWS, Wendy Fisher, 50416 Schoenharr #111, Shelby Twp., MI 48315, www.friendship-by-mail.com. 1993. Poetry, fiction, articles, art, photos, letters, news items, non-fiction. ''Digest-sized newsletter dedicated to women's friendship, pen pals, correspondence... written by pals for pals.'' circ. 1M. 6/yr. Pub'd 6 issues 2009; expects 6 issues 2010, 6-12 issues 2011. sub. price $20 USA, $30 International, $12 PDF issues sent via email; per copy $3; sample $3. Discounts: please write and inquire. 36 digest-sized pagespp. Simultaneous submissions accepted: yes. Publishes 80% of manuscripts submitted. Payment: copies only. Copyrighted, reverts to author. Pub's reviews. §Women, correspondence, seniors, journals, memories, crafts, how-to, gardening, collectors/antiques. Ads: $5 includes the issue (short ads). Subjects: Antiques, Collectibles, Crafts, Hobbies, Culture, Essays, Gardening, Genealogy, Newsletter, Newspapers, Postcards, Psychology, Short Stories, Travel, Women, Writers/Writing.

Inland Lighthouse Literary Press, Ned Haggard, Editor and Publisher, 13152 S. Cicero Avenue, PMB #110, Crestwood, IL 60445-1470, (708) 217-6377, Fax: (615) 526-5813, nedinwriting1@att.net. ''We are in the process of redesigning our publisher; the changes will be significant. Please watch online updates incorporated into the Small Press Review as we are not accepting submissions of any materials while the extensive remake is in process. When that changes, we will make an announcement in that forum.'' No titles listed in the *Small Press Record of Books in Print* (36th Edition, 2010-11). Does not copyright for author.

Inner City Books, Daryl Sharp, Victoria Cowan, Box 1271, Station Q, Toronto, ON M4T 2P4, Canada, 416-927-0355, FAX 416-924-1814, booksales@innercitybooks.net. 1980. Non-fiction. ''We publish *only* studies in Jungian psychology by Jungian analysts. Now 91 titles by 42 authors. Over a million books sold worldwide; over 200 other language editions. No unsolicited manuscripts.'' avg. press run 3M. Pub'd 6 titles 2009; expects 5 titles 2010, 6 titles 2011. 2 titles listed in the *Small Press Record of Books in Print* (36th Edition, 2010-11). Discounts: trade 40%/60 days or 50% prepaid (non-returnable); surface postage/handling, 15% of net. 160pp. Copyrights for author. Subject: Psychology.

Inner City Press (see also INNER CITY PRESS), Matthew Lee, P.O. Box 580188, Mount Carmel Station,

Bronx, NY 10458, Web: InnerCityPress.org Tel: 718-716-3540. 1987. Fiction, satire, news items, non-fiction. "Inner City Press / Community on the Move is a non-profit organization headquartered in the South Bronx of New York City since 1987. It began with a mimeographed newspaper, morphed into organizing the homesteading of long-abandoned buildings, then to fighting for fair access to finance, using the Community Reinvestment Act and combating predatory lending. While the work has gone nationwide, Inner City Press remains in and of The Bronx; its weekly Bronx Report goes online every Monday at www.innercitypress.org/bxreport.html ICP covers human rights, including beyond the U.S.. ICP's 2004 tome, "Predatory Bender," has been noted in The Times of London, the Washington Post, and elsewhere. A sequel is forthcoming." avg. press run 6000. Pub'd 3 titles 2009; expects 4 titles 2010, 5 titles 2011. No titles listed in the *Small Press Record of Books in Print* (36th Edition, 2010-11). Discounts: standard. 400pp. Reporting time: depends. Simultaneous submissions accepted: Yes. Payment: depends. Copyright depends. Subjects: African Literature, Africa, African Studies, Asian-American, Chicago, Chicano/a, China, Cities, Civil Rights, Human Rights, Latin America, Puerto Rico, South America, Tennessee, Washington, D.C.

INNER CITY PRESS, Inner City Press, Matthew Lee, P.O. Box 580188, Mount Carmel Station, Bronx, NY 10458, Web: InnerCityPress.org Tel: 718-716-3540. 1987. News items, non-fiction. "Inner City Press / Community on the Move is a non-profit organization headquartered in The Bronx since 1987. It began with a mimeographed newspaper, morphed into organizing the homesteading of long-abandoned buildings, then to fighting for fair access to finance, using the Community Reinvestment Act and combating predatory lending. While the work has gone nationwide, Inner City Press remains in and of The Bronx. Its weekly Reports (on community reinvestment, bank beat, the bronx, environmental justice, etc.) come out each week, and go online every Monday at www.innercitypress.org." 52/yr. Pub'd 52 issues 2009; expects 52 issues 2010, 52 issues 2011. Discounts: standard. 32pp. Reporting time: depends. Simultaneous submissions accepted: Yes. Payment: depends. depends. Pub's reviews: approx. 20 in 2009. §books about consumer issues, human rights, The Bronx, globalization, etc. Ads: depends / sliding scale. Subjects: Cities, Civil Rights, Human Rights, New York, Nicaragua.

•**INSIDE LEADERSHIP NEWSLETTER, Creative Creations Consulting Publishing Company,** DrTekemia Dorsey, P O Box 9671-4017, 5338 King Arthur Circle, Baltimore, MD 21237-4017, 410-391-3880 work; 443-413-5600 cell; 410-391-9036 fax; drdorsey@creativecreationsconsulting.com; www.creativecreationsconsulting.com. Pub's reviews.

•**InsideOut Press,** Kim Olver, PO Box 2666, Country Club Hills, IL 60478, 708-957-6047, fax: 708-957-8028, 800 number: 866-391-3034, info@insideoutpress.com, www.insideoutpress.com. 2006. Non-fiction. "We publish self-help non-fiction with a focus on spiritual and/or an internal therapeutic locus of control. Our mission is to publish authors who are making a positive difference in the world by showing people paths to InsideOut Empowerment." avg. press run 2500. Expects 1 title 2010, 3 titles 2011. No titles listed in the *Small Press Record of Books in Print* (36th Edition, 2010-11). Discounts: 2-4 copies 20% off5-9 copies 30% off10-24 copies 40% off25-49 copies 42% off50-74 copies 44% off100-199 copies 48% off200 or more copies 50% off. 240pp. Reporting time: two weeks. Simultaneous submissions accepted: Yes. Payment: No royalties or advances. We are essentially a self-publishing company. Copyrights for author. Subjects: Creative Non-fiction, Divorce, Family, Grieving, Human Rights, Inspirational, Leadership, Marriage, Mentoring/Coaching, Motivation, Success, Parenting, Psychology, Relationships, Self-Help, Spiritual.

Insight Press, 4064 N. Lincoln Ave. #264, Chicago, IL 60618, www.insight-press.com. 2004. Non-fiction. "There is a great need for critical and revolutionary thought. For thought that challenges received orthodoxies and what is deemed acceptablethat raises sights as to what is necessary and possible in todays worldthat opens pathways to deeper understanding of the world and radical social transformation.Insight Press joins with others in the publishing community seeking to meet the urgent and diverse needs of critical inquiry. We want to engage the timely conversations about taking responsibility for the future of this planet and the course of history. We want to influence contemporary discourse by bringing forward titles with a sharp Marxist-Leninist-Maoist edge, along with a broader mix of radical and innovative titles: from works of political theory, economics, history, science and environment, social and cultural theoryto fiction and poetryto reportage from the front lines.Insight Press is especially proud to feature the writings of Bob Avakian, Chairman of the Revolutionary Communist Party. It has been said about Bob Avakian that he is that "rare combination: a pathbreaking thinker and a conscious protagonist of history, someone who not only imparts a new knowledge but who also communicates and embodies a historical project that stirs and summons others."In a provocative and wide-ranging body of work, Avakian has addressed issues of philosophy; religion, atheism, and morality; the question of revolution, and the road to revolution, in todays world, including in the U.S.; the limits of classical democracy; and much, much more. He has been engaged in an ongoing project of critical examination of the experience of socialist revolution in the 20th centuryits great achievements, especially the profound lessons of the Cultural Revolution in China, as well as its setbacks, shortcomings, and mistakes. Importantly, Bob Avakian has been developing a far-reaching vision of socialism: a society full of dissent, diversity, and the critical spirit; of unseen and unheard of ferm." avg. press run 3000. No titles listed in the *Small Press Record of*

Books in Print (36th Edition, 2010-11). Discounts: Distributed by IPG, www.ipgbooks.com.Available at Ingram, Baker & Taylor and all major wholesalers.Free exam copies for educators. Subjects: African Literature, Africa, African Studies, African-American, Atheism, Autobiography, Civil Rights, Communism, Marxism, Leninism, Conservation, Counter-Culture, Alternatives, Communes, Culture, Non-Fiction, Political Science, Politics, Science, Social Movements, Vietnam.

Inspiring Teachers Publishing, Inc., Emma McDonald, Senior Editor; Dyan Hershman, Acquisitions Editor, 12655 N. Central Expressway, Suite 810, Dallas, TX 75243, 877-496-7633 (toll-free), 972-496-7633, Fax 972-763-0355, info@inspiringteachers.com, www.inspiringteachers.com. 1998. Articles, non-fiction. "We publish professional development and practical how-to books for teachers, specializing in materials for beginning educators." avg. press run 5M. Pub'd 4 titles 2009; expects 4 titles 2010, 4 titles 2011. 6 titles listed in the *Small Press Record of Books in Print* (36th Edition, 2010-11). Discounts: 40% for bookstores, Special Discounts for schools, districts, and other educators. Please call for details. 200pp. Reporting time: 6 months. Simultaneous submissions accepted: no. Payment: Typical royalties are 10% with no advance payment. Royalty payments are generally made 30 days after the end of each Quarter. Copyrights for author. Subject: Education.

INSURANCE, Chris Tokar, Kostas Anagnopoulos, 132 N. 1st Street #11, Brooklyn, NY 11211, ctokar@hotmail.com. 1999. Poetry, fiction, satire, parts-of-novels, long-poems, non-fiction. "Prefer to read at least 6 pages for submission; rarely take work more than 2,500 words (usually shorter). We take only previously unpublished work, lean toward experimental." 1/yr. Pub'd 1 issue 2009; expects 1 issue 2010, 1 issue 2011. sub. price $10; per copy $10. Back issues: $8. Reporting time: 1-6 months. Simultaneous submissions accepted: yes, but require notification immediately of submitted work accepted elsewhere. Publishes 5-10% of manuscripts submitted. Payment: $40 plus 2 copies of issue. Copyrighted, reverts to author. Ads: none. Subjects: Literature (General), Poetry, Prose.

Interalia/Design Books, G. Brown-M., PO Box 404, Oxford, OH 45056-0404, 513-523-1553 phone/Fax. 1989. Art, non-fiction. "It is the goal of Interalia/Design Books to make meaningful contributions to the art of the book as a container of knowledge—the textual manifestation of a culture's evolution—and to the book as an object by promoting the dissemination of quality design through an editorial focus on architecture, design/crafts, art criticism, art of the book, facsimiles of out-of-print primary sources on architecture, design/crafts and art criticism. Also by promoting quality in the art of bookmaking by experimenting with alternative structures for the production of books as objects, including alternative printing and binding methods, encouraging limited editions of experimental books and of books for the bibliophile, encouraging artist/writer/printer/binder collaborations." avg. press run 1M. Pub'd 1 title 2009; expects 1 title 2010, 4 titles 2011. 3 titles listed in the *Small Press Record of Books in Print* (36th Edition, 2010-11). Discounts: 40% for orders of 10+. 100pp. Reporting time: 4-6 weeks. Payment: varies. Copyrights for author. Subjects: Architecture, Arts, Book Arts, Criticism, Design, Visual Arts.

Intercultural Press, Inc., Patricia A. O'Hare, Publisher; Erika Heilman, Editorial Director, 20 Park Plz #1115A, Boston, MA 02116-4303, 617.523.3801, e-mail books@interculturalpress.com. 1980. Non-fiction. "Books on intercultural communication, intercultural education and cross-cultural training, especially practical materials for use in teaching and training; other areas: diversity, multicultural education, orientation for living abroad. Shipping address: 374 U.S. Route One, Yarmouth, ME 04096." avg. press run 2M. Pub'd 10 titles 2009; expects 12 titles 2010, 12 titles 2011. 75 titles listed in the *Small Press Record of Books in Print* (36th Edition, 2010-11). 200pp. Simultaneous submissions accepted: yes. Publishes 2% of manuscripts submitted. Payment: royalty. Copyrights for author. Subjects: Business & Economics, Communication, Journalism, Culture, Education, Moving/Relocation, Multicultural, Travel.

INTERCULTURE, Robert Vachon, Editor, Intercultural Institute of Montreal, 4730 Papineau Avenue, Montreal, Quebec H2H 1V3, Canada, 514-288-7229, FAX 514-844-6800, website:www.iim.gc.ca. 1968. Articles, reviews, non-fiction. "Printed in two separate editions: *Interculture* (English edition ISSN 0828-797X); *Interculture* (French edition ISSN 0712-1571). Length of material: 28M words average (each issue devoted to a particular theme). Material: cross-cultural understanding - themes include education, medicine, spirituality, communication, politics and law in an intercultural perspective. Recent titles: *The Shaman and the Ecologist, Dissolving Uniot Society Through Education and Money, Beyond Global Democracy, Africa-India: Contemporary Alternative Esocophies.* Recent contributors: Peter Raine, Derek Rasmussen, Ashis Nandy, John Clammer, Robert Vachon, Martinus L. Daneel, Cosmas Gonese and Vinay Lal." circ. 1M. 2/yr. Pub'd 2 issues 2009; expects 2 issues 2010, 2 issues 2011. 1 title listed in the *Small Press Record of Books in Print* (36th Edition, 2010-11). sub. price $20 individuals, $35 institutions in Canada; outside Canada $25 individuals, $40 institutions; per copy $9, instit. $11 including taxes for Canada or shipping outside Canada. Back issues: $4.50 older issues, $9 newer, instit. $11. Discounts: subscription agencies receive 15%. 60pp. Reporting time: 3 months. Copyrighted. §Cross-cultural issues. Subjects: Anthropology, Archaelogy, Community, Culture, Education, Human Rights, Immigration, Multicultural, Native American, Philosophy, Religion, Social Work, Society, Sociology, Third World, Minorities.

INTERIM, Claudia Keelan, Editor, English Department, Box 5011, University of Nevada, Las Vegas, NV 89154-5011. *"Interim* is the annual creative writing publication at the University of Nevada -Las Vegas. It features poetry, fiction and book reviews. Volume 26 is our largest issue to date, running nearly 300 pages. Including new translations of Holderlin by Paul Hoover and Maxine Chernoff."

Interlink Publishing Group, Inc., Michel Moushabeck, Pam Thompson, 46 Crosby Street, Northampton, MA 01060, 413 582 7054 tel, 413 582 7057 fax, www.interlinkbooks.com, info@interlinkbooks.com. 1987. Art, photos, non-fiction. "We specialize in world travel, world literature (translated fiction), world history, and ethnic cooking." avg. press run 10M. Pub'd 50 titles 2009; expects 50 titles 2010, 50 titles 2011. No titles listed in the *Small Press Record of Books in Print* (36th Edition, 2010-11). Discounts: trade 40% & up. 160pp. Reporting time: We aim to reply in 4-6 months. Simultaneous submissions accepted: Yes. Payment: annually, royalty varies. Copyrights for author. Subjects: African Literature, Africa, African Studies, Arts, Bilingual, Children, Youth, Civil Rights, Culture, Feminism, Fiction, History, Latin America, Middle East, Non-Fiction, Political Science, Sociology, Travel.

INTERNATIONAL ART POST, Banana Productions, Anna Banana, 3747 Highway 101, Roberts Creek, BC V0N 2W2, Canada, 604-885-7156. 1988. Art, photos. "ISSN 1202-8762. *IAP* is a cooperatively published periodical of stamps by artists (Artistamps), printed annually in November as a pre-Xmas edition of 700 copies in full color on gummed, glossy paper. All sheets are pin-hole perforated, and while the press sheet is divided into different sized blocks, there are generally 36 stamps/edition. After participants receive their 500 stamps and copies of the press sheet, Banana Productions distributes the remainder of the edition (approx. 200 sheets) through the International Mail-Art Network or in promotional mailings. Cost of participation is $170 for 500 stamps." circ. 500. 1/yr. Pub'd 1 issue 2009; expects 1 issue 2010, 1 issue 2011. sub. price $30; per copy $15; sample $16. Back issues: write for order form, it varies from issues to issue. Discounts: 50% wholesale. 2-7 blocks of stamps. Reporting time: 3-6 months, depending on how quickly a space or press sheet is sold. Simultaneous submissions accepted: yes. Payment: 500 copies their own stamp(s), 1 copy of the sheet on which it is printed, and 1 copy each of the blocks of stamps in the edition. Copyrighted. Ads: none. Subjects: Arts, Counter-Culture, Alternatives, Communes, Graphics, Philately, Photography, Visual Arts.

INTERNATIONAL ELECTRONIC JOURNAL FOR LEADERSHIP IN LEARNING, University of Calgary Press, K. Donlevy, Editor, Faculty of Education, Univ. of Calgary, 2500 University Drive NW, Calgary, AB T2N 1N4, Canada, 403-220-5675, Fax 403-282-3005, www.ucalgary.ca/~iejll/. 1997. Articles, reviews. *"IEJLL* is a refereed electronic journal that promotes the study and discussion of substantive leadership issues that are of current concern in education communities." 15-20 articles per volume year published as available. sub. price free access. Reporting time: 2 months. Publishes 40% of manuscripts submitted. Payment: none. Copyrighted, rights revert to author after 10 months. Pub's reviews: 3 in 2009. §Education. Ads: email for information. Subject: Education.

THE INTERNATIONAL FICTION REVIEW, Dr. Christoph Lorey, Culture & Language Studies, UNB, PO Box 4400, Fredericton, N.B. E3B 5A3, Canada, 506-453-4636, Fax 506-447-3166, e-mail ifr@unb.ca. 1973. "The *IFR* is an annual periodical devoted to international fiction. Mss are accepted in English and should be prepared in conformity with the *MLA Handbook for Writers of Research Papers*; articles: 10-20 typewritten pages; reviews: 600-800 words; spelling, hyphenation, and capitalization according to *Webster.*" circ. 600. 1/yr. Pub'd 1 issue 2009; expects 1 issue 2010, 1 issue 2011. sub. price $25 instit., $20 indiv.; per copy $15; sample $15. Back issues: $15. Discounts: 20% for agents and jobbers. 128pp. Reporting time: 6 weeks - 3 months. Simultaneous submissions accepted: NO. Publishes 20% of manuscripts submitted. Payment: none. Copyrighted. Pub's reviews: 25 in 2009. §Contemporary fiction and scholarly works on fiction. Subjects: Criticism, Fiction.

International Jewelry Publications, Louise Berlin, Beverly Newton, PO Box 13384, Los Angeles, CA 90013-0384, 626-282-3781, Fax 626-282-4807. 1987. Photos, interviews, non-fiction. "*Gemstone Buying Guide, 2nd Edition, Diamond Ring Buying Guide,* 7th edition, *Pearl Buying Guide,* 4th edition, *Gold & Platinum Jewelry Buying Guide, Ruby, Sapphire & Emerald Buying Guide, 3rd Edition* by Renee Newman. *Gem & Jewelry Pocket Guide,Diamond Handbook, 2nd Edition,Jewelry Handbook.*" avg. press run 6M. Pub'd 2 titles 2009; expects 2 titles 2010, 2 titles 2011. 11 titles listed in the *Small Press Record of Books in Print* (36th Edition, 2010-11). Discounts: 2-4 copies 30%, 5-11 40%, 12-24 42%, 25-49 45%, 50+ 48%. 170pp. Reporting time: 1 month, but call first before submitting manuscript. Copyrights for author. Subject: Jewelry, Gems.

INTERNATIONAL JOURNAL OF AMERICAN LINGUISTICS, University of Chicago Press, Keren Rice, University of Toronto, 130 St. George Street, Department of Linguistics, Toronto, Ontario M5S 3H1, Canada, http://www.journals.uchicago.edu/IJAL/home.html. 1917. *"International Journal of American Linguistics* is a world forum for the study of all the languages native to North, Central, and South America. Inaugurated by Franz Boas in 1917, *IJAL* concentrates on the investigation of linguistic data and on the presentation of grammatical fragments and other documents relevant to Amerindian languages." 4/yr. Pub's reviews.

INTERNATIONAL JOURNAL OF EDUCATIONAL POLICY, RESEARCH, AND PRACTICE: RECONCEPTUALIZING CHILDHOOD STUDIES, Caddo Gap Press, Marianne Bloch, Co-Editor; Gaile Cannella, Co-Editor, 3145 Geary Blvd. PMB 275, San Francisco, CA 94118, 415-666-3012, fax 415-666-3552, caddogap@aol.com, www.caddogap.com. 2000. Articles. circ. 200. 4/yr. Pub'd 4 issues 2009; expects 4 issues 2010, 4 issues 2011. sub. price $75 individuals; $175 institutions; per copy $30; sample free. Back issues: $20. Discounts: 15% to agents. 96pp. Reporting time: 3 months. Simultaneous submissions accepted: No. Publishes 25% of manuscripts submitted. No payment. Copyrighted, reverts to author. Ads: $200 per page. Subject: Education.

INTERNATIONAL POETRY REVIEW, Mark Smith-Soto, Dept of Romance Languages, Univ. of North Carolina, Greensboro, NC 27402-6170, 336-334-4433, mismiths@uncg.edu, http://www.uncg.edu/rom/IPR/IPRsubscription.htm. 1975. Poetry, art. "Our emphasis is on English translation of contemporary poets, presented in bilingual format. About a third of each issue is dedicated to original work in English. We are also interested in essays on the art/craft of translation. Some recent contributors are Alexis Levitin, Ana Istaru, Fred Chappell, Coleman Barks, Jorge Teillier, Mary Crow, Jascha Kessler, Bernhard Frank, Sarah Lindsay. Our reading period runs between September 1 and April 30. Beginning with the Spring 2006 issue, the magazine has been available online through EBSCO." circ. 300. 2/yr. Pub'd 2 issues 2009; expects 2 issues 2010, 2 issues 2011. sub. price $12 individuals; $20 libraries, institutions; per copy $6; sample $6. Back issues: varies. 100pp. Reporting time: 3-6 months. Simultaneous submissions accepted, but must be indicated. Publishes 2% of manuscripts submitted. Payment: copies. Copyrighted, reverts to author. Pub's reviews: 2 in 2009. §Poetry translation, poetry. Ads: $100/$50. Subjects: African Literature, Africa, African Studies, Armenian, Asia, Indochina, Bilingual, France, French, German, Greek, India, Language, Latin America, Literary Review, Poetry, Portugal, Spain, Translation.

International Publishers Co. Inc., Betty Smith, 235 West 23 Street FL8, New York, NY 10011, 212-366-9816, Fax 212-366-9820. 1924. Non-fiction. avg. press run 1M-4M. Pub'd 5 titles 2009; expects 4 titles 2010, 5 titles 2011. 4 titles listed in the *Small Press Record of Books in Print* (36th Edition, 2010-11). Discounts: trade and short discount. 200-400pp, some 96-150pp. Reporting time: 1 week to 2 months. Simultaneous submissions accepted: yes. Publishes 5% of manuscripts submitted. Payment: royalties. Copyrights for author. Subjects: African Literature, Africa, African Studies, Americana, Biography, Black, Business & Economics, Communism, Marxism, Leninism, Labor, Peace, Politics, Public Affairs, Socialist, Women, Worker.

International University Line (IUL), Gary Flint, PO Box 2525, La Jolla, CA 92038, Tel 858-457-0595, Fax 858-581-9073, email info@iul-press.com, http://www.iul-press.com. 1992. Non-fiction. avg. press run 3M. Pub'd 2 titles 2009; expects 1 title 2010, 2 titles 2011. 12 titles listed in the *Small Press Record of Books in Print* (36th Edition, 2010-11). Discounts: up to 40%. 400pp. Reporting time: 6 months. Payment: 5-10% royalty. Does not copyright for author. Subjects: Biotechnology, Non-Fiction, Psychology, Science.

INTERNATIONAL WOMEN'S WRITING GUILD, Elizabeth Julia Stoumen, Box 810, Gracie Station, New York, NY 10028, 212-737-7536, Fax 212-737-9469, iwwg@iwwg.org, www.iwwg.org. 1976. Interviews, reviews, news items. "A network for women who write, great variety of listings on where to submit work. New information every 2 months. Successes and questions of members. Lots more." circ. 3M. 4/yr. Pub'd 6 issues 2009; expects 6 issues 2010, 6 issues 2011. sub. price $45 (included in IWWG membership); sample $1. 32pp. Pub's reviews. Ads: $50 1/8 page. Subjects: Networking, Newsletter.

INTO THE TEETH WIND, Rimantos Ungalys, Laura Bradshaw, College of Creative Studies, University of California, Santa Barbara, Santa Barbara, CA 93106, www.ccs.ucsb.edu/windsteeth. 1999. Poetry, art. "We accept poetry and artwork (for cover). SASE must be included with submissions. Contributors receive one free copy in which their work appears. The editors reserve the right to publish poetry and artwork on the publication's website." 4/yr. Pub'd 4 issues 2009; expects 4 issues 2010, 4 issues 2011. sub. price $20; per copy $5.50; sample $5.50. Discounts: contributors $5 or $10 for a double-issue. 60pp. Reporting time: 1-3 months. Simultaneous submissions accepted: no. Publishes 5% of manuscripts submitted. Payment: 1 copy. Copyrighted, reverts to author. Subject: Poetry.

The Intrepid Traveler, Sally Scanlon, Editor-in-Chief, PO Box 531, Branford, CT 06405, 203-469-0214, Fax 203-469-0430, admin@intrepidtraveler.com. 1990. Non-fiction. "We publish specialized travel guidebooks (e.g., *Paris Movie Walks, America's Best Zoos*, and guides to the Orlando area) along with books on travel marketing, and some travel essay." avg. press run 5M. Pub'd 9 titles 2009; expects 3 titles 2010, 5 titles 2011. 18 titles listed in the *Small Press Record of Books in Print* (36th Edition, 2010-11). Discounts: per National Book Network, Inc. terms. 256pp. Reporting time: averages 3 months. Query before sending simultaneous submissions. Publishes 1% of manuscripts submitted. Copyrights for author. Subjects: Animals, Business & Economics, Disney, Family, Florida, How-To, Memoirs, Non-Fiction, Parenting, Quotations, Travel, Trivia.

Intuitive Moon Media (see also STARNOTES), Dominique Jones, 13170-B Central SE #191, Albuquerque, NM 87123, webmaster@intuitivemoon.com, 505-349-5993, 505-280-9667. 2008. Poetry, articles, non-fiction. "Intuitive Moon Media has two sides: One is a spiritual, metaphysical media company and the other is an eclectic media company focusing on arts, education, comics, music, fiction, and more. We publish high-quality works on metaphysics at intuitivemoon.com in e-book and DVD formats. Additionally, we can send bound books as well, but we very much attempt to use modern media to its fullest. On the eclectic side, we publish media at stemmamedia.com, using the same mediums." avg. press run 500. Expects 5 titles 2010, 50 titles 2011. 1 title listed in the *Small Press Record of Books in Print* (36th Edition, 2010-11). Discounts: We have wholesale prices available upon request and bulk prices as well. 200pp. Reporting time: 1 month. Simultaneous submissions accepted: Yes. Publishes 25% of manuscripts submitted. Payment: varies by agreement. Copyrights for author. Subjects: Alternative Medicine, Astrology, Audio/Video, Channelling, Creativity, Crystals, Humanism, Metaphysics, Novels, Occult, Psychology, Relationships, Self-Help, Supernatural, Tarot.

INVENTED LANGUAGES, Richard Harrison, PO Box 3105, High Springs, FL 32655-3105, 352-317-9068 www.InventedLanguages.com. 2008. Fiction, articles, interviews, non-fiction. "Small magazine about the craft/hobby of inventing new languages. Includes profiles of existing languages, articles about linguistic features that the readers might enjoy using (for example, onomatopoeia, tense-mood-aspect systems, polysynthetic morphology, etc), reviews of relevant books and other media. Open to short fiction in which an alien or artificial language plays a major role." circ. 400. 2/yr. Expects 2 issues 2010, 3 issues 2011. sub. price $10; per copy $6; sample $5. Back issues: inquire. Discounts: 5 or more copies 15%. 60pp. Reporting time: 3 months. Simultaneous submissions accepted: No. Publishes 25% of manuscripts submitted. Payment: Payment varies depending on length and uniqueness of material. Copyrighted, reverts to author. Pub's reviews: approx. 15 in 2009. §Books and periodicals about linguistics, artificial languages, fictional cultures. Ads: full page $50. Subjects: Crafts, Hobbies, Language, Reference, Science Fiction.

The Invisible College Press, LLC, Paul Mossinger, Business Manager; Phil Reynolds, Editor-in-Chief, PO Box 209, Woodbridge, VA 22194-0209, 703-590-4005, editor@invispress.com, www.invispress.com. 2002. Fiction, non-fiction. "The Invisible College Press is a small, independent publisher dedicated to bringing you literary-quality works in the fields of UFOs, Conspiracies, Secret Societies, the Paranormal, Anarchism, and other non-traditional, subversive topics that are underrepresented by mainstream, corporate media. Our titles are a blend of new, original fiction, and reprints of hard-to-find classics." avg. press run 1000. Pub'd 12 titles 2009; expects 12 titles 2010, 12 titles 2011. 26 titles listed in the *Small Press Record of Books in Print* (36th Edition, 2010-11). Simultaneous submissions accepted: Yes. Copyrights for author.

IODINE POETRY JOURNAL, Jonathan K. Rice, Editor, PO Box 18548, Charlotte, NC 28218-0548. 2000. Poetry. "Work in Iodine Poetry Journal has appeared in Best American Poetry 2006." circ. 350. 2/yr. Pub'd 2 issues 2009; expects 2 issues 2010, 2 issues 2011. sub. price $12 one year, $22 two years; per copy $7. Back issues: $4-$6. 80pp. Reporting time: 2 - 3 months. Simultaneous submissions accepted: no. Publishes 10% of manuscripts submitted. Payment: 1 copy. Copyrighted, reverts to author. Subject: Poetry.

Ion Imagination Publishing, Ion Imagination Entertainment, Inc., Keith Frickey, Program Director, PO Box 210943, Nashville, TN 37221-0943, 615-646-3644, Fax 615-646-6276, flumpa@aol.com, www.flumpa.com. 1994. Fiction, art, photos, music, non-fiction. "Children's only, science related topics ONLY. No unsolicited materials. Specifically looking for illustrators, *not* authors, for ongoing, already established series. We are also a children's music publisher - please DO NOT send any queries that are not elementary science related - we will not read them. Queries only with SASE for return." avg. press run 10M+. Pub'd 2 titles 2009; expects 2 titles 2010, 2 titles 2011. 4 titles listed in the *Small Press Record of Books in Print* (36th Edition, 2010-11). Discounts: please call for info. 40pp. Reporting time: 1 month to review. Simultaneous submissions accepted: no. Subjects: Animals, Audio/Video, Biology, Children, Youth, Science, Tapes & Records.

IOTA, Ragged Raven Press, Bob Mee, Janet Murch, 1 Lodge Farm, Snitterfield, Stratford-on-Avon, Warks CV37 0LR, England, 44-1789-730320, iotapoetry@aol.com, www.iotapoetry.co.uk. 1987. Poetry, reviews. "No line limit (but no room for epics), bias towards modern/contemporary." circ. 350. 4/yr. Pub'd 4 issues 2009; expects 4 issues 2010, 4 issues 2011. sub. price UK£18 for outside Europe inc p/h.Sterling only or credit card via website.; per copy UK£4.50 inc. p/h.; sample UK£4.50 inc. p/h. Back issues: UK£4.50 inc. p/h. 56pp. Reporting time: 1-2 months. Simultaneous submissions accepted: no. Publishes 15-20% of manuscripts submitted. Payment: 1 free copy. Copyrighted, reverts to author. Pub's reviews: 43 in 2009. §Poems and books about poetry. Ads: none. Subjects: Poetry, Reviews.

IOWA HERITAGE ILLUSTRATED, Ginalie Swaim, State Historical Society of Iowa, 402 Iowa Avenue, Iowa City, IA 52240, 319-335-3916, Fax 319-335-3935, ginalie-swaim@uiowa.edu. 1920. Articles, art, photos, interviews, letters, non-fiction. "*Iowa Heritage Illustrated* is Iowa's popular history magazine. It publishes manuscripts and edited documents on the history of Iowa and the Midwest that may interest a general reading audience. Submissions that focus on visual materials (photographs, maps, drawings) or on material culture are also welcomed. Originality and significance of the topic, as well as quality of research and writing, will determine acceptance. Manuscripts should be double-spaced, footnoted, and roughly 5-20 pages. Photographs or illustrations (or suggestions) are encouraged." circ. 2M. 4/yr. Pub'd 4 issues 2009; expects 4 issues 2010, 4 issues 2011. sub. price $50; per copy $9; sample free. Back issues: 1920-1972—50¢, 1973-June '84—$1, July '84-Dec. '86—$2.50, 1987—Summer '89 $3.50, fall 89 - winter 95 $4.50. Discounts: retailers get 40% off single issue cover price. 48pp. Reporting time: 3 months. Simultaneous submissions accepted: no. Publishes 35% of manuscripts submitted. Payment: 10 complimentary copies + $50-$500. Copyrighted, does not revert to author. Subjects: History, Iowa.

THE IOWA REVIEW, Russell Valentino, Editor, 308 EPB, Univ. Of Iowa, Iowa City, IA 52242, 319-335-0462. 1970. Poetry, fiction, interviews, reviews, non-fiction. "We welcome open submissions September 1-December 1. During the spring semester we concentrate on contest entries." circ. 2500. 3/yr. Pub'd 3 issues 2009; expects 3 issues 2010, 3 issues 2011. sub. price $25; per copy $9.95; sample $9.95. Back issues: $8. 208pp. Reporting time: 3-6 months. Simultaneous submissions accepted: yes. Publishes 5% of manuscripts submitted. Payment: $1.50/line for poetry ($40 minimum), $0.08/word for prose ($100 minimum). $50 for reviews. Copyrighted, reverts to author. Pub's reviews: 4 in 2009. §Poetry, fiction, creative nonfiction. Subjects: Book Reviewing, Criticism, English, Essays, Fiction, Literary Review, Literature (General), Non-Fiction, Poetry, Prose.

Iris Publishing Group, Inc (Iris Press / Tellico Books), Robert Cumming B, 969 Oak Ridge Turnpike, # 328, Oak Ridge, TN 37830-8832, Ph: 865-483-0837, Fx: 865-481-3793, rcumming@irisbooks.com, www.irisbooks.com. 1975. Poetry, fiction, criticism, long-poems, non-fiction. "Of our two book imprints, Iris Press is tho older and focuses on literary materal (Poems literary fiction and other literary prose.) Our other imprint, Tellico Books is broader in scope and more flexible in its approach." avg. press run 1500. Pub'd 4 titles 2009; expects 7 titles 2010, 7 titles 2011. No titles listed in the *Small Press Record of Books in Print* (36th Edition, 2010-11). Discounts: distributors & wholesalers: 55%Bookstores, retailers, institutions, classrooms : 40%. 120pp. Reporting time: 2 months. Simultaneous submissions accepted: Yes. Publishes 1% of manuscripts submitted. Payment: Varies according to the type of material. Copyrights for author. Subjects: Appalachia, Essays, Fiction, History, Kentucky, Language, Latin America, Nature, Non-Fiction, Peace, Poetry, Prose, Puerto Rico, South Carolina, Tennessee.

IRIS: A Journal About Women, Kimberley Roberts, Coordinating Editor, PO Box 800588, University of Virginia, Charlottesville, VA 22904, 434-924-4500, Fax 434-982-2901, iris@virginia.edu, http://womenscenter.virginia.edu/iris.htm. 1980. Poetry, fiction, articles, art, photos, interviews, reviews, music, long-poems, non-fiction. "We are a magazine for twenty-something women who want to make a difference in the world around them. We welcome submissions of high quality poetry, fiction, art, nonfiction, and reviews. We prefer submissions that represent a woman's experience or viewpoint. We also have features, which include 'Cool Women Profile' - Profiles of women young and old making a difference in their communities, but unknown to most; FYI - resource guide; 'Ask Iris' - A forum style discussion on an issue; 'Girl on the Street' - Composing a poll on a common issue/question. We do not accept email submissions. For sumission guidelines see http://iris.virginia.edu." circ. 2.5M. 2/yr. Pub'd 2 issues 2009; expects 2 issues 2010, 2 issues 2011. sub. price $9; per copy $5; sample $5. Back issues: $5. Discounts: 20% for trade or bulk. 70pp. Reporting time: 2-3 months. Simultaneous submissions accepted: yes. Publishes 5% of manuscripts submitted. Payment: a determined number of issues. Copyrighted, reverts to author. Pub's reviews: 4 in 2009. §Books about women or that are written by women and feminist theory, prefer nonfiction. Ads: $200/$140/$90 1/4 page. Subjects: African-American, Autobiography, Birth, Birth Control, Population, Bisexual, Black, Book Reviewing, Chicano/a, Community, Creativity, Education, Family, Feminism, Fiction, Food, Eating, Gender Issues.

IRISH FAMILY JOURNAL, Irish Genealogical Foundation, Michael C. O'Laughlin, Box 7575, Kansas City, MO 64116. 1978. Articles, art, photos, interviews, letters, news items, non-fiction. "Short articles, highlights, Irish American personalities, informal, tradition/history oriented. Time period: A) 1800's, B) current time for genealogy. Photos of Irish family castles, immigrants, lifestyle—1800's. Family names." circ. 2.5M+. 6 or 12/yr (12 issues to gold members). Pub'd 12 issues 2009; expects 12 issues 2010, 12 issues 2011. sub. price $59/$114; sample n/c. 8pp. Reporting time: 30 days. Payment: inquire. Copyrighted, reverts to author. Pub's reviews: 50 in 2009. §Irish genealogy, history, folklore, tradition. Ads: $1,000/$600. Subjects: Book Reviewing, Celtic, Genealogy, Ireland.

Irish Genealogical Foundation (see also IRISH FAMILY JOURNAL), Michael C. O'Laughlin, Box 7575, Kansas City, MO 64116, www.Irishroots.com. 1969. Articles, art, photos, interviews, letters, non-fiction. avg. press run 2M. Pub'd 10 titles 2009; expects 10 titles 2010, 10 titles 2011. 34 titles listed in the *Small Press Record of Books in Print* (36th Edition, 2010-11). Discounts: bulk purchases 10%-60%. 200pp. Reporting time: 30 days. Simultaneous submissions accepted: no. Payment: none. Does not copyright for author. Subjects: Celtic, Family, Folklore, Gaelic, Genealogy, Ireland, Missouri, Music, Reference, Reprints.

IRISH LITERARY SUPPLEMENT, Robert G. Lowery, Editor-Publisher; Maureen Murphy, Features Editor,

2592 N Wading River Road, Wading River, NY 11792-1404, 631-929-0224. 1982. Interviews, criticism, reviews, parts-of-novels, non-fiction. "Published in association with Boston College. All work assigned." circ. 4.5M. 2/yr. Pub'd 2 issues 2009; expects 2 issues 2010, 2 issues 2011. sub. price $6, $7.50 libraries, $12 foreign; per copy $3; sample $3. Back issues: $4. Discounts: only with subscription agencies. 32pp. Reporting time: varies. Payment: copies and book for review. Copyrighted, reverts to author. Pub's reviews: 140 in 2009. §Irish material. Ads: $500/$300. Subjects: Book Reviewing, Celtic, Criticism, Drama, Folklore, Ireland, Literary Review, Poetry, G.B. Shaw, Theatre.

IROL Press, LLC, James White, 547 McPherson Circle, Sagamore, OH 44067, www.irolpress.com. 2007. Non-fiction. avg. press run 1000. Expects 1 title 2010, 1 title 2011. 1 title listed in the *Small Press Record of Books in Print* (36th Edition, 2010-11). 300pp. Simultaneous submissions accepted: No. Publishes 1% of manuscripts submitted. Does not copyright for author. Subjects: Computers, Calculators, Technology.

IRON HORSE LITERARY REVIEW, Jill Patterson, Editor; Carrie Jerrell, Poetry Editor, Texas Tech University, English Dept., PO Box 43091, Lubbock, TX 79409-3091, 806-742-2500 X234. 1999. Poetry, fiction, photos, interviews, reviews, non-fiction. "Accepts literary fiction, poetry, and creative nonfiction as well as b&w photographs. We prefer not to publish commercial genres, including fantasy, science fiction, romance, horror, erotica, etc. No short-shorts." circ. 500. 6/yr. Pub'd 4 issues 2009; expects 6 issues 2010, 6 issues 2011. sub. price $15; per copy $5; sample $5. 40-60pp. Reporting time: 3 months. Simultaneous submissions accepted: yes. Publishes 1% of manuscripts submitted. Payment: $100 for fiction or nonfiction, $40 per poem. Copyrighted, reverts to author. Pub's reviews. §Literary fiction, poetry, creative nonfiction. Ads: ad-swap only. Subjects: African-American, Chicano/a, Fiction, Literary Review, Native American, Non-Fiction, Poetry, Texas.

Ironcroft Publishing, Brian Shureb, PO Box 630, Hartland, MI 48353. No titles listed in the *Small Press Record of Books in Print* (36th Edition, 2010-11).

Island Press, Barbara Dean, Executive Editor; Dan Sayre, Editor-In-Cheif; Chuck Savitt, Publisher, 1718 Connecticut Avenue NW #300, Washington, DC 20009, 202-232-7933; FAX 202-234-1328; e-mail info@islandpress.org; Website www.islandpress.org. 1978. Non-fiction. "Additional address: Box 7, Covelo, CA 95428. Books from original manuscripts on the environment, ecology, and natural resource management." avg. press run 3M. Pub'd 44 titles 2009; expects 48 titles 2010, 50 titles 2011. No titles listed in the *Small Press Record of Books in Print* (36th Edition, 2010-11). Discounts: trade 1-9 40%, 10-49 43%, 50-99 44%, 100-249 45%, 250+ 46%. 275pp. Reporting time: 3 weeks, sometimes less. Simultaneous submissions accepted: yes. Publishes 15% of manuscripts submitted. Payment: standard contracts, graduated royalties. Copyrights for author. Subjects: Biology, Conservation, Earth, Natural History, Ecology, Foods, Energy, Environment, Non-Fiction, Science, Water.

Islewest Publishing, Mary Jo Graham, 4242 Chavenelle Drive, Dubuque, IA 52002, 319-557-1500, Fax 319-557-1376. 1994. Non-fiction. avg. press run 1M-10M. Pub'd 2 titles 2009; expects 8 titles 2010, 15 titles 2011. 13 titles listed in the *Small Press Record of Books in Print* (36th Edition, 2010-11). Discounts: market norm. Reporting time: two weeks. Simultaneous submissions accepted: yes. Publishes 15% of manuscripts submitted. Copyrights for author. Subjects: Alcohol, Alcoholism, Gender Issues, Grieving, How-To, Men, Parenting, Psychology, Relationships, Self-Help, Sexual Abuse, Social Work, Vietnam.

ISSUES, Sue Perlman, PO Box 424885, San Francisco, CA 94142-4885, 415-864-4800 X136. 1978. Poetry, fiction, articles, art, photos, interviews, satire, reviews, non-fiction. "Messianic." circ. 40M. 6/yr. Pub'd 6 issues 2009; expects 6 issues 2010, 6 issues 2011. sub. price free; per copy free; sample 50¢. Back issues: 75¢ each. 8-12pp. Reporting time: 3-5 weeks. Payment: 10¢/word, minimum $25. Copyrighted, rights reverting to author is decided by contract. Pub's reviews: 5 in 2009. §Religion, Judaica, philosophy, Christianity. Ads: none. Subjects: Book Reviewing, Christianity, Interviews, Judaism, Poetry, Religion.

ISSUES IN TEACHER EDUCATION, Caddo Gap Press, Margaret Olebe, 3145 Geary Blvd. PMB 275, San Francisco, CA 94118, 415 666-3012. twice a year. sub. price $40 for individuals; $80 for institutions. 96pp. Subject: Education.

•ISTANBUL LITERARY REVIEW, Gloria Mindock, Editor; Susan Tepper, Assistant Editor; Etkin Getir, Founder, http://www.ilrmagazine.com/submissions/, http://www.ilrmagazine.net, Istanbul, Turkey. 2005. Poetry, fiction, articles, photos, interviews, reviews, plays. "The Istanbul Literary Review bridges the gaps in writing between countries. It is important for us to publish writers from all over the world." 3/yr. Pub'd 3 issues 2009; expects 3 issues 2010, 3 issues 2011. Reporting time: 2 months. Simultaneous submissions accepted: No. Publishes 5% of manuscripts submitted. Payment: Online Journal. Copyrighted. Pub's reviews: 2 in 2009. §poetry. Subjects: Absurdist, Avant-Garde, Experimental Art, Drama, Experimental, Fiction, Interviews, Poetry, Prose, Short Stories.

IT GOES ON THE SHELF, Purple Mouth Press, Ned Brooks, 4817 Dean Lane, Lilburn, GA 30047-4720, nedbrooks@sprynet.com. 1984. Art, reviews. "Art only, I write the text myself." circ. 350 paper, also at home.sprynet.com/~nedbrooks/home.htm. 1/yr. Pub'd 1 issue 2009; expects 1 issue 2010, 1 issue 2011. Discounts: trade, etc. 20pp. Reporting time: 1 week. Payment: copy. Not copyrighted, will copyright art if author wishes. Pub's reviews: 75 in 2009. §Science fiction, fantasy, typewriters, oddities. Subjects: Book Arts, Fantasy, Science Fiction.

ITALIAN AMERICANA, Carol Bonomo Albright, Editor; Bruno A. Arcudi, Associate Editor; John Paul Russo, Review Editor; Michael Palma, Poetry Editor, University of Rhode Island, 80 Washington Street, Providence, RI 02903-1803. 1974. Poetry, articles, reviews. "*Italian Americana,* a multi-disciplinary journal concerning itself with all aspects of the Italian experience in America, publishes articles, short stories, poetry, memoirs and book reviews. It is published in cooperation with the American Italian Historical Association. Submissions of 20 double-spaced pages maximum, following the latest MLA Style Sheet, are invited in the areas of Italian American history, sociology, political science, literature, art, folk art, anthropology, music, psychology, etc., and short stories. Book reviews of 1,000 words are assigned and poetry of no more than three pages is accepted. Submissions by historians, social scientists, literary critics, etc., of Italian are encouraged when related to Italian American studies. Comparative analysis is welcome when related to Italian American issues. Please submit materials in triplicate with an SASE. All submissions will be reviewed by the editor and two readers. Name should appear on the first page only with article title on subsequent pages. For poetry, one copy of each poem is acceptable." circ. 2.5M. 2/yr. Pub'd 2 issues 2009; expects 2 issues 2010, 2 issues 2011. 1 title listed in the *Small Press Record of Books in Print* (36th Edition, 2010-11). sub. price $20 indiv., $25 instit., $15 student, $35 foreign; per copy $8.50; sample $7. Back issues: $7 for issues starting Fall 1990; no copies available for Spring/Summer '93. Discounts: $35/2 years, $54/3 years. 150pp. Reporting time: 1-2 months. Simultaneous submissions accepted: no. Publishes 15% of manuscripts submitted. Payment: $500 for best historical article published each year and $1000 poetry prize annually, $250 for best fiction or memoir published each year. Copyrighted, reverts to author. Pub's reviews: 28 in 2009. §Significant books, films, plays, and art about Italian-American experience. Ads: $190/$100. Subjects: Anthropology, Archaelogy, Arts, History, Italian-American, Literature (General), Music, Philosophy, Political Science, Psychology, Short Stories, Sociology.

Italica Press, Inc., Ronald G. Musto, Eileen Gardiner, 595 Main Street, #605, New York, NY 10044, 212-935-4230; fax 212-838-7812; inquiries@italicapress.com. 1985. Poetry, fiction, art, letters, long-poems, plays, non-fiction. "We specialize in English translations of Italian and Latin works from the Middle Ages to the present. Primary interests are in history, literature, travel, and art. Published titles include Petrarch's *The Revolution of Cola di Rienzo*, the poet's letters to the revolutionary; *The Marvels of Rome*, a medieval guidebook to the city; and Theodorich's *Guide to the Holy Land*, written c. 1172; *The Fat Woodworker* by Antonio Manetti, a comic Renaissance tale about Brunelleschi and his circle; and new translations from Italian of twentieth-century novels, *Cosima* by Grazia Deledda and *Family Chronicle* by Vasco Pratolini, *The Wooden Throne* by Carlo Sgorlon, *Dolcissimo* by Guiseppe Bonaviri, and *Woman at War* by Dacia Maraina. Our audience is the general reader interested in works of lasting merit." avg. press run 1.5M. Pub'd 6 titles 2009; expects 8 titles 2010, 8 titles 2011. 29 titles listed in the *Small Press Record of Books in Print* (36th Edition, 2010-11). Discounts: trade single copy 20%, 25% 2 copies, 30% 3-4, 35% 5-9, 40% 10-25, 43% 26-50, 50% 100+; classroom 25% on adoptions of 5 or more; others are negotiable. 200pp. Reporting time: 6 weeks. Simultaneous submissions accepted: yes. Publishes 10% of manuscripts submitted. Payment: approx. 10% of net sales. Copyrights for author. Subjects: Architecture, Arts, Bilingual, Biography, Cities, Fiction, History, Italy, Literature (General), Medieval, Non-Fiction, Novels, Renaissance, Translation, Transportation.

Ithuriel's Spear, James Mitchell, 939 Eddy St., #102, San Francisco, CA 94109, http://www.ithuriel.com. 2004. Poetry, fiction, art, non-fiction. "We are open to all proposals which concern the literary arts." avg. press run 1000. Expects 4 titles 2010, 4 titles 2011. 14 titles listed in the *Small Press Record of Books in Print* (36th Edition, 2010-11). 84pp. Reporting time: Less than 30 days. Simultaneous submissions accepted: Yes. Publishes 12% of manuscripts submitted. Payment: Variable, please contact publisher. Does not copyright for author. Subjects: Arts, Buddhism, Fiction, Gay, Literature (General), Poetry, San Francisco, Zen.

•IT'S JUST THIS LITTLE CHROMIUM SWITCH HERE, Thomas Gedwillo, 3724 Baldwin Ave, Lincoln, NE 68504-2443, 402-817-9208, http://chromiumswitch.org. 1972. Articles, photos, cartoons, interviews, reviews, letters. circ. 150. 4/yr. Pub'd 1 issue 2009; expects 4 issues 2010, 4 issues 2011. price per copy $5.00; sample Free. Back issues: Inquire. 32pp. Reporting time: 1 week. Payment: Inquire. Not copyrighted. Pub's reviews: none in 2009. §Comedy, radio, theatre, broadcasting; specifically anything related to The Firesign Theatre. Ads: Inquire. Subjects: Absurdist, Broadcasting, Cartoons, Comics, Culture, Entertainment, Humor, Performing Arts, Radio, Reviews, Tapes & Records, Zines.

Ivy House Publishing Group, Janet Evans, Publisher; Anna Howland, Associate Director of Publishing; Ashley Hardin, Publishing Coordinator, 5122 Bur Oak Circle, Raleigh, NC 27612, 919-782-0281. 1993. Poetry, fiction, long-poems, non-fiction. "For more information, please visit *www.ivyhousebooks.com*." avg. press run

1000. Pub'd 20 titles 2009; expects 20 titles 2010, 10 titles 2011. 25 titles listed in the *Small Press Record of Books in Print* (36th Edition, 2010-11). Discounts: 1-4 35%, 5-99 40%, 100+ 45%. 200pp. Reporting time: 4-6 weeks. Simultaneous submissions accepted: Yes. Publishes 50% of manuscripts submitted. Payment: quarterly. Copyrights for author.

J

J & J Consultants, Inc. (see also NEW ALTERNATIVES), Walter Jones Jr., 603 Olde Farm Road, Media, PA 19063, 610-565-9692, Fax 610-565-9694, wjones13@juno.com, www.members.tripod.com/walterjones/. 1997. Poetry, articles, reviews, non-fiction. "Writers needed for magazine *New Alternatives.*" avg. press run 250. Pub'd 1 title 2009; expects 1 title 2010. 1 title listed in the *Small Press Record of Books in Print* (36th Edition, 2010-11). Discounts: 20% trade, 40% wholesale, 50% regional wholesale, 50% jobbers. 112pp. Reporting time: 2 months. Simultaneous submissions accepted: yes. Publishes 50% of manuscripts submitted. Payment: royalty 5% list price/flat fee. Does not copyright for author. Subjects: African-American, Non-Fiction, Poetry, Psychology.

J. Mark Press (see also WORLD POETRY SHOWCASE), Barbara Morris Fischer-Binstock Mrs., PO Box 24-3474, Boynton Beach, FL 33424, www.JMarkPress.com, jmpbooks@earthlink.net. 1963. Poetry. "3-16 lines, maximum 95 words. Stirring messages, picturesque phrases. No vulgarity. Prefer poets see prize-winning poems on our website. If you have no computer, ask your librarian to get it on the screen. Poems must be accompanied by a SASE or they won't be read and will be disposed of." avg. press run 500. Pub'd 3 titles 2009; expects 6 titles 2010, 6 titles 2011. 1 title listed in the *Small Press Record of Books in Print* (36th Edition, 2010-11). Discounts: 40%. 82pp. Reporting time: 1 week. Simultaneous submissions accepted: yes. Publishes 40% of manuscripts submitted. Payment: prizes. Copyrights for author. Subjects: Anthology, Family, Haiku, Internet, Poetry, Romance, Spiritual.

JACK MACKEREL MAGAZINE, Rowhouse Press, Greg Bachar, PO Box 23134, Seattle, WA 98102-0434. 1994. Poetry, fiction, articles, art, photos, interviews, criticism, reviews, music, letters, parts-of-novels, long-poems, collages, news items. "Recent contributors: Ann Paiva, William D. Waltz, John Rose, David Berman, Katie J. Kurtz." circ. 500-1M. 4/yr. Pub'd 4 issues 2009; expects 4 issues 2010, 4 issues 2011. sub. price $12; per copy $5; sample $5. Back issues: $5. 40-60pp. Reporting time: 2-4 weeks. Payment: copies. Copyrighted, reverts to author. Pub's reviews: 8 in 2009. §Fiction, poetry, art, artists, photography, physics. Ads: $25/$15/$5 1/4 page. Subjects: Arts, Biography, Book Reviewing, Comics, Dada, Dance, Electronics, Fiction, History, Holography, Language, Literature (General), Mental Health, Music, Philosophy.

Jacket Magazine, Kelly Writers House, 3805 Locust Walk, Philadelphia, PA 19104. 1997. Poetry, articles, photos, interviews, criticism, reviews, long-poems, news items. Three times per year, internet only. sub. price Jacket is free on the net at jacketmagazine.com. Back issues: All issues—over 30 in 2007—are available. 200pp. Payment: No payment, sorry. Pub's reviews: 100 in 2009. §Contemporary poetry.

Jackson Harbor Press, William H. Olson, RR 1, Box 107AA, 845 Jackson Harbor Road, Washington Island, WI 54246-9048. 1993. Poetry, fiction, non-fiction. "We intend to do primarily regional works (Door County, Wisconsin), but are unable to accept unsolicited manuscripts at this time." avg. press run 1M. Pub'd 3 titles 2009; expects 2 titles 2010, 2 titles 2011. 20 titles listed in the *Small Press Record of Books in Print* (36th Edition, 2010-11). Discounts: 2-4 20%, 5-9 30%, 10+ 40%. 64pp. Reporting time: 2 weeks. Payment: each arrangement will be individually negotiated. Copyrights for author. Subjects: Cooking, Great Lakes, Haiku, History, Novels, Poetry, Wisconsin.

Jako Books, Gablewoods South, PO Box VF665, Vieux Fort, St. Lucia, West Indies, 758-454-7839, info@jakoproductions.com, www.jakoproductions.com. 1999. Poetry, fiction, articles, art, photos, cartoons, interviews, criticism, reviews, music, letters, long-poems, news items, non-fiction. avg. press run 1000. Pub'd 1 title 2009; expects 2 titles 2010, 2 titles 2011. 1 title listed in the *Small Press Record of Books in Print* (36th Edition, 2010-11). Simultaneous submissions accepted: yes. Subjects: African Literature, Africa, African Studies, Arts, Black, Book Reviewing, Caribbean, Criticism, Culture, Current Affairs, Fiction, Literary Review, Literature (General), Multicultural, Non-Fiction, Poetry, Short Stories.

Jalmar Press/Innerchoice Publishing, Cathy Winch, Editor; Susanna Palomares, Editor, PO Box 370, Fawnskin, CA 92333, Fax 909 866 2961 Email: info@jalmarpress.com. 1973. Non-fiction. "Affiliated with B.L. Winch Group, Inc. Primarily interested in activity driven materials for school counselors, school psychologists and other child care givers to use with children to develop their social, emotional, and ethical skills. Topics include: Self Esteem, Conflict Resolution, Anger Management, Character Development,

Emotional Intelligence, etc. Have four series: 1) *Transactional Analysis for Everybody*, Warm Fuzzy Series, 2) *Conflict Resolution Series*, 3) *Right-Brain/Whole-Brain Learning Series*, 4) *Positive Self-Esteem Series*. Titles in *TA for Everybody Series*: Freed, Alvyn M. *TA for Tots (and Other Prinzes)*; Freed, Alvyn & Margaret *TA for Kids (and Grown-ups, too)*, 3rd edition newly revised and illustrated. Freed, Alvyn M. *TA for Teens (and Other Important People)*; Freed, Alvyn M. *TA for Tots Coloring Book. TA for Tots* Vol. II - Alvyn M. Freed. Steiner, Claude *Original Warm Fuzzy Tale*; *Songs of the Warm Fuzzy* cassette (all about your feelings)." avg. press run 1.5M. Pub'd 5 titles 2009; expects 6 titles 2010, 8 titles 2011. 109 titles listed in the *Small Press Record of Books in Print* (36th Edition, 2010-11). Discounts: trade 25-45%; agent/jobber 25-50%. 192pp. Reporting time: 4 weeks. Simultaneous submissions accepted: yes. Publishes 1% of manuscripts submitted. Payment: 7.5%-12.5% of net receipts. Copyrights for author. Subjects: Adolescence, Alcohol, Alcoholism, Children, Youth, Divorce, Drugs, Education, Ethics, Grieving, Guidance, Motivation, Success, Non-Fiction, Non-Violence, Parenting, Sexual Abuse, Young Adult.

Jamenair Ltd., Peter K. Studner, PO Box 241957, Los Angeles, CA 90024-9757, 310-470-6688. 1986. Non-fiction. "Books and software related to job search and career changing." avg. press run 10M. 3 titles listed in the *Small Press Record of Books in Print* (36th Edition, 2010-11). Discounts: depends on quantity. 352pp. Reporting time: 30 days. Payment: open, depends on material. Copyrights for author. Subjects: Business & Economics, Computers, Calculators, Education, Employment, How-To, Textbooks.

JAMES DICKEY REVIEW, English Department, Lynchburg College, 1501 Lakeside Drive, Lynchburg, VA 24501, 434-544-8732. 1984. Poetry, fiction, articles, interviews, satire, criticism, reviews, letters, parts-of-novels, long-poems, news items, non-fiction. "Mss. of all lengths are considered. All material should concern James Dickey/his work and includes comparative studies. We publish a few poems of *very* high caliber. Recent: Linda Roth, Gordon Van Ness, and John Van Peenen." 2/yr. Pub'd 2 issues 2009; expects 2 issues 2010, 2 issues 2011. sub. price $12 USA individuals, $14 institutions, outside USA: $12 indiv., $15 instit.; per copy $8; sample $8. Back issues: $8. Discounts: 25% to jobbers. 50pp. Simultaneous submissions accepted: no. Publishes a variable % of manuscripts submitted. Payment: 1 copy. Copyrighted, reverts to author. Pub's reviews: 2-4 in 2009. §southern/Applachian/nature writing; works about or embodying the themes (masculinity, war, nature, etc.) of James Dickey. Ads: full page flyer inserted $100—one time. Subjects: Appalachia, Book Reviewing, Creative Non-fiction, Criticism, James Dickey, Essays, Literary Review, Nature, Non-Fiction, Prose, South, Space, Travel, Virginia, War.

JAMES JOYCE BROADSHEET, Pieter Bekker, Editor; Richard Brown, Editor-in-Chief; Alistair Stead, Editor, School of English, University of Leeds, West Yorkshire LS2 9JT, England, 0113-233-4739. 1980. Poetry, articles, art, photos, cartoons, criticism, reviews, letters, news items. circ. 800. 3/yr. Pub'd 3 issues 2009; expects 3 issues 2010, 3 issues 2011. sub. price £7.50 Europe (£6 for students)/$15 (€15 for students elsewhere); per copy £2 plus 50p postage Europe ($6 including postage elsewhere); sample £2/$4. Back issues: at current annual subscription rate. Discounts: 33-1/3% to bookshops only. 4-6pp. Reporting time: 6 months-1 year. Payment: none. Copyrighted. Pub's reviews: 15 in 2009. §Modern literature, James Joyce, contemporary criticism. Ads: Please inquire. Subjects: Book Reviewing, Criticism, Ireland, James Joyce, Literary Review, Literature (General), Reviews, Translation, Visual Arts.

JAMES JOYCE QUARTERLY, TULSA STUDIES IN WOMEN'S LITERATURE, Sean Latham, Editor; Carol Kealiher, Managing Editor, University of Tulsa, 600 S. College, Tulsa, OK 74104, phone 918-631-2501, fax 918-631-2065, www.utulsa.edu/JJQ. 1963. Articles, criticism, reviews. "Academic criticism of Joyce's works; book reviews, notes, bibliographies; material relating to Joyce and Irish Renaissance and Joyce's relationship to other writers of his time. Articles should not normally exceed 20 pp. Notes should not excceed 6 pp. Please consult the Chicago Manual of Style and the "Special Note to Contributors" that appears on inside back cover of each issue of the *JJQ* regarding style and preparation of manuscript." circ. 1500. 4/yr. Pub'd 4 issues 2009; expects 4 issues 2010, 4 issues 2011. sub. price $22 U.S., $24 foreign; per copy $15.00; sample $15.00. Back issues: for back issues, write Swets & Zeitlinger, Heereweg 347b, Lisse, The Netherlands. 150pp. Reporting time: 4-5 months. Simultaneous submissions accepted: no. Publishes 40% of manuscripts submitted. Payment: contributors' copies & offprints. Copyrighted, does not revert to author. Pub's reviews: approx. 50 in 2009. §Joyce studies, modernism. Ads: $200. Subjects: James Joyce, Literary Review.

Jardin Publishing, Melissa Dragich, PO Box 6533, Portland, OR 97228. 2006. "As we are a small press, we are very careful about who we decide to partner with. At the moment, our focus is on business leadership books. Our latest title *The Secret Life of the Corporate Jester* is a great example of what we are looking for - a creative, fun, interesting read." Expects 2 titles 2010, 2 titles 2011. 1 title listed in the *Small Press Record of Books in Print* (36th Edition, 2010-11). Simultaneous submissions accepted: Yes. Does not copyright for author. Subjects: Business & Economics, Leadership.

•**JAVELINA BI-MONTHLY,** Eric Stone, Fort Worth, TX 76133, javelinabimonthly@hotmail.com. 2010. Poetry, fiction. "Javelina Bi-Monthly will publish magical realist fiction, (in the vein of Kafka, Marquez as two examples) and surrealist poetry (like Russell Edson's prose poems, James Tate, and Charles Simic.) Be sure you are familiar with what magical realism is. The poems that will be published do not have a particular "style" to them. Surrealist, Whitmanesque free verse is not required or discouraged, and form is welcome in syllabic, metered, and rhymed forms (but rhyme is hard to do well.)Fiction is 5000 words maximum. Poetry is 55 lines max. Email submissions to javelinabimonthly@hotmail.com." circ. 300. 6/yr. sub. price $8.45; per copy $2.95; sample $2.95. Back issues: $2.95. Reporting time: 7 weeks. Simultaneous submissions accepted: Yes. Copyrighted, reverts to author. §Magical Realist Fiction, Surrealist Poetry. Subjects: Absurdist, Dreams, Fiction, Poetry, Southwest, Texas, The West.

Jawbone Press, 1700 Fourth St., Berkeley, CA 94710, 510-809-3818, fax 510-809-3777, 877-528-1444, kevin@jawbonepress.com, www.jawbonepress.com. 2007. Music, non-fiction. "Jawbone is a leading independent music book publisher based in London and San Francisco." Pub'd 7 titles 2009; expects 11 titles 2010, 15 titles 2011. 20 titles listed in the *Small Press Record of Books in Print* (36th Edition, 2010-11).

J'ECRIS, Jean Guenot, BP 101, Saint-Cloud 92216, France, (1) 47-71-79-63. 1987. "Specialized on technical data concerning creative writing for French writers." circ. 2M. 4/yr. Pub'd 4 issues 2009; expects 4 issues 2010, 4 issues 2011. sub. price $47; per copy $12; sample free. Back issues: $10. 32pp. Payment: yes. Copyrighted, reverts to author. Pub's reviews: 15 in 2009. §Only books dealing with creative writing techniques. No ads. Subjects: Fiction, Literature (General), Printing, Writers/Writing.

‡JEWISH CURRENTS, Lawrence Bush, Editor, 45 E 33 Street 4th floor, New York, NY 10016, 212-889-2523, Fax 212-532-7518. 1946. Poetry, fiction, articles, art, photos, interviews, satire, criticism, reviews, letters, news items, non-fiction. "Articles of Jewish interest, progressive politics, Black-Jewish relations, 2M-3M words; reviews of books, records, plays, films, events, 1.8M-2M words; lively style, hard facts, secular p.o.v., pro-Israel/non-Zionist." circ. 14M. 6/yr. Pub'd 6 issues 2009; expects 6 issues 2010, 6 issues 2011. 3 titles listed in the *Small Press Record of Books in Print* (36th Edition, 2010-11). sub. price $30; per copy $5; Free sample. Back issues: $5. Discounts: 40% retail/25% subscription agency. 48pp—except March-April, 96 pp. Reporting time: 2 months. Simultaneous submissions accepted: no. Publishes 15% of manuscripts submitted. Payment: 6 copies + subscription; $54 to young writers. Copyrighted. Pub's reviews: 30 in 2009. §Jewish affairs, political & cultural, feminism, civil rights, labor history, Holocaust resistance, Black-Jewish relations, Yiddish culture, Mideast peace process. Ads: $250/180/120/50 - for 2 col. inch (greetings and memorials); $1000/800/750/450/400/300 2-1/2 col. inch (commercial ads). Subjects: History, Judaism, Middle East, Politics, Socialist.

Jewish Publication Society, Carol Hupping, Publishing Director, 2100 Arch Street, Philadelphia, PA 19103-1308, 215-802-0600, Fax 215-568-2017. 1888. Non-fiction. avg. press run 2M. Pub'd 12 titles 2009; expects 12 titles 2010, 10 titles 2011. No titles listed in the *Small Press Record of Books in Print* (36th Edition, 2010-11). Discounts: normal trade. 350pp. Reporting time: 6-9 months. Simultaneous submissions accepted: yes. Publishes less than 10% of manuscripts submitted. Payment: modest advance and royalties. Copyrights for author. Subjects: Judaism, Religion.

JEWISH WOMEN'S LITERARY ANNUAL, Henny Wenkart, National Council of Jewish Women NY Section, 820 Second Ave., New York, NY 10017-4504, 212-687-5030 ext.33/fax212-687-5032. 1994-95. "Poetry, fiction, art by Jewish women. No deadlines, we read continuously." 1/yr. sub. price $18 three issues; per copy $7.50. Back issues: available. 200pp. Simultaneous submissions accepted: yes. Payment: $15min., $5add.p.

Jigsaw Press, Mari Bushman, 784 US Highway 89, Vaughn, MT 59487-9535, 888-643-6455. 2006. Fiction. "We primarily publish fiction—paranormal thrillers, fantasy, and the like. We will entertain projects that entertain, but also encourage people to be more tolerant and accepting of the differences between us all." avg. press run 1500. Pub'd 3 titles 2009; expects 5 titles 2010, 5 titles 2011. 5 titles listed in the *Small Press Record of Books in Print* (36th Edition, 2010-11). Discounts: 25% off list price for any wholesaler, distributor, jobber, retailer, etc.—you pay shipping. 250-500pp. Reporting time: Responds in six to eight weeks. Simultaneous submissions accepted: Yes. Publishes 2% of manuscripts submitted. Payment: No advance. 50% royalty on profits above the print cost of each book to the author, paid monthly. Contact editor for details. Copyrights for author. Subjects: Children, Youth, Erotica, Fantasy, Fiction, Humor, Juvenile Fiction, Literature (General), Montana, Mystery, Novels, Picture Books, Spiritual, Supernatural.

JLA Publications, A Division Of Jeffrey Lant Associates, Inc., Dr. Jeffrey Lant, President, 50 Follen Street #507, Cambridge, MA 02138, 617-547-6372, drjlant@worldprofit.com, www.worldprofit.com and www.jeffreylant.com. 1979. Non-fiction. "We are interested in publishing books of particular interest to small businesses, entrepreneurs and independent professionals. To get an idea of what we publish, simply write us at the above address and request a current catalog. Up until now our titles have been all more than 100,000 words in length and are widely regarded as the most detailed books on their subjects. Recent books include Lant's *Multi Level Money*, Jeffrey Lant's Revised Third Edition of *Money Talks: The Complete Guide to Creating a Profitable Workshop or Seminar in any Field* and Lant's book *Cash Copy: How to Offer Your Products and*

Services So Your Prospects Buy Them...Now! We are now open, however, to shorter (though still very specific and useful) books in the 50,000-75,000 word length and titles in human development as well as business development. We are different because we pay royalties *monthly* and get our authors very involved in the publicity process. We do not pay advances for material but do promote strenuously." avg. press run 4M-5M. Pub'd 7 titles 2009; expects 2 titles 2010, 5 titles 2011. 12 titles listed in the *Small Press Record of Books in Print* (36th Edition, 2010-11). Discounts: 1-9 copies 20%, 10-99 40% (you pay shipping); thence negotiable up to 60% discount on major orders. 300+pp. Reporting time: 30-60 days. Payment: 10%, monthly. Copyrights for author. Subjects: Business & Economics, Communication, Journalism, How-To, Printing.

Joelle Publishing, Norman Russell, PO Box 91229, Santa Barbara, CA 93190, 805-692-1938. 1987. Non-fiction. avg. press run 5M. Expects 2 titles 2010, 3 titles 2011. 3 titles listed in the *Small Press Record of Books in Print* (36th Edition, 2010-11). Discounts: trade 40%, jobber 55%, library 20%. 140pp. Reporting time: 3 weeks. Simultaneous submissions accepted: yes. Payment: to be arranged. Copyrights for author. Subjects: Health, Psychology.

JONES AV, Paul Schwartz, 88 Dagmar Av, Toronto, Ontario M4M 1W1, Canada, www.interlog.com/~oel. 1994. Poetry, art, photos, concrete art. "We are a chap book size poetry journal. All styles, but no rhymed poetry unless it is really, really good." circ. 100. 4/yr. Pub'd 4 issues 2009; expects 4 issues 2010, 4 issues 2011. sub. price $12 for Canada and US. Please query for other countries.; per copy $3 for Canada and US. Please query for other countries.; sample $3 for Canada and US. Please query for other countries. Back issues: $2 or $3 (as per original price) for Canada and US. Please query for other countries. 24pp. Reporting time: 3 months. Simultaneous submissions accepted: No. Publishes 50% of manuscripts submitted. Payment: contributor's copy. Copyrighted, reverts to author. Pub's reviews: approx 16 in 2009. §poetry. Subjects: Arts, Poetry.

Jonkro Books, 244 Madison Ave., Suite 4200, New York, NY 10016, Tel: 866-588-0504, Fax: 866-219-4331, info@jonkrobooks.com, www.jonkrobooks.com. 2009. Pub'd 1 title 2009; expects 1 title 2011. 1 title listed in the *Small Press Record of Books in Print* (36th Edition, 2010-11).

Jon's Adventure Productions, Jon Frear, PO Box 901221, Sandy, UT 84090-1221, 801-647-5645. 2007. News items, non-fiction. "We publish a book each year detailing information from our production of "Jon's Adventure" Show. Episode and location info;dates; etc..." avg. press run 1000. Pub'd 1 title 2009; expects 1 title 2010, 1 title 2011. 1 title listed in the *Small Press Record of Books in Print* (36th Edition, 2010-11). Discounts: 10% off with Jon's Adventure Card. www.jonsadventureclub.com. 50pp. Reporting time: We do not accept manuscripts, only on-location prospects. Simultaneous submissions accepted: No. Publishes 1% of manuscripts submitted. Payment: In-house editors only. No outside submissions. Does not copyright for author. Subjects: Animals, Family, Handicapped, Nature, Utah.

Josiah Elisha Publishing, LLC, Denessa Luckett, P.O. Box 127, Indianapolis, IN 46206, 317 423-9484, fax 317 423-9480. 1 title listed in the *Small Press Record of Books in Print* (36th Edition, 2010-11).

THE JOURNAL, Kathy Fagan, Michelle Herman, OSU Dept. of English, 164 W. 17th Avenue, 421 Denney Hall, Columbus, OH 43210-1370, 614-292-4076, fax 614-292-7816, thejournal@osu.edu. 1973. Poetry, fiction, interviews, reviews, parts-of-novels, long poems, non-fiction. "We are looking for quality poetry, fiction, nonfiction, and reviews of poetry collections." circ. 1.6M. 2/yr. Pub'd 2 issues 2009; expects 2 issues 2010, 2 issues 2011. sub. price $12; per copy $7; sample $7. Back issues: $3. 140pp. Reporting time: 3 months. Simultaneous submissions accepted: yes, if informed. Publishes 2% of manuscripts submitted. Payment: $20. Copyrighted, reverts to author. Pub's reviews: 4 in 2009. §Poetry. Ads: $100/$50. Subjects: Essays, Fiction, Interviews, Ohio, Poetry, Reviews.

THE JOURNAL (once "of Contemporary Anglo-Scandinavian Poetry"), Original Plus, Sam Smith, 18 Oxford Grove, Flat 3, Devon. EX34 9HQ, England, 01271862708; e-mail smithsssj@aol.com. 1994. Poetry, reviews. "We publish all types and length of poetry, from a ten page narrative poem by Genista Lewes in #5 to occasional haiku." circ. 150. 3/yr. Pub'd 3 issues 2009; expects 3 issues 2010, 3 issues 2011. sub. price $11 US, £7 UK; per copy $5US, £2.50 UK; sample £3. Back issues: £2. Discounts: 25%. 40xA4pp. Reporting time: 2-4 weeks. Simultaneous submissions accepted: no (but will consider previously published material). Publishes 2% of manuscripts submitted. Payment: 1 copy. Copyrighted, reverts to author. Pub's reviews: 35 in 2009. §contemporary poetry.

THE JOURNAL OF AFRICAN TRAVEL-WRITING, Amber Vogel, PO Box 346, Chapel Hill, NC 27514. 1996. Poetry, fiction, articles, art, photos, interviews, reviews, letters, non-fiction. circ. 600. 1/yr. Pub'd 2 issues 2009; expects 1 issue 2010, 1 issue 2011. sub. price $10; per copy $6; sample $6. 192pp. Reporting time: 4-6 weeks. Simultaneous submissions accepted: no. Publishes 5% of manuscripts submitted. Payment: copies. Copyrighted, reverts to author. Pub's reviews: 6 in 2009. §Africa, travel. Subjects: African Literature, Africa, African Studies, Book Reviewing, Essays, Geography, Non-Fiction, Reviews, Short Stories, Transportation, Travel.

JOURNAL OF BRITISH STUDIES, University of Chicago Press, Anna Clark, University of Minnesota, Dept. of History, 614 Soc Sci Tower, 267 19th Ave., S., Minneapolis, MN 55445, http://www.journals.uchicago.edu/JBS/home.html. 1961. "The *Journal of British Studies* is the premier journal devoted to the study of British history and culture. Our editors and board give the journal an unparalleled sweep from the medieval to the early modern, eighteenth-century, Victorian and twentieth-century periods, and provide a new interdisciplinary range. Its extensive book review section and review essays also make it the journal of record for reviews." 4/yr. Pub's reviews.

THE JOURNAL OF CALIFORNIA AND GREAT BASIN ANTHROPOLOGY, Malki Museum Press, Debra Jenkins Garcia, P.O. Box 578, Banning, CA 92220, 951-849-7289, 951-849-3549, malkipress@aol.com, malkimuseum.org. 1974. Articles, interviews, non-fiction. "Quality articles dealing with ethnography, ethno history, languages, arts, archeology and prehistory of the Native peoples of Alta and Baja California and the Great Basin region." circ. 500. 2/yr. Pub'd 2 issues 2009; expects 2 issues 2010, 2 issues 2011. sub. price 40.00; per copy 20.00; sample 20.00. Back issues: 20.00. Discounts: 20% Museum Members. 270pp. Reporting time: 30-90 daus. Simultaneous submissions accepted: No. Publishes 90% of manuscripts submitted. Copyrighted, does not revert to author. Pub's reviews: 4 in 2009. §Anthropolgy, Archeology, Native American culture, lingusitics, ethnobotanicals, history. Ads: Full page $134.00, Half page $90.00, Quarter page $45.00. Subjects: Agriculture, Animals, Anthropology, Archaelogy, Language, Myth, Mythology, Native American, Weaving.

JOURNAL OF CANADIAN POETRY, Borealis Press Limited, Frank M. Tierney, Advertising Editor; W. Glenn Clever, Business Editor; David Staines, General Editor, 110 Bloomingdale Street, Ottawa, Ont. K2C 4A4, Canada, 613-797-9299, Fax 613-798-9747. 1976. Criticism, reviews. "Concerned solely with criticism and reviews of Canadian poetry. Does *not* publish poetry per se; we are a critical journal." circ. 500. 1/yr. Pub'd 1 issue 2009; expects 1 issue 2010, 1 issue 2011. sub. price $22.20 Canada, $20.95 others; $41.30/2 years Cdn., $39 others, $56.97/3 years Cdn. $53 others; per copy $12.95; sample $5. Back issues: $5. Discounts: book wholesalers 20%. 150pp. Reporting time: 4 months. Payment: none. Copyrighted, reverts to author. Pub's reviews: 40 in 2009. §Poetry only (Canadian). Ads: inquire. Subjects: Criticism, Poetry.

JOURNAL OF CHILD AND YOUTH CARE, Gerry Fewster, Editor; Thom Garfat, Editor, Malaspina University-College, Human Services, 900 5th Street, Nanaimo, BC V9R 5S5, Canada, 250-753-3245 X2207, Fax 250-741-2224, conlin@mala.bc.ca. 1981. Poetry, fiction, articles, art, photos, reviews, non-fiction. "This journal is primarily intended for child and youth care workers and all individuals who assume the responsibility for the well being of children." circ. 375. 4/yr. Pub'd 4 issues 2009; expects 4 issues 2010, 4 issues 2011. sub. price $49.50 indiv., $71.50 instit., in Canada add GST, outside Canada, price in U.S. dollars; per copy $18 + GST in Canada, outside Canada in US dollars. Back issues: $18 + GST in Canada, outside Canada in US dollars. 106pp. Reporting time: 8 months. Simultaneous submissions accepted: yes. Payment: none. Copyrighted, does not revert to author. Pub's reviews: 1 in 2009. §Child and youth care theory and practice. Ads: write for information. Subjects: Children, Youth, Community, Family, Sexual Abuse, Social Work.

JOURNAL OF CURRICULUM THEORIZING, Caddo Gap Press, Marla Morris, 3145 Geary Boulevard, PMB 275, San Francisco, CA 94118. Articles, art, photos, criticism, reviews. "Articles, commentary, art, opinion related to curriculum theory and practice." circ. 500. 4/yr. Pub'd 4 issues 2009; expects 4 issues 2010, 4 issues 2011. sub. price $75 ind., $150 inst.; per copy $20. Back issues: $20. Discounts: 15% to subscription agencies. 160pp. Reporting time: 2 months. Simultaneous submissions accepted: no. Publishes 50% of manuscripts submitted. Payment: none. Copyrighted, reverts to author. Pub's reviews. §Curriculum theory. Ads: $200 full page. Subject: Education.

JOURNAL OF MUSIC IN IRELAND (JMI), Toner Quinn, Edenvale, Esplanade, Bray, Co Wicklow, Ireland, 00-353-1-2867292 phone/Fax, editor@thejmi.com, www.thejmi.com. 2000. Articles, interviews, satire, criticism, reviews, music, letters, news items, non-fiction. "800-7,000 word articles. Articles by Ireland's most respected composers and musicians." circ. 6000. 6/yr. Pub'd 6 issues 2009; expects 6 issues 2010, 6 issues 2011. sub. price 35 euro; per copy 4.95 euro. Back issues: 5 euro plus postage. 44pp. Reporting time: 2 weeks. Simultaneous submissions accepted: yes. Publishes 50% of manuscripts submitted. Payment: negotiated. Copyrighted, reverts to author. Pub's reviews: 12 in 2009. §Music—contemporary/classical, jazz, folk/tradition. Subjects: Ireland, Music.

JOURNAL OF MUSICOLOGY, University of California Press, John Nadas, Editor, University of California Press, 2000 Center Street, Suite 303, Berkeley, CA 94704-1223, 510-643-7154. 1972. Articles, reviews, non-fiction. "Editorial address: CB #3320, Hill Hall, University of North Carolina, Chapel Hill, NC 27599-3320." circ. 651. 4/yr. Pub'd 4 issues 2009; expects 4 issues 2010, 4 issues 2011. sub. price $42 indiv., $141 instit., $27 students (+ $20 air freight); per copy $16 indiv., $40 instit., $16 students (+ $20 air freight); sample free. Back issues: same as single copy price. Discounts: foreign subs. agent 10%, one-time order 10+ 30%, standing orders (bookstores) 1-99 40%, 100+ 50%. 128pp. Reporting time: 1-2 months. Payment: varies. Copyrighted, does not revert to author. Pub's reviews: 8-10 in 2009. Ads: $295/$220. Subject: Music.

JOURNAL OF NEW JERSEY POETS, Sander Zulauf, Editor; Debra DeMattio, Associate Editor; Emily Birx, Associate Editor; Matthew Ayres, Associate Editor; Philip Chase, Associate Editor; Sharon Nolan, Editorial Assistant; Ellen Bastante, Layout Editor; Bunny Stetz, Business Manager, County College of Morris, 214 Center Grove Road, Randolph, NJ 07869-2086, 973-328-5471, szulauf@ccm.edu. 1976. Poetry, articles, reviews. "Open to submission of poetry from present and past residents of New Jersey; no biases concerning style or subject. Reviews of books by New Jersey poets. *First New Jersey Poets Prize awarded to Stephen Dobyns in 2010.*" circ. 1M. 1/yr. Pub'd 1 issue 2009; expects 1 issue 2010, 1 issue 2011. 1 title listed in the *Small Press Record of Books in Print* (36th Edition, 2010-11). sub. price $10/issue, $16/2 issues, $16/issue libraries and institutions; per copy $10. Back issues: limited availability, details on request. Discounts: 50% booksellers. 84-90pp. Reporting time: 1 year. We accept simultaneous submissions with notice of same and notification of acceptance elsewhere. Publishes 3% of manuscripts submitted. Payment: 2 copies plus 2 issue subscription. Copyrighted, reverts to author. Pub's reviews: 10 in 2009. §Poetry. Ads: upon request. Subject: Poetry.

JOURNAL OF ORDINARY THOUGHT, Hollen Reischer, Editor; Evin Rayford, Associate Editor; Carrie Spitler, Publisher, Neighborhood Writing Alliance, 1313 East 60th Street, Chicago, IL 60637, 773-684-2742 Voice, 773-684-2744 Fax. 1991. "The Neighborhood Writing Alliance (NWA) provokes dialogue and promotes change by creating opportunities for adults in low-income Chicago neighborhoods to write, publish, and perform works about their lives. These works are published in the award-winning *Journal of Ordinary Thought (JOT)* and presented at 25-30 special events each year. For more information, visit www.jot.org." 4/yr. sub. price $25. Discounts: Email editors@jot.org for information about educator and single-issue discounts.

JOURNAL OF PALESTINE STUDIES, University of California Press, Hisham Sharabi, Editor; Linda Butler, Managing Editor, University of California Press, 2000 Center St., Suite 303, Berkeley, CA 94704-1223, 510-643-7154. 1971. Articles, reviews, news items, non-fiction. "Editorial address: Institute for Palestine Studise, 3501 M St. NW, Washington DC 20007. Copyrighted by the Institute for Palestine Studies." circ. 2965. 4/yr. Pub'd 4 issues 2009; expects 4 issues 2010, 4 issues 2011. sub. price $45 indiv., $136 inst., $25 student; per copy $12 indiv., $38 inst., $12 student; sample same as single copy. Discounts: foreign subs. agents 10%, 10+ one-time orders 30%, standing orders (bookstores): 1-99 40%, 100+ 50%. 208pp. Copyrighted, does not revert to author. Pub's reviews: approx. 40 in 2009. Ads: $295/$220. Subjects: Middle East, Political Science.

•JOURNAL OF PAN AFRICAN STUDIES, Itibari M. Zulu, Senior Editor, PO Box 24194, Los Angeles, CA 90024-0194, www.jpanafrican.com. "*The Journal of Pan African Studies* is a trans-disciplinary peer reviewed scholarly journal devoted to the intellectual synthesis of research, scholarship and critical thought on the African experience. Since our inception in 1987, we have provided an international forum for diverse scholars to advance a plethora of perspectives and theoretical paradigms relevant to the social, political, economic and cultural issues that impact the African world community. Thus, the goal of the journal is to build a transnational community of scholars, theorists and practitioners who can ask questions and pose solutions to contemporary and historical issues, based upon an affirmative African centered logic and discourse of liberation. The complexity and dynamism of the African global community warrant discussion and multifaceted engagement, hence, this journal represents a resource for informed minds to address the challenges facing the African world. We welcome your participation in this process, thus join our subscription list at no cost, contribute an article, or simply inform your colleagues of our presence." No titles listed in the *Small Press Record of Books in Print* (36th Edition, 2010-11).

JOURNAL OF PSYCHOACTIVE DRUGS, Haight-Ashbury Publications, David E. Smith MD, Executive Editor; Terry Chambers, Managing Editor, 856 Stanyan Street, San Francisco, CA 94117, 415-752-7601, Fax 415-933-8674. 1967. Articles, art, photos, non-fiction. "The *Journal of Psychoactive Drugs* is a multidisciplinary forum for the study of drugs, every issue features a variety of articles by noted researchers and theorists. ISSN 0279-1072." circ. 700. 4/yr. Pub'd 4 issues 2009; expects 6 issues 2010, 6 issues 2011. sub. price $95 (indiv.), $195 (instit.), + $35/yr airmail postage outside U.S.; per copy $25; sample $10. Discounts: 5% subscription agency. 100pp. Reporting time: 60-90 days on articles; 30 days on art for cover or book reviews. Simultaneous submissions accepted: no. Payment: $50 for cover photo/art. Copyrighted, does not revert to author. Pub's reviews: 4 in 2009. §Alcohol and other drug-related topics. Ads: $350/$275. Subjects: Alcohol, Alcoholism, Drugs, Health, Mental Health, Psychiatry, Psychology, Self-Help, Social Work, Sociology.

THE JOURNAL OF PSYCHOHISTORY, Psychohistory Press, Lloyd deMause, 140 Riverside Drive, New York, NY 10024, 212-799-2294. 1973. Articles, reviews. "Psychohistory of individuals and groups, history of childhood and family." circ. 4M. 4/yr. Pub'd 4 issues 2009; expects 4 issues 2010. sub. price $54 individual, $129 organization; per copy $13; sample $13. Back issues: $13. 110pp. Reporting time: 2 weeks. Payment: none. Copyrighted, does not revert to author. Pub's reviews: 40 in 2009. §Psychology & history. Ads: $200/$100. Subjects: History, Psychology.

Journal of Pyrotechnics (see also JOURNAL OF PYROTECHNICS), Tom Smith, Publisher; Tom Smith, Managing Editor, 8 Aragon Place, Kimbolton, Huntingdon, Cambs PE28 0JD, United Kingdom, Phone: 44 1480 860124, FAX: 44 1480 861108, email: toms@davas.co.uk, web: www.jpyro.com. Founded by the Kosankes in 1995; transferred to Tom Smith in 2008. Articles, reviews, non-fiction. "The Journal of Pyrotechnics publishes peer-reviewed, technical literature. We have three different types of publications. The *Journal of Pyrotechnics* (cf) is a peer-reviewed, technical journal published twice a year with articles in the area of pyrotechnics, including fireworks, pyrotechnic special effects, rocketry and propellants, and civilian pyrotechnics. The Journal is dedicated to the advancement of pyrotechnics through the sharing of information.The Pyrotechnic Reference Series are technical books on various pyrotechnic topics. The current titles include *The Illustrated Dictionary of Pyrotechnics*, *Lecture Notes for Pyrotechnic Display Practices*, *Lecture Notes for Pyrotechnic Chemistry*, and *Pyrotechnic Chemistry*.The Pyrotechnic Literature Series are technical books that are collections of articles by a single author on a group of articles by several articles on a single topic. There are 7 in the series *Pyrotechnic Publications by K. L. and B. J. Kosanke*, and there are 4 in the series *Pyrotechnic Publications by Dr. Takeo Shimizu*." avg. press run 500. Pub'd 1 title 2009; expects 1 title 2010, 1 title 2011. 4 titles listed in the *Small Press Record of Books in Print* (36th Edition, 2010-11). Discounts: variable. 80-400pp. Reporting time: 1 to 10 days. Simultaneous submissions accepted: Yes. Publishes 75% of manuscripts submitted. Payment: There are no payments to authors and no royalties. Does not copyright for author. Subjects: Abstracts, Book Reviewing, Forensic Science, Research, Science, Textbooks.

JOURNAL OF PYROTECHNICS, Journal of Pyrotechnics, Tom Smith, Publisher; Tin Smith, Managing Editor; Bonnie Kosanke, Former Publisher; Ken Kosanke, Former Managing Editor, 8 Aragon Place, Kimbolton, Huntingdon, Cambs PE28 0JD, United Kingdom, 44 1480 860124, FAX: 44 1480 861108, email: toms@davas.co.uk, web: www.jpyro.com. 1995. Articles, reviews, non-fiction. "*The Journal of Pyrotechnics* is dedicated to the advancement of pyrotechnics through the sharing of information. We have had authors from around the world contribute to our publication. Additionally, the journal is distributed to many countries around the world." circ. 500. 1/yr. Pub'd 1 issue 2009; expects 1 issue 2010, 1 issue 2011. 15 titles listed in the *Small Press Record of Books in Print* (36th Edition, 2010-11). sub. price $50/yr - electronic only; $50/yr - print only; $85/yr electronic and print. Multiyear discounts available; per copy $60; sample $5 - US; $10 all other countries. Back issues: price varies - see web site - currently all back issues are available. Discounts: various. 80-200pp. Reporting time: 10 to 20 days. Simultaneous submissions accepted: No. Publishes 85% of manuscripts submitted. Payment: Articles are submitted gratis. There is no payment for articles. Copyrighted, reverts to author. Pub's reviews: approx 6 in 2009. §literature on pyrotechnics. We don't offer advertising. However, we do have "sponsors" that pay $160 per issue, and they receive a complimentary copy of the issue along with their name and contact information for their business published in the Journal and listed on the back cover. Subjects: Experimental, Forensic Science, Non-Fiction, Physics, Research, Science.

JOURNAL OF REGIONAL CRITICISM, Arjuna Library Press, Count Prof. Joseph A. Uphoff Jr., Director, 1404 East Bijou Street, Colorado Springs, CO 80909-5520. 1979. Poetry, art, photos, criticism, parts-of-novels, long-poems, plays, news items, non-fiction. "The processes of Experimental Surrealism derive Free Surrealism as a parameter that applies to Objects, Annotations, and Measures such that Experimental Philosophy limits the subject to Ethical Surrealism by the Adventure. This journal is an ongoing development of mathematical theories, with associated works, presented as the Contemporary Fine Arts. It is published as a xerox manuscript copy. We cannot, at this time, pay contributors except by enhancing their reputations, but we have plans for the future that include a fair return on the investment made by a literary or artistic career. we are not directing writers and artists to compete but to compose. Thus, it is not necessary to malpractice technical focus to emulate popular, economic misconceptions. The creation of beautiful images and essays should be a sufficient accomplishment to stand on its own merits. Previous contributions are considered on a priority basis. We present criticism by quotation or annotation. In the context of performance art and choreography, various manifestations are being documented with illustrative contributions that advance the system used to graph poetic and dynamic action. The ongoing focus is upon the Eshkol-Wachman System of Movement Notation. In reference to the concepts of Douglas Davis (Art In America, 2005) there are three kinds of curatorial potential, stable antiquity, transient production, and virtual projection. The fossils of our aspiration will become the valuable relics exhibited from museum storage and archives." circ. open. 6-12/yr. Pub'd 12 issues 2009; expects 12 issues 2010, 12 issues 2011. sample price at cost. Back issues: at current cost. 4pp. Reporting time: indefinite. Payment: none. Copyrighted, reverts to author. Subjects: Arts, Criticism, Dada, Mathematics, Metaphysics, Philosophy, Photography, Physics, Surrealism.

JOURNAL OF SCIENTIFIC EXPLORATION, Stephen Braude, Editor-in-Chief; Kathleen Erickson, Managing Editor, PO Box 1190, Tiburon, CA 94920, e-mail EricksonEditorial@att.net. 1987. "Publishes original multi-disciplinary research aimed at scientific advance and the expansion of human knowledge in areas falling outside the established scientific disciplines. It is a refereed journal, providing a neutral, professional forum for discussion and debate of anomalous phenomena." circ. 3M. 4/yr. Pub'd 4 issues 2009; expects 4 issues 2010, 4 issues 2011. sub. price $75 individuals, $135 institutions; sample $23.99 at Amazon. Back issues:

All back issues up until 2 years ago free online at scientificexploration.org. Current issues available to subscribers and members,. 200pp. Simultaneous submissions accepted: no. Publishes 40% of manuscripts submitted. Copyrighted, reverts to author. Pub's reviews: 40 in 2009. §Science. Subjects: AIDS, Alternative Medicine, Anthropology, Archaelogy, Artificial Intelligence, Astronomy, Channelling, Cosmology, Energy, Ethics, Experimental, Medicine, Philosophy, Physics, Science, Space.

JOURNAL OF THE AMERICAN MUSICOLOGICAL SOCIETY, University of California Press, Joseph H. Auner, Editor; Catherine Gjerdingen, Assistant Editor, University of California Press, 2000 Center St., Suite 303, Berkeley, CA 94704-1223, 510-643-7154. 1947. Articles, reviews. "Editorial office: JAMS, Department of Music, The State University of NY at Stony Brook, Stony Brook NY 11794-5475. Copyrighted by the American Musicological Association." circ. 3045. 3/yr. Pub'd 3 issues 2009; expects 3 issues 2010, 3 issues 2011. sub. price $100 indiv., $100 inst.; per copy $34 indiv., $34 inst.; sample same as single copy. Discounts: foreign subs. agents 10%, 10+ one-time orders 30%. 180pp. Copyrighted, does not revert to author. Pub's reviews: 15 in 2009. §musicology, music history, related fields. Ads: $405/$305. Subject: Music.

JOURNAL OF THE ASSOCIATION FOR RESEARCH ON MOTHERING (JARM), Association For Research On Mothering / Demeter Press, Andrea O'Reilly Ph.D, Rm 726, Atkinson College, York University, 4700 Keele Street, Toronto, Ontario M3J 1P3, Canada, 416-736-2100 x 60366; fax 416-736-5766; http://www.yorku.ca/arm.

JOURNAL OF THE HELLENIC DIASPORA, Pella Publishing Co., A. Kitroeff, 337 West 36th Street, New York, NY 10018, 212-279-9586. 1974. Fiction, articles, art, photos, cartoons, interviews, satire, criticism, reviews, music, parts-of-novels, long-poems, collages, plays. "The magazine is concerned with the entire spectrum of scholarly, critical, and artistic work that is based on contemporary Greece." circ. 1M. 2/yr. Pub'd 2 issues 2009; expects 2 issues 2010, 2 issues 2011. sub. price Individual: domestic $20, foreign $25; Institutions: domestic $30, foreign $35; per copy $12; sample free. Back issues: $15. Discounts: jobbers & bookstores-20%. 96-112pp. Reporting time: 12 weeks. Payment: 30 offprints for articles. Copyrighted, reverts to author. Pub's reviews: 8 in 2009. §Modern Greek studies and affairs. Ads: $125/$75. Subject: Greek.

JOURNAL OF THOUGHT, Caddo Gap Press, Douglas J. Simpson, 3145 Geary Boulevard #275, San Francisco, CA 94118, 415-392-1911. 1965. Articles. *"Journal of Thought* is an interdisciplinary scholarly journal focusing on educational philosophy, featuring articles by scholars and researchers." circ. 500. 4/yr. Pub'd 4 issues 2009; expects 4 issues 2010, 4 issues 2011. sub. price $50 individuals, $100 institutions; per copy $15. 96pp. Reporting time: 2 months. Publishes 25% of manuscripts submitted. Payment: none. Copyrighted, reverts to author. Ads: $200 per page. Subject: Education.

Journey Books Publishing, Edward Knight, Editor; Donnie Clemons, Editor, 3205 Highway 431, Spring Hill, TN 37174. 1997. Fiction. "We are dedicated to publishing quality Science Fiction and Fantasy as well as speculative poetry. We currently publish anthologies of short story and novella length works. All anthologies are themed and we do have reading periods. Submissions received outside the reading periods will be returned unread. Please read our guidelines on our website before submitting." Pub'd 1 title 2009; expects 3 titles 2010, 3 titles 2011. 8 titles listed in the *Small Press Record of Books in Print* (36th Edition, 2010-11). Trade discounts are available. Reporting time: 3 months. We publish 5% of the short story submissions made to us. Payment: Short story submissions are paid at a set price per word. Copyrights for author. Subjects: Fantasy, Fiction, Juvenile Fiction, Novels, Science Fiction.

J-Press Publishing, Sid Jackson, 4796 126th St. N., White Bear Lake, MN 55110, 651-429-1819, 651-429-1819 fax, 888-407-1723, sjackson@jpresspublishing.com, http://www.jpresspublishing.com. 1998. Fiction, non-fiction. "j-Press Publishing is an independent publisher of books of both fiction and non-fiction. Our goal is to bring to the reading public the best of both fictional and non-fictional works by top-notch authors. j-Press Publishing has been in business since 1998. We publish 1-3 books a year. We have published in a variety of subject-categories: history, biography, art, psychology, mystery,literary fiction, and we've even published a cookbook. Our books are distributed nationally through all the major wholesalers to bookstores, libraries, gift shops, etc., and we also sell to the academic community (colleges and universities). We publish our books under the imprint of j-Press. We invite you to browse through our listing of books shown on our web site." avg. press run 1000. Pub'd 1 title 2009; expects 1-2 titles 2010, 1-2 titles 2011. 6 titles listed in the *Small Press Record of Books in Print* (36th Edition, 2010-11). Discounts: 40% bookstores55-60% wholesalers20% classrooms. 250-350pp. Reporting time: 2-3 wks. Simultaneous submissions accepted: No. Payment: contractual. Copyrights for author. Subjects: Fiction, Mystery.

JPS Publishing Company, Janice Brown, 1141 Polo Run, Midlothian, TX 76065, 214-533-5685 (telephone), 972-775-5367 (fax), info@jpspublishing.com. 1998. Fiction, non-fiction. "Primarily a self-help publisher for women." avg. press run 20000. Pub'd 1 title 2009; expects 1 title 2010, 3 titles 2011. No titles listed in the *Small Press Record of Books in Print* (36th Edition, 2010-11). Discounts: 40% bookstores, 67% distributor, 55% online bookstore. 250pp. Reporting time: 3 months. Simultaneous submissions accepted: Yes. Publishes

1% of manuscripts submitted. Copyrights for author. Subjects: Alternative Medicine, Literature (General), Non-Fiction, Self-Help, Singles, Vegetarianism.

JUBILAT, Robert Casper, Publisher; Cathy Park Hong, Editor; Evie Shockley, Editor, English Dept., Bartlett Hall, University of Massachusetts, Amherst, MA 01003-0515, jubilat@english.umass.edu, www.jubilat.org. 2000. Poetry, art, interviews, letters, non-fiction. circ. 2000. 2/yr. Pub'd 2 issues 2009; expects 2 issues 2010, 2 issues 2011. sub. price $14/yr.; per copy $8; sample $6. Back issues: $6. 170pp. Reporting time: 3-6 months. We accept simultaneous submissions with notification; submit online only. Publishes 2% of manuscripts submitted. Payment: 2 copies plus 1 year subscription. Copyrighted, reverts to author. Ads: $200 full page. Subjects: Arts, Interviews, Literature (General), Non-Fiction, Poetry, Reprints, Visual Arts.

Judah Magnes Museum Publications, Rebecca Fromer, Editor; Paula Friedman, Editor; Nelda Cassuto, Editor, 2911 Russell Street, Berkeley, CA 94705. 1966. Art, non-fiction. "Consideration of new volumes is suspended through 2002. Primarily art, Judaica, Western Americana, and related. Query first." avg. press run 1M. Pub'd 3 titles 2009; expects 2 titles 2010, 2 titles 2011. 16 titles listed in the *Small Press Record of Books in Print* (36th Edition, 2010-11). Discounts: upon request - contact Order Department at address above. 150-200pp. Reporting time: 6 months. Simultaneous submissions accepted: no. Publishes 15% of manuscripts submitted. Payment: varies. We do not usually copyright for author, this may change ff. 2002. Subjects: Judaism, Middle East, Poetry.

Juel House Publishers and Literary Services, Laura Williams, P.O.Box 415, Riverton, IL 62561, (217)629-9026 juelhouse@familyonline.com. 2004. Fiction, reviews. "To offer opportunity to new voices wishing to be heard, so that they may realize their potential and goals. Our prime directive is to give the world a reason to smile. We accept women's and young adult fiction short stories or novels. Recent contributors include small businesses in Rochester, Illinois." avg. press run 100. Pub'd 1 title 2009; expects 3 titles 2010, 5 titles 2011. No titles listed in the *Small Press Record of Books in Print* (36th Edition, 2010-11). Discounts: 10 -20 copies 40% 5-10 copies 15%. 80pp. Reporting time: 60 days to 90 days. Simultaneous submissions accepted: Yes. Publishes 10% of manuscripts submitted. Payment: 10% upon acceptance,advance negotiable. Does not copyright for author. Subjects: Book Reviewing, Entertainment, Family, Fiction, Humor, Interviews, Juvenile Fiction, Literary Review, Publishing, Reviews, Satire, Short Stories, Women, Young Adult.

•**JUKED,** Online at: info@juked.com. "We are looking for works of fiction and creative non-fiction running at least 2,000 words long. If you have a story that is 1,999 words long, or something that is unconventional or otherwise special in its own way, write us and we'll see what we can do.We are also looking for poems, long poems, and poetic sequences. Send us a maximum of five poems, totalling no more than ten pages. If you have twenty one-line poems or other special formats e-mail us and we'll do our best to accommodate accordingly. To submit, send an attachment (we prefer .RTF, but .DOC and .DOCX are okay too) to print@juked.com. Indicate in the subject field: Print Submission: (fiction / non-fiction / poetry) by (your name). If it goes to the regular address, and without the right subject heading, it will not be read as a submission for the print issue. Simultaneous submissions are encouraged, but please e-mail us and let us know if your submission has been picked up elsewhere. If you have something that's more or less up our alley, send it to submissions@juked.com. Be sure to indicate Submission: (genre) by (your name) in the subject line, or it could very well end up bundled with the rest of our junk mail."

Jullundur Press, Aram T. Armenian, 1001 G St., Suite 301, Sacramento, CA 95814, phone 916-449-1300, fax 916-449-1320, email goldentemplepub.com, web: www.johnposwall.com. 2003. "Publish legal fiction works of John M. Poswall including *The Lawyers: Class of '69* and most recentlt *The Altar Boys.*" 2 titles listed in the *Small Press Record of Books in Print* (36th Edition, 2010-11). Copyrights for author. Subjects: Drama, Fiction, Law, Literature (General).

Junction Press, Mark Weiss, PO Box F, New York, NY 10034-0246, 212-942-1985. 1991. Poetry. "Modernist or postmodernist poetry, non-academic. Long, even book length poems welcomed. Recent books by Mervyn Taylor, Richard Elman, Susie Mee, Stephen Vincent, Ira Beryl Brakner, Rochelle Owens, Armand Schwerner, Gloria Gervitz (bilingual), and *Across the Line/ Al otro lado: The Poetry of Baja California*, a bilingual anthology. Increasingly interested in Latin American poetry." avg. press run 1M. Pub'd 1 title 2009; expects 3 titles 2010, 3 titles 2011. 16 titles listed in the *Small Press Record of Books in Print* (36th Edition, 2010-11). Discounts: bookstores 40%, standing orders 20%. 96pp. Reporting time: 3 months. Simultaneous submissions accepted: no. Payment: 10% paid in copies of first print, 8% thereafter. Copyrights for author. Subject: Poetry.

JUNIOR STORYTELLER, Storycraft Publishing, Vivian Dubrovin, PO Box 205, Masonville, CO 80541, 970-669-3755 phone/Fax, vivdub@aol.com, www.storycraft.com. 1994. Fiction, articles, non-fiction. "Shipping address: 8600 Firethorn Drive, Loveland, CO 80538. Newsletter/activity guide for young storytellers, age 9-12, in schools, libraries, camps and youth organizations. Each issue on theme, see website (Welcome Page) for upcoming themes. Purchased Pony Papers (for horse issue) and Meet the Fuzzybodies (for draw & tell) from Bea Caidy; Tandem Tale from Carol Rehme." circ. 500 in print edition. Also available in an online edition. 4/yr. Pub'd 4 issues 2009; expects 4 issues 2010, 4 issues 2011. sub. price $15.95 print edition. $9.95 online edition. $21.95 both editions.; per copy $4; sample $4 (plus 2 stamps postage). Back issues: see website for availability (About Us Page). Discounts: subscription discount for class and clubs 20%, single copy bulk rate (15+) $2. 8pp. Reporting time: query for assignment. Simultaneous submissions accepted: no. Payment: varies. Copyrighted, reverts to author. Pub's reviews: 2 in 2009. §Books for young readers on storytelling or related topics; no adult or teacher materials. Ads: do not currently use ads, but would be interested in storytelling products kids can use. Subjects: Children, Youth, Crafts, Hobbies, Education, Storytelling, Young Adult.

Juniper Creek Publishing, Inc., Ellen Hopkins, P.O. Box 2205, Carson City, NV 89702, 775 849-1637 (voice), 775 849-1707 (fax), jcpi@junipercreekpubs.com, www.junipercreekpubs.com. 2002. avg. press run 3500. Pub'd 1 title 2009; expects 2 titles 2010, 3 titles 2011. No titles listed in the *Small Press Record of Books in Print* (36th Edition, 2010-11). Discounts: retail discount 40%classroom, library discount 20%. 64pp.

Jupiter Scientific Publishing, Gezhi Weng, Stewart Allen, c/o Weng, 415 Moraga Avenue, Piedmont, CA 94611-3720, 510-420-1015, admin@jupiterscientific.org, www.jupiterscientific.org. 1996. Non-fiction. "Jupiter Scientific Publishing specializes in popular science books. For additional information check the website." avg. press run 2M. Expects 1 title 2011. 2 titles listed in the *Small Press Record of Books in Print* (36th Edition, 2010-11). Discounts: 2-3 20%, 4-7 25%, 8-11 30%, 12-15 35%, 16-47 40%, 48+ 45%. 300pp. Reporting time: 1 month. Simultaneous submissions accepted: yes. Publishes 2% of manuscripts submitted. Payment: 10%. Copyrights for author. Subject: Science.

Just Sisters Publications, Rhonda Rhea Byrd, P.O. Box 26071, Dayton, OH 45426, Telephone: (937) 369-7902; Fax: (937) 461-6865. 2007. Poetry, plays, non-fiction. "Just Sisters Publications publishes poetry and other African American historical material. It is our goal to tell the stories of unsung individuals from a historica perspective." Expects 1 title 2010, 2 titles 2011. No titles listed in the *Small Press Record of Books in Print* (36th Edition, 2010-11). Reporting time: 30 days. Simultaneous submissions accepted: Yes. Publishes 10% of manuscripts submitted. Copyrights for author. Subjects: African Literature, Africa, African Studies, African-American, Civil Rights, Civil War, Education, Family, History, Parenting, Poetry, Spiritual.

K

KABBALAH, Yehuda Berg, Michael Berg, 1062 S. Robertson Boulevard, Los Angeles, CA 90035, 310-657-5404, Fax 310-657-7774, kabbalahpublishing@kabbalah.com, www.kabbalah.com. 1996. Fiction, articles, photos, interviews, criticism, reviews, letters, news items, non-fiction. "Regular contributors are: Paul William Roberts, Mitch Sisskind, Kerry Madden-Lunsford, Barbara Einzig, and Ann Hirsch." circ. 8M. 4/yr. Pub'd 4 issues 2009; expects 4 issues 2010, 4 issues 2011. sub. price $12; per copy $5; sample free. Back issues: none. Discounts: available. 42pp. Simultaneous submissions accepted: no. Publishes 10% of manuscripts submitted. Payment: yes. Copyrighted, does not revert to author. Pub's reviews: 3 in 2009. §Spiritual, anti-aging medicine, immortality. Ads: $684/$363/$219 1/4 page/$164 1/8 page. Subjects: Business & Economics, Family, Motivation, Success, Relationships, Reviews, Self-Help, Spiritual, Women.

KAIROS, A Journal of Contemporary Thought and Criticism, Hermes House Press, Alan Mandell, Richard Mandell, 113 Summit Avenue, Brookline, MA 02446-2319. 1981. Poetry, fiction, articles, art, photos, interviews, criticism, reviews, long-poems, concrete art, non-fiction. "Not currently reading unsolicited material. Volume I, No. 3 focused on the meaning and experience of learning. Vol. I, No. 4 focused on German culture and society in America. Vol. II, No. 1 focused on the writings of Ernest Becker. Vol. II, No. 2 included materials on technology and poetry-in-translation. Poetry, fiction and artwork are encouraged. Please include SASE." circ. 500. 2/yr. Pub'd 2 issues 2009; expects 2 issues 2010, 2 issues 2011. sub. price $11 individual, $15 institutions; per copy $6 + $1 p/h; sample $6 + $1 p/h. Discounts: available upon request. 120pp. Reporting time: 4-8 weeks. Payment: copies. Copyrighted, reverts to author. Pub's reviews: 2 in 2009. §See past issues for tone, scope and direction. Ads: on exchange basis only. Subjects: Philosophy, Sociology.

Kakibubu Media Limited, Thomas Schmidt, 7A Willy Commercial Building, 28-36 Wing Kut Street, Sheung Wan, Hong Kong, +852 2557 3742, +852 2617 3742, tschmidt@kakibubu.com, www.kakibubu.com. 2006. Fiction, art, cartoons. "Kakibubu Media Limited publishes the "Bumbling Traveller" Adventure Series—a book series that seeks to promote environmental and cultural awareness through entertaining mysteries and adventures!" avg. press run 2000. Expects 2 titles 2010, 2 titles 2011. 2 titles listed in the *Small Press Record of Books in Print* (36th Edition, 2010-11). 100pp. Reporting time: Manuscripts not accepted at this time. Simultaneous submissions accepted: No. Publishes 1% of manuscripts submitted. Does not copyright for author.

Subjects: Anthropology, Archaelogy, Architecture, Asian-American, Cartoons, Conservation, Culture, Education, Environment, Global Affairs, Indigenous Cultures, Multicultural, Mystery, Sports, Outdoors, Travel, Wildlife.

KALDRON, An International Journal Of Visual Poetry, Karl Kempton, Karl Young, Harry Polkinhorn, 2740 Grell Lane, Oceano, Halcyon, CA 93445, 805-489-2770, www.thing.net/~grist/l&d/kaldron.htm. 1976. Poetry. "*KALDRON* is North America's longest running visual poetry magazine. Its on-line version opened on Bastille Day, 1997. Sections include 1) Selections from the Kaldron Archive: Number 21/22 and First Visualog Show, 1979; 2) Volume Two Continuing on-line issue of the magazine: samples from Fall, 1997 for Kaldron Wall Archives; 3) A Kaldron Wall Ancestor: Chumash Rock Painting showing a solar eclipse. 4) SURVEYS: A - Individual Poets: Avelino de Araujo; Doris Cross; Klaus Peter Dencker; Scott Helms; d.a.levy (includes visual poetry, book art, paintings, lexical poetry: a - holistic approach to this major figure); Hassan Massoudy; bpNichol (includes a wide variety of poems, continuation of TTA project, and commentary); Kenneth Patchen; Marilyn R. Rosenberg; Alain Satie; Carol Stetser; thalia; Edgardo Antonio Vigo (first instalments of a joint memorial to this great and typically unrecognized) Argentine polymath, shown in conjunction with Postypographika; B - Group Surveys: Lettriste Pages; A Collective Effort of Australian Visual Poets; A Workshop with Hungarian Visual Poets; U.S. and Canadian Pages for Nucleo Post Arte's VI Biennial; Festival of Experimental Art and Literature, Mexico City, November, 1998; FREE GRAPHZ: Meeting place for graffiti art and visual poetry. Much more including numerous essays by Karl Young who is also the site Webmaster. Policy change due to poets not paying attention to previous submission guidelines: by invitation only." circ. web-www. sub. price donations accepted; per copy $20; sample all back issues are $20 each, limit of 4 per order. Back issues: limited number of sets available, contact publisher. Reporting time: 2 weeks to 1 month. Simultaneous submissions accepted: yes. Publishes 2% of manuscripts submitted. Payment: none. Copyrighted, reverts to author. Pub's reviews. §Visual poetry, language art publications, art and poetry. No ads. Subjects: Arts, Avant-Garde, Experimental Art, Book Arts, Communication, Journalism, Criticism, Culture, Dada, Design, Futurism, Graphics, Language, Literary Review, Literature (General), Poetry, Visual Arts.

KALEIDOSCOPE: Exploring the Experience of Disability through Literature & the Fine Arts, Gail Willmott, Editor-in-Chief, United Disability Services, 701 S. Main Street, Akron, OH 44311-1019, 330-762-9755, 330-379-3349 (TDD), Fax 330-762-0912, mshiplett@udsakron.org, pboerner@udsakron.org, www.udsakron.org. 1979. Poetry, fiction, articles, art, photos, interviews, satire, reviews, parts-of-novels, non-fiction. "We publish fiction, poetry, and visual arts that capture and reflect the experience of disability. Also critical essays and book reviews, photo essays, interviews, personal experience narratives. Established writers/artists featured along with new promising writers. *Kaleidoscope* presents works that challenge stereotypical perceptions of people with disabilities by offering balanced realistic images." circ. 2M. 2/yr. Pub'd 2 issues 2009; expects 2 issues 2010, 2 issues 2011. sub. price $10 indiv., $20 instit., postage included - Distributed by The University of Akron Press - To subscribe call 1-800-247-6553 or uapress@uakron.edu; per copy $6 ($12 International, payable in US currency); sample $6 to cover p/h. Back issues: $6. Discounts: none. 64pp. Reporting time: acknowledgment of manuscripts within 2 weeks; status of manuscripts within 2 weeks of deadline dates, March 1 and August 1. Simultaneous submissions accepted: yes. Publishes 10% of manuscripts submitted. Payment: contributors receive two complimentary copies and $10-$25 and up to $150 for commissioned work. Copyrighted, reverts to author. Pub's reviews: none in 2009. §Disability-related short story, poetry, visual art, books. Subjects: Book Reviewing, Criticism, Disabled, Essays, Fiction, Humor, Non-Fiction, Poetry, Prose, Reviews.

Kali Press, Cynthia A. Bellini, Managing Director, PO Box 5491, Eagle, CO 81631-5491, ciao-cyn@yahoo.com. 1990. Poetry, fiction, art, photos, interviews, non-fiction. avg. press run 20-25M. Pub'd 2 titles 2009; expects 3 titles 2010, 4 titles 2011. 5 titles listed in the *Small Press Record of Books in Print* (36th Edition, 2010-11). Discounts: open for discussion. 100pp. Reporting time: 45 days. Simultaneous submissions accepted: yes. Publishes 5% of manuscripts submitted. Payment: open for discussion. Copyrights for author. Subjects: Australia, Disease, Environment, Health, How-To, Medicine, Non-Fiction, Pets, Reference, Water.

KALLIOPE, A Journal of Women's Literature and Art, Mary Sue Koeppel, Editor, FCCJ - South Campus, 11901 Beach Blvd., Jacksonville, FL 32246, 904-646-2081, www.fccj.org/kalliope. 1979. Poetry, fiction, articles, art, photos, interviews, criticism, reviews, plays. "*Kalliope* devotes itself to women in the arts by publishing their work and providing a forum for their ideas and opinions. Besides introducing the work of many new writers, *Kalliope* has published the work of established writers such as Marge Piercy, Denise Levertov, Susan Fromberg Schaffer, Kathleen Spivak, Enid Shomer, and Ruth Moon Kempher. Most issues include an interview with a prominent woman in the arts. Recent interviewees with *Kalliope* are Joyce Tenneson, Joy Harjo, Rosemary Daniell, Ruth Stone, and Eavan Boland. We have featured the photographs of Diane Farris, Joanne Leonard, Layle Silbert, and Anna Tomczak; the sculpture of Margaret Koscielny and Ella Tulin; the ceramics of Marilyn Taylor and Patti Warashina; and paintings and drawings by a large number of artists including Renee Faure, Marcia Isaacson, Mary Nash, Susan Zukowsky, and Mary Joan Waid. Theme issues have been devoted to women over 60; women under 30; women with disabilities; translations; Florida writers and artists; humor; women portraying men; the spiritual quest; women's body images; family; secrets; men speak to women; prose poetry and flash fiction; desire.'' circ. 1.6M. 2/yr. Pub'd 3 issues 2009; expects 2 issues 2010, 2 issues 2011. sub. price $16; per copy $7 recent issues before 2002; sample $4 pre-1987 issues, $7 issues (before 2002), $9 after 2002. Back issues: $7 recent, $4 pre-1987. Discounts: 40% to bookstores and distributors. 120pp. Reporting time: 3-6 months. Simultaneous submissions accepted: no. Publishes 10% of manuscripts submitted. Payment: copies or subscription, when possible, a small payment. Copyrighted, rights revert to author if requested for purposes of republication. Pub's reviews: 20 in 2009. §Books of poetry, novels, short stories. No ads. Subjects: Arts, Feminism, Women.

Kallisti Publishing, Anthony Michalski, 332 Center Street, Wilkes-Barre, PA 18702, 877-444-6188. 2000. Non-fiction. ""The Books You Need to Read to Succeed" - Kallisti Publishing specializes in the personal development books, e-books, and audio programs.'' avg. press run 2000. Pub'd 4 titles 2009; expects 8 titles 2010, 8 titles 2011. 13 titles listed in the *Small Press Record of Books in Print* (36th Edition, 2010-11). Discounts: Please contact Kallisti Publishing for a copy of our terms & conditions. 250pp. Reporting time: Two weeks. Simultaneous submissions accepted: Yes. 20. Copyrights for author. Subjects: Philosophy, Psychology, Self-Help.

Kamini Press, Henry Denander, Ringvagen 8, 4th floor, SE-11726 Stockholm, Sweden, editor@kamini-press.com, http://www.kaminipress.com. 2007. Poetry, art. ''Poetry collections by Glenn W. Cooper, Samuel Charters, Gerald Locklin, Ronald Baatz, Tom Kryss and t. kilgore splake are the first six titles by Kamini Press.'' avg. press run 200. Pub'd 2 titles 2009; expects 2 titles 2010, 2 titles 2011. 6 titles listed in the *Small Press Record of Books in Print* (36th Edition, 2010-11). 36pp. Reporting time: We don't take submissions at the moment. Copyrights for author. Subject: Poetry.

KARAMU, Olga Abella, Department of English, Eastern Illinois Univ., Charleston, IL 61920, 217-581-6297. 1966. Poetry, fiction, collages, non-fiction. ''Poems should be no longer than 3 pages; short stories no more than 3500 words. Submit no more than 5 poems or 1 story or essay at a time. We are looking for material that will interest a sophisticated, college-educated audience. We advise aspiring contributors to purchase and examine a sample issue ($8, $4) to see what kind of material we like. Some recent contributors, poetry: Jackie Bartley, Philip Williams, Barbara Daniels, Jae Newman, Bonnie Manion, Carlos Ponce-Melendez. Prose: Pappi Thomas, Patricia Brieschke, Richard Thieme, Mary Lynn Reed, Geer Austin, Kathleen Spivack.'' circ. 500. 1/yr. Pub'd 1 issue 2009; expects 1 issue 2010, 1 issue 2011. sub. price $8.00; per copy $8.00; sample $8.00. Back issues: $4. Discounts: $60 for 10 copies of current issue. 150pp. Reporting time: initial screening 4-6 months, promising material may be held up to 8 months for final decisions. We do get behind, so please be patient! Simultaneous submissions no longer accepted. Publishes 8-10% of manuscripts submitted. Payment: 1 contributor's copy, pre-publication discount on additional copies. Copyrighted, reverts to author. Subjects: Essays, Fiction, Poetry.

Kar-Ben Publishing, Inc., Joni Sussman, 241 First Avenue North, Minneapolis, MN 55401, 800-4KARBEN, www.karben.com. 1975. ''A division of Lerner Publishing Group. Juveniles on Jewish themes—fiction, holiday stories, preschool and primary level.'' avg. press run 10M. Pub'd 15 titles 2009; expects 15 titles 2010, 15 titles 2011. 47 titles listed in the *Small Press Record of Books in Print* (36th Edition, 2010-11). Discounts: 40% to trade; 25% on quantity orders to schools; up to 50% to major distributors. 32-48pp. Reporting time: 4-6 weeks. Simultaneous submissions accepted: yes. Publishes 1% of manuscripts submitted. Payment: flat rate or royalty based on net sales. Copyrights for author. Subjects: Children, Youth, Cooking, Folklore, Judaism, Religion.

Katabasis, 10 St Martins Close, London NW1 0HR, United Kingdom, Telephone and fax +44 (0)20 7485 3830. ''Katabasis has published pamphlets since 1967 and books since 1989, both poetry and prose. We publish English poetry and bilingual editions of Latin American poetry. The latter may have introductions, notes and pictures to set the poems in context. Besides publishing one of the best known Chilean poets now living in London, we are enthusiastic publishers of the poetry of Nicaragua, a country famous for its poets. Katabasis' latest Latin American title is from Mexico: Zapatista Stories by Subcomandante Marcos. As well as looking abroad, Katabasis is strongly attached to its home in London and to its native English landscape, language and radical tradition. We publish a distinctive list of English poetry We are local and internationalist, wanting down-to-Earth poetry, that is both rooted in a particular place and history, and speaks beyond them.'' No titles listed in the *Small Press Record of Books in Print* (36th Edition, 2010-11).

•**Kehot Publication Society,** 291 Kingston Ave., Brooklyn, NY 11213, 718 778 0226. 1942. ''Kehot Publication Society and Merkos Publications, the publishing divisions of the Lubavitch movement, were established in 1942 by the sixth Lubavitcher Rebbe, Rabbi Yosef Yitzchak Schneersohn. Under the leadership of his successor, Rabbi Menachem M. Schneerson, the Lubavitch publishing houses have brought Torah education to nearly every Jewish community in the world, and are the world's largest publisher of Jewish literature. More than 100,000,000 volumes have been disseminated to date in Hebrew, Yiddish, English, Russian, Spanish, French, Italian, Portuguese, Dutch, German, Farsi and Arabic.'' No titles listed in the *Small Press Record of Books in Print* (36th Edition, 2010-11).

Keiki O Ka Aina Press, Dr. Vicki Draeger, Editor-in-Chief; Dr. Gail Bellamy, Managing Editor; Linda Funk, Chair, Editorial Advisory Board; Momi Akana, Publisher; Dr. Ann Lee, Member, Editorial Advisory Board; Victoria Bence, Member, Editorial Advisory Board, P.O. Box 880887, Pukalani, HI 96788, 808-218-5300. 2000. Poetry, fiction, non-fiction. "Our press focuses on educational, inspirational, fiction, non-fiction, educational curriulum and poetry that appeals to children, youth, young adults their parents and grandparents. We are interested in intergenerational work, creative work that supports healthful living, as well as academic, physical, and social emotional development. No unsolicited manuscripts at this time, please." avg. press run 500. Pub'd 2 titles 2009; expects 4 titles 2010, 4 titles 2011. No titles listed in the *Small Press Record of Books in Print* (36th Edition, 2010-11). Discounts: Industry standard; contact us. 20pp. Reporting time: three months. Simultaneous submissions accepted: No. Payment: negotiated. Copyrights for author. Subjects: Adolescence, Aging, Ecology, Foods, Education, Family, Fiction, Food, Eating, Hawaii, Indigenous Cultures, Nutrition, Poetry, Young Adult.

•**Kelly Writers House,** 3805 Locust Walk, Philadekphia, PA 19104. No titles listed in the *Small Press Record of Books in Print* (36th Edition, 2010-11).

THE KELSEY REVIEW, Edward Carmien, Editor; Holly-Katharine Mathews, Editor, Mercer County Community College, PO Box B, Trenton, NJ 08690. 1988. Poetry, fiction, articles, art, cartoons, interviews, satire, criticism, parts-of-novels, long-poems, plays, non-fiction. "2,000 wds max/query. Must live or work in Mercer County, NJ to contribute." circ. 2000. 1/yr. Pub'd 1 issue 2009; expects 1 issue 2010, 1 issue 2011. sub. price free. 90pp. Reporting time: Annual deadline May 1; reads in mid-summer, reports no later than August. Simultaneous submissions accepted: no. Publishes 10% of manuscripts submitted. Payment: 5 copies of journal. Copyrighted, reverts to author. Pub's reviews: none in 2009. §Open. Ads: Sponsors welcome. Subjects: Fiction, Literary Review, Non-Fiction, Poetry.

Kelsey St. Press, Rena Rosenwasser, Editor,Founder; Patricia Dienstfry, Editor,Founder; Ramsay Breslin, Editor,Office Manager,Print Publicist; Hazel White, Editor,Bookkeeper,Book Fulfillment; Amber DiPietra, Editor,Blog Meister,E-publicist; Tiff Dressen, Editor,Public Relations Officer,Book Fulfillment, 2824 Kelsey St., Berkeley, CA 94705, 510-845-2260, Fax 510-548-9185, info@kelseyst.com, www.kelseyst.com. 1974. Poetry, fiction, art. "Kelsey Street publishes experimental poetry and fiction by women. We have in the past published collaborations between writers and visual artists. In terms of collaborations, we see ourselves moving in new directions to be announced on our website later in the year. In the meantime, we suggest you query us, preferably by email, after January first, 2009. By then we should have a better idea of when and whether we will be accepting unsolicited manuscripts. When the time comes, we will post our guidelines for submission on our website." avg. press run 1000. Pub'd 1 title 2009; expects 2 titles 2010, 2 titles 2011. 38 titles listed in the *Small Press Record of Books in Print* (36th Edition, 2010-11). Discounts: 40% to the trade. 48pp. Reporting time: 4 months. Payment: in copies or 10% of the gross price. Copyright retained by author unless otherwise agreed. Subjects: African-American, Arts, Asian-American, Avant-Garde, Experimental Art, Disabled, Feminism, Fiction, Literature (General), Poetry, Women.

The Kent State University Press, Susan Cash, Editor, PO Box 5190, 307 Lowry Hall, Kent, OH 44242-0001, 330-672-8098 phone, 330-672-3104 fax. 1965. Non-fiction. No titles listed in the *Small Press Record of Books in Print* (36th Edition, 2010-11).

Kenyette Productions, Kenyette Adrine-Robinson, 20131 Champ Drive, Euclid, OH 44117-2208, 216-486-0544. 1976. Poetry, art, photos. "Permanent address: 4209 E. 186th Street, Cleveland, OH 44122 (216) 752-4069. Past president, Urban Literary Arts Workshop (ULAW). Member: Verse Writers Guild of Ohio. Board member: Poets' & Writers' League of Greater Cleveland; past Treasurer of the Writers Center of Greater Cleveland 1999-2000." avg. press run 500. Expects 1 title 2010, 2 titles 2011. 4 titles listed in the *Small Press Record of Books in Print* (36th Edition, 2010-11). Discounts: non-profit organizations, bookstores, warehouses, vendors, public schools, artists, retail outlets. 48pp. Reporting time: 2 months. Simultaneous submissions accepted: yes. Publishes 10% of manuscripts submitted. Payment: negotiable. Copyrights for author. Subjects: African Literature, Africa, African Studies, Autobiography, Children, Youth, Haiku, Ohio, Photography, Poetry, Religion, Women.

THE KENYON REVIEW, David Lynn, Editor; Sergei Lobonov-Rostovsky, Associate Editor; David Baker, Poetry Editor; Geeta Kothari, Fiction Editor; John Kinsella, International Editor; G.C. Waldrep, Editor at Large, Finn House, 102 W. Wiggin Street, Gambier, OH 43022, 740-427-5208, Fax 740-427-5417, kenyonreview@kenyon.edu. 1939. Poetry, fiction, interviews, criticism, reviews, parts-of-novels, long-poems, plays, non-fiction. "We *strongly* discourage 'blind' submissions from writers who have not read a recent issue of the magazine. Bookstore distributors are Ingram and Media Solutions. Issue dates are Dec. (Winter), March (Spring), June (Summer), and Sept. (Fall). Reading period is September 15 - January 15 each year. Submissions must be sent using KR's online program at www.kenyonreview.org. Do not send submissions via email. Please note that unsolicited submissions will *not* be accepted through regular mail." circ. 6,500. 4/yr. Pub'd 4 issues 2009; expects 4 issues 2010, 4 issues 2011. sub. price $30 individuals, $35 libraries; per copy $10 single,$12 double issue includes domestic postage and handling. International shipping add $5. Back issues may be purchased online.; sample $12 includes postage. Back issues: Visit www.kenyonreview.org to purchase back issues. Discounts: agency 15%. 200pp. Reporting time: 3-4 months. Simultaneous submissions accepted: No. Publishes 3% of manuscripts submitted. Payment: $30 prose, $40 poetry (per printed page). Copyrighted, reverts to author. Pub's reviews: 3 in 2009. §Literature, criticism. Ads: $250 for half-page; $375 full-page; $450 for inside front or inside back cover. Frequency discounts available. 15% discount on ads for agencies and university presses. Subjects: Criticism, Culture, Drama, Essays, Experimental, Fiction, Interviews, Literary Review, Literature (General), Multicultural, Non-Fiction, Poetry, Reviews, Short Stories, Translation.

Keokee Co. Publishing, Inc. (see also **SANDPOINT MAGAZINE**), Billie Jean Plaster, Editor, PO Box 722, Sandpoint, ID 83864, 208-263-3573, www.keokee.com. 1990. Articles, art, photos, cartoons, interviews, news items, non-fiction. "Accept manuscripts. Interested in non-fiction, history, regional, outdoors, recreation guides. No fiction or poetry." avg. press run 5M. 17 titles listed in the *Small Press Record of Books in Print* (36th Edition, 2010-11). Discounts: STOP orders 40% retail 40%, wholesale/jobbers 50%. 224pp. Reporting time: 2 months. Simultaneous submissions accepted: yes. Publishes 1% of manuscripts submitted. Payment: depends, negotiable. Copyrights for author. Subjects: Conservation, Environment, History, Idaho, Montana, Non-Fiction, Pacific Northwest, Sports, Outdoors, Transportation.

KEREM: Creative Explorations in Judaism, Gilah Langner, Sara R. Horowitz, 3035 Porter Street, NW, Washington, DC 20008, 202-364-3006, langner@erols.com, www.kerem.org. 1992. Poetry, articles, art, photos, interviews, non-fiction. circ. 2M. 1/yr. Pub'd 1 issue 2009; expects 1 issue 2010, 1 issue 2011. sub. price $8.50; per copy $8.50; sample $8.50. 128pp. Reporting time: 3-5 months. Simultaneous submissions accepted: yes. Publishes 20% of manuscripts submitted. Payment: none. Copyrighted, reverts to author. Ads: $100/$50. Subjects: Ethics, Judaism, Literature (General), Religion, Spiritual.

THE KERF, Ken Letko, 883 W. Washington Boulevard, Crescent City, CA 95531, 707-465-2360, Fax 707-464-6867. 1995. Poetry. "The editors especially encourage themes related to humanity and/or environmental consciousness, but are open to diverse subjects. Poems: 1-2 pages, no more than 7 pages accepted. Contributors: George Keithley, John Bradley, Philip Dacey, Susan Clayton-Goldner, Meg Files, Ray Gonzalez, and Susan Thomas." circ. 300-400. 1/yr. Pub'd 1 issue 2009; expects 1 issue 2010, 1 issue 2011. sub. price $5; per copy $5; sample $5. Back issues: $5. Discounts: none. 54pp. Reporting time: 2 months. Simultaneous submissions accepted: no. Publishes 3% of manuscripts submitted. Payment: 1 copy. Copyrighted, reverts to author. Ads: none. Subjects: Environment, Poetry.

KESTREL: A Journal of Literature and Art, Donna J. Long, Editor; Charley Hively, Managing Editor; Elizabeth Savage, Poetry Editor; Suzanne Heagy, Fiction Editor; Donna J. Long, Non-Fiction Editor; Marian Hollinger, Art Editor; Kristin Scharnhorst, Media Editor, Fairmont State University, 1201 Locust Avenue, Fairmont, WV 26554-2451, 304-367-4809, Fax 304-367-4896, e-mail kestrel@fairmontstate.edu. 1993. Poetry, fiction, art, photos, interviews, parts-of-novels, long-poems, plays, non-fiction. "Send hard copy (regular post) submissions during our reading periods: November 1-January 31 (spring issue) and May 1-July 31 (fall issue); these are postmark deadlines. Submissions received outside our reading period will be returned unread. An SASE is required for response. Submissions should be typed, double spaced, in a conventional font. Only previously unpublished work will be considered. Contributors receive two copies. Additional copies may be purchased at a discount. Address your submission to the appropriate editor (fiction, poetry, nonfiction). Electronic submissions are accepted only with prior arrangement by the appropriate editor. Simultaneous submissions are grudgingly accepted; immediate notification of a manuscript accepted elsewhere is expected. Allow three months for our response before inquiring about your submission. Do not send additional work before receiving our response to your first submission. Multiple submissions will be returned unread. Submission Services are discouraged. Restrict yourself to one submission per calendar year unless we request additional work.Poetry: *Kestrel* welcomes poems of all genres, styles, and traditions, including experimental and hybrid forms. Send 3-5 of your best poems that work well together during one of our reading periods and restrict yourself to one set of offerings per calendar year. Fiction: *Kestrel* is open to any genre of short fiction that questions assumptions and moves us to reconsider everyday life. We enjoy stories with believable plots, developed characters, consistent points-of-view, vivid and symbolic settings, true dialogue, and thought-provoking themes, though we also enjoy experimental writing that makes new the expected conventions. 5,000 words maximum; the author's name and contact information must appear on page 1. Non-Fiction: Creative non-fiction, memoir, literary essay are preferred. Subject matter may vary but attention to writing as craft and art is paramount; the attention to diction, syntax, detail should delight and surprise. We appreciate writing that makes a subject's complexity understandable and its familiarity new. We expect non-fiction to be non-fiction. Reviews and scholarship are rarely published and only when solicited; you may query. The Mary Dillow Stewart Prize is awarded annually for a story, poem, or essay published in either the fall or spring issue by an emerging writer. Award is $250 and a subscription.Visual Art: Submissions to *Kestrel* may be made in any medium. Artists must send, electronically or by disk at least twenty (20) works for consideration. Please include a selective bibliography for each submission. Image resolution should be at least

300 dpi. This will enable our staff to view and to reproduce the work in the most professional manner possible. Thematic works or series are acceptable and should be labeled as such when submitted. If written material is routinely included with the work when it is exhibited, please include this for our staff. We will also need an artists statement. It may be possible to publish some or all of the written material with the works, but if this is not possible, it will, at the least, serve as a means for the staff to make selections of work for publication.It should be understood that *Kestrel* may use images for publicity purposes. Copyright of visual examples remains with the artist. Although color reproductions will occasionally be selected, budgetary constraints requires the staff to give precedence to black and white works." circ. 600. 2/yr. Pub'd 2 issues 2009; expects 2 issues 2010, 2 issues 2011. sub. price $20.00; per copy $12.00; sample $12.00. Back issues: $12.00. 100pp. Reporting time: 3 months. Simultaneous submissions accepted: yes. Payment: 2 copies of issue. Copyrighted. Ads: none. Subjects: Appalachia, Autobiography, Biography, Diaries, Essays, Fiction, Folklore, Interviews, Non-Fiction, Photography, Poetry, Short Stories, Translation, Visual Arts.

Kettering Foundation Press (see also KETTERING REVIEW), 200 Commons Road, Dayton, OH 45459-2799, 937-434-7300. 1983. Articles. avg. press run 7.5M. Expects 2 titles 2010, 2 titles 2011. 17 titles listed in the *Small Press Record of Books in Print* (36th Edition, 2010-11). 64pp. Reporting time: 2 months. Copyrights for author. Subjects: Education, Politics, Society.

KETTERING REVIEW, Kettering Foundation Press, Robert J. Kingston, Editor-in-Chief, 200 Commons Road, Dayton, OH 45459-2799, 937-434-7300. 1983. "Designed for the intelligent lay public with special interest in deliberative democracy and the relationships between peoples and their governments, individuals and their communities and civic institutions. Non-fiction only. Requirements: Manuscripts of approx. 3M words from those working in public politics and education who can address ideas of national and international importance in an interdisciplinary and popularly readable fashion. Read a sample before submitting. Articles must be exceptionally well-written; issues usually organized around a theme. Uses 5-6 articles per issue. No footnotes. Mss. must be accompanied by SASE. No responsibility is assumed for the return of unsolicited manuscripts." circ. 8M. 2/yr. Pub'd 2 issues 2009; expects 2 issues 2010, 2 issues 2011. 5 titles listed in the *Small Press Record of Books in Print* (36th Edition, 2010-11). price per copy $7; sample $7. 64pp. Payment: copies. Copyrighted, reverts to author. Subjects: Communication, Journalism, Community, Education, Government, Media, Newspapers, Political Science, Politics, Public Affairs, Society, Sociology.

Key Publications, PO Box 1064, Santa Monica, CA 90406, 818-613-7348. 1990. Non-fiction. "First book: *Parenting Your Aging Parents - How to Guarantee and Protect Their Quality of Life, and Yours!*. Second book: *Out on Your Own - Everything You Need to Know Before, During, and After Leaving the Nest*. Home Page URL: www.KeyPubs.com." avg. press run as needed. Expects 1 title 2010, 1 title 2011. 3 titles listed in the *Small Press Record of Books in Print* (36th Edition, 2010-11). Discounts: negotiable. 300pp. Reporting time: 4 weeks with SASE. Simultaneous submissions accepted: no. Publishes 1% of manuscripts submitted. Payment: negotiable. Copyrights for author.

THE KIDS' STORYTELLING CLUB WEBSITE, Storycraft Publishing, Vivian Dubrovin, PO Box 205, Masonville, CO 80541, 970-669-3755 phone/Fax, Vivian@storycraft.com, www.storycraft.com. 1996. "Designed for young storytellers, age 9-12, in language arts or computer classes, home schooling, computer camps, etc. Check website for upcoming themes (bottom of Welcome Page). Won the 2001 Pegasus Award for 'exemplary resource for young storytellers and for those working with youth.'" circ. 2.5M. 12/yr. Pub'd 12 issues 2009; expects 12 issues 2010, 6 issues 2011. sub. price free (online). Back issues: no longer available. Discounts: none. 7pp. Reporting time: query for assignment. Simultaneous submissions accepted: no. Payment: varies by contract. Not copyrighted. Ads: would be interested in talking to companies with storytelling products. Subjects: Children, Youth, Crafts, Hobbies, Education, Storytelling, Young Adult.

Kilmog Press, Dean Havard, 378 Princes Street, Dunedin, New Zealand, New Zealand, 0061 3 4792857. 2006. Poetry, fiction, art, non-fiction. "The Kilmog Press aspires to be New Zealand's answer to the Black Sparrow Press. I hand sew and use letterpress and woodcuts. I publish new and established writers of poetry. I also want to get into reprinting underrated NZ fiction and selling it to the world in a desirable package. Likewise, I would like to publish international poets. I would like to eventually move into novels." avg. press run 75. Pub'd 7 titles 2009; expects 10 titles 2010, 10 titles 2011. No titles listed in the *Small Press Record of Books in Print* (36th Edition, 2010-11). Discounts: 1-4 20% 5 or more 40% International negotiable. 24pp. Reporting time: a few weeks. Simultaneous submissions accepted: Yes. Publishes 10% of manuscripts submitted. Payment: 10% = of wholesale price of whole run, whether I sell them or not - upfront in cash or copies. first New Zealand rights. Subjects: Arts, Essays, Fiction, Philosophy, Poetry.

King Publishing, 1801 Bush Street, Suite 300, San Francisco, CA 94109, Fax 415-563-1467. No titles listed in the *Small Press Record of Books in Print* (36th Edition, 2010-11).

Kings Estate Press, Ruth Moon Kempher, 870 Kings Estate Road, St. Augustine, FL 32086, 800-249-7485, rmkkep@bellsouth.net. 1993. Poetry, fiction, art, long-poems. "No longer accepting unsolicited manuscripts, until further notice. Have published Wayne Hogan, Michael Hathaway, Joan Payne Kincaid, John Elsberg, among others; two anthologies.'' avg. press run 200-300. Pub'd 2 titles 2009; expects 3 titles 2010, 2 titles 2011. 12 titles listed in the *Small Press Record of Books in Print* (36th Edition, 2010-11). 50-80pp. Payment: negotiated. Copyrights for author. Subjects: Poetry, Short Stories.

Kirpan Press, Alan Horvath, PO Box 2943, Vancouver, WA 98668-2943, kirpan_press@msn.com. 41 titles listed in the *Small Press Record of Books in Print* (36th Edition, 2010-11).

KMT, A Modern Journal of Ancient Egypt, Dennis Forbes, NC 28787, 828-658-3353 phone/Fax. 1990. Articles, art, photos, interviews, reviews, collages. "Focus is *Ancient Egypt*: history, art, archaeology and culture." circ. 15M. 4/yr. Pub'd 4 issues 2009; expects 4 issues 2010, 4 issues 2011. sub. price $37; per copy $9.50; sample $10 (incl. p/h). Back issues: same. Discounts: distributor 40%-50%. 88pp. Reporting time: 60 days. Payment: $50-$400. Copyrighted, reverts to author. Pub's reviews: 16-20 in 2009. §History, culture, archaeology and art of Egypt. 4-color ads: $1,500 inside cover/$1,290 full page/ $1,000 2/3 page / $795 1/2 pge / $620 1/3 page / $420 1/4 page / $350 1/6 page; black/white ads:$1,300 inside cover/$920 full page / $690 2/3 page/ $545 1/2 page /$420 1/3 page/$275 1/4 page/$230 1/6 page; discounts for multiple insertions. Subjects: Anthropology, Archaelogy, Arts, Culture, History, Middle East.

Knife in the Toaster Publishing Company, LLC, PO Box 399, Cedar, MN 55011-0399, 763-434-2422, kittpubco.com. 2002. 2 titles listed in the *Small Press Record of Books in Print* (36th Edition, 2010-11).

KNOCK MAGAZINE, Bryan Tomasovich, Editor, Antioch University Seattle, 2326 Sixth Ave., Seattle, WA 98121-1814, 206.268.4420. 2004. Poetry, fiction, articles, art, photos, cartoons, interviews, parts-of-novels, plays, concrete art, news items, non-fiction. "*Knock* is a literary arts magazine published twice a year at Antioch University Seattle. *Knock* looks at what's ahead in writing, drama, and the visual arts. We publish fiction, essays, poetry, plays, cartoons, and contemporary art, along with interviews with artists, writers, and activists, and excerpts from books and other media just released or forthcoming." circ. 500. 2/year. sub. price $16; per copy $9. 100pp. Reporting time: 3-9 months. Simultaneous submissions accepted: yes. Publishes 3% of manuscripts submitted. Payment: copies. Copyrighted, reverts to author.

Allen A. Knoll Publishers, Abby Schott, 200 W. Victoria Street, 2nd Floor, Santa Barbara, CA 93101-3627, 805-564-3377, Fax 805-966-6657, bookinfo@knollpublishers.com. 1990. Fiction, photos, non-fiction. "Not looking for new submissions at this time." avg. press run 3-10M. Pub'd 3 titles 2009; expects 3 titles 2010, 3 titles 2011. 42 titles listed in the *Small Press Record of Books in Print* (36th Edition, 2010-11). Discounts: standard. 300pp. Payment: percentage different for each book. Copyrights for author. Subjects: California, Children, Youth, Fiction, Gardening, History, Humor, Literature (General), Los Angeles, Mystery, Newspapers, Novels, Photography, Reprints, Short Stories, Visual Arts.

Knowledge Concepts Publishing (see also GLOBAL ONE MAGAZINE), Ella Patterson, 136 South Laurel Springs Drive, DeSoto, TX 75115, 972-223-1558, fax: 214-988-2867. 1991. Articles, interviews, reviews, news items. "Magazines: To disseminate information to automotive manufacturers, suppliers and the consumer.Books: To provide all people with common knowledge about women issues." Pub'd 4 titles 2009. No titles listed in the *Small Press Record of Books in Print* (36th Edition, 2010-11). Discounts: 5- 10 copies 20%11-25 copies 25%26 and above 40%. 255pp. Reporting time: approximately 7 to 10 days. Simultaneous submissions accepted: No. Publishes 8% of manuscripts submitted. Payment: 15%. Copyrights for author. Subjects: Advertising, Self-Promotion, Aromatherapy, Comics, Education, Feminism, Food, Eating, How-To, Motivation, Success, Newsletter, Newspapers, Parenting, Peace, Self-Help, Sex, Sexuality, Women.

•Knowledge Power Books, Robinson Willa, 25379 Wayne Mills Place, Suite 131, Valencia, CA 91355, 661-513-0308, 661-513-0381, www.knowledgepowerinc.com. 2007. avg. press run 1000. Pub'd 1 title 2009; expects 2 titles 2010, 4 titles 2011. 2 titles listed in the *Small Press Record of Books in Print* (36th Edition, 2010-11). Discounts: 25-99 copies 20% 100-499 copies 40 % 500-999 copies 50% 1,000-14,999 copies 60%. 24pp.

KNUCKLE MERCHANT - The Journal of Naked Literary Aggression, Lost Prophet Press, Christopher Jones, 6101 Saintsbury Drive, Apt. 432, The Colony, TX 75056-5216, 505.256.4589 knucklemerchant@hotmail.com. 2001. Poetry, fiction, articles, art, photos, interviews, satire, criticism, reviews, non-fiction. circ. 500. 2/yr. Pub'd 2 issues 2009; expects 2 issues 2010, 2 issues 2011. sub. price $20; sample $5. Reporting time: 1 month. Simultaneous submissions accepted: yes. Publishes 1% of manuscripts submitted. Payment: 1-2 copies. Not copyrighted. Pub's reviews. Ads: $50/$25/$15. Subjects: Arts, Charles Bukowski, Celtic, Fiction, Poetry, Visual Arts.

Kobalt Books, Cedric Mixon, P.O. Box 1062, Bala Cynwyd, PA 19004, 314-503-5462. 2003. Poetry, fiction, non-fiction. "Journals." avg. press run 150. Pub'd 6 titles 2009; expects 3 titles 2010, 5 titles 2011. No titles listed in the *Small Press Record of Books in Print* (36th Edition, 2010-11). Discounts: 50% discount. 120pp. Reporting time: immediately. Simultaneous submissions accepted: Yes. Publishes 20% of manuscripts submitted. Payment: 50% net receipts. Does not copyright for author. Subjects: Advertising, Self-Promotion, African Literature, Africa, African Studies, African-American, Anthology, Biography, Motivation, Success, Public Relations/Publicity, Publishing, Religion, Romance.

KOBISENA, Prakalpana Literature, P40 Nandana Park, kolkata 700 034, W.B., India. 1/yr. Pub'd 1 issue 2009; expects 1 issue 2010, 1 issue 2011. price per copy 1 IRC. 8pp.

Kodiak Media Group, Grabenhorst Rhonda, Contact Person, PO Box 1029-DB, Wilsonville, OR 97070, Fax 503-625-4087. 1989. Non-fiction. "Specializing in deafness, disability, deaf education, deaf culture, parents of deaf children, ASL and sign language." avg. press run varies. Pub'd 1 title 2009; expects 2 titles 2010, 2 titles 2011. 5 titles listed in the *Small Press Record of Books in Print* (36th Edition, 2010-11). Discounts: 1-3 0%, 5+ 30%, 10+ 40% (non returnable) FOB Wilsonville, OR. 112pp. Reporting time: varies. Payment: negotiable. Copyrights are negotiable. Subjects: Culture, Disabled, Education, Newsletter, Parenting, Sexual Abuse.

KOKAKO, Patricia Prime Ms, 42 Flanshaw Road, Te Atatu South, Auckland 0610, New Zealand, pprime@ihug.co.nz. 2001. Poetry, reviews. "Our editorial mission is to publish the best work of New Zealand and overseas writers of the short Japanese form of poetry e.g. haiku, tanka and haibun.Recent contributors: Pamela A. Babusci, Catherine Mair, Bernard Gadd, Kirsty Karkow, Michael McKlintock, Andre Surridge." circ. 150. 2/yr. Pub'd 2 issues 2009; expects 2 issues 2010, 2 issues 2011. sub. price $20; per copy $10; sample $10. Back issues: $5. Discounts: no trade discounts. 64pp. Reporting time: one week to one month. Simultaneous submissions accepted: No. Publishes 80% of manuscripts submitted. Payment: no payment for authors. Copyrighted, reverts to author. Pub's reviews: 6 in 2009. §haiku or tanka collections. No advertising. Subjects: Poetry, Reviews.

KOKORO, Rebecca Knowlton, 454 N. Chugach, Palmer, AK 99645, http://www.kokoro-press.com. 2005. Fiction, articles, photos, cartoons, interviews, non-fiction. "Kokoro is a martial arts magazine covering all aspects of training in the lives of everyday warriors. Kokoro features individuals from all ranks and styles. Each issue includes sound health and stretching tips, particularly for the over 40 martial artist. And there are interactive features and stories especially geared to kids." circ. 1000. 4/yr. Expects 4 issues 2010, 4 issues 2011. sub. price $20; per copy $5.00; sample free. Back issues: $2.95. 12pp. Pub's reviews: 3 in 2009. §Kokoro is interested in publishing any work related to traditional martial arts. Ads: inquire.

KotaPress (see also DIFFERENT KIND OF PARENTING; KOTAPRESS ONLINE JOURNALS), Kara L.C. Jones, PO Box 514, Vashon Island, WA 98070-0514, editor@kotapress.com, www.kotapress.com. 1999. Poetry, articles, art, interviews, long-poems, non-fiction. "*We take e-mail submissions only.* We do not open any email attachments, so don't bother sending those. Please note, first and foremost, we are most interested in works (poetry included) written by parents after the death of a child. But not interested in religious oriented "make it better" takes on the experience. 1) For KotaPress Online Loss Journal, please see www.kotapress.com and www.kotapress.blogspot.com for current issues, full guidelines and archive. Please note that the Loss Journal and KOTA blog publish *non-fiction* poetry, essays, articles, short stories, etc. Please read current issue at least to make sure you really want to be published with us. 2) For our "Different Kind of Parenting" series, we are also looking for *non-fiction* works. This series posts as part of the KOTA blog now. Please query via email to editor@kotapress.com with "DIFF PARENT" in the subj line of your note for more information. Thanks!" Pub'd 12 titles 2009; expects 12 titles 2010, 12 titles 2011. 6 titles listed in the *Small Press Record of Books in Print* (36th Edition, 2010-11). 160-250pp. Reporting time: 1-6 months. Simultaneous submissions accepted: no. Publishes 25% of manuscripts submitted. Payment: Free access to e-book anthologies, online journals, and free author copies for print publication. One time electronic rights w/archive rights under Kota Press, then rights revert to author. Please note we ask for archive rights—this means we do not take down materials from the website after they are published, so don't ask us to do that for you! Subjects: Book Arts, Grieving, Literary Review, Anais Nin, Non-Violence, Pacific Northwest, Peace, Poetry.

KOTAPRESS ONLINE JOURNALS, KotaPress, Kara L. C. Jones, PO Box 514, Vashon Island, WA 98070-0514. 1999. "Email submissions only. We've archived all Journals except Loss Journal. Looking for works coming from real life grief, healing, loss, transformation experiences. Real death, dying, and grief are hard enough to deal with, so please don't send fictional pieces made up for entertainment purposes! We publish accepted works on either the main site and in 2008 the Kota Blog. We will let you know where the piece showcases once acceptance is made." 6 to 12/y. 1 title listed in the *Small Press Record of Books in Print* (36th Edition, 2010-11). sub. price free online. Back issues: Full archive available at KotaPress.com. Simultaneous submissions accepted: Yes. Copyrighted, reverts to author. Pub's reviews: approx. 4 in 2009. §Works about grief and healing based on real experiences.

KRAX, Andy Robson, 63 Dixon Lane, Leeds, Yorkshire LS12 4RR, England. 1971. Poetry, fiction, articles, art, photos, cartoons, interviews. "Prefer whimsical and amusing work by both writers and artists." 1/yr. Pub'd 1 issue 2009; expects 1 issue 2010, 1 issue 2011. 7 titles listed in the *Small Press Record of Books in Print* (36th Edition, 2010-11). sub. price £3.50 ($7) incl. Postage; per copy £3.50 ($7) incl. postage; sample $1. Back issues: on request. Discounts: trade 40%. 72pp. Reporting time: 6-8 weeks. Simultaneous submissions accepted: no. Publishes 8% of manuscripts submitted. Payment: cover design only £10 ($20). Copyrighted, reverts to author. Pub's reviews: 124 in 2009. §Light-hearted poetry. Subjects: Humor, Poetry.

Krhyme Publishing Inc., Johnnie Bunting Jr., PO Box 1090, Yonkers, NY 10704-9998, 914-665-1774. 2006. Poetry, fiction. "Accept poems and short stories or parts of novels as part of compilation for books." avg. press run 1,000. Pub'd 1 title 2009; expects 1 title 2010, expects 5 titles 2008 titles 2011. 2 titles listed in the *Small Press Record of Books in Print* (36th Edition, 2010-11). Discounts: 2-4 copies 20%, 5-9 copies 30%, 10-24 copies 40%, 25-49 copies 42%, 50-74 copies 44%, 75-99 copies 46%, 100-199 copies 48%, 200 or more copies 55%. 250pp. Reporting time: 4-6 weeks. Simultaneous submissions accepted: Yes. Publishes 85% of manuscripts submitted. Payment: Will purchase manuscript outright or pay author 8-12%. Copyrights for author.

Krill Press, Kent Lucas, P.O. Box 396, Rogue River, OR 97537, 541-582-1188, info@krillpress.com, http://www.krillpress.com. 2008. Fiction. "A small independent press showcasing some of today's most promising new authors in the mystery, suspense, thriller, and crime fiction genres. Our premier title of 2009, Oregon police chief Ken Lewis' crime fiction novel "LITTLE BLUE WHALES," has been been called "A taut, potent thriller, with a deeply creepy villain," by Bill Cameron, author of "LOST DOG," and "CHASING SMOKE," and "Authentic crime fiction at its best," by Robert W. Walker, author of "DEAD ON" and "CITY OF THE ABSENT."." avg. press run 2500. Pub'd 1 title 2009; expects 5 titles 2010, 10 titles 2011. 1 title listed in the *Small Press Record of Books in Print* (36th Edition, 2010-11). Discounts: 60% off retail to Libraries, Mystery Groups, Book Clubs, and Independent Bookstores using our in-house distribution program, "Krill Direct." Standard trade discounts are 40% - 50% off retail, depending on title. 300pp. Reporting time: Two weeks. Simultaneous submissions accepted: Yes. Publishes 5% of manuscripts submitted. Payment: Five free author's copies, author royalties of %40 of net (final) profits per book sold in print or electronic editions. Copyrights for author. Subjects: Crime, Fiction, Mystery, Novels, Oregon, Pacific Northwest.

Kriya Yoga Publications, 196 Mountain Road, PO Box 90, Eastman, Quebec J0E 1P0, Canada. 1989. avg. press run 3M. Pub'd 6 titles 2009. 17 titles listed in the *Small Press Record of Books in Print* (36th Edition, 2010-11). 250pp. Simultaneous submissions accepted: yes. Payment: 10% of net revenue.

Kumarian Press, John von Knorring, Publisher; Erica Flock, Head of Marketing and Production; Jim Lance, Associate Publisher and Editor; Andrea Ciecierski, Marketing Director, 22883 Quicksilver Drive, Sterling, VA 20166, Ph: 703-996-1042, Fax: 703-661-1501, Orders: 800-232-0223, Email: kpbooks@kpbooks.com, Web: www.kpbooks.com. 1977. Non-fiction. "We are an independent publisher of scholarly works that promote international engagement and an awareness of global connectedness. Our books look at current global issues, their social, ethical, cultural, political and economic context, and ways to overcome the problems they pose. Our publications deal with globalization, poverty, environment, health, the economy, and human rights. Please consult our website www.kpbooks.com for manuscript submission guidelines." avg. press run 2000. Pub'd 13 titles 2009; expects 16 titles 2010, 20 titles 2011. 84 titles listed in the *Small Press Record of Books in Print* (36th Edition, 2010-11). Discounts: Available for bookstores and bulk purchases. 288pp. Reporting time: 30-60 days. Simultaneous submissions accepted: yes. Copyrights for author in some instances. Subjects: Agriculture, Anthropology, Archaelogy, Business & Economics, Conservation, Environment, Gender Issues, Global Affairs, Government, Hunger, Immigration, Peace, Political Science, Politics, Sociology, Third World, Minorities.

KUMQUAT MERINGUE, Christian Nelson, PO Box 736, Pine Island, MN 55963-0736, Telephone 507-367-4430, moodyriver@aol.com, www.kumquatcastle.com. 1990. Poetry, fiction, art, photos, satire, reviews. "Recent contributors: Lynne Douglass, Mark Weber, Ianthe Brautigan, Denise Duhamel, Eugene McCarthy, and Lyn Lifshin. Mostly use short poetry, rare pieces of short prose. Looking for writings that 'remind' us of the same feeling we get from reading Richard Brautigan. Also like to read things 'about' Richard Brautigan. Never any reading fees or 'contests'." circ. 600. Irregular. Expects 1 issue 2010, 1 issue 2011. sub. price $12/3 issues; per copy $6; sample $6. Back issues: usually sold to collectors at high prices. 40pp. Reporting time: 30-120 days. Simultaneous submissions accepted, but please let us know. Publishes Less than 1% of manuscripts submitted. Payment: 1 copy for each issue they appear in. Copyrighted, reverts to author. Subjects: Beat, Ernest Hemingway, Sherlock Holmes, Humor, Indians, Japan, Minnesota, Montana, New Mexico, Poetry, Sex, Sexuality, Southwest.

KUUMBA, BLK Publishing Company, Inc., Mark Haile, PO Box 83912, Los Angeles, CA 90083-0912, 310-410-0808, fax 310-410-9250, e-mail newsroom@blk.com. 1991. Poetry, long-poems. circ. 1M. 2/yr. Expects 2 issues 2010, 2 issues 2011. sub. price $7.50; per copy $4.50; sample $5.50. Back issues: $5.50. 48pp. Reporting time: 4 weeks. Simultaneous submissions accepted: yes. Publishes 30% of manuscripts submitted. Payment: none. Copyrighted, rights reverting to author varies. Pub's reviews: 2 in 2009. §Black lesbian and gay community. Ads: $260. Subjects: African-American, Black, Gay, Lesbianism, Poetry.

KWC Press, Edmund August, Editor, 851 S. 4th Street #207, Louisville, KY 40203, eaugust@insightbb.com.

2002. Poetry, fiction, parts-of-novels, long-poems, non-fiction. "We publish three chapbooks each year:one in poetry, one in fiction, and one in creative non-fiction. All of the chapbooks are chosen through contests hosted by the Kentucky Writers' Coalition. www.kentuckywriters.org." No titles listed in the *Small Press Record of Books in Print* (36th Edition, 2010-11). Copyrights for author.

L

L&L Dreamspell, Linda Houle, Non-fiction Acquisitions Editor; Lisa Rene' Smith, Fiction Acquisitions Editor, P.O. Box 1984, Friendswood, TX 77546-1984, Administrator@lldreamspell.com, www.lldreams-pell.com. 2006. Fiction, articles, interviews, non-fiction. "We are a new micro-publishing company that enjoys working with first-time authors, to help them make their dreams of being published come true. We also work with established authors, especially those who would like to try a company that employs a friendly, teamwork approach to book promotion.We publish fiction in the genres of Mystery, Suspense, Romance, Paranormal themes, and Historical topics. We also publish non-fiction in the areas of Metaphysical and Paranormal topics, and self-improvement subjects. Sylvia Dickey Smith, John Foxjohn, and Diana L Driver are three of our new rising star authors! Pauline Baird Jones is an established author of seven books who decided she would love to work with us for book number eight—we're delighted to have her on our team." avg. press run 250. Pub'd 3 titles 2009; expects 12-18 titles 2010, 18-24 titles 2011. No titles listed in the *Small Press Record of Books in Print* (36th Edition, 2010-11). Discounts: Bookstores 40% Wholesalers 55%. 275pp. Reporting time: We respond to submissions within two weeks. Simultaneous submissions accepted: Yes. Publishes 25% of manuscripts submitted. Payment: We offer a 15% net royalty on print book sales and 40% on ebook sales. No advances at this time since we are just getting started! Does not copyright for author. Subjects: Anthropology, Archaelogy, Astrology, Channelling, Crystals, Dreams, Erotica, Fiction, Futurism, Hypnosis, Metaphysics, Mystery, New Age, Occult, Romance, Supernatural.

La Alameda Press, J.B. Bryan, 9636 Guadalupe Trail NW, Albuquerque, NM 87114, 505-897-0285, www.laalamedapress.com. 1991. Poetry, fiction, non-fiction. "We are a small press with an emphasis on literature: poetry, fiction, and creative non-fiction. Kate Horsley won the "1996 Western States Book Award for Fiction" for *A Killing in New Town*, which is now in its second printing. Several other titles are also in further editions. We are distributed by the University of New Mexico Press and Small Press Distribution. We do not accept unsolicited manuscripts becuase of our committment to regional writers and kindred spirits we know and work with. This simply happens to be our mission." avg. press run 1M. Pub'd 6 titles 2009; expects 6 titles 2010. 47 titles listed in the *Small Press Record of Books in Print* (36th Edition, 2010-11). Discounts: 40% bookstores, 55% distributors, 10% libraries or schools. 100-300pp. Simultaneous submissions accepted: no. Publishes 0% of manuscripts submitted. Payment: in books (10% of print run). Copyrights for author. Subjects: Agriculture, Culture, Ecology, Foods, Feminism, Fiction, Gardening, Haiku, Health, Literature (General), Native American, New Mexico, Non-Fiction, Poetry, Southwest, Zen.

La Familia Publishing, Lanae Rivers-Woods, Director; Emma Evans, Gallery Manager, 117 Prefontaine Place South, Seattle, WA 98104, 206-291-4608. 2005. Poetry, fiction, art, photos, non-fiction. avg. press run 5000. Pub'd 1 title 2009; expects 2 titles 2010, 5 titles 2011. 1 title listed in the *Small Press Record of Books in Print* (36th Edition, 2010-11). 300-500pp. Reporting time: 6 months. Simultaneous submissions accepted: Yes. Publishes 1% of manuscripts submitted. Copyrights for author. Subjects: African-American, Alaska, Arts, Asian-American, Feminism, Fiction, Global Affairs, Homelessness, Non-Fiction, Novels, Outdoor Adventure, Pacific Northwest, Photography, Poetry, Washington (state).

•**LA PETITE ZINE,** Melissa Broder, Editor-in-Chief; D.W. Lichtenberg, Managing Editor, ONLINE AT: lapetitezine@gmail.com. "We accept e-mail submissions only. Please paste your work directly into the e-mail. If you are greatly concerned about formatting, please send an attached document in addition to the pasted text. We accept visual files in pdf, jpeg, and gif format. Include a brief bio with your submission. Please send work in all genres. And all non- or anti-genres. We consider visual work of all types. We consider personal and academic essays."

LABOUR/LE TRAVAIL, Canadian Committee on Labour History, Bryan D. Palmer, Arts Publications, FM 2005, Memorial University, St. John's, NF A1C 5S2, Canada, 709-737-2144. 1976. Articles, reviews, non-fiction. "Articles 20-60 pages, reviews 1000 words. Alvin Finkel, History, Athabasca University." circ. 1M. 2/yr. Pub'd 2 issues 2009; expects 2 issues 2010, 2 issues 2011. sub. price $25CDN, $30 US; per copy $20 CDN, $20 US; sample free. Back issues: Complete set $960 (48 issues, new subscribers $540). Discounts: 5 or more 20%. 400pp. Reporting time: 4 months. Simultaneous submissions accepted: no. Publishes 40% of manuscripts submitted. Payment: none. Copyrighted, does not revert to author. Pub's reviews: 100 in 2009.

§Labour, history, especially social. Ads: $200/$150. Subjects: History, Labor.

LADY CHURCHILL'S ROSEBUD WRISTLET, 150 Pleasant St., #306, Easthampton, MA 01027. 1996. Poetry, fiction, articles. "We do not accept email, multiple, or simultaneous submissions. Response time is three to six months. We recommend you read *Lady Churchill's Rosebud Wristlet* before submitting. You can procure a copy from us or from assorted book shops. We accept fiction, non-fiction, poetry, and black and white art*. The fiction we publish most of tends toward but is not limited to the speculative. This does not mean only quietly desperate stories. We will consider items that fall out with regular categories. We do not publish gore, sword and sorcery or pornography. We can discuss these terms if you like. There are places for them all, this is not one of them." Twice per year. June and November. Pub'd 2 issues 2009; expects 2 issues 2010, 2 issues 2011. sub. price US/Canada: $20/4 issues. Add chocolate: $35/4 issues. Internation: $34/4 issues; per copy US/Canada: $5. International: $8.; sample US/Canada: $5. International: $8. Back issues: Some available: US/Canada: $5. International: $8. Discounts: Bookstores: 5+ copies/40% discount. 60pp. Reporting time: 6 months. Simultaneous submissions accepted: No. Payment: $20 fiction. $5 poetry. Ads: Yes. See website for rates: http://smallbeerpress.com/about/advertise/.

LADYBUG, the Magazine for Young Children, Marianne Carus, Editor-in-Chief; Paula Morrow, Executive Editor, 315 5th Street, PO Box 300, Peru, IL 61354, 815-224-5803, ext. 656, Fax 815-224-6615, mmiklavcic@caruspub.com. 1990. Poetry, fiction, art, music, non-fiction. "Fiction: 300-800 words. Poems: 20 lines maximum. Crafts/activities/games: 1-4 pages. Original finger plays (12 lines max.) and action rhymes (20 lines max.). *Ladybug* is for children ages 2-6 and their parents and caregivers. SASE is required for a response." circ. 130M. 12/yr. Pub'd 12 issues 2009; expects 12 issues 2010, 12 issues 2011. sub. price $35.97; per copy $5; sample $5. Back issues: $5. 36pp. Reporting time: 12 weeks, SASE required. Simultaneous submissions accepted: yes, please indicate. Publishes 1% of manuscripts submitted. Payment: 25¢/word (fiction); $3/line (poetry). Copyrighted. Rights vary. Ads: none.

Laguna Wilderness Press, Ronald Chilcote, PO Box 149, Laguna Beach, CA 92652-0149, 951-827-1571. 2002. Art, photos. "Founded in 2002 by environmentalists Ron Chilcote and Jerry Burchfield, Laguna Wilderness Press is a non-profit press dedicated to publishing books about the presence, preservation, and importance of wilderness environments. Established out of the founders concern for the preservation of the Laguna Wilderness in South Orange County, California, the press is especially interested in the protection and development of wilderness areas within or near urban centers. The press intends to play a role in redefining the term progress and help re-establish the connection between humanity and nature, as well as produce books that reassess the histories of specific environments by addressing misinformation and disinformation." avg. press run 1000. Pub'd 1 title 2009; expects 2 titles 2010, 2 titles 2011. No titles listed in the *Small Press Record of Books in Print* (36th Edition, 2010-11). Discounts: Retailer Discount 40%Distribution Companies 55%. 200-300pp. Reporting time: Within one month, enough time to fully consider the manuscript. Simultaneous submissions accepted: No. Publishes 50% of manuscripts submitted. Payment: 10%. Copyrights for author. Subjects: Agriculture, Book Arts, Environment, Geography, Photography, Picture Books, Travel, Wildlife, Wyoming.

Lahontan Images, Tim I. Purdy, PO Box 1592, 607 B Cottage Street, Susanville, CA 96130-1592, 530-257-6747. 1986. Non-fiction. "Primarily interested in the history and related topics of eastern California and Nevada. First title is Eric N. Moody's *Flanigan: Anatomy of a Railroad Ghost Town.*" avg. press run 2M. Expects 2 titles 2010, 4 titles 2011. 7 titles listed in the *Small Press Record of Books in Print* (36th Edition, 2010-11). Discounts: 5 or more 40%. 200pp. Reporting time: 1 month. Payment: percentage of sales. Copyrights for author. Subjects: Agriculture, California, History, The West.

Lake Claremont Press, Sharon Woodhouse, 1026 W. Van Buren St., 2nd Floor, Chicago, IL 60607, 312-226-8400, Fax 312-226-8420, lcp@lakeclaremont.com, www.lakeclaremont.com. 1994. Non-fiction. "Recent titles: *From Lumber Hookers to the Hooligan Fleet: A Treasury of Chicago Maritime History*; *On the Job: Behind the Stars of the Chicago Police Department*; *Rule 53: Capturing Hippies, Spies, Politicians, and Murderers in an American Courtroom*; *Finding Your Chicago Irish*; *For Members Only: A History and Guide to Chicago's Oldest Private Clubs*. Lake Claremont Press always welcomes book proposals for regional/nonfiction histories and guidebooks. Our focus is the Chicagoland area. If you have a query that fits these qualifications, we ask that you submit the following: 1)Book proposal/cover letter 2)Book outline 3)Author credentials 4)Brief marketing analysis 5)1-2 sample chapters (if not available send samples of previous writing). Please do not send a full manuscript until it is requested. Visit www.lakeclaremont.com for more information on our titles and authors." avg. press run 3M-6M. Pub'd 2 titles 2009; expects 7 titles 2010, 7 titles 2011. 44 titles listed in the *Small Press Record of Books in Print* (36th Edition, 2010-11). Discounts: 1-49 40%, 50-99 50%, 100+ 55%. 300pp. Reporting time: 3 weeks to 6 months. Simultaneous submissions accepted: yes. Publishes 1% of what we receive; 17% of what's appropriate for us% of manuscripts submitted. Payment: royalties 10-15% net. Copyrights for author. Subjects: Chicago, Cities, Entertainment, Folklore, Food, Eating, Great Lakes, History, Illinois, Movies, Non-Fiction, Reference, Supernatural, Travel.

LAKE EFFECT, George Looney, Editor-in-Chief, Penn State Erie, 4951 College Dr, Erie, PA 16563-1501, 814-898-6281. 2001. Poetry, fiction, long-poems, non-fiction. 1/yr. sub. price $6; per copy $6. 180pp. Reporting time: 1-4 months. Simultaneous submissions accepted: yes. Publishes 5% of manuscripts submitted. Payment: two copies. Subjects: Absurdist, Arts, Avant-Garde, Experimental Art, Criticism, Experimental, Fiction, Folklore, Gender Issues, Non-Fiction, Philosophy, Poetry, Post Modern, Short Stories.

•**Lake Street Press,** Hazel Dawkins, Editor; Anne Bengston, Editor, 4064 N. Lincoln Ave., #402, Chicago, IL 60618-3038, tel 773-525-3968, fax 773-525-1455, lsp@lakestreetpress.com, www.lakestreetpress.com. 2009. Fiction, non-fiction. "Lake Street Press publishes non-fiction and fiction titles by Midwestern authors. Our focus is personal growth, including a forthcoming title by intuitive and radio personality, Jillian Maas Backman, and teen historicals by Mary Osborne. Lake Street Press is a boutique publisher and is unable to accept manuscripts or queries at this time." avg. press run 5000. Pub'd 3 titles 2009; expects 2 titles 2010, 3 titles 2011. 1 title listed in the *Small Press Record of Books in Print* (36th Edition, 2010-11). Discounts: 1-4 books 20% 5-24 books 40% 25+ books 42% wholesalers 50%. 300pp. Reporting time: Lake Street Press is not accepting unsolicited manuscripts at this time. Simultaneous submissions accepted: No. Publishes 10% of manuscripts submitted. Payment: 10% of list price. Copyrights for author. Subjects: Fiction, Inspirational, Juvenile Fiction, Non-Fiction, Psychology, Relationships, Religion, Renaissance, Self-Help, Spiritual.

LAKE SUPERIOR MAGAZINE, Lake Superior Port Cities Inc., Konnie LeMay, Editor; Robert Berg, Managing Editor, Lake Superior Port Cities Inc., P.O. Box 16417, Duluth, MN 55816-0417, 218-722-5002, fax 218-722-4096, www.lakesuperior.com, e-mail: edit@lakesuperior.com. 1979. Fiction, articles, photos, cartoons, interviews, reviews, letters, news items, non-fiction. "We are a high-quality, glossy consumer magazine. We prefer manuscripts, but well-researched queries are attended to. We actively seek queries from writers in Lake Superior communities. Provide enough information on why the subject is important to the region and our readers, or why and how something is unique. We want details. The writer must have a thorough knowledge of the subject and how it relates to our region. We prefer a fresh, unused approach to the subject which provides the reader with an emotional involvement. Average 800-1,500 words, graphics/photos important." circ. 20M. 7/yr. Pub'd 7 issues 2009; expects 7 issues 2010, 7 issues 2011. sub. price $22.95; per copy $4.95 + p/h; sample same. Back issues: all issues $10, except current year—list available. 80pp. Reporting time: 3-5 months. Accept simultaneous submissions, but must know it is the case. Payment: up to $600, pix $20 (B&W), $50 (color), cover $125. Copyrighted, first rights for 90 days after publication. Pub's reviews: 12 in 2009. §Must be regional (Lake Superior) in topics covered. Ads: Full page $2,306 color; Full Page $1,844 B&W; Half page $1,546 color; Half Page $1,236 B&W; Marketplace classified listings available and display: 1/3 Page $692; 1/6 $464. Subjects: Antiques, Arts, Book Reviewing, Business & Economics, Culture, Environment, Folklore, Gardening, Great Lakes, History, Native American, Photography, Shipwrecks, Travel, Water.

Lake Superior Port Cities Inc. (see also LAKE SUPERIOR MAGAZINE), Paul L. Hayden, Publisher; Konnie LeMay, Editor; Robert Berg, Managing Editor, P.O. Box 16417, Duluth, MN 55816-0417, 888-244-5253, 218-722-5002, FAX 218-722-4096, www.lakesuperior.com, reader@lakesuperior.com. 1979. 22 titles listed in the *Small Press Record of Books in Print* (36th Edition, 2010-11).

THE LAKEVIEW REVIEW, Tanya Babcock, P.O. Box 428, Wayland, NY 14572, 585-645-2924. 2008. Fiction, art, interviews. "We publish fiction in many genres except mystery, children's stories, and romance. We look for fresh perspectives in the stories." circ. 2000. 4/yr. Expects 2000 issues 2010, 4000 issues 2011. sub. price $40; per copy $12.95; sample free. Back issues: $12.95. Discounts: Institutions and classrooms 20% off cover and subscription price. Bookstores 46% off cover price. 96pp. Reporting time: 6 weeks. Simultaneous submissions accepted: Yes. Publishes 22% of manuscripts submitted. Payment: Upon publication. Copyrighted, reverts to author. Ads: Print: 1 page(5x8) $1,750, 2/3 page (5x5-1/4) $725, 1/2 page island (2-1/2x8) $1,000, 1/2 page horizontal (5x4)$600, 1/3 page (5x2-3/4) $400, 1/8 page (1-1/4x2) $300, Cover 2 $1,150, Cover 3 $1,100, Cover 4 $1,200 Web: Leaderboard (728x90) $500, Box (300x250) $300, Vertical (120x240) $250, Sky Scraper (120x600) $350, Button (125x125) $150. Subject: Fiction.

LALITAMBA: An Uplifting Literary Experience, Swamini Sri Lalitambika Devi, Editor, P.O. Box 131, Planetarium Station, New York, NY 10024. 2004. Poetry, fiction, photos, interviews, parts-of-novels, non-fiction. "Lalitamba is a journal of modern devotional literature. It includes established and emerging writers from around the world. Contributors have been included in the Best American series, written award-winning novels, and received NEA grants. The journal was inspired by a devotional song sung on a trip through India. The name Lalitamba means Divine Mother. We are interested in bringing ancient spiritual ideals to bear with modern day life. Recent contributors include Shinjo Ito, Gregory Colbert, Carol Emshwiller, Julie Mars, and Bhau Kalchuri." circ. 1500. Pub'd 1 issue 2009; expects 1 issue 2010, 1 issue 2011. sub. price $10; per copy $12; sample $10. Back issues: $8. Discounts: 55%. 250pp. Copyrighted, reverts to author.

LAMBDA BOOK REPORT, Tony Valenzuela, Executive Director; Antonio Gonzalez, Chief Editor, Lambda Literary Foundation, 5482 Wilshire Avenue, #1595, Los Angeles, CA 90036, 213-568-3570. 1989. "LambdaLiterary.org (formerly "Lambda Book Report") is the country's most established review of contemporary LGBT literature. Though the journal used to appear four times a year - in January, April, July, and October - our reviews appear every week day on our website. Because of the volume of LGBT books published each year (this is a good thing!), we cannot review every book published. To submit a book to be reviewed on LambdaLiterary.org, please send one copy (finished book, bound galley, or bound manuscript) to our Chief Editor, Antonio Gonzalez at 152 Bank St. 4B £ New York, NY 10014.''

Lamp Light Press, A.C. Doyle, Founder, Publishing Division, PO Box 416, Denver, CO 80201-0416, 303-575-5676, Fax 303-575-1187. 1983. avg. press run 600. 4 titles listed in the *Small Press Record of Books in Print* (36th Edition, 2010-11). Discounts: distributed by Prosperity & Profits Unlimited, PO Box 416, Denver, CO 80201. 60pp. Reporting time: 6 weeks. Subjects: Alternative Medicine, Business & Economics, Cooking, Creativity, Education, Family, Food, Eating, Health, How-To, Inspirational, Motivation, Success, Poetry, Publishing, Spiritual, Textbooks.

Lancer Militaria, Box 1188, Mt. Ida, AR 71957-1188, 870-867-2232; www.warbooks.com. 1978. ''Specialize in reference type material for military collectors/historians.'' avg. press run 3M. Pub'd 2 titles 2009; expects 3 titles 2010. 6 titles listed in the *Small Press Record of Books in Print* (36th Edition, 2010-11). Discounts: 40-50% depending on quantity. 112pp. Copyrights for author. Subject: Military, Veterans.

THE LANGSTON HUGHES REVIEW, Valerie Babb, Editor; R. Baxter Miller, Executive Editor, Department of English, 254 Park Hall, Univ. of Georgia, Athens, GA 30602-6205, 706-542-1261. 1982. Articles, interviews, criticism, reviews, news items. ''Publishes articles on Langston Hughes, specifically, his cultural milieu and American modernism more generally. Also publishes special issues. Peer-reviewed.'' circ. 300-325. 2/yr. Pub'd 1 issue 2009; expects 2 issues 2010, 2 issues 2011. sub. price $20 ($25 foreign); per copy $14. Back issues: $9. 40-60pp. Reporting time: 6-8 weeks. Simultaneous submissions accepted: no. Publishes 3% of manuscripts submitted. Payment: none. Copyrighted, rights do not revert to author, but on request of author rights are assigned. Pub's reviews: 1 in 2009. §Langston Hughes and his contemporaries; African American literature and culture. Subject: Literary Review.

LANGUAGEANDCULTURE.NET, Liz Fortini, info@languageandculture.net. 2001. Poetry. ''Languageand-culture.net, an online poetry journal, welcomes original poetry and their English translation in the following languages: Spanish, French, German, Russian, Italian and the Slavic languages. Other languages are under review. We accept translations of known writers: please include the original language. Languageandculture.net also accepts original poetry in English. Please check online for submission guidelines, send 3-5 poems and a short bio and address inquiries to info@languageandculture.net.'' 2/yr. Pub'd 2 issues 2009; expects 2 issues 2010, 2 issues 2011. sample price 0. Reporting time: 9 weeks. Simultaneous submissions accepted: Yes. Payment: there is no paymnet. Copyrighted, reverts to author. Pub's reviews: 6 in 2009. §poetry. Subject: Poetry.

•LAPHAM'S QUARTERLY, Lewis Lapham Lapham, Editor, 33 Irving Place, Eighth Floor, New York, NY 10003. ''Laphams Quarterly does not accept unsolicited original work, but we invite readers to send along interesting, topical, unusual, or enlightening historical documents and articles for use in the Quarterly or online. You may send texts from authors on the order of Anas Nin, Herodotus, or Theodore Roosevelt; alternatively, you also can send lost drafts of the U.S. Constitution, stray Confederate specie, or still-pending Barbary ransom demands. Documents easily submitted electronically may be sent to editorial@laphamsquarterly.org.''

Laredo Publishing Co., Inc./Renaissance House, 465 Westview Ave, Englewood, NJ 07631. 1991. ''Children's/youth books.'' avg. press run 2M. Pub'd 15 titles 2009. No titles listed in the *Small Press Record of Books in Print* (36th Edition, 2010-11). Discounts: 40-45%. 32pp. Reporting time: 2-3 weeks. Simultaneous submissions accepted: yes. Publishes 20% of manuscripts submitted. Payment: 7%. Copyrights for author. Subject: Children, Youth.

LATIN AMERICAN LITERARY REVIEW, Latin American Literary Review Press, Yvette E. Miller, PO Box 17660, Pittsburgh, PA 15235-0860, 412-824-7903, www.lalrp.org, latinreview@hotmail.com. 1972. Fiction, articles, photos, interviews, criticism, reviews, music, non-fiction. ''Length of article varies from 10-20 pages in special issues. Some recent contributors: Roberto Gonzales Echevarria, Jose J. Arrom, Guillermo Cabrera Infante, John Updike, Alistair Reid, Robert Coles, Jorge de Sena, Harold de Campos, Joaquin de Sousa Andrade et al. Articles published in English, Spanish & Portuguese.'' circ. 1M. 2/yr. Pub'd 2 issues 2009; expects 2 issues 2010, 2 issues 2011. sub. price $47; per copy $25; sample $25. Back issues: $14. Discounts: 10% for subscription agencies. 150pp. Reporting time: within 12 weeks. Simultaneous submissions accepted: no. Copyrighted. Pub's reviews: 10 in 2009. §Recent Latin American Fiction, poetry, theatre, criticism. Ads: $250/$145/$100. Subjects: Latin America, Literature (General).

Latin American Literary Review Press (see also LATIN AMERICAN LITERARY REVIEW), Yvette E. Miller, PO Box 17660, Pittsburgh, PA 15235-0860, 412-824-7903, www.lalrp.org, editor@lalrp.org. 1980. Fiction, photos, criticism, plays, non-fiction. ''English translations of works by prominent L.A. writers.'' avg. press run 1.5M. Pub'd 8 titles 2009; expects 10 titles 2010, 10 titles 2011. 100 titles listed in the *Small Press*

Record of Books in Print (36th Edition, 2010-11). Discounts: negotiable. 160pp. Reporting time: 4 months. Simultaneous submissions accepted: no. Publishes 1% of manuscripts submitted. Payment: varies. Copyrights for author. Subjects: Bilingual, Latin America, Latino, Literary Review, Literature (General), Spain.

LATIN AMERICAN PERSPECTIVES, Ronald H. Chilcote, Managing Editor, PO Box 5703, Riverside, CA 92517-5703, 951-827-1571, fax 951-827-5685, laps@mail.ucr.edu, www.latinamericanperspectives.com. 1974. Articles, art, photos, interviews, reviews. "Obtain subscriptions through: Sage Publications, 2455 Teller Road, Thousand Oaks, Ca 91320." circ. 2M. 6/yr. Pub'd 6 issues 2009; expects 6 issues 2010, 6 issues 2011. sub. price Individual Subscription: $74 , Student Subscription: $25, Institutions Combined (Print & E-Access): $519, Institutions E-Access Only: $494, Institutions Print Only: $499; per copy $16; sample free on request. Back issues: $11. Discounts: 25% (5-10 copies) 30% (11-20 copies) 40% (21-40 copies) classroom & university bookstores. 128pp. Reporting time: 6-9 months. Simultaneous submissions accepted: no. Publishes 25% of manuscripts submitted. Payment: none. Copyrighted. Pub's reviews: 10 in 2009. §Latin America, radical theory, political economy. Ads: 1 Full Page Ad: $415, 3-5 Full Page Ads: $380, 6 or More Full Page Ads: $340, 1 Half Page Ad: $295, 3-5 Half Page Ads: $270, 6 or More Half Page Ads: $250. Subjects: Business & Economics, Latin America, Politics.

•**Latitude Press,** PO Box 603, Cardiff, CA 92007-0603, 760-536-6131. No titles listed in the *Small Press Record of Books in Print* (36th Edition, 2010-11).

The Latona Press, Marion K. Stocking, 24 Berry Cove Road, Lamoine, ME 04605. 1978. Non-fiction. "We are not looking for further manuscripts at the present time." avg. press run 1.5M. 1 title listed in the *Small Press Record of Books in Print* (36th Edition, 2010-11). Discounts: To bookstores and wholesalers: 1-4 copies 20%, 5 or more 40%. Postage and shipping extra. No discount on orders not paid for in 30 days. 200pp. Payment: royalties. Copyrights for author. Subjects: Biography, Biology, Conservation, Earth, Natural History, Ecology, Foods, History, Maine, New England.

LAUGHING BEAR NEWSLETTER, Tom Person, Editor, 1418 El Camino Real, Euless, TX 76040-6555, e-mail editor@laughingbear.com, www.laughingbear.com. 1976. "*LBN* has been serving the small press community with news, information, and inspiration since 1976. *LBN* is for small press writers and publishers. The emphasis is on limited budget publishing: design and strategies, alternative marketing techniques, and resources. The newsletter is being phased out and will cease publication with issue 150 (probably in 2006). However, our website will continue to offer articles and resources for independent publishers. *LBN* does NOT publish poetry, fiction or any other literary works, and will not consider submission of articles. We will also not be taking on any new subscribers - downloadable copies of the newsletter issues are immediately available on the web site." 4pp. Copyrighted, reverts to author. Pub's reviews: 30+ in 2009. §Small press publications of all kinds; publishing how-to especially. Subjects: How-To, Newsletter, Publishing, Reviews.

THE LAUGHING DOG, Subsynchronous Press, Hillary Lyon, Editor; Warren Andrle, Assistant Editor, #326, 4729 E. Sunrise, Tucson, AZ 85718, Subsyncpress.com, Subsyncpress@Gmail.com. 2000. Poetry. "Submit 3 poems at a time, maximum 30 lines each. No religious, political or pornographic poetry, please. No rhyming poems either. Recent contributors include: David Ray, Will Inman, and Gary Mex Glazner." circ. 150. 1/yr. Pub'd 2 issues 2009; expects 1 issue 2010, 1 issue 2011. price per copy $4; sample $3. Back issues: availability varies. Discounts: contributors get additional copies for $1 each. 26pp. Reporting time: 3 months to 6 months. Simultaneous submissions accepted: no. Publishes 20% of manuscripts submitted. Payment: 1 free copy, plus discount on additional copies. Copyrighted, reverts to author. Ads: none. Subject: Poetry.

Laureate Press, PO Box 8125, Bangor, ME 04402-8125, 800-946-2727. 1994. Non-fiction. "Not accepting submissions." avg. press run 5M. Pub'd 2 titles 2009; expects 2 titles 2010, 2 titles 2011. 7 titles listed in the *Small Press Record of Books in Print* (36th Edition, 2010-11). Trade Discount: 30%. 400pp. Copyrights for author. Subject: Sports, Outdoors.

THE LAUREL REVIEW, William Trowbridge, Associate Editor; David Slater, Associate Editor; Amy Benson, Editor; Nancy Mayer, Editor; Randall R. Freisinger, Associate Editor; Jeff Mock, Associate Editor; Leigh Allison Wilson, Associate Editor; Ann Cummins, Associate Editor, Department of English, Northwest Missouri State University, Maryville, MO 64468, 816-562-1265. 1960. Poetry, fiction, art, parts-of-novels, long-poems, non-fiction. "We read September through May. We have no regional, political, ethnic, or religious bias. We seek well-crafted poems, stories, and creative non-fiction accessible to a wide range of serious readers. Recent contributors: Nancy Van Winckel, Gary Finke, Albert Goldbarth, Charles Harper Webb, Katherine Soniat, Jonis Agee, Brendan Galvin, William Kloefkorn, Jim Daniels, Karla J. Kuban, Heather Ross Miller, Ian McMillan, Jonathan Holden." circ. 900. 2/yr. Pub'd 2 issues 2009; expects 2 issues 2010, 2 issues 2011. sub. price $10; per copy $7; sample $5. Back issues: $5. Discounts: 40%. 136pp. Reporting time: 1 week to 4 months. Simultaneous submissions accepted: no. Publishes less than 1% of manuscripts submitted. Payment: 2 copies, plus free one-year subscription. Copyrighted, reverts to author. Pub's reviews: 2 in 2009. Ads: $80/$40. Subjects: Essays, Fiction, Non-Fiction, Poetry.

LAW AND LITERATURE, University of California Press, Peter Goodrich, Editor, University of California Press, 2000 Center St., Suite 303, Berkeley, CA 94704-1223, 510-643-7154. 1989. Articles. "Editorial address: Cardozo School of Law, Brookdale Center, 55 Fifth Avenue, New York, NY 10003. Copyrighted by the Cardozo School of Law, Yeshiva University." circ. 446. 3/yr. Pub'd 3 issues 2009; expects 3 issues 2010, 3 issues 2011. sub. price $37 indiv., $149 inst., $27 student; per copy $15 indiv., $54 inst., $15 student; sample same as single copy. Discounts: foreign subs. agents 10%, 10+ one-time orders 30%. 168pp. Copyrighted, does not revert to author. Ads: $295/$220. Subjects: Law, Literature (General).

Lawells Publishing, Sherry A. Wells, PO Box 1338, Royal Oak, MI 48068-1338, 248-543-5297, fax 248-543-5683, lawells@tm.net. 1984. Fiction, non-fiction. "Law for Everyone series: "an ounce of prevention instead of a pound of court"; in plain-American-English such as *Michigan Law for Everyone*; Great Families: just completed subseries, each with 10 - 27 minibiographies honoring famous stepparents and stepchildren; other relatives forthcoming; *Father, Ford, $5 a Day*: in the spirit of Little House books, the Detroit area after Ford's 1914 offer of the five-dollar day—ages 8 and all the way up. Queries to email address." avg. press run 3000. Expects 4 titles 2010, 5-7 titles 2011. 6 titles listed in the *Small Press Record of Books in Print* (36th Edition, 2010-11). Discounts: Distribs. 55% case quantitiesBookstores 40%Classrooms 30%. 184pp. Reporting time: 2 weeks by email. Simultaneous submissions accepted: Yes. Payment: Royalty—10% retail price and Work for hire. Copyrights for author. Subjects: Biography, Consumer, Creative Non-fiction, Family, Feminism, Illinois, Indiana, Law, Michigan, Non-Fiction, Ohio, Parenting, Textbooks, Women, Young Adult.

Lawrence & Wishart, Ruth Kinna, European Thought, University of Loughborough, Loughborough LE11 3TU, United Kingdom, info@lwbooks.co.uk; www.lwbooks.co.uk/anarchiststudies. 1993. Pub'd 2 titles 2009; expects 2 titles 2010, 2 titles 2011. No titles listed in the *Small Press Record of Books in Print* (36th Edition, 2010-11). Discounts: trade terms - less 5% for cash with order, or payment before start of year of publication. 96pp. Reporting time: 3 months. Simultaneous submissions accepted: no. Publishes 25% of manuscripts submitted. Payment: none. Copyrights for author. Subject: Anarchist.

Nicholas Lawrence Books, Larry Thomas Ward, 932 Clover Avenue, Canon City, CO 81212, 719-276-0152, Fax 719-276-0154, icareinc@webtv.net. 1993. Photos, non-fiction. "We publish primarily celebrity biographies, autobiographies, and history." avg. press run 5,000. Pub'd 2 titles 2009; expects 3 titles 2010, 3 titles 2011. 3 titles listed in the *Small Press Record of Books in Print* (36th Edition, 2010-11). Discounts: 40% trade, etc. 175pp. Reporting time: 30 days. Simultaneous submissions accepted: yes. Publishes 50% of manuscripts submitted. Payment: $500 - $2000 advance, 10% royalty. Copyrights for author. Subjects: Autobiography, Biography.

LAYALAMA ONLINE MAGAZINE, Pushpa Ratna Tuladhar, 320 Phurkesalla Marg, Dhimelohan Swoyambhu,, P. O. Box 5146, Kathmandu, Nepal, Kathmandu 71100, Nepal, Tel: + 977 1 4274815, Fax: + 977 1 4274815, email:layalama@layalama.com, Website: http://www.layalama.com. 2002. Poetry, fiction. circ. 500. 4/yr. Pub'd 4 issues 2009; expects 4 issues 2010, 4 issues 2011. sub. price $16; per copy US$4.00; sample free. Back issues: inquire. Discounts: 25 copies - 30%. 16pp. Reporting time: Within 2-4 weeks. Simultaneous submissions accepted: Yes. Publishes 50% of manuscripts submitted. Payment: No contribution. Copyrighted, reverts to author. Ads: On request.

•Lazara Press, Box 2269, VMPO,, Vancouver, B.C. V6B 3W2, Canada, 604.872.1134. No titles listed in the *Small Press Record of Books in Print* (36th Edition, 2010-11).

Lazywood Press (see also MY TABLE: Houston's Dining Magazine), Teresa Byrne-Dodge, 1908 Harold Street, Houston, TX 77098-1502, 713-529-5500, teresa.byrnedodge@my-table.com, www.my-table.com. 1994. Non-fiction. "We publish only 1 or 2 new titles per year, in addition to a bimonthly magazine. All publications have a regional emphasis." avg. press run 15M. Pub'd 1 title 2009; expects 2 titles 2010, 1 title 2011. 2 titles listed in the *Small Press Record of Books in Print* (36th Edition, 2010-11). Discounts: please call for schedule. Pages vary. Reporting time: 1-2 months. Simultaneous submissions accepted: yes. Publishes a very small % of manuscripts submitted. Payment: varies. Copyrights for author. Subjects: Cooking, Dining, Restaurants, Food, Eating, Humor, Texas.

LDP, an occasional journal of aesthetics & language, Light Density Press, Yvette Johnson, Submission by EMAIL ONLY. Please state medium in content box, edit@lightdensitypress.com. 2007. Poetry, fiction, art, photos, cartoons, interviews, satire, criticism, music, letters, parts-of-novels, long-poems, collages, plays, concrete art, non-fiction. "LDP is an occasional journal of aesthetics & language, issuing 2 to 3 times a year. While the journal is largely a blank notebook for writing and sketching that may vary in construction, I also publish, as part of the front and back matter: poetry (especially soliciting vispo and/or concrete poetry), prose, short & short short fiction, "fictionalized fact," drawings, illustration, collages, cartoons, photography, mathematics, music and interviews. The intention of the published work is to serve as "inspiration" for the journal's user. The more varied & sundry the better." 2-3/yr. sub. price $45; per copy $20; sample $20. Back issues: Inquire. 160pp. Reporting time: fewer than 12 months. Simultaneous submissions accepted: Yes.

Payment: one subscription (3 issues). Copyrighted, reverts to author. Subjects: Abstracts, Absurdist, African Literature, Africa, African Studies, Anthropology, Archaelogy, Arts, Avant-Garde, Experimental Art, Birds, Book Arts, California, Color, Fashion, Fiction, Handwriting/Written, Poetry, Post Modern.

Leadership Education and Development, Inc., Donna Harrison, Joy Rhodes, Myra Curry J, 1116 West 7th Street, PMB 175, Columbia, TN 38401, 931-379-3799; 800-659-6135, www.leadershipdevelopment.com. 1987. Non-fiction. "Biases: ethical management. Recent contributor: Fred A. Manske, Jr., CEO of Purolator Courier." avg. press run 5-10M. Expects 1-2 titles 2010, 2-3 titles 2011. 2 titles listed in the *Small Press Record of Books in Print* (36th Edition, 2010-11). Discounts: distributors 50%, bookstores 40-45%, quantity retail discounts up to 35%. 200pp. Reporting time: 2-3 months. Copyrights are negotiable. Subjects: Business & Economics, Inspirational, Leadership.

LEAF GARDEN, Leaf Garden Press, Robert Henry, 1087 Harbin Rd., Dandridge, TN 37725, choicesreply@gmail.com. 2009. "Open-minded. The best art and best writing sent to us will be selected, regardless of publishing history. We publish things that surprise us; so surprise us." circ. 0. 2/yr. Expects 2 issues 2010, 2 issues 2011. price per copy 7.50; sample Free. Back issues: 7.50. 150pp. Reporting time: Less than a month. Simultaneous submissions accepted: Yes. Publishes 50% of manuscripts submitted. No payment. Copyrighted, reverts to author. Pub's reviews: none in 2009. §Music, writing, film. Subjects: Abstracts, Absurdist, Arts, Avant-Garde, Experimental Art, Biography, Creative Non-fiction, Dreams, Essays, Experimental, Fiction, Literature (General), Non-Fiction, Picture Books, Poetry, Prose.

Leaf Garden Press (see also LEAF GARDEN), Robert Henry, Poetry Editor, Co-editor; Melanie Browne, Prose Editor, Co-editor, choicesreply@gmail.com. 2009. Poetry, fiction, art, photos, interviews, satire, reviews, letters, parts-of-novels, collages, plays, concrete art, non-fiction. "Leaf Garden press is looking for fresh voices. We like people who dare be post-modern romantics, for example. We have a bias against genre fiction. We want gritty, pretty, and bold. If possible, all together. New writers are very welcomed." Pub'd 1 title 2009; expects 2 titles 2010, 3 titles 2011. 1 title listed in the *Small Press Record of Books in Print* (36th Edition, 2010-11). 100pp. Reporting time: Less than a month. Simultaneous submissions accepted: Yes. Publishes 33% of manuscripts submitted. Payment: None or negotiable. Does not copyright for author. Subjects: Abstracts, Absurdist, Beat, Creative Non-fiction, Diaries, Experimental, Fiction, Literature (General), Non-Fiction, Novels, Photography, Poetry, Surrealism, Visual Arts, Writers/Writing.

Leaf Press (see also THE CRAPSHOOTER), Larry Edell, Andrea Foote, PO Box 421440, San Diego, CA 92142, leafpress@aol.com. 1995. Non-fiction. "Gambling only." avg. press run 5M. Pub'd 2 titles 2009; expects 1 title 2010, 2 titles 2011. No titles listed in the *Small Press Record of Books in Print* (36th Edition, 2010-11). Discounts: 50% for distributors. 120pp. Reporting time: immediate. Simultaneous submissions accepted: yes. Publishes 20% of manuscripts submitted. Payment: varies. Copyright for author if requested. Subject: Games.

Leapfrog Press, Lisa Graziano, Tasha Enseki, PO Box 2110, Teaticket, MA 02536, 774-392-4384, email books@leapfrogpress.com, www.leapfrogpress.com. 1996. Fiction, non-fiction. "Our list is eclectic and represents quality fiction, poetry, audiobooks, non-fiction and memoir—books that are referred to by the large commercial publishers as midlist, but which we regard to be the heart and soul of literature. Please submit an email query letter telling us a little about your manuscript, and include no more than 40 pages from the beginning of the book, within the body of the email message. Online submissions only please. Authors published include Martin Espada, Marge Piercy, Theodore Roszak, Maureen McCoy, Toni Graham, Lev Raphael, and Pagan Kennedy. We are distributed by Consortium Book Sales & Distribution." avg. press run 3-5 thousand. Pub'd 4 titles 2009; expects 4 titles 2010, 4 titles 2011. No titles listed in the *Small Press Record of Books in Print* (36th Edition, 2010-11). 200-300pp. Reporting time: 1 month. Simultaneous submissions accepted: yes. Publishes less than 1% of manuscripts submitted. Payment: varies according to book. Copyrights for author. Subjects: Fiction, Literature (General), Memoirs, Poetry.

Leaping Dog Press (see also Asylum Arts), Jordan Jones, Editor and Publisher, PO Box 90473, Raleigh, NC 27675-0473, Phone/fax: (919) 809-9045 E-mail: editor@leapingdogpress.com, Web: www.leapingdog-press.com, Chapbooks and ephemera: www.cafepress.com/ldp/. 1990. Poetry, fiction, art, photos, criticism, letters, long-poems, collages, plays, non-fiction. "Manuscripts by invitation only, and only during the months of May-July. Leaping Dog Press publishes high-quality literary titles—fiction, plays, translations, essays, and poetry—in attractive trade paperback format. Recent books by Marie Redonnet, Eric Paul Shaffer, Greg Boyd, Mark Wisniewski, and Norberto Luis Romero. We are most interested in striking, clear, entertaining contemporary work and works in translation, especially from French and Spanish." avg. press run 1000. Pub'd 1 title 2009; expects 4 titles 2010, 5 titles 2011. 5 titles listed in the *Small Press Record of Books in Print* (36th Edition, 2010-11). Distributed to the book trade by AtlasBooks Distribution, 30 Amberwood Parkway, Ashland, OH 44805. Phone: (800) BookLog, Fax: (419) 281-6883. 144pp. Reporting time: 3-6 mos. Simultaneous submissions accepted: Yes. Publishes 2% of manuscripts submitted. Payment: in copies. Copyrights for author. Subjects: Absurdist, Arts, Avant-Garde, Experimental Art, Fiction, Poetry, Surrealism, Translation.

The Leaping Frog Press (see also Timson Edwards, Co.), Marlene McLauglin, Alex Gonzalez, PO Box 55-0898, Jacksonville, FL 32255-0898, Write to us (we all still write letters right?) PO Box 55-0898 Jacksonville, FL 32255-0898. http://www.short-fiction.com, www.timsonedwards.com, publisher@bell-south.net if you need to send email, do not send attachments, we will request the attachment. 1996. Fiction, photos. "Strictly limited to short (max. 2,500 words) fiction. Has 'Best Of' S.E., N.E. Midwest, S.W., N.W., regional anthologies competition for new and emerging writers held each year. All correspondence must have a SASE for return of anything sent or wanted. Currently seeking essays of up to 200 words regarding reading and windows, two separate topics and books. Also publishing poetry gift books illustrated with b/w photography." avg. press run Depending on the project, we will print as few as 200 to as many as 5M. Our magazine prints 500 and our anthologies will print about 1200 copies. Please enter our competitions and subscribe, this is how we manage to continue publishing the work of new writers... Pub'd 1 title 2009; expects 2 titles 2010, 5 titles 2011. No titles listed in the *Small Press Record of Books in Print* (36th Edition, 2010-11). Discounts: minimum 40% up to 50 + 20% with quantities and no returns. 128pp. Reporting time: 12 weeks minimum. Simultaneous submissions accepted: yes. Publishes 60% of manuscripts submitted. Payment: by prior arrangements. Does not copyright for author. Subjects: Christianity, Culture, Dreams, Essays, Family, Fiction, Humor, Inspirational, Literature (General), Mental Health, Motivation, Success, Mystery, Photography, Satire, Spiritual.

Leave No Sister Behind Publications, Carol Givner, 13 Pecan Ln, Long Beach, MS 39560-3620, 888-795-3570. 2008. Non-fiction. avg. press run 100. Expects 10 titles 2010, 15 titles 2011. 5 titles listed in the *Small Press Record of Books in Print* (36th Edition, 2010-11). Discounts: 10-or more copies 55%. 44-80pp. Reporting time: 1 -3 days. Simultaneous submissions accepted: No. Publishes 99% of manuscripts submitted. Payment: Authors receive all profits minus printing cost. This occurs on quarterly basis. Does not copyright for author. Subjects: Inspirational, Poetry, Self-Help.

THE LEDGE, Stacey Knecht, 8011 CE, Zwolle, The Netherlands, info@the-ledge.com, www.the-ledge.com. 2005. Poetry, fiction, articles, photos, interviews, music, letters, parts-of-novels, long-poems, plays, non-fiction. *"The Ledge* is a literary website, based in the Netherlands but aimed at an international audience. On the site, which can be viewed in both English and Dutch, visitors can read in-depth interviews with writers from around the world and hear them reading from their latest work, while reading along from 'a book'. There is also a built-in, ever-expanding reading guide: books to read 'before' and 'after'. The idea is, in time, to construct a worldwide-web of literature and a library/ archive of international, literary interviews. Visitors to the site can contribute to the database: comments, ideas for new 'before' and 'after' books, corrections, all suggestions are reviewed by the editors and, wherever possible, added to the site." Subjects: Anthology, Autobiography, Biography, Essays, Fiction, Interviews, Juvenile Fiction, Literature (General), Non-Fiction, Novels, Philosophy, Poetry, Reading, Short Stories, Zines.

THE LEDGE POETRY & FICTION MAGAZINE, Timothy Monaghan, Editor-in-Chief & Publisher, 40 Maple Avenue, Bellport, NY 11713-2011, www.theledgemagazine.com. 1988. Poetry, fiction. *"The Ledge Poetry & Fiction Magazine* features a wide and eclectic range of poems and stories by a diverse group of contemporary poets and writers. *The Ledge* is open to all styles and schools of writing. The Ledge seeks compelling stories that employ dramatic tension and complex characterization. We especially enjoy poignant stories with a sense of purpose. We dislike careless or contrived writing. We also seek passionate poems that utilize language and imagery in a fresh, original fashion and favor visceral poems that speak to the human experience. We want inspired, imaginative, well-crafted verse, and we are open to all styles and schools of writing, including formal poems. We realize how difficult a task it may seem to define exactly what we're looking for in a particular poem or story and simply encourage submitters to *The Ledge* to send us their best work. *The Ledge* welcomes work by both established and emerging poets and writers. We believe that superior work appeals to a wider audience than most journals endeavor to reach, and consider *The Ledge* a truly democratic publication in that regard. *The Ledge* also sponsors an annual fiction awards competition, an annual poetry awards competition, and an annual poetry chapbook competition. Please e-mail us at: info@theledgemagazine.com or tkmonaghan@aol.com or send SASE for competition guidelines. You may also visit us at www.theledgemagazine.com to purchase a copy of the magazine or for complete guidelines and additional information about our publication and press." circ. 1.2M. 1/yr. Pub'd 1 issue 2009; expects 1 issue 2010, 1 issue 2011. 5 titles listed in the *Small Press Record of Books in Print* (36th Edition, 2010-11). sub. price $20/2 issues or $35/4 issues or $45/6 issues. For subscriptions outside North America, please add $5 per issue.; per copy $12; sample $10. Back issues: $10. 240pp. Reporting time: 6-8 months. Simultaneous submissions accepted: yes. Publishes 2% of manuscripts submitted. Payment: 1 contributor's copy. Copyrighted, reverts to author. Pub's reviews: 1 in 2009. §At this time, The Ledge considers for review only poetry books and chapbooks. Subjects: Fiction, Poetry.

A.P. Lee & Co., Ltd., P.O. Box 340292, Columbus, OH 43234, 614-798-1998, www.APLeeCo.com, webmaster@APLeeCo.com. Fiction, non-fiction. "AP Lee & Co, Ltd publishes mind/body/spirit, spiritual, and self-improvement books, CDs and DVDs. We also publish mystery and detective books that do not have a lot of sex or violence. Our motto is: "Evolving mankind, one book at a time." We want only those works that further the spiritual evolution of humankind.'' Pub'd 8 titles 2009; expects 5 titles 2010, 5 titles 2011. 3 titles listed in the *Small Press Record of Books in Print* (36th Edition, 2010-11). 250pp. Reporting time: 10 days. Simultaneous submissions accepted: Yes. Publishes 50% of manuscripts submitted. Payment: varies by author. Copyrights for author. Subjects: Fiction, Grieving, Guidance, Inspirational, Metaphysics, Motivation, Success, Mystery, New Age, Non-Fiction, Novels, Philosophy, Religion, Self-Help, Spiritual, Theosophical.

Leete's Island Books, Peter Neill, Box 1, Sedgewick, ME 04676, 207-359-5054, 01-207-359-5054 (office), 01-207-610-0054 (mobile), pneill@thew2o.net. 1977. ''Fiction, essays, interesting reprints; for the moment, because of time, no unsolicited manuscripts accepted.'' avg. press run 2.5M. Pub'd 2 titles 2009; expects 3 titles 2010, 4 titles 2011. 3 titles listed in the *Small Press Record of Books in Print* (36th Edition, 2010-11). Discounts: 40%, distributed by: Independent Publishers Group, Chicago Review Press, 814 N. Franklin, 2nd FL., Chicago, Illinois 60610, 312-337-0747. 250pp. Payment: varies with title. Copyrights for author. Subjects: Literature (General), Translation.

LEFT CURVE, Csaba Polony, Editor; Jack Hirschman, Associate Editor; P.J. Laska, Associate Editor; Des McGuinness, Associate Editor; Agneta Falk, Associate Editor; Richard Olsen, Associate; John Hutnyk, Associate Editor; E. San Juan Jr., Associate Editor, PO Box 472, Oakland, CA 94604-0472, E-mail editor@leftcurve.org. 1974. Poetry, fiction, articles, art, photos, interviews, criticism, reviews, music, letters, long-poems, collages, non-fiction. ''*Left Curve* is an artist produced journal addressing the crises of modernity from an integrative social-historical context by publishing original visual and verbal art, as well as critical articles.'' circ. 2M. Irregular. Pub'd 1 issue 2009. sub. price $35 indiv, $50 instit (3 issues); per copy $12 indiv., $20 instit.; sample $12. Back issues: $10. Discounts: 30% trade. 144pp. Reporting time: max. 6 months. Simultaneous submissions accepted: no. Publishes 5% of manuscripts submitted. Payment: 2-5 copies dependent on length. Copyrighted. Pub's reviews: 2 in 2009. §Contemporary art, poetry, cultural politics, literature, cultural. Ads: $200/$125/$15 min; $1 per word. Subjects: Arts, Avant-Garde, Experimental Art, Criticism, Culture, Essays, Literature (General), Media, Photography, Poetry, Politics, Post Modern, Short Stories, Socialist, Third World, Minorities, Visual Arts.

Legacy Audio Books, Inc., Andrew Barnes L., P.O. Box 11183, Cincinnati, OH 45211, 866-499-2049. 2005. Non-fiction. ''Our MissionLegacy Audio Books, a division of The Voiceover Guy LLC, is dedicated to producing high quality audio books of primarily, but not exclusively, prominent historical figures. We seek to honor their literary works, and deliver outstanding vocal performances, to generate renewed interests in the authors' message.'' avg. press run 1000. Pub'd 4 titles 2009; expects 3 titles 2010, 5 titles 2011. No titles listed in the *Small Press Record of Books in Print* (36th Edition, 2010-11). 400pp. Reporting time: 7-10 Days. Simultaneous submissions accepted: Yes. Publishes 20% of manuscripts submitted. Payment: Quarterly payments. Legacy will copyright audio recordings of the title only. Subjects: African Literature, Africa, African Studies, African-American, Americana, Biography, Family, Folklore, Holocaust, Inspirational, Non-Violence, North America, Performing Arts, Political Science, Relationships, Religion, Self-Help.

LegacyForever, Porsha Starks J., 4930 Capri Avenue, Sarasota, FL 34235-4320, 941-358-3339. 2004. Poetry, fiction, music. Expects 2 titles 2010, 2 titles 2011. No titles listed in the *Small Press Record of Books in Print* (36th Edition, 2010-11). Discounts: 25 copies: 10%. 350pp. Reporting time: six weeks. Simultaneous submissions accepted: Yes. Publishes 50% of manuscripts submitted. Payment: Based upon work of author. Copyrights for author. Subjects: Fiction, Florida, Humor, Movies, Music, Mystery, Non-Fiction, Occult.

The Legal Center for People with Disabilities and Older People, Mary Anne Harvey, 455 Sherman Street, Suite 130, Denver, CO 80203-4403, (303) 722-0300, (303) 722-0720 fax, 1-800-288-1376, publications@thelegalcenter.org, www.thelegalcenter.org. 3 titles listed in the *Small Press Record of Books in Print* (36th Edition, 2010-11).

Lemieux International Ltd., William Lemieux, PO Box 170134, Milwaukee, WI 53217, 414-962-2844, FAX 414-962-2844, lemintld@msn.com. 1985. Fiction, non-fiction. avg. press run 1-3M. Pub'd 1 title 2009; expects 1 title 2010, 3 titles 2011. 8 titles listed in the *Small Press Record of Books in Print* (36th Edition, 2010-11). Discounts: trade. 200-300pp. Reporting time: 3 weeks. Simultaneous submissions accepted: yes. Publishes a variable % of manuscripts submitted. Payment: TBA. Copyrights for author. Subjects: Biography, Cooking, Fantasy, Gay, Health, History, How-To, Humor, Mental Health, Military, Veterans, Mystery, Spiritual, Travel.

Lemon Grove Press, Martine Ehrenclou, Publisher, Kristin Langenfeld, Sue Knopf, 1158 26th Street #502, Santa Monica, CA 90403, phone: (310)820-4779, fax: (310) 820-4771, www.criticalconditions.com, info@lemongrovepress.com. 2007. Non-fiction. ''The goal of Lemon Grove Press is to publish health/medical, self-help, and memoir titles. Our mission is to put good books into the world that enlighten, inspire and educate.'' avg. press run 5,000. Expects 2 titles 2010, 3 titles 2011. 1 title listed in the *Small Press Record of Books in Print* (36th Edition, 2010-11). Discounts: distribution through AtlasBooks Distribution—their discounts per arrangement with bookstores, retailers, wholesalers, distributors. 248pp. Reporting time: 2 months. Subjects: Aging, Autobiography, Children, Youth, Creative Non-fiction, Creativity, Disease, Family,

Health, Lifestyles, Medicine, Mental Health, Non-Fiction, Nursing, Psychology, Self-Help.

Lemon Shark Press, Darcy Mobraaten, 1604 Marbella Drive, Vista, CA 92081-5463, 760-727-2850, lemonsharkpress@yahoo.com, www.lemonsharkpress.com. 2003. Fiction, non-fiction. "Publishing literary novels set in Hawaii." avg. press run 1M. Expects 1 title 2010, 3 titles 2011. 3 titles listed in the *Small Press Record of Books in Print* (36th Edition, 2010-11). Discounts: 40% for bookstores. 300pp. Reporting time: 3 months. Simultaneous submissions accepted: no. Publishes 1% of manuscripts submitted. Payment: private. Copyrights for author. Subject: Literature (General).

The Lentz Leadership Institute LLC, The Refractive Thinker Press., Dr. Cheryl Lentz A, 9065 Big Plantation Ave, Las Vegas, NV 89143-5440, 702 719-9214, 877 298-5172, info@lentzleadership.com, www.lentzleadership.com. 2008. Non-fiction. "The Refractive Thinker series is an anthology that publishes individual chapters by doctoral scholars from various academic universities of higher learning across the globe. This series include *Volume I: Leadership, Vol. II: Research Methodology, Vol. III: Change Management*, and our soon to be released *Vol. IV: Ethics and Globalization in Leadership*. The Refractive Thinker family includes 40 chapters written by 25 unique authors from 19 states, and from 4 continents. We have been submitted for 5 awards. Our volumes are published in the Spring (April) and the Fall (October). Please visit our website for details http://www.refractivethinker.com. The Refractive Thinker Press is where the discriminating scholar publishes. As an institute, we also offer guest speaking, educational seminars, as well as thesis and dissertation coaching." avg. press run 1000. Pub'd 3 titles 2009; expects 3 titles 2010, 4 titles 2011. 4 titles listed in the *Small Press Record of Books in Print* (36th Edition, 2010-11). Please email for discounts and availability. 184pp. Reporting time: 48 hours. Simultaneous submissions accepted: No. Publishes 80% of manuscripts submitted. Payment: Personalized. Copyrights for author. Subjects: Abstracts, Anthology, Non-Fiction.

LEO Productions LLC., Linda E. Odenborg, PO Box 1333, Portland, OR 97207, 360-601-1379, Fax 360-210-4133. 1992. Fiction, art, letters, long-poems, plays, non-fiction. avg. press run 5M-10M. Pub'd 2 titles 2009; expects 3 titles 2010, 3 titles 2011. 4 titles listed in the *Small Press Record of Books in Print* (36th Edition, 2010-11). Discounts: yes. Reporting time: 3 months. Publishes 0% of manuscripts submitted. Payment: varies. Subjects: Arts, Bilingual, China, Diaries, Drama, Family, Fiction, France, French, History, Medieval, Oregon, Short Stories, Spiritual, Theatre, Young Adult.

Les Figues Press, Teresa Carmody, Co-Director; Vanessa Place, Co-Director, PO Box 7736, Los Angeles, CA 90007, info@lesfigues.com. 2005. Poetry, fiction, art, long-poems, plays. "Les Figues Press publishes new works of poetry and prose. We favor well-defined, innovative projects that may not fit within a specific genre, as well as works in translation or with an integral visual component. Most titles are published as part of our TrenchArt series, an annual series of new works selected and presented to draw connections between series titles. Authors are required to write an aesthetic essay as part of the submission process. Additional information about Les Figues Press and the TrenchArt series can be found on our website at www.lesfigues.com." avg. press run 1000. Pub'd 5 titles 2009; expects 7 titles 2010, 6 titles 2011. 6 titles listed in the *Small Press Record of Books in Print* (36th Edition, 2010-11). Discounts: Wholesale: 40% off. 80-200pp. Reporting time: 3-6 months. Simultaneous submissions accepted: Yes. Does not copyright for author. Subjects: Arts, Drama, Experimental, Feminism, Fiction, Literature (General), Poetry, Prose.

Lessiter Publications, Frank Lessiter, Editor & Publisher, PO Box 624, Brookfield, WI 53008-0624, 262-782-4480, Fax 262-782-1252. 1983. Photos, cartoons, interviews. avg. press run 2.5M. Pub'd 3 titles 2009; expects 5 titles 2010, 5 titles 2011. 8 titles listed in the *Small Press Record of Books in Print* (36th Edition, 2010-11). Discounts: trade, bulk. 150pp. Reporting time: 45 days. Simultaneous submissions accepted: no. Payment: yes. Copyrights for author. Subjects: Agriculture, Photography.

LETTER ARTS REVIEW, Christopher Calderhead, PO Box 9986, Greensboro, NC 27429, 800-369-9598, 336-272-6139, Fax 336-272-9015, lar@johnnealbooks.com. 1982. Articles, art, reviews. circ. 5M. 4/yr. Pub'd 4 issues 2009; expects 4 issues 2010, 4 issues 2011. 3 titles listed in the *Small Press Record of Books in Print* (36th Edition, 2010-11). sub. price $48 USA, $53 Canada, $70 all other countries; per copy $12.50; sample $12.50. Back issues: varied. Discounts: 60/40 for outlets, others negotiable. 64pp. Reporting time: 8 weeks or less. Publishes 60% of manuscripts submitted. Payment: on publication. Copyrighted, reverts to author. Pub's reviews: 10+ in 2009. §Calligraphy, graphic arts, typography, book arts, computer fonts. Ads: $550/$400/$25 classified/all one time/4x rate available. Subjects: Book Arts, Calligraphy.

LETTER X, Amy Christian, Publisher; Nicole Lowman, Editor, 9527 Wallingford Ave., N, Seattle, WA 98103, submit@letterxmag.com, www.letterxmag.com. 2004. Poetry, fiction, art, photos, cartoons, music. "Letter X is a semi-annual Creative Writing magazine independently published. We don't have a mission statement. We only want to make everyone's day a little better. All submissions should be 3,000 words or less. Please do not not send more than five poems or two short stories/personal essays per volume submission." circ. 8000. 2/yr. Pub'd 3 issues 2009; expects 2 issues 2010, 2 issues 2011. sub. price $10. Back issues: inquire. 24pp. Reporting time: 3-6 months, depending on when you submit. We accept submissions year round, but we have deadlines for each issue. If you submit directly after a deadline, we may take longer to respond as we want to consider all submissions for each issue before we make final decisions. Simultaneous submissions accepted: Yes. Payment: Contributor's Copies. Not copyrighted.

Level 4 Press, Inc., William Roetzheim Jr., 13518 Jamul Drive, Jamul, CA 91935-1635, 619-669-3100, 619-374-7311 fax, sales@level4Press.com, www.level4press.com. 2005. Poetry, fiction, plays. "We publish a wide variety of work. Our current catalog includes 5 poetry books, 15 poetry audio CDs, 4 fiction books, and several non-fiction titles." avg. press run 5000. Pub'd 7 titles 2009; expects 22 titles 2010, 5 titles 2011. 2 titles listed in the *Small Press Record of Books in Print* (36th Edition, 2010-11). 150-750pp. Reporting time: Query prior to submission. Simultaneous submissions accepted: Yes. Subjects: Audio/Video, Poetry.

Lexicus Press, Jacqueline Stewart, P.O. Box 1691, Palo Alto, CA 94301, 6507995602. 2003. Non-fiction. "Travel books with an emphasis on history and ecology. Undiscovered gems of nature. Color photographs on every page." Pub'd 1 title 2009; expects 1 title 2011. 1 title listed in the *Small Press Record of Books in Print* (36th Edition, 2010-11). Discounts: 1-5 copies 20%10+ copies 40%. 186pp. Reporting time: na. Does not copyright for author. Subject: Travel.

Libellum, Vincent Katz, 211 West 19th Street, #5, New York, NY 10011-4001, libellumbooks@gmail.com, 212-463-7598. 2004. Poetry, art, criticism, parts-of-novels, long-poems. "Libellum was founded to publish smaller-scale complete works, such as long poems or lectures, that might have a hard time getting published otherwise." avg. press run 500. Pub'd 2 titles 2009; expects 4 titles 2010, 2 titles 2011. 6 titles listed in the *Small Press Record of Books in Print* (36th Edition, 2010-11). Discounts: case sensitive. 50pp. Reporting time: I usually commission texts. Payment: Payment is in copies; authors share set of beliefs with publisher. Copyright is stated but not registered by publisher. Subjects: Anarchist, Anthropology, Archaelogy, Architecture, Chicago, Classical Studies, Essays, Experimental, F. Scott Fitzgerald, Non-Violence, Performing Arts, Poetry.

THE (LIBERTARIAN) CONNECTION, Erwin S. Strauss, 10 Hill Street #22-L, Newark, NJ 07102, 973-242-5999. 1968. Poetry, fiction, articles, art, photos, cartoons, interviews, satire, criticism, reviews, music, letters, parts-of-novels, long-poems, collages, plays, concrete art, news items, non-fiction. "Each subscriber is entitled to submit up to four pages of material to be printed in each issue. Additional pages run (unedited) for the cost of printing and mailing. Contributors you may have heard of include Bob ('The Abolition of Work') Black, Ace ('Twisted Image') Backwords, Robert ('Illuminatus!') Shea, Gerry ('Neutron Gun') Reith, Mike ('Loompanics') Hoy, Mike ('Factsheet Five') Gunderloy, Pat ('Salon') Hartman, Lev ('Anarchy') Chernyi, R.W. ('Liberty Magazine') Bradford." circ. 25. 8/yr. Pub'd 8 issues 2009; expects 8 issues 2010, 8 issues 2011. sub. price $10; per copy $1.25; sample $1.25. Back issues: $2.50. Discounts: none. 70pp. Reporting time: none. Simultaneous submissions accepted: yes. Publishes 100% of manuscripts submitted. Payment: none. Copyrighted, reverts to author. Pub's reviews: about 2 dozen in 2009. §Each contributor makes his/her own choices; works of socialist theory and of objectivist philosophy have been popular recently. Ads: ads may be submitted by subscribers as their four free pages, or as paid extra pages (current charge: $7 per extra page). Subjects: Anarchist, Counter-Culture, Alternatives, Communes, Libertarian, Philosophy, Politics.

Libertarian Press, Inc./American Book Distributors, Robert F. Sennholz, Lyn M. Sennholz, PO Box 309, Grove City, PA 16127-0309, 724-458-5861, Fax (724) 458-5962. 1952. Non-fiction. "LP publishes books and booklets on free market economics and political science. ABD is more diversified." avg. press run 2.5M-5M. Pub'd 2 titles 2009; expects 2 titles 2010, 4 titles 2011. No titles listed in the *Small Press Record of Books in Print* (36th Edition, 2010-11). Discounts: up to 60%, based on quantity, larger discounts available on booklets. 300pp. Reporting time: 30 days. Payment: negotable. Copyrights depend on contract. Subjects: Biography, Business & Economics, Children, Youth, Libertarian, Philosophy, Political Science, Reprints.

Libertas Press, LLC., Rob Hogan, P.O. Box 500399, Atlanta, GA 31150, 678-852-8110, contactus@libertas-press.net, http://www.libertaspress.net. 2006. Non-fiction. "Libertas Press, LLC. specializes in works of non-fiction in the fields of the social sciences with a particular emphasis on the importance of LIBERTY in human interaction." avg. press run 2000. Expects 2 titles 2010, 2 titles 2011. 2 titles listed in the *Small Press Record of Books in Print* (36th Edition, 2010-11). Discounts: 2-5 copies 20% 6-10 copies 30% 11-20 copies 40% 21-99 copies 50% 100 and more copies 55%. 300pp. Reporting time: One week. Simultaneous submissions accepted: Yes. Publishes 25% of manuscripts submitted. Payment: Subject to negotiation. Copyrights for author. Subjects: Anthropology, Archaelogy, Biography, Culture, Current Affairs, Geography, Global Affairs, Government, History, Human Rights, Liberal Arts, Libertarian, Non-Fiction, Philosophy, Political Science, Sociology.

LIBERTY, Stephen Cox, Editor, PO Box 20527, Rno, NV 89515-0527, 360-379-0242. 1987. Poetry, fiction, articles, art, cartoons, interviews, satire, criticism, reviews, non-fiction. "News and analysis, reviews, humor. Review of culture and politics from a classical liberal or libertarian perspective." circ. 10,000. 11/yr. Pub'd 11 issues 2009; expects 11 issues 2010, 11 issues 2011. sub. price $29.50; per copy $4; sample $4. Back issues: $4 each, up to $8 for select/rare issues. Discounts: 50%, minimum draw 10, fully returnable. 56pp. Reporting time: 2-4 weeks. Simultaneous submissions accepted: no. Payment: negotiable; most contributors write without remuneration. *Liberty* retains first print and cyberspace serial rights; copyright reverts to author on publication. Pub's reviews: 43 in 2009. §Current events, public policy, history, philosophy, economic theory, political theory, psychology, literature, etc. Ads: $300 full page, $163 half page, other sizes. Discounts: 5% for 3 insertions, 10% for 6, 15% for 12. Subjects: Anarchist, Business & Economics, Ethics, Human Rights, Libertarian, Philosophy, Political Science, Society.

Liberty Publishing Company, Inc., Jeffrey B. Little, Publisher, PO Box 4485, Deerfield Beach, FL 33442-4248, 561-395-3750. 1977. Non-fiction. "Nonfictn, business, horseracing, travel, computer software, video." avg. press run 4M-20M. Pub'd 3 titles 2009; expects 3 titles 2010, 3 titles 2011. 8 titles listed in the *Small Press Record of Books in Print* (36th Edition, 2010-11). Discounts: 40% - 5 or more assorted titles. 120pp. Reporting time: 6 weeks. Payment: 6-12% semi-annual. Will copyright only on request. Subjects: Business & Economics, Consumer, How-To, Non-Fiction, Short Stories, Sports, Outdoors, Travel.

Library Juice Press, Rory Litwin, PO Box 3320, Duluth, MN 55803, 218-260-6115. 2006. Non-fiction. "Library Juice Press specializes in theoretical and practical issues in librarianship from a critical perspective, for an audience of professional librarians and students of library science. Topics covered include library philosophy, information policy, library activism, and in general anything that can be placed under the rubric of "critical studies in librarianship."." avg. press run 400. Pub'd 6 titles 2009; expects 5 titles 2010, 5 titles 2011. 15 titles listed in the *Small Press Record of Books in Print* (36th Edition, 2010-11). Discounts: 25%, negotiable. 100-400pp. Reporting time: One week. Simultaneous submissions accepted: Yes. Publishes 25% of manuscripts submitted. Payment: 20% adjusted net; normally no advance; annual payment. Does not copyright for author. Subjects: Abstracts, Bibliography, Biography, Criticism, Dictionaries, Essays, Indexes & Abstracts, Libraries, Politics, Quotations, Reference, Research, Socialist, Sociology, Technology.

THE LIBRARY QUARTERLY, University of Chicago Press, John Carlo Bertot, Wayne A. Wiegand, Florida State University, School of Information Studies, 101 Shores Building, Tallahassee, FL 32306-2100. 1931. "Since it began publishing in 1931, *The Library Quarterly* has maintained its commitment to informed research in all areas of librarianship—historical, sociological, statistical, bibliographical, managerial, and educational. Combining traditional patterns of investigation with newer, interdisciplinary approaches, the *Quarterly* seeks to interpret relevant issues and current research for the librarian, educator, administrator, and others involved with the collection and history of books." 4/yr. Pub's reviews.

Life Energy Media, 11024 Balboa Blvd. Ste 420, Granada Hills, CA 91344, 818-995-3263. 1975. "Publishes and produces print, audio, and video materials on life energy concepts in the areas of organizations, massage, therapy, movement and dance, expressive arts, yoga, martial arts, spiritual evolution and other related areas." avg. press run 500-5M. Pub'd 1 title 2009; expects 3 titles 2010, 3 titles 2011. 6 titles listed in the *Small Press Record of Books in Print* (36th Edition, 2010-11). Discounts: trade, quantity, conferences, classroom, jobbers. 20-350pp. Reporting time: initial interest 1 month. Payment: negotiable. We can copyright for author. Subjects: Business & Economics, Dance, Health, Psychology, Spiritual.

Life Media (see also NATURAL LIFE), Wendy Priesnitz, B2-125 The Queensway, Suite 52, Toronto, Ontario M8Y 1H6, Canada, email publisher@lifemedia.ca, web www.lifemedia.ca. 1976. Articles, letters, news items, non-fiction. "*Natural Life magazine* has been providing information about natural family living since 1976. It covers all aspects of green living, including organic gardening, natural parenting, life learning, wellness, renewable energy and sustainable housing. Books to date deal with green living, home business and unschooling. See websites for guidelines." Pub'd 3 titles 2009; expects 3 titles 2010, 3 titles 2011. 6 titles listed in the *Small Press Record of Books in Print* (36th Edition, 2010-11). Discounts: retail 40%. 150pp. Reporting time: 1 month. Simultaneous submissions accepted: no. Publishes 2% of manuscripts submitted. Does not copyright for author. Subjects: Cooking, Co-ops, Ecology, Foods, Education, Energy, Environment, Family, Gardening, Society, Solar, Vegetarianism.

LifeCircle Press, Melissa Mosley, PO Box 805, Burlington, IA 52601, www.lifecircleent.com. 2001. Poetry, articles, art, photos, cartoons, letters, news items, non-fiction. "Poetry concerning caregiving and elderly issues. Articles should be concerning 50+ issues. Photos and cartoons for family and 50+ issues. Interested in subjects and formats not already published." Pub'd 2 titles 2009; expects 2 titles 2010, 2 titles 2011. 2 titles listed in the *Small Press Record of Books in Print* (36th Edition, 2010-11). Discounts: 40% wholesale/retail. 60pp. Reporting time: 2 months. Simultaneous submissions accepted: no. Publishes 10% of manuscripts submitted. Payment: 10% of retail price. Copyrights for author. Subjects: Adolescence, Aging, Alternative Medicine, Cartoons, Community, Cooking, Crafts, Hobbies, Creativity, Culture, Education, Family, Finances, Global Affairs, Government, Senior Citizens.

LifeSkill Institute, Inc., Sandra Spaulding Hughes, President; Mary Anne Mills, Editor, P.O. Box 302, Wilmington, NC 28402, 910-251-0665, 910-763-2494, 800-570-4009, lifeskill@earthlink.net, www.lifeskillinstitute.org. 2001. Non-fiction. "Prefer self-improvement/personal development titles." avg. press run 4000. Pub'd 1 title 2009; expects 3 titles 2010, 4 titles 2011. No titles listed in the *Small Press Record of Books in Print* (36th Edition, 2010-11). Discounts: Distributors/Wholesalers - 55%Bookstores/retailers - 40%Institutions/ Classrooms - 5 or more 25%. 200pp. Reporting time: 60 days. Simultaneous submissions accepted: Yes. Publishes 25% of manuscripts submitted. Payment: 10%, pay semi-annual, advance on cases by case basis. Does not copyright for author. Subjects: Metaphysics, New Age, Psychology, Self-Help.

LifeThread Publications, Susan M. Osborn, President, 7541 Wooddale Way, Citrus Heights, CA 95610-2621, 916-722-3452, E-mail susanosborn41@comcast.net Website www.susan.osborn.bz. 1996. 1 title listed in the *Small Press Record of Books in Print* (36th Edition, 2010-11).

LIFETIME MAGAZINE, American Carriage House Publishing, Mardie Caldwell, Editor-in-Chief; Heahter Featherston, Managing Editor, P.O. Box 1130, Nevada City, California, CA 95959, phone 530.432.8860, fax 530.432.7379. 1995. Articles, news items, non-fiction. "Articles can be used on the websites and/or in the magazine or adoption anthalogies, with written permission." circ. 500. 2/yr. Pub'd 1500 issues 2009; expects 2000 issues 2010, 2500 issues 2011. sub. price 25.00; per copy 4.95; sample 3.00. Back issues: Inquire. Discounts: 50% discount to the trade/distributors/agents, etc. 120pp. Reporting time: 6 months. Simultaneous submissions accepted: No. Publishes 10% of manuscripts submitted. Payment: net 30. Copyrighted. Pub's reviews: 20 in 2009. §Adoption Stories. Ads: 250.00 1/2 page175.00 1/4 page150.00 dqc. Subject: Adoption.

LIFTOUTS, Preludium Publishers, Barry Casselman, 520 5th Street SE #4, Minneapolis, MN 55414-1628, (612) 321-9044 barcass@mr.net. 1983. Poetry, fiction, criticism, reviews, parts-of-novels. "*Liftouts* is devoted primarily to reviews of new books and critical essays. Some short fiction and poetry is published, with an emphasis on translated works by foreign authors who have not previously been published in English. *Unsolicited submissions are not considered at this time.* Any inquiries should be accompanied by SASE. Translations of stories by Clarice Lispector, Luiz Vilela, Hans Christoph Buch, Sergio Sant'Anna and others have appeared in previous issues." circ. 5M. 1/yr. Expects 1 issue 2011. price per copy $5; sample $5. Back issues: $5. Discounts: negotiable. 40-75pp. Payment: varies. Copyrighted, reverts to author. Pub's reviews. §Poetry, fiction, plays, literary criticism, all literature in translation. Ads: $495/$275/$7.50 per column inch. Subjects: Book Reviewing, Criticism, Fiction, Poetry, Translation.

Light Density Press (see also LDP, an occasional journal of aesthetics & language), Yvette Johnson, 9162 West Pico Boulevard #15, Los Angeles, CA 90035, www.lightdensitypress.com. 2007. Poetry, fiction, art, photos, cartoons, interviews, music, letters, parts-of-novels, long-poems, collages, plays, concrete art, non-fiction. "Light Density Press publishes innovative small works of poetry, prose & art. Presently, the Press has 3 divisions: Joie Books & Pamphlets for longer works of 10 - 200 pages, LDP, an occasional journal of aesthetics & language, and the PLAIT "Chappy" Series for tiny works of 3 - 10 pages. Emphasis on style in publication." No titles listed in the *Small Press Record of Books in Print* (36th Edition, 2010-11). Reporting time: fewer than 12 weeks. Simultaneous submissions accepted: No. Payment: LDP: one subscription (3 issues); JOIE & PLAIT: ten copies. Copyrights for author. Subjects: Abstracts, Absurdist, African Literature, Africa, African Studies, African-American, Airplanes, Alternative Medicine, Animals, Anthropology, Archaelogy, Artificial Intelligence, Arts, Astronomy, Autobiography, Avant-Garde, Experimental Art, Black, Book Arts.

Light of New Orleans Publishing, Joshua Clark, 828 Royal Street #307, New Orleans, LA 70116, 504-523-4322, Fax 504-522-0688, editor@frenchquarterfiction.com, www.frenchquarterfiction.com. 2001. Fiction. "Published *French Quarter Fiction: The Newest Stories From America's Oldest Bohemia*, an anthology of the best works by living writers on the heart of New Orleans. Published Judy Conner's *Southern Fried Divorce* and Barry Gifford's *Back in America* in 2004." avg. press run 15,000. Pub'd 1 title 2009; expects 2 titles 2010, 2 titles 2011. 1 title listed in the *Small Press Record of Books in Print* (36th Edition, 2010-11). 350pp. Payment: varies. Does not copyright for author. Subjects: Anthology, Fiction, Literature (General), Short Stories.

LIGHT: The Quarterly of Light Verse, John Mella, Lisa Markwart, PO Box 7500, Chicago, IL 60680-7500, 800-285-4448 (Charge Orders only), 708-488-1388 (voice), www.lightquarterly.com (no submissions via fax or e-mail). 1992. Poetry, fiction, articles, art, cartoons, interviews, satire, criticism, reviews, letters, news items. "*Light* is the only magazine in the United States that publishes light verse exclusively. Write for guidelines. Contributors include John Updike, X.J. Kennedy, Donald Hall, Michael Benedikt, and Tom Disch. We also publish cartoons, satire, reviews, and humor. Fax by prior arrangement." circ. 1M. 4/yr. Pub'd 4 issues 2009; expects 4 issues 2010, 4 issues 2011. sub. price $24/4 issues, $36/8 issues, $40/4 issues international, $30/4 issues institutional; per copy $5 + $2 1st class mail; sample $4 + $2 1st class mail. Back issues: same. Discounts: jobber 10%. 64pp. Reporting time: 1-6 months. Simultaneous submissions accepted: no. Publishes 8% of manuscripts submitted. Payment: copies. Copyrighted, reverts to author. Pub's reviews: 60 in 2009. §Light verse, satire, cartoons. Ads: Write for ad card. Subjects: Cartoons, Comics, Essays, Fiction, Graphics, Literature (General), Poetry, Prose, Reviews.

Light-Beams Publishing, Mark Forman, 10 Toon Lane, Lee, NH 03861, Tel:603-659-1300, Tel:800-397-7641, Fax:603-659-3399, e-mail: mforman@light-beams.com. 1997. Fiction, photos. "Distribution to the book trade through IPG." avg. press run 10000. Pub'd 2 titles 2009; expects 2 titles 2010, 2 titles 2011. No titles listed in the *Small Press Record of Books in Print* (36th Edition, 2010-11). Discounts: 12 or more 45% 20 per item (case) 50%. 56pp. Subjects: Children, Youth, Family, Nature.

LightLines Publishing, 12 Wilson Street, Farmington, NH 03835-3428, 603-755-3091, Fax 603-755-3748, lightlinespublishing@yahoo.com, www.lightlinespublishing.com. 1996. Non-fiction. avg. press run 10M. Pub'd 2 titles 2009; expects 2 titles 2010, 4 titles 2011. 5 titles listed in the *Small Press Record of Books in Print* (36th Edition, 2010-11). Discounts: 40% to retailer, 55% to distributors. 175pp. Reporting time: variable. Simultaneous submissions accepted: no. Publishes 10% of manuscripts submitted. Payment: variable. Copyrights for author. Subjects: Alternative Medicine, Metaphysics, Self-Help, Spiritual.

•**Lightning Bug Learning Press,** Julie Rebboah, 16869 SW 65th Ave., #271, Lake Oswego, OR 97035, Phone 877-695-7312, Fax 971-250-2582, Email: mail@lightningbuglearning.com, web address: http://www.lightning-buglearningpress.com. 2008. Non-fiction. "Lightning Bug Learning Press is an educational publishing company. Some of our materials include learn-to-read books, literacy kits and learning aids." avg. press run 1500. Pub'd 4 titles 2009; expects 2 titles 2010, 2 titles 2011. No titles listed in the *Small Press Record of Books in Print* (36th Edition, 2010-11). Discounts: 1 copy 20% 2-4 copies 40% 5-9 copies 42% 10-100 copies 46% 100+ 50%. 90pp. Reporting time: 3 months. Simultaneous submissions accepted: No. Publishes 1% of manuscripts submitted. Payment: Negotiable. Does not copyright for author. Subjects: Education, Family, Juvenile Fiction, Libraries, Non-Fiction, Parenting, Reading, Textbooks.

LIGHTWORKS MAGAZINE, Charlton Burch, Designer and Editor; Andrea Martin, Managing Editor, PO Box 1202, Birmingham, MI 48012-1202, 248-626-8026, lightworks_mag@hotmail.com. 1975. Articles, art, photos, interviews, collages, concrete art. "Illuminating new and experimental art. A tribute issue devoted to the life and art of Ray Johnson (#22) was issued in 2001. The subject of mail art archives, personal and institutional collections of artists' publications and ephemera is planned for a future issue." circ. 2M. Irregular. Pub'd The magazine has been in a period of dormancy. However new issues arc planned for late 2009 and 2010 as well as a website. issues 2009. price per copy price varies; sample $5. Available back issues: #s 10, 13, 14/15, 16, 17, 18, 19 & 20/21 are $5 per copy. #22 (Ray Johnson issue w/audio CD) is $13 Mailing charge on all domestic orders is $5. Discounts: 30% on minimum orders of 12 copies of one issue. 64-96pp. Reporting time: usually quick. Publishes 50% of manuscripts submitted. Payment: none, other than a couple copies. Copyrighted. Pub's reviews. §Books, periodicals, and recordings which explore alternative & intermediate artforms, and artists' publications. No ads. Subjects: Arts, Avant-Garde, Experimental Art, Book Arts, Book Reviewing, Communication, Journalism, Counter-Culture, Alternatives, Communes, Creativity, Dada, Electronics, Graphics, Music, Networking, Photography, Visual Arts.

LILIES AND CANNONBALLS REVIEW, Daniel Connor, P.O. Box 702, Bowling Green Station, New York, NY 10274-0702, info@liliesandcannonballs.com, www.liliesandcannonballs.com. 2004. Poetry, fiction, art, photos, cartoons, interviews, satire, letters, parts-of-novels, long-poems, collages, plays, concrete art, non-fiction. "LCR seeks to create a space for the synthesis of contrary elements: aesthetically driven and socially conscious literature and art; traditional and experimental forms; crazy-man conservative and bleeding liberal views. Recent contributors include John Yau, Julio Cortazar, Albert Mobilio, Rob Phelps, Lynn Crawford, Matthew Thorburn, Inigo Garcia Ureta, and James Doyle. Reading period: May-June." circ. 300-500. 1-2/yr. Pub'd 1 issue 2009; expects 1 issue 2010, 1 issue 2011. sub. price $23; per copy $12; sample $12. Back issues: inquire. Discounts: inquire. 96pp. Reporting time: 1 to 6 months, give or take. Simultaneous submissions accepted: Yes. Publishes 5% of manuscripts submitted. Payment: 1 copy. Copyrighted, reverts to author. Ads: inquire.

LILITH, Susan W. Schneider, Editor-in-Chief, 250 West 57th, #2432, New York, NY 10107, 212-757-0818. 1976. Poetry, fiction, articles, art, photos, interviews, criticism, reviews, letters, parts-of-novels, long-poems, plays, news items, non-fiction. "independent, Jewish & frankly feminist. Published quarterly." circ. 10M. 4/yr. Pub'd 4 issues 2009; expects 4 issues 2010, 4 issues 2011. sub. price $25.97; per copy $4.50; sample $7, includes postage. Back issues: $7 for in-print back issues. Out-of-print $50. Discounts: through distributors: DeBoer's, Ingram, Koens, small changes, desert moon. 48pp. Reporting time: 3 months. Simultaneous submissions accepted, as long as we are told when another publication accepts. Payment: negotiable. Copyrighted, rights reverting to author negotiable. Pub's reviews: 20 in 2009. §Pertaining to the Jewish, female experience, history, biography/autobio., feminist, fiction, poetry. Ads: on request. Subjects: Judaism, Women.

LILLIPUT REVIEW, Don Wentworth, Editor, 282 Main Street, Pittsburgh, PA 15201. 1989. Poetry. "All poems must be 10 lines or *less*. All styles and forms considered. SASE or in the trash, period. 3 poems maximum per submissions. Any submission beyond the maximum will be returned unread." circ. 250-350. Irregular. Pub'd 8 issues 2009; expects 8 issues 2010, 8 issues 2011. 19 titles listed in the *Small Press Record of Books in Print* (36th Edition, 2010-11). sub. price $12; per copy $1; sample $1 or SASE. Back issues: $1.

Discounts: Individuals only: 6 issues=$5; 15 issues=$10. 16pp. Reporting time: 1-16 weeks. Simultaneous submissions accepted: no. Publishes 5% of manuscripts submitted. Payment: 2 copies. Copyrighted, reverts to author. Subjects: Haiku, Poetry, Translation.

Lilly Press (see also RIVER POETS JOURNAL), Judith Lawrence, 1848 Finch Dr, Bensalem, PA 19020-4406, 215-638-2493. 2007. Poetry, fiction, art, photos, parts-of-novels, non-fiction. "We seek poetry, fiction, non-fiction, essay, memoir, art and photography for our quarterly journals, special editions, anthologies and chapbooks. We welcome established writers, but actively seek new writers who show great promise. To see submission guidelines and samples of what we publish visit our website. www.riverpoetsjournal.com." Pub'd 6 titles 2009; expects 8 titles 2010, 10 titles 2011. 3 titles listed in the *Small Press Record of Books in Print* (36th Edition, 2010-11). Reporting time: Response to submissions is from 4 weeks to 6 months depending on type of submission, journal, anthology, chapbook or contest. Simultaneous submissions accepted: Yes. Payment: Payment is publication. All works are copyrighted. Subjects: Anthology, Arts, Fiction, Haiku, Memoirs, Mystery, Non-Fiction, Photography, Poetry, Prose, Publishing, Short Stories, Storytelling, Writers/Writing, Zines.

Lily Ruth Publishing, Jennifer Stone, Editor, PO Box 2067, Jacksonville, TX 75766, fax 888-602-6912; email lilyruthpublishing@yahoo.com; web site www.lilyruthpublishing.com. 2008. Fiction. "Lily Ruth Publishing is dedicated to fun children's literature. Our most recent contributor is child author J. K. Hawkins and her book, My Weird Family Series: My Werewolf Brothers. We look for compelling, yet fun, stories from our authors that will inspire children to develop a life-long love of reading." avg. press run 1000. Pub'd 1 title 2009; expects 3 titles 2010, 3 titles 2011. 3 titles listed in the *Small Press Record of Books in Print* (36th Edition, 2010-11). Discounts: 55% discount to wholesalers; 30% discount for quantities of 4 or less to retailers; 30% discount for quantities of 5 or more to retailers. 200pp. Reporting time: Lily Ruth Publishing currently responds to submissions within three months of the time the submission is received. Simultaneous submissions accepted: Yes. Please notify the editor of simultaneous submissions in a cover letter. Publishes 30% of manuscripts submitted. Copyrights for author. Subjects: Children, Youth, Fiction, Humor, Juvenile Fiction, Young Adult.

Limberlost Press, Rick Ardinger, Editor; Rosemary Ardinger, Editor, 17 Canyon Trail, Boise, ID 83716. 1976. Poetry, fiction, interviews, reviews. "*Limberlost Press* is devoted to the publication of fine, letterpress-printed, limited edition poetry chapbooks. Established in 1976 as a literary magazine, the magazine, *The Limberlost Review*, was suspended in the 1980s, when we began to letterpress chapbooks by individual authors. Since then, we have averaged three to four titles a year. Limberlost publishes work by nationally known writers, as well as established and emerging writers from the West (mostly). Noted writers in the Limberlost canon include Sherman Alexie, Edward Dorn, Lawrence Ferlinghetti, Gary Snyder, Gary Gildner, John Updike, Jim Harrison, Ed Sanders, Allen Ginsberg, John Haines, Jennifer Dunbar Dorn, Hayden Carruth, and others. Other poets include, Margaret Aho, William Studebaker, Judith Root, Nancy Takacs, Greg Keeler, Gino Sky, Chuck Guilford, Keith Wilson, Gary Holthaus, and others. Our books are printed on archival-quality papers, and sewn by hand in wrappers. A limited number of each title is bound by hand into cloth and boards as special signed/numbered editions. We try to keep the books affordable, typically between $15 to $25 (with signed copies priced higher). Occasionally, we publish full-length commercially printed books that are not letterpress printed, such as *Waltzing with the Captain: Remembeing Richard Brautigan*, a memoir by Montana writer Greg Keeler, *Coyote in the Mountains*, a collection of short stories by Idaho writer John Rember. Most of the time, we solicit manuscripts; however, sometimes a manuscript just arrives in the mail that just seems right for the canon. Because our methods are labor intensive, however, prospective contributors should be familiar with our books before considering. They should have held our books in their hands to truly understand what a Limberlost book is, and thus submit a collection for consideration that they feel is appropriate. A current list of titles in print is on our website at www.Limberlostpress.com." avg. press run 500. Pub'd 4 titles 2009; expects 4 titles 2010, 4 titles 2011. 18 titles listed in the *Small Press Record of Books in Print* (36th Edition, 2010-11). Discounts: 40% for 5 or more. 36pp. Reporting time: 1-2 months. Payment: in copies. Copyrights for author. Subjects: Literary Review, Poetry.

Limelight Editions, John Cerullo, Publisher, 19 West 21st Street, Suite 201, New York, NY 10010, 212-575-9265, fax 212-575-9270, info@limelighteditions.com, www.limelighteditions.com. 1984. Non-fiction. avg. press run 4M. Pub'd 10 titles 2009; expects 12 titles 2010, 14 titles 2011. 107 titles listed in the *Small Press Record of Books in Print* (36th Edition, 2010-11). Discounts: 1-4: 20%; 5-100: 47%; 100+: 50%. 300pp. Reporting time: 4-6 weeks. We do not usually accept simultaneous submissions. Publishes 10% of manuscripts submitted. Payment: generally 7-1/2% for paperback, 10% cloth. Does not copyright for author. Subjects: Autobiography, Biography, Criticism, Dance, Movies, Non-Fiction, Performing Arts, G.B. Shaw, Theatre.

LIMESTONE: A Literary Journal, Stacey Floyd, English Dept., Univ. of Kentucky, 1215 Patterson Office Tower, Lexington, KY 40506-0027, 859-257-6981, www.uky.edu/AS/English/Limestone. 1976. Poetry, fiction, art, photos, cartoons, interviews, plays, concrete art. "Since 1976, Limestone: A Literary Journal, ISSN 0899-5966, has published creative writing and art from around the world. We recently published Paul Muldoon,

Seamus Heaney, Evan Boland, and friends in a special Irish Poets issue. We accept only previously unpublished manuscripts from August to Dec. Final decisions are made by March. Please see our web site for jourbnal information.'' circ. 500-1M. 1-2/yr. Pub'd 1 issue 2009; expects 2 issues 2010, 1 issue 2011. sub. price $12; per copy $6; sample $6. Back issues: $4. 150pp. Reporting time: 6 months. Simultaneous submissions accepted: yes. Publishes 10% of manuscripts submitted. Payment: copy of the journal. Copyrighted, reverts to author. Pub's reviews: 2 in 2009. §We are most interested in reviews of works by Kentucky authors (or regional) - either poetry or fiction. Ads: $100/$50. Subject: Literature (General).

Lincoln Springs Press, 40 Post Avenue, Hawthorne, NJ 07506-1809. 1987. Poetry, fiction, photos. ''We have ceased accepting unsolicited poetry and fiction manuscripts for the time being.'' avg. press run 1M. Expects 4 titles 2010, 4 titles 2011. 9 titles listed in the *Small Press Record of Books in Print* (36th Edition, 2010-11). Discounts: 1-5 20%, 5-10 30%, 10+ 40%. 80pp. Reporting time: 6 months. Payment: 15% royalty. Copyrights for author. Subjects: Literature (General), Photography, Poetry, Prose.

LINES + STARS, Rachel Adams, Washington, DC 20009, www.linesandstars.com, editor@linesandstars.com. 2006. Poetry, fiction, art, long-poems. ''Lines + Stars began as a means of establishing a new creative forum in Washington, D.C.—a city that all-too-often coasts solely on its more mechanistic pursuits. While many of our contributors hail from the D.C. area, we've also expanded our writer-base to include national and international voices.Lines & Stars features poetry and short fiction of all types. In general, we commend the experimental and eschew the inane. Novice and seasoned writers are welcome; it is the quality and strength of the work that ultimately determines its inclusion in the journal.'' circ. 700. 4/yr. Pub'd 1 issue 2009; expects 2 issues 2010, 4 issues 2011. sub. price free; per copy $4; sample $4. Back issues: inquire. 30pp. Reporting time: 1-2 weeks. Simultaneous submissions accepted: Yes. Publishes 40% of manuscripts submitted. Payment: None. Copyrighted. Subjects: Literature (General), Photography, Poetry, Prose, Short Stories.

LINQ, Dr. Dosia Reichardt, General Editor, School of Humanities, James Cook Univ.-North Queensland, Townsville 4811, Australia, e-mail jcu.linq@jcu.edu.au. 1971. Poetry, fiction, articles, interviews, criticism, reviews, parts-of-novels, long-poems, plays. ''Critical articles about 3M words. Reviews 1M words.'' circ. 350. 2/yr. Pub'd 2 issues 2009; expects 2 issues 2010, 2 issues 2011. sub. price $30 indiv.; $40 instit. including postage, Australian, Overseas $50 Australian; per copy $15, Australian (including postage), $20 Australian overseas. Back issues: $3 prior to 1980. 140pp. Reporting time: 2 months. Simultaneous submissions accepted: yes. Payment: poetry $20 per poem, short fiction $50, reviews $30, articles $50 Australian dollars. Copyrighted, reverts to author. Pub's reviews: 8 in 2009. §Any area of contemporary interest, political, sociological, literary. Subjects: Arts, Bibliography, Book Reviewing, Criticism, Drama, Fiction, Literary Review, Poetry, Women.

Lintel, Naomi May Miller, Publisher, 24 Blake Lane, Middletown, NY 10940, 845-342-5224. 1978. Poetry, fiction, art, long-poems. ''Not currently accepting unsolicited manuscripts.'' 19 titles listed in the *Small Press Record of Books in Print* (36th Edition, 2010-11). Discounts: 40% to bookstores; 45% on 25 copies or more; 55% to wholesalers.

Lion Press, Norma L. Leone, PO Box 92541, Rochester, NY 14692, phone 585-381-6410; fax 585-381-7439; for orders only 800-597-3068. 1985. Non-fiction. avg. press run 1M-5M. Pub'd 3 titles 2009. 4 titles listed in the *Small Press Record of Books in Print* (36th Edition, 2010-11). Discounts: 20-50%. 1-200pp. Simultaneous submissions accepted: no. Publishes 0% of manuscripts submitted. Copyrights for author. Subjects: Computers, Calculators, Health, How-To, Transportation, Women.

Lion's Den Publishing, Kelly Cyr, 401 Sweetgrass Ct., Great Falls, MT 59405-1325, 406 453 4296. 2006. ''This press is for people who want to have a book based on their own lives or someone they know. We are accepting interest for personal histories, commemorative books, milestone books and business books of a personal nature. Memoirs and autobiographies welcomed. Please see www.lionsdenpublishing.com.'' Pub'd 1 title 2009. No titles listed in the *Small Press Record of Books in Print* (36th Edition, 2010-11). Discounts: 1-% 2-4 20% 5-99 40% 100 and up 50%. 528pp. Reporting time: within the week. Simultaneous submissions accepted: Yes. Payment: 15% of book sales. Copyrights for author. Subjects: Aging, Alcohol, Alcoholism, Autobiography, Book Reviewing, Cooking, Crafts, Hobbies, Death & Dying, Family, Genealogy, Journals, Literary Review, Memoirs, Montana, Non-Violence, Religion.

•**LIPS,** Laura Boss, Editor, 7002 Blvd. East, #2-26G, Guttenberg, NJ 07093. ''Submissions are being solicited for the next issue. We recommend that contributors send for a sample copy of Lips before submitting work to the magazine. Guidelines: Five poems unpublished, first rights, copyright reverts to the author upon publication. Please send poems with an S.A.S.E. with proper postage to the address below left. No submissions between March and September. *Lips* is published twice a year. We suggest seeing a copy of the magazine first, either at your library, or a back sample for $8 plus $2.50 postage and handling.''

Liquid Paper Press (see also NERVE COWBOY), Joseph Shields, Jerry Hagins, PO Box 4973, Austin, TX 78765, www.eden.com/~jwhagins/nervecowboy. 1995. Poetry. ''Recent books published by Liquid Paper Press include *The Active Ingredient, and Other Poems* and *The Back East Poems* by Gerald Locklin, *Sunday Ritual* by

Ralph Dranow, *Picking the Lock on the Door to Paradise* by Joan Jobe Smith, *Notes of a Human Warehouse Engineer* by Belinda Subraman, *E Pluribus Aluminum* by Thomas Michael McDade, and *Hoeing in High Heels* by Wilma Elizabeth McDaniel. We do not accept unsolicited manuscripts.'' avg. press run 150. Pub'd 4 titles 2009; expects 4 titles 2010, 4 titles 2011. 12 titles listed in the *Small Press Record of Books in Print* (36th Edition, 2010-11). Discounts: 40% on purchase of 3 or more copies. 32pp. We currently only accept solicited chapbook manuscripts, with the exception of our annual chapbook. Payment: 30 complimentary copies. Copyrights for author. Subject: Poetry.

THE LISTENING EYE, Grace Butcher, Editor; James Wohlken, Ass't Ed.; John McBratney, Ass't Ed., KSU Geauga Campus, 14111 Claridon-Troy Road, Burton, OH 44021, 440-286-3840, grace_butcher@msn.com. 1970. Poetry, fiction, art, photos, non-fiction. "5 x 7 vertical format, black & white or color. Make checks payable to Grace Butcher." circ. 250. 1/yr. Pub'd 1 issue 2009; expects 1 issue 2010, 1 issue 2011. sub. price $4; per copy $4; sample $4. Back issues: $4. Discounts: N/A. 60pp. Reporting time: 4 months max, sometimes sooner. Simultaneous submissions accepted: no. Publishes maybe 20% of manuscripts submitted. Payment: 2 free copies. Copyrighted, reverts to author. Subjects: Essays, Fiction, Photography, Poetry, Short Stories, Sports, Outdoors.

Listening Voice Media Ltd, Denise Gagne Williamson, P O Box 75032 RPO Cambrian, Calgary, Alberta T2K 1P0, Canada, 403-220-1166, 403-220-1162. 2004. Music, non-fiction. "Listening Voice Media publishes teacher resource guides to assist in second language instruction, whether French or English. These books include songs and games, an audio CD of the musical pieces, photocopy-ready activity sheets and many teaching suggestions." avg. press run 500. Pub'd 3 titles 2009; expects 3 titles 2010, 1 title 2011. 4 titles listed in the *Small Press Record of Books in Print* (36th Edition, 2010-11). Discounts: 2-10 copies 25% +11 copies 40%. 75pp. Subjects: Education, English, France, French, Language, Music, Non-Fiction.

LIT, Writing Program, Room 514, 66 West 12th Street, New York, NY 10011. "Poetry submissions should be no more than 5 poems or 10 pages. Prose submissions should be no longer than 25 pages, double-spaced, single-sided. All submissions must include a SASE for reply and a cover letter. Cover letters let us know that you're a real person who actually has some knowledge about LIT. We appreciate that sort of thing. Submissions without cover letters will NOT be considered. Contributors must receive a reply from LIT before submitting new work; additional submissions received before we have sent a reply to a previous submission will be returned unread! Our reading periods are from September to mid-December and January to May. Do not submit more than twice in either period. We do not consider submissions filed by professional coordinating services."

LITERAL: Latin American Voices, David Medina Portillo, Editor-in-Chief, 770 South Post Oak Lane, Suite 530, Houston, TX 77056. "*Literal*, Latin American Voices, winner of 2 CELJ Awards and three Lone Star Awards, offers its pages with a dual purpose: as a forum where the most important Latin American creative expressions converge and as a vehicle for the expression of new voices. Thus Literal provides a medium for the critique and diffusion of the Latin American literature and art, recognizing its potential strength as a point of departure for understanding that the broad cultural universe is not overshadowed by any single language, but is bathed in the light of a unified spirit."

LITERALLY HORSES/REMUDA, Laurie A. Cerny, 208 Cherry Hill Street, Kalamazoo, MI 49006-4221, 616-345-5915, literallyhorses@aol.com. 1999. Poetry, fiction, cartoons, reviews, music, parts-of-novels, long-poems. "Poems should be under 50 lines. Fiction (short story) under 3,500 words. All material should have a horse/rider, or western lifestyle theme. Recent contributors: Richard Wheeler, Maria Bailey, Rod Miller and Emery Mehok." circ. 1M. 2/yr. Pub'd 4 issues 2009; expects 4 issues 2010, 2 issues 2011. 1 title listed in the *Small Press Record of Books in Print* (36th Edition, 2010-11). sub. price $7.95; per copy $2.25; sample $2.50. Back issues: $2.50. Discounts: none. 46pp. Reporting time: 1 month. Simultaneous submissions accepted: yes. Publishes 50% of manuscripts submitted. Payment: contributor's copy/subscription. Copyrighted, reverts to author. Pub's reviews: 15 in 2009. §Topics must pertain to horses,showing of various disciplines like racing, rodeo, dressage, etc., cowboys, western lifestyle. Ads: none. Subjects: Animals, Fiction, Old West, Poetry, Prose, The West.

LITERARY HOUSE REVIEW, Skyline Publications, Victoria Valentine, P.O. Box 295, Stormville, NY 12582-0295, Website: http://www.literaryhouse.com, Email: literature@literaryhouse.com. 2006. Poetry, fiction, art, photos, long-poems, non-fiction. "Literary House Review is devoted to the promotion of fine literature, publishing Engaging Stories and Brilliant Poetry by International Authors and Poets, Online and in Print. We select six stories and/or poems from our online publication and other submissions to submit to Pushcart Prize each year, publishing the six nominees in an elegant annual print edition. A selection of other fine material is also published online and in our annual print edition. Visit us on www.LiteraryHouse.com for further information." One Print Annually. Quarterly Web Site Publication. Expects 1 issue 2011. 1 title listed in the *Small Press Record of Books in Print* (36th Edition, 2010-11). price per copy 16; sample $16. Back issues: inquire. Discounts: Universities, Libraries, Schools, 2-4 copies 10%. 80pp. Reporting time: 4 months. Due to the volume of mail we receive, not always able to respond. Follow up with status query after 2 months if you would like. Simultaneous submissions accepted: Yes. Publishes 25% of manuscripts submitted. Copyright notice of entire works, but not for each individual author. Author retains all rights and responsibilities for their personal copyright. Ads: no. Subjects: Creative Non-fiction, Drama, Essays, Inspirational, Literature (General), Motivation, Success, Mystery, Myth, Mythology, Nature, Non-Fiction, Poetry, Prose, Romance, Short Stories, Storytelling.

LITERARY IMAGINATION: The Review of the Association of Literary Scholars and Critics, Peter Campion, The Association of Literary Scholars and Critics, 650 Beacon Street, Suite 510, Boston, MA 02215, 617-358-1990, Fax 617-358-1995, alsc@bu.edu, www.bu.edu/literary. 1999. Poetry, fiction, articles, interviews, criticism, reviews, parts-of-novels. "Submissions only accepted ONLINE, http://litimag.oxfordjournals.org/." circ. 2,133. 3/yr. Pub'd 3 issues 2009; expects 3 issues 2010, 3 issues 2011. sub. price $70 individuals, $81 US institutions; sample free. 120pp. Reporting time: to 90 days. Simultaneous submissions accepted: no. Publishes 20% of manuscripts submitted. Payment: not usually. Copyrighted, reverts to author. Pub's reviews: 1 in 2009. Subjects: Criticism, Essays, Fiction, Literary Review, Literature (General), Poetry, Translation.

LITERARY MAGAZINE REVIEW, Jenny Brantley, Editor; Brian Fitch, Assistant Editor, Univ. of Wisconsin-River Falls, English Dept., 410 S. 3rd Street, River Falls, WI 54022, email: jennifer.s.brantley@uwrf.edu, web site: http://www.uwrf.edu/lmr/. 1981. Articles, art, interviews, criticism, reviews, news items. "*LMR* is devoted to providing critical appraisals of the specific contents of small, predominantly literary periodicals for the benefit of readers and writers. We print reviews of about 1.5M words that comment on the magazines' physical characteristics, on particular articles, stories, and poems featured, and on editorial preferences as evidenced in the selections. Recent contributors include John Pennington, D.E. Steward, Phil Miller, Kevin Prufer, Steve Heller, Maria Melendez, Stella Pope Duarte, and John McNally. We would be happy to entertain queries offering disinterested reviews and omnibus notices and pieces describing, explaining, or examining the current literary magazine scene. Subscription exchange inquiries are welcome." circ. 300. 4/yr. Pub'd 4 issues 2009; expects 4 issues 2010, 4 issues 2011. sub. price $16; per copy $5; sample $5. Back issues: $7 an issue. Discounts: 10% to subscription agencies. 48-52pp. Payment: copies. Copyrighted, rights revert on author's request. Pub's reviews: 70 in 2009. §Literary magazines. We are interested in magazines that publish at least some fiction, poetry, literary nonfiction, or all three. Ads: none. Subjects: Criticism, Literary Review, Magazines, Reviews.

LITERARY MAMA, Amy Hudock, Editor-in-Chief, Department of English, Pinewood Preparatory School, 1114 Orangeburg Road, Summerville, SC 29843, www.literarymam.com. "*Literary Mama*, an online literary magazine, features writing by mother writers about the complexities and many faces of motherhood. We publish fiction, poetry, creative nonfiction, literary criticism, book reviews, columns, and profiles about mother writers."

THE LITERARY REVIEW, Minna Proctor, Editor; Rene Steinke, Editor at Large; Walter Cummins, Editor Emeritus; Renee Ashley, Poetry Editor; David Daniel, Poetry Editor; Jena Salon, Review Editor, Fairleigh Dickinson University, 285 Madison Avenue, Madison, NJ 07940, 973-443-8564, Fax 973-443-8364. 1957. Poetry, fiction, articles, interviews, criticism, reviews, long-poems. "We consider fiction and poetry submissions of any type and of any length (within reason) from new and established writers. *TLR* has always had a special emphasis on contemporary writing abroad (in translation) and we welcome submissions from overseas, and new translations of contemporary foreign literature. We are particularly interested in receiving translations of and essays on ethnic writing abroad. We no longer read paper submissions; work to be considered should be submitted on line at theliteraryreview.org/submit.html." circ. 2M-2.5M. 4/yr. Pub'd 4 issues 2009; expects 4 issues 2010, 4 issues 2011. sub. price $24 U.S., $32 foreign; per copy $8 U.S., $8 foreign; sample $7 recent issues. Back issues: varies. 180-200pp. Reporting time: 4-5 months. Simultaneous submissions accepted: yes. Publishes 3% of manuscripts submitted. Payment: 2 free copies, additional copies at discount. Copyrighted, reverts to author. Pub's reviews: 10 in 2009. §Contemporary fiction, poetry, literary theory, US and world literature (contemporary). No ads. Subject: Literary Review.

Litmus Press (see also AUFGABE), Traccy E. Grinnell, Editor, PO Box 25526, Brooklyn, NY 11202-5526. "New experimental poetry and prose by established or new writers." No titles listed in the *Small Press Record of Books in Print* (36th Edition, 2010-11).

LITTLE BALKANS REVIEW, Ortolani Al, Editor; Hogard Mike, Editor; Watts Ted, Editor; Bockelman Wayne, Editor; Laflen John, Editor; Ortolani James, Editor; Blancho Chris, Editor; Burns Tom, Editor, 909 S. Olive, Pittsburg, KS 66762, littlebalkansreview@gmail.com. 1980. Poetry, fiction, articles, art, photos, cartoons, interviews, satire, music, letters, parts-of-novels, plays, concrete art, non-fiction. "The Little Balkans Review, a Southeast Kansas literary and graphics arts journal, uses poetry, fiction, non-fiction, photographs and art work. Under our current editorial policy, each issue of the magazine will have approximately ten pages of poetry, ten of graphics, thirty of fiction and thirty of non-fiction. Prime consideration is given to work by Kansans and former Kansans, as well as work set in the Little Balkans. Preference is given for non-fiction subjects related to the Little Balkans. At least half of the poetry of each issue will be devoted to poets who have had limited previous publication." circ. 1500. 2-4/yr. Expects 2 issues 2011. sub. price $20.00; per copy $10.00; sample $8.00. Back issues: inquire. Discounts: Free to libraries. Inquire directly for other discounts. 120pp. Reporting time: Six weeks. Simultaneous submissions accepted: No. Payment: Pays in contributor copies. Copyrighted, reverts to author. Subjects: Drama, Essays, Fiction, Haiku, History, Kansas, Literature (General), Memoirs, Non-Fiction, Photography, Poetry, Short Stories.

THE LITTLE MAGAZINE, Alifair Skebe, Michael Peters, Department of English, State Univ. of New York, University of Albany, Albany, NY 12222, website www.albany.edu/~litmag. 1965. Poetry, fiction. *"The Little Magazine* is an old literary journal revived under the editorship of UAlbany's faculty and graduate student writers. *TLM* is now a multi-media based journal published on the web and CD-ROM in effort to promote and display the creative opportunites that exist amongst literature, art, and new media. *We have no set guidelines.* We prefer work that lends itself to hypermedia/hypertext production. We like poetry and fiction that foregrounds language and is innovative in form, pushing its own limits and the limits of genre through sound, text, image. We'd like to see more work from minority writers. We do not read from May through August. Some recent contributors: Charles Bernstein, Raymond Federman, Christy Sheffield Sanford, Mark Amerika, Eduardo Kac, Juliana Spahr, Richard Kostelanetz. TLM can be found on line at www.albany.edu/~litmag." circ. 2M. 1/yr. Pub'd 1 issue 2009; expects 2 issues 2010, 2 issues 2011. sub. price $15 (for the CD-Rom); per copy $15 (for the CD-Rom); sample $15 (for the CD-Rom). Back issues: $6. Discounts: see website for details. Reporting time: 3 months. Simultaneous submissions accepted: yes. Publishes 20% of manuscripts submitted. Payment: 1 copy. Copyrighted, reverts to author. Ads: please inquire. Subjects: Fiction, Poetry.

Little Pear Press, Martha Manno, PO Box 343, Seekonk, MA 02771, Martha@LittlePearPress.com, www.LittlePearPress.com. 2003. Poetry. "Poetry by individuals, who have not previously published a book length work. Recent poets: James Cihlar, Barbara Schweitzer. Coming in 2009- 2010: Amanda Surkont, Eve Rivkah. Not reading unsolicited manuscripts at this time." avg. press run 500. Pub'd 1 title 2009; expects 3 titles 2010, 1 title 2011. 6 titles listed in the *Small Press Record of Books in Print* (36th Edition, 2010-11). Discounts: 40% discount 1+. 72pp. Payment: Small payment and payment in copies. Copyrights for author. Subjects: Anthology, Autobiography, Experimental, Juvenile Fiction, Memoirs, Poetry.

Little Poem Press, C. E. Laine, Editor, PO Box 185, Falls Church, VA 22040-0185, www.celaine.com/ LittlePoemPress. 2003. Poetry, fiction, long-poems. "We publish e-books and printed chapbooks (not to exceed 50 pages). No electronic submissions. Must include hardcopy and electronic file on disk/cd (.rtf/.doc/.txt only). Finished and polished manuscripts only. Please include author bio and acknowledgements. SASE required for returned work." avg. press run unlimited. Pub'd 4 titles 2009; expects 20 titles 2010, 30 titles 2011. 1 title listed in the *Small Press Record of Books in Print* (36th Edition, 2010-11). Discounts: 10%. 50pp. Reporting time: 90 days. Simultaneous submissions accepted: no. Publishes 5% of manuscripts submitted. Payment: 50-50 split after expenses. Author retains copyright. Subject: Poetry.

LITVISION, LITVISION PRESS, Patrick Simonelli, 7711 Greenback Lane #156, Citrus Heights, CA 95610.

Litwin Books, Rory Litwin, PO Box 3320, Duluth, MN 55803, 218-260-6115. 2006. Criticism, non-fiction. "Litwin Books specializes in scholarly books about media, communication, libraries, and related historical topics." avg. press run 500. Pub'd 4 titles 2009; expects 4 titles 2010, 4 titles 2011. 9 titles listed in the *Small Press Record of Books in Print* (36th Edition, 2010-11). Discounts: 20% negotiable. 150-400pp. Reporting time: One week. Simultaneous submissions accepted: Yes. Publishes 25% of manuscripts submitted. Payment: 20% adjusted net; normally no advance; annual payment. Does not copyright for author. Subjects: Anarchist, Bibliography, Biography, Book Collecting, Bookselling, Communication, Journalism, Criticism, Dictionaries, History, Language, Newspapers, Publishing, Reference, Socialist, Sociology, University Press.

LIVE MAG!, Jeffrey Cyphers Wright, 632 East 14th Street, #18, New York, NY 10009, 212-673-1152. 1976. Poetry, art, photos, cartoons, music, letters, collages. "The press is currently hosting LIVE MAG! events in New York City. LIVE MAG! is an art and poetry quarterly and so far has published Edward Field, Kimiko Hahn, Gary Indiana, Michael Andre, Robert C. Morgan, Norma Cole, Alex Lemon and others. Live Mag! was born to run at the Bowery Poetry Club. It was conceived by Bob Holman and Jeff Wright as a performance / publication dual event created specifically for the Bowery Poetry Club. The live events feature editors of other publications as guests. These guests read their own works, read some favorites and then solicit poems from the audience to read. The works that are read are considered "published" in Live Mag! This gives authors an extra chance to be published." circ. 500. Pub'd 4 issues 2009; expects 4 issues 2010, 4 issues 2011. 2 titles listed in the *Small Press Record of Books in Print* (36th Edition, 2010-11). Discounts: 40%. 24pp. Reporting time: 8 weeks. Simultaneous submissions accepted: No. Payment: 2% of copy. Copyrighted. Subjects: Arts, Poetry.

The Live Oak Press, LLC, David M. Hamilton, Editor-In-Chief, P.O. Box 60036, Palo Alto, CA 94306-0036, 650-853-0197, info@liveoakpress.com, www.liveoakpress.com. 1982. Non-fiction. "We publish regional books about California including California literary history. We also copublish Genny Smith Books titles." avg. press run 1M. Pub'd 1 title 2009; expects 1 title 2010, 2 titles 2011. 12 titles listed in the *Small Press Record of*

Books in Print (36th Edition, 2010-11). Discounts: 40% 3 or more. 96-250pp. Reporting time: 3 months. Simultaneous submissions accepted: yes. Publishes 5% of manuscripts submitted. Payment: Royalties on a sliding scale. No advances. Copyrights for author. Subjects: California, Jack London, San Francisco, Travel, Yosemite.

Liverpool University Press (see also BULLETIN OF HISPANIC STUDIES), Dorothy Sherman Severin, Professor; James Higgins, Professor, The University of Liverpool, 18 Oxford St., Liverpool L69 7ZN, England, 051 794 2774/5. 1923. Articles, reviews. "Specialist articles on the languages and literatures of Spain, Portugal and Latin America, in English, Spanish, Portuguese, and Catalan." avg. press run 1.2M. Expects 4 titles 2010. 17 titles listed in the *Small Press Record of Books in Print* (36th Edition, 2010-11). 112pp. Reporting time: 3 months. Payment: none. Does not copyright for author. Subject: Language.

LIVING CHEAP NEWS, Larry Roth, 7520 McGee St., Kansas City, MO 64114, 816-523-0224, livcheap@aol.com, www.livingcheap.com. 1992. "Usually, this is written in house, but we consider contributions (free), product recommendations, etc., from readers." circ. 2M. 10/yr. Pub'd 10 issues 2009; expects 10 issues 2010, 10 issues 2011. 4 titles listed in the *Small Press Record of Books in Print* (36th Edition, 2010-11). sub. price $12; per copy $1.20; sample $1.20. 4pp. Reporting time: varies. Payment: none. Copyrighted, does not revert to author. Pub's reviews: 30 in 2009. §Cheap and meaningful cooking, products, lifestyles, etc. Ads: none. Subject: Self-Help.

Livingston Press, Joe Taylor, University of West Alabama, Station 22, Department of Languages and Literature, Livingston, AL 35470, (205) 652-3470. 1983. Fiction. avg. press run 1000. Pub'd 8 titles 2009; expects 6 titles 2010, 7 titles 2011. 1 title listed in the *Small Press Record of Books in Print* (36th Edition, 2010-11). Discounts: 50%. 150pp. Reporting time: 6 months. Simultaneous submissions accepted: Yes, simply let us know if it's accepted elsewhere. Publishes 1% of manuscripts submitted. Payment: 8%. Author pays for copyrights registration. Subject: Literature (General).

LJW Publishing, Sarah Carter, 10457 E. Obispo Ave., Mesa, AZ 85212, www.larryjohnwrightpublishing.com. 2005. Fiction, non-fiction. "At LJW Publishing we publish Arizona authors who offer works that encourage readers to think. As the Pragmatic Press, LJW Publishing wants our titles to exhibit qualities of pragmatic thinking. Current titles include fiction and non-fiction from the following genres: philosophy, business, and young adult. LJW Publishing also features short pieces of writing by Arizona natives on their website on a monthly basis." avg. press run 1000. Pub'd 1 title 2009; expects 2 titles 2010, 3 titles 2011. No titles listed in the *Small Press Record of Books in Print* (36th Edition, 2010-11). Discounts: Wholesalers: 55% Discount on 40 or more books. 40% Discount on less than 40 books. 200pp. Reporting time: up to 3 months. Simultaneous submissions accepted: Yes. Publishes 20% of manuscripts submitted. Payment: to be determined. Copyrights for author. Subjects: Business & Economics, Construction, Juvenile Fiction, Young Adult.

Llumina Press, Deborah Greenspan, 7915 W. McNab Road, Tamarac, FL 33321, 866-229-9244, fax: 954 726-0902, web: www.llumina.com. 1997. Poetry, fiction, photos, cartoons, satire, criticism, reviews, long-poems, plays, non-fiction. "We publish anything that is well written and carefully edited, and offer editing services when needed." avg. press run 1000. Pub'd 370 titles 2009; expects 500 titles 2010, 800 titles 2011. No titles listed in the *Small Press Record of Books in Print* (36th Edition, 2010-11). Discounts: 35% to 55%. 200pp. Reporting time: one to two weeks. Simultaneous submissions accepted: Yes. Publishes 90% of manuscripts submitted. Payment: 10% of list to 30% of list. Copyrights: We can but we prefer that the author do it. Subjects: Advertising, Self-Promotion, Anthology, Autobiography, Experimental, Fantasy, Fiction, Finances, Food, Eating, Novels, Nutrition, Occult, Parenting, Philosophy, Picture Books, Romance.

LO STRANIERO: The Stranger, Der Fremde, L'Etranger, Ignazio Corsaro, Piazza Amedeo 8, Naples 80121, Italy, Tel: 0039-081-681238, fax: 0039-081-7611264, email: lostraniero85@libero.it. 1985. Poetry, articles, art, photos, interviews, satire, criticism, letters, collages, concrete art. "The Journal of the International Movement for the Interdisciplinary Study of Estrangement." circ. 10M. 2/yr. Pub'd 2 issues 2009; expects 2 issues 2010, 2 issues 2011. sub. price $50, Euro 15; per copy $25, Euro 10; sample $20, Euro 10. Back issues: $30, Euro 15. Discounts: distributor = $1/copy (at the order). 64pp. Payment: none. Registered at the Tribunal of Naples, Italy. §Politics, culture, sociology, avant gard/art, Italy, visual art, estrangement, literature & poetry, history and law, philosophy and anthropology. Ads: $200/$100/$20 ("spot" in the *network*). Subjects: Avant-Garde, Experimental Art, Culture, Italy, Politics, Sociology, Visual Arts.

Lockhart Press, Russell A. Lockhart, Editor; Franklyn B. Lockhart, Editor, 1717 Wetmore Avenue, Everett, WA 98201, 425-252-8882, ral@ralockhart.com, www.ralockhart.com. 1982. Poetry, fiction, long-poems, non-fiction. "Our aim is to publish books devoted to the direct expression of the psyche's restless search for place and value in our time. Our books will be crafted by hand in every particular: printing by handpress from handset type on handmade paper and handbound in limited editions. Inqiries invited. Inaugural Publication *Midnight's Daughter*, poems by Janet Dallett, winner of Letterpress Prize, Festival of the Arts, Seattle, 1983. New paperback editions began in 1991. Electronic editions began in 2000. On-Line Editions to begin 2010."

avg. press run 120-200. Pub'd 1 title 2009; expects 1 title 2010, 1 title 2011. 2 titles listed in the *Small Press Record of Books in Print* (36th Edition, 2010-11). Discounts: 20% to distributors & subscribers to the press on handmade; standard discounts on paperbacks. 80pp. Reporting time: 2 months. Simultaneous submissions accepted: yes. Payment: 15% after direct cost recovery. Does not copyright for author. Subjects: Folklore, Poetry, Psychology.

Logos Press, Yali Friedman, 3909 Witmer Rd #416, Niagara Falls, NY 14305. 2003. Non-fiction. "Logos Press is a niche publisher focusing on text and reference books guiding actions based on knowledge and experience." avg. press run 2000. Expects 1 title 2010, 2 titles 2011. 9 titles listed in the *Small Press Record of Books in Print* (36th Edition, 2010-11). Discounts: 1-5 copies 20%6+ copies 50% (wholesalers only). 300pp. Reporting time: 4 weeks. Subjects: Business & Economics, Science.

LONE STARS MAGAZINE, Milo Rosebud, 4219 Flinthill, San Antonio, TX 78230-1619, Website: www.lonestarsmagazine.net. 1990. Poetry, art, long-poems. "Published: Linda Amos, Michael Frey, Celine Mariotti, Cecil Boyce, and many more past and yet to come." circ. 200+. 3/yr. Expects 3 issues 2010, 3 issues 2011. sub. price $20; per copy $6; sample $5.50. Back issues: $5.5o. 25 to 32pppp. Reporting time: 4 - 6 weeks. Simultaneous submissions accepted: Yes. Publishes 60% of manuscripts submitted. Copyrighted, reverts to author. Ads: Quarter Page - $20.oo. Subjects: English, Networking, Poetry, Publishing.

Lone Willow Press, Fredrick Zydek, PO Box 31647, Omaha, NE 68131-0647, 402-551-9=0343. 1994. Poetry. "We publish chapbooks. Usually by invitation only. We will, however, give a fair reading to all typescripts that meet our guidelines. Poems must reflect a single theme." avg. press run 350 first edition, 300 second edition. Pub'd 27 titles 2009. No titles listed in the *Small Press Record of Books in Print* (36th Edition, 2010-11). Discounts: standard to bookstores (40%). 45-50pp. Reporting time: 2 months. Simultaneous submissions accepted: no. Publishes 3% of manuscripts submitted. Payment: 25 copies + 25% royalty once expenses are met, poets get 50% off additional copies. Copyrights for author. Subjects: AIDS, Gay, Nebraska, Poetry, Religion.

Long & Silverman Publishing, Inc., Rebecca Stein, 800 North Rainbow Boulevard, Suite 208, Las Vegas, NV 89107, Phone (702) 948-5073, Fax (702) 447-9733, www.lspub.com. 2003. Non-fiction. "Long & Silverman Publishing, Inc. is a highly regarded independent press committed to producing the very best in business, personal finance, and self-improvement books." avg. press run 5000. Pub'd 3 titles 2009; expects 3 titles 2010, 9 titles 2011. No titles listed in the *Small Press Record of Books in Print* (36th Edition, 2010-11). Discounts: See lspub.com for latest information. 250pp. Reporting time: 8 weeks for materials submitted by literary agent. Simultaneous submissions accepted: Yes. Publishes 5% of manuscripts submitted. Copyrights for author. Subjects: Business & Economics, Finances, Inspirational, Marketing, Motivation, Success, Real Estate, Self-Help, Taxes.

THE LONG STORY, R. Peter Burnham, Editor, 18 Eaton Street, Lawrence, MA 01843-1110, 978-686-7638, rpburnham@mac.com, http://web.me.com/rpburnham/Site/LongStory.html. 1982. Fiction. "Stories of 8,000-20,000 words, for serious educated literary people. We have very specific tastes and look for stories about common folk and committed fiction. Since we are the only journal devoted strictly to long stories, we do not close the door or anything completely (except detective fiction, sci-fi, romance and other forms of popular fiction). But the best way to save yourself time and postage is to be familiar with us. Sample copies are $7, and writers are strongly urged to buy a copy before submitting (orders are filled on the same day that they are received). No multiple submissions. No parts of novels; please note that we are a journal devoted to long stories, a literary form with a beginning, middle, and an end. Best length is 8,000-12,000 words since we are very unlikely to print a 20,000 word story unless it conforms exactly to our literary tastes. We are not particularly interested in the usual produce of the writing programs—stories that are merely about relationships without any reaching after higher significance, stories with a psychological core as opposed to a thematic, moral core, stories that are thinly disguised autobiography, stories about writers, etc." circ. 500. 1/yr. Pub'd 1 issue 2009; expects 1 issue 2010, 1 issue 2011. sub. price $13 (2 issues); per copy $7; sample $7. Back issues: $6. Discounts: 50% to bookstores. 160pp. Reporting time: 1-2 months, sometimes longer. Simultaneous submissions accepted if notified. Publishes 2-3% of manuscripts submitted. Payment: 2 copies and gift subscription. Copyrighted, reverts to author. No ads. Subject: Fiction.

THE LONG TERM VIEW: A Journal of Informed Opinion, Dean Lawrence R. Velvel, Editor-in-Chief; Holly Vietzke, Associate Editor, Massachusetts School of Law, 500 Federal Street, Andover, MA 01810, 978-681-0800. 1992. Articles, interviews. "Each issue is devoted to a balanced discussion of a single topic (usually one that has not received adequate/in-depth coverage in the mainstream press). Contributors range from academics to professionals, have included Eugene McCarthy, Alfred Malabre of the *Wall Street Journal*, Eliot Janeway, John Anderson, Harvey Mansfield, Alexandra Astin, Martha Nussbaum." circ. 5M. 3/yr. Pub'd 2 issues 2009; expects 2 issues 2010, 3 issues 2011. sub. price $10; per copy $4.95; sample free. Back issues: $3.95. Discounts: negotiable. 100pp. Reporting time: 3-5 weeks. Simultaneous submissions accepted: yes. Publishes (solicited) 75% of manuscripts submitted. Payment: none. Copyrighted, reverts to author. Subjects:

Business & Economics, Education, Government, Interviews, Law, Political Science, Politics, Public Affairs, Society.

Longhouse, Bob Arnold, 1604 River Road, Guilford, VT 05301, poetry@sover.net, www.Longhouse-Poetry.com. 1971. Poetry, long-poems, concrete art. "Longhouse is a bookshop as well as a publishing house of fine poetry titles. Under the Longhouse imprint we have published 350 titles of poetry including: *3*: poems by Bob Arnold, David Giannini and John Levy. Plus booklets and foldouts by Cid Corman, Theodore Enslin, Gerald Hausman, George Evans, David Huddle, Robert Creeley, Jean Pedrick, Robert Morgan, Lyle Glazier, James Koller, Barbara Moraff, Bill Bathurst, Ian Hamilton Finlay, Jane Brakhage, Hayden Carruth, Lorine Niedecker, Marcel Cohen, Janine Pommy Vega, Carson Arnold, Catherine Walsh, David Miller, Billy Mills, Bill Deemer, Keith Wilson, Andrew Schelling, Tim McNulty, Mike O'Conner, Edward Sanders, Joanne Kyger, Daisy Zamora, David Hinton, Joseph Massey, J.D. Whitney, Kent Johnson, Dale Smith, Hoa Nguyen, Jonathan Greene, Cralan Kelder, Alec Finlay, Gary Hotham, Laurie Clark, Franco Beltrametti, Rita Degali Esposti, Red Pine, Alan Chong Lau, Michael Casey, Jeffery Beam, Ce rosenow, Jermemy Seligson, Gael Turnbull, Andy Clauson, Bobby Byrd, John Taggart, John Martone, Greg Joly, Verandah Porche, David Budbill, Lars Amund Vaage, Robert Sund, Bob Arnold,Tsering Wangmo Dhompa, Patricia Smith, Stefan Hyner, J.P. Seaton, Thomas A. Clark, Louise Landes Levi, Henri Michaux, Rene Daumal, Han Shan offset with letterpress wraps. In 2006 we published our bibliography of 35 years of publishing from Longhouse. In 2007 Bob Arnold edited, on-line, the sixth series of Origin as a quartet of issues encompassing 1200 pages and gathering 125 poets & artists world-wide. A complete listing of publications may be obtained from our bookshop and catalog services: *Longhouse*: publishers and bookseller; same address." avg. press run 50-250. Pub'd 12 titles 2009; expects 12 titles 2010, 12 titles 2011. 18 titles listed in the *Small Press Record of Books in Print* (36th Edition, 2010-11). 8-75pp. Payment: copies. Subjects: Poetry, Translation.

Longleaf Press, Michael Colonnese, Managing Editor; Robin Greene, Editor; Celena Brock, Assistant Editor, Methodist University, English Dept., 5400 Ramsey Street, Fayetteville, NC 28311, 910-630-7110. 1997. Poetry. "A non-profit university press dedicated to publishing poetry chapbooks from writers in the Southeast. Annual chapbook contest deadline: January 31, 2008. Contest open to NC, SC, TN, FL, GA, VA and AL residents who have not yet published a full length collection of poetry. Starting in 2007, we now also publish chapbooks and short full-length poetry collections from poets in the Mid-Atlantic and Northeast. $20 reading fee required. Please write for guidelines first: rgreene@methodist.edu." avg. press run 300. Pub'd 2 titles 2009; expects 2 titles 2010, 2 titles 2011. 19 titles listed in the *Small Press Record of Books in Print* (36th Edition, 2010-11). Discounts: none. 30pp. Reporting time: 4 months. Simultaneous submissions accepted: yes. Publishes 2% of manuscripts submitted. Payment: honorarium to author. Copyrights for author.

Looking Beyond Publishing, Josh Mandrell, PO Box 2193, La Grange, IL 60525, www.lookingbeyond.org. 2009. Non-fiction. avg. press run 1850. Expects 2 titles 2010, 2 titles 2011. 1 title listed in the *Small Press Record of Books in Print* (36th Edition, 2010-11). Discounts: 1-2 Books No discount 3-5 Books 20% off 6-9 Books 30% off 10-29 Books 40% off 30-49 Books 42% off 50-99 Books 44% off 100-199 Books 46% off 200 or more Books 50% off. 130pp. Reporting time: 4-6 WEEKS. Simultaneous submissions accepted: Yes. Payment: per negotiation. Does not copyright for author. Subjects: Relationships, Religion.

Loom Press, Paul Marion, Box 1394, Lowell, MA 01853. 1978. Poetry. avg. press run 500-1M. Expects 1 title 2010, 1 title 2011. 6 titles listed in the *Small Press Record of Books in Print* (36th Edition, 2010-11). Discounts: trade 40%, libraries 20%. Pages vary. Reporting time: 60-90 days. Payment: individual negotiations. Copyrights for author. Subject: Poetry.

Loonfeather Press, Betty Rossi, Editor Publisher; Gail Rixen, Editor; Mart Lou Marchand, Editor, P.O. Box 1212, Bemidji, MN 56619, 218-444-4869 www.loonfeatherpress.com. 1979. Poetry, fiction, non-fiction. "Loonfeather Press publishes good writing by new and emerging writers as well as established writers. Most of our authors are regional, but we also publish writers from beyond our region. We are particularly interested in the work of Ojibwe authors. Recent contributors include Lynn Levin, Kimberly Blaeser, Louise Erdrich, Sharon Chmielarz, Greg Bernard, Jamie Parsley." avg. press run 700. Pub'd 4 titles 2009; expects 4 titles 2010, 4 titles 2011. No titles listed in the *Small Press Record of Books in Print* (36th Edition, 2010-11). Discounts: bookstores: 5 or more copies 40%institutions: 5 or more copies 40%classrooms: 5 or more copies 40% distributors: 55%. 115pp. Reporting time: Three months. Simultaneous submissions accepted: Yes. Publishes 25% of manuscripts submitted. Payment: 10% royalty paid semi-annually. Copyrights for author. Subjects: Fiction, Gardening, Juvenile Fiction, Native American, Nature, Novels, Poetry, Reprints, Short Stories.

Lord John Press, Herb Yellin, 19073 Los Alimos Street, Northridge, CA 91326, 818-360-5804. 1977. "Work only with established authors - our primary market is collectors and universities. Do not want unsolicited manuscripts. Published authors: John Updike, Norman Mailer, Robert B. Parker, Ray Bradbury, Ursula K. Le Guin, John Barth, Raymond Carver, Stephen King, Dan Simmons." avg. press run 300-500. Pub'd 3 titles 2009; expects 3 titles 2010. 13 titles listed in the *Small Press Record of Books in Print* (36th Edition, 2010-11). Discounts: trade 40%. 50pp. Subjects: Criticism, Fiction.

LOS, Virginia M. Geoffrey, Editor; I.B. Scrood, Managing Editor; P.N. Bouts, Art Editor; M. Peel, Poetry Editor; M. Hardy, Editor-at-large, 150 N. Catalina St., No. 2, Los Angeles, CA 90004, website: http://home.earthlink.net/~lospoesy, email: lospoesy@earthlink.net. 1991. "contemporary poesy & art."

LOST CARCOSA, Zirlinson Publishing, Shawn Tomlinson, 152 Stevers Mill Road, Broadalbin, NY 12025, 5i8-883-3055, harvor@lycos.com.

Lost Coast Press, Cynthia Frank, President; Joe Shaw, Editor, 155 Cypress Street, Fort Bragg, CA 95437, 800-773-7782, fax 707-964-7531, www.cypresshouse.com, joeshaw@cypresshouse.com. 1985. Poetry, fiction, art, non-fiction. "See listing for Cypress House." 8 titles listed in the *Small Press Record of Books in Print* (36th Edition, 2010-11). Simultaneous submissions accepted: Yes.

LOST GENERATION JOURNAL, Deloris Gray Wood, 6009 S Highway 19, Salem, MO 65560-8931, 314-729-2545, Fax 314-729-2545. 1973. Poetry, fiction, articles, art, photos, cartoons, interviews, criticism, reviews, letters, news items, non-fiction. "*LGJ* topics deal with Americans in Europe, chiefly Paris, between 1919 and 1939. Primary emphasis is placed on Americans who began making a name for themselves in literature, graphic and performing arts such as Pound, Stein and Hemingway. Article length can vary, but we prefer pieces between 800 and 2,500 words. Poetry should be 20 lines or less. Good photographs and art should relate to the theme in time and place as should the articles and poetry. Scholars must document their work with footnotes and bibliography. Lost Generation people (those who started in Paris) must state when they were abroad and supply evidence of their qualifications or cite references for confirmation. Authors should supply a passport-size photograph of themselves and a 200-word biographical blurb. Recent contributors: Mark Bassett, Robin Dormin, Mark Orwoll, John McCall, Jerry Rosco." circ. 400. 1/yr. Pub'd 1 issue 2009; expects 1 issue 2010, 1 issue 2011. sub. price $10; per copy $10; sample $10. Back issues: $10. Discounts: $9.50 per year to subscription agency. 32pp. Reporting time: 6 weeks, SASE earlier. Payment: 1¢ per word or 3 copies of issue article appears in. Copyrighted. Pub's reviews: 4 in 2009. §Twentieth Century literature, bibliography, biography, Americans in Paris, Hemingway, Pound, Stein, Miller. Ads: $150/$125/$85/$5 an inch. Subjects: African Literature, Africa, African Studies, Agriculture, Bibliography, Biography, Communication, Journalism, Dada, F. Scott Fitzgerald, France, French, Graphics, Ernest Hemingway, Literature (General), Magazines, Anais Nin, Photography, Printing.

Lost Hills Books, Bruce Henricksen, P.O. Box 3054, Duluth, MN 55803, info@losthillsbooks.com, www.losthillsbooks.com. 2008. Poetry, fiction. "Literary Fiction and Poetry. Submission by invitation. Recent contributors include Barbary Chaapel and Gibbons Ruark." avg. press run 1200. Expects 4 titles 2010. 3 titles listed in the *Small Press Record of Books in Print* (36th Edition, 2010-11). Discounts: 2-10 copies 40%. 125pp. Payment: Flexible.

Lost Horse Press, Christine Holbert, Publisher, 105 Lost Horse Lane, Sandpoint, ID 83864, 208-255-4410, Fax 208-255-1560, losthorsepress@mindspring.com, web: www.losthorsepress.org. 1998. Poetry. "Please check online (www.losthorsepress.org) for submission guidelines and to determine what genres Lost Horse Press is currently reading." avg. press run 500-2.5M. Pub'd 7 titles 2009; expects 5 titles 2010, 6 titles 2011. 42 titles listed in the *Small Press Record of Books in Print* (36th Edition, 2010-11). 100pp. Reporting time: 6 to 9 months. Simultaneous submissions accepted: yes. Publishes 5% of manuscripts submitted. Does not copyright for author. Subjects: Pacific Northwest, Poetry.

Lost Pond Press, Phil Brown, 40 Margaret St., Saranac Lake, NY 12983-1298, 518-891-3918 philbrown@juno.com. 2006. Fiction, non-fiction. "We publish primarily non-fiction about the Adirondack Mountains." avg. press run 5000. Pub'd 1 title 2009; expects 1 title 2010, 1 title 2011. 2 titles listed in the *Small Press Record of Books in Print* (36th Edition, 2010-11). Discounts: 40% discount to bookstores. Bulk and distributor sales negotiable. 128-334pp. Subjects: Adirondacks, Birds, Conservation, Environment, History, Outdoor Adventure.

Lost Prophet Press (see also KNUCKLE MERCHANT - The Journal of Naked Literary Aggression; THIN COYOTE), Christopher Jones, 4144 Office Pkwy, Apt. 2306, Dallas, TX 75204-2306, 505.256.4589. 1992. Poetry, fiction, art, photos, long-poems, collages, plays. avg. press run 200. Pub'd 2 titles 2009; expects 3 titles 2010, 4 titles 2011. 6 titles listed in the *Small Press Record of Books in Print* (36th Edition, 2010-11). Discounts: on request. 30pp. Reporting time: 1 month. Simultaneous submissions accepted: yes. Publishes 1% of manuscripts submitted. Payment: contributor copies. Does not copyright for author. Subjects: Fiction, Photography, Poetry.

Lotus Press, Inc., Naomi Madgett, Editor, PO Box 21607, Detroit, MI 48221, 313-861-1280, fax 313-861-4740, lotuspress@comcast.net. 1972. Poetry. "Annual Naomi Long Madgett Poetry Award for an outstanding book-length manuscript by an African American. Submissions from January 2 to March 31. Visit www.lotuspress.org for guidelines." avg. press run 800. Pub'd 2 titles 2009; expects 3 titles 2010, 2 titles 2011. 37 titles listed in the *Small Press Record of Books in Print* (36th Edition, 2010-11). Discounts: 30-40%; 50% for wholesalers. 80pp. Reporting time: 6-8 weeks. Simultaneous submissions accepted: no. Publishes 1% of manuscripts submitted. Payment: $500 in cash plus free copies and discounts. Copyrights for author. Subjects: African Literature, Africa, African Studies, Black, Literature (General), Literature (General), Poetry, Poetry, Third World, Minorities, Women.

•**LOUISIANA LITERATURE,** Jack Bedell, Editor, PO Box 10792, Hammond, LA 70402. "Submission Guidelines: Poetry should be typed, one poem per page, 3-5 poems per manuscript, addressed to: Jack B. Bedell, Editor. Short fiction should be typed, double-spaced. Include a brief cover letter with summary and bio addressed to: Norman German, Fiction Editor. Non-fiction and scholarly articles should be submitted only after query and should adhere to either the Chicago Style Manual or MLA form. Photo Essays and Fine Art should be submitted after query only. All submissions should include return postage. Simultaneous submissions are never welcome. We are currently unable to accept electronic submissions. All submissions and queries should be mailed to:Louisiana Literature, SLU Box 10792, Southeastern Louisiana University, Hammond, LA 70402."

THE LOUISIANA REVIEW, Billy Fontenot, Editor & Fiction Editor; Michael Alleman, Poetry Editor; Diane Langlois, Art Editor, Liberal Arts Div. PO Box 1129, Louisiana State Univ., Eunice, LA 70535, phone: 337-550-1315, email: bfonteno@lsue.edu Web: web.lsue.edu/la-review and www.myspace.com/louisianareview and www.facebook.com/louisiana.review. 1999. Poetry, fiction, art, photos, parts-of-novels, plays. "*The Louisiana Review* seeks to publish the best poetry, fiction, and black & white art it can get. While Louisiana writers and poets as well as those associated with or connected to the Gulf Coast get first consideration, the journal is becoming more national in scope. We like imagistic and metaphoric poetry as well as poetry with surprising language and excellent craft. We like a good story, any type except erotica. Only art that can be reproduced in black & white is considered. We read year round, but it may take a while to reply in summer." circ. 300-600. 1/yr. Pub'd 1 issue 2009; expects 1 issue 2010, 1 issue 2011. sub. price $5; per copy $5; sample $5. 80-120pp. Reporting time: between 6-12 weeks. Accept simultaneous submissions if noted. Publishes 5% of manuscripts submitted. Payment: 1 copy in which their work appears. Not copyrighted, author retains all rights. Subjects: Arts, Fiction, Louisiana, Poetry, Prose.

Louisiana State University Press, 3990 West Lakeshore Drive, Baton Rouge, LA 70803, 225-578-6294, Fax 225-578-6461. 1935. No titles listed in the *Small Press Record of Books in Print* (36th Edition, 2010-11).

THE LOUISVILLE REVIEW, Sena Jeter Naslund, Editor; Karen Mann, Managing Editor; Kathleen Driskell, Associate Editor, Spalding University, 851 S. 4th Street, Louisville, KY 40203, 502-585-9911 ext. 2777, louisvillereview@spalding.edu, www.louisvillereview.org. 1976. Poetry, fiction, parts-of-novels, long-poems, plays, non-fiction. "We now accept electronic submissions via an online submissions manager. Please visit website for complete guidelines. Some recent contributors: Maura Stanton, Wendy Bishop, Ursula Hegi, Maureen Morehead, Jhumpa Lahiri, Robin Lippincott, Virgil Suarez, Tony Hoagland, David Brendan Hopes, Greg Pape, and Claudia Emerson." circ. 500. 2/yr. Pub'd 2 issues 2009; expects 2 issues 2010, 2 issues 2011. sub. price $14; per copy $8; sample $5. Back issues: $5 each (postpaid). 128pp. Reporting time: 4-6 months. Simultaneous submissions accepted: yes. Publishes 5% of manuscripts submitted. Payment: 1 complimentary copy. Copyrighted, reverts to author. Swap ads. Subjects: Essays, Fiction, Non-Fiction, Poetry.

The Love and Logic Press, Inc., Nancy M. Henry, Publisher, 2207 Jackson Street, Golden, CO 80401, 303-278-7552. 1993. Non-fiction. "The Love and Logic Press, Inc. is a subsidiary of Cline/Fay Institute, Inc. CFI was founded in 1983 as a mail order publisher of audio and video tapes and books by Jim Fay and Foster W. Cline, M.D., internationally-recognized authorities on parenting, education and child psychiatry. CFI currently carries over 65 titles, available exclusively through mail order and catalog, www.loveandlogic.com. The Love and Logic Press, Inc. was started to publish audio, video and book titles for the general trade beginning in Fall 1994. LLPI will concentrate on titles dealing with parenting, psychology and current social trends." avg. press run 10M. Expects 12 titles 2010, 18 titles 2011. 8 titles listed in the *Small Press Record of Books in Print* (36th Edition, 2010-11). Discounts: 1 copy 20% prepaid, 2-4 20%, 5-24 40%, 25-99 42% free freight, 100-249 43%, 250-499 44%, 500+ 45%; 25 or more copies include free freight. 256pp. Reporting time: 90 days. Simultaneous submissions accepted: yes. Publishes 4% of manuscripts submitted. Payment: advance against royalties; 5-7.5% on net sales; royalties paid twice yearly. Copyrights for author. Subjects: Children, Youth, Family, Parenting, Psychology, Self-Help, Sociology.

Loving Healing Press, Inc., Victor Volkman, 5145 Pontiac Trail, Ann Arbor, MI 48105-9627, Phone 734-662-6864, http://www.LovingHealing.com. 2003. Non-fiction. "Publishing psychology, self-help, personal grown, and disability recovery. Our mission: redefining what is possible for healing mind and spirit." avg. press run 1000. Pub'd 6 titles 2009; expects 12 titles 2010, 18 titles 2011. 25 titles listed in the *Small Press Record of Books in Print* (36th Edition, 2010-11). Discounts: Distributors 55%, bookstores 40%, non-profits 30%. Others available depending on quantity ordered. Able to sell in UK and USA. 200pp. Reporting time: 30 days. Simultaneous submissions accepted: Yes. Publishes 20% of manuscripts submitted. Payment: 10% of List Price, paid twice yearly, no advances. Copyrights for author. Subjects: Acupuncture, Aging, Disabled, Disease, History, How-To, Medicine, Metaphysics, Non-Fiction, Psychiatry, Psychology, Self-Help, Sexual Abuse, Social Work, Textbooks.

LOVING MORE: New Models for Relationships, Robyn Trask, PO Box 4358, Boulder, CO 80306, 303-543-7540, lovingmore@lovemore.com. 1995. Articles, art, photos, cartoons, interviews, reviews, letters, news items, non-fiction. "Polyamorous themed between 750 and 2500 words for submissions." circ. 2M. 4/yr. Pub'd 4 issues 2009; expects 4 issues 2010, 4 issues 2011. sub. price $30; per copy $7; sample $7. Back issues: $7. Discounts: 55% to bookstores. 40pp. Reporting time: varies. Simultaneous submissions accepted: no. Publishes 50% of manuscripts submitted. Payment: copies. Copyrighted. Pub's reviews: 5 in 2009. §Polyamorous themed, Multi-partner or alternative relationships, new paradigms of relationships. Ads: $350/$125/$65. Subjects: Counter-Culture, Alternatives, Communes, Erotica, Experimental, Family, Futurism, Inspirational, New Age, Parenting, Relationships, Sex, Sexuality.

LOW BUDGET ADVENTURE, Cynic Press, PO Box 40691, Philadelphia, PA 19107. 2003. "Short stories and artwork - adventurous (western, mystery, spy, martial arts). Ceased publication as a separate title. Merged with Axe Factory. Back issues available." circ. 100. sub. price $20/6 issues; per copy $7; sample $6. 32pp. Reporting time: 3 weeks. Simultaneous submissions accepted: yes. Publishes 15% of manuscripts submitted. Payment: 1 year subscription. Copyrighted, reverts to author. Ads: $20/$10. Subjects: Audio/Video, Fiction, Martial Arts, Military, Veterans, Mystery, Old West.

LOW BUDGET SCIENCE FICTION, Cynic Press, Joseph Farley M., Editor, PO Box 40691, Philadelphia, PA 19107. 2002. Fiction, art, cartoons. "Make all checks to "Cynic Press". While back issues are still available, Low Budget Science Fiction is no longer published as a separate title. It merged with Axe Factory for Axe Factory's final year." circ. 100. 1/yr. sub. price $20/4 issues; per copy $7; sample $7. Back issues: $7. 32pp. Reporting time: 3 weeks. Simultaneous submissions accepted: yes. Publishes 15% of manuscripts submitted. Payment: 1 year subscription. Copyrighted, reverts to author. Ads: $20/$10. Subjects: Arthurian, Cartoons, Fantasy, Fiction, Horror, Science Fiction, Supernatural.

Low Fidelity Press, Bradley Armstrong, Editor; Tobin O'Donnell, Editor; Jeff Parker, Editor; Andrew Vernon, Editor, 1912 16th Ave South, Birmingham, AL 35205-5607. 2001. No titles listed in the *Small Press Record of Books in Print* (36th Edition, 2010-11).

Lowestoft Chronicle Press, Nicholas Litchfield, 1925 Massachusetts Avenue, Unit 8, Cambridge, MA 02140-1401. 2008. Fiction. 2 titles listed in the *Small Press Record of Books in Print* (36th Edition, 2010-11).

LP Publications (Teleos Institute) (see also EMERGING), Diane K. Pike, 7119 East Shea Boulevard, Suite 109, PMB 418, Scottsdale, AZ 85254, 480-948-1800, Fax 480-948-1870. 1972. Fiction, non-fiction. avg. press run 100. Expects 2 titles 2010, 1 title 2011. 15 titles listed in the *Small Press Record of Books in Print* (36th Edition, 2010-11). Discounts: available upon request. 250pp. Reporting time: variable. Copyrights for author. Subjects: Humanism, Metaphysics, Occult, Spiritual.

LPD Press (see also TRADICION REVISTA), Barbe Awalt, Paul Rhetts, 925 Salamanca NW, Los Ranchos de Albuquerque, NM 87107-5647, 505-344-9382, Fax 505-345-5129, info@nmsantos.com. 1994. Art, photos, non-fiction. "Actively seeking material on Southwestern art and culture, artists and arts. Ideal length of finished product with illustrations is 160-280pp. Recent contributions by Diana Pardue, Heard Museum, Rey Montez, Paul Pletka, Carmella Padilla, Father Thomas Steele, S.J., Dr. Charles Carrillo, Dr. Thomas Chavez, Joseph Sanchez, Pauline Chavez Bent, Dave DeWitt, Robert Bauver, Don Bullis Abe Pena, and Robert Torrez." avg. press run 8M. Pub'd 5 titles 2009; expects 2 titles 2010, 2 titles 2011. 28 titles listed in the *Small Press Record of Books in Print* (36th Edition, 2010-11). Discounts: Library/school 25%, 1-9 40%, 10+ 45%. 250pp. Reporting time: 2-3 months. Simultaneous submissions accepted: yes. Publishes 25% of manuscripts submitted. Payment: negotiable. Copyrights for author. Subjects: Americana, The Americas, Arizona, Arts, Catholic, Christianity, Christmas, Colorado, Culture, Latino, New Mexico, Religion, Southwest, Texas, U.S. Hispanic.

LrnIT Publishing Div. LRNIT CORPORATION, Philip N. Baldwin Jr., Dawn B. Barrett, Adalene Baldwin, Peggy Broussard, 1122 Samuel Pt., Colorado Springs, CO 80906-6310, 719-331-4510, Fax 760-946-7895, lrnit@consultant.com, PNB416@aol.com, www.lrnit.com. 1999. Non-fiction. avg. press run 2M. Pub'd 2 titles 2009; expects 1 title 2010, 2 titles 2011. 4 titles listed in the *Small Press Record of Books in Print* (36th Edition, 2010-11). Discounts: trade (-55%), bulk (-65%), agent/jobber (-60%), classroom (-65%), all FOB shipped. 230pp. Reporting time: 6 weeks. Simultaneous submissions accepted: yes. Publishes 15% of manuscripts submitted. Payment: negotiated. Copyrights for author. Subjects: Education, Engineering, Environment, Mathematics, Motivation, Success, Quotations, Textbooks.

Lucky Press, LLC, Janice P. Williams, Editor-in-Chief, PO Box 754, Athens, OH 45701-0754, Fax: 614-413-2820; Website: www.luckypress.com, Email: books@luckypress.com. 1999. Fiction, non-fiction. "Query first by MAIL with 1 page synopsis, author bio, 1 page marketing plan, Table of Contents (if nonfiction), and 2 sample chapters. Be sure to include an SASE for return of your materials. Include your email address for a quicker response. We are particularly interested in literary fiction and nonfiction categories of pets; special needs children and adults; inspirational; and topics of interest to women.For more information, visit www.luckypress.com/submissions.htm." Pub'd 2 titles 2009; expects 4 titles 2010, 6 titles 2011. 22 titles listed in the *Small Press Record of Books in Print* (36th Edition, 2010-11). 224pp. Reporting time: 3 months. Simultaneous submissions accepted: yes. Copyrights for author. Subjects: Alternative Medicine, Animals, Appalachia, Arts, Aviation, Birds, Creativity, Disabled, Family, Fiction, History, Nutrition, Ohio, Pets, Young Adult.

Ludlow Press, Jun Da, P.O. Box 575010, Whitestone, NY 11357. 2003. Fiction. "visit LudlowPress.com ... or visit: PermanentObscurity.com ... regarding the major title for 2010, Permanent Obscurity by Richard Perez, (full title is: Permanent Obscurity: Or a Cautionary Tale of Two Girls and Their Misadventures with Drugs, Pornography and Death) ... 464 pages; ISBN-13: 978-0971341548." avg. press run 3000. Expects 1 title 2011. 1 title listed in the *Small Press Record of Books in Print* (36th Edition, 2010-11). 200-464pp. Reporting time: Currently not viewing new material. Simultaneous submissions accepted: No. Publishes 3% of manuscripts submitted. Payment: private. Copyrights for author. Subject: Novels.

LULLABY HEARSE, Sarah Ruth Jacobs, 45-34 47th St. Apt. 6AB, Woodside, NY 11377, editor@lullabyhearse.com, www.lullabyhearse.com. 2002. Poetry, fiction, art, photos, cartoons, reviews, collages, concrete art. "Query for fiction over 6,000 words. Traditional horror themes, mystery, crime, and melodrama stand very little chance next to contemporary horror and dark experimental fiction subs. Approximately 5% of all subs are used, and short fiction must be exceptionally sharp since it pays the same flat fee as full length." circ. 200. 4/yr. Pub'd 1 issue 2009; expects 4 issues 2010, 4 issues 2011. sub. price $18; per copy $5; sample $4. 20pp. Reporting time: 4-6 weeks. Simultaneous submissions accepted: yes. Publishes 3% of manuscripts submitted. Payment: no payment. Copyrighted, reverts to author. Subjects: Avant-Garde, Experimental Art, Charles Bukowski, Creativity, Experimental, Horror, Poetry, Prose, Supernatural.

LULLWATER REVIEW, Laura Kochman, Editor in Chief, PO Box 122036, Emory University, Atlanta, GA 30322. 1990. Poetry, fiction, art, photos, cartoons, long-poems, plays, non-fiction. "*The Lullwater Review* is a trade-size journal for the literary arts, dedicated to presenting its readers with a wide variety of forms, styles, and perspectives in fiction, drama, and poetry. Recent contributors include: James Cushing, Denise Duhamel, Colette Inez, Aurel Rau, Josephine Humphreys (interview), Greg Grummer, Cindy Goff, Eve Shelnutt, and Charles Edward Eaton." circ. 2M-3M. 2/yr. Pub'd 2 issues 2009; expects 2 issues 2010, 2 issues 2011. sub. price $8-Individuals$10-Institutions; per copy $5; sample $5. Back issues: $5 per copy. Discounts: none. 74pp. Reporting time: 3-5 months, on average (longer during the summer). Simultaneous submissions accepted if we are notified upon submission and in the event that the work is published elsewhere. Please include a cover letter and SASE with sufficient postage. Payment: 3 copies of the issue in which author's work appears. Copyrighted, reverts to author. No ads. Subjects: Arts, Counter-Culture, Alternatives, Communes, Creativity, Culture, English, Fiction, Journals, Language, Literary Review, Literature (General), Novels, Poetry, Prose, Short Stories, Writers/Writing.

Luminous Epinoia Press, Edward Hunt, PO Box 2547, Sandpoint, ID 83864-0917, (800)786-1090 www.luminousepinoia.com. 2004. Non-fiction. "The concept is to encourage those writings that promote empowerment of the reader (soulfully, healthfully, creatively, emotionally, physically). Luminous Epinoia is Lighting Creative Consciousness!" avg. press run 5000. Expects 1 title 2010, 2 titles 2011. 2 titles listed in the *Small Press Record of Books in Print* (36th Edition, 2010-11). Discounts: see distributors. 250pp. Reporting time: 2-3 weeks. Simultaneous submissions accepted: Yes. Payment: Sliding scale as books sell, (more commission to author). Copyrights for author. Subjects: Alternative Medicine, Children, Youth, Creativity, Dreams, Energy, Humanism, Inspirational, Nutrition, Parenting, Relationships, Self-Help, Sex, Sexuality, Theosophical, Women, Young Adult.

THE LUMMOX JOURNAL, Lummox Press, RD Armstrong, Lummox PO Box 5301, San Pedro, CA 90733-5301, poetraindog@gmail.com, www.lummoxpress.com. 1995. Poetry, fiction, articles, art, photos, interviews, criticism, reviews, letters, long-poems, news items, non-fiction. "The Lummox Journal began as a monthly printed magazine in Oct. 1995 and evolved over the years to become a respected small press voice and observer. In 2007 it went online exclusively and it was hoped that it would continue to raise the expectations of what quality poetry and poetics is all about. In 2011 it will return as an annual. Recent contributors include Todd Moore, Leonard J. Cirino, Marie Lecrivain, Raindog and John Bennett." circ. 1000. 1/yr. Pub'd 1 issue 2009; expects 1 issue 2010, 1 issue 2011. 12 titles listed in the *Small Press Record of Books in Print* (36th Edition, 2010-11). sub. price $20; per copy $25; sample $25. Back issues: $15. 100pp. Reporting time: 1-2 months. Simultaneous submissions accepted: Yes. Publishes 5% of manuscripts submitted. Payment: one copy when published. Copyrighted, reverts to author. Pub's reviews: approx 20 in 2009. §small press poetry books & chapbooks. Ads: Full page (5 X 7) $100; Half page (5 X 3) $60; Quarter page (5 X 1.25) $30; Classified rates per column inch: $15; Classified rates per line: $3. Subjects: Book Reviewing, Charles Bukowski, Creative Non-fiction, Criticism, Essays, Graphics, Multicultural, Music, Non-Fiction, Photography, Poetry, Reviews, Short Stories, Writers/Writing, Zines.

Lummox Press (see also THE LUMMOX JOURNAL), RD Armstrong, Lummox PO Box 5301, San Pedro, CA 90733-5301, poetraindog@gmail.com, www.lummoxpress.com. 1994. Poetry, fiction, articles, art, photos, interviews, criticism, reviews, letters, non-fiction. "Lummox Press, along with its two publishing arms: DUFUS and Lummox Journal Online, seeks to raise the bar of micro-press publishing. The Lummox Press publishes the Little Red Book series with FIFTY NINE titles and counting. We publish known and unknown poets, including, most recently, Terry McCarty, W. S. Gainer, nila northSun, Pris Campbell, Todd Moore, John Yamrus and RD Armstrong. The Lummox Journal Online began publishing in 1995 as a print magazine, but evolved to an Ezine in 2007. DUFUS has always been online. In 2008, the Lummox Press began publishing trade paper books using POD technology and offers a line of titles (seven and counting)." avg. press run up to 1,000 copies. Pub'd 9 titles 2009; expects 8 titles 2010, 5 titles 2011. 7 titles listed in the *Small Press Record of Books in Print* (36th Edition, 2010-11). Discounts: 50%. pp varies (LRBs - 36 to 56; Trade Paper - 96 to 200)pp. Reporting time: 2 months. Simultaneous submissions accepted: No. Publishes 10% of manuscripts submitted. Payment: LRBs - 10 copies of print run in lieu of payment; Trade Paper - 20% of net sales per print run (royalty) + discount on title. we put the cee in the circle symbol on the info page. Subjects: Anthology, Book Reviewing, Charles Bukowski, Communication, Journalism, Essays, Fiction, Interviews, Los Angeles, Non-Fiction, Poetry, Reviews, Short Stories.

Luna Bisonte Prods, John M. Bennett, 137 Leland Ave, Columbus, OH 43214, 614-846-4126. 1974. Poetry, art, cartoons, satire, letters, collages, concrete art. "Interested in exchanges. We print broadsides and labels, chapbooks, poetry products, and books. Would like to see more material in Spanish." avg. press run 250. Pub'd 4 titles 2009; expects 4 titles 2010, 4 titles 2011. 137 titles listed in the *Small Press Record of Books in Print* (36th Edition, 2010-11). Discounts: 40% for resale. 56pp. Reporting time: 2 weeks. Publishes 5% of manuscripts submitted. Payment: copies. Copyrighted to author, but author must do own registering for copyright. Subjects: Arts, Avant-Garde, Experimental Art, Dada, Folklore, Graphics, Poetry, Visual Arts.

Lunar Offensive Publications, Stephen Fried, 1910 Foster Avenue, Brooklyn, NY 11230-1902. 1994. Poetry, fiction, art, photos, cartoons, parts-of-novels, collages, plays. "Doing a one-time book of violently erotic/erotically violent short short stories, graphics (line or halftone and color for 2 covers) poems or parts of poems under 100 lines, and short screenplays, as for a video under 15 minutes. No pedophiles, no torture. SASE required. We're not using work by anyone we know. Include email address of you have one. We've published books by Elliot Richman, John Wheatcroft, Joi Brozek, Susan Brennan and Letta Neely but this is something different. Deadline uncertain and if the input is disappointing the project dies. Surprise me." avg. press run 1600. Pub'd 1 title 2009; expects 2 titles 2010, 1 title 2011. 4 titles listed in the *Small Press Record of Books in Print* (36th Edition, 2010-11). Discounts: 10% on orders of 12 or more (+ $5 shipping + 10 copies). 100pp. Reporting time: 3 months with SASE. Simultaneous submissions accepted. Simultaneous submissions accepted: yes. Payment: 30 copies from first run, sales split 50/50 on agreed book price. Does not copyright for author. Subjects: Dada, Dreams, Erotica, Euthanasia, Death, Fantasy, Fiction, Photography, Poetry, Politics, Reviews, Sex, Sexuality, Surrealism, War, Weapons, Women.

LUNGFULL! MAGAZINE, Brendan Lorber, Editor-in-Chief, 316 23rd Street, Brooklyn, NY 11215-6409, lungfull@rcn.net. 1995. Poetry, fiction, articles, art, photos, cartoons, interviews, criticism, reviews, letters, parts-of-novels, long-poems, collages. "We print the rough drafts of contributor's work in addition to the final version so the readers can witness the creative process in action." circ. 1,000. 1/yr. Pub'd 1 issue 2009; expects 1 issue 2010, 1 issue 2011. sub. price $19.90/2 ISSUES $39.80/4 ISSUES; per copy $9.95; sample $13.50. Back issues: see http://www.lungfull.org for updated list. 200pp. Reporting time: 4-12 months. We accept simultaneous submissions with notification. Publishes 2% of manuscripts submitted. Payment: 2 copies. Copyrighted, reverts to author. §Poetry, experimental writing, fiction, essays. Ads: $100/$60/$35 1/4 page. Subjects: Essays, Experimental, Fiction, Literature (General), Poetry.

Luthers Publishing, Gary Luther, Alan Luther, 1009 North Dixie Freeway, New Smyrna Beach, FL 32168-6221, 386-423-1600 phone/Fax, www.lutherspublishing.com. 1988. "We are private publishers, specializing in limited-run books. Unless partnership arrangements have been made, the author pays to publish his/her work. We offer expertise in design, editing, art, and typography to produce a quality paperback/hardcover book. Marketing support includes copyright, generally registered in author's name. ISBN and Library of Congress number/CIP secured. UPC bar code provided as appropriate. Title entered into numerous indexes and data bases, as well as the Internet. News release/book review media package developed." avg. press run 500-1M. Pub'd 10 titles 2009; expects 7 titles 2010, 8 titles 2011. 55 titles listed in the *Small Press Record of Books in Print* (36th Edition, 2010-11). Discounts: 40% trade. 100+pp. Reporting time: 10 working days. Copyrights for author.

Lycanthrope Press, Rev. Victor C. Klein, Rev. Laurence Talbot, PO Box 9028, Metairie, LA 70005-9028, 504-866-9756. 1993. Poetry, fiction, criticism, plays, news items, non-fiction. "We are the publishing arm of Ordo Templi Veritatis. As such, our interest is theology, occult, etc." avg. press run 15M+. Pub'd 2 titles 2009; expects 6 titles 2010, 12 titles 2011. 9 titles listed in the *Small Press Record of Books in Print* (36th Edition, 2010-11). Discounts: as per fair market/industry standard. 150+pp. Reporting time: 1 month; solicited only; letter. Simultaneous submissions accepted: yes. Publishes 10% of manuscripts submitted. Payment: standard.

Copyrights for author. Subjects: Astrology, Atheism, Christianity, Erotica, Euthanasia, Death, Folklore, Humanism, Libertarian, Metaphysics, Myth, Mythology, New Age, Occult, Philosophy, Religion, Theosophical.

Lyceum Books, Inc., David Follmer, President, 5758 S. Blackstone, Chicago, IL 60637, 773-643-1902, Fax 773-643-1903, lyceum@lyceumbooks.com, www.lyceumbooks.com. 1989. Non-fiction. "Social Work is our only discipline." avg. press run 2M. Pub'd 6 titles 2009; expects 10 titles 2010, 10 titles 2011. 21 titles listed in the *Small Press Record of Books in Print* (36th Edition, 2010-11). Discounts: bookstores, wholesalers 20%. 300pp. Reporting time: 2 months. Simultaneous submissions accepted: yes. Payment: 10% net. Copyrights for author. Subject: Social Work.

Lynx House Press, Christopher Howell, 420 West 24th, Spokane, WA 99203. 1972. Poetry, fiction. "Lynx House Press publishes only highly literary material: books commercial presses would consider too literary. Authors include Yusef Komunyakaa, Patricia Goedicke, Madeline DeFrees, Vern Rutsala, Gillian Conoley, Bill Tremblay, Carolyne Wright, Valerie Martin, Carlos Reyes, James Grabill, Robert Abel, and Carole Oles." avg. press run 1.5M. Pub'd 6 titles 2009; expects 6 titles 2010, 6 titles 2011. No titles listed in the *Small Press Record of Books in Print* (36th Edition, 2010-11). Discounts: 1 book 10%, 2 20%, 3 30%, 4+ 40%, libraries 20%. 80pp. Reporting time: 3-6 months. Simultaneous submissions accepted: yes. Publishes 1% of manuscripts submitted. Payment: sometimes pay 10%, often copies. Copyrights for author. Subjects: Fiction, Poetry.

Lyons Publishing Limited, Judy Powell, 2704 Jerring Mews, Mississauga, Ontario L5L 2M8, Canada, info@judypowell.com. 2005. Fiction. "Area of focus: Romance novels, which must be written by African or Caribbean authors, or be set in an African or Caribbean country, or include African or Caribbean characters. May be written by writers of any culture or from any country, as long as there is some kind of link with Africa, the Caribbean or black people of the Third World." avg. press run 5000. Expects 2 titles 2010, 4 titles 2011. No titles listed in the *Small Press Record of Books in Print* (36th Edition, 2010-11). 260-320pp. Subjects: Black, Caribbean, Fiction, Jamaica, Novels, Romance.

THE LYRIC, Jean Mellichamp Milliken, Editor; Nancy Mellichamp Savo, Assistant Editor, PO Box 110, Jericho, VT 05465-0110. 1921. Poetry. "Rhymed verse in traditional forms preferred, about 40 lines maximum. We print poetry only. No Contemporary political or social themes; we do not seek to shock, confound, or embitter. Poems must be original, unpublished, and not under consideration elsewhere. Send SASE for reply." circ. 650. 4/yr. Pub'd 4 issues 2009; expects 4 issues 2010, 4 issues 2011. sub. price $12, $22/2 years $30/3 years, Canada and other foreign add $2 per year postage; per copy $3; sample $3. Back issues: depends on availability. 36pp. Reporting time: 2 months. Simultaneous submissions accepted: yes, grudgingly. Publishes 5% of manuscripts submitted. Payment: contributors receive complimentary copy of issue with their poem; quarterly and annual prizes for poetry published; $50 quarterly, $800 (total) annually. Copyrighted, reverts to author. No ads. Subject: Poetry.

•**LYRIC POETRY RVIEW,** PO Box 2494, Bloomington, IN 47402. *"Lyric* is an international journal of poetry and creative exchange published twice yearly. We work hard to present newer writers along with more established figures. However, writers are strongly encouraged to review a recent issue of the magazine before submitting their work. Unpublished work only. Simultaneous submissions okay if notified. Lyric does not accept emailed submissions. Poetry, essays, translation, interviews, reviews [query]."

M

MacAdam/Cage Publishing Inc., Patrick Walsh, Editor; Anika Streitfeld, Nonfiction Editor, 155 Sansome Street, Ste. 550, San Francisco, CA 94104-3615, 415-986-7502, Fax 415-986-7414, info@macadamcage.com. 1999. Fiction, non-fiction. "MacAdam/Cage publishes quality retail hardcover fiction and narrative nonfiction such as memoirs, nonfiction that reads like fiction." avg. press run 10M. Pub'd 6 titles 2009; expects 10 titles 2010, 10-20 titles 2011. 67 titles listed in the *Small Press Record of Books in Print* (36th Edition, 2010-11). Discounts: retail 1-9 copies 42% + freight, 10+ 46% + freight, 50% nonreturnable and free freight, no minimum. 300pp. Reporting time: 3-4 months. Simultaneous submissions accepted: yes. Payment: negotiated. Copyrights for author. Subjects: Fiction, Memoirs, Non-Fiction.

MacDonald/Sward Publishing Company, Catherine Snyder, 120 Log Cabin Lane, Greensburg, PA 15601, 724-832-7767. 1986. Fiction, articles, art, criticism, long-poems, plays, non-fiction. "Accepting no manuscripts at this time due to heavy schedule. We use historical material. Proceeds used for education. Now focusing on essays - mostly concerning Iraq invasion and occupation, and peace against torturous wars and torturous regimes." avg. press run 500-1M, also print on demand. Expects 2 titles 2011. 31 titles listed in the *Small Press*

Record of Books in Print (36th Edition, 2010-11). Discounts: 1-5 books 20%; 6+ 40%. 250pp. Publishes less than 19% of manuscripts submitted. Payment: varies. Does not copyright for author. Subjects: Civil War, Essays, History, Race, Religion, War.

THE MACGUFFIN, Steven Dolgin, Editor; Nicholle Cormier, Managing Editor; Elizabeth Kircos, Fiction Editor; Carol Was, Poetry Editor, Schoolcraft College, 18600 Haggerty Road, Livonia, MI 48152, (734) 462-4400 Ext. 5327, Fax: (734) 462-4679, Email: macguffin@schoolcraft.edu, Website: www.macguffin.org. 1984. Poetry, fiction, art, photos, parts-of-novels, long-poems, non-fiction. "Past contributors include Jim Daniels, Stuart Dybek, Michael Steinberg, Dawn McDuffie, Linda Nemec Foster, Terry Blackhawk, and Thomas Lynch. Sponsors the annual National Poet Hunt Contest ($500 first prize) April-June. For more details, visit www.macguffin.org." circ. 600. 3/yr. Pub'd 3 issues 2009; expects 3 issues 2010, 3 issues 2011. sub. price $22; per copy $9.00 (current issue); sample $6.00. Back issues: $6.00. Discounts: varies. 160-164pp. Reporting time: 12-16 weeks. Notify us regarding simultaneous submissions. Publishes 5% of manuscripts submitted. Payment: 2 contributor's copies. Copyrighted, reverts to author. Subjects: Arts, Creative Non-fiction, Fiction, Non-Fiction, Poetry, Short Stories.

B.B. Mackey Books, Betty Mackey, PO Box 475, Wayne, PA 19087-0475, www.mackeybooks.com. 1985. Non-fiction. "Not seeking submissions at this time." avg. press run 2M. Pub'd 2 titles 2009; expects 1 title 2010, 2 titles 2011. 7 titles listed in the *Small Press Record of Books in Print* (36th Edition, 2010-11). Discounts: Any 1-49 books 40%,Any 50 or more 50%. 180pp. Payment: royalty, small advance on royalty. Does not copyright for author. Subjects: Florida, Horticulture, Memoirs.

MACROBIOTICS TODAY, George Ohsawa Macrobiotic Foundation, Carl Ferre, Editor, PO Box 3998, Chico, CA 95927-3998, 530-566-9765, Fax 530-566-9768, gomf@ohsawamacrobiotics.com. 1970. Articles, interviews, reviews, non-fiction. "Length: 5-12 pages; double-spaced. Articles on macrobiotics, health, and nutrition accepted. Recent contributors include Verna Varona, David Briscoe, Meredith McCarty, and Julia Ferre." circ. 5M. 6/yr. Pub'd 6 issues 2009; expects 6 issues 2010, 6 issues 2011. sub. price $30; per copy $5.50; sample $1 ppd. Back issues: cover price. Discounts: 5-9 35%, 10-49 45%, 50+ 55%. 40pp. Reporting time: 6 weeks. Publishes 40% of manuscripts submitted. Payment: up to $50. Copyrighted, does not revert to author. Pub's reviews: 4 in 2009. §Macrobiotics, health, nutrition. Ads: $475/$270/$145 1/3 page/$90 1/6 pg/classifieds 50¢/frequency discounts. Subjects: Ecology, Foods, Health, Philosophy.

THE MAD HATTER, Ron Watson, 320 S. Seminary Street, Madisonville, KY 42431, 270-825-6000, Fax 270-825-6072, rwatson@hopkins.k12.ky.us, www.hopkins.k12.us/gifted/mad_hatter.htm. 1998. Poetry, art, photos, cartoons. "*The Mad Hatter* is an annual journal of creativity by students in grades four through 12. Established in 1998, TMH has featured distinguished work by students from across the United States and from around the world. Send copies only, including public, private, or home-school affiliation and a SASE. Recent contributors include Banah Gadbian, Kristy Chu, Amanda Wengert, Wan Chong Kim, Dong Gun Yoo, Zeke Pederson, Naomi Wolf, and others." circ. 600. 1/yr. Pub'd 1 issue 2009; expects 1 issue 2010, 1 issue 2011. sub. price $8; per copy $8; sample $8. Back issues: $8. Discounts: Classroom sets of 30, incased by pine bookracks that are hand-made and custom-decorated by students from Madisonville, Kentucky. Price: free to all secondary schools in Hopkins County District; $300 postage paid for schools outside of district. 60pp. Reporting time: 1 month. Simultaneous submissions accepted: yes. Publishes less than 10% of manuscripts submitted. Payment: 1 copy, additional copies for $8, postage paid. Copyrighted, reverts to author. Ads: none. Subjects: Adolescence, Lewis Carroll, Children, Youth, Education, Humor, Photography, Poetry, Visual Arts, Young Adult.

MAD HATTERS' REVIEW: Edgy & Englightened Literature, Art & Music in the Age of Dementia, Carol Novack, madhattersreview@gmail.com. 2005. Poetry, fiction, articles, art, photos, cartoons, interviews, satire, criticism, reviews, music, parts-of-novels, long-poems, collages, plays, concrete art, news items, non-fiction. "Please read our submission guidelines thoroughly before submitting *only during our reading periods,* and fill in your email address form on our front page to receive news of reading periods and contests. We consider *EMAIL SUBMISSIONS ONLY.* Through June 30th, 2010, we are running a fiction and poetry contest. MHR is for those with an appreciation for wit, whimsy, dark humor, satire, lyricism, rhythm, wild word plays and (just in general) post post postmodern post avant-gardey literature, art, music, politics, and comics.... and columns, book reviews, art reviews, interviews, mini-movies, scratch n sniff projects, collages, audios, etc. We love successful experiments and collaborations." Annual. Expects 1 issue 2010, 1 issue 2011. Reporting time: Average: 1 to 4 months. Simultaneous submissions accepted: Yes. Pub's reviews. §We are currently focusing on books by our contributors.

MAD POETS REVIEW, Eileen D'Angelo, Editor, PO Box 1248, Media, PA 19063-8248. 1990. Poetry. "Anxious for work with 'joie de vivre' that startles and inspires, *MPR* places no restrictions on subject matter, form, or style; The "Mad" in the magazine's name doesn't mean we want nonsensical ramblings or poets that are terminally ticked off. Assumes no responsibility for submissions received without adequate return postage. Submit original, unpublished work, limit 6 poems with a 3-4 sentence bio. We read submissions from Jan. 1 to

June 1. See website for details on annual competition: www.madpoetssociety.com." 1/yr. Pub'd 1 issue 2009; expects 1 issue 2010, 1 issue 2011. price per copy $12.00; sample $13.50. Discounts: negotiable. Approx. 175-200 pppp. Reporting time: 3 to 12 weeks. Although we try to respond as quickly as possible, we receive bags of mail weekly for the magazine. Please be patient. Simultaneous submissions accepted: yes. Payment: copy of issue that work appears in. Copyrighted, reverts to author. Ads: none.

Mad River Press, Barry Sternlieb, Maureen Sternlieb, State Road, Richmond, MA 01254, 413-698-3184. 1986. Poetry, long-poems. "Manuscripts always solicited. Recent contributors: Jack Gilbert, Gary Snyder, Linda Gregg, John Haines, Richard Wilbur, W.S. Merwin, C. Dale Young, Lee Gurga, Hayden Carruth, Samuel Green, Tom Sexton." avg. press run 125-200. Pub'd 3 titles 2009; expects 3 titles 2010, 2 titles 2011. 9 titles listed in the *Small Press Record of Books in Print* (36th Edition, 2010-11). 20-28pp. Payment: 10%-20% of press run. Copyrights for author. Subject: Poetry.

THE MADISON REVIEW, Meagan Walker, Managing Editor; Hillary Schroeder, Fiction Editor; Jason Harkleroad, Fiction Editor; Hannah Baker-Sority, Poetry Editor, Dept of English, H.C. White Hall, 600 N. Park Street, Madison, WI 53706, 263-3303. 1978. Poetry, fiction, art, photos, parts-of-novels, long-poems. "Short, short stories welcome." circ. 800. 2/yr. Pub'd 2 issues 2009; expects 2 issues 2010, 2 issues 2011. sub. price $8; per copy $5; sample $2.50. Back issues: $2.50. Discounts: $2/book for bulk orders be happy to trade copies. 80-150pp. Reporting time: replies given by Dec. 15th for Fall issue and by April 15th for Spring issue. Simultaneous submissions accepted: yes. Publishes 6% of manuscripts submitted. Payment: 2 copies. Copyrighted, reverts to author. §All subjects. Subjects: Fiction, Poetry.

The Madson Group, Inc., Madeline Bright Ogle, Editor; Stephen A. Mart, Editor, 13775 A Mono Way, Suite 224, Sonora, CA 95370, 360-446-5348, fax 360-446-5234, email madsongroup@earthlink.net, www.pet-groomer.com. 1987. Articles, non-fiction. "Business, career, vocation, education, pets, dog grooming, pet grooming." avg. press run 1M minimum. Expects 1 title 2010, 3 titles 2011. 1 title listed in the *Small Press Record of Books in Print* (36th Edition, 2010-11). 300pp. Reporting time: 30 days. Simultaneous submissions accepted: yes. Copyrights for author. Subjects: Animals, Business & Economics, Careers, Education, Management.

Madyfi Press, Catherine Blackford, 2131 Newton Road, Corydon, IA 50060, www.madyfipress.com. 2005. Fiction. "At this time, we publish only faith-based fiction." avg. press run 1000. Expects 1 title 2010, 2 titles 2011. 1 title listed in the *Small Press Record of Books in Print* (36th Edition, 2010-11). 175pp. Subjects: Christianity, Fiction.

MAELSTROM, Christine L. Reed, Editor, HC #1 Box 1624, Blakeslee, PA 18610. "For poetry submissions please send no more than four pieces at a time with name and address on the top of each page and a SASE sufficient for return of work. (Except in the case of e-mail submissions which are gladly accepted.) For short fiction please send no more than two pieces at a time unless it is very short. E-mail submissions are accepted at IMaelstrom@aol.com. If possible, please include submissions in the body of your e-mail. E-mail submissions are made at the author's own risk. Response time varies. Pay is 1 copy. We have no bias towards or against any form or genre, we look at everything. Simultaneous submissions o.k. Previously published, o.k. but you must state the name of the publication so that credit may be given. Also seeking black and white art, photographs, cartoons, etc. Maelstrom is seeking book reviews, send query. Maelstrom reviews poet's chapbooks, send query.All submissions should include a 2 line bio and mailing address."

Magic Circle Press, Valerie Harms, PO Box 1123, Bozeman, MT 59771. 1972. Fiction, art, photos, criticism, non-fiction. "Focus is now on book packaging for clients." avg. press run 2M. Expects 1 title 2010. 6 titles listed in the *Small Press Record of Books in Print* (36th Edition, 2010-11). Discounts: 40% trade, 15% library. 150pp. Reporting time: 2 months. Payment: depends. Copyrights for author. Subjects: Children, Youth, Diaries, Journals, Anais Nin, Poetry, Theatre, Women.

MAGNET MAGAZINE, Eric T. Miller, 1218 Chestnut Street, Suite 508, Philadelphia, PA 19107, 215-413-8570, fax 215-413-8569, magnetmag@aol.com. 1993. circ. 35M. 6/yr. Pub'd 6 issues 2009; expects 6 issues 2010, 6 issues 2011. sub. price $14.95; per copy $3.50; sample $4. Back issues: $4. 128pp. Reporting time: varies. Simultaneous submissions accepted: no. Publishes 0% of manuscripts submitted. Payment: varies. Copyrighted, does not revert to author. Pub's reviews: 10-12 in 2009. §Music and music criticism. Ads: $3,000/$2,100. Subjects: Criticism, Music.

•Magnifico Publications, Richard Di Giacomo, 2486 Aram Avenue, San Jose, CA 95128, (408)286-5179. 1998. Non-fiction. "We publish history publications for educators. All of our books are written by teachers for teachers. We specialize in filling the niche when we see an unfulfilled need in social studies curriculum. We feature books on historical role-playing games for a whole classroom to play together, activities for ELL students studying American History, teacher support books such as choosing and using films, historical humor, and special topics such as California Indians and Renaissance explorers." avg. press run 300. Pub'd 2 titles 2009; expects 2 titles 2010. 10 titles listed in the *Small Press Record of Books in Print* (36th Edition, 2010-11).

Discounts: 50% discount to distributors, retailers, & wholesalers 25% discount to bookstores. 100pp. Reporting time: 1-2 months. Simultaneous submissions accepted: Yes. Payment: We prefer to buy the rights to the materials from the contributor, and pay them upfront. Does not copyright for author. Subjects: The Americas, Business & Economics, California, Careers, Civil Rights, Civil War, Classical Studies, Communism, Marxism, Leninism, Education, England, Europe, History, Native American, Renaissance, World War II.

MAIN CHANNEL VOICES: A Dam Fine Literary Magazines, Nancy Kay Peterson, Co-editor; Carol Borzyskowski, Co-editor, P.O. Box 492, Winona, MN 55987-0492, http://www.mainchannelvocies.com. 2004. Poetry. "We have eclectic tastes and are looking for accessible poetry that triggers an "Aha!" response in the reader. We take rhymed verse, free verse, prose poems and experimental forms. We are not looking for greeting card verse or pornography. See our web site for samples of the kind of work we publish." circ. 100. 4/yr. Expects 4 issues 2010, 4 issues 2011. sub. price $25; per copy $7.50; sample $5. Back issues: $5. 38pp. Reporting time: 4 months. Simultaneous submissions accepted: Yes. Publishes 5% of manuscripts submitted. Payment: One copy. Copyrighted, reverts to author. Subject: Poetry.

MAIN STREET RAG, M. Scott Douglass, Publisher, Poetry Editor & Managing Editor, PO Box 690100, Charlotte, NC 28227-7001, 704-573-2516, editor@mainstreetrag.com, www.MainStreetRag.com. 1996. Poetry, fiction, articles, art, photos, cartoons, interviews, satire, criticism, reviews, letters, collages, non-fiction. "Any style or subject, we're eclectic, but we prefer things with an edge (even humor). Our submission guidelines will change starting in 2007. We will always read subscribers' manuscripts year round, but in 2007, we will have a restricted reading period for unsolicited poetry and short fiction. Please visit our website for current needs and submission guidelines before submitting." circ. 800. 4/yr. Pub'd 4 issues 2009; expects 4 issues 2010, 4 issues 2011. sub. price $24, $45/2 years; per copy $8 + $1 S&H; sample $7-8 + $1 S&H for recent. Back issues: prices vary—available online. 120pp. Reporting time: 3-6 weeks. Simultaneous submissions accepted: absolutely not—acceptance isn't finalized until a *publishing agreement* is signed. Publishes less than 10% of manuscripts submitted. Payment: 1 contributor's copy (and sometimes more). Copyrighted, reverts to author. Pub's reviews: 40 in 2009. §Mostly small press productions that don't get enough attention; must have a copyright date no older than the previous calendar year. Ads: mostly swap. Subjects: Americana, Essays, Global Affairs, Humor, Internet, Interviews, Non-Fiction, Poetry, Politics, Reviews, Short Stories.

THE MAINE EVENT, Liz Chandler, Janet Murphy, Rusheen, Firies, Co. Kerry, Ireland, 066-9763084 phone/Fax, maineevent@eircom.net, www.maineevent.net. 1999. Poetry. "Broad range of poetry considered." circ. 6M. 12/yr. Pub'd 12 issues 2009; expects 12 issues 2010, 24 issues 2011. sub. price E24; per copy E2.50; sample none. Back issues: none. 10pp. Simultaneous submissions accepted: yes. Payment: none. Copyrighted, reverts to author. Pub's reviews: 1 in 2009. Ads: E155/E90/E60 1/4 page. Subject: Poetry.

Maisonneuve Press, Robert Merrill, Dennis Crow, Institute for Advanced Cultural Studies, P. O. Box 426, College Park, MD 20741-0426, 301-277-7505, Fax 301-277-2467. 1987. Photos, criticism, non-fiction. "High quality library editions and paperbacks." avg. press run 1,500 - 4,000. Expects 4 titles 2010, 6 titles 2011. 23 titles listed in the *Small Press Record of Books in Print* (36th Edition, 2010-11). Discounts: Please order directly from the Press. Email orders are best—orders@maisonneuvepress.com. We give standard discounts to bookstores and library distributors. Send an email for more information. All of our books are available through standard library distributors (Blackwell, Baker and Taylor, etc.) and on-line bookstores. 280pp. Simultaneous submissions accepted: yes. Publishes 2-3% of manuscripts submitted. Payment: no advance, 5% of sales. Copyrights for author. Subjects: Cities, Criticism, Earth, Natural History, Education, History, Humanism, Labor, Literary Review, Literature (General), Philosophy, Political Science, Prison, Public Affairs, Socialist, Women.

•MAKE: A Literary Magazine, Sarah Dodson, Editor, www.makemag.com. "*Make* is telling of the times, of the people, of the story that is Chicago. Our bi-annual magazine features a series of fiction pieces, poetry, photography, and a nonfiction section, containing interviews, genre reviews, essays, and editorials. We sponsor author readings, short plays, and live music events in the Chicago area. MAKE circulates 2,000 copies twice yearly throughout Chicago and beyond. Find MAKE in Chicago area bookstores and making the rounds at special events, such as readings and festivals. MAKE is also available in neighboring states, as well as New York and California. MAKE is available anywhere, anytime, online."

Malafemmina Press, Rose Sorrentino, 4211 Fort Hamilton Parkway, Brooklyn, NY 11219. 1990. Poetry, plays. "Malafemmina Press is publishing a series of poetry chapbooks by Italian-American women on Italian-American themes. When ordering make checks payable to Rose Sorrentino." avg. press run 200. Pub'd 1 title 2009; expects 3 titles 2010. 2 titles listed in the *Small Press Record of Books in Print* (36th Edition, 2010-11). 20pp. Reporting time: 3 months. Simultaneous submissions accepted: no. Payment: 50 copies and 50% discount. Copyrights for author. Subjects: Italian-American, Women.

THE MALAHAT REVIEW, Marlene Cookshaw, Editor, PO Box 1700, Stn. CSC, Victoria, British Columbia V8W 2Y2, Canada. 1967. Poetry, fiction, art, photos, interviews, criticism, parts-of-novels, long-poems, plays.

"Short works preferred. Index available 1967-1977, $3.95; $4.95 overseas." circ. 1.2M. 4/yr. Pub'd 4 issues 2009. sub. price $30 in Canada, $40 other; per copy $10, special issues $12; sample $10. Back issues: $8. Discounts: 33-1/3%, agents and bookstores only, no returns policy. 128pp. Reporting time: 4-12 weeks. Simultaneous submissions accepted: no. Publishes approx. 3% of manuscripts submitted. Payment: $30 per magazine page, prose and poetry. Copyrighted. Pub's reviews: 20 in 2009. §Poetry, fiction (Canadian). Ads: full page: $150 single issue, $500 four consecutive issues, half page: $100 single issue, $300 four consecutive issues, quarter page: $50 single issue, $160 four consecutive issues. Subject: Literary Review.

Maledicta Press (see also MALEDICTA: The International Journal of Verbal Aggression), Reinhold A. Aman, Editor & Publisher, PO Box 14123, Santa Rosa, CA 95402-6123, Phone: (707) 795-8178 E-mail: aman@sonic.net Web site: http://www.sonic.net/maledicta/. 1975. Articles. "Stopped publishing *Maledicta* in 2005 after the final volume (13)." avg. press run 2M. 16 titles listed in the *Small Press Record of Books in Print* (36th Edition, 2010-11). Discounts: booksellers 20-40%, jobbers 40%. 160pp. Reporting time: 1 week. Simultaneous submissions accepted: no. Publishes 10% of manuscripts submitted. Payment: 10% paid annually, no advance. Copyrights for author. Subjects: Dictionaries, Folklore, Language, Reference.

MALEDICTA: The International Journal of Verbal Aggression, Maledicta Press, Reinhold A. Aman, Editor & Publisher, PO Box 14123, Santa Rosa, CA 95402-6123, Telephone: 707-795-8178 E-mail: aman@sonic.net Web site: http://www.sonic.net/maledicta/. 1975. Articles. "Stopped publishing *Maledicta* in 2005 after the final volume (13). Most back volumes (1978-2005) are still available." circ. 2M. 1/yr. sub. price $20; per copy $20; No sample copies available. Back issues: Price varies per volume. Discounts: booksellers 20-40%, jobbers 40%. 160pp. Reporting time: No further manuscripts accepted. Simultaneous submissions accepted: no. Publishes 10% of manuscripts submitted. Payment: 10 free offprints. Copyrighted, reverts to author. Pub's reviews: none in 2009. §Verbal aggression (insults, curses, slang, etc.). No ads. Subjects: Folklore, Humor, Language, Sex, Sexuality.

Malki Museum Press (see also THE JOURNAL OF CALIFORNIA AND GREAT BASIN ANTHROPOLOGY), Lynn H. Gamble, Editor; Thomas C. Blackburn, Associate Editor; Lowell John Bean, Associate Editor, P.O. Box 578, Banning, CA 92220, 951-849-7289, Fax 951 849-3549, E-Mail: malkipress@aol.com, www.malkimuseum.org. 1964. Poetry, articles, interviews, non-fiction. "Malki publishes books on Native American culture, linguistics (Native language dictionaries), ethnobotanicals, mythology, archeology, anthropology and some autobiographical text and poetry. Our mission is to preserve culture and linguistics." avg. press run 1500. Pub'd 2 titles 2009; expects 5 titles 2010, 5 titles 2011. 2 titles listed in the *Small Press Record of Books in Print* (36th Edition, 2010-11). Discounts: Wholesale 40%%Educational 20%Musuem Members 20%. 275pp. Reporting time: Editorial Board meets twice yearly. Simultaneous submissions accepted: Yes. Publishes 85% of manuscripts submitted. Payment: Decided on an individual basis. Malki retains most copyrights. Subjects: Agriculture, Animals, Anthropology, Archaelogy, Astronomy, Dictionaries, Earth, Natural History, Ecology, Foods, Horticulture, Indigenous Cultures, Language, Myth, Mythology, Native American, Nature, Non-Fiction, Storytelling.

Malki-Ballena Press, Katherine Siva Saubel, Chairman, Founder, Lowell John Bean, Thomas C. Blackburn, Lynn Gamble, Sylvia Vane, PO Box 578, Banning, CA 92220-0578, (951)849-7289, Fax (951)849-3549, E-mail: malkimuseummail@gmail.com. 1965. Non-fiction. "We publish works on the anthropology of the western United States, especially California and the Southwest. We are interested only in books demonstrating the highest level of scholarship. Unsolicited manuscripts are not used and will not be returned to the author." avg. press run 1M. Pub'd 1 title 2009; expects 2 titles 2010. 34 titles listed in the *Small Press Record of Books in Print* (36th Edition, 2010-11). Discounts: 40-45% retail/wholesale, 20% educational, 20% membership. 100-400pp. Reporting time: 1 month to 1 year. Simultaneous submissions accepted: no. Publishes a variable % of manuscripts submitted. Payment: varies. Copyrights for author. Subjects: Anthropology, Archaelogy, California, Folklore, Native American, Pacific Northwest, Religion, Southwest, The West.

Mama Incense Publishing, Lillian Powers, 5535 Westlawn Ave., Suite 164, Los Angeles, CA 90066, 310-490-9097, www.mamaincense.com. 2004. Poetry, fiction, music, long-poems, non-fiction. "The goal of Mama Incense Publishing is to put informative, meaningful and entertaining works in the hands of the people. Whether it be poetry, children's literature, or fiction - if it has the possibility to change people's lives in a positive way, Mama Incense Publishing wants to assist in getting the message heard. Our first sponsored work "girl Child (The Transition - In Poetic Form)", by author/poet lily is a poetry collection detailing the trials many women go through in becoming a woman. It is a book of empowerment, of learning to love oneself before seeking love in the arms of another. Currently Mama Incense Publishing acts as a sounding board and a provider of information for first time self-publishers." avg. press run 3000. Expects 1 title 2010, 1 title 2011. No titles listed in the *Small Press Record of Books in Print* (36th Edition, 2010-11). Discounts: 1 copy: no discount2-5 books: 15% 6-20 books: 25% 21-50 books: 40%51-100 books: 45%101+: 50%. 64-200pp. Reporting time: 30 days. Simultaneous submissions accepted: Yes. Publishes 25% of manuscripts submitted. Does not copyright for author. Subjects: Advertising, Self-Promotion, African Literature, Africa, African

Studies, African-American, Children, Youth, Family, Feminism, Fiction, Music, Non-Fiction, Novels.

MAMMOTH books, Antonio Vallone, President-Publisher; Robert McGovern, Editor, 7 Juniata Street, DuBois, PA 15801, avallone@psu.edu. 1998. Poetry, fiction, articles, long-poems, non-fiction. "We are not accepting manuscripts at this time." avg. press run 300 copies, but digital printing allows us to easily reprint. No titles listed in the *Small Press Record of Books in Print* (36th Edition, 2010-11). Discounts: 30%. Payment: copies.

MANDORLA: New Writing from the Americas / Nueva escritura de las Americas, Kristin Dykstra, Co-editor; Roberto Tejada, Co-editor; Gabriel Bernal Granados, Co-editor, ISU, Dept. of English, Campus Box 4240, Normal, IL 61790-4240, Publications Unit tel (309) 438-3025, Fax (309) 438-5414, email to mandorla-magazine@ilstu.edu, website at http://www.litline.org/Mandorla/. 1991. Poetry, fiction, articles, art, photos, criticism, parts-of-novels, long-poems, plays. "First published in Mexico City in 1991, Mandorla emphasizes innovative writing in its original language—most commonly English or Spanish—and high-quality translations of existing material. Visual art and short critical articles complement this work. The name of the magazine—mandorla , describing a space created by two intersecting circles—alludes to the notion of exchange and imaginative dialogue that is necessary now among the Americas.Some of our recent contributors include Jay Wright, Carlos Aguilera, Vera Kutzinski, Tamara Kamenszain, Eleni Sikelianos, Jaime Saenz, Jose Kozer, Eduardo Milan, Antonio Jose Ponte, Reina Maria Rodriguez, Jorge Guitart, Paul Vanouse, Maria Negroni, Forrest Gander, Esther Allen, Giannina Braschi, Rosmarie Waldrop, Consuelo Castaneda, Rosa Alcala, Michael Davidson." circ. 1000. 1/yr. Pub'd 1 issue 2009; expects 1 issue 2010, 1 issue 2011. sub. price $10; per copy $10; sample $10. Back issues: $10. Discounts: Distributed to U.S. bookstores via Ubiquity and Ingram. Different prices apply for Latin America: please inquire. 315pp. Copyrighted, reverts to author. Ads: Full page $500.Half page $250. Subjects: The Americas, Arts, Avant-Garde, Experimental Art, Experimental, Fiction, Latino, Literature (General), Multicultural, North America, Photography, Poetry, Prose, Translation, U.S. Hispanic, Visual Arts.

THE MANHATTAN REVIEW, Philip Fried, Founder and Editor, c/o Philip Fried, 440 Riverside Drive, #38, New York, NY 10027, 212-932-1854, phfried@earthlink.net. 1980. Poetry, articles, interviews, criticism, long-poems. "'My only prejudice is against those who lack ambition, believing there is no more to writing than purveying superficial ironies, jokes, or shared sentiments; or those who dedicate themselves to the proposition that poetry of a word, by a word and for a word shall not perish from this earth. A poem is not purely a verbal artifact. It must speak to and for human concerns. I welcome experiments, but poetry must ultimately communicate to an audience. It is not an unobserved wave in the vast ocean of language.' (quoted from preface to 1st issue). ISSN 0275-6889. In recent issues: Christopher Bursk, Peter Redgrove, Penelope Shuttle, Baron Wormser, D. Nurkse, Jeanne Marie Beaumont, Venus Khoury-Ghata, and Claire Malroux." circ. 500. 1/yr. Pub'd 1 issue 2009; expects 1 issue 2010, 1 issue 2011. sub. price 1 volume (2 issues) $15 individuals (U.S. and Canada), $18 libraries (U.S. and Canada), $24 libraries elsewhere; per copy $7.50 individuals, $9.00 libraries; sample $7.50 individuals, $9.00 libraries. Back issues: same, with 6 X 9 envelope and $2.10 postage. 128pp. Reporting time: 12-14 weeks. Simultaneous submissions accepted: yes with notification of simultaneous submission and any acceptances. Publishes .015% of manuscripts submitted. Payment: 2 copies. Copyrighted, reverts to author. Pub's reviews: 4 in 2009. §Poetry. Ads: $150/$75. Subjects: Literature (General), Poetry.

Manifold Press, Carol Frome, 102 Bridge Street, Plattsburgh, NY 12901, editormanifoldpress@msn.com, www.manifoldpress.com. 2003. Poetry, articles, art, interviews, criticism, long-poems. "We lean towards well-crafted free-verse poetry, but don't mind considering formal verse if it's handled in a fresh manner and does not rely only on rhyme. No doggeral, limericks, haiku, or language poetry. Also, we consider art, chapbooks, and essays for our website." avg. press run 1M. Expects 1 title 2011. No titles listed in the *Small Press Record of Books in Print* (36th Edition, 2010-11). 70pp. Reporting time: 3-4 months. Simultaneous submissions accepted: yes. Publishes 2-3% of manuscripts submitted. Payment: $500 advance for books (not e-chapbook). Copyrights for author. Subject: Poetry.

MANOA: A Pacific Journal of International Writing, Frank Stewart, Editor; Pat Matsueda, Managing Editor, Univ. of Hawaii English Department, 1733 Donaghho Road, Honolulu, HI 96822, 808-956-3070, Fax 808-956-3083, mjournal-l@hawaii.edu, http://manoajournal.hawaii.edu. 1988. Poetry, fiction, interviews, non-fiction. "Manoa publishes contemporary writing from Asia, the Pacific, and the Americas. In general, each issue is devoted to a single country. Past issues have presented new work from such places as China, Tibet, Indonesia, Korea, Japan, PNG, Malaysia, Viet Nam, the Philippines, Australia, New Zealand, Pacific island nations, Mexico, South American nations, Nepal, Taiwan, Cambodia, and French Polynesia. US contributors have included Arthur Sze, Linda Gregg, Barry Lopez, W.S. Merwin, and Ha Jin. Manoa has also published interviews with Kenzaburo Oe, Ma Yuan, Xue Di, Soth Polin, and other writers of international stature." circ. 2.5M (print edition); about 5M (electronic edition). 2/yr. Pub'd 2 issues 2009; expects 2 issues 2010, 2 issues 2011. sub. price $30; per copy $16; sample $12. Discounts: agency 10%, multiple orders: 10-19 20%, 20+ 30%. 220pp. Simultaneous submissions accepted: yes. Publishes 1% of manuscripts submitted. Payment: competitive, depends on material and length. Copyrighted, reverts to author. Ads: $200/$125. Subjects: Arts, Asia, Indochina, Asian-American, Autobiography, Earth, Natural History, Environment, Fiction, Hawaii, Literature (General), Non-Fiction, Novels, Poetry, Short Stories, Translation, Visual Arts.

MANTIS: A Journal of Poetry & Translation, Harris Feinsod, Managing Editor; Bronwen Tate, Poetry Editor, Mantis DLCL, Pigott Hall Bld. 260, Stanford University, Stanford, CA 94305, Web: http://mantisjournal.stanford.edu/index.html. "*Mantis* is a biannual a journal that focuses on poetry, poetics, and translation. *Mantis* is housed at the Division of Literatures, Cultures, and Languages at Stanford University and seeks out the work of talented poets, translators and critics around the world. On our website you can read and listen to sample poems and essays, order copies of *Mantis*, as well find out how to submit poetry, translations, and criticism."

Manuscript Press (see also COMICS REVUE), Rick Norwood, PO Box 336, Mountain Home, TN 37684-0336, 423-926-7495. 1976. "Comic strips." avg. press run 1000. Pub'd 1 title 2009; expects 1 title 2010, 1 title 2011. 7 titles listed in the *Small Press Record of Books in Print* (36th Edition, 2010-11). Discounts: 40% on 5 or more, 55% on 100 or more. 100-200pp. Reporting time: slow. Simultaneous submissions accepted: no. Publishes 0% of manuscripts submitted. Payment: by arrangement. Copyrights for author. Subjects: Comics, Science Fiction.

MANY MOUNTAINS MOVING, Naomi Horii, Editor-in-Chief; Debra Bokur, Poetry Editor; Steven Church, Essay Editor; David Rozgonyi, Book Review Editor, 549 Rider Ridge Drive, Longmont, CO 80501, 303-545-9942, Fax 303-444-6510. 1994. Poetry, fiction, articles, art, photos, cartoons, interviews, satire, reviews, letters, parts-of-novels, long-poems, non-fiction. "We invite fiction, poetry and essays from writers of all cultures. Contributors include Sherman Alexie, Isabel Allende, Amiri Baraka, Robert Bly, Lorna Dee Cervantes, Marge Piercy, Luis Urrea and many others. Poems have appeared in Best American Poetry and Pushcart. We are starting a poetry book contest and will print one book of poems per year." circ. 3M. 5/yr. Pub'd 3 issues 2009; expects 3 issues 2010, 6 issues 2011. sub. price $16/2 issues; per copy $9; sample $6. Back issues: $6. Discounts: negotiable. 80pp. Reporting time: usually within 1 month, but up to 4 months occasionally. Simultaneous submissions accepted: yes. Publishes .1% of manuscripts submitted. Payment: contributors' copies. Copyrighted, reverts to author. Pub's reviews: 2 in 2009. §fiction, poetry, creative nonfiction. Ads: $200/$100/no classifieds. Subjects: Essays, Feminism, Fiction, Poetry, Short Stories.

Mapletree Publishing Company, JB Howick, President, 72 N WindRiver Rd, Silverton, ID 83867-0446, 208-752-1836, info@windriverpublishing.com, www.mapletreepublishing.com. 2002. Fiction, non-fiction. "We publish books about homeschooling, child development, and family values. Mapletree Publishing Company is an imprint of WindRiver Publishing, Inc." Pub'd 4 titles 2009; expects 4 titles 2010, 8 titles 2011. 11 titles listed in the *Small Press Record of Books in Print* (36th Edition, 2010-11). Discounts: 2-4 copies 20%; 5-35 copies 40%; even case quantities 50%. 300pp. Reporting time: 4-6 months. Simultaneous submissions accepted: yes. Payment: 15% of net paid semi-annually. Copyrights for author. Subjects: Children, Youth, Education, Family, Parenting.

Marathon International Book Company, Jim Wortham, Publisher, Department SPR, PO Box 40, Madison, IN 47250-0040, 812-273-4672 phone/Fax, jwortham@seidata.com. 1969. "We are considering non-fiction and self help manuscripts. We are interested in considering other publishers' books for distribution. Please mail a sample copy of any title(s) you wish us to consider for distribution. We are also interested in purchasing small publishing companies. Contact us by mail, fax, or e-mail, please." avg. press run 3M. Pub'd 5 titles 2009; expects 5 titles 2010, 5 titles 2011. 20 titles listed in the *Small Press Record of Books in Print* (36th Edition, 2010-11). Discounts: 40% to trade; write for quantity and wholesale schedule. 64-300pp. Reporting time: 2-3 weeks. Simultaneous submissions accepted: yes. Publishes 5% of manuscripts submitted. Payment: 10% royalty or an outright purchase of the book rights. Copyright in author's name. Subjects: Drama, Poetry.

Peter Marcan Publications, Peter Marcan, PO Box 3158, London SEI 4RA, Great Britain, (020) 7357 0368. 1978. Non-fiction. "Has several titles in print including *The Lord's Prayer in Black & White*, *Music for Solo Violin* [a catalogue of published and unpublished works from the 17th century to 1989 with a 1997 supplement], and the *Marcan Visual Arts Handbook* [where to go for British contacts, expertise and specialty]." avg. press run 350-1M. Pub'd 1 title 2009; expects 2 titles 2010, 2 titles 2011. 10 titles listed in the *Small Press Record of Books in Print* (36th Edition, 2010-11). Discounts: 35% to book trade for two or more copies. 62-120pp. Subjects: Arts, Bibliography, Book Collecting, Bookselling, Cities, History, London, Music, Reference, Religion.

March Books, Elizabeth Marchand, P.O. Box 55, Sterling, CT 06377, 866-851-7621. 2008. Fiction. "March Books endeavors to offer quality fiction for all ages - from children to adults. For our adult and YA list especially, we try to publish stories that at least touch on the relevant social issues of our day. Some of our novels deal with the darker corners of our collective attic, in an attempt to bring some of these issues further into the daylight." avg. press run 8000. Expects 2-4 titles 2010, 2-7 titles 2011. No titles listed in the *Small*

Press Record of Books in Print (36th Edition, 2010-11). Discounts: 25-49 - 25% 50-99 - 35% 100+ - 45%. 150-350pp. Reporting time: One month. Simultaneous submissions accepted: Yes. Publishes 5% of manuscripts submitted. Payment: We will not be considering new submissions until 2010. Does not copyright for author. Subjects: Animals, Children, Youth, Death & Dying, Drugs, Environment, Fantasy, Food, Eating, Mental Health, Psychology, Relationships, Sex, Sexuality, Society, Storytelling, Supernatural, Young Adult.

March Street Press, Robert Bixby, 3413 Wilshire Drive, Greensboro, NC 27408-2923, 336 282 9754 fon and fax, rbixby@earthlink.net, http://www.marchstreetpress.com. 1988. Poetry, fiction. "Currently reading. I'm publishing a couple of books a month, including poetry, essays, short fiction, and novels. Please do not send novels without querying first as we will need to discuss whether March Street is a good fit for your needs. Please send a paper submission with cover letter and check for reading fee (reading fee: $20) and simultaneously send an rtf format electronic file of your complete work (not dozens of individual files containing the component poems or stories, for example)." avg. press run 50. Pub'd 15 titles 2009; expects 15 titles 2010, 15 titles 2011. 72 titles listed in the *Small Press Record of Books in Print* (36th Edition, 2010-11). Discounts: write. 70pp. Reporting time: 2-3 months. Simultaneous submissions are a bad idea even with presses that don't object to them. I'd prefer not to receive them, but if you really want me to look at a simultaneous submission, make sure you let me know that's what it is. I publish a high percentage—around 60 percent—of submissions because I have many regular authors who often send me a manuscript a year. Also, many of my new authors are referrals from my current authors and they are kind to me, making sure to only send me the work of truly promising authors. Most of my rejections are among the manuscripts I receive from complete strangers who have developed no relationship with me or the press. Payment: 10 free copies, 15% of sales. Does not copyright for author. Subjects: Fiction, Poetry.

Margaret Media, Inc., Mary Gehman, 618 Mississippi St., Donaldsonville, LA 70346, office phone: (225) 473-9319, cell phone: (225) 323-4559: orders@margaretmedia.com. 1981. Fiction, non-fiction. "We serve as a friend and business partner to our authors, offering basic publisher's services but depending on the author to make many of the decisions and help out with promotion. We are interested primarily in non-fiction about Louisiana and New Orleans. Some fiction with southern themes will be considered. See Publisher's Guidelines on our website." avg. press run 2M. Pub'd 4 titles 2009; expects 3 titles 2010, 5 titles 2011. 9 titles listed in the *Small Press Record of Books in Print* (36th Edition, 2010-11). Discounts: 40% to wholesalers. 250pp. Reporting time: 2 weeks. We accept simultaneous submissions, but query first. Publishes a variable % of manuscripts submitted. Payment: After publisher's cost to design, format and print the book is recouped, we split the rest of sales for that title with the author. Copyrighting for author depends on contract. Subjects: African-American, Biography, Children, Youth, Culture, Feminism, Folklore, History, Language, Leisure/Recreation, Louisiana, Multicultural, Race, South, Women.

Marick Press, Mariela Griffor, Publisher, P.O. Box 36253, Grosse Pointe Farms, MI 48236. No titles listed in the *Small Press Record of Books in Print* (36th Edition, 2010-11).

Markowski International Publishers, Marjorie L. Markowski, Editor, Michael A. Markowski, 1 Oakglade Circle, Hummelstown, PA 17036-9525, 717-566-0468, Fax 717-566-6423. 1981. Non-fiction. "Formerly Ultralight Publications, Inc. Publishes hardcover and trade paperback originals. Book catalog and ms guidelines for #10 SAE with two first class stamps. Publishes book on average of one year after acceptance. Simultaneous submissions OK. Primary focus is books on, human development, self-help, personal growth, sales and marketing, leadership training, network marketing, motivation and success. We are interested in how-to, motivational and instructional books of short to medium length that will serve recognized and emerging needs of society. Query or submit outline and three sample chapters. Reviews artwork/photos as part of ms package. Tips: 'We're very interested in publishing best sellers!'" avg. press run 5-50M. Pub'd 5 titles 2009; expects 10 titles 2010, 10 titles 2011. 31 titles listed in the *Small Press Record of Books in Print* (36th Edition, 2010-11). Discounts: 1-10, 2-4-20%, 5-9=30%, 10-24-40%, 25-49-42%, 50-74-45%, 75-99-47%, 100-499-50%, 500-999-55%, 1000 and up 60%. 108-192pp. Reporting time: 2 months. Simultaneous submissions accepted: yes. Publishes 1% of manuscripts submitted. Payment: 10%-12% royalty on wholesale price. Copyrights for author. Subjects: Motivation, Success, Psychology, Self-Help.

THE MARLBORO REVIEW, Ellen Dudley; Ruth Anderson Barnett, Poetry; Margaret Kaufman, Fiction; Helen Fremont, Fiction, PO Box 243, Marlboro, VT 05344, www.marlbororeview.com. 1995. Poetry, fiction, interviews, criticism, reviews, parts-of-novels, long-poems, non-fiction. "Longpoems okay, translations and reviews welcome. Recent contributors: Brenda Hillman, Yehuda Amichai, Stephen Dobyns, Heather McHugh, Dionision Martinez. No deadlines." circ. 1M. 2/yr. Pub'd 2 issues 2009; expects 2 issues 2010, 2 issues 2011. sub. price $16; per copy $8 + $1.30 postage; sample $8 + $1.30 postage. Back issues: none. Discounts: bookstores 40%. 100pp. Reporting time: 2-3 months. Simultaneous submissions accepted if notified. Publishes 6% of manuscripts submitted. Payment: copies. Copyrighted. Pub's reviews: 8 in 2009. §Poetry, fiction, and nonfiction. Ads: $150/$75/none. Subjects: Fiction, Interviews, Poetry, Reviews, Translation.

Marmot Publishing, Steven Laurens, 4652 Union Flat Creek Road, Endicott, WA 99125-9764, 509-657-3359,

294

marmot@wildblue.net. 1993. Non-fiction. "Please send queries only. We do not have the staff to read unsolicited manuscripts. Almost all general adult non-fiction subjects are welcome. Political material must be of a conservative or libertarian viewpoint. No pro-feminism or pro-multiculturalism." avg. press run 2M. Pub'd 1 title 2009; expects 1 title 2010, 1 title 2011. 2 titles listed in the *Small Press Record of Books in Print* (36th Edition, 2010-11). Discounts: bookstores-40%, wholesalers/distributors-55%. 300pp. Reporting time: 2 months. Simultaneous submissions accepted: yes. Payment: no advances, royalty negotiable. Copyrights for author. Subject: Non-Fiction.

MARQUEE, Steve Levin, York Theatre Building, 152 N. York Road, Suite 200, Elmhurst, IL 60126, 630-782-1800, Fax 630-782-1802, thrhistsoc@aol.com. 1969. Articles, photos, interviews, criticism. "Historical research on American Theatre buildings contributed by members. Recent article Metropolitan Opera House, Philadelphia and current article-history of Atlantic City theatres w/vintage pictures. Comprehensive study Chicago Theatre, Chicago, IL. Theatre Draperies Issue—1983 - Color issue - Fifth Avenue Th. Seattle, Washington. Special issue - 1984 - Preservation of OLD Theatres. 1985 Theatre Acoustics. 1976 Mastbaum Th. - Phila Pa; Earle Theatre, Philadelphia issue-1986; Al Ringling Th. Baraboo, WI - 1991. Michigan Thr, Detroit, 1995." circ. 1M. 5/yr. Pub'd 5 issues 2009; expects 5 issues 2010, 5 issues 2011. sub. price $45; per copy $6.50; sample $6.50. Back issues: $6.50. Discounts: library rate $35. 30pp. Reporting time: 3 months. Publishes 85% of manuscripts submitted. Copyrighted, reverts to author. Pub's reviews: 6 in 2009. §Theatre architecture. Ads: $200/$125. Subjects: Architecture, Theatre.

Marsh Hawk Press, Editorial Collective; Sandy McIntosh, Managing Editor, PO Box 206, East Rockaway, NY 11518-0206, mheditor@marshhawkpress.org, www.marshhawkpress.org. 2001. Poetry. "We like poets who have assimilated modern and postmodern traditions but expand from them, particularly toward connectons with the visual arts. Marsh Hawk Press currently accepts submissions only through its annual competition: the Marsh Hawk Press Prize. (See website for more information.)." avg. press run 1000. Pub'd 6 titles 2009; expects 6 titles 2010, 6 titles 2011. 4 titles listed in the *Small Press Record of Books in Print* (36th Edition, 2010-11). Discounts: standard 40% to wholesalers. 96pp. Copyrights for author. Subject: Poetry.

Maryland Historical Press (also MHPress), Vera Rollo, 2364 Sandell Drive, Dunwoody, GA 30338, 770-481-0912. 1964. Non-fiction. "We publish only non-fiction: histories, US history, US Presidential history, biographies, aviation law, aviation biographies, aviation histories." avg. press run 1000. Expects 2 titles 2010, 2 titles 2011. No titles listed in the *Small Press Record of Books in Print* (36th Edition, 2010-11). Discounts: 33%. 200pp. Reporting time: Month. Simultaneous submissions accepted: No. Publishes 10% of manuscripts submitted. Payment: After costs recouped, 10% royalties, paid every 6 months. Copyrights for author. Subjects: Airplanes, Americana, Anthropology, Archaelogy, Aviation, Biography, Government, History, Indians, Indigenous Cultures, Interviews, Thomas Jefferson, Native American, North America, Philosophy, Religion.

Marymark Press, Mark Sonnenfeld, 45-08 Old Millstone Drive, East Windsor, NJ 08520, 609-443-0646. 1994. Poetry, fiction, art, photos, cartoons, music, collages. "I prefer submissions that are in the experimental genre. Recent contributors are Spiel, Thomas Hays, Richard Kostelanetz, Jose Roberto Sechi, and Melanie Monterey." avg. press run 300-350+. Pub'd 50-75 titles 2009; expects 50-75 titles 2010, 50-75 titles 2011. 49 titles listed in the *Small Press Record of Books in Print* (36th Edition, 2010-11). Pages vary. Reporting time: 2 weeks maximum. Simultaneous submissions accepted: yes. Publishes 80-90% of manuscripts submitted. Payment: contributor's copies. Does not copyright for author. Subjects: Avant-Garde, Experimental Art, Beat, Poetry, Surrealism.

THE MASSACHUSETTS REVIEW, Corwin Ericson, Managing Editor, Editor; David Lenson, Editor; Ellen Watson, Editor, South College, University of Massachusetts, Amherst, MA 01003-7140, 413-545-2689. 1959. Poetry, fiction, articles, art, photos, interviews, satire, criticism, letters, long-poems, plays, non-fiction. "*A SASE must accompany each manuscript + query.* No fiction or poetry mss considered from June 1 to Oct 1." circ. 2M+. 4/yr. Pub'd 4 issues 2009; expects 4 issues 2010, 4 issues 2011. sub. price $25; per copy $8; sample $8. Back issues: $7-$14. Discounts: 15% on ads for adv. agencies; 40% bookstores; $50 full page ad for univ. and small presses. 172pp. Reporting time: 6-12 weeks. Publishes 10% of manuscripts submitted. Payment: $50 prose, $10 min. poetry, 35¢ per line. Copyrighted, rights revert to author on request. Ads: $125 full page. Subject: Literary Review.

Massey-Reyner Publishing, PO Box 323, Wallace, CA 95254, phone/fax 209-763-2590, e-mail reyners@comcast.net. 1996. Non-fiction. "We do not solicit manuscripts." avg. press run 5M. Pub'd 1 title 2009; expects 1 title 2010, 1 title 2011. 1 title listed in the *Small Press Record of Books in Print* (36th Edition, 2010-11). Discounts: 2-5 books 25%; 6-15 30%; 16-300 40%; 301-499 45%; 500 + up 50%. 150pp. Reporting time: 2 months. Simultaneous submissions accepted: no. Payment: bi-annual payment. Copyrights for author. Subjects: Autobiography, Disabled, Education, Handicapped, Motivation, Success, Non-Fiction, Religion.

THE MATCH, Fred Woodworth, PO Box 3012, Tucson, AZ 85702. 1969. Fiction, articles, cartoons, interviews, criticism, reviews, letters, parts-of-novels, news items. "Recent articles include 'Who the Police

Beat,' 'Freedom Eclipsed,'. Not seeking contributions." circ. 2M. 4/yr. Pub'd 1 issue 2009; expects 3 issues 2010, 4 issues 2011. sub. price $12/4 issues; per copy $2.50; sample $2. Discounts: 50%, payable on receipt of copies. 60pp. Pub's reviews: 17 in 2009. §Anarchism, government. No ads. Subjects: Anarchist, Book Reviewing.

MATCHBOOK, Debrie Stevens, 240 Edison Furlong Road, Doylestown, PA 18901-3013, Fax 215-340-3965. 1995. Poetry, reviews, long-poems. "Eclectic. Suggest reviewing sample copy before submitting." circ. internet. 2/yr. Pub'd 2 issues 2009; expects 2 issues 2010, 2 issues 2011. sub. price on internet. Discounts: inquire. 64-128 web pages. Reporting time: 2-4 weeks. Simultaneous submissions accepted if noted. Publishes 5% of manuscripts submitted. Copyrighted, reverts to author. Pub's reviews: 10-12 reviews in 2009. §Chapbooks, small press magazines featuring poetry. Ads: $50/$25 per banner on website. Subjects: Poetry, Reviews, Translation.

MATHEMATICAL SPECTRUM, Applied Probability Trust, D.W. Sharpe, School of Mathematics and Statistics, The University of Sheffield, Sheffield S3 7RH, England, tel: +44 (0)114 222-3922, fax: +44 (0)114 272-9782, email: spectrum@sheffield.ac.uk, web: http://www.appliedprobability.org. 1968. Articles, reviews, letters. circ. 2000. 3/yr. Pub'd 3 issues 2009; expects 3 issues 2010, 3 issues 2011. sub. price £13.00 (or $26.00 US or $27.00 Aus); free sample copy on request. Back issues: on request. Contact s.c.boyles@sheffield.ac.uk for details of discounts. 24pp. Simultaneous submission *not* accepted. Payment: Prizes awarded annually for best student contributions. Copyrighted, does not revert to author. Pub's reviews: 12 in 2009. §Books on mathematics suitable for senior students in schools and beginning undergraduates in colleges and universities. Ads: on request. Subjects: Education, Mathematics.

•**MATRIX MAGAZINE,** Jon Paul Fiorentino, Editor-in-Chief; Andy Brown, Senior Editor; Anne Stone, Senior Editor, 1400 de Maisonneuve Blvd. West, LB 658, Montreal, Quebec H3G 1M8, Canada. "Essays, fiction, poems, reviews. The 2010 Litpop Awards Competition is now open! Cant decide whether to be a pop star or a famous writer? Be both! Enter the 2010 Matrix/Pop Montreal Litpop Awards! The Pop Montreal International Music Festival and Matrix Magazine have once again teamed up to bring you Canadas most innovative and exciting literary competition."

Maui arThoughts Co., Victor C. Pellegrino, PO Box 967, Wailuku, HI 96793-0967, 808-244-0156 phone/Fax, booksmaui@hawaii.rr.com, www.booksmaui.com. 1987. Poetry, fiction, non-fiction. avg. press run 5M-25M. Pub'd 2 titles 2009; expects 2 titles 2010, 2 titles 2011. 8 titles listed in the *Small Press Record of Books in Print* (36th Edition, 2010-11). Discounts: 10% libraries and schools, 20% college bookstores, 40% retail, 40-55% major distributors. 160-220pp. Reporting time: 2 weeks. Simultaneous submissions accepted: no. Publishes 5% of manuscripts submitted. Payment: to be arranged. Copyrights for author. Subjects: Cooking, Fiction, Non-Fiction, Poetry, Writers/Writing.

Maupin House Publishing, Inc., 2416 NW 71st Place, Gainesville, FL 32607, 1-800-524-0634, Fax 352-373-5546. 1988. avg. press run 3M. Pub'd 8 titles 2009; expects 10 titles 2010, 10 titles 2011. 54 titles listed in the *Small Press Record of Books in Print* (36th Edition, 2010-11). Discounts: industry standard. Pages vary. Reporting time: 2 months. We accept simultaneous submissions with notice. Publishes 5-10% of manuscripts submitted. Payment: negotiable. Copyrights for author. Subjects: Communication, Journalism, Education, English, Reading.

Maverick Books, Josh Greene, Box 897, Woodstock, NY 12498, 866-478-9266 phone/Fax, maverickbooks@aol.com. 1998. Fiction, art, photos, reviews, non-fiction. avg. press run 1-2M. Expects 1 title 2010, 2 titles 2011. 1 title listed in the *Small Press Record of Books in Print* (36th Edition, 2010-11). Discounts: varies on circumstance. 250-375pp. Reporting time: 3 months. Simultaneous submissions accepted: yes. Publishes 1% of manuscripts submitted. Payment: varies. Author obtains own copyright. Subjects: Arts, Biography, Feminism, Fiction, Romance, Women.

Maverick Duck Press, Kendall Bell, Willingboro, NJ 08046, www.maverickduckpress.com, email: maverickduckpress@yahoo.com. 2005. Poetry. "Maverick Duck Press is a small chapbook press that publishes limited run, staple bound chapbooks. We look for fresh and innovative poems that capture the eye and resonate in the mind. We prefer shorter poems. Email submissions only." avg. press run 50. Pub'd 6 titles 2009; expects 8 titles 2010, 8 titles 2011. No titles listed in the *Small Press Record of Books in Print* (36th Edition, 2010-11). 24pp. Reporting time: 2-3 months. Simultaneous submissions accepted: No. Publishes 10% of manuscripts submitted. Payment: Author receives 20 copies and can buy additional copies at 50% off cover price. Acquires first publishing rights. Rights revert to poet after publication. Subject: Poetry.

Mayapple Press, Judith Kerman, Editor-Publisher, 408 N. Lincoln St., Bay City, MI 48708, 989-892-1429 (voice/fax), jbkerman@mayapplepress.com, www.mayapplepress.com. 1978. Poetry, fiction, art, parts-of-novels, long-poems. "$10 reading fee, payable by check or PayPal on website. *Please read the guidelines on our website before sending material.* We are closed to new submissions about half the year - information is on the website When we are open, email submissions OK with PayPal reading fee. Clear xeroxes OK, with name and address on every page; *please* number multi-page works and include TOC. No snailmail returns or responses without SASE. No free advice. We have a special interest in writing by women, Great Lakes regional writing, the Caribbean, translations, the immigrant experience, science fiction poetry, atypical Judaica - all sorts of things that cross typical category boundaries - as well as book arts and art/fine crafts. We have published poetry collections by Conrad Hilberry, Dennis Hinrichsen, Margo Solod, Susan Azar Porterfield, Gerry LaFemina, Pamela Miller, Hugh Fox, Judith Minty as well as an anthology of science fiction/fantasy poetry by leading genre authors and a multi-genre book about the Michigan cherry industry. We expect authors, especially poets, to take a major hand in distribution (terms are negotiable, but concept is, alas, inevitable!).'' avg. press run 400. Pub'd 7 titles 2009; expects 12 titles 2010, 12 titles 2011. 79 titles listed in the *Small Press Record of Books in Print* (36th Edition, 2010-11). Discounts: 1-5 copies to bookstores, jobbers & libraries 20%; 6 or more (mixed or same title) 30% consignment; 40% cash/returns; 50% no returns; 55% to wholesale distributors. Additional 5% discount for prepaid orders; include $2 for postage and handling per copy for first 3 copies, 75¢ per copy for additional copies. 60pp. Reporting time: up to 6 months. Simultaneous submissions accepted: OK - please inform us. We recommend sending an inquiry with sample section first. Payment: for poetry/fiction, 5% of run in lieu of royalties (minimum 10 copies) plus 50% discount on purchase of copies; for other projects, negotiable. Copyrights for author. Subjects: Book Arts, Caribbean, Great Lakes, Immigration, Judaism, Latin America, Literature (General), Michigan, Midwest, Poetry, Science Fiction, Translation, Women.

MAYFLY, Brooks Books, Randy Brooks, 3720 N. Woodridge Drive, Decatur, IL 62526, (217) 877-2966. 1986. Poetry. ''Mayfly is a small, square (5.5" X 5.5") haiku magazine published two times a year. Our goal is to be very selective, but then publish each haiku with dignity. In our opinion, haiku is best savored in small servings. We will publish only the very best, the most evocative haiku. Mayfly was first published in 1986 as a new approach to publishing haiku. We wanted to feature the individual haiku above all else, without embellishment nor distractions. To avoid any recurring mayfly haiku submissions, we opened with a mayfly contest, which resulted in the following winning haiku published in the first issue. a mayfly taps the screen warm beets slip their skins—Peggy LylesWe have not published another mayfly haiku since.We feel it is the duty of editors and writers to make careful selection and proper presentation of only the very best, the most evocative, the truly effective haiku. We publish only 14 or 15 haiku per issue, but each haiku is printed on its own page. The writer is paid $10.00 per haiku.We continue to strive for excellence in selective editing and publication design, and we hope that you enjoy each issue.Submissions to Mayfly are limited to five poems per issue. We screen submissions and place maybes on our kitchen counter where they are read and re-read over a period of time. Those haiku which continue to move us with repeated reading are selected for publication.We accept submissions by snail mail only.'' circ. 400. 2/yr. Pub'd 2 issues 2009; expects 2 issues 2010, 2 issues 2011. sub. price $8; per copy $4; sample $4. Back issues: $4. Discounts: none. 16pp. Reporting time: 6 months. Simultaneous submissions accepted: No. Publishes 2% of manuscripts submitted. Payment: $10 per poem. Copyrighted, reverts to author. Subject: Haiku.

Mayhaven Publishing, Inc., Doris R. Wenzel, PO Box 557, 803 Buckthorn Circle, Mahomet, IL 61853-0557, 217-586-4493; fax 217-586-6330. 1990. Poetry, fiction, art, photos, cartoons, interviews, satire, letters, non-fiction. ''We like variety in topic and style.'' avg. press run 2000. Pub'd 4 titles 2009; expects 8 titles 2010, 8 titles 2011. 112 titles listed in the *Small Press Record of Books in Print* (36th Edition, 2010-11). Discounts: Provided. 32-300pp. Reporting time: asap - many new submissions. Simultaneous submissions accepted: yes. Publishes less than 1% of manuscripts offered. Payment: Royalties: based on contract for: Traditional, Co-op, Awards for Fiction, Special Editions. Copyrights for author. Subjects: Biography, Children, Youth, Fiction, History, Humor, Illinois, Juvenile Fiction, Memoirs, Midwest, Mystery, New England, Non-Fiction, Novels, Poetry, Young Adult.

McBooks Press, Inc., Alexander G. Skutt, Owner, Publisher; Jackie Swift, Editorial Director, I. D. Booth Bldg, 520 North Meadow Street #2, Ithaca, NY 14850-3229, 607-272-2114, FAX 607-273-6068, mcbooks@mcbooks.com, www.mcbookspress.com. 1979. Fiction, photos, non-fiction. ''As a result of recent restructuring, we have scaled back our publishing for the foreseeable future. At this time, we are currently seeking a few extremely high-quality manuscripts, both fiction and non-fiction. In the current tough book market,it's important authors know how to self-promote. Show you know who your audience is and how to generate word-of-mouth. For nonfiction, we are looking for sports, nutrition/vegetarianism/veganism, and other topics that would compliment these areas. Submit a query letter first. For fiction, historical fiction is still of special interest, but currently we are open to almost any genre or style, except romance, science fiction/fantasy, and childrens. Send cover letter with a three-chapter excerpt.'' avg. press run 3M. Pub'd 15 titles 2009; expects 5 titles 2010, 7 titles 2011. 48 titles listed in the *Small Press Record of Books in Print* (36th Edition, 2010-11). Discounts: standard terms are available to bookstores, wholesalers, etc. 320pp. Reporting time: 3 months on query letters. Simultaneous submissions accepted: yes. Publishes less than 5% of manuscripts submitted. Payment: usual royalty basis with an advance. Copyrights for author. Subjects: Cooking, Ecology, Foods, Fiction, Food, Eating, Health, History, Military, Veterans, Nature, New York, Non-Fiction, Novels, Nutrition, Sports, Outdoors, Vegetarianism, World War II.

McGavick Field Publishing, Phyllis McGavick, Acquisitions, Anne Field, 118 North Cherry, Olathe, KS 66061, 913-782-1700, Fax 913-782-1765, fran@abcnanny.com, colleen@nationwidemedia.net, www.abc-nanny.com. 1996. Articles, non-fiction. avg. press run 30-50M. Pub'd 1 title 2009; expects 4 titles 2010, 8 titles 2011. 3 titles listed in the *Small Press Record of Books in Print* (36th Edition, 2010-11). Discounts: trade, bulk and jobber. 145pp. Reporting time: 6 months. Simultaneous submissions accepted: yes. Publishes 10% of manuscripts submitted. Payment: to be determined on individual basis. Copyrights for author. Subjects: Employment, Parenting, Women.

MCM Entertainment, Inc. Publishing Division, 177 Riverside Avenue, Suite F-1127, Newport Beach, CA 92663. 1990. Photos, letters, news items, non-fiction. 1 title listed in the *Small Press Record of Books in Print* (36th Edition, 2010-11). 495pp. Publishes 100% of manuscripts submitted. Copyrights for author. Subjects: Biography, California, Catholic, Divorce, Drama, Family, History, Italian-American, Italy, Los Angeles, Marriage, Non-Fiction, Performing Arts, Romance, World War II.

McPherson & Company Publishers, Bruce R. McPherson, PO Box 1126, 148 Smith Avenue, Kingston, NY 12402, 845-331-5807, toll free order #800-613-8219. 1973. Fiction, art, criticism, non-fiction. "Other imprints: Documentext, Treacle Press. Distributor of Saroff Editions. No unsolicited mss. Query. See www.mcpher-sonco.com before making query." avg. press run 2M. Pub'd 5 titles 2009; expects 5 titles 2010, 7 titles 2011. 93 titles listed in the *Small Press Record of Books in Print* (36th Edition, 2010-11). Discounts: 1 copy 20%, 2-4 30%, 5-25 40%, 26-99 42%, 100-199 copies 43%, 200+ copies 45%; prepaid STOP, 30%; non-returnable 50% 5+ copies; course adoptions 20% returnable; library discount 20% for orders $75+; shipping additional for all classes except library. 200pp. Reporting time: 2 weeks-3 months. Publishes 1% of manuscripts submitted. Payment: royalties and copies. Copyrights for author. Subjects: Anthology, Arts, Avant-Garde, Experimental Art, Criticism, Essays, Fiction, Literature (General), Music, Novels, Performing Arts, Post Modern, Reprints, Satire, Short Stories.

McQuinn Publishing, Debra Shah A, P.O. Box 667849, Charlotte, NC 28266-7849, phone no. 980-225-7661; fax no. 704-910-0717; www.McQuinn Publishing.com. 2007. Fiction. "Contemporary adult fiction." Expects 1 title 2010, 3 titles 2011. 1 title listed in the *Small Press Record of Books in Print* (36th Edition, 2010-11). Discounts: Discounts thru distributor AtlasBooks.Inc. 250pp. Reporting time: not accepting subbmissions at this time. Simultaneous submissions accepted: No. Copyrights for author. Subjects: African Literature, Africa, African Studies, African-American, Fantasy, Fiction, North Carolina, Novels, Race.

McRapperson Literary Enterprises, 15656 Main St., Bellevue, WA 98008. No titles listed in the *Small Press Record of Books in Print* (36th Edition, 2010-11).

ME MAGAZINE, Pittore Euforico, Carlo Pittore, PO Box 182, Bowdoinham, ME 04008, 207-666-8453. 1980. Poetry, art, criticism, reviews, collages, concrete art. "Important article on Maine's mighty artist, Bern Porter. Also, artwork-profusely illustrated. *An Artburst From Maine* by Carlo Pittore. ISSN 0272-5657." circ. 2M. Published at editor's discretion. Expects 5 issues 2010. sub. price $20; per copy $5; sample $5. Back issues: $5, $7.50 for ME IV (Audio Cassette). Discounts: 40%. 8pp. Reporting time: 2 months. Payment: copies. Not copyrighted. §Art movements, art, mail art. Ads: $140/$75. Subjects: Arts, Poetry.

THE MEADOW, Lindsay Wilson, Brad Summerhill, Revolving Faculty, 7000 Dandini Blvd, English Department, Reno, NV 89512-3999, 775-673-7092. 1994. Poetry, fiction, art, photos, cartoons, interviews, satire, letters, parts-of-novels, long-poems, plays, concrete art, non-fiction. "The Meadow is the literary arts magazine of Truckee Meadows Community College. We want to form a synergy between TMCC creative writing students and other writers (either established and emerging) who write about the west. Submissions should be from writers in the west, or from writers writing about the west. We publish poetry, fiction, non-fiction and art work. We will also except excerpts from long poems or novels, lyrical essays, prose poems or flash fiction. Writers who have appeared in our pages include Campbell McGrath, Kim Barnes, Nathan Graziano, Khaled Hosseini, C.C. Russell, Ellen Hopkins, Marilene Phipps, Suzanne Roberts, Leonard Cirino, Taylor Graham, and Krista Benjamin. All submissions should be sent via email to meadow@tmcc.edu. Snail mail submissions will NOT be accepted. We want quality writing and favor everything from the traditional to the experimental. A free verse, confessional, narrative poem could very well be published along side a traditional, rhyming, iambic, lyrical sonnet, but no Bukowski wannabes and no form for form's sake. Please see www.tmcc.edu/meadow for further information regarding submission guidelines, or query us at the email noted above." circ. 1000. 1/yr. Pub'd 1 issue 2009; expects 1 issue 2010, 1 issue 2011. price per copy None. Back issues: None. Discounts: None. 100-120pp. Reporting time: 2 to 5 months. Simultaneous submissions accepted: Yes. Publishes 5% of manuscripts submitted. Payment: Contributor copies. Not copyrighted. Ads: Ad exchange only. We are very interested in ad exchanges with like journals. Subjects: Arizona, California, Colorado, Comics, Creative Non-fiction, Essays, Fiction, Idaho, Interviews, Montana, Poetry, Short Stories, Southwest, The West, Wyoming.

MEAT FOR TEA: THE VALLEY REVIEW, Meaty Gonzales, 18 Orchard Street, Easthampton, MA 01027,

413-374-1486. 2006. Poetry, fiction, art, photos, cartoons, interviews, satire, criticism, reviews, music, long-poems, collages, plays. "Meat for Tea: The Northampton Review was created to provide a non-academically affiliated forum in which the plethora of talented local artists and musicians can publish their work. In this part of Massachusetts there is an active art, music, and literary scene but practically no publishing opportunities outside academe. We have filled this void. We seek to showcase new talent, but also publish more established authors, like Jon Mandel and Dorion Sagan. In each issue is an EP length CD featuring the work of local bands. We're Meat for Tea—giving the F.U. to P.C. everywhere." circ. 150. 4/yr. Expects 4 issues 2010, 4 issues 2011. sub. price $28; per copy $7; sample $6. Back issues: $7. Discounts: 2-10 copies 30%. 52pp. Reporting time: one week—max. Simultaneous submissions accepted: Yes. Publishes 60% of manuscripts submitted. Payment: Free copy of the magazine. Copyrighted. Pub's reviews: none in 2009. §Films, Music, Restaurants in Northampton, Books, Magazines. Ads: $200, $100, $75, $50, $25. Subjects: Absurdist, Advertising, Self-Promotion, Aromatherapy, Avant-Garde, Experimental Art, Beat, Book Reviewing, Lewis Carroll, Cartoons, Experimental, Fiction, Horror, Humor, Post Modern, Sex, Sexuality, Short Stories.

MEAT: A Journal of Writing and Materiality, Jacqueline Rhodes, Co-Editor; Jonathan Alexander, Co-Editor; Brian Bailie, Co-Editor, http://www.meatjournal.com. 2004. Poetry, fiction, articles, art, photos, cartoons, interviews, satire, criticism, reviews, music, letters, long-poems, collages, plays, concrete art, non-fiction. "In the rush toward digital space, what often gets left behind is the meat, the flesh, the working/breathing/paying-bills bodies that write.All of the folks responsible for the MeatJournal idea, have been (or still are) serious cyber-junkies, but all of us also worry that there's never enough critical attention to writing bodies, as those bodies are variously constructed/viewed/ interpreted/performed. The journal focuses less on high theory and practice and more on the people doing it. In each issue, we run a critical feature focusing on writers of various stripes and how they view their respective fields construction of their own body (flesh and body of work); think- (and feel-) pieces on new trends and possible consequences of those trends in writing; authors personal stories of how lack of money, time, and access have affected their own working theories and practices; poetry, prose, and digital performance art; and occasional rants and raves from different points on the political spectrum. Recent contributors: Erika Lpez, Ellen M. Gil-Gmez, Brian Bailie, Christi Rucker, Barclay Barrios, John Garcia." circ. 500. 2/yr. Pub'd 1 issue 2009; expects 2 issues 2010, 3 issues 2011. sub. price $0; per copy $0; sample Free. Back issues: inquire. Discounts: Online journal—it's all free! 25pp. Reporting time: 6 weeks. Simultaneous submissions accepted: No. Publishes 20% of manuscripts submitted. Copyrighted, reverts to author. Pub's reviews: approx. 2 in 2009. Subjects: Abstracts, African-American, Bisexual, Counter-Culture, Alternatives, Communes, Criticism, Essays, Experimental, Games, Gender Issues, Graphics, Philosophy, Politics, Post Modern, Reviews, Sex, Sexuality.

MEDICAL HISTORY, Wellcome Trust Centre for the History of Medicine at UCL, Caroline Tonson-Rye, Welcome Trust Centre for the History of Medicine at UCL, 183 Euston Road, London NW1 2BE, England, +44 (0)20 7679 8107, fax +44 (0)20 7679 8194, web: www.ucl.ac.uk/histmed. 1957. Articles, reviews, news items. circ. 900. 4/yr. Pub'd 4 issues 2009; expects 4 issues 2010. sub. price individuals worldwide £34/$54.50 USA, institutions (worldwide) £69, $107 USA; per copy £12. Back issues: £9 if available. 120pp. Reporting time: 3-4 months. Simultaneous submissions accepted: no. Publishes 35% of manuscripts submitted. Payment: none. Copyright The Trustee, The Wellcome Trust. Pub's reviews: 92 in 2009. §All aspects of history of medicine and allied sciences. Ads: £540/£370/£240. Subjects: Alternative Medicine, Disease, Health, History, Medicine, Nursing, Society.

Medi-Ed Press, Sherlyn Hogenson, Director, 523 Hunter Boulevard, Lansing, MI 48910, 800-500-8205, fax 517-882-0554. Medi.EdPress@verizon.net; www.Medi-EdPress.com. 1986. avg. press run 3M. Pub'd 2 titles 2009; expects 2 titles 2010. 7 titles listed in the *Small Press Record of Books in Print* (36th Edition, 2010-11). Discounts: bookstores and wholesalers 1-4 copies 20%, 5-9 30%, 10-49 40%, 50+ 50%. 350pp. Simultaneous submissions accepted: no. Publishes 20% of manuscripts submitted. Subjects: Medicine, Music, Science.

Medusa's Muse, Terena Scott, Publisher,editor; Jane Mackay, Copy-editor; Rick Wismar, Designer, P.O. Box 1021, Ukiah, CA 95482, www.medusasmuse.com. 2006. Fiction, non-fiction. "Medusa is the overwhelming fear when you're convinced you will drop dead from the weight of life. But instead of dropping, you look Medusa square in the eye and she blinks. That's the secret. Lock eyes with Medusa and you're free. We publish the stories of those who have used the power of Medusa's gaze to transform chaos into life, and in doing so, transform themselves. We are interested in memoir and creative non-fiction, as long as the emphasis is on transformation." avg. press run 500. Pub'd 1 title 2009; expects 2 titles 2010, 2 titles 2011. 3 titles listed in the *Small Press Record of Books in Print* (36th Edition, 2010-11). 250pp. Reporting time: 3 months. Simultaneous submissions accepted: Yes. Publishes 5% of manuscripts submitted. Payment: 30% royalty on net earnings (not sales), no advance. paid quarterly. Does not copyright for author. Subjects: Autobiography, Biography, Creative Non-fiction, Fiction, Grieving, Humor, Memoirs, Novels.

•**Meek Publishing,** Michael Stonebraker, 5110 Old Ellis Point, Roswell, GA 30076-3863, 770-740-8696, 770-751-7282, info@meekpublishing.com, www.meekpublishing.com. 2006. Non-fiction. "Drug and alcohol abuse, recovery, children's books, spirituality, relationships.'' avg. press run 1000. Pub'd 1 title 2009; expects 3 titles 2011. No titles listed in the *Small Press Record of Books in Print* (36th Edition, 2010-11). Discounts: 45%. 180pp. Reporting time: 1-3 months. Simultaneous submissions accepted: Yes. Publishes 5% of manuscripts submitted. Payment: 30%. Copyrights for author. Subjects: Adolescence, Alcohol, Alcoholism, Children, Youth, Drugs, Family, Guidance, Marriage, Mental Health, Parenting, Relationships, Self-Help.

Mehring Books, Inc., PO Box 48377, Oak Park, MI 48237-5977, 248-967-2924, 248-967-3023, sales@mehring.com. News items, non-fiction. ''Mehring Books, Inc. publishes 2-5 books and 5-10 pamphlets a year.'' Expects 3 titles 2010, 3 titles 2011. 23 titles listed in the *Small Press Record of Books in Print* (36th Edition, 2010-11). Discounts: trade 40%, library 20%, minimum order for discounts 5 titles/copies. Subjects: Anthropology, Archaelogy, Arts, Communism, Marxism, Leninism, Culture, History, Labor, Literary Review, Politics, Russia, Socialist, Third World, Minorities, U.S.S.R., Worker.

MELEE, Holmes Lisa, General Offices, PO Box 1619, Alexander City, AL 35111-1619, www.poetryme-lee.com, submissions@poetrymelee.com. 2006. Poetry, articles, art, cartoons, interviews, satire, letters, non-fiction. ''The editors of Melee are interested in poetry and essays that explore the symbiotic relationship between aesthetics and political/social activism. However, our intent is to publish the best work submitted to us regardless of topic. Poetry of any style or length and short essays on any topic will be considered. Content may or may not be of overtly political intent.'' circ. 5000. 4/yr. Expects 4 issues 2010, 4 issues 2011. Discounts: 10+ copies 10%. 36pp. Reporting time: 1 month. Simultaneous submissions accepted: Yes. Publishes 50% of manuscripts submitted. Payment: 5 copies and one year subscription. First serial rights to Mle. Reverts to author after publication. Subjects: African Literature, Africa, African Studies, Atheism, Avant-Garde, Experimental Art, Beat, Buddhism, Charles Bukowski, Cartoons, Essays, Experimental, Feminism, Haiku, Humanism, Philosophy, Poetry, Politics.

THE MELIC REVIEW, C.E. Chaffin, Editor, www.melicreview.com.

A Melody from an Immigrant's Soul, Dora Klinova, 5712 Baltimore Dr. #461, La Mesa, CA 91942, (619) 667-0925 E-mail: dorishka1@sbcglobal.net. 2004. Poetry, photos, satire, non-fiction. ''Klinova, Dora is an Award Winning Writer. The International Society of Poets awarded Dora by inscribed Silver Cup and a Medal "Poet of Merit Award". Klinova won several contests in newspapers. The theaters of San Diego, CA performed her stories. "The San Diego Union Tribune" and "The San Diego Jewish Times" published Klinova's articles many times. Also her stories were published in New York. The appearance of the book "A Melody from an Immigrant's Soul", written by Dora Klinova, a Russian-Jewish Immigrant, who recently came to America almost without any English, is an outstanding event. All readers who are interested in life itself, regardless of age, will be surprisingly pleased.'' avg. press run 500. Pub'd 1 title 2009; expects 1 title 2010, 1-2 titles 2011. No titles listed in the *Small Press Record of Books in Print* (36th Edition, 2010-11). Discounts: 2-10 copies 25%. 310pp. Reporting time: 2-3 weeks is enough for reprintng. Payment: payment by check or money order. Copyrights for author. Subjects: Cooking, Hawaii, Immigration, Inspirational, Nature, Parenting, Poetry, Sex, Sexuality, Short Stories, Spiritual, Tarot, U.S.S.R., World War II, Writers/Writing.

MEMOIR (AND): Prose, Poetry, Essay, Graphics, Lies and More, Joan Chapman E., Managing Editor; Candida Lawrence, Founding Editor, P.O. Box 1398, Sausalito, CA 94966-1398, (415)339-4130, admin@memoirjournal.com, www.memoirjournal.com. 2006. Poetry, art, photos, plays, non-fiction. ''MEMOIR (AND) is the only print journal committed to the exploration of memoir in multiple forms. The editors strive with each issue to include a selection of prose, poetry, narrative photography and graphic memoirs. They particularly invite submissions that push traditional boundaries of form and content in their exploration of the representation of self; they also just love a memoir well-told.With each issue, the editors award the MEMOIR (AND) Prize for Memoir in Prose or Poetry. The prize consists of $500 and publication the current issue. There is no entry fee. All works submitted are eligible for contest entry. Works that do not win the prize are still considered for publication, and works need not be entered in the contest in order to be published. For more information, visit http://memoirjournal.com.'' circ. 3500. 2/yr. Pub'd 1 issue 2009; expects 2 issues 2010, 2 issues 2011. sub. price $20; per copy $12; sample $12. Back issues: $12. 140pp. Reporting time: 16 weeks from close of reading period. Simultaneous submissions accepted: Yes. Publishes 5% of manuscripts submitted. Payment: no payment. Copyrighted, reverts to author. Ads: Currently placement of all ads is complimentary.

MEMORIOUS, Rebecca Morgan Frank, Editor-in-Chief, On-line magazine. http://www.memorious.org. ''*Memorious* does not consider previously published material. For all standard submissions, please send a cover letter in the body of the email (including a bio) and attach the submission itself as a separate file in plain text, Rich Text, or MS Word format. Please note any simultaneous submissions. Please be sure to send to the appropriate address as listed in the genre guidelines. Verse: Send 4-6 poems as one attached document, titled with your name (i.e. PabloNeruda.doc), to submit+poetry@memorious.org. Prose: Send one story or no more than three short shorts to submit+prose@memorious.org. Please do not submit more than once every six months.''

Menard Press, Anthony Rudolf, 8 The Oaks, Woodside Avenue, London N12 8AR, England. 1969. Poetry. "The press is in its final phase and no new manuscripts can be considered. Nuclear politics, poetry, poetics, translated poetry. The press's poetry books are distributed in the USA by Small Press Distribution Inc., Berkeley CA." avg. press run 1000. Pub'd 1 title 2009; expects 1 title 2010. 23 titles listed in the *Small Press Record of Books in Print* (36th Edition, 2010-11). Discounts: usual. Poetry 56pp; non-fiction 96; politics 24pp. Subjects: Anthropology, Archaelogy, Criticism, Literature (General), Poetry, Politics, Translation.

Menasha Ridge Press, Russell Helms, Acquisitions Editor, 2204 1st Ave. S. #102, Birmingham, AL 35233-2331, 205-322-0439, rhelms@menasharidge.com. 1982. Non-fiction. avg. press run 5M. Pub'd 23 titles 2009; expects 18 titles 2010, 28 titles 2011. 4 titles listed in the *Small Press Record of Books in Print* (36th Edition, 2010-11). Discounts: per catalogue. 200+pp. Reporting time: 90 days. Simultaneous submissions accepted: yes. Publishes 2-5% of manuscripts submitted. Payment: 10% royalty based on net. Copyrights for author. Subjects: Bicycling, Reference, Sports, Outdoors, Travel.

Mendham Publishing, Tim O'Brien, 515 S. Figueroa Street, Suite 1800, Los Angeles, CA 90071, Phone: (213) 622-0862, Fax: (213) 622-0842, liz@thepowerofpersonalbranding.com, www.thepowerofpersonal-branding.com. 2002. Non-fiction. avg. press run 5000. Expects 1 title 2010, 1 title 2011. No titles listed in the *Small Press Record of Books in Print* (36th Edition, 2010-11). 200-360pp. Subjects: Business & Economics, Marketing, Self-Help.

Mercer University Press, Marc Jolley, Director, 1400 Coleman Ave., Macon, GA 31207, (478) 301-2880, (478) 301-2585 fax. 1979. Fiction, art, criticism, letters, non-fiction. Pub'd 40 titles 2009; expects 40 titles 2010, 40 titles 2011. No titles listed in the *Small Press Record of Books in Print* (36th Edition, 2010-11). Discounts: Retail (returnable) - short - 30% / trade - 40% Retail(nonreturnable)- short - 40% Retail(nonreturnable)-trade - 45% 1-99 /50% 100+. 300pp. Subjects: African Literature, Africa, African Studies, African-American, Biography, Civil War, Culture, History, Immigration, Memoirs, Multicultural, Philosophy, Political Science, Politics, Religion, Mark Twain, War.

Mercury House, Jeremy Bigalke, Executive Director, PO BOX 192850, San Francisco, CA 94119-2858. No titles listed in the *Small Press Record of Books in Print* (36th Edition, 2010-11).

The Mercury Press, PO Box 672, Station P, Toronto, Ontario M5S 2Y4, Canada, PH: 416.531.4338, FAX: 416.531.0765. "The Mercury Press publishes poetry, fiction, murder mysteries, and culturally significant non-fiction by Canadian authors. The Mercury Press is dedicated to continuing the development of our essential mandate, the publication and dissemination of innovative Canadian fiction and poetry, which we believe rivals anything being written in English in the world today. Please note that we do not consider electronic submissions." No titles listed in the *Small Press Record of Books in Print* (36th Edition, 2010-11).

MERIDIAN, Jazzy Danziger, Editor, University of Virginia, P.O. Box 400145, Charlottesville, VA 22904-4145. 1998. "*Meridian* is a semiannual literary journal produced at the University of Virginia in conjunction with the university's M.F.A. Program in Creative Writing, whose students serve as the magazine's editors. However, as a magazine edited by young writers, we value nothing more than showcasing tomorrow's talent, often publishing a new author's first story or poem. We welcome—and carefully read—every submission we receive. Though a relatively young publication, Meridian poetry and prose has appeared in Best American Poetry, Best American Short Stories, Best American Essays, the Pushcart Prize anthology, and New Stories from the South. Our stories have also been short-listed for the O. Henry Prize, and our fine authors and poets have gone on to win many awards." price per copy $7; sample $7. Back issues: $6. Simultaneous submissions accepted: yes. Pub's reviews: 10 in 2009. Ads: Exchange ads only.

Meridien PressWorks, Jeanne Powell, Editor, Meridien PressWorks, PO Box 640024, San Francisco, CA 94164, 415-928-8904; 415-225-3265 c. 1996. Poetry, fiction, art, photos, non-fiction. "Poets and writers in California primarily. No unsolicited manuscripts." avg. press run 200-500. Pub'd 4 titles 2009; expects 3 titles 2010, 3 titles 2011. 27 titles listed in the *Small Press Record of Books in Print* (36th Edition, 2010-11). Discounts: wholesale price for booksellers and libraries. 50-200pp. Reporting time: 90 days. Simultaneous submissions accepted: yes. Publishes 10% of manuscripts submitted. Payment: all profits to authors. Copyrights for author. Subjects: Arts, Fiction, Photography, Poetry.

The Merion Press, Inc., PO Box 144, Merion Station, PA 19066-0144, 610-617-8919, Fax 610-617-8929, rjstern@merionpress.com, www.merionpress.com. 2001. Fiction. "We publish out-of-print, classic British detective stories." avg. press run 250. Pub'd 1 title 2009; expects 1 title 2010, 1 title 2011. No titles listed in the *Small Press Record of Books in Print* (36th Edition, 2010-11). 240pp. Does not copyright for author. Subject: Mystery.

Meritage Press, 256 North Fork Crystal Springs Road, St. Helena, CA 94574. "Meritage Press seeks to expand fresh ways of featuring literary and other art forms. Meritage expects to publish a wide range of artists poets, writers, visual artists, dancers, and performance artists. By acknowledging the multiplicity of aesthetic concerns, Meritages interests necessarily encompass a variety of disciplines politics, culture, identity, science, humor, religion, history, technology, philosophy and wine. Meritage includes an imprint BABAYLAN, which specializes in Filipino literature. The word "Babaylan" is a Bisayan word that can be translated to mean Poet-Priestess. As noted in the groundbreaking anthology BABAYLAN: An Anthology of Filipina and Filipina American Writers (Aunt Lute Press, 1999) co-edited by Eileen Tabios and Nick Carbo, the Babaylans were storytellers, healers and community leaders in the Philippines whose positions were disrupted by the invasion of Spanish colonizers over four centuries ago. BABAYLAN resurrects itself in the 21st century to facilitate the dissemination of Filipino literature a goal also addressed by Eileen Tabios when she edited The Anchored Angel: Selected Writings of Jose Garcia Villa (Kaya, 1999), recipient of the PEN/Oakland Josephine Miles National Literary Award." No titles listed in the *Small Press Record of Books in Print* (36th Edition, 2010-11).

Merkos Publications, Yonason Gordon, Marketing, 291 Kingston Ave., Brooklyn, NY 11213, 718-778-0226, fax: 718-778-4148, email: orders@kehotonline.com. 1 title listed in the *Small Press Record of Books in Print* (36th Edition, 2010-11).

Merl Publications, Cuauhtemoc Gallegos, 1658 N Milwaukee Ave # 242, Chicago, IL 60647, (708)445 8385 contact@merlpublications.com www.merlpublications.com. 1995. Non-fiction. "Publisher of Bilingual Legal dictionaries and glossaries." avg. press run 1000. Expects 2 titles 2010, 4 titles 2011. 2 titles listed in the *Small Press Record of Books in Print* (36th Edition, 2010-11). Discounts: 20%Bookstores25%-40%Distributors40%-50%Wholesalers. Subjects: Bilingual, Language, Latino, Law, Non-Fiction.

Merrimack Books, Wayne Edwards, P.O. Box 231229, Anchorage, AK 99523-1229, we21011@earthlink.net. 1989. avg. press run 1M+. Expects 2 titles 2011. 1 title listed in the *Small Press Record of Books in Print* (36th Edition, 2010-11). Discounts: 1-9 30%, 10-49 40%, 50 + 50%. 200-300pp. Reporting time: 4 weeks. Simultaneous submissions accepted: no. Publishes .0001% of manuscripts submitted. Payment: varies. Does not copyright for author. Subjects: Fantasy, Fiction, Horror, Literature (General), Poetry.

Merwood Books, Heather Dunne, 237 Merwood Lane, Ardmore, PA 19003, 215-947-3934, Fax 215-947-4229. 1997. Poetry, fiction, music. "Contemporary fiction and poetry with literary bent." avg. press run 1M. Pub'd 1 title 2009; expects 2 titles 2010, 2 titles 2011. 3 titles listed in the *Small Press Record of Books in Print* (36th Edition, 2010-11). Discounts: negotiable. 250-375pp. Reporting time: 3-6 months. Simultaneous submissions accepted: yes. Publishes 10% of manuscripts submitted. Payment: negotiable. Does not copyright for author. Subjects: Fiction, Music, Poetry.

Metacom Press, William Ferguson, Nancy Ferguson, 1 Tahanto Road, Worcester, MA 01602-2523, 508-757-1683. 1980. Poetry, fiction. "Booklets have ranged from 16 to 28 pages. Titles so far are by John Updike, William Heyen, Ann Beattie, James Tate, James Wright, Diane Wakoski, Raymond Carver, James Merrill, John McPhee, Edward Gorey. All titles to date have been published in a limited-edition format, using imported papers and hand-binding. Our intention is to establish ourselves financially with the limited editions and then to move to a more democratic, less exclusive type of publication. No unsolicited manuscripts." avg. press run 150-300. 3 titles listed in the *Small Press Record of Books in Print* (36th Edition, 2010-11). Discounts: 30% to dealers, 10% to libraries. 20pp. Payment: 10% of list value of the edition. Copyrights for author. Subjects: Fiction, Poetry.

Metallo House Publishers, Helene Andorre Hinson Staley, 170 E. River Road, Moncure, NC 27559-9617, 919-542-2908, Fax 919-774-5611. 1997. avg. press run 1M. Pub'd 1 title 2009. No titles listed in the *Small Press Record of Books in Print* (36th Edition, 2010-11). Discounts: available to libraries, bookstores, and direct from the publisher. 224pp. Reporting time: 2-3 months. Simultaneous submissions accepted: yes. Copyrights for author. Subjects: Law, Parenting, Sexual Abuse.

MEXICAN STUDIES/ESTUDIOS MEXICANOS, University of California Press, Jaime E. Rodriguez, Editor; Carla Duke, Editorial Assistant, University of California Press, 2000 Center Street, Suite 303, Berkeley, CA 94704-1223, 510-643-7154. 1985. Non-fiction. "Editorial address: 240 Krieger Hall, Univ. of CA, Irvine, CA 92697-3275." circ. 1350. 2/yr. Pub'd 2 issues 2009; expects 2 issues 2010, 2 issues 2011. sub. price $30 indiv., $107 instit., $18 students (+ $15 air freight); per copy $24 indiv. $55 instit., $24 students (+ $15 air freight); sample free. Back issues: $24 indiv.; $55 instit., $24 student (+ $15 air freight). Discounts: foreign subs. agent 10%, one-time orders 10+ 30%, standing orders (bookstores): 1-99 40%, 100+ 50%. 208pp. Copyrighted, does not revert to author. Ads: $295/$220. Subjects: Chicano/a, Political Science.

MGW (Mom Guess What) Newsmagazine, Jeffry Davis, Executive Publisher, 1123 21st St., Suite 200, Sacramento, CA 95814-4225, 916-441-6397, fax:916-441-6422, info@mgwnews.com, www.mgwnews.com. 1978. Poetry, articles, art, photos, cartoons, interviews, satire, criticism, reviews, music, letters, plays, news items. circ. 15,000 Bi-Monthly. 24/yr. Pub'd 24 issues 2009; expects 24 issues 2010, 24 issues 2011. sub. price $30; per copy Free; sample Free. Back issues: $1. Discounts: 5-25%. 32pp. Reporting time: 1 week. Simultaneous submissions accepted: yes. Publishes 25% of manuscripts submitted. Payment varies on submission type and length. Copyrighted, does not revert to author. Pub's reviews: 60 in 2009. §Politics, gay &

human rights, civil rights, music, fiction, non-fiction, childrens issues. Ads: Full Page - $1400, Half Page - $700, Quarter - $350, Eighth - $175. Subjects: Anarchist, Arts, Book Reviewing, Children, Youth, Civil Rights, Community, Computers, Calculators, Crafts, Hobbies, Gay, Lesbianism, Movies, Music, Sex, Sexuality, Social Work, Sports, Outdoors.

Miami University Press, Keith Tuma, Editor, English Dept., Miami University, Oxford, OH 45056, 513-529-5221, Fax 513-529-1392, E-mail tumakw@muohio.edu. 1992. Poetry, fiction. "Miami University Press has begun a second series featuring collections of short fiction and books of poetry. The first book of stories is Marianne Villanueva's *Mayor of the Roses*, edited by Brian Roley, and the first book of poems, edited by Keith Tuma, is an anthology of poems (and essays) from the Diversity in African American Poetry Festival of fall 2003: *Rainbow Darkness: an anthology of african american poetry*. The new series will emphasize multicultural and international writers, among others. Editorship will rotate among members of the creative writing faculty at Miami University. The Press also sponsors an annual novella contest." avg. press run 1,000. Pub'd 2 titles 2009; expects 3 titles 2010, 2 titles 2011. No titles listed in the *Small Press Record of Books in Print* (36th Edition, 2010-11). Discounts: 20% short, 40% full. 140pp. Reporting time: 3 months. Simultaneous submissions accepted: yes. Publishes 1% of manuscripts submitted. Payment: 6%. Copyrights for author. Subjects: African-American, Asian-American, Experimental, Fiction, Ireland, Latino, Native American, Poetry.

Mica Press - Paying Our Dues Productions, J.W. Grant; John F. Eastman, Fiction Editor; Chuck Miller, Poetry Editor, 1508 Crescent Road, Lawrence, KS 66044-3120, Only contact by E-mail jgrant@bookzen.com; website www.bookzen.com. 1990. Poetry, cartoons, reviews, non-fiction. "Do not submit manuscripts. Submit description only. As a service to small press authors and publishers we provide free space on our website (www.bookzen.com) to display books." avg. press run 2M. Pub'd 1 title 2009; expects 2 titles 2010, 2 titles 2011. 3 titles listed in the *Small Press Record of Books in Print* (36th Edition, 2010-11). 250-640pp. Payment: yes. Copyrights for author. Subjects: Cartoons, Jack Kerouac, Non-Fiction, Poetry, Reviews.

Micah Publications Inc., Robert Kalechofsky, Roberta Kalechofsky, 255 Humphrey Street, Marblehead, MA 01945, 781-631-7601. 1975. Fiction, articles, criticism. "Micah Publications publishes prose: scholarly, fictional, lyrical; a prose that addresses itself to issues without offending esthetic sensibilities, a prose that is aware of the esthetics of language without succumbing to esthetic solipsism. Three books a year. No unsolicited mss. Author must submit camera-ready copy of text - we'll do designs and illustrations. Author must also be involved in publicity." avg. press run 400. Pub'd 2 titles 2009; expects 4 titles 2010, 2-3 titles 2011. 30 titles listed in the *Small Press Record of Books in Print* (36th Edition, 2010-11). Discounts: 2-5 20%, 6-9 30%, 10-49 40%, 50+ 50%. 280pp. Reporting time: 3 months. Simultaneous submissions accepted: yes. Publishes 5% of manuscripts submitted. Payment: 10% to authors after primary expenses of printing and advertising is met from sale of books. Copyrights for author. Subjects: Animals, Fiction, Judaism, Vegetarianism.

MICHIGAN FEMINIST STUDIES, 1122 Lane Hall, Univ. of Michigan, 204 South State Street, Ann Arbor, MI 48109-1290, 734-761-4386, Fax 734-647-4943, e-mail mfseditors@umich.edu. 1978. Poetry, articles, art, photos, cartoons, interviews, reviews, news items. "A journal produced in conjunction with the Women's Studies Program at the University of Michigan." circ. 250. 1/yr. Pub'd 1 issue 2009; expects 1 issue 2010, 1 issue 2011. sub. price $25 institutions, $10 individuals; per copy same; sample same. Back issues: $75 for full print run (1987-present). 150pp. Reporting time: 2 months. Simultaneous submissions accepted: yes. Publishes 10% of manuscripts submitted. Payment: none. Copyrighted, reverts to author. Pub's reviews: none in 2009. §Current feminist scholarship. Ads: ad exchange. Subject: Feminism.

MICHIGAN QUARTERLY REVIEW, Jonathan Freedman, Editor; Michael Byers, Associate Editor; Vicki Lawrence, Managing Editor, 0576 Rackham, University of Michigan, 915 E. Washington St., Ann Arbor, MI 48109-1070, 734-764-9265. 1962. Poetry, fiction, articles, art, interviews, criticism, reviews, letters, parts-of-novels, long-poems. "We are not solely a literary magazine. In addition to poetry, fiction, and reviews, we include essays on a variety of topics in the humanities, arts & sciences. Writers are advised to refer to a sample back issue before submitting." circ. 1.8M. 4/yr. Pub'd 4 issues 2009; expects 4 issues 2010, 4 issues 2011. sub. price $25; per copy $7; sample $4. Back issues: $4 for regular issues, cover price for special issues. Discounts: agency rates - $30 for institution subscription; 15% for agent. 160pp. Reporting time: 6 weeks. Simultaneous submissions accepted: no. Publishes 1-2% of manuscripts submitted. Payment: $10/page of poetry, $10/page essays. Copyrighted, reverts to author. Pub's reviews: 14 in 2009. §Humanities, sciences, arts, literature. Ads: full page: $200: half page: $100; cover: $300-$350. Subjects: Literary Review, Literature (General).

Michigan State University Press (see also FOURTH GENRE: EXPLORATIONS IN NONFICTION), 1405 S. Harrison Road, #25, East Lansing, MI 48823-5245, 517-355-9543; fax 517-432-2611; E-mail journals@msu.edu. 1 title listed in the *Small Press Record of Books in Print* (36th Edition, 2010-11).

Micron Press, Anthony Jones, Marketing Director; Robert Hall, Executive Director, 71 Prince Street, #35, Boston, MA 02113, 617-301-2901, inquiries@micronpress.com. 2007. Fiction, non-fiction. avg. press run 3000.

Expects 5 titles 2010, 11 titles 2011. 2 titles listed in the *Small Press Record of Books in Print* (36th Edition, 2010-11). 200-350pp. Reporting time: 3 weeks. Simultaneous submissions accepted: Yes. Publishes ~ 8% of manuscripts submitted. Copyrights for author. Subjects: Fantasy, Fiction, History, Non-Fiction, Science, Science Fiction, Young Adult.

MID-AMERICAN REVIEW, Karen Craigo, Editor-in-Chief and Poetry Editor; Michael Czyzniejewski, Editor-in-Chief; Karen Babine, Associate Editor and Nonfiction Editor; George Looney, Translations Editor; Ashley Kaine, Fiction Editor, Dept of English, Bowling Green State University, Bowling Green, OH 43403-0191, 419-372-2725, www.bgsu.edu/midamericanreview. 1980. Poetry, fiction, articles, criticism, reviews, parts-of-novels, long-poems, non-fiction. "Recent Contributors: Hadara Bar-Nadav, Peter Conners, Kevin Griffith, W. Scott Olsen, Hilda Raz, David Shumate, George Singleton, Maura Stanton, J. David Stevens, Jean Thompson." circ. 2,200. 2/yr. Pub'd 2 issues 2009; expects 2 issues 2010, 2 issues 2011. sub. price $15; per copy $9; sample $5. Back issues: $10 for rare issues. Discounts: 20%/40%. 234pp. Reporting time: 1-5 months. Simultaneous submissions accepted: Yes, but please withdraw IMMEDIATELY if accepted elsewhere. Publishes 1% of manuscripts submitted. Payment: $10 per page up to $50 (when funding permits). Copyrighted, reverts to author. Pub's reviews: 24 in 2009. §Fiction, poetry, nonfiction, and criticism of contemporary literature. Ads: $85/$45/will exchange. Subjects: Book Reviewing, Criticism, Essays, Fiction, Literary Review, Literature (General), Non-Fiction, Ohio, Poetry, Prose, Reviews, Short Stories, Translation.

The Middle Atlantic Press, Blake Koen, Publisher, 10 Twosome Drive, Box 600, Moorestown, NJ 08057, 856-235-4444, orders 800-257-8481, fax 800-225-3840. 1968. "We are a trade book and educational materials publisher. Our material is oriented to the Middle Atlantic region, but all of our books are sold nation-wide. We accept unsolicited submissions with SASE." avg. press run varies. Pub'd 2 titles 2009; expects 4 titles 2010, 4-6 titles 2011. 19 titles listed in the *Small Press Record of Books in Print* (36th Edition, 2010-11). Pages vary with title. Reporting time: 1-2 months. Simultaneous submissions accepted: yes. Payment: 8% royalty on hardcover books, 5% + 10% on paperbacks to author, paid annually. Copyrights for author. Subjects: Folklore, Native American.

Middlebury College Publications (see also NEW ENGLAND REVIEW), Stephen Donadio, Editor, Middlebury College, Middlebury, VT 05753, 802-443-5075, Fax 802-443-2088, E-mail nereview@middle-bury.edu. 1978. Poetry, fiction, articles, interviews, criticism, reviews, parts-of-novels, long-poems. "Fiction, poetry, essays and reviews of the highest quality." avg. press run 2M. Pub'd 4 titles 2009; expects 4 titles 2010, 4 titles 2011. 2 titles listed in the *Small Press Record of Books in Print* (36th Edition, 2010-11). Discounts: 25% classroom. 184pp. Reporting time: 12 weeks. Simultaneous submissions accepted, if indicated. Payment: competitive. Does not copyright for author. Subjects: Literary Review, Literature (General).

Middleway Press, David McNeill, Managing Editor; Jason Henninger, Asst Book Editor, 606 Wilshire Boulevard, Attention: Mwende May, Marketing Associate, Santa Monica, CA 90401-1502, (310) 260-8900 ofc, (310) 260-8910 fax, middlewaypress@sgi-usa.org, www.middlewaypress.com. 2000. Non-fiction. "Religions—Nichiren Buddhism emphasis. No unsolicited manuscripts." avg. press run 5M. Pub'd 3 titles 2009; expects 3 titles 2010, 3 titles 2011. 16 titles listed in the *Small Press Record of Books in Print* (36th Edition, 2010-11). Discounts: via Independent Publishers Group. 250pp. Reporting time: 2 months. Subjects: Buddhism, Culture, Education, Inspirational, Peace, Self-Help.

Mid-List Press, Lane Stiles, Publisher, 4324 12th Avenue South, Minneapolis, MN 55407-3218, 612-822-3733, Fax 612-823-8387, guide@midlist.org, www.midlist.org. 1989. Poetry, fiction, non-fiction. "Please write or visit our website for guidelines before submitting. Since 1990 we have sponsored the First Series Awards in Poetry, the Novel, Short Fiction, and Creative Nonfiction for writers who have yet to publish a book-length work in that category. Notable authors include Alfred Corn and Dr. William Nolen." avg. press run 500-2.5M. Pub'd 6 titles 2009; expects 4 titles 2010, 5 titles 2011. 7 titles listed in the *Small Press Record of Books in Print* (36th Edition, 2010-11). Discounts: wholesale 3-4 books 20%, 5-9 30%, 10-50 40%, 50+ 50%. Poetry 80pp, others 200-300pp. Reporting time: 1-6 months. Simultaneous submissions accepted: yes. Publishes less than 1% of manuscripts submitted. Payment: by contract. Copyrights for author. Subjects: Fiction, Literature (General), Non-Fiction, Poetry, Reprints, Short Stories.

Midmarch Arts Press, Judy Seigel, Editor, 300 Riverside Drive, New York City, NY 10025, 212-666-6990. 1975. Art, photos, criticism, long-poems, non-fiction. avg. press run 2M-3M. Pub'd 4 titles 2009; expects 3 titles 2010, 3 titles 2011. 31 titles listed in the *Small Press Record of Books in Print* (36th Edition, 2010-11). Discounts: 20% for Institutional L.P, 20% for Jobber L.P. for single copies; 20% for 3-5 copies; 30% 6-9; 40% 10 and over, plus postage. 100-318pp. Reporting time: 4 weeks. Publishes 35% of manuscripts submitted. Payment: royalties to authors. Copyrights for author. Subjects: Architecture, Arts, Biography, California, Crafts, Hobbies, Drama, Electronics, New England, Photography, Poetry, Post Modern, South, Texas, Visual Arts, Women.

MIDNIGHT SHOWCASE: Romance Digest, Erotic-ahh Digest, Special Digest, Twin Souls Publications,

Jewel Adams, P.O. Box 726, Lusk, WY 82225, 307-334-3165, 727-848-5962, publisher@midnightshowcase.com, http://www.midnightshowcase.com.

MIDNIGHT STREET, Immediate Direction Publications, Trevor Denyer, Editor, 7 Mountview, Church Lane West, Aldershot, Hampshire GU11 3LN, England, tdenyer@ntlworld.com, www.midnightstreet.co.uk. 2004. Poetry, fiction, articles, interviews, reviews, non-fiction. "MS publishes horror, dark fantasy, science fiction and slipstream stories and small amount of poetry. It is currently open to submissions. MS is 56 pages, A4, stapled with full colour cover. Full details, including prices and writer guidelines, can be found on the website: www.midnightstreet.co.uk." 3/yr. sub. price £10.50, $32.00 US; per copy £3.80, $11.00 US. 56pp. Reporting time: 3 months average. Simultaneous submissions accepted: No. Publishes 10% of manuscripts submitted. Payment: £2.50 per 1,000 words + contributor's copy. Poetry, illustrations and interviews are different. Check: www.midnightstreet.co.uk. Copyrighted, reverts to author. Pub's reviews: 6 in 2009. §Fiction, short stories. Ads: Quarter A4 page ad with text and/or greyscale images: £6.00 ($9.00 US)Half A4 page ad with text and/or greyscale images: £12.00 ($18.00 US)Full A4 page ad with text and/or greyscale images: £24.00 ($36.00 US)Full Back Cover ad with text and colour images: £60.00 ($88.00 US)Please check space availability first.Submit electronically by e-mail or through the post on CD or disk, or hard copy for scanning.Use PayPal to pay or:Please make cheques payable to T. DENYER and send to:Immediate Direction Publications7 MountviewChurch Lane WestAldershotHampshireGU11 3LNEnglandUK. Subjects: Essays, Fantasy, Fiction, Graphics, Horror, Reviews, Science Fiction, Short Stories, Supernatural.

Midnight Whistler Publishers, Jon Batson, 3220 Shore View Road, #22, Raleigh, NC 27613, 919-327-5021. 1979. Non-fiction. "Award-winning author Beverly Eakman's book WALKING TARGETS is a non-fiction book that will change how you look at the educational process today. It is a well-documented, factually grounded work that will change the world. Midnight Whistler will consider nothing less." avg. press run 5000. Pub'd 1 title 2009; expects 1 title 2010, 1 title 2011. 2 titles listed in the *Small Press Record of Books in Print* (36th Edition, 2010-11). Discounts: 2-10 copies 40%. 300pp. Reporting time: Two months. Simultaneous submissions accepted: No. Publishes 1% of manuscripts submitted. Payment: Independently negotiated, usually outrageous. Does not copyright for author. Subjects: Children, Youth, Drugs, Education, Family, Society.

MIDWEST ART FAIRS, James W. Schiller, Publisher, PO Box 72, Pepin, WI 54759, 715-442-2022. 1990. "Bi-annual listing of art fairs and craft festivals with listings of organizations, businesses, services, suppliers." circ. 7.5M. 2/yr. Pub'd 2 issues 2009; expects 2 issues 2010, 2 issues 2011. sub. price $18.95; per copy $12.95; sample $12.95. Back issues: $12.95. 112pp. Reporting time: 4 weeks. Payment: none. Copyrighted, reverts to author. Ads: $575/$285. Subjects: Arts, Crafts, Hobbies, Iowa, Jewelry, Gems, Minnesota, Quilting, Sewing, Wisconsin.

MIDWEST POETRY REVIEW, Pariksith Singh, 7443 Oak Tree Lane, Spring Hill, FL 34607-2324. 1980. Poetry. circ. 246. 4/yr. Pub'd 4 issues 2009; expects 4 issues 2010, 4 issues 2011. sub. price $20; per copy $5; sample $6. Back issues: $6 (when available). 40pp. Reporting time: 4-6 weeks. Simultaneous submissions accepted: no. Publishes 10%-15% of manuscripts submitted. Payment: $5 to $20; contests $25 to $500. Copyrighted, reverts to author. Pub's reviews. §Poetry, literature. Ads: $100 full page. Subject: Poetry.

THE MIDWEST QUARTERLY, James B.M. Schick, Editor; Stephen Meats, Poetry; Tim Bailey, Book Reviews, Pittsburg State University, History Department, Pittsburg, KS 66762, 620-235-4369. 1959. Poetry, articles, interviews, criticism, reviews, non-fiction. "Scholarly articles on history, literature, the social sciences (especially political), art, music, the natural sciences (in non-technical language). Most articles run 4M to 5M words. Can use a brief note of 1M to 2M words once in a while. Chief bias is an aversion to jargon and pedantry. Instead of footnotes we use a minimum of parenthetical documentation. Reviews and interviews are assigned. Contributors: Walter McDonald, Jeanne Murray Walker, Lyn Lifshin, Charles Bukowski, William Kloefkorn, among others, have been represented in our pages. Will consider all poems submitted." circ. 1M. 4/yr. Pub'd 4 issues 2009; expects 4 issues 2010. sub. price $15 within U.S., otherwise $25; per copy $5; sample $5. Back issues: $5. Discounts: 10% to agencies. 110pp. Reporting time: 3-6 months. Simultaneous submissions accepted: no. Publishes 15% of manuscripts submitted. Payment: copies only, varies 3 usually. Copyrighted, reverts to author. Pub's reviews: 12 in 2009. §Poetry, non-fiction. No ads. Subjects: Criticism, History, Literary Review, Poetry, Society.

Midwest Villages & Voices, Gayla Ellis, PO Box 40214, St. Paul, MN 55104, 612-822-6878 or e-mail: midwestvillages@yahoo.com (e-mail preferred). 1981. "We are a publishing group and cultural organization for Midwestern writers and visual artists. Submission by invitation only. Unsolicited submissions not returned." 8 titles listed in the *Small Press Record of Books in Print* (36th Edition, 2010-11). Discounts: 40% for bookstores; 50% for nonprofits. Subjects: Literature (General), Poetry.

MIDWIFERY TODAY, Midwifery Today, Jan Tritten, Editor-in-Chief; Cheryl Smith K., Managing Editor, Box 2672, Eugene, OR 97402, 541-344-7438. 1985. "Birth information for midwives, doulas, childbirth educators and interested consumers. Photos, experiences, technical and non-technical articles." circ. 3M. 4/yr.

Pub'd 4 issues 2009; expects 4 issues 2010, 4 issues 2011. sub. price $55; per copy $13.95; sample $12.50. Back issues: $10. 72pp. Reporting time: 6 weeks. Simultaneous submissions accepted: no. Payment: subscription. Copyrighted, reverts to author. Pub's reviews: 23 in 2009. §Memoirs, fiction, essays, technical, how-to onmidwifery, pregnancy, birth, childbirth education, breastfeeding. Ads: $700/$1.25 per word classified, 10-word minimum. Subject: Medicine.

Midwifery Today (see also MIDWIFERY TODAY), Jan Tritten, Editor-in-Chief; Cheryl K. Smith, Managing Editor, PO Box 2672, Eugene, OR 97402, 541-344-7438; Fax 541-344-1422; editorial@midwiferytoday.com, www.midwiferytoday.com. 1986. Poetry, articles, interviews, letters, non-fiction. "Two books per year on the subject of midwifery which include articles on specialized topics such as shoulder dystocia, hemorrhage, normal birth. Query us first." avg. press run 1.5M. Pub'd 2 titles 2009; expects 2 titles 2010, 2 titles 2011. No titles listed in the *Small Press Record of Books in Print* (36th Edition, 2010-11). Discounts: send for information. 150pp. Reporting time: 1-6 months. Simultaneous submissions accepted: no. Publishes 50% of manuscripts submitted. Payment: send for information. We retain copyright. Subjects: Alternative Medicine, Birth, Birth Control, Population, Health, Medicine, Nursing.

Milkweed Editions, H. Emerson Blake, Editor in Chief; Ben Barnhart, Assistant Editor, 1011 Washington Ave. S., Ste. 300, Minneapolis, MN 55415, 612-332-3192, Fax 612-215-2550, www.milkweed.org. 1984. Poetry, fiction, non-fiction. "Milkweed Editions publishes in each of its genres with the intention of making a humane impact on society. Please familiarize yourself with our books before submitting manuscripts or queries." avg. press run 3M-5M. Pub'd 14 titles 2009; expects 17 titles 2010, 21 titles 2011. 113 titles listed in the *Small Press Record of Books in Print* (36th Edition, 2010-11). 250pp. Reporting time: 6 months. Simultaneous submissions accepted: yes. Publishes 1% of manuscripts submitted. Payment: advance against royalties, royalties payment varies by author. Copyrights for author. Subjects: Earth, Natural History, Environment, Fiction, Literature (General), Non-Fiction, Poetry, Prose.

Mille Grazie Press, David Oliveira, 967 Clover Lane, Hanford, CA 93230-2255. 1992. Poetry. "The focus of Mille Grazie Press is to publish the fine poets who live and work along California's Central Coast. Poets selected for publication are invited by the editors to submit manuscripts. No unsolicited manuscripts will be considered. The primary consideration for selection is the skillful use of language and strong vision of the poet. Mille Grazie Press publishes perfect bound chapbooks, from 24 to 40 pages. Current offerings include work by Glenna Luschei, Wilma Elizabeth McDaniel, and Will Inman." avg. press run 100. Pub'd 3 titles 2009; expects 4 titles 2010, 1 title 2011. 25 titles listed in the *Small Press Record of Books in Print* (36th Edition, 2010-11). 40pp. Payment: copies. Copyrights for author. Subject: Poetry.

Millennium Vision Press, Charles C. Hagan Jr., 401 West Main St., Suite 706, Louisville, KY 40202-2937, phone 502 5892607 fax 502 5896123. 2004. Poetry, non-fiction. "Millennium Vision Press is eagerly looking for inspirational and religious poetry submissions. We are also interested in non-ficiton works for the legal and business community:Recent contributors: NOT GUILTY EVERY TIME Keys To Courtoom Victory If I Could Only Write A Line: The Religious and Inspirational Poetry of Mary Southers." avg. press run 2000. Expects 4 titles 2010, 4 titles 2011. No titles listed in the *Small Press Record of Books in Print* (36th Edition, 2010-11). Discounts: national distributors 65% off listwholesalers 50 to 60% off listretail bookstores 45%college bookstores 25% off listlibraries 20% if requested3-199 copies -40%200-499 -50%500 and up -40%, -25%. 175-325pp. Reporting time: 30 days. Simultaneous submissions accepted: Yes. Publishes 5% of manuscripts submitted. Payment: 6 to 10% royalty on net. Copyrights for author. Subjects: African-American, Black, Civil Rights, Inspirational, Law, Motivation, Success, Poetry, Self-Help.

Mills Custom Services Publishing, Vicki Mills, Owner, Editor; Richard Mills, Owner, Editor, P.O. Box 866, Rancho Mirage, CA 92270, 760-250-1897, fax 760-406-6280, Vamills@aol.com, www.buybookscds.com. 2003. Poetry, fiction, satire, letters, non-fiction. "We have published self-help and instructional books on beginning use and success and enjoyment with computers. We have books in English and also have Spanish translations. With clear and basic, bold directions and illustrations, even the brand new beginning user can step into the computer age with confidance." avg. press run 150. Pub'd 1 title 2009; expects 1 title 2010, 2 titles 2011. 2 titles listed in the *Small Press Record of Books in Print* (36th Edition, 2010-11). Discounts: 40%. 190pp. Reporting time: 3 business days for initial response and confirmation of receipt. Simultaneous submissions accepted: Yes. Publishes 25% of manuscripts submitted. Payment: Varies depending on the amount of collaboration necessary and contractual agreement specifications. Initial consultation is done gratis to see how we can best serve the client's needs. We can do either, depends on client's preferences. Subjects: Adoption, Biography, Communication, Journalism, Computers, Calculators, Education, Family, Fiction, Libertarian, Libraries, Literary Review, Non-Fiction, Romance, Travel, Trivia, Writers/Writing.

The Kenneth G. Mills Foundation, Angela Wingfield, Mary Joy Leaper, P.O. Box 790, Station F, Toronto, Ontario M4Y 2N7, Canada, 800-437-1454, fax: 905-951-9712, email:news@kgmfoundation.org, www:kgmfoundation.org. 1975. Poetry, art, photos, interviews, reviews, music, long-poems, non-fiction. "Home office: PO Box 790, Station F, Toronto, Ontario M4Y 2N7, Canada, Tel: 416-410-0453, Fax

905-951-9712. Philosophical, educational. Primarily the works of Canadian philosopher, poet, composer and conductor, artist Kenneth George Mills. Prose, poetry, and spoken-word recordings. Poetry of Rolland G. Smith. Not currently accepting submissions." avg. press run 2M. Pub'd 6 titles 2009; expects 8 titles 2010, 9 titles 2011. 20 titles listed in the *Small Press Record of Books in Print* (36th Edition, 2010-11). Discounts: 40% to trade. 260pp. Subjects: Autobiography, Inspirational, Memoirs, Metaphysics, Non-Fiction, Philosophy, Poetry, Prose, Spiritual.

•**Milverstead Publishing LLC,** Christopher Finlan, 31 Rampart Drive, Wayne, PA 19087, (484)653-6205, info@milversteadpublishing.com. 2009. Fiction, photos, non-fiction. Pub'd 1 title 2009; expects 10-20 titles 2010, 20-25 titles 2011. 4 titles listed in the *Small Press Record of Books in Print* (36th Edition, 2010-11). 300pp. Reporting time: 4 weeks. Simultaneous submissions accepted: Yes. Payment: Varies. Copyrights for author.

Mind Power Publishing, Henry Kabaaga, 57 Elsinge Road, Enfield, London, EN1 4NS, England, +44(0)1992851158. 2004. Fiction, non-fiction. "Works of encouragement (motivational) for both adults and children. Works of mystery and adventure for children (fiction), all ages. Self help. Business, promoting entrepreneurship." avg. press run 3000. Expects 1 title 2010, 2 titles 2011. No titles listed in the *Small Press Record of Books in Print* (36th Edition, 2010-11). Discounts: 10-100 copies 10%100+ copies 25%. 150pp. Reporting time: 4 weeks. Simultaneous submissions accepted: Yes. This depends on the individual's piece of work. Subjects: Business & Economics, Careers, Children, Youth, Creativity, Education, English, Ethics, Finances, Guidance, Inspirational, Leadership, Literature (General), Management, Philosophy, Self-Help.

THE MINDERBINDER REVIEW OF BOOKS, Kenneth MacDonald, Editor; Bruce Pryor, Associate Editor, PO Box 236, Millbrae, CA 94030, website: www.minderbinderreview.com. 2009. Satire. "The Minderbinder Review of Books is the annual online literary review and subsidiary of Yossarian Univesal News Service, a parody news and disinformation syndicate. www.yunews.com." 1/yr. Expects 1 issue 2010, 1 issue 2011. Copyrighted. Subject: Satire.

•**MindGlow Media,** Leopold Peters, Suite 175, 75 East Fourth Street, New York, NY 10003. 2008. Fiction, art, non-fiction. "The board of MindGlow Media is made up of writers and free speech advocates who see in the current social climate an opportunity to combat the kind of scapegoating that has plagued the world since the beginning of recorded history. Dark skinned people, Jews, Irish, foreigners, homosexuals, the psychiatrically labeled, and Asians are but a few of the groups that have been demonized and subsequently elevated. Currently, one of the groups that is experiencing an especially egregious kind of calumny consists of men (and at times women) who have an intense love of boys. What was once celebrated in a number of cultures is, currently, unquestionably condemned without reflection or debate in the Western world.MindGlow Media is a publishing venture that has committed itself to examine social scapegoating by focusing on its most damaging manifestations in the modern world. Toward this end it will publish and advertise authors who challenge all forms of scapegoating, but special attention will be given to those who examine affectionate interactions between men and boys that, outside of the immediate family, today often bring suspicion and condemnation." avg. press run 3000. Pub'd 2 titles 2009; expects 1 title 2010, 2 titles 2011. No titles listed in the *Small Press Record of Books in Print* (36th Edition, 2010-11). Discounts: 2-9 copies 30% 10+ copies 50%. 110pp. Reporting time: one month. Simultaneous submissions accepted: Yes. Publishes 20% of manuscripts submitted. Payment: to be negotiated. Does not copyright for author. Subjects: Fantasy, Human Rights, Humanism, Humor, Novels, Poetry, Prison.

MINESHAFT, Everett Rand, Gioia Palmieri, P. O. Box 1226, Durham, NC 27702. 1999. Poetry, fiction, articles, art, photos, cartoons, interviews, satire, criticism, reviews, letters, parts-of-novels, non-fiction. "*Mineshaft* is a small independent art, literature, & comics magazine publishing some of the world's greatest artists and writers. It features comics, drawings, letters, fiction, poetry, photos & lots more! Regular contributors are R. Crumb, who designed our logos, Kim Deitch, Mary Fleener, Sophie Crumb, Jay Lynch, Andrei Codrescu, Nina Bunjevac, Bruce Simon, Simon Deitch, Pat Moriarity, Robert Armstrong, and many other amazing artists. Submissions are welcome. The mag was started in 1999, is published 2 times a year, and is printed on offset press. To find out more about *Mineshaft* & what it's all about check out the website at: www.mineshaftmagazine.com." circ. 1,000. 2/yr. Pub'd 2 issues 2009; expects 2 issues 2010, 2 issues 2011. sub. price $20; per copy $7.00. Back issues: Please inquire for details or check out the website. Discounts: 40% to bookstores. 48-52pp. Reporting time: 1 to 6 months. Simultaneous submissions accepted: yes. Payment: contributor copies. Copyrighted, reverts to author. Pub's reviews: two in 2009. Ads: occasional. Subjects: Cartoons, Comics, Essays, Fiction, Humor, Literary Review, Non-Fiction, Photography, Poetry, Prose, Reviews, Short Stories, Travel.

MINIATURE DONKEY TALK INC, Bonnie Gross, PO Box 982, Cripple Creek, CO 80813-0982, 719-689-2904, minidonk@qis.net, www.miniaturedonkeytalk.com. 1987. Non-fiction. circ. 5.5M. 4/yr. Pub'd 6 issues 2009; expects 4 issues 2010, 4 issues 2011. 1 title listed in the *Small Press Record of Books in Print* (36th Edition, 2010-11). sub. price $25; per copy $5; sample $5. Back issues: $5. 70pp. Simultaneous submissions accepted: yes. Publishes 80% of manuscripts submitted. Copyrighted, reverts to author. Ads: $220/$125/$65 1/4 page. Subjects: Agriculture, Animals, Non-Fiction, Pets.

Minnesota Historical Society Press (see also MINNESOTA HISTORY), Gregory M. Britton, Director; Ann Regan, Managing Editor, 345 Kellogg Blvd. West, St. Paul, MN 55102-1906, 651-297-2221. 1849. avg. press run 2M-8M. Pub'd 24 titles 2009; expects 22 titles 2010, 22 titles 2011. 50 titles listed in the *Small Press Record of Books in Print* (36th Edition, 2010-11). Discounts: 40% 1-9 books; 45% 10+ books. Reporting time: 3 months. Payment: negotiated. Copyrights for author. Subjects: African-American, Anthropology, Archaelogy, Architecture, Autobiography, Bibliography, Biography, Dictionaries, History, Indians, Minnesota, Native American, Non-Fiction, Women.

MINNESOTA HISTORY, Minnesota Historical Society Press, Anne Kaplan, Minnesota Historical Society Press, 345 Kellogg Blvd., St. Paul, MN 55102, 1651-297-2221.

THE MINNESOTA REVIEW, Jeffrey J. Williams, Dept. of English, Carnegie Mellon University, Baker Hall 259, Pittsburgh, PA 15213-3890, editors@theminnesotareview.org. 1960. Poetry, fiction, articles, art, photos, cartoons, interviews, satire, criticism, reviews, letters, parts-of-novels, long-poems, collages, non-fiction. "A journal of committed writing. We have a long tradition of publishing politically engaged work that deals with cultural politics. Our aim now is to publish the work of engaged younger critics and writers, such as Marc Bousquet, Robin Sowards, Katie Hogan, and Rita Felski in criticism; and Stefano Benni, Aimee Labrie, May Hall, and Amy Wilkinson in poetry and fiction. Many of our future issues will be organized around a special topic, such as our Fall 2004 issue on 'Smart Kids' and recent issues on 'The Legacy of Michael Sprinker' and '50s Culture.' In each issue, our aim is to present new writing that is *daring* and encroaches bounds, whether they be stylistic or conceptual. Theory's a good word here." circ. 1.5M. 2/yr. Pub'd 2 issues 2009; expects 2 issues 2010. sub. price $30/2yr individual, $60 institutions and/or overseas; per copy $15; sample $15. Back issues: $15. Discounts: 10%. 180-260pp. Reporting time: 1-3 months. Simultaneous submissions accepted: yes. Publishes 5% of manuscripts submitted. Payment: 2 copies. Copyrighted, reverts to author. Pub's reviews: 11 in 2009. §Poetry, fiction, very interested in Left literary & cultural criticism (feminist, marxist, poststructural, postcolonial), literary theory. Ads: $100/pg. Subjects: Feminism, Literature (General).

MIP Company, PO Box 27484, Minneapolis, MN 55427, 763-544-5915, mp@mipco.com, www.mipco.com. 1984. Poetry, fiction, non-fiction. Pub'd 3 titles 2009. 12 titles listed in the *Small Press Record of Books in Print* (36th Edition, 2010-11). Discounts: 40% when 10 or more copies purchased. Simultaneous submissions accepted: yes. Copyrights for author. Subjects: Erotica, Fiction, Poetry, Russia, Sex, Sexuality, Short Stories, U.S.S.R.

•Mishmish Press, Jean Grant, 1308 Jana Drive, Lawrence, KS 66049, 785-842-7552, info@mishmish-press.com, www.mishmishpress.com. 2009. Fiction, non-fiction. "This is a new press and will intentionally publish only a couple of books each year. We are interested primarily in offerings that will improve understanding of the Middle East." Expects 1 title 2010, 2 titles 2011. No titles listed in the *Small Press Record of Books in Print* (36th Edition, 2010-11). 150-300pp. Reporting time: One month for query. Simultaneous submissions accepted: No. Copyrights for author. Subjects: France, French, Middle East, Novels.

Miskwabik Press (see also THE CLIFFS "sounding"), Jikiwe, Editor, P.O. Box 7, 109 Fifth Street, Calumet, MI 49913-1608, 906-337-5970, www.miskwabikpress.com. 2005. Poetry, fiction, art, letters, non-fiction. "THE CLIFFS "sounding is published four times a year: winter, spring, summer and fall Short poems short stores and black and white art." avg. press run 100. Expects 6 titles 2010, 8 titles 2011. No titles listed in the *Small Press Record of Books in Print* (36th Edition, 2010-11). Discounts: 20%. 50pp. Reporting time: within 4 weeks. Simultaneous submissions accepted: No. Does not copyright for author. Subjects: Anarchist, Anthropology, Archaelogy, Antiques, Architecture, Arts, Biography, Black, Book Reviewing, Community, Criticism, Dada, Dance, Earth, Natural History, Ecology, Foods, Fiction.

Missing Man Press, Wayne Wirs, 1313 S. Military Trail, #193, Deerfield Beach, FL 33442, 954 263-5416, mmp@missingmanpress.com, http://missingmanpress.com. 2004. Photos, non-fiction. "Missing Man Press is a small, independent publishing house whose goal is to produce high quality books, greeting cards, and calendars which are centered around inspirational themes of expanded consciousness." avg. press run 3000. Expects 2 titles 2010, 4 titles 2011. No titles listed in the *Small Press Record of Books in Print* (36th Edition, 2010-11). Discounts: 6-299 copies: 40%, 300-499 copies: 50%, 500+ copies: 55%. 170pp. Reporting time: We are not currently accepting submissions. Subjects: Inspirational, Photography, Spiritual.

Missing Spoke Press (see also AMERICAN JONES BUILDING & MAINTENANCE), Von G. Binuia, PO Box 8645, Concord, NH 03303, 603-724-1158, Email:msp@singspeak.org. 1997. Poetry, fiction, art, photos, interviews, satire, parts-of-novels, long-poems, non-fiction. "Non-fiction essays about your community organizing experiences or plans (dreams); poems that are AS clear and illuminating when read drunk as when sober; short stories. No publishing plans for 2010. Web development in progress. If you yourself were delighted, then send it anyway." avg. press run 300. 3 titles listed in the *Small Press Record of Books in Print*

308

(36th Edition, 2010-11). 125pp. Reporting time: 3-4 months. Simultaneous submissions accepted: yes. Publishes 2% of manuscripts submitted. Payment: various and copies. Copyrights for author. Subjects: Absurdist, Americana, Creative Non-fiction, Culture, Current Affairs, Essays, Fiction, Human Rights, Labor, Literary Review, Poetry, Politics, Public Affairs, Worker, Zines.

MISSISSIPPI CROW, Cloud 9 Publishing, Nadia Giordana, Minneapolis, MN, mississippicrow@msn.com. 1992. Poetry, fiction, articles, art, photos, cartoons, collages, concrete art, non-fiction. "http://mississippi-crow.wordpress.com - Visit website for complete guidelines BEFORE submitting. Yes, we take submissions via email: MississippiCrow@msn.com. A highly visual and artistic magazine with a full color cover. Some of the best artwork will be featured on the front or back cover of each issue. We have published poetry ranging from both established and emerging or unknown poets, often giving a poet his/her first opportunity to be published in a quality magazine. We welcome submissions of articles on a variety of subjects, but especially about writing and the writing life and we love flash fiction. To buy a copy, go to http/stores.lulu.com/RiverMuse." circ. 250. 2-3/yr. Pub'd 2 issues 2009; expects 2 issues 2010, 2 issues 2011. Back issues: inquire for free ebook or go to http://stores.lulu.com/RiverMuse to order a print copy of any issue. 48pp. Reporting time: 2 weeks to 2 months. Publishes 50% of manuscripts submitted. Payment: PDF contributor copies. Copyrighted, reverts to author. Ads: negotiable. Subjects: Antiques, Arts, Avant-Garde, Experimental Art, Cartoons, Communication, Journalism, Crafts, Hobbies, Essays, Folklore, Humor, Photography, Poetry, Short Stories, Storytelling, Surrealism, Visual Arts.

MISSISSIPPI REVIEW, Frederick Barthelme, Executive Editor; Julia Johnson, Editor; Rie Fortenberry, Managing Editor, 118 College Dr., #5144, Hattiesburg, MS 39406-0001, 601-266-5600, www.mississippi-review.com. 1971. Poetry, fiction, parts-of-novels, long-poems. "Because we only publish 2 issues/year, we do not accept unsolicited manuscripts, except under the guidelines of the annual MR Prize: We award $1000 each in fiction and poetry; winners and finalists are published in print issue. Entry fee is $15 per entry and includes a complimentary copy of the prize issue. Deadline is October 1. Send entries to MR Prize, 118 College Dr., #5144, Hattiesburg, MS 39406. For more information e-mail contest coordinator at rief@mississippireview.com or visit our Web site, www.mississippireview.com." circ. 2000. 2/yr. Pub'd 2 issues 2009; expects 2 issues 2010, 2 issues 2011. sub. price $15/individuals; $32/libraries; per copy $9; sample $9. Back issues: $9. Discounts: none. 150-225pp. Simultaneous submissions accepted: yes. Payment: copies. Copyrighted, reverts to author. Ads: $100/$50/ Will consider trade-out. Subjects: Fiction, Poetry.

•MISSISSIPPIREVIEW.COM, The University of Southern Mississippi, PO Box 5144, Hattiesburg, MS 39406, rief@mississippireview.com. "In early 1995 we first put Mississippi Review on the Web. The idea was to make our literary magazine available free of charge to all who might be interested. Our second idea was to insist the magazine have fresh content distinct from the print edition of Mississippi Review. We've done that, more or less, with a couple of notable exceptions, and this archive page links to everything we've published online since we first posted on the internet in April 1995. These days we're seeing more than a quarter million visitors per year, so we thank you for making Mississippi Review one of the most highly regarded literary magazines on the Internet."

THE MISSOURI REVIEW, Speer Morgan, Editor; Richard Sowienski, Managing Editor; Evelyn Somers, Associate Editor; Katy Didden, Poetry Editor; Kristine Somerville, Promotions and Circulation, 357 McReynolds Hall, University of Missouri-Columbia, Columbia, MO 65211, 573-882-4474, Fax 573-884-4671, umcastmr@missouri.edu. 1978. Poetry, fiction, articles, art, cartoons, interviews, reviews, parts-of-novels, long-poems, non-fiction. "Overall excellence and freshness are priorities for us. We like fiction with a strong sense of story and essays that offer an intelligent perspective on compelling subjects or events. Emerging and established writers should take note of our Jeffrey E. Smith Editors' Prize contest, which awards $15,000 in prizes in fiction, poetry and essay. We read year-round and honor the best fiction of each volume year annually with our William Peden Prize in fiction ($1000 prize). Recently we've published prose by James McLaughlin, William Lychack, Dwight Allen, Jennifer Bryan and Margaret Malone." circ. 5.5M. 4/yr. Pub'd 4 issues 2009; expects 4 issues 2010, 4 issues 2011. 1 title listed in the *Small Press Record of Books in Print* (36th Edition, 2010-11). sub. price $24, $39/2 years, $48/3 years; per copy $8; sample $8. Back issues: call. Discounts: none. 175pp. Reporting time: 10-12 weeks. We accept simultaneous submissions with notification. Publishes 5% of manuscripts submitted. Payment: $30/page to $750 for prose and poetry; $300 for interviews and review essays. Copyrighted, author can reprint material without charge if author acknowledges mag. Pub's reviews: 4 in 2009. §Essay reviews only; query the associate editor. Ads: $400 or exchange. Subject: Literary Review.

The MIT Press, Ellen Faran, 55 Hayward Street, Cambridge, MA 02142-1315, 617-253-5646, 617-258-6779, 800-405-1619. 1932. Pub'd 230 titles 2009; expects 240 titles 2010, 240 titles 2011. No titles listed in the *Small Press Record of Books in Print* (36th Edition, 2010-11). Discounts: Trade discount to bookstores: 46%.

MOBILE BEAT: The Mobile Entertainer's Magazine, Daniel Walsh, Editor-in-Chief, PO Box 42365, Urbandale, IA 50323, 515-986-3300, webmaster@mobilebeat.com. 1991. Articles, photos, interviews, reviews, music, letters, news items. circ. 10,000. 7/yr. Pub'd 7 issues 2009; expects 7 issues 2010, 7 issues 2011. sub.

price $23; per copy $5; sample $5. Back issues: $5. 60pp. Simultaneous submissions accepted: NO. Publishes 80% assigned, unassigned 20% of manuscripts submitted. Copyrighted, does not revert to author. Pub's reviews: 6 in 2009. §Business/performance/technology-oriented publications; Sound/lighting/video equipment, music. Subjects: Advertising, Self-Promotion, Electronics, Entertainment, How-To, Insurance, Internet, Interviews, Magic, Music, Performing Arts, Public Relations/Publicity, Tapes & Records, Technology, Visual Arts.

MOBIUS, THE POETRY MAGAZINE, Juanita Torrence-Thompson, P.O. Box 671058, Flushing, NY 11367-1058, mobiusmag@earthlink.net, www.mobiuspoetry.com. 1982. Poetry. ''We publish imaginative, innovative, image-driven, high-quality poetry. Poems can be serious, thought-provoking, metaphorical, HUMOROUS, surreal... ALL poetic forms welcome, but especially free verse, sestina, haiku, tanka. Categories: Family & Relationships, Life Is..., Science & Nature, Conflicts & Disagreements, Emotions & Escapades, Spirituality, Art & Culture and The World About Us. We have published Rita Dove, Nikki Giovanni, Robert Bly, Toi Derricotte as well as gifted emerging poets from U.S. and abroad.'' 1/yr. Pub'd 1 issue 2009; expects 1 issue 2010, 1 issue 2011. sub. price $12; per copy $12; sample $12. Back issues: inquire. Discounts: 5 copies or more 17%. 92pp. Reporting time: It varies. Average 1-4 months. Simultaneous submissions accepted: No. Payment: one free copy to poets published in that issue of MOBIUS. Copyrighted, reverts to author. No advertising.

Mock Turtle Press (see also AMERICAN ROAD), Thomas Repp, Executive Editor, PO Box 46519, Mount Clemens, MI 48046, Orders 1-877-285-5434 x1. General information 586-468-7483, fax 877-285-5434, sales@mockturtlepress.com, www.mockturtlepress.com. 1998. ''Writers should request a copy of our guidelines and become familiar with American Road magazine prior to submitting queries. E-mail queries preferred. Be sure to include information on photographic support.'' Pub'd 1 title 2009; expects 1 title 2011. 3 titles listed in the *Small Press Record of Books in Print* (36th Edition, 2010-11). Wholesale discounts available on books—call publisher, Retail discount on books: Quantities: 1-2 @ 20%, 3-4 @ 30%, 5+ @ 40%. Shipping charges apply, American Road magazine is distributed by Disticor. 200pp. Reporting time: 6 months. Simultaneous submissions accepted: no. Publishes 1% of manuscripts submitted. Payment: 13¢ per word. Subjects: Americana, History, Non-Fiction, Transportation, Travel.

MODERN HAIKU, Charles Trumbull, Editor; Lidia Rozmus, Art Editor; Randy M. Brooks, Web Editor; Paul Miller, Book Review Editor; David Burleigh, Associate Editor, PO Box 7046, Evanson, IL 60204-7046. 1969. Poetry, articles, reviews. '''Best haiku magazine in North America'—Museum of Haiku Literature, Tokyo. International circulation. Good university and public library subscription list. Publishes haiku only, plus related book reviews and articles. No restrictions on article length. Contributors should enclose self-addressed, stamped return envelope.'' circ. 700. 3/yr. Pub'd 3 issues 2009; expects 3 issues 2010, 3 issues 2011. 5 titles listed in the *Small Press Record of Books in Print* (36th Edition, 2010-11). sub. price $23 in US; per copy $10; sample $10. Back issues: inquire. 100pp. Reporting time: 2 weeks. Simultaneous submissions accepted: no. Publishes 5% of manuscripts submitted. Payment: $1 for each haiku; $5 page for articles. Copyrighted, reverts to author. Pub's reviews: 40 in 2009. §Haiku, senryu, haibun. No ads. Subjects: Book Reviewing, Haiku.

THE MODERN LANGUAGE JOURNAL, Leo Van Lier, Editor, University of Wisconsin, Department of French and Italian, Madison, WI 53706-1558, 608-262-5010. 1916. Articles, reviews, news items. ''Sally S. Magnan, Editor, *The Modern Language Journal* (1994-present).'' circ. c. 5000. 4/yr. Pub'd 4 issues 2009; expects 4 issues 2010, 4 issues 2011. sub. price $38 indiv, $102 instit; per copy $12; sample free (indiv.). Back issues: $17 indiv., $23 instit. 150pp. Reporting time: 1-3 months. Simultaneous submissions accepted: no. Publishes 15-20% of manuscripts submitted. Payment: 2 copies of issue in which article appears. Copyrighted, does not revert to author. Pub's reviews: 138 in 2009. §Subjects of interest to language teachers and researchers. Ads: $375/$265/175 1/4 page. Subject: Language.

Modern Metrics Press, R. Nemo Hill, 328 East 6th Street #13, New York, NY 10003, www.modern-metrics.com. 2006. Poetry. ''Modern Metrics publishes high quality chapbooks and specializes in metrical poetry in a variety of traditional forms, though we are not obnoxiously dogmatic about it.'' avg. press run 100. Pub'd 5 titles 2009; expects 5 titles 2010, 5 titles 2011. No titles listed in the *Small Press Record of Books in Print* (36th Edition, 2010-11). Discounts: 35%. 25pp. Reporting time: 1 month. Simultaneous submissions accepted: Yes. Payment: 5 free copies / 35 %discount. Copyrights for author.

MODERN PHILOLOGY, University of Chicago Press, Richard Strier, University of Chicago, Wieboldt Hall 106, 1050 E. 59th Street, Chicago, IL 60637, 773-702-7600 (main #), 773-702-0694 (fax), http://www.journals.uchicago.edu/index.html. 1903. ''Founded in 1903, *Modern Philology* continues to set a high standard for investigations in literary scholarship, history, and criticism. Although *Modern Philology* publishes articles only in English (with rare exceptions), it welcomes innovative and scholarly work on literature in all modern languages, worldwide. Reviews of recent books appear in every regular issue; review articles, and archival notes and documents are also featured.'' 4/yr. Pub's reviews.

THE MODERN REVIEW, Simone dos Anjos, Editor-in-Chief, RPO P.O. Box 32659, Richmond Hill L4C 0A2CA, Canada. "Our desired end is sustained access to a relevant literature, one that refuses to oppose tradition to innovation, the personal to the objective."

MOJO ROSE, John Jacob, 808 S. Cuyler Avenue, Oak Park, IL 60304. 2006. Poetry, fiction, art, photos, criticism, non-fiction. "SASE required. Cover letter required (this means you Lyn Lifshin). All fiction right now is solicited. Essays are encouraged. This is the phoenix rising from the ashes of *Mojo Navigator*, which died in 1977. We hope to publish 2 issues per year, but make no promises. *Mojo* alumni are welcome. We are not considering book mss. right now. No "prose-poetry"." circ. 500. Irregular. Expects 2 issues 2010, 2 issues 2011. sub. price $12; per copy $6; sample $6. Discounts: library jobber 40%. 56-80pp. Reporting time: 3-6 weeks. Simultaneous submissions accepted: yes. Publishes an unknown % of manuscripts submitted. Payment: cash for art and photography; otherwise copies. Copyrighted, reverts to author. Ads: $200 full page.

Mojocastle Press, Stefani Kelsey, 94 N 200 E, Price, UT 84501, 435-630-6054. 2006. avg. press run 600. Pub'd 20 titles 2009; expects 40 titles 2010, 80 titles 2011. No titles listed in the *Small Press Record of Books in Print* (36th Edition, 2010-11). Discounts: ebooks. 300pp.

•Mondial, Andrew Moore, 203 West 107th street, #6C, New York, NY 10025, www.mondialbooks.com, Fax: 208-361-2863, Phone: 212-851-3252. 1996. Fiction, articles, reviews, plays, non-fiction. avg. press run 500. Pub'd 27 titles 2009; expects 18-25 titles 2010, 10-20 titles 2011. No titles listed in the *Small Press Record of Books in Print* (36th Edition, 2010-11). Discounts: distributors 55%; bookstores 45%; wholesalers 55%; retailers 45%; institutions 45%; classrooms 45%. 250pp. Reporting time: If no reply within 3 weeks, the manuscript is not accepted. Simultaneous submissions accepted: Yes. Payment: 10%. Copyright for author or publisher, depending on agreement. Subjects: Aging, Biography, Bisexual, Dictionaries, Erotica, Fiction, France, French, Gay, Language, Jack London, Men, Mystery, New York, Novels, Romance.

THE MONIST: An International Quarterly Journal of General Philosophical Inquiry, Barry Smith, Editor; Sherwood J.B. Sugden, Managing Editor, 315 Fifth Street, Peru, IL 61354, (815)224-6651, FAX:(815)223-4486, philomon1@netscape.net, http//monist.buffalo.edu. 1890. Articles, non-fiction. "THE MONIST, first published in 1890, is an international quarterly journal of general philosophical inquiry. Each issue (typically eight articles) is devoted to a single general topic in epistemology, metaphysics, aesthetics, or ethics selected by the Editor in advance. Recent contributors: Professors John Haldane (St. Andrews), John Hyman (The Queen's College, Oxford), Dominic Lopes (U. of British Columbia), Mark DeBellis (New York U.), Noel Carroll (U. of Wisconsin), Grace Yee (Monash U. Australia), Jennifer Church (Vassar), Mark Siebel (University of Leipzig). Editor: Barry Smith (SUNY)." circ. 1600. 4/yr. Pub'd 4 issues 2009; expects 4 issues 2010, 4 issues 2011. sub. price $30; per copy $12; sample $12. Back issues: $12. Discounts: Individual subscription: $30; institutional subscription: $50. 176pp. Reporting time: 3 months. Simultaneous submissions accepted: No. Publishes 40% of manuscripts submitted. Payment: copies and off-prints of article. Copyrighted, does not revert to author. §We list full bibliographic data as "Books Received" in philosophy, religion, science. Ads: Full page: $150Half-page: $80. Subjects: Philosophy, Religion.

MONKEY'S FIST, Robin Merrill, 6 Pearl St., Madison, ME 04950-1254. 2001. Poetry. "Open reading period Jan 1 - Feb 28 ONLY. Send 3 poems ONLY. Include SASE. Make checks payable to Robin Merrill." 1/yr. sub. price $6; sample $6. 32pp. Reporting time: 2 months. Simultaneous submissions accepted: yes. Publishes 3% of manuscripts submitted. Payment: 1 copy.

Monsoon Books, 52 Telok Blangah Road, #03-05 Telok Blangah House, Singapore 098829, Singapore, email: phil@monsoonbooks.com.sg, web: www.monsoonbooks.com.sg. Fiction, non-fiction. "We specialize in books with Southeast Asian content." Pub'd 12 titles 2009; expects 18 titles 2010, 24 titles 2011. 3 titles listed in the *Small Press Record of Books in Print* (36th Edition, 2010-11). 288pp. Reporting time: 60 days. Simultaneous submissions accepted: yes. Publishes 5% of manuscripts submitted.

MONTANA QUARTERLY, Nick Ehli, Editor-in-Chief, 2820 West College, Bozeman, MT 59718, TEL: 406-587-4491 or 800-275-0401. "Montana Quarterly welcomes story ideas and submissions. Our publishing goals are to cover the broad range of stories that make our state unique. Open the magazine and youll see the polarities of wide-open prairies and daunting peaks, suburban sprawl and pristine streams, wealthy and poor, environmental triumphs and tragedies, left- and right-wing politics and everything in between. All about Montana. Send detailed story and photo queries to:Megan Ault, Managing editor, 2820 West College, Bozeman, Mont., 59718//megan@themontanaquarterly.com."

Montemayor Press, Edward Myers, Publisher, PO Box 526, Millburn, NJ 07041, 973-761-1341, Fax 973-378-9749, mail@montemayorpress.com, montemayorpress.com. 1999. Fiction, plays, non-fiction. "Montemayor Press specializes in 1) middle-grade and young-adult fiction; 2) literary fiction and drama by Latino authors; and 3) literary fiction and nonfiction of a more general nature. No submissions accepted at this time." avg. press run 2M. Pub'd 3 titles 2009; expects 3 titles 2010, 4 titles 2011. 2 titles listed in the *Small Press Record of Books in Print* (36th Edition, 2010-11). Discounts: bookstores 40%, schools 25%. 180pp.

Publishes 0% of manuscripts submitted. Payment: standard. Copyrights for author. Subjects: Colorado, Fantasy, Fiction, Mexico, Multicultural, Non-Fiction, Novels, Poetry, South America, Women, Young Adult.

Montfort Publications (see also QUEEN OF ALL HEARTS), J. Patrick Gaffney, 26 South Saxon Avenue, Bay Shore, NY 11706, 516-665-0726, FAX 516-665-4349. 1947. avg. press run 5M. Pub'd 1 title 2009; expects 1 title 2010, 1 title 2011. 1 title listed in the *Small Press Record of Books in Print* (36th Edition, 2010-11). Does not copyright for author.

Moo-Cow Fan Club, Becky Ances, PO Box 165, Peterborough, NH 03458, 603-831-1386. 2001. Fiction, cartoons, non-fiction. "Moo-Cow Fan Club publishes "Children's Entertainment Both Funny & Smart." We only put out material for children that is educational, but also exciting and funny. Most of the material we release is created in house and features the Moo-Cow Fan Club characters, but we may branch out into other stories if the right one comes along. We are new to book publishing but published an award-winning educational magazine for 6 years. Some of our publications will be compilations of the articles from those with the possibility of room for new materials." avg. press run 3500. Pub'd 1 title 2009; expects 2 titles 2010, 4 titles 2011. 1 title listed in the *Small Press Record of Books in Print* (36th Edition, 2010-11). Discounts: 2-10 copies 30%10+ 40%. 80pp. Reporting time: 90 days. Simultaneous submissions accepted: Yes. Publishes 2% of manuscripts submitted. Payment: TBA. Copyrights for author. Subjects: Arts, China, Crafts, Hobbies, Creative Non-fiction, Education, Fiction, History, Multicultural, Non-Fiction, Reading, Science, Travel.

Mo'omana'o Press, Vicki Draeger, 3030 Kalihi St., Honolulu, HI 96818, 808-843-2502; (fax) 808-843-2572; email: clear@maui.net. 2004. Fiction, non-fiction. "'"Mo'omana'o" is Hawaiian for "the recording of thoughts." The editors of Mo'omana'o Press are all educators. Our regional interest publications have an educational component to promote intellectual, physical, and spiritual development. We are interested in material that preserves Hawaiian culture, tradition and values from a Christian perspective. Mo'omana'o Press is dedicated to publishing books for schools, churches, children and families." avg. press run 500. Expects 2 titles 2011. No titles listed in the *Small Press Record of Books in Print* (36th Edition, 2010-11). Discounts: 10 or more copies, 20%. 100pp. Reporting time: manuscripts submitted by invitation only; 3-4 months. Simultaneous submissions accepted: Yes. Payment: pays in contributors copies. Copyrights for author. Subjects: Adolescence, Children, Youth, Christmas, Community, Divorce, Ecology, Foods, Fiction, Folklore, Hawaii, Parenting, Relationships, Religion, Science, Women, Young Adult.

•MOON CITY REVIEW, Lanette Cadle, Editor; Marcus Cafaga, Editor, c/o Department of English, 901 South National Ave., Springfield, MO 65897.

Moon Pie Press, Alice Persons, Nancy A. Henry, 16 Walton Street, Westbrook, ME 04092, www.moonpiepress.com. 2003. Poetry. "We are a small press in Maine publishing poetry chapbooks. Books are generally 25 to 30 pages long, and we prefer poems no longer than two pages. The poets we have published so far are Nancy A. Henry, Alice Persons, Ted Bookey, Michael Macklin, Ellen M. Taylor, Jay Davis, Darcy Shargo, David Moreau, Jay Franzel, Robin Merrill, Ed Rielly, Eva M. Oppenheim, Thomas Edison (yes, him!), Marita O'Neill, Dennis Camire, Patrick Hicks, Kevin Sweeney, Don Moyer, and Tom Delmore. Our poets generally have at least 6 poems accepted for publication in journals and magazines before they put together a manuscript. We work with poets to help edit and design the chapbooks, which are stapled, not bound, of high quality. NOTE: We also have a perfect bound anthology of 11 Moon Pie Press Poets, called A MOXIE AND A MOON PIE: THE BEST OF MOON PIE PRESS, Volume I, $10. See our website for details and ordering." avg. press run 100. Pub'd 4 titles 2009; expects 7 titles 2010, 7 titles 2011. No titles listed in the *Small Press Record of Books in Print* (36th Edition, 2010-11). Discounts: 2-10 copies 20%. 30pp. Reporting time: a month if we can. Simultaneous submissions accepted: Yes. Publishes 75% of manuscripts submitted. Payment: This varies, but we help the poets with the expense of the books, and help market books. Email us for our submission guidelines. Copyright on book belongs to us; contents belong to poet. Subjects: Animals, Autobiography, Feminism, Gardening, Language, Maine, Newspapers, Peace, Pets, Poetry, Relationships, Translation, Travel, Women, Writers/Writing.

Moondance Press, Shari Maser, 4830 Dawson Drive, Ann Arbor, MI 48103, 734-426-1641, maser@mac.com, http://www.blessingway.net. 2004. Non-fiction. "Moondance Press publishes innovative non-fiction books about pregnancy, childbirth, and girlhood." avg. press run 5000. Expects 1 title 2010. No titles listed in the *Small Press Record of Books in Print* (36th Edition, 2010-11). 272pp. Subjects: Family, Non-Fiction, Parenting, Women.

Moonrise Press, Maja Trochimczyk, P.O.Box 4288, Sunland, CA 91041-4288, 818-352-4411; 818-384-8944. 2008. Poetry, articles, art, photos, criticism, non-fiction. avg. press run 100. Pub'd 2 titles 2009; expects 4 titles 2010, 4 titles 2011. No titles listed in the *Small Press Record of Books in Print* (36th Edition, 2010-11). 180pp. Reporting time: 1 month. Simultaneous submissions accepted: No. Publishes 10% of manuscripts submitted. Payment: individual per project. Copyrights for author. Subjects: Avant-Garde, Experimental Art, Criticism, Culture, Emily Dickinson, Eastern Europe, England, Europe, History, Liberal Arts, Music, Nature, Poetry,

Poland.

Morgan Quitno Corporation, Kathleen O'Leary Morgan, Scott Morgan, PO Box 1656, Lawrence, KS 66044, 785-841-3534, 785-841-3568, 800-457-0742, information@morganquitno.com, www.morganquitno.com. 1989. 6 titles listed in the *Small Press Record of Books in Print* (36th Edition, 2010-11).

Morgen Publishing Incorporated, M. Jean Rawson, PO Box 754, Naples, FL 34106, Fax 239-263-8472. 2000. Poetry, non-fiction. "Recent publications: *A Manual of Special Education Law* and *Mercy Me! Cancer Prayers, Poems, and Psalms*." Pub'd 1 title 2009; expects 1 title 2010, 1 title 2011. 2 titles listed in the *Small Press Record of Books in Print* (36th Edition, 2010-11). Discounts: contact for rates. 100-300pp. Reporting time: 3 months. Simultaneous submissions accepted: yes. Payment: negotiated. Copyrights for author. Subjects: Education, Law, Spiritual.

THE MORNING DEW REVIEW, Moreton's Harbour, NL A0G 3H0, Canada. Poetry, articles, cartoons, interviews, satire, criticism, reviews. "Forty percent of each issue is dedicated to haiku and other Japanese poetic forms. The rest is all types of open and closed forms of poetry." No titles listed in the *Small Press Record of Books in Print* (36th Edition, 2010-11). Subjects: Anarchist, Beat, Comics, Haiku, Poetry.

•**Morning Light Press,** 10881 North Boyer Road, Sandpoint, ID 83864, info@morninglightpress.com, 208-265-3626, Toll free 866-308-5200. "Morning Light Press publishes books that illuminate the spiritual searchworks of integrity that bring fresh insights to ageless questions. And as a division of a non-profit foundation, the Press is uniquely able to publish the words of authors whose insights might otherwise have remained unheard. Morning Light Press welcomes submissions from authors or agents. We are currently accepting non-fiction proposals, particularly in the areas of spirituality and transformation. Manuscripts related to body, mind, spirit topics are also welcome. Do not submit original materials. Under no circumstances will Morning Light Press be responsible for the safekeeping of original manuscripts. Sign and date the title page." No titles listed in the *Small Press Record of Books in Print* (36th Edition, 2010-11).

Morris Publishing, PO Box 2110, Kearney, NE 68848, 800-650-7888. 1 title listed in the *Small Press Record of Books in Print* (36th Edition, 2010-11). Simultaneous submissions accepted: yes. Copyrights for author.

•**MOSAIC LITERARY MAGAZINE,** Ron Kavanaugh, Executive Director, 314 West 231 St #470, Bronx, NY 10463, 718.530.9132. "Launched in 1998, *Mosaic* is a quarterly print magazine exploring the literary arts by writers of African descent. Each issue contains a unique blend of profiles, book reviews, and literature lesson plans. Mosaic is published by the Literary Freedom Project, a 501(c)3 tax-exempt not-for-profit arts organization that supports the literary arts through education, creative thinking, and new media."

MOTHER EARTH JOURNAL: An International Quarterly, Herman Berlandt, Editor, Publisher; Katherine Gallagher, Co-Editor; Rob Tricato, Assistant Editor, 934 Brannan St., San Francisco, CA 94103, 415-868-8865, 415-552-9261, info@internationalpoetrymuseum.org. 1990. Poetry. "*Mother Earth* is an international journal presenting the poet's perspective on the current political and ecological global crisis. Here poetry from six continents is represented in fine English translations. 'Let the voice of the poet be heard throughout the world' is our slogan. Among our contributors are Robert Bly, Gary Snyder, Anabel Torres, Marianne Larsen, Seamus Heaney, Kofi Awoonor, Wole Soyinka, Bei Dao, Mahmoud Darwish, Lawrence Ferlinghetti, etc." circ. 1M. 4/yr. Pub'd 4 issues 2009; expects 4 issues 2010, 4 issues 2011. sub. price $15; per copy $5; sample $3. Back issues: $3.50 each. Discounts: 50%. 40pp. Reporting time: 3 months. Simultaneous submissions accepted: yes. Publishes 15% of manuscripts submitted. Payment: 2 copies. Not copyrighted, rights revert to author on publication. Ads: $150/$100/$60 1/4 page. Subjects: Finances, Poetry.

MOTHERVERSE: A Journal of Contemporary Motherhood, Melanie Mayo-Laakso, Editor-in-Chief, 2663 Hwy 3, Two Harbors, MN 55616-1282, website www.motherverse.com, email editor@motherverse.com, submissions email submissions@motherverse.com, ordering email order@motherverse.com, advertising email ads@motherverse.com. 2005. Poetry, fiction, articles, art, photos, cartoons, interviews, satire, reviews, music, letters, parts-of-novels, long-poems, concrete art, news items, non-fiction. "MotherVerse prints smart, insightful and bold works of literature and art that explore and challenge mainstream ideals and reflect honest images of motherhood. We encourage the exploration of motherhood across geographical, political and cultural lines and reflect this by printing material from women around the globe. Recent contributers include Eugenia Chao, Sarojni Mehta-Lissak, Kate Haas, Suzanne Kamata and Bronmin Shumway. All submissions should be made electronically." 2/yr. Pub'd 4 issues 2009; expects 2 issues 2010, 2 issues 2011. sub. price Print $21.95, Digital $9; per copy Print $11.95; sample Print $11.95, Digital Free. Back issues: Print $11.95, Digital Back Issues Included with Digital Subscription. Bulk discounts available on orders of 3 or more issues or subscriptions. Free issues for review provided when available by special request. Contact order@motherverse.com. 120pp. Reporting time: 2-3 months. Simultaneous submissions accepted: Yes. Publishes 15% of manuscripts submitted. Payment: 1 contributer copy. Copyrighted, reverts to author. Pub's reviews: 20 in 2009. §Books, Magazines, Journals and Portfolios that examine contemporary or historical motherhood issues. We do not review material which could be considered parenting advice or instruction. Ads: Limited ad space available, rates vary.Contact ads@motherverse.com or visit www.motherverse.com/advertise. Subjects: Arts, Birth, Birth Control, Population, Family, Feminism, Gender Issues, Global Affairs, History, Homemaking, Human Rights, Interviews, Lesbianism, Literature (General), Multicultural, Parenting, Women.

Motom, Thomas Barber, 76 West 2100 South, Salt Lake City, UT 84115, (801)499-6021. 2005. Non-fiction. "As a new publisher we don't have an elaborate existing library, but we aim to. Currently, we are promoting, "Kick the Dealer...Not the Tires!" by Mark Marine. This non-fiction book takes the reader behind the scenes of the car buying process and and teaches them all they need to know in order to protect themselves when they buy a car." avg. press run 5000. Expects 1 title 2010, 3 titles 2011. No titles listed in the *Small Press Record of Books in Print* (36th Edition, 2010-11). Discounts: 1-5 33%6-49 40%50-99 45%100 or more 50%. 200pp. Reporting time: 1 week. Simultaneous submissions accepted: Yes. Publishes 25% of manuscripts submitted. Payment: Negotiable. Copyrights for author. Subjects: Abstracts, Absurdist, Adolescence, Advertising, Self-Promotion, Children, Youth, Christmas, Ethics, Fiction, How-To, Inspirational, Non-Fiction, Novels, Photography, Poetry, Zen.

Mount Ida Press, Diana S. Waite, 152 Washington Avenue, Albany, NY 12210-2203, Tel: 518-426-5935, Fax: 518-426-4116. 1984. Non-fiction. "Award-winning historical research, writing, editing, and indexing." avg. press run 1.5M-2M. Pub'd 1 title 2009; expects 2 titles 2010, 2 titles 2011. No titles listed in the *Small Press Record of Books in Print* (36th Edition, 2010-11). Discounts: 40% trade. 144pp. Reporting time: 2 months. Payment: royalty. Copyrights for author. Subjects: Architecture, Cities, History, Thomas Jefferson, New York, Textiles.

Mount Olive College Press (see also MOUNT OLIVE REVIEW), Pepper Worthington, Editor, Mount Olive College, 634 Henderson Street, Mount Olive, NC 28365. 1990. "The Mount Olive College Press accepts letters of inquiry year-round. If the Press is interested, the editor will request a complete manuscript." avg. press run 500-800. Pub'd 5-7 titles 2009; expects 5-7 titles 2010, 5-7 titles 2011. No titles listed in the *Small Press Record of Books in Print* (36th Edition, 2010-11). Poetry 70-110pp, others 30-210pp. Reporting time: 6 months to 1 year. Simultaneous submissions accepted: no. Publishes 5% of manuscripts submitted. Payment: negotiated. Copyrights for author.

MOUNT OLIVE REVIEW, Mount Olive College Press, Pepper Worthington, Editor, Department of Language and Literature, 634 Henderson Street, Mount Olive, NC 28365, 919-658-2502. 1987. Poetry, art, reviews, non-fiction. "Future themes include topics of travel, film, and metaphor in literature as well as a focus on North Carolina writers and major American writers. Recent contributors: Janet Lembke, Joseph Bathanti, Gladys Owings Hughes, James L. Abrahamson. Length of literary criticism as it relates to theme 1M-6M words. MLA style appropriate. Length of creative genres flexible." Publish 1 every 2 years. sub. price $25; per copy $25; sample $25. 394pp. Reporting time: varies, 6-10 months. Simultaneous submissions accepted: no. Publishes 20% of manuscripts submitted. Payment: none. Copyrighted, reverts to author. Pub's reviews. §Interviews, essays.

THE MOUNTAIN ASTROLOGER, Tem Tarriktar, PO Box 970, Cedar Ridge, CA 95924-0970, 530-477-8839, www.mountainastrologer.com. 1988. Poetry, articles, art, photos, cartoons, interviews, satire, reviews, letters, news items. "Any length; must have astrology content. Send SASE for return of materials." circ. print run 27M. 6/yr. Pub'd 6 issues 2009; expects 6 issues 2010, 6 issues 2011. sub. price $36 bulk rate, $48 1st class, $36US Canada; per copy $7 postpaid in U.S./Canada; sample $7 postpaid in U.S./Canada. Back issues: $6 postpaid in U.S./Canada and shipping charges. Discounts: available through distributors; write for a list of distributors. 132pp. Reporting time: varies. Simultaneous submissions accepted: no. Publishes 30% of manuscripts submitted. Payment: varies. Copyrighted, reverts to author. Pub's reviews: 30 in 2009. §Astrology only. Ads: $745/$395/subject to change. Subjects: Astrology, New Age, Philosophy.

Mountain Automation Corporation, Claude Wiatrowski, 6090 Whirlwind Dr, Colorado Springs, CO 80923-7560, 719-598-8256, Fax 719-598-8516, Order 800-345-6120, Order Fax 970-493-8781, Order Email mac@intrepidgroup.com, Order Address POB 2324 Ft Collins CO 80522-2324. 1976. 8 titles listed in the *Small Press Record of Books in Print* (36th Edition, 2010-11). Discounts: 50%. 64 pages books, 2 hours DVDspp. Subjects: Alaska, Arkansas, Canada, Catholic, Christianity, Colorado, Hawaii, History, The North, Old West, Religion, Transportation, Travel, The West.

Mountain Media, Wayne Murray, Kat Farmer, Rick Tompkins, PO box 271122, Las Vegas, NV 89127-1122, voice 702-656-3285, publisher@TheLibertarian.us, Web site http://www.LibertyBookShop.us. 1999. Fiction, non-fiction. "We publish a small number of libertarian and free-market titles in both fiction and non-fiction." avg. press run 5,000. Pub'd 1 title 2009; expects 2 titles 2011. 3 titles listed in the *Small Press Record of Books in Print* (36th Edition, 2010-11). Discounts: bookstore single-copy "STOP" 25 percent; 8-12 copies 30 percent plus shipping; 13-19 copies 40 percent plus shipping; 20-39 copies 50 percent plus shipping; 40+ copies 50 percent, free shipping. 600pp. Reporting time: 60-90 days. Simultaneous submissions accepted: Yes. Payment: negotiable. Copyrights for author. Subjects: Anarchist, Drugs, Fantasy, Fiction, Libertarian, Novels, Politics,

314

Science Fiction, Southwest, The West.

Mountain Press Publishing Co., Rob Williams, Business Manager; John Rimel, Publisher; Jeannie Painter, Production Coordinator; Gwen McKenna, History Editor; Jennifer Carey, Natural History Editor, PO Box 2399, Missoula, MT 59806, 406-728-1900. 1948 (became full time publisher in mid-70's - printing company prior to that). Non-fiction. "We publish primarily non-fiction. Besides our successful *Roadside Geology* series, we are publishing regional nature/outdoor guides such as *Wildflowers of Wyoming*. We also publish quality western history and western Americana. We also publish topical science books such as *Finding Fault in California*." avg. press run 5M. Pub'd 12 titles 2009; expects 12 titles 2010, 12 titles 2011. 192 titles listed in the *Small Press Record of Books in Print* (36th Edition, 2010-11). Discounts: bookstores 2-14 copies 40%, $4.00 shipping, 15+ 45% free freight. 150-360pp. Reporting time: 2-6 months. Payment: twice a year; royalty of 10-12% based on the amount the publisher receives from sales of the book. Copyrights for author. Subjects: Americana, Animals, Birds, Earth, Natural History, Geology, Montana, Reprints, Sports, Outdoors, Transportation, The West.

Mountain Publishing, PO Box 12720, Chandler, AZ 85248-0029, 800-879-8719, fax: 480-802-5644, email: info@mountainpublishingusa.com. 1989. Non-fiction. "Manuscripts: book-length dealing with business." avg. press run 5M. Pub'd 1 title 2009; expects 2 titles 2010, 1 title 2011. 1 title listed in the *Small Press Record of Books in Print* (36th Edition, 2010-11). 449pp. Reporting time: 60 days. Payment: negotiable. Copyrights for author. Subject: Business & Economics.

Mountain State Press, 2300 MacCorkle Avenue SE, Charleston, WV 25304-1099, 304-357-4767, msp1@mountainstatepress.org. 1978. Poetry, fiction, satire, criticism, plays. "We specialize in regional materials: Appalachian subjects and authors, primarily. We publish book-length mss. of fiction, nonfiction, and poetry. Book must either be written by a West Virginian or having to do with West Virginia." avg. press run 1.5M. Pub'd 1 title 2009; expects 1 title 2010, 1 title 2011. 32 titles listed in the *Small Press Record of Books in Print* (36th Edition, 2010-11). Discounts: 40% to bookstores, 25% gift shops, 10% libraries, schools and churches. 250pp. Reporting time: 2 months or more. Simultaneous submissions accepted: Yes, if informed. Publishes 2% of manuscripts submitted. Payment: negotiable. Copyrights for author. Subjects: Appalachia, Essays, Fiction, History, Novels, Short Stories.

Mountains and Rivers Press, Ce Rosenow, P.O. Box 5389, Eugene, OR 97405, http://mountainsandrivers-press.org, mtns_rivers@hotmail.com. 2001. Poetry. "Mountains and Rivers Press publishes books of poetry that are written in the traditions of Japanese poetry or Objectivist poetry as well as poetry reflecting the relationship between human beings and the natural world." avg. press run 200. Pub'd 2 titles 2009; expects 2 titles 2010, 2 titles 2011. 12 titles listed in the *Small Press Record of Books in Print* (36th Edition, 2010-11). Discounts: 60/40. 40-100pp. Reporting time: 4 months. Simultaneous submissions accepted: No. Payment: payment in author copies. Copyrights for author.

Mountainside Press, Alex Sophian, Publisher, PO Box 407, Shaftsbury, VT 05262, 802-447-7094, Fax 802-447-2611. 1991. "Focus on popular culture and the performing arts." avg. press run 500. Expects 1 title 2010, 2/3 titles 2011. 7 titles listed in the *Small Press Record of Books in Print* (36th Edition, 2010-11). Discounts: 2-4 40%, 5-25 42%, 26-49 46%, 50+ 50%. 288pp. Reporting time: 3 weeks. Simultaneous submissions accepted: yes. Publishes 20% of manuscripts submitted. Payment: 7%. Subjects: Americana, Arts, Culture, Leisure/Recreation, Performing Arts.

MOUSEION, Journal of the Classical Association of Canada/Revue de la Societe Canadienne des Etudes Classiques, University of Calgary Press, M. Joyal, Editor; J. Butrica, Editor; N. Kennell, Editor, University of Calgary Press, Univ. of Calgary, 2500 University Dr. N.W., Calgary, Alberta T2N 1N4, Canada, 403-220-3514, Fax 403-282-0085, ucpmail@ucalgary.ca. 1957. Articles, photos, reviews. "Formerly *Echoes du Monde Classique/Classical Views*. Reports on activities of Canadian classical archaeologists and articles on archaeological subjects, as well as articles and book reviews on classical history and literature." circ. 750. 3/yr. Pub'd 3 issues 2009; expects 3 issues 2010, 3 issues 2011. sub. price Instit. $40 + GST Canada, $40US outside Canada; indiv. $25 + GST Canada, $25US outside Canada; per copy $10 + GST. Back issues: Vol. 26-28 issues are $10 each and $15 per volume. Vol. 29 to present cost $10 each, $27/volume. 150pp. Reporting time: 6 weeks. Copyrighted, does not revert to author. Pub's reviews: 31 in 2009. §Classical studies. Ads: write for information. Subjects: Anthropology, Archaelogy, Classical Studies.

MOUTH: Voice of the Dis-Labeled Nation, Lucy Gwin, Mouth Magazine, 4201 SW 30th Street, Topeka, KS 66614-3203, Fax 785-272-7348. 1989. Articles, photos, cartoons, interviews, letters, news items, non-fiction. "(Send SASE for publishing schedule and guidelines. Only subscribers will be published.) *Mouth* speaks for 58 million Americans who are dis-labeled in one way or another. *Mouth* is known for its flaming exposes of charity's high rollers and bureaucracy's log jammers, for its consumer testing of deadening drugs and behavior modifiers, for its pride, its anger, its humor. *Mouth* is a crash course for Americans on the disability rights movement." circ. 4.2M. 6/yr. Pub'd 6 issues 2009; expects 6 issues 2010, 6 issues 2011. sub. price $16-32-48;

per copy $5; sample $3. Back issues: $5. Discounts: bulk: bundles of 100 $165. 40pp. Reporting time: 21 days. Simultaneous submissions accepted: yes. Publishes 5% of manuscripts submitted. Payment: Editor is unpaid, occasionally we pay $50-75 for items. Copyrighted, reverts to author. §Do-gooderism, eugenics, mercy killing and other helping professional euphemisms. De-institutionalization—or does that make freedom sound too complicated? Ads: none. Subjects: Bigotry, Civil Rights, Disabled, Disease, Euthanasia, Death, Human Rights, Law, Medicine, Politics, Resistance, Social Movements, Sociology.

Moving Parts Press, Felicia Rice, 10699 Empire Grade, Santa Cruz, CA 95060-9474, 408-427-2271. 1977. Poetry, fiction, art, letters, parts-of-novels, long-poems, collages. *"COSMOGONIE INTIME An Intimate Cosmogony*a French/English collaboration between Yves Peyre, Elizabeth R. Jackson, Ray Rice and Felicia Rice, limited edition artists' book published in 2006. *Codex Espangliensis: From Columbus to the Border Patrol* a bilingual collaboration between Enrique Chagoya, Guillermo Gomez-Pena and Felicia Rice, limited editon published by Moving Parts Press in 1998 and trade edition published by City Lights Books in 2000. Much more information at www.movingpartspress.com." avg. press run 75. 17 titles listed in the *Small Press Record of Books in Print* (36th Edition, 2010-11). Discounts: 30%. 45pp. Reporting time: 1-2 months. Payment: 10% copies. Copyrights for author. Subjects: Poetry, Politics.

MSLEXIA, Daneet Steffens, Editor, Mslexia Publications Limited, P.O. Box 656, Newcastle upon Tyne, NE99 1PZ, United Kingdom, +44 (0)191 233 3860. *"Mslexia* is a national magazine for woman writers that was launched in March 1999 with start-up funding from the National Lottery and Northern Arts. No other magazine provides *Mslexia's* unique mix of debate and analysis, advice and inspiration; news, reviews, interviews; competitions, events, courses, grants. All served up with a challenging selection of new poetry and prose.*Mslexia* is read by top authors and absolute beginners. A quarterly masterclass in the business and psychology of writing, it's the essential magazine for women who write." circ. 9000. Quarterly. sub. price Annual Subscriptions. UK: £21.75. Europe: £24. Rest of World: £30.; per copy UK: £5.50. Europe: £6. Rest of World: £7.50.

MUDFISH, Box Turtle Press, Jill Hoffman, Editor in Chief; Stephanie Dickinson, Associate Editor; Rob Cook, Associate Editor; Lawrence Applebaum, Associate Editor; Jennifer Belle, Associate Editor; Matt Sapio, Associate Editor; Paul Wuensche, Associate Editor; Marina Rubin, Associate Editor; Michael Montlack, Associate Editor, 184 Franklin Street, Ground Floor, New York, NY 10013, 212-219-9278, www.mudfish.org, mudfishmag@aol.com. 1983. Poetry, fiction, art, photos. "In addition to Mudfish, we publish Mudfish Individual Poet Series, and the latest issue is #6, marbles by Mary du Passage. Mudfish Poetry Prize awards the best poem, chosen by a judge, $1000 and publication in Mudfish; there are also 2nd and 3rd place poems published in the magazine. Every poem submitted is considered for publication. The 10th competition will be announced shortly." circ. 1.2M. 1/yr. Pub'd 1 issue 2009; expects 1 issue 2010, 1 issue 2011. 6 titles listed in the *Small Press Record of Books in Print* (36th Edition, 2010-11). sub. price $24 for 2 yr. subscription.$12 for Mudfish 16.; sample $12 plus $3.50 shipping and handling. Back issues: see website. 200pp. Reporting time: immediately to 6 months. Simultaneous submissions accepted: no. Publishes 5% of manuscripts submitted. Payment: 1 copy of magazine. Copyrighted, reverts to author. Ads: $250/$125. Subject: Poetry.

MUDLARK, William Slaughter, English Department, University of North Florida, Jacksonville, FL 32224-2645, mudlark@unf.edu, www.unf.edu/mudlark. 1995. Poetry, interviews, criticism, long-poems. "*Mudlark* is 'never in and never out of print.' As our full name, *Mudlark: An Electronic Journal of Poetry & Poetics*, suggests, we will consider accomplished work that locates itself anywhere on the spectrum of contemporary practice. We want poems, of course, but we want essays, too, that make us read poems (and write them?) differently somehow. Although we are not innocent, we do imagine ourselves capable of suprise. *Mudlark* has an ISSN (1081-3500), is refereed, copyrighted, archived and distributed free on the World Wide Web. Some recent contributors: John Allman, Denise Duhamel, Taylor Graham, Susan Kelly-DeWitt, Frederick Pollack, and Peter Waldor." 5M discrete visitors per month. Irregular but frequent. sub. price free (online); per copy free; sample free. Back issues: free. Pages vary. Reporting time: no less than one day, no more than one month. We'd rather not accept simultaneous submissions because our turn-around time is short, but we will if notified with submission. Payment: In *Mudlark* poetry is free. Our authors give us their work and we, in turn, give it to our readers. What is the coin of poetry's realm? Poetry is a gift economy. One of the things we can do at *Mudlark* to pay our authors for their work is point to it here and there, wherever else it is. We can tell our readers how to find it, how to subscribe to it, and how to buy it if it is for sale. Copyrighted, reverts to author. Subjects: Criticism, Essays, Interviews, Poetry, Translation.

MULTICULTURAL EDUCATION, Caddo Gap Press, Alan H. Jones, Editor; Heather L. Hazuka, Editor, 3145 Geary Boulevard, Ste. 275, San Francisco, CA 94118, 415-392-1911. 1993. Articles, art, photos, interviews, reviews, letters, news items, non-fiction. "*Multicultural Education* features articles, reviews, listings of resources, and a variety of other materials geared to assist with multicultural education programs in schools and with development and definition of the field." circ. 5M. 4/yr. Pub'd 3 issues 2009; expects 4 issues 2010, 4 issues 2011. sub. price $50 individuals, $100 institutions, $40 students; per copy $15; sample free. Back issues:

$10. Discounts: can be arranged. 40pp. Reporting time: 2 months. Publishes 25% of manuscripts submitted. Payment: only for solicited materials. Copyrighted, reverts to author. Pub's reviews: 12 in 2009. §Anything involved with multicultural education. Ads: $500/$300/$400 2/3 page/$200 1/3 page/$150 1/6 page/$50 1 inch. Subject: Education.

Multi-Media Publications Inc., Box 58043, Rosslynn RPO, Oshawa, Ontario L1J 8L6, Canada, Ph: (905) 986-5848; Toll-Free: (866) 721-1540 (Canada & USA Only); Fax: (905) 986-5777. Email: orders@mmpubs.com, Web: www.mmpubs.com. 1988. Fiction, photos, non-fiction. "Publishing business and careers-related non-fiction under the Multi-Media Publications imprint, entrepreneurship titles under the Impact Publications imprint, and both fiction (romance, sci-fi, mystery, etc.) and general trade non-fiction under the Crystal Dreams Publishing imprint. Formats include print books, ebooks, audiobooks (both downloadable and on CD), and DVDs. Manuscripts currently being accepted. Guidelines at www.mmpubs.com." Pub'd 20 titles 2009; expects 28 titles 2010, 25 titles 2011. 66 titles listed in the *Small Press Record of Books in Print* (36th Edition, 2010-11). 200-300pp. Reporting time: 2 weeks. Simultaneous submissions accepted: yes. Payment: 20% royalty. No author fees. Copyrights for author. Subjects: Audio/Video, Business & Economics, Careers, Consulting, Erotica, Fantasy, Fiction, Horror, Leadership, Management, Motivation, Success, Mystery, Romance, Science Fiction, Speaking.

Multnomah Publishers, Inc., Larry Libby, Rod Morris; David Webb, Editorial Director, David Kopp, 601 N. Larch St., Sisters, OR 97759-9320, 541-549-1144, Fax 541-549-8048. 1987. Fiction, non-fiction. "Imprints: Multnomah, Multnomah Gift, Multnomah Fiction." avg. press run 15M. Pub'd 100 titles 2009; expects 100 titles 2010, 100 titles 2011. No titles listed in the *Small Press Record of Books in Print* (36th Edition, 2010-11). Discounts: 40%. 225pp. Reporting time: 6 weeks. Simultaneous submissions accepted: yes. Publishes 1% of manuscripts submitted. Payment: varies. Copyrights for author. Subjects: Christianity, Fiction, Religion.

Munsey Music, T. Munsey, Box 511, Richmond Hill, Ontario L4C 4Y8, Canada, 905-737-0208; www.pathcom.com/~munsey. 1970. "Include SASE if return of submission is required. Only accept fantasy/science fiction." avg. press run 5M. Pub'd 1 title 2009; expects 2 titles 2010, 4 titles 2011. 7 titles listed in the *Small Press Record of Books in Print* (36th Edition, 2010-11). Discounts: 1-4 copies no discount, 5-10 20%, 11-20 30%, 21-40 35%, 41+ 40%. 250pp. Reporting time: 6-12 months. Simultaneous submissions accepted: yes. Payment: industry. Copyrights for author. Subjects: Fantasy, Fiction, Inspirational, Science Fiction, Spiritual, Young Adult.

MURDER CROWS, Osric Publishing, Chris Herdt, 1705 13th Ave S Unit A, Birmingham, AL 35205. 2009. Poetry, fiction. "All submissions should be sent via the Web. See www.murdercrows.com for details." circ. 100. 4/yr. Expects 1 issue 2010, 4 issues 2011. sub. price $12; per copy $4; sample $4. Back issues: $4. Discounts: 5+ copies 50%. 28pp. Reporting time: 3 months. Simultaneous submissions accepted: Yes. Publishes 2% of manuscripts submitted. Not copyrighted. Subjects: Fiction, Poetry, Prose.

Murder Slim Press (see also THE SAVAGE KICK LITERARY MAGAZINE), Steve Hussy, Richard White, 129 Trafalgar Road West, Gt. Yarmouth, Norfolk NR31 8AD, United Kingdom, www.murderslim.com/ publications.html. 2005. Fiction, articles, interviews, non-fiction. "CURRENT & UPCOMING AUTHORS: Mark SaFranko, Tommy Trantino, Robert McGowan, Steve Hussy. PLEASE SEND: Works dealing with any passionately held emotions and/or alternative viewpoints. These may well entail drink, sex, violence, bad language and any activity outside of the mainstream. Sleazy tales are very much encouraged and form the basis of Murder Slim Press.Real-life stories are preferred, unless work is distinctively extreme within the crime or war genres.We recommend that you have read 'The Savage Kick' before you submit. DO NOT SEND: Mainstream fiction or Oprah-style fiction. Internet/chat language or teen issues. Any genre fiction including horror, fantasy, sci-fi, western, erotica, etc. And please... no excessive Shakespearean language, surrealism or overworked irony. Also, we do not accept any poetry submissions." avg. press run 500. Pub'd 2 titles 2009; expects 3 titles 2010, 4 titles 2011. No titles listed in the *Small Press Record of Books in Print* (36th Edition, 2010-11). Discounts: 5-9 copies = 20% of RRP (no including postage)10+ copies = 25% of RRP (not including postage). 220pp. Reporting time: 1-4 weeks. Simultaneous submissions accepted: Yes. Publishes 2% of manuscripts submitted. Payment: For Murder Slim Press novels: Publisher's cut recoups per book printing cost & postage costs, then royalties are split 50/50 between author and publisher. Copyrights for author. Subjects: Alcohol, Alcoholism, Americana, Anarchist, Autobiography, Beat, Charles Bukowski, Comics, Crime, Death & Dying, Drugs, Fiction, Libertarian, Prose, Short Stories, War.

The Muse Media (see also THE GREAT AMERICAN POETRY SHOW, A SERIAL POETRY ANTHOLOGY), Larry Ziman, PO Box 69506, West Hollywood, CA 90069, 323-656-6126, www.tgaps.net. 2002. Poetry. "Recent contributors: Julie M. Tate, Alan Catlin, Pamela Miller, Doug Draime, Carrie Jerrell, Alan Britt, Sarah Brown Weitzman, Philip Wexler, Ellaraine Lockie, Fredrick Zydek, Stephanie Dickinson, Doug Ramspeck, Maureen Tolman Flannery, Leonard Orr, Regina Murray Brault, Robert Hoeft, Lyn Lifshin, Brad Johnson, Carol Carpenter, Kevin Pilkington, and Patricia Polak. We need to see a lot of poetry to find what we want to publish. So flood us with poems. We publish poems not poets. We'll accept good poems from new as well as established poets." avg. press run 1000. Expects 1 title 2010. 2 titles listed in the *Small Press Record of Books in Print* (36th Edition, 2010-11). Discounts: 40% for bookstores, retailers; 15% for agents, jobbers; wholesalers, distributors negotiable. 174pp. Reporting time: 1-12 weeks. Simultaneous submissions accepted: Yes. Publishes 1% of manuscripts submitted. Payment: Each contributor receives one copy of each issue he/she appears in. Does not copyright for author. Subject: Poetry.

Muse World Media Group, Roan Kaufman, PO Box 55094, Madison, WI 53705, 608-238-6681. 1990. Poetry, fiction, articles, interviews, news items, non-fiction. "We are actively seeking new titles. We also do subsiday publishing and co-publishing. In the past few years we've published books on commodity trading, business trade books, novels, and relationship books. So, we're open to publishing a variety of materials." avg. press run 2M - 10,000. Pub'd 2 titles 2009; expects 10 titles 2010. No titles listed in the *Small Press Record of Books in Print* (36th Edition, 2010-11). 150-250pp. Reporting time: 2 months. Simultaneous submissions accepted: yes. Publishes 10% of manuscripts submitted. Payment: 25% royalty. Copyrights for author. Subjects: Anarchist, Avant-Garde, Experimental Art, Engineering, How-To, Humor, Music, Novels, Nutrition, Occult, Reference, Relationships, Science, Sex, Sexuality, Writers/Writing.

MUSE: A Quarterly Journal of The Lit, Judith Mansour-Thomas, Editor; Ray McNiece, Poetry Editor; Peggy Latkovich, Assistant Editor; Alenka Banco, Art Editor, 2570 Superior Ave., Suite 203, Cleveland, OH 44114, phone: 216.694.0000, fax: 216.694.0003, website: www.the-lit.org, email; judith@the-lit.org, peggy@the-lit.org, art submissions: images4muse@the-lit.org, poetry/prose submissions: words4muse@the-lit.org, advertising; advertising4muse@the-lit.org. 1987. Poetry, fiction, articles, art, photos, interviews, satire, criticism, reviews, parts-of-novels, long-poems, plays, non-fiction. "Only service pieces published: poetry, fiction, essays, interviews of writers, focus on aspect of writing in Ohio, reviews of books, writer's conferences. Major piece 2,000 words; focus piece 1,500 words; column 800 words; book review 400-500 words. Annual writing contest for poetry, fiction, nonfiction and writers on writing, open to Ohio residents. Published by The Lit." circ. 1218. 4/yr. Pub'd 6 issues 2009; expects 4 issues 2010, 4 issues 2011. sub. price $35 individual, $45 institution; per copy $9; sample $5. Back issues: $5. 36pp. Reporting time: 1 month. Simultaneous submissions accepted: yes. Publishes 5% of manuscripts submitted. Copyrighted, reverts to author. Pub's reviews: 6 in 2009. §Books or magazines published in Ohio or by Ohio writers. Ads: Back cover: $500/ Nonprofit $400 Full page: $400/ Nonprofit $300 Half page: $200/ Nonprofit $150 Quarter page: $100/ Nonprofit $75 Discounts offered for repeat advertising. Subjects: Arts, Book Reviewing, Culture, Drama, Essays, Fiction, Journals, Literary Review, Literature (General), Magazines, Memoirs, Ohio, Poetry, Short Stories, Writers/Writing.

Museon Publishing, Borislav Stanic, P O Box 17095, Beverly Hills, CA 90209-2095, phone/fax: (323) 936-8151, www.museonbooks.com. 1996. Non-fiction. Expects 1 title 2010, 2 titles 2011. 1 title listed in the *Small Press Record of Books in Print* (36th Edition, 2010-11). Discounts: 2-4 copies 20%5-9 copies 40%10-49 copies 42%50-99 copies 44%100+ copies 46%. 300-500pp. Reporting time: 2 weeks. Simultaneous submissions accepted: Yes. Does not copyright for author. Subjects: Arts, California, North America, Travel.

Music City Publishing, P. Hunter, P.O. Box 41696, Nashville, TN 37204-1696, www.musiccitypublishing.com. 1987. Non-fiction. "Music City Publishing promotes Free Enterprise, Personal Responsibility, and Business Ownership. We support the Constitution of the United States and the Holy Bible, and publish works that promote them." Expects 1 title 2010, 3 titles 2011. No titles listed in the *Small Press Record of Books in Print* (36th Edition, 2010-11). Discounts: 25-99 35% discount. 100-499 45% discount. 500+ 55% discount. 272pp. Reporting time: One month. Simultaneous submissions accepted: Yes. Publishes 5% of manuscripts submitted. Payment: No advances. Author royalties: 15% of retail price. Quarterly payments. Copyrights for author. Subjects: Americana, Autobiography, Biography, Family, Finances, Humor, Inspirational, Memoirs, Mentoring/Coaching, Non-Fiction, Quotations, Relationships, Self-Help, Speaking, Storytelling.

MUSIC PERCEPTION, University of California Press, Lola L. Cuddy, Editor; Katie Spiller, Managing Editor, Univ of CA Press, 2000 Center Street, Suite 303, Berkeley, CA 94704-1223, 510-643-7154. 1983. Reviews, music, non-fiction. "Editorial address: Department of Psychology, Humphrey Hall, 62 Arch St., Room 232, Queen's University, Kingston, Ontario, K7L 3N6 Canada." circ. 699. 4/yr. Pub'd 4 issues 2009; expects 4 issues 2010, 4 issues 2011. sub. price $58 indiv., $233 instit., $35 student (+ $20 air freight); per copy $21 indiv., $63 instit., $21 student; sample free. Back issues: same as single copy price. Discounts: foreign subs. agents 10%, one-time orders 10+ 30%, standing orders (bookstores): 1-99 40%, 100+ 50%. 128pp. Copyrighted, does not revert to author. Pub's reviews: 20 in 2009. §Music, physical psychology, psychology of perception. Ads: $295/$220. Subjects: Mathematics, Music, Psychology.

MUSIC THEORY SPECTRUM, University of California Press, Brian Alegant, Editor; Brian Hyer, Reviews Editor, University of California Press, 2000 Center St., Suite 303, Berkeley, CA 94704-1223, 510-643-7154. 1978. Articles, reviews. "Editorial address: Oberlin College Conservatory, 77 West College Street, Oberlin, OH 44074-1449. Copyrighted by the Society for Music Theory." circ. 1458. 2/yr. Pub'd 2 issues 2009; expects 2 issues 2010, 2 issues 2011. sub. price $45 indiv., $104 inst., $20 student; per copy $32 indiv., $59 inst., $20 student; sample same as single copy. Discounts: foreign subs. agents 10%, 10+ one-time orders 30%. 144pp. Copyrighted, does not revert to author. Pub's reviews: approx. 8 in 2009. §musicology: aesthetics, the history of theory, linear analysis, atonal theory, networks, and narratology. Ads: $320. Subject: Music.

My Heart Yours Publishing, Tanya Davis, Jeannine Nyangira, PO Box 4975, Wheaton, IL 60187, (630) 452-2809, www.myheartyours.com, tanya@myheartyours.com, jeannine@myheartyours.com. 2004. Fiction, non-fiction. "Our purpose is to share our hearts in order to help form a wave of people walking in the Truth. As we truthfully deal with our inner beings and then share our hearts with others, both parties are then healed. Then those people will desire Truth on the inside, be healed, and then share with someone else. Eventually, this will create a healing wave—emotionally, spiritually, mentally, and physically. So far we have worked with memoir, fiction, and creative nonfiction. Our first book, *May I Please Speak with my Father,* was written by Tanya Davis and explores how women's relationships with their dads impacts their relationship with their heavenly Father. Several women contributed to this project, including editor Jeannine Nyangira." avg. press run 1800. Expects 2 titles 2010, 5 titles 2011. No titles listed in the *Small Press Record of Books in Print* (36th Edition, 2010-11). Discounts: 2-4 copies 20%, 5-9 copies 30%, 10-24 copies 40%, 25-49 copies 42%, 50-74 copies 44%, 100-199 copies 48%, 200+ copies 50%. 100-160pp. Reporting time: 2 months. Simultaneous submissions accepted: Yes. Publishes 70% of manuscripts submitted. Payment: To be discussed. Copyrights for author. Subjects: Children, Youth, Christianity, Essays, Family, Fiction, Journals, Memoirs, Non-Fiction, Religion, Spiritual.

MY TABLE: Houston's Dining Magazine, Lazywood Press, Teresa Byrne-Dodge, 1908 Harold Street, Houston, TX 77098-1502, 713-529-5500, teresa.byrnedodge@my-table.com, www.my-table.com. 1994. Articles, art, criticism, reviews, non-fiction. "We are region-specific (i.e. we write about food, wine and restaurants of interest to readers in greater Houston area)." circ. 22M. 6/yr. Pub'd 6 issues 2009; expects 6 issues 2010, 6 issues 2011. 1 title listed in the *Small Press Record of Books in Print* (36th Edition, 2010-11). sub. price $24; per copy $4.50; sample $7. Back issues: $7 each. Discounts: please call for schedule. 64-72pp. Reporting time: 2-3 weeks. Simultaneous submissions accepted: yes. Publishes 25% of manuscripts submitted. Payment: yes. Copyrighted, reverts to author. Pub's reviews: 25 in 2009. §Cookbooks, books on food, wine, and being at table. Ads: $1,980/$400. Subjects: Cooking, Dining, Restaurants, Essays, Food, Eating, Humor, Wine, Wineries.

Myriad Press, Gloria Stern, 12535 Chandler Blvd. #3, N. Hollywood, CA 91607-1934, 805-750-1423. 1993. Fiction, parts-of-novels. "Inquiry first." Pub'd 2 titles 2009. 2 titles listed in the *Small Press Record of Books in Print* (36th Edition, 2010-11). Volume discounts. 200pp. Reporting time: 10-12 weeks. Simultaneous submissions accepted: yes. Payment: via contract. Does not copyright for author. Subjects: Adolescence, Criticism, Culture, Family, Fiction, Novels, Publishing, Writers/Writing.

MYSTERY ISLAND MAGAZINE, Mystery Island Publications, Bradley Mason Hamlin, Publisher; Lucy Hell, Office Manager, Mystery Island, 384 Windward Way, Sacramento, CA 95831-2420, brad@mysteryisland.net, http://www.mysteryisland.net. Mystery Island began publishing in 2002. A new online MYSTERY ISLAND MAGAZINE is scheduled for Summer 2008. Poetry, fiction, articles, art, cartoons, interviews, criticism, reviews, music, non-fiction. "Mystery Island Publications publishes articles, interviews, reviews, poetry/fiction pertaining to: punk rock, comic books, classic TV/Film, pulps, monsters, and hot chicks." Back issues: see website. Reporting time: 1 week to 1 month. Simultaneous submissions accepted: No. Payment: varies. Copyrighted, reverts to author. Pub's reviews. Ads: Contact publisher. Subjects: Crime, Cults, Entertainment, Essays, Fiction, Horror, Literature (General), Metaphysics, Movies, Mystery, Non-Fiction, Poetry, Science Fiction, Short Stories, Supernatural.

Mystery Island Publications (see also MYSTERY ISLAND MAGAZINE), Brad Hamlin, 384 Windward Way, Sacramento, CA 95831-2420, blacksharkpress@mysteryisland.net www.mysteryisland.net. 2003. Poetry, fiction, articles, art, interviews, non-fiction. "Mystery Island Publications publishes three ongoing series: Monster Zipper, a metaphysical crime series created and written by Bradley Mason Hamlin (looking for art based on characters in the series, see website to order issues: www.mysteryisland.net/monster), Mystery Island Magazine (each issue different theme for poetry, short stories, and articles, see website: www.mysteryisland.net/magazine), and Mystery Island Double Feature (genre based short stories, publishing two writers/two stories each issue, see webiste: www.mysteryisland.net/double)." avg. press run 500. Pub'd 3 titles 2009; expects 10 titles 2010, 10 titles 2011. No titles listed in the *Small Press Record of Books in Print* (36th Edition, 2010-11). Discounts: 2 or more copies 20%. 20-24pp. Reporting time: Response time: 1 week to 1 month. Simultaneous submissions accepted: No. Payment: Mystery Island Double Feature pays $10.00 per short story + contributor copies. Copyright remains with author. Subjects: Anarchist, California, Comics, Cults, Fiction, Folklore, Haiku, Rudyard Kipling, Music, Occult, Poetry, Prison, Psychology, Religion, Science Fiction.

MYSTERY READERS JOURNAL, Janet A. Rudolph, PO Box 8116, Berkeley, CA 94707-8116, 510-845-3600, www.mysteryreaders.org. 1985. Articles, art, interviews, criticism, reviews, news items. "Each issue deals primarily with specific themes in mystery. 2001: New England Mysteries, Partners in Crime, Oxford, Cambridge. 2002: Pacific Northwest Mysteries, Culinary Crime, Southern Mysteries, Music and

Mystery.'' circ. 2M. 4/yr. Pub'd 4 issues 2009; expects 4 issues 2010, 4 issues 2011. sub. price $39 everyone in US/Canada, $50 overseas airmail; per copy $12; sample $12. Back issues: $12/issue US/Canada; $15 overseas. 88pp. Reporting time: 2 months. Simultaneous submissions accepted: yes. Publishes 80% of manuscripts submitted. Payment: free issue. Copyrighted, does not revert to author. Pub's reviews: 600 in 2009. §Mystery fiction, literary review magazines. No ads. Subjects: Book Collecting, Bookselling, Book Reviewing, Literary Review, Mystery.

THE MYSTERY REVIEW, Barbara Davey, PO Box 233, Colborne, Ont. K0K 1S0, Canada, 613-475-4440, Fax 613-475-3400, mystrev@reach.net, www.themysteryreview.com. 1992. Poetry, articles, art, interviews, criticism, reviews, letters. ''Magazine content is geared to the interests of mystery readers, reviews of mystery and suspense titles, interviews with mystery authors, word games and puzzles related to mystery.'' circ. 7M. 4/yr. Pub'd 4 issues 2009; expects 4 issues 2010, 4 issues 2011. sub. price $25 US in the United States; per copy $6.95; sample $7.50 (including p/h). Back issues: $5 + p/h charges (see website for details). 76pp. Reporting time: 1 month. Simultaneous submissions accepted: no. Payment: honorarium only. Copyrighted, does not revert to author. Pub's reviews: 50 in 2009. §Mystery, suspense, thrillers, adult. Ads: contact magazine (see website). Subjects: Crime, Sherlock Holmes, Interviews, Literary Review, Mystery, Reviews.

•**MYSTERY SCENE MAGAZINE,** 331 W. 57th Street, Suite 148, New York, NY 10019-3101, katestine@mysteryscenemag.com. ''Established in 1985, Mystery Scene Magazine is the oldest, largest, and most authoritative guide to the crime fiction genre. Our lively, expert coverage ranges from past mystery masters to today's top talents and tomorrow's bright new stars. We report on novels, of course, but also films, TV shows, audio-books, kid's mysteries, short stories, reference works, and much more.''

Mystic Jaguar Publishing, Robert Brooks, 10821 Margate Rd. Suite A, Silver Spring, MD 20901-1615, 301-385-6787, 800-590-7583, Fax 800-590-7583. 2007. Fiction. avg. press run 5000. Expects 1 title 2010, 1-2 titles 2011. 1 title listed in the *Small Press Record of Books in Print* (36th Edition, 2010-11). 40pp. Copyrights for author. Subject: Children, Youth.

N

N: NUDE & NATURAL, Lee Baxandall, Founder; Nicky Hoffman, Editor, PO Box 132, Oshkosh, WI 54903, 920-426-5009. 1981. Poetry, fiction, articles, art, photos, cartoons, letters, news items. ''Must relate to body acceptance and nude recreation.'' circ. 25M. 4/yr. Pub'd 4 issues 2009; expects 4 issues 2010, 4 issues 2011. sub. price $53; per copy $9 plus s/h; sample same. Back issues: same. Discounts: 40%, inquire. 124pp. Reporting time: 1 week. Simultaneous submissions accepted: no. Publishes 50% of manuscripts submitted. Payment: small. Copyrighted, reverts to author. Pub's reviews: 8 in 2009. §Issues on nudity. Ads: $975 4CP/$490 4C 1/2 page/$625 BWP/$350 bw 1/2 page. Subjects: Health, History, Lifestyles, New Age, Photography, Travel.

Nada Press (see also BIG SCREAM), David Cope, 2782 Dixie S.W., Grandville, MI 49418, 616-531-1442. 1974. Poetry, fiction, art. ''Poets and writers *must* include email address and SASE with their submissions and make sure there's enough postage on the envelope. I use email to ask authors accepted for publication to send electronic copies of their work.'' avg. press run 100. Pub'd 1 title 2009; expects 1 title 2010, 1 title 2011. 1 title listed in the *Small Press Record of Books in Print* (36th Edition, 2010-11). 60-70pp. Reporting time: 1-3 months. Simultaneous submissions accepted: yes. Publishes 2% of manuscripts submitted. Payment: copies. Subjects: Fiction, Poetry.

•**Naissance, chapbooks by chapbookpublisher.com,** Dan Waber, 443 Main Street, 2nd FL, Kingston, PA 18704, 570-762-6140. 2008. Poetry, fiction, articles, art, photos, cartoons, interviews, satire, criticism, reviews, letters, parts-of-novels, long-poems, collages, plays, concrete art, non-fiction. ''We are interested in the chapbook as a compositional unit. Just as some ideas are sonnet shaped, some ideas are novel shaped, and some ideas are blog shaped, we believe that some ideas are chapbook shaped, and we endeavor to publish the best of those that come our way.'' Pub'd 4 titles 2009; expects 8 titles 2010, 12 titles 2011. No titles listed in the *Small Press Record of Books in Print* (36th Edition, 2010-11). Discounts: 50%. 40pp. Reporting time: 24 hours. Simultaneous submissions accepted: Yes. Publishes 10% of manuscripts submitted. Payment: 10 payment copies, and authors can buy any title (including their own) for 1/2 off. Does not copyright for author.

NAMBLA BULLETIN, Joe Power, PO Box 174, Midtown Station, New York, NY 10018, 212-631-1194, arnoldschoen@yahoo.com. 1979. Poetry, fiction, articles, art, photos, cartoons, interviews, satire, criticism, reviews, letters, parts-of-novels, collages, news items, non-fiction. circ. 2.2M. 4/yr. Pub'd 4 issues 2009; expects 4 issues 2010, 4 issues 2011. sub. price $35 US & Canada, $50 international; per copy $5; sample $5.

Back issues: $5. Discounts: 50%. 24pp. Simultaneous submissions accepted: yes. Publishes 25% of manuscripts submitted. Payment: none. Copyrighted, reverts to author. Pub's reviews: 15 in 2009. §Gay, youth liberation, man/boy love. Subjects: Adolescence, Current Affairs, Gay, Politics, Sex, Sexuality, Young Adult.

Nanticoke Books, Hal Roth, Box 333, Vienna, MD 21869-0333, 410-376-2144. 1995. Fiction, photos, satire, non-fiction. "Regional - Chesapeake Bay/Delmarva history and folklore." avg. press run 3M. Pub'd 1 title 2009; expects 1 title 2010, 1 title 2011. 11 titles listed in the *Small Press Record of Books in Print* (36th Edition, 2010-11). Discounts: 40-50%. 224pp. Reporting time: We do not solicit manuscripts.

NARRATIVE MAGAZINE, Carol Edgarian, Editor; Tom Jenks, Editor, 2130 Fillmore Street #233, San Francisco, CA 94115. "Looking for submissions of previously unpublished mss of all lengths, from short-short stories to complete book-length works. Poetry, fiction, and nonfiction, including stories, novels, novellas, personal essays, humor, sketches, memoirs, literary biographies, commentary, reportage, interviews, and features of interest to readers who take pleasure in stroytelling and imaginative prose. On-line submissions only." No titles listed in the *Small Press Record of Books in Print* (36th Edition, 2010-11). Payment: 750-200 words: $150-$350; 2M to 10M words: $350-$1,000; book-length: $1,000+.

The Narrative Press, Vickie Zimmer, Editor; Michael Bond, Publisher, 2041 East A Street, Torrington, WY 82240, 800-315-9005, Fax 307-532-3495, service@narrativepress.com, www.narrativepress.com. 2001. Non-fiction. "The Narrative Press publishes true first person accounts of adventure and exploration." avg. press run 20-25. Expects 3 titles 2010, 4 titles 2011. 10 titles listed in the *Small Press Record of Books in Print* (36th Edition, 2010-11). Discounts: trade/classroom 20%. 350pp. Reporting time: 2-4 months. Publishes a variable % of manuscripts submitted. Copyrights for author. Subjects: Autobiography, Earth, Natural History, History, Marine Life, Military, Veterans, Nature, Non-Fiction, Travel.

National Economic Research Associates, Inc., Gregory Leonard, Lauren Stiroh, 50 Main Street, 14th Floor, White Plains, NY 10606, 617-621-6289. 1961. avg. press run 3000. Pub'd 1 title 2009; expects 1 title 2010, 1 title 2011. No titles listed in the *Small Press Record of Books in Print* (36th Edition, 2010-11). Discounts: 10+ copies 25%. 300pp.

NATIONAL MASTERS NEWS, Jerry Wojcik, Editor; Suzy Hess, Publisher, PO Box 1117, Orangevale, CA 95662-1117, 541-343-7716, Fax 541-345-2436, natmanews@aol.com. 1977. Articles, art, photos, interviews, satire, criticism, reviews, letters, news items, non-fiction. "The *National Masters News* is the bible of the Masters Athletics Program. It is the only national publication devoted exclusively to track & field, race walking and long distance running for men and women over age 30. An official publication of USA Track & Field, each month it delivers 32-48 pages of results, schedules, entry blanks, age records, rankings, photos, articles, training tips. Columns are about 1M words; anything of interest to over-age-30 performer/individual. Recent contributors: Mike Tymn, Hal Higdon, Dr. John Pagliano." circ. 8M. 12/yr. Pub'd 12 issues 2009; expects 12 issues 2010, 12 issues 2011. sub. price $28; per copy $3.00. Back issues: $3.00 plus $2.00 for each order. Discounts: http://www.nationalmastersnews.com. 37pp. Reporting time: 15-30 days. Simultaneous submissions accepted: yes. Publishes 60% of manuscripts submitted. Payment: none. Copyrighted, reverts to author. Pub's reviews: 3 in 2009. §Athletics for over-age-30 performer in track & field, long distance running, and racewalking. Ads: $630/$420/$2. Subject: Sports, Outdoors.

THE NATIONAL POETRY REVIEW, C.J. Sage, Editor; Ashley Capps, Assistant Editor; Jill Alexander Essbaum, Assistant Editor, PO Box 2080, Aptos, CA 95001-2080, website: www.nationalpoetryreview.com, Submissions: tnprsubmissions@yahoo.com, info: editor@nationalpoetryreview.com. 2002. Poetry, art, criticism, reviews. "TNPR READS UNSOLICITED SUBMISSIONS ONLY DURING DECEMBER, JANUARY, & FEBRUARY. CURRENT SUBSCRIBERS MAY SUBMIT OUTSIDE THE READING PERIOD SO LONG AS THEY DO NOT ABUSE THAT PRIVILEGE. TNPR CONSIDERS ONLY EMAILED SUBMISSIONS. Recent contributors include Martha Zweig, Larissa Szporluk, Jennifer Michael Hecht, Ted Kooser, Angela Vogel, Bob Hicok, C. Dale Young, Reginald Shepherd, Bruce Bond, Margot Schilpp, et cetera. TNPR YEARLY OFFERS THE ANNIE FINCH PRIZE FOR POETRY AND THE LAUREATE PRIZE FOR POETRY AS WELL AS THE NATIONAL POETRY REVIEW BOOK PRIZE SERIES. See website for complete guidelines." 1/yr. Pub'd 1 issue 2009; expects 1 issue 2010, 1 issue 2011. 8 titles listed in the *Small Press Record of Books in Print* (36th Edition, 2010-11). sub. price $15; per copy $15; sample $15. Discounts: for benefactors. 108pp. Reporting time: Up to 3 months. Simultaneous submissions accepted: Yes, with note to that effect in cover letter and immediate notice if work is accepted elsewhere. Publishes Less than 1% of manuscripts submitted. Payment: One copy. Also offers a yearly book prize through The National Poetry Review Book Prize series as well as single poem prizes via the Finch Prize for Poetry, and The Laureate Prize for Poetry. Please refer to website for guidelines and rules. Copyrights. TNPR acquires first serial rights; reprint rights, with acknowledgment to The National Poetry Review, revert to author on publication. Pub's reviews. §Books of poetry may be submitted to TNPR for short review consideration. See website for instructions on submitting book reviews and/or books for review consideration. Subject: Poetry.

National Writers Press, Anita E. Whelchel, President,C.E.O., 17011 Lincoln Ave., #421, Parker, CO 80134, 720-851-1944, Fax 303-841-2607, www.nationalwriters.com. 1970. Fiction, non-fiction. avg. press run 1M. Pub'd 2 titles 2009; expects 10 titles 2010, 12 titles 2011. 18 titles listed in the *Small Press Record of Books in Print* (36th Edition, 2010-11). Discounts: 55% for bulk orders. 150pp. Reporting time: 2 months. Simultaneous submissions accepted: yes. Publishes 50% of manuscripts submitted. Payment: none. Copyrights for author. Subjects: Alcohol, Alcoholism, Current Affairs, Fiction, How-To, Non-Fiction, Novels.

Native West Press, Yvette A. Schnoeker-Shorb, Editor; Terril L. Shorb, Editor, PO Box 12227, Prescott, AZ 86304, 928-771-8376, nativewestpres@cableone.net, www.nativewestpress.com. 1996. Poetry, art, photos, interviews, non-fiction. "We irregularly publish small collections that help to enhance awareness of natural biodiversity and particularly of noncharismatic creatures native to the American West. Poets and essayists are from the arts, sciences, social sciences, and education. Queries only. Include SASE. (Or see our website.) Unsolicited manuscripts for anthologies are read only in response to our Calls for Submissions in either *Small Press Review* or *Poets & Writers Magazine*. Recent contributors include Jeffrey A. Lockwood, Joanne E. Lauck, Robert Michael Pyle, Elisavietta Ritchie, Kenneth Pobo, Carol N. Kanter, Antler, CB Follett, Philip Miller, and Sara Littlecrow-Russell." avg. press run 1M. Pub'd 1 title 2009; expects 1 title 2010, 1 title 2011. 4 titles listed in the *Small Press Record of Books in Print* (36th Edition, 2010-11). Discounts: 40% trade (5+ copies), libraries 25%. 90pp. Reporting time: 6 months. Simultaneous submissions accepted: no. Publishes 2% of manuscripts submitted. Payment: contributor copies. Copyrights for author. Subjects: Animals, Anthology, Earth, Natural History, Nature, The West.

NATURAL BRIDGE, Kenneth E. Harrison Jr., Editor; Steven Schreiner, Editorial Board; Howard Schwartz, Editorial Board; Mary Troy, Editorial Board; Eamonn Wall, Editorial Board; Jennifer McKenzie, Editorial Board; Nanora Sweet, Editorial Board; John Dalton, Editorial Board, English Dept., Univ. of Missouri, One University Blvd., St. Louis, MO 63121, natural@umsl.edu, www.umsl.edu/~natural. 1999. Poetry, fiction, non-fiction. "Submit only during these two periods: July 1-August 31, and Nov. 1-Dec. 31. No electronic submissions." 2/yr. Pub'd 2 issues 2009; expects 2 issues 2010, 2 issues 2011. sub. price $15; per copy $8; sample $8. 200pp. Reporting time: 5 months. Simultaneous submissions accepted: yes. Publishes 5% of manuscripts submitted. Payment: two copies & 1 year subscription. Copyrighted, reverts to author. Ads: $100/$50/exchange. Subjects: Essays, Fiction, Non-Fiction, Poetry, Prose, Short Stories, Translation.

NATURAL LIFE, Life Media, Wendy Priesnitz, Box 112, Niagara Falls, NY 14304-0112, 416-260-0303, email: natural@life.ca, web: www.NaturalLifeMagazine.com. 1976. "An environmental lifestyles magazine that circulates in USA and Canada." circ. 35M. 6/yr. Pub'd 6 issues 2009; expects 6 issues 2010, 6 issues 2011. sub. price $27; per copy $4.95; sample $4.95. Back issues: $4.95. 44pp. Simultaneous submissions accepted: no. Publishes 10% of manuscripts submitted. Payment: none. Ads: $1200/page, no classifieds. Subjects: Business & Economics, Children, Youth, Community, Cooking, Ecology, Foods, Education, Solar.

NATURALLY, Bernard Loibl, PO Box 317, Newfoundland, NJ 07435, 973-697-3552. 1981. Poetry, articles, art, photos, cartoons, interviews, reviews, letters, news items, non-fiction. "NATURALLY is a nudist magazines for people who enjoy sans-clothing lifestyles and recreation. The magazine is dedicated to people who visit nudist parks, resorts, nude beaches, and enjoy nudist activities." circ. 20000. 4/yr. Pub'd 4 issues 2009; expects 4 issues 2010, 4 issues 2011. sub. price 32.95; per copy 9.95; sample 9.95. Back issues: 7. Discounts: 5-49 copies 40%50 + copies 50%. 68pp. Reporting time: We usually respond within two to six weeks after accepting a manuscript or photos. Simultaneous submissions accepted: Yes. Publishes 60% of manuscripts submitted. Payment: We pay $70 per published page, regardless if text or photos. Copyrighted, reverts to author. Pub's reviews: 3 in 2009. §Family nudism and items about nudists and naturists. Nude lifestyles and travel. Ads: $450 full page $295 half page $200 third page $90 sixth page. Subjects: Community, Counter-Culture, Alternatives, Communes, Cults, Culture, Eastern Europe, Environment, Health, Humanism, Leisure/Recreation, Liberal Arts, Lifestyles, Nature, Photography, Travel, Visual Arts.

Naturegraph Publishers, Barbara Brown, PO Box 1047, 3543 Indian Creek Road, Happy Camp, CA 96039, 530-493-5353, 530-493-5240, 1-800-390-5353. nature@isqtel.net, www.naturegraph.com. 1946. Non-fiction. avg. press run 2500. Expects 3 titles 2010, 2 titles 2011. 4 titles listed in the *Small Press Record of Books in Print* (36th Edition, 2010-11). Discounts: 1-4 copies 20%, 5-24 copies 40%, 25 - 49 copies 42%, 50-99 copies 43%, 100 copies 44%. 144pp. Reporting time: Within a week to up to two months depending on time and/or interest. Simultaneous submissions accepted: Yes. Publishes 1% of manuscripts submitted. Payment: No advances. Pays royalties once a year,. 10% of wholesale generally and 8% if bookis sold at discounts of 50% and up. Copyrights for author. Subjects: Americana, Anthropology, Archaelogy, Astronomy, Birds, Botany, Crafts, Hobbies, Earth, Natural History, Gardening, Indigenous Cultures, Marine Life, Multicultural, Native American, Nature, Quilting, Sewing, Southwest.

Nautilus Publishing Company, Lucy Baker-Dickey, 4807 Brighton Lakes Blvd., Boynton Beach, FL 33436-4836, 561 733 2920. 1985. Fiction, letters, plays, non-fiction. "We like historic novels and are publishing a book about William Grayson, a revolutionary war hero and the first senator from Virginia. We will also published a screen play about this gentleman and soon will publish "forgotten Patriot" a collection of letters and speeches to and from William Grayson.We are publishing a book about the history of Germany "Poppelsdorfer Allee" soon. This book follows the history of a German family that start during the reign of Charlemagne and run to the present day." avg. press run 5000. Expects 10 titles 2010. 2 titles listed in the *Small Press Record of Books in Print* (36th Edition, 2010-11). Discounts: 2-10 copies 25%. 300pp. Reporting time: one to two weeks. Simultaneous submissions accepted: No. Publishes 1% of manuscripts submitted. Payment: it varies according to the type and quality of the material. Copyrights for author. Subjects: Birds, Caribbean, Creative Non-fiction, Metaphysics, Non-Fiction, Novels, Occult, Political Science, Spiritual, Theatre.

NEBO, Andrew Geyer, Fiction Editor; Michael Ritchie, Poetry Editor, Department of English, Arkansas Tech University, Russellville, AR 72801, 479-968-0256. 1982. Poetry, fiction, articles, art, criticism, reviews, long-poems, non-fiction. "We are interested in quality poetry and fiction by both new and established writers. In fiction we are open to a wide range of styles. We seek poems whose rhythms are as compelling and memorable as their diction and images, and as a result we print a large number of formal poems (poems using meter and rhyme). We have published poems by Howard Nemerov, Timothy Steele, Julia Randall, Dana Gioia, Brenda Hillman, Turner Cassity, R. L. Barth, and many other excellent poets, many previously unknown to us. In addition, we are interested in well-written reviews and criticism of English language poetry. We encourage poetic translations from contemporary writers and personal essays about travel in other parts of the world." circ. 300. 1-2/yr. Pub'd 1 issue 2009; expects 2 issues 2010, 2 issues 2011. sub. price $10; per copy $6; sample $5. Back issues: $5. 48-60pp. Reporting time: 2 weeks to 4 months; between Aug 1 and Feb 1, issue is put together. Reporting time is March for year's submissions. Payment: 1 copy. Copyrighted, reverts to author. Pub's reviews: 6 in 2009. §Poetry, fiction, literature in translation. Ads: $75/$45. Subjects: Fiction, Poetry.

THE NEBRASKA REVIEW, Zoo Press, James Reed, Fiction; Coreen Wees, Poetry; John Price, Creative Nonfiction, FA 212, University of Nebraska-Omaha, Omaha, NE 68182-0324, 402-554-3159. 1972. Poetry, fiction, reviews. "Dedicated to the best contemporary fiction, essays and poetry. Previous contributors include Kelly Cherry, Jack Myers, Rebecca Seiferle, Tom Franklin, Stewart O'Nan, Cris Mazza, Patricia Goedicke, Leslie Pietrzyk, Jonis Agee, DeWitt Henry, Elaine Ford, Richard Jackson. Prefer fiction and poetry which shows control of form and an ear for language, and which transcends mere competence in technique. Closed April 30 - August 30." circ. 1M. 2/yr. Pub'd 2 issues 2009; expects 2 issues 2010, 2 issues 2011. sub. price $15; per copy $8; sample $4.50. Discounts: bookstores 60/40, distributors 55/45. 108pp. Reporting time: 3-6 months. Payment: 2 copies and 1 yr. subscription. Copyrighted, reverts to author. Ads: $100/$60. Subjects: English, Fiction, Poetry.

NEO: Literary Magazine, John Starkey, Editor, Departamento de Linguas e Literaturas, Universidade dos Acores, 9500 Ponta Delgada, Portugal, www.neomagazine.org. 2002. Poetry, fiction, interviews, reviews, parts-of-novels, non-fiction. "NEO, an international print magazine of poetry, fiction, and creative nonfiction, is published in association with the Department of Modern Languages and Literature, University of the Azores, Portugal. Recent North American contributors include Peter Makuck, Dara Wier, Mark Levine, Mark Cox, Frank X. Gaspar, Katherine Vaz, Paulo da Costa, William Trowbridge, Patricia Goedicke, Betty Adcock, and Colette Inez (among others). Some established European contributors include David Albahari, Luisa Villalta, Bjarte Breiteig, Rosa Lobato de Faria, Jose Martins Garcia, Pedro da Silveira, Urbano Bettencourt, Alamo Oliveira, Ivo Machado, and Pedro Javier Castaneda Garcia. Approximately half of the submissions are from Luso-American or Portuguese/Azorean authors." circ. 2000. 1/yr. Pub'd 1 issue 2009; expects 1 issue 2010, 1 issue 2011. sub. price $16/2 issues; per copy $10; sample $10. Back issues: $10. Discounts: 2-10 copies 20%, 11 or more 30%. 160pp. Reporting time: 3 to 5 months. Simultaneous submissions accepted: Yes. Publishes 5% of manuscripts submitted. Payment: in copies. Copyrighted, reverts to author. Pub's reviews: 3 in 2009. §Fiction, poetry, creative non-fiction. Subjects: Essays, Fiction, Interviews, Journals, Literary Review, Literature (General), Magazines, Memoirs, Multicultural, Non-Fiction, Novels, Poetry, Portugal, Short Stories, Travel.

THE NEO-COMINTERN, Joel Katelnikoff, 97 Maxwell Crescent, Saskatoon, Sask. S7L 3Y4, Canada, www.neo-comintern.com. 1998. Poetry, fiction, articles, art, cartoons, satire. circ. ~700. 2/yr. Pub'd 2 issues 2009; expects 2 issues 2010, 2 issues 2011. sub. price $10; per copy $4 ppd; sample $4 ppd. Back issues: $4 ppd. Discounts: $10 for 4 copies, $20 for 10 copies. 20pp. Simultaneous submissions accepted: no. Publishes 50% of manuscripts submitted. Payment: contributors receive complimentary copies. Copyrighted, reverts to author. Ads: none. Subjects: Absurdist, Creativity, Dada, Entertainment, Philosophy, Politics, Post Modern, Socialist.

NEROUP REVIEW, Michael LaPointe, 9129 National Blvd. #7, Los Angeles, CA 90034, www.neroupreview.com, submissions@neroupreview.com. 2004. Poetry, articles, art, photos, interviews, criticism, reviews, music, letters, long-poems, concrete art, non-fiction. "The Neroup Review publishes innovative science articles and poetry in the format of a Fine Arts magazine. Check the website for examples of our magazine. www.neroupreview.com." circ. 250. 4/yr. Expects 4 issues 2010, 4 issues 2011. sub. price $35; per copy $10;

sample $10. Back issues: inquire. 100pp. Reporting time: 1-4 months. Simultaneous submissions accepted: Yes. Publishes 30% of manuscripts submitted. Payment: Copies. Copyrighted, reverts to author. Pub's reviews: none in 2009. §All Science minus science fiction. Science Culture, Poetry, Fine Arts, etc... No advertising. Subjects: Agriculture, Anarchist, Anthropology, Archaelogy, Architecture, Arts, Biography, Book Reviewing, Classical Studies, Community, Computers, Calculators, Criticism, Dada, Earth, Natural History, Ecology, Foods, Energy.

NERVE COWBOY, Liquid Paper Press, Joseph Shields, Jerry Hagins, PO Box 4973, Austin, TX 78765, www.onr.com/user/jwhagins/nervecowboy.html. 1995. Poetry, fiction, art. "Open to all forms, styles and subject matter preferring writing that speaks directly and minimizes literary devices. Fiction (up to 5 pages), poetry, and black & white artwork submissions are welcome year round. Recent contributers include Gerald Locklin, Wilma Elizabeth McDaniel, Jennifer Jackson, Michael Estabrook, and Christopher Cunningham." circ. 250. 2/yr. Pub'd 2 issues 2009; expects 2 issues 2010, 2 issues 2011. sub. price $8; per copy $5; sample $5. Back issues: $4. Discounts: selected trades, 40% on 6 or more copies (bookstores). 64pp. Reporting time: 2 months. Simultaneous submissions accepted: no. Publishes 5% of manuscripts submitted. Payment: 1 copy. Copyrighted, reverts to author. Ads: trade ads with other small magazines. Subjects: Arts, Literature (General), Poetry.

Neshui Publishing, Neshui, neshui62@hotmail.com—online email. 1993. Poetry, fiction, art, cartoons, interviews, satire, music, letters, long-poems, plays, non-fiction. "neshui also produces films... neshui-flims.com—titles: dictatorship of taste, 9 toes in monte carlo, mosquite king, romeo and julliet, dirty cowboy dress(western)." avg. press run 100. Pub'd 3 titles 2009; expects 3 titles 2010, 3 titles 2011. 4 titles listed in the *Small Press Record of Books in Print* (36th Edition, 2010-11). Discounts: 55% wholesalers. 200pp. Reporting time: thirty two secounds. Simultaneous submissions accepted: yes. Publishes 1% of manuscripts submitted. Payment: zero cash payment—75 copies. Copyrights for author. Subjects: Fiction, Young Adult.

NEW ALTERNATIVES, J & J Consultants, Inc., Walter Jones, 603 Ole Farm Road, Media, PA 19063, 610-565-9692, Fax 610-565-9694, wjones13@juno.com, www.members.tripod/walterjones. 1993. Poetry, fiction, articles, cartoons, music, non-fiction. "Short: 100-200 words." circ. 250. 6/yr. Pub'd 6 issues 2009; expects 6 issues 2010, 6 issues 2011. sub. price $12; per copy $3. 8pp. Reporting time: 2 months. Simultaneous submissions accepted: yes. Publishes 75% of manuscripts submitted. Payment: none. Copyrighted, reverts to author. Pub's reviews. §Parenting, childcare. Subjects: Adolescence, Children, Youth, Mental Health, Poetry.

NEW AMERICAN IMAGIST, Michael McClintock, General Editor; Jean George, Special Assignments Editor; Val Cho, Copyeditor, PO Box 124, South Pasadena, CA 91031-0124. 2001; formerly Seer Ox, founded in 1971. Poetry, art, long-poems. "The New American Imagist is interested in neo-Imagist and post-modern impressionist poetry written in contemporary idiom, grounded in contemporary experience. We are not interested in still-life poetry in dead language or work that merely imitates the Imagist movement of the early twentieth century. Our special six-panel collector's editions are intended to be representative of a poet's finest work, and have included Alan Catlin, Cor van den Heuvel, Luis Cuauhtemoc Berriozabal, Leonard J. Cirino, Robert Edwards, and Akitsu Ei. We read all work submitted continuously, from both known and unknown poets; our editorial process can be lengthy for final selections; reporting time can vary from two weeks to several months; work accepted into the final selection phase receives regular updates back to the poet. It is always best to submit 10-20 poems at a time; poetry may be any length up to 200 lines for a single poem. All work accepted and published as part of The New American Imagist series will be anthologized in book form (about each five years), published by Hermitage West, a private foundation based in California." circ. Varies with each edition, from 200 to 1500. Currently ranges from 4 to 9 issues per year. sub. price $12 for 8 issues.; per copy $1.50; sample $1.50. Back issues: All editions remain in print indefinitely. Discounts: Generous discounts on copies are offered to published poets and to libraries. Reporting time: Varies greatly from two weeks to several months. Publishes 1% of manuscripts submitted. Payment: 30 copies to the poet. Copyrighted, reverts to author. Subjects: Arts, Asia, Indochina, Asian-American, Celtic, Chicano/a, Criticism, Gaelic, Haiku, Libraries, Philosophy, Poetry, Psychology, Religion, Reprints, Translation.

NEW AMERICAN WRITING, Paul Hoover, Maxine Chernoff, 369 Molino Avenue, Mill Valley, CA 94941, 415-389-1877, Fax 415-384-0364. 1971. Poetry, articles, criticism. "August to January submissions encouraged. Work by Cole Swensen, Nathaniel Mackey, Mahmoud Darwish, Rae Armantrout, Rusty Morrison, Charles Bernstein, Robert Hass, Brenda Hillman, Lyn Hejinian, Gillian Conoley, Tomaz Salamun, and others. Special issues: #4 Australian Poetry, #5 Censorship and the Arts, #9 New British Poetry, #18 Brazilian Poetry, #19 Clark Coolidge, #20 Russian Absurdist Poetry, #21 Poets Respond to Gerhard Richter, #22 Asian Poetry, Peret's Political Poems, #23 The New Canadian Poetry & Nine Contemporary Vietnamese Poets, #24 Nathaniel Mackey. Covers by Bill Viola, Enrique Chagoya, Arthur Dove." circ. 1.5M. 1/yr. Pub'd 1 issue 2009; expects 1 issue 2010, 1 issue 2011. sub. price $36 for three issues,individuals; see EBSCO, SWETS, and others for libraries; $6 postal surcharge per issue foreign mail.; per copy $15 domestic, $22 Canada; sample $15. Back issues: varies, please inquire. Discounts: 60/40 to bookstores. 175pp. Reporting time: 1-6 months. Simultaneous submissions accepted: Yes. Publishes 1-5% of manuscripts submitted. Payment: 2 copies. Copyrighted, reverts

324

to author. Ads: $250/full page, 4 x 7; $150 half-page 4 x 3.5. Subjects: Poetry, Translation.

New Atlantean Press, Nathan Wright, Publisher, PO Box 9638, Santa Fe, NM 87504-9638, 505-983-1856 phone/Fax, think@thinktwice.com, www.thinktwice.com. 1992. "Send for a free catalog or visit our website." avg. press run 5M. Pub'd 2 titles 2009; expects 2 titles 2010, 2 titles 2011. 9 titles listed in the *Small Press Record of Books in Print* (36th Edition, 2010-11). Discounts: 5+ 40%, 30+ 45%, case purchases 50%, higher discounts possible. 200pp. Reporting time: 3 weeks. Simultaneous submissions accepted: yes. Payment: yes. Copyrights for author. Subjects: Health, Parenting, Philosophy, Spiritual.

NEW BOOKS ON WOMEN, GENDER, & FEMINISM, Women's Studies Librarian, University of Wisconsin System, Phyllis Holman Weisbard, Linda Fain, 430 Memorial Library, 728 State Street, Madison, WI 53706, 608-263-5754. 1979. "A subject-arranged, indexed bibliography of new titles in women's studies, listing books and periodicals." circ. 1.1M. 2/yr. Pub'd 2 issues 2009; expects 2 issues 2010, 2 issues 2011. sub. price $35 individuals and women's programs, $65 institutions (includes subscriptions to *New Books On Women & Feminism*, *Feminist Collections*, and *Feminist Periodicals*) Please inquire about special prices in Wisconsin; per copy $10; sample $10. Back issues: $10. 75pp. Copyrighted. Subjects: Bibliography, Feminism, Indexes & Abstracts, Lesbianism, Libraries, Women.

New Canaan Publishing Company Inc., David Mittelstadt, 2384 N Highway 341, Rossville, GA 30741, 203-966-3408 phone, 203-548-9072 fax. 1995. Fiction, non-fiction. "Publisher of children's books for the Christian market and children's books with subject matter consistent with the Christian market." avg. press run 5M. Pub'd 2 titles 2009; expects 3 titles 2010, 4 titles 2011. 5 titles listed in the *Small Press Record of Books in Print* (36th Edition, 2010-11). Discounts: please call for rates. Pages vary. Reporting time: Due to volume of submissions, we do not guarantee to respond. Authors are encouraged to make simultaneous submissions. Simultaneous submissions accepted: yes. Publishes approx. 1% of manuscripts submitted. Payment: percentage royalty (4-10% depending on material) based on net cash. Copyright varies. We especially seek work for hire arangements. Subjects: Children, Youth, Christianity.

New Chapter Publisher, Chris Angermann, 1765 Ringling Blvd. Ste 300, Sarasota, FL 34236, Tel. 941.954.4690, Fax. 941.954.0111, www.newchapterpublisher.com. 2007. Poetry, fiction, photos, non-fiction. avg. press run 5000. Pub'd 1 title 2009; expects 4 titles 2010, 6 titles 2011. No titles listed in the *Small Press Record of Books in Print* (36th Edition, 2010-11). 200pp. Subjects: Fiction, Literature (General).

New Concept Press, Norman Beim, 425 West 57th Street Suite 2J, New York, NY 10019, 212-265-6284, Fax: 212-265-6659. 1993. Fiction, plays. "LiteratureNorman Beim." avg. press run 1000. Pub'd 1 title 2009; expects 1 title 2010, 1 title 2011. 11 titles listed in the *Small Press Record of Books in Print* (36th Edition, 2010-11). Discounts: 40%. 250-630pp. Subjects: Autobiography, Biography, Drama, Holocaust, Judaism, Literature (General), Memoirs, Novels, Performing Arts, Religion, Theatre.

New Creature Press (see also DRAMA GARDEN), Joseph Verrilli, PO Box 1158, Bridgeport, CT 06601-1158, 203-455-7285. 2006. Poetry, articles, art, photos, cartoons, satire, reviews, letters, long-poems, collages, non-fiction. "Some recent contributors: Marie Kazalia, Ana Christy, Laurel Speer, Lyn Lifshin, Colin Cross, D.J. Weston, Jonathan K. Rice, Laura Stamps, and Mark Sonnenfeld." avg. press run 50. Expects 3 titles 2010, 3 titles 2011. No titles listed in the *Small Press Record of Books in Print* (36th Edition, 2010-11). 21pp. Reporting time: 1 week. Simultaneous submissions accepted: yes. Publishes 95% of manuscripts submitted. Does not copyright for author. Subjects: Relationships, Religion, Society.

New Dawn Unlimited, Inc., Jerri Hardesty, 1830 Marvel Road, Brierfield, AL 35035, 205-665-7904; fax 205-665-2500; e-mail wytrabbit1@aol.com. 1997. Poetry, fiction, art, photos, cartoons, long-poems, plays, non-fiction. "Always accepting submissions! Annual theme issues. Please send 5-10 pieces! Also, for Annual Chapbook competition-send 20-50 pages/manuscript with a $10 entry fee. Pays 100-200 copies, services, advertising, and artistic input. PLEASE SEE NEWDAWNUNLIMITED.COM." avg. press run 300. Pub'd 3 titles 2009; expects 6-8 titles 2010, 6-8 titles 2011. No titles listed in the *Small Press Record of Books in Print* (36th Edition, 2010-11). Discounts: $2 each for 20 or more; will consider this price for any good cause. 40-50pp. Reporting time: Varies with volume; 3 months after deadline for chapbooks. Simultaneous submissions fine, except on chapbooks. Publishes 5% of manuscripts submitted. Payment: 1-2 copies magazines; 100-200 copies Annual Chapbook winner. Does not copyright for author.

New Day Publishing, Inc., Annie Galvin Teich, 26 Bluff Ridge Court, Greensboro, NC 27455, 336.545.1545. 2006. Non-fiction. "New Day Publishing publishes for teachers and parents of Christian children. Our goal is to infuse children with not only an excitement for learning and a love of reading, but with an appreciation of God's love for them. We currently focus on preschool through first grade children. Little learners need hands-on learning where they can see, hear, taste, and feel the lessons. Our activities channel that energy and help children use their God-given gifts on their journeys of faith." avg. press run 3000. Expects 10 titles 2010, 5 titles 2011. 10 titles listed in the *Small Press Record of Books in Print* (36th Edition, 2010-11). Discounts: 45-50%. 48pp. Reporting time: 1 month. Simultaneous submissions accepted: Yes. Publishes 25% of manuscripts submitted. Payment: No advance. 10% royalty. Does not copyright for author. Subjects: Catholic, Children, Youth, Christianity, Education, Parenting, Picture Books, Reading, Religion, Storytelling.

NEW DELTA REVIEW, Shane Noecker, Editor, New Delta Review, Louisiana State University, Department of English, 15 Allen Hall, Baton Rouge, LA 70803, 225-578-4079. 1984. Poetry, fiction, art, photos, interviews, reviews, long-poems, plays, non-fiction. *"New Delta Review* publishes new and established writers of poetry and fiction. We also accept literary interviews, reviews, essays, and art. For more information, please visit our Website: http://www.english.lsu.edu/journals/ndr." circ. 500. 2/yr. Pub'd 2 issues 2009; expects 2 issues 2010, 2 issues 2011. sub. price $12; per copy $7; sample $5 issue, $10 for 3. Back issues: $7 for any issue prior to the current one. 150pp. Reporting time: 3-5 months. Simultaneous submissions accepted: Yes, if noted in cover letter. We also ask that the author notify us if their work is accepted elsewhere. Publishes 1% of manuscripts submitted. Payment: 2 contributors' copies. Copyrighted, reverts to author. Pub's reviews: 7 in 2009. §Contemporary poetry, fiction and literary essays, popular culture, works on contemporary authors. Ads: $75/$40, one year contract (2 issues) $100/$60; mostly ad trades. Subjects: Essays, Fiction, Interviews, Poetry, Reviews.

•New Door Books, Douglas Gordon, 2115 Wallace Street, Philadelphia, PA 19130, 215-769-2525, info@newdoorbooks.com, http://www.newdoorbooks.com. 2009. Fiction. "New Door Books publishes original, innovative, book-length fiction. Its parent company, the packager P. M. Gordon Associates, has been producing books for other publishers since 1982. Editorially, New Door Books is an offshoot of the Working Writers Group (WWG), a Philadelphia-area group of writers who have been meeting monthly since 1985. We are not considering unsolicited submissions at this time." Pub'd 1 title 2009; expects 1 title 2010, 3 titles 2011. 1 title listed in the *Small Press Record of Books in Print* (36th Edition, 2010-11). 250pp. Subject: Fiction.

•NEW ENGLAND BY RAIL, Donald Adams, 4 Lincoln Street, Bruwick, ME 04011, 207-449-1486. 2009. Fiction, articles, art, photos, cartoons, interviews, reviews, letters, news items, non-fiction. "New England by Rail is a magazine for the Railroad Industry and will publish only related articles and items both for Freight, commuter and Tourist Rail Travel. Also interested in articles both fiction and non-fiction, photos, items for sale and any other related Rail industry items." circ. 4000. 12/yr. Expects 2 issues 2010, 12 issues 2011. sub. price $36.00; per copy $3.95; sample $3.95. Back issues: $3.95. Discounts: 18%. 12pp. Reporting time: three days. Simultaneous submissions accepted: Yes. Publishes 40% of manuscripts submitted. Payment: Company Check, Credit Card, PayPal, Direct transfer, personal check. Copyrighted. Pub's reviews: none in 2009. §Railroad. Ads: Half page - $50Full page - $100. Subjects: Antiques, Collectibles, Crafts, Hobbies, Creative Non-fiction, Family, Fiction, Folklore, History, Interviews, New England, Non-Fiction, Novels, Short Stories, Transportation, Travel.

New England Cartographics, Inc., Christopher J. Ryan, President; Valerie Vaughan, Editor, PO Box 9369, North Amherst, MA 01059-9369, 413-549-4124, toll free 888-995-6277, email: geolopes@comcast.net URL: www.necartographics.com. 1986. Non-fiction. "Specialize in outdoor recreation maps and guidebooks; hiking, backpacking, bicycling, mountain biking, paddling, rail-trails principally of areas in the North Eastern United States." avg. press run 3M-5M. Pub'd 2 titles 2009; expects 3 titles 2010, 4 titles 2011. 13 titles listed in the *Small Press Record of Books in Print* (36th Edition, 2010-11). Discounts: trade 40-45% retail, 45-55% wholesale/distributors. 178pp. Reporting time: 1 month. Simultaneous submissions accepted: yes. Publishes 25% of manuscripts submitted. Payment: 5-10% of cover price. Copyrights for author. Subjects: Adirondacks, Bicycling, Birds, Conservation, Geography, History, Leisure/Recreation, Maine, Maps, Nature, New England, New Hampshire, New York, Sports, Outdoors, Water.

THE NEW ENGLAND QUARTERLY, Linda Smith Rhoads, Editor, c/o Massachusetts Historical Society, 1154 Boylston St., Boston, MA 02215, 617-646-0543, fax: 617-859-0074, website: www.newenglandquarterly.org. 1928. Articles, criticism, reviews. *"The New England Quarterly,* a Historical Review of New England Life and Letters, publishes articles in the fields of literature, history, art, and culture; short memoranda and documents; and book reviews." circ. 2.5M. 4/yr. Pub'd 4 issues 2009; expects 4 issues 2010, 4 issues 2011. sub. price $35, individual; $25, student; $70, institution; per copy $10. Back issues: $12. 176pp. Reporting time: 6-8 weeks. Simultaneous submissions accepted: no. Publishes 20% of manuscripts submitted. Payment: 1-year free subscription. Copyrighted, does not revert to author. Pub's reviews: 45 in 2009. §American literature (with some connection to New England), New England history, art, culture, biography (all with some connection to New England). Ads: $200/$125. Subjects: Arts, Criticism, Culture, English, Feminism, History, Music, Native American, New England, Politics, Reviews, Sociology.

NEW ENGLAND REVIEW, Middlebury College Publications, Stephen Donadio, Editor; Carolyn Kuebler, Managing Editor; C. Dale Young, Poetry Editor, Middlebury College, Middlebury, VT 05753, 802-443-5075; toll-free 800-450-9571; fax 802-443-2088; e-mail NEReview@middlebury.edu; www.NEReview.com. 1978. Poetry, fiction, articles, interviews, criticism, reviews, letters, parts-of-novels, long-poems, plays, non-fiction. "Submissions must be postmarked between Sept. 1 and May 31 only; at this point no electronic submissions are accepted." circ. 2M. 4/yr. Pub'd 4 issues 2009; expects 4 issues 2010, 4 issues 2011. sub. price Individual $30

(1 yr) $50 (2 yrs) Institution $45 (1 yr) $85 (2 yrs); per copy $10; sample $10. Back issues: $6 or 3/$14. Discounts: 5% agency; 20% classroom. 210pp. Reporting time: 3-4 months. Simultaneous submissions accepted in PROSE ONLY, if indicated as such. No simultaneous submissions in poetry. Publishes 2% of manuscripts submitted. Payment: $10 per page, $20 minimum, plus 2 copies. Copyrighted, reverts to author. Pub's reviews: 4 in 2009. §Contemporary fiction, poetry, biography, autobiography, non-fiction. Ads: $200/$125/discounts for featured authors and books reviewed. Subjects: Arts, Book Reviewing, Classical Studies, Creative Non-fiction, Culture, Drama, Fiction, Literary Review, Literature (General), Memoirs, Non-Fiction, Poetry, Translation, Visual Arts, Writers/Writing.

NEW ENVIRONMENT BULLETIN, Harry Schwarzlander, 270 Fenway Drive, Syracuse, NY 13224, 315-446-8009. 1974. Articles, interviews, reviews, letters, news items. "Contains reports of activities of The New Environment Association, as well as articles and news items relating to the concerns of the Association, which are personal and social changes needed to achieve a sustainable society, and the creation of new communities which are humanly and environmentally sound. Content is contributed primarily by members and other readers." circ. 140. 10-11/yr. Pub'd 10 issues 2009; expects 10-11 issues 2010, 10-11 issues 2011. sub. price $12 (North America); sample free. Back issues: $5 for 2-year series (even-to-odd years). 6pp. Reporting time: not specified. Payment: none. Not copyrighted. Pub's reviews: 1 in 2009. §See above. Ads: none. Subjects: Agriculture, Community, Counter-Culture, Alternatives, Communes, Ecology, Foods, Energy, Environment, Futurism, Nature, New Age, Non-Violence, Peace.

New Falcon Publications, Frank Martin, 1753 E. Broadway Road, Suite 101-277, Tempe, AZ 85282, 602-708-1409 (phone), 602-708-1410 (fax), info@newfalcon.com (email), http://www.newfalcon.com (website). 1982. Fiction, satire, criticism, plays, non-fiction. Pub'd 8 titles 2009; expects 8 titles 2010, 8 titles 2011. 1 title listed in the *Small Press Record of Books in Print* (36th Edition, 2010-11). Discounts: 20% single copy, 30% 2-4 mix or match, 40% 5+ mix or match. Reporting time: 60-90 days. Simultaneous submissions accepted: yes. Publishes 3% of manuscripts submitted. Copyrights for author. Subjects: Anarchist, Biography, Criticism, Fiction, Folklore, Gay, Health, Lesbianism, Libertarian, Occult, Philosophy, Political Science, Psychology, Religion, Science Fiction.

THE NEW FORMALIST, The New Formalist Press, Leo Yankevich, Editor; David Castleman, Editor, P.O. Box 251, Dayton, WA 99328, thenewformalist@lycos.com, http://www.thenewformalist.com. 2000. Poetry, fiction, reviews. "We publish metrical poetry along with occasional essays, reviews, and stories. Recent contributors include Jared Carter, Moore Moran, Richard Moore, Tom Riley, and Joseph S. Salemi." circ. 1000. 1/yr. Pub'd 2 issues 2009; expects 2 issues 2010, 2 issues 2011. sub. price $20; per copy $10; sample $10. Back issues: inquiries welcome. 90pp. Reporting time: One week to one year. Publishes 1% of manuscripts submitted. Payment: copies. Copyrighted, reverts to author. Pub's reviews: 50 in 2009. §Most things except temporary enthusiasms. Ads: inquire. Subjects: Anthology, Arts, Essays, Ethics, Novels, Poetry, Storytelling, Dylan Thomas.

The New Formalist Press (see also THE NEW FORMALIST), Leo Yankevich, David Castleman, Lamon Cull, Box 251, Dayton, WA 99328-0251, thenewformalist@lycos.com, http://www.formalpoetry.com. 1990. Poetry, fiction, articles, interviews, satire, criticism, reviews, parts-of-novels, long-poems, non-fiction. "We appreciate the expansive humors of love, doubt, and joy, and we appreciate a conscionable belief. We appreciate laughter, and an intelligent responsibility. We appreciate the individual existence within the blessedness of continuity." avg. press run 250. Pub'd 2 titles 2009; expects 2 titles 2010, 2 titles 2011. No titles listed in the *Small Press Record of Books in Print* (36th Edition, 2010-11). 90pp. Reporting time: variable. Simultaneous submissions accepted: yes. Publishes 1% of manuscripts submitted. Payment: inquire. Copyrights for author. Subjects: Arts, Ethics.

NEW HOPE INTERNATIONAL REVIEW, New Hope International, Gerald England, 20 Werneth Avenue, Gee Cross, Hyde, Cheshire SK14 5NL, United Kingdom, www.geraldengland.co.uk. 1986. Reviews, music, letters. "Reviews of poetry books pamphlets and magazines. Unsolicited reviews not required but U.K. subscribers who can write fluently are welcome to join the reviewing team." circ. 1M. Continuously updated. Pub'd 2 issues 2009; expects 2 issues 2010, 2 issues 2011. price per copy $10 (includes postage) cash only. Back issues: $5 cash. 500pp. Simultaneous submissions accepted: no. Publishes (solicited only) 90% of manuscripts submitted. Payment: copies. Not copyrighted. Pub's reviews: 1000 in 2009. §Poetry, literary criticism. Ads: none. Subjects: Avant-Garde, Experimental Art, Beat, Biography, Book Reviewing, Haiku, Literary Review, Literature (General), Magazines, Poetry, Reviews, Tapes & Records, Textiles, Translation, Writers/Writing.

New Horizons Publishing, Jennifer Bishop, 5830 NW Expressway, Suite 225, Oklahoma City, OK 73132-5236, 405-823-9538, Fax 405-848-8118. 2001. Poetry, fiction, non-fiction. Expects 1 title 2010, 3 titles 2011. No titles listed in the *Small Press Record of Books in Print* (36th Edition, 2010-11). Discounts: contact for rates. 125pp. Reporting time: 3-4 months. Simultaneous submissions accepted: yes. Publishes 1-3% of manuscripts submitted. Does not copyright for author.

NEW INTERNATIONAL A magazine of Marxist politics and theory, Pathfinder Press, Mary-Alice Waters, P.O. Box 162767, Atlanta, GA 30321-2767, www.pathfinderpress.com.

New Issues Poetry & Prose, Marianne Swierenga, Managing Editor; William Olsen, Editor; Mark Halliday, Advisory Editor; Nancy Eimers, Advisory Editor; J. Allyn Rosser, Advisory Editor; Stuart Dybek, Advisory Editor, Western Michigan University, 1903 W. Michigan Avenue, Kalamazoo, MI 49008-5463, 269-387-8185, Fax 269-387-2562, new-issues@wmich.edu, www.wmich.edu/newissues. 1996. Poetry, fiction. "New Issues Poetry Prize, $2,000 and publication for a first book of poems. Deadline: Nov. 30. Judge to be named. The Green Rose Prize in Poetry, $2,000 and publication for a book of poems by an established poet. Deadline: Sept. 30. Send SASE for complete guidelines or visit our website. We do not read unsolicited manuscripts." avg. press run 1500. Pub'd 12 titles 2009; expects 12 titles 2010, 6-12 titles 2011. 90 titles listed in the *Small Press Record of Books in Print* (36th Edition, 2010-11). Discounts: individuals order through Amazon.com or www.spdbooks.com; bookstores may order through distributor, Partners 800-336-3137 or through Small Press Distribution: www.spdbooks.com. 72pp. Reporting time: 6 months. Simultaneous submissions accepted: yes. We publish 1 out of 250 manuscripts submitted for publication. Payment: poet receives 10% of press run in lieu of royalties. Copyrights for author. Subjects: Fiction, Literature (General), Poetry.

New Knowledge Press, Steven Weiss, 10556 Combie Rd., Suite 6360, Auburn, CA 95602, 530-320-4680 (tel), 530-268-7404 (fax), sweiss@newknowledgepress.com, http://www.newknowledgepress.com. 2007. Fiction, non-fiction. "We focus on personal growth and business/entrepreneur oriented non-fiction." avg. press run 1200. Expects 3-5 titles 2010, 7-10 titles 2011. No titles listed in the *Small Press Record of Books in Print* (36th Edition, 2010-11). Discounts: 1-25 copies 25%; 25-100 copies 30%; 100-250 copies 40%; more than 250: call for quote. 225pp. Reporting time: Varies. Simultaneous submissions accepted: No. Payment: Varies. We do not do advances. Does not copyright for author. Subjects: Alternative Medicine, Business & Economics, Consulting, Creative Non-fiction, Engineering, Finances, Health, Marketing, Motivation, Success, New Age, Non-Fiction, Psychology, Spiritual, Technology.

THE NEW LAUREL REVIEW, Lee Meitzen Grue, Editor; Andy Young, Poetry Editor; Lewis Schmidt, Managing Editor, 828 Lesseps Street, New Orleans, LA 70117, 504-947-6001. 1971. Poetry, fiction, articles, art, photos, reviews, non-fiction. "We want fresh work; shy away from dry academic articles with footnotes, and from poems with the guts cut out. Recently published: Julie Kane, P.B. Parris, James Nolan, Arthur Pfister III, Len Roberts, Marilyn Coffey, Billy Marshall-Stoneking, Dave Brinks, and Jared Carter." circ. 500. 1/yr. Pub'd 1 issue 2009. 3 titles listed in the *Small Press Record of Books in Print* (36th Edition, 2010-11). sub. price $12 individuals, $15 institutions, $15 foreign; per copy double issue $9; sample $8. Back issues: $8. Discounts: 5 copies for $40. 125pp. Reporting time: varies, longer time for interesting work; somewhat crowded with fiction & poetry—about 6 weeks; do not read in summer. We prefer to be informed of simultaneous submissions, but simultaneous submissions not good practice; must have immediate notification upon another acceptance. Publishes maybe 10% of manuscripts submitted. Payment: 1 copy of the magazine in which their work appears. Copyrighted. Pub's reviews: none in 2009. §Poetry and books about poets and related matter, collections of short fiction. Ads: none. Subjects: Literature (General), Poetry.

NEW LETTERS, Robert Stewart, Univ. of Missouri - Kansas City; University House, 5101 Rockhill Road, Kansas City, MO 64110, 816-235-1168, Fax 816-235-2611, www.newletters.org. 1971 (Predecessor, *University Review,* 1934). Poetry, fiction, articles, art, photos, satire, parts-of-novels, long-poems. "The best in contemporary fiction, poetry, personal essay, art, interviews, book reviews, and photography. Contributors include B.H. Fairchild, Willis Barnstone, Kevin Young, Thomas E. Kennedy, David Clewell, Maxine Kumin, John Barth, Padma Viswanathan, Marilyn Hacker." circ. 2.5M. 4/yr. Pub'd 3 issues 2009; expects 4 issues 2010, 4 issues 2011. 6 titles listed in the *Small Press Record of Books in Print* (36th Edition, 2010-11). sub. price $22; per copy $8-12, varies on length of issue; sample $10.00. Back issues: $10, rare issues $20. Discounts: 25% on contract of 4 ads. 140pp. Reporting time: 2-4 months. Simultaneous submissions accepted: yes. Publishes 2-5% of manuscripts submitted. Payment: small, upon publication. Copyrighted, reverts to author. Pub's reviews: 9 in 2009. §Collections of poetry, essays, and short stories. Ads: half page $250 / full page $450. Subjects: Arts, Fiction, Interviews, Non-Fiction, Poetry.

NEW MADRID, Ann Neelon, 7C Faculty Hall Murray State University, Department of English and Philosophy, Murray, KY 42071-3341, 270-809-4713. 2007. Poetry, fiction, art, interviews, reviews, parts-of-novels, long-poems, non-fiction. "New Madrid is the national journal of the low-residency MFA program at Murray State University. It takes its name from the New Madrid seismic zone, which falls within the central Mississippi Valley and extends through western Kentucky. Between 1811 and 1812, four earthquakes with magnitudes greater than 7.0 struck this region, changing the course of the Mississippi River, creating Reelfoot Lake in Tennessee and ringing church bells as far away as Boston." circ. 800. 2/yr. Expects 2 issues 2010, 2 issues 2011. sub. price $15.00 annually; two-year subscriptions $28.00; per copy $8; sample $8. Back issues: inquire. Discounts: inquire. 160pp. Reporting time: We read manuscripts on a rolling basis through each of our two annual submission periods, and as a rule, we respond after the close of the reading period. So if you've submitted during the January-April reading period, expect a response by May. If you've submitted during the August-November reading period, expect a response by December. Simultaneous submissions accepted: Yes. Payment: We pay only in copies. Copyrighted, reverts to author. Pub's reviews: About 10 in 2009. §Reviews of current literary works. Exchange ads welcome. Subjects: Chicago, Creative Non-fiction, Fiction, Illinois, Indiana, Kentucky, Midwest, Missouri, Poetry, Short Stories, South.

NEW MEXICO POETRY REVIEW, Kathleen Johnson, 44 Via Punto Nuevo, Santa Fe, NM 87508, E-mail: nmpr@live.com Web site: www.newmexicopoetryreview.com. 2009. Poetry, art, interviews, reviews, non-fiction. "NEW MEXICO POETRY REVIEW is dedicated to publishing strong, imaginative, well-crafted poems by both new talents and established writers. NMPR publishes poems, prose poems, poetry-related essays and interviews. New Mexico poets may send poetry books for review consideration." circ. 500. 2/yr. Pub'd 1 issue 2009; expects 2 issues 2010, 2 issues 2011. sub. price $22; per copy $12. 120pp. Payment: One copy of issue in which your work appears. Copyrighted, reverts to author. Pub's reviews. §poetry books by New Mexico poets. Subjects: Arts, Essays, Interviews, Literary Review, New Mexico, Poetry.

NEW MIRAGE QUARTERLY, GoodSAMARitan Press, Jerome Brooke, 95/31 Moo 10 Classic Village, T. Nongphure A. Banglamung, Chonburi 20150, Thailand, 66817177941. 1991. Poetry, fiction. circ. 60. 4/yr. Pub'd 4 issues 2009; expects 4 issues 2010, 4 issues 2011. sub. price $24; per copy $7; sample $7. Back issues: $7.00. Discounts: 50%. 12pp. Reporting time: 90 days. Simultaneous submissions accepted: Yes. Publishes 90% of manuscripts submitted. Payment: Copy payment. Copyrighted, reverts to author. Pub's reviews: 12 in 2009. §Poetry. Ads: $90.00. Subject: Poetry.

New Moon Publishing, Inc. (see also THE GROWING EDGE MAGAZINE), Tom Alexander, Executive Editor; Tom Weller, Editor, PO Box 1027, Corvallis, OR 97339-1027, 514-757-8477. 1980. 5 titles listed in the *Small Press Record of Books in Print* (36th Edition, 2010-11). Discounts: 40% to bookstores, newstands. 96pp. Subject: Drugs.

NEW MUSE OF CONTEMPT, Broken Jaw Press, Joe Blades, Box 596 Stn A, Fredericton, NB E3B 5A6, Canada, www.brokenjaw.com. 1987. Fiction, reviews, concrete art. "Experimental literary, mail art, culture mag. *New Muse of Contempt* publishes a wide range of new and established writers and visual artists from Canada and beyond. It has become a semiannual international forum for correspondence art and interesting creative writings. Submissions of pithy poetry (esp. visual/concrete poetry, found poetry and homolinguistic text translations), short fiction, essays, book reviews welcome by post if accompanied by a SASE with Canadian postage (not USA postage) or International Postal Reply Coupons. Contributions of correspondence art - from collage and rubber stamps, stickers, photos and drawings, to project and exhibition announcements are always welcome." circ. 200-500. 2/yr. Pub'd 2 issues 2009; expects 2 issues 2010, 2 issues 2011. sub. price $12; per copy $6; sample $6. 52pp. Reporting time: 2-6 months. Simultaneous submissions accepted: no. Publishes 5% of manuscripts submitted. Payment: copies. Copyrighted, reverts to author. Pub's reviews: 4 in 2009. §Poetry and art. Ads: $100/$50. Subjects: Canada, Dada, Fiction.

New Native Press, Thomas Rain Crowe, Publisher; Nan Watkins, Managing Editor, PO Box 661, Cullowhee, NC 28723, 828-293-9237. 1979. Poetry, art. "No unsolicited manuscripts considered." avg. press run varies. All books are 'print on demand' runs. Pub'd 2 titles 2009; expects 1 title 2010, 1 title 2011. 18 titles listed in the *Small Press Record of Books in Print* (36th Edition, 2010-11). Discounts: 40% for bookstore and vendor sales. 80pp. Payment: varies (usually 1/3 of run), 50% discount on additional copies. Copyrights for author. Subjects: Metaphysics, Myth, Mythology, Native American, Poetry, Post Modern, Spiritual, Surrealism.

NEW OHIO REVIEW, Jill Allyn Rosser, Editor, English Dept., 360 Ellis Hall, Ohio University, Athens, OH 45701, 740.597.1360, Web: www.ohiou.edu/nor. 2007. "We accept literary submissions in any genre. Translations are welcome if permission has been granted. We do not reprint previously published work. We accept general submissions Sept. 1 thru May 1, but accept submissions year-round from subscribers. Please include a brief cover letter with your submission. Poems should be individually typed, either single- or double-spaced, on one side of the page. Prose should be typed double-spaced on one side and be no longer than thirty pages. Cross-genre work or any work that is unusually formatted is welcome, but please be aware that our page width and font size are restricted. Simultaneous submissions to other journals are fine as long as you indicate so in your cover letter and inform us immediately if your work is accepted elsewhere." circ. 1,500. Biannual. sub. price See website.; per copy $9. Back issues: $5. 180-200pp. Reporting time: We aim for 12 weeks maximum. Simultaneous submissions accepted: Yes. Publishes 3-5% of manuscripts submitted. Payment: Yes. See website.

NEW ORLEANS REVIEW, Christopher Chambers, Editor, Box 195, Loyola University, New Orleans, LA 70118, 504-865-2295. 1968. Poetry, fiction, articles, art, photos, cartoons, interviews, satire, criticism, reviews, non-fiction. "Past contributors include Walker Percy, Pablo Neruda, Hunter S. Thompson, Alain Robbe-Grillet, Christopher Isherwood, Annie Dillard, William Matthews, Gordon Lish, William Kotzwinkle, Julio Cortazar, Michael Harper, Yusef Komunyaaka, Ed Skoog, and Michael Martone. Check us out and send your best work.

We privilege the language." circ. 1M. 2/yr. Pub'd 2 issues 2009; expects 2 issues 2010, 2 issues 2011. sub. price 2 issues - domestic $12 indiv, $20 instit, foreign $20; per copy $10 domestic, $12 foreign; sample $5 domestic, $10 foreign. Back issues: $5; inquire for availability. Discounts: none. 200pp. Reporting time: 3 months. Simultaneous submissions accepted: yes. Publishes 3% of manuscripts submitted. Payment: $25-$50 +copies. Copyrighted, reverts to author. Pub's reviews: 6 in 2009. §fiction, poetry, New Orleans. Subjects: Arts, Experimental, Fiction, Journals, Literary Review, Literature (General), Louisiana, Movies, Non-Fiction, Photography, Poetry.

New Orphic Publishers (see also THE NEW ORPHIC REVIEW), Ernest Hekkanen, Margrith Schraner, 706 Mill Street, Nelson, BC V1L 4S5, Canada, 250-354-0494, Fax 250-352-0743, web:www3.telus.net/ neworphicpublishers-hekkanen. 1995. Poetry, fiction, criticism, plays, non-fiction. "Recent contributors: Hillel Wright, Ed Roy, Margrith Schraner, Ernest Hekkanen. We don't look at unsolicited material." avg. press run 1.5M. Pub'd 5 titles 2009; expects 5 titles 2010, 4 titles 2011. 1 title listed in the *Small Press Record of Books in Print* (36th Edition, 2010-11). Discounts: 40%. 150-350pp. Simultaneous submissions accepted: no. Publishes 1% of manuscripts submitted. Payment: 10%. Copyrights for author. Subjects: Fiction, Literary Review, Novels, Poetry.

THE NEW ORPHIC REVIEW, New Orphic Publishers, Ernest Hekkanen, Editor-in-Chief; Margrith Schraner, Associate Editor, 706 Mill Street, Nelson, BC V1L 4S5, Canada, 250-354-0494. 1998. Poetry, fiction, articles, interviews, criticism, parts-of-novels, plays. "Stories, articles, and novel excerpts up to 10,000 words. I'm a harsh judge of poetry. Only send the best. Recent contributors: W.P. Kinsella, Jack Cady, Jana Harris, Catherine Owen, Chad Norman, and Michael Bullock. Send for full submission guidelines." circ. 500. 2/yr. Pub'd 2 issues 2009; expects 2 issues 2010, 2 issues 2011. sub. price $25 USD; per copy $15 USD; sample $15 USD. Back issues: we always sell out. Discounts: 30% break. 120pp. Reporting time: up to 4 months. Simultaneous submissions accepted: yes. Publishes 20% of manuscripts submitted. Payment: 1 complimentary copy. Copyrighted, reverts to author. Pub's reviews. §Fiction. Ads: $150/$75. Subjects: Fiction, Literary Review, Novels, Poetry.

New Paradigm Books, John Chambers, 22491 Vistawood Way, Boca Raton, FL 33428, 561-482-5971, 800-808-5179, Fax 561-852-8322, darbyc@earthlink.net, www.newpara.com. 1997. Non-fiction. "We publish 'New Age' books, but with a broader-than-usual literary and historical character, e.g. *The Chinese Roswell*, by Hartwig Hausdorf (ufology), *Conversations with Eternity: The Forgotten Masterpiece of Victor Hugo*, (channeling), *Father Ernetti's Chronovisor*, by Peter Krassa (time travel). We have expanded into wider areas of health and spirituality with titles on multiple sclerosis and Sufism." avg. press run 5,000. Expects 1 title 2010, 2 titles 2011. 9 titles listed in the *Small Press Record of Books in Print* (36th Edition, 2010-11). Copyrights negotiable. Subjects: Aging, Animals, Channelling, Inspirational, Literature (General), Medicine, Metaphysics, New Age, Occult, Philosophy, Self-Help, Spiritual, Sufism, Theosophical.

THE NEW RENAISSANCE, an international magazine of ideas & opinions, emphasizing literature & the arts, Louise T. Reynolds, Editor-in-Chief; Frank Finale, Poetry Editor, Patti J. D. Michaud, Olivera Sajkovic; James E. A. Woodbury, Consulting Editors, 26 Heath Road #11, Arlington, MA 02474-3645, Email: tnrlitmag@earthlink.net (inquiries only, send no manuscripts). 1968. Poetry, fiction, articles, photos, interviews, criticism, long-poems. "Since April 1995, our policy for fiction & poetry has required an entry fee, as both are tied to our award programs: $16.50 per submission for non-subscribers US; $11.50 per submission for subscribers US. Foreign submitters: $13.50 subscribers, $18.50 non-subscribers. Unless fiction is 4 pp or fewer, only one ms per submission. Ficton: mss from 2 to 36 pp. Poetry: 3-6 one-page poems; 2-4 two- page poems; only one long poem. Translations are welcome (include originals) EACH submission requires entry fee. Mss without the fee will be returned *unread*. The fourth awards will be announced in the Fall 2006. Submitting periods: January 2-June 30, & Sept. 1-Oct. 31 for fiction and nonfiction; poetry from Jan. 2-June 30. Only work published in a 3-issue *tnr* volume is eligible. All writers published in *tnr* receive a nominal payment, as well as the issue they're in. Independent judges. Fiction Awards: 1st place: $500; 2nd $250; 3rd $100; one honorable mention $50. *tnr* Poetry Awards: 1st place - $250; 2nd - $125; 3rd - $60; three or four honorable mentions - $25 ea. Send mss with entry fees. Current subscibers extend their subscription by an issue. Non-subscribers receive a recent issue. For those submitting non-fiction, ms must be accompanied by $10 for a recent issue. Non-fiction may be on literature, cinema, theatre, artwork, etc. Submitting periods—nonfiction: January 2 - November 30th each year. We are looking for writing that has something to say, says it with style or grace, & has a personalized voice. All submissions MUST be accompanied by a SASE or IRC. All queries re guidelines, questions about submissions, etc., *must* be accompanied by a SASE, IRC. Fiction submissions take 5-8 months; poetry 4-7 months; non-fiction 2-5 months. Writers recently published: Ann Struthers, M. E. McMullen, R. Tagore (trans. Wendy Barker, S. Tagore), Zoya Pavlovkis-Petit, Luis Miguel Aguilar (trans. Kathleen Snodgrass)." circ. 1.3M. 2/yr. Pub'd 1 issue 2009; expects 2 issues 2010, 2 issues 2011. sub. price individuals $38/3 issues USA, $42/3 issues Canada (air mail); all others $52/3 issues (air mail); institutions $42/3 issues USA, $45 Canada (air mail), $55 all others (air mail); per copy $14.50 USA, $16.00 Canada, $18.50 all others; sample $10.50 USA, $12.00 Canada, $14.00 all others. Discounts: subscription agents, etc. 20%; 20 or more copies for classroom use

330

25%, 35+ 30%; bookstores 40-60%, advance payment. 144-184pp. Reporting time: poetry 4-5 months, prose 5-8 months. Simultaneous submissions accepted: Reluctantly. Publishes up to 12-20+% of manuscripts submitted. Payment: $17-$55 poems, $48-$85 fiction, $65-$175 non-fiction, $25-$30 per drawing. Copyrighted, reverts to author after publication. Ads: $170/$95. Subjects: Criticism, Current Affairs, Essays, Fiction, Graphics, Poetry, Politics, Reviews, Short Stories, Theatre, Translation, Visual Arts.

New Rivers Press, Inc., Wayne Gudmundson, Director; Alan Davis, Senior Editor; Donna Carlson, Managing Editor, c/o MSUM, 1104 7th Avenue South, Moorhead, MN 56563-0178, contact@newriverspress.org, www.newriverspress.org. 1968. Poetry, fiction, art, photos, long-poems, concrete art. "New Rivers Press is a not for profit literary small press founded in 1968 by C.W. "Bill" Truesdale that has published over 320 books and is now a part of Minnesota State University Moorhead. Our dual mission is to publish enduring literature and provide academic learning opportunities for students. We publish new writing of merit and distinction—poetry, combinations of poetry and prose, short fiction, memoirs, and translations (mostly poetry). We are also involved in publishing such regional programs as the Minnesota Voices Project and the Many Minnesotas Project. The press is in a transitional state. Check our website for updates." avg. press run 1M-2.5M. Pub'd 10 titles 2009. 114 titles listed in the *Small Press Record of Books in Print* (36th Edition, 2010-11). Discounts: 1-5 copies 20%, 6+ 40% trade; 50% for outright purchases 1-4 20%, 5-24 42%, 24-99 43%, 100-249 44%, 250-499 45%, 500-750 46%, 750+ 47%. Bookstores order through Consortium Book Sales and Distribution 1045 Westgate Dr, Suite 90 St.Paul, MN 55114-1065, phone 800-283-3572, fax 612-221-0124. 96-300pp. Simultaneous submissions accepted: no. Copyrights for author. Subjects: African-American, Asian-American, Book Arts, Fiction, Literature (General), Poetry, Prose, Short Stories, Translation.

New Road Publishing, 3650 Rogers Rd., #328, Wake Forest, NC 27587, Phone # 919-453-2850 Fax # 888-957-8885. 2000. avg. press run 500 - 5000. 2 titles listed in the *Small Press Record of Books in Print* (36th Edition, 2010-11).

New Sins Press, Rane Arroyo, Co-Publisher; Glenn Sheldon, Co-Publisher; Dan Nowak, Editor; Melanie Dusseau, Editor; Stacia Fleegal, Editor; Teneice Delgado, Editor, 3925 Watson Avenue, Toledo, OH 43612-1113, web sites: www.newsinspress.com, www.myspace.com/newsinspress. 1985. Poetry. "New Sins Press used to publish poetry chapbooks. Some of our authors were: Barbara Hamby, Mark Magiera, Julie Parson-Nesbitt and Richard Collins. We published one full-length poetry collection by Amy Yanity. In 2007, we began publishing one full-length poetry collection annually through a poetry competition (deadline: May 1st). No Bones to Carry by James Penha was our first Editors' Prize winner." avg. press run 500-1000. Expects 1 title 2010, 1 title 2011. 4 titles listed in the *Small Press Record of Books in Print* (36th Edition, 2010-11). 70pp. Reporting time: 1-2 months. Simultaneous submissions accepted: Yes. Payment: in copies. Does not copyright for author. Subjects: Avant-Garde, Experimental Art, Bisexual, Drama, Experimental, Gay, Health, Latino, Lesbianism, Race.

NEW SOLUTIONS, Community Service, Inc., Pat Murphy, Editor, PO Box 243, Yellow Springs, OH 45387, 937-767-2161, info@communitysolution.org. 1940. Articles, reviews, letters, non-fiction. circ. 250. 4/yr. Pub'd 4 issues 2009; expects 4 issues 2010, 4 issues 2011. sub. price $25 includes membership; per copy $3.50; sample free. Back issues: $2. Discounts: write for schedule, 40% on 10 or more. 7pp. Reporting time: 2 weeks. Simultaneous submissions accepted: yes. Publishes 66% of manuscripts submitted. Payment: copies. Copyrighted, reverts to author. §Community, alternatives in community, society, local economy, education, land trusts and land reform, ecological concerns, family, simple living, sustainability issues, peak oil. Exchange ads. Subjects: Biography, Business & Economics, Community, Education, Family, Newsletter, Philosophy, Society, Sociology.

NEW STONE CIRCLE, Mary Hays, Karen Singer, 1185 E 1900 N Road, White Heath, IL 61884. 1994. Poetry, fiction, art, photos, interviews, satire, parts-of-novels, long-poems, non-fiction. circ. 100. 1-2/yr. Pub'd 1 issue 2009; expects 2 issues 2010, 2 issues 2011. sub. price $8; per copy $4.50; sample $4.50. Back issues: $4.50. 50pp. Reporting time: 3-6 months. We accept simultaneous submissions, but let us know. We don't for contests. Publishes 5% of manuscripts submitted. Payment: 1 copy. Copyrighted, reverts to author. Subjects: Fiction, Poetry.

NEW UNIONIST, Jeff Miller, 1301 Cambridge St., Ste. 102, Hopkins, MN 55343-1925, 651-646-5546, nup@minn.net. 1975. Articles, photos, cartoons, reviews, letters, news items. "No outside manuscripts." circ. 9M. 12/yr. Pub'd 12 issues 2009; expects 12 issues 2010, 12 issues 2011. sub. price 12 issues $7; per copy 30¢; sample free. Discounts: 15¢ each. 8pp. Payment: copies only. Not copyrighted. Pub's reviews: 4 in 2009. §Socialism, labor, politics, current affairs. Subjects: Labor, Socialist.

NEW VERSE NEWS, THE, James Penha, nvneditor@yahoo.com OR nvneditor@gmail.com. 2005. Poetry. "*The New Verse News* is an online journal [www.newversenews.com] that solicits and publishes poetry on topical issues and current events. It's a sort of poetic newspaper. Although the editor and thus the site have a clearly liberal political bias, we welcome a variety of views and verses. Recent and regular contributors:

Rochelle Owens, Mary Saracino, David Chorlton, Scott Siegel, David Feela, Howie Good, Earl Wilcox, Bill Costley, Andrew Hilbert, Alan Catlin, Louis Crew, Steve Hellyard Swartz. GUIDELINES: Submit previously unpublished poems to nvneditor@yahoo.com or to nvneditor@gmail.com for possible posting. Paste poems in the body of an email (no attachments) and write 'Verse News Submission' as the subject line. Send a brief bio too.'' Continually updated. Reporting time: 1-21 days. Simultaneous submissions accepted: Yes. Publishes 25% of manuscripts submitted. Payment: No payment. Copyrighted, reverts to author. Subjects: Current Affairs, Poetry, Politics, Writers/Writing.

New Victoria Publishers, Patricia Feuerhaken, PO Box 13173, Chicago, IL 60613-0173, 800-326-5297. 1976. Poetry, fiction, art, plays, non-fiction. Pub'd 2 titles 2009; expects 4 titles 2010, 6 titles 2011. 84 titles listed in the *Small Press Record of Books in Print* (36th Edition, 2010-11). Discounts: distributed by Bella Books, Tallahassee, Florida 32302. 200pp. Reporting time: 1 month. We'll possibly accept simultaneous submissions. Publishes 2-3% of manuscripts submitted. Payment: 10% of net. Copyrights for author. Subjects: Aging, Environment, Erotica, Fantasy, Feminism, Fiction, Humor, Lesbianism, Literature (General), Mystery, Novels, Science Fiction, Women.

New Voices Publishing, Rita Schiano, P.O. Box 560, Wilmington, MA 01887, 978-658-2131, www.kidsterrain.com. 2001. Fiction. ''Children's books.'' 5 titles listed in the *Small Press Record of Books in Print* (36th Edition, 2010-11). Subjects: Fiction, Picture Books.

NEW VOICES REVISITED: Poetry, Contests and Short Stories., Lorraine Moreau Laverriere, 75 Edgewood Ave Apt 38, Methuen, MA 01844, 978-688-5812. 1979. Poetry, non-fiction. ''I'm interested in new poets who are trying to see their work in print. Published poets are also welcome. I publish short poems that are well written. I don't accept anything vulgar or with four letter words that are not in the dictionary. I have published students throughout the years and accept mss. from teachers with their students work. Only mss. with a SASE will be returned. If your poetry is not accepted, it will not be rejected. If it is returned, it will include an editorial comment and positive criticism, if appropriate. There will be a poetry contest with cash prizes in 1997. Send a SASE to me for the rules.'' circ. 300. 1/yr. Expects 1 issue 2011. sub. price $7; per copy $7; sample $7. Back issues: inquire. Discounts: 2-10 copies 25%. 24pp. Reporting time: Two weeks. Simultaneous submissions accepted: Yes. Publishes 35% of manuscripts submitted. Payment: Contributor's copy. Copyrighted, reverts to author. Pub's reviews: none in 2009. §Poetry chapbooks. Subjects: Desktop Publishing, Emily Dickinson, Disabled, English, Nature, Non-Fiction, Non-Violence, The North, Poetry, Reading, Reference, Religion, Reviews, Writers/Writing, Young Adult.

New Win Publishing, Arthur Chou, 9682 Telstar Ave. Suite 110, El Monte, CA 91731, 626-448-3448, 626-602-3817, info@academiclearningcompany.com, www.newwinpublishing.com. 1978. Non-fiction. avg. press run 5,000. Pub'd 20 titles 2009; expects 25 titles 2010, 30 titles 2011. No titles listed in the *Small Press Record of Books in Print* (36th Edition, 2010-11). Discounts: 40-55%. Reporting time: 1-2 month. Simultaneous submissions accepted: Yes. Publishes 10% of manuscripts submitted. Payment: 10%. Copyrights for author. Subjects: Business & Economics, Careers, Collectibles, Employment, Finances, Health, How-To, Language, Latin America, Nature, Nutrition, Parenting, Self-Help, Spain, Sports, Outdoors.

New World Library, Marc Allen, Publisher, 14 Pamaron Way, Novato, CA 94949-6215. 1978. Fiction, non-fiction. avg. press run 15M. Pub'd 29 titles 2009; expects 32 titles 2010, 32 titles 2011. 55 titles listed in the *Small Press Record of Books in Print* (36th Edition, 2010-11). Discounts: 50-55% to distributors, 10% to individual consumers ordering 5 or more titles. 260pp. Reporting time: 15 weeks. Publishes less than 1% of manuscripts submitted. Payment: 12-16% of net royalty to authors, paid semi-annually. Copyrights for author. Subjects: Business & Economics, Creativity, Health, Inspirational, Metaphysics, Native American, New Age, Parenting, Psychology, Religion, Self-Help, Self-Help, Spiritual, Tapes & Records, Women.

New World Press (see also BLOODJET LITERARY MAGAZINE), Noni Howard Ph.D, Edd, MD, Littd,, Publisher, 20 Driftwood Trail, Half Moon Bay, CA 94019-2349, 650-726-5939; email: thepitheaisout@coast-side.net. 1974. Poetry, fiction, art, photos, letters, parts-of-novels, long-poems, collages. ''Length is 100 pages plus, prefer women writers, Jennifer Stone, Adrian Marcus and Evelyn Hickey are recent contributors. Persons able to write grants or obtain other funding especially considered. Telephone and leave number before writing. Send nothing by mail without telephoning first.'' avg. press run 1.2M. Expects 2 titles 2010, 1-3 titles 2011. 1 title listed in the *Small Press Record of Books in Print* (36th Edition, 2010-11). Discounts: 40% bulk or to educational institutions, schools, etc. 100-200pp. Reporting time: Send nothing by mail. Telephone first! Simultaneous submissions accepted: No. Publishes less than 2% of manuscripts submitted. Payment: 200 free copies. Copyrights for author. Subjects: Literature (General), Poetry.

New World Press, Inc, Steven Thedford, 5626 Platte Dr., Ellenwood, GA 30294, (404)512-6760. 1994. Poetry, fiction, non-fiction. avg. press run 750. Expects 1 title 2010, 2 titles 2011. No titles listed in the *Small Press Record of Books in Print* (36th Edition, 2010-11). Discounts: 2-10 25%. 50pp. Reporting time: 6 months. Simultaneous submissions accepted: Yes. Publishes 10% of manuscripts submitted. Payment: Industry

Standard. Does not copyright for author. Subjects: African Literature, Africa, African Studies, African-American, Autobiography, Children, Youth, Education, Egypt, Essays, Internet, Mystery.

THE NEW WRITER, Suzanne Ruthven, PO Box 60, Cranbrook, Kent TN17 2ZR, England, 01580-212626 admin@thenewwriter.com www.thenewwriter.com. 1996. Poetry, fiction, articles, interviews, reviews, letters, news items. "Monthly email News free of charge with annual subscription." 6/yr. Pub'd 6 issues 2009; expects 6 issues 2010, 6 issues 2011. sub. price £37.50; sample 6 IRCs for free sample. Discounts: negotiable. 56pp. Reporting time: 2-3 weeks. Simultaneous submissions accepted: yes. Publishes 5% of manuscripts submitted. Payment: varies. Copyrighted, reverts to author. Pub's reviews: 30 in 2009. §Short stories and writing techniques (but only if available in England). Ads: £150/£85/£50 1/4 page. Subjects: Fiction, Poetry, Writers/Writing.

THE NEW YORK QUARTERLY, Raymond Hammond, Editor, PO Box 2015, Old Chelsea Station, New York, NY 10113, info@nyquarterly.org, www.nyquarterly.org. 1969. Poetry, interviews. "*The New York Quarterly* is a magazine devoted to the craft of poetry. The editors are interested in seeing poems of any style or persuasion, so long as they are well-intentioned and well-written. Recent contributors include W. D. Snodgrass, David Lehman, Timothy Liu, Franz Wright and Charles Bukowski. Writers are strongly encouraged to read recent issues of *NYQ* before submitting." circ. 1000. 3/yr. Pub'd 1 issue 2009; expects 2 issues 2010, 3 issues 2011. sub. price $35/4 issues, $35 institutions, foreign orders add $15; per copy $10; sample $10. Back issues: $18. 176pp. Reporting time: 3 months. Simultaneous submissions accepted: yes. Publishes 5% of manuscripts submitted. Payment: issue copies. Copyrighted, reverts to author. Ads: $250/$150. Subjects: Interviews, Poetry.

•NEW YORK TYRANT, Giancarlo DiTrapano, Editor, 676A Ninth Avenue 153, New York, NY 10036. "*The New York Tyrant* is a tri-quarterly literary magazine based in Hells Kitchen, focusing on the immediacy of the short story. The pieces, coming from voices both new and seasoned, are concise, evocative, often humorous, and sometimes surreal. We believe in the power and urgency of the story and its ability to describe and illuminate the interior and exterior landscape. We believe in the power of narrative and its ability to make life more astonishingly alive."

NeWest Press, #201, 8540 - 109 Street, Edmonton AB T6G 1E6, Canada, (780) 432-9427 - phone, (780) 433-3179 - fax. "Since its inception, NeWest's literary division has generated numerous award-winning titles and made significant contributions to the Canadian literary scene through the Writer As Critic and Prairie Play Series, as well as through various anthologies of poetry, fiction and literary criticism. Today NeWest continues to thrive, publishing ten to twelve books annually. While still a western regional press in its focus, in recent years NeWest has expanded its mandate to publish work from British Columbia, in addition to the prairie provinces." No titles listed in the *Small Press Record of Books in Print* (36th Edition, 2010-11).

NewPages (see also NEWPAGES: Good Reading Starts Here), PO Box 1580, Bay City, MI 48706, www.newpages.com. No titles listed in the *Small Press Record of Books in Print* (36th Edition, 2010-11).

NEWPAGES: Good Reading Starts Here, NewPages, PO Box 1580, Bay City, MI 48706, www.newpages.com. 1979.

NEWS FROM NATIVE CALIFORNIA, Heyday Books, Malcolm Margolin, Publisher; Margaret Dubin, Managing Editor, PO Box 9145, Berkeley, CA 94709, 510-549-3564; FAX 510-549-1889. 1987. Articles, art, photos, interviews, criticism, reviews, letters, news items, non-fiction. "We are interested in material related to California Indians, past and present." circ. 10M. 4/yr. Pub'd 4 issues 2009; expects 4 issues 2010, 4 issues 2011. sub. price $19; per copy $4.95; sample $1. Back issues: range from $4 to $20. Discounts: 40% trade, call for other schedules. 56pp. Reporting time: 3 weeks. Simultaneous submissions accepted: yes. Payment: up to about $50/article. Copyrighted, does not revert to author. Pub's reviews: 5-10 in 2009. §Native American: culture, history, art, politics, literature. Ads: $545/$280/send for rate card. Subjects: Arts, Culture, History, Literature (General), Native American, Politics.

NewSage Press, Maureen Michelson, Publisher, PO Box 607, Troutdale, OR 97060-0607, 503-695-2211 www.newsagepress.com info@newsagepress.com. 1985. Non-fiction. "We are interested in publishing quality tradebooks—in content as well as production. NewSage only publishes nonfiction, specializing in books on grief and death, the animal/human bond, and social issues related to women, the environment, animals. No electronic submissions of materials without prior permission from the publisher. When sending submissions, include SASE for return of materials." avg. press run 7.5M. Pub'd 3 titles 2009; expects 4 titles 2010, 4 titles 2011. 30 titles listed in the *Small Press Record of Books in Print* (36th Edition, 2010-11). Discounts: For bookstores, purchase our books through our distributor for the U.S. and Canada, Publishers Group West (800-788-3123). All others may contact NewSage Press directly. On purchases of less than 12 books (mixed titles OK), there is a 20% discount. On orders of 12 books or more (mixed titles OK), discount is 40%. 190pp. Reporting time: 4 to 6 months. Simultaneous submissions accepted: yes. Publishes 10% of manuscripts submitted. Payment: Royalties paid, usually standard. Copyrights for author. Subjects: Animals, Environment, Euthanasia, Death, Feminism, Grieving, Marine Life, Memoirs, Multicultural, Non-Fiction, Non-Violence,

Peace, Pets, Whaling, Women.

NEWWITCH, Kenaz Filan, P.O. Box 641, Point Arena, CA 95468, Phone:888-724-3966, Fax:707-882-2793, website http://www.newwitch.com. 2002. Poetry, fiction, articles, art, photos, interviews, reviews, music, letters, non-fiction. 4/yr. Pub'd 4 issues 2009; expects 4 issues 2010, 4 issues 2011. sub. price $20. Back issues: inquire. Simultaneous submissions accepted: No. Copyrighted, reverts to author. Pub's reviews. Subjects: Counter-Culture, Alternatives, Communes, Magic, Multicultural, Myth, Mythology, Native American, Nature, New Age, Non-Fiction, Religion, Spiritual, Supernatural, Tarot, WICCA, Women.

Next Decade, Inc., Barbara Brooks Kimmel, 39 Old Farmstead Road, Chester, NJ 07930-2732, 908-879-6625, Fax 908-879-2920. 1990. "Publish nonfiction reference books (legal, financial, health and retirement) and sold to the trade, universities, corporations and libraries." avg. press run 5M-10M. Expects 2 titles 2010, 2 titles 2011. 10 titles listed in the *Small Press Record of Books in Print* (36th Edition, 2010-11). Discounts: 50% on distribution arrangements. 80-300pp. Reporting time: 1 month. Simultaneous submissions accepted: yes. Publishes 1% of manuscripts submitted. Payment: varies. Copyrights for author. Subject: Reference.

Niba Media Group, LLC, Nicole Hamer, 1555 Sherman Avenue #306, Evanston, IL 60201, info@nibaguides.com. 2007. Non-fiction. "The Niba Media Group publishes the Niba Guides series. Niba Guides are current affairs guidebooks to the ideas, events and people making news. Niba Guides integrate authoritative research and analysis, wit and a whimsical writing style to make challenging topics fascinating to read. We seek published writers able to write in a breezy manner but with flair and authority (style should be a cross between the Economist and the Lets Go series). The writer must also demonstrate excellent research and organizational skills. If a project goes well, we may add you to our stable of freelance writers. Please respond with an email or mail query. If your query is sent by email, please copy your query into the body of your email message. We do not accept attachments or unsolicited work. If we receive an attachment we will have to delete it, unopened. Serious inquiries only." avg. press run 1500. Expects 2-3 titles 2010, 10 titles 2011. No titles listed in the *Small Press Record of Books in Print* (36th Edition, 2010-11). 130pp. Reporting time: 1 to 2 weeks. Simultaneous submissions accepted: Yes. Payment: Work-for-hire agreements. Subject: Current Affairs.

NIBBLE, CT Press, Jeff Fleming, Oakland, CA, nibblepoems@gmail.com; http://nibblepoems.wordpress.com. 1995. Poetry. "*Nibble* is a new magazine from CT Press looking for great SHORT poetry (20 lines or less). Please visit our website for more information: http://nibblepoems.wordpress.com." circ. 200. 10/yr. Pub'd 4 issues 2009; expects 10 issues 2010, 10 issues 2011. sub. price $20; per copy $5; sample $4. Back issues: $4. 24pp. Reporting time: 2 weeks. Ads: Negotiable.

•Night Bomb Press (see also THE NIGHT BOMB REVIEW), Chris Ridenour, Editor and Publisher; Amber Ridenour, Editor and Publisher, 1812 NE 66th Avenue, #91, Portland, OR 97213, submissions@nightbomb-press.com, www.nightbombpress.com, (503)867-7270. 2008. Poetry, fiction. "We publish chapbooks, paperback volumes, and a review of poetry that embodies the idea of verse at the intersection of guts and craft. From promotion to every aspect of production, we operate completely independently, utilizing local materials and promoting local authors whenever possible. We sell our books to independent booksellers and try to promote unpublished poetry and flash fiction that has been overlooked by larger and more traditional/conservative publications. Recent contributors include Tommy Gaffney (Whiskey Days) Dennis McBride (Looking for Peoria) and Suzanne Burns (Misfits and Other Heroes)." avg. press run 200. Pub'd 3 titles 2009; expects 4-6 titles 2010, 4-6 titles 2011. 1 title listed in the *Small Press Record of Books in Print* (36th Edition, 2010-11). Discounts: average 30% off cover prices to wholesalers and/or independent consignment bookbuyers—details available on website. 20-200pp. Reporting time: We accept submissions to our chapbook contest from January-March. Response time is 6 weeks after March 31st. Reading fee:$10. We publish the winning chapbook and select poems from among the other entries for consideration in The Night Bomb Review. Simultaneous submissions accepted: Yes. Publishes 30% of manuscripts submitted. Payment: no advances; author gets 20% of profits. Copyrights for author. Subjects: Literary Review, Poetry, Prose.

•THE NIGHT BOMB REVIEW, Night Bomb Press, Chris Ridenour, 1812 NE 66th Avenue, #91, Portland, OR 97213, submissions@nightbombpress.com, www.nightbombpress.com, (503)867-7270. 2009. Poetry. "We're looking for poetry that pays an equal amount of attention to linguistics as it does to conceit. We're fans of innovation and enemies of most academic trends (like "poetry" that is actually prose with line breaks centered around one pity observation). Language poetry is fine, but it has to have a genuine emotional impact for us to consider publishing it. We tend to avoid poetry that rhymes, employs a great number of abstractions, does not contain tropes of any kind, and most socio-political rants or protest poems. Our goal is to produce a review that will still feel innovative, edgy, emotive, and just damn good ten years from now." circ. 200. 1/yr. Pub'd 1 issue 2009; expects 1 issue 2010, 1 issue 2011. sub. price $0; per copy $7.00; sample free. Back issues: $5.00. Discounts: $3-5 for wholesalers/retailers. 60pp. Reporting time: published in conjunction with chapbook contest ($10 reading fee); submission period Jan-March; 6 weeks response time after March 31. Simultaneous submissions accepted: Yes. Publishes 30% of manuscripts submitted. Payment: one copy of the review; winner recieves small prize $ and 5 copies of published chapbook. Copyrighted, reverts to author. Pub's reviews. Ads:

we don't advertise. Subjects: Poetry, Prose.

Night Horn Books, John Spilker, Co-Publisher; Robert Anbian, Co-Publisher, Editor, PO Box 424906, San Francisco, CA 94142-4906, 415-440-2442; nighthornb@aol.com. 1978. Poetry, articles, art, photos, interviews, satire, long-poems, collages. "Books can be purchased directly at www.protestworks.com/nighthorn.html. Also vailable from Amazon.com and other outlets. In-print poetry titles include Tomorrow Triumphant by Otto Rene Castillo, WE Parts 1 & 2 by Robert Anbian, plus work by Jack Hirschman, Katerina Gogou. Also distributes selected book titles by Ruddy Duck Press, War&Peace Press, and other small presses. Does not currently accept unsolicited mss." Pub'd 1 title 2009; expects 1 title 2010, 1 title 2011. 5 titles listed in the *Small Press Record of Books in Print* (36th Edition, 2010-11). Discounts: 40% to the trade direct or through distributions; 50% off for 9 or less copies, 55% off 10 or more to jobbers, wholesalers. 100-125pp. Reporting time: 8-12 weeks. Payment: negotiable. Copyrights for author. Subjects: Arts, Literature (General), Poetry.

•**Night Shade Books,** 1661 Tennessee Street, #3H, San Francisco, CA 94107, Phone: 415-206-1473. "Writing that inspires a sense of awe and wonder. Writing that explores the fantastic. vWriting that at once challenges and redefines a reader's expectations. Thse are the guiding editorial principles at Night Shaed Books." No titles listed in the *Small Press Record of Books in Print* (36th Edition, 2010-11).

NIGHT TRAIN, Rusty Barnes, Editor; Alicia Gifford, Fiction Editor, 212 Bellingham Ave., #2, Revere, MA 02151-4106, rustybarnes@nighttrainmagazine.com, www.nighttrainmagazine.com. 2002. Fiction, parts-of-novels. "*Night Train* (ISSN 1540-5494) welcomes submissions of flash fiction, short fiction, or self-contained novel excerpts in traditional or experimental styles. We do not consider poetry, criticism, book reviews or reprints. Please read *Night Train* to understand what we're all about. Visit our web site to see the latest information on submission guidelines, which can change. We're available through our website, at a growing number of independent book stores, and soon in some chains. Recent contributors: Robert Boswell, Steve Almond, Roy Kesey, Pia Ehrhardt, Jay Merill, DeWitt Henry, Terri Brown-Davidson." 2/yr. Pub'd 1 issue 2009; expects 2 issues 2010, 2 issues 2011. sub. price $17.95; per copy $9.95; sample $9.95. Back issues: $7. Discounts: 40%. 192pp. Reporting time: 3-6 months. Simultaneous submissions accepted: yes. Publishes 1-2% of manuscripts submitted. Payment: Pays in copies. Copyrighted. Ads: none. Subject: Literature (General).

Nightboat Books, Kazim Ali, Jennifer Chapis, Stephen Motika, 7 Fishkill Ave., Cold Spring, NY 10516-2303, info@nightboat.org, www.nightboat.org. 2003. Poetry, fiction. "Nightboat Books is a small, nonprofit publishing company dedicated to printing original books of poetry and prose, and bringing out-of-print treasures back to life. Nightboat seeks to publish cherished contemporary writers, as well as emerging and previously unknown poets and authors. Part of our inspiration comes from a desire to showcase new writers whose work may be otherwise underappreciated by the mainstream. Our mission is to distribute and promote beautifully crafted work that resists convention and transcends boundaries, books rich with poignancy, intelligence, and risk. Our authors include Fanny Howe, Juliet Patterson, Joshua Kryah, Nathalie Stephens, and Michael Burkard." avg. press run 1500. Pub'd 2 titles 2009; expects 3 titles 2010, 4 titles 2011. 4 titles listed in the *Small Press Record of Books in Print* (36th Edition, 2010-11). Discounts: Author's Discount. 100/300pp. Reporting time: 2 mos. for prose queries, 4 mos. for poetry manuscripts via contest. Simultaneous submissions accepted: Yes. Publishes less than 1% of manuscripts submitted. Payment varies depending on project. Copyrights for author.

NIGHTJAR REVIEW, Nightjar Press, Jeremy Rendina, Michael Klausman, P.O. Box 583, New York, NY 10002. 2005. Poetry, fiction, art, photos, long-poems, concrete art. "The featured writer of the inaugural issue is Lionel Ziprin, a legendary figureand lifelong resident of the Lower East Side whose curious body of writingincludes the one-thousand page epic poem, 'Sentencial Metaphrastic', as well as the highly off-kilter children's poems that make up 'Songs for Schizoid Siblings'. The Nightjar Review has excerpted the most ample selection from 'Songs' to date, which were composed in the mid 1950s at a time when Ziprin ran a greeting card company that employed such future luminaries as Bruce Conner, Jordan Belson, and Harry Smith. The 'Songs' were composed in the manner of Mother Goose rhymes and are infused with his own rendering of alchemy and the Kaballah. The first issue of The Nightjar Review is 144 pages perfect bound, with a silkscreened dust jacket featuring a new drawing by the artist Bruce Conner. Additonal contributions come from Anja Buechele, Dante Carfagna, Diane Cluck, inoli, Shannon Ketch, Michael Klausman, Angus MacLise, Peter Relic, Jeremy Rendina, John Fell Ryan, Dave Tompkins, and Yvonne." circ. 500. 2/yr. Expects 1 issue 2010, 2 issues 2011. sub. price $25; per copy $15. Discounts: 40% for 5 or more copies. 144pp. Reporting time: 1 month. Simultaneous submissions accepted: Yes. Payment: negotiable. Copyrighted, reverts to author. Subjects: Avant-Garde, Experimental Art, Photography, Poetry, Prose.

NIGHTLIFE MAGAZINE, Martine Desjardins, Publisher and Fashion Editor; Yann Fortier, Editor; Oliver Lalande, Music Editor; Sarah Levesque, Urban Culture Editor, 4200, Boulevard St. Laurent, Suite 1470, Montreal, Quebec H2W 2R2, Canada, 514.278.3222. 1999. Articles, art, photos, interviews, reviews, music, collages, news items. "Reference of activities and trends for Montrealers." circ. 40000. 10/yr. Pub'd 10 issues 2009; expects 10 issues 2010, 10 issues 2011. sub. price $35; per copy free; sample free. Back issues: $3,50.

100pp. Copyrighted. §Cosmetics and CDs. Ads: $2000 full page. Subjects: Arts, Bilingual, Canada, Dining, Restaurants, Entertainment, Fashion, Festivals, Music, Society, Visual Arts, Young Adult.

NIGHTSUN, Gerry LaFemina, Department of English, Frostburg State University, Frostburg, MD 21532-1099, nightsun@frostburg.edu. 1981. Poetry, fiction, criticism, long-poems. circ. 300. 1/yr. Expects 1 issue 2010, 1 issue 2011. sub. price $15; per copy $9; sample $5. Back issues: $3 per issue. Discounts: 10-19 copies 10%20-29 copies 20%30 + copies 40%. 100pp. Reporting time: 2 months. Simultaneous submissions accepted: No. Payment: small honorarium when possible; 2 copies of journal. Copyrighted, reverts to author. Ads: Full page: $120half page: $75quarter page: $40. Subject: Literary Review.

Nightsun Books, Ruth Wiley, 823 Braddock Road, Cumberland, MD 21502-2622, 301-722-4861. 1987. Poetry, fiction, cartoons, criticism, plays, non-fiction. "Please inquire before submitting manuscripts!" avg. press run 200-1M. Pub'd 5 titles 2009; expects 1 title 2010, 1 title 2011. 14 titles listed in the *Small Press Record of Books in Print* (36th Edition, 2010-11). Discounts: 1 0%, 2-4 20%, 5-24 40%, 25-49 43%, 50-99 46%, 100+ 50%. 30-200pp. Reporting time: varies. Payment: varies—inquire. Subjects: Anthology, Drama, Fiction, How-To, Philosophy, Philosophy, Poetry, Psychology, Visual Arts.

Nilgiri Press, PO Box 256, Tomales, CA 94971-0256, orders 800-475-2369, 707-878-2369, Fax 707-878-2375, info@nilgiri.org, www.nilgiri.org. No titles listed in the *Small Press Record of Books in Print* (36th Edition, 2010-11). Subjects: Inspirational, Philosophy, Relationships, Religion, Spiritual.

NIMROD INTERNATIONAL JOURNAL, Francine Ringold, 800 South Tucker Drive, Tulsa, OK 74104-3126. 1956. Poetry, fiction, articles, art, photos, interviews, parts-of-novels, long-poems, non-fiction. "Recent contributors: Gina Ochsner, Daniel Dusk, Natalie Diaz, Chloe Honum. Annual *Nimrod Literary* Awards: in poetry (Pablo Neruda Prize), in fiction (Katherine Anne Porter Prize). 1st prize in each category $2000, 2nd prize $1000. Submissions are accepted between January 1 and April 30 each year. Recent past judges include Mark Doty, Ron Carlson, Colum McCann, and Colleen McElroy. Please send business-size SASE for awards and guidelines." circ. 2,500. 2/yr. Pub'd 2 issues 2009; expects 2 issues 2010. 13 titles listed in the *Small Press Record of Books in Print* (36th Edition, 2010-11). sub. price $18.50/yr; $32/2 yrs.; outside US - $20/$35; per copy $11; sample $11. Back issues: varies; list of back issues available from *Nimrod*. Discounts: 10% orders over 20. 200pp. Reporting time: 3 months. Simultaneous submissions accepted: yes. Publishes 1% of manuscripts submitted. Payment: 2 copies of issue in which work is published and reduced cost on extra issues. Copyrighted, reverts to author. Ads: Exchange. Subjects: Fiction, Poetry.

nine muses books, margareta waterman, Publisher, 3541 Kent Creek Road, Winston, OR 97496, 541-679-6674, mw9muses@teleport.com. 1987. Poetry, fiction, parts-of-novels, long-poems. "nine muses is an artists' collective for the author-owned production of books and tapes. At this time 15 serious writers, highly esteemed by their colleagues, make up the list. a prime feature of nine muses books, in addition to the advantage of author ownership, is the design, which is done, not to a standard format, but with particular attention to each book as a work of art, so that illustration, color of paper and ink, balance of composition on each page, and so on, are fitted to the content and meaning of the book. submissions are by invitation." avg. press run 500. Pub'd 3 titles 2009; expects 4 titles 2010, 4 titles 2011. 67 titles listed in the *Small Press Record of Books in Print* (36th Edition, 2010-11). Discounts: trade to bookstores, bulk to libraries, etc. single orders no discount, prepay on first orders. 65 - 200pp. Payment: nine muses is an author's collective; see comments above. author owns books. Author owns copyrights and books. Subjects: Buddhism, Language, Literature (General), Magic, Myth, Mythology, Occult, Performing Arts, Poetry, Politics, Tapes & Records.

9N-2N-8N-NAA NEWSLETTER, G.W. Rinaldi, Robert R. Rinaldi Jr., PO Box 275, East Corinth, VT 05040-0275, www.n-news.com. 1985. Articles, art, photos, cartoons, interviews, criticism, reviews, letters, news items. "Magazine consists of 36-40 pages/3 columns, several photos, column pages, small print, equal to 50 in larger print." circ. 9M. 4/yr. Pub'd 4 issues 2009; expects 4 issues 2010, 4 issues 2011. sub. price $20 US, $23 Canada, $26 foreign; per copy $6.50; sample $6.50 + $1 p/h. Back issues: send for order form. Discounts: none. 36-40pp. Reporting time: 1 month. Publishes 80% of manuscripts submitted. Payment: none. Copyrighted, does not revert to author. Pub's reviews: 6-8 in 2009. §Agriculture, old tractors, farm memorabilia, farm equipment, farm lifestyle. Ads: free non-commercial classifieds for members; commercial: 90¢/word, display rates: POR.

1913, A Journal of Forms, Sandra Doller, Founder & Editrice; Ben Doller, Designer & Vice-Editor, Sandra Doller, Markstein Hall 126J, LTWR Department, CSU-San Marcos, 333 S. Twin Oaks Valley, San Marcos, CA 92096-0001. 2003. "Increasingly, small mags & presses depend upon support from individual donors who see the value in sustaining independent publishing projects of merit. *1913* is one such project. Committed to providing the finest in contemporary poetry, poetics, art, & their intersections, *1913* hopes to be able to continue its mission to publish in book-as-art-object form, with full-color images and the high quality printing, editing, and design readers have come to expect of *1913*." Discretionary intervals.

19TH-CENTURY LITERATURE, University of California Press, Joseph Bristow, Editor; Thomas

Wortham, Editor, University of California Press, 2000 Center Street, Suite 303, Berkeley, CA 94704-1223, 510-643-7154. 1946. Reviews, non-fiction. "Editorial address: Dept. of English, Box 951530, Rolfe Hall, Room 2225, 405 Hilgard, University of California, Los Angeles, CA 90095-1530." circ. 1913. 4/yr. Pub'd 4 issues 2009; expects 4 issues 2010, 4 issues 2011. sub. price $40 indiv., $112 instit., $25 students (+ $20 air freight); per copy $15 indiv., $33 instit., $15 students; sample free. Back issues: $15 indiv., $33 instit., $15 students. Discounts: foreign subs. agents 10%, one-time orders 10+, standing orders (bookstores): 1-99 40%, 100+ 50%. 144pp. Reporting time: 1-2 months. Copyrighted, does not revert to author. Pub's reviews: 4 in 2009. §19th-century literature, American and English. Ads: $295/$220. Subject: Literature (General).

19TH-CENTURY MUSIC, University of California Press, Larry Kramer, Editor; James Hepokoski, Editor; Christina Acosta, Managing Editor, University of California Press, 2000 Center Street, Suite 303, Berkeley, CA 94704-1223, 510-643-7154. 1977. Criticism, reviews, non-fiction. "Editorial address: Dept. of Music, One Shields Avenue, University of California, Davis, CA 95616." circ. 1326. 3/yr. Pub'd 3 issues 2009; expects 3 issues 2010, 3 issues 2011. sub. price $40 indiv., $139 instit., $25 student (+ $20 air freight); per copy $21 indiv.; $53 instit. (+ $20 air freight), $21 student; sample free. Back issues: same as single copy price. Discounts: foreign subs. agents 10%, one-time orders 10+ 30%, standing orders (bookstores): 1-99 40%, 100+ 50%. 96pp. Reporting time: 1-3 months. Copyrighted, does not revert to author. Pub's reviews: 3 in 2009. §19th-century music. Ads: $295/$220. Subject: Music.

Ninety-Six Press, Gilbert Allen, William Rogers, Furman University, 3300 Poinsett Highway, Greenville, SC 29613, 864-294-3152/6. 1991. Poetry. "Ninety-Six Press publishes books of poetry by authors from its region. The press reviews manuscripts only by invitation. No unsolicited manuscripts." avg. press run 500. Pub'd 1 title 2009; expects 1 title 2010, 1-2 titles 2011. 12 titles listed in the *Small Press Record of Books in Print* (36th Edition, 2010-11). Discounts: 40%. 50-70pp. Payment: copies. Copyrights for author. Subjects: Poetry, South.

NINTH LETTER, Jodee Stanley, Editor, 234 English Bldg., University of Illinois, 608 S. Wright St., Urbana, IL 61801, (217) 244-3145, fax (217)244-4147, www.ninthletter.com, ninthletter@uiuc.edu. 2004. Poetry, fiction, art, interviews, non-fiction. "Recent contributors include Sherman Alexie, Benjamin Percy, Viet Dinh, Angie Estes, Margot Livesey, D.A. Powell, Ander Monson, Marianne Boruch, Cathy Day, Stephan Clark, Amjad Nasser, Geri Doran, Tomaz Salamun, Robin Hemley, Douglas Glover, Stephen Marche, Katherine Vaz." circ. 2000. 2/yr. Pub'd 2 issues 2009; expects 2 issues 2010, 2 issues 2011. sub. price 21.95; per copy 14.95; sample 9.95. Back issues: 9.95. 200pp. Reporting time: 6-8 weeks. Simultaneous submissions accepted: OK. Payment: $25 per page, plus 2 copies, on publication. Copyrighted, reverts to author.

Nip and Tuck Publishing, 736 Wilson Avenue, Kelowna, BC V1Y 6X9, Canada, 250-762-7861, nipandtuck@shaw.ca. 1995. Non-fiction. avg. press run 1M. Pub'd 1 title 2009; expects 2 titles 2010, 5 titles 2011. 2 titles listed in the *Small Press Record of Books in Print* (36th Edition, 2010-11). Discounts: industry standard. 200pp. Simultaneous submissions accepted: no. Copyrights for author. Subjects: Biography, History, Immigration, Non-Fiction, The West, Women.

•NIS America, Inc., Mitsuharu Hiraoka, 1221 E. Dyer Rd., Suite 210, Santa Ana, CA 92705, 714-540-1122. 2003. Fiction. "NIS America Inc. is a wholly owned subsidiary of Nippon Ichi Software, Inc., a Japanese company famous for its unique line of strategy RPG video games including titles such as Disgaea, Phantom Brave, and Makai Kingdom. NIS America Inc. specializes in bringing excellent products (mainly from Japan)to the U.S. with the aim of enhancing the U.S. public's cultural experiences as well as enjoyment." avg. press run 5000. Expects 1 title 2010, 5 titles 2011. No titles listed in the *Small Press Record of Books in Print* (36th Edition, 2010-11). 36pp. Reporting time: We do not accept manuscripts. Simultaneous submissions accepted: No. Copyrights for author. Subjects: Children, Youth, Entertainment, Fantasy, Fiction, Humor, Japan, Nature, Picture Books.

•Nish Publishing Company, Dane Batty, 880 NE 25th Avenue, Suite 2-102, Hillsboro, OR 97124, 503-707-4132. 2008. Non-fiction. "Nish Publishing Company specializes in biographies and nonfiction and publish talented authors that tell true stories to the world and need help bringing their top-quality, professional, interesting and sales-worthy stories to readers. We believe in being a steward in the business world and contain honest and true values that were once found with a handshake. Nish Publishing Company start publishing authors starting at the end of 2010 and will be accepting submissions around that time." avg. press run 5000. Expects 1 title 2010, 1 title 2011. 1 title listed in the *Small Press Record of Books in Print* (36th Edition, 2010-11). Discounts: 2-4 copies 20% off; 5-9 copies 30% off; 10-24 copies 40% off; 25-49 copies 42% off; 50-99 copies 44% off; 100-199 copies 48% off; 200 or more copies 50% off. 218-350pp. Reporting time: 1-2 business days. Simultaneous submissions accepted: Yes. Payment: As negotiated. Copyrights for author. Subjects: Autobiography, Bibliography, Biography, Creative Non-fiction, Crime, Memoirs, Non-Fiction, Prison, Society, Sports, Outdoors, Storytelling.

NO JOURNAL, Kyle Peterson, Political Editor; Mike Young, Fiction & Poetry Editor, editors@noojournal.com, http://www.noojournal.com/index.htm. "*No Journal* began in 2005. We are a free literary and political print/online journal distributed all over, based out of California and Massachusetts. Our contributors range from emerging to award-winning. Our mission is to encourage mainstream readers to reconnect with literature and diverse critical thinking. To this end, we exhibit: 1) Short monologues and longer essays that reflect personal and honest reactions to political, social and philosophical issues. 2) Fiction and poetry from writers whose work is honest, well-crafted, modern and resonant. 3) Visual art of many stripes and flavors from artists who are aware they live today and that other people lived yesterday.''

No Starch Press, William Pollock, 555 De Haro Street, Suite 250, San Francisco, CA 94107-2365, 415-863-9900. 1994. Non-fiction. ''No Starch Press is one of the few remaining independent computer book publishers. We publish the finest in geek entertainment—unique books on technology, with a focus on Open Source, security, hacking, programming, alternative operating systems, and LEGO. Our titles have personality, our authors are passionate, and our books tackle topics that people care about.(And most No Starch Press books use RepKover, a lay-flat binding that won't snap shut.) Recent contributors include: Pete Goodliffe(*AACU.org*, columnist), and Michael Schrenk (author of *Webbots, Spiders, and Screen Scrapers*).Prospective authors may complete our book proposal form, http://nostarch.com/releases/book_proposal.pdf, and send it to editors@nostarch.com for consideration. If we are interested in publishing your book, an editor will contact you.'' avg. press run 7.5M. Pub'd 12 titles 2009; expects 20 titles 2010, 25 titles 2011. 6 titles listed in the *Small Press Record of Books in Print* (36th Edition, 2010-11). Standard trade discount schedule through O'Reilly. 300pp. Reporting time: 3-4 weeks. Simultaneous submissions accepted: yes. Publishes 10% of manuscripts submitted. Payment: 15% on all cash received from all sales. Copyrights for author. Subjects: Children, Youth, Computers, Calculators, Crafts, Hobbies, Family, Gardening, Humor, Judaism.

Noble Porter Press, Roger Karshner, 36-851 Palm View Road, Rancho Mirage, CA 92270, 760-770-6076, fax 760-770-4507. 1995. Non-fiction. ''Not soliciting manuscripts.'' avg. press run 5M. No titles listed in the *Small Press Record of Books in Print* (36th Edition, 2010-11). Discounts: trade 40%. 200pp. Payment: 10% cover. Does not copyright for author.

Noemi Press, Carmen Gimenez Smith, Publisher; Evan Lavender-Smith, Editor, Noemi Press, P.O. Box 1330, Mesilla Park, NM 88047. 2002. Poetry, fiction, art, criticism, plays. ''Noemi Press is a not-for-profit publisher of innovative poetry and fiction chapbooks. We primarily publish new and emerging writers with the hope of creating greater exposure for their work. In both poetry and fiction we look for work that tends toward linguistic, syntactic, and formal experimentation without sacrificing allegiance to audience and beauty. Recent authors include Matthew Kirby, John Chavez, Jenny Boully, Lila Zemborain and Claire Hero. www.noemipress.org. Annual fiction and poetry chapbook contests with deadlines in February.'' avg. press run 500. Pub'd 4 titles 2009; expects 8 titles 2010, 10 titles 2011. 20 titles listed in the *Small Press Record of Books in Print* (36th Edition, 2010-11). Discounts: independent bookstores, institutions, classrooms: 2-9 copies 20%, 10-24 copies 30%, 25 or more copies please email for more information. 18-40pp. Reporting time: 3-5 months. Simultaneous submissions accepted: Yes. Publishes 5% of manuscripts submitted. Payment: Author's copies. Copyrights revert to author upon publication. Subjects: Experimental, Fiction, Poetry.

THE NOISE, T Max, Publisher and Editor; Francis Dimenno, Senior Associate Editor; Lexi Kahn, Senior Associate Editor; Joe Coughlin, Associate Editor; Steve Gisselbretch, Associate Editor; Robin Umbley, Associate Editor; Kier Byrnes, Associate Editor; Joel Simches, Associate Editor; Shady, Associate Editor, 74 Jamaica Street, Jamaica Plain, MA 02130, 617-524-4735, tmax@thenoise-boston.com. 1981. Articles, photos, cartoons, interviews, reviews, music, news items. ''Interviews and articles - 1600 words. Live reviews (of bands) - 150 words per band. Reviews of LPs - 200 words. Reviews of singles - 150 words. Our bias is away from commercial rock and roll, focusing on underground music from New England.'' circ. 5M. 10/yr. Pub'd 10 issues 2009; expects 10 issues 2010, 10 issues 2011. sub. price $22; per copy $5; sample $5. Back issues: $5-$50. Discounts: none. 48pp. Reporting time: 1 month. Simultaneous submissions accepted: no. Publishes 95% of manuscripts submitted. Payment: none. Copyrighted, reverts to author. Pub's reviews: 4 in 2009. §New England based rock 'n' roll related. Ads: Biz rates: $340 (full), $200 (half), $125 (quarter), $75 (eighth)Band rate: $222 (full), $133 (half), $88 (quarter), $55 (eighth). Subjects: Arts, Cartoons, Music, New England, Radio.

NOLA-MAGICK Press, Keith Nicholson, CEO, Author, Bartender & Ne'er-do-well; Barnabas Collins, Senior Editor, 828 Royal Street # 214, New Orleans, LA 70116, 504-301-1080, (fax) 504-309-9004, info@nolamagick.org, www.nolamagick.org. 2004. Fiction, criticism, reviews, non-fiction. ''We are a nonprofit, occult publishing house. We also publish restaurant and nightclub reviews, concentrating on one city at a time.'' avg. press run 5000. Expects 2 titles 2010, 5 titles 2011. No titles listed in the *Small Press Record of Books in Print* (36th Edition, 2010-11). Discounts: 40-55%. Reporting time: 1 month. Simultaneous submissions accepted: Yes. Publishes 50% of manuscripts submitted. Payment: 40% minus production expenses. Copyrights for author. Subjects: Autobiography, Christianity, Dining, Restaurants, Fiction, Food, Eating, Louisiana, Magic, Metaphysics, New Age, Occult, Religion, Spiritual, Theosophical, Travel, WICCA.

Nolo Press Occidental, Charles Sherman, Owner; Sandra Borland, General Manager, 501 Mission Street, Suite 2, Santa Cruz, CA 95060, 831-466-9922, 800-464-5502, Fax: 831-466-9927, E-mail: inbox@nolotech.com,

Website: http://www.nolotech.com. 1971. Non-fiction. avg. press run 10M. Pub'd 3 titles 2009; expects 3 titles 2010, 3 titles 2011. 5 titles listed in the *Small Press Record of Books in Print* (36th Edition, 2010-11). Discounts: 10-19 20%, 20-99 40%, 100+ 50%. 260pp. Payment: 10% of retail paid quarterly. Copyrights for author. Subjects: California, Divorce, Family, How-To, Law, Marriage, Non-Fiction, Reference, Relationships, Self-Help, Texas.

Nonetheless Press, Marie-Christine Ebershoff, Acquisitions, 20332 W. 98th Street, Lenexa, KS 66220-2650, 913-254-7266, Fax 913-393-3245, info@nonethelesspress.com. 2002. Non-fiction. "Nonetheless Press imprint Looking Glass Press reviews memoirs, poetry, and fiction submissions. Contact person is Marcia Schutte." avg. press run 3M. Expects 10 titles 2010, 4/4 titles 2011. No titles listed in the *Small Press Record of Books in Print* (36th Edition, 2010-11). Reporting time: within 3 months. Simultaneous submissions accepted: yes. Publishes +/-5% of manuscripts submitted. Copyrights for author. Subjects: Arts, Autobiography, Biography, Business & Economics, Careers, Children, Youth, Consulting, Consumer, Current Affairs, Family, Fiction, Gardening, Global Affairs, Guidance, Health.

NOON, Diane Williams, 1324 Lexington Avenue Front 4, New York, NY 10128-1145, noonannual@yahoo.com. 2000. Fiction, articles, art, interviews. circ. 2M. 1/yr. Pub'd 1 issue 2009; expects 1 issue 2010, 1 issue 2011. sub. price $9; per copy $9. Back issues: none. Discounts: 55% distributor. 110pp. Reporting time: 1-2 months. Simultaneous submissions accepted: yes. Publishes 10% of manuscripts submitted. Payment: 2 copies of issue. Copyrighted, reverts to author. Ads: reciprocal ads with other magazines. Subjects: Arts, Fiction.

Noontide Press, PO Box 2719, Newport Beach, CA 92659, 949-631-1490, e-mail editor@noontidepress.com. 1962. Non-fiction. "Noontide Press sells a wide variety of special-interest books, including many that are 'politically incorrect.'" avg. press run 4M. Pub'd 10 titles 2009; expects 10 titles 2010. No titles listed in the *Small Press Record of Books in Print* (36th Edition, 2010-11). Discounts: 40% for book sellers. Pages vary. Reporting time: 4 weeks. Simultaneous submissions accepted: yes. Publishes 1% of manuscripts submitted. Payment: standard. Copyrights for author. Subjects: Americana, History, Holocaust, Middle East, Public Affairs, World War II.

NORTH AMERICAN REVIEW, Grant Tracey, Editor; Vince Gotera, Editor, University Of Northern Iowa, 1222 W. 27th Street, Cedar Falls, IA 50614-0516, 319-273-6455. 1815. Poetry, fiction, articles, satire, reviews, non-fiction. "We are especially interested in writing on the environment, race, ethnicity, gender, and class. The James Hearst Poetry Prize deadline (postmark) is October 31. The Kurt Vonnegut Fiction Prize deadline (postmark) is December 31. The Annual Student Cover Art Competition Deadline (postmark) is November 31. (Please visit our website for detailed entry information and required cover sheets at: http://webdelsol.com/NorthAmReview/NAR/) Please, no simultaneous or multiple submissions." circ. 2500. 4/yr. Pub'd 5 issues 2009; expects 4 issues 2010, 4 issues 2011. sub. price $22; per copy $5; sample $5. Back issues: $5. Discounts: agent 20%, bulk (10 or more) 30%. 52pp. Reporting time: 4 months. Simultaneous submissions accepted: no. Publishes 1-2% of manuscripts submitted. Payment: $5 per 350 words of prose, $1 a line for poetry ($20 minimum, $100 maximum). Copyrighted, reverts to author. Pub's reviews: 11 in 2009. §Drama, fiction, nonfiction, poetry, and popular culture. Ads: $125 and up. Subjects: Fiction, Non-Fiction, Poetry.

North Atlantic Books, 2526 Martin Luther King Jr. Way, Berkeley, CA 94704, 800-337-2665, 510-549-4270, fax 510-549-4276, www.northatlanticbooks.com. 1974. "We don't want poetry or fiction submissions - don't publish enough." avg. press run 3-5K. Pub'd 50 titles 2009; expects 50 titles 2010, 50 titles 2011. 4 titles listed in the *Small Press Record of Books in Print* (36th Edition, 2010-11). Discounts: trade 1-4 books 20%, 5+ 40%. 200pp. Reporting time: 4-8 weeks. Simultaneous submissions accepted: yes. Publishes .5-1% of manuscripts submitted. Payment: by contract. Only automatic copyrighting by publication.

NORTH CAROLINA LITERARY REVIEW, Margaret Bauer, English Department, East Carolina University, Greenville, NC 27858, 252-328-1537; Fax 252-328-4889. 1991. Poetry, fiction, articles, art, photos, interviews, satire, criticism, reviews, letters, plays, concrete art, news items, non-fiction. "Past contributors: Fred Chappell, Lee Smith, Janet Lembke; A.R. Ammons, Linda Beatrice Brown, James Applewhite, Charles Wright, Margaret Maron, Alan Shapiro. Length: 1,000-6,000 words. Biases: critical and historical essays about NC writers, usually directed to theme of special feature section; interviews with NC writers; contemporary creative work by NC writers; comprehensive essay reviews of recent books by NC writers; MLA style when appropriate." circ. 500. 1/yr. Pub'd 1 issue 2009; expects 1 issue 2010, 1 issue 2011. sub. price $25/2 years; per copy $15; sample $10-$20 depending on issue. Back issues: $10-$50. 200pp. Reporting time: 2-3 months. Simultaneous submissions accepted: no. Publishes 25% of manuscripts submitted. Payment: $25-$250 and/or subscriptions, extra copies, back issues. Copyrighted, rights revert to author on request. Pub's reviews: 5 in 2009. §North Carolina writers, literature, culture, history ONLY. Ads: $250/$150/$100 1/4 page. Subjects: Appalachia, Biography, Book Reviewing, Essays, Fiction, Food, Eating, Graphic Design, Literary Review, Non-Fiction, North Carolina, Photography, Poetry, Short Stories.

North Country Books, Inc., M. Sheila Orlin, 220 Lafayette St., Utica, NY 13502, 315-735-4877. 1965. Photos, non-fiction. "NY State, history, biography, nostalgia, heavy accent on Adirondacks and upstate." avg. press run 3M-5M. Pub'd 8 titles 2009; expects 8 titles 2010, 10 titles 2011. 79 titles listed in the *Small Press Record of Books in Print* (36th Edition, 2010-11). Discounts: 1-4 20%, 5 40%. 200pp. Reporting time: 3-6 months. Simultaneous submissions accepted: yes. Publishes 5% of manuscripts submitted. Payment: 8% retail price, 20% withheld against returns. Copyrights for author. Subjects: Adirondacks, Autobiography, Biography, Children, Youth, Crime, Environment, Folklore, History, Native American, Nature, New York, Non-Fiction, Photography, Supernatural, Tapes & Records.

NORTH DAKOTA QUARTERLY, UND Press, Robert W. Lewis, Editor; Elizabeth Harris Behling, Fiction Editor; Donald Junkins, Poetry Editor, Merrifield Hall Room 110, 276 Centennial Drive Stop 7209, Grand Forks, ND 58202-7209, 701-777-3322. 1910. Poetry, fiction, articles, art, photos, interviews, criticism, reviews, long-poems, non-fiction. "Recent contributors include Richard Wilbur, William Jay Smith, W. D. Snodgrass, and James Morrison." circ. 600. 4/yr. Pub'd 4 issues 2009; expects 4 issues 2010, 4 issues 2011. sub. price $25 individual, $30 institutional, $20 gifts, students, and seniors; per copy $10 and $16 for special (includes mailing); sample $10 (includes mailing). Back issues: $10 and $16 for special. 200pp. Reporting time: 1-4 months. Simultaneous submissions accepted: Only for fiction and essays (if noted in cover letter), not for poetry. Publishes 5% of manuscripts submitted. Payment: in copies. Copyrighted, reverts to author. Pub's reviews: approx. 45 in 2009. §Native American studies, Canadian studies, northern plains literature. Ads: $150/$100. Subjects: Book Reviewing, Criticism, Culture, Great Plains, Ireland, Literary Review, Literature (General), Native American.

North Star Books, PO Box 589, Pearblossom, CA 93553-0589, 661-944-1130, NSB@NorthStarBooks.com, http://www.NorthStarBooks.com. 1992. Non-fiction. "Since 1992, North Star Books has carefully built a reputation for integrity, professionalism, responsiveness, philanthropy, and most importantly, for quality titles that TOUCH THE WORLD, ONE FAMILY AT A TIME. This Los Angeles-based publisher has donated proceeds worldwide of its internationally sold health-related titles on dementia, caregiving, and Alzheimer's, for the past decade. During the next decade, North Star Books will focus on becoming a greater force in publishing with creatively executed titles for baby boomers (e.g., investing, sustainable retirement, quality of life, wilderness trekking, caregiving). Authors desiring to collaborate with a dependable publisher must bring passion for their message and an established audience." avg. press run 2-3M. Expects 1 title 2010, 2 titles 2011. 3 titles listed in the *Small Press Record of Books in Print* (36th Edition, 2010-11). Discounts: 50-55% wholesaler, 20-40% retail, 20% prepaid S.T.O.P. orders. 160-300pp. Reporting time: 4-8 weeks. Simultaneous submissions accepted: No. Copyrights for author. Subjects: Aging, Finances, Health, How-To, Humor, Lifestyles, Memoirs, Motivation, Success, Non-Fiction, Outdoor Adventure, Self-Help, Travel.

North Stone Editions (see also THE NORTH STONE REVIEW), PO Box 14098, Minneapolis, MN 55414. 1971. Poetry, fiction, criticism, reviews, letters. "At this point, these are the genres we're working with. More genres later, perhaps." avg. press run 1M-2M. Pub'd 1 title 2009; expects 1 title 2010, 2 titles 2011. No titles listed in the *Small Press Record of Books in Print* (36th Edition, 2010-11). Discounts: query, please, with proposal. Pages vary. Reporting time: 1 month to 6 weeks. Simultaneous submissions accepted: no. Publishes a small % of manuscripts submitted. Payment: after costs, yes. Copyrights for author. Subjects: Book Reviewing, Criticism, Dada, England, Fiction, Literary Review, Poetry, Reviews, Writers/Writing.

THE NORTH STONE REVIEW, North Stone Editions, James Naiden, Editor; Anne Duggan, Associate Editor; Sigrid Bergie, Contributing Editor; Richard Fournier, Contributing Editor; Eugene McCarthy, Contributing Editor; Michael Tjepkes, Contributing Editor; Jack Jarpe, Assistant Editor, PO Box 14098, Minneapolis, MN 55414. 1971. Poetry, fiction, articles, art, photos, interviews, reviews, long-poems, non-fiction. "Leslie Miller, Robert Bly, John Rezmerski, George T. Wright, Sigrid Bergie, etc., are among recent contributors." circ. 1.5M. 1+. Pub'd 1 issue 2009; expects 1 issue 2010, 1 issue 2011. sub. price $28/2 issues; per copy $14; sample $14. Back issues: query first. Discounts: depends—query first. 200-300+pp. Reporting time: 2-6 weeks or less. Simultaneous submissions accepted: no. Publishes 2-3% of manuscripts submitted. Payment: 2 copies. Copyrighted, reprint permission on written request. Pub's reviews: 15 in 2009. §Poetry, fiction, literary biography and theory, literary essay. Ads: $60/$35/$25 1/4 page, query first.

Northern Illinois University Press, Amy Farranto, Acquisitions Editor; Sara Hoerdeman, Acquisitions Editor; Linda Manning, Marketing Manager; J. Alex Schwartz, Director, 2280 Bethany Rd, University Press, DeKalb, IL 60115, (815) 753-1826 phone; (815) 753-1845 fax. 1965. Fiction, criticism, non-fiction. avg. press run 1000. Pub'd 16 titles 2009; expects 14 titles 2010, 15 titles 2011. No titles listed in the *Small Press Record of Books in Print* (36th Edition, 2010-11). Discounts: 1-4 copies 25%5-49 copies 40%50-99 copies 42%100 + copies 45%Text orders 25%. 230pp. Subjects: Chicago, Civil War, Eastern Europe, Illinois, Indigenous Cultures, Law, Literature (General), Political Science, Religion.

Northern Publishing, Tony Russ, PO BOx 871803, Wasilla, AK 99687, 907-376-6474, 907-373-6474, tony@TonyRuss.com, www.TonyRuss.com. 1994. Non-fiction. "Additional address: 574 Sarahs Way, Wasilla,

AK 99654." avg. press run 3M. Pub'd 1 title 2009; expects 1 title 2010, 2 titles 2011. 12 titles listed in the *Small Press Record of Books in Print* (36th Edition, 2010-11). Discounts: 40%, 50%, 55%. 256pp. Reporting time: 1 month. Simultaneous submissions accepted: yes. Publishes 30% of manuscripts submitted. Payment: 8%. Copyrights for author. Subjects: Alaska, Biography, Sports, Outdoors, Travel.

NORTHWEST REVIEW, Geri Doran, General Editor; Garrett Hongo, Poetry Editor; Ehud Havazelet, Fiction Editor, 5243 University of Oregon, Eugene, OR 97403-5243. 1957. Non-fiction. "Recent contributors: Yusef Komunyakaa, Charles Wright, Susan Wood, Brenda Hillman, W. Scott Olsen, Ron Carlson." circ. 1,000. 2/yr. Pub'd 3 issues 2009; expects 3 issues 2010, 2 issues 2011. 5 titles listed in the *Small Press Record of Books in Print* (36th Edition, 2010-11). sub. price $20; per copy $8; sample $8-$10. Back issues: $8 all except double issues or specially priced issues. Discounts: Author 40%; Book Distributor 40% (Bookstore 30%, Distributor 10%); Subscription Agencies 30%; Standing Order 40%. 190pp. Reporting time: Approximately 3 months. Simultaneous submissions accepted: Not accepted. Payment: 2 copies. Copyrighted, reverts to author. Subjects: Book Reviewing, Creative Non-fiction, Culture, Essays, Fiction, Journals, Literary Review, Non-Fiction, Oregon, Pacific Northwest, Poetry, Prose, Short Stories, University Press, Writers/Writing.

Northwestern University Press (see also TRIQUARTERLY), Henry Carrigan Jr., Senior Editor; Michael Levine, Acquisitions Editor, 629 Noyes Street, Evanston, IL 60208-4170, (847) 491-2046; fax (847)491-8150; www.nupress.northwestern.edu. 1893. Poetry, fiction, criticism, plays, non-fiction. "Northwestern University Press publishes in several disciplines including philosophy, Slavic studies, literature-in-translation, contemporary fiction and poetry, avant-garde and modernism studies, English-language Latino ficiton and memoirs, and theater and performance studies." Pub'd 40 titles 2009; expects 50 titles 2010, 50 titles 2011. No titles listed in the *Small Press Record of Books in Print* (36th Edition, 2010-11). Discounts: contact our sales department for discount schedule. Reporting time: Varies according to discipline. Simultaneous submissions accepted: No. Publishes 10% of manuscripts submitted. Payment: We pay royalties once a year. Copyrights for author. Subjects: Autobiography, Avant-Garde, Experimental Art, Biography, Chicago, Drama, Eastern Europe, Fiction, Latino, Literature (General), Non-Fiction, Performing Arts, Poetry, Theatre.

Norton Coker Press, Edward Mycue, PO Box 640543, San Francisco, CA 94164-0543, 415-922-0395. 1988. Poetry, fiction, art, satire, criticism, reviews, music, letters, plays, news items. avg. press run 150. Pub'd 22 titles 2009; expects 15 titles 2010, 10 titles 2011. 64 titles listed in the *Small Press Record of Books in Print* (36th Edition, 2010-11). Discounts: 5+ copies 40%. 44pp. Reporting time: 1-4 weeks. Payment: in copies. Copyrights for author. Subjects: Arts, Bibliography, Electronics, Literature (General), Music, Tapes & Records, Translation, Visual Arts.

NOSTOC MAGAZINE, Arts End Books, Marshall Brooks, Editor, PO Box 441, West Dover, VT 05356-0441. 1973. Poetry, fiction, articles, criticism, reviews, parts-of-novels. "A copy of our catalogue - detailing our past publications and describing our subscription package program is available upon request (please enclose a SASE). We read unsolicited mss. between October and December only." circ. 300. 2/yr. Pub'd 2 issues 2009; expects 2 issues 2010, 2 issues 2011. sub. price $10/4 issues; per copy $5; sample $5. Back issues: rates on request. Discounts: on request. 40pp. Simultaneous submissions accepted: no. Publishes 5% of manuscripts submitted. Payment: modest payment upon acceptance. Copyrighted, reverts to author. Pub's reviews: 5 in 2009. §Small press history, poetry, fiction & politics, bibliography. Ads: rates on request. Subjects: Bibliography, Book Reviewing, Poetry.

NoteBoat, Inc., Tom Serb, PO Box 6155, Woodridge, IL 60517, 630-697-7229, 630-910-4553. 1998. Music. "Educational works for guitar." avg. press run 3500. Pub'd 1 title 2009; expects 1 title 2010, 2 titles 2011. No titles listed in the *Small Press Record of Books in Print* (36th Edition, 2010-11). Discounts: 1-2 copies 20%3-4 copies 30%5-12 copies 40%13-34 copies 45%35+ copies 50%. 110pp. Reporting time: 4-8 weeks. Simultaneous submissions accepted: No. Payment: 8% on net sales. Copyrights for author. Subject: Music.

NOTES AND ABSTRACTS IN AMERICAN AND INTERNATIONAL EDUCATION, Caddo Gap Press, Alan H. Jones, Editor, 3145 Geary Boulevard #275, San Francisco, CA 94118, 415-392-1911. 1961. Articles. "A semi-annual bulletin featuring information, news, research, and abstracts in the social foundations of education." circ. 100. 2/yr. Pub'd 2 issues 2009; expects 2 issues 2010, 2 issues 2011. sub. price $30 indiv., $60 instit.; per copy $15. 24pp. Reporting time: 2 months. Publishes 25% of manuscripts submitted. Payment: none. Copyrighted, reverts to author. Ads: none. Subject: Education.

NOTRE DAME REVIEW, Kathleen Canavan, Executive Editor; William O'Rourke, Fiction Editor; John Matthias, Poetry Editor; Steve Tomasula, Senior Editor, 840 Flanner Hall, University of Notre Dame, Notre Dame, IN 46556, 574-631-6952, Fax 574-631-4795. 1995. Poetry, fiction, interviews, reviews, parts-of-novels. "Recent contributors: Edward Falco, Seamus Heaney, Richard Elman, Denise Levertov, and Czeslaw Milosz. Manuscripts submitted April-August will be returned to sender unread." circ. 2M. 2/yr. Pub'd 2 issues 2009; expects 2 issues 2010, 2 issues 2011. sub. price $15 individuals, $20 institutions; per copy $8; sample $6. Discounts: 10% for subscription agencies. 150pp. Reporting time: 3-4 months. Simultaneous submissions accepted: yes. Publishes 8% of manuscripts submitted. Payment: variable. Copyrighted, reverts to author. Pub's reviews: 7 in 2009. §Fiction, poetry, literary criticism/history. Ads: $165/$90/$75 1/3 page. Subjects: Fiction, Interviews, Literary Review, Literature (General), Poetry, Reviews.

NOUN VS. VERB, Christopher Bowen, Cleveland, OH 44217, http://www.burningriver.info. 2008. Poetry, fiction, satire, criticism, reviews, non-fiction. "accepts material for website." circ. 200. 1/yr. Expects 1 issue 2010, 1 issue 2011. price per copy $4; sample $4. Back issues: inquire. 80pp. Reporting time: one week. Simultaneous submissions accepted: Yes. Publishes 20% of manuscripts submitted. Payment: 2 author copies. Not copyrighted. Pub's reviews: none in 2009. §literary. Ads: none. Subjects: Arts, Book Arts, Book Reviewing, Criticism, Experimental, Literature (General), Poetry, Short Stories, Writers/Writing, Zines.

NOVA EXPRESS, Lawrence Person, PO Box 27231, Austin, TX 78755, E-mail lawrenceperson@jump.net. 1987. Poetry, fiction, articles, art, interviews, satire, criticism, reviews, letters, non-fiction. "We cover cutting edge science fiction, fantasy, horror, and slipstream literature, with an emphasis on post cyberpunk works." circ. 850. 2/yr. Pub'd 2 issues 2009; expects 2 issues 2010, 2 issues 2011. sub. price $12/4 issues; per copy $4; sample $4. Back issues: $4. Discounts: starts at 40% for 25 issues, write for rates. 48pp. Reporting time: 1-3 months, sometimes less. Simultaneous submissions accepted: no. Publishes 10% freelance, assigned 90% of manuscripts submitted. Payment: 2 contributor copies and 4-issue subscription. Copyrighted, reverts to author. Pub's reviews: 55 in 2009. §Science fiction, fantasy, horror, slipstream. Ads: $100/$60/$35 1/4 page. Subjects: Bibliography, Book Reviewing, Criticism, Fantasy, Fiction, Futurism, Interviews, Literary Review, H.P. Lovecraft, Science Fiction.

Nova House Press, Tim Gavin, 470 North Latch's Lane, Merion, PA 19066. 1998. Poetry. "Nova House Press concerns itself with publishing the best possible poetry without regard to school, form, or content. We are interested in not only what is being said, but in how it is being said. The how and what of poetry are important to use; therefore, we search for poetry the employs a range of poetic elements to support the content of the chapbook. The poets whose work we have published include, Margaret Holley, R. T. Smith, Lou McKee, Marcia Harlow, Jenn Bryant, Len Roberts, Ken Fifer, and David St. John. We only accept solicited manuscripts." avg. press run 100. Pub'd 1 title 2009; expects 2 titles 2010, 2 titles 2011. No titles listed in the *Small Press Record of Books in Print* (36th Edition, 2010-11). Discounts: 50% discount to all institutions interested in a chapbook. 28pp. Reporting time: Varies depending on the number of manuscripts reviewed. Simultaneous submissions accepted: Yes. Publishes 5% of manuscripts submitted. Payment: Author receives 1/2 of the press run; however, if the author desires more copies, he or she can cover the cost of printing. Does not copyright for author. Subject: Poetry.

Nova Press, Jeff Kolby, 11659 Mayfield Ave, Suite 1, Los Angeles, CA 90049, 310-207-4078, E-mail novapress@aol.com. 1993. "We publish only test prep books for college entrance exams such as the GRE, LSAT, SAT, GMAT, and MCAT, or closely related books such as college guides and vocabulary improvement. We are currently looking for TOFEL and ACT books to publish." avg. press run 3M. Pub'd 5 titles 2009; expects 5 titles 2010, 10 titles 2011. 5 titles listed in the *Small Press Record of Books in Print* (36th Edition, 2010-11). Discounts: 40%. 550pp. Payment: 10%-22.5% royalty. Subject: Education.

NOVA RELIGIO, University of California Press, Rebecca Moore, Editor; Catherine Wessinger, Editor, University of California Press, 2000 Center St., Suite 303, Berkeley, CA 94704-1223, 510-643-7154. 1997. Articles, reviews. "Editorial address: Dept. of Religious Studies, San Diego State University, 5500 Campanile Dr., San Diego, CA 92182-8143. Copyrighted by the Regents of the University of California." circ. 250. 3/yr. Pub'd 3 issues 2009; expects 3 issues 2010, 3 issues 2011. sub. price $47 indiv., $107 inst., $25 student; per copy $23 indiv., $42 inst., $23 student; sample same as single copy. Discounts: foreign subs. agents 10%, 10+ one-time orders 30%. 132pp. Copyrighted, does not revert to author. Pub's reviews: aprox. 30 in 2009. §Religious studies, history, literature, cultural studies, and sociology. Ads: $295/$220. Subjects: Culture, History, Literature (General), Religion, Sociology.

•Noved Audio, Debarkes Johnson, 4000 west 106th St., Ste#160-329, Carmel, IN 46032, (317)8764099. 2009. "We publish audio books on self-help, how-to, instructional audio and video." avg. press run 5000. Expects 5 titles 2011. No titles listed in the *Small Press Record of Books in Print* (36th Edition, 2010-11). Discounts: 2-10 copies 20% 10-20 copies 35% 20-100 copies 40% 100 or more copies 50%. 400pp. Reporting time: 6-12 weeks. Simultaneous submissions accepted: Yes. Publishes 40% of manuscripts submitted. Payment: We pay 10-15% royalties of retail price paid out every quarter. Copyrights for author. Subjects: Audio/Video, Business & Economics, How-To, Inspirational, Real Estate, Self-Help.

NOW AND THEN, Jane Harris Woodside, Editor-in-Chief; Nancy Fischman, Managing Editor; Linda Parsons, Poetry Editor; Sandra Ballard, Reviews Editor; Jo Carson, Poetry Editor, PO Box 70556, East Tennessee State University, Johnson City, TN 37614-0556, 423-439-5348; fax 423-439-6340; e-mail woodsidj@etsu.edu. 1984. Poetry, fiction, articles, art, photos, interviews, criticism, reviews, letters. "*Now and Then* is the publication of the Center for Appalachian Studies and Service of East Tennessee State University.

Each issue is divided between expository and imaginative material: studies of Appalachian nature and culture on the one hand, and visual art, imaginative writing on the other. Issues always have a thematic focus; for example, recent issues focused on food in Appalachia and photography. Each issue features juxtaposed visuals of an Appalachian locale now (present) and then (past). Photos, graphics, critical studies of Appalachian nature and culture, personal essays, poetry, fiction are welcomed for consideration on a continuing basis. 'Appalachia' is considered to cover the mountain region from New Yord State to Georgia. We'd like people to send for a free listing of upcoming issues and writer's guidelines." circ. 1.5M. 3/yr. Pub'd 3 issues 2009; expects 3 issues 2010, 3 issues 2011. sub. price $20; per copy $7; sample $5. Back issues: $4.50. 44pp. Reporting time: 4 months. We accept simultaneous submissions, but we must be notified where else it's been submitted. Payment: $15-$75 generally for articles and fiction; $10 per poem and per review + copies of the magazine. Copyrighted, does not revert to author. Pub's reviews: 12 in 2009. §Appalachian arts, history, culture, ecology. Subjects: Appalachia, Fiction, Poetry.

Now I See Publishing, Karl Trautwein, Box 352, Etiwanda, CA 91739, 909-922-7276, 909-899-6783. 2008. Non-fiction. avg. press run 2000. Expects 1 title 2011. 1 title listed in the *Small Press Record of Books in Print* (36th Edition, 2010-11). 216pp.

NSR Publications, Merry L. Gumm, 1482 51st Road, Douglass, KS 67039, 620-986-5472, e-mail: nsrpublications@nsrpublications.com, website: www.NSRpublications.com. 2004. Fiction, non-fiction. "Our primary focus is non-fiction for all ages and young-children's fiction. Our first published book titled *Help! I'm In Middle School...How Will I Survive?* is a lighthearted approach to the serious problems middle school children face in those tough pre-teen/teen years. For 2005 we have added *Let It Grow*, a plant activity book, *Dizzy Duck*, a children's book, *The Everything-You-Need-To-Know Writing Guide* and a series of "pocket books", small size books for children. Since 2006, we have added several titles including *151 Educational Games, Help! My Child's in Middle School*, and *America, the Beautiful, What to See and Do in All 50 States.*" avg. press run 3000. Pub'd 1 title 2009; expects 3 titles 2010, 5 titles 2011. 6 titles listed in the *Small Press Record of Books in Print* (36th Edition, 2010-11). Discounts: 3-9 copies 20%10-29 copies 30%30-99 40%100 or more 45%. non-fiction: 80-150pgs, children's fiction 15 pgs. Reporting time: 3 weeks. Simultaneous submissions accepted: No. Publishes 1% of manuscripts submitted. Payment: Authors provide the cost of printing up front. Fees for typesetting and cover design vary with each book. Does not copyright for author. Subjects: Adolescence, Children, Youth, Creative Non-fiction, Education, Family, Fiction, Non-Fiction, Young Adult.

Nunciata, A.C. Doyle, Publishing Division, PO Box 416, Denver, CO 80201-0416, 303-575-5676, Fax 303-575-1187. 1989. "Formerly Assoc. Advertisers Services." avg. press run 1.5M. Pub'd 3 titles 2009; expects 10 titles 2010. 9 titles listed in the *Small Press Record of Books in Print* (36th Edition, 2010-11). Discounts: standard to libraries + bookstores. 60pp. Subjects: Advertising, Self-Promotion, Business & Economics, Education, Homemaking, How-To, Self-Help, Singles, Textbooks.

Nushape Publication, Rashun Jones L, P.O. Box 36651, Oklahoma City,, OK 73136, Ph: 405 602-8447, Fax: 800 554-9718, PH: 800 550-9718 http://www.nushapebiz.com Email:rashun@nushapebiz.com. 2000. Poetry, fiction, articles, reviews, non-fiction. "The Mission of Nushape Publication is to provide books and speaker services that inspire, educate, inform, empower, entertain and support as many people as possible to achieve their greatest vision in a milieu of peace, love and joy." avg. press run 5000. Expects 1 title 2010, 2 titles 2011. 3 titles listed in the *Small Press Record of Books in Print* (36th Edition, 2010-11). Discounts: 2-10 20%11-20 30%21-49 40%50 or more 50%. 140-160pp. Reporting time: 24-48 hours. Simultaneous submissions accepted: Yes. Publishes 2% of manuscripts submitted. Copyrights for author. Subjects: African-American, Book Collecting, Bookselling, Book Reviewing, Creative Non-fiction, Disease, Feminism, How-To, Humor, Mental Health, Relationships, Women.

NUTHOUSE, Ludwig von Quirk, Chief of Staff, c/o Twin Rivers Press, PO Box 119, Ellenton, FL 34222, www.nuthousemagazine.com. 1993. Poetry, fiction, articles, cartoons, interviews, satire, non-fiction. "Humorous essays, stories, poetry and other amusements, preferably of 1,000 words or less. Recent contributors include Michael Fowler, Cornelia Snider Yarrington, John M. Floyd, Dale Andrew White." circ. 100+. 4-6/yr. Pub'd 4 issues 2009; expects 4 issues 2010, 4 issues 2011. 2 titles listed in the *Small Press Record of Books in Print* (36th Edition, 2010-11). sub. price $5 for 4 issues or $10 for 8 issues, checks must be payable to Twin Rivers Press; per copy $1.50; sample $1.50. Back issues: $1.50. 12pp. Reporting time: 1 month. Simultaneous submissions accepted: yes. Publishes 25% of manuscripts submitted. Payment: contributor's copy. Not copyrighted, all rights revert to author upon publication. Pub's reviews: approx. 4 in 2009. §humor, all genres. Ads: trade. Subject: Humor.

•NYQ Books, Raymond Hammond, PO Box 2015, Old Chelsea Station, New York, NY 10113, www.nyqbooks.org. 2009. Poetry, fiction, criticism, long-poems, non-fiction. "NYQ Books was established in 2009 as an imprint of The New York Quarterly Foundation, Inc. Its mission is to augment the New York Quarterly poetry magazine by providing an additional venue for poets who are already published in the magazine. Publication is by invitation only, we do not accept unsolicited manuscripts." Pub'd 12 titles 2009; expects 16 titles 2010, 20 titles 2011. 15 titles listed in the *Small Press Record of Books in Print* (36th Edition, 2010-11). Discounts: bookstores 40% discount, no returns. 100pp. Simultaneous submissions accepted: No. Payment: 15% royalties; paid annual; no advance; 10 copies. Copyrights for author.

O

O!!Zone (see also O!!ZONE, A LITERARY-ART ZINE), Harry Burrus, Editor & Publisher, Mexico. 1993. Poetry, fiction, articles, art, photos, interviews, criticism, reviews. avg. press run 50-300. 12 titles listed in the *Small Press Record of Books in Print* (36th Edition, 2010-11). Discounts: none. 40-80pp, visual poetry anthologies 180pp. Reporting time: ASAP. Simultaneous submissions accepted: yes. Payment: copies. Does not copyright for author. Subjects: Poetry, Surrealism.

O!!ZONE, A LITERARY-ART ZINE, O!!Zone, Harry Burrus, Editor & Publisher, Mexico. 1993. Poetry, fiction, art, photos, collages. *"O!!Zone* currently is in a dormant period. Future publication dates are uncertain. It will eventually resurface in some form. *O!!Zone* is not for prudes, the politically correct, ultra conservatives, the judgmental - those who believe they can decide what is right and proper for others. If easily offended by unusual lifestyles, nudity & provocative words...don't bother. *O!!Zone* is an international publication featuring poetry, visual poetry, reviews, interviews, manifestos, and art. I am particularly intrigued by poets who also do photography, college (or draw or paint or do line drawings). We welcome artists & visual poets. Send work that isn't taught in schools, words that lack in oral history, unspoken on any reading circuit. Time is a tyranny to be abolished. The writer expresses; the writer does not communicate - that's up to the reader. We are interested in D-I-S-C-O-V-E-R-Y and self-transcendence. Get Nakid! Submissions. *Do A Cover Letter.* Always include SASE or sufficient international coupons for return of work. No religious or when I was 12 poems or if you lack the energy of Isidore Ducasse. Poetry=2-4 poems; *expose yourself! Hit us! Bleed!* Photographic Submissions= 5 X 7 or 8 X 10 black and white prints. Desire nudes, surrealism, collage, & nude self-portraits. Yes, art brut. Liberate yourself. Do the unusal. *Can you shock? Enhance your chances!* Create & don't look over your shoulder. Inform your curious friends about *O!!Zone.* Share the word. Transform, mutate...SOAR! ...tempus edax rerum. *Rock us, don't bore."* Sporadic. Pub'd 10 issues 2009; expects 5 issues 2010, 4 issues 2011. price per copy $25; sample varies, depends on what is available. Back issues: depends. Discounts: none. 80-128pp. Reporting time: ASAP. Simultaneous submissions accepted: yes. Payment: copy. Copyrighted, reverts to author. Pub's reviews: 2 in 2009. §Poetry books, art, photography. Subjects: Avant-Garde, Experimental Art, Fiction, Poetry, Surrealism, Visual Arts.

Oak Knoll Press, 310 Delaware Street, New Castle, DE 19720-5038, 800-996-2556, 302-328-7232, fax 302-328-7274, oakknoll@oakknoll.com, www.oakknoll.com. 1976. Pub'd 30 titles 2009; expects 35 titles 2010, 40 titles 2011. 16 titles listed in the *Small Press Record of Books in Print* (36th Edition, 2010-11). Discounts: 1-4 20%, 5-25 40%, 26-99 45%, 100+ 50%, can mix titles. Pages vary. Reporting time: 1 month. Payment: 10% of income, quarterly payments. Copyrights for author. Subjects: Antiques, Arts, Bibliography, Biography, Book Collecting, Bookselling, Conservation, Crafts, Hobbies, Graphics, History, Indexes & Abstracts, Libraries, Literary Review, Literature (General), Printing, Reference.

Oak Tree Press, Billie Johnson, Publisher, 140 E. Palmer St., Taylorville, IL 62568, 217-824-6500, oaktreepub@aol.com, www.oaktreebooks.com. 1998. Fiction, non-fiction. "Three annual contests (mystery, law enforcement professional and romance) Winning entry in each is published." avg. press run 1M. Pub'd 3 titles 2009; expects 10 titles 2010, 10 titles 2011. 37 titles listed in the *Small Press Record of Books in Print* (36th Edition, 2010-11). Discounts: request schedule from publisher. 250pp. Reporting time: 1-3 months. Simultaneous submissions accepted: yes. Publishes less than 1% of manuscripts submitted. Payment: negotiable. Copyrights for author. Subjects: Business & Economics, Fiction, How-To, Humor, Marriage, Mystery, Romance, Self-Help.

Oberlin College Press (see also FIELD: Contemporary Poetry and Poetics), David Young, Co-editor; David Walker, Co-editor; Martha Collins, Editor-at-Large, 50 N. Professor St., Oberlin, OH 44074-1091, 440-775-8408, Fax 440-775-8124, E-mail oc.press@oberlin.edu. 1969. Poetry, long-poems. "Also essays on poetry and translations of poetry." avg. press run 1. Pub'd 3 titles 2009; expects 2 titles 2010, 2 titles 2011. 53 titles listed in the *Small Press Record of Books in Print* (36th Edition, 2010-11). Discounts: 1 copy 20%, 2+ 30%, bookstores and agencies. 80pp. Reporting time: 6-8 weeks. Simultaneous submissions accepted: yes. Publishes 0.25%- 0.50% of manuscripts submitted. Payment: $1,000 FIELD Poetry Prize Winner; royalty payments. Copyrights for author. Subjects: Poetry, Translation.

Obie Joe Media, Kelly Powers, Editor; Ellis L. Marsalis III, Editor, 3324 Ramona Avenue, Baltimore, MD 21213, 410-215-2262. 2004. Poetry, fiction, art, satire, long-poems, non-fiction. "Obie Joe Media is interested in titles intended to deconstruct societal myths while exampling a rigrorious scholarship. We pursue vigorious partnerships with our authors as they take their books to traditional and untraditional audiences." avg. press run 2000. Pub'd 1 title 2009; expects 2 titles 2010, 8 titles 2011. No titles listed in the *Small Press Record of Books in Print* (36th Edition, 2010-11). Discounts: More than 2 copies, 40% to distributors, bookstores, retailers. 60% for schools, nonprofits. 70pp. Reporting time: one month. Simultaneous submissions accepted: Yes. Publishes 20% of manuscripts submitted. Payment: each is specific to project. Copyrights for author. Subjects: African-American, Architecture, Arts, Civil Rights, Creative Non-fiction, Fiction, Food, Eating, Global Affairs, Government, Novels, Parenting, Philosophy, Photography, Poetry, Social Movements.

OBSIDIAN III: Literature in the African Diaspora, Thomas Lisk, Editor, Dept. of English, Box 8105, NC State University, Raleigh, NC 27695-8105, 919-515-4150. 1975. Poetry, fiction, articles, interviews, criticism, reviews, letters, parts-of-novels, long-poems, plays, news items. "Founded in 1975 by Alvin Aubert as *Obsidian: Black Literature in Review*, the journal was transferred to North Carolina State University in 1986 as *Obsidian II*. The journal publishes creative works in English by Black writers worldwide, or writers addressing black issues. with scholarly critical studies by all writers on Black literature in English. Contributors to *Obsidian* and *Obsidian II* (both creative and scholarly) have included Michael S. Harper, Jay Wright, Gayl Jones, Houston A. Baker, Jr., Eugenia Collier, Lloyd W. Brown, Gerald Early, Wanda Coleman, Jerry W. Ward, Nikki Grimes, Raymond R. Patterson, Akua Lezli Hope, Gary Smith, Bu-Buakei Jabbi, Yusef Komunyakaa, Jane Davis, Philip Royster." circ. 400. 2/yr. Pub'd 2 issues 2009; expects 2 issues 2010, 2 issues 2011. sub. price $22; per copy $10; sample $10. Back issues: $10. Discounts: 40% bookstores. 130pp. Reporting time: 3 months. Simultaneous submissions accepted: no. Publishes 15% of manuscripts submitted. Payment: 2 copies. Copyrighted, reverts to author. Pub's reviews: 2 in 2009. §Creative works by Black writers or writers who address black issues (poetry, fiction, drama); scholarship and criticism on same. Ads: $225 full page/$165 half page. Subjects: African Literature, Africa, African Studies, Black, Book Reviewing, Drama, Fiction, Poetry, Third World, Minorities.

Ocean Publishing, Frank Gromling, P.O. Box 1080, Flagler Beach, FL 32136-1080, 386-517-1600, Fax 386-517-2564, publisher@oceanpublishing.org, www.oceanpublishing.org. 2002. Non-fiction. "Authors include William Stewart, Mike Cavaliere, Kay Day, Victor DiGenti, Dorothy K. Fletcher, Sandra Wallus Sammons, Pete Davey, H. Steven Robertson, Jan Atchley Bevan, Alfred Nicol, Grahl Barkkoskie Neitz, Diane Till, Frank Gromling." avg. press run 2000. Pub'd 5 titles 2009; expects 3 titles 2010, 4 titles 2011. 18 titles listed in the *Small Press Record of Books in Print* (36th Edition, 2010-11). Discounts: bookstores: up to 40%, distributors/wholesalers: up to 55%, institutions/schools/corporations: 20%-30%. 200pp. Reporting time: 30-45 days. Simultaneous submissions accepted: Yes. Publishes 2% of manuscripts submitted. Payment: 8-15% of net, small advances, six month payment cycles. Copyrights for author. Subjects: Animals, Biography, Conservation, Earth, Natural History, Environment, Florida, Leadership, Marine Life, Nature, Non-Fiction, Oceanography, Whaling, Wildlife.

OCEAN YEARBOOK, University of Chicago Press, Aldo Chircop, Moira McConnell, Dalhousie Law School, 6061 University Avenue, Halifax, Nova Scotia B3H 4H9, Canada, 902-494-2955 (main #), 902-494-1316 (fax), http://www.journals.uchicago.edu/OY/home.html. 1978. "Since 1978, the *Ocean Yearbook* has published original, peer-reviewed articles and reference materials for students and practitioners of international law, ocean development, coastal zone management, foreign policy, and strategic studies. Coverage includes the global management of marine resources, international law, and environmental policy." 1/yr.

ODYSSEY: Adventures in Science, Cobblestone Publishing Company, Elizabeth E. Lindstrom, Editor, 30 Grove Street, Suite C, Peterborough, NH 03458, 603-924-7209, Fax 603-924-7380, custsvc@cobblestone.mv.com. 1979. Fiction, articles, art, photos, interviews, reviews, letters, non-fiction. "The magazine will accept freelance articles related to themes covered; write editor for guidelines." circ. 23M. 9/yr. Pub'd 9 issues 2009; expects 9 issues 2010, 9 issues 2011. sub. price $29.95 + $8 foreign, Canadian subs add 7% GST; per copy $6.95; sample $6.95. Back issues: $6.95. Discounts: 15% to agencies, bulk rate—3 subs $17.95 each/yr. 52pp. Reporting time: queries sent well in advance of deadline may not be answered for several months. Go-aheads usually sent 3 months prior to publication date. Simultaneous submissions accepted: yes. Payment: on publication. Copyrighted, *Odyssey* buys all rights. Pub's reviews: 10 in 2009. §Science, math, technology, space, astronomy, earth and physical sciences. Ads: none. Subjects: Astronomy, Space.

OFF OUR BACKS, Editorial Collective, 4201 Wilson Blvd., #110-487, Arlington, VA 22203, 202-234-8072, ww2w.offourbacks.com. 1970. Articles, art, photos, cartoons, interviews, criticism, reviews, letters, news items, non-fiction. "Consider ourselves a radical feminist *news* journal, with complete coverage of national and international news about women. Free to prisoners." circ. 22M. Quarterly. Pub'd 11 issues 2009; expects 6 issues 2010, 6 issues 2011. sub. price $29.95: Individual (US), $32.95: Individual (Canada and Mexico), $35.00: Individual (Other International), $75.00: Institutional (US), $80.00: Institutional (Canada and Mexico),

$85.00: Institutional (Other International); per copy $4.95 newstand price; sample $5. Back issues: $5. Discounts: 40% for 5 or more copies monthly; billed/paid quarterly. 80pp. Reporting time: 6 months. Simultaneous submissions accepted: No. Publishes 50% of manuscripts submitted. Payment: Free Contributing Copy of Issue. Copyrighted, reverts to author. Pub's reviews: 50 in 2009. §Women. Ads: $400/$210/40¢ (prepaid). Subjects: Birth, Birth Control, Population, Feminism, Gay, Health, Labor, Lesbianism, Politics, Third World, Minorities, Women.

OFF THE COAST, Valerie Lawson, Michael Brown, PO Box 14, 1175 US Route 1, Robbinston, ME 04671, 207-454-8026, poetrylane@hughes.net. 1994. Poetry. "Off the Coast is committed to publishing the finest poetry, any style or subject, featuring the work of Maine writers as well as an international community of poets and including poems from a select group of young writers in each issue. Contributors: Linda Buckmaster, Robert Chute, Susan Donnelly, Wes McNair, Betsy Scholl, Lewis Turco, Baron Wormser." circ. 250. 4/yr. Pub'd 3 issues 2009; expects 3 issues 2010, 4 issues 2011. sub. price $35; per copy $10. Back issues: inquire. Discounts: 20%. 85pp. Reporting time: maximum: 30 days after submissions close. Simultaneous submissions accepted: Yes. Publishes 5% of manuscripts submitted. Payment: Pays in contributor copy, additional copies 1/2 off cover price. Copyrighted, reverts to author. Pub's reviews: 12 in 2009. §Poetry Books. Ads: inquire. Subjects: Graphics, Poetry.

Off the Grid Press, Tam Lin Neville, Bert Stern, P.O. Box 84, Weld, ME 04285, (207)585-2218, (617)629-2541, info@offthegridprcss.net, www.offthegridpress.net. 2006. Poetry. "We publish good poetry by poets over sixty years of age. Our current two titles are Loyalty, by Henry Braun and A Darker, Sweeter String by Lee Sharkey." avg. press run 500. Pub'd 1 title 2009; expects 1 title 2010, 1 title 2011. No titles listed in the *Small Press Record of Books in Print* (36th Edition, 2010-11). Discounts: 2-10 copies 25%. 100pp. Reporting time: For first sample of ten pages, two weeks. For fulll manuscript, 1 month. Simultaneous submissions accepted: Yes. Publishes 10% of manuscripts submitted. Payment: Our authors pay the expenses for their own books. Copyrights for author.

OFFICE NUMBER ONE, Carlos B. Dingus, 2111 Quarry Road, Austin, TX 78703, 512-445-4489. 1989. Poetry, fiction, articles, cartoons, satire, letters. "*Office Number One* is a zine of satire or useful, unusual philosophical perspective. I need short (100 - 300 words) satirical news items, strange essays, or fiction. Poetry is limericks or haiku. Satire should have an upbeat point and make sense. Once in a while I print more serious words—400 or less on philosophy or religion—but it's got to be good." circ. 2M. 2/yr. Pub'd 1 issue 2009; expects 2 issues 2010, 2 issues 2011. sub. price $8.84/6 issues; per copy $2; sample $2. Discounts: 24 copies $12 postpaid (minimum order). 16pp. Reporting time: 6-12 weeks. Simultaneous submissions accepted: yes. We publish less than 10% of manuscripts submitted (so many submitted are poorly written!). Payment: contributor's copies. Copyrighted, reverts to author. §Reviews of other dimensions of existence are interesting. Ads: call for rates. Subjects: Cartoons, Christianity, Cults, Essays, Fiction, Fiction, Humor, Metaphysics, New Age, Philosophy, Religion.

‡**Ohio State University Press,** Kathy Edwards, Assistant Director, 180 Pressey Hall, 1070 Carmack Road, Columbus, OH 43210-1002, 614-292-6930. 1957. "The Ohio State University Press was established in 1957 and currently publishes 30 new books a year. We specialize in literary studies, including narrative theory, Victorian studies, medieval studies, and classics. We also publish annual winners of our short fiction and poetry prizes.Among the most notable titles published by the Press are Language Files, an introductory linguistics textbook now in its 10th edition; The Centenary Edition of the Works of Nathaniel Hawthorne, the definitive 23-volume edition of the American master's writings; Dickens' Journalism, a 4-volume collection; The Death of Contract, a classic in legal studies; and Listen to Me Good, a moving autobiography of an Alabama midwife. The Press was the original publisher of the Helen Hooven Santmyer blockbuster . . . And Ladies of the Club, which is now out of print. In addition to its books, the Press publishes a distinguished group of journals including the *Journal of Higher Education*, the leading scholarly journal on the institution of higher education. We also publish *American Periodicals*, and *Narrative*." No titles listed in the *Small Press Record of Books in Print* (36th Edition, 2010-11).

Ohio University Press/Swallow Press, David Sanders, The Ridges, Building 19, Athens, OH 45701, 740-593-1157, www.ohioswallow.com. 1964. Poetry, fiction, criticism. "We consider unsolicited poetry only through our annual Hollis Summers Poetry Prize competittion. We publish a little short fiction and practically no long fiction. As a scholarly press, we have special strengths in regional works including the Midwest, Appalachia, and Ohio; African studies; Victorian studies, as well as a number of specialized series." avg. press run 1000. Pub'd 50 titles 2009; expects 50 titles 2010, 55 titles 2011. No titles listed in the *Small Press Record of Books in Print* (36th Edition, 2010-11). Discounts: Retail trade discount is 1-2 copies 20%; 3-49, 40%; 50-99, 41%; 100-250, 43%; 250 or more, 46%; short discount books, 1-2, 20%; 3 or more, 40%. 250pp. Reporting time: four months. Simultaneous submissions accepted: No. Payment: 7% royalty on net sales. Copyrights for author. Subjects: African Literature, Africa, African Studies, Americana, Appalachia, Civil War, Feminism, Fiction, Great Lakes, History, Literature (General), Midwest, Ohio, Old West, Philosophy, Poetry,

Poland.

OHIOANA QUARTERLY, Beth Poley, Program Coordinator, 274 E. First Avenue, Suite 300, Columbus, OH 43201, 614-466-3831, Fax 614-728-6974, e-mail ohioana@ohioana.org. 1958. Criticism, reviews, news items. "Published by the Ohioana Library Association. Reviews by staff and guest reviewers. Length of review varies from 40 to 500 words. Ohio authors or books on Ohio only. Query first for articles on Ohio authors or Ohio subjects." circ. 2.5k. 4/yr. Pub'd 4 issues 2009; expects 4 issues 2010, 4 issues 2011. sub. price $35 (membership); per copy $6.50; sample gratis. Back issues: $6.50. Discounts: $35 to libraries. 112pp. Reporting time: 2-4 weeks. Simultaneous submissions accepted: no. Payment: copies only. Copyrighted, rights do not revert to author, but we grant permission for full use by author. Pub's reviews: 400 in 2009. §Books about Ohio or Ohioans, books by Ohioans or former Ohioans. Ads: none. Subjects: Arts, Book Reviewing, Literary Review, Midwest, Ohio.

George Ohsawa Macrobiotic Foundation (see also MACROBIOTICS TODAY), Carl Ferre, Editor, PO Box 3998, Chico, CA 95927-3998, 530-566-9765, Fax 530-566-9768, gomf@ohsawamacrobiotics.com. 1970. Articles, non-fiction. "Articles about macrobiotics and health. Books of at least 90 pages on macrobiotics, health, diet and nutrition. Special interest in cookbooks. Recent contributors include Julia Ferre, Natalie Buckley Rowland, Margaret Lawson, Rachel Albert, and Pam Henkel." avg. press run 3M-5M. Expects 1 title 2010, 1 title 2011. 25 titles listed in the *Small Press Record of Books in Print* (36th Edition, 2010-11). Discounts: 1 20%, 2-4 30%, 5+ 40%; distributors discount available. 192pp. Reporting time: 6 weeks. Publishes 10% of manuscripts submitted. Payment: 5% of gross retail sales, or 10% of net sales. Copyrights for author. Subjects: Cooking, Ecology, Foods, Health, Philosophy.

THE OLD RED KIMONO, Nancy Applegate, Faculty Advisor; Kimberly Yarborough, Editor; Derrick Lepard, Art Editor, Social & Cultural Studies,, Floyd College, Rome, GA 30162, 706-368-7623. 1972. Poetry, fiction. "*ORK* is looking for submissions of 1-5 short poems or one very short story (2,000 words max). A variety of literary styles are considered; free verse poems and short short stories are preferred. Recent contributors include Peter Huggins, John Cantey Knight, Ruth Moon Kempher, Al Braselton, Jessica Lindberg, and Matt Sunrich. Mss read September 1 - March 1." circ. 1400. 1/yr. Pub'd 1 issue 2009; expects 1 issue 2010. price per copy $4; sample $4. 72pp. Reporting time: 2 months. Simultaneous submissions accepted: Yes. Payment: 2 copies. Copyrighted, reverts to author. Subjects: Fiction, Poetry.

Old Sport Publishing Company, PO Box 2757, Stockbridge, GA 30281, 770-914-2237, Fax 770-914-9261, info@oldsportpublishing.com, www.oldsportpublishing.com. 2004. avg. press run 4M. Expects 1 title 2010, 2-4 titles 2011. No titles listed in the *Small Press Record of Books in Print* (36th Edition, 2010-11). Discounts: call for schedule. 536pp. Reporting time: 6 weeks (prefer detailed query letter; will not return unsolicited manuscripts). Simultaneous submissions accepted: yes. Publishes an unknown % of manuscripts submitted. Payment: negotiable. Will copyright for author upon request. Subjects: South, Sports, Outdoors.

Old Stage Publishing (see also THE BOOMERPHILE; BOULDER HERETIC; TOUCHSTONE), Dan Culberson, PO Box 17446, Boulder, CO 80308-0446, 303-444-3363, danculberson@juno.com. 1992. Articles, satire, criticism, reviews, news items, non-fiction. Pub'd 3 titles 2009; expects 3 titles 2010, 3 titles 2011. No titles listed in the *Small Press Record of Books in Print* (36th Edition, 2010-11). Reporting time: 1 week. Payment: 2 copies of issue for original work, 1 copy for reprinted work. Author retains all copyrights.

Olympic Mountain School Press, Jana Bourne, P.O. Box 1114, Gig Harbor, WA 98335, 253-858-4448. 2004. Photos, non-fiction. "We only publish photography books. Nearly all of our planned titles are how-to books. Authors include Rod Barbee, David Middleton, Carolyn Wright and Scott Bourne, all well-known photographers or experts in their fields." avg. press run 3000. Expects 2 titles 2010, 5 titles 2011. No titles listed in the *Small Press Record of Books in Print* (36th Edition, 2010-11). Discounts: Standard industry discounts available for wholesale buyers representing bookstores. Other bulk discounts are 2-10 copies 25% off 11-20 copies 35% off 21-30 copies 45% off. 128-180pp. Reporting time: six months. Simultaneous submissions accepted: Yes. Publishes 5% of manuscripts submitted. Payment: We negotiate royalty rates on a case by case basis. Copyrights for author. Subject: Photography.

OMEGA, Howling Dog Press / Brave New World Order Books, Michael Annis, P.O. Box 853, Berthoud, CO 80513-0853, WritingDangerously@msn.com, www.howlingdogpress.com, www.howlingdogpress.com/OMEGA. 2002. Poetry, fiction, articles, art, photos, cartoons, interviews, satire, reviews, parts-of-novels, long-poems, collages, plays, non-fiction. "Go online: www.howlingdogpress.com/OMEGA This will tell you everything you need to know. We are very open to many forms of expression, but we are closed to clones, imposters, and other crimes against criteria. The war, the imposter in office, and proselytizing through propaganda disgust us. Plagiarism will be prosecuted." 2-3/yr. Pub'd 2 issues 2009; expects 2 issues 2010, 2 issues 2011. sample price free online. Back issues: free archived. 120pp. Reporting time: Weeks to months. Simultaneous submissions accepted: Yes. Publishes 20% of manuscripts submitted. Payment: Online publication—non paying. Copyrighted, reverts to author. Pub's reviews. §poetry, philosophy, non-fiction,

fiction, novels, progressive political works. Ads: Links/advertising, negotiable, trades.

OmegaRoom Press, Radley Drew, 4041 Louisiana St #1, San Diego, CA 92104, omegaroom@yahoo.com. 2006. Fiction, cartoons. "Omega Room Press has two imprints: Omega Room Books specializes in Science Fiction and Fantasy (but will consider any fiction)and Omega Room Comics specializes comics and graphic novels. Please see www.omegaroom.com for more information and submission guidelines." Expects 10-15 titles 2010, 10-15 titles 2011. No titles listed in the *Small Press Record of Books in Print* (36th Edition, 2010-11). We offer a discount to retailers. For paper backs, we offer a 35% discount. For comics, we offer a 50% discount. 250-500pp. Reporting time: 1 week. Simultaneous submissions accepted: Yes. Does not copyright for author. Subjects: Fantasy, Fiction, Science Fiction.

Omnidawn Publishing, Ken Keegan, Rusty Morrison, 1632 Elm Avenue, Richmond, CA 94805-1614, Phone: (510) 237-5472, Fax: (510) 232-8525, web: http://www.omnidawn.com/contact.htm. 2001. "Omnidawn Publishing was founded by wife and husband team Rusty Morrison and Ken Keegan to create books that are most closely aligned with each author's vision, and to provide an interactive and rewarding publishing experience for poets and writers. We encourage authors to participate at every point in the decision making process of book design and book production, and thus far all have taken an active part, deciding on or providing cover art and assisting in the design of the interior of the books. Omnidawn has been publishing poetry since 2001, with Fabulist and New Fabulist Fiction added in 2006." No titles listed in the *Small Press Record of Books in Print* (36th Edition, 2010-11).

Omonomany, James Weeks, Editor, 5501 Murray Road, Memphis, TN 38119, 901-374-9027, Fax 901-374-0508, jimweeks12@gmail.com. "www.omonomany.com." No titles listed in the *Small Press Record of Books in Print* (36th Edition, 2010-11). Subjects: Fiction, Memoirs, Military, Veterans.

ON EARTH, Douglas Barasch, Editor-in-Chief, 40 West 20th Street, New York, NY 10011, 212-727-4412. 1979. Poetry, articles. "OnEarth, the award-winning environmental magazine, explores politics, nature, wildlife, science, the challenges that confront our planet, and the solutions that promise to heal and protect it. We publish original work by America's finest writers, including Elizabeth Kolbert, Bill Mckibben, Mary Oliver, and others." circ. 165,000. 4/yr. Pub'd 4 issues 2009; expects 4 issues 2010, 4 issues 2011. sub. price $15; per copy $2.95; sample $5. Back issues: $5. Discounts: none. 64pp. Reporting time: 2-3 months. Simultaneous submissions accepted: no. Publishes prose 10%, poetry 2% of manuscripts submitted. Payment: Negotiated with editor. Copyrighted, reverts to author. Pub's reviews: 10 in 2009. §Environment, energy, pollution, water, air, land conservation. Ads: Contact: adsales@onearth.org. Subjects: Conservation, Poetry.

ON SPEC, Diane Walton, Susan MacGregor, Barry Hammond, Robin Carson, Barb Galler-Smith, PO Box 4727, Edmonton, AB T6E 5G6, Canada, 403-413-0215, onspec@onspec.ca. 1989. Poetry, fiction. circ. 1.75M. 4/yr. Pub'd 4 issues 2009; expects 4 issues 2010, 4 issues 2011. sub. price 1-year subs: $24 CDN (in Canada), $25 USD (in USA), $35 USD (overseas); 2-year subs: $40 CDN (in Canada), $42 USD (in USA), $65 USD (overseas); 3-year subs: $54 CDN (in Canada), $56 USD (in USA), $90 USD (overseas); per copy $6.95 Cdn.; sample $8CDN, $8US. Back issues: Depends on buyer's mail address: $6 CAD (in Canada), $6.00 USD (in USA), $9 USD (overseas). Discounts: bookstore 40%. 112pp. Reporting time: 4-6 months. We accept simultaneous submissions, but please let us know. Publishes 5% of manuscripts submitted. Payment: $50-$200 depending on word count, two contributor copies and a 1-year subscription. Copyrighted, reverts to author. Ads: Please see our website - ads range from $50 to $500, depending on the type. Subjects: Fantasy, Science Fiction.

On The Rock Books, Rande Kessler, P.O. Box 9572, Dothan, AL 36304-9572, 334-702-9663. 2007. avg. press run 1000. Pub'd 1 title 2009; expects 5 titles 2010, 10 titles 2011. No titles listed in the *Small Press Record of Books in Print* (36th Edition, 2010-11). 500pp.

One Eyed Press, Caroline Smith, 272 Road 6Rt, Cody, WY 82414, one_eyed_press@yahoo.com, www.one-eyed-press.com. 1998. Poetry, fiction. "Accepts highest quality mainstream fiction and poetry-no genre or traditional poems. No simultaneous submissions. Query with S.A.S.E." avg. press run 3-5M. Pub'd 1 title 2009; expects 1 title 2010, 2 titles 2011. 3 titles listed in the *Small Press Record of Books in Print* (36th Edition, 2010-11). Discounts: complete schedule available by calling 1-800-247-6553. Pages vary. Reporting time: 6-8 weeks. Simultaneous submissions accepted: no. Publishes 1-2% of manuscripts submitted. Payment: negotiable. Copyrights for author. Subjects: Fiction, Poetry.

ONE Health Publishing, LLC, 2001 Wakefield Farm Road, Wildwood, MO 63038-1213, phone: 636-273-9032, fax: 636-273-9029, www.onehealthpublishing.com, publishers@onehealthpublishing.com. 2002. Non-fiction. Pub'd 2 titles 2009; expects 2 titles 2010, 2 titles 2011. 5 titles listed in the *Small Press Record of Books in Print* (36th Edition, 2010-11). Simultaneous submissions accepted: Yes.

One Horse Press/Rainy Day Press, Mike Helm, 1147 East 26th, Eugene, OR 97403, 541-484-4626. 1978. "History and culture of the Oregon country is the prime concern of Rainy Day Press and One Horse Press. Our first two books, Conversations with Pioneer Women and Conversations with Pioneer Men, are conversations with Oregon country pioneers. They are an oral history of life on the Oregon Trail and in the civilization building at its western end. Oregon's Ghosts and Monsters, by Mike Helm, is a collection of ghost stories and other local legends taken from towns throughout Oregon. Tracking Down Coyote tells of a search for the mythical and historical soul of Oregon. Though I refer to Rainy Day Press as 'we', it is still a one-horse show, and I am the horse. As I have a million ideas of my own for writing and publishing projects, I am not seeking manuscript submissions. Instead, send money.'' avg. press run 4M. 4 titles listed in the *Small Press Record of Books in Print* (36th Edition, 2010-11). Discounts: 1 book 0%, 2-5 10%, 6-24 40%, 25-49 42%, 50-74 44%, 75-99 46%, 100-149 48%, 150 or more 50%. 300+pp. Subjects: Americana, Creative Non-fiction, Folklore, History, Old West, Oregon, Outdoor Adventure, Pacific Northwest.

One Less Press (see also ONE LESS: Art on the Range), Nikki Widner, 6 Village Hill Road, Williamsburg, MA 01096-9706, onelessartontherange@yahoo.com, onelessmag.blogspot.com. 2004. Poetry, fiction, art, photos, cartoons, interviews, letters, parts-of-novels, collages, plays, concrete art, non-fiction. "We publish a collection of artistic works that challenge and engage in vision, concept, and constuction. Each issue is designated a specific theme which contributors respond to in some way with open interpretations. *One Less* evolves through its contributors building expression and discourse over a new theme. Recent contributors include: Eric Anderson, Eric Baus, Melissa Benham, Elizabeth Block, Mairead Byrne, Mei-Mei Chang, Bruce Covey, Marcus Civin, Catherine Daly, Patrick James Dunagan, Raymond Farr, Anne Heide, Stephanie Heit, Lisa Jarnot, Alexander Jorgensen, Jane Jortiz-Nakagawa, Sueyeun Juliette Lee, Gayle Mak, Nick-e Melville, Elizabeth Robinson, T.M. Roche-Kelley, Sharon Rogers, Michael Rothenberg, Ken Rumble, Mara Leigh Simmons, and Nico Vassilakis.'' avg. press run 200. Expects 2 titles 2010, 3 titles 2011. No titles listed in the *Small Press Record of Books in Print* (36th Edition, 2010-11). Discounts: 2-10 copies 25%. 150pp. Reporting time: Please check our blog for reading periods. Simultaneous submissions accepted: No. Publishes 30% of manuscripts submitted. Payment: Complimentary copy of the magazine. Copyrights revert back to authors/artists upon publication. Subjects: Avant-Garde, Experimental Art, Fiction, Non-Fiction, Photography, Poetry, Prose, Short Stories, Visual Arts.

ONE LESS: Art on the Range, One Less Press, Nikki Widner, 6 Village Hill Road, Williamsburg, MA 01096-9706, 413-268-7370, onelessartontherange@yahoo.com, onelessmag.blogspot.com. 2004. Poetry, fiction, art, photos, cartoons, letters, parts-of-novels, collages, plays, concrete art, non-fiction. circ. 300. 1/yr. Expects 2 issues 2010, 2 issues 2011. sub. price $18; per copy $10; sample $5. Back issues: $5. Discounts: 5 or more copies 25%. 150pp. Payment: One Contributor Copy of the Magazine. Ads: $50 (full page)/$25 (half page)no classifieds.

One Spirit Press, Suzanne Deakins Ph.D., Publisher; Alicia Prigmore, Administrative; Ethan Firpo, Art Director, One Spirit Press, 1815 SE Stark Street, Portland, OR 97214, spiritpresspublishing@gmail.com ; 1-503-954-0012 www.onespiritpress.com. 1997. Poetry, fiction, articles, art, photos, letters, long-poems. avg. press run 3M. Pub'd 3 titles 2009; expects 10 titles 2010, 15 titles 2011. 15 titles listed in the *Small Press Record of Books in Print* (36th Edition, 2010-11). Discounts: 40% to bookstores quanity discounts. 200pp. Reporting time: 30 days. Simultaneous submissions accepted: yes. Publishes 2% of manuscripts submitted. Payment: e-books every other month, paperbacks 2X a year. Copyrights for author. Subjects: Astrology, Buddhism, China, Creativity, Crystals, Gay, Jewelry, Gems, Lesbianism, Metaphysics, Philosophy, Sex, Sexuality, Spiritual, Sufism, Theosophical, Zen.

•**ONE STORY,** 232 3rd St. #A111, rooklyn, NY 11215. "*One Story* is a literary magazine that contains, simply, one story. Approximately every three weeks, subscribers are sent One Story in the mail. This story will be an amazing read. Each issue is artfully designed, lightweight, easy to carry, and ready to entertain on buses, in bed, in subways, in cars, in the park, in the bath, in the waiting rooms of doctors, on the couch in the afternoon or on line at the supermarket. One Story is available only by subscription. One Story does not accept submissions from June 1 through August 31.''

ONTHEBUS, Bombshelter Press, Jack Grapes, Bombshelter Press, P.O. Box 481266, Bicentennial Station, Los Angeles, CA 90048, http://www.bombshelterpress.com or http://www.jackgrapes.com. 1989. Poetry, fiction, art, interviews, reviews. "*ONTHEBUS* is a literary journal that includes work from poets and writers throughout the U.S. Guidelines for submission on copyright page of each issue. Editor expects those submitting work to have read a copy of our magazine and to be familliar with our guidelines printed on copyright page.'' circ. 3M. 1/yr. Pub'd 1 issue 2009; expects 1 issue 2010, 1 issue 2011. sub. price $30 for 2 double issues; $35 for 2 double issues to institutions; per copy $15; sample $15.00. Back issues: $13.50 for double issues #6/7, #8/9, #10/11; $11 for issues #12, #13, #14. $15.00 for double issues 15/16, 17/18, 19/20;. Discounts: 40% bookstores. Double Issues have 332 pages. Single issues have 275 pages. Reporting time: 1-12 months. Simultaneous submissions accepted: yes. Publishes 5% of manuscripts submitted. Payment: 1 copy, $ if available. Copyrighted, reverts to author. Pub's reviews: 14 in 2009. §Books of poetry. Ads: $300/$200/$125 1/4 page.

Oolichan Books, Ron Smith, Editor; Randal Mcnair, Publisher, PO Box 10, Lantzville, B.C., V0R 2H0,

Canada, 250-390-4839, oolichanbooks@telus.net, www.oolichan.com. 1975. Poetry, fiction, non-fiction. "Oolichan Books publishes books of poetry, creative non-fiction and fiction by Canadian writers only. See our website for submission guidelines. Query with sample writing and SASE. We attempt to maintain a balance between established and newer authors. Generally we are not interested in the mass market book, but rather in serious fiction and poetry which indicates how the writer sees through language. We produce books of excellent quality in content and design, and many of our authors have won prestigious awards. Recent contributors include: Bill New, Keith Harrison, Joanna Streetly, Rhona McAdam, Miranda Pearson and Michael Elcock." Pub'd 8 titles 2009; expects 8 titles 2010, 8 titles 2011. 95 titles listed in the *Small Press Record of Books in Print* (36th Edition, 2010-11). Discounts: trade: 40%. Reporting time: 1-3 months. Simultaneous submissions accepted: yes. Publishes 1% of manuscripts submitted. Copyrights for author. Subjects: Canada, Children, Youth, Fiction, Indigenous Cultures, Non-Fiction, Picture Books, Poetry.

OPEN CITY, Thomas Beller, Editor; Joanna Yas, Editor, 270 Lafayette Street, Suite 1412, New York, NY 10012. "*Open City Magazine* is published by Open City, Inc., a nonprofit corporation based in New York City. The editors, Thomas Beller and Joanna Yas, strive to keep the literary journal vital for each new generation by publishing a dynamic array of poetry and prose with a daring, youthful, spirit. We do not accept submissions via email. If you are outside of the U.S., either send International Reply Coupons for our response or provide an email address. We do not accept submissions via Fedex, UPS, or any other method that requires a signature. We do not accept art submissions. Please allow us up to six months to respond. Await a response before sending a new submission. Simultaneous submissions are okay; please notify us in writing (email or mail) if your story/poetry is accepted elsewhere, and let us know the date of your submission; this makes withdrawing the manuscript much easier."

Open Court Publishing Company, David Ramsay Steele, 70 East Lake St., Suite 300, Chicago, IL 60601, 312-701-1720, Fax 312-701-1728. 1887. Non-fiction. "Distributed by Perseus Book Group." avg. press run 3M. Pub'd 13 titles 2009; expects 13 titles 2010, 13 titles 2011. No titles listed in the *Small Press Record of Books in Print* (36th Edition, 2010-11). 300pp. Reporting time: 2-6 months. We will look at simultaneous submissions, but we give preference to exclusive submissions. Payment: varies. Copyrights for author. Subjects: Asia, Indochina, Education, Philosophy, Psychology, Religion, Sociology.

Open Hand Publishing LLC, Richard A. Koritz, PO Box 20207, Greensboro, NC 27420, 336-292-8585, Fax 336-292-8588, 866-888-9229; info@openhand.com; www.openhand.com. 1981. Non-fiction. "Open Hand is a literary/political press publishing multicultural books which will help to promote social change. We are not accepting unsolicited manuscripts at this time." avg. press run 2.5M. Pub'd 1 title 2009; expects 2 titles 2010, 2 titles 2011. 24 titles listed in the *Small Press Record of Books in Print* (36th Edition, 2010-11). Discounts: 40% to bookstores. 250pp. Reporting time: 4 weeks. Simultaneous submissions accepted: yes. Publishes 1% of manuscripts submitted. Copyrights for author. Subjects: African-American, Biography, British Columbia, Children, Youth, Civil Rights, History, Ireland, Labor, Multicultural, Pacific Northwest, Political Science, Theatre, War, Weaving, Women.

Open Horizons Publishing Company (see also BOOK MARKETING UPDATE), John Kremer, PO Box 2887, Taos, NM 87571-2887, 505-751-3398, Fax 505-751-3100; Email: johnkremer@bookmarket.com; Web: http://www.bookmarket.com. 1983. Articles, art, photos, cartoons, interviews, reviews, letters, news items, non-fiction. "Books on marketing, publishing, publicity, and anything that strikes the publisher's fancy. Jay Frederick Editions is an imprint." avg. press run 3M-5M. Pub'd 3 titles 2009; expects 3 titles 2010, 3 titles 2011. 7 titles listed in the *Small Press Record of Books in Print* (36th Edition, 2010-11). Discounts: 40%. 288pp. Reporting time: 2 weeks. Payment: 10% of list price. Copyrights for author. Subjects: Advertising, Self-Promotion, Bibliography, Book Arts, Book Collecting, Bookselling, Business & Economics, Children, Youth, Communication, Journalism, Entertainment, How-To, Language, Media, Motivation, Success, Movies, Publishing, Quotations.

•**Open Letter Books,** University of Rochester, Lattimore Hall 411, Box 270082, Rochester, NY 14267, 585 319 0823, [f] 585 273 1097, submissions@openletterbooks.org. "Open Letter is a literary press that publishes twelve books annually, mostly novels, collections of short stories, and literary essays. We only publish books in translation, and do not publish children's or young adult literature, plays, self-help books, or how-to guides, etc.Our editors are looking for contemporary literary fiction from around the world that is unique, distinctive, and that will have a significant impact on world literary conversation. It is strongly recommended that persons who intend to submit a query should familiarize themselves with Open Letter's publications before submitting. Translators and authors wishing to submit a query should include:* a one-page cover letter containing relevant autobiographical information about the author and the translator and a short description of the manuscript; * a sample translation of approximately 20 pages (more is appreciated) * a list of the author's published works, if available; and * a self-addressed, stamped envelope (SASE) for reply. We cannot take submissions of any kind by fax and we also do not accept disks." No titles listed in the *Small Press Record of Books in Print* (36th Edition, 2010-11).

OPEN MINDS QUARTERLY, Dinah Laprairie, Editor-Publisher, 680 Kirkwood Drive, Bldg. 1, Sudbury, ON P3E 1X3, Canada, 705-675-9193 ext. 8286, Fax 705-675-3501, openminds@nisa.on.ca, www.nisa.on.ca. 1998. Poetry, fiction, articles, reviews, letters, parts-of-novels, non-fiction. "*OMQ* publishes writing by mental health consumer/survivors (i.e. individuals who live with mental illness). We accept poetry, short fiction, book/movie reviews, and first-person accounts of living with mental illness. Submission guidelines available upon request." circ. 750. 4/yr. Pub'd 4 issues 2009; expects 4 issues 2010, 4 issues 2011. 1 title listed in the *Small Press Record of Books in Print* (36th Edition, 2010-11). sub. price Individuals: $24.95 Canada or US addresses; Organizations (two copies/issue): $49.95 Canada or US; Consumer/survivor/student: $12.95 Canada, $19.95 US.; sample $7 Cdn. Back issues: $7.00 Cdn. Discounts: negotiable. 28pp. Simultaneous submissions accepted: yes. Publishes 35% of manuscripts submitted. Payment: Complimentary copies. Copyrighted, reverts to author. Pub's reviews: 4-6 in 2009. §Mental health-related, recent fiction or nonfiction, novels, films, etc. Ads: $350/$200/$100 1/4 page/$60 1/8 page (funds in Canadian). Subjects: Autobiography, Disease, Essays, Mental Health, Non-Fiction, Poetry, Psychiatry, Short Stories, Social Work, Sociology.

OPEN RANGE MAGAZINE - The West's Premier Real Western Magazine, Dignified Designs, Amanda Smith, PO Box 1207, Glenrock, WY 82637, 307-436-5447, Editor@OpenRangeMagazine.com - www.OpenRangeMagazine.com. 1997. Poetry, fiction, articles, art, photos, cartoons, interviews, reviews, music, parts-of-novels, long-poems, news items, non-fiction. circ. 18000. 7/yr. Pub'd 7 issues 2009; expects 6 issues 2010, 7 issues 2011. sub. price $34.99; per copy $4.99; sample $4.99. Back issues: inquire. Discounts: Negotiable please inquire. 40pp. Reporting time: Less than one day. Simultaneous submissions accepted: Yes. Publishes 75% of manuscripts submitted. Payment: negotiable, please inquire. Copyrighted. Pub's reviews: 5 in 2009. §The West, Cowboys, Ranching. Ads: $900, $450, $225, $175.

OPEN SPACES QUARTERLY, PMB 134, 6327 C SW Capitol Hwy., Portland, OR 97239-1937, Fax: 503-227-3401, Ph: 503-313-4361. "Open Spaces is a quarterly which gives voice to the Northwest on issues that are regional, national and international in scope. Our readership is thoughtful, intelligent, widely read and appreciative of ideas and writing of the highest quality. With that in mind, we seek thoughtful, well-researched articles and insightful fiction, reviews and poetry on a variety of subjects from a number of different viewpoints. Although we take ourselves seriously, we appreciate humor as well."

Open University of America Press, Mary Rodgers, Dan Rodgers, 3916 Commander Drive, Hyattsville, MD 20782-1027, 301-779-0220 phone/Fax, openuniv@aol.com. 1965. Poetry, articles. "We publish literary work in our interests: poetry, the Catholic Italian-American experience, and distance learning using the latest information technologies. We prefer short pieces which we publish as collections, generally buying the writer's ms outright for preservation in our Literary Trust after one-time dissemination. English only. SASE required with query and submission. Recent contributor: Lucille Columbro, *Aurora Farm Revisited*, 1997 (Italian-American experience)." avg. press run 250. Pub'd 4 titles 2009; expects 4 titles 2010, 4 titles 2011. 10 titles listed in the *Small Press Record of Books in Print* (36th Edition, 2010-11). Discounts: 40%. 150pp. Reporting time: 3-4 weeks. Simultaneous submissions accepted: no. Publishes 1% of manuscripts submitted. Payment: by contract. We copyright for author if necessary. Subjects: Catholic, Education, Italian-American, Poetry, Technology.

Open Wide Books (see also OPEN WIDE MAGAZINE), James Quinton, Owner - Managing Editor; Elizabeth Roberts, Editor, 40 Wingfield Road, Lakenheath, Brandon, IP27 9HR, United Kingdom. 2001. Poetry, fiction, articles, interviews, criticism, music, letters. "Open Wide Books publishes the work of those poets and writers who have made a mark in Open Wide Magazine." avg. press run 600. Expects 7 titles 2010, 14 titles 2011. No titles listed in the *Small Press Record of Books in Print* (36th Edition, 2010-11). 100pp. Reporting time: Three months. Simultaneous submissions accepted: No. Publishes 5% of manuscripts submitted. Copyrights for author. Subjects: Criticism, Erotica, Fiction, Humanism, Libertarian, Literature (General), Henry Miller, Music, Novels, Philosophy, Poetry, Politics, Short Stories, Socialist, Tapes & Records.

OPEN WIDE MAGAZINE, Open Wide Books, James D Quinton, Managing Editor; Liz Roberts, Managing Editor, United Kingdom, www.openwidemagazine.co.uk. 2001. Poetry, fiction, interviews, reviews, music, parts-of-novels, long-poems. 80pp. Reporting time: It takes between one and two months for a submission to be considered. Publishes 10% of manuscripts submitted. Copyrighted. Pub's reviews: 10+ in 2009. §Music review both live gig reviews and album reviews. Film reviews, book reviews and theatre/play reviews. Subjects: Arts, Avant-Garde, Experimental Art, Beat, Charles Bukowski, Erotica, Feminism, Jack Kerouac, Libertarian, Media, Henry Miller, Movies, Music, Non-Fiction, Reviews, Writers/Writing.

ORACLE POETRY, Rising Star Publishers, Obi Harrison Ekwonna, PO Box 7413, Langley Park, MD 20787. 1989. Poetry, fiction, criticism, reviews, long-poems. "Only well-made poems with meanings will be considered. No lesbian and gay materials accepted." circ. 500. 4/yr. Pub'd 1 issue 2009; expects 2 issues 2010, 4 issues 2011. sub. price $50, $70 institutions; per copy $10; sample $10. Back issues: $10 plus $2.50 p/h. Discounts: 30%, but may consider 40% bulk orders. 50pp. Reporting time: 2 months. Simultaneous submissions accepted: no. Publishes 50% of manuscripts submitted. Payment: in copies. Copyrighted, does not revert to author. Pub's reviews: 1 in 2009. §Any kind or genre, especially poetry. Ads: $500/$300/others on request. Subject: Poetry.

Oracle Press, C. Sawall, PO Box 5491, Chicago, IL 60680. 1979. Poetry, fiction. "Published books by Paris Smith, Delbert Tibbs, Tracey Young, Rick Laveau. No biases." avg. press run varies. Pub'd 3 titles 2009; expects 3 titles 2010, 3 titles 2011. 2 titles listed in the *Small Press Record of Books in Print* (36th Edition, 2010-11). 100-150pp. Reporting time: 4-6 weeks. Simultaneous submissions accepted: yes. Payment: open for discussion. Copyrights for author. Subjects: Fiction, Poetry.

ORACLE STORY, Rising Star Publishers, Obi Harrison Ekwonna, PO Box 7413, Langley Park, MD 20787. 1989. Fiction, criticism, reviews, long-poems. "Only well-made short stories with meanings will be considered. No lesbian and gay materials accepted." circ. 500. 4/yr. Pub'd 1 issue 2009; expects 2 issues 2010, 4 issues 2011. sub. price $50, $70 institutions; per copy $10; sample $10. Back issues: $10 + $2.50 p/h. Discounts: 30%, but may consider 40% bulk orders. 50pp. Reporting time: 2 months. Simultaneous submissions accepted: no. Publishes 50% of manuscripts submitted. Payment: in copies. Copyrighted, does not revert to author. Pub's reviews: 1 in 2009. §Any kind or genre, especially short stories or short novels. Ads: $500/$300/others on request. Subjects: African Literature, Africa, African Studies, Short Stories.

Orage Publishing, Nannette Schmitt, 1460 Wren Ct, Punta Gorda, FL 33950, p-941-639-6144, fax-941-639-4144. 2003. Fiction. "historical novels-Remember Last Island-about 1856 Hurricane." avg. press run 2000. Pub'd 1 title 2009; expects 1 title 2010, 2 titles 2011. No titles listed in the *Small Press Record of Books in Print* (36th Edition, 2010-11). Discounts: distributors-55%bookstore -40%wholesalers-55%retailers -40%. 200-300pp. Simultaneous submissions accepted: No. Does not copyright for author. Subject: History.

ORAL HISTORY REVIEW, University of California Press, Andrew Dunar, Editor, University of California Press, 2000 Center St., Suite 303, Berkeley, CA 94704-1223, 510-643-7154. 1973. Articles, reviews. "Editorial address: Department of History, University of Alabama, Huntsville AL, 35899. Copyrighted by the Oral History Association." circ. 1057. 2/yr. Pub'd 2 issues 2009; expects 2 issues 2010, 2 issues 2011. sub. price $65 indiv., $119 inst., $35 student; per copy $30 indiv., $67 inst., $30 student; sample same as single copy. Discounts: foreign subs. agents 10%, 10+ one-time orders 30%. 198pp. Copyrighted, does not revert to author. Pub's reviews: approx. 24 in 2009. §genealogy, cultural preservation, history. Ads: $295/$220. Subjects: Genealogy, History.

Orange Alert Press, Jason Behrends, P.O. Box 3897, St. Charles, IL 60174, 630-301-1157. 2008. Fiction, letters. avg. press run 300. Expects 2 titles 2010, 3 titles 2011. 1 title listed in the *Small Press Record of Books in Print* (36th Edition, 2010-11). 160-200pp. Reporting time: 24 hours. Simultaneous submissions accepted: Yes. Payment: No advances, 25% royalty, paid monthly. Does not copyright for author. Subjects: Arts, Experimental, Fiction.

ORBIS, Carole Baldock, Editor, 17 Greenhow Avenue, West Kirby, Wirral CH48 5EL, England, +44 (0)151 625 1446, e-mail baldock.carole@googlemail.com, Websites, www.facebook.com/n/ ?group.php&gid=53636000056www.facebook.com/group.php?gid=187955986920 www.kudoswritingcompeti-tions.com. 1969. Poetry, fiction, articles, art, interviews, criticism, reviews, letters, news items. "Some longer poems, but mostly 40 lines. Prose: 500-1000 words. All types of material considered, and it should be the best it can be. 3 IRCs must be included with submissions overseas - *not* US-stamped addressed envelopes. NB, maximum of 4 poems per submission. 2 via email; no attachments. Brief covering letter preferred to CVs, press releases etc. Also Editor of *KUDOS*, formerly *Competitions Bulletin*, which includes a growing Overseas Section. Details of 50+ UK contests for poetry; about 40 for short stories; around $200,000 in prizes each issue. $7 per issue; $40/6 pa: www.kudoswritingcompetitions.wordpress.com." circ. 600. 4/yr. Pub'd 4 issues 2009; expects 4 issues 2010, 4 issues 2011. 3 titles listed in the *Small Press Record of Books in Print* (36th Edition, 2010-11). sub. price $46; per copy $14; sample varies. Back issues: 2/$15. Discounts: 30% to trade. 84pp. Reporting time: aim is within the month for initial submissions. Simultaneous submissions accepted: no objection, providing I am kept informed. Publishes 1% of manuscripts submitted. Payment: Each issue, £50/$88: Featured Writer; 3-4 poems or 2000 words. Plus Readers Award: £50/$88 for piece receiving the most votes and four winners selected for submission to Forward Poetry Prize, Single Poem Category; £50/$88 split between four, or more, runners-up. Copyrighted, reverts to author. Pub's reviews: 80 in 2009. §Mainly collections of poetry; some short stories. Also books of interest to writers. Magazine reviews appear in the Poetry Index Section. Ads: $100/$50. Subjects: Essays, Fiction, Humor, Literary Review, Myth, Mythology, Poetry, Prose, Translation, Women, Young Adult.

Orchard House Press, Cris DiMarco Ms, Senior Editor, 7419 Ebbert Drive SE, Port Orchard, WA 98367, www.orchardhousepress.com. 1989. Poetry, fiction, photos, satire, long-poems, plays. "Orchard House Press is a traditional publishing house dedicated to staying small, adaptable and innovative. We publish timeless books and games for all ages in more than a dozen genres. We excel at projects that push the envelope of expectation—projects created by impassioned authors. As an independent voice in publishing, we work with both new and established authors who are looking for a personal relationship with their publisher. We build careers, not over-night sensations. We do not backlist nor force results in a perform-or-be-canceled environment. We educate our authors in the industry and require that our staff be published authors. Orchard House Press is inclusive and diverse in celebration of this only green world and the endless variety of voices found here. We seamlessly integrate authors and staff from all walks of life and value their timeless stories. We are pro-child, pro-GLBT and pro-Christian. We are nonpartisan and owned and operated by women. We publish books that entertain and enrich; we do not publish agendas, doctrine or propaganda. We are not owned by a corporate interest nor do we answer to any force but our love of the arts.You must use our submission form and label and include a #10 envelope for our reply. We cannot return submissions over 12oz. due to USPS regulations. Do not send an entire mss. unless requested." avg. press run 10,000 copies. Pub'd 300 titles 2009; expects 200 titles 2010, 200 titles 2011. 5 titles listed in the *Small Press Record of Books in Print* (36th Edition, 2010-11). Discounts: For bookstores, libraries, schools, and other retail outlets we offer a 50% off retail, payment in 60 days; returns accepted within 60 day period. Late accounts will have discounts reduced to 10%. Distributor discounts are arranged individually. 250pp. Reporting time: Can be up to 6 months for full manuscripts. 3 months for queries. We accept simultaneous submissions with notification. Publishes 2-5% of manuscripts submitted. Payment: We do not offer advances. We pay a 15% royalty of gross monies received. We issue royalty statements twice a year in March and September. Does not copyright for author. Subjects: Arts, Black, Children, Youth, Comics, Fiction, Folklore, Gay, How-To, Lesbianism, Literature (General), Medieval, Mystery, Native American, Science Fiction.

Orchises Press, Roger Lathbury, PO Box 320533, Alexandria, VA 22320-4533, 703-683-1243. 1983. Poetry, fiction, articles, concrete art. avg. press run 1M. Pub'd 4 titles 2009; expects 4 titles 2010, 5 titles 2011. 104 titles listed in the *Small Press Record of Books in Print* (36th Edition, 2010-11). Discounts: 40% on no-return items to bookstores with some exceptions, distributors and jobbers; 20% if a return privilege is wanted; items under $20 shipped no return unless otherwise stipulated. 80pp. Reporting time: 1 month. Publishes .05% of manuscripts submitted. Payment: 36% royalty after costs recouped, generous free copy policy. Copyrights for author. Subjects: Fiction, Memoirs, Poetry, Science.

OREGON EAST, Daniel Harrington, Hoke 304, Eastern Oregon University, La Grande, OR 97850, (541) 962-3787, oe@eou.edu, www3.eou.edu/~oe. 1950. Poetry, fiction, art, non-fiction. "We accept fiction (under 3,000 words), poetry (less than 60 lines), and creative non-fiction (under 3,000 words). Reading from September to mid-March, with notification by June. No simultaneous or electronic submission." 1/yr. Pub'd 1 issue 2009; expects 1 issue 2010, 1 issue 2011. sub. price $5; per copy $5. 112pp. Simultaneous submissions accepted: No. Payment: payment is two copies of the magazine. Copyrighted, reverts to author. Subjects: Fiction, Poetry.

Oregon State University Press, Tom Booth, Associate Director; Mary Elizabeth Braun, Acquisitions Editor, 121 The Valley Library, Corvallis, OR 97331, 541-737-3166, OSU.Press@oregonstate.edu, http://oregonstate.edu/dept/press. 1961. Non-fiction. "We publish scholarly and general interest books about the history, cultures, literature, environment, and natural resources of the state and region. No fiction, no poetry. Author guidelines available upon request." Pub'd 15 titles 2009; expects 18 titles 2010, 25 titles 2011. No titles listed in the *Small Press Record of Books in Print* (36th Edition, 2010-11). Discounts: 20-50% depending on quantity. Reporting time: 1-3 months. Simultaneous submissions accepted: no. Payment: varies. Copyrights for author. Subjects: Americana, Biography, Biology, Conservation, Earth, Natural History, Ecology, Foods, History, Indians, Myth, Mythology, Native American, Nature, Pacific Northwest, Reprints, Water, The West.

Origin Press, Byron Belitsos, PO Box 151117, San Raphael, CA 94915. 1996. Non-fiction. "Favored topics: spirituality, "deep politics," esoterica, philosophy." avg. press run 3M. Expects 2-4 titles 2010, 2-4 titles 2011. 2 titles listed in the *Small Press Record of Books in Print* (36th Edition, 2010-11). Discounts: trade 20-40%, others negotiable. 250pp. Reporting time: 10 weeks. Simultaneous submissions accepted: yes. Publishes 2% of manuscripts submitted. Payment: 6% of list paid biannually. Copyrights for author. Subjects: Christianity, Culture, Global Affairs, Government, Health, Inspirational, Lifestyles, Metaphysics, Occult, Peace, Philosophy, Psychology, Religion, Self-Help, Spiritual.

Original Plus (see also THE JOURNAL (once "of Contemporary Anglo-Scandinavian Poetry")), Sam Smith, 17 High Street, Maryport, Cumbria, CA15 6BQ, England, 01900812194; email- smithsssj@aol.com. 1998. Poetry, fiction, articles, art, reviews, parts-of-novels, long-poems, plays, non-fiction. "22 poetry collections & 4 chapbooks to date." avg. press run 250. Pub'd 1 title 2009; expects 3 titles 2010, 1 title 2011. 21 titles listed in the *Small Press Record of Books in Print* (36th Edition, 2010-11). Discounts: 25%. 72pp. Payment: 10%. Copyrights for author.

ORNAMENT, Robert K. Liu, Co-Editor; Carolyn L.E. Benesh, Co-Editor, PO Box 2349, San Marcos, CA 92079, 760-599-0222, Fax 760-599-0228. 1974. Art, interviews, satire, criticism, letters, parts-of-novels, collages, news items. "Formerly published under the name of *The Bead Journal* which terminated with volume 3, #4. As of Volume 4, #1 published under the name of *Ornament*." circ. 40M. 5/yr. Pub'd 5 issues 2009;

expects 5 issues 2010, 5 issues 2011. sub. price $26 domestic, $41 foreign; per copy $6.78; sample $6.78. Back issues: write for information. Discounts: 40% on wholesale orders. 100pp. Reporting time: 8-12 weeks. Simultaneous submissions accepted: yes. Payment: copies of the magazine in which article appears, number depends on length of article; also per page payments. Copyrighted, reverts to author. Pub's reviews: none in 2009. §Jewelry, ancient, ethnic, contemporary, forms of personal adornment, costume, clothing, beads, textiles. Write for rates. Subjects: Arts, Clothing, Collectibles, Crafts, Hobbies, Jewelry, Gems, Jewelry, Gems, Native American, Textiles, Weaving.

THE ORPHAN LEAF REVIEW, James Paul Wallis, 26 Grove Park Terrace, Fishponds, Bristol, BS16 2BN, United Kingdom, www.orphanleaf.co.uk orphanleaf@jpwallis.co.uk. 2004. Poetry, fiction, art, photos, cartoons, interviews, music, letters, parts-of-novels, long-poems, collages, plays, non-fiction. "An "orphan leaf" is a single page written to appear as though it's been taken from a book. It can be from any kind of book (prose, poetry, non-fiction, music manuscript, illustration etc.) and from any part of a book. Each leaf is a different size, paper and design, hand cut and assembled. The magazine aims to engage its readers as much with the visual and tactile qualities as with the writing." circ. 200. 2/yr. Pub'd 1 issue 2009; expects 3 issues 2010, 3 issues 2011. sub. price $24; per copy $10. Back issues: $8. 56pp. Reporting time: 2-6 months. Simultaneous submissions accepted: Yes. Publishes 10% of manuscripts submitted. Payment: Complimentary copy. Copyrighted, reverts to author. Subjects: Biography, Cooking, Diaries, Essays, Fiction, Indexes & Abstracts, Interviews, Literature (General), Maps, Non-Fiction, Novels, Poetry, Prose, Short Stories, Textbooks.

OSIRIS, Andrea Moorhead, Osiris, PO Box 297, Deerfield, MA 01342-0297, rmoorhead@deerfield.edu. 1972. Poetry, interviews, long-poems. "*Osiris* is an international multi-lingual journal publishing contemporary poetry. English and French appear without translation. Poetry from other languages such as Spanish, Danish and Portuguese often appear with facing page English translation. Recent contributors: Abderrahmane Djelfaoui (Algeria), Anne Blonstein (Switzerland), Jurgen Kross (Germany), Astrid Cabral (Brazil), and Ingrid Swanberg (USA)." circ. 1M. 2/yr. Pub'd 2 issues 2009; expects 2 issues 2010, 2 issues 2011. sub. price $18 individuals and institutions; per copy $9.00; sample $4.00. 56pp. Reporting time: 4 weeks. Simultaneous submissions accepted: no. Publishes 15% of manuscripts submitted. Payment: 5 copies. Copyrighted, rights revert to author, with credit line to *Osiris*. Ads: query. Subjects: France, French, Language, Literary Review, Poetry.

Osric Publishing (see also MURDER CROWS), Christopher Herdt, 1705 13th Ave S Unit A, Birmingham, AL 35205. 1993. Poetry, fiction, art, photos, satire, letters, parts-of-novels, collages, non-fiction. "Submissions should be made via the Web site; see www.murdercrows.com for details." avg. press run 100. Expects 1 title 2010, 1 title 2011. No titles listed in the *Small Press Record of Books in Print* (36th Edition, 2010-11). 32pp. Reporting time: 6 months. Simultaneous submissions accepted: yes. Publishes 2% of manuscripts submitted. Payment: negotiable, contributors copies. Does not copyright for author. Subjects: Fiction, Poetry.

THE OTHER HERALD, Hidden Valley Farm, Publisher, T. F. Rice, P.O. Box 172, Perry, NY 14530, publisher.hiddenvalley@yahoo.com , theotherherald@yahoo.com , http://www.otherherald.com. 2006. Poetry, fiction, articles, art, photos, cartoons, interviews, satire, criticism, reviews, letters, parts-of-novels, collages, concrete art, news items, non-fiction. "We "herald" good writing, of all genres (if suitable for an audience of all ages), and other articles/info of interest to writers and creatives. Smaller pieces are appreciated because we are a small publication. Interesting art, sometimes experimental, graces each issue. Some issues are themed, but not all. See our web site for more info. Recent contributors are listed on web site: www.otherherald.com!" circ. 500. 4/yr. Pub'd 12 issues 2009; expects 8 issues 2010, 4 issues 2011. sub. price $10; per copy $3.00; monthly back-issue is free w/SASE (quarterly back-issue available for $3 each). Back issues: $0.50 or $3.00 per issue, depending on format of issue. Discounts: 2-9 copies 25% , 10+ copies 50%. 16pp. Reporting time: Normally less than 3 months. Simultaneous submissions accepted: No. Publishes 25% of manuscripts submitted. Payment: 1 copy of the issue your work appears in. Discounted copies if more copies desired. Copyrighted, reverts to author. Pub's reviews: 6 in 2009. §poetry, fiction, writers/writing, language, reference for writers. Ads: Typically no adv. Subjects: Adirondacks, Arts, Avant-Garde, Experimental Art, Book Reviewing, Experimental, Family, Fantasy, Fiction, Haiku, History, New York, Poetry, Prose, Quotations, Writers/Writing.

OTHER INVESTIGATIONS, Ilya Zaychik, 4 Ridgecrest Drive, West Roxbury, MA 02132. 2006. Non-fiction. "Please visit www.stationaery.com/oi, or http://otherinvestigations.blogspot.com and read the 'statement of purpose,' and/or the issue. We publish only personal, analytical non-fiction essays. One issue has been released so far, featuring Eli S. Evans, JD Smith, and Celia Lisset Alvarez." circ. 200. 1/yr. Expects 1 issue 2010, 1 issue 2011. sub. price $5; per copy $4; sample free. 40pp. Reporting time: A few days. Simultaneous submissions accepted: Yes. Publishes 12% of manuscripts submitted. Payment: Two copies of Other Investigations. Copyrighted, reverts to author. No ads. Subjects: Arts, Cities, Creative Non-fiction, Criticism, Culture, Essays, Handwriting/Written, History, Journals, Language, Memoirs, Non-Fiction, Reading, Society, Zines.

THE OTHER ISRAEL, Adam Keller, Beate Zilversmidt, PO Box 2542, Holon 58125 Israel, Israel, 972-3-5565804 phone/Fax. 1983. Articles, interviews, reviews, letters, news items, non-fiction. "Weekly email updating via otherisr@actcom.co.il is free - write "send me TOI-Billboard" in the subject line." circ. 3000. in principle 6/yr, but double issues. Pub'd 6 issues 2009; expects 6 issues 2010, 6 issues 2011. sub. price $30 regular, $50 institution; $15 students/senior/unemployed; per copy $5; sample free on request. Back issues: $5 - (free for subscribers / inst. subscribers - complete set). Discounts: agents 10% / retailers 33% / one-time bulk 90%. 14 (double issues 28)pp. Payment: none. Not copyrighted. Pub's reviews: approx. 0 in 2009. §Middle East politics, Economics, society, peace movement, conflict resolution. Subjects: Anarchist, Asia, Indochina, Civil Rights, Counter-Culture, Alternatives, Communes, History, Public Affairs, Third World, Minorities.

Other Press, 2 Park Avenue, 24th Floor, New York, NY 10016. "Other Press attracts authors who are guided by a passion to discover the limits of knowledge and imagination. We publish novels, short stories, poetry, and essays from America and around the world that represent literature at its best. Our nonfiction books—should they be history, current events, popular culture or memoir—explore how psychic, cultural, historical, and literary shifts inform our vision of the world and of each other. All editorial inquiries should be e-mailed to the editorial department: editor@otherpress.com. Sorry, but we do not accept unsolicited manuscript submissions." No titles listed in the *Small Press Record of Books in Print* (36th Edition, 2010-11).

Otoliths (see also OTOLITHS), Mark Young, 8 Kennedy St, Rockhampton, QLD 4700, Australia, otolitheditor@gmail.com, http://the-otolith.blogspot.com, http://stores.lulu.com/l_m_young. 2006. Poetry, fiction, interviews, concrete art, non-fiction. "The publishing arm of Otoliths began as print editions of the magazine of the same name, but has since expanded to include books & chapbooks, usually by authors associated with the journal. It focuses on postavant text & visual poetry. Authors include Nick Piombino, Sheila E. Murphy, Jordan Stempleman, Nico Vassilakis, Rochelle Ratner & Eileen Tabios." avg. press run 100. Pub'd 5 titles 2009; expects 20 titles 2010, 20 titles 2011. 1 title listed in the *Small Press Record of Books in Print* (36th Edition, 2010-11). Discounts: on request. 80-240pp. Reporting time: Within two weeks. Simultaneous submissions accepted: No. Publishes 25% of manuscripts submitted. Payment: Author's copies. Copyrights for author. Subjects: Literature (General), Poetry, Surrealism.

OTOLITHS, Otoliths, Mark Young, 8 Kennedy St, Rockhampton, QLD 4700, Australia, otolitheditor@gmail.com, http://the-otolith.blogspot.com, http://stores.lulu.com/l_m_young. 2006. Poetry, fiction, art, photos, long-poems, collages, concrete art, non-fiction. 4/yr. Pub'd 4 issues 2009; expects 4 issues 2010, 4 issues 2011. 240pp. Reporting time: Two weeks. Simultaneous submissions accepted: No. Publishes 25% of manuscripts submitted. Payment: Print copy of e-zine. Copyrighted, reverts to author. Subjects: Creative Non-fiction, Poetry, Prose.

OTTN Publishing, James Gallagher, 16 Risler Street, Stockton, NJ 08559, 609-397-4005, 609-397-4007 (fax), inquiries@ottnpublishing.com, www.ottnpublishing.com. 1998. Non-fiction. "We publish series nonfiction for juvenile/YA readers, which is primarily marketed to schools and libraries." avg. press run 2000. Pub'd 5 titles 2009; expects 8 titles 2010, 10-15 titles 2011. No titles listed in the *Small Press Record of Books in Print* (36th Edition, 2010-11). Discounts: 30% wholesale (returnable) or 40% (nonreturnable). 64pp. Reporting time: 4-6 months. Simultaneous submissions accepted: Yes.

Our Child Press, Carol Perrott, PO Box 4379, Philadelphia, PA 19118-8379, 610-308-8988. 1980. Fiction, non-fiction. "Adoption related materials." avg. press run 2000. Pub'd 1 title 2009; expects 2 titles 2010, 2 titles 2011. 4 titles listed in the *Small Press Record of Books in Print* (36th Edition, 2010-11). 32pp. Reporting time: 6 months to a year. Simultaneous submissions accepted: Yes. Publishes 1% of manuscripts submitted. Payment: 5% net sales. Does not copyright for author. Subjects: Adoption, Family.

OUR SCHOOLS/OUR SELVES, Erika Shaker, Editor, Canadian Centre for Policy Alternatives, 410-75 Albert Street, Ottawa, ON K1P 5E7, Canada, phone 613-563-1341, fax 613-233-1458, web: www.policyalternatives.ca. "Subscripers to OS/OS get 4 issues a year. Topics: education and labour, social justice, anti-racism, feminism, socialism, 'A magazine for Canadian education activists.'" circ. 1M. 4/yr. Pub'd 4 issues 2009; expects 4 issues 2010, 4 issues 2011. sub. price $48 (Canada), $60 Canadian (outside Canada); per copy $12; sample $12. Back issues: $9. 160pp. Simultaneous submissions accepted: yes. Publishes 50% of manuscripts submitted. Payment: none. Pub's reviews: at least 2 per issue in 2009. §Education. Ads: $350/$200. Subjects: Education, Labor.

•**OUR STORIES LITERARY JOURNAL,** Aleix E. Santi, Editor, 433 N Aurora Street, Apt 1S, Ithaca, NY 14850, Web site: www.ourstories.us Submission Guidelines: www.ourstories.us/submissions/. "Editorial Focus: *Our Stories Literary Journal* publishes short stories by some of the best emerging writers online and interviews. Our staff reviews every short story that is received and provides feedback to each submission.Tips from the Editor: Please send your stories as .doc files through our submission manager. Please know that we will read your story and give you tips, suggestions on how to improve it next time around. Please send stories under 7,000 words."

OUT OF LINE, Garden House Press, Sam Longmire, P.O. Box 321 Trenton, Ohio 45067, Trenton, OH 45067, 513-988-7183. 1998. Poetry, fiction, articles, non-fiction. "OUT OF LINE is an annual anthology of poetry, fiction, and nonficition with underlying themes of peace and justice. We look for works that deal with serious human issues such as tolerance, diversity, freedom, peace, healthy relationships, environmental justice, personal growth, and spirituality. Recent contributors include Michael Casey, Maureen Tolman Flannery, CB Follett, Paula Friedman, Lyn Lifshin, Karen Malpede, and Leza Lowitz OOL leans toward writers who bring a progressive and liberal perspective to their work. No hate literature.'' circ. 400. 500/yr. Pub'd 1 issue 2009; expects 1 issue 2010, 1 issue 2011. sub. price $12.50; per copy $12.50; sample free. Back issues: $5, all available. Discounts: 2-6 copies %5. 200pp. Reporting time: Two months. Simultaneous submissions accepted: Yes. Payment: Two free copies and the opportunity to purchase additional copies at cost. Copyrighted, reverts to author. No advertisements. Subjects: Alcohol, Alcoholism, Biography, Black, Community, Conservation, Ecology, Foods, Fiction, Gay, Humanism, Lesbianism, Poetry, Political Science, Politics, Religion, Spiritual.

OUT YOUR BACKDOOR: The Magazine of Do-It-Yourself Adventure and Homegrown Culture, Jeff Potter, Publisher, 4686 Meridian Road, Williamston, MI 48895, 517-347-1689; jeff@outyourbackdoor.com; outyourbackdoor.com. 1989. Poetry, fiction, articles, art, photos, cartoons, interviews, satire, criticism, reviews, music, letters, parts-of-novels, long-poems, collages, concrete art, news items, non-fiction. ''*OYB* is about thrifty, independent culture and exploration, the interface of art, action and hobby. *OYB* is an everyman's *Outside*—but it's a refreshing antidote to the elite fantasy consumerist aspect of that mag. I cover hard-to-find, quality, cultural, affordable projects, as presented by aficionados. With an emphasis on: boats, bikes, XC skis, unbestseller books, owner-operated restaurants and much else in indy-culture. I fight against fragmentation, go for sustainability, practical harmony and cross-training of the brain. I often use reprints that won't see the mainstream to achieve our tasty blend. Truly indy media is so rare that one has to see *OYB* to understand it. The paper mag only comes out annually, but I put up new web stories several times a week. The web is a likely place for an outside submission to appear. 90% of *OYB* is by me!'' circ. 5M. 1/yr. Pub'd 1 issue 2009; expects 1 issue 2010, 2 issues 2011. sub. price $5/1 issue; per copy $5; sample $5. Back issues: $5. Discounts: retail 1-10 40%, wholesalers 30+ 50%. 48-64pp. Reporting time: Eventually, with SASE. Simultaneous submissions accepted: yes. Publishes 10% of manuscripts submitted. Payment: Usually nothing, but *OYB* is growing so payment may not be far off. Copyrighted, reverts to author. Pub's reviews: 40 in 2009. §Alternative, subculture, unusual, bikes, boats, equipment, hunting, fishing, travel, culture, thrifty lifestyles, inside info on places/things. Ads: $200 full / $150 half / $100 quarter. Subjects: Architecture, Bicycling, Book Collecting, Bookselling, Community, Conservation, Counter-Culture, Alternatives, Communes, Crafts, Hobbies, Culture, Design, Ecology, Foods, Gardening, Homemaking, Networking, Reprints, Sports, Outdoors.

OUTER-ART, Dr. Florentin Smarandache, University of New Mexico, 200 College Road, Gallup, NM 87301, smarand@unm.edu, www.gallup.unm.edu/~smarandache/a/outer-art.htm. 2000. Articles, art, photos, interviews, criticism, reviews, collages, concrete art. ''Outer-Art is a movement set up by the editor in the 1990s (as a protest against random modern art, where anything could mean...art!) and consists of making art as ugly as possible, as wrong as possible, or as silly as possible, and generally as impossible as possible! It is an upside-down art!... to do art in the way it is not supposed to be done.'' 1/yr. Pub'd 1 issue 2009; expects 1 issue 2010, 1 issue 2011. Reporting time: 1 month. Simultaneous submissions accepted: yes. Copyrighted, reverts to author. Subjects: Arts, Avant-Garde, Experimental Art, Criticism, Essays, Multicultural, Post Modern, Visual Arts.

OUTLANDER, Robert Seaver Gebelein, PO Box 1546, Provincetown, MA 02657. 1994. ''My bias is new civilization.'' Irregular. Expects 1 issue 2010, 1 issue 2011. sub. price $10 for 10 issues; per copy $1; sample $1. Back issues: $1. Discounts: make me an offer. 10pp. Reporting time: not set. Publishes 0% of manuscripts submitted. Payment: none. Copyrighted, reverts to author.

OUTPOSTS POETRY QUARTERLY, Hippopotamus Press, Howard Sergeant, Founder, Editor; Roland John, Editor, 22, Whitewell Road, Frome, Somerset BA11 4EL, United Kingdom. 1943. Poetry, articles, criticism, reviews. ''*Outposts* is the longest-lived independent poetry magazine in the UK. It was founded to provide a satisfactory medium for those poets, recognised or unrecognised, who are concerned with the potentialities of the human spirit, and who are able to visualize the dangers and opportunites which confront the individual and the whole of humanity. Although recent contributors have included famous poets like Ted Hughes, Peter Porter, Roy Fuller, Vernon Scannell, Blake Morrison, Seamus Heaney, etc., the magazine makes a special point of introducing the work of new and unestablished poets to the public.'' circ. 1.9M. 4/yr. Pub'd 4 issues 2009; expects 4 issues 2010, 4 issues 2011. sub. price £14 or $24 (postage paid) for 1 year, £26 or $50 (postage paid) for 2 years; per copy £3.50, $7; sample $7. Back issues: price varies from £2-£10. Discounts: 35%. 80pp. Reporting time: 2 weeks, 4 weeks non-U.K. Simultaneous submissions accepted: yes. Payment: depends on length of poem. Copyrighted, reverts to author. Pub's reviews: 30 in 2009. §Poetry, criticism of poetry. Ads: £90 $120/£45 $70. Subjects: Criticism, Poetry.

Outrider Press, Whitney Scott, Senior Editor, 2036 Northwinds Drive, Dyer, IN 46311-1874, 219-322-7270, fax:219-322-7085 www.outriderpress.com, Email: outriderpress@sbcglobal.net. 1988. Poetry, fiction, art. ''Produces handmade, handbound, blank page books, 50-300 pp, suitable for journals or personal poetry as well as archival manuscript boxes. Our 2011 anthology will accept short fiction and creative nonfiction (to 2,500 words) and poetry (single-spaced up to 28 lines) on the theme of "A Bird in the Hand: Risk and Flight"—Flight, risk, gambling on the odds. Can be literal birds and literal flight as well as risktaking of all kinds. Email: outriderpress@sbcglobal.net for guidelines and entry forms or send SASE. We offer $1,000 in cash prizes - $500 in poetry and $500 in prose as determined by independent judges. Deadlines for manuscripts: Feb. 27 each year for our annual anthology/contest with a different theme every year." avg. press run 12M-13M. Pub'd 1 title 2009; expects 3 titles 2010, 4 titles 2011. 15 titles listed in the *Small Press Record of Books in Print* (36th Edition, 2010-11). Discounts: bookstores 60/40; others up to 50% off, depending upon # ordered. Annual anthology averages 200 pages. Reporting time: 2-3 months. Simultaneous submissions accepted: yes. Publishes a variable % of manuscripts submitted. Payment: negotiable. Copyrights for author. Subjects: Animals, Cooking, Creative Non-fiction, Ecology, Foods, Essays, Family, Fiction, Nature, Occult, Pets, Poetry, Romance, Travel, Wildlife, Women.

Outskirts Press Inc., Amy Booker, 10940 S. Parker Road #515, Parker, CO 80134, phone: 888-672-6657, fax: 888-672-6657, website http://outskirtspress.com/poemsfromtheheart. Poetry, fiction, articles, art, interviews, satire, criticism, reviews, letters, parts-of-novels, long-poems, plays, non-fiction. 1 title listed in the *Small Press Record of Books in Print* (36th Edition, 2010-11).

•THE OVAL LITERARY MAGAZINE, Samantha Steven, Editor-in-Chief, The University of Montana, 32 Campus Drive, Missoula, MT 59812, (406) 243-0211, email: oval.inquiries@mso.umt.edu. "The Oval began in autumn of 2007 with a simple goal: to start an undergraduate-run, non-profit literary journal publishing prose, poetry, and visual art. The name, Oval, is taken from the University of Montana campus promenades, where students can come together with equal representation for their ideologies and creativity, and, most importantly, to have fun. Like the location for which it is named, it is the goal of the Oval and its staff to provide a continuing nexus point for young writers, their ideologies, and creative pursuits. The Oval is published annually. It is sponsored by the University of Montana, the Associated Students of the University of Montana, and the Maureen and Mike Mansfield Library. Submissions are taken year round from current undergraduate college and university students."

OVERLAND JOURNAL, Robert Clark, Oregon-California Trails Association, PO Box 1019, Independence, MO 64051-0519, 816-252-2276, Fax 816-836-0989, octa@indepmo.org. 1983. Articles, photos, reviews, non-fiction. "Articles concerning the covered wagon migration to the American West in the 19th century: Oregon Trail, gold rush (various routes)." circ. 2.5M. 4/yr. Pub'd 4 issues 2009; expects 4 issues 2010, 4 issues 2011. sub. price $45; per copy $6.25; sample free to public libraries. Back issues: $6.25. Discounts: none. 36pp. Reporting time: 30 days. Simultaneous submissions accepted: no. Publishes 75% of manuscripts submitted. Payment: none. Copyrighted, reverts to author. Pub's reviews: 25 in 2009. §Covered wagon migration to the American West in the 19th century, gold rush. Ads: $275/$165/$95 1/4 page. Subjects: Book Reviewing, Diaries, Great Plains, Health, The West.

Owl Creek Press, Rich Ives, 2693 S. Camano Drive, Camano Island, WA 98282. 1979. Poetry, fiction, articles, long-poems. avg. press run 500-2M. Pub'd 4 titles 2009; expects 4 titles 2010, 4 titles 2011. 50 titles listed in the *Small Press Record of Books in Print* (36th Edition, 2010-11). Discounts: standard. Reporting time: 3-6 months. Simultaneous submissions accepted: yes. Payment: varies. Subjects: Fiction, Poetry.

The Owl Press, Albert Flynn DeSilver, PO Box 126, Woodacre, CA 94973-0126, 415-438-1539, asisowl@mindspring.com, www.theowlpress.com. 1997. Poetry, art, long-poems, concrete art. "Recent and forthcoming authors include Frank O'Hara, John Ashbery, Anne Waldman, Alice Notley, Joanne Kyger, Bill Berkson, Clark Coolidge, Bernadette Mayer, Anselm Berrigan, Edmund Berrigan, Brenda Coultas, Brendan Lorber, Lisa Jarnot and others." avg. press run 750. Pub'd 2 titles 2009; expects 3 titles 2010, 2 titles 2011. 7 titles listed in the *Small Press Record of Books in Print* (36th Edition, 2010-11). Discounts: 50-55%. 100pp. Reporting time: 1 month. Simultaneous submissions accepted: yes. Publishes .001% of manuscripts submitted. Payment: books. Copyrights for author. Subjects: Poetry, Prose.

THE OXFORD AMERICAN, Marc Smirnoff, Lisa Dixon, Bess Reed, J.E. Pitts, Sally Ann Cassady, 201 Donaghey Ave., #107, Conway, AR 72035-5001, www.oxfordamericanmag.com. 1992. Poetry, fiction, articles, art, photos, criticism, reviews, music, non-fiction. "*The Oxford American* is a general interest magazine covering all cultural aspects of the American South. *The Oxford American* is published by novelist John Grisham." circ. 50M+. 4/yr. Pub'd 6 issues 2009; expects 4 issues 2010, 4 issues 2011. sub. price $19.95; per copy call for rates; sample same. Back issues: varies, see website. Discounts: if you purchase 4 gift subscriptions, you receive the 5th one free of charge. 100+pp. Reporting time: 3-4 weeks, (high volume time) 3 months. We accept simultaneous submissions, but please notify of such. Publishes 10% of manuscripts submitted. Payment: varies, arrangements made after acceptance. Copyrighted, reverts to author. Pub's reviews: 30+ in 2009. §Books of fiction, poetry, nonfiction (Southern topics). Ads: contact our ad staff. Subjects: Fiction, Music, Non-Fiction, Poetry, Travel.

Oxford University Press, 198 Madison Avenue, New York, NY 10016. "Oxford University Press, Inc. (OUP USA), is Oxford University Presss second major publishing center, after Oxford (UK). It publishes works that further Oxford University's objective of excellence in research, scholarship, and education." No titles listed in the *Small Press Record of Books in Print* (36th Edition, 2010-11).

Oxford University Press (UK), Great Clarendon Street, Oxford OX2 6DP, United Kingdom. "Oxford University Press offers a wide range of scholarly and professional works in all academic disciplines, including science, humanities, law, medicine, and the social sciences. OUP has been voted as the UK's leading academic publisher by the Academic, Specialist and Professional Group of the UK Booksellers Association for the fourth year running." No titles listed in the *Small Press Record of Books in Print* (36th Edition, 2010-11).

OYEZ REVIEW, Janet Wondra Dr., School of Liberal Studies; Roosevelt University, 430 S. Michigan Avenue, Chicago, IL 60605, http://www.roosevelt.edu/oyezreview. 1965. Poetry, fiction, art, photos, concrete art, non-fiction. "Oyez Review is the literary magazine of the Creative Writing Program at Roosevelt University. It is published annually, edited by an all-student staff under the direction of a faculty member with professional experience in the publishing world. Founded in 1965, Oyez Review has featured work from such writers as Charles Bukowski, James McManus, Carla Panciera, Michael Onofrey, Tim Foley, John N. Miller, Gary Fincke, and Barry Silesky, and visual artists Vivian Nunley, C. Taylor, Jennifer Troyer, and Frank Spidale." circ. 800. 1/yr. Pub'd 1 issue 2009; expects 1 issue 2010, 1 issue 2011. sub. price $5; per copy $5; sample $5. Back issues: $5. Discounts: %40 off for bookstores. 100pp. Reporting time: 2 months on average. Simultaneous submissions accepted: No. Publishes 10% of manuscripts submitted. Payment: 2 copies and discount on more copies. Copyrighted, reverts to author. Subjects: Essays, Fiction, Non-Fiction, Poetry, Writers/Writing.

OYSTER BOY REVIEW, Damon Sauve, Fiction Editor; Jeffery Beam, Poetry Editor, PO Box 1483, Pacifica, CA 94044, email_2010@oysterboyreview.com, www.oysterboyreview.com. 1994. Poetry, fiction, art, photos, reviews. "Submissions closed for 2010." circ. 250. 3/yr. Pub'd 3 issues 2009; expects 3 issues 2010, 3 issues 2011. sub. price $12; per copy $4; sample $4. Back issues: $4. Discounts: 30% libraries and bookstores. 60pp. Reporting time: 1-2 months. Simultaneous submissions accepted: no. Publishes 1% of manuscripts submitted. Payment: 2 copies. Copyrighted, reverts to author. Pub's reviews: 10 in 2009. §First books, chapbooks, poetry collections, novels. Ads: $60/$30/$15 1/4 page/$20 1/3 page. Subjects: Fiction, North Carolina, Poetry, Reviews.

Oyster River Press, Cicely Buckley, Publisher, 36 Oyster River Road, Durham, NH 03824-3029, 603-868-5006, oysterriverpress@comcast.net, www.oysterriverpress.com. 1989. Poetry. "A cooperative press, editors, writers, and illustrators, working together. Average of 2 publications per year, suitable for a broad audience. Initially submit 6-10 poems or 2 chapters, no. of pages, synopsis, and a brief bio. Latestpublication is bilingual poems by 10 Swedish women: To CatchLife Anew. Upcoming is Chinese and English, poets Li Bai &Du Fu of the eighth century, and a new chapbook of poems by Robert Dunn, Portsmouth NH poet laureate." avg. press run 1000. Pub'd 3 titles 2009; expects 1 title 2010, 1 title 2011. 41 titles listed in the *Small Press Record of Books in Print* (36th Edition, 2010-11). 80-150pp. Reporting time: 1-6 months. Simultaneous submissions accepted: no. 7% of submitted manuscripts published. Translations a specialty; often bilingual presentation. Payment: Royalties 10% after production expenses are paid. Copyrights for author. Subjects: Bilingual, English, Inspirational, Language, Latin America, Nature, New England, New Hampshire, Non-Fiction, Peace, Poetry, Short Stories.

P

P.R.A. Publishing, Lucinda Clark, Managing Editor Publisher; Xavier Clark, Assistant Editor, P.O. Box 211701, Martinez, GA 30917-1701, (706) 855-6173, fax (210)855-6170, www.prapublishing.com, info@prapublishing.com, www.poetrymatterscelebration.com. 2002. Poetry, fiction, long-poems. "Interested in poetry, fiction and possibly non-fiction manuscripts. Strong interest in developing anthologies for poets." avg. press run 500. Pub'd 3 titles 2009; expects 3 titles 2010, 5 titles 2011. 12 titles listed in the *Small Press Record of Books in Print* (36th Edition, 2010-11). Discounts: Contact for more information. 115pp. Simultaneous submissions accepted: Yes. We have become very selective due to genre in which we publish. Chance of selection improves if author has developed a marketing platform. Payment: Royalties paid on titles. Poetry takes a little longer than most genres. Copyright filed for title published. Original rights remain with author. Subjects: African-American, Aging, Americana, Anthology, Bilingual, Careers, Culture, Family, Gender Issues, Homelessness, Human Rights, Myth, Mythology, Poetry, Relationships, Romance.

PACIFIC COAST JOURNAL, French Bread Publications, Stillson Graham, Editor; Stephanie Kylkis, Fiction Editor, PO Box 56, Carlsbad, CA 92018-0056, e-mail pcj@frenchbreadpublications.com. 1991. Poetry, fiction, articles, art, interviews, satire, criticism, reviews, parts-of-novels, plays, non-fiction. "We publish experimental and semi-experimental work that furthers the cause of artistic insolence. The best work will entertain as well as confuse. Query e-mail submissions, unsolicited regular mail submissions OK." circ. 200. 2-3/yr. Pub'd 2 issues 2009; expects 2 issues 2010, 2 issues 2011. 1 title listed in the *Small Press Record of Books in Print* (36th Edition, 2010-11). sub. price $15; per copy $4; sample $3. Back issues: $2.50- $4, depends on particular issue. 40pp. Reporting time: 6-9 months, sometimes longer. Simultaneous submissions accepted, just let us know. Payment: 1 copy. Copyrighted but not registered, author retains all rights. Pub's reviews: 1 in 2009. §Fiction, sciences, philosophy. Ads: $35/$20 or will trade with other publications. Subjects: Avant-Garde, Experimental Art, Essays, Poetry, Reviews, Short Stories, The West.

PACIFIC HISTORICAL REVIEW, University of California Press, David Johnson, Editor; Carl Abbot, Editor, Univ of California Press, 2000 Center Street, Suite 303, Berkeley, CA 94704-1223, 510-643-7154. 1931. Reviews, non-fiction. "Editorial address: Dept. of History, Portland State University, PO Box 751, Portland, OR 97207-0751." circ. 1448. 4/yr. Pub'd 4 issues 2009; expects 4 issues 2010, 4 issues 2011. sub. price $34 indiv., $123 instit., $22 students (+ $20 air freight); per copy $14 indiv., $36 instit., $14 students (+ $20 air freight); sample free. Back issues: $14 indiv., $36 instit., $14 students (+ $20 air freight). Discounts: foreign subs. agents 10%, one-time orders 10+ 30%, standing orders (bookstores): 1-99 40%, 100+ 50%. 170pp. Reporting time: 3 months. Payment: none. Copyrighted, does not revert to author. Pub's reviews: 100 in 2009. §Asia, American West, history, diplomatic history. Ads: $295/$220. Subjects: Asia, Indochina, Asian-American, The West.

Pacific Isle Publishing Company, Ronald W. Parkhurst, PO Box 827, Makawao, HI 96768, 808-572-9232 phone, book@bromes.com, www.bromes.com. 2000. Fiction, art, photos, cartoons, non-fiction. Pub'd 1 title 2009; expects 1 title 2010, 1 title 2011. 1 title listed in the *Small Press Record of Books in Print* (36th Edition, 2010-11). Discounts: industry standard/negotiable. 216pp. Reporting time: 30 days. Simultaneous submissions accepted: yes. Publishes 50% of manuscripts submitted. Payment: negotiable. Copyrights for author. Subject: Horticulture.

THE PACIFIC REVIEW, James Brown, Faculty Editor, Department of English, Calif State University, San Bernardino, CA 92407. 1982. Poetry, fiction, parts-of-novels, long-poems, plays, non-fiction. "While the *PR* attempts to reflect its unique geographic region—Southern California—material is not limited to the area; the *PR* invites excellence in poetry, fiction, drama, and essay. Do not submit more than three poems at a time, and please also include a short biographical statement with your entry." circ. 1M. 1/yr. Pub'd 1 issue 2009; expects 1 issue 2010, 1 issue 2011. sub. price $7; per copy $5; sample $5 (libraries $6.50). Back issues: $2. Discounts: 40%. 104pp. Reporting time: 3 months (mss are not read Feb.-Aug.). Simultaneous submissions accepted: yes. Publishes 20% of manuscripts submitted. Payment: in copies. Copyrighted, reverts to author. Ads: $150/$100. Subjects: Arts, Drama, Fiction, Literary Review, Literature (General), Poetry.

PADDLEFISH, Jim Reese, Mount Marty College 1105 W. 8th St., Yankton, SD 57078, office- (605)668-1362 Fax: (605)668-1607. 2006. Poetry, fiction, art, interviews, non-fiction. "PADDLEFISH, Mount Marty Colleges literary journal is now accepting submissions for its premiere issue. The editors are interested in poetry, fiction and nonfiction in all genres and styles." circ. 1000. 1/yr. Expects 1 issue 2011. sub. price $10; per copy $10; sample $10. Back issues: $10. Discounts: 2-10 copies 25%10-20 40%. 150pp. Reporting time: 2 months. Simultaneous submissions accepted: Yes. Publishes 10% of manuscripts submitted. Payment: payment in copies. Copyrighted, reverts to author. Ads: $90 display. Subjects: Arts, Fiction, Non-Fiction, Poetry.

Padishah Press, Richard Bronson, P.O.Box 528, Cold Spring Harbor, NY 11724, www.PadishahPress.com. 2006. Poetry. "A small, independent press devoted to the publication of poetry informed by the medical experience." avg. press run 250. Expects 1 title 2010. 2 titles listed in the *Small Press Record of Books in Print* (36th Edition, 2010-11). 90pp. Reporting time: 1 month. Simultaneous submissions accepted: No. Does not copyright for author. Subjects: Medicine, Poetry.

PAGAN AMERICA, Crescent Moon, Jeremy Robinson, Cassidy Hughes, PO Box 393, Maidstone, Kent ME14 5XU, United Kingdom. 1992. Poetry. "*Pagan America* is a bi-annual collection of poetry from North America and Canada. Many poets are unknown, others are well-established. One book each year features women's love poetry." circ. 200. 2/yr. Pub'd 2 issues 2009; expects 2 issues 2010, 2 issues 2011. sub. price $17; per copy $8.50; sample $6. Back issues: $6 for 1, $5 for 2+. Discounts: Trade: 20% single order, 35% 2+. 80pp. Reporting time: 3 months. We publish 5% or less of manuscripts submitted. Payment: to be negotiated. Copyrighted, reverts to author. Ads: $20/$10/$5 1/4 page. Subjects: Arts, Culture, Feminism, Literature (General), Myth, Mythology, Poetry, Prose, Religion, Sex, Sexuality, Women.

Pagan Press, John Lauritsen, 11 Elton St., Dorchester, MA 02125-1412, 617-282-2133, john_ lauritsen@post.harvard.edu. 1982. Articles, photos, interviews, non-fiction. "Founded to publish books of interest to intelligent gay men. Send query letter before submitting manuscript." avg. press run 2M. Expects 1 title 2010, 1 title 2011. 5 titles listed in the *Small Press Record of Books in Print* (36th Edition, 2010-11). 150pp. Does not copyright for author. Subject: Gay.

PageFree Publishing, Inc., Kim Blagg D, PO Box 60, Otsego, MI 49078-0060, 269-692-3926. 1998. Poetry, fiction, cartoons, interviews, criticism, music, parts-of-novels, long-poems, plays, non-fiction. "We publish for a variety of authors, particularly those targeting niche readers." avg. press run 1000. Pub'd 300 titles 2009; expects 600 titles 2010, 1000 titles 2011. No titles listed in the *Small Press Record of Books in Print* (36th Edition, 2010-11). Discounts: 30-55%. 250pp. Reporting time: 2 days. Simultaneous submissions accepted: Yes. Publishes 90% of manuscripts submitted. Payment: 7% royalty. Does not copyright for author.

PAINTED BRIDE QUARTERLY, Drexel University, Dept. of English and Philosophy, 3141 Chestnut Street, Philadelphia, PA 19104. "Painted Bride Quarterly accepts up to 5 poems, fiction up to 5000 words, and essays/reviews up to 3000 words, in any genre or school (occasional themed quarterly issues) All artwork: photographs, paintings, etchings, lithographs and line drawings are now accepted in black & white or color for our website and only black & white for publication in our print annual. If submitting art work for our website, please do so via pbq@drexel.edu. We appreciate photoshop files (psd.), or jpgs; size 600x600. Please note that we will not accept written submissions via e-mail." Pub's reviews.

PAJ NTAUB VOICE, Mai Neng Moua, Hmong American Institute for Learning (HAIL), 2654 Logan Avenue North, Minneapolis, MN 55411, Phone (651) 214-0955, Fax (612) 588-1534, mainengmoua@mn.rr.com. 1994. Poetry, fiction, art, photos, interviews, satire, criticism, letters, parts-of-novels, long-poems, plays, non-fiction. circ. 1000. 2/yr. sub. price $20 individual US, $30 individual international, 40 institution US, $50 institution international; per copy $10. Back issues: $5-$10 Loss and Separation; Becoming American; WAR; Art & Religion; Dating, Sex & Marriage; Visions for the Future; Gender & Identity; Silence. 80pp. Payment: $25 for publication, $25-$50 for reading at the public readings. Copyrighted, reverts to author. Subjects: Arts, Asia, Indochina, Asian-American, Fiction, Literature (General), Non-Fiction, Poetry.

•PALABRA: A Magazine of Chicano & Latino Literary Art, P. O. Box 86146, Los Angeles, CA 90086-0146, www.palabralitmag.com. "*Palabra* is about exploration, risk and ganasthe myriad intersections of thought, language, story and artel ms all of letters, symbols and spaces into meaning. Its about writing that cares as much about language and its structure as about content and storytellingand that shows awareness of and attention to the possibilities of both. Mostly it's about work with the emotional fiber that threads all honest art. Its purpose is to provide a portal for new threads of pensamiento, language and story, to reach from the past and present and dive headlong into the future of Chicano & Latino writingto push it, stretch it, keep it fresh, vibrant, honest and at the thumping edge of literary creativity and innovation. Its intent is to present an eclectic and adventurous array of thought and construct, alma y corazn, and a few carcajadas woven in for good measure. Submit only original, unpublished work (including work published online or in any other electronic form). English, Spanish, Spanglish or any combination thereof is welcome."

Paladin Enterprises, Inc., Peder C. Lund, President and Publisher; Donna Duvall, Editorial Director, Gunbarrel Tech Center, 7077 Winchester Circle, Boulder, CO 80301, 303-443-7250, Fax 303-442-8741, www.paladin-press.com. 1970. Non-fiction. "Non-fiction manuscripts on military related subjects are given first consideration. These include weaponry technology, police science, military tactics, martial arts, self-defense, espionage, survival. When accompanied with photos, mss are reviewed and returned within six weeks." avg. press run 1M-2M. Pub'd 40 titles 2009; expects 40 titles 2010, 40 titles 2011. 378 titles listed in the *Small Press Record of Books in Print* (36th Edition, 2010-11). Discounts: $50-$100 retail value - 20% all titles except supplementary list; $100-$500 40%; $500-$1000 45%; $1000-$5000, 50% both all titles except supplementary list. Over $5000 55% except supplementary list. 175pp. Reporting time: 6 weeks. Simultaneous submissions accepted: yes. Publishes 2% of manuscripts submitted. Payment: standard 10%, 12% & 15%. Copyrights for author. Subjects: Anarchist, Computers, Calculators, Counter-Culture, Alternatives, Communes, Crime, Drugs, History, How-To, Humor, Martial Arts, Military, Veterans, Non-Fiction, Reprints, Sports, Outdoors, War, Weapons.

Paladin Media Group, K Williamson, President; D King, Exec Prod; A Straka, Exec Edit, 673 Berkmar Court, Charlottesville, VA 22901, 434-817-2700, www.MyBigHeaven.com, www.PaladinMediaGroup.com. 2008. Fiction, non-fiction. "Our focus is on redemptive entertainment, both secular and sacred. We eschew labels." Expects 6 titles 2010, 12 titles 2011. No titles listed in the *Small Press Record of Books in Print* (36th Edition, 2010-11). 300pp. Reporting time: 2-6 Months. Simultaneous submissions accepted: Yes. Publishes 1% of manuscripts submitted. Payment: Varies. Copyrights for author. Subjects: Creative Non-fiction, Crime, Current Affairs, Fantasy, Fiction, Inspirational, Juvenile Fiction, Mystery, Non-Fiction, Novels, Reprints, Satire, Self-Help, Short Stories, Young Adult.

Palari Publishing, David Smitherman, PO Box 9288, Richmond, VA 23227-0288, phone/fax 866-570-6724, info@palaribooks.com, www.palaribooks.com. 1998. Fiction, non-fiction. Pub'd 2 titles 2009; expects 4 titles

2010, 6 titles 2011. 9 titles listed in the *Small Press Record of Books in Print* (36th Edition, 2010-11). Discounts: 2-4 copies 20%, 5-99 40%, 100+ 50%. 200pp. Reporting time: 1 month. Simultaneous submissions accepted: No simultaneous submissions accepted. Publishes 2% of manuscripts submitted. Payment: varies. Copyrights for author. Subjects: African-American, Bibliography, Business & Economics, Fiction, Gay, Health, Lifestyles, Non-Fiction.

PALO ALTO REVIEW, Ellen Shull, 1400 West Villaret Blvd., San Antonio, TX 78224-2499, 210-436-3249. 1992. Poetry, fiction, articles, art, photos, interviews, satire, reviews, letters, news items, non-fiction. "We have recently been downsized to one issue per year; however, it is enlarged at 88 pages." circ. 600. 1/yr. Pub'd 2 issues 2009; expects 1 issue 2010, 1 issue 2011. sub. price $10; per copy $10; sample $5. Back issues: $5. 88pp. Reporting time: maximum of 3 months. Simultaneous submissions accepted, if noted as such. Percent of mss submitted which are published: articles/essays 40%, poems 5%, stories 2-3%. Payment: 2 copies. Copyrighted, reverts to author. Pub's reviews: 2 in 2009. §Not interested in children's, gay & lesbian. Ads: $100/$50/$35 1/4 page. Subjects: Autobiography, Book Reviewing, Education, Essays, Fiction, Humor, Interviews, Journals, Memoirs, Multicultural, Nature, Non-Fiction, Poetry, Research, Travel.

Pancake Press, Patrick Smith, 163 Galewood Circle, San Francisco, CA 94131, 415-665 9215. 1973. Poetry, long-poems. "Not presently accepting unsolicited mss." avg. press run 1M. Expects 1 title 2010. 5 titles listed in the *Small Press Record of Books in Print* (36th Edition, 2010-11). Discounts: 40%. 35-50pp. Reporting time: 1 month. Payment: arranged by mutual consent. Does not copyright for author. Subjects: Arts, Poetry.

Pangaea, 226 South Wheeler Street, Saint Paul, MN 55105-1927, 651-690-3320 tel, info@pangaea.org, http://pangaea.org. 1991. "No unsolicited submissions accepted at this time." avg. press run 7.5M. Pub'd 3 titles 2009; expects 3 titles 2010, 3 titles 2011. 12 titles listed in the *Small Press Record of Books in Print* (36th Edition, 2010-11). Discounts: bookstores 1-4 20%, 5-9 25% 10-14 30% 15-24 35% 25+ 40%; wholesalers: Baker & Taylor, Follett, Quality, Lectorum, YBP, Blackwell's. 200pp. Copyrights for author. Subjects: African Literature, Africa, African Studies, The Americas, Animals, Anthropology, Archaelogy, Bilingual, Caribbean, Children, Youth, Conservation, Cuba, Earth, Natural History, Latin America, Nature, Poetry, Puerto Rico, Travel.

•**PANK MAGAZINE,** Walker Arts & Humanities Bldg., 1400 Townsend Dr., Houghton, MI 49931. "PANK, by which we mean PANK Magazine, Pankmagazine.com, and the PANK Little Book Series, is a nonprofit literary collective published daily, monthly, and annually, depending on your flavor. PANK was founded in 2006 by M. Bartley Seigel. In 2009, across print and digital platforms, PANK had more than 80,000 readers in 138 countries. The best definitions of the word pank can be found here and there, or you can make up your own and send it to us. Manuscripts and artwork submitted to PANK must be original and previously unpublished. Submissions are read year-round. There are few guidelines, but the ways and means for you to submit can be found at http://www.pankmagazine.com/submissions/."

Panther Books (see also GOODIE), Romy Ashby, 197 Seventh Avenue 4C, New York, NY 10011, www.goodie.org. 2001. Poetry, fiction, photos, interviews, letters. "Please see our website http://www.goodie.org. Authors include: Ira Cohen, Edgar Oliver, Marty Matz." avg. press run 1500. Pub'd 1 title 2009; expects 1 title 2010, 2 titles 2011. 3 titles listed in the *Small Press Record of Books in Print* (36th Edition, 2010-11). Discounts: 2-10 copies 40%11+ copies 50%. 150pp. Copyrights for author. Subjects: Beat, Fiction, Interviews, New York, Novels, Photography, Storytelling, Surrealism.

Panther Creek Press (see also TOUCHSTONE LITERARY JOURNAL), Guida Jackson, Publisher; Ted Walthen, Acquisitions Editor; Jerry Cooke, Editorial Assistant; Tucker Jackson, Webmaster; W. A. Jackson, Publicity Director; Adam Murphy, Graphic Designer, 104 Plum Tree Terrace #115, Houston, TX 77077, panthercreek3@hotmail.com, www.panthercreekpress.com. 1999. Poetry, fiction, non-fiction. "Fiction: 50,000-80,000 words, nonfiction same. Poetry: 100-200 pages. Recent authors: Paul Christensen, Robb Jackson, Dodie Meeks, Eric Muirhead, Omar Pound, Christopher Woods. We do not read unsolicited mss. We read queries only. If we request the manuscript, chances are good we will publish it. Due to the recent death of William Laufer, one of our principals, we will read no new submissions until 2008." avg. press run 1M. Pub'd 4 titles 2009; expects 5 titles 2010, 4-5 titles 2011. 15 titles listed in the *Small Press Record of Books in Print* (36th Edition, 2010-11). Discounts: trade 5+ 40%. 230pp. Reporting time: 4 weeks, queries only. We accept simultaneous submissions on queries only. If we request the manuscript, we expect an exclusive submission for 2 months. We do not accept unsolicited manuscripts. Publishes 1% of manuscripts submitted. Payment: 10% on list price, paid annually, no advance against royalties will be paid. Copyrights for author. Subjects: African Literature, Africa, African Studies, Classical Studies, Essays, Fiction, Genealogy, Latin America, Literature (General), Memoirs, Myth, Mythology, Native American, Novels, Poetry, Reference, Texas, Third World, Minorities.

Pantonne Press, Kitty Ciske Jr, 902 S Randall Rd. #C306, St. Charles, IL 60174, 630-587-1520, www.pantonnepress.com. 1992. Fiction. "Pantonne Press is committed to publishing quality works of fiction for the general market." avg. press run 5000. Pub'd 3 titles 2009; expects 2 titles 2010, 3 titles 2011. 1 title listed in the *Small Press Record of Books in Print* (36th Edition, 2010-11). Discounts: distributors 67 wholesalers 55 bookstores 40 college 25 2-4 books 20 5-9 books 30 10-24 books 40. 350pp. Reporting time: 3 months. Simultaneous submissions accepted: No. Publishes 2% of manuscripts submitted. Does not copyright for author. Subject: Fiction.

PAPERBACK PARADE, Gryphon Books, Gary Lovisi, PO Box 209, Brooklyn, NY 11228-0209. 1986. Articles, photos, interviews, criticism, reviews, letters, news items, non-fiction. "A quarterly digest magazine devoted to collectible vintage, rare paperbacks with articles, interviews, lists, on famous paperback authors, artists, publishers, and dozens of cover reproductions of scarce/rare books. Now with *color* covers!" circ. 1M. 5/yr. Pub'd 6 issues 2009; expects 6 issues 2010, 5 issues 2011. sub. price $35, $55 outside USA; per copy $10 + postage; sample $10 + postage. Back issues: $10 per issue + postage. Discounts: 40% on 5 or more of each issue. 100-110pp. Reporting time: 2-4 weeks. Simultaneous submissions accepted: no. Payment: copies and other arrangements. Copyrighted, reverts to author. Pub's reviews: dozens in 2009. §Non-fiction. Ads: $50/$25. Subjects: Arts, Bibliography, Book Arts, Book Collecting, Bookselling, Collectibles, Crime, Fantasy, Sherlock Holmes, H.P. Lovecraft, Mystery, Science Fiction, Writers/Writing.

PAPERPLATES, Bernard Kelly, Editor and Publisher; Tim Conley, Reviews Editor; Karen Belanger, Poetry Editor; Karl Buchner, Fiction Editor; Brenda Keble, Non-fiction Editor, 19 Kenwood Avenue, Toronto, ON M6C 2R8, Canada. 1991. Poetry, fiction, articles, art, photos, cartoons, interviews, satire, criticism, reviews, letters, parts-of-novels, plays, non-fiction. "Online only. Average length for secondary pieces (reviews, opinions, etc.) is 2,500 words. Maximum length for feature articles is 5,000 words. Maximum length for poetry is 1,500 words." 2/yr. Pub'd 2 issues 2009; expects 2 issues 2010, 2 issues 2011. 40pp. Reporting time: 6 months. Simultaneous submissions accepted: yes. Publishes 25% of manuscripts submitted. Payment: none. Copyrighted, reverts to author. Pub's reviews: 6 in 2009. §Fiction, poetry, essays. Ads: $300/$150/$100 1/3 page/$75 1/4 page/$50 1/6 page. Subjects: Book Reviewing, Essays, Fiction, Literary Review, Poetry, Short Stories, Storytelling.

Paperweight Press, L. H. Selman, 123 Locust Street, Santa Cruz, CA 95060-3907, 831-427-1177 or 1 800 538-0766. 1975. Art. avg. press run 3M. Pub'd 1 title 2009; expects 2 titles 2010, 3 titles 2011. 22 titles listed in the *Small Press Record of Books in Print* (36th Edition, 2010-11). Discounts: 6 or more copies, 40%; Distributor 200 or more, 60%. 200pp. Reporting time: 4-6 weeks. Payment: TBA. Copyrights for author. Subjects: Antiques, Arts.

Papillon Presse, Y. Darnell, P.O. Box 54502, Phoenix, AZ 85078-4502. 2008. Fiction, art, music, parts-of-novels, plays, news items, non-fiction. "Christian fiction (contemporary or historical) for teens, young adults, romance stories for women (both Contemporary and Historical), and non-fiction. Christian non-fiction and fiction are design to be entertaining as well a blessing for other Christians. We are also accepting stories involving married Christians. Stories of any race or interracial relationships are accepted as long that it does not go against the Word of God. We do not accept or read unsolicited manuscripts. The writer must submit a complete synopsis and the first three chapters of your work. If you want your submission to be returned to you, the writer must include a SASE (self addressed envelope with submission) along with the requested materials and the correct postage affixed to envelope. Otherwise, WE ARE NOT RESPONSIBLE FOR THESE SUBMISSIONS WITHOUT A SASE AND THEY WILL BE DISCARED. Also, we will not accept any submission without a returned address. We appreciate your cooperation and professionalism! Thanks!" avg. press run 1000. Expects 1 title 2010, 3 titles 2011. 3 titles listed in the *Small Press Record of Books in Print* (36th Edition, 2010-11). Discounts: 10-25%. 200pp. Reporting time: 30-90 days. Simultaneous submissions accepted: Yes. Publishes 25% of manuscripts submitted. Payment: standard. work-for-hire if accpeted and published. Subjects: African-American, Christianity, Creative Non-fiction, Family, Fiction, Inspirational, Juvenile Fiction, Latino, Multicultural, Novels, Picture Books, Romance, Short Stories, Singles, Young Adult.

Papoose Publishing, A. Anderson, 385 Main Street South, Suite 404-200, Southbury, CT 06488, 203-206-4838. 2008. Interviews, non-fiction. "Our mission is to support health (mental and physical) and how it affects aspects of life, family and success." Pub'd 1 title 2009; expects 1 title 2011. 1 title listed in the *Small Press Record of Books in Print* (36th Edition, 2010-11). Discounts: 40%. 350pp. Reporting time: 3 months. Simultaneous submissions accepted: Yes. Copyrights for author. Subjects: Family, Health, Parenting, Philosophy, Psychology, Reference, Self-Help, Sociology.

Para Publishing (see also PUBLISHING POYNTERS), Dan Poynter, Publisher, PO Box 8206 - Q, Santa Barbara, CA 93118-8206, 805-968-7277, Fax 805-968-1379, info@parapublishing.com, www.parapublishing.com. 1969. Photos, cartoons, news items, non-fiction. "Para Publishing specializes in non-fiction books on parachutes/skydiving and book writing/publishing/marketing. The technical parachute books and popular skydiving books have always been sold through non-traditional outlets. Publisher Dan Poynter is the author of 100+ books, 51 monographs and over 500 magazine articles, most of them on publishing. He serves as a consultant to the mail order and publishing industries and conducts workshops in Santa Barbara on book marketing, promotion and distribution. Poynter is a past Vice-President of the Publishers Marketing Association. No manuscripts, query first. Query regarding parachute and publishing books only. When offering a parachute manuscript, we want to know how many jumps you have made." avg. press run 5M-10M. Pub'd 7 titles 2009; expects 8 titles 2010, 8 titles 2011. 30 titles listed in the *Small Press Record of Books in Print* (36th Edition, 2010-11). Discounts: 6-199 40%, 200-499 50%, 500+ 55%. 250pp. Reporting time: 1 week. Simultaneous submissions accepted: yes. We publish 60% of manuscripts submitted, but we screen before submission. Payment: 6-8% of list price. Copyrights for author. Subjects: Publishing, Sports, Outdoors, Writers/Writing.

Paradigm Publications, Robert L. Felt, Acquisitions Editor; Nigel Wisemabn Ph.D., Senior Linguist; Eric Brand LAC, Clinical Editor, 202 Bendix Drive, Taos, NM 87571, 575 758 7758, Fax 575 758 7768, info@paradigm-pubs.com, www.paradigm-pubs.com. 1981. Non-fiction. "Scholarship and clinical excellence in acupuncture and oriental medicine." avg. press run 2M. Pub'd 4 titles 2009; expects 4 titles 2010, 4 titles 2011. 58 titles listed in the *Small Press Record of Books in Print* (36th Edition, 2010-11). Discounts: 40% net 30, library 20%. 500pp. Reporting time: 4-8 months. Simultaneous submissions accepted: yes. Publishes 1% of manuscripts submitted. Payment: 10%/15%/18% on net. Does not copyright for author. Subjects: Acupuncture, Alternative Medicine.

•Paradise Cay Publications, PO Box 29, Arcata, CA 95518-0029. "Paradise Cay Publications, Inc. is a small independent publisher specializing in nautical books, videos, and art prints. Our primary market is the US; however, we have distribution in many other countries. Our primary interest is in manuscripts that deal with the instructional and technical aspects of ocean sailing. We also publish and will consider fiction if it has a strong nautical theme. All manuscripts are be personally considered by the publisher, Matt Morehouse. To present your manuscript in the best possible way, submissions should include a cover letter containing a story synopsis and a short biography of the author, including any plans the author may have to promote their work. The cover letter should describe the book's subject matter, approach, distinguishing characteristics, intended audience, author's qualifications, and why the author thinks this book is appropriate for Paradise Cay." No titles listed in the *Small Press Record of Books in Print* (36th Edition, 2010-11).

Paradise Research Publications, Inc., Kenneth C. Burns, Box 837, Kihei, HI 96753-0837, 808-874-4876, dickb@dickb.com. 1994. avg. press run 3M. Pub'd 4 titles 2009; expects 4 titles 2010, 4 titles 2011. 30 titles listed in the *Small Press Record of Books in Print* (36th Edition, 2010-11). Discounts: 20% for 1 book, 40% for all over 1. 250pp. Reporting time: 1 week. Simultaneous submissions accepted: yes. Publishes 10% of manuscripts submitted. Does not copyright for author. Subject: Alcohol, Alcoholism.

Paradiso-Parthas Press (see also FEILE-FESTA), Robert Colvin, 214 Mulberry Street, New York, NY 10012. 2006. Poetry, fiction, photos. "We are interested in novels and poetry chapbooks/collections, especially writing that evokes some kind of Mediterranean and/or Celtic connection. We do not accept unsolicited manuscripts, but you may send a one page letter of inquiry with a SASE to:Paradiso-Parthas Press214 Mulberry StreetNew York, NY 10012." No titles listed in the *Small Press Record of Books in Print* (36th Edition, 2010-11). Simultaneous submissions accepted: Yes. Subjects: Celtic, Europe, Fiction, Italian-American, New York, Photography, Poetry.

PARADOXISM, Dr. Florentin Smarandache, Editor, 200 College Road, University of New Mexico, Gallup, NM 87301, 505-863-7647, fax 505-863-7532, smarand@unm.edu, www.gallup.unm.edu/~smarandache/a/paradoxism.htm. 1990. "*Paradoxism*, (formerly *The Paradoxist Literary Movement Journal*), is an annual journal of 'avant-garde poetry, experiments, poems without verses, literature beyond the words, anti-language, non-literature and its literature, as well as the sense of the non-sense; revolutionary forms of poetry.' We want avant-garde poetry, 1-2 pages, any subject, any style (lyrical experiments). *Paradoxism* was set up by the editor in 1980's as an anti-totalitarian protest, and it is based on an excessive use of contradictions, antitheses, antinomies, paradoxes in creation. No classical, fixed forms. We have published poetry by Paul Georgelin, Titu Popescu, Ion Rotaru, Michele de LaPlante, Claude LeRoy. Do not submit mss. in the summer." circ. 500. 1/yr. Pub'd 1 issue 2009; expects 1 issue 2010, 1 issue 2011. 52pp. Reporting time: 3-6 months. Simultaneous submissions accepted: no. Payment: 1 copy.

Paragon House Publishers, Rosemary Yokoi, 1925 Oakcrest Avenue, Suite 7, St. Paul, MN 55113-2619, Tel: (651) 644-3087, Fax: (651) 644-0997, www.paragonhouse.com. 1962. Non-fiction. avg. press run 3000. Pub'd 12 titles 2009; expects 11 titles 2010, 10-15 titles 2011. No titles listed in the *Small Press Record of Books in Print* (36th Edition, 2010-11). 280pp. Simultaneous submissions accepted: Yes. Publishes 2% of manuscripts submitted. Payment: Royalty payment twice yearly. Advance $1000. Copyrights for author. Subjects: Ethics, Holocaust, New Age, Philosophy, Political Science, Spiritual, Textbooks.

Parallax Press, Travis Masch Mr., Publisher; Rachel Neumann Mrs., Senior Editor, 2236B 6th St., Berkeley, CA 94710-2219, 510-525-0101; e-Mail info@parallax.org; web address http://www.parallax.org. 1986. "Buddhist and related books-especially how Buddhism might become more engaged in peace and social justice work. Primary author: Thich Nhat Hanh.'' avg. press run 4M. Pub'd 9 titles 2009; expects 8 titles 2010, 9 titles 2011. 24 titles listed in the *Small Press Record of Books in Print* (36th Edition, 2010-11). Discounts: standard. 200pp. Reporting time: 2 months. Publishes small % of manuscripts submitted. Payment: no advance, royalty. Copyrights for author. Subjects: Buddhism, Children, Youth, Non-Violence, Religion, Zen.

PARENTEACHER MAGAZINE, Carmen McGuinness, Editor-in-Chief; Michelle Banks, Managing Editor; Jennifer Bair, Managing Editor, PO Box 1246, Mount Dora, FL 32756, 352-385-1877, 800-732-3868, Fax 352-385-9424, rachat@aol.com. 1997. Poetry, fiction, articles, photos, interviews, criticism, reviews, letters, news items, non-fiction. ''500-1500 words. Mail or e-mail submissions attention Carmen McGuinness.'' circ. 50M. 6/yr. Pub'd 4 issues 2009; expects 6 issues 2010, 6 issues 2011. sub. price $9.99; per copy $2.50; sample free. Back issues: none. Discounts: $1 per copy, minimum of 50 copies. 30pp. Reporting time: 1 month. Simultaneous submissions accepted: yes. Publishes 85% of manuscripts submitted. Payment: negotiable. Copyrighted, rights reverting to author negotiable. Pub's reviews: 10 in 2009. §Literacy, education, family, children, health, nutrition, children's books. Ads: $675/$510/$585 2/3 page/$330 1/3 page/$280 1/4 page/$160 1/8 page. Subjects: Adolescence, Children, Youth, Education, How-To, Language, Literature (General), Non-Fiction, Parenting, Reading, Young Adult.

Parenting Press, Inc., Carolyn Threadgill, Publisher, PO Box 75267, Seattle, WA 98175-0267, 206-364-2900, Fax 206-364-0702. 1979. Non-fiction. ''Non-fiction; parent education.'' avg. press run 5M. Pub'd 1 title 2009; expects 3 titles 2010, 3 titles 2011. 86 titles listed in the *Small Press Record of Books in Print* (36th Edition, 2010-11). Discounts: contact publisher. 32pp childrens, 198pp parenting. Reporting time: 1-6 months. Simultaneous submissions accepted: yes. Publishes 1% of manuscripts submitted. Payment: case-by-case. Copyrights for author. Subjects: Children, Youth, Education, Family, Non-Fiction, Parenting, Picture Books, Sexual Abuse.

Pariah Press (see also HEELTAP/Pariah Press), Richard David Houff, 3070 Shields Drive #106, 3070 Shields Drive #106, Eagan, MN 55121. 1992. Poetry. ''Pariah Press is a non-profit chapbook publisher. Strictly solicited. We've lost most of our funding under the Bush administration ; future projects are on hold until further notice.'' avg. press run 500. Pub'd 2-4 titles 2009. 5 titles listed in the *Small Press Record of Books in Print* (36th Edition, 2010-11). Discounts: none as yet. 24pp. Reporting time: Usually, within 2 weeks. Simultaneous submissions accepted: yes. Publishes 1% of manuscripts submitted. Payment: 50 copies. Copyrights for author. Subjects: Anarchist, Avant-Garde, Experimental Art, Beat, Dada, Humor.

Paris Press, Jan Freeman, Executive Director, PO Box 487, Ashfield, MA 01330-0487, 413-628-0051, www.parispress.org. 1995. Poetry, fiction, letters, long-poems, plays, non-fiction. ''Paris Press publishes daring and beautiful literature by women writers who have been overlooked by the mainstream and independent publishing worlds. Recent authors include: Zdena Berger, Bryher, Virginia Woolf, Ruth Stone, and more. Please see our website, www.parispress.org, for more information.'' avg. press run 7000. Pub'd 2 titles 2009; expects 1 title 2010, 1 title 2011. No titles listed in the *Small Press Record of Books in Print* (36th Edition, 2010-11). 250pp. Reporting time: 6 months. Simultaneous submissions accepted: Yes. Subjects: Arts, Autobiography, Children, Youth, Creative Non-fiction, Essays, Fiction, Non-Fiction, Novels, Poetry, Prose, Short Stories, Theatre, Women, Young Adult.

THE PARIS REVIEW, Philip Gourevitch, Editor, 62 White Street, New York, NY 10013. ''*The Paris Review* does not accept e-mailed submissions. Short stories and nonfiction manuscripts should be sent by mail to the Fiction Editor and poetry should be sent to the Poetry Editor at the following address:The Paris Review62 White StreetNew York, NY 10013While the magazine welcomes unsolicited manuscripts, it cannot accept responsibility for their loss or damage. Rejected manuscripts will not be replied to or returned unless accompanied by a self-addressed, stamped envelope. Please remember that first-class postage is now $0.42. All submissions must be in English and previously unpublished. Please submit no more than six poems at a time. We do not accept poetry submissions from June through August. Translations are acceptable and should be accompanied by a copy of the original text. Simultaneous submissions are also acceptable as long as we are notified immediately if the manuscript is accepted for publication elsewhere. Be sure to include phone and (if possible) e-mail contact information. Please submit only one story manuscript at a time. We suggest to all who submit that they read several issues of The Paris Review to acquaint themselves with material the magazine has published. Discount subscriptions are available here.''

Park Place Publications, Kedron Bryson, Laurie Gibson, P.O. Box 829, Pacific Grove, CA 93950-0829, 831-649-6640, publishingbiz@sbcglobal.net, www.parkplacepublications.com, www.America-Healthy.com. 1991. Art, non-fiction. avg. press run 1M. Pub'd 4 titles 2009; expects 4 titles 2010, 4 titles 2011. 13 titles listed in the *Small Press Record of Books in Print* (36th Edition, 2010-11). Discounts: 40% bookstores; 20% single title. 150pp. Reporting time: 30 days. Simultaneous submissions accepted: yes. Publishes 1% of manuscripts submitted. Payment: varies. Copyrights for author. Subjects: Aging, Autobiography, Business & Economics, Children, Youth, Genealogy, Horticulture, Medicine, Pets, Travel.

Parkway Publishers, Inc., Rao Aluri, PO Box 3678, Boone, NC 28607, 828-265-3993. 1992. Non-fiction. "Book on the history, culture and tourism of western North Carolina; 250-400 pages double spaced; emphasis on marketability to tourists." avg. press run 1M. Pub'd 10 titles 2009; expects 15 titles 2010, 20 titles 2011. 22 titles listed in the *Small Press Record of Books in Print* (36th Edition, 2010-11). Discounts: bookstores 5+ copies 40%. 200pp. Reporting time: 6 weeks. Simultaneous submissions accepted: no. Publishes 25% of manuscripts submitted. Payment: 10% on first 1,000 copies, 15% afterward. Copyrights for author. Subjects: Appalachia, Autobiography, Biology, Civil War, Education, History.

PARNASSUS: Poetry in Review, Herbert Leibowitz, Editor & Publisher; Ben Downing, Co-Editor, 205 West 89th Street #8F, New York, NY 10024-1835, 212-362-3492, Fax 212-875-0148, parnew@aol.com, website www.parnassuspoetry.com. 1972. "Length varies from four pages to forty. Editorial policy is intentionally eclectic. Recent and forthcoming contributors: Adrienne Rich, David Barbe, Marilyn Chin, Tom Disch, Judith Gleason, Marjorie Perloff, Rafael Campo, Carl Phillips, Rikki Duconnet, Wayne Koestenbaum, Hayden Carruth, Seamus Heaney, Helen Vendler, William Logan, Eric Ormsby. Publish one or two unsolicited poems per year." circ. 1.75M. 1/yr. Pub'd 1 issue 2009; expects 1 issue 2010, 1 issue 2011. sub. price $27 individuals, $46 institutions; per copy $12-$15; sample $12-$15. Back issues: $10 per issue (indiv.), $20/issue (libraries). Discounts: 10% to magazine subscription agencies, 30% to bookstores. 350pp. Reporting time: 3 weeks to 2 months. Simultaneous submissions accepted: yes. Publishes 10% of manuscripts submitted. Payment: Essays: $200-$500; poems: $30/page. Copyrighted, rights revert to author on request. Pub's reviews: 60-80 in 2009. §Poetry, poetic fiction, non-academic poetry criticism, art, music, movies. Ads: $250/$150. Subjects: Literary Review, Poetry.

Parthian, Gwen Davies, Publishing Editor, The Old Surgery, Napier Street, Cardigan SA43 1ED, United Kingdom, parthianbooks@yahoo.co.uk, www.parthianbooks.co.uk. 1993. Fiction. ""While Parthian has only been publishing for a relatively short period, it has made a significant impact on the contemporary English language literary scene in Wales."World Literature Today." avg. press run 1000. Pub'd 8 titles 2009; expects 10 titles 2010, 12 titles 2011. No titles listed in the *Small Press Record of Books in Print* (36th Edition, 2010-11). Discounts: Negotiable. 150pp. Reporting time: Eight weeks. Simultaneous submissions accepted: Yes. Publishes 10% of manuscripts submitted. Payment: 10% of cover price. Copyrights for author. Subjects: Drama, Fiction, Gay, Writers/Writing.

Partisan Press (see also BLUE COLLAR REVIEW), Al Markowitz, PO Box 11417, Norfolk, VA 23517, e-mail: red-ink@earthlink.net, website: http:www.Partisanpress.org. 1993. Poetry, fiction, long-poems. "Looking for working class poetry or short stories-mostly poetry. Social/political focus but with a broad range. High quality writing, no polemics or screed." avg. press run 350. Pub'd 4 titles 2009; expects 3-4 titles 2010. No titles listed in the *Small Press Record of Books in Print* (36th Edition, 2010-11). 40-60pp. Reporting time: 3-6 weeks. Simultaneous submissions accepted: no. Publishes 4% of manuscripts submitted. Payment: 40 copies. Does not copyright for author. Subjects: Civil Rights, Culture, Environment, Feminism, Labor, Latino, Multicultural, Peace, Race, Reviews, Short Stories, Social Movements, Socialist, Society, Worker.

PASSAGER, Kendra Kopelke, Mary Azrael, 1420 N. Charles Street, Baltimore, MD 21201-5779, www.passagerpress.com. 1989. Poetry, fiction, interviews, non-fiction. "Fiction and memoir: 4,000 words maximum. Poetry: 40 lines max per poem, 5 poems maximum. No reprints. Please visit Web site or contact us for current guidelines. *Passager* publishes fiction, poetry, and memoir that give voice to human experience. We provide exposure for older writers, with a special interest in those who have recently discovered their creative self. We also act as a literary community for writers of all ages who are not connected to academic institutions or other organized groups." circ. 1500. 2/yr. Pub'd 2 issues 2009; expects 2 issues 2010, 2 issues 2011. 6 titles listed in the *Small Press Record of Books in Print* (36th Edition, 2010-11). sub. price $30 for 2 years (4 issues); overseas US $35; libraries/institutions $45; per copy $10; sample $10. Back issues: $10. 84pp. Reporting time: 3 months from close of submission period. Simultaneous submissions accepted: OK; Please notify if work is accepted elsewhere. Payment: 1 copy of issue in which work appears. Copyrighted, reverts to author. No ads. Subjects: Aging, Americana, Arts, Autobiography, Book Arts, Creativity, Fiction, Language, Literature (General), Memoirs, Men, Mental Health, Poetry, Translation, Women.

PASSAGES NORTH, Kate Myers Hanson, Editor-in-Chief, English Dept., N. Michigan Univ., 1401 Presque Isle Avenue, Marquette, MI 49855, 906-227-1203, Fax 906-227-1096, passages@nmu.edu, http://myweb.nmu.edu/~passages. 1979. Poetry, fiction, interviews, parts-of-novels, long-poems, non-fiction. "*Passages North*'s primary interest is high quality poetry and short fiction, interviews and creative non-fiction. Contributors: Established and emerging writers; encourages students in writing programs. Recently published: Steve Almond, Carrie Jerrell, Tracy Winn, John McNally, David Dodd Lee, Aimee LaBrie, Ralph Black and Alison Stine. Send SASE for submission guidelines. Submit all prose double-spaced with ample margins; use paper clips, not staples. Name and address on top right corner of top page; submissions returned only if an SASE (w/adequate postage) is included." circ. 1500. 1/yr. Pub'd 1 issue 2009; expects 1 issue 2010, 1 issue 2011. sub. price $13/yr, $23/2 yrs; per copy $13; sample $13. Back issues: $3 (single back issues 1999 and earlier). Discounts: contact us. 225pp. Reporting time: 3 months. Simultaneous submissions accepted: yes. Publishes 5-10% of manuscripts submitted. Payment: 2 copies. Copyrighted, reverts to author. Ads: exchange ads only. Subjects: Fiction, Literary Review, Literature (General), Non-Fiction, Poetry, Prose, Short Stories.

PASSAIC REVIEW, Rich Quatrone, c/o Ah! Sunflower Theater, 410-1/2 Morris Avenue, Spring Lake, NJ 07762-1320. 1979. Poetry, fiction, articles, art, photos, interviews, satire, criticism, reviews, long-poems. "Passaic Review goes through evolutions. Its most recent was Passaic Review Ezine, which documented the period from Sept 11, 2001 until the invasion and occupation of Iraq. If and when someone sends us work that knocks us off our feet, we'll publish it in some form. Until then we rest. We do not wish to be another drop in an ocean of magazines which publish poems that say little or nothing. We are not interested in writers who think more of their careers than of their work. We are not interested in the schools of John Ashbery or Gerald Stern, et al. We have always sought poetry that is an intelligent, courageous pouring out of hearts, minds, souls, to an audience of hungry men and women who struggle in the real world. Erotic poetry that is open and revelatory is always welcomed." We don't circulation know at this point. when the work demands publication. Pub'd we don't know issues 2009. sub. price to be determined; per copy to be determined; sample $5, included postage. Back issues: $10. Discounts: inquire. Pages vary. Reporting time: immediate to indefinite. Simultaneous submissions accepted only if indicated. Publishes 2% of manuscripts submitted. Payment: copies of magazine. Not copyrighted. Pub's reviews: none in 2009. §We'll review anything if its worthy. Ads: $80/$40/$20/$10. Subjects: Literary Review, Poetry.

Passeggiata Press, Inc., Donald Herdeck, Editor and Publisher; Norman Ware, Int'l Editor, 420 West 14th Street, Pueblo, CO 81003-2708, 719-544-1038, Fax 719-546-7889; e-mail Passeggia@aol.com. 1997. Poetry, fiction, criticism, long-poems, plays. "Publishers of Third World literature (Africa, Caribbean, Middle East, Pacific, Asia), and the scholarship thereof: recently bio-lingual poetry collections (one poet per vol.) English language, English-Russian, English-Bulgaria, English-Hungarian and some architective books." avg. press run 1M-2M. Pub'd 15 titles 2009; expects 10-15 titles 2010. 46 titles listed in the *Small Press Record of Books in Print* (36th Edition, 2010-11). Discounts: 30% prepaid by retailers and wholesalers; 20% prepaid by libraries; 20% not prepaid, university bookstores. No discounts on single-copy orders 40% on prepaid 100 copies, 10 titles min. 175-250pp. Reporting time: 5-6 weeks, but often much longer or shorter. Simultaneous submissions accepted: yes. Publishes 3-5% of manuscripts submitted. Payment: usually 7.5% with small advance. Copyrights for author. Subjects: African Literature, Africa, African Studies, Architecture, Bibliography, Biography, Black, Business & Economics, Criticism, Drama, Fiction, Folklore, Indexes & Abstracts, Middle East, Music, Poetry, Theatre.

Passing Through Publications, Fiona Rock, 1918 23rd Street, San Francisco, CA 94107. 1996. Poetry, fiction, art, photos. "Our business is dedicated to publishing works of odd fiction." avg. press run 2M. Pub'd 1 title 2009; expects 2-3 titles 2010, 2-3 titles 2011. 3 titles listed in the *Small Press Record of Books in Print* (36th Edition, 2010-11). Discounts: 5+ copies 40%. 100pp. Reporting time: immediate. Simultaneous submissions accepted: no. Publishes less than 1% of manuscripts submitted. Payment: individual agreements. Copyrights for author. Subjects: Anarchist, Counter-Culture, Alternatives, Communes, Fiction, Lifestyles, Prose, Short Stories, Transportation, Women.

PASSION, Crescent Moon, Jeremy Robinson, PO Box 393, Maidstone, Kent ME14 5XU, United Kingdom. 1994. Poetry, articles, art, photos, interviews, criticism, reviews, music, letters, parts-of-novels. "Shortish mss. prefered; literature, media, cultural studies, feminism, arts topics." circ. 200. 4/yr. Pub'd 4 issues 2009; expects 4 issues 2010, 4 issues 2011. sub. price $17; per copy $4; sample $4. Back issues: $3 for 1, $2.50 for 2 or more. Discounts: Trade 20% on single order, 35% on 2+. 50pp. Reporting time: 2 months. Simultaneous submissions accepted: yes. Publishes 3% of manuscripts submitted. Payment: to be negotiated. Copyrighted, reverts to author. Pub's reviews: 100 in 2009. §Arts, literature, media, cultural studies, poetry. Ads: $20/$10/$5 1/4 page. Subjects: Arts, Biography, Book Reviewing, Creativity, Criticism, Culture, Emily Dickinson, Electronics, Feminism, Interviews, D.H. Lawrence, Literary Review, Literature (General), Magic, Media.

Passion Power Press, Inc, Jamie Binder, PO 127, Indianapolis, IN 46206-0127, 317-356-6885 or 317-357-8821. 2004. Poetry, fiction, satire, long-poems, non-fiction. "We specialize in first-time authors with a passion to communicate." avg. press run 5000. Pub'd 1 title 2009; expects 3 titles 2010, 5 titles 2011. 1 title listed in the *Small Press Record of Books in Print* (36th Edition, 2010-11). Discounts: 40-55%. 300pp. Reporting time: 90 days. Simultaneous submissions accepted: Yes. Publishes 75% of manuscripts submitted. Payment: no advances, 12%-50% return to author based on sales volume. Copyrights for author. Subjects: Children, Youth, Erotica, Essays, Feminism, Fiction, Gay, Gender Issues, Lesbianism, Multicultural, Non-Fiction, Poetry, Sex, Sexuality, Social Work, Wine, Wineries, Women.

The Passion Profit Company, Walt Goodridge, PO Box 618, Church Street Station, New York, NY 10008-0618, (646)219-3565, walt@passionprofit.com, www.passionprofit.com. 1992. Poetry, non-fiction. "We are interested in non-fiction. Primarily business "how to" which helps people discover, develop or profit from their passions." Pub'd 3 titles 2009; expects 3 titles 2010, 5 titles 2011. 10 titles listed in the *Small Press*

366

Record of Books in Print (36th Edition, 2010-11). Discounts: 1 book15% discount2-4 books = 20% Discount5-9 books = 30% Discount1O + BOOKS = 40%. 200pp. Reporting time: 120 days. Simultaneous submissions accepted: Yes. Publishes 20% of manuscripts submitted. Payment: Varies. Call for details. Does not copyright for author. Subjects: African-American, Business & Economics, Caribbean, Entertainment, Finances, Inspirational, New Age, Poetry, Public Relations/Publicity, Publishing.

Passport Press, Jack Levesque, Miranda d'Hauteville, PO Box 2543, Champlain, NY 12919-2543, 514-937-3868, Fax 514-931-0871, e-mail travelbook@bigfoot.com. 1976. "Travel and children's items." avg. press run 10M. Pub'd 4 titles 2009; expects 6 titles 2010, 4 titles 2011. 6 titles listed in the *Small Press Record of Books in Print* (36th Edition, 2010-11). Discounts: 20% with payment (small orders); 6 copies, 40%. 400pp. Payment: as negotiated. Does not copyright for author. Subjects: Children, Youth, Latin America, Transportation.

Past Times Publishing Co., Jordan R. Young, Editorial Director, 271 N. Milford Road, Orange, CA 92867-7849, 714-997-1157; jordanyoung50@sbcglobal.net, www.actingsolo.com. 1980. "Formerly Moonstone Press. Although we're not soliciting manuscripts, Past Times Publishing is not strictly a self-publishing operation. Have been in business 27 years and have titles by four authors, with books in the works." Pub'd 1 title 2009; expects 1 title 2010, 1 title 2011. 8 titles listed in the *Small Press Record of Books in Print* (36th Edition, 2010-11).

THE PATERSON LITERARY REVIEW, The Poetry Center, Maria Mazziotti Gillan, Editor, Passaic County Community College, One College Boulevard, Paterson, NJ 07505-1179, 973-684-6555. 1979. Poetry, fiction, art. "Stories should be short. Poems: under 60 lines preferred. Poetry, fiction, reviews. 6 x 9 size for art work. Clear photocopies acceptable. *No unsolicited reviews.*" circ. 1M. 1/yr. Pub'd 1 issue 2009; expects 1 issue 2010, 1 issue 2011. sub. price $13; per copy $13; sample $13. Back issues: $10. Discounts: 40% for orders of 10 or more. 380pp. Reporting time: 6 months. Simultaneous submissions accepted: yes. Publishes 5% of manuscripts submitted. Payment: contributor's copies. Copyrighted, reverts to author. Pub's reviews: 4 in 2009. §Poetry, short stories, novels (particularly African American, Latino, Asian American, Native American), critical books on literature. Ads: $300/$150/$75 1/4 page. Subjects: Literary Review, Poetry.

Path Press, Inc., Bennett J. Johnson, President, PO Box 2925, Chicago, IL 60690-2925, 847-492-0177. 1969. Poetry, fiction, non-fiction. "Path Press, Inc. has merged its operations with Third World Press, Inc., 7822 South Dobson Avenue, Chicago, IL 60619." avg. press run 5M. Expects 1 title 2010, 6-10 titles 2011. 7 titles listed in the *Small Press Record of Books in Print* (36th Edition, 2010-11). Usual trade discounts. 300pp. Reporting time: 90-120 days. Simultaneous submissions accepted: Yes. Payment: no advance, 10% royalty for first 5M copies, staggered rate to 15% after that. Copyrights for author. Subjects: African Literature, Africa, African Studies, Biography, Black, Chicago, Children, Youth, Civil Rights, Fiction, Literature (General), Non-Fiction, Non-Violence, Politics, Third World, Minorities, World War II.

Pathfinder Press (see also NEW INTERNATIONAL A magazine of Marxist politics and theory), Steve Clark, Editorial Director, Mary-Alice Waters, P.O. Box 162767, Atlanta, GA 30321-2767, www.pathfinder-press.com; orders@pathfinderpress.com (orders); pathfinder@pathfinderpress.com (editorial); permis-sions@pathfinderpress.com (permissions). 1928. "Publisher of books on current events, history, economics, Marxism, Black studies, labor, women's liberation, Cuba, South Africa. Authors include Malcolm X, Nelson Mandela, Che Guevara, Fidel Castro, V.I. Lenin, Karl Marx, and Leon Trotsky. Accounts by participants and leaders of the Cuban Revolution; primary source material on Marxism, Russian Revolution, working-class movement. Distributor of New International, a magazine of Marxist politics and theory." Pub'd 4 titles 2009; expects 8 titles 2010, 5 titles 2011. 47 titles listed in the *Small Press Record of Books in Print* (36th Edition, 2010-11). Discounts: retail bookstores 40-42%; textbooks 25%; libraries pay full price. 300pp. Subjects: African Literature, Africa, African Studies, The Americas, Black, Communism, Marxism, Leninism, Cuba, Current Affairs, History, Labor, Latin America, Political Science, Politics, Socialist, Third World, Minorities, U.S.S.R., Women.

Pathwise Press (see also BATHTUB GIN), Christopher Harter, 2311 Broadway Street, New Orleans, LA 70125-4127, pathwisepress@hotmail.com. 1997. Poetry, fiction, articles, art, photos, interviews, satire, criticism, reviews, non-fiction. "Looking to publish poetry or short fiction chapbooks of around 40-48 pages. Strong imagery desired. Nothing overly academic or Bukowskiesque. Query first to see if accepting new manuscripts. If so, send manuscript and cover letter. Will work with author to match their ideas/design to ours. Submission time: June 1 to September 15. NOTE: Currently on hiatus until 2010." avg. press run 150-200 initial run. Pub'd 1 title 2009. 8 titles listed in the *Small Press Record of Books in Print* (36th Edition, 2010-11). Discounts: sliding scale. 48pp. Reporting time: 1-2 months. Simultaneous submissions accepted: yes. Payment: author receives 15 author copies up front, 10% royalties on sales over initial 100. Copyrights for author. Subjects: Absurdist, Dada, Literary Review, Literature (General), Poetry, Prose.

PAVEMENT SAW, Pavement Saw Press, David Baratier, Editor, 321 Empire Street, Montpelier, OH

43543-1301, 419-485-0524, info@pavementsaw.org, www.pavementsaw.org. 1994. Poetry, art, photos, interviews, reviews, concrete art. "Five poems, clean photocopy (prefer type quality) with cover letter. One page prose or 1-2 pages short fiction, are acceptable also. Always send attention getting devices with submissions. *Pavement Saw* seeks unusual poetry and prose. There is one featured writer or section (20 pages or so) each issue and often a theme. #8 is the all unfinished male author interview issue, #9 is a special double Visual Poetry issue, #10 Low Carb Issue: Roy Bentley, #11 Sells Out: Candice Kaucher. Odd themes are sprung inside each issue including The Minty Fresh Pirate Issue, The Man Po(etry), The Whitey Issue, The Ultimate (superhero) Issue and so on. Issues 1-7 are sold out. We are one of the few journals who focus on the prose poem & letter boundaries. Guidelines are in issue #10 or 11." circ. 551. irregular. Expects 1 issue 2011. sub. price $15/2 issues; per copy $8; sample $8. Back issues: $8. Discounts: 40% for 5 copies. 88pp. Reporting time: 1-4 months, we only read from June 1st to the end of August. Simultaneous submissions accepted, only from writers who have not had their first full length collection published. Publishes less than 1% of manuscripts submitted. Payment: 4 or more copies. Copyrighted, reverts to author. Pub's reviews: none in 2009. §Books of poetry by contemporary authors, and anthologies. Subjects: Avant-Garde, Experimental Art, Construction, Dada, Labor, Poetry, Prose, Short Stories, Surrealism.

Pavement Saw Press (see also PAVEMENT SAW), David Baratier, Editor, 321 Empire Street, Montpelier, OH 43543-1301, 419-485-0524, info@pavementsaw.org, www.pavementsaw.org. 1994. Poetry. "Often, material for the full length books are chosen from authors previously published in Pavement Saw. Reading the journal and submitting pieces before sending material to the press would be more than necessary for full length titles. We have an annual chapbook competition and our we are the only publisher to have our chapbooks recently reviewed in Poets & Writers and Publishers Weekly. We also have a full-length book competition in July and August. Previous judges include Judith Vollmer, Bin Ramke, David Bromige and others. The winner receives $1,000. Query before sending for guidelines or contest rules. The 2nd Edition of *Hands Collected: The Poems of Simon Perchik 1949-1999*, 612pp was released in 2003. *Drunk & Disorderly: Selected Poems* by Alan Catlin, 186pp, was also released in 2003.Our catalog also includes Errol Miller, Gordon Massman, Richard Blevins, Dana Curtis, Jeffrey Levine, Rachel Simon, Julie Otten, Garin Cycholl, Steve Davenport, Rodney Koeneke, Kaya Oakes, Sheila E. Murphy and 42 other books." avg. press run 1M for full length books, 400 copies for chapbooks. Pub'd 5 titles 2009; expects 4 titles 2010, 5 titles 2011. 60 titles listed in the *Small Press Record of Books in Print* (36th Edition, 2010-11). Discounts: 40% for 5 copies or more. 80-612pp books, 32-40pp chapbooks. Simultaneous submissions accepted: yes. Publishes less than 1% of manuscripts submitted. Payment: negotiable. Copyrights for author. Subjects: Avant-Garde, Experimental Art, Construction, Dada, Gender Issues, Handwriting/Written, Labor, Poetry, Prose, Sports, Outdoors, Surrealism.

Paycock Press (see also GARGOYLE), Richard Myers Peabody, Editor, 3819 N. 13th Street, Arlington, VA 22201, Fax 703-525-9296, hedgehog2@erols.com. 1976. Poetry, fiction, art, photos, satire, reviews, long-poems. "Poetry titles: *Collected Poems* by Ed Cox. Fiction titles: *In Praise of What Persists* by Joyce Renwick. Anthologies: *Grace and Gravity: Fiction by Washington Area Women* ed. by Richard Peabody. Nonfiction: *Mavericks: Nine Independent Publishers* ed. by Richard Peabody." avg. press run 1M. Expects 1 title 2010, 1 title 2011. 9 titles listed in the *Small Press Record of Books in Print* (36th Edition, 2010-11). Dealer discount available. 60-100pp. Reporting time: 1 month. Payment: 10% of press run plus 50/50 split on sales if/when we break even. Copyrights for author. Subjects: Fiction, Poetry.

PEACEWORK, Sara Burke, Co-Editor; Sam Diener, Co-Editor, 2161 Massachusetts Avenue, Cambridge, MA 02140, 617-661-6130. 1972. Articles, art, photos, cartoons, interviews, satire, reviews, letters, news items, non-fiction. "*Peacework* focuses on 'global thought and local action for nonviolent social change.'" circ. 2K. 10/yr. Pub'd 10 issues 2009; expects 10 issues 2010, 10 issues 2011. sub. price $23, $14 student-low income, $1 prisoners; per copy $2; sample free. 24pp. Reporting time: 2 weeks - 1 month. Payment: free subscription. Copyrighted under a Creative Commons Attribution-Noncommercial-ShareAlike License unless author wishes to retain copyright. Pub's reviews: 14 in 2009. §Peace and social justice. Paid advertising not accepted. Subjects: African-American, AIDS, Anarchist, Chicano/a, Civil Rights, Counter-Culture, Alternatives, Communes, Environment, Feminism, Gay, Global Affairs, Human Rights, Multicultural, Non-Violence, Peace, War.

Peachtree Publishers, Ltd., Helen Harris, Submissions Editor, 1700 Chattahoochee Avenue, Atlanta, GA 30318, 404-876-8761, www.peachtree-online.com. 1977. Non-fiction. "Peachtree Publishers, Ltd. is interested in quality childrens fiction and non-fiction for all ages, and adult non-fiction and guides for the Southeast. To submit a manuscript, send complete manuscript(required for children's picture books) or an outline and 3 sample chapters, along with biographical information on the author, and a SASE large enough to hold the material. Please mark to the attention of Helen Harriss." avg. press run 5M-25M. Pub'd 30 titles 2009; expects 35 titles 2010, 35 titles 2011. No titles listed in the *Small Press Record of Books in Print* (36th Edition, 2010-11). Discounts: retail 12+ copies 50% non-returnable; 1-4 20%, 5-10 40%, 11-24 42%, 25-49 43%, 50-199 44%, 200-499 45%, 500+ 46% returnable; jobbers 50% on 50 or more assorted. Pages vary. Reporting time: 4-6 months. Simultaneous submissions accepted: yes. Payment: individual basis subject to contractual terms. Copyrights for author. Subjects: Children, Youth, Health, Parenting, Picture Books, Self-Help, Young Adult.

PEARL, Pearl Editions, Joan Jobe Smith, Marilyn Johnson, Barbara Hauk, 3030 E. Second Street, Long Beach, CA 90803-5163, 562-434-4523 phone/fax or 714-968-7530, PearlMag@aol.com, www.pearlmag.com. 1987. Poetry, fiction, art, cartoons. ''We are interested in accessible, humanistic poetry and short fiction that communicates and is related to real life. Humor and wit are welcome, along with the ironic and serious. No taboos stylistically or subject-wise. Prefer poems up to 35 lines and short stories up to 1200 words. Submissions accepted September through May *only*. Our purpose is to provide a forum for lively, readable poetry and prose that reflects a wide variety of contemporary voices, viewpoints, and experiences and that speaks to *real* people about *real* life in direct, living language, from the profane to the sublime. Have recently published poetry by Kim Addonizio, Jim Daniels, Gerald Locklin, Lisa Glatt, and David Hernandez.'' circ. 600. 2/yr. Pub'd 2 issues 2009; expects 2 issues 2010, 2 issues 2011. sub. price $21 (2 issues)+ 1 poetry book; per copy $10; sample $8. Discounts: 2+ 40%. 128pp. Reporting time: 6-8 weeks. Simultaneous submissions accepted: yes. Publishes 5% of manuscripts submitted. Payment: 1 copy. Copyrighted, reverts to author. Subjects: Poetry, Short Stories.

Pearl Editions (see also PEARL), Joan Jobe Smith, Marilyn Johnson, Barbara Hauk, 3030 E. Second Street, Long Beach, CA 90803-5163, 562-434-4523 phone/fax or 714-968-7530, PearlMag@aol.com, www.pearl-mag.com. 1989. Poetry. ''Currently only publish solicited authors and winner of our annual poetry book contest.'' avg. press run 500. Pub'd 1 title 2009; expects 1 title 2010, 1 title 2011. 29 titles listed in the *Small Press Record of Books in Print* (36th Edition, 2010-11). Discounts: 2+ 40%. 80pp. Reporting time: 4-5 months (contest). We accept simultaneous submissions for our contest. Publishes less than 1% of manuscripts submitted. Payment: $1,000 + 25 copies (contest winners), 25 copies (solicited authors). Copyrights for author. Subject: Poetry.

Pearl's Book'em Publisher, Pearlie Harris, Shonia Brown, Keisha Whitehorn, Yvette Appiah, 614 Parker Ave, Decatur, GA 30032, 678-368-6657, bookpearl@yahoo.com, www.book-pearl.com. 2000. Poetry, art, photos, cartoons, satire, reviews, music, long-poems. Expects 1 title 2010, 3 titles 2011. 10 titles listed in the *Small Press Record of Books in Print* (36th Edition, 2010-11). Discounts: bulk,library,wholesalers, institutions, classrooms. 100pp. Reporting time: 4 weeks. Payment: advances, royalty. Copyrights for author. Subjects: African-American, Arts, Audio/Video, Children, Youth, Christianity, Comics, Creativity, Culture, English, Essays, Graphics, Haiku, Literature (General), Music.

Pearl-Win Publishing Co., Barbara Fitz Vroman, N4721 9th Drive, Hancock, WI 54943-7617, 715-249-5407. 1980. Poetry, fiction, non-fiction. ''We are not enouraging submissions at this time since we have a backlog of good material.'' avg. press run 3M. Pub'd 2 titles 2009; expects 2 titles 2010. 8 titles listed in the *Small Press Record of Books in Print* (36th Edition, 2010-11). Discounts: 40% trade; 20% libraries. Poetry 64pp, prose 250pp. Reporting time: reasonable. Payment: 10% hard, 7.5% paper. Copyrights for author. Subjects: Fiction, Poetry.

Peartree Books & Music, Barbara Birenbaum, PO Box 14533, Clearwater, FL 33766-4533, P/ F 727-531-4973. 1985. ''No pre-k picture books. Accept manuscripts and queries for GRL-S that lend themselves to pen + ink drawings. Also subsidy works w/full color illustrations all levels Pre K-Gr. 8.'' avg. press run 1M-3M. Expects 5 titles 2010, 5+ titles 2011. 17 titles listed in the *Small Press Record of Books in Print* (36th Edition, 2010-11). Discounts: 20% libraries, retail 40% paper, 30% cloth, jobbers 50%+. 50pp. Reporting time: 6 weeks. Simultaneous submissions accepted: yes. Payment: percent of sales of book based on profit margin. Copyrights for author. Subjects: Animals, Birds, Children, Youth, Creative Non-fiction, Festivals, Fiction, Folklore, History, Juvenile Fiction, Law, Multicultural, Nature, Sports, Outdoors.

Pebble Press, Inc., Robert Piepenburg, 1610 Longshore Drive, Ann Arbor, MI 48105. 1957. Art, photos. avg. press run 4M. Expects 1 title 2010, 1 title 2011. 4 titles listed in the *Small Press Record of Books in Print* (36th Edition, 2010-11). Discounts: 40%. 159pp. Reporting time: 2 months. Payment: to be arranged. Copyrights for author. Subjects: Arts, Crafts, Hobbies.

Pecan Grove Press, H. Palmer Hall, St. Mary's University, 1 Camino Santa Maria, San Antonio, TX 78228, 210-436-3441. 1985. Poetry. ''Pecan Grove Press publishes contemporary poetry with an emphasis on first book poets and with roots grounded in its origins in Texas, though not limited to regional authors.'' avg. press run 375. Pub'd 4 titles 2009; expects 5 titles 2010, 5 titles 2011. 41 titles listed in the *Small Press Record of Books in Print* (36th Edition, 2010-11). Discounts: 30% Discount to Booksellers45% Discount to Baker and Taylor. 60-70pp. Reporting time: 2-3 months. Simultaneous submissions accepted: Yes. Publishes 3% of manuscripts submitted. Payment: 50% after cost of printing is recovered. Copyrights for author. Subject: Poetry.

THE PEDESTAL MAGAZINE.COM, John Amen, Editor in Chief; Nathan Leslie, Fiction Editor, 704-889-2787, pedestalmagazine@aol.com, www.thepedestalmagazine.com. 2000. Poetry, fiction, art, photos, interviews, non-fiction. ''On-line only journal. Previously featured writers include Maxime Kumin, Sharon Olds, W.S. Merwin, Ai, and Thomas Lux. Other prominent features include an interactive Forum, an online Art

Gallery and Bookstore." circ. 11,000 per month. 6/yr. Expects 6 issues 2010, 6 issues 2011. sub. price free. Back issues: archived on the website, no charge. 30pp. Reporting time: 1-2 months. Simultaneous submissions accepted: yes. Publishes 2% of manuscripts submitted. Payment: poetry: $30/poem, Fiction and Nonfiction: 5¢/word, 6,000 word max. Copyrighted, rights revert to author, however we retain the right to republish in subsequent issue or anthology. Pub's reviews: 2 in 2009. §See submit page on website for instructions. Ads: banner ads $150 per month on prominent pages. Subjects: Arts, Fiction, Internet, Interviews, Magazines, Non-Fiction, Poetry, Visual Arts.

PEDIATRICS FOR PARENTS, Richard J. Sagall, 35 Starknaught Hts., P.O. Box 219, Gloucester, MA 01931, 215-253-4543, richsagall@pedsforparents.com, www.pedsforparents.com. 1981. Non-fiction. "Pediatrics for Parent is the newsletter for parents and others who care for children. Our articles are aimed at parents. We view ourselves as the pediatric journal for parents and other who care for children. Our writers are healthcare professionals and healthcare writers." circ. 150,000. 6/yr. Pub'd 12 issues 2009; expects 12 issues 2010, 12 issues 2011. sub. price $25 for one year, $47 for two years, and $70 for three years. Add $15 per year for outside USA.; per copy $5; sample $5. Back issues: $5. Discounts: write for details. 32pp. Reporting time: 30-60 days. Simultaneous submissions accepted: yes. Publishes 50% of manuscripts submitted. Payment: $25-$50. Copyrighted, reverts to author. Ads: none. Subjects: Health, Parenting.

Peepal Tree Press, Jeremy Poynting, Managing Editor, 7 King's Avenue, Leeds LS6 1QS, United Kingdom, telephone +44 (0)113 2451703. No titles listed in the *Small Press Record of Books in Print* (36th Edition, 2010-11).

PEGASUS, M.E. Hildebrand, Pegasus Publishing, PO Box 61324, Boulder City, NV 89006-1324. 1986. Poetry. circ. 200. 4/yr. Pub'd 4 issues 2009; expects 4 issues 2010, 4 issues 2011. sub. price $20, int'l add $5 postage; per copy $6 includes postage; sample $6 includes postage. Back issues: $6 includes postage. 32pp. Reporting time: 2 weeks. Simultaneous submissions accepted: no. Publishes 10-15% of manuscripts submitted. Payment: publication. Copyrighted, reverts to author. §Poetry publishing. Subject: Poetry.

THE PEGASUS REVIEW, Art Bounds, PO Box 88, Henderson, MD 21640-0088, 410-482-6736. 1980. Poetry, fiction, art, cartoons, satire. "Upon publication writer will receive two copies of *The Pegasus Review*. Occasional book awards throughout the year. Recommend purchasing a sample copy to better understand format ($2.50) for 2003 themes - request by SASE. Upcoming 2003 themes: Jan./Feb. Books/Music/Art, Mar./Apr. Humor, May/June Memories/Dreams, July/Aug. Nature, Sept./Oct. Men & Women, Nov./Dec. The Written Word. Occasionally comments on returned manuscripts. Publishes 10 new writers a year. Recently published work by Jane Stuart, Peggy Fitzgerald, Michael Keshigian, and Robert Deluty, to mention a few. Advice: Read and write; write and read. Read what has been written in the past as well as what is current. Keep your work circulating. Get involved with a 'critiquing' group. Persevere." circ. 130. 6/yr + special issues. Pub'd 6 issues 2009; expects 6 issues 2010, 6 issues 2011. sub. price $12; per copy $2.50; sample $2.50. Back issues: $2.50. 10-12pp. Reporting time: 4-10 weeks. Simultaneous submissions accepted: yes. Publishes 35% of manuscripts submitted. Payment: 2 copies and additional book awards (throughout year). Copyrighted, reverts to author. Subjects: Fiction, Poetry.

•**Pelican Publishing Company,** Nina Kooij, Editor-in-Chief, 1000 Burmaster Street, Gretna, LA 70053, Tel: 800-843-1724, 504-368-1175, eb: www.pelicanpub.com. 1926. "Committed to publishing books of quality and permanence that enrich the lives of those who read them, Pelican Publishing Company has been in operation since 1926. The New Orleans area based company publishes general trade and childrens books. With a backlist of more than 2,500 titles, Pelican produces art and architecture books, travel guides, holiday books, local and international cookbooks, motivational and inspirational works, business titles, picture books, and a growing number of social commentary and history titles." No titles listed in the *Small Press Record of Books in Print* (36th Edition, 2010-11).

Pella Publishing Co. (see also THE CHARIOTEER; JOURNAL OF THE HELLENIC DIASPORA), Leandros Papathanasiou, Publisher, President, 337 West 36th Street, New York, NY 10018, 212-279-9586. 1976. Poetry, fiction, articles, art, criticism, reviews, letters, plays, non-fiction. "We are interested in Modern Greek studies and culture, but also have a general list composed of new fiction and poetry by young writers and books on contemporary society and politics. We also publish books on the work of young artists." avg. press run 3M. Pub'd 4 titles 2009; expects 10 titles 2010, 10 titles 2011. 57 titles listed in the *Small Press Record of Books in Print* (36th Edition, 2010-11). Discounts: jobbers 30%, bookstores 20%. 176pp. Reporting time: 4-6 weeks. Simultaneous submissions accepted: no. Publishes 1% of manuscripts submitted. Payment: standard royalty arrangements. Copyrights for author. Subject: Greek.

Pellingham Casper Communications (see also THE ART OF ABUNDANCE), Paula Langguth Ryan, 1121 Annapolis Road, Suite 120, Odenton, MD 21113, 800-507-9244; 208-545-8164 (fax), www.ArtOfAbundance.com. 1998. Non-fiction. "Personal finance self-help inspirational titles." avg. press run 10000. Pub'd 1 title 2009; expects 2 titles 2010, 4 titles 2011. No titles listed in the *Small Press Record of Books in Print* (36th

Edition, 2010-11). Discounts: 2-10 copies 25% bookstores/retailersdistributors 55% no returnsdistributors 40% returns allowed. 176-224pp. Reporting time: 3 months on queries, does not accept unsolicited manuscripts. Query first. Simultaneous submissions accepted: Yes. Publishes 25% of manuscripts submitted. Payment: 12%-15% royalty, paid quarterly. Does not copyright for author. Subjects: Finances, Inspirational, Marketing, Spiritual.

PEMBROKE MAGAZINE, Shelby Stephenson, Editor; Norman Macleod, Founding Editor, UNCP, Box 1510, Pembroke, NC 28372-1510, 910-521-6433 ext 6433. 1969. Poetry, fiction, articles, art, photos, criticism, reviews. "Contributors: Felix Pollak, Fred Chappell, A.R. Ammons, Betty Adcock, Robert Morgan, Barbara Guest, Fleda Jackson, Judson Crews, Reinhold Grimm, Gerald Barrax, Ronald H. Bayes, Lee Smith, John Ehle, Michael Martin, Jill McCorkle, Leslie Ullman, Jaki Shelton Green, Glenna Luschei, Lenard Moore." circ. 500. 1/yr. Pub'd 2 issues 2009; expects 1 issue 2010. sub. price $10; per copy $10 (overseas $14.03); sample $8. Discounts: 40% bookstores. 275pp. Reporting time: 1-4 months. Simultaneous submissions accepted: no. Payment: copy. Copyrighted, rights revert to author, except for right of editor to reprint the magazine and to issue a *PM* anthology. Pub's reviews: 6 in 2009. §Native American poetry and novels. Ads: $40/$25. Subjects: Fiction, Literary Review, Poetry.

PEMMICAN, Pemmican Press, Robert Edwards, Co-editor; Ben Howard, Co-editor, No longer accepting hard copy submissions, only email., www.pemmicanpress.com. 1992. Poetry, articles, interviews, criticism, reviews, long-poems. "Our bias is toward literature that directly confronts the political and social issues of our time. We also would like to see poetry of imagery and imagination. We have published Sherman Alexie, Al Markowitz, and Marilyn Zuckerman." circ. 1200 approx. Ongoing. Pub'd We were down during 2007 because we were hacked. As part of the recovery process we will only put out one "issue" during 2008. issues 2009. sub. price Internet magazine "free" for the reading, however any and all contributions are welcome. Reporting time: 1 month. Simultaneous submissions accepted: yes. Payment: none. yes/yes. Pub's reviews: 8 in 2009. §Political, poetry of "witness", social, feminist, working class, blue collar, erotica, prose poems, poetry of imagination, revolutionary. Also collections of essays, short fiction and creative non-fiction that are working class or political in nature. Ads: none. Subjects: Civil Rights, Communism, Marxism, Leninism, Erotica, Experimental, Literary Review, Literature (General), Pacific Northwest, Poetry, Politics, Socialist, Surrealism.

Pemmican Press (see also PEMMICAN), Robert Edwards, Ben Howard, Pemmican no longer has a physical contract address, Email contact only, thebenhoward@yahoo.com, www.pemmicanpress.com. 1992. Poetry, long-poems. avg. press run 300. Pub'd 2 titles 2009; expects 1 title 2010, 1 title 2011. No titles listed in the *Small Press Record of Books in Print* (36th Edition, 2010-11). Discounts: varies. Pages vary. Reporting time: 1 month, approximately. Simultaneous submissions accepted: yes. Publishes less than 5% of manuscripts submitted. Payment: none. Copyrights for author. Subject: Poetry.

PEN AMERICA: A Journal for Writers & Readers, 588 Broadway, Room 303, New York, NY 10012-3229, 212-334-1660 x115, Fax 212-334-2181, journal@pen.org, www.pen.org/journal. 2000. Poetry, fiction, articles, art, photos, interviews, criticism, letters, parts-of-novels, long-poems, plays, non-fiction. "*PA* publishes transcripts of PEN events and forums, as well as the work of PEN's award winners and members. *PA* does not accept unsolicited submissions except from members of PEN American Center." circ. 4M. 2/yr. Pub'd 1 issue 2009; expects 2 issues 2010, 2 issues 2011. sub. price $18 individual, $28 institute; per copy $10. Discounts: bookstore/classroom 40%. 212pp. Copyrighted, reverts to author. Ads: $600/$300.

Pendant Publishing Inc., Elaine Benes, PO Box 2933, Grand Junction, CO 81502, 970-243-6465. 1982. Non-fiction. No titles listed in the *Small Press Record of Books in Print* (36th Edition, 2010-11). Reporting time: 3 months. Simultaneous submissions accepted: no. Publishes 3% of manuscripts submitted. Payment: 10% net. Copyrights for author. Subjects: Business & Economics, Crafts, Hobbies, Motivation, Success, Public Affairs, Travel.

Pendragonian Publications (see also PENNY DREADFUL: Tales and Poems of Fantastic Terror; SONGS OF INNOCENCE), Michael Pendragon, PO Box 719, New York, NY 10101-0719, mmpendragon@aol.com. 1995. Poetry, fiction, articles, art, interviews, criticism, reviews, letters, long-poems, non-fiction. "Poetry up to 5 pages (rhymed, metered, lyrical preferred), stories set in the 19th century or earlier. *Penny Dreadful* publishes tales and poems which celebrate the darker aspects of Man, the World and their Creator (Gothic/Romantic Horror). *Songs of Innocence* publishes tales and poems which celebrate the nobler aspects of mankind and the human experience. Recent contributors to *Penny Dreadful* include: John B. Ford, Laurel Robertson, Scott Thomas, Paul Bradshaw, Nancy Bennett, K.S. Hardy, Louise Webster, Karen R. Porter, James S. Dorr, Kevin N. Roberts, Charlee Jacob, Tamera Latham, Dennis Saleh, Ann K. Schwader, and Susan E. Abramski." avg. press run 200. Pub'd 4 titles 2009; expects 3 titles 2010, 2 titles 2011. 2 titles listed in the *Small Press Record of Books in Print* (36th Edition, 2010-11). Discounts: 1 year subscription (3 issues) $25. 200+pp. Reporting time: up to 1 year. Simultaneous submissions accepted: yes. Publishes 5% of manuscripts submitted. Payment: 1 copy. Does not copyright for author. Subjects: Essays, Fantasy, Fiction, Literary Review, Literature (General), Myth, Mythology, Poetry, Reviews, Short Stories.

PENNINE INK MAGAZINE, Laura Sheridan, Editor, The Gallery, Yorke Street, Burnley, Lancs. BB11 1HD, England, sheridansdandl@yahoo.co.uk. 1983. Poetry, fiction, articles, parts-of-novels, non-fiction. "Quality poetry up to 40 lines. Prose/short stories up to 1,000 words. We publish once a year around December, so please do not send material until around August/September." circ. 400. 1/yr. price per copy £3, $6; sample £3, $6. Back issues: £2, $4. 48pp. Reporting time: 2 months. Simultaneous submissions accepted: yes. Publishes 10% of manuscripts submitted. Payment: free copy of magazine. Copyrighted, reverts to author. Ads: none. Subjects: Fiction, Poetry, Prose.

PENNINE PLATFORM, Nicholas Bielby, Editor, Frizingley Hall, Frizinghall Road, Bradford BD9 4LD, England, 01274 541015, nicholas.bielby@virgin.net, www.pennineplatform.co.uk. 1966. Poetry, criticism, reviews. "The magazine depends entirely on subscriptions. Tries to keep a high standard. Copyrighted for contributors who retain copyright. Submit hard copy with SAE and/or email. No email submissions. Any poetry but concrete, prose poems or haiku. Religious (but not religiose) poetry accepted. Craft and intelligence preferred. Crit. given." circ. 300. 2/yr. Pub'd 2 issues 2009; expects 2 issues 2010, 2 issues 2011. sub. price £8.50 UK, £10 Europe, £12 elsewhere in world. Payable only in sterling. Payment by Paypal possible; per copy £4.50 UK, £6 abroad; sample £4.50 UK, £6 abroad. Back issues: £2.50 UK, £4 abroad. Discounts: bulk orders by agreement. 60pp. Reporting time: submissions usually considered Sept-Oct and Jan-March. Simultaneous submissions accepted: no. Publishes 10% of manuscripts submitted. Payment: contributor copy. Copyrighted. Pub's reviews: 8 in 2009. §Poetry. Subjects: Literary Review, Poetry, Reviews, Translation.

•PENNSYLVANIA ENGLISH, Antonio Vallone, Editor, Penn State DuBois, College Place, DuBois, PA 15801-3199, Office: 814-375-4785, Fax: 814-375-4785. "The Pennsylvania English Association in association with Penn State DuBois publishes Pennsylvania English once a year in the fall. Essays, poetry, fiction."

Pennsylvania State University Press (see also THE CHAUCER REVIEW: A Journal of Medieval Studies and Literary Criticism; SHAW: THE ANNUAL OF BERNARD SHAW STUDIES), Fred D. Crawford, Penn State Press, Suite C, 820 N. University Drive, University Park, PA 16802-1711, 814-865-1327. 1951. Articles. "As the publishing arm of the Pennsylvania State University and a division of the Penn State University Libraries and Scholarly Communications, Penn State University Press is dedicated to serving the University community, the citizens of Pennsylvania, and scholars worldwide by publishing books and journals of the highest quality. The Press promotes the advance of scholarship by disseminating knowledgenew information, interpretations, methods of analysiswith an emphasis on core fields of the humanities and social sciences." avg. press run 2M. Pub'd 1 title 2009; expects 1 title 2010, 1 title 2011. No titles listed in the *Small Press Record of Books in Print* (36th Edition, 2010-11). Discounts: short-20%. 265pp. Reporting time: 2 months. Payment: 1 copy of the volume. Copyrights for author in name of publisher. Subjects: English, Literary Review, G.B. Shaw.

PENNY DREADFUL: Tales and Poems of Fantastic Terror, Pendragonian Publications, Michael Pendragon, PO Box 719, New York, NY 10101-0719, mmpendragon@aol.com. 1996. Poetry, fiction, articles, art, interviews, criticism, reviews, letters, long-poems, non-fiction. "Art: black and white line art only. All must be in the Gothic/Horror genre." circ. 200. 1-2/yr. Pub'd 1 issue 2009; expects 1 issue 2010, 1 issue 2011. sub. price $25/3 issues; per copy $10; sample $10. Back issues: usually sells out the first month. 200+pp. Reporting time: up to 1 year. Simultaneous submissions accepted: yes. Publishes 5% of manuscripts submitted. Payment: 1 free issue. Not copyrighted. Pub's reviews: 30 in 2009. §Gothic, horror, romantic, literary. Subjects: Essays, Fantasy, Fiction, Literary Review, Literature (General), Myth, Mythology, Poetry, Reviews, Short Stories.

PENNY-A-LINER, Redrosebush Press, Ella M. Dillon, PO Box 2163, Wenatchee, WA 98807-2163, 509-662-7858. 1995. Poetry, fiction, articles, art, photos, cartoons, interviews, satire, criticism, reviews, letters, non-fiction. "Prefer poetry 30 lines or less, other writings 500-1,500 words. Short stories, anecdotes, articles, essays, some poetry, puzzles, word games, jokes, cartoons all being accepted now. No pornography. Original work only. Please put name and address on each page. Please type all submissions, double-spaced. Send SASE if you desire an answer." circ. 1M+. 3/yr. Pub'd 3 issues 2009; expects 3 issues 2010, 3 issues 2011. sub. price $21; per copy $7.50; sample free. Back issues: $3.25. 52pp. Reporting time: when published. Simultaneous submissions accepted: yes. Payment: 1¢/word and copy. Copyrighted, reverts to author. Pub's reviews: 5 in 2009. §No pornography. Ads: $300/$200/$25 and up.

Penthe Publishing, Arthur Ward, PO Box 1066, Middletown, CA 95461-1066, 800-649-5954, 707-987-3470, penthpub@earthlink.net, penthepub.com. 1996. Poetry, fiction. avg. press run 5000. Expects 1 title 2010. No titles listed in the *Small Press Record of Books in Print* (36th Edition, 2010-11). Discounts: Retailers/Bookstores 40%Distributors 65%. 350pp. Reporting time: We are not accepting unsolicited mss at this time. Subjects: Birds, Birth, Birth Control, Population, Counter-Culture, Alternatives, Communes, Earth, Natural History, Ecology, Foods, Environment, Fiction, Humor, Literature (General), Men, Religion, Science Fiction, Singles, Sports, Outdoors, Women.

Penworth Publishing, Carmen Wisenbaker, 6942 FM 1960 East, #152, Humble, TX 77346, 281-404-5019,

FAX 713-893-6107, Email: carmen@penworth.com, Website: www.penworth.com. 2002. Non-fiction. "We publish Non-Fiction, Business and How-To books." avg. press run 1500. Pub'd 2 titles 2009; expects 4 titles 2010, 6 titles 2011. 2 titles listed in the *Small Press Record of Books in Print* (36th Edition, 2010-11). Discounts: 1-2 books No discount 3-9 books 20% off 10-50 books 30% off 51-100 books 40% off 101-199 books 45% off 200 or more books 50% off. 200pp. Reporting time: 6-8 weeks. Simultaneous submissions accepted: Yes. Publishes 5% of manuscripts submitted. Payment: Varies per project. Copyrights for author. Subjects: Business & Economics, Consulting, Creative Non-fiction, How-To, Leadership, Management, Marketing, Motivation, Success, Public Relations/Publicity, Publishing, Self-Help.

The People's Press, Shirley Richburg, 4810 Norwood Avenue, Baltimore, MD 21207-6839, (410)448-0254 phone/fax, (800)517-4475, biblio@talkamerica.net, http://thepeoplespress.info. Poetry, fiction, non-fiction. "We aim to move readers to try and make the world a better place than when we inherited it. "Excellence" with a human rights/dignity theme is the major criterion for publication. UNTOUCHABLE JIVAN, published in 2006, is our most recent release. This wonderful work chronicles Aasha Sunar's journey out of low caste life in Nepal, where young women are frequently regarded as chattel, to the United States of America where she is a free, naturalized citizen, appreciative of life, liberty and the pursuit...." 15 titles listed in the *Small Press Record of Books in Print* (36th Edition, 2010-11). Discounts: 40%. Reporting time: Usually within a month or two. Simultaneous submissions accepted: Yes. Payment: Royalties are paid, along with copies of author's publication(s). Copyrights for author. Subjects: Adolescence, Aging, Community, Family, Fiction, Human Rights, Humanism, Lifestyles, Multicultural, Non-Fiction, Non-Violence, Novels, Peace, Poetry, Society.

•**PERMAFROST,** Dept. of English, PO Box 755720, Fairbanks, AK 99775-5720.

The Permanent Press/The Second Chance Press, Martin Shepard, Judith Shepard, 4170 Noyac Road, Sag Harbor, NY 11963, 631-725-1101. 1979. Fiction, satire, news items. "We publish original material and specialize in quality fiction." avg. press run 2M. Expects 12 titles 2010, 12 titles 2011. 136 titles listed in the *Small Press Record of Books in Print* (36th Edition, 2010-11). Discounts: 20-50%. 250pp. Reporting time: 8-12 weeks. Simultaneous submissions accepted: yes. Publishes .17% of manuscripts submitted. Payment: 10% net, small standard advances, for all writers. Copyrights for author. Subjects: Fiction, Literature (General).

Perpetual Press, Matthew Lucas, PO Box 3956, Seattle, WA 98124-3956, 800-807-3030. 1993. Photos, non-fiction. avg. press run 5-7M. Pub'd 2 titles 2009; expects 3 titles 2010. 9 titles listed in the *Small Press Record of Books in Print* (36th Edition, 2010-11). 300pp. Simultaneous submissions accepted: yes. Subjects: Business & Economics, Careers, Guidance, How-To, Japan, Non-Fiction, Pacific Northwest, Self-Help, Sports, Outdoors, Transportation.

Perrin Press, David Moncur, 1700 W Big Beaver Rd Ste 315, Troy, MI 48084, 248.649.8071, fax 248.649.8087, www.perrinpress.com. 2004. Fiction. "At Perrin Press, we believe that children's creativity is limitless, and our goal is to encourage this creativity by producing wonderful books that fuel young minds and let imaginations soar. We are committed to publishing well-written books that can be enjoyed by children and the adults who read to them." avg. press run 5000. Pub'd 1 title 2009; expects 2 titles 2010, 5 titles 2011. No titles listed in the *Small Press Record of Books in Print* (36th Edition, 2010-11). Discounts: 2-4 copies 20%5-9 copies 30%10-24 copies 40%25-49 copies 42%50-99 copies 44%100-199 copies 48%200+ copies 50%. 32pp. Reporting time: 2-3 weeks. Simultaneous submissions accepted: Yes. Copyrights for author. Subjects: Adolescence, Children, Youth, Dreams, Family, Fantasy, Fiction, Folklore, Magic, Myth, Mythology, Picture Books, Reading, Storytelling.

•**Persea Books,** 853 Broadway, Suite 601, New York, NY 10003, info@perseabooks.com, (212) 260-9256 phone, (212) 260-1902 fax. "We are pleased to receive query letters from authors and literary agents for fiction and nonfiction manuscripts, including those for novels, novellas, short story collections, biography, essays, literary anthologies, literary criticism, literature in translation, memoir, contemporary issues, travel writing, and works for a young adult readership. Queries should include a cover letter, author background and publication history, a detailed synopsis of the proposed work, and a sample chapter. Please indicate if the work is simultaneously submitted. Our aim is to respond to proposals within eight weeks and to requested manuscripts within ten weeks. While we appreciate the interest of all of the dedicated writers who propose and submit their work to us, our small staff can't always adhere to these time frames or provide as comprehensive a response to the works as we would like. If you would like your manuscript returned to you, please enclose a self-addressed, stamped envelope with sufficient postage; otherwise, we will recycle it." No titles listed in the *Small Press Record of Books in Print* (36th Edition, 2010-11).

Persephone Press (see also Scots Plaid Press), Tom Tolnay, Editor-Publisher, PO Box 81, Delhi, NY 13753. 1987. Poetry, art, photos, long-poems. "Persephone Press is now an adjunct to Birch Brook Press, PO Box 81, Delhi, NY 13753 and is exclusively for poetry. Poetry Book Publication Award Endowment series is for up coming workshop leaders or career poets who have published but no more than 2 books or chapbooks. No entry fee, no application process; must be nominated 24pg. ms. recommended *by university instructors or editors*."

avg. press run 250-500-1000. Pub'd 2 titles 2009; expects 5 titles 2010, 4 titles 2011. No titles listed in the *Small Press Record of Books in Print* (36th Edition, 2010-11). Discounts: orders of 5 copies 30%; of 10 copies 40%. 32-64-320pp. Reporting time: 1-6 months. Simultaneous submissions accepted: yes. Publishes 10% of manuscripts submitted. Payment: Persephone Press Award Series now endowed; no entry fee; 80-90% of edition paid as royalties in advance. Copyrights for author. Subjects: Haiku, Poetry.

Personhood Press, Cathy Winch, PO Box 370, Fawnskin, CA 92333-0370, 909-866-2912, Fax 909-866-2961, 800 429 1192, www.personhoodpress.com. 2003. Non-fiction. "Personhood Press publishes "Books for All that You ARE", primarily focusing on personal and/or spiritual growth and development. Recent publications include "Parenting Well in a Media Age" which provides parents with tools to teach kids to be discerning media viewers; "Coming Home: Community, Creativity and Consciousness" describes the value of "community" and how to create a healthy communities at work, locally, etc. "The Gentle Art of Blessing" offers lessons for living your spirituality in everyday life. "Modern Medicine: The New World Religion" shows how beliefs secretly influence medical dogmas and practices. "Love is Not a Game, But You Should Know the Odds" shows you how to search for a quality love relationship. "I Thought I Was the Crazy One" 201 ways to identify and deal with toxic people." avg. press run 2000. Pub'd 17 titles 2009; expects 2 titles 2010, 4 titles 2011. No titles listed in the *Small Press Record of Books in Print* (36th Edition, 2010-11). Discounts: 50% prepaid non-returnable Bookstores purchase through IPG (exclusive distributor for trade sales). 200-300pp. Reporting time: 1-4 weeks. Simultaneous submissions accepted: Yes. Publishes 10% of manuscripts submitted. Payment: 10% royalties, no advances usually, payment bi-annually. Copyrights for author. Subject: Non-Fiction.

Perugia Press, Susan Kan, PO Box 60364, Florence, MA 01062-0364, info@perugiapress.com, www.perugiapress.com. 1997. Poetry. "Perugia Press Prize: An award of $1000 and publication is given annually for a first or second unpublished poetry collection by a woman. Submit 48 to 72 pages with a $25 entry fee between August 1 and November 15. Send an e-mail, SASE, or visit the web site for complete guidelines. The winner of the contest is the only book we publish each year." avg. press run 1000. Pub'd 1 title 2009; expects 1 title 2010, 1 title 2011. 11 titles listed in the *Small Press Record of Books in Print* (36th Edition, 2010-11). Discounts: standard. Reporting time: by April 1 for the annual contest. Simultaneous submissions accepted: yes. Copyrights for author. Subjects: Poetry, Women.

Petroglyph Press, Ltd., 160 Kamehameha Avenue, Hilo, HI 96720-2834, 808-935-6006, Fax 808-935-1553, PetroglyphPress@hawaiiantel.net, www.PetroglyphPress.com. 1962. Non-fiction. avg. press run 2M. Pub'd 2 titles 2009; expects 2 titles 2010, 2 titles 2011. No titles listed in the *Small Press Record of Books in Print* (36th Edition, 2010-11). Discounts: 40% trade, 50% jobber, 55% 500+ books. 90pp. Payment: paid quarterly. Does not copyright for author. Subjects: Crafts, Hobbies, Ecology, Foods, Folklore, Gardening, Hawaii, Health, History, Language, Poetry.

•**PHANTASMAGORIA,** English Dept - Century College, 3300 Century Ave N., White Bear Lake, MN 55110, (651)779-3410. "Our mission is to publish the very best literary fiction, poetry and non-fiction available to us."

Phelps Publishing Company, PO Box 22401, Cleveland, OH 44122, 216-433-2531, 216-752-4938. 1993. Art, cartoons, non-fiction. avg. press run 3M. Expects 2 titles 2010, 3 titles 2011. 5 titles listed in the *Small Press Record of Books in Print* (36th Edition, 2010-11). Discounts: jobber 50-55%, trade 30-40%, bulk 65-70%. 80pp. Reporting time: 6-8 weeks. We Publish art instruction books and graphic novels. Send non-returnable samples for consideration. Copyrights for author. Subjects: African-American, Arts, Asian-American, Book Arts, Children, Youth, Comics, Fantasy, How-To, Multicultural, Native American, Visual Arts.

PHILADELPHIA POETS, Rosemary Cappello, 1919 Chestnut Street, Apartment 1721, Philadelphia, PA 19103-3430, redrose108@comcast.net. 1980. Poetry, art, reviews. "*Philadelphia Poets* does not publish poets from Philadelphia only. The editor believes in the humanistic ideals of those who founded Philadelphia, and since it originates from that city, thus the name. Although it wishes to publish the works of current poets, tribute is paid to those of the past as well. Volume 9 Number 2 featured a special section on Writers and Readers Showcase, a group that was active in Philadelphia in the early 1980's. Volume 10 Number 1 contains ten pages of poetry by the late Jim Marinell. Volume 10 Number 2 pays homage to the late Almitra David with 12 pages of her poetry. Contributors have been Gerald Stern, Kate Northrop, Louis McKee, Ann Menebroker, Joan Jobe Smith, Fred Voss, Eileen Spinelli, Mbali Umoja, Beth Philips Brown, Lamont Steptoe, Aschak, Tommi Avicolli Mecca, Janet Mason, Michael C Ford, Ann E. Michael, Anne Kaier, and many other fine poets, approximately 50 poets per issue. Cover artists have been the late Sid Shupak, Sean Wholey, Barbara Barasch Rosin, Peter Quarracino, Lynn Liberman, Clifford Ward, Nina Nocella, Al Tacconelli, and Karl Hagedorn." circ. 350. 1/yr. Pub'd 1 issue 2009; expects 1 issue 2010, 1 issue 2011. price per copy $12; sample $6. Back issues: $6. Discounts: Negotiable. 175pp. Reporting time: Six weeks. Simultaneous submissions accepted: No. Publishes 50% of manuscripts submitted. Payment: One copy. Copyrighted, reverts to author. Pub's reviews: 4 in 2009. §Poetry and creative non-fiction. No advertising.

PHILADELPHIA STORIES, Carla Spataro, Publisher-Fiction Editor; Christine Weiser, Publisher-Poetry

Editor, 2021 S. 11th Street, Philadelphia, PA 19148.

Philomel Books, Patricia Lee Gauch, Vice President and Editor at Large; Michael Green, Associate Publisher and Editorial Director; Emily Heath, Editor; Courtenay Lewis, Associate Editor, 345 Hudson Street, New York, NY 10014, 212-414-3610. 1980. Poetry, fiction, non-fiction. "We are a hardcover children's trade book list. Our primary emphasis is on picturebooks, with a small number of young adult novels and middle grade novels. We publish some poetry. We look for fresh and innovative books imbued with a child's spirit and crafted with fine writing and art. Recent selections include *Mister Seahorse* by Eric Carle, *Rakkety Tam* by Brian Jacques, *An Orange for Frankie* by Patricia Polacco, and *Eagle Strike* by Anthony Horowitz." avg. press run 5M-10M. Expects 25 titles 2010. No titles listed in the *Small Press Record of Books in Print* (36th Edition, 2010-11). Novels 200pp, picturebooks 32pp. Reporting time: 2 months on queries, 3 months on manuscripts. Simultaneous submissions accepted: yes. Publishes 1% of manuscripts submitted. Payment: varies. Does not copyright for author. Subject: Children, Youth.

Philos Press, Laura Beausoleil, 8038-A N. Bicentennial Loop SE, Lacey, WA 98503-1708, 360-456-5106, sales@philospress.org, www.philospress.org. 2000. Poetry, fiction, art, long-poems, collages. "Philos Press is a woman owned small press. When asked for the Greek word for friends the Greek poet Nanos Valaoritis answered, Philos. Accordingly, Philos Press will publish books by "friends" whose work, poetry, prose and visual arts has been overlooked by other presses. It is pure joy to be able to present work by artists and writers of the first order who, more than being just "friends", are friends of the written and spoken word." avg. press run 500. Pub'd 1 title 2009; expects 1 title 2010, 1 title 2011. 3 titles listed in the *Small Press Record of Books in Print* (36th Edition, 2010-11). Discounts: 40% trade discounts to distributors, bookstores, wholesalers, retailers, institutions, classrooms. 75-100pp. Reporting time: We do not accept unsolicited works. Simultaneous submissions accepted: No. Payment: Arranged on a book-by-book basis. Copyrights for author. Subjects: Hawaii, Poetry, Prose, Visual Arts.

Phi-Psi Publishers, Sean O'Connell, Box 75198, Ritchie P.O., Edmonton, AB T6E 6K1, Canada, phipsibk@netscape.net. 1999. Plays. avg. press run 500. Pub'd 2 titles 2009; expects 2 titles 2010, 1 title 2011. 4 titles listed in the *Small Press Record of Books in Print* (36th Edition, 2010-11). Discounts: 20-40%. 110pp. Reporting time: 2-3 months. Simultaneous submissions accepted: yes. Publishes 10-20% of manuscripts submitted. Payment: 10-15% of net. Copyrights for author. Subjects: Drama, Philosophy.

Phlare, Inc., Theresa DeGroote, PO Box 1400, Arvada, CO 80001-1400, 303-513-1565, 888-731-6950, www.phlare.com. 2003. avg. press run 3000. Pub'd 1 title 2009; expects 2 titles 2010, 2 titles 2011. No titles listed in the *Small Press Record of Books in Print* (36th Edition, 2010-11). Discounts: Please contact us for discount pricing information, as it is dependent upon whether you are a distributor, bookstore or end customer as well as volume. 25pp.

PHOEBE: A Journal of Literature and Art, Nat Foster, Editor; Wade Fletcher, Poetry Editor; Ryan Call, Fiction Editor, MSN 2D6, 4400 University Drive, George Mason University, Fairfax, VA 22030, www.gmu.edu.pubs/phoebe/, phoebejournal.blogspot.com. 1971. Poetry, fiction, art, interviews, reviews. circ. 1.5M. 2/yr. Pub'd 2 issues 2009; expects 2 issues 2010, 2 issues 2011. sub. price $12; per copy $6; sample $6. Back issues: $6. Discounts: none. 128pp. Reporting time: 3-5 months, longer during summer. Simultaneous submissions accepted: yes. Publishes 3% of manuscripts submitted. Payment: two copies or subscription. Copyrighted, reverts to author. Pub's reviews: 2 in 2009. Ads: exchange ads accepted. Subjects: Avant-Garde, Experimental Art, Fiction, Literature (General), Poetry.

PHOEBE: Journal of Gender & Cultural Critiques, Kathleen O'Mara, Women's & Gender Studies Department, State University of New York, Oneonta, NY 13820-4015, Phone (607) 436-2014, Fax (607) 436-2656, phoebe@oneonta.edu, http://www.oneonta.edu/academics/womens/Phoebe_Small.htm. 1989. Poetry, fiction, articles, reviews. "Phoebe focuses on feminist scholarship, theory, and aesthetics in this international literary journal. Appearing in each issue are short stories, essays, poetry, and articles that enrich critical thinking about women's lives in the U.S. and around the world." circ. 100. 2/yr. Pub'd 2 issues 2009; expects 2 issues 2010, 2 issues 2011. sub. price $35; per copy $17.50; sample $7.50. Back issues: $7.50. 128pp. Reporting time: 4-6 months. Simultaneous submissions accepted: No. Publishes 85% of manuscripts submitted. Payment: No payment. Provide two contributor's copies for Essays, one copy for short stories and poetry. Copyrighted. Pub's reviews: 7 in 2009.

Phoenix Illusion, Shay Phoenix R, Publisher, c/o Shay R. Phoenix, 208 South Sixth St., Newark, NJ 07103, (862) 902-6457. 2005. Poetry, fiction, parts-of-novels, long-poems. "Currently we only publish poetry and fiction (novels)." avg. press run 500. Expects 2 titles 2010, 5 titles 2011. 3 titles listed in the *Small Press Record of Books in Print* (36th Edition, 2010-11). Discounts: 1 book No discoun t2-4 books 20% off 5-9 books 30% off 10-24 books 40% off 25-49 books 42% off 50-74 books 44% off 100-199 books 48% off 200 Or more books 50% off. 200pp. Reporting time: 1 to 2 months. Simultaneous submissions accepted: No. Publishes 10% of manuscripts submitted. Copyrights for author. Subjects: Fiction, Novels, Reviews, Short Stories.

PhoeniX in Print, Patricia Arnold, P. O. Box 81234, Chicago, IL 60681-0234, 312-698-9817, 312-946-9698 fax, info@phoenixinprint.com, www.phoenixinprint.com. 2004. Non-fiction. "PhoeniX in Print publishes "books that make the spirit soar". Seeking uplifting, empowering, superbly written prose that is not preachy and does not promote fear." avg. press run 5000. Expects 1 title 2010, 2 titles 2011. 2 titles listed in the *Small Press Record of Books in Print* (36th Edition, 2010-11). Discounts: General 40% discount on orders placed directly with publisher. 300pp. Reporting time: One month. Simultaneous submissions accepted: Yes. Payment: Varies. Copyrights for author. Subjects: African-American, Inspirational, Metaphysics, Non-Fiction, Relationships, Spiritual.

Phrygian Press (see also ZYX), Arnold Skemer, 58-09 205th Street, Bayside, NY 11364, PhrygianZYX @ AOL.COM. 1984. Fiction. "Focus is on innovative fiction. Presently engaged in long term project: Arnold Skemer's *ABCDEFGHIJKLMNOPQRSTUVWXYZ*, a novella-continuum (=a series of novellae constituting a unity). Approximate completion in 2025. This and other works published in microeditions of 100. Binding done in house. Recent publications: Leonard Cirino's *The Ability to Dream* in 2007, Guy R. Beining's *Inrue*, Arnold Skemer's *Of The Extinction Of The Hittites*, Jonathan Hayes' *T(HERE)* in 2008, Jon Cone's *Family Portrait With Two Dogs Bleeding*, Geof Huth's *Carl Ornery, Mississippi. Carl Doddering, Mississippi.* in 2009, *G* by Skemer in 2009. Planned for 2010, Bob Grumman's *Poems, Diverging*, Arnold Skemer's *Sexptych*. Chapbook publication originates out of initial publication in *ZYX*. If a contributor's work sufficiently intrigues us, a chapbook offer will be made.This is a spartan micropress with stark covers, low overhead, no frills, accepting no subsidies or grants, in full samizdat spirit of publishing. Member: POETSHOUSE, Finnegans Wake Society of New York." avg. press run 100. Pub'd 3 titles 2009; expects 3 titles 2010, 3 titles 2011. 18 titles listed in the *Small Press Record of Books in Print* (36th Edition, 2010-11). Discounts: libraries and institutions 20%; wholesalers and bookstores 1-4 30%. 60pp; chapbooks 20pp. Reporting time: timely. Simultaneous submissions accepted: no. Payment: negotiable. Does not copyright for author. Subjects: Avant-Garde, Experimental Art, Dada, Fiction, Poetry, Post Modern, Surrealism.

Piano Press, Elizabeth C. Axford, PO Box 85, Del Mar, CA 92014-0085, pianopress@pianopress.com, www.pianopress.com, 619-884-1401. 1998. Poetry, fiction, music, long-poems, non-fiction. "Publish songbooks and CD's for music teachers and students, music teaching materials and some poetry. All work is original and/or public domain. All manuscripts are computer typeset." avg. press run 500-1M. Pub'd 13 titles 2009; expects 12 titles 2010, 10 titles 2011. 10 titles listed in the *Small Press Record of Books in Print* (36th Edition, 2010-11). Discounts: 40%-55% wholesale. 36-112pp. Reporting time: 2-3 months. Simultaneous submissions accepted: yes. Publishes 25% of manuscripts submitted. Payment: copies of chapbook or anthology for poetry, short stories and essays, standard print music and/or mechanical royalty for sheet music, songbooks and/or CDs. Copyrights for author. Subjects: Children, Youth, Music, Poetry, Tapes & Records, Technology.

Piccadilly Books, Ltd., Leslie Fife, PO Box 25203, Colorado Springs, CO 80936, 719-550-9887. 1985. Non-fiction. "Email orders to: orders@piccadillybooks.com." avg. press run 3M. Pub'd 4 titles 2009; expects 3 titles 2010, 3 titles 2011. 45 titles listed in the *Small Press Record of Books in Print* (36th Edition, 2010-11). Discounts: 6-23 45%, 24-99 50%, 100-199 55%, 200+ 60%. 150pp. Reporting time: 8 weeks. Simultaneous submissions accepted: yes. Payment: negotiable. Copyrights for author. Subjects: Alternative Medicine, Business & Economics, Health, How-To, Non-Fiction, Nutrition.

Pictorial Histories Pub. Co., Stan Cohen, 713 S. 3rd Street, Missoula, MT 59801, 406-549-8488, www.pictorialhistoriespublishing.com, fax 406-718-9280. 1976. Non-fiction. "Only do history books, mainly military." avg. press run 2-3M. Pub'd 6 titles 2009; expects 5 titles 2010, 5 titles 2011. 1 title listed in the *Small Press Record of Books in Print* (36th Edition, 2010-11). Discounts: trade 40%, distributor 55%. 180pp. Reporting time: 1 month. Simultaneous submissions accepted: no. Publishes 10% of manuscripts submitted. Payment: 10%. Copyrights for author. Subject: History.

Pierian Press, C. Edward Wall, PO Box 1808, Ann Arbor, MI 48106, 734-434-5530, Fax 734-434-5582. 1968. "Biographies, reference books, resources on information literacy." 126 titles listed in the *Small Press Record of Books in Print* (36th Edition, 2010-11).

PIG IRON, Pig Iron Press, Jim Villani, Editor, 26 North Phelps Street, PO Box 237, Youngstown, OH 44501-0237, 330-747-6932, Fax 330-747-0599. 1974. Poetry, fiction, articles, art, photos, cartoons, criticism, parts-of-novels, long-poems, collages, plays, concrete art, non-fiction. "Compiled creative and investigative examinations of popular social themes. Energetic and inclusive of marginal insight. Length: open. Style/bias: open. Recent contributors: Winona Baker, Jeanne Carney, Joel Harris, Lyn Lifshin, Ed Meek, Leonard Moskovit, Dirk van Nouhuys, Julia Older, Jack Remick, Ed Schwartz, Laurel Speer, Karl Tierney." circ. 1M. 1/yr. Pub'd 1 issue 2009; expects 1 issue 2010, 1 issue 2011. price per copy $18.95; sample $5.00. Back issues: write for backlist. Discounts: 20% for I or 2copies, 40% for 3+ copies. 175pp. Reporting time: 90 days. Simultaneous submissions accepted: no. Publishes 2% of manuscripts submitted. Payment: 2 copies, $5 per page fiction, $5 per poem. Copyrighted, reverts to author. §Forthcoming: Jazz Tradition; Frontier: Custom & Archetype; Years of Rage: 1960s; Religion in Modernity; 20th Century. No ads. Subjects: Arts, Avant-Garde,

Experimental Art, Comics, Counter-Culture, Alternatives, Communes, Criticism, Culture, Culture, Dada, Design, Family, Feminism, Fiction, Graphics, Photography, Poetry.

Pig Iron Press (see also PIG IRON), Jim Villani, Publisher, 26 North Phelps Street, PO Box 237, Youngstown, OH 44501, 330-747-6932, Fax 330-747-0599. 1973. Poetry, fiction, art, photos, collages, non-fiction. "Want marginal and emphatic voices. We sponsor the Kenneth Patchen Competition -reading fee = $5." avg. press run 1M. Pub'd 1 title 2009; expects 2 titles 2010, 2 titles 2011. 24 titles listed in the *Small Press Record of Books in Print* (36th Edition, 2010-11). Discounts: 20%/40% for 3+ copies. Pages vary. Reporting time: 4 months. Simultaneous submissions accepted: no. Payment: 10% annually. Copyrights for author. Subjects: Anarchist, Arts, Dada, Fiction, Poetry, Politics, Science Fiction.

The Pikestaff Press, Robert D. Sutherland, Editor; James R. Scrimgeour, Editor, P.O. Box 127, Normal, IL 61761, (309) 452-4831, e-mail: staff@pikestaffpress.com website: http://www.pikestaffpress.com. 1977. Poetry, fiction, long-poems. "We publish traditional and experimental poetry and prose fiction by established and non-established writers. We subscribe to no specific "school" of poetry or fiction, and are particularly interested in giving launchpad exposure to new writers and to those who might have difficulty in getting a hearing. Authors must query first by e-mail or letter (in the latter case, supplying SASE for reply) before sending a manuscript. Unsolicited manuscripts will be sent back without comment if the author supplies sufficient postage for return; otherwise they will be recycled unread. The query should provide full particulars of the manuscript's length, contents, aims, and intended audience, as well as a brief biographical sketch of the author. Response will be forthcoming within one month. Recent authors include Jeff Gundy, Lucia Cordell Getsi, J. W. Rivers, Frannie Lindsay." avg. press run 500. Pub'd 1 title 2009; expects 2 titles 2010, 2 titles 2011. 8 titles listed in the *Small Press Record of Books in Print* (36th Edition, 2010-11). Discounts: Bookstores 40%, Distributors 50%. 25-40pp. Reporting time: Within one month. Simultaneous submissions accepted: No. Payment: Authors receive 20% of press run. We print author's copyright notice on book. Authors are responsible for registering their copyrights with the U.S. Copyright Office.

•**PILGRIMAGE,** Maria Melendez, Editor & Publisher, PO BOX 9110, Pueblo, CO 81008, info@pilgrimage-press.org, www.pilgrimagepress.org. "*Pilgrimage*, founded in 1976, is published three times a year. Pilgrimage is dedicated to serving a community of artists, writers, adventurers, naturalists, contemplatives, activists, seekers and tricksters in and beyond the American Southwest. We welcome literary nonfiction and poetry, and favor writing on themes related to soul, spirit, place, and social justice." No titles listed in the *Small Press Record of Books in Print* (36th Edition, 2010-11).

•**PILGRIMAGE,** PO box 9110, Pueble, CO 81008. "A small magazine living the big questions. A community-in-print serving an eclectic fellowship of readers, writers, artists, naturalists, contemplatives, activists, seekers, adventurers, and other kindred spirits. A place to tell the stories that matter. An invitation to inward and outward exploration. And an appreciation of the way home."

Pilgrims Book House, Rama Nand Tiwari, Founder, MD; John Snyder, Executive Editor; Christopher N Burchett, Editor, Thamel, PO Box 3872, Kathmandu, Nepal, 977-1-4700942, Fax 977-1-4700943, pilgrims@wlink.com.np, www.pilgrimsbooks.com. 2000. Non-fiction. avg. press run 1.5-3M. Expects 60 titles 2010. 18 titles listed in the *Small Press Record of Books in Print* (36th Edition, 2010-11). Discounts: 40%. 350pp. Reporting time: 60 days. Simultaneous submissions accepted: yes. Publishes 15% of manuscripts submitted. Payment: 10% annually in July. Does not copyright for author. Subjects: Asia, Indochina, Buddhism, Non-Fiction, Religion, Third World, Minorities, Transportation.

THE PINCH, Kristen Iversen, Editor-in-Chief, University of Memphis, Department of English, 435 Patterson Hall, Memphis, TN 38152-6176, 901-678-4591, www.thepinchjournal.com, editor@thepinchjournal.com. 1980. Poetry, fiction, articles, art, photos, interviews, non-fiction. "*The Pinch* publishes fiction, poetry, essays, and visual art. Please do not send unsolicited manuscripts during the summer. Length under 7,000 words. No genre fiction or literary criticism. Send complete mss. Poetry: free verse, traditional, experimental. Submit maximum of 5 poems. Annual fiction contest: $1,500 first place. Annual poetry contest: $1,000 first place. Check website for guidelines. It's a good idea to see an issue of *The Pinch* before submitting." circ. 1,500. 2/yr. Pub'd 2 issues 2009; expects 2 issues 2010, 2 issues 2011. sub. price $22; per copy $12; sample $12. Back issues: $6 for issues more than two years old. 160pp. Reporting time: 2 weeks to 3 months. Simultaneous submissions accepted: Yes. Publishes 5% of manuscripts submitted. Payment: 2 copies. Copyrighted, reverts to author. Ads: exchange ads for other publications. Subjects: Arts, Creative Non-fiction, English, Fiction, Literary Review, Literature (General), Non-Fiction, Poetry, Short Stories, Storytelling, Visual Arts, Writers/Writing.

PINE ISLAND JOURNAL OF NEW ENGLAND POETRY, Linda Porter, PO Box 317, West Springfield, MA 01090. 1998. Poetry. "Submissions limited to poets currently residing in New England. Up to thirty lines, haiku and other forms welcome, no horror, no erotica, no previously published material. Please include cover letter with current bio. and SASE." circ. 200. 2/yr. Pub'd 2 issues 2009; expects 2 issues 2010, 2 issues 2011. sub. price $10; per copy $5; sample $5. Discounts: library discount available. 50pp. Reporting time: 6-8 weeks.

Simultaneous submissions accepted: no. Publishes 10% of manuscripts submitted. Payment: $1 per poem, plus one copy. Copyrighted, reverts to author. Pub's reviews. §books of poetry by New England poets/editors published within the last twelve months. Subjects: Haiku, New England, Poetry.

Pineapple Press, Inc., June Cussen, PO Box 3889, Sarasota, FL 34230-3889, 941-739-2219, FAX: 941-739-2296. 1982. Fiction, non-fiction. "We publish hard and soft cover adult trade fiction and nonfiction, as well as hard and soft cover books for children and young adults—all with a focus on the Southeast, and in particular, Florida." avg. press run 3M+. Pub'd 22 titles 2009; expects 20 titles 2010, 20 titles 2011. 255 titles listed in the *Small Press Record of Books in Print* (36th Edition, 2010-11). Discounts: trade 1-3 copies 20%, 4-15 40%, 16-49 42%, 50-99 43%, 100-199 44%, 200+ 46%. 300pp. Reporting time: 3 months. Simultaneous submissions accepted: yes. Publishes less than 1% of manuscripts submitted. Payment: negotiable. Copyrights for author. Subjects: Animals, Birds, Conservation, Cooking, Environment, Fiction, Florida, Gardening, Ernest Hemingway, History, Nature, Reference, Senior Citizens, Travel, Young Adult.

PINYON, Randy Phillis, Editor; Carol Christ, Poetry Editor; John Nizalowski, Fiction Editor; TJ Gerlach, Fiction Editor; Jennifer Hancock, Poetry Editor, Dept. of Languages, Lit., & Comm., Mesa State College, 1100 North Ave., Grand Junction, CO 81502-2647, 970-248-1740. 1996. Poetry, fiction, long-poems, non-fiction. "No bias other than quality, though we appreciate a strong voice. Name, address and email on each poem and story." circ. 300. 1/yr. Pub'd 1 issue 2009; expects 1 issue 2010, 1 issue 2011. sub. price $8; per copy $9; sample $3.50. Back issues: $3.50. Discounts: standard. 120pp. Reporting time: reading period Aug. 1 to Dec. 1, report in March. Simultaneous submissions accepted: Okay with notification. Publishes 5% of manuscripts submitted. Payment: copies. Copyrighted, reverts to author. Subjects: Colorado, Fiction, Poetry, Prose.

PIPERS MAGAZINE, Aircraft Owners Group, Joe Jones, Publisher, PO Box 5000, Iola, WI 54945, 715-445-5000; e-mail piper@aircraftownergroup.com. Articles, photos, interviews. "Aimed at owners and pilots of Piper aircraft." circ. 5000. 12/yr. Pub'd 12 issues 2009; expects 12 issues 2010, 12 issues 2011. sub. price $49.95, includes membership in Piper Owner Society. 60pp. Reporting time: varies. Payment: 5¢/word and up, on publication. Copyrighted. Pub's reviews: 6 in 2009. §Aviation, pilot's skills and experiences. Ads: call for media kit. Subjects: Airplanes, Aviation.

Pirate Publishing International, Sarah Jane Kaserman, 6323 St. Andrews Circle South, Fort Myers, FL 33919-1719, 239-939-4845 phone/Fax, superK@juno.com. 1999. Fiction, articles, non-fiction. avg. press run 5M. Pub'd 2 titles 2009; expects 1 title 2010, 1 title 2011. 5 titles listed in the *Small Press Record of Books in Print* (36th Edition, 2010-11). Discounts: 45-55%. 300+pp. Reporting time: 3 months. Simultaneous submissions accepted: yes. Publishes 3% of manuscripts submitted. Payment: varies. Copyrights for author. Subjects: Children, Youth, Fiction, History.

PITCHFORK POETRY MAGAZINE, Pitchfork Press, Chris Gibson, Editor, 2002A Guadalupe #461, Austin, TX 78705.

•**Pixiu Press,** Picott Camille, P.O. Box 183, Healdsburg, CA 95448, www.pixiupress.com. 2008. Fiction, art. "Submissions for Heritage Tale Books: Heritage Tale stories are speculative fiction books for juveniles. Each book is a "Coming to America" story told using myths and/or legends from the native culture. The first in this series is Raggedy Chan: A Chinese Heritage Tale. We will grow this series to include other Tales, such as An Italian Heritage Tale, A Mexican Heritage Tale, A Jewish Heritage Tale, An African Heritage Tale, etc. The intent of this series to help children explore themes of immigration while exposing them to myths, legends, and fairy tales they might not come across in general text books. Required length is 8,000 to 12,000 words. Stories must lend themselves to strong visuals. Selected stories will be published as stand-alone, fully illustrated books.Heritage Tale books are marketed to schools, libraries, and educators. PIXIU Press works with two California-credentialed teachers to develop free teaching curricula for each of these stories. All curricula are available online for free download. We attend teaching conferences and encourage classroom visits. We hope to increase the amount of speculative fiction used in learning environments." avg. press run 500. Pub'd 1 title 2009; expects 1 title 2010, 1 title 2011. No titles listed in the *Small Press Record of Books in Print* (36th Edition, 2010-11). Discounts: Industry standard. 80pp. Reporting time: 2 months. Simultaneous submissions accepted: Yes. Publishes 5% of manuscripts submitted. Payment: 15% - 25% net profit, bi-annual payment. Does not copyright for author. Subjects: Comics, Fantasy, Fiction, Folklore, Immigration, Juvenile Fiction, Magic, Multicultural, Science Fiction.

The Place In The Woods (see also READ, AMERICA!), Roger A. Hammer, Editor & Publisher, 3900 Glenwood Avenue, Golden Valley, MN 55422-5302, Tel: 763-374-2120. 1980. Poetry, fiction, photos, interviews, criticism, reviews, letters, news items, non-fiction. "SAN 689-058X. Primarily interested in short biographies (and art) on significant achievements by American minorities—African-American, Women, Native People, Seniors, Handicapped/Disabled, Hispanic, War Vets, Gay/Lesbians, Young Achievers, Business Person, Asian/Pacific, other minority persons with significant but *little-known* contributions to the American culture. Well-documented personalities (such as African-Americans in sports or entertainment) are unacceptable.

Interested in developing role models for minorities (adults and children). Need talented illustrators at whatever level, age who speak for their minority. Bios can run 50 to 500 words. Pays for completed work or leads. Queries recommended. Also looking for new material with themes appealing to elementary through seconday educational levels. Should be creative and original—subjects not found in general textbooks, yet of interest to mainstream Americans, young and adult." avg. press run 2M. Pub'd 1 title 2009; expects 2 titles 2010, 4 titles 2011. 10 titles listed in the *Small Press Record of Books in Print* (36th Edition, 2010-11). Discounts: 40% wholesaler/distributor; 40% to RIF programs; quantity rates on request. 30-80pp. Reporting time: 1 week-1 month. Simultaneous submissions accepted: no. Publishes 10% of manuscripts submitted. Payment: royalties vary with material, buys all rights with liberal reprint permission. Does not copyright for author. Subjects: African-American, Asian-American, Biography, Black, Book Reviewing, Chicano/a, Children, Youth, Civil Rights, Disabled, Education, Handicapped, Native American, Poetry, Third World, Minorities, Women.

PLAIN BROWN WRAPPER (PBW), Richard Freeman, 513 N. Central Avenue, Fairborn, OH 45324-5209, 513-878-5184. 1988. Poetry, fiction, articles, art, criticism, reviews, parts-of-novels, long-poems, non-fiction. "*PBW* comes out on floppy disc for Macintosh computers, so the only limitation is what can go onto a floppy disc. However, I can put in computer art if sent to me via floppy disc, and can print very long pieces if sent on floppy. Some contributors: Lisa B. Herskovits, Jennifer Blowdryer, Marie Markoe, Art Snyder, Danielle Willis, Anni Roberts." circ. 80 + several computer bulletin boards. 2/yr. Pub'd 2 issues 2009; expects 2 issues 2010, 2 issues 2011. price per copy $2. Back issues: $2. Discounts: none. 5-600pp. Reporting time: 1 week. Payment: 1 copy. Not copyrighted. Pub's reviews: 60 in 2009. §I will send material to my reviewers; prefer underground zines. Will trade. Subjects: Arts, Autobiography, Avant-Garde, Experimental Art, Book Reviewing, Computers, Calculators, Culture, Dada, Diaries, Dreams, Electronics, Erotica, Humor, James Joyce, Jack Kerouac, Los Angeles.

Plain Philosophy Center, Mark Plain, 310 - 8870 Citation Drive, Richmond, BC V6Y 3A3, Canada, 1-604-276-8272. 1998. Non-fiction. "General Philosophy, Christian Philosophy, Philosophy of Science." avg. press run 2000. Expects 2 titles 2010, 5 titles 2011. 2 titles listed in the *Small Press Record of Books in Print* (36th Edition, 2010-11). Discounts: please contact us. 150pp. Reporting time: 3 months. Simultaneous submissions accepted: Yes. Publishes 2% of manuscripts submitted. Payment: please contact us. Copyrights for author. Subjects: Philosophy, Religion, Self-Help.

Plain View Press, Susan Bright, PO Box 42255, Austin, TX 78704, sb@plainviewpress.net. 1975. Poetry, fiction, art, photos, letters, long-poems, plays, non-fiction. "Plain View Press is a 35-year-old issue-based literary publishing house. We have published 350 titles presenting the work of almost 500 national and international writers. Despite evidence that relentless violence has taken root worldwide, there is hope and there are artists to show the human face of it. We publish contemporary literature poetry, fiction, memoir and nonfiction.Our books result from artistic collaboration between writers, artists and editors. Over the years we have become a far-flung community of activists whose energies bring humanitarian enlightenment and hope to individuals and communities grappling with the major issues of our time—peace, justice, the environment, education and gender. This is a humane and highly creative group of people committed to art and social change." avg. press run 700, offset, 100 POD. Pub'd 40 titles 2009; expects 60 titles 2010, 60 titles 2011. No titles listed in the *Small Press Record of Books in Print* (36th Edition, 2010-11). Discounts: library discounts vary, standard bookstore rates, for info: sbpvp@sbcglobal.net, new titles filed with Lightning Source, Ingram International, Baker and Taylor. 80-500ppspp. Reporting time: varies. Simultaneous submissions accepted: Yes. Publishes 5% of manuscripts submitted. Payment: Non-traditional profit and cost structure. We copyright in author's name. Subjects: African Literature, Africa, African Studies, African-American, Aging, Arts, Environment, Experimental, Family, Feminism, Fiction, Indigenous Cultures, Memoirs, Non-Violence, Peace, Poetry, Women.

Plan B Press, Steven May, PO Box 4067, Alexandria, VA 22303, 215-732-2663. 1998. Poetry. "Plan B Press publishes work from new voices in the poetry scene and generally under-published authors. We also value experimentation and the use of visuals with poetry. See our website for more information: www.planbpress.com." avg. press run 75. Pub'd 8 titles 2009; expects 8 titles 2010, 10 titles 2011. 32 titles listed in the *Small Press Record of Books in Print* (36th Edition, 2010-11). Discounts: bookstores and colleges get the standard 40% discount; all other organizations are negotiable. 40pp. Reporting time: We read mss. for most of the year with the exception of the period from Jan 1 through May 1 which is set aside for our poetry contest. Simultaneous submissions accepted: Yes. Publishes 10% of manuscripts submitted. Payment: 20-30% of profit from book sales. Author keeps all rights to material except for design and cover work. Author retains copyright. Subjects: Absurdist, Experimental, Poetry.

Plank Road Publishing, Judith Cook Tucker, Publisher, Editor-in-Chief; Claudia Chapman, Art Director, Assoc. Editor; Belongia Nancy, Managing Editor; Schill Candy, Multicultural Editor, PO Box 26627, Wauwatosa, WI 53226-0627, phone 800-437-0832 or 262-790-5210; fax 888-272-0212 or 262-781-8818; e-mail Lynn@MusicK8.com; website www.MusicK8.com. 1990. Photos, music, plays, non-fiction. "Plank

Road Publishing publishes quality educational vocal and recorder music for elementary and middle schools. In 2009, Plank Road Publishing purchased World Music Press, which consists of multicultural music and incorporates the other arts with some history of the country/area. Many World Music Press products are for all ages, some just for high schools, and some for young children." Pub'd 7 titles 2009; expects 7 titles 2010, 6 titles 2011. 19 titles listed in the *Small Press Record of Books in Print* (36th Edition, 2010-11). Discounts: If you purchase products for resale at a store, please contact us for the discount schedule, and we would be happy to set you up as a dealer. Copyrights for author. Subjects: African Literature, Africa, African Studies, Asia, Indochina, Audio/Video, Bilingual, Caribbean, Cuba, Dance, Education, Folklore, Latin America, Multicultural, Music, Native American, Poland, Vietnam.

Plantagenet Productions (see also PLANTAGENET PRODUCTIONS, Libraries of Spoken Word Recordings and of Stagescripts), Westridge (Open Centre), Highclere, Nr. Newbury, Berkshire RG20 9PJ, England. Pub'd 1 title 2009; expects 1 title 2011. 40 titles listed in the *Small Press Record of Books in Print* (36th Edition, 2010-11).

PLANTAGENET PRODUCTIONS, Libraries of Spoken Word Recordings and of Stagescripts, Plantagenet Productions, Dorothy Rose Gribble, Director of Productions, Westridge (Open Centre), Star Lane, Highclere, Newbury RG20 9PJ, England. 1964. "Recordings of poetry, philosophy, narrative and light work on cassette, tape, LP. Family history: *Gribble Annals 1* by Charles Besly Gribble, Captain East India Company, Besly 1986, £2.25 plus postage; *Gribble Annals 2* by Henry Gribble, Captain, East India Company, 1988, £4.50 + p/h. *Milton Traditions*, compiled by F.G.M. Milton and D.R. Gribble, £10.50 + p/h (direct sales), 1990. *Gribble Annals 3: Family Letters 1822-1940*, 1992, £12.75 + p/h (direct sales). *Gribble Annals 4: Kinship* £16.50 + p/h (direct sales)." Erratic. Pub'd 1 issue 2009; expects 3 issues 2010. price per copy LP-£2.25, £2, £1 cassette £2.25, £1.75 postage extra. Subject: Tapes & Records.

THE PLASTIC TOWER, Carol Dyer, Roger Kyle-Keith, PO Box 702, Bowie, MD 20718. 1989. Poetry, art, reviews. "Prefer poems of two pages or shorter. No style or subject biases; our only 'no-no' is fiction. We just don't have the space to print stories right now! We read throughout the year, but typically are slowest in December." circ. 200. 4/yr. Pub'd 4 issues 2009; expects 4 issues 2010, 4 issues 2011. sub. price $8; per copy $2.50; sample $2.50. Back issues: free for large SASE with 3 stamps postage. Discounts: schools, libraries and bulk; write for details. 48pp. Reporting time: 6 months. Simultaneous submissions accepted: yes. Publishes 5% of manuscripts submitted. Payment: in copies. Copyrighted, reverts to author. Pub's reviews: 20 in 2009. §Poetry chapbooks and literary magazines. Subject: Poetry.

Platinum Dreams Publishing, Jactesha Childress, P.O. Box 320693, Flint, MI 48532, jacki@InspiredToPublish.com, (810)720-3390, www.PlatinumDreamsPublishing.com. 2006. Fiction, non-fiction. Expects 1 title 2010, 3 titles 2011. 1 title listed in the *Small Press Record of Books in Print* (36th Edition, 2010-11). 250pp. Reporting time: 6-8 weeks. Simultaneous submissions accepted: No. Copyrights for author. Subjects: African-American, Christianity, Creative Non-fiction, Fiction, Mentoring/Coaching, Motivation, Success, Non-Fiction, Novels, Publishing, Relationships, Self-Help, Spiritual, Writers/Writing, Young Adult.

Platinum One Publishing, J. Shailander, Copy Editor; Jean Church, Editor Advisor, 30 Cooper Lake Road Suite A7, Mableton, GA 30126, www.platinumonepublishing.com, fax:1-203-651-1825, Email:customerservice@platinumonepublishing.com. 2003. Fiction, non-fiction. "Fiction or non Fiction, we tend to focus on the market for a particular manuscript first, its feasability and the companys' ROI. Once we acknowledge the solicited manascript market we will partner with the author. There will be a collaborative effort on the entire project." avg. press run 3000. Pub'd 1 title 2009; expects 1 title 2010, 2 titles 2011. No titles listed in the *Small Press Record of Books in Print* (36th Edition, 2010-11). Discounts: 3-10-20% or 55% for no returns and net 60. 250-350pp. Reporting time: two weeks. Simultaneous submissions accepted: No. Publishes 100% of manuscripts submitted. Payment: Royalty payments will consist of 15% of net sales asside from the resources allocated in the project. Copyrights for author. Subjects: Advertising, Self-Promotion, Children, Youth, Consulting, Cooking, Creativity, Divorce, Drama, Fiction, Health.

Platte Purchase Publishers, Jacqueline Lewin, PO Box 8096, 3406 Frederick Ave., St. Joseph, MO 64508-8096, (816) 232-8471, fax.(816) 232-8482, sjm@stjosephmuseum.org. 1992. Pub'd 2 titles 2009; expects 4 titles 2010, 4 titles 2011. 9 titles listed in the *Small Press Record of Books in Print* (36th Edition, 2010-11). Discounts: 40% discount for wholesale customers and educational institutions. Payment: Net 30. Subjects: Book Collecting, Bookselling, Civil War, Research, The West.

Playdate Kids Publishing, Tena Fanning, P.O. 2785, Malibu, CA 90265, 310-456-6400. 2006. Cartoons. "Playdate Kids Publishing specializes in social and developemental behaviors for children ages three to six. The colorful, 32 page books are entertaining for both parent and child. All books and DVDs are writeen to American Psychological Standards to ensure the advice is sound and trustworthy. All books contain interactivite activities and tips at the end of each book. The music books all include a catchy CD and sheet music to ensure the fun lives on at home, in the car or at school." avg. press run 5000. Pub'd 4 titles 2009; expects 7 titles 2010,

7 titles 2011. 11 titles listed in the *Small Press Record of Books in Print* (36th Edition, 2010-11). Discounts: Book Stores & Retailers: 50% off RP. 60% for Non-Returnables. Gift Shops: 50% off RP. Libraries & Schools: 30-50% discount Pending order amount. Wholesalers: 50% off RP. 60% for Non-Returnables. 32pp. Reporting time: Thirty Days. Simultaneous submissions accepted: No. Payment: New Authors, $1000 advance, 8% royalty. Copyrights for author. Subjects: Adoption, Animals, Audio/Video, Bilingual, Family, France, French, Juvenile Fiction, Parenting, Picture Books, Psychiatry, Publishing, Television.

Players Press, Inc., Robert W. Gordon, Vice President Editorial, PO Box 1132, Studio City, CA 91614-0132, 818-789-4980. 1965. Plays, non-fiction. avg. press run 2M-15M. Pub'd 28 titles 2009; expects 35 titles 2010, 35-50 titles 2011. 510 titles listed in the *Small Press Record of Books in Print* (36th Edition, 2010-11). Discounts: 20%-45% trade. 200pp. Reporting time: 3-6 months. Simultaneous submissions accepted: no. Publishes performing arts 12%, general 3% of manuscripts submitted. Payment: varies, dependent on material. Copyrights for author. Subjects: Arts, Avant-Garde, Experimental Art, Drama, Education, Entertainment, Shakespeare, Theatre.

PLEASANT LIVING, 5 South 1st St., Richmond, VA 23219-3716, 804-644-3091. 1989. Poetry, fiction, articles, photos, reviews, letters, non-fiction. "Material must be regionally oriented. Read a copy of our publication before submitting. Our readers are a diverse group, from 30-80 years of age, educated, interested in the Bay and its preservation and interested in reading clear, readable prose." circ. 30,000. 6/yr. Pub'd 6 issues 2009; expects 6 issues 2010, 6 issues 2011. sub. price $18; sample $5. Back issues: $5. Discounts: 50%. 40pp. Reporting time: 10 weeks. Simultaneous submissions accepted: yes. Publishes 25% of manuscripts submitted. Payment: varies. Copyrighted, reverts to author. Pub's reviews: 8 in 2009. §Nonfiction, fiction, poetry. Ads: $200 and up. Subjects: Environment, Family, Food, Eating, Gardening, History, Interviews, Leisure/Recreation, Lifestyles, Non-Fiction, Poetry, Reviews, Short Stories, Travel, Virginia, Wildlife.

Pleasure Boat Studio: A Literary Press (including imprints Caravel Books and Aequitas Books, and the division Empty Bowl Press), Jack Estes, 201 West 89 Street, New York, NY 10024-1848, 888-810-5308 fax, pleasboat@nyc.rr.com, www.pleasureboatstudio.com. 1996. Poetry, fiction, satire, criticism, non-fiction. "Pleasure Boat Studio is a publisher, primarily in trade paperback editions (occasional chapbooks), of the best poetry, fiction, and non-fiction (in English language original and translation) that it can find. Query via email only with sample and cover letter. But please read what we publish before submitting a query. So much of what we get really doesn't fit. Also a new imprint: Aequitas Books. Also a new division: Empty Bowl Press." avg. press run 300-5000. Pub'd 12 titles 2009; expects 12 titles 2010, 12 titles 2011. 47 titles listed in the *Small Press Record of Books in Print* (36th Edition, 2010-11). Discounts: 1 copy 0%, 2-4 20%, 5+ 40%. Poetry 64-96pp, fiction and non-fiction 180-300pp. Reporting time: Not always very fast. Sometimes six months or longer. Much better if you submit electronically. Simultaneous submissions accepted: yes. We are a very small press. Chances of publication with us are correspondingly small. Payment: standard royalty contract. Copyrights for author. Subjects: African-American, Alaska, Buddhism, China, Culture, Environment, Fiction, Gay, Non-Fiction, Novels, Philosophy, Poetry, Satire, Sociology, Translation.

PLEIADES: A Journal of New Writing, Wayne Miller, Editor; Phong Nguyen, Editor, Department of English, University of Central Missouri, Warrensburg, MO 64093. circ. 3000. 2 issues per year. sub. price $16/yr; per copy $8; sample $6. 240-280pp. Reporting time: 3 months, longer in summer. Simultaneous submissions accepted: yes. Publishes less than 1% of manuscripts submitted. Pub's reviews: 80+ in 2009. §We only publish reviews of poetry or small/university press fiction, criticism, and nonfiction. We publish more reviews than any other journal. We regularly feature 150+ pages of reviews in every issue. Ads: exchange ads, or price per page on query.

Plexus Publishing, Inc. (see also BIOLOGY DIGEST), Thomas H. Hogan, 143 Old Marlton Pike, Medford, NJ 08055, 609-654-6500. 1977. Non-fiction. "Publish a limited number of books on biology and natural history." avg. press run 2M. Expects 4 titles 2010, 4 titles 2011. 32 titles listed in the *Small Press Record of Books in Print* (36th Edition, 2010-11). Discounts: 40%. 200pp. Reporting time: 60 days. Payment: $500 advance against royalty of 10-15%. Copyrights for author. Subject: Science.

Pliant Press, 1943 Walnute Street, St. Paul, MN 55113. No titles listed in the *Small Press Record of Books in Print* (36th Edition, 2010-11).

PLOPLOP, Geekspeak Unique Press, John Clark; Kit Andis, Contributing Editor, ploplopt@yahoo.com. 1991. Poetry, fiction, articles, art, cartoons, interviews, satire, reviews, music, letters, parts-of-novels, collages, plays, concrete art, non-fiction. "Bukowski, Vonnegut, Fielding, Dawson, Eileen Myles, Kit Andis, Gerald Locklin, Edward Field, Hal Sirowitz, Ferlinghetti, Kuda LaBranch, and Dan Grossman. pLopLop prefers poetry that is witty and brief, concise and with impact. Open to most forms except for the extremely conventional and academic. Future issues will focus on surrealist collaborations, also known as Flap Action Brain Splashes. On-line submissions only to ploplopt@yahoo.com." circ. 300-500. 1/yr. Pub'd 1 issue 2009; expects 1 issue 2010, 1 issue 2011. sub. price $10; per copy $5; sample $5. Discounts: 20%. 50pp. Reporting time: 6-8 weeks.

Simultaneous submissions accepted: yes. Publishes 5% of manuscripts submitted. Payment: 1 copy. Copyrighted. Pub's reviews. §Avant-garde, experimental, humor, music-pop/rock, surrealist collaborations, dada experiments, fluxus elaborations. Subjects: Book Arts, Jack Kerouac, Henry Miller, Surrealism.

PLOUGHSHARES, Ladette Randolph, Editor; Andrea Drygas, Managing Editor, Emerson College, 120 Boylston Street, Boston, MA 02116, 617-824-8753. 1971. Poetry, fiction, parts-of-novels, long-poems. "Maximum length for prose is 30 doublespaced pages. Read an issue or two before submitting. In the past, we announced specific themes for issues, but we no longer restrict submissions to thematic topics. Some past contributors: Joseph Brodsky, Rita Dove, Garrett Kaoru Hongo, Seamus Heaney, Carol Frost, Sharon Olds, Joyce Carol Oates, Michael S. Harper, Mary Oliver, Phillip Lopate, Sue Miller, Gerald Stern. Reading period: June 1 to January 15(Postmark dates)." circ. 6M. 3/yr. Pub'd 3 issues 2009; expects 3 issues 2010, 3 issues 2011. 2 titles listed in the *Small Press Record of Books in Print* (36th Edition, 2010-11). sub. price $30/3 issues (individual), $27/3 issues (institutional), Add $1/yr for international. $50/6 issues (individual).; per copy $14. Back issues: prices vary. Discounts: 40% trade (6 copies or more); 10% agent. 224pp. Reporting time: 3-5 months. Simultaneous submissions accepted: yes. Publishes 1% of manuscripts submitted. Payment: $25/page prose, $50 minimum, $250 max. per author. Copyrighted, rights released on publication. Pub's reviews: 11 in 2009. §Quality literary poetry, fiction, non-fiction. We do not accept unsolicited reviews. Ads: $400/$275. Subjects: Criticism, Fiction, Literary Review, Poetry.

Pluma Productions, 1421 N Causeway Blvd., #200, Metairie, LA 70001-4144, email pluma@earthlink.net. 1992. Poetry. "Will only consider works by Southern Dominicans - a Roman Catholic Order of Religious priests and brothers." avg. press run 1.5M. Expects 1 title 2010, 1 title 2011. 2 titles listed in the *Small Press Record of Books in Print* (36th Edition, 2010-11). Discounts: 40%. 96pp. Simultaneous submissions accepted: no. Copyrights for author. Subject: Poetry.

PMS POEMMEMOIRSTORY, Tina Harris, Editor-in-Chief, English Dept., HB 217, 1530 3rd Avenue South, Birmingham, AL 35294-1260, 205-934-5380, Fax 205-975-8125, lfrost@uab.edu, www.pms-journal.org. 2001. Poetry, fiction, non-fiction. "Our three principle genres are those listed in our title: poetry, memoir, and short stories. We publish exclusively work by women (and those posing as women), and look simply for the best and most catchy work we receive to print. We are *not* a goddess-promoting, menses-celebrating, chick-flick revering publication; we do *not* favor work *about* PMS. On the other hand, we're not afraid to be politicized. In an attempt to enhance the arts in our home state, we make it a point to publish at least some work by writers from Alabama, although we are by no means a regional journal. In each issue, we feature one memoir that we solicit (although suggestions here are welcome) from a woman who would not describe herself as a writer, but who has experienced something of national and historic significance (e.g., our first issue featured a memoir by Emily Lyons, the nurse critically injured in the 1998 bombing of the women's clinic in Birmingham). Writers we have published include Cathleen Calbert, Vicki Covington, Denise Duhamel, Elaine Equi, Nikky Finney, Amy Gerstler, Honoree Fanonne Jeffers, Allison Joseph, MaryJo Mahoney, Kat Meads, Lucia Perillo, Molly Peacock, Paisley Rekdal, Carly Sachs, Sonia Sanchez, Lori Soderlind, Ruth Stone, Natasha Trethewey, and Harriet Zinnes. We love the up-and-coming as much as we do the established and famous. Work from PMS has been republished in Best American Poetry (twice), Best American Essays (twice), New Stories from the South, Best Creative Nonfiction (twice), and has recieved honorable mention in the Pushcart Prize. PMS is distributed by Ubiquity and Ingram Periodicals, Inc. We ask that submitters send up to five poems *or* fifteen pages of prose; not both. Our reading period each year is from January 1 through March 31." circ. 1000. 1/yr. Pub'd 1 issue 2009; expects 1 issue 2010, 1 issue 2011. sub. price $7; per copy $7; sample $7. Back issues: $6. 120pp. Reporting time: 2-8 weeks. Simultaneous submissions accepted: yes. Publishes 12% of manuscripts submitted. Payment: 2 copies and a 1-year subscription. Copyrighted, reverts to author. Subject: Poetry.

Pocahontas Press, Inc., Mary C. Holliman, President & Publisher, PO Drawer F, Blacksburg, VA 24063-1020, 540-951-0467, 800-446-0467. 1984. Poetry, non-fiction. "Our first trade book was the true story of the Golden Hill Indians of Connecticut told in the words of Chief Big Eagle. We are publishing a series of books for middle-school age children and teen-agers, short story length, in both Spanish and English with black-and-white illustrations; these are historical and biographical topics and most will be in the series Tales of the Virginia Wilderness. We are also interested in memoirs, family histories, poetry collections, and scientific monographs. We do not publish fiction unless it is closely tied to historical events and real people are main characters." avg. press run poetry 500, other 1M-3M. Pub'd 6 titles 2009; expects 3 titles 2010, 3 titles 2011. 40 titles listed in the *Small Press Record of Books in Print* (36th Edition, 2010-11). Discounts: for prepayment 5%, wholesalers: 1 20%, 2-50 40%, 51+ 50%. 80-180pp. Reporting time: 3 months or more. Simultaneous submissions accepted: yes. Publishes probally no more than 1% of manuscripts submitted. Payment: 10% royalty. Copyrights for author. Subjects: Americana, Appalachia, Autobiography, Bilingual, Biography, Children, Youth, Fiction, Folklore, History, Memoirs, Native American, Science, Virginia, Weather.

POCKETS, Lynn Gilliam, PO Box 340004, Nashville, TN 37203-0004, 615-340-7333, pockets@upper-room.org, www.pockets.org. 1978. Poetry, fiction, articles, art, photos, non-fiction. "The purpose of Pockets is the help children, ages six through twelve, grow in their relationship with God. Pockets is an interdenominational devotional magazine, with readers representing many cultures and ethnic backgrounds. Content reflects a variety of cultural backgrounds, rural and urban settings, and a variety of family units.The magazine presents an understanding of God that is whole and mature. We want to help children wrap themselves in Christian tradition and envision themselves in the light of that tradition. Through scripture, fiction, poetry, prayer, art, graphics, and activities, children see a Christian lifestyle that portrays an openness to the continuing revelation of God's will. The magazine emphasizes that God loves us and that God's grace calls us into community. Through this commuinty of God's people we experience God's love in our daily lives.Content encompasses a wide variety of concerns and needs. Each issue is thematic, based on issues faced by today's children. Pockets affirms children as persons created and loved by God. We strive to provide ways for them to experience God's love, to communicate with God, and to enable them to relate to people, to make decisions, and to learn how to show the love of God to others." 11/yr. Pub'd 11 issues 2009; expects 11 issues 2010, 11 issues 2011. sub. price $21.95; per copy $3.50; sample 9x12 SASE with 4 first-class stamps. Back issues: 9x12 SASE with 4 1st-class stamps. Discounts: 10 copies $17.50/issue20 copies $35.00/issue30 copies $52.50/issue. 48pp. Reporting time: maximum of 8 weeks. Simultaneous submissions accepted: No. Publishes 5% of manuscripts submitted. Payment: made at the time of acceptance. Copyrighted, rights are returned to author one year after publication and upon request of rights from the author. No advertising. Subject: Children, Youth.

Pocol Press, J. Thomas Hetrick, Box 411, Clifton, VA 20124-1333, 703-870-9611, chrisandtom@erols.com, www.pocolpress.com. 1999. Fiction, art, photos, interviews, non-fiction. "Pocol Press is the leader in short fiction collections and baseball history and fiction from first-time, non-agented authors. Expert storytellers welcome. Recent fiction contributors include Stephan Solberg with *The Last of One*, Brock Adams with *Gulf*, and *A Good Death* by David E. Lawrence. Other recent baseball books are *A Baseball Family Album* by Gene Carney, *The Fade-away* by George Jansen, and *A Whole New Ballgame: The 1969 Washington Senators* by Stephen Walker. Please see our website for more details, especially on purchasing and submissions. No electronic submissions, please. Distributed by Baker & Taylor." avg. press run 500. Pub'd 6 titles 2009; expects 3 titles 2010, 5 titles 2011. 45 titles listed in the *Small Press Record of Books in Print* (36th Edition, 2010-11). Discounts: 70% of cover price for bulk purchase from bookstores, 70% for classroom. 210pp. Reporting time: 1-3 months. Simultaneous submissions accepted: no. Payment: 1-2 payments per annum, 10% net. Copyrights for author. Subjects: Family, Fiction, Florida, Homelessness, Horror, India, Judaism, Memoirs, Poetry, Religion, San Francisco, Short Stories, Sports, Outdoors, Vietnam, World War II.

POEM, Rebecca Harbor, Editor; Georgette Perry, Assistant Editor; Nancy Compton Williams, Assistant Editor, P.O. Box 2006, Huntsville, AL 35804. 1967. Poetry. circ. 500. 2/yr. Pub'd 2 issues 2009; expects 2 issues 2010, 2 issues 2011. sub. price $20; per copy $10. Back issues: $7. 85pp. Reporting time: 1-2 months. Simultaneous submissions accepted: no. Publishes 5-6 % of manuscripts submitted. Payment: 2 copies. Copyrighted, reverts to author. Ads: none. Subject: Poetry.

POEMELEON: A Journal of Poetry, Cati Porter, Founder & Editor, Riverside, CA, Online at http://www.poemeleon.org/. "*Poemeleon: A Journal of Poetry* was founded in December of 2005. Each issue is devoted to a specific kind of poetry and features relevant poems, essays, book reviews and interviews. Themes so far have included the poetry of place, ekphrastic poetry, poems in form, the prose poem, the persona poem, humor, and gender. We have published poems by Sherman Alexie, Tony Barnstone, Richard Garcia, Eloise Klein Healy, Bob Hicok, Charles Harper Webb, Cecilia Woloch, and many others. Poemeleon is edited by Cati Porter (founder & editor-in-chief), Maureen Alsop, Judy Kronenfeld and Ren Powell (associate editors), and Tom Hunley (book review editor), and published twice per year. Submissions accepted via the online submission form only. No snail mail submissions, please." circ. Greater than 10,000 unique visitors per year. 2/yr. Yes. Pub's reviews: approx. 10 in 2009. §Individual collections of poetry as well as anthologies relevant to the theme of the issue. Subjects: Criticism, Essays, Interviews, Poetry, Reviews.

POEMS & PLAYS, Gaylord Brewer, Department of English, Middle Tennessee State University, Murfreesboro, TN 37132, 615-898-2712. 1993. Poetry, art, plays. "Recent contributors include Rane Arroyo, Nancy Naomi Carlson, and Robert Collins. Short plays (10-15 pgs.) have a better chance of publication. We *read* for this spring annual from Oct. 1-Nov. 30, either open submissions or 20-24 page manuscripts for the Tennessee Chapbook Prize. Contest entries can be any combo of poetry and drama. Winner is published as interior chapbook in *Poems & Plays*. Recent winners are Laura Maria Censabella (drama) and Julie Lechevsky (poetry). Author receives 50 copies of issue. For contest, SASE and $15 (for reading fee and one copy of issue) required. *Poems & Plays* was awarded a Pipistrelle, Best of the Small Presses Award in 2000." circ. 800. 1/yr. Pub'd 1 issue 2009; expects 1 issue 2010, 1 issue 2011. sub. price $10/2 issues; per copy $6; sample $6. Back issues: please call or write for availability. Discounts: please call/write. 80+pp. Reporting time: 1-2 months. Publishes 2% of manuscripts submitted. Payment: 1 copy. Copyrighted, reverts to author. Ads: none. Subjects: Drama, Poetry.

POESY, Brian Morrisey, Publisher; Doug Holder, Boston Editor; Melissa Pereria, Copy Editor, P.O. Box 7823, Santa Cruz, CA 95061, www.poesy.org, info@poesy.org. 1990. Poetry, articles, art, photos, interviews, criticism, reviews. "POESY MAGAZINE IS AN ANTHOLOGY for poets across the country. Poesy's main concentration is Boston, MA and Santa Cruz, CA, two thriving homesteads for poets and artists. Eastern and western poets rarely collaborate on publications. Our goal is to unite the two scenes, updating poets on what's happening across the country. Poesy is based in Santa Cruz, we have a Boston editor, Doug Holder, covering the Boston area. We publish inspirational poetry, reviews, interviews, articles, readings, and whatever fits best. Poesy is published biannually.The original intentions of Poesy is to bring a lighter notion to the table that promotes interesting and active verse that strays away from the dark and dry stereotypes that exist when referring to poetry by society. To achieve this goal, we have incorporated photography throughout our pages of each issue, that not only relate to the poems, but draw the eye into the page while discovering the words. The poems and photos compliment one another. Poesy strives to be the best literary journal on the market while remaining true to publishing poetry and art that pushes creative aura to its limits. Poetry is a breathtaking, artistic venture into the world of the unknown. It is about finding your voice and letting it be heard through outlets like Poesy." circ. 500. 2/yr. Pub'd 2 issues 2009; expects 2 issues 2010, 2 issues 2011. 1 title listed in the *Small Press Record of Books in Print* (36th Edition, 2010-11). sub. price $12.00; per copy $3; sample $3. Back issues: $3.00-5.00. 40pp. Reporting time: 6-8 weeks. Simultaneous submissions accepted: Yes, if extremely powerful. Publishes 5% of manuscripts submitted. Payment: A copy of the issue your work appears in and addition issues at cost. Copyrighted, reverts to author. Pub's reviews: 15 in 2009. §Poetry. Ads: $75 Full /$50 Half /$35 Quarter. Subjects: Photography, Poetry.

POET LORE, The Writer's Center, Jody Bolz, Executive Editor; E. Ethelbert Miller, Executive Editor; Caitlin Hill, Managing Editor; Jean Nordhaus, Book Review Editor, Poet Lore, 4508 Walsh Street, Bethesda, MD 20815-6006, 301-654-8664. 1889. Poetry, reviews, long-poems. "All material submitted for possible publication must include a SASE." circ. 1,000. 2/yr. Pub'd 2 issues 2009; expects 2 issues 2010, 2 issues 2011. sub. price $18 indiv., $28 instit., $12 Writer's Center members; per copy $9, $5 foreign postage; sample $5.50 plus $1 shipping. Back issues: $9 for double issues; $4.50 for earlier single issues. Discounts: agency 5%. 144pp. Reporting time: 2-4 months. Simultaneous submissions accepted: yes *indicate in cl*. Publishes 5% of manuscripts submitted. Payment: 2 copies of issue and 1 yr subscription. Copyrighted, reverts to author. Pub's reviews: 14 in 2009. §Small press poetry books, and poetry books published by major publishers & university presses. Ads: full pg$100/half pg$55. Subjects: Poetry, Reviews.

Poet Tree Press, Tom Worthen PhD, 1488 North 200 West, Logan, UT 84341-6803, 888-618-8444, Fax 435-713-4422, editor@poettreepress.com, www.poettreepress.com. 2000. Poetry. avg. press run 15M. Expects 2 titles 2010, 2 titles 2011. 1 title listed in the *Small Press Record of Books in Print* (36th Edition, 2010-11). Discounts: 40% trade. 248pp. Simultaneous submissions accepted: no. Publishes 10% of manuscripts submitted. Copyrights for author. Subjects: Children, Youth, Poetry.

POETALK, Bay Area Poets Coalition, Maggie Morley, Editor, PO Box 11435, Berkeley, CA 94712-2435, poetalk@aol.com, www.bayareapoetscoalition.org. 1974. Poetry. circ. 400. 2-4/yr. Pub'd 1 issue 2009; expects 2 issues 2010, 2 issues 2011. sub. price $15 membership (includes subscription and discount on contest entry fees); $5 subscription for two issues (please inquire for foreign rates); per copy $3; sample $2. Back issues: Most issues available from 1998 to present. 36pp. Reporting time: 2-6 months (sometimes longer). Simultaneous submissions accepted: yes. Publishes 20-30% of manuscripts submitted. Payment: one contributor's copy. Copyrighted, reverts to author. Ads: none. Subject: Poetry.

Poetic Matrix Press, John Peterson, Publisher, P.O. Box 1223, Madera, CA 93639, www.poeticmatrix.com, www.poeticmatrixpress.com, email- poeticmatrix@yahoo.com. 1997. Poetry, long-poems. "Poetic Matrix Press is a poetry press dedicated to publishing high quality poetry by poets who have something to say and the craft to say it. To peruse the Poetic Matrix Website go to www.poeticmatrix.com. The site includes poetry, essays and information on publications." Pub'd 4 titles 2009; expects 8 titles 2010, 6 titles 2011. No titles listed in the *Small Press Record of Books in Print* (36th Edition, 2010-11). Discounts: 40% retailers, 55% distributors, 55% wholesalers, 55% institutions, 55% classrooms. 88-160pp. Reporting time: 1-3 months. Payment: Royalty on books. Subjects: Buddhism, Haiku, Poetry, Yosemite, Zen.

POETICA MAGAZINE, Reflections of Jewish Thought, Michal Mahgerefteh, P.O.Box 11014, Norfolk, VA 23517, www.poeticamagazine.com. 2003. Poetry, fiction, art, photos, long-poems, non-fiction. "The goal of Poetica is to publish poetry, essays, and short stories (2-3 pages if well written) pertaining to Jewish subjects or presenting a Jewish point of view. We like poetry that builds around real experiences, and real characters, and that avoids abstractions and over philosophizing. Recent contributors are Ronald Pies, Rachel Barenblat, Judy Belsky, Ed Galing, Rochelle Mass, and Gilda Kreuter." circ. 250. 3/yr. Pub'd 3 issues 2009; expects 3 issues 2010, 3 issues 2011. sub. price $19.50; per copy $10.00; sample no charge. Back issues: inquire. 64pp. Reporting time: 2-3 month. Simultaneous submissions accepted: Yes. Payment: 1 copy per published piece. writers retain all rights to their work. Ads: $36.00 half page $54.00 full page. Subjects: Essays, Holocaust,

Judaism, Poetry, Prose, Reviews, Short Stories.

POETICS TODAY: International Journal for Theory and Analysis of Literature and Communication, Duke University Press, Meir Sternberg, Box 90660, Duke University, Durham, NC 27708-0660. *"Poetics Today* brings scholars from throughout the world who are concerned with developing systematic approaches to the study of literature (e.g. semiotics, structuralism, narratology) and with applying such approaches to the interpretation of literary works. *Poetics Today* presents a remarkable diversity of methodologies and examines a wide range of literary and critical topics. Several thematic review sections or special issues are published with each volume, and each issue contains a book review section, with article-length review essays. Send review copies to the Book Review Editor, *Poetics Today,* Porter Institute for Poetics and Semiotics, Tel Aviv University, Tel Aviv 69978, Israel." circ. 950. 4/yr. Pub'd 4 issues 2009; expects 4 issues 2010, 4 issues 2011. sub. price $92 institutions, $34 individuals, $17 students with photocopy of current I.D., additional $12 foreign. Pub's reviews. Ads: $225/$175.

POETRY, Christian Wiman, Editor, 444 North Michigan Ave., Suite 1850, Chicago, IL 60611-4034, tel 312-787-7070, fax 312-787-6650, email poetry@poetrymagazine.org, www.poetrymagazine.org, https:/ /submissions.poetrymagazine.org. 1912. Poetry, articles, criticism, reviews, letters, long-poems. circ. 30,000. 11/yr. Pub'd 11 issues 2009; expects 11 issues 2010, 11 issues 2011. 3 titles listed in the *Small Press Record of Books in Print* (36th Edition, 2010-11). sub. price individuals $35, $47 outside USA, institutions $38, $50 outside USA; per copy $3.75 plus $1.75 postage; sample $3.75 plus $1.75 postage. Back issues: $4.25 plus $1.75 postage. 92pp. Reporting time: 8 weeks. Simultaneous submissions accepted: no. Publishes less than 1% of manuscripts submitted. Payment: $150/page prose, $10/line verse. First serial rights. All rights revert to author upon publication. Pub's reviews: 70 in 2009. §Poetry, Criticism/Essays, and poetry-related novels and non-fiction. Ads: Full page $800; Half page $500; Quarter page $375. Subject: Poetry.

Poetry, Katheryn Sims, 22 Harris Rd, Salisbury East, South Australia, Australia, 08/ 8182 4117 or 0415 271 093. 2006. Poetry. "poetry all kinds from the heart." Pub'd 12 titles 2009; expects 50-100 titles 2010, 100-200 titles 2011. No titles listed in the *Small Press Record of Books in Print* (36th Edition, 2010-11). Discounts: Poetry. Subjects: Family, Fantasy, Lifestyles, Relationships.

The Poetry Center (see also THE PATERSON LITERARY REVIEW), Maria Mazziotti Gillan, Passaic County Community College, One College Boulevard, Paterson, NJ 07505-1179, 973-684-6555. 1977. Poetry, fiction, long-poems. 1 title listed in the *Small Press Record of Books in Print* (36th Edition, 2010-11). Simultaneous submissions accepted: YES. Subjects: Arts, Essays, Juvenile Fiction, Literary Review, Literature (General), Magazines, Multicultural, Poetry, Short Stories, Writers/Writing.

The Poetry Center Press/Shoestring Press, P.M. Morrison; Bill Johnson, Associate Editor, 3 Monte Vista Road, Orinda, CA 94563, 925-254-6639. 1986. Poetry, fiction, non-fiction. "Have published fine limited letter-press editions as well as modest chapbooks and hardcover and perfect bound editions. Professional consultation and assistance to self-publishers." avg. press run 250-5M. Pub'd 5 titles 2009; expects 6 titles 2010, 8 titles 2011. 9 titles listed in the *Small Press Record of Books in Print* (36th Edition, 2010-11). Discounts: trade, wholesale. Payment: negotiated. Copyrights for author. Subjects: Book Arts, How-To, Humor, Inspirational, Motivation, Success, Poetry, Printing, Self-Help, Senior Citizens.

POETRY DAILY, Don Selby, Editor; Diane Boller, Editor, PO Box 1306, Charlottesville, VA 22902-1306, Phone & Fax: 434-971-4001. *"Poetry Daily* is an online anthology of poetry published by The Daily Poetry Association. Poems featured on *Poetry Daily* are chosen from books or journals currently or imminently available in print or online. We do not publish previously unpublished work and cannot accept unsolicited manuscripts of original poetry."

POETRY DEPTH QUARTERLY, Joyce Odam, Editor; G. Elton Warrick, Publisher, 5836 North Haven Drive, North Highlands, CA 95660, 916-331-3512, e-mail: poetrydepthquarterly.com NO download or attached files accepted. Prefers postal submissions with S.A.S.E. Magazine established in 1995. For Art guidelines and submissions of photographs and original art,: Art Editors, Carol and Gerald Wheeler, e mail: csw@houston.rr.com Postal address: 1811 Brookchester Street, Katy, Texas 77450. Poetry, art. "Cover letter *required* with short 3-10 line biography. All poems must be in English, typewritten and presented exactly as you would like them to appear. Due to the page size, only 52 characters will fit across the page, including spaces. Poems of any length are considered, but each work must be the original property of the submitting poet. Send 3-5 poems. Your name and address must appear on each page submitted. For non e-mail submissions: include an SASE." circ. 200. 4/yr. Pub'd 4 issues 2009; expects 4 issues 2010, 4 issues 2011. sub. price $20/yr; $38/2 years, $56/3 years; add $12 a year for foreign postage; per copy $5.50; sample $5.50. Back issues: $5.50. 35-60pp. Reporting time: 2 weeks to 3 months. Simultaneous submissions accepted: no. Publishes 5-10% of manuscripts submitted. Payment: author/contributor receives 1 copy. Copyrighted, reverts to author.

Poetry Direct, Brian Levison, Rip Bulkeley, 6 Princes Street, Oxford, OX4 1DD, United Kingdom, ++44-1865791202 :: editors@poetry-direct.com :: http://www.poetry-direct.com. 2003. Poetry, long-poems.

"Poetry Direct is a regionally focussed 'not-for-loss' publisher (central southern England) and we do not read or respond to totally unsolicited complete MSS. That said, we are already building a reputation for good poetry and very high production values. So if you really are the next Derek Walcott, by all means send us a sample of your work by email (maximum 6 shortish poems) and we will certainly get back to you." avg. press run 200. Pub'd 3 titles 2009; expects 1-2 titles 2010, 1-2 titles 2011. No titles listed in the *Small Press Record of Books in Print* (36th Edition, 2010-11). Discounts: Retailers - 33%. 90pp. Reporting time: Eight weeks. Simultaneous submissions accepted: No. Publishes 25% of manuscripts submitted. Payment: Informal - profits will be shared equitably if there are any, and authors have access to our accounts. Does not copyright for author. Subject: Poetry.

•**Poetry Dispatch,** Norbert Blei Editor, http://poetrydispatch.wordpress.com/. "The online column began in August of 2005 at 6:52 in the morning and the poems have kept coming at me (dispatched to you) ever since, whenever time allows. Im not sure what inspired the first one, except no doubt a poem I had read the night before that worked its way inside me and begged to be passed on to others come daylight.Poetry Dispatch elicits none of my own writing but for occasional commentary on the poet or poem at hand. My role is to disseminate, to call attention to the work of others. Which hopefully might garner enough interest in the poets work to read more of it, purchase a book, even write or refine ones own poems."

POETRY EAST, Richard Jones, Editor; Meredith Ferrill, Assistant Editor, Dept. of English, DePaul Univ., 802 West Belden Avenue, Chicago, IL 60614-3214, 773-325-7487, www.poetryeast.org. 1980. Poetry, fiction, articles, art, photos, interviews, criticism, reviews, letters, collages, concrete art, news items. "The journal is published twice each year, in the spring and autumn. We are open to all subject areas - the political, the spiritual, the personal. Our only criterion for selection is excellence, but we are partial to poems that have some fire to them." 2/yr. Pub'd 2 issues 2009; expects 2 issues 2010, 2 issues 2011. sub. price $15; per copy $10, $15 for anthologies; sample $8. Back issues: #9/10 *Art & Guns: Political Poetry* $20; #19 *The Inward Eye: the Photographs of Ed Roseberry* $10; #43 *Origins* $15. Discounts: bookstores 20%. 100pp for single issue, 200pp for double issue. Reporting time: 4 months. Simultaneous submissions accepted: Yes. Publishes less than 5% of manuscripts submitted. Payment: Copies of issue. Copyrighted, reverts to author. Ads: none. Subjects: Fiction, Literary Review, Literature (General), Poetry, Translation.

THE POETRY EXPLOSION NEWSLETTER (THE PEN), Arthur C. Ford, PO Box 4725, Pittsburgh, PA 15206-0725, 1-866-234-0297, wewuvpoetry@hotmail.com. 1985. Poetry. "We use poetry of max. length 30 lines, and prose max. 200-300 words. Rhyme and non-rhyme. Submit a max. of 5 poems, SASE and $1 reading fee." circ. 350. 4/yr. Pub'd 4 issues 2009; expects 4 issues 2010, 4 issues 2011. sub. price $20; sample $4. Back issues: $4. 10-15pp. Reporting time: 2-4 weeks. Simultaneous submissions accepted: yes. Publishes 10-15% of manuscripts submitted. Payment: copies. Copyrighted, reverts to author. Pub's reviews: 2 in 2009. §Poetry, prose. Ads: $100/$50/$25 1/4 page/$10 bus. card. Subject: Poetry.

POETRY FLASH, Joyce Jenkins, Publisher & Editor; Richard Silberg, Associate Editor, 1450 Fourth Street #4, Berkeley, CA 94710, 510-525-5476, Fax 510-525-6752. 1972. Poetry, articles, art, photos, interviews, criticism, reviews, collages, news items. "*Poetry Flash*, A Poetry Review & Literary Calendar for the West, publishes reviews, essays, interviews, poems, and calls for submissions. Our primary editorial focus is poetry, but we do review literary and experimental fiction, interview fiction writers, and cover every genre and kind of literary event in our event calendar. The intention is to review and publish high quality work of interest to writers in California, the Northwest, Southwest and beyond. We publish established and emerging poets and writers who may live in any geographical location. Queries should be made for reviews and interviews; poems may be sent with SASE. Occasional double-numbered issues." circ. 22M. 4/yr. Pub'd 4 issues 2009; expects 4 issues 2010, 4 issues 2011. sub. price $12 for four issues, $22 for eight.; per copy free at bookstores, libraries, cafes, art centers or by subscription; sample one copy free on request. Back issues: $2-$5 depending on year. 52-60pp. Reporting time: 4 months. Simultaneous submissions accepted: Yes, with notification. Publishes 10% of manuscripts submitted. Payment: 2-year subscription for poems, payment for articles. Copyrighted, reverts to author. Pub's reviews: 150 in 2009. §Poetry, experimental or literary fiction, criticism or biography, especially poetry related. Ads: $630/$315/$15.75 column inch. Subjects: Book Reviewing, Criticism, Poetry.

Poetry Harbor (see also NORTH COAST REVIEW), Patrick McKinnon, Ellie Schoenfeld, PO Box 202, Kailua Kona, HI 96745-0202. 1992. avg. press run 1M. Pub'd 2 titles 2009; expects 2 titles 2010, 2 titles 2011. 9 titles listed in the *Small Press Record of Books in Print* (36th Edition, 2010-11). Discounts: 40% booksellers; 55% wholesalers. 56pp. Reporting time: 1-6 months. Simultaneous submissions accepted: yes. Publishes 20% of manuscripts submitted. Payment: $10 + copies. Copyrights for author. Subjects: Michigan, Minnesota, Native American, The North, Poetry, Wisconsin.

POETRY INTERNATIONAL, Ilya Kaminsky, Editor; Jenny Minniti-Shippey, Managing Editor, Dept. of English and Comparative Literature, SDSU, 5500 Campanile Drive, San Diego, CA 92182-6020, Telephone: (619) 594-1522, Fax: (619) 594-4998. "New poems from emerging and well established poets. Translations from around the world translated into English. Our translators have included the late John Frederick Nims, W.S.

Merwin, Robert Bly, Lisa Katz, Mark Weiss and Martha Collins. A feature section showcasing the poetry of one nation, such as Russia, Israel, Vietnam, and Cuba or the work of a single poet such as William Matthews. Book reviews offering commentary on poetry anthologies, books by individual poets, and poetic criticism. Art from around the world. The Inaugural Poetry International Prize - $1,000. We do not accept email submissions." Annual. sub. price $15/year. $30/2years. $45/3years.; per copy $15. Back issues: See website: http://poetryinternational.sdsu.edu/Bookstore.htm. 350pp. Simultaneous submissions accepted: Yes. Please notify us when accepted elsewhere. Payment: Pays 1 copy. Pub's reviews.

POETRY KANTO, Alan Botsford, Co-editor; Nishihara Katsumasa, Co-editor, Kanto Gakuin University, Kamariya Minami 3-22-1, Kanazawa-Ku, Yokohama 236-8502, Japan. 1984. Poetry. "Poetry Kanto has both a cross-cultural and literary mission. Seeks well-crafted original poems in English, as well as Japanese poems in English translation (for translations, include Japanese originals/or query first: alan@kanto-gakuin.ac.jp). Some recent contributors include: Patricia Smith, Gwyneth Lewis, Vijay Seshadri, Harryette Mullen, Rigoberto Gonzalez, Ellen Bass, Tamura Ryuichi, Taguchi Inuo, Masayo Koike. Reads between December through April. (check website at: http://home.kanto-gakuin.ac.jp/~kg061001/." circ. 800. 1/yr. Pub'd 1 issue 2009; expects 1 issue 2010, 1 issue 2011. 2 titles listed in the *Small Press Record of Books in Print* (36th Edition, 2010-11). Back issues: send reply coupons to cover air mail or sea mail. 130pp. Simultaneous submissions accepted: no. Publishes 10% of manuscripts submitted. Payment: 5 contributor's copies. Not copyrighted. Ads: none. Subject: Poetry.

Poetry London, Maurice Riordan, Poetry Editor, 6 Daniels Road, London SE15 3LR, United Kingdom. "*Poetry London* is an international poetry magazine where new poets share pages with acclaimed contemporary poets. We also publish a wide range of poetry in translation. Send a maximum of six poems."

THE POETRY MISCELLANY, Richard Jackson, 423-425-4238, Richard-Jackson@utc.edu. 1971. Poetry, interviews, criticism, reviews, long-poems. "David Wagoner, Denise Levertov, Tomaz Salamun, Mark Strand, Laura Jensen, Richard Wilbur, Donald Justice, James Tate, Dara Wier, Carol Muske, Maxine Kumin, Robert Penn Warren, Marvin Bell, Jean Valentine, David St. John, A.R. Ammons, Stanley Kunitz, Charles Simic, John Hollander, Linda Pastan, William Stafford, John Haines, Pamela Stewart, Galway Kinnell, W. S. Merwin, William Meredith, Laurence Raab, Cynthia MacDonald, Robert Pack, Carolyn Forche, Anthony Hecht, John Ashbery, Donald Finkel, Michael Harper, Robert Creeley, David Ignatow, Donald Hall, Heather McHugh, Sharon Olds, Stanley Plumly, William Matthews. Review essays 1M words must be assigned/approved in advance. We use translations too." Now published mainly online. 1/yr. Pub'd 1 issue 2009; expects 1 issue 2010, 1 issue 2011. sub. price $10 for hard copies; per copy $10 for hard copy; sample $10 look online at English department, UT-Chattanooga. Back issues: Limited, same price as current issues + postage. 60pp. Reporting time: 3 months. Simultaneous submissions accepted: yes. Publishes 1% of manuscripts submitted. Payment: 1 copy. Copyrighted, rights revert to author upon request as for re-publication. Pub's reviews: 4 in 2009. §Poetry, poetics. Ads: $50 1/2 page. Subjects: Criticism, Poetry, Translation.

•**POETRY NORTHWEST,** Everett Community collge, 2000 Tower St., Everett, WA 98201. "*Poetry Northwest* is published semi-annually in April and October. We also publish new work on our website, between our print editions. All work submitted to us during our reading period will be considered for the print editions, the website, or both, at the editors discretion.We welcome unsolicited submissions of poetry only, original or in translation, at this time. Please submit no more than five poems at a time, and no more than one submission per reading period. Simultaneous submissions are accepted with advance indication and prompt notice upon acceptance elsewhere.Please note that our reading period begins on September 15 and ends on April 15. Manuscripts submitted outside this period will be returned unread. We understand that getting a decision quickly is important, and our goal is to respond to unsolicited submissions in 6-8 weeks. Please be patient. We read everything carefully. Enclose an SASE for notification. Manuscripts will be recycled. We cannot consider anything that has been previously published or accepted for publication in any form, including work that has appeared online. Due to the large volume of submissions we receive, we cannot offer individual criticism. Poems submitted should be in English. When submitting translations, please include both English and origianl versions."

POETRY NOW, Sacramento's Literary Review and Calendar, Heather Hutcheson, 1719 25th St., Sacramento, CA 95816, 916-441-7395, poetrynow@sacramentopoetrycenter.org, www.sacramentopoetry-center.org. 1994. Poetry, articles, photos, interviews, criticism, reviews. circ. 1M + website. 12/yr. Pub'd 12 issues 2009; expects 12 issues 2010, 12 issues 2011. sub. price $25; per copy $3; sample $3. Back issues: n/a. Discounts: call for information. 8pp. Reporting time: 1-3 months. Simultaneous submissions accepted: yes. Publishes 20% of manuscripts submitted. Payment: none. Not copyrighted. Pub's reviews: 4+ in 2009. §Poetry, performance or reading of poetry. Ads: call for information/3 X 5=$20/month. Subjects: Poetry, Reviews.

The Poetry Project (see also THE POETRY PROJECT NEWSLETTER; THE WORLD), Editorial Staff, St. Mark's Church, 131 East 10th Street, New York, NY 10003, 212-674-0910, poproj@thorn.net. 1966. Poetry, fiction, art, photos, long-poems, non-fiction. "We mainly publish solicited work." avg. press run

4,000'/800 respectively. Pub'd 1 title 2009; expects 1 title 2010, 1 title 2011. No titles listed in the *Small Press Record of Books in Print* (36th Edition, 2010-11). Discounts: none. 128pp. Reporting time: 6 months. Simultaneous submissions accepted: yes. Publishes 5% of manuscripts submitted. Payment: copies. Does not copyright for author. Subject: Poetry.

THE POETRY PROJECT NEWSLETTER, The Poetry Project, St. Mark's Church, 131 East 10th Street, New York, NY 10003, 212-674-0910, poproj@thorn.net. 1966. Poetry, fiction, articles, art, interviews, criticism, reviews, letters. "We also list events scheduled at the Poetry Project and publications received." circ. 4M. 5/yr. Pub'd 5 issues 2009; expects 5 issues 2010, 5 issues 2011. sub. price $20; per copy $5; sample $5. Back issues: $5 if available. Discounts: none. 32pp. Reporting time: 2 months. Simultaneous submissions accepted: no. Publishes 5% of manuscripts submitted. Payment: copies. Copyrighted, reverts to author. Pub's reviews: 40 in 2009. §Poetry. Ads: $250/$160/$60-250. Subjects: Avant-Garde, Experimental Art, Literary Review, Literature (General), Poetry.

POETRY REVIEW, Fiona Sampson Dr, 22 Betterton Street, London WC2H 9BX, England. 1912. Poetry, articles, photos, interviews, criticism, reviews, letters, long-poems. circ. 5M. 4/yr. Pub'd 4 issues 2009; expects 4 issues 2010. sub. price $56 individuals, $70 institutions, all airmail; per copy $10 surface; $15 airmail; sample $10 surface, $15 airmail. Back issues: $10 surface, $15 airmail. Discounts: 1/3 to trade. 128pp. Reporting time: 3 months. Payment: £40- £120 per poem, up to £250 per esay, dependent on length. Copyrighted, reverts to author. Pub's reviews: 120 in 2009. §Poetry, criticism, relevant novels, biographies/autobiographies, belle-lettres, etc. Ads: £250/£170/£300 back page/£85 1/4 page/£275 3,500 loose inserts. Subject: Poetry.

POETRYREPAIRS: Contemporary International Poetry, John Horvath Jr, 222 Melrose Drive, Jackson, MS 39211. 1997. Poetry, articles, interviews, criticism, reviews, letters, long-poems. "new and established international poets who write social narrative in which persona is a type or representative of broader group. Bias against rhymed, strictly biographical, and religious (visionary) poems. Poets know good poetry, its traditions and devices, and when to break rules. Essays 500-1000 words, related to fine arts, expecially the art of writing. Since 1997 at http://www.poetryrepairs.com. Lyn Lifshin, Gabor Gyukics, Elisha Porat, Pia Taavila, Anjana Basu, Garland Strother, Christina Pacosz." circ. 1000. 12/yr. Pub'd 12 issues 2009; expects 12 issues 2010, 12 issues 2011. 36pp. Reporting time: 1 to 3 months. Simultaneous submissions accepted: Yes. Publishes 25% of manuscripts submitted. No payment. Copyrighted, reverts to author. Subjects: Arts, Bilingual, Criticism, Culture, Disabled, Human Rights, Humanism, Indigenous Cultures, Literary Review, Multicultural, Philosophy, Poetry, Social Movements, Society, Third World, Minorities.

POETS & WRITERS MAGAZINE, Poets & Writers, Inc., Kevin Larimer, Editor, 90 Broad Street, Suite 2100, New York, NY 10004, 212-226-3586, Fax 212-226-3963, www.pw.org. 1973. Articles, photos, interviews, letters, concrete art, news items, non-fiction. "Subscription orders: Poets & Writers Magazine, PO Box 422460, Palm Coast, FL 32142-2460, 386-246-0106, email poets&writers@emailcustomerservice.com. *Poets & Writers Magazine* publishes factual articles of interest to writers, editors, publishers, and all others interested in contemporary American literature. It also publishes essays, interviews with writers, and news and comments on publishing, political issues, grants and awards, and requests for submissions. Most articles are written by freelance writers. Always send a letter of inquiry to the editor prior to submitting a manuscript. *Poets & Writers Magazine* has a Letters column and encourages comments from readers. *Poets & Writers Magazine* does not review poetry or fiction." circ. 60,000. 6/yr. Pub'd 6 issues 2009; expects 6 issues 2010, 6 issues 2011. sub. price $19.95, $38/2 yrs for individuals; per copy $5.95; sample $5.95. Back issues: $3.95 prior to 1999, after $4.95. Discounts: bookstores, min. 10 copies, 40%; to distributors, min. 10 copies, 50%; to teachers, for bulk subscriptions, min. 20, 20% to one address. 120pp. Reporting time: 2 months. Simultaneous submissions accepted: yes. Publishes 10% of manuscripts submitted. Payment: $150-$500. Copyrighted, reverts to author. Ads: $2,600/$1,475, less 20% at 6X rate; classifieds $120 up to 50 words, over 50 $2.50 per add'l word. Subjects: Creative Non-fiction, Fiction, Poetry.

Poets & Writers, Inc. (see also POETS & WRITERS MAGAZINE), Thesese Eiben, Editor, 72 Spring Street, New York, NY 10012, 212-226-3586, Fax 212-226-3963, www.pw.org. 1970. Articles, photos, interviews, letters, concrete art, news items, non-fiction. "Poets & Writers publishes *A Directory of American Poets and Fiction Writers*, 2001-2002 Edition, a listing of contact names, addresses, phone numbers, e-mail and website addresses and publications for over 7,400 poets, fiction writers, and performance writers." avg. press run 3M. Expects 1 title 2010. 1 title listed in the *Small Press Record of Books in Print* (36th Edition, 2010-11). Discounts: distributed through Small Press Distribution, 1341 7th Street, Berkeley, CA 94710-1403, 510-524-1668. Pages vary. Subjects: Fiction, Literature (General), Poetry, Reference.

POETS AT WORK, Jessee Poet Publications, Jessee Poet, PO Box 232, Lyndora, PA 16045. 1985. Poetry. "Length—about 20 lines and under. I publish everyone who writes in good taste. William Middleton, Ralph Hammond, Ann Gasser, and at least 300 other poets. I am a marvelous market for unpublished poets." circ. 300+. 6/yr. Pub'd 6 issues 2009; expects 6 issues 2010, 6 issues 2011. sub. price $23; per copy $4; sample $4. Back issues: $4 when available. 40pp. Reporting time: 2 weeks. Simultaneous submissions accepted and I accept previously published material (poetry). Publishes nearly 100% of manuscripts submitted. Payment: none. Copyrighted, reverts to author. Ads: negotiable. Subject: Poetry.

POETS ON THE LINE, Linda Lerner, PO Box 20292, Brooklyn, NY 11202-0292, 718-596-0137. 1995. Poetry, interviews, non-fiction. *"No unsolicited manuscripts.* Nos. 9&10 came out 1/2000 (double millennium issue) and will be the last regular issue to come out. There may be an occasional special issue of *POTL,* no plans as of yet. In this issue are: W.D. Ehrhart, Lynne Savitt, Kell Robertson, Janine Pommy Vega, Tony Moffat, Jack Micheline, Todd Moore, and others.)." 2/yr. Pub'd 1-2 issues 2009; expects 1 issue 2010, 1 issue 2011. 31pp. Payment: none. Copyrighted, reverts to author. Subject: Poetry.

POETS' ROUNDTABLE, Esther Alman, 3172 South Offield Monument Road, Crawfordsville, IN 47933-6933, 812-234-0819. 1939. Poetry, news items. *"Poets' Rountable* is a bulletin published bimonthly for members of Poets' Study Club. It is not an open market for poetry. Open contests: One annual open competition—The International Contest, with awards of $25 and $15 in three categories: serious poems, light verse, traditional haiku. No entry fees. Deadline is February 1st each year. Send entries to Annual International Contest, Esther Alman, 826 South Center Street, Terre Haute, IN 47807. We use *only* material by members for publication, but annual contest is open to everyone. We keep manuscripts in a file, but will return on request, for publication of poems *by members only."* circ. 2M. 6/yr. Pub'd 6 issues 2009; expects 6 issues 2010, 6 issues 2011. sub. price $15 membership; sample free. 12pp. Payment: none. Copyrighted, reverts to author. Pub's reviews: 25 in 2009. No ads. Subjects: Haiku, Magazines, Poetry.

Poets Wear Prada, Roxanne Hoffman, 533 Bloomfield Street, 2nd Floor, Hoboken, NJ 07030, (201)795-3810. 2006. Poetry, art, cartoons, long-poems, collages. "Small press based in Hoboken, New Jersey devoted to introducing new authors through limited edition, high-quality chaplets and chapbooks, primarily of poetry. Currently, all chapbook submissions are by invitation only. However, unsolicited submissions are accepted for annual anthology. 2010/2011 Topic for Anthology: Rituals. Please visit our blog spot (http://pwpbooks.blogspot.com) for submission guidelines." avg. press run 200. Pub'd 6 titles 2009; expects 8 titles 2010, 8 titles 2011. 25 titles listed in the *Small Press Record of Books in Print* (36th Edition, 2010-11). Discounts: 10 or more copies 10%. 20pp. Reporting time: 3 months. Simultaneous submissions accepted: Yes. Payment: For chapbooks. 10 free copies as payment. Additional author copies at 1/2 off cover. For Anthologies. 1 Free Copy as payment. 25% Discount on Author Copies. 1st North American Rights. Returned to author after publication. Subject: Poetry.

POETSWEST ONLINE, Barbara A. Evans, Editor; J. Glenn Evans, Poetry Editor, 1100 University St., #17A, Seattle, WA 98101, 206-682-1268, JGE@poetswest.com, www.poetswest.com. 1988. Poetry. "General poetry published online. Submit 6 poems not to exceed 50 lines each. Poetry changes quarterly. Unscheduled hard copy anthology of poems selected from previously published online poems from time to time. Author contacted for permission. Publishes 25% of poems submitted. Simultaneous and previous published poems okay. Include previous publication credits. Publish one to four book reviews per year. No payment other than exposure. Reporting time two months. Copyright reverts to author." Back issues: 1998-2002 issues in print: 3 or more $2 each. Simultaneous submissions accepted: yes. Publishes 25% of manuscripts submitted. Authors retain copyrights. Pub's reviews: 4 in 2009. §Poetry books and chapbooks. Ads: none. Subject: Poetry.

Pogo Press, Incorporated, Moira F. Harris, 4 Cardinal Lane, St. Paul, MN 55127, 651-483-4692, fax 651-483-4692, E-mail pogopres@minn.net. 1986. Art, non-fiction. "Submission by prearrangement only." avg. press run 3M. Pub'd 3 titles 2009; expects 3 titles 2010, 3 titles 2011. 22 titles listed in the *Small Press Record of Books in Print* (36th Edition, 2010-11). Discounts: query. Pages vary. Reporting time: 60 days. Simultaneous submissions accepted: no. Payment: negotiable. Copyrights for author. Subjects: Architecture, Arts, Culture, Essays, Florida, History, Humor, Military, Veterans, Minnesota, Music, Native American, Theatre, Travel.

POGO STICK, Lillian Kopaska-Merkel, 1300 Kicker Road, Tuscaloosa, AL 35404, 553-2284, uniquewish@juno.com. 2004. Poetry, fiction, art, cartoons. "Only work by people under 17." circ. 100. 4/yr. Expects 1 issue 2010, 4 issues 2011. sub. price $12; per copy $4; sample $4. Back issues: $4. 19pp. Reporting time: up to 2 months. Simultaneous submissions accepted: yes. Publishes 70% of manuscripts submitted. Payment: 1 copy of magazine. Not copyrighted. Ads: $2/$1.50/$1. Subjects: Fantasy, Fiction, Juvenile Fiction, Poetry, Science Fiction, Short Stories, Visual Arts, Young Adult.

POIESIS, Propaganda Press, Leah Angstman, PO Box 398058, Cambridge, MA 02139, alt-current.com, alt.current@gmail.com. 2007. Poetry, art, long-poems, collages. "This litzine is a poetry-only various-author chapbook. We accept poetry of all types, genres, lengths, subjects, styles. No bios or author photos, no cover letters with tremendous resumes; we don't care where you have been published, just that your words are awesome. Pick your one or two favorite poem(s) and send it/them to us. We do not want to be inundated with poems, as this litzine comes out twice a year with only one poem published per author per issue. Save a tree: one or two poems, short hello letter telling us your submission wishes. No homophobic or racist material, but mostly uncensored and open to submissions all year long. Deadlines are June 1st and December 1st of each year to go into the next issues that will be printed in January and July of each year. Subscriptions are $5 US for one-year, $9 US for two-year, and $22 US for five-year; $9 out-of-US for one-year; $16 out-of-US for two-year; $35 out-of-US for five-year. Authors do not receive royalties; all profits go back into the press. Black and white cover artwork submissions accepted. One free copy for authors if work appears in the issue." circ. 500. 2/yr. Pub'd 1 issue 2009; expects 2 issues 2010, 2 issues 2011. sub. price $5; per copy $3. Back issues: $3. Discounts: Free copy for distributors/reviewers/retailers to check out for possible distribution or review. Free copies for libraries and zine archives. Distribution discount prices are available and vary depending on page numbers and at-cost price. 50pp. Reporting time: We respond to all submissions immediately, usually within a day or two. Please provide an email address for quickest response. Simultaneous submissions accepted: Yes. Publishes 50% of manuscripts submitted. We do not officially purchase a copyright, but all material is listed as copyrighted to the authors, and the magazine is copyrighted to the press. All authors retain their own copyrights and can use their materials elsewhere at any time. Ads: No advertising in this litzine. Subject: Poetry.

POINT OF CONTACT, The Journal of Verbal & Visual Arts, Pedro Cuperman, Owen Shapiro, 216 H.B. Crouse Building, Syracuse University, Syracuse, NY 13244-1160, 315-443-2247, Fax 315-443-5376, cfawcett@syr.edu, www.pointcontact.org. 1975. Poetry, photos, interviews, criticism, parts-of-novels, long-poems, concrete art, non-fiction. "Journal of creative scholarship in the arts. Some recent contributors include: Robert Ashley, Alicia Borinsky, Trisha Brown, Pedro Cuperman, Elka Krajewska, Marco Maggi, Jeffrey Mehlman, Nam June Paik, Raimon Panikkar, Liliana Porter, Izhar Patkin, Ana Tiscornia, Owen Shapiro, Andy Waggoner, Wayne Wang. Text and art contributions by invitation only." circ. 200. 2/yr. Expects 2 issues 2010, 2 issues 2011. sub. price $40, $60 institutions; per copy $20; sample $10. Back issues: $20. Discounts: negotiable. 100pp. Reporting time: 3-6 months. Simultaneous submissions accepted: no. Payment: none. Copyrighted, does not revert to author. Ads: $300/$175. Subjects: Arts, Avant-Garde, Experimental Art, Caribbean, Culture, Electronics, English, Feminism, Language, Latin America, Latino, Literature (General), Multicultural, Puerto Rico, Translation, U.S. Hispanic.

Poisoned Pen Press, 6962 E. First Avenue #103, Scottsdale, AZ 85251, 480-945-3375, Fax 480-949-1707, info@poisonedpenpress.com. 1997. Fiction. "Only interested in mystery-fiction." No titles listed in the *Small Press Record of Books in Print* (36th Edition, 2010-11). Copyrights for author.

Polar Bear & Company, Paul Cornell du Houx, Editor, PO Box 311, Solon, ME 04979-0311, 207-643-2795, www.polarbearandco.com, polarbear@polarbearandco.com. 1991. Poetry, fiction, articles, art, photos, cartoons, satire, criticism, letters, long-poems, plays, news items, non-fiction. "Understanding how truth is projected by fiction and how nonfiction can develop the imagination is a key to our publishing philosophy. We are looking for the clarity that tends to enhance the natural environment and our sense of equal opportunity. For example, we have published David Cook's *Above the Gravel Bar: The Native Canoe Routes of Maine*, which, in the words of James Eric Francis, Sr., tribal historian of the Penobscot Nation, puts the true ancestral landscape into perspective. Likewise, in his memoir, *My Tainted Blood*, professor emeritus of German, Hubert C. Kueter, gives us the perspective of foraging to feed family and friends while being half-Jewish under Nazi rule and after WWII: a picaresque adventure filled with unexpected hilarity against such a background. The title of Prof. Charles A. Ferguson's new translation, *Venice and the Water: A Model for the Planet* speaks for itself as well as for Polar Bear & Company." Pub'd 3 titles 2009; expects 7 titles 2010, 7 titles 2011. 25 titles listed in the *Small Press Record of Books in Print* (36th Edition, 2010-11). Simultaneous submissions accepted: Yes. Payment: individual. Copyrights for author. Subjects: Autobiography, Biography, Crime, Essays, Fiction, Juvenile Fiction, Literature (General), Maine, Memoirs, Mystery, Myth, Mythology, Non-Fiction, Novels, Poetry, Short Stories.

Polka Dot Publishing, Stanley F. Schmidt, 9034 Western Skies Drive, Reno, NV 89521-5236, 775-852-2690 phone, LifeofFred@yahoo.com. 2001. Non-fiction. avg. press run 2M. Pub'd 3 titles 2009; expects 3 titles 2010, 2 titles 2011. 13 titles listed in the *Small Press Record of Books in Print* (36th Edition, 2010-11). 544pp. Reporting time: 1 month. Simultaneous submissions accepted: yes. Payment: to be arranged. Copyrights for author. Subjects: Christianity, Mathematics.

Poltroon Press, Alastair Johnston, PO Box 5476, Berkeley, CA 94705-0476, 510-845-8097. 1974. Poetry, fiction, art, photos, interviews, satire, criticism, concrete art, non-fiction. "Do not read unsolicited work. Recent books: Mark Coggins, Vulture Capital (Detective fiction, 2002) ISBN: 0-918395-21-6; Philip Whalen, Prose [Out] Takes (poetry, 2002); Alastair Johnston, Zephyrus Image: A Bibliography, with photos by Rob Rusk, illustrated by Michael Myers (2003) ISBN: 0-918395-22-4." avg. press run 200-1000. Pub'd 4 titles 2009; expects 5 titles 2010, 4 titles 2011. 8 titles listed in the *Small Press Record of Books in Print* (36th Edition, 2010-11). Discounts: distributor: Small Press Distribution, or visit us on line at www.poltroonpress.com. 64pp. Payment: 15%. Copyrights for author. Subjects: African Literature, Africa, African Studies, Bibliography, Design, Poetry, Printing.

Polygonal Publishing House, Michael Weinstein, PO Box 357, Washington, NJ 07882, 908-689-3894. 1976. Non-fiction. "We publish books on mathematics." avg. press run 1M. Expects 1 title 2010, 1 title 2011. 17

titles listed in the *Small Press Record of Books in Print* (36th Edition, 2010-11). Discounts: 20% trade & bulk. 200pp. Payment: 17%. Subject: Mathematics.

Poor Richard's Press, Richard Doyle, 17854 Lyons St. NE, Forest Lake, MN 55025-8107, www.mensdefense.org. 1972. Non-fiction. "Books dealing with gender issues." avg. press run 1000. Pub'd 1 title 2009; expects 1 title 2010, 1 title 2011. 1 title listed in the *Small Press Record of Books in Print* (36th Edition, 2010-11). Discounts: 10+ copies 20%. 265pp. Reporting time: Not accepting submissions. Simultaneous submissions accepted: No. Payment: Not applicable. Does not copyright for author. Subjects: Civil Rights, Divorce, Feminism, Gender Issues, Marriage, Men, Sociology.

Poor Souls Press/Scaramouche Books (see also THE BROADSIDER: An Annual Magazine of Rescued Poems), Paul Fericano, Editor; C. P. Chase, Associate Editor; Bruce Pryor, Managing Editor, PO Box 236, Millbrae, CA 94030, www.yunews.com. 1974. Poetry, satire. "Sorry, but Poor Souls Press cannot accept unsolicited material. If you're a poet and/or satirist, we encourage self-publishing and close contact with others doing like work. We do exchanges. "The Broadsider" is our annual publication of broadsides published by our press during the year. In addition we publish two online journals, "Giuseppe" and "The Minderbinder Review of Books." Poor Souls Press is the book publishing subsidiary of Yossarian Universal (YU) News Service, the world's only parody news and disinformation syndicate founded in 1980 with bureaus in 37 cities worldwide. We publish broadsides, postcards, chapbooks, pamphlets, and dispatches." avg. press run Chapbooks: 1000 copies; Mini-Chapbooks: 100-300 copies; Post Cards: 2000 copies; Limited Edition Broadsides, Numbered and Signed by the Author: 100 Copies; Regular Issue Broadsides: 50 copies; Dispatches: Millions. Pub'd 3 titles 2009; expects 20 titles 2010, 20 titles 2011. 147 titles listed in the *Small Press Record of Books in Print* (36th Edition, 2010-11). For our broadside series ("The Broadsider") we publish poems that have been previously published only. By solicitation and invitation only. Payment: We pay our authors with half the print run. Copyrights for author. Subjects: Poetry, Satire.

Poplar Leaf Press, Derek Cressman, 2320 D St #203, Sacramento, CA 95816, 916-760-1519. 2007. Non-fiction. "We are interested in investigative reporting/muckraking of money in politics, ethics, and election issues and policy analysis of democratic reform proposals that will interest both academic, opinion-leader, and mainstream audiences." avg. press run 3000. Pub'd 1 title 2009; expects 1-2 titles 2010, 1-2 titles 2011. 1 title listed in the *Small Press Record of Books in Print* (36th Edition, 2010-11). Discounts: 55 percent to distributors 40 percent to bookstore/retail 40 percent to non-profit/educational. 350pp. Reporting time: Two months. Simultaneous submissions accepted: Yes. Publishes 10% of manuscripts submitted. Payment: Varies, but we are a non-profit organization and publish primarily for public education, not anyone's private gain. Copyrights for author. Subjects: California, Community, Fundraising, Government, Thomas Jefferson, Leadership, Non-Fiction, Political Science, Politics, Social Movements.

Poptritus Press (see also CAUSE & EFFECT MAGAZINE), Ben J. Biesek, PO Box 15329, San Luis Obispo, CA 93406-5329, (805) 748-3521. 2008. Poetry, fiction, interviews, criticism, non-fiction. "Poptritus Press publishes fiction, poetry, essays, and non-fiction, with a focus on the human condition and the modern world." avg. press run 100. Expects 3-5 titles 2010, 10-20 titles 2011. No titles listed in the *Small Press Record of Books in Print* (36th Edition, 2010-11). Discounts: Up to 10 copies at 10%. 32pp. Reporting time: 1-2 weeks. Simultaneous submissions accepted: Yes. Publishes 25% of manuscripts submitted. Payment: 50% royalties. Payments on a monthly basis. Copyrights for author. Subjects: Current Affairs, Dreams, Drugs, Essays, Ethics, Fiction, Liberal Arts, Metaphysics, Music, Non-Fiction, Philosophy, Poetry, Post Modern, Zines.

Portal Press, Darick Allan, 1327 Irving Street, NE, Washington, DC 20017-2453, 202-529-4950 (phone), 202-529-4950 (fax), editor@theportalpress.com (e-mail), www.theportalpress.com (website). 2005. Fiction, art, non-fiction. "We specialize in unusual fiction and memoirs, with an emphasis on multicultural themes." avg. press run 2100. Expects 2 titles 2010, 2 titles 2011. 3 titles listed in the *Small Press Record of Books in Print* (36th Edition, 2010-11). Discounts: distributors, wholesalers 55%. 200pp. Reporting time: 2-4 months. Simultaneous submissions accepted: Yes. Publishes 5% of manuscripts submitted. Payment: 10% of the net. Copyrights for author. Subjects: Autobiography, Buddhism, Conservation, Cooking, Ecology, Foods, Fiction, Literature (General), Memoirs, Multicultural, Novels, Picture Books, Vegetarianism.

PORTALS, Redrosebush Press, Ella M. Dillon, PO Box 2163, Wenatchee, WA 98807-2163, 509-662-7858. 1991. Poetry, fiction, articles, art, photos, cartoons, interviews, satire, criticism, reviews, letters, non-fiction. "Prefer poetry 30 lines or less, other writings 500-1,500 words." circ. 1M+. 4/yr. Pub'd 4 issues 2009; expects 4 issues 2010, 4 issues 2011. sub. price $18; per copy $6; sample free. Back issues: $2.50. Discounts: none. 52pp. Reporting time: when published. Simultaneous submissions accepted: yes. Payment: none. Copyrighted, reverts to author. Pub's reviews: 5 in 2009. §No pornography. Ads: $300/$200/$25 and up.

Portals Press, John P. Travis, 4411 Fontainebleau Drive, New Orleans, LA 70125, 504-821-5404, travport@bellsouth.net, www.portalspress.com. 1992. Poetry, fiction, long-poems. "Authors we have published: Kay Murphy, Ralph Adamo, Chris Champagne, John Gery, Maxine Cassin, Richard Katrovas, James

Knudsen, Tom Whalen, Everett Maddox, William S. Maddox, Nancy Harris, Grace Bauer, Brad Richard, Yictove, Chris Chandler, and H.R. Stoneback." avg. press run 500-1M. Pub'd 1 title 2009; expects 1 title 2010, 1 title 2011. 13 titles listed in the *Small Press Record of Books in Print* (36th Edition, 2010-11). Discounts: 40%. 128pp. Reporting time: 1 month. Simultaneous submissions accepted: okay. Publishes 1% of manuscripts submitted. Payment: 10-20%. Copyrights for author. Subjects: Fiction, Poetry, Science Fiction.

PORTLAND REVIEW, Chris Cottrell, PO BOX 347, Portland, OR 97207-0347. 1956. Poetry, fiction, art, photos, long-poems, non-fiction. "The editor for 2008-09 is on the lookout for astounding and previously unpublished works of fiction, creative non-fiction, poetry and art from anywhere on Earth. Previously unpublished authors and experimental writers are encouraged to submit mind-blowing poetry and prose. Prose submissions of greater than 6,500 are less likely to be accepted. Newest issue includes work by B.J. Best, Jeff Alessandrelli and Jenni Hanning. MS returned only at request and adequate postage. Reviews handled in-house, please only send creative work." 3/yr. Pub'd 1500 issues 2009; expects 1500 issues 2010, 1500 issues 2011. sub. price $28; per copy $9; sample TBD. Back issues: $4. Discounts: 2-10 copies: 20%, 10-20 copies: 30%, 20+ copies: 40%. 120pp. Reporting time: 3-6 mos. Simultaneous submissions accepted: Yes. Publishes 2% of manuscripts submitted. Payment: Unpaid. 1st NA rights-revert after 3mos. Pub's reviews. §Recently released poetry, fiction, creative non-fiction, flash fiction, etc. Genre unimportant, material reviewed on merit. Ads: Full Page, single issue: $150, full year (3 issues): $400; 1/2 Page, single issue: $80, full year: $200; 1/4 Page, single issue: $60, full year: $120. Ads must be relevant to literature. Subjects: Arts, Avant-Garde, Experimental Art, Creative Non-fiction, Fiction, Language, Non-Fiction, Poetry, Prose, Reviews, Short Stories.

PORTRAIT, Susan T. Landry, Melissa Shook, 11 Robeson St., Jamaica Plain, MA 02130. 2003. Art, photos, long-poems, non-fiction. "PORTRAIT is a quarterly publication that explores the realm of biography through art and literature. Each issue features one artist and one writer in an intimate 5 x 7 portable format. PORTRAIT continues under new editors to function as a collectible publication as well as a forum for the ongoing discussion of our interests in one another." 4/yr. Pub'd 6 issues 2009; expects 4 issues 2010, 4 issues 2011. sub. price $18.00; per copy $5.00; sample $5.00. Back issues: inquire. Discounts: inquire. 15pp. Reporting time: 4-5 weeks. Simultaneous submissions accepted: Yes. Payment: Complimentary issues. Copyrighted, reverts to author.

The Post-Apollo Press, Simone Fattal, 35 Marie Street, Sausalito, CA 94965, 415-332-1458, fax 415-332-8045. 1982. Poetry, fiction. "No longer taking unsolicited manuscripts." Pub'd 4 titles 2009; expects 4 titles 2010, 4 titles 2011. 28 titles listed in the *Small Press Record of Books in Print* (36th Edition, 2010-11). Discounts: Bookstores: 20% returnable; 40% non-returnable. Simultaneous submissions accepted: no. Payment: percentage after all expenses are met. Copyrights for author. Subjects: Fiction, History, Literature (General), Middle East, Poetry, Visual Arts.

POSTCARD CLASSICS (formerly DELTIOLOGY), Dr. James Lewis Lowe, Deltiologists of America, PO Box 132, Norwood, PA 19074-0008, 610-485-8572. 1960. "No hardcopy." sample price $2.00 in USA funds postpaid to USA addresses. Outside USA: write for shipping estimate to your country. USA checks and money orders from USA buyers; PayPal accepted worldwide. Back issues: 10 *POSTCARD CLASSICS* back issues: $10.00 plus $4.00 USA shipping. 50 *DELTIOLOGY* back issues: $30 plus $6.00 Media Mail shipping USA only. Outside USA: write for shipping estimate to your country. USA checks and money orders from USA buyers; PayPal accepted worldwide. Copyrighted. Pub's reviews: 2 in 2009. §Books about picture postcards and postcard collecting only. Ads: No. Subject: Postcards.

Samuel Powell Publishing Company, 2201 I Street, #D, Sacramento, CA 95816, 916-443-1161. 1978. Fiction. avg. press run 750. Expects 1-2 titles 2010, 1-2 titles 2011. 6 titles listed in the *Small Press Record of Books in Print* (36th Edition, 2010-11). Discounts: 55% distributors, 40% bookstores. 105pp. Copyrights for author. Subject: Fiction.

The Power Within Institute, Inc., Joni Maki, P.O. Box 595, Matlacha, FL 33993, 239-989-9000. 1987. Music. 2 titles listed in the *Small Press Record of Books in Print* (36th Edition, 2010-11).

Practically Shameless Press, Alyce Barry, 2120 West Farragut Ave, Chicago, IL 60625-1244, 773-728-0209, info@practicallyshameless.com, www.practicallyshameless.com. 2007. Non-fiction. "We publish books for the general and professional reader about practical applications for archetypal psychology, written by practitioners of experiential personal growth work based on Jungian psychology. Recent contributors include Alyce Barry and Shadow Work(r) founder Cliff Barry." avg. press run 1500. Expects 1 title 2010, 1 title 2011. 2 titles listed in the *Small Press Record of Books in Print* (36th Edition, 2010-11). We offer discounts to bookstores, distributors, wholesalers, institutions and specialty stores. Please contact us for details at info@practicallyshameless.com. 216pp. Reporting time: Three weeks. We do not expect to accept many manuscripts from the general public. We publish works by experienced facilitators. Simultaneous submissions accepted: No. Payment: To be agreed upon. Copyrights for author. Subjects: Adolescence, Christmas, Grieving, Humor, Leadership, Non-Fiction, Parenting, Philosophy, Psychology, Relationships, Religion, Self-Help, Sexual Abuse,

Spiritual, Young Adult.

THE PRAIRIE JOURNAL OF CANADIAN LITERATURE, Prairie Journal Press, A. Burke, PO Box 68073, 28 Crowfoot Terrace NW, Calgary, Alberta T3G 3N8, Canada, prairiejournal@yahoo.com, www.prairiejournal.org. 1983. Poetry, fiction, interviews, criticism, reviews, long-poems. "Recent contributors: Laurie Anne Whitt, Fred Cogswell, interviews with poet Lorna Crozier, playwright James Reaney. Literary biases for reviews of Canadian prairie literature; also one act plays. Poems of the Month is a feature being launched by our brand-new website. Submit up to 4 poems with $1 reading fee by snail mail, reply by e-mail or return with SASE." circ. 650+. 2/yr. Pub'd 2 issues 2009; expects 2 issues 2010, 2 issues 2011. 1 title listed in the *Small Press Record of Books in Print* (36th Edition, 2010-11). sub. price $10, $20 institutions; per copy $6; sample $3. Back issues: $5. Discounts: negotiable. 58-62pp. Reporting time: 2 weeks. Payment: copies and honoraria. Copyrighted. Pub's reviews: 12 in 2009. §Western, prairie, literary, Canadian Query first with clips. Ads: $50/$25/exchange. Subjects: Canada, Criticism, English, Fiction, Great Plains, Humor, Libraries, Literary Review, Literature (General), Magazines, Midwest, Poetry, Theatre, Women.

Prairie Journal Press (see also THE PRAIRIE JOURNAL OF CANADIAN LITERATURE), A. Burke, Brentwood P.O., Calgary, Alberta T2L 2K6, Canada, prairiejournal@yahoo.com, www.geocities.com/prairiejournal. 1983. Poetry, fiction, interviews, criticism, reviews, long-poems, plays. "Recent publication of an anthology of short fiction by six authors and a collection of poetry by one author. *Prairie Journal Fiction* $6 and for $6 *A Vision of Birds* by Ronald Kurt. Potential contributors please send samples of work with IRC and envelope for reply, covering letter." avg. press run 600+. Pub'd 1 title 2009; expects 2 titles 2010, 1 title 2011. 22 titles listed in the *Small Press Record of Books in Print* (36th Edition, 2010-11). Discounts: negotiable. 40-60pp. Reporting time: 2 weeks - 6 months. Publishes 20% of manuscripts submitted. Payment: copies. Copyrights for author. Subjects: Canada, Criticism, English, Fiction, Humor, Literature (General), Poetry, Women.

PRAIRIE MARGINS, Amanda Papenfus, Department of English, Bowling Green State University, Bowling Green, OH 43403, debrab@bgnet.bgsu.edu http://www.bgsu.edu/departments/creative-writing/home.html (under BFA).

PRAIRIE SCHOONER, Hilda Raz, Editor-in-Chief; James Engelhardt, Managing Editor, 201 Andrews Hall, PO Box 880334, Univ. of Nebraska, Lincoln, NE 68588-0334, 402-472-0911. 1926. Poetry, fiction, art, interviews, reviews, parts-of-novels, long-poems, non-fiction. "Manuscripts are read from September 1st through May 1st only." circ. 2.0M. 4/yr. Pub'd 4 issues 2009; expects 4 issues 2010, 4 issues 2011. sub. price $28; per copy $9; sample $6. Write for information on back issue prices. Write for information on discounts. 200pp. Reporting time: 3-4 months. Simultaneous submissions accepted: no. Publishes 1% of manuscripts submitted. Payment: copies of magazine, and annual prizes; payments depend on grants rec'd. Copyrighted, rights revert to author upon request. Pub's reviews: 20 in 2009. §Current literature. Ads: $200 for full page, 50% discount to university, literary, and independent presses. Subjects: Essays, Fiction, Literary Review, Poetry, Reviews, Short Stories.

PRAIRIE WINDS, Derric Ludens, Editor, Dakota Wesleyan University, DWU Box 536, Mitchell, SD 57301, 605-995-2814. 1946. Poetry, fiction, art, photos, long-poems, plays. "Annual literary review. All submissions must have SASE. Art and photos—preferably black and white; deadline end of January." circ. 500. 1/yr. Pub'd 1 issue 2009; expects 1 issue 2010, 1 issue 2011. 1 title listed in the *Small Press Record of Books in Print* (36th Edition, 2010-11). sub. price $7; per copy $7; sample $7. Back issues: $10. 50-70pp. Reporting time: 2 months from deadline. Simultaneous submissions accepted: no. Publishes 18% of manuscripts submitted. Payment: 2 copies each. Copyrighted, reverts to author. Ads: none. Subjects: Arts, Fiction, Photography, Poetry.

Prakalpana Literature (see also KOBISENA; PRAKALPANA SAHITYA/PRAKALPANA LITERA-TURE), Vattacharja Chandan, P40 Nandana Park, Kolkata 700034, Kolkata, West Bengal, India, +9831714756. Email:prakalpana@yours.com Blog:http://vattacharjachandan.blogspot.com. 1972. Poetry, articles. "Biases: we invite in English or in Bengali: 1) experimental poem, having definitely visual, sonorous & mathematical dimensions, and also Sarbangin poetry; 2) Prakalpana (=P for prose, poetry + R for story + A for art, essay + K for kinema, kinetic + L for play + N for song, novel...)—which is a mixed composition using the above forms appropriately as per need of the composition; 3) also articles on Prakalpana literature. If selected, at first we publish the work in our mags, then we may include it in our future anthology; 4) mail art works. Submissions not returnable. Reply of snailmail with International Reply Coupons or thru email only. Submissions with full name and address & email Id OK. Length of material: in any case within 2,400 words or upto 4 artworks at a time. Before submission it is better to look at our enttirely different kind of writing by grabbing a sample copy @ 6 IRC or checking out our blog.We are open to new artists & unsolicited works. No fixed route for queries/ proposals; only that must be within our biases as described above. We read throughout the year. No fixed period of publication or reply, as we are 100% non profitable and independent organization dedicated only to create non-prevailing literature and art and not to recreate prevailing literature and art. We want them who want us! International contributors include Dilip Gupta, John M. Bennett, Syamoli Mukherjee,

Mark Sonenfeld, Holden, Vattacharja Chandan, Carla Bertola, Nikhil Bhowmik, Mick Cusimano, Christian Burgaud, Ramratan Mukhopadhyay, Margarita Engle, Utpal, Gerald England, John Light, Giovanni Malito, Jorge Ignacio Nazavel Cowan.....and many others." avg. press run 500. 8 titles listed in the *Small Press Record of Books in Print* (36th Edition, 2010-11). Discounts: 20%. 64pp. Reporting time: No fixed time. Simultaneous submissions accepted: no. Payment: One copy.We reserve the right to publish or republish the selected material and the writer/artist may also publish that elsewhere. Does not copyright for author. Subjects: Literature (General), Poetry.

PRAKALPANA SAHITYA/PRAKALPANA LITERATURE, Prakalpana Literature, Vattacharja Chandan, P-40 Nandana Park, Kolkata-700034, West Bengal, India. 1977. Poetry, articles, reviews, letters, news items. "Biases: we invite in English or in Bengali: 1) only experimental poem, having definitely visual, sonorous & mathematical dimensions—which we call Sarbangin poetry, 2) Prakalpana (=P for prose, poetry + R for story + A for art, essay + K for kinema, kinetic + L for play + N for song, novel...)—which is a composition using the above forms appropriately; 3) also criticism, essay & letters on Prakalpana literature. Submissions not returnable. Length of material: in any case within 2,400 words. Some recent contributors: Dilip Gupta, Vattacharja Chandan, Norman J. Olson, Shyamali Mukhopadhyay Bhattacharya, Sheila Murphy, and Jessica Manack." circ. 1M. 1/yr. Pub'd 1 issue 2009; expects 1 issue 2010, 1 issue 2011. sub. price 30 rupees; per copy 30 rupees. Overseas: 6 IRCs or exhcnage of little mags; sample 30 rupees. Overseas: 6 IRCs or exchange of little mags. Back issues: 30 rupees. Discounts: 20%. 64pp. Simultaneous submissions accepted: no. Payment: One copy. Not copyrighted. Pub's reviews: 4 in 2009. §Alternative literary & art books and magazines. Ads: 500 rupees/300 rupees/800 rupees (2nd, 3rd, 4th cover pages). Subjects: Arts, Avant-Garde, Experimental Art, Bilingual, Book Reviewing, Creativity, Experimental, Fiction, Graphics, Literary Review, Literature (General), Poetry, Reviews, Zines.

Preludium Publishers (see also LIFTOUTS), Barry Casselman, 520 5th Street SE #4, Minneapolis, MN 55414-1628, 612-321-9044, Fax 612-305-0655, barcass@mr.net. 1971. Poetry, fiction, criticism, plays. "Preludium Publishers is interested in experimental work in poetry and fiction, and in the translation of new writing which has not previously been published in English. *Unsolicited manuscripts are not considered at this time.* Translators should make inquiry before sending any manuscript, and must include an SASE for a reply." avg. press run 1M. Expects 2 titles 2011. No titles listed in the *Small Press Record of Books in Print* (36th Edition, 2010-11). Payment: negotiable; some payment to all authors. Copyrights for author. Subjects: Fiction, Poetry, Theatre, Translation.

Premium Press America, George Schnitzer Jr., 2606 Eugenia Avenue, Suite C, Nashville, TN 37211, 615-256-8484. 1986. Fiction, photos, non-fiction. "Specialize in gift/souvenir books to gift shops, book stores and speciality outlets—state and federal parks, souvenir stores, museums, historical sites and the like.Added romance novels (352 pgs)in 2006." avg. press run 10,000-20,000. Pub'd 6 titles 2009; expects 9 titles 2010, 9 titles 2011. No titles listed in the *Small Press Record of Books in Print* (36th Edition, 2010-11). Discounts: 55-60% to distributors and wholesalers, 12 copies, 45-50% to retailers. 128pp. Reporting time: 2 to 3 weeks. Simultaneous submissions accepted: Yes. Payment: Small advance against 15% of collected money paid quarterly. Copyrights for author. Subjects: Arkansas, Children, Youth, Christmas, Civil War, Florida, Inspirational, Native American, Romance, South Carolina, Sports, Outdoors, Tennessee, Texas, Virginia, Wine, Wineries, Women.

PREMONITIONS, Tony Lee, 13 Hazely Combe, Arreton, Isle of Wight, PO30 3AJ, United Kingdom, http://www.pigasuspress.co.uk. 1992. Poetry, fiction, art, cartoons, satire, long-poems. "The most important piece of advice we can offer is - study copies of our magazine first! Because reading what we have already published is the best way to learn what sort of writings may be suitable for Premonitions." 1/yr. Pub'd 1 issue 2009. price per copy $13; sample $13. Back issues: 4.10. 60pp. Reporting time: 1 to 6 months. Simultaneous submissions accepted: No. Payment: 5 or US$5 per 1,000 words, for stories + copy of the magazine, copy only for poetry, artwork, and shorter fiction or prose. Copyrighted. §cutting-edge science fiction and horror stories. Subjects: Absurdist, Artificial Intelligence, Experimental, Fantasy, Fiction, Futurism, Poetry, Science Fiction, Short Stories.

PREP Publishing, Anne McKinney, 1110 1/2 Hay Street, Suite C, Fayetteville, NC 28305, 910-483-6611, Fax 910-483-2439. 1994. Fiction, non-fiction. "Street address: 1110-1/2 Hay Street, Fayetteville, NC 28305." avg. press run 5M+. Pub'd 6 titles 2009; expects 6 titles 2010, 8 titles 2011. 44 titles listed in the *Small Press Record of Books in Print* (36th Edition, 2010-11). Discounts: 20%-50%. 250-350pp. Reporting time: 12 weeks. Simultaneous submissions accepted: yes. Publishes 5% of manuscripts submitted. Payment: 6%. Copyrights for author. Subjects: Careers, Caribbean, Fiction, How-To, Inspirational, Management, Motivation, Success, North Carolina, Novels, Religion, Romance, Spiritual.

PRESA, Presa Press, Roseanne Ritzema, PO Box 792, Rockford, MI 49341, presapress@aol.com. 2005. Poetry, art, photos, criticism, reviews. "Imagistic bias. If it's political, it better be more than just bitching. Surrealism, experimental & personal poetry. We don't think that cutting prose into lines necessarily makes it a good poem. Something magical, some kind of intuitive leap in the last line is preferred. Imagery is essential. Contributors include Antler, John Amen, Harry Smith, Kirby Condgon, Hugh Fox, Eric Greinke, Stanley Nelson, Kerry Shawn Keys, AD Winans, Lyn Lifshin, Charles P. Ries, Glenna Luschei, Richard Kostelanetz,Donald Lev, Ingrid Swanberg, Simon Perchik, Doug Holder, Linda Lerner, BZ Niditch, Arthur Winfield Knight,Guy Beining, Ellaraine Lockie, Alan Catlin.'' circ. 500-1000. 2/yr. Pub'd 2 issues 2009; expects 2 issues 2010, 2 issues 2011. sub. price $15.00; per copy $8.50; sample $8.50. Back issues: $4.00; $20/set. Discounts: 50% discount to the trade. 48-64pp. Reporting time: Up to three months. Simultaneous submissions accepted: No. Payment: Pays in copies. Copyright, reverts to author on publication, except we retain the right to reprint. Pub's reviews. §Poetry books & chapbooks. Ads: half page - $35.00full page - $60.00. Subjects: Avant-Garde, Experimental Art, Essays, Experimental, Poetry, Reviews, Surrealism.

Presa Press (see also PRESA), Roseanne Ritzema, PO Box 792, Rockford, MI 49341, presapress@aol.com. 2002. Poetry, non-fiction. ''Prefers imagistic poetry where form is extension of content. Biases against overtly political or didactic material.Recently published authors include Stanley Nelson, Harry Smith, Glenna Luschei, Eric Greinke, Kirby Congdon, Leslie H. Whitten Jr., Richard Kostelanetz, Kerry Shawn Keys, Louis E. Bourgeois, Lyn Lifshin, Hugh Fox, AD Winans, Linda Lerner, Lynne Savitt & John Amen.'' Pub'd 7 titles 2009; expects 6 titles 2010, 6 titles 2011. 19 titles listed in the *Small Press Record of Books in Print* (36th Edition, 2010-11). Discounts: Library: 33%; Bookstores: 50%; Wholesalers: 50%. 100-200pp. Reporting time: varies. Simultaneous submissions accepted: No. Payment: flat fee or copies. Individual works in author's name, anthologies in publisher's name. Acquires perpetual rights to print works in anthologies. Subjects: Avant-Garde, Experimental Art, Experimental, Memoirs.

The Preservation Foundation, Inc., J. Richard Loller, Editor, 2213 Pennington Bend Road, Nashville, TN 37214, 800-228-8517, 615-269-2433, preserve@storyhouse.org, www.storyhouse.org. 1976. Non-fiction. 1 title listed in the *Small Press Record of Books in Print* (36th Edition, 2010-11).

•**Press 53,** PO Box 30314, Winston-Salem, NC 27130. ''Press 53 is a small independent publisher of literary fiction, poetry, and nonfiction that was founded in October 2005. Kevin Morgan Watson is the founder, owner and Fiction Editor; Tom Lombardo is Poetry Editor; and Robin Miura is Novel/Memoir Editor. Press 53 is located in Winston-Salem, North Carolina, and publishes full-length books by established writers. In addition to finding and showcasing new writers in our Press 53 Open Awards Anthology and established writers in our short story and poetry collections, novels, and creative nonfiction books, we also have a fondness for bringing back great books that are out of print, which we re-issue under our Press 53 Classics imprint.'' No titles listed in the *Small Press Record of Books in Print* (36th Edition, 2010-11).

The Press at Foggy Bottom, Mike Rosenthal, 35 Linden Lane, 2nd Floor, Princeton, NJ 08540, 609-921-1782. 1994. Fiction, cartoons, criticism, music, plays. ''The Press at Foggy Bottom publishes, on an ongoing basis, short run, reprintable trade books of anthologies of interest to children, young adults and the young at heart. Selected materials are also expressed as examples of the Book Arts in limited editions. We are interested in the whole range of literary expression including but not necessarily limited to short stories, humor, folk tales, plays, music, poetry, picture books, cartoons and even literary criticism which can be enjoyed by everyone including adults who are concerned with what children and young adults read. Our efforts, produced in either trade book or Book Art form, are intended to contain offerings children, young adults and parents can share, if not together, than separately within each volume. Great emphasis is placed on non-violence, where characters think up clever ways of besting the tribulations of any and all types of injustice and unfairness using the mental agility of matching wits and the understanding of people coupled with a concomitant, unstated message of ethical conduct. Lightheartedness, humor and good, clean fun are certainly always welcome! As always, we are interested in good secular material, but we are also more focused now, in Judaism. To this purpose, The Havurah for Jewish Storypeople: Tellers, Writers, Illustrators, & Scholars is performing free outreach services. We seek to help those who would like to publish while enjoying the benefits of a supportive, social, scholary and religious extended community. Please write to the Editor for details.'' avg. press run 500. Pub'd 1 title 2009; expects 3 titles 2010, 3-4 titles 2011. No titles listed in the *Small Press Record of Books in Print* (36th Edition, 2010-11). Discounts: by agreement. 100pp. Reporting time: 1-2 months. Simultaneous submissions accepted: yes. Publishes 25% of manuscripts submitted. Payment: by agreement. We copyright for author by agreement. Subjects: Cartoons, Children, Youth, Education, Fiction, Folklore, Humor, Judaism, Non-Violence, Religion, Short Stories, Social Work, Storytelling, Theatre.

Press Here (see also TUNDRA), Michael Dylan Welch, Editor & Publisher, 22230 NE 28th Place, Sammamish, WA 98074-6408, WelchM@aol.com. 1989. Poetry, articles, interviews, satire, criticism. ''Press Here publishes books of poetry, primarily haiku and related forms. Query before sending manuscripts. Authors include Paul O. Williams, William J. Higginson, Lee Gurga, Edward J. Rielly, Randy Brooks, Jeanne Emrich, Michael Dylan Welch and others. Books have won ten Merit Book Awards from the Haiku Society of America (including two first-place prizes). Manuscripts preferred only by those widely published in the leading haiku magazines. If the editor does not already know your work from leading haiku magazines, do not submit your manuscript. Especially interested in books of criticism on or about haiku, or small-book-length interviews with established haiku poets." avg. press run 200-1M. Pub'd 1 title 2009; expects 2 titles 2010, 1 title 2011. 28 titles listed in the *Small Press Record of Books in Print* (36th Edition, 2010-11). Discounts: at least 10% for 5-9 books (all one title); discounts negotiable. 28-112pp. Reporting time: usually 1-4 weeks for queries, 2-6 months for manuscripts (query first please). Simultaneous submissions accepted: no. Publishes 5% of manuscripts submitted. Payment: usually in copies. Copyrights for author. Subjects: Anthology, Lewis Carroll, Criticism, Haiku, Japan, Nature, Poetry, Zen.

Pressarius Publishing, Robert Schecter, 15 Mountain Laurel, Dove Canyon, CA 92679-4216, 949-842-6301. 2009. Non-fiction. "Pressarius Publishing (founded in 2009) is a boutique publisher focusing on parenting, health, nutrition, self-help, and personal finance. Forthcoming titles include: A History of Vaccination in America, The Fluoride Fact Book and What's Wrong with Wall Street." avg. press run 5000. Expects 5 titles 2010, 5 titles 2011. No titles listed in the *Small Press Record of Books in Print* (36th Edition, 2010-11). Discounts: 2-10 copies 25%. 250pp. Reporting time: Responds in 1 month to queries: 3 months to mss. Simultaneous submissions accepted: Yes. Publishes 5% of manuscripts submitted. Payment: Advances are based upon perceived sales potential while royalties are generally calculated on a sliding scale based on unit volume. Copyrights for author.

PRETEXT, Pen & Inc Press, Katri Skala, Managing Editor; Jon Cook, General Editor, Pen & Inc Press, School of Literature & Creative Writing, Norwich, Norfolk NR4 7TJ, United Kingdom, +44 (0)1603 592783, Fax + 44 (0)1603 507728, info@penandinc.co.uk, www.inpressbooks.co.uk/penandinc. 1999. Poetry, fiction, photos, interviews, criticism, letters, parts-of-novels, long-poems, plays. "Recent contributors include: Michle Roberts, Patricia Duncker, Christopher Hope, Paul Bailey, J G Ballard, Maureen Duffy, Michael Holroyd, Blake Morrison, Seamus Heaney, Iain Sinclair." circ. 700. 2/yr. Pub'd 2 issues 2009; expects 2 issues 2010, 3 issues 2011. sub. price £14 UK, £16 Europe, £18 ROW; per copy £7.99 UK, £8.99 Europe, £9.99 Rest of World. Back issues: £7.99 UK, £8.99 Europe, £9.99 ROW. 200pp. Reporting time: 3 months. Simultaneous submissions accepted: yes. Publishes 2% of manuscripts submitted. Payment: £50 per contribution. Copyrighted, reverts to author. Ads: apply for details. Subjects: Arts, Essays, Fiction, Literature (General), Non-Fiction, Photography, Poetry, Prose, Writers/Writing.

Price World Publishing, Rob Price, 1300 W. Belmont Ave., Suite 20G, Chicago, IL 60657, p 888-234-6896 x 713, f 216-803-0350, email publishing@PriceWorldPublishing.com, www.PriceWorldPublishing.com. 2002. Non-fiction. "We publish Sports and Fitness Training Books." avg. press run 2000. Pub'd 3 titles 2009; expects 4 titles 2010, 5-10 titles 2011. 35 titles listed in the *Small Press Record of Books in Print* (36th Edition, 2010-11). Discounts: 50% discount to retailers. 20% discount to schools and institutions. 176-224pp. Reporting time: One Week. Simultaneous submissions accepted: Yes. Publishes 25% of manuscripts submitted. Payment: Contract by contract basis. Subjects: Bicycling, Health, Sports, Outdoors.

PRICK OF THE SPINDLE, Cynthia Reeser, Editor-in-Chief, 1500 Beville Rd. Ste. 606-144, Daytona Beach, FL 32114-5644, Journal: http://www.prickofthespindle.com. "*Prick of the Spindle* is an on-line journal that publishes poetry, fiction (from flash to novella-length), drama, creative and academic nonfiction, and literary reviews. Though we do not publish genre fiction, we are open to different forms. It is the goal of the journal both to recognize new talent and to include those who have one or more feet planted in the writing community."

Princess Publishing, Cheryl A. Matschek, Editor, PO Box 1781, North Plains, OR 97133, 503-647-5754, fax: 503-647-7620, www.matschek.com, www.soaringhorizons.com. 1987. Non-fiction. avg. press run 5M. Pub'd 1 title 2009; expects 2 titles 2010, 2 titles 2011. 6 titles listed in the *Small Press Record of Books in Print* (36th Edition, 2010-11). 150-200pp. Reporting time: 1 month. Simultaneous submissions accepted: no. Publishes 1-5% of manuscripts submitted. Payment: variable. Copyrights for author. Subjects: Alternative Medicine, Business & Economics, Christianity, Food, Eating, Health, Leadership, Motivation, Success, Nutrition, Pets, Self-Help, Vegetarianism.

Princess Tides Publishing LLC, Carol Heston, 3 Gerry Street, Marblehead, MA 01945-3029, www.princesstides.com. 2004. Fiction. "Princess Tides Publishing was formed to publish selected works of fiction and non-fiction for readers who seek creative, stimulating entertainment, knowledge and insight. As a woman-owned business, we are particularly interested in works that portray strong women in challenging roles. On February 1, 2005, we released our first book, Absolute Values, a novel by Andrew R Menard (HC, 386 pages, $24.95). See www.princesstides.com." avg. press run 5000. Expects 2-3 titles 2010, 4-6 titles 2011. No titles listed in the *Small Press Record of Books in Print* (36th Edition, 2010-11). Discounts: Normal discount structure by distribution channel. 400pp. Reporting time: 4 to 8 weeks. Simultaneous submissions accepted: Yes. Payment: TBA. Copyrights for author.

Printed Matter Press (Tokyo), Hillel Wright, Taylor Mignon, Joseph Zanghi, Yagi Bldg. 4F, 2-10-13 Shitaya,, Taito-ku, Tokyo, Japan, 110-0004, Japan, Fax: 81-03-3871-4964 email:info@printedmatterpress.com, http://www.printedmatterpress.com. 1976. Poetry, fiction. "Recent contributors: Cid Corman, Kazuko Shiraishi, Shuntaro Tanikawa, Malinda Markham, Ralph Alfonso, Crad Kilodney, and Donald Richie." avg. press run 1M. Pub'd 1 title 2009; expects 1 title 2010, 2 titles 2011. 1 title listed in the *Small Press Record of Books in Print* (36th Edition, 2010-11). 212pp. Reporting time: 3 months. Simultaneous submissions accepted: no. Publishes 25% of manuscripts submitted. Payment: case by case. Copyrights for author. Subjects: Fiction, Poetry.

PRISM INTERNATIONAL, Jamella Hagen, Executive Editor; Kellee Ngan, Executive Editor; Sheryda Warrener, Poetry Editor; Claire Tacon, Fiction Editor, E462-1866 Main Mall, University of British Columbia, Vancouver BC V6T 1Z1, Canada, 604-822-2514, Fax 604-822-3616, prism@interchange.ubc.ca, www.prism-magazine.ca. 1959. Poetry, fiction, art, parts-of-novels, long-poems, plays, non-fiction. *"Prism* publishes translations of poetry and fiction from languages other than English. No reviews or scholarly essays." circ. 1.25M. 4/yr. Pub'd 4 issues 2009; expects 4 issues 2010, 4 issues 2011. sub. price $28 for 1-yr/$46 for 2-yr indiv., $35/$55 libraries, outside Canada pay US funds.; per copy $10 (bookstores and in person); sample $11 (covers mailing costs). Back issues: varies. 80pp. Reporting time: 12-16 weeks. Simultaneous submissions accepted: no. Publishes 3-5% of manuscripts submitted. Payment: per page: $40 poetry, $20 prose, $10 web + 1-year subscription. Selected authors get an additional $10/printed page for publication on the World Wide Web;. Copyrighted, reverts to author. Ads: $300/$200. Subjects: Drama, Fiction, Literature (General), Non-Fiction, Poetry, Translation, Visual Arts.

PRISON LEGAL NEWS, Paul Wright, P.O. Box 2420, West Brattleboro, VT 05303-2420, 802-257-1342, pln@prisonlegalnews.org. 1990. Articles, interviews, satire, criticism, reviews, letters, news items, non-fiction. *"PLN* reports on court decisions affecting the rights of prisoners, we cover news and analysis of prisons from around the world. The majority of each issue is written by prisoners and former prisoners and is uncensored by prison officials. *PLN* has a progressive point of view and seeks to educate its readers concerning racism, homophobia and sexism within the prison community and organize its readers into a force for progressive change within the penal system." circ. 7,000. 12/yr. Pub'd 12 issues 2009; expects 12 issues 2010, 12 issues 2011. sub. price $30 individuals, $80 institutions; per copy $5; sample $3.50. Back issues: $80 per year for 12 issues. $7.50 single issues. Discounts: contact editors to make special arrangements. 56pp. Reporting time: 6-8 weeks depending on timeliness. Simultaneous submissions accepted: yes. Publishes 20% of manuscripts submitted. Payment: $50 for articles over 1,500 words, $10 for anything under 1,500 words. Copyrighted, reverts to author. Pub's reviews: 60 in 2009. §Prisons, criminal justice, revolutionary struggle/politics, law, etc. Ads: $850/$450, classified rates are $60 for two months, 185 characters. Subjects: Civil Rights, Crime, Government, Human Rights, Immigration, Law, Prison.

PRISONERS' SPEAK!, Anthony Rayson, PO Box 721, Homewood, IL 60430, 708-534-1334, anthonyrayson@hotmail.com. 1998. Poetry, fiction, articles, art, photos, cartoons, satire, criticism, reviews, letters, parts-of-novels, collages, news items, non-fiction. *"Thought Bombs* is a literary anarchist, activist, 60-paged digest-sized zine. I also write other zines and edit still others. I mostly include the work of myself, prisoners, and activists." circ. 500. 3/yr. Pub'd 3 issues 2009; expects 3 issues 2010, 3 issues 2011. 1 title listed in the *Small Press Record of Books in Print* (36th Edition, 2010-11). sub. price donation; per copy $2; sample $2. Back issues: 20% off orders over $5. Discounts: willing to entertain offers. 60pp. We will possibly accept simultaneous submissions. Publishes 50% of manuscripts submitted. Payment: do not pay contributors. Not copyrighted. Pub's reviews: a few in 2009. Ads: none. Subjects: Anarchist, Feminism, Prison.

PRIVACY JOURNAL, Robert Ellis Smith, PO Box 28577, Providence, RI 02908, 401-274-7861, fax 401-274-4747, orders@privacyjournal.net, www.privacyjournal.net. 1974. Articles, cartoons, reviews, letters, news items. 12/yr. Pub'd 12 issues 2009; expects 12 issues 2010, 12 issues 2011. 10 titles listed in the *Small Press Record of Books in Print* (36th Edition, 2010-11). sub. price $125/$165 overseas; per copy $10; sample free. Back issues: $70 per whole year. Discounts: $35 to individuals if paid in advance. 8pp. Reporting time: 1 month. Publishes 25% of manuscripts submitted. Payment: negotiable. Copyrights negotiable. Pub's reviews. §Privacy, computers and society, surveillance. No ads. Subjects: Computers, Calculators, Consumer, Law, Newsletter.

Pro musica press, Edward Foreman, 8725 Promenade Lane, Apt 329, Woodbury, MN 55125-9622. 1967. Criticism, music, non-fiction. "We specialize in vocal pedagogy, translations of classics and reprints of important more recent contributions to the field. Author submissions are welcome." avg. press run 500. Expects 2 titles 2010. No titles listed in the *Small Press Record of Books in Print* (36th Edition, 2010-11). Discounts: Trade: 10%. 300pp. Reporting time: 2-4 weeks. Payment: Usual royalty 10% of published price. Negotiable. Most of our titles are copyrighted for the press. Subject: Music.

Profile Press, Ann & Deidre Woodward, Silhouettes, How to Cut for Fun and Money, 6051 Greenway Court, Manassas, VA 20112-3049, 703-730-0642. 1988. Non-fiction. avg. press run 5M. Pub'd 1 title 2009. 1 title listed in the *Small Press Record of Books in Print* (36th Edition, 2010-11). Discounts: 5-20 copies, 40% - all over 50%. 100pp. Reporting time: 3 months. Simultaneous submissions accepted: no. Copyrights for author.

Subject: Crafts, Hobbies.

Progressive Press; Tree of Life Publications, John Leonard, PO Box 126, Joshua Tree, CA 92252, 760-366-3695, fax 760-366-2937. 1972. Non-fiction. "Progressive Press publishes books on alternative views of politics and history. Tree of Life imprint has the backlist of New Age books." avg. press run 3000. Pub'd 5 titles 2009; expects 10 titles 2010, 6 titles 2011. No titles listed in the *Small Press Record of Books in Print* (36th Edition, 2010-11). Discounts: 40%. 300pp. Reporting time: A few days. Simultaneous submissions accepted: Yes. Publishes 50% of manuscripts submitted. Payment: 6 - 10% of list price, depending on volume. Copyrights for author. Subjects: African-American, Alternative Medicine, Animals, Christianity, Ecology, Foods, New Age, Politics, Sufism, Translation, War.

Prologue Press, 375 Riverside Drive #14-C, New York, NY 10025. No titles listed in the *Small Press Record of Books in Print* (36th Edition, 2010-11).

Proof Press (see also RAW NERVZ HAIKU), D. Howard, 67 Court Street, Aylmer, QC J9H 4M1, Canada. 1994. Poetry. "Haiku, renga." avg. press run 200. Pub'd 7 titles 2009; expects 10 titles 2010, 10 titles 2011. No titles listed in the *Small Press Record of Books in Print* (36th Edition, 2010-11). 6-40pp. Reporting time: 6 weeks to 3 months. Simultaneous submissions accepted: no. Publishes 10% of manuscripts submitted. Payment: 10% of run. Copyrights for author.

Propaganda Press (see also POIESIS), Leah Angstman, PO Box 398058, Cambridge, MA 02139, alt-current.com, alt.current@gmail.com. 1994. Poetry, fiction, articles, art, cartoons, interviews, music, parts-of-novels, long-poems, collages, plays, concrete art, news items, non-fiction. "Propaganda Press is the small press portion of the Alternating Current Arts Co-op. The mission of the Alternating Current Arts Co-op is to bring fresh, innovative art projects of all kinds from the small stream to the mainstream to a world that desperately needs it, while always providing the lowest prices, the most exposure, the best networking, and the most updated information we can possibly offer; to make art more than a luxurious afterthought; and to provide artists of all kinds with the opportunity to promote themselves. We publish zines, litzines, art, poetry chapbooks, short story chapbooks, and almost anything you can imagine. We won't take racist or homophobic material, as we just plain deem it unnecessary, but we are really very uncensored and open. We are open to submissions and proposals all year long, just drop us a line first so we can get some idea of with whom we are dealing. We like cutting edge, previously unpublished works, not really big into lovely-dovey Valentine poems, but we will consider everything evenly and fairly. Some recent and future contributors are B.Z. Niditch, Michael Kriesel, Joseph Verrilli, Marie Kazalia, Iris Berry, Christopher Cunningham, justin.barrett, Kevin M. Hibshman, Alan Catlin, David S. Pointer, Nathan Graziano, Ed Galing, Hosho McCreesh, Don Winter, A.D. Winans, and oh, so many more!" Pub'd 3 titles 2009; expects 30 titles 2010, 35-45 titles 2011. No titles listed in the *Small Press Record of Books in Print* (36th Edition, 2010-11). Discounts: All books are available at a discounted price for distribution, which varies depending on page numbers and at-cost prices. One free copy always available for distributors/retailers/reviewers/etc. to check out, upon request, for chapbooks. Free copies available for libraries and zine archives. 40-60pp. Reporting time: We respond immediately. Usually within a couple of days. Turnaround time is usually less than a month for the first proof. Simultaneous submissions accepted: Yes. Publishes 60% of manuscripts submitted. Payment: All authors decide their own royalties on our press. We mail out royalties quarterly. Authors receive two free copies of everything printed on our press and can purchase additional copies at a discounted author price in any quantity. We do not officially purchase a copyright for the author, but we list the material as copyrighted to the author, and we list the book as copyrighted to the press. All authors retain their rights and can use their material elsewhere at any time.

Prospect Press (see also CELEBRATION), William Sullivan, 2707 Lawina Road, Baltimore, MD 21216-1608, (410) 542-8785. 1975. Poetry. "Seldom use poems that rhyme, otherwise we are open to most forms. Sheila E. Murphy; Lyn Lifshin; Laurie Calhoun; George Gott; David Sapp; Timothy Houghton; Austin Straus." avg. press run 300. Expects 1 title 2010, 1 title 2011. No titles listed in the *Small Press Record of Books in Print* (36th Edition, 2010-11). 25pp. Reporting time: six months. Simultaneous submissions accepted: No. Publishes 5% of manuscripts submitted. Payment: one copy of issue in which work appears. Each issue is copyrighted by the editor. Subject: Poetry.

Protean Press, Terry Horrigan, 1190 Sacramento St., #4, San Francisco, CA 94108-1946, 415.931-8484, cell:415.260-5527, proteanpress@sbcglobal.net, www.califiabooks.com/finepress/p/protean.html. 1982. Poetry, articles, art, letters, non-fiction. "Recent publication: The China I Knew by Rose Covarrubias. Piece in progress: Aeolian Island, wind-force scales by Petersen and Beaufort." avg. press run 60. Expects 1 title 2010, 2 titles 2011. 15 titles listed in the *Small Press Record of Books in Print* (36th Edition, 2010-11). Discounts: 1-4 25%, 5-9 35%. Pages vary. Simultaneous submissions accepted: no. Publishes 0% of manuscripts submitted. Payment: varies. Copyrights for author. Subjects: The Americas, Anthropology, Archaelogy, Biography, History, Language, Poetry.

PROVINCETOWN ARTS, Provincetown Arts Press, Christopher Busa, 650 Commercial Street,

Provincetown, MA 02657, 508-487-3167, web: www.provincetownarts.com. 1985. Poetry, fiction, articles, art, photos, cartoons, interviews, criticism, reviews, collages, non-fiction. "Published annually in July, *Provincetown Arts* focuses broadly on the artists and writers, emerging and established, who inhabit or visit the tip of Cape Cod. Previous cover subjects have included Norman Mailer, Robert Motherwell, and Annie Dillard, Stanley Kunitz, Mark Doty, Mary Oliver, and Karen Finley. Placing contemporary creative activity in a context that draws upon a 75-year tradition of literature, visual art, and theatre, *Provincetown Arts* seeks to consolidate the voices and images of the nation's foremost summer art colony. Some recent contributors include Olga Broumas, Douglas Huebler, Michael Klein, Susan Mitchell, Martha Rhodes, and Anne-Marie Levine." circ. 8M. 1/yr. Pub'd 1 issue 2009; expects 1 issue 2010, 1 issue 2011. sub. price $10; per copy $10; sample $10. Back issues: $10. Discounts: 40% for resale. 184pp. Reporting time: 2 months. Simultaneous submissions discouraged. Publishes 2% of manuscripts submitted. Payment: prose $100-300, poetry $25-125, art $25-300. Copyrighted, reverts to author. Pub's reviews: 20 in 2009. §Biographies of artists, exhibition catalogues, poetry, fiction. Ads: $950/$550/color available. Subjects: Arts, Literature (General), Poetry, Visual Arts.

Provincetown Arts Press (see also PROVINCETOWN ARTS), Christopher Busa, Editorial Director, PO Box 35, 650 Commercial Street, Provincetown, MA 02657, 508-487-3167; FAX 508-487-8634. "A non-profit press for artists and poets." avg. press run artbooks-3M, poetry-1.5M. Pub'd 3 titles 2009; expects 4 titles 2010, 4 titles 2011. 11 titles listed in the *Small Press Record of Books in Print* (36th Edition, 2010-11). Discounts: 40%. Art books 150pp, poetry 70pp. Reporting time: 4 months. Simultaneous submissions accepted: no. Publishes 2% of manuscripts submitted. Payment: $500 advance, 10% royalties.

Pruett Publishing Company, Jim Pruett, Publisher, PO Box 2140, Boulder, CO 80306-2140, 303-449-4919, toll free: 1-800-247-8224. 1959. Art, photos, non-fiction. "Publisher of books pertaining to outdoor travel and recreation, fishing, and the West. Books include *A Climbing Guide to Colorado's Fourteeners: 20th Anniversry Edition, Colorado Nature Almanac,* and *The Earth is Enough.*" avg. press run varies per book. Pub'd 6 titles 2009; expects 12 titles 2010, 7-10 titles 2011. 67 titles listed in the *Small Press Record of Books in Print* (36th Edition, 2010-11). Discounts: write for a copy of our complete schedule. Pages vary. Reporting time: 4-6 weeks. Simultaneous submissions accepted: yes. Publishes about 10% of manuscripts submitted. Payment: generally a royalty basis for authors. Copyrights for author. Subjects: Alaska, Anthropology, Archaelogy, Arizona, Bicycling, Colorado, Cooking, Environment, History, Montana, Nature, New Mexico, Southwest, Sports, Outdoors, Wine, Wineries, Wyoming.

PSYCHE, Eros Books, Mary Nicholaou, 463 Barlow Avenue, Staten Island, NY 10308, 718-317-7484. 2002. Fiction, articles, cartoons, criticism, reviews, letters, parts-of-novels, non-fiction. "*Psyche* is a postmodern newsletter of literary fiction and nonfiction. We provide a forum for experiments in open forms that interrogate the canon." 4/yr. Expects 4 issues 2010, 4 issues 2011. sub. price $3; per copy 75¢; sample 50¢. Back issues: 50¢. Discounts: 25%-40%. 16-20pp. Reporting time: 2 months. Simultaneous submissions accepted: yes. Publishes 50% of manuscripts submitted. Payment: currently 10 contributor's copies. Copyrighted, reverts to author. Pub's reviews. §Postmodern novellas, novels, short stories, graphic novels, nonfiction and romance. Ads: $15/$10/$5 1/3 page. Subjects: Biography, Criticism, Education, Essays, Gender Issues, Language, Lifestyles, Literary Review, Myth, Mythology, New Age, Philosophy, Post Modern, Psychology, Relationships.

•Psychedelic Literature (see also BLACK MAGNOLIAS LITERARY JOURNAL), C. Liegh McInnis, 203 Lynn Lane, Clinton, MS 39056, (601) 383-0024, psychedeliclit@bellsouth.net, www.psychedelicliterature.com. 1996. Poetry, fiction, articles, interviews, satire, criticism, reviews, music, parts-of-novels, long-poems, plays, non-fiction. "The journal uses poetry, fiction, and essays to examine and celebrate the social, political, economic, and aesthetic accomplishments of African Americans with an emphasis on Afro-Mississippians and Afro-Southerners. Past contributors include Dr. Jerry Ward, Dr. Reginald Martin, Ahmos Zu-Bolton, Kalamu ya Salaam, Dr. Julius Thompson, Sterling Plump, Charlie Braxton, David Brian Williams, Jolivette Anderson, Kenneth Earl Stiggers, Sheree Rence Thomas, Dr. Howard Rambsy, Lenard D. Moore, Ronda Penrice, Marcus Uganda White, Waurene Roberson, Carlton Turner, and many others. We are seeking an equal amount of essays, poetry, and fiction. We welcome pieces on a variety of African American and Afro-Southern culture, including history, politics, education, incidents/events, social life, and literature. We also accept essays/critical analyses on literary works by white authors that have some significance or relevance to African American culture." avg. press run 2000. Pub'd 4 titles 2009; expects 4 titles 2010, 4 titles 2011. 7 titles listed in the *Small Press Record of Books in Print* (36th Edition, 2010-11). 120pp. Reporting time: Sixty Days. Simultaneous submissions accepted: Yes. Payment: Contributors to the literary journal receive one copy of the journal. Authors of books that we publish receive 50% of profits on a quarterly payment. Does not copyright for author. Subjects: African Literature, Africa, African Studies, African-American, Beat, Black, Book Reviewing, Caribbean, Creativity, Criticism, Feminism, Fiction, Literary Review, Literature (General), Music, Novels, Poetry.

Psychohistory Press (see also THE JOURNAL OF PSYCHOHISTORY), Lloyd deMause, Editor, 140 Riverside Drive, New York, NY 10024, 212-799-2294. 1973. Articles. avg. press run 3M. Pub'd 2 titles 2009;

expects 3 titles 2010. No titles listed in the *Small Press Record of Books in Print* (36th Edition, 2010-11). Discounts: 20%. 300pp. Reporting time: 4 weeks. Copyrights for author. Subjects: Anthropology, Archaelogy, History, Psychology.

PTOLEMY/BROWNS MILLS REVIEW, David C. Vajda, PO Box 252, Juliustown, NJ 08042. 1979. Poetry, fiction, articles, satire, criticism, parts-of-novels, long-poems, concrete art. circ. 100-250. 1-2/yr. Expects 3-4 issues 2010, 2 issues 2011. 9 titles listed in the *Small Press Record of Books in Print* (36th Edition, 2010-11). sub. price $4; per copy $2; sample $1-$2. Back issues: $1-$2. No discounts per se. 16pp. Reporting time: 1 week to 1 month. Payment: 5 copies per acceptance. Copyrighted, rights revert to author with permission. No ads. Subjects: Fiction, Poetry.

THE PUBLIC EYE, Abby Scher, 1310 Broadway, Suite 201, Somerville, MA 02144, 6176665300, www.publiceye.org. 1982. Articles, non-fiction. "Political Research Associates publishes The Public Eye, our signature quarterly, presenting insightful reports by scholars and journalists on trends within the US Right." 4/yr. Pub'd 4 issues 2009; expects 4 issues 2010, 4 issues 2011. sub. price $21.00; per copy $5.25. 24pp. Pub's reviews: 8 in 2009. §non-fiction. Ads: Full page $350, Half-page Horizontal $250, One-third Page Vertical $200, One-third Page Horizontal $200, One-sixth Page Horizontal $100. Subjects: Current Affairs, Feminism, Human Rights, Political Science, Politics, Race.

THE PUBLIC HISTORIAN, University of California Press, Ann Plane, Editor; Lindsey Reed, Managing Editor, University of California Press, 2000 Center Street, Suite 303, Berkeley, CA 94704-1223, 510-643-7154. 1978. Articles, interviews, reviews, news items, non-fiction. "Editorial address: Dept. of History, University of California, Santa Barbara, CA 93106." circ. 1514. 4/yr. Pub'd 4 issues 2009; expects 4 issues 2010, 4 issues 2011. sub. price $60 indiv., $128 instit., $25 students (+ $20 air freight); per copy $15 indiv.; $38 instit., $15 students; sample free. Back issues: same as single copy price. Discounts: foreign subs. agents 10%, one-time orders 10+ 30%, standing orders (bookstores): 1-99 40%, 100+ 50%. 144pp. Reporting time: 2-3 months. Copyrighted, does not revert to author. Pub's reviews: 50 in 2009. §History. Ads: $295/$220. Subject: History.

PublishAmerica, LLLP., Miranda Prather, Executive Director; Miranda Richmond, Acquisitions Manager; Brenda Swope, Cover Design Manager; Sophie Lewis, Text Production Manager, PO Box 151, Frederick, MD 21705-0151, 240-529-1031, Fax 301-631-9073, writers@publishamerica.com, www.publishamerica.com. 1999. Poetry, fiction, articles, satire, parts-of-novels. "Publish America, Inc. is interested in submissions from talented new authors. Manuscripts should be a minimum of 20,000 words. We pay special attention to authors, plots, and subjects overcoming challenges and obstacles. Mailed or emailed submissions are both acceptable." avg. press run print on demand. Pub'd 500 titles 2009; expects 800 titles 2010, 800 titles 2011. No titles listed in the *Small Press Record of Books in Print* (36th Edition, 2010-11). Discounts: 40% to retailers, 55% to wholesalers. 200pp. Reporting time: 1-2 months. Simultaneous submissions accepted: yes. Publishes 60% of manuscripts submitted. Payment: 8% minimum on royalties. Does not copyright for author. Subjects: Biography, Christianity, Drama, Fiction, Humor, Juvenile Fiction, Military, Veterans, Mystery, Philosophy, Poetry, Romance, Science Fiction, Short Stories, Spiritual.

PUBLISHING POYNTERS, Para Publishing, Dan Poynter, PO Box 8206-Q, Santa Barbara, CA 93118-8206, 805-968-7277, Fax 805-968-1379, info@parapublishing.com, www.parapublishing.com. 1986. News items. "Book marketing news and ideas from Dan Poynter. *Publishing Poynters* is full of non-fiction book marketing, promotion and distribution leads." circ. 16,000+. 26/yr. Pub'd 26 issues 2009; expects 26 issues 2010, 26 issues 2011. sub. price $9.95/2 years; sample free. Back issues: free. 20pp. Reporting time: 2 weeks. Simultaneous submissions accepted: yes. Payment: none. Copyrighted. Pub's reviews: 15 in 2009. §Non-fiction book marketing, promotion or distribution *only*. Subjects: Printing, Publishing.

PublishingWorks, Inc., Jeremy Townsend, 151 Epping Road, Exeter, NH 03833-2029, 603-778-9883, Fax 603-772-1980, email: jeremy@publishingworks.com. 2003. Fiction, photos, non-fiction. "We are interested in non-mainstream titles, debut fiction as well as literary fiction, high quality nonfiction, and projects that are perhaps too quirky for the major houses. But we demand strong author participation and must see a clear market and audience for the books." avg. press run 3000-5000 copies. Pub'd 10 titles 2009. 2 titles listed in the *Small Press Record of Books in Print* (36th Edition, 2010-11). Discounts: 40%-55%. 250pp. Reporting time: 1-2 months. Simultaneous submissions accepted: yes. Publishes 5% of manuscripts submitted. Payment: varies. Copyrights for author. Subjects: Animals, Arts, Bilingual, Children, Youth, Fiction, History, Literature (General), Nature, Pets.

Pudding House Publications (see also PUDDING MAGAZINE: The International Journal of Applied Poetry), Jennifer Bosveld, Editor,President; Fred Kirchner, Publications Director; Steve Abbott, Associate Editor; Kathleen Burgess, Associate Editor; Doug Swisher, Assistant Editor; Bob Pringle, Associate Editor; Mark Hartenbach, Associate Editor; Carol Schott Martino, Columnist, Assistant Editor; Bennett Rader, Assistant Editor; Sandra Feen-Diehl, Assistant Editor, 81 Shadymere Lane, Columbus, OH 43213-1568, 614-986-1881, info@puddinghouse.com, www.puddinghouse.com. 1979. Poetry, non-fiction. "Will not return manuscripts for which SASE is not enclosed. $10.00 reading fee for chapbooks, outside of competition 10-40 pages, $15 over 40 pages.'' avg. press run 400 chapbooks (that might be several reprints); 3000 anthologies. Pub'd 130 titles 2009; expects 130 titles 2010, 130 titles 2011. 308 titles listed in the *Small Press Record of Books in Print* (36th Edition, 2010-11). Discounts: 10% for single copies to classrooms, teachers, bookstores, non-profit or charity organizations; 35% on 10 or more copies 40% 25 or more, 50% on 50+. 24-32pp for chapbooks; 200pp for anthologies. Reporting time: 2 weeks except for competition submissions; sometimes overnight. Simultaneous submissions accepted: no. Publishes less than 1% of manuscripts submitted. Payment: 20 copies of the book; deep discount on additionals, but no expectations for authors to buy extras. Copyrights for author, but we don't register the copyright. Subjects: Poetry, Psychology.

PUDDING MAGAZINE: The International Journal of Applied Poetry, Pudding House Publications, Jennifer Bosveld, Editor; Steve Abbott, Associate Editor; Doug Swisher, Associate Editor; Kathleen Burgess, Associate Editor; Mark Hartenbach, Associate Editor; Robert Pringle, Associate Editor, 81 Shadymere Lane, Columbus, OH 43213-1568, 614-986-1881, info@puddinghouse.com, www.puddinghouse.com. 1979. Poetry, articles, art, photos, cartoons, interviews, criticism, reviews, letters, non-fiction. ''All styles and forms of poetry considered. Looking for the wildly different and the subtly profound. We recommend: reflections of intense human situations, conflict, and closure poems on popular culture, politics, social concern, quirky character, and the contemporary scene; concrete images and specific detail; artful expressions of unique situations; or the shock of recognition in things perhaps felt before (or almost felt) but never spoken. No trite comparisons, please. No cliches. No religious verse or sentimentality. Mini-Articles: by poets who share their craft in the human services; about *applied poetry* experiences either from clients/patients or from psychiatrists, teachers, or other professionals and paraprofesionals who put the art of poetry to use in helping others. Reviews of poetry books and chapbooks, how-to-write-poetry books, methodology books, and other relevant publications that would be beneficial to groups or individual readers. Likes dense, rich short short stories, 1-2 pages.'' circ. 1M. Irregular. Pub'd 2 issues 2009; expects 2 issues 2010, 2 issues 2011. sub. price $29.95/4 issues; per copy $8.95; sample $8.95. Back issues: $8.95, $455 for back set. Discounts: 20% on 5+ copies to classrooms, teachers, independent bookstores, non-profit or charity organizations; 35% on 10-49, 50% on 50+. 45-95pp. Reporting time: usually overnight; if held, we're traveling. Simultaneous submissions accepted: no. Publishes way less than 1% of manuscripts submitted. Payment: 1 copy, featured poets receive 4 copies and $10. Copyrighted, rights revert to author, with Pudding House retaining permission to reprint. Pub's reviews: 15 in 2009. §Poetry, 'applied poetry', popular culture and the arts, social justice. Ads: $200/$135 only in our priorties no classifieds. Subjects: Poetry, Psychology.

Puddin'head Press, David Gecic, PO Box 477889, Chicago, IL 60647, 708-656-4900. 1985. Poetry, fiction. ''We publish two or three books a year and have many submissions. We get to choose from high quality material. Please only submit work if you are a serious writer. Visit www.puddinheadpress.com.'' 2 titles listed in the *Small Press Record of Books in Print* (36th Edition, 2010-11).

PUERTO DEL SOL, Carmen Gimenez-Smith, Poetry Editor, Editor in Chief; Evan Lavender-Smith, Prose Editor, New Mexico State University, MSC 3E, Box 30001, Las Cruces, NM 88003, contact@puertodelsol.org, www.puertodelsol.org. 1961. Poetry, fiction, art, photos, interviews, criticism, reviews, parts-of-novels, long-poems, plays, non-fiction. ''Features Southwestern Chicano, Nat. Am. The primary emphasis, however, is on *top quality writing*, wherever it comes from. Translations are welcome, provided the translator has the author's permission.'' 2/yr. Pub'd 2 issues 2009; expects 2 issues 2010, 2 issues 2011. sub. price $20; per copy $8; sample $8. Back issues: Back issues available for $8; email for specific issue information. Issues older than 25 years may be more expensive. 200pp. Reporting time: 18 weeks. Simultaneous submissions accepted: yes. Publishes 3-5% of manuscripts submitted. Payment: copies. Copyrighted, reverts to author. Pub's reviews: 8 in 2009. §Chicano, Native American, poetry, fiction, Southwestern, anthologies. Ads: $120/$75; Interested in exchange ads- email for more information. Subjects: Fiction, Poetry.

PULSAR POETRY WEBZINE, David Pike, 34 Lineacre, Grange Park, Swindon, Wiltshire SN5 6DA, United Kingdom, 01793-875941, e-mail pulsar.ed@btopenworld.com, web: www.pulsarpoetry.com. 1994. Poetry, articles, art, photos, cartoons, reviews, long-poems, news items. ''Please note now a webzine only, www.pulsarpoetry.com. We post selected poems to the Pulsar web on a quarterly basis. Not keen on religious poetry. Will not advertise vanity press.'' Now a Webzine only. There are 4 quarterly postings of poems and reviews to Pulsar Poetry Webzine, namely in, March, June, September, December. Pub'd 2 issues 2009; expects 4 issues 2010, 4 issues 2011. Subscription not applicable. Back issues: $9.00/copy - if we have enough spare old stock to permit. Discounts: Subscriptions are not applicable. Reporting time: Usually reply within approx 30 days, for posting of selected poems to the next issue of Pulsar Poetry Webzine. Book review posts will take longer. Simultaneous submissions accepted: No. Publishes 1 in 50?% of manuscripts submitted. Payment: None, but selected poems will be posted to Pulsar Poetry Webzine with a photograph of the poet. Photographs not mandatory though. Copyrighted, reverts to author. Pub's reviews: 20 in 2009. §Poetry only, also poetry CDs. Ads: We can publicise poetry books on Pulsar Poetry Webzine,UK, cost by negotiation. Subjects: Arts, Book Reviewing, England, Language, Literary Review, Literature (General), Poetry, Quotations, Tapes &

Puna Press, Lesli Bandy, Marketing Director, P.O. Box 7790, San Diego, CA 92107, 619.278.8089, www.punapress.com. 1995. Poetry, art. avg. press run 500. Pub'd 2 titles 2009; expects 2 titles 2010, 4 titles 2011. 5 titles listed in the *Small Press Record of Books in Print* (36th Edition, 2010-11). Discounts: 40%-50%. 50-200pp. Reporting time: 4 to 6 months. Accepts simultaneous submissions. Does not copyright for author. Subjects: Arts, Poetry, Visual Arts.

•**PUNKIN HOUSE DIGEST, Punkin House Press,** Amy Ferrell, 9824 Mar Largo Cr, Fort Myers, FL 33919, http://www.punkinhousepress.com, ContactUs@punkinhousepress.org. 2009. Poetry, fiction, art, photos, cartoons, satire, long-poems, non-fiction. "Every author is different.So is Punkin House.Punkin House is on a mission to help the artist.Unlike other publishing companies, our number one priority is to take care of our authors, helping guide them through a process that produces quality material.We make it our goal to personally know our authors. This allows them to exercise as much control over their creative output as they desire.If an author's manuscript is accepted for publication they are completely represented by Punkin House.There are no fees, ever, for our authors. Our dedicated staff will edit, design, publish, and market their work at absolutely no cost to them.The author, as well as the entire creative team, is on a royalty-based system. Punkin House has an incredible staff who have made it their personal goal to make our writers household names.Our secondary goal is to be as "green" as possible. So along with your piece being on a bookshelf, it will also be digitally available for download as an e-book." 4/yr. Reporting time: Less than three months. Simultaneous submissions accepted: Yes. Subjects: Arts, Creative Non-fiction, Creativity, Fantasy, Fiction, Liberal Arts, Literature (General), Memoirs, Non-Fiction, Novels, Poetry, Prose, Romance, Science Fiction, Young Adult.

•**Punkin House Press (see also PUNKIN HOUSE DIGEST),** Amy Ferrell, 9824 Mar Largo Cr, Fort Myers, FL 33919, http://www.punkinhousepres.com, ContactUs@punkinhousepress.org. 2009. Poetry, fiction, art, photos, cartoons, satire, music, long-poems, non-fiction. "Punkin House Press is on a mission to help the artist. Unlike other publishing companies, our number one priority is to take care of our authors, helping guide them through a process that produces quality material.Our secondary goal is to be as "green" as possible. So along with your piece being on a bookshelf, it will also available as an e-book." No titles listed in the *Small Press Record of Books in Print* (36th Edition, 2010-11). Reporting time: Less than three months. Simultaneous submissions accepted: Yes. Copyrights for author. Subjects: Arts, Avant-Garde, Experimental Art, Creativity, Essays, Fantasy, Fiction, Literature (General), Magazines, Non-Fiction, Poetry, Prose, Reading, Satire, Science Fiction, Short Stories.

Purple Mouth Press (see also IT GOES ON THE SHELF), Ned Brooks, 4817 Dean Lane, Lilburn, GA 30047-4720, nedbrooks@sprynet.com, http://home.sprynet.com/~nedbrooks/home.htm. 1975. Fiction, art, satire. avg. press run 500. 5 titles listed in the *Small Press Record of Books in Print* (36th Edition, 2010-11). Discounts: 40% for 5 or more. 60pp. Reporting time: 1 week. Payment: yes. Copyrights for author. Subjects: Fantasy, Science Fiction.

PURPLE PATCH, Geoff Stevens, 25 Griffiths Road, West Bromwich, B71 2EH, England. 1976. Poetry, fiction, articles, art, reviews, news items. "Mainly poetry. Fiction should be short.We occasionally publish a free supplement of poetry to subscribers only)." circ. 200. 3/yr. Pub'd 3 issues 2009; expects 5 issues 2010, 3 issues 2011. 1 title listed in the *Small Press Record of Books in Print* (36th Edition, 2010-11). sub. price £6 for 3 issues; per copy £2-00; $6 check made out to G.Wall and sent to our Purple Patch address(for American purchasers or £20 check for 3 issue subscription.); sample £1.50, $5 bill. 24+pp. Reporting time: 1 month. Simultaneous submissions accepted: yes. Publishes 5% of manuscripts submitted. Payment: none. Copyrighted, reverts to author. Pub's reviews: 150 in 2009. §Poetry, short stories, biographies of writers, art. Ads: inquire. Subjects: Fiction, Literary Review, Poetry.

Pushcart Press, Bill Henderson, PO Box 380, Wainscott, NY 11975, 631-324-9300, www.pushcartprize.com. 1973. "Each year we will publish *The Pushcart Prize: Best of the Small Presses*, with the help of our distinguished contributing editors. We also sponsor the annual Editors' Book Award for manuscripts overlooked by commercial publishers. (All manuscripts must be nominated by an editor.)." avg. press run varies. Pub'd 8 titles 2009; expects 8 titles 2010, 9 titles 2011. 47 titles listed in the *Small Press Record of Books in Print* (36th Edition, 2010-11). Discounts: 1-9, 20%; 10+, 40%. 200-600pp. Reporting time: varies. Payment: 10%. Copyrights for author. Subjects: How-To, Literature (General).

Pussywillow, Birdie Newborn, 1212 Punta Gorda Street, #13, Santa Barbara, CA 93103-3568, 805-899-2145 phone/Fax. 2002. Fiction, art, cartoons, interviews, parts-of-novels. "Pussywillow is for women who feel good about sexualityy." avg. press run 1M. Expects 1 title 2010, 2 titles 2011. No titles listed in the *Small Press Record of Books in Print* (36th Edition, 2010-11). None, no returns. 80pp. Reporting time: 2 months. Simultaneous submissions accepted: yes. Publishes 3% of manuscripts submitted. Payment: by agreement. Copyrights for author. Subjects: Autobiography, Comics, Erotica, Fiction, Graphics, Interviews, Lifestyles, Memoirs, Romance, Sex, Sexuality, Short Stories, Singles, Women.

Pygmy Forest Press, Leonard Cirino, 1125 Mill St, Springfield, OR 97477-3729, 541-747-9734. 1987. Poetry, fiction, art, reviews, non-fiction. "Query with 10-15 pages." avg. press run 200. Pub'd 2 titles 2009; expects 3 titles 2010, 4 titles 2011. 12 titles listed in the *Small Press Record of Books in Print* (36th Edition, 2010-11). Discounts: 1/3 off to retail and institutional prisoners; libraries full price. 20-80pp. Reporting time: immediate to 1 month. Simultaneous submissions accepted: yes. Publishes 3-5% of manuscripts submitted. Payment: new format is that author must subsidy 90% of printing costs and will receive like in copies. Copyrights for author. Subjects: Anarchist, Arts, Asian-American, John Berryman, Black, California, Chicano/a, Fiction, Native American, Pacific Northwest, Poetry, Prison, Short Stories, Tapes & Records, Translation.

Pyncheon House, David Rhodes, 6 University Drive, Suite 105, Amherst, MA 01002. 1991. Poetry, fiction, criticism. "Recent contributors: F.D. Reeve, Jonathan Edward, Rebecca Scott and James Cole." avg. press run 2M-3M. Pub'd 4 titles 2009; expects 4 titles 2010, 4 titles 2011. 3 titles listed in the *Small Press Record of Books in Print* (36th Edition, 2010-11). Discounts: 1-5 10%, 6-15 15%, 16-25 20%; direct to library 20%, 26-100 30% 101+ negotiable. 150pp. Reporting time: 3-6 months. Publishes 5% of manuscripts submitted. Payment: 10% and/or free books. Copyrights for author. Subjects: Criticism, Fiction, Literature (General), Novels, Poetry, Short Stories.

Q

QED Press, Cynthia Frank, President, Managing Editor; Joe Shaw, Editor, 155 Cypress Street, Fort Bragg, CA 95437, 707-964-9520, Fax 707-964-7531, qedpress@mcn.org. 1986. Fiction, art, non-fiction. "QED Press is a small, Mendocino-based publishing house whose vision is to publish fiction and non-fiction that inspires readers to transcend national, racial and ethnic boundaries through appreciation of world literature and art. Each year QED publishes selected titles of uncommon interest and quality." avg. press run 3M. Pub'd 1 title 2009; expects 5 titles 2010, 5 titles 2011. 22 titles listed in the *Small Press Record of Books in Print* (36th Edition, 2010-11). Discounts: 1-2 books list, 3-5 33%, 6+ 40%. 224pp. Reporting time: 3 months. Simultaneous submissions accepted: yes. Publishes less than 3% of manuscripts submitted. Payment: varies. Copyrights for author. Subjects: African-American, Biography, Careers, Fiction, Health, History, How-To, Literature (General), Memoirs, Mental Health, Pacific Northwest, Political Science, Printing, Self-Help, Women.

QP Publishing (see also QUALITY QUIPS NEWSLETTER), Nancy Sue Swoger, PO Box 18281, Pittsburgh, PA 15236-0281, phone/Fax. 1990. Non-fiction. "Primary focus is quality/technical non-fiction. Will consider other works in the non-fiction field. Also interested in any business publications." avg. press run 1M. Pub'd 2 titles 2009; expects 3 titles 2010. 3 titles listed in the *Small Press Record of Books in Print* (36th Edition, 2010-11). Discounts: 1-4 books 20%, 5-9 30%, 10-24 40%, 25-49 45%, 50+ 50%. 184pp. Publishes 50% of manuscripts submitted. Payment: negotiable. Copyrights for author. Subject: Business & Economics.

QRL POETRY SERIES, Quarterly Review of Literature Press, Theodore Weiss, Renee Weiss, Princeton University, 185 Nassau Street, Princeton, NJ 08540, 609-258-4703. 1943. Poetry, long-poems. "4-6 books under one cover and listed by volume number." sub. price 2 volumes paper $20, single $12, $20 institutional & hardback per volume; per copy $20/cl, $10/pa, anniversary double volume $20/pa, $25/cl; sample $10. Back issues: roughly $20 per volume, cloth; $10 per volume paper; write for catalog for complete list. Discounts: non-returnable—bookstores 40% on 5+ copies, 10% on 1 copy; agency 10%; 20% for returnable arrangements. 250-350pp. Copyrighted, does not revert to author. Subjects: Poetry, Translation.

Quail Ridge Press, PO Box 123, Brandon, MS 39043, kgrissom@quailridge.com. No titles listed in the *Small Press Record of Books in Print* (36th Edition, 2010-11).

Quale Press, Gian Lombardo, P.O. Box 511, Williamsburg, MA 01096, 413-268-7911, central@quale.com. 1997. "No unsolicited work. Press will publish prose poetry, experimental fiction and literary criticism on a solicited basis only. Also interested mainly in scientific, engineering and computer-related books emphasizing the humanistic aspect and effects of technology. Query first. Occasionally will publish reprints of exceptional but overlooked literary work currently not in print." avg. press run Titles being published print-on-demand. Advance copies number from 75 to 125. Pub'd 4 titles 2009; expects 6 titles 2010, 4 titles 2011. 34 titles listed in the *Small Press Record of Books in Print* (36th Edition, 2010-11). Discounts: 20% agent/jobber on more than 10 copies. 64-152pp. Payment: Author receives net sales royalty. Copyrights for author. Subjects: Computers, Calculators, Criticism, Engineering, Experimental, Fiction, Literature (General), Poetry, Science, Socialist, Surrealism.

QUALITY QUIPS NEWSLETTER, QP Publishing, Nancy Sue Swoger, PO Box 18281, Pittsburgh, PA 15236-0281, phone/Fax. 1991. "This quarterly newsletter deals with quality, customer service and team issues (non-fiction business). Book reviews are a regular feature (6-8 reviews per issue). Distribution is to quality managers, customer service managers and representatives, and quality engineers, to companies of all sizes." circ. 5M. 4/yr. Pub'd 4 issues 2009; expects 4 issues 2010, 4 issues 2011. sub. price $30. 10pp. Payment: free 1 year subscription. Pub's reviews: 24-32 in 2009. Subject: Business & Economics.

QUARTER AFTER EIGHT, Wendy Walker, Editor-in-Chief, Ellis Hall, Ohio University, Athens, OH 45701. 1993. Fiction, articles, interviews, satire, criticism, letters, parts-of-novels, plays, non-fiction. "*QAE* seeks dynamic prose works—short fiction, prose-poetry, letters, drama, essays, memoirs, translations—that eschew the merely prosaic across a range of genres. Although *QAE* does not publish traditional verse and/or lyric poetry, the editors do welcome work that provocatively explores—even challenges—the prose/poetry distinction." circ. 1M. 1/yr. Pub'd 1 issue 2009; expects 1 issue 2010, 1 issue 2011. sub. price $10; per copy $10; sample $10. Back issues: reduced price. Discounts: 25+ copies 30%, distributed by Bernhard DeBoer, Ingram. 200pp. Reporting time: 4-6 months. We accept simultaneous submissions if stated in cover letter. Publishes 7% of manuscripts submitted. Payment: 2 copies of upcoming issue. Copyrighted, reverts to author. Pub's reviews: 5 in 2009. §Cutting edge prose and poetry books. Subjects: Criticism, Culture, Essays, Fiction, Interviews, Prose.

Quarterly Committee of Queen's University (see also QUEEN'S QUARTERLY: A Canadian Review), Boris Castel, Queen's University, Kingston, Ontario K7L 3N6, Canada, 613-533-2667, qquarter@post.queensu.ca, http://info.queensu.ca/quarterly. 1893. Poetry, fiction, articles, interviews, satire, criticism, parts-of-novels, plays. "Articles: 20-25 double-spaced pages plus copy on disk in Wordperfect. Recent contributors: Marlene Brant Castellano, Jerry S. Grafstein, Sylvia Ostry, Janice Gross Stein, Michael Ignatieff, Conor Cruise O'Brien." avg. press run 3.5M. Expects 1 title 2010. No titles listed in the *Small Press Record of Books in Print* (36th Edition, 2010-11). 224pp. Reporting time: 2-3 months. Payment: yes. Copyrights for author. Subjects: Arts, Biography, Book Reviewing, Business & Economics, Criticism, Earth, Natural History, Education, History, Literature (General), Philosophy, Politics, Psychology, Science.

Quarterly Review of Literature Press (see also QRL POETRY SERIES), Theodore Weiss, Renee Weiss, 900 Hollingshead Spring Road, Apt J-300, Skillman, NJ 08558-2075, 609-921-6976, Fax 609-258-2230, qrl@princeton.edu. 1943. Poetry. avg. press run 3M-5M. Pub'd 4-6 titles 2009. 78 titles listed in the *Small Press Record of Books in Print* (36th Edition, 2010-11). Discounts: 10%. 350pp. Reporting time: 1-3 months. Simultaneous submissions accepted: yes. Payment: $1000 and 100 copies for each manuscript printed. Copyright by QRL. Subject: Poetry.

QUARTERLY WEST, Mike White, Editor; Paul Ketzle, Editor, 255 South Central Campus Drive, Dept. of English, LNCO 3500/University of Utah, Salt Lake City, UT 84112-9109, 801-581-3938. 1976. Poetry, fiction, interviews, criticism, reviews, parts-of-novels, long-poems, non-fiction. "We publish quality fiction, poetry, nonfiction and reviews in experimental or traditional forms, by new or established writers. We solicit our reviews but do read unsolicited ones. Since 1982 we have sponsored a biennial novella competition with cash prizes for the two winners. We read unsolicited MSS from *Sept. 1-May 1 only* and will accept simultaneous submissions (make this clear in your cover letter). Contributors: Ai, Kate Braverman, Ron Carlson, Andre Dubus, Stephen Dunn, Allen Ginsberg, Albert Goldbarth, Eamon Grennan, Barry Hannah, Tess Gallagher, Patricia Goedicke, Philip Levine, Larry Levis, Lynne McMahon, Lucia Perillo, Francine Prose, Dave Smith, George Saunders, Eleanor Wilner." circ. 1700. 2/yr. Pub'd 2 issues 2009; expects 2 issues 2010, 2 issues 2011. sub. price $14.00; per copy $8.50; sample $7.50. Back issues: $5. Discounts: agents 25%, bookstores 40%. 144pp. Reporting time: 3-6 months. Simultaneous submissions accepted: yes. Publishes less than 1% of manuscripts submitted. Payment: 2 copies; $25-$100 fiction, $25-100 poetry, $500 novella competition. Copyrighted, does not revert to author. Pub's reviews: 5 in 2009. §Fiction, poetry, and non-fiction. Ads: $150/$85. Subjects: Fiction, Poetry, Reviews.

QUARTZ HILL JOURNAL OF THEOLOGY:A Journal of Bible and Contemporary Theological Thought, Quartz Hill Publishing House, R.P. Nettelhorst, Editor; Dandi Moyers, Assistant Editor, 43543 51st Street West, Quartz Hill, CA 93536, 661-722-0891, 661-943-3484, E-mail robin@theology.edu. 1993. Poetry, articles, interviews, criticism, reviews, non-fiction. "*Quartz Hill Journal of Theology* is the official journal of Quartz Hill School of Theology, a ministry of Quartz Hill Community Church. Quartz Hill Community Church is associated with the Southern Baptist Convention. We accept as our doctrinal statement *The Baptist Faith and Message*, adopted by the SBC in 1963. Length: 25,000 words max.; prefer 5,000-10,000. Submit complete manuscript. Enclose SASE for response. Submissions without SASE will be disposed of unread." circ. 200. 4/yr. Pub'd 2 issues 2009; expects 4 issues 2010, 4 issues 2011. sub. price $40; per copy $10.95; sample $10.95. Back issues: $10.95. Discounts: none. 100pp. Reporting time: 30 days. Simultaneous submissions accepted: yes. Publishes 10% of manuscripts submitted. Payment: 1 contributor's copy. Copyrighted, does not revert to author. Pub's reviews: 12 in 2009. §Bible, theology, science, literature, poetry. Ads: $50/$25/will trade ads with other publishers. Subjects: Christianity, Religion.

Quartz Hill Publishing House (see also QUARTZ HILL JOURNAL OF THEOLOGY:A Journal of Bible

and Contemporary Theological Thought), R.P. Nettelhorst, Editor; Dandi Moyers, Assistant Editor, 43543 51st Street West, Quartz Hill, CA 93536, 661-722-0891, 661-943-3484, E-mail robin@theology.edu. 1993. Non-fiction. "Quartz Hill Publishing House is the official publishing arm of Quartz Hill School of Theology, a ministry of Quartz Hill Community Church. Quartz Hill Community Church is associated with the Southern Baptist Convention. We accept as our doctrinal statement *The Baptist Faith and Message*, adopted by the SBC in 1963. Length: 500,000 words max. for books. Query first. Must enclose SASE for response. Submissions without SASE will be disposed of unread." avg. press run 200. Pub'd 5 titles 2009; expects 5 titles 2010, 5 titles 2011. 29 titles listed in the *Small Press Record of Books in Print* (36th Edition, 2010-11). 200pp. Reporting time: 30 days. Publishes 1% of manuscripts submitted. Payment: no advance; 10% royalty. Copyrights for author. Subjects: Christianity, Religion.

QUEEN OF ALL HEARTS, Montfort Publications, J. Patrick Gaffney, Editor; Roger M. Charest, Managing Editor, 26 South Saxon Avenue, Bay Shore, NY 11706, info@montfortmissionaries.com, www.montfortmissionaries.com. 1950. Poetry, fiction, articles, art, non-fiction. "*Queen of all Hearts* Magazine promotes knowledge of and devotion to the Mother of God, by explaining the Scriptural basis as well as the traditional teaching of the Church concerning the Mother of Jesus; her place in theology, the apostolate and spiritual life of the Roman Catholic Church; to make known her influence, over the centuries, in the fields of history, literature, art, music, poetry, etc., and to keep our readers informed of the happenings and recent developments in all fields of Marian endeavors around the world. Length of article: 1500 to 2500 words. Authors: Roman Ginn, o.c.s.o., Viola Ward, Joseph Tusiani, etc." circ. 1.5M. 6/yr. Pub'd 6 issues 2009; expects 6 issues 2010, 6 issues 2011. sub. price $22; per copy $2; sample $2. Back issues: 50% discount plus postage. Discounts: schedules upon request. 48pp. Reporting time: less than a month. Simultaneous submissions accepted: no. Publishes approx. 25% of manuscripts submitted. Payment: yes, most of the time. Not copyrighted. Pub's reviews: about 18 in 2009. §Marian topics. Ads: none. Subject: Religion.

QUEEN'S QUARTERLY: A Canadian Review, Quarterly Committee of Queen's University, Boris Castel, Queen's University, Kingston, Ontario K7L 3N6, Canada, 613-533-2667, queens.quarterly@queensu.ca, www.queensu.ca/quarterly. 1893. Poetry, fiction, articles, interviews, satire, criticism, parts-of-novels, plays. "Articles 2000 - 3000 words by email or regular mail. Recent contributors include Michael Ignatieff, Mavis Gallant, Mark Kingwell, Leslie Millin, Michael Posner." circ. 3.5M. 4/yr. Pub'd 4 issues 2009; expects 4 issues 2010, 4 issues 2011. sub. price $20 Canada, $25 U.S.; per copy $6.50; sample $6.50. Back issues: depends on age, min. $4, max. $6. Discounts: none. 160pp. Reporting time: 1 month. Simultaneous submissions accepted: no. Payment: up to $300 (short stories), $80 per poem, copies, subscriptions. Copyrighted, reverts to author. Pub's reviews: 60 in 2009. §Serious books only, history, science, politics, philosophy, social science, literary studies, music, art, etc. Not interested in unsolicited reviews. Ads: none. Subjects: Arts, Biography, Book Reviewing, Business & Economics, Criticism, Earth, Natural History, Education, History, Literature (General), Philosophy, Politics, Psychology, Science.

QUERCUS REVIEW, Sam Pierstorff, Modesto Junior College, 435 College Avenue, Modesto, CA 95350, 209-575-6183, pierstorffs@mjc.edu, www.quercusreview.com. 2000. Poetry, fiction, art, photos. "Established in 1999, *Quercus Review (QR)* has quickly become a prominent literary arts journal, publishing numerous nationally recognized, award-winning authors and artists from all across the nation. Additionally, *QR* continues to discover new voices and reflect the lyricism of California's Great Central Valley. However, our main goal has always been simply to publish the best work we can find. Recent contributors: X.J. Kennedy, Amiri Baraka, Gerald Locklin, Lawrence Raab, Naomi Shihab Nye, Steve Kowit, Alan Catlin, Lyn Lifshin, Charles Harper Webb, Stellasue Lee, Wilma McDaniel. In addition to publishing our annual literary arts journal, Quercus Review Press publishes one full-length collection of poetry by a single author every year through our annual book award contest. More info about the Quercus Review Press Poetry Series can be found at our website." circ. 500. 1/yr. Pub'd 1 issue 2009; expects 2 issues 2010, 2 issues 2011. sub. price $20 for 1yr. (2 books); $35 for 2 yrs. (4 books); per copy $8; sample $8. Back issues: $6. Discounts: Additional contributor copies are $5. Other discounts available for orders of 10 or more. 200pp. Reporting time: 3 weeks to 6 months. Simultaneous submissions accepted: no. Publishes 5% of manuscripts submitted. Payment: 1 copy + $5 for additional copies. Copyrighted, reverts to author. Subjects: Fiction, Poetry.

QUICKSILVER, D. Brian Anderson, General Editor; Michelle Primeau, General Editor, El Paso, TX 79968, academics.utep.edu/quicksilver, quicksilver@utep.edu. 2008. Poetry, fiction, photos, interviews, non-fiction. "Quicksilver is an online literary magazine affiliated with the online MFA program at the University of Texas at El Paso. Quicksilver invites quality submissions of prose and poetry from emerging and established writers. Submit prose and poetry that demands reading and rereading. Quicksilver only accepts previously unpublished and electronic submissions. Submissions must be submitted electronically. Cover letters are welcomed; include a third-person biography of less than 50 words. Simultaneous submissions are accepted as long as work is so noted during initial submission and writers inform us if work is accepted elsewhere. We are unable to offer payment beyond publication in the magazine, our heartfelt thanks, and the best web hype we can manage. We currently accept less than 5% of all submissions; much good work is sent our way, but we like to keep our house small and clean. At the present time we do not consider plays, screenplays, or novellas. Recent contributors include Gary Fincke, Brian Doyle, and Blake Butler.'' 2/yr. Pub'd 1 issue 2009; expects 2 issues 2010. Reporting time: 1-3 months. Simultaneous submissions accepted: Yes. Publishes 5% of manuscripts submitted.

Quicksilver Productions, Jim Maynard, P.O.Box 340, 559 S Mountain Avenue, Ashland, OR 97520-3241, 541-482-5343, Fax 541-482-0960. 1973. ''Not accepting manuscripts at this time.'' avg. press run 30M. Pub'd 5 titles 2009; expects 6 titles 2010, 6 titles 2011. 9 titles listed in the *Small Press Record of Books in Print* (36th Edition, 2010-11). Discounts: trade and jobbers, (trade from 40% at 5 copies to 50% at 1,000 mixed titles). Prepaid orders receive 5% extra discount plus free shipping. Copyrights for author. Subjects: Astrology, Cooking, Occult.

THE QUIET FEATHER, Taissa Csaky, Dominic Hall, Tim Major, St. Mary's Cottage, Church Street, Dalton-In-Furness, Cumbria, LA15 8BA, ENGLAND, United Kingdom. 2004. Poetry, fiction, articles, art, photos, cartoons, interviews, music, plays, non-fiction. circ. 200. 4/yr. Pub'd 3 issues 2009; expects 4 issues 2010, 4 issues 2011. sub. price 9; per copy 2.50; sample 2.50. Back issues: 2.50. 24pp. Reporting time: 2 weeks. Simultaneous submissions accepted: Yes. Publishes 5% of manuscripts submitted. Payment: Profit-sharing when circulation gets larger - see http://www.thequietfeather.co.uk/QFworks.htm. Not copyrighted. Subjects: Arts, Cartoons, Creativity, Current Affairs, Environment, Fiction, Non-Fiction, Poetry, Politics, Prose, Short Stories, Travel.

Quiet Tymes, Inc., Roger J. Wannell, Founder, 1400 Downing Street, Denver, CO 80218, 303-839-8628, Fax 720-488-2682. 1979. ''Quiet Tymes, Inc. holds trademark for The Baby Soother.'' 2 titles listed in the *Small Press Record of Books in Print* (36th Edition, 2010-11). We sometimes copyright for author. Subjects: Family, Parenting, Tapes & Records.

Quill Driver Books, Sorsky Kent, Publisher, 2006 S. Mary, Fresno, CA 93711-3311, 559-233-6633, Fax 559-233-6933, 800-345-4447. 1993. Non-fiction. ''Additional imprint is Word Dancer Press. Quill Driver Books publishes hardcover and trade paperback originals and reprints with national appeal. Word Dancer Press imprint is used for regional and special market hardcover and trade paperback books. Unagented submissions welcome. Please query before submitting manuscripts. Send SASE.'' avg. press run 4M-10M. Pub'd 10 titles 2009; expects 15 titles 2010, 15 titles 2011. 18 titles listed in the *Small Press Record of Books in Print* (36th Edition, 2010-11). Discounts: retailers 1 book 20%, 2-9 40%, 10-49 43%, 50+ 46% libraries and schools 20%. Special discounts apply to reference titles, please inquire. 200pp. Reporting time: 30 days. Simultaneous submissions accepted: yes. Publishes 1/4 of 1% of manuscripts submitted. Payment: royalties negotiated. Copyrights for author. Subjects: California, History, How-To, Self-Help, Senior Citizens, Writers/Writing.

THE QUILLDRIVER, Donna Schillinger, P.O. Box 573, Clarksville, AR 72830, 479.497-0321, www.thequilldriver.com, info@thequilldriver.com. 2006. Non-fiction. ''*The Quilldriver* is a small independent press of inspirational non-fiction. Our focus is books that bolster the faith of young adults during the transition from living with their family to living on their own.'' circ. 4000. Expects 1 issue 2010, 3 issues 2011. 3 titles listed in the *Small Press Record of Books in Print* (36th Edition, 2010-11). Discounts: 3 to 10 copies - 25% discount; bulk orders 50% discount, distributors - call for pricing. 200pp. Reporting time: 8 to 10 weeks. Simultaneous submissions accepted: Yes. Publishes 2% of manuscripts submitted. Payment: $1000 advance with 15% royalties on the actual sale price (not on retail price). Copyrighted. Subjects: Autobiography, Catholic, Christianity, Creative Non-fiction, Diaries, Inspirational, Latin America, Motivation, Success, Non-Fiction, Spiritual, Young Adult.

Quincannon Publishing Group, Alan Quincannon, Editor-in-Chief; Holly Benedict, Editor, Compass Point Mysteries, Patricia Drury, Loretta Bolger, Jeanne Wilcox, PO Box 8100, Glen Ridge, NJ 07028, 973-380-9942, editors@quincannongroup.com, www.quincannongroup.com. 1990. ''Imprints: Compass Point Mysteries; Tory Corner Editions; Learning & Coloring Books.'' Pub'd 5 titles 2009; expects 5 titles 2010, 5 titles 2011. 15 titles listed in the *Small Press Record of Books in Print* (36th Edition, 2010-11). Copyrights for author.

Quinn Entertainment, 7535 Austin Harbour Drive, Cumming, GA 30041, Phone (770) 356-3847, Fax (770) 886-1475, info@quinnentertainment.com, www.quinnentertainment.com. Fiction, plays, non-fiction. ''Quinn Entertainment is dedicated to the promotion of fun and educational books that enrich the lives of children.'' 4 titles listed in the *Small Press Record of Books in Print* (36th Edition, 2010-11). Discounts: 55% Discount. 150pp.

R

Rabeth Publishing Company, Raymond Quigley, Elizabeth Quigley, 3515 NE 61st St., Gladstone, MO 64119-1931, email: qurabeth@kvmo.net. 1990. Poetry, fiction, non-fiction. avg. press run 400-2M. Pub'd 2 titles 2009; expects 3 titles 2010, 3-4 titles 2011. 7 titles listed in the *Small Press Record of Books in Print* (36th Edition, 2010-11). Discounts: 40% to trade. 100-125pp. Reporting time: 2-4 weeks. Simultaneous submissions accepted: yes. Publishes 30-50% of manuscripts submitted. Payment: negotiable. Copyrights for author. Subjects: Fiction, Non-Fiction, Poetry, Religion.

Rada Press, Inc., Daisy Pellant, 1277 Fairmount Avenue, St. Paul, MN 55105-7052, phone: 651-554-7645; fax: 651-455-6975. 1975. Non-fiction. "Our publishing focus is education. We produce books for students in their middle and high school years. Our special area is history." avg. press run 500. Pub'd 13 titles 2009; expects 1 title 2010, 1 title 2011. 3 titles listed in the *Small Press Record of Books in Print* (36th Edition, 2010-11). 100pp. Reporting time: 30 days. Simultaneous submissions accepted: Yes. Payment: 10% of cover price; no advances. Subjects: Communication, Journalism, Education, Geography, History, Media, Non-Fiction, Political Science, Technology.

•Ragamuffin Heart Publishing, Kenneth Grie, 8011 Anchor Drive, Longmont, CO 80504, 720-494-1374. 2010. Poetry, fiction, cartoons. "Ragamuffin Heart Publishers are interested in books with colorful illustrations that tap into the curiosity of young children, and explore their tender emotions. As well RHP is looking for books full of excitement and adventure. RHP accepts picture books, books for young and middle readers.We have published Gracies Return." avg. press run 500. Expects 2 titles 2010, 1 title 2011. No titles listed in the *Small Press Record of Books in Print* (36th Edition, 2010-11). Discounts: 2-10 copies 25%11-99 copies 40%100-up 50%. 32pp. Reporting time: 3-4 months. Simultaneous submissions accepted: Yes. Payment: 7.5 % of wholesale price. We offer a $1,000 advance. Does not copyright for author. Subjects: Adoption, Aging, Animals, Cartoons, Children, Youth, Dance, Family, Fantasy, Festivals, Fiction, Gardening, Music, Nature, Parenting.

Ragged Edge Press, Harold E. Collier, Acquisitions Editor, PO Box 708, 73 West Burd Street, Shippensburg, PA 17257, 717-532-2237, Fax 717-532-6110. 1994. Non-fiction. "Ragged Edge Press makes a difference in people's lives with topics that focus on religion and relationships." avg. press run 2M-3M. Expects 4 titles 2010, 10 titles 2011. 13 titles listed in the *Small Press Record of Books in Print* (36th Edition, 2010-11). Discounts: available on request. 200pp. Reporting time: 30 days for proposals, 90 days for full manuscripts, proposal guidelines upon request. Simultaneous submissions accepted: yes. Payment: twice yearly. Copyrights for author. Subjects: Christianity, Non-Fiction, Religion, Society.

Ragged Raven Press (see also IOTA), Bob Mee, Janet Murch, 1 Lodge Farm, Snitterfield, Stratford-upon-Avon, Warwickshire CV37 0LR, England, 44-1789-730320, raggedravenpress@aol.com, www.raggedraven.co.uk. 1998. Poetry, non-fiction. "Poetry - Submissions welcome for individual collections. Annual anthology linked to international competition. Nonfiction - schedule currently full." avg. press run 400. Pub'd 2 titles 2009; expects 2 titles 2010, 2 titles 2011. 15 titles listed in the *Small Press Record of Books in Print* (36th Edition, 2010-11). Discounts: 33%. 84pp. Reporting time: 1 month. Simultaneous submissions accepted: no. Publishes 5% of manuscripts submitted. Payment: negotiated individually with authors of collections, 1 free copy for anthology. Copyrights for author. Subjects: Non-Fiction, Poetry.

Ragged Sky Press, Ellen Foos, Editor, PO Box 312, Annandale, NJ 08801. "Ragged Sky Press, founded in 1992, has published fiction, nonfiction, and poetry books. In 2005, Ellen Foos decided to publish five poetry collections simultaneously: the Ragged Sky Poetry Series, launched in February 2006." Pub'd 1 title 2009; expects 1 title 2010, 1 title 2011. 9 titles listed in the *Small Press Record of Books in Print* (36th Edition, 2010-11).

THE RAGING FACE: Goofball Prose, Otis Barry, Editor, 448 14th Street, Brooklyn, NY 11215, 718 938 0013. 2002. Fiction, satire, non-fiction. "The Raging Face is a community of goofs who like to write, read and talk nonsense. In our quarterly magazine, we publish original prose that is clever, clean and short. Most of the time, the work is made up of humor pieces, absurd fiction and oddball travel essays. We also collect resources for authors and enjoyers of this kind of work. Submissions should be no longer than 1000 words. *Our Motto:* Scribo absurdos ut sim pulcher (I write absurdities so that I may be beautiful). *Our Mission:* To form a gang with other nonsense writers and take over the world. *Our Team:* We are, at least in the fantasies that come to life in our pages, adventurers, scamps, wretches, lowlifes, rascals, rapscallions, knaves, reprobates, swindlers, outlaws, louses, cads, malfeasors, derelicts, sad sacks, beggars, fools, loons, black sheep, lost souls, the dregs of society, bad eggs, degenerates, heroes and gods.'' 4/yr. Pub'd 4 issues 2009; expects 4 issues 2010, 4 issues 2011. Reporting time: 0-2 months. Simultaneous submissions accepted: yes. Publishes 5% of manuscripts submitted. Payment: No payment at this time, though we have been known to provide Raging Face t-shirts to our regular writers. Copyrighted, reverts to author. Subjects: Absurdist, Experimental, Fiction, Humor, Prose, Satire, Zines.

Rain Mountain Press Collective, 63 East Third Street, Suite 16, New York, NY 10003, web:www.rainmountainpress.com. No titles listed in the *Small Press Record of Books in Print* (36th Edition, 2010-11).

RAIN TAXI REVIEW OF BOOKS, Eric Lorberer, PO Box 3840, Minneapolis, MN 55403, 612-825-1528 tel/Fax, info@raintaxi.com, www.raintaxi.com. 1995. Articles, interviews, reviews. ''Book reviews run from 400 words to 1500 words. Interview lengths vary widely. Feature articles from 850 to 3000 words. Manuscripts are usually solicited.'' circ. 18,000. 4/yr. Pub'd 4 issues 2009; expects 4 issues 2010, 4 issues 2011. sub. price $15 domestic/ $23 Canada or Mexico/$30 overseas international; per copy $5. Back issues: $5. Discounts: distributed free of charge in bookstores & literary centers. 56pp. Reporting time: 30 days. Simultaneous submissions accepted: no. Publishes 10% of manuscripts submitted. Payment: copies of magazine, otherwise none. Copyrighted, reverts to author. Pub's reviews: 240 in 2009. §Books and audio- literary fiction & nonfiction, poetry, cultural studies, art. Ads: $800full/$550 2/3 page/$400half/$300 1/3 page/$250 1/4 page/$150 1/8 page. Contract pricing available. Subjects: Avant-Garde, Experimental Art, Book Reviewing, Essays, Interviews, Literary Review, Reviews.

Rainbow Books, Inc., Betsy Wright-Lampe, PO Box 430, Highland City, FL 33846-0430, 863-648-4420, 863-647-5951, rbibooks@aol.com, www.RainbowBooksInc.com. 1979. Fiction, non-fiction. ''Writers' guidelines for first-class, self-addressed, stamped envelope or can be found online on our website under "submissions"; No work under 64 pages. No religious material; no biographies/autobiographies unless a celebrity or marketable, no diet books or business books at all. Looking for how-to and self-help books for adults; self-help books for kids—both adult and children's nonfiction by credentialled authors, please. Being the parent of a successful child does NOT qualify as credentials for a parenting book. We seek active authors who give lectures, seminars and who otherwise assist in promotion of themselves and their books. We enjoy discovering first-time authors. Please be professional in your approach. If you haven't already done so, research and learn about being an author and working with a publisher. Read The Writer magazine, read The Self-Publishing Manual by Dan Poynter and 1001 Ways to Market Your Books by John Kremer. Understand the industry through those two books. We do not offer big advances, and we do not contract on incomplete works. Please, no email queries.'' avg. press run 10M. Pub'd 10 titles 2009; expects 16 titles 2010, 20 titles 2011. 14 titles listed in the *Small Press Record of Books in Print* (36th Edition, 2010-11). Discounts: Single-copy orders must be pre-paid, you pay S&H. Our wholesale terms are 50% (returnable), 55% (nonreturnable), no minimum order. Our VOR is Ingram, but we also work with Baker & Taylor, Book Clearing House and a boatload of jobbers. Our titles are available new through Amazon.com's Advantage Program and used (bookstore returns) through the Marketplace Program. Our 1-800 order number (Book Clearing House) is 1-800-431-1579 (all major cards accepted). We cannot process credit card orders at our editorial offices; those orders must go through Book Clearing House. 250pp. Reporting time: 4 weeks (only with SASE). Simultaneous submissions accepted: yes. Publishes 5% of manuscripts submitted. Payment: Contract depends on material, usually $500 advance, 6% royalty, but we are flexible. We can go with no advance for a higher royalty. Payment twice yearly. Copyrights for author. Subjects: Appalachia, Armenian, Aviation, Black, Children, Youth, How-To, Men, Mystery, Native American, Non-Fiction, Parenting, Psychology, Relationships, Science, Self-Help.

RAINBOW CURVE, Julianne Bonnet, Poetry Editor; Daphne Young, Fiction Editor, P.O. Box 93206, Las Vegas, NV 89193-3206, rainbowcurve@sbcglobal.net, www.rainbowcurve.com. 2002. Poetry, fiction, photos, parts-of-novels, long-poems. ''Rainbow Curve is a segment of highway which bridges two halves of the city of Las Vegas - the affluence of the "new" Las Vegas with their sparkling new developments, to the old downtown and the struggles of an aging tradition. Similarly, Rainbow Curve hopes to uphold the fundamentals of some old literary traditions while, at the same time, paving the way for work that speaks to a new and diverse audience. Recent contributors include: Catherine Ryan Hyde, Virgil Suarez, Terry Ehret and Rob Carney.'' circ. 250. 2/yr. Pub'd 2 issues 2009; expects 2 issues 2010, 2 issues 2011. sub. price $16; per copy $8; sample $6. Back issues: inquire. Discounts: inquire. 100pp. Reporting time: Maximum of three months. Simultaneous submissions accepted: Yes. Publishes 2% of manuscripts submitted. Payment: One contributor copy upon publication. Copyrighted, reverts to author. Ads: Advertise for trade. Subjects: Absurdist, Arts, Avant-Garde, Experimental Art, Essays, Experimental, Feminism, Haiku, Humor, Memoirs, Poetry, Post Modern, Prose, Satire, Short Stories, Storytelling.

RALPH'S REVIEW, Ralph Cornell, 129-A Wellington Avenue, Albany, NY 12203-2637. 1988. Poetry, fiction, art, cartoons, letters. ''No heavy racial, political, rape stories. No slasher stories. Up to 1,000 words; poems to 2 pages. Recent contributors: R. Cornell, Dan Buck, Frederick Zydek, Joseph Danoski, Joyce Frohn,

Brendan J. McDonald, and Joanne Tolson. There is now a $2 reading fee for all stories and $.50 each for poems." circ. 100+. 2+. Pub'd 3 issues 2009; expects 3 issues 2010, 3 issues 2011. sub. price $15; per copy $5; sample $3. Back issues: varies. 35pp. Reporting time: 2-4 weeks. Simultaneous submissions accepted: yes. Publishes 50-60% of manuscripts submitted. Payment: 1 copy. Copyrighted, reverts to author. Ads: $18/$10/$3 1''/$7 3x5/$5 business card. Subjects: Anthropology, Archaelogy, Antiques, Artificial Intelligence, Birds, Book Collecting, Bookselling, Collectibles, Conservation, Dreams, Folklore, Gardening, H.P. Lovecraft, Occult, Philately, Poetry, Science Fiction.

Ram Press (see also CATAMARAN SAILOR), Amelia Norlin, PO Box 2060, Key Largo, FL 33037, 305-451-3287, Fax 305-453-0255, rick@catsailor.comt, www.rambooks.com, www.catsailor.com. 1991. Fiction, non-fiction. Expects 4 titles 2010, 6 titles 2011. 3 titles listed in the *Small Press Record of Books in Print* (36th Edition, 2010-11). Discounts: 2-4 20%, 5-99 40%, 100+ 60%. 352pp. Reporting time: 60 days. Payment: standard. Subjects: Fiction, How-To, Non-Fiction, Sports, Outdoors, Water.

RAMBUNCTIOUS REVIEW, Nancy Lennon, Co-editor; Elizabeth Hausler, Co-editor, Rambunctious Press, Inc., 1221 West Pratt Blvd., Chicago, IL 60626, Rambupress@aol.com. 1984. Poetry, fiction, art, photos. *"Rambunctious Review* accepts submissions from September through May. Length of material: poems 100 lines, fiction 12 pages. No biases. Recent contributors: Maureen Flannery, B.Z. Niditch, Ruth Hull Chatlien, Ron Offen." circ. 600. 1/yr. Pub'd 1 issue 2009; expects 1 issue 2010, 1 issue 2011. sub. price $15/3 issues; per copy $5; sample $4. Back issues: $4. Discounts: none. 48pp. Reporting time: 9 months. Publishes 10% of manuscripts submitted. Payment: 2 free copies of the magazine. Copyrighted, reverts to author. Ads: none. Subjects: Fiction, Poetry.

Peter E. Randall Publisher, Deidre Randall, PO Box 4726, Portsmouth, NH 03802-4726, 603-431-5667, deidre@perpublisher.com, www.perpublisher.com. 1970. Poetry, photos, non-fiction. "We are subsidy publishers, working with many communities, historical societies, businesses, and individuals to produce quality cloth and paperbound books. Catalogue at perpublisher.com." avg. press run varies from 500 up. Pub'd 20 titles 2009; expects 20 titles 2010, 20 titles 2011. No titles listed in the *Small Press Record of Books in Print* (36th Edition, 2010-11). Reporting time: one month. Copyrights for author. Subjects: Biography, History, Maine, New England, New Hampshire, Photography, Picture Books.

•**Rapacious Press,** Jay Rusovich, 3311 Virginia, Houston, TX 77098, 713.417.9381. 2009. Fiction, art, photos, satire, criticism, non-fiction. avg. press run 2500. Pub'd 1 title 2009; expects 2 titles 2010, 2 titles 2011. No titles listed in the *Small Press Record of Books in Print* (36th Edition, 2010-11). 128pp. Subjects: Absurdist, Adolescence, Aging, Alcohol, Alcoholism, Arts, Culture, Erotica, Feminism, Fiction, Gay, Photography, Picture Books, Women, Writers/Writing, Yoga.

Rarach Press, Ladislav R. Hanka, 1005 Oakland Drive, Kalamazoo, MI 49008. 1981. Poetry, art, long-poems. "This is essentially a vehicle for my art and rather personal and idiosyncratic notions of what I wish to print: i.e. occasional small books, poems set into an etching, wood engravings, handbills, posters for exhibitions, and one substantial book of 100 pp. containing 5 long poems in Czech. This is labor-intensive hand-done bibliophilia. My bread and butter is printing my own artwork often as suites of etchings or wood engravings sometimes with a bit of type-set commentary, titles or description. The bibliophilia is an amusement appearing irregularly. I am essentially uninterested in unsolicited manuscripts, unless someone wants me to illustrate something I like." avg. press run 20-30. Pub'd 1 title 2009; expects 1 title 2010, 1 title 2011. 7 titles listed in the *Small Press Record of Books in Print* (36th Edition, 2010-11). Discounts: 40% off for dealers. 10-100pp. Payment: done individually, generally in copies of print. Does not copyright for author. Subjects: Book Arts, Folklore, Poetry.

RARITAN: A Quarterly Review, Jackson Lears, Editor-in-Chief; Stephanie Volmer, Managing Editor, 31 Mine Street, New Brunswick, NJ 08903, 732-932-7887, Fax 732-932-7855, rqr@rci.rutgers.edu. 1981. Poetry, articles, interviews, criticism, reviews, non-fiction. *"Raritan* specializes in literary and cultural criticism. In addition to essays, *Raritan* prints a *small* quantity of poetry and fiction. Contributors include Adam Phillips, Carlo Rotella, Victoria Nelson, Richard White, Marina Warner, John Hollander, and Georgina Kleege." circ. 3.5M. 4/yr. Pub'd 4 issues 2009; expects 4 issues 2010. sub. price $24 individuals, $35 institutions; per copy $8; sample $8 where applicable. Back issues: $6 per copy. Discounts: available for bookstores, distributors, and subscription agencies. 160pp. Reporting time: 4-6 months. Simultaneous submissions accepted: no. Payment: $100. Copyrighted. Pub's reviews: 23 in 2009. §Literary criticism, philosophy, pol. sci., fine arts, history. Ads: $275/$180. Subjects: Arts, Book Reviewing, Criticism, Literature (General).

Raspberry Press Limited, Betty J. Schultz, 1989 Grand Detour Road, Dixon, IL 61021-9520, 815-288-4910, email: raspberrypresslimited@yahoo.com, Url: www.raspberrypresslimited.com. 1988. "Additional address: 1989 Grand Detour Road, Dixon, IL 61021." 5 titles listed in the *Small Press Record of Books in Print* (36th Edition, 2010-11). Reporting time: Not accepting manuscripts at this time. Simultaneous submissions accepted: yes. Subject: Children, Youth.

RATTAPALLAX, Flavia Rocha, Editor; Edwin Torres, Editor; Catherine Fletcher, Editor; Idra Novey, Editor, 217 Thompson Street, Suite 353, New York, NY 10012, info@rattapallax.com. 1998. Poetry, fiction, art, photos, satire, criticism, long-poems, concrete art, non-fiction. "Some recent contributors: Martin Espada, Anthony Hecht, Billy Collins, MC Solaar, Lou Reed, Marilyn Hacker, Glyn Maxwell, and Yusef Komunyakaa. Journal of contemporary poetry, prose and art. First issue comes with an attached CD featuring the poets from that edition." circ. 2M. 2/yr. Pub'd 2 issues 2009; expects 2 issues 2010, 2 issues 2011. 2 titles listed in the *Small Press Record of Books in Print* (36th Edition, 2010-11). price per copy $7.95; sample $7.95. Back issues: $7.95. 128pp. Reporting time: 2 weeks. Simultaneous submissions accepted: no. Copyrighted, reverts to author. Ads: $300/$150. Subjects: Arts, Criticism, Essays, Fiction, Haiku, Literature (General), Non-Fiction, Poetry, Prose, Short Stories, Visual Arts.

RATTLE, Alan Fox, Editor-in-Chief; Timothy Green, Editor, 12411 Ventura Blvd., Studio City, CA 91604, 818-505-6777. 1993. Poetry, art, interviews, criticism, reviews, long-poems. "Essays on writing 2500 words or less. See website for special themes." circ. 4000. 2/yr. Pub'd 2 issues 2009; expects 2 issues 2010, 2 issues 2011. sub. price $18; per copy $10; sample $10. Back issues: $6. Discounts: Half-off for Libraries, otherwise negotiable. 196pp. Reporting time: 6-8 weeks. Simultaneous submissions accepted: Yes. Publishes 1% of manuscripts submitted. Payment: 2 copies. Copyrighted, reverts to author. Pub's reviews: 70 in 2009. §Poetry books, chapbooks, and anthologies; essay books on poetry. No advertising. Subject: Poetry.

Rattlesnake Press (see also RATTLESNAKE REVIEW), Kathy Kieth, P.O. Box 762, Pollock Pines, CA 95726-0762, kathykieth@hotmail.com or rattlesnakepress.com. 2004. No titles listed in the *Small Press Record of Books in Print* (36th Edition, 2010-11). Reporting time: 3-5 days. Simultaneous submissions accepted: No.

RATTLESNAKE REVIEW, Rattlesnake Press, Kathy Kieth, P.O. Box 762, Pollock Pines, CA 95726-0762, kathykieth@hotmail.com or rattlesnakepress.com. 2004. Poetry, articles, art, photos, interviews, reviews, letters. "Preference given to submissions from Northern California." circ. approx. 200. Quarterly. Pub'd 4 issues 2009; expects 4 issues 2010, 4 issues 2011. price per copy free; sample free. Back issues: $2. 60pp. Reporting time: 3-5 days. Simultaneous submissions accepted: no. Payment: contributor's copy. Copyrighted, reverts to author. Pub's reviews: 30 in 2009. §poetry. Subject: Poetry.

Raular Publishing, Eileen Sheehan, PO Box, 5786, Goodyear, AZ 85338, www.raularpublishing.com; editor@raularpublishing.com. 2008. Fiction, plays, non-fiction. "We are dedicated to providing an avenue for the up and coming writer's work to reach the millions of eager readers on this planet." Expects 10-15 titles 2011. 7 titles listed in the *Small Press Record of Books in Print* (36th Edition, 2010-11). Discounts: website; wholesale. 250-400pp. Simultaneous submissions accepted: No. Payment: twice per year. Copyrights for author. Subjects: Alternative Medicine, Autobiography, Bisexual, Book Reviewing, Buddhism, Fantasy, Fiction, Gay, Horror, Lesbianism, Literature (General), Non-Fiction, Romance, Short Stories, Spiritual.

THE RAVEN CHRONICLES, Phoebe Bosche, Managing Editor & Co-Publisher; Phil Red Eagle, Co-Publisher; Kathleen Alcala, Fiction Editor; Elizabeth Myhr, Poetry Editor; Anna Balint, Non-Fiction Editor; Stephanie Lawyer, Reviews Editor; Phoebe Bosche, Spoken Word Editor; Elizabeth Myhr, Nature Writing Online Editor; Anne Fraser, Food & Culture Online Editor, 12346 Sand Point Way N.E., Seattle, WA 98125, 206-364-2045, editors@ravenchronicles.org, www.ravenchronicles.org. 1991. Poetry, fiction, articles, art, photos, cartoons, interviews, satire, criticism, reviews, music, letters, parts-of-novels, long-poems, plays, concrete art, non-fiction. "Raven Chronicles publishes and promotes work which documents the profound contribution of art and literature created at the community level. Raven publications reflect the cultural diversity and multitude of viewpoints of writers from the Pacific Northwest, the US, and beyond. SASE required. Check web site for submission periods and themes. Recent contributors include: Diane Glancy, Dina Ben-Lev, Carolyn Lei-lani Lau, Abe Blashko, Charles Johnson, Elizabeth Woody, Sherman Alexie, Rita Chavez, Stacey Levine." circ. 1,000. 2/yr. Pub'd 2 issues 2009; expects 2 issues 2010, 2 issues 2011. sub. price $20, $35 foreign; per copy $8-$9; sample $6.24, including postage=past issues; $10.24, including postage, recent issue. Back issues: Check website for prices, or write, or e-mail for information. Discounts: 50% to distributors; 30% to educators ordering 50 or more. 84-100pp. Reporting time: 1-6 months. Simultaneous submissions accepted: A few: but write editors first. Publishes 7-9% of manuscripts submitted. Payment: $0-$40 and/or copies. Copyrighted, reverts to author. Pub's reviews: 30 & more online in 2009. §Poetry, Fiction, Non-fiction, essays: reviews published in print and on our web site. Ads: $30-$300; inquire. Subjects: African-American, Bilingual, Experimental, Fiction, Indigenous Cultures, Literary Review, Literature (General), Multicultural, Non-Fiction, Poetry, Reviews, Short Stories, Storytelling, Translation, Visual Arts.

Raven Publishing, Inc., Janet Hill, P.O. Box 2866, Norris, MT 59745, 406-685-3545, 866-685-3545, fax: 406-685-3599. 2001. Fiction. "Raven Publishing, Inc. specializes in True Fiction (emotionally true stories that confront true-to-life issues via fictional characters) for children ages 8 14. We prefer submissions in the form of a query letter and the first chapter by e-mail to our editor (fore@3rivers.net) or our publisher (janet@ravenpublishing.net) Following are the criteria we look for:1. A story so interesting that children will prefer reading to watching TV2. A hook on the first page of the novel that will compel the reader to continue. 3.

410

Confront important issues that children face. 4. Esteem-building and encouraging lessons in the story without the slightest hint of didacticism or religiosity. 5. Authentic portrayal of natural human emotion and reactions. 6. No downgrading implications to any culture, lifestyle, or group of people. 7. Fully developed characters that todays children will care about. 8. A satisfying ending that makes the reader feel good about the book, the characters, and themselves. 9. Concise writing in an active voice with one point of view. 10. Contains 20,000 to 50,000 words." Pub'd 1 title 2009; expects 1 title 2010, 2 titles 2011. No titles listed in the *Small Press Record of Books in Print* (36th Edition, 2010-11). 180pp. Reporting time: usually report in one month. Simultaneous submissions accepted: Yes. Payment: Royalty, no advance. Copyrights for author. Subjects: Adolescence, Animals, Family, Fiction, Homelessness, Juvenile Fiction, Kansas, Kentucky, Literature (General), Montana, Multicultural, Native American, Prison, Social Work, Washington (state).

Raven Rocks Press, John Morgan, 53650 Belmont Ridge Road, Beallsville, OH 43716, 614-926-1705. 1972. Fiction, non-fiction. "In addition to re-publishing classic children's books by Ethel Cook Eliot, Raven Rocks Press has published Warren Stetzel's book, *School for the Young* (explores some of our assumptions about our human nature and the nature of our world), and reprinted *Hollingsworth's Vision*, a first-person account by a 19th-century Quaker. We expect to publish materials which touch on a variety of fields: education, economics and social organization, environmental issues, solar and underground construction. Those involved in Raven Rocks Press are members of Raven Rocks, Inc., an organization which is engaged in these and other fields, and much of what we publish will be out of our own experience. We will hope, too, to publish relevant material from elsewhere. No exact price is set for *School for the Young*. Rather, contributions are accepted from those able to make them. With this policy, it has been possible for some to secure the book at little or no cost. Others have been able to contribute enough to make up the difference." avg. press run 5M. Expects 1 title 2010, 1 title 2011. 3 titles listed in the *Small Press Record of Books in Print* (36th Edition, 2010-11). Discounts: bookstores & jobbers 1 copy 15%, 2-3 copies 30%, 4+ 40%. 244pp. Copyrights for author. Subjects: Children, Youth, Education, Environment, Psychology.

Raven Tree Press, A Division of Delta Systems Inc, Dawn Jeffers, 1400 Miller Pkwy, McHenry, IL 60050-1906, 877-256-0579, 800-909-9901, raven@delta-systems.com, www.raventreepress.com. 2000. "Raven Tree Press publishes children's bilingual (English/Spanish) picture books." Pub'd 10 titles 2009; expects 10 titles 2010, 10 titles 2011. 7 titles listed in the *Small Press Record of Books in Print* (36th Edition, 2010-11). Discounts: See web site for distributor and wholesaler information.Contact raven@raventree-press.com for more info on discounts. 32pp. Submission information can be obtained from the web site, ww.raventreepress.com. Payment: Advance and royalties are contracted on a title-by-title basis. Copyrights for author. Subjects: Bilingual, Picture Books.

Ravenhawk Books, Hans Jr. Shepherd, Carl Lasky, 7739 E. Broadway Boulevard #95, Tucson, AZ 85710, 520-296-4491, Fax 520-296-4491, ravenhawk6dof@yahoo.com. 1999. Fiction, non-fiction. "No unsolicited materials are accepted at this time." avg. press run 2.5M. Expects 5 titles 2010, 6 titles 2011. 5 titles listed in the *Small Press Record of Books in Print* (36th Edition, 2010-11). Discounts: 55% off cover retail. 65% off if title is ordered 60 days prior to publication date. 320pp. Simultaneous submissions accepted: no. Publishes .005% of manuscripts submitted. Payment: graduated royalty schedule 35%-45%-55% calculated from gross profits. Copyrights for author. Subjects: Anthology, Fiction, Non-Fiction, Novels, Self-Help.

RAVING DOVE, Jo-Ann Moss, Editor, PO Box 28, West Linn, OR 97068. "*Raving Dove* is an on-line journal that publishes original poetry, nonfiction essays, fiction, photography, and art with (universal) anti-war, anti-violence, peace-related, and human rights themes. Original means that you are the author. Fiction may be up to 2,000 words (shorter submissions are preferred), nonfiction may be up to 1,000 words, and multiple submissions are welcome. Poetry content is more important than technical perfection, and free verse is preferred over other forms. Depending on the material received, some editions may not feature all categories of writing and art. International submissions are encouraged. Do not send material to physical address. Send to: editor@ravingdove.org."

Raw Dog Press, R. Gerry Fabian, 151 S. West Street, Doylestown, PA 18901, 215-345-6838. 1977. Poetry. "We are now doing only our Post Poem Series. We publish in the summer. Submit any time. The type of poetry that we are looking for is short (2-10) lines. We want 'people-oriented' work. We'll send samples for $4.00. You MUST enclose a short note and a SASE. Neatness and professionalism really count with us. Visit web page http://rawdogpress.bravehost.com for current information." avg. press run 100. Pub'd 1 title 2009; expects 1 title 2010, 1 title 2011. 28 titles listed in the *Small Press Record of Books in Print* (36th Edition, 2010-11). Discounts: will negotiate and haggle with anyone; will exchange. 12-15pp. Reporting time: 1 month. Simultaneous submissions accepted: no. Publishes 10% of manuscripts submitted. Payment: varies with the material but we will work something out (copies +). Copyright is agreed upon. Subjects: Humor, Inspirational, Poetry, Postcards.

RAW NERVZ HAIKU, Proof Press, Dorothy Howard, 67 Court Street, Aylmer, QC J9H 4M1, Canada, dhoward@aix1.uottawa.ca. 1994. Poetry, fiction, articles, art, reviews, letters, collages. "Haiku, senryu, renga, tanka, haibun, haiga." circ. 260. 4/yr. Pub'd 4 issues 2009; expects 4 issues 2010, 4 issues 2011. sub. price Canada $25, US US$22, elsewhere US$24; per copy Canada $7, US US$6, elsewhere US$7; sample Canada $7, US US$6, elsewhere US$7. Back issues: $5 to contributors. 52pp. Reporting time: 4-6 weeks. Simultaneous submissions accepted: no. Payment: none. Copyrighted, reverts to author. Pub's reviews: 3 in 2009. §Haiku, etc.

Rayve Productions Inc., Norm Ray, Barbara Ray, PO Box 726, Windsor, CA 95492, 707-838-6200, Fax 707-838-2220, E-mail rayvepro@aol.com. 1989. Pub'd 3 titles 2009; expects 3 titles 2010, 2 titles 2011. 37 titles listed in the *Small Press Record of Books in Print* (36th Edition, 2010-11). Subjects: Business & Economics, California, Careers, Folklore, Food, Eating, Genealogy, Health, History, How-To, Journals, Parenting, Reference, Senior Citizens, Transportation, Wine, Wineries.

Razor7 Publishing, Coleman Andre, PO Box 6746, Altadena, CA 91003-6746, (626) 205-3154. 2005. Poetry, fiction, satire. "Books with a cutting edge that are not afraid to cross genres. We like stuff that is not afraid to say "Here I am, now think about what I am saying."Fiction, we expect big things from Blackbirds a our volume fictional series wrapped around real events in 2006. Check out our first title "A Liar's Tale."." avg. press run 1500. Expects 1 title 2010, 3 titles 2011. No titles listed in the *Small Press Record of Books in Print* (36th Edition, 2010-11). Discounts: 1- No discount2-4 20%5-9 30%10-24 40%25-49 42%50-74 44%75-99-46%100-199-48%200 or more 50%. 300pp. Does not copyright for author. Subjects: African-American, Fantasy, Fiction, Political Science, Science Fiction.

REACTIONS, Pen & Inc Press, Clare Pollard, Editor, Pen & Inc Press, School of Literature & Creative Writing, Norwich, Norfolk NR4 7TJ, United Kingdom. 1999. Poetry. "*Reactions* is an annual anthology of contemporary poetry, which is published in book format. It is a specific national and international showcase for up-and-coming poets who have had a first collection published or who are about to reach that stage. It includes the work of around 20 new poets every year, and provides an exclusive preview of the next generation of poetry stars. Any theme/format allowed, we just want *good poetry*." 1/yr. Pub'd 1 issue 2009; expects 1 issue 2010, 1 issue 2011. price per copy £7.99; sample £7.99. 200pp. Reporting time: 3 months. Simultaneous submissions accepted: yes. Payment: £50. Copyrighted. Subject: Poetry.

READ, AMERICA!, The Place In The Woods, Roger A. Hammer, Editor & Publisher, 3900 Glenwood Avenue, Golden Valley, MN 55422. 1982. Reviews. "A quarterly newsletter to Libraries, Reading Is Fundamental, Head Start, and migrant education programs. ISSN-0891-4214. Looking for professional children's librarians to do regular reviews. Three feature sections: powtry for children and adults, short stories for children, trends and case histories in education, literacy." circ. 10M. 4/yr. Pub'd 4 issues 2009; expects 4 issues 2010, 4 issues 2011. sub. price $25; per copy $7.50; sample $7.50. Back issues: $5. Discounts: 15% to qualified book suppliers & librarians. 16pp. Reporting time: 1 week to 6 months. Simultaneous submissions accepted: no. Publishes 20% of manuscripts submitted. Payment: 50 per review or article. Copyrighted, does not revert to author. Pub's reviews: 8 in 2009. §Children's books, P/K - 12, stories on trends, ideas, problem solving. Ads: use flier inserts—rates on request. Subjects: Bilingual, Book Collecting, Bookselling, Chicano/a, Children, Youth, Publishing, Reading, Reviews.

Reading Connections, Mary Howard Ms., P.O. Box 52426, Tulsa, OK 74152-0426, 818-902-0278 contact number of Marketing Manager. 2003. Non-fiction. "Educational products; reading, literacy. Dr. Mary Howard is a passionate advocate for the struggling reader and provides clear strategies in her books (one with 4 CDs, one with DVD) for building effective elementary-school literacy programs." avg. press run 10000. Pub'd 3 titles 2009; expects 1 title 2010. No titles listed in the *Small Press Record of Books in Print* (36th Edition, 2010-11). Discounts: 2-4 copies 10%5-9 copies 20%10-14 copies 30%15+ copies 40%for book with CD. 152pp. Reporting time: 7 days. Simultaneous submissions accepted: Yes. Publishes 5% of manuscripts submitted. Does not copyright for author. Subjects: Education, Non-Fiction, Reading.

THE READING ROOM, Great Marsh Press, Barbara Probst Solomon, Editor-in-Chief & Publisher, P.O. Box 2144, Lenox Hill Station, New York, NY 10021. "*The Reading Room* is proud to offer readers the best fiction, essays, smart argument, art portfolios and poetry of the moment. Little magazines have always provided the intelligent literary glue for society, and are needed today more than ever. RR brings you strong individual voices from the US and around the world.*The Reading Room*welcomes submissions by new writers. We cannot accept responsibility of their loss or delay, or engage in related correspondence. Unless accompanied by a stamped, self-addressed envelope, manuscripts will not be returned. *The Reading Room* is published by Great Marsh Press, which is a sponsored organization of The New York Foundation of the Arts and a member of the Council of Literary Magazines and Presses."

RealPeople Press, 1221 Lefthand Canyon Drive, Boulder, CO 80302-9344. No titles listed in the *Small Press Record of Books in Print* (36th Edition, 2010-11).

Reconstruction Books Publishing LLC, PO Box 1427, Mitchellville, MD 20721, info@reconstruction-books.com. "Reconstruction Books is dedicated to the promotion of quality literature created by authors of works that have not previously found an outlet. While our primary goal is to provide an avenue by which authors of African descent can express their artistry, RB is exclusive only in regard to talent. Reconstruction Books has accepted an element of responsibility for exposing readers to poetry and prose that is determined to be not just unique, but decidedly enduring. We publish poetry and prose. Verse that demonstrates evidence of the poet's awareness of tradition as a genesis for innovation. Fiction that is literate with attention paid by the writer to writing as an art form. Non-fiction that has an unusual perspective and is equally literate. All manuscripts received will be given careful consideration." No titles listed in the *Small Press Record of Books in Print* (36th Edition, 2010-11).

Red Alder Books, David Steinberg, P.O. Box 641312, San Francisco, CA 94109, 415-674-1618, david@davidsteinberg.us. 1974. Poetry, fiction, art, photos, letters, long-poems, non-fiction. "Our present emphasis is fine art sexual photography." avg. press run 3M. Expects 1 title 2010, 1 title 2011. 6 titles listed in the *Small Press Record of Books in Print* (36th Edition, 2010-11). Discounts: 2-4 books 20%, 5+ 40%. 150pp. Reporting time: 2-6 weeks. Simultaneous submissions accepted: yes. Publishes a very small % of manuscripts submitted. Payment: varies. Copyrights for author. Subjects: Biography, Community, Drugs, Erotica, Feminism, Fiction, Men, Photography, Poetry, Psychology, Sex, Sexuality, Society, Women.

Red Candle Press (see also CANDELABRUM POETRY MAGAZINE), M.L. McCarthy, Mr, 1 Chatsworth Court, Outram Rd., Southsea PO5 1RA, England, 02392753696, rcp@poetry7.fsnet.co.uk, www.members.tripod.com/redcandlepress. 1970. Poetry. "Poetry. The Red Candle Press is a fringe-press. It provides a (free) service to poets and does not aim to make a profit. Contributors to *Candelabrum Poetry Magazine* receive one free copy." avg. press run 1M for magazine. 1 title listed in the *Small Press Record of Books in Print* (36th Edition, 2010-11). Discounts: 1/3 to booksellers. Reporting time: 1-2 months. Simultaneous submissions accepted: no. Payment: free copy to magazine contributors. Copyrights for author. Subject: Poetry.

Red Coyote Press, Suzanne Flaig, Susan Budavari, P.O. Box 60582, Phoenix, AZ 85082, 602-454-7815, info@redcoyotepress.com, www.redcoyotepress.com. 2004. "Specializing in high quality mysteries, Red Coyote Press currently publishes short story anthologies. Beginning in 2008, we plan to publish 2-3 novels per year. Queries may be submitted via email or snail mail; submissions accepted by mail only. Any sub-genre will be considered, including amateur sleuth, cozy, hard-boiled, police procedural, suspense, romantic intrigue, and psychological thriller." avg. press run 700-1000. Pub'd 1 title 2009; expects 2 titles 2010, 2-3 titles 2011. 4 titles listed in the *Small Press Record of Books in Print* (36th Edition, 2010-11). 200-250pp. Reporting time: 3-4 weeks for queries; 2-3 months for manuscripts. Payment: For short stories: flat fee, complimentary copy and scaled discounts on additional copies. For novels: pays variable royalty. Subjects: Fiction, Mystery, Short Stories.

Red Cygnet Press, Bruce Glassman, 2245 Enterprise St., Suite 110, Escondido, CA 92029, tel: 760-839-2273, fax: 760-839-2258, web: http://www.redcygnet.com, e: jgravin@redcygnet.com. 2005. Fiction. "To discover and nurture the next generation of America's most talented children's author/illustrators and to provide them with their first opportunity to be published." Pub'd 8 titles 2009; expects 10 titles 2010, 12 titles 2011. 18 titles listed in the *Small Press Record of Books in Print* (36th Edition, 2010-11). 32pp. Subjects: Animals, Children, Youth, Family, Fiction, Literature (General).

Red Dragon Press, Laura Qa, Editor-Publisher, PO Box 320301, Alexandria, VA 22320-4301, 703-683-5877. 1993. Poetry, fiction, long-poems. "Red Dragon Press is an independent publisher undertaking to promote authors who aspire to evoke the emotions of the reader by stressing the symbolic value of language, and in the creation of meaningful new ideas, forms, and methods. We are proponents of works that utilize androgynous literary characterization, psychological and parapsychological topics, and progress in virtue of self determination and individual achievement." avg. press run 500. Expects 2 titles 2010, 2 titles 2011. 17 titles listed in the *Small Press Record of Books in Print* (36th Edition, 2010-11). 64pp. Reporting time: 6 months or less. Simultaneous submissions accepted: yes. Publishes 5% of manuscripts submitted. Does not copyright for author. Subjects: Poetry, Short Stories.

Red Dragonfly Press, Scott King, Editor & Publisher, 307 Oxford Street, Northfield, MN 55057. "Red Dragonfly Press, press-in-residence at the Anderson Center since the fall of 1999, is a small literary press that produces letterpress printed limited edition books of poetry.." No titles listed in the *Small Press Record of Books in Print* (36th Edition, 2010-11).

Red Dust, Joanna Gunderson, 1148 5th Ave., Apt.12-B, New York, NY 10028, 212-348-4388. 1963. Poetry, fiction. "Short works, once accepted, must be sent on disk. In general, authors get 30 copies. There is no advance." avg. press run 300 short works. Pub'd 2 titles 2009; expects 2 titles 2010, 2 titles 2011. 72 titles listed in the *Small Press Record of Books in Print* (36th Edition, 2010-11). Discounts: libraries 20%; wholesalers & booksellers 1 copy-30%, 2 or more-40%, paperback 1-4 copies-20%, 5 or more-40%. 140pp, short works 16-32pp. Reporting time: 2 months. Simultaneous submissions accepted: yes. Publishes 10% of manuscripts submitted. Payment: $300 advance against royalty for full-length works, for short works we pay nothing and claim no rights. Copyrights for author. Subjects: Drama, Fiction, Poetry, Translation.

Red Eye Press, James Goodwin, PO Box 65751, Los Angeles, CA 90065-0751, 323-225-3805. 1988. Art, photos, non-fiction. "We do not accept unsolicited manuscripts or proposals." avg. press run 5M-18M. Pub'd 2 titles 2009; expects 2 titles 2010, 1 title 2011. 5 titles listed in the *Small Press Record of Books in Print* (36th Edition, 2010-11). Discounts: 37%-63%. 360pp. Reporting time: 8 weeks. Simultaneous submissions accepted: yes. Publishes 5% of manuscripts submitted. Payment: 10%. Copyrights for author. Subjects: Counter-Culture, Alternatives, Communes, Drugs, Horticulture, How-To, Quotations, Reference.

•**RED FEZ ENTERTAINMENT,** Michele McDannold, Managing Editor; Leopold McGinnis, Owner; Rob Taylor, Poetry Editor; R.W. Watkins, Poetry Editor; Pat Simonelli, Head Fiction Editor; Aidan Hailes, Fiction Editor; Michael D Grover, Head Poetry Editor, 5 Morningside Drive, Jacksonville, IL 62650, www.redfez.net. 2002. Poetry, fiction, photos, cartoons, parts-of-novels, long-poems, plays, non-fiction. "We are currently ONLINE ONLY. Our main goal is to bring light to underground and under-recognized writers and writing. We've categorized our journal in database style, so readers can search for work in their interest area from mystery to sex to subversion. Though our main submissions seem to be in the realm of so-called literature, Red Fez was founded with the expectation that we would accept and publish interesting and original fiction and poetry in all categories (even new and undiscovered ones!) from Science Fiction, to Drama, to Literary. Past contributors include: MK Chavez, Paul Corman-Roberts, Christina Hoag, Karl Koweski." 4/yr. Pub'd 4 issues 2009; expects 4 issues 2010, 4 issues 2011. sub. price free; per copy free; sample free. Back issues: free. 40pp. Reporting time: 2-8 wks. Simultaneous submissions accepted: Yes. Publishes 20% of manuscripts submitted. Payment: No Payment. All creative content Copyright the respective authors. Subjects: Absurdist, Audio/Video, Comics, Creative Non-fiction, Drugs, Experimental, Fiction, Literature (General), Memoirs, Novels, Poetry, Prose, Relationships, Sex, Sexuality, Short Stories.

RED HAWK, Suburban Wilderness Press, Linda Erickson, Patrick McKinnon, Bud Backen, 730 Linda Vista St., San Jose, CA 95127-1126. 1984. Poetry, fiction, art, photos, interviews, satire, criticism, long-poems, collages. "We tend toward work that brings an interesting story. We prefer characters other than 'you' & 'me' & 'I.' We consider rhythm the element lacking in most of the work we pass up. We have published Ron Androla, Adrian C. Louis, Todd Moore, Albert Huffstickler and Linda Wing recently." circ. 900. Published every 260 days. Pub'd 2 issues 2009; expects 1 issue 2010, 2 issues 2011. sub. price $26/3 issues, $99 lifetime sub.; per copy $9.95; sample $9.95. Back issues: not available. Discounts: none. 36pp. Reporting time: 1 week to never. Simultaneous submissions accepted: yes. Publishes a variable % of manuscripts submitted. Payment: varies. Copyrighted, reverts to author. Ads: none. Subjects: Arts, Fiction, Literary Review, Literature (General), Magazines, Minnesota, Poetry.

Red Hen Press, Mark Cull, PO Box 3537, Granada Hills, CA 91394, 626-356-476, Fax 818-831-6659, E-mail: marketing@redhen.org. 1994. Poetry, fiction, non-fiction. avg. press run 1M. Pub'd 10 titles 2009; expects 10 titles 2010, 20 titles 2011. 15 titles listed in the *Small Press Record of Books in Print* (36th Edition, 2010-11). Discounts: 40% bookstores, 20% classroom. 100pp. Reporting time: 2 months. Simultaneous submissions accepted: yes. Publishes 5% of manuscripts submitted. Payment: 10%. Copyrights for author. Subjects: Essays, Fiction, Poetry.

•**Red Honor Press,** PO Box 166677, Irving, TX 75016, 214-616-0161, www.redhonor.com, dscott@redhonor.com. "Red Honor Press and Red Honor Media are divisions of Red Honor Ventures, a limited partnership company located in Irving, Texas. Formed in 2006, our company offers a distinctive suite of books and media products for today's demanding markets. Red Honor works closely with authors, private and public institutions, organizations and groups seeking to successfully communicate and promote programs, message, subject and mission to an increasingly knowledgeable and discriminating readership. Red Honor balances vision and creativity with traditional and new media to derive maximum value from every publication." No titles listed in the *Small Press Record of Books in Print* (36th Edition, 2010-11).

RED LAMP, Brad Evans, Editor, 6 Madras Road, Cambridge, Cambs CB1 3PX, United Kingdom. 1998. Poetry, articles, cartoons, interviews, criticism, reviews, long-poems, concrete art. circ. Semi-Annual. 2 issues yearly. 1 title listed in the *Small Press Record of Books in Print* (36th Edition, 2010-11). sub. price £2; per copy £2; sample Free (excl. postage). Back issues: £1. 60-70pp. Reporting time: Between 2-4 weeks. Simultaneous submissions accepted: Yes. Payment: CC. Copyrighted, reverts to author. Pub's reviews: none in 2009. §Poetry anthologies, films. Subjects: Arts, Australia, Communism, Marxism, Leninism, Counter-Culture, Alternatives, Communes, History, Human Rights, Humanism, Interviews, Poetry, Politics, Resistance, Reviews, Socialist, Sociology, Writers/Writing.

Red Letter Press, Helen Gilbert, Managing Editor, 4710 University Way NE #100, Seattle, WA 98105-4427, 206-985-4621, Fax 206-985-8965, redletterpress@juno.com. 1990. Non-fiction. "No unsolicited manuscripts." avg. press run 3M. Pub'd 1 title 2009; expects 1 title 2010, 1-2 titles 2011. 20 titles listed in the *Small Press Record of Books in Print* (36th Edition, 2010-11). Discounts: bookstores 40%, wholesalers/distributors negotiable, classes 20%. 200pp. Subjects: Feminism, Gay, Labor, Lesbianism, Politics, Socialist, Third World, Minorities.

•RED MARE, X Su Zi, PO Box 831544, Ocala, FL 34483, X.SuZi@Live.com. 2008. Poetry, long-poems. "Red Mare is a hand-bound(usually sewn) print publication, with a numbered block print for the cover. It is a serial monograph, publishing only one author per issue: in 2008 , a single long poem by Marie C Jones; in 2009, three connected poems by Lola Haskins. All editions are under 50 copies and are numbered. It is available through the publisher directly, or , variably, through Amazon or Alibris via third party seller. Currently, author payment is contributor copies." circ. 30-50. 1-2/yr. Pub'd 1 issue 2009; expects 1 issue 2010, 1 issue 2011. sub. price $7; per copy $7; sample $7. Back issues: $5. Discounts: negotiable. 10-20pp. Reporting time: one week to one month. Simultaneous submissions accepted: Yes. Payment: contributor's copies—more hoped for later. ISSN . Copyright through Library of Congress registration. Ads: No advertising. Subjects: Animals, Avant-Garde, Experimental Art, Beat, Book Arts, Environment, Feminism, Florida, Folklore, Gay, Gender Issues, Indigenous Cultures, Literature (General), Occult, Post Modern, Supernatural.

Red Moon Press, PO Box 2461, Winchester, VA 22604-1661, Tel: 540-722-2156. 1993. "Red Moon Press was founded in 1993 as the publishing arm of the international journal South by Southeast. It was named for an apocalyptic song written by the owner of the press during his stint in Nashville as a singer/songwriter. In 1996 RMP produced its first books: The Red Moon Anthology of English-Language Haiku 1996, which has endured as our signature series, and endgrain, an individual collection of work by Dee Evetts, which has become a minor classic. Since those days RMP has produced more than 100 volumes: 14 years of the Red Moon Anthology series, 11 volumes of contemporary haibun, 6 volumes of A New Resonance: Emerging Voices in English-Language Haiku, and scores of individual collections, theoretical and critical volumes, haiku-related novels and smaller anthologies. Our goal is to continue to publish the best in English-language haiku from around the world." No titles listed in the *Small Press Record of Books in Print* (36th Edition, 2010-11). 64-120pp. Publishes 5% of manuscripts submitted. Copyrights for author.

Red Morning Press, Andrew Brown, Editor; Dennis Campbell, Editor; Chris Perkowski, Editor. "Our mailing address is changing and will be updated soon! Red Morning Press accepts unsolicited poetry manuscripts year-round. We are equally interested in the work of published and unpublished poets. RMP will accept electronic submissions ONLY; manuscripts received by regular mail will not be read and will not be returned. Electronic submissions should follow the below guidelines as closely as possible. Please send manuscripts and any questions to submissions@redmorningpress.com. Manuscripts should be at least 48 pages long, excluding front matter." No titles listed in the *Small Press Record of Books in Print* (36th Edition, 2010-11).

RED MOUNTAIN REVIEW, 1800 Eighth Avenue North, Birmingham, AL 35203. "We have a simple goal to produce a fine literary magazine that gets noticed, and to do so with Birminghams roots in mind. The Magic City has a long history of working hard and of grappling with hard truths. In addition to publishing great individual poems, stories, and essays, we are the champions of the chapbook. Every issue will feature the winning collection from our chapbook contest, which is free to enter and is judged independently by a poet of national reputation. The contest winner recieves a $250 honorarium and publication in the magazine."

Red Rock Press, Ilene Barth, Creative Director, 459 Columbus Avenue, Ste. 114, New York, NY 10024, 212-362-8304, Fax 212-362-6216, redrockprs@aol.com, www.redrockpress.com. 1999. Poetry, concrete art, non-fiction. "We have one series, Virtue Victorious, that publishes 1500-2000 word first person essays and poems. Each volume has its own editor; please check *www.virtuevictorious.com* for submission guidelines and addresses. At our New York office, we review submissions for nonfiction books only. Each submission must be accompanied by sophisticated marketing plan. We are particularly interested in books with crossover potential to the gift market. Most of our authors have previously published books; some are very well known." avg. press run 5M-8M. Pub'd 2 titles 2009; expects 3 titles 2010, 3 titles 2011. 12 titles listed in the *Small Press Record of Books in Print* (36th Edition, 2010-11). Discounts: contact Richard Barth at above addresses for schedules. Reporting time: 4-6 weeks. Simultaneous submissions accepted: no. Publishes 10% of manuscripts submitted. Payment: varies. Copyrights for author. Subjects: Dining, Restaurants, Fashion, Food, Eating, Humor, Inspirational, Literature (General), Memoirs, Sex, Sexuality.

RED ROCK REVIEW, Richard Logsdon, 6375 W. Charleston Blvd., Las Vegas, NV 89146, 1-702-651-5634. 1995. Poetry, fiction, interviews, reviews, non-fiction. "Red Rock Review is dedicated to publishing the finest poetry and fiction available. Because we are based in Las Vegas, we do give slight preference to works published by Southwestern writers. Recent contributors include Diane Thiel, Jack Hirschman, Tony Barnstone, Dean Kostos, H Lee Barnes, and Jim Daniels. Submissions must be online: redrockreview@csn.nev." circ. 2250. 2/yr. Pub'd 2 issues 2009; expects 2 issues 2010, 2 issues 2011. sub. price $12.00/2 issues; per copy $6.50; sample $6.50. Back issues: inquire. Discounts: none. 110pp. Reporting time: 2-3 months. Simultaneous submissions accepted: Yes. Publishes 5% of manuscripts submitted. Payment: 2 copies. Copyrighted, reverts to author. Pub's reviews: approx. 8 in 2009. §Books of poetry and fiction. Subjects: Book Reviewing, Creativity, Experimental, Fiction, Interviews, Literary Review, Literature (General), Poetry, Post Modern, Prose, Reviews, Short Stories, Southwest, Storytelling, The West.

Red Tiger Press (see also ARTISTIC RAMBLINGS), A.D. Beache, P.O. Box 2907, Thomasville, NC 27361,

PH: 832-634-7012, Fax: 530-323-8251, email: RedTigerPress@gmail.com. 2005. Poetry, fiction, articles, art, photos, interviews, satire, music, letters, long-poems, concrete art, non-fiction. Expects 2 titles 2010, 8 titles 2011. No titles listed in the *Small Press Record of Books in Print* (36th Edition, 2010-11). Discounts: 3-10 copies 25%. Simultaneous submissions accepted: Yes. Subjects: Creativity, Erotica, Fantasy, Feminism, Fiction, Folklore, Futurism, Non-Fiction, Occult, Performing Arts, Photography, Poetry, Prose, Short Stories, Writers/Writing.

RED WHEELBARROW, Ken Weisner, 21250 Stevens Creek Blvd., De Anza College, Cupertino, CA 95014, Phone: 408-864-5797, 831-252-3958, weisnerken@fhda.edu. 1976. Poetry, fiction, art, photos, cartoons, interviews, plays, non-fiction. "Formerly known as *Bottomfish*. Seeks excellence, diversity, authenticity, daring, and conviction. Recent contributors include Stephanie Dickinson, Joseph Millar, Karen Tei Yamashita, Bill Minor, Ed Pavlic, Al Young, Ellen Bass, Debra Spencer, Nils Peterson; interviews with Alfredo Vea, Adrienne Rich, Khaled Hosseini, Tracy Kidder, Persis Karim, Azin Arefi, Marilyn Chin, Regie Cabico, Kim Addonizio. Submissions accepted between Sept. 1 and Jan. 31 only. Magazine published annually." circ. 250-500. 1/yr. Pub'd 1 issue 2009; expects 1 issue 2010, 1 issue 2011. price per copy $12 (current issue); sample $8. Back issues: $5-$10. 160pp. Reporting time: 3-6 months. Simultaneous submissions accepted: yes. Publishes 5-10% of manuscripts submitted. Payment: one copy of magazine. Copyrighted, reverts to author. Ads: $150 full page. Subjects: California, Drama, Essays, Fiction, Interviews, Literature (General), Poetry, Short Stories.

RedBone Press, Lisa C. Moore, PO Box 15571, Washington, DC 20003-0571, Phone 202-667-0392, Fax 301-588-0588, Email info@redbonepress.com, www.redbonepress.com. 1997. Fiction, non-fiction. "Accepts ms celebrating culture of black lesbians and gay men, and work that promotes understanding between black gays/lesbians and black mainstream." avg. press run 1M. Pub'd 3 titles 2009; expects 4 titles 2010, 4 titles 2011. 15 titles listed in the *Small Press Record of Books in Print* (36th Edition, 2010-11). Discounts: 40% trade. 215pp. Reporting time: 3-6 months. Simultaneous submissions accepted: yes. Publishes 1% of manuscripts submitted. Payment: varies. Copyrights for author. Subjects: Black, Gay, Lesbianism.

Redgreene Press (see also Anderson Publishing; also RC Anderson Books; REDGREENE REVIEW; Spring Grass), Rosemary Anderson C., Editor & Publisher, 1401 Hodgkiss St., Pittsburgh, PA 15212-2719, Out-of-country authors may submit poems by e-mail: anderson_rc1@earthlink.net with the word poem or poetry in the subject line. 1990. Poetry, art, photos, long-poems. "Always reading for the REDGREENE POETRY PRIZE ($100): enclose SASE for reply and $10 reading fee; send up to 24 pages of poetry—any style or subject plus table of contents and bio; no manuscripts returned. Entrants will receive a free copy of a previous winner's chapbook. Future ANTHOLOGIES are planned on subjects such as America (all viewpoints), portraits (people, places, things), art/color/artists, seasons and nature, animals, life and death, music, parent/child/primal experiences, spiritual/religion, women, sex, and on writing/writers. I like quality poetry, and remain open to new writers, subjects, and styles. Authors include John Sokol, Samuel Hazo, Andrew T. Roy (Collected Poems), Jay Udall, Marjorie Maddox, Marilyn E. Johnston, Sharon Scholl. Spring Grass Press has published unknown poets and handsewn haiku books (Andrew T. Roy: My Chinese Haiku). RC Anderson Books has also published selected books in which the author bears half or all of the costs. Fine editing and design a priority. Query first with self-addressed stamped envelope and three pages of writing. *Redgreene Review* journal takes quality work of any form or length; biannual,$6 sample." 8 titles listed in the *Small Press Record of Books in Print* (36th Edition, 2010-11). Reporting time: varies greatly. Simultaneous submissions accepted: Yes. Payment: Contest winner paid $100 plus publication and royalties. Magazine and anthology authors paid one copy and royalties. Can copyright for author if requested. Subjects: Haiku, Literary Review, Poetry, Writers/Writing.

REDGREENE REVIEW, Redgreene Press, Rosemary Anderson C., PO Box 22322, Pittsburgh, PA 15222, 412-231-0436, anderson_rc1@earthlink.net (only for use by out-of-country authors.)

REDIVIDER, Laura van den Berg, Department of Writing, Literature, and Publishing, Emerson College, 120 Boylston Street, Boston, MA 02116. 2003. Poetry, fiction, art, photos, parts-of-novels, collages, plays, concrete art, non-fiction. "Redivider, a journal of international literature and art, is run by the graduate students of the Writing, Literature, and Publishing Department of Emerson College in Boston. The journal, formerly known as the Beacon Street Review, made its debut at the 2004 AWP Conference in Chicago, and features a fresh and eclectic selection of poetry, fiction, creative non-fiction, plays and art by both emerging and established artists. Recent contributors include Steve Almond, Benjamin Percy, A. Van Jordan, Peter Jay Shippy, Pauls Toutonghi, Timothy Liu, Bob Hicok, M. Allen Cunningham, Gerry LaFemina, Dorianne Laux, Julianna Baggott, Paul Yoon, Kim Chinquee, Kyle Minor, Marilyn Nelson, Tracy K. Smith, and Felicia C. Sullivan. Redivider has also published interviews with celebrated contemporary authors, such as Richard Russo, Antonya Nelson, and Kelly Link. Poetry from the most recent issue was selected for Verse Daily on four occasions and a story from the fall 2006 issue will be reprinted in Best American Fantasy." 2/yr. Pub'd 2 issues 2009; expects 2 issues 2010, 2 issues 2011. sub. price $10; per copy $6; sample $6. Back issues: inquire. 150pp. Reporting time: 2-5 months. Simultaneous submissions accepted: Yes. Payment: Two copies of the issue in which a contributor appears.

Copyrighted, reverts to author. Ads: yes. Subjects: Absurdist, Arts, Experimental, Fiction, Non-Fiction, Photography, Poetry.

RedJack, Heidi Lampietti, P.O. Box 633, Bayside, CA 95524, (707) 825-7817, redjackbooks@gmail.com, www.redjackbooks.com. 1998. Fiction. "RedJack publishes books of science fiction, humor, humorous science fiction, and science-fiction-related blank notebooks. Our fiction titles to date include: *The Adventures of Damion Koehkh, MD, Space Doctor (Original Scripts and Photos from the Series)*; *X and Y, and Other Like Stories* (Sept. 2005); and the Liquid Laughter Collaborative Writing Project. At this time, we are not accepting unsolicited manuscripts." avg. press run 1000. Pub'd 2 titles 2009; expects 2 titles 2010, 2 titles 2011. 6 titles listed in the *Small Press Record of Books in Print* (36th Edition, 2010-11). Discounts: 45%. 200pp. Subjects: Absurdist, Biography, Experimental, Fiction, Humor, Science Fiction, Self-Help, Space, Television.

Redrosebush Press (see also PENNY-A-LINER; PORTALS), Ella M. Dillon, PO Box 2163, Wenatchee, WA 98807-2163, 509-662-7858. 1991. Poetry, fiction, articles, art, photos, cartoons, interviews, satire, criticism, reviews, letters, non-fiction. avg. press run 500-3.1M. Pub'd 3 titles 2009; expects 1-3 titles 2010, 1-3 titles 2011. 4 titles listed in the *Small Press Record of Books in Print* (36th Edition, 2010-11). 60-260pp. Reporting time: asap. Simultaneous submissions accepted: yes. Publishes 100% of manuscripts submitted. Payment: customer pays printing costs, retains all proceeds. Copyrights for author.

Redwood Creek Publishing, Penny Hastings, P.O. Box 368, Santa Rosa, CA 95402, 707 579-3479, penny@sonic.net, www.winasportsscholarship.com. 2006. Non-fiction. avg. press run 3000. Expects 1 title 2010, 2 titles 2011. 1 title listed in the *Small Press Record of Books in Print* (36th Edition, 2010-11). Discounts: 5-10 copies 20%; 25-55% on larger orders. 200pp. Subjects: Business & Economics, Education, Parenting, Sports, Outdoors.

The Reed Edwards Company, Reed Edward, P.O. Box 434, Sturbridge, MA 01566, 508-347-7237. 2007. Fiction, non-fiction. "Reed Edwards is a small independent publisher dedicated to new and emerging writers. We look for authors whose words both inspire and entertain. We publish only a handful of books each year, keeping our concentration and our commitment to our authors focused." avg. press run 1500. Pub'd 1 title 2009; expects 2 titles 2010, 1 title 2011. 4 titles listed in the *Small Press Record of Books in Print* (36th Edition, 2010-11). 300-500pp. Reporting time: 10-12 weeks. Simultaneous submissions accepted: Yes. Payment: 10%-12%-15%. Copyrights for author. Subjects: Fiction, Memoirs, Novels, Short Stories.

•**REED MAGAZINE,** San Jose State University, English Department, One Washington Square, San Jose, CA 95192-0090. "Reed Magazine is sponsored by San Jose State University. Reed is produced annually in the spring. We welcome submissions of fiction, poetry, and non-fiction. Please do not submit any pornographic material. We do not publish translations or previously published material. We do accept simultaneous submissions, but we request that you notify us immediately if your piece is accepted elsewhere. All prose and poetry submissions must be in either .doc or .rtf format. We are unable to read other formats. Submit your short story for the Steinbeck Award, which awards a prize of $1,000 to the winner! Runners up may also be chosen for publication (with the author's permission). There is a $15.00 processing fee. Submission dates are the same as for regular submissions."

•**Reedy Press,** Josh Stevens, Editor, PO Box 5131, St. Louis, MO 63139, 314-644-3400, www.reedypress.com. "Founded in 2003, Reedy Press, LLC, publishes cultural, historical, and sports books of premium quality. Reedy Press develops, produces, and markets its own titles and series. We also specialize in co-publishingworking with colleges and universities, secondary schools, cultural/social institutions (museums, nonprofit organizations, historical societies, etc.), and companies to make trade and commemorative books that reflect a unique, inspired vision." No titles listed in the *Small Press Record of Books in Print* (36th Edition, 2010-11).

Reference Service Press, R. David Weber, Sandra Hirsh, Gail Schlachter, 5000 Windplay Drive, Suite 4, El Dorado Hills, CA 95762-9319, (916) 939-9620, fax: (916) 939-9626, email: info@rspfunding.com, web site: www.rspfunding.com. 1975. Non-fiction. "Reference Service Press is a library-oriented reference publishing company. We specialize in the development of directories of financial aid for special needs groups (e.g. women, minorities, the disabled)." avg. press run 5M. Pub'd 10 titles 2009; expects 14 titles 2010, 12 titles 2011. 20 titles listed in the *Small Press Record of Books in Print* (36th Edition, 2010-11). Discounts: up to 20%. 375pp. Reporting time: 60 days or less. Payment: 10% and up, depending upon sales; royalties paid annually. Copyrights for author. Subjects: Asian-American, Awards, Foundations, Grants, Black, Chicano/a, Education, Native American, Reference, Women.

REFLECTIONS LITERARY JOURNAL, Dawn E. Langley, Managing Editor and Dean, General Education, PO Box 1197, Roxboro, NC 27573, 336-599-1181, reflect@piedmontcc.edu. 1999. Poetry, fiction, non-fiction. "The journal is now only available online. We will consider submissions from North Carolina authors only. Poetry (each poem one page or less), short fiction and personal essays (up to 4000 words) by established and emerging writers at all levels. Local, regional, international (in English). Submit 1-5 poems, or 1 story, or 1 essay. Send two copies of ms, one with name and address, one without. Include biog information in brief cover letter. Will consider all accessible forms of poetry, including traditional forms. Annual deadline Dec. 31." circ. 200. 1/yr. Pub'd 1 issue 2009; expects 1 issue 2010. Back issues: $3. 120pp. Reporting time: up to 12 months, we read Sept.-Feb. and notify writers Mar.-Apr. We accept simultaneous submissions if notified immediately upon acceptance elsewhere. Publishes 5-10% of manuscripts submitted. Copyrighted, reverts to author. Subjects: Essays, Fiction, Poetry, Short Stories, South.

Regent Press (see also Defiant Times Press), Mark B. Weiman, 2747 Regent St., Oakland, CA 94705, 510-845-1196, fax: 510-704-1543, web: www.regentpress.net. 1978. Poetry, fiction, non-fiction. avg. press run 300 - 1,000. Pub'd 10 titles 2009; expects 10 titles 2010, 10 titles 2011. 134 titles listed in the *Small Press Record of Books in Print* (36th Edition, 2010-11). Discounts: 1 copy 20%, 2-3 30%, 4+ 40%. 200pp. Reporting time: varies. Payment: varies, % of gross. Copyrights for author. Subject: Literature (General).

Re-invention UK Ltd, Stephen Kuta Mr, Primrose Cottage, Lakes Farm, Braintree Green, Rayne, Braintree, United Kingdom, (0044) 1245 332147. 2004. Poetry, fiction, art, photos, cartoons, parts-of-novels, long-poems, plays, concrete art, non-fiction. "Our mission is to challenge important issues and target controversial topics. All of our publications help raise money for charity." avg. press run 1000. Pub'd 4 titles 2009; expects 15 titles 2010, 25 titles 2011. No titles listed in the *Small Press Record of Books in Print* (36th Edition, 2010-11). Discounts: Trade discounts: 2 - 25 copies 25%26 copies or more - 35%. 200pp. Reporting time: 2 - 4 weeks. Simultaneous submissions accepted: Yes. Payment: We don't necessarily pay an advance but on a royalty basis we allow 25%, unless arranged otherwise. Subjects: Abstracts, Adolescence, African Literature, Africa, African Studies, AIDS, Avant-Garde, Experimental Art, Bisexual, Creativity, Disabled, Erotica, Gay, Juvenile Fiction, Lesbianism, Memoirs, Photography, Poetry.

THE REJECTED QUARTERLY, Daniel Weiss, Editor, PO Box 1351, Cobb, CA 95426, bplankton@yahoo.com; rejectedq.com. 1998. Fiction, articles, satire. "Five rejection slips must accompany each manuscript. Prefer offbeat, but always quality fiction. Accept only rejection-related poetry. Accept only nonfiction articles dealing with literary rejection." 2/yr. sub. price $20.00 (4 issues); per copy $7.50. Back issues: $7.50. 40pp. Reporting time: 1-6 Months. Simultaneous submissions accepted: Yes. Payment: $15 (per story).

Reliance Books, Sarah Webber, 208 E. Oak Crest Drive, Ste. 250, Wales, WI 53183-9700, 262-968-9857, Fax 262-968-9854, contact@reliancebooks.com, www.reliancebooks.com. 2002. Non-fiction. "Please see website for more information. Query required prior to submission." avg. press run 5M. Expects 2 titles 2010, 4-6 titles 2011. 2 titles listed in the *Small Press Record of Books in Print* (36th Edition, 2010-11). Discounts: quantity discounts available by volume. 200pp. Reporting time: 90 days. Simultaneous submissions accepted: yes. Publishes a variable % of manuscripts submitted. Payment: by agreement. Copyrights for author. Subjects: Business & Economics, Ethics, Finances, Leadership, Management.

RELIGION & AMERICAN CULTURE, University of California Press, Thomas J. Davis, Managing Editor, University of California Press, 2000 Center St., Suite 303, Berkeley, CA 94704-1223, 510-643-7154. 1990. Articles. "Editorial address: CSRAC, 425 University Blvd., Room 341, Indiana University-Purdue University, Indianapolis, IN 46202-5140. Copyrighted by the Center for the Study of Religion and American Culture." circ. 726. 2/yr. Pub'd 2 issues 2009; expects 2 issues 2010, 2 issues 2011. sub. price $29 indiv., $88 inst., $18 student; per copy $15 indiv., $51 inst., $15 student; sample same as single copy. Discounts: foreign subs. agents 10%, 10+ one-time orders 30%. 130pp. Copyrighted, does not revert to author. Ads: $295/$220. Subjects: Culture, History, Literature (General), Religion, Sociology.

REMARK, Kathleen Paul-Flanagan, 1104 Indian Trail, Apex, NC 27502-1520, www.remarkpoetry.net remarkpoetry@gmail.com. 1998. Poetry. ""remark." contains mostly poetry, with a flash fiction piece once in a while. (Submissions for fiction are not taken. I find pieces of flash fiction on my own.) I prefer free verse over traditional rhymed forms. Email submissoins only. The PO Box is for subscription payments only. "remark." is handmade. No two issues are alike. Some recent contributors- Lyn Lifshin, Christopher Cunningham, Brian McGettrick, Sheila Knowles, William Taylor, Jr. and Nescher Pyscher." circ. 55. 10/yr. Pub'd 10 issues 2009; expects 10 issues 2010, 10 issues 2011. sub. price $30; per copy $6; sample $4. Back issues: inquire. Discounts: 5 or more copies drops the prices to $4 an issue. 40pp. Reporting time: Three weeks. Simultaneous submissions accepted: Yes. Publishes 10% of manuscripts submitted. Payment: one copy of the issue the poet appears in. Not copyrighted. Pub's reviews: approx. 8 in 2009. §Poetry Chapbooks. Ads: A removable postcard ad costs $25 for three issues.

REMS Publishing & Publicity, Dr. Maureen Stephenson, 25852 McBean Parkway #714, Valencia, CA 91355-2004, 800-915-0048, 661-287-3309, Fax 661-287-4443, remesbookdoctor@ca.rr.com, www.remspublishingpublicity.com, www.makemoneywritingsite.com. 1998. Fiction, satire, non-fiction. "If manuscript is over 150 pages, please send only story line, synopsis, and chapter headings for consideration. In addition, we also accept "teen" readers' manuscripts published under our Books for Young People division. Send all manuscripts with SASE and cover letter with contact information." avg. press run 50-500. Pub'd 4 titles 2009; expects 3 titles 2010, 2 titles 2011. 1 title listed in the *Small Press Record of Books in Print* (36th Edition, 2010-11). 150pp. Reporting time: 6-12 weeks. Simultaneous submissions accepted: yes. Publishes 5% of manuscripts submitted. Payment: negotiated per author. Copyrights for author. Subjects: Advertising, Self-Promotion, Autobiography, Avant-Garde, Experimental Art, Biography, Business & Economics, Careers, Inspirational, Inspirational, Ireland, Non-Fiction.

RENDITIONS, Research Centre for Translation, Chinese University of Hong Kong, Eva Hung, Editor, Chinese University of Hong Kong, Shatin, NT, Hong Kong, 852-26097407; fax 852-26035110; e-mail renditions@cuhk.hk. 1973. "A Chinese-English translation magazine. Publishes translations only of Chinese poetry, prose and fiction, classical and contemporary. Also welcomes articles on related topics dealing with Chinese language, literature and arts, or on translation. All submitted translations must be accompanied by Chinese text; require *pinyin* romanization. Special issues include: Contemporary Women Writers; Hong Kong Writing; Middlebrow Fiction; Drama; Classical Prose; Taiwan literature." 2/yr. price per copy US $17. Back issues: same as current prices. Discounts: trade discount for agents and bookstores. 160pp. Simultaneous submissions accepted: no. Payment: honoraria and 2 free copies to contributors. Copyrighted, does not revert to author. Ads: full page $280 US/1/2 page $170 US/inside back cover (full page only) $380 US. Subjects: Literature (General), Translation.

REPORTS OF THE NATIONAL CENTER FOR SCIENCE EDUCATION, Andrew Petto, Editor, NCSE, Box 9477, Berkeley, CA 94709, 510-601-7203, Fax 510-601-7204. 1980. Articles, criticism, reviews, letters, news items, non-fiction. "Scientists review creationist arguments and also report on developments in evolutionary science." circ. 3.5M. 6/yr. Pub'd 6 issues 2009; expects 6 issues 2010, 6 issues 2011. sub. price $30, foreign $37, foreign air $39; per copy $5; sample same. Back issues: $5 each. Discounts: complete set $450 (all pubs), $150 *Creation Evolution Journal* only. 44pp. Reporting time: 1 month. Simultaneous submissions accepted: yes. Payment: none; free issues are provided. Copyrighted, reverts to author. Pub's reviews: 12 in 2009. §The creation/evolution controversy. Ads: contact editor. Subjects: Anthropology, Archaelogy, Education, Humanism, Philosophy, Religion, Science.

REPRESENTATIONS, University of California Press, Catherine Gallagher, Co-Chair; Tom Laqueur, Co-Chair; Jean Day, Managing Editor, University of California Press, 2000 Center Street, Suite 303, Berkeley, CA 94704-1223, 510-643-7154. 1982. Art, photos, criticism, non-fiction. "Editorial address: *Representations*, 322 Wheeler Hall, MC 1030, University of California, Berkeley, CA 94720." circ. 1244. 4/yr. Pub'd 4 issues 2009; expects 4 issues 2010, 4 issues 2011. sub. price $42 individual, $173 institution, $28 students (+ $20 air freight); per copy $12 indiv.; $46 instit., $12 students (+ $20 air freight); sample free. Back issues: same as single copy price. Discounts: foreign subs. agent 10%, one-time orders 10+ 30%, standing orders (bookstores): 1-99 40%, 100+ 50%. 96pp. Reporting time: 1 month. Copyrighted, does not revert to author. Ads: $325/$225. Subjects: Anthropology, Archaelogy, Arts, Criticism, Culture, English, History.

Research Centre for Translation, Chinese University of Hong Kong (see also RENDITIONS), Eva Hung, General Editor, Research Centre for Translation, Chinese University of Hong Kong, Shatin, NT, Hong Kong, 852-26097407; e-Mail renditions@cuhk.hk. 1973. Poetry, articles, long-poems, plays. avg. press run 2M. 19 titles listed in the *Small Press Record of Books in Print* (36th Edition, 2010-11). Discounts: trade discount to distributors and bookstores. 160pp. Reporting time: 3 months. Simultaneous submissions accepted: no. Publisher owns copyright. Subjects: Literature (General), Translation.

A RESOURCE FOR EMBEDDED HAIKU, Martin Wasserman, P.O. Box 35, Pilot Knob, NY 12844, 518-743-2258. 2009. Poetry. "I believe that the spirit of haiku is present in most great poetry. If you support this point of view, please send me some inspiring haiku which you have uncovered and extracted from the works of the poets you admire. The poems need not be 17 syllables, but they certainly should depict a little picture that aims towards enlightenment. You should send along at least 5 examples of embedded haiku which were taken from the same author." circ. 300. 2/yr. Expects 2 issues 2010, 2 issues 2011. sub. price $10; per copy $5; sample Free. Back issues: Inquire. Discounts: None. 30pp. Reporting time: Two weeks. Simultaneous submissions accepted: Yes. Payment: Three complimentary copies. Copyrighted, reverts to author. No advertising. Subjects: Haiku, Poetry.

RESOURCES FOR FEMINIST RESEARCH/DOCUMENTATION SUR LA RECHERCHE FEMIN-ISTE, Philinda Masters, Editor, 252 Bloor Street W., Toronto, Ontario M5S 1V6, Canada, 416-978-2033, Fax 416-926-4725, E-mail rfrdrf@oise.utoronto.ca. 1972. Articles, interviews, criticism, reviews. "Articles, abstracts, bibliographies, resource guides. Thematic issues regularly. Bilingual (English and French)." circ. 2M. 2/yr. Pub'd 2 issues 2009; expects 2 issues 2010, 2 issues 2011. sub. price $38 Canadian, $58 foreign, $105 institution (Canada), $128 institution (outside Canada), student $27 (with school & student no.); per copy $20 individual; sample free to institutions and libraries. Back issues: individuals: $7-20 each, $38 volume, $58 outside Canada/vol; institutions: $20 each, $105 vol./Canada, $128 outside Canada. Discounts: write for details. 250pp. Reporting time: 1 week. Simultaneous submissions accepted: no. Publishes 50% of manuscripts submitted. Payment: none. Copyrighted. Pub's reviews: 30 in 2009. §Women's studies, feminist research. Ads: $300 full page/$150 1/2 page. Subjects: Book Reviewing, Education, Feminism, Women.

•REVERIE: MIDWEST AFRICAN AMERICAN LITERATURE, Aquarius Press, Heather Buchanan, Editor & Publisher; Randall Horton, Editor; Patricia Biela, Assistant Poetry Editor, PO Box 23096, Detroit, MI 48223, 877-979-3639, aquariuspress@gmail.com, www.aquariuspressbookseller.net. 2007. Poetry, fiction, photos, interviews, reviews, parts-of-novels, plays, non-fiction. "We publish the work of African American writers with ties to the American Midwest." 1/yr. Pub'd 2 issues 2009; expects 1 issue 2010, 1 issue 2011. Reporting time: 3 months. Simultaneous submissions accepted: Yes. Copyrighted, reverts to author. Pub's reviews. Ads: inquire. Subjects: African-American, Drama, Essays, Fiction, Midwest, Non-Fiction, Poetry, Reviews.

THE REVIEW OF CONTEMPORARY FICTION, Dalkey Archive Press, John O'Brien, University of Illinois, 1805 S. Wright Street, MC-011, Champaign, IL 61820, 217-244-5700. 1981. Articles, interviews, criticism, reviews. "No unsolicited manuscripts. First twenty issues devoted to Gilbert Sorrentino, Paul Metcalf, Hubert Selby, Douglas Woolf, Wallace Markfield, William Gaddis, Coleman Dowell, Nicholas Mosley, Paul Bowles, William Eastlake, Aidan Higgins, Jack Kerouac, Robert Pinget, Julio Cortazar, John Hawkes, William S. Burroughs, Ishmael Reed, Juan Goytisolo, Camilo Jose Cela, Charles Bukowski. Recent contributors: Gilbert Sorrentino, Robert Creeley, William S. Burroughs, Carlos Fuentes, Paul Metcalf, Edward Dorn, Edmund White, Thom Gunn, Luisa Valenzuela, Juan Goytisolo, Samuel Beckett, Gabriel Garcia Marquez." circ. 3.5k. 3/yr. Pub'd 3 issues 2009; expects 3 issues 2010, 3 issues 2011. sub. price $17 indiv., $26 instit.; per copy $8; sample $8. Back issues: $8. Discounts: 10% to agencies; 45% to bookstores with a minimum order of 5 units. 180pp. Payment: copy. Copyrighted, reverts to author. Pub's reviews: 150 in 2009. §Fiction, criticism. Ads: $250/exchange. Subjects: Fiction, Literary Review.

RFD, RFD Collective, PO Box 68, Liberty, TN 37095, 615-536-5176. 1974. Poetry, fiction, articles, art, photos, cartoons, interviews, reviews, letters, news items, non-fiction. "*RFD* is a country journal by gay men, for gay men. Any material relevant to building our community is considered. A networking tool for radical faeries." circ. 2.5M. 4/yr. Pub'd 4 issues 2009; expects 4 issues 2010, 4 issues 2011. sub. price $25 2nd Class mailing, $37 1st Class, $30 foreign; per copy $7.75; sample $7.75. Back issues: $2 each when available over 1 year old. Discounts: bookstores 40%. 52pp. Reporting time: 3 months minimum. Payment: 1 copy of the issue in which their work appears. Copyrighted, reverts to author. Pub's reviews: 33 in 2009. §Country concerns, spiritual realities, gay men, poetry, alternatives (new age), radical faeries. Ads: $350/$175. Subjects: Agriculture, Community, Counter-Culture, Alternatives, Communes, Fiction, Gardening, Gay, Health, Men, New Age, Peace, Poetry, Politics, Prison, Spiritual.

RFF Press / Resources for the Future, Don Reisman, 1616 P Street NW, Washington, DC 20036-1400, 202-328-5086, 202-328-5002, 1-800-537-5487, rffpress@rff.org, www.rffpress.org. 1999. Non-fiction. "RFF Press extends the mission of Resources for the Future by publishing books that make a distinct and original contribution to scholarship, teaching, debate, and decisionmaking about important issues in environmental and natural resource policy and in risk analysis. Since its founding, Resources for the Future has published groundbreaking works about natural resources and the environment. Works of economic analysis such as Allen Kneese's *Measuring the Benefits of Clean Air and Water* and Krutilla and Fisher's *The Economics of Natural Environments* helped establish the identity of RFF. They influenced a generation of scholarship outside of RFF and had an important impact on public policy. Created as a new publishing imprint in late 1999, RFF Press expands upon this tradition by producing books that present a broad range of social science approaches to the study of natural resources and the environment. Authors of RFF Press books include RFF staff and leading researchers at universities and NGOs around the world. To ensure their quality and objectivity, publications are subject to a peer review process equal to that employed by the most rigorous university presses. RFF Press books are issued in both print and electronic (e-book) formats. They are marketed by the Press itself, by a distribution arrangement with Johns Hopkins University Press, and by select, overseas partners." avg. press run 1000. Pub'd 15 titles 2009; expects 18 titles 2010, 20 titles 2011. No titles listed in the *Small Press Record of Books in Print* (36th Edition, 2010-11). Discounts: Contact Meg Keller keller@rff.org for complete discount schedules. 250pp. Reporting time: 1-3 months. Simultaneous submissions accepted: No. Publishes 10% of manuscripts submitted. Payment: Varies; contact us for more information. Copyright varies; contact us for more information. Subjects: Agriculture, Business & Economics, Conservation, Earth, Natural History, Ecology, Foods, Environment, Nature, Non-Fiction, Political Science, Public Affairs, Textbooks.

RHAPSODY MAGAZINE, John Riddick, Editor, PO Box 2443, Durham, NC 27715-2443. "*Rhapsody* is a quarterly literary magazine that is a compilation of poetry, prose, commentary and artwork. We showcase the talents of nationally selected writers and artists based on originality and content. Our goal is to publish a diverse and creative array of works to promote both the artists and this publication. *Rhapsody* is a soapbox of sorts upon which visual and literary artists express themselves. The artists retain all rights of the works submitted and authorial anonymity is preserved throughout the review process. The opinions and beliefs of the artists are not necessarily a reflection of our staff. Our purpose is to stimulate consciousness.''

RHETORICA: A Journal of the History of Rhetoric, University of California Press, Harvey Yunis, Editor, Univ of California Press, 2000 Center Street, Suite 303, Berkeley, CA 94704-1223, 510-643-7154. "Publication of and copyrighted by the International Society for the History of Rhetoric. Editorial address: Dept. of Classical Studies, Rice University, 6100 Main Street, Houston, TX 77005-1892.'' circ. 1062. 4/yr. Pub'd 4 issues 2009; expects 4 issues 2010, 4 issues 2011. sub. price $44 indiv., $140 instit., $18 students; per copy $12 indiv., $37 instit., $12 students; sample free. Back issues: same as single copy price. Discounts: foreign subs. agents 10%, one-time orders 10+ 30%, standing orders (bookstores): 1-99 40%, 100+ 50%. 112pp. Reporting time: 2 months. Payment: none. Copyrighted, does not revert to author. Ads: $295/$220. Subject: Language.

Rhiannon Press, Mary Sue Koeppel, Editor, P.O. Box 140310, Gainesville, FL 32614, skoeppel@fscj.edu ; contact@writecorner.com. 1977. Poetry, long-poems. "New editor as of 2003. Concentration on women's poetry. Editor lines up authors for new chapbooks. *See Writecorner.com for other chances to work with this new editor.*'' avg. press run 500. Pub'd 1 title 2009; expects 1 title 2010, 1 title 2011. 9 titles listed in the *Small Press Record of Books in Print* (36th Edition, 2010-11). 25-35pp. Payment: copies of work or percentage of copies. Copyrights for author. Subjects: Poetry, Women.

RHINO: THE POETRY FORUM, Jackie K. White, Deborah Nodler Rosen, Helen Degen Cohen, Ralph Hamilton, PO Box 591, Evanston, IL 60204, www.rhinopoetry.org. 1976. Poetry, fiction, photos. "RHINO is looking for compelling poetry, short-short fiction (2-3 pp), and translations. We encourage regional talent while listening to voices from around the world. Editors are partial to adventurous work in love with language. Submit 3-5 poems with SASE between April-October 1 only. Read excerpts and contest info on our website at www.rhinopoetry.org.'' circ. 1M. 1/yr. Pub'd 1 issue 2009; expects 1 issue 2010, 1 issue 2011. sub. price $12/1year; $20/2yrs; per copy $12; sample $6. Back issues: $6. 150pp. Reporting time: 4-6 months. Simultaneous submissions accepted: yes. Publishes 5% of manuscripts submitted. Payment: 2 copies. Copyrighted, reverts to author. Subjects: African-American, Asian-American, Experimental, Fiction, Poetry, Third World, Minorities, Translation, U.S. Hispanic, Women.

Ridenbaugh Press, Randy Stapilus, P.O. Box 834, Carlton, OR 97111, 503-852-0010. 1988. Articles, reviews, news items, non-fiction. Pub'd 2 titles 2009; expects 6 titles 2010, 4 titles 2011. 2 titles listed in the *Small Press Record of Books in Print* (36th Edition, 2010-11). 250-300pp. Reporting time: 3 weeks. Simultaneous submissions accepted: Yes. Subjects: Government, History, Idaho, Oregon, Pets, Politics, Washington (state), Water, The West.

Ridgeway Press of Michigan, M.L. Liebler, PO Box 120, Roseville, MI 48066, 313-577-7713 / E-mail mlliebler@aol.com. 1973. "No unsolicited manuscripts.'' avg. press run 300-1M. Pub'd 1 title 2009; expects 1 title 2010, 1 title 2011. 12 titles listed in the *Small Press Record of Books in Print* (36th Edition, 2010-11). Discounts: 20% to college bookstores, 40% to others. 30-60pp. Simultaneous submissions accepted: no. Publishes less than 5% of manuscripts submitted. Payment: authors get 50 copies of book. Does not copyright for author. Subjects: Christianity, Drama, Fiction, Labor, Poetry, Surrealism.

Rising Star Publishers (see also ORACLE POETRY; ORACLE STORY), Obi Harrison Ekwonna, 7510 Lake Glen Drive, Glenn Dale, MD 20769, 301-352-2533, Fax 301-352-2529. 1989. "We are fulltime book publishers: fiction and non-fiction: novels, criticisms, biographies, memoirs histories etc.'' 4 titles listed in the *Small Press Record of Books in Print* (36th Edition, 2010-11). Simultaneous submissions accepted: Send your submissions in hard copies and file(s)in diskette and or CDs or file attachment(s).

Rising Tide Press New Mexico, Pamela Tree, Publisher; Eva Correlli, Assoc. Publisher, PO Box 6136, Santa Fe, NM 87502-6136, 505-983-8484, Fax 505-983-8484. 1991. Poetry. "We publish environmental books plus belle lettres plus prose poetry. A division of American-Canadian Publishers, Inc., a non-profit corporation. Our latest book title says it all: *Every Person's Little Book of P=L=U=T=O=N=I=U=M* by Stanley Berne with Arlene Zekowski. This popular book, written for just plain folks, is a study of the Department of Energy and the Nuclear Power Industry, which demonstrates a U.S. Government out of control. Why should our own government agency poison us all? We are going to be hammering away on environmental issues, before it's too late! Please do *not* send unsolicited materials.'' avg. press run 6M. Expects 2 titles 2010, 2 titles 2011. 5 titles listed in the *Small Press Record of Books in Print* (36th Edition, 2010-11). Discounts: 40% to all bookstores, 50% on 10—not one bookstore has returned this book. 200pp. Payment: yes. Copyrights for author. Subjects: Environment, Nuclear Energy.

Rivendell Books, Butch Drury, PO Box 9306, Richmond Heights, MO 63117-0306, 1-314-609-6534, butch@rivendellbooks.com. 2007. Non-fiction. "Rivendell Books is a very narrowly focused, niche publisher for a select group of authors who write nonfiction books that deal with freeing mankind from the tyranny of sincere ignorance, the ego and the destructive side of our animal natures, through a conscious union with soul.—We do not publish fiction or any other books that do not meet these criteria.'' Expects 1 title 2011. 1 title listed in the *Small Press Record of Books in Print* (36th Edition, 2010-11). 300pp. Reporting time: One to two months, depending on work load. Simultaneous submissions accepted: No. Copyrights for author. Subjects: Creative Non-fiction, Memoirs.

River City Publishing, Jim Gilbert, Editor, 1719 Mulberry Street, Montgomery, AL 36106. 1988. Fiction, non-fiction. avg. press run 1500-3000. No titles listed in the *Small Press Record of Books in Print* (36th Edition, 2010-11).

RIVER KING POETRY SUPPLEMENT, Wayne Lanter, Co-Editor; Donna Biffar, Co-Editor; Emily Lambeth-Climaco, Associate Editor; Phil Miller, Art Editor, PO Box 122, Freeburg, IL 62243. 1995. circ. 6M. 2/yr. Pub'd 2 issues 2009; expects 2 issues 2010, 2 issues 2011. sub. price free; per copy free; sample free. Back issues: none. 12pp. Reporting time: 6 months. Simultaneous submissions accepted: no. Publishes 10% of manuscripts submitted. Payment: 10 copies. Copyrighted, reverts to author. Ads: none. Subject: Poetry.

RIVER POETS JOURNAL, Lilly Press, Judith Lawrence, 1848 Finch Dr, Bensalem, PA 19020-4406, 215-638-2493. 2007. Poetry, fiction, art, photos, parts-of-novels, plays, non-fiction. "Quarterly Journal plus one special themed edition yearly. We are seeking work that is memorable. Prefer email submissions, but will accept mailed submissions if writer does not use a pc, although there is a longer respose time to mailed submissions due to large number of submissions. Please check our website and journal for the type of work we publish." 5/yr. Pub'd 5 issues 2009; expects 5 issues 2010, 5 issues 2011. 3 titles listed in the *Small Press Record of Books in Print* (36th Edition, 2010-11). sub. price $35 for 4 issues - $40 including themed issue; per copy $10. Back issues: Available. 28-36pp. Reporting time: 3 to 6 months. Simultaneous submissions accepted: Yes. Payment: Payment is publication. Copyrighted, reverts to author. Subjects: Arts, Creative Non-fiction, Creativity, Drama, Fiction, Haiku, Memoirs, Mystery, Non-Fiction, Photography, Poetry, Prose, Short Stories, Zines.

River Press, Paul Marks, 499 Islip Avenue, Islip, NY 11751-1826, 631-277-8618, Fax 631-277-8660, rivpress@aol.com. 1995. Non-fiction. "We publish self-help and self-improvement books and a/c tapes." avg. press run 5M. Expects 4 titles 2010, 6 titles 2011. No titles listed in the *Small Press Record of Books in Print* (36th Edition, 2010-11). 200pp. Reporting time: 60 days. Simultaneous submissions accepted: yes. Payment: to be determined. Copyrights for author. Subjects: Divorce, Marriage, Psychology, Relationships, Self-Help.

RIVER STYX, Richard Newman, Editor; Shanie Latham, Managing Editor, 3547 Olive St., Suite 107, St. Louis, MO 63103-1014, 314-533-4541, www.riverstyx.org. 1975. Poetry, fiction, art, photos, long-poems, plays, non-fiction. "*River Styx* is an award-winning multi-cultural journal of literature and art. Recent issues have featured Alan Shapiro, Yusef Komunyakaa, Julia Alvarez, Andrew Hudgins, R.S. Gwynn, Reginald Shepherd, Catherine Bowman, Marilyn Hacker, Ha Jin, and Rodney Jones. Art/photography by Deborah Luster, Tim Rollins, and K.O.S. Unsolicited submissions are accepted only between May 1 and November 30. *River Styx* holds a poetry contest and a micro-fiction contest each year. See web site for complete details about entry fees and submission periods for contests." circ. 2,000. 3/yr. Pub'd 3 issues 2009; expects 3 issues 2010, 3 issues 2011. sub. price $20 individuals, $28 institutions; per copy $9; sample $9. Back issues: complete set, issues 5-78: $7-30. Discounts: 33% to stores, 40% with orders of 10 or more. 108pp. Reporting time: 3-5 months. Simultaneous submissions accepted: Yes. Publishes 1% of manuscripts submitted. Payment: 2 contributor's copies, 1 year subscription, $8/page if funds available. Copyrighted, reverts to author. Ads: $250/$175. Subjects: Arts, Fiction, Graphics, Literature (General), Photography, Poetry, Translation.

RIVER TEETH: A Journal of Nonfiction Narrative, University of Nebraska Press, Joe Mackall, Dan Lehman, University of Nebraska Press, 1111 Lincoln Mall #400, Lincoln, NE 68588-0630, www.nebraska-press.unl.edu. 1999. Articles, interviews, criticism, non-fiction. "The editors seek the best creative nonfiction, including narrative reporting, essay, memoir, and critical essays on nonfiction. Recent contributors include Kim Barnes, David James Duncan, Madeleine Blais, Philip Gerard, Jon Franklin, Nancy Mairs, Leon Dash, Susan Sheehan, Mark Kramer, and Wil Haygood." circ. 1M. 2/yr. Pub'd 2 issues 2009; expects 2 issues 2010, 2 issues 2011. sub. price Individuals: $20 per year; Institutions $55 per year; Foreign Subscriptions add $15; per copy $15; sample $15. Back issues: $15. 190pp. Reporting time: 2-4 months. Simultaneous submissions accepted: yes. Publishes 1-5 percent% of manuscripts submitted. Payment: 2 copies. Copyrighted, reverts to author. Ads: Contact University of Nebraska Press. Subjects: Communication, Journalism, Essays, Memoirs, Non-Fiction, Storytelling.

RIVERBED HAIKU, Brock Peoples, 2524 Leeper Drive #B, Champaign, IL 61822-6802, 2178988867, http://www.riverbedhaiku.com/index.html. 2008. Poetry, articles, criticism, reviews. "Riverbed Haiku is an online English-language haiku journal, publishing new material online quarterly, and in print annually. Please see our website for submission criteria. I recommend that you read our journal, Modern Haiku, Frogpond, and Mayfly to get a feel for the kind of poetry we look for." 1/yr. Expects 1 issue 2010, 1 issue 2011. sub. price $35; per copy $35; sample $35. Back issues: inquire. Discounts: 10+ copies 25% off list. 125pp. Reporting time: 1 month. Simultaneous submissions accepted: No. Payment: none. Copyrighted, reverts to author on publication. Author agrees that any submitted material may be used in any Riverbed publication at any time. Pub's reviews. §English-language haiku books, journals, magazines, and online magazines. Subjects: English, Haiku, Illinois, Literary Review, Midwest, North America, Poetry.

RIVERSEDGE, The University of TX-Pan American Press, Antonio A. Reyna, Editor, TheUniversity of Texas Pan American, 1201 W. University, Lamar Bldg., Room 9A, Edinburg, TX 78539, 956-381-3638, bookworm@utpa.edu. 1983. Poetry, fiction, art, photos, non-fiction. circ. 400. 2/yr. Pub'd 2 issues 2009; expects 2 issues 2010, 2 issues 2011. sub. price $16; per copy $8. Back issues: $8. 120pp. Reporting time: 6-9 months. Simultaneous submissions accepted: yes. Payment: 2 complimentary copies. Copyrighted, reverts to author. Subjects: Arts, Fiction, Non-Fiction, Poetry.

Riverstone, A Press for Poetry, PO Box 1421, Carefree, AZ 85377-1421. 1992. Poetry. "We are a chapbook press only. Any style. Not accepting submissions in 2010." avg. press run 300. Pub'd 1 title 2009. 10 titles listed in the *Small Press Record of Books in Print* (36th Edition, 2010-11). Discounts: 40% to the author and to bookstores. 20-36pp. Reporting time: 2 months from deadline. Simultaneous submissions accepted: yes. Publishes 1% of manuscripts submitted. Payment: copies (50) and award of $100. Copyrights for author. Subject: Poetry.

RIVERWIND, Bonnie Proudfoot, Editor; Jeff Hanson, Editor, Arts & Sciences, Oakley 312, Hocking College, Nelsonville, OH 45764. 1975. Poetry, fiction, art, photos, interviews, reviews, plays, non-fiction. "Open to new and established writers. Story/play/interview length: not to exceed 15 manuscript pages, double-spaced. On poetry: batches of 3-6, any subject, any length, but typed. We enjoy both imagistic and lyric poems. We do not read manuscripts during the summer. Recent contributors include Gerald Wheeler, Larry Smith, Roy Bentley, Jill Rosser, and Mark Halliday." circ. 400. 1/yr. Pub'd 1 issue 2009; expects 1 issue 2010, 1 issue 2011. sub. price $10; per copy $5; sample $5. Back issues: $5. 112-156pp. Reporting time: 1-3 months. Simultaneous submissions accepted: no. Payment: 2 copies. Copyrighted, reverts to author. Pub's reviews: 1 in 2009. §Contemporary American poetry, essay, creative non-fiction, and fiction. Ads: open. Subjects: Literary Review, Midwest, Ohio.

Riverwinds Publishing, John Bond, 109 Cromwell Court, Woodbury, NJ 08096, 856-845-1250. 2005. Non-fiction. avg. press run 1500. Expects 1 title 2010, 1 title 2011. No titles listed in the *Small Press Record of Books in Print* (36th Edition, 2010-11). 160pp. Simultaneous submissions accepted: No. Copyrights for author. Subjects: How-To, Writers/Writing.

RIVET MAGAZINE, Leah Baltus, 3518 Fremont Avenue N. #118, Seattle, WA 98103, editor@rivetmaga-zine.org, www.rivetmagazine.org. 2001. Poetry, fiction, articles, art, photos, cartoons, interviews, satire, reviews, parts-of-novels, long-poems, plays, non-fiction. "Rivet is a panoramic magazine that uses themes to reveal intersections of art and culture. Literary and glossy at once, Rivet turns the notion of niche inside out: Its broad collection of ideas, styles and forms favors a big-picture perspective rooted in a way of thinking, rather than a specific interest. Recent contributors include Elizabeth Knaster, Kelly Igoe, Kynan Antos, Rain Grimes, Melissa Sands, Jeremy Richards, Matt Neyens, Emily Mannion, Michael Dylan Welch." circ. 1500. 4/yr. Pub'd 4 issues 2009; expects 4 issues 2010, 4 issues 2011. sub. price $16; per copy $5; sample $3. Back issues: inquire. Discounts: Distributors: 10%; Wholesalers, retailers, bookstores: 40%; Other: negotiable. 72pp. Reporting time: 1-3 months. Simultaneous submissions accepted: No. Publishes 10% of manuscripts submitted. Payment: Pro-bono. Copyrighted, rights revert to author on publication. Rivet reserves the right, however, to re-publish all work on its Web site and in future collections or anthologies. Pub's reviews: 20 in 2009. §Independent music, writing, art, film, etc. Ads: $225 full/$150 half. Subjects: Arts, Autobiography, Bibliography, Cities, Culture, Essays, Experimental, Fiction, Humor, Liberal Arts, Lifestyles, Multicultural, Non-Fiction, Photography, Poetry.

THE ROANOKE REVIEW, Paul Hanstedt, Roanoke College, 221 College Lane, Salem, VA 24153, 540-375-2380. 1968. Poetry, fiction. "Poems to 100 lines, fiction to 7,500 words. Recent contributors include Robert Morgan, Charles Wright, and Lucy Ferriss." circ. 200-300. 1/yr. Pub'd 1 issue 2009; expects 1 issue 2010, 1 issue 2011. sub. price $13/2 years; per copy $8; sample $5. Back issues: $5. Discounts: $5 to libraries and agencies. 176pp. Reporting time: 12-16 weeks. Simultaneous submissions accepted: yes. Payment: 2 copies. Copyrighted, rights revert to author but acknowledgement of original publisher demanded.

Roaring Lion Publishing, Olutunde Olufemi, Po Box 10505, Atlanta, GA 30310-0505, 678-663-3570. 2007. Poetry. avg. press run 600. Pub'd 3 titles 2009; expects 1 title 2010, 3 titles 2011. No titles listed in the *Small Press Record of Books in Print* (36th Edition, 2010-11). 200pp. Publishes 3% of manuscripts submitted. Subjects: African Literature, Africa, African Studies, African-American, Black, Caribbean, Creativity, Culture, Folklore, Holocaust, Performing Arts, Poetry, Relationships, Romance, Spiritual, Storytelling, Theatre.

Rock Island Press, Louis Skipper, 3411 West Circle Drive, Pearland, TX 77581, 281-744-1681. 2006. Poetry, fiction, non-fiction. avg. press run 200. Expects 2 titles 2010, 3 titles 2011. 3 titles listed in the *Small Press Record of Books in Print* (36th Edition, 2010-11). 150pp. Reporting time: two weeks. Simultaneous submissions accepted: No. Publishes 100% of manuscripts submitted. Copyrights for author.

Rock Spring Press Inc., Alice Platt, 6015 Morrow Street East Suite 106, Jacksonville, FL 32217, editor@rockspringpress.com. 2004. Non-fiction. "Rock Spring Press is interested in publishing non-fiction writing about the outdoors, nature, the environment, and travel - preferably travel in natural places. Historical is also acceptable if it is related to nature/environment. Manuscripts covering regions east of the Mississippi River in the United States are preferred. Anthologies and/or essay collections will not be considered." avg. press run 2000. Expects 2 titles 2010, 3 titles 2011. No titles listed in the *Small Press Record of Books in Print* (36th Edition, 2010-11). 275pp. Reporting time: Three months. Simultaneous submissions accepted: Yes. Publishes 10% of manuscripts submitted. Payment: 12-14% of the wholesale price. Small advance possible. Royalties paid biannually. Copyrights for author. Subjects: Adirondacks, Americana, Appalachia, Biography, Conservation, Culture, Earth, Natural History, Ecology, Foods, Environment, Florida, History, Kentucky, Louisiana, Nature, South Carolina.

THE ROCKFORD REVIEW, Rosangela Taylor, Editor, PO Box 858, Rockford, IL 61105-0858, www.RockfordWritersGuild.com, rosangela.taylor@rockfordwritersguild.com. 1971. Poetry, fiction, art, satire, plays. "*Rockford Review*, a literary arts magazine, is published by the Rockford Writers' Guild each summer and winter as a 100-page perfectbound book. *Review* seeks experimental or traditional poetry of up to 50 lines (shorter works are preferred). Short fiction, essays, and satire are welcome—in the 250 to 1300-word range. We also publish one-acts and other dramatic forms (1300 words). We are always on the lookout for black and white illustrations and glossy photos in a vertical format. We look for writing that explores the range of human emotions and that would appeal to a general readership." circ. 350. 2/yr. sub. price $35; per copy $12 (free shipping within USA). Back issues: $12 (free shipping within USA). Discounts: none. 70pp. Reporting time: For submissions, please check out the guidelines at www.RockfordWritersGuild.com. Simultaneous submissions accepted: yes. Publishes 15% to 20% of manuscripts submitted. Payment: copies, Editor's Choice $25 prizes 1) prose, 2) poetry. Copyrighted, reverts to author. Pub's reviews: 6 in 2009. §poetry, fiction, creative non-fiction. Ads: none. Subjects: Avant-Garde, Experimental Art, Drama, Fiction, Poetry, Prose, Satire.

ROCKY MOUNTAIN KC NEWS, Rocky Mountain KC Publishing Co., John Frear, PO Box 901221, Sandy, UT 84090-1221, 801-574-0618 (Apollo Enterprises), getproducts@juno.com, www.dream4u.us, www.aim2get.com, www.jonfrear.com. 1993. Fiction, satire, reviews, parts-of-novels, news items. "Subsidiary: Excaliber Publishing, Apollo Mini Books,. *Enclose self-addressed stamped envelope for return. If none is supplied, then manuscript will not be returned and will be destroyed." circ. 242M. 6/yr. Pub'd 6 issues 2009; expects 6 issues 2010, 6 issues 2011. sub. price $36; per copy $6; sample $5. Back issues: $5 each. Discounts: 2% off the top. 50pp. Reporting time: 60 days. Simultaneous submissions accepted: no. Publishes 25% of manuscripts submitted. Payment: $20-$100 per submission, based on content and length. Copyrighted, does not revert to author. Pub's reviews: 6 in 2009. §Animals, business, how-to, pets, self-help, adventure. Ads: $2,500/$1,250/$625 1/4 page. Subjects: Animals, Business & Economics, Fiction, Folklore, Pets, Publishing, Supernatural.

Rocky Mountain KC Publishing Co. (see also ROCKY MOUNTAIN KC NEWS), John Frear, PO Box 901221, Sandy, UT 84090-1221, 801-574-0618 (Apollo Enterprises), getproducts@juno.com , www.getproducts.us, www.dream4u.us, www.aim2get.com, www.jonfrear.com . 801-647-5645 Jon's Adventure Productions ; www.jonsadventure.com , www.jonsadventureclub.com. 1993. Fiction, satire, reviews, parts-of-novels, news items. "Subsidiary: Excaliber Publishing Co., Apollo Mini Books, * Enclose self-addressed stamped envelope for return. If none is supplied, then manuscript will not be returned and will be destroyed. Jon's Adventure Productions (children's educational series)." Pub'd 23 titles 2009; expects 20 titles 2010, 25 titles 2011. 2 titles listed in the *Small Press Record of Books in Print* (36th Edition, 2010-11). Discounts: 2% off the top. 50pp. Reporting time: 60 days. Simultaneous submissions accepted: no. Publishes 25% of manuscripts submitted. Payment: based on projected sales. We copyright for author, if needed. Subjects: Animals, Business & Economics, Fiction, Folklore, Pets, Publishing, Supernatural.

ROCTOBER COMICS AND MUSIC, Jake Austen, 1507 East 53rd Street #617, Chicago, IL 60615, 773 875 6470. 1992. Fiction, articles, photos, cartoons, interviews, reviews, music, collages, news items, non-fiction. "*Roctober* is commited to a joyful exploration into the history of popular music and it's most colorful characters." circ. 5,000. 3/yr. Pub'd 3 issues 2009; expects 3 issues 2010, 3 issues 2011. sub. price $10; per copy $4; sample $4. Back issues: $4. 96pp. Reporting time: 2 weeks from receipt. Publishes 10% of manuscripts submitted. Payment: lifetime subscription. Copyrighted, reverts to author. Pub's reviews: 1500 in 2009. §Music, film, baseball related themes, monsters. Ads: $170/$90. Subjects: Americana, Chicago, Comics, Counter-Culture, Alternatives, Communes, Fantasy, Feminism, Folklore, Movies, Music, Storytelling, Television.

Rodnik Publishing Co., Robert Powers, Senior Editor; Lidiya Zabokritskaya, Editor; Lillian Levy Guevara, Editor; Steve Pallady, Editor, PO Box 46956, Seattle, WA 98146-0956, Tel 206-937-5189 Fax 206-937-3554, URL: www.rodnikpublishing.com. 1994. avg. press run 3-5M. Expects 3 titles 2010, 2 titles 2011. 8 titles listed in the *Small Press Record of Books in Print* (36th Edition, 2010-11). Discounts: max. 55%. 400pp. Simultaneous submissions accepted: yes. Payment: by contract. Copyrights for author. Subjects: Dictionaries, English, Language, Relationships, Russia, Sex, Sexuality, Vietnam.

ROGER, an art & literary magazine, Renee Soto, Department of Creative Writing / Roger Williams University, One Old Ferry, Bristol, RI 02809, (401) 254-3860. 2006. Poetry, fiction, long-poems. "http://roger.rwu.edu." 1/yr. Pub'd 1 issue 2009; expects 1 issue 2010, 1 issue 2011. sub. price $7.00; per copy $7.00. Discounts: to contributors. 128pp. Reporting time: 3-5 months. Simultaneous submissions accepted: yes. Publishes 5% of manuscripts submitted. Payment: complimentary issues. 1st time serial rights. Ads: exchange ads. Subjects: Arts, Fiction, Poetry, Prose, Translation.

•**Rogue Scholars Press,** C. D. Johnson, Editor-In-Chief; Miriam Stanley, Senior Submissions Editor, 228 East 25th Street, #2, New York, NY 10010. 1997. "A modest little enterprise supported by the current members of the Rogue scholars Collective, a literary organization based in the East Village, New York City, dedicated to the promotion of poetry and the arts on the world wide web." No titles listed in the *Small Press Record of Books in Print* (36th Edition, 2010-11).

Rollaway Bay Publications, Inc., Rick Elliott, 6334 S. Racine Circle, Suite 202, Centennital, CO 80111-6405, Tel=303 799-8320, Fax=303 799-4220, email publisher@rollawaybay.com. 2003. Non-fiction. "We at Rollaway Bay Publications are dedicated to independent production of high stanard interesting (not boring) business titles. We expect our readers to enjoy reading our books while learning something new and valuable in the process." avg. press run 3000. Expects 2-5 titles 2010, 5-10 titles 2011. 4 titles listed in the *Small Press Record of Books in Print* (36th Edition, 2010-11). Discounts: Bookstores & Libraries - Credit card or prepaid orders = 45% discount; invoiced order (with approved credit) = 40% discount. 350pp. Reporting time: 3 to 4 weeks. Simultaneous submissions accepted: Yes. Publishes 5% of manuscripts submitted. Copyrights for author. Subject: Business & Economics.

Rolling Hills Publishing, Michael Gray, 242 Eagle Flight, Ozark, MO 65721-7868, Ph: 800-918-7323, Fax: 888-329-2747, info@rollinghillspublishing.com, www.rollinghillspublishing.com. 2003. Non-fiction. "Educational and How to books." avg. press run 5000. Pub'd 2 titles 2009; expects 1 title 2010, 2 titles 2011. 2 titles listed in the *Small Press Record of Books in Print* (36th Edition, 2010-11). 192pp. Reporting time: 10 days. Simultaneous submissions accepted: Yes. Subjects: Autos, Construction, Consumer, Crafts, Hobbies, Education, Finances, How-To, Marriage, Non-Fiction, Real Estate, Wood Engraving/Woodworking.

Ronin Publishing, Inc., Beverly A. Potter, Publisher, Box 22900, Oakland, CA 94609, 510-420-3669, Fax 510-420-3672, ronin@roninpub.com, www.roninpub.com. 1983. Non-fiction. "No unsolicited material." avg. press run 5-7,000. Pub'd 5 titles 2009; expects 5 titles 2010, 5 titles 2011. 83 titles listed in the *Small Press Record of Books in Print* (36th Edition, 2010-11). Pages vary, average is 192. Simultaneous submissions accepted: yes. Payment: 10% net, some advances. Copyrights for author. Subjects: Careers, Counter-Culture, Alternatives, Communes, Self-Help, Spiritual.

Ronsdale Press, R. Hatch, Director, 3350 West 21st Avenue, Vancouver, B.C. V6S 1G7, Canada, 604-738-4688, toll free 888-879-0919, Fax 604-731-4548. 1988. Poetry, fiction, art, photos, satire, parts-of-novels, long-poems, collages, plays, concrete art, non-fiction. avg. press run 1.2M-2M. Pub'd 10 titles 2009; expects 11 titles 2010, 9 titles 2011. 163 titles listed in the *Small Press Record of Books in Print* (36th Edition, 2010-11). Discounts: trade 40%, libraries 20%, wholesale (bulk) 50%. 108pp. Reporting time: 2 months. Simultaneous submissions accepted, but must be stated so. Publishes 10% of manuscripts submitted. Payment: 10% of retail, royalties negotiated at contract signing. Copyrights for author. Subjects: Autobiography, Bilingual, Biography, British Columbia, British Columbia, Canada, Children, Youth, Criticism, Drama, Fiction, History, Literature (General), Non-Fiction, Photography, Poetry.

ROOM, John Perlman, 24450 Sisters Lane, Millsboro, DE 19966-2818. 1987. Poetry. "*Room* will publish single author chapbooks when and if a ms. so moves and impresses the editor that he would be remiss in not publishing the work." circ. 150. Frequency varies. sub. price gratis. Pages vary. Reporting time: ASAP. Simultaneous submissions accepted: no. Publishes 1% of manuscripts submitted. Payment: copies. Not copyrighted. Subject: Poetry.

ROOM MAGAZINE, PO Box 46160, Station D, Vancouver, BC V6J 5G5, Canada. 1975. Poetry, fiction, art, photos, cartoons, interviews, reviews, music, parts-of-novels, long-poems, plays. "Good quality literary material by, for and about women. Payment in Canadian funds only." circ. 3000. 4/yr. Pub'd 4 issues 2009; expects 4 issues 2010, 4 issues 2011. sub. price Individuals - $27 if in Canada; $39 if in US; $49.50 if outside of North America. Institutions - $36 if in Canada; $48 if in US; $58.50 if outside of North America. Note: All prices in Canadian funds.; per copy $9 Canada, US$10 US and foreign; sample $5 Canada, US$5 US and foreign. Back issues: In Canada: $10; In the US: $13; Outside North America: $18. 112pp. Reporting time: 9 months. Simultaneous submissions accepted: no. Publishes 8% of manuscripts submitted. Payment: $50-$75, plus 1-year sub. Copyrighted, reverts to author. Pub's reviews: 8-10 in 2009. §Literature, women. Ads:

$60/$30/$20 1/3 page. Subjects: Literary Review, Literature (General), Women.

Rose Alley Press, David D. Horowitz, 4203 Brooklyn Avenue NE #103A, Seattle, WA 98105-5911, 206-633-2725, rosealleypress@juno.com, www.rosealleypress.com. 1995. Poetry, non-fiction. "Rose Alley Press primarily publishes books featuring rhymed metrical verse. We have published books by poets Victoria Ford, William Dunlop, Michael Spence, David D. Horowitz, Douglas Schuder, Joannie K. Stangeland, and Donald Kentop. We do *not* accept or read unsolicited manuscripts." avg. press run 1M. Pub'd 1 title 2009; expects 1 title 2010, 1 title 2011. 13 titles listed in the *Small Press Record of Books in Print* (36th Edition, 2010-11). Discounts: bookstores 40%, libraries 10%, distributors 55%; possible discount for bulk purchase. 28-164pp. Payment: 1-10 copies, percentage of profit from sales of book after earning back printing and marketing expenses. Copyrights for author. Subjects: Poetry, Writers/Writing.

Rose Metal Press, Kathleen Rooney, Abby Beckel, PO Box 1956, Brookline, MA 02446, (617) 548.9145. 2006. Poetry, fiction, long-poems, non-fiction. "We are dedicated to the publication of work in hybrid genres such as prose poetry, flash fiction, and novels-in-verse." avg. press run 1000. Pub'd 3 titles 2009; expects 3 titles 2010, 3 titles 2011. 6 titles listed in the *Small Press Record of Books in Print* (36th Edition, 2010-11). Discounts: We offer discounts for course adoptions. 120pp. Reporting time: A few weeks to a few months. Simultaneous submissions accepted: Yes.

ROSEBUD, Roderick Clark, N 3310 Asje Rd., Cambridge, WI 53523, 608-423-4750. 1993. Poetry, fiction, articles, art, interviews, satire, parts-of-novels, long-poems, plays, non-fiction. "*Rosebud* is a magazine designed 'for people who enjoy good writing.' Each issue features five rotating themes, such as 'Songs of Suburbia' and 'Mothers Daughters, Wives.' Stories, articles, profiles and poems of love, alienation, travel, humor, nostalgia, and unexpected revelation. Send a SASE for guidelines or check www.rsbd.net. *Rosebud* is looking for interesting voices and discerning readers." circ. 12M. 4/yr. Expects 3 issues 2010, 4 issues 2011. sub. price $20/3 issues; per copy $7.95; sample $7.95. Back issues: $7.95 or 3 for $18. Discounts: upon request. 136pp. Reporting time: 14 weeks. Simultaneous submissions accepted: yes. Publishes 5% of manuscripts submitted. Payment: $15 per piece. Copyrighted, reverts to author. Ads: $500/$300. Subjects: Fiction, Literary Review, Poetry, Prose, Writers/Writing.

ROUND, George Pedersen, www.roundonline.com. "We are based in Boston (with a tiny little bit of us in New York City). We used to publish a print issue quarterly, but now it's pretty much an internet thing with plans for annual print "Best of" compilations. Each issue we have a different theme. Your job is to come up with something based on that theme that people will want to spend time reading or looking at or being distracted/engaged by. If you do that, we'll put you in our magazine. All material will be considered for publication on www.roundonline.com, with the best material later being published in our printed version. Please email all submissions to: isubmit at roundonline.com."

Rowan Mountain Press, PO Box 10111, Blacksburg, VA 24062-0111, 540-449-6178, e-mail faulkner@bev.net, web www.rowanmountain.com. 1988. Poetry, non-fiction. "Appalachian poetry and short stories. Manuscript submission by invitation. Recent authors: R. Franklin Pate, Jim Wayne Miller, Sharyn McCrumb, Bennie Lee Sinclair, Harry Dean, Earl S. Zehr, Norman M. Bowman." avg. press run 300. Pub'd 1 title 2009; expects 2 titles 2010, 1 title 2011. 9 titles listed in the *Small Press Record of Books in Print* (36th Edition, 2010-11). Discounts: 2-4 copies 20%, 5+ 40%; 40% any quantity and s/h if prepaid. 75pp. Payment: 10% of press run. Copyrights for author. Subjects: Appalachia, Education, Mystery, Poetry, Scotland, Short Stories, Vietnam, War.

Rowan Press, Inc., Joan Robinson-Blumit, 4414 North 35th St., Phoenix, AZ 85018, 602-380-9213. 1997. Fiction, non-fiction. avg. press run 100. Expects 1 title 2010, 1 title 2011. No titles listed in the *Small Press Record of Books in Print* (36th Edition, 2010-11). 100-300pp.

Rowhouse Press (see also JACK MACKEREL MAGAZINE), Greg Bachar, PO Box 23134, Seattle, WA 98102-0434. 1992. Poetry, fiction, art, photos, criticism, music, parts-of-novels, long-poems, non-fiction. "Send money orders (cash only) to Greg Bachar." avg. press run varies. Pub'd 1 title 2009; expects 3-4 titles 2010, 7-8 titles 2011. 7 titles listed in the *Small Press Record of Books in Print* (36th Edition, 2010-11). Pages vary. Reporting time: 2-4 weeks. Payment: copies. Copyrights for author. Subjects: Arts, Biography, Book Reviewing, Comics, Criticism, Dada, Dance, Electronics, Fiction, History, Holography, Language, Literature (General), Music, Philosophy.

RTMC Organization, LLC, Kenneth Besser, Post Office Box 15105, Baltimore, MD 21282-5105, 410-900-7834, krb@rtmc.org. 2005. Fiction, non-fiction. "At RTMC, we are 'Reaching to motivate change.' Change in ourselves, change in others, and change in the circumstances that perplex us all. As a social entrepreneurial enterprise, our goal is not to employ people to publish books. Rather, our mission is to publish good books from new authors and make them available to booksellers who want to employ themselves. Our genres are diverse and comprise fiction (legal thrillers and other commercial novels), young reader's (grades 6-12) fiction (we are publishing a new series of children's adventures titled the Arnie Carver Adventures), and

426

nonfiction (body, mind, spirit, community; motivational; health; legal; business)." avg. press run 5000. Pub'd 2 titles 2009; expects 6 titles 2010, 12 titles 2011. 2 titles listed in the *Small Press Record of Books in Print* (36th Edition, 2010-11). Discounts: 2 books - less than a caselot 40% off; Caselots 45% off; Multiple cases 50% off. 300pp. Reporting time: Prompt reports to well written, interesting initial query letters; immediate reports to bad ones. Please query prior to submitting manuscripts. Will consider e-mail submissions. Simultaneous submissions accepted: Yes. Publishes 1% of manuscripts submitted. Payment: Generous royalty arrangements, but no advances. Prompt royalty payment schedules. Copyrights for author. Subjects: Business & Economics, Consulting, Food, Eating, Health, Law, Motivation, Success, Non-Fiction, Novels, Parenting, Philosophy, Picture Books, Psychology, Romance, Young Adult.

RUBBERSTAMPMADNESS, Roberta Sperling, PO Box 610, Corvallis, OR 97339-0610. 1980. Articles, art, photos, interviews, reviews, letters. circ. 8M. 4/yr. Pub'd 6 issues 2009; expects 4 issues 2010, 4 issues 2011. sub. price $21.95; per copy $5.99; sample $7. Back issues: $7 USA/Canada $12 overseas. Discounts: $7. 84pp. Payment: $100-$200 depending on size of article. Copyrighted. Pub's reviews: 36 in 2009. §Rubberstamping, paper arts, creative ideas, book arts, mail art. Ads: $1050/$550/$1.75 per word. Subjects: Arts, Visual Arts.

RUBIES IN THE DARKNESS, Peter Geoffrey Paul Thompson, Editor, 41 Grantham Road, Manor Park, London E12 5LZ, England. 1991. Poetry. "We run an annual poetry competition. Traditional, romantic, lyrical and spiritually inspired poetry (international). Recent contributors include Pamela Constantine, Peter Geoffrey Paul Thompson, Philip Higson, Pamela Harvey, Jack Clubb (USA), Dr. K. Ikeda (Japan), Tim Cloudsley (Columbia), and Dr. A. Schedchikov (Russia). Submissions in traditional form especially welcome!" circ. 250. 2/yr. Expects 2 issues 2010, 2 issues 2011. sub. price £15, $40; per copy £5, $10; sample £5, $10. Back issues: £5, $10. Discounts: none. 36pp. Reporting time: 1 month maximum. Simultaneous submissions accepted: no. Publishes 20% of manuscripts submitted. Payment: by arrangement for individual anthologies; mag: one free copy only. Copyrighted. Small ads free for subscribers, no other ads accepted. Subject: Poetry.

THE RUE BELLA, Nigel Bird, Geoff Bird, 40, Jordangate, Macclesfield SK10 1EW, England, www.ruebella.co.uk. 1998. Poetry, fiction. circ. 350-400. 2/yr. Pub'd 2 issues 2009; expects 2 issues 2010, 2 issues 2011. sub. price £10/4 issues; per copy £3.50. Back issues: £1.50. 120pp. Reporting time: 6-8 weeks. Simultaneous submissions accepted: yes. Publishes 10% of manuscripts submitted. Payment: free copy. Copyrighted, reverts to author. Subjects: Poetry, Short Stories.

RUMINATE MAGAZINE, Brianna VanDyke, Editor, 140 North Roosevelt Ave., Fort Collins, CO 80521. "*Ruminate Magazine* is brought to you from Fort Collins, Colorado. It was created by a few fellow writers and believers who wanted to develop a space for the thoughtful expressions of those who are nudged forward, backward, and sideways by a faith in God. *Ruminate* is a quarterly magazine of short stories, poetry, creative nonfiction, and visual art that resonate with the complexity and truth of the Christian faith."

RUMINATIONS: The Nigerian Dwarf & Mini Dairy Goat Magazine, Cheryl Smith, 22705 Hwy 36, Cheshire, OR 97419, 541 998-6081. 1993. Poetry, fiction, articles, photos, cartoons, interviews, reviews, letters, news items, non-fiction. "Ruminations is dedicated to the free exchange of ideas, knowledge and opinions relevant to Nigerian Dwarf and other miniature dairy goats." circ. 200. 4/yr. Pub'd 6 issues 2009; expects 4 issues 2010, 4 issues 2011. 1 title listed in the *Small Press Record of Books in Print* (36th Edition, 2010-11). sub. price $24; per copy $6.50; sample $5.00. Back issues: $4.00. 32pp. Reporting time: 1 day to 4 weeks. Simultaneous submissions accepted: No. Publishes 90% of manuscripts submitted. Payment: No payment; ad exchanges. Copyrighted. Pub's reviews: approx 6 in 2009. §goats, poison plants, videos, livestock, health. Ads: Classified—$25/wordDisplay—$25/%30/$40/$60/$80/$100/$115. Subjects: Agriculture, Book Reviewing, How-To, Pets, Reviews.

The Runaway Spoon Press, Bob Grumman, 1708 Hayworth Road, Port Charlotte, FL 33952, 941-629-8045. 1987. Poetry, art, cartoons, satire, criticism, reviews, long-poems, collages, plays, non-fiction. "My press is in its second decade and slowing down. I'm no longer as open to new authors as I once was. I'm definitely not interested in the kind of thing commercial and academic presses publish. I've recently published Clemente Padin, Karl Kempton and Carla Bertola." avg. press run 100. Pub'd 4 titles 2009; expects 5 titles 2010, 6 titles 2011. 149 titles listed in the *Small Press Record of Books in Print* (36th Edition, 2010-11). Discounts: 40% off for purchase of 5 or more copies of a book, 40% retailers' discount. 48pp. Reporting time: indefinite. Simultaneous submissions accepted: yes. Publishes 10% of manuscripts submitted. Payment: author gets 25% of each printing. Does not copyright for author. Subjects: Arts, Avant-Garde, Experimental Art, Comics, Criticism, Drama, Graphics, Humor, Poetry, Psychology, Visual Arts.

Rural Messengers Press (see also SIDE OF GRITS), Michele McDannold, 5 Morningside Drive, Jacksonville, IL 62650, rmp@theliteraryunderground.org, http://theliteraryunderground.org/rmp/grits. 2006. Poetry, fiction, art, photos, interviews, reviews. "RMP is a publisher of unique mailers, specializing in limited edition collections. Our focus is on poetry by underpublished or under-recognized authors. Contributors include F.N. Wright, Stephen Morse, Aleathia Drehmer and David Blaine." avg. press run 50. Pub'd 3 titles 2009;

427

expects ? titles 2010, ? titles 2011. 4 titles listed in the *Small Press Record of Books in Print* (36th Edition, 2010-11). Subjects: Avant-Garde, Experimental Art, Book Arts, Book Collecting, Bookselling, Experimental, Interviews, Photography, Poetry, Postcards, Printing, Short Stories, Zines.

Russet Press, Kathleen Millman, 3442 Capland Ave., Clermont, FL 34711-5738. 1995. 2 titles listed in the *Small Press Record of Books in Print* (36th Edition, 2010-11).

Russian Information Services (see also RUSSIAN LIFE), Paul Richardson, Stephanie Ratmeyer, PO Box 567, Montpelier, VT 05601-0567, 802-223-4955. 1990. Non-fiction. "Publish Russian Life magazine, Chtenia literary quarterly, maps, calendar and 2-3 works of fiction and non-fiction on Russia each year." avg. press run 5M. Pub'd 5 titles 2009; expects 5 titles 2010, 5+ titles 2011. 7 titles listed in the *Small Press Record of Books in Print* (36th Edition, 2010-11). Discounts: case by case. 200pp. Reporting time: 1 month. Payment: case by case. Copyrights for author. Subjects: Business & Economics, Russia, Travel, U.S.S.R.

RUSSIAN LIFE, Russian Information Services, Paul Richardson, Publisher & Editorial Director, PO Box 567, Montpelier, VT 05601-0567. 1956. Photos, non-fiction. "Bi-monthly magazine on Russian history, culture, travel." 6/yr. Pub'd 6 issues 2009; expects 6 issues 2010, 6 issues 2011. sub. price $33 US, $38 foreign; per copy $8. Back issues: $8. 64pp. Reporting time: 1 month. Publishes less than 10% of manuscripts submitted. Copyrighted, rights do not revert if WFH. Pub's reviews: 6-8 in 2009. §History, culture. Ads: contact for rates. Subject: Russia.

S

•**S4N Books,** Tim Miller, Jenny Miller, 6904 Colonial Road, #28, Brooklyn, NY 11220. 2005. "To save you postage and to get a quicker response, we only accept submissions (attached or in the body of an email) sent to s4nbooks@gmail.com.Full guidelines are at http://www.s4nbooks.com/contact.html, but briefly: we want new epic poems, new long poems, new poem sequences, new poetry that assumes poetry's epic and bardic tradition should remain as alive as the (to us) more lifeless modern poetry that seems theoretical, cold, and lacking the courage to believe words can and do carry meaning. Our ideal antecedents are usually religious/mythological: the Biblical prophets, the Hindu scriptures, Egyptian funerary texts, Gilgamesh, the Norse Eddas, Dante, Arthurian literature, the Kalevala, etc. As much of the above these are expressed in prose just as well as poetry, we will also look at novels of any length." Pub'd 1 title 2009; expects 1 title 2010, 2 titles 2011. 2 titles listed in the *Small Press Record of Books in Print* (36th Edition, 2010-11). 100pp. Reporting time: One month at most, usually within a week. Simultaneous submissions accepted: Yes. We are writers too, and understand this is necessary nowadays. No need to inform us of a simultaneous submission—we assume it! Publishes Maybe 5%, probably less% of manuscripts submitted. Payment: Advance and royalties, negotiated. Copyrights for author. Subjects: Anthropology, Archaelogy, Arthurian, Buddhism, Celtic, Christianity, Classical Studies, Death & Dying, Robinson Jeffers, Myth, Mythology, Native American, Poetry, Religion, Spiritual, Sufism, Walt Whitman.

Sabellapress, Ed Parris, 11014 19th Avenue SE, Suite 8, Box 314, Everett, WA 98208. 1987. Poetry, fiction, non-fiction. "Sabellapress seeks to find good writing and produce good books; to respect the artistic integrity of its authors; to help its authors promote their careers; and to cultivate new markets for well written, well designed books." avg. press run 5000. Expects 10 titles 2010, 10 titles 2011. No titles listed in the *Small Press Record of Books in Print* (36th Edition, 2010-11). Discounts are available to authors and retailers. 150-400pp. Reporting time: 30-60 days. Simultaneous submissions accepted: Yes. Payment: 15% of list; paid quarterly, no advance. Does not copyright for author. Subjects: African-American, Anthology, Fiction, Folklore, Government, Leadership, Literature (General), Multicultural, Non-Fiction, Novels, Pacific Northwest, Performing Arts, Poetry, Prose, Young Adult.

Saber Press, Michael Conti, 268 Main Street, PMB 138, North Reading, MA 01864, Tel./Fax. 978-749-3731, Email: admin@sabergroup.com, Website: www.saber-press.com. 2006. Non-fiction. "We are currently accepting manuscripts for consideration. All submissions will be handled with great care to ensure your privacy. We are interested in non-fiction training and informational material that will be of interest to our particular audience, the law enforcement, military, and corporate security sectors.We offer full publishing services as well as consultation services to assist you in making your project a reality." 1 title listed in the *Small Press Record of Books in Print* (36th Edition, 2010-11). Special discounts are available. Contact Booksales@sabergroup.com for more information! 150-400pp. Reporting time: 1-2 weeks. Simultaneous submissions accepted: Yes. Payment: Industry standard (and better) arrangements are available. Copyrights for author. Subjects: Non-Fiction, Safety, Textbooks.

SABLE LITMAG, Kadija George, Founder-Editor, PO Box 33504, London E9 7YE, United Kingdom. "Additional address: PO Box 2803, Upper Darby, PA 19082. *Sable LItMag* is a 132 page black and white international publication, for writers of colour. *Sable* also offers training through e-internships, professional development for writers through its courses and workshops, and a Reading Series, that brings *Sable LitMag* 'live and off the page' with regular performances and readings around the globe including an annual LitFest. The mag provides a space for new writers to showcase their work and to receive critical feedback in their chosen written language of expression. It provides readers with an opportunity to read new work by published and unpublished authors and provides useful and interesting literary information in a format that is aesthetically as important as the written word."

The Sacred Beverage Press, Amelie Frank, Matthew Niblock, PO Box 10312, Burbank, CA 91510-0312, Fax 818-780-1912, sacredbev@aol.com. 1994. Poetry, art, long-poems. "The press is currently on hiatus. Sole editorial bias: Quality. Contributors: The Carma Bums, The Valley Contemporary Poets, FrancEyE, Nelson Gary, Richard Osborn Hood, and Diane DiPrima." avg. press run 500-1M. Pub'd 3 titles 2009; expects 3 titles 2010, 4 titles 2011. 7 titles listed in the *Small Press Record of Books in Print* (36th Edition, 2010-11). Discounts: 40% retail. 100pp. Reporting time: 2-3 months. Simultaneous submissions accepted: no. Publishes 5% of manuscripts submitted. Payment: % of sales after costs are met; 40% of consignment sales; 25 free author's copies; author's expenses. Copyrights for author. Subject: Poetry.

SACS Consulting, Timothy A. Dimoff, 520 South Main St., Suite 2512, Akron, OH 44311-1073, tadimoff@sacsconsulting.com, www.sacsconsulting.com 330-255-1101. 1990. Non-fiction. "Focus on business topics including high risk and security issues,human resource issues, and entrepreneurship." avg. press run 3M. Pub'd 3 titles 2009; expects 1 title 2010, 2 titles 2011. 1 title listed in the *Small Press Record of Books in Print* (36th Edition, 2010-11). Discounts: 40% to bookstores, 50% wholesale/distributors, 20% libraries & schools, 2-4 quantities 20%, 5-99 40%, 100+ 50%. 125pp. Simultaneous submissions accepted: yes. Payment: negotiable. Copyrights for author. Subjects: Business & Economics, Careers, Management.

Sadorian Publications, PO Box 2443, Durham, NC 27715-2443, 919-599-3038, Fax 309-431-4387, sadorianllc@aol.com, www.Sadorianonline.com. 2000. Poetry, fiction, art, non-fiction. "The preferred range for novels is from 60,000 to 80,000 words. We do not publish hate related, pornographic material. Submissions are not returned, they are shred, please do not send your only copy. All submissions must include a SASE and a stamped postcard for confirmation of receipt. Due to the volume of submissions we receive, we cannot discuss or provide the status of your manuscript via email or telephone. Please include a SASE to be notified with regards to your submission. No SASE, no response." avg. press run 3000. Pub'd 12 titles 2009; expects 12 titles 2010, 18 titles 2011. 1 title listed in the *Small Press Record of Books in Print* (36th Edition, 2010-11). Discounts: less than 10 units 0%, 10-49 40%, 50-249 45%, 250+ 50%. 275pp. Reporting time: 2-3 months. Simultaneous submissions accepted: yes. Publishes 5-10% of manuscripts submitted. Copyrights for author. Subjects: African-American, Children, Youth, Fiction, Inspirational, Memoirs, Poetry.

Sagamore Publishing, 804 N. Neil St, Champaign, IL 61820, 217-359-5940, 217-359-5975 (fax), HTTP://www.sagamorepub.com. 1974. Non-fiction. "For the past 33 years, Sagamore Publishing has been doing materials for the parks, recreation and leisure industry. Each quarter, we publish the prestigious Journal of the Parks and Recreation Administration. Well-known in their respective fields, some of our recent authors are: Ruth V. Russell, Ted Cable, Tom Griffiths, Chris Edginton, Thomas Sawyer, Linda Jean Carpenter, David Austin, Norma Stumbo H. Ken Cordell and Joseph J. Bannon." Pub'd 8 titles 2009; expects 8 titles 2010, 8 titles 2011. 1 title listed in the *Small Press Record of Books in Print* (36th Edition, 2010-11). Discounts: Trade discounts are negotiable. Standard volume discounts are: 1-9 10%, 10-49 20%, 50-99 30%, 100+ 35%. Add 5% if books are non-returnable. 345pp. Reporting time: 1-2 months. Payment: We pay royalties every six months. Subjects: Business & Economics, Children, Youth, Conservation, Education, Environment, Health, Journals, Music, Psychology, Reference, Self-Help, Senior Citizens, Sports, Outdoors, Storytelling, Third World, Minorities.

Sage Hill Press, Thomas Caraway, 1024 N. Summit Blvd., Spokane, WA 99201, 509-413-1184, sagehillpress@yahoo.com. 2004. Poetry, criticism, long-poems, non-fiction. "I tend to favor non-experimental writing, environmental themes, narrative, meditative, or dramatic lyric poetry, but above all, good writing. Also interested in poetry in translation." avg. press run 500-1000. Expects 1 title 2010, 3 titles 2011. 1 title listed in the *Small Press Record of Books in Print* (36th Edition, 2010-11). Discounts: 40% wholesale. 88pp. Reporting time: 3 months. Simultaneous submissions accepted: Yes, if notified. Copyrights for author. Subjects: Criticism, Environment, Poetry, Surrealism, Translation, Writers/Writing.

SAGE OF CONSCIOUSNESS E-ZINE, Michelle Williams, PO Box 1209, Ocala, FL 34478-1209, sageofcon@gmail.com http://www.sageofcon.com. 2004. Poetry, fiction, articles, art, photos, interviews, satire, criticism, reviews, music, letters, parts-of-novels, long-poems, collages, plays, concrete art, non-fiction. "We look for innovative, ground breaking—perhaps even glancing the edges of the taboo—poetry, short stories, photography, plays, digital media, and art that speaks to a reader's soul in some fashion. Our mission is to publish art, photography, short fiction and non-fiction, poetry, essay, articles, plays, paintings, digital media, and more, to give artists and writers an outlet to present their work. Sage of Consciousness editors are from different backgrounds, upbringings, and have different tastes, points of view, and political affiliations; we do not select pieces based on political, religious, or geographical bias. Each piece submitted stands on its own merits. We also delve further into the writing and art world by offering helpful articles for writers and artists, links to writing communities, and offer to put links to artists and writers' web sites. ISSN 1555 - 192X.'' circ. 4,367. 4/yr. Expects 4 issues 2010, 4 issues 2011. sub. price free; per copy free; sample free. Back issues: free. Discounts: free. 60pp. Reporting time: Notification of submission received within 21 days. Simultaneous submissions accepted: Yes. Publishes 47% of manuscripts submitted. Copyrighted, reverts to author. Pub's reviews: 2 in 2009. §All areas open. Subjects: Arts, Avant-Garde, Experimental Art, Essays, Fiction, Graphic Design, Haiku, Internet, Non-Fiction, Photography, Poetry, Prose, Short Stories, Visual Arts, Writers/Writing, Zines.

SAGEWOMAN, Anne Newkirk Niven, Editor in Chief, PO Box 687, Forest Grove, OR 97116. 1986. Articles, art, photos, interviews, reviews, music. circ. 21M. 4/yr. Pub'd 4 issues 2009; expects 4 issues 2010, 4 issues 2011. sub. price $22; per copy $7.50; sample $7.50. Back issues: $7.50 except reprint editions at $10. Discounts: none. 96pp. Reporting time: 1-2 months. We rarely accept simultaneous submissions. Publishes 20% of manuscripts submitted. Payment: minimum 2¢ per word, sometimes higher. Copyrighted, reverts to author. Pub's reviews: 40 in 2009. §Women's spirituality, ecology, feminism. Ads: $625/$325/$1.50 per word. Subjects: Astrology, Celtic, Metaphysics, Myth, Mythology, New Age, Occult, Spiritual, Tarot, Women.

St. Andrews College Press (see also CAIRN: The New St. Andrews Review), Caitlin Johnson, Managing Editor; Ronald Bayes, Executive Editor; Edna Ann Loftus, Consulting Editor; Ted Wojtasik, Consulting Editor; Thomas Heffernan, Consulting Editor, 1700 Dogwood Mile, Laurinburg, NC 28352-5598, 910-277-5310. 1969. Poetry, fiction, long-poems, plays. ''The Press does not accept unsolicited manuscripts. The Managing Editor may be queried at the address given. The size and nature of the publication should be described. As a rule we publish only poetry and short fiction. The magazine accepts unsolicited MSS. Hard copy preferred, with SASE.'' avg. press run 400. Pub'd 6 titles 2009; expects 4 titles 2010, 3 titles 2011. 29 titles listed in the *Small Press Record of Books in Print* (36th Edition, 2010-11). Discounts: 40%. 100pp. Reporting time: 3-4 months, usually sooner. Publishes 2% of manuscripts submitted. Payment: 2 copies, 50% discount on extra copies. Copyrights for author. Subjects: Drama, Fiction, Literary Review, Poetry.

THE SAINT ANN'S REVIEW, Beth Bosworth, Editor, 129 Pierrepont Street, Brooklyn, NY 11201, ph: 718-522-1660 x317, fax:718-522-2599. *''The Saint Ann's Review*, now in its eighth year, celebrates the arts. We select from hundreds of submissions to bring you two issues annually of fine fiction, poetry, reviews, translations, art, and the occasional musical score. We aim, in so doing, for a certain transparency: to let you open the gorgeous cover of a given issue and connect directly with the works within. Material offered for first publication only is considered. Simultaneous submissions are accepted with notification upon publication elsewhere. We consider short fiction and essays (up to 6000 words), poetry (up to 10 pages), plays (up to 25 pages) and excerpts (up to 25 pages) from larger works; also translations of poetry and short prose. The original-language work must accompany the translation and the translator is responsible for author's permission. We read submissions September-July.''

Saint Bob Press, Richard Murff, 2095 Poplar Avenue, Suite 54, Memphis, TN 38104, 901.412.7362, www.saintbobpress.com. 2007. Fiction, non-fiction. ''Saint Bob Press focuses on modern fiction and its Saint Bob Classics imprint. Fiction has to date focused on thrillers and mainstream fiction. Saint Bob Classics publishes ancient classics as they relate to the modern world and topical events of the day.'' avg. press run 5000. Expects 3 titles 2010, 10 titles 2011. No titles listed in the *Small Press Record of Books in Print* (36th Edition, 2010-11). Discounts: standard 55%. 250pp. Reporting time: two months. Simultaneous submissions accepted: Yes. Copyrights for author. Subjects: Alcohol, Alcoholism, Audio/Video, Fiction, Greek, Horror, Humor, Literature (General), Novels, Philosophy, Politics, Reprints, Society, South.

St. John's Publishing, Inc., Timothy Montgomery, Editor-in-Chief; Donna L. Montgomery, President, 6824 Oaklawn Avenue, Edina, MN 55435, 952-920-9044. 1986. Fiction, non-fiction. ''Trade paperback publisher of quality nonfiction. No manuscripts accepted for review without prior approval based on query letter and synopsis with SASE.'' avg. press run 5M. Pub'd 1 title 2009; expects 3 titles 2010, 3 titles 2011. 13 titles listed in the *Small Press Record of Books in Print* (36th Edition, 2010-11). Discounts: per quantity for individuals, schools, libraries, government agencies; up to 42% for bookstores; 50% for wholesalers and jobbers. 200pp. Reporting time: 3 weeks or less. Payment: standard royalty; minimal advance; payments semi-annual. Copyrights for author. Subject: Parenting.

Saint Mary's Press, Brian Singer-Towns, Steven McGlaun, Maura Thompson Hagarty, Gloria Shahin, 702 Terrace Heights, Winona, MN 55987, 800-533-8095, http://www.smp.org, smpress@smp.org. 1943. Fiction, non-fiction. ''Saint Mary's Press is a contemporary expression of the Catholic Church's mission to proclaim the Good News of Jesus Christ and the Lasallian mission to provide a human and Christian education for young people, including those who are economically deprived. We publish Bibles for teens ages 10-19, as well as Catholic textbooks, parish religious education programs, and Catholic youth ministry resources." avg. press run 7.5M. Pub'd 20 titles 2009; expects 20 titles 2010, 20 titles 2011. No titles listed in the *Small Press Record of Books in Print* (36th Edition, 2010-11). 150pp. Reporting time: 3 months. Simultaneous submissions accepted: yes. Copyrights for author. Subjects: Adolescence, Catholic, Children, Youth, Christianity, Fiction, Guidance, Non-Fiction, Religion, Spiritual, Textbooks, Young Adult.

ST. VITUS PRESS & POETRY REVIEW, Theron Moore, Editor, 7408 Estes Park Avenue NW, Albuquerque, NM 87114, www.saintvituspress.com. 2002. "Outlaw poetry." We update our website on average, every two weeks. We are now a website and no longer a print magazine. Back issues: Back issues of the print mag are available. Simultaneous submissions accepted: Not accepted / encouraged. Payment: Sorry. We do not pay our writers. Pub's reviews: 50+ in 2009. §Strictly Outlaw Poetry. Ads: Ads are accepted. Please e-mail stvitusfan@aol.com for more info.

SALAMANDER, Jennifer Barber, Editor-in-Chief; Catherine Parnell, Fiction Editor; Valerie Duff-Strautmann, Poetry Editor, Salamander/Suffolk University English Dept., 41 Temple Street, Boston, MA 02114. 1992. Poetry, fiction, art, parts-of-novels, non-fiction. "We publish outstanding new and established writers, and works in translation. Recent contributors: Siobhan Fallon, Jessica Greenbaum, Paul Yoon, Fred Marchant, Laura Kasischke, Major Jackson, Oona Patrick, Chase Twichell, Yiyun Li, Mary O'Donoghue, George Kalogeris, Daniel Tobin, Christine Dwyer Hickey, Geoff Kronik." circ. 1M. 2/yr. Pub'd 2 issues 2009; expects 2 issues 2010, 2 issues 2011. sub. price $13; per copy $7; sample $3. Back issues: $3 when available. Discounts: write for details. 140pp. Reporting time: 3-4 months. Simultaneous submissions accepted: yes. Publishes 5% of manuscripts submitted. Payment: 2 copies of magazine; $200 per story; $35 per poem honoraria. Copyrighted, reverts to author. Pub's reviews: 6 in 2009. §primarily poetry. Ads: $150. Subjects: Fiction, Memoirs, Poetry, Short Stories, Translation.

SALMAGUNDI, Robert Boyers, Editor; Peg Boyers, Executive Editor; Marc Woodworth, Associate Editor; Tom Lewis, Associate Editor, Skidmore College, 815 North Broadway, Saratoga Springs, NY 12866-1632, 518-584-5186. 1965. Poetry, fiction, articles, photos, interviews, satire, criticism, reviews, letters, parts-of-novels, non-fiction. "Recent contributors: Rick Moody, Carolyn Forch, Nadine Gordimer, George Steiner, Seamus Heaney, Robert Pinsky, Carl Dennis, Tzvetan Todorov, Adam Zagajewski, Bernard-Henri Levi, Ben Barber, Martha Nussbaum, Peter Singer, Jean Elshtain, Mary Gordon, Orlando Patterson and Joyce Carol Oates. For the time being unsolicited manuscripts are not being considered. We anticipate returning to a normal reading pattern in October, 2010. After that the annual reading period will begin as before, on October 15th, and end on April 1. Any mss. received before October 2009 and later, outside that reading period, will not be returned." circ. 4500- 6M. 3-4/yr. Pub'd 4 issues 2009; expects 4 issues 2010, 4 issues 2011. sub. price Individuals: $20-1 year $30-2 yrs $40-3 yrs $60-5 yrs Institutions: $32-1 year $50-2 yrs $70 -3 yrs $100-5 yrs; per copy $8; sample $5. Back issues: send SASE for the list. Discounts: 40% to stores/ 2 yr. subs.: $30./ 5 yr. sub.: $60. 200pp. Reporting time: 6-9 months. Simultaneous submissions accepted: yes. Payment: none. Copyrighted, reverts to author. Pub's reviews: 8 in 2009. §Politics, social sciences, literary crit, poetry, fiction, essays. Ads: $150/$200/$250 cover. Subjects: Arts, Biography, Book Reviewing, Communism, Marxism, Leninism, Criticism, Culture, Dance, Electronics, Electronics, English, Fiction, Judaism, Latin America, Philosophy, Poetry.

Salmon Poetry Ltd., Jessie Lendennie, Knockeven, Cliffs of Moher, Co. Clare, Ireland, 011-353-65-7081941, info@salmonpoetry.com, www.salmonpoetry.com. 1981. Poetry, non-fiction. "Salmon has an extensive list of Irish, American, Canadian and British poets." avg. press run 1,000. Pub'd 15 titles 2009; expects 15 titles 2010, 15 titles 2011. No titles listed in the *Small Press Record of Books in Print* (36th Edition, 2010-11). Discounts: distributed in the U.S. by Dufour Editions, who have their own pricing system. 80pp. Reporting time: Email queries: Reply within One day. Mail queries: One to Two months. In fact, I don't encourage mail submissions since the process takes so much longer (and there are still people who don't include return envelopes and postage). Simultaneous submissions accepted: yes. Publishes 1% of manuscripts submitted. Payment: 10% of retail cover price. Copyrights for author. Subjects: Non-Fiction, Poetry, Publishing.

Salmon Run Press, John E. Smelcer, Chief Editor, PO Box 671236, Chugiak, AK 99567-1236. 1991. Poetry, fiction, art, non-fiction. "Recently published work by X.J. Kennedy, Joy Harjo, Denise Duhamel, John Haines, Ursula K. LeGuin, Molly Peacock, R.L. Barth, Phillip Levine, Denise Levertov, and Moore Moran." avg. press run 500-1M. Pub'd 5 titles 2009; expects 3-5 titles 2010, 3-5 titles 2011. 8 titles listed in the *Small Press Record of Books in Print* (36th Edition, 2010-11). Discounts: 40% to retailers, 50-55% to distributors, 30% to libraries. 68-156pp. Reporting time: 1-3 months. Simultaneous submissions accepted: yes. Publishes 1-2% of manuscripts submitted. Payment: 5-10% royalties and copies. Copyrights for author.

SALT HILL, English Department, Syracuse University, Syracuse, NY 13244-1170. 1994. Poetry, fiction, articles, art, interviews, criticism, reviews, parts-of-novels, long-poems, non-fiction. "Address your submission to specific genre editor: Poetry Editor, Fiction Editor, etc. Fiction: 6,000 word maximum; poems - send 3-5.

Recent contributers include: Dean Young, Brian Evenson, Kim Addonizio, Terese Svoboda, James Tate, Steve Almond, and Nin Andrews. We hold annual poetry and short short fiction contests. Deadline - January 15th. For more information visit our web site at http://students.syr.edu/salthill." circ. 1M. 2/yr. Pub'd 2 issues 2009; expects 2 issues 2010, 2 issues 2011. sub. price $15; per copy $8; sample $8. Back issues: $5. 120-150pp. Reporting time: 2-6 months. Simultaneous submissions accepted: yes. Publishes 5% of manuscripts submitted. Payment: 2 copies. Copyrighted, reverts to author. Pub's reviews: 4 in 2009. §Poetry, short story, fiction, hypertext. Ads: $125/$75. Ad swaps welcome.

Salt Publishing, Chris Hamilton-Emery, Director; Jen Hamilton-Emery, Director, 14a High Street, Fulbourn, Cambridge CB21 5DH, United Kingdom, +44 (0)1223 882220 chris@saltpublishing.com. 2002. Poetry, fiction, interviews, criticism, long-poems, non-fiction. "Salt Publishing offers a growing list of internationally acclaimed poetry, essays, and short fiction. Series include The Salt Companion series, which presents intelligent and evocative guides to such luminaries as Harold Bloom and Carter Revard. The award-winning Earthworks series, edited by Janet McAdams, offers Native American writing and includes work by Heid Erdrich, Kimberly Blaeser, and Diane Glancy. Salt authors appear at festivals and conferences the world over and their work continues to receive major critical attention." avg. press run 1500. Pub'd 70 titles 2009; expects 80 titles 2010, 90 titles 2011. No titles listed in the *Small Press Record of Books in Print* (36th Edition, 2010-11). Discounts: 1-4 copies 20%5-249 copies 45%250-499 copies 46%500+ copies 47%. 144pp. Reporting time: Four months. Simultaneous submissions accepted: Yes. Publishes 1% of manuscripts submitted. Payment: 5%-10%, no advance, paid annually in June, first full year after publication on amounts exceeding $75. Copyrights for author. Subjects: Black, Essays, Experimental, Feminism, Gay, Indigenous Cultures, Interviews, Latin America, Literature (General), Native American, Non-Fiction, Poetry, Short Stories, Women, Writers/Writing.

THE SALT RIVER REVIEW, James Cervantes, 448 N. Matlock, Mesa, AZ 85203-7222, http://www.poetserv.org/. 1997. Poetry, fiction, articles, criticism, reviews, letters, long-poems, non-fiction. "The Salt River Review is an eclectic and high-quality online publication. We have published work by Tess Gallagher, David Graham, Laura Jensen, Dara Wier, Carlos Reyes, Paul Howell, Halvard Johnson, Wendy Taylor Carlisle, Greg Simon, and John Morgan." circ. 500. 3/yr. Pub'd 3 issues 2009; expects 3 issues 2010, 3 issues 2011. sample price $0. 50pp. Reporting time: Three days to three months. Simultaneous submissions accepted: Yes. Publishes 2% of manuscripts submitted. Payment: None. Copyrighted, reverts to author. Pub's reviews: 2 in 2009. §These are done in-house.

Sand and Sable Publishing, Joyce Hyndman, Publisher; Brandy Wilson, Editor; Ronald Hyndman, Creative Designer, P.O. Box 744, Jonesboro, GA 30237, 404-509-3352. 2005. Non-fiction. "Sand and Sable publishing offers adult fictional romances, ppetry and romantic. Within the next year we are expecting to expand our publishing capacity to include children and teen self awarness books, puzzles and straight talk informationals. Our focus is tapping into talent from varied backgrounds and experiences. All writtenn work is a form of self expression and art. We cater to individuals who have a story to tell, but lack the platform to do so." avg. press run 5000. Expects 2 titles 2010, 5 titles 2011. 1 title listed in the *Small Press Record of Books in Print* (36th Edition, 2010-11). Discounts: For independant bookstores, a 30% discount for orders over 5. For wholesalers, a 40% discount for orders over 20 and 30% for orders under 20. 304pp. Reporting time: the average reporting time is three weeks. Simultaneous submissions accepted: Yes. Publishes 50% of manuscripts submitted. Payment: All contracts are negotiable based on the type of involvement and creative control author wants to have with publishing thier product. Based on the needs of the author. Subjects: Adolescence, Advertising, Self-Promotion, African Literature, Africa, African Studies, Black, Family, Fantasy, Fashion, Feminism, Festivals, Fiction, Gaelic, Magazines, Novels, Nursing, Peace.

Sand River Press, Bruce W. Miller, 1319 14th Street, Los Osos, CA 93402, 805-543-3591. 1987. Non-fiction. avg. press run 3M. Pub'd 2 titles 2009; expects 3 titles 2010, 1 title 2011. 7 titles listed in the *Small Press Record of Books in Print* (36th Edition, 2010-11). Discounts: 3+ 40%, 100+ 42%, 200+ 43%. 132pp. Reporting time: 8 weeks, must send return postage. Payment: standard. Copyrights for author. Subjects: California, Earth, Natural History, History, Literature (General), Native American, The West.

SANDPOINT MAGAZINE, Keokee Co. Publishing, Inc., Billie Jean Plaster, Editor; Chris Bessler, Publisher, PO Box 722, Sandpoint, ID 83864, 208-263-3573, info@keokee.com. 1990. Fiction, articles, art, photos, cartoons, interviews, criticism, reviews, parts-of-novels, long-poems, news items, non-fiction. "Physical Address: 307 N. 2nd Avenue, Sandpoint, ID 83864. *Sandpoint Magazine* is a regional magazine for North Idaho." circ. 25M. 2/yr. Pub'd 2 issues 2009; expects 2 issues 2010, 2 issues 2011. sub. price $7; per copy $3; sample $3.50. Back issues: $3.50. Discounts: negotiable. 48pp. Reporting time: 2 months. Simultaneous submissions accepted: yes. Publishes 25% of manuscripts submitted. Payment: negotiable. Copyrighted. Ads: 1720/110/$45 for 25 words. Subjects: Conservation, Entertainment, Essays, Idaho, Lifestyles, Pacific Northwest, Sports, Outdoors, Travel.

Santa Fe Writers Project, Andrew Gifford, 369 Montezuma Ave, #350, Santa Fe, NM 87501, info@sfwp.com, www.sfwp.com. 1998. Poetry, fiction, articles, interviews, satire, criticism, reviews, parts-of-novels, non-fiction. "SFWP maintains an online literary journal at www.sfwp.com dedicated to new authors. Submission details can be found on the webpage. We also maintain an independent publishing house, releasing work from Ray Robertson, Alan Cheuse, Pagan Kennedy and Richard Currey. Every year, we sponsor a contest open to fiction and creative nonfiction of any genre. In 2007, the contest judge is Robert Olen Butler. Submissions details can be found at www.sfwp.com." Expects 2 titles 2010, 4 titles 2011. 4 titles listed in the *Small Press Record of Books in Print* (36th Edition, 2010-11). 330pp. Reporting time: 60 days. Simultaneous submissions accepted: Yes. Copyrights for author. Subjects: Americana, Counter-Culture, Alternatives, Communes, Erotica, Experimental, Fantasy, Fiction, History, Literature (General), Memoirs, Mystery, Occult, Prose, Satire, Science Fiction, Southwest.

Santa Monica Press, PO Box 1076, Santa Monica, CA 90406-1076, 310-230-7759, Fax 310-230-7761. 1991. Photos, non-fiction. "At Santa Monica Press, we're not afraid to cast a wide editorial net. Our vision extends from lively and modern how-to books to offbeat looks at popular culture, from film history to literature. Recent titles include "Elvis Presley Passed Here," "Atomic Wedgies, Wet Willies, & Other Acts of Roguery," "L.A. Noir," "Calculated Risk," "Loving Through Bars," and "Can a Dead Man Strike Out?" Please see the "Author Guidelines" page on our website (www.santamonicapress.com) for submission instructions." Pub'd 14 titles 2009; expects 10 titles 2010, 12 titles 2011. 7 titles listed in the *Small Press Record of Books in Print* (36th Edition, 2010-11). Reporting time: 2-3 months. Simultaneous submissions accepted: yes. Payment: 4%-10% net royalty; $0-$2500 advance. Copyrights for author. Subjects: Arts, Culture, Entertainment, Folklore, How-To, Humor, Los Angeles, Movies, Music, Non-Fiction, Performing Arts, Reference, Theatre, Travel, Visual Arts.

THE SANTA MONICA REVIEW, Andrew Tonkovich, 1900 Pico Boulevard, Santa Monica, CA 90405-1628, www.smc.edu/sm_review. 1988. Fiction, parts-of-novels, non-fiction. "Recent contributors: Amy Gerstler, Judith Grossman, Jim Krusoe, Bernard Cooper, Michelle Latiolais. Looking for literary fiction and creative nonfiction." circ. 1M. 2/yr. Pub'd 1 issue 2009; expects 2 issues 2010, 2 issues 2011. sub. price $12; per copy $7; sample $7. Back issues: varies. 200pp. Reporting time: 1 month. Simultaneous submissions accepted: yes. Publishes 1% of manuscripts submitted. Payment: 2 copies plus subscription. Copyrighted, reverts to author. Ads: $200/$100. Subject: Literary Review.

SAPONIFIER, Kathy Tarbox, P.O. Box 280, Silvana, WA 98287, saponifier@gmail.com, phone 425-760-1004, http://www.saponifier.com. 1998. Articles, photos, interviews, reviews, news items, non-fiction. "Saponifier magazine has been the leading trade publication to the industry for the past 9 years. Every other month, soap, toiletry and candle makers, both large and small, look to Saponifier to provide the information they need to run their businesses. From formulating, packaging, regulations, marketing and establishing industry connections. With their May issue, Saponifier brings onboard their 9th editor, Mr. Tony Burfield, consultant to the aroma industry, as their Aromatic Materials editor. Within each article, of every issue, Saponifier's mission shines through.... they are dedicated to the success of the handcrafted soapmaker!" circ. 4,000. 6/yr. Pub'd 6 issues 2009; expects 6 issues 2010, 6 issues 2011. sub. price $33; per copy $7.95; sample $7.95. Back issues: $7.95. 44pp. Reporting time: 5-7 days. Simultaneous submissions accepted: No. Publishes 40% of manuscripts submitted. Payment: 2.5 cents per word. Copyrighted, reverts to author 6 months after publication. Pub's reviews: 6 in 2009. §Trade books on soap, toiletries and candlemaking. Ads: $350 full page/$225 half page/$160 1/3 page. Subjects: Alternative Medicine, Aromatherapy, Book Reviewing, Festivals, Folklore, Insurance, Internet, Interviews, Marketing, Motivation, Success, Public Relations/Publicity, Reviews, Trade.

•**SAPPHIRE MAGAZINE,** A2EO Media, Inc., 853 Broadway, suite 1516, New York, NY 10003, info@sapphire-magazine.com, Telephone: 212-358-3725, Fax: 360-237-0543. "As a lifestyle magazine, Sapphire caters to upscale black men and women (professionals) who live in the surburbs, the New York metropolitan area and surrounding areas. These professionals are seeking a magazine that empowers, entertains and informs them about New York. The magazine exists primarily to provide distinct lifestyle content that is engaging, in-depth and timely about the New York metropolitan area to upscale blacks."

Saqi Books Publisher, 26 Westbourne Grove, London W2 5RH, England, 020 7221 9347, fax 020 7229 7492. 1983. "Main focus is on works dealing with the Middle East, Islam and the Third World. Saqi's authors include some of the major European experts on the Middle East, as well as writers from the region itself: Germaine Tillion, Jacques Berque, Maxime Rodinson." avg. press run 3.5M. Pub'd 8 titles 2009; expects 8 titles 2010, 10 titles 2011. 23 titles listed in the *Small Press Record of Books in Print* (36th Edition, 2010-11). Discounts: as arranged by U.S. distributors—St. Martin's Press, Scholarly & Reference Div., 175 Fifth Avenue, New York, NY 10010, tel: 212-982-3900, Fax: 212-777-6359. 224pp. Reporting time: 8 weeks. Payment: annually (March). Copyrights for author. Subjects: Arts, Bibliography, Bilingual, Biography, Fiction, History, Language, Literature (General), Middle East, Poetry, Political Science, Politics, Religion, Reprints, Third World, Minorities.

Sarabande Books, Sarah Gorham, Editor-in-Chief; Kirby Gann, Managing Editor; Kristina McGrath, Associate Editor, 2234 Dundee Road Suite 200, Louisville, KY 40205, www.sarabandebooks.org. 1994. Poetry, fiction, non-fiction. avg. press run 2500. Pub'd 10 titles 2009; expects 10 titles 2010, 10 titles 2011. No titles listed in the *Small Press Record of Books in Print* (36th Edition, 2010-11). Discounts: contact Consortium Book Sales and Distribution: 800/283-3572. 224pp. Reporting time: Three months. Simultaneous submissions accepted: Yes. Publishes 1% of manuscripts submitted. Payment: standard royalty contract. Copyrights for author. Subjects: Essays, Fiction, Literature (General), Poetry.

THE SARANAC REVIEW, J.L. Torres, Co-Editor-Managing Editor; Michael Carrino, Co-Editor-Poetry Editor, CVH, Dept of English, SUNY Plattsburgh, 101 Broad St, Plattsburgh, NY 12901. "*The Saranac Review* aims to be a textual clearing in which a space is opened for cross-pollination between American and Canadian writers. In that way, we aim to be a textual river reflecting diverse voices, a literal "cluster of stars," an illumination of the Iroquois roots of our namesake, the word, Saranac. We believe in a vision of shared governance, of connection, and in the power of art. We accept poetry, fiction, non-fiction, inter genre pieces and translations. We are also very interested in publishing Canadian writers. We read from Sept 1 to February 15. We do not accept online submissions."

Saskatchewan Writers Guild (see also GRAIN MAGAZINE), PO Box 67, Saskatoon, SK S7K 3K1, Canada, 306-244-2828, grainmag@sasktel.net, www.grainmagazine.ca. 1973. Poetry, fiction, art, long-poems, non-fiction. "Grain Magazine, published four times per year, is an internationally acclaimed literary journal that publishes engaging, surprising, eclectic, and challenging writing and art by Canadian and international writers and artists." avg. press run 1000. Pub'd 4 titles 2009; expects 4 titles 2010, 4 titles 2011. No titles listed in the *Small Press Record of Books in Print* (36th Edition, 2010-11). 128pp. Reporting time: 3-6 months. Simultaneous submissions accepted: no. Publishes 5% of manuscripts submitted. Payment: $50/page up to a maximum of $225, plus 2 contributor copies. Grain purchases first Canadian serial rights only. Copyright remains with the writer or artist.

Sasquatch Books, Chad Haight, Publisher, 119 S. Main Street, Suite 400, Seattle, WA 98104-2555, 206-467-4300, 800-775-0817, Fax 206-467-4301, books@SasquatchBooks.com. 1986. Pub'd 34 titles 2009; expects 41 titles 2010, 45 titles 2011. 169 titles listed in the *Small Press Record of Books in Print* (36th Edition, 2010-11). Reporting time: 6-8 weeks. Simultaneous submissions accepted: yes. Copyrights for author. Subjects: Alaska, California, Children, Youth, Cooking, Cooking, Earth, Natural History, Gardening, Native American, Native American, Nature, Nature, Pacific Northwest, Transportation, Travel.

Sassy Sunflower Books, Donna Hedley, PO Box 67106, 421 Richmond Road, Ottawa, ON K2A 4E4, Canada, 613-799-1017. 2009. Poetry, fiction, articles, interviews, satire, letters, long-poems, plays, non-fiction. "The mission of Sassy Sunflower Books is to create a partnership environment that will give the authors as much control over their work as possible." avg. press run 100. Expects 8 titles 2010, 10 titles 2011. 4 titles listed in the *Small Press Record of Books in Print* (36th Edition, 2010-11). Discounts: 20%. 200pp. Reporting time: 1 month. Simultaneous submissions accepted: Yes. Publishes 80% of manuscripts submitted. Payment: no advances, high percent of revenue to go to author, terms may vary. Copyrights for author. Subjects: Autobiography, Canada, Consulting, Family, Fantasy, Fiction, Health, How-To, Motivation, Success, Novels, Poetry, Science Fiction, Self-Help, Storytelling, Young Adult.

Saturday Press, Charlotte Mandel, Editor, PO Box 43534, Upper Montclair, NJ 07043, 973-239-0436, fax: 973-239-0427. 1975. Poetry. "Sponsor of Eileen W. Barnes Award for women poets over forty. Not reading new submissions at this time." avg. press run 1M. 12 titles listed in the *Small Press Record of Books in Print* (36th Edition, 2010-11). Discounts: 40% to bookstores and jobbers. 64-102pp. Reporting time: responds to queries in 2 weeks. Publishes less than 1% of manuscripts submitted. Payment: individual arrangement. Copyrights for author. Subject: Poetry.

Saturnalia Books, Henry Israeli, Publisher, 105 Woodside Rd, Ardmore, PA 19003, www.saturnalia-books.com. 2002. "Saturnalia Books mission is to publish literary works, primarily poetry, of high merit, by new and established writers; to encourage collaboration between poets and visual artists, particularly in book form; and to encourage the publication of literature of a non-commercial and challenging nature. At present, Saturnalia Books publishes two book series per year: the Artist/Poet Collaboration Series, and the winner of the Saturnalia Books Poetry Prize. We regret that we do not take unsolicited submissions." Pub'd 4 titles 2009; expects 4 titles 2010, 4 titles 2011. No titles listed in the *Small Press Record of Books in Print* (36th Edition, 2010-11). 80pp. Copyrights for author. Subjects: Arts, Poetry.

Saturno Press, Anton Haardt, 1220 South Hull Street, Montgomery, AL 36104, 334-414-0745. 2003. avg. press run 4500. Expects 1 title 2010, 2 titles 2011. 1 title listed in the *Small Press Record of Books in Print* (36th Edition, 2010-11). 100pp.

THE SAVAGE KICK LITERARY MAGAZINE, Murder Slim Press, Steve Hussy, Richard White, 129 Trafalgar Road West, Gt. Yarmouth, Norfolk NR31 8AD, United Kingdom, www.murderslim.com/publications.html. 2005. Fiction, articles, interviews. "RECENT CONTRIBUTORS: Dan Fante, Mark SaFranko, Doug Stanhope, Jim Goad, Joe R. Lansdale, Tony O'Neill, Joe Matt, Tommy Trantino, Steve Hussy,

Zsolt Alapi, Robert McGowan and more...PLEASE SEND: Works dealing with any passionately held emotions and/or alternative viewpoints. These may well entail drink, sex, violence, bad language and any activity outside of the mainstream. Sleazy tales are very much encouraged and form the basis of 'The Savage Kick'.Real-life stories are preferred, unless work is distinctively extreme within the crime genre.We recommend that you have read 'The Savage Kick' before you submit. Ideal for fans of Dan Fante John Fante Charles Bukowski. DO NOT SEND: Mainstream fiction or Oprah-style fiction. Internet/chat language or teen issues. Any genre fiction including horror, fantasy, sci-fi, western, erotica, etc. And please... no excessive Shakespearean language, surrealism or overworked irony. We do not accept any poetry submissions.'' circ. 200. 1/yr. Pub'd 1 issue 2009; expects 1 issue 2010, 1 issue 2011. sub. price 12; per copy 12; sample Inquire. Back issues: 12. Discounts: Inquire. 76pp. Reporting time: 1-4 weeks. Simultaneous submissions accepted: Yes. Publishes 2% of manuscripts submitted. Payment: Stories: 20 (in UK) or $35 (International) for each accepted story. Articles: 15 (in UK) or $25 (International) for each accepted article. We will pay within two weeks of publication. Upon acceptance, advance payment may be requested and considered. Copyrighted. Ads: 'The Savage Kick' carries no advertising. Subjects: Alcohol, Alcoholism, Anarchist, Atheism, Autobiography, Beat, Biography, Charles Bukowski, Comics, Crime, Death & Dying, Drugs, Fiction, Henry Miller, Short Stories, War.

Savant Garde Workshop, Vilna Jorgen II, Publisher & Editor-in-Chief; Artemis Smith, Artistic Director, PO Box 1650, Sag Harbor, NY 11963-0060, 631-725-1414; website www.savantgarde.org. 1964. Poetry, fiction, criticism, long-poems, plays, concrete art, non-fiction. "We have suspended operations waiting upon major funding for expansion. Don't expect a reply unless your SASE query is accepted. DO NOT SEND MS until invited upon query, as it will be returned unopened. Focus on multinational intelligentsia. Looking for people who have eventual Nobel Prize potential. Publish limited signed editions and their overruns, ON DEMAND.'' On Demand. Expects 1 title 2010, 1 title 2011. 2 titles listed in the *Small Press Record of Books in Print* (36th Edition, 2010-11). Discounts: 25% rare bookdealers, bookdealers, wholesalers, art galleries & print shops. 300pp. Simultaneous submissions accepted: no. Publishes 1+% of manuscripts submitted. Payment: varies. Copyrights for author. Subjects: Arts, Atheism, Creativity, Dada, Drama, Ethics, Fiction, Humanism, Literature (General), Music, Philosophy, Poetry, Science, Science Fiction, Society.

Savor Publishing House, Inc., Carol Anderson, 6020 Broken Bow Dr., Citrus Heights, CA 95621, 916 729-3664, 866 762-7898. 2002. Poetry, fiction, non-fiction. "Savor Publishing House is the creator of the Smarties series. This is a medically based multicultural picture book series designed to develop early readers and educate in the field of medicine.'' avg. press run 3000. Expects 2 titles 2010, 1 title 2011. No titles listed in the *Small Press Record of Books in Print* (36th Edition, 2010-11). Discounts: Trade discounts are based on the number of books purchased.1-5 books 20%6-25 books 30%26 or more books 40%. 33pp. Reporting time: We do not accept submissions. Simultaneous submissions accepted: No. Payment: $3000 to $5000 advance with 10% royalty. Copyrights for author. Subjects: Health, Medicine, Multicultural, Picture Books, Storytelling.

SB&F (SCIENCE BOOKS & FILMS), Heather Malcomson, Editor, 1200 New York Avenue NW, Washington, DC 20005, 202-326-6646. 1965. Articles, interviews, reviews, news items. "Reviews books, films, videos, and software in all the sciences for all ages. We do not accept unsolicited reviews or articles.'' circ. 4.5M. 6/yr. Pub'd 6 issues 2009; expects 6 issues 2010, 6 issues 2011. sub. price $45; per copy $7 + $1.50 p/h; sample free. Back issues: $7, plus $1.50 p/h. Discounts: agents 10%. 48pp. Payment: none. Copyrighted, reverts to author. Pub's reviews: 898 in 2009. §Sciences. Ads: $900/$635. Subject: Science.

•**Scapegoat Press,** PO Box 410962, Kansas City, MO 64141. "Shining a light on remarkable writing from America's diverse communities.'' No titles listed in the *Small Press Record of Books in Print* (36th Edition, 2010-11).

Scarlet Tanager Books, Lucille L. Day, PO Box 20906, Oakland, CA 94620, 510-763-3874. 1999. Poetry, fiction, long-poems, non-fiction. "Web site: www.scarlettanager.com. Length of material: 64-160 pages. West Coast writers only (California, Oregon, Washington, Alaska, Hawaii). Recent contributors: Anne Coray, Daniel Hawkes, Judy Wells, Naomi Ruth Lowinsky, Lucille Lang Day, Jack Foley, Marc Elihu Hofstadter, Risa Kaparo, and Zack Rogow. We are not currently reading submissions.'' avg. press run 1M. 12 titles listed in the *Small Press Record of Books in Print* (36th Edition, 2010-11). Discounts: bookstores 40%, wholesalers 55%. 100pp. Reporting time: 3 months. Simultaneous submissions accepted: yes. Publishes 1% of manuscripts submitted. Payment: 10% of press run. Copyrights for author. Subjects: Fiction, Non-Fiction, Poetry.

Scars Publications (see also CHILDREN, CHURCHES AND DADDIES, A Non Religious, Non Familial Literary Magazine; DOWN IN THE DIRT LITERARY MAGAZINE, the prose & poetry magazine revealing all your dirty little secrets; FREEDOM AND STRENGTH PRESS FORUM), Janet Kuypers, Attn: Janet Kuypers, 829 Brian Court, Gurnee, IL 60031-3155, Editor@scars.tv, http://scars.tv. 1993. Poetry, fiction, art, photos, letters, long-poems, collages, non-fiction. "Scars Publications was created originally for the magazine *Children, Churches and Daddies*, and the magazine *Down In the Dirt*, but now extends itself to printing perfect bound paperback collection volumes from the magazine and also for publishing an occasional book or 24-page special highlighting one or two authors alone. If you submit work, please let me know whether you want a single piece published in the magazine or are looking for a collection of your own work being published. A cover letter is appreciated. If you're published in a book, please be prepared to try to sell copies to your friends and in stores in your area. That's how we succeed. Otherwise, look at the guidelines for *Children, Churches and Daddies*. We also run a book/chapbook contest. Contact Sears for more infomation. Electronic submissions (e-mail or text format, Macintash prefered) appreciated. Issues are available in print only as books (paid only), electronic format, and on the World Wide Web at above address.'' avg. press run determined individually. Pub'd 6 titles 2009; expects 12 titles 2010, 12 titles 2011. 68 titles listed in the *Small Press Record of Books in Print* (36th Edition, 2010-11). Books 200pp, chapbooks 24-32pp. Reporting time: We'll get back to you in a week if there is a SASE in it; if not, you'll never hear from us. Simultaneous submissions accepted: yes. Publishes 40% of manuscripts submitted. Payment: none for collection volumes; contact me about printing larger volumes of individual artist's works. Does not copyright for author. Subjects: Arts, Beat, Book Arts, Chicago, Counter-Culture, Alternatives, Communes, Culture, Feminism, Fiction, Graphics, Language, Literature (General), Magazines, Photography, Poetry, Women.

Scentouri, Publishing Division, A.C. Doyle, c/o Prosperity + Profits Unlimited, PO Box 416, Denver, CO 80201-0416, 303-575-5676, Fax 303-575-1187. 1982. avg. press run 1.5M. 10 titles listed in the *Small Press Record of Books in Print* (36th Edition, 2010-11). Discounts: 25% to libraries, bookstores, etc. 60pp. Reporting time: 6 weeks. Subjects: Biography, Crafts, Hobbies, Education, How-To, Refcrence, Textbooks.

SCHOLAR-PRACTITIONER QUARTERLY, Caddo Gap Press, Patrick Jenlink Dr., Coeditor; Raymond Horn Dr., Co-editor, 3145 Geary Blvd. PMB 275, San Francisco, CA 94118, 415 666-3012. sub. price $60 individuals, $120 institutions. 96pp.

School for Advanced Research Press, Lynn Baca, Director, PO Box 2188, Santa Fe, NM 87504-2188, 505-954-7206, Fax 505-954-7241, bkorders@sarsf.org, baca@sarsf.org, www.sarpress.sarweb.org. 125 titles listed in the *Small Press Record of Books in Print* (36th Edition, 2010-11). Subjects: Anthropology, Archaelogy, Arts, Culture, Environment, Europe, Gender Issues, Global Affairs, History, Latin America, Native American, New Mexico, North America, Science, Sociology, Southwest.

Schreiber Publishing, Morry Schreiber, 51 Monroe Street, Suite 101, Rockville, MD 20850-4193, 301-424-7737, Fax 301-424-2336, spbooks@aol.com, www.schreiberNet.com. 1957. ''Languages, Judaica.'' Expects 10 titles 2010. 17 titles listed in the *Small Press Record of Books in Print* (36th Edition, 2010-11). Pages vary. Reporting time: 30-90 days. Simultaneous submissions accepted: yes. Publishes 20% of manuscripts submitted. Payment: negotiable. Copyrights for author.

Schuylkill Living (see also SCHUYLKILL LIVING MAGAZINE), Erica Ramus, 115 S Centre St., Pottsville, PA 17901-3000, 570-622-8625. 1997. Fiction, articles, photos, interviews, reviews, news items, non-fiction. ''Must be related to Schuylkill County Pennsylvania. This is a regional title.'' avg. press run 5000. Pub'd 1 title 2009; expects 1 title 2010, 1 title 2011. No titles listed in the *Small Press Record of Books in Print* (36th Edition, 2010-11). Discounts: 20% discount to bookstores & distributors. 64pp. Reporting time: 4 weeks. Simultaneous submissions accepted: No. Payment: Pays upon publication. Does not copyright for author.

SCHUYLKILL LIVING MAGAZINE, Schuylkill Living, Erica Ramus, 1 One Norwegian Plz, Pottsville, PA 17901-4400, 570-622-8625, Fax 570-622-2143, eramus@comcast.net, www.schuylkillliving.com. 1997. Poetry, articles, art, photos, interviews, reviews, news items, non-fiction. circ. 5M. 4/yr. Pub'd 4 issues 2009; expects 4 issues 2010, 4 issues 2011. sub. price $20; per copy $4.95; sample $5. Back issues: $5. 64pp. Reporting time: 3 weeks. Simultaneous submissions accepted: no. Publishes 25% of manuscripts submitted. Payment: $50-100. Copyrighted, reverts to author. Pub's reviews: 2 in 2009. §Only publishes LOCAL INTEREST information and poetry. Ads: $1600/$800. Subject: Gardening.

SCHUYLKILL VALLEY JOURNAL, Peter Krok, Editor-in-Chief &Non-Fiction Editor; Bill Wunder, Poetry Editor; Fran Metzman, Fiction Editor; Anna Evans, Online Editor & Contributing Editor; Joseph "Hoagie" Hauser, Film Writer; Kate DeBevois, Contributing Editor; Michael Cohen, Contributing Editor; Elisha Darville, Production Editor; Peter Campbell, Graphic Designer, 240 Golf Hills Road, Havertown, PA 19083-1026, (h) 610-789-4692, macpoet1@aol.com, www.svjlit.com (online SVJ journal), www.manayunkartcenter.org. Readings are held at Maynayunk/Roxborough Art Center at 419 Green Lane in Philadelphia (phone - 215-482-3363). 1990. Poetry, fiction, articles, photos, interviews, criticism, non-fiction. ''The journal includes poetry, a featured poet from the region, accessible criticism, short essays, articles with some kind of regional but not currently popular themes, tips on the craft of writing, creative non-fiction, etc. Past featured poets (such as Lou McKee, Nathalie Anderson, Joe Chelius, Lynn Levin, Dan Maguire, Bill Van Buskirk, and Bill Wunder) represent a good sampling of work we like to see in our journal. Online poetry submissions are encouraged and should be sent to svjpoetry@yahoo.com. Material in the print SVJ will also be considered for the online edition of the SVJ. The nonfiction portion of the journal is often connected to themes. The editor particularly likes material dealing with the Philadelphia area (rivers, statues, history and writers) and articles related to themes (for example celebrating Lincoln or Poe, Philadelphia statues or Indians from the Delaware Valley). Articles are frequently solicited since material is often based on themes. The editors prefer to respond via email." circ. 250. 2/yr. Pub'd 2 issues 2009; expects 2 issues 2010, 2 issues 2011. 2 titles listed in the *Small Press Record of Books in Print* (36th Edition, 2010-11). sub. price $15; per copy $7; sample $6. 130pp. Reporting time: varies. Simultaneous submissions accepted: yes. Publishes a variable % of manuscripts submitted. Payment: 1 copy. Copyrighted, reverts to author. Pub's reviews: 2 in 2009. §I prefer reviews on current area writers. The reviews are mostly considered for the online journal. Subjects: Arts, Beat, Creativity, Culture, English, Essays, Fiction, Humanism, Literature (General), Non-Fiction, Poetry, Walt Whitman.

SCIENCE AND TECHNOLOGY, Univelt, Inc., R.H. Jacobs, Series Editor, PO Box 28130, San Diego, CA 92198, 760-746-4005, Fax 760-746-3139, sales@univelt.com, www.univelt.com. 1964. "Space and related fields. An irregular serial. Publishers for the American Astronautical Society. Standing orders accepted. Vols. 1-110 published." circ. 400. Irregular. Pub'd 5 issues 2009; expects 5 issues 2010, 5 issues 2011. sub. price varies. Back issues: no. Discounts: 20%, or more by arrangement; special prices for classroom use. 200-700pp. Reporting time: 60 days. Payment: 10% (if the volume author). Copyrighted, authors may republish material with appropriate credits given and authorization from publishers. Ads: none. Subjects: Engineering, Political Science, Science, Sociology, Space.

Scienter Press, David Leightty, 2308 Fallsview Road, Louisville, KY 40207, Fax 502-415-7130, dleightty@earthlink.net. 2003. Poetry. "Scienter is a publisher of small books, chiefly by invitation. The goal of the press is to publish poems that manifest meaning—poems that show the poet had something in mind. Our strong preference is for poems having measure." avg. press run 100. Pub'd 2 titles 2009; expects 2 titles 2010, 2 titles 2011. 19 titles listed in the *Small Press Record of Books in Print* (36th Edition, 2010-11). 16pp. Payment: copies only. Copyrights for author. Subject: Poetry.

Scientia Press, Kenneth Dillon, 4115 Wisconsin Avenue, N.W. #507, Washington, DC 20016, 202-364-8742, kendillon@verizon.net, www.scientiapress.com. 1997. avg. press run 1000. Expects 1 title 2010, 1 title 2011. No titles listed in the *Small Press Record of Books in Print* (36th Edition, 2010-11). 250pp.

Scientia Publishing, LLC, Cynthia McNeill, P. O. Box 5495, Chatsworth, CA 91313, 1-818-620-0433, www.scientiapublishingllc.com. 2001. Non-fiction. "Scientia Publishing, LLC welcomes fresh and innovative ideas for the subjects of our nonfiction books. We prefer natural history, environment, and subjects of general science for consideration." Expects 1-2 titles 2011. No titles listed in the *Small Press Record of Books in Print* (36th Edition, 2010-11). Discounts: Provided upon request. 300pp. Reporting time: We respond within 72 hours upon receipt of a manuscript. Simultaneous submissions accepted: No. Payment: These are determined individually. Copyrights for author. Subjects: Alaska, Anthropology, Archaelogy, Artificial Intelligence, Astronomy, Biology, Biotechnology, Birds, Earth, Natural History, Ecology, Foods, Environment, Nature, Non-Fiction, Oceanography, Research, Science.

Scots Plaid Press (see also Persephone Press), Jeff Farr, President, 600 Kelly Road, Carthage, NC 28327, 910-947-2587; Fax 910-947-5112. 1987. Poetry. "Archival handbound chapbook. *Query first*; describe MS & PC include bio/vita, SASE. *Do not submit ms.* no more than 3 page sample. Accept no unsolicited ms." avg. press run 500-1.5M. Pub'd 9 titles 2009; expects 12 titles 2010, 24 titles 2011. No titles listed in the *Small Press Record of Books in Print* (36th Edition, 2010-11). Discounts: 30% on orders of 5 copies; 40% for 10 copies. 40pp. Reporting time: 1 day to 1 month. Simultaneous submissions accepted: yes. Publishes 1% of manuscripts submitted. Payment: 10%. Does not copyright for author. Subject: Poetry.

Andrew Scott Publishers, E.S. Lev, 15023 Tierra Alta, Del Mar, CA 92014, 858-461-0089 andrewscottpublishers@juno.com. 1998. Fiction. "Dedicated to advance informative, realistic mysteries. *Prescription for Terror* is our debut novel." avg. press run 2M. Expects 2 titles 2010, 1 title 2011. 1 title listed in the *Small Press Record of Books in Print* (36th Edition, 2010-11). Discounts: 50% non-returnable, 40% returnable plus freight. 240pp. Reporting time: 2 weeks. Simultaneous submissions accepted: no. Publishes 1% of manuscripts submitted. Copyrights for author. Subject: Mystery.

Scottwall Associates, Publishers, James Heig, 95 Scott Street, San Francisco, CA 94117, 415-861-1956. 1982. Non-fiction. "We publish books on California history, biographies." avg. press run 5M-10M. Pub'd 2 titles 2009; expects 2 titles 2010, 2-3 titles 2011. 5 titles listed in the *Small Press Record of Books in Print* (36th Edition, 2010-11). Discounts: 40% to bookstores in quantity orders; 40% to prepaid STOP orders; 30% single copy orders; 20% to schools & libraries. 200-500pp. Reporting time: indefinite. Payment: 8% royalty on all books sold and paid for. Copyrights for author. Subjects: Airplanes, Americana, Biography, California, History, Ireland, Native American, San Francisco.

SCP JOURNAL, Tal Brooke, President and Editor, PO Box 4308, Berkeley, CA 94704. 1975. Articles, interviews, reviews, letters, news items, non-fiction. "*SCP* is a non-profit organization that researches and publishes information on new religious cult movements and spiritual trends. No unsolicited Mss." circ. 18M. 4 journals, 4 newsletters published per year. Pub'd 4 issues 2009; expects 4 issues 2010, 4 issues 2011. sub. price $25/year; per copy $5; sample free - newsletter only. Back issues: $5-6. Discounts: 40% for retailers. 40pp single journals; 60pp for double journals. Reporting time: 3-6 weeks, only after telephone approval, do not submit before phone inquiry. Payment: varies. Copyrighted, does not revert to author. Pub's reviews: 4 in 2009. §Religion, metaphysics, cults, sociology and psychology of religion. Subjects: Religion, Spiritual.

THE SCRIBIA, Danielle B. Otero, Uju Ifeanyi, PO Box 68, Grambling State University, Grambling, LA 71245, 318-274-2190, oterod@gram.edu. 1966. Poetry, fiction, articles, art, interviews, criticism, reviews, letters, parts-of-novels, long-poems, plays, concrete art, non-fiction. "Emphasis on GSU student and alumni work, multi-culturalism, southern culture. Recent contributors: X.J. Kennedy, Pinkie Gordon Lane, Errol Miller, Mary Winters, Christopher Pressfield, Maitaika Favorite." circ. 800. 1/yr. Pub'd 1 issue 2009; expects 1 issue 2010, 1 issue 2011. sub. price cops; per copy cops; sample cops. Back issues: cops. Discounts: none. 72pp. Reporting time: 3-6 months. Simultaneous submissions accepted with notices. Publishes 20% of manuscripts submitted. Payment: 2 copies. Copyrighted, reverts to author. Pub's reviews: 2 in 2009. §Contemparary literature, multi-cultural issues. Ads: trade. Subjects: African-American, Literature (General), Poetry.

Scripta Humanistica, Bruno Damiani, Editor, 1383 Kersey Lane, Potomac, MD 20854, 301-294-7949, 301-340-1095. avg. press run 500. Pub'd 15 titles 2009. 4 titles listed in the *Small Press Record of Books in Print* (36th Edition, 2010-11). Discounts: 20%. 200pp. Reporting time: 4 weeks. Simultaneous submissions accepted: no. Publishes 35% of manuscripts submitted. Payment: 5% of gross sales. Does not copyright for author. Subjects: James Joyce, Poetry.

SCRIVENER, Meredith Needham, Coordinating Editor; Anca Szilagyi, Coordinating Editor; Matthew Frassica, Fiction Editor; Kristie LeBlanc, Fiction Editor; Addy Litfin, Poetry Editor; Dan Huffateer, Poetry Editor; Kristie LeBlanc, Book Review Editor; Lukas Rieppel, Photography Editor; Pablo Rodriguez, Photography Editor, McGill University, 853 Sherbrooke Street W., Montreal, P.Q. H3A 2T6, Canada, scrivenermag@hotmail.com. 1980. Poetry, fiction, art, photos, interviews, criticism, reviews, non-fiction. "Recent book reviews only. Prose less than 30 pages typed; creative shorts. Poetry 5-10 pages. Black & white photos and graphics. Please send international reply coupon (not U.S. stamps) + self-addressed envelopes. New material only—no reprints. Does not report from May to August." circ. 500. 1/yr. Pub'd 1 issue 2009; expects 1 issue 2010, 1 issue 2011. sub. price $7 + $2 p/h; per copy same; sample same. Back issues: same. Discounts: 40% commission for 10 or more copies. 100pp. Reporting time: 4-6 months. We accept simultaneous submissions, but submitters must list the other journals to which they have made submissions. Payment: 1 free copy, more upon request. Copyrighted, reverts to author. Pub's reviews: 3 in 2009. §Canadian and American prose, poetry, criticism. Ads: currently under review. Subjects: Arts, Book Reviewing, Criticism, English, Fiction, Literature (General), Poetry.

SCULPTURAL PURSUIT MAGAZINE, Nancy DeCamillis, P.O. Box 749, Littleton, CO 80160, 303-738-9892, www.sculpturalpursuit.com, publishersp@sculpturalpursuit.com. 2002. Poetry, articles, art, photos, interviews, criticism, reviews, letters, long-poems, concrete art, news items, non-fiction. "Sculptural Pursuit, a quarterly publication, explores the world of sculpture and its creative and technical processes in order to enlighten and inform sculptors, collectors, and the curious. While Sculptural Pursuit emphasizes three-dimensional art, it also features poetry and two-dimensional art through their annual Art/Literary competition and feature sculpture only in a 2nd annual competition. Articles providing information on the world of sculpture include: art history, techniques and processes, health and safety issues, and interviews with current three-dimensional artists. These enhance the readers' knowledge base; allow the reader to envision what a career in art entails; and provide motivation and encouragement, regardless of the creative endeavors undertaken by the reader. HPP offers 2 free monthly publications: an e-zine, CREATIVE WISDOM, and a calendar of calls for entry, ON THE LOOKOUT." circ. 12,000. 4/yr. Pub'd 4 issues 2009; expects 4 issues 2010, 4 issues 2011. sub. price $28 for U.S., $37 for International; per copy $9; sample $9. Back issues: $9. Discounts: Distributors - 50%Bulk sales - no returns:5 - 15 copies 38%16-35 copies 41%36-55 copies 44%56-75 copies 47%over 75 copies 50%. 100pp. Reporting time: 4-6 weeks. Simultaneous submissions accepted: Yes. Publishes 30% of manuscripts submitted. Payment is done with ad space, or variable fee. Copyrighted, reverts to author. Pub's reviews: 8 in 2009. §Art books & magazines, particularly ones that focus on three-dimensional art and artists. Ads: Color: $1,499/$899/$540/$1,834/$2,900(full/half/quarter/inside front & back covers/back cover). Subjects: Abstracts, Advertising, Self-Promotion, Architecture, Arts, Book Arts, Design, Inspirational, Interviews, Liberal Arts, Motivation, Success, Photography, Poetry, Renaissance, Visual Arts, Writers/Writing.

Sea Fog Press (see also HARMONY: Voices for a Just Future), Rose Evans, 447 20th Avenue, San Francisco, CA 94121, 415-221-8527. 1982. Non-fiction. "2 children's books published, 1 bimonthly magazine." avg. press run 5M. Expects 1 title 2010. 2 titles listed in the *Small Press Record of Books in Print* (36th Edition, 2010-11). Discounts: bookstores 4+ copies, 40%. 200pp. Reporting time: 1 month. Simultaneous submissions accepted: yes. Publishes .03% of manuscripts submitted. Payment: standard. Copyrights for author. Subjects: Children, Youth, Education.

SEA KAYAKER, Christopher Cunningham, Editor; Leslie Forsberg, Executive Editor, PO Box 17029, Seattle,

WA 98107-0729, 206-789-1326, Fax 206-781-1141, mail@seakayakermag.com. 1984. Fiction, articles, art, photos, cartoons, interviews, reviews, letters, non-fiction. "1M-3M words; specializing in sea kayaking; bias towards education and environmental." circ. 27M+. 6/yr. Pub'd 6 issues 2009; expects 6 issues 2010, 6 issues 2011. sub. price $23.95; per copy $4.95; sample $7.30. Back issues: 1-2 issues $7.30, 3+ $6.30 each. Discounts: 5-9 copies 35%, 10+ 45%, no returns. 82+pp. Reporting time: 2 months. Simultaneous submissions rarely accepted. Publishes 15% of manuscripts submitted. Payment: approx. $120 per publ. page, on publication. Copyrighted, reverts to author. Pub's reviews: 6 in 2009. §Sea kayaking. Ads: call for current rates 206-789-6413. Subjects: Environment, Geology, How-To, Marine Life, Sports, Outdoors, Travel, Water.

SeaCrab Publishing (see also THE ENGLISH CLARION), David Searle, Editor, 2 Nuffield Close, Shaw, Swindon SN5 5WT, England, +44 (0)1793 330420, seacrabart@googlemail.com. 2007. Poetry, articles, photos, interviews, reviews, music, letters, news items, non-fiction. "SeaCrab Publishing offers niche magazines and books of various types in small runs for specialist interests. Open to original, positive ideas. Always interested in photo articles on English history and culture as well as English rock bands." avg. press run 100. Expects 1 title 2010, 5 titles 2011. No titles listed in the *Small Press Record of Books in Print* (36th Edition, 2010-11). 60-400pp. Reporting time: 1 month maximum, often less than a week. Simultaneous submissions accepted: Yes. Publishes 50% of manuscripts submitted. Payment: As the press has just started we are not offering payment, just the thrill of seeing your work published. If we accidentally start making any money, we'll share it out fairly between all contributors. Fame or greed merchants need not apply, only those with a genuine interest in the subject. We always attribute copyright in our magazines to the author. We assume all articles are the original work of the person sending it to us unless otherwise stated. Subjects: Arthurian, Channelling, Christianity, Cities, Culture, England, Festivals, Folklore, History, London, Medieval, Music, Photography, Religion, World War II.

Search Institute, Bill Kauffmann, 615 First Ave. NE, Ste. 125, Minneapolis, MN 55413-2254, 612-692-5527 direct phone, 612-692-5553 fax, 877-240-7251 toll free orders. 1958. Non-fiction. "Search Institute publishes practical and hope-filled books to create a world where all young people are valued and thrive. At the heart of the institute's work is the 40 Developmental Assets. Search Institute has surveyed more than 1,000,000 students in grades 6 -12 in more than 2,000 communities. This scientific research is the basis for the creation of our framework for healthy youth development known as the 40 Developmental Assets. "Assets," as they are commonly known, represent simple wisdom about the kinds of positive experiences and characteristics young people need to succeed." avg. press run 4,000. Pub'd 14 titles 2009; expects 14 titles 2010, 15 titles 2011. No titles listed in the *Small Press Record of Books in Print* (36th Edition, 2010-11). Discounts: Distributed to the trade by Independent Publishers Group; toll free 800-888-4741; www.ipgbook.com. 225pp. Reporting time: 10 -12 weeks. Simultaneous submissions accepted: Yes. Publishes 10% of manuscripts submitted. Subjects: Adolescence, Adoption, Awards, Foundations, Grants, Children, Youth, Family, Mentoring/Coaching, Non-Fiction, Parenting, Relationships, Trade.

THE SEATTLE REVIEW, Andrew Feld, Editor-in-Chief, P.O. Box 354330, University of Washington, Seattle, WA 98195, ph. 206 543 2302. "*The Seattle Review* awards the Editors Choice Prize in Nonfiction, the Nelson Bentley Prize in Fiction and Poetry, and the Perry Lee and Ann Belle Prize for the best work published in its pages the preceding year. Recently, The Seattle Review Annual Fiction and Poetry Contest was established as an open contest by submission. We only accept submissions between October 1 and May 31. No simultaneous submissions. Guidelines for Poetry Submissions: Mail 3-5 poems to the above address, attention: Poetry Editor. Submissions must be typed on white, 8 1/2 x 11 paper. The authors name and address should appear in the upper right hand corner."

Second Aeon Publications, Peter Finch, 19 Southminster Road, Roath, Cardiff, Wales CF23 5AT, Great Britain, 029-2049-3093, secondaeon@peterfinch.co.uk. 1967. Poetry, art, long-poems, collages, concrete art. avg. press run 300-1M. Pub'd 1 title 2009. 1 title listed in the *Small Press Record of Books in Print* (36th Edition, 2010-11). Discounts: by arrangement. 50pp. Reporting time: 2 weeks. Publishes 10% of manuscripts submitted. Payment: by arrangement. Does not copyright for author. Subject: Poetry.

Second Coming Press, A.D. Winans, PO Box 31249, San Francisco, CA 94131. 1972. Poetry, fiction. "Not accepting manuscripts at this time." avg. press run 1M-1.5M. Pub'd 1 title 2009; expects 1 title 2011. 7 titles listed in the *Small Press Record of Books in Print* (36th Edition, 2010-11). Discounts: 20% library only if this listed source is quoted; bookstores 5+ books 40%. 64-72pp. anthologies 200-240pp. Reporting time: 30 days. Payment: 10% of press run, 50% of any profit after expenses are met. Only copyrights for author upon arrangement. Subjects: Literature (General), Poetry.

SECRETUM MEUM MIHI, Secretum Meum Mihi Press, Kristen McGuire, P.O. Box 1501, Great Falls, MT 59403-1501, info@mysecretismine.com www.MySecretisMine.com. 2006. Poetry, articles, interviews, reviews, news items. "Currently reprinting back issues online only. Published authors with clips, and a particular expertise in theology, literature, history, biblical exegesis or compelling personal narratives related to same can submit if there is a particular topic you would want to cover as a series. The newsletter is tightly themed, and content is decided upon about four months in advance. (All theme essays are turned into books for study groups of Catholic women.).'' circ. 250. 52 weekly emails. Pub'd 9 issues 2009; expects 12 issues 2011. only free online version now available; price per copy n/a; sample free. Back issues: $2.50. 12pp. Reporting time: 30 days. Simultaneous submissions accepted: No. Publishes 2% of manuscripts submitted. Payment: $25, or 5% of book sales if bound into a book. copyrighted, unless reprinting an article from a previous publication. Pub's reviews: 12 in 2009. §Classics, Catholic, or titles of interest to women, probing the relationship between faith, reason and love. Ads: E-Letter: $50 Website: $25 quarter page display: $25. Subjects: Book Reviewing, Catholic, Essays, History, Inspirational, Religion, Spiritual, Women, Zines.

Secretum Meum Mihi Press (see also SECRETUM MEUM MIHI), Kristen McGuire, P.O. Box 1501, Great Falls, MT 59403-1501, info@mysecretismine.com www.MySecretisMine.com. 2006. ''Spirituality titles for Catholic women. Secretum Meum Mihi means "my secret is mine" in Latin. The German philosopher and convert Dr. Edith Stein wrote this on a piece of paper when her best friend asked why she converted. We try to help all women to discover the special secret they have that keeps them persevering. We do not print original short stories or poetry. Our editorial needs are limited right now. Content for the newsletter (book reviews, bible studies, historical sketches, and theme essays) is rebundled into books for parish women's study groups. Also published online for free.'' avg. press run 500. Pub'd 1 title 2009; expects 1 title 2011. 1 title listed in the *Small Press Record of Books in Print* (36th Edition, 2010-11). Discounts: universal discount of 20% for more than 6 copies.Free shipping on orders of more than $25. 100pp. Reporting time: 30 days. Simultaneous submissions accepted: No. Publishes 2% of manuscripts submitted. Payment: 5% IF the work is included in a compilation book. reprints previously published work of established authors, with attribution. Subjects: Book Reviewing, Catholic, History, Inspirational, Newsletter, Religion, Spiritual, Women.

SEDUCTIVE SELLING, Craig Garber, 3959 Van Dyke Road #253, Lutz, FL 33558, 813-909-2214. 2006. Interviews, news items, non-fiction. ''Seductive Selling is a monthly newsletter for entrepreneurs and business-owners which shows you unconventional copywriting and marketing strategies (based on emotional direct-response marketing) that make you an absolute KILLING in business! Along with the newsletter, every month you also get an Audio Success CD Interview of the month. This is a 60-minute plus Audio CD interview with another successful entrepreneur, who reveals their own unusual or interesting direct-marketing methods and how you can profit from them.'' 12/yr. Pub'd 12 issues 2009; expects 12 issues 2010, 12 issues 2011. 1 title listed in the *Small Press Record of Books in Print* (36th Edition, 2010-11). sub. price $600; per copy $49.95; sample $5.95 from website alone at http:www.kingofcopy.com/ssnl. Back issues: $49.95. 18pp. Reporting time: no submissions accepted. Copyrighted. Pub's reviews: 3 in 2009. §marketing, copywriting, self-development, business growth, unusual success stories. No advertising. Subjects: Advertising, Self-Promotion, Americana, How-To, Internet, Interviews, Marketing, Mentoring/Coaching, Motivation, Success, Newsletter, Non-Fiction, Public Relations/Publicity, Publishing.

See Sharp Press, Charles Bufe, Publisher, PO Box 1731, Tucson, AZ 85702-1731, 520-628-8720, info@seesharppress.com, www.seesharppress.com. 1984. Non-fiction. ''Length is unimportant—quality is the deciding factor; our published works range from a 4,000 word pamphlet to a 200,000-word classic reprint. Biases are towards works with anarchist and/or atheist views and toward works providing practical information, especially in the area of music.'' avg. press run 1M for pamphlets, 3M for books. Pub'd 5 titles 2009; expects 2 titles 2010, 2 titles 2011. 57 titles listed in the *Small Press Record of Books in Print* (36th Edition, 2010-11). Discounts: books exclusively distributed by Independent Publisher Group. Books 192pp, pamphlets 32pp. Reporting time: 1 month. Simultaneous submissions accepted: no. Publishes 1% to 2% of manuscripts submitted. Payment: for books - normally 7% of cover first run, 8.5% to 10% thereafter; quarterly payments; for pamphlets - 10% of press run in lieu of royalties. Sometimes copyright for author if author overseas, otherwise no, but will provide info to authors on how to do it. Subjects: Alcohol, Alcoholism, Anarchist, Atheism, H.L. Mencken, Music, Non-Fiction, Philosophy, Politics, Psychology, Self-Help.

SEED SAVERS EXCHANGE, Kent Whealy, 3094 North Winn Road, Decorah, IA 52101, 563-382-5990, Fax 563-382-5872. 1975. Articles, photos, interviews, letters, non-fiction. ''Seed Exchange of Heirloom Vegetable & Fruit Varieties.'' circ. 8M. 3/yr. Pub'd 3 issues 2009; expects 3 issues 2010, 3 issues 2011. 4 titles listed in the *Small Press Record of Books in Print* (36th Edition, 2010-11). sub. price $35 US, $40 Canada and Mexico, $50 overseas. Back issues: not available. 200pp. Payment: none. Copyrighted. Ads: none accepted. Subjects: Conservation, Gardening.

SEEMS, Karl Elder, Editor, c/o Lakeland College, Box 359, Sheboygan, WI 53082-0359. 1971. Poetry, fiction, parts-of-novels, long-poems, non-fiction. ''No. 14, *What Is the Future of Poetry?*, in its third printing, contains essays by Cutler, Dacey, Dunn, Evans, Elliott, Etter, Flaherty, Gildner, Hathaway, Heffernan, Hershon, Heyen, Hilton, Matthews, McKeown, Morgan, Oliphant, Rice, Scott, Sobin, Stryk, and Zimmer. ($5) Samples of back issues, detailed guidelines, etc., are available at www1.lakeland.edu/seems/. For insight concerning the editor's own work and aesthetic inclinations see pages and links at www.karlelder.com.'' circ. 500. Irregular. Pub'd 1 issue 2009; expects 2 issues 2010, 2 issues 2011. 3 titles listed in the *Small Press Record of Books in Print* (36th

Edition, 2010-11). sub. price $20/4 issues; per copy $5; sample $5. Discounts: 25%. 40pp. Reporting time: 1-4 months. Simultaneous submissions accepted: no. Publishes less than .5% of manuscripts submitted. Payment: copies. Copyrighted, reverts to author. Subjects: Fiction, Non-Fiction, Poetry.

The Seer Press, Alexander J Cuthbert; Suzanne Muir Scott, Dr, PO Box 29313, Glasgow, Lanarkshire, Scotland, G20 2AE, United Kingdom. 2004. Poetry. avg. press run 200. Expects 2 titles 2010, 2 titles 2011. No titles listed in the *Small Press Record of Books in Print* (36th Edition, 2010-11). Discounts: 0-10 35%11-100% 40%. 28-40pp. Simultaneous submissions accepted: No. Copyrights for author. Subject: Poetry.

The Sektor Co., Joseph Crest, PO Box 501005, San Diego, CA 92150, 858 485-7550. 1994. Non-fiction. "Inspirational biography, patriotic and American heritage, military history, Japanese history, adventure, poker." avg. press run 3M-10M. Pub'd 1 title 2009; expects 3 titles 2010, 6 titles 2011. 2 titles listed in the *Small Press Record of Books in Print* (36th Edition, 2010-11). Discounts: 20-55%. 250pp. Reporting time: 1 month. Simultaneous submissions accepted: yes. Publishes 20% of manuscripts submitted. Payment: flexible. Does not copyright for author. Subjects: Americana, Biography, History, Military, Veterans, Vietnam, World War II.

Selah Publishing Co. Inc., David P. Schaap, PO Box 98066, Pittsburgh, PA 15227-0466, 845-338-2816, Fax 845-338-2991, customerservice@selahpub.com. 1988. Poetry, music. "Publish primarily in the field of Church Music and Hymnology. Books vary in length from small to large publications." avg. press run 5M. Pub'd 2 titles 2009; expects 2 titles 2010, 3-4 titles 2011. 14 titles listed in the *Small Press Record of Books in Print* (36th Edition, 2010-11). Discounts: trade 1-3 copies 20%, 4-up 40%. 200pp. Reporting time: 1-2 months. Simultaneous submissions accepted: yes. Payment: generally 10% of retail sales price. Copyrights for author. Subjects: Music, Reference.

SelectiveHouse Publishers, Inc., Gerilynne Seigneur, PO Box 10095, Gaithersburg, MD 20898, 301-990-2999; email sr@selectivehouse.com; www.selectivehouse.com. 1997. Fiction, non-fiction. "See our web page for the types of books published. Primarily mainstream fiction with science fiction and/or spiritual overtones." avg. press run 2M. Pub'd 2 titles 2009; expects 2 titles 2010, 3 titles 2011. 4 titles listed in the *Small Press Record of Books in Print* (36th Edition, 2010-11). 300pp. Reporting time: 6-8 weeks. Simultaneous submissions accepted: yes. Publishes less than 1% of manuscripts submitted. Copyrights for author. Subjects: Christianity, Fiction, Mystery, New Age, Novels, Religion, Science Fiction, Spiritual.

Semprove/Learning, 228 Park Ave. South, Suite 32135, New York, NY 10003. No titles listed in the *Small Press Record of Books in Print* (36th Edition, 2010-11).

SENECA REVIEW, David Weiss, Editor; John D'Agata, Associate Editor for Creative Nonfiction; Karl Parker, Associate Editor for Poetry, Hobart & William Smith Colleges, Geneva, NY 14456, 315-781-3392, Fax 315-781-3348, senecareview@hws.edu. 1970. Poetry, long-poems, non-fiction. "Lyric Essays and innovative poetry; we have a history of publishing translations. Recent contributors: Wayne Koestenbaum, Joe Wenderoth, Donald Platt, Thalia Field, Mary Ruefle, Steve Kuusisto." circ. 1M. 2/yr. Pub'd 2 issues 2009; expects 2 issues 2010, 2 issues 2011. sub. price $8.00/issue, $15.00/one year, & $28.00/two years; per copy $8.00 + $1.00 shipping; sample $8.00 + $1.00 shipping. Back issues: $7.00 + $1.00 shipping. Discounts: 40% trade for stores. 100pp. Reporting time: 10-14 weeks. Simultaneous submissions accepted: No. Please make only one submission during our annual reading period (September through May). Publishes 1% of manuscripts submitted. Payment: 2 copies and a 2-year subscription. Copyrighted, reverts to author. Ads: $75.00, special small press rates, exchange. Subjects: Criticism, Essays, Non-Fiction, Poetry, Translation.

SENSATIONS MAGAZINE, David Messineo, P.O. Box 132, Lafayette, NJ 07848-0132, www.sensations-mag.com. 1987. Poetry, fiction. "Sensations Magazine concludes a six-issue, three-year series of American Century theme issues, ending with Issue 48, "21st Century America," in Fall/Winter 2010. For 2011, we are seeking poetry about the U.S. Presidents. Go to www.sensationsmag.com, "Submit Poems/Stories" button, for more details, including submission requirements and timeline of events. Sensations Magazine is a three-time winner in the American Literary Magazine Awards, celebrating 25 years of independent, non-grant-funded publication. Please note any checks, whether subscribing or submitting, must be made out to "The Six Centuries Club" ONLY, and 2011 submissions/subscriptions must be received before June 30, 2011." circ. 125. 2/yr. Pub'd 2 issues 2009; expects 2 issues 2010, 2 issues 2011. sub. price $30 individual, $40 institutional, $50 outside U.S./Canada; per copy $20; sample $20. Back issues: Inquire. 100pp. Reporting time: Two months after posted deadline. Simultaneous submissions accepted: Yes. Publishes 20% of manuscripts submitted. Payment: Payment upon acceptance (top poems/stories only). Copyrighted, reverts to author. Pub's reviews: 1 in 2009. §Poetry books, by active subscribers only. Ads: No advertising accepted. Subjects: African-American, Americana, Civil Rights, Civil War, Community, Creativity, Education, English, Fiction, Gay, History, Poetry, Publishing, Women, Writers/Writing.

THE $ENSIBLE SOUND, Karl Nehring, 403 Darwin Drive, Snyder, NY 14226, 716-833-0930. 1976. Articles, art, photos, cartoons, interviews, satire, criticism, reviews, music, letters, news items, non-fiction. "We run mainly audio equipment reviews, musical recording reviews, audio semi-technical articles, and audio and music industry news." circ. 14M. 6/yr. Pub'd 6 issues 2009; expects 6 issues 2010, 6 issues 2011. sub. price $29; per copy $6; sample $3. Back issues: 5 each $3 each after one year old. Discounts: 5 or more 20%. 96pp. Reporting time: 2 weeks. Simultaneous submissions accepted: no. Publishes 30% of manuscripts submitted. Payment: yes. Copyrighted, reverts to author. Pub's reviews: 14 in 2009. §Technical, music related, audio related, Hi Fi, Stereo, Home theater. Ads: b&w $1200/$750, color $1500/$900, no classifieds. Subjects: Crafts, Hobbies, Music.

SENTENCE, A Journal of Prose Poetics, Firewheel Editions, Brian Clements, Editor, Box 7, Western Connecticut State University, 181 White St., Danbury, CT 06810. 2003. "Our mission: To continue the tradition of publishing excellent prose poems established by Peter Johnson's *The Prose Poem: an International Journal* (currently dormant). To publish reviews and essays (personal, critical, experimental, etc.) about the prose poem, prose poets, and the poetics of the prose poem. To continue the discussion about the distinction between the prose poem and "poetic prose." One issue per nine months. sub. price http://firewheel-editions.org/sentence/subscriptions.htm; per copy $12 (plus $3 shipping; additional $6 outside North American and Caribbean). Back issues: $10 (shipping included; additional $6 outside North American and Carribean). 300pp. Reporting time: immediately to 6 months. Simultaneous submissions accepted: Yes. Payment: contributor copy. Copyrighted, reverts to author on publication, but we reserve the right to republish work in Firewheel Editions anthologies, with author's permission. Pub's reviews: 12 in 2009. §Prose poetry, poetics of the prose poem, genre studies. Ads: $100 for full page ad at back of issue.

Sentient Publications, LLC, Connie Shaw, 1113 Spruce Street, Boulder, CO 80302, 303-443-2188, Fax 303-381-2538, www.sentientpublications.com. 2001. Non-fiction. "Sentient Publications, LLC publishes books on cultural creativity, experimental education, transformative spirituality, holistic health, new science, ecology, and a variety of other topics, approached from an integral viewpoint. Our authors are intensely interested in exploring the nature of life from fresh perspectives, addressing life's great questions, and fostering the full expression of the human potential. Sentient Publication's books arise from the spirit of inquiry and the richness of the inherent dialogue between writer and reader.Our Culture Tools series is designed to give social catalyzers and cultural entrepreneurs the essential information, technology, and inspiration to forge a sustainable, creative, and compassionate world." avg. press run 3M. Pub'd 13 titles 2009; expects 15 titles 2010, 18 titles 2011. No titles listed in the *Small Press Record of Books in Print* (36th Edition, 2010-11). Discounts: Trade discounts are through our distributor, National Book Network. 200pp. Reporting time: 1-2 months. Simultaneous submissions accepted: yes. Publishes 3% of manuscripts submitted. Payment: varies. Copyrights for author. Subjects: Aging, Alternative Medicine, Culture, Current Affairs, Education, Health, How-To, Non-Fiction, Parenting, Psychology, Publishing, Relationships, Sex, Sexuality, Spiritual, Theatre.

Serpent & Eagle Press, Jo Mish, 10 Main Street, Laurens, NY 13796, 607-432-2990. 1981. Poetry, fiction, art, photos, non-fiction. "I've shifted emphasis to short book-length work on historical & folk-lore oriented subjects. I'll put out an occasional book of poetry. Not accepting submissions during 2002-03." avg. press run 200. Expects 1 title 2011. No titles listed in the *Small Press Record of Books in Print* (36th Edition, 2010-11). Discounts: 40%. 30pp. Simultaneous submissions accepted: no. Payment: varies. Does not copyright for author. Subjects: Folklore, Poetry.

•**Serving House Books (see also SERVING HOUSE: A Journal of the Arts),** editors@servinghouse-press.com. "Serving House Books is an imprint dedicated to selecting memorable poetry, fiction, and essays from throughout the world. Most of our authors already have significant publishing histories, winning many grants and awards. At the same time, we take pride in introducing new writers at the start of careers that will be equally successful. Our initial publications include poetry, fiction, and memoirs by Claire Bateman, Steve Heller, Rita Signorelli-Pappas, Gladys Swan, Susan Tekulve, and William Zander. Scheduled for 2010 are books by Supriya Bhatnagar. Mark Hillringhouse, Steve Kowit, Liam Mac Mac Sheinn, Thomas McCarthy, and Elisabeth Murawski, as well as The Book of Worst Meals, more than 20 writers telling of their food disasters. All titles are available through Amazon.com.Serving House Books is an imprint dedicated to selecting memorable poetry, fiction, and essays from throughout the world. Most of our authors already have significant publishing histories, winning many grants and awards. At the same time, we take pride in introducing new writers at the start of careers that will be equally successful. Our initial publications include poetry, fiction, and memoirs by Claire Bateman, Steve Heller, Rita Signorelli-Pappas, Gladys Swan, Susan Tekulve, and William Zander. Scheduled for 2010 are books by Supriya Bhatnagar. Mark Hillringhouse, Steve Kowit, Liam Mac Mac Sheinn, Thomas McCarthy, and Elisabeth Murawski, as well as The Book of Worst Meals, more than 20 writers telling of their food disasters. All titles are available through Amazon.com." No titles listed in the *Small Press Record of Books in Print* (36th Edition, 2010-11).

•**SERVING HOUSE: A Journal of the Arts, Serving House Books,** duffbrenna@servinghousejournal.com, www.duffbrenna.com. "*ServingHouse* endeavors to publish fiction, non-fiction (essays, memoirs, interviews), and poetry that will surprise, rivet, amuse, charm, enchantelectrifyits readers. Our mission is to play an international role in fostering and preserving the best of what the literary arts are capable of doing: writing that may impel others to become writers themselves; writing that will add to and enhance the dialogue of the arts; writing that reaffirms our belief in the inspiring possibilities of the written word.''

Set Sail Productions, LLC, Eric Holmes, 621 Wills Point, Allen, TX 75013, 972 369 3574, www.setsailmotivation.com, eric@setsailforsuccess.com. 2003. Non-fiction. ''Set Sail Productions specializes in personal development, self-help and motivation.'' avg. press run 5500. Pub'd 1 title 2009; expects 5 titles 2010, 10 titles 2011. No titles listed in the *Small Press Record of Books in Print* (36th Edition, 2010-11). 152pp. Reporting time: 2-4 weeks. Simultaneous submissions accepted: Yes. Publishes 20% of manuscripts submitted. Copyrights for author. Subjects: Careers, Current Affairs, Ethics, Finances, Health, Inspirational, Leadership, Management, Marketing, Mentoring/Coaching, Motivation, Success, Non-Fiction, Quotations, Sports, Outdoors, Taxes.

Seven Buffaloes Press, Art Coelho, Box 249, Big Timber, MT 59011. 1973. Poetry, fiction, art, photos, interviews, reviews, parts-of-novels, long-poems, collages. ''Book-length manuscripts are not being accepted at this time. I do publish some books, even novels, but the authors are those that have had work in my magazines.'' avg. press run 750. Pub'd 8 titles 2009; expects 2 titles 2010. 55 titles listed in the *Small Press Record of Books in Print* (36th Edition, 2010-11). Discounts: 1-4 0%, 5 copies or more 30%. 80pp. Reporting time: within a week; sometimes same day. Payment: negotiable. Copyrights for author. Subjects: Fiction, Poetry.

Seven Stories Press, Dan Simon, Publisher, 140 Watts Street, New York, NY 10013. ''Seven Stories Press is an independent book publisher based in New York City, with distribution throughout the United States, Canada, England, Australia, and New Zealand. We publish works of the imagination by such writers as Nelson Algren, Kate Braverman, Octavia Butler. Under the direction of publisher Dan Simon, perhaps no other small independent house in America has consistently attracted so many important voices away from the corporate publishing sector.'' No titles listed in the *Small Press Record of Books in Print* (36th Edition, 2010-11).

74th Street Productions, L.L.C., Nigel Loring, Editor, 350 North 74th Street, Seattle, WA 98103, 206-781-1447, info@74thstreet.com, www.74thstreet.com, www.writersatthepodium.com. 1996. Fiction, art, photos, non-fiction. ''*No* unsolicited manuscripts - e-mail for guidelines. Shakespeare For Young Adults (7-14) plays retold in story form. Theatre oriented topics for young people. Presentation skills for writers.'' avg. press run 3M. Pub'd 1 title 2009; expects 1 title 2010, 1 title 2011. 5 titles listed in the *Small Press Record of Books in Print* (36th Edition, 2010-11). 100pp. Reporting time: varies. Simultaneous submissions accepted: yes. Subjects: Marketing, Motivation, Success, Performing Arts, Prose, Shakespeare, Speaking, Theatre, Theatre, Writers/Writing.

SEWANEE REVIEW, George Core, Editor; Leigh Anne Couch, Managing Editor, University of the South, 735 University Avenue, Sewanee, TN 37383-1000, 931-598-1246, email:lcouch@sewanee.edu. 1892. Poetry, fiction, articles, criticism, reviews, letters, non-fiction. ''Publish book reviews, but books and reviewers are selected by editor. No electronic submissions or queries are accepted at this time. Our reading period extends from September 1 to June 1.'' circ. 2.5M. 4/yr. Pub'd 4 issues 2009; expects 4 issues 2010, 4 issues 2011. sub. price $34 instit., $25 indiv.; per copy $8.50; sample $8.50. Back issues: $9 for issues 1964-2002 (some vary); before 1964 inquire. Discounts: 5% to subscription agents. 192pp. Reporting time: 4-6 weeks after receipt. Simultaneous submissions accepted: no. Publishes approximately 1% of manuscripts submitted. Payment: $12-$14/printed page for prose; $.80-$1/line for poetry. Copyrighted in the author's name except book reviews. Pub's reviews: approx. 100 in 2009. §New fiction & poetry; literary criticism; biography, memoirs, and general nonfiction. Ads: $350/$245. Subjects: Book Reviewing, Criticism, English, Essays, Fiction, Literary Review, Literature (General), Memoirs, Non-Fiction, Poetry, Reviews, Short Stories, Writers/Writing.

Shadow Poetry (see also SP QUILL MAGAZINE; WHITE LOTUS), Marie Summers, 1209 Milwaukee Street, Excelsior Springs, MO 64024, Fax: (208) 977-9114, shadowpoetry@shadowpoetry.com, http://www.shadowpoetry.com. 2000. 69 titles listed in the *Small Press Record of Books in Print* (36th Edition, 2010-11).

THE SHAKESPEARE NEWSLETTER, John W. Mahon, Thomas A. Pendleton, English Department, Iona College, New Rochelle, NY 10801. 1951. Poetry, articles, criticism, reviews, letters, news items. circ. 2.5M. 4/yr. Pub'd 4 issues 2009; expects 4 issues 2010, 4 issues 2011. sub. price indiv. $15, instit. $15, $17 foreign; per copy $4; sample $4. Back issues: $4. Discounts: none. 20pp. Reporting time: 1-2 months. Payment: 3 copies. Not copyrighted. Pub's reviews: 30+ in 2009. §Scholarly and any interesting Shakespeareana and related material. Ads: $210/$125, discounts for multiple insertions. Subjects: Criticism, Drama, English, Shakespeare, Theatre.

SHAMAN'S DRUM: A Journal of Experiential Shamanism, Timothy White, PO Box 270, Williams, OR 97544, 541-846-1313. 1985. Poetry, articles, art, photos, interviews, reviews, letters, news items, non-fiction. ''We seek contributions directed to a general but well-informed audience. Past contributors have included

Jeanne Achterberg, Brooke Medicine Eagle, Richard Erdoes. We see *Shaman's Drum* as an ongoing effort to expand, challenge, and refine our readers' and our own understanding of shamanism in practice. In the process, we cover a wide range of related topics—from indigenous medicineway practices to contemporary shamanic psychotherapies, from transpersonal healing ceremonies to ecstatic spiritual practices. Our focus is on experiential shamanism. We prefer original material that is based on, or illustrated with, firsthand knowledge and personal experience. Articles should, however, be well documented with descriptive examples and pertinent background information. We are looking for examples of not only how shamanism has transformed individual lives but also practical ways it can help ensure the survival of life on this planet. We want material that captures the heart and feeling of shamanism and that can inspire people to direct action and participation.'' circ. 12M. 4/yr. Pub'd 4 issues 2009; expects 4 issues 2010, 4 issues 2011. sub. price $19; per copy $6.95; sample $7. Back issues: $7 each or 4 for $19. Discounts: retail 30%, classroom 30%, wholesale 50%. 80+pp. Reporting time: 3 months. Simultaneous submissions accepted: no. Publishes 5% of manuscripts submitted. Payment: 5¢ per word. Copyrighted, rights reverting to author is optional. Pub's reviews: 24 in 2009. §Shamanism, Native American spirituality, Entheogens. Ads: $990/$450/$330 1/3 page. Subjects: Anthropology, Archaelogy, Dreams, Native American, Religion, Spiritual.

Shambling Gate Press, Lawrence Paulson, 3314 Rosemary Lane, Hyattsville, MD 20782-1032, 301-779-6863, 301-779-9263. 1995. Poetry, fiction, non-fiction. avg. press run 2000. Expects 1 title 2010, 1 title 2011. No titles listed in the *Small Press Record of Books in Print* (36th Edition, 2010-11). Discount to bookstores and other retailers 50% on 2 copies or more. 100-400pp. Copyrights for author.

Shangri-La Publications, Sheldon Gosline, Publisher; Lester Ness, Chief Editor, #3 Coburn Hill Rd., POB 65, Warren Center, PA 18851-0065, telephone 607-272-6156, toll free 866-966-6288, email gosline@hotmail.com, web http://shangri-la.0catch.com. 1998. Fiction, articles, art, photos, cartoons, criticism, music, long-poems, plays, news items, non-fiction. "We publish advanced academic research with a cross cultural focus in our Marco Polo Monographs Series. The most recent volume is #9, *FUNDING EXPLORATION*. We publish political topics, such as *MUSLIMS IN THE WEST* and mystery novels such as *LILAC MOON*. We have a children's book series under the imprint Panda Print, with *ZOONAUTS: THE SECRET OF ANIMALVILLE*. In 2004, we are beginning a new joint venture with a number of Chinese universities and research institutes to publish the latest Chinese scientific research. In 2004 we are beginning a new journal called *Chinese Agriculture and Life Sciences (CALS)*. We have an Egyptian Language series called *HIERATIC PALEOGRAPHY*.'' avg. press run 2000 to 5000. Pub'd 4 titles 2009; expects 3 titles 2010, 12 titles 2011. 16 titles listed in the *Small Press Record of Books in Print* (36th Edition, 2010-11). Discounts: 20 academic / 45 trade. 200 to 400pp. Reporting time: 1 to 2 months. Simultaneous submissions accepted: no. Publishes 34% of manuscripts submitted. Payment: 7% royalty. Copyrights for author. Subjects: African Literature, Africa, African Studies, Anthropology, Archaelogy, Antiques, Architecture, Bibliography, Biography, Book Collecting, Bookselling, Book Reviewing, Classical Studies, Communism, Marxism, Leninism, Community, Computers, Calculators, Conservation, Crafts, Hobbies, Dada.

SHARE INTERNATIONAL, Benjamin Creme, PO Box 5668, Santa Monica, CA 90409, 818-785-6300, Fax 818-904-9132, sisubscriptions@cs.com. 1982. Articles, photos, interviews, reviews, letters, news items, non-fiction. "Combines socially-conscious and spiritual perspectives on world events and news about emergence of Maitreya, the World Teacher.Editorial office: PO Box 3677, London NW5 1RU, UK.'' circ. 5M. 10/yr. Pub'd 10 issues 2009; expects 10 issues 2010, 10 issues 2011. sub. price $30; per copy $3.50; sample $3.50. Back issues: $3.50. Discounts: USA library subscription $20. 28-40pp. Payment: none. Copyrighted. Pub's reviews: Apx 6 in 2009. §Subjects we cover. Ads: none. Subjects: Birth, Birth Control, Population, Book Reviewing, Business & Economics, Environment, Futurism, Humanism, Hunger, Inspirational, Interviews, New Age, Peace, Politics, Society, Spiritual, Third World, Minorities.

•**Shared Roads Press,** Diane Kistner, 75 Henson Road SW, Cave Spring, GA 30124, dkistner@shared-roads.net, www.sharedroads.net. 2009. Poetry, fiction, non-fiction. "We are a small, collaborative press with high standards for content and production. We aim to straddle the popular and the academic, to meld the best of both to spark creative new thought. *Poetry and Fiction:* We are interested in exploring our place in the context of larger systems, especially the complex natural world. We are eclectic, even a little eccentric, in our tastes. We favor work that modestly yet inexorably asserts its worth and beauty, much as a tomato plant does. We are not interested in the rarified or formulaic, whether academic or popular. Metaphorically speaking, we prefer books that are more like gardens than cities. *Non-Fiction:* We are interested in how humankind can *practically* bring itself back into harmony with the rest of the world. We value both sustainability and transcendence. We would like to help preserve the simple wisdom of the old-timers before this information is lost to us for good. *Book Example: The Gravedigger's Roots* by Robert S. King. *Submission Guidelines:* We invite submissions only post-query, and any submission not adhering strictly to our online guidelines and reading time frames will be returned without comment.'' avg. press run 001. Expects 3 titles 2010, 6 titles 2011. 2 titles listed in the *Small Press Record of Books in Print* (36th Edition, 2010-11). Discounts: Our books are print-on-demand, subject to the discounts offered by our POD printer (Lulu.com). 88pp. Reporting time: Up to three months. Simultaneous submissions accepted: Yes. Publishes 2% of manuscripts submitted. Copyrights for author. Subjects: Anthology, Community, Co-ops, Counter-Culture, Alternatives, Communes, Creative Non-fiction, Ecology, Foods, Fiction, Horticulture, How-To, Non-Fiction, Poetry, Prose, Short Stories, Zen.

SHATTERED WIG REVIEW, Sonny Bodkin, 425 East 31st Street, Baltimore, MD 21218, 410-243-6888. 1988. Poetry, fiction, articles, art, cartoons, satire, letters, parts-of-novels, collages, concrete art. "Do you take medicine? I take 3 "Joan Crawfords In a Wheelchair". Like Gertrude said it's in the telling, not necessarily what's told. Or as Serge Gainsbourg said: "Beauty ages and fades, while ugliness endures" (or words to that effect). We have a penchant for hardboiled surreal absurdity, but will accept anything that hits the target with a solid twang." circ. 500. 2/yr. Pub'd 2 issues 2009; expects 2 issues 2010, 2 issues 2011. sub. price $12.00; per copy $6; sample $5. Back issues: $5. Discounts: 10%. 66pp. Reporting time: 4 months. Simultaneous submissions accepted: Yes. Payment: One contributor's copy. Not copyrighted. Subjects: Alcohol, Alcoholism, Anarchist, Arts, Biography, William Blake, Lewis Carroll, Cities, Comics, Dada, Folklore, James Joyce, Literature (General), H.P. Lovecraft, Music, Poetry.

‡**SHAW: THE ANNUAL OF BERNARD SHAW STUDIES, Pennsylvania State University Press,** MaryAnn K. Crawford, Co-Editor; Michel Pharand, Co-Editor., Penn State Press, Suite C, 820 N. University Drive, University Park, PA 16802-1711, 814-865-1327. 1951. Articles, interviews, criticism, reviews, letters. "*Shaw* publishes general articles on Shaw and his milieu, reviews, notes, and the authoritative Continuing Checklist of Shaviana, the bibliography of Shaw studies. Every other issue is devoted to a special theme." circ. 2M. 1/yr. Pub'd 1 issue 2009; expects 1 issue 2010, 1 issue 2011. sub. price $35; per copy $35. 265pp. Reporting time: 2 months. Simultaneous submissions accepted: no. Publishes 25-30% of manuscripts submitted. Payment: 1 copy of the volume. Copyrighted, does not revert to author. Pub's reviews: 3 in 2009. §Shaw. Ads: none. Subjects: English, Literary Review, G.B. Shaw.

Shearer Publishing, Katherine Shearer, President, 406 Post Oak Road, Fredericksburg, TX 78624, 830-997-6529. 1981. Non-fiction. avg. press run 2M-40M. Pub'd 2 titles 2009; expects 4 titles 2010, 4 titles 2011. 18 titles listed in the *Small Press Record of Books in Print* (36th Edition, 2010-11). 250pp. Reporting time: average is 3 months. Payment: depends on book. Copyrights for author. Subjects: Fiction, Gardening, Texas.

SHEARSMAN, Tony Frazer, Editor, 58 Velwell Road, Exeter EX4 4LD, United Kingdom, Tel: 01392-434511. 1981. Poetry. "From Editor Tony Frazer: In terms of the magazine's position with regard to contemporary poetry, there is a clear inclination towards the more exploratory end of the current spectrum. Notwithstanding this, however, quality work of a more conservative kind will always be considered seriously, provided that the work is well-written. What I do not like at all is sloppy writing of any kind; I always look for some rigour in the work, though I will be more forgiving of failure in this regard if the writer is trying to push out the boundaries." 2 double-issues, in paperback format. These appear annually in April and October. Pub'd 2 issues 2009; expects 2 issues 2010, 2 issues 2011. sub. price £13.; per copy £8.50 / $13.50; sample As for single copies. Back issues: As for single copies. Bulk orders will be supplied at subscription rates. 108 per double-issue.pp. Reporting time: Up to 3 months. Simultaneous submissions accepted: Permitted. Publishes 5% of manuscripts submitted. Payment: 2 copies of the issue in which work appears. Copyrighted, reverts to author.

SHENANDOAH NEWSLETTER, Scan Doa, 736 West Oklahoma Street, Appleton, WI 54914. 1973. Poetry, articles, criticism, reviews, letters, news items, non-fiction. "All material must relate to American Indian by Indians. Editor holds strict rights on this." circ. 1M. 12/yr. Pub'd 12 issues 2009; expects 12 issues 2010, 12 issues 2011. sub. price $17.50; per copy $1.75; sample $1.75. 21pp. Reporting time: material must be into office by 24th of previous month. Payment: none. Not copyrighted. Pub's reviews: 30 in 2009. §Material relating to Native Peoples and their struggles/history. Ads: none. Subjects: Indians, Native American, Third World, Minorities.

SHENANDOAH: The Washington and Lee University Review, R.T. Smith, Editor; Lynn L. Leech, Managing Editor, Mattingly House / 2 Lee Avenue, Washington and Lee University, Lexington, VA 24450-2116, 540-458-8765; http://shenandoah.wlu.edu. 1950. Poetry, fiction, art, reviews, non-fiction. "For over half a century *Shenandoah* has published splendid poems, stories, essays and reviews that display passionate understanding, formal accomplishment and serious mischief. Reading period Sept through May 15; work received mid-May through August will be returned unread. Will become online in 2011." circ. 1.3M. 3/yr. Pub'd 3 issues 2009; expects 3 issues 2010, 3 issues 2011. sub. price $25 individual, $27 institution; Canadian subscribers/institutions add $7/yr for postage; all other countries add $13/yr; per copy $12; sample $12. Back issues: $10. Discounts: 50% bulk rate to bookstores. 200pp. Reporting time: 3 weeks. Publishes less than 1% of manuscripts submitted. Payment: $25/page prose ($250 cap); $2.50/line poetry ($200 cap); $300/cover art + 1 free copy of issue in which work appears and 1 year free subscription. Copyrighted, rights revert to author. Pub's reviews: 20 in 2009. §Short fiction/poetry—solicited reviews only. Ads: $300/$200. Subjects: Book Reviewing, Essays, Fiction, Literary Review, Literature (General), Non-Fiction, Poetry.

Shen's Books, 1547 Palos Verdes Mall #291, Walnut Creek, CA 94597, 925-262-8108, www.shens.com. No titles listed in the *Small Press Record of Books in Print* (36th Edition, 2010-11).

Sherian Publishing, Brian McClellan, 2700 Braselton Highway Suite 10-390, Dacula, GA 30019-3207, 888-276-6730. 2006. Non-fiction. Pub'd 1 title 2009; expects 4 titles 2010, 8 titles 2011. No titles listed in the *Small Press Record of Books in Print* (36th Edition, 2010-11). Subjects: How-To, Inspirational, Motivation, Success, Non-Fiction.

Sherman Asher Publishing, Jim Mafchir, P.O. Box 31725, Santa Fe, NM 87501-0172, 505-988-7214, Fax 505-988-7214, westernedge@santa-fe.net, www.shermanasher.com. 1994. Poetry, fiction, non-fiction. "Writers with proven track record who actively promote their books." avg. press run 1M. Pub'd 2 titles 2009; expects 2 titles 2010, 1 title 2011. 12 titles listed in the *Small Press Record of Books in Print* (36th Edition, 2010-11). Discounts: 20% library, 40% trade, 50% bulk. Book length. Reporting time: 6 months. Simultaneous submissions accepted: Only if advised. Publishes 2% of manuscripts submitted. Copyrights for author. Subjects: Arizona, Bilingual, Colorado, Cooking, Essays, Fiction, Literature (General), Memoirs, Native American, Nature, New Mexico, Old West, Poetry, Wildlife, Writers/Writing.

Shining Mountain Publishing, 2268 Spinnaker Circle, Longmont, CO 80503, Telephone 303-651-6230, email info@shiningmountain.net, website www.shiningmountain.net. 2002. Pub'd 1 title 2009; expects 2 titles 2010, 2 titles 2011. 2 titles listed in the *Small Press Record of Books in Print* (36th Edition, 2010-11). 175pp.

Shipyard Press, LC, Marilyn Brown, Editor; Ana Melisa Brown, Publisher, 191 Brightwater Falls Road, Henderson, NC 28739-7171, 828-808-8768. 2005. Fiction, non-fiction. avg. press run 1085. Expects 1 title 2010, 2 titles 2011. 1 title listed in the *Small Press Record of Books in Print* (36th Edition, 2010-11). Discounts: 2-31 copies 30%, case of 32 45%, prepaid orders free shipping. 212pp. Copyrights for author. Subjects: Architecture, Aviation, Fiction, Florida.

SHIRIM, Marc Steven Dworkin, 259 Saint Joseph Avenue, Long Beach, CA 90803-1733. 1982. Poetry. "*Shirim* seeks poetry (original + translated) of Jewish reference. Such known poets as Yehuda Amichai, Robert Mezey, Deena Metzger, Karl Shapiro, Irving Layton, Jerome Rothenberg, and Howard Schwartz have had poetry appear in the magazine. All submissions are welcome." circ. 250. 2/yr. Expects 1 issue 2010, 2 issues 2011. sub. price $7; per copy $4; sample $4. 36pp. Reporting time: 2 months. Payment: copies. Copyrighted, reverts to author. Pub's reviews: 2 in 2009. Subjects: Judaism, Poetry.

THE SHOP: A Magazine of Poetry, John Wakeman, Editor; Hilary Wakeman, Editor, c/o Skeagh, Schull, County Cork, Ireland, Tel: +353 28 28263 Email: theshop@theshop-poetry-magazine.ie Website: www.theshop-poetry-magazine.ie. 3/yr. sub. price In Ireland: 25 euro Rest of the world: 35 euro or £25 or $40. 80pp. Payment: Discretionary.

SHORT FUSE, Holden, PO Box 90436, Santa Barbara, CA 93190. 1983. Poetry, fiction, articles, art, photos, cartoons, interviews, satire, criticism, music, letters, parts-of-novels, long-poems, collages, plays, concrete art, non-fiction. "Some recent contributors: Lyn Lifshin, Blair Wilson, Richard Kostelanetz, Hector, Frank Moore, Annie Sprinkle, Dragon Mangan, and Bob Zark. *Short Fuse* is open to anyone's participation and material from people from all walks of life is included. The physical form of the magazine is adaptable to the requirements of the pieces included. Its sociological and ideological context is antiauthoritarian-populist. Esthetically, there's an openness to the avant-garde and experimental but no single aesthetic theory is endorsed to the exclusion of others. However, some ideas derived from dada, surrealism, and punk are of lingering interest." circ. 500+. 4/yr. Pub'd 4 issues 2009; expects 4 issues 2010, 4 issues 2011. sub. price free to institutionalized persons, $9 for 6 issues otherwise; per copy $1; sample $1. Back issues: $1. 20pp. Reporting time: 1 week. Payment: copies. Copyrighted, reverts to author. Subjects: Anarchist, Arts, Avant-Garde, Experimental Art, Cartoons, Counter-Culture, Alternatives, Communes, Creativity, Criticism, Dada, Dreams, Erotica, Essays, Fiction, Folklore, Haiku, Libertarian.

SHORT STORY, PO Box 50567, Columbia, SC 29250. Fiction. "*Short Story* is published twice yearly in spring and fall. We welcome submissions of short stories* (1,000-7,000 words) between August 1st - February 29th. A self-addressed stamped envelope must be supplied for reply. Submissions sent between March and July will be returned unread if sufficient postage is included. All submissions should be clean double-spaced typed copy and be sure to put your name on each page of the manuscript. *Short Story* does not accept personal essays, poetry or literary criticisms." Subjects: Fiction, Short Stories.

SHORTRUNS, Shirley Copperman, Sr.Editor; Dana Sigmund, Editor, 720 Wesley Ave. #10, Tarpon Springs, FL 34689, 727-942-2218. 1986. Fiction, articles, cartoons, interviews, satire, criticism, music, parts-of-novels, news items, non-fiction. "We read ALL submitted work. You must be flexible if we require additional editing by you/us. Only material with return postage included will be returned." circ. 18M & several special issues. 4/yr. Pub'd 4 issues 2009; expects 4 issues 2010, 4 issues 2011. sub. price Only sent to qualified user. 32-64pp. Reporting time: 2 weeks. Simultaneous submissions accepted: Yes. Publishes 15% of manuscripts submitted.

446

Payment: By copies. Copyrighted, reverts to author. Pub's reviews: 15-20 in 2009. §Fiction, poetry, essays, creative non-fiction. We also review @ 80 music CD's. Ads: We will add this to our new music edition. Subjects: Book Reviewing, Comics, Cooking, Crafts, Hobbies, Experimental, Festivals, Fiction, Food, Eating, Magazines, Music, Newsletter, Occult, Sex, Sexuality, Singles, Tapes & Records.

Sibyl Publications, Inc, Miriam Selby, 2505 Reuben Boise road, Dallas, OR 97338, 503-623-3438, fax 503-623-2943. 1993. Non-fiction. "Not accepting mss. at this time. Small press of women's books. Nonfiction, positive themes. No poetry or fiction. Topics are: cooking, women and change, aging, women in midlife, mythology, spirituality, health, other women's issues. No manuscripts accepted. *Inventing Ourselves Again: Woman Face Middle Age, Sacred Myths: Stories of World Religion, The Goddess Speaks,* revised edition and *Mythmaking: Heal Your Past, Claim Your Future, Spirited Threads, Oh Boy, Oh Boy, Oh Boy!, Love, Loss & Healing: A Woman's Guide to Transforming Grief, Food No Matter What! Stories & Recipes for Perfect Dining in an Imperfect World,* and *Classic Liqueurs.*" avg. press run 7.5M. Pub'd 2 titles 2009; expects 5 titles 2010, 5 titles 2011. 6 titles listed in the *Small Press Record of Books in Print* (36th Edition, 2010-11). Discounts: trade 40%, schools 25%. 200pp. Payment: 10-12% of net (minus discounts and returns). Copyrights for author. Subjects: Cooking, Feminism, Myth, Mythology, Parenting, Psychology, Spiritual, Women.

SIDE OF GRITS, Rural Messengers Press, Michele McDannold, Managing Editor; Wayne Mason, Editor, 5 Morningside Drive, Jacksonville, IL 62650, rmp@theliteraryunderground.org, http://theliteraryunderground.org/rmp/grits. 2008. Poetry, fiction, articles, art, photos, interviews, criticism, reviews, letters, parts-of-novels, long-poems, news items, non-fiction. "Currently CLOSED to submissions. We DO NOT accept submissions by postal mail. Address is for queries only. Please see website for submission guidelines. *http://theliteraryunderground.org/rmp/grits/guidelines.html* . Recent contributors include: Hugh Fox, Mathias Nelson, AD Winans and Shaindel Beers." 4/yr. Pub'd 1 issue 2009. Reporting time: 4-8 weeks. Simultaneous submissions accepted: Yes. Publishes 27% of manuscripts submitted. Copyrighted, reverts to author. Pub's reviews: 3 in 2009. §online literary journals, fiction novels. Subjects: Americana, Audio/Video, Avant-Garde, Experimental Art, Beat, Dada, Humor, Literature (General), Photography, Poetry, Post Modern, Prose, Reviews, Satire, Short Stories, Stoicism.

Sidebrow, 912 Cole St., #162, San Francisco, CA 94117. No titles listed in the *Small Press Record of Books in Print* (36th Edition, 2010-11).

Sidran Institute, 200 E. Joppa Road, Suite 207, Towson, MD 21286, 410-825-8888, Fax 410-337-0747, sidran@sidran.org, www.sidran.org. 1991. Non-fiction. "Division of Sidran Traumatic Stress Foundation. Our focus is on mental health, primarily in the area of trauma (sexual abuse, child abuse, war, violent crime, etc.)." avg. press run 1M-2M. Pub'd 4 titles 2009; expects 4 titles 2010, 2 titles 2011. No titles listed in the *Small Press Record of Books in Print* (36th Edition, 2010-11). Discounts: trade 1-2 copies 20%, 3-49 40%, 50-99 41%, 100+ 42%. 300pp. Simultaneous submissions accepted: no. Payment: varies. Subjects: Mental Health, Psychology, Self-Help, Sexual Abuse.

THE SIENESE SHREDDER, 344 West 23rd Street # 4D, New York, NY 10011, 212-431-1714 phone, 212-431-1714 fax.

•Signalman Publishing, John McClure, 3209 Stonehurst Cir., Kissimmee, FL 34741, (407)343-4853/ info@signalmanpublishing.com/ http://www.signalmanpublishing.com. 2008. Fiction, non-fiction. "Signalman Publishing started out publishing non-fiction classics excusively for the Amazon Kindle. In 2009, we expanded into some fiction and also into paperback. Signalman is a member of the Christian Small Publishers Association and the Small Publishers Association of North America." avg. press run 500. Pub'd 14 titles 2009; expects 14 titles 2010, 16 titles 2011. 4 titles listed in the *Small Press Record of Books in Print* (36th Edition, 2010-11). Discounts: 30-50%. 300pp. Reporting time: 4 weeks. Simultaneous submissions accepted: Yes. Publishes 25% of manuscripts submitted. Payment: Royalty is 5% of book's retail price paid semi-annually. Typically no advance is paid. Will in some cases. Depends on the author preference. Subjects: Business & Economics, Careers, Christianity, Fiction, Government, Juvenile Fiction, Non-Fiction, Relationships, Religion, Technology, Trade, Young Adult.

SIGNALS, Frederick Moe, 36 West Main Street, Warner, NH 03278. 2006. Articles, interviews, reviews, letters, non-fiction. "SIGNALS is a homegrown, small zine devoted to education and discourse related to independent media with an emphasis on radio including: shortwave listening, low power FM, pirate radio, and the vanishing world of non-commercial, community radio. Also includes content on zines, films, music, radio programs, and related material." circ. 120. 2/yr. Pub'd 2 issues 2009; expects 2 issues 2010. sub. price 7.00; per copy 4.00; sample $3. 32pp. Reporting time: 2 days to 23 months. Simultaneous submissions accepted: Yes. Publishes 40% of manuscripts submitted. Payment: one copy of issue in which work appears - no other payment. Not copyrighted. Pub's reviews: 4 in 2009. §books / journals / dvds / mp3s / cds / music related to media in general and radio in specific. Subjects: Counter-Culture, Alternatives, Communes, Creative Non-fiction, Culture, Electronics, Media, Zines.

Signpost Press Inc. (see also BELLINGHAM REVIEW), Brenda Miller, Editor-in-Chief, Mail Stop 9053, WWU, Bellingham, WA 98225, 360-650-4863. 1975. Poetry, fiction, non-fiction. "Not accepting book mss. at present." avg. press run 500. 15 titles listed in the *Small Press Record of Books in Print* (36th Edition, 2010-11). Discounts: 40% on 5 or more copies. 24-68pp. Reporting time: 1-3 months. Payment: varies. Copyrights for author. Subject: Poetry.

SIGNS, University of Chicago Press, Mary Hawkesworth, Rutgers University, Voorhees Chapel, Room 8, 5 Chapel Drive, New Brunswick, NJ 08901, 732-932-2841 (main #), 732-932-5732 (fax), http://www.journals.uchicago.edu/Signs/home.html. "Founded in 1975, *Signs* is recognized as the leading international journal in women's studies. *Signs* publishes articles from a wide range of disciplines in a variety of voices, articles engaging gender, race, culture, class, sexuality, and / or nation. The focus of essays ranges from cross-disciplinary theorizing and methodologies to specific disciplinary issues, framed to enter conversations of interest across disciplines." 4/yr. Pub's reviews.

Silenced Press (see also SILENCED PRESS), Michael J. Alfaro, 449 Vermont Place, Columbus, OH 43201, http://silencedpress.com. 2007. Poetry, fiction, interviews, music, parts-of-novels, long-poems, concrete art, news items, non-fiction. "Silenced Press is an independent publisher and international online literary journal based out of Columbus, Ohio. We are dedicated to giving a voice to artists that must be heard and highlighting writers from Ohio. Work that first appeared in our journal has been nominated for The Micro Award, The Donald Murray Prize and The Pushcart Prize. Our journal is ad-free with an aesthetic design to showcase the finest work that comes our way. Enjoy!" avg. press run 1000. Expects 3-10 titles 2010, 10-15 titles 2011. No titles listed in the *Small Press Record of Books in Print* (36th Edition, 2010-11). Contact directly for discount. Reporting time: Same day-3 months. Simultaneous submissions accepted: Yes. Publishes 8% of manuscripts submitted. Payment: 10% royalties for print publications + author copies. Copyrights for author. Subjects: Buddhism, Creative Non-fiction, Dada, Experimental, Fiction, Haiku, Humor, Literature (General), Memoirs, Music, Ohio, Poetry, Prose, Short Stories, Surrealism.

SILENCED PRESS, Silenced Press, Michael J. Alfaro, 449 Vermont Place, Columbus, OH 43201, http://silencedpress.com. 2007. Poetry, fiction, interviews, music, parts-of-novels, long-poems, concrete art, news items, non-fiction. Contact directly for discounts. Simultaneous submissions accepted: Yes.

Silk Pages Publishing, PO Box 385, Deerwood, MN 56444, Fax 218-534-3949. No titles listed in the *Small Press Record of Books in Print* (36th Edition, 2010-11).

SILVER WINGS, Jackson Wilcox, PO Box 2340, Clovis, CA 93613-2340, 661-264-3726. 1983. Poetry. "Poems with Christian foundation focusing on the realities of faith." circ. 250-300. 6/yr. Pub'd 6 issues 2009; expects 6 issues 2010, 6 issues 2011. sub. price $10; per copy $2; sample $2. Back issues: $2 as available. Discounts: 20%. 16-32pp. Reporting time: 4 weeks. We rarely accept simultaneous submissions. Publishes 10% of manuscripts submitted. Payment: 1 copy. Not copyrighted. Pub's reviews: 4 in 2009. §Poetry books only. Ads: none. Subjects: Community, Family, Reference.

Silverfish Review Press, Rodger Moody, Editor, PO Box 3541, Eugene, OR 97403, 503-344-5060. 1979. Poetry. "Guidelines for the annual Gerald Cable Book Award for a first book by a poet are available from the website: www.silverfishreviewpress.com." avg. press run 1M. Pub'd 2 titles 2009; expects 3 titles 2010, 3 titles 2011. 35 titles listed in the *Small Press Record of Books in Print* (36th Edition, 2010-11). Discounts: 40% wholesale for bookstores. 80pp. Reporting time: 16-20 weeks. Simultaneous submissions accepted: yes. Payment: $1,000 to winner of annual poetry book contest (for author who has yet to publish a book) plus publication by Silverfish Review Press and 25 copies of the book. Copyrights for author. Subject: Poetry.

SIMPLYWORDS, Ruth Niehaus, 605 Collins Avenue #23, Centerville, GA 31028, simplywords@hotmail.com. 1991. Poetry, fiction, articles, letters, non-fiction. 4/yr. Pub'd 4 issues 2009; expects 4 issues 2010, 4 issues 2011. sub. price $18.50; per copy $5; sample $5. Back issues: none. Discounts: none. 38pp. Reporting time: 2-3 weeks. Simultaneous submissions accepted: no. Publishes 80% of manuscripts submitted. Payment: none. Not copyrighted, all rights revert to author on publication. Pub's reviews: 1-2 in 2009. Ads: must write for rates.

SINISTER WISDOM, Fran Day, Editor; Susan Levinkind, Administrator, PO Box 3252, Berkeley, CA 94703. 1976. Poetry, fiction, articles, art, photos, cartoons, interviews, satire, criticism, reviews, letters, parts-of-novels, long-poems, collages, plays, concrete art, non-fiction. "*Sinister Wisdom* is a magazine for the lesbian imagination in the arts and politics. Contributors range from 'famous' writers to first-time submitters—quality and original voice are what count. Subject matter may be anything that expresses depth of vision. Multi-cultural: writing by lesbians of color, Jewish, disabled, fat, ethnic, working class, older and younger lesbians encouraged." circ. 3M. 3/yr. Pub'd 3 issues 2009; expects 3 issues 2010, 3 issues 2011. sub. price $20, $25 foreign, $33 institutions and libraries; per copy $7.50 (pp); sample $7.50 (pp). Back issues: $5-$6. Discounts: 40% to bookstores, 45-50% for bulk sales of 50 or more. 128-144pp. Reporting time: 3-9 months. We prefer not to receive simultaneous submissions. Payment: 2 copies. Copyrighted, reverts to author. Pub's reviews: 10 in 2009. §Lesbian poetry, fiction, theatre, arts and non-fiction, especially with radical emphasis. Ads: $200/$100/$50 1/4/write for classified. Subjects: Feminism, Lesbianism, Literature (General), Women.

Six Ft. Swells Press (see also CHEAP SHOTS: Poetry Series), Todd Cirillo, Julie Valin, 417 Neal Street, Grass Valley, CA 95945, 530-271-0662, sixfootswells@yahoo.com, www.myspace.com/sixftswells. 2006. Poetry. "We specialize in "After Hours" poetry. Our mission is to bring poetry to places its not used to going, like bar rooms, bowling alleys, truck stops and rock and roll shows. We look for young, fresh, alternative, "hip", edgy poetry that tells it like it is. We don't believe in academic poetry that needs a dictionary to glean meaning. We want the raw, simple, straightforward stuff that breaks a heart or two, or encourages another round of drinks." avg. press run 100. Expects 3 titles 2010, 3 titles 2011. No titles listed in the *Small Press Record of Books in Print* (36th Edition, 2010-11). 30pp. Reporting time: 1 month. Simultaneous submissions accepted: Yes. Does not copyright for author. Subjects: Alcohol, Alcoholism, Beat, Charles Bukowski, Erotica, Food, Eating, Ernest Hemingway, Jack Kerouac, D.H. Lawrence, Henry Miller, Music, Anais Nin, Poetry, Sex, Sexuality, Dylan Thomas, Travel.

Sixteen Rivers Press, Jacqueline Kudler, Collective Member; Terry Ehret, Collective Member; Carolyn Miller, Collective Member; Margaret Kaufman, Collective Member; Gerald Fleming, Collective Member; Murray Silverstein, Collective Member; Sharon Olson, Supporting Member; Nina Lindsay, Supporting Member; Helen Wickes, Collective Member; Dan Bellm, Collective Member; Gillian Wegener, Collective Member; Lynne Knight, Collective Member; Valerie Berry, Supporting Member; Susan Sibbet, Supporting Member; Jeanne Wagner, Collective Member; Christina Hutchins, Collective Member, P.O. Box 640663, San Francisco, CA 94164-0663, 415-273-1303. 1999. Poetry. "Sixteen Rivers Press is a shared-work, nonprofit poetry collective dedicated to providing an alternative publishing avenue for San Francisco Bay Area poets. We are open to many diverse styles provided the manuscript is of the highest quality. Poets, on acceptance, must be prepared to become working members of the press for three years." avg. press run 1000. Pub'd 2 titles 2009; expects 2 titles 2010, 2 titles 2011. No titles listed in the *Small Press Record of Books in Print* (36th Edition, 2010-11). 96pp. Reporting time: Four months. Simultaneous submissions accepted: Yes. Publishes 15% of manuscripts submitted. Payment: This is a nonprofit press. All proceeds go to publishing the next year's selections. Copyrights for author. Subject: Poetry.

SKEPTICAL INQUIRER, Kendrick Frazier, Editor; Benjamin Radford, Managing Editor, PO Box 703, Amherst, NY 14226, 716-636-1425, info@csicop.org. 1976. Articles, art, photos, cartoons, criticism, reviews, letters, news items, non-fiction. "Articles 2,000-3,500 words, reviews 600-1,200 words, news and comments 250-1,000 words, letters and forum 250-1,000 words. Contributors: Martin Gardner, Paul Kurtz, Joe Nickell, and Richard Dawkins. We investigate science, paranormal, and pseudo science claims from a skeptical point of view." circ. 40M. 6/yr. Pub'd 6 issues 2009; expects 6 issues 2010, 6 issues 2011. sub. price $19.95 intro.; per copy $4.95; sample free. Back issues: $4.95. Discounts: 50% off 10 or more copies. 68pp. Reporting time: 2 months. Simultaneous submissions accepted: no. Payment: issues. Copyrighted, does not revert to author. Pub's reviews: 25-30 in 2009. §Science, paranormal, psychology, popular culture, fringe science. Ads: none. Subjects: Education, Newsletter, Psychology, Science.

SKIDROW PENTHOUSE, Rob Cook, Stephanie Dickinson, 44 Four Corners Road, Blairstown, NJ 07825, 212-614-9505 (hm). 1998. Poetry, fiction, articles, art, photos, cartoons, interviews, parts-of-novels, long-poems, collages, non-fiction. "Skidrow Penthouse is published to give emerging and idiocyncratic writers a new forum. We're looking for authentic voices, surreal, experimental, New York School, formal or free verse. We want poets and fiction writers who sound like themselves, not workshop professionals. We showcase a poet in each issue by publishing a full-length collection within the magazine. We have published poetry by Andrew Kaufman, Maya Hebert, Gil Fagiani, John Colburn, Lisa Jarnot, Aase Berg, Johannes Goransson, Marc DePalo, Hilary Melton, Ronald Wardall, and James Grinwis." circ. 500. 1/yr. Pub'd 1 issue 2009; expects 1 issue 2010, 1 issue 2011. 1 title listed in the *Small Press Record of Books in Print* (36th Edition, 2010-11). sub. price $20; per copy $12.50. Back issues: Inquire. Discounts: 2-10 copies 25%. 275pp. Reporting time: Three to four months. Simultaneous submissions accepted: Yes. Payment: Contributor's copy. Copyrighted, reverts to author. Pub's reviews. §Poetry, fiction, non-fiction collections, criticism. Ads: Full page $90Half page $45. Subjects: Arts, Experimental, Fiction, Non-Fiction, Photography, Poetry, Post Modern.

Skullvines Press, S.D. Hintz, 585 Chippewa Trail, Lino Lakes, MN 55014, http://skullvines.com, mail@skullvines.com. 2007. Poetry, fiction, long-poems, plays, non-fiction. "We are the "Publisher of Whatever the Fuck We Want"!" No titles listed in the *Small Press Record of Books in Print* (36th Edition, 2010-11). Simultaneous submissions accepted: Yes. Payment: Author receives 50% of net profits. Does not copyright for author. Subjects: Euthanasia, Death, Fantasy, Fiction, Horror, Literature (General), Myth, Mythology, Non-Fiction, Novels, Poetry, Science Fiction, Sex, Sexuality, Short Stories, Supernatural, Theatre.

SKYLINE LITERARY MAGAZINE, Skyline Publications, Victoria Valentine, Publisher; Phaedra Valentine, Executive Editor, PO Box 295, Stormville, NY 12582-0295, skylineeditor@aol.com, http://www.skylinemagazines.com. 2001. Poetry, fiction, articles, art, photos, parts-of-novels, non-fiction.

"International publisher of previously published and novice authors and artists. Publishes multiple titles under Skyline Publications. Short stories up to 4000 words. Poetry of any length and style. Quarterly Print Magazines and WebSite publication. Ongoing competitions; cash and other prizes. Nominates for Pushcart Prize." circ. 45,000 *electronic circ* Quarterly Print Magazine circ to be determined during the next few issues. 4/yr. Pub'd 12 issues 2009; expects 6 issues 2010, 4 issues 2011. price per copy $16.00 covers the price of one 80 page magazine, including Continental USA shipping. Will ship Internationally but must receive payment in USD.; sample See Website for information on special print issues (dates & availability) Sample issues $8.00 shipped when available. Back issues: Pay shipping. Issues older than 6 months are free if available. Current issues sell out quickly. See website for details. 80pp. Reporting time: Up to 4 months. We try but cannot always repond to every submission due to high volume of submissions we receive. Feel free to email us to check status if you have not heard back in 2 months. Simultaneous submissions accepted: Yes. Just let us know if your work has been accepted elsewhere so we can remove from our files. Email Submissions Only. Submit *inside* EMAIL, NO attachments. Read website guidelines on *how to submit*. Publishes 20% of manuscripts submitted. Copyright notice of entire works, but not for each individual author. Author retains all rights and responsibilities for their personal copyright. Pub's reviews: 2 in 2009. §On website & in print - we publish your professional book reviews online, and in print if magazine space permits. In 2007 Skyline will have a staff book reviewer available who will review one book per issue, which will appear in print. Ads: Website Banner Advertising. Header Banner Advertising. E-Magazine OR Web Site hyperlinks: $10.00 Full page: $50.00 All color. Low cost ads. All prices on Website. Print advertising also available. Contact SkyWriterr@aol.com for details. Subjects: Arts, Entertainment, Fiction, Literature (General), Magazines, Non-Fiction, Poetry, Prose, Publishing, Short Stories, Storytelling, Writers/Writing.

Skyline Publications (see also A HUDSON VIEW POETRY DIGEST; LITERARY HOUSE REVIEW; SKYLINE LITERARY MAGAZINE), Victoria Valentine, Editor, PO Box 295, Stormville, NY 12582-0295, website: http://www.skylinepublications.com, Email: skylineeditor@aol.com. 2001. Poetry, fiction, art, photos, non-fiction. "Please see each individual website for further information, guidelines and publishing calendar. No previously published material. No attachments will be opened. We try to reply to every query, however, due to the volume of mail we receive, we cannot always do so. Please accept our apologies. You may drop us a note in 2 months to check status. Main site: http://www.skylinepublications.com." Pub'd 2 titles 2009; expects 4 titles 2010, 5 titles 2011. 1 title listed in the *Small Press Record of Books in Print* (36th Edition, 2010-11). pp varies with each title we publish. Can be from 48 in our digests to 120 in magazines and bookspp. Reporting time: At least 4 months. Due to the overwhelming amount of submissions we receive, we are at times only able to reply to accepted authors. Simultaneous submissions accepted: yes. Publishes 20% of manuscripts submitted. Copyright notice of entire works, but not for each individual author. Author retains all rights and responsibilities for their personal copyright. Subjects: Erotica, Fantasy, Fiction, Haiku, Horror, Humor, Literature (General), Magazines, Memoirs, Mystery, Non-Fiction, Poetry, Romance, Science Fiction, Short Stories.

Skyline West Press/Wyoming Almanac, Philip J. Roberts, 1409 Thomes, Laramie, WY 82072, 307-745-8205. 1982. Non-fiction. "Considers only manuscripts dealing with history, politics and culture of Wyoming or reference works on that geographic area." avg. press run 2M. Pub'd 1 title 2009; expects 1 title 2010, 2 titles 2011. 3 titles listed in the *Small Press Record of Books in Print* (36th Edition, 2010-11). Discounts: 40% to recognized dealers. 140-576pp. Reporting time: 4-5 weeks. Simultaneous submissions accepted: no. Publishes 10% of manuscripts submitted. Payment: varies with author (negotiable). Copyrights vary. Subjects: Great Plains, The West, Wyoming.

SLAB, Francine Maitland, Managing Editor; Kim Galvin, Managing Editor, Dept. of English, 314 SWC, Slippery Rock University, Slippery Rock, PA 16057. "Submit your works of: sudden fiction, poetry, and traditional or web-based art via surface mail or online form. Submissions will not be returned unless accompanied by a SASE. Please include full contact information with submission."

SLANT: A Journal of Poetry, James Fowler, University of Central Arkansas, PO Box 5063, Conway, AR 72035-5000, 501-450-5107. 1987. Poetry. "We use traditional and 'modern' poetry, even experimental, moderate length, any subject on approval of Board of Readers. Our purpose is to publish a journal of fine poetry from all regions. No haiku, no translations. No previously published poems. No multiple submissions. Recent contributors include Gaylord Brewer, Linda Dyer, Carolyn Gregory, Marc Jampole, Donna Pucciani, and Peter Swanson. Submission deadline is November 15 for annual late-spring publication." circ. 175. 1/yr. Pub'd 1 issue 2009; expects 1 issue 2010, 1 issue 2011. sub. price $10; per copy $10; sample $10. Back issues: $8. Discounts: negotiable. 112pp. Reporting time: 3-4 months from deadline. Simultaneous submissions accepted: no. Publishes 8% of manuscripts submitted. Payment: 1 copy on publication. Copyrighted, reverts to author. Ads: none. Subject: Poetry.

Slapering Hol Press, Margo Stever, Suzanne Cleary, 300 Riverside Drive, Sleepy Hollow, NY 10591-1414, 914-332-5953, Fax 914-332-4825, info@writerscenter.org, www.writerscenter.org. 1990. Poetry. "We publish emerging poets who have never published in book form, and thematic anthologies. 2008, *A Thirst That's Partly*

Mine, Liz Ahl; *Poems in Conversation and a Conversation*, Elizabeth Alexander and Lyrae Van Clief-Stefanon; 2007, *The Heart That Lies Outside the Body*, Stephanie Lenox; 2006, *Falling Into Velazquez*, Mary Kaiser; 2005, *A House That Falls*, Sean Nevin; 2003, *Days When Nothing Happens*, David Tucker; 2002, *The Scottish Cafe*, Susan H. Case; 2001, *The Landscape of Mind*, Jianqing Zheng; 1998, *The Last Campaign*, Rachel Loden; 1994, 1999, *What's Become of Eden: Poems of Family at Century's End*; 1992, *River Poems*. Annual chapbook competition deadline May 15th; send SASE or see website for guidelines." avg. press run 500. Pub'd 2 titles 2009; expects 1 title 2010, 2 titles 2011. 21 titles listed in the *Small Press Record of Books in Print* (36th Edition, 2010-11). Discounts: standard. 28-36pp. Reporting time: 3-4 months. Simultaneous submissions accepted: yes. Annual chapbook competition winner is paid $1000 plus 10 copies. Copyrights for author. Subject: Poetry.

Sligo Press, 4 Willow Drive, Apt. 2, Provincetown, MA 02657-1638, 508-487-5113, Fax 508-487-5113, dplennon@comcast.net. 2000. Fiction, criticism. "Sligo Press was established to publish scholarly/critical work on Norman Mailer. *Norman Mailer: Works and Days* by J. Michael & Donna Pedro Lennon, a bio-bibliography, illus., 280 pp., published Fall 2000. *Norman Mailer's Letters on An American Dream, 1963-69* consisting of 76 letters, a critical introduction, appendices, bibliography and index published June 2004 in a limited edition of 110 copies. Edited by J. Michael Lennon. Norman Mailer's Provincetown: The Wild West of the East, published in a limited edition August 2005." avg. press run 500. Pub'd 1 title 2009; expects 1 title 2010, 2 titles 2011. 3 titles listed in the *Small Press Record of Books in Print* (36th Edition, 2010-11). 295pp. Simultaneous submissions accepted: yes. Payment: yes. Copyrights for author. Subjects: Bibliography, Biography, Criticism, Literature (General).

Slipdown Mountain Publications LLC, Walt Shiel, 28151 Quarry Lake Rd, Lake Linden, MI 49945, (phone) 906-523-4118, (toll-free phone/fax) 866-341-3705, (email) Books@SlipdownMountain.com, (website) http://www.SlipdownMountain.com. 2003. Fiction, art, non-fiction. "Our books, although intended for adults, contain no graphic sexual content, excessive violence or gratuitous profanity. You can safely share them with your family...teens to great-grandparents. Our goal is your satisfaction.Topics include: historical fiction, SciFi/Speculative Fiction, Aviation/Military History, Cryptozoology, Reprints of Military Flight ManualsActive Series: Cessna Warbirds, Human Origins, Backyard Bigfoot, Dawn of AviationAuthors: Walt Shiel, Lisa A. Shiel, Jan Forsgren, Mike Little, James R. McConnell." Pub'd 1 title 2009; expects 2 titles 2010, 3 titles 2011. 9 titles listed in the *Small Press Record of Books in Print* (36th Edition, 2010-11). Discounts: For all books except ISBN 978-0-9746553-3-3: 1 Copy - 10% 2-5 Copies - 20% 6-19 Copies - 30% 20+ Copies - 40% For ISBN 978-0-9746553-3-3: 1-5 Copies - 10% 6-19 Copies - 20% 20+ Copies - 30%. Reporting time: 2 weeks (provided online submission requirements are met, anything else is ignored). Simultaneous submissions accepted: Yes. Publishes 1% of manuscripts submitted. Payment: No advance, variable royalty paid quarterly. Copyrights for author. Subjects: Airplanes, Ancient Astronauts, Anthropology, Archaelogy, Arts, Aviation, Fiction, Great Lakes, Memoirs, Michigan, Military, Veterans, Novels, Reprints, Science Fiction, Short Stories, World War II.

SLIPSTREAM, Slipstream Productions, Dan Sicoli, Robert Borgatti, Livio Farallo, Box 2071, New Market Station, Niagara Falls, NY 14301, 716-282-2616 (after 5 p.m., E.S.T.). 1980. Poetry, art, photos, long-poems, collages, concrete art. "Submissions are completely open. Query for themes. Reading through 2010 for a general issue as well as a theme issue on SEX-FOOD-DEATH (Visit our web site for details: www.slipstreampress.org). NO LONGER READING FICTION. Some recent contributors are Gerald Locklin, Joan E. Bauer, Jim Daniels, Ron Koertge, Terry Godbey, Donna Pucciani, and Patrick Carrington." circ. 600. 1/yr. Pub'd 1 issue 2009; expects 1 issue 2010, 1 issue 2011. 4 titles listed in the *Small Press Record of Books in Print* (36th Edition, 2010-11). sub. price $20; per copy $10; sample $10. Back issues: available upon request. 100pp. Reporting time: 4-10 weeks. Payment: presently only in copies. Copyrighted, reverts to author. Subjects: Photography, Poetry.

Slipstream Productions (see also SLIPSTREAM), Dan Sicoli, Robert Borgatti, Livio Farallo, Box 2071, New Market Station, Niagara Falls, NY 14301. 1980. Poetry, fiction, art, photos, long-poems, collages. avg. press run 500. Pub'd 2 titles 2009; expects 3 titles 2010, 2 titles 2011. 16 titles listed in the *Small Press Record of Books in Print* (36th Edition, 2010-11). 40pp. Simultaneous submissions accepted: yes.

SLOPE, Lucas Farrell, Editor; Brandon Shimoda, Editor, On-line journal at: http://www.slope.org. "*Slope* has always been committed to presenting the finest in both experimental and traditonal lyric poetry, working within a multitude of pressing themes and concerns. Poems by Gregory Brooker, Julie Carr, Wynn Cooper. and others.Future issues of Slope may include critical, audio, video and visual work. If you want to propose a particular project, please query the editors at: slope.editors@gmail.com. Please include the word "INQUIRY" in the subject line."

THE SMALL BUSINESS ADVISOR, Joseph Gelb, 11 Franklin Avenue, Hewlett, NY 11557-2034, 516-374-1387, Fax 516-374-1175, smalbusadv@aol.com, www.smallbusinessadvice.com. 1974. Poetry, articles, cartoons, reviews, letters. "Length of material 900-1500 words." circ. 1M. 12/yr. Pub'd 2 issues 2009;

expects 12 issues 2010, 12 issues 2011. sub. price $45; per copy $7.25; sample $3. Back issues: $8. Discounts: Bulk rate to be negotiated. 16pp. Reporting time: 2 months. Simultaneous submissions accepted: yes. Publishes 60% of manuscripts submitted. Payment: copies 2 times. Copyrighted. Pub's reviews: 1 in 2009. §Business management, marketing, human resources, cash management. Subjects: Business & Economics, Insurance, Labor, Law, Management.

Small Dogma Publishing, Inc., Matthew Porricelli, PO Box 91023, Lakeland, FL 33804, 863-838-7251. 2006. Poetry, fiction, non-fiction. "Small Dogma Publishing is a company looking for authors who desire to come to voice. We are dedicated to making a difference and are always looking for new manuscripts that entertain, teach, challenge, inform or inspire. *Please note- We do not accept material with gratuitous violence or sexual content." avg. press run 500. Pub'd 21 titles 2009; expects 30 titles 2010, 30 titles 2011. 1 title listed in the *Small Press Record of Books in Print* (36th Edition, 2010-11). Discounts: Varies by quantity. Usually 55%. 220pp. Reporting time: 2-3 months. Simultaneous submissions accepted: Yes. Publishes 3% of manuscripts submitted. Payment: 23% paid semiannually. Author holds copyright. Subjects: Biography, Christianity, Creative Non-fiction, Family, Fantasy, Fiction, History, Inspirational, Juvenile Fiction, Literature (General), Mentoring/Coaching, Motivation, Success, Non-Fiction, Poetry, Young Adult.

Small Helm Press, Pearl Evans, 4235 Porte de Palmas, Unit 182, San Diego, CA 92122-5123, 858-546-0140, smallhelm@san.rr.com. 1986. Non-fiction. "Small Helm Press is unable to receive unsolicited manuscripts at this time." Expects 1 title 2011. 5 titles listed in the *Small Press Record of Books in Print* (36th Edition, 2010-11). Discounts: 3 up 40%, 25 up 50% for bookstores. 128pp. Payment: individual basis. Copyrights for author. Subjects: China, Christianity, Culture, Education, Non-Fiction, Public Affairs.

THE SMALL PRESS REVIEW/SMALL MAGAZINE REVIEW, Dustbooks, Len Fulton, Editor-Publisher; Bob Grumman, Contributing Editor (Experioddica); Michael Andre, Contributing Editor (New York Letter); Richard Lauson, Associate Editor, PO Box 100, Paradise, CA 95967-9999, 530-877-6110, fax: 530-877-0222, email: publisher@dustbooks.com, Website: http://www.dustbooks.com/. 1966. Articles, cartoons, interviews, reviews, letters, news items. "Now published on-line only. However, a subscription gives you on-line access to issues back to March, 2006. The *Small Press Review* seeks to study and promulgate the small press and little magazine (i.e. the *independent* publisher) worldwide. It was started in 1966 as part of an effort by its publisher to get a grip on small press/mag information since no one at the time (or for some years thereafter) seemed interested in doing it. It is also designed to promote the small press in a variety of ways. *SPR/SMR* publishes reviews, guest editorials and other material related to BOTH books and magazines published by small publishers. We are always on the lookout for competently written reviews (yes, we have a 'style sheet'), as long as they hold to a page in length and review a title published by a small press or magazine. *SPR/SMR* has regular 'News Notes' sections which give info about small press activities, manuscript needs (*and there are many!*), contests, prizes and so on. We print full-info listings bi-monthly on many new small presses and many new magazines which come into our database throughout the year. A particularly popular feature of the magazine is the 'Free Sample Mart' which lists about two dozen free samples of small magazines and books available each issue." circ. 3.5M. 6/yr. Pub'd 6 issues 2009; expects 6 issues 2010, 6 issues 2011. sub. price individuals $35/yr, $49/2 yrs; sample free. Back issues: inquire. Discounts: schedule available for agents. 24pp. Reporting time: 3-6 weeks. Publishes 85% of manuscripts submitted. Not copyrighted. Pub's reviews: 200 in 2009. §Anything published by a small press. Ads: $150/$90/$75/$50/(display). Subjects: Book Reviewing, Magazines, Publishing, Reference, Reviews.

SMARANDACHE NOTIONS JOURNAL, Staring Media, Dr. Sabin Tabirca, J. McGray, Box 141, Rehoboth, NM 87322, m_l_perez@yahoo.com, http://www.gallup.unm.edu/~smarandache/. 1990. Articles. "Research papers on Smarandache Notions such as: Smarandache type functions, sequences, numbers, primes, constants, classes of paradoxes and quantum paradoxes, paradoxist geometries (partially Euclidean and partially non-Euclidean), manifolds, algebraic structures and neutrosophic algebraic structures, neutrosophy (a generalization of dialectics), neutrosophic logic (generalization of fuzzy logic), neutrosophic set (generalization of fuzzy set), neutrosophic probability and statistics (generalization of classical and imprecise probabilities), Smarandache hypothesis that there is no speed barrier in the universe, unmatter (a new form of matter), tautologies, Dezert-Smarandache Theory of plausible and paradoxist reasoning in information fusion (DSmT), etc." circ. 5M. 1-2/yr. Pub'd 1 issue 2009; expects 1 issue 2010, 1-2 issues 2011. sub. price $39.95; per copy $39.95; sample $39.95. Back issues: none available. 250-300pp. Reporting time: 1 month. Simultaneous submissions accepted: yes. Publishes 80% of manuscripts submitted. Payment: free copies of the magazine. Copyrighted, reverts to author. Pub's reviews: 4 in 2009. §Papers, books, etc. about Smarandache Notions. Ads: $20/page. Subject: Mathematics.

Smart Publications, John Morgenthaler, P.O. 4667, Petaluma, CA 94955, 1-800-976-2793, 888-998-6889(Fax), www.smart-publications.com. No titles listed in the *Small Press Record of Books in Print* (36th Edition, 2010-11).

SMARTISH PACE, Stephen Reichert, PO Box 22161, Baltimore, MD 21203, www.smartishpace.com. 1999.

Poetry, articles, interviews, criticism, reviews, long-poems. "We welcome unsolicited submissions. However, we strongly suggest that you read selections from a recent issue of *Smartish Pace*, or at least some of the sample work displayed on this site, before submitting. Submit no more than 6 poems. Type your name, address, e-mail and phone (preferred) in an upper corner of each poem that you submit. We will consider poems of any length, style and subject matter. We accept only electronic submissions at www.smartishpace.com; we no longer accept postal submission, except for our two prizes. Currently accepting submissions throughout the year. Recent contributors: Paul Muldoon, Stephen Dunn, Maxine Kumin, Carl Dennis, Sherman Alexie, Campbell McGrath, and Carol Muske-Dukes." circ. 750. 2/yr. Pub'd 2 issues 2009; expects 2 issues 2010, 2 issues 2011. sub. price $20; per copy $10; sample $10. Back issues: $10; Issues 1 through 16. Discounts: none. 145pp. Reporting time: upto 6 months. Simultaneous submissions accepted: yes. Publishes 1-3% of manuscripts submitted. Payment: copies of issue. Copyrighted, reverts to author. Pub's reviews: 15 in 2009. §Recent books of poetry. Ads: inquire. Subjects: Book Reviewing, Creativity, Criticism, Haiku, Interviews, Journals, Literary Review, Literature (General), Magazines, Poetry, Reviews, Translation, Writers/Writing.

Smirk Books, Agnes Franz, 833 Alpha Lane, Prescott, AZ 86303, (928) 778-6788. 1987. Satire. "We are looking for original or attributed quotes, quips or cliches with a snarky, satirical and/or whimsical tone. A single one-liner is acceptable for submission. Humor will keep this project rolling along...let's see what YOU have. Thanx. AF." Pub'd 1 title 2009; expects 1 title 2010. No titles listed in the *Small Press Record of Books in Print* (36th Edition, 2010-11). 200pp. Reporting time: 3 weeks. Simultaneous submissions accepted: Yes. Publishes 50% of manuscripts submitted. Payment: We must discuss...depends on submission. We ARE fair and reasonable. Does not copyright for author. Subjects: Adolescence, Advertising, Self-Promotion, Aging, The Americas, Fashion, Folklore, Gardening, Humor, Marketing, H.L. Mencken, Old West, Parenting, Philosophy, Romance, Satire.

The Smith (subsidiary of The Generalist Assn., Inc.), Harry Smith, Publisher, 999 Sawyer Road, Cape Elizabeth, ME 04107-9638. 1964. Poetry, fiction. "Not currently reading unsolicited mss. For book orders only please contact: Arts End Books, POB 441, W. Dover VT 05356 or artsendbooks.com." avg. press run 1.5M. 65 titles listed in the *Small Press Record of Books in Print* (36th Edition, 2010-11). Discounts: varies to bookstores and wholesalers. 80pp. Copyrights for author. Subjects: Essays, Fiction, Non-Fiction, Novels, Poetry, Prose, Short Stories.

Genny Smith Books, Genny Smith, Editor, Publisher, 23100 Via Esplendor, Villa 44, Cupertino, CA 95014, 650-964-4071, www.liveoakpress.com. 1976. Articles, photos, non-fiction. "I specialize in publications on the Eastern Sierra region of California—to date, guidebooks, natural history, regional history, and sets of historic postcards. My guidebooks (I edit and coauthor them) to this mountain-and-desert vacation area include chapters on roads, trails, natural history and history. Best known localities in this region are Owens Valley and Mammoth Lakes. These guidebooks are for sightseers, campers, hikers, fishermen, nature lovers and history buffs. Alternate address: PO Box 1060, Mammoth Lakes, CA 93546 (summer only). All my books are now published by The Live Oak Press, LLC PO Box 60036, Palo Alto, CA 94306, (650) 853-0197." avg. press run 7M. Pub'd 1 title 2009; expects 1 title 2010, 1 title 2011. 5 titles listed in the *Small Press Record of Books in Print* (36th Edition, 2010-11). 224pp. Reporting time: 3 months. Payment: Varies from sharing of royalties to flat payment for material. Copyrights for author. Subjects: Americana, Autobiography, California, Conservation, Earth, Natural History, Geology, History, Native American, Non-Fiction, Sports, Outdoors, Mark Twain, Water, The West, Women.

Gibbs Smith, Publisher, Madge Baird, V.P. Managing Editor; Suzanne Taylor, V.P. Development Editor; Linda Nimori, Editor; Monica Weeks, Editor; Holly Venables, Editorial Assistant; Melissa Mikesell, Editorial Assistant, PO Box 667, Layton, UT 84041, 801-544-9800, Fax 801-544-5582, info@GibbsSmith.com. 1969. Poetry, fiction, art, criticism, non-fiction. "Additional address: 1877 E. Gentile Street, Layton, UT 84040. Books on architecture, arts, reprints, guide books, natural environment, poetry, children's, inspirational, cookbooks, nonfiction." avg. press run 5M-7M. Pub'd 45 titles 2009; expects 36 titles 2010. No titles listed in the *Small Press Record of Books in Print* (36th Edition, 2010-11). Discounts: 49.5% average. 144-160pp. Reporting time: 12 weeks. Simultaneous submissions accepted: yes. Publishes 1% of manuscripts submitted. Payment: 10% on net. Copyrights for author. Subjects: Animals, Architecture, Arts, Biography, California, Collectibles, Earth, Natural History, Environment, Fiction, New York, Novels, Short Stories, Southwest, Textbooks, Utah.

Smith-Johnson Publisher, Irwin Gray, 175-14 73rd Avenue, Flushing, NY 11366-1502, 718-969-0665 irwingray@hotmail.com. 2001. Non-fiction. "Business/management/entrepreneurial." avg. press run 4500. Pub'd 1 title 2009. 1 title listed in the *Small Press Record of Books in Print* (36th Edition, 2010-11). Discounts: 50% discount to the trade. 300pp. Reporting time: 2 months. Simultaneous submissions accepted: Yes. Publishes 10% of manuscripts submitted. Payment: individual arrangements. Copyright: individual arrangements. Subjects: Business & Economics, Consulting, Education, Engineering, Leadership, Management, Motivation, Success.

SMOKE, Windows Project, Dave Ward, Liver House, 96 Bold Street, Liverpool L1 4HY, England. 1974. Poetry, fiction, art, photos, cartoons, long-poems, collages, concrete art. "Tom Pickard, Jim Burns, Dave Calder, Roger McGough, Frances Horovitz." circ. 500. 2/yr. sub. price £3/6 issues incl. postage; per copy 50p plus post; sample 50p plus post. 24pp. Reporting time: as quickly as possible. Publishes 1.28% of manuscripts submitted. Payment: none. Not copyrighted. No ads. Subjects: Fiction, Poetry.

Smyrna Press, Dan Georgakas, Barbara Saltz, 6 University Drive, Suite 206, PMB 161, Amherst, MA 01002-3820, Fax 201-617-0203, smyrnapress@hotmail.com. 1964. Poetry, fiction, art, parts-of-novels, collages, plays, non-fiction. "We try to publish 1-3 books a year which combine the latest technical breakthroughs with a concern for social change that is essentially Marxist but undogmatic. Our current projects combine art and politics as well as themes of sexual liberation. We can use good line drawings or woodcuts. We also distribute books for Intervention Press, Pella Publishing, and some titles of Lake View Press. Query before sending any material. Sample copies of literary books, $2; sample copies of art books, $3." avg. press run 2M. Pub'd 2 titles 2009; expects 2 titles 2010, 2 titles 2011. 24 titles listed in the *Small Press Record of Books in Print* (36th Edition, 2010-11). Discounts: 40% bookstores, 10% education, bulk by arrangement, 30% prepaid bookstores. 60-250pp. Reporting time: 2-3 weeks, query before submitting. Simultaneous submissions accepted: no. Publishes 1% of manuscripts submitted. Payment: copies and 10% net. Copyrights for author. Subjects: Anarchist, Arts, Bibliography, Bilingual, Cuba, Drama, Feminism, Fiction, Graphics, Labor, Middle East, Poetry, Socialist, Third World, Minorities, Women.

SNAKE NATION REVIEW, Roberta George, Founding Editor; Jean Arambula, Managing Editor, 110 #2 West Force, Valdosta, GA 31601, 912-249-8334. 1989. Poetry, fiction, art, photos. circ. 1M. 3/yr. Pub'd 3 issues 2009; expects 3 issues 2010, 3 issues 2011. sub. price $20; per copy $6; sample $6 (includes mailing). Back issues: $6 (includes mailing). Discounts: 40% to bookstores, jobbers. 110pp. Reporting time: 3-6 months. Simultaneous submissions accepted: yes. Publishes 10% of manuscripts submitted. Payment: 2 copies or prize money. Copyrighted, reverts to author. Ads: $100/$50/$25.

Snapshot Press, John Barlow, PO Box 132, Waterloo, Liverpool L22 8WZ, United Kingdom, info@snapshotpress.co.uk, www.snapshotpress.co.uk. 1997. Poetry. "Snapshot Press specializes in haiku, tanka and short poetry, publishing anthologies, individual collections, and *The Haiku Calendar*. Please see the website for further details. (N.B. Publication of the journals *Snapshots* (haiku) and *Tangled Hair* (tanka) ceased in 2006.)." Pub'd 3 titles 2009; expects 6 titles 2010, 8 titles 2011. 1 title listed in the *Small Press Record of Books in Print* (36th Edition, 2010-11). Discounts: 33%. 64-320pp. Simultaneous submissions accepted: no. Publishes 2% of manuscripts submitted. Payment: Royalties paid annually on individual collections. Subjects: Haiku, Poetry.

SNOW MONKEY, Kathryn Rantala, John Burgess, www.ravennapress.com/snowmonkey, snowmonkey.editor@comcast.net. 1999. Poetry. "We welcome original, unpublished submissions of poetry and micro-prose (500 word maximum).Please send your submissions as text-only in the body of your e-mail. Include your last name in the subject line." Online. Updated 10 times a year, September thru June. Pub'd 1 issue 2009; expects 1 issue 2010, 1 issue 2011. Reporting time: varies, try for no longer than 3 months. We accept simultaneous submissions if advised. Publishes 10-20% of manuscripts submitted. Copyrighted, reverts to author. Subjects: Avant-Garde, Experimental Art, Experimental, Haiku, Poetry, Prose, Translation, Washington (state).

SNOWY EGRET, Philip Repp, Editor; Karl Barnebey, Publisher, PO Box 9265, Terre Haute, IN 47808, www.snowyegret.net. 1922. Poetry, fiction, articles, art, interviews, satire, criticism, reviews, letters, parts-of-novels, long-poems, non-fiction. "Emphasis on natural history and human beings in relation to nature from literary, artistic, philosophical, and historical points of view. Prose generally not more than 3M words but will consider up to 10M; poetry generally less than page although long poems will be considered. Interested in works that celebrate the abundance and beauty of nature and examine the variety of ways, both positive and negative, through which human beings connect psychologically and spiritually with the natural world and living things. Looking for nature-oriented original graphics (offset prints, lithographs, woodcuts, etc) that can be editioned as part of an issue. Review copies of books desired. Originality of material or originality of treatment and literary quality and readability important. Payment on publication plus 2 contributor's copies. Recent contributors: Conrad Hilberry, David Abrams, James Armstrong, Justin D'Ath, Patricia Hooper. Send #10 SASE for writer's guidelines." circ. 500. 2/yr. Pub'd 2 issues 2009; expects 2 issues 2010, 2 issues 2011. 1 title listed in the *Small Press Record of Books in Print* (36th Edition, 2010-11). sub. price $15/1 year, $25/2 years; per copy $8; sample $8. Back issues: available on request. 56pp. Reporting time: 2 months. Simultaneous submissions accepted: yes. Publishes less than 5% of manuscripts submitted. Payment: prose, $2 mag page; poetry, $4/poem, $4 mag page. Copyrighted, reverts to author. Pub's reviews: none in 2009. §Review essays only. Ads: none. Subjects: Animals, Biology, Birds, Earth, Natural History, Fiction, Nature, Poetry.

SNREVIEW, Conlin Joseph, 197 Fairchild Ave., Fairfield, CT 06825-4856, 203 366-5991. 1999. Poetry, fiction, non-fiction. "Authors must submit via e-mail: editor@snreview.org. Label the e-mail: SUB: Name of Story. In the case of poetry, put SUB: Poetry in the subject line. You may include a cover letter, but it is unnecessary. Do not include attachments (we will not open them). If your e-mail service will not allocate enough space for an entire story (many services will not transmit e-mail with more than 5000 words), break the story into two parts and send part one and part two in two separate e-mails. You will hear from us within eight weeks. We will respond to your e-mail address. (Therefore use an email address at which we can locate you three months from the day you send it.) Should we accept your submission, we will ask for a biography of less than 200 words, which should include the citations of previous published works.Guidelines are simple:Short stories should be less than 7000 words. Be original. Catch our attention with your characters, plot, theme, style of writing, imagery, and point of view. No romance, mystery, science fiction, fantasy, or horror genre fiction. Not interested in short stories that start or end with a scene that includes an alarm clock ringing.'' circ. 50,000 page views per issue. 4/yr. Pub'd 4 issues 2009; expects 4 issues 2010, 4 issues 2011. sub. price 60; per copy 15; sample $15. Back issues: 15. 200pp. Reporting time: Six to eight months. Simultaneous submissions accepted: Yes. Publishes 20% of manuscripts submitted. Payment: None. Copyrighted, reverts to author. Subjects: Creative Non-fiction, Essays, Fiction, Literary Review, Literature (General), Non-Fiction, Poetry.

•**SNReview,** editor@snreview.org. ''SNReview is a quarterly literary e-zine created for writers of non-genre fiction, non-fiction, and poetry. It is edited and published by Joseph Conlin. Short stories should be less than 7000 words. Be original. Catch our attention with your characters, plot, theme, style of writing, imagery, and point of view. No romance, mystery, science fiction, fantasy, or horror genre fiction.''

SO TO SPEAK: A Feminist Journal of Language & Art, Jen Daniels, Editor; Alison Strub, Managing Editor; Suzanne DeSaix, Art Editor; Lisa Hill Corley, Fiction Editor; Warren Ciabattoni, Nonfiction Editor; Ellie Tipton, Poetry Editor, So To Speak, George Mason University, 4400 University Drive, MS 2D6, Fairfax, VA 22030-4444, sts@gmu.edu, www.gmu.edu/sts. 1991. Poetry, fiction, art, photos, interviews, reviews, long-poems, plays, non-fiction. ''*So to Speak* aims to feature work that addresses issues of significance to women's lives and movements for women's equality. We are especially interested in pieces that explore issues of race, class, and sexuality in relation to gender. We publish work by emerging and established writers that lives up to a high standard of language, form, and meaning. *So to Speak* offers annual Poetry, Fiction, and Nonfiction Contests (see our website for details).'' circ. 1.3M. 2/yr. Pub'd 2 issues 2009; expects 2 issues 2010, 2 issues 2011. sub. price $12; per copy $7; sample $7. Back issues: $3. 100pp. Reporting time: 3-4 months. Simultaneous submissions accepted: yes. Publishes 10% of manuscripts submitted. Payment: 2 copies. Copyrighted, reverts to author. Ads: $50/$25-negotiable, also exchange ads. Subjects: Arts, Book Reviewing, Creativity, Feminism, Fiction, Interviews, Lesbianism, Multicultural, Non-Fiction, Photography, Poetry, Visual Arts, Women, Writers/Writing.

SO YOUNG!, Anti-Aging Press, Julia M. Busch, PO Box 142174, Coral Gables, FL 33114, 305-662-3928, Fax 305-661-4123. 1996. Poetry, articles, reviews, letters, news items, non-fiction. ''Positive, very up-paced. 200-500 words. Aromatherapy, cosmetics, acupressure, short subjects also, short *up* poetry. Recent contributors: Nancy Dahlberg, Joe Polansky, astrologers, experts in fields, Phil Breman investigative reporter. Milton Feher, Relaxation/Dance, therapist, Lisa Curtis, president Sophrological Society.'' 4/yr. Pub'd 6 issues 2009; expects 4 issues 2010, 4 issues 2011. sub. price $35 USA, Canada; per copy $9 USA, Canada; sample same. Back issues: $6 before issue #45, #45 and after $9. Discounts: 25-49 20%, 50-100 30%, 100-499 40%, 500-999 50%, 1000+ 55%. 12pp. Reporting time: 1 month. Simultaneous submissions accepted: yes. Payment: newsletter copies. Copyrighted, reverts to author. Pub's reviews: 30+ in 2009. §Anti-aging, positive thought, holistic health, spiritual, cutting-edge medical breakthrough. Subjects: Alcohol, Alcoholism, Conservation, Energy, Health, How-To, Humor, Men, Poetry, Safety, Self-Help, Senior Citizens, Singles, Spiritual, Tapes & Records, Women.

SOCIAL ANARCHISM: A Journal of Practice and Theory, Howard J. Ehrlich, 2743 Maryland Avenue, Baltimore, MD 21218, 410-243-6987. 1980. Fiction, articles, art, photos, cartoons, interviews, satire, criticism, reviews, letters, non-fiction. ''Essays should be between 1,000 and 15,000 words. Book reviews: 500-2,000 words. Recent contributors: Neala Schleuning, Kingsley Widmer, Brian Martin, Colin Ward, Elaine Leeder, Gaetano Piluso, David Bouchier, Murray Bookchin, Jane Myerding.'' circ. 1.2M. 2/yr. Pub'd 2 issues 2009; expects 2 issues 2010, 2 issues 2011. sub. price $16 for 4 issues; per copy $5; sample $5. Back issues: $5. Discounts: 40%. 96pp. Reporting time: 6 weeks. Payment: 3 copies. Not copyrighted. Pub's reviews: 40 in 2009. §Anarchism, feminism, ecology, radical arts and culture. Subjects: Anarchist, Community, Counter-Culture, Alternatives, Communes, Environment, Feminism, Non-Violence.

SOCIAL JUSTICE: A JOURNAL OF CRIME, CONFLICT, & WORLD ORDER, Global Options, Gregory Shank, PO Box 40601, San Francisco, CA 94140, 415-550-1703, socialjust@aol.com, www.socialjusticejournal.org. 1974. Poetry, articles, interviews, satire, reviews, letters, news items, non-fiction. ''Maximum length: 30 double-spaced ms pages, including footnotes. Recent authors: Edward Herman, Tony Platt, Samir Amin, Elaine Kim, Nancy Sheper-Hughes. A journal of progressive criminology, international law, human rights, and social conflicts.'' circ. 3M. 4/yr. Pub'd 4 issues 2009; expects 4 issues 2010, 4 issues 2011. sub. price $45 individual, $80 institution; per copy $12.95 individual, $20 institutions; sample $10. Back issues: same as single copy price or available from University Microfilms, Ann Arbor, MI. Discounts: agency 15%, trade discount to stores, distribution handled through De Boer, Ingram, Ubiquity. 180-200pp. Reporting time: 90 days. Simultaneous submissions accepted: no. Payment: none. Copyrighted, does not revert to author. Pub's reviews: 3 in 2009. §Criminology, international law, civil liberties, minority issues, pedagogy, women, human rights. Ads: $125/$75. Subjects: Book Reviewing, Civil Rights, Community, Crime, Drugs, Human Rights, Labor, Law, Prison, Race, Socialist, Society, Sociology, Third World, Minorities.

SOCIAL PROBLEMS, University of California Press, James Holstein, Editor; Stephen L. Franzois, Associate Editor, University of California Press, 2000 Center Street, Suite 303, Berkeley, CA 94704-1223, 510-643-7154. 1953. Articles, reviews, non-fiction. "Editorial address: P.O. Box 1881, Milwaukee WI, 53201-1881. Copyrighted by Society for the Study of Social Problems." circ. 3747. 4/yr. Pub'd 4 issues 2009; expects 4 issues 2010, 4 issues 2011. sub. price $136 (+ $20 air freight); per copy $36; sample free. Back issues: same as single copy price. Discounts: foreign subs. agent 10%, one-time order 10+ 30%, standing orders (bookstores): 1-99 40%, 100+ 50%. 160pp. Copyrighted, does not revert to author. Ads: $295/$220. Subjects: Society, Sociology.

SOCIOLOGICAL PERSPECTIVES, University of California Press, Peter M. Nardi, Editor, University of California Press, 2000 Center St., Suite 303, Berkeley, CA 94704-1223, 510-643-7154. 1957. Articles. "Editorial Address: Sociology Dept., Pitzer College, The Claremont Colleges, 1050 N. Mills Ave., Claremont, CA 91711. Copyrighted by the Pacific Sociological Association." circ. 1736. 4/yr. Pub'd 4 issues 2009; expects 4 issues 2010, 4 issues 2011. sub. price Inst. $251; per copy Inst. $67. Discounts: foreign subs. agents 10%, 10+ one-time orders 30%. 170pp. Copyrighted, does not revert to author. Ads: $295/$220. Subject: Sociology.

THE SOCIOLOGICAL QUARTERLY, University of California Press, Kevin Leicht, Editor; Beth Lyman, Managing Editor, University of California Press, 2000 Center St., Suite 303, Berkeley, CA 94704-1223, 510-643-7154. 1959. Articles. "Editorial address: Dept. of Sociology, Univ. of Iowa, W505 Seashore Hall, Iowa City, IA 52242. Copyrighted by the Midwest Sociological Society." circ. 2214. 4/yr. Pub'd 4 issues 2009; expects 4 issues 2010, 4 issues 2011. sub. price $75 indiv., $255 inst.; per copy $25 indiv., $67 inst.; sample same as single copy. Discounts: foreign subs. agents 10%, 10+ one-time orders 30%. 192pp. Copyrighted, does not revert to author. Ads: $295/$220. Subjects: Education, Psychology, Research, Social Work, Sociology.

Socratic Consulting Group, Jill Schatz, PO Box 70162, Rochester, MI 48307-0003. 2004. Fiction, non-fiction. "We are actively looking for outstanding educational titles within a defined marketing niche, through our non-fiction imprint The Socratic Press. Our fiction imprint The Black Boot Press is seeking gritty pulp in areas of crime, cyberpunk and spiritual horror." avg. press run 500. Expects 5 titles 2010, 9 titles 2011. 1 title listed in the *Small Press Record of Books in Print* (36th Edition, 2010-11). Discounts: 1+ copies 40%. 250-350pp. Reporting time: 3 Months. Simultaneous submissions accepted: Yes. Subjects: Education, Fiction, Inspirational, Libertarian, Non-Fiction, Occult, Philosophy, Self-Help, Spiritual, Zen.

Soft Skull Press, Richard Nash, Editorial Director, 2117 Fourth Street, Suite D, Berkeley, CA 94710, 212-673-2502, Fax 212-673-0787, sander@softskull.com, www.softskull.com. 1992. Poetry, fiction, art, photos, cartoons, satire, music, plays, news items, non-fiction. "Press recently acquired by Counterpoint will be publishing books ranging from Josh MacPhee and Favianna Rodriguez's illustrated documentary of political street art, and Jack Sargeant's definitive guide to underground trash cinema, to a memoir on creative resistance by Erick Lyle (a.k.a. Iggy Scam)." avg. press run 3M. Pub'd 10 titles 2009; expects 12 titles 2010, 18 titles 2011. No titles listed in the *Small Press Record of Books in Print* (36th Edition, 2010-11). Discounts: distributed wholesale for fundraisers, 55% for 10+ copies. 120pp. Reporting time: 3 weeks. Simultaneous submissions accepted: no. Publishes 3% of manuscripts submitted. Payment: advance negotiable (most under $1,000), 7/8/9% royalty per 5,000 sold. Copyrights for author. Subjects: Absurdist, African-American, AIDS, Anarchist, Artificial Intelligence, Avant-Garde, Experimental Art, Beat, Biotechnology, Bisexual, Business & Economics, Civil Rights, Communism, Marxism, Leninism, Counter-Culture, Alternatives, Communes, Culture, Zines.

Soho Press, Inc., Laura Hruska, Editor-in-Chief, 853 Broadway, New York, NY 10003, Tel: 212.260.1900, Fax: 212.260.1902. "Soho Press primarily publishes fiction, with the occasional autobiography or cultural historical account. Completed manuscripts should be 60,000 words or more. While many of our published works arrive here through agents, we place a high priority on publishing quality unsolicited materials from new writers. Though eager to accept a wide range of literary fiction, we are generally unenthusiastic about publishing formula fiction, young adult dramas, stock romances, juvenile literature, short story collections, cookbooks, how-to books, self-help, fantasy, and anything that might recommend itself as a "quick read." Further, we do not consider electronic submissions. A query letter accompanied by three chapters of a completed work (preferably the first three) and a brief outline of plot events should precede the submission of an entire manuscript. A cover letter listing previous publishing credits should be included with your work. We accept submissions year round." No titles listed in the *Small Press Record of Books in Print* (36th Edition, 2010-11).

456

SOJOURN: A Journal of the Arts, Diane McGurren, Editor; Jon Hart, Editor, School of Arts and Humanities, UT Dallas, Box 830688, JO 31, Richardson, TX 75083-0688, Email: sojourn@utdallas.edu Web site: http://sojourn.utdallas.edu. 1986. Poetry, fiction, art, photos, satire, parts-of-novels, long-poems, collages, plays, non-fiction. circ. 800. 1/yr. Pub'd 1 issue 2009; expects 1 issue 2010, 1 issue 2011. sub. price $10.00; per copy $10.00; sample $10.00. Back issues: $7.50 if available. 168pp. Reporting time: Annual deadline Dec. 1; reporting in late March, early April. Simultaneous submissions accepted: yes, but inform immediately upon publication elsewhere. Publishes 5% of manuscripts submitted. Payment: 1 copy. Copyrighted, reverts to author. Ads: yes-see website. Subjects: Arts, Creative Non-fiction, Drama, Experimental, Fiction, Non-Fiction, Photography, Poetry, Short Stories, Translation.

SOLO CAFE, Glenna Luschei, Founding Editor & Editor-in-Chief; Kevin Patrick Sullivan, Co-Editor; Elizabeth Carmo, Co-Editor, 5146 Foothill Road, Carpinteria, CA 93013, berrypress@aol.com. 2005. Poetry, criticism, reviews, long-poems. "Recent contributors include: Fred Chappell, Jane Hirshfield, Linda Pastan, Ronald Bayes, Forest Gander, Ron Koertge, Robert Creeley, Robert Bly and Poet Laureates Al Young and Ted Kooser." circ. 1M. 1/yr. Pub'd 2 issues 2009; expects 2 issues 2010, 2 issues 2011. sub. price $20/2 issues; per copy $12; sample $12. Back issues: $10 for old Solo and Cafe Solo. Discounts: tradition. 130pp. Reporting time: 1 month. Simultaneous submissions accepted: no. Publishes 75% of manuscripts submitted. Payment: copies. Copyrighted, rights reverting negotiable. Pub's reviews: 1 book of poetry review, 4 small book review(s) notes in 2009. §Poetry, criticism. Subjects: Criticism, Poetry.

SOLO FLYER, David B. McCoy, 1112 Minuteman Avenue NW, Massillon, OH 44646. 1979. Poetry. "Three or more 4-page flyers will be published a year, each by an individual author. For the near future, we will be publishing prose poetry only. Also, accepting only email submissions. dbmccoy@eudoramail.com." circ. 100. 3/yr. Pub'd 3 issues 2009; expects 3 issues 2010, 3 issues 2011. sample price free with SASE. 4pp. Reporting time: 1-3 months. Simultaneous submissions accepted: yes. Publishes 5-10% of manuscripts submitted. Payment: 20-25 copies. Copyrighted, reverts to author. Subject: Poetry.

$olvency International Inc., Publishing, Olga Favrow, PO Box 4433, Clearwater, FL 33758-4433, www.solvencyinternational.com, 727-447-3138 wk., 403-2130 cell, 461-5483 fx, : solvencyint@gmail.com. 1996. Fiction, non-fiction. Pub'd 3 titles 2009; expects 4 titles 2010, 5 titles 2011. 3 titles listed in the *Small Press Record of Books in Print* (36th Edition, 2010-11). Discounts: book trade 55%. 250pp. Reporting time: 60 days. Simultaneous submissions accepted: yes. Publishes 1% of manuscripts submitted. Payment: 10% of list price. Copyrights for author. Subjects: Fiction, Non-Fiction.

SOM Publishing, division of School of Metaphysics (see also THRESHOLDS JOURNAL), Dr. Barbara Condron, CEO & Editor-in-Chief, 163 Moon Valley Road, Windyville, MO 65783, 417-345-8411, www.som.org. 1973. "Educational, inspirational, uplifting books designed to raise the consciousness of humanity." avg. press run 5M. Pub'd 1 title 2009; expects 4 titles 2010, 4 titles 2011. 25 titles listed in the *Small Press Record of Books in Print* (36th Edition, 2010-11). Discounts: 40% trade, 50% jobbers, 20% organizations, churches, groups without sales tax number. 180-224pp. Payment: none. SOM holds copyright. Subjects: Dreams, Health, How-To, Metaphysics, New Age, Science Fiction, Spiritual.

SONG OF THE SAN JOAQUIN, Cleo Griffith, PO Box 1161, Modesto, CA 95353-1161, (209) 543-1776, cleor36@yahoo.com. 2003. Poetry. "We concentrate on the lifestyles pertinent to the California Central Valley, but publish poets from all over the United States. Geographical references must be of the valley, but other poetry needs only to be representative of the human condition. No vulgarity, rants, sexism. Recent contributors include Ed Bearden, Carol Frith, Lyn Lifshin, Joyce Odam, Fredrick Zydek." circ. 60. 4/yr. Pub'd 4 issues 2009; expects 4 issues 2010, 4 issues 2011. sub. price $18; per copy $5.00; sample $5.00. Back issues: inquire. Discounts: 5 copies free. 44pp. Reporting time: up to three months. Simultaneous submissions accepted: No. Publishes 40% of manuscripts submitted. Payment: One copy. Not copyrighted. Ads: none. Subjects: Aging, Agriculture, Americana, Animals, Birds, California, Creativity, Culture, Environment, Indians, Native American, Nature, Poetry, Relationships, Wildlife.

SONGS OF INNOCENCE, Pendragonian Publications, Michael Pendragon, Editor & Publisher, PO Box 719, New York, NY 10101-0719, mmpendragon@aol.com. 1999. Poetry, fiction, articles, art, interviews, criticism, reviews, letters, long-poems, non-fiction. "Poetry, short stories (3,500 word maximum), essays and b/w artwork which celebrate the nobler aspects of mankind and the human experience. Rhymed, metered, lyrical verse preferred. Publishes literary poetry and prose in the tradition of Blake, Shelley, Keats, Whitman, Emerson, Wordsworth, Thoreau and Twain." circ. 200. 1-2/yr. Pub'd 2 issues 2009; expects 2 issues 2010, 2 issues 2011. sub. price $25/3 issues; per copy $10; sample $10. Back issues: $5. 150+pp. Reporting time: up to 1 year. Simultaneous submissions accepted: yes. Publishes 5% of manuscripts submitted. Payment: 1 copy. Not copyrighted. Pub's reviews: 25 in 2009. §Romantic poetry, the Bardic tradition, prophetic verse. Subjects: Essays, Fantasy, Fiction, Literary Review, Literature (General), Myth, Mythology, Poetry, Reviews, Short Stories.

SONORA REVIEW, PR Griffis, Co-Editor-in-Chief; Amy Knight, Co-Editor-in-Chief, Dept. of English, University of Arizona, Tucson, AZ 85721, 520-624-9192. 1980. Poetry, fiction, articles, interviews, satire, criticism, reviews, letters, parts-of-novels, non-fiction. "We publish poetry, fiction, and creative non-fiction, as well as interviews and book reviews. Submissions should be accompanied by an SASE. Editors change every year. Please address work to the appropriate genre editor: Fiction, Poetry, etc. Business or subscription matters and any questions or forms should be addressed to the Managing Editor. Revisions only upon editorial request. Simultaneous submissions accepted." circ. 800. 2/yr. Pub'd 2 issues 2009; expects 2 issues 2010, 2 issues 2011. sub. price $16; per copy $8; sample $6. Discounts: 40% to bookstores. 120pp. Reporting time: 3-6 months. Simultaneous submissions accepted: yes. Publishes 1% of manuscripts submitted. Payment: 2 contributor's copies. Copyrighted, reverts to author. Pub's reviews: 2 in 2009. Ads: $90/$45. Subject: Literary Review.

Sonoran Publishing, George A. Fathauer, 6503 W. Frye Rd, Suite 3, Chandler, AZ 85226-3337, 480-961-5176. 1994. Art, non-fiction. "Books on history of radio and electronics, for historians and collectors of radios. Purchased existing inventory and publishing rights to several titles from another publisher." avg. press run 3M. Pub'd 1 title 2009; expects 2 titles 2010, 1 title 2011. 10 titles listed in the *Small Press Record of Books in Print* (36th Edition, 2010-11). Discounts: 6-24 copies 40%, 25-49 copies 42%, 50-99 44%, 100+ 46%. 250pp. Reporting time: 60 days. Simultaneous submissions accepted: yes. Publishes 20% of manuscripts submitted. Payment: usually 10% royalty. Does not copyright for author. Subjects: Antiques, Collectibles, Electronics, History, Radio.

Soto Publishing Company, Pedro Soto, P.O. Box 10, Dade City, FL 33526, 352-567-5256 (fax 7279), www.sotopublishingcompany.com. 2008. Fiction, art, photos, non-fiction. "Soto Publishing is a small independent trade publishing company located in the rolling hills of west central Florida. Our main focus is young adult and children's literature. We seek to provide high quality works that capture and inspire the mind and imagination of young readers. It's our goal to help you reap the benefits of your creativity. If your manuscript is selected, we finance your book and you share equally in the financial rewards." avg. press run 2500. Pub'd 3 titles 2009; expects 8 titles 2010, 6-8 titles 2011. 7 titles listed in the *Small Press Record of Books in Print* (36th Edition, 2010-11). Discounts: 35-50% to Distributors; 35-40% to bookstores and retailers, min 10 copies; 10%+ to Institutions and Classrooms; Others, on a per case basis... 200pp. Reporting time: 3-6 months. Simultaneous submissions accepted: Yes. Publishes less than 1% of manuscripts submitted. Payment: 50/50 split on royalties; Rights released to Publisher; Publisher provides all services: in-house editing, illustrations, book design/layout, copyrights (authors name); printing and marketing... Copyrights for author. Subjects: Autobiography, Biology, Education, Family, Fiction, Humor, Medicine, Non-Fiction, Parenting, Picture Books, Science Fiction, Self-Help, Short Stories, Women, Young Adult.

SOUL, Soul, Aisha Johnson, 806 8th Street Thomas, Birmingham, AL 35214, Soul@delimaehowar.org. 2006. Poetry, fiction, long-poems, non-fiction. circ. 500. 1000/yr. Expects 2 issues 2011. sub. price 20.00; per copy 10.00; sample 10.00. Back issues: inquire. Discounts: 5 copies of 10% off. 125pp. Reporting time: varies. Simultaneous submissions accepted: No. Publishes 25% of manuscripts submitted. Payment: varies. Copyrighted. Ads: 25.00 half50.00 whole page.

Soul Care Publishing, 106-6198 Kathleen Ave., Burnaby, BC V5H257, Canada. No titles listed in the *Small Press Record of Books in Print* (36th Edition, 2010-11).

•**Soul Inscriptions Press,** Toronto, Ontario, Canada, www.SoulInscriptionsPress.com, info@soulinscriptions-press.com. "Soul Inscriptions Press recognizes the power of the arts to help people express themselves, become empowered, and heal. Our books feature poems, short stories, songs, and personal essays by individuals who have discovered this gift through writing and desire to share this special part of themselves with others. These people come from diverse populations and have much to offer the world. However, they haven't always been given a fair chance to be heard because of personal challenges they have faced along with others' preconceived notions about where they come from, their circumstances, how they look, and/or whether they deserve an equal chance at a normal life. In finding their voice and sharing their writings through our books, they are able to connect with each other as well as to the readers, igniting sparks of inspiration, understanding, education, and healing. It is our hope that, over time, the ripples formed by their words will continue to flow outward, uniting others through movements toward positive changes in themselves and the world around them." 1 title listed in the *Small Press Record of Books in Print* (36th Edition, 2010-11).

•**Soulstice Media,** Kayse Gehret, P.O. Box 2436, Sausalito, CA 94965, 415.331.2895. 2009. 1 title listed in the *Small Press Record of Books in Print* (36th Edition, 2010-11).

•**Sound Enterprises Publishing,** Richard Zerbey, 970 Cornwallis Drive, West Chester, PA 19380, 610-696-1715, richzerbey@zerbey.com , www.soundenterprisespublishing.com , hell-thscare.com. 1985. Non-fiction. "Our current interest is in the healthcare profession." Expects 1 title 2011. No titles listed in the *Small Press Record of Books in Print* (36th Edition, 2010-11). Discounts: 25-55%. 128pp. Reporting time: 1 week. Simultaneous submissions accepted: Yes. Payment: on a per project basis. Copyrights for author.

Subjects: Aging, Death & Dying, Disease, Health, Music, Nursing, Politics, Senior Citizens.

Sound View Publishing, Inc., James Green, P.O. Box 696, Shoreham, NY 11786-0696, 631-899-2481, Fax 631-899-2487, 1-888-529-3496, info@SoundViewPublishing.com, www.SoundViewPublishing.com. 2003. Non-fiction. "We deal in Self Help books designed to serve as platforms for speakers." avg. press run 3000. Expects 1 title 2010, 1 title 2011. No titles listed in the *Small Press Record of Books in Print* (36th Edition, 2010-11). Discounts: Distributors/Wholesalers—55%.Institutions/Classrooms—40%.Retail Bookstores—2-4 20%, 5-99 40%, 100+ 50%.Libraries—3 or more 20%.Outside Sales—3 or more 20%, even case lots 40%. 280pp. Reporting time: We do not take unsolicited manuscripts. Simultaneous submissions accepted: No. Publishes 0% of manuscripts submitted. Does not copyright for author. Subjects: Inspirational, Non-Fiction, Self-Help.

Soundboard Books, 933 Exmoor Way, Sunnyvale, CA 94087, 408-738-1705, sboardbooks@sbcglobal.net. 1990. Non-fiction. avg. press run 2M. Expects 1 title 2010, 1 title 2011. 3 titles listed in the *Small Press Record of Books in Print* (36th Edition, 2010-11). Discounts: 2-15 20%, 16+ 40%. 48pp. Copyrights for author. Subject: Biography.

SOUNDINGS EAST, Rod Kessler, Advisory Editor; James Connatser, Editor, English Dept., Salem State College, 352 Lafayette St., Salem, MA 01970, 978-542-6205. 1973. Poetry, fiction, non-fiction. "Publishes poetry, fiction and creative non-fiction. We read Sept. 1-Feb. 15." circ. 1.5M. 1/yr. Pub'd 1 issue 2009; expects 1 issue 2010, 1 issue 2011. sub. price $10; per copy $5; sample $3. Back issues: usually $3 per copy. 80pp. Reporting time: 2-3 months. Simultaneous submissions accepted: yes. Publishes 5% of manuscripts submitted. Not copyrighted. Subjects: Fiction, Poetry.

SOUNDINGS REVIEW, Marian Blue, P.O. BOX 639, Freeland, WA 98249, 360-331-6719, soundings@whidbey.com, www.writeonwhidbey.org/Publications. 2008. Poetry, fiction, articles, art, photos, cartoons, interviews, satire, letters, long-poems, plays, concrete art, non-fiction. "Open to different styles and voices, Soundings Review is passionate about accessibility and depth, stories that make an impression on the first read, and with subsequent readings continue to elicit thought and understanding. We want readers to be as diverse as the writers we publish; we include new writers, including some students, and are open to genre bending work." circ. 400. 2/yr. Expects 1 issue 2010, 2 issues 2011. sub. price $12.50; per copy $6.50; sample $6.50. Back issues: inquire. Discounts: 15 or more copies $20%. 80pp. Reporting time: 8 - 10 weeks. Simultaneous submissions accepted: Yes. Publishes 20% of manuscripts submitted. Payment: 2 copies. Stipends as budget allows. Copyrighted, reverts to author. Ads: $300 full page/ $175 1/2 page/$125 1/3 page/$80 1/4 page. Subjects: Absurdist, Creative Non-fiction, Experimental, Family, Fantasy, Fiction, Humor, Mystery, Nature, Pacific Region, Post Modern, Prose, Science Fiction, Short Stories, Surrealism.

Sourcebooks, Inc., Mark Warda, Todd Stocke, 1935 Brookdale Road, Ste. 139, Naperville, IL 60563, 630-961-3900; Fax 630-961-2168. 1987. Non-fiction. "Shipping Address: 1725 Clearwater/Largo Rd. S., Clearwater, FL 33756. Also publish under the imprint of Sphinx Publishing." Pub'd 15 titles 2009; expects 65 titles 2010, 65 titles 2011. 111 titles listed in the *Small Press Record of Books in Print* (36th Edition, 2010-11). 130pp. Reporting time: 3 months. Copyrights for author. Subjects: Business & Economics, How-To, Law, Real Estate.

Sources (see also THE SOURCES HOTLINK), Ulli Diemer, 489 College Street, Suite 305, Toronto ON M6G 1A5, Canada, Phone: 416-964-7799. Fax: 416-964-8763. 1977. Articles, reviews, news items, non-fiction. "We publish materials related to journalism, media, media criticism, research, skepticism, propaganda, public relations, public speaking, communications.Recent contributors include Dean Tudor, Lynn Fenske, Allan Bonner, Ann Douglas, Cathleen Fillmore, Mark LaVigne, Barbara Florio Graham, Ulli Diemer, Steve Slaunwhite, Peter Urs Bender, Barrie Zwicker." avg. press run 3000. Pub'd 5 titles 2009; expects 6 titles 2010, 6 titles 2011. 3 titles listed in the *Small Press Record of Books in Print* (36th Edition, 2010-11). Discounts: Distributors 50%Retailers & Bookstores 40%Insitutions & classrooms - negotiated. 280pp. Reporting time: 1 month. Simultaneous submissions accepted: Yes. Publishes 50% of manuscripts submitted. Payment: Royalty varies per title. No advances. Payments quarterly. Copyrights for author. Subjects: Awards, Foundations, Grants, Canada, Communication, Journalism, Marketing, Media, Public Relations/Publicity, Reference.

THE SOURCES HOTLINK, Sources, Ulli Diemer, 489 College Street, Suite 305, Toronto ON M6G 1A5, Canada, Phone: 416-964-7799. Fax: 416-964-8763. 1996. Articles, interviews, reviews, news items, non-fiction. "Articles, interviews, case studies, reviews, personal experiences related to media relations, public relations, and getting publicity." circ. 1200. 4/yr. Pub'd 4 issues 2009; expects 4 issues 2010, 4 issues 2011. sub. price $20; per copy $5; sample $2. Back issues: inquire. 8pp. Reporting time: 1 month. Simultaneous submissions accepted: Yes. Publishes 70% of manuscripts submitted. Copyrighted, reverts to author. Pub's reviews: 12 in 2009. §Books, periodicals and Web sites related to media, public relations, communications, self-promotion, public speaking, publicity. Ads: Full page $6752/3 page $5401/2 page $4351/3 page $3501/4 page $2901/6 page $195. Subjects: Advertising, Self-Promotion, Communication, Journalism, Internet, Media, Public

Relations/Publicity, Reviews.

SOUTH CAROLINA REVIEW, Wayne Chapman, Editor, Ctr. for Electronic & Digital Publishing, Clemson University, 611 Strode Tower, Box 340522, Clemson, SC 29634-0522, 864-656-3151; 864-656-5399. 1968. Poetry, fiction, articles, interviews, satire, criticism, reviews, non-fiction. "Past contributors: Steve Almond, Alberto Rios, Jane Marcus, George Will, Mary Gordon, Tim O'Brien, Richard Rodriguez, Christopher Dickey." circ. 500. 2/yr. Pub'd 2 issues 2009. sub. price $22 + $3 s/h; per copy $15; sample $15. Back issues: $15. 192-256pp. Reporting time: 4-9 weeks. Simultaneous submissions accepted: no. Payment: copies. Copyrighted. Pub's reviews: 18 in 2009. §Poetry, literary history, criticism, contemporary fiction. Subjects: Fiction, Poetry.

SOUTH DAKOTA REVIEW, Brian Bedard, Editor, Department of English / University of South Dakota, 414 East Clark St., Vermillion, SD 57069, 605-677-5184, 605-677-5966, email: sdreview@usd.edu, website: http://www.usd.edu/sdreview. 1963. Poetry, fiction, articles, interviews, criticism, parts-of-novels, non-fiction. "Issues vary in content; not every type of material will be in each issue. Still committed to Western subjects and focuses as primary interest, though all regions considered if awareness of natural world is reflected." circ. 500. 4/yr. Pub'd 4 issues 2009; expects 4 issues 2010, 4 issues 2011. sub. price $30, $45/2 years; international: $38, $61/2 years; per copy $10; sample $5. Back issues: $8 single / $12 double (if available). Discounts: 40% to bookstores. 120-150pp. Reporting time: 8-10 weeks, except during summer. Simultaneous submissions accepted: yes, as long as noted on cover letter. Publishes 1%-3% of manuscripts submitted. Payment: 2 copies plus 1 year subscription. We reserve first and reprint rights, all others revert to writer upon publication. Ads: none. Subjects: Biography, Criticism, Essays, Fiction, Great Plains, Literature (General), Midwest, Native American, Nature, Non-Fiction, Poetry, Short Stories, Southwest, The West.

South End Press, Jocelyn Burrell, Alexander Dwinell, Asha Tall, Alex Straaik, Medgar Evers College, 1650 Bedford Ave, Brooklyn, NY 11225, email: southend@southendpress.org. 1977. Criticism, non-fiction. "At South End Press—a POC majority, collectively managed, independent publisher of nonfiction—we provide books to encourage critical thinking and constructive action, thereby helping to create fundamental social change. Since 1977, we have released over 200 titles addressing the key issues of the day, focusing on political, economic, cultural, gender, race, and ecological dimensions of life in the United States and the world." Average press run 3500-7000. Pub'd 6 titles 2009; expects 8 titles 2010, 8 titles 2011. 89 titles listed in the *Small Press Record of Books in Print* (36th Edition, 2010-11). Discounts: bookstores 20-50%. 250pp. Reporting time: 3 months, no calls please. Simultaneous submissions accepted: yes. Publishes 1-5% of manuscripts submitted. Payment: 11% of discount price. Copyrights for author. Subjects: African-American, Anarchist, Asian-American, Environment, Feminism, Gender Issues, Labor, Latino, Media, Middle East, Native American, Peace, Politics, Race, Social Movements.

•SOUTH LOOP REVIEW, ReLynn Hansen, Editor, Columbia College Chicago, English Dept., 600 South Michigan Avenue, Chicago, IL 60605, 312-369-8106 or 312-369-8212. "South Loop Review: Creative Nonfiction + Art is a magazine publishing nonfiction in lyric and narrative forms. We give greater emphasis to non-linear work, including blended genres. We look for personal essays and memoir with fresh voices and new takes on presentation and form. As well, we look for narrative photography and art that blends image and word."

Southeast Missouri State University Press (see also BIG MUDDY: Journal of the Mississippi River Valley), Susan Swartwout, MS 2650, One University Plaza, Cape Girardeau, MO 63701, (573) 651-2044, fax (573)651-5188, upress@semo.edu, www6.semo.edu/universitypress. 2002. Poetry, fiction, articles, art, photos, interviews, reviews, news items, non-fiction. "We don't publish children's literature, romance, westerns. We do have a special fondness for material from or about the Mississippi River Valley, but have and will publish good literature outside that focus. Recent authors include Morley Swingle, Alan Terry Wright, Joanna Beth Tweedy, and Tom Cushman." avg. press run 2500. Pub'd 4 titles 2009; expects 4 titles 2010, 4 titles 2011. No titles listed in the *Small Press Record of Books in Print* (36th Edition, 2010-11). Discounts: Distributors 55%Bookstores 40%Classrooms 40%. 300pp. Reporting time: book manuscript: 6 - 9 months. Simultaneous submissions accepted: Yes. Publishes 8% of manuscripts submitted. Payment: We pay royalties. Copyrights for author. Subjects: African-American, Americana, Biography, Civil Rights, Civil War, Essays, Fiction, History, Kentucky, Multicultural, Non-Fiction, Novels, Poetry, Reviews, Short Stories.

THE SOUTHEAST REVIEW, Katie Cortese, Editor, Department of English, Florida State University, Tallahassee, FL 32306. 1979. "The mission of *The Southeast Review* is to present emerging writers on the same stage as well-established ones. In each semi-annual issue, we publish literary fiction, creative nonfiction, poetry, interviews, book reviews and art. With nearly sixty members on our editorial staff who come from throughout the country and the world, we strive to publish work that is representative of our diverse interests and aesthetics, and we celebrate the eclectic mix this produces." 2/yr. sub. price $15; per copy $8; sample $6. Reporting time: 2-4 months. Simultaneous submissions accepted: Yes. Payment: 2 contributor copies. Pub's reviews: 10 in 2009. §fiction, poetry, essays, and creative nonfiction.

SOUTHERN CALIFORNIA REVIEW, Annlee Ellingson, Editor-in-Chief, Master of Professional Writing Program, 3501 Trousdale Parkw, University of Southern California, Los Angeles, CA 90089-0355, 213-740-3253. 1983. Poetry, fiction, parts-of-novels, long-poems, plays, non-fiction. "The editors encourage submissions from new and emerging writers while continuing to publish established writers. Fiction: We accept short shorts but rarely use stories more than 8,000 words. Novel excerpts are acceptable if they can stand alone. We do consider genre work (horror, mystery, romance, sci-fi) if it transcends the boundaries of the genre. Poetry: We accept poems in traditional and experimental styles. Nonfiction: We accept memoir, personal essay, and creative nonfiction. Stageplays: We occasionally publish one-act plays or scenes. Please format according to the standard unpublished playwriting format. Screenplays: We occasionally publish short films or scenes. Please format according to the standard unpublished screenwriting format. Format for all submissions: All manuscripts must be typed (double-spaced for fiction and nonfiction; poetry may be single-spaced). Print on standard-size white paper and staple. Address your envelope to the proper editor (Fiction, Poetry, etc.). Please include a cover letter. Be sure your full name and contact information (address, phone, and email) appear on the first page of the manuscript. No electronic or email submissions are accepted. Every submission MUST include a self-addressed stamped envelope (SASE). Do not send more than one piece at a time. Up to three poems are accepted simultaneously. Please wait until we have responded to your first piece before sending another. Query letters are unnecessary. Please send the entire manuscript. We accept simultaneous submissions, but please note this in the cover letter and notify us immediately if your submission is accepted for publication elsewhere. We consider only previously unpublished work. Payment upon publication is two copies of the issue containing your work. Author retains copyright. Author is asked to cite appearance in Southern California Review when the work is published elsewhere." circ. 1,000. 2/yr. Expects 2 issues 2010, 2 issues 2011. sub. price $20; per copy $10. 140pp. Reporting time: 3 to 6 months. Simultaneous submissions accepted: yes. Payment: 2 copies. Copyrighted, reverts to author. Subjects: Fiction, Non-Fiction, Poetry.

SOUTHERN HUMANITIES REVIEW, Dan R. Latimer, Co-Editor; Chantel Acevedo, Co-Editor, 9088 Haley Center, Auburn University, AL 36849, 334-844-9088, www.auburn.edu/shr. 1967. Poetry, fiction, articles, interviews, satire, criticism, reviews, parts-of-novels, non-fiction. "No e-mail submissions. Recent contributors: Roald Hoffmann, Juliana Gray, Kathleen Rooney, Wayne Flynt, Richard Dokey, Kate Krautkramer." circ. 700. 4/yr. Pub'd 4 issues 2009; expects 4 issues 2010, 4 issues 2011. sub. price $15 U.S., $20 foreign; per copy $5 U.S.; $7 foreign; sample $5 U.S.; $7 foreign. Back issues: same as single copy price/or complete volumes, $15 US $20 foreign. Discounts: none. 100pp. Reporting time: 1-3 months. Simultaneous submissions accepted: no. Publishes poetry 2%, fiction 1%, essays 12% of manuscripts submitted. Payment: $100 best essay, $100 best story, $50 best poem *published* each volume. Copyrighted, reverts to author. Pub's reviews: 27 in 2009. §Criticism, fiction, poetry. Ads: $100 inside back cover, full page only, arranged well in advance. Subjects: Book Reviewing, Criticism, Fiction, Literary Review, Poetry.

Southern Illinois University Press, John Stetter, 1915 University Press Drive #MC6806, Carbondale, IL 62901-4323, 618-453-6615 (phone) 618-453-1221 (FAX). 1955. Poetry, non-fiction. "SIU Press publishes books in rhetoric and composition, poetry, Civil War and regional history, film studies, theater studies, criminology, aviation, and related fields. All poetry should be submitted to Allison Joseph, Editor, The Crab Orchard Review, English Dept. Southern Illinois University, Carbondale, IL 62902. Please query Dr. Joseph before submitting poetry manuscripts. As a scholarly publisher SIU Press follows the standard external peer review process for all manuscripts." avg. press run 800. Pub'd 50 titles 2009; expects 56 titles 2010, 58 titles 2011. No titles listed in the *Small Press Record of Books in Print* (36th Edition, 2010-11). Discounts: Standard trade discounts apply. 300-500pp. Reporting time: 2 - 4 months. Simultaneous submissions accepted: No. Payment: Depends on the kind of book submitted. We will copyright in the name of the author on request, otherwise in the name of the university. Subjects: African-American, Audio/Video, Aviation, Botany, Crime, Great Plains, History, Illinois, Jack Kerouac, Movies, Nature, Non-Fiction, Performing Arts, Scandinavia.

SOUTHERN INDIANA REVIEW, Ron Mitchell, Editor, College of Liberal Arts, Univ. of Southern Indiana, 8600 University Blvd., Evansville, IN 47712, 812-461-5202, Fax 812-465-7152, email sir@usi.edu. 1994. Poetry, fiction, articles, art, photos, interviews, criticism, reviews, letters, parts-of-novels, long-poems, plays, non-fiction. circ. 1000. 2/yr. Pub'd 2 issues 2009; expects 2 issues 2010, 2 issues 2011. sub. price $16; per copy $10; sample $10. Back issues: $6. 150pp. Reporting time: 2 months. Simultaneous submissions accepted: yes. Publishes 10% of manuscripts submitted. Payment: 2 copies of magazine. Copyrighted, reverts to author. Pub's reviews: 6 in 2009. §Midwestern themes.

Southern Methodist University Press, Kathryn Lang, PO Box 750415, Dallas, TX 75275-0415, 214-768-1433, 214-768-1428 (fax), 800-826-8911 (orders), klang@mail.smu.edu, www.tamu.edu/upress. 1937. Fiction, non-fiction. "The SMU Press is known nationally as a publisher of books of the highest quality for the "educated general reader." We publish 10-12 titles a year in the areas of creative nonfiction, ethics and human values, literary fiction, medical humanities, performing arts, Southwestern studies, and sport. June, 2010: Operations have been temporarily suspended until Fall, 2010." avg. press run 1500-2500. Pub'd 7 titles 2009; expects 7 titles 2010, 8 titles 2011. No titles listed in the *Small Press Record of Books in Print* (36th Edition,

2010-11). Discounts: Wholesale discounts (returnable accounts): 1 or more copies 50%.Wholesale discounts (non-returnable accounts): 1 or more 55%.Retail discounts (returnable accounts): 1 or more copies 45%.Retail discounts (non-returnable accounts): 50%. 288pp. Reporting time: 6-8 months. Simultaneous submissions accepted: Yes. Publishes 10% of manuscripts submitted. Payment: 10% net royalties; $500 advance; annual payment. Copyrights for author. Subjects: Medicine, Non-Fiction, Novels, Short Stories, Southwest, Sports, Outdoors, Texas.

SOUTHERN POETRY REVIEW, Robert Parham, Editor; James Smith, Associate Editor, Dept. of LLP, Armstrong Atlantic State University, 11935 Abercorn Street, Savannah, GA 31419-1997, 912-344-3196, Fax 912-344-3494, James.Smith@armstrong.edu, www.spr.armstrong.edu. 1958. Poetry. "No restrictions on form, style, or content. SASE required." 2/yr. Pub'd 2 issues 2009; expects 2 issues 2010, 2 issues 2011. sub. price $14, individual; $17, institutional; per copy $7; sample $7. Back issues: $7. 80pp. Reporting time: 6-8 weeks. Simultaneous submissions accepted: Yes, but please indicate. Publishes 5% of manuscripts submitted. Payment: publication; 2 contributor copies. SPR retains right to reprint work on its Web site, in a special issue of the journal, in an anthology or other book project. Ads: Exchange ads with other journals. Subject: Poetry.

THE SOUTHERN QUARTERLY: A Journal of the Arts in the South, Douglas Chambers, Editor; Ann Branton, Managing Editor, 118 College Drive #5078, The University of Southern Mississippi, Hattiesburg, MS 39406-5078, 601-266-4350, Fax 601-266-6033, www.usm.edu/soq. 1962. Articles, art, photos, interviews, criticism, reviews, music, letters. "We are commited to the interdisciplinary study of southern culture through reasoned consideration of the arts. We define "the arts" broadly to include literature, poetry, folklore, anthropology and history, as well as the traditional arts. Likewise, we take an expansive view of "the South" to incorporate the circum-Caribbean. We will continue to publish articles based on original research or new critical analysis, and will seek to address the wide range of interests of our audience. We are continuing the annual "Bibliography of the Visual Arts and Architecture in the South," and will feature more extensive reviews of recent books and films. The *Quarterly* encourages submissions from all disciplines, though you will see a slight shift in emphasis from literature to history. Inquiries and manuscripts should be addressed to *The Southern Quarterly* at the above address." circ. 650. 4/yr. Expects 4 issues 2010, 4 issues 2011. sub. price $25/yr individual; $35/yr institutions, add $15 for international mailing; per copy $18. includes shipping and handling; sample upon request. Back issues: vary, price list available. Discounts: subscription agency $20/individual subscriptions; $30 institutional subscriptions, add $15 for int'l mailing. 200pp. Reporting time: 3-5 months. Simultaneous submissions accepted: no. Payment: 2 copies of journal and 1 yr. subscription. Copyrighted, does not revert to author. Pub's reviews. §Studies of the arts in the South: literature, history, music, art, architecture, popular and folk arts, theatre and dance. Ads: 100/$100 or exchange free. Subjects: African-American, Anthropology, Archaelogy, Architecture, Arts, Book Reviewing, Criticism, Folklore, History, Interviews, Music, Performing Arts, Photography, South, Theatre, Visual Arts.

THE SOUTHERN REVIEW, Bret Lott, Editor, Old Presidents' House, Louisiana State University, Baton Rouge, LA 70803-5005, 225-578-5108. 1965 new series (1935 original series). Poetry, fiction, articles, art, photos, interviews, criticism, reviews, letters, parts-of-novels, non-fiction. "We emphasize craftsmanship and intellectual content. We favor articles on contemporary literature and on the history and culture of the South. Recent contributors: Lewis P. Simpson, W.D. Snodgrass, Seamus Heaney, Reynolds Price, Lee Smith, Mary Oliver, Medbh McGuckian, Eavan Boland, Andrea Barrett, Ann Beattie, and B.H. Fairchild." circ. 3.1M. 4/yr. Pub'd 4 issues 2009; expects 4 issues 2010, 4 issues 2011. sub. price $25 ind., $50 inst.; per copy $8 ind., $16 inst.; sample $8 ind., $16 inst. Back issues: same. 250pp. Reporting time: 6-8 weeks. Publishes 1% or less of manuscripts submitted. Payment: $30 per page. Copyrighted, reverts to author. Pub's reviews: 12 in 2009. §Contemporary literature, fiction, poetry, culture of the South. Ads: $250/$150. Subjects: Fiction, Literary Review, Literature (General), Poetry.

SOUTHWEST COLORADO ARTS PERSPECTIVE, Heather Leavitt, Art Director, Publisher; Sonja Horoshko, Editor, P.O. Box 843, Mancos, CO 81328-0843, 970-739-3200, 970-533-0642, www.artsperspective.com. 2004. Poetry, articles, art, photos, cartoons, interviews, music, letters, collages. "Arts Perspective is a venue for artists in Southwest Colorado. We strive to share the lives of artists with our readers by bringing them into the artists' life, their studio, share their vision, their passion and their world. We use freelance writers and do not have a staff. We have published works by Leanne Goebel, Sonja Horoshko, Jeff Mannix and Jonathan Thompson. Each issue features 2-4 in-depth articles about artists, a studio visit, poem, exhibition and events listings, an opinion, resources for artists and an image gallery of fine artworks." circ. 8,000-10,000 per quarter. Quarterly. Pub'd 4 issues 2009; expects 4 issues 2010, 4 issues 2011. sub. price $20; sample Free. Back issues: $5. 32pp. Reporting time: 2-14 days. Simultaneous submissions accepted: No. Payment: $75 for 750-1000 words, $15 for poetry. Copyrighted. §Fine art of Southwest Colorado communities. Ads: $700/$400/$250/$85/$25/(display). Subjects: Arts, Avant-Garde, Experimental Art, Awards, Foundations, Grants, Book Arts, Calligraphy, Festivals, Graphics, Haiku, Music, Performing Arts, Photography, Poetry, Politics, Prose, Theatre.

Southwest Research and Information Center (see also VOICES FROM THE EARTH), Annette Aguayo,

Editor, PO Box 4524, Albuquerque, NM 87196-4524, 505-262-1862; Fax 505-262-1864; Info@sric.org; www.sric.org. 1974. Articles, reviews, news items. "Resource information for citizen action of all kinds. Review of small and 'alternative' press publications in more than 30 categories of environmental justice and social change issues." avg. press run 2.5M. Pub'd 4 titles 2009; expects 4 titles 2010, 4 titles 2011. 5 titles listed in the *Small Press Record of Books in Print* (36th Edition, 2010-11). Discounts: 40% to distributors. 48pp. Reporting time: 1 month. Payment: occasional funding secured. Does not copyright for author. Subjects: Book Reviewing, Energy, Environment, Health, Indigenous Cultures, New Mexico, Newsletter, Nuclear Energy, Society, Southwest, Water.

SOUTHWEST REVIEW, Willard Spiegelman, Editor-in-Chief; Jennifer Cranfill, Senior Editor, Southern Methodist University, P.O. Box 750374, Dallas, TX 75275-0374, 214-768-1037, www.smu.edu/southwestreview. 1915. Poetry, fiction, articles, criticism, parts-of-novels, long-poems, non-fiction. "The fourth oldest, continuously published literary quarterly in the country. The *Southwest Review* tries to discover works by new writers and publish them beside those of more established authors. Manuscripts accepted through web site or by mail. Mailed submissions should be typed neatly on white paper and include a stamped, self-addressed envelope for reply. Manuscripts will not be returned unless SASE includes sufficient postage. *SWR* prefers not to receive simultaneous or fax submissions, and does not consider work that has been published previously. Manuscripts are not accepted during the months of June, July, and August. We have no specific limitations as to theme. Preferred length for articles and fiction is 3,500 to 7,000 words. We demand very high quality in poetry; we accept both traditional and experimental writing; we place no arbitrary limits on length. Morton Marr Poetry Prize contest awards $1,000, first prize, and $500, second prize, to poem by a writer who has not yet published a first book. David Nathan Meyerson Prize for Fiction awards $1,000 to a story by a writer who has not published a first book. See web site for entry fees and guidelines, or send a SASE." circ. 1,500. 4/yr. Pub'd 4 issues 2009; expects 4 issues 2010, 4 issues 2011. sub. price 1 yr $24; 2 yrs $42; 3 yrs $65.; per copy $6; sample $6. Back issues: Available on request. Discounts: 15% to agencies. 144pp. Reporting time: 6 weeks. Simultaneous submissions accepted: no. Publishes 3% of manuscripts submitted. Payment: Yes. Amount varies. Copyrighted, reverts to author. Ads: Full page: $250; Half Page: $150; Covers 2 & 3: $300; Cover 4: $400. Subjects: Essays, Fiction, Literature (General), Non-Fiction, Poetry.

Southwestern Michigan Publications, Roderick Rasmussen, P.O. Box 916, Coloma, MI 49038, 269-468-9337 fax269-468-3889 email rick@swmichiganstore.com website swmichiganstore.com. 1994. "Historical books about Southwest Michigan with an emphasis on photographs and non fiction." avg. press run 1500. Expects 1 title 2011. No titles listed in the *Small Press Record of Books in Print* (36th Edition, 2010-11). 128pp. Simultaneous submissions accepted: No. Does not copyright for author. Subject: History.

SOU'WESTER, Allison Funk, Co-Editor; Geoff Schmidt, Co-Editor, Southern Illinois University, Edwardsville, IL 62026-1438. 1960. Poetry, fiction, interviews, reviews, long-poems, non-fiction. "We have no particular editorial biases or taboos. We publish the best poetry and fiction we can find." circ. 500. 2/yr. Pub'd 2 issues 2009; expects 2 issues 2010, 2 issues 2011. sub. price $12; per copy $6; sample $6. Back issues: price varies. 128pp. Reporting time: 3 months. Simultaneous submissions accepted: yes. Publishes 2% of manuscripts submitted. Payment: 2 copies; 1 year subscription. Copyrighted, reverts to author. Pub's reviews. §Books of poems and short fiction. Ads: $90/$50. Subjects: Fiction, Poetry.

THE SOW'S EAR POETRY REVIEW, The Sow's Ear Press, Robert G. Lesman, Managing Editor; Kristin Camitta Zimet, Editor, P.O. Box 127, Millwood, VA 22646-0127, Email: rglesman@gmail.comWebsite: http://sows-ear.kitenet.net. 1989. Poetry, art, photos, interviews, reviews. "No length limits on poems. We try to be eclectic. We look for work which 'makes the familiar strange, or the strange familiar,' which shines the light of understanding on the particular, and which uses sound and rhythms to develop meaning. Recent contributors: Penelope Scambly Schott, Virgil Suarez, Susan Terris, Madeline Tiger, and Steven Lautermilch." circ. 600. 4/yr. Pub'd 4 issues 2009; expects 4 issues 2010, 4 issues 2011. sub. price $27; per copy $8; sample $8. Back issues: $8 when available. Discounts: trade 30%. 32pp. Reporting time: 3-4 months. Simultaneous submissions accepted: yes. Publishes 5% of manuscripts submitted. Payment: 2 copies. Copyrighted, reverts to author. Pub's reviews: 3 in 2009. §Any poetry. Ads: none. Subjects: Poetry, Visual Arts.

The Sow's Ear Press (see also THE SOW'S EAR POETRY REVIEW), Kristin Zimet, Editor; Robert G. Lesman, Managing Editor, 217 Brookneil Drive, Winchester, VA 22602, sowsearpoetry@yahoo.com. 1989. Poetry, art, photos, reviews, long-poems. "Our main focus is *The Sow's Ear Poetry Review*. We also hold an annual chapbook contest (March-April) with a May 1 deadline and a poetry contest (September-October) with a November 1 deadline. Each is judged by a poet of national renown, and the prize is $1000, publication, and copies. Recent judges have been Sam Rasnake, Eleanor Wilner, Marge Piercy, Gregory Orr, and Henry Taylor. For guidelines, see our website, email us at rglesman@gmail.com, or send a SASE to Robert G. Lesman, Managing Editor, PO Box 127, Millwood, VA 22646. For the review we look for poems that are carefully crafted, keenly felt, and freshly perceived. We like poems with voice, a sense of place, delight in language, and a meaning that unfolds." avg. press run 700. 6 titles listed in the *Small Press Record of Books in Print* (36th

Edition, 2010-11). 32pp. Reporting time: 3 months for non-contest submissions, varied for contest submissions. Simultaneous submissions accepted: yes. Publishes 2% of manuscripts submitted. Copyrights for author. Subject: Poetry.

SP QUILL MAGAZINE, Shadow Poetry, Marie Summers, 1209 Milwaukee Street, Excelsior Springs, MO 64024, Fax: (208) 977-9114, spquill@shadowpoetry.com, http://www.shadowpoetry.com/magazine/spquill.html. 2004. Poetry, fiction, articles, art, interviews, reviews, letters. "Wants high-quality poetry, short/flash stories, and quotes. Does not want anything in poor taste, or poorly crafted poetry. Cinquain and Etheree for special spring and fall issues." Biannually. Pub'd 4 issues 2009; expects 2 issues 2010. price per copy $15.00 USA; $20.00 International; sample $15.00 USA; $20.00 International. 60-150pp. Reporting time: Three weeks before printing or sooner. Simultaneous submissions accepted: No. Publishes 8% of manuscripts submitted. Copyrighted, reverts to author. Pub's reviews: 12 in 2009. §Poetry. Subjects: Arts, Creativity, Essays, Literary Review, Literature (General), Poetry, Short Stories.

SP Turner Group, Chase Turner, 8306 Wilshire Boulevard, Suite 1213, Beverly Hills, CA 90211, 866 604 3852. 2007. Photos. "SP Turner Group is a small press based in Beverly Hills, California publishing works significant to the public. We publish photography books which reflect important artistic and biographical stories or information. Self-help books are also of interest to our company. Our award-winning books reflect our attention to detail and storyline. Inquiries may be submitted to our editorial offices." avg. press run Varies. Pub'd 3 titles 2009; expects 3 titles 2010, 3 titles 2011. 5 titles listed in the *Small Press Record of Books in Print* (36th Edition, 2010-11). Discounts: Total 1-9,30% discount Total 10-24, 40% discount Total 25-49, 47% discount Total 50+, 50% discount. pp varies. Reporting time: one month. Simultaneous submissions accepted: Yes. Publishes 20% of manuscripts submitted. Payment: each are different; negotiation. Copyrights for author. Subjects: Arts, Autobiography, Biography, Entertainment, Erotica, Experimental, Music, Photography, Poetry.

SPACE AND TIME, Space and Time Press, Hildy Silverman, Editor-in-Chief; Gerard Houarner, Fiction Editor; Linda D. Addison, Poetry Editor; Diane Weinstein, Art Editor, 1308 Centennial Avenue, Suite 101, Piscataway, NJ 08854, www.spaceandtimemagazine.com. 1966. Poetry, fiction, art, cartoons. "*Space and Time* is a fantasy, horror, and science fiction magazine, we have a very broad definition of these genres, and we aren't fussy about sub-genre barriers, but we don't want anything that obviously falls outside of speculative fiction(i.e. straight mystery, mainstream, etc.). Prefer under 10K words." circ. 2K. 4/yr. Pub'd 2 issues 2009; expects 4 issues 2010, 4 issues 2011. sub. price $20; per copy $5 + 1.50 p/h; sample $5 + 1.50 p/h. Back issues: 2.50. Discounts: 40% off on orders of 5 or more copies of an issue. 48pp. Reporting time: 6-8 weeks. Simultaneous submissions accepted: no. Publishes 1% of manuscripts submitted. Payment: 1¢ per word on acceptance. Copyrighted, reverts to author. Pub's reviews. §Occasionally review new fiction. Ads: $150/$75/50¢ per word ($10 min.). Subjects: Fantasy, Horror, Science Fiction.

Space and Time Press (see also SPACE AND TIME), Gordon Linzner, Publisher & Editor, 138 West 70th Street 4-B, New York, NY 10023-4468. 1984. Fiction. "Not actively soliciting at this time (overstocked). Fantasy and science fiction novels—preferably ones that don't fit neatly into a sub-genre. Interested in seeing borderline fantasy-mysteries, along lines of George Chesbro's *Mongo* series. We are still overstock and not considering new book proposals for the indefinite future. We *are* looking for short stories for the magazine." avg. press run 1M. Expects 1 title 2010, 1 title 2011. 14 titles listed in the *Small Press Record of Books in Print* (36th Edition, 2010-11). Discounts: 1 30%, 2-4 35%, 5-24 40%. 160pp. Payment: 10% of cover price, based on print run, within 3 months of publication. Copyrights for author. Subjects: Fantasy, Science Fiction.

SPARE CHANGE NEWS, Emily Johnson, Executive Publisher, 1151 Massachusetts Avenue, Cambridge, MA 02138, 617-497-1595, sceditor@homelessempowerment.org. 1992. circ. 8,000 every two weeks. 26/year. Pub'd 26 issues 2009; expects 26 issues 2010, 26 issues 2011. sub. price $60; per copy $1; sample $1. 20pp. Payment: $50 for homeless and formerly homeless writers per article; vendors are independent contractors and purchase copies of Spare Change News for 25 cents apiece, sell them on the street for $1, and keep 100% of the profit. Rights revert to author but articles are available for NASNA members. Pub's reviews: 50 in 2009. §Issues regarding homelessness and other social justice issues. Ads: http://www.homelessempowerment.org.

SPEAK UP, Speak Up Press, PO Box 100506, Denver, CO 80250, 303-715-0837, Fax 303-715-0793, info@speakuppress.org, www.speakuppress.org. 1999. Poetry, fiction, art, photos, plays, non-fiction. "Original work by Teens (13-19 years old) Only. Written work: 2500 words max. See web site for submission information or contact Speak Up Press for required submission forms." circ. 2M. 1/yr. Pub'd 1 issue 2009; expects 1 issue 2010, 1 issue 2011. sub. price $10; per copy $10; sample free. Discounts: classroom 50%, bookstores 50%, libraries 50%. 128pp. Reporting time: up to 4 months. Simultaneous submissions accepted: yes. Publishes 10% of manuscripts submitted. Payment: 2 copies. Copyrighted, reverts to author. Ads: none. Subjects: Arts, Fiction, Young Adult.

Speak Up Press (see also SPEAK UP), PO Box 100506, Denver, CO 80250, 303-715-0837, Fax 303-715-0793, info@speakuppress.org, www.speakuppress.org. 1999. Fiction, non-fiction. "Only Young Adult

Fiction and Nonfiction. See web site for submission information." avg. press run 1M. No titles listed in the *Small Press Record of Books in Print* (36th Edition, 2010-11). Reporting time: 2 months. Simultaneous submissions accepted: yes. Payment: negotiable. Copyrights for author. Subject: Young Adult.

SPECIALTY TRAVEL INDEX, Larry Boggs, Editor, PO BOX 458, San Anselmo, CA 94979-0458, 415-455-1643, Fax 415-455-1648, advertiser@specialtytravel.com, www.specialtytravel.com. 1980. Articles, photos, non-fiction. "The Special Interest and Adventure Travel Directory." circ. 23K. 2/yr. Pub'd 2 issues 2009; expects 2 issues 2010, 2 issues 2011. 68pp. Simultaneous submissions accepted: yes. Publishes 5% of manuscripts submitted. Copyrighted. Ads: $4,600/$1,100. Subjects: Sports, Outdoors, Transportation, Travel.

Speck Press, Derek Lawrence, Publisher, 4690 Table Mountain Drive, Ste. 100, Golden, CO 80403, 303-277-1623, FAX 303-279-7111, books@speckpress.com, www.speckpress.com. 2002. Art, non-fiction. avg. press run 5-10M. Pub'd 8 titles 2009; expects 8 titles 2010, 8 titles 2011. No titles listed in the *Small Press Record of Books in Print* (36th Edition, 2010-11). 200+pp. Reporting time: 3-5 months. Simultaneous submissions accepted: yes. Publishes less than 1% of manuscripts submitted. Payment: varies. Copyrights for author. Subjects: Arts, Culture, Law, Lifestyles, Music, Non-Fiction, Performing Arts, Sex, Sexuality, Travel.

SPECS, Vidhu Aggarwal, Rollins College specs Journal, 1000 Holt Avenue - 705, Winter Park, FL 32789, 407-646-2666. 2007. Poetry, fiction, art, photos, cartoons, criticism, long-poems, non-fiction. "specs (specifications, speculations, spectacle . . .) is a journal that aims to produce a charged atmosphere around artistic and critical approaches. Hence, specs is willing to live in a constant state of flux, with the mission of propagating strange and involved sympathies between disparate genres and forms. We want to break down hierarchies between poems, fictions, and critical writing. We hope for seepages, warped conversations, and misappropriations between areas of content.We accept simultaneous submission of creative work if indicated on the cover letter. Please inform us immediately if work is accepted elsewhere. The deadline for fiction, creative non-fiction, and poetry is December 2008. The theme for volume 2 of specs is "Faux Histories"—more information to come.Please send all submissions in an .rft or .doc file in Times New Roman Font to editors@specsjournal.org. Include a brief cover letter and indicate whether you wish to be considered for the print edition, the web edition, or both. Please also indicate the type/genre of submission in the subject heading (Poetry, Cultural Criticism, etc.). Please limit poetry submissions to 10-12 pages. Visit www.specsjournal.org for more information." 1/yr. Expects 1 issue 2010, 1 issue 2011. sub. price $10; per copy $10. Back issues: $10. 152pp. Reporting time: Maximum of three months. Simultaneous submissions accepted: Yes. Publishes 10% of manuscripts submitted. Payment: Two copies of the journal. Copyrighted, reverts to author. Ads: specs does not publish advertisements. Subjects: Culture, Electronics, English, Experimental, Fiction, History, Humanism, Literature (General), Magazines, Prose, Religion, Writers/Writing.

•**SPECTACULAR SPECULATIONS,** Colin Neilson, 13804-114 St., Edmonton, Alberta, T5X 4J1, Canada, 780-456-1646, admin@speculativefictionstories.com, http://www.speculativefictionstories.com. 2009. Poetry, fiction, photos, reviews, long-poems, plays. "We publish speculative fiction, which includes fantasy, science fiction, some types of horror, magic realism and other genres where the unreal happens. We are most interested in whether a story is entertaining and well crafted from the criteria of characterization, setting design, narrative, dialogue and plot. We accept manuscripts from established and starting authors. Email authors@speculativefictionstories.com for more information." 12/yr. Expects 2 issues 2010, 12 issues 2011. sub. price $24 CDN; per copy $5.00 CDN. Back issues: inquire. Discounts: 25%. 225pp. Reporting time: 1-2 weeks. Simultaneous submissions accepted: Yes. Payment: Free authors copy of magazine, no monetary pay at this time. The magazine is copyrighted, however contributors retain the rights to their work and are allowed to submit to other publications. Pub's reviews: none in 2009. §Speculative Fiction only. Subjects: Arthurian, Biotechnology, Children, Youth, Comics, Cosmology, Fantasy, Fiction, Folklore, Futurism, Horror, Juvenile Fiction, Occult, Science Fiction, Young Adult.

Spectrum Productions, Oscar Mandel, 979 Casiano Road, Los Angeles, CA 90049. 1974. Plays. "We are interested in receiving inquiries (not mss.) in the field of translations of European drama before the twentieth century." 7 titles listed in the *Small Press Record of Books in Print* (36th Edition, 2010-11). Copyrights for author. Subject: Drama.

The Speech Bin, Inc., Jan J. Binney, Senior Editor, PO Box 922668, Norcross, GA 30010-2668, 772-770-0007, FAX 772-770-0006; website: www.speechbin.com. 1984. "The Speech Bin publishes educational materials and books in speech-language pathology, audiology, occupational and physical therapy, special education, and treatment of communication disorders in children and adults. One publication is *Getting Through: Communicating When Someone You Care For Has Alzheimer's Disease*, a unique book written for caregivers (both family members and professionals) of Alzheimer's victims. Most Speech Bin authors are specialists in communication disorders, rehabilitation, or education although we are eager to receive queries for new books and materials from all authors who write for our specialized market. Please study our market before submitting fiction. The Speech Bin also publishes educational card sets and games plus novelties. We do not accept faxed submissions or telephone inquiries." avg. press run varies. Pub'd 8-10 titles 2009; expects 10-12

465

titles 2010, 10-12 titles 2011. 59 titles listed in the *Small Press Record of Books in Print* (36th Edition, 2010-11). Discounts: 20%. 40-400pp. Reporting time: 2-3 months. Simultaneous submissions accepted: no. Publishes 2-5% of manuscripts submitted. Payment: varies. Copyrights for author. Subjects: Bilingual, Communication, Journalism, Education.

SPEX (SMALL PRESS EXCHANGE), Margaret Speaker Yuan, PO Box E, Corte Madera, CA 94976, 866-622-1325. 1979. Articles, reviews, letters, news items. "This is the newsletter of the Bay Area Independent Publishers Association, a non-profit public benefit organization." circ. 300. 10/yr. Pub'd 12 issues 2009; expects 10 issues 2010, 10 issues 2011. sub. price Included in membership in BAIPA, $40 yearly; sample SASE. 8pp. Payment: none. Copyrighted, reverts to author. Ads: $80/$60/$40 1/4 page/$20 1/8 page/classifieds $3 per 4 lines. Subjects: Book Collecting, Bookselling, Book Reviewing, How-To, Printing.

SPIDER, Marianne Carus, Editor-in-Chief; Heather Delabre, Associate Editor, PO Box 300, Peru, IL 61354, 815-224-5803, ext 656, Fax 815-224-6615, mmiklavcic@caruspub.com. 1994. "Word limit for fiction - 1000 words, nonfiction - 800 words. Include bibliography with nonfiction. SASE required for response." circ. 80M. 12/yr. Pub'd 12 issues 2009; expects 12 issues 2010, 12 issues 2011. sub. price $35.97; per copy $5; sample $5. Back issues: $5. 34pp. Reporting time: approx. 3 months. We accept simultaneous submissions, but please indicate as such. Publishes 1% of manuscripts submitted. Payment: stories and articles up to 25¢ per word, poems up to $3 per line. Copyrighted, does not revert to author. Pub's reviews: 8 in 2009. §Chapter books, middle grade fiction, poetry, younger nonfiction, joke, craft, or puzzle collections. Ads: none. Subjects: Children, Youth, Literature (General), Magazines.

SPILLWAY, Tebot Bach, Susan Terris, Editor, Box 7887, Huntington Beach, CA 92615-7887, 714-968-0905. 1993. Poetry, photos, criticism, reviews, long-poems. "Recent contributors: John Balaban, Eleanor Wilner, Richard Jones, David St. John, M.L. Liebler, Allison Joseph, Sam Hamill, Jody Azzouni, Jan Wesley, Jeanette Clough, Amy Uyematsu. Dorianne Laux .Eleanor Wilner, Pushcart Winner for her poem *Sidereal* in *Spillway 10*." 2/yr. Pub'd 2 issues 2009; expects 1 issue 2010, 2 issues 2011. sub. price Single copy: $12 post paid; subscription: $21 postpaid for 2issues , $33 postpaid for 4 issues.; per copy $13 postpaid; sample $13 postpaid. Back issues: $8 postpaid. Discounts: by arrangement. 135pp. Reporting time: 2 weeks to 6 months. Simultaneous submissions accepted: only rarely. Publishes 2% of manuscripts submitted. Payment: 1 copy. Copyrighted, reverts to author. Pub's reviews. §Poetry related material. Subjects: Criticism, Photography, Poetry.

SPINDRIFT ART & LITERARY JOURNAL, Shoreline Community College, 16101 Greenwood Avenue North, Shoreline, WA 98133. "*Spindrift* is the award-winning, nationally recognized art and literary journal of Shoreline Community College in Shoreline, Washington. *Spindrift* accepts essays and fiction with a maximum of 4,500 words, Short plays or dialogues with a maximum of 15 typed pages, Poetry with a maximum of 6 poems, and musical scores. Two typed, double-spaced copies are required to be included with each submission, with the exception that poetry need not be double-spaced. The authors name should not appear on the work. Due to volume received, literary work will not be returned."

Spinifex Press, Susan Hawthorne, PO Box 212, North Melbourne VIC 3051, Australia, +61-3-9329 6088, Fax +61-3-9329 9238. 1991. Poetry, fiction, art, photos, cartoons, long-poems, plays, non-fiction. "Our mission is to publish innovatiive and controversial feminist books with an optimistic edge. Our range is diverse and includes authors from Australia, USA, Canada, Botswana, India, Bangladesh, Lebanon, Japan, Philippines, New Zealand, Germany and elsewhere. We now have an eBookstore with a growing number of Spinifex eBooks available in electronic formats such as DX Reader, Mobipocket, Microsoft Reader and Adobe Reader. Go to www.spinifexpress.com.au and click on the eBookstore and follow the leads." avg. press run 3000. Pub'd 10 titles 2009; expects 5 titles 2010, 4 titles 2011. 172 titles listed in the *Small Press Record of Books in Print* (36th Edition, 2010-11). All books sold in North America go through our distributors, Independent Publishers Group (IPG). We offer standard trade discounts in Australia of 40% to booksellers. Book with prices in Australian dollars are not available in the USA through IPG, but can be ordered directly over our website: www.spinifexpress.com.au. 250pp. Reporting time: We are currently not accepting unsolicited manuscripts. Simultaneous submissions accepted: No. Publishes 1% of manuscripts submitted. Copyrights for author. Subjects: Arts, Crime, Feminism, Health, Indigenous Cultures, Lesbianism, Literature (General), Memoirs, Multicultural, Myth, Mythology, Non-Violence, Peace, Poetry, Theatre, Women.

SPINNING JENNY, Black Dress Press, C.E. Harrison, P.O. Box 1067, New York, NY 10014-1067, www.spinning-jenny.com. 1994. Poetry. circ. 1M. 1/yr. Pub'd 1 issue 2009; expects 1 issue 2010, 1 issue 2011. sub. price $15/2 years; per copy $8; sample $8. Back issues: $8, if available. Discounts: refer to Ubiquity Distributors. 96pp. Reporting time: 1-4 months. Simultaneous submissions accepted: no. Publishes Less than 5% of manuscripts submitted. Payment: contributors' copies. Copyrighted, reverts to author. Ads: none. Subject: Poetry.

SPINNINGS...INTENSE TALES OF LIFE MAGAZINE, Victoria Valentine, PO Box 295, Stormville, NY

12582-0295, http://www.spinningsmagazine.com email: spinningsmag@aol.com. 2000. Poetry, fiction, photos. "80 pages filled with intense stories, poems and art/illustrations,*SpinningS* is precisely what the title implies: intense!! Publishing hard-hitting fiction: detective, mystery, sensual, thriller, horror, suspense, romance, gothic romance, sci fi: stories and poems and of course art and illustrations, *SpinningS*, intense tales of life is intended for a mature audience. Electronic submissions only." Temporarily on hold. Enjoy our web site archives while we reorganize. Expects 1 issue 2010, 1 issue 2011. sample price unavailable at this time. Back issues: 10.00. 80pp. Reporting time: 4 months. Simultaneous submissions accepted: Yes. Publishes 25% of manuscripts submitted. Copyrighted, reverts to author. Subjects: Diaries, Drama, Erotica, Fiction, Horror, Inspirational, Memoirs, Mystery, Poetry, Publishing, Relationships, Romance, Science Fiction, Short Stories, Supernatural.

The Spirit That Moves Us Press, Inc., Morty Sklar, Editor, Publisher; Marcela Bruno, Technical Consultant, PO Box 720820-DB, Jackson Heights, Queens, NY 11372-0820, 718-426-8788, msklar@mindspring.com. 1974. Poetry, fiction, art, photos, long-poems, collages, non-fiction. "We ceased publishing in 2008. Our entire list available for $200. Write for complete catalog or/and download it from http://home.mindspring.com/~the.spirit.that.moves.us.press." avg. press run 1M-4.2M. Expects 1 title 2010. 22 titles listed in the *Small Press Record of Books in Print* (36th Edition, 2010-11). Discounts: 60% or entire list for $200. Ask for our complete catalog or download it at http://home.mindspring.com/~the.spirit.that.moves.us.press. 208-504pp. Publishes 1.5% poetry, fiction 2% of manuscripts submitted. Copyrights for author. Subjects: Anthology, Essays, Multicultural, Photography, Poetry, Short Stories.

SPIRITCHASER, Elizabeth Hundley, 3183 Sharon-Copley Road, Medina, OH 44256, 330-722-1561. 1994. Articles. "After my sister and her husband died of cancer 23 days apart, I began my spiritual search. I interview people I am drawn to, of different faiths. Naomi Judd was my first subscriber. I've interviewed Deepak Chopra, Bernie Siegel, Cece Winans, Dave Dravecky, Dr. Joyce Brothers, Sonya Friedman, Bob Greene (Oprah's trainer). He mentioned me in his journal on the Oprah website. Spiritchaser is a labor of love." circ. 20. Pub'd 1 issue 2009; expects 3 issues 2010, 3 issues 2011. sub. price $20; per copy $5; sample $5. Back issues: $5. Discounts: none. 8pp. Publishes 0% of manuscripts submitted. Copyrighted, reverts to author. Subjects: Inspirational, Newsletter, Spiritual.

SPITBALL: The Literary Baseball Magazine, Mike Shannon, Editor-in-Chief; William J. McGill, Managing Editor & Poetry Editor; Mark Schraf, Fiction Editor; Tom Eckel, Contributing Editor, 5560 Fox Road, Cincinnati, OH 45239-7271, 513-385-2268. 1981. Poetry, fiction, articles, art, cartoons, interviews, satire, criticism, reviews, parts-of-novels, long-poems, collages, plays, concrete art, non-fiction. "*Spitball* is a unique litarary magazine devoted to baseball. We publish primarily poetry & fiction, with no biases concerning style or technique or genre. We strive to publish only what we consider to be good work, however, and using baseball as subject matter does not guarantee acceptance. We have no big backlog of accepted material, nevertheless, and good baseball poetry and fiction submitted to us can be published reasonably quickly. If one has never written about baseball, it would probably help a great deal to read the magazine or our book, *The Best of Spitball*, an anthology, published by Pocket Books, March 1988. We try to give considerate fair treatment to everything we receive. We occasionally publish special issues. First issue of 1989 was devoted entirely to David Martin's sequence of poems connecting one-time Milwaukee Brewers outfielder Gorman Thomas to Wisconsin lorre and mythology. A $6 payment must accompany submissions from writers submitting to *Spitball* for the first time. We will send a sample copy in return. The $6 is a one-time charge. Once you have paid it, you may submit additional material as often as you like at no charge." circ. 1M. 2/yr. Pub'd 2 issues 2009; expects 2 issues 2010, 2 issues 2011. sub. price $12; per copy $6; sample $6. Back issues: many sold out, write for prices and availability. Discounts: can be negotiated. 96pp. Reporting time: from 1 week to 3 months. Simultaneous submissions accepted: no. Payment: copies. Not copyrighted. Pub's reviews: 60 in 2009. §We would love to receive review copies of any small press publications dealing with baseball, especially baseball poetry and fiction. Ads: $100/$60. Subjects: Fiction, Kentucky, Poetry, Sports, Outdoors.

Split Oak Press, James Stafford, P.O. Box 700, Vestal, NY 13851, 607-748-5834 splitoakpress.com. 2009. Poetry. "Poetry chapbooks so far. Publication of novels possible in the future. Visit splitoakpress.com." avg. press run 150. Expects 6 titles 2010, 6 titles 2011. No titles listed in the *Small Press Record of Books in Print* (36th Edition, 2010-11). Discounts: 2-10 copies 25%. 30-35pp. Simultaneous submissions accepted: Yes. Publishes 8% of manuscripts submitted. Payment: Visit website, splitoakpress.com. Copyrights for author. Subjects: Abstracts, Poetry.

SPOKEWRITE: The Spokane/Coeur d'Alene Journal of Art and Writing, Gray Dog Press, Russel Davis, 2727 S. Mt. Vernon #4, Spokane, WA 99223, P:509-768-6206, F:509-533-1897, editor@graydogpress.com, www.graydogpress.com. 2009. Poetry, fiction, art, photos, interviews, reviews, non-fiction. circ. 2500. 4/yr. Expects 10000 issues 2010, 10000 issues 2011. sub. price $40.00; per copy $10.00; sample $5.00. Back issues: $5.00. 160pp. Reporting time: 5-10 business days. Simultaneous submissions accepted: No. Publishes 60% of manuscripts submitted. Payment: None. Copyrighted, reverts to author.

Spoon River Poetry Press, David R. Pichaske, PO Box 6, Granite Falls, MN 56241. 1976. Poetry. "We do not, as a rule, solicit book-length manuscripts. Mostly we favor Midwest writers working with Midwest subjects and themes.'' avg. press run 1.5M. Pub'd 6 titles 2009; expects 3 titles 2010, 3 titles 2011. No titles listed in the *Small Press Record of Books in Print* (36th Edition, 2010-11). Discounts: 2-5 20%, 6+ 40% to bookstores; textbook orders 20%; 20% if payment accompanies order to individuals and libraries. 32-400+pp. Payment: 50% of receipts over set, print, bind costs. Copyrights for author.

SPOON RIVER POETRY REVIEW, Kirstin Hotelling Zona, Editor, Department of English 4241, Illinois State University, Normal, IL 61790-4241, 309-438-3025. 1976. Poetry. circ. 1.5M. 2/yr. Pub'd 2 issues 2009; expects 2 issues 2010, 2 issues 2011. sub. price $15 ($18 institutions); per copy $10; sample $10. Back issues: $5-$10. Discounts: 30%. 128pp. Reporting time: 3 months. Simultaneous submissions accepted. Please notify us promptly if your work is accepted elsewhere. Publishes 2% of manuscripts submitted. Payment: year's subscription. Copyrighted, reverts to author. Pub's reviews: 2 in 2009. §Books of poems, poetry translations, anthologies of poems, criticism and poetics. Ads: $150/$75. Subjects: Poetry, Reviews.

SPORE, Score, Crag Hill, 1111 E. Fifth Street, Moscow, ID 83843, schneider-hill@adelphia.com, http://scorecard.typepad.com/spore/. 1983. Articles, art, photos, interviews, criticism, reviews, letters, concrete art. ''Our primary focus is the visual poem—creative, historical, theoretical—but we're also interested in any work pushing back boundaries, verse or prose. Subscription price includes 1 issues of *SPORE* plus occasional publications such as broadsides and postcards that I can fit into the envelope.'' circ. 150-250. 1/yr. Pub'd 1 issue 2009; expects 1 issue 2010, 1 issue 2011. sub. price $12 per issue; per copy $12; sample $12. Back issues: query. 80pp. Reporting time: 2 weeks to 6 months. Simultaneous submissions accepted: Yes, but make sure to let us know. Publishes 5-10% of manuscripts submitted. Payment: 1 copy. Not copyrighted. Pub's reviews: 1 in 2009. §We would be interested in books and magazines with a visual/literal basis. Ads: none. Subjects: Arts, Avant-Garde, Experimental Art, Language, Literature (General), Poetry.

•**SPOT LITERARY MAGAZINE,** 4729 E. Sunrise Dr., PO Box 254, Tucson, AZ 85718-4535, susan.hansell@gmail.com. ''SLM accepts submissions from January 15 through February 15 for spring issues, and from August 15 to September 15 for fall issues. Submissions are considered for acceptance via email only: Texts must be sent as Microsoft Word files in (simple) TIMES (or Times New Roman if you do not have TIMES CE) font. Send black and white photos or art work in grayscale JPEG file format. Send two or three poems, and/or one short story or short play, essay, etc., as word.doc or attachments to *susan.hansell@gmail.com* with the subject header: Spot Lit Mag. Send each text as a separate word.doc attachment, but send the separate attachments in the same email. Please type your name, snail-mail address, and your phone number in the regular email body window to which you are attaching your work/s.''

•**SPOTops Books,** Joseph Jones, 337 Hickory Bluff, Johnson City, TN 37601-1327, 423-610-8464. 2009. Poetry, fiction, satire, parts-of-novels, long-poems, non-fiction. ''From the SPOTops welcome page: The SPOTops slogan arises from Ernst Cassirer's observation, in his Philosophy of Symbolic Forms, that the fundamental task of every individual is "to make sense of the senses." So, you see, SPOT Operations embraces it all, from the innermost whisper of private prospect to fully comprehensive dimensions of all there is, was or ever may be. Both extensional and intentional aspects of consciousness, the entire universe of imaginal being. Visit http://www.spotops.net/ for further information about SPOT media.'' avg. press run 10. Expects 1 title 2010, 2 titles 2011. No titles listed in the *Small Press Record of Books in Print* (36th Edition, 2010-11). Discounts: 25%. 500pp. Reporting time: Query first, will acknowledge immediately and provide estimated timeline, given current projects, if any. Simultaneous submissions accepted: Yes. Publishes 10% of manuscripts submitted. Payment: Negotiable. Does not copyright for author. Subjects: Appalachia, Artificial Intelligence, Arts, Avant-Garde, Experimental Art, Cosmology, Culture, Fiction, Metaphysics, Myth, Mythology, Novels, Philosophy, Satire, Science, Science Fiction, Zen.

SPOUT, Spout Press, John Colburn, Chris Watercott, Michelle Filkins, PO BOX 581067, Minneapolis, MN 55458-1067, http://www.spoutpress.org. 1989. Poetry, fiction, articles, art, cartoons, interviews, letters, collages, non-fiction. ''Accepts poetry, prose, and fiction for publication. Submission should include SASE. Looking for the unique voice, for someone with something to say in an offbeat way.'' circ. 200+. 1-2/yr. Pub'd 3 issues 2009; expects 2 issues 2010, 3 issues 2011. sub. price $15; per copy $5; sample $5. Back issues: $3. 56pp. Reporting time: Varies. Simultaneous submissions accepted: yes. Publishes 10% of manuscripts submitted. Payment: copy. Copyrighted, reverts to author. Subjects: Essays, Fiction, Non-Fiction, Poetry.

•**SPOUT, Spout Press,** Carrie Eidem, PO Box 581067, Minneapolis, MN 55458-1067. 1989. Poetry, fiction, art, photos, cartoons, long-poems, collages, non-fiction. ''We accept materials September 1 through May 1. We are open to many types of writing. Our mission is to publish and promote the finest in contemporary experimental writing—mentoring young writers and bringing new and/or under-appreciated voices to the attention of a larger audience. This is accomplished through both the publishing of books and the production of live events within the community. Both strive to combine artistic genres to facilitate dialogue between the film, music, visual art and literary communities creating synergy that expands possibilities for both artists and audiences.'' circ. 150. 2/yr. Pub'd 1 issue 2009; expects 2 issues 2010, 2 issues 2011. sub. price $30; per copy

$5; sample $5. Back issues: $4. 50-80pp. Reporting time: 6 months. Simultaneous submissions accepted: No. Payment: Payment is in the form of copies of the journal. Subjects: Anthology, Charles Bukowski, Experimental, Mystery, Non-Fiction, Visual Arts.

Spout Press (see also SPOUT), John Colburn, Michelle Filkins, Chris Watercott, PO Box 581067, Minneapolis, MN 55458-1067. 1996. Poetry, fiction, non-fiction. "Recent anthology includes Jim Northrup, Jonis Agee, and Alison McGhee. Tend to put out calls for anthologies or theme-related books rather than publish single-author manuscripts." avg. press run 500. Expects 2 titles 2010, 2 titles 2011. 3 titles listed in the *Small Press Record of Books in Print* (36th Edition, 2010-11). 110pp. Reporting time: 2-3 months. Simultaneous submissions accepted: yes. Publishes 5% of manuscripts submitted. Payment: varies. Copyrights for author. Subjects: Essays, Fiction, Non-Fiction, Poetry.

•**Spout Press (see also SPOUT),** Carrie Eidem, PO Box 581067, Minneapolis, MN 55458-1067. 1989. Poetry, fiction, art, satire, long-poems, non-fiction. "We do not take unsolicited manuscripts at this time. Our missions is to publish and promote the finest in contemporary experimental writing—mentoring young writers and bringing new and/or under-appreciated voices to the attention of a larger audience. This is accomplished through both the publishing of books and the production of live events within the community. Both strive to combine artistic genres to facilitate dialogue between the film, music, visual art and literary communities creating synergy that expands possibilities for both artists and audiences." avg. press run 500. Expects 1 title 2010, 2 titles 2011. No titles listed in the *Small Press Record of Books in Print* (36th Edition, 2010-11). 50-150pp. Reporting time: We do not accept unsolicited manuscipts at this time. Simultaneous submissions accepted: No.

Spring Grass (see also Redgreene Press), RC Anderson, PO Box 22322, Pittsburgh, PA 15222, 412-231-0436. 1999. Poetry, long-poems. "Up-and-coming poets with talent and haiku/tanka are published, usually paid for by the author, who receives most of the edition and ongoing support. One author made all her money back AND 133% more by selling her chapbook in person. Books of haiku-type poetry may be handbound, sewn with Japanese stab binding, on fine paper; style and size of book varies - these are Artists Books often designed by the editor, an exhibited artist. Unsolicited work welcome - send up to three sheets of written or typed work with SASE for reply; response time varies. Recent authors include Jessica Bigi (*Through Emily's Window*) and Andrew T. Roy (*My Chinese Haiku*)." 2 titles listed in the *Small Press Record of Books in Print* (36th Edition, 2010-11). Simultaneous submissions accepted: yes. Payment: 10% royalties once I sell more than 300 copies of their book. May copyright for author, or advise. Subjects: Animals, Autobiography, Book Arts, Creativity, Experimental, Haiku, Handicapped, Memoirs, Mental Health, Miniature Books, Nature, Poetry, Religion, Visual Arts, Women.

•**Spring Journal Books (see also SPRING JOURNAL, Inc.),** 627 Ursulines Street #7, New Orleans, LA 70116, (504)524-5117, submissions@springjournalandbooks.com. "Spring Journal publishes books in the fields of archetypal psychology, mythology, and Jungian psychology under the imprint of Spring Journal Books. All manuscripts must be typewritten, double-spaced, on one side only of good quality, white 8 1/2" x 11" paper, unbound, with one-inch margins on all sides and numbered consecutively; hand numbering is acceptable. For correct punctuation, capitalization, organization of material, usage and the like, we recommend the comprehensive guide, The Chicago Manual of Style, 15th edition (University of Chicago Press, 2003).Take particular care with footnotes and bibliographies. In general, follow the form given in The Chicago Manual of Style." No titles listed in the *Small Press Record of Books in Print* (36th Edition, 2010-11).

•**SPRING JOURNAL, Inc., Spring Journal Books,** Nancy Cater, Editor, 627 Ursulines Street #7, New Orleans, LA 70116, (504)524-5117, submissions@springjournalandbooks.com. "Each issue of *Spring Journal* is organized around a theme. Past themes have included, for example, MUSES, ORPHEUS, and BODY AND SOUL. Spring Journal welcomes submissions of essays or commentaries relating to all aspects of analytical and archetypal psychology and its relation to aspects of world culture. Contributions may be theoretical, critical, historical, or personal. All articles must be related to the theme of the issue. Spring Journal Book and Film Reviews. Spring welcomes the submission of film reviews. Spring usually commissions book reviews.Spring Journal Fiction and Poetry Spring Journal rarely publishes fiction or poetry and then only if it is interwoven with the text of the journal article."

SQUARE ONE, Jennifer Dunbar Dorn, Campus Box 226, University of Colorado, Boulder, CO 80309-0001, 303-492-8890, square1@colorado.edu, http://www.colorado.edu/English/squareone/index.htm. 2003. circ. 600. 1/yr. Pub'd 1 issue 2009; expects 1 issue 2010, 1 issue 2011. sub. price $10; per copy $7; sample $7 or free. Back issues: $10. Discounts: 2-10 copies 25%. 100pp.

Square One Publishers, Inc., Rudy Shur, Publisher, 115 Herricks Road, Garden City Park, NY 11040, 516-535-2010, Fax 516-535-2014, sq1info@aol.com, www.squareonepublishers.com. 1999. Non-fiction. "Here at Square One Publishers, we produce books that provide reliable information on a range of meaningful, as well as intriguing, topics. Square One is the best place to start! When submitting a proposal, please include only: a cover letter that includes some biographical info on the author and indicates the book's potential audience; 2-3 page overview of the book; table of contents; and SASE for return of your material." avg. press run 8-10M. Pub'd 20 titles 2009; expects 25 titles 2010, 25 titles 2011. 2 titles listed in the *Small Press Record of Books in Print* (36th Edition, 2010-11). Discounts: trade 20%-45%. 225pp. Reporting time: 4 weeks. Simultaneous submissions accepted: yes. Publishes 2% of manuscripts submitted. Payment: 10% of net, paid semi-annually. Copyrights for author. Subjects: Alternative Medicine, Collectibles, Cooking, Crafts, Hobbies, Environment, Finances, Grieving, Health, How-To, New Age, Non-Fiction, Parenting, Religion, Vegetarianism, Writers/Writing.

Squire Press, David Squire, 411 4th Ave, Melbourne Beach, FL 32951, 3217256827. 2007. Fiction, non-fiction. "Contemporary, mainstream adult literary fiction: David Johansson's new novel, Skin of Sunset, Squire Press, 2009.Creative non-fiction: In the Nation of the Heart: War Stories, coming in 2010, by David Johansson." avg. press run 1000. Pub'd 1 title 2009; expects 1 title 2010, 1 title 2011. No titles listed in the *Small Press Record of Books in Print* (36th Edition, 2010-11). Discounts: 50% discount. 370pp. Reporting time: Four weeks. Simultaneous submissions accepted: No. Publishes 1% of manuscripts submitted. Payment: lump sum advance, 10% royalty. Does not copyright for author. Subjects: Alcohol, Alcoholism, Buddhism, Charles Bukowski, Fiction, Humor, Non-Fiction, Novels, Sex, Sexuality, Women, Zen.

SRLR Press (see also SULPHUR RIVER LITERARY REVIEW), James Michael Robbins, PO Box 19228, Austin, TX 78760. 1997. Poetry, fiction, articles, art, photos, interviews, satire, criticism, non-fiction. "We have published books by Errol Miller, Frances Neidhardt, James Scofield, Albert Huffstickler, Nola Perez, Willie James King, Ben Norwood, Lee Slonimsky, and Joe Ahearn. We publish by invitation only. No unsolicited manuscripts are accepted." avg. press run 250-500. Pub'd 1 title 2009; expects 2 titles 2010, 2 titles 2011. 9 titles listed in the *Small Press Record of Books in Print* (36th Edition, 2010-11). Discounts: varies. 80pp. Payment: 50/50 split once printing is paid for. Copyrights for author. Subjects: Fiction, Poetry.

Staghorn Press, Dian Kennedy, 5906 Etiwanda Ave. #27, Tarzana, CA 91356, 818-342-3823. 2007. Fiction. Expects 1 title 2010, 1 title 2011. 1 title listed in the *Small Press Record of Books in Print* (36th Edition, 2010-11). Discounts: 1-6 copies 20%7-11 copies 25%1-5 cases (case of 12 copies) 40%6-11 cases (case of 12 copies) 45%12 cases + (case of 12 copies) 50%Wholesalers 55%. 320pp. Copyrights for author.

STAND MAGAZINE, Michael Hulse, John Kinsella, School of English, Univeristy of Leeds, Leeds LS2 9JT, England. 1952. Poetry, interviews, criticism, reviews, letters. circ. 4.5M. 4/yr. Pub'd 4 issues 2009; expects 4 issues 2010. sub. price $49.50; per copy $13; sample $5. Back issues: $10. 120pp. Reporting time: 1-2 months. Simultaneous submissions accepted: no. Publishes 5% of manuscripts submitted. Payment: $45/poem, $45/1,000 words prose. Copyrighted, reverts to author. Pub's reviews: 30 in 2009. §Literature. Ads: $225/$112/$56 1/4 page. Subject: Literary Review.

Standard Publications, Inc., PO Box 2226, Champaign, IL 61825, 217-898-7825, spi@standardpublications.com. 2 titles listed in the *Small Press Record of Books in Print* (36th Edition, 2010-11).

Standish Press, Olga Rothschild, 105 Standish Street, Duxbury, MA 02332-5027, 781-934-9570, Fax 781-934-9570, duxroth@verizon.net. 1999. Non-fiction. "Publishes health and fitness, self-help, medical care, writing, home improvement, humor, business, travel for an educated adult audience. Recent title: *Better Health, Simple, Sensible Strategies* by Dick Rothschild. *No poetry, please.*" avg. press run 3M-5M. Expects 1 title 2011. No titles listed in the *Small Press Record of Books in Print* (36th Edition, 2010-11). Discounts: 2-4 books 20%, 5-99 40%, 100+ 50%; short 20%. 192pp. Reporting time: 1 month, query before submitting. We accept simultaneous submissions, but please query before submission. Publishes 10% of manuscripts submitted. Payment: 5-10% royalty on retail price. Does not copyright for author. Subjects: Business & Economics, Construction, Health, How-To, Humor, Medicine, Nursing, Travel, Writers/Writing.

THE STAR BEACON, Earth Star Publications, Ann Ulrich Miller, Publisher, 216 Sundown Circle, Pagosa Springs, CO 81147, TEL 970-759-2983, starbeacon@gmail.com, www.earthstarpublications.com. 1987. Poetry, articles, art, photos, cartoons, interviews, reviews, letters, long-poems, news items, non-fiction. "*Star Beacon* readers are looking for the latest information on UFOs and related phenomena, as most of them are UFO percipients of various degrees, searching for answers. Because science, for the most part, has rejected them, *Star Beacon* readers are turning to metaphysics (the science of higher mind) for such answers as why are we here, where are we going, how can we make our world and the universe better." circ. 500+. 12/yr. Pub'd 8 issues 2009; expects 12 issues 2010, 12 issues 2011. sub. price $27 print US, $30 Canada, $36 foreign, $12 PDF; per copy $2.50; sample $2. Back issues: $1.50. Discounts: 50% to retailers. 16pp. Reporting time: 2 weeks. Simultaneous submissions accepted: yes. Publishes 80% of manuscripts submitted. Payment: copies, subscription, small honorarium in some cases. Copyrighted, reverts to author. Pub's reviews: 12 in 2009. §UFOs, metaphysics, psychic phenomena, New Age living, astrology, shamanism. Ads: $80/$40/$20 1/4 page/$10 1/8 page/$3 per column inch/20 cents per word classifieds. Subjects: Newsletter, Space, Spiritual.

Star Publish LLC, T.C. McMullen, Owner and Director of Operations; Janet Elaine Smith, Head Editor,

Marketing Director, PO Box 122, Loretto, PA 15940, 814-421-5142. 2003. Fiction, non-fiction. *"Do you want to self publish but don't want to spend your valuable time learning how to do so? Star Publish LLC has the expertise to produce a quality book that you can be proud to present to the world. What makes Star Publish different than other publishing houses? We work with you one-on-one. We listen to your desires and wishes for your manuscript while providing you with our expertise in turning it into a quality book. Star Publish LLC - changing the publishing world one book at a time!*Queries required. Send by email to submissions@starpublishllc.com. Recent writers whose manuscripts were accepted at Star Publish LLC: Dr. Cal Hunter, L. Lee Parmeter, JC Marino, and Holly Weiss."* Pub'd 12 titles 2009; expects 10 titles 2010, 15 titles 2011. No titles listed in the *Small Press Record of Books in Print* (36th Edition, 2010-11). Discounts: 40% to bookstores. 200pp. Reporting time: 1 to 2 weeks. Simultaneous submissions accepted: No. Publishes 50% of manuscripts submitted. Payment: from 50% to 70% royalties paid on a quarterly basis. Does not copyright for author. Subjects: Erotica, Fantasy, Fiction, Humor, Juvenile Fiction, Literature (General), Memoirs, Non-Fiction, Romance, Science Fiction, Self-Help, Writers/Writing, Young Adult.

Starcherone Books, PO Box 303, Buffalo, NY 14201-0303, www.starcherone.com. 2000. Fiction. "Looking for innovative fiction, new stuff, work which renews our faith in the form. We read unsolicited manuscripts August-September. Always query first, listing your literary accomplishments, publications, etc." avg. press run 1000. Pub'd 2 titles 2009; expects 4 titles 2010, 4 titles 2011. 12 titles listed in the *Small Press Record of Books in Print* (36th Edition, 2010-11). Discounts: wholesale 40%. 200pp. Reporting time: 6-10 months. We accept simultaneous submissions if author makes it clear it is under consideration elsewhere. Publishes 1% of manuscripts submitted. Payment: $500 advance; 10% royalties. Copyrights for author. Subjects: Absurdist, Anarchist, Dada, Experimental, Fiction, Futurism, Literature (General), Novels, Post Modern, Prose, Satire, Storytelling, Surrealism.

Stardate Publishing Company, John Cothran, P. O. Box 112302, Carrollton, TX 75011-2302, voice-972-898-8349, fax-1-866-728-6500, jcothran@stardatepublishing.com, www.stardatepublishing.com. 1984. Art, photos, non-fiction. "I am interested in culture." avg. press run 4000. Expects 1 title 2010. 1 title listed in the *Small Press Record of Books in Print* (36th Edition, 2010-11). Discounts: 2-10 copies 25%. 382pp. Reporting time: A week. Simultaneous submissions accepted: No. Publishes 50% of manuscripts submitted. Payment: Varies. Copyrights for author. Subjects: Adolescence, African-American, The Americas, Avant-Garde, Experimental Art, Civil Rights, Civil War, Culture, Education, Entertainment, Literature (General), Military, Veterans, Movies, Music, Non-Fiction, World War II.

Starik Publishing, Stacie Craig, Executive Editor, PO Box 307, Slaton, TX 79364, web:www.starikpublishing.com. 2006. avg. press run 2000. Pub'd 1 title 2009; expects 1 title 2010, 2 titles 2011. 2 titles listed in the *Small Press Record of Books in Print* (36th Edition, 2010-11). Booksellers Discount: 1-4 copies 20% 5-24 copies 40% 25+ copies 45% Case quantity discount for 32 copies, or a multiple of 32 copies, of a single title is 50%.Distributors Discount: 55%. 288pp. Reporting time: 6 weeks. Simultaneous submissions accepted: yes. Publishes 2% of manuscripts submitted. Copyrights for author. Subjects: Adoption, Christianity, Family, Fiction, Inspirational, Non-Fiction, Novels, Religion, Romance, Young Adult.

Staring Media (see also SMARANDACHE NOTIONS JOURNAL), Joanne McGray, Box 141, Rehoboth, NM 87322, m_l_perez@yahoo.com, http://fs.gallup.unm.edu//eBooks-otherformats.htm and http://fs.gallup.unm.edu//eBooksLiterature.htm. avg. press run 50. 240 titles listed in the *Small Press Record of Books in Print* (36th Edition, 2010-11).

Starlight Press, Ira Rosenstein, Box 3102, Long Island City, NY 11103. 1980. Poetry. "Anthology published in 1992. No immediate publishing plans." avg. press run 300. 6 titles listed in the *Small Press Record of Books in Print* (36th Edition, 2010-11). Discounts: normal trade. 35pp. Reporting time: 2 months. Payment: 2 free copies & 50% discount on further Starlight copies (any title). Copyrights for author. Subject: Poetry.

STARNOTES, Intuitive Moon Media, Dominique Jones, 13170-B Central SE #191, Albuquerque, NM 87123, webmaster@intuitivemoon.com, 505-349-5993, 505-280-9667. 2008. Articles, interviews, reviews. circ. 50000. 24/yr. Pub'd 24 issues 2009; expects 24 issues 2010, 24 issues 2011. Back issues: inquire. 4pp. Reporting time: 1 month. Simultaneous submissions accepted: Yes. Publishes 10% of manuscripts submitted. Payment: varies by agreement. Copyrighted, reverts to author. Pub's reviews: approx 25 in 2009. §tarot decks, astrology books, tarot books, metaphysical books, self-improvement, videos, podcasts, blogs, etc. Ads: $125 full page /$75 half page /$40 quarter page /$5 classified/$. Subjects: Astrology, Cosmology, Dreams, Interviews, Magic, Mentoring/Coaching, Metaphysics, Motivation, Success, New Age, Occult, Psychology, Self-Help, Spiritual, Supernatural, Tarot.

Starry Night Publishing, Richard Goldstein, 904 Broad Street, Collingdale, PA 19023, www.starrynightpublishing.com. 2005. Satire, non-fiction. "Our primary focus is non-fiction." avg. press run 1000. Pub'd 1 title 2009; expects 6 titles 2010, 25 titles 2011. 1 title listed in the *Small Press Record of Books in Print* (36th Edition, 2010-11). 200-300pp. Reporting time: 2 weeks. Simultaneous submissions accepted: Yes. Publishes

5% of manuscripts submitted. Payment: Varies on material, level of expertise, amount of work required and type of market. Varies on Sitution. Subjects: Family, History, Humor, Non-Fiction, Nutrition, Public Affairs, Relationships, Self-Help, Senior Citizens, Women.

STATE AND LOCAL GOVERNMENT REVIEW, Michael J. Scicchitano, Editor; Ann Allen, Contact Person, Carl Vinson Institute of Government, 201 N. Milledge Ave., Univ. of GA, Athens, GA 30602, 706-542-2736. 1968. "A journal of research and viewpoints on state, local, and intergovernmental issues." circ. 1.4M. 3/yr. Pub'd 3 issues 2009; expects 3 issues 2010, 3 issues 2011. sub. price $26 individual, $75 library; electronic subscription: $22 individual, $70 library; per copy $8.70 plus shipping. Back issues: volumes 1-7 $1/copy plus shipping, all other $8.70/copy plus shipping. 72pp. Reporting time: 10 weeks. Publishes 25% of manuscripts submitted. Copyrighted. Pub's reviews. Subject: Political Science.

STATE OF CALIFORNIA LABOR, University of California Press, Ruth Milkman, Editor; Rebecca Frazier, Managing Editor, University of California Press, 2000 Center St., Suite 303, Berkeley, CA 94704-1223, 510-634-7154. 2001. Articles. "Editorial address: UC Institute for Labor and Employment, 2310 Hershey Hall, UCLA, Box 951478, Los Angeles, CA 90095-1478. Copyrighted by the Regents of the University of California." circ. 2500. 1/yr. Pub'd 1 issue 2009; expects 1 issue 2010, 1 issue 2011. sub. price $25 indiv., $70 inst., $25 student; per copy $25 indiv., $70 inst., $25 student; sample same as single copy. Discounts: foreign subs. agents 10%, one-time orders 30%. 236pp. Copyrighted, does not revert to author. Ads: $295/$220. Subjects: Labor, Research.

State University of New York Press, Gary Dunham, Executive Director; Jane Bunker, Associate Director and Editor-in-Chief; Daniel Flynn, Associate Director and Director of Sales and Business Development, 194 Washington Avenue, Suite 305, Albany, NY 12210-2384, main editorial 518-472-5000, orders 877-204-6073, website www.sunypress.edu. 1966. Non-fiction. "Editorial Program: Scholarly titles and serious works of general interest with special interest in Continental Philosophy; Transpersonal Psychology; African American studies; Gender/Sexuality Studies; American Indian Studies; Museum/Archival Science; Asian Studies; Religious Studies; and New York State." avg. press run 700. Pub'd 209 titles 2009; expects 180 titles 2010, 180 titles 2011. No titles listed in the *Small Press Record of Books in Print* (36th Edition, 2010-11). Discounts: Trade Titles-Hardcover & Paper: T follows price, 40%; Short Titles-Cloth & Paper: 20%; Classroom adoption: 20%Trade sales may earn higher discount on short paperbacks if placed through sales reps or through SUNY Press Director of Sales and Business Development. 256pp. Reporting time: one to two months. Simultaneous submissions accepted: Yes, at proposal stage. Publishes less than 5% of manuscripts submitted. Payment: royalties after 1000 sold depending on contract. Copyrights for author. Subjects: Adirondacks, African-American, Anthropology, Archaelogy, Asia, Indochina, Buddhism, Feminism, Gender Issues, Indigenous Cultures, Native American, New York, Philosophy, Psychology, Race, Religion, Spiritual.

Steel Balls Press, R. Don Steele, Box 807, Whittier, CA 90608, E-mail don@steelballs.com. 1986. Non-fiction. "No unsolicited m/s! 1 page. Query letters only. Specialize in controversial how-to/self help. *Absolutely* no New Age, poetry, fiction." avg. press run 20M. Pub'd 2 titles 2009; expects 2 titles 2010, 2 titles 2011. 4 titles listed in the *Small Press Record of Books in Print* (36th Edition, 2010-11). Discounts: normal trade; STOP 25%. 224pp. Reporting time: 6 weeks. Simultaneous submissions accepted: yes. Publishes 2% of manuscripts submitted. Payment: 10% retail cover price after 500 copies. Does not copyright for author. Subjects: Drugs, Health, How-To, Men, Romance, Self-Help, Sex, Sexuality, Singles.

Steel Toe Books, Tom C. Hunley Ph.D., English Department / Western Kentucky University, 1906 College Heights Blvd. #11086, Bowling Green, KY 42101-1086, (270) 745-5769 tom.hunley@wku.edu www.steeltoe-books.com. 2003. Poetry. "Among our titles are Einstein Considers a Sand Dune by James Doyle, winner of the 2003 Steel Toe Books Prize in Poetry, selected by David Kirby, Diary of a Cell by Jennifer Gresham, winner of the 2004 Steel Toe Books Prize in Poetry, selected by Charles Harper Webb, Becoming the Villainess by Jeannine Hall Gailey, Blue Collar Eulogies by Michael Meyerhofer, and My Father's Kites by Allison Joseph. We only read unsolicited manuscripts during advertised open reading periods, usually held in January. There is no fee, but we ask that everyone submitting to us purchase one of our books ($12)." avg. press run 500. Pub'd 3 titles 2009; expects 3 titles 2011. No titles listed in the *Small Press Record of Books in Print* (36th Edition, 2010-11). Discounts: 40%. 90pp. Reporting time: one to three months. Simultaneous submissions accepted: Yes. Publishes 1% of manuscripts submitted. Payment: standard royalties contract. Copyrights for author. Subject: Poetry.

Steerforth Press, L.C., Thomas Powers, Senior Editor; Michael Moore, Senior Editor; Alan Lelchuk, Senior Editor; Chip Fleischer, Publisher, 25 Lebanon St., Hanover, NH 03755-2143, 603-643-4787. 1993. Fiction, non-fiction. "No unsolicited manuscripts accepted." avg. press run 5M. Pub'd 15 titles 2009; expects 15 titles 2010, 20 titles 2011. 14 titles listed in the *Small Press Record of Books in Print* (36th Edition, 2010-11). 275pp. Reporting time: query first. Payment: standard cuts for clothbound and paperbacks. Copyrights for author. Subjects: Biography, Essays, History, Literature (General), Memoirs, Novels.

Stellaberry Press, Edward Cervinski, P.O. Box 18217, St. Paul, MN 55118, http://www.stellaberry.com. 2005. Poetry, fiction, cartoons, music, parts-of-novels, non-fiction. avg. press run 3000. Expects 3 titles 2010, 3 titles 2011. 1 title listed in the *Small Press Record of Books in Print* (36th Edition, 2010-11). 50-300pp. Simultaneous submissions accepted: Yes. Subjects: Children, Youth, Fiction, Music, Non-Fiction, Poetry.

Stemmer House Publishers, Inc., David Eisenstadter, Editor, 4 White Brook Road, P.O. Box 89, Gilsum, NH 03448-0089. 1975. Fiction, art, non-fiction. avg. press run 5M. Pub'd 20 titles 2009; expects 15 titles 2010, 15 titles 2011. 18 titles listed in the *Small Press Record of Books in Print* (36th Edition, 2010-11). Discounts: 40% for 5 assorted titles or more to retailers. 170pp. Reporting time: 4 weeks. Simultaneous submissions accepted: yes. Publishes .1% of manuscripts submitted. Payment: royalty and advance. Copyrights for author. Subjects: Arts, Design, Earth, Natural History, Fiction.

Sterli Publishing, James Rives, 2202 Coathbridge Dr, Germantown, TN 38139, 901-351-6849. 2006. Fiction, photos. Expects 2 titles 2010, 4 titles 2011. No titles listed in the *Small Press Record of Books in Print* (36th Edition, 2010-11). Subjects: Christmas, Juvenile Fiction.

SterlingHouse Publisher, Cynthia Sterling, Publisher & CEO, 3468 Babcock Blvd., Pittsburgh, PA 15237, Phone: 412-837-2423, www.sterlinghousepublisher.com. 1998. Poetry, fiction, non-fiction. avg. press run 3M-3.5M. Pub'd 64 titles 2009; expects 50 titles 2010, 50 titles 2011. No titles listed in the *Small Press Record of Books in Print* (36th Edition, 2010-11). Discounts: call distributor for trade and bookstore discounts: Partners (800) 336-3137; direct sales and special sales call for pricing: (888) 542-BOOK. 245pp. Reporting time: 2-6 months. Simultaneous submissions accepted: yes. Publishes less than 10% of manuscripts submitted. Payment: 10-12% royalty, royalties paid bi-yearly. Copyrights for author. Subjects: Biotechnology, Christianity, Essays, Fantasy, Fiction, Holocaust, Memoirs, Metaphysics, Mystery, New Age, Poetry, Politics, Religion, Science Fiction, Sex, Sexuality.

Chuck Stewart, Chuck Stewart, 3722 Bagley Ave. #19, Los Angeles, CA 90034-4113, www.StewartEducationServices.com. 2000. Non-fiction. "Eclectic mix from "Bankrupt Your Student Loans," "Lead Hazards in Residential Real Estate," "Mold Hazards in Residential Real Estate," to "Queer Word Puzzles," "Queer History and Politics Word Games," and "Queer Pop Culture Word Games.".'' avg. press run 500. Pub'd 3 titles 2009; expects 3 titles 2010, 2 titles 2011. No titles listed in the *Small Press Record of Books in Print* (36th Edition, 2010-11). Discounts: negotiated. 300pp. Reporting time: 30 days. Simultaneous submissions accepted: No. Publishes 1% of manuscripts submitted. Payment: 10%. Copyrights for author. Subjects: Environment, Finances, Gay, Lesbianism, Safety.

Stewart Publishing & Printing, Robert Stewart, 17 Sir Constantine Drive, Markham, Ontario L3P 2X3, Canada, www.stewartbooks.com 905-294-4389; robert@stewartbooks.com. 1992. Poetry, fiction, letters, non-fiction. Pub'd 33 titles 2009; expects 40 titles 2010, 45 titles 2011. 6 titles listed in the *Small Press Record of Books in Print* (36th Edition, 2010-11). Copyrights for author. Subjects: Biography, Business & Economics, England, Genealogy, History, How-To, Ireland, Miniature Books, New Age, Printing, Scotland, Self-Help, Spiritual, Textbooks.

Still Waters Press, Shirley Lake, 459 South Willow Avenue, Galloway, NJ 08205-4633. 1985. Poetry, non-fiction. "Still Waters Press of Galloway, New Jersey, officially concluded all publishing operations on January 1, 2007. No manuscripts will be read, accepted, or invited. Some chapbooks on the SWP booklist remain in print and are available until further notice. Authors of SWP chapbooks are invited to contact the editor to arrange for acquisition or disposition of the "masters" of their chapbooks. Gratitude to all poets, now, and always." No titles listed in the *Small Press Record of Books in Print* (36th Edition, 2010-11). Discounts: 40%. 32pp. Please do not submit manuscripts. Simultaneous submissions accepted: No. Publishes 0% of manuscripts submitted. Payment: No longer publishing new works.

THE STINGING FLY, Declan Meade, Publisher-Editor; Eabhan Ni Shuileabhain, Poetry Editor, PO Box 6016, Dublin 8, Ireland, stingingfly@gmail.com, www.stingingfly.org. 1997. Poetry, fiction, articles, art, photos, cartoons, interviews, criticism, reviews, letters, parts-of-novels, long-poems, collages, plays, news items, non-fiction. "The Stinging Fly is dedicated to promoting new Irish and international writing. It has a particular interest in discovering and fostering new writing talent. We operate an open submission policy, with submissions accepted January to March each year. No email submissions are accepted but we can respond to international postal submissions by email. Full submission guidelines on our web site." circ. 1000. 3/yr. Pub'd 3 issues 2009; expects 3 issues 2010, 3 issues 2011. 2 titles listed in the *Small Press Record of Books in Print* (36th Edition, 2010-11). sub. price 25 euro (International); per copy 10 euro (International); sample 10 euro (International). 128pp. Reporting time: 3 months. Simultaneous submissions accepted: No. Publishes 10% of manuscripts submitted. Payment: Two copies plus 25 euro. Copyrighted, reverts to author. Pub's reviews: 10 in 2009. §Fiction and poetry, Irish and international. Ads: Full Page 250 euro, half page 150 euro. Subjects: Interviews, Ireland, Literary Review, Literature (General), Poetry, Prose, Reviews, Short Stories, Translation, Writers/Writing.

Stone and Scott, Publishers, Les Boston, PO Box 56419, Sherman Oaks, CA 91413-1419, 818-904-9088 Fax 818-787-1431 www.StoneandScott.com. 1990. Poetry, fiction, non-fiction. "Also publish wordplay: spponnerisms, puns, and such. *Stoopnagle's Tale Is Twisted: Spoonerisms Run Amok* has been a staple for four years. *The Giant Book of Animal Jokes: Beastly Humor for Grownups* by Richard Lederer and James Ertner with Illustrations by James McLean is new for 2006. *Hawk,* a novel by William Wallis, won PMA's 2006 Benjamin Franklin Award in Fiction. We have too much work in process to consider new material." avg. press run 2,000 - 3,000. 7 titles listed in the *Small Press Record of Books in Print* (36th Edition, 2010-11).

•**STONE CANOE,** Robert Colley, Editor, 700 University Avenue, Suite 326, Syracuse, NY 13244-2530, Phone: 315-443-1082/3225, Fax: 315-443-4174, e-mail: rmcolley@uc.syr.edu. "*Stone Canoe*, a journal of arts and ideas from Upstate New York, is published annually, each spring, by University College of Syracuse University, 700 University Avenue, Syracuse, New York 13244-2530. Address all correspondence to the above address, or to stonecanoe@syr.edu. Stone Canoe showcases the work of a diverse mix of emerging and well-established artists and writers with connections to Upstate New York. In doing so, the journal supports Syracuse University's ongoing efforts to nurture creative community partnerships and seeks to promote a greater awareness of the cultural and intellectual richness that characterizes life in the region." No titles listed in the *Small Press Record of Books in Print* (36th Edition, 2010-11).

Stone Cottage Press, Kevin Diaz, 2020 S. Mission Street, Suite 232, Mount Pleasant, MI 48858-4425, 989-773-1570, editor@stonecottagepress.com. 2008. Poetry, fiction. "Our mission is to publish good, literary fiction." avg. press run 200. Expects 3 titles 2010, 4 titles 2011. No titles listed in the *Small Press Record of Books in Print* (36th Edition, 2010-11). Discounts: 2-10 copies 25%. 100pp. Reporting time: Two weeks. Simultaneous submissions accepted: Yes. Payment: Standard royalty arrangements. Does not copyright for author. Subject: Fiction.

STONE SOUP, The Magazine By Young Writers and Artists, Gerry Mandel, William Rubel, Box 83, Santa Cruz, CA 95063, 831-426-5557, Fax 831-426-1161, e-mail editor@stonesoup.com, www.stonesoup.com. 1973. Poetry, fiction, art, photos, reviews, letters, parts-of-novels, long-poems, plays. "All material written & drawn by children 8-13." circ. 20M. 6/yr. Pub'd 6 issues 2009; expects 6 issues 2010, 6 issues 2011. sub. price $37; per copy $6.50; sample $6.50, or free online. Back issues: prices upon request. Discounts: schedule available upon request. 48pp. Reporting time: 4 weeks. Simultaneous submissions accepted: no. Publishes .5% of manuscripts submitted. Payment: 2 copies, $40 plus certificate. Copyrighted, does not revert to author. Pub's reviews: 12 in 2009. §Children's books. Ads: none. Subjects: Children, Youth, Education, Magazines.

STONE TABLE REVIEW, Bradley J. Stiles Ph.D., Editor; Leigh J. Harbin Ph.D, Co-Editor, Contact: editors@stonetablereview.com. "*Stone Table Review* is an online journal publishing new works in traditional or new media formats by emerging and established writers in October and April of each year. We look for work that contributes something significant to the ongoing human discoursework that brings something to the table, as it wereand all voices and styles are considered equally. STR is not affiliated with any organization and is not supported by subscriptions. Each issue is a labor of love, driven by the editors' desire to let sincere and talented voices be heard. All readers are invited to sit, read, and converse freely. We provide the table, but every contributor provides the feast. Submission Deadline: March 15, 2008.Reading Period: August 15 - June 15. We only accept e-mail submissions.. Send to editors@stonetable-review.com." Bi-annually (October & April).

Stonehorse Publishing, LLC, Rainer Kohrs Ph.D., Marketing Director, 6521 East 101 St., Ste. D1, Room 296, Tulsa, OK 74133, 1.888.867.1927, Fax: 1.888.867.1927, generalinfo@stonehorsepublishing.com, www.stone-horsepublishing.com. 2004. Fiction, non-fiction. avg. press run 7500. Expects 1 title 2010, 2 titles 2011. 3 titles listed in the *Small Press Record of Books in Print* (36th Edition, 2010-11). Discounts: 1 copy 40%, 2-100 copies 50%, 101 or more 55%. 55% Nonreturn option: If a buyer is willing to purchase nonreturnable books, discount is a flat 55% for 10 or more books, plus free freight. 32pp. Copyrights for author. Subjects: Children, Youth, Fantasy, Fiction, Non-Fiction, Picture Books.

Stonemark Publishing, Jon Iverson, P.O. Box 8854, 312 S. Ivy Street, Medford, OR 97501, 541-772-3477. 1997. Non-fiction. Expects 1 title 2010, 1 title 2011. 1 title listed in the *Small Press Record of Books in Print* (36th Edition, 2010-11). 250pp. Subjects: Law, Wine, Wineries.

Storm Publishing Group, Debarkes Johnson, 8117 Birchfield Dr, Indianapolis, IN 46268, stormpublishing@sbcglobal.net, www.stormpublishinggroup.com. 2005. Non-fiction. "we publish NONFICTION: How-to, cookbooks, gardening, travel guides and travel related books." avg. press run 3000. Expects 16 titles 2010, 30 titles 2011. No titles listed in the *Small Press Record of Books in Print* (36th Edition, 2010-11). 150pp. Reporting time: 2-6 months. Simultaneous submissions accepted: Yes. Publishes 55% of manuscripts submitted. Payment: 5-7% of retail for royalties, advances very from book to book. Copyrights for author. Subjects: Animals, Cooking, Finances, Gardening, How-To, Non-Fiction, Parenting, Pets, Publishing, Quilting, Sewing, Real Estate, Travel, Wood Engraving/Woodworking.

Stormline Press, Inc., Raymond Bial S., P. O. Box 593, Urbana, IL 61803, 217-328-2665. 1985. Poetry, fiction, art, photos, satire, non-fiction. "Stormline Press publishes works of literary and artistic distinction, with emphasis upon rural and small town life in the American Midwest. Notable titles include Living With Lincoln by Dan Guillory and Silent Friends by Margaret Lacey. No unsolicited queries or manuscripts are accepted. Stormline Press publishes by invitation only." avg. press run 1. Expects 1 title 2010, 1 title 2011. No titles listed in the *Small Press Record of Books in Print* (36th Edition, 2010-11). Discounts: 40% discount; no charge for shipping on orders of five or more books. 100-250pp. Reporting time: One month. Simultaneous submissions accepted: No. Payment: 15% of net sales price. 1. Subjects: Agriculture, Americana, Amish Culture, Fiction, History, Humor, Indiana, Literature (General), Mystery, Non-Fiction, North America, Photography, Short Stories, Storytelling, Writers/Writing.

STORMWARNING!, PO Box 21604, Seattle, WA 98111, 206-374-2215 phone/Fax, vvawai@oz.net, www.oz.net/~vvawai/. 1986. Poetry, articles, art, photos, cartoons, criticism, reviews, letters, news items, non-fiction. "Vets, Vietnam veterans especially encouraged. Anti-war, peace, justice issues, revolution, people's struggles. Veterans of all eras. Young people. Radical thinking." circ. 3M. 2-3/yr. Pub'd 2 issues 2009; expects 2 issues 2010, 2 issues 2011. sub. price $10; per copy $2; sample free. Back issues: 1/2 cover price. Discounts: bookstores/newstands 50%, outposts 3+ 70%. 16pp. Simultaneous submissions accepted: yes. Payment: none. Not copyrighted. Pub's reviews: 4 in 2009. §Books, Vietnam War, history, fiction by Nam vets, Gulf War, social issues. Ads: none. Subjects: Book Reviewing, Civil Rights, Communism, Marxism, Leninism, Counter-Culture, Alternatives, Communes, Crime, Criticism, Current Affairs, History, Human Rights, Military, Veterans, Peace, Politics, Vietnam, War, Young Adult.

Story County Books, Theresa Pappas, Co-Editor; Michael Martone, Co-Editor, PO Box 21179, Tuscaloosa, AL 35402-1179. 1984. Fiction. "Story County Books was published in Story County, Iowa. We publish one story chapbooks in formats that vary with each story. We publish cheap chapbooks, and we try to keep the price under $1. Our first book was Michael Wilkerson's *Can This Story Be Saved?* a take-off of the *Ladies Home Journal* piece. We chose a Dell Purse Book format to complement the 'self-improvement' parody of the piece. We are interested in clever stories, regional stories, stories with a voice." avg. press run 100. Pub'd 1 title 2009; expects 1 title 2010, 1 title 2011. 8 titles listed in the *Small Press Record of Books in Print* (36th Edition, 2010-11). Discounts: 50%. Pages vary. Reporting time: 14 months. Simultaneous submissions accepted: no. Publishes 1% of manuscripts submitted. Payment: by arrangement. Copyrights for author. Subject: Fiction.

STORYBOARD, Robert Alan Burns, General Editor, Christopher S. Lobban, 25 Slab City Road, Lincolnville, ME 04849, storybd@uog.edu, rburns@uog9.uog.edu. 1991. Poetry, fiction, art, photos, interviews, parts-of-novels, long-poems, non-fiction. "Material should have Pacific regional focus or be written by a resident of this region." circ. 200. 1/yr. Pub'd 1 issue 2009; expects 1 issue 2010, 1 issue 2011. sub. price $7.50; per copy $7.50; sample $4. Back issues: $5. Discounts: 30% retail; 50% distributor. 100pp. Reporting time: 4-6 months, SASE required. Simultaneous submissions accepted: no. Publishes 30% of manuscripts submitted. Payment: 2 copies. Copyrighted, reverts to author. Ads: $150/$100/$50 1/3 page. Subject: Pacific Region.

Storycraft Publishing (see also JUNIOR STORYTELLER; THE KIDS' STORYTELLING CLUB WEBSITE), Vivian Dubrovin, PO Box 205, Masonville, CO 80541, 970-669-3755 phone/Fax, JrStoryteller@storycraft.com, www.storycraft.com. 1993. Fiction, articles, non-fiction. "Shipping address: 8600 Firethorn Drive, Loveland, CO 80538. We are a narrow niche publisher of books and periodicals for young (age 9-12) storytellers. Interested in feature articles on young tellers and programs for young storytellers. We are expanding into related areas. Query only. No unsolicited material accepted." avg. press run 3M. Expects 1-3 titles 2010, 1-3 titles 2011. 6 titles listed in the *Small Press Record of Books in Print* (36th Edition, 2010-11). Discounts: library 20%, bookstore 40%, distributor 50%, other by contract. 80-204pp. Reporting time: query only. Simultaneous submissions accepted: no. Payment: varies. Copyrights for author vary. Subjects: Children, Youth, Crafts, Hobbies, Education, Storytelling, Young Adult.

STORYQUARTERLY, P. O. Box 29272, San Francisco, CA 94129, www.storyquarterly.com, narrativemaga-zine.com, 415-346-4477. 1975. Fiction, parts-of-novels, non-fiction. "Accept submissions only online. No Reading Fee. Needs: Literary stories of any type or style, serious or humorous. No preferred length. Short-shorts as well as longer. No genre work. Publish prominent and first-time authors in each issue. Recently published: Joyce Carol Oates, Richard Bausch, T. Coraghessan Boyle, Robert Olen Butler, Stuart Dybek, Tom Grimes, Lore Segal, Janet Burroway, Alice Hoffman, and Pamela Painter. Publishes online and one large print anthology annually." circ. 30,000. One large print anthology published annually; ongoing online issues. Pub'd 2 issues 2009; expects 4 issues 2010, 3 issues 2011. sub. price online free; per copy $35/donation for the hard copy annual; sample $35/donation for hard copy issue. Back issues: $35/donation for hard copy issue. Discounts: contact Editor. 400pp. Reporting time: 4 to 16 weeks. Simultaneous submissions accepted: yes. Publishes .05% of manuscripts submitted. Payment: Between $150 and $750. Copyrighted, reverts to author. Subjects: Fiction, Literature (General), Non-Fiction.

Strata Publishing, Inc., Kathleen Domenig, PO Box 1303, State College, PA 16804, 814-234-8545, Fax

814-238-7222, www.stratapub.com. 1990. Non-fiction. "We publish mid-level and advanced textbooks for college courses in communication and journalism. Authors are professors who teach such courses." Pub'd 2 titles 2009; expects 3 titles 2010, 2 titles 2011. 12 titles listed in the *Small Press Record of Books in Print* (36th Edition, 2010-11). Reporting time: 1-3 months. Simultaneous submissions accepted: yes. Payment: varies. varies with circumstances. Subjects: Civil Rights, Communication, Journalism, Communication, Journalism, Criticism, Editing, Language, Law, Media, Media, Political Science, Speaking, Writers/Writing.

Strawberry Patchworks, Susan A. McCreary, Box 3, Green Mansion, North, VA 23128, 804-725-7560, berrybookssam@gmail.com. 1982. Non-fiction. "We specialize in one subject cookbooks, softcover using 4 color process on cover. Emphasis on originality of subject and exploring every aspect of the subject. Poetry, art and history are incorporated throughout books." avg. press run 2M-4M. Pub'd 1 title 2009; expects 1 title 2010, 1 title 2011. 5 titles listed in the *Small Press Record of Books in Print* (36th Edition, 2010-11). Discounts: trade 40%, wholesaler 50%. 100-200pp. Reporting time: 1 month or less. Payment: negotiable, no advances. Copyrights for author. Subjects: Cooking, Ecology, Foods.

STRINGTOWN, Polly Buckingham, Editor; Jenny Heard, Associate Editor, PO Box 1406, Medical Lake, WA 99022-1406, stringtown@earthlink.net, http://www.home.earthlink.net/~stringtown/index.html. 1998. Poetry, fiction, parts-of-novels, long-poems, plays, non-fiction. "Submissions determine the content. We prefer to read manuscripts Sept.-April. We've published work from Peter Meinke, Judith Skillman, James Bertolino, and James Nolan." circ. 1M. 1/yr. Pub'd 1 issue 2009; expects 1 issue 2010, 1 issue 2011. sub. price $6.00; per copy $6.00; sample $6.00 or $3.00 for any back issue. Back issues: $3. Discounts: $4 wholesale or $4.50 consignment for independent bookstores. 56pp. Average reporting time is three to six months. We accept simultaneous submissions with notification upon acceptance elsewhere. Publishes 10-15% of manuscripts submitted. Payment: 5 copies. Copyrighted, reverts to author. Subjects: Fiction, Poetry.

STRUGGLE: A Magazine of Proletarian Revolutionary Literature, Tim Hall, PO Box 28536, Detroit, MI 48228. 1985. Poetry, fiction, articles, art, cartoons, satire, criticism, reviews, music, letters, collages, plays. "We want literature and art of rebellion against the ruling class." 4/yr, sub extended if 4 not published. Pub'd 3 issues 2009; expects 4 issues 2010, 4 issues 2011. sub. price $10, $12 to institutions, $15 overseas, $5 to prisoners, exchanges possible with similar publications; per copy $2, $4 for a double issue; sample $3.00 via mail, $5 for a double issue. Back issues: by arrangement (vol. 1 available, photocopied at extra charge), $120 for full set (19 years). Discounts: by arrangement. 36pp in a single issue, 72pp in a double, we usually issue a double. Reporting time: 3 months. We encourage simultaneous submissions. Publishes 10% of manuscripts submitted. Payment: 1 copy. Not copyrighted. Ads: none. Subjects: Astronomy, Black, Chicano/a, Communism, Marxism, Leninism, Drama, Fiction, Humor, Labor, Native American, Poetry, Satire, Short Stories, Socialist, Third World, Minorities, Women.

Studio 4 Productions An imprint of Quick Publishing, LC, 1610 Long Leaf Circle, Saint Louis, MO 63146, 888publish (782-5474), Fax 314-993-4485, www.studio4productions.com. 1972. "Length: +/-200 pages. Most recent publications: *The Wisdom to Choose* and *Shadowdad*." avg. press run 3M-6M. Pub'd 3 titles 2009; expects 3 titles 2010, 3 titles 2011. 8 titles listed in the *Small Press Record of Books in Print* (36th Edition, 2010-11). 200pp. Reporting time: 30 days. Simultaneous submissions accepted: Not currently accepting submissions. Payment: 10% list paid annually. We hold copyrights on most books. Subjects: Parenting, Self-Help, Senior Citizens, Social Work, Travel.

STUDIO - A Journal of Christians Writing, Paul Grover, Managing Editor, Kate Lumley, 727 Peel Street, Albury, N.S.W. 2640, Australia, email: studio00@bigpond.net.au. 1980. Poetry, fiction, articles, reviews, letters. "Published poets by reputable Australian publishing houses have been represented. Material varies from short poems to short stories of 2M to 5M words." circ. 300. 4/yr. Pub'd 4 issues 2009; expects 4 issues 2010, 4 issues 2011. sub. price $AUD60; per copy $AUD15; sample $AUD10 (air mail). Discounts: order of 20 or more in advance of printing receives 10%. 36pp. Reporting time: 3 weeks. Simultaneous submissions accepted: yes. Publishes 30% of manuscripts submitted. Payment: for contests $AUD50, no payment for ordinary submissions but free copy posted for submissions. Copyrighted, reverts to author. Pub's reviews: 30 in 2009. §Poetry, fiction, books for children. Ads: $AUD100/$AUD50/no classified. Subjects: Australia, Book Reviewing, Fiction, Graphics, Literary Review, Literature (General), Poetry, Religion.

STUDIO ONE, College of St. Benedict, Haehn Campus Center, St. Joseph, MN 56374. 1976. Poetry, fiction, art, photos, satire, long-poems. "Short fiction should generally be fewer than 5,000 words. *Studio One* accepts submissions of literary and visual art from across the nation, but contributors from the Midwest are especially encouraged to submit. Art should reproduce well in black and white. Now accept color visual art." circ. 900. 1/yr. Pub'd 1 issue 2009; expects 1 issue 2010, 1 issue 2011. sub. price $6 check or money order with SASE. 70-100pp. Reporting time: we try to send out acceptance/rejection letters within 1 month of the deadline. Simultaneous submissions accepted: no. Publishes 10% of manuscripts submitted. Payment: none. Copyrighted, reverts to author. Subjects: Arts, Essays, Fiction, Photography, Poetry, Short Stories.

476

Stunt Publishing, Michael Kewley, 22287 Mulholland Hwy, #281, Calabasas, CA 91302, ph:818-312-5157, fax:818-312-5157, www.stuntpublishing.com, stuntpublishing@stuntpublishing.com. 2003. Fiction, art, collages. "children's books." Pub'd 1 title 2009; expects 1-2 titles 2010, 1-2 titles 2011. No titles listed in the *Small Press Record of Books in Print* (36th Edition, 2010-11). 32pp. Simultaneous submissions accepted: Yes. Subjects: Children, Youth, Family, Picture Books.

STYLUS, Peter Bates, 65 Westbourne Street, Roslindale, MA 02131, peterbates01@yahoo.com. 1990. Reviews. "We are a Web-only publisher. Please query with any ideas you may have. We do not pay for submissions, but you are allowed to keep books and software that you review. Hardware may be subject to return to the manufacturer after the evaluation period. Typically we request that reviewers keep their reviews down to under 500 words.The Web URL is www.stylus.batescommunications.net." circ. 4000. 3/yr. Pub'd 3 issues 2009; expects 3 issues 2010, 3 issues 2011. 12pp. Reporting time: 1 month. Simultaneous submissions accepted: Yes. Publishes 25% of manuscripts submitted. Payment: No cash payment. Copyrighted, reverts to author. Pub's reviews: approx. 12 in 2009. §We are most interested in music reviews of concerts in the Greater Boston area. We also publish gadget reviews, i.e. life-enhancing gadgets such as software, hardware, pet tools, and household items. Subjects: Computers, Calculators, Consumer, Media, Movies, Music, Photography, Visual Arts.

Subsynchronous Press (see also THE LAUGHING DOG), Hillary Lyon, Editor; Warren Andrle, Assistant Editor, 4729 E. Sunrise #326, Tucson, AZ 85718, Subsyncpress.com, Subsyncpress@CS.com. 2000. "Submissions read all year round." avg. press run 150. Pub'd 1 title 2009; expects 1 title 2010, 1 title 2011. No titles listed in the *Small Press Record of Books in Print* (36th Edition, 2010-11). 30pp. Reporting time: 2-6 months. Simultaneous submissions accepted: *No.* Payment: Contributors recieve one free copy of the issue their poem(s) appears in. Copyrights for author.

•**Subsynchronuos Press (see also VEIL: Journal of Darker Musings),** Hillary Lyon, 4729 E. Sunrise, #326, Tucson, AZ 85718, Subsyncpress.com. 2002. Poetry. "We are looking for all your darker musings: serious Gothic, modern speculative, and comically-spooky poems. Length is no issue; quality is. Free verse stands a better chance with us than rhyme." avg. press run 50. Pub'd 1 title 2009; expects 1 title 2010, 1 title 2011. No titles listed in the *Small Press Record of Books in Print* (36th Edition, 2010-11). 34pp. Reporting time: 3-6 months. Simultaneous submissions accepted: No. Publishes 25% of manuscripts submitted. Payment: Contributors recieve one free copy of the issue their work apears in; additional copies are discounted. Copyrights for author. Subjects: Ancient Astronauts, Experimental, Haiku, Horror, Magic, Mystery, Myth, Mythology, Science Fiction, Surrealism.

SUB-TERRAIN, Anvil Press, Brian Kaufman, Publisher, Senior Editor; Patrick Mackenzie, Managing Editor, P.O. Box 3008, Main Post Office, Vancouver, BC V6B 3X5, Canada, 604-876-8710, subter@portal.ca, www.subterrain.ca. 1988. Poetry, fiction, articles, photos, interviews, satire, criticism, reviews, non-fiction. "subTerrain no longer accepts unsolicited poetry submissions." circ. 4M. 3/yr. Pub'd 3 issues 2009; expects 3 issues 2010, 3 issues 2011. sub. price $15; per copy $5.95 Can., $4.95 US; sample $5 to cover post. Back issues: $5. 56pp. Reporting time: 4-6 months. Simultaneous submissions are accepted, but please inform us if the work has been accepted for publication elsewhere. Publishes 5% of manuscripts submitted. Payment: Prose: $25 per page; Poetry: $20 per poem; photography/illustration: $25 - $100; plus complimentary 1-year subscription + 5 contributor copies of issue in which your work appears. Copyrighted, reverts to author. Pub's reviews: 30 in 2009. §Poetry, fiction, social issues (primarily releases from small to med. size publishers not receiving attention they deserve). Send review copies Attn: Review Column. Ads: $900 (full col., back cover); $800 (full col. inside front/back); $700 (full page b/w); $475 1/2 page; Publishing, book, art, or literary related *only.* Subjects: Avant-Garde, Experimental Art, Creative Non-fiction, Erotica, Essays, Experimental, Fiction, Non-Fiction, Prose, Satire, Short Stories, Socialist, Theatre, Writers/Writing.

SUBTROPICS, David Leavitt, Editor, P.O. Box 112075, 4008 Turlington Hall, University of Florida, Gainesville, FL 32611-2075. "*Subtropics* seeks to publish the best literary fiction, essays, and poetry being written today, both by established and emerging authors. We will consider works of fiction of any length, from short shorts to novellas and self-contained novel excerpts. We give the same latitude to essays. We appreciate work in translation and, from time to time, republish important and compelling stories, essays, and poems that have lapsed out of print. For stories and essays, *Subtropics* pays a flat fee of $1,000 ($500 for a short short) for North American first serial rights. Poets are paid $100 per poem. Subtropics pays upon acceptance for prose; for poetry, we pay after the publication of the issue preceding the one in which the authors work will appea."

Suburban Wilderness Press (see also RED HAWK), PO Box 202, Kailua-Kona, HI 96745. 1984. Poetry, fiction, art, photos, collages. "Broadsides." avg. press run 150. Pub'd 40 titles 2009; expects 40 titles 2010, 40 titles 2011. No titles listed in the *Small Press Record of Books in Print* (36th Edition, 2010-11). Discounts: none. 1 page broadsides. Reporting time: 1 week to never. Publishes a variable % of manuscripts submitted. Payment: varies. Copyrights for author. Subjects: Minnesota, Poetry.

Success Publishing, Allan H. Smith, 3419 Dunham Drive, Box 263, Warsaw, NY 14569. 1978. Non-fiction. "How to make money. How to start in business. How to market your product. How to publish. Sewing, craft, business." avg. press run 2M-5M. Pub'd 6 titles 2009; expects 4 titles 2010, 6 titles 2011. 14 titles listed in the *Small Press Record of Books in Print* (36th Edition, 2010-11). Discounts: 1 10%, 2-6 25%, 7-15 40%, 16-50 50%, 50-100 53%; library 25%. 150pp. Reporting time: 90-120 days. Payment: varies. Copyrights for author. Subjects: Crafts, Hobbies, Education, Family, How-To, Printing, Quilting, Sewing.

Successful Kids Publishing, AnnaMarie Squailia, P.O. Box 34025, Reno, NV 89533, info@successfulkidspublishing.com, 775-351-4368. 2008. Articles, non-fiction. "Successful Kids Publishing produces childrens book that weaves self-help material into the questions and activities in the Character Building Section. There are both easy and hard questions and low cost activities, which makes them perfect for a wide age range. This helps builds the foundation of communication which every parent wants when their children reaches those turbulent teenage years. Like every other skill, it takes practice. The books provided by Successful Kids Publishing will help adults start conversations with the children they love, helping them develop effective communication skills. After the Character Building Section, there is a section of possible answers to the questions. This acts like a springboard to help adults dive into a conversation with their children. Tough times require strong communication skills for all of us." Expects 1 title 2010, 4 titles 2011. 1 title listed in the *Small Press Record of Books in Print* (36th Edition, 2010-11). Discounts: 2-4 copies 20%5-9 copies 30%10-24 copies 40%25-49 copies 42%50-74 Copies 44%100-199 copies 48%200 or more 50%. 40-80pp. Subjects: Children, Youth, Family, Picture Books, Self-Help.

Sugar Loaf Press, 343 North Pearl Street, Granville, OH 43023-1334, 740-507-2704. 2000. Pub'd 1 title 2009; expects 1 title 2010, 1 title 2011. No titles listed in the *Small Press Record of Books in Print* (36th Edition, 2010-11). Reporting time: 1 month.

SUGAR MULE, M.L. Weber, Editor, Online publication., Email: misc@marclweber.com. Website: http://www.marclweber.com/sugarmule/. "A literary magazine with eccentric buddhist leanings. *Sugar Mule* does not pay for accepted work(s) at this time. *Sugar Mule* wishes to use only new material not seen before elsewhere on the internet. As to rights, you retain all rights to your work; we retain none. Before submitting, please check the reading schedule of upcoming issues (on the 2nd page of the website), as there are periods when we do not read submissions for some time. Otherwise, we welcome submissions of poetry, fiction, and all genres of non-fiction. Submit only via email or by email file attachment if by file attachment be sure to include your name and email address on every page of the attached file."

Sherwood Sugden & Company, Publishers, Sherwood Sugden, 315 Fifth Street, Peru, IL 61354, 815-224-6651, Fax 815-223-4486, philomon1@netscape.net www.geocities.com/sugdenpublishers/ (or) www.sugdenpublishers.com. 1975. Non-fiction. avg. press run 3M. Pub'd 3 titles 2009; expects 3 titles 2010, 3 titles 2011. 29 titles listed in the *Small Press Record of Books in Print* (36th Edition, 2010-11). Discounts: 40% STOP; otherwise 20%-1 copy, 25% 2-3 copies, 40%-5+ copies. 300pp. Reporting time: 2-3 months. Payment: 8%-12%. Copyrights for author. Subjects: Biography, Christianity, Criticism, Education, English, History, History, Literature (General), Philosophy, Religion, Reprints, South, Textbooks.

SUMMER ACADEME: A Journal of Higher Education, Caddo Gap Press, David Schejbal, Editor, 3145 Geary Boulevard #275, San Francisco, CA 94118, 415-392-1911. 1997. Articles. "An annual journal of college and university summer session administrators." circ. 1M. 1/yr. Pub'd 1 issue 2009; expects 1 issue 2010, 1 issue 2011. sub. price $30 indiv., $60 instit.; per copy $30. 96pp. Reporting time: 2 months. Publishes 25% of manuscripts submitted. Payment: none. Copyrighted, reverts to author. Ads: none. Subject: Education.

Summer Stream Press, David Duane Frost, Editor, PO Box 6056, Santa Barbara, CA 93160-6056, 805-962-6540. 1978. Poetry, non-fiction. "This press is now producing and marketing a series of cassette tapes under the general title: Poetic Heritage. #102180 Elinor Wylie/Amy Lowell; #103010 Sara Teadsale/Margaret Widdemer; #103150 Edna St. Vincent Millay; #103290 Emily Dickinson/Lizette Woodworth Reese." avg. press run 5M. Expects 1 title 2011. 3 titles listed in the *Small Press Record of Books in Print* (36th Edition, 2010-11). Discounts: 50% no returns. 450pp. Reporting time: 6 months to 1 year. Simultaneous submissions accepted: yes. Publishes 2% of manuscripts submitted. Payment: 15% - paid annually January 1st. Copyrights for author. Subjects: Non-Fiction, Poetry.

Summerland Publishing, Jolinda Pizzirani, 21 Oxford Drive, Lompoc, CA 93436, PH/Fax: 8057355241, www.summerlandpublishing.com. 2003. Poetry, fiction, photos, cartoons, non-fiction. "Our goal at Summerland Publishing is to publish books that will help make the world a better place. One of our most recent releases, "Kid Ethics 2: From A to Z" by James "Bud" Bottoms is a workbook that teaches ethics to young children. This book has been widely accepted by educational institutions as a great way to educate our youngsters on proper behavior as they mature." avg. press run 5000. Pub'd 4 titles 2009; expects 6 titles 2010, 6 titles 2011. No titles listed in the *Small Press Record of Books in Print* (36th Edition, 2010-11). Discounts: 40%. 150pp. Reporting time: Within two weeks. Simultaneous submissions accepted: No. Publishes 10% of manuscripts submitted. Payment: We pay royalties quarterly. Does not copyright for author. Subjects: Aging, Channelling, Creative Non-fiction, Ethics, Family, Fiction, Guidance, Inspirational, Metaphysics, Motivation, Success, New Age, Parenting, Philosophy, Self-Help, Spiritual.

Summerset Press, Brooks Robards, Jim Kaplan, 20 Langworthy Road, Northampton, MA 01060, 413-586-3394 phone/FAX, BrooksRoba@aol.com. 1994. avg. press run 1M. Expects 1 title 2010. 6 titles listed in the *Small Press Record of Books in Print* (36th Edition, 2010-11). Discounts: 60-40%. 100pp. Reporting time: 30 days. Simultaneous submissions accepted: yes. Payment: individually negotiated. Does not copyright for author. Subjects: Poetry, Sports, Outdoors, Travel.

THE SUMMERSET REVIEW, Joseph Levens, Editor; Amy Leigh Owen, Associate Editor, 25 Summerset Drive, Smithtown, NY 11787. 2002. Poetry, fiction, non-fiction. Quarterly (online) Annually (print). price per copy $10. 150pp. Simultaneous submissions accepted: Yes. Publishes 1% of manuscripts submitted. Payment: Complimentary print copy. Ads: No.

Summit Crossroads Press, Eileen Haavik, 9329 Angelina Circle, Columbia, MD 21045-5109, Phone/fax 410-290-7058, sumcross@aol.com, www.parentsuccess.com. 1993. Non-fiction. "Publishes books relating to parenting, family and school." avg. press run 5M. 5 titles listed in the *Small Press Record of Books in Print* (36th Edition, 2010-11). Discounts: wholesaler/distributor 55%, bookstores 40%. 250pp. Reporting time: 2 weeks. Simultaneous submissions accepted: yes. Payment: 10% of net receipts. Copyrights for author. Subjects: Children, Youth, Family, Parenting.

Sun Dog Press, Al Berlinski, 22058 Cumberland Drive, Northville, MI 48167, 248-449-7448, Fax 248-449-4070, sundogpr@voyager.net. 1987. Poetry, fiction, letters. "Hard-edged and innovative fiction, poetry, letters. Book length manuscripts considered." avg. press run 500-1M. Pub'd 2 titles 2009; expects 2 titles 2010, 2 titles 2011. 15 titles listed in the *Small Press Record of Books in Print* (36th Edition, 2010-11). Discounts: 20%-48%. 250pp. Reporting time: 8 weeks. Simultaneous submissions accepted: yes. Payment: royalty on sales. Copyrights for author. Subjects: Fantasy, Fiction, Memoirs, Poetry.

THE SUN, A Magazine of Ideas, Sy Safransky, Editor, 107 North Roberson Street, Chapel Hill, NC 27516, 919-942-5282. 1974. Poetry, fiction, articles, art, photos, cartoons, interviews, satire, letters, parts-of-novels, long-poems, collages, non-fiction. "A monthly magazine of ideas in its twenty-eighth year of publication, *The Sun* celebrates good writing—and the warmth of shared intimacies—in essays, fiction, interviews, and poetry. People write in the magazine of their struggle to understand their lives, often baring themselves with remarkable candor. Recent contributors: Poe Ballantine, Derrick Jensen, Alison Luterman, Stephen J. Lyons, and Sybil Smith." circ. 50M. 12/yr. Pub'd 12 issues 2009; expects 12 issues 2010, 12 issues 2011. sub. price $34; per copy $3.95; sample $5. Back issues: complete set of all available back issues for $300. Discounts: 50% for distributors. 48pp. Reporting time: 3 months. Simultaneous submissions accepted: no. Publishes 1% of manuscripts submitted. Payment: essays and interviews $300-$1,000; short stories $300-$500; poetry $50-$200; photos $50-$300. Copyrighted, reverts to author. Ads: none. Subjects: Essays, Fiction, Interviews, Journals, Non-Fiction, Photography, Poetry.

SunandShade Publications, Gini Coover, Editor, PO Box 22, Shade, OH 45776, 740-594-4147, www.SunandShadePublications.com. 1 title listed in the *Small Press Record of Books in Print* (36th Edition, 2010-11).

Sunbelt Publications, Lowell Lindsay, CEO; Jennifer Redmond, Editor-in-Chief, 1256 Fayette Street, El Cajon, CA 92020-1511, 619-258-4911, Fax 619-258-4916, editor@sunbeltpub.com, www.sunbeltbooks.com. 1988. Fiction, non-fiction. "We accept proposals for nonfiction books with camera-ready supporting materials (e.g., photos, maps, artwork) that would have a broad, general market appeal in our genre, which is outdoor recreation, cultural heritage, history, pictorials and guidebooks to California, Mexico, and the Southwest U.S. Also memoir and fiction by established authors or those with an established "platform" and audience; No poetry." avg. press run 3M-5M. Pub'd 14 titles 2009; expects 6 titles 2010, 6 titles 2011. 54 titles listed in the *Small Press Record of Books in Print* (36th Edition, 2010-11). Discounts: (40-50% to booksellers with resale #, 55% to AWBA-listed wholesalers). 250-300pp. Reporting time: 1 month on queries, 90 days on MS. Simultaneous submissions accepted: yes. Payment: royalties based on net sales. Copyright will be registered for author, but may assigned to author or publisher. Subjects: Bicycling, California, Dictionaries, Earth, Natural History, Folklore, Geology, History, Maps, Mexico, Native American, Non-Fiction, Sports, Outdoors, Travel, U.S. Hispanic, The West.

Sunlight Publishers, Joseph Kent, Poetry Editor, PO Box 640545, San Francisco, CA 94109, 415-776-6249. 1989. Poetry. "Some bias toward poetic consciousness of an evolutionary nature and organic poetry in the modernist vein based on experience of the perceiver." avg. press run 700. Expects 3 titles 2010. 4 titles listed in the *Small Press Record of Books in Print* (36th Edition, 2010-11). Discounts: 2-4 30%, 5-100 40%. 64pp. Reporting time: 1 month. Payment: 10% royalty on all sales, paid twice yearly. Copyrights for author. Subject: Poetry.

sunnyoutside, David McNamara, PO Box 911, Buffalo, NY 14207, www.sunnyoutside.com. 2005. Poetry, fiction, non-fiction. No titles listed in the *Small Press Record of Books in Print* (36th Edition, 2010-11). Simultaneous submissions accepted: No. Does not copyright for author.

Sunnyside Press, Richard Triumpho, 297 Triumpho Road, St. Johnsville, NY 13452-4003, 518-568-7853 phone/Fax, triglade@telenet.net. 2001. Non-fiction. avg. press run 1M. Pub'd 2 titles 2009; expects 2 titles 2010, 4 titles 2011. 4 titles listed in the *Small Press Record of Books in Print* (36th Edition, 2010-11). Discounts: trade 40%. 248pp. Reporting time: 6 weeks. Simultaneous submissions accepted: yes. Publishes 10% of manuscripts submitted. Payment: negotiable. Copyrights for author. Subjects: Adirondacks, Agriculture, Alaska, Americana, Amish Culture, Business & Economics, Folklore, Non-Fiction.

Sunrise Health Coach Publications, Jan DeCourtney, PO Box 21132, Boulder, CO 80308, Phone and fax: 303-527-2886, info@sunrisehealthcoach.com, http://sunrisehealthcoach.com. 1996. Non-fiction. "Alternative medicine books for symptom relief, pain relief, natural healing, physical, emotional, and mental health. Books focusing on self-help for chronic illness and optimal health." avg. press run 3000. Expects 1 title 2010, 2 titles 2011. 2 titles listed in the *Small Press Record of Books in Print* (36th Edition, 2010-11). Discounts: See website at http://sunrisehealthcoach.com. 100-440pp. Reporting time: 2 months. Simultaneous submissions accepted: Yes. Payment: TBA. TBA. Subjects: Alternative Medicine, Health, Self-Help.

SunShine Press Publications, Inc., Jackie Hofer, Publisher, 6 Gardner Court, Longmont, CO 80501, 303-772-3556, jlhof1@yahoo.com, www.sunshinepress.com. 1986. Poetry, photos, non-fiction. "Will be publishing books and chapbooks in CD format *only* for reading and viewing in Adobe Reader. All will be in full color including any photographs, art or illustrations. They will be sold primarily on the Internet and other online sources. Recent publication: *Tree Magic: Nature's Antennas* 450 pages in full color, 169 authors (poems and short stories) and 115 photos and paintings. Authors include Kirby Congdon, Jim Fisher, John Fitzpatrick, Laurie Klein, Jacqueline Marcus, Reg Saner, Howard Rheingold and others. (see www.sunshinepress.com) Currently working on a CD of nature poems, photographs and paintings. Watch *Small Press Review* and *Poets and Writers* for requests for submissions." avg. press run 1,000. Pub'd 1 title 2009; expects 2 titles 2010, 3 titles 2011. 17 titles listed in the *Small Press Record of Books in Print* (36th Edition, 2010-11). 200pp. Reporting time: 3 months SASE. Simultaneous submissions accepted: yes. Copyrights for author. Subjects: Animals, Anthology, Arts, Color, Essays, Nature, Non-Fiction, Poetry, Prose, Short Stories, Spiritual.

Sunstone Press, James Clois Smith Jr., President, PO Box 2321, Santa Fe, NM 87504-2321, 505-988-4418, fax 505-988-1025, jsmith@sunstonepress.com. 1971. Fiction, non-fiction. "Primarily southwestern US subjects; prefers non-fiction." avg. press run 3M. Pub'd 24 titles 2009; expects 24 titles 2010, 30 titles 2011. 128 titles listed in the *Small Press Record of Books in Print* (36th Edition, 2010-11). Discounts: standard. 160pp. Reporting time: 90 days or less. Simultaneous submissions accepted: no. Payment: royalty only. Copyrights for author. Subjects: Crafts, Hobbies, History, Southwest.

SUPERIOR CHRISTIAN NEWS, Superior Christian Press, Ed Chaberek, Guna Chaberek, PO Box 424, Superior, MT 59872. 1995. Poetry, articles. "Recent contributors include Arthur Winfield Knight, Robert Kimm, Simon Perchik, John Grey, and Ronald Scott. Poetry, 40 lines or less, emphasis on originality. Very important - we want translations of poetry from any language. Magazine is now a Christian publication, please consider this when submitting." circ. 100-150. 4/yr. Pub'd 4 issues 2009; expects 4 issues 2010, 4 issues 2011. sub. price $6; per copy $6; sample $6. Back issues: none. Discounts: classroom 10 copies $50. 24-40pp. Reporting time: within 6 months. Simultaneous submissions accepted: yes. Publishes 10% of manuscripts submitted. Payment: 1 copy. Not copyrighted, all rights except 1st always with author. No ads. Subjects: Poetry, Translation.

Superior Christian Press (see also SUPERIOR CHRISTIAN NEWS), Ed Chaberek, Guna Chaberek, PO Box 424, Superior, MT 59872. 1995. Poetry, articles. "We are looking for more inspirational, factual, research-oriented prose (nonfiction) pieces of a Christian nature. No biases. But must be sound intellectually. Though we believe in Jesus absolutely and in the literal Resurrection we, like the writers of the Gospels and Paul, maintain that faith must be supported by intellect." avg. press run 100-150. Pub'd 4 titles 2009; expects 4 titles 2010, 4 titles 2011. No titles listed in the *Small Press Record of Books in Print* (36th Edition, 2010-11). 24-40pp. Reporting time: within 6 months. We accept simultaneous submissions, but want to be informed. Publishes less than 10% of manuscripts submitted. Payment: 1 copy on publication. Does not copyright for author. Subjects: Philosophy, Poetry, Religion, Sociology.

George Suttton Publishing Co., Sutton George, 54 Crawford Drive, Aurora, Ontario, Canada L4G 4R4, Canada, georgesutton2005@yahoo.com. 2004. Fiction, articles, interviews, criticism, reviews, letters, parts-of-novels. "Some recent contributors:1. Recently re-discovered works/letters/diaries by Leo Tolstoy, one of the world 's best novelists2. Seniors Yearbook and Directory with many Health, Longevity, Retirement Tips, etc." avg. press run 500. Pub'd 2 titles 2009; expects 5 titles 2010, 10 titles 2011. No titles listed in the *Small Press Record of Books in Print* (36th Edition, 2010-11). Discounts: 2-10 copies 25%. 250pp. Reporting time: 2

months. Simultaneous submissions accepted: No. Publishes 1% of manuscripts submitted. Payment: 10 percent. Does not copyright for author. Subjects: Family, Health, Language, Literature (General).

Swamp Press (see also TIGHTROPE), Ed Rayher, 15 Warwick Avenue, Northfield, MA 01360-1105. 1975. Poetry, art, long-poems. "We make limited edition letterpress books which live up to the standards of the fine-crafted poem. We're open to almost anything, as long as it's the best...to last 1,000 years. Recent contributors: Chuck Zerby, L.A. Davidson, vincent tripi, Robert Bensen." avg. press run 300. Pub'd 2 titles 2009; expects 2 titles 2010, 2 titles 2011. 10 titles listed in the *Small Press Record of Books in Print* (36th Edition, 2010-11). Discounts: dealers and booksellers 40%, continuing collectors 40%, libraries 20%. 60pp. Reporting time: 8 weeks. Simultaneous submissions accepted: no. Publishes 1% of manuscripts submitted. Payment: 10% press run. Does not copyright for author. Subject: Poetry.

Swan Duckling Press (see also THE BLUE MOUSE), Mark Bruce, PO Box 8317, Eureka, CA 95502-8317. 1999. Poetry. avg. press run 300. Pub'd 3 titles 2009. 2 titles listed in the *Small Press Record of Books in Print* (36th Edition, 2010-11). 40pp. Reporting time: 3-6 months. Simultaneous submissions accepted: no. Publishes 20% of manuscripts submitted. Payment: authors retain copyright, pays in copies. We do not copyright for author unless chapbook.

Swan Scythe Press, James DenBoer, Director, 515 P Street #804, Sacramento, CA 95814-6320, 916 492 8917. 2000. Poetry. "Swan Scythe Press, a publishing group located in Sacramento, California, discovers and publishes some of the best new poets in America today. Swan Scythe Press has focussed on publishing poetry by emerging poets, of any age, race, ethnicity, gender or sexual orientation. Each year we open a chapbook competition, usually between April 1 and June 1. We are also beginning two chapbook series: one called Poetas:Puentes, with English translations from poets writing in Spanish from North, Central and South America; the other named New Native American Poets. To date, we have published 26 chapbooks." No titles listed in the *Small Press Record of Books in Print* (36th Edition, 2010-11).

Swedenborg Foundation, Morgan Beard, 320 North Church Street, West Chester, PA 19380, (610) 430-3222 (Phone), (610) 430-7982 Fax, 1-800-355-3222 (Phone), info@swedenborg.com, www.swedenborg.com. 1850. Fiction, articles, interviews, non-fiction. "We only accept for publication books that contain Swedenborgian content consistent with out mission. Most of our books are by or about Swedenborg's life and work. Our annual Chrysalis Reader is an anthology of short prose pieces and poems." Pub'd 4 titles 2009; expects 4 titles 2010, 7 titles 2011. No titles listed in the *Small Press Record of Books in Print* (36th Edition, 2010-11). Discounts: Retail discount schedule:(all books combine for discounts whether single or assorted titles)1- 4 copies 20%5- 24 copies 40%25-99 copies 42%. 220pp. Reporting time: three months. Simultaneous submissions accepted: Yes. Publishes 5% of manuscripts submitted. Copyrights for author. Subjects: Non-Fiction, Religion, Self-Help, Spiritual.

Sweet People Publishing, Alfred Moore, 14175 W. Indian School Road, Ste B4, PMB 506, Goodyear, AZ 85395, 866-824-9843, info@sweetpeoplepublishing.com, www.sweetpeoplepublishing.com. 2005. Fiction, photos, plays, non-fiction. "Sweet People Publishing focuses on writings that inspire, motivate and empower its readers. Selections can be inspirational, spiritual or wellness related. The primary focus is they provide upliftment. Ours is a positive publishing company that desires to be in partnership with our authors to generate a product that publisher and author are proud of. We are energetic and creative in our marketing efforts. We seek to get our authors the maximum exposure, but require they promote the book as diligently as we do." avg. press run 2000. Expects 2 titles 2010, 6 titles 2011. 1 title listed in the *Small Press Record of Books in Print* (36th Edition, 2010-11). Discounts: 1 book No Discount2-4 books 20% off5-9 books 30% off10-24 books 40% off25-49 books 42% off50-74 books 44% off100-199 books 48% off200 or more books 50% off. 100-400pp. Reporting time: 15 days. Simultaneous submissions accepted: No. Publishes 15% of manuscripts submitted. Payment: Varies. Copyrights for author. Subjects: African-American, Aging, Alcohol, Alcoholism, Alternative Medicine, Family, Fiction, Food, Eating, Fundraising, How-To, Inspirational, Motivation, Success, Nutrition, Relationships, Religion, Self-Help.

SWILL, Rob Pierce, Editor-in-Chief; Sean Craven, Assistant Editor, Art & Design, editors@swillmagazine.com, www.swillmagazine.com. 2006. Poetry, fiction, satire, parts-of-novels, plays. "We like stories where things actually happen, stories where someone might die. We prefer the Shakespeare approach to existentialism: question the meaning of life, then litter the stage with corpses. We accept submissions via e-mail only. Attachments (.doc or .rtf) are preferred. Contributors have included John Shirley, W.G. Kelly, Steve Young, Craig Hartglass, Brian Haycock, Gene Hines, Sam J. Miller, William Peacock, Ben Cheetham, Ross Cavins, Robert N. Jennings, Mark Vanner, Andrew Killmeier, Jen Michalski, Nina Alvarez, Doug Draime, Owen Roberts, Giano Cromley, Samantha Roman, Bucky Sinister, Corey Mesler, Dan Donche, Delphine LeCompte, Keith Rutledge, Mark Scheel, Rob Pierce, Russell Bittner, Sean Craven, and Spencer Dew." 1/yr. Pub'd 1 issue 2009; expects 1 issue 2010, 1 issue 2011. sub. price $5; per copy $5; sample $5. Back issues: $5. 62pp. Reporting time: We usually reply in 3 to 6 months, faster toward the end of our reading period. Simultaneous submissions accepted: Yes. Publishes 3% of manuscripts submitted. Payment: Payment is 2 copies of issue in which the writer is published. Copyrighted, reverts to author. Subjects: Absurdist, Crime, Experimental, Fantasy, Fiction, Horror, Humor, Literature (General), Poetry, Prose, Satire, Science Fiction, Short Stories, Surrealism.

Swing-Hi Press, Barbara Moroney, 3045 S. Ponte Vedra Blvd., Ponte Vedra Beach, FL 32082, 904-819-9115, fax:904-825-0820, toll free:1-877-315-8638, barbara@naturalbodyshape.com, www.NaturalBodyShape.com. 2003. Expects 1 title 2010, 1 title 2011. 2 titles listed in the *Small Press Record of Books in Print* (36th Edition, 2010-11). Subject: Yoga.

SWINK, Leelila Strogov, 244 Fifth Ave. #2722, New York, NY 10001, 212-591-1651, 212-658-9995, www.swinkmag.com. 2004. Poetry, fiction, art, photos, cartoons, parts-of-novels, long-poems, non-fiction. "Swink is a biannual print magazine dedicated to identifying and promoting literary talent in both established and emerging writers. We're interested in writing that pushes the boundaries of the traditionalwriting that is new in concept, form or execution; that reflects a diversity of thought, experience or perspective; that provokes or entertains. Recent authors include Amy Bloom, Charles D'Ambrosio, Neal Pollack, Chris Offutt, Jonathan Ames, Steve Almond, Bob Hicok, Lucia Perillo, Beckian Fritz Goldberg and D. Nurkse, among others.Swink publishes fiction, non-fiction, poetry and interviews, and sponsors frequent readings and events in New York City and Los Angeles. Online theme issues of fiction, essays and poetry will also be available exclusively on our website." circ. 3000. 2/yr. Expects 2 issues 2010, 2 issues 2011. sub. price $16; per copy $10; sample $10. Back issues: $10. Discounts: 40% discount. 224pp. Reporting time: 3 months. Simultaneous submissions accepted: Yes. Publishes 1% of manuscripts submitted. Payment: $100 for fiction; $25 for poetry. Copyrighted, reverts to author. §Fiction, essays, poetry, artwork, photography. Ads: $400 full page. Subjects: Arts, Cartoons, Essays, Experimental, Fiction, Non-Fiction, Photography, Poetry, Short Stories.

Switchback Books, Brandi Homan, Editor-in-Chief, PO Box 478868, Chicago, IL 60647. "Switchback Books is a feminist press publishing poetry by women. Our definition of "women" is broad and includes transsexual, transgender, genderqueer, and female-identified individuals. Founded in 2006 by a group of students at Columbia College Chicago, Switchback Books publishes two books a year, one of which is the winner of the Gatewood Prize for a first book of poetry by a woman aged 18 through 39. Switchback Books welcomes young women writers who aren't afraid to look for answers in all directions." No titles listed in the *Small Press Record of Books in Print* (36th Edition, 2010-11).

SYCAMORE REVIEW, Anthony Cook, Editor-in-Chief, Purdue University, Department of English, 500 Oval Drive, West Lafayette, IN 47907, 765-494-3783. 1988. Poetry, fiction, art, photos, cartoons, interviews, satire, criticism, reviews, letters, parts-of-novels, long-poems, plays, non-fiction. "Sycamore Review accepts personal essays, short fiction, translations, drama (one act or standalone pieces) and quality poetry in any form. We are a journal devoted to contemporary literature, publishing both traditional and experimental forms. Submissions read between Aug. 1 and March 31 (the academic year).Please remember SR's WABASH PRIZES in poetry and fiction. Visit http://www.sycamorereview.com for more information." circ. 1000. 2/yr. Pub'd 2 issues 2009; expects 2 issues 2010, 2 issues 2011. sub. price $14; per copy $7; sample $7. Back issues: $5. Discounts: call for info. 160pp. Reporting time: 3-4 months. Simultaneous submissions accepted: yes. Publishes .6% of manuscripts submitted. Payment: 2 copies. Copyrighted, reverts to author. Pub's reviews: approx. 10 in 2009. §Poetry collections, short story and essay collections, novels, nonfiction that would appeal to readers of literature. Ads: Will participate in adswaps. Contact for paid advertisements. Subjects: Arts, Book Reviewing, Drama, English, Essays, Fiction, Interviews, Literary Review, Literature (General), Non-Fiction, Poetry, Reviews, Short Stories, Writers/Writing.

Symbios, Sanford R. Wilbur, 4367 S.E. 16th, Gresham, OR 97080-9178, 503-667-0633, home.netcom.com/~symbios. 1994. Expects 1 title 2010. 4 titles listed in the *Small Press Record of Books in Print* (36th Edition, 2010-11). Discounts: 1 copy 20%; 2-9 copies 50%; 10+ 70%.

SYMBOLIC INTERACTION, University of California Press, Simon Gottschalk, Editor, University of California Press, 2000 Center St., Suite 303, Berkeley, CA 94704-1223, 510-643-7154. 1977. Articles. "Editorial address: Dept of Sociology, University of Nevada, Las Vegas, 4505 Maryland Parkway, Las Vegas, NV 89154-5033. Copyrighted by the Society for the Study of Symbolic Interaction." circ. 787. 4/yr. Pub'd 4 issues 2009; expects 4 issues 2010, 4 issues 2011. sub. price $80 indiv., $251 inst., $27 student; per copy $21 indiv., $67 inst., $21 student; sample same as single copy. Discounts: foreign subs. agents 10%, 10+ one-time orders 30%. 170pp. Copyrighted, does not revert to author. Ads: $295/$220. Subjects: Social Work, Sociology.

SYMPLOKE: A Journal for the Intermingling of Literary, Cultural and Theoretical Scholarship, Jeffrey R. Di Leo, c/o J. Di Leo, Univ. of Houston, 3007 N. Ben Wilson, Victoria, TX 77901, Fax 361-570-4207, editor@symploke.org. 1993. Articles, interviews, criticism, non-fiction. "*Symploke* has no theoretical bias, and supports scholarship on any aspect of the intermingling of discourses and/or disciplines." circ. 650. 2/yr. Pub'd 2 issues 2009; expects 2 issues 2010, 2 issues 2011. sub. price $30; per copy $15; sample $10. Back issues: $40 per volume (2 issues). 130pp. Reporting time: 3 months. Simultaneous submissions accepted: yes. Publishes

10% of manuscripts submitted. Payment: none. Copyrighted, does not revert to author. Pub's reviews: 30 in 2009. §literary theory and criticism; cultural studies; philosophy; contemporary fiction. Ads: $100/$75/ exchanges. Subjects: Arts, Criticism, Culture, English, Ethics, Feminism, Fiction, History, Humanism, Non-Fiction, Novels, Philosophy, Politics, Race, Reading.

SYMPOSIUM, Augustus Pallotta, Editor; Elizabeth Foxwell, Managing Editor, Heldref Publications, 1319 18th St NW, Washington, DC 20036-1802, 202-296-6267 X275, Fax 202-293-6130, www.heldref.org. 1946. Articles, criticism, reviews. *"Symposium,* a journal in modern foreign literatures, includes research on authors, themes, periods, genres, works, and theory, frequently through comparative studies. Works are cited, and often discussed, in the original language. Submissions are approx. 15-25 double-spaced pages." circ. 500. 4/yr. Pub'd 4 issues 2009; expects 4 issues 2010, 4 issues 2011. sub. price $51; per copy $27; sample $27. 56pp. Simultaneous submissions accepted: no. Payment: 2 contributor's copies. Copyrighted, does not revert to author. Pub's reviews: 11 in 2009. §Books pertaining to modern foreign literatures. Ads: $155 full page. Subjects: Biography, France, French, Italy, Journals, Latin America, Literature (General), Spain.

synaesthesia press, Jim Camp, 3113 Beverly BLVD, Los Angeles, CA 90057, jim@synaesthesia.net, www.synaesthesia.net. 1995. Poetry, fiction, letters, parts-of-novels, long-poems, non-fiction. "Query first, always, no matter what. SASE gets replies." avg. press run 125. Pub'd 4 titles 2009; expects 3-4 titles 2010, 4 titles 2011. 1 title listed in the *Small Press Record of Books in Print* (36th Edition, 2010-11). Discounts: contact me. 16pp. Reporting time: 6 months. Simultaneous submissions accepted: yes. Publishes 1% of manuscripts submitted. Payment: usually $200 and 6 copies. We can copyright for author. Subjects: Fiction, Poetry.

Synergetic Press, Deborah Parrish Snyder, 1 Bluebird Court, Santa Fe, NM 87508-1531, Tel. 505-424-0237 Fax. 505 424 3336 e-mail: tango@synergeticpress.com website: www.synergeticpress.com. 1971. Poetry, fiction, art, cartoons, long-poems, plays, non-fiction. "50-450 pages in length. New and classic works in biospherics, Biosphere 2, ethnobotany, psychedelic culture, feng-shui, drama, fiction, culturology, and poetry." avg. press run 2M. Pub'd 4 titles 2009; expects 3 titles 2010, 3 titles 2011. 26 titles listed in the *Small Press Record of Books in Print* (36th Edition, 2010-11). Discounts: bookstores: 1-4 35% + postage, 5-10 40% post free, 11-25 42% postage-free, 26-50 43%, 51-99 44%. 200pp. Reporting time: 1-3 months. Payment: 7% authors royalty. Sometimes copyrights for author. Subjects: Arts, Avant-Garde, Experimental Art, China, Comics, Drama, Earth, Natural History, Metaphysics, Poetry, Visual Arts.

Synergistic Press, Bud Johns, 3965 Sacramento St., San Francisco, CA 94118, 415-EV7-8180, Fax 415-751-8505; website www.synergisticbooks.com; e-mail goodreading@synergisticbooks.com. 1968. Articles, art, letters, non-fiction. "Synergistic Press focuses its activity on nonfiction but in 2000 published its first novel, *Baby's Breath.* Its eclectic list of nonfiction shows the firm's wide-ranging interests including *Old Dogs Remembered* (an anthology of nonfiction and poems by 46 writers reminiscing about a much-loved dog), *Dying Unafraid* (the stories of people who did just that, told without pop psychology or religious intonations), *My ABC Book of Cancer* (written and drawn by a 10-year-old cancer patient, with supplemental text about her and childhood cancer), and art-focused titles such as *Not a Station But a Place, Paris Alive, Last Look at the Old Met* and *The Ecotopian Sketchbook.* Most of our titles have been developed internally and that probably will continue to be the case." avg. press run 3M-5M. Pub'd 2 titles 2009; expects 1 title 2010, 1 title 2011. 13 titles listed in the *Small Press Record of Books in Print* (36th Edition, 2010-11). Discounts: trade: single copies, 20%; 2-5, 35%, 6-11, 37%; 12-49, 40%, 50 or more, 44%; wholesaler/jobber discounts upon request. Pages vary, have published from 52-240pp. Reporting time: 1 month. Payment: varies with title. Copyrights for author. Subjects: Architecture, Arts, Bilingual, Biography, Fiction, France, French, Humor, Literature (General), Sports, Outdoors, Transportation.

Synergy Press, Sally Miller, POB 8, Flemington, NJ 08822-0008, 908.782.7101, Synergy@SynergyBookService, www.SynergyBookService.com. 1985. Fiction, non-fiction. "Our main subjects are health and sexuality. With a several-year hiatus for personal health reasons, we're back with a cookbook and a memoir; in 2006, a newly discovered author of short fiction (12,000 words) Mykola Dementiuk was featured. More of Mykola's work, of novel length, was published 2007-9, while other projects were set aside, though we did manage to get out a new cookbook and a compilation of essays in 2009, also.A new age dawns in 2010, with the final book of Mykola's we will publish, 100 Whores. See our website for other titles.Then I plan to get back to writing and publishing my own work as my life draws to a close." avg. press run 100-2500. Pub'd 3 titles 2009; expects 2 titles 2010, 2 titles 2011. No titles listed in the *Small Press Record of Books in Print* (36th Edition, 2010-11). Discounts: varies with book, 40-50%. 70-250pp. Reporting time: 1-2 weeks if phone number included. Simultaneous submissions accepted: Yes. Payment: Varies with chapbook. $1-200 plus $1/book sold. Does not copyright for author. Subjects: Adolescence, Alternative Medicine, Bisexual, Erotica, Fiction, Gay, Gender Issues, Health, Libertarian, Nutrition, Relationships, Sex, Sexuality, Sexual Abuse, Short Stories, Spiritual.

Syracuse Cultural Workers/Tools for Change, Dik Cool, Publisher, PO Box 6367, Syracuse, NY 13217, 315-474-1132, free fax 877-265-5399, scw@syracuseculturalworkers.com, SyracuseCulturalWorkers.com. 1982. Art, photos, cartoons, collages. "SCW publishes and distributes the annual Peace Calendar, the Women

Artists Datebook, posters, notecards, postcards, T-shirts, and selected books. We are a multicultural, visual arts publisher and distributor. Our images, in general, relate to peace and social justice, personal or social liberation and feminism. We sell wholesale and by direct mail." avg. press run 5-17M. Pub'd 20 titles 2009; expects 25 titles 2010, 25 titles 2011. No titles listed in the *Small Press Record of Books in Print* (36th Edition, 2010-11). Discounts: 40% returnable, 50% nonreturnable calendars; posters and cards 50%; books 40%, t-shirts 40%. 28pp. Reporting time: 3-6 months. Simultaneous submissions accepted: yes. Payment: 6%, one time calendar payment $100-200, cover $400. Does not copyright for author. Subjects: Arts, Black, Counter-Culture, Alternatives, Communes, Feminism, Feminism, Gay, Human Rights, Labor, Latin America, Lesbianism, Native American, Peace, Peace, Politics, Visual Arts.

Syracuse University Press, 621 Skytop Road Suite 110, Syracuse, NY 13244-5290, 1-800-365-8929. No titles listed in the *Small Press Record of Books in Print* (36th Edition, 2010-11).

Syukhtun Editions, Theo Radic, Odengatan 8, 114 24 Stockholm, Sweden, (468)6124988, theoradic@yahoo.com, http://www.syukhtun.net. 1987. Poetry, art, satire, music, long-poems, collages, plays, non-fiction. "Syukhtun Editions publishes non-fiction, poetry, plays, sheet music for guitar and fine arts prints. We give special emphasis to Native Californian cultures, and view the arts of writing and reading as ways to better understand Reality. Translations of prose and poetry from other languages are also of special interest, as in our bilingual Swedish-English edition, Selected Poetry of Edith Sodergran. Please contact us by regular mail or email before submitting anything." avg. press run 300. Pub'd 3 titles 2009; expects 3 titles 2010, 5 titles 2011. 7 titles listed in the *Small Press Record of Books in Print* (36th Edition, 2010-11). Discounts: 5-10 copies 20%. 200pp. Reporting time: 2 weeks. Simultaneous submissions accepted: No. Payment: negotiable. Copyrights for author. Subjects: Arts, Autobiography, California, Drama, Music, Myth, Mythology, Native American, Non-Fiction, Poetry, Prose, Satire, T'ai Chi, Visual Arts.

T

THE TABBY: A CHRONICLE OF THE ARTS AND CRAFTS MOVEMENT, Bruce Smith, 3085 Buckingham Drive SE, Port Orchard, WA 98366, (360) 871-7707. 1996. Articles, criticism, reviews, non-fiction. "Letterpress printed and hand bound, THE TABBY chronicles both the historic Arts & Crafts movement and its current-day revival. It provides a forum for new research, for analysis and throughtful historical narrative, for well-founded criticism, and the occasional wandering contemplation. Past articles can be seen on the website at www.artsandcraftspress.com/tabby." circ. 480. 4/yr. Pub'd 1 issue 2009; expects 4 issues 2010, 4 issues 2011. sub. price $65; per copy $20; sample $20. Back issues: inquire. Discounts: three or more copies: 40%. 108pp. Reporting time: two weeks. Simultaneous submissions accepted: Yes. Publishes 40% of manuscripts submitted. Payment: payment upon publication; $100 to $500 per piece. Copyrighted, reverts to author. Pub's reviews: approx. 8 in 2009. §Any essays, theses, books, or catalogues relating to the turn-of-the-century Arts and Crafts movement. No advertising. Subjects: Antiques, Architecture, Arts, Book Arts, Culture, History.

TABOO: Journal of Education & Culture, Caddo Gap Press, Shirley R. Steinberg, Editor, 3145 Geary Boulevard #275, San Francisco, CA 94118, 415-392-1911. 1995. Poetry, articles, art, reviews. "Articles, commentary, research, opinion about education and culture." circ. 300. 2/yr. Pub'd 2 issues 2009; expects 2 issues 2010, 2 issues 2011. sub. price $50 ind., $100 inst.; per copy $25. Back issues: $20 each. Discounts: 15% to subscription agencies. 150pp. Reporting time: 2 months. Simultaneous submissions accepted: no. Publishes 50% of manuscripts submitted. Payment: none. Copyrighted, reverts to author. Pub's reviews. §Education and culture. Ads: $200 full page. Subject: Education.

T'AI CHI, Wayfarer Publications, Marvin Smalheiser, Editor, PO Box 39938, Los Angeles, CA 90039, 323-665-7773, www.tai-chi.com. 1977. Articles, interviews, reviews, letters, news items. "Articles about Tai Chi Chuan, Chinese internal martial arts, Chi kung, meditation, health about 700-5M words each." circ. 50M. 4/yr. Pub'd 4 issues 2009; expects 4 issues 2010, 4 issues 2011. sub. price $20; per copy $5.99; sample $5.99. 68pp. Reporting time: 3 weeks. Simultaneous submissions accepted: no. Publishes 80% of manuscripts submitted. Payment: up to $500. Copyrighted. Ads: $825 BW Full Page/$1,030 for 4 color. Subjects: Health, New Age, Philosophy, Spiritual.

TAJ MAHAL REVIEW, Cyberwit.net, Santosh Kumar, 4/2 B Lig Govindpur Colony, Allahabad, India, 91-9415091004. 2001. Poetry, fiction, articles, art, photos, cartoons, interviews, satire, criticism, reviews, letters, parts-of-novels, long-poems, concrete art, news items, non-fiction. "Our main aim is to publish the poets and writers in English all over the world. The critical articles, essays, and poems should exhibit the post-modern trends, without obscurity, artificiality and violation of laws of criticism. Taj Mahal Review does not accept compositions founded on violent self-pity, or feelings of egocentricity. We will accept published, unpublished and also simultaneous creations, but Taj Mahal Review does not publish anonymous writings.Adam Donaldson Powell, Albert Russo, Banya Natsuishi, Bhuwan Thapaliya, Casimiro de Brito, Dimitris P. Kraniotis, Floriana Hall, Geert Verbeke, Helen Bar-Lev, Henry Victor, Janet K. Brennan, Jan Oscar Hansen, Maria Cristina Azcona, Mary Barnet, Oliver Rice.'' circ. 300. 2/yr. Pub'd 2 issues 2009; expects 2 issues 2010, 2 issues 2011. 1 title listed in the *Small Press Record of Books in Print* (36th Edition, 2010-11). sub. price 40; per copy 20; sample 12. Back issues: 15. Discounts: 2-10 copies 25. 500pp. Reporting time: We acknowledge at once. Final confirmation in Nov. for Dec. issues and in May for June issue. Simultaneous submissions accepted: Yes. Publishes 75% of manuscripts submitted. Copyrighted, reverts to author. Pub's reviews: 6 in 2009. §Fiction, Short Stories and Poetry.

Talent House Press, Paul Hadella, 1306 Talent Avenue, Talent, OR 97540, talhouse@mcleodusa.net. 1992. Poetry, fiction, art, photos, cartoons, satire, non-fiction. ''Projects vary but never stem from unsolicited mss.'' avg. press run 150-300. Pub'd 5 titles 2009; expects 5 titles 2010, 5 titles 2011. No titles listed in the *Small Press Record of Books in Print* (36th Edition, 2010-11). 40pp. Reporting time: 6 weeks. Payment: varies. Does not copyright for author.

Tales Press, 2609 N. High Croass Road, Urbana, IL 61802. No titles listed in the *Small Press Record of Books in Print* (36th Edition, 2010-11).

Talisman House, Publishers, Edward Foster, PO Box 3157, Jersey City, NJ 07303-3157, 201-938-0698. 1993. Poetry, fiction, interviews, criticism. avg. press run 1M-2M. Pub'd 2 titles 2009; expects 7 titles 2010, 7 titles 2011. 14 titles listed in the *Small Press Record of Books in Print* (36th Edition, 2010-11). Discounts: negotiated individually. 60-250pp. Reporting time: 3 months. Payment: negotiated individually. Copyrights for author. Subjects: Criticism, Fiction, Interviews, Literature (General), Novels, Poetry.

TALKING RIVER REVIEW, Lewis-Clark State College, 500 8th Avenue, Lewiston, ID 83501, Email: triver@lcsc.edu, www.lcsc.edu/TalkingRiverReview/. 1994. Poetry, fiction, art, photos, parts-of-novels, long-poems, non-fiction. ''*The Talking River Review* may cease publication after the Winter 2002 issue, but a final decision has not been made. Please see our website for updated information. Maximum length of prose is 7,500 words. Up to 5 poems may be submitted, any length or style. Recent contributers include: William Kittredge, Pattiann Rogers, Stephen Dunn, and Dorianne Laux.'' circ. 500. 2/yr. Pub'd 2 issues 2009; expects 2 issues 2010, 2 issues 2011. sub. price $14; per copy $5; sample $5. Back issues: $5. Discounts: 40% to bookstores. 140pp. Reporting time: 3 months. We accept simultaneous submissions with notification. Publishes 2% of manuscripts submitted. Payment: 2 copies and a year's subscription. Copyrighted, reverts to author. Ads: none. Subject: Literature (General).

TalSan Publishing/Distributors, Sandi J. Lloyd, 7614 W. Bluefield Avenue, Glendale, AZ 85308, 602-843-1119, fax 602-843-3080. 1995. Fiction, non-fiction. ''Mysteries, sci-fi, fantasy, history, romance, etc. All categories, all genres no poetry.'' avg. press run 1M. Expects 10 titles 2010, 20 titles 2011. 6 titles listed in the *Small Press Record of Books in Print* (36th Edition, 2010-11). Discounts: returnable: 1-4 20%, 5-24 40%, 25-49 42%, 50-99 43%, 100-999 45%, 1000+ 57%. Libraries: 1-9 10%, 10+ 15%. Reporting time: 2-3 weeks. Payment: standard 7-10%. Copyrights for author. Subjects: Fiction, Non-Fiction.

Tamal Vista Publications, Wayne de Fremery, 222 Madrone Ave., Larkspur, CA 94939-1913, www.tamalvista.com, 617-492-7234. 1976. Poetry, fiction, criticism, non-fiction. ''Tamal Vista Publications is a family-run business with roots in the book printing and publishing industry that go back three generations. Tamal Vista's publications have always reflected the passions of the family members running the company. Founder Peter de Fremery brought together his knowledge of printing, gained while working for his father as a printer's representative, with a passion for woodworking and the outdoors to create Tamal Vista's original line of books on woodworking and boatbuilding. Now owned by his son Wayne de Fremery, Tamal Vista reflects both the company's history and Wayne's passion for East Asian literature, particularly Korean poetry.'' 8 titles listed in the *Small Press Record of Books in Print* (36th Edition, 2010-11). Discounts: 1-4 copies 20%, must have CWO; 5+ 40%. Reporting time: 1 month. Copyrights for author. Subjects: Asia, Indochina, Bilingual, Botany, Buddhism, California, Crafts, Hobbies, How-To, Pacific Region, Poetry, Sports, Outdoors, Translation.

Tameme, C.M. Mayo, 300 3rd Street, #9, Los Altos, CA 94022, www.tameme.org. 1999. Poetry, fiction, parts-of-novels, long-poems, non-fiction. ''*Tameme* is now publishing bilingual (Spanish/English) chapbooks of new writing from North America: Canada, the US, and Mexico. Please do not submit without first consulting the guidelines on the website. Tameme is the Nahautl word for messenger or porter. Pronounced 'ta-may-may.''' Pub'd 1 title 2009; expects 1 title 2010, 1 title 2011. 2 titles listed in the *Small Press Record of Books in Print* (36th Edition, 2010-11). Discounts: please contact us for more info. Reporting time: varies. Simultaneous submissions accepted: yes. Publishes 2% of manuscripts submitted. Payment: varies depending on funding. We are now a press. Depends on contract. Subjects: Bilingual, Canada, Fiction, Mexico,

Non-Fiction, Poetry, Translation.

TAMPA REVIEW, University of Tampa Press, Richard B. Mathews, Editor; Elizabeth Winston, Nonfiction Editor; Don Morrill, Poetry Editor; Lisa Birnbaum, Fiction Editor; Martha Serpas, Poetry Editor; Kathleen Ochshorn, Fiction Editor, 401 W. Kennedy Boulevard, University of Tampa-19F, Tampa, FL 33606-1490, (813) 253-6266, Email: utpress@ut.edu, http://utpress.ut.edu, http://tampareview.ut.edu. 1988. Poetry, fiction, art, photos, interviews, non-fiction. *"Tampa Review* Tampa Review is a literary magazine dedicated to the integration of contemporary literature and visual arts. Each issue features contemporary writing and art from Florida and the world, emphasizing connections between the Tampa Bay region and the international literary community. Publishing in a hardcover format, the editors strive to produce a physically beautiful magazine that presents words in meaningful aesthetic relationship with world-class visual art. We consider submissions between September 1 and December 31 each year. The annual DANAHY FICTION PRIZE awards $1,000 and publication for a previously unpublished short story, 500-5,000 words; $15 reading fee includes one-year subscription, with Nov. 1 postmark deadline. The annual TAMPA REVIEW PRIZE FOR POETRY awards $2,000 plus book publication in hardcover and quality paperback. Reading fee: $25; submission deadline, Dec. 31. See guidelines at *http://tampareview.ut.edu*. Recent contributors: Peter Meinke, Naomi Nye, Richard Chess, Julia B. Levine, Ron De Maris, Sarah Maclay, and Richard Terrill." circ. 750. 2/yr. Pub'd 2 issues 2009; expects 2 issues 2010, 2 issues 2011. sub. price $15; per copy $9.95; sample $6. Back issues: $9.95. Discounts: retail booksellers: cash, 1-4 copies 20% off cover price, 5 or more 40%. 80-96pp. Reporting time: we read from September through December; report January through March. Simultaneous submissions accepted: NO. Publishes 4% of manuscripts submitted. Payment: $10 per printed page. Copyrighted, reverts to author. Exchange ads only.

Tanest Publishing House, Taj Starr, 626 S. 41st Court, Springfield, OR 97478. 2006. Fiction. Expects 1 title 2010, 3 titles 2011. 1 title listed in the *Small Press Record of Books in Print* (36th Edition, 2010-11). 20pp.

Tangerine Press (see also DWANG: Outsider poetry and prose), Michael Curran, 23 Khartoum Road, Tooting, London SW17 0JA, England, www.eatmytangerine.com. 2006. Poetry, fiction, art, cartoons, parts-of-novels. "Tangerine Press publishes outsider writing, including neglected poet-thinkers such as William Wantling, but also the best of the current wave. Recent contributors include Dan Fante, Billy Childish, Neil Rollinson, Geoff Hattersley, Fred Voss, Steve Richmond, Adelle Stripe, Salena Godden, Jim Burns, Edward Lucie-Smith, Peter Finch, Trevor Reeves, Tony O'Neill, Mike Daily, Rob Plath, Adrian Manning, Tim Wells." avg. press run 126. Expects 2 titles 2010, 2-3 titles 2011. 2 titles listed in the *Small Press Record of Books in Print* (36th Edition, 2010-11). Discounts: Please contact for details. 150pp. Reporting time: 2 weeks - 2 months. Simultaneous submissions accepted: No. Payment: contact for details. Copyrights for author. Subjects: Beat, Counter-Culture, Alternatives, Communes, England, Fiction, Poetry, Prose.

Tantalus Books, Rick Griggs, 4529 Idledale Drive, Fort Collins, CO 80526-5152, www.tantalusbooks.com. 1989. "Special emphasis on *Balanced Mastery* for combining life balance with career achievement. Tantalus Books provides titles for the 10-Month *Mastery Academy* leadership training series." avg. press run 5M. Pub'd 3 titles 2009; expects 3 titles 2010, 3 titles 2011. 5 titles listed in the *Small Press Record of Books in Print* (36th Edition, 2010-11). Simultaneous submissions accepted: no. Publishes 1-2% of manuscripts submitted.

TAPESTRIES, Patricia Casentino, Editor, Mount Wachusett Community College, 444 Green St., Gardner, MA 01440, 978-630-9176, alanahb@earthlink.net, life@mwcc.mass.edu. 2000. Poetry, fiction, non-fiction. "30 line limit for poetry, any form, 1200 words flash fiction, nonfiction. Avoid didactic, be creative by using figurative language. Avoid first person (I) point of view. *Strict* guidelines. Spiritual poems, non-sectarian okay. No political, pornographic materials. Looking for universality in themes. Think how young we are as a country. Death and dying should be avoided (ha!), celebrate life." circ. 1K. 1/yr. Pub'd 1 issue 2009. price per copy $10. 116pp. Reporting time: 6 months. Simultaneous submissions accepted: yes. Publishes 15% of manuscripts submitted. Payment: none, tear sheets. Copyrighted, reverts to author.

TAPROOT LITERARY REVIEW, Taproot Press Publishing Co., Tikvah Feinstein, Editor Publisher; Tina Forbes, Associate Editor; Marc and Amy Rosenberg, Technology; Candace Austin, Publicity Editor; Monte Wilkinson, Consulting Editor, PO Box 204, Ambridge, PA 15003, 724-266-8476, taproot10@aol.com. 1984. Poetry, fiction, art, photos, reviews. "International Literary Review looking for the best quality poetry and short fiction available. We enjoy diversity and multinational themes and varied formats by both new and established writers. We also conduct an annual writing contest and publish winners and best of entries and submissions alike." circ. 500. 1/yr. Pub'd 2 issues 2009; expects 2 issues 2010, 3 issues 2011. 1 title listed in the *Small Press Record of Books in Print* (36th Edition, 2010-11). sub. price $7.50; per copy $8.95; sample $5. Back issues: $5. Discounts: contributor copy $6.50 each, plus $2 p/h. 94pp. Reporting time: 6-8 months. Simultaneous submissions accepted: no. Publishes 23% of manuscripts submitted. Payment: copies. Copyrighted, reverts to author. Pub's reviews: 2 in 2009. §Ask us first if we are interested. Ads: ask for rates. Subjects: Fiction, Literary Review, Literature (General), Poetry, Short Stories, Storytelling.

Taproot Press Publishing Co. (see also TAPROOT LITERARY REVIEW), Tikvah Feinstein, Editor Publisher; Tina Forbes, Associate Editor; Candace Austin, Publicity Editor, Box 204, Ambridge, PA 15003, taproot10@aol.com. 1985. Poetry, fiction, art, photos. "Taproot Press is a subsidiary of Taproot Writer's Workshop Inc., a non-profit group with its goal to assist fine writers. We sponsor an annual contest. Recently published: Ran Huntsberry, B.Z. Niditch, Zan Gay, Lila Julius, Lyn Lifshin, and T. Anders Carson." avg. press run 500-1M. Pub'd 3 titles 2009; expects 3 titles 2010, 4 titles 2011. 8 titles listed in the *Small Press Record of Books in Print* (36th Edition, 2010-11). Discounts: 50% retailers, libraries, schools. 98pp. Reporting time: 3-6 months. Simultaneous submissions accepted: no. Publishes 10-20% of manuscripts submitted. Payment: books. Copyrights for author. Subjects: Poetry, Short Stories.

TAPROOT, a journal of older writers, Philip W. Quigg, Editor; Joan Martin, Associate Editor, PO Box 841, University at Stony Brook, Stony Brook, NY 11790-0841, 631-689-0668. 1974. Poetry, articles, art, photos, non-fiction. "Poetry, prose and art by elder writers. Publication limited to Taproot Workshop members." circ. 1M. 2/yr. Pub'd 2 issues 2009; expects 2 issues 2010, 2 issues 2011. sub. price $18; per copy $8; sample $8. Back issues: variable $3-$6. Discounts: please inquire. 100pp. Reporting time: 2 months. Payment: 1 copy. Copyrighted, reverts to author. Ads: $1,000/$500/negotiable. Subjects: Aging, Literature (General), Poetry, Public Affairs, Senior Citizens.

TAR RIVER POETRY, Luke Whisnant, Editor, Erwin Building Mail Room, East Carolina University, Greenville, NC 27858-4353, 252-328-6046. 1978. Poetry, reviews. "Among recent featured contributors have been Laurence Lieberman, Tom Reiter, Leslie Norris, Brendan Galvin, Betty Adcock, Louis Simpson, Julie Suk, Mark Jarman, Deborah Cummins, Elizabeth Dodd, Susan Elizabeth Howe, Henry Taylor, Mark Cox, Debra Kang Dean, Thom Ward, David Mason, Gray Jacobik, Jeffrey Harrison, Robert Cording, Larry Woiwode, Kimberly Meyer, Fred Chappell, Natasha Saje, Susan Cohen, Jonathan Holden, James Harms, Bruce Bennett, and Al Maginnes." circ. 700. 2/yr. Pub'd 2 issues 2009; expects 2 issues 2010, 2 issues 2011. sub. price $12, $20/2 yrs; per copy $6.50; sample $6.50. Back issues: $6.50. Discounts: 40% to bookstores. 64pp. Reporting time: 4-6 weeks. Simultaneous submissions accepted: no. Publishes 5% of manuscripts submitted. Payment: contributor's copies. Rights reassigned to author upon request. Pub's reviews: 6 in 2009. §Poetry. Ads: we swap ads. Subject: Poetry.

TARPAULIN SKY, Tarpaulin Sky Press, Christian Peet, Publisher & Co-Editor; Elena Georgiou, Co-Editor, PO Box 189, Grafton, VT 05146. "*Tarpaulin Sky* focuses on cross-genre / trans genre / hybrid forms as well as innovative poetry and prose. The journal emphasizes experiments with language and form, but holds no allegiance to any one style or school or network of writers."

Tarpaulin Sky Press (see also TARPAULIN SKY), Christian Peet, Publisher & Co-Editor, PO Box 189, Grafton, VT 05146. "We will read chapbook manuscripts in August 2008, full-length manuscripts in October 2008. Details are forthcoming." No titles listed in the *Small Press Record of Books in Print* (36th Edition, 2010-11).

THE TARPEIAN ROCK, Arx Publishing LLC, PO Box 1333, Merchantville, NJ 08109. 2003. Poetry, fiction, cartoons, reviews. Annual. 16pp. Simultaneous submissions accepted: No. Publishes Less than 10% of manuscripts submitted. Ads: Back cover: $250, Inside front/back cover: $200, Full page: $150, 1/2 page: $80, 1/4 page: $60, 1/8 page: $40. Subjects: Arts, Cartoons, Essays, Fantasy, Fiction, Literature (General), Poetry, Science Fiction, Short Stories.

Tarragon Books, 1424 E. Maplewood Ave., Bellingham, WA 98225, tel: 360-738-7875. "Tarragon Books publishes Pacific Northwest novelists with lively stories and distinctive voices. Our readers agree that "entertaining" and "thought-provoking" need not be mutually exclusive." No titles listed in the *Small Press Record of Books in Print* (36th Edition, 2010-11).

Taurean Horn Press, Bill Vartnaw, PO Box 526, Petaluma, CA 94953-0526. 1974. Poetry. "I go to a lot of readings in the SF Bay Area. I keep my ears open. I like what I like. Each book has its own history. Overall, I document what I think is among the best happening here. There are a lot of deserving poets and seemingly fewer publishers than there used to be. I do the best I can. Publications in print: *In Concern: for Angels* by Bill Vartnaw, *from spirit to matter* by carol lee sanchez, *Spectacles* by Tom Sharp, *On the Good Red Interstate, Truck Stop Tellings and Other Poems* by Lee Francis, *Whose Really Blues* by q. r. hand, jr. No submissions accepted." avg. press run 500. Expects 1 title 2010, 1 title 2011. 5 titles listed in the *Small Press Record of Books in Print* (36th Edition, 2010-11). Discounts: 40% to book trade. 100pp. Publishes 0% of manuscripts submitted. Payment: copies and/or other arrangements agreed upon prior to publication. Copyrights for author. Subject: Poetry.

Tax Property Investor, Inc., F. Marea, PO Box 4602, Winter Park, FL 32793, 407-671-0004. 1989. Non-fiction. "Publishing for real estate investors." avg. press run 5M. Expects 1 title 2010, 3 titles 2011. 1 title listed in the *Small Press Record of Books in Print* (36th Edition, 2010-11). Discounts: trade 3-99 40%; 100-199 45%; 200499 50%, 500+ 55%. 160pp. Reporting time: 30 days. Payment: to be negotiated. Subjects: How-To,

Real Estate, Taxes.

TEACHER EDUCATION QUARTERLY, Caddo Gap Press, Thomas Nelson, Editor, 3145 Geary Boulevard #275, San Francisco, CA 94118, 415-392-1911. 1971. Articles. "The quarterly journal of the California Council on the Education of Teachers." circ. 900. 4/yr. Pub'd 4 issues 2009; expects 4 issues 2010, 4 issues 2011. sub. price $75 indiv., $150 instit., $50 students; per copy $25. 96pp. Reporting time: 2 months. Publishes 25% of manuscripts submitted. Payment: none. Copyrighted, reverts to author. Ads: $200 full page. Subject: Education.

TEACHERS & WRITERS, Teachers & Writers Collaborative, Susan Karwoska, Editor, 520 Eighth Ave., Suite 2020, New York, NY 10018-6507, 212-691-6590, www.twc.org. 1967. Articles, interviews, reviews, letters. "No poetry." circ. 3M. 4/yr. Pub'd 5 issues 2009; expects 4 issues 2010, 4 issues 2011. sub. price $20; per copy $5; sample same. Back issues: $5. Discounts: none. 40pp. Reporting time: varies. Simultaneous submissions accepted: no. Publishes 5% of manuscripts submitted. Payment: varies. Copyrighted, reverts to author. Ads: none. Subjects: Arts, Education, Literature (General), Poetry, Writers/Writing.

Teachers & Writers Collaborative (see also TEACHERS & WRITERS), Amy Swauger, Director, 520 Eighth Ave., Suite 2020, New York, NY 10018, 212-691-6590, 212-675-0171. 1967. Articles, interviews, reviews. "No poetry." avg. press run 3M. Pub'd 1 title 2009; expects 2 titles 2011. 45 titles listed in the *Small Press Record of Books in Print* (36th Edition, 2010-11). Discounts: varies. 230pp. Reporting time: varies. Simultaneous submissions accepted: no. Publishes 2% of manuscripts submitted. Payment: varies. Copyrights for author. Subjects: Arts, Education.

THE TEACHER'S VOICE: A Literary Magazine for Poets and Writers in Education, Andres Castro, Founder & Managing Editor, P.O. Box 150384, Kew Gardens, NY 11415, Email: editor@the-teachers-voice.org. "*The Teachers Voice* was founded as an experimental hardcopy literary magazine in 2004 and is now free and online. We publish creative nonfiction, poetry, short stories, and essays that reflect the many different American teacher experiences. We ask to see critical creative writing that takes risks without being overly self-indulgent or inaccessible."

Tears in the Fence (see also TEARS IN THE FENCE), David Caddy, 38 Hod View Stourpaine, Blandford Forum, Dorset DT11 8TN, United Kingdom. 1995. Poetry, fiction. "Recent contributors include: Damian Furniss, Gerald Locklin, Gregory Warren Wilson, K.V. Skene, Joan-Jobe Smith." avg. press run 300. Pub'd 8 titles 2009; expects 6 titles 2010, 10 titles 2011. 2 titles listed in the *Small Press Record of Books in Print* (36th Edition, 2010-11). 48pp. Reporting time: no unsolicited submissions. Payment: yes. Copyrights for author. Subjects: Poetry, Prose.

TEARS IN THE FENCE, Tears in the Fence, David Caddy, Sarah Hopkins, 38 Hod View, Stourpaine, Blandford Forum, Dorset DT11 8TN, England. 1984. Poetry, fiction, art, interviews, criticism, reviews. circ. 1.5M. 3/yr. Pub'd 3 issues 2009; expects 3 issues 2010, 3 issues 2011. sub. price £18 for three or £30 for six issues, $20 cash for four issues, including postage; per copy £7, $8 cash including postage; sample £6, $8 cash. Back issues: variable amounts from issues 27 - 49. 160pp. Reporting time: 3-6 weeks. Simultaneous submissions accepted: no. Publishes 1-2% of manuscripts submitted. Payment: 1 copy. Copyrighted, reverts to author. Pub's reviews: 60 in 2009. §Essays and reviews on and of modern, contemporary, underground and postmodern poetry. Subjects: Criticism, Poetry, Prose.

Tebot Bach (see also SPILLWAY), Mifanwy Kaiser, Editor, Box 7887, Huntington Beach, CA 92615-7887, 714-968-0905. 1998. Poetry. "Books by individual authors published include: Jeannette Clough, Richard Jones, Richard Fox, Robin Chapman, Marjorie Becker, Sam Pereira, Michael Clifton, Kate Buckley, Carroll C.Kearley, Marcia Cohee, Bruce Boston, Michael Miller, Bruce Williams, Marjorie Becker, Jonathan Harris, Glover Davis, Paul Tayyar, Sallie Bingham, Joan Stepp Smith." Pub'd 3 titles 2009; expects 3 titles 2010, 3 titles 2011. 10 titles listed in the *Small Press Record of Books in Print* (36th Edition, 2010-11). Discounts: by arrangement. 96pp. Reporting time: 3-6 months. Simultaneous submissions accepted: yes. Payment: per author contract. Subject: Poetry.

Technics Publications, LLC, Steve Hoberman, PO Box 161, Bradley Beach, NJ 07720, dbooks@technics-pub.com. 2005. Non-fiction. "We focus on business and computer books." avg. press run 5000. Expects 1 title 2010, 2 titles 2011. No titles listed in the *Small Press Record of Books in Print* (36th Edition, 2010-11). Discounts: 2-10 copies 25%10-20 copies 35%More than 20 40%. 150pp. Subject: Computers, Calculators.

Tecolote Publications, Carol Bowers, 4761 Niagara Avenue, San Diego, CA 92107-2206, telephone (619)222-6066, e-mail tecopubs@earthlink.net, website tecolotepublications.com. 1986. Poetry, fiction, non-fiction. "Main publications are local history books (San Diego County) nature books, novels, poetry; author - subsidize." avg. press run 1-5M. Pub'd 11 titles 2009; expects 10 titles 2010, 10 titles 2011. 25 titles listed in the *Small Press Record of Books in Print* (36th Edition, 2010-11). Discounts: trade - 40%; wholesalers - 50%. 150pp. Copyrights for author.

TEEN VOICES MAGAZINE, Rebecca Steinitz, Managing Editor, 80 Summer St. #300, Boston, MA 02110-1218, 617-426-5505, Fax 617-426-5577, teenvoices@teenvoices.com, www.teenvoices.com. 1988. Poetry, fiction, articles, art, photos, cartoons, interviews, satire, criticism, reviews, music, letters, news items, non-fiction. "Additional address: PO Box 120-027, Boston, MA 02112-0027. We publish the writing of teenage girls *only*." circ. 54,000. 2 print issues, monthly online content. Pub'd 2 issues 2009; expects 2 issues 2010, 2 print; 12/12/12 online issues 2011. sub. price $20 one-year membership; $35 two-year membership; per copy $3.50 US, $5.45 Canada; sample $5. Back issues: $5-$10 depending on issue. Discounts: bulk, human service agencies, classrooms. 60pp. Reporting time: 6 months. Simultaneous submissions accepted: yes. Publishes 30% of manuscripts submitted. Payment: 5 copies of magazine. Copyrighted, non-exclusive rights revert to author. Pub's reviews: 12 in 2009. §Teenage girls or teenagers in general might want to know about. Ads: b+w: $1,200/$750; color: $2100/$1,275. Subjects: Poetry, Race, Sexual Abuse, Women, Young Adult.

The Teitan Press, Inc., Franklin C. Winston, President, PO Box 1972, Bolingbrook, IL 60440, e-mail editor@teitanpress.com, http://www.teitanpress.com. 1985. Fiction, non-fiction. "We only use in-house material; we do not accept submissions." avg. press run 1M. Expects 1 title 2010, 1 title 2011. 6 titles listed in the *Small Press Record of Books in Print* (36th Edition, 2010-11). Discounts: 50% to wholesalers, 20%-40% to retail outlets depending on quantity; 10% to libraries postpaid. 200pp. Copyrights for author. Subjects: History, Occult, Poetry, Short Stories, Theosophical.

Telephone Books, Maureen Owen, 2358 South Bannnock St., Denver, CO 80223, (303) 698-7837, pomowen@ix.netcom.com. 1971. Poetry, fiction, plays. "Press will do 2 books a year, but titles remain available. Books: *The Amerindian Coastline Poem* by Fanny Howe; *Hot Footsteps* by Yuki Hartman; *Ciao Manhattan* by Rebecca Wright; *Delayed: Not Postponed* by Fielding Dawson; *The Secret History of the Dividing Line* by Susan Howe; *The Temple* by Janet Hamill; *No More Mr. Nice Guy* by Sam Kashner; *Audrey Hepburn's Symphonic Salad and the Coming of Autumn* by Tom Weigel; *The Telephone Book* by Ed Friedman; *3-Way Split* by Rebecca Brown; *Hot* by Joe Johnson; *The Celestial Splendor Shining Forth From Geometric Thought* and *On the Motion of the Apparently Fixed Stars* by Britt Wilkie. No unsolicited ms." avg. press run 750-1M. Pub'd 2 titles 2009. 20 titles listed in the *Small Press Record of Books in Print* (36th Edition, 2010-11). 40-80pp. Simultaneous submissions accepted: no. Payment: in copies. Copyrights for author. Subject: Poetry.

TELOS, Telos Press, Russell Berman, Editor; David Pan, Review Editor; Robert Richardson, Managing Editor, 431 East 12th Street, New York, NY 10009, 212-228-6479. 1968. Articles, criticism, reviews, non-fiction. "For additional information, please visit our website, www.telospress.com." circ. 1000. 4/yr. Pub'd 4 issues 2009; expects 4 issues 2010, 4 issues 2011. sub. price *Invididuals*: $60/one year, $100/two years; *Institutions*: $189/year, print (US); $227/year, print (international); $230/year, online only; $290/year, print and online (US); $328/year, print and online (international).; per copy $15 US; $18 International. Back issues: Individuals: $20/each; Institutions: $50/each. Discounts: 30% bulk orders, 10% agent, 30% bookstores. 192pp. Reporting time: 3-6 months. Payment: none. Copyrighted. Pub's reviews: approx. 12 in 2009. §Politics, philosophy, critical and social theory, law, religion, culture, and the arts. Ads: Please inquire. Subjects: Arts, Criticism, Current Affairs, Europe, Global Affairs, Government, History, Journals, Law, Literature (General), Philosophy, Political Science, Politics, Religion.

Telos Press (see also TELOS), Russell Berman, Editor; David Pan, Review Editor; Robert Richardson, Managing Editor, 431 East 12th Street, New York, NY 10009, 212-228-6479. 1968. Articles, criticism, reviews, non-fiction. "For more information, please visit our website, www.telospress.com." 17 titles listed in the *Small Press Record of Books in Print* (36th Edition, 2010-11). Discounts: usual is 30%, other can be arranged. Reporting time: 6 months. Payment: Negotiated. Subjects: Arts, Criticism, Culture, Europe, Journals, Law, Literature (General), Philosophy, Politics, Post Modern, Translation.

•Templar Poetry, Alex McMillen, Managing Editor, PO BOX 7082, Bakewell, Derbyshire DE45 9AF, United Kingdom, info@templarpoetry.co.uk. "Templar Poetry is delighted to be one of four poetry publishers in the 2010 shortlist for the Publishing category of the awards. The final results will be announced at the awards event at the British Library on Wednesday 16th June. The Michael Marks Awards for Poetry Pamphlets recognise the enormous contribution that pamphlets make to the world of poetry and the wider cultural life of the United Kingdom. Explore the thriving world of the poetry pamphlet with readings from some of the most innovative contemporary voices, chosen by Ali Smith, Jo Shapcott and Richard Price." No titles listed in the *Small Press Record of Books in Print* (36th Edition, 2010-11).

Temple Inc., Charles Potts, PO Box 100, Walla Walla, WA 99362-0033, order@thetemplebookstore.com. 1995. Poetry, non-fiction. "The Temple has suspended publication. Back issues available for $5. Do not send unsolicited manuscripts." avg. press run 500-1.2M. Pub'd 2 titles 2009; expects 3 titles 2010, 4 titles 2011. 12 titles listed in the *Small Press Record of Books in Print* (36th Edition, 2010-11). Discounts: 40% trade. 120pp. Reporting time: varies. Simultaneous submissions accepted: No submissions of any kind. Publishes 1% of manuscripts submitted. Payment: 10%. Copyrights for author. Subjects: History, Poetry, Political Science.

1097 MAGAZINE, Ian Rose, 1427 NW Highland Drive, Corvallis, OR 97330, http://www.1097mag.com. 2007. Poetry, fiction, art, photos, music, long-poems, plays, concrete art. circ. 100. 12/yr. Expects 3 issues 2010, 12 issues 2011. sub. price $25; per copy $3; sample $1.50. Back issues: inquire. Discounts: 5+ copies 30%. 24pp. Reporting time: 2 weeks - 2 months. Simultaneous submissions accepted: Yes. Publishes 10% of manuscripts submitted. Payment: Small payment plus free year's subscription to all contributors. Copyrighted, reverts to author. Pub's reviews. Ads: Full page $75. Subjects: Absurdist, Arts, Graphic Design, Journals, North America, Photography, Poetry, Prose, Short Stories.

Ten Penny Players, Inc. (see also WATERWAYS: Poetry in the Mainstream), Barbara Fisher, Co-Editor; Richard Spiegel, Co-Editor, 393 St. Pauls Avenue, Staten Island, NY 10304-2127, 718-442-7429, www.tenpennyplayers.org. 1975. Poetry, fiction, plays. "Books: Age range is child to adult. Varying lengths: 8pp-150pp. We stress an integration of language and picture so that the material can be used either as a book to read or a book to perform. Also child + young adult poets published monthly in literary magazines and picture books from NYC elementary & high schools including incarcerated youths. No unsolicited manuscripts, please. Selected publications published at tenpennyplayers.org; in the process of publishing the 31 year archive of our publications on SCRIBD." avg. press run 200. Pub'd 2 titles 2009; expects 2 titles 2010, 3 titles 2011. 37 titles listed in the *Small Press Record of Books in Print* (36th Edition, 2010-11). Discounts: standard 60/40. 60pp. Simultaneous submissions accepted: no. Payment: negotiable. Copyrights for author. Subjects: Arts, Drama, Poetry.

10x3 PLUS, Sue Ann Simar, 1077 Windsor Avenue, Morgantown, WV 26505-3325. 2007. Poetry, long-poems. "Each issue features 10 poets x 3 poems plus additional poems, prose-poems, and features. George Szirtes, Dzvinia Orlowsky, Ron Padgett, Grace Cavalieri, Caleb Barber, Ralph Culver, Jefferson Carter, Michael Wurster, Wendy Mooney, and Llewelyn McKernon will be the ten writers showcased in the upcoming #4 issue. John Kay, Michael Gessner, Jesse Weiner, Martin Turner, Lisa Zimmerman, Tomas de Faoite, and Fredrick Zydek were among the poets featured in the first three issues. The editor reads at all times of the year except during the month of December. Submission details are included on the 10x3 plus website. Please review the web site and blog site carefully before submitting. In 2009, 10x3 plus and Beginner's Mind will publish its first book. The tile is PHANTOM OF THE APPLE by John Kay. Support of the magazine is needed and necessary to keep publishing. Please buy an issue, and hopefully, you will be hooked on buying the next issue, too. Please submit your best work and please note that simultaneous submissions are not acceptable. Professionally printed with cover art work by artists such as Laura den Hertog and Dan Casado. Artwork is by invitation only." circ. 250. 2/yr. Pub'd 2 issues 2009; expects 2 issues 2010, 2 issues 2011. sub. price $20 any three issues.; per copy $8. Back issues: first issue is limited. Discounts: inquire. 56pp. Reporting time: 1-8 months. Simultaneous submissions accepted: No. Payment: Contributor's copies. First rights reserved by 10x3 plus. Future rights revert to the individual contributors. No advertising.

Tendre Press, Ann Kreilkamp, 134 N. Overhill Dr., Bloomington, IN 47408, 812-337-0193, 812-334-1987 (fax), 866-489-4727 (toll free), ann@tendrepress.com, www.tendrepress.com. 2006. Non-fiction. avg. press run 3000. Expects 1 title 2010, 1 title 2011. No titles listed in the *Small Press Record of Books in Print* (36th Edition, 2010-11). 250pp.

Tennyson Press, Janet Barnes, P.O. Box 105, Reading, MA 01867, publisher@tennysonpress.com. 2008. Poetry, criticism, long-poems. "Tennyson Press publishes literature by new voices—with a particular emphasis on poetry. We also publish literary criticism and theory by poets who are intellectually engaged in a conversation about their craft and its vital role in our culture. We value rigorous study of the literary canon as a way of entering into a conversation about its evolution and the writer's craft. Tennyson Press will be discriminating in the authors we choose to publish, with the intention of bringing the best new literary voices to a broader audience. We are particularly interested in poetry that is written in traditional poetic forms, as well as the ironic manipulation of traditional poetic forms. We also have a preference for poetry that requires some unpacking to get at its full meaning. As Helen Vendler has asserted, poems give readers pleasure through our ability to uncover the ways in which they convey their layers of meaning.Western Civilization has arrived at a fragile moment. We face great difficulties. We bear great responsibilities. The mission of Tennyson Press is to cultivate a literature that, like the great literature of the past, will be strong enough to help." Expects 1 title 2010, 4 titles 2011. 1 title listed in the *Small Press Record of Books in Print* (36th Edition, 2010-11). Reporting time: 4 - 6 weeks. Simultaneous submissions accepted: Yes. Copyrights for author.

TERMINUS: A Magazine of the Arts, Travis Denton, Editor, 1034 Hill Street, Atlanta, GA 30315. "While we want to push the boundaries of general aesthetics and standards, we also want to publish writing that is accessible to a wide audience. We seek to live up to the highest standards in publishing, always growing and reaching new levels of understanding and awareness both within our immediate community and within the greater community of our country and world. For prose, poetry, and visual art, simultaneous submissions are fine. Please notify us by email, phone or postcard if work is accepted elsewhere. No previously published work."

490

TERRA INCOGNITA: A Bilingual Journal of Literature, Art and Commentary, Robert J. Lavigna, Editor; Alexandra van de Kamp, Editor; William Glenn, Editor, APDO. 14401, 28080 Madrid, Spain.

Tesseract Publications, Janet Leih, PO Box 164, Canton, SD 57013-0164, 605-987-5070, Fax same, call ahead, it is a one-liner information@tesseractpublications.com, www.tesseractpublications.com. 1981. Poetry, fiction, non-fiction. "Prefer feminist, non-fiction, poetry." avg. press run 300-500. Pub'd 1 title 2009; expects 2 titles 2010, 2 titles 2011. 29 titles listed in the *Small Press Record of Books in Print* (36th Edition, 2010-11). Discounts: available on request. 60pp. Reporting time: 3 months. Simultaneous submissions accepted: yes. Payment: subsidized publications only. Copyrights for author if asked. Subjects: Feminism, Poetry.

TEXAS POETRY JOURNAL, Smith Steven Ray, 6205 Carrington Drive, Austin, TX 78749-5206, 512-779-6202, www.texaspoetryjournal.com, submissions@texaspoetryjournal.com. 2004. Poetry, interviews, criticism, non-fiction. "Texas Poetry Journal publishes poetry and poets from around the world in a quality and affordable format, perfect for readers at home or on-the-go. Our goal is to add poetry to the lives of busy people, to bring a touch of extraordinary language to each day.Texas Poetry Journal publishes poetry, interviews with poets, criticism for a general audience, and black and white photography. The print edition is published semi-annually. We also publish a Feature Poem on our web site each week." circ. 400. 2/yr. Expects 2 issues 2010, 2 issues 2011. sub. price 12; per copy 7.50; sample 7.50. Back issues: 7.50. Discounts: Bookstores 40%Jobbers 5%Distributors 55%. 100pp. Reporting time: 3 months. Simultaneous submissions accepted: Yes. Publishes 8% of manuscripts submitted. Payment: One copy. Copyrighted, reverts to author. Ads: Half Page $40Full Page $75. Subjects: Interviews, Photography, Poetry.

THE TEXAS REVIEW, Texas Review Press, Paul Ruffin, Editor, English Department, Sam Houston State University, Huntsville, TX 77341-2146. 1976. Poetry, fiction, articles, photos, interviews, reviews. "Because of the size of our magazine, we do not encourage the submission of long poems or exceptionally long short stories. Now accept photography, critical essays on literature and culture, etc. Each year we publish the *The Texas Review* Poetry Award Chapbook. We will no longer read during June through August." circ. 750-1M. 2/yr. Pub'd 2 issues 2009; expects 2 issues 2010. sub. price $20; 2 years $35; 3 years $50; per copy $10; sample $5. Back issues: $5. Discounts: 40% to libraries. 160pp. Reporting time: 8 weeks-6 months. Simultaneous submissions accepted: no. Publishes 2% of manuscripts submitted. Payment: copies, subscription (1 year). Copyrighted, rights revert to author on request. Pub's reviews: 24 in 2009. §Poetry, fiction, history, art, literary criticism, informal essays. Ads: exchange ads only. Subject: Literary Review.

Texas Review Press (see also THE TEXAS REVIEW), Paul Ruffin, Editor, English Department, Sam Houston State University, Huntsville, TX 77341-2146. 1976. "We do not read June-August." avg. press run 500. Pub'd 3 titles 2009. 20 titles listed in the *Small Press Record of Books in Print* (36th Edition, 2010-11). 160pp. Reporting time: 2-6 months. Simultaneous submissions accepted: no. Publishes 1% of manuscripts submitted. Payment: copies plus 1 year subscription. Copyrights for author.

Texas Tech University Press, Judith Keeling, Editor-in-chief, Box 41037, Lubbock, TX 79409-1037, 806-742-2982, fax 806-742-2979. 1971. Fiction, art, photos, criticism, letters, non-fiction. "TTUP publishes scholarly, trade, and crossover books in the natural sciences and natural history; environmental studies and literature of place; history and culture of Texas, the Southwest, and the Great Plains; Western Americana; Vietnam War and Southeast Asian studies; eighteenth-century studies; Joseph Conrad studies; costume and textile history and conservation; regional fiction." avg. press run 1500. Pub'd 18 titles 2009; expects 24 titles 2010, 24 titles 2011. No titles listed in the *Small Press Record of Books in Print* (36th Edition, 2010-11). Discounts: 1-2 copies 20%3-9 copies 40%10-24 copies 41%25-49 copies 42%50-99 copies 44%100+ copies 45%1-9 nonreturnable copies 40%10+ nonreturnable copies 50%. 250pp. Reporting time: queries, 1 week; proposals, 1 month; manuscripts, 2 months. Simultaneous submissions accepted: No. Publishes 6% of manuscripts submitted. Payment: 10% of net on trade and promising crossover titles. Copyrights for author. Subjects: Asia, Indochina, Biography, Botany, Clothing, Environment, Fiction, Great Plains, Literature (General), Native American, Nature, Photography, Texas, Textiles, Vietnam, The West.

THALIA: Studies in Literary Humor, Jacqueline Tavernier-Courbin, Editor, English Dept.,University of Ottawa, 70 Laurier East, Ottawa, Ontario, K1N 6N5, Canada, thaliahumor@hotmail.com. 1978. Articles, art, cartoons, interviews, satire, criticism, reviews, letters, collages, non-fiction. "the last volume published is vol 21 (2004)." circ. 500. 2/yr or 1 double issue. sub. price $25 individuals, $30 libraries, discounts for 2 or 3 year subs.; sample varies with the issue requested. Back issues: most back-issues are still available; the cost varies with the issues requested and their number. send E-mail to editor for questions and requests. Discounts: by direct query only. 75-125pp. Reporting time: varies with ms. content. We are not currently accepting submissions. Publishes 25-30% of manuscripts submitted. Payment: none. Copyrighted, copyrights contract signed prior to publication. Pub's reviews: 2 in 2009. §Any area connected to humor. Ads: $150/$75. Subjects: Criticism, Humor, Literary Review, Literature (General).

Thatch Tree Publications, K. Jones, Kathy Alba PhD, 2250 N. Rock Road, Suite 118-169, Wichita, KS 67226,

316-687-6629, thatchtreepub@aol.com, www.kathyalba.com. 2001. Fiction, art, photos, non-fiction. "Full length novels - generally wholesome or Christian. Nonfiction works of any subject except the occult or negative." avg. press run 1M. Pub'd 2 titles 2009; expects 2 titles 2010, 2 titles 2011. 10 titles listed in the *Small Press Record of Books in Print* (36th Edition, 2010-11). Discounts: 10-20% for bulk, 50% for distributors. 220pp. Reporting time: 2-3 weeks. Publishes 100% of manuscripts submitted. Payment: the authors pay for everything and retain total rights. Copyrights for author. Subjects: Arts, Christianity, Crafts, Hobbies, Education, English, Fiction, Futurism, Health, How-To, Inspirational, Interviews, Language, Literature (General), Medicine, Non-Fiction.

THEECLECTICS, Creative With Words Publications (CWW), Brigitta Geltrich, Editor & Publisher; Bert Hower, Editor, PO Box 223226, Carmel, CA 93922, fax 831-655-8627; e-mail cwwpub@usa.net; website http://members.tripod.com/~CreativeWithWords. 1998. Poetry, fiction, cartoons, satire. "On any topic, written by adults only (20 and older), poetry preferred." 2/yr. Pub'd 2 issues 2009; expects 2 issues 2010, 2 issues 2011. price per copy $6. Discounts: authors 20%; offices, schools, libraries, clubs 10%; legitimate shutins get a one time only free copy. 16+pp. Reporting time: 2-4 weeks after set deadline. Simultaneous submissions accepted: no. Publishes 90% of manuscripts submitted. Payment: 20% discount. Copyrighted, reverts to author. Ads: $125/$70/$35/$16. Subject: Poetry.

THEMA, Virginia Howard, PO Box 8747, Metairie, LA 70011-8747, Telephone: 504-940-7156; e-mail: thema@cox.net; website address: http://members.cox.net/thema. 1988. Poetry, fiction, art, cartoons. "Each issue is related to a unique central premise. Publication dates and themes [*submission deadline in brackets*]: June 2011, *About Two Miles Down the Road* [*7-1-10*]; Sept. 2011, *One Thing Done Superbly* [*11-1-10*]; Feb 2012, *Your Reality or Mine?* [*3-1-11*]." circ. 300. 3/yr. Pub'd 3 issues 2009; expects 3 issues 2010, 3 issues 2011. sub. price $20; per copy $10; sample $10. Back issues: $10. Discounts: 10%. 180pp. Reporting time: 5-6 months after manuscript submission deadline of specific issue. Simultaneous submissions accepted: yes, but must fit upcoming theme. Publishes 10% of manuscripts submitted. Payment: $25 short stories, $10 poetry, $10 b/w artwork and photography, $25 color cover art/photography, $10 short-short pieces. Copyrighted, reverts to author. §Fiction. Ads: $150/$100/$50 1/4 page. Subjects: Fiction, Literature (General).

THE2NDHAND, Todd Dills, 1430 Roberts Ave., Nashville, TN 37206, 205-907-2481. 2000. Fiction, articles, art, cartoons, interviews, satire, reviews, letters, news items, non-fiction. "We accept prose for our print edition, a broadsheet that focuses on the work of a single writer, of up to 5,000 words in length and pay a nominal fee. Our online magazine publishes weekly and accepts work of up to 2,500 words in length. Recent contributors include Patrick Somerville, Spencer Dew, Al Burian, Anne Elizabeth Moore, Todd Dills, Joe Meno, Mickey Hess, Doug Milam, Tao Lin, Jill Summers, Kate Duva, Lauren Pretnar, Paul A. Toth, and many more. . . ." circ. 2M. 4/yr. Pub'd 4 issues 2009; expects 4 issues 2010, 4 issues 2011. We offer lifetime subscriptions to the printed broadsheet for a donation of $30 or more; price per copy $1 or 2 stamps; sample write us. Back issues: write and send $1. Four pages, or 1 large 11"-by-17" page printed both sides.pp. Reporting time: 1-2 months. Simultaneous submissions accepted: yes. Publishes 30% of manuscripts submitted. Payment: We pay up to $300 for our single-author broadsheets. Copyrighted, reverts to author. Pub's reviews: 2 in 2009. §Fiction, politics, culture. Ads: $350 for printed issue—7-by-2-inch banner style or other comparable size. Web $30 for three months or $50 for six months—rotation on splash page at www.the2ndhand.com. Subjects: Absurdist, Comics, Hypnosis, Storytelling, T'ai Chi, Taxes.

Theytus Books Ltd., Greg Young-Ing, Manager, Green Mountain Road, Lot 45, RR #2, Site 50, Comp. 8, Penticton, B.C. V2A 6J7, Canada, 250-493-7181, fax: 250-493-5302, Web: www.theytusbooks.com, order email: order@theytusbooks.ca, general inquiries: info@theytusbooks.ca. 1980. Poetry, fiction, photos, non-fiction. "We publish indigenous voices. Recent contributors: Jeannette Armstrong, Beth Cuthand, Douglas Cardinal, Ruby Slipperjack, Lee Maracle, and Drew Hayden Taylor. USA address: PO Box 2089, Oroville, WA 98844." avg. press run 4M. Pub'd 4 titles 2009; expects 4 titles 2010, 4 titles 2011. 41 titles listed in the *Small Press Record of Books in Print* (36th Edition, 2010-11). 150pp. Reporting time: 6 months to 1 year. Payment: 8-10% 2 times a year. Copyrights for author. Subjects: Anthropology, Archaelogy, Children, Youth, Electronics, Fiction, History, Native American, Poetry.

THIN COYOTE, Lost Prophet Press, Christopher Jones, 6101 Saintsbury Drive, Apt. 432, The Colony, TX 75056-5216, 505.256.4589 knucklemerchant@hotmail.com. 1992. Poetry, fiction, art, photos, interviews, satire, collages, plays. "When we are able to stop guzzling whiskey long enough to read submissions, we tend to favor the work of scofflaws, muleskinners, seers, witchdoctors, maniacs, alchemists, giant-slayers, and their ilk." circ. 200-300. 3/yr. Pub'd 2 issues 2009; expects 3 issues 2010, 3 issues 2011. sub. price $18; per copy $6; sample $7. Back issues: available on request. Discounts: on request. 45pp. Reporting time: 1 month. Simultaneous submissions accepted: yes. Publishes 2-3% of manuscripts submitted. Payment: 1 copy of issue in which they appear. Copyrighted, reverts to author. Pub's reviews: §Poetry, fiction, artwork. Ads: $100/$50/$25. Subjects: Arts, Celtic, Fiction, Photography, Poetry.

THINK Journal, Christine Yurick, P.O. Box 454, Downingtown, PA 19335. 2008. Poetry, fiction, art, criticism, letters, parts-of-novels, long-poems. "Think Journal is a literary journal that focuses on words that have meaning, that are presented in a clear way, and that exhibit the skills demanded by craft. The journal prints work that achieves a balance between form and content. The most important traits that will be considered are form, structure, clarity, content, imagination and style." 4/yr. Expects 4 issues 2010, 4 issues 2011. sub. price $20.00; per copy $7; sample $6. Back issues: inquire. 55pp. Reporting time: 3 months. Simultaneous submissions accepted: No. Copyrighted, reverts to author.

THIRD COAST, Laura Donnelley, Editor, Department of English, Western Michigan University, Kalamazoo, MI 49008-5331, editors@thirdcoastmagazine.com (preferred), 269-387-2675, Fax 269-387-2562, www.third-coastmagazine.com. 1995. Poetry, fiction, interviews, parts-of-novels, long-poems, non-fiction. "*Third Coast* publishes poetry, fiction (including traditional and experimental fiction, shorts, and novel excerpts, but not genre fiction), creative nonfiction (including reportage, essay, memoir, and fragments) and translations. We encourage new as well as established writers. We recommend you look at an issue before submitting. You may order single issues (a current issue is $9; a back issue is $6) by sending a check made out to *Third Coast.* Write Sample Current Issue or Sample Back Issue on the envelope. All submissions should be sent via the online submission system. Any attachments sent to our e-mail address will be deleted. The link to the online submission system is below.For all submissions, we accept simultaneous submissions, but not multiple submissions. Please submit no more than one manuscript at a time. Also, we do not accept previously published works. For Fiction and Nonfiction: Submit manuscripts of up to 9,000 words; authors wishing to submit longer manuscripts should query the editors at editors@thirdcoastmagazine.com. As for short shorts, we accept up to five at a time. Fiction and nonfiction submissions should be typed, double-spaced, openly margined, and printed clearly. The author's name, address, email address, and phone number should be included on the first page. Each subsequent page should have a page number and the author's name or title of the piece. Poetry: Poetry should be typed and single-spaced, with the author's name and contact info on the first page. Stanza breaks should be double-spaced. Please send no more than five poems at a time (with a maximum of fifteen pages total per submission). Save all poems in one document before submitting. For Drama: Please submit short plays and excerpts of no more than 20 pages. Plays must be unpublished, but not necessarily unperformed. Please submit in standard play format. For Book Reviews: If you are interested in writing book reviews for *Third Coast,* please submit a writing sample via the online submission system. Choose "Book Review" under genre. If you are interested in interviewing an author for a future issue of *Third Coast,* please send a query to the editors: editors@thirdcoastmagazine.com. Before submitting your work, please save it as an RTF file (most word processing programs allow you to save as .rtf). If you are using a Mac, add the extension .rtf. Also, remember to include the title of the work, your name, and contact info on the first page of your manuscript. We do not accept submissions from May 1st through August 1st. For instructions and to submit your work, visit http://www.thirdcoastmagazine.com/submissions. In general, submissions will be accepted or declined within four months. Please use e-mail only to inquire about the status of your submission and please wait a minimum of four months to send follow-up inquiries. Write "Submission Inquiry-Fiction," "Submission Inquiry-Poetry," or "Submission Inquiry-Creative Nonfiction," or "Submission Inquiry-Drama" in the Subject line of your e-mail and send to editors@thirdcoastmagazine.com. Recent contributors include: Keith Banner, Moira Crone, Sean Thomas Dougherty, Albert Goldbarth, Mark Halliday, Terrance Hayes, Bob Hicok, Major Jackson, Trudy Lewis, John McNally, Mary Morris, Peter Orner, Tim Seibles, and Nance Van Winckel. Authors whose work in *Third Coast* has been recently anthologized: Ted Kooser, *Best American Poetry 2003*, Alan Shapiro, *Best American Poetry 2003*, Sharon Dilworth, 2002 Pushcart Prize in Fiction." circ. 1500. 2/yr. Pub'd 2 issues 2009; expects 2 issues 2010, 2 issues 2011. sub. price $16; per copy $9; sample $9. Back issues: $6. Discounts: classroom - $6/issue. 176pp. Reporting time: 16 weeks. Simultaneous submissions accepted: yes. Publishes 1% of manuscripts submitted. Payment: 2 copies, discounted copies, 1-year subscription. Not copyrighted, rights revert to author upon publication. Pub's reviews: approx. 20 in 2009. §Poetry, fiction, creative nonfiction and drama. Ads: negotiable; will consider ad swaps. Subjects: Essays, Fiction, Poetry, Short Stories.

Third Dimension Publishing, Teri Washington, President; Maxine Clayton, Editor, evangtw@hotmail.com, takeoffthemask.com. 2003. Poetry, fiction, plays, non-fiction. "Spirituality, Christian Living, Empowerment books. christian Greeting Cards." avg. press run 2000. Expects 5 titles 2010, 5 titles 2011. 1 title listed in the *Small Press Record of Books in Print* (36th Edition, 2010-11). Discounts: 15%. 100pp. Reporting time: 1 Week. Simultaneous submissions accepted: No. Publishes 95% of manuscripts submitted. Payment: 15%. Copyrights for author. Subjects: Family, Relationships, Religion, Women.

Third Dimension Publishing, Jeff Compton, PO Box 1845, Calhoun, GA 30703-1845, 706-602-0398. 2004. Fiction, non-fiction. "Third Dimension Publishing publishes non-fiction self help books, non-fiction humor and children's fiction." avg. press run 5000. Pub'd 1 title 2009; expects 1-3 titles 2010, 5-10 titles 2011. No titles listed in the *Small Press Record of Books in Print* (36th Edition, 2010-11). Discounts: 2-10 copies 25%. 96-300pp. Reporting time: 1 month. Simultaneous submissions accepted: Yes. Publishes 1% of manuscripts submitted. Payment: We pay ywice a year, most royalties are 10%, no advances. Does not copyright for author. Subjects: Business & Economics, Children, Youth, Humor, Mentoring/Coaching, Philosophy, Self-Help.

THIRDEYE MAGAZINE, Thirdeye Publications, Jason Glover Mr., PO Box 8911, Portland, OR 97201, 231-218-6126 www.thirdeyemag.com. 2004. Poetry, fiction, articles, art, photos, interviews, satire, reviews, letters, news items, non-fiction. "Thirdeye magazine judges submissions on creativity, composition, and social message. We welcome submissions of all mediums. Submissions will not be returned. For more information visit www.thirdeyemag.com/submissions.htm." 6/yr. Pub'd 6 issues 2009; expects 6 issues 2010, 6 issues 2011. sub. price $15; per copy free plus shipping; sample free plus shipping. Back issues: inquire. 32pp. Reporting time: one month for magazine submissions. Simultaneous submissions accepted: Yes. Publishes 50% of manuscripts submitted. Payment: $25 for 1200 word features. Copyrighted. Pub's reviews: approx. 10 in 2009. §Social/political nonfictionExperimental fictionMusic/Film. Ads: www.thirdeyemag.com/advertising.htm. Subjects: Anarchist, Arts, Avant-Garde, Experimental Art, Essays, Ethics, Fiction, Graphic Design, Human Rights, Non-Fiction, Non-Violence, Philosophy, Poetry, Prose, Short Stories, Social Movements.

Thirdeye Publications (see also THIRDEYE MAGAZINE), Jason Glover Mr., PO Box 8911, Portland, OR 97201, 231-218-6126 www.thirdeyepublications.com. 2004. Poetry, fiction. "Thirdeye Publications will publish experimental fiction, with its first release being a novel written by the editor of Thirdeye Magazine, Jason M Glover. We are not currently accepting unsolicited manuscripts." avg. press run 1000. Expects 1 title 2011. 1 title listed in the *Small Press Record of Books in Print* (36th Edition, 2010-11). Discounts: 40 percent less for retail, 55 less for wholesale. 350pp. Simultaneous submissions accepted: No. Currently only publishing work by Jason Glover. Subjects: Culture, Experimental, Fiction, Human Rights, Magazines, Novels, Philosophy, Poetry, Post Modern, Short Stories.

Thirsty Turtle Press, Daniel Rogers, CEO; Nina B. Rogers, Editor, PO Box 402, Maggie Valley, NC 28751, Phone 828-926-6472, FAX 828-926-8851, dan@thirstyturtlepress.com, www.thirstyturtlepress.com. 2003. Fiction, non-fiction. avg. press run 500 - 1000. Expects 1 title 2010, 2 titles 2011. No titles listed in the *Small Press Record of Books in Print* (36th Edition, 2010-11). 225pp. Reporting time: 10 Days. Simultaneous submissions accepted: Yes. Publishes 90% of manuscripts submitted. Copyrights for author. Subjects: Autobiography, History, Non-Fiction, Ohio, Outdoor Adventure, Travel.

Thirteen Colonies Press, John F. Millar, 710 South Henry Street, Williamsburg, VA 23185, 757-229-1775. 1986. Art, music, non-fiction. "We specialize in popular history (non-fiction) from the period of the Renaissance up to 1800." avg. press run 3M. Pub'd 2 titles 2009; expects 3 titles 2010, 3 titles 2011. 3 titles listed in the *Small Press Record of Books in Print* (36th Edition, 2010-11). Discounts: retailer 40% up to 24 copies, 45% 24+ copies; wholesaler 20% up to 6 copies, 50% up to 24 copies, 60% 24+ copies; libraries 10% 1 book, 2+ books 30%. 200pp. Payment: 10% gross sales, paid quarterly on previous quarter's sales. Copyrights for author. Subjects: Americana, The Americas, Architecture, Biography, Canada, Christianity, Crafts, Hobbies, Dance, Europe, History, Music, New England, Religion.

13TH MOON, Judith E. Johnson, Editor, The 13th Moon Press, 2 Horizon Road, Apt G20, Fort Lee, NJ 07024, : 518 320-8581; Website: www.albany.edu/13thMoon. 1973. Poetry, fiction, articles, art, photos, interviews, criticism, reviews, parts-of-novels, long-poems, plays, news items, non-fiction. "Current issues include work by Josephine Jacobsen, Lyn Lifshin, Lori Anderson, Kim Vaseth, Carolyn Beard Whitlow, Nell Altizer, Toi Derricotte, Judith Barrington, Ethel Schwabacher, Sallie Bingham, Lavonne Mueller, Star Olderman, Cassandra Medley, Courtland Jessup, Alicia Ostriker, Laurel Speer, Kathleene West, Ursula K. LeGuin, Chitra Divakaruni, E.M. Broner, Susan Montez and Frances Sherwood. Volume XI, Nos. 1 & 2, features translations of the work of Italian women writers and a special sectin on Feminist Fiction(s). Future issues will feature work by Eastern European and Caribbean women writers and feminist politics." circ. 1.5M. 1 double-issue per year. Pub'd 1 issue 2009; expects 1 issue 2010. sub. price $10 for 1 double issue; per copy $10; sample $10. Back issues: $10. Discounts: varies. 275pp. Reporting time: 2 weeks to 4 months. Payment: copies. Copyrighted, reverts to author. Pub's reviews: 3 in 2009. §Poetry by women small press books by women/literature by women/women's literary history by women. Ads: $200/$125. Subjects: Criticism, Essays, Feminism, Fiction, Graphics, Journals, Lesbianism, Literary Review, Literature (General), Magazines, Poetry, Reviews, Short Stories, Visual Arts, Women.

The Thirty First Bird Press (see also THE THIRTY FIRST BIRD REVIEW: The Committed, Critical, and Creative Journal of Religion and Literature), Edward Simon, Pittsburgh, PA 15213, www.thirtyfirst-bird.com. 2009. Poetry, fiction, articles, art, photos, interviews, criticism, reviews, letters, parts-of-novels, long-poems, plays, non-fiction. "We are interested in work that critically examines the relationship between literature and religion. We are not interested in apologetics, or new age self-help articles. We are interested in creative works about religion, from both the perspective of faith and disbelief." avg. press run 100. Expects 2 titles 2010, 5 titles 2011. No titles listed in the *Small Press Record of Books in Print* (36th Edition, 2010-11). 100pp. Reporting time: A week to a month. Simultaneous submissions accepted: Yes. Payment: We are unable to pay at this time. Does not copyright for author. Subjects: Americana, William Blake, Experimental, Fantasy, Fiction, Folklore, Kafka, Language, Liberal Arts, Poetry, Prose, Religion.

THE THIRTY FIRST BIRD REVIEW: The Committed, Critical, and Creative Journal of Religion and

Literature, The Thirty First Bird Press, Edward Simon, Pittsburgh, PA 15213, www.thirtyfirstbird.com. 2009. Poetry, fiction, articles, art, photos, interviews, criticism, reviews, letters, parts-of-novels, long-poems, plays, non-fiction. circ. 500. 3/yr. Expects 3 issues 2011. sub. price $30; per copy $12. Back issues: $10. 150pp. Pub's reviews: N/A in 2009. Ads: Full Page: $75Half Page: $50.

32 POEMS, Deborah Ager, Publisher & Editor; John Poch, Editor, Texas Tech University, Lubbock, TX 79409-3091. "We do not read from May 1 to August 31. Submissions sent during that time will be returned unread. Please submit poems of 32 lines or fewer. Email submissions are not accepted unless requested. Include a brief bio with your submission. Simultaneous submissions are not accepted. Please include an SASE to receive a response. We prefer submissions in #10 envelopes. Translations are not currently accepted." 32 Poems is published 2 times per year in April and November.

THIS IS IMPORTANT, F.A. Nettelbeck, Editor, PO Box 69, Beatty, OR 97621, 541-533-2486, www.fanettelbeck.com. 1980. Poetry. "Patterned after a religious tract and features one poem from six different poets each issue. The pamphlets are distributed on buses, subways, toilet floors, in laundromats, bars, theaters, etc., with the aim being to get poetry out to non-literary types and others. Some of the featured poets have included: William S. Burroughs, Richard Kostelanetz, Wanda Coleman, Todd Moore, Tom Clark, John Giorno, Lyn Lifshin, David Fisher, James Bertolino, John M. Bennett, Jack Micheline, Ann Menebroker, Judson Crews, Anselm Hollo, Flora Durham, Charles Bernstein, Robin Holcomb, Michael McClure, Douglas Blazek, James Grauerholz, Nila Northsun, Allen Ginsberg...as well as many others. Send poems. We want it *all* as long as it's *small*...but, *make me cry*. Make checks payable to F.A. Nettelbeck." circ. 1M. 4/yr. Pub'd 2 issues 2009; expects 2 issues 2010, 2 issues 2011. sub. price $10; per copy SASE; sample $1. Back issues: individual issues vary in price, when available. Limited complete sets of Issues #1-#16 are available for $100 per set. Discounts: none. 8pp. Reporting time: immediate. Simultaneous submissions accepted: yes. Publishes 20% of manuscripts submitted. Payment: 50 copies. Copyrighted, reverts to author. Subject: Poetry.

THIS MAGAZINE, Jessica Johnston, Editor, 401 Richmond St. W. #396, Toronto, ON, M5V 3A8, Canada, (877) 999-8447 or (416) 979-9429 or email circ@thismagazine.ca. "*This Magazine* focuses on Canadian politics, pop culture and the arts, but in keeping with its radical roots never pulls punches. Subversive, edgy and smart, *This Magazine* is the real alternative to that. Praised for integrating commentary and investigative reporting with in-depth arts coverage, *This Magazine* has been instrumental in trumpeting the new works of young Canadian writers and artists. *This Magazine* has introduced the early work of Canada's most notable writers, critics and artists, including Margaret Atwood, Dionne Brand, Tomson Highway, Naomi Klein and Michael Ondaatje."

Thorp Springs Press, Paul Foreman, Editor; Foster Robertson, Editor; Terri Vaughn, Associate Editor, 1400 Cullen Avenue, Austin, TX 78757-2527, thorpsprings@ymail.com. 1971. Poetry, fiction, plays. "Looking for quality poetry. SASE required." Expects 3 titles 2010, 5 titles 2011. 24 titles listed in the *Small Press Record of Books in Print* (36th Edition, 2010-11). Discounts: bookstores 40%, 10 or more copies; jobbers 10%, 3-10 copies; 20%, 11-50 copies. 150-200pp. Reporting time: 9 months. Simultaneous submissions accepted: yes. Copyrights for author. Subjects: English, Language, Literature (General), Poetry, Public Affairs.

THOUGHTS FOR ALL SEASONS: The Magazine of Epigrams, Michel Paul Richard, Editor-in-Chief, 86 Leland Road, Becket, MA 01223, 413-623-0174. 1976. Poetry, satire. "Dedicated to preserving the epigram as a literary form. Guidelines for writing epigrams available on request without charge (with SASE). Poetry: rhyming quatrains, limericks; nonsense verse with good imagery; no haiku. Each issue has a commemorative theme, e.g. "The Devil's Dictionary: Ambrose Bierce after 100 Years", Vol. 7." circ. 1M. Irregular, special issues. Expects 1 issue 2010. sub. price $5 + $1.50 p/h; per copy $5 + $1.50 p/h; sample $5 + $1.50 p/h. Back issues: Vol. 2,3,4 & 5 available $3.75 + $1.25 p/h. Discounts: none. 80pp. Reporting time: 1 week. Simultaneous submissions accepted: yes. Publishes 15% of manuscripts submitted. Payment: 1 free copy of magazine. Copyrighted, reverts to author. Ads: $125/$80. Subjects: Humor, Society.

Three Bean Press, Seneca Clark Francione, Editor, Author, Publisher, Owner; Julie Decedue, Illustrator, Publisher, Owner; Sandy Giardi, Editor, Author, Publisher, Owner, P.O. Box 301711, Jamaica Plain, MA 02130, phone: 617.584.5759, email: info@threebeanpress.com, web: www.threebeanpress.com. 2005. Fiction, art, photos, cartoons, non-fiction. "Three Bean Press, LLC is a custom publish, offering a broad range of asssistance on publishing books of all types. Owned by Seneca Clark Francione, Julie Decedue, and Sandy Giardi, the Boston-based company creates, edits, designs, publishes, markets, and sells books. Three Bean Press is young and eager, with an eye for visually dramatic book design and clean, pleasing writing. The company's first books are "Lily + the Imaginary Zoo," "The Yellowest Yellow Lab," and "Frankie Goes to Fenway: The Tale of the Faithful, Red Sox-Loving Mouse," all by Seneca Clark and Sandy Giardi, illustrated by Julie Decedue. Three Bean Press also published a cookbook for Chef Peter Davis, and is currently working on several titles for other authors." avg. press run 5000. Pub'd 1 title 2009; expects 3 titles 2010, 10 titles 2011. 5 titles listed in the *Small Press Record of Books in Print* (36th Edition, 2010-11). Discounts: 1-2 copies no discount3-5 copies 25%6-20 copies 40%21-300 copies 50%301-up copies 55%. 70pp. Reporting time: 1 week.

Copyrights for author. Subjects: Animals, Arts, Children, Youth, Cooking, Design, Fiction, Food, Eating, Juvenile Fiction, North America, Novels, Nutrition, Photography, Picture Books, Printing, Short Stories.

Three Bears Publishing, Ashley, 690 Community Row, Winnipeg, Manitoba Canada R3R 1H7, Canada, Tel. 1 (204) 783-7966, Email: info@ThreeBearsPublishing.com, Website: www.ThreeBearsPublishing.com. 2005. Fiction, art. "Publishes Children's books for ages 5 and up." Expects 1 title 2010, 3 titles 2011. No titles listed in the *Small Press Record of Books in Print* (36th Edition, 2010-11). 32pp. Reporting time: Due to the large number of submissions we receive, we may only respond to manuscripts we are interested in publishing. Simultaneous submissions accepted: Yes. Subjects: Children, Youth, Fiction, Humor.

Three Dog Press, Jeff Herman, PO Box 1522, Stockbridge, MA 01262, 413-298-0077. 2005. "Books for writers about writing and publishing." Pub'd 1 title 2009; expects 2 titles 2010, 3 titles 2011. No titles listed in the *Small Press Record of Books in Print* (36th Edition, 2010-11). Discounts: 50%. 1,000pppp. Reporting time: Not sure. Simultaneous submissions accepted: Yes. Payment: negotiable. Copyrights for author. Subjects: August Derleth, Editing, Writers/Writing.

Three Pyramids Publishing, John F. Simone, E-mail JFS999@mindspring.com. 1989. Non-fiction. "Trade paperbacks on New Age, occult, metaphysics, tarot, spiritual and associated topics. Practical advice, how-to information. 64-200 pages average. Manuscripts must be on IBM-compatible disks. Will read submissions, prefer query letter & sample chapter first." avg. press run 500-3M. Pub'd 1 title 2009; expects 3 titles 2010, 3 titles 2011. 3 titles listed in the *Small Press Record of Books in Print* (36th Edition, 2010-11). Discounts: trade 3-299 40%, 300-499 50%, 500+ 55%. 200pp. Reporting time: 2 weeks to 1 month. We accept simultaneous submissions if noted when submitting. Payment: 5-10% net; no advance. Copyrights for author. Subjects: Astrology, Crystals, Dreams, England, How-To, Magic, Metaphysics, Myth, Mythology, New Age, Occult, Spiritual, Supernatural, Tarot.

THE THREEPENNY REVIEW, Wendy Lesser, Editor; John Berger, Consulting Editor; Frank Bidart, Consulting Editor; Anne Carson, Consulting Editor; Jonathan Franzen, Consulting Editor; Louise Gluck, Consulting Editor; Ian McEwan, Consulting Editor; Gore Vidal, Consulting Editor; Lawrence Weschler, Consulting Editor; Tobias Wolff, Consulting Editor; Kathryn Crim, Deputy Editor, PO Box 9131, Berkeley, CA 94709-0131, 510-849-4545. 1979. Poetry, fiction, art, interviews, criticism, reviews. "Length of material: Reviews should be 1M-3M words, covering several books or an author in depth, or dealing with a whole topic (e.g., the current theater season in one city, or the state of jazz clubs in another). Fiction should be under 5M words; poems should be under 100 lines. Special features: Though primarily a literary and performing arts review, *The Threepenny Review* will contain at least one essay on a topic of current social or political concern in each issue. Interested essayists should first submit a letter of inquiry. Recent Contributors: John Berger, Thom Gunn, Amy Tan. *SASE must accompany all manuscripts.*" circ. 8M. 4/yr. Pub'd 4 issues 2009; expects 4 issues 2010, 4 issues 2011. sub. price $25, $45/2 years, $50/yr foreign; per copy $7; sample $12 (includes shipping). Back issues: variable (price list available). 36pp. Reporting time: 1 to 2 months (but we do NOT read in the fall months). Simultaneous submissions accepted: No. Payment: $200-$400. Copyrighted, reverts to author. Pub's reviews: 20 in 2009. §Fiction, poetry, essays, philosophy, social theory, visual arts and architecture, history, criticism. Ads: $1800/$1100/$600 (full/half/quarter page). Subjects: Arts, Criticism, Electronics, Fiction, Literary Review, Literature (General), Poetry, Theatre.

THRESHOLDS JOURNAL, SOM Publishing, division of School of Metaphysics, Dr. Barbara Condron, Editor-in-Chief, 163 Moon Valley Road, Windyville, MO 65783, 417-345-8411, www.som.org. 1975. "Print version is an annual publication which serves as a voice for School of Metaphysics teachings. Educational, inspirational, and visionary. On-line publication accepts articles that are uplifting, educational, inspirational, and visionary. Need sort pieces, under 1000 words. Includes on-line interviews with well-known people who are successful in their fields. Recent interviews with Bernie Siegel, Diane Stein, Fred Pryor, Raymond Moody, Deena Metzger, Barbara Max Hubbard, Swami Beyondananda, Dalai Lama." circ. 5M+. 1/yr. Pub'd 1 issue 2009; expects 1 issue 2010, 1 issue 2011. sub. price online publication only. Back issues: $5 for available issues. Discounts: available only through SOMA. Reporting time: 5 weeks-3 months. Payment: if accepted, international exposure, membership to SOMA ($60 value). Copyrighted, does not revert to author. Classified only, by donation to School of Metaphysics. Subjects: Arts, Dreams, Education, Fiction, Health, Humor, Inspirational, Magazines, Metaphysics, Religion, Science Fiction, Spiritual.

Thunder Rain Publishing Corp., Katherine (Rhi) Tracy, Editor, 603 Hickory St., Thibodaux, LA 70301, rhi@thunder-rain.com, www.thunder-rain.com, www.lintrigue.org. 1996. Poetry, fiction, articles, art, photos, satire, criticism, reviews, long-poems, non-fiction. "Contest discontinued." Publishes 1-2 online issues a year. Pub'd 1 title 2009; expects 2 titles 2010, 2 titles 2011. 3 titles listed in the *Small Press Record of Books in Print* (36th Edition, 2010-11). Reporting time: 3-6 months. Simultaneous submissions accepted: yes. Copyrights for author. Subjects: Anthology, Creative Non-fiction, Essays, Experimental, Fiction, Folklore, Gender Issues, History, Literary Review, Non-Fiction, Poetry, Prose, Reviews, Short Stories, Zines.

Thundercloud Books, Laurel Tesoro, Press Contact, PO Box 97, Aspen, CO 81612, (970) 925-1588, fax (970) 920-9361, web: www.ThundercloudBooks.com, www.WakingThe Ancients.com. 2003. Fiction. "Novels for adults involving southwestern United States, prehistoric civilizations, outdoors and recreation, women's concerns." Expects 1 title 2011. 1 title listed in the *Small Press Record of Books in Print* (36th Edition, 2010-11). Copyrights for author. Subjects: Arizona, Colorado, Fiction, History, Indigenous Cultures, Literature (General), Native American, New Mexico, Society, Travel, Utah.

Tia Chucha Press, Luis J. Rodriguez, PO Box 328, San Fernando, CA 91341, 818-898-0013. 1989. Poetry, fiction. "A project of Tia Chucha's Centro Cultural, a not-for-profit corporation. Distributed by: Northwestern University Press, 625 Colfax, Evanston, IL 60208; 800-621-2736; FAX 800-621-8476." avg. press run 1M. Pub'd 1 title 2009; expects 2 titles 2010, 3 titles 2011. 28 titles listed in the *Small Press Record of Books in Print* (36th Edition, 2010-11). 64pp. Reporting time: 6 weeks to 6 months. We accept simultaneous submissions, but we must be informed if another publisher is interested. Publishes .05% of manuscripts submitted. Payment: 10% royalties, discount on books. Copyrights for author. Subjects: Literature (General), Multicultural, Poetry.

TIFERET: A Journal of Spiritual Literature, Eryon Press, Cynthia Brown, PO Box 309, Gladstone, NJ 07934.

Tiger Moon, Terry Reis Kennedy, 3-882 Coconut Grove, Prasanthi Nilayam A.P. India 515134, India, cosmicpowerpress@yahoo.co.in AND treiskennedy@gmail.com. 1991. "Self publish at lowest rates: Poetry, fiction, and literary essays, biography, Tibetan-related material, and doctoral dissertations. For more information contact Terry Reis Kennedy by email at cosmicpowrepress@yahoo.co.in." avg. press run 1M. 5 titles listed in the *Small Press Record of Books in Print* (36th Edition, 2010-11). 100-200pp. Reporting time: 2 months. Simultaneous submissions accepted: yes. Payment: varies with each project. Copyrights for author.

TIGHTROPE, Swamp Press, Ed Rayher, 15 Warwick Avenue, Northfield, MA 01360. 1975. Poetry, art, long-poems. "Fine poetry and graphic art printed by letterpress in artistic and sometimes unconventional formats. Recent contributors: Greg Joly, Chuck Zerby, Carolyn Cushing." circ. 350. 2/yr. Pub'd 2 issues 2009; expects 2 issues 2010, 2 issues 2011. sub. price $10; per copy $6; sample $6. Back issues: $6. Discounts: bookstores and dealers 40%. 60pp. Reporting time: 8 weeks. Simultaneous submissions accepted: No. Publishes 1% of manuscripts submitted. Payment: copies. Copyrighted, reverts to author. Subjects: Graphics, Haiku, Poetry.

Tilbury House, Publishers, Jennifer Bunting, Publisher, 103 Brunswick Avenue, Gardiner, ME 04345, Tel: 207-582-1899, Web Site: http://www.tilburyhouse.com. "Tilbury House narrowed its editorial focus several years ago, and we would appreciate receiving only queries and manuscripts that fit within our current areas of interest. We receive hundreds of unsolicited manuscripts each year; it's a time-consuming task to read and answer them all-although we sometimes find a gem! If you are connected to the Internet, please take a moment to visit our web site at www.tilburyhouse.com to familiarize yourself with our catalog and the kinds of books we publish. We look forward to seeing your manuscript and appreciate your interest in Tilbury House." No titles listed in the *Small Press Record of Books in Print* (36th Edition, 2010-11).

TIMBER CREEK REVIEW, J.M. Freiermuth, Editor; Willa Schmidt, Associate Editor, c/o J.M. Freiermuth, PO Box 16542, Greensboro, NC 27416. 1994. Poetry, fiction, articles, photos, cartoons, satire, letters, plays, non-fiction. "*Timber Creek Review* is a quarterly collection of short stories with a few poems. Contributors in the 13th year include John Campbell, Dennis Vannatta, Joel Ensana, Roslyn Willett, Rafael Weinstein, Candace Lyons, Vickie Weaver, Louy Castonguay, and Willa Schmidt. Send all correspondence and make all checks payable to: J.M. Freiermuth. (Do not mention the magazine on your check, or it will be returned.) Published 31 stories in 08 and expect 32 stories in 2009. We do not accept reprints." circ. 150-180. 4/yr. Pub'd 4 issues 2009; expects 4 issues 2010, 4 issues 2011. sub. price $16 individuals, $18 institutions and Canada, $22 international; per copy $4.75; sample $4.75. Discounts: 50% for creative writing classes and groups. 76-88pp. Reporting time: from the next mail to 4 months. Simultaneous submissions accepted: yes. Publishes 8-12% of manuscripts submitted. Payment: 1 year subscription for first story, 1 copy for poems, additional short stories and short-short stories to 2 pages. Pays $35 to $60 for stories, including annual subscription. Not copyrighted, rights revert to author upon publication. Pub's reviews: 2 in 2009. §Books of short stories or poems that include stories or poems published in TCR would be considered for review. Ads: none.

•Timber Gap Publishers, Matthew Taylor, 1825 Roche Drive, Pleasant Hill, CA 94523, 925-349-5074, mtaylor@timbergap.com, www.timbergap.com. 2009. Fiction, non-fiction. avg. press run 5000. Expects 1 title 2010, 5 titles 2011. 1 title listed in the *Small Press Record of Books in Print* (36th Edition, 2010-11). 380pp.

Timberline Press, Clarence Wolfshohl, 6281 Red Bud, Fulton, MO 65251, 573-642-5035. 1975. Poetry, non-fiction. "Print chapbooks of 20-50 pages (prefer shorter 20-30 pp). We look at all poetry sent, but lean toward nature poetry with a sense of place or good lyrical, imagistic poetry. Actually, our taste is eclectic with quality being our primary criterion. We also publish short essays of natural history (under 20 pages) which will be printed in a reduced size format (not miniature). No set preference, but possible contributors should be familiar with better contemporary writers of natural history." avg. press run 200. Pub'd 2 titles 2009; expects 2 titles 2011. 27 titles listed in the *Small Press Record of Books in Print* (36th Edition, 2010-11). Discounts: 1-4 books 25%, 5+ 40%. 25-45pp. Reporting time: 30 days. Payment: 50-50 split after expenses. Does not copyright for author. Subjects: Earth, Natural History, Poetry.

Time Barn Books, Klyd Watkins, 529 Barrywood Drive, Nashville, TN 37220-1636, www.thetimegarden.com. 2000. Poetry, music, long-poems. "I publish stuff that I believe in that might not get out there otherwise, much of it my own work. I am not seeking manuscripts and have a short pile on hand that I may never get around to reading." avg. press run 300. Pub'd 2 titles 2009; expects 3 titles 2010. 3 titles listed in the *Small Press Record of Books in Print* (36th Edition, 2010-11). Discounts: 40%. 40pp. Reporting time: My first response will be quick but my final answer may never come. Simultaneous submissions accepted: No. Publishes 33% of manuscripts submitted. Payment: The authors pay the publishing costs and own all the books. I take 40% for any that I sell. I add the symbol for the author but do not send to Library of Congress. Subject: Poetry.

TIME FOR RHYME, Richard W. Unger, Editor, c/o Richard Unger, PO Box 1055, Battleford SK S0M 0E0, Canada, 306-445-5172. 1995. Poetry. "This is a handcrafted, pocket-sized quarterly magazine that publishes *only* rhyming poetry. Writer's guidelines or advertisers guidelines available with SASE (IRC or $1US acceptable from non-Canadians without Canadian postage)." circ. 83. 4/yr. Pub'd 4 issues 2009; expects 4 issues 2010, 4 issues 2011. sub. price $12 Cdn. for Canadians, $12US for Americans, $19 Cdn. for overseas; per copy $3.25 with SASE, Americans use either Canadian postage or IRCs, $5 Cdn. overseas; sample $3.25 Cdn. for Canadians, $3.25 US for Americans, $5 Cdn. overseas. Back issues: same. 32pp. Reporting time: as quickly as possible. Simultaneous submissions accepted: no. Publishes less than 1% of manuscripts submitted. Payment: 1 copy (when financially viable, will consider cash payment). Copyrighted, reverts to author. Pub's reviews: 4 in 2009. §Those mostly or entirely containing rhyming poetry (either new or old with artwork). Ads: classifieds 15¢/word. Subject: Poetry.

Timeless Books (see also ASCENT), Clea McDougall, Editor, PO Box 9, 527 Walker's Landing Rd, Kootenay Bay BC V0B 1X0, Canada, 1-800-661-8711, 250-227-9224contact@timeless.org, www.timeless.org. 1978. Non-fiction. "Timeless publications are for those who seek a deeper meaning and purpose to their lives. Our focus is on the ancient teachings of yoga and Buddhism. Inspiration is combined with practical tools for living a life of quality and to bring out the best in ourselves and others." avg. press run 2000. Pub'd 4 titles 2009; expects 4 titles 2010, 4/ titles 2011. 22 titles listed in the *Small Press Record of Books in Print* (36th Edition, 2010-11). Discounts: 1-5 titles 20%, 5 or more 40%. 250pp. Reporting time: one to three months. Copyrights for author. Subjects: Autobiography, Biography, Buddhism, Inspirational, Memoirs, Metaphysics, Non-Fiction, Religion, Self-Help, Spiritual, Tapes & Records, Yoga.

TIN HOUSE MAGAZINE, Win McCormack, Publisher, PO Box 469049, Escondido, CA 92046. "A journal of sex, saints and satellite convulsions! Each issue includes fiction, non-fiction, New Voices, Author Interviews, Lost and Found (underappreciated books), profound Pilgrimages, a Readable Feast (memorable dishes and the events that inspired them), Blithe Spirits (signature drinks). We set out to capture the energy and vitality of the best new writers in fiction and poetry from around the world and showcase their work in a format that's elegant, inspired and inviting."

TINY LIGHTS: A Journal of Personal Narrative, Susan Bono, PO Box 928, Petaluma, CA 94953, 707-762-3208, sbono@tiny-lights.com, www.tiny-lights.com. 1995. Non-fiction. "*Tiny Lights* celebrates the power of personal essay with a biannual journal devoted to short essay. The annual essay contest, which offers $1500 in prizes, provides the material for the summer issue, along with much of the winter Flashpoints issue (flash essays of 1,000 words or less). Past contributors include Rebecca Lawton, Gerald Haslam, Jean Hegland, Suzanne LaFetra, Ron Franscell, Pat Schneider, Kevin Holdsworth, Sheila Bender. *TL*'s website at www.tiny-lights.com features additional venues for narrative non-fiction." circ. approx. 800. 2/yr. Pub'd 2 issues 2009; expects 2 issues 2010, 2 issues 2011. sub. price $10; per copy $5. Back issues: $3. Discounts: contact us. 20 (newsletter format)pp. Reporting time: 3 months. Simultaneous submissions accepted: yes. Publishes 10% of manuscripts submitted. Payment: contest issue only. Not copyrighted. Ads: Go to "Literary Services Directory" at www.tiny-lights.com for rates. Subjects: Essays, Memoirs.

Titan Press, Stefanya Wilson, Publisher, PO Box 17897, Encino, CA 91416-7897. 1980. Poetry, fiction, photos, non-fiction. "We look only at high quality manuscripts. If it also embodies socially redeeming commentary, terrific. Very 'current' styles are preferred. We have strong liaisons in the entertainment industry and are thusly somewhat media oriented. Only strong writers with some sort of track record should submit. We sponsor the 'Masters Literary Award', and publish the results, et al. Professionalism, style and quality are the keys to submission here. We are not interested in simply the good, but rather the great. To know us, read something by: Milan Kundera, Scott Alixander Sonders, Tom Robbins, Chaim Potok, or John Irving." avg. press run 3K-10K poetry, 50K calendars, 5-50K novels. Pub'd 6 titles 2009; expects 6 titles 2010, 6 titles 2011. 5 titles listed in the *Small Press Record of Books in Print* (36th Edition, 2010-11). Discounts: trade 2-4 20%,

5-9 30%, 10-24 40%, 25-49 45%, 50-99 50%; schools and libraries less added 5%. 112pp. Reporting time: 2-6 months. Payment: 5-10% on sales + guarantee and expenses, see Standard Writers Union Contract. Copyrights for author. Subjects: Awards, Foundations, Grants, Fiction, Health, Photography, Poetry, Science, Sex, Sexuality, Spiritual.

Titlewaves Publishing; Writers Direct, Rob Sanford, Cathy Crary, 4330 Kauai Beach Drive, Suite G21, Lihue, HI 96766, orders 800-867-7323. 1989. Fiction, articles, photos, cartoons, interviews, satire, news items, non-fiction. avg. press run print-on-demand (200). Pub'd 1 title 2009; expects 3 titles 2010, 4 titles 2011. 4 titles listed in the *Small Press Record of Books in Print* (36th Edition, 2010-11). Discounts: 3-299 40%, 300-499 50%, 500+ 55%, STOP orders 40% + $2.75/order. 235pp. Reporting time: 30 days. Simultaneous submissions accepted: yes. Payment: varies; better than standard. Copyrights for author. Subjects: Ecology, Foods, Ethics, Finances, Hawaii, Health, How-To, Humor, Inspirational, Marketing, Motivation, Success, Nature, Non-Fiction, Quotations, Spiritual, Travel.

Titus Home Publishing, Carolena Lapierre, 204 N. Main, Rogersville, MO 65742-6574, 417-753-3449. 2006. Photos, non-fiction. "Titus Home Publishing "Books to Pass On" Wholesome books on Family History, Life Stories, Cookbooks, Special family helps and advice, Children's books." Expects 2 titles 2010, 2 titles 2011. No titles listed in the *Small Press Record of Books in Print* (36th Edition, 2010-11). Discounts: 2-10 copies 20%11+ copies 40%. 130pp. Reporting time: 60 Days. Copyrights for author. Subjects: Adoption, Aging, Amish Culture, Autobiography, Biography, Children, Youth, Cooking, Family, Genealogy, History, Journals, Memoirs, Picture Books, Poetry, Storytelling.

TMC Books LLC (see also WILDERNESS MEDICINE NEWSLETTER), Frank Hubbell, 731 Tasker Hill Rd., Conway, NH 03818, 603-447-5589, info@tmcbooks.com, www.tmcbooks.com. 2002. Articles, non-fiction. "TMC Books is a specialty publisher, we supply textbooks to Stonehearth Open Learning Opportunities (SOLO), the well known education school in the White Mountains of New Hampshire, we also publish the online magazine Wilderness Medicine Newsletter, guide books, and some non-fiction titles." avg. press run 8000. Pub'd 1 title 2009; expects 1 title 2010, 1 title 2011. 5 titles listed in the *Small Press Record of Books in Print* (36th Edition, 2010-11). 120pp. Reporting time: Due to a backlog of projects we are not looking for manuscript submissions at this time. Simultaneous submissions accepted: No. Does not copyright for author. Subjects: Architecture, Education, Medicine, Nature, New England, Non-Fiction.

TnT Classic Books, Linda Reynolds, Francine L. Trevens, 360 West 36 Street #2NW, New York, NY 10018-6412, 212-736-6279, Fax 212-695-3219, tntclassics@aol.com, www.tntclassicbooks.com. 1994. Fiction, plays. "We handle old JH Press gay play series and their gay novels. We are moving into a children's line called the Happy Task Series. Overstocked and not reading until mid-2005." avg. press run 2M. Expects 1 title 2010, 1 title 2011. 17 titles listed in the *Small Press Record of Books in Print* (36th Edition, 2010-11). Discounts: 40% commercial bookstores, 30% college bookstores, none for orders under 5 books. 100pp. Simultaneous submissions accepted: no. Payment: 10% semi-annually. Copyrights for author. Subjects: Drama, Fiction, Gay, Lesbianism, Novels.

Toad Press International Chapbook Series, Genevieve Kaplan, Sean Bernard, Claremont, CA 91711-0159, www.toadpress.blogspot.com, toadpress@hotmail.com. 2003. Poetry, fiction, parts-of-novels, long-poems, collages, plays. "We publish literary translations only." avg. press run 200. Pub'd 2 titles 2009; expects 1 title 2010, 2 titles 2011. 9 titles listed in the *Small Press Record of Books in Print* (36th Edition, 2010-11). 30pp. Reporting time: see website for submission period. Simultaneous submissions accepted: Yes. Payment: pays in copies only. Subjects: Avant-Garde, Experimental Art, Experimental, Literature (General), Poetry, Prose, Surrealism, Translation.

Toadlily Press, Myrna Goodman Editor, Meredith Trede Editor, P O. Box 2, Chappaqua, NY 10514, mgoodman@toadlilypress.com, www.toadlilypress.com. 2005. Poetry. "The Quartet Series presents four poets each represented by a chapbook, in one handsome, perfect-bound volume. Toadlily publications are as artful and imaginative as the words within them." avg. press run 1000. Pub'd 1 title 2009; expects 1 title 2010, 1/ titles 2011. 5 titles listed in the *Small Press Record of Books in Print* (36th Edition, 2010-11). Discounts: 30-40%. 80pp. Reporting time: 2-3 months. Simultaneous submissions accepted: Yes. Payment: cash and copies of book. Author retains rights of his/her individual work, we copyright the Quartet Series. Subject: Poetry.

Toca Family Publishing, div. of Toca Family Communications Group, LLC (see also EQUAL CONSTRUCTION RECORD), Heather Loveridge, 2483 Heritage Drive, Suite 16-184, Snellville, GA 30078, 404-348-4065 x5, 404-348-4469, info@tocafamilypublishing.com, www.tocafamilypublishing.com. 2007. Articles, non-fiction. "We publish informational books targeted to the small and medium-sized business community that are industry independent." avg. press run 5000. Expects 1-3 titles 2010, 3-5 titles 2011. 1 title listed in the *Small Press Record of Books in Print* (36th Edition, 2010-11). Discounts: 2-10 copies, 25% 10-50 copies, 30% 50-100 copies, 40% 100 copies, 55%. 150-250pp. Reporting time: 10-20 days. Simultaneous submissions accepted: Yes. Publishes 15% of manuscripts submitted. Payment: Royalty: 15%, no advance payments; payments made every 30 days. Does not copyright for author. Subjects: Advertising, Self-Promotion, Business & Economics, Careers, Construction, Consulting, Finances, How-To, Internet, Newspapers, Non-Fiction.

Tomart Publications, Tom Tumbusch, Publisher, President; Amber Henry, Editor, Production; Amanda Spicer, Customer Service, Advertising; Chris Hall, Photographer, Editor; Heather Bentley, Graphic Designer, 3300 Encrete Lane, Dayton, OH 45439-1944, 937-294-2250; Fax 937-294-1024. 1977. Non-fiction. "We are publishers of antique & collectible photo price guides for Disneyana (any Disney product), radio premiums, character glasses, space adventure collectibles, etc. Other non-fiction on related subjects. Books on musical theatre." avg. press run 6M-10M. Pub'd 3 titles 2009; expects 6 titles 2010, 5 titles 2011. 7 titles listed in the *Small Press Record of Books in Print* (36th Edition, 2010-11). Discounts: booksellers 25%, distributors up to 50%. 220pp. Reporting time: 30 days. Payment: 50% advance. Copyrights for author. Subjects: Antiques, Biography, Book Collecting, Bookselling, Collectibles, Crafts, Hobbies, Disney, Theatre.

Tombouctou Books, Michael Wolfe, 1472 Creekview Lane, Santa Cruz, CA 95062, 831-476-4144. 1975. Poetry, fiction, interviews, long-poems. "No unsolicited manuscripts will be returned. Distributed to the trade by Small Press Distribution, 1341 Seventh StreetBerkeley, CA 94710-1409." avg. press run 500-2M. Pub'd 4 titles 2009; expects 4 titles 2010, 4 titles 2011. 17 titles listed in the *Small Press Record of Books in Print* (36th Edition, 2010-11). Discounts: inquire publisher. 48-200pp. Simultaneous submissions accepted: no. Publishes 1% of manuscripts submitted. Payment: varies. Copyrights for author. Subjects: African Literature, Africa, African Studies, Fiction, Poetry.

Top Shelf Productions, Inc., Chris Staros, Publisher; Brett Warnock, Publisher, PO Box 1282, Marietta, GA 30061-1282, 770-425-0551, Fax: 770-427-6395, Email: chris@topshelfcomix.com. 1997. "Top Shelf Productions is the graphic novel and comics publisher best known for its ability to discover and showcase the vanguard of the alternative comics scene. Since forming in 1997, Top Shelf Productions has published over one-hundred graphic novels and comic books that have helped to revitalize interest in comics as a literary art form. Most notably, Craig Thompsons *Blankets* and Alan Moore & Eddie Campbell's *From Hell*, both of which have garnered critical accolades from the likes of Time Magazine, Entertainment Weekly, Publishers Weekly, The New Yorker, and the New York Times Book Review. Perennial favorites also include: Craig Thompson's *Good-bye, Chunky Rice*; Alan Moore's *Voice of the Fire*, Jeffrey Brown's *Clumsy* and *Unlikely*; James Kochalka's *Monkey vs. Robot*; Doug TenNapel's *Creature Tech*; Alex Robinsons *Box Office Poison*; Rich Koslowski's *Three Fingers*, Scott Morse's *The Barefoot Serpent*; and Jon B. Cooke's award-winning *Comic Book Artist* magazine." No titles listed in the *Small Press Record of Books in Print* (36th Edition, 2010-11).

Top 20 Press, Paul Bernabei, 1873 Standord Avenue, St. Paul, MN 55105, 651-690-5758. 2003. Non-fiction. "To provide books and materials to help people develop their potential." Expects 1 title 2011. No titles listed in the *Small Press Record of Books in Print* (36th Edition, 2010-11). Discounts: 2-10 copies 25%. 230pp. Subjects: Adolescence, Children, Youth, Family, Leadership, Non-Fiction, Relationships, Self-Help, Young Adult.

TORRE DE PAPEL, Eduardo Guizar Alvarez, 111 Phillips Hall, The University of Iowa, Iowa City, IA 52242, 319-335-0487. 1991. Poetry, fiction, articles, art, interviews, criticism, reviews. circ. 400. 3/yr. Pub'd 2 issues 2009; expects 3 issues 2010, 3 issues 2011. sub. price $30; per copy $10; sample $10. Back issues: $15. 110pp. Reporting time: 2 months (may vary). Payment: none. Copyrighted, rights revert to author and publisher. Pub's reviews. §Latin American literature (Hispanic and Brazilian), Caribbean literature, Spanish literature, Portuguese literature, Chicano/Puerto Rican/Cuban American/Afro-American literature, translations and linguistics. Subjects: Caribbean, Criticism, Journals, Latin America, Latino, Literary Review, Literature (General), Portugal, Puerto Rico, Spain, Translation, Women, Writers/Writing.

Tortuga Books, Carolyn Gloeckner, 108 Paradox Point Drive, Aurora, NC 27806-9304, 800-345-6665 (orders), 305-745-8709, Fax 305-745-2704, www.tortugabooks.com. 1998. Non-fiction. avg. press run 5M. Pub'd 3 titles 2009; expects 1 title 2010, 2 titles 2011. No titles listed in the *Small Press Record of Books in Print* (36th Edition, 2010-11). Discounts: 2-3 10%, 4-10 20%, 11-20 30%, 21-100 40%, 100+ 50%. 200pp. Reporting time: 2 months. Simultaneous submissions accepted: no. Payment: cash. Does not copyright for author. Subjects: Caribbean, Children, Youth, Environment, Florida, Marine Life, Non-Fiction, Picture Books, Puerto Rico, Sports, Outdoors, Travel.

Total Cardboard Publishing, John Mansfield, 70 Mount Barker Road, Stirling, SA 5152, Australia, www.totalcardboard.com. 2003. Poetry, fiction, articles. "Books that are too flammable for bookstores." avg. press run 300. Pub'd 3 titles 2009; expects 2 titles 2010, 3 titles 2011. 3 titles listed in the *Small Press Record of Books in Print* (36th Edition, 2010-11). Discounts: 40% trade discount. 200pp. Reporting time: 1 month. Simultaneous submissions accepted: Yes. Publishes 20% of manuscripts submitted. Payment: Split all profits 50-50. Copyrights for author. Subjects: Anarchist, Australia, Avant-Garde, Experimental Art, Experimental, Fiction, Gaelic, Genealogy, Paper, Psychiatry, Zen.

Total Package Publications, LLC, David L. Henry, P.O. Box 3237, Mount Vernon, NY 10553, website: www.totalpackagepublications.com, email: contacttpp@totalpackagepublications.com. 2006. Fiction. "Mission Statement: At Total Package Publications, LLC, the overall vision is well-constructed fictional content, reader satisfaction, and overall sense of self-worth after completion of a project. The company name was crafted to enhance the publishing process by providing the general public with a "package deal" for their purchase: INTEGRITY - SINCERITY - CONSISTENCY in it's quality of work and ability to maximize reader satisfaction at all levels of the reading experience." Expects 1 title 2010, 2 titles 2011. 4 titles listed in the *Small Press Record of Books in Print* (36th Edition, 2010-11). Reporting time: 1 - 7 days. Simultaneous submissions accepted: Yes. Publishes 1% of manuscripts submitted. Payment: to be determined. Does not copyright for author. Subjects: African-American, Fiction, Juvenile Fiction, Multicultural, Relationships, Young Adult.

TOUCHSTONE, Old Stage Publishing, Dan Culberson, PO Box 17446, Boulder, CO 80308-0446, 303-444-3363, danculberson@juno.com. 1996. Articles, interviews, criticism, news items, non-fiction. *"Touchstone* is an e-mail distributed free newsletter that is also published on the Internet at http://www.forums.delphiforums.com/touchstone and is concerned with political activism." circ. 300. 12/yr. Pub'd 12 issues 2009; expects 12 issues 2010, 12 issues 2011. sub. price free; per copy free; sample free. Back issues: $1. 10pp. Reporting time: 1 week. Simultaneous submissions accepted: yes. Publishes 25% of manuscripts submitted. Payment: 2 copies. Copyrighted, reverts to author. Pub's reviews: none in 2009. §Politics, elections, political activism, government. Ads: none. Subjects: Birth, Birth Control, Population, Black, Business & Economics, Civil Rights, Colorado, Communism, Marxism, Leninism, Community, Conservation, Counter-Culture, Alternatives, Communes, Crime, Cuba, Culture, Current Affairs, Earth, Natural History, Education.

Touchstone Center Publications, 141 East 88th Street, New York, NY 10128, rlewis212@aol.com. 1969. "At present Touchstone Center Publications is primarily concerned with documenting and publishing the work of the The Touchstone Center - particularly its work with children and teachers in the area of arts education, poetry and the nature of the imaginative experience." 7 titles listed in the *Small Press Record of Books in Print* (36th Edition, 2010-11).

TOUCHSTONE LITERARY JOURNAL, Panther Creek Press, Guida Jackson, Publisher & Editor; T.E. Walthen, Poetry Editor, 104 Plum Tree Terrace, #115, Houston, TX 77077-5375. 1976. Poetry, fiction, interviews, criticism, reviews, non-fiction. "No line limit for good poetry, prose." circ. 500. 1/yr, plus book-length collections. Pub'd 2 issues 2009; expects 2 issues 2010, 2 issues 2011. 8 titles listed in the *Small Press Record of Books in Print* (36th Edition, 2010-11). sub. price contribution: 1 book postage stamps; per copy same; sample same. Back issues: same. 80pp. Reporting time: 6 weeks. Payment: 1 copy. Copyrighted, reverts to author. Pub's reviews: 6 in 2009. §Poetry, short story collections. Subjects: Fiction, Poetry, Reviews, Translation.

TOWER POETRY, Tower Poetry Society, Jeff Seffinga, Editor-in-Chief, c/o McMaster University, 1280 Main Street W Box 1021, Hamilton, Ontario, L8S 1CO, Canada, http://www.towerpoetry.ca; tps@tower-poetry.ca. 1950. Poetry. "Tower Poetry welcomes submissions from poets everywhere. Submissions of not more than four(4) poems please, must be accompanied by a self-addressed, stamped envelope, and should arrive only during the months of February and August. Late submissions will be kept until the next reading period but will not be acknowledged. Please include your name and address on each page. We request first print publication and electronic rights only. Payment, should your work be accepted, will be one(1) copy of the issue in which your poem appears." circ. 250. 2/yr. Pub'd 2 issues 2009; expects 2 issues 2010, 2 issues 2011. sub. price $15 North America, $18 abroad (Canadian funds; includes postage); per copy $8 North America; $9 abroad (Can. Funds); sample $5 North America; $6 abroad (Can. Funds). Back issues: $5 North America; $6 abroad (Can. Funds). Discounts: 40%. 44pp. Reporting time: four months. Simultaneous submissions accepted: no. Publishes 15-20% of manuscripts submitted. Payment: 1 copy. Copyrighted, reverts to author.

Tower Poetry Society (see also TOWER POETRY), Jeff Seffinga, Editor-in-chief, c/o McMaster University, 1280 Main Street W. Box 1021, Hamilton, Ontario, L8S 1CO, Canada. 1950. Poetry. avg. press run 250. Pub'd 2 titles 2009; expects 2 titles 2010, 2 titles 2011. No titles listed in the *Small Press Record of Books in Print* (36th Edition, 2010-11). 44pp. Reporting time: 2 months for submissions in Feb. + Aug. Simultaneous submissions accepted: no. Publishes 20% of manuscripts submitted. Payment: one copy of publication in which poem appears. Copyright reverts to author upon publication.

TRADICION REVISTA, LPD Press, Paul Rhetts, Barbe Awalt, 925 Salamanca NW, Los Ranchos de Albuquerque, NM 87107-5647, 505-344-9382, Fax 505-345-5129, info@nmsantos.com. 1995. Articles, art, photos, non-fiction. "A journal on contemporary and traditional Spanish Colonial art and culture." circ. 5-10M per issue. 2/yr; Summer (July) and Winter (December). Pub'd 4 issues 2009; expects 4 issues 2010, 4 issues 2011. sub. price $15; per copy $10; sample $10. Back issues: $10. 64-72pp. Reporting time: 1-2 months. Simultaneous submissions accepted: yes. Publishes 80% of manuscripts submitted. Payment: negotiable. Copyrighted. Pub's reviews: 40 in 2009. §Southwest art and culture; Hispanic topics. Ads: b/w:

$360/$240/$160, 4-color: $975/$650/$475. Subjects: Anthropology, Archaelogy, Arizona, Arts, Catholic, Colorado, Latin America, Latino, New Mexico, Southwest, Texas, Textiles, Weaving.

Trafford Publishing, 2657 Wilfert Road, Victoria, BC V9B 5c3, Canada, 888-232-4444, Fax 250-383-6804, info@trafford.com, www.trafford.com. 1995. "Trafford Publishing has provided self-publishing services to thousands of authors worldwide since 1995. If you have finished manuscript you can now have it published and available worldwide in just weeks!" Pub'd 2200 titles 2009; expects 3100 titles 2010, 4500 titles 2011. 3 titles listed in the *Small Press Record of Books in Print* (36th Edition, 2010-11). Discounts: 40% for booksellers, 15% for libraries and colleges and 60% for our authors. 50-700pp. Simultaneous submissions accepted: yes. Publishes 99% of manuscripts submitted. Payment: author makes 60% of gross margin. Subjects: Fiction, Non-Fiction.

Trafton Publishing, Rick Singer, 109 Barcliff Terrace, Cary, NC 27518-8900. 1993. Cartoons, satire, music. "We look for well conceived how to manuals/books/cassettes or videos for music lovers. Also, we need clean and original humor of any length, from a joke to a complete book." Pub'd 3 titles 2009; expects 3-5 titles 2010, 3-5 titles 2011. No titles listed in the *Small Press Record of Books in Print* (36th Edition, 2010-11). Discounts: 30%-65%, depending on book and quantity. 150pp. Reporting time: 1-3 months. Publishes 5% of manuscripts submitted. Payment: varies. Does not copyright for author. Subjects: Aging, How-To, Humor, Music, North Carolina, Wine, Wineries.

Transcending Mundane, Inc., Tommy Kirchhoff, 3434 E. 7800 South, Salt Lake City, UT 84121, 435-901-2546, tommy@paracreative.com, www.paracreative.com. 1998. Poetry, fiction, articles, art, photos, cartoons, satire, reviews, letters, plays, concrete art, non-fiction. "Our policy is "no news." It must either be funny, witty, off the wall or out of the norm. We accept unsolicited work, but can't always read all of it; we only respond to the stuff that really tickles us." avg. press run 15-3M. Pub'd 1 title 2009; expects 1-3 titles 2010, 3-5 titles 2011. 2 titles listed in the *Small Press Record of Books in Print* (36th Edition, 2010-11). Discounts: commercial-40% off "Utah or Bust" orders over ten booksno more discounts on "Nuts in the Woodwork". 150pp. Reporting time: not set yet. Simultaneous submissions accepted: yes. Payment: not set yet. Copyrights for author. Subjects: Arts, Colorado, Counter-Culture, Alternatives, Communes, Humor, Philosophy, Satire, Sex, Sexuality, Surrealism.

TRANSLATION REVIEW, Rainer Schulte, Editor; Dennis Kratz, Editor, Univ. of Texas-Dallas, 800 W. Campbell Rd.,- JO51, Richardson, TX 75080-3201, 972-883-2093, Fax 972-883-6303. 1978. Poetry, fiction, articles, interviews, criticism, reviews, news items, non-fiction. "*Translation Review* is a publication of The Center for Translation Studies at The University of Texas at Dallas and the American Literary Translators Association (ALTA). The journal is distributed to ALTA members and subscribing libraries. *Translation Review* focuses on the theory, practice, and evaluation of literary works in translation." circ. 1,000. 2/yr. Pub'd 2 issues 2009; expects 2 issues 2010, 2 issues 2011. Subscription by membership to ALTA only:$80 for US and Canada Individual Memberships$100 for International Individual Memberships$20 for Student Individual Memberships$60 for Senior Individual Memberships$100 for Joint Household Memberships$100 for US or Canada Library Membership$125 for International Library Membership$150 for Institutional Membership$1,500 for Lifetime Membership; price per copy N/A; sample $20. Back issues: $20 each. 90pp. Reporting time: 8-12 weeks. Simultaneous submissions accepted: no. Publishes 30% of manuscripts submitted. Payment: copies. Copyrighted. Pub's reviews: 2 in 2009. §Any literary work in recent English translation. Ads: $250 Full Page, $160 Half Page, $100 Quarter Page. Subjects: Literary Review, Translation.

TREATING YOURSELF: The Alternative Medicine Journal, Marco Renda, 250 The East Mall, P.O. Box 36531, Etobicoke, Ontario M9B 3Y8, Canada, Phone 416 620 1951, Fax 416 620 0698, weedmaster@treatingyourself.com , http://www.treatingyourself.com. 2005. Poetry, articles, art, photos, cartoons, interviews, satire, criticism, reviews, music, letters, news items. circ. 25000. 6/yr. Pub'd 4 issues 2009; expects 6 issues 2010, 6 issues 2011. sub. price $45USD/CAD $75USD Int.; per copy $7.99USD/CAD; sample free. Back issues: $10. Discounts: 12-1500 50%. 128 plus cover plus 8 page posterpp. Reporting time: 48 - 72 hours. Simultaneous submissions accepted: Yes. Payment: negotiable. Copyrighted. Pub's reviews: aprox. 10 in 2009. Ads: Centerfold poster $5000USD Back Cover $3000USD Inside Cover $2500USD Full Page $2000USD PG 3 $2300 1/2 Page $1250USD 1/4 Page $750USD. Subjects: AIDS, Alternative Medicine, Cartoons, Festivals, Food, Eating, Gardening, Gay, Health, Human Rights, Humor, Inspirational, Magazines, Nutrition, Poetry, Reviews.

Trellis Publishing, Inc., Mary Koski, Rachel Ellen, PO Box 16141-D, Duluth, MN 55816. 1997. "We will be taking on a few, high-quality children's picture books; however, we need to wait a year before taking submissions." avg. press run 10M. Pub'd 1 title 2009; expects 2 titles 2010, 2 titles 2011. 9 titles listed in the *Small Press Record of Books in Print* (36th Edition, 2010-11). Discounts: yes. Cloth 32pp, workbooks 16pp. Simultaneous submissions accepted: yes. Payment: 10% paid to author/illustrator on retail price. Copyrights for author. Subjects: Children, Youth, Picture Books, Public Relations/Publicity.

Tres Chicas Books, PO Box 417, El Rito, NM 87530. No titles listed in the *Small Press Record of Books in Print* (36th Edition, 2010-11).

Tres Picos Press, Jim Brumfield, PO Box 932, Freedom, CA 95019, 831 254-7447; email: submissions@trespicospress.com. 2003. Fiction, non-fiction. "We are new and small but will consider anything that we think can successfully be marketed. Before submitting anything, ask yourself one question: can you convince me that your book will sell at least 3,000 copies?" avg. press run 5000. 3 titles listed in the *Small Press Record of Books in Print* (36th Edition, 2010-11). Discounts: Our books are distributed by Biblio distribution, a sister company of the National Book Network. email orders@trespicospress.com for information on discounts. 320pp. Reporting time: 1 - 2 months. Simultaneous submissions accepted: Yes. Publishes 1% of manuscripts submitted. Payment: negotiable. Does not copyright for author. Subjects: Agriculture, Anthropology, Archaelogy, Australia, California, Caribbean, Fiction, Libertarian, Mexico, New Zealand, Old West, Real Estate, Sports, Outdoors, Mark Twain, The West, Yosemite.

Trickle Creek Books, Toni Albert, 500 Andersontown Rd, Mechanicsburg, PA 17055-6055, 717-766-2638, fax 717-766-1343, 800-353-2791. 1994. Fiction, non-fiction. "We publish books that teach kids to care for the Earth. Our books are used by teachers in classrooms across the nation, as well as by parents and homeschoolers. All of our books are written by Toni Albert, M.Ed., author of more than forty books that help children explore nature and love our environment." avg. press run 4000. Expects 1 title 2010. 9 titles listed in the *Small Press Record of Books in Print* (36th Edition, 2010-11). Discounts: Retailers - 2 copies 20%, 3-4 copies 30%, 5-99 copies 40%; Wholesalers - 50%; Distributors - 65%; Libraries - 20%. 48pp. Subjects: Animals, Biology, Birds, Education, Environment, Gardening, Marine Life, Nature, Non-Fiction, Oceanography, Science.

TRICYCLE: The Buddhist Review, James Shaheen, 92 Vandam Street, New York, NY 10013-1007. 1991. Poetry, fiction, articles, art, photos, cartoons, interviews, satire, letters, parts-of-novels, news items, non-fiction. circ. 50M. 4/yr. Pub'd 4 issues 2009; expects 4 issues 2010, 4 issues 2011. sub. price $24; per copy $7.95; sample $7.95. Back issues: $15.95. 104pp. Reporting time: 3 months. Simultaneous submissions accepted: no. Publishes 10% of manuscripts submitted. Payment: varies. Copyrighted, reverts to author. Pub's reviews: 32 in 2009. §Buddhism, religion, philosophy, Asian studies. Ads: Contact Goodfellows at: 510-548-1680. Subject: Buddhism.

Trinity University Press, Barbara Ras, Director; Claudia Guerra, Marketing Manager, One Trinity Place, San Antonio, TX 78212-7200, www.trinity.edu/tupress, general number: (210)999-8884, fax: (210)999-8838, books@trinity.edu. "Trinity University Press focuses primarily on the following areas: *Books on Texas, Mexico, and the Southwest-* Work that increases literacy about our own particular place in the world while celebrating local culture, history, and people. *Books on Landscape-* Work that explores how the land informs who we are and how we, in turn, shape the places we inhabit. *Books by Writers on Writing-* Work that peers into the creative process and, in the bargain, explains how we understand and portray our world. We do not publish fiction or poetry. We welcome a written proposal for projects that might fit our publishing program." 9 titles listed in the *Small Press Record of Books in Print* (36th Edition, 2010-11).

•Triple Crown Publications, PO Box 247378, Columbus, OH 43224. "Triple Crown Publications is an Urban and Hip-Hop Literature publishing company that services urban readers. The company purchases quality Urban and Hip-Hop manuscripts, publishes and distributes them throughout the urban community and within mainstream literary circles. The company continues to grow and hopes to continually uplift and enlighten readers from around the world. In 2009, Triple Crown signed a deal with Ingram Publisher Services, who now is the sole distributor of Triple Crown's titles. This agreement will bring Triple Crown even further to the forefront of the Urban Literature renaissance, and will ensure that Triple Crown's world-famous catalog continues to reach its readers everywhere. All manuscripts which are not considered urban street fiction according to the TCP Editorial Department will be recycled and will not be reviewed. Your submission must clearly display your name, address, phone number(s) and email address (if applicable) so we may easily contact you. The title page must display the word count of the entire manuscript. We only accept completed novels. Incomplete submissions will not be reviewed." No titles listed in the *Small Press Record of Books in Print* (36th Edition, 2010-11).

TRIQUARTERLY, Northwestern University Press, Susan Betz, 629 Noyes Street, Evanston, IL 60208, (847) 491-2046; fax (847)491-8150; www.nupress.northwestern.edu. 1958. Poetry, fiction. circ. 2000. 3/yr. Pub'd 3 issues 2009; expects 3 issues 2010, 3 issues 2011. sub. price $24; per copy 11.95; sample free. Back issues: inquire. 288pp. Ads: inquire for advertising rates.

Triskelion Publishing, Terese Ramin, Print & Media Liaison; Kristi Studts, Publisher; Gail Northman, Executive Editor; Kathi Troyer, Inspiration Editor; Brynna Ramin, SF&F Editor, 15508 W. Bell Road #101, PMB #205, Surprise, AZ 85374, Contact: 517-294-0765, Sales: 602-509-8582, Fax: 623-561-0250, sales@triskelionpublishing.com, www.triskelionpublishing.net. 2004. Fiction. "Triskelion Publishing is: All about women. All about extraordinary. We publish fiction for and about women, including romance, sf/f, futuristic, paranormal, gothic-horror, erotic romance in our Sister O imprint, inspirational romance fiction, action-adventure, suspense-thriller, mystery, etc. Romance is an element in almost all of our fiction, but doesn't necessarily always play in the forefront.We publish full-length novels (45,000 words to 80,000 words), as well as anthologies, and we also publish some novellas in our e-publishing products (where we publish over 100 novels, anthologies & novellas every year.) We also do novel reprints. Submission guidelines are available at the website: www.triskelionpublishing.net. Queries should be made in the body of an email to submissions@triskelionpublishing.com. Inspirational submissions should be made to submissions@triskelion-publishing.com ATTN: Kathi Troyer.'' avg. press run 750-2500. Pub'd 10 titles 2009; expects 36-50 titles 2010, 50-75 titles 2011. No titles listed in the *Small Press Record of Books in Print* (36th Edition, 2010-11). 300-350pp. Reporting time: 14 - 45 days. Simultaneous submissions accepted: No. Publishes 50% of manuscripts submitted. Payment: ebook royalties are paid monthly beginning 45 days after the work's first appearance; print royalties are paid quarterly as soon as the distributors pay us. Does not copyright for author. Subjects: Erotica, Fantasy, Fiction, Gay, Inspirational, Lesbianism, Mystery, Occult, Romance, Science Fiction, Supernatural.

Triumvirate Publications, Vladimir Chernozemsky, Publisher, 497 West Avenue 44, Los Angeles, CA 90065-3917, 818-340-6770 Phone/Fax, Triumpub@aol.com, www.Triumpub.com. 1985. Fiction. ''Publisher of genre fiction: Science Fiction/Fantasy, Mystery, Thriller/Suspense, Horror/Occult, Adventure.'' avg. press run 8M. Pub'd 3 titles 2009; expects 3 titles 2010, 5 titles 2011. 5 titles listed in the *Small Press Record of Books in Print* (36th Edition, 2010-11). Discounts: retail: 1 copy 20%, 2-3 30%, 4+ 40%, wholesale: 1-2 copies 30%, 3-4 40%, 5+ 50%, quantity stocking orders 55%. 500pp. Reporting time: 2 months. Simultaneous submissions accepted: yes. Payment: trade standard. Copyrights for author. Subjects: Crime, Fantasy, Fiction, Horror, Mystery, Science Fiction.

Trost Publishing, Katherine Moody, 509 Octavia St., New Orleans, LA 70115, 504-680-6754, www.trostpublishing.com. 2004. Non-fiction. avg. press run 20000. Expects 1 title 2010, 2 titles 2011. No titles listed in the *Small Press Record of Books in Print* (36th Edition, 2010-11). 150-200pp. Simultaneous submissions accepted: Yes. Does not copyright for author. Subject: Business & Economics.

The True Bill Press, Antony E. Simpson, P.O. Box 0349, Lambertville, NJ 08530-0349, (212) 927-5898, Tony@TheTrueBillPress.com, http://www.TheTrueBillPress.com. 2006. Fiction, non-fiction. ''We are primarily in the business of reprinting classic 19th century works of social investigation and also some fiction from the same period.'' Expects 3 titles 2011. 2 titles listed in the *Small Press Record of Books in Print* (36th Edition, 2010-11). Discounts: None. 250pp. Reporting time: We are not soliciting manuscripts at this time. Simultaneous submissions accepted: No. Does not copyright for author. Subjects: Civil War, Communication, Journalism, Crime, Diaries, Charles Dickens, England, English, History, Literature (General), London, Memoirs, Military, Veterans, Non-Fiction, Sex, Sexuality.

TRUE POET MAGAZINE, Michelle True. 2003. Poetry, articles. ''We are a webzine dedicated to publishing the best in poetry by new or published writers. Our mission is to help promote poetry and provide a voice for gifted poets.'' circ. 10,000. 12/yr. Pub'd 12 issues 2009; expects 12 issues 2010, 12 issues 2011. 10pp. Reporting time: 3-4 weeks. Simultaneous submissions accepted: Yes. Publishes 3% of manuscripts submitted. We do not currently have advertising. Subjects: Poetry, Publishing, Writers/Writing.

Truly Fine Press, Jerry Madson, PO Box 891, Bemidji, MN 56619. 1973. ''Truly Fine Press has in the past published a pamphlet series, and also published Minnesota's first tabloid novel. Must query first. Only publish ulra limited edition visual poetry that gravitates toward art. Currently studying print-on demand options.'' avg. press run varies. 19 titles listed in the *Small Press Record of Books in Print* (36th Edition, 2010-11). Pages vary. Reporting time: 2 weeks to 6 months. Copyrights for author.

Truman State University Press, Nancy Rediger, Director-Editor in Chief, 100 East Normal Avenue, Kirksville, MO 63501, 660-785-7336, Fax 660-785-4480, http://tsup.truman.edu. 1986. Poetry, art, photos, criticism, non-fiction. ''Early modern studies, American studies, poetry series.'' avg. press run 1000. Pub'd 10 titles 2009; expects 13 titles 2010, 13 titles 2011. 144 titles listed in the *Small Press Record of Books in Print* (36th Edition, 2010-11). Discounts: 20%, 2-9 copies 30%, 10+ 40%, 100+ 50%. 300pp. Reporting time: 3 months. Simultaneous submissions accepted: no. Publishes 10% of manuscripts submitted. Payment: 6%-10%. Copyrights for author. Subjects: Civil War, Environment, History, Midwest, Non-Fiction, North America, Poetry, Presidents, Religion, Renaissance.

TRUTH SEEKER, Bonnie Lange, Publisher-Editor, 239 S. Juniper Street, Escondido, CA 92025-0550, 760-489-5211, Fax 760-489-5311, tseditor@aol.com, www.truthseeker.com. 1873. Articles, interviews, criticism, reviews, letters, news items. ''Length of material: 400-1,600 words. Past contributors: Steve Allen, Gerald LaRue, Howard Blume, Arthur Melville, David Icke, Jon Rappoport, Louis Turi, Zecharia Sitchin, and Angela Brown Miller.'' circ. 2,000. 1/yr. Pub'd 1 issue 2009; expects 1 issue 2010, 1 issue 2011. sub. price $20; per copy $10; sample $10. Back issues: $20. 40-220pp. Simultaneous submissions accepted: yes. Publishes 20%

of manuscripts submitted. Payment: $75 per article plus 1 year subscription. Copyrighted, reverts to author. Pub's reviews: 10 in 2009. §Freethought, religion, government. Ads: none. Subjects: Atheism, Education, Ethics, Euthanasia, Death, Government, History, Human Rights, Metaphysics, New Age, Philosophy, Religion, Reviews, Shaker, Taxes, Women.

TSAR Publications, Nurjehan Aziz, PO Box 6996, Station A, Toronto, Ontario M5W 1X7, Canada, www.tsarbooks.com. 1985. Poetry, fiction, interviews, criticism, plays, non-fiction. "TSAR Publications is dedicated to bringing to the reading public fresh new writing from Canada and across the world that reflects the diversity of our rapidly globalizing world, particularly in Canada and the United States. Our focus is on works that can loosely be termed "multicultural" and particularly those that pertain to Asia and Africa." 27 titles listed in the *Small Press Record of Books in Print* (36th Edition, 2010-11). Copyrights for author. Subjects: African Literature, Africa, African Studies, African-American, Asia, Indochina, Bilingual, Canada, Caribbean, Criticism, Fiction, India, Literature (General), Multicultural, Poetry, Prose, Publishing, Women.

TU REVIEW, Vincent Moore, Editor, Tiffin University, 155 Miami St., Tiffin, OH 44883, 419-448-3299, Fax 419-443-5009, TUReview@tiffin.edu, http://bruno.tiffin.edu/tureview/. 2004. Poetry, fiction, non-fiction. "We are an online literary journal that accepts both poetry and prose. Fiction, essays, prose poems, or any type of poetry, all should be characterized by being original and using vivid, specific imagery. Submission guidelines and more specific writing tips can be found at our website. Submissions accepted Sept. 1 to April 6, maximum length 4,500 words." 2/yr. Simultaneous submissions accepted: no. Payment: satisfaction and byline. Copyrighted, reverts to author.

TUESDAY: An Art Project, Jennifer Flscher, Editor, P.O. Box 1074, Arlington, MA 02474. 2006. "Submit up to five poems via e-mail or regular mail. E-mail is preferred. We accept work all year round. We are very small, though (in staff and issues), so our response and print times may vary. You can always e-mail with questions. As for an aesthetic . . . Send us your favorite poems." Pub'd 2 issues 2009; expects 2 issues 2010, 2 issues 2011. sub. price $25; per copy $13. 17pp. Reporting time: 3 months. Simultaneous submissions accepted: Yes. Payment: 2 copies.

THE TULE REVIEW, Jane Blue, Sacramento Poetry Center, 1719 25th St., Sacramento, CA 95816-5813, 916-441-7395, blueattule@yahoo.com, www.sacramentopoetrycenter.org. 1998. Poetry. "Regional magazine published by Sacramento Poetry Center. Recent contributors: Doug Blazek, Ann Menebroker, Dennis Schmitz, and Muriel Zeller. Revived in 1998 in chapbook format. Sacramento-San Joaquin bias, but consider others." circ. 500. 2/yr. Pub'd 2 issues 2009; expects 2 issues 2010, 2 issues 2011. sub. price w/SPC membership; per copy $5; sample $5. 28-32pp. Reporting time: 2-4 months. Simultaneous submissions accepted: no. Payment: 2 copies. Copyrighted, reverts to author. Subject: Poetry.

TULSA STUDIES IN WOMEN'S LITERATURE, JAMES JOYCE QUARTERLY, Holly Laird, Editor; Sarah Theobald-Hall, Managing Editor, 600 S. College, Tulsa, OK 74104-3189, 918-631-2503, Fax 918-631-2065, sarah-theobald-hall@utulsa.edu. 1982. Articles, criticism, reviews, letters. circ. 1M. 2/yr. Pub'd 2 issues 2009; expects 2 issues 2010, 2 issues 2011. sub. price U.S. individuals $12/1 yr, $23/2 yrs, $34/3 yrs, institutions $14/$27/$40, other individuals $15/$29/$43, institutions $16/$31/$46, U.S. students $10/$19/$28, elsewhere students $12/$23/$34, airmail surcharge $10; per copy $7 US/$8 elsewhere; sample $7US/$8 elsewhere. Back issues: $10. 150pp. Reporting time: 6 months. Simultaneous submissions accepted: no. Payment: none. Copyrighted, does not revert to author. Pub's reviews: 25 in 2009. §Women's literature—critical studies. Ads: $150/$75. Subjects: Literary Review, Women.

TUNDRA, Press Here, Michael Dylan Welch, 22230 NE 28th Place, Sammamish, WA 98074-6408, welchm@aol.com. 1999. Poetry, interviews, criticism, reviews. "*Tundra* is a journal for short poetry, 13 lines or fewer in length (especially, but not limited to, haiku, senryu, and tanka). See http://sites.google.com/site/tundrashortpoem/ for full submission guidelines and publication news." circ. 650. 1/yr. Expects 1 issue 2010, 1 issue 2011. sub. price $21; per copy $10; sample $10. Back issues: Available at the single copy price. 128pp. Reporting time: Usually 1-3 months. Simultaneous submissions accepted: no. Publishes 0.5% of manuscripts submitted. Payment: 1 contributor's copy. Copyrighted, reverts to author. Pub's reviews: 2-4 in 2009. §Short poetry or criticism about short poetry. Ads: none. Subjects: Criticism, Haiku, Poetry.

Tuns Press, Faculty of Architecture and Planning, Dalhousie University, Box 1000 Central Station, Halifax, Nova Scotia B3J 2X4, Canada, 902-494-3925, Fax 902-423-6672, tuns.press@dal.ca, tunspress.dal.ca. 1989. Non-fiction. "Faculty press. Publishes books on architecture and planning." avg. press run 1M-2M. 14 titles listed in the *Small Press Record of Books in Print* (36th Edition, 2010-11). Discounts: trade. Subjects: Architecture, Canada, Design, History.

Tupelo Press, Jeffrey Levine, Editor-in-Chief; Margaret Donovan, Managing Editor; Susan Williamson, Associate Publisher, PO Box 539, Dorset, VT 05251, Telephone 802-366-8185, Fax 802-362-1883. 1999. Poetry, fiction, letters, non-fiction. avg. press run 5000. Pub'd 9 titles 2009; expects 14 titles 2010, 15 titles 2011. No titles listed in the *Small Press Record of Books in Print* (36th Edition, 2010-11). Reporting time: 3

months. Simultaneous submissions accepted: yes. Payment: standard royalty contract and some advances. Copyrights for author. Subjects: Memoirs, Non-Fiction, Novels, Poetry, Prose, Short Stories.

TURNING THE TIDE: Journal of Anti-Racist Action, Research & Education, Michael Novick, PO Box 1055, Culver City, CA 90232-1055, 310-495-0299, antiracistaction_la@yahoo.com. 1987. Poetry, articles, photos, cartoons, interviews, satire, criticism, reviews, news items, non-fiction. "prefer short piece, no more than 1 poem per issue." circ. 8,000. 4/yr. Pub'd 5 issues 2009; expects 5 issues 2010, 4 issues 2011. sub. price $18 individuals, $28 institutional/foreign payable to "Michael Novick"; sample $2. Back issues: $3, inquire on availability. 8pp. Reporting time: 1-2 months. Simultaneous submissions accepted: yes. Publishes 6-8% of manuscripts submitted. Payment: 5 free copies. Not copyrighted. §Racism, sexism, homophobia, liberation movements. Ads: $100/$65/$35 1/4 page. Subjects: African-American, Anarchist, Chicano/a, Children, Youth, Ecology, Foods, Feminism, Gay, Hawaii, Human Rights, Native American, Prison, Puerto Rico, Race, Third World, Minorities, War.

TURNING WHEEL, Susan Moon, PO Box 3470, Berkeley, CA 94703. 1980. Poetry, articles, art, photos, cartoons, interviews, criticism, reviews, letters, news items, non-fiction. *"Turning Wheel* is about 'engaged' Buddhism, or Buddhism and social activism. We print articles, art, poetry, etc. about nonviolent protest, about issues of activism, sexism, human rights, etc. in American Buddhist communities and Asian Buddhist countries. We print Gary Snyder, Thich Nhat Hanh, grassroots activists." circ. 7M. 4/yr. Pub'd 4 issues 2009; expects 4 issues 2010, 4 issues 2011. sub. price $45 membership, $20 low-income; per copy $5 newstand; sample $6 by mail. 48pp. Reporting time: about 1 month. Simultaneous submissions accepted: yes. Publishes 20% of manuscripts submitted. Payment: 2 copies of magazine, one year subscription. Copyrighted, reverts to author. Pub's reviews: about 20 in 2009. §Buddhism and social activism, engaged spirituality, deep ecology, social ecology. Ads: $345/$190/50¢. Subjects: Asian-American, Buddhism, Community, Ecology, Foods, Education, Euthanasia, Death, Human Rights, Non-Violence, Spiritual, Zen.

TurnKey Press, Michael Odom; Cody Goehring, Project Consultant, 2100 Kramer Lane Suite 300, Austin, TX 78758-4094, 512.478.2028, cgoehring@bookpros.com. 2002. Poetry, fiction, satire, criticism, parts-of-novels, long-poems, non-fiction. "We provide a free media analysis for all works submitted. This analysis, in addition to serving as a service to the authors, aids in our decision-making process as to whether or not we feel the book is a good fit for TurnKey Press. The process is competitive and not all submissions are accepted." No titles listed in the *Small Press Record of Books in Print* (36th Edition, 2010-11). Reporting time: 2-3 business days. Simultaneous submissions accepted: Yes. Payment: Authors pay individually for the services they recieve. Authors are paid 100% of net receipts on sales made through retail outlets. After wholesale discount and printing costs are taken off of the retail price, everything else goes to the author. Copyrights for author.

TURNROW, Jack Heflin, William Ryan, Univ. of Louisiana at Monroe, English Dept., 700 University Ave., Monroe, LA 71209, 318-342-1520, Fax 318-342-1491, ryan@ulm.edu, heflin@ulm.edu, http://turn-row.ulm.edu. 2001. Poetry, fiction, articles, art, photos, cartoons, criticism, letters, parts-of-novels, long-poems, plays, non-fiction. "Seeks nonfiction of a general interest. Interested also in publishing the works of authors written in genres different from what they usually publish." circ. 1M. 2/yr. Pub'd 2 issues 2009; expects 2 issues 2010, 2 issues 2011. sub. price $12; per copy $7; sample $7. Back issues: $5. 200pp. Reporting time: 3 months. Simultaneous submissions accepted: no. Publishes .01% of manuscripts submitted. Payment: $50 poem, $15/page for prose, $150-$250 features. Copyrighted, reverts to author. Ads: $200 full page. Subjects: Arts, Essays, Fiction, Non-Fiction, Photography, Poetry, Translation.

Turnstone Press, Todd Besant, Managing Editor; Kelly Stifora, Marketing Director, 607-100 Arthur Street, Winnipeg R3B 1H3, Canada, 204-947-1555, info@turnstonepress.com. 1976. Poetry, fiction, criticism, long-poems. "Contemporary Canadian writing." avg. press run 1M. Pub'd 12 titles 2009; expects 12 titles 2010, 12 titles 2011. 166 titles listed in the *Small Press Record of Books in Print* (36th Edition, 2010-11). Discounts: bookstores 1-9 copies 20%, 10+ 40%; schools & libraries 40%; wholesalers 45%. Poetry 80pp, fiction & criticism 220pp. Reporting time: 4 months. Query first before sending simultaneous submissions. Publishes .8% of manuscripts submitted. Payment: 10% paid annually. Copyrights for author. Subjects: Criticism, Fiction, Literature (General), Memoirs, Mystery, Novels, Poetry, Short Stories, Travel.

Turtle Press, division of S.K. Productions Inc., Cynthia Kim, PO Box 34010, Santa Fe, NM 87594-4010, 860-721-1198. 1990. Non-fiction. "We publish primarily non-fiction titles of interest to martial artists and those readers interested in self-protection. We are especially interested in new, unique or previously unpublished facets of the arts. Will also consider topics related to Asian culture, such as Zen, philosophy, etc." avg. press run 3M-4M. Pub'd 4 titles 2009; expects 5 titles 2010, 5 titles 2011. 11 titles listed in the *Small Press Record of Books in Print* (36th Edition, 2010-11). 300pp. Reporting time: 1 month. Simultaneous submissions accepted: yes. Publishes 2-3% of manuscripts submitted. Payment: 10% on gross (royalties), advance of $500-$1000. Copyrights for author. Subjects: Martial Arts, Philosophy, Zen.

Tuscarora Books Inc., Bruce Battaglia, POB 987 Falls Station, Niagara Falls, NY 14303, 716-284-5595, fax

716-284-5597. 2007. Non-fiction. avg. press run 3000. Pub'd 1 title 2009; expects 2 titles 2010, 3 titles 2011. No titles listed in the *Small Press Record of Books in Print* (36th Edition, 2010-11). Discounts: 25-50%. 140pp. Subjects: Communication, Journalism, Crime, History, Memoirs, Music, New York, Newspapers.

Tuumba Press, Lyn Hejinian, Editor, 2639 Russell Street, Berkeley, CA 94705-2131, 510-548-1817, 510-704-8350. 1976. Poetry, fiction, articles, long-poems, plays. "In its current manifestation, Tuumba Press publishes work by invitation only." avg. press run 750. 3 titles listed in the *Small Press Record of Books in Print* (36th Edition, 2010-11).

Tuvela Press, Linda Lakeland, P.O.Box 877913, Wasilla, AK 99687-7913, TuvelaPress.com, contact@tuvela-press.com. 2008. Poetry, reviews, plays. "Currently publishing the series 'Innovations of Inner Space Poetry', a new avant garde form using color, speech, and the 'inner poem', a parenthetical interwoven stream. Book 1: "Quartet with Two Voices & Counterpoint on the Horizon", Ranger Doolac & Betty Baud, 2008 Book 2: "Progressions in Arctic Light", Betty Baud, 2010. We do not read unsolicited work, but will accept proposals and questions emailed to tuvela@mtaonline.net." avg. press run 1100. 2 titles listed in the *Small Press Record of Books in Print* (36th Edition, 2010-11). 75pp. Subjects: Alaska, Astronomy, Dada, Experimental, Grieving, Metaphysics, Myth, Mythology, New Age, Philosophy, Poetry, Psychology, Relationships, Religion, Romance, Science Fiction.

TWENTY-EIGHT PAGES LOVINGLY BOUND WITH TWINE, Christoph Meyer, PO Box 106, Danville, OH 43014. 2001. Poetry, fiction, art, photos, cartoons, letters, collages, non-fiction. "No unsolicited submissions except art. I do use illustrators and artist and cartoonist. Anyone interested in doing art for *28PLBWT* should write w/samples of drawings (b/w only)." circ. 756. 2-5/yr. Pub'd 3 issues 2009; expects 4 issues 2010, 3-4 issues 2011. sub. price $10/6 issues; per copy $2; sample $2. Back issues: $2, $3 for 5. 28pp. Payment: subscription, contributor's copies, a little bit of $. Not copyrighted. Ads: no ads. Subjects: Autobiography, Non-Fiction, Ohio.

24th Street Irregular Press, Richard Hansen, 1008 24th Street, Sacramento, CA 95816. 2000. No titles listed in the *Small Press Record of Books in Print* (36th Edition, 2010-11).

twentythreebooks, Douglas Mowbray, 3029 Arizona Avenue, Baltimore, MD 21234, 410-882-5783. 2006. Poetry, fiction, satire, letters, long-poems, plays, non-fiction. avg. press run 500. Pub'd 2 titles 2009; expects 3 titles 2010, 2 titles 2011. 9 titles listed in the *Small Press Record of Books in Print* (36th Edition, 2010-11). 100pp. Simultaneous submissions accepted: No. Copyrights for author. Subjects: Experimental, Literature (General), Poetry, Prose, Satire, Writers/Writing.

The Twickenham Press, Karla Kraus, Publisher; D. Charles Rosenberg, Editor; Susan Walker, Editor, 302A West 12th Street, #339, New York, NY 10014-6025, 917-282-6657. 1980. Fiction. "Our orientation has been and will remain literary, feminist, and politically liberal; we are interested only in serious novels for adults. After being dormant for a long time, we now have a website for folks to visit with audio on: http://www.twickenhampress.com. And we are actively engaging in publishing operations again. We still find e-books fascinating and see them in the long term as a viable alternative to paper-waste. Queries should include a paragraph about yourself, a brief description of the work you would like to submit, and a word-count—nothing else. An SASE would be appreciated. Agents and other strictly commercial types need NOT apply." avg. press run 1M. Expects 1 title 2010, 1-2 titles 2011. 5 titles listed in the *Small Press Record of Books in Print* (36th Edition, 2010-11). Discounts: 20% to libraries; 40-50% to dealers; returns to 99 years. 250pp. Reporting time: long. Simultaneous submissions accepted: yes. Payment: 10-15% of list. Copyrights for author. Subjects: Feminism, Fiction, Gay, Lesbianism, Literature (General), Poetry.

Twilight Tales, Inc., Tina Jens, VP, Publications; Tes La Loggia, Director, Book Publications, 2339 Commonwealth Ave., #4C, Chicago, IL 60614, 1-888-763-READ, 312-222-9185, Publications@Twilight-Tales.com, www.TwilightTales.com. 1993. Poetry, fiction, non-fiction. "The mission of Twilight Tales' Books Publication is to foster professional author development and publish superior fiction in a variety of genres, including mystery, crime & detective, sci-fi, fantasy, horror, humor, and others. In 2005, we published *Something to Build Upon*, a mystery graphic novel by Tim Broderick; and *The Occult Detective*, a collection of short stories by Robert Weinberg. In 2006, we published *Ex Cathedra*, a collection of spec-/sci-fi short stories by Rebecca Maines; and will publish *My Lolita Complex and other Tales of Sex and Violence*, by Max Allan Collins and Matthew V. Clemens. In 2007, we will publish two anthologies; a writing "how to" book by Chelsea Quinn Yarbro; and a collection of short stories by Jay Bonansinga." avg. press run 500. Pub'd 2 titles 2009; expects 2 titles 2010, 4 titles 2011. 11 titles listed in the *Small Press Record of Books in Print* (36th Edition, 2010-11). 200pp. Reporting time: 2-4 months. Simultaneous submissions accepted: Yes. Payment: The amount varies for each book, but our authors receive an advance for each story or book-length work, and either a % royalty (single-author publications) or a scheduled royalty payment (anthologies). Does not copyright for author. Subjects: Crime, Fantasy, Fiction, Horror, How-To, Humor, Magic, Mystery, Myth, Mythology, Novels, Poetry, Publishing, Science Fiction, Short Stories, Writers/Writing.

Twilight Times Books, Lida E. Quillen, PO Box 3340, Kingsport, TN 37664-0340, 423-323-0183 phone/Fax, publisher@twilighttimesbooks.com, www.twilighttimesbooks.com. 1999. Fiction, non-fiction. "Open to submissions July 15 to August 5th. Be sure to check the web site for current submission guidelines." Pub'd 18 titles 2009; expects 16 titles 2010, 10 titles 2011. 11 titles listed in the *Small Press Record of Books in Print* (36th Edition, 2010-11). 250pp. Reporting time: 2 months. Simultaneous submissions accepted: no. Publishes 5% of manuscripts submitted. Payment: standard. Does not copyright for author. Subjects: Fantasy, Fiction, Humor, Literature (General), Metaphysics, Military, Veterans, Mystery, New Age, Non-Fiction, Science Fiction, Self-Help, Translation, Women, Writers/Writing, Young Adult.

Twin Souls Publications (see also MIDNIGHT SHOWCASE: Romance Digest, Erotic-ahh Digest, Special Digest), Jewel Adams, P.O. Box 726, Lusk, WY 82225, 307-334-3165, 727-848-5962, publisher@midnightshowcase.com, http://www.midnightshowcase.com. 2005. Fiction. "Midnight Showcase publishes Romance and Erotic-ahh Romance Digest, which are themed collections of short stories to 25,000 word novellas in each digest. We also publish full novels as Special Editions in all the Romance and Erotic-ahh Romance genres." Expects 15 titles 2010, 30 titles 2011. No titles listed in the *Small Press Record of Books in Print* (36th Edition, 2010-11). 250pp. Reporting time: Three to Four Weeks. Simultaneous submissions accepted: No. Publishes 25% of manuscripts submitted. Payment: Royalty is based on word count and is the same for print and ebook formats. Author retains the copyright of their work, contract is for exclusive rights for one year with renewal, contract is on site to review. Subjects: Erotica, History, Romance.

Twinteum Artist, Inc., Teo Tioliendo, P.O. Box 15016, St. Louis, MO 63110. 2006. Poetry, fiction, articles, art, photos, interviews, music, letters, long-poems, plays, non-fiction. "New Title 2007-Dolphin, (Poem, Paintings, Drawings), Saxy Poems, Amazing Spirit' (Epic Poem) 'Amazing Spirit' the play, 'Cajun On The Pits, Learn all types of valuable facts about pitbulls in these creative story poems from an expert whose profession involves handling dog attacks daily. (Poems include deft drawings, by the artist author-drawings without erasing using Pen-Ink) The lyrical, spicey poems tell the stories of his Cajun Pits, cajun music loving pitbulls in all their variety, fun, and their battles with the fighter Pitpits.(The book also features this front line Pitman's-Lessons From Warrior Dogs, Pitman's Protection From Dog Attacks, and Pit Puppies Remember, tips on understanding the psychology of pitbulls from puppies to maturity). Saxy Poems, Drawings, Paintings, Art Of Tioliendo-(Memior-autobiographical about the artist as sharpened and refined by artist encounters, revelations of the artist from being self taught, to learning from art and art teachers at the university). These art shows, artist story, anecdotes, travel experiences and poetry are in the artist, author, Tioliendo's own words. See Paintings, Drawings, Sculpture from his naive art to published masterpiece, and get inspiration from quotations, and personal experiences of the Artist. (Subtitle-Honor Of A Self Taught Artist, includes inspirational thoughts for artist, artist's philosophy towards paintings, and futuristic IAfriqan subject matter, autobiogaphical stories of celebrities whom the Artist met and/or paid tributes to, and his approach to a new style and originality in art." avg. press run 2000. Pub'd 3 titles 2009; expects 7 titles 2010, 30 titles 2011. No titles listed in the *Small Press Record of Books in Print* (36th Edition, 2010-11). 50% discount to distributors, bookstores, wholesalers, retailers, and Libraries, discounts to book buyers making purchases direct from the publisher, Twinteum Artist, Inc. 50-250pp. Reporting time: 1-3 months. Simultaneous submissions accepted: Yes. Publishes 10% of manuscripts submitted. Payment: 5-15. New authors need to copyright their work before submitting manuscripts to our publication. Copyright consultations are free to beginning writers. Minimal fees charged for consultations on Copyrighting artworks from professional Art Agent/Art Manager. Subjects: African Literature, Africa, African Studies, Fiction, Futurism, How-To, Humor, Latino, Martial Arts, Performing Arts, Pets, Philosophy, Photography, Poetry, Spiritual, Visual Arts, Writers/Writing.

Twisted Spoon Press, Howard Sidenberg, PO Box 21, Preslova 12, Prague 5, 150 00, Czech Republic, www.twistedspoon.com. 1992. Poetry, fiction, art, photos, letters, non-fiction. "No unsolicited manuscripts." avg. press run 1.5M-2M. Pub'd 4 titles 2009; expects 5 titles 2010, 6 titles 2011. No titles listed in the *Small Press Record of Books in Print* (36th Edition, 2010-11). Discounts: distributor takes care of this. 200pp. Reporting time: 6 months. Simultaneous submissions accepted: no. Payment: by contract. Copyrights for author. Subjects: Dada, Essays, Fiction, Poetry, Prose, Surrealism, Translation.

Two Canoes Press, C.W. Duncan, PO Box 256, Upton, MA 01568, 508-529-6034, www.TwoCanoes-Press.com. 1998. Fiction. "I want to publish fiction that will make a difference, deepen spirituality, cause the reader to think. But the book must be good fiction first and the message must be part of the story....not preachy." avg. press run 5000. Expects 1 title 2010, 2 titles 2011. No titles listed in the *Small Press Record of Books in Print* (36th Edition, 2010-11). Discounts: 65% discount to distributor, Partners Publishing Group. 50% when I sell directly to bookstores or institutions. 300pp. Reporting time: A month. Simultaneous submissions accepted: No. Copyrights for author.

Two Dog Press, Karen Kaiser, PO Box 164, Brooklin, ME 04616-0164, http://www.twodogpress.com/index.html; tel: 1.207.359.8967 Tollfree: 1.888.310.2DOG. 1997. Poetry, fiction, art, photos, non-fiction. "We publish books about dogs. Our preference is for material that features dogs without getting sentimental. We're looking for fresh, innovative prose and poetry, art and interesting non-fiction about dogs." avg. press run 8M. Pub'd 1 title 2009; expects 1 title 2010, 1 title 2011. 3 titles listed in the *Small Press Record of Books in Print* (36th Edition, 2010-11). Discounts: jobber 55%, bookstores: 1 10%, 2-4 20%, 5 or more 40%. 100pp. Reporting time: 3 months. Simultaneous submissions accepted: no. Publishes 2% of manuscripts submitted. Payment: varies. Copyrights for author. Subjects: Animals, Folklore, Pets, Poetry.

Two Eagles Press International, Dr. Paul E. Huntsberger, 1029 Hickory Drive, Las Cruces, NM 88005, 575-523-7911, Fax 575-523-1953, Cell 575-644-5436, twoeaglespress@comcast.net, twoeaglespress.com. 1991. Non-fiction. "Additional address: 1029 Hickory Drive, Las Cruces, NM 88005. Multicultural/ international oriented materials prferred; book length 50-200 pages; will consider bilingual English/Spanish submissions." avg. press run 3.0M. 3 titles listed in the *Small Press Record of Books in Print* (36th Edition, 2010-11). 240pp. Reporting time: 6 weeks. Simultaneous submissions accepted: No. Payment: 10%, payable biannually. Copyrights for author. Subjects: Bilingual, Business & Economics, Chicano/a, Culture, Latin America, Latino, Management, Mexico, Multicultural, New Mexico, Non-Fiction, Southwest, Texas, U.S. Hispanic.

2L Publishing, LLC, LaShaune Stitt-Clemons, Editor, Publisher, Author; Lonice Eversely, Editor, Publisher, Author, 1525 Split Oak Lane #F, Henrico, VA 23229, 804-971-6367. 2009. Fiction, long-poems. Expects 2 titles 2010, 2 titles 2011. No titles listed in the *Small Press Record of Books in Print* (36th Edition, 2010-11). Reporting time: One Week. Simultaneous submissions accepted: No. Publishes 10% of manuscripts submitted. Does not copyright for author. Subjects: African-American, Black, Erotica, Fiction, Lifestyles, Poetry, Relationships, Sex, Sexuality, Short Stories, Women.

TWO LINES: World Writing in Translation, Olivia E. Sears, Founding Editor, Center for the Art of Translation, 35 Stillman Street, Suite 201, San Francisco, CA 94107, 415-512-8812 (phone) /415-512-8824 (fax), web: www.catranslation.org. 1995. Poetry, fiction, articles, art, interviews, satire, criticism, letters, parts-of-novels, long-poems, plays, non-fiction. "*Two Lines* publishes an annual anthology of world writing in English translation. All genres of literature are considered as long as the work is previously unpublished. Each submission must be accompanied by a copy of the original language text, as well as a translator's introduction that comments on the original work, author, and translation process. (The author cannot be the translator.) Detailed submission guidelines are available on the website. Published annually in the spring. Email submissions to: submissions@catranslation.org." circ. 1500. 1/yr. Pub'd 1 issue 2009; expects 1 issue 2010, 1 issue 2011. 1 title listed in the *Small Press Record of Books in Print* (36th Edition, 2010-11). price per copy $14.95 + $2.50 s/h domestic, $7 Canada/Mexico, $9 s/h int'l; sample same. Back issues: $5-11. Discounts: 20% libraries, 40% bookstores. 250pp. Reporting time: 3 months after submission deadline. Simultaneous submissions accepted: Yes. Publishes 15% of manuscripts submitted. Payment: $35. Copyrighted, rights revert to author/translator; world rights requested. §Although we do not publish reviews, we do collect world literature titles of poetry and fiction translated into English for The Center for the Art of Translation's library. Ads: None. Subjects: Literature (General), Translation.

Two Thousand Three Associates, 4180 Saxon Drive, New Smyrna Beach, FL 32169-3851, 386-690-2503. 1994. Non-fiction. "No unsolicited manuscripts. *Proposals only.*" avg. press run 5M. Pub'd 3 titles 2009; expects 4 titles 2010, 4 titles 2011. 6 titles listed in the *Small Press Record of Books in Print* (36th Edition, 2010-11). Discounts: IPG (Independent Publishers Group) distributes our books and sets discount rate. 144pp. Reporting time: 1 month. Simultaneous submissions accepted: yes. Payment: per author/individual basis. Copyrights for author. Subjects: Aging, Caribbean, Caribbean, Children, Youth, Family, Florida, Florida, Humor, Humor, Romance, Sports, Outdoors, Sports, Outdoors, Travel.

Two-Handed Engine Press, Peter Nash, Editor; Cesca Janece Waterfield, Editor, PO Box 803, Richmond, VA 23219, 9175686184, www.myspace.com/twohandedenginepress. 2005. Poetry, fiction, photos, satire, criticism, plays, non-fiction. "The editorial focus of Two-Handed Engine Press: Contemporary Literature, including Poetry, Collected Short Fiction, Drama, Novellas; Other genres with a clearly-defined niche, including regional unique travel, alternative history, and cookbooks. While each marketing campaign is personalized according to the author, subject, ETC, consistent means of marketing and promotion include, but are not limited to: Extensive Book Tours supported by press releases to regional media and targeted media of major metropolitan areas. Advance Copies to renowned authors among our friends. Advance Copies to academic writers with whom we've studied and published. Advance Copies to Writers Organizations. Postcards to targeted universities and appropriate alumni associations. Book Signings. Posters to key bookstores. Radio Interviews. Mailing List . Announcements. Promotional items." avg. press run 1000. Pub'd 1 title 2009; expects 2 titles 2010, 4 titles 2011. 2 titles listed in the *Small Press Record of Books in Print* (36th Edition, 2010-11). Discounts: 2-12, 25%13-33, 35%34 and more, 45%. 120pp. Reporting time: 2-4 weeks. Simultaneous submissions accepted: Yes. Publishes 20% of manuscripts submitted. Payment: Each is negotiable. Copyrights for author. Subjects: Anarchist, Appalachia, Arts, Creative Non-fiction, Essays, Experimental, Fantasy, Feminism, Gay, Novels, Peace, Performing Arts, Philosophy, Photography, Poetry.

2River (see also THE 2RIVER VIEW), Richard Long, 7474 Drexel Dr., University City, MO 63130, 314-721-7393, www.2River.org. 1996. Poetry. "Since 1996, 2River has been a site of poetry, art, and theory, quarterly publishing The 2River View and occasionally publishing individual authors in the 2River Chapbook Series. All publications appear online and afterwards in print." avg. press run 100. Pub'd 4 titles 2009; expects 4 titles 2010, 4 titles 2011. No titles listed in the *Small Press Record of Books in Print* (36th Edition, 2010-11). 32pp. Reporting time: A couple of months at most for submissions to The 2River View, and a few week for submissions to the 2River Chapbook Series. Simultaneous submissions accepted: No. Publishes 1% of manuscripts submitted. Payment: Copies. Does not copyright for author. Subject: Poetry.

THE 2RIVER VIEW, 2River, Richard Long, 7474 Drexel Dr., University City, MO 63130, 314-721-7393, www.2River.org, long@2River.org. 1996. Poetry. "Since 1996, 2River has been a site of poetry, art, and theory, quarterly publishing The 2River View and occasionally publishing individual authors in the 2River Chapbook Series. All publications appear online and afterwards in print." circ. 200. 4/yr. Pub'd 4 issues 2009; expects 4 issues 2010, 4 issues 2011. sub. price Free; per copy Free; sample PDF is online. Back issues: None. 32pp. Reporting time: A couple of months at most. Simultaneous submissions accepted: No. Publishes 1% of manuscripts submitted. Payment: Copy. Copyrighted, reverts to author. Ads: None. Subject: Poetry.

Typographia Press. Pub'd 1 title 2009; expects 4 titles 2010, 8 titles 2011. No titles listed in the *Small Press Record of Books in Print* (36th Edition, 2010-11). 268pp. Simultaneous submissions accepted: No. Copyrights for author.

Tyr Publishing, Paul Massell, PO Box 9189, Santa Rosa, CA 95405-1189, 623-298-7235, Fax 480-323-2177, info@tyrpublishing.com, www.tyrpublishing.com. 2002. Fiction, non-fiction. "We are looking for high quality materials from authors with an enthusiasm to promote their work over the long haul. We are especially interested in working with authors who are considered experts on their subject matter and/or have a target audience with whom they have a special way to reach." avg. press run 10M. Pub'd 1 title 2009; expects 2 titles 2010, 5 titles 2011. No titles listed in the *Small Press Record of Books in Print* (36th Edition, 2010-11). 325pp. Simultaneous submissions accepted: no. Copyrights for author. Subjects: Catholic, Christianity, Cooking, Cosmology, Non-Fiction, Philosophy, Religion, Science, Spiritual, J.R.R. Tolkien.

Tyrannosaurus Press (see also THE ILLUMINATA), Roxanne Reiken, 5486 Fairway Dr., Zachary, LA 70791, 225.287.8885, Fax 206-984-0448, info@tyrannosauruspress.com, www.tyrannosauruspress.com. 2002. Fiction. "We are interested in novel length speculative fiction (science fiction, fantasy, and horror)." avg. press run 2000. Pub'd 2 titles 2009; expects 1 title 2010, 1 title 2011. 4 titles listed in the *Small Press Record of Books in Print* (36th Edition, 2010-11). 400pp. Simultaneous submissions accepted: yes. Payment: varies. Copyrights for author. Subjects: Fantasy, Science Fiction.

U

U.S.1 WORKSHEETS, Nancy Scott, Managing Editor; Betty Lies, Rotating Editor; Linda Arntzenius, Rotating Editor; Wanda Praisner, Rotating Editor, PO Box 127, Kingston, NJ 08528-0127. 1973. Poetry, fiction, satire. "We primarily publish poetry, but will consider exceptional fiction or creative non-fiction up to 1000 words. Submit up to five poems, single-spaced, but not more than seven pages in total. No previously published poems. A wide range of tastes represented in the rotating panel of editors. No restriction on subject or point of view. We read unsolicited mss. Reading period April 15 through June 30. All inquiries and mss should be sent to U.S.1 Worksheets, P.O. Box 127, Kingston, NJ 08528-0127. SASE (no postcards, please) for notification." circ. 500. 1/yr. Pub'd 1 issue 2009; expects 1 issue 2010, 1 issue 2011. sub. price $15 (two years); per copy $8; sample $5. Back issues: inquire. Discounts: bulk back issues available, inquire. 105pp. Reporting time: two to three months, after June 30. Simultaneous submissions accepted: yes, but must notify if accepted elsewhere. Publishes 10% of manuscripts submitted. Payment: 1 copy. Copyrighted, reverts to author. Ads: none. Subjects: Creative Non-fiction, Fiction, Haiku, Poetry, Prose.

UBC Press, R. Peter Milroy, 2029 West Mall, Vancouver, BC V6T 1Z2, Canada, Phone 604-822-5959, 1-877-377-9378; Fax 604-822-6083, 1-800-668-0821; info@ubcpress.ca; www.ubcpress.ca. 1971. Non-fiction. "Publisher, distributor of scholarly books, some general trade and text, non-fiction. Canadian agent for US, Canadian and British academic publishers." Pub'd 54 titles 2009; expects 55-60 titles 2010, 55-60 titles 2011. No titles listed in the *Small Press Record of Books in Print* (36th Edition, 2010-11). Reporting time: One month or less. Simultaneous submissions accepted: No. Subjects: Agriculture, Anthropology, Archaelogy, Architecture, Asia, Indochina, Canada, Education, Health, History, Language, Law, Native American, Political Science, Politics, Public Affairs, Society.

UCLA Chicano Studies Research Center Press (see also AZTLAN: A Journal of Chicano Studies), Chon A. Noriega, Editor; Rebecca Frazier, Senior Editor, University of California-Los Angeles, 193 Haines Hall, Los Angeles, CA 90095-1544, 310-825-2642, press@chicano.ucla.edu, www.chicano.ucla.edu. 1970. Articles, criticism, reviews, letters, non-fiction. "Original research and analysis related to Chicano and Latino populations." avg. press run 1M. Pub'd 3 titles 2009; expects 3 titles 2010, 3 titles 2011. 18 titles listed in the *Small Press Record of Books in Print* (36th Edition, 2010-11). Discounts: for classroom use only. 300pp. Reporting time: 6 months. Simultaneous submissions accepted: no. Publishes 15% of manuscripts submitted. Payment: books in quantity. Copyrights for author. Subjects: Chicano/a, Society.

Ugly Duckling Presse, The Old American Can Factory, 232 Third Street, #E002 (corner Third Avenue), Brooklyn, NY 11215, Tel: 718-852-5529. "Ugly Duckling Presse is a nonprofit art & publishing collective producing small to mid-size editions of new poetry, translations, lost works, and artist's books. The Presse favors emerging, international, and "forgotten" writers with well-defined formal or conceptual projects that are difficult to place at other presses. Its full-length books, chapbooks, artists books, broadsides, magazine and newspaper all contain handmade elements, calling attention to the labor and history of bookmaking." No titles listed in the *Small Press Record of Books in Print* (36th Edition, 2010-11).

•**Ultra Media Publications,** Beth Holderman-Blonski, 177 Main Street, Suite D, East Brunswick, NJ 08816, www.ultramediapublications.com. 2009. Fiction. No titles listed in the *Small Press Record of Books in Print* (36th Edition, 2010-11). Simultaneous submissions accepted: No. Copyrights for author. Subjects: Fantasy, Fiction, Juvenile Fiction, Storytelling.

Ultramarine Publishing Co., Inc., Christopher P. Stephens, PO Box 303, Hastings-on-Hudson, NY 10706, 914-478-1339. 1965. Poetry, fiction. "We rescue books. We primarily distribute titles for authors (a major publisher has remaindered). The author buys some of the stock and we sell it for the author and split the proceeds." avg. press run 500-2.5M. Pub'd 20 titles 2009; expects 25 titles 2010, 30 titles 2011. No titles listed in the *Small Press Record of Books in Print* (36th Edition, 2010-11). Discounts: 1-4 20%; 5-9 30%; 10+ 40%. 250pp. Reporting time: 60 days. We have never published an unsolicited manuscript. Payment: varies. Copyrights for author. Subjects: Fantasy, Fiction, Poetry, Science Fiction.

UmbraProjects Publishing, Visit www.umbraprojects.com and please send your submissions to submissions@umbraprojects.com. 2004. Poetry, fiction, articles, cartoons, satire, parts-of-novels, long-poems, plays. "Manuscripts submitted by e-mail are exceptable and will be seen as a normal submission. We prefer fiction (fiction, sci-fi, humor, and fantasy). It can be as macabre as you want to write it, or not, your choice. We also publish comics (perferably in Japanese manga style). All materials submitted and/or published will remain the property of the author(s) as specified in the contract which will be supplied upon acceptence." avg. press run 100. Pub'd 2 titles 2009; expects 7 titles 2010, 20 titles 2011. No titles listed in the *Small Press Record of Books in Print* (36th Edition, 2010-11). 30-350pp. Reporting time: Within a week. Simultaneous submissions accepted: yes. Publishes 50% of manuscripts submitted. Payment: Author receives 50% royalties unless otherwise specified or aranged. Does not copyright for author. Subjects: Cartoons, Fantasy, Fiction, Graphic Design, Japan, Juvenile Fiction, Magazines, Medieval, Miniature Books, Myth, Mythology, Picture Books, Romance, Writers/Writing, Young Adult, Zines.

UND Press (see also NORTH DAKOTA QUARTERLY), Robert W. Lewis, Editor; William Borden, Fiction Editor; Jay Meek, Poetry Editor, University of North Dakota, PO Box 7209, Grand Forks, ND 58202, 701-777-3321. 1910. Poetry, fiction, articles, art, photos, interviews, satire, criticism, reviews, long-poems, non-fiction. Pub'd 80 titles 2009; expects 80 titles 2010, 80 titles 2011. 4 titles listed in the *Small Press Record of Books in Print* (36th Edition, 2010-11). 175pp. Reporting time: 1-4 months. We accept simultaneous submissions for fiction and essays if noted in cover letter, but not for poetry. Publishes 5% of manuscripts submitted. Payment: in copies. Copyrights for author. Subjects: Book Reviewing, Criticism, Culture, Great Plains, Ireland, Literary Review, Literature (General), Native American.

UNDER THE SUN, Heidemarie Z. Weidner, Editor, English Dept., Box 5053, Tennessee Technological University, Cookeville, TN 38505, 931-372-3768, hweidner@tntech.edu, www.tntech.edu/underthesun. 1995. Non-fiction. "'An essay,' it has been said, 'is a short piece of prose in which the author reveals himself in relation to any subject under the sun.' Hence, the name of our magazine. It is devoted exclusively to the publication of a form that began with Montaigne and that continues, despite neglect, to thrive today. No academic articles, reviews, feature stories, or excerpts. An essay from our inauguual issue was chosen for inclusion in the 1997 volume of Best American Essays. We have had "Notables" every year since then." 1/yr. Pub'd 1 issue 2009; expects 1 issue 2010, 1 issue 2011. sub. price $12.00; per copy $12.00; sample $7.00. Back issues: From $7.00 to $2.00, depending on the year. 200-250pp. Reporting time: 1-4 months. Simultaneous submissions accepted: yes. Publishes 10% of manuscripts submitted. Payment: 1 copy, 50% for additional copies. Copyrighted, reverts to author. Ads: none.

UNDERSTANDING MAGAZINE, Dionysia Press Ltd., Denise Smith, Thom Nairn, 20 A Montgomery

Street, Edinburgh, EH7 5JS, United Kingdom, 0131-4780680. 1989. Poetry, fiction, articles, art, photos, satire, criticism, reviews, parts-of-novels, long-poems, plays. circ. 500. 1/yr. Pub'd 1 issue 2009; expects 1 issue 2010, 1 issue 2011. sub. price £10 overseas; per copy £3.50 + £1.50 p/h; sample £2.50 + £1.50 p/h. Back issues: same. Discounts: 2 mags for £8. 150pp. Reporting time: 8 months. Simultaneous submissions accepted: no. Publishes 20% of manuscripts submitted. Payment: free copy. Not copyrighted. Pub's reviews: 4 in 2009. §Poetry, short stories, novels. Ads: £100/£50/25pp per word. Subjects: African Literature, Africa, African Studies, African-American, William Blake, Lewis Carroll, Classical Studies, Criticism, Kafka, Rudyard Kipling, Literature (General), Philosophy, Reviews, Satire, Surrealism, Tennessee, Writers/Writing.

Underwhich Editions, Paul Dutton, Steven Smith, PO Box 262, Adelaide Street Station, Toronto, Ontario M5C 2J4, Canada, 536-9316. 1978. Poetry, fiction, art, interviews, music, long-poems, collages, plays, concrete art, non-fiction. "Dedicated to presenting, in diverse and appealing physical formats, new works by contemporary creators, focusing on formal invention and encompassing the expanded frontiers of literary and musical endeavor. Recent contributors include: Bob Cobbing, Gerry Gilbert, Gerry Shikatani, Lia Pas." avg. press run 200-500. Expects 2 titles 2010, 3 titles 2011. 44 titles listed in the *Small Press Record of Books in Print* (36th Edition, 2010-11). Discounts: 40% to retailers, 20% to educational institutions and libraries, 20% to radio stations on audiocassettes only. 30-50pp. Payment: 10% (copies or sales). Copyright remains with author. Subjects: Avant-Garde, Experimental Art, Literature (General), Music, Poetry, Short Stories, Tapes & Records.

United Artists Books, Lewis Warsh, Publisher, 114 W. 16th Street, 5C, New York, NY 10011. "United Artists Books (formerly Angel Hair Books) was founded in 1967. It is one of the oldest independent publishing companies in the United States that focuses primarily on publishing books of poetry." No titles listed in the *Small Press Record of Books in Print* (36th Edition, 2010-11).

United Lumbee Nation (see also UNITED LUMBEE NATION TIMES), Jackie Deerheart, PO Box 115, Ravendale, CA 96123, 916-336-6701. 1977. Art. "We have 3 copyrighted books out: *United Lumbee Indian Ceremonies*, an Indian cookbook, *Over The Cooking Fires*, and *United Lumbee Deer Clan Cook Book*, all edited and compiled by Princess Silver Star Reed." avg. press run 100. Pub'd 1 title 2009; expects 1 title 2011. 1 title listed in the *Small Press Record of Books in Print* (36th Edition, 2010-11). Discounts: 20% per copy. 20-25pp. Payment: none. Does not copyright for author. Subjects: Ecology, Foods, Folklore, Native American.

UNITED LUMBEE NATION TIMES, United Lumbee Nation, Jackie Deerheart, P.O. Box 115, Ravendale, CA 96123, 530-336-6701. 1979. circ. 2M. 3-4/yr. Pub'd 3 issues 2009; expects 3 issues 2010, 4 issues 2011. sub. price $8/4 issues; per copy $3; sample $3. 8-12pp. Reporting time: no set time, write for press time of next issue. Payment: none. Not copyrighted. Pub's reviews: 1-3 in 2009. §Native American Indian Heritage and Native American Indians today. Ads: $120/$60/Business card size $12/10% discount if put in four issues. Subjects: Book Reviewing, Crafts, Hobbies, Ecology, Foods, Education, Folklore, Native American, Reprints.

United Nations University Press, Robert Davis, United Nations University, 53-70 Jingumae 5-chome, Shibuya-ku, Tokyo, Japan, Tel: +81-3499-2811, Fax: +81-3-3406-7345, sales@hq.unu.edu, http://www.unu.edu/unupress. 1990. Articles. "scholary publications in the fields of political science and international relations, environment and sustainable development." avg. press run 800. Pub'd 16 titles 2009; expects 17 titles 2010, 18 titles 2011. No titles listed in the *Small Press Record of Books in Print* (36th Edition, 2010-11). Discounts: 2-20 copies 25% 21-50 copies 35%. 350pp. Reporting time: 6 weeks. Simultaneous submissions accepted: No. Publishes 33% of manuscripts submitted. Payment: no royalty payments are made to authors/editors. UN University holds copyright to all publications. Subjects: African Literature, Africa, African Studies, Asia, Indochina, Business & Economics, Education, Environment, Ethics, Europe, Finances, Geography, Japan, Multicultural, Non-Fiction, Peace, Political Science, Politics.

Unity House (see also DAILY WORD; UNITY MAGAZINE), Stephanie Oliver, Editorial Director, 1901 NW Blue Parkway, Unity Village, MO 64065-0001, 816-524-3550, fax 816-347-5518. 1889. Non-fiction. "Types of books sought: spiritual, metaphysical, Christian, self-help, motivational, healing, mysticism." Pub'd 9 titles 2009; expects 6 titles 2010, 6 titles 2011. 82 titles listed in the *Small Press Record of Books in Print* (36th Edition, 2010-11). Discounts: wholesalers 52%, retailers 40%. 200pp. Reporting time: 6 months. Simultaneous submissions accepted: no. Publishes 1% of manuscripts submitted. Payment: upon acceptance. Copyrights for author. Subjects: Health, History, Inspirational, Metaphysics, Motivation, Success, Non-Fiction, Religion, Self-Help, Spiritual.

UNITY MAGAZINE, Unity House, Toni Lapp, 1901 NW Blue Parkway, Unity Village, MO 64065-0001, 816-524-3550. 1889. Poetry, articles, photos, non-fiction. "Types of materials sought: spiritual, metaphysical, Christian, self-help, motivational, healing, mysticism." circ. 40M. 6/yr. Pub'd 6 issues 2009; expects 6 issues 2010, 6 issues 2011. sub. price $19.95; per copy $3.50; sample free. 48pp. Reporting time: 3 months. Simultaneous submissions accepted: no. Payment: upon acceptance. Copyrighted, reverts to author. Pub's reviews: 4 in 2009. Ads: none. Subjects: Health, History, Metaphysics, Motivation, Success, Non-Fiction, Religion, Self-Help, Spiritual.

512

Univelt, Inc. (see also AAS HISTORY SERIES; ADVANCES IN THE ASTRONAUTICAL SCIENCES; SCIENCE AND TECHNOLOGY), Robert H. Jacobs, Series Editor, PO Box 28130, San Diego, CA 92198-0130, voice:760-746-4005; Fax:760-746-3139; Email:sales@univelt.com, Web Site: http://www.univelt.com. 1970. "We are publishing books on space, astronomy, veterinary medicine (esp. first aid for animals). *To Catch a Flying Star: A Scientific Theory of UFOs*; *Realm of the Long Eyes* (astronomy); *General First Aid for Dogs* (veterinary medicine); *The Case for Mars*; *Spacecraft Tables 1957-1990*; *The Human Quest in Space* (space). Publishers for the American Astronautical Society." avg. press run 500-2M. Pub'd 10 titles 2009; expects 10 titles 2010, 10 titles 2011. 50 titles listed in the *Small Press Record of Books in Print* (36th Edition, 2010-11). Discounts: 20%; special discounts for classroom use; larger discounts by arrangement. 100-700pp. Reporting time: 60 days. Payment: 10% for a volume author. Copyright held by Society or Univelt but obtained by Univelt. Subjects: Adirondacks, Animals, Astronomy, Communication, Journalism, Engineering, Graphics, Indexes & Abstracts, Language, Political Science, Printing, Reference, Science, Science Fiction, Sociology.

University of Akron Press, Akron, OH 44325-1703. No titles listed in the *Small Press Record of Books in Print* (36th Edition, 2010-11). Subjects: Environment, History, Law, Ohio, Poetry, Politics, Technology, University Press.

University of Alabama Press (see also ALABAMA HERITAGE), Donna Cox, Box 870342, 500 Margaret Drive, Tuscaloosa, AL 35487-0342, 205-348-7434, www.AlabamaHeritage.com. No titles listed in the *Small Press Record of Books in Print* (36th Edition, 2010-11). Subject: University Press.

University of Alaska Press, Erica Hill, Editor, PO Box 756240, Fairbanks, AK 99775-6240, 907.474.5831, 907.474.5502 fax, 888.252.6657, fypress@uaf.edu. www.uaf.edu/uapress. 1969. Non-fiction. "University of Alaska Press publishes scholarly nonfiction about Alaska and the circumpolar North." avg. press run 1500. Pub'd 11 titles 2009; expects 10 titles 2010. No titles listed in the *Small Press Record of Books in Print* (36th Edition, 2010-11). 300pp. Simultaneous submissions accepted: Yes. Publishes 10% of manuscripts submitted. Subjects: Alaska, Anthropology, Archaelogy, Native American, The North, Pacific Region.

University of Arkansas Press, Larry Malley, McIlroy House, 105 N. McIlroy Avenue, Fayetteville, AR 72701, 1-479-575-3246. 1980. Poetry, non-fiction. "The Press has a Poetry Series edited by Enid Shomer that publishes four poetry collections each year, two in the fall, two in the spring. The Press awards the $5000 Miller Williams Arkansas Poetry Prize to one finalist each year. (Check our website for submission requirements:www.uapress.com." avg. press run 1500. Pub'd 10 titles 2009; expects 12 titles 2010, 12 titles 2011. No titles listed in the *Small Press Record of Books in Print* (36th Edition, 2010-11). Discounts: 1-2 copies 20% 3-24 copies 40% 25-49 copies 41% 50-99 copies 42% 100-249 copies 44% 250+ 46%. 240pp. Reporting time: Usually around 4-6 months. Simultaneous submissions accepted: Yes. Publishes 3% of manuscripts submitted. Payment: No advance, standard royalty rates. Copyrights for author. Subjects: African-American, Americana, Arkansas, Biography, Civil War, Communication, Journalism, Criticism, Folklore, History, Middle East, Non-Fiction, Poetry, Political Science, South, Trade, University Press.

University of Calgary Press (see also ARIEL, A Review of International English Literature; CANADIAN JOURNAL OF COUNSELLING; CANADIAN JOURNAL OF LATIN AMERICAN AND CARIBBEAN STUDIES/Revue canadienne des etudes latino-americaines et caraibes; CANADIAN JOURNAL OF PHILOSOPHY; CANADIAN JOURNAL OF PROGRAM EVALUATION; CURRENTS: New Scholarship in the Human Services; INTERNATIONAL ELECTRONIC JOURNAL FOR LEADER-SHIP IN LEARNING; MOUSEION, Journal of the Classical Association of Canada/Revue de la Societe Canadienne des Etudes Classiques), John King, Senior Editor; Donna Livingstone, Director, 2500 University Drive NW, Calgary, Alberta T2N 1N4, Canada, 403-220-7578, Fax 403-282-0085, www.uofcpress.com. 1981. Poetry, criticism, non-fiction. "The University of Calgary Press (UC Press) is a non-profit, scholarly publisher committed to producing high-calibre academic and trade books and journals on a wide range of subjects, including art and architecture, the Canadian North, and international topics such as African studies and Latin American studies. As the heartland publisher, we are also particularly known for our focus on Alberta and the North American west. The University of Calgary Press seeks to: publish works that give voice to the heartland of the continent, with a special emphasis on Alberta; publish works that are innovative, experimental, and offer alternative perspectives; publish works that offer diverse views on international themes; help new writers break into academic and trade markets and nurture their careers; and link the creation and dissemination of new knowledge. Orders and inquiries: IN CANADA: Canada uniPRESSES, Georgetown Terminal Warehouses, 34 Armstrong Ave., Georgetown, ON, L7G 4R9. Telephone: 877-864-8477, Fax 877-864-4272, e-mail orders@gtwcanada.com IN THE U.S.: Michigan State University Press, 1405 S. Harrison Road, Ste. 25, Manly Miles Bldg., E. Lansing, MI 48823-5245. Phone 517-355-9543, Fax 517-432-2611, e-mail msupress@msu.edu IN THE U.K. AND EUROPE: Gazelle Book Services, White Cross Mills, High Town, Lancaster LA1 4XS, U.K.. Phone 1524-68765, Fax 1524-63232, e-mail sales@gazellebooks.co.uk." Pub'd 31 titles 2009; expects 30 titles 2010, 30 titles 2011. 283 titles listed in the *Small Press Record of Books in Print* (36th Edition, 2010-11). Discounts: Booksellers: 20-46% Libraries: 10% College and University bookstores: 20-46%. 250pp.

Simultaneous submissions accepted: no. Payment: No advances, royalties 5% net sales after costs are recovered. Copyrights for author. Subjects: African Literature, Africa, African Studies, Anthropology, Archaelogy, Arts, Biography, Canada, Environment, History, Holocaust, Indigenous Cultures, Native American, The North, Political Science, University Press, The West, Women.

University of California Press (see also AGRICULTURAL HISTORY; ASIAN SURVEY; CLASSICAL ANTIQUITY; CONTEXTS: UNDERSTANDING PEOPLE IN THEIR SOCIAL WORLDS; FEDERAL SENTENCING REPORTER; FILM QUARTERLY; GASTRONOMICA: The Journal of Food and Culture; HISTORICAL STUDIES IN THE PHYSICAL & BIOLOGICAL SCIENCES; HUNTINGTON LIBRARY QUARTERLY; INDEX TO FOREIGN LEGAL PERIODICALS; JOURNAL OF MUSICOLOGY; JOURNAL OF PALESTINE STUDIES; JOURNAL OF THE AMERICAN MUSICOLOGICAL SOCIETY; LAW AND LITERATURE; MEXICAN STUDIES/ESTUDIOS MEXICANOS; MUSIC PERCEPTION; MUSIC THEORY SPECTRUM; 19TH-CENTURY LITERA-TURE; 19TH-CENTURY MUSIC; NOVA RELIGIO; ORAL HISTORY REVIEW; PACIFIC HISTORICAL REVIEW; THE PUBLIC HISTORIAN; RELIGION & AMERICAN CULTURE; REPRESENTATIONS; RHETORICA: A Journal of the History of Rhetoric; SOCIAL PROBLEMS; SOCIOLOGICAL PERSPECTIVES; THE SOCIOLOGICAL QUARTERLY; STATE OF CALI-FORNIA LABOR; SYMBOLIC INTERACTION), Rebecca Simon, Assistant Director, Journals, 2000 Center Street, Suite 303, Berkeley, CA 94704-1223, 510-643-7154, e-mail journals@ucpress.edu. 1893. Articles, photos, interviews, criticism, reviews. avg. press run varies. Pub'd 28 titles 2009; expects 31 titles 2010, 31 titles 2011. No titles listed in the *Small Press Record of Books in Print* (36th Edition, 2010-11). Pages vary. Reporting time: varies widely. Payment: none. Copyrights in the name of Regents of the University of California (see individual listings). Subject: University Press.

University of Chicago Press (see also CRITICAL INQUIRY; INTERNATIONAL JOURNAL OF AMERICAN LINGUISTICS; JOURNAL OF BRITISH STUDIES; THE LIBRARY QUARTERLY; MODERN PHILOLOGY; OCEAN YEARBOOK; SIGNS), Paula Barker Duffy, Director, 1427 E. 60th Street, Chicago, IL 60437-2954, 773-702-7700, http://www.press.uchicago.edu/. 1891. Poetry, fiction, art, photos, criticism, music, long-poems, news items, non-fiction. "The University of Chicago Press, a non-profit university publisher founded in 1891, publishes ground breaking books and cutting edge journals in the humanities, sciences, and social sciences for a global community of scholars, researchers, professionals, and educated readers. Often ranked as the largest university press in the United States, Chicago has developed an internationally respected list of academic, professional, and writing reference books, as well as a premier list of Chicago regional titles. Through its Chicago Distribution Services division, the Press also distributes books for more than four dozen not-for-profit scholarly presses and maintains the Chicago Digital Distribution Center with its unique digital printing center adjacent to the warehouse and the BiblioVault repository for book files. Also, the Journals Division of the Press currently distributes nearly 50 journals and hardcover serials, presenting original research from international scholars in the social sciences, humanities, education, biological and medical sciences, and physical sciences. A complete list of books and journals published by Chicago can be found at: www.press.uchicago.edu." Pub'd 210 titles 2009; expects 188 titles 2010, 200 titles 2011. No titles listed in the *Small Press Record of Books in Print* (36th Edition, 2010-11). Payment: Once a year, after fiscal close. Copyright is usually in the name of the Press. Subjects: African Literature, Africa, African Studies, Agriculture, Anthropology, Archaelogy, Architecture, Arts, Bibliography, Cities, Conservation, Criticism, Earth, Natural History, Education, Gay, History, Labor, Lesbianism.

University of Iowa Press, Holly Carver, Director, 119 Weast Park Road, 100 Kuhl House, Iowa City, IA 52242-1000. "Submission Guidelines: The University of Iowa Press seeks proposals to add to its strong lists in the following areas: literary studies, including Whitman studies and poetics; letters and diaries; American studies; literary nonfiction and thematic edited anthologies, particularly poetry anthologies; the craft of writing; literature and medicine; theatre studies; archaeology; the natural history of the Upper Midwest; and regional history and cuture. We publish single-author short fiction and poetry through series only." No titles listed in the *Small Press Record of Books in Print* (36th Edition, 2010-11). Subject: University Press.

University of Massachusetts Press, Bruce Wilcox, Director; Clark Dougan, Senior Editor, Box 429, Amherst, MA 01004, 413-545-2217; fax 413-545-1226; orders 1-800-537-5487. 1963. Poetry, fiction, criticism, non-fiction. "Scholarly books and serious nonfiction, with an emphasis on American studies, broadly construed. We also publish the annual winners of the Juniper Prize for Poetry, the AWP Grace Paley Prize in Short Fiction, and the Juniper Prize for Fiction. Information is available at our website—www.umass.edu/umpress." Pub'd 36 titles 2009; expects 34 titles 2010, 35 titles 2011. No titles listed in the *Small Press Record of Books in Print* (36th Edition, 2010-11). Discounts: For discount terms, please contact our distributor, Hopkins Fulfillment Service, at 1-800-537-5487. Reporting time: preliminary response within two weeks, followed by formal review process. Simultaneous submissions accepted: Yes. Payment: royalties vary. Copyrights for author. Subjects: African-American, Architecture, Arts, Biography, Civil Rights, Criticism, Current Affairs, Environment, History, Memoirs, Multicultural, New England, Non-Fiction, University Press, Vietnam.

University of Michigan Press, LeAnn Fields, 839 Greene Street, Ann Arbor, MI 48104-3209, Phone 734-764-4388, Fax 734-615-1540, http://www.press.umich.edu/. 1930. Pub'd 160 titles 2009; expects 160 titles 2010, 160 titles 2011. No titles listed in the *Small Press Record of Books in Print* (36th Edition, 2010-11). Subject: University Press.

University of Nebraska Press (see also RIVER TEETH: A Journal of Nonfiction Narrative), Ladette Randolph Ms, 1111 Lincoln Mall #400, Lincoln, NE 68508-3905, 402 472 3581, 402 472 6214, 800 755 1105, pressmail@unl.edu, www.nebraskapress.unl.edu, www.bisonbooks.com. 1941. "The University of Nebraska Press, founded in 1941, seeks to encourage, develop, publish, and disseminate research, literature, and the publishing arts. The Press is the largest academic publisher in the Great Plains and a major publisher of books about that region. It is the states largest repository of the knowledge, arts, and skills of publishing and advises the University and the people of Nebraska about book publishing. Reporting to the Vice-Chancellor for Research and having a faculty advisory board, the Press maintains scholarly standards and fosters innovations guided by refereed evaluations." avg. press run 2000. Pub'd 141 titles 2009; expects 160 titles 2010, 170 titles 2011. No titles listed in the *Small Press Record of Books in Print* (36th Edition, 2010-11). Discounts: Discount schedule available on request or through ABA Handbook. 280pp. Reporting time: 1-2 weeks. Simultaneous submissions accepted: No. Publishes 20% of manuscripts submitted. Payment: varies. Copyrights for author. Subjects: African-American, Anthropology, Archaelogy, Civil War, Feminism, Great Plains, History, Indigenous Cultures, Literature (General), Midwest, Native American, Nebraska, Non-Fiction, Old West, University Press, World War II.

University of Nevada Press, Joanne O'Hare, Mail Stop 0166, Reno, NV 89557-0166, 775-784-6573, www.unpress.nevada.edu. No titles listed in the *Small Press Record of Books in Print* (36th Edition, 2010-11). Subject: University Press.

University of Pittsburgh Press, 3400 Forbes Avenue, 5th Floor, Eureka Bldg., Pittsburgh, PA 15260, 412-383-2456. 1936. 19 titles listed in the *Small Press Record of Books in Print* (36th Edition, 2010-11). Subject: University Press.

University of Scranton Press, Patricia Mecadon, 445 Madison Ave., Scranton, PA 18510, 1-800-941-3081, 1-800-941-8804, www.scrantonpress.com. No titles listed in the *Small Press Record of Books in Print* (36th Edition, 2010-11). Subject: University Press.

University of South Carolina Press, Linda Fogle, Assistant Director for Operations; Alex Moore, Acquisitions Editor; Jim Denton, Acquisitions Editor, 1600 Hampton Street, 5th Floor, Columbia, SC 29208, 803-777-5245; 803-777-0160; www.sc.edu/uscpress. 1944. Art, photos, criticism, letters, non-fiction. avg. press run 1000. Pub'd 53 titles 2009; expects 74 titles 2010, 75 titles 2011. No titles listed in the *Small Press Record of Books in Print* (36th Edition, 2010-11). 200-500pp. Reporting time: 3-6 months for full proposal or manuscript. Simultaneous submissions accepted: Yes. Publishes 15% of manuscripts submitted. Payment: Varies widely. Copyright in name of university negotiable. Subjects: African-American, Architecture, Arts, Civil Rights, Civil War, Folklore, Food, Eating, Gardening, History, Literature (General), Memoirs, Nature, Religion, South Carolina, University Press.

University of Tampa Press (see also TAMPA REVIEW), Richard Mathews, 401 W Kennedy Blvd, Tampa, FL 33606, (813) 253-6266, Email: utpress@ut.edu, http://utpress.ut.edu, http://tampareview.ut.edu. 1952. Poetry, photos, interviews, criticism, letters, plays, non-fiction. "The University of Tampa Press publishes a limited number of books related to local and regional history as well as hardcover and quality paperback books by the annual winners of the Tampa Review Prize for Poetry. Recent poetry winners are Jordan Smith, Julia B. Levine, Sarah Maclay, and Lance Larsen. Other UT Press poets are Jenny Browne, Richard Chess, Kathleen Jesme, Lisa Steinman, and Richard Terrill, winner of the 2004 Minnesota Book Award for poetry. Winners in drama are Brian Silberman (MANIFEST), Susan Miller (A MAP OF DOUBT AND RESCUE) and J.T. Rogers (MADAGASCAR). The press also publishes two journals, TAMPA REVIEW, a hardcover literary magazine issued twice yearly, and PINTER REVIEW, a scholarly annual collection of essays on the work of Harold Pinter.The press does not currently accept unsolicited work except through its annual book award competitions and by direct submission to each journal, following published guidelines." avg. press run 750. Pub'd 7 titles 2009; expects 6-8 titles 2010, 6-8 titles 2011. 35 titles listed in the *Small Press Record of Books in Print* (36th Edition, 2010-11). Discounts: 1-4 copies 20%5+ copies 40%Some titles are on short discount. 88-450pp. Reporting time: Poetry and drama are accepted only via contest submission (see guidelines at http://pinter.ut.edu and http://tampareview.ut.edu/tr_prize.html). Simultaneous submissions accepted: No. Publishes 1% of manuscripts submitted. Payment: varies. Copyrights for author. Subjects: Book Arts, Criticism, Drama, English, Essays, Florida, History, Interviews, Literary Review, Literature (General), Non-Fiction, Poetry, Printing, Prose, Theatre, University Press.

The University of TX-Pan American Press (see also RIVERSEDGE), Desirae Aguirre Ms., Editor, The University of TX-Pan American Press, 1201 W. Univ. Drive, Lamar Bldg., Room 9A, Edinburg, TX 78541,

956-381-3638, Fax 956-381-3697, bookworm@panam.edu. 4 titles listed in the *Small Press Record of Books in Print* (36th Edition, 2010-11). 120pp. Payment: Payment is 2 complimentary copies. After printing copyrights revert to the author. Subject: University Press.

University of Utah Press, J. Willard Marriott Library, Suite 5400, 295 South 1500 East, Salt Lake City, UT 84112, 800-621-2736, Fax 800-621-8471, UofUpress.com. 1949. Pub'd 26 titles 2009; expects 23 titles 2010, 30 titles 2011. No titles listed in the *Small Press Record of Books in Print* (36th Edition, 2010-11). Subjects: The Americas, Anthropology, Archaelogy, Language, Memoirs, Middle East, Mormon, Native American, Non-Fiction, Southwest, Trade, University Press, Utah, The West, Women, World War II.

University of Virginia Press, Richard Holway, Acquisitions Editor; Boyd Zenner, Acquisitions Editor; Cathie Brettschneider, Acquisitions Editor, P.O. Box 400318, Charlottesville, VA 22904-4318, 800-831-3406, 877-288-6400, vapress@virginia.edu, www.upress.virginia.edu. 1963. Poetry, art, photos, criticism, letters, non-fiction. "The University of Virginia Press was founded in 1963 to advance the intellectual interests not only of the University of Virginia, but of institutions of higher learning throughout the state. A member of the Association of American University Presses, UVaP currently publishes fifty to sixty new titles annually. New titles are approved by the Board of Directors after a rigorous process of peer review. The UVaP editorial program focuses primarily on the humanities and social sciences with special concentrations in American history, African American studies, southern studies, literature, ecocriticism, and regional books. While it continuously pursues new titles, UVaP also maintains a backlist of over 1,000 titles in print. Some recent titles are *Pocahontas, Powhatan, Opechancanough*, *Equity and Excellence in American Higher Education*, *Bitter Fruits of Bondage* and *Schooling and Riding the Sport Horse*." avg. press run 1,500. Pub'd 57 titles 2009; expects 53 titles 2010, 60 titles 2011. No titles listed in the *Small Press Record of Books in Print* (36th Edition, 2010-11). Discounts: 1:20% 2-25:40% 26-100:42% 101-200:43% 201 or more:46%. 256pp. Reporting time: Anywhere from 2 months to a year if the author is still revising the manuscript. Simultaneous submissions accepted: Yes. Payment: Royalty is only given under special arrangements for certain books. We maintain copyright of all books unless there is a special case. Subjects: African Literature, Africa, African Studies, Architecture, Biography, Caribbean, Civil War, France, French, Gardening, History, Thomas Jefferson, Literature (General), Non-Fiction, Poetry, Sports, Outdoors, Translation, University Press, Virginia.

UNIVERSITY OF WINDSOR REVIEW, Marty Gervais, 2124 Chrysler Hall North, University of Windsor, Windsor, Ontario N9B 3P4, Canada, 519-293-3000 X2290; Fax 519-973-7050; uwrevu@uwindsor.ca. 1965. Poetry, fiction, articles, art, photos, cartoons, interviews, satire, criticism, parts-of-novels, long-poems, collages, plays, concrete art, non-fiction. "The journal was established in 1965 by Eugene McNamara, the well-known poet and short story writer and a former professor in the Department of English at the University of Windsor. Poets and short story writers who have seen their work published in the Windsor Review include Irving Layton, Gwendolen MacEwen, Frances Itani and W.D. Valgardson. Visual artists whose works have been featured in the journal include Jane Ash Poitras and Robert Fortin.The Windsor Review welcomes submissions from both new and established artists." circ. 250. 2/yr. Pub'd 2 issues 2009; expects 2 issues 2010, 2 issues 2011. sub. price $29.95 CDN. (+ 7% GST) and $29.95 U.S. per year; per copy $15 Cdn; sample $8 Cdn. Back issues: please write. Discounts: n/a at present. 100pp. Reporting time: 6 weeks. Simultaneous submissions accepted: no. Payment: $25 for story or essay, $10 for poem. Copyrighted, reverts to author. Ads: no paid ads at present, though possibly in near future; same for exchange ads—please write. Subjects: Arts, Fiction, Literary Review, Poetry.

University of Wisconsin Press, Andrea Christofferson, Marketing Manager; Raphael Kadushin, Acquisitions Editor; Gwen Walker, Acquisitions Editor, 1930 Monroe Street, 3rd Floor, Madison, WI 53711-2059, (608)263-0814, fax (608)263-1132. 1947. Fiction, criticism, non-fiction. "UW Press publishes books and journals valued by a world-wide scholarly community, which are an extension of the university's teaching and research missions. We also publish books that serve to doument the regional heritage of the Great Lakes region. Areas of special inerest include: Jewish Studies, African Studies, Gay & Lesbian Studies, Environmental Studies, Anthropology, and History.UW Press publishes a few poetry and fiction titles each season." Pub'd 85 titles 2009; expects 75 titles 2010, 70 titles 2011. No titles listed in the *Small Press Record of Books in Print* (36th Edition, 2010-11). Subject: University Press.

University Press of Colorado, Darrin Pratt, 5589 Arapahoe Avenue, Suite 206C, Boulder, CO 80303, Orders: 800-627-7377, Editorial: 720-406-8849, Fax: 720-406-3443. 1965. Non-fiction. "We publish non-fiction books with a focus on anthropology, archaeology, history, natural history, and the state of Colorado and Rocky Mountain Region." avg. press run 750. Pub'd 34 titles 2009; expects 28 titles 2010, 20 titles 2011. No titles listed in the *Small Press Record of Books in Print* (36th Edition, 2010-11). 268-340pp. Reporting time: 2-4 weeks. Simultaneous submissions accepted: Yes. Publishes less than 5% of manuscripts submitted. Copyrights for author. Subjects: The Americas, Animals, Anthropology, Archaelogy, Astronomy, Biology, Birds, Botany, Colorado, History, Law, Mexico, Non-Fiction, Political Science, South America, University Press, The West.

UnKnownTruths.com Publishing Company, Walter Parks, 8815 Conroy Windermere Rd., Suite 190,

Orlando, FL 32835, Ph 407-929-9207, Fax 407-876-3933, info@unknowntruths.com. 2003. Fiction, non-fiction. "Publishes books and produces Television Programing of true stories of the unusual or of the previously unexplained. The 56 stories currently in development or already published are grouped into seven catagories: Religious and Philosophical, Health and Medical, Historical, Psychic, Children-Young Adults-Nature, Travel and Leisure, and Fact Based Novels." avg. press run 5000. Pub'd 1 title 2009; expects 4 titles 2010, 9 titles 2011. 8 titles listed in the *Small Press Record of Books in Print* (36th Edition, 2010-11). Discounts: Standard. 304pp. Simultaneous submissions accepted: no. Copyrights for author. Subjects: Aging, Christianity, Earth, Natural History, History, Metaphysics, Myth, Mythology, Philosophy, Physics, Religion, Science, Spiritual, Supernatural, Technology, Treasure.

Unlimited Publishing LLC, P.O. Box 3007, Bloomington, IN 47402, Please visit http://www.unlimitedpublishing.com for contact info. We strongly recommend reviewing UP's submission policies online before sending a manuscript. 2000. Non-fiction. "Specializing in re-publishing out-of-print books formerly from well known imprints, and publishing short nonfiction by professional writers. We also co-publish with many smaller presses and a growing number of charitable and educational institutions. We focus on POD books with appeal in specialty or niche outlets, rather than conventional book trade channels. UP does not accept unagented submissions by post or return unsolicited manuscripts. New writers are welcome to query by e-mail *after careful review of submission guidelines at http://www.unlimitedpublishing.com at any time.*" Pub'd 50 titles 2009; expects 100 titles 2010, 200 titles 2011. No titles listed in the *Small Press Record of Books in Print* (36th Edition, 2010-11). Discounts: Long discounts, non-returnable; short discounts, returnable. UP also customizes books for bulk buyers at attractive rates. 250pp. Reporting time: Prompt. Simultaneous submissions accepted: No. Publishes 5% of manuscripts submitted. Payment: Modest advances possible, royalties of 10% or better. Subjects: Adolescence, Advertising, Self-Promotion, Aging, Airplanes, Biography, Business & Economics, Communication, Journalism, Entertainment, Family, Fiction, How-To, Non-Fiction, Pets, Sociology, Speaking.

UNMUZZLED OX, ZerOX Books, Michael Andre, '304 Pine Street, (1R), Philadelphia, PA 19107, 718-448-3395, 212-226-7170, MAndreOX@aol.com. 1971. Poetry, fiction, articles, art, photos, interviews, criticism, reviews, music, letters, parts-of-novels. "It's helpful if contributors already understand pre-anti-post-modernism. Tabloid. We do not publish reviews, but we review books elsewhere and love to get them. We become ever more esoteric. Following the editing and publication of W.H. Auden's translation of an 18th century opera libretto, we plan an *Ox* of neo-baroque comapct disks. 2010: I'm re-organizing as usual. Thinking of doing an UnmuzzledOX.blogspot Daily starting in the autumn but it requires some considerable organizing. Most every Unmuzzled OX printed is still for sale and available at 105 Hudson NYC 10013. I'm still computerphobic but what can you do? The machines won.—Michael." circ. 20M. 2/yr. sub. price $20; per copy $12; sample $12. Back issues: 1-6: $20 each 7-21 cover price. Discounts: 40%. 140pp. Reporting time: 2 weeks. Payment: none. Copyrighted. §Art, literature, music, politics. Ads: $65/$35. Subjects: Arts, Literary Review.

UNSPLENDID, Douglas Basford, Editor; Jason Gray, Editor; Natalie Shapero, Editor; Erin Sweeten, Editor, Web: www.unsplendid.com. "*Unsplendid*, we believe, is a dazzling new cabochon on the Web's necklace: there are not many websites at present devoted to new poetry in received forms, and many of those that are are either sputtering to a halt, cursed with unattractive websites, behind the curve in some way, more interested in reviewing books of "formal" poetry than publishing new work, or some combination thereof. We view this venture not as a partisan-like imposition of a particular aesthetic, but as establishing something akin to the radio station that "listeners" will turn to when they are in the mood to "hear" top-notch poetry written in meter and traditional or nonce forms."

•**Upheaval Media,** Ida Byrd-Hill, 19170 Huntington Avenue, Harper Woods, MI 48225, 877-429-2370, 313-221-9494, info@upheavalmedia.net. 2008. Non-fiction. "Non fiction self help, Journals." avg. press run 2500. Pub'd 1 title 2009; expects 4 titles 2010, 10 titles 2011. 3 titles listed in the *Small Press Record of Books in Print* (36th Edition, 2010-11). Discounts: 10 books 10% Discount50 books 20% Discount100 books 30% Discount250 books 40% Discount500 books 50% Discount1000 books 60% Discount. 150pp. Reporting time: 30 days. Simultaneous submissions accepted: Yes. Publishes 20% of manuscripts submitted. Payment: 25% of profit generated. Subjects: Adolescence, African-American, Aging, Artificial Intelligence, Careers, Cooking, Family, Futurism, Journals, Non-Fiction, Parenting, Self-Help, Travel, Young Adult.

Upper Access Inc. Book Publishers, Steve Carlson, 87 Upper Access Road, Hinesburg, VT 05461, 800-310-8320 (orders only), 802-482-2988, Fax 802-304-1005, info@upperaccess.com. 1987. Non-fiction. "*No* genre focus. We are looking for unique non-fiction to improve the quality of life. We also publish business software for the book publishing industry. Our primary software programs are *Publishers' Assistant* (Invoicing and office management) and *Couplet* (title and contact management, including creating ONIX databases)." avg. press run 5000. Pub'd 1 title 2009; expects 3 titles 2010, 3 titles 2011. 15 titles listed in the *Small Press Record of Books in Print* (36th Edition, 2010-11). Discounts: Trade discounts set our distributor, Midpoint. 195-603pp. Reporting time: 2 weeks, usually. Simultaneous submissions accepted: Yes, but send proposal, not full MS.

Publishes 5% of manuscripts submitted. Payment: 10% of net sales to 5,000 books, 15% thereafter, modest advance for finished mss. Copyrights for author. Subjects: Consumer, Ecology, Foods, Environment, Ethics, Food, Eating, Grieving, Health, Non-Fiction, Peace, Politics, Real Estate, Reference, Self-Help, Taxes.

UPSTAIRS AT DUROC, Barbara Beck, Editor, WICE, Upstairs at Duroc, 7 Cite Falguiere, 75015 Paris, France, wice@wice-paris.org (attention:Upstairs at Duroc submissions). 1999. Poetry, fiction, art, photos, parts-of-novels, non-fiction. "We publish innovative poetry, fiction and cross-genre work and a few pages of artwork/photography. New as well as established writers from the Paris, France area and around the world. Recent issues contain work by Lisa Fishman, Cole Swensen, Stephen Ratcliffe, Laynie Browne, Jennifer K. Dick, Marilyn Hacker, George Szirtes, Susana Gardner, Michelle Noteboom and many more.." circ. 170. 1/yr. Pub'd 1 issue 2009; expects 1 issue 2010, 1 issue 2011. price per copy Euros 10; sample 10 Euros. Back issues: inquire. No discounts. 100pp. Reporting time: 4 months. Simultaneous submissions accepted: Yes. Publishes 10% of manuscripts submitted. Payment: 1 contributor's copy. Not copyrighted. Ads: no advertising. Subjects: Avant-Garde, Experimental Art, Fiction, Non-Fiction, Poetry, Prose, Short Stories.

•**Upstart Crow Literary,** P.O. Box 25404, Brooklyn, NY 11202, info@upstartcrowliterary.com. "Upstart Crow Literary is an entirely green company, and we accept submissions only via email. We do not accept submissions via hard copy and the US Mail. Mailed submissions will be tossed unread into the recycle bin. (Is this because were eco-conscious? Or because we hate messing about with giant stacks of paper and letter openers and having to lick envelopes and stick stamps and make frequent trips to the post office? Perhaps it is for both reasons.)." No titles listed in the *Small Press Record of Books in Print* (36th Edition, 2010-11).

UPSTREET, Vivian Dorsel, Editor; Robin Oliveira, Fiction Editor; Harrison Candelaria Fletcher, Creative Nonfiction Editor, PO Box 105, Richmond, MA 01254-0105, Tel: (413) 441-9702, blog: http://upstreetfanclub.blogspot.com/. 2005. "*upstreet*, based in the Berkshires of Western Massachusetts, is an annual literary anthology containing the best new fiction, poetry, and creative nonfiction available. We invite you to submit your poetry, fiction, and creative nonfiction (including prose poems) for the fifth issue of *upstreet*. See website for submission guidelines. We expect the fifth issue of *upstreet* to appear in mid-June of 2009. Each author will receive a complimentary copy, and will be able to purchase more copies at a special author rate." one. sub. price $14.50; per copy $14.50; sample $12.50. 224pp. Simultaneous submissions accepted: yes. Payment: one author copy.

•**URBAN REFLECTIONS MAGAZINE,** Shanea Patterson, New York, NY 10003. 2010. Fiction, interviews, reviews, parts-of-novels. sub. price 35.00; per copy 9.99; sample 3.95. Back issues: inquire. Discounts: inquire. 110pp. Reporting time: MSS responds in 2-3 weeks. Simultaneous submissions accepted: Yes. Publishes 50% of manuscripts submitted. Payment: No payment is being offered at this time. Not copyrighted. Pub's reviews. §Materials surrounding the ethnic/multi-cultural experience in a positive light. Ads: $50-half page display$75-quarter page display$150-full page display. Subjects: Drama, Erotica, Novels, Reviews, Romance, Women.

The Urbana Free Library, Debra Lissak, 210 West Green Street, Urbana, IL 61801, 217-367-4057. 1874. Articles, photos, non-fiction. "Currently, all the library's publications are on the history and people of east central Illinois." avg. press run 500-1,500. 7 titles listed in the *Small Press Record of Books in Print* (36th Edition, 2010-11). Discounts: retail and wholesale schedules are available on request. *History of Champaign County; Combined 1893, 1913, and 1929 Atlases of Champaign County*, and *From Salt Fork to Chickamauga* are short-discounted. Pages vary. Payment: usually 15% of net. Subjects: Genealogy, Geography, Government, History, Illinois, Indexes & Abstracts, Libraries, Midwest, Military, Veterans, Photography, Transportation.

Urion Press, Alan Rosenus, PO Box 10085, San Jose, CA 95157, 408-867-7695 phone/Fax. 1972. Fiction. "Reprints, fiction, history. Please send letter of inquiry first." avg. press run 2.5M. Expects 1 title 2010. 6 titles listed in the *Small Press Record of Books in Print* (36th Edition, 2010-11). Discounts: bookstores 40% on orders over 3, jobbers 50% on orders over 10. 250pp. Reporting time: 1 month. Copyrights for author. Subjects: Fiction, History, Literature (General).

Utah State University Press, Michael Spooner, John Alley, 3078 Old Main Hill, Logan, UT 84322-3078, 435-797-1362, Fax 435-797-0313, michael.spooner@usu.edu (editorial) web: www.USUPress.org. 1972. "Scholarly books." avg. press run 1-2K. Pub'd 16 titles 2009; expects 16 titles 2010, 16 titles 2011. No titles listed in the *Small Press Record of Books in Print* (36th Edition, 2010-11). Discounts: retail, wholesale, educ. 200pp. Reporting time: 6 weeks. Simultaneous submissions accepted: no. Publishes 10% of manuscripts submitted. Payment: yes. Does not copyright for author. Subjects: Education, English, Environment, Folklore, History, Mormon, Native American, Nature, Poetry, Southwest, Utah, The West, Wildlife.

The Utility Company LLC, Kenneth Massie, 15893 Northgate Drive, Dumfries, VA 22025-1704, 703 583.4408. 2002. Non-fiction. Expects 1 title 2010, 1 title 2011. No titles listed in the *Small Press Record of Books in Print* (36th Edition, 2010-11). 100-250pp. Simultaneous submissions accepted: No. Publishes 1% of manuscripts submitted. Does not copyright for author. Subjects: Business & Economics, Consulting, Energy,

Leadership, Management, Mentoring/Coaching, Motivation, Success.

UTNE READER, Nina Utne, Chair; David Schimke, Executive Editor; Keith Goetzman, Senior Editor; Julie Hanus, Assistant Editor; Hannah Lobel, Assistant Editor, 12 North 12th St., Suite 400, Minneapolis, MN 55403, 612-338-5040, www.utne.com. 1984. Articles, art, photos, cartoons, interviews, satire, criticism, reviews, letters, news items, non-fiction. "*Utne Reader* is a digest of alternative ideas and material reprinted from alternative and independent media. We don't accept unsolicited reviews, but we do accept unsolicited essays and cartoons." circ. 228M. 6/yr. Pub'd 6 issues 2009; expects 6 issues 2010, 6 issues 2011. sub. price $19.97; per copy $4.99; sample $7 (includes p/h). Back issues: $7, some older issues are $25. Discounts: inquire. 104pp. Reporting time: 2 months. Payment: varies. Copyrighted, reverts to author. Pub's reviews: 60-80 in 2009. §All independently-published books and periodicals welcome. Ads: $16,080/$9,650/$4.70 classified word. Subjects: Culture, Current Affairs, Society.

V

Vagabond Press, Richard Kendrick, PO Box 4830, Austin, TX 78765-4830, (512) 343-1540, vagabondpress@sbcglobal.net, vagabondpress.com. 2004. Poetry, fiction. "Publishing vital, innovative literary works." avg. press run 1000. Pub'd 1 title 2009; expects 2 titles 2010, 1 title 2011. 5 titles listed in the *Small Press Record of Books in Print* (36th Edition, 2010-11). Reporting time: 3-4 weeks. Simultaneous submissions accepted: Yes. Copyrights for author. Subjects: Fiction, Poetry.

VALLUM: CONTEMPORARY POETRY, Joshua Auerbach, Helen Zisimatos, PO Box 48003, Montreal, QC H2V 4S8, Canada, info@vallummag.com, www.vallummag.com. 2000. Poetry, articles, art, photos, interviews, criticism, reviews, long-poems, concrete art, non-fiction. "We publish poetry that's fresh and edgy, contemporary and well-crafted. Send 4-7 unpublished poems. Recent contributors: Paul Muldoon, Stephen Dunn, John Kinsella, Anne Simpson, Charles Bernstein, Erin Moure." circ. 2500. 2/yr. Pub'd 2 issues 2009; expects 2 issues 2010, 2 issues 2011. sub. price $17 CDN (Canada); $15.50 US (United States); $23 USD (outside North America); per copy $9 CDN (Canada); $7.95 US (United States); $12 USD (outside North America). 100pp. Reporting time: 6 - 12 months. Simultaneous submissions accepted: no. Publishes less than 2% of manuscripts submitted. Payment: rates vary, honorarium and 1 copy. Copyrighted, reverts to author. Pub's reviews: 10 in 2009. §Poetry books, chapbooks, essays on poetry and poetics. Ads: $225 (CDN) full page, $125 (CDN) half page. Subjects: Arts, Book Reviewing, Essays, Interviews, Literary Review, Photography, Poetry, Reviews, Translation, Visual Arts, Writers/Writing.

•Valuable Quality Publishing Company, Gwyndolyn McClellan, 4930 Capri Avenue, Sarasota,, FL 34235-4320, 941-351-8581. 2006. Poetry, fiction, cartoons, non-fiction. "Children's Books." avg. press run 500. Expects 4 titles 2010, 10 titles 2011. No titles listed in the *Small Press Record of Books in Print* (36th Edition, 2010-11). Discounts: 55%. 300pp. Reporting time: 30 days. Simultaneous submissions accepted: Yes. Publishes 5% of manuscripts submitted. Payment: industry standrad. Does not copyright for author. Subjects: Inspirational, Non-Fiction.

Van Cleave Publishing, Erik Fortman, 1712 Riverside Dr. #93, Austin, TX 78741, 5126655451. 2004. Fiction, non-fiction. "Van Cleave Publishing seeks to promote two types of books. Fiction books will be creative and progressive. We appreciate the work of the Lost Generation forward.Non-Fiction books will be the base of the company. We are concentrating on books concerning politics, World & American History, and government. VCP concentrates on conspiracy theory and history revision." avg. press run 10000. Expects 3 titles 2010, 10 titles 2011. No titles listed in the *Small Press Record of Books in Print* (36th Edition, 2010-11). Discounts: 2-4 copies 20%5-9 copies 30%10-19 copies 40%20-49 copies 50%100+ copies 60%. 300pp. Reporting time: 6-12 weeks. Simultaneous submissions accepted: No. Publishes 10% of manuscripts submitted. Payment: Up to $500 in advance, and 15% of net. Copyrights for author. Subjects: Anarchist, Beat, Civil War, Communism, Marxism, Leninism, Counter-Culture, Alternatives, Communes, Drugs, History, Holocaust, Libertarian, Literature (General), Military, Veterans, Political Science, Politics, Science Fiction, Texas.

Vanderbilt University Press, Sue Havlish, VU Station B #351813, 2301 Vanderbilt Place, Nashville, TN 37235-1813, 615-343-2446. 1940. Criticism, letters, non-fiction. "The Press's primary mission is to select, produce, market, and disseminate scholarly publications of outstanding quality and originality. In conjunction with the long-term development of its editorial program, the Press draws on and supports the intellectual activities of the University and its faculty. Although its main emphasis falls in the area of scholarly publishing, the Press also publishes books of substance and significance that are of interest to the general public, including regional books. In this regard, the Press also supports Vanderbilt's service and outreach to the larger local and national community.'' Pub'd 15 titles 2009; expects 20 titles 2010, 30 titles 2011. No titles listed in the *Small Press Record of Books in Print* (36th Edition, 2010-11). Reporting time: 1 month. Simultaneous submissions accepted: Yes. Publishes 5% of manuscripts submitted. Payment: small royalties. We usually copyright in the name of the press, but will copyright in the name of the author if asked. Subjects: Arts, Black, Chicano/a, Children, Youth, Cities, Criticism, English, Folklore, Health, Labor, Language, Latin America, Literary Review, Literature (General), Men.

VanderWyk & Burnham, PO Box 2789, Acton, MA 01720, 978-263-7595, FAX:866-614-7405, email:info@VandB.com, www.VandB.com. 1994. Non-fiction. avg. press run 3M. Pub'd 6 titles 2009; expects 4 titles 2010, 4 titles 2011. 27 titles listed in the *Small Press Record of Books in Print* (36th Edition, 2010-11). 182pp. Reporting time: 1-6 months. Simultaneous submissions accepted: yes. Publishes 2% of manuscripts submitted. Payment: advances $0-2000; royalty 5-10%. Copyrights for author. Subjects: Aging, Autobiography, Education, Family, Humanism, Non-Fiction, Psychology, Self-Help, Social Work, Women.

Vanguard Press, Steve Parker M.D., Editor & CEO, PO Box 1198, Higley, AZ 85236, Phone: 480-695-3192, Web: www.VanguardPress.us, Email: info@vanguardpress.us. 2007. Non-fiction. ''We focus on issues related to human health.'' avg. press run 2000. Expects 1 title 2010, 2 titles 2011. 1 title listed in the *Small Press Record of Books in Print* (36th Edition, 2010-11). 300pp. Reporting time: 30 days. Manuscript will not be returned. Simultaneous submissions accepted: Yes. Subjects: Aging, AIDS, Alternative Medicine, Arizona, Disabled, Disease, Drugs, Health, Nursing, Nutrition, Psychiatry, Science.

Vanilla Heart Publishing, Kimberlee Williams, Managing Editor, 10121 Evergreen Way, Bldg 25, Suite 156, Everett, WA 98204, 425-609-4718, VHP1@vanillaheartbooksandauthors.com, http://www.vanillaheartbooksandauthors.com. 2006. Fiction, non-fiction. ''romance, horror, thriller, suspense, mystery, paranormal, and LGBT, writing and publishing non-fiction to assist authors in improving style.Chelle Cordero, Smoky Trudeau, Victoria Howard, Marilyn C. Morris, Robert Hays, Brenda Hill, L.E. Harvey, Collin Kelley, Kate Evans, Mary Quast, Jeffrey Martin, Vila SpiderHawk, Eva Gordon, Kelsey Chasen, Misha Crews, K.D Richardson, Ryan Callaway, Sarah Natalia Lee, Kimberly McKay.'' avg. press run 1750. Pub'd 26 titles 2009; expects 32 titles 2010, 30 titles 2011. 62 titles listed in the *Small Press Record of Books in Print* (36th Edition, 2010-11). Discounts: standard trade discounts through Ingram, Baker & Taylor, Gardner's, Bertram's and Follett.Indie booksellers without trade distribution accounts receive 30-35% discount with prepay. 300pp. Reporting time: 3 weeks. Simultaneous submissions accepted: Yes. Publishes 27% of manuscripts submitted. Payment: July and October royalty payments. depends on previous copyrights obtained prior to contract; in general, publisher copyrights for author in author's name upon receipt of required forms. Subjects: Anthology, Crime, Fantasy, Fiction, Folklore, Gay, History, How-To, Lifestyles, Mystery, Prose, Relationships, Romance, Science Fiction, Supernatural.

VANITAS, Vincent Katz, 211 West 19th Street, #5, New York, NY 10011-4001, vanitas@el.net. 2005. Poetry, fiction, art, photos, criticism, parts-of-novels. ''VANITAS was founded to add a voice in a time of crisis; also as a means of collective inquiry or discovery into current problems, using primarily voices of artists. A conversation among the arts is stimulated; poets combined with artists in other fields. Contributors to the first two issues include: Tom Clark, Kate Colby, Nada Gordon, Richard Hell, Fannie Howe, Joanne Kyger, Ann Lauterbach, Brendan Lorber, Judith Malina, Ange Mlinko, Laura Moriarty, Jeni Olin, Akilah Oliver, Nick Piombino, Jerome Sala, Ed Sanders, Ron Silliman, Anne Waldman, Peter Lamborn Wilson, Stephanie Young. Featured artists in first two issues: Jim Dine and Kiki Smith.'' circ. 750. 1/yr. Expects 1 issue 2010, 1 issue 2011. 1 title listed in the *Small Press Record of Books in Print* (36th Edition, 2010-11). sub. price One issue $10/Two issues $18; per copy $10. Discounts: case sensitive. 140pp. Simultaneous submissions accepted: No. Copyrighted, reverts to author. Pub's reviews: approx. 2 in 2009. §poetry, literary history. Ads: For ads contact vanitas@el.net. Subjects: Experimental, Performing Arts, Poetry.

Vantage Press, Inc., Richard Fairbanks, 419 Park Ave. S., New York, NY 10016, Ph:212-736-1767, F: 212-736-2273, 1-800-882-3273. 1949. Poetry, fiction, satire, criticism, parts-of-novels, long-poems, plays, non-fiction. avg. press run 450. No titles listed in the *Small Press Record of Books in Print* (36th Edition, 2010-11). Simultaneous submissions accepted: Yes. Copyrights for author.

VARIOUS ARTISTS, Tony Lewis-Jones, 24, Northwick Road, Bristol BS7 0UG, England. 1992. Poetry, fiction, articles, interviews, music, letters, non-fiction. ''Circulation is by email to a select list of subscribers, including the ground-breaking publishers Rattapallax of New York and nthposition of London. We also have good links with Haiku Ireland & Poetry Scotland. Subscriptions are US $12/year, $20 Canadian etc., cheques please to A Lewis-Jones. Please send no more than 6 poems in the body of an email to: tonylj@firewater.fsworld.co.uk.'' Pub'd 150 issues 2009. Reporting time: 1 week. Payment: Some commissioned work by arrangement. Copyrighted, reverts to author. Pub's reviews: 5 in 2009. §Any poetry which meets the criteria above. Ads: none. Subjects: Arts, Culture, Haiku, Literary Review, Literature (General), Media, Poetry, Wales, Women, Writers/Writing.

Varro Press, Michael Nossaman, PO Box 8413, Shawnee Mission, KS 66208, 913-385-2034, Fax 913-385-2039, varropress@aol.com. 1992. Non-fiction. "Publisher of law enforcement, security, executive protection training manuals, handbooks, etc." avg. press run 1M. Pub'd 1 title 2009; expects 1 title 2010, 1 title 2011. 13 titles listed in the *Small Press Record of Books in Print* (36th Edition, 2010-11). Discounts: 10+ 20%. Pages vary. Reporting time: 120 days. Simultaneous submissions accepted: no. Payment: 10%+ Author royalty, paid semi-annually. No advance. Copyrights for author. Subjects: Safety, Weapons.

Vedanta Press, R. Adjemian, 1946 Vedanta Place, Hollywood, CA 90068-3996, 323-960-1728, e-mail address: bob@vedanta.org, web address: www.vedanta.com, web page shows our online catalog. Note that titles with an asterisk by the title in the catalog are not wholesale titles. 1947. Non-fiction. "Although I am open to 'that special title', we generally do not print from outside our organization. As a matter of fact, we are mainly keeping our previous titles in print. Rarely is a 'new' title published." avg. press run 3M. Pub'd 2 titles 2009; expects 1 title 2010, 3 titles 2011. 16 titles listed in the *Small Press Record of Books in Print* (36th Edition, 2010-11). Discounts: 5+ 40%. 150pp. Payment: no royalty to authors - no payments. Copyrights are usually to Vedanta Society or Vedanta Press. Subject: Religion.

VEGETARIAN JOURNAL, The Vegetarian Resource Group, Debra Wasserman, Managing Editor; Keryl Cryer, Senior Editor, P.O. Box 1463, Baltimore, MD 21203, 410-366-VEGE (8343). 1982. Articles, art, cartoons, interviews, reviews, letters, news items, non-fiction. circ. 20M. 4/yr. Pub'd 4 issues 2009; expects 4 issues 2010, 4 issues 2011. sub. price $20; per copy $4.50; sample $4. Back issues: inquire. Discounts: inquire. 36pp. Reporting time: 1 month. Simultaneous submissions accepted: no. Payment: inquire. Copyrighted, we retain reprint rights. Pub's reviews: 16 in 2009. §Vegetarianism, animal rights, scientific nutrition, recipes. Ads: none. Subjects: Animals, Consumer, Cooking, Ecology, Foods, Health, Vegetarianism.

The Vegetarian Resource Group (see also VEGETARIAN JOURNAL), Debra Wasserman, Charles Stahler, P.O. Box 1463, Baltimore, MD 21203, 410-366-8343. 1982. avg. press run 8M. Pub'd 3 titles 2009; expects 3 titles 2010, 3 titles 2011. 14 titles listed in the *Small Press Record of Books in Print* (36th Edition, 2010-11). Discounts: 40% bookstores. 224pp. Subjects: Cooking, Ecology, Foods, Vegetarianism.

Vehicule Press, Simon Dardick, General Editor; Carmine Starnino, Poetry Editor; Andrew Steinmetz, Fiction Editor, PO Box 125, Place du Parc Station, Montreal, Quebec H2X 4A3, Canada, 514-844-6073, FAX 514-844-7543, vp@vehiculepress.com, www.vehiculepress.com. 1973. Poetry, fiction, non-fiction. "Publishers of Canadian literary works with occasional titles in the area of urban social history and feminism. Actively publish fiction in translation (French [Quebec] to English). Recent publications: *The Rent Collector* by B. Glen Rotchin, *The New Canon: An Anthology of Canadian Poetry* edited by Carmine Starnino, *How We All Swiftly: The First Six Books* by Don Coles, *Out to Dry in Cape Breton* by Anita Lahey, *Dr. Delicious: Memoirs of a Life in CanLit* by Robert Lecker." avg. press run 1M-1.5M. Pub'd 12 titles 2009; expects 15 titles 2010, 14 titles 2011. 167 titles listed in the *Small Press Record of Books in Print* (36th Edition, 2010-11). Discounts: jobbers 20%; bookstores 40%; occasional short-discounted title 20%; please inquire. Poetry 76pp, other 300pp. Reporting time: 3 months. Simultaneous submissions accepted: no. Payment: generally 10-12%. Copyrights for author. Subjects: Canada, Cities, Dining, Restaurants, Fiction, Multicultural, Non-Fiction, Poetry, Short Stories, Translation.

VEIL: Journal of Darker Musings, Subsynchronuos Press, Hillary Lyon, 4729 E. Sunrise, #326, Tucson, AZ 85718, Subsyncpress.com. 2002. Poetry. "We are looking for your darker poetic musings—whether Gothic, sci-fi, or comically spooky. Free verse stands a better chance with us than rhyme. Length is no issue; quality is. Recent contributors include: David Stone, Lyn Lifshin, Gary Every, Cardinal Cox." 50/yr. Pub'd 1 issue 2009; expects 1 issue 2010, 1 issue 2011. price per copy 5.00; sample 3. Back issues: inquire. 34pp. Reporting time: 3 to 6 months. Simultaneous submissions accepted: No. Publishes 20% of manuscripts submitted. Payment: Contriburs receive one free copy of the issue their work appears in; additional copies are discounted. Copyrighted, reverts to author. Subjects: Experimental, Haiku, Horror, Science Fiction, Surrealism.

Velazquez Press, Claudia P. Huesca, 9682 Telstar Ave. Suite 110, El Monte, CA 91731, 626-448-3448, 626-602-3817, info@academiclearningcompany.com, www.velazquezpress.com. 2003. Non-fiction. "Velazquez Press prides itself on publishing bilingual reference and language education material." avg. press run 10,000. Pub'd 4 titles 2009; expects 3 titles 2010, 12 titles 2011. 1 title listed in the *Small Press Record of Books in Print* (36th Edition, 2010-11). Discounts: 40-55%. Reporting time: 1 month. Simultaneous submissions accepted: Yes. Publishes 10% of manuscripts submitted. Payment: The author usually receives 10 % of the retail sales of the book. Copyrights for author. Subjects: Bilingual, Dictionaries, Education, Language, Reference.

VERB: An Audioquarterly, Daren Wang, Publisher & Editor, PO Box 2684, Decatur, GA 30031. "Original fiction, poetry and music exclusively in audio."

VERBATIM: The Language Quarterly, Erin McKean, Editor, PO Box 597302, Chicago, IL 60659. "We look for articles that explain and illuminate without condescending; that are funny; that are moving; that are fascinating; that are less than 3,000 words; that are all of the above. There are some kinds of articles we are always interested in: Articles on the insider jargons of professions: best boys, dental hygienists, taxidermists, sous-chefs, prison wardens. Articles about the history of grammar "rules." Articles about bygone language theories. Payment is made at the time of publication, and ranges from $25 to $500, depending on length, wit, and other merit."

VERSAL, Megan M. Garr, Editor; Sarah Ream, Managing Editor; Robert Glick, Fiction Editor, Amsterdam, Holland, versaljournal@wordsinhere.com (queries only), http://versal.wordsinhere.com. 2002. Poetry, fiction, art, photos, letters, long-poems, plays. "We look for writers with an instinct for language and line break, for the urgent, involved, and unexpected. Recent contributors include Sawako Nakayasu, Russell Edson, Marilyn Hacker, David Miller, B.J. Hollars, Jeffery Beam, Naomi Shihab Nye, Myronn Hardy, Alissa Nutting and Andrew Michael Roberts. Reading Period: Sept 15-Jan 15. We only accept submissions through an online submission system, which is available through our website during the reading period." circ. 750. 1/yr. Pub'd 1 issue 2009; expects 1 issue 2010, 1 issue 2011. sub. price 2 yr: USD 27; 3 yr: USD 39; per copy USD 15. 100pp. Reporting time: 1-3 months. Simultaneous submissions accepted: yes. Publishes 8% of manuscripts submitted. Payment: copy. Copyrighted, reverts to author. Ads: Interested in exchange ads with other literary journals. Subjects: Fiction, Literature (General), Multicultural, Poetry, Prose, Short Stories, Visual Arts.

VERSE, Andrew Zawacki, Brian Henry, Department of English, University of Georgia, Athens, GA 30602. 1984. Poetry, articles, interviews, criticism, reviews. "Articles on contemporary, 10 to 20 pages long, most suitable. We publish a large number of translations of poetry, and poetry by British, American, Australian and international writers. Recent contributors: Kenneth Koch, Allen Grossman, Peter Porter, Medbh McGuckian, Charles Wright, Kevin Hart, Karen Volkman, James Tate, August Kleinzahler, John Kinsella, Penelope Shuttle, Charles Bernstein, and John Ashbery. Translations of Tomaz Salamun, Ales Debeljak, Eugen Jebeleanu." circ. 1M. 3/yr. Pub'd 3 issues 2009; expects 3 issues 2010, 3 issues 2011. sub. price $18 individual, $30 institution; per copy $8; sample $6. Back issues: $5. 128-256pp. Reporting time: 3-6 months. Simultaneous submissions accepted: yes. Publishes about 1% of manuscripts submitted. Payment: 2 copies and 1-year subscription. Copyrighted, reverts to author. Pub's reviews: 60 in 2009. §Poetry, poetry criticism, interviews with poets. Ads: $150 full page.

Verve Press, Jenny Goldfisher, Assistant Editor, PO Box 1997, Huntington Beach, CA 92647, fax: 714-840-8335. 1986. avg. press run 4M. Pub'd 1 title 2009; expects 1 title 2010, 1 title 2011. 2 titles listed in the *Small Press Record of Books in Print* (36th Edition, 2010-11). Discounts: bookstores less than 4 20%, more 50% non-returnable; 40% returnable, 20% college textbook stores. 216pp. Does not copyright for author. Subjects: Creativity, Writers/Writing.

Vestibular Disorders Association, Lisa Haven PhD, PO Box 13305, Portland, OR 97213-0305, 503-229-7705, Fax 503-229-8064, toll-free 1-800-837-8428, veda@vestibular.org, www.vestibular.org. 1983. Articles, interviews, reviews, news items, non-fiction. "Please do not send unsolicited manuscripts." Pub'd 3 titles 2009; expects 3 titles 2010, 3 titles 2011. 3 titles listed in the *Small Press Record of Books in Print* (36th Edition, 2010-11). Discounts: none. Simultaneous submissions accepted: no. Payment: negotiated. Copyrights for author. Subjects: Aging, Disabled, Disease, Health, Medicine, Newsletter, Psychology, Research, Social Security.

Village Lane Press, Dean Unger, 10024 Wilson Rd., Winfield, Canada, 250-870-8278. 2005. Art, photos, non-fiction. "At Village Lane Press our mandate is to seek out, preserve and present good books that promote skill and intellect in a concise, thoughtful manner that we hope will entertain and inform. We strive to acquire and publish the otherwise unobtainable lost classics and undiscovered works in the practical arts. From hunting & fishing, archery, wilderness survival, homesteading and fine crafts, to ranching, farming, and animal husbandry, to techniques of the masters in fine arts, and traditional medicine, we are building and preserving a library of significant historic and practical importance. Recent titles published in the Traditional Archery Collection: Essay on Archery, by Walter Moseley; How To Train in Archery, by Maurice Thompson; Treatise on Archery, Thomas Waring; Archers' Complete Guide or Instructions for Use of the Long Bow, etc." avg. press run 1000. Pub'd 6 titles 2009; expects 10 titles 2010, 15 titles 2011. 6 titles listed in the *Small Press Record of Books in Print* (36th Edition, 2010-11). Discounts: depending on number of units ordered and order frequency, we offer 40-50% trade discounts to distributors, 35-40% to bookstores and institutions. Please contact with any questions. 150pp. Reporting time: approx. 4-6 weeks. Simultaneous submissions accepted: Yes. Payment: usually 10%. Advance negotiable. Copyrights for author. Subjects: Architecture, Arthurian, Arts, Aviation, Conservation, Construction, Crafts, Hobbies, Creativity, Engineering, Forensic Science, History, How-To, Massage, Medicine, Reprints.

Vintage Romance Publishing, LLC, Dawn Carrington, Editor and Business Manager, 2520 Atlantic Palms Lane #908, N. Charleston, SC 29406-9298, (843) 270-3742, www.vrpublishing.com, submissions@vrpublishing.com. 2004. Poetry, fiction, non-fiction. "Vintage Romance Publishing is interested in publishing nostalgic romances set anytime before 1969. We have several lines of historical romance including romantic suspense, era romances, comedy, inspirational, and coming soon, we will debut our Mystique line specifically for African-American historicals and Spanish Eyes specifically for Hispanic historicals. We publish a select amount of non-fiction dealing with romance, i.e., true love stories, and we will be publishing anthologies each year with different types of short stories." Expects 5-10 titles 2010, 10-15 titles 2011. No titles listed in the *Small Press Record of Books in Print* (36th Edition, 2010-11). Discounts: 2-10 copies 25%11-15 copies 27%. 200pp. Reporting time: Within one week for query, one month for partial submission and three months for full. Simultaneous submissions accepted: No. Publishes 5% of manuscripts submitted. Payment: Authors receive 40% of the download price and we pay royalties every three months. Does not copyright for author. Subjects: Family, Fiction, History, Non-Fiction, Novels, Poetry, Prose, Romance, Vietnam, World War II.

Virginia City Publishing Co. LLC, Leland Cross, P.O. Box 51389, Sparks, NV 89435, 775-359-8453. 2006. Fiction, non-fiction. "We primarily publish fiction; historical fiction, science fiction, fantasy, alternate history.Two non-fiction historical works are planned for 2008." avg. press run 500. Pub'd 2 titles 2009; expects 1 title 2010. No titles listed in the *Small Press Record of Books in Print* (36th Edition, 2010-11). Discounts: Until our website is set up in August, all distribution is through Lightning Source. 235pp. Reporting time: Indeterminate. Simultaneous submissions accepted: No. Payment: Indeterminate. Copyrights for author. Subjects: Civil War, Fiction, Folklore, History, Novels, Science Fiction, Self-Help, World War II.

THE VIRGINIA QUARTERLY REVIEW, Ted Genoways, Editor, One West Range, University of Virginia, PO Box 400223, Charlottesville, VA 22904-4223, Email: vqr@vwronline.org, ph: 434-924-3124, web: www.vqronline.org. 1925. Poetry, fiction, articles, art, photos, satire, criticism, reviews, long-poems, non-fiction. "Only accepts submissions online at http://www.vqronline.org/submission/; does not accept submissions via mail or email." circ. 6,000+. 4/yr. Pub'd 4 issues 2009; expects 4 issues 2010, 4 issues 2011. sub. price $32 individual, $36 institution; per copy $14; sample $14. 288pp. Reporting time: 1-3 months. Simultaneous submissions accepted: yes, but notify us immediately if work is accepted elsewhere. Publishes less than 1% of manuscripts submitted. Payment: Fiction & Nonfiction: $100/typeset page; Poetry: $5/line, $200 minimum per poem. Exclusive first serial rights in North America, nonexclusive online rights. Pub's reviews: 200 in 2009. §All. Ads: $300 full-page, $180 half-page. Subjects: Book Reviewing, Culture, Current Affairs, Fiction, Global Affairs, Government, History, Literature (General), Poetry, Politics, Reprints, Short Stories.

•**Visible Ink Press,** 43311 Joy Road #414, Canton, MI 48187-2075. "Visible Ink Press publishes mega-works that inform and entertain in the areas of popular culture, science, history, religion, and government. Packed with facts, handsomely illustrated, and armed with great indexes, these big bold beautiful books are built by experts to satisfy that lust for information, whatever the intensity or level of social acceptance. Aside from the usual work-release interns, the Visible Ink Press editorial and design community brings decades of unique information manipulation skills, second only to professional politicians." No titles listed in the *Small Press Record of Books in Print* (36th Edition, 2010-11).

Vision Works Publishing, Dr. Joseph Rubino, PO Box 217, Boxford, MA 01921, 888-821-3135, Fax 630-982-2134, visionworksbooks@email.com. 1999. Fiction, non-fiction. "We focus on personal development, leadership, self-improvement titles that champion the human spirit and enhance productivity and communication." avg. press run 4M. Pub'd 4 titles 2009; expects 4 titles 2010, 4 titles 2011. 4 titles listed in the *Small Press Record of Books in Print* (36th Edition, 2010-11). 180pp. Reporting time: 60 days. Simultaneous submissions accepted: yes. Publishes 10% of manuscripts submitted. Payment: negotiable. Will copyright for author if desired. Subjects: Business & Economics, Self-Help, Young Adult.

VISIONHOPE NEWSLETTER, BELIEVERS EXCHANGE NEWSLETTER, Annagail Lynes, 3540 East Amelia Avenue, Phoenix, AZ 85018, 206-350-2237, publisher@annagaillynes.net, www.annagaillynes.net. 2000. Articles, non-fiction. "Although geared toward young adults, it is enjoyed by those young and those more mature alike." 6/yr. Pub'd 6 issues 2009; expects 6 issues 2010, 6 issues 2011. sub. price $15; per copy $3; sample $3. Back issues: $3. 12pp. Reporting time: 1 month. Simultaneous submissions accepted: yes. Publishes 50% of manuscripts submitted. Payment: complimentary copy. Copyrighted, reverts to author. Subject: Young Adult.

VISIONS-INTERNATIONAL, The World Journal of Illustrated Poetry, Black Buzzard Press, Bradley R. Strahan, Publisher, Poetry Editor; Shirley G. Sullivan, Associate Editor; Melissa Bell, Review Editor; Jeff Minor, Art Editor; Lane Jennings, Circulation, 3503 Ferguson Lane, Austin, TX 78754. 1979. Poetry, art, photos, reviews. "We are looking for poetry that excites the imagination, that says things in fascinating new ways (even if they are the same old things), that hits people 'where they live.' We are open minded about poetry styles but send us *only your best*. You may include matching pen and ink illustrations. We don't care if you're a big name but we do expect poetry that is well worked (no poetasters please). We are always looking for good translations, particularly of work not previously rendered into English and from unusual languages such as Catalan, Celtic languages, Malayan (please include original language version when submitting). Prefer poems under 60 lines (but will consider longer). Recent contributors: Louis Simpson, Naomi Shihab-Nye, Lawrence

523

Ferlinghetti, Marilyn Hacker, Michael Mott, Ai, Sharon Olds, Charles Wright, Miller Williams, Eamon Grennan, Andrei Codrescu, T. Alan Broughton and Marilyn Krysl. Please don't submit more than 6, or less than 3 poems at a time (not more than once a year unless requested). Strongly recommend getting a sample copy (cost $4.95) before submitting material. *Submissions without SASE will be trashed!* We are indexed in *The Index of American Periodical Verse*, the *Roths Periodical Index*, the *American Humanities Index*, and *Roths Index of Poetry Periodicals*. We are also in *Ulrich's* periodicals listings.'' circ. 750. 2/yr. Pub'd 2 issues 2009; expects 2 issues 2010, 2 issues 2011. 3 titles listed in the *Small Press Record of Books in Print* (36th Edition, 2010-11). We now only offer a 4 issue subscription for $25. Special LIBRARY rates, Please inquire; price per copy $6.50. add $3 per copy for Europe Airmail, $4 for airmail to Asia, Africa and the South Pacific or $2.50 for Airmail to Latin America and the Carribean; sample $4.95 plus same postage as single copy. Back issues: quoted on request (a full backrun is still available). Discounts: bulk 30+ copies 30%. 48pp. Reporting time: 3 days to 3 weeks, unless we are out of the country. Publishes 1% of manuscripts submitted. Payment: 1 contributor's copy, we hope to get money to pay contributors at least $5 per poem in future. Copyrighted, reverts to author. Ads: none. Subjects: Literary Review, Poetry, Translation.

•**Visual Arts Press,** Missy Loewe, PO Box 10621, Gaithersburg, MD 20898, 301-661-6590. 2009. Non-fiction. ''Small press publishing business and how-to books concerning art, for artists and their buyers. Recent projects include an art markeing guide for artists, a how-to guide for brides when choosing a photographer, and a how-to book for those breaking into print modeling.'' avg. press run 1000. Expects 1 title 2010, 3 titles 2011. No titles listed in the *Small Press Record of Books in Print* (36th Edition, 2010-11). Discounts: 2-5 copies, 30% 6-99 copies, 40% 100+ copies, 50%. 300pp. Reporting time: 60 days. Simultaneous submissions accepted: Yes. Publishes 10% of manuscripts submitted. Payment: varies. Copyrights for author. Subjects: Advertising, Self-Promotion, Arts, How-To, Marketing, Photography, Public Relations/Publicity.

Visual Studies Workshop (see also AFTERIMAGE), Tate Shaw, Director, Tate Shaw, Tate Shaw, 31 Prince Street, Rochester, NY 14607, 585-442-8676, www.vsw.org. 1972. Art, photos, interviews, criticism, reviews, concrete art, news items. avg. press run 1M. Pub'd 12 titles 2009; expects 12 titles 2010, 12 titles 2011. 34 titles listed in the *Small Press Record of Books in Print* (36th Edition, 2010-11). Discounts: 20% to bookstores. Pages vary. Payment: varies. Copyrights for author. Subjects: Arts, Book Arts, Photography.

VITAE SCHOLASTICAE: The Journal of Educational Biography, Caddo Gap Press, Patricia Inman, Editor; Naomi Norquay, Editor, 3145 Geary Boulevard #275, San Francisco, CA 94118, 415-392-1911. 1980. Articles. ''The annual journal of the International Society of Educational Biography.'' circ. 200. 2/yr. Pub'd 2 issues 2009; expects 2 issues 2010, 2 issues 2011. sub. price $50 indiv., $100 instit.; per copy $50. 96pp. Reporting time: 2 months. Publishes 25% of manuscripts submitted. Payment: none. Copyrighted, reverts to author. Ads: $200 per page. Subject: Education.

VIVIPAROUS BLENNY, Douglas Mowbray, 3029 Arizona Avenue, Baltimore, MD 21234. 2007. Poetry, fiction, art, photos, cartoons, interviews, satire, criticism, reviews, letters, collages, non-fiction. ''Viviparous Blenny is the newest endeavor of twentythreebooks, publisher of Omar Shapli. Each year we will put out one issue centered around a theme. All high quality work that speaks to the theme will be considered. Volume I's theme is "Synchronicity." Reading period is March-July.'' circ. 500. 1/yr. Expects 1 issue 2010, 1 issue 2011. sub. price $23; per copy $23; sample $23. Back issues: $23. 200pp. Reporting time: 1-3 months. Simultaneous submissions accepted: No. Publishes 46% of manuscripts submitted. Payment: Payment is one free contributor's copy. Copyrighted, reverts to author. Pub's reviews. Ads: Full: 150Half: 75. Subjects: Absurdist, Americana, Avant-Garde, Experimental Art, Beat, Charles Bukowski, Cartoons, Comics, Creative Non-fiction, Criticism, Culture, Dada, Experimental, Fiction, Philosophy, Poetry.

VLQ (Verse Libre Quarterly), Artisan Studio Design, C.E. Laine, PO Box 185, Falls Church, VA 22040-0185, Fax 703-852-3906, editor@vlqpoetry.com, http://vlqpoetry.com. 2000. Poetry, art, photos, long-poems. ''*VLQ* looks for quality poetry of any length or style (except rhymed poetry). Past contributors include Janet Buck, Dorothy D. Mienko, Michael Meyerhofer, Ward Kelley, Lyn Lifshin, Pris Campbell, Nick Antosca, T.E. Ballard, Kristy Bown, kris t kahn, Erin Elizabeth, Michelle Cameron, David Mascellani, Jane Fenton Keane, Brett Hursey, Debrah Kayla Sterling and contributing editor C.E. Laine. *VLQ* nominates for the Pushcart Prize.'' circ. electronic, POD. Pub'd 4 issues 2009; expects 4 issues 2010, 4 issues 2011. price per copy free; sample free. 20pp. Reporting time: 60 days. Simultaneous submissions accepted: yes. Publishes 5% of manuscripts submitted. Payment: none. Not copyrighted. Subjects: Experimental, Photography, Poetry.

•**VOICE(S), Disparate Voices,** Stephanie Hicks, Los Angeles, CA 90028, editorial@disparatevoices.com, www.disparatevoices.com. 2009. Photos, letters, non-fiction. ''*Voice(s)* is looking for literary nonfiction and black and white photography that celebrates the nuances of the world and the people in it. For additional information, please see our website.'' circ. 50. 1/yr. Expects 1 issue 2010, 1 issue 2011. sample price free. Back issues: Inquire. Discounts: Not-for-profit; by donation only. 35pp. Reporting time: Expect to hear back no sooner than a couple weeks to a month after the stated deadline. Simultaneous submissions accepted: No. Publishes 2% of manuscripts submitted. Payment: A complimentary copy is sent to all selected contributors.

Copyrighted, reverts to author. Ads: no advertisements. Subjects: Creative Non-fiction, Creativity, Desktop Publishing, How-To, Humanism, Humor, Los Angeles, Magazines, Memoirs, Non-Fiction, Photography, Printing, Satire, Short Stories, Storytelling.

VOICES FROM THE EARTH, Southwest Research and Information Center, Annette Aguayo, Editor, PO Box 4524, Albuquerque, NM 87196, 505-262-1862, Fax 505-262-1864. 2000. Articles, reviews, news items. "Activist oriented. Environmental views, news and reviews on issues primarily, but not limited to, the Southwest." circ. 2.5M. 3/yr. Pub'd 3 issues 2009; expects 3 issues 2010, 3 issues 2011. sub. price $10.00 students and senior citizens, $15 individuals, $30 institutions; per copy $4.50; sample $2. Back issues: $2.50. Discounts: 40% to distributors. 12pp. Reporting time: 1 month. Payment: occasional. Copyrighted by Southwest Research & Information Center. Pub's reviews: 14 in 2009. §Environmental, consumer & social problems. Subjects: Book Reviewing, Energy, Environment, Health, New Mexico, Nuclear Energy, Southwest, Water.

VOICES ISRAEL, Michael Dickel, Co-Editor; Sheryl Abbey, Co-Editor, 9 Shalom Yehuda 7, Jerusalem, 93395, Israel, Voices_Israel_2010@me.com. 1972. Poetry. "The Voices Israel Group of Poets in English annually publishes an annual anthology of poetry, *Voices Israel*. Volume 35 of the Voices Israel Anthology, for the year 2009, is now at the printers. Submissions for volume 36, to be published in 2010, are welcome until 7 October 2009. Poems received after that date will be considered for the 2011 Anthology. *Anyone, anywhere, is welcome to submit a maximum of 4 poems in English to the anthology. Poems should not exceed 40 lines.*" circ. 400. 1/yr. Expects 1 issue 2010, 1 issue 2011. sub. price $15 / $20 postpaid advance order / after publication; per copy $20 postpaid; sample $20 postpaid. Back issues: $15-$20 as available (postpaid). Discounts: 33-1/3% off to recognized booksellers only. No library discounts. 200 - 250pp. Reporting time: report in fall/winter each year. Simultaneous submissions accepted: no. Payment: none. Copyrighted, reverts to author. Subjects: Arts, Experimental, Family, Feminism, Humor, Judaism, Marriage, Middle East, Multicultural, Non-Violence, Peace, Poetry, Religion, Spiritual, War.

Volcano Press, Inc, Ruth Gottstein, Publisher Emerita; Adam Gottstein, Publisher, PO Box 270, Volcano, CA 95689, 209-296-4991, fax 209-296-4995, Credit card or check orders only: 1-800-879-9636, e-mail sales@volcanopress.com, website http://www.volcanopress.com. 1976. News items, non-fiction. "All materials published in book form, posters, audio tapes." avg. press run 3M-5M. Pub'd 2 titles 2009; expects 4 titles 2010, 4 titles 2011. 12 titles listed in the *Small Press Record of Books in Print* (36th Edition, 2010-11). Discounts: 1-9 copies: full price, 10-24 copies: 20% discount, 25-49 copies: 25%, 50-99 copies: 30%, 100+ copies: 35%. Reporting time: 3 months. Payment: Royalties. Copyrights for author. Subjects: Asian-American, Chicano/a, Children, Youth, Community, Folklore, Health, History, Indexes & Abstracts, Lesbianism, Psychology, Public Affairs, Reference, Religion, Society, Tapes & Records.

Vonpalisaden Publications Inc., 60 Saddlewood Drive, Hillsdale, NJ 07642-1336, 201-664-4919. 1986. Non-fiction. "Currently pet/hobby (dogs) animal book publisher (so far non-fiction only). *The Rottweiler: An International Study of the Breed,* by Dr. Dagmar Hodinar." avg. press run 5M. Pub'd 1 title 2009. 1 title listed in the *Small Press Record of Books in Print* (36th Edition, 2010-11). Discounts: for resale: 1-9 copies 20%, 10-25 30%, 26-50 40%, 51-99 45%, 100+ 50% plus addit. 10% on net if displayed in catalogue. 350+pp. Subjects: Animals, Pets.

VOX, VOX Press, Louis Bourgeois, P.O Box 527, Oxford, MS 38655-0527, (662) 801-2167. 2004. Poetry, fiction, interviews, criticism, reviews, collages, plays, non-fiction. "*Vox* is an avant-garde journal that seeks to publish the most extreme forms of literature being written in the 21st century." circ. 500. 1-2/yr. Pub'd 1 issue 2009; expects 1 issue 2010, 2 issues 2011. price per copy $6.00; sample $5.00. Back issues: $5.00. Discounts: 300. 100pp. Reporting time: 3 months. Simultaneous submissions accepted: Yes. Payment: Publication is payment. Copyrighted, reverts to author. Pub's reviews: 4 in 2009. §Experimental novel. Ads: None. Subjects: Absurdist, Anarchist, Surrealism.

•Vox Humana Books, Philip Hyams, 7 Rivka Guber Street, 2, Kfar Sava, 44471, Israel, 972.54.4.803.163, publisher@voxhumana-books.com, www.voxhumana-books.com. 2009. Poetry, fiction, criticism, non-fiction. "Eclectic literature with a human voiceVox Humana Books is an independent, small literary publisher founded in 2009. The press maintains a strong focus on the publication of works by new and established international, Israeli, Palestinian and other Middle-Eastern writers and artists. Vox Humana Books will be debuting in the Fall of 2010 with a number of quality titles in fiction, non-fiction and poetry. Vox Humana Books unique emphasis is on disseminating creative work which adheres to the principles of the Human Voice in content, form and without intentional racism and discrimination, regardless of any inherent artistic or political messaging by the writer or artist themselves. We believe there is room for all differing opinions and stories that can be related while still veering away from the propagation of deliberate anti-life, inhuman diatribe.Vox Humana Books unique emphasis is on disseminating creative work which adheres to the principles of the Human Voice in content, form and without intentional racism and discrimination, regardless of any inherent artistic or political messaging by the writer or artist themselves. We believe there is room for all differing opinions and stories that can be related while still veering away from the propagation of deliberate anti-life, inhuman diatribe." Pub'd 7 titles 2009. No titles listed in the *Small Press Record of Books in Print* (36th Edition, 2010-11). 275pp. Reporting time: two weeks. Simultaneous submissions accepted: No. Publishes 2% of manuscripts submitted. Payment: 15% royalties. Does not copyright for author. Subjects: Fiction, Holocaust, Human Rights, Judaism, Literature (General), Multicultural, Non-Fiction, Novels, Philosophy, Poetry, Writers/Writing.

VOX Press (see also VOX), Louis E. Bourgeois, P.O Box 527, Oxford, MS 38655, (662) 801-2167. 2004. Poetry, fiction, interviews, criticism, reviews, plays, non-fiction. "Vox Press publishes *Vox Journal*, an avant-garde journal that seeks to publish the most extreme forms of literature being written in the 21st century." avg. press run 500. Pub'd 1 title 2009; expects 1 title 2010, 2 titles 2011. No titles listed in the *Small Press Record of Books in Print* (36th Edition, 2010-11). 100pp. Reporting time: 3 months. Simultaneous submissions accepted: Yes. Payment: Publication is Payment. First rights. Subjects: Absurdist, Anarchist, Atheism, Autobiography, Dada, Diaries, Disabled, Euthanasia, Death, Experimental, Holocaust, Homelessness, Post Modern, Surrealism.

Vulgar Marsala Press, Lisa Flowers, Norfolk, VA 23507. 2008. Poetry. "Vulgar Marsala Press was founded in Norfolk, VA, in 2008. In a nutshell, we are interested in satire, verse that deals with mythology and folklore, visual/imagist poetry, and work that explores philosophical, theological, and multi-dimensional issues. VM welcomes epic poetry and plays in verse, in the Bardic or contemporary tradition. Though our only true criteria is talent, and we do not espouse adherence to traditional forms, please note that we do not publish spoken word, political poetry, or any work that puts undisciplined spontaneity before fine-toothed comb editing and craftsmanship. We generally publish no more than 4 authors a year. Submissions will open in December of 2009." avg. press run 200. Expects 4 titles 2010, 4 titles 2011. 1 title listed in the *Small Press Record of Books in Print* (36th Edition, 2010-11). 80pp. Reporting time: 4 weeks. Simultaneous submissions accepted: Yes. Publishes 5% of manuscripts submitted. Payment: disclosed upon acceptance. Copyrights for author. Subjects: Arthurian, Avant-Garde, Experimental Art, Lewis Carroll, Geoffrey Chaucer, Classical Studies, Emily Dickinson, Rudyard Kipling, D.H. Lawrence, H.L. Mencken, Metaphysics, Myth, Mythology, Philosophy, Satire, Surrealism, Theosophical.

W

W.W. Norton, 500 Fifth Avenue, New York, NY 10110, 212-354-5500. 1923. No titles listed in the *Small Press Record of Books in Print* (36th Edition, 2010-11).

W.W. Publications (see also MINAS TIRITH EVENING-STAR), Philip W. Helms, PO Box 373, Highland, MI 48357-0373, 727-585-0985 phone/Fax. 1967. Poetry, fiction, articles, art, photos, cartoons, interviews, satire, criticism, reviews, music, letters, long-poems, news items, non-fiction. "Send questions to: Paul S. Ritz, PO Box 901, Clearwater, FL 33757." avg. press run 200-500. Pub'd 2 titles 2009; expects 1 title 2010, 3 titles 2011. 7 titles listed in the *Small Press Record of Books in Print* (36th Edition, 2010-11). 200pp. Reporting time: 2 months. Payment: 5 free copies. Copyrights for author. Subject: J.R.R. Tolkien.

John Wade, Publisher, John Wade, P. O. Box 303, Phillips, ME 04966, 1-888-211-1381. 1989. Poetry, fiction, art, non-fiction. avg. press run 3000. Pub'd 1 title 2009; expects 1 title 2010, 1 title 2011. 16 titles listed in the *Small Press Record of Books in Print* (36th Edition, 2010-11). Discounts: 50% booksellers, 55% wholesalers, No minimum copies. 250pp. Subjects: Animals, Arts, Biography, Crafts, Hobbies, Fiction, Geology, Handicapped, How-To, D.H. Lawrence, Maine, New Age, Occult, Poetry, Sports, Outdoors.

Wafer Mache Publications, Donna Horn, 16 Elmgate Road, Marlton, NJ 08053-2402, (856)983-5360 http://www.WaferMache.com. 1982. Non-fiction. "publish confectionery art, cake decorating how-to articles, and how-to craft books and articles on edible sculpture, edible party and holiday decorations." avg. press run 3000. Pub'd 2 titles 2009; expects 3 titles 2010, 3 titles 2011. No titles listed in the *Small Press Record of Books in Print* (36th Edition, 2010-11). Discounts: 2-10 copies 25%. 100pp. Reporting time: 4-6 weeks. Simultaneous submissions accepted: No. Publishes 5% of manuscripts submitted. Payment: varies. Copyrights for author. Subjects: Arts, Food, Eating, How-To.

THE WAKING, Ethan Lewis, 488 Brookens Hall, UIS, Springfield, IL 62792-9243, elewis@uis.edu, www.geocities.com/uis_the_waking/. 2003. Poetry. "New on-line journal to begin-print journal in near future. See website for guidelines." 6/yr. Expects 6 issues 2010, 12 issues 2011. Reporting time: 6-8 weeks. Simultaneous submissions accepted: yes. Publishes 1% of manuscripts submitted. Payment: free copy. Copyrighted, reverts to author. Pub's reviews. §Poetry, fiction and art. Subject: Poetry.

THE WALLACE STEVENS JOURNAL, The Wallace Stevens Society Press, John N. Serio, Editor; Joseph

Duemer, Poetry Editor, Clarkson University Box 5750, 8 Clarkson Avenue, Potsdam, NY 13699-5750, 315-268-6410, serio@clarkson.edu, www.wallacestevens.com. 1977. Poetry, articles, criticism, reviews, letters, news items. *"The Wallace Stevens Journal* publishes criticism on the poetry of Wallace Stevens. It also publishes archival material, Stevensesque poems, a current bibliography, and book reviews. Recent contributors have been: Eleanor Cook, Alan Filreis, Diane Wakoski, B.J. Leggett, Albert Gelpi, Helen Vendler, and Milton Bates." circ. 600. 2/yr. Pub'd 2 issues 2009; expects 2 issues 2010, 2 issues 2011. sub. price $30 1yr, $50 2yrs individuals; $40 US & $50 foreign institutions; per copy $10; sample $5 (postage). Back issues: $7 per number. 120pp. Reporting time: 6 weeks. Simultaneous submissions accepted: no. Publishes 25% of manuscripts submitted. Payment: copies. Copyrighted, reverts to author. Pub's reviews: 5 in 2009. §Wallace Stevens. Ads: $200/$150. Subjects: Biography, Criticism, Culture, Literature (General), Philosophy, Poetry, Post Modern.

The Wallace Stevens Society Press (see also THE WALLACE STEVENS JOURNAL), John N. Serio, Series Editor, Box 5750 Clarkson University, Potsdam, NY 13699-5750, 315-268-3987, Fax 268-3983, serio@clarkson.edu, www.wallacestevens.com. 1992. Poetry. "We initiated a poetry series with the publication of *Inhabited World: New & Selected Poems 1970-1995* by John Allman (166pp). We hope to publish a book of poetry each year." avg. press run 900. Pub'd 1 title 2009; expects 1 title 2010, 1 title 2011. 2 titles listed in the *Small Press Record of Books in Print* (36th Edition, 2010-11). Discounts: 20-30% depending on quantity. 80pp. Reporting time: 6-8 weeks. Simultaneous submissions accepted: no. Publishes 5% of manuscripts submitted. Payment: 10%. Copyrights for author. Subject: Poetry.

WALT WHITMAN QUARTERLY REVIEW, Ed Folsom, 308 EPB The University of Iowa, Iowa City, IA 52242-1492, 319-335-0454, 335-0592, Fax 319-335-2535, wwqr@uiowa.edu. 1983. Articles, criticism, letters, non-fiction. "The *Walt Whitman Quarterly Review* is a literary quarterly begun in the summer of 1983. *WWQR* features previously unpublished letters and documents written by Whitman, critical essays dealing with Whitman's work and its place in American literature, thorough reviews of Whitman-related books, and an ongoing Whitman bibliography—one of the standard reference sources for Whitman studies. The journal is edited by Ed Folsom and published at The University of Iowa and the editorial board is made up of some of the most distinguished Whitman scholars including Betsy Erkkila, Harold Aspiz, Arthur Golden, Jerome Loving, James E. Miller Jr., Roger Asselineau, and M. Wynn Thomas. We also offer for sale selected back issues of the *Walt Whitman Review* (1955-1982). Please write for details." circ. 1M. 4/yr. Pub'd 4 issues 2009; expects 4 issues 2010, 4 issues 2011. sub. price $12 individuals, $15 institutions ($3 postage charge on foreign subs); per copy $3; sample $3. Back issues: $3 each. Discounts: 10% to agencies for subscriptions, 40% to bookstores, 25% to classroom. 56pp. Reporting time: 1-3 months. Payment: contributor copies. Copyrighted, reverts to author. Pub's reviews: 8 in 2009. §Whitman scholarship, 19th and 20th American and World literature that discusses Whitman, poetry collections that reveal Whitman influences. Ads: $100/$50. Subjects: Criticism, Walt Whitman.

WAR, LITERATURE & THE ARTS: An International Journal of the Humanities, Donald Anderson, 2354 Fairchild Drive, Suite 6D149, Department of English & Fine Arts, United States Air Force Academy, CO 80840, 719-333-8465, website: WLAjournal.com. 1989. Poetry, fiction, articles, art, photos, interviews, satire, criticism, reviews, letters, parts-of-novels, long-poems, plays, concrete art, non-fiction. "From time immemorial, war and art have reflected one another. It is this intersection of war and art that WLA seeks to illuminate. If one of the functions of art is to disturb the status quo, to force us to view the world anew, to consider our capacities to build or tear down, then we welcome those disturbances. Before we made fire, before we made tools, before we made weapons, we made images. Art, at its deepest level is about preserving the world. Recent contributors include Paul West, Philip Caputo, Robert Pinsky, Dana Gioia, Carolyn Forche, Wendy Bishop, Robert Morgan, Ellen Bass." circ. 600. 1/yr. Pub'd 1 issue 2009; expects 1 issue 2010, 1 issue 2011. Journal provided free of charge to libraries and serious scholars. Back issues: free if in print. 350pp. Reporting time: 6 months. Simultaneous submissions accepted: No. Publishes 25% of manuscripts submitted. Payment: Two copies of the journal. Public Domain. Pub's reviews: 20 in 2009. §Works from any time or culture that explore the intersection of war and art. Subjects: Arts, Biography, Book Reviewing, Civil War, Fiction, Holocaust, Literary Review, Literature (General), Memoirs, Photography, Poetry, Vietnam, Visual Arts, War, Weapons.

WASCANA REVIEW OF CONTEMPORARY POETRY AND SHORT FICTION, Michael Trussler, Editor; Marcel De Coste, Fiction Editor; Nick Ruddick, Poetry Editor, Department of English, University of Regina, Regina, Sask S4S 0A2, Canada, 584-4302. 1966. Poetry, fiction, articles, reviews. circ. 300-500. 2/yr. Pub'd 2 issues 2009; expects 2 issues 2010, 2 issues 2011. sub. price $12 ($10 Canadian); per copy $5; sample $5. Discounts: 20% for subscription agencies. 90pp. Reporting time: 2-3 months. Simultaneous submissions accepted: no. Publishes 10% of manuscripts submitted. Payment: poetry $10 per page; fiction, reviews, critical articles $3 per page. Copyrighted, reverts to author. Pub's reviews: 2 in 2009. §Canadian literature, modern literature,contemporary world literature in English, short fiction, poetry.

WASHINGTON SQUARE, Martin Rock, Editor-in-Chief; Angelo Nikolopolous, Managing Editor, Creative

Writing Program, New York University, 58 West 10th St., New York, NY 10011. *"Washington Square* is an innovative, internationally-distributed literary journal publishing fiction and poetry by emerging and established writers. Edited and produced biannually by the students of the NYU Graduate Creative Writing Program, Washington Square also sponsors an annual literary contest judged by eminent poets and writers (poet Nick Flynn and novelist Darin Strauss were the 2007 judges), and hosts a series of readings in NYC. *Washington Square* invites you to enter the 2008 Washington Square competition. Winners (one in Fiction and one in Poetry) receive $500 and publication in a forthcoming issue of Washington Square. Selected runners-up will also receive publication." Biannual. sub. price check current deals on website; 10$ per copy. Back issues: Contact us. We may be able to offer free back issues. 160pp. Reporting time: 90 days. Simultaneous submissions accepted if notified immediately upon acceptance elsewhere. Payment: contributor copy. Ads: Contact us. Willing to trade ads. Also available for purchase.

Washington State University Press, Glen Lindeman, PO Box 645910, Pullman, WA 99164-5910, 509-335-7880, 509-335-8568 (fax), 800-354-7360, wsupress@wsu.edu, wsupress.wsu.edu. No titles listed in the *Small Press Record of Books in Print* (36th Edition, 2010-11).

WASHINGTON TRAILS, Andrew Engelson, Managing Editor, 2019 3rd Ave., Suite #100, Seattle, WA 98121-2430, 206-625-1367, www.wta.org. 1966. Articles, art, photos, cartoons, interviews, reviews, letters, news items, non-fiction. "Editorial content is heavily weighted for *Pacific Northwest backpackers*, ski tourers, snow shoers, etc. We frequently purchase outside material, but pay not more than $25.00 per manuscript." circ. 6,000. 10/yr. Pub'd 10 issues 2009; expects 10 issues 2010, 10 issues 2011. sub. price $35; per copy $3.50; sample n/c. Back issues: $3.50. 40pp. Reporting time: 2 months. Copyrighted, reverts to author. Pub's reviews: 6 in 2009. §Hiking, backpacking, cross-country skiing, snowshoeing, nature study and related activities—all with NW focus where applicable. Ads: $285/$143/50¢-wd. $12 min. Subjects: Environment, Nature, Pacific Northwest, Sports, Outdoors.

Washington Writers' Publishing House, Carly Sachs, President; Elisavietta Ritchie, Fiction President; Elizabeth Bruce, Treasurer; Sid Gold, Distribution Coordinator; Piotr Gwiazda, Publicity and Distribution, PO Box 15271, Washington, DC 20003, website: www.wwph.org, carly.sachs@gmail.com, gwiazda@umbc.edu (Gwiazda), elisavietta@xchesapeake.net (Ritchie), terry galvin (treasurer) 301-652-5636. 1975. Poetry, fiction. "Open to poets and fiction writers in the Greater Washington and Baltimore area only (a 60-mile radius from the Capitol). A *cooperative* press. Minimum of two year commitment to Press required. Annual deadline is November 1." avg. press run 750-1000. Pub'd 3 titles 2009; expects 3 titles 2010, 3 titles 2011. 56 titles listed in the *Small Press Record of Books in Print* (36th Edition, 2010-11). Discounts: bulk orders-5 or more titles 40%; bookstores 20%. 64-72pp (poetry), 250pp (fiction). Reporting time: about 3-4 months, submissions are accepted only during submission period, July 1 to October 15, decisions made by end of year. Simultaneous submissions accepted: yes. Publishes 2-3% of manuscripts submitted. Payment: authors receive 50 copies and $500. Does not copyright for author. Subjects: Fiction, Poetry.

Water Mark of Lyons PPP: papers press and permaculture, Coco Gordon, 523 5th Ave., PO Box 225, Lyons, CO 80540, 303-823-5585, 917-774-3538, cocogord@mindspring.com, http://www.galerie.kultur.at/coco/base/core.htm, http://transitioncolorado.ning.com/group/transitiontownlyonsco, http://transitioncolorado.ning.com/profile/CocoGordon. 1978. Poetry, art, photos, interviews, music, long-poems, collages, concrete art. "Works that are artist-book based with the artist book concept, merging avant garde, fluxist, indigenous, ecoventionist, and performance based writing, art, visuals, photos, music, poetry. 2003 did an anthology of 45 artists and bioregionalists from 16 nations in *Visioning Life Systems* as an artist book in edition of 144 copies.TIKYSK (Things I Know You Should Know) now a subdivision of Water Mark Press for Permaculture/Bioregionally based projects and art. New Interactiv' collaborative project, a sculptural book planned for 2011, new website and guidelines coming in fall of 2010. May also have a Local Lyons LIPS (Lyons Itinerant Poetry Society) poetry chapbook come out in 2010." avg. press run 75, may do new on demand books in 2011. Expects 2 titles 2011. 15 titles listed in the *Small Press Record of Books in Print* (36th Edition, 2010-11). Discounts: 40% more than 3 copies for 1980's series, 20% on handmade paper and special editions for more than 3 copies. Pages vary. Simultaneous submissions accepted: no. Payment: varies. varies. Subjects: Audio/Video, Avant-Garde, Experimental Art, Book Arts, Dada, Dreams, Ecology, Foods, Environment, Experimental, Indigenous Cultures, Interviews, Poetry, Visual Arts, Water, Zen.

Water Row Press (see also WATER ROW REVIEW), Cisco Harland, PO Box 438, Sudbury, MA 01776. 1985. Poetry, fiction, interviews, criticism, plays. "Our main focus are books and broadsides relative to the understanding and appreciation of the writings and times of 'Beat' writers. We are also seeking poetry and fiction from second generation 'Beats' and 'Outsiders'. Editions include signed limitations. Some recent contributors include Tom Clark, Arthur Knight, R. Crumb, Joy Walsh, William Burroughs. Any manuscripts which add to the understanding of Kerouac, Ginsberg, Bukowski are welcome. Tributes, poetry, dissertations, artwork. New poets' submissions always welcome." avg. press run 500-1M. Pub'd 5 titles 2009; expects 10 titles 2010, 10 titles 2011. 11 titles listed in the *Small Press Record of Books in Print* (36th Edition, 2010-11).

528

Discounts: 2-5 copies 25%, 6 or more 40%, distributors inquire. Reporting time: 4-8 weeks. Payment: copies of work and additional payment on publication to be arranged. Copyrights for author. Subjects: Fiction, Jack Kerouac, Poetry.

WATER ROW REVIEW, Water Row Press, Cisco Harland, PO Box 438, Sudbury, MA 01776. 1986. Poetry, fiction, articles, interviews, criticism, reviews, parts-of-novels. "Recent contributors: William Burroughs, Charles Bukowski, Jeffrey Weinberg." circ. 2.5M. 4/yr. Pub'd 4 issues 2009; expects 4 issues 2010, 4 issues 2011. sub. price $24; per copy $6; sample $6. Discounts: 2-10 20%, 11 or more 40%. 100pp. Copyrighted. Pub's reviews: 12 in 2009. §Literature, fiction, poetry. Subjects: Jack Kerouac, Literary Review, Literature (General), Poetry.

WATER~STONE REVIEW, Mary Rockcastle, Editor; Sheila O'Connor, Prose Editor; Patricia Kirkpatrick, Poetry Editor, MS-A1730, 1536 Hewitt Avenue, Saint Paul, MN 55104-1284, water-stone@gw.hamline.edu. 1998. Poetry, fiction, interviews, reviews, non-fiction. circ. 2,000. 1/yr. sub. price $15; per copy $15. 275pp. Reporting time: 1-3 months. Simultaneous submissions accepted: Yes. Payment: Two copies of magazine. Pub's reviews: 2 in 2009. §We review poetry and creative nonfiction. We have our own reviewers and do not accept submissions for reviews. Ads: Full page, $250Half page, $150.

Watermark Publishing, 1088 Bishop St., Suite 310, Honolulu, HI 96813, 808-587-7766, toll-free: 866-900-BOOK, fax: 808-521-3461. "Specializing in books about Hawaii and the Pacific. Humor, entertainment, children's titles, history - from pocket guides to coffee table books, biographies to cookbooks." 8 titles listed in the *Small Press Record of Books in Print* (36th Edition, 2010-11).

WATERMEN, Thomas Lockie, 2428 Gramercy Ave, Torrance, CA 90501, 310 850 6431. 2005. Poetry, fiction, articles, art, photos, music, non-fiction. "Ocean based, Sport based, Lifestyle based, Surfing, Diving, Paddlesports, Underwater Hunting, Lifeguarding, Underwater Photography, Underwater Videography." circ. 7500. 1500/yr. Pub'd 2 issues 2009; expects 2 issues 2010, 2 issues 2011. sub. price $12.00; per copy $6; sample Free. Back issues: inquire. Discounts: Consign+ 50% split. 32pp. Pub's reviews: 1 in 2009. §poems short fiction histories(all ocean based).

Waters Edge Press, 8 Venado Drive, Tiburon, CA 94920, 415-435-2837, Fax 415-435-2404, anderson-gram@comcast.net. 1996. Art, photos, non-fiction. avg. press run 2.5M-10M. Expects 1 title 2010, 2 titles 2011. 2 titles listed in the *Small Press Record of Books in Print* (36th Edition, 2010-11). Discounts: 55% gift stores, (bookstores, libraries, gift stores through distributors), also Amazon.com, Barnes and Noble.com, Borders.com. 64pp. Simultaneous submissions accepted: yes. Copyrights for author.

•WATER-STONE REVIEW, Graduate School of Liberal Studies, MS-A1730, 1536 Hewitt Ave., Hamline University, St. Paul, MN 55104. "Fiction and Creative NonFiction work should be typed, printed on white paper, one side only, double-spaced, and paginated, with your name, address, phone number, and e-mail address on the first page, title on subsequent pages. We are unable to read submissions of more than 8,000 words. Novels and memoir excerpts are acceptable as long as they stand on their own. Poems (one to three poems per submissionplease only submit once per reading period) should be typed with your name, address, phone number, and e-mail address on the first page of each."

WATERWAYS: Poetry in the Mainstream, Bard Press, Ten Penny Players, Inc., Barbara Fisher, Co-Editor; Richard Spiegel, Co-Editor, 393 St. Pauls Avenue, Staten Island, NY 10304-2127, 718-442-7429, www.tenpennyplayers.org, bfisher@si.rr.com or rspiegel@si.rr.com. 1978. Poetry. "Our themes and sample issues are posted at our web site, at SCRIBD and should be used as guides before submitting. e-mail submissions can be sent as text and usually are answered more quickly. Recently published poets include Richard Kostelanetz, Ida Fasel, Sylvia Manning & John Grey." circ. 100-200. 11/yr. Pub'd 11 issues 2009; expects 11 issues 2010, 11 issues 2011. 4 titles listed in the *Small Press Record of Books in Print* (36th Edition, 2010-11). sub. price $45; per copy $5.00; sample $5.00. Back issues: $5.00 (includes postage). 40pp. Reporting time: 1 month. Simultaneous submissions accepted: yes. Publishes 50% of manuscripts submitted. Payment: copies. Copyrighted, reverts to author.

WAV MAGAZINE: Progressive Music Art Politics Culture, Wasim Muklashy, 3253 S. Beverly Dr., Los Angeles, CA 90034, (310) 876-0490. 2004. Poetry, fiction, articles, art, photos, cartoons, interviews, satire, criticism, reviews, music, non-fiction. "we're very interested in socially conscious artists in the fields of rock, hip-hop and electronic music, as well as artists, poets and writers with similar themes. We're trying to help build and nurture an environmentally conscious and globally cooperative society." circ. 20000. 4/yr. Pub'd 2 issues 2009; expects 4 issues 2010, 6 issues 2011. sub. price $14.99; per copy $3.99; sample free. Back issues: inquire. Discounts: inquire. 68pp. Reporting time: within a month. Simultaneous submissions accepted: Yes. Publishes 15% of manuscripts submitted. Payment: inquire. Copyrighted, reverts to author. Pub's reviews: approx. 20 in 2009. §books, music, dvds of a progressive nature. Ads: inquire. Subjects: Alternative Medicine, Anarchist, Arts, Audio/Video, Comics, Environment, Feminism, Global Affairs, Government, Human Rights, Humor, Media, Music, Non-Violence, Photography.

Wave Books, Joshua Beckman, Editor; Matthew Zapruder, Editor, 1938 Fairview Avenue East, Suite 201, Seattle, WA 98102, info@wavepoetry.com, www.wavepoetry.com. 2000. Poetry. "Wave Books is an independent poetry press based in Seattle, Washington. Dedicated to publishing the best in American poetry by new and established authors, Wave Books was founded in 2005, joining forces with already-established publisher Verse Press. Wave Books seeks to build on and expand the mission of Verse Press by publishing strong innovative work and encouraging our authors to expand and interact with their readership through nationwide readings and events, affirming our belief that the audience for poetry is larger and more diverse than commonly thought. We do have a reading period for unsolicited mss; please consult http://www.wavepoetry.com/special section/7 for guidelines." avg. press run varies. Pub'd 8 titles 2009; expects 6 titles 2010, 6 titles 2011. 22 titles listed in the *Small Press Record of Books in Print* (36th Edition, 2010-11). Reporting time: 4 months. Payment: varies. Copyrights for author. Subject: Poetry.

Wave Publishing, Carol Doumani, 4 Yawl Street, Marina del Rey, CA 90292-7159, 310-306-0699. 1994. Fiction, non-fiction. "Our goal is to create the highest quality hardcover books." avg. press run 4M. Pub'd 1 title 2009; expects 1 title 2011. 7 titles listed in the *Small Press Record of Books in Print* (36th Edition, 2010-11). Discounts: 1-2 books 0%, 3-9 books 40%, 10-19 books 45%, 20+ books 50%. 360pp. Simultaneous submissions accepted: no. Publishes 0% of manuscripts submitted. Subjects: Cooking, Fiction.

Wayfarer Press, LLC, Robert Halmo, P.O. Box 948, Waterford, MI 48387-0948, www.wayfarerbooks.com. 2006. Fiction, non-fiction. "We're a new small publishing house, launching with a line of children's picture books. As we grow, we'll be branching into other areas, such as non-fiction and fiction." avg. press run 3000. Expects 1-5 titles 2011. 4 titles listed in the *Small Press Record of Books in Print* (36th Edition, 2010-11). 24pp. Reporting time: We're not accepting submissions at this time. Payment: Negotiated on an individual basis. Copyrights for author. Subject: Children, Youth.

Wayfarer Publications (see also T'AI CHI), Marvin Smalheiser, PO Box 39938, Los Angeles, CA 90039, 323-665-7773. 1981. Articles, interviews, reviews, letters, news items, non-fiction. avg. press run 10M. Pub'd 1 title 2009; expects 2 titles 2010, 3 titles 2011. 1 title listed in the *Small Press Record of Books in Print* (36th Edition, 2010-11). Simultaneous submissions accepted: no. Subjects: Health, Spiritual.

Wayside Publications, N. Nottingham, PO Box 318, Goreville, IL 62939, n.nottingham@violet.toler.com. 2004. Articles. "Wayside publishes Childrens books, Puppet books, and *Teacher Tips* books for religious teachers of children. These books feature all aspects of children's worship (i.e. Bible lessons, puzzles, games, activities, crafts, puppets, songs, prayer, discipline, and more). Submissions must be original, unpublished material, written in a clear, concise manner. Artistic ability is not required, but rough sketches are encouraged, if necessary to portray an idea. We are looking for fresh, easy, fun activities and lessons that are not limited to a specific denomination. Email submission preferred. This is a great opportunity for new authors to obtain writing credits. Recent contributors: PattyAnn and Violet Toler." avg. press run 1000. Pub'd 2 titles 2009; expects 4 titles 2010, 4-6 titles 2011. 6 titles listed in the *Small Press Record of Books in Print* (36th Edition, 2010-11). 55pp. Reporting time: 4 weeks. Payment: $10 and one copy of the book for each published idea. Does not copyright for author. Subjects: Children, Youth, Crafts, Hobbies, How-To, Religion.

The Waywiser Press (see also Between The Lines), Philip Hoy, Managing Editor, The Cottage, 14 Lyncroft Gardens, Ewell, Surrey KT17 1UR, United Kingdom, Tel: +44 (0)20 8393 7055, W: www.waywiser-press.com, E: waywiserpress@aol.com. "U.S. address: P.O. Box 6205, Baltimore, MD 21206. The Waywiser Press is a small independent company, with its main office in the UK, and a subsidiary in the USA. It was founded in late 2001, and started publishing in 2002. Waywiser is a literary press, first and foremost, with a special interest in modern poetry and fiction. From time to time, however, we also issue books belonging to other literary genres e.g. memoir, criticism, history. We are keen to promote the work of new as well as established authors, and would like to rescue still others from undeserved neglect." No titles listed in the *Small Press Record of Books in Print* (36th Edition, 2010-11).

Weber State University (see also WEBER: The Contemporary West), Brad L. Roghaar, Weber State University, 1214 University Circle, Ogden, UT 84408-1214, 801-626-6616, 801-262-6473, weberstudies@weber.edu, http://weberstudies.weber.edu. No titles listed in the *Small Press Record of Books in Print* (36th Edition, 2010-11).

WEBER: The Contemporary West, Weber State University, Michael Wutz, Editor; Kathryn MacKay, Associate Editor; Brad Roghaar, Associate Poetry Editor, Weber State University, 1405 University Circle, Ogden, UT 84408-1405, 801-626-6473. 1984. Poetry, fiction, articles, art, photos, interviews, parts-of-novels, long-poems, non-fiction. "Recent Contributors: Billy Collins, Carolyn Forche, Stephen Dunn, Robert Dana, Ken Burns, Robert Pinsky, Waddie Mitchell, Ken Brewer, Michael Schumacher, Gary Gildner, Maxine Hong Kingston, Carlos Fuentes, Amy Ling, William Kloefkorn, Dipti Ranjan Pattanaik, David James Duncan, Max Oelschlaeger, James Welch, David Lee, Katharine Coles, Raquel Valle-Senties, Robert Hodgson Wagoner, Stephen Trimble, Kate Wheeler, Nancy Kline, David Quammen, Peggy Shumaker, Pattiann Rogers, Terry

Tempest Williams, Joseph M. Ditta, Ron McFarland, Daniel R. Schwarz, Barry Lopez, and Chitra Banervee Divakaruni. Length of articles: 2,000 to 5,000 words. We are known for our fiction/interview series in which we feature original work by an author followed by an interview with her/him in the same issue. We like to publish 2-3 pages of poetry per poet in order to give a genuine flavor of the poet to our readers. Generally we ask for about 3-5 poems for submission. We like manuscripts that inform the culture and environment (both broadly defined) of the contemporary Western United States." circ. 1K-1.2K. 3/yr. Pub'd 3 issues 2009; expects 3 issues 2010, 3 issues 2011. sub. price $30 institutions, $20 individuals; per copy $8; sample $8. Back issues: $10. Discounts: 15%. 132pp. Reporting time: 3-4 months. Simultaneous submissions accepted: yes. Publishes 5% of manuscripts submitted. Payment: $100-$300 or more depending on our grant monies and length of mss. Copyrighted, reverts to author. Ads: none. Subjects: Conservation, Environment, Essays, Fiction, History, Interviews, Multicultural, Native American, Nature, Non-Fiction, Poetry, Short Stories, Southwest, Utah, The West.

WEIRD TALES, George Scithers, Editor; Darrell Schweitzer, Editor, PO Box 4001, Rockville, MD 20849-4001. 1923. Poetry, fiction. "Weird fiction up to 10K words. We're looking for the best in fantasy-based horror, heroic fantasy, and exotic mood pieces plus the occasional odd story that won't fit anywhere else." circ. 9M. 4/yr. Pub'd 4 issues 2009; expects 4 issues 2010, 4 issues 2011. sub. price $16; per copy $5.95; sample $6. Discounts: inquire. 58pp. Reporting time: 1-2 months. Simultaneous submissions accepted: no. Publishes 5% of manuscripts submitted. Payment: 3¢-6¢ on acceptance. Copyrighted. Pub's reviews. §Horror, fantasy, related criticism.

Wellcome Trust Centre for the History of Medicine at UCL (see also MEDICAL HISTORY), 183 Euston Road, London NW1 2BE, England. 26 titles listed in the *Small Press Record of Books in Print* (36th Edition, 2010-11). Subjects: Alternative Medicine, Disease, Health, History, Medicine, Nursing, Society.

Wellington House Publishing Company, Joyce Costigan, Editor, P.O. Box 1451, Lowell, MA 01854, 978-397-0005. 2007. Criticism. "Generally we publish education related books: "thought pieces" on criticism and educ. reform. However, we will also consider works of fiction and non fiction." avg. press run 1000. Pub'd 1 title 2009; expects 3 titles 2010, 5 titles 2011. 1 title listed in the *Small Press Record of Books in Print* (36th Edition, 2010-11). 40% discount off retail price. 225pp. Reporting time: Two weeks. Simultaneous submissions accepted: No. Publishes 25% of manuscripts submitted. Payment: negotiable. Copyrights for author. Subjects: Adolescence, Communication, Journalism, Creative Non-fiction, Criticism, Education, Fiction, Government, Juvenile Fiction, Mentoring/Coaching, Motivation, Success, Poetry, Politics, Prose, Public Affairs.

The Wellsweep Press, John Cayley, Harold Wells, Unit 3 Ashburton Centre276 Cortis Road, 276 Cortis Road, London SW15 3AY, United Kingdom, ws@shadoof.net. 1988. Poetry, fiction, non-fiction. "Specializes in literary translation from Chinese literature." avg. press run 750-1M. Pub'd 4 titles 2009; expects 5 titles 2010, 5-6 titles 2011. No titles listed in the *Small Press Record of Books in Print* (36th Edition, 2010-11). Discounts: trade 35%. 96pp. Reporting time: can be 2 months. Payment: by arrangement, up to 6%. Subjects: China, Essays, Fiction, Literature (General), Non-Fiction.

Wesleyan University Press, Suzanna Tamminen, Director, Editor-in-Chief; Parker Smathers, Acquisitions Editor, 215 Long Lane, Middletown, CT 06459, 860-685-7711. 1957. avg. press run 1500. Pub'd 24 titles 2009; expects 25 titles 2010, 24 titles 2011. No titles listed in the *Small Press Record of Books in Print* (36th Edition, 2010-11). 256pp. Reporting time: 3-4 months. We only occasionally accept simultaneous submissions. Publishes 5% of manuscripts submitted. Payment: dependent on author. Copyrights for author.

The Wessex Collective, Sandra Shwayder Sanchez, POB 1088, Nederland, CO 80466-1088, 303-258-3004, sss@wessexcollective.com, www.wessexcollective.com. 2004. Fiction. "we publish fiction that deals sensitively with social issues." avg. press run 250. Pub'd 3 titles 2009; expects 3 titles 2010, 3 titles 2011. 14 titles listed in the *Small Press Record of Books in Print* (36th Edition, 2010-11). Discounts: our distributor offers the standard discounts to wholesalers and bookstores. 150-250pp. Does not copyright for author. Subjects: Feminism, Fiction, Holocaust, Literature (General), Maine, Memoirs, Mystery, Myth, Mythology, Novels, Race, Society, Spiritual, Storytelling, Surrealism, Yoga.

WEST BRANCH, Paula Closson Buck, Editor; Andrew Ciotola, Managing Editor, Bucknell Hall, Bucknell University, Lewisburg, PA 17837, 570-577-1853, westbranch@bucknell.edu. 1977. Poetry, fiction, articles, criticism, reviews, parts-of-novels, long-poems, non-fiction. "*West Branch* publishes fiction, poetry, nonfiction, and reviews in a range of styles from the traditional to the innovative. We are open to work from both new and established writers." circ. 1M. 2/yr. Pub'd 2 issues 2009; expects 2 issues 2010, 2 issues 2011. sub. price $10; per copy $6; sample $3. Back issues: $4. Discounts: 20-40% to bookstores. 118-140pp. Reporting time: 6-10 weeks. We accept simultaneous submissions if marked as such. Publishes less than 1% of manuscripts submitted. Payment: Poetry: $20/poem + $10/additional page. Prose: $10/page. Minimum payment: $30. Maximum payment: $100. Copyrighted, reverts to author. Pub's reviews: 4 in 2009. §Poetry from university and independent presses. Ads: exchange ads only. Subjects: Essays, Fiction, Literary Review, Non-Fiction,

531

Poetry.

WEST COAST LINE: A Journal of Contemporary Writing and Criticism, Miriam Nichols, Editor; Roger Farr, Managing Editor, 2027 EAA, Simon Fraser University, Burnaby, B.C. V5A 1S6, Canada. 1990. Interviews, criticism. "Criticism, bibliography, reviews, and interviews concerned with contemporary writing, poetry and short fiction." circ. 500. 3/yr. Pub'd 3 issues 2009; expects 3 issues 2010, 3 issues 2011. sub. price $25 individuals, $40 libraries; per copy $10; sample $10. Back issues: $8. Discounts: $7 agents & jobbers. 128-144pp. Reporting time: 6-8 months. Simultaneous submissions accepted: no. Publishes 20% of manuscripts submitted. Payment: 2 contributor's copies & modest royalty fee. Copyrighted, reverts to author. Pub's reviews: 3 in 2009. §Experimental postmodern poetry, prose, criticism, cultural studies, art history, poetics, aesthetics. Subjects: Avant-Garde, Experimental Art, Canada, Criticism, Language, Multicultural, Poetry, Post Modern, Race.

West Coast Paradise Publishing, Robert G. Anstey, PO Box 2093, Sardis Sta. Main, Sardis, B.C. V2R 1A5, Canada, 604-824-9528, Fax 604-824-9541, web:http://rg.anstey.ca/. 1993. Poetry, fiction, non-fiction. avg. press run 100. Pub'd 12 titles 2009; expects 12 titles 2010, 12 titles 2011. 77 titles listed in the *Small Press Record of Books in Print* (36th Edition, 2010-11). Reporting time: 1 week. Simultaneous submissions accepted: yes. Publishes 90% of manuscripts submitted. Copyrights for author. Subjects: Autobiography, Biography, Fiction, Music, Non-Fiction, Poetry.

West End Press, PO Box 27334, Albuquerque, NM 87125. 1976. Poetry, fiction, art, music, long-poems, plays, non-fiction. "Politically progressive material favored." avg. press run 500-2,000. Pub'd 4 titles 2009; expects 2 titles 2010, 3 titles 2011. 62 titles listed in the *Small Press Record of Books in Print* (36th Edition, 2010-11). Discounts: write for info. 48-192pp. Reporting time: 2 to 3 months. Simultaneous submissions accepted: no. Publishes 1% of manuscripts submitted. Payment: in copies, 10% of run; 6% cash payment for initial print run; rest is negotiable. Copyrights for author. Subjects: African-American, Asian-American, Chicano/a, Feminism, Humanism, Native American, Politics, Socialist, Women, Worker.

WEST GOES SOUTH, McQuade Amanda, 4024 Providence Rd. #C, Charlotte, NC 28211, 419-565-2059. 2008. Poetry, fiction, art, photos, interviews, long-poems, non-fiction. "West Goes South is located in the elbow of Los Angeles and the hip of Charlotte, NC, and as any new independent journal, we are still finding our voice along this waterfall of free presses, so feel free to send us anything from the experimental, to the witty - even literature. As our name suggests, we are an eclectic mix of the modern and the traditional, the out there and the familiar. That being said, we strive to avoid typical images associated with rain, clouds, weather, nature, animals, love, and death. Fresh is king!" circ. 200. 4/yr. Expects 4 issues 2010, 4 issues 2011. Discounts: Discounts to colleges and independent bookstores. 25pp. Reporting time: 3-4 months. Simultaneous submissions accepted: No. Publishes 10% of manuscripts submitted. Payment: Copies. Copyrighted, reverts to author. Pub's reviews: none in 2009. Ads: $250 web, $175 print. Subjects: Abstracts, Adirondacks, African Literature, Africa, African Studies, Alaska, Alternative Medicine, The Americas, Animals, Appalachia, Architecture, Astronomy, Genealogy, North Carolina, Politics, Religion, Shipwrecks.

West Virginia University Press, Patrick Conner, P.O. Box 6295, G3 White Hall, Morgantown, WV 26506, Office (304) 293-8400, Toll free for orders (866) 988-7737, Fax (304) 293-6585. 1963. Poetry, fiction, art, photos, criticism, music, parts-of-novels, non-fiction. "The mission of the WVU Press is to publish scholarly works on a wide variety of subjects and to publish books of interest to the general reader with a focus on Appalachia." avg. press run 3000. Pub'd 7 titles 2009; expects 12 titles 2010, 12-14 titles 2011. No titles listed in the *Small Press Record of Books in Print* (36th Edition, 2010-11). Discounts: Retail trade discounts 1-4 copies 20%, 5+ 40% except short discount titles (s) which are 20% regardless of quantity. 300pp. Reporting time: One month. Simultaneous submissions accepted: No. Publishes 25% of manuscripts submitted. Payment: Varies. Copyrights for author. Subjects: African Literature, Africa, African Studies, Agriculture, Arts, Black, Civil War, Classical Studies, Fiction, Gay, Literature (General), Music, Native American, Poetry, Political Science, Politics, Race.

WESTERN AMERICAN LITERATURE, Melody Graulich, Editor; Jennifer Sinor, Book Review Editor; Sabine Barcatta, Managing Editor, English Dept., Utah State Univ., 3200 Old Main Hill, Logan, UT 84322-3200, 435-797-1603, Fax 435-797-4099, wal@cc.usu.edu. 1966. Articles, art, photos, cartoons, interviews, criticism, reviews. "Send books for review to Book Review Editor. No unsolicited reviews." circ. 1M+. 4/yr. Pub'd 4 issues 2009; expects 4 issues 2010, 4 issues 2011. sub. price subscriptions to individuals: $25 US/$40 Canada+Mexico/$50 overseas, institutions: $65 US/$80 Canada+Mexico/$90 overseas. Individual memberships for the Western Literature Association: $30 US/$45 Canada+Mexico/$55 overseas; memberships for students and retirees: $25 US/$40 Canada+Mexico/$55 overseas.; per copy $7.50 indiv., $13 libraries; sample free back issues (based on availability). Back issues: $7.50 indiv., $13 libraries. Discounts: 20% agency. 112pp. Reporting time: 2 months. Simultaneous submissions accepted: no. Publishes 10% of manuscripts submitted. Payment: 5 copies, tear sheets (for articles); tear sheets only for reviewers. Copyrighted, does not revert to author. Pub's reviews: 100-120 in 2009. §Books by western authors, about western authors or western literature, or books that focus on the West. Ads: $150/$90/no classifieds. Subjects: Folklore, Great Plains, Robinson Jeffers, Jack Kerouac, Literary Review, Literature (General), Jack London, Southwest, Texas, Visual Arts, The West.

WESTERN HUMANITIES REVIEW, Barry Weller, Editor; Karen Brennan, Fiction Editor; Richard Howard, Poetry Editor; dawn lonsinger, Managing Editor, University of Utah, Salt Lake City, UT 84112, 801-581-6070. 1947. Poetry, fiction, articles, art, interviews, satire, criticism, reviews, music, letters, parts-of-novels, long-poems, plays, concrete art, non-fiction. "We prefer 2-3M words; We print articles in the humanities, fiction, poetry, and film and book reviews. Recent contributors: Joseph Brodsky, Christine Hume, Cris Mazza, Kristy Bowen, Allen Grossman, David Shields, Bin Ramke, Jean McGarry, Lucie Brock-Broido, Lidia Yuknavitch, Richard Pairier, Helen Vendler." circ. 1.5M. 3/yr. Pub'd 3 issues 2009; expects 3 issues 2010. sub. price $26 (institutions) $20 (individuals); per copy $10; sample $10. Back issues: $10. Discounts: 25% to agents. 150pp. Reporting time: 4-6 months. Simultaneous submissions accepted: yes. Publishes less than 1% of manuscripts submitted. Payment: contributor copies. Copyrighted, rights revert to author on request. We don't use ads. Subjects: Literary Review, Literature (General).

Westgate Press, Lorraine Chandler, Editor, 176 Helen Garland Drive, Opelousas, LA 70570-6874. 1979. Art, photos, collages, non-fiction. "Metaphysical material, occult science and philosophy, esoteric mss. in related areas. Presently we are publishing *The Book Of Azrael* by Leilah Wendell, 'an intimate and first person encounter with the True Personification of Death! This dark and melancholy Angel is revealed through the writings of His Earthbound 'Bride' as well as direct communications with the Angel of Death Himself! Never before and never again will a book of this nature be offered. *This is not fiction.* But rather an account of the journey of an ancient spirit from the beginning of time to the present and beyond!...A Divine Dance Macabre!' That should give you an idea of what we are interested in. We request that *only queries* be sent at this time with appropriate SASE." avg. press run 500-5M. Pub'd 3 titles 2009; expects 3 titles 2010, 5 titles 2011. 3 titles listed in the *Small Press Record of Books in Print* (36th Edition, 2010-11). Discounts: 1-5 books 20%, 6-25 40%, 26-50 43%, 51-100 46%, 100+ 50%, discount applies to booksellers and others. 200+pp. Reporting time: 1 month on ms., 2 weeks on query. Simultaneous submissions accepted: yes. Publishes 20% of manuscripts submitted. Payment: negotiable on a project to project basis; no advance at present. Copyrights for author. Subjects: Arts, Euthanasia, Death, Fantasy, Folklore, Graphics, Metaphysics, New Age, Non-Fiction, Occult, Philosophy, Postcards, Prose, Supernatural, Surrealism, Visual Arts.

•**Westholme Publishing,** Bruce Franklin, Publisher; Lucina Bartley, Editor, 904 Edgewood Road, Yardley, PA 19067. "WESTHOLME is an independent publisher of American and world history and culture, military history, sports, arts, science, and regional interest. Book proposals in American, military, and world history, sports, natural history, science, and arts are welcome. Please email a brief description of the project to editorial@westholmepublishing.com Posted material will not be returned unlessrequested and accompanied by a SASE." No titles listed in the *Small Press Record of Books in Print* (36th Edition, 2010-11).

WESTVIEW, James Silver, Editor; Kevin Collins, Managing Editor; Kelly Moor, Assistant Editor; Joel Kendall, Publications Manager; Helen Maxson, Electronic Submissions Editor, SW Oklahoma State University, 100 Campus Dr., Weatherford, OK 73096, 580-774-3242, Fax 580-774-7111, james.silver@swosu.edu. 1981. Poetry, fiction, articles, art, photos, interviews, criticism, reviews, parts-of-novels, long-poems, plays, non-fiction. "*Westview* publishes fiction, poetry, drama, nonfiction, book reviews, scholarly work, literary criticism, and artwork. *Westview* holds the first rights for all works published unless otherwise specified. Recent contributors: Miller Williams, Carolyne Wright, Walter McDonald, and Alicia Ostriker." circ. 300. 2/yr. Pub'd 2 issues 2009; expects 2 issues 2010, 2 issues 2011. sub. price $15/2 years within US, $25 all others; per copy $6; sample $6. Back issues: $5. Discounts: inquire. 70pp. Reporting time: 2-6 months. Simultaneous submissions accepted if notified should poem be taken elsewhere. Publishes 5% of manuscripts submitted. Payment: copies. Copyrighted, reverts to author. Pub's reviews. §The journal has a traditional focus on regional works and themes but publishes a diverse range of material. Ads: $450/$300/$150 1/4 page/$75 1/8 page (all prices are for 4 issues.

WeWrite LLC, Delores Palmer, Publisher, 11040 Alba Road, Ben Lomond, CA 95005-9220, dpalmer@wewrite.net, www.wewrite.net. 1993. Poetry, fiction, art, cartoons. "Physical address: 11040 Alba Rd, Ben Lomond, California 95005. Publisher: specializing in books by kids, for kids called WeWrite Kids. Created within a workshop setting. An illustrator sketches while children brainstorm and act out story ideas." avg. press run 1M-15M. Pub'd 1 title 2009; expects 4 titles 2010, 20 titles 2011. No titles listed in the *Small Press Record of Books in Print* (36th Edition, 2010-11). Discounts: jobber 40%. 60pp. Reporting time: Less than 6 months. Simultaneous submissions accepted: yes. Publishes 80% of manuscripts submitted. Payment: none, prepaid by client quantity purchase. Copyright for author, and we own most copyrights. Subjects: Business & Economics, Cartoons, Children, Youth, Education, Finances, Marketing, Prison.

•**Wexford & Barrow, Publishers,** John Barrow, 4145 Woodman Ave., Sherman Oaks, CA 91423, 818-326-9810 / wexfordandbarrow@yahoo.com. 1994. Poetry, fiction, photos, interviews, plays, non-fiction.

"Photo directories and publications of regional interest. Rarely fiction." avg. press run 1000. Pub'd 2 titles 2009; expects 3 titles 2010, 3 titles 2011. No titles listed in the *Small Press Record of Books in Print* (36th Edition, 2010-11). Discounts: 2-10 copies 20%10-50 copies 30%50 copies and over 45%. 200-400pp. Reporting time: 4 weeks. Simultaneous submissions accepted: Yes. Publishes 2% of manuscripts submitted. Payment: no advance; 7-15% royalty based on sales. Does not copyright for author. Subjects: Biography, California, Catholic, Fiction, Los Angeles, Henry Miller, Novels, Old West, Poetry, The West, Yoga.

The WhaleInn Publishing House (1998) (see also ATLANTIC PACIFIC PRESS), Christine Walen, Editor; Crystal K. Walen, Graphic Design Editor; Luke Walen, Photography Editor, 279 Gulf Rd., South Dartmouth, MA 02748-1580, 508-994-7869 Query via regular mail with a SASE for reply. Questions? Call or Email: lyrics_songs@yahoo.com. Est. 1998. Poetry, fiction, art, photos, parts-of-novels, plays, non-fiction. "ATLANTIC PACIFIC PRESS. Est. 2008. Poetry, fiction, art, photos, parts-of-novels, plays. "Atlantic Pacific Press is a quarterly literary journal of creative writing, art and photography. Publishes fiction, non-ficion, science fiction, children's stories, poetry, lyrics, prose poetry, flash fiction, drama, veterans/military, mystery, horror, romance, fantasy, art and photography. Recent contributors include Florence Appleseed, Robert Ludlow, Deborah Valianti, John Brantingham, Marjorie Bixler, M. Seamus Briscoe, Suzanne Del Sarto, Ray Greenblatt, Mediha F. Saliba, Eugene Carrington, Lynn Veach Sadler, Doug Bolling, Kendra E.S. Adams, Randall Brock, Mary Kipps, Simon Perchik, Laura A. Steeb, Brian C. Felder, Cathy Porter, D. Davis Philips, Claudia Barnett, David Radavich, Jason Wilkinson, Michael Foster, Michael Ceraolo, Jon Wesick, James Fowler, J.W. Major, J.P. Andreason, T. Anders Carson, Mark D. Cohen, Ron Koppelberger, Dena Mallory, John Marvin, Diane Webster, Greg Moglia,James Hoggard, Robert Cooperman, George Gott, John Grey, George W. Hayden, Lewis Horton, Mark Katrinak, Pamela L. Laskin, Sheryl L. Nelms, Charles Rammelkamp, Samantha R. Reiser, Ted Richer, Art Schwartz, Laurence Snydal, Vincent Tomeo, A.D. Winans, Yoseph Leibowitz-Shultz 1st and Arthur Winfield Knight. Artists include Jenna Walen (sculpture), Dennis Dreher, Guy R. Beining, Eric Walen, and Mary P. Leimbach. Photographers include Luke Walen, Crystal Walen, Max Buckley and U.S. Navy (1940's). Lois Shapley Bassen's The End of Shakespeare & Co. won the 2009 ATLANTIC PACIFIC PRESS DRAMA PRIZE. Ms. Bassen's play was published as a special edition of ATLANTIC PACIFIC PRESS. Query for copies. 2010 Drama Prize was cancelled. 2011 Drama prize submission deadline: January 30th. George W. Hayden will judge. Snail mail with a SASE for guidelines. Email queries to: lyrics_songs@yahoo.com." circ. 40. 4/yr. Pub'd 5 issues 2009; expects 4 issues 2010, 5 issues 2011. 1 title listed in the Small Press Record of Books in Print. sub. price $30; per copy $8 newstand; sample $10 postpaid. Back issues: $10 postpaid. Discounts: 2-10 copies 25%. 100pp. Reporting time: 1-3 months. Simultaneous submissions accepted: No. Publishes 80% of manuscripts submitted. Payment: Free contributor copy, publishes author bio with acknowledgements, contributors posted on web page. Copyright and international copyright notices are published on title pages for all contributors. Buy first North American and World serial rights. Rights revert to author upon publication. Ads: $35/180 character, $250 bus card, $500 half page, $1000 full page. Subjects: Arts, Avant-Garde, Experimental Art, Creative Non-fiction, Drama, Fantasy, Fiction, Humor, Military, Veterans, Mystery, Non-Fiction, Photography, Poetry, Vietnam, War, World War II." avg. press run 30-50. Pub'd 5 titles 2009; expects 4 titles 2010, 5 titles 2011. 1 title listed in the *Small Press Record of Books in Print* (36th Edition, 2010-11). Discounts: 2-10 copies 25%. 100pp. Reporting time: 1-3 months. Simultaneous submissions accepted: No. Publishes 80% of manuscripts submitted. Payment: Free contributor copy, publishes author bio with acknowledgements, contributors posted on webpage. Copyright and international copyright notices published on title pages for all contributors. Does not accept material previously published on the Internet. Subjects: Cartoons, Creative Non-fiction, Crime, Drama, Fiction, Juvenile Fiction, Military, Veterans, Mystery, Non-Fiction, Poetry, Romance, Science Fiction, Short Stories, World War II, Young Adult.

Whalesback Books, W.D. Howells, Box 9546, Washington, DC 20016, 202-333-2182. 1988. Art, photos, non-fiction. "Books of interest to museums: art, architecture and graphic presentations." avg. press run 2M-5M. Pub'd 1 title 2009; expects 1-2 titles 2010, 2 titles 2011. 4 titles listed in the *Small Press Record of Books in Print* (36th Edition, 2010-11). Discounts: standard. 200-300pp. Payment: negotiable. Copyrights for author. Subjects: Anthropology, Archaelogy, Antiques, Architecture, Arts, Photography.

Wharton Publishing, Inc., T. Losasso, 2683 Via De La Valle, Suite G #210, Del Mar, CA 92014, 760-931-8977, Fax 858-759-7097, e-mail marketingtina@aol.com. 1991. Non-fiction. "Effective and easy to apply information that impacts people's wealth, health, relationships, time or attitude. Books with commercial tie-ins to products or services." Pub'd 1 title 2009; expects 2 titles 2010, 4 titles 2011. 2 titles listed in the *Small Press Record of Books in Print* (36th Edition, 2010-11). 140pp. Reporting time: 30 days or less. Simultaneous submissions accepted: no. Payment: varies. Copyrights for author. Subjects: Health, How-To, Non-Fiction.

WHAT IS ENLIGHTENMENT?, EnlightenNext, Andrew Cohen, Editor in Chief; Carter Phipps, Managing Editor, PO Box 2360, Lenox, MA 01240-5360, 413-637-6000, Fax 413-637-6015, wie@wie.org. 1991. Articles, photos, cartoons, interviews, criticism, reviews, letters, non-fiction. "Recent contributors: Ken Wilber, Dalai Lama, Howard Bloom." circ. 65K. 4/yr. Pub'd 2 issues 2009; expects 4 issues 2010, 4 issues 2011. sub. price $19.95; per copy $7.50; sample $7.50. Back issues: $9. Discounts: 40%. 140pp. Simultaneous submissions accepted: No. Copyrighted, rights possibly revert to author on publication. Pub's reviews: 10 in 2009. §Spirituality. Ads: $1340/$820 color; $970/600 B&W. Subjects: Book Reviewing, Environment, Ethics, Futurism, Inspirational, Judaism, Philosophy, Politics, Post Modern, Psychology, Religion, Science, Spiritual, Theosophical, Zen.

What The Heck Press, Jenny Stein, PO Box 149, Ithaca, NY 14851-0149, 607-275-0806, Fax 607-275-0702. 1992. Poetry, fiction, non-fiction. "Childrens audio. Currently not accepting submissions." avg. press run 5M. 3 titles listed in the *Small Press Record of Books in Print* (36th Edition, 2010-11). Discounts: trade 40%, call or write for discounts on large or special orders. 100pp. Payment: confidential. Copyrights for author. Subject: Children, Youth.

Wheatmark Book Publishing, Atilla Vekony, Publishing Consultant, 610 East Delano Street, Suite 104, Tucson, AZ 85705-5210, 520-798-0888, 520-798-3394 (fax), http://www.wheatmark.com. 1999. Fiction, non-fiction. "If you would like Wheatmark to consider your book for publication, visit http:/ /www.wheatmark.com/go." No titles listed in the *Small Press Record of Books in Print* (36th Edition, 2010-11). Discounts: Booksellers = 40% Wholesalers = 55% Fully returnable. Reporting time: Quickly. Payment: 20-40% royalties are paid quarterly, no advances offered. Will officially copyright as per author's wishes. Subjects: Advertising, Self-Promotion, Arizona, Business & Economics, Christianity, Literature (General), Management, Memoirs, Non-Fiction, Parenting, Politics, Real Estate, Religion, Research, Self-Help, Speaking.

WHEELHOUSE MAGAZINE, David Wolach M, Eden Shulz, Andrew Csank, 1414 Madison, Olympia, WA 98502, 248.298.9424. 2006. Poetry, fiction, articles, art, photos, cartoons, interviews, criticism, reviews, music, long-poems, collages, plays, concrete art, news items, non-fiction. "Wheelhouse, a progressive arts and politics magazine, appears online 6 times per year and in-print annually. Our online debut was in January, 2007, and our print volume will debut in August of 2007. We seek to promote new writers and artists, as well as to offer a form for progressive politics and ideas, with a bent towards organized labor and civil rights." circ. 500. 6/yr. Expects 1 issue 2010, 1 issue 2011. sub. price $12; per copy $12; sample $12. Back issues: inquire. Discounts: Free copies to contributors,; sample copies to wholesalers, retailers, bookstores. 150pp. Reporting time: 1-3 months. Simultaneous submissions accepted: Yes. Payment: $5-30 dollars per printed page. Copyrighted, reverts to author. Pub's reviews: 1 in 2009. §Wheelhouse rarely publishes reviews. We only review journals, small presses, new media works, and recently released/forthcoming books of poetry. Query the the editors first. Subjects: Anarchist, Audio/Video, Avant-Garde, Experimental Art, Civil Rights, Experimental, Fiction, Labor, Literary Review, Literature (General), Photography, Poetry, Politics, Publishing, Social Movements, Worker.

Whelks Walk Press, Marianne Mitchell, Publisher; Joan Peternel, Editor, 37 Harvest Lane, Southampton, NY 11968, whelkswalk@aol.com. 1995. Poetry, fiction, articles, art, photos, interviews, criticism, reviews. "The *Whelks Walk Review* has ceased publication. Two books were published by the Press: *Howl and Hosanna*, poems (1997) and *Nintotem: Indiana Stories* (1999), both by Joan Peternel. The Press has been inactive since 2000, but do check us again in 2006." 2 titles listed in the *Small Press Record of Books in Print* (36th Edition, 2010-11). Copyrights for author. Subjects: Arts, Culture, Fiction, Movies, Performing Arts, Poetry, Prose, Television.

Whiskey Creek Press, Debra Womack, Publisher & Executive Editor; Jan Janssen, Executive Editor - Torrid Romance Division; Marsha Briscoe, Senior Editor; Chere Gruver, Senior Editor - Torrid Romance Division, P.O. Box 51052, Casper, WY 82605-1052, 307-265-8585 (fax only), email: publisher@whiskeycreek-press.com, websites: www.whiskeycreekpress.com, www.whiskeycreekpresstorrid.com. 2003. Fiction, non-fiction. "Our editorial mission is to bring quality works of Fiction and Non-Fiction by outstanding authors to our reading public." Pub'd 100 titles 2009; expects 150 titles 2010, 150 titles 2011. 194 titles listed in the *Small Press Record of Books in Print* (36th Edition, 2010-11). Discounts: Up to 40% for qualified wholesale orders. 280pp. Reporting time: 90-120 days, depending on the number of received submissions. Simultaneous submissions accepted: No. Publishes 10% of manuscripts submitted. Payment: 2 year contract required, royalties paid to authors quarterly at 30% for ebooks and 7.5% for paperbacks. No advances. Does not copyright for author. Subjects: Anthology, Erotica, Fantasy, Fiction, Horror, Humor, Inspirational, Mystery, Non-Fiction, Old West, Romance, Science Fiction, Self-Help, Supernatural, Young Adult.

Whispering Pine Press, Matthew Wilson, Director of Marketing and Sales, 507 N. Sullivan Rd. Ste. A-7, Spokane Valley, WA 99037-8531, Phone: (509) 927-0404, Fax: (509) 927-1550, Web: www.whisperingpine-press.com, E-Mail: whisperingpinepressinc@hotmail.com. 2000. Poetry, non-fiction. "We specialize in publication of wholesome, family-oriented reading material. Our line of titles includes cookbooks, regional humor, children's literature, Christian-themed books and journals, books about and for foster and adopted children, juvenile horse-themed activity and coloring books, etc..." avg. press run 500. Pub'd 5 titles 2009; expects 10 titles 2010, 12 titles 2011. 7 titles listed in the *Small Press Record of Books in Print* (36th Edition, 2010-11). Discounts: 2 copies 40%. 300pp. Simultaneous submissions accepted: No. Subjects: Adolescence, Adoption, African Literature, Africa, African Studies, African-American, Americana, Animals, Cooking,

535

Family, Folklore, Gardening, Gender Issues, Pacific Northwest, Picture Books, Poetry, Washington (state).

Whit Press, 4701 SW Admiral Way, #125, Seattle, WA 98116. "Whit Press exists as an oasis to nurture and promote the rich diversity of literary work from women writers, writers from ethnic, social, and economic minorities, young writers, and first-time authors. We publish stories of creative discovery, cultural insight, human experience, spiritual exploration and more." No titles listed in the *Small Press Record of Books in Print* (36th Edition, 2010-11).

White Buck Publishing, David J. Thomas, Editor-in-Chief; Rebekka K. Nielson, Poetry Editor, 1143 U.S. Highway 99, Waynesboro, TN 38485-3014, 931-722-3586 phone/fax, submissions@whitebuckpublishing.com. 1996. Poetry, art, photos, criticism, long-poems, non-fiction. "Accept only material which reflect Christian theology, ethics, and morals. Work with book length manuscripts only. Poetry, non-fiction, apologetics, etc. are solicited." avg. press run 10-25M. Expects 2 titles 2010, 4 titles 2011. 1 title listed in the *Small Press Record of Books in Print* (36th Edition, 2010-11). Discounts: retail base 40%, wholesale 50-55%, distribution 60-65%; sliding scale on basis of single order quantity. 225pp. Reporting time: 12-18 months. Simultaneous submissions accepted: yes. Publishes 1-3% of manuscripts submitted. Payment: as circumstances dictate. Copyrights for author if requested. Subjects: Catholic, Christianity, Grieving, Poetry, Religion, Spiritual, Theosophical.

White Cliffs Media, Inc., Lawrence Aynesmith, PO Box 6083, Incline Village, NV 89450. 1985. Poetry, art, photos, music. "Current emphasis is on innovative publications in world and popular music. Compact Discs, cassettes often included. General trade titles also considered. Current title: *The Healing Power of the Drum* by Robert Lawrence Friedman." avg. press run varies. Pub'd 12 titles 2009; expects 3 titles 2010, 10 titles 2011. 12 titles listed in the *Small Press Record of Books in Print* (36th Edition, 2010-11). Discounts: follow industry standards. 180pp. Reporting time: 1-3 months. Publishes 10% of manuscripts submitted. Payment: varies. Copyrights for author. Subjects: African Literature, Africa, African Studies, Anthropology, Archaelogy, Arts, Biography, Black, Caribbean, Chicano/a, Computers, Calculators, Cults, Folklore, Music, Third World, Minorities.

White Crosslet Publishing Co, Marc Anthony Hatsis, 456 West Lake Road, tuxedo park, NY 10987, 845 351 3345 (fax&telephone). 2006. Poetry, fiction, articles, art, photos, interviews, satire, criticism, reviews, parts-of-novels, collages, plays, non-fiction. "White Crosslet Publishing Co is committed to publishing works which combine an aesthetic foundation (art, poetry, fiction, contemporary artist monographs), with a marked esoteric or symbolic element. For 2006 White Crosslet is publishing two cookbooks on raw foods which are heavily illustrated throughout with symbolic line drawings by Marc-Anthony Hatsis. Other titles deal with esoteric vegetarianism, the tarot, and elaborately illustrated limited edition books of poetry. One forthcoming work of poetry entitled "tempestad" is by Spanish poet and critic Ilia Galan, the book will be illustrated by Marc Anthony Hatsis." avg. press run 15000. Expects 10 titles 2010, 15 titles 2011. No titles listed in the *Small Press Record of Books in Print* (36th Edition, 2010-11). Discounts: 2-10 copies 25%10-49 copies 40%50-99 copies 46%100+copies 50%. 200pp. Reporting time: one week. Simultaneous submissions accepted: Yes. Payment: we usually purchase works on a "work for hire" basis, but could entertain possible royalty contract arrangements. Copyrights for author. Subjects: Absurdist, Arts, Astrology, Avant-Garde, Experimental Art, Cults, Dada, Drama, Experimental, Hypnosis, Magic, New Age, Non-Fiction, Occult, Tarot, Vegetarianism.

WHITE FUNGUS, Ron Hanson, Room 3, Floor 16, No. 566 13, Sec. 2, Wunsin Road, Situn District, Taichung City 407, Taiwan, 64(4)3829113, 64 274819660, whitefungusmail@yahoo.com. 2004. Poetry, fiction, articles, art, photos, interviews, satire, criticism, music, letters, collages, news items, non-fiction. "White Fungus is an experimental arts magazine based in Taichung City, Taiwan. Featuring writing on art, music, history and politics, plus original artworks, poetry, fiction and comics, White Fungus is an ongoing experiment incommunity media art. As the spores have been released its creators look forward to seeing which way the wind blows. The only thing more uncertain than its future is its past." circ. 3000. 2/yr. Pub'd 2 issues 2009; expects 2 issues 2010, 2 issues 2011. sub. price $40(four issues); per copy $8.99; sample free. Back issues: $15. 128pp. Simultaneous submissions accepted: yes. Copyrighted. §articles on art or experimental music, history, comics, poetry, non-fiction and fiction, original artwork. Ads: yes. Subjects: Anarchist, Arts, Asia, Indochina, Avant-Garde, Experimental Art, Biography, Book Arts, Charles Bukowski, Comics, Bob Dylan, Experimental, Jack Kerouac, New Zealand, Performing Arts, Post Modern, Visual Arts.

WHITE LOTUS, Shadow Poetry, Marie Summers, Editor, 1209 Milwaukee Street, Excelsior Springs, MO 64024, (208) 977-9114. 2005. Poetry, photos, interviews, reviews. "White Lotus accepts high quality submissions of these forms: haiku, senryu and tanka. Haiga, taiga, sumi-e, and haiku related articles and/or book reviews are welcome. Send up to ten pieces per poet for review with the appropriate seasonal theme in accordance with the next issue to be released by mail, email to whitelotus@shadowpoetry.com, or submit via online forms. Originality is a requirement. We reserve the right to reject submissions as a whole that do not contain original pieces or thoughts. Name of the poet, address, and email address (if applicable) must accompany all submissions, no exceptions. If submitting by mail, please supply a #10 SASE, no postcards. All work, if accepted, must be the original work(s) of the poet/author/artist and previously unpublished. No web published material considered." 2/yr. Pub'd 2 issues 2009; expects 2 issues 2010. sub. price $15.00/year US; $20.00/year International; per copy $10.00/US & International; sample $10.00/US & International. Back issues: $10.00/US & International. 32-60pp. Reporting time: 2-3 weeks. Simultaneous submissions accepted: No. Publishes 2-5% of manuscripts submitted. Payment: None. Copyrighted, reverts to author. Pub's reviews: 4 in 2009. §haiku, tanka, haibun, haiga. Ads: None.

White Mane Publishing Company, Inc., Harold Collier, Acquisitions Editor, 73 West Burd Street, PO Box 708, Shippensburg, PA 17257, 717-532-2237, Fax 717-532-6110, email:marketing@whitemane.com. 1987. Non-fiction. "White Mane Books emphasizes the importance of fine quality non-fiction adult military history. White Mane Kids is historically based fiction for children and young adults." avg. press run 3M-5M. Pub'd 30 titles 2009; expects 40 titles 2010, 50 titles 2011. 142 titles listed in the *Small Press Record of Books in Print* (36th Edition, 2010-11). Discounts: available on request. 200-300pp. Reporting time: 120 days with guideline and manuscript, proposal guidelines available on request. Simultaneous submissions accepted: yes. Payment: twice yearly statements. Copyrights for author. Subjects: Americana, Biography, Children, Youth, Civil War, History, Military, Veterans, Non-Fiction, War, Women, World War II.

White Pine Press, Dennis Maloney, Editor; Elaine LaMattina, Editor, PO Box 236, Buffalo, NY 14201-0236, 716-627-4665 phone/Fax, wpine@whitepine.org, www.whitepine.org. 1973. Poetry, fiction, long-poems, non-fiction. "Do not send unsolicited ms without querying first. We read unsolicited American poetry only as part of our annual competition. White Pine Press has published fine works of poetry, fiction, essays, non-fiction, and literature in translation from many languages. We are not presently reading new American fiction." avg. press run 1M-2M. Pub'd 10 titles 2009; expects 9 titles 2010, 8 titles 2011. 135 titles listed in the *Small Press Record of Books in Print* (36th Edition, 2010-11). Discounts: 2-4 copies 20%, 5+ 40%. 150-250pp. Reporting time: 1-3 months. Simultaneous submissions accepted: yes. Publishes 1% of manuscripts submitted. Payment: copies, honorarium, royalties. Does not copyright for author. Subjects: Asia, Indochina, Essays, Fiction, Latin America, Novels, Poetry, Short Stories, Translation, Zen.

White Thread Press, Abdur Mangera R, 480 Whitman Street #102, Goleta, CA 93117, 805 968 4666. 2004. Non-fiction. "We publish classical and traditional works by Muslim scholars on Islam and related sciences." avg. press run 4000. Expects 5 titles 2010, 5 titles 2011. No titles listed in the *Small Press Record of Books in Print* (36th Edition, 2010-11). Discounts: 2-4 copies 35%5-9 copies 40%10-99 copies 42%100-499 copies 45%500+ copies call for priceExceptions are possible. 145pp. Copyrights for author. Subjects: Autobiography, Biography, Ethics, History, Law, Philosophy, Spiritual, Sufism.

White Urp Press (see also ABBEY), 5360 Fallriver Row Court, Columbia, MD 21044. avg. press run 200. 6 titles listed in the *Small Press Record of Books in Print* (36th Edition, 2010-11). 15-20pp. Simultaneous submissions accepted: no. Does not copyright for author.

WHITEWALL OF SOUND, Jim Clinefelter, 411 NE 22nd #21, Portland, OR 97232-3270, jcline@tele-port.com. 1983. Poetry, fiction, articles, art, photos, interviews, criticism, long-poems, collages, concrete art, non-fiction. "This magazine originated in NE Ohio, and is reflective of publications that have been produced in that area. And please note that it's *Whitewall* not *White Wall*. The title is a reference to automobile tires. Please request a sample issue before submitting your work or check the listings on www.printedmatter.org." circ. 100-250. 1-4/yr. Pub'd 1 issue 2009; expects 3 issues 2010, 3 issues 2011. price per copy varies; sample $10 ink-jet printer. Back issues: varies. Discounts: Special prices available to libraries and schools, please inquire via e-mail. 30pp. Simultaneous submissions accepted: yes. Publishes a variable % of manuscripts submitted. Payment: 1 copy. Copyrighted, reverts to author. Ads: none. Subjects: Avant-Garde, Experimental Art, Bibliography, Ohio, Pacific Northwest.

Whitston Publishing Co., PO Box 38263, Albany, NY 12203-8263, 518-869-9110, fax: 518-452-2154. 1969. "For UPS/FedEx delivery: 220 Walnut Lane, Slingerlands, NY 12159." Pub'd 15 titles 2009; expects 15 titles 2010, 15 titles 2011. No titles listed in the *Small Press Record of Books in Print* (36th Edition, 2010-11). Reporting time: 120-180 days. Copyrights for author. Subjects: African Literature, Africa, African Studies, Architecture, Bibliography, Biography, Business & Economics, Charles Dickens, Emily Dickinson, English, Indexes & Abstracts, Literary Review, Medieval, Native American, Poetry, Political Science, Sports, Outdoors.

Whole Person Associates Inc., Carlene Sippola, 210 West Michigan Street, Duluth, MN 55802-1908, 218-727-0500, Fax 218-727-0505. 1977. avg. press run 200 - 1000. Pub'd 5 titles 2009. 67 titles listed in the *Small Press Record of Books in Print* (36th Edition, 2010-11). Discounts: normal trade for some books/professional discounts. 192pp. Simultaneous submissions accepted: yes. Copyrights for author. Subjects: Health, Lifestyles, Men, Mental Health, Mentoring/Coaching, Psychology, Relationships, Self-Help, Women, Yoga.

WHOLE TERRAIN - REFLECTIVE ENVIRONMENTAL PRACTICE, Rowland Russell, Managing Director, 40 Avon Street, Antioch University New England, Keene, NH 03431-3552, 603-283-2377. 1992. Poetry, fiction, art, interviews, non-fiction. "Fiction, nonfiction, and personal essay manuscripts on specific yearly themes should be no longer than 2,000 words. Poetry submissions also accepted. Recent contributors include: Kathleen Dean Moore, Charles Siebert, Lynn Margulis, Terry Tempest Williams, Thomas Moore, Simon Ortiz, David James Duncan, and Ann Zwinger. New theme guidelines are posted each summer on our website (www.wholeterrain.org); they may also be requested from our office via phone or email.'' circ. 2000. 1/yr. Pub'd 1 issue 2009; expects 1 issue 2010, 1 issue 2011. sub. price $20 for 3 years; $30 for 5 years; per copy $8; sample $5. Back issues: $8. Discounts: Discounts are offered on multiple-year subscriptions, and to wholesalers. 52pp. Reporting time: 6-8 weeks after annual submission deadline. We are not able to reply to unsolicited material that is off theme. Simultaneous submissions accepted: yes. Publishes 15% of manuscripts submitted. Payment: None. Contributors are compensated with copies of their issue, and a lifetime subscription to Whole Terrain. Copyrighted, reverts to author. §Environmental topics, nature related fiction and non-fiction. Subjects: Environment, Essays, Fiction, Nature, Non-Fiction, Poetry.

Wide World Publishing, Elvira Monroe, PO Box 476, San Carlos, CA 94070, 650-593-2839, Fax 650-595-0802. 1976. Articles, photos, non-fiction. ''Imprint—Wide World Publishing/Tetra wegsite: http://www.wideworldpublishing.com.'' avg. press run varies. Pub'd 4 titles 2009; expects 3 titles 2010, 3 titles 2011. 44 titles listed in the *Small Press Record of Books in Print* (36th Edition, 2010-11). Discounts: 2-4 books 20%, 5-24 40%, 25-49 42%, 50-99 44%, 100+ 48%. 200 to 300pp. Reporting time: 2 weeks. Payment: 10%. Copyrights for author. Subjects: California, Ecology, Foods, Greek, Hawaii, Mathematics, Travel.

WILD DUCK REVIEW, Casey Walker, P.O. Box 335, Davenport, CA 95017, www.wildduckreview.com / casey@wildduckreview.com. 1994. Poetry, fiction, articles, art, photos, interviews, satire, criticism, reviews, letters, news items, non-fiction. ''Recent contributors include: Jim Dodge, Jerry Martien, Gary Snyder, Galway Kinnell, Bill Joy, Nelson Foster, Florence Shepard, Ed Casey, Marilynne Robinson, Wendell Berry, Martha Herbert, Stuart Newman, Richard Strohman, David Noble, Jim Harrison, Jack Turner, Terry Tempest Williams, Freeman House, Keekok Lee, Bill McKibben, Elizabeth Herron, Lewis Lapham, Todd Gitlin, Suzanne Romaine, Catherine Keller. Does not read unsolicited manuscripts.'' circ. global www.wildduckreview.com. Please sign up for E-newsletter at www.instituteforinquiry.org/enewsletter.php?email= to stay abreast of publishing schedule. price per copy $8; sample free back issues available at www.wildduckreview.com. Back issues: Free back issue contents available at www.wildduckreview.com. Discounts: 30% discount on orders of 15 copies or more of each issue used for educational purposes. 44 10x14" pp. Payment: copies. Copyrighted, reverts to author. Subjects: Arts, Biology, Environment, Interviews, Literary Review, Nature, Philosophy, Physics, Politics, Writers/Writing.

WILD PLUM, Constance Campbell, Founding Editor, PO Box 4282, Austin, TX 78765. 2003. Poetry. 1/yr. Pub'd 1 issue 2009; expects 1 issue 2010, 1 issue 2011. sub. price $9; per copy $9; sample $9. 48pp. Reporting time: 2 months, unless work is under consideration. Simultaneous submissions accepted: no. Publishes 5% of manuscripts submitted. Payment: 1 copy. Copyrighted, reverts to author. Subject: Poetry.

Wilde Publishing, David Wilde, PO Box 4581, Albuquerque, tel 504-810-2241, wilde@unm.edu, http://www.artmajeur.com/davidwilde. 1989. Poetry, fiction, articles, interviews, satire, music, letters, long-poems, plays. ''Depending on the type of work to be published we will look at just about anything.'' avg. press run 50. Pub'd 1 title 2009; expects 1 title 2010, 4 titles 2011. 5 titles listed in the *Small Press Record of Books in Print* (36th Edition, 2010-11). Discounts: 40%. 129pp. Reporting time: 6 weeks to 12 months, no guarantees. Simultaneous submissions accepted: Yes. Publishes 1% of manuscripts submitted. Payment: depends on the work. Depends on the work. Subjects: Absurdist, African Literature, Africa, African Studies, Aging, Americana, Anarchist, Beat, Bilingual, English, Europe, Euthanasia, Death, France, French, Motivation, Success, New Mexico, Novels, World War II.

Zelda Wilde Publishing, John Lehman F., 315 Water St., Cambridge, WI 53523, 608-423-9609. 2003. Poetry, non-fiction. ''We specialize in literary and business books that have clearly defined audiences and efficient means to reach them.'' avg. press run 2000. Pub'd 2 titles 2009; expects 3 titles 2010, 5 titles 2011. No titles listed in the *Small Press Record of Books in Print* (36th Edition, 2010-11). Discounts: 2-10 copies 25%. 136pp. Reporting time: We are currently not accepting unsolicited manuscripts. Simultaneous submissions accepted: No. Publishes 1% of manuscripts submitted. Payment: Authors receive a percent of sales. Copyrights for author. Subjects: Biography, Buddhism, How-To, Leadership, Liberal Arts, Non-Fiction, North America, Prose, Public Relations/Publicity, Trade, Wisconsin, Zen.

Wilderness Adventure Books, Erin Sims Howarth, Po Box 856, Manchester, MI 48158-0856, www.wildernessbooks.org. 1983. Photos, non-fiction. ''We publish mostly how to guides of the Great Lakes outdoors. Recent books include: *Edible Medicinal Plants of the Great Lakes Region*.'' avg. press run 3M. Pub'd 4 titles 2009; expects 4 titles 2010, 4 titles 2011. 5 titles listed in the *Small Press Record of Books in Print* (36th Edition, 2010-11). Discounts: 30-50%. 300pp. Reporting time: 6 weeks. Simultaneous submissions accepted: yes. Publishes 5% of manuscripts submitted. Payment: 5-10% of retail/every 6 months. Copyrights for author. Subjects: Bicycling, Botany, Great Lakes, How-To, Michigan, Shipwrecks, Sports, Outdoors.

•**WILDERNESS HOUSE LITERARY REVIEW, Wilderness House Press,** Steve Glines, Editor & Publisher, 145 Foster St., Littleton, MA 01460. *"The Wilderness House Literary Review* is a publication devoted to excellence in literature and the arts. The WHL Review is published online quarterly with a best of annual print edition."

•**Wilderness House Press (see also WILDERNESS HOUSE LITERARY REVIEW),** Steve Glines, Editor, 145 Foster Street, Littleton, MA 01460, voice 978-800-1625, fax 978-522-3753. 2005. "Wilderness House Press seeks new fiction, non-fiction and poetry. In general we publish authors that have first appeared in Wilderness House Literary Review but that is not a prerequisite.We are interested in any work of literary value from a chapbook through a full length novel or non-fiction work. Our publishing schedule is completely contingent on operating funds. That means one of two things: We will publish new works only when the last work published has broken even financially OR sooner if the author or their sponsors wish to subsidize the publication of a new work. We hope to publish the equivalent of 3- 5 full length works each year.Queries for works of poetry should include a completed manuscript and be sent electronically. Included works should be in a form readable by Microsoft Word. Fiction and non-fiction queries should include a synopsis as well as a chapter of (at least) 25 pages. We are willing to work with developing authors as long as we feel there is a reasonable chance that a publishable book will result from our efforts." Pub'd 1 title 2009; expects 3 titles 2010, 5 titles 2011. 1 title listed in the *Small Press Record of Books in Print* (36th Edition, 2010-11).

WILDERNESS MEDICINE NEWSLETTER, TMC Books LLC, Peter Lewis, 731 Tasker Hill Rd., Conway, NH 03818, 603-447-5589, info@tmcbooks.com www.tmcbooks.com. 2002. Non-fiction. "ISSN-1059-6518." 6/yr. Pub'd 6 issues 2009; expects 6 issues 2010, 6 issues 2011. sub. price $15; sample Free Online at www.tmcbooks.com. Back issues: can be ordered through TMC Books either by phone or email info@tmcbooks.com. 10pp. Payment: Check or online c/c. Copyrighted. Subject: Medicine.

Wilderness Ministries, Paul L. Prough Jr., PO Box 225, Mount Union, PA 17066, 814-542-8668. 1975. Fiction, photos, non-fiction. avg. press run 2M. Pub'd 3 titles 2009; expects 3 titles 2010, 4 titles 2011. 1 title listed in the *Small Press Record of Books in Print* (36th Edition, 2010-11). 75pp. Reporting time: 6-12 months. Simultaneous submissions accepted: no. Publishes 1% of manuscripts submitted. Payment: negotiated. Does not copyright for author. Subjects: Christianity, Inspirational, Juvenile Fiction, Motivation, Success, Religion, Spiritual.

Wilderness Press, Roslyn Bullas, Associate Publisher, 1200 5th Street, Berkeley, CA 94710-1453, 510-558-1666; e-mail mail@wildernesspress.com; website www.wildernesspress.com. 1966. Non-fiction. "Conservation, environmental bias. Bias for accuracy. Bias against sloppy writing." avg. press run 5M. Pub'd 10 titles 2009; expects 15 titles 2010, 15 titles 2011. 17 titles listed in the *Small Press Record of Books in Print* (36th Edition, 2010-11). 180pp. Reporting time: 2 weeks. Simultaneous submissions accepted: yes. Publishes 5% of manuscripts submitted. Payment: competitive royalty paid quarterly or semi-annually. Copyrights for author. Subject: Sports, Outdoors.

THE WILDWOOD READER, Timson Edwards, Co., Marlene McLauglin, Alex Gonzalez, PO Box 55-0898, Jacksonville, FL 32255-0898, 904-705-6806; gonz2171@bellsouth.net; www.short-fiction.com. 1995. Fiction, photos. "Short short fiction, essays, stream of conscience prose and anything creative - especially if the material matches the photography. We would prefer writings in the traditional literary realm. However, any material may be sent except erotica, western, sci-fi and horror. We would like to see collaborations of new or emerging writers and new fine art photographers." circ. 500. 4/yr. Pub'd 2 issues 2009; expects 4 issues 2010, 4 issues 2011. sub. price $15; per copy $6; sample $8. Discounts: trade 30% no returns; bulk 50% no returns; agents 5-10% commission on any sale; bonafide school/classroom orders 50%. 48pp. Reporting time: 3 months. Simultaneous submissions accepted: yes. Publishes 60% of manuscripts submitted. Payment: $10-$25. Copyrighted, reverts to author. Pub's reviews: 1-4 in 2009. §Short fiction, essays, photography. Ads: $250/$100/$25. Subjects: Essays, Fiction, Interviews, Literature (General), Magazines, New Age, Photography, Satire.

Willfam Publishing Co., Wayne Williams, P.O.Box 60455, Harrisburg, PA 17106-0455, 717-592-9407, willfampub@verizon.net, willfampublishing.com. 2004. Fiction, music, parts-of-novels, plays. avg. press run 1200. Pub'd 1 title 2009; expects 1 title 2010, 2 titles 2011. 1 title listed in the *Small Press Record of Books in Print* (36th Edition, 2010-11). Discounts: 50% off list price (distributor, wholesalers 55% off list price, retailers 40% off list price, institutions 55% off list price, agents and jobbers 40% off list price. 285pp. Simultaneous submissions accepted: Yes. Copyrights for author. Subjects: Business & Economics, Comics, Crime, Family, Fantasy, Fiction, Finances, How-To, Humor, Inspirational, Relationships, Science Fiction, Self-Help, Sex, Sexuality, Supernatural.

WILLIAM AND MARY REVIEW, Editors rotate yearly, Campus Center, PO Box 8795, Williamsburg, VA 23187-8795, 757-221-3290, Fax 757-221-3451. 1962. Poetry, fiction, art, photos, satire, long-poems, non-fiction. "The Review is an internationally circulated literary magazine published annually by The College of William and Mary. In past issues, we have published works by Cornelius Eady, Dana Gioia, Eric Paul Shaffer, Lyn Lifshin, David Bergman, Walta Borawski, Minnie Bruce Pratt, among others. Please send SASE for our reply. Address submissions to appropriate editor (prose/poetry/art). We do not accept previously published work. Email review@wm.edu with questions ONLY; no submissions accepted via email." circ. 1200. 1/yr. Pub'd 1 issue 2009; expects 1 issue 2010, 1 issue 2011. sub. price $5.50; per copy $5.50 includes shipping; $1.50 surcharge for international shipping; sample $5.50. Back issues: $5.50 per issue. Discounts: 40% off list for trade. 100pp. Reporting time: 4-5 months. Simultaneous submissions accepted, but not preferred. Publishes 3% of manuscripts submitted. Payment: 5 copies of issue. Copyrighted, reverts to author. Subjects: Photography, Poetry, Prose.

William Joseph K Publications, Lisa Ball, 150 Fisher Court, Clawson, MI 48017, 2485890056. 2007. Poetry, fiction, art, cartoons, music, parts-of-novels, long-poems, non-fiction. avg. press run 200. Pub'd 1 title 2009; expects 3 titles 2010, 2 titles 2011. 1 title listed in the *Small Press Record of Books in Print* (36th Edition, 2010-11). Discounts: 50%. 60pp. Reporting time: 1 week. Simultaneous submissions accepted: No. Publishes 5% of manuscripts submitted. Payment: currently only accepting donated works for Anthology 50% of proceeds to Autism Society. Subjects: Abstracts, Adolescence, Anthology, Experimental, Feminism, Picture Books.

WILLOW REVIEW, Michael Latza, College of Lake County, 19351 W. Washington, Grayslake, IL 60030, 847-543-2956, com426@clcillinois.edu, www.clcillinois.edu/community/willowreview.asp. 1969. Poetry, fiction, interviews, reviews, non-fiction. "Willow Review is a non-profit journal published annually at the College of Lake County and partially supported by a grant from the Illinois Arts Council (a state agency), College of Lake County Publications, and private contributions and sales. Submissions are invited Sept. 1st to May 1st. Send a maximum of five poems or short fiction and creative non-fiction up to 7,000 words. All work should be unpublished and accompanied by a self-addressed stamped envelope. Manuscripts will not be returned unless requested. We will accept simultaneous submissions if indicated in the cover letter. At this time we are not accepting electronic submissions. As part of our mission Willow Review also publishes reviews of books written by Midwestern writers or published by Midwestern presses.Recent Contributors: Patricia Smith, Lisel Mueller, Li-Young Lee." circ. 1000. 1/yr. Pub'd 1 issue 2009; expects 1 issue 2010, 1 issue 2011. sub. price one year, $7 / 3 years, $18 / 6 years, $30.; per copy $7; sample $5. Back issues: inquire. 110pp. Reporting time: 12-16 weeks. Simultaneous submissions accepted: Yes. Publishes 5% of manuscripts submitted. Payment: 2 copies of magazine. Copyrighted, reverts to author. Pub's reviews: 1 in 2009. §Poetry Books. Subjects: Fiction, Non-Fiction, Poetry.

WILLOW SPRINGS, Samuel Ligon, Editor; O'Connor Rodriguez Adam, Managing Editor, Eastern Washington University, 501 North Riverpoint Blvd., Spokane, WA 99202-2410, 509-623-4349. 1977. Poetry, fiction, interviews, criticism, reviews, parts-of-novels, long-poems, non-fiction. "Michael Burkard, Russell Edson, Alison Baker, Thomas Lux, Alberto Rios, Carolyn Kizer, Madeline DeFrees, Peter Cooley, Yusef Komunyakaa, Donald Revell, William Stafford, Lee Upton, Paisley Rekdal, and Robert Gregory. We encourage the submissions of translations from all languages and periods, as well as essays and essay-reviews." circ. 1,700. 2/yr. Pub'd 2 issues 2009; expects 2 issues 2010, 2 issues 2011. sub. price $13.00; per copy $7; sample $5. Back issues: varies. Discounts: 40%. 144pp. Reporting time: 1-3 months. Simultaneous submissions accepted: Yes. Publishes .5% of manuscripts submitted. Payment: 2 contributor copies. Copyrighted, reverts to author. Pub's reviews: none in 2009. §Poetry, fiction, nonfiction. Ads: Exchange only. Subjects: Criticism, Essays, Fiction, Interviews, Non-Fiction, Poetry, Prose, Translation.

Willowood Press, Judith Greenwood, Publisher, 1209 Lincoln St., Alamosa, CO 81101, 719-589-3052. 1980. "Press is in state of transition to new subjects and new formats to be self-published only." No titles listed in the *Small Press Record of Books in Print* (36th Edition, 2010-11). Subjects: Children, Youth, Colorado, Inspirational, Libraries, Miniature Books, Spiritual, Storytelling, Visual Arts.

Wilshire Books Inc., 9731 Variel Ave., Chatsworth, CA 91311-4315, 818-700-1522 [tel], 818-700-1527 [fax], website: www.mpowers.com. 1947. avg. press run 5M. Pub'd 25 titles 2009; expects 25 titles 2010, 25 titles 2011. No titles listed in the *Small Press Record of Books in Print* (36th Edition, 2010-11). 224pp. Reporting time: 2 months. Simultaneous submissions accepted: yes. Publishes a variable % of manuscripts submitted. Payment: varies. Copyrights for author. Subjects: How-To, Humor, Hypnosis, Magic, Marketing, Metaphysics, Motivation, Success, Non-Fiction, Psychology, Publishing, Self-Help, Sex, Sexuality.

WIN NEWS, Fran P. Hosken, Editor & Publisher, 69 Payson Road, Chestnut Hill, MA 02467-3218, 781-862-9431, Fax 781-862-1734. 1975. "*WIN News (Women's International Network)* has ongoing columns on women and health, women and development, women and media, environment, violence, united nations and more. International career opportunities are listed; an investigation on genital/sexual mutilations regularly reports; news from Africa, the Middle East, Asia & Pacific, Europe and the Americas are featured in every issue. You are invited to send news and participate! *WIN* is a non-profit organization. Contributions tax-deductible. We hope to hear from you soon. Deadline (next issue): July." circ. 1M-1.1M. 4/yr. Pub'd 4 issues 2009; expects 4 issues 2010, 4 issues 2011. 7 titles listed in the *Small Press Record of Books in Print*

(36th Edition, 2010-11). sub. price $48 institution, $35 individual, add $4/yr postage abroad, add $10/yr air abroad; per copy $5; sample $5. Back issues: $15/year. Discounts: available on request. 80pp. Simultaneous submissions accepted, but must be 1-2 pages of facts, documented reports, and no fiction. Payment: none. Copyrighted. Pub's reviews: 18-20+ in 2009. §Women and international development, women's right world-wide. Ads: $300/$150/$75 1/4 page. Subjects: Health, Women.

Wind Eagle Press, Steve Wingeier, P.O. Box 5379, Atlanta, GA 31107, 404/378-6815, WindEagle-Press@yahoo.com. 2008. Fiction. "Founded with the goal of "environmental education through literary excellence," Wind Eagle Press publishes titles which not only inform readers about the ecological crisis facing this planet but inspire them to help turn it around. We are committed to preserving Earth's forests by using paper with the highest post-consumer recycled content we can afford." avg. press run 1000. Expects 1 title 2010, 1 title 2011. 1 title listed in the *Small Press Record of Books in Print* (36th Edition, 2010-11). Standard discounts to bookstores and wholesalers; contact us for volume discounts. Reporting time: We are not accepting manuscripts at this time. Does not copyright for author. Subjects: Animals, Environment, Fiction, Inspirational, Spiritual.

Wind Publications, 600 Overlook Drive, Nicholasville, KY 40356. No titles listed in the *Small Press Record of Books in Print* (36th Edition, 2010-11).

Wind River Institute Press/Wind River Broadcasting, Jim McDonald, 117 East 11th, Loveland, CO 80537, 970-669-3442, Fax 970-663-6081, 800-669-3993. 1985. Non-fiction. "Technical regulatory in broadcast industry." avg. press run 5M. Pub'd 1 title 2009; expects 2 titles 2010, 2 titles 2011. 1 title listed in the *Small Press Record of Books in Print* (36th Edition, 2010-11). Discounts: 2+ 20%. 200pp. Subjects: Engineering, Government, Law, Radio.

WINDHOVER: A Journal of Christian Literature, Audell Shelburne, UMHB Box 8008, 900 College Street, Belton, TX 76513, 254-295-4561. 1995. Poetry, fiction, art, interviews, reviews, long-poems, plays, non-fiction. "*Windhover* is devoted to promoting writers and literature with a Christian perspective. The journal accepts a broad definition of that perspective while remaining committed to its identity as a journal of Christian literature. The journal accepts unsolicited submissions of poetry, short fiction, non-fiction, and creative non-fiction. Please send no more than four poems per issue. Items longer than 3,000 words (approximately 10 double-spaced pages) are not ordinarily considered. The deadline for submissions is June 1st. The editorial team reads only during summer. Final decisions will be made by August 1st. Please include a stamped postcard for acknowledgement. Manuscripts will be recycled and will not be returned. Manuscripts received after June 1st will be considered for the next annual issue. We do not accept submissions via email." circ. 500. 1/yr. Pub'd 1 issue 2009; expects 1 issue 2010, 1 issue 2011. sub. price $15; per copy $15; sample $8. Back issues: $8. 148pp. Reporting time: 3 months, sometimes longer. Simultaneous submissions accepted: yes. Publishes 10% of manuscripts submitted. Payment: 2 copies. Copyrighted, reverts to author. Pub's reviews: 4 in 2009. §Collections of stories or poetry by Christian writers. Subject: Literary Review.

Windows Project (see also SMOKE), Dave Ward, Liver House, 96 Bold Street, Liverpool L1 4HY, England. 1974. Poetry, fiction, art, photos, cartoons, long-poems, collages, concrete art. avg. press run 500. Pub'd 1 title 2009; expects 1 title 2010. 28 titles listed in the *Small Press Record of Books in Print* (36th Edition, 2010-11). Discounts: 33%. 24pp. Reporting time: as quickly as possible. Publishes 1.28% of manuscripts submitted. Payment: 1 copy. Subject: Poetry.

WindRiver Publishing, JB Howick, President, 72 N WindRiver Rd, Silverton, ID 83867-0446, Phone: 208-752-1836, FAX: 208-752-1876, http://www.windriverpublishing.com. 2003. Fiction, non-fiction. "WindRiver Publishing publishes general fiction with a focus on historical fiction, mystery/thriller, and sci-fi/fantasy; and non-fiction history, general religion, and self-help." Pub'd 2 titles 2009; expects 4 titles 2010, 8 titles 2011. No titles listed in the *Small Press Record of Books in Print* (36th Edition, 2010-11). Discounts: 40% to bookstores, 55% to distributors, 40% to libraries. No minimum order. 300pp. Reporting time: 4-6 months. Simultaneous submissions accepted: Yes. Payment: 15% of net sales. Copyrights for author. Subjects: Christianity, Fantasy, Fiction, Futurism, How-To, Juvenile Fiction, Mystery, Picture Books, Political Science, Politics, Publishing, Religion, Romance, Science Fiction, Self-Help.

Windward Publishing, An Imprint of Finney Company (see also Finney Company, Inc.), Alan Krysan, President, 8075 215th Street West, Lakeville, MN 55044, (952) 469-6699, Fax: (952) 469-1968, (800) 846-7027, Fax: (800) 330-6232, feedback@finneyco.com, www.finneyco.com. 1973. Non-fiction. "This imprint of Finney Company offers trade books for both children and adults with and educational base. Most recent releases are Wild Beach, Through Endangered Eyes, Let's Meet a Marine Educator!, and Nightlight." avg. press run 5000. Pub'd 5 titles 2009; expects 2-7 titles 2010, 5-10 titles 2011. No titles listed in the *Small Press Record of Books in Print* (36th Edition, 2010-11). Discounts: 1-9 copies 20%; 10-24 copies 40%; 25-49 copies 45%; 50 or more copies 50%. Reporting time: 8-10 weeks. Simultaneous submissions accepted: Yes. Payment: varies. Subjects: Animals, Children, Youth, Florida, Leisure/Recreation, Marine Life, Nature,

Non-Fiction, Picture Books, Space, Trade, Travel, Whaling.

Wineberry Press, Elisavietta Ritchie, P.O. Box 298, Broomes Island, MD 20615, 410-586-3086, 202-363-8036, elisavietta.ritchie@gmail.com. 1983. Poetry. "To order books: Wineberry Press, PO Box 298, Broomes Island, MD 20615, 410-586-3086. Send check or money order. Press formed as collaborative to publish anthology *Finding The Name*, 1983. *Get With It, Lord*, chapbook by Beatrice Murphy, 1990; *Horse and Cart: Stories from the Country*, fiction by Elisabeth Stevens, 1990; *Listening For Wings* by Maxine Combs, 2002. Can't handle unsolicited manuscripts—already have plenty I'd like to publish." avg. press run 500-2M. Pub'd 2 titles 2009; expects 1 title 2010, 1 title 2011. 5 titles listed in the *Small Press Record of Books in Print* (36th Edition, 2010-11). Discounts: 40% to booksellers. 32-200pp. Reporting time: ASAP. Simultaneous submissions accepted: no. Publishes 1% of manuscripts submitted. Payment: copies (as many as they need), some free, some discounted. Does not copyright for author. Subjects: Conservation, Fiction, Poetry.

WinePress Publishing, Adam Cothes, Solutions Advistor, PO Box 428, Enumclaw, WA 98022, 360-802-9758, Fax 360-802-9992, info@winepresspub.com. 1993. "Most titles are Christian based messages." avg. press run 2.5M. Pub'd 77 titles 2009; expects 90 titles 2010, 100 titles 2011. 1 title listed in the *Small Press Record of Books in Print* (36th Edition, 2010-11). Discounts: 1-5 books 30%, 6+ 40%, case lots 50%. 168pp. Reporting time: 2-3 days. Simultaneous submissions accepted: yes. Publishes 25% of manuscripts submitted. Payment: author pays for production, keeps all profits from sales. Copyrights for author. Subjects: Christianity, Inspirational, Religion.

Wings Press, Bryce Milligan, 627 E. Guenther, San Antonio, TX 78210, 210-271-7805 (phone and fax). 1975. Poetry, fiction, art, plays, non-fiction. "Wings Press publishes a wide array of multicultural literature. We very very rarely accept unsolicited submissions, and we never publish "poets" who do not read poetry. *The Bloomsbury Review* called Wings Press "the best little publishing house in Texas."." avg. press run 3000. Pub'd 17 titles 2009; expects 16 titles 2010, 12 titles 2011. No titles listed in the *Small Press Record of Books in Print* (36th Edition, 2010-11). Discounts: trade—40%distributors—55%textbook use—20%. 150pp. Reporting time: avg 3 months. Simultaneous submissions accepted: Yes. Publishes 2% of manuscripts submitted. Payment: Royalties but no advances. Copyrights for author. Subjects: African-American, Anthology, Bilingual, Black, Celtic, Chicano/a, Fiction, Latino, Literature (General), Native American, Non-Fiction, Poetry, Texas, U.S. Hispanic, Young Adult.

•**Winoca Books & Media,** 1923 29th Street, Suite 2, Lubbock, TX 79411. "Winoca Books & Media titles represent a symbiotic partnership between publisher and author. As publishers, we bring our full range of editorial, packaging, and marketing expertise to each titlewhile as author, you exercise your unique understanding of your particular readers. The author's financial subvention distributes up-front risk, allowing us to publish deserving books for niche markets and to print quantities of copies only as needed. It also provides the opportunity for revision or correction when an update is called for. As with traditional publishing channels, however, the manuscript consideration process at Winoca is selective. Every project is rigorously reviewed, and a title is accepted only if the quality of its content warrants publication. We do not publish works of a gratuitously violent, discriminatory, or erotic nature, and we reserve the right to reject any project according to our discretion." No titles listed in the *Small Press Record of Books in Print* (36th Edition, 2010-11).

Winslow Publishing, Michelle West, Box 38012, 550 Eglinton Avenue West, Toronto, Ontario M5N 3A8, Canada, 416-789-4733, winslow@interlog.com, www.winslowpublishing.com. 1981. Non-fiction. "After publishing for mail order only since 1981, we moved into book stores in 1986. Title range from *The Complete Guide To Companion Advertising* to *The No-Bull Guide To Getting Published And Making It As A Writer*. At present, most business is still in mail order, and we are always looking for new reps to drop ship for. Please send *Queries only* (no mss)—non-fiction only, which can be marketed through the mail. Books do *not* have to have Canadian content - we are well represented in the U.S., and will be expanding greatly in the next couple of years. (Someday we'll be a *Big* Press!) We are completely computerized, and would appreciate mss on disk." avg. press run 1M-5M (mail order), 5M (bookstore). Pub'd 4 titles 2009; expects 4 titles 2010, 4 titles 2011. 8 titles listed in the *Small Press Record of Books in Print* (36th Edition, 2010-11). Discounts: 40% on 5 or more copies of a title. 160pp. Reporting time: 1-2 weeks. Payment: usual royalties, or purchase ms. outright. Copyrights for author. Subjects: Business & Economics, Communication, Journalism, Consumer, How-To, Printing.

•**Wintertree Press,** Sheila Sundquist, Editor; Roger Furst, Editor, P.O. Box 7818, Wilmington, DE 19803, 302-691-8331, www.wintertreepress.com. 2009. Poetry, fiction, art, photos, long-poems, plays, non-fiction. "We seek a major share of a nich market composed of educated readers who demand excellence in writing and intelligent content. Submissions must exceed the traditional bounds of genre. We expect writers to show, not ask, how that is done." avg. press run 3000. Pub'd 1 title 2009; expects 4 titles 2010, 5 titles 2011. No titles listed in the *Small Press Record of Books in Print* (36th Edition, 2010-11). Discounts: Major distributors =55% off retail. For direct sales to bookstores and retailers: 2-4 copies = 20% off 5-99 copies = 40% off 100 and up in case lots = 50%off. 300pp. Reporting time: Three to six weeks. Simultaneous submissions accepted: Yes.

Publishes 8% of manuscripts submitted. Payment: Highly variable. 15% plus or minus 7%. Copyrights for author. Subjects: Amish Culture, Biography, Creative Non-fiction, Fiction, History, Horror, How-To, Literature (General), Mystery, Novels, Poetry, Prose, Satire, Science, Science Fiction.

WISCONSIN ACADEMY REVIEW, Joan Fischer, Editor, 1922 University Ave., Madison, WI 53705, 608-263-1692. 1954. Poetry, fiction, articles, art, photos, interviews, criticism, reviews. "We use poetry, short fiction, art and literary history, and book reviews that have Wisconsin connected author or subject, as well as scientific articles or political essays which have Wisconsin tie-in. Quarterly journal of the Wisconsin Academy of Sciences, Arts and Letters. If not Wisconsin return address, include Wisconsin connection with submission or query. Include SASE." circ. 1.5M. 4/yr. Pub'd 4 issues 2009; expects 4 issues 2010, 4 issues 2011. sub. price none available, free to members or available for $5 purchase; per copy $5; sample $5. Back issues: none. Discounts: none. 56pp. Reporting time: 8-10 weeks. Simultaneous submissions accepted: no. Payment: 2 copies. Copyrighted. Pub's reviews: 24 in 2009. §Wisconsin connected books by author or subject. Ads: none. Subjects: Culture, Wisconsin.

WISCONSIN TRAILS, Cristy Garcia-Thomas, Publisher; Harriet Brown, Editor; Andrea Bahe, Assistant Editor, 4101 West Burnham St., Milwaukee, WI 53215-2055, e-mail editor@wistrails.com. 1960. Poetry, articles, art, photos, interviews, satire, criticism, reviews, letters, news items, non-fiction. "*Wisconsin Trails* at present is interested in articles about Wisconsin: nature and the environment, heritage, folklore, travel, art and the arts, personality profiles, history, food and restaurants, outdoor sports. Magazine submissions should contain detailed outline plus clips. No phone calls please." circ. 40-45M. 6/yr. Pub'd 6 issues 2009; expects 6 issues 2010, 6 issues 2011. sub. price $24.95; per copy $4.95; sample $4.95 + $3 p/h. Back issues: $7. Discounts: subscription agency, all other universal schedule. 84+pp. Reporting time: 1-3 months. We accept simultaneous submissions, but must be clearly indicated. Publishes 5% of manuscripts submitted. Payment: on publication. Copyrighted, rights revert to author after 60 days. Pub's reviews: 6 in 2009. §Outdoor sports, activities, food and restaurants, travel, arts events, anything dealing w/Wisconsin, photography. Ads: frequency discounts available; contact Erika Baer, ebaer@wistrails.com, for information. Subjects: Agriculture, Animals, Arts, Bicycling, Conservation, Cooking, Environment, Essays, Folklore, History, Non-Fiction, Performing Arts, Sports, Outdoors, Travel, Wisconsin.

Wisdom Publications, Inc., Timothy McNeill, Publisher; David Kittelstrom, Editor; Josh Bartok, Editor, 199 Elm Street, Somerville, MA 02144-3129, 617-776-7416; Fax 617-776-7841. 1975. Non-fiction. "Wisdom Publications is dedicated to making available authentic Buddhist works for the benefit of all. We publish translations of the sutras and tantras, commentaries and teachings of past and contemporary Buddhist masters, and original works by the world's leading Buddhist scholars. We publish our titles with the appreciation of Buddhism as a living philosophy and with the special commitment to preserve and transmit important works from all the major Buddhist traditions. Wisdom Publications is a 501(c)3 nonprofit charitable organization, and all profits are reinvested into the creation of new works. Our titles are distributed worldwide and have been translated into more than thirty foreign languages. We have a backlist of over two hundred titles in print, with over twenty new titles appearing each year." avg. press run 5M. Pub'd 12 titles 2009; expects 12 titles 2010, 14 titles 2011. 16 titles listed in the *Small Press Record of Books in Print* (36th Edition, 2010-11). Discounts: Trade sales thru Publishers Group West. 224pp. Reporting time: 3 months. Simultaneous submissions accepted: yes. Publishes 5% of manuscripts submitted. Payment: once a year based on net sales. We sometimes copyright for author. Subjects: Asia, Indochina, Buddhism, Philosophy, Psychology, Religion, Self-Help, Spiritual.

Wise Press, Line Wise, 8794 Rolling Acres Trail, Fair Oaks, TX 78015-4015, Fax 619-437-4160, lwise@san.rr.com, www.wisepress.com. 1999. Long-poems, non-fiction. avg. press run 5M. Expects 1 title 2010, 2 titles 2011. 1 title listed in the *Small Press Record of Books in Print* (36th Edition, 2010-11). Discounts: 40%, buyer pays shipping. 188pp. Reporting time: 3 months. Simultaneous submissions accepted: yes. Publishes 5-10% of manuscripts submitted. Payment: 2 books. Copyrights for author. Subjects: Grieving, Poetry, Senior Citizens, Short Stories.

THE WISE WOMAN, Ann Forfreedom, 2441 Cordova Street, Oakland, CA 94602, 510-536-3174. 1980. Poetry, articles, art, photos, cartoons, interviews, reviews, music, news items, non-fiction. "No longer accepting unsolicited submissions. Focus of *The Wise Woman*: feminist spirituality, feminist witchcraft, feminist issues. Includes articles, columns (such as *The War Against Women* and *The Rising of Women*). Annotated songs appropriate to subject, interviews, poems, art, wise sayings, cartoons by Bulbul, photos. Also available on microfilm through University Microfilms International." circ. small but influential. 4/yr. Pub'd 2 issues 2009; expects 2 issues 2010, 4 issues 2011. sub. price $15; per copy $4; sample $4. Back issues: $4. 20pp. Reporting time: varies, try to reply promptly when SASE is included. Simultaneous submissions accepted: no. Payment: copy of the issue. Copyrighted, rights revert to author, but TWW reserves the right to reprint. Subjects: Feminism, Occult, Spiritual.

Wish Publishing, Holly Kondras, President, PO Box 10337, Terra Haute, IN 47801, 812-299-5700, email:holly@wishpublishing.com. 1999. Non-fiction. "We are a women's sports publishing company. We publish books by and for women in sports." avg. press run 3M. Pub'd 8 titles 2009; expects 8 titles 2010, 8 titles 2011. 3 titles listed in the *Small Press Record of Books in Print* (36th Edition, 2010-11). 224pp. Reporting time: 6-8 weeks. Simultaneous submissions accepted: yes. Publishes 10% of manuscripts submitted. Payment: arranged on a title by title basis. Copyrights for author. Subjects: Health, Sports, Outdoors, Women.

Wizard Works, Jan O'Meara, PO Box 1125, Homer, AK 99603, 907-235-8757 phone/Fax, toll free 877-210-2665, wizard@xyz.net. 1988. Poetry, fiction, art, photos, cartoons, reviews, non-fiction. "Alaska subjects only. No unsolicited manuscripts without query first." avg. press run 1M. Pub'd 2 titles 2009; expects 2 titles 2010, 2 titles 2011. 11 titles listed in the *Small Press Record of Books in Print* (36th Edition, 2010-11). Discounts: library 20%, wholesale 1-5 20%, 6-99 40%, 100+ 50%. 130pp. Payment: negotiable. Copyrights for author. Subject: Alaska.

The Wolf Pirate Project Inc., Catherine Rudy, 4801 SW 164 Terrace, Fort Lauderdale, FL 33331, www.wolf-pirate.com. 2007. Fiction. "The Wolf Pirate Project is an innovative, nonprofit organization for the eductation of writers and readers in the pursuit of developing an appreciation for literary merit in all types of literature. The Wolf Pirate Project does not publish authors in a traditional sense but works extensively with them with the hopes of preparing them for their career as a writer and to promote a limited number of outstanding authors to the publishing industry. The Project does not charge for any of its programs and receives no remittance from promotion. Visit our website at wolf-pirate.com to learn more about our mission and requirements. Proceeds from the sales of limited quantities of selected author works supports the endeavors of the project." Expects 3 titles 2010, 4 titles 2011. 6 titles listed in the *Small Press Record of Books in Print* (36th Edition, 2010-11). 370 pages originally 6x9 trade paperback size, but all books now printed at 5.5x8.5 digest size.pp. Reporting time: Authors are solicited through workshop scouting. Not entertaining unsolicited queries at this time. Yes. Publishes we promote no more than four authors annually.% of manuscripts submitted. Payment: Selected authors for promotion receive significant number of copies of their work for distribution as they see fit. Copyrights for author. Subjects: Crime, Experimental, Fantasy, Fiction, Horror, Humor, Juvenile Fiction, Mystery, Myth, Mythology, Novels, Occult, Romance, Satire, Science Fiction, Supernatural.

WOMEN AND LANGUAGE, Patricia Sotirin, Editor, Humanities Dept, Michigan Technological University, Houghton, MI 49931-1295. 1975. Articles, cartoons, interviews, criticism, reviews, news items, non-fiction. "*Women and Language* is an interdisciplinary research periodical. WL attends to communication, language, gender and women's issues. It reports books, journals, articles and research in progress; publishes short articles and speeches." circ. 400+. 2/yr. Pub'd 2 issues 2009; expects 2 issues 2010, 2 issues 2011. sub. price $40 (US) all international institutions; $30 all US institutions; $15 U.S., Canadian and Mexican individuals; $25 other international individuals.; per copy $7.50. Back issues: A few issues are available in photocopy only; additional charge applies for international shipping. 70pp. Reporting time: 2-3 months. Publishes 35% of manuscripts submitted. Payment: none. Copyrighted, does not revert to author. Pub's reviews: 10 in 2009. §Women's studies, language, gender, linguistics, communication, speech, public address. No ads. Subjects: Communication, Journalism, Feminism, Gender Issues, Language, Speaking, Women.

Women and Men Books, Marilyn Nodiff, P.O. Box 98, Bethlehem, CT 06751-0098, 203.266.7118, publisher@womenandmenbooks.com, www.womenandmenbooks.com. 2006. Fiction, non-fiction. "Serious literary works that explore the relationship between women and men. Recent contributor: Marilyn Jane Babcock. Title: Equality Ascended." Pub'd 1 title 2009; expects 1 title 2010. 1 title listed in the *Small Press Record of Books in Print* (36th Edition, 2010-11). Discounts: 40% discount any quantity, no returns. 455pp. Subjects: Divorce, Family, Fiction, Men, Novels, Prose, Women.

WOMEN IN THE ARTS BULLETIN/NEWSLETTER, Women In The Arts Foundation, Inc., Erin Butler, 32-35 30th Street #D24, Astoria, NY 11106, 718-545-9337. 1971. Articles, photos, interviews, letters, news items. "Length: 200 to 1,000 words—must be on women's art movement or topics relevant to women artists." circ. 1M. 3/yr. Pub'd 3 issues 2009; expects 3 issues 2010, 3 issues 2011. sub. price $9, $15 institution, $19 foreign; per copy $1; sample free. 6pp. Reporting time: 2-3 months. Payment: none. Copyrighted, reverts to author. Pub's reviews: 1 in 2009. §Women's visual art & writing. Ads: $110/$60. Subjects: Arts, Women.

Women In The Arts Foundation, Inc. (see also WOMEN IN THE ARTS BULLETIN/NEWSLETTER), Erin Butler, Editor, 32-35 30th Street #D24, Astoria, NY 11106. 1971. 1 title listed in the *Small Press Record of Books in Print* (36th Edition, 2010-11). Payment: none. Does not copyright for author.

Women of Diversity Productions, Inc., 5790 Park Street, Las Vegas, NV 89149-2304, 702-341-9807; fax 702-341-9828; E-mail dvrsty@aol.com. 1995. Art, photos, cartoons, non-fiction. avg. press run 3.5M. Pub'd 1 title 2009; expects 1 title 2010, 2 titles 2011. 3 titles listed in the *Small Press Record of Books in Print* (36th Edition, 2010-11). Discounts: 40% trade; 50% for 100 or more bulk, agent, author; 20% classroom. 150pp. Reporting time: 1-2 months. Simultaneous submissions accepted: yes. Publishes less than 50% of manuscripts submitted. Payment: 8% first 1000, increasing increments. Copyrights for author. Subjects: Health, Mental Health, Parenting, Psychology, Self-Help, Self-Help, Women.

WOMEN'S REVIEW OF BOOKS, Amy Hoffman, 628 North 2nd Street, Philadelphia, PA 19123, 215-925-4390. 1983. Poetry, fiction, articles, art, photos, cartoons, interviews, criticism, reviews, letters, news items. circ. 7500. 6/yr. Pub'd 11 issues 2009; expects 3 issues 2010, 6 issues 2011. sub. price $38; per copy $6; sample free. Back issues: $5. Discounts: 5% to subscription agents on instituional subscriptions. 32pp. Reporting time: Contact Editor. Simultaneous submissions accepted: No. Payment: Contact Editor. Copyrighted. Pub's reviews: 50 in 2009. §Books by and about women. Ads: Contact publisher info@oldcitypublishing.com for rate card information.

Women's Studies Librarian, University of Wisconsin System (see also FEMINIST COLLECTIONS: A QUARTERLY OF WOMEN'S STUDIES RESOURCES; FEMINIST PERIODICALS: A CURRENT LISTING OF CONTENTS; NEW BOOKS ON WOMEN, GENDER, & FEMINISM), Phyllis Holman Weisbard, JoAnne Lehman, Linda Fain, Heather Shimon, 430 Memorial Library, 728 State Street, Madison, WI 53706, 608-263-5754. 1977. Articles, interviews, criticism, reviews, non-fiction. "In addition to the three periodicals listed above, we publish a series *Wisconsin Bibliographies in Women's Studies.*" avg. press run 1.1M. Pub'd 1 title 2009. No titles listed in the *Small Press Record of Books in Print* (36th Edition, 2010-11). Reporting time: 1-2 weeks. Simultaneous submissions accepted: no. Payment: none. Does not copyright for author. Subjects: Bibliography, Book Collecting, Bookselling, Book Reviewing, Feminism, Indexes & Abstracts, Lesbianism, Libraries, Printing, Wisconsin, Women.

WOOD COIN: An Online Magazine of Literature & Liberal Arts, James Beach, Wood Coin Press, 551 W. Cordova Rd., #369, Santa Fe, NM 87505, http://www.woodcoin.net. 2008. Poetry, fiction, articles, art, photos, cartoons, interviews, satire, criticism, reviews, music, letters, parts-of-novels, long-poems, collages, plays, concrete art, news items, non-fiction. "For ages 12 & up. An introduction to literature & the liberal arts. Themed issues." circ. 1000. 6/yr. Pub'd 1 issue 2009; expects 6 issues 2010, 6 issues 2011. sample price free. Back issues: inquire. Discounts: please inquire. 37pp. Reporting time: Response within 2 weeks to any submission of up to 10 pages. Simultaneous submissions accepted: Yes. Payment: Wood Coin offers no monetary compensation at this time. Copyrighted, reverts to author. Pub's reviews: none in 2009. §open.

Wood Thrush Books, Walt McLaughlin, Publisher, Editor; Judy Ashley, Associate Editor, 85 Aldis Street, St. Albans, VT 05478, 802-524-6606. 1985. Non-fiction. "Currently looking at booklength collections of nature-related essays and non-fiction narratives. No longer publishing chapbooks of poetry." avg. press run 200. Pub'd 1 title 2009; expects 1 title 2010, 1 title 2011. 20 titles listed in the *Small Press Record of Books in Print* (36th Edition, 2010-11). Discounts: 40%. 72-128pp. Reporting time: 3 months. Publishes 2% of manuscripts submitted. Payment: copies. Copyrights for author. Subjects: Earth, Natural History, Essays, Nature, Non-Fiction, Philosophy, Sports, Outdoors.

Wood Works, Paul Hunter, 4131 Greenwood Ave. N., Seattle, WA 98103-7017, www.woodworkspress.com. 1994. Poetry, fiction, long-poems. avg. press run 400-500. Pub'd 1 title 2009; expects 2 titles 2010, 2 titles 2011. No titles listed in the *Small Press Record of Books in Print* (36th Edition, 2010-11). Discounts: 40% on trade paper, no discount on signed hardbound. 32pp. Reporting time: 3-6 months. Simultaneous submissions accepted: no. Publishes 1-5% of manuscripts submitted. Payment: 50 copies plus the first signed hardback. Copyrights for author. Subject: Poetry.

Woodland Press, LLC and Woodland Gospel Publishing, Cheryl Davis, Aquisitions; Davis Keith, CEO; Mike Collins, Associate, 118 Woodland Drive, Chapmanville, WV 25508, 304-752-7152, Fax 304-752-9002; woodlandpressllc@mac.com. 2002. Non-fiction. "We focus on Appalachian History, non-fiction. We also emphasize inspirational titles through our Woodland Gospel Publishing imprint." avg. press run 5000. Pub'd 6 titles 2009; expects 6 titles 2010, 10 titles 2011. 2 titles listed in the *Small Press Record of Books in Print* (36th Edition, 2010-11). Discounts: 40% -55% based upon quantity. Simultaneous submissions accepted: Yes. Publishes 10% of manuscripts submitted. Payment: 60 - 90-days.

WOODWORKER'S JOURNAL, Rob Johnstone, Editor in Chief; Joanna Takes, Senior Editor; Chris Marshall, Field Editor, 4365 Willow Drive, Medina, MN 55340, 763-478-8306, Fax 763-478-8396, editor@woodworkersjournal.com. 1976. Articles. "Woodworking articles." circ. 243,716. 6/yr. Pub'd 6 issues 2009; expects 6 issues 2010, 6 issues 2011. sub. price $19.95; per copy $5.99. 98pp. Reporting time: 6 months. Simultaneous submissions accepted: no. Publishes less than 5% of manuscripts submitted. Payment: 25¢/word. Copyrighted, does not revert to author. Pub's reviews: 3 in 2009. §Woodworking. Ads: full-page $9,880 4-color 1X, $7,870 4-color 12X; half-page $5,145 4-color 1X, half-page $4,125 4-color 12X. Subjects: Crafts, Hobbies, Wood Engraving/Woodworking.

THE WORCESTER REVIEW, Rodger Martin, 1 Ekman St., Worcester, MA 01607-1513, 978-797-4770, www.theworcesterreview.org. 1973. Poetry, fiction, art, photos, satire, criticism. "Submit up to five poems. Fiction to 4,000 words maximum. Literary articles and criticism should have a central New England connection. Photography: black and white glossy, minimum 5''x 7''. Graphic art: black and white, minimum 5''x 7''. Starting in 2010, we will look at limited color artwork. (Author's name should appear in upper left of each page." circ. 750. 1/yr. Pub'd 1 issue 2009; expects 1 issue 2010, 1 issue 2011. sub. price $30 membership in Worcester County Poetry Assoc.; per copy $15; sample $8 plus $2.50 shipping and handling. Back issues: see website listing. Discounts: 20% on orders of 10 or more of current issues. 150pp. Reporting time: 9-12 months. Simultaneous submissions accepted: yes with notice and notification if a piece has been accepted elsewehere. Payment: 2 contributor's copies plus very small honorarium. Copyrighted, reverts to author. Pub's reviews: 2 in 2009. §Central New England writers (primarily poets). Ads: $150 benefactors/$75 patrons; Full page per issue $250/1/2 pg. $150. Subjects: Criticism, Fiction, Graphics, Literary Review, New England, Photography, Poetry.

Word Forge Books, Mary Shafer, Almost Perfect: Disabled Pets and the People Who Love Them; Rebecca Valentine, Devastation on the Delaware: Stories and Images of the Deadly Flood of 1955, Mission: Murder, PO Box 97, Ferndale, PA 18921, Tel 610-847-2456, email admin@wordforgebooks.com, URL www.wordforge-books.com. 2005. Fiction, art, photos, non-fiction. "Word Forge Books is an independent publisher of quality nonfiction and fiction titles about the following subjects: National and MidAtlantic regional history, American folkways & folklore, weather & the environment, nature, animals & habitat, and mind/body/spirit. More than ever, our world can be a dangerous and frightening place. People are bombarded daily with dark, scary and cynical messages and images. We believe what's really needed now are messages of hope, of positive vision, and of genuine caring for all living creatures. Our mission is to provide a platform for some of today's most forward-thinking, constructive voices in ideas and literature. We seek out authors and artists whose sincere wish is to help make a better world for us all. Many of our products carry a give-back, meaning that a portion of the sale of each item is donated to a related charity or independent project. Word Forge Books is constantly searching for products that will help our customers adopt and live with such constructive ideas and visions. Our lines include: BOOKS, Audiobooks, Interactive titles on DVD, eBooks; ARTWORK: Original 2D & 3D works, Limited edition prints, Stationery, greeting & blank note cards; RELATED PRODUCTS: Calendars, Tins, licensed character figures and other unique gift items. We hope readers find Word Forge Books an oasis of what's best about our world, and a sense of comfort and connectedness in our community of readers and doers." avg. press run 2500. Expects 2 titles 2010, 2 titles 2011. 3 titles listed in the *Small Press Record of Books in Print* (36th Edition, 2010-11). Discounts: All: 5 copy min.; shipping via media mail $2.50 1st copy, $0.75 ea. add'l, all prepaid. Booksellers: 40% returnable, 50% non-returnable. Retailers: 50% non-returnable. Classrooms & Libraries: 1-4 copies full retail; 5-9 copies 10%; 10+ 15%.Wholesalers & jobbers: negotiable. 300pp. Reporting time: 12-18 months. Simultaneous submissions accepted: Yes. Publishes 30% of manuscripts submitted. Payment: At this point, everything is negotiable, depending on the needs of the creator and our needs as a publisher. We register our books and other products with the copyright office, in whose name the contract stipulates holds the copyright. That could be us or the author, depending on our negotiations. Subjects: Alternative Medicine, Americana, Animals, Anthology, Arts, Creativity, Fiction, Gay, Grieving, Health, History, Nature, Photography, Picture Books, Weather.

WORD RIOT, Jackie Corley, Publisher; Kevin O'Cuinn, Fiction Editor; Martha Clarkson, Poetry Editor, PO Box 414, Middletown, NJ 07748, online journal at: http://www.wordriot.org. 2002. "Word Riot published its first issue in March 2002. Each month we provide readers with book reviews, author interviews, and, most importantly, writing from some of the best and brightest making waves on the literary scene. We accept submissions of experimental and literary fiction, non-fiction, and poetry. Prose should be emailed to wr.submissions@gmail.com, submissions of poetry to wr.poetry@gmail.com, and creative non-fiction to wr.submissions@gmail.com with the piece submitted in the body of the email or, in the case of fictional prose, as a Microsoft Word document. No snail mail please." 12/yr. 2 titles listed in the *Small Press Record of Books in Print* (36th Edition, 2010-11). Pub's reviews: approx. 25 in 2009. §Fiction, poetry and creative non-fiction.

The Word Works, Nancy White, President, Co-Editor-in-Chief; Karren Alenier, Co-Editor-in-Chief, PO Box 42164, Washington, DC 20015, fax: 301-581-9443, editor@wordworksdc.com, www.wordworksdc.com. 1974. Poetry. "The Word Works publishes contemporary poetry in single author volumes and, occasionally, in anthologies. Our annual Washington Prize has awarded book publication to such noted authors as Enid Shomer, Christopher Bursk, Fred Marchant, Nathalie Anderson, Miles Waggener, Ron Mohring, Frannie Lindsay, and Richard Lyons. We only read unsolicited work through our Washington Prize. Guidelines for the Washington Prize are available on our web site." avg. press run 1000. Pub'd 4 titles 2009; expects 4 titles 2010, 2 titles 2011. 13 titles listed in the *Small Press Record of Books in Print* (36th Edition, 2010-11). Discounts: 5+ copies 40% but buyer pays shipping. 72pp. Reporting time: 5 months. Simultaneous submissions accepted: Yes. Publishes Less than 1% of manuscripts submitted. Payment: 100 author copies, author support, review copies, and distribution through both Ingram and SPD are provided. Does not copyright for author. Subjects: Experimental, Literature (General), Translation.

Wordcraft of Oregon, LLC, David Memmott, P.O. Box 3235, La Grande, OR 97850, 541-912-8261. 1987. Poetry, fiction. "Preference is for poetry collections, novels and story collections with emphasis on Pacific Northwest. Only occasionally publish non-fiction but only with editor's invitation. Currently closed to unsolicited submissions as we have projects planned through 2011. Most recent authors include John Griswold, Linda Lappin, Alex Kuo, Matt Schumacher, Ellen Waterston, Leslie What and Lars Nordstrom's translations of

Harry Martinson. In 2010 will see books by David Axelrod, Peter Donahue, Dan Raphael and Bette Husted." avg. press run 500-1000. Pub'd 5 titles 2009; expects 5 titles 2010, 5 titles 2011. 21 titles listed in the *Small Press Record of Books in Print* (36th Edition, 2010-11). Discounts: Standard 40% discount to bookstores for all orders. See website for more ordering info. 60-300pp. Reporting time: two months. Simultaneous submissions accepted: No. Payment: standard 10% royalty on net sales. Depends on what is arranged with author, either copyrights for author or copyright reverts to author. Subjects: Experimental, Fantasy, Fiction, Novels, Pacific Northwest, Poetry, Reprints, Satire, Science Fiction, Short Stories, Writers/Writing.

WordFarm, Marci Johnson, 2816 E Spring St., Seattle, WA 98122, info@wordfarm.net. 2002. Poetry, fiction, non-fiction. avg. press run 1500. Pub'd 2 titles 2009; expects 4 titles 2010, 4 titles 2011. No titles listed in the *Small Press Record of Books in Print* (36th Edition, 2010-11). 112pp. Reporting time: 3-6 months. Simultaneous submissions accepted: yes.

WORDKNOT AUDIO: A Literary Podcast Magazine, Ramona Broussard, 515 Krebs Lane #102, Austin, TX 78704, wordknot@gmail.com, www.wordknot.com. 2006. Fiction, satire, long-poems, plays. "This is an audio magazine for literary readers. We are seeking stories that make a reader laugh, cry, or both. Genre fiction is likely not for us, though we are interested in experimental work. Check www.wordknot.com for our full guidelines." circ. 100. 48/yr. Expects 10 issues 2010, 48 issues 2011. sub. price $0; per copy $0; sample free. Back issues: free. Discounts: This is a free podcast magazine. 3pp. Reporting time: 1 month. Simultaneous submissions accepted: Yes. Publishes 10% of manuscripts submitted. Payment: $20 for over 1500 words, $5 for under 700 words. We are buying the rights to produce stories in an audio format only. Stories will be distributed using the Creative Commons Attribution/Noncommercial/No Derivative Works license. §Literature. Ads: No advertising right now. Subjects: Absurdist, Biography, Creative Non-fiction, Experimental, Fiction, Gender Issues, History, Humor, Literature (General), Politics, Race, Reprints.

Words Without Borders, Susan Harris, Editor, PO Box 1658, New York, NY 10276, info@wordswithoutborders.org, http://wordswithoutborders.org. 2003. Poetry, fiction, articles, cartoons, criticism, parts-of-novels, long-poems, plays, non-fiction. "We accept translations only and the author must be a native speaker of the original language. We do not publish work originally written in English or by native English speakers writing in another language." Pub'd 12 titles 2009; expects 12 titles 2010, 12 titles 2011. No titles listed in the *Small Press Record of Books in Print* (36th Edition, 2010-11). Simultaneous submissions accepted: yes.

The WordShed, LLC (see also THE APUTAMKON REVIEW), Les Simon, Post Office Box 190, Jonesboro, ME 04648-0190, 207/434-5661, thewordshed@tds.net. 2005. Poetry, fiction, articles, art, photos, cartoons, interviews, satire, criticism, music, letters, parts-of-novels, collages, plays, concrete art, news items, non-fiction. "DO NOT SUBMIT UNLESS YOU LIVE FULL OR PART TIME IN DOWNEAST MAINE OR THE CANADIAN MARITIMES." avg. press run 500. Pub'd 1 title 2009; expects 1 title 2010, 1 title 2011. No titles listed in the *Small Press Record of Books in Print* (36th Edition, 2010-11). Discounts: 25%. 160pp. Reporting time: Between May 1 and July 31 each year. Simultaneous submissions accepted: Yes. Publishes 90% of submissions coming from Downeast Maine and the Canadian Maritimes% of manuscripts submitted. Payment: First North American Serial Rights.

Wordsonthestreet, Tony O'Dwyer, Gerardine Burke, Six San Antonio Park, Salthill, Galway, Ireland, publisher@wordsonthestreet.com, www.wordsonthestreet.com. 2005. Poetry, fiction, non-fiction. "Quality fiction and poetry plus non-fiction (memoir, biography, local history) under imprint 6th House." 12 titles listed in the *Small Press Record of Books in Print* (36th Edition, 2010-11). Discounts: 35%-50%. Reporting time: Closed for submissions but see website www.wordsonthestreet.com. Simultaneous submissions accepted: Prefer not. Publishes 20% of manuscripts submitted. Payment: Generally 10% royalties on net sales. Copyrights for author. Subjects: Catholic, Creative Non-fiction, Drama, Education, Fiction, Literature (General), Memoirs, Non-Fiction, Novels, Poetry, Short Stories, Textbooks, Young Adult.

Wordwrights Canada, Susan Ioannou, PO Box 456, Station O, Toronto, Ontario M4A 2P1, Canada, wordwrights@sympatico.ca, www.wordwrights.ca. 1985. avg. press run 100-1M. Pub'd 1 title 2009; expects 1 title 2010. 4 titles listed in the *Small Press Record of Books in Print* (36th Edition, 2010-11). Discounts: please request schedule. 28-260pp. Reporting time: 1 month. Simultaneous submissions accepted: no. Publishes less than 1% of manuscripts submitted. Payment/honorarium on publication plus copies. Author owns copyright. Subjects: Creativity, Criticism, Fiction, Poetry, Short Stories, Writers/Writing.

WORKERS WRITE!, David LaBounty, P.O. Box 250382, Plano, TX 75025-0382, 9728240646, www.workerswritejournal.com. 2005. Poetry, fiction, plays. "Workers Write! is an annual literary journal—theme-oriented collections of the best stories from the workplace." circ. 1500. 1/yr. Pub'd 1 issue 2009; expects 1 issue 2010, 1 issue 2011. sub. price $15 - includes 6 copies of Overtime; per copy $8; sample $8. Back issues: inquire. 140pp. Reporting time: 6 to 8 weeks. Simultaneous submissions accepted: Yes. Publishes 5% of manuscripts submitted. Payment: $5 - $50 depending on length and rights requested. Copyrighted, reverts to author. Subject: Worker.

547

WORKERS WRITE!, Blue Cubicle Press, LLC, David LaBounty, P.O. Box 250382, Plano, TX 75025-0382, 9728240646. 2005. Poetry, fiction, cartoons, satire, plays. "Workers Write! is an annual literary journal—theme-oriented collections of the best stories from the workplace." circ. 1500. 1/yr. Pub'd 1 issue 2009; expects 1 issue 2010, 1 issue 2011. sub. price $15; per copy $8; sample $8. Back issues: $8. 160pp. Reporting time: 6-8 weeks. Simultaneous submissions accepted: Yes. Publishes 10% of manuscripts submitted. Payment: $5-$50. Copyrighted, reverts to author. Subjects: Fiction, Labor, Poetry, Prose, Short Stories, Worker.

WORKING WRITER, Maggie Frisch, PO Box 6943, Libertyville, IL 60048, workingwriters@aol.com. 2000. Articles, criticism, letters, non-fiction. "*Working Writer Newsletter* is for writers of all genres, at all levels. Submissions on writing topics (how-to, how-not-to, tips, shared experience) are always welcome. Request guidelines by e-mail, or simply e-mail article to workingwriters@aol.com (not as attachment). *WW* offers "solid information with a sense of humor and a spirit of writing camraderie." circ. 200. 6/yr. Pub'd 6 issues 2009; expects 6 issues 2010, 6 issues 2011. sub. price $12.95 by mail, $24.95/2 years, $6 by e-mail (PDF); per copy $2.00 regular mail, $1.00 by e-mail; sample free by e-mail, on request. Back issues: $2 by regular mail, $1 by e-mail. Discounts: $11.95/year for seniors, students; quantities provided at cost for conferences, classrooms, etc. 12pp. Reporting time: immediate (upon receipt). Simultaneous submissions accepted: yes. Publishes 90% of manuscripts submitted. Payment: byline, short bio with plug for books, copies of article, link to WW website. Copyrighted, reverts to author. Ads: none. Subject: Writers/Writing.

THE WORLD, The Poetry Project, Staff of the Poetry Project, St. Marks Church/The Poetry Project, 131 East 10th Street, New York, NY 10003, poproj@thorn.net. 1966. Poetry, fiction, interviews, long-poems. "Recent contributors: Alice Notley, John Ashbery, Amiri Baraka, Diane de Prima, Wang Ping, Ron Padgett, Paul Beatty, Eric Bogosian, Wanda Coleman, Harryette Mullen, Brenda Coultas, Tracie Morris, Jamie Manrique." circ. 750. 1/yr. Pub'd 1 issue 2009; expects 1 issue 2010, 1 issue 2011. sub. price $25/4 issues; per copy $7; sample $7. Back issues: on request. Discounts: none. 128pp. Reporting time: 6 months. Simultaneous submissions accepted: yes. Publishes 5% of manuscripts submitted. Payment: copies. Copyrighted, reverts to author. Ads: $125/$75. Subjects: Fiction, Poetry.

World Audience, M. Stefan Strozier, 303 Park Avenue South, Suite 1440, New York, NY 10010-3657, (646) 620-7406; http://www.worldaudience.org; http://www.worldaudience.co.uk; http://www.worldaudience.mobi; http://www.mstefanstrozier.org. "World Audience, Inc. is an independent press in New York with nearly 200 titles and we are growing every month. Get the latest issue of our literary journal, "audience"—http://www.worldaudience.org/pubs_aud_mag_issues.html." 126 titles listed in the *Small Press Record of Books in Print* (36th Edition, 2010-11).

World Changing Books, Jason Wolf, Justin Pahio, Northview Hotel BRGY 46, Condo #9, Laoag, Ilocos Norte, Philippines, 808-934-7942. 1993. Non-fiction. "Second address: 489 Ocean View Dr., Hilo, HI 96720. Our primary concern this year is with the book *Never 'Old': The Ultimate Success Story* by Jesse Anson Dawn. This book is the product of 24 years of study and research, and presents unprecedented breakthroughs in health and anti-aging - all presented in a lively and delightful style." avg. press run 5M. Pub'd 1 title 2009; expects 3-4 titles 2010, 1 title 2011. 2 titles listed in the *Small Press Record of Books in Print* (36th Edition, 2010-11). Discounts: 40-50% for wholesale and bookstores. 250pp. Reporting time: 1-2 weeks. Payment: negotiable. Copyrights for author. Subjects: Aging, Health, Human Rights, Humor.

World Gumbo Publishing, Douglas Barkley, 7801 Alma Suite 105-323, Plano, TX 75025-3483, 1-888-318-2911, dbarkley@worldgumbo.com, www.worldgumbo.com. 2004. Non-fiction. "Information is Yummy!!! At World Gumbo Publishing, we are commited to providing vital, hip, and fresh business and personal growth information to savvy readers. Think COOL Business Books.Publishers of Cracking the Networking CODE - 4 Steps to Priceless Business Relationships by Dean Lindsay." avg. press run 10,000. Expects 3 titles 2011. 1 title listed in the *Small Press Record of Books in Print* (36th Edition, 2010-11). Discounts: Special Trade Discounts Available!!! contact Toll Free: 1-800-346-5566. 160-192pp. Reporting time: 6 weeks. Simultaneous submissions accepted: Yes. Publishes 2% of manuscripts submitted. Payment: Varies Greatly. Copyrighting is available but not a deal breaker. Subjects: Advertising, Self-Promotion, Business & Economics, Consulting, Humor, Inspirational, Leadership, Mentoring/Coaching, Multicultural, Networking, Non-Fiction, Public Relations/Publicity, Scandinavia, Self-Help, Speaking, Trivia.

World Love Press Publishing, Dan S. Leyrer, 1028 Joliet Street, New Orleans, LA 70118, 504-866-4476 phone/Fax, worldlovepress@aol.com. 2000. Poetry, fiction, satire, non-fiction. avg. press run 3M. Expects 1 title 2010, 2 titles 2011. 1 title listed in the *Small Press Record of Books in Print* (36th Edition, 2010-11). Discounts: 2-4 books 20%, 5-9 30%, 10-24 40%, 25-49 42%, 50-74 44%, 75-199 48%, 200+ 50%, classroom 1-12 books 20%, 13+ 40%. 112pp. Reporting time: 30 days. Publishes -30% of manuscripts submitted. Payment: varies. Copyrights for author. Subjects: Fiction, Humor, Metaphysics, Poetry, The West, Zen.

•World Parade Books, 5267 Warner Ave., #191, Huntington Beach, CA 92649-4079. "Founded in 2007, World Parade Books is dedicated to publishing authors from all over the globe whose work captires the beauty, energy and complexity of the American experience based in Southern California. We are a press that is interested in promoting original, accessible narratives that embody the independent, free-spirited ethos that has long been a vital strand in our country's artistic growth and success. Poetry, crime, young adult, memoir, fiction." No titles listed in the *Small Press Record of Books in Print* (36th Edition, 2010-11).

WORLD POETRY SHOWCASE, J. Mark Press, Barbara Morris Fischer, PO Box 24-3474, Boynton Beach, FL 33424, www.JMarkPress.com. 2005. Articles, letters, non-fiction. "An ongoing, online poetry contest." Ongoing. Reporting time: Same day. Simultaneous submissions accepted: yes. Publishes 60% of manuscripts submitted. Copyrighted, reverts to author. Subjects: Advertising, Self-Promotion, The Americas, Asia, Indochina, Australia, Cities, Dining, Restaurants, Entertainment, Europe, Festivals, Leisure/Recreation, Lighthouses, Portugal, Reviews, Shipwrecks, Travel.

•**WORN FASHION JOURNAL, The House of Worn,** Serah-Marie McMahon, Editor-in-pants & Publisher, 77 Maynard Ave., #3, Toronto, Ontario, Canada, 416-531-3145. 2005. "Discusses the cultures, subcultures, histories, and personal stories of fashion. We strive to embody a place between pop culture magazine and academic journal that opens new avenues in art and fashion theory by hovering where these two ideas intersect, connecting with fashion scholars and artists. We pay attention to how what is worn is made, interpreted, transformed, disseminated, and copied." circ. 4000. Pub'd 2 issues 2009. 48pp. Reporting time: 6 months (deadlines posted on website). Payment: honorariums and donations. Subjects: Clothing, Crafts, Hobbies, Fashion, Textiles.

Write Now Publishing Company, Mark Christian, P.O. Box 40297, Redford, MI 48240, Phone (313) 887-5153 Website www.writenowpublishingcompany.com. 2006. Poetry, fiction, articles, non-fiction. avg. press run 5000. Pub'd 1 title 2009; expects 4 titles 2010, 4 titles 2011. 1 title listed in the *Small Press Record of Books in Print* (36th Edition, 2010-11). Discounts: 10-100 copies 25% discount. 136pp. Reporting time: 4-12 weeks. Simultaneous submissions accepted: Yes. Publishes 10% of manuscripts submitted. Payment: 10-15%. Copyrights for author. Subjects: How-To, Marriage, Non-Fiction, Self-Help, Short Stories, Spiritual, Women.

•**The Write Place At the Write Time,** Nicole M. Bouchard, Editor-in-Chief, http://www.thewriteplaceatthewritetime.org/. "L*The Write Place At the Write Time* is an online literary publication which features fiction, poetry, "Our Stories"- non-fiction, a Writers' Craft Box of writing essays and resources from professionals in the field, an Exploration of Theme page, Archives of past issues, A Writers' Contest, fine artwork from artists whose backgrounds include having done work for The New York Times, and best-selling author interviews such as Janet Fitch (White Oleander) and Alice Hoffman (Practical Magic), both of whom have had their work made into major motion pictures. Other interviews with literary professionals include Director of the Oscar Wilde Centre for Creative Writing in Dublin, Ireland, Nancy Slonim Aronie- founder of the famed Chilmark Writing Workshop, Washington Post Book Editor and award-winning author- Carolyn See, internationally known author, interior designer, and lifestyle philosopher- Alexandra Stoddard, Random House V.P. of Children's Books- Michelle Poploff, Terri Windling, internationally acclaimed author and editor who helped to establish major publishing imprints Ace and Tor, Jeff Herman of The Jeff Herman Agency, Loreena McKennitt- a cultured, Celtic Grammy-nominated musician whose sold over 14 million albums and incorporates storytelling into her work, successful debut novelist Erica Bauermeister (School of Essential Ingredients) hailed by Publisher's Weekly, best-selling author Joan Anderson (A Year by the Sea), hit debut novelist Kathleen Flinn (The Sharper Your Knife, The Less You Cry) who details her journey through Le Cordon Bleu in Paris and most recently New York Times best-selling authors Frances Mayes (Under the Tuscan Sun) and Arthur Golden (Memoirs of a Geisha)."

Writecorner.com Press, Robert B. Gentry, Mary Sue Koeppel, P.O. Box 140310, Gainesville, FL 32614-0310, www.writecorner.com. 2002. Fiction, criticism, reviews, parts-of-novels, non-fiction. "Writecorner Press at www.writecorner.com features the annual E.M. Koeppel Short Fiction Award - first prize $1,100; Editors' choices - $100; and the P.L. Titus Short Fiction Scholarship - $500. Fiction contest submissions postmarked between Oct. 1 and April 30. See website for guidelines and past winners. (Also sponsors the Writecorner Press $500 Poetry Prize; Editors' Choice $100. Poetry contest submisssions Oct. 1 - Mar. 31. See website for guidelines.) Site also features Fresh & Ripe pages of short fiction, criticism, as well as book reviews. Send books for review on the site. (Editors - Mary Sue Koeppel was the longtime editor of *Kalliope, a Journal of Women's Literature & Art* and Robert B. Gentry is an award-winning fiction writer)." No titles listed in the *Small Press Record of Books in Print* (36th Edition, 2010-11). Payment: $1,100.00 annual E.M. Koeppel Short Fiction Award. Copyrights for author. Subjects: Fiction, Literary Review, Literature (General).

The Writers Block, Inc., Sandra Thomas Wales, President, POB 821, Franklin, KY 42135-0821, cell: 270-791-6252, fax: 270-586-9840; HEGwritersbl@aol.com, HaleyElizabethGarwood.com. 1994. Fiction. "Historical novels run about 450 pages. That is our main interest, but we do publish good mystery novels, very little romance, and some mainstream is in the works. We are operating slowly to remain debt free. Note: No unsolicited or unagented materials." avg. press run 5-10M. Pub'd 1 title 2009; expects 2 titles 2010, 3 titles 2011. 2 titles listed in the *Small Press Record of Books in Print* (36th Edition, 2010-11). Discounts: 2-4 20%,

5-99 40%, 100+ in even case lots 55%. 450pp. Reporting time: 3 months. Simultaneous submissions accepted: yes. Publishes 1% of manuscripts submitted. Payment: 10%, no advance. Copyrights for author. Subject: Fiction.

The Writer's Center (see also THE CAROUSEL; POET LORE), 4508 Walsh Street, Bethesda, MD 20815-6006, 301-654-8664, www.writer.org. 1977. 4 titles listed in the *Small Press Record of Books in Print* (36th Edition, 2010-11).

WRITER'S CHRONICLE, David Fenza, Editor-in-Chief; Supriya Bhatnagar, Editor, Mail Stop 1E3, George Mason University, Fairfax, VA 22030-4444, 703-993-4301, http://awpwriter.org. 1967. Articles, interviews, criticism, news items. "Articles pertaining to contemporary literature, writing, and the teaching of writing welcome. News items, grants & awards, magazine submission notices. Interviews in every issue." circ. 26M. 6 issues each academic year. Pub'd 6 issues 2009; expects 6 issues 2010, 6 issues 2011. sub. price $20-6 editions/$34-12 issues. Contact the office for international rates.; per copy $4.95; sample $5.00. Back issues: $5.00. 72pp. Reporting time: 3 months. Simultaneous submissions accepted: yes/please notify if accepted elsewhere. Publishes 5% of manuscripts submitted. Payment: honorarium and copies, $10/100 words, no kill fees. Copyrighted, reverts to author. Ads: Display - $1,040 - Full Page/$695 - Half Page/$590 - Junior Page/$485 - Third Page/$375 - Quarter Page/$250 - Ninth Page/Classifieds: $70 for up to 50 words, $1 per each additional word. Subjects: Criticism, Editing, Education, Essays, Fiction, Literature (General), Non-Fiction, Poetry, Women, Writers/Writing.

•**Writers House Press (see also BEGINNING MAGAZINE),** Bro. John-Paul Ignatius Mary, 1111 S. Sheridan Ave., Ottumwa, IA 52501-5350, editor.office@writers-house-press.org. 1983. Poetry, articles, letters, long-poems, non-fiction. "Manuscripts accepted only between January and April." Expects 1 title 2011. No titles listed in the *Small Press Record of Books in Print* (36th Edition, 2010-11). 84pp. Reporting time: one month. Simultaneous submissions accepted: Yes. Publishes 10% of manuscripts submitted. Copyrights for author. Subjects: Biography, Catholic, Christianity, Essays, Fiction, History, Inspirational, Interviews, Non-Fiction, Philosophy, Poetry, Political Science, Prison, Prose, Short Stories.

WRITERS INK, Writers Ink Press, Writers Unlimited Agency, Inc, David B. Axelrod, 1104 Jacaranda Avenue, Daytona Beach, FL 32118, 631-451-0478, Fax 631-451-0478, http://www.writersunlimited.org. 1975. Articles, art, photos, cartoons, interviews, satire, criticism, reviews, collages. "We have changed to an on-line format. Consult our website and contact us to suggest material. http://www.writersunlimited.org." circ. 2M. 0-4/yr. Pub'd 1 issue 2009; expects 2 issues 2010, 1 issue 2011. sub. price $6; per copy $1; No samples. Back issues: specific issues by request, free if available. Discounts: none-but free to worthy folks or groups—sold, $6 yearly rate direct by 1st class mail from WI. 4-12pp. Reporting time: immediate (maximum 2 weeks) only if we are interested; no reply means "no thanks" Payment: 50¢/col. inch or $2/photo. Copyrighted, reverts to author. Pub's reviews: 1 in 2009. §All aids to writers, general interest and of course, L.I. works, mags, books. Ads: $15/$8/25¢. Subject: Book Reviewing.

Writers Ink Press (see also WRITERS INK), David B. Axelrod, 1104 Jacaranda Avenue, Daytona Beach, FL 32118, 386-337-4567 axelrodthepoet@yahoo.com. 1975. Poetry. "No unsolicited mss. at this time." avg. press run 800. Pub'd 12 titles 2009; expects 3 titles 2010, 5 titles 2011. 27 titles listed in the *Small Press Record of Books in Print* (36th Edition, 2010-11). Discounts: 30% bookstores & distributors. Chapbooks 24-48pp, perfectbound 72-128pp. Payment: 50% profit over cost, varies. Copyrights for author. Subject: Poetry.

WRITERS' JOURNAL, Leon Ogroske, Editor; John Ogroske, Publisher-Managing Editor, PO Box 394, Perham, MN 56573-0394, Phone 218-346-7921, Fax 218-346-7924, E-mail writersjournal@writersjournal.com, Web site www.writersjournal.com. 1980. Poetry, fiction, articles, photos, reviews. "Articles on the art of writing - inspirational and informative - 500-2000 words. Especially interested in articles discussing unusual freelance writing markets. Markets Report. *Writers' Journal* is a bi-monthly journal for writers and poets. We sponsor a 5000 word Fiction contest, 2000 word Short Story, Romance, Science Fiction/Fantasy, and Horror/Ghost contests with cash prizes up to $500.00. We also sponsor three Poetry contests and two Photo contests each year. We have six 'Write to Win!' contests where a starter phrase is given. See our Web site www.writersjournal.com or send an SASE for contest guidelines." circ. 10M. 6/yr. Pub'd 6 issues 2009; expects 6 issues 2010, 6 issues 2011. 1 title listed in the *Small Press Record of Books in Print* (36th Edition, 2010-11). sub. price $19.97; per copy $5.99; sample $5. Back issues: $5. Discounts: varies. 64pp. Reporting time: Up to six months. Simultaneous submissions accepted: yes. Publishes 20% of manuscripts submitted. Payment: $10-$50 and copies. Copyrighted, reverts to author. Ads: Full page $477, Half page $287, Classifieds $1.50 per word. Subjects: Desktop Publishing, Editing, Fiction, Poetry, Publishing, Writers/Writing.

Writers Unlimited Agency, Inc (see also WRITERS INK), David B. Axelrod, 1104 Jacaranda Avenue, Daytona Beach, FL 32118, 386-337-4567, email: writersunlimitedagency@yahoo.com http://www.writersunlimited.org. 1975. "We are not both a NYS and Florida corporation. Daniel E. Axelrod has become our NY/Northeastern Director. David B. Axelrod will coordinate the Florida programs.We keep an active file of poets' work and can sometimes provide referals for publication and/or readings. No unsolicited mss.'' avg. press run 800. Pub'd 2 titles 2009; expects 3 titles 2010, 3 titles 2011. 1 title listed in the *Small Press Record of Books in Print* (36th Edition, 2010-11). Discounts: 30% distributor/bookseller. 40pp. Payment: varies. Copyrights for author. Subject: Poetry.

Writer's World Press, Lavern Hall, Publisher & Publishing Consultant, PO Box 284, Aurora, OH 44202-0284, WritersWorld@juno.com, www.writersworldpress.com. 1991. Non-fiction. ''Through our consulting division, Books by Design, we offer consulting and editorial services for writers seeking publication, authors who wish to self-publish, or those wanting to produce family histories/memoirs.'' No titles listed in the *Small Press Record of Books in Print* (36th Edition, 2010-11).

WSQ (formerly WOMEN'S STUDIES QUARTERLY), The Feminist Press at the City University of New York, Florence Howe, Publisher; Anjoli Roy, Managing Editor; Cindi Katz, General Editor; Nancy Miller, General Editor, The Feminist Press at CUNY, 365 Fifth Avenue, Suite 5406, New York, NY 10016, 212-817-7915, 212-817-1593, aroy@gc.cuny.edu, www.feministpress.org/wsq. 1972. Poetry, fiction, articles, art, photos, cartoons, interviews, satire, criticism, reviews, letters, collages, news items, non-fiction. circ. 1200. 2/yr. Pub'd 2 issues 2009; expects 2 issues 2010, 2 issues 2011. sub. price $40 individuals, $60 institutions, foreign $55 individuals, $75 institutions; per copy $22 (double issue). Back issues: $18 per copy. Discounts: See Consortium or our catalog on line at www.feministpress.org. 400pp. Pub's reviews: 8 in 2009. §Women's studies. Ads: $175/$100/$75. Subjects: Criticism, Education, Essays, Feminism, Gender Issues, History, Lesbianism, Reviews, Sociology, Third World, Minorities, Women.

WWW.HOTMETALPRESS.NET, Carolina Sineni, Co-Editor; Martin Willitts Jr., Co-Editor, 1173 Sea Eagle Watch, Charleston, SC 29413, On-line address: www.hotmetalpress.net, email: sea7@comcast.net. ''Additional address for Martin Willitts Jr, co-editor: P.O. Box 4322, Rome, NY 13422. mwillitts01@yahoo.com. VMagazine needs: We publish poems, occasional short stories and articles, and we will write reviews of books if you send your published book/chapbooks (you only need to send to one of us). We also publish artwork, digital artwork, and music. We are unpredictable in our selections ranging from nature to language poems. We are both are published writers, and we have been through the joy of publishing and the agony of rejection. Our first chapbook winner was Peter Nash (Tracks) and we have had many best poem winners including recently Julia Hastain and Shaindel Beers. We have published: Lewis Turco, Frederick Lord, PD Lyons, John Gray, Ong Muslim, Allison Joseph. Artwork by: Florin Mahai, Jan Kristein, Erin McElroy, Joel Haber, Martin Willitts, Carolina Sineni. How to submit: We publish three times a year. We are an online magazine so submissions are by email for our magazine. We have best poem contests and a chapbook contest. We always consider 3-5 poems, or 1 short story. You must send a short bio and a digital photograph of yourself (we include this as a part of your page). You must send to both Carolina and Martin. We do not consider rhyme poetry, pornographic, or offensive poems. Advice: The best way to know when we are having a contest or a deadline is to check our site. We are getting better all of the time. We do publish many poems by an individual poet, usually at our request.''

Wytherngate Press, Pamela Mogen, P O Box 3134, Couer d Alene, ID 83816, 208-818-3078, 208-661-4566, wytherngatepress@gmail.com, after 4/30/2006: info@wytherngate.com. 2003. Fiction. ''Fiction and non-fiction written for the discerning reader. Mild "language" acceptable if appropriate for context. No explicit sexual descriptions.'' Pub'd 1 title 2009; expects 3 titles 2010, 3 titles 2011. 1 title listed in the *Small Press Record of Books in Print* (36th Edition, 2010-11). Discounts: 35%. Reporting time: 1 month. Simultaneous submissions accepted: Yes. Payment: 55% profit after editing, production, shipping costs. Manuscripts will be edited at $25 per hour. Copyrights for author. Subjects: Christianity, Fantasy, Fiction, History, Inspirational, Mystery, Religion, Romance.

X

XAVIER REVIEW, Ralph Adamo, Editor; Nicole Pepinster Greene, Managing Editor, Box 110C, Xavier University, New Orleans, LA 70125, 504-520-5245 Adamo, 504-520-5246 Greene, Fax 504-520-7944. 1980. Poetry, fiction, photos, criticism, reviews, parts-of-novels. circ. 300. 2/yr. Pub'd 2 issues 2009; expects 2 issues 2010, 2 issues 2011. sub. price $10 individuals, $15 institutions; per copy $5; sample $5. Back issues: inquire. Discounts: inquire. 75pp. Reporting time: 1 month. Simultaneous submissions accepted: Yes, if notified. Publishes 5% of manuscripts submitted. Payment: 2 copies of issue. Copyrighted, rights reassigned to author upon request. Pub's reviews: 10 in 2009. §Southern ethnic, and Latin-American culture, African-American. Ads: $40/$20. Subjects: The Americas, Black, Book Reviewing, Caribbean, Essays, Fiction, Literary Review, Literature (General), Louisiana, Poetry, Short Stories, South.

XCP: CROSS-CULTURAL POETICS, Mark Nowak, Rose O'Neill Literary House/Washington College, 300 Washington Avenue, Chestertown, MD 21620, website: http://lithouse.washcoll.edu/. 1997. "Seeks to address the increasingly untenable boundaries between poetry, politics, and cultural studies. Recent issues on "South Africa: Literature and Social Movements" and "Public Language & Dreamstories"; recent contributors include Amiri Baraka, Kamau Brathwaite, Grace Lee Boggs, Kimiko Hahn, and Adrienne Rich." circ. 500. 2/yr. sub. price $18 indivduals, $40 institutions, foreign add $5; checks payable to College of St. Catherine.; per copy $10; sample $9. Back issues: Back issues are available for $6 each (our double issue, no. 15/16, is available for $12). 176pp. Reporting time: 1-2 months. Simultaneous submissions accepted: no. Payment: 2 copies. Copyrighted, reverts to author. Pub's reviews: 30 in 2009. §"News that stays news"; cultural and performance studies; labor history; anti-globalization/social movement theory; international and cross-cultural poetry and poetics; politics; race/whiteness; CLR James. Ads: $125. Subjects: African-American, Anthropology, Archaelogy, Asian-American, Avant-Garde, Experimental Art, Bilingual, Black, Culture, Experimental, Folklore, Latin America, Multicultural, Native American, Resistance, Reviews.

Xenos Books, Karl Kvitko, Box 16433, Las Cruces, NM 88004, 505-523-8798, E-mail info@xenosbooks.com, www.xenosbooks.com. 1986. Poetry, fiction, art, satire, long-poems, plays, non-fiction. avg. press run 200-500. Pub'd 3 titles 2009; expects 3 titles 2010, 3 titles 2011. 26 titles listed in the *Small Press Record of Books in Print* (36th Edition, 2010-11). Discounts: 20-40%. 120-250pp. Reporting time: 1-3 months. Simultaneous submissions accepted: yes. Publishes 5% of manuscripts submitted. Payment: individual agreements. Copyrights for author. Subjects: Autobiography, Bilingual, Drama, Fiction, Non-Fiction, Novels, Poetry, Prose, Surrealism, Translation, U.S.S.R.

•X-Peri Press (see also X-PERI: Experimental Journal), Koronas Irene, Mindock Gloria, P.O. Box 440357, West Somerville, MA 02144-3222. 2010. Poetry. "We publish and solicit experimental poetry only. We are interested in seeing work that takes risks.Any unsolicited work received will be returned." avg. press run 500. Expects 2 titles 2010, 2 titles 2011. No titles listed in the *Small Press Record of Books in Print* (36th Edition, 2010-11). No discounts. 70pp. Reporting time: 3 months. Simultaneous submissions accepted: No. Payment: Contributors receive one complimentary copy. Copyrights for author. Subjects: Experimental, Poetry.

•X-PERI: Experimental Journal, X-Peri Press, Gloria Mindock, P.O. Box 440357, West Somerville, MA 02144. 2010. Poetry. "We publish and solicit experimental poetry only. We are interested in seeing work that takes risks. Any unsolicited work received will be returned." circ. 500. 2/yr. Expects 2 issues 2010, 2 issues 2011. sub. price $18.00; per copy $9.00; sample $6.00. Back issues: $6.00. Discounts: 20-40 copies 20%. 70pp. Reporting time: 3 months. Simultaneous submissions accepted: No. Payment: one comlimentary copy. Copyrighted, reverts to author. Subjects: Absurdist, Dada, Experimental.

XPLOITED ZINE, 2600 18th St., Suite 9, San Francisco, CA 94110.

X-RAY, Johnny Brewton, Po Box 170488, San Francisco, CA 94117, xraybookco@gmail.com. 1993. Poetry, fiction, art, photos, cartoons, interviews, satire, music, collages, concrete art. "*X-Ray* is an Art/ literary magazine or sorts. Sometimes bound like a book and sometimes loose leaf in a letterpress box. Recent contributors include Ruth Weiss, Wanda Gleman, Dan Fante, Bern Porter, A.D. Winans, Allen Ginsberg, Jaime Hernandez, Charles Bukowski, August Kleinzahler, Neeli Cherkovski, Jack Micheline and Hunter S. Thompson. Correspondence artists are encouraged to contribute. Accepting short fiction, poetry, erotica, prose, found poems, experimental poetry, found objects, assemblage, original art, comics, interviews, photography, etc. Materials range from Chinese telephone directory, sheet music from the early 1900's to hemp and colored craft paper. Every page a different paper. Chapbooks can be found within the pages stuffed into envelopes and fold-out broadsides also grace the pages. Guidelines vary depending upon the issue. Send one completed suggested piece for approval. After approval send at least 126 pieces as the edition is limited to 126. 100 numbered and 26 lettered copies + 4 proofs. Send SASE for exact guideline information." circ. 126. 100 numbered copies and 26 lettered A-Z and signed. 2/yr. Pub'd 2 issues 2009; expects 2 issues 2010, 2 issues 2011. sub. price none; per copy $55. Back issues: Available: visit www.xraybookco.com. 80pp. Reporting time: 2 weeks. Simultaneous submissions accepted: no. Publishes 25% of manuscripts submitted. Payment: 1 copy. Copyrighted, reverts to author. Pub's reviews. §Novels, poetry, music, zines, art, whatever... Ads: none. Subjects: Arts, Literature (General).

X-Ray Book Co. (see also BAGAZINE), Johnny Brewton, P.O. Box 170488, San Francisco, CA 94117. 2005. Poetry, fiction, articles, art, photos, cartoons, interviews, letters, parts-of-novels, collages, concrete art. "X-Ray seeks original work and ideas. Contributors include:Mark Mothersbaugh, Billy Childish, Charles Bukowski, Hunter S. Thompson, Allen Ginsberg, Thurston Moore, Michael Montfort, Mark Faigenbaum, Johnny Brewton, Michael Napper, F.N. Wright, Timothy Leary and more." avg. press run 100. Expects 2 titles 2010, 2 titles 2011. No titles listed in the *Small Press Record of Books in Print* (36th Edition, 2010-11). Discounts: contact publisher for more information. 50pp. Reporting time: 10 Days. Simultaneous submissions accepted: No. Payment: (1) copy unless specifed in mutual agreement. Copyright reverts to authors with permission to reprint all works in collection of past issues book. Subjects: Abstracts, Absurdist, Architecture, Avant-Garde,

Experimental Art, Beat, Charles Bukowski, Chicano/a, Experimental, Jack Kerouac, Music, Photography, Poetry, Short Stories, Tapes & Records, Zines.

XTRAS, From Here Press, William J. Higginson, Penny Harter, PO Box 1402, Summit, NJ 07902-1402. 1975. Poetry, fiction, criticism, parts-of-novels, long-poems, plays, non-fiction. "*Xtras*, a cooperative chapbook series, features writing in both verse and prose. Issues of *Xtras* are devoted to the work of one or a related group of writers who cooperate in publishing their own chapbooks, and receive a substantial number of copies in payment. Individual *Xtras* chapbooks feature poems by Penny Harter, W.J. Higginson, and Ruth Stone, haiku and sequences by Alan Pizzarelli, W.J. Higginson, Adele Kenny, and Elizabeth Searle Lamb, workshop writings by teens and elderly, haiku and short poems by Allen Ginsberg, diary in haiku-prose by Rod Tulloss, essays and long poems by WJH. Not reading unsolicited mss now." circ. 200-500. 0-1/yr. Pub'd 1 issue 2009; expects 1 issue 2011. price per copy $3-$9. Discounts: 40% to trade (5 mixed titles; titles can be mixed with From Here Press books). 28-72pp. Reporting time: 1 month. Payment: a substantial number of copies. Copyrighted, reverts to author. No ads. Subjects: Haiku, Poetry.

Y

•**Yaldah Publishing,** Sheyna Galyan, PO Box 18662, Saint Paul, MN 55118-0662, Tel: 651-470-3853, Fax: 651-224-7447, Email: info@yaldahpublishing.com, Web: http://www.yaldahpublishing.com. 2003. Fiction, non-fiction. "Yaldah Publishing is an independent publisher specializing in books written from a Jewish perspective with a preference for those written by women. We encourage work that reflects the diversity of Jews and Jewish practice. We will consider adult fiction and non-fiction, children's chapter books, and both adult and children's Jewish liturgy resources such as siddurim and haggadot. At this time, we do not publish children's picture books or books entirely in Hebrew. If your manuscript is fiction for adults or children, your story should be unique and original, with interesting, believable characters and situations. It should have well-paced action and engaging dialogue. Children's chapter books should be a minimum of 10,000 words. We do not accept unsolicited manuscripts, but we do accept unagented manuscripts.Recent authors include children's book expert Barbara Bietz and award-winning author Sylvia Rouss." avg. press run 1000. Expects 2 titles 2011. 3 titles listed in the *Small Press Record of Books in Print* (36th Edition, 2010-11). Discounts: Resellers—Hardcover 1-4 copies 20%, Hardcover 5+ copies 35%, Softcover 1-4 copies 20%, Softcover 5+ copies 40%, Schools/non-profits—Hardcover 1-4 copies 20%, Hardcover 5-49 copies 30%, Hardcover 50+ copies 35%, Softcover 1-4 copies 20%, Softcover 5-49 copies 30%, Softcover 50+ copies 40%. 100-400pp. Reporting time: Please allow up to two months for a reply, especially during Jewish holidays. Usually it is sooner. Simultaneous submissions accepted: No. Publishes 10% of manuscripts submitted. Payment: Better-than-competitive royalties paid every six months, starting six months after publication. No advances. Copyrights for author. Subjects: Creative Non-fiction, Ethics, Family, Fiction, Food, Eating, Judaism, Juvenile Fiction, Middle East, Mystery, Non-Fiction, Novels, Parenting, Religion, Women, Young Adult.

THE YALE REVIEW, J.D. McClatchy, Editor; Susan Bianconi, Associate Editor, Yale University, PO Box 208243, New Haven, CT 06520-8243. 1911. Poetry, fiction, articles, criticism, reviews, letters, long-poems, plays, non-fiction. "The editors of *The Yale Review* have established no formal writers' guidelines. We recommend instead that you become acquainted with the magazine in order to see the kinds of work we publish. We ask only that each submission or group of submissions be typed, double-spaced (with the exception of poetry, which may be single-spaced), and accompanied by a stamped, addressed return envelope. Consideration of manuscripts usually requires one to three months." circ. 6M. 4/yr. Pub'd 4 issues 2009; expects 4 issues 2010. sub. price $65 institutions, $27 individuals; per copy $10 (includes postage and handling); sample $10 (includes postage and handling). Back issues: on request. Discounts: distributor, 50%, agent 20% bookstores 10%. 160pp plus 16-24pp front matter. Reporting time: 1-2 months. Simultaneous submissions accepted: no. Publishes less than 5% of manuscripts submitted. Payment: on publication. Copyright Yale University, remaining so on publication by agreement with author or transfer of copyright to author. Pub's reviews: 12 in 2009. §Literature, history, fiction, poetry, economics, biography, arts & architecture, politics, foreign affairs. Ads: on request. Subjects: Criticism, English, Literary Review.

Yale University Press, Jonathan Brent, Larisa Heimert, John Kulka, Mary Jane Peluso, Jean Thompson Black, Patricia Fidler, Michael O'Malley, Lauren Shapiro, Keith Condon, PO Box 209040, New Haven, CT 06520, 203-432-0960, 203-432-0948 [fax], www.yalebooks.com. 1908. Poetry, art, photos, criticism, music, letters, plays, non-fiction. "By publishing serious works that contribute to a global understanding of human affairs, Yale University Press aids in the discovery and dissemination of light and truth, lux et veritas, which is a central purpose of Yale University. The publications of the Press are books and other materials that further scholarly investigation, advance interdisciplinary inquiry, stimulate public debate, educate both within and outside the classroom, and enhance cultural life. Through the distribution of works that combine excellence in scholarship with skillful editing, design, production, and marketing, the Press demonstrates its commitment to increasing the range and vigor of intellectual pursuits within the university and elsewhere. With an innovative and entrepreneurial spirit, Yale University Press continually extends its horizons to embody university press publishing at its best." No titles listed in the *Small Press Record of Books in Print* (36th Edition, 2010-11).

THE YALOBUSHA REVIEW, Neal Walsh, Editor, English Dept, Univ. of Mississippi, PO Box 1848, University, MS 38677-1848, 662-915-3175, yalobusha@olemiss.edu, www.olemiss.edu/yalobusha. 1995. Poetry, fiction, art, photos, interviews, parts-of-novels, long-poems, plays, non-fiction. *"The Yalobusha Review* is an annual small-press publication whose main goal is promoting quality writing, regardless of subject matter, genre, or type. Each year we feature prominent or emerging writers alongside new and often unpublished writers. Previous editions have featured stories and poems by Barry Hannah, Charles Wright, Tom Chandler, George Singleton, Janisse Ray, Shay Youngblood, Alan Michael Parker, and National Book Award finalist Dan Chaon, as well as interviews with Lee Smith (*Saving Grace, The Last Girls*), Jill McCorkle Youngblood (*Black Girl in Paris*), and Steve Almond (*My Life in Heavy Metal, Candy Freak*). Reading period: July 15 - Nov. 15. Please see the website for full submissions guidelines. CONTEST: Second Annual Barry Hannah Fiction Prize. Winner receives $500 & publication in 2005 *Yalobusha Review*. Deadline is September 30. Include SASE and $10 reading fee (cash or check made out to Yalobusha Review). Please see our website for full details." circ. 1000. 1/yr. Pub'd 1 issue 2009; expects 1 issue 2010, 1 issue 2011. sub. price $8/yr for multiple years; per copy $10; sample $5. Back issues: $5. Discounts: Please contact us for bulk discount information. 125pp. Reporting time: 1-3 months to manuscripts. Simultaneous submissions accepted: no. Publishes 3-5% of manuscripts submitted. Payment: Small honorarium & 2 contributor's copies. Copyrighted, reverts to author. Ads: for swap.

YA'SOU/Skyline Productions, David D. Bell, Editor, PO Box 77463, Columbus, OH 43207. Poetry. "No profanity, no excess violence. Poetry 26 lines or less. Reading fee: $1.50 per poem." circ. 60. 4/yr. Pub'd 4 issues 2009; expects 4 issues 2010, 4 issues 2011. Publishes 80% of manuscripts submitted. Payment: free copy. Not copyrighted. Ads: none.

YCD Press, Stephanie St. Pierre MDiv, MPH, 45 Park Place South # 240, Morristown, NJ 07960, 917-690-0029. 2005. Non-fiction. "Business/ self help books and interactive training Cdroms with an emphasis on leadership, influencing, negotiating and career development." avg. press run 10,000. Pub'd 4 titles 2009; expects 3 titles 2010, 3 titles 2011. 1 title listed in the *Small Press Record of Books in Print* (36th Edition, 2010-11). Discounts: 1-10 20%10-50 30%over 50 40%. 200pp. Reporting time: 60 days. Simultaneous submissions accepted: No. Payment: 15% books, 5 % cdroms. Copyrights for author. Subjects: Business & Economics, Ethics.

Ye Olde Font Shoppe, Victoria Rivas, PO Box 8328, New Haven, CT 06530, e-mail varivas@yahoo.com; website www.webcom.com/yeolde. 1995. Poetry. "Chapbooks and perfect bound poetry books. Recent authors: Linda Lerner, A.D. Winana, Lynne Savitt, Tony Moffeit. Ye Olde Font Shoppe is finally once more accepting Open Submissions for chapbooks only. We still produce bound books but all bound books are solicited by the press. POETRY CHAPBOOKS: Books may be submitted either on diskette or hard copy. However, if the book is accepted, it must be submitted in MSWord format. Submissions should include from 20 - 30 pages of poetry.MARTIAL ARTS CHAPBOOKS: Ye Olde Font Shoppe is expanding to include books about martial arts, or aimed at martial artists. Books can include photos or images and should be 20-30 pages including images and text." avg. press run 500. Pub'd 8 titles 2009; expects 15 titles 2010, 30 titles 2011. No titles listed in the *Small Press Record of Books in Print* (36th Edition, 2010-11). Discounts: 40% off author and reseller. 40 and 80pp. Reporting time: 6-8 weeks. Simultaneous submissions accepted: no. Publishes 25% of manuscripts submitted. Payment: 10% of retail, once a year. Copyrights for author. Subject: Poetry.

Yellow Moon Press, Robert B. Smyth, PO Box 381316, Cambridge, MA 02238-0001, 617-776-2230, Fax 617-776-8246, E-mail story@yellowmoon.com, www.yellowmoon.com. 1978. Poetry, music, non-fiction. "Authors/Storytellers include: Coleman Barks, Robert Bly, Rafe Martin, Michael Meade, Elizabeth McKim, Lorraine Lee Hammond, Doug Lipman, Maggi Peirce, Ruth Stone, and Dovie Thomason. *Yellow Moon* is committed to publishing material related to the oral tradition. It is our goal to make available material that explores the history of the oral tradition while breathing new life into it." avg. press run varies with title. Pub'd 3 titles 2009; expects 3 titles 2010, 3-4 titles 2011. 49 titles listed in the *Small Press Record of Books in Print* (36th Edition, 2010-11). Distributed to the trade through Ingram, Baker & Taylor, and Amazon. 32-56pp. Reporting time: 6-8 weeks. Simultaneous submissions accepted: no. Publishes 1% of manuscripts submitted. Payment: varies according to book. Copyrights for author. Subjects: Folklore, Men, Music, Myth, Mythology, Native American, New England, Poetry, Storytelling, Tapes & Records, Translation, Women.

•**Yellowstone Publishing, LLC,** Michael Lininger, 5335 South Grant Street, Littleton, CO 80121, (406) 371-1175, www.etiquettescholar.com. 2007. Non-fiction. "Reference. Dining etiquette, wine etiquette, business etiquette, international etiquette, everyday etiquette." avg. press run 3000. Expects 2 titles 2010, 2 titles 2011. 1

title listed in the *Small Press Record of Books in Print* (36th Edition, 2010-11). Discounts: distributors 50%, bookstores 40-45%, quantity retail discounts up to 35%. 42pp. Reporting time: 3-4 months. Simultaneous submissions accepted: No. Copyrights are negotiable. Subjects: Dining, Restaurants, Wine, Wineries.

YEMASSEE, Darien Cavanaugh, Co-Editor; Jonathan Maricle, Co-Editor, Dept. of English, University of South Carolina, Columbia, SC 29208. *"Yemassee* publishes all genres and forms of writing, including poetry, fiction, drama, nonfiction, reviews, and interviews. We publish in the fall and spring, printing three to five stories and twelve to fifteen poems per issue. We tend to solicit reviews, essays, and interviews but welcome unsolicited queries. We do not favor any particular aesthetic or school of writing. Quality of writing is our only concern.''

Yes International Publishers (see also HIMALAYAN PATH), Theresa King, 1317 Summit Avenue, St. Paul, MN 55105, 651-645-6808, Fax 651-645-7935, yes@yespublishers.com, www.yespublishers.com. 1988. Non-fiction. "Books for self-transformation. Yoga, wellness, spirituality, personal transformation, yoga psychology.'' avg. press run 2M. Pub'd 3 titles 2009; expects 2 titles 2010, 2 titles 2011. 30 titles listed in the *Small Press Record of Books in Print* (36th Edition, 2010-11). Discounts: 40% no returns. 200pp. Reporting time: 2 weeks to 2 months. Simultaneous submissions accepted: no. Publishes 1% of manuscripts submitted. Copyrights for author. Subjects: Autobiography, Catholic, Christianity, Health, Non-Fiction, Philosophy, Poetry, Psychology, Self-Help, Spiritual, Women, Yoga.

YMAA Publication Center, James O'Leary, Editor; Jwing-Ming Yang, President; David Ripianzi, Director, 4354 Washington Street, Roslindale, MA 02131, 617-323-7215, Fax 617-323-7417, ymaa@aol.com, www.ymaa.com. 1982. Non-fiction. "Publication categories: Traditional Asian martial arts, Taijiquan, Qigong, Eastern thought, Oriental healing, East/West synthesis, Fitness grounded in an Asian tradition.'' avg. press run 4M. Pub'd 8 titles 2009; expects 10 titles 2010, 10 titles 2011. 54 titles listed in the *Small Press Record of Books in Print* (36th Edition, 2010-11). 180pp. Reporting time: 3 months. Simultaneous submissions accepted: yes. Publishes 20% of manuscripts submitted. Payment: no advance, royalty on books sold. Copyrights for author. Subjects: Alternative Medicine, Asia, Indochina, Health, How-To, Martial Arts, Spiritual, Sports, Outdoors, T'ai Chi.

YogaVidya.com, Brian Dana Akers, PO Box 569, Woodstock, NY 12498-0569, 845-679-9619, Fax 586-283-4680, info@yogavidya.com, www.yogavidya.com. 2001. Photos, non-fiction. "YogaVidya.com is dedicated to publishing excellent and affordable books about Yoga. It is independent of all other commercial, governmental, educational, and religious institutions.'' 1 title listed in the *Small Press Record of Books in Print* (36th Edition, 2010-11). Reporting time: Less than 48 hours. Simultaneous submissions accepted: No. Payment: Royalties paid quarterly. Copyrights for author. Subject: Yoga.

Youthful Wisdom Press, Colston Andrea, 2343 W. Claremont St, Phoenix, AZ 85015, 888-241-2062. 2008. Poetry, fiction, long-poems. "short story collections, novellas, poetry collections, blog stories, full-length novels (fiction only).WERE DOWN WITH THESE: action/adventure, contemporary, fantasy, humor/satire, mystery/suspense, multicultural, romance, science fiction, paranormal, inspirational/spiritual, gay/lesbian.BUT KICK THESE TO THE CURB: comic books, historical, graphic novels, picture books, photography, horror, erotica, plays/scripts, essays, coffee table books, cookbooks, political, full-color and/or illustrated books, or any type of violent content (rape, murder, sodomy, incest, etc).'' avg. press run 100. No titles listed in the *Small Press Record of Books in Print* (36th Edition, 2010-11). Discounts: PRE-PAID, NO INVOICING~ 40% discount per unit, no minimum quantity~ 50% discount for case quantities. 200pp. Reporting time: 2-4 weeks for queries, 8-12 weeks for fulls and partials. Simultaneous submissions accepted: Yes. Publishes 40% of manuscripts submitted. Payment: No advance, 12% royalties, paid quarterly. Copyrights for author. Subjects: Bisexual, Black, Crime, Diaries, Disabled, Fantasy, Fiction, Lesbianism, Mystery, Novels, Science Fiction, Supernatural, Young Adult.

YUKHIKA—LATUHSE, Jim Stevens, P.O. Box 365, Oneida Nation Arts Program, Oneida, WI 54155-0365, jstevens@ez-net.com. 2005. Poetry, fiction, articles, interviews, criticism, reviews, parts-of-novels, plays, non-fiction. "Editorial board: Jim Stevens, Richie Plass, Jody Barnes. We publish work by Native American writers only. Our mission is to publish as wide a range of writing by Native American writers as we can. We usually publish early in July. Deadline for submissions in 2007 is May 18. Recent contibutors: Kimberly Blaeser, Jose Boner, Denise Sweet, Ed Two Rivers, Maurice Kenny.'' circ. 500. 1/yr. Pub'd 1 issue 2009; expects 1 issue 2010, 1 issue 2011. sub. price $12.00 for 2 issues.; per copy $6.00; sample $6.00. Back issues: inquire. 48pp. Reporting time: 1 month. Simultaneous submissions accepted: No. Publishes 50% of manuscripts submitted. Payment in copies. Not copyrighted. Pub's reviews: none in 2009. Subjects: Essays, Fiction, Native American, Non-Fiction, Poetry.

Z

Zagier & Urruty Publications, Sergio Zagier, Dario Urruty, PO Box 94 Sucursal 19, Buenos Aires 1419, Argentina, +54-11-4572-1050, info@zagier.com, www.patagonishop.com. 1985. Articles, photos, reviews, letters, news items, non-fiction. "We publish basically about travel and tourism (books, maps, guides, magazines) and about science. Manuscripts about traveling through South America and Antarctica are welcome. Spanish, English, German and French. We also are interested in photographies travel and adventour-oriented. Any length of manuscripts are considered." avg. press run 1M. Pub'd 6 titles 2009; expects 6 titles 2010, 12 titles 2011. 10 titles listed in the *Small Press Record of Books in Print* (36th Edition, 2010-11). Discounts: 50% distributor, 30% bookstores, 20% travel companies. 256pp. Reporting time: 6 weeks. Payment: on an individual basis depending on the kind of work. Copyrights for author. Subjects: The Americas, Animals, Anthropology, Archaelogy, Birds, Book Reviewing, Conservation, Earth, Natural History, Ethics, Geography, History, Judaism, Latin America, Native American, Physics, Sports, Outdoors.

ZAHIR: A Journal of Speculative Fiction, Sheryl Tempchin, 315 South Coast Hwy. 101 Suite U8, Encinitas, CA 92024, stempchin@zahirtales.com, http://www.zahirtales.com. 2003. Fiction, art. "Zahir is a quarterly online journal of speculative fiction. Perhaps more than any other type of literature, speculative fiction gives voice to the collective, mythic dream that is at the center of human existence. Zahir's goal is twofold: to find and bring to light new speculative fiction of literary quality, and to encourage emerging writers by providing them with an audience for their work. Since Zahir's debut in 2003 we have published a wide variety of speculative short stories, from science fiction to fantasy to magical realism and beyond. Each issue includes six to eight stories, some by established writers, but many by those with few or no publishing credits. We are always thrilled and honored to be the first to publish the work of a promising new writer." 4/yr. Pub'd 3 issues 2009; expects 4 issues 2010, 4 issues 2011. sub. price free. Reporting time: 4 to 8 weeks. Simultaneous submissions accepted: Yes, but please inform us immediately if accepted elsewhere. Publishes 6% of manuscripts submitted. Payment: $10 flat fee upon publication. Copyrighted, reverts to author. Subjects: Fantasy, Science Fiction, Supernatural, Surrealism.

Zante Publishing, Steve Johnson, P.O. Box 35404, Greensboro, NC 27425, (336) 605-7900. 2004. Non-fiction. "We specialize in high quality titles, heavily promoted for the national market. Authors must commit to taking active participation in promoting their titles." avg. press run 5000. Pub'd 1 title 2009; expects 2 titles 2010, 2 titles 2011. 1 title listed in the *Small Press Record of Books in Print* (36th Edition, 2010-11). 200pp. Reporting time: 30 days. Simultaneous submissions accepted: No. Publishes 30% of manuscripts submitted. Copyrights for author. Subjects: Europe, Travel.

ZAUM - The Literary Review of Sonoma State University, Julie Reid, Senior Editor; Kay Elliott, Assistant Editor, English Department, SSU, 1801 E. Cotati Avenue, Rohnert Park, CA 94928, 707-664-2140. 1996. Poetry, fiction, art, photos, criticism, collages. "All prose max. 10 pages, 5 poems max. All color artwork in slide form, b&w prints ok. We only accept submissions from students currently enrolled in an undergraduate or graduate degree program." circ. 500. 1/yr. Pub'd 1 issue 2009; expects 1 issue 2010, 1 issue 2011. sub. price $9.50; per copy $7.51 + p/h; sample $7.51 + p/h. Back issues: 4 for $20, 5 for $25. 100pp. Reporting time: 3-6 months. We accept simultaneous submissions, but let us know. Publishes 7% of manuscripts submitted. Payment: 1 copy. Copyrighted, reverts to author. Ads: none. Subject: Avant-Garde, Experimental Art.

ZAWP, Rabah Seffal, PO Box 411, Mossville, IL 61552-0411, 309-310-7709 Tel, 217-717-0779, Fax http://zighen-aym.site.voila.fr/order.html, azawp@yahoo.com. 2005. Fiction, criticism. "Ethnic ProfilingNorth African literatureHistory of North Africa." avg. press run 1000. Expects 1 title 2010, 2 titles 2011. 1 title listed in the *Small Press Record of Books in Print* (36th Edition, 2010-11). Discounts: 2-10 copies 10%11-20 copies 15%20-50 copies 20%. 70pp. Reporting time: One week. Simultaneous submissions accepted: No. Publishes 1% of manuscripts submitted. Payment: 15%. Copyrights for author. Subjects: African Literature, Africa, African Studies, Criticism, Indigenous Cultures, Literature (General), Non-Fiction, Translation.

ZEEK: A Jewish Journal of Thought & Culture, Jo Ellen Green Kaiser, Editor-in-Chief, P. O. Box 1342, New York, NY 10016. "Submissions are accepted via email only to zeek@zeek.net. *Zeek: A Journal of Jewish Thought and Culture* is a publication of Zeek Media Inc., a nonprofit organization. In its print journal, online magazine, public events, and multimedia content, Zeek Media builds community, identity, and culture for the next generation of American Jews. By creating and promoting new Jewish culture with the sophistication and breadth of the best of contemporary culture, Zeek builds a bridge between religious and secular, connects Israeli creativity with the diaspora, and helps to create a vital, inclusive Judaism for the 21st century."

ZerOX Books (see also UNMUZZLED OX), Michael Andre, 1304 Pine St., #1R, Philadelphia, PA 19107. 1971. "ZerOx Books is an occasional imprint of Unmuzzled Ox Books." avg. press run 105. 7 titles listed in the *Small Press Record of Books in Print* (36th Edition, 2010-11).

Zerx Press, Mark Weber, 725 Van Buren Place SE, Albuquerque, NM 87108, zerxpress@aol.com, www.zerxrecords.com. 1983. Poetry, fiction, art, photos. "61 chapbooks since 1983. Contributors: Gerald Locklin, Judson Crews, Todd Moore, Ann Menebroker, Ron Androla, Hugh Fox, Kurt Nimmo, Kell Robertson, Cheryl Townsend, and Brent Leake. Am not really in the market financially for unsolicited mss." avg. press run 200-500. Pub'd 5 titles 2009; expects 6 titles 2010, 2+ titles 2011. 15 titles listed in the *Small Press Record of Books in Print* (36th Edition, 2010-11). 44pp. Reporting time: less than a week. Payment: we've never made back initial printing costs but think it'd be like 10% or 15% after 1000 sold; author usually gets 25-35 copies and is able to buy extra at Zerx cost. Copyrights for author. Subjects: Poetry, Prose, Short Stories.

ZINE WORLD: A Reader's Guide to the Underground Press, Jerianne Thompson, PO Box 330156, Murfreesboro, TN 37133-0156, www.undergroundpress.org. 1996. Art, reviews, letters, news items. "Short reviews of underground or alternative lit, books, newsletters, etc." circ. 1.2M. 3/yr. Pub'd 3 issues 2009; expects 3 issues 2010, 3 issues 2011. sub. price $14; per copy $4; sample $4. 64pp. Reporting time: staff only. Simultaneous submissions accepted: no. Publishes 0% of manuscripts submitted. Payment: none. Copyrighted, reverts to author. Pub's reviews: 1,200+ in 2009. §Self-published and/or counterculture, "anything that's not mainstream corporate-controlled crap" Ads: $130/$65. Subjects: Counter-Culture, Alternatives, Communes, Publishing, Reviews, Writers/Writing, Zines.

Zirlinson Publishing (see also LOST CARCOSA), Shawn Tomlinson, 97 Charlton Road, Ballston Lake, NY 12019, Ballston Lake, NY 12019, 518-631-9119, tomlinson.shawn@gmail.com. 1983. Poetry, fiction, photos, interviews, satire, long-poems, non-fiction. "We are a small press publishing company established in 1983. We publish poetry chapbooks, fiction chapbooks, non-fiction chapbooks, magazines, PDF publications and other materials. We are launching a Web site in 2011. Our newest publication is *Lost Carcosa,* a science fiction/horror/dark fantasy/surreal/speculative magazine in the tradition of Robert W. Chambers, H.P. Lovecraft, Clark Ashton Smith, Weird Tales, Unknown Worlds and other publications. We also accept illustrations and illustrated stories. Please make all submissions and inquiries to lostcarcosamag@aol.com." avg. press run 100. Pub'd 2 titles 2009; expects 2 titles 2010, 6-10 titles 2011. 5 titles listed in the *Small Press Record of Books in Print* (36th Edition, 2010-11). Discounts: 25% to 40%. 64pp. Reporting time: one to two months. Simultaneous submissions accepted: No. Payment: copies. First North American Serial Rights. Subjects: Absurdist, Creative Non-fiction, August Derleth, Design, Desktop Publishing, Essays, Experimental, Fantasy, Fiction, Horror, H.P. Lovecraft, Non-Fiction, Poetry, Satire, Science Fiction.

ZOETROPE: ALL-STORY, Michael Ray, Editor, 916 Kearny Street, San Francisco, CA 94133-5107, www.all-story.com, info@all-story.com. 1997. Fiction, plays. "Short stories and one-act plays under 7,000 words. A submission must be accompanied by an SASE. Recent contributors: Mary Gaitskill, John Hughes, Woody Allen, Elizabeth McCracken, David Means, Ha Jin, Ethan Coen, Ryu Murakami." circ. 25,000. 4/yr. Pub'd 4 issues 2009; expects 4 issues 2010, 4 issues 2011. sub. price $24; per copy $8; sample $8 + shipping. 112pp. Reporting time: 6 months. Simultaneous submissions accepted: yes. Publishes 0.3% of manuscripts submitted. Payment: $1,000 and 5 copies of magazine. Copyrighted, buy 1st serial rights. Ads: $3,500 full page, with discounts for multi-issue commitments. Subject: Fiction.

Zoilita Grant MS CCHt., Attn: Zoilita Grant, 200 Lincoln Street, Longmont, CO 80501, 303-776-6103, Fax 303-682-2384, info@zoilitagrant.net, www.zoilitagrant.net. 1997. avg. press run 2.7M. Pub'd 7 titles 2009; expects 5 titles 2010, 5 titles 2011. 22 titles listed in the *Small Press Record of Books in Print* (36th Edition, 2010-11). 175pp. Simultaneous submissions accepted: yes. Payment: yes. Copyrights for author. Subjects: New Age, Psychology, Self-Help.

Zon International Publishing Co., William Manns, PO Box 6459, Santa Fe, NM 87502, 505-995-0102, Email zon@nets.com, Web, zonbooks.com. 1985. Art. "We publish photo books on Americana." avg. press run 15M. Pub'd 1 title 2009; expects 3 titles 2010, 6 titles 2011. 4 titles listed in the *Small Press Record of Books in Print* (36th Edition, 2010-11). Discounts: 4-9 40%, 10-49 45%, 50+ 50%. 250pp. Publishes almost 0% of manuscripts submitted. Payment: flat fee and royalty. Does not copyright for author. Subjects: Armenian, Arts, Photography, The West.

ZONE 3, Blas Falconer, Poetry Editor; Barry Kitterman, Fiction Editor; Susan Wallace, Mg. Editor, Austin Peay State University, P.O. Box 4565, Clarksville, TN 37044, 931-221-7031/7878. 1986. Poetry, fiction, reviews, non-fiction. "*Zone 3* is a poetry and fiction journal published in Tennessee but seeking submissions and readership nationwide and beyond. Editors want poems that are deeply rooted in place, mind, heart, experience, rage, imagination, laughter, etc. Published fall and spring. Issues include work by A. Van Jordan, David Keplinger, Michael Blumenthal, Gina Ochsner, Phil Dacey, Tamas Dobozy, E.G. Burrows, Paulette Roeske, Eric Torgersen, Virgil Suarez, Joan Frank, Gerry LaFemina, Rose Marie Kinder, James Iredell, Lara

Tupper, Andrew Kozma, Leigh Anne Couch, Jim Daniels, Paul Gibbons, and Maria Melendez." circ. 1.2M. 2/yr. Pub'd 2 issues 2009; expects 2 issues 2010, 2 issues 2011. sub. price $10/yr, $12 to libraries & institutions; per copy $5; sample $5. Back issues: $4. Discounts: 33%. 125pp. Reporting time: 1-3 months. Simultaneous submissions accepted: Yes. Payment: copies. Copyrighted, reverts to author. Pub's reviews. §Poetry, fiction, and creative nonfiction. Subjects: Fiction, Non-Fiction, Poetry, Translation.

Zoo Press (see also THE NEBRASKA REVIEW), Neil Azevedo, Publisher; K. Caitlin Phelps, Assistant Editor, 15511 Marcy Circle, Omaha, NE 68154-2740, 402-770-8104, editors@zoopress.org, http://zoopress.org. 2000. Poetry, fiction, criticism, plays. "We currently publish The Paris Review Prize in Poetry, The Kenyon Review Prize in Poetry for a First Book, The Angela Marie Ortiz Award for the Novel, The Zoo Press Award for Short Fiction and The Parnassus Prize in Poetry Criticism. See our website for submission guidelines. Recent authors include Christopher Cessac, Eric Charles LeMay, Kate Light and Judith Taylor." avg. press run varies. Pub'd 3 titles 2009; expects 8 titles 2010, 12 titles 2011. No titles listed in the *Small Press Record of Books in Print* (36th Edition, 2010-11). Discounts: standard discounts set by our distributor, the Univ. of Nebraska Press (800) 755-1105. 80pp. Reporting time: varies. Simultaneous submissions accepted: yes. Publishes 1% of manuscripts submitted. Payment: standard. Copyrights for author. Subjects: Criticism, Drama, Fiction, Literature (General), Poetry.

Zookeeper Publications, Allan Falk, Jacqueline DeRouin, 2010 Cimarron Drive, Okemos, MI 48864-3908, 517-347-4697. 1991. Non-fiction. avg. press run 1.5M. Pub'd 3 titles 2009; expects 2 titles 2010. 6 titles listed in the *Small Press Record of Books in Print* (36th Edition, 2010-11). Discounts: 50% wholesale, 40% consignment. 165-240pp. Reporting time: 1 month. Payment: negotiable; principally self-funded. Copyrights for author. Subject: Games.

Zumaya Publications LLC, Elizabeth Burton, 3209 S. IH35, #1086, Austin, TX 78741-6905, 512-402-5298, 235-660-2009. 2000. Fiction, non-fiction. "Zumaya publishes full-length works of fiction and nonfiction. Preferred minimum word count for adult fiction is 65,000 words, with preference for 85,000-135,000 words. We will read works of 40,000 words and up; however, the author will likely be encouraged to expand it or combine it with other short works before the manuscript will be accepted. For Young Adult, teen fiction and childrens chapter books, minimum word count is 35,000 with a preferred maximum of 60,000 words. In fiction, we look for well-written, professional presented manuscripts that extend the boundaries of the usual genre definitions. We want the kind of books people can't put down and can't get enough of. While we don't necessarily turn down well-crafted stories that fall into the standard formulas for their genre, our first choice will always be the one that moves beyond those formulas, whether because of unique characters or new plot twists. We require of literary fiction the same thing we look for in genre works: a solid plot and believable characters. Books for children and young adults should first and foremost be first-rate stories, with lessons and morals implicit rather than explicit. We do not publish children's picture books at this time. In nonfiction, we look for books that will potentially have or develop a wide audience in the areas of paranormal phenomena, true crime, self-help, history/cultural and inspirational/New Age. While we have no objection to Christian works, we don't feel we are suited to properly marketing them, and encourage Christian writers to exhaust those publishers noted for that area first. We will consider memoirs if they contain a self-help element, give insight into a particular era of history or if the author has a unique view that has broad appeal." avg. press run 1. Pub'd 20 titles 2009; expects 37 titles 2010, 34 titles 2011. No titles listed in the *Small Press Record of Books in Print* (36th Edition, 2010-11). Discounts: Invoiced, 40%; Author Consignment: 30%; Publisher consignment: 35%; Prepaid: 50%. 250pp. Reporting time: Average response time is 6-9 months. Simultaneous submissions accepted: Yes. Publishes 2% of manuscripts submitted. Payment: We do not pay advances at this time. Authors receive 20% of publisher's net on all retail and third-party sales and 20 copies of the book at straight wholesale. They may purchase additional copies at 52% discount. Royalties are paid twice annually in February and August provided a minimum of $50 is attained. All royalties due in a calendar year are paid the following February. Royalties on all ebooks sales are 50% of publisher's net. Does not copyright for author. Subjects: Anthology, Dreams, Fiction, History, Inspirational, Literature (General), Memoirs, Native American, Occult, Reprints, Science Fiction, Self-Help, Spiritual, Tarot, WICCA.

Zygote Publishing, Tate Young, 913, 390 Queens Quay West, Toronto, ON M5V3A6, Canada, www.zygotepublishing.com. 2004. Poetry, fiction, long-poems. "Zygote Publishing is a collective of highly motivated, like-minded, literature-loving, Western Canadian individuals who are dedicated to presenting literary works in a manner that captivates and entices new audiences.Our first book, Nunt, is the shocking story of a man who walks out on his wife and embarks on a ferocious two year odyssey of womanizing and alcohol-fuelled violence. Tourette roars across a barbaric America in this savage tale of murderous fist fights and molotov cocktails, doing battle with malevolent priests, falling in love with obsessed prostitutes, and desperately trying to exorcise the ghosts of his failed marriage." avg. press run 2000. Expects 1 title 2010, 1 title 2011. No titles listed in the *Small Press Record of Books in Print* (36th Edition, 2010-11). Discounts: 46% to distributors, jobbers, wholesalers40% to bookstores20% to institutions. 112pp. Reporting time: 6 weeks. Simultaneous submissions accepted: Yes. Publishes 1% of manuscripts submitted. Payment: No advances so far. Does not copyright for author. Subjects: Charles Bukowski, Erotica, Fiction, Haiku, Ernest Hemingway, James Joyce, Kafka, Jack Kerouac, Henry Miller, Anais Nin, Poetry, Religion, Sex, Sexuality, Weapons, Zen.

ZYX, Phrygian Press, Arnold Skemer, 58-09 205th Street, Bayside, NY 11364-1712, PhrygianZYX @ AOL.COM, 718-428-9368. 1990. Criticism, reviews. "Essays and commentary on innovative/experimental fiction. We are interested in tendencies in avant-garde fiction, useful techniques and stratagems that a fictioneer can avail himself of, author resources (self-publishing, technological changes and publishing empowerment).Predelictions: dark humor,cosmic focus, nihilism, existential dispair, the emptiness of historical experience, misanthropy, bemused contempt,general hippopotomonstrosesquippedaliophilia.Newsletter format.*ZYX* on occasion is the object of condescension by "the carriage trade." Just be aware. Some reviews. Accepting original fiction, but make it compact, ideally 1-2 pages. Poetry accepted. Recent contributors: Christopher Mulrooney, James Chapman, Spencer Selby, Luis Cuauhtemoc Berriozabal, Richard Kostelanetz, Geof Huth, Randall Brock, John Crouse, T. Kilgore Splake, Leonard J. Cirino, Florentin Smarandache, Jon Cone, Jonathan Hayes, John Grey, Thomas Lowe Taylor, Crag Hill, Alan Catlin, Nathan Whiting, Normal, Kevin Higgins, Jonathan Hayes, Doreen King, Bob Grumman, Guy R. Beining, Mark Sonnenfeld, Daneen Wardrop, Jnana Hodson, Robert Michael O'Hearn, Edward Mycue, Michael S. Begnal, Gerald England, B.Z. Niditch, Susan Maurer, Spiel, Louis E. Bourgeois, R.W. Watkins, Cardinal Cox, Robert Pomerhn, Dan Weber, George Kuntzman, David Madgalene, George Gott, Dick Bentley, Daniel F. Bradley, James Babbs, McArthur Gunter, Doug Draime, William Wolak, Glenn W. Cooper, David Chorlton, A.D. Winans, Charles Bryant, Simon Perchik. Member: POETSHOUSE, Finnegans Wake Society of New York. Chapbook publication by *Phrygian Press* derives from initial appearances in *ZYX* Reading period of January 1-December 31 of each year strictly observed. Current issue as of 04/2010: #53." circ. 333. 3/yr. Pub'd 3 issues 2009; expects 3 issues 2010, 3 issues 2011. Subscriptions in multiples of the then prevailing 1st class base rate if you wish issues periodically. Will send up to one pound of back issues for $3.00 which would contain approximately 15 issues; up to 2 pounds, $4.00.; price per copy gratis; send return postage appropriate for .44, .61, .78 etc.; sample same. Back issues: Send $3.00 for just under one pound of back issues. Send $4.00 for just under 2 pounds. 10pp. Reporting time: 4-5 months. Simultaneous submissions accepted: no. Payment: copies. Copyrighted, reverts to author. Pub's reviews: 30 in 2009. §Innovative fiction and criticism, poetry. Subjects: Avant-Garde, Experimental Art, Book Reviewing, Dada, Post Modern, Publishing, Surrealism, Writers/Writing.

ZYZZYVA, Howard Junker, PO Box 590069, San Francisco, CA 94159-0069, Tel 415-752-4393, editor@zyzzyva.org, www.zyzzyva.org. 1985. Poetry, fiction, art, photos, satire, letters, plays, concrete art, non-fiction. "Only writers who live on West Coast." circ. 3M. 3/yr. Pub'd 3 issues 2009; expects 3 issues 2010, 3 issues 2011. sub. price $24/44; per copy $11; sample $6. Back issues: $10. 160pp. Reporting time: prompt. Simultaneous submissions accepted: no. Publishes 1% of manuscripts submitted. Payment: $50. Copyrighted, reverts to author. Ads: $500 full/$300 half/$200 quarter page.

Regional Index

ALABAMA

MELEE, General Offices, PO Box 1619, Alexander City, AL 35111-1619, www.poetrymelee.com, submissions@poetryme-lee.com

SOUTHERN HUMANITIES REVIEW, 9088 Haley Center, Auburn University, AL 36849, 334-844-9088, www.auburn.edu/shr

AURA LITERARY ARTS REVIEW, HUC 135, 1530 3rd Avenue South, Birmingham, AL 35294, 205-934-3216

BIRMINGHAM POETRY REVIEW, English Department HB 205 UAB, 1530 3rd Ave. S., Birmingham, AL 35294, 205-934-8573

Fitness Press, 2112-A Montreat Lane, Birmingham, AL 35216, 205-637-7838; 205-999-5595, fitness9@mindspring.com

Low Fidelity Press, 1912 16th Ave South, Birmingham, AL 35205-5607

Menasha Ridge Press, 2204 1st Ave. S. #102, Birmingham, AL 35233-2331, 205-322-0439, rhelms@menasharidge.com

MURDER CROWS, 1705 13th Ave S Unit A, Birmingham, AL 35205

Osric Publishing, 1705 13th Ave S Unit A, Birmingham, AL 35205

PMS POEMMEMOIRSTORY, English Dept., HB 217, 1530 3rd Avenue South, Birmingham, AL 35294-1260, 205-934-5380, Fax 205-975-8125, lfrost@uab.edu, www.pms-journal.org

RED MOUNTAIN REVIEW, 1800 Eighth Avenue North, Birmingham, AL 35203

SOUL, 806 8th Street Thomas, Birmingham, AL 35214, Soul@delimaehowar.org

New Dawn Unlimited, Inc., 1830 Marvel Road, Brierfield, AL 35035, 205-665-7904; fax 205-665-2500; e-mail wytrabbit1@aol.com

On The Rock Books, P.O. Box 9572, Dothan, AL 36304-9572, 334-702-9663

Cypress Creek Publishing, P.O. Box 731, Florence, AL 35631, 256-767-9055

POEM, P.O. Box 2006, Huntsville, AL 35804

Livingston Press, University of West Alabama, Station 22, Department of Languages and Literature, Livingston, AL 35470, (205) 652-3470

Hot Box Press / Southern Roots Publishing, PO Box 161078, Mobile, AL 36616, 251-645-9018, info@hotboxpress.com

River City Publishing, 1719 Mulberry Street, Montgomery, AL 36106

Saturno Press, 1220 South Hull Street, Montgomery, AL 36104, 334-414-0745

Doctor Jazz Press, 119 Pintail Drive, Pelham, AL 35124

ALABAMA LITERARY REVIEW, Smith 253, Troy State University, Troy, AL 36082, 334-670-3971, Fax 334-670-3519

ALABAMA HERITAGE, Box 870342, 500 Margaret Drive, Tuscaloosa, AL 35487-0342, 205-348-7434, www.AlabamaHeri-tage.com

BLACK WARRIOR REVIEW, PO Box 862936, University of Alabama, Tuscaloosa, AL 35486-0027, 205-348-4518

POGO STICK, 1300 Kicker Road, Tuscaloosa, AL 35404, 553-2284, uniquewish@juno.com

Story County Books, PO Box 21179, Tuscaloosa, AL 35402-1179

University of Alabama Press, Box 870342, 500 Margaret Drive, Tuscaloosa, AL 35487-0342, 205-348-7434, www.AlabamaHeritage.com

ALASKA

ALASKA QUARTERLY REVIEW, University of Alaska-Anchorage, 3211 Providence Drive, Anchorage, AK 99508, 907-786-6916

Capalo Press, 3705 Arctic PMB 2571, Anchorage, AK 99503, 907-322-7105

Edenscape Publishing Company, P.O. Box 110650, Anchorage, AK 99511-0650, Phone:(907) 223-3624, Email:info@edensca-pepublishing.com, Web Site:www.edenscapepublishing.com

Fathom Publishing Co., PO Box 200448, Anchorage, AK 99520-0448, 907-272-3305

Greatland Graphics, PO Box 141414, Anchorage, AK 99514, 907-337-1234, fax 907-337-4567, info@alaskacalendars.com, www.alaskacalendars.com

Merrimack Books, P.O. Box 231229, Anchorage, AK 99523-1229, we21011@earthlink.net

Salmon Run Press, PO Box 671236, Chugiak, AK 99567-1236

Alaska Native Language Center, University of Alaska, PO Box 757680, Fairbanks, AK 99775-7680, 907-474-7874, Fax 907-474-6586

PERMAFROST, Dept. of English, PO Box 755720, Fairbanks, AK 99775-5720

University of Alaska Press, PO Box 756240, Fairbanks, AK 99775-6240, 907.474.5831, 907.474.5502 fax, 888.252.6657, fypress@uaf.edu. www.uaf.edu/uapress

Wizard Works, PO Box 1125, Homer, AK 99603, 907-235-8757 phone/Fax, toll free 877-210-2665, wizard@xyz.net

The Denali Press, PO Box 21535, Juneau, AK 99802, 907-586-6014, Fax 907-463-6780, denalipress@alaska.com

THE FIT CHRISTIAN A Christian Health & Fitness Magazine, P.O. Box 5732, Ketchikan, AK 99901, phone 206-274-8474, fax 614-388-0664, email editor@hisworkpub.com, website http://www.hisworkpub.com

His Work Christian Publishing, P.O. Box 5732, Ketchikan, AK 99901, phone 206-274-8474, fax 614-388-0664, email editor@hisworkpub.com, website http://www.hisworkpub.com

KOKORO, 454 N. Chugach, Palmer, AK 99645, http://www.kokoro-press.com

Northern Publishing, PO BOx 871803, Wasilla, AK 99687, 907-376-6474, 907-373-6474, tony@TonyRuss.com, www.TonyRuss.com

Tuvela Press, P.O.Box 877913, Wasilla, AK 99687-7913, TuvelaPress.com, contact@tuvelapress.com

ARIZONA

Riverstone, A Press for Poetry, PO Box 1421, Carefree, AZ 85377-1421

Five Star Publications, Inc., PO Box 6698, Chandler, AZ 85246-6698, 480-940-8182

Mountain Publishing, PO Box 12720, Chandler, AZ 85248-0029, 800-879-8719, fax: 480-802-5644, email: info@mountain-publishingusa.com

Sonoran Publishing, 6503 W. Frye Rd, Suite 3, Chandler, AZ 85226-3337, 480-961-5176

Holbrook Street Press, PO Box 399, Cortaro, AZ 85652-0399, 520-616-7643, fax 520-616-7519, hsp@triconet.org, www.copshock.com www.writingpublishing.com

ALMOST NORMAL COMICS and Other Oddities, Almost Normal Comics, PO Box 12822, Ft. Huachuca, AZ 85670, info@almostnormalcomics.com, http://almostnormalcomics.com

Blue Planet Books Inc., 4619 W. McRae Way, Glendale, AZ 85308, Phone: 602-769-2066, Fax 623-780-0468, www.blueplanetbooksandsaudio.com

Delaney Day Press, 14014 North 64th Drive, Glendale, AZ 85306-3706, Tel:623-810-7590, Fax:623-486-8662, stoben1@cox.net

GRAY AREAS, PMB 624, 5838 West Olive Ave., STE C105, Glendale, AZ 85302-3155, www.grayarea.com

TalSan Publishing/Distributors, 7614 W. Bluefield Avenue, Glendale, AZ 85308, 602-843-1119, fax 602-843-3080

Raular Publishing, PO Box, 5786, Goodyear, AZ 85338, www.raularpublishing.com; editor@raularpublishing.com

Sweet People Publishing, 14175 W. Indian School Road, Ste B4, PMB 506, Goodyear, AZ 85395, 866-824-9843, info@sweetpeoplepublishing.com, www.sweetpeoplepublishing.com

Vanguard Press, PO Box 1198, Higley, AZ 85236, Phone: 480-695-3192, Web: www.VanguardPress.us, Email: info@vanguardpress.us

Andros Books, P. O. Box 2887, Mesa, AZ 85204, androsbks@aol.com

LJW Publishing, 10457 E. Obispo Ave., Mesa, AZ 85212, www.larryjohnwrightpublishing.com

THE SALT RIVER REVIEW, 448 N. Matlock, Mesa, AZ 85203-7222, http://www.poetserv.org/

Arizona Master Gardener Press, 4341 E. Broadway Road, Phoenix, AZ 85040-8807, 602-470-8086 ext. 312, Fax 602-470-8092

BELIEVERS EXCHANGE NEWSLETTER, 3540 East Amelia Avenue, Phoenix, AZ 85018, 206-350-2237, publisher@anna-gaillynes.net, www.annagaillynes.net

FLUENT ASCENSION, c/o FIERCE Concepts, PO Box 14581, Phoenix, AZ 85063-4581, submissions@fluentascension.com, www.fluentascension.com

Papillon Presse, P.O. Box 54502, Phoenix, AZ 85078-4502

Red Coyote Press, P.O. Box 60582, Phoenix, AZ 85082, 602-454-7815, info@redcoyotepress.com, www.redcoyotepress.com

Rowan Press, Inc., 4414 North 35th St., Phoenix, AZ 85018, 602-380-9213

VISIONHOPE NEWSLETTER, 3540 East Amelia Avenue, Phoenix, AZ 85018, 206-350-2237, publisher@annagaillynes.net, www.annagaillynes.net

Youthful Wisdom Press, 2343 W. Claremont St, Phoenix, AZ 85015, 888-241-2062

Hohm Press, PO Box 2501, Prescott, AZ 86302, 928-778-9189, 800-381-2700, hppublisher@cableone.net

Native West Press, PO Box 12227, Prescott, AZ 86304, 928-771-8376, nativewestpres@cableone.net, www.nativewest-press.com

Smirk Books, 833 Alpha Lane, Prescott, AZ 86303, (928) 778-6788

EMERGING, 7119 East Shea Blvd., Suite 109, PMB 418, Scottsdale, AZ 85254, 480-948-1800, Fax 480-948-1870, teleosinst@aol.com

Footsteps Media, #621, 6929 N. Hayden Road, Suite C4, Scottsdale, AZ 85250, footstepsadventures@cox.net

LP Publications (Teleos Institute), 7119 East Shea Boulevard, Suite 109, PMB 418, Scottsdale, AZ 85254, 480-948-1800, Fax 480-948-1870

Poisoned Pen Press, 6962 E. First Avenue #103, Scottsdale, AZ 85251, 480-945-3375, Fax 480-949-1707, info@poisonedpenpress.com

Best Life Media, 6560 Highway 179, Suite 114, Sedona, AZ 86351, 928.204.1106, http://www.bestlifemedia.com, moh@bestlifemedia.com

Triskelion Publishing, 15508 W. Bell Road #101, PMB #205, Surprise, AZ 85374, Contact: 517-294-0765, Sales: 602-509-8582, Fax: 623-561-0250, sales@triskelionpublishing.com, www.triskelionpublishing.net

Bilingual Review Press, Hispanic Research Center, Arizona State Univ., Box 875303, Tempe, AZ 85287-5303

BILINGUAL REVIEW/Revista Bilingue, Hispanic Research Center, Arizona State Univ., Box 875303, Tempe, AZ 85287-5303

BRB Publications, Inc., PO Box 27869, Tempe, AZ 85285-7869, 800-929-3811, Fax 800-929-4981, brb@brbpub.com, www.brbpub.com

CHASQUI, School of International Languages and Cultures, Arizona State University, Tempe, AZ 85287-0202, 480-965-3752, fax: 480-965-0135, web: www.public.asu.edu/~atdwf.

Facts on Demand Press, PO Box 27869, Tempe, AZ 85285-7869, 800-929-3811, Fax 800-929-4981, brb@brbpub.com, www.brbpub.com

HAYDEN'S FERRY REVIEW, Box 875002, Arizona State University, Tempe, AZ 85287-5002, 480-965-1337

New Falcon Publications, 1753 E. Broadway Road, Suite 101-277, Tempe, AZ 85282, 602-708-1409 (phone), 602-708-1410 (fax), info@newfalcon.com (email), http://www.newfalcon.com (website)

Act on Wisdom, PO Box 12484, Tucson, AZ 85732-2484, 520-326-4674(voice), 773-661-7447 (fax)

California Bill's Automotive Handbooks, PO Box 91858, Tucson, AZ 85752-1858, 520-547-2462, Fax 888-511-1501, web: www.californiabills.com www.goodyearbooks.com www.nononsenseguides.com

Chax Press, 101 W. Sixth St., Tucson, AZ 85701-1000, 520-620-1626, http://chax.org

Cheops Books, 8746 E. Wallen Ridge Drive, Tucson, AZ 85710-6235, (520)232-2152, occultus@cox.net, www.cheops-books.org

Desert Bloom Press, 7170 N. Harold Drive, Tucson, AZ 85743-8614, 520-572-1597 phone, 520-572-1597 fax, pub@desertbloompress.com

DIAGRAM, English Department, University of Arizona, ML 445, PO Box 210067, Tucson, AZ 85721

DISSE: Directory of inmate shopping services and e-commerce, P.O. Box 91008, Tucson, AZ 85752, 1-877-884-7639, vanessa@disse.biz, www.disse.biz

Galen Press, Ltd., PO Box 64400, Tucson, AZ 85728-4400, 520-577-8363, Fax 520-529-6459

Great West Publishing, P. O. Box 31631, Tucson, AZ 85751-1631, Tel: 520-396-1081, Fax: 520-514-9336, URL: www.sentrybooks.com

Imago Press, 3710 East Edison Street, Tucson, AZ 85716, 520-327-0540, ljoiner@dakotacom.net, www.ImagoBooks.com

THE LAUGHING DOG, #326, 4729 E. Sunrise, Tucson, AZ 85718, Subsyncpress.com, Subsyncpress@Gmail.com

THE MATCH, PO Box 3012, Tucson, AZ 85702

Ravenhawk Books, 7739 E. Broadway Boulevard #95, Tucson, AZ 85710, 520-296-4491, Fax 520-296-4491, ravenhawk6dof@yahoo.com

See Sharp Press, PO Box 1731, Tucson, AZ 85702-1731, 520-628-8720, info@seesharppress.com, www.seesharppress.com

SONORA REVIEW, Dept. of English, University of Arizona, Tucson, AZ 85721, 520-624-9192

SPOT LITERARY MAGAZINE, 4729 E. Sunrise Dr., PO Box 254, Tucson, AZ 85718-4535, susan.hansell@gmail.com

Subsynchronous Press, 4729 E. Sunrise #326, Tucson, AZ 85718, Subsyncpress.com, Subsyncpress@CS.com

Subsynchronuos Press, 4729 E. Sunrise, #326, Tucson, AZ 85718, Subsyncpress.com

VEIL: Journal of Darker Musings, 4729 E. Sunrise, #326, Tucson, AZ 85718, Subsyncpress.com
Wheatmark Book Publishing, 610 East Delano Street, Suite 104, Tucson, AZ 85705-5210, 520-798-0888, 520-798-3394 (fax), http://www.wheatmark.com

ARKANSAS

THE QUILLDRIVER, P.O. Box 573, Clarksville, AR 72830, 479.497-0321, www.thequilldriver.com, info@thequilldriver.com
THE OXFORD AMERICAN, 201 Donaghey Ave., #107, Conway, AR 72035-5001, www.oxfordamericanmag.com
SLANT: A Journal of Poetry, University of Central Arkansas, PO Box 5063, Conway, AR 72035-5000, 501-450-5107
AQUATERRA, METAECOLOGY & CULTURE, 5473 Highway 23N, Eureka Springs, AR 72631
University of Arkansas Press, McIlroy House, 105 N. McIlroy Avenue, Fayetteville, AR 72701, 1-479-575-3246
Best Books Plus, 2901 Skinner Heights, Greenwood, AR 72936, 479-650-5546, bestbooksplus@cox.net, www.best-booksplus.com
Lancer Militaria, Box 1188, Mt. Ida, AR 71957-1188, 870-867-2232; www.warbooks.com
NEBO, Department of English, Arkansas Tech University, Russellville, AR 72801, 479-968-0256
ARKANSAS REVIEW, Arkansas State University, PO Box 1890, State University, AR 72467, phone numbers: 870-972-3043, fax: 870-972-3045, email address: delta@astate.edu, www: www.clt.astate.edu/arkreview

CALIFORNIA

Hunter House Inc., Publishers, PO Box 2914, Alameda, CA 94501, 510-865-5282, Fax 510-865-4295, info@hunterhouse.com, www.hunterhouse.com
Business Coach Press, PO Box 301, Alamo, CA 94507-0301, 877-782-6226
Razor7 Publishing, PO Box 6746, Altadena, CA 91003-6746, (626) 205-3154
THE AMERICAN POETRY JOURNAL, PO Box 2080, Aptos, CA 95001-2080, editor@americanpoetryjournal.com, www.americanpoetryjournal.com
Chatoyant, PO Box 832, Aptos, CA 95003, 831-662-3047 phone/Fax, books@chatoyant.com, www.chatoyant.com
Dream Horse Press, PO Box 2080, Aptos, CA 95001-2080, dreamhorsepress@yahoo.com, www.dreamhorsepress.com
THE NATIONAL POETRY REVIEW, PO Box 2080, Aptos, CA 95001-2080, website: www.nationalpoetryreview.com, Submissions: tnprsubmissions@yahoo.com, info: editor@nationalpoetryreview.com
Paradise Cay Publications, PO Box 29, Arcata, CA 95518-0029
Impact Publishers, Inc., PO Box 6016, Atascadero, CA 93423-6016, 805-466-5917, info@impactpublishers.com, www.impactpublishers.com
New Knowledge Press, 10556 Combie Rd., Suite 6360, Auburn, CA 95602, 530-320-4680 (tel), 530-268-7404 (fax), sweiss@newknowledgepress.com, http://www.newknowledgepress.com
THE JOURNAL OF CALIFORNIA AND GREAT BASIN ANTHROPOLOGY, P.O. Box 578, Banning, CA 92220, 951-849-7289, 951-849-3549, malkipress@aol.com, malkimuseum.org
Malki Museum Press, P.O. Box 578, Banning, CA 92220, 951-849-7289, Fax 951-849-3549, E-Mail: malkipress@aol.com, www.malkimuseum.org
Malki-Ballena Press, PO Box 578, Banning, CA 92220-0578, (951)849-7289, Fax (951)849-3549, E-mail: malkimuseum-mail@gmail.com
ARCATA ARTS, P.O.B. 800, Bayside, CA 95524, 707 822 5839, 707 826 2002 fax, 888 687 8962, pub@arcata-arts.com, http://arcata-arts.com
RedJack, P.O. Box 633, Bayside, CA 95524, (707) 825-7817, redjackbooks@gmail.com, www.redjackbooks.com
Cadmus Editions, PO Box 126, Belvedere Tiburon, CA 94920-0126, 707-762-0510
WeWrite LLC, 11040 Alba Road, Ben Lomond, CA 95005-9220, dpalmer@wewrite.net, www.wewrite.net
AGRICULTURAL HISTORY, University of California Press, 2000 Center Street, Suite 303, Berkeley, CA 94704-1223, 510-643-7154
ANARCHY: A Journal of Desire Armed, PO Box 3448, Berkeley, CA 94703, editor@anarchymag.org
Apogee Press, 2308 Sixth Street, Berkeley, CA 94710, Email: editors@ApogeePress.com
ASIAN SURVEY, University of California Press, 2000 Center Street, Suite 303, Berkeley, CA 94704-1223, 510-643-7154
Bay Area Poets Coalition, POETALK, PO Box 11435, Berkeley, CA 94712-2435, poetalk@aol.com, www.bayareapoetscoalition.org
THE BERKELEY FICTION REVIEW, 10-B Eshleman Hall, University of California, Berkeley, CA 94720
THE BERKELEY REVIEW OF BOOKS, 1731 10th Street, Apt. A, Berkeley, CA 94710
Carousel Press, PO Box 6038, Berkeley, CA 94706-0038, 510-527-5849, carous4659@aol.com, www.carousel-press.com
CC. Marimbo, PO Box 933, Berkeley, CA 94701-0933
CLASSICAL ANTIQUITY, Univ of California Press, 2000 Center Street, Suite 303, Berkeley, CA 94704-1223, 510-643-7154
Command Performance Press, 28 Hopkins Court, Berkeley, CA 94706-2512, 510-524-1191
CONTEXTS: UNDERSTANDING PEOPLE IN THEIR SOCIAL WORLDS, University of California Press, 2000 Center St., Suite 303, Berkeley, CA 94704-1223, 510-643-7154
Counterpoint, 2117 Fourth Street, Suite D, Berkeley, CA 94710
Creative Arts Book Company, 833 Bancroft Way, Berkeley, CA 94710, staff@creativeartsbooks.com
FEDERAL SENTENCING REPORTER, University of California Press, 2000 Center Street, Suite 303, Berkeley, CA 94704-1223, 510-643-7154
FILM QUARTERLY, University of California Press, 2000 Center Street, Suite 303, Berkeley, CA 94704-1223, 510-643-7154
GASTRONOMICA: The Journal of Food and Culture, 2000 Center Street, Suite 303, Journals Division, Berkeley, CA 94704-1223, 510-643-7154, Fax 510-642-9917, journals@ucpress.edu
The Gutenberg Press, c/o Fred Foldvary, 1920 Cedar Street, Berkeley, CA 94709, 510-843-0248, e-mail gutenbergpress@po-box.com
Heyday Books, PO Box 9145, Berkeley, CA 94709, 510-549-3564, Fax 510-549-1889
HISTORICAL STUDIES IN THE PHYSICAL & BIOLOGICAL SCIENCES, University of California Press, 2000 Center Street, Suite 303, Berkeley, CA 94704-1223, 510-643-7154
HUNTINGTON LIBRARY QUARTERLY, University of California Press, 2000 Center St., Suite 303, Berkeley, CA 94704-1223, 626-405-2174
INDEX TO FOREIGN LEGAL PERIODICALS, University of California Press, 2000 Center Street, Suite 303, Berkeley, CA 94704-1223, 510-643-7154
Jawbone Press, 1700 Fourth St., Berkeley, CA 94710, 510-809-3818, fax 510-809-3777, 877-528-1444, kevin@jawbone-press.com, www.jawbonepress.com
JOURNAL OF MUSICOLOGY, University of California Press, 2000 Center Street, Suite 303, Berkeley, CA 94704-1223,

510-643-7154

JOURNAL OF PALESTINE STUDIES, University of California Press, 2000 Center St., Suite 303, Berkeley, CA 94704-1223, 510-643-7154

JOURNAL OF THE AMERICAN MUSICOLOGICAL SOCIETY, University of California Press, 2000 Center St., Suite 303, Berkeley, CA 94704-1223, 510-643-7154

Judah Magnes Museum Publications, 2911 Russell Street, Berkeley, CA 94705

Kelsey St. Press, 2824 Kelsey St., Berkeley, CA 94705, 510-845-2260, Fax 510-548-9185, info@kelseyst.com, www.kelseyst.com

LAW AND LITERATURE, University of California Press, 2000 Center St., Suite 303, Berkeley, CA 94704-1223, 510-643-7154

MEXICAN STUDIES/ESTUDIOS MEXICANOS, University of California Press, 2000 Center Street, Suite 303, Berkeley, CA 94704-1223, 510-643-7154

MUSIC PERCEPTION, Univ of CA Press, 2000 Center Street, Suite 303, Berkeley, CA 94704-1223, 510-643-7154

MUSIC THEORY SPECTRUM, University of California Press, 2000 Center St., Suite 303, Berkeley, CA 94704-1223, 510-643-7154

MYSTERY READERS JOURNAL, PO Box 8116, Berkeley, CA 94707-8116, 510-845-3600, www.mysteryreaders.org

NEWS FROM NATIVE CALIFORNIA, PO Box 9145, Berkeley, CA 94709, 510-549-3564; FAX 510-549-1889

19TH-CENTURY LITERATURE, University of California Press, 2000 Center Street, Suite 303, Berkeley, CA 94704-1223, 510-643-7154

19TH-CENTURY MUSIC, University of California Press, 2000 Center Street, Suite 303, Berkeley, CA 94704-1223, 510-643-7154

North Atlantic Books, 2526 Martin Luther King Jr. Way, Berkeley, CA 94704, 800-337-2665, 510-549-4270, fax 510-549-4276, www.northatlanticbooks.com

NOVA RELIGIO, University of California Press, 2000 Center St., Suite 303, Berkeley, CA 94704-1223, 510-643-7154

ORAL HISTORY REVIEW, University of California Press, 2000 Center St., Suite 303, Berkeley, CA 94704-1223, 510-643-7154

PACIFIC HISTORICAL REVIEW, Univ of California Press, 2000 Center Street, Suite 303, Berkeley, CA 94704-1223, 510-643-7154

Parallax Press, 2236B 6th St., Berkeley, CA 94710-2219, 510-525-0101; e-Mail info@parallax.org; web address http://www.parallax.org

POETALK, PO Box 11435, Berkeley, CA 94712-2435, poetalk@aol.com, www.bayareapoetscoalition.org

POETRY FLASH, 1450 Fourth Street #4, Berkeley, CA 94710, 510-525-5476, Fax 510-525-6752

Poltroon Press, PO Box 5476, Berkeley, CA 94705-0476, 510-845-8097

THE PUBLIC HISTORIAN, University of California Press, 2000 Center Street, Suite 303, Berkeley, CA 94704-1223, 510-643-7154

RELIGION & AMERICAN CULTURE, University of California Press, 2000 Center St., Suite 303, Berkeley, CA 94704-1223, 510-643-7154

REPORTS OF THE NATIONAL CENTER FOR SCIENCE EDUCATION, NCSE, Box 9477, Berkeley, CA 94709, 510-601-7203, Fax 510-601-7204

REPRESENTATIONS, University of California Press, 2000 Center Street, Suite 303, Berkeley, CA 94704-1223, 510-643-7154

RHETORICA: A Journal of the History of Rhetoric, Univ of California Press, 2000 Center Street, Suite 303, Berkeley, CA 94704-1223, 510-643-7154

SCP JOURNAL, PO Box 4308, Berkeley, CA 94704

SINISTER WISDOM, PO Box 3252, Berkeley, CA 94703

SOCIAL PROBLEMS, University of California Press, 2000 Center Street, Suite 303, Berkeley, CA 94704-1223, 510-643-7154

SOCIOLOGICAL PERSPECTIVES, University of California Press, 2000 Center St., Suite 303, Berkeley, CA 94704-1223, 510-643-7154

THE SOCIOLOGICAL QUARTERLY, University of California Press, 2000 Center St., Suite 303, Berkeley, CA 94704-1223, 510-643-7154

Soft Skull Press, 2117 Fourth Street, Suite D, Berkeley, CA 94710, 212-673-2502, Fax 212-673-0787, sander@softskull.com, www.softskull.com

STATE OF CALIFORNIA LABOR, University of California Press, 2000 Center St., Suite 303, Berkeley, CA 94704-1223, 510-634-7154

SYMBOLIC INTERACTION, University of California Press, 2000 Center St., Suite 303, Berkeley, CA 94704-1223, 510-643-7154

THE THREEPENNY REVIEW, PO Box 9131, Berkeley, CA 94709-0131, 510-849-4545

TURNING WHEEL, PO Box 3470, Berkeley, CA 94703

Tuumba Press, 2639 Russell Street, Berkeley, CA 94705-2131, 510-548-1817, 510-704-8350

University of California Press, 2000 Center Street, Suite 303, Berkeley, CA 94704-1223, 510-643-7154, e-mail journals@ucpress.edu

Wilderness Press, 1200 5th Street, Berkeley, CA 94710-1453, 510-558-1666; e-mail mail@wildernesspress.com; website www.wildernesspress.com

Museon Publishing, P O Box 17095, Beverly Hills, CA 90209-2095, phone/fax: (323) 936-8151, www.museonbooks.com

SP Turner Group, 8306 Wilshire Boulevard, Suite 1213, Beverly Hills, CA 90211, 866 604 3852

Hole In The Head Press, P.O. Box 807, Bodega Bay, CA 94923-0807, 707-875-3928

Adamantine Publishing House, PO Box 6338, Burbank, CA 91510-6338, 818-843-3427

CHIMERA, 921 N. Frederic Street, Burbank, CA 91505, 818 846 8700

The Sacred Beverage Press, PO Box 10312, Burbank, CA 91510-0312, Fax 818-780-1912, sacredbev@aol.com

Buddhist Text Translation Society, 1777 Murchison Drive, Burlingame, CA 94010-4504, (707) 468-9112, e-mail EileenHu@drba.org

Stunt Publishing, 22287 Mulholland Hwy, #281, Calabasas, CA 91302, ph:818-312-5157, fax:818-312-5157, www.stuntpublishing.com, stuntpublishing@stuntpublishing.com

American Carriage House Publishing, P.O. Box 1130, Nevada City, California, CA 95959, phone 530.432.8860, fax 530.432.7379

LIFETIME MAGAZINE, P.O. Box 1130, Nevada City, California, CA 95959, phone 530.432.8860, fax 530.432.7379

Latitude Press, PO Box 603, Cardiff, CA 92007-0603, 760-536-6131

Craftsman Book Company, 6058 Corte Del Cedro, Carlsbad, CA 92011, 760-438-7828

French Bread Publications, P.O. Box 56, Carlsbad, CA 92018

Gurze Books, PO Box 2238, Carlsbad, CA 92018, 800-756-7533; 760-434-7533; Fax 760-434-5476; email: info@gurze.net

PACIFIC COAST JOURNAL, PO Box 56, Carlsbad, CA 92018-0056, e-mail pcj@frenchbreadpublications.com

Creative With Words Publications (CWW), PO Box 223226, Carmel, CA 93922-3226, Fax: 831-655-8627; e-mail: cwwpub@usa.net; http://members.tripod.com/~creativewithwords

Fisher King Press, P.O. Box 222321, Carmel, CA 93922-2321, 831-238-7799, 800-228-9316, queries@fisherkingpress.com, www.fisherkingpress.com

THEECLECTICS, PO Box 223226, Carmel, CA 93922, fax 831-655-8627; e-mail cwwpub@usa.net; website http://members.tripod.com/~CreativeWithWords

Dry Creek Press, 5753 Cada Circle, Carmichael, CA 95608, 916-531-1249, 916-218-6036, www.drycreekpress.com

Brown Fox Books, 1090 Eugenia Place, Carpinteria, CA 93013, 805-684-5951, Fax 805-684-1628, Manager@Brownfox-books.com, www.Brownfoxbooks.com

SOLO CAFE, 5146 Foothill Road, Carpinteria, CA 93013, berrypress@aol.com

The Infinity Group, 22516 Charlene Way, Castro Valley, CA 94546, 510-581-8172; kenandgenie@yahoo.com

Dharma Publishing, 35788 Hauser Bridge Road, Cazadero, CA 95421, 707-847-3717, fax: 707-847-3380, web: www.dharmapublishing.com, email: dp@dharmapublishing.com

THE MOUNTAIN ASTROLOGER, PO Box 970, Cedar Ridge, CA 95924-0970, 530-477-8839, www.mountainastrologer.com

Scientia Publishing, LLC, P. O. Box 5495, Chatsworth, CA 91313, 1-818-620-0433, www.scientiapublishingllc.com

Wilshire Books Inc., 9731 Variel Ave., Chatsworth, CA 91311-4315, 818-700-1522 [tel], 818-700-1527 [fax], website: www.mpowers.com

Flume Press, California State University, Chico, 400 W. First Street, Chico, CA 95929-0830, 530-898-5983

Heidelberg Graphics, 2 Stansbury Court, Chico, CA 95928-9410, 530-342-6582

MACROBIOTICS TODAY, PO Box 3998, Chico, CA 95927-3998, 530-566-9765, Fax 530-566-9768, gomf@ohsawamacro-biotics.com

George Ohsawa Macrobiotic Foundation, PO Box 3998, Chico, CA 95927-3998, 530-566-9765, Fax 530-566-9768, gomf@ohsawamacrobiotics.com

LifeThread Publications, 7541 Wooddale Way, Citrus Heights, CA 95610-2621, 916-722-3452, E-mail susanosborn41@comcast.net Website www.susan.osborn.bz

LITVISION, 7711 Greenback Lane #156, Citrus Heights, CA 95610

Savor Publishing House, Inc., 6020 Broken Bow Dr., Citrus Heights, CA 95621, 916 729-3664, 866 762-7898

Toad Press International Chapbook Series, Claremont, CA 91711-0159, www.toadpress.blogspot.com, toadpress@hotmail.com

HEALMB Publishing, P.O. Box 4005, Clovis, CA 93613-4005, 559-291-4387, 559-297-7077, comments@nailcareinfo.com, http://www.nailcareinfo.com

SILVER WINGS, PO Box 2340, Clovis, CA 93613-2340, 661-264-3726

THE REJECTED QUARTERLY, PO Box 1351, Cobb, CA 95426, bplankton@yahoo.com; rejectedq.com

Bear Star Press, 185 Hollow Oak Drive, Cohasset, CA 95973, 530-891-0360, www.bearstarpress.com

C & T Publishing, 1651 Challenge Drive, Concord, CA 94520-5206, 925-677-0377

SPEX (SMALL PRESS EXCHANGE), PO Box E, Corte Madera, CA 94976, 866-622-1325

THE KERF, 883 W. Washington Boulevard, Crescent City, CA 95531, 707-465-2360, Fax 707-464-6867

EquiLibrium Press, 10736 Jefferson Blvd. #680, Culver City, CA 90230

TURNING THE TIDE: Journal of Anti-Racist Action, Research & Education, PO Box 1055, Culver City, CA 90232-1055, 310-495-0299, antiracistaction_la@yahoo.com

Happy About, 20660 Stevens Creek Blvd, Suite 210, Cupertino, CA 95014, 408-257-3000, info@happyabout.info, http://www.happyabout.info

RED WHEELBARROW, 21250 Stevens Creek Blvd., De Anza College, Cupertino, CA 95014, Phone: 408-864-5797, 831-252-3958, weisnerken@fhda.edu

Genny Smith Books, 23100 Via Esplendor, Villa 44, Cupertino, CA 95014, 650-964-4071, www.liveoakpress.com

WILD DUCK REVIEW, P.O. Box 335, Davenport, CA 95017, www.wildduckreview.com / casey@wildduckreview.com

Piano Press, PO Box 85, Del Mar, CA 92014-0085, pianopress@pianopress.com, www.pianopress.com, 619-884-1401

Andrew Scott Publishers, 15023 Tierra Alta, Del Mar, CA 92014, 858-461-0089 andrewscottpublishers@juno.com

Wharton Publishing, Inc., 2683 Via De La Valle, Suite G #210, Del Mar, CA 92014, 760-931-8977, Fax 858-759-7097, e-mail marketingtina@aol.com

Front Row Experience, 540 Discovery Bay Boulevard, Discovery Bay, CA 94514, 925-634-5710

Pressarius Publishing, 15 Mountain Laurel, Dove Canyon, CA 92679-4216, 949-842-6301

HAPA NUI, East Palo Alto, CA 94303, www.hapanui.com

Sunbelt Publications, 1256 Fayette Street, El Cajon, CA 92020-1511, 619-258-4911, Fax 619-258-4916, editor@sunbelt-pub.com, www.sunbeltbooks.com

The Glencannon Press, PO Box 1428, El Cerrito, CA 94530-4428, 510-528-4216, fax 510-528-3194

Cloudland Books, 585 Encina Drive, El Dorado Hills, CA 95762, www.cloudlandbooks.com

Reference Service Press, 5000 Windplay Drive, Suite 4, El Dorado Hills, CA 95762-9319, (916) 939-9620, fax: (916) 939-9626, email: info@rspfunding.com, web site: www.rspfunding.com

New Win Publishing, 9682 Telstar Ave. Suite 110, El Monte, CA 91731, 626-448-3448, 626-602-3817, info@academiclearningcompany.com, www.newwinpublishing.com

Velazquez Press, 9682 Telstar Ave. Suite 110, El Monte, CA 91731, 626-448-3448, 626-602-3817, info@academiclearning-company.com, www.velazquezpress.com

Heritage Library Press, 8772 Boysenberry Way, Elk Grove, CA 95624, 916-689-6806, Fax 916-689-6683, jaysonlee@frontier-net.net, www.heritagelibrarypress.com

ZAHIR: A Journal of Speculative Fiction, 315 South Coast Hwy. 101 Suite U8, Encinitas, CA 92024, stempchin@zahir-tales.com, http://www.zahirtales.com

Titan Press, PO Box 17897, Encino, CA 91416-7897

Red Cygnet Press, 2245 Enterprise St., Suite 110, Escondido, CA 92029, tel: 760-839-2273, fax: 760-839-2258, web: http://www.redcygnet.com, e: jgravin@redcygnet.com

TIN HOUSE MAGAZINE, PO Box 469049, Escondido, CA 92046

TRUTH SEEKER, 239 S. Juniper Street, Escondido, CA 92025-0550, 760-489-5211, Fax 760-489-5311, tseditor@aol.com, www.truthseeker.com

Now I See Publishing, Box 352, Etiwanda, CA 91739, 909-922-7276, 909-899-6783

THE BLUE MOUSE, PO Box 8317, Eureka, CA 95502-8317

FINE BOOKS & COLLECTIONS, PO Box 106, Eureka, CA 95502, 707-443-9562, Fax 707-443-9572, scott@finebooksmagazine.com, www.finebooksmagazine.com

Swan Duckling Press, PO Box 8317, Eureka, CA 95502-8317
Adams-Blake Publishing, 8041 Sierra Street, Fair Oaks, CA 95628, 916-962-9296
GINOSKO LITERARY JOURNAL, PO Box 246, Fairfax, CA 94978, www.GinoskoLiteraryJournal.com
Encore Publishing, 124 S. Mercedes Rd, Fallbrook, CA 92028, (909) 437-7015, (760) 451-8670 fax
Jalmar Press/Innerchoice Publishing, PO Box 370, Fawnskin, CA 92333, Fax 909 866 2961 Email: info@jalmarpress.com
Personhood Press, PO Box 370, Fawnskin, CA 92333-0370, 909-866-2912, Fax 909-866-2961, 800 429 1192, www.personhoodpress.com
Floreant Press, 6195 Anderson Rd, Forestville, CA 95436, 7078877868
Cypress House, 155 Cypress Street, Fort Bragg, CA 95437, 707-964-9520, Fax 707-964-7531, publishing@cypresshouse.com
Lost Coast Press, 155 Cypress Street, Fort Bragg, CA 95437, 800-773-7782, fax 707-964-7531, www.cypresshouse.com, joeshaw@cypresshouse.com
QED Press, 155 Cypress Street, Fort Bragg, CA 95437, 707-964-9520, Fax 707-964-7531, qedpress@mcn.org
Tres Picos Press, PO Box 932, Freedom, CA 95019, 831 254-7447; email: submissions@trespicospress.com
Adventure Books Inc., PO Box 5196, Fresno, CA 93755, 559-294-8781, adventurebooks@juno.com
Quill Driver Books, 2006 S. Mary, Fresno, CA 93711-3311, 559-233-6633, Fax 559-233-6933, 800-345-4447
Elite Books, PO Box 442, Fulton, CA 95439, 707-525-9292, Fax 800-330-9798, deb@authorspublishing.com, www.elitebooks.biz
Energy Psychology Press, PO Box 442, Fulton, CA 95439, 707-525-9292, Fax 800-330-9798, dawson@authorspublishing.com, www.energypsychologypress.com
Balcony Media, Inc., 512 E. Wilson Avenue, Suite 213, Glendale, CA 91206, 818-956-5313(T), web: www.balconypress.com, email: alexi@formmag.net
FORM: pioneering design, 512 E. Wilson Avenue, Suite 213, Glendale, CA 91206
White Thread Press, 480 Whitman Street #102, Goleta, CA 93117, 805 968 4666
Life Energy Media, 11024 Balboa Blvd. Ste 420, Granada Hills, CA 91344, 818-995-3263
Red Hen Press, PO Box 3537, Granada Hills, CA 91394, 626-356-476, Fax 818-831-6659, E-mail: marketing@redhen.org
CHEAP SHOTS: Poetry Series, 417 Neal Street, Grass Valley, CA 95945, 530-271-0662, sixfootswells@yahoo.com, www.myspace.com/sixftswells
Comstock Bonanza Press, 18919 William Quirk Memorial Drive, Grass Valley, CA 95945-8611, 530-263-2906
Six Ft. Swells Press, 417 Neal Street, Grass Valley, CA 95945, 530-271-0662, sixfootswells@yahoo.com, www.myspace.com/sixftswells
KALDRON, An International Journal Of Visual Poetry, 2740 Grell Lane, Oceano, Halcyon, CA 93445, 805-489-2770, www.thing.net/~grist/l&d/kaldron.htm
BLOODJET LITERARY MAGAZINE, 20 Driftwood Trail, Half Moon Bay, CA 94019-2349, 650-726-5939
New World Publishing, 20 Driftwood Trail, Half Moon Bay, CA 94019-2349, 650-726-5939; email: thepitheaisout@coastside.net
Mille Grazie Press, 967 Clover Lane, Hanford, CA 93230-2255
Naturegraph Publishers, PO Box 1047, 3543 Indian Creek Road, Happy Camp, CA 96039, 530-493-5353, 530-493-5240, 1-800-390-5353. nature@isqtel.net, www.naturegraph.com
ARROYO LITERARY REVIEW, Dept/English MB 2579, CSU-East Bay, 25800 Carlos Bee Blvd., Hayward, CA 94542
Pixiu Press, P.O. Box 183, Healdsburg, CA 95448, www.pixiupress.com
Vedanta Press, 1946 Vedanta Place, Hollywood, CA 90068-3996, 323-960-1728, e-mail address: bob@vedanta.org, web address: www.vedanta.com, web page shows our online catalog. Note that titles with an asterisk by the title in the catalog are not wholesale titles
SPILLWAY, Box 7887, Huntington Beach, CA 92615-7887, 714-968-0905
Tebot Bach, Box 7887, Huntington Beach, CA 92615-7887, 714-968-0905
Verve Press, PO Box 1997, Huntington Beach, CA 92647, fax: 714-840-8335
World Parade Books, 5267 Warner Ave., #191, Huntington Beach, CA 92649-4079
Academy Press of America, 19700 Fairchild Road, Suite 300, Irvine, CA 92612-2512, telephone: 1-949-720-3860, toll free: 1-800-935-6020, Email address: orders@academypressofamerica.com, web site: www.academypressofamerica.com
FAULTLINE, Department of English, University of California, Irvine, Irvine, CA 92697-2650, (949) 824-1573
Level 4 Press, Inc., 13518 Jamul Drive, Jamul, CA 91935-1635, 619-669-3100, 619-374-7311 fax, sales@level4press.com, www.level4press.com
Progressive Press; Tree of Life Publications, PO Box 126, Joshua Tree, CA 92252, 760-366-3695, fax 760-366-2937
BLUE UNICORN, 22 Avon Road, Kensington, CA 94707, 510-526-8439
International University Line (IUL), PO Box 2525, La Jolla, CA 92038, Tel 858-457-0595, Fax 858-581-9073, email info@iul-press.com, http://www.iul-press.com
A Melody from an Immigrant's Soul, 5712 Baltimore Dr. #461, La Mesa, CA 91942, (619) 667-0925 E-mail: dorishka1@sbcglobal.net
BEGGARS & CHEESEBURGERS, La Palma, CA 90623, submitbeggars@gmail.com
Laguna Wilderness Press, PO Box 149, Laguna Beach, CA 92652-0149, 951-827-1571
Frontline Publications, PO Box 815, Lake Forest, CA 92609, 949-837-6258
Info Net Publishing, 21142 Canada Road Unit 1-C, Lake Forest, CA 92630-6714, 949-462-0224, Fax 949-462-9595, herb@infonetpublishing.com
Tamal Vista Publications, 222 Madrone Ave., Larkspur, CA 94939-1913, www.tamalvista.com, 617-492-7234
Auromere Books and Imports, 2621 W. US Highway 12, Lodi, CA 95242-9200, 800-735-4691, 209-339-3710, Fax 209-339-3715, books@auromere.com, www.auromere.com
Summerland Publishing, 21 Oxford Drive, Lompoc, CA 93436, PH/Fax: 8057355241, www.summerlandpublishing.com
FMA Publishing, 1920 Pacific Ave, #16152, Long Beach, CA 90746, (T)310-438-3483, (F)310-438-3486, (E)info@fmapublishing.com, www.fmapublishing.com
PEARL, 3030 E. Second Street, Long Beach, CA 90803-5163, 562-434-4523 phone/fax or 714-968-7530, PearlMag@aol.com, www.pearlmag.com
Pearl Editions, 3030 E. Second Street, Long Beach, CA 90803-5163, 562-434-4523 phone/fax or 714-968-7530, PearlMag@aol.com, www.pearlmag.com
SHIRIM, 259 Saint Joseph Avenue, Long Beach, CA 90803-1733
BeachSide Press, 115 Doud Dr, Los Altos, CA 94022, 650-714-3069
Tameme, 300 3rd Street, #9, Los Altos, CA 94022, www.tameme.org
AAIMS Publishers, 11000 Wilshire Boulevard, PO Box 241777, Los Angeles, CA 90024-0777, 480-243-9022, 888-490-2276, fax 213-931-7217, email aaims1@aol.com
AMERICAN INDIAN CULTURE AND RESEARCH JOURNAL, UCLA, 3220 Campbell Hall, Los Angeles, CA 90095-1548,

565

310-825-7315, Fax 310-206-7060, www.sscnet.ucla.edu/esp/aisc/index.html
American Indian Studies Center, 3220 Campbell Hall, Box 951458, UCLA, Los Angeles, CA 90095-1548, 310-825-7315, Fax 310-206-7060, www.sscnet.ucla.edu/esp/aisc/index.html
Ariko Publications, 8513 Venice Blvd #201, Los Angeles, CA 90034
AZTLAN: A Journal of Chicano Studies, University of California-Los Angeles, 193 Haines Hall, Los Angeles, CA 90095-1544, 310-825-2642, press@chicano.ucla.edu, www.chicano.ucla.edu
BLACK LACE, PO Box 83912, Los Angeles, CA 90083-0912, 310-410-0808, fax 310-410-9250, e-mail newsroom@blk.com
BLACKFIRE, PO Box 83912, Los Angeles, CA 90083-0912, 310-410-0808, fax 310-410-9250, e-mail newsroom@blk.com
BLK, PO Box 83912, Los Angeles, CA 90083-0912, 310-410-0808, fax 310-410-9250, e-mail newsroom@blk.com
BLK Publishing Company, Inc., PO Box 83912, Los Angeles, CA 90083-0912, 310-410-0808, Fax 310-410-9250, newsroom@blk.com
BLOOM: Queer Fiction, Art, Poetry and more, 5482 Wilshire Blvd, #1616, Los Angeles, CA 90036
Bombshelter Press, P.O Box 481266, Bicentennial Station, Los Angeles, CA 90048, 310-651-5488, jgrapes@bombshelter-press.com, http://www.bombshelterpress.com
Burning Books Press, PO Box 41053, Los Angeles, CA 90041-0053
Cloverfield Press, 1430 Cerro Gordo Street, Los Angeles, CA 90026-2010, submissions@cloverfieldpress.com, www.cloverfieldpress.com
Cotsen Institute of Archaeology Publications, Univ. of California-Los Angeles, A210 Fowler, Los Angeles, CA 90095-1510, 310-825-7411
Disparate Voices, Los Angeles, CA 90028, editorial@disparatevoices.com, www.disparatevoices.com
THE DUCKBURG TIMES, 3010 Wilshire Blvd., #362, Los Angeles, CA 90010-1146, 213-388-2364
ELECTRONIC GREEN JOURNAL, UCLA Charles E. Young Library, UCLA - Box 951575, Los Angeles, CA 90095-1575, e-mail majanko@uidaho.edu, http://repositories.cdlib.org/uclalib/egj/
Everflowing Publications, PO Box 191536, Los Angeles, CA 90019, 323-993-8577, everflowing@nycmail.com
Heat Press, PO Box 26218, Los Angeles, CA 90026, 213-482-8902, heatpresseditions@yahoo.com
Hollywood Creative Directory, 5055 Wilshire Blvd., Los Angeles, CA 90036, 800-815-0503, 323-525-2369, Fax 323-525-2393, www.hcdonline.com
Ignite! Entertainment, P.O. Box 641131, Los Angeles, CA 90064-1980, 310-806-0325, jeffkrell@ignite-ent.com, www.ignite-ent.com
International Jewelry Publications, PO Box 13384, Los Angeles, CA 90013-0384, 626-282-3781, Fax 626-282-4807
Jamenair Ltd., PO Box 241957, Los Angeles, CA 90024-9757, 310-470-6688
JOURNAL OF PAN AFRICAN STUDIES, PO Box 24194, Los Angeles, CA 90024-0194, www.jpanafrican.com.
KABBALAH, 1062 S. Robertson Boulevard, Los Angeles, CA 90035, 310-657-5404, Fax 310-657-7774, kabbalahpublishing@kabbalah.com, www.kabbalah.com
KUUMBA, PO Box 83912, Los Angeles, CA 90083-0912, 310-410-0808, fax 310-410-9250, e-mail newsroom@blk.com
LAMBDA BOOK REPORT, Lambda Literary Foundation, 5482 Wilshire Avenue, #1595, Los Angeles, CA 90036, 213-568-3570
Les Figues Press, PO Box 7736, Los Angeles, CA 90007, info@lesfigues.com
Light Density Press, 9162 West Pico Boulevard #15, Los Angeles, CA 90035, www.lightdensitypress.com
LOS, 150 N. Catalina St., No. 2, Los Angeles, CA 90004, website: http://home.earthlink.net/~lospoesy, email: lospoesy@earthlink.net
Mama Incense Publishing, 5535 Westlawn Ave., Suite 164, Los Angeles, CA 90066, 310-490-9097, www.mamaincense.com
Mendham Publishing, 515 S. Figueroa Street, Suite 1800, Los Angeles, CA 90071, Phone: (213) 622-0862, Fax: (213) 622-0842, liz@thepowerofpersonalbranding.com, www.thepowerofpersonalbranding.com
NEROUP REVIEW, 9129 National Blvd. #7, Los Angeles, CA 90034, www.neroupreview.com, submissions@neroupreview.com
Nova Press, 11659 Mayfield Ave, Suite 1, Los Angeles, CA 90049, 310-207-4078, E-mail novapress@aol.com
ONTHEBUS, Bombshelter Press, P.O. Box 481266, Bicentennial Station, Los Angeles, CA 90048, http://www.bombshelterpress.com or http://www.jackgrapes.com
PALABRA: A Magazine of Chicano & Latino Literary Art, P. O. Box 86146, Los Angeles, CA 90086-0146, www.palabralitmag.com
Red Eye Press, PO Box 65751, Los Angeles, CA 90065-0751, 323-225-3805
SOUTHERN CALIFORNIA REVIEW, Master of Professional Writing Program, 3501 Trousdale Parkw, University of Southern California, Los Angeles, CA 90089-0355, 213-740-3253
Spectrum Productions, 979 Casiano Road, Los Angeles, CA 90049
Chuck Stewart, 3722 Bagley Ave. #19, Los Angeles, CA 90034-4113, www.StewartEducationServices.com
synaesthesia press, 3113 Beverly BLVD, Los Angeles, CA 90057, jim@synaesthesia.net, www.synaesthesia.net
T'AI CHI, PO Box 39938, Los Angeles, CA 90039, 323-665-7773, www.tai-chi.com
Triumvirate Publications, 497 West Avenue 44, Los Angeles, CA 90065-3917, 818-340-6770 Phone/Fax, Triumpub@aol.com, www.Triumpub.com
UCLA Chicano Studies Research Center Press, University of California-Los Angeles, 193 Haines Hall, Los Angeles, CA 90095-1544, 310-825-2642, press@chicano.ucla.edu, www.chicano.ucla.edu
VOICE(S), Los Angeles, CA 90028, editorial@disparatevoices.com, www.disparatevoices.com
WAV MAGAZINE: Progressive Music Art Politics Culture, 3253 S. Beverly Dr., Los Angeles, CA 90034, (310) 876-0490
Wayfarer Publications, PO Box 39938, Los Angeles, CA 90039, 323-665-7773
Sand River Press, 1319 14th Street, Los Osos, CA 93402, 805-543-3591
Poetic Matrix Press, P.O. Box 1223, Madera, CA 93639, www.poeticmatrix.com, www.poeticmatrixpress.com, email-poeticmatrix@yahoo.com
Playdate Kids Publishing, P.O. 2785, Malibu, CA 90265, 310-456-6400
East West Discovery Press, PO Box 3585, Manhattan Beach, CA 90266, 310-545-3730, Fax 310-545-3731, info@eastwestdiscovery.com, web www.eastwestdiscovery.com
Wave Publishing, 4 Yawl Street, Marina del Rey, CA 90292-7159, 310-306-0699
Fithian Press, PO Box 2790, McKinleyville, CA 95519-2790, 805-962-1780, Fax 805-962-8835, dandd@danielpublishing.com
Penthe Publishing, PO Box 1066, Middletown, CA 95461-1066, 800-649-5954, 707-987-3470, penthpub@earthlink.net, penthepub.com
NEW AMERICAN WRITING, 369 Molino Avenue, Mill Valley, CA 94941, 415-389-1877, Fax 415-384-0364
THE BROADSIDER: An Annual Magazine of Rescued Poems, PO Box 236, Millbrae, CA 94030, website: www.thebroadsider.com

566

GIUSEPPE: A Magazine of Literature and Impersonation, PO Box 236, Millbrae, CA 94030, website: www.giuseppemaga-zine.com

THE MINDERBINDER REVIEW OF BOOKS, PO Box 236, Millbrae, CA 94030, website: www.minderbinderreview.com

Poor Souls Press/Scaramouche Books, PO Box 236, Millbrae, CA 94030, www.yunews.com

Booksmart Publications, 19 Bolero, Mission Viejo, CA 92692, 949 462 0076

QUERCUS REVIEW, Modesto Junior College, 435 College Avenue, Modesto, CA 95350, 209-575-6183, pierstorffs@mjc.edu, www.quercusreview.com

SONG OF THE SAN JOAQUIN, PO Box 1161, Modesto, CA 95353-1161, (209) 543-1776, cleor36@yahoo.com

Barney Press, 2550 Honolulu Avenue Ste. 104, Montrose, CA 91020-1859, 805-871-9118

Assilem 9 Publications, 23838 Mark Twain, Moreno Valley, CA 92557, 310-412-1266

Myriad Press, 12535 Chandler Blvd. #3, N. Hollywood, CA 91607-1934, 805-750-1423

Calaca Press, P.O. Box 2309, National City, CA 91951, (619) 434-9036, calacapress@cox.net, www.calacapress.com

Blue Dolphin Publishing, Inc., PO Box 8, Nevada City, CA 95959, 530-477-1503

Dawn Publications, 12402 Bitney Springs Rd., Nevada City, CA 95959, 530-274-7775, toll free 800-545-7475, fax 530-274-7778, nature@dawnpub.com

Gateways Books And Tapes, Box 370, Nevada City, CA 95959-0370, 530-477-8101, fax 530-272-0184, orders 530-271-2239, info@gatewaysbooksandtapes.com, www.gatewaysbooksandtapes.com

MCM Entertainment, Inc. Publishing Division, 177 Riverside Avenue, Suite F-1127, Newport Beach, CA 92663

Noontide Press, PO Box 2719, Newport Beach, CA 92659, 949-631-1490, e-mail editor@noontidepress.com

POETRY DEPTH QUARTERLY, 5836 North Haven Drive, North Highlands, CA 95660, 916-331-3512, e-mail: poetrydepthquarterly.com NO download or attached files accepted. Prefers postal submissions with S.A.S.E.

4AM POETRY REVIEW, 10631 Lindley Ave., Apt. 118, Northridge, CA 91326-3271, fourampoetryreview@gmail.com http://fourampoetryreview.i8.com

Lord John Press, 19073 Los Alimos Street, Northridge, CA 91326, 818-360-5804

BIGFOOT TIMES, 10926 Milano Avenue, Norwalk, CA 90650, www.bigfoottimes.net

Chandler & Sharp Publishers, Inc., 11 Commercial Blvd.Suite A, Novato, CA 94949, 415-883-2353, FAX 415-440-5004, www.chandlersharp.com

New World Library, 14 Pamaron Way, Novato, CA 94949-6215

AK Press, 674-A 23rd Street, Oakland, CA 94612, 415-864-0892, FAX 415-864-0893, akpress@org.org

THE BLACK SCHOLAR: Journal of Black Studies and Research, PO Box 2869, Oakland, CA 94609, 510-547-6633

Broken Shadow Publications, 472 44th Street, Oakland, CA 94609-2136, 510 594-2200

COLORLINES, PMB 319, 4096 Piedmont Ave, Oakland, CA 94609, 510-653-3415

Defiant Times Press, 6020-A Adeline, Oakland, CA 94608, defianttimespress@lycos.com

580 SPLIT, Mills College, P.O. Box 9982, Oakland, CA 94613-0982

GRASSROOTS FUNDRAISING JOURNAL, 1904 Franklin St Ste 705, Oakland, CA 94612, 510-452-4520, Fax 510-452-2122, info@grassrootsfundraising.org, www.grassrootsfundraising.org

LEFT CURVE, PO Box 472, Oakland, CA 94604-0472, E-mail editor@leftcurve.org

Regent Press, 2747 Regent St., Oakland, CA 94705, 510-845-1196, fax: 510-704-1543, web: www.regentpress.net

Ronin Publishing, Inc., Box 22900, Oakland, CA 94609, 510-420-3669, Fax 510-420-3672, ronin@roninpub.com, www.roninpub.com

Scarlet Tanager Books, PO Box 20906, Oakland, CA 94620, 510-763-3874

THE WISE WOMAN, 2441 Cordova Street, Oakland, CA 94602, 510-536-3174

CALIFORNIA QUARTERLY (CQ), CSPS/CQ, PO Box 7126, Orange, CA 92863, 949-854-8024, jipalley@aol.com

Past Times Publishing Co., 271 N. Milford Road, Orange, CA 92867-7849, 714-997-1157; jordanyoung50@sbcglobal.net, www.actingsolo.com

NATIONAL MASTERS NEWS, PO Box 1117, Orangevale, CA 95662-1117, 541-343-7716, Fax 541-345-2436, natmanews@aol.com

Hip Pocket Press, 5 Del Mar Court, Orinda, CA 94563, 925-386-0611

The Poetry Center Press/Shoestring Press, 3 Monte Vista Road, Orinda, CA 94563, 925-254-6639

Park Place Publications, P.O. Box 829, Pacific Grove, CA 93950-0829, 831-649-6640, publishingbiz@sbcglobal.net, www.parkplacepublications.com, www.America-Healthy.com

BIG BRIDGE: A Webzine of Poetry and Everything Else, 2000 Highway 1, Pacifica, CA 94044, www.bigbridge.org

OYSTER BOY REVIEW, PO Box 1483, Pacifica, CA 94044, email_2010@oysterboyreview.com, www.oysterboyreview.com

ETC Publications, 1456 Rodeo Road, Palm Springs, CA 92262, 760-316-9695, fax 760-316-9681

Accendo Publishing, 4211 Rickeys Way Unit G, Palo Alto, CA 94306, 408-406-6697 phone

Lexicus Press, P.O. Box 1691, Palo Alto, CA 94301, 6507995602

The Live Oak Press, LLC, P.O. Box 60036, Palo Alto, CA 94306-0036, 650-853-0197, info@liveoakpress.com, www.liveoakpress.com

Dustbooks, PO Box 100, Paradise, CA 95967-0100, 530-877-6110, Fax 530-877-0222, email: publisher@dustbooks.com, Website: http://www.dustbooks.com/

THE SMALL PRESS REVIEW/SMALL MAGAZINE REVIEW, PO Box 100, Paradise, CA 95967-9999, 530-877-6110, fax: 530-877-0222, email: publisher@dustbooks.com, Website: http://www.dustbooks.com/

BAGAZINE, Po Box 2234, Pasadena, CA 91102

Gorilla Dreamz Publishing, 3579 East Foothill Blvd., #593, Pasadena, CA 91107, Viki@GorillaDreamz.com, www.GorillaDreamz.com

Hope Publishing House, PO Box 60008, Pasadena, CA 91116, 626-792-6123; fax 626-792-2121

Hunter Publishing Corporation, 115 West California Boulevard, Suite 411, Pasadena, CA 91105, tel: 626 792 3316, fax: 626 792 7077, email: info@hpcwww.com, website: www.hpcwww.com

INDEFINITE SPACE, PO Box 40101, Pasadena, CA 91114, www.indefinitespace.net

North Star Books, PO Box 589, Pearblossom, CA 93553-0589, 661-944-1130, NSB@NorthStarBooks.com, http://www.NorthStarBooks.com

R.L. Crow Publications, P.O. Box 262, Penn Valley, CA 95946, Fax and Message: (530) 432-8195, info@rlcrow.com

Smart Publications, P.O. 4667, Petaluma, CA 94955, 1-800-976-2793, 888-998-6889(Fax), www.smart-publications.com

Taurean Horn Press, PO Box 526, Petaluma, CA 94953-0526

TINY LIGHTS: A Journal of Personal Narrative, PO Box 928, Petaluma, CA 94953, 707-762-3208, sbono@tiny-lights.com, www.tiny-lights.com

Jupiter Scientific Publishing, c/o Weng, 415 Moraga Avenue, Piedmont, CA 94611-3720, 510-420-1015, admin@jupiterscienti-fic.org, www.jupiterscientific.org

Bluestocking Press, PO Box 1014, Placerville, CA 95667-1014, 530-622-8586, Fax 530-642-9222, 1-800-959-8586 (orders only), website: www.bluestockingpress.com

Hot Pepper Press, 3541 Wildwood Lane, Placerville, CA 95667

Timber Gap Publishers, 1825 Roche Drive, Pleasant Hill, CA 94523, 925-349-5074, mtaylor@timbergap.com, www.timbergap.com

CKO UPDATE, PO Box 10757, Pleasanton, CA 94588, 925-425-9513, Fax 1-800-605-2914, 1-800-605-2913, editor@blueprintbooks.com, blueprintbooks.com

NEWWITCH, P.O. Box 641, Point Arena, CA 95468, Phone:888-724-3966, Fax:707-882-2793, website http://www.newwitch.com

Rattlesnake Press, P.O. Box 762, Pollock Pines, CA 95726-0762, kathykieth@hotmail.com or rattlesnakepress.com

RATTLESNAKE REVIEW, P.O. Box 762, Pollock Pines, CA 95726-0762, kathykieth@hotmail.com or rattlesnakepress.com

QUARTZ HILL JOURNAL OF THEOLOGY:A Journal of Bible and Contemporary Theological Thought, 43543 51st Street West, Quartz Hill, CA 93536, 661-722-0891, 661-943-3484, E-mail robin@theology.edu

Quartz Hill Publishing House, 43543 51st Street West, Quartz Hill, CA 93536, 661-722-0891, 661-943-3484, E-mail robin@theology.edu

DREAM FANTASY INTERNATIONAL, 411 14th Street #H1, Ramona, CA 92065-2769

Dramaline Publications, 36851 Palm View Road, Rancho Mirage, CA 92270-2417, 760-770-6076, FAX 760-770-4507, drama.line@verizon.net

Mills Custom Services Publishing, P.O. Box 866, Rancho Mirage, CA 92270, 760-250-1897, fax 760-406-6280, Vamills@aol.com, www.buybookscds.com

Noble Porter Press, 36-851 Palm View Road, Rancho Mirage, CA 92270, 760-770-6076, fax 760-770-4507

United Lumbee Nation, PO Box 115, Ravendale, CA 96123, 916-336-6701

UNITED LUMBEE NATION TIMES, P.O. Box 115, Ravendale, CA 96123, 530-336-6701

DayDream Publishing, 808 Vincent ST, Redondo Beach, CA 90277, www.daydreampublishers.com

Brason-Sargar Publications, PO Box 872, Reseda, CA 91337, 818-994-0089, Fax 305-832-2604, sonbar@bigfoot.com

Bay Tree Publishing, 32 Harbor View Drive, Richmond, CA 94804-6400, telephone 510-526-2916, fax 510-525-0842

Omnidawn Publishing, 1632 Elm Avenue, Richmond, CA 94805-1614, Phone: (510) 237-5472, Fax: (510) 232-8525, web: http://www.omnidawn.com/contact.htm

Aquila Ink Publishing, P.O. Box 160, Rio Nido, CA 95471, 707-799-5981

EPICENTER: A LITERARY MAGAZINE, PO Box 367, Riverside, CA 92502, www.epicentrermagazine.org

LATIN AMERICAN PERSPECTIVES, PO Box 5703, Riverside, CA 92517-5703, 951-827-1571, fax 951-827-5685, laps@mail.ucr.edu, www.latinamericanperspectives.com

ZAUM - The Literary Review of Sonoma State University, English Department, SSU, 1801 E. Cotati Avenue, Rohnert Park, CA 94928, 707-664-2140

FINANCIAL FOCUS, 2140 Professional Drive Ste. 105, Roseville, CA 95661-3734, 916-791-1447, Fax 916-791-3444, jeverett@quiknet.com

Athanor Books, P.O.Box 22309, Sacramento, CA 95820-0309, 916-424-4355

Casperian Books LLC, PO Box 161026, Sacramento, CA 95816-1026

EKPHRASIS, PO Box 161236, Sacramento, CA 95816-1236, www.ekphrasisjournal.com

Frith Press, PO Box 161236, Sacramento, CA 95816-1236, www.ekphrasisjournal.com

HUMOR TIMES, PO Box 162429, Sacramento, CA 95816-2429, 916-455-1217, www.humortimes.com, info@humortimes.com

Jullundur Press, 1001 G St., Suite 301, Sacramento, CA 95814, phone 916-449-1300, fax 916-449-1320, email goldentemplepub.com, web: www.johnposwall.com

MGW (Mom Guess What) Newsmagazine, 1123 21st St., Suite 200, Sacramento, CA 95814-4225, 916-441-6397, fax:916-441-6422, info@mgwnews.com, www.mgwnews.com

MYSTERY ISLAND MAGAZINE, Mystery Island, 384 Windward Way, Sacramento, CA 95831-2420, brad@mysteryisland.net, http://www.mysteryisland.net

Mystery Island Publications, 384 Windward Way, Sacramento, CA 95831-2420, blacksharkpress@mysteryisland.net www.mysteryisland.net

POETRY NOW, Sacramento's Literary Review and Calendar, 1719 25th St., Sacramento, CA 95816, 916-441-7395, poetrynow@sacramentopoetrycenter.org, www.sacramentopoetrycenter.org

Poplar Leaf Press, 2320 D St #203, Sacramento, CA 95816, 916-760-1519

Samuel Powell Publishing Company, 2201 I Street, #D, Sacramento, CA 95816, 916-443-1161

Swan Scythe Press, 515 P Street #804, Sacramento, CA 95814-6320, 916 492 8917

THE TULE REVIEW, Sacramento Poetry Center, 1719 25th St., Sacramento, CA 95816-5813, 916-441-7395, blueattule@yahoo.com, www.sacramentopoetrycenter.org

24th Street Irregular Press, 1008 24th Street, Sacramento, CA 95816

SPECIALTY TRAVEL INDEX, PO BOX 458, San Anselmo, CA 94979-0458, 415-455-1643, Fax 415-455-1648, advertiser@specialtytravel.com, www.specialtytravel.com

THE PACIFIC REVIEW, Department of English, Calif State University, San Bernardino, CA 92407

AzurAlive, 751 Laurel Street, Suite 808, San Carlos, CA 94070, 650-276-0448, http://azuralive.com

Wide World Publishing, PO Box 476, San Carlos, CA 94070, 650-593-2839, Fax 650-595-0802

AAS HISTORY SERIES, PO Box 28130, San Diego, CA 92198, 760-746-4005, Fax 760-746-3139, sales@univelt.com, www.univelt.com

ADVANCES IN THE ASTRONAUTICAL SCIENCES, PO Box 28130, San Diego, CA 92198, 760-746-4005, Fax 760-746-3139, sales@univelt.com, www.univelt.com

Altair Publications, PO Box 221000, San Diego, CA 92192-1000, 858-453-2342, e-mail altair@astroconsulting.com

Birth Day Publishing Company, PO Box 7722, San Diego, CA 92167

Brenner Information Group, PO Box 721000, San Diego, CA 92172-1000, 858-538-0093

Caernarvon Press, 4435 Marlborough Ave. #3, San Diego, CA 92116, (619) 284-0411, terryh@cts.com

THE CRAPSHOOTER, PO Box 421440, San Diego, CA 92142, larryedell@aol.com

Culturelink Press, P.O. Box 3538, San Diego, CA 92163, Tel. (619) 501-9873, www.culturelinkpress.com; Fax purchase and school orders: Tel(619) 501-1369

Dawn Sign Press, 6130 Nancy Ridge Drive, San Diego, CA 92121-3223, 858-625-0600[v], 858-768-0478 [vp], www.dawnsign.com

GRASSLIMB, P.O. Box 420816, San Diego, CA 92142-0816, editor@grasslimb.com, http://www.grasslimb.com

Leaf Press, PO Box 421440, San Diego, CA 92142, leafpress@aol.com

OmegaRoom Press, 4041 Louisiana St #1, San Diego, CA 92104, omegaroom@yahoo.com
POETRY INTERNATIONAL, Dept. of English and Comparative Literature, SDSU, 5500 Campanile Drive, San Diego, CA 92182-6020, Telephone: (619) 594-1522, Fax: (619) 594-4998
Puna Press, P.O. Box 7790, San Diego, CA 92107, 619.278.8089, www.punapress.com
SCIENCE AND TECHNOLOGY, PO Box 28130, San Diego, CA 92198, 760-746-4005, Fax 760-746-3139, sales@univelt.com, www.univelt.com
The Sektor Co., PO Box 501005, San Diego, CA 92150, 858 485-7550
Small Helm Press, 4235 Porte de Palmas, Unit 182, San Diego, CA 92122-5123, 858-546-0140, smallhelm@san.rr.com
Tecolote Publications, 4761 Niagara Avenue, San Diego, CA 92107-2206, telephone (619)222-6066, e-mail tecopubs@earth-link.net, website tecolotepublications.com
Univelt, Inc., PO Box 28130, San Diego, CA 92198-0130, voice:760-746-4005; Fax:760-746-3139; Email:sales@univelt.com, Web Site: http://www.univelt.com
Tia Chucha Press, PO Box 328, San Fernando, CA 91341, 818-898-0013
Alan Wofsy Fine Arts, PO Box 2210, San Francisco, CA 94126, 415-292-6500, www.art-books.com, order@art-books.com
ALEHOUSE, PO Box 31655, San Francisco, CA 94131
Androgyne Books, 930 Shields, San Francisco, CA 94132, 415-586-2697
Artifact, 2921B Folsom St., San Francisco, CA 94110, 415-647-7689
Aspermont Press, 1249 Hayes Street, San Francisco, CA 94117, 415-863-2847
Aunt Lute Books, PO Box 410687, San Francisco, CA 94141, 415-826-1300; FAX 415-826-8300
BALLOT ACCESS NEWS, PO Box 470296, San Francisco, CA 94147, 415-922-9779, fax 415-441-4268, e-Mail ban@igc.apc.org, www.ballot-access.org
BOOKS TO WATCH OUT FOR, PO Box 882554, San Francisco, CA 94188-2554, 415-642-9993, editor at BooksToWatchOutFor dot com, www.BooksToWatchOutFor.com
Caddo Gap Press, 3145 Geary Boulevard, Suite 275, San Francisco, CA 94118, 415-666-3012 telephone, 415-666-3552 fax, caddogap@aol.com, www.caddogap.com
City Lights Books, Attn: Bob Sharrard, Editor, 261 Columbus Avenue, San Francisco, CA 94133, 415-362-8193
ClearPoint Press, PO Box 170658, San Francisco, CA 94117, 415-386-5377 phone/Fax
The Communication Press, PO Box 22541, San Francisco, CA 94122, 415-386-0178
CONCEIT MAGAZINE, P. O. Box 884223, San Francisco, CA 94188-4223, http://www.myspace.com/conceitmagazine, conceitmagazine2007@yahoo.com
Down There Press, 938 Howard St., #101, San Francisco, CA 94103-4100, 415-974-8985 x 205, fax 415-974-8989, 800-289-8423, downtherepress@excite.com, www.goodvibes.com/dtp/dtp.html
EDUCATIONAL FOUNDATIONS, 3145 Geary Boulevard, Suite 275, San Francisco, CA 94118, 415-666-3012
EDUCATIONAL LEADERSHIP & ADMINISTRATION, 3145 Geary Boulevard #275, San Francisco, CA 94118, 415-392-1911
FAULTLINE, 300 Boadway, Suite 28, San Francisco, CA 94133
FOURTEEN HILLS: The SFSU Review, Creative Writing Dept., SFSU, 1600 Holloway Avenue, San Francisco, CA 94132, 415-338-3083, fax 415-338-0504, E-mail hills@sfsu.edu
GLB Publishers, 1028 Howard Street #503, San Francisco, CA 94103-2868, 415-621-8307, www.GLBpubs.com
Global Options, PO Box 40601, San Francisco, CA 94140, 415-550-1703
HAIGHT ASHBURY LITERARY JOURNAL, 558 Joost Avenue, San Francisco, CA 94127
Haight-Ashbury Publications, 856 Stanyan Street, San Francisco, CA 94117, 415-752-7601, Fax 415-933-8674
HARMONY: Voices for a Just Future, PO Box 210056, San Francisco, CA 94121-0056, 415-221-8527
Heritage House Publishers, PO Box 194242, San Francisco, CA 94119, 415-776-3156
INTERNATIONAL JOURNAL OF EDUCATIONAL POLICY, RESEARCH, AND PRACTICE: RECONCEPTUALIZING CHILDHOOD STUDIES, 3145 Geary Blvd. PMB 275, San Francisco, CA 94118, 415-666-3012, fax 415-666-3552, caddogap@aol.com, www.caddogap.com
ISSUES, PO Box 424885, San Francisco, CA 94142-4885, 415-864-4800 X136
ISSUES IN TEACHER EDUCATION, 3145 Geary Blvd. PMB 275, San Francisco, CA 94118, 415 666-3012
Ithuriel's Spear, 939 Eddy St., #102, San Francisco, CA 94109, http://www.ithuriel.com
JOURNAL OF CURRICULUM THEORIZING, 3145 Geary Boulevard, PMB 275, San Francisco, CA 94118
JOURNAL OF PSYCHOACTIVE DRUGS, 856 Stanyan Street, San Francisco, CA 94117, 415-752-7601, Fax 415-933-8674
JOURNAL OF THOUGHT, 3145 Geary Boulevard #275, San Francisco, CA 94118, 415-392-1911
King Publishing, 1801 Bush Street, Suite 300, San Francisco, CA 94109, Fax 415-563-1467
MacAdam/Cage Publishing Inc., 155 Sansome Street, Ste. 550, San Francisco, CA 94104-3615, 415-986-7502, Fax 415-986-7414, info@macadamcage.com
Mercury House, PO BOX 192850, San Francisco, CA 94119-2858
Meridien PressWorks, Meridien PressWorks, PO Box 640024, San Francisco, CA 94164, 415-928-8904; 415-225-3265 c
MOTHER EARTH JOURNAL: An International Quarterly, 934 Brannan St., San Francisco, CA 94103, 415-868-8865, 415-552-9261, info@internationalpoetrymuseum.org
MULTICULTURAL EDUCATION, 3145 Geary Boulevard, Ste. 275, San Francisco, CA 94118, 415-392-1911
NARRATIVE MAGAZINE, 2130 Fillmore Street #233, San Francisco, CA 94115
Night Horn Books, PO Box 424906, San Francisco, CA 94142-4906, 415-440-2442; nighthornb@aol.com
Night Shade Books, 1661 Tennessee Street, #3H, San Francisco, CA 94107, Phone: 415-206-1473
No Starch Press, 555 De Haro Street, Suite 250, San Francisco, CA 94107-2365, 415-863-9900
Norton Coker Press, PO Box 640543, San Francisco, CA 94164-0543, 415-922-0395
NOTES AND ABSTRACTS IN AMERICAN AND INTERNATIONAL EDUCATION, 3145 Geary Boulevard #275, San Francisco, CA 94118, 415-392-1911
Pancake Press, 163 Galewood Circle, San Francisco, CA 94131, 415-665 9215
Passing Through Publications, 1918 23rd Street, San Francisco, CA 94107
Protean Press, 1190 Sacramento St., #4, San Francisco, CA 94108-1946, 415.931-8484, cell:415.260-5527, protean-press@sbcglobal.net, www.califiabooks.com/finepress/p/protean.html
Red Alder Books, P.O. Box 641312, San Francisco, CA 94109, 415-674-1618, david@davidsteinberg.us
SCHOLAR-PRACTITIONER QUARTERLY, 3145 Geary Blvd. PMB 275, San Francisco, CA 94118, 415 666-3012
Scottwall Associates, Publishers, 95 Scott Street, San Francisco, CA 94117, 415-861-1956
Sea Fog Press, 447 20th Avenue, San Francisco, CA 94121, 415-221-8527
Second Coming Press, PO Box 31249, San Francisco, CA 94131
Sidebrow, 912 Cole St., #162, San Francisco, CA 94117

Sixteen Rivers Press, P.O. Box 640663, San Francisco, CA 94164-0663, 415-273-1303
SOCIAL JUSTICE: A JOURNAL OF CRIME, CONFLICT, & WORLD ORDER, PO Box 40601, San Francisco, CA 94140, 415-550-1703, socialjust@aol.com, www.socialjusticejournal.org
STORYQUARTERLY, P. O. Box 29272, San Francisco, CA 94129, www.storyquarterly.com, narrativemagazine.com, 415-346-4477
SUMMER ACADEME: A Journal of Higher Education, 3145 Geary Boulevard #275, San Francisco, CA 94118, 415-392-1911
Sunlight Publishers, PO Box 640545, San Francisco, CA 94109, 415-776-6249
Synergistic Press, 3965 Sacramento St., San Francisco, CA 94118, 415-EV7-8180, Fax 415-751-8505; website www.synergisticbooks.com; e-mail goodreading@synergisticbooks.com
TABOO: Journal of Education & Culture, 3145 Geary Boulevard #275, San Francisco, CA 94118, 415-392-1911
TEACHER EDUCATION QUARTERLY, 3145 Geary Boulevard #275, San Francisco, CA 94118, 415-392-1911
TWO LINES: World Writing in Translation, Center for the Art of Translation, 35 Stillman Street, Suite 201, San Francisco, CA 94107, 415-512-8812 (phone) /415-512-8824 (fax), web: www.catranslation.org.
VITAE SCHOLASTICAE: The Journal of Educational Biography, 3145 Geary Boulevard #275, San Francisco, CA 94118, 415-392-1911
XPLOITED ZINE, 2600 18th St., Suite 9, San Francisco, CA 94110
X-RAY, Po Box 170488, San Francisco, CA 94117, xraybookco@gmail.com
X-Ray Book Co., P.O. Box 170488, San Francisco, CA 94117
ZOETROPE: ALL-STORY, 916 Kearny Street, San Francisco, CA 94133-5107, www.all-story.com, info@all-story.com
ZYZZYVA, PO Box 590069, San Francisco, CA 94159-0069, Tel 415-752-4393, editor@zyzzyva.org, www.zyzzyva.org
ABLE MUSE, 467 Saratoga Avenue #602, San Jose, CA 95129, www.ablemuse.com, editor@ablemuse.com
Anancybooks, PO Box 28677, San Jose, CA 95159-8677, 408-286-0726, Fax 408-947-0668, info@anancybooks.com, www.anancybooks.com
R.J. Bender Publishing, PO Box 23456, San Jose, CA 95153, 408-225-5777, Fax 408-225-4739, order@bender-publishing.com
Ibexa Press, P.O. Box 611732, San Jose, CA 95161, www.ibexa.com, info@ibexa.com
INDIA CURRENTS, Box 21285, San Jose, CA 95151, 408-324-0488, Fax 408-324-0477, e-Mail editor@indiacurrents.com
Magnifico Publications, 2486 Aram Avenue, San Jose, CA 95128, (408)286-5179
RED HAWK, 730 Linda Vista St., San Jose, CA 95127-1126
REED MAGAZINE, San Jose State University, English Department, One Washington Square, San Jose, CA 95192-0090
Urion Press, PO Box 10085, San Jose, CA 95157, 408-867-7695 phone/Fax
Five Fingers Press, PO Box 4, San Leandro, CA 94577-0100
FIVE FINGERS REVIEW, PO Box 4, San Leandro, CA 94577-0100
CAUSE & EFFECT MAGAZINE, PO Box 15329, San Luis Obispo, CA 93406-5329, (805) 748-3521
Poptritus Press, PO Box 15329, San Luis Obispo, CA 93406-5329, (805) 748-3521
1913, A Journal of Forms, Sandra Doller, Markstein Hall 126J, LTWR Department, CSU-San Marcos, 333 S. Twin Oaks Valley, San Marcos, CA 92096-0001
ORNAMENT, PO Box 2349, San Marcos, CA 92079, 760-599-0222, Fax 760-599-0228
Golden West Books, PO Box 80250, San Marino, CA 91118-8250, 626-458-8148
Huntington Library Press, 1151 Oxford Road, San Marino, CA 91108, 626-405-2172, Fax 626-585-0794, e-mail booksales@huntington.org
In Print Publishing, PO Box 6966, San Pedro, CA 90734-6966, 928-284-5298, Fax 928-284-5283
THE LUMMOX JOURNAL, Lummox PO Box 5301, San Pedro, CA 90733-5301, poetraindog@gmail.com, www.lummox-press.com
Lummox Press, Lummox PO Box 5301, San Pedro, CA 90733-5301, poetraindog@gmail.com, www.lummoxpress.com
Origin Press, PO Box 151117, San Raphael, CA 94915
NIS America, Inc., 1221 E. Dyer Rd., Suite 210, Santa Ana, CA 92705, 714-540-1122
Aegean Publishing Company, PO Box 6790, Santa Barbara, CA 93160, 805-964-6669
Artamo Press, 11 W. Anapamu Street, Santa Barbara, CA 93101, phone(805) 568-1400, fax (805) 568-1400, contact@artamopress.com, www.artamopress.com
Bandanna Books, 1212 Punta Gorda Street #13, Santa Barbara, CA 93103-3568, Phone 805-899-2145, Fax 805-899-2145, bandanna@cox.net, www.bandannabooks.com
Green River Press, PO Box 6905, Santa Barbara, CA 93160, 805-964-4475, Fax 805-967-6208, narob@cox.net
INTO THE TEETH WIND, College of Creative Studies, University of California, Santa Barbara, Santa Barbara, CA 93106, www.ccs.ucsb.edu/windsteeth
Joelle Publishing, PO Box 91229, Santa Barbara, CA 93190, 805-692-1938
Allen A. Knoll Publishers, 200 W. Victoria Street, 2nd Floor, Santa Barbara, CA 93101-3627, 805-564-3377, Fax 805-966-6657, bookinfo@knollpublishers.com
Para Publishing, PO Box 8206 - Q, Santa Barbara, CA 93118-8206, 805-968-7277, Fax 805-968-1379, info@parapublish-ing.com, www.parapublishing.com
PUBLISHING POYNTERS, PO Box 8206-Q, Santa Barbara, CA 93118-8206, 805-968-7277, Fax 805-968-1379, info@parapublishing.com, www.parapublishing.com
Pussywillow, 1212 Punta Gorda Street, #13, Santa Barbara, CA 93103-3568, 805-899-2145 phone/Fax
SHORT FUSE, PO Box 90436, Santa Barbara, CA 93190
Summer Stream Press, PO Box 6056, Santa Barbara, CA 93160-6056, 805-962-6540
Aristata Publishing, 16429 Lost Canyon Rd., Santa Clarita, CA 91387, Ph (661) 600-5011, Fx (661) 299-9478, general@aristatapublishing.com, www.aristatapublishing.com
Alcatraz Editions, 3965 Bonny Doon Road, Santa Cruz, CA 95060
GREENHOUSE REVIEW, 3965 Bonny Doon Road, Santa Cruz, CA 95060
Greenhouse Review Press, 3965 Bonny Doon Road, Santa Cruz, CA 95060-9706, 831-426-4355
Moving Parts Press, 10699 Empire Grade, Santa Cruz, CA 95060-9474, 408-427-2271
Nolo Press Occidental, 501 Mission Street, Suite 2, Santa Cruz, CA 95060, 831-466-9922, 800-464-5502, Fax: 831-466-9927, E-mail: inbox@nolotech.com, Website: http://www.nolotech.com
Paperweight Press, 123 Locust Street, Santa Cruz, CA 95060-3907, 831-427-1177 or 1 800 538-0766
POESY, P.O. Box 7823, Santa Cruz, CA 95061, www.poesy.org, info@poesy.org
STONE SOUP, The Magazine By Young Writers and Artists, Box 83, Santa Cruz, CA 95063, 831-426-5557, Fax 831-426-1161, e-mail editor@stonesoup.com, www.stonesoup.com
Tombouctou Books, 1472 Creekview Lane, Santa Cruz, CA 95062, 831-476-4144
Archer Books, PO Box 1254, Santa Maria, CA 93456, 805-878-8279 phone, email: jtc@archer-books.com, web site:

www.archer-books.com

Atelier Press, 1112 Montana Ave., #270, Santa Monica, CA 90403, info@atelierpress.com, www.atelierpress.com

Bonus Books, Inc., 1223 Wilshire Blvd., #597, Santa Monica, CA 90403-5400, www.bonusbooks.com

Clover Park Press, PO Box 5067, Santa Monica, CA 90409-5067, 310-452-7657, info@cloverparkpress.com, http://www.cloverparkpress.com

Key Publications, PO Box 1064, Santa Monica, CA 90406, 818-613-7348

Lemon Grove Press, 1158 26th Street #502, Santa Monica, CA 90403, phone: (310)820-4779, fax: (310) 820-4771, www.criticalconditions.com, info@lemongrovepress.com

Middleway Press, 606 Wilshire Boulevard, Attention: Mwende May, Marketing Associate, Santa Monica, CA 90401-1502, (310) 260-8900 ofc, (310) 260-8910 fax, middlewaypress@sgi-usa.org, www.middlewaypress.com

Santa Monica Press, PO Box 1076, Santa Monica, CA 90406-1076, 310-230-7759, Fax 310-230-7761

THE SANTA MONICA REVIEW, 1900 Pico Boulevard, Santa Monica, CA 90405-1628, www.smc.edu/sm_review

SHARE INTERNATIONAL, PO Box 5668, Santa Monica, CA 90409, 818-785-6300, Fax 818-904-9132, sisubscriptions@cs.com

Clamshell Press, 160 California Avenue, Santa Rosa, CA 95405

Golden Door Press, 6450 Stone Bridge Road, Santa Rosa, CA 95409, (707) 538-5018

IN OUR OWN WORDS, P. O. Box 4658, Santa Rosa, CA 95402-4658, http://www.bbbooks.com

Maledicta Press, PO Box 14123, Santa Rosa, CA 95402-6123, Phone: (707) 795-8178 E-mail: aman@sonic.net Web site: http://www.sonic.net/maledicta/

MALEDICTA: The International Journal of Verbal Aggression, PO Box 14123, Santa Rosa, CA 95402-6123, Telephone: 707-795-8178 E-mail: aman@sonic.net Web site: http://www.sonic.net/maledicta/

Redwood Creek Publishing, P.O. Box 368, Santa Rosa, CA 95402, 707 579-3479, penny@sonic.net, www.winasportsscholarship.com

Tyr Publishing, PO Box 9189, Santa Rosa, CA 95405-1189, 623-298-7235, Fax 480-323-2177, info@tyrpublishing.com, www.tyrpublishing.com

THE FREEFALL REVIEW, Saratoga, CA 95070, http://www.freefallreview.t35.com

Arctos Press, PO Box 401, Sausalito, CA 94966-0401, 415-331-2503, Fax 415-331-3092, runes@aol.com, http://members.aol.com/runes

E & E Publishing, 1001 Bridgeway, No. 227, Sausalito, CA 94965, Tel: 415-331-4025, Fax: 415-331-4023, www.EandEGroup.com/Publishing

In Between Books, PO Box 790, Sausalito, CA 94966, 415 383-8447

MEMOIR (AND): Prose, Poetry, Essay, Graphics, Lies and More, P.O. Box 1398, Sausalito, CA 94966-1398, (415)339-4130, admin@memoirjournal.com, www.memoirjournal.com

The Post-Apollo Press, 35 Marie Street, Sausalito, CA 94965, 415-332-1458, fax 415-332-8045

Soulstice Media, P.O. Box 2436, Sausalito, CA 94965, 415.331.2895

Stone and Scott, Publishers, PO Box 56419, Sherman Oaks, CA 91413-1419, 818-904-9088 Fax 818-787-1431 www.StoneandScott.com

Wexford & Barrow, Publishers, 4145 Woodman Ave., Sherman Oaks, CA 91423, 818-326-9810 / wexfordandbarrow@yahoo.com

Crystal Press, 4212 E. Los Angeles Avenue # 42, Simi Valley, CA 93063-3308, 805-527-4369, Fax 805-527-3949, crystalpress@aol.com

Datamaster Publishing, LLC, 1750 Orr Avenue, Simi Valley, CA 93065, Phone:805-527-4369 Fax:805-527-3949, www.CrystalPress.org

Cuore Libre Publishing, 19201 Sonoma Hwy #125, Sonoma, CA 95476, Tel: 707-320-4274 Fax: 707-320-0572

The Madson Group, Inc., 13775 A Mono Way, Suite 224, Sonora, CA 95370, 360-446-5348, fax 360-446-5234, email madsongroup@earthlink.net, www.petgroomer.com

Blue Lupin Press, c/o Anita Thomas, 1919 Apache Avenue, South Lake Tahoe, CA 96150, (530) 573-1452

NEW AMERICAN IMAGIST, PO Box 124, South Pasadena, CA 91031-0124

China Books & Periodicals, Inc., 360 Swift Ave., Suite #48, South San Francisco, CA 94080-6220, 800-818-2017 [tel], 650-872-7808 [fax], email: orders@chinabooks.com, website: www.chinabooks.com

Meritage Press, 256 North Fork Crystal Springs Road, St. Helena, CA 94574

Hoover Institution Press, Stanford University, Stanford, CA 94305-6010, 650-723-3373, e-mail bliss@hoover.stanford.edu

MANTIS: A Journal of Poetry & Translation, Mantis DLCL, Pigott Hall Bld. 260, Stanford University, Stanford, CA 94305, Web: http://mantisjournal.stanford.edu/index.html

Choice Point Editions, 7883 N. Pershing Ave., Stockton, CA 95207, 209-952-7108, 866-952-7108, FAX 209-951-3216, choicepointeditions.com, info@choicepointeditions.com

Abigon Press, 12135 Valley Spring Lane, Studio City, CA 91604, ascap@pacbell.net

Empire Publishing Service, PO Box 1344, Studio City, CA 91614-0344

Players Press, Inc., PO Box 1132, Studio City, CA 91614-0132, 818-789-4980

RATTLE, 12411 Ventura Blvd., Studio City, CA 91604, 818-505-6777

Moonrise Press, P.O.Box 4288, Sunland, CA 91041-4288, 818-352-4411; 818-384-8944

Soundboard Books, 933 Exmoor Way, Sunnyvale, CA 94087, 408-738-1705, sboardbooks@sbcglobal.net

Lahontan Images, PO Box 1592, 607 B Cottage Street, Susanville, CA 96130-1592, 530-257-6747

dreamslaughter, PO Box 571454, Tarzana, CA 91357, 8183216708, http://www.dreamslaughter.com

Staghorn Press, 5906 Etiwanda Ave. #27, Tarzana, CA 91356, 818-342-3823

The Center Press, PO Box 6936, Thousand Oaks, CA 91361, 818-889-7071, Fax 818-889-7072

JOURNAL OF SCIENTIFIC EXPLORATION, PO Box 1190, Tiburon, CA 94920, e-mail EricksonEditorial@att.net

Waters Edge Press, 8 Venado Drive, Tiburon, CA 94920, 415-435-2837, Fax 415-435-2404, anderson-gram@comcast.net

BLUE MOUNTAIN, PO Box 256, Tomales, CA 94971, 707-878-2369, 800-475-2369, Fax 707-878-2375, info@nilgiri.org, www.nilgiri.org

Nilgiri Press, PO Box 256, Tomales, CA 94971-0256, orders 800-475-2369, 707-878-2369, Fax 707-878-2375, info@nilgiri.org, www.nilgiri.org

WATERMEN, 2428 Gramercy Ave, Torrance, CA 90501, 310 850 6431

Medusa's Muse, P.O. Box 1021, Ukiah, CA 95482, www.medusasmuse.com

BLACK CLOCK, Black Clock / CalArts, 24700 McBean Parkway, Valencia, CA 91355, info@blackclock.org, www.blackclock.org

Knowledge Power Books, 25379 Wayne Mills Place, Suite 131, Valencia, CA 91355, 661-513-0308, 661-513-0381, www.knowledgepowerinc.com

REMS Publishing & Publicity, 25852 McBean Parkway #714, Valencia, CA 91355-2004, 800-915-0048, 661-287-3309, Fax 661-287-4443, remesbookdoctor@ca.rr.com, www.remspublishingpublicity.com, www.makemoneywritingsite.com

Gain Publications, PO Box 2204, Van Nuys, CA 91404, 818-981-1996

88: A Journal of Contemporary American Poetry, PO Box 2872, Venice, CA 90294, 310-712-1238, Fax 310-828-4860, t88ajournal@aol.com, guidelines at www.hollyridgepress.com

Hollyridge Press, PO Box 2872, Venice, CA 90294, 310-712-1238, Fax 310-828-4860, hollyridgepress@aol.com, http://www.hollyridgepress.com

Borden Publishing Co., 2244 S. Santa Fe Ave. Unit B-12, Vista, CA 92084, 760-594-0918, bordenpub@roadrunner.com, featured on www.amazon.com

Lemon Shark Press, 1604 Marbella Drive, Vista, CA 92081-5463, 760-727-2850, lemonsharkpress@yahoo.com, www.lemonsharkpress.com

Volcano Press, Inc, PO Box 270, Volcano, CA 95689, 209-296-4991, fax 209-296-4995, Credit card or check orders only: 1-800-879-9636, e-mail sales@volcanopress.com, website http://www.volcanopress.com

Massey-Reyner Publishing, PO Box 323, Wallace, CA 95254, phone/fax 209-763-2590, e-mail reyners@comcast.net

AltaMira Press, 1630 N. Main Street #367, Walnut Creek, CA 94596, 301-459-3366, Fax 925-933-9720

Devil Mountain Books, PO Box 4115, Walnut Creek, CA 94596, 925-939-3415, Fax 925-937-4883, cbsturges@aol.com

Empyrean Hill Books, Inc., 1541 3rd Ave., Walnut Creek, CA 94597, submissions@empyreanhillbooks.com, www.empyreanhillbooks.com, 925-588-6083

Shen's Books, 1547 Palos Verdes Mall #291, Walnut Creek, CA 94597, 925-262-8108, www.shens.com

THE GREAT AMERICAN POETRY SHOW, A SERIAL POETRY ANTHOLOGY, P.O. Box 69506, West Hollywood, CA 90069-0506, 1-323-656-6126

The Muse Media, PO Box 69506, West Hollywood, CA 90069, 323-656-6126, www.tgaps.net

Steel Balls Press, Box 807, Whittier, CA 90608, E-mail don@steelballs.com

Rayve Productions Inc., PO Box 726, Windsor, CA 95492, 707-838-6200, Fax 707-838-2220, E-mail rayvepro@aol.com

The Owl Press, PO Box 126, Woodacre, CA 94973-0126, 415-438-1539, asisowl@mindspring.com, www.theowlpress.com

City Life Books, LLC, 21417 Providencia St, Woodland Hills, CA 91364

The Heyeck Press, 25 Patrol Court, Woodside, CA 94062, 650-851-7491, Fax 650-851-5039, heyeck@ix.netcom.com

COLORADO

Willowood Press, 1209 Lincoln St., Alamosa, CO 81101, 719-589-3052

Phlare, Inc., PO Box 1400, Arvada, CO 80001-1400, 303-513-1565, 888-731-6950, www.phlare.com

Thundercloud Books, PO Box 97, Aspen, CO 81612, (970) 925-1588, fax (970) 920-9361, web: www.Thundercloud-Books.com, www.WakingThe Ancients.com

CLARK STREET REVIEW, PO Box 1377, Berthoud, CO 80513, clarkreview@earthlink.net, http://home.earthlink.net/~clarkreview/

Howling Dog Press / Brave New World Order Books, P.O. Box 853, Berthoud, CO 80513-0853, WritingDangerously@msn.com, www.howlingdogpress.com, www.howlingdogpress.com/OMEGA

OMEGA, P.O. Box 853, Berthoud, CO 80513-0853, WritingDangerously@msn.com, www.howlingdogpress.com, www.howlingdogpress.com/OMEGA

Bauu Press, PO Box 4445, Boulder, CO 80306, http://www.bauuinstitute.com, 303-827-6365

BOMBAY GIN, Naropa University, Writing & Poetics Dept., 2130 Arapahoe Avenue, Boulder, CO 80302

THE BOOMERPHILE, PO Box 17446, Boulder, CO 80308-0446, 303-444-3363, www.forums.delphiforums.com/boomer

BOULDER HERETIC, PO Box 17446, Boulder, CO 80308-0446, 303-444-3363, danculberson@juno.com

Cassandra Press, Inc., PO Box 228, Boulder, CO 80306, 303 444 2590

Devenish Press, 1425 Blue Sage Court, Boulder, CO 80305, 303-926-0378 phone/fax, books@devenishpress.com, www.devenishpress.com

DIVIDE: Journal of Literature, Arts, and Ideas, Univ. of Colorado, Boulder / UCB 317, Boulder, CO 80309, www.colorado.edu/journals/divide

Gemstone House Publishing, PO Box 19948, Boulder, CO 80308, sthomas170@aol.com

LOVING MORE: New Models for Relationships, PO Box 4358, Boulder, CO 80306, 303-543-7540, lovingmore@love-more.com

Old Stage Publishing, PO Box 17446, Boulder, CO 80308-0446, 303-444-3363, danculberson@juno.com

Paladin Enterprises, Inc., Gunbarrel Tech Center, 7077 Winchester Circle, Boulder, CO 80301, 303-443-7250, Fax 303-442-8741, www.paladin-press.com

Pruett Publishing Company, PO Box 2140, Boulder, CO 80306-2140, 303-449-4919, toll free: 1-800-247-8224

RealPeople Press, 1221 Lefthand Canyon Drive, Boulder, CO 80302-9344

Sentient Publications, LLC, 1113 Spruce Street, Boulder, CO 80302, 303-443-2188, Fax 303-381-2538, www.sentientpublications.com

SQUARE ONE, Campus Box 226, University of Colorado, Boulder, CO 80309-0001, 303-492-8890, square1@colorado.edu, http://www.colorado.edu/English/squareone/index.htm

Sunrise Health Coach Publications, PO Box 21132, Boulder, CO 80308, Phone and fax: 303-527-2886, info@sunrisehealthcoach.com, http://sunrisehealthcoach.com

TOUCHSTONE, PO Box 17446, Boulder, CO 80308-0446, 303-444-3363, danculberson@juno.com

University Press of Colorado, 5589 Arapahoe Avenue, Suite 206C, Boulder, CO 80303, Orders: 800-627-7377, Editorial: 720-406-8849, Fax: 720-406-3443

Clearwater Publishing Co., PO Box 778, Broomfield, CO 80038-0778, 303-436-1982, fax 917-386-2769, e-mail wordguise@aol.com

Nicholas Lawrence Books, 932 Clover Avenue, Canon City, CO 81212, 719-276-0152, Fax 719-276-0154, icareinc@webtv.net

Glenbridge Publishing Ltd., 19923 E. Long Avenue, Centennial, CO 80016-1969, 720-870-8381, fax: 720-870-5598, website: www.glenbridgepublishing.com, email: glenbridge@qwest.net

Rollaway Bay Publications, Inc., 6334 S. Racine Circle, Suite 202, Centennital, CO 80111-6405, Tel=303 799-8320, Fax=303 799-4220, email publisher@rollawaybay.com

Aaron Communications III, P.O. Box 63270, Colorado Springs, CO 80962-3270, 719-487-0342

Arjuna Library Press, 1025 Garner St., D, Space 18, Colorado Springs, CO 80905-1774, Email address pfuphoff@earthlink.net Website address http://home.earthlink.net/~pfuphoff/

COOK PARTNERS, David C. Cook, 4050 Lee Vance View, Colorado Springs, CO 80918-7100, 719-536-0100, Fax 719-536-3266

HANG GLIDING & PARAGLIDING, U.S. Hang Gliding & Paragliding Assoc., Inc., PO Box 1330, Colorado Springs, CO

80901-1330, 719-632-8300, fax 719-632-6417

JOURNAL OF REGIONAL CRITICISM, 1404 East Bijou Street, Colorado Springs, CO 80909-5520

LrnIT Publishing Div. LRNIT CORPORATION, 1122 Samuel Pt., Colorado Springs, CO 80906-6310, 719-331-4510, Fax 760-946-7895, lrnit@consultant.com, PNB416@aol.com, www.lrnit.com

Mountain Automation Corporation, 6090 Whirlwind Dr, Colorado Springs, CO 80923-7560, 719-598-8256, Fax 719-598-8516, Order 800-345-6120, Order Fax 970-493-8781, Order Email mac@intrepidgroup.com, Order Address POB 2324 Ft Collins CO 80522-2324

Piccadilly Books, Ltd., PO Box 25203, Colorado Springs, CO 80936, 719-550-9887

Alpine Publications, Inc., 38262 Linman Road, Crawford, CO 81415-9326, 970-921-5005, Fax 970-921-5081, alpinepubl@aol.com, www.alpinepub.com

MINIATURE DONKEY TALK INC, PO Box 982, Cripple Creek, CO 80813-0982, 719-689-2904, minidonk@qis.net, www.miniaturedonkeytalk.com

Affinity Publishers Services, c/o Continuous, PO Box 416, Denver, CO 80201-0416, 303-575-5676, email: email-street@gmail.com

Arden Press, Inc., PO Box 418, Denver, CO 80201, 303-697-6766

THE BLOOMSBURY REVIEW, 1553 Platte Street, Suite 206, Denver, CO 80202-1167, 303-455-3123, Fax 303-455-7039

Center For Self-Sufficiency, PO Box 416, Denver, CO 80201-0416, 305-575-5676

THE COPPER NICKEL, Campus Box 175, PO Box 173364, Denver, CO 80217-3364

Counterpath Press, P.O. Box 18351, Denver, CO 80218, www.counterpathpress.org

COUNTERPATH REVIEW, P.O. Box 18351, Denver, CO 80218, www.counterpathpress.org

DENVER QUARTERLY, University of Denver, Denver, CO 80208, 303-871-2892

DEVIL'S ADVOCATE, 2123 S. Fulton Circle, Unit #202, Denver, CO 80247, 785-840-7348, rluthye@devilsad.net, http://www.devilsad.net

ELIXIR, PO Box 27029, Denver, CO 80227, www.elixirpress.com

Elixir Press, PO Box 27029, Denver, CO 80227-0029, www.elixirpress.com

Face to Face Press, 3419 Fillmore St., Denver, CO 80205-4257, slevart@face2facepress.com, www.face2facepress.com

HEARTLODGE: Honoring the House of the Poet, P.O. Box 370627, Denver, CO 80237, email: heartlodgepoets@gmail.com web site: heartlodge.org

Lamp Light Press, Publishing Division, PO Box 416, Denver, CO 80201-0416, 303-575-5676, Fax 303-575-1187

The Legal Center for People with Disabilities and Older People, 455 Sherman Street, Suite 130, Denver, CO 80203-4403, (303) 722-0300, (303) 722-0720 fax, 1-800-288-1376, publications@thelegalcenter.org, www.thelegalcenter.org

Nunciata, Publishing Division, PO Box 416, Denver, CO 80201-0416, 303-575-5676, Fax 303-575-1187

Quiet Tymes, Inc., 1400 Downing Street, Denver, CO 80218, 303-839-8628, Fax 720-488-2682

Scentouri, Publishing Division, c/o Prosperity + Profits Unlimited, PO Box 416, Denver, CO 80201-0416, 303-575-5676, Fax 303-575-1187

SPEAK UP, PO Box 100506, Denver, CO 80250, 303-715-0837, Fax 303-715-0793, info@speakuppress.org, www.speakuppress.org

Speak Up Press, PO Box 100506, Denver, CO 80250, 303-715-0837, Fax 303-715-0793, info@speakuppress.org, www.speakuppress.org

Telephone Books, 2358 South Bannnock St., Denver, CO 80223, (303) 698-7837, pomowen@ix.netcom.com

Alpine Guild, Inc., PO Box 4848, Dillon, CO 80435, Fax 970-262-9378, information@alpineguild.com

CUTTHROAT, A JOURNAL OF THE ARTS, P.O. Box 2414, Durango, CO 81302, 970-903-7914, www.cutthroatmag.com, cutthroatmag@gmail.com

Kali Press, PO Box 5491, Eagle, CO 81631-5491, ciaocyn@yahoo.com

Advanced Learning Press, 317 Inverness Way South, Suite 150, Englewood, CO 80112, 303-504-9312, 303-504-9417, 800-844-6599

Dreams Due Media Group, Inc., P.O. Box 1018, Firestone, CO 80520, Phone 303.241.3155, Fax 303.682.2695, Toll Free 877.462.1710, info@dreamsdue.com, www.dreamsdue.com

Center for Literary Publishing, Colorado Review / Dept of English, 9105 Campus Delivery / Colorado State University, Fort Collins, CO 80523-9105, 970-491-5449, creview@colostate.edu, http://coloradoreview.colostate.edu

COLORADO REVIEW, Dept of English, Colorado State University, 9105 Campus Delivery, Fort Collins, CO 80523-9105, 970-491-5449, creview@colostate.edu, http://coloradoreview.colostate.edu

Cottonwood Press, Inc., 109-B Cameron Drive, Fort Collins, CO 80525, 970-204-0715

Paul Dilsaver, Publisher, 2802 Clydesdale Court, Fort Collins, CO 80526-1155

Grace Creek Press, 3806 Bromley Drive, Fort Collins, CO 80525, telephone 970-282-0600 GraceCreekPress.books.office-live.com

RUMINATE MAGAZINE, 140 North Roosevelt Ave., Fort Collins, CO 80521

Tantalus Books, 4529 Idledale Drive, Fort Collins, CO 80526-5152, www.tantalusbooks.com

Fulcrum, Inc., 16100 Table Mountain Pkwy #300, Golden, CO 80403-1672, 303-277-1623, website:www.fulcrumpoetry.com/reviews

The Love and Logic Press, Inc., 2207 Jackson Street, Golden, CO 80401, 303-278-7552

Speck Press, 4690 Table Mountain Drive, Ste. 100, Golden, CO 80403, 303-277-1623, FAX 303-279-7111, books@speckpress.com, www.speckpress.com

Pendant Publishing Inc., PO Box 2933, Grand Junction, CO 81502, 970-243-6465

PINYON, Dept. of Languages, Lit., & Comm., Mesa State College, 1100 North Ave., Grand Junction, CO 81502-2647, 970-248-1740

Cladach Publishing, PO Box 336144, Greeley, CO 80633, 970.371.9530, fax 970.351.8240, office@cladach.com, http://www.cladach.com

Communication Creativity, 4542 Melbourne Way, Highlands Ranch, CO 80130-6866, 720-344-4388, bookstore@Communica-tionCreativity.com, www.communicationcreativity.com

GLASS ART, PO Box 630377, Highlands Ranch, CO 80163-0377, 303-791-8998

Grace Acres Press, PO Box 22, Larkspur, CO 80118, (303)681-9995, (303) 681-9996, 888-700-GRACE (4722), Anne@GraceAcresPress.com, www.GraceAcresPress.com

Anchor Cove Publishing, Inc., PO Box 270588, Littleton, CO 80128, Tel 303-972-0099, Fax 303-265-9119

SCULPTURAL PURSUIT MAGAZINE, P.O. Box 749, Littleton, CO 80160, 303-738-9892, www.sculpturalpursuit.com, publishersp@sculpturalpursuit.com

Yellowstone Publishing, LLC, 5335 South Grant Street, Littleton, CO 80121, (406) 371-1175, www.etiquettescholar.com

MANY MOUNTAINS MOVING, 549 Rider Ridge Drive, Longmont, CO 80501, 303-545-9942, Fax 303-444-6510

Ragamuffin Heart Publishing, 8011 Anchor Drive, Longmont, CO 80504, 720-494-1374

Shining Mountain Publishing, 2268 Spinnaker Circle, Longmont, CO 80503, Telephone 303-651-6230, email info@shiningmountain.net, website www.shiningmountain.net

SunShine Press Publications, Inc., 6 Gardner Court, Longmont, CO 80501, 303-772-3556, jlhof1@yahoo.com, www.sunshinepress.com

Zoilita Grant MS CCHt., Attn: Zoilita Grant, 200 Lincoln Street, Longmont, CO 80501, 303-776-6103, Fax 303-682-2384, info@zoilitagrant.net, www.zoilitagrant.net

Wind River Institute Press/Wind River Broadcasting, 117 East 11th, Loveland, CO 80537, 970-669-3442, Fax 970-663-6081, 800-669-3993

Water Mark of Lyons PPP: papers press and permaculture, 523 5th Ave., PO Box 225, Lyons, CO 80540, 303-823-5585, 917-774-3538, cocogord@mindspring.com, http://www.galerie.kultur.at/coco/base/core.htm, http://transitioncolorado.ning.com/group/transitiontownlyonsco, http://transitioncolorado.ning.com/profile/CocoGordon

SOUTHWEST COLORADO ARTS PERSPECTIVE, P.O. Box 843, Mancos, CO 81328-0843, 970-739-3200, 970-533-0642, www.artsperspective.com

JUNIOR STORYTELLER, PO Box 205, Masonville, CO 80541, 970-669-3755 phone/Fax, vivdub@aol.com, www.storycraft.com

THE KIDS' STORYTELLING CLUB WEBSITE, PO Box 205, Masonville, CO 80541, 970-669-3755 phone/Fax, Vivian@storycraft.com, www.storycraft.com

Storycraft Publishing, PO Box 205, Masonville, CO 80541, 970-669-3755 phone/Fax, JrStoryteller@storycraft.com, www.storycraft.com

The Wessex Collective, POB 1088, Nederland, CO 80466-1088, 303-258-3004, sss@wessexcollective.com, www.wessexcollective.com

Earth Star Publications, 216 Sundown Circle, Pagosa Springs, CO 81147, TEL 970-759-2983, starbeacon@gmail.com, www.earthstarpublications.com

THE STAR BEACON, 216 Sundown Circle, Pagosa Springs, CO 81147, TEL 970-759-2983, starbeacon@gmail.com, www.earthstarpublications.com

AARO Publishing,Inc., Post Office Box 1281, Palisade, CO 81526, 970 314 7690, 970 985 4018, 1 877 766 9333, carolynwhite@snowff.com, www.snowff.com

HIGH COUNTRY NEWS, PO Box 1090, 119 Grand Avenue, Paonia, CO 81428, 970-527-4898, editor@hcn.org

National Writers Press, 17011 Lincoln Ave., #421, Parker, CO 80134, 720-851-1944, Fax 303-841-2607, www.nationalwriters.com

Outskirts Press Inc., 10940 S. Parker Road #515, Parker, CO 80134, phone: 888-672-6657, fax: 888-672-6657, website http://outskirtspress.com/poemsfromtheheart

PILGRIMAGE, PO box 9110, Pueble, CO 81008

Passeggiata Press, Inc., 420 West 14th Street, Pueblo, CO 81003-2708, 719-544-1038, Fax 719-546-7889, e-mail Passeggia@aol.com

PILGRIMAGE, PO BOX 9110, Pueblo, CO 81008, info@pilgrimagepress.org, www.pilgrimagepress.org

Bardsong Press, PO Box 775396, Steamboat Springs, CO 80477, 970-819-9728, Fax 970-879-2657, bard@bardsongpress.com, www.bardsongpress.com

WAR, LITERATURE & THE ARTS: An International Journal of the Humanities, 2354 Fairchild Drive, Suite 6D149, Department of English & Fine Arts, United States Air Force Academy, CO 80840, 719-333-8465, website: WLAjournal.com

CONNECTICUT

Women and Men Books, P.O. Box 98, Bethlehem, CT 06751-0098, 203.266.7118, publisher@womenandmenbooks.com, www.womenandmenbooks.com

The Intrepid Traveler, PO Box 531, Branford, CT 06405, 203-469-0214, Fax 203-469-0430, admin@intrepidtraveler.com

Anomaly Press, 85 Ferris Street, Bridgeport, CT 06605, 203-576-9168

DRAMA GARDEN, PO Box 1158, Bridgeport, CT 06601-1158, 203-455-7285

New Creature Press, PO Box 1158, Bridgeport, CT 06601-1158, 203-455-7285

Firewheel Editions, Box 7, WCSU, 181 White St., Danbury, CT 06810, http://firewheel-editions.org

SENTENCE, A Journal of Prose Poetics, Box 7, Western Connecticut State University, 181 White St., Danbury, CT 06810

FRESHWATER, 170 Elm Street, Enfield, CT 06082-3873, 860-253-3105, freshwater@acc.commnet.edu, www.acc.commnet.edu/freshwater.htm

SNREVIEW, 197 Fairchild Ave., Fairfield, CT 06825-4856, 203 366-5991

Chicory Blue Press, Inc., 795 East Street North, Goshen, CT 06756, 860-491-2271, Fax 860-491-8619

Higganum Hill Books, PO Box 666, Higganum, CT 06441, rcdebold@connix.com

Falk Art Reference, PO Box 833, Madison, CT 06443, 203-245-2246, peterfalk@comcast.net, www.falkart.com, www.illuminario.com

Wesleyan University Press, 215 Long Lane, Middletown, CT 06459, 860-685-7711

Cooper Hill Press, 92 Naugatuck Ave., Milford, CT 06460, 203-387-7236 phone/Fax, editor@cooperhill.com, www.cooperhill.com

CONNECTICUT REVIEW, SCSU, 501 Crescent Street, New Haven, CT 06515, 203-392-6737, Fax 203-392-5748

THE YALE REVIEW, Yale University, PO Box 208243, New Haven, CT 06520-8243

Yale University Press, PO Box 209040, New Haven, CT 06520, 203-432-0960, 203-432-0948 [fax], www.yalebooks.com

Ye Olde Font Shoppe, PO Box 8328, New Haven, CT 06530, e-mail varivas@yahoo.com; website www.webcom.com/yeolde

THE CONNECTICUT POET, PO Box 596, Newtown, CT 06470-0596, 203-426-3388, Fax 203-426-3398, hanoverpress@faithvicinanza.com, www.poetz.com/connecticut

Biographical Publishing Company, 95 Sycamore Drive, Prospect, CT 06712-1493, 203-758-3661, Fax 253-793-2618, biopub@aol.com

FRIENDS OF PEACE PILGRIM, PO Box 2207, Shelton, CT 06484

Papoose Publishing, 385 Main Street South, Suite 404-200, Southbury, CT 06488, 203-206-4838

Hannacroix Creek Books, Inc, 1127 High Ridge Road, #110, Stamford, CT 06905-1203, 203-321-8674, Fax 203-968-0193, hannacroix@aol.com

March Books, P.O. Box 55, Sterling, CT 06377, 866-851-7621

Antrim House, PO Box 111, Tariffville, CT 06081, 860-217-0023 [phone]

Grayson Books, PO Box 270549, W. Hartford, CT 06127, 860-523-1196 phone/Fax, GraysonBooks@aol.com, www.GraysonBooks.com

Fine Tooth Press, PO Box 11512, Waterbury, CT 06703, kolchak@snet.net, http://www.finetoothpress.com

Blue Lion Books, 45 Ravenwood Road, West Hartford, CT 06107-1539
The Bold Strummer Ltd., 110-C Imperial Avenue, PO Box 2037, Westport, CT 06880-2037, 203-227-8588, toll free 866-518-9991 (orders only), Fax 203-227-8775, theboldstrummer@msn.com, www.boldstrummerltd.com
Curbstone Press, 321 Jackson St., Willimantic, CT 06226
BOTTLE ROCKETS: A collection of short verse, PO Box 189, Windsor, CT 06095, e-mail address: bottlerockets_99@yahoo.com

DELAWARE

BOTTLE, 902 Wilson Dr, Dover, DE 19904, bill@bospress.net, www.bospress.net
Bottle of Smoke Press, 902 Wilson Drive, Dover, DE 19904-2437, bill@bospress.net, www.bospress.net
Fruitbearer Publishing, LLC, P.O. Box 777, Georgetown, DE 19947, 302-856-6649, 302-856-7742 (fax), cfa@candyab-bott.com, www.fruitbearer.com
DELAWARE POETRY REVIEW, Cape Gazette, PO Box 213, Lewes, DE 19958, (302) 645-7700
Birdsong Books, 1322 Bayview Road, Middletown, DE 19709, birdsong@birdsongbooks.com, www.birdsongbooks.com
ROOM, 24450 Sisters Lane, Millsboro, DE 19966-2818
THE BROADKILL REVIEW: A Journal of Literature, c/o John Milton and Company Quality Used Books, 104 Federal Street, Milton, DE 19968, (302) 684-3514, the_broadkill_review@earthlink.net
Oak Knoll Press, 310 Delaware Street, New Castle, DE 19720-5038, 800-996-2556, 302-328-7232, fax 302-328-7274, oakknoll@oakknoll.com, www.oakknoll.com
BLADES, Poporo Press, 335 Paper Mill Road, Newark, DE 19711-2254
Wintertree Press, P.O. Box 7818, Wilmington, DE 19803, 302-691-8331, www.wintertreepress.com

DISTRICT OF COLUMBIA

AERIAL, PO Box 25642, Washington, DC 20007, 202-362-6418, aerialedge@aol.com
AMERICAN FORESTS, PO Box 2000, Washington, DC 20013, 202-737-1944
ANQ: A Quarterly Journal of Short Articles, Notes, and Reviews, 1319 18th Street NW, Washington, DC 20036, 202-296-6267 x275, Fax 202-293-6130, www.heldref.org
Azul Editions, 2013 Park Rd., NW, Washington, DC 20010, 703.861.1298, info@azuleditions.com, www.azuleditions.com
BELTWAY POETRY QUARTERLY, 626 Quebec Place NW, Washington, DC 20010-1609, http://www.beltwaypoetry.com
CONSCIENCE: The Newsjournal of Catholic Opinion, Catholics for Choice, 1436 U Street NW #301, Washington, DC 20009-3997, 202-986-6093, Fax 202-332-7995, conscience@catholicsforchoice.org, www.conscience-magazine.org
Cotton Tree Press, 2710 Ontario Road NW, Washington, DC 20009, 202-527-3991, 231 (6) 528 840, info@cottontree-press.com, www.cottontreepress.com
Del Sol Press, 2020 Pennsylvania Ave., Ste. 443, Washington, DC 20006
THE DEL SOL REVIEW, 2020 Pennsylvania Ave., Ste. 443, Washington, DC 20006
FOLIO: A Literary Journal of American University, Dept. of Literature, American University, Washington, DC 20016, folio.editors@gmail.com, www.american.edu/cas/literature/folio
Gallaudet University Press, 800 Florida Avenue NE, Washington, DC 20002-3695, 202-651-5488
Island Press, 1718 Connecticut Avenue NW #300, Washington, DC 20009, 202-232-7933; FAX 202 234-1328; e-mail info@islandpress.org; Website www.islandpress.org
KEREM: Creative Explorations in Judaism, 3035 Porter Street, NW, Washington, DC 20008, 202-364-3006, langner@erols.com, www.kerem.org
LINES + STARS, Washington, DC 20009, www.linesandstars.com, editor@linesandstars.com
Portal Press, 1327 Irving Street, NE, Washington, DC 20017-2453, 202-529-4950 (phone), 202-529-4950 (fax), editor@theportalpress.com (e-mail), www.theportalpress.com (website)
RedBone Press, PO Box 15571, Washington, DC 20003-0571, Phone 202-667-0392, Fax 301-588-0588, Email info@redbonepress.com, www.redbonepress.com
RFF Press / Resources for the Future, 1616 P Street NW, Washington, DC 20036-1400, 202-328-5086, 202-328-5002, 1-800-537-5487, rffpress@rff.org, www.rffpress.org
SB&F (SCIENCE BOOKS & FILMS), 1200 New York Avenue NW, Washington, DC 20005, 202-326-6646
Scientia Press, 4115 Wisconsin Avenue, N.W. #507, Washington, DC 20016, 202-364-8742, kendillon@verizon.net, www.scientiapress.com
SYMPOSIUM, Heldref Publications, 1319 18th St NW, Washington, DC 20036-1802, 202-296-6267 X275, Fax 202-293-6130, www.heldref.org
Washington Writers' Publishing House, PO Box 15271, Washington, DC 20003, website: www.wwph.org, carly.sachs@gmail.com, gwiazda@umbc.edu (Gwiazda), elisavietta@xchesapeake.net (Ritchie), terry galvin (treasurer) 301-652-5636
Whalesback Books, Box 9546, Washington, DC 20016, 202-333-2182
The Word Works, PO Box 42164, Washington, DC 20015, fax: 301-581-9443, editor@wordworksdc.com, www.wordworksdc.com

FLORIDA

HARP-STRINGS, PO Box 640387, Beverly Hills, FL 34464
New Paradigm Books, 22491 Vistawood Way, Boca Raton, FL 33428, 561-482-5971, 800-808-5179, Fax 561-852-8322, darbyc@earthlink.net, www.newpara.com
J. Mark Press, PO Box 24-3474, Boynton Beach, FL 33424, www.JMarkPress.com, jmpbooks@earthlink.net
Nautilus Publishing Company, 4807 Brighton Lakes Blvd., Boynton Beach, FL 33436-4836, 561 733 2920
WORLD POETRY SHOWCASE, PO Box 24-3474, Boynton Beach, FL 33424, www.JMarkPress.com
A2Z Publications LLC, POB 101163, Bradenton, FL 34211, 941-322-2739
Peartree Books & Music, PO Box 14533, Clearwater, FL 33766-4533, P/ F 727-531-4973
$olvency International Inc., Publishing, PO Box 4433, Clearwater, FL 33758-4433, www.solvencyinternational.com, 727-447-3138 wk., 403-2130 cell, 461-5483 fx, : solvencyint@gmail.com
Russet Press, 3442 Capland Ave., Clermont, FL 34711-5738
Anti-Aging Press, Box 142174, Coral Gables, FL 33114, 305-662-3928, juliabusch@att.net
SO YOUNG!, PO Box 142174, Coral Gables, FL 33114, 305-662-3928, Fax 305-661-4123
Soto Publishing Company, P.O. Box 10, Dade City, FL 33526, 352-567-5256 (fax 7279), www.sotopublishingcompany.com
PRICK OF THE SPINDLE, 1500 Beville Rd. Ste. 606-144, Daytona Beach, FL 32114-5644, Journal: http://www.prickofthespindle.com

WRITERS INK, 1104 Jacaranda Avenue, Daytona Beach, FL 32118, 631-451-0478, Fax 631-451-0478, http://www.writersunlimited.org

Writers Ink Press, 1104 Jacaranda Avenue, Daytona Beach, FL 32118, 386-337-4567 axelrodthepoet@yahoo.com

Writers Unlimited Agency, Inc, 1104 Jacaranda Avenue, Daytona Beach, FL 32118, 386-337-4567, email: writersunlimitedagency@yahoo.com http://www.writersunlimited.org

Garrett Publishing, Inc., 368 S. Military Trail, Deerfield Beach, FL 33442-6320, 561-953-1322, Fax 954-834-0295

Liberty Publishing Company, Inc., PO Box 4485, Deerfield Beach, FL 33442-4248, 561-395-3750

Missing Man Press, 1313 S. Military Trail, #193, Deerfield Beach, FL 33442, 954 263-5416, mmp@missingmanpress.com, http://missingmanpress.com

BEACHCOMBER MAGAZINE, PO Box 2255, Delray Beach, FL 33445, 561-734-5428, Fax 561-276-0931, Autelitano@aol.com, www.AuteliMedia.com

NUTHOUSE, c/o Twin Rivers Press, PO Box 119, Ellenton, FL 34222, www.nuthousemagazine.com

Ocean Publishing, P.O. Box 1080, Flagler Beach, FL 32136-1080, 386-517-1600, Fax 386-517-2564, publisher@oceanpublishing.org, www.oceanpublishing.org

Consumer Press, 13326 SW 28th Street, Ste. 102, Fort Lauderdale, FL 33330-1102, 954-370-9153, info@consumerpress.com

The Wolf Pirate Project Inc., 4801 SW 164 Terrace, Fort Lauderdale, FL 33331, www.wolf-pirate.com

Pirate Publishing International, 6323 St. Andrews Circle South, Fort Myers, FL 33919-1719, 239-939-4845 phone/Fax, superK@juno.com

PUNKIN HOUSE DIGEST, 9824 Mar Largo Cr, Fort Myers, FL 33919, http://www.punkinhousepress.com, ContactUs@punkinhousepress.org

Punkin House Press, 9824 Mar Largo Cr, Fort Myers, FL 33919, http://www.punkinhousepres.com, ContactUs@punkinhousepress.org

Children Of Mary, PO Box 350333, Ft. Lauderdale, FL 33335-0333, 954-583-5108 phone/fax, mascmen8@bellsouth.net, www.catholicbook.com

FIDELIS ET VERUS, PO Box 350333, Ft. Lauderdale, FL 33335-0333, Phone/fax 954-583-5108 E-mail: mascmen7@yahoo.com Website: http://www.catholicbook.com

Brain Injury Success Books, 7025 NW 52nd Drive, Gainesville, FL 32653-7014, 352-672-6672, info@braininjurysuccess.org, www.braininjurysuccess.org

COUNTERPOISE: For Social Responsibilities, Liberty and Dissent, 1716 SW Williston Road, Gainesville, FL 32608-4049, 352-335-2200, editor@counterpoise.info, www.counterpoise.info.

Florida Academic Press, PO Box 540, Gainesville, FL 32602-0540, 352-332-5104, Fax 352-331-6003, FAPress@gmail.com, web: www.FloridaAcademicPress.com

Maupin House Publishing, Inc., 2416 NW 71st Place, Gainesville, FL 32607, 1-800-524-0634, Fax 352-373-5546

Rhiannon Press, P.O. Box 140310, Gainesville, FL 32614, skoeppel@fscj.edu ; contact@writecorner.com

SUBTROPICS, P.O. Box 112075, 4008 Turlington Hall, University of Florida, Gainesville, FL 32611-2075

Writecorner.com Press, P.O. Box 140310, Gainesville, FL 32614-0310, www.writecorner.com

Good Life Products, PO Box 170070, Hialeah, FL 33017-0070, 305-362-6998, Fax 305-557-6123

INVENTED LANGUAGES, PO Box 3105, High Springs, FL 32655-3105, 352-317-9068 www.InventedLanguages.com

Rainbow Books, Inc., PO Box 430, Highland City, FL 33846-0430, 863-648-4420, 863-647-5951, rbibooks@aol.com, www.RainbowBooksInc.com

BR Anchor Publishing, 4596 Capital Dome Drive, Jacksonville, FL 32246-7457, 904-641-1140

Dumouriez Publishing, PO Box 12849, Jacksonville, FL 32209, 904.536.8910, http://www.dpublishing1.com, admin@dpublishing1.com, tocca@dpublishing1.com

Famaco Publishers (Qalam Books), PO Box 440665, Jacksonville, FL 32244-0665, 904-434-5901, Fax 904-777-5901, famapub@aol.com

FOTOTEQUE, PO Box 55-0898, Jacksonville, FL 32255-0898, 904-705-6806, htpp://www.fototeque.com (must inquire prior to adding portfolios)

KALLIOPE, A Journal of Women's Literature and Art, FCCJ - South Campus, 11901 Beach Blvd., Jacksonville, FL 32246, 904-646-2081, www.fccj.org/kalliope

The Leaping Frog Press, PO Box 55-0898, Jacksonville, FL 32255-0898, Write to us (we all still write letters right?) PO Box 55-0898 Jacksonville, FL 32255-0898. http://www.short-fiction.com, www.timsonedwards.com, publisher@bellsouth.net if you need to send email, do not send attachments, we will request the attachment.

MUDLARK, English Department, University of North Florida, Jacksonville, FL 32224-2645, mudlark@unf.edu, www.unf.edu/mudlark

Rock Spring Press Inc., 6015 Morrow Street East Suite 106, Jacksonville, FL 32217, editor@rockspringpress.com

THE WILDWOOD READER, PO Box 55-0898, Jacksonville, FL 32255-0898, 904-705-6806; gonz2171@bellsouth.net; www.short-fiction.com

CATAMARAN SAILOR, PO Box 2060, Key Largo, FL 33037, 05-451-3287, Fax 305-453-0255, rick@catsailor.comt, www.catsailor.com

Foodnsport Press, 609 N Jade Drive, Key Largo, FL 33037, 541-688-8809, www.foodnsport.com

Ram Press, PO Box 2060, Key Largo, FL 33037, 305-451-3287, Fax 305-453-0255, rick@catsailor.comt, www.rambooks.com, www.catsailor.com

Signalman Publishing, 3209 Stonehurst Cir., Kissimmee, FL 34741, (407)343-4853/info@signalmanpublishing.com/ http://www.signalmanpublishing.com

Small Dogma Publishing, Inc., PO Box 91023, Lakeland, FL 33804, 863-838-7251

SEDUCTIVE SELLING, 3959 Van Dyke Road #253, Lutz, FL 33558, 813-909-2214

The Power Within Institute, Inc., P.O. Box 595, Matlacha, FL 33993, 239-989-9000

Squire Press, 411 4th Ave, Melbourne Beach, FL 32951, 3217256827

Cantadora Press, 5406 Persimmon Hollow Rd., Milton, FL 32583-6700

COGNITIO: A Graduate Humanities Journal, 5406 Persimmon Hollow Rd., Milton, FL 32583-6700

PARENTEACHER MAGAZINE, PO Box 1246, Mount Dora, FL 32756, 352-385-1877, 800-732-3868, Fax 352-385-9424, rachat@aol.com

Morgen Publishing Incorporated, PO Box 754, Naples, FL 34106, Fax 239-263-8472

Luthers Publishing, 1009 North Dixie Freeway, New Smyrna Beach, FL 32168-6221, 386-423-1600 phone/Fax, www.lutherspublishing.com

Two Thousand Three Associates, 4180 Saxon Drive, New Smyrna Beach, FL 32169-3851, 386-690-2503

GULF STREAM MAGAZINE, English Department FIU, Biscayne Bay Campus, 3000 NE 151 Street, North Miami, FL 33181-3000, http://www.gulfstreamlitmag.com

576

Atlantic Publishing Group, Inc., 1210 SW 23rd Place, Ocala, FL 34474-7014, 800-814-1132, Fax 352-622-1875, sales@atlantic-pub.com, www.atlantic-pub.com

RED MARE, PO Box 831544, Ocala, FL 34483, X.SuZi@Live.com

SAGE OF CONSCIOUSNESS E-ZINE, PO Box 1209, Ocala, FL 34478-1209, sageofcon@gmail.com http://www.sageof-con.com

THE FLORIDA REVIEW, Department of English, Univeristy of Central Florida, PO Box 161346, Orlando, FL 32816-1346, 407-823-2038, flreview@mail.ucf.edu, www.flreview.com

UnKnownTruths.com Publishing Company, 8815 Conroy Windermere Rd., Suite 190, Orlando, FL 32835, Ph 407-929-9207, Fax 407-876-3933, info@unknowntruths.com

Cycad Press, PO Box 10407, Panama City, FL 32404, 850-532-3106

BAYOU, The University of West Florida/English Dept., 11000 University Parkway, Pensacola, FL 32514-5751, 904-474-2923

Ethos Publishing, 4224 Spanish Trail Place, Pensacola, FL 32504-8561

Swing-Hi Press, 3045 S. Ponte Vedra Blvd., Ponte Vedra Beach, FL 32082, 904-819-9115, fax:904-825-0820, toll free:1-877-315-8638, barbara@naturalbodyshape.com, www.NaturalBodyShape.com

The Runaway Spoon Press, 1708 Hayworth Road, Port Charlotte, FL 33952, 941-629-8045

THE INK SLINGER REVIEW, 3895 Esplanade Ave, Port Orange, FL 32129, 386-290-2435

Orage Publishing, 1460 Wren Ct, Punta Gorda, FL 33950, p-941-639-6144, fax-941-639-4144

A Cappela Publishing, P.O. Box 3691, Sarasota, FL 34230-3691, 941-351-4735, 941-351-2050, acappub@aol.com, www.acappela.com

Ageless Press, 3759 Collins St., Sarasota, FL 34232-3201, 941-365-1367, irishope@comcast.net

Barefoot Press, 1012 Danny Drive, Sarasota, FL 34243-4409, 941-751-3200, fax 941-751-3244

Goss Press, 5353 Creekside Trail, Sarasota, FL 34243

LegacyForever, 4930 Capri Avenue, Sarasota, FL 34235-4320, 941-358-3339

New Chapter Publisher, 1765 Ringling Blvd. Ste 300, Sarasota, FL 34236, Tel. 941.954.4690, Fax. 941.954.0111, www.newchapterpublisher.com

Pineapple Press, Inc., PO Box 3889, Sarasota, FL 34230-3889, 941-739-2219, FAX: 941-739-2296

Valuable Quality Publishing Company, 4930 Capri Avenue, Sarasota,, FL 34235-4320, 941-351-8581

MIDWEST POETRY REVIEW, 7443 Oak Tree Lane, Spring Hill, FL 34607-2324

Kings Estate Press, 870 Kings Estate Road, St. Augustine, FL 32086, 800-249-7485, rmkkep@bellsouth.net

Anhinga Press, PO Box 10595, Tallahassee, FL 32302, 850-442-1408, Fax 850-442-6323, info@anhinga.org, www.anhinga.org

APALACHEE REVIEW, PO Box 10469, Tallahassee, FL 32302

FUTURECYCLE POETRY, 354 Dreadnaught Ct, Tallahassee, FL 32312, 850-559-1405, 1-800-755-7332, rsking@futurecy-cle.org, http://www.futurecycle.org

THE LIBRARY QUARTERLY, Florida State University, School of Information Studies, 101 Shores Building, Tallahassee, FL 32306-2100

THE SOUTHEAST REVIEW, Department of English, Florida State University, Tallahassee, FL 32306

Llumina Press, 7915 W. McNab Road, Tamarac, FL 33321, 866-229-9244, fax: 954 726-0902, web: www.llumina.com.

TAMPA REVIEW, 401 W. Kennedy Boulevard, University of Tampa-19F, Tampa, FL 33606-1490, (813) 253-6266, Email: utpress@ut.edu, http://utpress.ut.edu, http://tamparcview.ut.edu

University of Tampa Press, 401 W Kennedy Blvd, Tampa, FL 33606, (813) 253-6266, Email: utpress@ut.edu, http://utpress.ut.edu, http://tamparcview.ut.edu

SHORTRUNS, 720 Wesley Ave. #10, Tarpon Springs, FL 34689, 727-942-2218

Heritage Global Publishing, 908 Innergary Place, Valrico, FL 33594, 813-643-6029

Common Boundaries, 2895 Luckie Road, Weston, FL 33331-3047, 954-385-8434, Fax 954-385-8652, www.commonboundar-ies.com, info@commonboundaries.com

SPECS, Rollins College specs Journal, 1000 Holt Avenue - 705, Winter Park, FL 32789, 407-646-2666

Tax Property Investor, Inc., PO Box 4602, Winter Park, FL 32793, 407-671-0004

GEORGIA

BearManor Media, PO Box 71426, Albany, GA 31708-1426, 580-252-3547, Fax: 814-690-1559, benohmart@gmail.com, www.bearmanormedia.com

A Child Called Poor, P O Box 5716, Albany, GA 31706, 229-291-7556, 229-435-8224, ACHILDCALLEDPOOR.COM

Dervla Publishing, LLC, P.O. Box 1401, Alpharetta, GA 30009-1401, 678-521-4173, 678-521-4160-fax, info@dervlapublish-ing.com, dervlapublishing.com

DISCGOLFER, 3828 Dogwood Lane, Appling, GA 30802-0312, 816.471.3472, email rickrothstein@pdga.com

THE GEORGIA REVIEW, 285 S. Jackson St., Rm. 125, University of Georgia, Athens, GA 30602-9009, 706-542-3481

THE LANGSTON HUGHES REVIEW, Department of English, 254 Park Hall, Univ. of Georgia, Athens, GA 30602-6205, 706-542-1261

STATE AND LOCAL GOVERNMENT REVIEW, Carl Vinson Institute of Government, 201 N. Milledge Ave., Univ. of GA, Athens, GA 30602, 706-542-2736

VERSE, Department of English, University of Georgia, Athens, GA 30602

Allwrite Advertising and Publishing, P.O. Box 1071, Atlanta, GA 30301, 678-691-9005

ATLANTA REVIEW, PO Box 8248, Atlanta, GA 31106

The Chicot Press, Box 53198, Atlanta, GA 30355, 770-640-9918, Fax 770-640-9819, info@cypressmedia.net

Clarity Press, Inc., 3277 Roswell Road NE, Suite 469, Atlanta, GA 30305, 877-613-1495; www.claritypress.com

FIVE POINTS, P.O. Box 3999, Georgia State University, Atlanta, GA 30302-3999, 404.413.5812

Libertas Press, LLC., P.O. Box 500399, Atlanta, GA 31150, 678-852-8110, contactus@libertaspress.net, http://www.libertaspress.net

LULLWATER REVIEW, PO Box 122036, Emory University, Atlanta, GA 30322

NEW INTERNATIONAL A magazine of Marxist politics and theory, P.O. Box 162767, Atlanta, GA 30321-2767, www.pathfinderpress.com

Pathfinder Press, P.O. Box 162767, Atlanta, GA 30321-2767, www.pathfinderpress.com; orders@pathfinderpress.com (orders); pathfinder@pathfinderpress.com (editorial); permissions@pathfinderpress.com (permissions)

Peachtree Publishers, Ltd., 1700 Chattahoochee Avenue, Atlanta, GA 30318, 404-876-8761, www.peachtree-online.com

Roaring Lion Publishing, Po Box 10505, Atlanta, GA 30310-0505, 678-663-3570

TERMINUS: A Magazine of the Arts, 1034 Hill Street, Atlanta, GA 30315

Wind Eagle Press, P.O. Box 5379, Atlanta, GA 31107, 404/378-6815, WindEaglePress@yahoo.com

Harbor House, 111 Tenth Street, Augusta, GA 30901, 706-738-0354(phone), 706-823-5999(fax), harborhouse@harborhousebooks.com, www.harborhousebooks.com

Third Dimension Publishing, PO Box 1845, Calhoun, GA 30703-1845, 706-602-0398

Shared Roads Press, 75 Henson Road SW, Cave Spring, GA 30124, dkistner@sharedroads.net, www.sharedroads.net

SIMPLYWORDS, 605 Collins Avenue #23, Centerville, GA 31028, simplywords@hotmail.com

Brentwood Christian Press, 4000 Beallwood Avenue, Columbus, GA 31904

Brick Road Poetry Press, P.O. Box 751, Columbus, GA 31902

Dream Catcher Publishing, 3260 Keith Bridge Road #343, Cumming, GA 30041-4058, 770-887-7058, fax 888-771-2800, dcp@dreamcatcherpublishing.net, www.dreamcatcherpublishing.net

Quinn Entertainment, 7535 Austin Harbour Drive, Cumming, GA 30041, Phone (770) 356-3847, Fax (770) 886-1475, info@quinnentertainment.com, www.quinnentertainment.com

Sherian Publishing, 2700 Braselton Highway Suite 10-390, Dacula, GA 30019-3207, 888-276-6730

Pearl's Book'em Publisher, 614 Parker Ave, Decatur, GA 30032, 678-368-6657, bookpearl@yahoo.com, www.book-pearl.com

VERB: An Audioquarterly, PO Box 2684, Decatur, GA 30031

THE CHATTAHOOCHEE REVIEW, Georgia Perimeter College, 2101 Womack Road, Dunwoody, GA 30338-4497, 770-274-5145

Maryland Historical Press (also MHPress), 2364 Sandell Drive, Dunwoody, GA 30338, 770-481-0912

New World Press, Inc, 5626 Platte Dr., Ellenwood, GA 30294, (404)512-6760

Sand and Sable Publishing, P.O. Box 744, Jonesboro, GA 30237, 404-509-3352

IT GOES ON THE SHELF, 4817 Dean Lane, Lilburn, GA 30047-4720, nedbrooks@sprynet.com

Purple Mouth Press, 4817 Dean Lane, Lilburn, GA 30047-4720, nedbrooks@sprynet.com, http://home.sprynet.com/~nedbrooks/home.htm

Platinum One Publishing, 30 Cooper Lake Road Suite A7, Mableton, GA 30126, www.platinumonepublishing.com, fax:1-203-651-1825, Email:customerservice@platinumonepublishing.com

Mercer University Press, 1400 Coleman Ave., Macon, GA 31207, (478) 301-2880, (478) 301-2585 fax

FutureCycle Press, P. O. Box 680695, Marietta, GA 30068, 404-805-6039, 1-800-755-7332 (FAX), rsking@futurecycle.org, http://www.futurecycle.org

Top Shelf Productions, Inc., PO Box 1282, Marietta, GA 30061-1282, 770-425-0551, Fax: 770-427-6395, Email: chris@topshelfcomix.com

P.R.A. Publishing, P.O. Box 211701, Martinez, GA 30917-1701, (706) 855-6173, fax (210)855-6170, www.prapublishing.com, info@prapublishing.com, www.poetrymatterscelebration.com

ARTS & LETTERS: Journal of Contemporary Culture, Georgia College & State University, Campus Box 89, Milledgeville, GA 31061-0490, 478-445-1289, al@gcsu.edu, http://al.gcsu.edu

The Speech Bin, Inc., PO Box 922668, Norcross, GA 30010-2668, 772-770-0007, FAX 772-770-0006; website: www.speechbin.com

Gallopade International, 665 Highway 74 South #600, Peachtree City, GA 30269-3036, customerservice@gallopade.com

THE OLD RED KIMONO, Social & Cultural Studies,, Floyd College, Rome, GA 30162, 706-368-7623

New Canaan Publishing Company Inc., 2384 N Highway 341, Rossville, GA 30741, 203-966-3408 phone, 203-548-9072 fax

Black Dolphin Publishing, PO Box 768931, Roswell, GA 30076

Meek Publishing, 5110 Old Ellis Point, Roswell, GA 30076-3863, 770-740-8696, 770-751-7282, info@meekpublishing.com, www.meekpublishing.com

SOUTHERN POETRY REVIEW, Dept. of LLP, Armstrong Atlantic State University, 11935 Abercorn Street, Savannah, GA 31419-1997, 912-344-3196, Fax 912-344-3494, James.Smith@armstrong.edu, www.spr.armstrong.edu

EQUAL CONSTRUCTION RECORD, 2483 Heritage Drive, Suite 16-184, Snellville, GA 30078, 404-348-4065, 404-348-4469, info@equalconstruction.com, www.equalconstruction.com

5th Street Books, 1691 Norris landing Drive, Suite A, Snellville, GA 30039-0028, 678-413-9100, www.5thstreetbooks.com

Toca Family Publishing, div. of Toca Family Communications Group, LLC, 2483 Heritage Drive, Suite 16-184, Snellville, GA 30078, 404-348-4065 x5, 404-348-4469, info@tocafamilypublishing.com, www.tocafamilypublishing.com

Old Sport Publishing Company, PO Box 2757, Stockbridge, GA 30281, 770-914-2237, Fax 770-914-9261, info@oldsportpublishing.com, www.oldsportpublishing.com

Aspen Mountain Publishing, 5885 Cumming Highway Suite 108, PMB 254, Sugar Hill, GA 30518, www.aspenmtnpublishing.com, www.whiteelkpress.com

Anvil Publishers, Inc., PO Box 2694, Tucker, GA 30085-2694, 770-938-0289, Fax 770-493-7232, anvilpress@aol.com, www.anvilpub.com

SNAKE NATION REVIEW, 110 #2 West Force, Valdosta, GA 31601, 912-249-8334

HAWAII

THE EAST HAWAII OBSERVER, P.O. Box 10247, Hilo, HI 96721, eho7148@hotmail.com, http://easthawaiiobserver.blogspot.com

Petroglyph Press, Ltd., 160 Kamehameha Avenue, Hilo, HI 96720-2834, 808-935-6006, Fax 808-935-1553, PetroglyphPress@hawaiiantel.net, www.PetroglyphPress.com

Bamboo Ridge Press, PO Box 61781, Honolulu, HI 96839-1781, 808-626-1481 phone/Fax, brinfo@bambooridge.com

BAMBOO RIDGE, Journal of Hawai'i Literature and Arts, PO Box 61781, Honolulu, HI 96839-1781

The Bess Press, 3565 Harding Avenue, Honolulu, HI 96816, 808-734-7159

CHINA REVIEW INTERNATIONAL, Center for Chinese Studies, Univ of Hawaii, 1890 East-West Road, Rm. 417, Honolulu, HI 96822-2318, 808-956-8891, Fax 808-956-2682

HAWAI'I REVIEW, 1755 Pope Road, Ka Leo Bldg. 31-D, Honolulu, HI 96822, 808-956-3030

HAWAI'I PACIFIC REVIEW, 1060 Bishop Street, Hawai'i Pacific University, Honolulu, HI 96813, 808-544-1108

MANOA: A Pacific Journal of International Writing, Univ. of Hawaii English Department, 1733 Donaghho Road, Honolulu, HI 96822, 808-956-3070, Fax 808-956-3083, mjournal-l@hawaii.edu, http://manoajournal.hawaii.edu

Mo'omana'o Press, 3030 Kalihi St., Honolulu, HI 96818, 808-843-2502; (fax) 808-843-2572; email: clear@maui.net

Watermark Publishing, 1088 Bishop St., Suite 310, Honolulu, HI 96813, 808-587-7766, toll-free: 866-900-BOOK, fax: 808-521-3461

Poetry Harbor, PO Box 202, Kailua Kona, HI 96745-0202

Suburban Wilderness Press, PO Box 202, Kailua-Kona, HI 96745

ARTELLA: the waltz of words and art, P.O. Box 44418, Kamuela, HI 96743, www.ArtellaWordsandArt.com

Good Book Publishing Company, PO Box 837, Kihei, HI 96753-0837, 808-874-4876, dickb@dickb.com, www.dickb.com/index.shtml

Paradise Research Publications, Inc., Box 837, Kihei, HI 96753-0837, 808-874-4876, dickb@dickb.com

Titlewaves Publishing; Writers Direct, 4330 Kauai Beach Drive, Suite G21, Lihue, HI 96766, orders 800-867-7323
Pacific Isle Publishing Company, PO Box 827, Makawao, HI 96768, 808-572-9232 phone, book@bromes.com, www.bromes.com
Keiki O Ka Aina Press, P.O. Box 880887, Pukalani, HI 96788, 808-218-5300
First Journey Publishing Company, Waianae, HI 96792, 808.548.5148 (office)
Maui arThoughts Co., PO Box 967, Wailuku, HI 96793-0967, 808-244-0156 phone/Fax, booksmaui@hawaii.rr.com, www.booksmaui.com

IDAHO

Ahsahta Press, Boise State University, 1910 University Drive, Boise, ID 83725-1525, 208-426-3134, ahsahta@boisestate.edu, http://ahsahtapress.boisestate.edu
COLD-DRILL, 1910 University Drive, Boise, ID 83725, 208-426-3862
Idaho Center for the Book, 1910 University Drive, Boise, ID 83725-1525, 208-426-1999, Fax 208-426-4373, www.lili.org/icb
THE IDAHO REVIEW, Boise State University, 1910 University Drive/English Dept., Boise, ID 83725, 208-426-1002, http://english.boisestate.edu/idahoreview/
Limberlost Press, 17 Canyon Trail, Boise, ID 83716
The Caxton Press, 312 Main Street, Caldwell, ID 83605, 208-459-7421
Wytherngate Press, P O Box 3134, Couer d Alene, ID 83816, 208-818-3078, 208-661-4566, wytherngatepress@gmail.com, after 4/30/2006: info@wytherngate.com
TALKING RIVER REVIEW, Lewis-Clark State College, 500 8th Avenue, Lewiston, ID 83501, Email: triver@lcsc.edu, www.lcsc.edu/TalkingRiverReview/
FUGUE, Brink Hall, Room 200, Engl. Dept., University of Idaho, Moscow, ID 83844-1102, 208-885-6156
SPORE, 1111 E. Fifth Street, Moscow, ID 83843, schneider-hill@adelphia.com, http://scorecard.typepad.com/spore/
Blue Scarab Press, PO Box 4966, Pocatello, ID 83205-4966
The Great Rift Press, 1135 East Bonneville, Pocatello, ID 83201, Phone 208-232-6857, Fax 208-233-0410
Keokee Co. Publishing, Inc., PO Box 722, Sandpoint, ID 83864, 208-263-3573, www.keokee.com
Lost Horse Press, 105 Lost Horse Lane, Sandpoint, ID 83864, 208-255-4410, Fax 208-255-1560, losthorse-press@mindspring.com, web: www.losthorsepress.org
Luminous Epinoia Press, PO Box 2547, Sandpoint, ID 83864-0917, (800)786-1090 www.luminousepinoia.com
Morning Light Press, 10881 North Boyer Road, Sandpoint, ID 83864, info@morninglightpress.com, 208-265-3626, Toll free 866-308-5200
SANDPOINT MAGAZINE, PO Box 722, Sandpoint, ID 83864, 208-263-3573, info@keokee.com
Mapletree Publishing Company, 72 N WindRiver Rd, Silverton, ID 83867-0446, 208-752-1836, info@windriverpublishing.com, www.mapletreepublishing.com
WindRiver Publishing, 72 N WindRiver Rd, Silverton, ID 83867-0446, Phone: 208-752-1836, FAX: 208-752-1876, http://www.windriverpublishing.com

ILLINOIS

Cozy Cat Press, 2452 Reflections Drive, Aurora, IL 60502, 630-820-1945
The Teitan Press, Inc., PO Box 1972, Bolingbrook, IL 60440, e-mail editor@teitanpress.com, http://www.teitanpress.com
CRAB ORCHARD REVIEW, SIUC Dept. of English - Mail Code 4503, 1000 Faner Drive, Carbondale, IL 62901, 618-453-6833, www.siu.edu/~crborchd
Southern Illinois University Press, 1915 University Press Drive #MC6806, Carbondale, IL 62901-4323, 618-453-6615 (phone) 618-453-1221 (FAX)
Button Press, 1518 W. Park Ave., Champaign, IL 61821, buttonpressbooks@gmail.com
Dalkey Archive Press, University of Illinois, 1805 S. Wright Street, MC-011, Champaign, IL 61820, 217-244-5700
THE REVIEW OF CONTEMPORARY FICTION, University of Illinois, 1805 S. Wright Street, MC-011, Champaign, IL 61820, 217-244-5700
RIVERBED HAIKU, 2524 Leeper Drive #B, Champaign, IL 61822-6802, 2178988867, http://www.riverbedhaiku.com/index.html
Sagamore Publishing, 804 N. Neil St, Champaign, IL 61820, 217-359-5940, 217-359-5975 (fax), HTTP://www.sagamore-pub.com
Standard Publications, Inc., PO Box 2226, Champaign, IL 61825, 217-898-7825, spi@standardpublications.com
KARAMU, Department of English, Eastern Illinois Univ., Charleston, IL 61920, 217-581-6297
Adonis Designs Press, P.O. Box 202, Chatham, IL 62629, info@adonisdesignspress.com, www.adonisdesignspress.com
African American Images, 1909 West 95th Street, Chicago, IL 60643-1105, 773-445-0322, Fax 773-445-9844
ALTERNATIVE PRESS INDEX, Alternative Press Center, Inc., PO Box 47739, Chicago, IL 60647, 312-451-8133, altpress-AT-altpress.org
ANOTHER CHICAGO MAGAZINE(ACM), 3709 North Kenmore, Chicago, IL 60613, 312-248-7665, www.anotherchicago-mag.com
CHICAGO REVIEW, 5801 South Kenwood, Chicago, IL 60637
Chicago Review Press, 814 North Franklin Street, Chicago, IL 60610, 312-337-0747
COLUMBIA POETRY REVIEW, English Department, Columbia College Chicago, 600 South Michigan Avenue, Chicago, IL 60605, 312/344-8212, 312/344-8001 (fax), columbiapoetryreview@colum.edu, http://english.colum.edu/cpr/
CONTRARY, 3133 S. Emerald Avenue, Chicago, IL 60616, (312) 264-0744, Accepts submissions online only: www.contrarymagazine.com.
CORNERSTONE, 939 W. Wilson Avenue, Chicago, IL 60640, 773-561-2450 ext. 2080, Fax 773-989-2076
COURT GREEN, Columbia College Chicago, English Dept., 600 South Michigan Ave., Chicago, IL 60605, 312/369-8212
CRICKET, 70 E. Lake St., Suite 300, Chicago, IL 60601, Phone: 312-701-1720. Fax: 312-701-1728. Website: www.cricketmag.com
CRITICAL INQUIRY, University of Chicago, Wieboldt Hall 202, 1050 East 59th Street, Chicago, IL 60637, Telephone: (773) 702-8477; Fax: (773) 702-3397, http://www.journals.uchicago.edu/CI/home.html
EbonyEnergy Publishing, Inc., P.O. Box 43476, Chicago, IL 60643-0476, 773-445-4946; e-mail to: cheryl@ebonyenergy.com
EUPHONY, 5706 University Avenue, Room 001, Chicago, IL 60637
Featherproof Books, 2725 N Troy St 1, Chicago, IL 60647
4 Your Spirit Productions, P.O. Box 201718, Chicago, IL 60620-1718, 773.817.4161, 773.435.6335-Fax, cbronson@4yourspir-it.com, www.4yourspirit.com
GEM Literary Foundation Press, P.O. Box 43476, Chicago, IL 60643-0476, 773-445-4946

HOTEL AMERIKA, Columbia College, English Department, 600 S. Michigan Ave., Chicago, IL 60605-1996, 740-597-1360, editors@hotelamerika.net, www.hotelamerika.net
Insight Press, 4064 N. Lincoln Ave. #264, Chicago, IL 60618, www.insight-press.com
JOURNAL OF ORDINARY THOUGHT, Neighborhood Writing Alliance, 1313 East 60th Street, Chicago, IL 60637, 773-684-2742 Voice, 773-684-2744 Fax
Lake Claremont Press, 1026 W. Van Buren St., 2nd Floor, Chicago, IL 60607, 312-226-8400, Fax 312-226-8420, lcp@lakeclaremont.com, www.lakeclaremont.com
Lake Street Press, 4064 N. Lincoln Ave., #402, Chicago, IL 60618-3038, tel 773-525-3968, fax 773-525-1455, lsp@lakestreetpress.com, www.lakestreetpress.com
LIGHT: The Quarterly of Light Verse, PO Box 7500, Chicago, IL 60680-7500, 800-285-4448 (Charge Orders only), 708-488-1388 (voice), www.lightquarterly.com (no submissions via fax or e-mail)
Lyceum Books, Inc., 5758 S. Blackstone, Chicago, IL 60637, 773-643-1902, Fax 773-643-1903, lyceum@lyceumbooks.com, www.lyceumbooks.com
Merl Publications, 1658 N Milwaukee Ave # 242, Chicago, IL 60647, (708)445 8385 contact@merlpublications.com www.merlpublications.com
MODERN PHILOLOGY, University of Chicago, Wieboldt Hall 106, 1050 E. 59th Street, Chicago, IL 60637, 773-702-7600 (main #), 773-702-0694 (fax), http://www.journals.uchicago.edu/index.html
New Victoria Publishers, PO Box 13173, Chicago, IL 60613-0173, 800-326-5297
Open Court Publishing Company, 70 East Lake St., Suite 300, Chicago, IL 60601, 312-701-1720, Fax 312-701-1728
Oracle Press, PO Box 5491, Chicago, IL 60680
OYEZ REVIEW, School of Liberal Studies; Roosevelt University, 430 S. Michigan Avenue, Chicago, IL 60605, http://www.roosevelt.edu/oyezreview
Path Press, Inc., PO Box 2925, Chicago, IL 60690-2925, 847-492-0177
PhoeniX in Print, P. O. Box 81234, Chicago, IL 60681-0234, 312-698-9817, 312-946-9698 fax, info@phoenixinprint.com, www.phoenixinprint.com
POETRY, 444 North Michigan Ave., Suite 1850, Chicago, IL 60611-4034, tel 312-787-7070, fax 312-787-6650, email poetry@poetrymagazine.org, www.poetrymagazine.org, https://submissions.poetrymagazine.org
POETRY EAST, Dept. of English, DePaul Univ., 802 West Belden Avenue, Chicago, IL 60614-3214, 773-325-7487, www.poetryeast.org
Practically Shameless Press, 2120 West Farragut Ave, Chicago, IL 60625-1244, 773-728-0209, info@practicallyshameless.com, www.practicallyshameless.com
Price World Publishing, 1300 W. Belmont Ave., Suite 20G, Chicago, IL 60657, p 888-234-6896 x 713, f 216-803-0350, email publishing@PriceWorldPublishing.com, www.PriceWorldPublishing.com
Puddin'head Press, PO Box 477889, Chicago, IL 60647, 708-656-4900
RAMBUNCTIOUS REVIEW, Rambunctious Press, Inc., 1221 West Pratt Blvd., Chicago, IL 60626, Rambupress@aol.com
ROCTOBER COMICS AND MUSIC, 1507 East 53rd Street #617, Chicago, IL 60615, 773 875 6470
SOUTH LOOP REVIEW, Columbia College Chicago, English Dept., 600 South Michigan Avenue, Chicago, IL 60605, 312-369-8106 or 312-369-8212
Switchback Books, PO Box 478868, Chicago, IL 60647
Twilight Tales, Inc., 2339 Commonwealth Ave., #4C, Chicago, IL 60614, 1-888-763-READ, 312-222-9185, Publications@TwilightTales.com, www.TwilightTales.com
University of Chicago Press, 1427 E. 60th Street, Chicago, IL 60437-2954, 773-702-7700, http://www.press.uchicago.edu/
VERBATIM: The Language Quarterly, PO Box 597302, Chicago, IL 60659
InsideOut Press, PO Box 2666, Country Club Hills, IL 60478, 708-957-6047, fax: 708-957-8028, 800 number: 866-391-3034, info@insideoutpress.com, www.insideoutpress.com
Inland Lighthouse Literary Press, 13152 S. Cicero Avenue, PMB #110, Crestwood, IL 60445-1470, (708) 217-6377, Fax: (615) 526-5813, nedinwriting1@att.net
Brooks Books, 3720 N. Woodridge Drive, Decatur, IL 62526, (217) 877-2966
MAYFLY, 3720 N. Woodridge Drive, Decatur, IL 62526, (217) 877-2966
Northern Illinois University Press, 2280 Bethany Rd, University Press, DeKalb, IL 60115, (815) 753-1826 phone; (815) 753-1845 fax
Ara Pacis Publishers, PO Box 1202, Des Plaines, IL 60017-1202
Raspberry Press Limited, 1989 Grand Detour Road, Dixon, IL 61021-9520, 815-288-4910, email: raspberrypresslimited@yahoo.com, Url: www.raspberrypresslimited.com
DRUMVOICES REVUE, Southern Illinois University, English Dept., Box 1431, Edwardsville, IL 62026-1431, 618-650-3991; Fax 618-650-3509; eredmon@siue.edu; www.siue/ENGLISH/dvr/
SOU'WESTER, Southern Illinois University, Edwardsville, IL 62026-1438
MARQUEE, York Theatre Building, 152 N. York Road, Suite 200, Elmhurst, IL 60126, 630-782-1800, Fax 630-782-1802, thrhistsoc@aol.com
MODERN HAIKU, PO Box 7046, Evanson, IL 60204-7046
Niba Media Group, LLC, 1555 Sherman Avenue #306, Evanston, IL 60201, info@nibaguides.com
Northwestern University Press, 629 Noyes Street, Evanston, IL 60208-4170, (847) 491-2046; fax (847)491-8150; www.nupress.northwestern.edu
RHINO: THE POETRY FORUM, PO Box 591, Evanston, IL 60204, www.rhinopoetry.org
TRIQUARTERLY, 629 Noyes Street, Evanston, IL 60208, (847) 491-2046; fax (847)491-8150; www.nupress.northwestern.edu
Allium Press of Chicago, 1530 Elgin Avenue, Forest Park, IL 60130, emvic@alliumpress.com
RIVER KING POETRY SUPPLEMENT, PO Box 122, Freeburg, IL 62243
Wayside Publications, PO Box 318, Goreville, IL 62939, n.nottingham@violet.toler.com
WILLOW REVIEW, College of Lake County, 19351 W. Washington, Grayslake, IL 60030, 847-543-2956, com426@clcillinois.edu, www.clcillinois.edu/community/willowreview.asp
CHILDREN, CHURCHES AND DADDIES, A Non Religious, Non Familial Literary Magazine, Attn: Janet Kuypers, 829 Brian Court, Gurnee, IL 60031-3155, ccandd96@scars.tv, http://scars.tv
DOWN IN THE DIRT LITERARY MAGAZINE, the prose & poetry magazine revealing all your dirty little secrets, Scars Publications, 829 Brian Court, Gurnee, IL 60031-3155, AlexRand@scars.tv, http://scars.tv
FREEDOM AND STRENGTH PRESS FORUM, Scars Publications, 829 Brian Court, Gurnee, IL 60031-3155, Editor@scars.tv, http://scars.tv to forum: http://www.quicktopic.com/5/H/xp9RaQTGMyH7EUeK5ZrQ
Scars Publications, Attn: Janet Kuypers, 829 Brian Court, Gurnee, IL 60031-3155, Editor@scars.tv, http://scars.tv

PRISONERS' SPEAK!, PO Box 721, Homewood, IL 60430, 708-534-1334, anthonyrayson@hotmail.com
RED FEZ ENTERTAINMENT, 5 Morningside Drive, Jacksonville, IL 62650, www.redfez.net
Rural Messengers Press, 5 Morningside Drive, Jacksonville, IL 62650, rmp@theliteraryunderground.org, http://theliteraryunderground.org/rmp/grits
SIDE OF GRITS, 5 Morningside Drive, Jacksonville, IL 62650, rmp@theliteraryunderground.org, http://theliteraryunderground.org/rmp/grits
Bronze Girl Productions, Inc., 1106 Sable Ridge Drive, Joliet, IL 60421-8853, fax 916-922-1989, bronzegirl.com
Looking Beyond Publishing, PO Box 2193, La Grange, IL 60525, www.lookingbeyond.org
WORKING WRITER, PO Box 6943, Libertyville, IL 60048, workingwriters@aol.com
FIFTH WEDNESDAY JOURNAL, PO Box 4033, Lisle, IL 60532-9033
Mayhaven Publishing, Inc., PO Box 557, 803 Buckthorn Circle, Mahomet, IL 61853-0557, 217-586-4493; fax 217-586-6330
Raven Tree Press, A Division of Delta Systems Inc, 1400 Miller Pkwy, McHenry, IL 60050-1906, 877-256-0579, 800-909-9901, raven@delta-systems.com, www.raventreepress.com
ZAWP, PO Box 411, Mossville, IL 61552-0411, 309-310-7709 Tel, 217-717-0779, Fax http://zighen-aym.site.voila.fr/order.html, azawp@yahoo.com
Sourcebooks, Inc., 1935 Brookdale Road, Ste. 139, Naperville, IL 60563, 630-961-3900; Fax 630-961-2168
MANDORLA: New Writing from the Americas / Nueva escritura de las Americas, ISU, Dept. of English, Campus Box 4240, Normal, IL 61790-4240, Publications Unit tel (309) 438-3025, Fax (309) 438-5414, email to mandorla-magazine@ilstu.edu, website at http://www.litline.org/Mandorla/
The Pikestaff Press, P.O. Box 127, Normal, IL 61761, (309) 452-4831, e-mail: staff@pikestaffpress.com website: http://www.pikestaffpress.com
SPOON RIVER POETRY REVIEW, Department of English 4241, Illinois State University, Normal, IL 61790-4241, 309-438-3025
MOJO ROSE, 808 S. Cuyler Avenue, Oak Park, IL 60304
AFTERTOUCH: New Music Discoveries & Gifts For Your Creative Imagination, 1024 West Willcox Avenue, Peoria, IL 61604-2675, 309-685-4843
DOWNSTATE STORY, 1825 Maple Ridge, Peoria, IL 61614, 309-688-1409, email ehopkins7@prodigy.net http://www.wiu.edu/users/mfgeh/dss
LADYBUG, the Magazine for Young Children, 315 5th Street, PO Box 300, Peru, IL 61354, 815-224-5803, ext. 656, Fax 815-224-6615, mmiklavcic@caruspub.com
THE MONIST: An International Quarterly Journal of General Philosophical Inquiry, 315 Fifth Street, Peru, IL 61354, (815)224-6651, FAX:(815)223-4486, philomon1@netscape.net, http//monist.buffalo.edu
SPIDER, PO Box 300, Peru, IL 61354, 815-224-5803, ext 656, Fax 815-224-6615, mmiklavcic@caruspub.com
Sherwood Sugden & Company, Publishers, 315 Fifth Street, Peru, IL 61354, 815-224-6651, Fax 815-223-4486, philomon1@netscape.net www.geocities.com/sugdenpublishers/ (or) www.sugdenpublishers.com
The Hosanna Press, 203 Keystone, River Forest, IL 60305, 708-771-8259
Juel House Publishers and Literary Services, P.O.Box 415, Riverton, IL 62561, (217)629-9026 juelhouse@familyonline.com
Helm Publishing, 3923 Seward Ave., Rockford, IL 61108-7658, work: 815-398-4660, dianne@publishersdrive.com, www.publishersdrive.com
THE ROCKFORD REVIEW, PO Box 858, Rockford, IL 61105-0858, www.RockfordWritersGuild.com, rosangela.taylor@rockfordwritersguild.com
THE WAKING, 488 Brookens Hall, UIS, Springfield, IL 62792-9243, elewis@uis.edu, www.geocities.com/uis_the_waking/
Orange Alert Press, P.O. Box 3897, St. Charles, IL 60174, 630-301-1157
Pantonne Press, 902 S Randall Rd. #C306, St. Charles, IL 60174, 630-587-1520, www.pantonnepress.com
Oak Tree Press, 140 E. Palmer St., Taylorville, IL 62568, 217-824-6500, oaktreepub@aol.com, www.oaktreebooks.com
NINTH LETTER, 234 English Bldg., University of Illinois, 608 S. Wright St., Urbana, IL 61801, (217) 244-3145, fax (217)244-4147, www.ninthletter.com, ninthletter@uiuc.edu
Stormline Press, Inc., P. O. Box 593, Urbana, IL 61803, 217-328-2665
Tales Press, 2609 N. High Croass Road, Urbana, IL 61802
The Urbana Free Library, 210 West Green Street, Urbana, IL 61801, 217-367-4057
Crossway, 1300 Crescent Street, Wheaton, IL 60187, 630-682-4300
My Heart Yours Publishing, PO Box 4975, Wheaton, IL 60187, (630) 452-2809, www.myheartyours.com, tanya@myheartyours.com, jeannine@myheartyours.com
NEW STONE CIRCLE, 1185 E 1900 N Road, White Heath, IL 61884
BLACK BOOK PRESS: The Poetry Zine id, Black Book Press (id), 1608 Wilmette Ave., Wilmette, IL 60091, 847-302-9547
NoteBoat, Inc., PO Box 6155, Woodridge, IL 60517, 630-697-7229, 630-910-4553

INDIANA

Cottontail Publications, 9641 Drakes Ridge Rd, Bennington, IN 47011-1960, 812-427-3921, info@cottontailpublications.com
Banta & Pool Literary Properties, 1020 Greenwood Avenue, Bloomington, IN 47401, writerpool@aol.com
FROZEN WAFFLES, The Writer's Group, 329 West 1st St., Apt. 5, Bloomington, IN 47403-2474, 812-333-6304 c/o Rocky
Frozen Waffles Press/Shattered Sidewalks Press; 45th Century Chapbooks, The Writer's Group, 329 West 1st Street #5, Bloomington, IN 47403-2474
INDIANA REVIEW, Ballantine Hall 465, Indiana University, 1020 E. Kirkwood Avenue, Bloomington, IN 47405-7103, 812-855-3439
LYRIC POETRY RVIEW, PO Box 2494, Bloomington, IN 47402
Tendre Press, 134 N. Overhill Dr., Bloomington, IN 47408, 812-337-0193, 812-334-1987 (fax), 866-489-4727 (toll free), ann@tendrepress.com, www.tendrepress.com
Unlimited Publishing LLC, P.O. Box 3007, Bloomington, IN 47402, Please visit http://www.unlimitedpublishing.com for contact info. We strongly recommend reviewing UP's submission policies online before sending a manuscript.
Noved Audio, 4000 west 106th St., Ste#160-329, Carmel, IN 46032, (317)8764099
POETS' ROUNDTABLE, 3172 South Offield Monument Road, Crawfordsville, IN 47933-6933, 812-234-0819
Outrider Press, 2036 Northwinds Drive, Dyer, IN 46311-1874, 219-322-7270, fax:219-322-7085 www.outriderpress.com, Email: outriderpress@sbcglobal.net
EVANSVILLE REVIEW, Univ. of Evansville, English Dept., 1800 Lincoln Avenue, Evansville, IN 47722, 812-488-1042
SOUTHERN INDIANA REVIEW, College of Liberal Arts, Univ. of Southern Indiana, 8600 University Blvd., Evansville, IN 47712, 812-461-5202, Fax 812-465-7152, email sir@usi.edu
FIRST CLASS, PO Box 86, Friendship, IN 47021, christopherm@four-sep.com, www.four-sep.com

581

Four-Sep Publications, PO Box 86, Friendship, IN 47021, christopherm@four-sep.com, www.four-sep.com
AIS Publications, PO Box 42603, Indianapolis, IN 46242-0603, Office: (317) 856-8942, Cell: (317) 292-2615
GENRE: WRITER AND WRITINGS, PO Box 42603, Indianapolis, IN 46242-0603, Office: (317) 856-8942, Cell: (317) 292-2615
Josiah Elisha Publishing, LLC, P.O. Box 127, Indianapolis, IN 46206, 317 423-9484, fax 317 423-9480
Passion Power Press, Inc, PO 127, Indianapolis, IN 46206-0127, 317-356-6885 or 317-357-8821
Storm Publishing Group, 8117 Birchfield Dr, Indianapolis, IN 46268, stormpublishing@sbcglobal.net, www.stormpublishing-group.com
Bordighera, Inc., PO Box 1374, Lafayette, IN 47902-1374, 818-205-1266, via1990@aol.com
Marathon International Book Company, Department SPR, PO Box 40, Madison, IN 47250-0040, 812-273-4672 phone/Fax, jwortham@seidata.com
Cornerstone Publishing, Inc., PO Box 707, New Albany, IN 47151, 267-975-7676, 770-842-8877, books@cornerstonepublishing.com, www.cornerstonepublishing.com
NOTRE DAME REVIEW, 840 Flanner Hall, University of Notre Dame, Notre Dame, IN 46556, 574-631-6952, Fax 574-631-4795
Wish Publishing, PO Box 10337, Terra Haute, IN 47801, 812-299-5700, email:holly@wishpublishing.com
GRASSLANDS REVIEW, Department of English, Indiana State University, Terre Haute, IN 47809
SNOWY EGRET, PO Box 9265, Terre Haute, IN 47808, www.snowyegret.net
SYCAMORE REVIEW, Purdue University, Department of English, 500 Oval Drive, West Lafayette, IN 47907, 765-494-3783

IOWA

FLYWAY: A Journal of Writing and Environment, 206 Ross Hall, Iowa State University, Ames, IA 50011, 515-294-8273, FAX 515-294-6814, flyway@iastate.edu
LifeCircle Press, PO Box 805, Burlington, IA 52601, www.lifecircleent.com
NORTH AMERICAN REVIEW, University Of Northern Iowa, 1222 W. 27th Street, Cedar Falls, IA 50614-0516, 319-273-6455
COE REVIEW, 1220 1st Ave NE, Cedar Rapids, IA 52402
Madyfi Press, 2131 Newton Road, Corydon, IA 50060, www.madyfipress.com
SEED SAVERS EXCHANGE, 3094 North Winn Road, Decorah, IA 52101, 563-382-5990, Fax 563-382-5872
Islewest Publishing, 4242 Chavenelle Drive, Dubuque, IA 52002, 319-557-1500, Fax 319-557-1376
BOOK MARKETING UPDATE, PO Box 205, Fairfield, IA 52556-0205, 641-472-6130, Fax 641-472-1560, e-mail johnkremer@bookmarket.com
THE ANNALS OF IOWA, 402 Iowa Avenue, Iowa City, IA 52240, 319-335-3931, fax 319-335-3935, e-mail marvin-bergman@uiowa.edu
CESUM MAGAZINE, 102 Clapp St, Iowa City, IA 52245-3306, 319-210-0951, cesiummagazine@gmail.com, www.cesium-online.com
IOWA HERITAGE ILLUSTRATED, State Historical Society of Iowa, 402 Iowa Avenue, Iowa City, IA 52240, 319-335-3916, Fax 319-335-3935, ginalie-swaim@uiowa.edu
THE IOWA REVIEW, 308 EPB, Univ. Of Iowa, Iowa City, IA 52242, 319-335-0462
TORRE DE PAPEL, 111 Phillips Hall, The University of Iowa, Iowa City, IA 52242, 319-335-0487
University of Iowa Press, 119 Weast Park Road, 100 Kuhl House, Iowa City, IA 52242-1000
WALT WHITMAN QUARTERLY REVIEW, 308 EPB The University of Iowa, Iowa City, IA 52242-1492, 319-335-0454, 335-0592, Fax 319-335-2535, wwqr@uiowa.edu
Ice Cube Press, 205 North Front Street, North Liberty, IA 52317, 1-319-626-2055, fax 1-413-451-0223, steve@icecubepress.com, www.icecubepress.com
BEGINNING MAGAZINE, 1111 S. Sheridan Ave., Ottumwa, IA 52501-5350, beginning.editor@writers-house-press.org
Writers House Press, 1111 S. Sheridan Ave., Ottumwa, IA 52501-5350, editor.office@writers-house-press.org
THE BRIAR CLIFF REVIEW, 3303 Rebecca St., Sioux City, IA 51104, 712-279-1651
Five Bucks Press, PO Box 31, Stacyville, IA 50476-0031, 641-710-9953, fivebuckspress@omnitelcom.com, www.fivebuckspress.com
MOBILE BEAT: The Mobile Entertainer's Magazine, PO Box 42365, Urbandale, IA 50323, 515-986-3300, webmaster@mobilebeat.com

KANSAS

NSR Publications, 1482 51st Road, Douglass, KS 67039, 620-986-5472, e-mail: nsrpublications@nsrpublications.com, website: www.NSRpublications.com
FLINT HILLS REVIEW, 1200 Commercial Street, 404 Plumb Hall Campus Box 4019, Emporia, KS 66801
Aura Productions, LLC, 106 West 17th St, Hays, KS 67601, 785.259.6962
FREETHOUGHT HISTORY, Box 5224, Kansas City, KS 66119, 913-588-1996
COTTONWOOD, Room 400, Kansas Union, 1301 Jayhawk Blvd., University of Kansas, Lawrence, KS 66045, 785-864-2528 (Lorenz) 785-864-3777 (Wedge)
Cottonwood Press, 400 Kansas Union, Box J, Univ. of Kansas, Lawrence, KS 66045, 785-864-2528
GROWING FOR MARKET, PO Box 3747, Lawrence, KS 66046, 785-748-0605, 800-307-8949, growing4market@earthlink.net, www.growingformarket.com
Hill Song Press, P.O. Box 486, Lawrence, KS 66044, (785) 749-3660
Mica Press - Paying Our Dues Productions, 1508 Crescent Road, Lawrence, KS 66044-3120, Only contact by E-mail jgrant@bookzen.com; website www.bookzen.com
Mishmish Press, 1308 Jana Drive, Lawrence, KS 66049, 785-842-7552, info@mishmishpress.com, www.mishmishpress.com
Morgan Quitno Corporation, PO Box 1656, Lawrence, KS 66044, 785-841-3534, 785-841-3568, 800-457-0742, information@morganquitno.com, www.morganquitno.com
Nonetheless Press, 20332 W. 98th Street, Lenexa, KS 66220-2650, 913-254-7266, Fax 913-393-3245, info@nonetheless-press.com
ENVIRONMENTAL & ARCHITECTURAL PHENOMENOLOGY NEWSLETTER, 211 Seaton Hall, Architecture Dept., Kansas State University, Manhattan, KS 66506-2901, 913-532-1121
McGavick Field Publishing, 118 North Cherry, Olathe, KS 66061, 913-782-1700, Fax 913-782-1765, fran@abcnanny.com, colleen@nationwidemedia.net, www.abcnanny.com
LITTLE BALKANS REVIEW, 909 S. Olive, Pittsburg, KS 66762, littlebalkansreview@gmail.com
THE MIDWEST QUARTERLY, Pittsburg State University, History Department, Pittsburg, KS 66762, 620-235-4369

Varro Press, PO Box 8413, Shawnee Mission, KS 66208, 913-385-2034, Fax 913-385-2039, varropress@aol.com
CHIRON REVIEW, 522 E South Ave, St. John, KS 67576-2212, 620-786-4955, editor@chironreview.com, chironreview.com.
MOUTH: Voice of the Dis-Labeled Nation, Mouth Magazine, 4201 SW 30th Street, Topeka, KS 66614-3203, Fax 785-272-7348
Al-Galaxy Publishing Corporation, PO Box 2591, Wichita, KS 67201, 316-651-0464, Fax 316-651-0461, email: sales@algalaxypress.com
Thatch Tree Publications, 2250 N. Rock Road, Suite 118-169, Wichita, KS 67226, 316-687-6629, thatchtreepub@aol.com, www.kathyalba.com

KENTUCKY

FLOWERS & VORTEXES, CREATIVE MAGAZINE, PO Box 11, Bedford, KY 40006, 502-663-1654 www.promiseo-flight.com
APPALACHIAN HERITAGE, CPO 2166, Berea, KY 40404-3699, 859-985-3699, 859-985-3903, george_brosi@berea.edu, www.berea.edu/appalachianheritage
Steel Toe Books, English Department / Western Kentucky University, 1906 College Heights Blvd. #11086, Bowling Green, KY 42101-1086, (270) 745-5769 tom.hunley@wku.edu www.steeltoebooks.com
The Writers Block, Inc., POB 821, Franklin, KY 42135-0821, cell: 270-791-6252, fax: 270-586-9840; HEGwritersbl@aol.com, HaleyElizabethGarwood.com
Finishing Line Press, PO Box 1626, Georgetown, KY 40324, 859-514-8966, finishingbooks@aol.com, www.finishingline-press.com
GEORGETOWN REVIEW, 400 East College St., Box 227, Georgetown, KY 40324, email: gtownreview@georgetowncol-lege.edu http://georgetownreview@georgetowncollege.edu
HORTIDEAS, 750 Black Lick Road, Gravel Switch, KY 40328, 859-332-7606
Apex Book Company, P.O. Box 24323, Lexington, KY 40524, (859) 312-3974
APEX Magazine, PO Box 24323, Lexington, KY 40524, 859-312-3974, http://www.apexbookcompany.com, apex.submis-sion@gmail.com
LIMESTONE: A Literary Journal, English Dept., Univ. of Kentucky, 1215 Patterson Office Tower, Lexington, KY 40506-0027, 859-257-6981, www.uky.edu/AS/English/Limestone
Chicago Spectrum Press, 4824 Brownsboro Center, Louisville, KY 40207-2342, 502-899-1919; Fax 502-896-0246; editor@evanstonpublishing.com; www.evanstonpublishing.com
Green River Writers, Inc./Grex Press, 103 Logsdon Court, Louisville, KY 40243-1161, 502-245-4902
KWC Press, 851 S. 4th Street #207, Louisville, KY 40203, eaugust@insightbb.com
THE LOUISVILLE REVIEW, Spalding University, 851 S. 4th Street, Louisville, KY 40203, 502-585-9911 ext. 2777, louisvillereview@spalding.edu, www.louisvillereview.org
Millennium Vision Press, 401 West Main St., Suite 706, Louisville, KY 40202-2937, phone 502 5892607 fax 502 5896123
Sarabande Books, 2234 Dundee Road Suite 200, Louisville, KY 40205, www.sarabandebooks.org
Scienter Press, 2308 Fallsview Road, Louisville, KY 40207, Fax 502-415-7130, dleightty@earthlink.net
THE MAD HATTER, 320 S. Seminary Street, Madisonville, KY 42431, 270-825-6000, Fax 270-825-6072, rwatson@hopkins.k12.ky.us, www.hopkins.k12.us/gifted/mad_hatter.htm
NEW MADRID, 7C Faculty Hall Murray State University, Department of English and Philosophy, Murray, KY 42071-3341, 270-809-4713
Wind Publications, 600 Overlook Drive, Nicholasville, KY 40356
Francis Asbury Press, PO Box 7, Wilmore, KY 40390, 859-858-4222, web: www.francisasburysociety.com

LOUISANA

Claitor's Law Books & Publishing Division, Inc., 3165 S. Acadian, PO Box 261333, Baton Rouge, LA 70826-1333, 225-344-0476; FAX 225-344-0480; claitors@claitors.com; www.claitors.com
Gothic Press, 2272 Quail Oak, Baton Rouge, LA 70808-9023, 225-766-2906 www.gothicpress.com gothicpt12@aol.com
Louisiana State University Press, 3990 West Lakeshore Drive, Baton Rouge, LA 70803, 225-578-6294, Fax 225-578-6461
NEW DELTA REVIEW, New Delta Review, Louisiana State University, Department of English, 15 Allen Hall, Baton Rouge, LA 70803, 225-578-4079
THE SOUTHERN REVIEW, Old Presidents' House, Louisiana State University, Baton Rouge, LA 70803-5005, 225-578-5108
Margaret Media, Inc., 618 Mississippi St., Donaldsonville, LA 70346, office phone: (225) 473-9319, cell phone: (225) 323-4559: orders@margaretmedia.com
THE LOUISIANA REVIEW, Liberal Arts Div. PO Box 1129, Louisiana State Univ., Eunice, LA 70535, phone: 337-550-1315, email: bfonteno@lsue.edu Web: web.lsue.edu/la-review and www.myspace.com/louisianareview and www.facebook.com/louisiana.review
THE SCRIBIA, PO Box 68, Grambling State University, Grambling, LA 71245, 318-274-2190, oterod@gram.edu
Pelican Publishing Company, 1000 Burmaster Street, Gretna, LA 70053, Tel: 800-843-1724, 504-368-1175, eb: www.pelicanpub.com
LOUISIANA LITERATURE, PO Box 10792, Hammond, LA 70402
DESIRE STREET, 257 Bonnabel Boulevard, Metairie, LA 70005-3738, 504-835-8472 (Andrea), 504-467-9034 (Jeanette), Fax 504-834-2005, ager80@worldnet.att.net, Fax 504-832-1116, neworleanspoetryforum@yahoo.com
Lycanthrope Press, PO Box 9028, Metairie, LA 70005-9028, 504-866-9756
Pluma Productions, 1421 N Causeway Blvd., #200, Metairie, LA 70001-4144, email pluma@earthlink.net
THEMA, PO Box 8747, Metairie, LA 70011-8747, Telephone: 504-940-7156; e-mail: thema@cox.net; website address: http://members.cox.net/thema
TURNROW, Univ. of Louisiana at Monroe, English Dept., 700 University Ave., Monroe, LA 71209, 318-342-1520, Fax 318-342-1491, ryan@ulm.edu, heflin@ulm.edu, http://turnrow.ulm.edu
H-NGM-N, Natchitoches, LA 71457, nathanpritts@hotmail.com, www.h-ngm-n.com
H_NGM_N B_ _KS, NSU/Dept. of Language & Communication, Natchitoches, LA 71497, editor@h-ngm-n.com
The American Zen Association, 748 Camp St, New Orleans, LA 70130, Phone 504-525-3533, Fax 504-565-4690, info@nozt.org, www.nozt.org
BATHTUB GIN, 2311 Broadway Street, New Orleans, LA 70125-4127, pathwisepress@hotmail.com
HERE AND NOW, 748 Camp St, New Orleans, LA 70130, info@nozt.org, www.nozt.org
THE ILLUMINATA, PO Box 8337, New Orleans, LA 70182-8337, Illuminata@tyrannosauruspress.com, www.Tyrannosaur-usPress.com
Light of New Orleans Publishing, 828 Royal Street #307, New Orleans, LA 70116, 504-523-4322, Fax 504-522-0688,

editor@frenchquarterfiction.com, www.frenchquarterfiction.com
THE NEW LAUREL REVIEW, 828 Lesseps Street, New Orleans, LA 70117, 504-947-6001
NEW ORLEANS REVIEW, Box 195, Loyola University, New Orleans, LA 70118, 504-865-2295
NOLA-MAGICK Press, 828 Royal Street # 214, New Orleans, LA 70116, 504-301-1080, (fax) 504-309-9004, info@nolamagick.org, www.nolamagick.org
Pathwise Press, 2311 Broadway Street, New Orleans, LA 70125-4127, pathwisepress@hotmail.com
Portals Press, 4411 Fontainebleau Drive, New Orleans, LA 70125, 504-821-5404, travport@bellsouth.net, www.portals-press.com
Spring Journal Books, 627 Ursulines Street #7, New Orleans, LA 70116, (504)524-5117, submissions@springjournaland-books.com
SPRING JOURNAL, Inc., 627 Ursulines Street #7, New Orleans, LA 70116, (504)524-5117, submissions@springjournaland-books.com
Trost Publishing, 509 Octavia St., New Orleans, LA 70115, 504-680-6754, www.trostpublishing.com
World Love Press Publishing, 1028 Joliet Street, New Orleans, LA 70118, 504-866-4476 phone/Fax, worldlovepress@aol.com
XAVIER REVIEW, Box 110C, Xavier University, New Orleans, LA 70125, 504-520-5245 Adamo, 504-520-5246 Greene, Fax 504-520-7944
Westgate Press, 176 Helen Garland Drive, Opelousas, LA 70570-6874
4AllSeasons Publishing, P.O. Box 6473, Shreveport, LA 71136, 504-715-3094
Thunder Rain Publishing Corp., 603 Hickory St., Thibodaux, LA 70301, rhi@thunder-rain.com, www.thunder-rain.com, www.lintrigue.org
Tyrannosaurus Press, 5486 Fairway Dr., Zachary, LA 70791, 225.287.8885, Fax 206-984-0448, info@tyrannosauruspress.com, www.tyrannosauruspress.com

MAINE

Laureate Press, PO Box 8125, Bangor, ME 04402-8125, 800-946-2727
Dancing Bridge Publishing, 45 Green Street, Bath, ME 04530, 207 443-6084
Colerith Press, 175 Dickey Mill Rd., Belmont, ME 04952, 207-342-2619
Heartsong Books, PO Box 370, Blue Hill, ME 04614-0370, publishers/authors phone: 207-266-7673, e-mail maggie@downeast.net, http://heartsongbooks.com
ME MAGAZINE, PO Box 182, Bowdoinham, ME 04008, 207-666-8453
Brook Farm Books, PO Box 246, Bridgewater, ME 04735, 506-375-4680
Two Dog Press, PO Box 164, Brooklin, ME 04616-0164, http://www.twodogpress.com/index.html; tel: 1.207.359.8967 Tollfree: 1.888.310.2DOG
Coyote's Journal, PO Box 629, Brunswick, ME 04011, http://www.coyotesjournal.com
NEW ENGLAND BY RAIL, 4 Lincoln Street, Bruwick, ME 04011, 207-449-1486
Downeast Books, PO Box 679, Camden, ME 04843, 207-594-9544, Fax 207-594-0147, books@downeast.com, www.downeastbooks.com, www.countrysportpress.com
The Smith (subsidiary of The Generalist Assn., Inc.), 999 Sawyer Road, Cape Elizabeth, ME 04107-9638
Clamp Down Press, PO Box 7270, Cape Porpoise, ME 04014-7270, 207-967-2605
Deerbrook Editions, P.O. Box 542, Cumberland, ME 04021, phone & FAX: 207-829-5038, http://www.deerbrookeditions.com
Alice James Books, University of Maine at Farmington, 238 Main Street, Farmington, ME 04938-1911, 207-778-7071 phone/Fax, ajb@umf.maine.edu
THE AUROREAN, PO Box 187, Farmington, ME 04938, 207-778-0467
BELOIT POETRY JOURNAL, P.O. Box 151, Farmington, ME 04938, (207) 778-0020, bpj@bpj.org, www.bpj.org
Tilbury House, Publishers, 103 Brunswick Avenue, Gardiner, ME 04345, Tel: 207-582-1899, Web Site: http://www.tilburyhouse.com
THE APUTAMKON REVIEW, Post Office Box 190, Jonesboro, ME 04648-0190, 207/434-5661, thewordshed@tds.net
The WordShed, LLC, Post Office Box 190, Jonesboro, ME 04648-0190, 207/434-5661, thewordshed@tds.net
The Latona Press, 24 Berry Cove Road, Lamoine, ME 04605
STORYBOARD, 25 Slab City Road, Lincolnville, ME 04849, storybd@uog.edu, rburns@uog9.uog.edu
MONKEY'S FIST, 6 Pearl St., Madison, ME 04950-1254
John Wade, Publisher, P. O. Box 303, Phillips, ME 04966, 1-888-211-1381
THE CAFE REVIEW, c/o Yes Books, 589 Congress Street, Portland, ME 04101, caferevieweditors@mailcity.com, www.thecafereview.com
OFF THE COAST, PO Box 14, 1175 US Route 1, Robbinston, ME 04671, 207-454-8026, poetrylane@hughes.net
Leete's Island Books, Box 1, Sedgewick, ME 04676, 207-359-5054, 01-207-359-5054 (office), 01-207-610-0054 (mobile), pneill@thew2o.net
Polar Bear & Company, PO Box 311, Solon, ME 04979-0311, 207-643-2795, www.polarbearandco.com, polarbear@polarbearandco.com
Goose River Press, 3400 Friendship Road, Waldoboro, ME 04572-6337, Telephone: 207-832-6665, e mail: gooseriverpress@roadrunner.com, web:www.gooseriverpress.com
Off the Grid Press, P.O. Box 84, Weld, ME 04285, (207)585-2218, (617)629-2541, info@offthegridpress.net, www.offthegridpress.net
Moon Pie Press, 16 Walton Street, Westbrook, ME 04092, www.moonpiepress.com
Abernathy House Publishing, PO Box 1109, Yarmouth, ME 04096-1109, 207-838-6170, info@abernathyhousepub.com, www.abernathyhousepub.com

MARYLAND

Back House Books, 1703 Lebanon Street, Adelphi, MD 20783
CAFE NOIR REVIEW, 1703 Lebanon Street, Adelphi, MD 20783
The Bunny & The Crocodile Press/Forest Woods Media Productions, Inc, 1821 Glade Court, Annapolis, MD 21403-1945, 410-267-7432
Abecedarian books, Inc., 2817 Forest Glen Drive, Baldwin, MD 21013, 410-692-6777, fax 410-692-9175, toll free 877-782-2221, books@abeced.com, www.abeced.com
American Literary Press, 8019 Belair Road #10, Baltimore, MD 21236, 410-882-7700, 800-873-2003, Fax 410-882-7703, amerlit@americanliterarypress.com, www.americanliterarypress.com
Bancroft Press, PO Box 65360, Baltimore, MD 21209-9945, 410-358-0658, Fax 410-764-1967
BLACKBIRD, PO Box 16235, Baltimore, MD 21210, e-mail chocozzz2@aol.com

584

BrickHouse Books, Inc., 306 Suffolk Road, Baltimore, MD 21218, 410-235-7690, 410-704-2869
CELEBRATION, 2707 Lawina Road, Baltimore, MD 21216-1608, (410) 542-8785, e-mail wjspoet@jhu.edu
DIRTY LINEN, PO Box 66600, Baltimore, MD 21239-6600, 410-583-7973, Fax 410-337-6735
The Hopkins review, The Johns Hopkins University Press, 2715 North Charles Street, Baltimore, MD 21218-4363
Icarus Press, 1015 Kenilworth Drive, Baltimore, MD 21204, 410-821-7807, www.icaruspress.com
INSIDE LEADERSHIP NEWSLETTER, P O Box 9671-4017, 5338 King Arthur Circle, Baltimore, MD 21237-4017, 410-391-3880 work; 443-413-5600 cell; 410-391-9036 fax; drdorsey@creativecreationsconsulting.com; www.creativecrea-tionsconsulting.com
Obie Joe Media, 3324 Ramona Avenue, Baltimore, MD 21213, 410-215-2262
PASSAGER, 1420 N. Charles Street, Baltimore, MD 21201-5779, www.passagerpress.com
The People's Press, 4810 Norwood Avenue, Baltimore, MD 21207-6839, (410)448-0254 phone/fax, (800)517-4475, biblio@talkamerica.net, http://thepeoplespress.info
Prospect Press, 2707 Lawina Road, Baltimore, MD 21216-1608, (410) 542-8785
RTMC Organization, LLC, Post Office Box 15105, Baltimore, MD 21282-5105, 410-900-7834, krb@rtmc.org
SHATTERED WIG REVIEW, 425 East 31st Street, Baltimore, MD 21218, 410-243-6888
SMARTISH PACE, PO Box 22161, Baltimore, MD 21203, www.smartishpace.com
SOCIAL ANARCHISM: A Journal of Practice and Theory, 2743 Maryland Avenue, Baltimore, MD 21218, 410-243-6987
twentythreebooks, 3029 Arizona Avenue, Baltimore, MD 21234, 410-882-5783
VEGETARIAN JOURNAL, P.O. Box 1463, Baltimore, MD 21203, 410-366-VEGE (8343)
The Vegetarian Resource Group, P.O. Box 1463, Baltimore, MD 21203, 410-366-8343
VIVIPAROUS BLENNY, 3029 Arizona Avenue, Baltimore, MD 21234
Gryphon House, Inc., PO Box 207, Beltsville, MD 20704-0207, 800-638-0928
HAND PAPERMAKING, PO Box 1070, Beltsville, MD 20704-1070, 800-821-6604, Fax 301-220-2394, info@handpapermak-ing.org
THE CAROUSEL, 4508 Walsh Street, Bethesda, MD 20815-6006, 301-654-8664
THE FUTURIST, World Future Society, 7910 Woodmont Avenue, Suite 450, Bethesda, MD 20814-3032, 301-656-8274
Ibex Publishers, Inc., PO Box 30087, Bethesda, MD 20824, toll free 888-718-8188, 301-718-8188, Fax 301-907-8707
POET LORE, Poet Lore, 4508 Walsh Street, Bethesda, MD 20815-6006, 301-654-8664
The Writer's Center, 4508 Walsh Street, Bethesda, MD 20815-6006, 301-654-8664, www.writer.org
THE PLASTIC TOWER, PO Box 702, Bowie, MD 20718
Wineberry Press, P.O. Box 298, Broomes Island, MD 20615, 410-586-3086, 202-363-8036, elisavietta.ritchie@gmail.com
Cornell Maritime Press/Tidewater Publishers, P.O. Box 456, Centreville, MD 21620, 1-800-638-7641, www.cmptp.com
XCP: CROSS-CULTURAL POETICS, Rose O'Neill Literary House/Washington College, 300 Washington Avenue, Chestertown, MD 21620, website: http://lithouse.washcoll.edu/
First Chance Publishing, 76 Cranbrook Road #232, Cockeysville, MD 21030, 443-912-8719
FEMINIST STUDIES, 0103 Taliaferro, University of Maryland, College Park, MD 20742-7726, 301-405-7415, Fax 301-405-8395, creative@feministstudies.org; www.feministstudies.org
Maisonneuve Press, Institute for Advanced Cultural Studies, P. O. Box 426, College Park, MD 20741-0426, 301-277-7505, Fax 301-277-2467
ABBEY, 5360 Fallriver Row Court, Columbia, MD 21044-1910, e-mail at greisman@aol.com
Summit Crossroads Press, 9329 Angelina Circle, Columbia, MD 21045-5109, Phone/fax 410-290-7058, sumcross@aol.com, www.parentsuccess.com
White Urp Press, 5360 Fallriver Row Court, Columbia, MD 21044
Nightsun Books, 823 Braddock Road, Cumberland, MD 21502-2622, 301-722-4861
A COMPANION IN ZEOR, 1622-B Swallow Crest Drive, Sunrise Villas Apartments, Edgewood, MD 21040-1751, Fax 410-676-0164, Klitman323@aol.com, cz@simegen.com www.simegen.com/sgfandom/rimonslibrary/cz/
PublishAmerica, LLLP., PO Box 151, Frederick, MD 21705-0151, 240-529-1031, Fax 301-631-9073, writers@publishamer-ica.com, www.publishamerica.com
NIGHTSUN, Department of English, Frostburg State University, Frostburg, MD 21532-1099, nightsun@frostburg.edu
Bob & Bob Publishing, Bob & Bob Associates, Inc., P.O. Box 10246, Gaithersburg, MD 20898-0246, 301-518-9835, Fax 301-515-0962, bobandbobinc@comcast.net, www.bobandbob.com
SelectiveHouse Publishers, Inc., PO Box 10095, Gaithersburg, MD 20898, 301-990-2999; email sr@selectivehouse.com; www.selectivehouse.com
Visual Arts Press, PO Box 10621, Gaithersburg, MD 20898, 301-661-6590
Rising Star Publishers, 7510 Lake Glen Drive, Glenn Dale, MD 20769, 301-352-2533, Fax 301-352-2529
THE PEGASUS REVIEW, PO Box 88, Henderson, MD 21640-0088, 410-482-6736
Open University of America Press, 3916 Commander Drive, Hyattsville, MD 20782-1027, 301-779-0220 phone/Fax, openuniv@aol.com
Shambling Gate Press, 3314 Rosemary Lane, Hyattsville, MD 20782-1032, 301-779-6863, 301-779-9263
ORACLE POETRY, PO Box 7413, Langley Park, MD 20787
ORACLE STORY, PO Box 7413, Langley Park, MD 20787
GERMAN LIFE, 1068 National Highway, LaVale, MD 21502-7501, 301-729-6190, Fax 301-729-1720, editor@german-life.com
Creative Creations Consulting Publishing Company, P O Box 9671-4017, 617 Middle River Rd, Middle River, MD 21220, 410-391-3880 work; 443-413-5600 cell; 410-391-9036 fax; drdorsey@creativecreationsconsulting.com; www.creativecrea-tionsconsulting.com
Reconstruction Books Publishing LLC, PO Box 1427, Mitchellville, MD 20721, info@reconstructionbooks.com
THE ART OF ABUNDANCE, 1121 Annapolis Road, Suite 120, Odenton, MD 21113, 800-507-9244; 208-545-8164 (fax), www.ArtOfAbundance.com
Pellingham Casper Communications, 1121 Annapolis Road, Suite 120, Odenton, MD 21113, 800-507-9244; 208-545-8164 (fax), www.ArtOfAbundance.com
Scripta Humanistica, 1383 Kersey Lane, Potomac, MD 20854, 301-294-7949, 301-340-1095
Schreiber Publishing, 51 Monroe Street, Suite 101, Rockville, MD 20850-4193, 301-424-7737, Fax 301-424-2336, spbooks@aol.com, www.schreiberNet.com
WEIRD TALES, PO Box 4001, Rockville, MD 20849-4001
AMERICAN HIKER, 1422 Fenwick Lane, Silver Spring, MD 20910-2160, 301-565-6704
American Hiking Society, 1422 Fenwick Lane, Silver Spring, MD 20910-2160, 301-565-6704
Beckham Publications Group, PO Box 4066, Silver Spring, MD 20914, phone: 301-384-7995; fax: 413-702-5632;

editor@beckhamhouse.com, jv@beckhamhouse.com; www.beckhamhouse.com
Mystic Jaguar Publishing, 10821 Margate Rd. Suite A, Silver Spring, MD 20901-1615, 301-385-6787, 800-590-7583, Fax 800-590-7583
THE BALTIMORE REVIEW, PO Box 36418, Towson, MD 21286, www.BaltimoreReview.org
Sidran Institute, 200 E. Joppa Road, Suite 207, Towson, MD 21286, 410-825-8888, Fax 410-337-0747, sidran@sidran.org, www.sidran.org
The Galileo Press Ltd., 3637 Black Rock Road, Upperco, MD 21155-9322
Nanticoke Books, Box 333, Vienna, MD 21869-0333, 410-376-2144
ACME Press, PO Box 1702, Westminster, MD 21158, 410-848-7577
Heritage Books, Inc., 65 E. Main Street, Westminster, MD 21157-5026, 410-876-6101, Fax 410-871-2674, info@heritage-books.com

MASSACHUSETTS

VanderWyk & Burnham, PO Box 2789, Acton, MA 01720, 978-263-7595, FAX:866-614-7405, email:info@VandB.com, www.VandB.com
Amherst Writers & Artists Press, Inc., PO Box 1076, Amherst, MA 01004, 413-253-7764 phone/Fax, awapress@aol.com, www.amherstwriters.com
JUBILAT, English Dept., Bartlett Hall, University of Massachusetts, Amherst, MA 01003-0515, jubilat@english.umass.edu, www.jubilat.org
THE MASSACHUSETTS REVIEW, South College, University of Massachusetts, Amherst, MA 01003-7140, 413-545-2689
Pyncheon House, 6 University Drive, Suite 105, Amherst, MA 01002
Smyrna Press, 6 University Drive, Suite 206, PMB 161, Amherst, MA 01002-3820, Fax 201-617-0203, smyrnapress@hot-mail.com
University of Massachusetts Press, Box 429, Amherst, MA 01004, 413-545-2217; fax 413-545-1226; orders 1-800-537-5487
THE LONG TERM VIEW: A Journal of Informed Opinion, Massachusetts School of Law, 500 Federal Street, Andover, MA 01810, 978-681-0800
THE NEW RENAISSANCE, an international magazine of ideas & opinions, emphasizing literature & the arts, 26 Heath Road #11, Arlington, MA 02474-3645, Email: tnrlitmag@earthlink.net (inquiries only, send no manuscripts)
TUESDAY: An Art Project, P.O. Box 1074, Arlington, MA 02474
Paris Press, PO Box 487, Ashfield, MA 01330-0487, 413-628-0051, www.parispress.org
History Compass, LLC, 25 Leslie Rd., Auburndale, MA 02466, www.historycompass.com, 617 332 2202 (O), 617 332 2210 (F)
THOUGHTS FOR ALL SEASONS: The Magazine of Epigrams, 86 Leland Road, Becket, MA 01223, 413-623-0174
AGNI, Boston University, 236 Bay State Road, Boston, MA 02215, 617-353-7135, agni@bu.edu
BAY WINDOWS, 46 Plympton Street Suite 5, Boston, MA 02118-4201, 617-266-6670, X211
Beacon Press, 25 Beacon Street, Boston, MA 02108, 617-742-2110
Black Widow Press, c/o Commonwealth Books, Inc, 9 Spring Lane, Boston, MA 02109
D.B.A. Books, 291 Beacon Street #8, Boston, MA 02116, 617-262-0411
THE EUGENE O'NEILL REVIEW, Department of English, Suffolk University, 41 Temple Street, Boston, MA 02114-4280, 617-573-8272
Intercultural Press, Inc., 20 Park Plz #1115A, Boston, MA 02116-4303, 617.523.3801, e-mail books@interculturalpress.com
LITERARY IMAGINATION: The Review of the Association of Literary Scholars and Critics, The Association of Literary Scholars and Critics, 650 Beacon Street, Suite 510, Boston, MA 02215, 617-358-1990, Fax 617-358-1995, alsc@bu.edu, www.bu.edu/literary
Micron Press, 71 Prince Street, #35, Boston, MA 02113, 617-301-2901, inquiries@micronpress.com
THE NEW ENGLAND QUARTERLY, c/o Massachusetts Historical Society, 1154 Boylston St., Boston, MA 02215, 617-646-0543, fax: 617-859-0074, website: www.newenglandquarterly.org
PLOUGHSHARES, Emerson College, 120 Boylston Street, Boston, MA 02116, 617-824-8753
REDIVIDER, Department of Writing, Literature, and Publishing, Emerson College, 120 Boylston Street, Boston, MA 02116
SALAMANDER, Salamander/Suffolk University English Dept., 41 Temple Street, Boston, MA 02114
TEEN VOICES MAGAZINE, 80 Summer St. #300, Boston, MA 02110-1218, 617-426-5505, Fax 617-426-5577, teenvoices@teenvoices.com, www.teenvoices.com
Vision Works Publishing, PO Box 217, Boxford, MA 01921, 888-821-3135, Fax 630-982-2134, visionworksbooks@email.com
Brookline Books, 34 University Rd, Brookline, MA 02445, 617-834-6772
Hermes House Press, 113 Summit Avenue, Brookline, MA 02446-2319, 617-566-2468
KAIROS, A Journal of Contemporary Thought and Criticism, 113 Summit Avenue, Brookline, MA 02446-2319
Rose Metal Press, PO Box 1956, Brookline, MA 02446, (617) 548.9145
THE HARVARD ADVOCATE, 21 South Street, Cambridge, MA 02138, Fax 617-496-9740, contact@theharvardadvocate.com
HARVARD JOURNAL OF LAW AND GENDER, Publications Center, Harvard Law School, Cambridge, MA 02138, 617-495-3726
HARVARD REVIEW, Lamont Library, Harvard University, Cambridge, MA 02138, 617-495-9775
JLA Publications, A Division Of Jeffrey Lant Associates, Inc., 50 Follen Street #507, Cambridge, MA 02138, 617-547-6372, drjlant@worldprofit.com, www.worldprofit.com and www.jeffreylant.com
Lowestoft Chronicle Press, 1925 Massachusetts Avenue, Unit 8, Cambridge, MA 02140-1401
The MIT Press, 55 Hayward Street, Cambridge, MA 02142-1315, 617-253-5646, 617-258-6779, 800-405-1619
PEACEWORK, 2161 Massachusetts Avenue, Cambridge, MA 02140, 617-661-6130
POIESIS, PO Box 398058, Cambridge, MA 02139, alt-current.com, alt.current@gmail.com
Propaganda Press, PO Box 398058, Cambridge, MA 02139, alt-current.com, alt.current@gmail.com
SPARE CHANGE NEWS, 1151 Massachusetts Avenue, Cambridge, MA 02138, 617-497-1595, sceditor@homelessempower-ment.org
Yellow Moon Press, PO Box 381316, Cambridge, MA 02238-0001, 617-776-2230, Fax 617-776-8246, E-mail story@yellowmoon.com, www.yellowmoon.com
WIN NEWS, 69 Payson Road, Chestnut Hill, MA 02467-3218, 781-862-9431, Fax 781-862-1734
THE AMERICAN DISSIDENT, 1837 Main Street, Concord, MA 01742-3811, todslone@yahoo.com
OSIRIS, Osiris, PO Box 297, Deerfield, MA 01342-0297, rmoorhead@deerfield.edu
Pagan Press, 11 Elton St., Dorchester, MA 02125-1412, 617-282-2133, john_lauritsen@post.harvard.edu
Standish Press, 105 Standish Street, Duxbury, MA 02332-5027, 781-934-9570, Fax 781-934-9570, duxroth@verizon.net
Ash Lad Press, PO Box 294, East Orleans, MA 02643, 508-255-2301 phone/Fax

Adastra Press, 16 Reservation Rd., Easthampton, MA 01027-1227
LADY CHURCHILL'S ROSEBUD WRISTLET, 150 Pleasant St., #306, Easthampton, MA 01027
MEAT FOR TEA: THE VALLEY REVIEW, 18 Orchard Street, Easthampton, MA 01027, 413-374-1486
Perugia Press, PO Box 60364, Florence, MA 01062-0364, info@perugiapress.com, www.perugiapress.com
TAPESTRIES, Mount Wachusett Community College, 444 Green St., Gardner, MA 01440, 978-630-9176, alanahb@earth-link.net, life@mwcc.mass.edu
Atlantic Path Publishing, 17 Hammond St., Gloucester, MA 01930, 978-283-1531, Fax 866-640-1412, contactus@atlanticpath-publishing.com, www.atlanticpathpublishing.com
PEDIATRICS FOR PARENTS, 35 Starknaught Hts., P.O. Box 219, Gloucester, MA 01931, 215-253-4543, richsagall@pedsforparents.com, www.pedsforparents.com
ASKEW REVIEWS, P.O. Box 684, Hanover, MA 02339
Bone Print Press, P.O. Box 684, Hanover, MA 02339
Asphodel Press, 12 Simonds Hill Road, Hubbardston, MA 01452, 978-928-4198
THE NOISE, 74 Jamaica Street, Jamaica Plain, MA 02130, 617-524-4735, tmax@thenoise-boston.com
PORTRAIT, 11 Robeson St., Jamaica Plain, MA 02130
Three Bean Press, P.O. Box 301711, Jamaica Plain, MA 02130, phone: 617.584.5759, email: info@threebeanpress.com, web: www.threebeanpress.com
THE LONG STORY, 18 Eaton Street, Lawrence, MA 01843-1110, 978-686-7638, rpburnham@mac.com, http://web.me.com/rpburnham/Site/LongStory.html
EnlightenNext, PO Box 2360, Lenox, MA 01240-5360, 413-637-6000, Fax 415-637-6015, info@enlightennext.org
WHAT IS ENLIGHTENMENT?, PO Box 2360, Lenox, MA 01240-5360, 413-637-6000, Fax 413-637-6015, wie@wie.org
WILDERNESS HOUSE LITERARY REVIEW, 145 Foster St., Littleton, MA 01460
Wilderness House Press, 145 Foster Street, Littleton, MA 01460, voice 978-800-1625, fax 978-522-3753
Loom Press, Box 1394, Lowell, MA 01853
Wellington House Publishing Company, P.O. Box 1451, Lowell, MA 01854, 978-397-0005
Blanket Fort Publishing, 117 Lakeview Avenue, Lynn, MA 01904, 781-632-1824
Micah Publications Inc., 255 Humphrey Street, Marblehead, MA 01945, 781-631-7601
Princess Tides Publishing LLC, 3 Gerry Street, Marblehead, MA 01945-3029, www.princesstides.com
NEW VOICES REVISITED: Poetry, Contests and Short Stories., 75 Edgewood Ave Apt 38, Methuen, MA 01844, 978-688-5812
W.S. Beetle & Company, 732 County Street, New Bedford, MA 02740, 774-202-1285 phone, 774-202-1293 fax, info@wsbeetle.com, www.wsbeetle.com
Coastal 181, 29 Water Street, Newburyport, MA 01950, 978-462-2436, 978 462-9198 (fax), 877-907-8181, www.coastal181.com
Focus Publishing/R. Pullins Co., PO Box 369, Newburyport, MA 01950, 800-848-7236, Fax 978-462-9035, pullins@pullins.com, www.pullins.com
New England Cartographics, Inc., PO Box 9369, North Amherst, MA 01059-9369, 413-549-4124, toll free 888-995-6277, email: geolopes@comcast.net URL: www.necartographics.com
AT-HOME DAD, 61 Brightwood Avenue, North Andover, MA 01845, athomedad@aol.com, www.athomedad.com
Saber Press, 268 Main Street, PMB 138, North Reading, MA 01864, Tel./Fax. 978-749-3731, Email: admin@sabergroup.com, Website: www.saber-press.com
BATEAU, PO Box 1584, Northampton, MA 01061-1584, www.bateaupress.org
Bateau Press, PO Box 1584, Northampton, MA 01061-1584, www.bateaupress.org
Interlink Publishing Group, Inc., 46 Crosby Street, Northampton, MA 01060, 413 582 7054 tel, 413 582 7057 fax, www.interlinkbooks.com, info@interlinkbooks.com
Summerset Press, 20 Langworthy Road, Northampton, MA 01060, 413-586-3394 phone/FAX, BrooksRoba@aol.com
Swamp Press, 15 Warwick Avenue, Northfield, MA 01360-1105
TIGHTROPE, 15 Warwick Avenue, Northfield, MA 01360
Annedawn Publishing, PO Box 247, Norton, MA 02766-0247, 508-222-9069
OUTLANDER, PO Box 1546, Provincetown, MA 02657
PROVINCETOWN ARTS, 650 Commercial Street, Provincetown, MA 02657, 508-487-3167, web: www.provincetownarts.com
Provincetown Arts Press, PO Box 35, 650 Commercial Street, Provincetown, MA 02657, 508-487-3167; FAX 508-487-8634
Sligo Press, 4 Willow Drive, Apt. 2, Provincetown, MA 02657-1638, 508-487-5113, Fax 508-487-5113, dplennon@comcast.net
Tennyson Press, P.O. Box 105, Reading, MA 01867, publisher@tennysonpress.com
NIGHT TRAIN, 212 Bellingham Ave., #2, Revere, MA 02151-4106, rustybarnes@nighttrainmagazine.com, www.nighttrainmagazine.com
Mad River Press, State Road, Richmond, MA 01254, 413-698-3184
UPSTREET, PO Box 105, Richmond, MA 01254-0105, Tel: (413) 441-9702, blog: http://upstreetfanclub.blogspot.com/
STYLUS, 65 Westbourne Street, Roslindale, MA 02131, peterbates01@yahoo.com
YMAA Publication Center, 4354 Washington Street, Roslindale, MA 02131, 617-323-7215, Fax 617-323-7417, ymaa@aol.com, www.ymaa.com
SOUNDINGS EAST, English Dept., Salem State College, 352 Lafayette St., Salem, MA 01970, 978-542-6205
Little Pear Press, PO Box 343, Seekonk, MA 02771, Martha@LittlePearPress.com, www.LittlePearPress.com
HAPPENINGNOW!EVERYWHERE, 22 Dell Street, Somerville, MA 02145, happeningmagazine@yahoo.com, www.happeningnoweverywhere.com
IBBETSON ST., 25 School Street, Somerville, MA 02143, dougholder@post.harvard.edu
Ibbetson St. Press, 25 School Street, Somerville, MA 02143-1721, dougholder@post.harvard.edu
THE PUBLIC EYE, 1310 Broadway, Suite 201, Somerville, MA 02144, 6176665300, www.publiceye.org
Wisdom Publications, Inc., 199 Elm Street, Somerville, MA 02144-3129, 617-776-7416; Fax 617-776-7841
BOSTON REVIEW, 35 Medford St., Suite 302, Someville, MA 02143, 617-591-0505, Fax 617-591-0440, website: bostonreview.net
ATLANTIC PACIFIC PRESS, 279 Gulf Rd., South Dartmouth, MA 02748-1580, 508-994-7869
The WhaleInn Publishing House (1998), 279 Gulf Rd., South Dartmouth, MA 02748-1580, 508-994-7869 Query via regular mail with a SASE for reply. Questions? Call or Email: lyrics_songs@yahoo.com.
Harvest Shadows Publications, PO Box 378, Southborough, MA 01772-0378, Prefer contact by email. dbharvest@harvestshadows.com, www.harvestshadows.com

Three Dog Press, PO Box 1522, Stockbridge, MA 01262, 413-298-0077
Anthony Publishing Company, 206 Gleasondale Road, Stow, MA 01775-1356, 978-897-7191
The Reed Edwards Company, P.O. Box 434, Sturbridge, MA 01566, 508-347-7237
Compact Clinicals, 40 Tall Pine Dr, Sudbury, MA 01776, 800-832-0034, 800-408-8830, Fax 978-443-8000
Water Row Press, PO Box 438, Sudbury, MA 01776
WATER ROW REVIEW, PO Box 438, Sudbury, MA 01776
Leapfrog Press, PO Box 2110, Teaticket, MA 02536, 774-392-4384, email books@leapfrogpress.com, www.leapfrogpress.com
Agityne Corp, PO Box 690, Upton, MA 01568, 508-529-4135, www.agityne.com/
Two Canoes Press, PO Box 256, Upton, MA 01568, 508-529-6034, www.TwoCanoesPress.com
Cloudkeeper Press, P.O. Box 440357, W. Somerville, MA 02144-3222, http://www.cloudkeeperpress.com, editor@cloudkee-perpress.com
EASTGATE QUARTERLY REVIEW OF HYPERTEXT, 134 Main Street, Watertown, MA 02472, 617-924-9044, info@eastgate.com, www.eastgate.com
Eastgate Systems Inc., 134 Main Street, Watertown, MA 02472, 617-924-9044, info@eastgate.com, www.eastgate.com
Branden Books, PO Box 812094, Wellesley, MA 02482, 781-235-3634, Fax 781-790-1056, branden@brandenbooks.com, www.brandenbooks.com
The B & R Samizdat Express, 33 Gould Street, West Roxbury, MA 02132, 617-469-2269, seltzer@samizdat.com, main content site http://www.samizdat.com online store http://store.yahoo.com/samizdat
OTHER INVESTIGATIONS, 4 Ridgecrest Drive, West Roxbury, MA 02132
Cervena Barva Press, P. O. Box 440357, West Somerville, MA 02144-3222, editor@cervenabarvapress.com, http://www.cervenabarvapress.com
X-Peri Press, P.O. Box 440357, West Somerville, MA 02144-3222
X-PERI: Experimental Journal, P.O. Box 440357, West Somerville, MA 02144
PINE ISLAND JOURNAL OF NEW ENGLAND POETRY, PO Box 317, West Springfield, MA 01090
BUTTON, PO Box 77, Westminster, MA 01473, sally@moonsigns.net
One Less Press, 6 Village Hill Road, Williamsburg, MA 01096-9706, onelessartontherange@yahoo.com, onelessmag.blogs-pot.com
ONE LESS: Art on the Range, 6 Village Hill Road, Williamsburg, MA 01096-9706, 413-268-7370, onelessartontherange@yahoo.com, onelessmag.blogspot.com
Quale Press, P.O. Box 511, Williamsburg, MA 01096, 413-268-7911, central@quale.com
New Voices Publishing, P.O. Box 560, Wilmington, MA 01887, 978-658-2131, www.kidsterrain.com
Metacom Press, 1 Tahanto Road, Worcester, MA 01602-2523, 508-757-1683
THE WORCESTER REVIEW, 1 Ekman St., Worcester, MA 01607-1513, 978-797-4770, www.theworcesterreview.org

MICHIGAN

BRIDGES: A Jewish Feminist Journal, 4860 Washtenaw Ave., #I-165, Ann Arbor, MI 48108, E-mail clare@bridgesjournal.org
Burns Park Publishers, P.O. Box 4239, Ann Arbor, MI 48106, 734 663 5435, www.burnsparkpublishers.com
Center for Japanese Studies, The University of Michigan, 1007 E. Huron St., Ann Arbor, MI 48104-1690, 734-647-8885, Fax 734-647-8886
HOBART, PO Box 1658, Ann Arbor, MI 48103, info@hobartpulp.com, submit@hobartpulp.com, http://www.hobartpulp.com
Loving Healing Press, Inc., 5145 Pontiac Trail, Ann Arbor, MI 48105-9627, Phone 734-662-6864, http://www.LovingHeal-ing.com
MICHIGAN FEMINIST STUDIES, 1122 Lane Hall, Univ. of Michigan, 204 South State Street, Ann Arbor, MI 48109-1290, 734-761-4386, Fax 734-647-4943, e-mail mfseditors@umich.edu
MICHIGAN QUARTERLY REVIEW, 0576 Rackham, University of Michigan, 915 E. Washington St., Ann Arbor, MI 48109-1070, 734-764-9265
Moondance Press, 4830 Dawson Drive, Ann Arbor, MI 48103, 734-426-1641, maser@mac.com, http://www.blessingway.net
Pebble Press, Inc., 1610 Longshore Drive, Ann Arbor, MI 48105
Pierian Press, PO Box 1808, Ann Arbor, MI 48106, 734-434-5530, Fax 734-434-5582
University of Michigan Press, 839 Greene Street, Ann Arbor, MI 48104-3209, Phone 734-764-4388, Fax 734-615-1540, http://www.press.umich.edu/
Mayapple Press, 408 N. Lincoln St., Bay City, MI 48708, 989-892-1429 (voice/fax), jbkerman@mayapplepress.com, www.mayapplepress.com
NewPages, PO Box 1580, Bay City, MI 48706, www.newpages.com
NEWPAGES: Good Reading Starts Here, PO Box 1580, Bay City, MI 48706, www.newpages.com
LIGHTWORKS MAGAZINE, PO Box 1202, Birmingham, MI 48012-1202, 248-626-8026, lightworks_mag@hotmail.com
ILLOGICAL MUSE, 115 Liberty St. Apt. 1, Buchanan, MI 49107, illogicalmuse@yahoo.com, http://geocities.com/illogicalmuse
THE CLIFFS "sounding", P.O. Box 7, 109 Fifth Street, Calumet, MI 49913-1608, 906-337-5970
Miskwabik Press, P.O. Box 7, 109 Fifth Street, Calumet, MI 49913-1608, 906-337-5970, www.miskwabikpress.com
Visible Ink Press, 43311 Joy Road #414, Canton, MI 48187-2075
William Joseph K Publications, 150 Fisher Court, Clawson, MI 48017, 2485890056
Southwestern Michigan Publications, P.O. Box 916, Coloma, MI 49038, 269-468-9337 fax269-468-3889 email rick@swmichiganstore.com website swmichiganstore.com
Aquarius Press, PO Box 23096, Detroit, MI 48223, 877-979-3639, aquariuspress@gmail.com, www.aquariuspressbookseller.net
Lotus Press, Inc., PO Box 21607, Detroit, MI 48221, 313-861-1280, fax 313-861-4740, lotuspress@comcast.net
REVERIE: MIDWEST AFRICAN AMERICAN LITERATURE, PO Box 23096, Detroit, MI 48223, 877-979-3639, aquariuspress@gmail.com, www.aquariuspressbookseller.net
STRUGGLE: A Magazine of Proletarian Revolutionary Literature, PO Box 28536, Detroit, MI 48228
FOURTH GENRE: EXPLORATIONS IN NONFICTION, Dept. of Writing, Rhetoric, & American Cultures, 229 Bessey, Michigan State University, East Lansing, MI 48824, 517-432-2556; fax 517-353-5250; e-mail fourthgenre@cal.msu.edu
HYPATIA: A Journal of Feminist Philosophy, 503 South Kedzie Hall, Michigan State University, East Lansing, MI 48824
Michigan State University Press, 1405 S. Harrison Road, #25, East Lansing, MI 48823-5245, 517-355-9543; fax 517-432-2611; E-mail journals@msu.edu
ABSINTHE: New European Writing, P.O. Box 2297, Farmington Hills, MI 48333-2297, www.absinthenew.com, dhayes@absinthenew.com, http://absinthenew.blogspot.com/
FIFTH ESTATE, PO Box 201016, Ferndale, MI 48220-9016

BlackBerry Fields Press, 2712 North Saginaw Street, Suite 103, Flint, MI 48505, Phone: (810) 275-8316, Fax (810)234-8593 web:www.bblit.info, www.myspace.com/bblit, email:bblit@hotmail.com

Platinum Dreams Publishing, P.O. Box 320693, Flint, MI 48532, jacki@InspiredToPublish.com, (810)720-3390, www.PlatinumDreamsPublishing.com

Blue Mouse Studio, 26829 37th Street, Gobles, MI 49055, 616-628-5160; fax 616-628-4970

Wm.B. Eerdmans Publishing Co., 2140 Oak Industrial Drive NE, Grand Rapids, MI 49505-6014, 616-459-4591

BIG SCREAM, 2782 Dixie S.W., Grandville, MI 49418, 616-531-1442

Nada Press, 2782 Dixie S.W., Grandville, MI 49418, 616-531-1442

Marick Press, P.O. Box 36253, Grosse Pointe Farms, MI 48236

Dream Publishing Co., 1304 Devonshire, Grosse Pointe Park, MI 48230, 313-882-6603, Fax 313-882-8280

Avery Color Studios, 511 D Avenue, Gwinn, MI 49841, 800-722-9925

Upheaval Media, 19170 Huntington Avenue, Harper Woods, MI 48225, 877-429-2370, 313-221-9494, info@upheaval-media.net

Ironcroft Publishing, PO Box 630, Hartland, MI 48353

W.W. Publications, PO Box 373, Highland, MI 48357-0373, 727-585-0985 phone/Fax

PANK MAGAZINE, Walker Arts & Humanities Bldg., 1400 Townsend Dr., Houghton, MI 49931

WOMEN AND LANGUAGE, Humanities Dept, Michigan Technological University, Houghton, MI 49931-1295

Flowerfield Enterprises, LLC, 10332 Shaver Road, Kalamazoo, MI 49024, 269-327-0108, www.wormwoman.com

LITERALLY HORSES/REMUDA, 208 Cherry Hill Street, Kalamazoo, MI 49006-4221, 616-345-5915, literally-horses@aol.com

New Issues Poetry & Prose, Western Michigan University, 1903 W. Michigan Avenue, Kalamazoo, MI 49008-5463, 269-387-8185, Fax 269-387-2562, new-issues@wmich.edu, www.wmich.edu/newissues

Rarach Press, 1005 Oakland Drive, Kalamazoo, MI 49008

THIRD COAST, Department of English, Western Michigan University, Kalamazoo, MI 49008-5331, editors@thirdcoastmaga-zine.com (preferred), 269-387-2675, Fax 269-387-2562, www.thirdcoastmagazine.com

Slipdown Mountain Publications LLC, 28151 Quarry Lake Rd, Lake Linden, MI 49945, (phone) 906-523-4118, (toll-free phone/fax) 866-341-3705, (email) Books@SlipdownMountain.com, (website) http://www.SlipdownMountain.com

Medi-Ed Press, 523 Hunter Boulevard, Lansing, MI 48910, 800-500-8205, fax 517-882-0554. Medi.EdPress@verizon.net; www.Medi-EdPress.com.

THE MACGUFFIN, Schoolcraft College, 18600 Haggerty Road, Livonia, MI 48152, (734) 462-4400 Ext. 5327, Fax: (734) 462-4679, Email: macguffin@schoolcraft.edu, Website: www.macguffin.org

Free Books Inc., 1787 Rhoda, Lowell, MI 49331

Wilderness Adventure Books, Po Box 856, Manchester, MI 48158-0856, www.wildernessbooks.org

PASSAGES NORTH, English Dept., N. Michigan Univ., 1401 Presque Isle Avenue, Marquette, MI 49855, 906-227-1203, Fax 906-227-1096, passages@nmu.edu, http://myweb.nmu.edu/~passages

Humanergy, 213 West Mansion Street, Marshall, MI 49068, www.humanergy.com

AMERICAN ROAD, PO Box 46519, Mont Clemens, MI 48046, Orders 1-877-285-5434 x1. General information 586-468-7483, fax 877-285-5434, sales@americanroadmagazine.com, www.americanroadmagazine.com, General Manager Becky Repp 206-369-5782.

Mock Turtle Press, PO Box 46519, Mount Clemens, MI 48046, Orders 1-877-285-5434 x1. General information 586-468-7483, fax 877-285-5434, sales@mockturtlepress.com, www.mockturtlepress.com

Stone Cottage Press, 2020 S. Mission Street, Suite 232, Mount Pleasant, MI 48858-4425, 989-773-1570, editor@stonecottage-press.com

Sun Dog Press, 22058 Cumberland Drive, Northville, MI 48167, 248-449-7448, Fax 248-449-4070, sundogpr@voyager.net

Mehring Books, Inc., PO Box 48377, Oak Park, MI 48237-5977, 248-967-2924, 248-967-3023, sales@mehring.com

Zookeeper Publications, 2010 Cimarron Drive, Okemos, MI 48864-3908, 517-347-4697

PageFree Publishing, Inc., PO Box 60, Otsego, MI 49078-0060, 269-692-3926

AMERICAN WRITER, 509 Woodlake Ln, Pontiac, MI 48340, 810-625-6221 witherscraig@gmail.com

Write Now Publishing Company, P.O. Box 40297, Redford, MI 48240, Phone (313) 887-5153 Website www.writenowpublish-ingcompany.com

Socratic Consulting Group, PO Box 70162, Rochester, MI 48307-0003

PRESA, PO Box 792, Rockford, MI 49341, presapress@aol.com

Presa Press, PO Box 792, Rockford, MI 49341, presapress@aol.com

CONTROLLED BURN, Kirtland Community College, 10775 N. St. Helen Road, Roscommon, MI 48653, 989-275-5000, Fax 989-275-8219, cburn@kirtland.edu, http://www2.kirtland.edu/cburn/

Ridgeway Press of Michigan, PO Box 120, Roseville, MI 48066, 313-577-7713 / E-mail mlliebler@aol.com

ALARM CLOCK, PO Box 1551, Royal Oak, MI 48067, 248-442-8634

Doorjamb Press, P.O. Box 1296, Royal Oak, MI 48068-1296, Email: Editor@doorjambpress.org.

Lawells Publishing, PO Box 1338, Royal Oak, MI 48068-1338, 248-543-5297, fax 248-543-5683, lawells@tm.net

INKY TRAIL NEWS, 50416 Schoenharr #111, Shelby Twp., MI 48315, www.friendship-by-mail.com

Arbutus Press, 2364 Pinehurst Trail, Traverse City, MI 49686, phone 231-946-7240, FAX 231-946-4196, editor@arbutus-press.com, www.Arbutuspress

Book Marketing Solutions, 10300 E. Leelanau Court, Traverse City, MI 49684, p. 231-939-1999, f. 231-929-1993, info@bookmarketingsolutions.com

DUNES REVIEW, Michigan Writers Inc., PO Box 1505, Traverse City, MI 49685

Eighth Sea Books, 223 West 7th Street, Traverse City, MI 49684-2426, 231-946-0678, info@8thSeaBooks.com, www.8thSeaBooks.com

FOREWORD, 129 1/2 East Front Street, Traverse City, MI 49684, 231-933-3699

INDEPENDENT PUBLISHER ONLINE, 1129 Woodmere Ave., Ste. B, Traverse City, MI 49686, 231-933-0445, Fax 231-933-0448, jimb@bookpublishing.com, www.independentpublisher.com

Perrin Press, 1700 W Big Beaver Rd Ste 315, Troy, MI 48084, 248.649.8071, fax 248.649.8087, www.perrinpress.com

Wayfarer Press, LLC, P.O. Box 948, Waterford, MI 48387-0948, www.wayfarerbooks.com

OUT YOUR BACKDOOR: The Magazine of Do-It-Yourself Adventure and Homegrown Culture, 4686 Meridian Road, Williamston, MI 48895, 517-347-1689; jeff@outyourbackdoor.com; outyourbackdoor.com

MINNESOTA

Loonfeather Press, P.O. Box 1212, Bemidji, MN 56619, 218-444-4869 www.loonfeatherpress.com

Truly Fine Press, PO Box 891, Bemidji, MN 56619

Knife in the Toaster Publishing Company, LLC, PO Box 399, Cedar, MN 55011-0399, 763-434-2422, kittpubco.com
Cloud 9 Publishing, PO Box 338, Champlin, MN 55316, mississippicrow@msn.com
BTW Press, LLC, PO Box 554, Chanhassen, MN 55317, 1-866-818-8029, www.btwpress.com
Silk Pages Publishing, PO Box 385, Deerwood, MN 56444, Fax 218-534-3949
Clover Valley Press, LLC, 6286 Homestead Rd., Duluth, MN 55804-9621, 218-525-4552, charlene@clovervalleypress.com, http://clovervalleypress.com
Holy Cow! Press, PO Box 3170, Mount Royal Station, Duluth, MN 55803, 218-724-1653 phone/Fax
LAKE SUPERIOR MAGAZINE, Lake Superior Port Cities Inc., P.O. Box 16417, Duluth, MN 55816-0417, 218-722-5002, fax 218-722-4096, www.lakesuperior.com, e-mail: edit@lakesuperior.com.
Lake Superior Port Cities Inc., P.O. Box 16417, Duluth, MN 55816-0417, 888-244-5253, 218-722-5002, FAX 218-722-4096, www.lakesuperior.com, reader@lakesuperior.com.
Library Juice Press, PO Box 3320, Duluth, MN 55803, 218-260-6115
Litwin Books, PO Box 3320, Duluth, MN 55803, 218-260-6115
Lost Hills Books, P.O. Box 3054, Duluth, MN 55803, info@losthillsbooks.com, www.losthillsbooks.com
Trellis Publishing, Inc., PO Box 16141-D, Duluth, MN 55816
Whole Person Associates Inc., 210 West Michigan Street, Duluth, MN 55802-1908, 218-727-0500, Fax 218-727-0505
HEELTAP/Pariah Press, c/o Richard D. Houff, 3070 Shields Drive #106, Eagan, MN 55121
Pariah Press, 3070 Shields Drive #106, 3070 Shields Drive #106, Eagan, MN 55121
Beaver's Pond Press, Inc., 7104 Ohms Lane, Suite 216, Edina, MN 55439-2129, 952-829-8818, email: BeaversPondPress@integra.net, www.beaverspondpress.com
St. John's Publishing, Inc., 6824 Oaklawn Avenue, Edina, MN 55435, 952-920-9044
Poor Richard's Press, 17854 Lyons St. NE, Forest Lake, MN 55025-8107, www.mensdefense.org
The Place In The Woods, 3900 Glenwood Avenue, Golden Valley, MN 55422-5302, Tel: 763-374-2120
READ, AMERICA!, 3900 Glenwood Avenue, Golden Valley, MN 55422
Spoon River Poetry Press, PO Box 6, Granite Falls, MN 56241
NEW UNIONIST, 1301 Cambridge St., Ste. 102, Hopkins, MN 55343-1925, 651-646-5546, nup@minn.net
Anacus Press, An Imprint of Finney Company, 8075 215th Street West, Lakeville, MN 55044, (952) 469-6699, Fax: (952) 469-1968, (800) 326-9272, Fax: (800) 330-6232 feedback@finneyco.com, www.anacus.com
Ecopress, An Imprint of Finney Company, 8075 215th Street West, Lakeville, MN 55044, Phone: 952-469-6699 or (800) 846-7027, Fax: 952-469-1968 or (800) 330-6232, feedback@finneyco.com, www.ecopress.com
Finney Company, Inc., 8075 215th Street West, Lakeville, MN 55044, (952) 469-6699, Fax: (952) 469-1968, (800)846-7027, Fax: (800) 330-6232, feedback@finneyco.com, www.finneyco.com
Galde Press, Inc., PO Box 460, Lakeville, MN 55044, phone: 9528915991, email: galde@galdepress.com, web: www.galdepress.com
Hobar Publications, A Division of Finney Company, 8075 215th Street West, Lakeville, MN 55044, (952) 469-6699, Fax:(952) 469-1968, (800)846-7027, Fax: (800) 330-6232, feedback@finney-hobar.com, www.finney-hobar.com
Windward Publishing, An Imprint of Finney Company, 8075 215th Street West, Lakeville, MN 55044, (952) 469-6699, Fax: (952) 469-1968, (800) 846-7027, Fax: (800) 330-6232, feedback@finneyco.com, www.finneyco.com
Skullvines Press, 585 Chippewa Trail, Lino Lakes, MN 55014, http://skullvines.com, mail@skullvines.com
The Creative Company, PO Box 227, Mankato, MN 56002
WOODWORKER'S JOURNAL, 4365 Willow Drive, Medina, MN 55340, 763-478-8306, Fax 763-478-8396, editor@woodworkersjournal.com
GREY SPARROW JOURNAL, 812 Hilltop Road, Mendota Heights, MN 55118, 651-452-5066
Grey Sparrow Press, 812 Hilltop Road, Mendota Heights, MN 55118, 651-452-5066
Blue Raven Press, 219 S.E. Main St., Suite 506, Minneapolis, MN 55414, 612-331-8039, 612-331-8115, www.blueravenpress.com
Coffee House Press, 79 13th Avenue NE Suite 110, Minneapolis, MN 55413-1073, 612-338-0125, Fax 612-338-4004, fish@coffeehousepress.org, www.coffeehousepress.org
DISLOCATE, 207 Church Street, 207 Lind Hall, Minneapolis, MN 55455
ILLUMINATIONS LITERARY JOURNAL, Illuminations Publications, P.O. Box 52049, Minneapolis, MN 55402
INDUSTRY MINNE-ZINE, 12 Vincent Avenue South, Minneapolis, MN 55405, 612.308.2467
JOURNAL OF BRITISH STUDIES, University of Minnesota, Dept. of History, 614 Soc Sci Tower, 267 19th Ave., S., Minneapolis, MN 55445, http://www.journals.uchicago.edu/JBS/home.html
Kar-Ben Publishing, Inc., 241 First Avenue North, Minneapolis, MN 55401, 800-4KARBEN, www.karben.com
LIFTOUTS, 520 5th Street SE #4, Minneapolis, MN 55414-1628, (612) 321-9044 barcass@mr.net
Mid-List Press, 4324 12th Avenue South, Minneapolis, MN 55407-3218, 612-822-3733, Fax 612-823-8387, guide@midlist.org, www.midlist.org
Milkweed Editions, 1011 Washington Ave. S., Ste. 300, Minneapolis, MN 55415, 612-332-3192, Fax 612-215-2550, www.milkweed.org
MIP Company, PO Box 27484, Minneapolis, MN 55427, 763-544-5915, mp@mipco.com, www.mipco.com
North Stone Editions, PO Box 14098, Minneapolis, MN 55414
THE NORTH STONE REVIEW, PO Box 14098, Minneapolis, MN 55414
PAJ NTAUB VOICE, Hmong American Institute for Learning (HAIL), 2654 Logan Avenue North, Minneapolis, MN 55411, Phone (651) 214-0955, Fax (612) 588-1534, mainengmoua@mn.rr.com
Preludium Publishers, 520 5th Street SE #4, Minneapolis, MN 55414-1628, 612-321-9044, Fax 612-305-0655, barcass@mr.net
RAIN TAXI REVIEW OF BOOKS, PO Box 3840, Minneapolis, MN 55403, 612-825-1528 tel/Fax, info@raintaxi.com, www.raintaxi.com
Search Institute, 615 First Ave. NE, Ste. 125, Minneapolis, MN 55413-2254, 612-692-5527 direct phone, 612-692-5553 fax, 877-240-7251 toll free orders
SPOUT, PO BOX 581067, Minneapolis, MN 55458-1067, http://www.spoutpress.org
SPOUT, PO Box 581067, Minneapolis, MN 55458-1067
Spout Press, PO Box 581067, Minneapolis, MN 55458-1067
Spout Press, PO Box 581067, Minneapolis, MN 55458-1067
UTNE READER, 12 North 12th St., Suite 400, Minneapolis, MN 55403, 612-338-5040, www.utne.com
ASCENT, Department of English, Concordia College, Moorhead, MN 56562, E-mail Ascent@cord.edu
New Rivers Press, Inc., c/o MSUM, 1104 7th Avenue South, Moorhead, MN 56563-0178, contact@newriverspress.org, www.newriverspress.org
Red Dragonfly Press, 307 Oxford Street, Northfield, MN 55057

WRITERS' JOURNAL, PO Box 394, Perham, MN 56573-0394, Phone 218-346-7921, Fax 218-346-7924, E-mail writersjournal@writersjournal.com, Web site www.writersjournal.com

KUMQUAT MERINGUE, PO Box 736, Pine Island, MN 55963-0736, Telephone 507-367-4430, moodyriver@aol.com, www.kumquatcastle.com

GREAT RIVER REVIEW, PO Box 406, Red Wing, MN 55066, 651-388-2009, info@andersoncenter.org, www.anderson-center.org

CONDUIT, 788 Osceola Avenue, Saint Paul, MN 55105, www.conduit.org, info@conduit.org

Pangaea, 226 South Wheeler Street, Saint Paul, MN 55105-1927, 651-690-3320 tel, info@pangaea.org, http://pangaea.org

WATER~STONE REVIEW, MS-A1730, 1536 Hewitt Avenue, Saint Paul, MN 55104-1284, water-stone@gw.hamline.edu

Yaldah Publishing, PO Box 18662, Saint Paul, MN 55118-0662, Tel: 651-470-3853, Fax: 651-224-7447, Email: info@yaldahpublishing.com, Web: http://www.yaldahpublishing.com

STUDIO ONE, College of St. Benedict, Haehn Campus Center, St. Joseph, MN 56374

Ally Press, 524 Orleans St., St. Paul, MN 55107, 651-291-2652, pferoe@comcast.net

Fieldstone Alliance, 60 Plato Boulevard East, Suite 150, St. Paul, MN 55107, 800-274-6024, Fax 651-556-4517, books@fieldstonealliance.org, www.fieldstonealliance.org

Graywolf Press, 2402 University Avenue #203, St. Paul, MN 55114

HIMALAYAN PATH, 1317 Summit Ave., St. Paul, MN 55105, 651-645-6808, fax 651-645-7935, yes@yespublishers.com, www.yespublishers.com

Midwest Villages & Voices, PO Box 40214, St. Paul, MN 55104, 612-822-6878 or e-mail: midwestvillages@yahoo.com (e-mail preferred)

Minnesota Historical Society Press, 345 Kellogg Blvd. West, St. Paul, MN 55102-1906, 651-297-2221

MINNESOTA HISTORY, Minnesota Historical Society Press, 345 Kellogg Blvd., St. Paul, MN 55102, 1651-297-2221

Paragon House Publishers, 1925 Oakcrest Avenue, Suite 7, St. Paul, MN 55113-2619, Tel: (651) 644-3087, Fax: (651) 644-0997, www.paragonhouse.com

Pliant Press, 1943 Walnute Street, St. Paul, MN 55113

Pogo Press, Incorporated, 4 Cardinal Lane, St. Paul, MN 55127, 651-483-4692, fax 651-483-4692, E-mail pogopres@minn.net

Rada Press, Inc., 1277 Fairmount Avenue, St. Paul, MN 55105-7052, phone: 651-554-7645; fax: 651-455-6975

Stellaberry Press, P.O. Box 18217, St. Paul, MN 55118, http://www.stellaberry.com

Top 20 Press, 1873 Standord Avenue, St. Paul, MN 55105, 651-690-5758

WATER-STONE REVIEW, Graduate School of Liberal Studies, MS-A1730, 1536 Hewitt Ave., Hamline University, St. Paul, MN 55104

Yes International Publishers, 1317 Summit Avenue, St. Paul, MN 55105, 651-645-6808, Fax 651-645-7935, yes@yespublishers.com, www.yespublishers.com

MOTHERVERSE: A Journal of Contemporary Motherhood, 2663 Hwy 3, Two Harbors, MN 55616-1282, website www.motherverse.com, email editor@motherverse.com, submissions email submissions@motherverse.com, ordering email order@motherverse.com, advertising email ads@motherverse.com

J-Press Publishing, 4796 126th St. N., White Bear Lake, MN 55110, 651-429-1819, 651-429-1819 fax, 888-407-1723, sjackson@jpresspublishing.com, http://www.jpresspublishing.com

PHANTASMAGORIA, English Dept - Century College, 3300 Century Ave N., White Bear Lake, MN 55110, (651)779-3410

MAIN CHANNEL VOICES: A Dam Fine Literary Magazines, P.O. Box 492, Winona, MN 55987-0492, http://www.mainchannelvocies.com

Saint Mary's Press, 702 Terrace Heights, Winona, MN 55987, 800-533-8095, http://www.smp.org, smpress@smp.org

Pro musica press, 8725 Promenade Lane, Apt 329, Woodbury, MN 55125-9622

MISSISSIPPI

Quail Ridge Press, PO Box 123, Brandon, MS 39043, kgrissom@quailridge.com

BLACK MAGNOLIAS LITERARY JOURNAL, 203 Lynn Lane, Clinton, MS 39056, (601) 383-0024, psychedeliclit@bellsouth.net, www.psychedelicliterature.com

Psychedelic Literature, 203 Lynn Lane, Clinton, MS 39056, (601) 383-0024, psychedeliclit@bellsouth.net, www.psychedelicliterature.com

MISSISSIPPI REVIEW, 118 College Dr., #5144, Hattiesburg, MS 39406-0001, 601-266-5600, www.mississippireview.com

MISSISSIPPIREVIEW.COM, The University of Southern Mississippi, PO Box 5144, Hattiesburg, MS 39406, rief@mississippireview.com

THE SOUTHERN QUARTERLY: A Journal of the Arts in the South, 118 College Drive #5078, The University of Southern Mississippi, Hattiesburg, MS 39406-5078, 601-266-4350, Fax 601-266-6033, www.usm.edu/soq

POETRYREPAIRS: Contemporary International Poetry, 222 Melrose Drive, Jackson, MS 39211

Leave No Sister Behind Publications, 13 Pecan Ln, Long Beach, MS 39560-3620, 888-795-3570

VOX, P.O Box 527, Oxford, MS 38655-0527, (662) 801-2167

VOX Press, P.O Box 527, Oxford, MS 38655, (662) 801-2167

THE YALOBUSHA REVIEW, English Dept, Univ. of Mississippi, PO Box 1848, University, MS 38677-1848, 662-915-3175, yalobusha@olemiss.edu, www.olemiss.edu/yalobusha

MISSOURI

Cornerstone Press, 1825 Bender Lane, Arnold, MO 63010-1269, (314)608-4175

BIG MUDDY: Journal of the Mississippi River Valley, MS 2650, One University Plaza, Cape Girardeau, MO 63701, (573) 651-2044, fax (573)651-5188, upress@semo.edu, www6.semo.edu/universitypress

THE CAPE ROCK, English Dept, Southeast Missouri State Univ., Cape Girardeau, MO 63701, 314-651-2500

Southeast Missouri State University Press, MS 2650, One University Plaza, Cape Girardeau, MO 63701, (573) 651-2044, fax (573)651-5188, upress@semo.edu, www6.semo.edu/universitypress

CENTER: A Journal of the Literary Arts, 107 Tate Hall, University of Missouri, Columbia, MO 65211-1500, Phone: (573) 882-4971

Columbia Alternative Library Press, PO Box 1446, Columbia, MO 65205-1446, 573-442-4352 jmcquinn@calpress.org

THE MISSOURI REVIEW, 357 McReynolds Hall, University of Missouri-Columbia, Columbia, MO 65211, 573-882-4474, Fax 573-884-4671, umcastmr@missouri.edu

Shadow Poetry, 1209 Milwaukee Street, Excelsior Springs, MO 64024, Fax: (208) 977-9114, shadowpoetry@shadowpoetry.com, http://www.shadowpoetry.com

SP QUILL MAGAZINE, 1209 Milwaukee Street, Excelsior Springs, MO 64024, Fax: (208) 977-9114, spquill@shadowpoetry.com, http://www.shadowpoetry.com/magazine/spquill.html

WHITE LOTUS, 1209 Milwaukee Street, Excelsior Springs, MO 64024, (208) 977-9114
Timberline Press, 6281 Red Bud, Fulton, MO 65251, 573-642-5035
Rabeth Publishing Company, 3515 NE 61st St., Gladstone, MO 64119-1931, email: qurabeth@kvmo.net
OVERLAND JOURNAL, Oregon-California Trails Association, PO Box 1019, Independence, MO 64051-0519, 816-252-2276,
    Fax 816-836-0989, octa@indepmo.org
ADVENTURES, 6401 The Paseo, Kansas City, MO 64131, 816-333-7000
BkMk Press, University of Missouri-Kansas City, 5101 Rockhill, University House, Kansas City, MO 64110, 816-235-2558,
    FAX 816-235-2611, bkmk@umkc.edu
Helicon Nine Editions, Box 22412, Kansas City, MO 64113, 816-753-1095, Fax 816-753-1016, helicon9@aol.com,
    www.heliconnine.com
IRISH FAMILY JOURNAL, Box 7575, Kansas City, MO 64116
Irish Genealogical Foundation, Box 7575, Kansas City, MO 64116, www.Irishroots.com
LIVING CHEAP NEWS, 7520 McGee St., Kansas City, MO 64114, 816-523-0224, livcheap@aol.com, www.livingcheap.com
NEW LETTERS, Univ. of Missouri - Kansas City; University House, 5101 Rockhill Road, Kansas City, MO 64110,
    816-235-1168, Fax 816-235-2611, www.newletters.org
Scapegoat Press, PO Box 410962, Kansas City, MO 64141
CHARITON REVIEW, Truman State University Press, 100 East Normal Avenue, Kirksville, MO 63501, 800-916-6802
THE GREEN HILLS LITERARY LANTERN, Truman State University, Department of English, McClain Hall, Kirksville, MO
    63501-4221, 660-785-4119, adavis@truman.edu, jksmith@grm.net, jbeneven@truman.edu, ll.truman.edu/ghllweb
Truman State University Press, 100 East Normal Avenue, Kirksville, MO 63501, 660-785-7336, Fax 660-785-4480,
    http://tsup.truman.edu
Images Unlimited and Snaptail Press, a Division of Images Unlimited Publishing, PO Box 305, Maryville, MO 64468,
    660-582-4279, info@imagesunlimitedpub.com, www.imagesunlimitedpub.com
THE LAUREL REVIEW, Department of English, Northwest Missouri State University, Maryville, MO 64468, 816-562-1265
Rolling Hills Publishing, 242 Eagle Flight, Ozark, MO 65721-7868, Ph: 800-918-7323, Fax: 888-329-2747,
    info@rollinghillspublishing.com, www.rollinghillspublishing.com
BOULEVARD, 6614 Clayton Road, PMB 325, Richmond Heights, MO 63117, 314-862-2643
Rivendell Books, PO Box 9306, Richmond Heights, MO 63117-0306, 1-314-609-6534, butch@rivendellbooks.com
Titus Home Publishing, 204 N. Main, Rogersville, MO 65742-6574, 417-753-3449
COMMUNITIES, RR 1 Box 156, Rutledge, MO 63563-9720, 660-883-5545 (editorial), 828-669-0997 (advertising), editor
    AT(sub) ic.org (editorial), ads AT(sub) ic.org (advertising), www.ic.org, store.ic.org
Studio 4 Productions An imprint of Quick Publishing, LC, 1610 Long Leaf Circle, Saint Louis, MO 63146, 888publish
    (782-5474), Fax 314-993-4485, www.studio4productions.com
LOST GENERATION JOURNAL, 6009 S Highway 19, Salem, MO 65560-8931, 314-729-2545, Fax 314-729-2545
GINGKO TREE REVIEW, Drury University, 900 North Benton Ave., Springfield, MO 65802
MOON CITY REVIEW, c/o Department of English, 901 South National Ave., Springfield, MO 65897
Platte Purchase Publishers, PO Box 8096, 3406 Frederick Ave., St. Joseph, MO 64508-8096, (816) 232-8471, fax.(816)
    232-8482, sjm@stjosephmuseum.org
AFRICAN AMERICAN REVIEW, Saint Louis University, Adorjan Hall 317, 3800 Lindell Boulevard, St. Louis, MO
    63108-3414, 314-977-3688, FAX 314-977-1514, ngrant2@slu.edu, keenanam@slu.edu, http://aar.slu.edu
Earthshaker Books, P.O. Box 300184, St. Louis, MO 63130-4602, (Tel)314-862-8177, earthshakerbooks.com
NATURAL BRIDGE, English Dept., Univ. of Missouri, One University Blvd., St. Louis, MO 63121, natural@umsl.edu,
    www.umsl.edu/~natural
Reedy Press, PO Box 5131, St. Louis, MO 63139, 314-644-3400, www.reedypress.com
RIVER STYX, 3547 Olive St., Suite 107, St. Louis, MO 63103-1014, 314-533-4541, www.riverstyx.org
Twinteum Artist, Inc., P.O. Box 15016, St. Louis, MO 63110
Gorilla Convict Publications, 1019 Willott Road, St. Peters, MO 63376, www.gorillaconvict.com
DAILY WORD, 1901 NW Blue Parkway, Unity Village, MO 64065, 816-524-3550, fax 816-251-3553
Unity House, 1901 NW Blue Parkway, Unity Village, MO 64065-0001, 816-524-3550, fax 816-347-5518
UNITY MAGAZINE, 1901 NW Blue Parkway, Unity Village, MO 64065-0001, 816-524-3550
2River, 7474 Drexel Dr., University City, MO 63130, 314-721-7393, www.2River.org
THE 2RIVER VIEW, 7474 Drexel Dr., University City, MO 63130, 314-721-7393, www.2River.org, long@2River.org
Cave Hollow Press, P. O. Drawer J, Warrensburg, MO 64093, 660-441-2500
PLEIADES: A Journal of New Writing, Department of English, University of Central Missouri, Warrensburg, MO 64093
ONE Health Publishing, LLC, 2001 Wakefield Farm Road, Wildwood, MO 63038-1213, phone: 636-273-9032, fax:
    636-273-9029, www.onehealthpublishing.com, publishers@onehealthpublishing.com
SOM Publishing, division of School of Metaphysics, 163 Moon Valley Road, Windyville, MO 65783, 417-345-8411,
    www.som.org
THRESHOLDS JOURNAL, 163 Moon Valley Road, Windyville, MO 65783, 417-345-8411, www.som.org

MONTANA

Seven Buffaloes Press, Box 249, Big Timber, MT 59011
Cattpigg Press, PO Box 565, Billings, MT 59103, 406-248-4875, e-mail starbase@mcn.net, website www.mcn.net/~starbase/
    dawn
Council For Indian Education, 1240 Burlington Avenue, Billings, MT 59102-4224, 406-248-3465 phone, 1-5 pm Mtn.time,
    FAX: (406)-248-1297 www.cie-mt.org., cie@cie-mt.org.
GoldenHouse Publishing Group, 290 Energy Boulevard, Billings, MT 59102-6806, 406-655-1224, groadifer@msn.com
BIG SKY JOURNAL, 1050 E. Main St., Suite 3, Bozeman, MT 59715
CORONA, Dept. of Hist. & Phil., Montana State Univ., PO Box 172320, Bozeman, MT 59717-2320, 406-994-5200
Magic Circle Press, PO Box 1123, Bozeman, MT 59771
MONTANA QUARTERLY, 2820 West College, Bozeman, MT 59718, TEL: 406-587-4491 or 800-275-0401
Lion's Den Publishing, 401 Sweetgrass Ct., Great Falls, MT 59405-1325, 406 453 4296
SECRETUM MEUM MIHI, P.O. Box 1501, Great Falls, MT 59403-1501, info@mysecretismine.com www.MySecretis-
    Mine.com
Secretum Meum Mihi Press, P.O. Box 1501, Great Falls, MT 59403-1501, info@mysecretismine.com www.MySecretis-
    Mine.com
AMERICAN JUROR (formerly FIJACTIVIST, 1989-2007), PO Box 5570, Helena, MT 59604-5570, 406-442-7800
Farcountry Press, PO Box 5630, Helena, MT 59604, 406-444-5111

Farcountry Press, PO Box 5630, Helena, MT 59604, 406-444-5128, 406-443-5480 fax, 800-821-3874
CUTBANK, English Department—LA 133, University of Montana, Missoula, MT 59812, cutbank@umontana.edu, www.cutbankonline.org
Mountain Press Publishing Co., PO Box 2399, Missoula, MT 59806, 406-728-1900
THE OVAL LITERARY MAGAZINE, The University of Montana, 32 Campus Drive, Missoula, MT 59812, (406) 243-0211, email: oval.inquiries@mso.umt.edu
Pictorial Histories Pub. Co., 713 S. 3rd Street, Missoula, MT 59801, 406-549-8488, www.pictorialhistoriespublishing.com, fax 406-718-9280
Raven Publishing, Inc., P.O. Box 2866, Norris, MT 59745, 406-685-3545, 866-685-3545, fax: 406-685-3599
SUPERIOR CHRISTIAN NEWS, PO Box 424, Superior, MT 59872
Superior Christian Press, PO Box 424, Superior, MT 59872
Jigsaw Press, 784 US Highway 89, Vaughn, MT 59487-9535, 888-643-6455

NEBRASKA

Morris Publishing, PO Box 2110, Kearney, NE 68848, 800-650-7888
Black Oak Press, PO Box 4663, University Place Stn., Lincoln, NE 68504, 402-467-4608
IT'S JUST THIS LITTLE CHROMIUM SWITCH HERE, 3724 Baldwin Ave, Lincoln, NE 68504-2443, 402-817-9208, http://chromiumswitch.org
PRAIRIE SCHOONER, 201 Andrews Hall, PO Box 880334, Univ. of Nebraska, Lincoln, NE 68588-0334, 402-472-0911
RIVER TEETH: A Journal of Nonfiction Narrative, University of Nebraska Press, 1111 Lincoln Mall #400, Lincoln, NE 68588-0630, www.nebraskapress.unl.edu
University of Nebraska Press, 1111 Lincoln Mall #400, Lincoln, NE 68508-3905, 402 472 3581, 402 472 6214, 800 755 1105, pressmail@unl.edu, www.nebraskapress.unl.edu, www.bisonbooks.com
Addicus Books, Inc., PO Box 45327, Omaha, NE 68145, 402-330-7493
The Backwaters Press, 3502 N 52nd St, Omaha, NE 68104-3506, 402-451-4052e-mail: gkosmicki@cox.net..comWebsite: www.thebackwaterspress.homestead.com
CERISE PRESS, P O Box 241187, Omaha, NE 68124, editors@cerisepress.com
Holmes House, 530 North 72nd Avenue, Omaha, NE 68114
Lone Willow Press, PO Box 31647, Omaha, NE 68131-0647, 402-551-9=0343
THE NEBRASKA REVIEW, FA 212, University of Nebraska-Omaha, Omaha, NE 68182-0324, 402-554-3159
Zoo Press, 15511 Marcy Circle, Omaha, NE 68154-2740, 402-770-8104, editors@zoopress.org, http://zoopress.org

NEVADA

PEGASUS, Pegasus Publishing, PO Box 61324, Boulder City, NV 89006-1324
America West Publishers, PO Box 2208, Carson City, NV 89702, 800-729-4131
Juniper Creek Publishing, Inc., P.O. Box 2205, Carson City, NV 89702, 775 849-1637 (voice), 775 849-1707 (fax), jcpi@junipercreekpubs.com, www.junipercreekpubs.com
Carapace Books, Carapace Publishing Group, 1450 West Horizon Ridge Parkway, Suite B304 #278, Henderson, NV 89012
White Cliffs Media, Inc., PO Box 6083, Incline Village, NV 89450
ART:MAG, PO Box 70896, Las Vegas, NV 89170, 702-734-8121
Brooke-Richards Press, 10713 Paradise Point Drive, Las Vegas, NV 89134, phone 702 982 6942; fax 702 254 8003
Crystal Publishers, Inc., 3460 Lost Hills Drive, Las Vegas, NV 89122, 702-434-3037 phone/Fax
Dash-Hill, LLC, 3540 W. Sahara Avenue #O94, Las Vegas, NV 89102-5816, 212-591-0384, www.dashhillpress.com
Huntington Press, 3665 S. Procyon Avenue, Las Vegas, NV 89103, 702-252-0655; Fax 702-252-0675; editor@huntington-press.com; http://www.huntingtonpress.com; http://www.lasvegasadvisor.com
INTERIM, English Department, Box 5011, University of Nevada, Las Vegas, NV 89154-5011
The Lentz Leadership Institute LLC, The Refractive Thinker Press., 9065 Big Plantation Ave, Las Vegas, NV 89143-5440, 702 719-9214, 877 298-5172, info@lentzleadership.com, www.lentzleadership.com
Long & Silverman Publishing, Inc., 800 North Rainbow Boulevard, Suite 208, Las Vegas, NV 89107, Phone (702) 948-5073, Fax (702) 447-9733, www.lspub.com
Mountain Media, PO box 271122, Las Vegas, NV 89127-1122, voice 702-656-3285, publisher@TheLibertarian.us, Web site http://www.LibertyBookShop.us
RAINBOW CURVE, P.O. Box 93206, Las Vegas, NV 89193-3206, rainbowcurve@sbcglobal.net, www.rainbowcurve.com
RED ROCK REVIEW, 6375 W. Charleston Blvd., Las Vegas, NV 89146, 1-702-651-5634
Women of Diversity Productions, Inc., 5790 Park Street, Las Vegas, NV 89149-2304, 702-341-9807; fax 702-341-9828; E-mail dvrsty@aol.com
Beagle Bay Books / Creative Minds Press, 14120 Saddlebow Drive, Reno, NV 89511, 775-827-8654, Fax 775-827-8633, info@beaglebay.com, www.beaglebay.com
THE MEADOW, 7000 Dandini Blvd, English Department, Reno, NV 89512-3999, 775-673-7092
Polka Dot Publishing, 9034 Western Skies Drive, Reno, NV 89521-5236, 775-852-2690 phone, LifeofFred@yahoo.com
Successful Kids Publishing, P.O. Box 34025, Reno, NV 89533, info@successfulkidspublishing.com, 775-351-4368
University of Nevada Press, Mail Stop 0166, Reno, NV 89557-0166, 775-784-6573, www.unpress.nevada.edu
LIBERTY, PO Box 20527, Rno, NV 89515-0527, 360-379-0242
Virginia City Publishing Co. LLC, P.O. Box 51389, Sparks, NV 89435, 775-359-8453

NEW HAMPSHIRE

Igneus Press, 310 N. Amherst Road, Bedford, NH 03110, 603-472-3466
Hobblebush Books, 17-A Old Milford Road, Brookline, NH 03033, Ph./Fax: 603-672-4317, E-mail: hobblebush@charter.net, Web: www.hobblebush.com
COMPASS ROSE, Chester College of New England, 40 Chester Street, Chester, NH 03036, 603-887-7432, compass.rose@chestercollege.edu, http://compassroseonline.wordpress.com
AMERICAN JONES BUILDING & MAINTENANCE, P.O. Box 4014, Concord, NH 03302, Tel:603-708-0093; Email: von@spokepress.com
Missing Spoke Press, PO Box 8645, Concord, NH 03303, 603-724-1158, Email:msp@singspeak.org
TMC Books LLC, 731 Tasker Hill Rd., Conway, NH 03818, 603-447-5589, info@tmcbooks.com, www.tmcbooks.com
WILDERNESS MEDICINE NEWSLETTER, 731 Tasker Hill Rd., Conway, NH 03818, 603-447-5589, info@tmcbooks.com www.tmcbooks.com
Oyster River Press, 36 Oyster River Road, Durham, NH 03824-3029, 603-868-5006, oysterriverpress@comcast.net,

www.oysterriverpress.com

PublishingWorks, Inc., 151 Epping Road, Exeter, NH 03833-2029, 603-778-9883, Fax 603-772-1980, email: jeremy@publishingworks.com

LightLines Publishing, 12 Wilson Street, Farmington, NH 03835-3428, 603-755-3091, Fax 603-755-3748, lightlinespublishing@yahoo.com, www.lightlinespublishing.com

Stemmer House Publishers, Inc., 4 White Brook Road, P.O. Box 89, Gilsum, NH 03448-0089

Chase Publishing, PO Box 1200, Glen, NH 03838-1200, 603-383-4166, achase@chasepublishing.com, www.chasepublishing.com

Nicolin Fields Publishing, Inc., 861 Lafayette Rd Unit 2A, Hampton, NH 03842-1232, 603-758-6363, Fax 603-758-6366, nfpi@comcast.net

Steerforth Press, L.C., 25 Lebanon St., Hanover, NH 03755-2143, 603-643-4787

WHOLE TERRAIN - REFLECTIVE ENVIRONMENTAL PRACTICE, 40 Avon Street, Antioch University New England, Keene, NH 03431-3552, 603-283-2377

GUD MAGAZINE (Greatest Uncommon Denominator), PO Box 1537, Laconia, NH 03247

Light-Beams Publishing, 10 Toon Lane, Lee, NH 03861, Tel:603-659-1300, Tel:800-397-7641, Fax:603-659-3399, e-mail: mforman@light-beams.com

The Ark, 51 Pleasant Street, Marlborough, NH 03455-2532, 603-876-4160, anarkiss@mindspring.com

FREELANCE WRITER'S REPORT, PO Box A, North Stratford, NH 03590, 603-922-8338, editor@writers-editors.com, www.writers-editors.com

APPLESEEDS, 30 Grove Street, Suite C, Peterborough, NH 03458, 603-924-7209, Fax 603-924-7380, custsvc@cobblestone.mv.com

Bauhan Publishing, LLC, 7 Main Street, 2nd Floor, Peterborough, NH 03458, 603-567-4430

CALLIOPE: Exploring World History, 30 Grove Street, Suite C, Peterborough, NH 03458, 603-924-7209, Fax 603-924-7380, custsvc@cobblestone.mv.com

Cobblestone Publishing Company, 30 Grove Street, Suite C, Peterborough, NH 03458, 603-924-7209, Fax 603-924-7380, www.cricketmag.com (click on Customer Service)

COBBLESTONE: Discover American History, 30 Grove Street, Suite C, Peterborough, NH 03458, 603-924-7209, Fax 603-924-7380, custsvc@cobblestone.mv.com

DIG, 30 Grove Street, Suite C, Peterborough, NH 03458, 800-821-0115, digstuff@caruspub.com, www.digonsite.com

FACES: People, Places, and Culture, 30 Grove Street, Suite C, Peterborough, NH 03458, 603-924-7209, Fax 603-924-7380, custsvc@cobblestone.mv.com

Moo-Cow Fan Club, PO Box 165, Peterborough, NH 03458, 603-831-1386

ODYSSEY: Adventures in Science, 30 Grove Street, Suite C, Peterborough, NH 03458, 603-924-7209, Fax 603-924-7380, custsvc@cobblestone.mv.com

Peter E. Randall Publisher, PO Box 4726, Portsmouth, NH 03802-4726, 603-431-5667, deidre@perpublisher.com, www.perpublisher.com

SIGNALS, 36 West Main Street, Warner, NH 03278

NEW JERSEY

Ragged Sky Press, PO Box 312, Annandale, NJ 08801

SKIDROW PENTHOUSE, 44 Four Corners Road, Blairstown, NJ 07825, 212-614-9505 (hm)

Technics Publications, LLC, PO Box 161, Bradley Beach, NJ 07720, dbooks@technicspub.com

Next Decade, Inc., 39 Old Farmstead Road, Chester, NJ 07930-2732, 908-879-6625, Fax 908-879-2920

CHRISTIAN*NEW AGE QUARTERLY, PO Box 276, Clifton, NJ 07015-0276, www.christiannewage.com, info@christiannewage.com

Homa & Sekey Books, PO Box 103, Dumont, NJ 07628, 201-384-6692, Fax 201-384-6055, info@homabooks.com, www.homabooks.com

Ultra Media Publications, 177 Main Street, Suite D, East Brunswick, NJ 08816, www.ultramediapublications.com

Marymark Press, 45-08 Old Millstone Drive, East Windsor, NJ 08520, 609-443-0646

The Fire!! Press, 241 Hillside Road, Elizabeth, NJ 07208-1432, 908-289-3714 phone/Fax, tw@firepress.com, www.firepress.com

Laredo Publishing Co., Inc./Renaissance House, 465 Westview Ave, Englewood, NJ 07631

EXIT 13 MAGAZINE, PO Box 423, Fanwood, NJ 07023, Exit13magazine@yahoo.com (no attachments)

Synergy Press, POB 8, Flemington, NJ 08822-0008, 908.782.7101, Synergy@SynergyBookService, www.SynergyBookService.com

13TH MOON, The 13th Moon Press, 2 Horizon Road, Apt G20, Fort Lee, NJ 07024, : 518 320-8581; Website: www.albany.edu/13thMoon

Still Waters Press, 459 South Willow Avenue, Galloway, NJ 08205-4633

Edin Books, Inc., 102 Sunrise Drive, Gillette, NJ 07933-1944

Eryon Press, PO Box 309, Gladstone, NJ 07934, (908)246-8665

TIFERET: A Journal of Spiritual Literature, PO Box 309, Gladstone, NJ 07934

Quincannon Publishing Group, PO Box 8100, Glen Ridge, NJ 07028, 973-380-9942, editors@quincannongroup.com, www.quincannongroup.com

Great Little Books, LLC, PMB 139, 233 Rock Road, Glen Rock, NJ 07452, www.greatlittlebooksllc.com

LIPS, 7002 Blvd. East, #2-26G, Guttenberg, NJ 07093

Lincoln Springs Press, 40 Post Avenue, Hawthorne, NJ 07506-1809

Vonpalisaden Publications Inc., 60 Saddlewood Drive, Hillsdale, NJ 07642-1336, 201-664-4919

Poets Wear Prada, 533 Bloomfield Street, 2nd Floor, Hoboken, NJ 07030, (201)795-3810

Abaton Book Company, 100 Gifford Avenue, Jersey City, NJ 07304-1704, web: www.abatonbookcompany.com

GOOD FOOT, 44 West Hamilton Place, Jersey City, NJ 07302

Talisman House, Publishers, PO Box 3157, Jersey City, NJ 07303-3157, 201-938-0698

PTOLEMY/BROWNS MILLS REVIEW, PO Box 252, Juliustown, NJ 08042

U.S.1 WORKSHEETS, PO Box 127, Kingston, NJ 08528-0127

SENSATIONS MAGAZINE, P.O. Box 132, Lafayette, NJ 07848-0132, www.sensationsmag.com

The True Bill Press, P.O. Box 0349, Lambertville, NJ 08530-0349, (212) 927-5898, Tony@TheTrueBillPress.com, http://www.TheTrueBillPress.com

Broken Rifle Press, 33 Morton Drive, Lavallette, NJ 08735-2826, 732-830-7014, grgioglio@verizon.net

THE LITERARY REVIEW, Fairleigh Dickinson University, 285 Madison Avenue, Madison, NJ 07940, 973-443-8564, Fax

973-443-8364
AMERICAN VEGAN, 56 Dinshah Lane, PO Box 369, Malaga, NJ 08328-0908, 856/694-2887, www.americanvegan.org
Hamilton Stone Editions, PO Box 43, Maplewood, NJ 07040, web: www.hamiltonstone.org
HAMILTON STONE REVIEW, P.O. Box 43, Maplewood, NJ 07040
Wafer Mache Publications, 16 Elmgate Road, Marlton, NJ 08053-2402, (856)983-5360 http://www.WaferMache.com
BIOLOGY DIGEST, 143 Old Marlton Pike, Medford, NJ 08055, 609-654-6500
Plexus Publishing, Inc., 143 Old Marlton Pike, Medford, NJ 08055, 609-654-6500
Arx Publishing LLC, PO Box 1333, Merchantville, NJ 08109, 856-486-1310, Fax 856-665-0170, info@arxpub.com, www.arxpub.com
Evolution Publishing, PO Box 13333, Merchantville, NJ 08109, 856-486-1310, Fax 856-665-0170, info@evolpub.com, www.evolpub.com
THE TARPEIAN ROCK, PO Box 1333, Merchantville, NJ 08109
WORD RIOT, PO Box 414, Middletown, NJ 07748, online journal at: http://www.wordriot.org
Montemayor Press, PO Box 526, Millburn, NJ 07041, 973-761-1341, Fax 973-378-9749, mail@montemayorpress.com, montemayorpress.com
Benchmark Publications Inc., Montclair, NJ 07042, 203-966-6653, Fax 973-718-4606 [secure], www.benchpress.com, BPIsmallpress@benchpress.com
The Middle Atlantic Press, 10 Twosome Drive, Box 600, Moorestown, NJ 08057, 856-235-4444, orders 800-257-8481, fax 800-225-3840
YCD Press, 45 Park Place South # 240, Morristown, NJ 07960, 917-690-0029
RARITAN: A Quarterly Review, 31 Mine Street, New Brunswick, NJ 08903, 732-932-7887, Fax 732-932-7855, rqr@rci.rutgers.edu
SIGNS, Rutgers University, Voorhees Chapel, Room 8, 5 Chapel Drive, New Brunswick, NJ 08901, 732-932-2841 (main #), 732-932-5732 (fax), http://www.journals.uchicago.edu/Signs/home.html
THE (LIBERTARIAN) CONNECTION, 10 Hill Street #22-L, Newark, NJ 07102, 973-242-5999
Phoenix Illusion, c/o Shay R. Phoenix, 208 South Sixth St., Newark, NJ 07103, (862) 902-6457
NATURALLY, PO Box 317, Newfoundland, NJ 07435, 973-697-3552
THE PATERSON LITERARY REVIEW, Passaic County Community College, One College Boulevard, Paterson, NJ 07505-1179, 973-684-6555
The Poetry Center, Passaic County Community College, One College Boulevard, Paterson, NJ 07505-1179, 973-684-6555
Hug The Earth Publications, 42 Greenwood Avenue, Pequannock, NJ 07440
HUG THE EARTH, A Journal of Land and Life, 42 Greenwood Avenue, Pequannock, NJ 07440
SPACE AND TIME, 1308 Centennial Avenue, Suite 101, Piscataway, NJ 08854, www.spaceandtimemagazine.com
BIG HAMMER, PO Box 527, Point Pleasant, NJ 08742-0527, iniquitypress@hotmail.com (no email submissions)
Iniquity Press/Vendetta Books, PO Box 527, Point Pleasant, NJ 08742-0527, 732 664 3901 iniquitypress@hotmail.com
The Press at Foggy Bottom, 35 Linden Lane, 2nd Floor, Princeton, NJ 08540, 609-921-1782
QRL POETRY SERIES, Princeton University, 185 Nassau Street, Princeton, NJ 08540, 609-258-4703
JOURNAL OF NEW JERSEY POETS, County College of Morris, 214 Center Grove Road, Randolph, NJ 07869-2086, 973-328-5471, szulauf@ccm.edu
Crandall, Dostie & Douglass Books, Inc., 245 West 4th Avenue, Roselle, NJ 07203-1135, Phone: 908.241.5439, Fax: 908.245.4972, Email: Publisher@CDDbooks.com, www.CDDbooks.com
Quarterly Review of Literature Press, 900 Hollingshead Spring Road, Apt J-300, Skillman, NJ 08558-2075, 609-921-6976, Fax 609-258-2230, qrl@princeton.edu
PASSAIC REVIEW, c/o Ah! Sunflower Theater, 410-1/2 Morris Avenue, Spring Lake, NJ 07762-1320
OTTN Publishing, 16 Risler Street, Stockton, NJ 08559, 609-397-4005, 609-397-4007 (fax), inquiries@ottnpublishing.com, www.ottnpublishing.com
From Here Press, PO Box 1402, Summit, NJ 07902-1402
XTRAS, PO Box 1402, Summit, NJ 07902-1402
THE KELSEY REVIEW, Mercer County Community College, PO Box B, Trenton, NJ 08690
THE CLASSICAL OUTLOOK, Department of Classics and General Humanities, Dickson Hall, Montclair State University, Upper Montclair, NJ 07043
Saturday Press, PO Box 43534, Upper Montclair, NJ 07043, 973-239-0436, fax: 973-239-0427
Polygonal Publishing House, PO Box 357, Washington, NJ 07882, 908-689-3894
Down The Shore Publishing, PO Box 100, West Creek, NJ 08092, 609-978-1233; fax 609-597-0422
Maverick Duck Press, Willingboro, NJ 08046, www.maverickduckpress.com, email: maverickduckpress@yahoo.com
Riverwinds Publishing, 109 Cromwell Court, Woodbury, NJ 08096, 856-845-1250

NEW MEXICO

BLUE MESA REVIEW, University of New Mexico, Creative Writing Program, MSC03-2170, Humanities 274, Albuquerque, NM 87131-0001, 505-277-6347
Central Avenue Press, PO Box 2132-A, #144, Albuquerque, NM 87106, (505) 323-9953 www.centralavepress.com
Health Press NA Inc., PO Box 37470, Albuquerque, NM 87176-7470, goodbooks@healthpress.com
Intuitive Moon Media, 13170-B Central SE #191, Albuquerque, NM 87123, webmaster@intuitivemoon.com, 505-349-5993, 505-280-9667
La Alameda Press, 9636 Guadalupe Trail NW, Albuquerque, NM 87114, 505-897-0285, www.laalamedapress.com
ST. VITUS PRESS & POETRY REVIEW, 7408 Estes Park Avenue NW, Albuquerque, NM 87114, www.saintvituspress.com
Southwest Research and Information Center, PO Box 4524, Albuquerque, NM 87196-4524, 505-262-1862; Fax 505-262-1864; Info@sric.org; www.sric.org
STARNOTES, 13170-B Central SE #191, Albuquerque, NM 87123, webmaster@intuitivemoon.com, 505-349-5993, 505-280-9667
VOICES FROM THE EARTH, PO Box 4524, Albuquerque, NM 87196, 505-262-1862, Fax 505-262-1864
West End Press, PO Box 27334, Albuquerque, NM 87125
Zerx Press, 725 Van Buren Place SE, Albuquerque, NM 87108, zerxpress@aol.com, www.zerxrecords.com
The Heather Foundation, 713 W. Spruce #48, Deming, NM 88030, 915-261-0502, sm@look.net
Tres Chicas Books, PO Box 417, El Rito, NM 87530
OUTER-ART, University of New Mexico, 200 College Road, Gallup, NM 87301, smarand@unm.edu, www.gallup.unm.edu/~smarandache/a/outer-art.htm
PARADOXISM, 200 College Road, University of New Mexico, Gallup, NM 87301, 505-863-7647, fax 505-863-7532,

smarand@unm.edu, www.gallup.unm.edu/~smarandache/a/paradoxism.htm

BEATLICK NEWS, 1300 El Paseo Road, Suite G #308, Las Cruces, NM 88001, 505-496-8729

BEATLICK NEWS POETRY & ARTS NEWSLETTER, 1300 El Paseo Road, Suite G #308, Las Cruces, NM 88001-2222, 575-621-9694

PUERTO DEL SOL, New Mexico State University, MSC 3E, Box 30001, Las Cruces, NM 88003, contact@puertodelsol.org, www.puertodelsol.org

Two Eagles Press International, 1029 Hickory Drive, Las Cruces, NM 88005, 575-523-7911, Fax 575-523-1953, Cell 575-644-5436, twoeaglespress@comcast.net, twoeaglespress.com

Xenos Books, Box 16433, Las Cruces, NM 88004, 505-523-8798, E-mail info@xenosbooks.com, www.xenosbooks.com

LPD Press, 925 Salamanca NW, Los Ranchos de Albuquerque, NM 87107-5647, 505-344-9382, Fax 505-345-5129, info@nmsantos.com

TRADICION REVISTA, 925 Salamanca NW, Los Ranchos de Albuquerque, NM 87107-5647, 505-344-9382, Fax 505-345-5129, info@nmsantos.com

Noemi Press, Noemi Press, P.O. Box 1330, Mesilla Park, NM 88047

SMARANDACHE NOTIONS JOURNAL, Box 141, Rehoboth, NM 87322, m_l_perez@yahoo.com, http://www.gallup.unm.edu/~smarandache/

Staring Media, Box 141, Rehoboth, NM 87322, m_l_perez@yahoo.com, http://fs.gallup.unm.edu//eBooks-otherformats.htm and http://fs.gallup.unm.edu//eBooksLiterature.htm

Cleanan Press, Inc., 106 North Washington Avenue, Roswell, NM 88201, 575-420-4064

American Canadian Publishers, Inc., PO Box 4595, Santa Fe, NM 87502-4595, 505-983-8484, Fax 505-983-8484

AWAREing Press, 551 W. Cordova Rd., #369, Santa Fe, NM 87505

Azro Press, PMB 342, 1704 Llano Street B, Santa Fe, NM 87505, gae@nets.com, www.azropress.com

Burning Books, PO Box 2638, Santa Fe, NM 87504, Fax 505-820-6216, brnbx@nets.com, burningbooks.org

COALITION FOR PRISONERS' RIGHTS NEWSLETTER, PO Box 1911, Santa Fe, NM 87504, 505-982-9520

Russell Dean and Company, 141 Tesuque Village Road #12, Santa Fe, NM 87506-0023, 505-988-7153 phone and fax. Email: topdogrdc@peoplepc.com, www.RDandCo.com

New Atlantean Press, PO Box 9638, Santa Fe, NM 87504-9638, 505-983-1856 phone/Fax, think@thinktwice.com, www.thinktwice.com

NEW MEXICO POETRY REVIEW, 44 Via Punto Nuevo, Santa Fe, NM 87508, E-mail: nmpr@live.com Web site: www.newmexicopoetryreview.com

Rising Tide Press New Mexico, PO Box 6136, Santa Fe, NM 87502-6136, 505-983-8484, Fax 505-983-8484

Santa Fe Writers Project, 369 Montezuma Ave, #350, Santa Fe, NM 87501, info@sfwp.com, www.sfwp.com

School for Advanced Research Press, PO Box 2188, Santa Fe, NM 87504-2188, 505-954-7206, Fax 505-954-7241, bkorders@sarsf.org, baca@sarsf.org, www.sarpress.sarweb.org

Sherman Asher Publishing, P.O. Box 31725, Santa Fe, NM 87501-0172, 505-988-7214, Fax 505-988-7214, westernedge@santa-fe.net, www.shermanasher.com

Sunstone Press, PO Box 2321, Santa Fe, NM 87504-2321, 505-988-4418, fax 505-988-1025, jsmith@sunstonepress.com

Synergetic Press, 1 Bluebird Court, Santa Fe, NM 87508-1531, Tel. 505-424-0237 Fax. 505 424 3336 e-mail: tango@synergeticpress.com website: www.synergeticpress.com

Turtle Press, division of S.K. Productions Inc., PO Box 34010, Santa Fe, NM 87594-4010, 860-721-1198

WOOD COIN: An Online Magazine of Literature & Liberal Arts, Wood Coin Press, 551 W. Cordova Rd., #369, Santa Fe, NM 87505, http://www.woodcoin.net

Zon International Publishing Co., PO Box 6459, Santa Fe, NM 87502, 505-995-0102, Email zon@nets.com, Web, zonbooks.com

Alamo Square Press, 103 FR 321, Tajique, NM 87016, 505-384-9766, alamosquare@earthlink.net

Open Horizons Publishing Company, PO Box 2887, Taos, NM 87571-2887, 505-751-3398, Fax 505-751-3100; Email: johnkremer@bookmarket.com; Web: http://www.bookmarket.com

Paradigm Publications, 202 Bendix Drive, Taos, NM 87571, 575 758 7758, Fax 575 758 7768, info@paradigm-pubs.com, www.paradigm-pubs.com

NEW YORK

A & U AMERICA'S AIDS MAGAZINE, 25 Monroe Street, Suite 205, Albany, NY 12210-2729, 518-426-9010, Fax 518-436-5354, mailbox@aumag.org

FENCE, New Library 320, University at Albany, Albany, NY 12222, www.fenceportal.org

THE LITTLE MAGAZINE, Department of English, State Univ. of New York, University of Albany, Albany, NY 12222, website www.albany.edu/~litmag.

Mount Ida Press, 152 Washington Avenue, Albany, NY 12210-2203, Tel: 518-426-5935, Fax: 518-426-4116

RALPH'S REVIEW, 129-A Wellington Avenue, Albany, NY 12203-2637

State University of New York Press, 194 Washington Avenue, Suite 305, Albany, NY 12210-2384, main editorial 518-472-5000, orders 877-204-6073, website www.sunypress.edu

Whitston Publishing Co., PO Box 38263, Albany, NY 12203-8263, 518-869-9110, fax: 518-452-2154

BYLINE, PO Box 111, Albion, NY 14411-0111, 585-355-8172

SKEPTICAL INQUIRER, PO Box 703, Amherst, NY 14226, 716-636-1425, info@csicop.org

AXES & ALLEYS, 25-26 44th Street #A1, Astoria, NY 11103, 718-204-0313, jeremy@danielbester.com

WOMEN IN THE ARTS BULLETIN/NEWSLETTER, 32-35 30th Street #D24, Astoria, NY 11106, 718-545-9337

Women In The Arts Foundation, Inc., 32-35 30th Street #D24, Astoria, NY 11106

Aspicomm Media, PO Box 1212, Baldwin, NY 11510, Phone (516) 642-5976, Fax (516) 489-1199, www.aspicomm.com

Zirlinson Publishing, 97 Charlton Road, Ballston Lake, NY 12019, Ballston Lake, NY 12019, 518-631-9119, tomlinson.shawn@gmail.com

Barrytown/Station Hill Press, 124 Station Hill Road, Barrytown, NY 12507, 845-340-4300, fax: 845-339-0780, web: www.stationhill.org, email: publisher@stationhill.org

Montfort Publications, 26 South Saxon Avenue, Bay Shore, NY 11706, 516-665-0726, FAX 516-665-4349

QUEEN OF ALL HEARTS, 26 South Saxon Avenue, Bay Shore, NY 11706, info@montfortmissionaries.com, www.montfortmissionaries.com

BEGINNINGS - A Magazine for the Novice Writer, PO Box 214-R, Bayport, NY 11705-0214, 631-472-1143, jenineb@optonline.net, www.scbeginnings.com

Phrygian Press, 58-09 205th Street, Bayside, NY 11364, PhrygianZYX @ AOL.COM

ZYX, 58-09 205th Street, Bayside, NY 11364-1712, PhrygianZYX @ AOL.COM, 718-428-9368

THE LEDGE POETRY & FICTION MAGAZINE, 40 Maple Avenue, Bellport, NY 11713-2011, www.theledgemagazine.com
HARPUR PALATE, English Dept., PO Box 6000, Binghamton University, Binghamton, NY 13902-6000, http://harpurpalate.binghamton.edu
LOST CARCOSA, 152 Stevers Mill Road, Broadalbin, NY 12025, 5i8-883-3055, harvor@lycos.com
Bronx River Press, 3915 Dyre Ave. PMB #98, Bronx, NY 10466, info@bronxriverpress.com, http://www.bronxriverpress.com
Fordham University Press, 2546 Belmont Avenue, University Box L, Bronx, NY 10458, 718-817-4781
Inner City Press, P.O. Box 580188, Mount Carmel Station, Bronx, NY 10458, Web: InnerCityPress.org Tel: 718-716-3540
INNER CITY PRESS, P.O. Box 580188, Mount Carmel Station, Bronx, NY 10458, Web: InnerCityPress.org Tel: 718-716-3540
MOSAIC LITERARY MAGAZINE, 314 West 231 St #470, Bronx, NY 10463, 718.530.9132
ABRAMELIN: a Journal of Poetry and Magick, Box 337, Brookhaven, NY 11719, 631 803-2211
ADVANCES IN THANATOLOGY, 391 Atlantic Ave., Brooklyn, NY 11217-1708, 718-858-3026, 718-852-1846, no 800, rhalporn@pipeline.com, thanatology.org
Archipelago Books, 232 3rd St., #A111, Brooklyn, NY 11215
AUFGABE, PO Box 25526, Brooklyn, NY 11202-5526
Bad Noise Productions, 25 Kingsland Ave. #3L, Brooklyn, NY 11211-1530, www.badnoiseproductions.com, saburo@badnoiseproductions.com
Bird Brain Press, 37 Greenpoint Avenue, 4th Floor, Brooklyn, NY 11222
BOMB MAGAZINE, 80 Hanson Place #703, Brooklyn, NY 11217-1505, 718-636-9100, email:generalinquiries@bombsite.com
CABINET, 181 Wyckoff Street, Brooklyn, NY 11217
Center for Thanatology Research & Education, Inc., 391 Atlantic Ave., Brooklyn, NY 11217-1708, 718-858-3026, 718-852-1846, no 800, rhalporn@pipeline.com, thanatology.org
THE CRIER, 220 DeKalb Ave., Brooklyn, NY 11205
DOWNTOWN BROOKLYN: A Journal of Writing, English Department; Long Island Univ., Brooklyn Campus, 1 University Plaza, Brooklyn, NY 11201
GRAMMAR CRISIS, 248 McKibbin St. #2T, Brooklyn, NY 11206-3577, www.badnoiseproductions.com, saburo@badnoiseproductions.com
Gryphon Books, PO Box 209, Brooklyn, NY 11228-0209
HANGING LOOSE, 231 Wyckoff Street, Brooklyn, NY 11217, www.hangingloosepress.com
Hanging Loose Press, 231 Wyckoff Street, Brooklyn, NY 11217, www.hangingloosepress.com
HARDBOILED, PO Box 209, Brooklyn, NY 11228
IAMBS & TROCHEES, 6801 19th Avenue #5H, Brooklyn, NY 11204, 718-232-9268
INSURANCE, 132 N. 1st Street #11, Brooklyn, NY 11211, ctokar@hotmail.com
Kehot Publication Society, 291 Kingston Ave., Brooklyn, NY 11213, 718 778 0226
Litmus Press, PO Box 25526, Brooklyn, NY 11202-5526
Lunar Offensive Publications, 1910 Foster Avenue, Brooklyn, NY 11230-1902
LUNGFULL! MAGAZINE, 316 23rd Street, Brooklyn, NY 11215-6409, lungfull@rcn.net
Malafemmina Press, 4211 Fort Hamilton Parkway, Brooklyn, NY 11219
Merkos Publications, 291 Kingston Ave., Brooklyn, NY 11213, 718-778-0226, fax: 718-778-4148, email: orders@kehotonline.com
PAPERBACK PARADE, PO Box 209, Brooklyn, NY 11228-0209
POETS ON THE LINE, PO Box 20292, Brooklyn, NY 11202-0292, 718-596-0137
THE RAGING FACE: Goofball Prose, 448 14th Street, Brooklyn, NY 11215, 718 938 0013
S4N Books, 6904 Colonial Road, #28, Brooklyn, NY 11220
THE SAINT ANN'S REVIEW, 129 Pierrepont Street, Brooklyn, NY 11201, ph: 718-522-1660 x317, fax:718-522-2599.
South End Press, Medgar Evers College, 1650 Bedford Ave, Brooklyn, NY 11225, email: southend@southendpress.org
Ugly Duckling Presse, The Old American Can Factory, 232 Third Street, #E002 (corner Third Avenue), Brooklyn, NY 11215, Tel: 718-852-5529
Upstart Crow Literary, P.O. Box 25404, Brooklyn, NY 11202, info@upstartcrowliterary.com
Blowtorch Press, 55 Lark Street, Buffalo, NY 14211, webmaster@blowtorchpress.com
BUCKLE &, PO Box 1653, Buffalo, NY 14205
BUFFALO SPREE, 6215 Sheridan Drive, Buffalo, NY 14221-4837, 716-634-0820, fax 716-810-0075
EARTH'S DAUGHTERS: Feminist Arts Periodical, PO Box 41, Central Park Station, Buffalo, NY 14215-0041, 716-627-9825, http://bfn.org/~edaught
Starcherone Books, PO Box 303, Buffalo, NY 14201-0303, www.starcherone.com
sunnyoutside, PO Box 911, Buffalo, NY 14207, www.sunnyoutside.com
White Pine Press, PO Box 236, Buffalo, NY 14201-0236, 716-627-4665 phone/Fax, wpine@whitepine.org, www.whitepine.org
Brookview Press, 901 Western Road, Castleton-on-Hudson, NY 12033, 518-732-7093 phone/Fax, info@brookviewpress.com, www.brookviewpress.com
Passport Press, PO Box 2543, Champlain, NY 12919-2543, 514-937-3868, Fax 514-931-0871, e-mail travelbook@bigfoot.com
Break Free Publishing, PO Box 975, Routing 101, Chappaqua, NY 10514-0975, 914-773-4307, Jill.Schmidt@BreakFreePub.com, www.BreakFreePublishing.com
Toadlily Press, P O. Box 2, Chappaqua, NY 10514, mgoodman@toadlilypress.com, www.toadlilypress.com
Highest Hurdle Press, 660 Cleveland Drive, Suite 3, Cheektowaga, NY 14225
Cherry Valley Editions, PO Box 303, Cherry Valley, NY 13320, cveds@cherryvalley.com
Chicken Soup Press, Inc., PO Box 164, Circleville, NY 10919-0164, 845-692-6320, Fax 845-692-7574, poet@hvc.rr.com
Nightboat Books, 7 Fishkill Ave., Cold Spring, NY 10516-2303, info@nightboat.org, www.nightboat.org
Padishah Press, P.O.Box 528, Cold Spring Harbor, NY 11724, www.PadishahPress.com
Berry Hill Press, 2349 State Route 12-B, Deansboro, NY 13328, 315-821-6188 phone/fax; dls@berryhillbookshop.com
Birch Brook Press, PO Box 81, Delhi, NY 13753, phone/fax orders & sales inquiries: 607-746-7453, email: birchbrook@copper.net, website: www.birchbrookpress.info
Persephone Press, PO Box 81, Delhi, NY 13753
Marsh Hawk Press, PO Box 206, East Rockaway, NY 11518-0206, mheditor@marshhawkpress.org, www.marshhawkpress.org
BITTER OLEANDER, 4983 Tall Oaks Drive, Fayetteville, NY 13066-9776, Fax 315-637-5056, info@bitteroleander.com, www.bitteroleander.com
MOBIUS, THE POETRY MAGAZINE, P.O. Box 671058, Flushing, NY 11367-1058, mobiusmag@earthlink.net, www.mobiuspoetry.com

Smith-Johnson Publisher, 175-14 73rd Avenue, Flushing, NY 11366-1502, 718-969-0665 irwingray@hotmail.com

Howln Moon Press, 7222 State Highway 357, Franklin, NY 13775-3100, 607-829-2187 (office), 888-349-9438 (ordering), email: bmueller@hmpress.com

Athanata Arts, Ltd., P.O. Box 321, Garden City, NY 11530-0321

Square One Publishers, Inc., 115 Herricks Road, Garden City Park, NY 11040, 516-535-2010, Fax 516-535-2014, sq1info@aol.com, www.squareonepublishers.com

SENECA REVIEW, Hobart & William Smith Colleges, Geneva, NY 14456, 315-781-3392, Fax 315-781-3348, senecareview@hws.edu

CONFRONTATION, English Department, C.W. Post of Long Island Univ., Greenvale, NY 11548, 516-299-2720

Ultramarine Publishing Co., Inc., PO Box 303, Hastings-on-Hudson, NY 10706, 914-478-1339

Black Dome Press Corp., 1011 Route 296, Hensonville, NY 12439, 518-734-6357, Fax 518-734-5802

THE SMALL BUSINESS ADVISOR, 11 Franklin Avenue, Hewlett, NY 11557-2034, 516-374-1387, Fax 516-374-1175, smalbusadv@aol.com, www.smallbusinessadvice.com

HOME PLANET NEWS, PO Box 455, High Falls, NY 12440, 845-687-4084, homeplanetnews@yahoo.com

Home Planet Publications, PO Box 455, High Falls, NY 12440, 845-687-4084, homeplanetnews@yahoo.com

The Groundwater Press, PO Box 704, Hudson, NY 12534, 516-767-8503

River Press, 499 Islip Avenue, Islip, NY 11751-1826, 631-277-8618, Fax 631-277-8660, rivpress@aol.com

Blue Hull Press, 225 Warren Place, Ithaca, NY 14850, 607 351 6615

EPOCH MAGAZINE, 251 Goldwin Smith Hall, Cornell University, Ithaca, NY 14853-3201, 607-255-3385, Fax 607-255-6661

McBooks Press, Inc., I. D. Booth Bldg, 520 North Meadow Street #2, Ithaca, NY 14850-3229, 607-272-2114, FAX 607-273-6068, mcbooks@mcbooks.com, www.mcbookspress.com

OUR STORIES LITERARY JOURNAL, 433 N Aurora Street, Apt 1S, Ithaca, NY 14850, Web site: www.ourstories.us Submission Guidelines: www.ourstories.us/submissions/

What The Heck Press, PO Box 149, Ithaca, NY 14851-0149, 607-275-0806, Fax 607-275-0702

The Spirit That Moves Us Press, Inc., PO Box 720820-DB, Jackson Heights, Queens, NY 11372-0820, 718-426-8788, msklar@mindspring.com

Fantail, PO Box 145, Johnson City, NY 13790-0145, http://www.fantail.com, liz@fantail.com

THE TEACHER'S VOICE: A Literary Magazine for Poets and Writers in Education, P.O. Box 150384, Kew Gardens, NY 11415, Email: editor@the-teachers-voice.org

McPherson & Company Publishers, PO Box 1126, 148 Smith Avenue, Kingston, NY 12402, 845-331-5807, toll free order #800-613-8219

ADIRONDAC, 814 Goggins Road, Lake George, NY 12845-4117, 518-668-4447, e-mail ADKinfo@adk.org

Adirondack Mountain Club, Inc., 814 Goggins Road, Lake George, NY 12845-4117, 518-668-4447, FAX 518-668-3746, e-mail pubs@adk.org

Serpent & Eagle Press, 10 Main Street, Laurens, NY 13796, 607-432-2990

The Edwin Mellen Press, PO Box 450, Lewiston, NY 14092, 716-754-2266

The Edwin Mellen Press, PO Box 450, 415 Ridge Street, Lewiston, NY 14092-0450, 716-754-2266, Fax 716-754-4056, editor@mellenpress.com, www.mellenpress.com

Starlight Press, Box 3102, Long Island City, NY 11103

Cross-Cultural Communications, 239 Wynsum Ave., Merrick, NY 11566-4725, Tel: 516-868-5635 Fax: 516-379-1901 E: cccpoetry@aol.com, www.cross-culturalcommunications.com

Lintel, 24 Blake Lane, Middletown, NY 10940, 845-342-5224

BOOK/MARK QUARTERLY REVIEW, PO Box 516, Miller Place, NY 11764-0516, 631-331-4118, cyberpoet@msn.com, www.writernetwork.com

Demarche Publishing LLC, P.O. Box 36, Mohegan Lake, NY 10547, www.demarchepublishing.com, info@demarchepublishing.com

ICONOCLAST, 1675 Amazon Road, Mohegan Lake, NY 10547-1804

ART TIMES, PO Box 730, Mount Marion, NY 12456-0730, 845-246-6944, info@arttimesjournal.com, www.arttimesjournal.com

Total Package Publications, LLC, P.O. Box 3237, Mount Vernon, NY 10553, website: www.totalpackagepublications.com, email: contacttpp@totalpackagepublications.com

THE SHAKESPEARE NEWSLETTER, English Department, Iona College, New Rochelle, NY 10801

A Midsummer Night's Press, 16 West 36th Street, 2nd Floor, New York, NY 10018, www.amidsummernightspress.com

THE ADIRONDACK REVIEW, New York, NY 10003, editors@theadirondackreview.com

Affluent Publishing Corp., 1040 Ave. of the Americas, 24th floor, New York, NY 10018, Phone: (888) 488-9517, Fax: (888) 861-3175, Email: info@Affluent-Publishing.com, Website: http://wwww.Affluent-Publishing.com

Akashic Books, PO Box 1456, New York, NY 10009, 212-433-1875, 212-414-3199, Akashic7@aol.com, www.akashic-books.com

ALIMENTUM - The Literature of Food, P. O. Box 776, New York, NY 10163, info@alimentumjournal.com www.alimentumjournal.com

Allworth Press, 10 East 23rd Street, Suite 510, New York, NY 10010, 212-777-8395, Fax 212-777-8261, Pub@allworth.com, www.allworth.com

Amadeus Press, 19 West 21st Street, Suite 201, New York, NY 10010, 212-575-9265, fax 212-575-9270, www.amadeuspress.com

AMERICA, 106 West 56th Street, New York, NY 10019, 212-581-4640

American Poet, The Academy of American Poets, 584 Broadway, Suite 604, New York, NY 10012, 212-274-0343, fax 212-274-9427, www.poets.org

ANDERBO.COM, 270 Lafayette St., Suite 1412, New York, NY 10012, editors@anderbo.com

ARARAT, 55 E 59th Street, New York, NY 10022-1112

The Asian American Writers' Workshop, 110-112 West 27th Street, Sixth Floor, New York, NY 10001, p) 212.494.0061, (f) 212.494.0062

THE ASIAN PACIFIC AMERICAN JOURNAL, 16 West 32nd Street, Suite 10A, New York, NY 10001-3814, 212-494-0061

The Avery Anthology, 3657 Broadway, Apt. 1E, New York, NY 10031

BARROW STREET, PO Box 1831, Murray Hill Stn., New York, NY 10156, 212-937-1970, www.barrowstreet.org

Barrow Street Press, PO Box 1831, Murray Hill Stn., New York, NY 10156, 212-937-1970, info@barrowstreet.org, www.barrowstreet.org

Bellevue Literary Press, Dept. of Medicine, NYU School of Medicine, 550 First Avenue OBV 612, New York, NY 10016, 212-263-7802, FAX:212-263-7803, egoldman@BLReview.org

BELLEVUE LITERARY REVIEW, NYU School of Medicine, Dept. of Medicine, 550 First Avenue, OBV-A612, New York, NY 10016, www.BLReview.org, info@BLReview.org

BIGNEWS MAGAZINE, 484 West 43rd St., Apt. 24D, New York, NY 10036-6341, 212-679-4535, Fax 212-679-4573, bignewsmag@aol.com, www.mainchance.org

Black Dress Press, P.O. Box 1067, New York, NY 10014, www.blackdresspress.com

Bowery Poetry Books, 310 Bowery, New York, NY 10012, www.bowerypoetry.com, 212-334-6414

Box Turtle Press, 184 Franklin Street, New York, NY 10013

Calliope Press, PO Box 2408, New York, NY 10108-2408, 212-564-5068

Cantarabooks LLC, New York, NY 10003, 917.674.7560, editor@cantarabooks.com, www.cantarabooks.com

Channel Lake, Inc., P.O. Box 1771, New York, NY 10156, Phone #347.329.5576, e-mail:info@channellake.com

THE CHARIOTEER, 337 West 36 Street, New York, NY 10018, 212-279-9586

Chelsea Editions, Box 125 Cooper Station, New York, NY 10276-0125, 212-989-3083, fax:212-989-3083, e:chelseaeditions@aol.com, web:www.chelseaeditionsbooks.org

Cheshire House Books, Attn: Joanna Rees, PO Box 2484, New York, NY 10021, 212-861-5404 phone/Fax, publisher@samthecat.com/www.samthecat.com

CINEASTE MAGAZINE, 243 Fifth Ave., #706, New York, NY 10016-8703, 212-366-5720

COLUMBIA: A Journal of Literature & Art, 415 Dodge Hall, Columbia University, 2960 Broadway, New York, NY 10027, www.columbiajournal.org (online submissions only!)

CONCRETE JUNGLE JOURNAL, 163 Third Avenue #130, New York, NY 10003, 718-465-8573 URL: www.concretejunglepress.com

Concrete Jungle Press, 163 Third Avenue #130, New York, NY 10003, Tel: 718-465-8573, Fax: 718-468-3007, URL: www.concretejunglepress.com

CONJUNCTIONS, 21 East 10th Street #3E, New York, NY 10003-5924, Phone: 845-758-1539, fax: 845-758-2660, e-mail: conjunctions@bard.edu, URL: www.conjunctions.com

THE CORTLAND REVIEW, 35 Grove Street, 5D, New York, NY 10014, http://www.cortlandreview.com, tcr@cortlandreview.com

Creative Roots, Inc., 140 Riverside Drive, New York, NY 10024, 212-799-2294

CROSS CURRENTS, 475 Riverside Drive, Suite 1945, New York, NY 10115, 212-870-2544, Fax: 212-870-2539

THE DIRTY GOAT, 277 Broadway, Suite 210, New York, NY 10007, Phone: 212-905-2365, FAX: 212-905-2369, www.hostpublications.com, www.thedirtygoat.com, jbratcher@hostpublications.com

DLite Press, P.O. Box 1644, New York, NY 10150, 718-379-0612

THE DRAMATIST, The Dramatists Guild of America Inc., 1501 Broadway Suite 701, New York, NY 10036

Dramatists Play Service, 440 Park Ave. S, New York, NY 10016, (212) 683-8960[ph], 212) 213-1539[f]

Edgewise Press, 24 Fifth Avenue #224, New York, NY 10011-8815, 212-982-4818, Fax 212-982-1364

Encounter Books, 900 Broadway, Ste.400, New York, NY 10003-1239, 415-538-1460, Fax 415-538-1461, read@encounterbooks.com, www.encounterbooks.com

EPIPHANY, A Literary Journal, 71 Bedford Street, New York, NY 10014, 212-633-7987

Falls Media, 1 Astor Place, PH K, New York, NY 10003, 917-667-2269, www.wouldyourather.com

FEILE-FESTA, Mediterranaean Celtic Cultural Association, PO Box 436, Prince Street Station, New York, NY 10012

The Feminist Press at the City University of New York, The Graduate Center, 365 Fifth Avenue, Suite 5406, New York, NY 10016, 212-817-7915, Fax 212-817-1593, www.feministpress.org

FICTION, c/o Dept. of English, City College, 138th Street & Convent Ave., New York, NY 10031, 212-650-6319

Fotofolio, Inc., 561 Broadway, 2nd Floor, New York, NY 10012-3918, 212-226-0923

Four Way Books, PO Box 535, Village Station, New York, NY 10014, www.fourwaybooks.com editors@fourwaybooks.com

Fugue State Press, PO Box 80, Cooper Station, New York, NY 10276, 212-673-7922

A GATHERING OF THE TRIBES, PO Box 20693, Tompkins Square, New York, NY 10009, 212-674-3778, Fax 212-674-5576, info@tribes.org, www.tribes.org

GAYELLOW PAGES, Box 533 Village Station, New York, NY 10014-0533, 646-213-0263 http://gayellowpages.com, gypages@gmail.com

GOODIE, 197 7th Avenue #4C, New York, NY 10011, www.goodie.org, romy@goodie.org, foxy@goodie.org

Great Marsh Press, P.O. Box 2144, Lenox Hill Station, New York, NY 10021

Guarionex Press Ltd., 201 West 77th Street, New York, NY 10024, 212-724-5259

GUERNICA: A Magazine of Art & Politics, 403 East 69th Street #3D, New York, NY 10021

HEARING HEALTH, 641 Lexington Ave. 15th Floor, New York, NY 10022, 866-454-3924, TTY 888-435-6104

Emma Howard Books, Attn: Armando H. Luna, PO Box 385, Planetarium Stn., New York, NY 10024-0385, 212-996-2590 phone/Fax, emmahowardbooks@verizon.net, www.eelgrassgirls.com

THE HUDSON REVIEW, 684 Park Avenue, New York, NY 10021, 212-650-0020, Fax 212-774-1911

Ikon Inc., 151 First Ave. #46, New York, NY 10003

THE INDEPENDENT SHAVIAN, The Bernard Shaw Society, PO Box 1159 Madison Square Stn., New York, NY 10159-1159, 212-982-9885

International Publishers Co. Inc., 235 West 23 Street FL8, New York, NY 10011, 212-366-9816, Fax 212-366-9820

INTERNATIONAL WOMEN'S WRITING GUILD, Box 810, Gracie Station, New York, NY 10028, 212-737-7536, Fax 212-737-9469, iwwg@iwwg.org, www.iwwg.org

Italica Press, Inc., 595 Main Street, #605, New York, NY 10044, 212-935-4230; fax 212-838-7812; inquiries@italicapress.com

JEWISH CURRENTS, 45 E 33 Street 4th floor, New York, NY 10016, 212-889-2523, Fax 212-532-7518

JEWISH WOMEN'S LITERARY ANNUAL, National Council of Jewish Women NY Section, 820 Second Ave., New York, NY 10017-4504, 212-687-5030 ext.33/fax212-687-5032

Jonkro Books, 244 Madison Ave., Suite 4200, New York, NY 10016, Tel: 866-588-0504, Fax: 866-219-4331, info@jonkrobooks.com, www.jonkrobooks.com

THE JOURNAL OF PSYCHOHISTORY, 140 Riverside Drive, New York, NY 10024, 212-799-2294

JOURNAL OF THE HELLENIC DIASPORA, 337 West 36th Street, New York, NY 10018, 212-279-9586

Junction Press, PO Box F, New York, NY 10034-0246, 212-942-1985

LALITAMBA: An Uplifting Literary Experience, P.O. Box 131, Planetarium Station, New York, NY 10024

LAPHAM'S QUARTERLY, 33 Irving Place, Eighth Floor, New York, NY 10003

Libellum, 211 West 19th Street, #5, New York, NY 10011-4001, libellumbooks@gmail.com, 212-463-7598

LILIES AND CANNONBALLS REVIEW, P.O. Box 702, Bowling Green Station, New York, NY 10274-0702, info@liliesandcannonballs.com, www.liliesandcannonballs.com

LILITH, 250 West 57th, #2432, New York, NY 10107, 212-757-0818

Limelight Editions, 19 West 21st Street, Suite 201, New York, NY 10010, 212-575-9265, fax 212-575-9270, info@limelighteditions.com, www.limelighteditions.com
LIT, Writing Program, Room 514, 66 West 12th Street, New York, NY 10011
LIVE MAG!, 632 East 14th Street, #18, New York, NY 10009, 212-673-1152
THE MANHATTAN REVIEW, c/o Philip Fried, 440 Riverside Drive, #38, New York, NY 10027, 212-932-1854, phfried@earthlink.net
MindGlow Media, Suite 175, 75 East Fourth Street, New York, NY 10003
Modern Metrics Press, 328 East 6th Street #13, New York, NY 10003, www.modern-metrics.com
Mondial, 203 West 107th street, #6C, New York, NY 10025, www.mondialbooks.com, Fax: 208-361-2863, Phone: 212-851-3252
MUDFISH, 184 Franklin Street, Ground Floor, New York, NY 10013, 212-219-9278, www.mudfish.org, mudfish-mag@aol.com
MYSTERY SCENE MAGAZINE, 331 W. 57th Street, Suite 148, New York, NY 10019-3101, katestine@mysteryscene-mag.com
NAMBLA BULLETIN, PO Box 174, Midtown Station, New York, NY 10018, 212-631-1194, arnoldschoen@yahoo.com
New Concept Press, 425 West 57th Street Suite 2J, New York, NY 10019, 212-265-6284, Fax: 212-265-6659
THE NEW YORK QUARTERLY, PO Box 2015, Old Chelsea Station, New York, NY 10113, info@nyquarterly.org, www.nyquarterly.org
NEW YORK TYRANT, 676A Ninth Avenue 153, New York, NY 10036
NIGHTJAR REVIEW, P.O. Box 583, New York, NY 10002
NOON, 1324 Lexington Avenue Front 4, New York, NY 10128-1145, noonannual@yahoo.com
NYQ Books, PO Box 2015, Old Chelsea Station, New York, NY 10113, www.nyqbooks.org
ON EARTH, 40 West 20th Street, New York, NY 10011, 212-727-4412
OPEN CITY, 270 Lafayette Street, Suite 1412, New York, NY 10012
Other Press, 2 Park Avenue, 24th Floor, New York, NY 10016
Oxford University Press, 198 Madison Avenue, New York, NY 10016
Panther Books, 197 Seventh Avenue 4C, New York, NY 10011, www.goodie.org
Paradiso-Parthas Press, 214 Mulberry Street, New York, NY 10012
THE PARIS REVIEW, 62 White Street, New York, NY 10013
PARNASSUS: Poetry in Review, 205 West 89th Street #8F, New York, NY 10024-1835, 212-362-3492, Fax 212-875-0148, parnew@aol.com, website www.parnassuspoetry.com
The Passion Profit Company, PO Box 618, Church Street Station, New York, NY 10008-0618, (646)219-3565, walt@passionprofit.com, www.passionprofit.com
Pella Publishing Co., 337 West 36th Street, New York, NY 10018, 212-279-9586
PEN AMERICA: A Journal for Writers & Readers, 588 Broadway, Room 303, New York, NY 10012-3229, 212-334-1660 x115, Fax 212-334-2181, journal@pen.org, www.pen.org/journal
Pendragonian Publications, PO Box 719, New York, NY 10101-0719, mmpendragon@aol.com
PENNY DREADFUL: Tales and Poems of Fantastic Terror, PO Box 719, New York, NY 10101-0719, mmpendra-gon@aol.com
Persea Books, 853 Broadway, Suite 601, New York, NY 10003, info@perseabooks.com, (212) 260-9256 phone, (212) 260-1902 fax
Philomel Books, 345 Hudson Street, New York, NY 10014, 212-414-3610
Pleasure Boat Studio: A Literary Press (including imprints Caravel Books and Aequitas Books, and the division Empty Bowl Press), 201 West 89 Street, New York, NY 10024-1848, 888-810-5308 fax, pleasboat@nyc.rr.com, www.pleasureboat-studio.com
The Poetry Project, St. Mark's Church, 131 East 10th Street, New York, NY 10003, 212-674-0910, poproj@thorn.net
THE POETRY PROJECT NEWSLETTER, St. Mark's Church, 131 East 10th Street, New York, NY 10003, 212-674-0910, poproj@thorn.net
POETS & WRITERS MAGAZINE, 90 Broad Street, Suite 2100, New York, NY 10004, 212-226-3586, Fax 212-226-3963, www.pw.org
Poets & Writers, Inc., 72 Spring Street, New York, NY 10012, 212-226-3586, Fax 212-226-3963, www.pw.org
Prologue Press, 375 Riverside Drive #14-C, New York, NY 10025
Psychohistory Press, 140 Riverside Drive, New York, NY 10024, 212-799-2294
Rain Mountain Press Collective, 63 East Third Street, Suite 16, New York, NY 10003, web:www.rainmountainpress.com
RATTAPALLAX, 217 Thompson Street, Suite 353, New York, NY 10012, info@rattapallax.com
THE READING ROOM, P.O. Box 2144, Lenox Hill Station, New York, NY 10021
Red Dust, 1148 5th Ave., Apt.12-B, New York, NY 10028, 212-348-4388
Red Rock Press, 459 Columbus Avenue, Ste. 114, New York, NY 10024, 212-362-8304, Fax 212-362-6216, redrockprs@aol.com, www.redrockpress.com
Rogue Scholars Press, 228 East 25th Street, #2, New York, NY 10010
SAPPHIRE MAGAZINE, A2EO Media, Inc., 853 Broadway, suite 1516, New York, NY 10003, info@sapphire-magazine.com, Telephone: 212-358-3725, Fax: 360-237-0543
Semprove/Learning, 228 Park Ave. South, Suite 32135, New York, NY 10003
Seven Stories Press, 140 Watts Street, New York, NY 10013
THE SIENESE SHREDDER, 344 West 23rd Street # 4D, New York, NY 10011, 212-431-1714 phone, 212-431-1714 fax
Soho Press, Inc., 853 Broadway, New York, NY 10003, Tel: 212.260.1900, Fax: 212.260.1902
SONGS OF INNOCENCE, PO Box 719, New York, NY 10101-0719, mmpendragon@aol.com
Space and Time Press, 138 West 70th Street 4-B, New York, NY 10023-4468
SPINNING JENNY, P.O. Box 1067, New York, NY 10014-1067, www.spinning-jenny.com
SWINK, 244 Fifth Ave. #2722, New York, NY 10001, 212-591-1651, 212-658-9995, www.swinkmag.com
TEACHERS & WRITERS, 520 Eighth Ave., Suite 2020, New York, NY 10018-6507, 212-691-6590, www.twc.org
Teachers & Writers Collaborative, 520 Eighth Ave., Suite 2020, New York, NY 10018, 212-691-6590, 212-675-0171
TELOS, 431 East 12th Street, New York, NY 10009, 212-228-6479
Telos Press, 431 East 12th Street, New York, NY 10009, 212-228-6479
TnT Classic Books, 360 West 36 Street #2NW, New York, NY 10018-6412, 212-736-6279, Fax 212-695-3219, tntclassics@aol.com, www.tntclassicbooks.com
Touchstone Center Publications, 141 East 88th Street, New York, NY 10128, rlewis212@aol.com
TRICYCLE: The Buddhist Review, 92 Vandam Street, New York, NY 10013-1007

The Twickenham Press, 302A West 12th Street, #339, New York, NY 10014-6025, 917-282-6657
United Artists Books, 114 W. 16th Street, 5C, New York, NY 10011
URBAN REFLECTIONS MAGAZINE, New York, NY 10003
VANITAS, 211 West 19th Street, #5, New York, NY 10011-4001, vanitas@el.net
Vantage Press, Inc., 419 Park Ave. S., New York, NY 10016, Ph:212-736-1767, F: 212-736-2273, 1-800-882-3273
W.W. Norton, 500 Fifth Avenue, New York, NY 10110, 212-354-5500
WASHINGTON SQUARE, Creative Writing Program, New York University, 58 West 10th St., New York, NY 10011
Words Without Borders, PO Box 1658, New York, NY 10276, info@wordswithoutborders.org, http://wordswithoutborders.org
THE WORLD, St. Marks Church/The Poetry Project, 131 East 10th Street, New York, NY 10003, poproj@thorn.net
World Audience, 303 Park Avenue South, Suite 1440, New York, NY 10010-3657, (646) 620-7406; http://www.worldaudience.org; http://www.worldaudience.co.uk; http://www.worldaudience.mobi; http://www.mstefanstrozier.org.
WSQ (formerly WOMEN'S STUDIES QUARTERLY), The Feminist Press at CUNY, 365 Fifth Avenue, Suite 5406, New York, NY 10016, 212-817-7915, 212-817-1593, aroy@gc.cuny.edu, www.feministpress.org/wsq
ZEEK: A Jewish Journal of Thought & Culture, P. O. Box 1342, New York, NY 10016
Midmarch Arts Press, 300 Riverside Drive, New York City, NY 10025, 212-666-6990
Logos Press, 3909 Witmer Rd #416, Niagara Falls, NY 14305
NATURAL LIFE, Box 112, Niagara Falls, NY 14304-0112, 416-260-0303, email: natural@life.ca, web: www.NaturalLifeMagazine.com
SLIPSTREAM, Box 2071, New Market Station, Niagara Falls, NY 14301, 716-282-2616 (after 5 p.m., E.S.T.)
Slipstream Productions, Box 2071, New Market Station, Niagara Falls, NY 14301
Tuscarora Books Inc., POB 987 Falls Station, Niagara Falls, NY 14303, 716-284-5595, fax 716-284-5597
PHOEBE: Journal of Gender & Cultural Critiques, Women's & Gender Studies Department, State University of New York, Oneonta, NY 13820-4015, Phone (607) 436-2014, Fax (607) 436-2656, phoebe@oneonta.edu, http://www.oneonta.edu/academics/womens/Phoebe_Small.htm
Avocet Press Inc., 19 Paul Court, Pearl River, NY 10965, 212-754-6300, oopc@interport.net, www.avocetpress.com
Hidden Valley Farm, Publisher, P.O. Box 172, Perry, NY 14530, publisher.hiddenvalley@yahoo.com , theotherherald@yahoo.com , http://www.otherherald.com
THE OTHER HERALD, P.O. Box 172, Perry, NY 14530, publisher.hiddenvalley@yahoo.com , theotherherald@yahoo.com , http://www.otherherald.com
Bloated Toe Publishing, PO Box 324, Peru, NY 12972, (518)563-9469, info@bloatedtoe.com, www.bloatedtoe.com
A RESOURCE FOR EMBEDDED HAIKU, P.O. Box 35, Pilot Knob, NY 12844, 518-743-2258
Manifold Press, 102 Bridge Street, Plattsburgh, NY 12901, editormanifoldpress@msn.com, www.manifoldpress.com
THE SARANAC REVIEW, CVH, Dept of English, SUNY Plattsburgh, 101 Broad St, Plattsburgh, NY 12901
Chatterley Press International, 19 Dorothy Street, Port Jefferson Station, NY 11776, 631-928-9074 phone/Fax, info@chatterleypress.com
BLUELINE, State University College, English Dept., Potsdam, NY 13676, 315-267-2043
THE WALLACE STEVENS JOURNAL, Clarkson University Box 5750, 8 Clarkson Avenue, Potsdam, NY 13699-5750, 315-268-6410, serio@clarkson.edu, www.wallacestevens.com
The Wallace Stevens Society Press, Box 5750 Clarkson University, Potsdam, NY 13699-5750, 315-268-3987, Fax 268-3983, serio@clarkson.edu, www.wallacestevens.com
INKWELL, Manhattanville College, 2900 Purchase Street, Purchase, NY 10577, www.inkwelljournal.org
AFTERIMAGE, 31 Prince Street, Rochester, NY 14607, 585/442.8676, fax 585.442.1992, afterimage@vsw.org, www.vsw.org/afterimage/
BOA Editions, Ltd., 250 Goodman St, N., Suite 306, Rochester, NY 14607-1190, 585-546-3410, www.boaeditions.org
HAZMAT REVIEW, PO Box 30507, Rochester, NY 14603
Lion Press, PO Box 92541, Rochester, NY 14692, phone 585-381-6410; fax 585-381-7439; for orders only 800-597-3068
Open Letter Books, University of Rochester, Lattimore Hall 411, Box 270082, Rochester, NY 14267, 585 319 0823, [f] 585 273 1097, submissions@openletterbooks.org
Visual Studies Workshop, 31 Prince Street, Rochester, NY 14607, 585-442-8676, www.vsw.org
Butcher Shop Press, 529 Beach 132nd St., Rockaway Park, NY 11694-1413
FULLOSIA PRESS, RPPS, PO Box 280, Ronkonkoma, NY 11779, deanofrpps@aol.com, http://rpps_fullosia_press.tripod.com
ONE STORY, 232 3rd St. #A111, rooklyn, NY 11215
ALTERNATIVE EDUCATION RESOURCE ORGANIZATION, 417 Roslyn Road, Roslyn Heights, NY 11577, 516-621-2195, Fax 516-625-3257, jerryaero@aol.com
The Bookman Press, PO Box 1892, Sag Harbor, NY 11963, 631-725 1115
The Permanent Press/The Second Chance Press, 4170 Noyac Road, Sag Harbor, NY 11963, 631-725-1101
Savant Garde Workshop, PO Box 1650, Sag Harbor, NY 11963-0060, 631-725-1414; website www.savantgarde.org
Lost Pond Press, 40 Margaret St., Saranac Lake, NY 12983-1298, 518-891-3918 philbrown@juno.com
SALMAGUNDI, Skidmore College, 815 North Broadway, Saratoga Springs, NY 12866-1632, 518-584-5186
Allbook Books, P.O. Box 562, Selden, NY 11784, (631)716-1385, www.allbook-books.com
HELIOTROPE, A JOURNAL OF POETRY, P.O Box 456, Shady, NY 12409, www.heliopoems.com
Sound View Publishing, Inc., P.O. Box 696, Shoreham, NY 11786-0696, 631-899-2481, Fax 631-899-2487, 1-888-529-3496, info@SoundViewPublishing.com, www.SoundViewPublishing.com
Slapering Hol Press, 300 Riverside Drive, Sleepy Hollow, NY 10591-1414, 914-332-5953, Fax 914-332-4825, info@writerscenter.org, www.writerscenter.org
THE SUMMERSET REVIEW, 25 Summerset Drive, Smithtown, NY 11787
THE $ENSIBLE SOUND, 403 Darwin Drive, Snyder, NY 14226, 716-833-0930
Whelks Walk Press, 37 Harvest Lane, Southampton, NY 11968, whelkswalk@aol.com
Sunnyside Press, 297 Triumpho Road, St. Johnsville, NY 13452-4003, 518-568-7853 phone/Fax, triglade@telenet.net
Bard Press, 393 St. Pauls Avenue, Staten Island, NY 10304-2127, 718-442-7429
Blood Moon Productions, 75 Saint Marks Place, Staten Island, NY 10301-1606, Tel. 718/556-9410, FAX 718/816-4092
DESIRE, 463 Barlow Avenue, Staten Island, NY 10308, 718-317-7484, marynicholaou@aol.com, www.geocities.com/marynicholaou/classic_blue.html
Eros Books, 463 Barlow Avenue, Staten Island, NY 10308, 718-317-7484
PSYCHE, 463 Barlow Avenue, Staten Island, NY 10308, 718-317-7484
Ten Penny Players, Inc., 393 St. Pauls Avenue, Staten Island, NY 10304-2127, 718-442-7429, www.tenpennyplayers.org
WATERWAYS: Poetry in the Mainstream, 393 St. Pauls Avenue, Staten Island, NY 10304-2127, 718-442-7429,

www.tenpennyplayers.org, bfisher@si.rr.com or rspiegel@si.rr.com
TAPROOT, a journal of older writers, PO Box 841, University at Stony Brook, Stony Brook, NY 11790-0841, 631-689-0668
Celebrity Profiles Publishing, PO Box 344, Stonybrook, NY 11790, 631-862-8555, Fax 631-862-0139, celebpro4@aol.com, rgrudens1@aol.com
A HUDSON VIEW POETRY DIGEST, P.O. Box 295, Stormville, NY 12582-0295, http://www.hudsonview.us, email: hudsonviewpoetry@gmail.com
LITERARY HOUSE REVIEW, P.O. Box 295, Stormville, NY 12582-0295, Website: http://www.literaryhouse.com, Email: literature@literaryhouse.com
SKYLINE LITERARY MAGAZINE, PO Box 295, Stormville, NY 12582-0295, skylineeditor@aol.com, http://www.skylinemagazines.com
Skyline Publications, PO Box 295, Stormville, NY 12582-0295, website: http://www.skylinepublications.com, Email: skylineeditor@aol.com
SPINNINGS...INTENSE TALES OF LIFE MAGAZINE, PO Box 295, Stormville, NY 12582-0295, http://www.spinningsmagazine.com email: spinningsmag@aol.com
THE COMSTOCK REVIEW, Comstock Writers' Group, Inc., 4956 St. John Drive, Syracuse, NY 13215, www.comstockreview.org
COMSTOCK REVIEW, 4956 St. John Drive, Syracuse, NY 13215
NEW ENVIRONMENT BULLETIN, 270 Fenway Drive, Syracuse, NY 13224, 315-446-8009
POINT OF CONTACT, The Journal of Verbal & Visual Arts, 216 H.B. Crouse Building, Syracuse University, Syracuse, NY 13244-1160, 315-443-2247, Fax 315-443-5376, cfawcett@syr.edu, www.pointcontact.org
SALT HILL, English Department, Syracuse University, Syracuse, NY 13244-1170
STONE CANOE, 700 University Avenue, Suite 326, Syracuse, NY 13244-2530, Phone: 315-443-1082/3225, Fax: 315-443-4174, e-mail: rmcolley@uc.syr.edu
Syracuse Cultural Workers/Tools for Change, PO Box 6367, Syracuse, NY 13217, 315-474-1132, free fax 877-265-5399, scw@syracuseculturalworkers.com, SyracuseCulturalWorkers.com
Syracuse University Press, 621 Skytop Road Suite 110, Syracuse, NY 13244-5290, 1-800-365-8929
Bright Hill Press, PO Box 193, Treadwell, NY 13846-0193, 607-829-5055, fax 607-829-5054, wordthur@stny.rr.com. web: www.brighthillpress.org
Dwarf Lion Press, P.O. Box 436, Trumansburg, NY 14886, 607/387-9100, 607/387-9100, dwarflionpress@yahoo.com
White Crosslet Publishing Co, 456 West Lake Road, tuxedo park, NY 10987, 845 351 3345 (fax&telephone)
North Country Books, Inc., 220 Lafayette St., Utica, NY 13502, 315-735-4877
THE BROOME REVIEW, PO Box 900, Vestal, NY 13851
Split Oak Press, P.O. Box 700, Vestal, NY 13851, 607-748-5834 splitoakpress.com
IRISH LITERARY SUPPLEMENT, 2592 N Wading River Road, Wading River, NY 11792-1404, 631-929-0224
Pushcart Press, PO Box 380, Wainscott, NY 11975, 631-324-9300, www.pushcartprize.com
Beekman Books, Inc., 300 Old All Angels Hill Road, Wappingers Falls, NY 12590, 845-297-2690
Success Publishing, 3419 Dunham Drive, Box 263, Warsaw, NY 14569
HEAVEN BONE MAGAZINE, 62 Woodcock Mt. Dr., Washingtonville, NY 10992-1828, 845-496-4109
Heaven Bone Press, 62 Woodcock Mtn. Dr., Washingtonville, NY 10992, 845-496-4109
THE LAKEVIEW REVIEW, P.O. Box 428, Wayland, NY 14572, 585-645-2924
Gingerbread House, 602 Montauk Highway, Westhampton Beach, NY 11978, 631-288-5119, Fax 631-288-5179, ghbooks@optonline.net, www.gingerbreadbooks.com
National Economic Research Associates, Inc., 50 Main Street, 14th Floor, White Plains, NY 10606, 617-621-6289
Ludlow Press, P.O. Box 575010, Whitestone, NY 11357
Alms House Press, PO Box 218, Woodbourne, NY 12788-0218
Celtic Heritage Books, PO Box 770637, Woodside, NY 11377-0637, Tel/Fax: 718-478-8162; Toll Free 1-877-215-7861
LULLABY HEARSE, 45-34 47th St. Apt. 6AB, Woodside, NY 11377, editor@lullabyhearse.com, www.lullabyhearse.com
Ash Tree Publishing, PO Box 64, Woodstock, NY 12498, 845-246-8081
Ceres Press, PO Box 87, Woodstock, NY 12498, tel/fax: 845-679-5573, web: www.HealthyHighways.com
Maverick Books, Box 897, Woodstock, NY 12498, 866-478-9266 phone/Fax, maverickbooks@aol.com
YogaVidya.com, PO Box 569, Woodstock, NY 12498-0569, 845-679-9619, Fax 586-283-4680, info@yogavidya.com, www.yogavidya.com
Krhyme Publishing Inc., PO Box 1090, Yonkers, NY 10704-9998, 914-665-1774

NORTH CAROLINA

KMT, A Modern Journal of Ancient Egypt, NC 28787, 828-658-3353 phone/Fax
REMARK, 1104 Indian Trail, Apex, NC 27502-1520, www.remarkpoetry.net remarkpoetry@gmail.com
DTS Group, Inc., P.O. Box 4217, Asheboro, NC 27204-4217, DTSgroupinc@aol.com, DTSGroupInc.com
Black Mountain Press or Black Mountain College Museum + Arts Ctr, PO Box 18912, Asheville, NC 28814, Tel: 828-350-8484 email: bmcmac@bellsouth.net
Brave Ulysses Books, POB 1877, Asheville, NC 28802, 828-713-8840, cecil@braveulysses.com, www.braveulysses.com
THE FRONT STRIKER BULLETIN, The Retskin Report, PO Box 18481, Asheville, NC 28814-0481, 828-254-4487
Tortuga Books, 108 Paradox Point Drive, Aurora, NC 27806-9304, 800-345-6665 (orders), 305-745-8709, Fax 305-745-2704, www.tortugabooks.com
Appalachian Consortium Press, University Hall, Appalachian State University, Boone, NC 28608, 704-262-2064, fax 704-262-6564
CORRECTION(S): A Literary Journal for Inmate Writing, PO Box 1326, Boone, NC 28607-1326
Parkway Publishers, Inc., PO Box 3678, Boone, NC 28607, 828-265-3993
Celo Valley Books, 160 Ohle Road, Burnsville, NC 28714, 828-675-5918
Scots Plaid Press, 600 Kelly Road, Carthage, NC 28327, 910-947-2587; Fax 910-947-5112
Trafton Publishing, 109 Barcliff Terrace, Cary, NC 27518-8900
Blink Chapbooks, CB #3520, Greenlaw Hall, UNC, Chapel Hill, NC 27599-3520
Canonymous Press, PO Box 1328, Chapel Hill, NC 27514-1328, e-mail press@canonymous.com, www.canonymous.com
THE CAROLINA QUARTERLY, CB# 3520 Greenlaw Hall, Univ of N. Carolina, Chapel Hill, NC 27599-3520, 919-962-0244, Fax 919-962-3520
Cockeyed Press, PO Box 3669, Chapel Hill, NC 27515
THE JOURNAL OF AFRICAN TRAVEL-WRITING, PO Box 346, Chapel Hill, NC 27514
THE SUN, A Magazine of Ideas, 107 North Roberson Street, Chapel Hill, NC 27516, 919-942-5282

Black Hawk Press, P.O. Box 10324, Charlotte, NC 28212, Website: www.blackhawkpress.com, Email: info@blackhawk-press.com

A. Borough Books, 3901 Silver Bell Drive, Charlotte, NC 28211, 704-364-1788, 800-843-8490 (orders only), humorbooks@aol.com

IODINE POETRY JOURNAL, PO Box 18548, Charlotte, NC 28218-0548

MAIN STREET RAG, PO Box 690100, Charlotte, NC 28227-7001, 704-573-2516, editor@mainstreetrag.com, www.MainStreetRag.com

McQuinn Publishing, P.O. Box 667849, Charlotte, NC 28266-7849, phone no. 980-225-7661; fax no. 704-910-0717; www.McQuinn Publishing.com

WEST GOES SOUTH, 4024 Providence Rd. #C, Charlotte, NC 28211, 419-565-2059

Granite Publishing Group, PO Box 1429, Columbus, NC 28722, 828-894-8444, Fax 828-894-8454, GraniteP@aol.com, www.5thworld.com

New Native Press, PO Box 661, Cullowhee, NC 28723, 828-293-9237

AMERICAN LITERATURE, Box 90660, Duke University, Durham, NC 27708-0660, 919-684-3948

THE BLOTTER MAGAZINE, Inc., 1010 Hale St., Durham, NC 27705

Carolina Academic Press, 700 Kent Street, Durham, NC 27701, 919-489-7486, fax:919-493-5668

Carolina Wren Press, 120 Morris Street, Durham, NC 27701, 919-560-2738; www.carolinawrenpress.org

Duke University Press, Box 90660, Durham, NC 27708-0660, 919-687-3600; Fax 919-688-4574, www.dukeupress.edu

MINESHAFT, P. O. Box 1226, Durham, NC 27702

POETICS TODAY: International Journal for Theory and Analysis of Literature and Communication, Box 90660, Duke University, Durham, NC 27708-0660

RHAPSODY MAGAZINE, PO Box 2443, Durham, NC 27715-2443

Sadorian Publications, PO Box 2443, Durham, NC 27715-2443, 919-599-3038, Fax 309-431-4387, sadorianllc@aol.com, www.Sadorianonline.com

Bright Mountain Books, 206 Riva Ridge Drive, Fairview, NC 28730-9764, booksbmb@charter.net

GREEN PRINTS, "The Weeder's Digest", PO Box 1355, Fairview, NC 28730, 828-628-1902, www.greenprints.com, patstone@atlantic.net

Longleaf Press, Methodist University, English Dept., 5400 Ramsey Street, Fayetteville, NC 28311, 910-630-7110

PREP Publishing, 1110 1/2 Hay Street, Suite C, Fayetteville, NC 28305, 910-483-6611, Fax 910-483-2439

Avisson Press, Inc., 3007 Taliaferro Road, Greensboro, NC 27408, 336-288-6989 phone/FAX

CAVE WALL, Cave Wall Press LLC, PO Box 29546, Greensboro, NC 27429-9546

ELT Press, English Dept., Univ of N. Carolina, PO Box 26170, Greensboro, NC 27402-6170, 336-273-5507, Fax 336-334-3281, eltpress@gmail.com

ENGLISH LITERATURE IN TRANSITION, 1880-1920, English Department/U of North Carolina, P.O. Box 26170, Greensboro, NC 27402-6170, 336-273-5507, Fax 336-334-3281; eltpress@gmail.com

THE GREENSBORO REVIEW, Greensboro Review, MFA Program, 3302 MHRA, PO Box 26170, Univ. of North Carolina Greensboro, Greensboro, NC 27402-6170, 336-334-5459, Fax 336-256-1470, jlclark@uncg.edu, www.greensbororeview.org

INTERNATIONAL POETRY REVIEW, Dept of Romance Languages, Univ. of North Carolina, Greensboro, NC 27402-6170, 336-334-4433, mismiths@uncg.edu, http://www.uncg.edu/rom/IPR/IPRsubscription.htm

LETTER ARTS REVIEW, PO Box 9986, Greensboro, NC 27429, 800-369-9598, 336-272-6139, Fax 336-272-9015, lar@johnnealbooks.com

March Street Press, 3413 Wilshire Drive, Greensboro, NC 27408-2923, 336 282 9754 fon and fax, rbixby@earthlink.net, http://www.marchstreetpress.com

New Day Publishing, Inc., 26 Bluff Ridge Court, Greensboro, NC 27455, 336.545.1545

Open Hand Publishing LLC, PO Box 20207, Greensboro, NC 27420, 336-292-8585, Fax 336-292-8588, 866-888-9229; info@openhand.com; www.openhand.com

TIMBER CREEK REVIEW, c/o J.M. Freiermuth, PO Box 16542, Greensboro, NC 27416

Zante Publishing, P.O. Box 35404, Greensboro, NC 27425, (336) 605-7900

NORTH CAROLINA LITERARY REVIEW, English Department, East Carolina University, Greenville, NC 27858, 252-328-1537; Fax 252-328-4889

TAR RIVER POETRY, Erwin Building Mail Room, East Carolina University, Greenville, NC 27858-4353, 252-328-6046

Shipyard Press, LC, 191 Brightwater Falls Road, Henderson, NC 28739-7171, 828-808-8768

CAIRN: The New St. Andrews Review, St. Andrews Prebyterian College, 1700 Dogwood Mile, Laurinburg, NC 28352, 910-277-5310

St. Andrews College Press, 1700 Dogwood Mile, Laurinburg, NC 28352-5598, 910-277-5310

Thirsty Turtle Press, PO Box 402, Maggie Valley, NC 28751, Phone 828-926-6472, FAX 828-926-8851, dan@thirstyturtle-press.com, www.thirstyturtlepress.com

Metallo House Publishers, 170 E. River Road, Moncure, NC 27559-9617, 919-542-2908, Fax 919-774-5611

Explorer Press, 1501 Edgewood Drive, Mount Airy, NC 27030-5215, 336-789-6005, Fax 336-789-6005, E-mail terryleecollins@hotmail.com

Mount Olive College Press, Mount Olive College, 634 Henderson Street, Mount Olive, NC 28365

MOUNT OLIVE REVIEW, Department of Language and Literature, 634 Henderson Street, Mount Olive, NC 28365, 919-658-2502

PEMBROKE MAGAZINE, UNCP, Box 1510, Pembroke, NC 28372-1510, 910-521-6433 ext 6433

Dancing Lemur Press, L.L.C., P.O. Box 383, Pikeville, NC 27863-0383, 919-273-0939, 888-502-1117fax, www.dancinglemur-press.com, inquiries@dancinglemurpress.com

DRT Press, PO Box 427, Pittsboro, NC 27312-0427, 1-919-542-1763 (phone/fax), editorial@drtpress.com, www.drtpress.com

Asylum Arts, c/o Leaping Dog Press, PO Box 90437, Raleigh, NC 27675-0473, Phone/fax: (877) 570-6873 E-mail: editor@leapingdogpress.com, Web: www.leapingdogpress.com, Chapbooks and ephemera: www.cafepress.com/ldp/

C & M Online Media Inc., 3905 Meadow Field Lane, Raleigh, NC 27606-4470, 919-233-8164, nancy@cmonline.com, www.bosonbooks.com

Ivy House Publishing Group, 5122 Bur Oak Circle, Raleigh, NC 27612, 919-782-0281

Leaping Dog Press, PO Box 90473, Raleigh, NC 27675-0473, Phone/fax: (919) 809-9045 E-mail: editor@leapingdogpress.com, Web: www.leapingdogpress.com, Chapbooks and ephemera: www.cafepress.com/ldp/

Midnight Whistler Publishers, 3220 Shore View Road, #22, Raleigh, NC 27613, 919-327-5021

OBSIDIAN III: Literature in the African Diaspora, Dept. of English, Box 8105, NC State University, Raleigh, NC 27695-8105, 919-515-4150

REFLECTIONS LITERARY JOURNAL, PO Box 1197, Roxboro, NC 27573, 336-599-1181, reflect@piedmontcc.edu

Ammons Communications; Imprint: Catch the Spirit of Appalachia, 29 Regal Ave, Amy, Sylva, NC 28779-2877, v.ammons@mchsi.com

ARTISTIC RAMBLINGS, P.O. Box 2907, Thomasville, NC 27361, PH: 832-634-7012, Fax: 530-323-8251, email: ArtisticRamblings@gmail.com

Red Tiger Press, P.O. Box 2907, Thomasville, NC 27361, PH: 832-634-7012, Fax: 530-323-8251, email: RedTiger-Press@gmail.com

New Road Publishing, 3650 Rogers Rd., #328, Wake Forest, NC 27587, Phone # 919-453-2850 Fax # 888-957-8885

ECOTONE: Reimagining Place, UNCW Dept. of Creative Writing, 601 South College Road, Wilmington, NC 28403-3297, 910-962-3070

Etched Press, Box 3063, Wilmington, NC 28406, www.etchedpress.com, submit@etchedpress.com

LifeSkill Institute, Inc., P.O. Box 302, Wilmington, NC 28402, 910-251-0665, 910-763-2494, 800-570-4009, lifeskill@earth-link.net, www.lifeskillinstitute.org

CRUCIBLE, Office of the Vice President for Academic Affairs, Barton College, Wilson, NC 27893, 252-399-6344

John F. Blair, Publisher, 1406 Plaza Drive, Winston-Salem, NC 27103, 336-768-1374

Press 53, PO Box 30314, Winston-Salem, NC 27130

NORTH DAKOTA

Ephemera Bound Publishing, 719 9th St N, Fargo, ND 58102, 701-306-6458

NORTH DAKOTA QUARTERLY, Merrifield Hall Room 110, 276 Centennial Drive Stop 7209, Grand Forks, ND 58202-7209, 701-777-3322

UND Press, University of North Dakota, PO Box 7209, Grand Forks, ND 58202, 701-777-3321

HEALTHY WEIGHT JOURNAL, 402 South 14th Street, Hettinger, ND 58639, 701-567-2646, Fax 701-567-2602, e-mail fmberg@healthyweight.net

OHIO

KALEIDOSCOPE: Exploring the Experience of Disability through Literature & the Fine Arts, United Disability Services, 701 S. Main Street, Akron, OH 44311-1019, 330-762-9755, 330-379-3349 (TDD), Fax 330-762-0912, mshiplett@udsakron.org, pboerner@udsakron.org, www.udsakron.org

SACS Consulting, 520 South Main St., Suite 2512, Akron, OH 44311-1073, tadimoff@sacsconsulting.com, www.sacsconsulting.com 330-255-1101

University of Akron Press, Akron, OH 44325-1703

The Ashland Poetry Press, 401 College Avenue, Ashland, OH 44805, 419-289-5957, app@ashland.edu, www.ashland.edu/aupoetry

Lucky Press, LLC, PO Box 754, Athens, OH 45701-0754, Fax: 614-413-2820; Website: www.luckypress.com, Email: books@luckypress.com

NEW OHIO REVIEW, English Dept., 360 Ellis Hall, Ohio University, Athens, OH 45701, 740.597.1360, Web: www.ohiou.edu/nor

Ohio University Press/Swallow Press, The Ridges, Building 19, Athens, OH 45701, 740-593-1157, www.ohioswallow.com

QUARTER AFTER EIGHT, Ellis Hall, Ohio University, Athens, OH 45701

Writer's World Press, PO Box 284, Aurora, OH 44202-0284, WritersWorld@juno.com, www.writersworldpress.com

Raven Rocks Press, 53650 Belmont Ridge Road, Beallsville, OH 43716, 614-926-1705

MID-AMERICAN REVIEW, Dept of English, Bowling Green State University, Bowling Green, OH 43403-0191, 419-372-2725, www.bgsu.edu/midamericanreview

PRAIRIE MARGINS, Department of English, Bowling Green State University, Bowling Green, OH 43403, debrab@bgnet.bgsu.edu http://www.bgsu.edu/departments/creative-writing/home.html (under BFA)

Faded Banner Publications, PO Box 101, Bryan, OH 43506-0101, 419-636-3807, 419-636-3807 (fax), 888-799-3787, fadedbanner.com

THE LISTENING EYE, KSU Geauga Campus, 14111 Claridon-Troy Road, Burton, OH 44021, 440-286-3840, grace_butcher@msn.com

Indigo Ink Press, Inc., 150 35th Street NW, Canton, OH 44709, 330-417-7715

CYBERFICT, English Department, Wright State Univ - Lake Campus, 7600 State Routem 703, Celina, OH 45822, www.wright.edu/~martin.kich/

GRAND LAKE REVIEW, Wright State University-Lake Campus, 7600 State Route 703, Celina, OH 45822, 419-586-0374, Fax 419-586-0368, martin.kich@wright.edu, www.wright.edu/~martin.kich/

THE CINCINNATI REVIEW, Dept. of English & Comparative Lit; University of Cincinnati, McMicken Hall, Room 369; PO Box 210069, Cincinnati, OH 45221-0069, (513) 556-3954

Legacy Audio Books, Inc., P.O. Box 11183, Cincinnati, OH 45211, 866-499-2049

SPITBALL: The Literary Baseball Magazine, 5560 Fox Road, Cincinnati, OH 45239-7271, 513-385-2268

Chapultepec Press, 4222 Chambers, Cincinnati, Ohio 45223, OH 45223, chapultepecpress@hotmail.com http://www.tokyorosecords.com

Cleveland State Univ. Poetry Center, Cleveland State University, 2121 Euclid Avenue, Cleveland, OH 44115-2214, 216-687-3986; 888-278-6473 toll-free; Fax 216-687-6943; poetrycenter@csuohio.edu; www.csuohio.edu/poetrycenter

deep cleveland press, PO Box 14248, Cleveland, OH 44114-0248, 216-706-3725, press@deepcleveland.com, www.deepcleveland.com

ERASED, SIGH, SIGH, 701 East Schaaf Road, Cleveland, OH 44131-1227, ViaDolorosaPress@sbcglobal.net, www.angelfire.com/oh2/dolorosa/erased.html

Green Square Publishing, 3718 Normandy Road, Cleveland, OH 44120, 216-283-2309, www.greensquarepublishing.com

MUSE: A Quarterly Journal of The Lit, 2570 Superior Ave., Suite 203, Cleveland, OH 44114, phone: 216.694.0000, fax: 216.694.0003, website: www.the-lit.org, email: judith@the-lit.org, peggy@the-lit.org, art submissions: images4muse@the-lit.org, poetry/prose submissions: words4muse@the-lit.org, advertising: advertising4muse@the-lit.org

NOUN VS. VERB, Cleveland, OH 44217, http://www.burningriver.info

Phelps Publishing Company, PO Box 22401, Cleveland, OH 44122, 216-433-2531, 216-752-4938

THE FUNNY TIMES, PO Box 18530, Cleveland Heights, OH 44118, 216-371-8600, Fax 216-371-8696, www.funnytimes.com, ft@funnytimes.com

Ecrivez!, Columbus, OH 43219-2002, 614-253-0773

THE JOURNAL, OSU Dept. of English, 164 W. 17th Avenue, 421 Denney Hall, Columbus, OH 43210-1370, 614-292-4076, fax 614-292-7816, thejournal@osu.edu

A.P. Lee & Co., Ltd., P.O. Box 340292, Columbus, OH 43234, 614-798-1998, www.APLeeCo.com, webmas-

ter@APLeeCo.com
Luna Bisonte Prods, 137 Leland Ave, Columbus, OH 43214, 614-846-4126
Ohio State University Press, 180 Pressey Hall, 1070 Carmack Road, Columbus, OH 43210-1002, 614-292-6930
OHIOANA QUARTERLY, 274 E. First Avenue, Suite 300, Columbus, OH 43201, 614-466-3831, Fax 614-728-6974, e-mail ohioana@ohioana.org
Pudding House Publications, 81 Shadymere Lane, Columbus, OH 43213-1568, 614-986-1881, info@puddinghouse.com, www.puddinghouse.com
PUDDING MAGAZINE: The International Journal of Applied Poetry, 81 Shadymere Lane, Columbus, OH 43213-1568, 614-986-1881, info@puddinghouse.com, www.puddinghouse.com
Silenced Press, 449 Vermont Place, Columbus, OH 43201, http://silencedpress.com
SILENCED PRESS, 449 Vermont Place, Columbus, OH 43201, http://silencedpress.com
Triple Crown Publications, PO Box 247378, Columbus, OH 43224
YA'SOU/Skyline Productions, PO Box 77463, Columbus, OH 43207
TWENTY-EIGHT PAGES LOVINGLY BOUND WITH TWINE, PO Box 106, Danville, OH 43014
Just Sisters Publications, P.O. Box 26071, Dayton, OH 45426, Telephone: (937) 369-7902; Fax: (937) 461-6865
Kettering Foundation Press, 200 Commons Road, Dayton, OH 45459-2799, 937-434-7300
KETTERING REVIEW, 200 Commons Road, Dayton, OH 45459-2799, 937-434-7300
Tomart Publications, 3300 Encrete Lane, Dayton, OH 45439-1944, 937-294-2250; Fax 937-294-1024
Evening Street Press, 7652 Sawmill Road, #352, Dublin, OH 43016-9296, 614-847-1780, editor@eveningstreetpress.com, eveningstreetpress.com
EVENING STREET REVIEW, 7652 Sawmill Road, #352, Dublin, OH 43016-9296, 614-847-1780, editor@eveningstreet-press.com, eveningstreetpress.com
Kenyette Productions, 20131 Champ Drive, Euclid, OH 44117-2208, 216-486-0544
PLAIN BROWN WRAPPER (PBW), 513 N. Central Avenue, Fairborn, OH 45324-5209, 513-878-5184
AMERICAN TANKA, 57 Fawn Drive, Fairfield, OH 45014, americantanka@earthlink.net, www.americantanka.com
THE KENYON REVIEW, Finn House, 102 W. Wiggin Street, Gambier, OH 43022, 740-427-5208, Fax 740-427-5417, kenyonreview@kenyon.edu
Sugar Loaf Press, 343 North Pearl Street, Granville, OH 43023-1334, 740-507-2704
HIRAM POETRY REVIEW, Box 162, Hiram, OH 44234, 330-569-5331, Fax 330-569-5166, poetryreview@hiram.edu
Bottom Dog Press / Bird Dog Publishing, PO Box 425, Huron, OH 44839, 419-433-5560, x20784 http://smithdocs.net
Drinian Press, P.O. Box 63, Huron, OH 44839, www.DrinianPress.com, rob@smithwrite.net
The Kent State University Press, PO Box 5190, 307 Lowry Hall, Kent, OH 44242-0001, 330-672-8098 phone, 330-672-3104 fax
Cooperative Press, 13000 Athens Ave C288, Lakewood, OH 44107, 216-712-7667, http://www.cooperativepress.com, info@cooperativepress.com
Dos Madres Press, PO Box 294, Loveland, OH 45140
SOLO FLYER, 1112 Minuteman Avenue NW, Massillon, OH 44646
SPIRITCHASER, 3183 Sharon-Copley Road, Medina, OH 44256, 330-722-1561
PAVEMENT SAW, 321 Empire Street, Montpelier, OH 43543-1301, 419-485-0524, info@pavementsaw.org, www.pavement-saw.org
Pavement Saw Press, 321 Empire Street, Montpelier, OH 43543-1301, 419-485-0524, info@pavementsaw.org, www.pavementsaw.org
Equine Graphics Publishing Group: New Concord Press, SmallHorse Press, SunDrop, P.O. Box 35, Nashport, OH 43830-9045, 740-828-2445, http://www.equinegraphicspublishing.com, writerone@newconcordpress.com, http://www.newconcord-press.com
RIVERWIND, Arts & Sciences, Oakley 312, Hocking College, Nelsonville, OH 45764
FIELD: Contemporary Poetry and Poetics, 50 N. Professor St., Oberlin, OH 44074-1091, 440-775-8408, Fax 440-775-8124, oc.press@oberlin.edu
Oberlin College Press, 50 N. Professor St., Oberlin, OH 44074-1091, 440-775-8408, Fax 440-775-8124, E-mail oc.press@oberlin.edu
Interalia/Design Books, PO Box 404, Oxford, OH 45056-0404, 513-523-1553 phone/Fax
Miami University Press, English Dept., Miami University, Oxford, OH 45056, 513-529-5221, Fax 513-529-1392, E-mail tumakw@muohio.edu
IROL Press, LLC, 547 McPherson Circle, Sagamore, OH 44067, www.irolpress.com
SunandShade Publications, PO Box 22, Shade, OH 45776, 740-594-4147, www.SunandShadePublications.com
TU REVIEW, Tiffin University, 155 Miami St., Tiffin, OH 44883, 419-448-3299, Fax 419-443-5009, TUReview@tiffin.edu, http://bruno.tiffin.edu/tureview/
Glass Tower Press, 506 Ogden Ave., Toledo, OH 43609, Phone: (419)377-1361 E-mail: gtp.editor@gmail.com
New Sins Press, 3925 Watson Avenue, Toledo, OH 43612-1113, web sites: www.newsinspress.com, www.myspace.com/newsinspress
Garden House Press, P.O. Box 321 Trenton, Ohio 45067, Trenton, OH 45067, 513-988-7183
OUT OF LINE, P.O. Box 321 Trenton, Ohio 45067, Trenton, OH 45067, 513-988-7183
Holy Macro! Books, 13386 Judy Avenue NW, PO Box 82, Uniontown, OH 44685-9310, 330-715-2875, Fax 707-220-4510, consult@MrExcel.com, www.HolyMacroBooks.com
Halo Publishing International, 5549 Canal Road, Valley View, OH 44125, 216-255-6756
ICON, Kent State University/ Trumbull campus, 4314 Mahoning Ave., Warren, OH 44483, 330-847-0571
ARTFUL DODGE, Department of English, College of Wooster, Wooster, OH 44691, 330-263-2577, artfuldodge@wooster.edu, www3.wooster.edu/artfuldodge
THE ANTIOCH REVIEW, PO Box 148, Yellow Springs, OH 45387, 937-769-1365
Community Service, Inc., PO Box 243, Yellow Springs, OH 45387-0243, 937-767-2161, www.smallcommunity.org
NEW SOLUTIONS, PO Box 243, Yellow Springs, OH 45387, 937-767-2161, info@communitysolution.org
PIG IRON, 26 North Phelps Street, PO Box 237, Youngstown, OH 44501-0237, 330-747-6932, Fax 330-747-0599
Pig Iron Press, 26 North Phelps Street, PO Box 237, Youngstown, OH 44501, 330-747-6932, Fax 330-747-0599

OKLAHOMA

BLINK: A little little magazine of little poems, English Department, Box 184, University of Central Oklahoma, 100 N. University Drive, Edmond, OK 73003
The Colbert House LLC, PO Box 786, Mustang, OK 73064-0786, 405-329-7999, FAX 405-329-6977, 800-698-2644,

customerservice@greatbargainbooks.com, www.greatbargainbooks.com
Arthur H. Clark Co., 2800 Venture Dr., Norman, OK 73069, 405-325-2000
Devi Press, Inc., 126 W. Main, Norman, OK 73069, (405) 447-0364
New Horizons Publishing, 5830 NW Expressway, Suite 225, Oklahoma City, OK 73132-5236, 405-823-9538, Fax 405-848-8118
Nushape Publication, P.O. Box 36651, Oklahoma City,, OK 73136, Ph: 405 602-8447, Fax: 800 554-9718, PH: 800 550-9718 http://www.nushapebiz.com Email:rashun@nushapebiz.com
CIMARRON REVIEW, 205 Morrill Hall, Oklahoma State University, Stillwater, OK 74078-4069, (405) 744-9476, cimarronreview@yahoo.com, http://cimarronreview.okstate.edu
COFFEESPOONS, 1104 E. 38th Place, Tulsa, OK 74105, 918-712-9278
Hawk Publishing Group, Inc., 7107 S. Yale Avenue, PMB 345, Tulsa, OK 74136-6308, 918-492-3677, www.hawkpub.com
IMOCO Publishing, PO Box 471721, Tulsa, OK 74147-1721, 918-814-4174, imoco@officefunnies.com, www.officefunnies.com
JAMES JOYCE QUARTERLY, University of Tulsa, 600 S. College, Tulsa, OK 74104, phone 918-631-2501, fax 918-631-2065, www.utulsa.edu/JJQ
NIMROD INTERNATIONAL JOURNAL, 800 South Tucker Drive, Tulsa, OK 74104-3126
Reading Connections, P.O. Box 52426, Tulsa, OK 74152-0426, 818-902-0278 contact number of Marketing Manager
Stonehorse Publishing, LLC, 6521 East 101 St., Ste. D1, Room 296, Tulsa, OK 74133, 1.888.867.1927, Fax: 1.888.867.1927, generalinfo@stonehorsepublishing.com, www.stonehorsepublishing.com
TULSA STUDIES IN WOMEN'S LITERATURE, 600 S. College, Tulsa, OK 74104-3189, 918-631-2503, Fax 918-631-2065, sarah-theobald-hall@utulsa.edu
WESTVIEW, SW Oklahoma State University, 100 Campus Dr., Weatherford, OK 73096, 580-774-3242, Fax 580-774-7111, james.silver@swosu.edu

OREGON

AB, c¢o Lisa Ahne, PO Box 181, Alsea, OR 97324-0181
DWELLING PORTABLY, Light Living Library, c/o Lisa Ahne, PO Box 181, Alsea, OR 97324-0181
Idylls Press, PO Box 3219, Ashland, OR 97520, phones: 541-905-1386, fax: 213-402-8967, idyllspress@gmail.com, www.idyllspress.com
Quicksilver Productions, P.O.Box 340, 559 S Mountain Avenue, Ashland, OR 97520-3241, 541-482-5343, Fax 541-482-0960
The Bacchae Press, c/o The Brown Financial Group, 10 Sixth Street, Suite 215, Astoria, OR 97103-5315, 503-325-7972; FAX 503-325-7959; 800-207-4358; E-mail brown@pacifier.com
THIS IS IMPORTANT, PO Box 69, Beatty, OR 97621, 541-533-2486, www.fanettelbeck.com
HIGH DESERT JOURNAL, P.O. BOX 7647, Bend, OR 97708
Ridenbaugh Press, P.O. Box 834, Carlton, OR 97111, 503-852-0010
Backcountry Publishing, 3303 Dick George Road, Cave Junction, OR 97523-9623, 541-955-5650
RUMINATIONS: The Nigerian Dwarf & Mini Dairy Goat Magazine, 22705 Hwy 36, Cheshire, OR 97419, 541 998-6081
Camp Colton, 30000 S Camp Colton Dr., Colton, OR 97017, 503-824-2267
Calyx Books, PO Box B, Corvallis, OR 97330, 541-753-9384, Fax 541-753-0515, calyx@calyxpress.com, www.calyxpress.com
CALYX: A Journal of Art and Literature by Women, PO Box B, Corvallis, OR 97339, 541-753-9384, Fax 541-753-0515, info@calyxpress.org, www.calyxpress.org
CLOUDBANK, PO Box 610, Corvallis, OR 97339-0610, 541 752-0075, 877 762-6762, Fax 541 752-5475, michael@cloudbankbooks.com, www.cloudbankbooks.com
The Fiction Works, 2070 SW Whiteside Drive, Corvallis, OR 97333, 541-730-2044, 541-738-2648, fictionworks@comcast.com, http://www.fictionworks.com
THE GROWING EDGE MAGAZINE, PO Box 1027, Corvallis, OR 97339-1027, 514-757-8477
New Moon Publishing, Inc., PO Box 1027, Corvallis, OR 97339-1027, 514-757-8477
Oregon State University Press, 121 The Valley Library, Corvallis, OR 97331, 541-737-3166, OSU.Press@oregonstate.edu, http://oregonstate.edu/dept/press
RUBBERSTAMPMADNESS, PO Box 610, Corvallis, OR 97339-0610
1097 MAGAZINE, 1427 NW Highland Drive, Corvallis, OR 97330, http://www.1097mag.com
Sibyl Publications, Inc, 2505 Reuben Boise road, Dallas, OR 97338, 503-623-3438, fax 503-623-2943
Hood Press, 19130 SE Hwy 212, Damascus, OR 97089-8704
ERDC Publishing, PO Box 1096, Drain, OR 97435, www.erdc.com
Cornucopia Press, 1056 Green Acres Rd. #102-212, Eugene, OR 97408, www.CornucopiaPress.com, query@cornucopiapress.com, 541-337-8088
GREEN ANARCHY, PO Box 11331, Eugene, OR 97440, collective@greenanarchy.org, www.greenanarchy.org
MIDWIFERY TODAY, Box 2672, Eugene, OR 97402, 541-344-7438
Midwifery Today, PO Box 2672, Eugene, OR 97402, 541-344-7438; Fax 541-344-1422; editorial@midwiferytoday.com, www.midwiferytoday.com
Mountains and Rivers Press, P.O. Box 5389, Eugene, OR 97405, http://mountainsandriverspress.org, mtns_rivers@hotmail.com
NORTHWEST REVIEW, 5243 University of Oregon, Eugene, OR 97403-5243
One Horse Press/Rainy Day Press, 1147 East 26th, Eugene, OR 97403, 541-484-4626
Silverfish Review Press, PO Box 3541, Eugene, OR 97403, 503-344-5060
SAGEWOMAN, PO Box 687, Forest Grove, OR 97116
Symbios, 4367 S.E. 16th, Gresham, OR 97080-9178, 503-667-0633, home.netcom.com/~symbios
Beyond Words Publishing, Inc., 20827 NW Cornell Road, Ste. 500, Hillsboro, OR 97124-9808, 503-531-8700, Fax 503-531-8773, www.beyondword.com
Ellechor Publishing House, P.O. Box 5693, Hillsboro, OR 97124, 559-744-ELLE, acquisitions@ellechor.org, http://www.ellechorpublishing.com
Nish Publishing Company, 880 NE 25th Avenue, Suite 2-102, Hillsboro, OR 97124, 503-707-4132
BASALT, School of Arts and Sciences, Eastern Oregon University, La Grande, OR 97850, 541-962-3633
The Bear Wallow Publishing Company, 809 South 12th Street, La Grande, OR 97850, 541-962-7864, bearwallow@uwtc.net, www.bear-wallow.com
OREGON EAST, Hoke 304, Eastern Oregon University, La Grande, OR 97850, (541) 962-3787, oe@eou.edu, www3.eou.edu/~oe
Wordcraft of Oregon, LLC, P.O. Box 3235, La Grande, OR 97850, 541-912-8261

Lightning Bug Learning Press, 16869 SW 65th Ave., #271, Lake Oswego, OR 97035, Phone 877-695-7312, Fax 971-250-2582, Email: mail@lightningbuglearning.com, web address: http://www.lightningbuglearningpress.com
Stonemark Publishing, P.O. Box 8854, 312 S. Ivy Street, Medford, OR 97501, 541-772-3477
Airlie Press, PO Box 434, Monmouth, OR 97361, 541-344-7403, www.airliepress.org
The Apostolic Press, 547 NW Coast Street, Newport, OR 97365, 541 264-0452
Princess Publishing, PO Box 1781, North Plains, OR 97133, 503-647-5754, fax: 503-647-7620, www.matschek.com, www.soaringhorizons.com.
Elderberry Press, Inc., 1393 Old Homestead Drive, Second Floor,, Oakland, OR 97462-9506, Tel: 541-459-6043, Email: editor@elderberrypress.com Site: elderberrypress.com
CLACKAMAS LITERARY REVIEW, 19600 South Molalla Avenue, Oregon City, OR 97045
DIET SOAP, 1321 Monroe St, Oregon City, OR 97405
ALCHEMY, Portland Community College P.O Box 19000, Portland, OR, 97280-0990, (503) 977-4793
THE AMERICAN DRIVEL REVIEW, 3561 SE Cora Drive, Portland, OR 97202, 503-236-6377 info@americandrivelreview.com www.americandrivelreview.com
ART BUREAU, 3321 SW Kelly Ave, Portland, OR 97239, 415-759-1788, www.artbureau.org
THE BEAR DELUXE MAGAZINE, PO Box 10342, Portland, OR 97296, 503-242-1047, Fax 503-243-2645, bear@orlo.org
Beynch Press Publishing Company, 1928 S.E. Ladd Avenue, Portland, OR 97214, 503-232-0433
Blue Unicorn Press, Inc., PO Box 40300, Portland, OR 97240-0300, 503-423-7781
BURNSIDE REVIEW, P.O. BOX 1782, Portland, OR 97207, sid@burnsidereview.org, www.burnsidereview.org
Collectors Press, Inc., PO Box 230986, Portland, OR 97281, 503-684-3030, Fax 503-684-3777
Continuing Education Press, Portland State University, Continuing Education Press, PO Box 1394, Portland, OR 97207-1394, www.cep.pdx.edu
Crooked Hills Publishing, PO Box 83066, Portland, OR 97283, www.crookedhills.com
The Eighth Mountain Press, 624 Southeast 29th Avenue, Portland, OR 97214, 503-233-3936, ruth@eighthmountain.com
First Books, 6750 SW Franklin, # A, Portland, OR 97223-2542, 503-968-6777
GERTRUDE, PO Box 83948, Portland, OR 97283, www.gertrudepress.org
Gertrude Press, PO Box 83948, Portland, OR 97283, www.gertrudepress.org
Glimmer Train Press, Inc., 1211 NW Glisan St., Suite 207, Portland, OR 97209, Ph: 503/221-0836 Web site address: www.glimmertrain.org
GLIMMER TRAIN STORIES, 1211 NW Glisan St., Suite 207, Portland, OR 97209, Ph: 503/221-0836 Web site address: www.glimmertrain.org
Global Learning, 1001 SE Water Avenue, Suite 310, Portland, OR 97214, www.1night1flight.com
Gloger Family Books, 2020 NW Northrup Street #311, Portland, OR 97209-1679
THE GROVE REVIEW, 1631 NE Broadway, PMB #137, Portland, OR 97232, editor@thegrovereview.org, www.thegrovereview.org
HUBBUB, 5344 S.E. 38th Avenue, Portland, OR 97202, 503-775-0370
Inkwater Press, 6750 SW Franklin Street, Suite A, Portland, OR 97223-2542, Phone: 503.968.6777; Fax: 503.968.6779; Web: www.inkwaterpress.com
Jardin Publishing, PO Box 6533, Portland, OR 97228
LEO Productions LLC., PO Box 1333, Portland, OR 97207, 360-601-1379, Fax 360-210-4133
Night Bomb Press, 1812 NE 66th Avenue, #91, Portland, OR 97213, submissions@nightbombpress.com, www.nightbombpress.com, (503)867-7270
THE NIGHT BOMB REVIEW, 1812 NE 66th Avenue, #91, Portland, OR 97213, submissions@nightbombpress.com, www.nightbombpress.com, (503)867-7270
One Spirit Press, One Spirit Press, 1815 SE Stark Street, Portland, OR 97214, spiritpresspublishing@gmail.com ; 1-503-954-0012 www.onespiritpress.com
OPEN SPACES QUARTERLY, PMB 134, 6327 C SW Capitol Hwy., Portland, OR 97239-1937, Fax: 503-227-3401, Ph: 503-313-4361
PORTLAND REVIEW, PO BOX 347, Portland, OR 97207-0347
THIRDEYE MAGAZINE, PO Box 8911, Portland, OR 97201, 231-218-6126 www.thirdeyemag.com
Thirdeye Publications, PO Box 8911, Portland, OR 97201, 231-218-6126 www.thirdeyepublications.com
Vestibular Disorders Association, PO Box 13305, Portland, OR 97213-0305, 503-229-7705, Fax 503-229-8064, toll-free 1-800-837-8428, veda@vestibular.org, www.vestibular.org
WHITEWALL OF SOUND, 411 NE 22nd #21, Portland, OR 97232-3270, jcline@teleport.com
Krill Press, P.O. Box 396, Rogue River, OR 97537, 541-582-1188, info@krillpress.com, http://www.krillpress.com
Deep Well Publishing Company, 1371 Peace Street SE #12, Salem, OR 97302-2572, 503-581-6339
EDGZ, Edge Publications, PO Box 618, Scappoose, OR 97056
Flying Pencil Publications, 33126 SW Callahan Road, Scappoose, OR 97056, 503-543-7171, fax: 503-543-7172
Health Plus Publishers, PO Box 1027, Sherwood, OR 97140, 503-625-0589, Fax 503-625-1525
Multnomah Publishers, Inc., 601 N. Larch St., Sisters, OR 97759-9320, 541-549-1144, Fax 541-549-8048
Pygmy Forest Press, 1125 Mill St, Springfield, OR 97477-3729, 541-747-9734
Tanest Publishing House, 626 S. 41st Court, Springfield, OR 97478
Talent House Press, 1306 Talent Avenue, Talent, OR 97540, talhouse@mcleodusa.net
NewSage Press, PO Box 607, Troutdale, OR 97060-0607, 503-695-2211 www.newsagepress.com info@newsagepress.com
Accent On Music, LLC, PMB 252, 19363 Willamette Drive, West Linn, OR 97068, (503)699-1814, (503)699-1813(FAX), (800)313-4406, info@accentonmusic.com
RAVING DOVE, PO Box 28, West Linn, OR 97068
SHAMAN'S DRUM: A Journal of Experiential Shamanism, PO Box 270, Williams, OR 97544, 541-846-1313
Kodiak Media Group, PO Box 1029-DB, Wilsonville, OR 97070, Fax 503-625-4087
nine muses books, 3541 Kent Creek Road, Winston, OR 97496, 541-679-6674, mw9muses@teleport.com

PENNSYLVANIA

TAPROOT LITERARY REVIEW, PO Box 204, Ambridge, PA 15003, 724-266-8476, taproot10@aol.com
Taproot Press Publishing Co., Box 204, Ambridge, PA 15003, taproot10@aol.com
Merwood Books, 237 Merwood Lane, Ardmore, PA 19003, 215-947-3934, Fax 215-947-4229
Saturnalia Books, 105 Woodside Rd, Ardmore, PA 19003, www.saturnaliabooks.com
Black Lawrence Press, 115 Center Ave, Aspinwall, PA 15215, www.blacklawrencepress.com
Kobalt Books, P.O. Box 1062, Bala Cynwyd, PA 19004, 314-503-5462

Disclosure Research and Publishing, PO Box 262, Bartonsville, PA 18321-0262, 570-619-5271, www.disclosurepublish-ing.com
Chistell Publishing, 2500 Knights Road, Suite 19-01, Bensalem, PA 19020-3429
Lilly Press, 1848 Finch Dr, Bensalem, PA 19020-4406, 215-638-2493
RIVER POETS JOURNAL, 1848 Finch Dr, Bensalem, PA 19020-4406, 215-638-2493
MAELSTROM, HC #1 Box 1624, Blakeslee, PA 18610
Appalachian House, P.O. Box 627, Boiling Springs, PA 17007, (717) 609-6234, apphouse@pa.net
Dufour Editions Inc., PO Box 7, Chester Springs, PA 19425-0007, 610-458-5005, Fax 610-458-7103
Starry Night Publishing, 904 Broad Street, Collingdale, PA 19023, www.starrynightpublishing.com
Black Bear Publications, 1916 Lincoln Street, Croydon, PA 19021-8026, bbreview@earthlink.net, www.blackbearreview.com
BLACK BEAR REVIEW, Black Bear Publications, 1916 Lincoln Street, Croydon, PA 19021, bbreview@earthlink.net, www.blackbearreview.com
THE AGUILAR EXPRESSION, 1329 Gilmore Avenue, Donora, PA 15033, 724-379-8019, www.wordrunner.com/xfaguilar
THINK Journal, P.O. Box 454, Downingtown, PA 19335
MATCHBOOK, 240 Edison Furlong Road, Doylestown, PA 18901-3013, Fax 215-340-3965
Raw Dog Press, 151 S. West Street, Doylestown, PA 18901, 215-345-6838
MAMMOTH books, 7 Juniata Street, DuBois, PA 15801, avallone@psu.edu
PENNSYLVANIA ENGLISH, Penn State DuBois, College Place, DuBois, PA 15801-3199, Office: 814-375-4785, Fax: 814-375-4785
LAKE EFFECT, Penn State Erie, 4951 College Dr, Erie, PA 16563-1501, 814-898-6281
Word Forge Books, PO Box 97, Ferndale, PA 18921, Tel 610-847-2456, email admin@wordforgebooks.com, URL www.wordforgebooks.com
THE GETTYSBURG REVIEW, Gettysburg College, Gettysburg, PA 17325, 717-337-6770
FAT TUESDAY, 560 Manada Gap Road, Grantville, PA 17028, 717-469-7159
MacDonald/Sward Publishing Company, 120 Log Cabin Lane, Greensburg, PA 15601, 724-832-7767
Libertarian Press, Inc./American Book Distributors, PO Box 309, Grove City, PA 16127-0309, 724-458-5861, Fax (724) 458-5962
Faith Builders Resource Group, PO Box 125, Guys Mills, PA 16327, 814-789-4769, 814-789-3396, 877-222-4769, clr@fbep.org, www.christianlearning.org
Cider Press Review, A Journal of Contemporary Poetry, 777 Braddock Lane, Halifax, PA 17032
Willfam Publishing Co., P.O.Box 60455, Harrisburg, PA 17106-0455, 717-592-9407, willfampub@verizon.net, willfampub-lishing.com
Art of Living, PrimaMedia,Inc, 1250 Bethlehem Pike, Suite #241, Hatfield, PA 19440, 215-660-5045; Fax: 734-448-4125; 1-800-581-9020; primamedia4@yahoo.com
SCHUYLKILL VALLEY JOURNAL, 240 Golf Hills Road, Havertown, PA 19083-1026, (h) 610-789-4692, mac-poet1@aol.com, www.svjlit.com (online SVJ journal), www.manayunkartcenter.org. Readings are held at Maynayunk/ Roxborough Art Center at 419 Green Lane in Philadelphia (phone - 215-482-3363).
Himalayan Institute Press, 952 Bethany TPKE, Honesdale, PA 18341, 570-253-5551
EARTHSHINE, P.O. Box 245, Hummelstown, PA 17036, 717.645.2908, poetry@ruminations.us, http://www.ruminations.us/esIndex.htm
Markowski International Publishers, 1 Oakglade Circle, Hummelstown, PA 17036-9525, 717-566-0468, Fax 717-566-6423
GROUP Publishing, 93 Old York Road Suite 1-406, Jenkintown, PA 19046, 267 258-7967
HOT FLASHES: Not a Menopause Thang, 93 Old York Road Suite 1-406, Jenkintown, PA 19046, 267 258-7967
Naissance, chapbooks by chapbookpublisher.com, 443 Main Street, 2nd FL, Kingston, PA 18704, 570-762-6140
WEST BRANCH, Bucknell Hall, Bucknell University, Lewisburg, PA 17837, 570-577-1853, westbranch@bucknell.edu
Star Publish LLC, PO Box 122, Loretto, PA 15940, 814-421-5142
POETS AT WORK, PO Box 232, Lyndora, PA 16045
Bookhaven Press, LLC, 249 Field Club Circle, McKees Rocks, PA 15136-1034, 412-494-6926, Fax 412-494-5749, bookhaven@aol.com, http://federaljobs.net
THE ALLEGHENY REVIEW, Box 32, Allegheny College, Meadville, PA 16335, 814-332-6553
Trickle Creek Books, 500 Andersontown Rd, Mechanicsburg, PA 17055-6055, 717-766-2638, fax 717-766-1343, 800-353-2791
J & J Consultants, Inc., 603 Olde Farm Road, Media, PA 19063, 610-565-9692, Fax 610-565-9694, wjones13@juno.com, www.members.tripod.com/walterjones/
MAD POETS REVIEW, PO Box 1248, Media, PA 19063-8248
NEW ALTERNATIVES, 603 Ole Farm Road, Media, PA 19063, 610-565-9692, Fax 610-565-9694, wjones13@juno.com, www.members.tripod/walterjones
Nova House Press, 470 North Latch's Lane, Merion, PA 19066
The Merion Press, Inc., PO Box 144, Merion Station, PA 19066-0144, 610-617-8919, Fax 610-617-8929, rjstern@merion-press.com, www.merionpress.com
Wilderness Ministries, PO Box 225, Mount Union, PA 17066, 814-542-8668
Camel Press, Box 212, Needmore, PA 17238, 717-573-4526
DUST (From the Ego Trip), Box 212, Needmore, PA 17238, 717-573-4526
THE FREEDONIA GAZETTE: The Magazine Devoted to the Marx Brothers, 335 Fieldstone Drive, New Hope, PA 18938-1224, 215-862-9734
POSTCARD CLASSICS (formerly DELTIOLOGY), PO Box 132, Norwood, PA 19074-0008, 610-485-8572
Book Garden Publishing,LLC, 147 A Roesch Avenue, Oreland, PA 19075, 215-576-5544
The Elevator Group, PO Box 207, Paoli, PA 19301-0207
Kelly Writers House, 3805 Locust Walk, Philadekphia, PA 19104
AMERICAN POETRY REVIEW, 1700 Sansom St., Suite 800, Philadelphia, PA 19103-5214, 215-496-0439
Authentic Publishing LLC, PO Box 8486, Philadelphia, PA 19101, 215-495-7300, www.AuthenticPublishingLLC.com, ContactUs@AuthenticPublishingLLC.com
AXE FACTORY REVIEW, PO Box 40691, Philadelphia, PA 19107
CYNIC BOOK REVIEW, PO Box 40691, Philadelphia, PA 19107
Cynic Press, PO Box 40691, Philadelphia, PA 19107
Paul Dry Books, 1616 Walnut St., Suite 808, Philadelphia, PA 19103, 215-231-9939, fax:215-231-9942, website: www.@pauldrybooks.com
The Haworth Press, 325 Chestnut St., Philadelphia, PA 19106-1580, Tel.: (607)722-5857, Fax: (607)722-8465, Web:

http://www.HaworthPress.com
HOLY ROLLERS, PO Box 40691, Philadelphia, PA 19107
Ika, LLC, 4630 Sansom Street, 1st Floor, Philadelphia, PA 19139-4630, 215-327-7341
Jacket Magazine, Kelly Writers House, 3805 Locust Walk, Philadelphia, PA 19104
Jewish Publication Society, 2100 Arch Street, Philadelphia, PA 19103-1308, 215-802-0600, Fax 215-568-2017
LOW BUDGET ADVENTURE, PO Box 40691, Philadelphia, PA 19107
LOW BUDGET SCIENCE FICTION, PO Box 40691, Philadelphia, PA 19107
MAGNET MAGAZINE, 1218 Chestnut Street, Suite 508, Philadelphia, PA 19107, 215-413-8570, fax 215-413-8569, magnetmag@aol.com
New Door Books, 2115 Wallace Street, Philadelphia, PA 19130, 215-769-2525, info@newdoorbooks.com, http://www.newdoorbooks.com
Our Child Press, PO Box 4379, Philadelphia, PA 19118-8379, 610-308-8988
PAINTED BRIDE QUARTERLY, Drexel University, Dept. of English and Philosophy, 3141 Chestnut Street, Philadelphia, PA 19104
PHILADELPHIA POETS, 1919 Chestnut Street, Apartment 1721, Philadelphia, PA 19103-3430, redrose108@comcast.net
PHILADELPHIA STORIES, 2021 S. 11th Street, Philadelphia, PA 19148
UNMUZZLED OX, '304 Pine Street, (1R), Philadelphia, PA 19107, 718-448-3395, 212-226-7170, MAndreOX@aol.com
WOMEN'S REVIEW OF BOOKS, 628 North 2nd Street, Philadelphia, PA 19123, 215-925-4390
ZerOX Books, 1304 Pine St., #1R, Philadelphia, PA 19107
Anderson Publishing; also RC Anderson Books, PO Box 22322, Pittsburgh, PA 15222, 412-231-0436
Autumn House Press, P.O. Box 60100, Pittsburgh, PA 15211, 412-381-4261, www.autumnhouse.org
Bellday Books, P.O. Box 3687, Pittsburgh, PA 15230, 1-866-790-4041
CAKETRAIN, PO Box 82588, Pittsburgh, PA 15218-1540, www.caketrain.org, caketrainjournal@hotmail.com
Caketrain Journal and Press, PO Box 82588, Pittsburgh, PA 15218, www.caketrain.org, caketrainjournal@hotmail.com
Carnegie Mellon University Press, Carnegie Mellon University, English Department, Pittsburgh, PA 15213, 412-268-6446
COAL HILL REVIEW, www.coalhillreview.com, 87 1/2 Westwood Street, Autumn House Press, Pittsburgh, PA 15211, 412-381-4261
CREATIVE NONFICTION, 5501 Walnut Street #202, Pittsburgh, PA 15232-2329, 412-688-0304, fax 412-688-0262
Harobed Publishing Creations, P.O.Box 8195, Pittsburgh, PA 15217-0915, 412-243-9299 fax/phone(if beeps redial fax in use)
LATIN AMERICAN LITERARY REVIEW, PO Box 17660, Pittsburgh, PA 15235-0860, 412-824-7903, www.lalrp.org, latinreview@hotmail.com
Latin American Literary Review Press, PO Box 17660, Pittsburgh, PA 15235-0860, 412-824-7903, www.lalrp.org, editor@lalrp.org
LILLIPUT REVIEW, 282 Main Street, Pittsburgh, PA 15201
THE MINNESOTA REVIEW, Dept. of English, Carnegie Mellon University, Baker Hall 259, Pittsburgh, PA 15213-3890, editors@theminnesotareview.org
THE POETRY EXPLOSION NEWSLETTER (THE PEN), PO Box 4725, Pittsburgh, PA 15206-0725, 1-866-234-0297, wewuvpoetry@hotmail.com
QP Publishing, PO Box 18281, Pittsburgh, PA 15236-0281, phone/Fax
QUALITY QUIPS NEWSLETTER, PO Box 18281, Pittsburgh, PA 15236-0281, phone/Fax
Redgreene Press, 1401 Hodgkiss St., Pittsburgh, PA 15212-2719, Out-of-country authors may submit poems by e-mail: anderson_rc1@earthlink.net with the word poem or poetry in the subject line.
REDGREENE REVIEW, PO Box 22322, Pittsburgh, PA 15222, 412-231-0436, anderson_rc1@earthlink.net (only for use by out-of-country authors.
Selah Publishing Co. Inc., PO Box 98066, Pittsburgh, PA 15227-0466, 845-338-2816, Fax 845-338-2991, customerservice@selahpub.com
Spring Grass, PO Box 22322, Pittsburgh, PA 15222, 412-231-0436
SterlingHouse Publisher, 3468 Babcock Blvd., Pittsburgh, PA 15237, Phone: 412-837-2423, www.sterlinghousepublisher.com
The Thirty First Bird Press, Pittsburgh, PA 15213, www.thirtyfirstbird.com
THE THIRTY FIRST BIRD REVIEW: The Committed, Critical, and Creative Journal of Religion and Literature, Pittsburgh, PA 15213, www.thirtyfirstbird.com
University of Pittsburgh Press, 3400 Forbes Avenue, 5th Floor, Eureka Bldg., Pittsburgh, PA 15260, 412-383-2456
Schuylkill Living, 115 S Centre St., Pottsville, PA 17901-3000, 570-622-8625
SCHUYLKILL LIVING MAGAZINE, 1 One Norwegian Plz, Pottsville, PA 17901-4400, 570-622-8625, Fax 570-622-2143, eramus@comcast.net, www.schuylkillliving.com
University of Scranton Press, 445 Madison Ave., Scranton, PA 18510, 1-800-941-3081, 1-800-941-8804, www.scrantonpress.com
Burd Street Press, PO Box 708, 73 W. Burd Street, Shippensburg, PA 17257, 717-532-2237, Fax 717-532-6110
Ragged Edge Press, PO Box 708, 73 West Burd Street, Shippensburg, PA 17257, 717-532-2237, Fax 717-532-6110
White Mane Publishing Company, Inc., 73 West Burd Street, PO Box 708, Shippensburg, PA 17257, 717-532-2237, Fax 717-532-6110, email:marketing@whitemane.com
SLAB, Dept. of English, 314 SWC, Slippery Rock University, Slippery Rock, PA 16057
Avari Press, P.O. Box 285, Smoketown, PA 17576, editorial@avaripress.com, http://www.avaripress.com
5 AM, Box 205, Spring Church, PA 15686
Strata Publishing, Inc., PO Box 1303, State College, PA 16804, 814-234-8545, Fax 814-238-7222, www.stratapub.com
THE CHAUCER REVIEW: A Journal of Medieval Studies and Literary Criticism, 820 North University Drive, University Support Building 1, Suite C, University Park, PA 16802
Pennsylvania State University Press, Penn State Press, Suite C, 820 N. University Drive, University Park, PA 16802-1711, 814-865-1327
SHAW: THE ANNUAL OF BERNARD SHAW STUDIES, Penn State Press, Suite C, 820 N. University Drive, University Park, PA 16802-1711, 814-865-1327
Shangri-La Publications, #3 Coburn Hill Rd., POB 65, Warren Center, PA 18851-0065, telephone 607-272-6156, toll free 866-966-6288, email gosline@hotmail.com, web http://shangri-la.0catch.com
B.B. Mackey Books, PO Box 475, Wayne, PA 19087-0475, www.mackeybooks.com
Milverstead Publishing LLC, 31 Rampart Drive, Wayne, PA 19087, (484)653-6205, info@milversteadpublishing.com
COLLEGE LITERATURE, 210 East Rosedale Avenue, West Chester University, West Chester, PA 19383, 610-436-2901, fax 610-436-2275, collit@wcupa.edu, www.collegeliterature.org
Sound Enterprises Publishing, 970 Cornwallis Drive, West Chester, PA 19380, 610-696-1715, richzerbey@zerbey.com ,

www.soundenterprisespublishing.com , hell-thscare.com
Swedenborg Foundation, 320 North Church Street, West Chester, PA 19380, (610) 430-3222 (Phone), (610) 430-7982 Fax, 1-800-355-3222 (Phone), info@swedenborg.com, www.swedenborg.com
Infinity Publishing, 1094 New Dehaven St, Suite 100, West Conshohocken, PA 19428, info@infinitypublishing.com
Kallisti Publishing, 332 Center Street, Wilkes-Barre, PA 18702, 877-444-6188
BRILLIANT CORNERS: A Journal of Jazz & Literature, Lycoming College, Williamsport, PA 17701, 570-321-4279
Westholme Publishing, 904 Edgewood Road, Yardley, PA 19067

RHODE ISLAND

EZRA: An Online Journal of Translation, Roger Williams University, Bristol, RI 02809
ROGER, an art & literary magazine, Department of Creative Writing / Roger Williams University, One Old Ferry, Bristol, RI 02809, (401) 254-3860
THE ALEMBIC, English Department, Providence College, Providence, RI 02918
Burning Deck Press, 71 Elmgrove Avenue, Providence, RI 02906
Copper Beech Press, P O Box 2578, English Department, Providence, RI 02906, 401-351-1253
ITALIAN AMERICANA, University of Rhode Island, 80 Washington Street, Providence, RI 02903-1803
PRIVACY JOURNAL, PO Box 28577, Providence, RI 02908, 401-274-7861, fax 401-274-4747, orders@privacyjournal.net, www.privacyjournal.net
BRYANT LITERARY REVIEW, Faculty Suite F, Bryant University, Smithfield, RI 02917, website http://bryant2.bryant.edu/~blr/

SOUTH CAROLINA

GenNext Publishing, 103 Elliott Circle, Anderson, SC 29621, 864-260-9818
APOSTROPHE: USCB Journal of the Arts, 801 Carteret Street, Beaufort, SC 29902, 843-521-4158, sjtombe@gwm.sc.edu
CRAZYHORSE, Dept. of English College of Charleston, 66 George Street, Charleston, SC 29424, crazyhorse@cofc.edu, http://www.crazyhorsejournal.org
ILLUMINATIONS, English Dept., 66 George Street, College of Charleston, Charleston, SC 29424-0001, Tel: 843-953-1920, Fax: 843-953-1924, Web: www.cofc.edu/illuminations
WWW.HOTMETALPRESS.NET, 1173 Sea Eagle Watch, Charleston, SC 29413, On-line address: www.hotmetalpress.net, email: sea7@comcast.net
CLEMSON POETRY REVIEW, Clemson, SC 29630
Clemson University Digital Press, 611 Strode Tower, Box 340522, Clemson University, Clemson, SC 29634-0522
SOUTH CAROLINA REVIEW, Ctr. for Electronic & Digital Publishing, Clemson University, 611 Strode Tower, Box 340522, Clemson, SC 29634-0522, 864-656-3151; 864-656-5399
SHORT STORY, PO Box 50567, Columbia, SC 29250
University of South Carolina Press, 1600 Hampton Street, 5th Floor, Columbia, SC 29208, 803-777-5245; 803-777-0160; www.sc.edu/uscpress
YEMASSEE, Dept. of English, University of South Carolina, Columbia, SC 29208
Banks Channel Books, 2435 East North St. #245, Greenville, SC 29615, Order phone 215-589-5032; E-mail bankschan@aol.com
EMRYS JOURNAL, PO Box 8813, Greenville, SC 29601, www.emrys.org
Emrys Press, PO Box 8813, Greenville, SC 29601, www.emrys.org
Ninety-Six Press, Furman University, 3300 Poinsett Highway, Greenville, SC 29613, 864-294-3152/6
Bel Canto Press, 555 Westham Dr., Murrells Inlet, SC 29576-9160, 843-685-3711, 843-650-6267, editor@belcantopress.com, www.belcantopress.com
Vintage Romance Publishing, LLC, 2520 Atlantic Palms Lane #908, N. Charleston, SC 29406-9298, (843) 270-3742, www.vrpublishing.com, submissions@vrpublishing.com
LITERARY MAMA, Department of English, Pinewood Preparatory School, 1114 Orangeburg Road, Summerville, SC 29843, www.literarymam.com

SOUTH DAKOTA

Tesseract Publications, PO Box 164, Canton, SD 57013-0164, 605-987-5070, Fax same, call ahead, it is a one-liner information@tesseractpublications.com, www.tesseractpublications.com
Dog's Eye View Media, PO Box 888, Hot Springs, SD 57747, 605 745-4350
PRAIRIE WINDS, Dakota Wesleyan University, DWU Box 536, Mitchell, SD 57301, 605-995-2814
Blue Owl Press, 3700 S. Westport Ave, #1876, Sioux Falls, SD 57106, 5207051239, howard@blueowlpress.com, www.blueowlpress.com
SOUTH DAKOTA REVIEW, Department of English / University of South Dakota, 414 East Clark St., Vermillion, SD 57069, 605-677-5184, 605-677-5966, email: sdreview@usd.edu, website: http://www.usd.edu/sdreview
PADDLEFISH, Mount Marty College 1105 W. 8th St., Yankton, SD 57078, office- (605)668-1362 Fax: (605)668-1607

TENNESSEE

Cold Tree Publishing, 214 Overlook Court, Ste. 253, Brentwood, TN 37027, 615.309.4984, http://coldtreepublishing.com
BABYSUE, PO Box 15749, Chattanooga, TN 37415
BABYSUE MUSIC REVIEW, PO Box 15749, Chattanooga, TN 37415
C&R Press, 1844 Knickerbocker Ave., Chattanooga, TN 37405-2216, www.crpress.org
ZONE 3, Austin Peay State University, P.O. Box 4565, Clarksville, TN 37044, 931-221-7031/7878
Leadership Education and Development, Inc., 1116 West 7th Street, PMB 175, Columbia, TN 38401, 931-379-3799; 800-659-6135, www.leadershipdevelopment.com
UNDER THE SUN, English Dept., Box 5053, Tennessee Technological University, Cookeville, TN 38505, 931-372-3768, hweidner@tntech.edu, www.tntech.edu/underthesun
LEAF GARDEN, 1087 Harbin Rd., Dandridge, TN 37725, choicesreply@gmail.com
Sterli Publishing, 2202 Coathbridge Dr, Germantown, TN 38139, 901-351-6849
AETHLON, Sport Literature Association, Box 70270 ETSU, Johnson City, TN 37614
CENTAUR MAGAZINE: The Online Literary Journal of Equine Inspiration, Johnson City, TN 37604, becky@centaurlit.com, www.centaurlit.com
NOW AND THEN, PO Box 70556, East Tennessee State University, Johnson City, TN 37614-0556, 423-439-5348; fax 423-439-6340; e-mail woodsidj@etsu.edu

610

SPOTops Books, 337 Hickory Bluff, Johnson City, TN 37601-1327, 423-610-8464

Twilight Times Books, PO Box 3340, Kingsport, TN 37664-0340, 423-323-0183 phone/Fax, publisher@twilighttimes-books.com, www.twilighttimesbooks.com

RFD, PO Box 68, Liberty, TN 37095, 615-536-5176

HEAL Foundation Press, PO Box 241209, Memphis, TN 38002, www.healfoundation.org, info@healfoundation.org, (901) 320-9179

Omonomany, 5501 Murray Road, Memphis, TN 38119, 901-374-9027, Fax 901-374-0508, jimweeks12@gmail.com

THE PINCH, University of Memphis, Department of English, 435 Patterson Hall, Memphis, TN 38152-6176, 901-678-4591, www.thepinchjournal.com, editor@thepinchjournal.com

Saint Bob Press, 2095 Poplar Avenue, Suite 54, Memphis, TN 38104, 901.412.7362, www.saintbobpress.com

Black Forest Press and The Tennessee Publishing House, Belle Arden Run Estate, 496 Mountain View Drive, Mosheim, TN 37818-3524, 423-422-4711, ; E-mail: authorinfo@blackforestpress.net, web: www.blackforestpress.net

COMICS REVUE, PO Box 336 -Manuscript Press, Mountain Home, TN 37684-0336, 432-926-7495

Manuscript Press, PO Box 336, Mountain Home, TN 37684-0336, 423-926-7495

POEMS & PLAYS, Department of English, Middle Tennessee State University, Murfreesboro, TN 37132, 615-898-2712

ZINE WORLD: A Reader's Guide to the Underground Press, PO Box 330156, Murfreesboro, TN 37133-0156, www.undergroundpress.org

AFRO-HISPANIC REVIEW, The Bishop Joseph Johnson Black Cultural Center, Vanderbilt University, VU Station B #351666, Nashville, TN 37235-1666

Ion Imagination Publishing, Ion Imagination Entertainment, Inc., PO Box 210943, Nashville, TN 37221-0943, 615-646-3644, Fax 615-646-6276, flumpa@aol.com, www.flumpa.com

Music City Publishing, P.O. Box 41696, Nashville, TN 37204-1696, www.musiccitypublishing.com

POCKETS, PO Box 340004, Nashville, TN 37203-0004, 615-340-7333, pockets@upperroom.org, www.pockets.org

Premium Press America, 2606 Eugenia Avenue, Suite C, Nashville, TN 37211, 615-256-8484

The Preservation Foundation, Inc., 2213 Pennington Bend Road, Nashville, TN 37214, 800-228-8517, 615-269-2433, preserve@storyhouse.org, www.storyhouse.org

THE2NDHAND, 1430 Roberts Ave., Nashville, TN 37206, 205-907-2481

Time Barn Books, 529 Barrywood Drive, Nashville, TN 37220-1636, www.thetimegarden.com

Vanderbilt University Press, VU Station B #351813, 2301 Vanderbilt Place, Nashville, TN 37235-1813, 615-343-2446

Iris Publishing Group, Inc (Iris Press / Tellico Books), 969 Oak Ridge Turnpike, # 328, Oak Ridge, TN 37830-8832, Ph: 865-483-0837, Fx: 865-481-3793, rcumming@irisbooks.com, www.irisbooks.com

SEWANEE REVIEW, University of the South, 735 University Avenue, Sewanee, TN 37383-1000, 931-598-1246, email:lcouch@sewanee.edu

Journey Books Publishing, 3205 Highway 431, Spring Hill, TN 37174

White Buck Publishing, 1143 U.S. Highway 99, Waynesboro, TN 38485-3014, 931-722-3586 phone/fax, submissions@white-buckpublishing.com

TEXAS

Set Sail Productions, LLC, 621 Wills Point, Allen, TX 75013, 972 369 3574, www.setsailmotivation.com, eric@setsailforsuccess.com

Future Horizons, Inc., 721 West Abram Street, Arlington, TX 76013-6995, 817-277-0727, 1-800-4890727, Fax 817-277-2270, info@futurehorizons-autism.com

American Short Fiction, PO Box 301209, Austin, TX 78703, 512.538.1305 (voice), 512.538.1306 (fax), web: americanshortfiction.org, email: editors@americanshortfiction.org, subscriptions@americanshortfiction.org

Argo Press, PO Box 4201, Austin, TX 78765-4201, charspot01@austin.rr.com

BAT CITY REVIEW, Dept. of English, The University of Texas at Austin, 1 University Station B5000, Austin, TX 78712

Black Buzzard Press, 3503 Ferguson Lane, Austin, TX 78754

BORDERLANDS: Texas Poetry Review, PO Box 33096, Austin, TX 78764, borderlandspoetry@sbcglobal.net, www.borderlands.org

CHARLTON SPOTLIGHT, PO Box 4201, Austin, TX 78765-4201, charspot01@austin.rr.com

Erespin Press, 6906 Colony Loop Drive, Austin, TX 78724-3749

Host Publications, Inc., 1000 East 7th St., Suite 201, Austin, TX 78702-1953, Phone 212-905-2365; FAX 212-905-2369; jbratcher@hostpublications.com

Liquid Paper Press, PO Box 4973, Austin, TX 78765, www.eden.com/~jwhagins/nervecowboy

NERVE COWBOY, PO Box 4973, Austin, TX 78765, www.onr.com/user/jwhagins/nervecowboy.html

NOVA EXPRESS, PO Box 27231, Austin, TX 78755, E-mail lawrenceperson@jump.net

OFFICE NUMBER ONE, 2111 Quarry Road, Austin, TX 78703, 512-445-4489

PITCHFORK POETRY MAGAZINE, 2002A Guadalupe #461, Austin, TX 78705

Plain View Press, PO Box 42255, Austin, TX 78704, sb@plainviewpress.net

SRLR Press, PO Box 19228, Austin, TX 78760

TEXAS POETRY JOURNAL, 6205 Carrington Drive, Austin, TX 78749-5206, 512-779-6202, www.texaspoetryjournal.com, submissions@texaspoetryjournal.com

Thorp Springs Press, 1400 Cullen Avenue, Austin, TX 78757-2527, thorpsprings@ymail.com

TurnKey Press, 2100 Kramer Lane Suite 300, Austin, TX 78758-4094, 512.478.2028, cgoehring@bookpros.com

Vagabond Press, PO Box 4830, Austin, TX 78765-4830, (512) 343-1540, vagabondpress@sbcglobal.net, vagabondpress.com

Van Cleave Publishing, 1712 Riverside Dr. #93, Austin, TX 78741, 5126655451

VISIONS-INTERNATIONAL, The World Journal of Illustrated Poetry, 3503 Ferguson Lane, Austin, TX 78754

WILD PLUM, PO Box 4282, Austin, TX 78765

WORDKNOT AUDIO: A Literary Podcast Magazine, 515 Krebs Lane #102, Austin, TX 78704, wordknot@gmail.com, www.wordknot.com

Zumaya Publications LLC, 3209 S. IH35, #1086, Austin, TX 78741-6905, 512-402-5298, 235-660-2009

WINDHOVER: A Journal of Christian Literature, UMHB Box 8008, 900 College Street, Belton, TX 76513, 254-295-4561

THE CARETAKER GAZETTE, 3 Estancia Lane, Boerne, TX 78006, 830-755-2300, www.caretaker.org

Benecton Press, 9001 Grassbur Road, Bryan, TX 77808, 979-589-2665

Stardate Publishing Company, P. O. Box 112302, Carrollton, TX 75011-2302, voice-972-898-8349, fax-1-866-728-6500, jcothran@stardatepublishing.com, www.stardatepublishing.com

CALLALOO, MS 4212 TAMU, Texas A&M University,, College Station, TX 77843-4212, Phone: 979-458-3108, Fax: 979-458-3275, Web: http://callaloo.tamu.edu, e-mail: callaloo@tamu.edu

611

Historical Resources Press, 2104 Post Oak Court, Corinth / Denton, TX 76210-1900, 940-321-1066, fax 940-497-1313, www.booksonhistory.com
THE AFRICAN HERALD, PO Box 132394, Dallas, TX 75313-2394
Behavioral Sciences Research Press, Inc., 12803 Demetra Drive, Ste. 100, Dallas, TX 75234, 972-243-8543, Fax 972-243-6349
Brown Books Publishing Group, 16200 N. Dallas Parkway, Suite 170, Dallas, TX 75248-2616, 972-381-0009, fax: 972-248-4336, publishing@brownbooks.com, www.brownbooks.com
CARVE MAGAZINE, P.O. Box 701510, Dallas, TX 75370
Good Hope Enterprises, Inc., PO Box 132394, Dallas, TX 75313-2394, 214-823-7666, fax 214-823-7373
Inspiring Teachers Publishing, Inc., 12655 N. Central Expressway, Suite 810, Dallas, TX 75243, 877-496-7633 (toll-free), 972-496-7633, Fax 972-763-0355, info@inspiringteachers.com, www.inspiringteachers.com
Lost Prophet Press, 4144 Office Pkwy, Apt. 2306, Dallas, TX 75204-2306, 505.256.4589
Southern Methodist University Press, PO Box 750415, Dallas, TX 75275-0415, 214-768-1433, 214-768-1428 (fax), 800-826-8911 (orders), klang@mail.smu.edu, www.tamu.edu/upress
SOUTHWEST REVIEW, Southern Methodist University, P.O. Box 750374, Dallas, TX 75275-0374, 214-768-1037, www.smu.edu/southwestreview
AMERICAN LITERARY REVIEW, PO Box 311307, University of North Texas, Denton, TX 76203-1307, 940-565-2755
GLOBAL ONE MAGAZINE, 136 South Laurel Springs Drive, DeSoto, TX 75115, 972-223-1558
Knowledge Concepts Publishing, 136 South Laurel Springs Drive, DeSoto, TX 75115, 972-223-1558, fax: 214-988-2867
HILL COUNTRY SUN, 100 Commons Road, Suite 7, Number 319, Dripping Springs, TX 78620, 512-569-8212, melissa@hillcountrysun.com, www.hillcountrysun.com
RIVERSEDGE, TheUniversity of Texas Pan American, 1201 W. University, Lamar Bldg., Room 9A, Edinburg, TX 78539, 956-381-3638, bookworm@utpa.edu
The University of TX-Pan American Press, The University of TX-Pan American Press, 1201 W. Univ. Drive, Lamar Bldg., Room 9A, Edinburg, TX 78541, 956-381-3638, Fax 956-381-3697, bookworm@panam.edu
Cinco Puntos Press, 701 Texas, El Paso, TX 79901, Phone: (915) 838-1625, Fax: (915) 838-1635
QUICKSILVER, El Paso, TX 79968, academics.utep.edu/quicksilver, quicksilver@utep.edu
LAUGHING BEAR NEWSLETTER, 1418 El Camino Real, Euless, TX 76040-6555, e-mail editor@laughingbear.com, www.laughingbear.com
Wise Press, 8794 Rolling Acres Trail, Fair Oaks, TX 78015-4015, Fax 619-437-4160, lwise@san.rr.com, www.wisepress.com
DESCANT, English Department, TCU, Box 297270, Fort Worth, TX 76129
JAVELINA BI-MONTHLY, Fort Worth, TX 76133, javelinabimonthly@hotmail.com
Shearer Publishing, 406 Post Oak Road, Fredericksburg, TX 78624, 830-997-6529
Gemini Publishing Company, 3102 West Bay Area Blvd., Suite 707, Friendswood, TX 77546, Phone: 281-316-4275, website: www.getgirls.com, email: getgirls@getgirls.com
L&L Dreamspell, P.O. Box 1984, Friendswood, TX 77546-1984, Administrator@lldreamspell.com, www.lldreamspell.com
Immunizations for Public Health, 301 University Blvd., Galveston, TX 77555-0350, 4097720199, 4097725208, nnii@i4ph.org, www.i4ph.org
Armadillo Publishing Corporation, PO Box 2052, Georgetown, TX 78627-2052, 512-863-8660
CRITICAL REVIEW, Critical Review Foundation, P.O. Box 869, Helotes, TX 78023, edcritrev@gmail.com
Cookbook Resources, LLC, 541 Doubletree Drive, Highland Village, TX 75077, 972-317-0245
Arte Publico Press, University of Houston, 452 Cullen Performance Hall, Houston, TX 77204-2004, 713-743-2999, fax 713-743-2847, www.artepublicopress.com
Bear House Publishing, 14781 Memorial Drive #10, Houston, TX 77079-5210
CIRCLE INC., THE MAGAZINE, PO Box 670096, Houston, TX 77267-0096, 281-580-8634
Circle of Friends Books, PO Box 670096, Houston, TX 77267-0096, 281-580-8634
Dominion Global Publishing, P.O. Box 630372, Houston, TX 77263, 281-277-6626, info@positiontoreceive.com
ELEMENTS, PO Box 88086, Houston, TX 77288-0086, 713-252-5816, bWashington53@hotmail.com
GULF COAST, Dept. of English, University of Houston, Houston, TX 77204-3013
Lazywood Press, 1908 Harold Street, Houston, TX 77098-1502, 713-529-5500, teresa.byrnedodge@my-table.com, www.my-table.com
LITERAL: Latin American Voices, 770 South Post Oak Lane, Suite 530, Houston, TX 77056
MY TABLE: Houston's Dining Magazine, 1908 Harold Street, Houston, TX 77098-1502, 713-529-5500, teresa.byrne-dodge@my-table.com, www.my-table.com
Panther Creek Press, 104 Plum Tree Terrace #115, Houston, TX 77077, panthercreek3@hotmail.com, www.panthercreek-press.com
Rapacious Press, 3311 Virginia, Houston, TX 77098, 713.417.9381
TOUCHSTONE LITERARY JOURNAL, 104 Plum Tree Terrace, #115, Houston, TX 77077-5375
All That Productions,Inc., P.O. Box 1594, Humble, TX 77347, 281-878-2062
Penworth Publishing, 6942 FM 1960 East, #152, Humble, TX 77346, 281-404-5019, FAX 713-893-6107, Email: carmen@penworth.com, Website: www.penworth.com
THE TEXAS REVIEW, English Department, Sam Houston State University, Huntsville, TX 77341-2146
Texas Review Press, English Department, Sam Houston State University, Huntsville, TX 77341-2146
Authorlink.com, PO Box 140278, Irving, TX 75014-0278, http://www.authorlink.com, (972) 402-0101 /Fax 1-866-381-1587
Red Honor Press, PO Box 166677, Irving, TX 75016, 214-616-0161, www.redhonor.com, dscott@redhonor.com
Lily Ruth Publishing, PO Box 2067, Jacksonville, TX 75766, fax 888-602-6912; email lilyruthpublishing@yahoo.com; web site www.lilyruthpublishing.com
Camino Bay Books, 331 Old Blanco Road, Kendalia, TX 78027-1901, 830-336-3636, 800-463-8181
Falcon Publishing, LTD, P O Box 6099, Kingwood, TX 77345-6099, 713-417-7600, 281-360-8284, sales@falconpublishing.com, www.falconpublishing.com
IRON HORSE LITERARY REVIEW, Texas Tech University, English Dept., PO Box 43091, Lubbock, TX 79409-3091, 806-742-2500 X234
Texas Tech University Press, Box 41037, Lubbock, TX 79409-1037, 806-742-2982, fax 806-742-2979
32 POEMS, Texas Tech University, Lubbock, TX 79409-3091
Winoca Books & Media, 1923 29th Street, Suite 2, Lubbock, TX 79411
GIN BENDER POETRY REVIEW, PO Box 150932, Lufkin, TX 75915-0932, ginbender@yahoo.com, www.ginbender.com
JPS Publishing Company, 1141 Polo Run, Midlothian, TX 76065, 214-533-5685 (telephone), 972-775-5367 (fax), info@jpspublishing.com
Rock Island Press, 3411 West Circle Drive, Pearland, TX 77581, 281-744-1681

Blue Cubicle Press, LLC, P.O. Box 250382, Plano, TX 75025-0382, 9728240646

THE FIRST LINE, PO Box 250382, Plano, TX 75025-0382, 972-824-0646, submission@thefirstline.com, www.thefirst-line.com

WORKERS WRITE!, P.O. Box 250382, Plano, TX 75025-0382, 9728240646, www.workerswritejournal.com

WORKERS WRITE!, P.O. Box 250382, Plano, TX 75025-0382, 9728240646

World Gumbo Publishing, 7801 Alma Suite 105-323, Plano, TX 75025-3483, 1-888-318-2911, dbarkley@worldgumbo.com, www.worldgumbo.com

Friendly Oaks Publications, 227 Bunker Hill, PO Box 662, Pleasanton, TX 78064-0662, 830-569-3586, Fax 830-281-2617, E-mail friendly@docspeak.com

SOJOURN: A Journal of the Arts, School of Arts and Humanities, UT Dallas, Box 830688, JO 31, Richardson, TX 75083-0688, Email: sojourn@utdallas.edu Web site: http://sojourn.utdallas.edu

TRANSLATION REVIEW, Univ. of Texas-Dallas, 800 W. Campbell Rd.,- JO51, Richardson, TX 75080-3201, 972-883-2093, Fax 972-883-6303

Blue Moose Press, 1319 E Logan Street, Round Rock, TX 78664, 512-923-0475, 512-244-0140 fax, http://www.thebluemoosepress.com

CONCHO RIVER REVIEW, English Department, Angelo State University, San Angelo, TX 76909, 915-942-2269, me.hartje@angelo.edu

AMERICAN LETTERS & COMMENTARY, Dept. of English, Univ. of Texas at San Antonio, One UTSA Circle, San Antonio, TX 78249, amerletters@satx.rr.com, www.amleters.org

Candlestick Publishing, PO Box 39241, San Antonio, TX 78218-1241

Hill Country Books, 1302 Desert Links, San Antonio, TX 78258, 830-980-5425

LONE STARS MAGAZINE, 4219 Flinthill, San Antonio, TX 78230-1619, Website: www.lonestarsmagazine.net

PALO ALTO REVIEW, 1400 West Villaret Blvd., San Antonio, TX 78224-2499, 210-436-3249

Pecan Grove Press, St. Mary's University, 1 Camino Santa Maria, San Antonio, TX 78228, 210-436-3441

Trinity University Press, One Trinity Place, San Antonio, TX 78212-7200, www.trinity.edu/tupress, general number: (210)999-8884, fax: (210)999-8838, books@trinity.edu

Wings Press, 627 E. Guenther, San Antonio, TX 78210, 210-271-7805 (phone and fax)

ANHEDONIA, 4227 Elderwood Drive, Seabrook, TX 77586

Starik Publishing, PO Box 307, Slaton, TX 79364, web:www.starikpublishing.com

Absey & Co., 23011 Northcrest Drive, Spring, TX 77389, 888-412-2739, Fax 281-251-4676, abseyland@aol.com

KNUCKLE MERCHANT - The Journal of Naked Literary Aggression, 6101 Saintsbury Drive, Apt. 432, The Colony, TX 75056-5216, 505.256.4589 knucklemerchant@hotmail.com

THIN COYOTE, 6101 Saintsbury Drive, Apt. 432, The Colony, TX 75056-5216, 505.256.4589 knucklemerchant@hot-mail.com

BOTH SIDES NOW, 10547 State Highway 110 North, Tyler, TX 75704-3731, 903-592-4263; web site: www.bothsides-now.info. email: editor@bothsidesnow.info

FAQs Press, PO Box 130115, Tyler, TX 75713, 903-565-6653 phone/Fax, www.FAQsPress.com

Free People Press, 10547 State Hwy 110 N, Tyler, TX 75704-3731

BOOKS OF THE SOUTHWEST, 2508 Garner Field Road, Uvalde, TX 78801-6250, e-mail richter@hilconet.com

AMERICAN BOOK REVIEW, University of Houston-Victoria, School of Arts & Science, Victoria, TX 77901, 361-570-4101, Fax

Fiction Collective Two (FC2), Fiction Collective Two, 3007 N. Ben Wilson, Victoria, TX 77901-5731, 361-570-4118, Fax 361-580-5501

SYMPLOKE: A Journal for the Intermingling of Literary, Cultural and Theoretical Scholarship, c/o J. Di Leo, Univ. of Houston, 3007 N. Ben Wilson, Victoria, TX 77901, Fax 361-570-4207, editor@symploke.org

Eakins Press, PO Box 21235, Waco, TX 76702-1235, www.eakinpress.com, sales@eakinpress.com, phone: 1-254-235-6161, Fax: 254-235-6230

UTAH

American Legacy Media, 1544 W 1620 N STE 1-G, Clearfield, UT 84015-8243, 801-774-5472, 1-866-233-8165, info@americanlegacymedia.com, http://americanlegacymedia.com

Gibbs Smith, Publisher, PO Box 667, Layton, UT 84041, 801-544-9800, Fax 801-544-5582, info@GibbsSmith.com

Eagle's View Publishing, 6756 North Fork Road, Liberty, UT 84310, 801-393-4555 (orders), editorial phone 801-745-0905

Poet Tree Press, 1488 North 200 West, Logan, UT 84341-6803, 888-618-8444, Fax 435-713-4422, editor@poettreepress.com, www.poettreepress.com

Utah State University Press, 3078 Old Main Hill, Logan, UT 84322-3078, 435-797-1362, Fax 435-797-0313, michael.spooner@usu.edu (editorial) web: www.USUPress.edu

WESTERN AMERICAN LITERATURE, English Dept., Utah State Univ., 3200 Old Main Hill, Logan, UT 84322-3200, 435-797-1603, Fax 435-797-4099, wal@cc.usu.edu

DREAM NETWORK, PO Box 1026, Moab, UT 84532-3031, 435-259-5936; Publisher@DreamNetwork.net http:dreamne-twork.net http://DreamNetwork.com

Weber State University, Weber State University, 1214 University Circle, Ogden, UT 84408-1214, 801-626-6616, 801-262-6473, weberstudies@weber.edu, http://weberstudies.weber.edu

WEBER: The Contemporary West, Weber State University, 1405 University Circle, Ogden, UT 84408-1405, 801-626-6473

Bladestar Publishing, 1499 North 950 West, Orem, UT 84057, www.BladestarPublishing.com

Mojocastle Press, 94 N 200 E, Price, UT 84501, 435-630-6054

THE DEFENDER - Rush Utah's Newsletter, Eborn Books, Box 559, Roy, UT 84067

American Book Publishing, PMB 146, 5442 South 900 East, Salt Lake City, UT 84117-7204, info@american-book.com, http://www.american-book.com

Cedars Press, LLC, PO Box 581470, Salt Lake City, UT 84158, tel:(801)631-7811; fax(801)363-2945

ELLIPSIS, Westminster College, 1840 South 1300 East, Salt Lake City, UT 84105

Forest Dale Publishing Company, 2277 Windsor St., Salt Lake City, UT 84106, 801-883-9574, www.forestdalepublishing.com

Motom, 76 West 2100 South, Salt Lake City, UT 84115, (801)499-6021

QUARTERLY WEST, 255 South Central Campus Drive, Dept. of English, LNCO 3500/University of Utah, Salt Lake City, UT 84112-9109, 801-581-3938

Transcending Mundane, Inc., 3434 E. 7800 South, Salt Lake City, UT 84121, 435-901-2546, tommy@paracreative.com, www.paracreative.com

University of Utah Press, J. Willard Marriott Library, Suite 5400, 295 South 1500 East, Salt Lake City, UT 84112,

800-621-2736, Fax 800-621-8471, UofUpress.com
WESTERN HUMANITIES REVIEW, University of Utah, Salt Lake City, UT 84112, 801-581-6070
Jon's Adventure Productions, PO Box 901221, Sandy, UT 84090-1221, 801-647-5645
ROCKY MOUNTAIN KC NEWS, PO Box 901221, Sandy, UT 84090-1221, 801-574-0618 (Apollo Enterprises), getproducts@juno.com, www.dream4u.us, www.aim2get.com, www.jonfrear.com
Rocky Mountain KC Publishing Co., PO Box 901221, Sandy, UT 84090-1221, 801-574-0618 (Apollo Enterprises), getproducts@juno.com , www.getproducts.us, www.dream4u.us, www.aim2get.com, www.jonfrear.com . 801-647-5645 Jon's Adventure Productions ; www.jonsadventure.com , www.jonsadventureclub.com
Academic Innovations, 929 West Sunset Boulevard, St. George, UT 84770-4865, 800-967-8016, 800-967-4027
Eborn Books, 3601 S. 2700 W. B120, West Valley City, UT 84119, 801-965-9410, ebornbk@doitnow.com

VERMONT

Tupelo Press, PO Box 539, Dorset, VT 05251, Telephone 802-366-8185, Fax 802-362-1883
9N-2N-8N-NAA NEWSLETTER, PO Box 275, East Corinth, VT 05040-0275, www.n-news.com
TARPAULIN SKY, PO Box 189, Grafton, VT 05146
Tarpaulin Sky Press, PO Box 189, Grafton, VT 05146
Longhouse, 1604 River Road, Guilford, VT 05301, poetry@sover.net, www.LonghousePoetry.com
Upper Access Inc. Book Publishers, 87 Upper Access Road, Hinesburg, VT 05461, 800-310-8320 (orders only), 802-482-2988, Fax 802-304-1005, info@upperaccess.com
THE LYRIC, PO Box 110, Jericho, VT 05465-0110
Gihon River Review, Johnson State College, Johnson, VT 05656
GREEN MOUNTAINS REVIEW, Johnson State College, Johnson, VT 05656, 802-635-1350
THE MARLBORO REVIEW, PO Box 243, Marlboro, VT 05344, www.marlbororeview.com
Middlebury College Publications, Middlebury College, Middlebury, VT 05753, 802-443-5075, Fax 802-443-2088, E-mail nereview@middlebury.edu
NEW ENGLAND REVIEW, Middlebury College, Middlebury, VT 05753, 802-443-5075; toll-free 800-450-9571; fax 802-443-2088; e-mail NEReview@middlebury.edu; www.NEReview.com
HUNGER MOUNTAIN, The VCFA Journal of Arts, Vermont College of Fine Arts, 36 College Street, Montpelier, VT 05602, 802-828-8517, hungermtn@vermontcollege.edu, www.hungermtn.org
Russian Information Services, PO Box 567, Montpelier, VT 05601-0567, 802-223-4955
RUSSIAN LIFE, PO Box 567, Montpelier, VT 05601-0567
Black Thistle Press, 165 Wiswall Hill Road, Newfane, VT 05345-9548, 212-219-1898
Bear & Company, One Park Street, Rochester, VT 05767-0388, Tel: 802-767-3174, Toll Free: 1-800-246-8648, Fax: 802-767-3726, Email: info@innertraditions.com
Mountainside Press, PO Box 407, Shaftsbury, VT 05262, 802-447-7094, Fax 802-447-2611
Wood Thrush Books, 85 Aldis Street, St. Albans, VT 05478, 802-524-6606
PRISON LEGAL NEWS, P.O. Box 2420, West Brattleboro, VT 05303-2420, 802-257-1342, pln@prisonlegalnews.org
Arts End Books, PO Box 441, West Dover, VT 05356-0441, www.artsendbooks.com
NOSTOC MAGAZINE, PO Box 441, West Dover, VT 05356-0441
Chelsea Green Publishing Company, PO Box 428, White River Junction, VT 05001-0428, 802-295-6300

VIRGIN ISLANDS

THE CARIBBEAN WRITER, University of the Virgin Islands, RR 1, Box 10,000, Kingshill, St. Croix, VI 00850, Phone: 340-692-4152, Fax: 340-692-4026, e-mail: qmars@uvi.edu, submit@thecaribbeanwriter.org, orders@thecaribbeanwriter.org, website: www.TheCaribbeanWriter.org

VIRGINIA

CORRECTIONS TODAY, American Correctional Association, 206 North Washington Street, Suite 200, Alexandria, VA 22314, 703-224-0000
EDUCATION IN FOCUS, PO Box 2, Alexandria, VA 22313, 703-548-0457
EEI Press, 66 Canal Center Plaza #200, Alexandria, VA 22314, 703-683-0683
firefall editions, 4905 Tunlaw Street, Alexandria, VA 22312, 5105492461, www.firefallmedia.com
Orchises Press, PO Box 320533, Alexandria, VA 22320-4533, 703-683-1243
Plan B Press, PO Box 4067, Alexandria, VA 22303, 215-732-2663
Red Dragon Press, PO Box 320301, Alexandria, VA 22320-4301, 703-683-5877
AD/VANCE, 1593 Colonial Terrace #206, Arlington, VA 22209-1430
ALTERNATIVE PRESS REVIEW, PO Box 6245, Arlington, VA 22206
American Homeowners Foundation Press, 6776 Little Falls Road, Arlington, VA 22213, 703-536-7776, www.americanhomeowners.org
Bogg Publications, 422 North Cleveland Street, Arlington, VA 22201
BOGG: A Journal of Contemporary Writing, 422 N Cleveland Street, Arlington, VA 22201-1424
CONTEMPORARY POETRY REVIEW, PO Box 5222, Arlington, VA 22205
GARGOYLE, 3819 North 13th Street, Arlington, VA 22201-4922, Phone/Fax 703-525-9296, hedgehog2@erols.com, gargoylemagazine@comcast.com, www.gargoylemagazine.com
Gival Press, PO Box 3812, Arlington, VA 22203, 703-351-0079 phone, givalpress@yahoo.com, www.givalpress.com
OFF OUR BACKS, 4201 Wilson Blvd., #110-487, Arlington, VA 22203, 202-234-8072, ww2w.offourbacks.com
Paycock Press, 3819 N. 13th Street, Arlington, VA 22201, Fax 703-525-9296, hedgehog2@erols.com
Pocahontas Press, Inc., PO Drawer F, Blacksburg, VA 24063-1020, 540-951-0467, 800-446-0467
Rowan Mountain Press, PO Box 10111, Blacksburg, VA 24062-0111, 540-449-6178, e-mail faulkner@bev.net, web www.rowanmountain.com
Cedar Creek Publishing, PO Box 115, Bremo Bluff, VA 23022
dbS Productions, PO Box 1894, University Station, Charlottesville, VA 22903-0594, 800-745-1581, Fax 434-293-5502, info@dbs-sar.com, www.dbs-sar.com
IRIS: A Journal About Women, PO Box 800588, University of Virginia, Charlottesville, VA 22904, 434-924-4500, Fax 434-982-2901, iris@virginia.edu, http://womenscenter.virginia.edu/iris.htm
MERIDIAN, University of Virginia, P.O. Box 400145, Charlottesville, VA 22904-4145
Paladin Media Group, 673 Berkmar Court, Charlottesville, VA 22901, 434-817-2700, www.MyBigHeaven.com, www.PaladinMediaGroup.com

POETRY DAILY, PO Box 1306, Charlottesville, VA 22902-1306, Phone & Fax: 434-971-4001
University of Virginia Press, P.O. Box 400318, Charlottesville, VA 22904-4318, 800-831-3406, 877-288-6400, vapress@virginia.edu, www.upress.virginia.edu
THE VIRGINIA QUARTERLY REVIEW, One West Range, University of Virginia, PO Box 400223, Charlottesville, VA 22904-4223, Email: vqr@vwronline.org, ph: 434-924-3124, web: www.vqronline.org
Grace House Publishing, Grace House & Associates, LLC., P.O. Box 2265, Chesapeake, VA 23327, www.gracehousepublishing.com or www.cadipspress.com
Pocol Press, Box 411, Clifton, VA 20124-1333, 703-870-9611, chrisandtom@erols.com, www.pocolpress.com
CHRYSALIS READER, Box 4510, Route 1, Dillwyn, VA 23936, 1-434-983-3021
The Utility Company LLC, 15893 Northgate Drive, Dumfries, VA 22025-1704, 703 583.4408
PHOEBE: A Journal of Literature and Art, MSN 2D6, 4400 University Drive, George Mason University, Fairfax, VA 22030, www.gmu.edu.pubs/phoebe/, phoebejournal.blogspot.com
SO TO SPEAK: A Feminist Journal of Language & Art, So To Speak, George Mason University, 4400 University Drive, MS 2D6, Fairfax, VA 22030-4444, sts@gmu.edu www.gmu.edu/org/sts
WRITER'S CHRONICLE, Mail Stop 1E3, George Mason University, Fairfax, VA 22030-4444, 703-993-4301, http://awpwriter.org
ANCIENT PATHS, PO Box 7505, Fairfax Station, VA 22039, ssburris@cox.net http://www.editorskylar.com
EROSHA, PO Box 185, Falls Church, VA 22040-0185, Fax 703-852-3906, editor@erosha.net, http://erosha.net
Little Poem Press, PO Box 185, Falls Church, VA 22040-0185, www.celaine.com/LittlePoemPress
VLQ (Verse Libre Quarterly), PO Box 185, Falls Church, VA 22040-0185, Fax 703-852-3906, editor@vlqpoetry.com, http://vlqpoetry.com
Briery Creek Press, Department of English, Longwood University, Farmville, VA 23909, www.brierycreekpress.org
THE DOS PASSOS REVIEW, Department of English, Longwood University, Farmville, VA 23909
Blackwater Publications, PO Box 595, Flint Hill, VA 22627-0595, 540/987-9536; www.blackwaterpublications.com
Glen Allen Press, 4036-D Cox Road, Glen Allen, VA 23060, 804-747-1776, Fax 804-273-0500, mail@glenallenpress.com, www.glenallenpress.com
THE BEACON: Journal of Special Education Law & Practice, PO Box 480, Hartfield, VA 23071, 804-758-8400, Fax 202-318-3239, info@harborhouselaw.com, www.harborhouselaw.com
Harbor House Law Press, Inc., PO Box 480, Hartfield, VA 23071, 804-758-8400, Fax 202-318-3239, info@harborhouselaw.com, www.harborhouselaw.com
2L Publishing, LLC, 1525 Split Oak Lane #F, Henrico, VA 23229, 804-971-6367
THE HOLLINS CRITIC, PO Box 9538, Hollins University, VA 24020
SHENANDOAH: The Washington and Lee University Review, Mattingly House / 2 Lee Avenue, Washington and Lee University, Lexington, VA 24450-2116, 540-458-8765; http://shenandoah.wlu.edu
JAMES DICKEY REVIEW, English Department, Lynchburg College, 1501 Lakeside Drive, Lynchburg, VA 24501, 434-544-8732
Bereshith Publishing, 7200 Danny Lane, Manassas, VA 20112-3658, 703-222-9387, Fax 707-922-0875, info@bereshith.com
Profile Press, 6051 Greenway Court, Manassas, VA 20112-3049, 703-730-0642
CHANTEH, the Iranian Cross-Cultural Quarterly, 7229 Vistas Lane, McLean, VA 22101, saideh_pakravan@yahoo.com, www.saideh-pakravan.com
DOLLS UNITED INTERACTIVE MAGAZINE, 6360 Camille Drive, Mechanicsville, VA 23111, http://www.dollsunited.com, 804-339-8579, editor@dollsunited.com
THE SOW'S EAR POETRY REVIEW, P.O. Box 127, Millwood, VA 22646-0127, Email: rglesman@gmail.comWebsite: http://sows-ear.kitenet.net
August Press LLC, 108 Terrell Road, P.O. Box 6693, Newport News, VA 23606, wdawkins4bj@aol.com, www.augustpress.net
BLUE COLLAR REVIEW, PO Box 11417, Norfolk, VA 23517, red-ink@earthlink.net
Partisan Press, PO Box 11417, Norfolk, VA 23517, e-mail: red-ink@earthlink.net, website: http:www.Partisanpress.org
POETICA MAGAZINE, Reflections of Jewish Thought, P.O.Box 11014, Norfolk, VA 23517, www.poeticamagazine.com
Vulgar Marsala Press, Norfolk, VA 23507
Strawberry Patchworks, Box 3, Green Mansion, North, VA 23128, 804-725-7560, berrybookssam@gmail.com
BRIDGES: An Interdisciplinary Journal of Theology, Philosophy, History, and Science, PO Box 3075, Oakton, VA 22124-3075, 703-281-4722, Fax 703-734-1976, E-mail Bridges23@aol.com
Grateful Press, 11654 Plaza America Drive #123, Reston, VA 20190-4700, 877-588-7753, www.gratefulpress.com, info@gratefulpress.com
Brandylane Publishers, Inc., 5 S. 1st St., Richmond, VA 23219-3716, 804-644-3090, Fax 804-644-3092
FAILBETTER.COM, 2022 Grove Avenue, Richmond, VA 23220
FOLK ART MESSENGER, PO Box 17041, Richmond, VA 23226, 804-285-4532, 1-800-527-3655, fasa@folkart.org
Palari Publishing, PO Box 9288, Richmond, VA 23227-0288, phone/fax 866-570-6724, info@palaribooks.com, www.palaribooks.com
PLEASANT LIVING, 5 South 1st St., Richmond, VA 23219-3716, 804-644-3091
Two-Handed Engine Press, PO Box 803, Richmond, VA 23219, 9175686184, www.myspace.com/twohandedenginepress
THE ROANOKE REVIEW, Roanoke College, 221 College Lane, Salem, VA 24153, 540-375-2380
Kumarian Press, 22883 Quicksilver Drive, Sterling, VA 20166, Ph: 703-996-1042, Fax: 703-661-1501, Orders: 800-232-0223, Email: kpbooks@kpbooks.com, Web: www.kpbooks.com
Golden Quill Press, P.O. Box 83, Troutville, VA 24175-7130, 540 777 3700 thewritesource@pobox.com, goldenquillpress@mindspring.com, www.goldenquillpress.com
Books for All Times, Inc., PO Box 202, Warrenton, VA 20188, 540-428-3175, staff@bfat.com
All Nations Press, P.O. Box 601, White Marsh, VA 23183, 757-581-4063, www.allnationspress.com
HAMPTON ROADS HEALTH JOURNAL, 4808 Courthouse Street, Suite 204, Williamsburg, VA 23188, 757-645-4475
THE HEALTH JOURNALS, 4808 Courthouse Street, Suite 204, Williamsburg, VA 23188, 757-645-4475
Thirteen Colonies Press, 710 South Henry Street, Williamsburg, VA 23185, 757-229-1775
WILLIAM AND MARY REVIEW, Campus Center, PO Box 8795, Williamsburg, VA 23187-8795, 757-221-3290, Fax 757-221-3451
Red Moon Press, PO Box 2461, Winchester, VA 22604-1661, Tel: 540-722-2156
The Sow's Ear Press, 217 Brookneil Drive, Winchester, VA 22602, sowsearpoetry@yahoo.com
Don Carmichael, P.O. Box 1602, Woodbridge, VA 22193, 7035779051
The Invisible College Press, LLC, PO Box 209, Woodbridge, VA 22194-0209, 703-590-4005, editor@invispress.com, www.invispress.com

615

Corvus Publishing Company, 6021 South Shore Road, Anacortes, WA 98221-8915, 360-293-6068, DP@CorvusBooks.com, www.CorvusBooks.com

ABLAZE Publishing, 2800 122nd Place NE, Bellevue, WA 98005-1520, 877-624-0230, Fax 509-275-5817, welcome@family-pearls.org www.familypearls.org

Illumination Arts, PO Box 1865, Bellevue, WA 98009, 425-644-7185

McRapperson Literary Enterprises, 15656 Main St., Bellevue, WA 98008

BELLINGHAM REVIEW, Mail Stop 9053, WWU, Bellingham, WA 98225, 360-650-4863, bhreview@cc.wwu.edu

GREATCOAT, 3228 Peabody St., Bellingham, WA 98225, submissions@greatcoat.net, www.greatcoat.net

Signpost Press Inc., Mail Stop 9053, WWU, Bellingham, WA 98225, 360-650-4863

Tarragon Books, 1424 E. Maplewood Ave., Bellingham, WA 98225, tel: 360-738-7875

Owl Creek Press, 2693 S. Camano Drive, Camano Island, WA 98282

Crane Press, Suite #172, 3510 NE 3rd Avenue, Camas, WA 98607, 360-210-5982, fax 360-210-5983, 800-745-6273, Info@CranePress.com

ANIMAL PEOPLE, PO Box 960, Clinton, WA 98236-0960

THE NEW FORMALIST, P.O. Box 251, Dayton, WA 99328, thenewformalist@lycos.com, http://www.thenewformalist.com

The New Formalist Press, Box 251, Dayton, WA 99328-0251, thenewformalist@lycos.com, http://www.formalpoetry.com

Marmot Publishing, 4652 Union Flat Creek Road, Endicott, WA 99125-9764, 509-657-3359, marmot@wildblue.net

Global Sports Productions, Ltd., 16810 Crystal Drive East, Enumclaw, WA 98022, 310-454-9480, www.sportsbooksem-pire.com, globalnw@earthlink.net, Fax (253) 874-1027

WinePress Publishing, PO Box 428, Enumclaw, WA 98022, 360-802-9758, Fax 360-802-9992, info@winepresspub.com

Lockhart Press, 1717 Wetmore Avenue, Everett, WA 98201, 425-252-8882, ral@ralockhart.com, www.ralockhart.com

POETRY NORTHWEST, Everett Community collge, 2000 Tower St., Everett, WA 98201

Sabellapress, 11014 19th Avenue SE, Suite 8, Box 314, Everett, WA 98208

Vanilla Heart Publishing, 10121 Evergreen Way, Bldg 25, Suite 156, Everett, WA 98204, 425-609-4718, VHP1@vanillaheart-booksandauthors.com, http://www.vanillaheartbooksandauthors.com

SOUNDINGS REVIEW, P.O. BOX 639, Freeland, WA 98249, 360-331-6719, soundings@whidbey.com, www.writeonwhid-bey.org/Publications

Hamster Huey Press, 7627 84th Avenue Ct. NW, Gig Harbor, WA 98335-6237, Phone 253-851-7839 http://www.hamsterhueypress.com

Olympic Mountain School Press, P.O. Box 1114, Gig Harbor, WA 98335, 253-858-4448

Dunamis House, 19801 SE 123rd Street, Issaquah, WA 98027, 425-255-5274, fax 425-277-8780

Hexagon Blue, PO Box 1790, Issaquah, WA 98027-0073, 425-890-5351, www.hexagonblue.com

Concrete Wolf Press, PO Box 1808, Kingston, WA 98346-1808, ConcreteWolf@yahoo.com, http://concretewolf.com

CRAB CREEK REVIEW, PO Box 1524, Kingston, WA 98346, crabcreekreview@gmail.com, crabcreekeditors@gmail.com, www.crabcreekreview.org

Dixon-Price Publishing, PO Box 1360, Kingston, WA 98346-1360, 360-710-2936, Fax 360-297-8702, dixonpr@dixon-price.com, www.dixonprice.com

THE BELTANE PAPERS: A Journal of Women's Mysteries, 11506 NE 113th Pl., Kirkland, WA 98033, 425-827-7004, editor@thebeltanepapers.net, www.thebeltanepapers.net

Philos Press, 8038-A N. Bicentennial Loop SE, Lacey, WA 98503-1708, 360-456-5106, sales@philospress.org, www.philospress.org

J. M. Entrikin Publishing, 351 Birch Bay Lynden Rd., Lynden, WA 98264, 360-201-8506, tianji@tianjishorserace.com

STRINGTOWN, PO Box 1406, Medical Lake, WA 99022-1406, stringtown@earthlink.net, http://www.home.earthlink.net/~stringtown/index.html

Black Heron Press, PO Box 13396, Mill Creek, WA 98082, 425-355-4929

AIM MAGAZINE, PO Box 390, Milton, WA 98354-0390

CMP Publishing Group LLC, 27657 Highway 97, Okanogan, WA 98840, Web: www.cmppg.com; email: edna@cmppg.org

WHEELHOUSE MAGAZINE, 1414 Madison, Olympia, WA 98502, 248.298.9424

Church Leadership Library (US Office), PO Box 1477, Point Roberts, WA 98281, 604-952-0050, 604-952-4650, admin@churchleadershiplibrary.org, www.churchleadershiplibrary.com

Hartley & Marks, Publishers, PO Box 147, Point Roberts, WA 98281, (800) 277-5887

Orchard House Press, 7419 Ebbert Drive SE, Port Orchard, WA 98367, www.orchardhousepress.com

THE TABBY: A CHRONICLE OF THE ARTS AND CRAFTS MOVEMENT, 3085 Buckingham Drive SE, Port Orchard, WA 98366, (360) 871-7707

Copper Canyon Press, PO Box 271, Port Townsend, WA 98368, poetry@coppercanyonpress.org, www.coppercanyonpress.org, 360-385 4925 (tel)

THE HERON'S NEST, 816 Taft Street, Port Townsend, WA 98368, www.theheronsnest.com

Washington State University Press, PO Box 645910, Pullman, WA 99164-5910, 509-335-7880, 509-335-8568 (fax), 800-354-7360, wsupress@wsu.edu, wsupress.wsu.edu

Infinite Love Publishing, 15127 N.E. 24th St., #341, Redmond, WA 98052

Blue Brush Media, 851 Monroe Ave. NE, Renton, WA 98056, 425-818-8850, Fax: 425-228-6775, info@sikulu.com, www.sikulu.com

Building Blocks Press, 129 Bremmer St, Richland, WA 99352, (509) 374-7606, Fax: (815) 346-2486, Toll-free (877) 422-2386, jpayne@buildingblockspress.com, www.buildingblockspress.com

Press Here, 22230 NE 28th Place, Sammamish, WA 98074-6408, WelchM@aol.com

TUNDRA, 22230 NE 28th Place, Sammamish, WA 98074-6408, welchm@aol.com

Balanced Books Publishing, PO Box 14957, Seattle, WA 98144, 206-328-3995, fax 206-328-1339, toll free 877-838-4858, info@balancedbookspub.com, www.balancedbookspub.com

BARNWOOD, 4604 47th Ave., South, Seattle, WA 98118

The Barnwood Press, 4604 47th Ave., South, Seattle, WA 98118

Bay Press, 1411 4th Avenue, Suite 830, Seattle, WA 98101-2225, 206-284-5913

CHRYSANTHEMUM, 2012 18th Ave. South, Seattle, WA 98144-4324, 206-329-5566, nooknoow@aol.com

CUNE MAGAZINE, PO Box 31024, Seattle, WA 98103, Fax (206) 782-1330; www.cunemagazines.com; www.cunepress.net; magazines@cunepress.com

Cune Press, PO Box 31024, Seattle, WA 98103, Fax 206-774-0592, Tel 206-789-7055, www.cunepress.net, www.cunepress.com, www.cunemagazines.com, cunepress@gmail.com, cune@aol.com

FIVE WILLOWS MAGAZINE, 202 6th Avenue South #1105, Seattle, WA 98104-2303, 202-682-3851

Floating Bridge Press, PO Box 18814, Seattle, WA 98118, www.floatingbridgepress.org. E-mail: floatingbridgepress@yahoo.com

Florentia Press, 4616 25th Avenue NE #174, Seattle, WA 98105, 206-524-7084, kathy@discoverlavender.com, www.discoverlavender.com

GLOBAL VEDANTA, 2716 Broadway Avenue East, Seattle, WA 98102-3909, 206-323-1228, Fax 206-329-1791, global@vedanta-seattle.org, www.vedanta-seattle.org

Goldfish Press, 2012 18th Ave. South, Seattle, WA 98144-4324, 206-329-5566, nooknoow@aol.com

IMAGE: ART, FAITH, MYSTERY, 3307 Third Avenue West, Seattle, WA 98119-1940, phone 206-281-2988, fax 206-281-2979

Impassio Press, PO Box 31905, Seattle, WA 98103, 206-632-7675, Fax 775-254-4073, books@impassio.com, www.impassio.com

JACK MACKEREL MAGAZINE, PO Box 23134, Seattle, WA 98102-0434

KNOCK MAGAZINE, Antioch University Seattle, 2326 Sixth Ave., Seattle, WA 98121-1814, 206.268.4420

La Familia Publishing, 117 Prefontaine Place South, Seattle, WA 98104, 206-291-4608

LETTER X, 9527 Wallingford Ave., N, Seattle, WA 98103, submit@letterxmag.com, www.letterxmag.com

Parenting Press, Inc., PO Box 75267, Seattle, WA 98175-0267, 206-364-2900, Fax 206-364-0702

Perpetual Press, PO Box 3956, Seattle, WA 98124-3956, 800-807-3030

POETSWEST ONLINE, 1100 University St., #17A, Seattle, WA 98101, 206-682-1268, JGE@poetswest.com, www.poetswest.com

THE RAVEN CHRONICLES, 12346 Sand Point Way N.E., Seattle, WA 98125, 206-364-2045, editors@ravenchronicles.org, www.ravenchronicles.org

Red Letter Press, 4710 University Way NE #100, Seattle, WA 98105-4427, 206-985-4621, Fax 206-985-8965, redletterpress@juno.com

RIVET MAGAZINE, 3518 Fremont Avenue N. #118, Seattle, WA 98103, editor@rivetmagazine.org, www.rivetmagazine.org

Rodnik Publishing Co., PO Box 46956, Seattle, WA 98146-0956, Tel 206-937-5189 Fax 206-937-3554, URL: www.rodnikpublishing.com

Rose Alley Press, 4203 Brooklyn Avenue NE #103A, Seattle, WA 98105-5911, 206-633-2725, rosealleypress@juno.com, www.rosealleypress.com

Rowhouse Press, PO Box 23134, Seattle, WA 98102-0434

Sasquatch Books, 119 S. Main Street, Suite 400, Seattle, WA 98104-2555, 206-467-4300, 800-775-0817, Fax 206-467-4301, books@SasquatchBooks.com

SEA KAYAKER, PO Box 17029, Seattle, WA 98107-0729, 206-789-1326, Fax 206-781-1141, mail@seakayakermag.com

THE SEATTLE REVIEW, P.O. Box 354330, University of Washington, Seattle, WA 98195, ph. 206 543 2302

74th Street Productions, L.L.C., 350 North 74th Street, Seattle, WA 98103, 206-781-1447, info@74thstreet.com, www.74thstreet.com, www.writersatthepodium.com

STORMWARNING!, PO Box 21604, Seattle, WA 98111, 206-374-2215 phone/Fax, vvawai@oz.net, www.oz.net/~vvawai/

WASHINGTON TRAILS, 2019 3rd Ave., Suite #100, Seattle, WA 98121-2430, 206-625-1367, www.wta.org

Wave Books, 1938 Fairview Avenue East, Suite 201, Seattle, WA 98102, info@wavepoetry.com, www.wavepoetry.com

Whit Press, 4701 SW Admiral Way, #125, Seattle, WA 98116

Wood Works, 4131 Greenwood Ave. N., Seattle, WA 98103-7017, www.woodworkspress.com

WordFarm, 2816 E Spring St., Seattle, WA 98122, info@wordfarm.net

BELLOWING ARK, PO Box 55564, Shoreline, WA 98155, e-mail bellowingark@bellowingark.org

Bellowing Ark Press, PO Box 55564, Shoreline, WA 98155, 206-440-0791

Clearbridge Publishing, PO Box 33772, Shoreline, WA 98133, 206-533-9357, Fax 206-546-9756, beckyw@clearbridge.com, www.clearbridge.com

SPINDRIFT ART & LITERARY JOURNAL, Shoreline Community College, 16101 Greenwood Avenue North, Shoreline, WA 98133

SAPONIFIER, P.O. Box 280, Silvana, WA 98287, saponifier@gmail.com, phone 425-760-1004, http://www.saponifier.com

Eastern Washington University Press, 534 E. Spokane Falls Blvd. Suite 203, Spokane, WA 99202, Main line: 509-368-6574, Fax: 509-368-6596, 1-800-508-6596, Email: ewupress@mail.ewu.edu, Website: http://ewupress.ewu.edu

Gray Dog Press, 2727 S. Mt. Vernon #4, Spokane, WA 99223, P:509-534-0372, F:509-533-1897, editor@graydogpress.com, www.graydogpress.com

Lynx House Press, 420 West 24th, Spokane, WA 99203

Sage Hill Press, 1024 N. Summit Blvd., Spokane, WA 99201, 509-413-1184, sagehillpress@yahoo.com

SPOKEWRITE: The Spokane/Coeur d'Alene Journal of Art and Writing, 2727 S. Mt. Vernon #4, Spokane, WA 99223, P:509-768-6206, F:509-533-1897, editor@graydogpress.com, www.graydogpress.com

WILLOW SPRINGS, Eastern Washington University, 501 North Riverpoint Blvd., Spokane, WA 99202-2410, 509-623-4349

Whispering Pine Press, 507 N. Sullivan Rd. Ste. A-7, Spokane Valley, WA 99037-8531, Phone: (509) 927-0404, Fax: (509) 927-1550, Web: www.whisperingpinepress.com, E-Mail: whisperingpinepressinc@hotmail.com

Kirpan Press, PO Box 2943, Vancouver, WA 98668-2943, kirpan_press@msn.com

DIFFERENT KIND OF PARENTING, PO Box 514, Vashon Island, WA 98070-0514

KotaPress, PO Box 514, Vashon Island, WA 98070-0514, editor@kotapress.com, www.kotapress.com

KOTAPRESS ONLINE JOURNALS, PO Box 514, Vashon Island, WA 98070-0514

Brooding Heron Press, Bookmonger Row, Waldron Island, WA 98294, 360-420-8181

Temple Inc., PO Box 100, Walla Walla, WA 99362-0033, order@thetemplebookstore.com

Ho Logos Press, 2311 G St, Washougal, WA 98671, 360-835-7838, 360-835-0785 (fax), hlpressmarketing@yahoo.com, hlpress@aol.com

PENNY-A-LINER, PO Box 2163, Wenatchee, WA 98807-2163, 509-662-7858

PORTALS, PO Box 2163, Wenatchee, WA 98807-2163, 509-662-7858

Redrosebush Press, PO Box 2163, Wenatchee, WA 98807-2163, 509-662-7858

WEST VIRGINIA

Woodland Press, LLC and Woodland Gospel Publishing, 118 Woodland Drive, Chapmanville, WV 25508, 304-752-7152, Fax 304-752-9002; woodlandpressllc@mac.com

Mountain State Press, 2300 MacCorkle Avenue SE, Charleston, WV 25304-1099, 304-357-4767, msp1@mountainstatepress.org

BIBLIOPHILOS, 200 Security Building, Fairmont, WV 26554, 304-366-8107

KESTREL: A Journal of Literature and Art, Fairmont State University, 1201 Locust Avenue, Fairmont, WV 26554-2451, 304-367-4809, Fax 304-367-4896, e-mail kestrel@fairmontstate.edu

ABZ A Magazine of Poetry, John McKernan, Editor Marshall University, One John Marshall Drive, Huntington, WV 25755-2646

ABZ Poetry Press, PO Box 2746, Huntington, WV 25727-2746, www.abzpress.com, editorial@abzpress.com

Enlightened Living Publishing, LLC, P O Box 7291, Huntington, WV 25775-7291, telephone 304-486-9000, fax 304-486-5815, toll free 866-896-2665, e-mail: info@enlightenedlivingpublishing.com, www.enlightenedlivingpublishing.com

10x3 PLUS, 1077 Windsor Avenue, Morgantown, WV 26505-3325

West Virginia University Press, P.O. Box 6295, G3 White Hall, Morgantown, WV 26506, Office (304) 293-8400, Toll free for orders (866) 988-7737, Fax (304) 293-6585

WISCONSIN

Green Hut Press, 1015 Jardin Street East, Appleton, WI 54911, 920-734-9728, janwfcloak@uspower.net

SHENANDOAH NEWSLETTER, 736 West Oklahoma Street, Appleton, WI 54914

Lessiter Publications, PO Box 624, Brookfield, WI 53008-0624, 262-782-4480, Fax 262-782-1252

Cable Publishing, 14090 E Keinenen Rd, Brule, WI 54820, 715-372-8499, nan@cablepublishing.com

ROSEBUD, N 3310 Asje Rd., Cambridge, WI 53523, 608-423-4750

Zelda Wilde Publishing, 315 Water St., Cambridge, WI 53523, 608-423-9609

Foremost Press, 7067 Cedar Creek Rd., Cedarburg, WI 53012, 262.377.3180, mary@foremostpress.com, http://foremostpress.com

Michael E. Coughlin, Publisher, PO Box 205, Cornucopia, WI 54827

THE DANDELION, PO Box 205, Cornucopia, WI 54827

BEAUTY/TRUTH: A Journal of Ekphrastic Poetry, N8 W31309 Concord Lane, Delafield, WI 53018, http://www.BeautyTruthPoetry.com, JamesGapinski@BeautyTruthPoetry.com

Canvas Press, N8 W31309 Concord Lane, Delafield, WI 53018

COLLECTION, N8 W31309 Concord Lane, Delafield, WI 53018

Blue Tiger Press, 2016 Hwy 67, Dousman, WI 53118, 262-965-2751

Pearl-Win Publishing Co., N4721 9th Drive, Hancock, WI 54943-7617, 715-249-5407

Aircraft Owners Group, PO Box 5000, Iola, WI 54945-5000, 800-331-0038, e-mail cessna@aircraftownergroup.com or piper@aircraftownergroup.com

CESSNA OWNER MAGAZINE, PO Box 5000, Iola, WI 54945-5000, 715-445-5000; E-mail cessna@aircraftownergroup.com

PIPERS MAGAZINE, PO Box 5000, Iola, WI 54945, 715-445-5000; e-mail piper@aircraftownergroup.com

Big Valley Press, S2104 Big Valley Road, La Farge, WI 54639, 608 489 3525

ABRAXAS, PO Box 260113, Madison, WI 53726-0113, 608-238-0175, abraxaspress@hotmail.com

EXTRA INNINGS: The Writer's Home Encouragement, 4337 Felton Place, Madison, WI 53705, 608-238-4007, mcook@dcs.wisc.edu

FEMINIST COLLECTIONS: A QUARTERLY OF WOMEN'S STUDIES RESOURCES, 430 Memorial Library, 728 State Street, Madison, WI 53706, 608-263-5754

FEMINIST PERIODICALS: A CURRENT LISTING OF CONTENTS, 430 Memorial Library, 728 State Street, Madison, WI 53706, 608-263-5754

Ghost Pony Press, PO Box 260113, Madison, WI 53726-0113, 608-238-0175, ghostponypress@hotmail.com, www.thing.net/~grist/l&d/dalevy/dalevy.htm, www.thing.net/~grist/ld/saiz/saiz.htm

THE MADISON REVIEW, Dept of English, H.C. White Hall, 600 N. Park Street, Madison, WI 53706, 263-3303

THE MODERN LANGUAGE JOURNAL, University of Wisconsin, Department of French and Italian, Madison, WI 53706-1558, 608-262-5010

Muse World Media Group, PO Box 55094, Madison, WI 53705, 608-238-6681

NEW BOOKS ON WOMEN, GENDER, & FEMINISM, 430 Memorial Library, 728 State Street, Madison, WI 53706, 608-263-5754

University of Wisconsin Press, 1930 Monroe Street, 3rd Floor, Madison, WI 53711-2059, (608)263-0814, fax (608)263-1132

WISCONSIN ACADEMY REVIEW, 1922 University Ave., Madison, WI 53705, 608-263-1692

Women's Studies Librarian, University of Wisconsin System, 430 Memorial Library, 728 State Street, Madison, WI 53706, 608-263-5754

ANTHILLS, PO Box 170322, Milwaukee, WI 53217-8026, www.centennialpress.com, chuck@centennialpress.com

Centennial Press, PO Box 170322, Milwaukee, WI 53217-8026

THE CREAM CITY REVIEW, PO Box 413, English Dept, Curtin Hall, Univ. of Wisconsin, Milwaukee, WI 53201, 414-229-4708

Creative Writing and Publishing Company, PO Box 511848, Milwaukee, WI 53203-0311, (414) 507-9677, (414) 447-7810 for Fax Machine

Grip Publishing, PO Box 091882, Milwaukee, WI 53209, 414-807-6403

Lemieux International Ltd., PO Box 170134, Milwaukee, WI 53217, 414-962-2844, FAX 414-962-2844, lemintld@msn.com

WISCONSIN TRAILS, 4101 West Burnham St., Milwaukee, WI 53215-2055, e-mail editor@wistrails.com

Goblin Fern Press, 1288 Summit Ave, Suite 107, PMB 115, Oconomowoc, WI 53066, tel: 262-567-5915, fax 262-567-0091, www.goblinfernpress.com, info@goblinfernpress.com

YUKHIKA—LATUHSE, P.O. Box 365, Oneida Nation Arts Program, Oneida, WI 54155-0365, jstevens@ez-net.com

N: NUDE & NATURAL, PO Box 132, Oshkosh, WI 54903, 920-426-5009

MIDWEST ART FAIRS, PO Box 72, Pepin, WI 54759, 715-442-2022

LITERARY MAGAZINE REVIEW, Univ. of Wisconsin-River Falls, English Dept., 410 S. 3rd Street, River Falls, WI 54022, email: jennifer.s.brantley@uwrf.edu, web site: http://www.uwrf.edu/lmr/

SEEMS, c/o Lakeland College, Box 359, Sheboygan, WI 53082-0359

Colgate Press, P.O.Box 597, Sussex, WI 53089, 414-477-8686

Reliance Books, 208 E. Oak Crest Drive, Ste. 250, Wales, WI 53183-9700, 262-968-9857, Fax 262-968-9854, contact@reliancebooks.com, www.reliancebooks.com

Jackson Harbor Press, RR 1, Box 107AA, 845 Jackson Harbor Road, Washington Island, WI 54246-9048

The Film Instruction Company of America, 5928 W. Michigan Street, Wauwatosa, WI 53213-4248, 414-258-6492

Plank Road Publishing, PO Box 26627, Wauwatosa, WI 53226-0627, phone 800-437-0832 or 262-790-5210; fax 888-272-0212 or 262-781-8818; e-mail Lynn@MusicK8.com; website www.MusicK8.com

AT THE LAKE MAGAZINE, 93 West Geneva St., P.O. Box 1080, Williams Bay, WI 53191, phone 262-245-1000; fax 262-245-2000; toll free 800-386-3228; e-mail jrhodes@ntmediagroup.com; web www.ntmediagroup.com

WYOMING

Whiskey Creek Press, P.O. Box 51052, Casper, WY 82605-1052, 307-265-8585 (fax only), email: publisher@whiskeycreek-press.com, websites: www.whiskeycreekpress.com, www.whiskeycreekpresstorrid.com
Crazy Woman Creek Press, 3073 Hanson, Cheyenne, WY 82001, 707-829-8568, www.jewsofwyoming.org
One Eyed Press, 272 Road 6Rt, Cody, WY 82414, one_eyed_press@yahoo.com, www.one-eyed-press.com
High Plains Press, Box 123, 403 Cassa Road, Glendo, WY 82213, 307-735-4370, Fax 307-735-4590, 800-552-7819
Dignified Designs, PO Box 1207, Glenrock, WY 82637, 307-436-5447, Editor@OpenRangeMagazine.com - www.OpenRange-Magazine.com
OPEN RANGE MAGAZINE - The West's Premier Real Western Magazine, PO Box 1207, Glenrock, WY 82637, 307-436-5447, Editor@OpenRangeMagazine.com - www.OpenRangeMagazine.com
Agathon Books, PO Box 630, Lander, WY 82520-0630, 307-332-5252, Fax 307-332-5888, agathon@rmisp.com, www.rmisp.com/agathon/
Skyline West Press/Wyoming Almanac, 1409 Thomes, Laramie, WY 82072, 307-745-8205
MIDNIGHT SHOWCASE: Romance Digest, Erotic-ahh Digest, Special Digest, P.O. Box 726, Lusk, WY 82225, 307-334-3165, 727-848-5962, publisher@midnightshowcase.com, http://www.midnightshowcase.com
Twin Souls Publications, P.O. Box 726, Lusk, WY 82225, 307-334-3165, 727-848-5962, publisher@midnightshowcase.com, http://www.midnightshowcase.com
Alpine Press, PO Box 1930, Mills, WY 82644, 307-234-1990
The Narrative Press, 2041 East A Street, Torrington, WY 82240, 800-315-9005, Fax 307-532-3495, service@narrative-press.com, www.narrativepress.com

ARGENTINA

Zagier & Urruty Publications, PO Box 94 Sucursal 19, Buenos Aires 1419, Argentina, +54-11-4572-1050, info@zagier.com, www.patagonishop.com

AUSTRALIA

STUDIO - A Journal of Christians Writing, 727 Peel Street, Albury, N.S.W. 2640, Australia, email: studio00@bigpond.net.au
DARK ANIMUS, PO Box 750, Katoomba, NSW 2780, Australia, skullmnky@hotmail.com, www.darkanimus.com
BLAST poetry and critical writing, 2008/22 Jane Bell Lane, Melbourne, VIC 3000, Australia, blastpoetry[at]gmail[dot]com, www.blastpoetry.com
Spinifex Press, PO Box 212, North Melbourne VIC 3051, Australia, +61-3-9329 6088, Fax +61-3-9329 9238
Otoliths, 8 Kennedy St, Rockhampton, QLD 4700, Australia, otolitheditor@gmail.com, http://the-otolith.blogspot.com, http://stores.lulu.com/l_m_young
OTOLITHS, 8 Kennedy St, Rockhampton, QLD 4700, Australia, otolitheditor@gmail.com, http://the-otolith.blogspot.com, http://stores.lulu.com/l_m_young
Poetry, 22 Harris Rd, Salisbury East, South Australia, Australia, 08/ 8182 4117 or 0415 271 093
HECATE, School of English, Media Studies & Art History, The University of Queensland, St. Lucia, Queensland 4072, Australia, phone: 07 336 53146, fax: 07 3365 2799, web: www.emsah.uq.edu.au/awsr, email: c.ferrier@mailbox.uq.edu.au
Hecate Press, School of English, Media Studies and Art History, The University of Queensland, St. Lucia, Queensland 4072, Australia
Total Cardboard Publishing, 70 Mount Barker Road, Stirling, SA 5152, Australia, www.totalcardboard.com
LINQ, School of Humanities, James Cook Univ.-North Queensland, Townsville 4811, Australia, e-mail jcu.linq@jcu.edu.au
Galaxy Press, 71 Recreation Street, Tweed Heads, N.S.W. 2485, Australia, (07) 5536-1997

BELIZE

Axios Newletter, Inc., 16 Maxi Street, PO Box 90, Santa Elena, Cayo, Belize, Belize, 501-824-2382 Daxgor@Yahoo.com

CANADA

THE ANTIGONISH REVIEW, St Francis Xavier University, PO Box 5000, Antigonish, Nova Scotia B2G 2W5, Canada, Phone: 902-867-3962; Email: TAR@stfx.ca; Website: www.antigonishreview.com
George Suttton Publishing Co., 54 Crawford Drive, Aurora, Ontario, Canada L4G 4R4, Canada, georgesutton2005@yahoo.com
Proof Press, 67 Court Street, Aylmer, QC J9H 4M1, Canada
RAW NERVZ HAIKU, 67 Court Street, Aylmer, QC J9H 4M1, Canada, dhoward@aix1.uottawa.ca
CANADIAN MONEYSAVER, Box 370, 5540 Bath Road, Bath, Ontario K0H 1G0, Canada, www.canadianmoneysaver.ca, moneyinfo@canadianmoneysaver.ca
TIME FOR RHYME, c/o Richard Unger, PO Box 1055, Battleford SK S0M 0E0, Canada, 306-445-5172
Bayhampton Publications, 54 Mozart Crescent, Brampton, ON L6Y 2W7, Canada, 905-455-7331, Fax 905-455-0207, www.bayhampton.com
WEST COAST LINE: A Journal of Contemporary Writing and Criticism, 2027 EAA, Simon Fraser University, Burnaby, B.C. V5A 1S6, Canada
Soul Care Publishing, 106-6198 Kathleen Ave., Burnaby, BC V5H257, Canada
ESPERANTIC STUDIES, 8888 University Drive, Faculty of Education, Burnaby, BC, V5A 1S6, Canada, Contact: jclark@esperantic.org, www.esperantic.org
ALBERTA HISTORY, 95 Holmwood Ave NW, Calgary Alberta T2K 2G7, Canada, 403-289-8149
CANADIAN JOURNAL OF COUNSELLING, University of Calgary Press, 2500 University Drive NW, Calgary, AB T2N 1N4, Canada, 613-237-1099, toll-free 877-765-5565, Fax 613-237-9786, info@ccacc.ca, www.ccacc.ca/
CURRENTS: New Scholarship in the Human Services, Faculty of Social Work, Univ. of Calgary, 2500 University Drive NW, Calgary, AB T2N 1N4, Canada, 403-220-7550, Fax 403-282-7269, currents@ucalgary.ca, www.uofcpress.com/journals/currents
HISTORY OF INTELLECTUAL CULTURE, Faculty of Education, EDT 722, Univ. of Calgary, 2500 Univ. Drive NW, Calgary, AB T2N 1N4, Canada, 403-220-6296, Fax 403-282-8479, elpanayo@ucalgary.ca, pjstortz@ucalgary.ca, www.ucalgary.ca/hic/
INTERNATIONAL ELECTRONIC JOURNAL FOR LEADERSHIP IN LEARNING, Faculty of Education, Univ. of Calgary, 2500 University Drive NW, Calgary, AB T2N 1N4, Canada, 403-220-5675, Fax 403-282-3005, www.ucalgary.ca/~iejll/
EDGE Science Fiction and Fantasy Publishing, PO Box 1714, Calgary, AB T2P 2L7, Canada, 403-254-0160
FREEFALL MAGAZINE, 922 9th Ave. S.E., Calgary, Alberta T2G 0S4, Canada
Listening Voice Media Ltd, P O Box 75032 RPO Cambrian, Calgary, Alberta T2K 1P0, Canada, 403-220-1166, 403-220-1162

Historical Society of Alberta, 95 Holmwood Ave. NW, Calgary, Alberta T2K 2G7, Canada

Prairie Journal Press, Brentwood P.O., Calgary, Alberta T2L 2K6, Canada, prairiejournal@yahoo.com, www.geocities.com/prairiejournal

ARIEL, A Review of International English Literature, The University of Calgary, 2500 University Drive NW, Calgary, Alberta T2N 1N4, Canada, 403-220-4657, Fax 403-289-1123, ariel@ucalgary.ca, www.english.ucalgary.ca/ariel/

CANADIAN JOURNAL OF PHILOSOPHY, University of Calgary Press, Univ. of Calgary, 2500 University Dr. N.W., Calgary, Alberta T2N 1N4, Canada, 403-220-3514, Fax 403-282-0085, ucpmail@ucalgary.ca

MOUSEION, Journal of the Classical Association of Canada/Revue de la Societe Canadienne des Etudes Classiques, University of Calgary Press, Univ. of Calgary, 2500 University Dr. N.W., Calgary, Alberta T2N 1N4, Canada, 403-220-3514, Fax 403-282-0085, ucpmail@ucalgary.ca

University of Calgary Press, 2500 University Drive NW, Calgary, Alberta T2N 1N4, Canada, 403-220-7578, Fax 403-282-0085, www.uofcpress.com

Aardvark Enterprises (Sole Proprietorship of J. Alvin Speers), 204 Millbank Drive S.W., Calgary, Alberta T2Y 2H9, Canada, 403-256-4639

THE PRAIRIE JOURNAL OF CANADIAN LITERATURE, PO Box 68073, 28 Crowfoot Terrace NW, Calgary, Alberta T3G 3N8, Canada, prairiejournal@yahoo.com, www.prairiejournal.org

THE MYSTERY REVIEW, PO Box 233, Colborne, Ont. K0K 1S0, Canada, 613-475-4440, Fax 613-475-3400, mystrev@reach.net, www.themysteryreview.com

Church Leadership Library (Canadian Office), 2 - 7201 72nd Street, Delta, British Columbia V4G 1M5, Canada, Phone: 604-952-0050, Fax: 604-952-4650, contact@outreach.ca, www.churchleadershiplibrary.org

Kriya Yoga Publications, 196 Mountain Road, PO Box 90, Eastman, Quebec J0E 1P0, Canada

NeWest Press, #201, 8540 - 109 Street, Edmonton AB T6G 1E6, Canada, (780) 432-9427 - phone, (780) 433-3179 - fax

Canadian Committee on Labour History, Athabasca University Press, Peace Hills Trust Tower, 1200, 10011 - 109 Street, Edmonton, AB T5J 3S8, Canada, 709-737-2144

ON SPEC, PO Box 4727, Edmonton, AB T6E 5G6, Canada, 403-413-0215, onspec@onspec.ca

Phi-Psi Publishers, Box 75198, Ritchie P.O., Edmonton, AB T6E 6K1, Canada, phipsibk@netscape.net

EXCEPTIONALITY EDUCATION CANADA, Department of Educational Psychology, 6-102 Education North, University of Alberta, Edmonton, AB T6G 2G5, Canada, Telephone: (780) 492-2198/7471, Fax: (780) 492-1318, E-mail: eecj@ualberta.ca, judy.lupart@ualberta.ca, christina.rinaldi@ualberta.ca

SPECTACULAR SPECULATIONS, 13804-114 St., Edmonton, Alberta, T5X 4J1, Canada, 780-456-1646, admin@speculativefictionstories.com, http://www.speculativefictionstories.com

TREATING YOURSELF: The Alternative Medicine Journal, 250 The East Mall, P.O. Box 36531, Etobicoke, Ontario M9B 3Y8, Canada, Phone 416 620 1951, Fax 416 620 0698, weedmaster@treatingyourself.com , http://www.treatingyourself.com

THE INTERNATIONAL FICTION REVIEW, Culture & Language Studies, UNB, PO Box 4400, Fredericton, N.B. E3B 5A3, Canada, 506-453-4636, Fax 506-447-3166, e-mail ifr@unb.ca

THE FIDDLEHEAD, Campus House, PO Box 4400, University of New Brunswick, Fredericton, NB E3B 5A3, Canada, 506-453-3501

Broken Jaw Press, PO Box 596 Stn A, Fredericton, NB E3B 5A6, Canada, ph/fax 506-454-5127, jblades@nbnet.nb.ca, www.brokenjaw.com

NEW MUSE OF CONTEMPT, Box 596 Stn A, Fredericton, NB E3B 5A6, Canada, www.brokenjaw.com

BRADY MAGAZINE, 165 Old Muskoka Road, Suite 306, Gravenhurst, Ontario P1P 1N3, Canada, 705-687-3963 [phone], 705-687-8736 [fax], editor@bradymagazine.com [e-mail], http://www.bradymagazine.com [website]

CAPCAT, 8 Karen Drive, Guelph, Ontario N1G 2N9, Canada, 519-824-7423

ATLANTIS: A Women's Studies Journal/Revue d'etudes sur les femmes, Institute for the Study of Women, Mt. Saint Vincent University, Halifax, N.S. B3M 2J6, Canada, 902-457-6319, Fax 902-443-1352, atlantis@msvu.ca, www.msvu.ca/atlantis

THE DALHOUSIE REVIEW, Dalhousie University, Halifax, Nova Scotia B3H 3J5, Canada, 902-494-2541, fax 902-494-3561, email dalhousie.review@dal.ca

OCEAN YEARBOOK, Dalhousie Law School, 6061 University Avenue, Halifax, Nova Scotia B3H 4H9, Canada, 902-494-2955 (main #), 902-494-1316 (fax), http://www.journals.uchicago.edu/OY/home.html

Tuns Press, Faculty of Architecture and Planning, Dalhousie University, Box 1000 Central Station, Halifax, Nova Scotia B3J 2X4, Canada, 902-494-3925, Fax 902-423-6672, tuns.press@dal.ca, tunspress.dal.ca

TOWER POETRY, c/o McMaster University, 1280 Main Street W Box 1021, Hamilton, Ontario, L8S 1CO, Canada, http://www.towerpoetry.ca; tps@towerpoetry.ca

Tower Poetry Society, c/o McMaster University, 1280 Main Street W. Box 1021, Hamilton, Ontario, L8S 1CO, Canada

Nip and Tuck Publishing, 736 Wilson Avenue, Kelowna, BC V1Y 6X9, Canada, 250-762-7861, nipandtuck@shaw.ca

Quarterly Committee of Queen's University, Queen's University, Kingston, Ontario K7L 3N6, Canada, 613-533-2667, qquarter@post.queensu.ca, http://info.queensu.ca/quarterly

QUEEN'S QUARTERLY: A Canadian Review, Queen's University, Kingston, Ontario K7L 3N6, Canada, 613-533-2667, queens.quarterly@queensu.ca, www.queensu.ca/quarterly

Callawind Publications / Custom Cookbooks / Children's Books, 3551 St. Charles Blvd., Suite 179, Kirkland, Quebec H9H 3C4, Canada, 514-685-9109, Fax 514-685-7952, info@callawind.com

ASCENT, PO Box 9, Kootenay Bay BC V0B 1X0, Canada, 250-227-9224, Fax 514-499-3904, info@ascentmagazine.com, www.ascentmagazine.com

Timeless Books, PO Box 9, 527 Walker's Landing Rd, Kootenay Bay BC V0B 1X0, Canada, 1-800-661-8711, 250-227-9224contact@timeless.org, www.timeless.org

Oolichan Books, PO Box 10, Lantzville, B.C., V0R 2H0, Canada, 250-390-4839, oolichanbooks@telus.net, www.oolichan.com

Hochelaga Press, 8140 Ogilvie, LaSalle, QC H8P 3R4, Canada, 514-366-5655, Fax 514-364-5655, hochelaga@sympatico.ca

Enigmatic Ink, 654 Grosvenor St, London, Ontario N5Y 3T4, Canada, www.enigmaticink.com

CANADIAN POETRY, Department of English, University of Western Ontario, London, Ontario N6A 3K7, Canada, 519 661 2111 x85834

Canadian Poetry Press, Department of English, University of Western Ontario, London, Ontario N6A 3K7, Canada

Stewart Publishing & Printing, 17 Sir Constantine Drive, Markham, Ontario L3P 2X3, Canada, www.stewartbooks.com 905-294-4389; robert@stewartbooks.com

Canadian Educators' Press, 100 City Centre Drive, PO Box 2094, Mississauga, ON L5B 3C6, Canada, 905-826-0578

Lyons Publishing Limited, 2704 Jerring Mews, Mississauga, Ontario L5L 2M8, Canada, info@judypowell.com

SCRIVENER, McGill University, 853 Sherbrooke Street W., Montreal, P.Q. H3A 2T6, Canada, scrivenermag@hotmail.com

GOOD GIRL, 837 rue Gilford, Montreal, QB H2J 1P1, Canada, 514-288-5626, Fax 514-499-3904, info@goodgirl.ca, www.goodgirl.ca

VALLUM: CONTEMPORARY POETRY, PO Box 48003, Montreal, QC H2V 4S8, Canada, info@vallummag.com, www.vallummag.com
CANADIAN JOURNAL OF LATIN AMERICAN AND CARIBBEAN STUDIES/Revue canadienne des etudes latino-americaines et caraibes, CALACS, CCASLS SB-115, Concordia University, 1455 de Maisonneuve Ouest, Montreal, QC H3G 1M8, Canada, calacs@concordia.ca
INTERCULTURE, Intercultural Institute of Montreal, 4730 Papineau Avenue, Montreal, Quebec H2H 1V3, Canada, 514-288-7229, FAX 514-844-6800, website:www.iim.gc.ca
NIGHTLIFE MAGAZINE, 4200, Boulevard St. Laurent, Suite 1470, Montreal, Quebec H2W 2R2, Canada, 514.278.3222
Vehicule Press, PO Box 125, Place du Parc Station, Montreal, Quebec H2X 4A3, Canada, 514-844-6073, FAX 514-844-7543, vp@vehiculepress.com, www.vehiculepress.com
Black Rose Books Ltd., C.P. 1258, Succ. Place du Parc, Montreal, Quebec H2X 4A7, Canada, 514-844-4076, Fax 514-849-4797, blakrose@web.net, http://www.blackrosebooks.net
MATRIX MAGAZINE, 1400 de Maisonneuve Blvd. West, LB 658, Montreal, Quebec H3G 1M8, Canada
CELLAR, PO Box 111, Moreton's Harbour, NL A0G 3H0, Canada
CONTEMPORARY GHAZALS, PO Box 111, Moreton's Harbour, NL A0G 3H0, Canada
THE MORNING DEW REVIEW, Moreton's Harbour, NL A0G 3H0, Canada
JOURNAL OF CHILD AND YOUTH CARE, Malaspina University-College, Human Services, 900 5th Street, Nanaimo, BC V9R 5S5, Canada, 250-753-3245 X2207, Fax 250-741-2224, conlin@mala.bc.ca
New Orphic Publishers, 706 Mill Street, Nelson, BC V1L 4S5, Canada, 250-354-0494, Fax 250-352-0743, web:www3.telus.net/neworphicpublishers-hekkanen
THE NEW ORPHIC REVIEW, 706 Mill Street, Nelson, BC V1L 4S5, Canada, 250-354-0494
EVENT, Douglas College, PO Box 2503, New Westminster, B.C. V3L 5B2, Canada, 604-527-5293, Fax 604-527-5095, event@douglas.bc.ca, http://event.douglas.bc.ca
THE CAPILANO REVIEW, 2055 Purcell Way, North Vancouver, B.C. V7J 3H5, Canada, 604-984-1712
Multi-Media Publications Inc., Box 58043, Rosslynn RPO, Oshawa, Ontario L1J 8L6, Canada, Ph: (905) 986-5848; Toll-Free: (866) 721-1540 (Canada & USA Only); Fax: (905) 986-5777. Email: orders@mmpubs.com, Web: www.mmpubs.com
Crystal Dreams Publishing, Box 58043, Rosslynn RPO, Oshawa, Ontario, L1J 8L6, Canada, Phone: (905) 986-5848Toll-Free: 1-866-721-1540 (Canada and USA only)Fax: (905) 986-5777
Betelgeuse Books, Suite 604, 71 Somerset West, Ottawa Ottawa K2P 2G2, Canada, betelgeuse@sympatico.ca, http://maxpages.com/betelgeuse
OUR SCHOOLS/OUR SELVES, Canadian Centre for Policy Alternatives, 410-75 Albert Street, Ottawa, ON K1P 5E7, Canada, phone 613-563-1341, fax 613-233-1458, web: www.policyalternatives.ca
CANADIAN JOURNAL OF PROGRAM EVALUATION, Canadian Evaluation Society, 1485 Laperriere Avenue, Ottawa, ON K1Z 7S8, Canada, 613-725-2526, Fax 613-729-6206, ces@thewillowgroup.com
Sassy Sunflower Books, PO Box 67106, 421 Richmond Road, Ottawa, ON K2A 4E4, Canada, 613-799-1017
Borealis Press Limited, 110 Bloomingdale Street, Ottawa, Ont. K2C 4A4, Canada, 613-798-9299, Fax 379-897-4747
JOURNAL OF CANADIAN POETRY, 110 Bloomingdale Street, Ottawa, Ont. K2C 4A4, Canada, 613-797-9299, Fax 613-798-9747
Book Coach Press, 14 Moorside Private, Ottawa, Ontario K2C 3P4, Canada, (613) 226-4850, 1-877-GGR-RUNE, www.gentlegiantrunes.com, gentlegiantrunes@sympatico.ca
Canadian Library Association, 1150 Morrison Drive, Suite 400, Ottawa, Ontario K2H 8S9, Canada, 613-232-9625 X322, fax: 613-563-9895, www.cla.ca
FELICITER, 328 Frank Street, Ottawa, Ontario K2P 0X8, Canada, 613-232-9625, ext. 322
THALIA: Studies in Literary Humor, English Dept.,University of Ottawa, 70 Laurier East, Ottawa, Ontario, K1N 6N5, Canada, thaliahumor@hotmail.com
Theytus Books Ltd., Green Mountain Road, Lot 45, RR #2, Site 50, Comp. 8, Penticton, B.C. V2A 6J7, Canada, 250-493-7181, fax: 250-493-5302, Web: www.theytusbooks.com, order email: order@theytusbooks.ca, general inquiries: info@theytus-books.ca.
WASCANA REVIEW OF CONTEMPORARY POETRY AND SHORT FICTION, Department of English, University of Regina, Regina, Sask S4S 0A2, Canada, 584-4302
Coteau Books, 2517 Victoria Ave., Regina, Sask. S4P 0T2, Canada, 306-777-0170, e-mail coteau@coteaubooks.com
THE MODERN REVIEW, RPO P.O. Box 32659, Richmond Hill L4C 0A2CA, Canada
Munsey Music, Box 511, Richmond Hill, Ontario L4C 4Y8, Canada, 905-737-0208; www.pathcom.com/~munsey
Asteroid Publishing, Inc., P.O. Box 3, Richmond Hill, Ontario, Canada L4X 4X9, Canada, 416-319-5911, 416-352-1561
Plain Philosophy Center, 310 - 8870 Citation Drive, Richmond, BC V6Y 3A3, Canada, 1-604-276-8272
BANANA RAG, 3747 Highway 101, Roberts Creek, B.C. V0N 2W2, Canada, 604-885-7156
Banana Productions, 3747 Highway 101, Roberts Creek, BC V0N 2W2, Canada, 604-885-7156, no fax #
INTERNATIONAL ART POST, 3747 Highway 101, Roberts Creek, BC V0N 2W2, Canada, 604-885-7156
West Coast Paradise Publishing, PO Box 2093, Sardis Sta. Main, Sardis, B.C. V2R 1A5, Canada, 604-824-9528, Fax 604-824-9541, web:http://rg.anstey.ca/
THE NEO-COMINTERN, 97 Maxwell Crescent, Saskatoon, Sask. S7L 3Y4, Canada, www.neo-comintern.com
CROSSCURRENTS, 516 Ave K South, Saskatoon, Sask. S7M 2E2, Canada, Fax 306-244-0795, green@webster.sk.ca—www.webster.sk.ca/greenwich/xc.htm
BLACKFLASH Magazine, PO Box 7381 Station Main, Saskatoon, Saskatchewan S7K 4J3, Canada, 306-374-5115, editor@blackflash.ca
GRAIN MAGAZINE, PO Box 67, Saskatoon, SK S7K 3K1, Canada, 306-244-2828, grainmag@sasktel.net
Saskatchewan Writers Guild, PO Box 67, Saskatoon, SK S7K 3K1, Canada, 306-244-2828, grainmag@sasktel.net, www.grainmagazine.ca
LABOUR/LE TRAVAIL, Arts Publications, FM 2005, Memorial University, St. John's, NF A1C 5S2, Canada, 709-737-2144
OPEN MINDS QUARTERLY, 680 Kirkwood Drive, Bldg. 1, Sudbury, ON P3E 1X3, Canada, 705-675-9193 ext. 8286, Fax 705-675-3501, openminds@nisa.on.ca, www.nisa.on.ca
BLUELINES, #202, 7027-134 Street, Surrey, BC V3W 4T1, Canada, 604-596-1601, lpwordsolutions@hotmail.com; www.lpwordsolutions.com
ECLECTICA MAGAZINE, #102, 7575-140th Street, Surrey, BC V3W-5J9, Canada, Phone: (604) 543-1957 / (604) 590-2735
Sources, 489 College Street, Suite 305, Toronto ON M6G 1A5, Canada, Phone: 416-964-7799. Fax: 416-964-8763
THE SOURCES HOTLINK, 489 College Street, Suite 305, Toronto ON M6G 1A5, Canada, Phone: 416-964-7799. Fax: 416-964-8763
DESCANT, PO Box 314, Station P, M5S 2S8, Toronto, ON, Canada, phone: 416 593 2557, fax: 416 593 9362, email general:

info@descant.on.ca, email subscriptions/back issues: circulation@descant.on.ca, web: www.descant.on.ca

Annick Press Ltd., 15 Patricia Avenue, Toronto, ON M2M 1H9, Canada, 416-221-4802, Fax 416-221-8400, annickpress@annickpress.com

Inner City Books, Box 1271, Station Q, Toronto, ON M4T 2P4, Canada, 416-927-0355, FAX 416-924-1814, booksales@innercitybooks.net

Coach House Books, 401 Huron, on bpNichol Lane, Toronto, ON M5S 2G5, Canada, t: 800-367-6360, f: 416-977-1158, website: www.chbooks.com

BRICK, A Literary Journal, Box 609, Station P, Toronto, ON M5S 2Y4, Canada, www.brickmag.com, info@brickmag.com, orders@brickmag.com

Zygote Publishing, 913, 390 Queens Quay West, Toronto, ON M5V3A6, Canada, www.zygotepublishing.com

PAPERPLATES, 19 Kenwood Avenue, Toronto, ON M6C 2R8, Canada

THIS MAGAZINE, 401 Richmond St. W. #396, Toronto, ON, M5V 3A8, Canada, (877) 999-8447 or (416) 979-9429 or email circ@thismagazine.ca

Fuse Magazine, Artons Cultural Affairs Society, 454-401 Richmond Street West, Toronto, Ont., M5V 3A8, Canada

The House of Worn, 77 Maynard Ave., #3, Toronto, Ontario, Canada

Soul Inscriptions Press, Toronto, Ontario, Canada, www.SoulInscriptionsPress.com, info@soulinscriptionspress.com

WORN FASHION JOURNAL, 77 Maynard Ave., #3, Toronto, Ontario, Canada, 416-531-3145

Association For Research On Mothering / Demeter Press, Rm 726, Atkinson College, York University, 4700 Keele Street, Toronto, Ontario M3J 1P3, Canada, 416-736-2100 x 60366; fax 416-736-5766; http://www.yorku.ca/arm

CANADIAN WOMAN STUDIES/les cahiers de la femme, 210 Founders College, York Univ., 4700 Keele Street, Toronto, Ontario M3J 1P3, Canada, 416-736-5356, fax 416-736-5765, e-mail cwscf@yorku.ca

JOURNAL OF THE ASSOCIATION FOR RESEARCH ON MOTHERING (JARM), Rm 726, Atkinson College, York University, 4700 Keele Street, Toronto, Ontario M3J 1P3, Canada, 416-736-2100 x 60366; fax 416-736-5766; http://www.yorku.ca/arm

Wordwrights Canada, PO Box 456, Station O, Toronto, Ontario M4A 2P1, Canada, wordwrights@sympatico.ca, www.wordwrights.ca

JONES AV, 88 Dagmar Av, Toronto, Ontario M4M 1W1, Canada, www.interlog.com/~oel

The Kenneth G. Mills Foundation, P.O. Box 790, Station F, Toronto, Ontario M4Y 2N7, Canada, 800-437-1454, fax: 905-951-9712, email:news@kgmfoundation.org, www:kgmfoundation.org

Underwhich Editions, PO Box 262, Adelaide Street Station, Toronto, Ontario M5C 2J4, Canada, 536-9316

Winslow Publishing, Box 38012, 550 Eglinton Avenue West, Toronto, Ontario M5N 3A8, Canada, 416-789-4733, winslow@interlog.com, www.winslowpublishing.com

RESOURCES FOR FEMINIST RESEARCH/DOCUMENTATION SUR LA RECHERCHE FEMINISTE, 252 Bloor Street W., Toronto, Ontario M5S 1V6, Canada, 416-978-2033, Fax 416-926-4725, E-mail rfrdrf@oise.utoronto.ca

FROGPOND: Journal of the Haiku Society of America, PO Box 279, Station P, Toronto, Ontario M5S 2S8, Canada, gswede@ryerson.ca

Haiku Society of America, PO Box 279, Station P, Toronto, Ontario M5S 2S8, Canada, gswede@ryerson.ca/http://www.hsa-haiku.org/frogpond.htm

The Mercury Press, PO Box 672, Station P, Toronto, Ontario M5S 2Y4, Canada, PH: 416.531.4338, FAX: 416.531.0765

INTERNATIONAL JOURNAL OF AMERICAN LINGUISTICS, University of Toronto, 130 St. George Street, Department of Linguistics, Toronto, Ontario M5S 3H1, Canada, http://www.journals.uchicago.edu/IJAL/home.html

TSAR Publications, PO Box 6996, Station A, Toronto, Ontario M5W 1X7, Canada, www.tsarbooks.com

CONNEXIONS DIGEST, 489 College Street, Suite 305, Toronto, Ontario M6G 1A5, Canada, 416-964-1511, www.connexions.org

Connexions Information Services, Inc., 489 College Street, Suite 305, Toronto, Ontario M6G 1A5, Canada, 416-964-1511, www.connexions.org

Gesture Press, 623 Christie St., #4, Toronto, Ontario M6G 3E6, Canada

Guernica Editions, Inc., 11 Mount Royal Avenue, Toronto, Ontario M6H 2S2, Canada, 416-658-9888, Fax 416-657-8885, guernicaeditions@cs.com

The Emergency Response Unit, 517 Runnymede Rd. Second Floor, Toronto, Ontario M6S 2Z8, Canada, http://theemergencyresponseunit.wordpress.com/

Clark-Nova Books, 2812 Bloor St.W Suite 2, Toronto, Ontario M8X 1A7, Canada, www.clarknovabooks.com

Life Media, B2-125 The Queensway, Suite 52, Toronto, Ontario M8Y 1H6, Canada, email publisher@lifemedia.ca, web www.lifemedia.ca

CANADIAN JOURNAL OF COMMUNICATION, Canadian Centre for Studies in Publishing, Simon Fraser Univ., 515 West Hastings St., Vancouver BC V6B 5K3, Canada, (778) 782-5116

PRISM INTERNATIONAL, E462-1866 Main Mall, University of British Columbia, Vancouver BC V6T 1Z1, Canada, 604-822-2514, Fax 604-822-3616, prism@interchange.ubc.ca, www.prismmagazine.ca

Anvil Press, 278 East First Avenue, Vancouver, B.C. V5T 1A6, Canada, 604-876-8710, info@anvilpress.com, www.anvilpress.com

Lazara Press, Box 2269, VMPO,, Vancouver, B.C. V6B 3W2, Canada, 604.872.1134

Ronsdale Press, 3350 West 21st Avenue, Vancouver, B.C. V6S 1G7, Canada, 604-738-4688, toll free 888-879-0919, Fax 604-731-4548

CANADIAN LITERATURE, University of British Columbia, Buchanan E158, 1866 Main Mall, Vancouver, B.C. V6T 1Z1, Canada, 604-822-2780, fax 604-822-5504

Iconoclast Press, 3495 Cambie Street, Suite 144, Vancouver, BC V5Z 4R3, Canada, 604-682-3269 X8832, admin@iconoclastpress.com

GEIST MAGAZINE, 341 Water Street,#200, Vancouver, BC V6B 1B8, Canada, (604) 681-9161, 1-888-Geist-eh, Fax: (604) 669-8250

SUB-TERRAIN, P.O. Box 3008, Main Post Office, Vancouver, BC V6B 3X5, Canada, 604-876-8710, subter@portal.ca, www.subterrain.ca

ROOM MAGAZINE, PO Box 46160, Station D, Vancouver, BC V6J 5G5, Canada

UBC Press, 2029 West Mall, Vancouver, BC V6T 1Z2, Canada, Phone 604-822-5959, 1-877-377-9378; Fax 604-822-6083, 1-800-668-0821; info@ubcpress.ca; www.ubcpress.ca

Good Times Publishing Co., #217 - 1027 Davie St., Vancouver, BC, V6E 4L2, Canada, 604-736-1045

CANADIAN JOURNAL OF COMMUNICATION, Simon Fraser University, 515 West Hastings Street, Vancouver, British Columbia V6B 5K3, Canada, T.778-782-5243, F.778-782-5239, ccsp-info@sfu.ca, www.ccsppress.com

CCSP Press, Simon Fraser University, 515 West Hastings Street, Vancouver, British Columbia V6B 5K3, Canada,

T.778-782-5243, F.778-782-5239, ccsp-info@sfu.ca, www.ccsppress.com
Arias Press, Vancouver, Canada V6T 2H2, Canada, www.ariaspress.com
EcceNova Editions, 308-640 Dallas Road, Victoria, BC V8V 1B6, Canada, Fax: 250-595-8401 email: info@eccenova.com
    URL: www.eccenova.com
Horned Owl Publishing, 4605 Bearwood Court, Victoria, BC V8Y 3G1, Canada, fax 250-414-4987; e-mail
    hornowl@islandnet.com
Trafford Publishing, 2657 Wilfert Road, Victoria, BC V9B 5c3, Canada, 888-232-4444, Fax 250-383-6804, info@trafford.com,
    www.trafford.com
Brindle and Glass Publishing, 6-356 Simcoe Street, Victoria, BC, V8V 1L1, Canada
THE MALAHAT REVIEW, PO Box 1700, Stn. CSC, Victoria, British Columbia V8W 2Y2, Canada
UNIVERSITY OF WINDSOR REVIEW, 2124 Chrysler Hall North, University of Windsor, Windsor, Ontario N9B 3P4,
    Canada, 519-293-3000 X2290; Fax 519-973-7050; uwrevu@uwindsor.ca
Village Lane Press, 10024 Wilson Rd., Winfield, Canada, 250-870-8278
Hopeace Press, 188 Morley Ave, Winnepeg, MB R3L 0Y1, Canada, 250 335 0535, palesurface@hopeace.ca,
    www.palesurfaceofthings.com
Turnstone Press, 607-100 Arthur Street, Winnipeg R3B 1H3, Canada, 204-947-1555, info@turnstonepress.com
Three Bears Publishing, 690 Community Row, Winnipeg, Manitoba Canada R3R 1H7, Canada, Tel. 1 (204) 783-7966, Email:
    info@ThreeBearsPublishing.com, Website: www.ThreeBearsPublishing.com
CONTEMPORARY VERSE 2: the Canadian Journal of Poetry and Critical Writing, 207-100 Arthur Street, Winnipeg,
    Manitoba R3B 1H3, Canada, (204) 949-1365, cv2@mb.sympatico.ca, www.contemporaryverse2.ca

PEOPLE'S REPUBLIC OF CHINA

CHINESE LITERATURE, 24 Baiwanzhuang Road, Beijing 100037, People's Republic of China, 892554
Chinese Literature Press, 24 Baiwanzhuang Road, Beijing 100037, People's Republic of China

CZECH REPUBLIC

Twisted Spoon Press, PO Box 21, Preslova 12, Prague 5, 150 00, Czech Republic, www.twistedspoon.com

ENGLAND

Immediate Direction Publications, 7 Mountview, Church Lane West, Aldershot, Hampshire GU11 3LN, England,
    tdenyer@ntlworld.com, www.midnightstreet.co.uk
MIDNIGHT STREET, 7 Mountview, Church Lane West, Aldershot, Hampshire GU11 3LN, England, tdenyer@ntlworld.com,
    www.midnightstreet.co.uk
PENNINE PLATFORM, Frizingley Hall, Frizinghall Road, Bradford BD9 4LD, England, 01274 541015, nicholas.bielby@vir-
    gin.net, www.pennineplatform.co.uk
VARIOUS ARTISTS, 24, Northwick Road, Bristol BS7 0UG, England
PENNINE INK MAGAZINE, The Gallery, Yorke Street, Burnley, Lancs. BB11 1HD, England, sheridansdandl@yahoo.co.uk
THE NEW WRITER, PO Box 60, Cranbrook, Kent TN17 2ZR, England, 01580-212626 admin@thenewwriter.com
    www.thenewwriter.com
THE JOURNAL (once "of Contemporary Anglo-Scandinavian Poetry"), 18 Oxford Grove, Flat 3, Devon. EX34 9HQ, England,
    01271862708; e-mail smithsssj@aol.com
TEARS IN THE FENCE, 38 Hod View, Stourpaine, Blandford Forum, Dorset DT11 8TN, England
Hippopotamus Press, 22 Whitewell Road, Frome, Somerset BA11 4EL, England, 0373-466653
Flapjack Press, 6 Chiffon Way, Trinity Riverside, Gtr Manchester M3 6AB, England, +4407814570441, paul@mucusart.co.uk,
    www.mucusart.co.uk/press.htm
STAND MAGAZINE, School of English, Univeristy of Leeds, Leeds LS2 9JT, England
KRAX, 63 Dixon Lane, Leeds, Yorkshire LS12 4RR, England
SMOKE, Liver House, 96 Bold Street, Liverpool L1 4HY, England
Windows Project, Liver House, 96 Bold Street, Liverpool L1 4HY, England
BULLETIN OF HISPANIC STUDIES, The University of Liverpool, 18 Oxford St., Liverpool L69 7ZN, England, 051 794
    2774/5
Liverpool University Press, The University of Liverpool, 18 Oxford St., Liverpool L69 7ZN, England, 051 794 2774/5
GOLD DUST, 55 Elmdale Road, London E17 6PN, England
Menard Press, 8 The Oaks, Woodside Avenue, London N12 8AR, England
MEDICAL HISTORY, Welcome Trust Centre for the History of Medicine at UCL, 183 Euston Road, London NW1 2BE,
    England, +44 (0)20 7679 8107, fax +44 (0)20 7679 8194, web: www.ucl.ac.uk/histmcd
Wellcomc Trust Centre for the History of Medicine at UCL, 183 Euston Road, London NW1 2BE, England
DWANG: Outsider poetry and prose, 23 Khartoum Road, Tooting, London SW17 0JA, England, www.eatmytangerine.com
Tangerine Press, 23 Khartoum Road, Tooting, London SW17 0JA, England, www.eatmytangerine.com
Hole Books, 2 Hailsham Avenue, London SW2 3AH, England, (0) 208 677 3121, fax (0) 208 677 3121, email
    holebooks@yahoo.co.uk, web www.holebooks.com
Saqi Books Publisher, 26 Westbourne Grove, London W2 5RH, England, 020 7221 9347, fax 020 7229 7492
AQUARIUS, Flat 4, Room B, 116 Sutherland Avenue, Maida-Vale, London W9, England
POETRY REVIEW, 22 Betterton Street, London WC2H 9BX, England
Mind Power Publishing, 57 Elsinge Road, Enfield, London, EN1 4NS, England, +44(0)1992851158
AMBIT, 17 Priory Gardens, London, N6 5QY, England, 0181-340-3566
THE RUE BELLA, 40, Jordangate, Macclesfield SK10 1EW, England, www.ruebella.co.uk
The Association of Freelance Writers, Sevendale House, 7 Dale Street, Manchester, M1 1JB, England, 0161-228-2362, Fax
    0161-236-9440
FREELANCE MARKET NEWS, Sevendale House, 7 Dale Street, Manchester, M1 1JB, England, 0161-228-2362, Fax
    0161-228-3533
RUBIES IN THE DARKNESS, 41 Grantham Road, Manor Park, London E12 5LZ, England
Original Plus, 17 High Street, Maryport, Cumbria, CA15 6BQ, England, 01900812194; email- smithsssj@aol.com
PLANTAGENET PRODUCTIONS, Libraries of Spoken Word Recordings and of Stagescripts, Westridge (Open Centre), Star
    Lane, Highclere, Newbury RG20 9PJ, England
Plantagenet Productions, Westridge (Open Centre), Highclere, Nr. Newbury, Berkshire RG20 9PJ, England
FOURTH WORLD REVIEW, 26 High Street, Purton, Wiltshire SN5 9AE, England, 01793-772214
Applied Probability Trust, School of Mathematics and Statistics, University of Sheffield, Sheffield S3 7RH, England, tel: +44

623

(0)114 222-3920; fax: +44 (0)114 272-9782; email: apt@sheffield.ac.uk; web: http://www.appliedprobability.org
MATHEMATICAL SPECTRUM, School of Mathematics and Statistics, The University of Sheffield, Sheffield S3 7RH, England, tel: +44 (0)114 222-3922, fax: +44 (0)114 272-9782, email: spectrum@sheffield.ac.uk, web: http://www.appliedprobability.org
CANDELABRUM POETRY MAGAZINE, 1 Chatsworth Court, Outram Rd., Southsea PO5 1RA, England, tel: 02392 753696, rcp@poetry7.fsnet.co.uk, www.members.tripod.com/redcandlepress
Red Candle Press, 1 Chatsworth Court, Outram Rd., Southsea PO5 1RA, England, 02392753696, rcp@poetry7.fsnet.co.uk, www.members.tripod.com/redcandlepress
IOTA, 1 Lodge Farm, Snitterfield, Stratford-on-Avon, Warks CV37 0LR, England, 44-1789-730320, iotapoetry@aol.com, www.iotapoetry.co.uk
THE ENGLISH CLARION, 2 Nuffield Close, Shaw, Swindon SN5 5WT, England, seacrabart@googlemail.com
SeaCrab Publishing, 2 Nuffield Close, Shaw, Swindon SN5 5WT, England, +44 (0)1793 330420, seacrabart@googlemail.com
Ragged Raven Press, 1 Lodge Farm, Snitterfield, Stratford-upon-Avon, Warwickshire CV37 0LR, England, 44-1789-730320, raggedravenpress@aol.com, www.raggedraven.co.uk
Comrades Press, 23 George Street, Stockton, Southam, Warwickshire CV47 8JS, England, editor@comrade.org.uk, www.comrade.org.uk/press
PURPLE PATCH, 25 Griffiths Road, West Bromwich, B71 2EH, England
DATA DUMP, 4 Nowell Place, Almondbury, Huddersfield, West Yorkshire HD5 8PB, England
Hilltop Press, 4 Nowell Place, Almondbury, Huddersfield, West Yorkshire HD5 8PB, England
JAMES JOYCE BROADSHEET, School of English, University of Leeds, West Yorkshire LS2 9JT, England, 0113-233-4739
ORBIS, 17 Greenhow Avenue, West Kirby, Wirral CH48 5EL, England, +44 (0)151 625 1446, e-mail baldock.carole@googlemail.com, Websites, www.facebook.com/n/?group.php&gid=53636000056www.facebook.com/group.php?gid=187955986920 www.kudoswritingcompetitions.com
IMPress, 26 Oak Road, Withington, Manchester M2O 3DA, England, +44(0)161-2837636

FINLAND

BOOKS FROM FINLAND: Online literature journal of writing from and about Finland, P.O.Box 259, FI-00171 Helsinki, Finland, 358 201 131345, www.booksfromfinland.fi, booksfromfinland@finlit.fi

FRANCE

Buenos Books, 35 Avenue Ernest Reyer, 75014 PARIS, France, www.buenosbooks.fr
UPSTAIRS AT DUROC, WICE, Upstairs at Duroc, 7 Cite Falguiere, 75015 Paris, France, wice@wice-paris.org (attention:Upstairs at Duroc submissions)
FRANK: AN INTERNATIONAL JOURNAL OF CONTEMPORARY WRITING AND ART, 32 rue Edouard Vaillant, 93100 Montreuil Sous Bois, France, (33) 1 48596658, e-mail david@paris-anglo.com
Handshake Editions, Atelier A2, 83 rue de la Tombe-Issoire, Paris 75014, France, 01-4327-1767, jim_haynes@wanadoo.fr, jim@jim-haynes.com, www.jim-haynes.com
J'ECRIS, BP 101, Saint-Cloud 92216, France, (1) 47-71-79-63
Hotel des Bains Editions, 28, rue du Pont Perce, 27130, Verneuil sur Avre, France, 33-(0)2 32 32 46 15

GREAT BRITAIN

Second Aeon Publications, 19 Southminster Road, Roath, Cardiff, Wales CF23 5AT, Great Britain, 029-2049-3093, secondaeon@peterfinch.co.uk
Peter Marcan Publications, PO Box 3158, London SEI 4RA, Great Britain, (020) 7357 0368

GERMANY

Expanded Media Editions, Diezstr. 8, 53113 Bonn, Germany, 0228/22 95 83, FAX 0228/21 95 07
Edition Gemini, Juelichstrasse 7, Huerth-Efferen D-50354, Germany, 02233/63550, Fax 02233/65866

GREECE

Anagnosis, Deliyianni 3, Maroussi 15122, Greece, +302106254654, Fax:+302106254089, www.anagnosis.gr

HOLLAND

VERSAL, Amsterdam, Holland, versaljournal@wordsinhere.com (queries only), http://versal.wordsinhere.com

HONG KONG

RENDITIONS, Chinese University of Hong Kong, Shatin, NT, Hong Kong, 852-26097407; fax 852-26035110; e-mail renditions@cuhk.hk
Research Centre for Translation, Chinese University of Hong Kong, Research Centre for Translation, Chinese University of Hong Kong, Shatin, NT, Hong Kong, 852-26097407; e-Mail renditions@cuhk.hk
Kakibubu Media Limited, 7A Willy Commercial Building, 28-36 Wing Kut Street, Sheung Wan, Hong Kong, +852 2557 3742, +852 2617 3742, tschmidt@kakibubu.com, www.kakibubu.com
Fountain Publisher Limited, Flat 'C', 33/F, Block 10, Metro Harbour View, 8 Fuk Lee Stre, Tai Kok Tsui, Kowloon, Hong Kong, www.fountainpublisher.com

INDIA

TAJ MAHAL REVIEW, 4/2 B Lig Govindpur Colony, Allahabad, India, 91-9415091004
Cyberwit.net, 4/2 B Lig, Govindpur Colony, Allahabad (UP) 211004, India, 91-9415091004
Dnar Kaker Basa, Akunji Bagan, 1ST Lane, Palpara, Chandannagore, Hoogly, West Bengal, India. Pin: 712136., India, 033-26851666
DNAR KAKER BASA, Akunji Bagan, 1ST Lane, Palpara, Chandannagore, Hoogly, West Bengal, India. Pin: 712136., India, 033-26851666
KOBISENA, P40 Nandana Park, kolkata 700 034, W.B., India
ABOL TABOL, 7/1 d Kalicharan Ghosh Road, Kolkata, W. Bengal, India, 033-25571767, babychowin@yahoo.co.in
Prakalpana Literature, P40 Nandana Park, Kolkata 700034, Kolkata, West Bengal, India, +9831714756. Email:prakalpana@yours.com Blog:http://vattacharjachandan.blogspot.com
Tiger Moon, 3-882 Coconut Grove, Prasanthi Nilayam A.P. India 515134, India, cosmicpowerpress@yahoo.co.in AND treiskennedy@gmail.com

PRAKALPANA SAHITYA/PRAKALPANA LITERATURE, P-40 Nandana Park, Kolkata-700034, West Bengal, India

IRELAND

JOURNAL OF MUSIC IN IRELAND (JMI), Edenvale, Esplanade, Bray, Co Wicklow, Ireland, 00-353-1-2867292 phone/Fax, editor@thejmi.com, www.thejmi.com

Salmon Poetry Ltd., Knockeven, Cliffs of Moher, Co. Clare, Ireland, 011-353-65-7081941, info@salmonpoetry.com, www.salmonpoetry.com

THE SHOP: A Magazine of Poetry, c/o Skeagh, Schull, County Cork, Ireland, Tel: +353 28 28263 Email: theshop@theshop-poetry-magazine.ie Website: www.theshop-poetry-magazine.ie

THE STINGING FLY, PO Box 6016, Dublin 8, Ireland, stingingfly@gmail.com, www.stingingfly.org

THE MAINE EVENT, Rusheen, Firies, Co. Kerry, Ireland, 066-9763084 phone/Fax, maineevent@eircom.net, www.mainee-vent.net

CRANNOG, Galway Language Center, Bridge Mills, Galway, Ireland, editor@crannogmagazine.com, www.crannogmaga-zine.com

Wordsonthestreet, Six San Antonio Park, Salthill, Galway, Ireland, publisher@wordsonthestreet.com, www.wordsonthes-treet.com

ISRAEL

Espretto, 10 Ehad Haam St., P.O. Box 11, Azur 58015, Israel, +972 3 550 9000 www.espretto.com

THE OTHER ISRAEL, PO Box 2542, Holon 58125 Israel, Israel, 972-3-5565804 phone/Fax

Ibis Editions, P.O. Box 8074, German Colony, Jerusalem 91080, Israel, Phone 972-2-627-7035, Fax 972-2-627-6058

VOICES ISRAEL, 9 Shalom Yehuda 7, Jerusalem, 93395, Israel, Voices_Israel_2010@me.com

Vox Humana Books, 7 Rivka Guber Street, 2, Kfar Sava, 44471, Israel, 972.54.4.803.163, publisher@voxhumana-books.com, www.voxhumana-books.com

ARC, PO Box 39385, Tel Aviv 61393, Israel, iawe_mailbox@yahoo.com

ITALY

LO STRANIERO: The Stranger, Der Fremde, L'Etranger, Piazza Amedeo 8, Naples 80121, Italy, Tel: 0039-081-681238, fax: 0039-081-7611264, email: lostraniero85@libero.it

JAPAN

POETRY KANTO, Kanto Gakuin University, Kamariya Minami 3-22-1, Kanazawa-Ku, Yokohama 236-8502, Japan

United Nations University Press, United Nations University, 53-70 Jingumae 5-chome, Shibuya-ku, Tokyo, Japan, Tel: +81-3499-2811, Fax: +81-3-3406-7345, sales@hq.unu.edu, http://www.unu.edu/unupress

Printed Matter Press (Tokyo), Yagi Bldg. 4F, 2-10-13 Shitaya,, Taito-ku, Tokyo, Japan, 110-0004, Japan, Fax: 81-03-3871-4964 email:info@printedmatterpress.com, http://www.printedmatterpress.com

MEXICO

O!!Zone, Mexico

O!!ZONE, A LITERARY-ART ZINE, Mexico

Citiria Publishing, Paseo de los Sabinos 3701, Del Paseo, Monterrey, NL. 64920, Mexico, fiction1st@yahoo.co.uk, www.citiria.com

NEPAL

Pilgrims Book House, Thamel, PO Box 3872, Kathmandu, Nepal, 977-1-4700942, Fax 977-1-4700943, pil-grims@wlink.com.np, www.pilgrimsbooks.com

LAYALAMA ONLINE MAGAZINE, 320 Phurkesalla Marg, Dhimelohan Swoyambhu,, P. O. Box 5146, Kathmandu, Nepal, Kathmandu 71100, Nepal, Tel: + 977 1 4274815, Fax: + 977 1 4274815, email:layalama@layalama.com, Website: http://www.layalama.com

THE NETHERLANDS

THE LEDGE, 8011 CE, Zwolle, The Netherlands, info@the-ledge.com, www.the-ledge.com

Amsterdam University Press, Prinsengracht 747-751, 1017 JX, Amsterdam, The Netherlands, T 0031 (0)20 4200050, F 0031 (0)20 4203412, www.aup.nl

NEW ZEALAND

KOKAKO, 42 Flanshaw Road, Te Atatu South, Auckland 0610, New Zealand, pprime@ihug.co.nz

Hallard Press, 43 Landscape Rd, Papatoetoe, Auckland 1701, New Zealand, 64 09 2782731, 64 09 2782731

DEEP SOUTH, Department of English, University of Otago, P.O. Box 56, Dunedin, New Zealand, email: deepsouthjournal@gmail.com

Kilmog Press, 378 Princes Street, Dunedin, New Zealand, New Zealand, 0061 3 4792857

BRAVADO, PO Box 13-533, Grey Street, Tauranga 3001, New Zealand, 07 576 3040, fax:07 570 2446

PHILIPPINES

World Changing Books, Northview Hotel BRGY 46, Condo #9, Laoag, Ilocos Norte, Philippines, 808-934-7942

REPUBLIC OF PANAMA

Caribbean Books-Panama, Apdo. 0301-01249, Colon, Republic of Panama, +507-433-0349, http://www.caribbeanbooks-pub.com, publisher@caribbeanbookspub.com

PORTUGAL

NEO: Literary Magazine, Departamento de Linguas e Literaturas, Universidade dos Acores, 9500 Ponta Delgada, Portugal, www.neomagazine.org

SCOTLAND

CHAPMAN, Chapman Publishing Ltd., 4 Broughton Place, Edinburgh EH1 3RX, Scotland, 0131-557-2207

SINGAPORE

Monsoon Books, 52 Telok Blangah Road, #03-05 Telok Blangah House, Singapore 098829, Singapore, email: phil@monsoonbooks.com.sg, web: www.monsoonbooks.com.sg

SPAIN

TERRA INCOGNITA: A Bilingual Journal of Literature, Art and Commentary, APDO. 14401, 28080 Madrid, Spain

SWEDEN

Syukhtun Editions, Odengatan 8, 114 24 Stockholm, Sweden, (468)6124988, theoradic@yahoo.com, http://www.syukhtun.net
Kamini Press, Ringvagen 8, 4th floor, SE-11726 Stockholm, Sweden, editor@kaminipress.com, http://www.kaminipress.com

TAIWAN

WHITE FUNGUS, Room 3, Floor 16, No. 566 13, Sec. 2, Wunsin Road, Situn District, Taichung City 407, Taiwan, 64(4)3829113, 64 274819660, whitefungusmail@yahoo.com

THAILAND

GoodSAMARitan Press, 95/31 Moo 10 Classic Village, T. Nongphure A. Banglamung, Chonburi 20150, Thailand, 66817177941
NEW MIRAGE QUARTERLY, 95/31 Moo 10 Classic Village, T. Nongphure A. Banglamung, Chonburi 20150, Thailand, 66817177941

TURKEY

ISTANBUL LITERARY REVIEW, http://www.ilrmagazine.com/submissions/, http://www.ilrmagazine.net, Istanbul, Turkey

UNITED KINGDOM

OPEN WIDE MAGAZINE, United Kingdom, www.openwidemagazine.co.uk
Accent Press Ltd, The Old School, Upper High Street, Bedlinog CF46 6SA, United Kingdom, info@accentpress.co.uk www.accentpress.co.uk
THE CANNON'S MOUTH, 22 Margaret Grove, Harborne, Birmingham B17 9JH, United Kingdom, [+44] 121 449 3866
Re-invention UK Ltd, Primrose Cottage, Lakes Farm, Braintree Green, Rayne, Braintree, United Kingdom, (0044) 1245 332147
Open Wide Books, 40 Wingfield Road, Lakenheath, Brandon, IP27 9HR, United Kingdom
THE ORPHAN LEAF REVIEW, 26 Grove Park Terrace, Fishponds, Bristol, BS16 2BN, United Kingdom, www.orphanleaf.co.uk orphanleaf@jpwallis.co.uk
Salt Publishing, 14a High Street, Fulbourn, Cambridge CB21 5DH, United Kingdom, +44 (0)1223 882220 chris@saltpublishing.com
RED LAMP, 6 Madras Road, Cambridge, Cambs CB1 3PX, United Kingdom
Parthian, The Old Surgery, Napier Street, Cardigan SA43 1ED, United Kingdom, parthianbooks@yahoo.co.uk, www.parthianbooks.co.uk
THE QUIET FEATHER, St. Mary's Cottage, Church Street, Dalton-In-Furness, Cumbria, LA15 8BA, ENGLAND, United Kingdom
Templar Poetry, PO BOX 7082, Bakewell, Derbyshire DE45 9AF, United Kingdom, info@templarpoetry.co.uk
Tears in the Fence, 38 Hod View Stourpaine, Blandford Forum, Dorset DT11 8TN, United Kingdom
Dionysia Press Ltd., 127 Milton Road West, 7, Duddingston House Courtyard, Edinburgh, EH15 1Jg, United Kingdom, 0131-6611153 [tel/fax, 0131 6614853 [tel]
UNDERSTANDING MAGAZINE, 20 A Montgomery Street, Edinburgh, EH7 5JS, United Kingdom, 0131-4780680
SHEARSMAN, 58 Velwell Road, Exeter EX4 4LD, United Kingdom, Tel: 01392-434511
OUTPOSTS POETRY QUARTERLY, 22, Whitewell Road, Frome, Somerset BA11 4EL, United Kingdom
NEW HOPE INTERNATIONAL REVIEW, 20 Werneth Avenue, Gee Cross, Hyde, Cheshire SK14 5NL, United Kingdom, www.geraldengland.co.uk
Journal of Pyrotechnics, 8 Aragon Place, Kimbolton, Huntingdon, Cambs PE28 0JD, United Kingdom, Phone: 44 1480 860124, FAX: 44 1480 861108, email: toms@davas.co.uk, web: www.jpyro.com
JOURNAL OF PYROTECHNICS, 8 Aragon Place, Kimbolton, Huntingdon, Cambs PE28 0JD, United Kingdom, 44 1480 860124, FAX: 44 1480 861108, email: toms@davas.co.uk, web: www.jpyro.com
PREMONITIONS, 13 Hazely Combe, Arreton, Isle of Wight, PO30 3AJ, United Kingdom, http://www.pigasuspress.co.uk
The Seer Press, PO Box 29313, Glasgow, Lanarkshire, Scotland, G20 2AE, United Kingdom
Peepal Tree Press, 7 King's Avenue, Leeds LS6 1QS, United Kingdom, telephone +44 (0)113 2451703
Deborah Charles Publications, 173 Mather Avenue, Liverpool L18 6JZ, United Kingdom, phone 44-151-724-2500 from outside UK
BAD PRESS SERIALS, 21 Portland Rise, Finsbury Park, London, United Kingdom, Email: badpress@gmail.com Web: http://badpress.infinology.net
SABLE LITMAG, PO Box 33504, London E9 7YE, United Kingdom
FEMINIST REVIEW, c/o Women's Studies, London North Campus, London Metropolitan University, 166-220 Holloway Road, London N7 8DB, United Kingdom
Katabasis, 10 St Martins Close, London NW1 0HR, United Kingdom, Telephone and fax +44 (0)20 7485 3830
Poetry London, 6 Daniels Road, London SE15 3LR, United Kingdom
Marion Boyars Publishers, 24 Lacy Road, London SW15 1NL, United Kingdom
The Wellsweep Press, Unit 3 Ashburton Centre276 Cortis Road, 276 Cortis Road, London SW15 3AY, United Kingdom, ws@shadoof.net
GRANTA, Granta Publications, 12 Addison Avenue, London W11 4QR, United Kingdom, +44(0)20 7605 1360, www.granta.com
Lawrence & Wishart, European Thought, University of Loughborough, Loughborough LE11 3TU, United Kingdom, info@lwbooks.co.uk; www.lwbooks.co.uk/anarchiststudies
Crescent Moon, PO Box 393, Maidstone, Kent ME14 5XU, United Kingdom
PAGAN AMERICA, PO Box 393, Maidstone, Kent ME14 5XU, United Kingdom
PASSION, PO Box 393, Maidstone, Kent ME14 5XU, United Kingdom
MSLEXIA, Mslexia Publications Limited, P.O. Box 656, Newcastle upon Tyne, NE99 1PZ, United Kingdom, +44 (0)191 233 3860

Abbey Press, Northern Ireland, Courtenay Hill, Newry, Country Down BT34 2ED, United Kingdom, 01693-63142, Fax 01693-62514, Molly71Freeman@aol.com, www.geocities.com/abbeypress/

Murder Slim Press, 129 Trafalgar Road West, Gt. Yarmouth, Norfolk NR31 8AD, United Kingdom, www.murderslim.com/publications.html

THE SAVAGE KICK LITERARY MAGAZINE, 129 Trafalgar Road West, Gt. Yarmouth, Norfolk NR31 8AD, United Kingdom, www.murderslim.com/publications.html

PRETEXT, Pen & Inc Press, School of Literature & Creative Writing, Norwich, Norfolk NR4 7TJ, United Kingdom, +44 (0)1603 592783, Fax + 44 (0)1603 507728, info@penandinc.co.uk, www.inpressbooks.co.uk/penandinc

REACTIONS, Pen & Inc Press, School of Literature & Creative Writing, Norwich, Norfolk NR4 7TJ, United Kingdom

The Alembic Press, Hyde Farm House, Marcham, Abingdon, Oxford, Oxford OX13 6NX, United Kingdom

Oxford University Press (UK), Great Clarendon Street, Oxford OX2 6DP, United Kingdom

Poetry Direct, 6 Princes Street, Oxford, OX4 1DD, United Kingdom, ++44-1865791202 :: editors@poetry-direct.com :: http://www.poetry-direct.com

ACUMEN, 6 The Mount, Higher Furzeham, Brixham, South Devon TQ5 8QY, United Kingdom

Between The Lines, The Cottage, 14 Lyncroft Gardens, Ewell, Surrey KT17 1UR, United Kingdom, T/F: +44 (0)20 8393 7055, W: www.waywiser-press.com/imprints/.

The Waywiser Press, The Cottage, 14 Lyncroft Gardens, Ewell, Surrey KT17 1UR, United Kingdom, Tel: +44 (0)20 8393 7055, W: www.waywiser-press.com, E: waywiserpress@aol.com.

PULSAR POETRY WEBZINE, 34 Lineacre, Grange Park, Swindon, Wiltshire SN5 6DA, United Kingdom, 01793-875941, e-mail pulsar.ed@btopenworld.com, web: www.pulsarpoetry.com

Snapshot Press, PO Box 132, Waterloo, Liverpool L22 8WZ, United Kingdom, info@snapshotpress.co.uk, www.snapshotpress.co.uk

AESTHETICA MAGAZINE, PO Box 371, York, United Kingdom, +441904 527560

WEST INDIES

Jako Books, Gablewoods South, PO Box VF665, Vieux Fort, St. Lucia, West Indies, 758-454-7839, info@jakoproductions.com, www.jakoproductions.com

627

Subject Index

Myriad Press
NAMBLA BULLETIN
NEW ALTERNATIVES
NSR Publications
PARENTEACHER MAGAZINE
The People's Press
Perrin Press
Practically Shameless Press
Rapacious Press
Raven Publishing, Inc.
Re-invention UK Ltd
Saint Mary's Press
Sand and Sable Publishing
Search Institute
Smirk Books
Stardate Publishing Company
Synergy Press
Top 20 Press
Unlimited Publishing LLC
Upheaval Media
Wellington House Publishing Company
Whispering Pine Press
William Joseph K Publications

ADOPTION

American Carriage House Publishing
Chicago Review Press
Colerith Press
Creative Arts Book Company
CURRENTS: New Scholarship in the Human Services
Dreams Due Media Group, Inc.
DRT Press
Green River Press
LIFETIME MAGAZINE
Mills Custom Services Publishing
Our Child Press
Playdate Kids Publishing
Ragamuffin Heart Publishing
Search Institute
Starik Publishing
Titus Home Publishing
Whispering Pine Press

ADVERTISING, SELF-PROMOTION

AD/VANCE
Atlantic Publishing Group, Inc.
Banana Productions
Bay Tree Publishing
BlackBerry Fields Press
Bonus Books, Inc.
BOOK MARKETING UPDATE
Communication Creativity
Creative Creations Consulting Publishing Company
Cypress Creek Publishing
D.B.A. Books
Dnar Kaker Basa
Dominion Global Publishing
ELEMENTS
GEM Literary Foundation Press
Happy About
Info Net Publishing
Knowledge Concepts Publishing
Kobalt Books
Llumina Press
Mama Incense Publishing
MEAT FOR TEA: THE VALLEY REVIEW
MOBILE BEAT: The Mobile Entertainer's Magazine
Motom
Nunciata
Open Horizons Publishing Company
Platinum One Publishing
REMS Publishing & Publicity
Sand and Sable Publishing
SCULPTURAL PURSUIT MAGAZINE
SEDUCTIVE SELLING
Smirk Books
THE SOURCES HOTLINK
Toca Family Publishing, div. of Toca Family Communica-

tions Group, LLC
Unlimited Publishing LLC
Visual Arts Press
Wheatmark Book Publishing
World Gumbo Publishing
WORLD POETRY SHOWCASE

AFRICAN LITERATURE, AFRICA, AFRICAN STUDIES

AAIMS Publishers
AFRICAN AMERICAN REVIEW
AIM MAGAZINE
Ariko Publications
The B & R Samizdat Express
Back House Books
BLACK MAGNOLIAS LITERARY JOURNAL
THE BLACK SCHOLAR: Journal of Black Studies and Research
Blue Brush Media
Chicago Spectrum Press
Clover Park Press
COLLEGE LITERATURE
Cotton Tree Press
Cyberwit.net
THE DIRTY GOAT
DRUMVOICES REVUE
The Edwin Mellen Press
EPICENTER: A LITERARY MAGAZINE
EPIPHANY, A Literary Journal
Fantail
The Feminist Press at the City University of New York
FEMINIST STUDIES
First Journey Publishing Company
Florida Academic Press
GEM Literary Foundation Press
GHOTI MAGAZINE
Good Hope Enterprises, Inc.
Hood Press
Host Publications, Inc.
Imago Press
Inner City Press
Insight Press
Interlink Publishing Group, Inc.
INTERNATIONAL POETRY REVIEW
International Publishers Co. Inc.
Jako Books
THE JOURNAL OF AFRICAN TRAVEL-WRITING
Just Sisters Publications
Kenyette Productions
Kobalt Books
LDP, an occasional journal of aesthetics & language
Legacy Audio Books, Inc.
Light Density Press
LOST GENERATION JOURNAL
Lotus Press, Inc.
Mama Incense Publishing
McQuinn Publishing
MELEE
Mercer University Press
New World Press, Inc
OBSIDIAN III: Literature in the African Diaspora
Ohio University Press/Swallow Press
ORACLE STORY
Pangaea
Panther Creek Press
Passeggiata Press, Inc.
Path Press, Inc.
Pathfinder Press
Plain View Press
Plank Road Publishing
Poltroon Press
Psychedelic Literature
Re-invention UK Ltd
Roaring Lion Publishing
Sand and Sable Publishing
Shangri-La Publications
Tombouctou Books
TSAR Publications

Twinteum Artist, Inc.
UNDERSTANDING MAGAZINE
United Nations University Press
University of Calgary Press
University of Chicago Press
University of Virginia Press
WEST GOES SOUTH
West Virginia University Press
Whispering Pine Press
White Cliffs Media, Inc.
Whitston Publishing Co.
Wilde Publishing
ZAWP

AFRICAN-AMERICAN

Abernathy House Publishing
Affluent Publishing Corp.
All Nations Press
American Literary Press
Aquarius Press
Aspicomm Media
Bancroft Press
BEATLICK NEWS
BIG MUDDY: Journal of the Mississippi River Valley
BLACK LACE
BLACK MAGNOLIAS LITERARY JOURNAL
BlackBerry Fields Press
BLACKFIRE
BLK
Blue Brush Media
BRILLIANT CORNERS: A Journal of Jazz & Literature
Bronze Girl Productions, Inc.
C & M Online Media Inc.
Cable Publishing
Cantadora Press
Center for Thanatology Research & Education, Inc.
CIRCLE INC., THE MAGAZINE
Circle of Friends Books
Clarity Press, Inc.
COALITION FOR PRISONERS' RIGHTS NEWSLETTER
COGNITIO: A Graduate Humanities Journal
The Colbert House LLC
COLORLINES
THE COMSTOCK REVIEW
CONCEIT MAGAZINE
Cornerstone Publishing, Inc.
Creative Writing and Publishing Company
Demarche Publishing LLC
Dominion Global Publishing
Dream Publishing Co.
DRUMVOICES REVUE
EbonyEnergy Publishing, Inc.
Ecrivez!
ELEMENTS
Everflowing Publications
The Feminist Press at the City University of New York
The Fire!! Press
First Journey Publishing Company
Fotofolio, Inc.
4AllSeasons Publishing
GEM Literary Foundation Press
GenNext Publishing
GOOD GIRL
Gorilla Convict Publications
Grip Publishing
Heritage Books, Inc.
Hole Books
Ika, LLC
IN OUR OWN WORDS
Insight Press
IRIS: A Journal About Women
IRON HORSE LITERARY REVIEW
J & J Consultants, Inc.
Just Sisters Publications
Kelsey St. Press
Kobalt Books
KUUMBA
La Familia Publishing

Legacy Audio Books, Inc.
Light Density Press
Mama Incense Publishing
Margaret Media, Inc.
McQuinn Publishing
MEAT: A Journal of Writing and Materiality
Mercer University Press
Miami University Press
Millennium Vision Press
Minnesota Historical Society Press
New Rivers Press, Inc.
New World Press, Inc
Nushape Publication
Obie Joe Media
Open Hand Publishing LLC
P.R.A. Publishing
Palari Publishing
Papillon Presse
The Passion Profit Company
PEACEWORK
Pearl's Book'em Publisher
Phelps Publishing Company
PhoeniX in Print
The Place In The Woods
Plain View Press
Platinum Dreams Publishing
Pleasure Boat Studio: A Literary Press (including imprints Caravel Books and Aequitas Books, and the division Empty Bowl Press)
Progressive Press; Tree of Life Publications
Psychedelic Literature
QED Press
THE RAVEN CHRONICLES
Razor7 Publishing
REVERIE: MIDWEST AFRICAN AMERICAN LITERATURE
RHINO: THE POETRY FORUM
Roaring Lion Publishing
Sabellapress
Sadorian Publications
THE SCRIBIA
SENSATIONS MAGAZINE
Soft Skull Press
South End Press
Southeast Missouri State University Press
Southern Illinois University Press
THE SOUTHERN QUARTERLY: A Journal of the Arts in the South
Stardate Publishing Company
State University of New York Press
Sweet People Publishing
Total Package Publications, LLC
TSAR Publications
TURNING THE TIDE: Journal of Anti-Racist Action, Research & Education
2L Publishing, LLC
UNDERSTANDING MAGAZINE
University of Arkansas Press
University of Massachusetts Press
University of Nebraska Press
University of South Carolina Press
Upheaval Media
West End Press
Whispering Pine Press
Wings Press
XCP: CROSS-CULTURAL POETICS

AGING

Abernathy House Publishing
Anti-Aging Press
Bay Tree Publishing
Blue Dolphin Publishing, Inc.
BLUE MOUNTAIN
Bonus Books, Inc.
Bronze Girl Productions, Inc.
Colerith Press
DTS Group, Inc.
Dunamis House

Ethos Publishing
Fitness Press
Forest Dale Publishing Company
HAMPTON ROADS HEALTH JOURNAL
The Haworth Press
THE HEALTH JOURNALS
Keiki O Ka Aina Press
Lemon Grove Press
LifeCircle Press
Lion's Den Publishing
Loving Healing Press, Inc.
Mondial
New Paradigm Books
New Victoria Publishers
North Star Books
P.R.A. Publishing
Park Place Publications
PASSAGER
The People's Press
Plain View Press
Ragamuffin Heart Publishing
Rapacious Press
Sentient Publications, LLC
Smirk Books
SONG OF THE SAN JOAQUIN
Sound Enterprises Publishing
Summerland Publishing
Sweet People Publishing
TAPROOT, a journal of older writers
Titus Home Publishing
Trafton Publishing
Two Thousand Three Associates
UnKnownTruths.com Publishing Company
Unlimited Publishing LLC
Upheaval Media
VanderWyk & Burnham
Vanguard Press
Vestibular Disorders Association
Wilde Publishing
World Changing Books

AGRICULTURE

AGRICULTURAL HISTORY
Alpine Press
Art of Living, PrimaMedia,Inc
BANANA RAG
Beekman Books, Inc.
THE BLOOMSBURY REVIEW
THE CARETAKER GAZETTE
The Chicot Press
China Books & Periodicals, Inc.
Dignified Designs
Elderberry Press, Inc.
THE GROWING EDGE MAGAZINE
GROWING FOR MARKET
The Haworth Press
Hobar Publications, A Division of Finney Company
HORTIDEAS
THE JOURNAL OF CALIFORNIA AND GREAT BASIN
    ANTHROPOLOGY
Kumarian Press
La Alameda Press
Laguna Wilderness Press
Lahontan Images
Lessiter Publications
LOST GENERATION JOURNAL
Malki Museum Press
MINIATURE DONKEY TALK INC
NEROUP REVIEW
NEW ENVIRONMENT BULLETIN
RFD
RFF Press / Resources for the Future
RUMINATIONS: The Nigerian Dwarf & Mini Dairy Goat
    Magazine
SONG OF THE SAN JOAQUIN
Stormline Press, Inc.
Sunnyside Press
Tres Picos Press

UBC Press
University of Chicago Press
West Virginia University Press
WISCONSIN TRAILS

AIDS

A & U AMERICA'S AIDS MAGAZINE
Abernathy House Publishing
Bay Press
Biographical Publishing Company
BLK
Brookline Books
CONSCIENCE: The Newsjournal of Catholic Opinion
GEM Literary Foundation Press
GERTRUDE
Gertrude Press
GOOD GIRL
JOURNAL OF SCIENTIFIC EXPLORATION
Lone Willow Press
PEACEWORK
Re-invention UK Ltd
Soft Skull Press
TREATING YOURSELF: The Alternative Medicine Journal
Vanguard Press

AIRPLANES

R.J. Bender Publishing
Brick Road Poetry Press
Cable Publishing
CESSNA OWNER MAGAZINE
The Film Instruction Company of America
GLOBAL ONE MAGAZINE
Ho Logos Press
Light Density Press
Maryland Historical Press (also MHPress)
PIPERS MAGAZINE
Scottwall Associates, Publishers
Slipdown Mountain Publications LLC
Unlimited Publishing LLC

ALASKA

Alaska Native Language Center
Council For Indian Education
Cypress Creek Publishing
The Denali Press
Edenscape Publishing Company
Fathom Publishing Co.
Greatland Graphics
Heyday Books
His Work Christian Publishing
La Familia Publishing
Mountain Automation Corporation
Northern Publishing
Pleasure Boat Studio: A Literary Press (including imprints
    Caravel Books and Aequitas Books, and the division
    Empty Bowl Press)
Pruett Publishing Company
Sasquatch Books
Scientia Publishing, LLC
Sunnyside Press
Tuvela Press
University of Alaska Press
WEST GOES SOUTH
Wizard Works

ALCOHOL, ALCOHOLISM

Assilem 9 Publications
Capalo Press
Colerith Press
Devil Mountain Books
GEM Literary Foundation Press
Good Book Publishing Company
GROUP Publishing
Haight-Ashbury Publications
HAMPTON ROADS HEALTH JOURNAL
THE HEALTH JOURNALS
Hope Publishing House

ILLUMINATIONS LITERARY JOURNAL
Islewest Publishing
Jalmar Press/Innerchoice Publishing
JOURNAL OF PSYCHOACTIVE DRUGS
Lion's Den Publishing
Meek Publishing
Murder Slim Press
National Writers Press
OUT OF LINE
Paradise Research Publications, Inc.
Rapacious Press
Saint Bob Press
THE SAVAGE KICK LITERARY MAGAZINE
See Sharp Press
SHATTERED WIG REVIEW
Six Ft. Swells Press
SO YOUNG!
Squire Press
Sweet People Publishing

ALTERNATIVE MEDICINE

Accendo Publishing
Act on Wisdom
Anderson Publishing; also RC Anderson Books
Best Life Media
Brookline Books
Capalo Press
Cooperative Press
Cuore Libre Publishing
Elite Books
Energy Psychology Press
Fitness Press
GOOD GIRL
Granite Publishing Group
HAMPTON ROADS HEALTH JOURNAL
THE HEALTH JOURNALS
Himalayan Institute Press
Hohm Press
Hunter House Inc., Publishers
ILLUMINATIONS LITERARY JOURNAL
IN OUR OWN WORDS
Intuitive Moon Media
JOURNAL OF SCIENTIFIC EXPLORATION
JPS Publishing Company
Lamp Light Press
LifeCircle Press
Light Density Press
LightLines Publishing
Lucky Press, LLC
Luminous Epinoia Press
MEDICAL HISTORY
Midwifery Today
New Knowledge Press
Paradigm Publications
Piccadilly Books, Ltd.
Princess Publishing
Progressive Press; Tree of Life Publications
Raular Publishing
SAPONIFIER
Sentient Publications, LLC
Square One Publishers, Inc.
Sunrise Health Coach Publications
Sweet People Publishing
Synergy Press
TREATING YOURSELF: The Alternative Medicine Journal
Vanguard Press
WAV MAGAZINE: Progressive Music Art Politics Culture
Wellcome Trust Centre for the History of Medicine at UCL
WEST GOES SOUTH
Word Forge Books
YMAA Publication Center

AMERICANA

AMERICAN JONES BUILDING & MAINTENANCE
AMERICAN ROAD
Ammons Communications; Imprint: Catch the Spirit of Appalachia

Anvil Publishers, Inc.
Aspen Mountain Publishing
Avery Color Studios
Bauhan Publishing, LLC
BIBLIOPHILOS
BIG MUDDY: Journal of the Mississippi River Valley
Blackwater Publications
Blue Mouse Studio
THE BOOMERPHILE
Bordighera, Inc.
Branden Books
The Caxton Press
CESUM MAGAZINE
Channel Lake, Inc.
Command Performance Press
Cornucopia Press
COSMOPSIS QUARTERLY
Cottontail Publications
Crazy Woman Creek Press
Culturelink Press
Deep Well Publishing Company
Devil Mountain Books
Down The Shore Publishing
Eagle's View Publishing
Eborn Books
EXIT 13 MAGAZINE
firefall editions
Fotofolio, Inc.
Gallopade International
Glenbridge Publishing Ltd.
Harbor House
Heritage Books, Inc.
Huntington Library Press
Ice Cube Press
International Publishers Co. Inc.
Legacy Audio Books, Inc.
LPD Press
MAIN STREET RAG
Maryland Historical Press (also MHPress)
Missing Spoke Press
Mock Turtle Press
Mountain Press Publishing Co.
Mountainside Press
Murder Slim Press
Music City Publishing
Naturegraph Publishers
Noontide Press
Ohio University Press/Swallow Press
One Horse Press/Rainy Day Press
Oregon State University Press
P.R.A. Publishing
PASSAGER
Pocahontas Press, Inc.
Rock Spring Press Inc.
ROCTOBER COMICS AND MUSIC
Santa Fe Writers Project
Scottwall Associates, Publishers
SEDUCTIVE SELLING
The Sektor Co.
SENSATIONS MAGAZINE
SIDE OF GRITS
Genny Smith Books
SONG OF THE SAN JOAQUIN
Southeast Missouri State University Press
Stormline Press, Inc.
Sunnyside Press
Thirteen Colonies Press
The Thirty First Bird Press
University of Arkansas Press
VIVIPAROUS BLENNY
Waters Edge Press
Whispering Pine Press
White Mane Publishing Company, Inc.
Wilde Publishing
Word Forge Books

THE AMERICAS

Allbook Books

BEGINNING MAGAZINE
Cantadora Press
COGNITIO: A Graduate Humanities Journal
COLORLINES
Culturelink Press
CUTTHROAT, A JOURNAL OF THE ARTS
THE DIRTY GOAT
The Edwin Mellen Press
EXIT 13 MAGAZINE
Host Publications, Inc.
LPD Press
Magnifico Publications
MANDORLA: New Writing from the Americas / Nueva
    escritura de las Americas
Pangaea
Pathfinder Press
Protean Press
Smirk Books
Stardate Publishing Company
Thirteen Colonies Press
University of Utah Press
University Press of Colorado
WEST GOES SOUTH
WORLD POETRY SHOWCASE
XAVIER REVIEW
Zagier & Urruty Publications

AMISH CULTURE

Stormline Press, Inc.
Sunnyside Press
Titus Home Publishing
Wintertree Press

ANARCHIST

ABRAMELIN: a Journal of Poetry and Magick
AK Press
ALTERNATIVE PRESS INDEX
THE AMERICAN DISSIDENT
THE AMERICAN DRIVEL REVIEW
ANARCHY: A Journal of Desire Armed
Bad Noise Productions
BLACK BOOK PRESS: The Poetry Zine id
Black Rose Books Ltd.
BOTH SIDES NOW
CAFE NOIR REVIEW
CESUM MAGAZINE
City Lights Books
Columbia Alternative Library Press
Michael E. Coughlin, Publisher
THE DANDELION
DIET SOAP
Dnar Kaker Basa
EPICENTER: A LITERARY MAGAZINE
Fine Tooth Press
GOOD GIRL
GoodSAMARitan Press
GRAMMAR CRISIS
GRAY AREAS
GREEN ANARCHY
The Heather Foundation
HEELTAP/Pariah Press
Highest Hurdle Press
Hole Books
Iniquity Press/Vendetta Books
Lawrence & Wishart
Libellum
THE (LIBERTARIAN) CONNECTION
LIBERTY
Litwin Books
THE MATCH
MGW (Mom Guess What) Newsmagazine
Miskwabik Press
THE MORNING DEW REVIEW
Mountain Media
Murder Slim Press
Muse World Media Group
Mystery Island Publications
NEROUP REVIEW

New Falcon Publications
THE OTHER ISRAEL
Paladin Enterprises, Inc.
Pariah Press
Passing Through Publications
PEACEWORK
Pig Iron Press
PRISONERS' SPEAK!
Pygmy Forest Press
THE SAVAGE KICK LITERARY MAGAZINE
See Sharp Press
SHATTERED WIG REVIEW
SHORT FUSE
Smyrna Press
SOCIAL ANARCHISM: A Journal of Practice and Theory
Soft Skull Press
South End Press
Starcherone Books
THIRDEYE MAGAZINE
Total Cardboard Publishing
TURNING THE TIDE: Journal of Anti-Racist Action,
    Research & Education
Two-Handed Engine Press
Van Cleave Publishing
VOX
VOX Press
WAV MAGAZINE: Progressive Music Art Politics Culture
WHEELHOUSE MAGAZINE
WHITE FUNGUS
Wilde Publishing

ANCIENT ASTRONAUTS

EcceNova Editions
GoodSAMARitan Press
Granite Publishing Group
Slipdown Mountain Publications LLC
Subsynchronuos Press

ANIMALS

Abernathy House Publishing
Alpine Publications, Inc.
ANIMAL PEOPLE
Avery Color Studios
Biographical Publishing Company
Birdsong Books
Bloated Toe Publishing
Brick Road Poetry Press
Brookline Books
Camino Bay Books
Chelsea Green Publishing Company
City Life Books, LLC
Corvus Publishing Company
Dawn Publications
Dixon-Price Publishing
Dog's Eye View Media
DTS Group, Inc.
E & E Publishing
Equine Graphics Publishing Group: New Concord Press,
    SmallHorse Press, SunDrop
Farcountry Press
First Books
FISH DRUM MAGAZINE
Flowerfield Enterprises, LLC
Fotofolio, Inc.
Hobar Publications, A Division of Finney Company
Howln Moon Press
The Intrepid Traveler
Ion Imagination Publishing, Ion Imagination Entertainment,
    Inc.
Jon's Adventure Productions
THE JOURNAL OF CALIFORNIA AND GREAT BASIN
    ANTHROPOLOGY
Light Density Press
LITERALLY HORSES/REMUDA
Lucky Press, LLC
The Madson Group, Inc.
Malki Museum Press
March Books

Micah Publications Inc.
MINIATURE DONKEY TALK INC
Moon Pie Press
Mountain Press Publishing Co.
Native West Press
New Paradigm Books
NewSage Press
Ocean Publishing
Outrider Press
Pangaea
Peartree Books & Music
Pineapple Press, Inc.
Playdate Kids Publishing
Progressive Press; Tree of Life Publications
PublishingWorks, Inc.
Ragamuffin Heart Publishing
Raven Publishing, Inc.
Red Cygnet Press
RED MARE
ROCKY MOUNTAIN KC NEWS
Rocky Mountain KC Publishing Co.
Gibbs Smith, Publisher
SNOWY EGRET
SONG OF THE SAN JOAQUIN
Spring Grass
Storm Publishing Group
SunShine Press Publications, Inc.
Three Bean Press
Trickle Creek Books
Two Dog Press
Univelt, Inc.
University Press of Colorado
VEGETARIAN JOURNAL
Vonpalisaden Publications Inc.
John Wade, Publisher
WEST GOES SOUTH
Whispering Pine Press
Wind Eagle Press
Windward Publishing, An Imprint of Finney Company
WISCONSIN TRAILS
Word Forge Books
Zagier & Urruty Publications

ANTHOLOGY

A Midsummer Night's Press
Accendo Publishing
Allbook Books
Allium Press of Chicago
ARC
Bancroft Press
Central Avenue Press
Cornerstone Press
Coteau Books
Cotton Tree Press
Cyberwit.net
Russell Dean and Company
Elite Books
Equine Graphics Publishing Group: New Concord Press, SmallHorse Press, SunDrop
Goss Press
Hidden Valley Farm, Publisher
Ika, LLC
Imago Press
In Print Publishing
Indigo Ink Press, Inc.
The Infinity Group
J. Mark Press
Kobalt Books
THE LEDGE
The Lentz Leadership Institute LLC, The Refractive Thinker Press.
Light of New Orleans Publishing
Lilly Press
Little Pear Press
Llumina Press
Lummox Press
McPherson & Company Publishers
Native West Press

THE NEW FORMALIST
Nightsun Books
P.R.A. Publishing
Press Here
Ravenhawk Books
Sabellapress
Shared Roads Press
The Spirit That Moves Us Press, Inc.
SPOUT
SunShine Press Publications, Inc.
Thunder Rain Publishing Corp.
Vanilla Heart Publishing
Whiskey Creek Press
William Joseph K Publications
Wings Press
Word Forge Books
Zumaya Publications LLC

ANTHROPOLOGY, ARCHAELOGY

AB
Anagnosis
Arjuna Library Press
The B & R Samizdat Express
Bauu Press
Bear & Company
THE BELTANE PAPERS: A Journal of Women's Mysteries
THE BLOOMSBURY REVIEW
Blue Dolphin Publishing, Inc.
Blue Unicorn Press, Inc.
Celtic Heritage Books
Center for Japanese Studies
Chandler & Sharp Publishers, Inc.
THE CLASSICAL OUTLOOK
Cotsen Institute of Archaeology Publications
CROSSCURRENTS
THE DALHOUSIE REVIEW
The Denali Press
DIG
DREAM NETWORK
Eborn Books
FACES: People, Places, and Culture
Faded Banner Publications
Fine Tooth Press
Galde Press, Inc.
Glenbridge Publishing Ltd.
The Heather Foundation
Hopeace Press
Horned Owl Publishing
INTERCULTURE
ITALIAN AMERICANA
THE JOURNAL OF CALIFORNIA AND GREAT BASIN ANTHROPOLOGY
JOURNAL OF SCIENTIFIC EXPLORATION
Kakibubu Media Limited
KMT, A Modern Journal of Ancient Egypt
Kumarian Press
L&L Dreamspell
LDP, an occasional journal of aesthetics & language
Libellum
Libertas Press, LLC.
Light Density Press
Malki Museum Press
Malki-Ballena Press
Maryland Historical Press (also MHPress)
Mehring Books, Inc.
Menard Press
Minnesota Historical Society Press
Miskwabik Press
MOUSEION, Journal of the Classical Association of Canada/Revue de la Societe Canadienne des Etudes Classiques
Naturegraph Publishers
NEROUP REVIEW
Pangaea
Protean Press
Pruett Publishing Company
Psychohistory Press

RALPH'S REVIEW
REPORTS OF THE NATIONAL CENTER FOR SCIENCE
EDUCATION
REPRESENTATIONS
S4N Books
School for Advanced Research Press
Scientia Publishing, LLC
SHAMAN'S DRUM: A Journal of Experiential Shamanism
Shangri-La Publications
Slipdown Mountain Publications LLC
THE SOUTHERN QUARTERLY: A Journal of the Arts in
the South
State University of New York Press
Theytus Books Ltd.
TRADICION REVISTA
Tres Picos Press
UBC Press
University of Alaska Press
University of Calgary Press
University of Chicago Press
University of Nebraska Press
University of Utah Press
University Press of Colorado
Whalesback Books
White Cliffs Media, Inc.
XCP: CROSS-CULTURAL POETICS
Zagier & Urruty Publications

ANTIQUES

C & T Publishing
Cattpigg Press
China Books & Periodicals, Inc.
Downeast Books
DTS Group, Inc.
INKY TRAIL NEWS
LAKE SUPERIOR MAGAZINE
Miskwabik Press
MISSISSIPPI CROW
NEW ENGLAND BY RAIL
Oak Knoll Press
Paperweight Press
RALPH'S REVIEW
Shangri-La Publications
Sonoran Publishing
THE TABBY: A CHRONICLE OF THE ARTS AND
CRAFTS MOVEMENT
Tomart Publications
Whalesback Books

APPALACHIA

Ammons Communications; Imprint: Catch the Spirit of
Appalachia
Appalachian Consortium Press
APPALACHIAN HERITAGE
Appalachian House
APPLE VALLEY REVIEW: A Journal of Contemporary
Literature
BIBLIOPHILOS
Bright Mountain Books
THE COMSTOCK REVIEW
DTS Group, Inc.
ECOTONE: Reimagining Place
Iris Publishing Group, Inc (Iris Press / Tellico Books)
JAMES DICKEY REVIEW
KESTREL: A Journal of Literature and Art
Lucky Press, LLC
Mountain State Press
NORTH CAROLINA LITERARY REVIEW
NOW AND THEN
Ohio University Press/Swallow Press
Parkway Publishers, Inc.
Pocahontas Press, Inc.
Rainbow Books, Inc.
Rock Spring Press Inc.
Rowan Mountain Press
SPOTops Books
Two-Handed Engine Press
WEST GOES SOUTH

ARCHITECTURE

Art of Living, PrimaMedia,Inc
Balcony Media, Inc.
Bauhan Publishing, LLC
Bay Press
Beekman Books, Inc.
Black Dome Press Corp.
THE BLOOMSBURY REVIEW
China Books & Periodicals, Inc.
Clover Park Press
Craftsman Book Company
Downeast Books
ENVIRONMENTAL & ARCHITECTURAL PHENOMEN-
OLOGY NEWSLETTER
Hopeace Press
Interalia/Design Books
Italica Press, Inc.
Kakibubu Media Limited
Libellum
MARQUEE
Midmarch Arts Press
Minnesota Historical Society Press
Miskwabik Press
Mount Ida Press
NEROUP REVIEW
Obie Joe Media
OUT YOUR BACKDOOR: The Magazine of Do-It-
Yourself Adventure and Homegrown Culture
Passeggiata Press, Inc.
Pogo Press, Incorporated
SCULPTURAL PURSUIT MAGAZINE
Shangri-La Publications
Shipyard Press, LC
Gibbs Smith, Publisher
THE SOUTHERN QUARTERLY: A Journal of the Arts in
the South
Synergistic Press
THE TABBY: A CHRONICLE OF THE ARTS AND
CRAFTS MOVEMENT
Thirteen Colonies Press
TMC Books LLC
Tuns Press
UBC Press
University of Chicago Press
University of Massachusetts Press
University of South Carolina Press
University of Virginia Press
Village Lane Press
WEST GOES SOUTH
Whalesback Books
Whitston Publishing Co.
X-Ray Book Co.

ARIZONA

Chax Press
Arthur H. Clark Co.
Eborn Books
Five Star Publications, Inc.
LPD Press
THE MEADOW
Pruett Publishing Company
Sherman Asher Publishing
Thundercloud Books
TRADICION REVISTA
Vanguard Press
Wheatmark Book Publishing

ARKANSAS

GHOTI MAGAZINE
Mountain Automation Corporation
Premium Press America
University of Arkansas Press

ARMENIAN

ARARAT
INTERNATIONAL POETRY REVIEW
Rainbow Books, Inc.

Zon International Publishing Co.

AROMATHERAPY

THE ART OF ABUNDANCE
Cuore Libre Publishing
HAMPTON ROADS HEALTH JOURNAL
THE HEALTH JOURNALS
Knowledge Concepts Publishing
MEAT FOR TEA: THE VALLEY REVIEW
SAPONIFIER

ARTHURIAN

THE ENGLISH CLARION
Fisher King Press
LOW BUDGET SCIENCE FICTION
S4N Books
SeaCrab Publishing
SPECTACULAR SPECULATIONS
Village Lane Press
Vulgar Marsala Press

ARTIFICIAL INTELLIGENCE

Ageless Press
Blue Owl Press
JOURNAL OF SCIENTIFIC EXPLORATION
Light Density Press
PREMONITIONS
RALPH'S REVIEW
Scientia Publishing, LLC
Soft Skull Press
SPOTops Books
Upheaval Media

ARTS

A & U AMERICA'S AIDS MAGAZINE
Aaron Communications III
THE ADIRONDACK REVIEW
AERIAL
AFTERIMAGE
AK Press
Alan Wofsy Fine Arts
Glen Allen Press
Allworth Press
ALMOST NORMAL COMICS and Other Oddities
American Canadian Publishers, Inc.
THE AMERICAN DISSIDENT
THE AMERICAN DRIVEL REVIEW
Ammons Communications; Imprint: Catch the Spirit of Appalachia
APOSTROPHE: USCB Journal of the Arts
ARC
Aristata Publishing
Arjuna Library Press
ART BUREAU
ART TIMES
ART:MAG
ARTELLA: the waltz of words and art
ARTS & LETTERS: Journal of Contemporary Culture
ASCENT
Asylum Arts
Athanata Arts, Ltd.
ATLANTIC PACIFIC PRESS
BABYSUE MUSIC REVIEW
Back House Books
Balcony Media, Inc.
THE BALTIMORE REVIEW
Banana Productions
BANANA RAG
Bancroft Press
Barrytown/Station Hill Press
Bauhan Publishing, LLC
Bay Press
BEACHCOMBER MAGAZINE
THE BEAR DELUXE MAGAZINE
The Bear Wallow Publishing Company
BearManor Media
BEATLICK NEWS
BEAUTY/TRUTH: A Journal of Ekphrastic Poetry

Beekman Books, Inc.
BEGGARS & CHEESEBURGERS
BEGINNING MAGAZINE
Bel Canto Press
BIGNEWS MAGAZINE
Black Dome Press Corp.
Black Dress Press
BLACK WARRIOR REVIEW
BLACKFLASH Magazine
THE BLOOMSBURY REVIEW
BLUE UNICORN
BOMB MAGAZINE
BOOK/MARK QUARTERLY REVIEW
Borden Publishing Co.
BORDERLANDS: Texas Poetry Review
BOSTON REVIEW
BOULEVARD
Branden Books
THE BRIAR CLIFF REVIEW
BRILLIANT CORNERS: A Journal of Jazz & Literature
THE BROADKILL REVIEW: A Journal of Literature
Brookline Books
Burning Books
BURNSIDE REVIEW
C & T Publishing
CAIRN: The New St. Andrews Review
Camp Colton
CANADIAN POETRY
Canvas Press
THE CAPILANO REVIEW
CAUSE & EFFECT MAGAZINE
Center for Thanatology Research & Education, Inc.
CERISE PRESS
CESUM MAGAZINE
CHANTEH, the Iranian Cross-Cultural Quarterly
Chatoyant
Chax Press
CHICAGO REVIEW
Chicago Review Press
CHILDREN, CHURCHES AND DADDIES, A Non Religious, Non Familial Literary Magazine
China Books & Periodicals, Inc.
CIMARRON REVIEW
Clamshell Press
COLLECTION
CONDUIT
CONJUNCTIONS
CORONA
Coteau Books
COTTONWOOD
Cottonwood Press
Creative Writing and Publishing Company
Crescent Moon
CROSSCURRENTS
Cypress Creek Publishing
THE DALHOUSIE REVIEW
Dawn Sign Press
Deerbrook Editions
DENVER QUARTERLY
DESCANT
DIET SOAP
THE DIRTY GOAT
THE DMQ REVIEW
DOLLS UNITED INTERACTIVE MAGAZINE
DOWN IN THE DIRT LITERARY MAGAZINE, the prose & poetry magazine revealing all your dirty little secrets
Downeast Books
Dumouriez Publishing
E & E Publishing
THE EAST HAWAII OBSERVER
Edgewise Press
EKPHRASIS
ELEMENTS
Empire Publishing Service
Enigmatic Ink
ENVIRONMENTAL & ARCHITECTURAL PHENOMEN-OLOGY NEWSLETTER
EPICENTER: A LITERARY MAGAZINE

Ethos Publishing
Falk Art Reference
Fine Tooth Press
First Books
580 SPLIT
FIVE POINTS
FLUENT ASCENSION
Fotofolio, Inc.
FRANK: AN INTERNATIONAL JOURNAL OF CON-
TEMPORARY WRITING AND ART
FREEDOM AND STRENGTH PRESS FORUM
GASTRONOMICA: The Journal of Food and Culture
Gateways Books And Tapes
Gertrude Press
Glenbridge Publishing Ltd.
Global Learning
GOOD GIRL
Goss Press
Green Hut Press
Grey Sparrow Press
GUD MAGAZINE (Greatest Uncommon Denominator)
HAPA NUI
HAWAI'I REVIEW
HAYDEN'S FERRY REVIEW
HEAVEN BONE MAGAZINE
Heaven Bone Press
Helicon Nine Editions
Hidden Valley Farm, Publisher
HILL COUNTRY SUN
Hollywood Creative Directory
Homa & Sekey Books
The Hosanna Press
Host Publications, Inc.
THE HUDSON REVIEW
Hunter Publishing Corporation
Huntington Library Press
HUNTINGTON LIBRARY QUARTERLY
IMAGE: ART, FAITH, MYSTERY
Indigo Ink Press, Inc.
INDUSTRY MINNE-ZINE
The Infinity Group
Interalia/Design Books
Interlink Publishing Group, Inc.
INTERNATIONAL ART POST
ITALIAN AMERICANA
Italica Press, Inc.
Ithuriel's Spear
JACK MACKEREL MAGAZINE
Jako Books
JONES AV
JOURNAL OF REGIONAL CRITICISM
JUBILAT
KALDRON, An International Journal Of Visual Poetry
KALLIOPE, A Journal of Women's Literature and Art
Kelsey St. Press
Kilmog Press
KMT, A Modern Journal of Ancient Egypt
KNUCKLE MERCHANT - The Journal of Naked Literary
Aggression
La Familia Publishing
LAKE EFFECT
LAKE SUPERIOR MAGAZINE
LDP, an occasional journal of aesthetics & language
LEAF GARDEN
Leaping Dog Press
LEFT CURVE
LEO Productions LLC.
Les Figues Press
Light Density Press
LIGHTWORKS MAGAZINE
Lilly Press
LINQ
LIVE MAG!
THE LOUISIANA REVIEW
LPD Press
Lucky Press, LLC
LULLWATER REVIEW
Luna Bisonte Prods

THE MACGUFFIN
MANDORLA: New Writing from the Americas / Nueva
escritura de las Americas
MANOA: A Pacific Journal of International Writing
Peter Marcan Publications
Maverick Books
McPherson & Company Publishers
ME MAGAZINE
Mehring Books, Inc.
Meridien PressWorks
MGW (Mom Guess What) Newsmagazine
Midmarch Arts Press
MIDWEST ART FAIRS
Miskwabik Press
MISSISSIPPI CROW
Moo-Cow Fan Club
MOTHERVERSE: A Journal of Contemporary Motherhood
Mountainside Press
MUSE: A Quarterly Journal of The Lit
Museon Publishing
NEROUP REVIEW
NERVE COWBOY
NEW AMERICAN IMAGIST
THE NEW ENGLAND QUARTERLY
NEW ENGLAND REVIEW
THE NEW FORMALIST
The New Formalist Press
NEW LETTERS
NEW MEXICO POETRY REVIEW
NEW ORLEANS REVIEW
NEWS FROM NATIVE CALIFORNIA
Night Horn Books
NIGHTLIFE MAGAZINE
THE NOISE
Nonetheless Press
NOON
Norton Coker Press
NOUN VS. VERB
Oak Knoll Press
Obie Joe Media
OHIOANA QUARTERLY
OPEN WIDE MAGAZINE
Orange Alert Press
Orchard House Press
ORNAMENT
THE OTHER HERALD
OTHER INVESTIGATIONS
OUTER-ART
THE PACIFIC REVIEW
PADDLEFISH
PAGAN AMERICA
PAJ NTAUB VOICE
Pancake Press
PAPERBACK PARADE
Paperweight Press
Paris Press
PASSAGER
PASSION
Pearl's Book'em Publisher
Pebble Press, Inc.
THE PEDESTAL MAGAZINE.COM
Phelps Publishing Company
PIG IRON
Pig Iron Press
THE PINCH
PLAIN BROWN WRAPPER (PBW)
Plain View Press
Players Press, Inc.
The Poetry Center
POETRYREPAIRS: Contemporary International Poetry
Pogo Press, Incorporated
POINT OF CONTACT, The Journal of Verbal & Visual
Arts
PORTLAND REVIEW
PRAIRIE WINDS
PRAKALPANA   SAHITYA/PRAKALPANA   LITERA-
TURE
PRETEXT

PROVINCETOWN ARTS
PublishingWorks, Inc.
PULSAR POETRY WEBZINE
Puna Press
PUNKIN HOUSE DIGEST
Punkin House Press
Pygmy Forest Press
Quarterly Committee of Queen's University
QUEEN'S QUARTERLY: A Canadian Review
THE QUIET FEATHER
RAINBOW CURVE
Rapacious Press
RARITAN: A Quarterly Review
RATTAPALLAX
RED HAWK
RED LAMP
REDIVIDER
REPRESENTATIONS
RIVER POETS JOURNAL
RIVER STYX
RIVERSEDGE
RIVET MAGAZINE
ROGER, an art & literary magazine
Rowhouse Press
RUBBERSTAMPMADNESS
The Runaway Spoon Press
SAGE OF CONSCIOUSNESS E-ZINE
SALMAGUNDI
Santa Monica Press
Saqi Books Publisher
Saturnalia Books
Savant Garde Workshop
Scars Publications
School for Advanced Research Press
SCHUYLKILL VALLEY JOURNAL
SCRIVENER
SCULPTURAL PURSUIT MAGAZINE
SHATTERED WIG REVIEW
SHORT FUSE
SKIDROW PENTHOUSE
SKYLINE LITERARY MAGAZINE
Slipdown Mountain Publications LLC
Gibbs Smith, Publisher
Smyrna Press
SO TO SPEAK: A Feminist Journal of Language & Art
SOJOURN: A Journal of the Arts
THE SOUTHERN QUARTERLY: A Journal of the Arts in
    the South
SOUTHWEST COLORADO ARTS PERSPECTIVE
SP QUILL MAGAZINE
SP Turner Group
SPEAK UP
Speck Press
Spinifex Press
SPORE
SPOTops Books
Stemmer House Publishers, Inc.
STUDIO ONE
SunShine Press Publications, Inc.
SWINK
SYCAMORE REVIEW
SYMPLOKE: A Journal for the Intermingling of Literary,
    Cultural and Theoretical Scholarship
Synergetic Press
Synergistic Press
Syracuse Cultural Workers/Tools for Change
Syukhtun Editions
THE TABBY: A CHRONICLE OF THE ARTS AND
    CRAFTS MOVEMENT
THE TARPEIAN ROCK
TEACHERS & WRITERS
Teachers & Writers Collaborative
TELOS
Telos Press
1097 MAGAZINE
Ten Penny Players, Inc.
Thatch Tree Publications
THIN COYOTE

THIRDEYE MAGAZINE
Three Bean Press
THE THREEPENNY REVIEW
THRESHOLDS JOURNAL
TRADICION REVISTA
Transcending Mundane, Inc.
TURNROW
Two-Handed Engine Press
University of Calgary Press
University of Chicago Press
University of Massachusetts Press
University of South Carolina Press
UNIVERSITY OF WINDSOR REVIEW
UNMUZZLED OX
VALLUM: CONTEMPORARY POETRY
Vanderbilt University Press
VARIOUS ARTISTS
Village Lane Press
Visual Arts Press
Visual Studies Workshop
VOICES ISRAEL
John Wade, Publisher
Wafer Mache Publications
WAR, LITERATURE & THE ARTS: An International
    Journal of the Humanities
WATERWAYS: Poetry in the Mainstream
WAV MAGAZINE: Progressive Music Art Politics Culture
West Virginia University Press
Westgate Press
Whalesback Books
Whelks Walk Press
White Cliffs Media, Inc.
White Crosslet Publishing Co
WHITE FUNGUS
WILD DUCK REVIEW
WISCONSIN TRAILS
WOMEN IN THE ARTS BULLETIN/NEWSLETTER
Word Forge Books
X-RAY
Zon International Publishing Co.

ASIA, INDOCHINA

Anthony Publishing Company
ASIAN SURVEY
AXE FACTORY REVIEW
China Books & Periodicals, Inc.
Chinese Literature Press
Cross-Cultural Communications
Cynic Press
Eastern Washington University Press
Homa & Sekey Books
Hoover Institution Press
INDIA CURRENTS
INTERNATIONAL POETRY REVIEW
MANOA: A Pacific Journal of International Writing
NEW AMERICAN IMAGIST
Open Court Publishing Company
THE OTHER ISRAEL
PACIFIC HISTORICAL REVIEW
PAJ NTAUB VOICE
Pilgrims Book House
Plank Road Publishing
State University of New York Press
Tamal Vista Publications
Texas Tech University Press
TSAR Publications
UBC Press
United Nations University Press
WHITE FUNGUS
White Pine Press
Wisdom Publications, Inc.
WORLD POETRY SHOWCASE
YMAA Publication Center

ASIAN-AMERICAN

THE ASIAN PACIFIC AMERICAN JOURNAL
Back House Books
Bamboo Ridge Press

638

BAMBOO RIDGE, Journal of Hawai'i Literature and Arts
The Bess Press
CAIRN: The New St. Andrews Review
Carolina Wren Press
Center for Thanatology Research & Education, Inc.
Chandler & Sharp Publishers, Inc.
Chax Press
China Books & Periodicals, Inc.
COLORLINES
Comstock Bonanza Press
Cynic Press
East West Discovery Press
Fine Tooth Press
First Journey Publishing Company
FIVE WILLOWS MAGAZINE
FROZEN WAFFLES
Fulcrum, Inc.
Goldfish Press
HAWAI'I REVIEW
Homa & Sekey Books
INDIA CURRENTS
Inner City Press
Kakibubu Media Limited
Kelsey St. Press
La Familia Publishing
MANOA: A Pacific Journal of International Writing
Miami University Press
NEW AMERICAN IMAGIST
New Rivers Press, Inc.
PACIFIC HISTORICAL REVIEW
PAJ NTAUB VOICE
Phelps Publishing Company
The Place In The Woods
Pygmy Forest Press
Reference Service Press
RHINO: THE POETRY FORUM
South End Press
TURNING WHEEL
Volcano Press, Inc
West End Press
XCP: CROSS-CULTURAL POETICS

ASTROLOGY

ABRAMELIN: a Journal of Poetry and Magick
Altair Publications
Aquila Ink Publishing
Bear & Company
THE BELTANE PAPERS: A Journal of Women's Mysteries
Blue Dolphin Publishing, Inc.
BOTH SIDES NOW
Cassandra Press, Inc.
Cuore Libre Publishing
EcceNova Editions
Granite Publishing Group
Helm Publishing
Himalayan Institute Press
Hood Press
Intuitive Moon Media
L&L Dreamspell
Lycanthrope Press
THE MOUNTAIN ASTROLOGER
One Spirit Press
Quicksilver Productions
SAGEWOMAN
STARNOTES
Three Pyramids Publishing
White Crosslet Publishing Co

ASTRONOMY

ABRAMELIN: a Journal of Poetry and Magick
Granite Publishing Group
JOURNAL OF SCIENTIFIC EXPLORATION
Light Density Press
Malki Museum Press
Naturegraph Publishers
ODYSSEY: Adventures in Science
Scientia Publishing, LLC

STRUGGLE: A Magazine of Proletarian Revolutionary Literature
Tuvela Press
Univelt, Inc.
University Press of Colorado
WEST GOES SOUTH

ATHEISM

Bandanna Books
BLACK BOOK PRESS: The Poetry Zine id
BOULDER HERETIC
Dwarf Lion Press
GHOTI MAGAZINE
Insight Press
Lycanthrope Press
MELEE
THE SAVAGE KICK LITERARY MAGAZINE
Savant Garde Workshop
See Sharp Press
TRUTH SEEKER
VOX Press

AUDIO/VIDEO

ABLAZE Publishing
AFTERIMAGE
BLUE MOUNTAIN
CKO UPDATE
COUNTERPOISE: For Social Responsibilities, Liberty and Dissent
Creative Creations Consulting Publishing Company
Flowerfield Enterprises, LLC
Intuitive Moon Media
Ion Imagination Publishing, Ion Imagination Entertainment, Inc.
Level 4 Press, Inc.
LOW BUDGET ADVENTURE
Multi-Media Publications Inc.
Noved Audio
Pearl's Book'em Publisher
Plank Road Publishing
Playdate Kids Publishing
RED FEZ ENTERTAINMENT
Saint Bob Press
SIDE OF GRITS
Southern Illinois University Press
Water Mark of Lyons PPP: papers press and permaculture
WAV MAGAZINE: Progressive Music Art Politics Culture
WHEELHOUSE MAGAZINE

AUSTRALIA

BOGG: A Journal of Contemporary Writing
Galaxy Press
Kali Press
RED LAMP
STUDIO - A Journal of Christians Writing
Total Cardboard Publishing
Tres Picos Press
WORLD POETRY SHOWCASE

AUTOBIOGRAPHY

A Cappela Publishing
Aaron Communications III
Academy Press of America
Accendo Publishing
AIS Publications
Alaska Native Language Center
American Legacy Media
American Literary Press
Aquarius Press
Art of Living, PrimaMedia,Inc
Assilem 9 Publications
Bear & Company
BearManor Media
BIBLIOPHILOS
Biographical Publishing Company
Blue Lupin Press
Bonus Books, Inc.
Bright Mountain Books

Celo Valley Books
China Books & Periodicals, Inc.
Coastal 181
Coteau Books
Crane Press
Creative Arts Book Company
Creative Creations Consulting Publishing Company
Devil Mountain Books
Equine Graphics Publishing Group: New Concord Press, SmallHorse Press, SunDrop
The Feminist Press at the City University of New York
THE FLORIDA REVIEW
Gallaudet University Press
Green River Press
HAPA NUI
Harbor House
Historical Resources Press
Hobblebush Books
Impassio Press
In Print Publishing
Insight Press
IRIS: A Journal About Women
Kenyette Productions
KESTREL: A Journal of Literature and Art
Nicholas Lawrence Books
THE LEDGE
Lemon Grove Press
Light Density Press
Limelight Editions
Lion's Den Publishing
Little Pear Press
Llumina Press
MANOA: A Pacific Journal of International Writing
Massey-Reyner Publishing
Medusa's Muse
The Kenneth G. Mills Foundation
Minnesota Historical Society Press
Moon Pie Press
Murder Slim Press
Music City Publishing
The Narrative Press
New Concept Press
New World Press, Inc
Nish Publishing Company
NOLA-MAGICK Press
Nonetheless Press
North Country Books, Inc.
Northwestern University Press
OPEN MINDS QUARTERLY
PALO ALTO REVIEW
Paris Press
Park Place Publications
Parkway Publishers, Inc.
PASSAGER
PLAIN BROWN WRAPPER (PBW)
Pocahontas Press, Inc.
Polar Bear & Company
Portal Press
Pussywillow
THE QUILLDRIVER
Raular Publishing
REMS Publishing & Publicity
RIVET MAGAZINE
Ronsdale Press
Sassy Sunflower Books
THE SAVAGE KICK LITERARY MAGAZINE
Genny Smith Books
Soto Publishing Company
SP Turner Group
Spring Grass
Syukhtun Editions
Thirsty Turtle Press
Timeless Books
Titus Home Publishing
TWENTY-EIGHT PAGES LOVINGLY BOUND WITH TWINE
VanderWyk & Burnham
VOX Press

West Coast Paradise Publishing
White Thread Press
Xenos Books
Yes International Publishers

AUTOS

Brown Fox Books
California Bill's Automotive Handbooks
Coastal 181
GLOBAL ONE MAGAZINE
Rolling Hills Publishing

AVANT-GARDE, EXPERIMENTAL ART

A & U AMERICA'S AIDS MAGAZINE
ABRAMELIN: a Journal of Poetry and Magick
ABRAXAS
AD/VANCE
AFTERIMAGE
ALMOST NORMAL COMICS and Other Oddities
Androgyne Books
ARC
Arjuna Library Press
ART BUREAU
ARTELLA: the waltz of words and art
Asylum Arts
ATLANTIC PACIFIC PRESS
BAGAZINE
BANANA RAG
BATHTUB GIN
BEGGARS & CHEESEBURGERS
BLACK BEAR REVIEW
Black Radish Books
BLACKBIRD
Brookline Books
Burning Books
BUST DOWN THE DOOR AND EAT ALL THE CHICKENS: A Journal of Absurd and Surreal Fiction
Camp Colton
CANADIAN POETRY
Canvas Press
THE CAPILANO REVIEW
Cervena Barva Press
Chax Press
Cloud 9 Publishing
COLLECTION
CONDUIT
DARK GOTHIC RESURRECTED
THE DIRTY GOAT
DOLLS UNITED INTERACTIVE MAGAZINE
DWANG: Outsider poetry and prose
EbonyEnergy Publishing, Inc.
ELIXIR
Enigmatic Ink
EROSHA
Everflowing Publications
Fiction Collective Two (FC2)
Five Fingers Press
FIVE FINGERS REVIEW
THE FLORIDA REVIEW
FLUENT ASCENSION
FRANK: AN INTERNATIONAL JOURNAL OF CONTEMPORARY WRITING AND ART
GERTRUDE
Gertrude Press
Ghost Pony Press
GHOTI MAGAZINE
GOOD GIRL
Goss Press
GRAMMAR CRISIS
HAWAI'I REVIEW
HEAVEN BONE MAGAZINE
Heaven Bone Press
HEELTAP/Pariah Press
Helicon Nine Editions
Hidden Valley Farm, Publisher
Highest Hurdle Press
Host Publications, Inc.
Hotel des Bains Editions

ILLOGICAL MUSE
ILLUMINATIONS
INDEFINITE SPACE
Indigo Ink Press, Inc.
INDUSTRY MINNE-ZINE
ISTANBUL LITERARY REVIEW
KALDRON, An International Journal Of Visual Poetry
Kelsey St. Press
LAKE EFFECT
LDP, an occasional journal of aesthetics & language
LEAF GARDEN
Leaping Dog Press
LEFT CURVE
Light Density Press
LIGHTWORKS MAGAZINE
LO STRANIERO: The Stranger, Der Fremde, L'Etranger
LULLABY HEARSE
Luna Bisonte Prods
MANDORLA: New Writing from the Americas / Nueva
escritura de las Americas
Marymark Press
McPherson & Company Publishers
MEAT FOR TEA: THE VALLEY REVIEW
MELEE
MISSISSIPPI CROW
Moonrise Press
Muse World Media Group
NEW HOPE INTERNATIONAL REVIEW
New Sins Press
NIGHTJAR REVIEW
Northwestern University Press
O!!ZONE, A LITERARY-ART ZINE
One Less Press
OPEN WIDE MAGAZINE
THE OTHER HERALD
OUTER-ART
PACIFIC COAST JOURNAL
Pariah Press
PAVEMENT SAW
Pavement Saw Press
PHOEBE: A Journal of Literature and Art
Phrygian Press
PIG IRON
PLAIN BROWN WRAPPER (PBW)
Players Press, Inc.
THE POETRY PROJECT NEWSLETTER
POINT OF CONTACT, The Journal of Verbal & Visual
Arts
PORTLAND REVIEW
PRAKALPANA SAHITYA/PRAKALPANA LITERA-
TURE
PRESA
Presa Press
Punkin House Press
RAIN TAXI REVIEW OF BOOKS
RAINBOW CURVE
RED MARE
Re-invention UK Ltd
REMS Publishing & Publicity
THE ROCKFORD REVIEW
The Runaway Spoon Press
Rural Messengers Press
SAGE OF CONSCIOUSNESS E-ZINE
SHORT FUSE
SIDE OF GRITS
SNOW MONKEY
Soft Skull Press
SOUTHWEST COLORADO ARTS PERSPECTIVE
SPORE
SPOTops Books
Stardate Publishing Company
SUB-TERRAIN
Synergetic Press
THIRDEYE MAGAZINE
Toad Press International Chapbook Series
Total Cardboard Publishing
Underwhich Editions
UPSTAIRS AT DUROC

VIVIPAROUS BLENNY
Vulgar Marsala Press
Water Mark of Lyons PPP: papers press and permaculture
WEST COAST LINE: A Journal of Contemporary Writing
and Criticism
WHEELHOUSE MAGAZINE
White Crosslet Publishing Co
WHITE FUNGUS
WHITEWALL OF SOUND
XCP: CROSS-CULTURAL POETICS
X-Ray Book Co.
ZAUM - The Literary Review of Sonoma State University
ZYX

AVIATION

AB
The Bear Wallow Publishing Company
Beekman Books, Inc.
Bright Mountain Books
Burd Street Press
Cable Publishing
CESSNA OWNER MAGAZINE
The Film Instruction Company of America
GLOBAL ONE MAGAZINE
HANG GLIDING & PARAGLIDING
Lucky Press, LLC
Maryland Historical Press (also MHPress)
PIPERS MAGAZINE
Rainbow Books, Inc.
Shipyard Press, LC
Slipdown Mountain Publications LLC
Southern Illinois University Press
Village Lane Press

AWARDS, FOUNDATIONS, GRANTS

Creative Creations Consulting Publishing Company
Reference Service Press
Search Institute
Sources
SOUTHWEST COLORADO ARTS PERSPECTIVE
Titan Press

BEAT

ABRAMELIN: a Journal of Poetry and Magick
ALMOST NORMAL COMICS and Other Oddities
THE AMERICAN DISSIDENT
Androgyne Books
BEATLICK NEWS
Bottle of Smoke Press
THE CAFE REVIEW
COMPASS ROSE
THE DIRTY GOAT
DWANG: Outsider poetry and prose
Frozen Waffles Press/Shattered Sidewalks Press; 45th
Century Chapbooks
HEELTAP/Pariah Press
Hole Books
Host Publications, Inc.
Iniquity Press/Vendetta Books
KUMQUAT MERINGUE
Leaf Garden Press
Marymark Press
MEAT FOR TEA: THE VALLEY REVIEW
MELEE
THE MORNING DEW REVIEW
Murder Slim Press
NEW HOPE INTERNATIONAL REVIEW
OPEN WIDE MAGAZINE
Panther Books
Pariah Press
Psychedelic Literature
RED MARE
THE SAVAGE KICK LITERARY MAGAZINE
Scars Publications
SCHUYLKILL VALLEY JOURNAL
SIDE OF GRITS
Six Ft. Swells Press
Soft Skull Press

Tangerine Press
Van Cleave Publishing
VIVIPAROUS BLENNY
Wilde Publishing
X-Ray Book Co.

JOHN BERRYMAN

Pygmy Forest Press

BIBLIOGRAPHY

Absey & Co.
AMERICAN LITERATURE
ANQ: A Quarterly Journal of Short Articles, Notes, and
    Reviews
Appalachian Consortium Press
Arden Press, Inc.
Arts End Books
Athanor Books
BIBLIOPHILOS
Bottle of Smoke Press
CANADIAN POETRY
Cantadora Press
Center for Japanese Studies
COUNTERPOISE: For Social Responsibilities, Liberty and
    Dissent
Crane Press
The Denali Press
Dustbooks
Ecrivez!
Edition Gemini
ELEMENTS
ELT Press
ENGLISH LITERATURE IN TRANSITION, 1880-1920
FEMINIST COLLECTIONS: A QUARTERLY OF WO-
    MEN'S STUDIES RESOURCES
FEMINIST PERIODICALS: A CURRENT LISTING OF
    CONTENTS
The Great Rift Press
GROUP Publishing
Gryphon Books
Hoover Institution Press
Library Juice Press
LINQ
Litwin Books
LOST GENERATION JOURNAL
Peter Marcan Publications
Minnesota Historical Society Press
NEW BOOKS ON WOMEN, GENDER, & FEMINISM
Nish Publishing Company
Norton Coker Press
NOSTOC MAGAZINE
NOVA EXPRESS
Oak Knoll Press
Open Horizons Publishing Company
Palari Publishing
PAPERBACK PARADE
Passeggiata Press, Inc.
Poltroon Press
RIVET MAGAZINE
Saqi Books Publisher
Shangri-La Publications
Sligo Press
Smyrna Press
University of Chicago Press
WHITEWALL OF SOUND
Whitston Publishing Co.
Women's Studies Librarian, University of Wisconsin
    System

BICYCLING

AB
Anacus Press, An Imprint of Finney Company
Appalachian House
DWELLING PORTABLY
Nicolin Fields Publishing, Inc.
Heyday Books
Info Net Publishing
Menasha Ridge Press

New England Cartographics, Inc.
OUT YOUR BACKDOOR: The Magazine of Do-It-
    Yourself Adventure and Homegrown Culture
Price World Publishing
Pruett Publishing Company
Sunbelt Publications
Wilderness Adventure Books
WISCONSIN TRAILS

BIGOTRY

COLORLINES
MOUTH: Voice of the Dis-Labeled Nation

BILINGUAL

A Midsummer Night's Press
Alaska Native Language Center
THE AMERICAN DISSIDENT
BEATLICK NEWS
Bilingual Review Press
BILINGUAL REVIEW/Revista Bilingue
Branden Books
Calaca Press
The Chicot Press
China Books & Periodicals, Inc.
Cross-Cultural Communications
Dawn Sign Press
THE DIRTY GOAT
East West Discovery Press
FEMINIST STUDIES
FLUENT ASCENSION
Helicon Nine Editions
Host Publications, Inc.
Hotel des Bains Editions
Interlink Publishing Group, Inc.
INTERNATIONAL POETRY REVIEW
Italica Press, Inc.
Latin American Literary Review Press
LEO Productions LLC.
Merl Publications
NIGHTLIFE MAGAZINE
Oyster River Press
P.R.A. Publishing
Pangaea
Plank Road Publishing
Playdate Kids Publishing
Pocahontas Press, Inc.
POETRYREPAIRS: Contemporary International Poetry
PRAKALPANA SAHITYA/PRAKALPANA LITERA-
    TURE
PublishingWorks, Inc.
THE RAVEN CHRONICLES
Raven Tree Press, A Division of Delta Systems Inc
READ, AMERICA!
Ronsdale Press
Saqi Books Publisher
Sherman Asher Publishing
Smyrna Press
The Speech Bin, Inc.
Synergistic Press
Tamal Vista Publications
Tameme
TSAR Publications
Two Eagles Press International
Velazquez Press
Wilde Publishing
Wings Press
XCP: CROSS-CULTURAL POETICS
Xenos Books

BIOGRAPHY

Aaron Communications III
Affinity Publishers Services
AIS Publications
AK Press
Allwrite Advertising and Publishing
American Legacy Media
Anderson Publishing; also RC Anderson Books
Androgyne Books

THE ANNALS OF IOWA
ANQ: A Quarterly Journal of Short Articles, Notes, and
 Reviews
Appalachian Consortium Press
Aquarius Press
Archer Books
Arden Press, Inc.
Avisson Press, Inc.
Bancroft Press
Banta & Pool Literary Properties
Bauhan Publishing, LLC
Bear & Company
BearManor Media
Beekman Books, Inc.
W.S. Beetle & Company
BELLOWING ARK
Black Dome Press Corp.
Blackwater Publications
Bloated Toe Publishing
THE BLOOMSBURY REVIEW
Blue Unicorn Press, Inc.
Bonus Books, Inc.
Branden Books
Brooke-Richards Press
Brown Fox Books
Burd Street Press
Cable Publishing
Calliope Press
Camel Press
Celebrity Profiles Publishing
Celo Valley Books
Chelsea Green Publishing Company
Chicago Spectrum Press
China Books & Periodicals, Inc.
Arthur H. Clark Co.
Clover Park Press
Coastal 181
Community Service, Inc.
Comstock Bonanza Press
Coteau Books
COTTONWOOD
Cottonwood Press
Crescent Moon
Cypress Creek Publishing
Cypress House
Deep Well Publishing Company
DESIRE
Devil Mountain Books
Downeast Books
Paul Dry Books
DUST (From the Ego Trip)
Dustbooks
Earth Star Publications
ELT Press
Encounter Books
ENGLISH LITERATURE IN TRANSITION, 1880-1920
ENGLISH LITERATURE IN TRANSITION, 1880-1920
Equine Graphics Publishing Group: New Concord Press,
 SmallHorse Press, SunDrop
Eros Books
ETC Publications
Explorer Press
Faith Builders Resource Group
The Feminist Press at the City University of New York
Fine Tooth Press
Five Star Publications, Inc.
Foremost Press
THE FREEDONIA GAZETTE: The Magazine Devoted to
 the Marx Brothers
Fulcrum, Inc.
Galde Press, Inc.
Gallaudet University Press
Garden House Press
GENRE: WRITER AND WRITINGS
Glenbridge Publishing Ltd.
Good Book Publishing Company
The Great Rift Press
Harbor House

HAWAI'I REVIEW
Heidelberg Graphics
Helm Publishing
Heritage House Publishers
Historical Resources Press
History Compass, LLC
Hohm Press
Hole Books
Hope Publishing House
Hot Box Press / Southern Roots Publishing
Icarus Press
Iconoclast Press
In Print Publishing
International Publishers Co. Inc.
Italica Press, Inc.
JACK MACKEREL MAGAZINE
KESTREL: A Journal of Literature and Art
Kobalt Books
The Latona Press
Lawells Publishing
Nicholas Lawrence Books
LEAF GARDEN
THE LEDGE
Legacy Audio Books, Inc.
Lemieux International Ltd.
Libertarian Press, Inc./American Book Distributors
Libertas Press, LLC.
Library Juice Press
Limelight Editions
Litwin Books
LOST GENERATION JOURNAL
Margaret Media, Inc.
Maryland Historical Press (also MHPress)
Maverick Books
Mayhaven Publishing, Inc.
MCM Entertainment, Inc. Publishing Division
Medusa's Muse
Mercer University Press
Midmarch Arts Press
Mills Custom Services Publishing
Minnesota Historical Society Press
Miskwabik Press
Mondial
Music City Publishing
NEROUP REVIEW
New Concept Press
New Falcon Publications
NEW HOPE INTERNATIONAL REVIEW
NEW SOLUTIONS
Nip and Tuck Publishing
Nish Publishing Company
Nonetheless Press
NORTH CAROLINA LITERARY REVIEW
North Country Books, Inc.
Northern Publishing
Northwestern University Press
Oak Knoll Press
Ocean Publishing
Open Hand Publishing LLC
Oregon State University Press
THE ORPHAN LEAF REVIEW
OUT OF LINE
Passeggiata Press, Inc.
PASSION
Path Press, Inc.
The Place In The Woods
Pocahontas Press, Inc.
Polar Bear & Company
Protean Press
PSYCHE
PublishAmerica, LLLP.
QED Press
Quarterly Committee of Queen's University
QUEEN'S QUARTERLY: A Canadian Review
Peter E. Randall Publisher
Red Alder Books
RedJack
REMS Publishing & Publicity

Rock Spring Press Inc.
Ronsdale Press
Rowhouse Press
SALMAGUNDI
Saqi Books Publisher
THE SAVAGE KICK LITERARY MAGAZINE
Scentouri, Publishing Division
Scottwall Associates, Publishers
The Sektor Co.
Shangri-La Publications
SHATTERED WIG REVIEW
Sligo Press
Small Dogma Publishing, Inc.
Gibbs Smith, Publisher
Soundboard Books
SOUTH DAKOTA REVIEW
Southeast Missouri State University Press
SP Turner Group
Steerforth Press, L.C.
Stewart Publishing & Printing
Sherwood Sugden & Company, Publishers
SYMPOSIUM
Synergistic Press
Texas Tech University Press
Thirteen Colonies Press
Timeless Books
Titus Home Publishing
Tomart Publications
University of Arkansas Press
University of Calgary Press
University of Massachusetts Press
University of Virginia Press
Unlimited Publishing LLC
John Wade, Publisher
THE WALLACE STEVENS JOURNAL
WAR, LITERATURE & THE ARTS: An International
　Journal of the Humanities
West Coast Paradise Publishing
Wexford & Barrow, Publishers
White Cliffs Media, Inc.
WHITE FUNGUS
White Mane Publishing Company, Inc.
White Thread Press
Whitston Publishing Co.
Zelda Wilde Publishing
Wintertree Press
WORDKNOT AUDIO: A Literary Podcast Magazine
Writers House Press

BIOLOGY

dbS Productions
The Denali Press
Dog's Eye View Media
Flowerfield Enterprises, LLC
Hobar Publications, A Division of Finney Company
Ion Imagination Publishing, Ion Imagination Entertainment,
　Inc.
Island Press
The Latona Press
Oregon State University Press
Parkway Publishers, Inc.
Scientia Publishing, LLC
SNOWY EGRET
Soto Publishing Company
Trickle Creek Books
University Press of Colorado
WILD DUCK REVIEW

BIOTECHNOLOGY

CONSCIENCE: The Newsjournal of Catholic Opinion
Hobar Publications, A Division of Finney Company
International University Line (IUL)
Scientia Publishing, LLC
Soft Skull Press
SPECTACULAR SPECULATIONS
SterlingHouse Publisher

BIRDS

Annedawn Publishing
Birdsong Books
Chelsea Green Publishing Company
CONCRETE JUNGLE JOURNAL
Corvus Publishing Company
Dog's Eye View Media
Hobar Publications, A Division of Finney Company
LDP, an occasional journal of aesthetics & language
Lost Pond Press
Lucky Press, LLC
Mountain Press Publishing Co.
Naturegraph Publishers
Nautilus Publishing Company
New England Cartographics, Inc.
Peartree Books & Music
Penthe Publishing
Pineapple Press, Inc.
RALPH'S REVIEW
Scientia Publishing, LLC
SNOWY EGRET
SONG OF THE SAN JOAQUIN
Trickle Creek Books
University Press of Colorado
Zagier & Urruty Publications

BIRTH, BIRTH CONTROL, POPULATION

AT-HOME DAD
Cassandra Press, Inc.
Ceres Press
Children Of Mary
China Books & Periodicals, Inc.
CONSCIENCE: The Newsjournal of Catholic Opinion
Dreams Due Media Group, Inc.
FIDELIS ET VERUS
GOOD GIRL
THE HEALTH JOURNALS
IRIS: A Journal About Women
Midwifery Today
MOTHERVERSE: A Journal of Contemporary Motherhood
OFF OUR BACKS
Penthe Publishing
SHARE INTERNATIONAL
TOUCHSTONE

BISEXUAL

A Midsummer Night's Press
Assilem 9 Publications
BOOKS TO WATCH OUT FOR
Broken Jaw Press
GAYELLOW PAGES
GERTRUDE
Gertrude Press
GLB Publishers
Grip Publishing
GROUP Publishing
HOT FLASHES: Not a Menopause Thang
IRIS: A Journal About Women
MEAT: A Journal of Writing and Materiality
Mondial
New Sins Press
Raular Publishing
Re-invention UK Ltd
Soft Skull Press
Synergy Press
Youthful Wisdom Press

BLACK

AAIMS Publishers
African American Images
AFRICAN AMERICAN REVIEW
AFRO-HISPANIC REVIEW
AIM MAGAZINE
Aquarius Press
Ariko Publications
Aspicomm Media
Assilem 9 Publications

Back House Books
BLACK LACE
BLACK MAGNOLIAS LITERARY JOURNAL
THE BLACK SCHOLAR: Journal of Black Studies and Research
BLACKFIRE
BLK
Blue Brush Media
CAFE NOIR REVIEW
Carolina Wren Press
Clarity Press, Inc.
COTTONWOOD
Cottonwood Press
Creative Arts Book Company
Dominion Global Publishing
The Edwin Mellen Press
Everflowing Publications
The Feminist Press at the City University of New York
The Fire!! Press
Garden House Press
Goldfish Press
Gorilla Convict Publications
Grip Publishing
GROUP Publishing
History Compass, LLC
International Publishers Co. Inc.
IRIS: A Journal About Women
Jako Books
KUUMBA
Light Density Press
Lotus Press, Inc.
Lyons Publishing Limited
Millennium Vision Press
Miskwabik Press
OBSIDIAN III: Literature in the African Diaspora
Orchard House Press
OUT OF LINE
Passeggiata Press, Inc.
Path Press, Inc.
Pathfinder Press
The Place In The Woods
Psychedelic Literature
Pygmy Forest Press
Rainbow Books, Inc.
RedBone Press
Reference Service Press
Roaring Lion Publishing
Salt Publishing
Sand and Sable Publishing
STRUGGLE: A Magazine of Proletarian Revolutionary Literature
Syracuse Cultural Workers/Tools for Change
TOUCHSTONE
2L Publishing, LLC
Vanderbilt University Press
West Virginia University Press
White Cliffs Media, Inc.
Wings Press
XAVIER REVIEW
XCP: CROSS-CULTURAL POETICS
Youthful Wisdom Press

WILLIAM BLAKE

ALMOST NORMAL COMICS and Other Oddities
THE ENGLISH CLARION
SHATTERED WIG REVIEW
The Thirty First Bird Press
UNDERSTANDING MAGAZINE

BOOK ARTS

AFTERIMAGE
ART BUREAU
ARTELLA: the waltz of words and art
ARTISTIC RAMBLINGS
BAGAZINE
BIBLIOPHILOS
BOOK ARTS CLASSIFIED
BOOK MARKETING UPDATE

BOOK/MARK QUARTERLY REVIEW
Branden Books
Bright Hill Press
Chax Press
Clamp Down Press
Deerbrook Editions
EEI Press
Enigmatic Ink
FINE BOOKS & COLLECTIONS
Goss Press
Gryphon Books
HAND PAPERMAKING
The Hosanna Press
Hotel des Bains Editions
Idaho Center for the Book
Interalia/Design Books
IT GOES ON THE SHELF
KALDRON, An International Journal Of Visual Poetry
KotaPress
Laguna Wilderness Press
LDP, an occasional journal of aesthetics & language
LETTER ARTS REVIEW
Light Density Press
LIGHTWORKS MAGAZINE
Mayapple Press
New Rivers Press, Inc.
NOUN VS. VERB
Open Horizons Publishing Company
PAPERBACK PARADE
PASSAGER
Phelps Publishing Company
PLOPLOP
The Poetry Center Press/Shoestring Press
Rarach Press
RED MARE
Rural Messengers Press
Scars Publications
SCULPTURAL PURSUIT MAGAZINE
SOUTHWEST COLORADO ARTS PERSPECTIVE
Spring Grass
THE TABBY: A CHRONICLE OF THE ARTS AND CRAFTS MOVEMENT
University of Tampa Press
Visual Studies Workshop
Water Mark of Lyons PPP: papers press and permaculture
WHITE FUNGUS

BOOK COLLECTING, BOOKSELLING

BIBLIOPHILOS
Blackwater Publications
BOOK ARTS CLASSIFIED
BOOK MARKETING UPDATE
Bottle of Smoke Press
Chicago Spectrum Press
Children Of Mary
COOK PARTNERS
FINE BOOKS & COLLECTIONS
Gallopade International
Gryphon Books
Harobed Publishing Creations
INDEPENDENT PUBLISHER ONLINE
Litwin Books
Peter Marcan Publications
MYSTERY READERS JOURNAL
Nushape Publication
Oak Knoll Press
Open Horizons Publishing Company
OUT YOUR BACKDOOR: The Magazine of Do-It-Yourself Adventure and Homegrown Culture
PAPERBACK PARADE
Platte Purchase Publishers
RALPH'S REVIEW
READ, AMERICA!
Rural Messengers Press
Shangri-La Publications
SPEX (SMALL PRESS EXCHANGE)
Tomart Publications
Women's Studies Librarian, University of Wisconsin

System

BOOK REVIEWING

THE ADIRONDACK REVIEW
AFRICAN AMERICAN REVIEW
AIM MAGAZINE
ALABAMA LITERARY REVIEW
THE ANNALS OF IOWA
ANQ: A Quarterly Journal of Short Articles, Notes, and Reviews
Anti-Aging Press
THE ANTIGONISH REVIEW
Arts End Books
ASCENT
AT-HOME DAD
AXE FACTORY REVIEW
THE BALTIMORE REVIEW
Bancroft Press
THE BEAR DELUXE MAGAZINE
THE BELTANE PAPERS: A Journal of Women's Mysteries
BIBLIOPHILOS
Black Rose Books Ltd.
BLK
THE BLOOMSBURY REVIEW
BLUE MESA REVIEW
BOOK MARKETING UPDATE
BOOK/MARK QUARTERLY REVIEW
BOOKS FROM FINLAND: Online literature journal of writing from and about Finland
BORDERLANDS: Texas Poetry Review
BRIDGES: An Interdisciplinary Journal of Theology, Philosophy, History, and Science
C&R Press
THE CAROUSEL
Children Of Mary
CKO UPDATE
THE CLASSICAL OUTLOOK
COLLEGE LITERATURE
CONCEIT MAGAZINE
COSMOPSIS QUARTERLY
COTTONWOOD
Cottonwood Press
COUNTERPOISE: For Social Responsibilities, Liberty and Dissent
Creative Creations Consulting Publishing Company
Crescent Moon
THE DALHOUSIE REVIEW
DARK GOTHIC RESURRECTED
The Denali Press
DREAM NETWORK
ELEMENTS
Ellechor Publishing House
ENGLISH LITERATURE IN TRANSITION, 1880-1920
FEMINIST COLLECTIONS: A QUARTERLY OF WO-MEN'S STUDIES RESOURCES
FIDELIS ET VERUS
THE FLORIDA REVIEW
FOURTH GENRE: EXPLORATIONS IN NONFICTION
FROZEN WAFFLES
Global Options
GOLD DUST
GRAY AREAS
GREEN MOUNTAINS REVIEW
Harobed Publishing Creations
HEAVEN BONE MAGAZINE
Heaven Bone Press
Helm Publishing
HOME PLANET NEWS
ICONOCLAST
Immediate Direction Publications
INDEPENDENT PUBLISHER ONLINE
THE IOWA REVIEW
IRIS: A Journal About Women
IRISH FAMILY JOURNAL
IRISH LITERARY SUPPLEMENT
ISSUES
JACK MACKEREL MAGAZINE

Jako Books
JAMES DICKEY REVIEW
JAMES JOYCE BROADSHEET
THE JOURNAL OF AFRICAN TRAVEL-WRITING
Journal of Pyrotechnics
Juel House Publishers and Literary Services
KALEIDOSCOPE: Exploring the Experience of Disability through Literature & the Fine Arts
LAKE SUPERIOR MAGAZINE
LIFTOUTS
LIGHTWORKS MAGAZINE
LINQ
Lion's Den Publishing
THE LUMMOX JOURNAL
Lummox Press
THE MATCH
MEAT FOR TEA: THE VALLEY REVIEW
MGW (Mom Guess What) Newsmagazine
MID-AMERICAN REVIEW
Miskwabik Press
MODERN HAIKU
MUSE: A Quarterly Journal of The Lit
MYSTERY READERS JOURNAL
NEROUP REVIEW
NEW ENGLAND REVIEW
NEW HOPE INTERNATIONAL REVIEW
NORTH CAROLINA LITERARY REVIEW
NORTH DAKOTA QUARTERLY
North Stone Editions
NORTHWEST REVIEW
NOSTOC MAGAZINE
NOUN VS. VERB
NOVA EXPRESS
Nushape Publication
OBSIDIAN III: Literature in the African Diaspora
OHIOANA QUARTERLY
THE OTHER HERALD
OVERLAND JOURNAL
PALO ALTO REVIEW
PAPERPLATES
PASSION
The Place In The Woods
PLAIN BROWN WRAPPER (PBW)
POETRY FLASH
PRAKALPANA SAHITYA/PRAKALPANA LITERA-TURE
Psychedelic Literature
PULSAR POETRY WEBZINE
Quarterly Committee of Queen's University
QUEEN'S QUARTERLY: A Canadian Review
RAIN TAXI REVIEW OF BOOKS
RARITAN: A Quarterly Review
Raular Publishing
RED ROCK REVIEW
RESOURCES FOR FEMINIST RESEARCH/DOCUMEN-TATION SUR LA RECHERCHE FEMINISTE
Rowhouse Press
RUMINATIONS: The Nigerian Dwarf & Mini Dairy Goat Magazine
SALMAGUNDI
SAPONIFIER
SCRIVENER
SECRETUM MEUM MIHI
Secretum Meum Mihi Press
SEWANEE REVIEW
Shangri-La Publications
SHARE INTERNATIONAL
SHENANDOAH: The Washington and Lee University Review
SHORTRUNS
THE SMALL PRESS REVIEW/SMALL MAGAZINE REVIEW
SMARTISH PACE
SO TO SPEAK: A Feminist Journal of Language & Art
SOCIAL JUSTICE: A JOURNAL OF CRIME, CONFLICT, & WORLD ORDER
SOUTHERN HUMANITIES REVIEW
THE SOUTHERN QUARTERLY: A Journal of the Arts in

the South
Southwest Research and Information Center
SPEX (SMALL PRESS EXCHANGE)
STORMWARNING!
STUDIO - A Journal of Christians Writing
SYCAMORE REVIEW
UND Press
UNITED LUMBEE NATION TIMES
VALLUM: CONTEMPORARY POETRY
THE VIRGINIA QUARTERLY REVIEW
VOICES FROM THE EARTH
WAR, LITERATURE & THE ARTS: An International Journal of the Humanities
WHAT IS ENLIGHTENMENT?
Women's Studies Librarian, University of Wisconsin System
WRITERS INK
XAVIER REVIEW
Zagier & Urruty Publications
ZYX

BOTANY

AB
BANANA RAG
Birdsong Books
CONCRETE JUNGLE JOURNAL
Granite Publishing Group
Naturegraph Publishers
Southern Illinois University Press
Tamal Vista Publications
Texas Tech University Press
University Press of Colorado
Waters Edge Press
Wilderness Adventure Books

BRITISH COLUMBIA

Hopeace Press
Open Hand Publishing LLC
Ronsdale Press
Ronsdale Press

BROADCASTING

BearManor Media
Bonus Books, Inc.
D.B.A. Books
EEI Press
IT'S JUST THIS LITTLE CHROMIUM SWITCH HERE

BUDDHISM

ABRAMELIN: a Journal of Poetry and Magick
Arias Press
Beacon Press
BLUE MOUNTAIN
BOULDER HERETIC
Center for Japanese Studies
China Books & Periodicals, Inc.
ClearPoint Press
Dharma Publishing
Fisher King Press
FLUENT ASCENSION
Frozen Waffles Press/Shattered Sidewalks Press; 45th Century Chapbooks
Granite Publishing Group
HEAVEN BONE MAGAZINE
Heaven Bone Press
Himalayan Institute Press
Hohm Press
INDIA CURRENTS
Ithuriel's Spear
MELEE
Middleway Press
nine muses books
One Spirit Press
Parallax Press
Pilgrims Book House
Pleasure Boat Studio: A Literary Press (including imprints Caravel Books and Aequitas Books, and the division Empty Bowl Press)

Poetic Matrix Press
Portal Press
Raular Publishing
S4N Books
Silenced Press
Squire Press
State University of New York Press
Tamal Vista Publications
Timeless Books
TRICYCLE: The Buddhist Review
TURNING WHEEL
Zelda Wilde Publishing
Wisdom Publications, Inc.

CHARLES BUKOWSKI

ALMOST NORMAL COMICS and Other Oddities
AMERICAN JONES BUILDING & MAINTENANCE
Bandanna Books
BEGGARS & CHEESEBURGERS
BOTTLE
Bottle of Smoke Press
DWANG: Outsider poetry and prose
Iniquity Press/Vendetta Books
KNUCKLE MERCHANT - The Journal of Naked Literary Aggression
LULLABY HEARSE
THE LUMMOX JOURNAL
Lummox Press
MELEE
Murder Slim Press
OPEN WIDE MAGAZINE
THE SAVAGE KICK LITERARY MAGAZINE
Six Ft. Swells Press
SPOUT
Squire Press
VIVIPAROUS BLENNY
WHITE FUNGUS
X-Ray Book Co.
Zygote Publishing

BUSINESS & ECONOMICS

A Cappela Publishing
Adams-Blake Publishing
Addicus Books, Inc.
Affinity Publishers Services
AIS Publications
Aspen Mountain Publishing
AT-HOME DAD
Bay Tree Publishing
Beekman Books, Inc.
Behavioral Sciences Research Press, Inc.
Benchmark Publications Inc.
Black Rose Books Ltd.
Blue Owl Press
Bluestocking Press
Book Marketing Solutions
BOOK MARKETING UPDATE
Bookhaven Press, LLC
THE BOOMERPHILE
Break Free Publishing
Brenner Information Group
Burns Park Publishers
Business Coach Press
CANADIAN MONEYSAVER
Center for Japanese Studies
Center For Self-Sufficiency
The Chicot Press
China Books & Periodicals, Inc.
CKO UPDATE
Clearwater Publishing Co.
Communication Creativity
Community Service, Inc.
Craftsman Book Company
Crane Press
Crystal Press
D.B.A. Books
Dash-Hill, LLC
Datamaster Publishing, LLC

DOLLS UNITED INTERACTIVE MAGAZINE
Dominion Global Publishing
Edenscape Publishing Company
Encore Publishing
Encounter Books
Enlightened Living Publishing, LLC
EQUAL CONSTRUCTION RECORD
ETC Publications
FINANCIAL FOCUS
Five Star Publications, Inc.
Fountain Publisher Limited
Frontline Publications
Gain Publications
Gallopade International
Gemstone House Publishing
GENRE: WRITER AND WRITINGS
Glenbridge Publishing Ltd.
Good Hope Enterprises, Inc.
Happy About
The Heather Foundation
Helm Publishing
Hobar Publications, A Division of Finney Company
Hoover Institution Press
IMOCO Publishing
Info Net Publishing
Intercultural Press, Inc.
International Publishers Co. Inc.
The Intrepid Traveler
Jamenair Ltd.
Jardin Publishing
JLA Publications, A Division Of Jeffrey Lant Associates, Inc.
KABBALAH
Kumarian Press
LAKE SUPERIOR MAGAZINE
Lamp Light Press
LATIN AMERICAN PERSPECTIVES
Leadership Education and Development, Inc.
Libertarian Press, Inc./American Book Distributors
LIBERTY
Liberty Publishing Company, Inc.
Life Energy Media
LJW Publishing
Logos Press
Long & Silverman Publishing, Inc.
THE LONG TERM VIEW: A Journal of Informed Opinion
The Madson Group, Inc.
Magnifico Publications
Mendham Publishing
Mind Power Publishing
Mountain Publishing
Multi-Media Publications Inc.
NATURAL LIFE
New Knowledge Press
NEW SOLUTIONS
New Win Publishing
New World Library
Nonetheless Press
Noved Audio
Nunciata
Oak Tree Press
Open Horizons Publishing Company
Palari Publishing
Park Place Publications
Passeggiata Press, Inc.
The Passion Profit Company
Pendant Publishing Inc.
Penworth Publishing
Perpetual Press
Piccadilly Books, Ltd.
Princess Publishing
QP Publishing
QUALITY QUIPS NEWSLETTER
Quarterly Committee of Queen's University
QUEEN'S QUARTERLY: A Canadian Review
Rayve Productions Inc.
Redwood Creek Publishing
Reliance Books

REMS Publishing & Publicity
RFF Press / Resources for the Future
ROCKY MOUNTAIN KC NEWS
Rocky Mountain KC Publishing Co.
Rollaway Bay Publications, Inc.
RTMC Organization, LLC
Russian Information Services
SACS Consulting
Sagamore Publishing
SHARE INTERNATIONAL
Signalman Publishing
THE SMALL BUSINESS ADVISOR
Smith-Johnson Publisher
Soft Skull Press
Sourcebooks, Inc.
Standish Press
Stewart Publishing & Printing
Sunnyside Press
Third Dimension Publishing
Toca Family Publishing, div. of Toca Family Communications Group, LLC
TOUCHSTONE
Trost Publishing
Two Eagles Press International
United Nations University Press
Unlimited Publishing LLC
The Utility Company LLC
Vision Works Publishing
WeWrite LLC
Wheatmark Book Publishing
Whitston Publishing Co.
Willfam Publishing Co.
Winslow Publishing
World Gumbo Publishing
YCD Press

CALIFORNIA

Androgyne Books
BeachSide Press
Borden Publishing Co.
Carousel Press
Arthur H. Clark Co.
Clover Park Press
Command Performance Press
Comstock Bonanza Press
Creative Arts Book Company
Cuore Libre Publishing
Devil Mountain Books
East West Discovery Press
Fisher King Press
Heritage House Publishers
Heyday Books
Huntington Library Press
Iconoclast Press
IN OUR OWN WORDS
Allen A. Knoll Publishers
Lahontan Images
LDP, an occasional journal of aesthetics & language
The Live Oak Press, LLC
Magnifico Publications
Malki-Ballena Press
MCM Entertainment, Inc. Publishing Division
THE MEADOW
Midmarch Arts Press
Museon Publishing
Mystery Island Publications
Nolo Press Occidental
Poplar Leaf Press
Pygmy Forest Press
Quill Driver Books
Rayve Productions Inc.
RED WHEELBARROW
Sand River Press
Sasquatch Books
Scottwall Associates, Publishers
Genny Smith Books
Gibbs Smith, Publisher
SONG OF THE SAN JOAQUIN

Sunbelt Publications
Syukhtun Editions
Tamal Vista Publications
Tres Picos Press
Waters Edge Press
Wexford & Barrow, Publishers
Wide World Publishing

CALLIGRAPHY

BOOK ARTS CLASSIFIED
China Books & Periodicals, Inc.
firefall editions
LETTER ARTS REVIEW
SOUTHWEST COLORADO ARTS PERSPECTIVE

CANADA

Aardvark Enterprises (Sole Proprietorship of J. Alvin Speers)
ASCENT
Betelgeuse Books
Black Rose Books Ltd.
BOGG: A Journal of Contemporary Writing
Borealis Press Limited
Broken Jaw Press
Canadian Educators' Press
CANADIAN JOURNAL OF COMMUNICATION
CANADIAN LITERATURE
CANADIAN POETRY
THE CAPILANO REVIEW
CONNEXIONS DIGEST
Connexions Information Services, Inc.
Coteau Books
DESCANT
The Edwin Mellen Press
Mountain Automation Corporation
NEW MUSE OF CONTEMPT
NIGHTLIFE MAGAZINE
Oolichan Books
THE PRAIRIE JOURNAL OF CANADIAN LITERATURE
Prairie Journal Press
Ronsdale Press
Sassy Sunflower Books
Sources
Tameme
Thirteen Colonies Press
TSAR Publications
Tuns Press
UBC Press
University of Calgary Press
Vehicule Press
WEST COAST LINE: A Journal of Contemporary Writing and Criticism

CAREERS

THE ART OF ABUNDANCE
Aspen Mountain Publishing
Bluestocking Press
Bookhaven Press, LLC
Crane Press
Finney Company, Inc.
Galen Press, Ltd.
GLOBAL ONE MAGAZINE
Global Sports Productions, Ltd.
The Madson Group, Inc.
Magnifico Publications
Mind Power Publishing
Multi-Media Publications Inc.
New Win Publishing
Nonetheless Press
P.R.A. Publishing
Perpetual Press
PREP Publishing
QED Press
Rayve Productions Inc.
REMS Publishing & Publicity
Ronin Publishing, Inc.
SACS Consulting
Set Sail Productions, LLC

Signalman Publishing
Toca Family Publishing, div. of Toca Family Communications Group, LLC
Upheaval Media

CARIBBEAN

Aspicomm Media
CANADIAN JOURNAL OF LATIN AMERICAN AND CARIBBEAN STUDIES/Revue canadienne des etudes latino-americaines et caraibes
THE CARIBBEAN WRITER
Demarche Publishing LLC
DLite Press
The Edwin Mellen Press
Jako Books
Lyons Publishing Limited
Mayapple Press
Nautilus Publishing Company
Pangaea
The Passion Profit Company
Plank Road Publishing
POINT OF CONTACT, The Journal of Verbal & Visual Arts
PREP Publishing
Psychedelic Literature
Roaring Lion Publishing
TORRE DE PAPEL
Tortuga Books
Tres Picos Press
TSAR Publications
Two Thousand Three Associates
Two Thousand Three Associates
University of Virginia Press
White Cliffs Media, Inc.
XAVIER REVIEW

LEWIS CARROLL

THE MAD HATTER
MEAT FOR TEA: THE VALLEY REVIEW
Press Here
SHATTERED WIG REVIEW
UNDERSTANDING MAGAZINE
Vulgar Marsala Press

CARTOONS

ABLAZE Publishing
Allworth Press
THE AMERICAN DISSIDENT
THE AMERICAN DRIVEL REVIEW
ART BUREAU
AXE FACTORY REVIEW
Bad Noise Productions
BANANA RAG
BEGGARS & CHEESEBURGERS
BLACK WARRIOR REVIEW
BLK
Brenner Information Group
Brick Road Poetry Press
BUTTON
CONTRARY
Creative Writing and Publishing Company
Dnar Kaker Basa
DWANG: Outsider poetry and prose
THE FIT CHRISTIAN A Christian Health & Fitness Magazine
GROUP Publishing
HUMOR TIMES
Ignite! Entertainment
ILLOGICAL MUSE
INDUSTRY MINNE-ZINE
IT'S JUST THIS LITTLE CHROMIUM SWITCH HERE
Kakibubu Media Limited
LifeCircle Press
LIGHT: The Quarterly of Light Verse
LOW BUDGET SCIENCE FICTION
MEAT FOR TEA: THE VALLEY REVIEW
MELEE
Mica Press - Paying Our Dues Productions

MINESHAFT
MISSISSIPPI CROW
THE NOISE
OFFICE NUMBER ONE
The Press at Foggy Bottom
THE QUIET FEATHER
Ragamuffin Heart Publishing
SHORT FUSE
SWINK
THE TARPEIAN ROCK
TREATING YOURSELF: The Alternative Medicine Journal
UmbraProjects Publishing
VIVIPAROUS BLENNY
WeWrite LLC
The WhaleInn Publishing House (1998)

CATHOLIC

Bear & Company
Bel Canto Press
Blackwater Publications
BOULDER HERETIC
Cantadora Press
Central Avenue Press
COGNITIO: A Graduate Humanities Journal
CONSCIENCE: The Newsjournal of Catholic Opinion
Dwarf Lion Press
Gingerbread House
Halo Publishing International
Idylls Press
LPD Press
MCM Entertainment, Inc. Publishing Division
Mountain Automation Corporation
New Day Publishing, Inc.
Open University of America Press
THE QUILLDRIVER
Saint Mary's Press
SECRETUM MEUM MIHI
Secretum Meum Mihi Press
TRADICION REVISTA
Tyr Publishing
Wexford & Barrow, Publishers
White Buck Publishing
Wordsonthestreet
Writers House Press
Yes International Publishers

EDGAR CAYCE

Granite Publishing Group

CELTIC

Bardsong Press
Blackwater Publications
Blue Moose Press
Celtic Heritage Books
DIRTY LINEN
Dufour Editions Inc.
The Edwin Mellen Press
Helm Publishing
Horned Owl Publishing
IRISH FAMILY JOURNAL
Irish Genealogical Foundation
IRISH LITERARY SUPPLEMENT
KNUCKLE MERCHANT - The Journal of Naked Literary Aggression
NEW AMERICAN IMAGIST
Paradiso-Parthas Press
S4N Books
SAGEWOMAN
THIN COYOTE
Waters Edge Press
Wings Press

CHANNELLING

Arias Press
Granite Publishing Group
Intuitive Moon Media
JOURNAL OF SCIENTIFIC EXPLORATION

L&L Dreamspell
New Paradigm Books
SeaCrab Publishing
Summerland Publishing

GEOFFREY CHAUCER

Blue Moose Press
Vulgar Marsala Press

CHICAGO

Allium Press of Chicago
Chicago Review Press
CHILDREN, CHURCHES AND DADDIES, A Non Religious, Non Familial Literary Magazine
DOWN IN THE DIRT LITERARY MAGAZINE, the prose & poetry magazine revealing all your dirty little secrets
EbonyEnergy Publishing, Inc.
FREEDOM AND STRENGTH PRESS FORUM
Inner City Press
Lake Claremont Press
Libellum
NEW MADRID
Northern Illinois University Press
Northwestern University Press
Path Press, Inc.
ROCTOBER COMICS AND MUSIC
Scars Publications

CHICANO/A

Arte Publico Press
AZTLAN: A Journal of Chicano Studies
Back House Books
Bilingual Review Press
BILINGUAL REVIEW/Revista Bilingue
THE BLOOMSBURY REVIEW
Bronze Girl Productions, Inc.
Calaca Press
Carolina Wren Press
THE COMSTOCK REVIEW
THE CREAM CITY REVIEW
The Denali Press
The Feminist Press at the City University of New York
First Journey Publishing Company
IN OUR OWN WORDS
Inner City Press
IRIS: A Journal About Women
IRON HORSE LITERARY REVIEW
MEXICAN STUDIES/ESTUDIOS MEXICANOS
NEW AMERICAN IMAGIST
PEACEWORK
The Place In The Woods
Pygmy Forest Press
READ, AMERICA!
Reference Service Press
STRUGGLE: A Magazine of Proletarian Revolutionary Literature
TURNING THE TIDE: Journal of Anti-Racist Action, Research & Education
Two Eagles Press International
UCLA Chicano Studies Research Center Press
Vanderbilt University Press
Volcano Press, Inc
West End Press
White Cliffs Media, Inc.
Wings Press
X-Ray Book Co.

CHILDREN, YOUTH

Aaron Communications III
Abernathy House Publishing
Absey & Co.
Adirondack Mountain Club, Inc.
ADVENTURES
Allwrite Advertising and Publishing
American Carriage House Publishing
AMERICAN FORESTS
Amherst Writers & Artists Press, Inc.
Annick Press Ltd.

Aquarius Press
AT-HOME DAD
Auromere Books and Imports
Authentic Publishing LLC
Azro Press
The B & R Samizdat Express
BeachSide Press
Beekman Books, Inc.
Beyond Words Publishing, Inc.
Birdsong Books
THE BLOOMSBURY REVIEW
Blue Brush Media
Blue Mouse Studio
Book Garden Publishing,LLC
Book Marketing Solutions
Booksmart Publications
Borealis Press Limited
Bronze Girl Productions, Inc.
Callawind Publications / Custom Cookbooks / Children's Books
Carolina Wren Press
Center for Thanatology Research & Education, Inc.
The Center Press
Chicago Review Press
Chicken Soup Press, Inc.
CMP Publishing Group LLC
COBBLESTONE: Discover American History
The Colbert House LLC
Cornell Maritime Press/Tidewater Publishers
Cornerstone Publishing, Inc.
Coteau Books
Council For Indian Education
Creative Creations Consulting Publishing Company
Creative With Words Publications (CWW)
Creative Writing and Publishing Company
CRICKET
CURRENTS: New Scholarship in the Human Services
Cypress Creek Publishing
Dawn Publications
Dawn Sign Press
Delaney Day Press
Demarche Publishing LLC
Dharma Publishing
Downeast Books
Dream Publishing Co.
Dreams Due Media Group, Inc.
Dufour Editions Inc.
E & E Publishing
Eagle's View Publishing
East West Discovery Press
EbonyEnergy Publishing, Inc.
Ecrivez!
Wm.B. Eerdmans Publishing Co.
ELEMENTS
Ellechor Publishing House
EXCEPTIONALITY EDUCATION CANADA
Faith Builders Resource Group
Falcon Publishing, LTD
Farcountry Press
First Chance Publishing
First Journey Publishing Company
THE FIT CHRISTIAN A Christian Health & Fitness Magazine
Five Star Publications, Inc.
Flowerfield Enterprises, LLC
Fotofolio, Inc.
4 Your Spirit Productions
Front Row Experience
Fruitbearer Publishing, LLC
Fulcrum, Inc.
Future Horizons, Inc.
Galde Press, Inc.
The Galileo Press Ltd.
Gallaudet University Press
Gallopade International
Gingerbread House
Goose River Press
Grace House Publishing

Great West Publishing
Gryphon House, Inc.
Guarionex Press Ltd.
Halo Publishing International
Hannacroix Creek Books, Inc
HAPPENINGNOW!EVERYWHERE
The Haworth Press
Heartsong Books
Helm Publishing
Hidden Valley Farm, Publisher
His Work Christian Publishing
History Compass, LLC
Hood Press
Horned Owl Publishing
Hunter House Inc., Publishers
Illumination Arts
Images Unlimited and Snaptail Press, a Division of Images Unlimited Publishing
Impact Publishers, Inc.
In Between Books
Interlink Publishing Group, Inc.
Ion Imagination Publishing, Ion Imagination Entertainment, Inc.
Jalmar Press/Innerchoice Publishing
Jigsaw Press
JOURNAL OF CHILD AND YOUTH CARE
JUNIOR STORYTELLER
Kar-Ben Publishing, Inc.
Kenyette Productions
THE KIDS' STORYTELLING CLUB WEBSITE
Allen A. Knoll Publishers
Laredo Publishing Co., Inc./Renaissance House
Lemon Grove Press
Libertarian Press, Inc./American Book Distributors
Light-Beams Publishing
Lily Ruth Publishing
The Love and Logic Press, Inc.
Luminous Epinoia Press
THE MAD HATTER
Magic Circle Press
Mama Incense Publishing
Mapletree Publishing Company
March Books
Margaret Media, Inc.
Mayhaven Publishing, Inc.
Meek Publishing
MGW (Mom Guess What) Newsmagazine
Midnight Whistler Publishers
Mind Power Publishing
Mo'omana'o Press
Motom
My Heart Yours Publishing
Mystic Jaguar Publishing
NATURAL LIFE
NEW ALTERNATIVES
New Canaan Publishing Company Inc.
New Day Publishing, Inc.
New World Press, Inc
NIS America, Inc.
No Starch Press
Nonetheless Press
North Country Books, Inc.
NSR Publications
Oolichan Books
Open Hand Publishing LLC
Open Horizons Publishing Company
Orchard House Press
Pangaea
Parallax Press
PARENTEACHER MAGAZINE
Parenting Press, Inc.
Paris Press
Park Place Publications
Passion Power Press, Inc
Passport Press
Path Press, Inc.
Peachtree Publishers, Ltd.
Pearl's Book'em Publisher

Peartree Books & Music
Perrin Press
Phelps Publishing Company
Philomel Books
Piano Press
Pirate Publishing International
The Place In The Woods
Platinum One Publishing
Pocahontas Press, Inc.
POCKETS
Poet Tree Press
Premium Press America
The Press at Foggy Bottom
PublishingWorks, Inc.
Ragamuffin Heart Publishing
Rainbow Books, Inc.
Raspberry Press Limited
Raven Rocks Press
READ, AMERICA!
Red Cygnet Press
Ronsdale Press
Sadorian Publications
Sagamore Publishing
Saint Mary's Press
Sasquatch Books
Sea Fog Press
Search Institute
SPECTACULAR SPECULATIONS
SPIDER
Stellaberry Press
STONE SOUP, The Magazine By Young Writers and Artists
Stonehorse Publishing, LLC
Storycraft Publishing
Stunt Publishing
Successful Kids Publishing
Summit Crossroads Press
Theytus Books Ltd.
Third Dimension Publishing
Three Bean Press
Three Bears Publishing
Titus Home Publishing
Top 20 Press
Tortuga Books
Trellis Publishing, Inc.
TURNING THE TIDE: Journal of Anti-Racist Action, Research & Education
Two Thousand Three Associates
Vanderbilt University Press
Volcano Press, Inc
Wayfarer Press, LLC
Wayside Publications
WeWrite LLC
What The Heck Press
White Mane Publishing Company, Inc.
Willowood Press
Windward Publishing, An Imprint of Finney Company

CHINA

China Books & Periodicals, Inc.
CHINA REVIEW INTERNATIONAL
Cynic Press
Inner City Press
LEO Productions LLC.
Moo-Cow Fan Club
One Spirit Press
Pleasure Boat Studio: A Literary Press (including imprints Caravel Books and Aequitas Books, and the division Empty Bowl Press)
Small Helm Press
Synergetic Press
The Wellsweep Press

SRI CHINMOY

INDIA CURRENTS

CHRISTIANITY

Aaron Communications III

ABLAZE Publishing
All That Productions,Inc.
Allwrite Advertising and Publishing
American Literary Press
ANCIENT PATHS
Aura Productions, LLC
Beacon Press
BEGINNING MAGAZINE
BELIEVERS EXCHANGE NEWSLETTER
Blue Dolphin Publishing, Inc.
Book Marketing Solutions
BOULDER HERETIC
Brentwood Christian Press
Brick Road Poetry Press
Candlestick Publishing
Children Of Mary
CHRISTIAN*NEW AGE QUARTERLY
Church Leadership Library (Canadian Office)
Church Leadership Library (US Office)
Cladach Publishing
CORNERSTONE
Crossway
Cyberwit.net
Dancing Lemur Press, L.L.C.
Delaney Day Press
Dominion Global Publishing
Dunamis House
Dwarf Lion Press
Eborn Books
Edenscape Publishing Company
Wm.B. Eerdmans Publishing Co.
Elderberry Press, Inc.
Ellechor Publishing House
Faith Builders Resource Group
Falcon Publishing, LTD
FIDELIS ET VERUS
THE FIT CHRISTIAN A Christian Health & Fitness Magazine
4 Your Spirit Productions
Fruitbearer Publishing, LLC
FULLOSIA PRESS
Galaxy Press
Gingerbread House
Good Book Publishing Company
Goose River Press
Grace Acres Press
Grace House Publishing
Gray Dog Press
Halo Publishing International
HEALMB Publishing
The Heather Foundation
Heidelberg Graphics
His Work Christian Publishing
Ho Logos Press
Hope Publishing House
ISSUES
The Leaping Frog Press
LPD Press
Lycanthrope Press
Madyfi Press
Mountain Automation Corporation
Multnomah Publishers, Inc.
My Heart Yours Publishing
New Canaan Publishing Company Inc.
New Day Publishing, Inc.
NOLA-MAGICK Press
OFFICE NUMBER ONE
Origin Press
Papillon Presse
Pearl's Book'em Publisher
Platinum Dreams Publishing
Polka Dot Publishing
Princess Publishing
Progressive Press; Tree of Life Publications
PublishAmerica, LLLP.
QUARTZ HILL JOURNAL OF THEOLOGY:A Journal of Bible and Contemporary Theological Thought
Quartz Hill Publishing House

THE QUILLDRIVER
Ragged Edge Press
Ridgeway Press of Michigan
S4N Books
Saint Mary's Press
SeaCrab Publishing
SelectiveHouse Publishers, Inc.
Signalman Publishing
Small Dogma Publishing, Inc.
Small Helm Press
Starik Publishing
SterlingHouse Publisher
Sherwood Sugden & Company, Publishers
Thatch Tree Publications
Thirteen Colonies Press
Tyr Publishing
UnKnownTruths.com Publishing Company
Wheatmark Book Publishing
White Buck Publishing
Wilderness Ministries
WindRiver Publishing
WinePress Publishing
Writers House Press
Wytherngate Press
Yes International Publishers

CHRISTMAS

City Life Books, LLC
DTS Group, Inc.
Halo Publishing International
LPD Press
Mo'omana'o Press
Motom
Practically Shameless Press
Premium Press America
Sterli Publishing
Waters Edge Press

CITIES

AMERICAN HIKER
Authentic Publishing LLC
Barney Press
BeachSide Press
Black Rose Books Ltd.
Cantarabooks LLC
Carousel Press
Chandler & Sharp Publishers, Inc.
Clover Park Press
CONCRETE JUNGLE JOURNAL
ENVIRONMENTAL & ARCHITECTURAL PHENOMEN-
   OLOGY NEWSLETTER
Gallopade International
Gemini Publishing Company
GREEN ANARCHY
GROUP Publishing
Heritage House Publishers
Inner City Press
INNER CITY PRESS
Italica Press, Inc.
Lake Claremont Press
Maisonneuve Press
Peter Marcan Publications
Mount Ida Press
OTHER INVESTIGATIONS
RIVET MAGAZINE
SeaCrab Publishing
SHATTERED WIG REVIEW
University of Chicago Press
Vanderbilt University Press
Vehicule Press
WORLD POETRY SHOWCASE

CIVIL RIGHTS

AIS Publications
BALLOT ACCESS NEWS
Beacon Press
BLK
THE BOOMERPHILE

Cantadora Press
Clarity Press, Inc.
COALITION FOR PRISONERS' RIGHTS NEWSLETTER
COLORLINES
Demarche Publishing LLC
First Journey Publishing Company
Global Options
GROUP Publishing
IN OUR OWN WORDS
Inner City Press
INNER CITY PRESS
Insight Press
Interlink Publishing Group, Inc.
Just Sisters Publications
Magnifico Publications
MGW (Mom Guess What) Newsmagazine
Millennium Vision Press
MOUTH: Voice of the Dis-Labeled Nation
Obie Joe Media
Open Hand Publishing LLC
THE OTHER ISRAEL
Partisan Press
Path Press, Inc.
PEACEWORK
PEMMICAN
The Place In The Woods
Poor Richard's Press
PRISON LEGAL NEWS
SENSATIONS MAGAZINE
SOCIAL JUSTICE: A JOURNAL OF CRIME, CONFLICT,
   & WORLD ORDER
Soft Skull Press
Southeast Missouri State University Press
Stardate Publishing Company
STORMWARNING!
Strata Publishing, Inc.
TOUCHSTONE
University of Massachusetts Press
University of South Carolina Press
WHEELHOUSE MAGAZINE

CIVIL WAR

Blackwater Publications
John F. Blair, Publisher
Bright Mountain Books
Burd Street Press
Chicago Spectrum Press
Arthur H. Clark Co.
Cornell Maritime Press/Tidewater Publishers
DTS Group, Inc.
Faded Banner Publications
FULLOSIA PRESS
Galen Press, Ltd.
Harbor House
Historical Resources Press
Just Sisters Publications
MacDonald/Sward Publishing Company
Magnifico Publications
Mercer University Press
Northern Illinois University Press
Ohio University Press/Swallow Press
Parkway Publishers, Inc.
Platte Purchase Publishers
Premium Press America
SENSATIONS MAGAZINE
Southeast Missouri State University Press
Stardate Publishing Company
The True Bill Press
Truman State University Press
University of Arkansas Press
University of Nebraska Press
University of South Carolina Press
University of Virginia Press
Van Cleave Publishing
Virginia City Publishing Co. LLC
WAR, LITERATURE & THE ARTS: An International
   Journal of the Humanities
West Virginia University Press

White Mane Publishing Company, Inc.

CLASSICAL STUDIES

ABLAZE Publishing
APOSTROPHE: USCB Journal of the Arts
The B & R Samizdat Express
Barrytown/Station Hill Press
BeachSide Press
BIBLIOPHILOS
Branden Books
THE BROADKILL REVIEW: A Journal of Literature
Cantadora Press
CLASSICAL ANTIQUITY
THE CLASSICAL OUTLOOK
CONTEMPORARY GHAZALS
THE DALHOUSIE REVIEW
Dufour Editions Inc.
The Edwin Mellen Press
The Edwin Mellen Press
Erespin Press
Evolution Publishing
Focus Publishing/R. Pullins Co.
Horned Owl Publishing
Libellum
Magnifico Publications
MOUSEION, Journal of the Classical Association of Canada/Revue de la Societe Canadienne des Etudes Classiques
NEROUP REVIEW
NEW ENGLAND REVIEW
Panther Creek Press
S4N Books
Shangri-La Publications
UNDERSTANDING MAGAZINE
Vulgar Marsala Press
West Virginia University Press

CLOTHING

AB
Cooperative Press
Eagle's View Publishing
GROUP Publishing
Hunter Publishing Corporation
Ibexa Press
INDUSTRY MINNE-ZINE
ORNAMENT
Texas Tech University Press
WORN FASHION JOURNAL

COLLECTIBLES

Borden Publishing Co.
C & T Publishing
Cattpigg Press
Celebrity Profiles Publishing
Cottontail Publications
DTS Group, Inc.
FOLK ART MESSENGER
Gryphon Books
INKY TRAIL NEWS
NEW ENGLAND BY RAIL
New Win Publishing
ORNAMENT
PAPERBACK PARADE
RALPH'S REVIEW
Gibbs Smith, Publisher
Sonoran Publishing
Square One Publishers, Inc.
Tomart Publications

COLOR

DOLLS UNITED INTERACTIVE MAGAZINE
Green Hut Press
LDP, an occasional journal of aesthetics & language
SunShine Press Publications, Inc.

COLORADO

City Life Books, LLC
Cottonwood Press, Inc.

LPD Press
THE MEADOW
Montemayor Press
Mountain Automation Corporation
PINYON
Pruett Publishing Company
Sherman Asher Publishing
Thundercloud Books
TOUCHSTONE
TRADICION REVISTA
Transcending Mundane, Inc.
University Press of Colorado
Willowood Press

COMICS

Alan Wofsy Fine Arts
Allworth Press
ALMOST NORMAL COMICS and Other Oddities
THE AMERICAN DRIVEL REVIEW
Argo Press
ART BUREAU
BABYSUE
BABYSUE MUSIC REVIEW
BEGGARS & CHEESEBURGERS
Brick Road Poetry Press
CHARLTON SPOTLIGHT
COMICS REVUE
THE DUCKBURG TIMES
Enigmatic Ink
Explorer Press
FAT TUESDAY
Fine Tooth Press
FISH DRUM MAGAZINE
Five Star Publications, Inc.
THE FLORIDA REVIEW
Fotofolio, Inc.
Hidden Valley Farm, Publisher
HUMOR TIMES
Ignite! Entertainment
INDIANA REVIEW
IT'S JUST THIS LITTLE CHROMIUM SWITCH HERE
JACK MACKEREL MAGAZINE
Knowledge Concepts Publishing
LIGHT: The Quarterly of Light Verse
Manuscript Press
THE MEADOW
MINESHAFT
THE MORNING DEW REVIEW
Murder Slim Press
Mystery Island Publications
Orchard House Press
Pearl's Book'em Publisher
Phelps Publishing Company
PIG IRON
Pixiu Press
Pussywillow
RED FEZ ENTERTAINMENT
ROCTOBER COMICS AND MUSIC
Rowhouse Press
The Runaway Spoon Press
THE SAVAGE KICK LITERARY MAGAZINE
SHATTERED WIG REVIEW
SHORTRUNS
SPECTACULAR SPECULATIONS
Synergetic Press
THE2NDHAND
VIVIPAROUS BLENNY
WAV MAGAZINE: Progressive Music Art Politics Culture
WHITE FUNGUS
Willfam Publishing Co.

COMMUNICATION, JOURNALISM

Allworth Press
ALTERNATIVE PRESS REVIEW
Arjuna Library Press
Assilem 9 Publications
Bay Tree Publishing
BEACHCOMBER MAGAZINE

Beekman Books, Inc.
Best Books Plus
Blackwater Publications
Bonus Books, Inc.
CANADIAN JOURNAL OF COMMUNICATION
THE CAROUSEL
Chicory Blue Press, Inc.
CKO UPDATE
Communication Creativity
COOK PARTNERS
D.B.A. Books
EEI Press
ELEMENTS
ESPERANTIC STUDIES
FREELANCE WRITER'S REPORT
Gallopade International
Global Sports Productions, Ltd.
GROUP Publishing
Guarionex Press Ltd.
Intercultural Press, Inc.
JLA Publications, A Division Of Jeffrey Lant Associates, Inc.
KALDRON, An International Journal Of Visual Poetry
KETTERING REVIEW
LIGHTWORKS MAGAZINE
Litwin Books
LOST GENERATION JOURNAL
Lummox Press
Maupin House Publishing, Inc.
Mills Custom Services Publishing
MISSISSIPPI CROW
Open Horizons Publishing Company
Rada Press, Inc.
RIVER TEETH: A Journal of Nonfiction Narrative
Sources
THE SOURCES HOTLINK
The Speech Bin, Inc.
Strata Publishing, Inc.
Strata Publishing, Inc.
The True Bill Press
Tuscarora Books Inc.
Univelt, Inc.
University of Arkansas Press
Unlimited Publishing LLC
Wellington House Publishing Company
Winslow Publishing
WOMEN AND LANGUAGE

COMMUNISM, MARXISM, LENINISM

ALTERNATIVE PRESS INDEX
Back House Books
Beekman Books, Inc.
BLUE COLLAR REVIEW
Bordighera, Inc.
Children Of Mary
FIDELIS ET VERUS
Hoover Institution Press
Insight Press
International Publishers Co. Inc.
Magnifico Publications
Mehring Books, Inc.
Pathfinder Press
PEMMICAN
RED LAMP
SALMAGUNDI
Shangri-La Publications
Soft Skull Press
STORMWARNING!
STRUGGLE: A Magazine of Proletarian Revolutionary Literature
TOUCHSTONE
Van Cleave Publishing

COMMUNITY

AFRICAN AMERICAN REVIEW
AMERICAN JONES BUILDING & MAINTENANCE
ARTELLA: the waltz of words and art
Bay Tree Publishing

Bear & Company
THE BELTANE PAPERS: A Journal of Women's Mysteries
Black Rose Books Ltd.
BLUE MOUNTAIN
Bottom Dog Press / Bird Dog Publishing
Church Leadership Library (Canadian Office)
Church Leadership Library (US Office)
COMMUNITIES
Community Service, Inc.
FRIENDS OF PEACE PILGRIM
Garden House Press
Global Options
GOOD GIRL
GROUP Publishing
The Heather Foundation
Ice Cube Press
INDUSTRY MINNE-ZINE
INTERCULTURE
IRIS: A Journal About Women
JOURNAL OF CHILD AND YOUTH CARE
KETTERING REVIEW
LifeCircle Press
MGW (Mom Guess What) Newsmagazine
Miskwabik Press
Mo'omana'o Press
NATURAL LIFE
NATURALLY
NEROUP REVIEW
NEW ENVIRONMENT BULLETIN
NEW SOLUTIONS
OUT OF LINE
OUT YOUR BACKDOOR: The Magazine of Do-It-Yourself Adventure and Homegrown Culture
The People's Press
Poplar Leaf Press
Red Alder Books
RFD
SENSATIONS MAGAZINE
Shangri-La Publications
Shared Roads Press
SILVER WINGS
SOCIAL ANARCHISM: A Journal of Practice and Theory
SOCIAL JUSTICE: A JOURNAL OF CRIME, CONFLICT, & WORLD ORDER
TOUCHSTONE
TURNING WHEEL
Volcano Press, Inc

COMPUTERS, CALCULATORS

Adams-Blake Publishing
Ageless Press
Benchmark Publications Inc.
Brenner Information Group
Frontline Publications
Gallopade International
GRAY AREAS
Happy About
Holy Macro! Books
IROL Press, LLC
Jamenair Ltd.
Lion Press
MGW (Mom Guess What) Newsmagazine
Mills Custom Services Publishing
NEROUP REVIEW
No Starch Press
Paladin Enterprises, Inc.
PLAIN BROWN WRAPPER (PBW)
PRIVACY JOURNAL
Quale Press
Shangri-La Publications
STYLUS
Technics Publications, LLC
White Cliffs Media, Inc.

CONSERVATION

ADIRONDAC
Adirondack Mountain Club, Inc.

AMERICAN FORESTS
AMERICAN HIKER
American Hiking Society
AMERICAN JONES BUILDING & MAINTENANCE
AQUATERRA, METAECOLOGY & CULTURE
Atlantic Publishing Group, Inc.
BANANA RAG
Beacon Press
Bear & Company
THE BEAR DELUXE MAGAZINE
BIG MUDDY: Journal of the Mississippi River Valley
THE BLOOMSBURY REVIEW
Chelsea Green Publishing Company
Downeast Books
DWELLING PORTABLY
ECOTONE: Reimagining Place
ELECTRONIC GREEN JOURNAL
Fulcrum, Inc.
Garden House Press
Granite Publishing Group
HIGH COUNTRY NEWS
Hobar Publications, A Division of Finney Company
Insight Press
Island Press
Kakibubu Media Limited
Keokee Co. Publishing, Inc.
Kumarian Press
The Latona Press
Lost Pond Press
New England Cartographics, Inc.
Oak Knoll Press
Ocean Publishing
ON EARTH
Oregon State University Press
OUT OF LINE
OUT YOUR BACKDOOR: The Magazine of Do-It-
    Yourself Adventure and Homegrown Culture
Pangaea
Pineapple Press, Inc.
Portal Press
RALPH'S REVIEW
RFF Press / Resources for the Future
Rock Spring Press Inc.
Sagamore Publishing
SANDPOINT MAGAZINE
SEED SAVERS EXCHANGE
Shangri-La Publications
Genny Smith Books
SO YOUNG!
TOUCHSTONE
University of Chicago Press
Village Lane Press
WEBER: The Contemporary West
Wineberry Press
WISCONSIN TRAILS
Zagier & Urruty Publications

CONSTRUCTION

BLUE COLLAR REVIEW
Consumer Press
EQUAL CONSTRUCTION RECORD
Hobar Publications, A Division of Finney Company
LJW Publishing
PAVEMENT SAW
Pavement Saw Press
Rolling Hills Publishing
Standish Press
Toca Family Publishing, div. of Toca Family Communica-
    tions Group, LLC
Village Lane Press

CONSULTING

Adams-Blake Publishing
Book Marketing Solutions
Burns Park Publishers
CKO UPDATE
EQUAL CONSTRUCTION RECORD
Finney Company, Inc.

Friendly Oaks Publications
Goblin Fern Press
Happy About
Multi-Media Publications Inc.
New Knowledge Press
Nonetheless Press
Penworth Publishing
Platinum One Publishing
RTMC Organization, LLC
Sassy Sunflower Books
Smith-Johnson Publisher
Toca Family Publishing, div. of Toca Family Communica-
    tions Group, LLC
The Utility Company LLC
World Gumbo Publishing

CONSUMER

Affinity Publishers Services
Art of Living, PrimaMedia,Inc
Bay Tree Publishing
BeachSide Press
CANADIAN MONEYSAVER
Center For Self-Sufficiency
Communication Creativity
Consumer Press
DWELLING PORTABLY
Guarionex Press Ltd.
Happy About
HEARING HEALTH
Lawells Publishing
Liberty Publishing Company, Inc.
Nonetheless Press
PRIVACY JOURNAL
Rolling Hills Publishing
STYLUS
Upper Access Inc. Book Publishers
VEGETARIAN JOURNAL
Winslow Publishing

COOKING

ABLAZE Publishing
ALIMENTUM - The Literature of Food
Art of Living, PrimaMedia,Inc
Avery Color Studios
BANANA RAG
Banta & Pool Literary Properties
BELIEVERS EXCHANGE NEWSLETTER
The Bess Press
Blue Dolphin Publishing, Inc.
Bright Mountain Books
Bronze Girl Productions, Inc.
Callawind Publications / Custom Cookbooks / Children's
    Books
Chicago Review Press
Chicago Spectrum Press
Cookbook Resources, LLC
Cooperative Press
Cornell Maritime Press/Tidewater Publishers
Espretto
Fantail
Farcountry Press
Nicolin Fields Publishing, Inc.
First Books
Five Star Publications, Inc.
Florentia Press
Goose River Press
Grace Creek Press
GROUP Publishing
His Work Christian Publishing
ILLUMINATIONS LITERARY JOURNAL
Images Unlimited and Snaptail Press, a Division of Images
    Unlimited Publishing
Info Net Publishing
Jackson Harbor Press
Kar-Ben Publishing, Inc.
Lamp Light Press
Lazywood Press
Lemieux International Ltd.

656

Life Media
LifeCircle Press
Lion's Den Publishing
Maui arThoughts Co.
McBooks Press, Inc.
A Melody from an Immigrant's Soul
MY TABLE: Houston's Dining Magazine
NATURAL LIFE
George Ohsawa Macrobiotic Foundation
THE ORPHAN LEAF REVIEW
Outrider Press
Pineapple Press, Inc.
Platinum One Publishing
Portal Press
Pruett Publishing Company
Quicksilver Productions
Sasquatch Books
Sasquatch Books
Sherman Asher Publishing
SHORTRUNS
Sibyl Publications, Inc
Square One Publishers, Inc.
Storm Publishing Group
Strawberry Patchworks
Three Bean Press
Titus Home Publishing
Tyr Publishing
Upheaval Media
VEGETARIAN JOURNAL
The Vegetarian Resource Group
Wave Publishing
Whispering Pine Press
WISCONSIN TRAILS

CO-OPS

Hobar Publications, A Division of Finney Company
Life Media
Shared Roads Press

COSMOLOGY

Chax Press
Dawn Publications
Granite Publishing Group
Himalayan Institute Press
JOURNAL OF SCIENTIFIC EXPLORATION
SPECTACULAR SPECULATIONS
SPOTops Books
STARNOTES
Tyr Publishing

COUNTER-CULTURE, ALTERNATIVES, COMMUNES

ABRAMELIN: a Journal of Poetry and Magick
Act on Wisdom
Allbook Books
ALMOST NORMAL COMICS and Other Oddities
ALTERNATIVE PRESS REVIEW
THE AMERICAN DISSIDENT
ASCENT
Bear & Company
BLACK BOOK PRESS: The Poetry Zine id
THE BOOMERPHILE
BOTH SIDES NOW
Cantarabooks LLC
Cassandra Press, Inc.
CHILDREN, CHURCHES AND DADDIES, A Non Religious, Non Familial Literary Magazine
COMMUNITIES
COUNTERPOISE: For Social Responsibilities, Liberty and Dissent
The Denali Press
DOWN IN THE DIRT LITERARY MAGAZINE, the prose & poetry magazine revealing all your dirty little secrets
Down There Press
DWANG: Outsider poetry and prose
DWELLING PORTABLY
The Edwin Mellen Press
FIRST CLASS

Four-Sep Publications
FREEDOM AND STRENGTH PRESS FORUM
Granite Publishing Group
GRAY AREAS
THE GROWING EDGE MAGAZINE
Higganum Hill Books
Insight Press
INTERNATIONAL ART POST
THE (LIBERTARIAN) CONNECTION
LIGHTWORKS MAGAZINE
LOVING MORE: New Models for Relationships
LULLWATER REVIEW
MEAT: A Journal of Writing and Materiality
NATURALLY
NEW ENVIRONMENT BULLETIN
NEWWITCH
THE OTHER ISRAEL
OUT YOUR BACKDOOR: The Magazine of Do-It-Yourself Adventure and Homegrown Culture
Paladin Enterprises, Inc.
Passing Through Publications
PEACEWORK
Penthe Publishing
PIG IRON
Red Eye Press
RED LAMP
RFD
ROCTOBER COMICS AND MUSIC
Ronin Publishing, Inc.
Santa Fe Writers Project
Scars Publications
Shared Roads Press
SHORT FUSE
SIGNALS
SOCIAL ANARCHISM: A Journal of Practice and Theory
Soft Skull Press
STORMWARNING!
Syracuse Cultural Workers/Tools for Change
Tangerine Press
TOUCHSTONE
Transcending Mundane, Inc.
Van Cleave Publishing
ZINE WORLD: A Reader's Guide to the Underground Press

CRAFTS, HOBBIES

Affinity Publishers Services
Allworth Press
ARTELLA: the waltz of words and art
Backcountry Publishing
BAGAZINE
The Bess Press
BUTTON
C & T Publishing
Camp Colton
Cattpigg Press
Center For Self-Sufficiency
Chicago Review Press
Cooperative Press
Cornell Maritime Press/Tidewater Publishers
Cottontail Publications
Council For Indian Education
DOLLS UNITED INTERACTIVE MAGAZINE
Downeast Books
DWELLING PORTABLY
Eagle's View Publishing
ETC Publications
THE FRONT STRIKER BULLETIN
Global Sports Productions, Ltd.
Guarionex Press Ltd.
Hidden Valley Farm, Publisher
Hobar Publications, A Division of Finney Company
Hood Press
Ibexa Press
INKY TRAIL NEWS
INVENTED LANGUAGES
JUNIOR STORYTELLER
THE KIDS' STORYTELLING CLUB WEBSITE
LifeCircle Press

657

Lion's Den Publishing
MGW (Mom Guess What) Newsmagazine
Midmarch Arts Press
MIDWEST ART FAIRS
MISSISSIPPI CROW
Moo-Cow Fan Club
Naturegraph Publishers
NEW ENGLAND BY RAIL
No Starch Press
Oak Knoll Press
ORNAMENT
OUT YOUR BACKDOOR: The Magazine of Do-It-Yourself Adventure and Homegrown Culture
Pebble Press, Inc.
Pendant Publishing Inc.
Petroglyph Press, Ltd.
Profile Press
Rolling Hills Publishing
Scentouri, Publishing Division
THE $ENSIBLE SOUND
Shangri-La Publications
SHORTRUNS
Square One Publishers, Inc.
Storycraft Publishing
Success Publishing
Sunstone Press
Tamal Vista Publications
Thatch Tree Publications
Thirteen Colonies Press
Tomart Publications
UNITED LUMBEE NATION TIMES
Village Lane Press
John Wade, Publisher
Wayside Publications
WOODWORKER'S JOURNAL
WORN FASHION JOURNAL

CREATIVE NON-FICTION

A Cappela Publishing
ATLANTIC PACIFIC PRESS
Aura Productions, LLC
Authentic Publishing LLC
Bandanna Books
W.S. Beetle & Company
BEGINNING MAGAZINE
BLACK MAGNOLIAS LITERARY JOURNAL
BLUE COLLAR REVIEW
BLUE MESA REVIEW
BOGG: A Journal of Contemporary Writing
Brain Injury Success Books
THE BROADKILL REVIEW: A Journal of Literature
C&R Press
Calaca Press
Clark-Nova Books
Colerith Press
Cornerstone Press
COSMOPSIS QUARTERLY
Cotton Tree Press
Creative Creations Consulting Publishing Company
Dervla Publishing, LLC
Dominion Global Publishing
Dry Creek Press
DTS Group, Inc.
THE EAST HAWAII OBSERVER
Eastern Washington University Press
EbonyEnergy Publishing, Inc.
Edenscape Publishing Company
Ellechor Publishing House
EPIPHANY, A Literary Journal
Equine Graphics Publishing Group: New Concord Press, SmallHorse Press, SunDrop
Etched Press
EVANSVILLE REVIEW
Evening Street Press
EVENING STREET REVIEW
Florida Academic Press
Forest Dale Publishing Company
THE FREEFALL REVIEW

GHOTI MAGAZINE
Gingerbread House
Goblin Fern Press
Gray Dog Press
Green Square Publishing
HAPA NUI
ICONOCLAST
ILLOGICAL MUSE
THE INK SLINGER REVIEW
InsideOut Press
JAMES DICKEY REVIEW
Lawells Publishing
LEAF GARDEN
Leaf Garden Press
Lemon Grove Press
LITERARY HOUSE REVIEW
THE LUMMOX JOURNAL
THE MACGUFFIN
THE MEADOW
Medusa's Muse
Missing Spoke Press
Moo-Cow Fan Club
Nautilus Publishing Company
NEW ENGLAND BY RAIL
NEW ENGLAND REVIEW
New Knowledge Press
NEW MADRID
Nish Publishing Company
NORTHWEST REVIEW
NSR Publications
Nushape Publication
Obie Joe Media
One Horse Press/Rainy Day Press
OTHER INVESTIGATIONS
OTOLITHS
Outrider Press
Paladin Media Group
Papillon Presse
Paris Press
Peartree Books & Music
Penworth Publishing
THE PINCH
Platinum Dreams Publishing
POETS & WRITERS MAGAZINE
PORTLAND REVIEW
PUNKIN HOUSE DIGEST
THE QUILLDRIVER
RED FEZ ENTERTAINMENT
Rivendell Books
RIVER POETS JOURNAL
Shared Roads Press
SIGNALS
Silenced Press
Small Dogma Publishing, Inc.
SNREVIEW
SOJOURN: A Journal of the Arts
SOUNDINGS REVIEW
SUB-TERRAIN
Summerland Publishing
Thunder Rain Publishing Corp.
Two-Handed Engine Press
U.S.1 WORKSHEETS
VIVIPAROUS BLENNY
VOICE(S)
Wellington House Publishing Company
The WhaleInn Publishing House (1998)
Wintertree Press
WORDKNOT AUDIO: A Literary Podcast Magazine
Wordsonthestreet
Yaldah Publishing
Zirlinson Publishing

CREATIVITY

Absey & Co.
Act on Wisdom
Allbook Books
ARTELLA: the waltz of words and art
ARTISTIC RAMBLINGS

658

BEGGARS & CHEESEBURGERS
Bel Canto Press
BLACK MAGNOLIAS LITERARY JOURNAL
C&R Press
THE CANNON'S MOUTH
THE CAROUSEL
Crescent Moon
Dnar Kaker Basa
DOLLS UNITED INTERACTIVE MAGAZINE
ECOTONE: Reimagining Place
Edenscape Publishing Company
Granite Publishing Group
Green Hut Press
Grey Sparrow Press
GROUP Publishing
The Heather Foundation
Hidden Valley Farm, Publisher
Hunter Publishing Corporation
ILLOGICAL MUSE
INDUSTRY MINNE-ZINE
Intuitive Moon Media
IRIS: A Journal About Women
Lamp Light Press
Lemon Grove Press
LifeCircle Press
LIGHTWORKS MAGAZINE
Lucky Press, LLC
LULLABY HEARSE
LULLWATER REVIEW
Luminous Epinoia Press
Mind Power Publishing
THE NEO-COMINTERN
New World Library
One Spirit Press
PASSAGER
PASSION
Pearl's Book'em Publisher
Platinum One Publishing
PRAKALPANA   SAHITYA/PRAKALPANA   LITERA-
    TURE
Psychedelic Literature
PUNKIN HOUSE DIGEST
Punkin House Press
THE QUIET FEATHER
RED ROCK REVIEW
Red Tiger Press
Re-invention UK Ltd
RIVER POETS JOURNAL
Roaring Lion Publishing
Savant Garde Workshop
SCHUYLKILL VALLEY JOURNAL
SENSATIONS MAGAZINE
SHORT FUSE
SMARTISH PACE
SO TO SPEAK: A Feminist Journal of Language & Art
SONG OF THE SAN JOAQUIN
SP QUILL MAGAZINE
Spring Grass
Verve Press
Village Lane Press
VOICE(S)
Word Forge Books
Wordwrights Canada

CRIME

Addicus Books, Inc.
CIRCLE INC., THE MAGAZINE
Circle of Friends Books
COALITION FOR PRISONERS' RIGHTS NEWSLETTER
CORRECTIONS TODAY
Creative Arts Book Company
Dash-Hill, LLC
FMA Publishing
FULLOSIA PRESS
Global Options
Gorilla Convict Publications
GRASSLIMB
GRAY AREAS

GROUP Publishing
Gryphon Books
HARDBOILED
Holbrook Street Press
Krill Press
Murder Slim Press
MYSTERY ISLAND MAGAZINE
THE MYSTERY REVIEW
Nish Publishing Company
North Country Books, Inc.
Paladin Enterprises, Inc.
Paladin Media Group
PAPERBACK PARADE
Polar Bear & Company
PRISON LEGAL NEWS
THE SAVAGE KICK LITERARY MAGAZINE
SOCIAL JUSTICE: A JOURNAL OF CRIME, CONFLICT,
    & WORLD ORDER
Southern Illinois University Press
Spinifex Press
STORMWARNING!
SWILL
TOUCHSTONE
Triumvirate Publications
The True Bill Press
Tuscarora Books Inc.
Twilight Tales, Inc.
Vanilla Heart Publishing
The WhaleInn Publishing House (1998)
Willfam Publishing Co.
The Wolf Pirate Project Inc.
Youthful Wisdom Press

CRITICISM

AFRICAN AMERICAN REVIEW
AFTERIMAGE
ALABAMA LITERARY REVIEW
American Canadian Publishers, Inc.
AMERICAN LITERATURE
THE ANTIGONISH REVIEW
Arjuna Library Press
Authentic Publishing LLC
Barrytown/Station Hill Press
Bay Press
Bilingual Review Press
BLACK MAGNOLIAS LITERARY JOURNAL
BOGG: A Journal of Contemporary Writing
BOOK/MARK QUARTERLY REVIEW
BORDERLANDS: Texas Poetry Review
Borealis Press Limited
BOULEVARD
CANADIAN LITERATURE
THE CANNON'S MOUTH
CAUSE & EFFECT MAGAZINE
Center for Japanese Studies
CINEASTE MAGAZINE
Clamshell Press
Clark-Nova Books
COUNTERPOISE: For Social Responsibilities, Liberty and
    Dissent
Crescent Moon
CROSSCURRENTS
THE DALHOUSIE REVIEW
THE DALHOUSIE REVIEW
DESCANT
DESIRE
Edgewise Press
88: A Journal of Contemporary American Poetry
ELT Press
Encounter Books
ENGLISH LITERATURE IN TRANSITION, 1880-1920
FEMINIST STUDIES
Fine Tooth Press
Florida Academic Press
From Here Press
FUGUE
Galaxy Press
THE GEORGIA REVIEW

Gothic Press
Graywolf Press
GREEN MOUNTAINS REVIEW
Hippopotamus Press
HOME PLANET NEWS
Host Publications, Inc.
Interalia/Design Books
THE INTERNATIONAL FICTION REVIEW
THE IOWA REVIEW
IRISH LITERARY SUPPLEMENT
Jako Books
JAMES DICKEY REVIEW
JAMES JOYCE BROADSHEET
JOURNAL OF CANADIAN POETRY
JOURNAL OF REGIONAL CRITICISM
KALDRON, An International Journal Of Visual Poetry
KALEIDOSCOPE: Exploring the Experience of Disability
    through Literature & the Fine Arts
THE KENYON REVIEW
LAKE EFFECT
LEFT CURVE
Library Juice Press
LIFTOUTS
Limelight Editions
LINQ
LITERARY IMAGINATION: The Review of the Associa-
    tion of Literary Scholars and Critics
LITERARY MAGAZINE REVIEW
Litwin Books
Lord John Press
THE LUMMOX JOURNAL
MAGNET MAGAZINE
Maisonneuve Press
McPherson & Company Publishers
MEAT: A Journal of Writing and Materiality
Menard Press
MID-AMERICAN REVIEW
THE MIDWEST QUARTERLY
Miskwabik Press
Moonrise Press
MUDLARK
Myriad Press
NEROUP REVIEW
NEW AMERICAN IMAGIST
THE NEW ENGLAND QUARTERLY
New Falcon Publications
THE NEW RENAISSANCE, an international magazine of
    ideas & opinions, emphasizing literature & the arts
NORTH DAKOTA QUARTERLY
North Stone Editions
NOUN VS. VERB
NOVA EXPRESS
Open Wide Books
OTHER INVESTIGATIONS
OUTER-ART
OUTPOSTS POETRY QUARTERLY
Passeggiata Press, Inc.
PASSION
PIG IRON
PLOUGHSHARES
POEMELEON: A Journal of Poetry
POETRY FLASH
THE POETRY MISCELLANY
POETRYREPAIRS: Contemporary International Poetry
THE PRAIRIE JOURNAL OF CANADIAN LITERATURE
Prairie Journal Press
Press Here
PSYCHE
Psychedelic Literature
Pyncheon House
Quale Press
QUARTER AFTER EIGHT
Quarterly Committee of Queen's University
QUEEN'S QUARTERLY: A Canadian Review
RARITAN: A Quarterly Review
RATTAPALLAX
REPRESENTATIONS
Ronsdale Press

Rowhouse Press
The Runaway Spoon Press
Sage Hill Press
SALMAGUNDI
SCRIVENER
SENECA REVIEW
SEWANEE REVIEW
THE SHAKESPEARE NEWSLETTER
SHORT FUSE
Sligo Press
SMARTISH PACE
SOLO CAFE
SOUTH DAKOTA REVIEW
SOUTHERN HUMANITIES REVIEW
THE SOUTHERN QUARTERLY: A Journal of the Arts in
    the South
SPILLWAY
STORMWARNING!
Strata Publishing, Inc.
Sherwood Sugden & Company, Publishers
SYMPLOKE: A Journal for the Intermingling of Literary,
    Cultural and Theoretical Scholarship
Talisman House, Publishers
TEARS IN THE FENCE
TELOS
Telos Press
THALIA: Studies in Literary Humor
13TH MOON
THE THREEPENNY REVIEW
TORRE DE PAPEL
TSAR Publications
TUNDRA
Turnstone Press
UND Press
UNDERSTANDING MAGAZINE
University of Arkansas Press
University of Chicago Press
University of Massachusetts Press
University of Tampa Press
Vanderbilt University Press
VIVIPAROUS BLENNY
THE WALLACE STEVENS JOURNAL
WALT WHITMAN QUARTERLY REVIEW
Wellington House Publishing Company
WEST COAST LINE: A Journal of Contemporary Writing
    and Criticism
WILLOW SPRINGS
THE WORCESTER REVIEW
Wordwrights Canada
WRITER'S CHRONICLE
WSQ (formerly WOMEN'S STUDIES QUARTERLY)
THE YALE REVIEW
ZAWP
Zoo Press

CRYSTALS

Cuore Libre Publishing
ELEMENTS
Granite Publishing Group
Intuitive Moon Media
L&L Dreamspell
One Spirit Press
Three Pyramids Publishing

CUBA

A Midsummer Night's Press
Pangaea
Pathfinder Press
Plank Road Publishing
Smyrna Press
TOUCHSTONE

CULTS

BLACK BOOK PRESS: The Poetry Zine id
BOULDER HERETIC
Dwarf Lion Press
firefall editions
MYSTERY ISLAND MAGAZINE

Mystery Island Publications
NATURALLY
OFFICE NUMBER ONE
White Cliffs Media, Inc.
White Crosslet Publishing Co

CULTURE

AERIAL
AFTERIMAGE
Alaska Native Language Center
ARC
Archer Books
Ariko Publications
ARTS & LETTERS: Journal of Contemporary Culture
Balcony Media, Inc.
Bay Press
Birch Brook Press
BLACK BOOK PRESS: The Poetry Zine id
Black Lawrence Press
BLUE COLLAR REVIEW
Blue Lupin Press
BOOK/MARK QUARTERLY REVIEW
THE BOOMERPHILE
Borealis Press Limited
BOSTON REVIEW
BRIDGES: An Interdisciplinary Journal of Theology,
   Philosophy, History, and Science
CAUSE & EFFECT MAGAZINE
Cave Hollow Press
Chandler & Sharp Publishers, Inc.
THE CHARIOTEER
Chax Press
CHILDREN, CHURCHES AND DADDIES, A Non
   Religious, Non Familial Literary Magazine
CONTEXTS: UNDERSTANDING PEOPLE IN THEIR
   SOCIAL WORLDS
CORONA
Coteau Books
Cotton Tree Press
Crescent Moon
Culturelink Press
Dawn Sign Press
DESCANT
DESIRE
THE DIRTY GOAT
DOWN IN THE DIRT LITERARY MAGAZINE, the prose
   & poetry magazine revealing all your dirty little secrets
Down There Press
Dumouriez Publishing
THE EAST HAWAII OBSERVER
East West Discovery Press
EbonyEnergy Publishing, Inc.
ECOTONE: Reimagining Place
Encounter Books
THE ENGLISH CLARION
Espretto
Etched Press
Everflowing Publications
FACES: People, Places, and Culture
Falls Media
Five Fingers Press
FIVE FINGERS REVIEW
Florida Academic Press
FREEDOM AND STRENGTH PRESS FORUM
FULLOSIA PRESS
GASTRONOMICA: The Journal of Food and Culture
THE GEORGIA REVIEW
GREEN ANARCHY
GREEN MOUNTAINS REVIEW
Grey Sparrow Press
Heartsong Books
HISTORY OF INTELLECTUAL CULTURE
Hope Publishing House
Host Publications, Inc.
Ika, LLC
INKY TRAIL NEWS
Insight Press
Intercultural Press, Inc.

INTERCULTURE
Interlink Publishing Group, Inc.
IT'S JUST THIS LITTLE CHROMIUM SWITCH HERE
Jako Books
Kakibubu Media Limited
KALDRON, An International Journal Of Visual Poetry
THE KENYON REVIEW
KMT, A Modern Journal of Ancient Egypt
Kodiak Media Group
La Alameda Press
LAKE SUPERIOR MAGAZINE
The Leaping Frog Press
LEFT CURVE
Libertas Press, LLC.
LifeCircle Press
LO STRANIERO: The Stranger, Der Fremde, L'Etranger
LPD Press
LULLWATER REVIEW
Margaret Media, Inc.
Mehring Books, Inc.
Mercer University Press
Middleway Press
Missing Spoke Press
Moonrise Press
Mountainside Press
MUSE: A Quarterly Journal of The Lit
Myriad Press
NATURALLY
THE NEW ENGLAND QUARTERLY
NEW ENGLAND REVIEW
NEWS FROM NATIVE CALIFORNIA
NORTH DAKOTA QUARTERLY
NORTHWEST REVIEW
NOVA RELIGIO
Origin Press
OTHER INVESTIGATIONS
OUT YOUR BACKDOOR: The Magazine of Do-It-
   Yourself Adventure and Homegrown Culture
P.R.A. Publishing
PAGAN AMERICA
Partisan Press
PASSION
Pearl's Book'em Publisher
PIG IRON
PIG IRON
PLAIN BROWN WRAPPER (PBW)
Pleasure Boat Studio: A Literary Press (including imprints
   Caravel Books and Aequitas Books, and the division
   Empty Bowl Press)
POETRYREPAIRS: Contemporary International Poetry
Pogo Press, Incorporated
POINT OF CONTACT, The Journal of Verbal & Visual
   Arts
QUARTER AFTER EIGHT
Rapacious Press
RELIGION & AMERICAN CULTURE
REPRESENTATIONS
RIVET MAGAZINE
Roaring Lion Publishing
Rock Spring Press Inc.
SALMAGUNDI
Santa Monica Press
Scars Publications
School for Advanced Research Press
SCHUYLKILL VALLEY JOURNAL
SeaCrab Publishing
Sentient Publications, LLC
SIGNALS
Small Helm Press
Soft Skull Press
SONG OF THE SAN JOAQUIN
Speck Press
SPECS
SPOTops Books
Stardate Publishing Company
SYMPLOKE: A Journal for the Intermingling of Literary,
   Cultural and Theoretical Scholarship
THE TABBY: A CHRONICLE OF THE ARTS AND

CRAFTS MOVEMENT
Telos Press
Thirdeye Publications
TOUCHSTONE
Two Eagles Press International
UND Press
UTNE READER
VARIOUS ARTISTS
THE VIRGINIA QUARTERLY REVIEW
VIVIPAROUS BLENNY
THE WALLACE STEVENS JOURNAL
Whelks Walk Press
WISCONSIN ACADEMY REVIEW
XCP: CROSS-CULTURAL POETICS

CURRENT AFFAIRS

Archer Books
Bancroft Press
Bluestocking Press
Bonus Books, Inc.
BOOK/MARK QUARTERLY REVIEW
Caribbean Books-Panama
CAUSE & EFFECT MAGAZINE
Clarity Press, Inc.
CONSCIENCE: The Newsjournal of Catholic Opinion
Crandall, Dostie & Douglass Books, Inc.
Culturelink Press
Elderberry Press, Inc.
Encounter Books
Florida Academic Press
THE FREEFALL REVIEW
GREEN ANARCHY
Ho Logos Press
IN OUR OWN WORDS
Jako Books
Libertas Press, LLC.
Missing Spoke Press
NAMBLA BULLETIN
National Writers Press
THE NEW RENAISSANCE, an international magazine of ideas & opinions, emphasizing literature & the arts
NEW VERSE NEWS, THE
Niba Media Group, LLC
Nonetheless Press
Paladin Media Group
Pathfinder Press
Poptritus Press
THE PUBLIC EYE
THE QUIET FEATHER
Sentient Publications, LLC
Set Sail Productions, LLC
STORMWARNING!
TELOS
TOUCHSTONE
University of Massachusetts Press
UTNE READER
THE VIRGINIA QUARTERLY REVIEW

DADA

AD/VANCE
AK Press
American Canadian Publishers, Inc.
THE AMERICAN DRIVEL REVIEW
Androgyne Books
Arjuna Library Press
Asylum Arts
Bad Noise Productions
BANANA RAG
Black Oak Press
BLADES
BUST DOWN THE DOOR AND EAT ALL THE CHICKENS: A Journal of Absurd and Surreal Fiction
Chax Press
CHILDREN, CHURCHES AND DADDIES, A Non Religious, Non Familial Literary Magazine
Enigmatic Ink
FAT TUESDAY
FROZEN WAFFLES

Frozen Waffles Press/Shattered Sidewalks Press; 45th Century Chapbooks
GRAMMAR CRISIS
HEELTAP/Pariah Press
Highest Hurdle Press
Host Publications, Inc.
JACK MACKEREL MAGAZINE
JOURNAL OF REGIONAL CRITICISM
KALDRON, An International Journal Of Visual Poetry
LIGHTWORKS MAGAZINE
LOST GENERATION JOURNAL
Luna Bisonte Prods
Lunar Offensive Publications
Miskwabik Press
THE NEO-COMINTERN
NEROUP REVIEW
NEW MUSE OF CONTEMPT
North Stone Editions
Pariah Press
Pathwise Press
PAVEMENT SAW
Pavement Saw Press
Phrygian Press
PIG IRON
Pig Iron Press
PLAIN BROWN WRAPPER (PBW)
Rowhouse Press
Savant Garde Workshop
Shangri-La Publications
SHATTERED WIG REVIEW
SHORT FUSE
SIDE OF GRITS
Silenced Press
Starcherone Books
Tuvela Press
Twisted Spoon Press
VIVIPAROUS BLENNY
VOX Press
Water Mark of Lyons PPP: papers press and permaculture
White Crosslet Publishing Co
X-PERI: Experimental Journal
ZYX

DANCE

AFRICAN AMERICAN REVIEW
Amherst Writers & Artists Press, Inc.
Emrys Press
Everflowing Publications
Ibexa Press
IMAGE: ART, FAITH, MYSTERY
JACK MACKEREL MAGAZINE
Life Energy Media
Limelight Editions
Miskwabik Press
Plank Road Publishing
Ragamuffin Heart Publishing
Rowhouse Press
SALMAGUNDI
Thirteen Colonies Press

DANISH

ABSINTHE: New European Writing
BeachSide Press
Blue Dolphin Publishing, Inc.

DEATH & DYING

ANHEDONIA
Bad Noise Productions
Disparate Voices
DTS Group, Inc.
Gingerbread House
GRAMMAR CRISIS
HEALMB Publishing
Himalayan Institute Press
Lion's Den Publishing
March Books
Murder Slim Press
S4N Books

662

THE SAVAGE KICK LITERARY MAGAZINE
Sound Enterprises Publishing

AUGUST DERLETH

Three Dog Press
Zirlinson Publishing

DESIGN

Aegean Publishing Company
Allworth Press
APOSTROPHE: USCB Journal of the Arts
ART BUREAU
Art of Living, PrimaMedia,Inc
Balcony Media, Inc.
Banana Productions
Ceres Press
Cuore Libre Publishing
DOLLS UNITED INTERACTIVE MAGAZINE
ENVIRONMENTAL & ARCHITECTURAL PHENOMEN-
    OLOGY NEWSLETTER
Hunter Publishing Corporation
Ibexa Press
INDUSTRY MINNE-ZINE
Interalia/Design Books
KALDRON, An International Journal Of Visual Poetry
OUT YOUR BACKDOOR: The Magazine of Do-It-
    Yourself Adventure and Homegrown Culture
PIG IRON
Poltroon Press
SCULPTURAL PURSUIT MAGAZINE
Stemmer House Publishers, Inc.
Three Bean Press
Tuns Press
Zirlinson Publishing

DESKTOP PUBLISHING

Allworth Press
Brenner Information Group
Chicago Spectrum Press
CKO UPDATE
COOK PARTNERS
Disparate Voices
Equine Graphics Publishing Group: New Concord Press,
    SmallHorse Press, SunDrop
NEW VOICES REVISITED: Poetry, Contests and Short
    Stories.
VOICE(S)
WRITERS' JOURNAL
Zirlinson Publishing

DIARIES

BLACK BOOK PRESS: The Poetry Zine id
Bloated Toe Publishing
Burd Street Press
Arthur H. Clark Co.
Disparate Voices
Impassio Press
In Between Books
KESTREL: A Journal of Literature and Art
Leaf Garden Press
LEO Productions LLC.
Magic Circle Press
THE ORPHAN LEAF REVIEW
OVERLAND JOURNAL
PLAIN BROWN WRAPPER (PBW)
THE QUILLDRIVER
SPINNINGS...INTENSE TALES OF LIFE MAGAZINE
The True Bill Press
VOX Press
Youthful Wisdom Press

CHARLES DICKENS

THE ENGLISH CLARION
The True Bill Press
Whitston Publishing Co.

JAMES DICKEY

JAMES DICKEY REVIEW

EMILY DICKINSON

BIBLIOPHILOS
Chatterley Press International
Crescent Moon
EPIPHANY, A Literary Journal
Moonrise Press
NEW VOICES REVISITED: Poetry, Contests and Short
    Stories.
PASSION
Vulgar Marsala Press
Whitston Publishing Co.

DICTIONARIES

The Bess Press
Celo Valley Books
Library Juice Press
Litwin Books
Maledicta Press
Malki Museum Press
Minnesota Historical Society Press
Mondial
Rodnik Publishing Co.
Sunbelt Publications
Velazquez Press

DINING, RESTAURANTS

The Bess Press
Callawind Publications / Custom Cookbooks / Children's
    Books
Lazywood Press
MY TABLE: Houston's Dining Magazine
NIGHTLIFE MAGAZINE
NOLA-MAGICK Press
Red Rock Press
Vehicule Press
WORLD POETRY SHOWCASE
Yellowstone Publishing, LLC

DISABLED

Alpine Guild, Inc.
Brain Injury Success Books
Brookline Books
Future Horizons, Inc.
HEARING HEALTH
KALEIDOSCOPE: Exploring the Experience of Disability
    through Literature & the Fine Arts
Kelsey St. Press
Kodiak Media Group
Loving Healing Press, Inc.
Lucky Press, LLC
Massey-Reyner Publishing
MOUTH: Voice of the Dis-Labeled Nation
NEW VOICES REVISITED: Poetry, Contests and Short
    Stories.
The Place In The Woods
POETRYREPAIRS: Contemporary International Poetry
Re-invention UK Ltd
Vanguard Press
Vestibular Disorders Association
VOX Press
Youthful Wisdom Press

DISEASE

BELLEVUE LITERARY REVIEW
Carolina Wren Press
Flowerfield Enterprises, LLC
THE HEALTH JOURNALS
Hunter House Inc., Publishers
Kali Press
Lemon Grove Press
Loving Healing Press, Inc.
MEDICAL HISTORY
MOUTH: Voice of the Dis-Labeled Nation
Nushape Publication
OPEN MINDS QUARTERLY
Sound Enterprises Publishing
Vanguard Press

Vestibular Disorders Association
Wellcome Trust Centre for the History of Medicine at UCL

DISNEY

BearManor Media
CELLAR
THE DUCKBURG TIMES
The Intrepid Traveler
Tomart Publications

DIVORCE

Brick Road Poetry Press
Disparate Voices
Fruitbearer Publishing, LLC
HAMPTON ROADS HEALTH JOURNAL
HEALMB Publishing
THE HEALTH JOURNALS
Impact Publishers, Inc.
InsideOut Press
Jalmar Press/Innerchoice Publishing
MCM Entertainment, Inc. Publishing Division
Mo'omana'o Press
Nolo Press Occidental
Platinum One Publishing
Poor Richard's Press
River Press
Women and Men Books

DRAMA

ALASKA QUARTERLY REVIEW
THE ALLEGHENY REVIEW
ANQ: A Quarterly Journal of Short Articles, Notes, and
    Reviews
APOSTROPHE: USCB Journal of the Arts
Arjuna Library Press
Artamo Press
Arte Publico Press
ARTS & LETTERS: Journal of Contemporary Culture
Asylum Arts
Athanata Arts, Ltd.
ATLANTIC PACIFIC PRESS
The B & R Samizdat Express
BATHTUB GIN
Bilingual Review Press
Black Dress Press
BOMB MAGAZINE
Borealis Press Limited
Branden Books
THE BROADKILL REVIEW: A Journal of Literature
C & M Online Media Inc.
CAPCAT
CONCEIT MAGAZINE
Cottonwood Press, Inc.
Dawn Sign Press
DESCANT
THE DIRTY GOAT
Dramaline Publications
Empire Publishing Service
ENGLISH LITERATURE IN TRANSITION, 1880-1920
THE EUGENE O'NEILL REVIEW
EVANSVILLE REVIEW
Everflowing Publications
The Fiction Works
Gallopade International
HARVARD REVIEW
Host Publications, Inc.
IRISH LITERARY SUPPLEMENT
ISTANBUL LITERARY REVIEW
Jullundur Press
THE KENYON REVIEW
LEO Productions LLC.
Les Figues Press
LINQ
LITERARY HOUSE REVIEW
LITTLE BALKANS REVIEW
Marathon International Book Company
MCM Entertainment, Inc. Publishing Division
Midmarch Arts Press

MUSE: A Quarterly Journal of The Lit
New Concept Press
NEW ENGLAND REVIEW
New Sins Press
Nightsun Books
Northwestern University Press
OBSIDIAN III: Literature in the African Diaspora
THE PACIFIC REVIEW
Parthian
Passeggiata Press, Inc.
Phi-Psi Publishers
Platinum One Publishing
Players Press, Inc.
POEMS & PLAYS
PRISM INTERNATIONAL
PublishAmerica, LLLP.
Red Dust
RED WHEELBARROW
REVERIE: MIDWEST AFRICAN AMERICAN LITERA-
    TURE
Ridgeway Press of Michigan
RIVER POETS JOURNAL
THE ROCKFORD REVIEW
Ronsdale Press
The Runaway Spoon Press
St. Andrews College Press
Savant Garde Workshop
THE SHAKESPEARE NEWSLETTER
Smyrna Press
SOJOURN: A Journal of the Arts
Spectrum Productions
SPINNINGS...INTENSE TALES OF LIFE MAGAZINE
STRUGGLE: A Magazine of Proletarian Revolutionary
    Literature
SYCAMORE REVIEW
Synergetic Press
Syukhtun Editions
Ten Penny Players, Inc.
TnT Classic Books
University of Tampa Press
URBAN REFLECTIONS MAGAZINE
The WhaleInn Publishing House (1998)
White Crosslet Publishing Co
Wordsonthestreet
Xenos Books
Zoo Press

DREAMS

Asylum Arts
THE BELTANE PAPERS: A Journal of Women's
    Mysteries
CONCEIT MAGAZINE
DIET SOAP
DREAM FANTASY INTERNATIONAL
DREAM NETWORK
Enigmatic Ink
THE HEALTH JOURNALS
Iconoclast Press
In Between Books
Iniquity Press/Vendetta Books
JAVELINA BI-MONTHLY
L&L Dreamspell
LEAF GARDEN
The Leaping Frog Press
Luminous Epinoia Press
Lunar Offensive Publications
Perrin Press
PLAIN BROWN WRAPPER (PBW)
Poptritus Press
RALPH'S REVIEW
SHAMAN'S DRUM: A Journal of Experiential Shamanism
SHORT FUSE
SOM Publishing, division of School of Metaphysics
STARNOTES
Three Pyramids Publishing
THRESHOLDS JOURNAL
Water Mark of Lyons PPP: papers press and permaculture
Zumaya Publications LLC

664

DRUGS

Addicus Books, Inc.
Bad Noise Productions
BLACK BOOK PRESS: The Poetry Zine id
CAUSE & EFFECT MAGAZINE
Consumer Press
Devil Mountain Books
Global Options
GRAMMAR CRISIS
GRAY AREAS
Haight-Ashbury Publications
Health Press NA Inc.
Iniquity Press/Vendetta Books
Jalmar Press/Innerchoice Publishing
JOURNAL OF PSYCHOACTIVE DRUGS
March Books
Meek Publishing
Midnight Whistler Publishers
Mountain Media
Murder Slim Press
New Moon Publishing, Inc.
Paladin Enterprises, Inc.
Poptritus Press
Red Alder Books
Red Eye Press
RED FEZ ENTERTAINMENT
THE SAVAGE KICK LITERARY MAGAZINE
SOCIAL JUSTICE: A JOURNAL OF CRIME, CONFLICT,
    & WORLD ORDER
Steel Balls Press
Van Cleave Publishing
Vanguard Press

BOB DYLAN

AMERICAN JONES BUILDING & MAINTENANCE
GRAY AREAS
WHITE FUNGUS

EARTH, NATURAL HISTORY

ADIRONDAC
Adirondack Mountain Club, Inc.
Alpine Publications, Inc.
America West Publishers
AMERICAN FORESTS
AMERICAN HIKER
American Hiking Society
AQUATERRA, METAECOLOGY & CULTURE
AzurAlive
Beacon Press
Birdsong Books
Black Dome Press Corp.
THE BLOOMSBURY REVIEW
Camino Bay Books
Caribbean Books-Panama
Chelsea Green Publishing Company
Clover Park Press
Dawn Publications
Downeast Books
ETC Publications
EXIT 13 MAGAZINE
Flowerfield Enterprises, LLC
Fulcrum, Inc.
GREEN ANARCHY
Heartsong Books
Heyday Books
Island Press
The Latona Press
Maisonneuve Press
Malki Museum Press
MANOA: A Pacific Journal of International Writing
Milkweed Editions
Miskwabik Press
Mountain Press Publishing Co.
The Narrative Press
Native West Press
Naturegraph Publishers
NEROUP REVIEW

Ocean Publishing
Oregon State University Press
Pangaea
Penthe Publishing
Quarterly Committee of Queen's University
QUEEN'S QUARTERLY: A Canadian Review
RFF Press / Resources for the Future
Rock Spring Press Inc.
Sand River Press
Sasquatch Books
Scientia Publishing, LLC
Genny Smith Books
Gibbs Smith, Publisher
SNOWY EGRET
Stemmer House Publishers, Inc.
Sunbelt Publications
Synergetic Press
Timberline Press
TOUCHSTONE
University of Chicago Press
UnKnownTruths.com Publishing Company
Wood Thrush Books
Zagier & Urruty Publications

EASTERN EUROPE

Cross-Cultural Communications
THE DIRTY GOAT
Florida Academic Press
Moonrise Press
NATURALLY
Northern Illinois University Press
Northwestern University Press

ECOLOGY, FOODS

ADIRONDAC
Anomaly Press
AQUATERRA, METAECOLOGY & CULTURE
Art of Living, PrimaMedia,Inc
Ash Tree Publishing
AzurAlive
Beacon Press
Bear & Company
Beekman Books, Inc.
Black Rose Books Ltd.
THE BLOOMSBURY REVIEW
Blue Dolphin Publishing, Inc.
Cassandra Press, Inc.
Chelsea Green Publishing Company
City Lights Books
DWELLING PORTABLY
ENVIRONMENTAL & ARCHITECTURAL PHENOMEN-
    OLOGY NEWSLETTER
ETC Publications
Fine Tooth Press
Flowerfield Enterprises, LLC
Garden House Press
GASTRONOMICA: The Journal of Food and Culture
Granite Publishing Group
Island Press
Keiki O Ka Aina Press
La Alameda Press
The Latona Press
Life Media
MACROBIOTICS TODAY
Malki Museum Press
McBooks Press, Inc.
Miskwabik Press
Mo'omana'o Press
NATURAL LIFE
NEROUP REVIEW
NEW ENVIRONMENT BULLETIN
George Ohsawa Macrobiotic Foundation
Oregon State University Press
OUT OF LINE
OUT YOUR BACKDOOR: The Magazine of Do-It-
    Yourself Adventure and Homegrown Culture
Outrider Press
Penthe Publishing

Petroglyph Press, Ltd.
Portal Press
Progressive Press; Tree of Life Publications
RFF Press / Resources for the Future
Rock Spring Press Inc.
Scientia Publishing, LLC
Shared Roads Press
Strawberry Patchworks
Titlewaves Publishing; Writers Direct
TURNING THE TIDE: Journal of Anti-Racist Action,
    Research & Education
TURNING WHEEL
United Lumbee Nation
UNITED LUMBEE NATION TIMES
Upper Access Inc. Book Publishers
VEGETARIAN JOURNAL
The Vegetarian Resource Group
Water Mark of Lyons PPP: papers press and permaculture
Wide World Publishing

EDITING

Brenner Information Group
C&R Press
CANADIAN POETRY
THE CAROUSEL
COOK PARTNERS
Cooper Hill Press
Strata Publishing, Inc.
Three Dog Press
WRITER'S CHRONICLE
WRITERS' JOURNAL

EDUCATION

AARO Publishing,Inc.
Absey & Co.
Academic Innovations
Adirondack Mountain Club, Inc.
Advanced Learning Press
African American Images
AFRICAN AMERICAN REVIEW
Alaska Native Language Center
Alpine Guild, Inc.
AltaMira Press
ALTERNATIVE EDUCATION RESOURCE ORGANIZA-
    TION
THE AMERICAN DISSIDENT
Anderson Publishing; also RC Anderson Books
Andros Books
Applied Probability Trust
AQUATERRA, METAECOLOGY & CULTURE
Ash Lad Press
Atlantic Publishing Group, Inc.
ATLANTIS: A Women's Studies Journal/Revue d'etudes
    sur les femmes
Authentic Publishing LLC
Bayhampton Publications
THE BEACON: Journal of Special Education Law &
    Practice
Beekman Books, Inc.
BILINGUAL REVIEW/Revista Bilingue
Black Forest Press and The Tennessee Publishing House
Blue Dolphin Publishing, Inc.
BLUE MOUNTAIN
Books for All Times, Inc.
Branden Books
Break Free Publishing
Brook Farm Books
Brookline Books
Building Blocks Press
Caddo Gap Press
Canadian Educators' Press
Center for Thanatology Research & Education, Inc.
Church Leadership Library (US Office)
THE CLASSICAL OUTLOOK
Clearwater Publishing Co.
Clover Valley Press, LLC
Community Service, Inc.
Continuing Education Press

Cooper Hill Press
CORRECTIONS TODAY
Cottonwood Press, Inc.
Council For Indian Education
Creative Creations Consulting Publishing Company
Crystal Press
D.B.A. Books
Dawn Publications
Dawn Sign Press
DESIRE
DREAM NETWORK
Dream Publishing Co.
dreamslaughter
East West Discovery Press
EDUCATION IN FOCUS
EDUCATIONAL FOUNDATIONS
EDUCATIONAL LEADERSHIP & ADMINISTRATION
Empire Publishing Service
ETC Publications
EXCEPTIONALITY EDUCATION CANADA
The Feminist Press at the City University of New York
Finney Company, Inc.
First Journey Publishing Company
Flowerfield Enterprises, LLC
Fountain Publisher Limited
Friendly Oaks Publications
Front Row Experience
Fulcrum, Inc.
Gallaudet University Press
Gallopade International
Garden House Press
Global Learning
Gryphon House, Inc.
Guarionex Press Ltd.
Harbor House Law Press, Inc.
The Haworth Press
THE HEALTH JOURNALS
Heartsong Books
Higganum Hill Books
History Compass, LLC
Hoover Institution Press
Hunter House Inc., Publishers
Hunter Publishing Corporation
ILLUMINATIONS LITERARY JOURNAL
Inspiring Teachers Publishing, Inc.
Intercultural Press, Inc.
INTERCULTURE
INTERNATIONAL ELECTRONIC JOURNAL FOR LEA-
    DERSHIP IN LEARNING
INTERNATIONAL JOURNAL OF EDUCATIONAL PO-
    LICY, RESEARCH, AND PRACTICE: RECONCEP-
    TUALIZING CHILDHOOD STUDIES
IRIS: A Journal About Women
ISSUES IN TEACHER EDUCATION
Jalmar Press/Innerchoice Publishing
Jamenair Ltd.
JOURNAL OF CURRICULUM THEORIZING
JOURNAL OF THOUGHT
JUNIOR STORYTELLER
Just Sisters Publications
Kakibubu Media Limited
Keiki O Ka Aina Press
Kettering Foundation Press
KETTERING REVIEW
THE KIDS' STORYTELLING CLUB WEBSITE
Knowledge Concepts Publishing
Kodiak Media Group
Lamp Light Press
Life Media
LifeCircle Press
Lightning Bug Learning Press
Listening Voice Media Ltd
THE LONG TERM VIEW: A Journal of Informed Opinion
LrnIT Publishing Div. LRNIT CORPORATION
THE MAD HATTER
The Madson Group, Inc.
Magnifico Publications
Maisonneuve Press

Mapletree Publishing Company
Massey-Reyner Publishing
MATHEMATICAL SPECTRUM
Maupin House Publishing, Inc.
Middleway Press
Midnight Whistler Publishers
Mills Custom Services Publishing
Mind Power Publishing
Moo-Cow Fan Club
Morgen Publishing Incorporated
MULTICULTURAL EDUCATION
NATURAL LIFE
New Day Publishing, Inc.
NEW SOLUTIONS
New World Press, Inc
NOTES AND ABSTRACTS IN AMERICAN AND INTERNATIONAL EDUCATION
Nova Press
NSR Publications
Nunciata
Open Court Publishing Company
Open University of America Press
OUR SCHOOLS/OUR SELVES
PALO ALTO REVIEW
PARENTEACHER MAGAZINE
Parenting Press, Inc.
Parkway Publishers, Inc.
The Place In The Woods
Plank Road Publishing
Players Press, Inc.
The Press at Foggy Bottom
PSYCHE
Quarterly Committee of Queen's University
QUEEN'S QUARTERLY: A Canadian Review
Rada Press, Inc.
Raven Rocks Press
Reading Connections
Redwood Creek Publishing
Reference Service Press
REPORTS OF THE NATIONAL CENTER FOR SCIENCE EDUCATION
RESOURCES FOR FEMINIST RESEARCH/DOCUMEN-TATION SUR LA RECHERCHE FEMINISTE
Rolling Hills Publishing
Rowan Mountain Press
Sagamore Publishing
Scentouri, Publishing Division
Sea Fog Press
SENSATIONS MAGAZINE
Sentient Publications, LLC
SKEPTICAL INQUIRER
Small Helm Press
Smith-Johnson Publisher
THE SOCIOLOGICAL QUARTERLY
Socratic Consulting Group
Soto Publishing Company
The Speech Bin, Inc.
Stardate Publishing Company
STONE SOUP, The Magazine By Young Writers and Artists
Storycraft Publishing
Success Publishing
Sherwood Sugden & Company, Publishers
SUMMER ACADEME: A Journal of Higher Education
TABOO: Journal of Education & Culture
TEACHER EDUCATION QUARTERLY
TEACHERS & WRITERS
Teachers & Writers Collaborative
Thatch Tree Publications
THRESHOLDS JOURNAL
TMC Books LLC
TOUCHSTONE
Trickle Creek Books
TRUTH SEEKER
TURNING WHEEL
UBC Press
UNITED LUMBEE NATION TIMES
United Nations University Press

University of Chicago Press
Utah State University Press
VanderWyk & Burnham
Velazquez Press
VITAE SCHOLASTICAE: The Journal of Educational Biography
Wellington House Publishing Company
WeWrite LLC
Wordsonthestreet
WRITER'S CHRONICLE
WSQ (formerly WOMEN'S STUDIES QUARTERLY)

EGYPT

New World Press, Inc

ELECTRONICS

AD/VANCE
Bancroft Press
BLK
BOMB MAGAZINE
CELLAR
Children Of Mary
CINEASTE MAGAZINE
Crescent Moon
dbS Productions
FIDELIS ET VERUS
Future Horizons, Inc.
JACK MACKEREL MAGAZINE
LIGHTWORKS MAGAZINE
Midmarch Arts Press
MOBILE BEAT: The Mobile Entertainer's Magazine
Norton Coker Press
PASSION
PLAIN BROWN WRAPPER (PBW)
POINT OF CONTACT, The Journal of Verbal & Visual Arts
Rowhouse Press
SALMAGUNDI
SALMAGUNDI
SIGNALS
Sonoran Publishing
SPECS
Theytus Books Ltd.
THE THREEPENNY REVIEW

EMPLOYMENT

Aspen Mountain Publishing
Atlantic Publishing Group, Inc.
Black Forest Press and The Tennessee Publishing House
BLUE COLLAR REVIEW
Bookhaven Press, LLC
THE CARETAKER GAZETTE
CORRECTIONS TODAY
Finney Company, Inc.
Galen Press, Ltd.
Global Sports Productions, Ltd.
Inkwater Press
Jamenair Ltd.
McGavick Field Publishing
New Win Publishing

ENERGY

Accendo Publishing
Adams-Blake Publishing
AQUATERRA, METAECOLOGY & CULTURE
Blue Dolphin Publishing, Inc.
DWELLING PORTABLY
The Film Instruction Company of America
HIGH COUNTRY NEWS
Island Press
JOURNAL OF SCIENTIFIC EXPLORATION
Life Media
Luminous Epinoia Press
NEROUP REVIEW
NEW ENVIRONMENT BULLETIN
SO YOUNG!
Southwest Research and Information Center
The Utility Company LLC

VOICES FROM THE EARTH

ENGINEERING

A2Z Publications LLC
Adams-Blake Publishing
ADVANCES IN THE ASTRONAUTICAL SCIENCES
Aegean Publishing Company
AQUATERRA, METAECOLOGY & CULTURE
LrnIT Publishing Div. LRNIT CORPORATION
Muse World Media Group
New Knowledge Press
Quale Press
SCIENCE AND TECHNOLOGY
Smith-Johnson Publisher
Univelt, Inc.
Village Lane Press
Wind River Institute Press/Wind River Broadcasting

ENGLAND

BeachSide Press
BOGG: A Journal of Contemporary Writing
THE CANNON'S MOUTH
DWANG: Outsider poetry and prose
THE ENGLISH CLARION
Magnifico Publications
Moonrise Press
North Stone Editions
PULSAR POETRY WEBZINE
SeaCrab Publishing
Stewart Publishing & Printing
Tangerine Press
Three Pyramids Publishing
The True Bill Press

ENGLISH

Absey & Co.
ANQ: A Quarterly Journal of Short Articles, Notes, and Reviews
APOSTROPHE: USCB Journal of the Arts
ATLANTIS: A Women's Studies Journal/Revue d'etudes sur les femmes
Bandanna Books
Borealis Press Limited
CANADIAN POETRY
THE CANNON'S MOUTH
Cantadora Press
THE CAROUSEL
Chatterley Press International
CIMARRON REVIEW
Clark-Nova Books
COGNITIO: A Graduate Humanities Journal
Cooper Hill Press
Cottonwood Press, Inc.
CREATIVE NONFICTION
THE DALHOUSIE REVIEW
THE DIRTY GOAT
THE ENGLISH CLARION
Fine Tooth Press
Flapjack Press
FULLOSIA PRESS
Galaxy Press
Gallaudet University Press
Gallopade International
Gingerbread House
Host Publications, Inc.
THE IOWA REVIEW
Listening Voice Media Ltd
LONE STARS MAGAZINE
LULLWATER REVIEW
Maupin House Publishing, Inc.
Mind Power Publishing
THE NEBRASKA REVIEW
THE NEW ENGLAND QUARTERLY
NEW VOICES REVISITED: Poetry, Contests and Short Stories.
Oyster River Press
Pearl's Book'em Publisher
Pennsylvania State University Press

THE PINCH
POINT OF CONTACT, The Journal of Verbal & Visual Arts
THE PRAIRIE JOURNAL OF CANADIAN LITERATURE
Prairie Journal Press
REPRESENTATIONS
RIVERBED HAIKU
Rodnik Publishing Co.
SALMAGUNDI
SCHUYLKILL VALLEY JOURNAL
SCRIVENER
SENSATIONS MAGAZINE
SEWANEE REVIEW
THE SHAKESPEARE NEWSLETTER
SHAW: THE ANNUAL OF BERNARD SHAW STUDIES
SPECS
Sherwood Sugden & Company, Publishers
SYCAMORE REVIEW
SYMPLOKE: A Journal for the Intermingling of Literary, Cultural and Theoretical Scholarship
Thatch Tree Publications
Thorp Springs Press
The True Bill Press
University of Tampa Press
Utah State University Press
Vanderbilt University Press
Whitston Publishing Co.
Wilde Publishing
THE YALE REVIEW

ENTERTAINMENT

AK Press
THE AMERICAN DRIVEL REVIEW
BANANA RAG
BEACHCOMBER MAGAZINE
BLK
THE BOOMERPHILE
Cave Hollow Press
Celebrity Profiles Publishing
Empire Publishing Service
Fotofolio, Inc.
IT'S JUST THIS LITTLE CHROMIUM SWITCH HERE
Juel House Publishers and Literary Services
Lake Claremont Press
MOBILE BEAT: The Mobile Entertainer's Magazine
MYSTERY ISLAND MAGAZINE
THE NEO-COMINTERN
NIGHTLIFE MAGAZINE
NIS America, Inc.
Open Horizons Publishing Company
The Passion Profit Company
Players Press, Inc.
SANDPOINT MAGAZINE
Santa Monica Press
SKYLINE LITERARY MAGAZINE
SP Turner Group
Stardate Publishing Company
Unlimited Publishing LLC
WORLD POETRY SHOWCASE

ENVIRONMENT

Act on Wisdom
ADIRONDAC
AK Press
ALTERNATIVE PRESS INDEX
AMERICAN FORESTS
AMERICAN HIKER
American Hiking Society
AMERICAN VEGAN
Art of Living, PrimaMedia,Inc
AzurAlive
Bauu Press
Bay Tree Publishing
THE BEAR DELUXE MAGAZINE
BLUE MOUNTAIN
BLUELINE
Bookhaven Press, LLC
Brave Ulysses Books

668

Brookview Press
CAPCAT
THE CARETAKER GAZETTE
Ceres Press
Cornell Maritime Press/Tidewater Publishers
THE CREAM CITY REVIEW
CROSSCURRENTS
Cuore Libre Publishing
CUTTHROAT, A JOURNAL OF THE ARTS
Dawn Publications
DWELLING PORTABLY
Ecopress, An Imprint of Finney Company
ECOTONE: Reimagining Place
ELECTRONIC GREEN JOURNAL
ENVIRONMENTAL & ARCHITECTURAL PHENOMEN-
    OLOGY NEWSLETTER
FOURTH WORLD REVIEW
THE FREEFALL REVIEW
FRIENDS OF PEACE PILGRIM
GREEN ANARCHY
Heartsong Books
HIGH COUNTRY NEWS
Hope Publishing House
Ice Cube Press
Island Press
Kakibubu Media Limited
Kali Press
Keokee Co. Publishing, Inc.
THE KERF
Kumarian Press
Laguna Wilderness Press
LAKE SUPERIOR MAGAZINE
Life Media
Lost Pond Press
LrnIT Publishing Div. LRNIT CORPORATION
MANOA: A Pacific Journal of International Writing
March Books
Milkweed Editions
NATURALLY
NEW ENVIRONMENT BULLETIN
New Victoria Publishers
NewSage Press
North Country Books, Inc.
Ocean Publishing
Partisan Press
PEACEWORK
Penthe Publishing
Pineapple Press, Inc.
Plain View Press
PLEASANT LIVING
Pleasure Boat Studio: A Literary Press (including imprints
    Caravel Books and Aequitas Books, and the division
    Empty Bowl Press)
Pruett Publishing Company
THE QUIET FEATHER
Raven Rocks Press
RED MARE
RFF Press / Resources for the Future
Rising Tide Press New Mexico
Rock Spring Press Inc.
Sagamore Publishing
Sage Hill Press
School for Advanced Research Press
Scientia Publishing, LLC
SEA KAYAKER
SHARE INTERNATIONAL
Gibbs Smith, Publisher
SOCIAL ANARCHISM: A Journal of Practice and Theory
SONG OF THE SAN JOAQUIN
South End Press
Southwest Research and Information Center
Square One Publishers, Inc.
Chuck Stewart
Texas Tech University Press
Tortuga Books
Trickle Creek Books
Truman State University Press
United Nations University Press

University of Akron Press
University of Calgary Press
University of Massachusetts Press
Upper Access Inc. Book Publishers
Utah State University Press
VOICES FROM THE EARTH
WASHINGTON TRAILS
Water Mark of Lyons PPP: papers press and permaculture
WAV MAGAZINE: Progressive Music Art Politics Culture
WEBER: The Contemporary West
WHAT IS ENLIGHTENMENT?
WHOLE TERRAIN - REFLECTIVE ENVIRONMENTAL
    PRACTICE
WILD DUCK REVIEW
Wind Eagle Press
WISCONSIN TRAILS

EROTICA

Abecedarian books, Inc.
ABRAMELIN: a Journal of Poetry and Magick
Accendo Publishing
Anderson Publishing; also RC Anderson Books
Asylum Arts
AXE FACTORY REVIEW
Bad Noise Productions
Bandanna Books
THE BOOMERPHILE
CAFE NOIR REVIEW
Creative Arts Book Company
Crystal Dreams Publishing
DARK GOTHIC RESURRECTED
DIET SOAP
Ephemera Bound Publishing
EROSHA
GLB Publishers
GRAMMAR CRISIS
Host Publications, Inc.
Jigsaw Press
L&L Dreamspell
LOVING MORE: New Models for Relationships
Lunar Offensive Publications
Lycanthrope Press
MIP Company
Mondial
Multi-Media Publications Inc.
New Victoria Publishers
Open Wide Books
OPEN WIDE MAGAZINE
Passion Power Press, Inc
PEMMICAN
PLAIN BROWN WRAPPER (PBW)
Pussywillow
Rapacious Press
Red Alder Books
Red Tiger Press
Re-invention UK Ltd
Santa Fe Writers Project
SHORT FUSE
Six Ft. Swells Press
Skyline Publications
SP Turner Group
SPINNINGS...INTENSE TALES OF LIFE MAGAZINE
Star Publish LLC
SUB-TERRAIN
Synergy Press
Triskelion Publishing
Twin Souls Publications
2L Publishing, LLC
URBAN REFLECTIONS MAGAZINE
Whiskey Creek Press
Zygote Publishing

ESSAYS

AERIAL
AGNI
ALASKA QUARTERLY REVIEW
Allbook Books
THE AMERICAN DISSIDENT

AMERICAN INDIAN CULTURE AND RESEARCH JOURNAL
American Indian Studies Center
AMERICAN JONES BUILDING & MAINTENANCE
AMERICAN LETTERS & COMMENTARY
AMERICAN LITERARY REVIEW
APPLE VALLEY REVIEW: A Journal of Contemporary Literature
ART:MAG
Artamo Press
ARTS & LETTERS: Journal of Contemporary Culture
Asylum Arts
AXE FACTORY REVIEW
THE BALTIMORE REVIEW
Bancroft Press
BATHTUB GIN
BEATLICK NEWS
BELLINGHAM REVIEW
THE BELTANE PAPERS: A Journal of Women's Mysteries
BIG MUDDY: Journal of the Mississippi River Valley
BITTER OLEANDER
BkMk Press
BLACK MAGNOLIAS LITERARY JOURNAL
BLACK WARRIOR REVIEW
BOGG: A Journal of Contemporary Writing
BORDERLANDS: Texas Poetry Review
Bordighera, Inc.
Brave Ulysses Books
BRILLIANT CORNERS: A Journal of Jazz & Literature
THE BROADKILL REVIEW: A Journal of Literature
Broken Shadow Publications
Brookview Press
Caketrain Journal and Press
Cantarabooks LLC
CERISE PRESS
CHANTEH, the Iranian Cross-Cultural Quarterly
CHAPMAN
Chelsea Green Publishing Company
CIMARRON REVIEW
Cleveland State Univ. Poetry Center
Clover Valley Press, LLC
Coffee House Press
COLORADO REVIEW
CONNECTICUT REVIEW
CONTRARY
COSMOPSIS QUARTERLY
Cotton Tree Press
THE CREAM CITY REVIEW
CREATIVE NONFICTION
Culturelink Press
Cynic Press
DESIRE
Devil Mountain Books
THE DIRTY GOAT
Paul Dry Books
Dwarf Lion Press
EASTGATE QUARTERLY REVIEW OF HYPERTEXT
ECOTONE: Reimagining Place
Edgewise Press
The Eighth Mountain Press
Elderberry Press, Inc.
Emrys Press
EPICENTER: A LITERARY MAGAZINE
EROSHA
EVANSVILLE REVIEW
Evening Street Press
EVENING STREET REVIEW
Five Fingers Press
FIVE FINGERS REVIEW
FLUENT ASCENSION
FOLIO: A Literary Journal of American University
FOURTH GENRE: EXPLORATIONS IN NONFICTION
THE FREEFALL REVIEW
THE GEORGIA REVIEW
THE GETTYSBURG REVIEW
Gival Press
GREEN ANARCHY

HARVARD REVIEW
HAWAI'I REVIEW
HAWAI'I PACIFIC REVIEW
HEAVEN BONE MAGAZINE
Heaven Bone Press
Helicon Nine Editions
Hidden Valley Farm, Publisher
Highest Hurdle Press
Host Publications, Inc.
Hotel des Bains Editions
IAMBS & TROCHEES
ICON
ICONOCLAST
ILLOGICAL MUSE
Imago Press
Immediate Direction Publications
Impassio Press
IMPress
Iniquity Press/Vendetta Books
INKY TRAIL NEWS
THE IOWA REVIEW
Iris Publishing Group, Inc (Iris Press / Tellico Books)
JAMES DICKEY REVIEW
THE JOURNAL
THE JOURNAL OF AFRICAN TRAVEL-WRITING
KALEIDOSCOPE: Exploring the Experience of Disability through Literature & the Fine Arts
KARAMU
THE KENYON REVIEW
KESTREL: A Journal of Literature and Art
Kilmog Press
THE LAUREL REVIEW
LEAF GARDEN
The Leaping Frog Press
THE LEDGE
LEFT CURVE
Libellum
Library Juice Press
LIGHT: The Quarterly of Light Verse
THE LISTENING EYE
LITERARY HOUSE REVIEW
LITERARY IMAGINATION: The Review of the Association of Literary Scholars and Critics
LITTLE BALKANS REVIEW
THE LOUISVILLE REVIEW
THE LUMMOX JOURNAL
Lummox Press
LUNGFULL! MAGAZINE
MacDonald/Sward Publishing Company
MAIN STREET RAG
MANY MOUNTAINS MOVING
McPherson & Company Publishers
THE MEADOW
MEAT: A Journal of Writing and Materiality
MELEE
MID-AMERICAN REVIEW
MIDNIGHT STREET
MINESHAFT
Missing Spoke Press
MISSISSIPPI CROW
Mountain State Press
MUDLARK
MUSE: A Quarterly Journal of The Lit
My Heart Yours Publishing
MY TABLE: Houston's Dining Magazine
MYSTERY ISLAND MAGAZINE
NATURAL BRIDGE
NEO: Literary Magazine
NEW DELTA REVIEW
THE NEW FORMALIST
NEW MEXICO POETRY REVIEW
THE NEW RENAISSANCE, an international magazine of ideas & opinions, emphasizing literature & the arts
New World Press, Inc
NORTH CAROLINA LITERARY REVIEW
NORTHWEST REVIEW
OFFICE NUMBER ONE
OPEN MINDS QUARTERLY

ORBIS
THE ORPHAN LEAF REVIEW
OTHER INVESTIGATIONS
OUTER-ART
Outrider Press
OYEZ REVIEW
PACIFIC COAST JOURNAL
PALO ALTO REVIEW
Panther Creek Press
PAPERPLATES
Paris Press
Passion Power Press, Inc
Pearl's Book'em Publisher
Pendragonian Publications
PENNY DREADFUL: Tales and Poems of Fantastic Terror
POEMELEON: A Journal of Poetry
POETICA MAGAZINE, Reflections of Jewish Thought
The Poetry Center
Pogo Press, Incorporated
Polar Bear & Company
Poptritus Press
PRAIRIE SCHOONER
PRESA
PRETEXT
PSYCHE
Punkin House Press
QUARTER AFTER EIGHT
RAIN TAXI REVIEW OF BOOKS
RAINBOW CURVE
RATTAPALLAX
Red Hen Press
RED WHEELBARROW
REFLECTIONS LITERARY JOURNAL
REVERIE: MIDWEST AFRICAN AMERICAN LITERA-
TURE
RIVER TEETH: A Journal of Nonfiction Narrative
RIVET MAGAZINE
SAGE OF CONSCIOUSNESS E-ZINE
Salt Publishing
SANDPOINT MAGAZINE
Sarabande Books
SCHUYLKILL VALLEY JOURNAL
SECRETUM MEUM MIHI
SENECA REVIEW
SEWANEE REVIEW
SHENANDOAH: The Washington and Lee University
Review
Sherman Asher Publishing
SHORT FUSE
The Smith (subsidiary of The Generalist Assn., Inc.)
SNREVIEW
SONGS OF INNOCENCE
SOUTH DAKOTA REVIEW
Southeast Missouri State University Press
SOUTHWEST REVIEW
SP QUILL MAGAZINE
The Spirit That Moves Us Press, Inc.
SPOUT
Spout Press
Steerforth Press, L.C.
SterlingHouse Publisher
STUDIO ONE
SUB-TERRAIN
THE SUN, A Magazine of Ideas
SunShine Press Publications, Inc.
SWINK
SYCAMORE REVIEW
THE TARPEIAN ROCK
THIRD COAST
THIRDEYE MAGAZINE
13TH MOON
Thunder Rain Publishing Corp.
TINY LIGHTS: A Journal of Personal Narrative
TURNROW
Twisted Spoon Press
Two-Handed Engine Press
University of Tampa Press
VALLUM: CONTEMPORARY POETRY

WEBER: The Contemporary West
The Wellsweep Press
WEST BRANCH
White Pine Press
WHOLE TERRAIN - REFLECTIVE ENVIRONMENTAL
PRACTICE
THE WILDWOOD READER
WILLOW SPRINGS
WISCONSIN TRAILS
Wood Thrush Books
WRITER'S CHRONICLE
Writers House Press
WSQ (formerly WOMEN'S STUDIES QUARTERLY)
XAVIER REVIEW
YUKHIKA—LATUHSE
Zirlinson Publishing

ETHICS

Aardvark Enterprises (Sole Proprietorship of J. Alvin
Speers)
Glen Allen Press
THE AMERICAN DISSIDENT
AMERICAN VEGAN
Beacon Press
Cantadora Press
COGNITIO: A Graduate Humanities Journal
Wm.B. Eerdmans Publishing Co.
Galen Press, Ltd.
HYPATIA: A Journal of Feminist Philosophy
Jalmar Press/Innerchoice Publishing
JOURNAL OF SCIENTIFIC EXPLORATION
KEREM: Creative Explorations in Judaism
LIBERTY
Mind Power Publishing
Motom
THE NEW FORMALIST
The New Formalist Press
Paragon House Publishers
Poptritus Press
Reliance Books
Savant Garde Workshop
Set Sail Productions, LLC
Summerland Publishing
SYMPLOKE: A Journal for the Intermingling of Literary,
Cultural and Theoretical Scholarship
THIRDEYE MAGAZINE
Titlewaves Publishing; Writers Direct
TRUTH SEEKER
United Nations University Press
Upper Access Inc. Book Publishers
WHAT IS ENLIGHTENMENT?
White Thread Press
Yaldah Publishing
YCD Press
Zagier & Urruty Publications

EUROPE

ABSINTHE: New European Writing
Art of Living, PrimaMedia,Inc
AzurAlive
Carousel Press
THE DIRTY GOAT
Faith Builders Resource Group
Fisher King Press
GERMAN LIFE
Heyday Books
Host Publications, Inc.
Magnifico Publications
Moonrise Press
Paradiso-Parthas Press
School for Advanced Research Press
TELOS
Telos Press
Thirteen Colonies Press
United Nations University Press
Wilde Publishing
WORLD POETRY SHOWCASE
Zante Publishing

671

EUTHANASIA, DEATH

ADVANCES IN THANATOLOGY
BOULDER HERETIC
Center for Thanatology Research & Education, Inc.
ERASED, SIGH, SIGH
Galen Press, Ltd.
GENRE: WRITER AND WRITINGS
Grateful Press
Lunar Offensive Publications
Lycanthrope Press
MOUTH: Voice of the Dis-Labeled Nation
NewSage Press
Skullvines Press
TRUTH SEEKER
TURNING WHEEL
VOX Press
Westgate Press
Wilde Publishing

EXPERIMENTAL

A Cappela Publishing
THE AMERICAN DRIVEL REVIEW
AMERICAN LETTERS & COMMENTARY
Artamo Press
ARTELLA: the waltz of words and art
AXES & ALLEYS
Bad Noise Productions
BAGAZINE
BANANA RAG
BITTER OLEANDER
Black Radish Books
Bogg Publications
BOGG: A Journal of Contemporary Writing
THE BROADKILL REVIEW: A Journal of Literature
Bronx River Press
CAIRN: The New St. Andrews Review
CAKETRAIN
Caketrain Journal and Press
Canvas Press
THE CAPILANO REVIEW
Chax Press
COLLECTION
COMPASS ROSE
Comrades Press
CONJUNCTIONS
Cornerstone Press
COSMOPSIS QUARTERLY
Counterpath Press
COUNTERPATH REVIEW
CUTTHROAT, A JOURNAL OF THE ARTS
DIET SOAP
Dnar Kaker Basa
THE EAST HAWAII OBSERVER
ELIXIR
Enigmatic Ink
EPICENTER: A LITERARY MAGAZINE
EROSHA
580 SPLIT
THE FLORIDA REVIEW
Gertrude Press
GHOTI MAGAZINE
GRAMMAR CRISIS
GRASSLIMB
Grey Sparrow Press
HAPA NUI
Highest Hurdle Press
HOBART
Hole Books
In Between Books
Iniquity Press/Vendetta Books
ISTANBUL LITERARY REVIEW
JOURNAL OF PYROTECHNICS
JOURNAL OF SCIENTIFIC EXPLORATION
THE KENYON REVIEW
LAKE EFFECT
LEAF GARDEN
Leaf Garden Press

Les Figues Press
Libellum
Little Pear Press
Llumina Press
LOVING MORE: New Models for Relationships
LULLABY HEARSE
LUNGFULL! MAGAZINE
MANDORLA: New Writing from the Americas / Nueva escritura de las Americas
MEAT FOR TEA: THE VALLEY REVIEW
MEAT: A Journal of Writing and Materiality
MELEE
Miami University Press
NEW ORLEANS REVIEW
New Sins Press
Noemi Press
NOUN VS. VERB
Orange Alert Press
THE OTHER HERALD
PEMMICAN
Plain View Press
Plan B Press
PRAKALPANA   SAHITYA/PRAKALPANA LITERA-TURE
PREMONITIONS
PRESA
Presa Press
Quale Press
THE RAGING FACE: Goofball Prose
RAINBOW CURVE
THE RAVEN CHRONICLES
RED FEZ ENTERTAINMENT
RED ROCK REVIEW
REDIVIDER
RedJack
RHINO: THE POETRY FORUM
RIVET MAGAZINE
Rural Messengers Press
Salt Publishing
Santa Fe Writers Project
SHORTRUNS
Silenced Press
SKIDROW PENTHOUSE
SNOW MONKEY
SOJOURN: A Journal of the Arts
SOUNDINGS REVIEW
SP Turner Group
SPECS
SPOUT
Spring Grass
Starcherone Books
Subsynchronuos Press
SUB-TERRAIN
SWILL
SWINK
Thirdeye Publications
The Thirty First Bird Press
Thunder Rain Publishing Corp.
Toad Press International Chapbook Series
Total Cardboard Publishing
Tuvela Press
twentythreebooks
Two-Handed Engine Press
VANITAS
VEIL: Journal of Darker Musings
VIVIPAROUS BLENNY
VLQ (Verse Libre Quarterly)
VOICES ISRAEL
VOX Press
Water Mark of Lyons PPP: papers press and permaculture
WHEELHOUSE MAGAZINE
White Crosslet Publishing Co
WHITE FUNGUS
William Joseph K Publications
The Wolf Pirate Project Inc.
The Word Works
Wordcraft of Oregon, LLC
WORDKNOT AUDIO: A Literary Podcast Magazine

XCP: CROSS-CULTURAL POETICS
X-Peri Press
X-PERI: Experimental Journal
X-Ray Book Co.
Zirlinson Publishing

FAMILY

AAIMS Publishers
Aardvark Enterprises (Sole Proprietorship of J. Alvin Speers)
Abernathy House Publishing
Academic Innovations
Academy Press of America
ADVANCES IN THANATOLOGY
Affluent Publishing Corp.
African American Images
All That Productions,Inc.
Allwrite Advertising and Publishing
American Carriage House Publishing
Ammons Communications; Imprint: Catch the Spirit of Appalachia
Anderson Publishing; also RC Anderson Books
APPLE VALLEY REVIEW: A Journal of Contemporary Literature
Art of Living, PrimaMedia,Inc
Aspicomm Media
AT-HOME DAD
BeachSide Press
BELIEVERS EXCHANGE NEWSLETTER
Big Valley Press
BlackBerry Fields Press
BLUE MOUNTAIN
Booksmart Publications
THE BOOMERPHILE
Brain Injury Success Books
Cable Publishing
Carousel Press
City Life Books, LLC
Clover Valley Press, LLC
Colerith Press
Community Service, Inc.
CONCEIT MAGAZINE
Cornerstone Publishing, Inc.
Creative Writing and Publishing Company
CURRENTS: New Scholarship in the Human Services
CUTTHROAT, A JOURNAL OF THE ARTS
Cyberwit.net
Datamaster Publishing, LLC
Delaney Day Press
Dominion Global Publishing
Dream Publishing Co.
Dreams Due Media Group, Inc.
DRT Press
Faith Builders Resource Group
First Journey Publishing Company
THE FIT CHRISTIAN A Christian Health & Fitness Magazine
Forest Dale Publishing Company
4 Your Spirit Productions
Friendly Oaks Publications
Front Row Experience
Fruitbearer Publishing, LLC
Future Horizons, Inc.
Gallopade International
Gingerbread House
GLOBAL ONE MAGAZINE
GoodSAMARitan Press
Grace Acres Press
Grace Creek Press
Grace House Publishing
Grayson Books
Guarionex Press Ltd.
Halo Publishing International
HARVARD JOURNAL OF LAW AND GENDER
The Haworth Press
His Work Christian Publishing
Hood Press
Hope Publishing House

Images Unlimited and Snaptail Press, a Division of Images Unlimited Publishing
Impact Publishers, Inc.
In Between Books
InsideOut Press
The Intrepid Traveler
IRIS: A Journal About Women
Irish Genealogical Foundation
J. Mark Press
Jon's Adventure Productions
JOURNAL OF CHILD AND YOUTH CARE
Juel House Publishers and Literary Services
Just Sisters Publications
KABBALAH
Keiki O Ka Aina Press
Lamp Light Press
Lawells Publishing
The Leaping Frog Press
Legacy Audio Books, Inc.
Lemon Grove Press
LEO Productions LLC.
Life Media
LifeCircle Press
Light-Beams Publishing
Lightning Bug Learning Press
Lion's Den Publishing
The Love and Logic Press, Inc.
LOVING MORE: New Models for Relationships
Lucky Press, LLC
Mama Incense Publishing
Mapletree Publishing Company
MCM Entertainment, Inc. Publishing Division
Meek Publishing
Midnight Whistler Publishers
Mills Custom Services Publishing
Moondance Press
MOTHERVERSE: A Journal of Contemporary Motherhood
Music City Publishing
My Heart Yours Publishing
Myriad Press
NEW ENGLAND BY RAIL
NEW SOLUTIONS
No Starch Press
Nolo Press Occidental
Nonetheless Press
NSR Publications
THE OTHER HERALD
Our Child Press
Outrider Press
P.R.A. Publishing
Papillon Presse
Papoose Publishing
Parenting Press, Inc.
The People's Press
Perrin Press
PIG IRON
Plain View Press
Playdate Kids Publishing
PLEASANT LIVING
Pocol Press
Poetry
Quiet Tymes, Inc.
Ragamuffin Heart Publishing
Raven Publishing, Inc.
Red Cygnet Press
Sand and Sable Publishing
Sassy Sunflower Books
Search Institute
SILVER WINGS
Small Dogma Publishing, Inc.
Soto Publishing Company
SOUNDINGS REVIEW
Starik Publishing
Starry Night Publishing
Stunt Publishing
Success Publishing
Successful Kids Publishing
Summerland Publishing

Summit Crossroads Press
George Suttton Publishing Co.
Sweet People Publishing
Third Dimension Publishing
Titus Home Publishing
Top 20 Press
Two Thousand Three Associates
Unlimited Publishing LLC
Upheaval Media
VanderWyk & Burnham
Vintage Romance Publishing, LLC
VOICES ISRAEL
Whispering Pine Press
Willfam Publishing Co.
Women and Men Books
Yaldah Publishing

FANTASY

A Midsummer Night's Press
Abecedarian books, Inc.
Adamantine Publishing House
Adventure Books Inc.
American Literary Press
Apex Book Company
Aquila Ink Publishing
Argo Press
ARTISTIC RAMBLINGS
Arx Publishing LLC
Atelier Press
ATLANTIC PACIFIC PRESS
Avari Press
AXE FACTORY REVIEW
Bereshith Publishing
Bladestar Publishing
Blue Moose Press
Blue Planet Books Inc.
BUST DOWN THE DOOR AND EAT ALL THE
    CHICKENS: A Journal of Absurd and Surreal Fiction
Caernarvon Press
Caribbean Books-Panama
Casperian Books LLC
CELLAR
Central Avenue Press
Citiria Publishing
CMP Publishing Group LLC
Cornerstone Press
Creative Writing and Publishing Company
Crystal Dreams Publishing
DARK GOTHIC RESURRECTED
Demarche Publishing LLC
DIET SOAP
Dnar Kaker Basa
Dream Catcher Publishing
DREAM FANTASY INTERNATIONAL
EASTGATE QUARTERLY REVIEW OF HYPERTEXT
EDGE Science Fiction and Fantasy Publishing
Empyrean Hill Books, Inc.
Enigmatic Ink
Ephemera Bound Publishing
Equine Graphics Publishing Group: New Concord Press,
    SmallHorse Press, SunDrop
The Fiction Works
Flapjack Press
Fountain Publisher Limited
Glass Tower Press
GoodSAMARitan Press
Gothic Press
Gryphon Books
GUD MAGAZINE (Greatest Uncommon Denominator)
Halo Publishing International
Helm Publishing
Hood Press
Idylls Press
THE ILLUMINATA
Imago Press
Immediate Direction Publications
In Between Books
IT GOES ON THE SHELF

Jigsaw Press
Journey Books Publishing
Lemieux International Ltd.
Llumina Press
LOW BUDGET SCIENCE FICTION
Lunar Offensive Publications
March Books
McQuinn Publishing
Merrimack Books
Micron Press
MIDNIGHT STREET
MindGlow Media
Montemayor Press
Mountain Media
Multi-Media Publications Inc.
Munsey Music
New Victoria Publishers
NIS America, Inc.
NOVA EXPRESS
OmegaRoom Press
ON SPEC
THE OTHER HERALD
Paladin Media Group
PAPERBACK PARADE
Pendragonian Publications
PENNY DREADFUL: Tales and Poems of Fantastic Terror
Perrin Press
Phelps Publishing Company
Pixiu Press
Poetry
POGO STICK
PREMONITIONS
PUNKIN HOUSE DIGEST
Punkin House Press
Purple Mouth Press
Ragamuffin Heart Publishing
Raular Publishing
Razor7 Publishing
Red Tiger Press
ROCTOBER COMICS AND MUSIC
Sand and Sable Publishing
Santa Fe Writers Project
Sassy Sunflower Books
Skullvines Press
Skyline Publications
Small Dogma Publishing, Inc.
SONGS OF INNOCENCE
SOUNDINGS REVIEW
SPACE AND TIME
Space and Time Press
SPECTACULAR SPECULATIONS
Star Publish LLC
SterlingHouse Publisher
Stonehorse Publishing, LLC
Sun Dog Press
SWILL
THE TARPEIAN ROCK
The Thirty First Bird Press
Triskelion Publishing
Triumvirate Publications
Twilight Tales, Inc.
Twilight Times Books
Two-Handed Engine Press
Tyrannosaurus Press
Ultra Media Publications
Ultramarine Publishing Co., Inc.
UmbraProjects Publishing
Vanilla Heart Publishing
Westgate Press
Whiskey Creek Press
Willfam Publishing Co.
WindRiver Publishing
The Wolf Pirate Project Inc.
Wordcraft of Oregon, LLC
Wytherngate Press
Youthful Wisdom Press
ZAHIR: A Journal of Speculative Fiction
Zirlinson Publishing

674

FASHION

AMERICAN VEGAN
BLK
CAUSE & EFFECT MAGAZINE
CESUM MAGAZINE
Cyberwit.net
Fotofolio, Inc.
GLOBAL ONE MAGAZINE
Harobed Publishing Creations
Hunter Publishing Corporation
Ibexa Press
INDUSTRY MINNE-ZINE
LDP, an occasional journal of aesthetics & language
NIGHTLIFE MAGAZINE
Red Rock Press
Sand and Sable Publishing
Smirk Books
WORN FASHION JOURNAL

FEMINISM

AK Press
ALTERNATIVE PRESS INDEX
American Literary Press
Anderson Publishing; also RC Anderson Books
ANHEDONIA
Anomaly Press
ATLANTIS: A Women's Studies Journal/Revue d'etudes
    sur les femmes
Aunt Lute Books
Beacon Press
Bear & Company
THE BELTANE PAPERS: A Journal of Women's
    Mysteries
Black Rose Books Ltd.
BLUE COLLAR REVIEW
Blue Dolphin Publishing, Inc.
BOOKS TO WATCH OUT FOR
THE BOOMERPHILE
Bordighera, Inc.
BRIDGES: A Jewish Feminist Journal
CANADIAN WOMAN STUDIES/les cahiers de la femme
Center for Thanatology Research & Education, Inc.
Chax Press
Chicory Blue Press, Inc.
CHILDREN, CHURCHES AND DADDIES, A Non
    Religious, Non Familial Literary Magazine
City Life Books, LLC
Clark-Nova Books
COLLEGE LITERATURE
COLORLINES
CONSCIENCE: The Newsjournal of Catholic Opinion
Cooperative Press
Crescent Moon
Cyberwit.net
Deep Well Publishing Company
Dnar Kakcr Basa
DOWN IN THE DIRT LITERARY MAGAZINE, the prose
    & poetry magazine revealing all your dirty little secrets
The Eighth Mountain Press
Ephemera Bound Publishing
Evening Street Press
FEMINIST COLLECTIONS: A QUARTERLY OF WO-
    MEN'S STUDIES RESOURCES
FEMINIST PERIODICALS: A CURRENT LISTING OF
    CONTENTS
The Feminist Press at the City University of New York
FEMINIST STUDIES
FREEDOM AND STRENGTH PRESS FORUM
GAYELLOW PAGES
GERTRUDE
Gertrude Press
GHOTI MAGAZINE
GLB Publishers
GOOD GIRL
HARVARD JOURNAL OF LAW AND GENDER
Hope Publishing House
HYPATIA: A Journal of Feminist Philosophy

Interlink Publishing Group, Inc.
IRIS: A Journal About Women
KALLIOPE, A Journal of Women's Literature and Art
Kelsey St. Press
Knowledge Concepts Publishing
La Alameda Press
La Familia Publishing
Lawells Publishing
Les Figues Press
Mama Incense Publishing
MANY MOUNTAINS MOVING
Margaret Media, Inc.
Maverick Books
MELEE
MICHIGAN FEMINIST STUDIES
THE MINNESOTA REVIEW
Moon Pie Press
MOTHERVERSE: A Journal of Contemporary Motherhood
NEW BOOKS ON WOMEN, GENDER, & FEMINISM
THE NEW ENGLAND QUARTERLY
New Victoria Publishers
NewSage Press
Nushape Publication
OFF OUR BACKS
Ohio University Press/Swallow Press
OPEN WIDE MAGAZINE
PAGAN AMERICA
Partisan Press
PASSION
Passion Power Press, Inc
PEACEWORK
PIG IRON
Plain View Press
POINT OF CONTACT, The Journal of Verbal & Visual
    Arts
Poor Richard's Press
PRISONERS' SPEAK!
Psychedelic Literature
THE PUBLIC EYE
RAINBOW CURVE
Rapacious Press
Red Alder Books
Red Letter Press
RED MARE
Red Tiger Press
RESOURCES FOR FEMINIST RESEARCH/DOCUMEN-
    TATION SUR LA RECHERCHE FEMINISTE
ROCTOBER COMICS AND MUSIC
Salt Publishing
Sand and Sable Publishing
Scars Publications
Sibyl Publications, Inc
SINISTER WISDOM
Smyrna Press
SO TO SPEAK: A Feminist Journal of Language & Art
SOCIAL ANARCHISM: A Journal of Practice and Theory
South End Press
Spinifex Press
State University of New York Press
SYMPLOKE: A Journal for the Intermingling of Literary,
    Cultural and Theoretical Scholarship
Syracuse Cultural Workers/Tools for Change
Syracuse Cultural Workers/Tools for Change
Tesseract Publications
13TH MOON
TURNING THE TIDE: Journal of Anti-Racist Action,
    Research & Education
The Twickenham Press
Two-Handed Engine Press
University of Nebraska Press
VOICES ISRAEL
WAV MAGAZINE: Progressive Music Art Politics Culture
The Wessex Collective
West End Press
William Joseph K Publications
THE WISE WOMAN
WOMEN AND LANGUAGE
Women's Studies Librarian, University of Wisconsin

675

System
WSQ (formerly WOMEN'S STUDIES QUARTERLY)

FESTIVALS

Dnar Kaker Basa
THE ENGLISH CLARION
GEM Literary Foundation Press
NIGHTLIFE MAGAZINE
Peartree Books & Music
Ragamuffin Heart Publishing
Sand and Sable Publishing
SAPONIFIER
SeaCrab Publishing
SHORTRUNS
SOUTHWEST COLORADO ARTS PERSPECTIVE
TREATING YOURSELF: The Alternative Medicine Journal
WORLD POETRY SHOWCASE

FICTION

A Cappela Publishing
Aaron Communications III
Abecedarian books, Inc.
Accendo Publishing
ACME Press
THE ADIRONDACK REVIEW
Adventure Books Inc.
Affluent Publishing Corp.
AFRICAN AMERICAN REVIEW
Ageless Press
AGNI
THE AGUILAR EXPRESSION
AIM MAGAZINE
AK Press
ALABAMA LITERARY REVIEW
ALASKA QUARTERLY REVIEW
All That Productions,Inc.
THE ALLEGHENY REVIEW
Allium Press of Chicago
Allwrite Advertising and Publishing
AMBIT
American Indian Studies Center
AMERICAN JONES BUILDING & MAINTENANCE
AMERICAN LETTERS & COMMENTARY
American Literary Press
Ammons Communications; Imprint: Catch the Spirit of Appalachia
ANCIENT PATHS
Androgyne Books
ANOTHER CHICAGO MAGAZINE(ACM)
ANQ: A Quarterly Journal of Short Articles, Notes, and Reviews
THE ANTIGONISH REVIEW
THE ANTIOCH REVIEW
Apex Book Company
APEX Magazine
APOSTROPHE: USCB Journal of the Arts
Aquarius Press
Aquila Ink Publishing
ART:MAG
Artamo Press
Arte Publico Press
ARTELLA: the waltz of words and art
ARTFUL DODGE
ARTISTIC RAMBLINGS
ARTS & LETTERS: Journal of Contemporary Culture
Arx Publishing LLC
Aspicomm Media
Assilem 9 Publications
Asteroid Publishing, Inc.
Asylum Arts
Atelier Press
Athanata Arts, Ltd.
ATLANTIC PACIFIC PRESS
Authentic Publishing LLC
Autumn House Press
Avari Press
Avery Color Studios

Avocet Press Inc.
AXE FACTORY REVIEW
The B & R Samizdat Express
The Bacchae Press
Bad Noise Productions
THE BALTIMORE REVIEW
Bancroft Press
Bandanna Books
Banks Channel Books
Bardsong Press
Barrytown/Station Hill Press
BAYOU
BeachSide Press
THE BEAR DELUXE MAGAZINE
BEAUTY/TRUTH: A Journal of Ekphrastic Poetry
BEGINNING MAGAZINE
BEGINNINGS - A Magazine for the Novice Writer
Bel Canto Press
Bellevue Literary Press
BELLEVUE LITERARY REVIEW
BELLINGHAM REVIEW
BELLOWING ARK
Bellowing Ark Press
BIBLIOPHILOS
BIG MUDDY: Journal of the Mississippi River Valley
BIG SCREAM
Big Valley Press
Bilingual Review Press
Birch Brook Press
BITTER OLEANDER
BkMk Press
Black Dress Press
Black Forest Press and The Tennessee Publishing House
Black Heron Press
Black Lawrence Press
BLACK MAGNOLIAS LITERARY JOURNAL
Black Thistle Press
BLACK WARRIOR REVIEW
BlackBerry Fields Press
Bladestar Publishing
Blowtorch Press
Blue Cubicle Press, LLC
Blue Hull Press
Blue Lupin Press
BLUE MESA REVIEW
Blue Moose Press
BLUELINE
BOA Editions, Ltd.
BOGG: A Journal of Contemporary Writing
BOMB MAGAZINE
Book Marketing Solutions
Books for All Times, Inc.
BOOKS FROM FINLAND: Online literature journal of writing from and about Finland
Borealis Press Limited
Bottle of Smoke Press
Bottom Dog Press / Bird Dog Publishing
BOULEVARD
Branden Books
THE BRIAR CLIFF REVIEW
BrickHouse Books, Inc.
BRILLIANT CORNERS: A Journal of Jazz & Literature
THE BROADKILL REVIEW: A Journal of Literature
Bronx River Press
BRYANT LITERARY REVIEW
BUFFALO SPREE
Burning Books
Burning Deck Press
BUST DOWN THE DOOR AND EAT ALL THE CHICKENS: A Journal of Absurd and Surreal Fiction
BUTTON
BYLINE
C & M Online Media Inc.
C&R Press
Cable Publishing
Cadmus Editions
Caernarvon Press
CAFE NOIR REVIEW

676

CAIRN: The New St. Andrews Review
CAKETRAIN
Caketrain Journal and Press
Calaca Press
Calyx Books
CALYX: A Journal of Art and Literature by Women
Cantarabooks LLC
Canvas Press
CAPCAT
Caribbean Books-Panama
THE CAROLINA QUARTERLY
Carolina Wren Press
Casperian Books LLC
CAUSE & EFFECT MAGAZINE
Celo Valley Books
Center for Japanese Studies
CENTER: A Journal of the Literary Arts
Central Avenue Press
CERISE PRESS
Cervena Barva Press
CHANTEH, the Iranian Cross-Cultural Quarterly
CHAPMAN
CHARITON REVIEW
Chase Publishing
Chatterley Press International
Cheops Books
Cherry Valley Editions
Chicory Blue Press, Inc.
CHILDREN, CHURCHES AND DADDIES, A Non Religious, Non Familial Literary Magazine
CHIRON REVIEW
CIMARRON REVIEW
CIRCLE INC., THE MAGAZINE
Circle of Friends Books
Citiria Publishing
City Life Books, LLC
City Lights Books
Cladach Publishing
Clamp Down Press
Clark-Nova Books
Clearwater Publishing Co.
Cleveland State Univ. Poetry Center
Cloudkeeper Press
Cloudland Books
Clover Valley Press, LLC
CMP Publishing Group LLC
Coffee House Press
The Colbert House LLC
COLD-DRILL
COLORADO REVIEW
Communication Creativity
COMPASS ROSE
Comrades Press
CONCEIT MAGAZINE
CONCRETE JUNGLE JOURNAL
CONJUNCTIONS
CONNECTICUT REVIEW
CONTRARY
Copper Beech Press
Cornerstone Press
Cornucopia Press
CORRECTIONS TODAY
THE CORTLAND REVIEW
COSMOPSIS QUARTERLY
Cotton Tree Press
COTTONWOOD
Cottonwood Press
Cozy Cat Press
CRAB CREEK REVIEW
CRAB ORCHARD REVIEW
Crane Press
CRANNOG
CRAZYHORSE
THE CREAM CITY REVIEW
Creative Arts Book Company
CRUCIBLE
Crystal Dreams Publishing
CUTBANK

CUTTHROAT, A JOURNAL OF THE ARTS
CYBERFICT
Cyberwit.net
Cynic Press
Cypress Creek Publishing
Cypress House
THE DALHOUSIE REVIEW
Dalkey Archive Press
Dancing Bridge Publishing
Dancing Lemur Press, L.L.C.
DARK ANIMUS
DARK GOTHIC RESURRECTED
Russell Dean and Company
Demarche Publishing LLC
DESCANT
DESCANT
Desert Bloom Press
DESIRE
DIET SOAP
Dignified Designs
Paul Dilsaver, Publisher
THE DIRTY GOAT
DLite Press
Dnar Kaker Basa
Dominion Global Publishing
DOWN IN THE DIRT LITERARY MAGAZINE, the prose & poetry magazine revealing all your dirty little secrets
Down The Shore Publishing
Down There Press
Downeast Books
Dream Catcher Publishing
DREAM FANTASY INTERNATIONAL
Dreams Due Media Group, Inc.
Drinian Press
Paul Dry Books
Dufour Editions Inc.
DWANG: Outsider poetry and prose
Earth Star Publications
EARTH'S DAUGHTERS: Feminist Arts Periodical
Earthshaker Books
Eastern Washington University Press
EASTGATE QUARTERLY REVIEW OF HYPERTEXT
ECOTONE: Reimagining Place
Ecrivez!
Edenscape Publishing Company
The Eighth Mountain Press
Elderberry Press, Inc.
ELIXIR
Elixir Press
Ellechor Publishing House
ELT Press
Empyrean Hill Books, Inc.
EMRYS JOURNAL
Emrys Press
Ephemera Bound Publishing
EPICENTER: A LITERARY MAGAZINE
EPIPHANY, A Literary Journal
EPOCH MAGAZINE
Equine Graphics Publishing Group: New Concord Press, SmallHorse Press, SunDrop
Eros Books
Ethos Publishing
EVANSVILLE REVIEW
Evening Street Press
EVENING STREET REVIEW
EVENT
Expanded Media Editions
Falcon Publishing, LTD
FAT TUESDAY
FICTION
Fiction Collective Two (FC2)
The Fiction Works
Fine Tooth Press
First Books
FISH DRUM MAGAZINE
Fisher King Press
Fithian Press
580 SPLIT

Five Fingers Press
FIVE FINGERS REVIEW
FIVE POINTS
Five Star Publications, Inc.
Floreant Press
Florida Academic Press
THE FLORIDA REVIEW
FLUENT ASCENSION
Flume Press
FLYWAY: A Journal of Writing and Environment
FMA Publishing
FOLIO: A Literary Journal of American University
Foremost Press
Fountain Publisher Limited
4 Your Spirit Productions
FOURTEEN HILLS: The SFSU Review
FRANK: AN INTERNATIONAL JOURNAL OF CON-
   TEMPORARY WRITING AND ART
Free People Press
FREEDOM AND STRENGTH PRESS FORUM
French Bread Publications
FROZEN WAFFLES
Frozen Waffles Press/Shattered Sidewalks Press; 45th
   Century Chapbooks
Fruitbearer Publishing, LLC
FUGUE
Fugue State Press
Galde Press, Inc.
The Galileo Press Ltd.
Gallaudet University Press
Gallopade International
Garden House Press
GARGOYLE
GEM Literary Foundation Press
GenNext Publishing
THE GEORGIA REVIEW
GERTRUDE
Gertrude Press
Gesture Press
THE GETTYSBURG REVIEW
GHOTI MAGAZINE
GIN BENDER POETRY REVIEW
Gival Press
Glass Tower Press
GLB Publishers
The Glencannon Press
Glimmer Train Press, Inc.
GLIMMER TRAIN STORIES
GOLD DUST
Golden Quill Press
GoodSAMARitan Press
Goose River Press
Goss Press
Gothic Press
GRASSLIMB
Gray Dog Press
Graywolf Press
GREAT RIVER REVIEW
GREEN MOUNTAINS REVIEW
Green River Press
Green Square Publishing
THE GREENSBORO REVIEW
Grey Sparrow Press
Grip Publishing
Gryphon Books
GUD MAGAZINE (Greatest Uncommon Denominator)
GULF COAST
Halo Publishing International
HANGING LOOSE
Hanging Loose Press
HAPA NUI
HAPPENINGNOW!EVERYWHERE
HARVARD REVIEW
Harvest Shadows Publications
HAWAI'I REVIEW
HAWAI'I PACIFIC REVIEW
HAYDEN'S FERRY REVIEW
HEAVEN BONE MAGAZINE

Heaven Bone Press
Heidelberg Graphics
Helicon Nine Editions
Helm Publishing
Heritage Library Press
Hermes House Press
The Heyeck Press
HOBART
Hole Books
Hollyridge Press
Homa & Sekey Books
HOME PLANET NEWS
Hood Press
Host Publications, Inc.
HOT FLASHES: Not a Menopause Thang
A HUDSON VIEW POETRY DIGEST
ICON
ICONOCLAST
THE IDAHO REVIEW
Idylls Press
ILLOGICAL MUSE
ILLUMINATIONS
ILLUMINATIONS LITERARY JOURNAL
IMAGE: ART, FAITH, MYSTERY
Imago Press
Immediate Direction Publications
Impassio Press
IMPress
IN OUR OWN WORDS
INDIANA REVIEW
The Infinity Group
THE INK SLINGER REVIEW
Inkwater Press
Interlink Publishing Group, Inc.
THE INTERNATIONAL FICTION REVIEW
THE IOWA REVIEW
Iris Publishing Group, Inc (Iris Press / Tellico Books)
IRIS: A Journal About Women
IRON HORSE LITERARY REVIEW
ISTANBUL LITERARY REVIEW
Italica Press, Inc.
Ithuriel's Spear
JACK MACKEREL MAGAZINE
Jako Books
JAVELINA BI-MONTHLY
J'ECRIS
Jigsaw Press
THE JOURNAL
Journey Books Publishing
J-Press Publishing
Juel House Publishers and Literary Services
Jullundur Press
KALEIDOSCOPE: Exploring the Experience of Disability
   through Literature & the Fine Arts
KARAMU
Keiki O Ka Aina Press
THE KELSEY REVIEW
Kelsey St. Press
THE KENYON REVIEW
KESTREL: A Journal of Literature and Art
Kilmog Press
Allen A. Knoll Publishers
KNUCKLE MERCHANT - The Journal of Naked Literary
   Aggression
Krill Press
L&L Dreamspell
La Alameda Press
La Familia Publishing
LAKE EFFECT
Lake Street Press
THE LAKEVIEW REVIEW
THE LAUREL REVIEW
LDP, an occasional journal of aesthetics & language
LEAF GARDEN
Leaf Garden Press
Leapfrog Press
Leaping Dog Press
The Leaping Frog Press

THE LEDGE
THE LEDGE POETRY & FICTION MAGAZINE
A.P. Lee & Co., Ltd.
LegacyForever
LEO Productions LLC.
Les Figues Press
LIFTOUTS
Light of New Orleans Publishing
LIGHT: The Quarterly of Light Verse
Lilly Press
Lily Ruth Publishing
LINQ
THE LISTENING EYE
LITERALLY HORSES/REMUDA
LITERARY IMAGINATION: The Review of the Associa-
  tion of Literary Scholars and Critics
LITTLE BALKANS REVIEW
THE LITTLE MAGAZINE
Llumina Press
THE LONG STORY
Loonfeather Press
Lord John Press
Lost Prophet Press
THE LOUISIANA REVIEW
THE LOUISVILLE REVIEW
LOW BUDGET ADVENTURE
LOW BUDGET SCIENCE FICTION
Lucky Press, LLC
LULLWATER REVIEW
Lummox Press
Lunar Offensive Publications
LUNGFULL! MAGAZINE
Lynx House Press
Lyons Publishing Limited
MacAdam/Cage Publishing Inc.
THE MACGUFFIN
THE MADISON REVIEW
Madyfi Press
Mama Incense Publishing
MANDORLA: New Writing from the Americas / Nueva
  escritura de las Americas
MANOA: A Pacific Journal of International Writing
MANY MOUNTAINS MOVING
March Street Press
THE MARLBORO REVIEW
Maui arThoughts Co.
Maverick Books
Mayhaven Publishing, Inc.
McBooks Press, Inc.
McPherson & Company Publishers
McQuinn Publishing
THE MEADOW
MEAT FOR TEA: THE VALLEY REVIEW
Medusa's Muse
Meridien PressWorks
Merrimack Books
Merwood Books
Metacom Press
Miami University Press
Micah Publications Inc.
Micron Press
MID-AMERICAN REVIEW
Mid-List Press
MIDNIGHT STREET
Milkweed Editions
Mills Custom Services Publishing
MINESHAFT
MIP Company
Miskwabik Press
Missing Spoke Press
MISSISSIPPI REVIEW
Mondial
Montemayor Press
Moo-Cow Fan Club
Mo'omana'o Press
Motom
Mountain Media
Mountain State Press

Multi-Media Publications Inc.
Multnomah Publishers, Inc.
Munsey Music
MURDER CROWS
Murder Slim Press
MUSE: A Quarterly Journal of The Lit
My Heart Yours Publishing
Myriad Press
MYSTERY ISLAND MAGAZINE
Mystery Island Publications
Nada Press
National Writers Press
NATURAL BRIDGE
NEBO
THE NEBRASKA REVIEW
NEO: Literary Magazine
Neshui Publishing
New Chapter Publisher
NEW DELTA REVIEW
New Door Books
NEW ENGLAND BY RAIL
NEW ENGLAND REVIEW
New Falcon Publications
New Issues Poetry & Prose
NEW LETTERS
NEW MADRID
NEW MUSE OF CONTEMPT
NEW ORLEANS REVIEW
New Orphic Publishers
THE NEW ORPHIC REVIEW
THE NEW RENAISSANCE, an international magazine of
  ideas & opinions, emphasizing literature & the arts
New Rivers Press, Inc.
NEW STONE CIRCLE
New Victoria Publishers
New Voices Publishing
THE NEW WRITER
Nightsun Books
NIMROD INTERNATIONAL JOURNAL
NIS America, Inc.
Noemi Press
NOLA-MAGICK Press
Nonetheless Press
NOON
NORTH AMERICAN REVIEW
NORTH CAROLINA LITERARY REVIEW
North Stone Editions
NORTHWEST REVIEW
Northwestern University Press
NOTRE DAME REVIEW
NOVA EXPRESS
NOW AND THEN
NSR Publications
O!!ZONE, A LITERARY-ART ZINE
Oak Tree Press
Obie Joe Media
OBSIDIAN III: Literature in the African Diaspora
OFFICE NUMBER ONE
OFFICE NUMBER ONE
Ohio University Press/Swallow Press
THE OLD RED KIMONO
OmegaRoom Press
Omonomany
One Eyed Press
One Less Press
Oolichan Books
Open Wide Books
Oracle Press
Orange Alert Press
ORBIS
Orchard House Press
Orchises Press
OREGON EAST
THE ORPHAN LEAF REVIEW
Osric Publishing
THE OTHER HERALD
OUT OF LINE
Outrider Press

Scars Publications
SCHUYLKILL VALLEY JOURNAL
SCRIVENER
SEEMS
SelectiveHouse Publishers, Inc.
SENSATIONS MAGAZINE
Seven Buffaloes Press
SEWANEE REVIEW
Shared Roads Press
Shearer Publishing
SHENANDOAH: The Washington and Lee University Review
Sherman Asher Publishing
Shipyard Press, LC
SHORT FUSE
SHORT STORY
SHORTRUNS
Signalman Publishing
Silenced Press
SKIDROW PENTHOUSE
Skullvines Press
SKYLINE LITERARY MAGAZINE
Skyline Publications
Slipdown Mountain Publications LLC
Small Dogma Publishing, Inc.
The Smith (subsidiary of The Generalist Assn., Inc.)
Gibbs Smith, Publisher
SMOKE
Smyrna Press
SNOWY EGRET
SNREVIEW
SO TO SPEAK: A Feminist Journal of Language & Art
Socratic Consulting Group
SOJOURN: A Journal of the Arts
$olvency International Inc., Publishing
SONGS OF INNOCENCE
Soto Publishing Company
SOUNDINGS EAST
SOUNDINGS REVIEW
SOUTH CAROLINA REVIEW
SOUTH DAKOTA REVIEW
Southeast Missouri State University Press
SOUTHERN CALIFORNIA REVIEW
SOUTHERN HUMANITIES REVIEW
THE SOUTHERN REVIEW
SOUTHWEST REVIEW
SOU'WESTER
SPEAK UP
SPECS
SPECTACULAR SPECULATIONS
SPINNINGS...INTENSE TALES OF LIFE MAGAZINE
SPITBALL: The Literary Baseball Magazine
SPOTops Books
SPOUT
Spout Press
Squire Press
SRLR Press
Star Publish LLC
Starcherone Books
Starik Publishing
Stellaberry Press
Stemmer House Publishers, Inc.
SterlingHouse Publisher
Stone Cottage Press
Stonehorse Publishing, LLC
Stormline Press, Inc.
Story County Books
STORYQUARTERLY
STRINGTOWN
STRUGGLE: A Magazine of Proletarian Revolutionary Literature
STUDIO - A Journal of Christians Writing
STUDIO ONE
SUB-TERRAIN
Summerland Publishing
Sun Dog Press
THE SUN, A Magazine of Ideas
Sweet People Publishing

SWILL
SWINK
SYCAMORE REVIEW
SYMPLOKE: A Journal for the Intermingling of Literary, Cultural and Theoretical Scholarship
synaesthesia press
Synergistic Press
Synergy Press
Talisman House, Publishers
TalSan Publishing/Distributors
Tameme
Tangerine Press
TAPROOT LITERARY REVIEW
THE TARPEIAN ROCK
Texas Tech University Press
Thatch Tree Publications
THEMA
Theytus Books Ltd.
THIN COYOTE
THIRD COAST
THIRDEYE MAGAZINE
Thirdeye Publications
13TH MOON
The Thirty First Bird Press
Three Bean Press
Three Bears Publishing
THE THREEPENNY REVIEW
THRESHOLDS JOURNAL
Thunder Rain Publishing Corp.
Thundercloud Books
Titan Press
TnT Classic Books
Tombouctou Books
Total Cardboard Publishing
Total Package Publications, LLC
TOUCHSTONE LITERARY JOURNAL
Trafford Publishing
Tres Picos Press
Triskelion Publishing
Triumvirate Publications
TSAR Publications
TURNROW
Turnstone Press
The Twickenham Press
Twilight Tales, Inc.
Twilight Times Books
Twinteum Artist, Inc.
Twisted Spoon Press
2L Publishing, LLC
U.S.1 WORKSHEETS
Ultra Media Publications
Ultramarine Publishing Co., Inc.
UmbraProjects Publishing
UNIVERSITY OF WINDSOR REVIEW
Unlimited Publishing LLC
UPSTAIRS AT DUROC
Urion Press
Vagabond Press
Vanilla Heart Publishing
Vehicule Press
VERSAL
Vintage Romance Publishing, LLC
Virginia City Publishing Co. LLC
THE VIRGINIA QUARTERLY REVIEW
VIVIPAROUS BLENNY
Vox Humana Books
John Wade, Publisher
WAR, LITERATURE & THE ARTS: An International Journal of the Humanities
Washington Writers' Publishing House
Water Row Press
Wave Publishing
WEBER: The Contemporary West
Wellington House Publishing Company
The Wellsweep Press
The Wessex Collective
WEST BRANCH
West Coast Paradise Publishing

West Virginia University Press
Wexford & Barrow, Publishers
The WhaleInn Publishing House (1998)
WHEELHOUSE MAGAZINE
Whelks Walk Press
Whiskey Creek Press
White Pine Press
WHOLE TERRAIN - REFLECTIVE ENVIRONMENTAL
PRACTICE
THE WILDWOOD READER
Willfam Publishing Co.
WILLOW REVIEW
WILLOW SPRINGS
Wind Eagle Press
WindRiver Publishing
Wineberry Press
Wings Press
Wintertree Press
The Wolf Pirate Project Inc.
Women and Men Books
THE WORCESTER REVIEW
Word Forge Books
Wordcraft of Oregon, LLC
WORDKNOT AUDIO: A Literary Podcast Magazine
Wordsonthestreet
Wordwrights Canada
WORKERS WRITE!
THE WORLD
World Love Press Publishing
Writecorner.com Press
The Writers Block, Inc.
WRITER'S CHRONICLE
Writers House Press
WRITERS' JOURNAL
Wytherngate Press
XAVIER REVIEW
Xenos Books
Yaldah Publishing
Youthful Wisdom Press
YUKHIKA—LATUHSE
Zirlinson Publishing
ZOETROPE: ALL-STORY
ZONE 3
Zoo Press
Zumaya Publications LLC
Zygote Publishing

FINANCES

THE ART OF ABUNDANCE
Bancroft Press
Bay Tree Publishing
BlackBerry Fields Press
Blue Owl Press
Bluestocking Press
CANADIAN MONEYSAVER
CKO UPDATE
Communication Creativity
Dominion Global Publishing
EQUAL CONSTRUCTION RECORD
Fountain Publisher Limited
Garrett Publishing, Inc.
Gemstone House Publishing
GENRE: WRITER AND WRITINGS
Grace Creek Press
Happy About
LifeCircle Press
Llumina Press
Long & Silverman Publishing, Inc.
Mind Power Publishing
MOTHER EARTH JOURNAL: An International Quarterly
Music City Publishing
New Knowledge Press
New Win Publishing
North Star Books
The Passion Profit Company
Pellingham Casper Communications
Reliance Books
Rolling Hills Publishing

Set Sail Productions, LLC
Square One Publishers, Inc.
Chuck Stewart
Storm Publishing Group
Titlewaves Publishing; Writers Direct
Toca Family Publishing, div. of Toca Family Communications Group, LLC
United Nations University Press
WeWrite LLC
Willfam Publishing Co.

F. SCOTT FITZGERALD

Libellum
LOST GENERATION JOURNAL

FLORIDA

BEACHCOMBER MAGAZINE
Cantadora Press
COGNITIO: A Graduate Humanities Journal
IN OUR OWN WORDS
THE INK SLINGER REVIEW
The Intrepid Traveler
LegacyForever
B.B. Mackey Books
Ocean Publishing
Pineapple Press, Inc.
Pocol Press
Pogo Press, Incorporated
Premium Press America
RED MARE
Rock Spring Press Inc.
Shipyard Press, LC
Tortuga Books
Two Thousand Three Associates
Two Thousand Three Associates
University of Tampa Press
Windward Publishing, An Imprint of Finney Company

FOLKLORE

Alaska Native Language Center
AMERICAN FORESTS
Ammons Communications; Imprint: Catch the Spirit of Appalachia
Anagnosis
Ariko Publications
Avery Color Studios
Black Dome Press Corp.
John F. Blair, Publisher
THE BLOOMSBURY REVIEW
Blue Lupin Press
Borealis Press Limited
Celtic Heritage Books
Center for Thanatology Research & Education, Inc.
Cloud 9 Publishing
Cotton Tree Press
Council For Indian Education
Creative With Words Publications (CWW)
Dervla Publishing, LLC
THE ENGLISH CLARION
EXIT 13 MAGAZINE
Fulcrum, Inc.
Galde Press, Inc.
Gray Dog Press
GUD MAGAZINE (Greatest Uncommon Denominator)
HAPA NUI
Harbor House
Hood Press
Ice Cube Press
Irish Genealogical Foundation
IRISH LITERARY SUPPLEMENT
Kar-Ben Publishing, Inc.
KESTREL: A Journal of Literature and Art
Lake Claremont Press
LAKE EFFECT
LAKE SUPERIOR MAGAZINE
Legacy Audio Books, Inc.
Lockhart Press
Luna Bisonte Prods

Lycanthrope Press
Maledicta Press
MALEDICTA: The International Journal of Verbal Aggression
Malki-Ballena Press
Margaret Media, Inc.
The Middle Atlantic Press
MISSISSIPPI CROW
Mo'omana'o Press
Mystery Island Publications
NEW ENGLAND BY RAIL
New Falcon Publications
North Country Books, Inc.
One Horse Press/Rainy Day Press
Orchard House Press
Passeggiata Press, Inc.
Peartree Books & Music
Perrin Press
Petroglyph Press, Ltd.
Pixiu Press
Plank Road Publishing
Pocahontas Press, Inc.
The Press at Foggy Bottom
RALPH'S REVIEW
Rarach Press
Rayve Productions Inc.
RED MARE
Red Tiger Press
Roaring Lion Publishing
ROCKY MOUNTAIN KC NEWS
Rocky Mountain KC Publishing Co.
ROCTOBER COMICS AND MUSIC
Sabellapress
Santa Monica Press
SAPONIFIER
SeaCrab Publishing
Serpent & Eagle Press
SHATTERED WIG REVIEW
SHORT FUSE
Smirk Books
THE SOUTHERN QUARTERLY: A Journal of the Arts in the South
SPECTACULAR SPECULATIONS
Sunbelt Publications
Sunnyside Press
The Thirty First Bird Press
Thunder Rain Publishing Corp.
Two Dog Press
United Lumbee Nation
UNITED LUMBEE NATION TIMES
University of Arkansas Press
University of South Carolina Press
Utah State University Press
Vanderbilt University Press
Vanilla Heart Publishing
Virginia City Publishing Co. LLC
Volcano Press, Inc
Waters Edge Press
WESTERN AMERICAN LITERATURE
Westgate Press
Whispering Pine Press
White Cliffs Media, Inc.
WISCONSIN TRAILS
XCP: CROSS-CULTURAL POETICS
Yellow Moon Press

FOOD, EATING

ALIMENTUM - The Literature of Food
AMERICAN VEGAN
Atlantic Publishing Group, Inc.
Aura Productions, LLC
BANANA RAG
Beagle Bay Books / Creative Minds Press
THE BELTANE PAPERS: A Journal of Women's Mysteries
BlackBerry Fields Press
Brick Road Poetry Press
Cable Publishing

Cookbook Resources, LLC
Creative Writing and Publishing Company
DWELLING PORTABLY
THE ENGLISH CLARION
Equine Graphics Publishing Group: New Concord Press, SmallHorse Press, SunDrop
THE FIT CHRISTIAN A Christian Health & Fitness Magazine
Florentia Press
GROWING FOR MARKET
Ika, LLC
Images Unlimited and Snaptail Press, a Division of Images Unlimited Publishing
IRIS: A Journal About Women
Keiki O Ka Aina Press
Knowledge Concepts Publishing
Lake Claremont Press
Lamp Light Press
Lazywood Press
Llumina Press
March Books
McBooks Press, Inc.
MY TABLE: Houston's Dining Magazine
NOLA-MAGICK Press
NORTH CAROLINA LITERARY REVIEW
Obie Joe Media
PLEASANT LIVING
Princess Publishing
Rayve Productions Inc.
Red Rock Press
RTMC Organization, LLC
SHORTRUNS
Six Ft. Swells Press
Sweet People Publishing
Three Bean Press
TREATING YOURSELF: The Alternative Medicine Journal
University of South Carolina Press
Upper Access Inc. Book Publishers
Wafer Mache Publications
Yaldah Publishing

FORENSIC SCIENCE

Galen Press, Ltd.
GENRE: WRITER AND WRITINGS
GUD MAGAZINE (Greatest Uncommon Denominator)
Journal of Pyrotechnics
JOURNAL OF PYROTECHNICS
Village Lane Press

FRANCE, FRENCH

ABSINTHE: New European Writing
THE ADIRONDACK REVIEW
AzurAlive
Barrytown/Station Hill Press
Black Lawrence Press
The Chicot Press
Cross-Cultural Communications
FRANK: AN INTERNATIONAL JOURNAL OF CONTEMPORARY WRITING AND ART
INTERNATIONAL POETRY REVIEW
LEO Productions LLC.
Listening Voice Media Ltd
LOST GENERATION JOURNAL
Mishmish Press
Mondial
OSIRIS
Playdate Kids Publishing
SYMPOSIUM
Synergistic Press
University of Virginia Press
Wilde Publishing

FUNDRAISING

Atlantic Publishing Group, Inc.
Bonus Books, Inc.
First Journey Publishing Company
GRASSROOTS FUNDRAISING JOURNAL

Poplar Leaf Press
Sweet People Publishing

FUTURISM

ARTISTIC RAMBLINGS
BAGAZINE
CAUSE & EFFECT MAGAZINE
CONJUNCTIONS
Crane Press
Crystal Press
DIET SOAP
Dnar Kaker Basa
Enigmatic Ink
THE FUTURIST
Gallopade International
Heartsong Books
KALDRON, An International Journal Of Visual Poetry
L&L Dreamspell
LOVING MORE: New Models for Relationships
NEW ENVIRONMENT BULLETIN
NOVA EXPRESS
PREMONITIONS
Red Tiger Press
SHARE INTERNATIONAL
SPECTACULAR SPECULATIONS
Starcherone Books
Thatch Tree Publications
Twinteum Artist, Inc.
Upheaval Media
WHAT IS ENLIGHTENMENT?
WindRiver Publishing

GAELIC

Celtic Heritage Books
Irish Genealogical Foundation
NEW AMERICAN IMAGIST
Sand and Sable Publishing
Total Cardboard Publishing

GAMES

Carousel Press
THE CRAPSHOOTER
Dawn Sign Press
DISCGOLFER
East West Discovery Press
Falls Media
Front Row Experience
Gallopade International
Gateways Books And Tapes
GRAMMAR CRISIS
Guarionex Press Ltd.
Hunter House Inc., Publishers
Huntington Press
Leaf Press
MEAT: A Journal of Writing and Materiality
Zookeeper Publications

GARDENING

Affinity Publishers Services
AMERICAN VEGAN
Annedawn Publishing
Arizona Master Gardener Press
Atlantic Publishing Group, Inc.
BeachSide Press
Blue Dolphin Publishing, Inc.
Center For Self-Sufficiency
Chelsea Green Publishing Company
Chicago Review Press
The Chicot Press
Cladach Publishing
Downeast Books
Equine Graphics Publishing Group: New Concord Press, SmallHorse Press, SunDrop
Fulcrum, Inc.
Gallopade International
Garden House Press
GREEN PRINTS, ''The Weeder's Digest''
THE GROWING EDGE MAGAZINE

GROWING FOR MARKET
Hobar Publications, A Division of Finney Company
HORTIDEAS
INKY TRAIL NEWS
Allen A. Knoll Publishers
La Alameda Press
LAKE SUPERIOR MAGAZINE
Life Media
Loonfeather Press
Moon Pie Press
Naturegraph Publishers
No Starch Press
Nonetheless Press
OUT YOUR BACKDOOR: The Magazine of Do-It-Yourself Adventure and Homegrown Culture
Petroglyph Press, Ltd.
Pineapple Press, Inc.
PLEASANT LIVING
Ragamuffin Heart Publishing
RALPH'S REVIEW
RFD
Sasquatch Books
SCHUYLKILL LIVING MAGAZINE
SEED SAVERS EXCHANGE
Shearer Publishing
Smirk Books
Storm Publishing Group
TREATING YOURSELF: The Alternative Medicine Journal
Trickle Creek Books
University of South Carolina Press
University of Virginia Press
Waters Edge Press
Whispering Pine Press

GAY

A Midsummer Night's Press
AD/VANCE
Alamo Square Press
Allbook Books
ALTERNATIVE PRESS INDEX
Assilem 9 Publications
Avari Press
Back House Books
Banta & Pool Literary Properties
Bay Press
BAY WINDOWS
Beacon Press
BLACK LACE
BLACKFIRE
BLK
BOOKS TO WATCH OUT FOR
Bordighera, Inc.
Broken Jaw Press
Carolina Wren Press
Casperian Books LLC
CESUM MAGAZINE
CHIRON REVIEW
THE CREAM CITY REVIEW
DARK GOTHIC RESURRECTED
Down There Press
The Fire!! Press
FLUENT ASCENSION
Garden House Press
GAYELLOW PAGES
GERTRUDE
Gertrude Press
Gival Press
GLB Publishers
GOOD GIRL
Grip Publishing
Holmes House
Ignite! Entertainment
IN OUR OWN WORDS
Ithuriel's Spear
KUUMBA
Lemieux International Ltd.
Lone Willow Press

MGW (Mom Guess What) Newsmagazine
Mondial
NAMBLA BULLETIN
New Falcon Publications
New Sins Press
OFF OUR BACKS
One Spirit Press
Orchard House Press
OUT OF LINE
Pagan Press
Palari Publishing
Parthian
Passion Power Press, Inc
PEACEWORK
Pleasure Boat Studio: A Literary Press (including imprints Caravel Books and Aequitas Books, and the division Empty Bowl Press)
Rapacious Press
Raular Publishing
Red Letter Press
RED MARE
RedBone Press
Re-invention UK Ltd
RFD
Salt Publishing
SENSATIONS MAGAZINE
Chuck Stewart
Synergy Press
Syracuse Cultural Workers/Tools for Change
TnT Classic Books
TREATING YOURSELF: The Alternative Medicine Journal
Triskelion Publishing
TURNING THE TIDE: Journal of Anti-Racist Action, Research & Education
The Twickenham Press
Two-Handed Engine Press
University of Chicago Press
Vanilla Heart Publishing
West Virginia University Press
Word Forge Books

GENDER ISSUES

APPLE VALLEY REVIEW: A Journal of Contemporary Literature
ATLANTIS: A Women's Studies Journal/Revue d'etudes sur les femmes
Bandanna Books
BOOKS TO WATCH OUT FOR
CANADIAN POETRY
Cantarabooks LLC
CESUM MAGAZINE
COLLEGE LITERATURE
CONSCIENCE: The Newsjournal of Catholic Opinion
CURRENTS: New Scholarship in the Human Services
DESIRE
Down There Press
Ephemera Bound Publishing
Eros Books
EROSHA
Forest Dale Publishing Company
Gertrude Press
GREEN ANARCHY
The Haworth Press
HYPATIA: A Journal of Feminist Philosophy
IRIS: A Journal About Women
Islewest Publishing
Kumarian Press
LAKE EFFECT
MEAT: A Journal of Writing and Materiality
MOTHERVERSE: A Journal of Contemporary Motherhood
P.R.A. Publishing
Passion Power Press, Inc
Pavement Saw Press
Poor Richard's Press
PSYCHE
RED MARE
School for Advanced Research Press

South End Press
State University of New York Press
Synergy Press
Thunder Rain Publishing Corp.
Whispering Pine Press
WOMEN AND LANGUAGE
WORDKNOT AUDIO: A Literary Podcast Magazine
WSQ (formerly WOMEN'S STUDIES QUARTERLY)

GENEALOGY

Alaska Native Language Center
Assilem 9 Publications
Cantadora Press
COGNITIO: A Graduate Humanities Journal
Colerith Press
Cottontail Publications
Crazy Woman Creek Press
Guarionex Press Ltd.
Heritage Books, Inc.
INKY TRAIL NEWS
IRISH FAMILY JOURNAL
Irish Genealogical Foundation
Lion's Den Publishing
ORAL HISTORY REVIEW
Panther Creek Press
Park Place Publications
Rayve Productions Inc.
Stewart Publishing & Printing
Titus Home Publishing
Total Cardboard Publishing
The Urbana Free Library
WEST GOES SOUTH

GEOGRAPHY

The Denali Press
EXIT 13 MAGAZINE
THE JOURNAL OF AFRICAN TRAVEL-WRITING
Laguna Wilderness Press
Libertas Press, LLC.
New England Cartographics, Inc.
Rada Press, Inc.
United Nations University Press
The Urbana Free Library
Zagier & Urruty Publications

GEOLOGY

America West Publishers
Black Dome Press Corp.
Mountain Press Publishing Co.
SEA KAYAKER
Genny Smith Books
Sunbelt Publications
John Wade, Publisher

GERMAN

A2Z Publications LLC
ABSINTHE: New European Writing
THE ADIRONDACK REVIEW
R.J. Bender Publishing
Black Lawrence Press
Dufour Editions Inc.
The Edwin Mellen Press
GERMAN LIFE
Green Hut Press
Ignite! Entertainment
INTERNATIONAL POETRY REVIEW

GLOBAL AFFAIRS

Academy Press of America
Accendo Publishing
ALTERNATIVE PRESS INDEX
Cantarabooks LLC
Dervla Publishing, LLC
FEMINIST STUDIES
Global Learning
Ho Logos Press
Hope Publishing House
Kakibubu Media Limited

Kumarian Press
La Familia Publishing
Libertas Press, LLC.
LifeCircle Press
MAIN STREET RAG
MOTHERVERSE: A Journal of Contemporary Motherhood
Nonetheless Press
Obie Joe Media
Origin Press
PEACEWORK
School for Advanced Research Press
TELOS
THE VIRGINIA QUARTERLY REVIEW
WAV MAGAZINE: Progressive Music Art Politics Culture

GOVERNMENT

Academy Press of America
Benchmark Publications Inc.
Bluestocking Press
Bookhaven Press, LLC
Borealis Press Limited
CESUM MAGAZINE
Chandler & Sharp Publishers, Inc.
Children Of Mary
CKO UPDATE
Comstock Bonanza Press
Encore Publishing
FIDELIS ET VERUS
Florida Academic Press
Ho Logos Press
KETTERING REVIEW
Kumarian Press
Libertas Press, LLC.
LifeCircle Press
THE LONG TERM VIEW: A Journal of Informed Opinion
Maryland Historical Press (also MHPress)
Obie Joe Media
Origin Press
Poplar Leaf Press
PRISON LEGAL NEWS
Ridenbaugh Press
Sabellapress
Signalman Publishing
TELOS
TRUTH SEEKER
The Urbana Free Library
THE VIRGINIA QUARTERLY REVIEW
WAV MAGAZINE: Progressive Music Art Politics Culture
Wellington House Publishing Company
Wind River Institute Press/Wind River Broadcasting

GRAPHIC DESIGN

Allworth Press
ART BUREAU
Best Books Plus
Brenner Information Group
Cypress Creek Publishing
EEI Press
ERDC Publishing
INDUSTRY MINNE-ZINE
NORTH CAROLINA LITERARY REVIEW
SAGE OF CONSCIOUSNESS E-ZINE
1097 MAGAZINE
THIRDEYE MAGAZINE
UmbraProjects Publishing

GRAPHICS

ART BUREAU
Banana Productions
Barefoot Press
BOOK MARKETING UPDATE
BrickHouse Books, Inc.
Bright Hill Press
CHILDREN, CHURCHES AND DADDIES, A Non Religious, Non Familial Literary Magazine
DOWN IN THE DIRT LITERARY MAGAZINE, the prose & poetry magazine revealing all your dirty little secrets
EDGZ

THE ENGLISH CLARION
FREEDOM AND STRENGTH PRESS FORUM
HAPA NUI
The Hosanna Press
Immediate Direction Publications
INDUSTRY MINNE-ZINE
INTERNATIONAL ART POST
KALDRON, An International Journal Of Visual Poetry
LIGHT: The Quarterly of Light Verse
LIGHTWORKS MAGAZINE
LOST GENERATION JOURNAL
THE LUMMOX JOURNAL
Luna Bisonte Prods
MEAT: A Journal of Writing and Materiality
MIDNIGHT STREET
THE NEW RENAISSANCE, an international magazine of ideas & opinions, emphasizing literature & the arts
Oak Knoll Press
OFF THE COAST
Pearl's Book'em Publisher
PIG IRON
PRAKALPANA SAHITYA/PRAKALPANA LITERA-TURE
Pussywillow
RIVER STYX
The Runaway Spoon Press
Scars Publications
Smyrna Press
SOUTHWEST COLORADO ARTS PERSPECTIVE
STUDIO - A Journal of Christians Writing
13TH MOON
TIGHTROPE
Univelt, Inc.
Westgate Press
THE WORCESTER REVIEW

GREAT LAKES

Allium Press of Chicago
Anacus Press, An Imprint of Finney Company
Arbutus Press
Cable Publishing
Wm.B. Eerdmans Publishing Co.
Farcountry Press
Farcountry Press
Jackson Harbor Press
Lake Claremont Press
LAKE SUPERIOR MAGAZINE
Mayapple Press
Ohio University Press/Swallow Press
Slipdown Mountain Publications LLC
Wilderness Adventure Books

GREAT PLAINS

Eagle's View Publishing
Farcountry Press
Farcountry Press
NORTH DAKOTA QUARTERLY
OVERLAND JOURNAL
THE PRAIRIE JOURNAL OF CANADIAN LITERATURE
Skyline West Press/Wyoming Almanac
SOUTH DAKOTA REVIEW
Southern Illinois University Press
Texas Tech University Press
UND Press
University of Nebraska Press
WESTERN AMERICAN LITERATURE

GREEK

ABSINTHE: New European Writing
Anagnosis
THE CHARIOTEER
Dwarf Lion Press
Focus Publishing/R. Pullins Co.
Hopeace Press
Horned Owl Publishing
INTERNATIONAL POETRY REVIEW
JOURNAL OF THE HELLENIC DIASPORA
Pella Publishing Co.

Saint Bob Press
Wide World Publishing

GRIEVING

Center for Thanatology Research & Education, Inc.
City Life Books, LLC
Dumouriez Publishing
ERASED, SIGH, SIGH
Forest Dale Publishing Company
Fruitbearer Publishing, LLC
Galen Press, Ltd.
HEALMB Publishing
Imago Press
Impact Publishers, Inc.
InsideOut Press
Islewest Publishing
Jalmar Press/Innerchoice Publishing
KotaPress
A.P. Lee & Co., Ltd.
Medusa's Muse
NewSage Press
Practically Shameless Press
Square One Publishers, Inc.
Tuvela Press
Upper Access Inc. Book Publishers
White Buck Publishing
Wise Press
Word Forge Books

GUIDANCE

Aaron Communications III
Academy Press of America
THE ART OF ABUNDANCE
Black Forest Press and The Tennessee Publishing House
Church Leadership Library (US Office)
Forest Dale Publishing Company
Hopeace Press
Impact Publishers, Inc.
Jalmar Press/Innerchoice Publishing
A.P. Lee & Co., Ltd.
Meek Publishing
Mind Power Publishing
Nonetheless Press
Perpetual Press
Saint Mary's Press
Summerland Publishing

HAIKU

AIS Publications
Allbook Books
THE AUROREAN
BLACK BEAR REVIEW
Bogg Publications
BOGG: A Journal of Contemporary Writing
Brooks Books
THE CANNON'S MOUTH
CELLAR
Cloud 9 Publishing
COMPASS ROSE
CONCRETE JUNGLE JOURNAL
Devenish Press
DREAM FANTASY INTERNATIONAL
Drinian Press
FROGPOND: Journal of the Haiku Society of America
From Here Press
FROZEN WAFFLES
Frozen Waffles Press/Shattered Sidewalks Press; 45th Century Chapbooks
GENRE: WRITER AND WRITINGS
GIN BENDER POETRY REVIEW
Haiku Society of America
HAPA NUI
THE HERON'S NEST
A HUDSON VIEW POETRY DIGEST
ILLUMINATIONS LITERARY JOURNAL
J. Mark Press
Jackson Harbor Press
Kenyette Productions

La Alameda Press
LILLIPUT REVIEW
Lilly Press
LITTLE BALKANS REVIEW
MAYFLY
MELEE
MODERN HAIKU
THE MORNING DEW REVIEW
Mystery Island Publications
NEW AMERICAN IMAGIST
NEW HOPE INTERNATIONAL REVIEW
THE OTHER HERALD
Pearl's Book'em Publisher
Persephone Press
PINE ISLAND JOURNAL OF NEW ENGLAND POETRY
Poetic Matrix Press
POETS' ROUNDTABLE
Press Here
RAINBOW CURVE
RATTAPALLAX
Redgreene Press
A RESOURCE FOR EMBEDDED HAIKU
RIVER POETS JOURNAL
RIVERBED HAIKU
SAGE OF CONSCIOUSNESS E-ZINE
SHORT FUSE
Silenced Press
Skyline Publications
SMARTISH PACE
Snapshot Press
SNOW MONKEY
SOUTHWEST COLORADO ARTS PERSPECTIVE
Spring Grass
Subsynchronuos Press
TIGHTROPE
TUNDRA
U.S.1 WORKSHEETS
VARIOUS ARTISTS
VEIL: Journal of Darker Musings
XTRAS
Zygote Publishing

HANDICAPPED

ABLAZE Publishing
Alpine Guild, Inc.
Brain Injury Success Books
CONCRETE JUNGLE JOURNAL
Creative Arts Book Company
The Edwin Mellen Press
Forest Dale Publishing Company
HEARING HEALTH
Jon's Adventure Productions
Massey-Reyner Publishing
The Place In The Woods
Spring Grass
John Wade, Publisher

HANDWRITING/WRITTEN

Continuing Education Press
ILLOGICAL MUSE
LDP, an occasional journal of aesthetics & language
OTHER INVESTIGATIONS
Pavement Saw Press

HAWAII

Bamboo Ridge Press
BAMBOO RIDGE, Journal of Hawai'i Literature and Arts
The Bess Press
THE EAST HAWAII OBSERVER
HAWAI'I REVIEW
Keiki O Ka Aina Press
MANOA: A Pacific Journal of International Writing
A Melody from an Immigrant's Soul
Mo'omana'o Press
Mountain Automation Corporation
Petroglyph Press, Ltd.
Philos Press
Titlewaves Publishing; Writers Direct

TURNING THE TIDE: Journal of Anti-Racist Action, Research & Education
Wide World Publishing

HEALTH

AB
Abecedarian books, Inc.
Abigon Press
ABLAZE Publishing
Act on Wisdom
Addicus Books, Inc.
Ageless Press
Allwrite Advertising and Publishing
Alpine Guild, Inc.
AMERICAN VEGAN
Anomaly Press
Anti-Aging Press
ARCATA ARTS
Ash Tree Publishing
Balanced Books Publishing
BeachSide Press
Bear & Company
Beekman Books, Inc.
Beyond Words Publishing, Inc.
BLUE MOUNTAIN
Bonus Books, Inc.
THE BOOMERPHILE
Brain Injury Success Books
Branden Books
Cable Publishing
Cassandra Press, Inc.
Cladach Publishing
Consumer Press
Creative Writing and Publishing Company
Cuore Libre Publishing
Cypress Creek Publishing
Cypress House
DAILY WORD
Dash-Hill, LLC
Delaney Day Press
Demarche Publishing LLC
Dharma Publishing
Down There Press
Dream Publishing Co.
THE EAST HAWAII OBSERVER
Encore Publishing
Enlightened Living Publishing, LLC
Nicolin Fields Publishing, Inc.
Fitness Press
Flowerfield Enterprises, LLC
Foodnsport Press
Forest Dale Publishing Company
Front Row Experience
Future Horizons, Inc.
Galde Press, Inc.
Galen Press, Ltd.
Garden House Press
Glenbridge Publishing Ltd.
Golden West Books
GoldenHouse Publishing Group
Good Book Publishing Company
Gurze Books
Haight-Ashbury Publications
HAMPTON ROADS HEALTH JOURNAL
HEALMB Publishing
THE HEALTH JOURNALS
Health Plus Publishers
Health Press NA Inc.
HEALTHY WEIGHT JOURNAL
HEARING HEALTH
Heritage Global Publishing
Hill Country Books
Hope Publishing House
Howln Moon Press
Hunter House Inc., Publishers
Immunizations for Public Health
Impact Publishers, Inc.
IN OUR OWN WORDS

Joelle Publishing
JOURNAL OF PSYCHOACTIVE DRUGS
Kali Press
La Alameda Press
Lamp Light Press
Lemieux International Ltd.
Lemon Grove Press
Life Energy Media
Lion Press
MACROBIOTICS TODAY
McBooks Press, Inc.
MEDICAL HISTORY
Midwifery Today
N: NUDE & NATURAL
NATURALLY
New Atlantean Press
New Falcon Publications
New Knowledge Press
New Sins Press
New Win Publishing
New World Library
Nonetheless Press
North Star Books
OFF OUR BACKS
George Ohsawa Macrobiotic Foundation
Origin Press
OVERLAND JOURNAL
Palari Publishing
Papoose Publishing
Peachtree Publishers, Ltd.
PEDIATRICS FOR PARENTS
Petroglyph Press, Ltd.
Piccadilly Books, Ltd.
Platinum One Publishing
Price World Publishing
Princess Publishing
QED Press
Rayve Productions Inc.
RFD
RTMC Organization, LLC
Sagamore Publishing
Sassy Sunflower Books
Savor Publishing House, Inc.
Sentient Publications, LLC
Set Sail Productions, LLC
SO YOUNG!
SOM Publishing, division of School of Metaphysics
Sound Enterprises Publishing
Southwest Research and Information Center
Spinifex Press
Square One Publishers, Inc.
Standish Press
Steel Balls Press
Sunrise Health Coach Publications
George Suttton Publishing Co.
Synergy Press
T'AI CHI
Thatch Tree Publications
THRESHOLDS JOURNAL
Titan Press
Titlewaves Publishing; Writers Direct
TREATING YOURSELF: The Alternative Medicine Journal
UBC Press
Unity House
UNITY MAGAZINE
Upper Access Inc. Book Publishers
Vanderbilt University Press
Vanguard Press
VEGETARIAN JOURNAL
Vestibular Disorders Association
VOICES FROM THE EARTH
Volcano Press, Inc
Wayfarer Publications
Wellcome Trust Centre for the History of Medicine at UCL
Wharton Publishing, Inc.
Whole Person Associates Inc.
WIN NEWS

Wish Publishing
Women of Diversity Productions, Inc.
Word Forge Books
World Changing Books
Yes International Publishers
YMAA Publication Center

ERNEST HEMINGWAY

Broken Jaw Press
KUMQUAT MERINGUE
LOST GENERATION JOURNAL
Pineapple Press, Inc.
Six Ft. Swells Press
Zygote Publishing

HISTORY

A2Z Publications LLC
Aardvark Enterprises (Sole Proprietorship of J. Alvin Speers)
AAS HISTORY SERIES
Academy Press of America
AFRICAN AMERICAN REVIEW
AK Press
ALBERTA HISTORY
Allium Press of Chicago
Allwrite Advertising and Publishing
AltaMira Press
AMERICAN FORESTS
American Legacy Media
AMERICAN ROAD
Ammons Communications; Imprint: Catch the Spirit of Appalachia
Anagnosis
THE ANNALS OF IOWA
Anvil Publishers, Inc.
Appalachian Consortium Press
Appalachian House
Arden Press, Inc.
Atelier Press
ATLANTIS: A Women's Studies Journal/Revue d'etudes sur les femmes
Aura Productions, LLC
Avari Press
Avery Color Studios
Axios Newletter, Inc.
The B & R Samizdat Express
BANANA RAG
Bauhan Publishing, LLC
The Bear Wallow Publishing Company
Beekman Books, Inc.
W.S. Beetle & Company
BEGINNING MAGAZINE
R.J. Bender Publishing
Betelgeuse Books
BIBLIOPHILOS
BIG MUDDY: Journal of the Mississippi River Valley
Biographical Publishing Company
Black Dome Press Corp.
Blackwater Publications
Bloated Toe Publishing
THE BLOOMSBURY REVIEW
Blue Hull Press
Blue Unicorn Press, Inc.
Bluestocking Press
THE BOOMERPHILE
Borealis Press Limited
A. Borough Books
Branden Books
Brentwood Christian Press
THE BRIAR CLIFF REVIEW
Brick Road Poetry Press
BRIDGES: An Interdisciplinary Journal of Theology, Philosophy, History, and Science
Bright Mountain Books
Broken Jaw Press
Broken Rifle Press
Brooke-Richards Press
Brookline Books

Buenos Books
Burd Street Press
Cable Publishing
CALLIOPE: Exploring World History
Camel Press
Canadian Committee on Labour History
Candlestick Publishing
CAPCAT
Casperian Books LLC
Celtic Heritage Books
Center for Japanese Studies
Center for Thanatology Research & Education, Inc.
Chelsea Green Publishing Company
Cheops Books
CINEASTE MAGAZINE
Arthur H. Clark Co.
Clark-Nova Books
CMP Publishing Group LLC
Coastal 181
COBBLESTONE: Discover American History
COGNITIO: A Graduate Humanities Journal
Colerith Press
Command Performance Press
Communication Creativity
Comstock Bonanza Press
Cornucopia Press
Cotsen Institute of Archaeology Publications
Cottontail Publications
Cottonwood Press, Inc.
Creative Roots, Inc.
CROSSCURRENTS
Cypress Creek Publishing
Cypress House
DAILY WORD
THE DALHOUSIE REVIEW
Deep Well Publishing Company
The Denali Press
Dharma Publishing
Down The Shore Publishing
Downeast Books
Paul Dry Books
Dufour Editions Inc.
DUST (From the Ego Trip)
Dwarf Lion Press
Eagle's View Publishing
East West Discovery Press
Edition Gemini
The Edwin Mellen Press
The Edwin Mellen Press
Wm.B. Eerdmans Publishing Co.
ELEMENTS
Ephemera Bound Publishing
Equine Graphics Publishing Group: New Concord Press, SmallHorse Press, SunDrop
Erespin Press
Evolution Publishing
Faith Builders Resource Group
Fantail
Farcountry Press
Farcountry Press
The Feminist Press at the City University of New York
FEMINIST STUDIES
Florida Academic Press
Forest Dale Publishing Company
Fotofolio, Inc.
Fulcrum, Inc.
Galde Press, Inc.
Gallaudet University Press
Garden House Press
GERMAN LIFE
The Glencannon Press
Global Learning
Golden Quill Press
Golden West Books
Good Book Publishing Company
The Gutenberg Press
Heartsong Books
Heidelberg Graphics

Heritage Books, Inc.
Heritage House Publishers
Heyday Books
Hidden Valley Farm, Publisher
High Plains Press
Hill Country Books
Historical Resources Press
Historical Society of Alberta
HISTORICAL STUDIES IN THE PHYSICAL & BIOLO-
  GICAL SCIENCES
History Compass, LLC
HISTORY OF INTELLECTUAL CULTURE
Ho Logos Press
Hole In The Head Press
Homa & Sekey Books
Hoover Institution Press
Horned Owl Publishing
Hot Box Press / Southern Roots Publishing
Huntington Library Press
HUNTINGTON LIBRARY QUARTERLY
Icarus Press
Info Net Publishing
Interlink Publishing Group, Inc.
IOWA HERITAGE ILLUSTRATED
Iris Publishing Group, Inc (Iris Press / Tellico Books)
ITALIAN AMERICANA
Italica Press, Inc.
JACK MACKEREL MAGAZINE
Jackson Harbor Press
JEWISH CURRENTS
THE JOURNAL OF PSYCHOHISTORY
Just Sisters Publications
Keokee Co. Publishing, Inc.
KMT, A Modern Journal of Ancient Egypt
Allen A. Knoll Publishers
LABOUR/LE TRAVAIL
Lahontan Images
Lake Claremont Press
LAKE SUPERIOR MAGAZINE
The Latona Press
Lemieux International Ltd.
LEO Productions LLC.
Libertas Press, LLC.
LITTLE BALKANS REVIEW
Litwin Books
Lost Pond Press
Loving Healing Press, Inc.
Lucky Press, LLC
MacDonald/Sward Publishing Company
Magnifico Publications
Maisonneuve Press
Peter Marcan Publications
Margaret Media, Inc.
Maryland Historical Press (also MHPress)
Mayhaven Publishing, Inc.
McBooks Press, Inc.
MCM Entertainment, Inc. Publishing Division
MEDICAL HISTORY
Mehring Books, Inc.
Mercer University Press
Micron Press
THE MIDWEST QUARTERLY
Minnesota Historical Society Press
Mock Turtle Press
Moo-Cow Fan Club
Moonrise Press
MOTHERVERSE: A Journal of Contemporary Motherhood
Mount Ida Press
Mountain Automation Corporation
Mountain State Press
N: NUDE & NATURAL
The Narrative Press
NEW ENGLAND BY RAIL
New England Cartographics, Inc.
THE NEW ENGLAND QUARTERLY
NEWS FROM NATIVE CALIFORNIA
Nip and Tuck Publishing
Noontide Press

North Country Books, Inc.
NOVA RELIGIO
Oak Knoll Press
Ohio University Press/Swallow Press
One Horse Press/Rainy Day Press
Open Hand Publishing LLC
Orage Publishing
ORAL HISTORY REVIEW
Oregon State University Press
THE OTHER HERALD
OTHER INVESTIGATIONS
THE OTHER ISRAEL
Paladin Enterprises, Inc.
Parkway Publishers, Inc.
Pathfinder Press
Peartree Books & Music
Petroglyph Press, Ltd.
Pictorial Histories Pub. Co.
Pineapple Press, Inc.
Pirate Publishing International
PLEASANT LIVING
Pocahontas Press, Inc.
Pogo Press, Incorporated
The Post-Apollo Press
Protean Press
Pruett Publishing Company
Psychohistory Press
THE PUBLIC HISTORIAN
PublishingWorks, Inc.
QED Press
Quarterly Committee of Queen's University
QUEEN'S QUARTERLY: A Canadian Review
Quill Driver Books
Rada Press, Inc.
Peter E. Randall Publisher
Rayve Productions Inc.
RED LAMP
RELIGION & AMERICAN CULTURE
REPRESENTATIONS
Ridenbaugh Press
Rock Spring Press Inc.
Ronsdale Press
Rowhouse Press
Sand River Press
Santa Fe Writers Project
Saqi Books Publisher
School for Advanced Research Press
Scottwall Associates, Publishers
SeaCrab Publishing
SECRETUM MEUM MIHI
Secretum Meum Mihi Press
The Sektor Co.
SENSATIONS MAGAZINE
Small Dogma Publishing, Inc.
Genny Smith Books
Sonoran Publishing
Southeast Missouri State University Press
Southern Illinois University Press
THE SOUTHERN QUARTERLY: A Journal of the Arts in
  the South
Southwestern Michigan Publications
SPECS
Starry Night Publishing
Steerforth Press, L.C.
Stewart Publishing & Printing
Stormline Press, Inc.
STORMWARNING!
Sherwood Sugden & Company, Publishers
Sherwood Sugden & Company, Publishers
Sunbelt Publications
Sunstone Press
SYMPLOKE: A Journal for the Intermingling of Literary,
  Cultural and Theoretical Scholarship
THE TABBY: A CHRONICLE OF THE ARTS AND
  CRAFTS MOVEMENT
The Teitan Press, Inc.
TELOS
Temple Inc.

Theytus Books Ltd.
Thirsty Turtle Press
Thirteen Colonies Press
Thunder Rain Publishing Corp.
Thundercloud Books
Titus Home Publishing
The True Bill Press
Truman State University Press
TRUTH SEEKER
Tuns Press
Tuscarora Books Inc.
Twin Souls Publications
UBC Press
Unity House
UNITY MAGAZINE
University of Akron Press
University of Arkansas Press
University of Calgary Press
University of Chicago Press
University of Massachusetts Press
University of Nebraska Press
University of South Carolina Press
University of Tampa Press
University of Virginia Press
University Press of Colorado
UnKnownTruths.com Publishing Company
The Urbana Free Library
Urion Press
Utah State University Press
Van Cleave Publishing
Vanilla Heart Publishing
Village Lane Press
Vintage Romance Publishing, LLC
Virginia City Publishing Co. LLC
THE VIRGINIA QUARTERLY REVIEW
Volcano Press, Inc
WEBER: The Contemporary West
Wellcome Trust Centre for the History of Medicine at UCL
White Mane Publishing Company, Inc.
White Thread Press
Wintertree Press
WISCONSIN TRAILS
Word Forge Books
WORDKNOT AUDIO: A Literary Podcast Magazine
Writers House Press
WSQ (formerly WOMEN'S STUDIES QUARTERLY)
Wytherngate Press
Zagier & Urruty Publications
Zumaya Publications LLC

SHERLOCK HOLMES

THE ENGLISH CLARION
ENGLISH LITERATURE IN TRANSITION, 1880-1920
Gryphon Books
KUMQUAT MERINGUE
THE MYSTERY REVIEW
PAPERBACK PARADE

HOLOCAUST

A Midsummer Night's Press
Absey & Co.
AIS Publications
BLACKBIRD
Book Marketing Solutions
BRIDGES: An Interdisciplinary Journal of Theology, Philosophy, History, and Science
Creative Arts Book Company
Cross-Cultural Communications
GENRE: WRITER AND WRITINGS
Legacy Audio Books, Inc.
New Concept Press
Noontide Press
Paragon House Publishers
POETICA MAGAZINE, Reflections of Jewish Thought
Roaring Lion Publishing
SterlingHouse Publisher
University of Calgary Press
Van Cleave Publishing

Vox Humana Books
VOX Press
WAR, LITERATURE & THE ARTS: An International Journal of the Humanities
The Wessex Collective

HOLOGRAPHY

JACK MACKEREL MAGAZINE
Rowhouse Press

HOMELESSNESS

Calyx Books
HEALMB Publishing
Iniquity Press/Vendetta Books
La Familia Publishing
P.R.A. Publishing
Pocol Press
Raven Publishing, Inc.
VOX Press

HOMEMAKING

Affinity Publishers Services
BLUE COLLAR REVIEW
Center For Self-Sufficiency
MOTHERVERSE: A Journal of Contemporary Motherhood
Nunciata
OUT YOUR BACKDOOR: The Magazine of Do-It-Yourself Adventure and Homegrown Culture

HORROR

ALMOST NORMAL COMICS and Other Oddities
Apex Book Company
APEX Magazine
ARTISTIC RAMBLINGS
AXE FACTORY REVIEW
BUST DOWN THE DOOR AND EAT ALL THE CHICKENS: A Journal of Absurd and Surreal Fiction
Cheops Books
Crystal Dreams Publishing
DARK GOTHIC RESURRECTED
Ephemera Bound Publishing
The Fiction Works
Flapjack Press
Foremost Press
Glass Tower Press
Gothic Press
GUD MAGAZINE (Greatest Uncommon Denominator)
Harbor House
Harvest Shadows Publications
Immediate Direction Publications
LOW BUDGET SCIENCE FICTION
LULLABY HEARSE
MEAT FOR TEA: THE VALLEY REVIEW
Merrimack Books
MIDNIGHT STREET
Multi-Media Publications Inc.
MYSTERY ISLAND MAGAZINE
Pocol Press
Raular Publishing
Saint Bob Press
Skullvines Press
Skyline Publications
SPACE AND TIME
SPECTACULAR SPECULATIONS
SPINNINGS...INTENSE TALES OF LIFE MAGAZINE
Subsynchronuos Press
SWILL
Triumvirate Publications
Twilight Tales, Inc.
VEIL: Journal of Darker Musings
Whiskey Creek Press
Wintertree Press
The Wolf Pirate Project Inc.
Zirlinson Publishing

HORTICULTURE

Arizona Master Gardener Press
Bright Mountain Books

Focus Publishing/R. Pullins Co.
Huntington Library Press
B.B. Mackey Books
Malki Museum Press
Pacific Isle Publishing Company
Park Place Publications
Red Eye Press
Shared Roads Press

HOW-TO

AB
Absey & Co.
Academy Press of America
Addicus Books, Inc.
Affinity Publishers Services
Affinity Publishers Services
Alaska Native Language Center
Allworth Press
American Literary Press
Anderson Publishing; also RC Anderson Books
Annedawn Publishing
Anti-Aging Press
Arden Press, Inc.
Assilem 9 Publications
Atlantic Publishing Group, Inc.
Backcountry Publishing
Barney Press
Beagle Bay Books / Creative Minds Press
Benchmark Publications Inc.
The Bess Press
Beynch Press Publishing Company
Blue Dolphin Publishing, Inc.
Bonus Books, Inc.
Bookhaven Press, LLC
A. Borough Books
Brain Injury Success Books
Brenner Information Group
Bronze Girl Productions, Inc.
BYLINE
C & T Publishing
Camp Colton
Cassandra Press, Inc.
Center For Self-Sufficiency
Chelsea Green Publishing Company
Chicago Review Press
Chicago Spectrum Press
The Chicot Press
Church Leadership Library (US Office)
Communication Creativity
The Communication Press
Consumer Press
Cookbook Resources, LLC
Cottonwood Press, Inc.
Crandall, Dostie & Douglass Books, Inc.
Crane Press
Crystal Dreams Publishing
Cypress House
D.B.A. Books
Dash-Hill, LLC
Disparate Voices
Dixon-Price Publishing
Dog's Eye View Media
DOLLS UNITED INTERACTIVE MAGAZINE
Dominion Global Publishing
Downeast Books
Dunamis House
Dustbooks
DWELLING PORTABLY
Eagle's View Publishing
Ecrivez!
ETC Publications
Ethos Publishing
Famaco Publishers (Qalam Books)
Fitness Press
Flowerfield Enterprises, LLC
Foremost Press
Gemini Publishing Company
Glenbridge Publishing Ltd.

GLOBAL ONE MAGAZINE
Goblin Fern Press
Good Life Products
Good Times Publishing Co.
Grace Creek Press
Green Square Publishing
Guarionex Press Ltd.
Heidelberg Graphics
Howln Moon Press
Hunter Publishing Corporation
Ibexa Press
Images Unlimited and Snaptail Press, a Division of Images
    Unlimited Publishing
In Print Publishing
Info Net Publishing
The Intrepid Traveler
Islewest Publishing
Jamenair Ltd.
JLA Publications, A Division Of Jeffrey Lant Associates,
    Inc.
Kali Press
Knowledge Concepts Publishing
Lamp Light Press
LAUGHING BEAR NEWSLETTER
Lemieux International Ltd.
Liberty Publishing Company, Inc.
Lion Press
Loving Healing Press, Inc.
MOBILE BEAT: The Mobile Entertainer's Magazine
Motom
Muse World Media Group
National Writers Press
New Win Publishing
Nightsun Books
Nolo Press Occidental
North Star Books
Noved Audio
Nunciata
Nushape Publication
Oak Tree Press
Open Horizons Publishing Company
Orchard House Press
Paladin Enterprises, Inc.
PARENTEACHER MAGAZINE
Penworth Publishing
Perpetual Press
Phelps Publishing Company
Piccadilly Books, Ltd.
The Poetry Center Press/Shoestring Press
PREP Publishing
Pushcart Press
QED Press
Quill Driver Books
Rainbow Books, Inc.
Ram Press
Rayve Productions Inc.
Red Eye Press
Riverwinds Publishing
Rolling Hills Publishing
RUMINATIONS: The Nigerian Dwarf & Mini Dairy Goat
    Magazine
Santa Monica Press
Sassy Sunflower Books
Scentouri, Publishing Division
SEA KAYAKER
SEDUCTIVE SELLING
Sentient Publications, LLC
Shared Roads Press
Sherian Publishing
SO YOUNG!
SOM Publishing, division of School of Metaphysics
Sourcebooks, Inc.
SPEX (SMALL PRESS EXCHANGE)
Square One Publishers, Inc.
Standish Press
Steel Balls Press
Stewart Publishing & Printing
Storm Publishing Group

Success Publishing
Sweet People Publishing
Tamal Vista Publications
Tax Property Investor, Inc.
Thatch Tree Publications
Three Pyramids Publishing
Titlewaves Publishing; Writers Direct
Toca Family Publishing, div. of Toca Family Communications Group, LLC
Trafton Publishing
Twilight Tales, Inc.
Twinteum Artist, Inc.
Unlimited Publishing LLC
Vanilla Heart Publishing
Village Lane Press
Visual Arts Press
VOICE(S)
John Wade, Publisher
Wafer Mache Publications
Wayside Publications
Wharton Publishing, Inc.
Zelda Wilde Publishing
Wilderness Adventure Books
Willfam Publishing Co.
Wilshire Books Inc.
WindRiver Publishing
Winslow Publishing
Wintertree Press
Write Now Publishing Company
YMAA Publication Center

HUMAN RIGHTS

AB
ABRAMELIN: a Journal of Poetry and Magick
AIS Publications
AMERICAN JONES BUILDING & MAINTENANCE
Anderson Publishing; also RC Anderson Books
Archer Books
Bauu Press
Beacon Press
BLUE COLLAR REVIEW
CAIRN: The New St. Andrews Review
Calaca Press
Candlestick Publishing
CESUM MAGAZINE
Clarity Press, Inc.
COALITION FOR PRISONERS' RIGHTS NEWSLETTER
COLORLINES
COUNTERPOISE: For Social Responsibilities, Liberty and Dissent
Crandall, Dostie & Douglass Books, Inc.
CROSSCURRENTS
DREAM NETWORK
The Edwin Mellen Press
FEMINIST STUDIES
FOURTH WORLD REVIEW
FRIENDS OF PEACE PILGRIM
GENRE: WRITER AND WRITINGS
GLB Publishers
Global Options
Inner City Press
INNER CITY PRESS
InsideOut Press
INTERCULTURE
Libertas Press, LLC.
LIBERTY
MindGlow Media
Missing Spoke Press
MOTHERVERSE: A Journal of Contemporary Motherhood
MOUTH: Voice of the Dis-Labeled Nation
P.R.A. Publishing
PEACEWORK
The People's Press
POETRYREPAIRS: Contemporary International Poetry
PRISON LEGAL NEWS
THE PUBLIC EYE
RED LAMP
SOCIAL JUSTICE: A JOURNAL OF CRIME, CONFLICT,

& WORLD ORDER
STORMWARNING!
Syracuse Cultural Workers/Tools for Change
THIRDEYE MAGAZINE
Thirdeye Publications
TREATING YOURSELF: The Alternative Medicine Journal
TRUTH SEEKER
TURNING THE TIDE: Journal of Anti-Racist Action, Research & Education
TURNING WHEEL
Vox Humana Books
WAV MAGAZINE: Progressive Music Art Politics Culture
World Changing Books

HUMANISM

AIS Publications
ASCENT
ATLANTIS: A Women's Studies Journal/Revue d'etudes sur les femmes
BELLEVUE LITERARY REVIEW
Black Rose Books Ltd.
Blue Lupin Press
BOULDER HERETIC
Cantarabooks LLC
COSMOPSIS QUARTERLY
Dharma Publishing
Disparate Voices
Dufour Editions Inc.
EMERGING
Erespin Press
Fine Tooth Press
FOURTH WORLD REVIEW
THE FREEFALL REVIEW
Garden House Press
GENRE: WRITER AND WRITINGS
Green Hut Press
Intuitive Moon Media
LP Publications (Teleos Institute)
Luminous Epinoia Press
Lycanthrope Press
Maisonneuve Press
MELEE
MindGlow Media
NATURALLY
Open Wide Books
OUT OF LINE
The People's Press
POETRYREPAIRS: Contemporary International Poetry
RED LAMP
REPORTS OF THE NATIONAL CENTER FOR SCIENCE EDUCATION
Savant Garde Workshop
SCHUYLKILL VALLEY JOURNAL
SHARE INTERNATIONAL
SPECS
SYMPLOKE: A Journal for the Intermingling of Literary, Cultural and Theoretical Scholarship
VanderWyk & Burnham
VOICE(S)
West End Press

HUMOR

A Midsummer Night's Press
Abecedarian books, Inc.
ACME Press
Ageless Press
All That Productions,Inc.
THE AMERICAN DRIVEL REVIEW
American Literary Press
ARTISTIC RAMBLINGS
Aspen Mountain Publishing
AT-HOME DAD
ATLANTIC PACIFIC PRESS
The B & R Samizdat Express
BABYSUE
BANANA RAG
Bancroft Press

Beagle Bay Books / Creative Minds Press
BEGGARS & CHEESEBURGERS
BEGINNING MAGAZINE
BEGINNINGS - A Magazine for the Novice Writer
The Bess Press
BLADES
Blue Dolphin Publishing, Inc.
Blue Lupin Press
Blue Mouse Studio
THE BOOMERPHILE
A. Borough Books
Brave Ulysses Books
Brick Road Poetry Press
Bright Mountain Books
Brook Farm Books
BUST DOWN THE DOOR AND EAT ALL THE CHICKENS: A Journal of Absurd and Surreal Fiction
C&R Press
THE CANNON'S MOUTH
CAPCAT
CAUSE & EFFECT MAGAZINE
The Center Press
Cloud 9 Publishing
The Communication Press
CONJUNCTIONS
COSMOPSIS QUARTERLY
Cottonwood Press, Inc.
Crystal Dreams Publishing
Dawn Sign Press
Disparate Voices
Dog's Eye View Media
Downeast Books
Dreams Due Media Group, Inc.
Eagle's View Publishing
Falls Media
FAT TUESDAY
First Books
Fotofolio, Inc.
4 Your Spirit Productions
THE FREEDONIA GAZETTE: The Magazine Devoted to the Marx Brothers
THE FREEFALL REVIEW
Fulcrum, Inc.
THE FUNNY TIMES
Gateways Books And Tapes
Gingerbread House
Glass Tower Press
GLOBAL ONE MAGAZINE
Grace Creek Press
HEELTAP/Pariah Press
Hobblebush Books
Hood Press
HUMOR TIMES
Ignite! Entertainment
IMOCO Publishing
IT'S JUST THIS LITTLE CHROMIUM SWITCH HERE
Jigsaw Press
Juel House Publishers and Literary Services
KALEIDOSCOPE: Exploring the Experience of Disability through Literature & the Fine Arts
Allen A. Knoll Publishers
KRAX
KUMQUAT MERINGUE
Lazywood Press
The Leaping Frog Press
LegacyForever
Lemieux International Ltd.
Lily Ruth Publishing
THE MAD HATTER
MAIN STREET RAG
MALEDICTA: The International Journal of Verbal Aggression
Mayhaven Publishing, Inc.
MEAT FOR TEA: THE VALLEY REVIEW
Medusa's Muse
MindGlow Media
MINESHAFT
MISSISSIPPI CROW

Muse World Media Group
Music City Publishing
MY TABLE: Houston's Dining Magazine
New Victoria Publishers
NIS America, Inc.
No Starch Press
North Star Books
Nushape Publication
NUTHOUSE
Oak Tree Press
OFFICE NUMBER ONE
ORBIS
Paladin Enterprises, Inc.
PALO ALTO REVIEW
Pariah Press
Penthe Publishing
PLAIN BROWN WRAPPER (PBW)
The Poetry Center Press/Shoestring Press
Pogo Press, Incorporated
Practically Shameless Press
THE PRAIRIE JOURNAL OF CANADIAN LITERATURE
Prairie Journal Press
The Press at Foggy Bottom
PublishAmerica, LLLP.
THE RAGING FACE: Goofball Prose
RAINBOW CURVE
Raw Dog Press
Red Rock Press
RedJack
RIVET MAGAZINE
The Runaway Spoon Press
Saint Bob Press
Santa Monica Press
SIDE OF GRITS
Silenced Press
Skyline Publications
Smirk Books
SO YOUNG!
Soto Publishing Company
SOUNDINGS REVIEW
Squire Press
Standish Press
Star Publish LLC
Starry Night Publishing
Stormline Press, Inc.
STRUGGLE: A Magazine of Proletarian Revolutionary Literature
SWILL
Synergistic Press
THALIA: Studies in Literary Humor
Third Dimension Publishing
THOUGHTS FOR ALL SEASONS: The Magazine of Epigrams
Three Bears Publishing
THRESHOLDS JOURNAL
Titlewaves Publishing; Writers Direct
Trafton Publishing
Transcending Mundane, Inc.
TREATING YOURSELF: The Alternative Medicine Journal
Twilight Tales, Inc.
Twilight Times Books
Twinteum Artist, Inc.
Two Thousand Three Associates
Two Thousand Three Associates
VOICE(S)
VOICES ISRAEL
WAV MAGAZINE: Progressive Music Art Politics Culture
Whiskey Creek Press
Willfam Publishing Co.
Wilshire Books Inc.
The Wolf Pirate Project Inc.
WORDKNOT AUDIO: A Literary Podcast Magazine
World Changing Books
World Gumbo Publishing
World Love Press Publishing

694

HUNGER

Bad Noise Productions
Kumarian Press
SHARE INTERNATIONAL

HYPNOSIS

Act on Wisdom
Borden Publishing Co.
Capalo Press
Dumouriez Publishing
L&L Dreamspell
THE2NDHAND
White Crosslet Publishing Co
Wilshire Books Inc.

IDAHO

COLD-DRILL
Eastern Washington University Press
Farcountry Press
The Great Rift Press
Idaho Center for the Book
Keokee Co. Publishing, Inc.
THE MEADOW
Ridenbaugh Press
SANDPOINT MAGAZINE

ILLINOIS

Allium Press of Chicago
BLACK BOOK PRESS: The Poetry Zine id
Chicago Review Press
Lake Claremont Press
Lawells Publishing
Mayhaven Publishing, Inc.
NEW MADRID
Northern Illinois University Press
RIVERBED HAIKU
Southern Illinois University Press
The Urbana Free Library

IMMIGRATION

A2Z Publications LLC
AB
Athanata Arts, Ltd.
Banta & Pool Literary Properties
Bay Tree Publishing
Bordighera, Inc.
Calaca Press
COLORLINES
East West Discovery Press
Heritage Books, Inc.
INDIA CURRENTS
INTERCULTURE
Kumarian Press
Mayapple Press
A Melody from an Immigrant's Soul
Mercer University Press
Nip and Tuck Publishing
Pixiu Press
PRISON LEGAL NEWS

INDEXES & ABSTRACTS

ALTERNATIVE PRESS INDEX
Anderson Publishing; also RC Anderson Books
COLLEGE LITERATURE
CONNEXIONS DIGEST
Connexions Information Services, Inc.
THE DALHOUSIE REVIEW
The Denali Press
FEMINIST PERIODICALS: A CURRENT LISTING OF CONTENTS
Heritage Books, Inc.
HORTIDEAS
Library Juice Press
NEW BOOKS ON WOMEN, GENDER, & FEMINISM
Oak Knoll Press
THE ORPHAN LEAF REVIEW
Passeggiata Press, Inc.

Univelt, Inc.
The Urbana Free Library
Volcano Press, Inc
Whitston Publishing Co.
Women's Studies Librarian, University of Wisconsin System

INDIA

ASCENT
Biographical Publishing Company
CONTEMPORARY GHAZALS
Erespin Press
Iconoclast Press
INDIA CURRENTS
INTERNATIONAL POETRY REVIEW
Pocol Press
TSAR Publications

INDIANA

Banta & Pool Literary Properties
Frozen Waffles Press/Shattered Sidewalks Press; 45th Century Chapbooks
Lawells Publishing
NEW MADRID
Stormline Press, Inc.

INDIANS

Alaska Native Language Center
Bauu Press
DTS Group, Inc.
Eagle's View Publishing
Heyday Books
KUMQUAT MERINGUE
Maryland Historical Press (also MHPress)
Minnesota Historical Society Press
Oregon State University Press
SHENANDOAH NEWSLETTER
SONG OF THE SAN JOAQUIN

INDIGENOUS CULTURES

AIS Publications
Allbook Books
ALTERNATIVE PRESS INDEX
Bauu Press
Beagle Bay Books / Creative Minds Press
Book Marketing Solutions
Calaca Press
Caribbean Books-Panama
Chandler & Sharp Publishers, Inc.
COLLEGE LITERATURE
COLORLINES
THE COMSTOCK REVIEW
THE FREEFALL REVIEW
GENRE: WRITER AND WRITINGS
Grey Sparrow Press
HAWAI'I REVIEW
Kakibubu Media Limited
Keiki O Ka Aina Press
Malki Museum Press
Maryland Historical Press (also MHPress)
Naturegraph Publishers
Northern Illinois University Press
Oolichan Books
Plain View Press
POETRYREPAIRS: Contemporary International Poetry
THE RAVEN CHRONICLES
RED MARE
Salt Publishing
Southwest Research and Information Center
Spinifex Press
State University of New York Press
Thundercloud Books
University of Calgary Press
University of Nebraska Press
Water Mark of Lyons PPP: papers press and permaculture
ZAWP

INSPIRATIONAL

Aaron Communications III
American Literary Press
Ammons Communications; Imprint: Catch the Spirit of Appalachia
Anderson Publishing; also RC Anderson Books
THE ART OF ABUNDANCE
ASCENT
THE AUROREAN
Best Life Media
Beyond Words Publishing, Inc.
Big Valley Press
Biographical Publishing Company
BLUE MOUNTAIN
Burns Park Publishers
THE CANNON'S MOUTH
Celo Valley Books
Church Leadership Library (Canadian Office)
City Life Books, LLC
Cladach Publishing
Crane Press
Dancing Lemur Press, L.L.C.
Delaney Day Press
Dharma Publishing
Dream Publishing Co.
Dreams Due Media Group, Inc.
DTS Group, Inc.
Dumouriez Publishing
Dwarf Lion Press
EbonyEnergy Publishing, Inc.
Ellechor Publishing House
Nicolin Fields Publishing, Inc.
Fountain Publisher Limited
4 Your Spirit Productions
Friendly Oaks Publications
Fruitbearer Publishing, LLC
Gingerbread House
Good Book Publishing Company
Goose River Press
Grey Sparrow Press
Halo Publishing International
Heartsong Books
The Heather Foundation
Himalayan Institute Press
Hope Publishing House
A HUDSON VIEW POETRY DIGEST
Hunter Publishing Corporation
Illumination Arts
In Print Publishing
Inkwater Press
InsideOut Press
Lake Street Press
Lamp Light Press
Leadership Education and Development, Inc.
The Leaping Frog Press
Leave No Sister Behind Publications
A.P. Lee & Co., Ltd.
Legacy Audio Books, Inc.
LITERARY HOUSE REVIEW
Long & Silverman Publishing, Inc.
LOVING MORE: New Models for Relationships
Luminous Epinoia Press
A Melody from an Immigrant's Soul
Middleway Press
Millennium Vision Press
The Kenneth G. Mills Foundation
Mind Power Publishing
Missing Man Press
Motom
Munsey Music
Music City Publishing
New Paradigm Books
New World Library
Nilgiri Press
Noved Audio
Origin Press
Oyster River Press

Paladin Media Group
Papillon Presse
The Passion Profit Company
Pellingham Casper Communications
PhoeniX in Print
The Poetry Center Press/Shoestring Press
Premium Press America
PREP Publishing
THE QUILLDRIVER
Raw Dog Press
Red Rock Press
REMS Publishing & Publicity
REMS Publishing & Publicity
Sadorian Publications
SCULPTURAL PURSUIT MAGAZINE
SECRETUM MEUM MIHI
Secretum Meum Mihi Press
Set Sail Productions, LLC
SHARE INTERNATIONAL
Sherian Publishing
Small Dogma Publishing, Inc.
Socratic Consulting Group
Sound View Publishing, Inc.
SPINNINGS...INTENSE TALES OF LIFE MAGAZINE
SPIRITCHASER
Starik Publishing
Summerland Publishing
Sweet People Publishing
Thatch Tree Publications
THRESHOLDS JOURNAL
Timeless Books
Titlewaves Publishing; Writers Direct
TREATING YOURSELF: The Alternative Medicine Journal
Triskelion Publishing
Unity House
Valuable Quality Publishing Company
WHAT IS ENLIGHTENMENT?
Whiskey Creek Press
Wilderness Ministries
Willfam Publishing Co.
Willowood Press
Wind Eagle Press
WinePress Publishing
World Gumbo Publishing
Writers House Press
Wytherngate Press
Zumaya Publications LLC

INSURANCE

Bay Tree Publishing
GLOBAL ONE MAGAZINE
MOBILE BEAT: The Mobile Entertainer's Magazine
SAPONIFIER
THE SMALL BUSINESS ADVISOR

INTERNET

Atlantic Publishing Group, Inc.
Brenner Information Group
C & T Publishing
Cooperative Press
DOLLS UNITED INTERACTIVE MAGAZINE
EEI Press
Encore Publishing
EQUAL CONSTRUCTION RECORD
The Fiction Works
Frontline Publications
Happy About
J. Mark Press
MAIN STREET RAG
MOBILE BEAT: The Mobile Entertainer's Magazine
New World Press, Inc
THE PEDESTAL MAGAZINE.COM
SAGE OF CONSCIOUSNESS E-ZINE
SAPONIFIER
SEDUCTIVE SELLING
THE SOURCES HOTLINK
Toca Family Publishing, div. of Toca Family Communica-

ITALY

ABSINTHE: New European Writing
Art of Living, PrimaMedia,Inc
Blue Dolphin Publishing, Inc.
Bordighera, Inc.
Cross-Cultural Communications
Desert Bloom Press
Fisher King Press
Italica Press, Inc.
LO STRANIERO: The Stranger, Der Fremde, L'Etranger
MCM Entertainment, Inc. Publishing Division
SYMPOSIUM

JAMAICA

Demarche Publishing LLC
DLite Press
Lyons Publishing Limited

JAPAN

Center for Japanese Studies
Cyberwit.net
KUMQUAT MERINGUE
NIS America, Inc.
Perpetual Press
Press Here
UmbraProjects Publishing
United Nations University Press

ROBINSON JEFFERS

S4N Books
WESTERN AMERICAN LITERATURE

THOMAS JEFFERSON

Bluestocking Press
Maryland Historical Press (also MHPress)
Mount Ida Press
Poplar Leaf Press
University of Virginia Press

JEWELRY, GEMS

DTS Group, Inc.
Eagle's View Publishing
International Jewelry Publications
MIDWEST ART FAIRS
One Spirit Press
ORNAMENT
ORNAMENT

JOURNALS

BORDERLANDS: Texas Poetry Review
Chatterley Press International
CHILDREN, CHURCHES AND DADDIES, A Non
  Religious, Non Familial Literary Magazine
CREATIVE NONFICTION
DREAM NETWORK
580 SPLIT
FLUENT ASCENSION
FREEDOM AND STRENGTH PRESS FORUM
The Haworth Press
Impassio Press
Lion's Den Publishing
LULLWATER REVIEW
Magic Circle Press
MUSE: A Quarterly Journal of The Lit
My Heart Yours Publishing
NEO: Literary Magazine
NEW ORLEANS REVIEW
NORTHWEST REVIEW
OTHER INVESTIGATIONS
PALO ALTO REVIEW
Rayve Productions Inc.
Sagamore Publishing
SMARTISH PACE
THE SUN, A Magazine of Ideas
SYMPOSIUM
TELOS
Telos Press

1097 MAGAZINE
13TH MOON
Titus Home Publishing
TORRE DE PAPEL
Upheaval Media

JAMES JOYCE

Barrytown/Station Hill Press
JAMES JOYCE BROADSHEET
JAMES JOYCE QUARTERLY
PLAIN BROWN WRAPPER (PBW)
Scripta Humanistica
SHATTERED WIG REVIEW
Zygote Publishing

JUDAISM

ARC
Beacon Press
BOULDER HERETIC
BRIDGES: A Jewish Feminist Journal
Chicago Spectrum Press
Cross-Cultural Communications
Dwarf Lion Press
The Edwin Mellen Press
The Eighth Mountain Press
Florida Academic Press
Gloger Family Books
IN OUR OWN WORDS
ISSUES
JEWISH CURRENTS
Jewish Publication Society
Judah Magnes Museum Publications
Kar-Ben Publishing, Inc.
KEREM: Creative Explorations in Judaism
LILITH
Mayapple Press
Micah Publications Inc.
New Concept Press
No Starch Press
Pocol Press
POETICA MAGAZINE, Reflections of Jewish Thought
The Press at Foggy Bottom
SALMAGUNDI
SHIRIM
VOICES ISRAEL
Vox Humana Books
WHAT IS ENLIGHTENMENT?
Yaldah Publishing
Zagier & Urruty Publications

JUVENILE FICTION

A Cappela Publishing
Aaron Communications III
Absey & Co.
Aquila Ink Publishing
Authentic Publishing LLC
Bel Canto Press
Bronze Girl Productions, Inc.
Cladach Publishing
Creative Arts Book Company
Creative Writing and Publishing Company
Dancing Lemur Press, L.L.C.
Delaney Day Press
Demarche Publishing LLC
DLite Press
Earthshaker Books
Ecrivez!
Ellechor Publishing House
Empyrean Hill Books, Inc.
4 Your Spirit Productions
Gingerbread House
Great West Publishing
Illumination Arts
Images Unlimited and Snaptail Press, a Division of Images
  Unlimited Publishing
THE INK SLINGER REVIEW
Inkwater Press
Jigsaw Press

Journey Books Publishing
Juel House Publishers and Literary Services
Lake Street Press
THE LEDGE
Lightning Bug Learning Press
Lily Ruth Publishing
Little Pear Press
LJW Publishing
Loonfeather Press
Mayhaven Publishing, Inc.
Paladin Media Group
Papillon Presse
Peartree Books & Music
Pixiu Press
Playdate Kids Publishing
The Poetry Center
POGO STICK
Polar Bear & Company
PublishAmerica, LLLP.
Raven Publishing, Inc.
Re-invention UK Ltd
Signalman Publishing
Small Dogma Publishing, Inc.
SPECTACULAR SPECULATIONS
Star Publish LLC
Sterli Publishing
Three Bean Press
Total Package Publications, LLC
Ultra Media Publications
UmbraProjects Publishing
Wellington House Publishing Company
The WhaleInn Publishing House (1998)
Wilderness Ministries
WindRiver Publishing
The Wolf Pirate Project Inc.
Yaldah Publishing

KAFKA

BUST DOWN THE DOOR AND EAT ALL THE CHICKENS: A Journal of Absurd and Surreal Fiction
The Thirty First Bird Press
UNDERSTANDING MAGAZINE
Zygote Publishing

KANSAS

Arthur H. Clark Co.
COTTONWOOD
Cottonwood Press
LITTLE BALKANS REVIEW
Raven Publishing, Inc.

KENTUCKY

Chicago Spectrum Press
Iris Publishing Group, Inc (Iris Press / Tellico Books)
NEW MADRID
Raven Publishing, Inc.
Rock Spring Press Inc.
Southeast Missouri State University Press
SPITBALL: The Literary Baseball Magazine

JACK KEROUAC

THE BOOMERPHILE
Creative Arts Book Company
FRANK: AN INTERNATIONAL JOURNAL OF CON-TEMPORARY WRITING AND ART
Frozen Waffles Press/Shattered Sidewalks Press; 45th Century Chapbooks
Mica Press - Paying Our Dues Productions
OPEN WIDE MAGAZINE
PLAIN BROWN WRAPPER (PBW)
PLOPLOP
Six Ft. Swells Press
Southern Illinois University Press
Water Row Press
WATER ROW REVIEW
WESTERN AMERICAN LITERATURE
WHITE FUNGUS
X-Ray Book Co.

Zygote Publishing

RUDYARD KIPLING

ENGLISH LITERATURE IN TRANSITION, 1880-1920
Mystery Island Publications
UNDERSTANDING MAGAZINE
Vulgar Marsala Press

LABOR

AMERICAN JONES BUILDING & MAINTENANCE
ATLANTIS: A Women's Studies Journal/Revue d'etudes sur les femmes
Beekman Books, Inc.
Black Rose Books Ltd.
THE BLOOMSBURY REVIEW
BLUE COLLAR REVIEW
Blue Cubicle Press, LLC
Canadian Committee on Labour History
Global Options
History Compass, LLC
Iniquity Press/Vendetta Books
International Publishers Co. Inc.
LABOUR/LE TRAVAIL
Maisonneuve Press
Mehring Books, Inc.
Missing Spoke Press
NEW UNIONIST
OFF OUR BACKS
Open Hand Publishing LLC
OUR SCHOOLS/OUR SELVES
Partisan Press
Pathfinder Press
PAVEMENT SAW
Pavement Saw Press
Red Letter Press
Ridgeway Press of Michigan
THE SMALL BUSINESS ADVISOR
Smyrna Press
SOCIAL JUSTICE: A JOURNAL OF CRIME, CONFLICT, & WORLD ORDER
South End Press
STATE OF CALIFORNIA LABOR
STRUGGLE: A Magazine of Proletarian Revolutionary Literature
Syracuse Cultural Workers/Tools for Change
University of Chicago Press
Vanderbilt University Press
WHEELHOUSE MAGAZINE
WORKERS WRITE!

LANGUAGE

Absey & Co.
AERIAL
Alaska Native Language Center
Ariko Publications
Bad Noise Productions
Bilingual Review Press
BILINGUAL REVIEW/Revista Bilingue
BULLETIN OF HISPANIC STUDIES
CANADIAN POETRY
Center for Japanese Studies
Chax Press
The Chicot Press
Clamshell Press
THE CLASSICAL OUTLOOK
COLLEGE LITERATURE
DESIRE
DOWN IN THE DIRT LITERARY MAGAZINE, the prose & poetry magazine revealing all your dirty little secrets
EEI Press
Eros Books
ESPERANTIC STUDIES
Evolution Publishing
Focus Publishing/R. Pullins Co.
FREEDOM AND STRENGTH PRESS FORUM
Gallaudet University Press
GRAMMAR CRISIS
HEAVEN BONE MAGAZINE

Heaven Bone Press
Ibex Publishers, Inc.
INTERNATIONAL POETRY REVIEW
INVENTED LANGUAGES
Iris Publishing Group, Inc (Iris Press / Tellico Books)
JACK MACKEREL MAGAZINE
THE JOURNAL OF CALIFORNIA AND GREAT BASIN
    ANTHROPOLOGY
KALDRON, An International Journal Of Visual Poetry
Listening Voice Media Ltd
Litwin Books
Liverpool University Press
LULLWATER REVIEW
Maledicta Press
MALEDICTA: The International Journal of Verbal Aggres-
    sion
Malki Museum Press
Margaret Media, Inc.
Merl Publications
THE MODERN LANGUAGE JOURNAL
Mondial
Moon Pie Press
New Win Publishing
nine muses books
Open Horizons Publishing Company
OSIRIS
OTHER INVESTIGATIONS
Oyster River Press
PARENTEACHER MAGAZINE
PASSAGER
Petroglyph Press, Ltd.
POINT OF CONTACT, The Journal of Verbal & Visual
    Arts
PORTLAND REVIEW
Protean Press
PSYCHE
PULSAR POETRY WEBZINE
RHETORICA: A Journal of the History of Rhetoric
Rodnik Publishing Co.
Rowhouse Press
Saqi Books Publisher
Scars Publications
SPORE
Strata Publishing, Inc.
George Suttton Publishing Co.
Thatch Tree Publications
The Thirty First Bird Press
Thorp Springs Press
UBC Press
Univelt, Inc.
University of Utah Press
Vanderbilt University Press
Velazquez Press
WEST COAST LINE: A Journal of Contemporary Writing
    and Criticism
WOMEN AND LANGUAGE

LAPIDARY

Cynic Press

LATIN AMERICA

AFRO-HISPANIC REVIEW
THE BLOOMSBURY REVIEW
CANADIAN JOURNAL OF LATIN AMERICAN AND
    CARIBBEAN STUDIES/Revue canadienne des etudes
    latino-americaines et caraibes
CHASQUI
Cross-Cultural Communications
Fine Tooth Press
Garden House Press
Hoover Institution Press
Hope Publishing House
Inner City Press
Interlink Publishing Group, Inc.
INTERNATIONAL POETRY REVIEW
Iris Publishing Group, Inc (Iris Press / Tellico Books)
LATIN AMERICAN LITERARY REVIEW
Latin American Literary Review Press

LATIN AMERICAN PERSPECTIVES
Mayapple Press
New Win Publishing
Oyster River Press
Pangaea
Panther Creek Press
Passport Press
Pathfinder Press
Plank Road Publishing
POINT OF CONTACT, The Journal of Verbal & Visual
    Arts
THE QUILLDRIVER
SALMAGUNDI
Salt Publishing
School for Advanced Research Press
SYMPOSIUM
Syracuse Cultural Workers/Tools for Change
TORRE DE PAPEL
TRADICION REVISTA
Two Eagles Press International
Vanderbilt University Press
White Pine Press
XCP: CROSS-CULTURAL POETICS
Zagier & Urruty Publications

LATINO

A Midsummer Night's Press
Archer Books
BILINGUAL REVIEW/Revista Bilingue
Calaca Press
THE COMSTOCK REVIEW
Dream Publishing Co.
Latin American Literary Review Press
LPD Press
MANDORLA: New Writing from the Americas / Nueva
    escritura de las Americas
Merl Publications
Miami University Press
New Sins Press
Northwestern University Press
Papillon Presse
Partisan Press
POINT OF CONTACT, The Journal of Verbal & Visual
    Arts
South End Press
TORRE DE PAPEL
TRADICION REVISTA
Twinteum Artist, Inc.
Two Eagles Press International
Wings Press

LAW

Allworth Press
AMERICAN JUROR (formerly FIJACTIVIST, 1989-2007)
Atlantic Publishing Group, Inc.
THE BEACON: Journal of Special Education Law &
    Practice
Bluestocking Press
Buenos Books
Claitor's Law Books & Publishing Division, Inc.
EQUAL CONSTRUCTION RECORD
Fathom Publishing Co.
Frontline Publications
Global Options
GRAY AREAS
Harbor House Law Press, Inc.
HARVARD JOURNAL OF LAW AND GENDER
INDEX TO FOREIGN LEGAL PERIODICALS
Jullundur Press
LAW AND LITERATURE
Lawells Publishing
THE LONG TERM VIEW: A Journal of Informed Opinion
Merl Publications
Metallo House Publishers
Millennium Vision Press
Morgen Publishing Incorporated
MOUTH: Voice of the Dis-Labeled Nation
Nolo Press Occidental

Northern Illinois University Press
Peartree Books & Music
PRISON LEGAL NEWS
PRIVACY JOURNAL
RTMC Organization, LLC
THE SMALL BUSINESS ADVISOR
SOCIAL JUSTICE: A JOURNAL OF CRIME, CONFLICT,
& WORLD ORDER
Sourcebooks, Inc.
Speck Press
Stonemark Publishing
Strata Publishing, Inc.
TELOS
Telos Press
UBC Press
University of Akron Press
University Press of Colorado
White Thread Press
Wind River Institute Press/Wind River Broadcasting

D.H. LAWRENCE

Chatterley Press International
Crescent Moon
PASSION
Six Ft. Swells Press
Vulgar Marsala Press
John Wade, Publisher

LEADERSHIP

Advanced Learning Press
Alpine Guild, Inc.
Book Marketing Solutions
Burns Park Publishers
Church Leadership Library (Canadian Office)
Church Leadership Library (US Office)
Common Boundaries
Dancing Lemur Press, L.L.C.
Edenscape Publishing Company
Falcon Publishing, LTD
Famaco Publishers (Qalam Books)
Finney Company, Inc.
Goblin Fern Press
InsideOut Press
Jardin Publishing
Leadership Education and Development, Inc.
Mind Power Publishing
Multi-Media Publications Inc.
Ocean Publishing
Penworth Publishing
Poplar Leaf Press
Practically Shameless Press
Princess Publishing
Reliance Books
Sabellapress
Set Sail Productions, LLC
Smith-Johnson Publisher
Top 20 Press
The Utility Company LLC
Zelda Wilde Publishing
World Gumbo Publishing

LEISURE/RECREATION

Anacus Press, An Imprint of Finney Company
Anchor Cove Publishing, Inc.
BEACHCOMBER MAGAZINE
Brookview Press
THE FREEFALL REVIEW
Margaret Media, Inc.
Mountainside Press
NATURALLY
New England Cartographics, Inc.
PLEASANT LIVING
Windward Publishing, An Imprint of Finney Company
WORLD POETRY SHOWCASE

LESBIANISM

A Midsummer Night's Press
Alamo Square Press

Anomaly Press
Assilem 9 Publications
ATLANTIS: A Women's Studies Journal/Revue d'etudes
sur les femmes
Aunt Lute Books
Back House Books
BAY WINDOWS
Beacon Press
BLACK LACE
BLK
BOOKS TO WATCH OUT FOR
Bordighera, Inc.
Broken Jaw Press
Carolina Wren Press
Clover Valley Press, LLC
THE CREAM CITY REVIEW
Down There Press
The Eighth Mountain Press
Ephemera Bound Publishing
FEMINIST COLLECTIONS: A QUARTERLY OF WO-
MEN'S STUDIES RESOURCES
FEMINIST PERIODICALS: A CURRENT LISTING OF
CONTENTS
The Feminist Press at the City University of New York
FEMINIST STUDIES
Fine Tooth Press
Garden House Press
GAYELLOW PAGES
GERTRUDE
Gertrude Press
GLB Publishers
KUUMBA
MGW (Mom Guess What) Newsmagazine
MOTHERVERSE: A Journal of Contemporary Motherhood
NEW BOOKS ON WOMEN, GENDER, & FEMINISM
New Falcon Publications
New Sins Press
New Victoria Publishers
OFF OUR BACKS
One Spirit Press
Orchard House Press
OUT OF LINE
Passion Power Press, Inc
Raular Publishing
Red Letter Press
RedBone Press
Re-invention UK Ltd
SINISTER WISDOM
SO TO SPEAK: A Feminist Journal of Language & Art
Spinifex Press
Chuck Stewart
Syracuse Cultural Workers/Tools for Change
13TH MOON
TnT Classic Books
Triskelion Publishing
The Twickenham Press
University of Chicago Press
Volcano Press, Inc
Women's Studies Librarian, University of Wisconsin
System
WSQ (formerly WOMEN'S STUDIES QUARTERLY)
Youthful Wisdom Press

LIBERAL ARTS

ATLANTIS: A Women's Studies Journal/Revue d'etudes
sur les femmes
Bandanna Books
Bel Canto Press
Blue Lupin Press
BURNSIDE REVIEW
Libertas Press, LLC.
Moonrise Press
NATURALLY
Poptritus Press
PUNKIN HOUSE DIGEST
RIVET MAGAZINE
SCULPTURAL PURSUIT MAGAZINE
The Thirty First Bird Press

Zelda Wilde Publishing

LIBERTARIAN

A2Z Publications LLC
ANARCHY: A Journal of Desire Armed
Axios Newletter, Inc.
Books for All Times, Inc.
Candlestick Publishing
City Lights Books
Columbia Alternative Library Press
Michael E. Coughlin, Publisher
THE DANDELION
Elderberry Press, Inc.
Garden House Press
Handshake Editions
The Heather Foundation
Iconoclast Press
THE (LIBERTARIAN) CONNECTION
Libertarian Press, Inc./American Book Distributors
Libertas Press, LLC.
LIBERTY
Lycanthrope Press
Mills Custom Services Publishing
Mountain Media
Murder Slim Press
New Falcon Publications
Open Wide Books
OPEN WIDE MAGAZINE
SHORT FUSE
Socratic Consulting Group
Synergy Press
Tres Picos Press
Van Cleave Publishing

LIBRARIES

Big Valley Press
Canadian Library Association
COUNTERPOISE: For Social Responsibilities, Liberty and Dissent
The Denali Press
FELICITER
FEMINIST COLLECTIONS: A QUARTERLY OF WO-MEN'S STUDIES RESOURCES
FEMINIST PERIODICALS: A CURRENT LISTING OF CONTENTS
Happy About
The Haworth Press
INDEPENDENT PUBLISHER ONLINE
Library Juice Press
Lightning Bug Learning Press
Mills Custom Services Publishing
NEW AMERICAN IMAGIST
NEW BOOKS ON WOMEN, GENDER, & FEMINISM
Oak Knoll Press
THE PRAIRIE JOURNAL OF CANADIAN LITERATURE
The Urbana Free Library
Willowood Press
Women's Studies Librarian, University of Wisconsin System

LIFESTYLES

AB
Callawind Publications / Custom Cookbooks / Children's Books
Colerith Press
COMMUNITIES
DESIRE
DWELLING PORTABLY
Fountain Publisher Limited
THE FREEFALL REVIEW
GAYELLOW PAGES
GLOBAL ONE MAGAZINE
HAMPTON ROADS HEALTH JOURNAL
Lemon Grove Press
N: NUDE & NATURAL
NATURALLY
North Star Books
Origin Press

Palari Publishing
Passing Through Publications
The People's Press
PLEASANT LIVING
Poetry
PSYCHE
Pussywillow
RIVET MAGAZINE
SANDPOINT MAGAZINE
Speck Press
2L Publishing, LLC
Vanilla Heart Publishing
Whole Person Associates Inc.

LIGHTHOUSES

WORLD POETRY SHOWCASE

LITERARY REVIEW

ABRAMELIN: a Journal of Poetry and Magick
THE ADIRONDACK REVIEW
AFRICAN AMERICAN REVIEW
ALASKA QUARTERLY REVIEW
ALCHEMY
THE ALLEGHENY REVIEW
AMERICAN BOOK REVIEW
THE AMERICAN DISSIDENT
AMERICAN LETTERS & COMMENTARY
ANQ: A Quarterly Journal of Short Articles, Notes, and Reviews
THE ANTIGONISH REVIEW
APOSTROPHE: USCB Journal of the Arts
ARC
ARIEL, A Review of International English Literature
ATLANTIS: A Women's Studies Journal/Revue d'etudes sur les femmes
AURA LITERARY ARTS REVIEW
Back House Books
THE BALTIMORE REVIEW
Bancroft Press
BEATLICK NEWS
BELLEVUE LITERARY REVIEW
BELLINGHAM REVIEW
BIG MUDDY: Journal of the Mississippi River Valley
Black Dress Press
BLACK MAGNOLIAS LITERARY JOURNAL
BLUELINE
BOOK/MARK QUARTERLY REVIEW
BOOKS FROM FINLAND: Online literature journal of writing from and about Finland
BOSTON REVIEW
THE BRIAR CLIFF REVIEW
Brooding Heron Press
CANADIAN LITERATURE
THE CAPILANO REVIEW
CENTER: A Journal of the Literary Arts
CHAPMAN
CHARITON REVIEW
CHASQUI
THE CHATTAHOOCHEE REVIEW
CHICAGO REVIEW
CONFRONTATION
CONTROLLED BURN
CORRECTIONS TODAY
COTTONWOOD
Cottonwood Press
CRAB ORCHARD REVIEW
THE CREAM CITY REVIEW
Crescent Moon
CRUCIBLE
THE DALHOUSIE REVIEW
DESCANT
DESIRE
DOWN IN THE DIRT LITERARY MAGAZINE, the prose & poetry magazine revealing all your dirty little secrets
EVANSVILLE REVIEW
THE FIDDLEHEAD
Five Fingers Press
FIVE FINGERS REVIEW

THE FLORIDA REVIEW
FRANK: AN INTERNATIONAL JOURNAL OF CON-
    TEMPORARY WRITING AND ART
THE GEORGIA REVIEW
GHOTI MAGAZINE
GRAND LAKE REVIEW
THE GREEN HILLS LITERARY LANTERN
GULF COAST
Harobed Publishing Creations
THE HARVARD ADVOCATE
HARVARD REVIEW
THE HOLLINS CRITIC
HOME PLANET NEWS
Home Planet Publications
THE HUDSON REVIEW
ICONOCLAST
THE IDAHO REVIEW
INDEPENDENT PUBLISHER ONLINE
INDIANA REVIEW
THE INK SLINGER REVIEW
INTERNATIONAL POETRY REVIEW
THE IOWA REVIEW
IRISH LITERARY SUPPLEMENT
IRON HORSE LITERARY REVIEW
Jako Books
JAMES DICKEY REVIEW
JAMES JOYCE BROADSHEET
JAMES JOYCE QUARTERLY
Juel House Publishers and Literary Services
KALDRON, An International Journal Of Visual Poetry
THE KELSEY REVIEW
THE KENYON REVIEW
KotaPress
THE LANGSTON HUGHES REVIEW
Latin American Literary Review Press
Limberlost Press
LINQ
Lion's Den Publishing
LITERARY IMAGINATION: The Review of the Associa-
    tion of Literary Scholars and Critics
LITERARY MAGAZINE REVIEW
THE LITERARY REVIEW
LULLWATER REVIEW
Maisonneuve Press
THE MALAHAT REVIEW
THE MASSACHUSETTS REVIEW
Mehring Books, Inc.
MICHIGAN QUARTERLY REVIEW
MID-AMERICAN REVIEW
Middlebury College Publications
THE MIDWEST QUARTERLY
Mills Custom Services Publishing
MINESHAFT
Missing Spoke Press
THE MISSOURI REVIEW
MUSE: A Quarterly Journal of The Lit
MYSTERY READERS JOURNAL
THE MYSTERY REVIEW
NEO: Literary Magazine
NEW ENGLAND REVIEW
NEW HOPE INTERNATIONAL REVIEW
NEW MEXICO POETRY REVIEW
NEW ORLEANS REVIEW
New Orphic Publishers
THE NEW ORPHIC REVIEW
Night Bomb Press
NIGHTSUN
NORTH CAROLINA LITERARY REVIEW
NORTH DAKOTA QUARTERLY
North Stone Editions
NORTHWEST REVIEW
NOTRE DAME REVIEW
NOVA EXPRESS
Oak Knoll Press
OHIOANA QUARTERLY
ORBIS
OSIRIS
THE PACIFIC REVIEW

PAPERPLATES
PARNASSUS: Poetry in Review
PASSAGES NORTH
PASSAIC REVIEW
PASSION
THE PATERSON LITERARY REVIEW
Pathwise Press
PEMBROKE MAGAZINE
PEMMICAN
Pendragonian Publications
PENNINE PLATFORM
Pennsylvania State University Press
PENNY DREADFUL: Tales and Poems of Fantastic Terror
THE PINCH
PLOUGHSHARES
The Poetry Center
POETRY EAST
THE POETRY PROJECT NEWSLETTER
POETRYREPAIRS: Contemporary International Poetry
THE PRAIRIE JOURNAL OF CANADIAN LITERATURE
PRAIRIE SCHOONER
PRAKALPANA   SAHITYA/PRAKALPANA   LITERA-
    TURE
PSYCHE
Psychedelic Literature
PULSAR POETRY WEBZINE
PURPLE PATCH
RAIN TAXI REVIEW OF BOOKS
THE RAVEN CHRONICLES
RED HAWK
RED ROCK REVIEW
Redgreene Press
THE REVIEW OF CONTEMPORARY FICTION
RIVERBED HAIKU
RIVERWIND
ROOM MAGAZINE
ROSEBUD
St. Andrews College Press
THE SANTA MONICA REVIEW
SEWANEE REVIEW
SHAW: THE ANNUAL OF BERNARD SHAW STUDIES
SHENANDOAH: The Washington and Lee University
    Review
SMARTISH PACE
SNREVIEW
SONGS OF INNOCENCE
SONORA REVIEW
SOUTHERN HUMANITIES REVIEW
THE SOUTHERN REVIEW
SP QUILL MAGAZINE
STAND MAGAZINE
THE STINGING FLY
STUDIO - A Journal of Christians Writing
SYCAMORE REVIEW
TAPROOT LITERARY REVIEW
THE TEXAS REVIEW
THALIA: Studies in Literary Humor
13TH MOON
THE THREEPENNY REVIEW
Thunder Rain Publishing Corp.
TORRE DE PAPEL
TRANSLATION REVIEW
TULSA STUDIES IN WOMEN'S LITERATURE
UND Press
University of Tampa Press
UNIVERSITY OF WINDSOR REVIEW
UNMUZZLED OX
VALLUM: CONTEMPORARY POETRY
Vanderbilt University Press
VARIOUS ARTISTS
VISIONS-INTERNATIONAL, The World Journal of Illus-
    trated Poetry
WAR, LITERATURE & THE ARTS: An International
    Journal of the Humanities
WATER ROW REVIEW
WEST BRANCH
WESTERN AMERICAN LITERATURE
WESTERN HUMANITIES REVIEW

WHEELHOUSE MAGAZINE
Whitston Publishing Co.
WILD DUCK REVIEW
WINDHOVER: A Journal of Christian Literature
THE WORCESTER REVIEW
Writecorner.com Press
XAVIER REVIEW
THE YALE REVIEW

LITERATURE (GENERAL)

A & U AMERICA'S AIDS MAGAZINE
A Cappela Publishing
Absey & Co.
THE ADIRONDACK REVIEW
AERIAL
Affluent Publishing Corp.
AK Press
ALASKA QUARTERLY REVIEW
Allium Press of Chicago
THE AMERICAN DISSIDENT
THE AMERICAN DRIVEL REVIEW
ANCIENT PATHS
Androgyne Books
Anhinga Press
ANQ: A Quarterly Journal of Short Articles, Notes, and Reviews
APOSTROPHE: USCB Journal of the Arts
Appalachian Consortium Press
Aquarius Press
ARC
ARIEL, A Review of International English Literature
ARTS & LETTERS: Journal of Contemporary Culture
ASCENT
Asylum Arts
Atelier Press
Athanata Arts, Ltd.
AURA LITERARY ARTS REVIEW
Bamboo Ridge Press
BAMBOO RIDGE, Journal of Hawai'i Literature and Arts
Bandanna Books
Banta & Pool Literary Properties
Barrytown/Station Hill Press
BASALT
BATHTUB GIN
Beacon Press
THE BEAR DELUXE MAGAZINE
BEATLICK NEWS
BEAUTY/TRUTH: A Journal of Ekphrastic Poetry
Beekman Books, Inc.
BEGGARS & CHEESEBURGERS
BEGINNING MAGAZINE
Bel Canto Press
BIBLIOPHILOS
BIGNEWS MAGAZINE
Birch Brook Press
BkMk Press
Black Dress Press
Black Heron Press
Black Lawrence Press
BLACK MAGNOLIAS LITERARY JOURNAL
BLOODJET LITERARY MAGAZINE
Blue Cubicle Press, LLC
Blue Lupin Press
BOOK/MARK QUARTERLY REVIEW
BORDERLANDS: Texas Poetry Review
Bordighera, Inc.
Borealis Press Limited
Bottle of Smoke Press
BOULEVARD
Branden Books
THE BRIAR CLIFF REVIEW
Brick Road Poetry Press
Broken Jaw Press
Bronx River Press
Brookline Books
Brookview Press
Burning Books
BUST DOWN THE DOOR AND EAT ALL THE

CHICKENS: A Journal of Absurd and Surreal Fiction
Caketrain Journal and Press
Calaca Press
Calyx Books
CALYX: A Journal of Art and Literature by Women
Canvas Press
THE CAROLINA QUARTERLY
Casperian Books LLC
Central Avenue Press
Chatterley Press International
Chicago Spectrum Press
CHILDREN, CHURCHES AND DADDIES, A Non Religious, Non Familial Literary Magazine
Chinese Literature Press
CIMARRON REVIEW
City Lights Books
Clamp Down Press
Clark-Nova Books
Coffee House Press
COLD-DRILL
COLLECTION
COLLEGE LITERATURE
COMPASS ROSE
CONDUIT
CONJUNCTIONS
COSMOPSIS QUARTERLY
Coteau Books
CRAB CREEK REVIEW
CRANNOG
CRAZYHORSE
Creative Arts Book Company
CREATIVE NONFICTION
Crescent Moon
CRICKET
CRUCIBLE
Cypress House
Dalkey Archive Press
Deep Well Publishing Company
DESCANT
DESIRE
THE DIRTY GOAT
Down The Shore Publishing
Downeast Books
Drinian Press
DRUMVOICES REVUE
Dufour Editions Inc.
EARTH'S DAUGHTERS: Feminist Arts Periodical
Earthshaker Books
Eastern Washington University Press
EASTGATE QUARTERLY REVIEW OF HYPERTEXT
EbonyEnergy Publishing, Inc.
ECOTONE: Reimagining Place
Edition Gemini
ELT Press
Empyrean Hill Books, Inc.
ENGLISH LITERATURE IN TRANSITION, 1880-1920
Ephemera Bound Publishing
EPICENTER: A LITERARY MAGAZINE
EPIPHANY, A Literary Journal
Eros Books
EVANSVILLE REVIEW
The Feminist Press at the City University of New York
FICTION
Fiction Collective Two (FC2)
FIRST CLASS
THE FIRST LINE
FISH DRUM MAGAZINE
Fisher King Press
Fithian Press
FOLIO: A Literary Journal of American University
Four-Sep Publications
FOURTEEN HILLS: The SFSU Review
THE FREEFALL REVIEW
The Galileo Press Ltd.
THE GETTYSBURG REVIEW
Glimmer Train Press, Inc.
GLIMMER TRAIN STORIES
GOLD DUST

Goss Press
GRASSLIMB
Graywolf Press
Grey Sparrow Press
Guernica Editions, Inc.
GULF COAST
HAIGHT ASHBURY LITERARY JOURNAL
Harobed Publishing Creations
THE HARVARD ADVOCATE
Heyday Books
The Heyeck Press
Hobblebush Books
THE HOLLINS CRITIC
Hollyridge Press
Holy Cow! Press
Homa & Sekey Books
HOME PLANET NEWS
A HUDSON VIEW POETRY DIGEST
Huntington Library Press
HUNTINGTON LIBRARY QUARTERLY
ICON
ICONOCLAST
ILLOGICAL MUSE
ILLUMINATIONS
Impassio Press
In Between Books
Indigo Ink Press, Inc.
The Infinity Group
THE INK SLINGER REVIEW
INKWELL
INSURANCE
THE IOWA REVIEW
ITALIAN AMERICANA
Italica Press, Inc.
Ithuriel's Spear
JACK MACKEREL MAGAZINE
Jako Books
JAMES JOYCE BROADSHEET
J'ECRIS
Jigsaw Press
JPS Publishing Company
JUBILAT
Jullundur Press
KALDRON, An International Journal Of Visual Poetry
Kelsey St. Press
THE KENYON REVIEW
KEREM: Creative Explorations in Judaism
Allen A. Knoll Publishers
La Alameda Press
LATIN AMERICAN LITERARY REVIEW
Latin American Literary Review Press
LAW AND LITERATURE
LEAF GARDEN
Leaf Garden Press
Leapfrog Press
The Leaping Frog Press
THE LEDGE
Leete's Island Books
LEFT CURVE
Lemon Shark Press
Les Figues Press
Light of New Orleans Publishing
LIGHT: The Quarterly of Light Verse
LIMESTONE: A Literary Journal
Lincoln Springs Press
LINES + STARS
LITERARY HOUSE REVIEW
LITERARY IMAGINATION: The Review of the Associa-
   tion of Literary Scholars and Critics
LITTLE BALKANS REVIEW
Livingston Press
LOST GENERATION JOURNAL
Lotus Press, Inc.
Lotus Press, Inc.
LULLWATER REVIEW
LUNGFULL! MAGAZINE
Maisonneuve Press
MANDORLA: New Writing from the Americas / Nueva

escritura de las Americas
THE MANHATTAN REVIEW
MANOA: A Pacific Journal of International Writing
Mayapple Press
McPherson & Company Publishers
Menard Press
Merrimack Books
MICHIGAN QUARTERLY REVIEW
MID-AMERICAN REVIEW
Middlebury College Publications
Mid-List Press
Midwest Villages & Voices
Milkweed Editions
Mind Power Publishing
THE MINNESOTA REVIEW
MOTHERVERSE: A Journal of Contemporary Motherhood
MUSE: A Quarterly Journal of The Lit
MYSTERY ISLAND MAGAZINE
NEO: Literary Magazine
NERVE COWBOY
New Chapter Publisher
New Concept Press
NEW ENGLAND REVIEW
NEW HOPE INTERNATIONAL REVIEW
New Issues Poetry & Prose
THE NEW LAUREL REVIEW
NEW ORLEANS REVIEW
New Paradigm Books
New Rivers Press, Inc.
New Victoria Publishers
New World Press
NEWS FROM NATIVE CALIFORNIA
Night Horn Books
NIGHT TRAIN
nine muses books
19TH-CENTURY LITERATURE
NORTH DAKOTA QUARTERLY
Northern Illinois University Press
Northwestern University Press
Norton Coker Press
NOTRE DAME REVIEW
NOUN VS. VERB
NOVA RELIGIO
Oak Knoll Press
Ohio University Press/Swallow Press
Open Wide Books
Orchard House Press
THE ORPHAN LEAF REVIEW
Otoliths
THE PACIFIC REVIEW
PAGAN AMERICA
PAJ NTAUB VOICE
Panther Creek Press
PARENTEACHER MAGAZINE
PASSAGER
PASSAGES NORTH
PASSION
Path Press, Inc.
Pathwise Press
Pearl's Book'em Publisher
PEMMICAN
Pendragonian Publications
PENNY DREADFUL: Tales and Poems of Fantastic Terror
Penthe Publishing
The Permanent Press/The Second Chance Press
PHOEBE: A Journal of Literature and Art
THE PINCH
The Poetry Center
POETRY EAST
THE POETRY PROJECT NEWSLETTER
Poets & Writers, Inc.
POINT OF CONTACT, The Journal of Verbal & Visual
   Arts
Polar Bear & Company
Portal Press
The Post-Apollo Press
THE PRAIRIE JOURNAL OF CANADIAN LITERATURE
Prairie Journal Press

Prakalpana Literature
PRAKALPANA SAHITYA/PRAKALPANA LITERA-
TURE
PRETEXT
PRISM INTERNATIONAL
PROVINCETOWN ARTS
Psychedelic Literature
PublishingWorks, Inc.
PULSAR POETRY WEBZINE
PUNKIN HOUSE DIGEST
Punkin House Press
Pushcart Press
Pyncheon House
QED Press
Quale Press
Quarterly Committee of Queen's University
QUEEN'S QUARTERLY: A Canadian Review
RARITAN: A Quarterly Review
RATTAPALLAX
Raular Publishing
THE RAVEN CHRONICLES
Raven Publishing, Inc.
Red Cygnet Press
RED FEZ ENTERTAINMENT
RED HAWK
RED MARE
Red Rock Press
RED ROCK REVIEW
RED WHEELBARROW
Regent Press
RELIGION & AMERICAN CULTURE
RENDITIONS
Research Centre for Translation, Chinese University of
Hong Kong
RIVER STYX
Ronsdale Press
ROOM MAGAZINE
Rowhouse Press
Sabellapress
Saint Bob Press
Salt Publishing
Sand River Press
Santa Fe Writers Project
Saqi Books Publisher
Sarabande Books
Savant Garde Workshop
Scars Publications
SCHUYLKILL VALLEY JOURNAL
THE SCRIBIA
SCRIVENER
Second Coming Press
SEWANEE REVIEW
SHATTERED WIG REVIEW
SHENANDOAH: The Washington and Lee University
Review
Sherman Asher Publishing
SIDE OF GRITS
Silenced Press
SINISTER WISDOM
Skullvines Press
SKYLINE LITERARY MAGAZINE
Skyline Publications
Sligo Press
Small Dogma Publishing, Inc.
SMARTISH PACE
SNREVIEW
SONGS OF INNOCENCE
SOUTH DAKOTA REVIEW
THE SOUTHERN REVIEW
SOUTHWEST REVIEW
SP QUILL MAGAZINE
SPECS
SPIDER
Spinifex Press
SPORE
Star Publish LLC
Starcherone Books
Stardate Publishing Company

Steerforth Press, L.C.
THE STINGING FLY
Stormline Press, Inc.
STORYQUARTERLY
STUDIO - A Journal of Christians Writing
Sherwood Sugden & Company, Publishers
George Suttton Publishing Co.
SWILL
SYCAMORE REVIEW
SYMPOSIUM
Synergistic Press
Talisman House, Publishers
TALKING RIVER REVIEW
TAPROOT LITERARY REVIEW
TAPROOT, a journal of older writers
THE TARPEIAN ROCK
TEACHERS & WRITERS
TELOS
Telos Press
Texas Tech University Press
THALIA: Studies in Literary Humor
Thatch Tree Publications
THEMA
13TH MOON
Thorp Springs Press
THE THREEPENNY REVIEW
Thundercloud Books
Tia Chucha Press
Toad Press International Chapbook Series
TORRE DE PAPEL
The True Bill Press
TSAR Publications
Turnstone Press
twentythreebooks
The Twickenham Press
Twilight Times Books
TWO LINES: World Writing in Translation
UND Press
UNDERSTANDING MAGAZINE
Underwhich Editions
University of Nebraska Press
University of South Carolina Press
University of Tampa Press
University of Virginia Press
Urion Press
Van Cleave Publishing
Vanderbilt University Press
VARIOUS ARTISTS
VERSAL
THE VIRGINIA QUARTERLY REVIEW
Vox Humana Books
THE WALLACE STEVENS JOURNAL
WAR, LITERATURE & THE ARTS: An International
Journal of the Humanities
WATER ROW REVIEW
The Wellsweep Press
The Wessex Collective
West Virginia University Press
WESTERN AMERICAN LITERATURE
WESTERN HUMANITIES REVIEW
Wheatmark Book Publishing
WHEELHOUSE MAGAZINE
THE WILDWOOD READER
Wings Press
Wintertree Press
The Word Works
WORDKNOT AUDIO: A Literary Podcast Magazine
Wordsonthestreet
Writecorner.com Press
WRITER'S CHRONICLE
XAVIER REVIEW
X-RAY
ZAWP
Zoo Press
Zumaya Publications LLC

LONDON

THE ENGLISH CLARION

706

Peter Marcan Publications
SeaCrab Publishing
The True Bill Press

JACK LONDON

The Live Oak Press, LLC
Mondial
WESTERN AMERICAN LITERATURE

LOS ANGELES

Balcony Media, Inc.
Clover Park Press
East West Discovery Press
Allen A. Knoll Publishers
Lummox Press
MCM Entertainment, Inc. Publishing Division
PLAIN BROWN WRAPPER (PBW)
Santa Monica Press
VOICE(S)
Wexford & Barrow, Publishers

LOUISIANA

The Chicot Press
Claitor's Law Books & Publishing Division, Inc.
DESIRE STREET
THE LOUISIANA REVIEW
Margaret Media, Inc.
NEW ORLEANS REVIEW
NOLA-MAGICK Press
Rock Spring Press Inc.
XAVIER REVIEW

H.P. LOVECRAFT

ALMOST NORMAL COMICS and Other Oddities
Gryphon Books
NOVA EXPRESS
PAPERBACK PARADE
RALPH'S REVIEW
SHATTERED WIG REVIEW
Zirlinson Publishing

MAGAZINES

ALTERNATIVE PRESS REVIEW
THE AMERICAN DISSIDENT
BABYSUE
BOGG: A Journal of Contemporary Writing
BOOK MARKETING UPDATE
CHAPMAN
CHILDREN, CHURCHES AND DADDIES, A Non
   Religious, Non Familial Literary Magazine
CONFRONTATION
COUNTERPOISE: For Social Responsibilities, Liberty and
   Dissent
CRICKET
DARK ANIMUS
DOWN IN THE DIRT LITERARY MAGAZINE, the prose
   & poetry magazine revealing all your dirty little secrets
DREAM NETWORK
Dustbooks
EEI Press
FEMINIST PERIODICALS: A CURRENT LISTING OF
   CONTENTS
FIDELIS ET VERUS
FRANK: AN INTERNATIONAL JOURNAL OF CON-
   TEMPORARY WRITING AND ART
FREEDOM AND STRENGTH PRESS FORUM
THE FREEFALL REVIEW
GRAY AREAS
Gryphon Books
Heidelberg Graphics
A HUDSON VIEW POETRY DIGEST
ICONOCLAST
Info Net Publishing
LITERARY MAGAZINE REVIEW
LOST GENERATION JOURNAL
MUSE: A Quarterly Journal of The Lit
NEO: Literary Magazine
NEW HOPE INTERNATIONAL REVIEW

THE PEDESTAL MAGAZINE.COM
The Poetry Center
POETS' ROUNDTABLE
THE PRAIRIE JOURNAL OF CANADIAN LITERATURE
Punkin House Press
RED HAWK
Sand and Sable Publishing
Scars Publications
SHORTRUNS
SKYLINE LITERARY MAGAZINE
Skyline Publications
THE SMALL PRESS REVIEW/SMALL MAGAZINE
   REVIEW
SMARTISH PACE
SPECS
SPIDER
STONE SOUP, The Magazine By Young Writers and
   Artists
Thirdeye Publications
13TH MOON
THRESHOLDS JOURNAL
TREATING YOURSELF: The Alternative Medicine Jour-
   nal
UmbraProjects Publishing
VOICE(S)
THE WILDWOOD READER

MAGIC

ABRAMELIN: a Journal of Poetry and Magick
THE BELTANE PAPERS: A Journal of Women's
   Mysteries
Crescent Moon
DARK GOTHIC RESURRECTED
EcceNova Editions
Empyrean Hill Books, Inc.
Horned Owl Publishing
MOBILE BEAT: The Mobile Entertainer's Magazine
NEWWITCH
nine muses books
NOLA-MAGICK Press
PASSION
Perrin Press
Pixiu Press
STARNOTES
Subsynchronuos Press
Three Pyramids Publishing
Twilight Tales, Inc.
White Crosslet Publishing Co
Wilshire Books Inc.

MAINE

Bauhan Publishing, LLC
The Latona Press
Moon Pie Press
New England Cartographics, Inc.
Polar Bear & Company
Peter E. Randall Publisher
John Wade, Publisher
The Wessex Collective

MANAGEMENT

Adams-Blake Publishing
Alpine Guild, Inc.
Behavioral Sciences Research Press, Inc.
Benchmark Publications Inc.
Burns Park Publishers
Canadian Educators' Press
Church Leadership Library (Canadian Office)
Dancing Bridge Publishing
Dash-Hill, LLC
Edenscape Publishing Company
EQUAL CONSTRUCTION RECORD
Famaco Publishers (Qalam Books)
Finney Company, Inc.
Frontline Publications
Goblin Fern Press
GoldenHouse Publishing Group
Happy About

The Madson Group, Inc.
Mind Power Publishing
Multi-Media Publications Inc.
Penworth Publishing
PREP Publishing
Reliance Books
SACS Consulting
Set Sail Productions, LLC
THE SMALL BUSINESS ADVISOR
Smith-Johnson Publisher
Two Eagles Press International
The Utility Company LLC
Wheatmark Book Publishing

MAPS

CONCRETE JUNGLE JOURNAL
New England Cartographics, Inc.
THE ORPHAN LEAF REVIEW
Sunbelt Publications

MARINE LIFE

Abernathy House Publishing
Birdsong Books
Dixon-Price Publishing
The Narrative Press
Naturegraph Publishers
NewSage Press
Ocean Publishing
SEA KAYAKER
Tortuga Books
Trickle Creek Books
Windward Publishing, An Imprint of Finney Company

MARKETING

Adams-Blake Publishing
Bay Tree Publishing
Best Books Plus
Brenner Information Group
Burns Park Publishers
C&R Press
Cuore Libre Publishing
D.B.A. Books
Dash-Hill, LLC
DOLLS UNITED INTERACTIVE MAGAZINE
Dominion Global Publishing
Encore Publishing
GoldenHouse Publishing Group
Happy About
The Haworth Press
Info Net Publishing
Long & Silverman Publishing, Inc.
Mendham Publishing
New Knowledge Press
Pellingham Casper Communications
Penworth Publishing
SAPONIFIER
SEDUCTIVE SELLING
Set Sail Productions, LLC
74th Street Productions, L.L.C.
Smirk Books
Sources
Titlewaves Publishing; Writers Direct
Visual Arts Press
WeWrite LLC
Wilshire Books Inc.

MARRIAGE

APPLE VALLEY REVIEW: A Journal of Contemporary
    Literature
Blue Dolphin Publishing, Inc.
THE FIT CHRISTIAN A Christian Health & Fitness
    Magazine
Fruitbearer Publishing, LLC
HEALMB Publishing
Impact Publishers, Inc.
InsideOut Press
MCM Entertainment, Inc. Publishing Division
Meek Publishing

Nolo Press Occidental
Oak Tree Press
Poor Richard's Press
River Press
Rolling Hills Publishing
VOICES ISRAEL
Write Now Publishing Company

MARTIAL ARTS

Arjuna Library Press
Best Life Media
LOW BUDGET ADVENTURE
Paladin Enterprises, Inc.
Turtle Press, division of S.K. Productions Inc.
Twinteum Artist, Inc.
YMAA Publication Center

MASSAGE

ARCATA ARTS
Best Life Media
Dharma Publishing
Himalayan Institute Press
Village Lane Press

MATHEMATICS

Applied Probability Trust
Arjuna Library Press
Blue Owl Press
Clearwater Publishing Co.
First Books
Gingerbread House
Huntington Press
JOURNAL OF REGIONAL CRITICISM
LrnIT Publishing Div. LRNIT CORPORATION
MATHEMATICAL SPECTRUM
MUSIC PERCEPTION
Polka Dot Publishing
Polygonal Publishing House
SMARANDACHE NOTIONS JOURNAL
Wide World Publishing

MEDIA

Bay Press
BLACK BOOK PRESS: The Poetry Zine id
BOOK MARKETING UPDATE
Cottonwood Press, Inc.
Crescent Moon
D.B.A. Books
HAPPENINGNOW!EVERYWHERE
Hollywood Creative Directory
ILLOGICAL MUSE
KETTERING REVIEW
LEFT CURVE
Open Horizons Publishing Company
OPEN WIDE MAGAZINE
PASSION
Rada Press, Inc.
SIGNALS
Sources
THE SOURCES HOTLINK
South End Press
Strata Publishing, Inc.
Strata Publishing, Inc.
STYLUS
VARIOUS ARTISTS
WAV MAGAZINE: Progressive Music Art Politics Culture

MEDICINE

Abigon Press
Adams-Blake Publishing
Alpine Guild, Inc.
America West Publishers
Bellevue Literary Press
BELLEVUE LITERARY REVIEW
Blowtorch Press
Brain Injury Success Books
Cable Publishing
Carolina Academic Press

Citiria Publishing
Consumer Press
dbS Productions
Devil Mountain Books
firefall editions
Flowerfield Enterprises, LLC
Future Horizons, Inc.
Galen Press, Ltd.
The Haworth Press
Health Press NA Inc.
HEALTHY WEIGHT JOURNAL
HEARING HEALTH
Immunizations for Public Health
JOURNAL OF SCIENTIFIC EXPLORATION
Kali Press
Lemon Grove Press
Loving Healing Press, Inc.
MEDICAL HISTORY
Medi-Ed Press
MIDWIFERY TODAY
Midwifery Today
MOUTH: Voice of the Dis-Labeled Nation
New Paradigm Books
Padishah Press
Park Place Publications
Savor Publishing House, Inc.
Soto Publishing Company
Southern Methodist University Press
Standish Press
Thatch Tree Publications
TMC Books LLC
Vestibular Disorders Association
Village Lane Press
Wellcome Trust Centre for the History of Medicine at UCL
WILDERNESS MEDICINE NEWSLETTER

MEDIEVAL

Avari Press
BIBLIOPHILOS
Blue Moose Press
Blue Planet Books Inc.
Blue Unicorn Press, Inc.
THE BROADKILL REVIEW: A Journal of Literature
CONTEMPORARY GHAZALS
Erespin Press
Fine Tooth Press
Helm Publishing
Italica Press, Inc.
LEO Productions LLC.
Orchard House Press
SeaCrab Publishing
UmbraProjects Publishing
Whitston Publishing Co.

MEMOIRS

A Cappela Publishing
Accendo Publishing
AGNI
Alaska Native Language Center
ALASKA QUARTERLY REVIEW
All Nations Press
American Legacy Media
APPLE VALLEY REVIEW: A Journal of Contemporary
   Literature
Archer Books
Bancroft Press
Bauhan Publishing, LLC
Black Lawrence Press
Bloated Toe Publishing
BLUELINE
Brain Injury Success Books
Bright Mountain Books
BRILLIANT CORNERS: A Journal of Jazz & Literature
C&R Press
Cantarabooks LLC
Chicory Blue Press, Inc.
Cladach Publishing
Clover Valley Press, LLC

Colerith Press
COLORADO REVIEW
Comstock Bonanza Press
Cornerstone Press
Cotton Tree Press
THE CREAM CITY REVIEW
Creative Arts Book Company
Cypress House
Delaney Day Press
DESIRE
Disparate Voices
DLite Press
Drinian Press
Elderberry Press, Inc.
Emrys Press
Eros Books
First Books
Fithian Press
THE FLORIDA REVIEW
Foremost Press
Forest Dale Publishing Company
FOURTH GENRE: EXPLORATIONS IN NONFICTION
Fruitbearer Publishing, LLC
Goblin Fern Press
HAPA NUI
Ice Cube Press
IMAGE: ART, FAITH, MYSTERY
Imago Press
Impassio Press
The Infinity Group
THE INK SLINGER REVIEW
Inkwater Press
The Intrepid Traveler
Leapfrog Press
Lilly Press
Lion's Den Publishing
LITTLE BALKANS REVIEW
Little Pear Press
MacAdam/Cage Publishing Inc.
B.B. Mackey Books
Mayhaven Publishing, Inc.
Medusa's Muse
Mercer University Press
The Kenneth G. Mills Foundation
MUSE: A Quarterly Journal of The Lit
Music City Publishing
My Heart Yours Publishing
NEO: Literary Magazine
New Concept Press
NEW ENGLAND REVIEW
NewSage Press
Nish Publishing Company
North Star Books
Omonomany
Orchises Press
OTHER INVESTIGATIONS
PALO ALTO REVIEW
Panther Creek Press
PASSAGER
Plain View Press
Pocahontas Press, Inc.
Pocol Press
Polar Bear & Company
Portal Press
Presa Press
PUNKIN HOUSE DIGEST
Pussywillow
QED Press
RAINBOW CURVE
RED FEZ ENTERTAINMENT
Red Rock Press
The Reed Edwards Company
Re-invention UK Ltd
Rivendell Books
RIVER POETS JOURNAL
RIVER TEETH: A Journal of Nonfiction Narrative
Sadorian Publications
SALAMANDER

709

Santa Fe Writers Project
SEWANEE REVIEW
Sherman Asher Publishing
Silenced Press
Skyline Publications
Slipdown Mountain Publications LLC
Spinifex Press
SPINNINGS...INTENSE TALES OF LIFE MAGAZINE
Spring Grass
Star Publish LLC
Steerforth Press, L.C.
SterlingHouse Publisher
Sun Dog Press
Timeless Books
TINY LIGHTS: A Journal of Personal Narrative
Titus Home Publishing
The True Bill Press
Tupelo Press
Turnstone Press
Tuscarora Books Inc.
University of Massachusetts Press
University of South Carolina Press
University of Utah Press
VOICE(S)
WAR, LITERATURE & THE ARTS: An International
  Journal of the Humanities
The Wessex Collective
Wheatmark Book Publishing
Wordsonthestreet
Zumaya Publications LLC

MEN

AFRICAN AMERICAN REVIEW
AT-HOME DAD
Beacon Press
Bear & Company
BLK
Ecrivez!
Fine Tooth Press
Gemini Publishing Company
GLB Publishers
Ika, LLC
Islewest Publishing
Mondial
PASSAGER
Penthe Publishing
Poor Richard's Press
Rainbow Books, Inc.
Red Alder Books
RFD
SO YOUNG!
Steel Balls Press
Vanderbilt University Press
Whole Person Associates Inc.
Women and Men Books
Yellow Moon Press

H.L. MENCKEN

FULLOSIA PRESS
See Sharp Press
Smirk Books
Vulgar Marsala Press

MENTAL HEALTH

ABLAZE Publishing
Act on Wisdom
AIS Publications
American Legacy Media
ANHEDONIA
BLUE MOUNTAIN
Carolina Wren Press
Compact Clinicals
Consumer Press
CURRENTS: New Scholarship in the Human Services
Delaney Day Press
Gallaudet University Press
GENRE: WRITER AND WRITINGS
Haight-Ashbury Publications

HAMPTON ROADS HEALTH JOURNAL
The Haworth Press
Holbrook Street Press
Hunter House Inc., Publishers
JACK MACKEREL MAGAZINE
JOURNAL OF PSYCHOACTIVE DRUGS
The Leaping Frog Press
Lemieux International Ltd.
Lemon Grove Press
March Books
Meek Publishing
NEW ALTERNATIVES
Nushape Publication
OPEN MINDS QUARTERLY
PASSAGER
QED Press
Sidran Institute
Spring Grass
Whole Person Associates Inc.
Women of Diversity Productions, Inc.

MENTORING/COACHING

THE ART OF ABUNDANCE
Church Leadership Library (Canadian Office)
Church Leadership Library (US Office)
The Fiction Works
Finney Company, Inc.
Hopeace Press
InsideOut Press
Music City Publishing
Platinum Dreams Publishing
Search Institute
SEDUCTIVE SELLING
Set Sail Productions, LLC
Small Dogma Publishing, Inc.
STARNOTES
Third Dimension Publishing
The Utility Company LLC
Wellington House Publishing Company
Whole Person Associates Inc.
World Gumbo Publishing

METAPHYSICS

Allbook Books
Altair Publications
Anderson Publishing; also RC Anderson Books
Aquila Ink Publishing
Arias Press
Arjuna Library Press
THE ART OF ABUNDANCE
AT-HOME DAD
Bear & Company
THE BELTANE PAPERS: A Journal of Women's
  Mysteries
Best Life Media
Beyond Words Publishing, Inc.
BLUE MOUNTAIN
Borden Publishing Co.
BOTH SIDES NOW
Cuore Libre Publishing
Devi Press, Inc.
Dharma Publishing
EcceNova Editions
Edin Books, Inc.
EMERGING
Free People Press
Galde Press, Inc.
Gateways Books And Tapes
Heartsong Books
HEAVEN BONE MAGAZINE
Heaven Bone Press
Himalayan Institute Press
Horned Owl Publishing
In Print Publishing
Intuitive Moon Media
JOURNAL OF REGIONAL CRITICISM
L&L Dreamspell
A.P. Lee & Co., Ltd.

LifeSkill Institute, Inc.
LightLines Publishing
Loving Healing Press, Inc.
LP Publications (Teleos Institute)
Lycanthrope Press
The Kenneth G. Mills Foundation
MYSTERY ISLAND MAGAZINE
Nautilus Publishing Company
New Native Press
New Paradigm Books
New World Library
NOLA-MAGICK Press
OFFICE NUMBER ONE
One Spirit Press
Origin Press
PhoeniX in Print
Poptritus Press
SAGEWOMAN
SOM Publishing, division of School of Metaphysics
SPOTops Books
STARNOTES
SterlingHouse Publisher
Summerland Publishing
Synergetic Press
Three Pyramids Publishing
THRESHOLDS JOURNAL
Timeless Books
TRUTH SEEKER
Tuvela Press
Twilight Times Books
Unity House
UNITY MAGAZINE
UnKnownTruths.com Publishing Company
Vulgar Marsala Press
Westgate Press
Wilshire Books Inc.
World Love Press Publishing

MEXICO

Calaca Press
Montemayor Press
Sunbelt Publications
Tameme
Tres Picos Press
Two Eagles Press International
University Press of Colorado

MICHIGAN

Avery Color Studios
Wm.B. Eerdmans Publishing Co.
Glass Tower Press
Lawells Publishing
Mayapple Press
Poetry Harbor
Slipdown Mountain Publications LLC
Wilderness Adventure Books

MIDDLE EAST

Academy Press of America
ARC
Bluestocking Press
Clarity Press, Inc.
CONTEMPORARY GHAZALS
Florida Academic Press
Hoover Institution Press
Ibex Publishers, Inc.
Interlink Publishing Group, Inc.
JEWISH CURRENTS
JOURNAL OF PALESTINE STUDIES
Judah Magnes Museum Publications
KMT, A Modern Journal of Ancient Egypt
Mishmish Press
Noontide Press
Passeggiata Press, Inc.
The Post-Apollo Press
Saqi Books Publisher
Smyrna Press
South End Press

University of Arkansas Press
University of Utah Press
VOICES ISRAEL
Yaldah Publishing

MIDWEST

Allium Press of Chicago
THE ANNALS OF IOWA
Aquarius Press
Avery Color Studios
BIG MUDDY: Journal of the Mississippi River Valley
Blackwater Publications
THE BRIAR CLIFF REVIEW
Cave Hollow Press
Chicago Review Press
CHILDREN, CHURCHES AND DADDIES, A Non
    Religious, Non Familial Literary Magazine
Clover Valley Press, LLC
CMP Publishing Group LLC
DRUMVOICES REVUE
Farcountry Press
FREEDOM AND STRENGTH PRESS FORUM
Glass Tower Press
Mayapple Press
Mayhaven Publishing, Inc.
NEW MADRID
Ohio University Press/Swallow Press
OHIOANA QUARTERLY
THE PRAIRIE JOURNAL OF CANADIAN LITERATURE
REVERIE: MIDWEST AFRICAN AMERICAN LITERA-
    TURE
RIVERBED HAIKU
RIVERWIND
SOUTH DAKOTA REVIEW
Truman State University Press
University of Nebraska Press
The Urbana Free Library

MILITARY, VETERANS

AAIMS Publishers
American Legacy Media
ATLANTIC PACIFIC PRESS
R.J. Bender Publishing
Bookhaven Press, LLC
Broken Rifle Press
Cantadora Press
COGNITIO: A Graduate Humanities Journal
Cypress Creek Publishing
Elderberry Press, Inc.
Faded Banner Publications
FULLOSIA PRESS
Galde Press, Inc.
The Glencannon Press
Historical Resources Press
History Compass, LLC
Lancer Militaria
Lemieux International Ltd.
LOW BUDGET ADVENTURE
McBooks Press, Inc.
The Narrative Press
Omonomany
Paladin Enterprises, Inc.
Pogo Press, Incorporated
PublishAmerica, LLLP.
The Sektor Co.
Slipdown Mountain Publications LLC
Stardate Publishing Company
STORMWARNING!
The True Bill Press
Twilight Times Books
The Urbana Free Library
Van Cleave Publishing
The WhaleInn Publishing House (1998)
White Mane Publishing Company, Inc.

HENRY MILLER

Fisher King Press
Open Wide Books

711

OPEN WIDE MAGAZINE
PLOPLOP
THE SAVAGE KICK LITERARY MAGAZINE
Six Ft. Swells Press
Wexford & Barrow, Publishers
Zygote Publishing

MINIATURE BOOKS

Clamp Down Press
Disparate Voices
DWELLING PORTABLY
Spring Grass
Stewart Publishing & Printing
UmbraProjects Publishing
Willowood Press

MINNESOTA

Blackwater Publications
Blue Unicorn Press, Inc.
THE BRIAR CLIFF REVIEW
Clover Valley Press, LLC
CMP Publishing Group LLC
Galde Press, Inc.
Grey Sparrow Press
INDUSTRY MINNE-ZINE
KUMQUAT MERINGUE
MIDWEST ART FAIRS
Minnesota Historical Society Press
Poetry Harbor
Pogo Press, Incorporated
RED HAWK
Suburban Wilderness Press

MISSOURI

Cave Hollow Press
Irish Genealogical Foundation
NEW MADRID

MONTANA

Arthur H. Clark Co.
Farcountry Press
The Great Rift Press
Jigsaw Press
Keokee Co. Publishing, Inc.
KUMQUAT MERINGUE
Lion's Den Publishing
THE MEADOW
Mountain Press Publishing Co.
Pruett Publishing Company
Raven Publishing, Inc.

MORMON

American Legacy Media
BOULDER HERETIC
THE DEFENDER - Rush Utah's Newsletter
Eborn Books
University of Utah Press
Utah State University Press

MOTIVATION, SUCCESS

A Cappela Publishing
Aaron Communications III
Accendo Publishing
Allwrite Advertising and Publishing
Arden Press, Inc.
Behavioral Sciences Research Press, Inc.
Bronze Girl Productions, Inc.
City Life Books, LLC
DAILY WORD
DREAM NETWORK
Dumouriez Publishing
Edenscape Publishing Company
Elite Books
Finney Company, Inc.
InsideOut Press
Jalmar Press/Innerchoice Publishing
KABBALAH
Knowledge Concepts Publishing

Kobalt Books
Lamp Light Press
The Leaping Frog Press
A.P. Lee & Co., Ltd.
LITERARY HOUSE REVIEW
Long & Silverman Publishing, Inc.
LrnIT Publishing Div. LRNIT CORPORATION
Markowski International Publishers
Massey-Reyner Publishing
Millennium Vision Press
Multi-Media Publications Inc.
New Knowledge Press
North Star Books
Open Horizons Publishing Company
Pendant Publishing Inc.
Penworth Publishing
Platinum Dreams Publishing
The Poetry Center Press/Shoestring Press
PREP Publishing
Princess Publishing
THE QUILLDRIVER
RTMC Organization, LLC
SAPONIFIER
Sassy Sunflower Books
SCULPTURAL PURSUIT MAGAZINE
SEDUCTIVE SELLING
Set Sail Productions, LLC
74th Street Productions, L.L.C.
Sherian Publishing
Small Dogma Publishing, Inc.
Smith-Johnson Publisher
STARNOTES
Summerland Publishing
Sweet People Publishing
Titlewaves Publishing; Writers Direct
Unity House
UNITY MAGAZINE
The Utility Company LLC
Wellington House Publishing Company
Wilde Publishing
Wilderness Ministries
Wilshire Books Inc.

MOVIES

ALMOST NORMAL COMICS and Other Oddities
Blue Lupin Press
Brick Road Poetry Press
Cantarabooks LLC
CELLAR
Fotofolio, Inc.
THE FREEDONIA GAZETTE: The Magazine Devoted to
   the Marx Brothers
FULLOSIA PRESS
HAPPENINGNOW!EVERYWHERE
IMAGE: ART, FAITH, MYSTERY
Lake Claremont Press
LegacyForever
Limelight Editions
MGW (Mom Guess What) Newsmagazine
MYSTERY ISLAND MAGAZINE
NEW ORLEANS REVIEW
Open Horizons Publishing Company
OPEN WIDE MAGAZINE
ROCTOBER COMICS AND MUSIC
Santa Monica Press
Southern Illinois University Press
Stardate Publishing Company
STYLUS
Whelks Walk Press

MOVING/RELOCATION

ECOTONE: Reimagining Place
First Books
Intercultural Press, Inc.

MULTICULTURAL

Allbook Books
APPLE VALLEY REVIEW: A Journal of Contemporary

Literature
Aquarius Press
ARTS & LETTERS: Journal of Contemporary Culture
Bay Tree Publishing
THE BELTANE PAPERS: A Journal of Women's Mysteries
BkMk Press
BLUE COLLAR REVIEW
BOOK/MARK QUARTERLY REVIEW
Calaca Press
Calyx Books
Carolina Wren Press
Casperian Books LLC
Church Leadership Library (Canadian Office)
Church Leadership Library (US Office)
Clark-Nova Books
COLLEGE LITERATURE
COLORLINES
THE COMSTOCK REVIEW
Cornerstone Publishing, Inc.
Coteau Books
Crandall, Dostie & Douglass Books, Inc.
Cross-Cultural Communications
Dawn Sign Press
Demarche Publishing LLC
DESIRE
Dream Publishing Co.
dreamslaughter
East West Discovery Press
Eastern Washington University Press
Face to Face Press
FEMINIST STUDIES
First Journey Publishing Company
Five Fingers Press
FIVE FINGERS REVIEW
A GATHERING OF THE TRIBES
GERTRUDE
Gertrude Press
Gingerbread House
Grey Sparrow Press
HAWAI'I REVIEW
Himalayan Institute Press
A HUDSON VIEW POETRY DIGEST
Ibexa Press
Ika, LLC
Illumination Arts
INDIA CURRENTS
Intercultural Press, Inc.
INTERCULTURE
Jako Books
Kakibubu Media Limited
THE KENYON REVIEW
THE LUMMOX JOURNAL
MANDORLA: New Writing from the Americas / Nueva escritura de las Americas
Margaret Media, Inc.
Mercer University Press
Montemayor Press
Moo-Cow Fan Club
MOTHERVERSE: A Journal of Contemporary Motherhood
Naturegraph Publishers
NEO: Literary Magazine
NewSage Press
NEWWITCH
Open Hand Publishing LLC
OUTER-ART
PALO ALTO REVIEW
Papillon Presse
Partisan Press
Passion Power Press, Inc
PEACEWORK
Peartree Books & Music
The People's Press
Phelps Publishing Company
Pixiu Press
Plank Road Publishing
The Poetry Center
POETRYREPAIRS: Contemporary International Poetry

POINT OF CONTACT, The Journal of Verbal & Visual Arts
Portal Press
THE RAVEN CHRONICLES
Raven Publishing, Inc.
RIVET MAGAZINE
Sabellapress
Savor Publishing House, Inc.
SO TO SPEAK: A Feminist Journal of Language & Art
Southeast Missouri State University Press
Spinifex Press
The Spirit That Moves Us Press, Inc.
Tia Chucha Press
Total Package Publications, LLC
TSAR Publications
Two Eagles Press International
United Nations University Press
University of Massachusetts Press
Vehicule Press
VERSAL
VOICES ISRAEL
Vox Humana Books
WEBER: The Contemporary West
WEST COAST LINE: A Journal of Contemporary Writing and Criticism
World Gumbo Publishing
XCP: CROSS-CULTURAL POETICS

MUSIC

Act on Wisdom
AD/VANCE
AFRICAN AMERICAN REVIEW
AFTERTOUCH: New Music Discoveries & Gifts For Your Creative Imagination
ALARM CLOCK
Allworth Press
ALMOST NORMAL COMICS and Other Oddities
Amadeus Press
Atelier Press
BABYSUE
BABYSUE MUSIC REVIEW
Bad Noise Productions
BAGAZINE
Barrytown/Station Hill Press
Bel Canto Press
Black Dress Press
BLACK MAGNOLIAS LITERARY JOURNAL
The Bold Strummer Ltd.
Brick Road Poetry Press
BRILLIANT CORNERS: A Journal of Jazz & Literature
Building Blocks Press
Burning Books
BUTTON
Celebrity Profiles Publishing
Clearwater Publishing Co.
Creative Arts Book Company
CROSSCURRENTS
Crystal Publishers, Inc.
DARK GOTHIC RESURRECTED
Dignified Designs
DIRTY LINEN
The Edwin Mellen Press
Faith Builders Resource Group
Glenbridge Publishing Ltd.
GRAMMAR CRISIS
GRAY AREAS
HAPPENINGNOW!EVERYWHERE
HILL COUNTRY SUN
Hollywood Creative Directory
IMAGE: ART, FAITH, MYSTERY
Iniquity Press/Vendetta Books
Irish Genealogical Foundation
ITALIAN AMERICANA
JACK MACKEREL MAGAZINE
JOURNAL OF MUSIC IN IRELAND (JMI)
JOURNAL OF MUSICOLOGY
JOURNAL OF THE AMERICAN MUSICOLOGICAL SOCIETY

LegacyForever
LIGHTWORKS MAGAZINE
Listening Voice Media Ltd
THE LUMMOX JOURNAL
MAGNET MAGAZINE
Mama Incense Publishing
Peter Marcan Publications
McPherson & Company Publishers
Medi-Ed Press
Merwood Books
MGW (Mom Guess What) Newsmagazine
MOBILE BEAT: The Mobile Entertainer's Magazine
Moonrise Press
Muse World Media Group
MUSIC PERCEPTION
MUSIC THEORY SPECTRUM
Mystery Island Publications
THE NEW ENGLAND QUARTERLY
NIGHTLIFE MAGAZINE
19TH-CENTURY MUSIC
THE NOISE
Norton Coker Press
NoteBoat, Inc.
Open Wide Books
OPEN WIDE MAGAZINE
THE OXFORD AMERICAN
Passeggiata Press, Inc.
Pearl's Book'em Publisher
Piano Press
Plank Road Publishing
Pogo Press, Incorporated
Poptritus Press
Pro musica press
Psychedelic Literature
Ragamuffin Heart Publishing
ROCTOBER COMICS AND MUSIC
Rowhouse Press
Sagamore Publishing
Santa Monica Press
Savant Garde Workshop
SeaCrab Publishing
See Sharp Press
Selah Publishing Co. Inc.
THE $ENSIBLE SOUND
SHATTERED WIG REVIEW
SHORTRUNS
Silenced Press
Six Ft. Swells Press
Sound Enterprises Publishing
THE SOUTHERN QUARTERLY: A Journal of the Arts in
    the South
SOUTHWEST COLORADO ARTS PERSPECTIVE
SP Turner Group
Speck Press
Stardate Publishing Company
Stellaberry Press
STYLUS
Syukhtun Editions
Thirteen Colonies Press
Trafton Publishing
Tuscarora Books Inc.
Underwhich Editions
WAV MAGAZINE: Progressive Music Art Politics Culture
West Coast Paradise Publishing
West Virginia University Press
White Cliffs Media, Inc.
X-Ray Book Co.
Yellow Moon Press

MYSTERY

A Cappela Publishing
A Midsummer Night's Press
Abecedarian books, Inc.
Absey & Co.
Accendo Publishing
Adventure Books Inc.
Affluent Publishing Corp.
Ageless Press

Allium Press of Chicago
Aquila Ink Publishing
Aspicomm Media
ATLANTIC PACIFIC PRESS
Avari Press
Avocet Press Inc.
BEGINNINGS - A Magazine for the Novice Writer
Booksmart Publications
C & M Online Media Inc.
CAPCAT
Caribbean Books-Panama
Cave Hollow Press
CELLAR
Central Avenue Press
Clover Valley Press, LLC
CMP Publishing Group LLC
CONCEIT MAGAZINE
Cornell Maritime Press/Tidewater Publishers
Cornerstone Press
Cozy Cat Press
Creative Arts Book Company
Demarche Publishing LLC
DESIRE
DTS Group, Inc.
Ecrivez!
Falcon Publishing, LTD
The Fiction Works
FMA Publishing
Foremost Press
GenNext Publishing
Gryphon Books
HARDBOILED
Helm Publishing
Idylls Press
Imago Press
Jigsaw Press
J-Press Publishing
Kakibubu Media Limited
Allen A. Knoll Publishers
Krill Press
L&L Dreamspell
The Leaping Frog Press
A.P. Lee & Co., Ltd.
LegacyForever
Lemieux International Ltd.
Lilly Press
LITERARY HOUSE REVIEW
LOW BUDGET ADVENTURE
Mayhaven Publishing, Inc.
The Merion Press, Inc.
Mondial
Multi-Media Publications Inc.
MYSTERY ISLAND MAGAZINE
MYSTERY READERS JOURNAL
THE MYSTERY REVIEW
New Victoria Publishers
New World Press, Inc
Oak Tree Press
Orchard House Press
Paladin Media Group
PAPERBACK PARADE
Polar Bear & Company
PublishAmerica, LLLP.
Rainbow Books, Inc.
Red Coyote Press
RIVER POETS JOURNAL
Rowan Mountain Press
Santa Fe Writers Project
Andrew Scott Publishers
SelectiveHouse Publishers, Inc.
Skyline Publications
SOUNDINGS REVIEW
SPINNINGS...INTENSE TALES OF LIFE MAGAZINE
SPOUT
SterlingHouse Publisher
Stormline Press, Inc.
Subsynchronuos Press
Triskelion Publishing

Triumvirate Publications
Turnstone Press
Twilight Tales, Inc.
Twilight Times Books
Vanilla Heart Publishing
The Wessex Collective
The WhaleInn Publishing House (1998)
Whiskey Creek Press
WindRiver Publishing
Wintertree Press
The Wolf Pirate Project Inc.
Wytherngate Press
Yaldah Publishing
Youthful Wisdom Press

MYTH, MYTHOLOGY

A Midsummer Night's Press
Agathon Books
Allbook Books
Arjuna Library Press
Bear & Company
THE BELTANE PAPERS: A Journal of Women's Mysteries
Blue Moose Press
BOULDER HERETIC
Bright Mountain Books
Caribbean Books-Panama
CONJUNCTIONS
Cornerstone Press
Coteau Books
Dervla Publishing, LLC
DESIRE
DREAM NETWORK
Flapjack Press
Focus Publishing/R. Pullins Co.
Heyday Books
Horned Owl Publishing
A HUDSON VIEW POETRY DIGEST
Immediate Direction Publications
In Between Books
THE JOURNAL OF CALIFORNIA AND GREAT BASIN ANTHROPOLOGY
LITERARY HOUSE REVIEW
Lycanthrope Press
Malki Museum Press
New Native Press
NEWWITCH
nine muses books
ORBIS
Oregon State University Press
P.R.A. Publishing
PAGAN AMERICA
Panther Creek Press
Pendragonian Publications
PENNY DREADFUL: Tales and Poems of Fantastic Terror
Perrin Press
Polar Bear & Company
PSYCHE
S4N Books
SAGEWOMAN
Sibyl Publications, Inc
Skullvines Press
SONGS OF INNOCENCE
Spinifex Press
SPOTops Books
Subsynchronuos Press
Syukhtun Editions
Three Pyramids Publishing
Tuvela Press
Twilight Tales, Inc.
UmbraProjects Publishing
UnKnownTruths.com Publishing Company
Vulgar Marsala Press
The Wessex Collective
The Wolf Pirate Project Inc.
Yellow Moon Press

NATIVE AMERICAN

Abernathy House Publishing
ABRAXAS
AIS Publications
Alaska Native Language Center
ALBERTA HISTORY
Allbook Books
AMERICAN INDIAN CULTURE AND RESEARCH JOURNAL
American Indian Studies Center
Avery Color Studios
The B & R Samizdat Express
Backcountry Publishing
Bauu Press
Beagle Bay Books / Creative Minds Press
The Bess Press
BIG MUDDY: Journal of the Mississippi River Valley
Black Dome Press Corp.
Borealis Press Limited
THE BRIAR CLIFF REVIEW
Bright Hill Press
Bright Mountain Books
Calaca Press
Cantadora Press
Carolina Wren Press
Clarity Press, Inc.
COLORLINES
Comstock Bonanza Press
THE COMSTOCK REVIEW
CONCEIT MAGAZINE
Coteau Books
Council For Indian Education
THE CREAM CITY REVIEW
Cross-Cultural Communications
Deep Well Publishing Company
The Denali Press
Dervla Publishing, LLC
Dream Catcher Publishing
DREAM NETWORK
Eagle's View Publishing
Eastern Washington University Press
ETC Publications
Evolution Publishing
Faith Builders Resource Group
First Journey Publishing Company
Fisher King Press
FROZEN WAFFLES
Frozen Waffles Press/Shattered Sidewalks Press; 45th Century Chapbooks
Fulcrum, Inc.
FULLOSIA PRESS
GENRE: WRITER AND WRITINGS
Goldfish Press
Granite Publishing Group
Heartsong Books
Heidelberg Graphics
Heyday Books
HIGH COUNTRY NEWS
Historical Society of Alberta
History Compass, LLC
Imago Press
INTERCULTURE
IRON HORSE LITERARY REVIEW
THE JOURNAL OF CALIFORNIA AND GREAT BASIN ANTHROPOLOGY
La Alameda Press
LAKE SUPERIOR MAGAZINE
Loonfeather Press
Magnifico Publications
Malki Museum Press
Malki-Ballena Press
Maryland Historical Press (also MHPress)
Miami University Press
The Middle Atlantic Press
Minnesota Historical Society Press
Naturegraph Publishers
THE NEW ENGLAND QUARTERLY

New Native Press
New World Library
NEWS FROM NATIVE CALIFORNIA
NEWWITCH
North Country Books, Inc.
NORTH DAKOTA QUARTERLY
Orchard House Press
Oregon State University Press
ORNAMENT
Panther Creek Press
Phelps Publishing Company
The Place In The Woods
Plank Road Publishing
Pocahontas Press, Inc.
Poetry Harbor
Pogo Press, Incorporated
Premium Press America
Pygmy Forest Press
Rainbow Books, Inc.
Raven Publishing, Inc.
Reference Service Press
S4N Books
Salt Publishing
Sand River Press
Sasquatch Books
Sasquatch Books
School for Advanced Research Press
Scottwall Associates, Publishers
SHAMAN'S DRUM: A Journal of Experiential Shamanism
SHENANDOAH NEWSLETTER
Sherman Asher Publishing
Genny Smith Books
SONG OF THE SAN JOAQUIN
SOUTH DAKOTA REVIEW
South End Press
State University of New York Press
STRUGGLE: A Magazine of Proletarian Revolutionary Literature
Sunbelt Publications
Syracuse Cultural Workers/Tools for Change
Syukhtun Editions
Texas Tech University Press
Theytus Books Ltd.
Thundercloud Books
TURNING THE TIDE: Journal of Anti-Racist Action, Research & Education
UBC Press
UND Press
United Lumbee Nation
UNITED LUMBEE NATION TIMES
University of Alaska Press
University of Calgary Press
University of Nebraska Press
University of Utah Press
Utah State University Press
WEBER: The Contemporary West
West End Press
West Virginia University Press
Whitston Publishing Co.
Wings Press
XCP: CROSS-CULTURAL POETICS
Yellow Moon Press
YUKHIKA—LATUHSE
Zagier & Urruty Publications
Zumaya Publications LLC

NATURE

Adirondack Mountain Club, Inc.
AMERICAN FORESTS
AzurAlive
Birdsong Books
Brookview Press
Cable Publishing
CANADIAN POETRY
Clover Park Press
CONCRETE JUNGLE JOURNAL
Concrete Jungle Press
Coteau Books

Dawn Publications
Dog's Eye View Media
Down The Shore Publishing
Ecopress, An Imprint of Finney Company
ECOTONE: Reimagining Place
THE FREEFALL REVIEW
GIN BENDER POETRY REVIEW
Greatland Graphics
Hobar Publications, A Division of Finney Company
Ice Cube Press
Iris Publishing Group, Inc (Iris Press / Tellico Books)
JAMES DICKEY REVIEW
Jon's Adventure Productions
Light-Beams Publishing
LITERARY HOUSE REVIEW
Loonfeather Press
Malki Museum Press
McBooks Press, Inc.
A Melody from an Immigrant's Soul
Moonrise Press
The Narrative Press
Native West Press
NATURALLY
Naturegraph Publishers
New England Cartographics, Inc.
NEW ENVIRONMENT BULLETIN
NEW VOICES REVISITED: Poetry, Contests and Short Stories.
New Win Publishing
NEWWITCH
NIS America, Inc.
North Country Books, Inc.
Ocean Publishing
Oregon State University Press
Outrider Press
Oyster River Press
PALO ALTO REVIEW
Pangaea
Peartree Books & Music
Pineapple Press, Inc.
Press Here
Pruett Publishing Company
PublishingWorks, Inc.
Ragamuffin Heart Publishing
RFF Press / Resources for the Future
Rock Spring Press Inc.
Sasquatch Books
Sasquatch Books
Scientia Publishing, LLC
Sherman Asher Publishing
SNOWY EGRET
SONG OF THE SAN JOAQUIN
SOUNDINGS REVIEW
SOUTH DAKOTA REVIEW
Southern Illinois University Press
Spring Grass
SunShine Press Publications, Inc.
Texas Tech University Press
Titlewaves Publishing; Writers Direct
TMC Books LLC
Trickle Creek Books
University of South Carolina Press
Utah State University Press
WASHINGTON TRAILS
WEBER: The Contemporary West
WHOLE TERRAIN - REFLECTIVE ENVIRONMENTAL PRACTICE
WILD DUCK REVIEW
Windward Publishing, An Imprint of Finney Company
Wood Thrush Books
Word Forge Books

NEBRASKA

THE BRIAR CLIFF REVIEW
Holmes House
Lone Willow Press
University of Nebraska Press

NETWORKING

AQUATERRA, METAECOLOGY & CULTURE
Black Forest Press and The Tennessee Publishing House
Church Leadership Library (Canadian Office)
CONNEXIONS DIGEST
Connexions Information Services, Inc.
EQUAL CONSTRUCTION RECORD
Finney Company, Inc.
INTERNATIONAL WOMEN'S WRITING GUILD
LIGHTWORKS MAGAZINE
LONE STARS MAGAZINE
OUT YOUR BACKDOOR: The Magazine of Do-It-Yourself Adventure and Homegrown Culture
World Gumbo Publishing

NEW AGE

A Cappela Publishing
Act on Wisdom
Al-Galaxy Publishing Corporation
Allworth Press
American Literary Press
Anderson Publishing; also RC Anderson Books
Aquila Ink Publishing
Athanor Books
Balanced Books Publishing
BOTH SIDES NOW
Brason-Sargar Publications
CHRISTIAN*NEW AGE QUARTERLY
Cuore Libre Publishing
Devi Press, Inc.
Dharma Publishing
DOWN IN THE DIRT LITERARY MAGAZINE, the prose & poetry magazine revealing all your dirty little secrets
DREAM NETWORK
EcceNova Editions
Edin Books, Inc.
Elite Books
Foremost Press
Free People Press
Guarionex Press Ltd.
Guarionex Press Ltd.
HEAL Foundation Press
HEAVEN BONE MAGAZINE
Heaven Bone Press
Himalayan Institute Press
Hood Press
Ika, LLC
Imago Press
In Print Publishing
L&L Dreamspell
A.P. Lee & Co., Ltd.
LifeSkill Institute, Inc.
LOVING MORE: New Models for Relationships
Lycanthrope Press
THE MOUNTAIN ASTROLOGER
N: NUDE & NATURAL
NEW ENVIRONMENT BULLETIN
New Knowledge Press
New Paradigm Books
New World Library
NEWWITCH
NOLA-MAGICK Press
OFFICE NUMBER ONE
Paragon House Publishers
The Passion Profit Company
Progressive Press; Tree of Life Publications
PSYCHE
RFD
SAGEWOMAN
SelectiveHouse Publishers, Inc.
SHARE INTERNATIONAL
SOM Publishing, division of School of Metaphysics
Square One Publishers, Inc.
STARNOTES
SterlingHouse Publisher
Stewart Publishing & Printing
Summerland Publishing

T'AI CHI

Three Pyramids Publishing
TRUTH SEEKER
Tuvela Press
Twilight Times Books
John Wade, Publisher
Westgate Press
White Crosslet Publishing Co
THE WILDWOOD READER
Zoilita Grant MS CCHt.

NEW ENGLAND

AMERICAN JONES BUILDING & MAINTENANCE
THE AUROREAN
Bauhan Publishing, LLC
BLUELINE
Chelsea Green Publishing Company
Cookbook Resources, LLC
Nicolin Fields Publishing, Inc.
The Latona Press
Mayhaven Publishing, Inc.
Midmarch Arts Press
NEW ENGLAND BY RAIL
New England Cartographics, Inc.
THE NEW ENGLAND QUARTERLY
THE NOISE
Oyster River Press
PINE ISLAND JOURNAL OF NEW ENGLAND POETRY
Peter E. Randall Publisher
Thirteen Colonies Press
TMC Books LLC
University of Massachusetts Press
THE WORCESTER REVIEW
Yellow Moon Press

NEW HAMPSHIRE

AMERICAN JONES BUILDING & MAINTENANCE
Bauhan Publishing, LLC
Crystal Press
Nicolin Fields Publishing, Inc.
New England Cartographics, Inc.
Oyster River Press
Peter E. Randall Publisher

NEW MEXICO

BEATLICK NEWS
Farcountry Press
firefall editions
KUMQUAT MERINGUE
La Alameda Press
LPD Press
NEW MEXICO POETRY REVIEW
Pruett Publishing Company
School for Advanced Research Press
Sherman Asher Publishing
Southwest Research and Information Center
Thundercloud Books
TRADICION REVISTA
Two Eagles Press International
VOICES FROM THE EARTH
Wilde Publishing

NEW YORK

Adirondack Mountain Club, Inc.
Black Dome Press Corp.
Bronx River Press
Chelsea Green Publishing Company
CONCRETE JUNGLE JOURNAL
Concrete Jungle Press
Fotofolio, Inc.
Goss Press
IN OUR OWN WORDS
INNER CITY PRESS
McBooks Press, Inc.
Mondial
Mount Ida Press
New England Cartographics, Inc.
North Country Books, Inc.

THE OTHER HERALD
Panther Books
Paradiso-Parthas Press
Gibbs Smith, Publisher
State University of New York Press
Tuscarora Books Inc.

NEW ZEALAND

BOGG: A Journal of Contemporary Writing
Tres Picos Press
WHITE FUNGUS

NEWSLETTER

Affinity Publishers Services
Anti-Aging Press
AQUATERRA, METAECOLOGY & CULTURE
Black Forest Press and The Tennessee Publishing House
Center For Self-Sufficiency
Community Service, Inc.
THE CONNECTICUT POET
Downeast Books
Eborn Books
EEI Press
THE EUGENE O'NEILL REVIEW
FIDELIS ET VERUS
Harobed Publishing Creations
Heidelberg Graphics
INKY TRAIL NEWS
INTERNATIONAL WOMEN'S WRITING GUILD
Knowledge Concepts Publishing
Kodiak Media Group
LAUGHING BEAR NEWSLETTER
NEW SOLUTIONS
PRIVACY JOURNAL
Secretum Meum Mihi Press
SEDUCTIVE SELLING
SHORTRUNS
SKEPTICAL INQUIRER
Southwest Research and Information Center
SPIRITCHASER
THE STAR BEACON
Vestibular Disorders Association

NEWSPAPERS

BOOK MARKETING UPDATE
Children Of Mary
Deep Well Publishing Company
FIDELIS ET VERUS
THE FREEFALL REVIEW
Heritage Books, Inc.
INKY TRAIL NEWS
KETTERING REVIEW
Allen A. Knoll Publishers
Knowledge Concepts Publishing
Litwin Books
Moon Pie Press
Toca Family Publishing, div. of Toca Family Communications Group, LLC
Tuscarora Books Inc.

NICARAGUA

INNER CITY PRESS

ANAIS NIN

Chatterley Press International
KotaPress
LOST GENERATION JOURNAL
Magic Circle Press
Six Ft. Swells Press
Zygote Publishing

NON-FICTION

A Cappela Publishing
Aaron Communications III
Abecedarian books, Inc.
Absey & Co.
Accendo Publishing
Adventure Books Inc.

Ageless Press
AIS Publications
AK Press
Alaska Native Language Center
ALASKA QUARTERLY REVIEW
All Nations Press
Glen Allen Press
THE AMERICAN DRIVEL REVIEW
American Legacy Media
AMERICAN ROAD
Anacus Press, An Imprint of Finney Company
Anti-Aging Press
Appalachian House
Aquarius Press
Archer Books
Arden Press, Inc.
Ariko Publications
Artamo Press
ARTS & LETTERS: Journal of Contemporary Culture
Asteroid Publishing, Inc.
ATLANTIC PACIFIC PRESS
Atlantic Publishing Group, Inc.
Aura Productions, LLC
Authentic Publishing LLC
Avari Press
Avery Color Studios
AXE FACTORY REVIEW
AzurAlive
Balanced Books Publishing
THE BALTIMORE REVIEW
Bancroft Press
Bay Press
Bayhampton Publications
THE BEAR DELUXE MAGAZINE
The Bear Wallow Publishing Company
BearManor Media
BEATLICK NEWS
W.S. Beetle & Company
Bel Canto Press
Bellevue Literary Press
BELLEVUE LITERARY REVIEW
BELLINGHAM REVIEW
Benchmark Publications Inc.
R.J. Bender Publishing
Benecton Press
The Bess Press
Beyond Words Publishing, Inc.
BIG MUDDY: Journal of the Mississippi River Valley
Biographical Publishing Company
Birdsong Books
Black Dome Press Corp.
Black Forest Press and The Tennessee Publishing House
Black Lawrence Press
BLACK MAGNOLIAS LITERARY JOURNAL
Black Thistle Press
BLACK WARRIOR REVIEW
BlackBerry Fields Press
John F. Blair, Publisher
Blowtorch Press
Blue Lupin Press
Blue Owl Press
Bluestocking Press
Bonus Books, Inc.
Book Marketing Solutions
Books for All Times, Inc.
Brain Injury Success Books
THE BRIAR CLIFF REVIEW
Bright Mountain Books
BRILLIANT CORNERS: A Journal of Jazz & Literature
THE BROADKILL REVIEW: A Journal of Literature
Broken Rifle Press
Bronze Girl Productions, Inc.
Brookview Press
Buenos Books
BUFFALO SPREE
Burd Street Press
BYLINE
C & M Online Media Inc.

C&R Press
CAKETRAIN
Caketrain Journal and Press
Cantadora Press
Caribbean Books-Panama
The Caxton Press
Celo Valley Books
CENTER: A Journal of the Literary Arts
Central Avenue Press
CHAPMAN
Chase Publishing
Chelsea Green Publishing Company
Chicago Spectrum Press
Children Of Mary
CHIRON REVIEW
Church Leadership Library (Canadian Office)
Church Leadership Library (US Office)
CIMARRON REVIEW
Citiria Publishing
CKO UPDATE
Cladach Publishing
Clark-Nova Books
CMP Publishing Group LLC
COGNITIO: A Graduate Humanities Journal
Colerith Press
COLORADO REVIEW
Communication Creativity
COMPASS ROSE
Comrades Press
Comstock Bonanza Press
CONCEIT MAGAZINE
CONJUNCTIONS
Consumer Press
Continuing Education Press
CONTRARY
Cornell Maritime Press/Tidewater Publishers
Cornerstone Press
Cornerstone Publishing, Inc.
CORRECTIONS TODAY
THE CORTLAND REVIEW
Cotton Tree Press
CRAB ORCHARD REVIEW
Crane Press
CRAZYHORSE
THE CREAM CITY REVIEW
CREATIVE NONFICTION
Crossway
Crystal Dreams Publishing
Culturelink Press
CUTBANK
Cyberwit.net
Cypress Creek Publishing
DAILY WORD
Dancing Bridge Publishing
Dancing Lemur Press, L.L.C.
Datamaster Publishing, LLC
Dawn Publications
Russell Dean and Company
Delaney Day Press
Dervla Publishing, LLC
Devenish Press
DIET SOAP
Dignified Designs
Disparate Voices
DLite Press
Dominion Global Publishing
Dream Catcher Publishing
dreamslaughter
DTS Group, Inc.
Dufour Editions Inc.
Dumouriez Publishing
Dunamis House
Dwarf Lion Press
Eastern Washington University Press
EbonyEnergy Publishing, Inc.
EcceNova Editions
Ecopress, An Imprint of Finney Company
Ecrivez!

Edenscape Publishing Company
Wm.B. Eerdmans Publishing Co.
Elderberry Press, Inc.
Ellechor Publishing House
EMRYS JOURNAL
Emrys Press
Ephemera Bound Publishing
EPICENTER: A LITERARY MAGAZINE
Eros Books
EVANSVILLE REVIEW
Evening Street Press
EVENING STREET REVIEW
EVENT
Evolution Publishing
Faith Builders Resource Group
Fathom Publishing Co.
The Feminist Press at the City University of New York
The Fiction Works
FIDELIS ET VERUS
Nicolin Fields Publishing, Inc.
Finney Company, Inc.
First Books
First Journey Publishing Company
Fisher King Press
THE FIT CHRISTIAN A Christian Health & Fitness
    Magazine
FIVE POINTS
Florida Academic Press
FLUENT ASCENSION
FLYWAY: A Journal of Writing and Environment
FMA Publishing
Focus Publishing/R. Pullins Co.
FOLIO: A Literary Journal of American University
Foremost Press
Forest Dale Publishing Company
Fountain Publisher Limited
THE FREEFALL REVIEW
Front Row Experience
FUGUE
Galde Press, Inc.
Galen Press, Ltd.
The Galileo Press Ltd.
Gallaudet University Press
Gateways Books And Tapes
GENRE: WRITER AND WRITINGS
THE GEORGIA REVIEW
GERTRUDE
Gertrude Press
Gival Press
Glass Tower Press
GLB Publishers
The Glencannon Press
Goblin Fern Press
Good Book Publishing Company
Goose River Press
Grace House Publishing
Graywolf Press
The Great Rift Press
GREEN ANARCHY
THE GREEN HILLS LITERARY LANTERN
Green Hut Press
Green River Press
Green Square Publishing
Gryphon Books
GUD MAGAZINE (Greatest Uncommon Denominator)
GULF COAST
Halo Publishing International
Harbor House
HAWAI'I REVIEW
Heartsong Books
Heidelberg Graphics
Helm Publishing
His Work Christian Publishing
Historical Resources Press
Hobar Publications, A Division of Finney Company
Holbrook Street Press
Hoover Institution Press
Hot Box Press / Southern Roots Publishing

Howln Moon Press
A HUDSON VIEW POETRY DIGEST
Ibexa Press
ICON
Idylls Press
Ika, LLC
IMAGE: ART, FAITH, MYSTERY
Imago Press
Immediate Direction Publications
Impact Publishers, Inc.
Impassio Press
INDIANA REVIEW
THE INK SLINGER REVIEW
Inkwater Press
INKWELL
Insight Press
Interlink Publishing Group, Inc.
International University Line (IUL)
The Intrepid Traveler
THE IOWA REVIEW
Iris Publishing Group, Inc (Iris Press / Tellico Books)
IRON HORSE LITERARY REVIEW
Island Press
Italica Press, Inc.
J & J Consultants, Inc.
Jako Books
Jalmar Press/Innerchoice Publishing
JAMES DICKEY REVIEW
THE JOURNAL OF AFRICAN TRAVEL-WRITING
JOURNAL OF PYROTECHNICS
JPS Publishing Company
JUBILAT
KALEIDOSCOPE: Exploring the Experience of Disability
    through Literature & the Fine Arts
Kali Press
THE KELSEY REVIEW
THE KENYON REVIEW
Keokee Co. Publishing, Inc.
KESTREL: A Journal of Literature and Art
La Alameda Press
La Familia Publishing
Lake Claremont Press
LAKE EFFECT
Lake Street Press
THE LAUREL REVIEW
Lawells Publishing
LEAF GARDEN
Leaf Garden Press
THE LEDGE
A.P. Lee & Co., Ltd.
LegacyForever
Lemon Grove Press
The Lentz Leadership Institute LLC, The Refractive Thinker
    Press.
Libertas Press, LLC.
Liberty Publishing Company, Inc.
Lightning Bug Learning Press
Lilly Press
Limelight Editions
Listening Voice Media Ltd
LITERARY HOUSE REVIEW
LITTLE BALKANS REVIEW
THE LOUISVILLE REVIEW
Loving Healing Press, Inc.
THE LUMMOX JOURNAL
Lummox Press
MacAdam/Cage Publishing Inc.
THE MACGUFFIN
MAIN STREET RAG
Malki Museum Press
Mama Incense Publishing
MANOA: A Pacific Journal of International Writing
Marmot Publishing
Massey-Reyner Publishing
Maui arThoughts Co.
Mayhaven Publishing, Inc.
McBooks Press, Inc.
MCM Entertainment, Inc. Publishing Division

Merl Publications
Mica Press - Paying Our Dues Productions
Micron Press
MID-AMERICAN REVIEW
Mid-List Press
Milkweed Editions
Mills Custom Services Publishing
The Kenneth G. Mills Foundation
MINESHAFT
MINIATURE DONKEY TALK INC
Minnesota Historical Society Press
Mock Turtle Press
Montemayor Press
Moo-Cow Fan Club
Moondance Press
Motom
Music City Publishing
My Heart Yours Publishing
MYSTERY ISLAND MAGAZINE
The Narrative Press
National Writers Press
NATURAL BRIDGE
Nautilus Publishing Company
NEO: Literary Magazine
NEW ENGLAND BY RAIL
NEW ENGLAND REVIEW
New Knowledge Press
NEW LETTERS
NEW ORLEANS REVIEW
NEW VOICES REVISITED: Poetry, Contests and Short
    Stories.
NewSage Press
NEWWITCH
Nip and Tuck Publishing
Nish Publishing Company
Nolo Press Occidental
NORTH AMERICAN REVIEW
NORTH CAROLINA LITERARY REVIEW
North Country Books, Inc.
North Star Books
NORTHWEST REVIEW
Northwestern University Press
NSR Publications
Ocean Publishing
One Less Press
Oolichan Books
OPEN MINDS QUARTERLY
OPEN WIDE MAGAZINE
THE ORPHAN LEAF REVIEW
OTHER INVESTIGATIONS
THE OXFORD AMERICAN
OYEZ REVIEW
Oyster River Press
PADDLEFISH
PAJ NTAUB VOICE
Paladin Enterprises, Inc.
Paladin Media Group
Palari Publishing
PALO ALTO REVIEW
PARENTEACHER MAGAZINE
Parenting Press, Inc.
Paris Press
PASSAGES NORTH
Passion Power Press, Inc
Path Press, Inc.
THE PEDESTAL MAGAZINE.COM
The People's Press
Perpetual Press
Personhood Press
PhoeniX in Print
Piccadilly Books, Ltd.
Pilgrims Book House
THE PINCH
Platinum Dreams Publishing
PLEASANT LIVING
Pleasure Boat Studio: A Literary Press (including imprints
    Caravel Books and Aequitas Books, and the division
    Empty Bowl Press)

720

Polar Bear & Company
Poplar Leaf Press
Poptritus Press
PORTLAND REVIEW
Practically Shameless Press
PRETEXT
PRISM INTERNATIONAL
PUNKIN HOUSE DIGEST
Punkin House Press
THE QUIET FEATHER
THE QUILLDRIVER
Rabeth Publishing Company
Rada Press, Inc.
Ragged Edge Press
Ragged Raven Press
Rainbow Books, Inc.
Ram Press
RATTAPALLAX
Raular Publishing
THE RAVEN CHRONICLES
Ravenhawk Books
Reading Connections
Red Tiger Press
REDIVIDER
REMS Publishing & Publicity
REVERIE: MIDWEST AFRICAN AMERICAN LITERA-
    TURE
RFF Press / Resources for the Future
RIVER POETS JOURNAL
RIVER TEETH: A Journal of Nonfiction Narrative
RIVERSEDGE
RIVET MAGAZINE
Rolling Hills Publishing
Ronsdale Press
RTMC Organization, LLC
Sabellapress
Saber Press
SAGE OF CONSCIOUSNESS E-ZINE
Saint Mary's Press
Salmon Poetry Ltd.
Salt Publishing
Santa Monica Press
Scarlet Tanager Books
SCHUYLKILL VALLEY JOURNAL
Scientia Publishing, LLC
Search Institute
SEDUCTIVE SELLING
See Sharp Press
SEEMS
SENECA REVIEW
Sentient Publications, LLC
Set Sail Productions, LLC
SEWANEE REVIEW
Shared Roads Press
SHENANDOAH: The Washington and Lee University
    Review
Sherian Publishing
Signalman Publishing
SKIDROW PENTHOUSE
Skullvines Press
SKYLINE LITERARY MAGAZINE
Skyline Publications
Small Dogma Publishing, Inc.
Small Helm Press
The Smith (subsidiary of The Generalist Assn., Inc.)
Genny Smith Books
SNREVIEW
SO TO SPEAK: A Feminist Journal of Language & Art
Socratic Consulting Group
SOJOURN: A Journal of the Arts
$olvency International Inc., Publishing
Soto Publishing Company
Sound View Publishing, Inc.
SOUTH DAKOTA REVIEW
Southeast Missouri State University Press
SOUTHERN CALIFORNIA REVIEW
Southern Illinois University Press
Southern Methodist University Press

SOUTHWEST REVIEW
Speck Press
SPOUT
SPOUT
Spout Press
Square One Publishers, Inc.
Squire Press
Star Publish LLC
Stardate Publishing Company
Starik Publishing
Starry Night Publishing
Stellaberry Press
Stonehorse Publishing, LLC
Storm Publishing Group
Stormline Press, Inc.
STORYQUARTERLY
SUB-TERRAIN
Summer Stream Press
THE SUN, A Magazine of Ideas
Sunbelt Publications
Sunnyside Press
SunShine Press Publications, Inc.
Swedenborg Foundation
SWINK
SYCAMORE REVIEW
SYMPLOKE: A Journal for the Intermingling of Literary,
    Cultural and Theoretical Scholarship
Syukhtun Editions
TalSan Publishing/Distributors
Tameme
Thatch Tree Publications
THIRDEYE MAGAZINE
Thirsty Turtle Press
Thunder Rain Publishing Corp.
Timeless Books
Titlewaves Publishing; Writers Direct
TMC Books LLC
Toca Family Publishing, div. of Toca Family Communica-
    tions Group, LLC
Top 20 Press
Tortuga Books
Trafford Publishing
Trickle Creek Books
The True Bill Press
Truman State University Press
Tupelo Press
TURNROW
TWENTY-EIGHT PAGES LOVINGLY BOUND WITH
    TWINE
Twilight Times Books
Two Eagles Press International
Tyr Publishing
United Nations University Press
Unity House
UNITY MAGAZINE
University of Arkansas Press
University of Massachusetts Press
University of Nebraska Press
University of Tampa Press
University of Utah Press
University of Virginia Press
University Press of Colorado
Unlimited Publishing LLC
Upheaval Media
Upper Access Inc. Book Publishers
UPSTAIRS AT DUROC
Valuable Quality Publishing Company
VanderWyk & Burnham
Vehicule Press
Vintage Romance Publishing, LLC
VOICE(S)
Vox Humana Books
Waters Edge Press
WEBER: The Contemporary West
The Wellsweep Press
WEST BRANCH
West Coast Paradise Publishing
Westgate Press

The WhaleInn Publishing House (1998)
Wharton Publishing, Inc.
Wheatmark Book Publishing
Whiskey Creek Press
White Crosslet Publishing Co
White Mane Publishing Company, Inc.
WHOLE TERRAIN - REFLECTIVE ENVIRONMENTAL
  PRACTICE
Zelda Wilde Publishing
WILLOW REVIEW
WILLOW SPRINGS
Wilshire Books Inc.
Windward Publishing, An Imprint of Finney Company
Wings Press
WISCONSIN TRAILS
Wood Thrush Books
Wordsonthestreet
World Gumbo Publishing
Write Now Publishing Company
WRITER'S CHRONICLE
Writers House Press
Xenos Books
Yaldah Publishing
Yes International Publishers
YUKHIKA—LATUHSE
ZAWP
Zirlinson Publishing
ZONE 3

NON-VIOLENCE

Aaron Communications III
Abernathy House Publishing
Act on Wisdom
BLUE MOUNTAIN
Broken Rifle Press
CAIRN: The New St. Andrews Review
Celo Valley Books
Crandall, Dostie & Douglass Books, Inc.
dreamslaughter
First Journey Publishing Company
Fotofolio, Inc.
Free People Press
FRIENDS OF PEACE PILGRIM
HARMONY: Voices for a Just Future
HEAL Foundation Press
Heartsong Books
Hope Publishing House
Hunter House Inc., Publishers
Ika, LLC
Jalmar Press/Innerchoice Publishing
KotaPress
Legacy Audio Books, Inc.
Libellum
Lion's Den Publishing
NEW ENVIRONMENT BULLETIN
NEW VOICES REVISITED: Poetry, Contests and Short
  Stories.
NewSage Press
Parallax Press
Path Press, Inc.
PEACEWORK
The People's Press
Plain View Press
The Press at Foggy Bottom
SOCIAL ANARCHISM: A Journal of Practice and Theory
Spinifex Press
THIRDEYE MAGAZINE
TURNING WHEEL
VOICES ISRAEL
WAV MAGAZINE: Progressive Music Art Politics Culture

THE NORTH

Betelgeuse Books
Clover Valley Press, LLC
COLORLINES
Mountain Automation Corporation
NEW VOICES REVISITED: Poetry, Contests and Short
  Stories.

Poetry Harbor
University of Alaska Press
University of Calgary Press

NORTH AMERICA

BearManor Media
BEGGARS & CHEESEBURGERS
Birdsong Books
Blue Hull Press
Cable Publishing
Cyberwit.net
Faith Builders Resource Group
Fisher King Press
GAYELLOW PAGES
Heritage Books, Inc.
Legacy Audio Books, Inc.
MANDORLA: New Writing from the Americas / Nueva
  escritura de las Americas
Maryland Historical Press (also MHPress)
Museon Publishing
RIVERBED HAIKU
School for Advanced Research Press
Stormline Press, Inc.
1097 MAGAZINE
Three Bean Press
Truman State University Press
Zelda Wilde Publishing

NORTH CAROLINA

Ammons Communications; Imprint: Catch the Spirit of
  Appalachia
Banks Channel Books
John F. Blair, Publisher
Bright Mountain Books
C & M Online Media Inc.
Cyberwit.net
Explorer Press
McQuinn Publishing
NORTH CAROLINA LITERARY REVIEW
OYSTER BOY REVIEW
PREP Publishing
Trafton Publishing
WEST GOES SOUTH

NOVELS

A Cappela Publishing
Absey & Co.
ACME Press
Affluent Publishing Corp.
ALASKA QUARTERLY REVIEW
Allwrite Advertising and Publishing
American Literary Press
Ammons Communications; Imprint: Catch the Spirit of
  Appalachia
Aquarius Press
Aquila Ink Publishing
Artamo Press
Arx Publishing LLC
Asteroid Publishing, Inc.
Asylum Arts
Atelier Press
Athanata Arts, Ltd.
Avari Press
THE BALTIMORE REVIEW
Banks Channel Books
Bardsong Press
Barney Press
Bayhampton Publications
Bel Canto Press
BIG MUDDY: Journal of the Mississippi River Valley
Black Heron Press
Black Lawrence Press
Black Oak Press
BlackBerry Fields Press
Bladestar Publishing
Blanket Fort Publishing
Blue Hull Press
Blue Planet Books Inc.

Bordighera, Inc.
Bronx River Press
Brookline Books
C&R Press
Cable Publishing
Cantarabooks LLC
Caribbean Books-Panama
Casperian Books LLC
Celo Valley Books
Central Avenue Press
Citiria Publishing
City Life Books, LLC
Cladach Publishing
Clark-Nova Books
Clover Valley Press, LLC
CMP Publishing Group LLC
Coffee House Press
CONCRETE JUNGLE JOURNAL
Concrete Jungle Press
Cornerstone Press
Cornucopia Press
COSMOPSIS QUARTERLY
Cotton Tree Press
Cozy Cat Press
Crystal Dreams Publishing
Cyberwit.net
Demarche Publishing LLC
Eastern Washington University Press
Edenscape Publishing Company
Ellechor Publishing House
Ephemera Bound Publishing
Eros Books
First Books
Fisher King Press
Fithian Press
Foremost Press
Fountain Publisher Limited
4 Your Spirit Productions
Fruitbearer Publishing, LLC
The Galileo Press Ltd.
GEM Literary Foundation Press
GenNext Publishing
Global Learning
Goblin Fern Press
GOLD DUST
GoodSAMARitan Press
Goss Press
Grip Publishing
HAPA NUI
Harbor House
Helm Publishing
Hole Books
Hopeace Press
Idylls Press
ILLUMINATIONS
Imago Press
IMPress
In Between Books
Indigo Ink Press, Inc.
Intuitive Moon Media
Italica Press, Inc.
Jackson Harbor Press
Jigsaw Press
Journey Books Publishing
Allen A. Knoll Publishers
Krill Press
La Familia Publishing
Leaf Garden Press
THE LEDGE
A.P. Lee & Co., Ltd.
Llumina Press
Loonfeather Press
Ludlow Press
LULLWATER REVIEW
Lyons Publishing Limited
Mama Incense Publishing
MANOA: A Pacific Journal of International Writing
Mayhaven Publishing, Inc.

McBooks Press, Inc.
McPherson & Company Publishers
McQuinn Publishing
Medusa's Muse
MindGlow Media
Mishmish Press
Mondial
Montemayor Press
Motom
Mountain Media
Mountain State Press
Muse World Media Group
Myriad Press
National Writers Press
Nautilus Publishing Company
NEO: Literary Magazine
New Concept Press
NEW ENGLAND BY RAIL
THE NEW FORMALIST
New Orphic Publishers
THE NEW ORPHIC REVIEW
New Victoria Publishers
Obie Joe Media
Open Wide Books
THE ORPHAN LEAF REVIEW
Paladin Media Group
Panther Books
Panther Creek Press
Papillon Presse
Paris Press
The People's Press
Phoenix Illusion
Platinum Dreams Publishing
Pleasure Boat Studio: A Literary Press (including imprints Caravel Books and Aequitas Books, and the division Empty Bowl Press)
Polar Bear & Company
Portal Press
PREP Publishing
Psychedelic Literature
PUNKIN HOUSE DIGEST
Pyncheon House
Ravenhawk Books
RED FEZ ENTERTAINMENT
The Reed Edwards Company
RTMC Organization, LLC
Sabellapress
Saint Bob Press
Sand and Sable Publishing
Sassy Sunflower Books
SelectiveHouse Publishers, Inc.
Skullvines Press
Slipdown Mountain Publications LLC
The Smith (subsidiary of The Generalist Assn., Inc.)
Gibbs Smith, Publisher
Southeast Missouri State University Press
Southern Methodist University Press
SPOTops Books
Squire Press
Starcherone Books
Starik Publishing
Steerforth Press, L.C.
SYMPLOKE: A Journal for the Intermingling of Literary, Cultural and Theoretical Scholarship
Talisman House, Publishers
Thirdeye Publications
Three Bean Press
TnT Classic Books
Tupelo Press
Turnstone Press
Twilight Tales, Inc.
Two-Handed Engine Press
URBAN REFLECTIONS MAGAZINE
Vintage Romance Publishing, LLC
Virginia City Publishing Co. LLC
Vox Humana Books
The Wessex Collective
Wexford & Barrow, Publishers

White Pine Press
Wilde Publishing
Wintertree Press
The Wolf Pirate Project Inc.
Women and Men Books
Wordcraft of Oregon, LLC
Wordsonthestreet
Xenos Books
Yaldah Publishing
Youthful Wisdom Press

NUCLEAR ENERGY

Hole In The Head Press
Rising Tide Press New Mexico
Southwest Research and Information Center
VOICES FROM THE EARTH

NUMISMATICS

C & M Online Media Inc.
Edenscape Publishing Company

NURSING

Adams-Blake Publishing
Bonus Books, Inc.
Center for Thanatology Research & Education, Inc.
Delaney Day Press
Dream Publishing Co.
Galen Press, Ltd.
HAMPTON ROADS HEALTH JOURNAL
THE HEALTH JOURNALS
Lemon Grove Press
MEDICAL HISTORY
Midwifery Today
Sand and Sable Publishing
Sound Enterprises Publishing
Standish Press
Vanguard Press
Wellcome Trust Centre for the History of Medicine at UCL

NUTRITION

AB
Abigon Press
Allwrite Advertising and Publishing
Consumer Press
Cookbook Resources, LLC
Creative Creations Consulting Publishing Company
Cuore Libre Publishing
Delaney Day Press
Dream Publishing Co.
THE FIT CHRISTIAN A Christian Health & Fitness Magazine
Foodnsport Press
GLOBAL ONE MAGAZINE
HAMPTON ROADS HEALTH JOURNAL
HEALMB Publishing
THE HEALTH JOURNALS
Hohm Press
Hunter House Inc., Publishers
ILLUMINATIONS LITERARY JOURNAL
Keiki O Ka Aina Press
Llumina Press
Lucky Press, LLC
Luminous Epinoia Press
McBooks Press, Inc.
Muse World Media Group
New Win Publishing
Piccadilly Books, Ltd.
Princess Publishing
Starry Night Publishing
Sweet People Publishing
Synergy Press
Three Bean Press
TREATING YOURSELF: The Alternative Medicine Journal
Vanguard Press

OCCULT

Alamo Square Press

ALMOST NORMAL COMICS and Other Oddities
Aquila Ink Publishing
Arias Press
ARTISTIC RAMBLINGS
Athanor Books
Auromere Books and Imports
The B & R Samizdat Express
Bad Noise Productions
Barrytown/Station Hill Press
Borden Publishing Co.
BOTH SIDES NOW
Cassandra Press, Inc.
Crystal Dreams Publishing
DARK GOTHIC RESURRECTED
Dwarf Lion Press
EcceNova Editions
EMERGING
Ephemera Bound Publishing
Flapjack Press
Free People Press
Galde Press, Inc.
GoodSAMARitan Press
GRAMMAR CRISIS
Harbor House
Heartsong Books
Hood Press
Iconoclast Press
Intuitive Moon Media
L&L Dreamspell
LegacyForever
Llumina Press
LP Publications (Teleos Institute)
Lycanthrope Press
Muse World Media Group
Mystery Island Publications
Nautilus Publishing Company
New Falcon Publications
New Paradigm Books
nine muses books
NOLA-MAGICK Press
Origin Press
Outrider Press
Quicksilver Productions
RALPH'S REVIEW
RED MARE
Red Tiger Press
SAGEWOMAN
Santa Fe Writers Project
SHORTRUNS
Socratic Consulting Group
SPECTACULAR SPECULATIONS
STARNOTES
The Teitan Press, Inc.
Three Pyramids Publishing
Triskelion Publishing
John Wade, Publisher
Westgate Press
White Crosslet Publishing Co
THE WISE WOMAN
The Wolf Pirate Project Inc.
Zumaya Publications LLC

OCEANOGRAPHY

Ocean Publishing
Scientia Publishing, LLC
Trickle Creek Books

OHIO

The Bacchae Press
Drinian Press
Faded Banner Publications
Glass Tower Press
ICON
THE JOURNAL
Kenyette Productions
Lawells Publishing
Lucky Press, LLC
MID-AMERICAN REVIEW

MUSE: A Quarterly Journal of The Lit
Ohio University Press/Swallow Press
OHIOANA QUARTERLY
RIVERWIND
Silenced Press
Thirsty Turtle Press
TWENTY-EIGHT PAGES LOVINGLY BOUND WITH TWINE
University of Akron Press
WHITEWALL OF SOUND

OLD WEST

The Bear Wallow Publishing Company
C & M Online Media Inc.
Arthur H. Clark Co.
Cornucopia Press
Deep Well Publishing Company
Dervla Publishing, LLC
Dignified Designs
Eagle's View Publishing
Farcountry Press
The Fiction Works
High Plains Press
Ho Logos Press
LITERALLY HORSES/REMUDA
LOW BUDGET ADVENTURE
Mountain Automation Corporation
Ohio University Press/Swallow Press
One Horse Press/Rainy Day Press
Sherman Asher Publishing
Smirk Books
Tres Picos Press
University of Nebraska Press
Wexford & Barrow, Publishers
Whiskey Creek Press

OREGON

BURNSIDE REVIEW
Arthur H. Clark Co.
Deep Well Publishing Company
Flying Pencil Publications
Krill Press
LEO Productions LLC.
NORTHWEST REVIEW
One Horse Press/Rainy Day Press
Ridenbaugh Press

OUTDOOR ADVENTURE

Appalachian House
AzurAlive
Dervla Publishing, LLC
Dignified Designs
Edenscape Publishing Company
La Familia Publishing
Lost Pond Press
North Star Books
One Horse Press/Rainy Day Press
Thirsty Turtle Press

PACIFIC NORTHWEST

Anacus Press, An Imprint of Finney Company
Arthur H. Clark Co.
CMP Publishing Group LLC
Continuing Education Press
Cookbook Resources, LLC
Deep Well Publishing Company
Dunamis House
DWELLING PORTABLY
Eastern Washington University Press
Farcountry Press
Florentia Press
Flying Pencil Publications
Iconoclast Press
Idylls Press
Keokee Co. Publishing, Inc.
KotaPress
Krill Press
La Familia Publishing

Lost Horse Press
Malki-Ballena Press
NORTHWEST REVIEW
One Horse Press/Rainy Day Press
Open Hand Publishing LLC
Oregon State University Press
PEMMICAN
Perpetual Press
Pygmy Forest Press
QED Press
Sabellapress
SANDPOINT MAGAZINE
Sasquatch Books
WASHINGTON TRAILS
Whispering Pine Press
WHITEWALL OF SOUND
Wordcraft of Oregon, LLC

PACIFIC REGION

The Bess Press
THE EAST HAWAII OBSERVER
HAWAI'I REVIEW
SOUNDINGS REVIEW
STORYBOARD
Tamal Vista Publications
University of Alaska Press

PAPER

EEI Press
Total Cardboard Publishing

PARENTING

Glen Allen Press
Andros Books
APPLE VALLEY REVIEW: A Journal of Contemporary Literature
AT-HOME DAD
Atlantic Publishing Group, Inc.
Bancroft Press
Bayhampton Publications
THE BEACON: Journal of Special Education Law & Practice
Beyond Words Publishing, Inc.
BlackBerry Fields Press
Bronze Girl Productions, Inc.
Cladach Publishing
Clover Valley Press, LLC
Consumer Press
Cornerstone Publishing, Inc.
Creative Creations Consulting Publishing Company
Datamaster Publishing, LLC
Delaney Day Press
Dreams Due Media Group, Inc.
Dumouriez Publishing
East West Discovery Press
First Books
THE FIT CHRISTIAN A Christian Health & Fitness Magazine
Forest Dale Publishing Company
Future Horizons, Inc.
Gallaudet University Press
GLB Publishers
Grace Acres Press
Grace Creek Press
Green River Press
Gurze Books
Harbor House Law Press, Inc.
Heritage Global Publishing
Hohm Press
Hopeace Press
Images Unlimited and Snaptail Press, a Division of Images Unlimited Publishing
Impact Publishers, Inc.
InsideOut Press
The Intrepid Traveler
Islewest Publishing
Jalmar Press/Innerchoice Publishing
Just Sisters Publications

Knowledge Concepts Publishing
Kodiak Media Group
Lawells Publishing
Lightning Bug Learning Press
Llumina Press
The Love and Logic Press, Inc.
LOVING MORE: New Models for Relationships
Luminous Epinoia Press
Mapletree Publishing Company
McGavick Field Publishing
Meek Publishing
A Melody from an Immigrant's Soul
Metallo House Publishers
Mo'omana'o Press
Moondance Press
MOTHERVERSE: A Journal of Contemporary Motherhood
New Atlantean Press
New Day Publishing, Inc.
New Win Publishing
New World Library
Obie Joe Media
Papoose Publishing
PARENTEACHER MAGAZINE
Parenting Press, Inc.
Peachtree Publishers, Ltd.
PEDIATRICS FOR PARENTS
Playdate Kids Publishing
Practically Shameless Press
Quiet Tymes, Inc.
Ragamuffin Heart Publishing
Rainbow Books, Inc.
Rayve Productions Inc.
Redwood Creek Publishing
RTMC Organization, LLC
St. John's Publishing, Inc.
Search Institute
Sentient Publications, LLC
Sibyl Publications, Inc
Smirk Books
Soto Publishing Company
Square One Publishers, Inc.
Storm Publishing Group
Studio 4 Productions An imprint of Quick Publishing, LC
Summerland Publishing
Summit Crossroads Press
Upheaval Media
Wheatmark Book Publishing
Women of Diversity Productions, Inc.
Yaldah Publishing

PEACE

Academy Press of America
Act on Wisdom
American Literary Press
Best Life Media
BLUE COLLAR REVIEW
BLUE MOUNTAIN
Branden Books
Broken Rifle Press
CAUSE & EFFECT MAGAZINE
Free People Press
FRIENDS OF PEACE PILGRIM
Halo Publishing International
HARMONY: Voices for a Just Future
Heartsong Books
The Heather Foundation
IN OUR OWN WORDS
International Publishers Co. Inc.
Iris Publishing Group, Inc (Iris Press / Tellico Books)
Knowledge Concepts Publishing
KotaPress
Kumarian Press
Middleway Press
Moon Pie Press
NEW ENVIRONMENT BULLETIN
NewSage Press
Origin Press
Oyster River Press

Partisan Press
PEACEWORK
The People's Press
Plain View Press
RFD
Sand and Sable Publishing
SHARE INTERNATIONAL
South End Press
Spinifex Press
STORMWARNING!
Syracuse Cultural Workers/Tools for Change
Syracuse Cultural Workers/Tools for Change
Two-Handed Engine Press
United Nations University Press
Upper Access Inc. Book Publishers
VOICES ISRAEL

PERFORMING ARTS

Aaron Communications III
Ammons Communications; Imprint: Catch the Spirit of Appalachia
Athanata Arts, Ltd.
Bel Canto Press
Blue Lupin Press
BRILLIANT CORNERS: A Journal of Jazz & Literature
Clark-Nova Books
Cornerstone Press
DIET SOAP
Everflowing Publications
GLOBAL ONE MAGAZINE
Harobed Publishing Creations
Hollywood Creative Directory
IMAGE: ART, FAITH, MYSTERY
INDUSTRY MINNE-ZINE
IT'S JUST THIS LITTLE CHROMIUM SWITCH HERE
Legacy Audio Books, Inc.
Libellum
Limelight Editions
MCM Entertainment, Inc. Publishing Division
McPherson & Company Publishers
MOBILE BEAT: The Mobile Entertainer's Magazine
Mountainside Press
New Concept Press
nine muses books
Northwestern University Press
Red Tiger Press
Roaring Lion Publishing
Sabellapress
Santa Monica Press
74th Street Productions, L.L.C.
Southern Illinois University Press
THE SOUTHERN QUARTERLY: A Journal of the Arts in the South
SOUTHWEST COLORADO ARTS PERSPECTIVE
Speck Press
Twinteum Artist, Inc.
Two-Handed Engine Press
VANITAS
Whelks Walk Press
WHITE FUNGUS
WISCONSIN TRAILS

PETS

Alpine Publications, Inc.
Biographical Publishing Company
Bronze Girl Productions, Inc.
City Life Books, LLC
Creative Writing and Publishing Company
Cypress Creek Publishing
Dancing Bridge Publishing
Howln Moon Press
ILLUMINATIONS LITERARY JOURNAL
Kali Press
Lucky Press, LLC
MINIATURE DONKEY TALK INC
Moon Pie Press
NewSage Press
Outrider Press

Park Place Publications
Princess Publishing
PublishingWorks, Inc.
Ridenbaugh Press
ROCKY MOUNTAIN KC NEWS
Rocky Mountain KC Publishing Co.
RUMINATIONS: The Nigerian Dwarf & Mini Dairy Goat
  Magazine
Storm Publishing Group
Twinteum Artist, Inc.
Two Dog Press
Unlimited Publishing LLC
Vonpalisaden Publications Inc.

PHILATELY

Banana Productions
INTERNATIONAL ART POST
RALPH'S REVIEW

PHILOSOPHY

ABRAMELIN: a Journal of Poetry and Magick
Academy Press of America
Agathon Books
AK Press
Glen Allen Press
Anagnosis
Anthony Publishing Company
THE ART OF ABUNDANCE
ASCENT
Auromere Books and Imports
The B & R Samizdat Express
Barrytown/Station Hill Press
Bauu Press
BEGINNING MAGAZINE
Best Life Media
Black Rose Books Ltd.
BOTH SIDES NOW
BOULDER HERETIC
Brason-Sargar Publications
BRIDGES: An Interdisciplinary Journal of Theology,
  Philosophy, History, and Science
Buenos Books
Burning Books
Camino Bay Books
CANADIAN JOURNAL OF PHILOSOPHY
Cantadora Press
CAUSE & EFFECT MAGAZINE
Cherry Valley Editions
Children Of Mary
Community Service, Inc.
CONDUIT
Crane Press
CRITICAL REVIEW
THE DALHOUSIE REVIEW
Devenish Press
Dharma Publishing
Dominion Global Publishing
dreamslaughter
Paul Dry Books
Dufour Editions Inc.
Dwarf Lion Press
Edition Gemini
The Edwin Mellen Press
Elderberry Press, Inc.
EPICENTER: A LITERARY MAGAZINE
Eros Books
Faith Builders Resource Group
FAT TUESDAY
FIDELIS ET VERUS
Florida Academic Press
Focus Publishing/R. Pullins Co.
Free People Press
FREETHOUGHT HISTORY
Glenbridge Publishing Ltd.
Goldfish Press
GRAMMAR CRISIS
The Gutenberg Press
Handshake Editions

The Heather Foundation
Ho Logos Press
HYPATIA: A Journal of Feminist Philosophy
Iconoclast Press
Impassio Press
INTERCULTURE
ITALIAN AMERICANA
JACK MACKEREL MAGAZINE
JOURNAL OF REGIONAL CRITICISM
JOURNAL OF SCIENTIFIC EXPLORATION
KAIROS, A Journal of Contemporary Thought and
  Criticism
Kallisti Publishing
Kilmog Press
LAKE EFFECT
THE LEDGE
A.P. Lee & Co., Ltd.
THE (LIBERTARIAN) CONNECTION
Libertarian Press, Inc./American Book Distributors
Libertas Press, LLC.
LIBERTY
Llumina Press
Lycanthrope Press
MACROBIOTICS TODAY
Maisonneuve Press
Maryland Historical Press (also MHPress)
MEAT: A Journal of Writing and Materiality
MELEE
Mercer University Press
The Kenneth G. Mills Foundation
Mind Power Publishing
THE MONIST: An International Quarterly Journal of
  General Philosophical Inquiry
THE MOUNTAIN ASTROLOGER
THE NEO-COMINTERN
NEW AMERICAN IMAGIST
New Atlantean Press
New Falcon Publications
New Paradigm Books
NEW SOLUTIONS
Nightsun Books
Nightsun Books
Nilgiri Press
Obie Joe Media
OFFICE NUMBER ONE
Ohio University Press/Swallow Press
George Ohsawa Macrobiotic Foundation
One Spirit Press
Open Court Publishing Company
Open Wide Books
Origin Press
Papoose Publishing
Paragon House Publishers
Phi-Psi Publishers
Plain Philosophy Center
Pleasure Boat Studio: A Literary Press (including imprints
  Caravel Books and Aequitas Books, and the division
  Empty Bowl Press)
POETRYREPAIRS: Contemporary International Poetry
Poptritus Press
Practically Shameless Press
PSYCHE
PublishAmerica, LLLP.
Quarterly Committee of Queen's University
QUEEN'S QUARTERLY: A Canadian Review
REPORTS OF THE NATIONAL CENTER FOR SCIENCE
  EDUCATION
Rowhouse Press
RTMC Organization, LLC
Saint Bob Press
SALMAGUNDI
Savant Garde Workshop
See Sharp Press
Smirk Books
Socratic Consulting Group
SPOTops Books
State University of New York Press
Sherwood Sugden & Company, Publishers

727

Summerland Publishing
Superior Christian Press
SYMPLOKE: A Journal for the Intermingling of Literary,
    Cultural and Theoretical Scholarship
T'AI CHI
TELOS
Telos Press
Third Dimension Publishing
THIRDEYE MAGAZINE
Thirdeye Publications
Transcending Mundane, Inc.
TRUTH SEEKER
Turtle Press, division of S.K. Productions Inc.
Tuvela Press
Twinteum Artist, Inc.
Two-Handed Engine Press
Tyr Publishing
UNDERSTANDING MAGAZINE
UnKnownTruths.com Publishing Company
VIVIPAROUS BLENNY
Vox Humana Books
Vulgar Marsala Press
THE WALLACE STEVENS JOURNAL
Westgate Press
WHAT IS ENLIGHTENMENT?
White Thread Press
WILD DUCK REVIEW
Wisdom Publications, Inc.
Wood Thrush Books
Writers House Press
Yes International Publishers

PHOTOGRAPHY

AFTERIMAGE
ALABAMA LITERARY REVIEW
THE ALLEGHENY REVIEW
Allworth Press
AMERICAN FORESTS
Ammons Communications; Imprint: Catch the Spirit of
    Appalachia
ANOTHER CHICAGO MAGAZINE(ACM)
Appalachian Consortium Press
Arjuna Library Press
ARTISTIC RAMBLINGS
ASCENT
ATLANTIC PACIFIC PRESS
Avery Color Studios
BAGAZINE
Banana Productions
Barefoot Press
Barrytown/Station Hill Press
BATHTUB GIN
Bay Press
The Bear Wallow Publishing Company
BEAUTY/TRUTH: A Journal of Ekphrastic Poetry
BEGINNING MAGAZINE
BLACK BOOK PRESS: The Poetry Zine id
BLACKFLASH Magazine
THE BRIAR CLIFF REVIEW
THE CAPE ROCK
CERISE PRESS
CHILDREN, CHURCHES AND DADDIES, A Non
    Religious, Non Familial Literary Magazine
CIMARRON REVIEW
COTTONWOOD
Cottonwood Press
Crazy Woman Creek Press
CUTBANK
Cypress Creek Publishing
Dawn Sign Press
DESCANT
Dignified Designs
Disparate Voices
DOLLS UNITED INTERACTIVE MAGAZINE
DOWN IN THE DIRT LITERARY MAGAZINE, the prose
    & poetry magazine revealing all your dirty little secrets
Down There Press
East West Discovery Press

EEI Press
THE ENGLISH CLARION
EPIPHANY, A Literary Journal
EROSHA
Farcountry Press
Farcountry Press
firefall editions
580 SPLIT
FOLIO: A Literary Journal of American University
Fotofolio, Inc.
FOTOTEQUE
Free Books Inc.
FREEDOM AND STRENGTH PRESS FORUM
THE FREEFALL REVIEW
FROZEN WAFFLES
Gesture Press
Ghost Pony Press
GLOBAL ONE MAGAZINE
Greatland Graphics
Grey Sparrow Press
GUD MAGAZINE (Greatest Uncommon Denominator)
HAYDEN'S FERRY REVIEW
Historical Resources Press
HOT FLASHES: Not a Menopause Thang
ICON
Iconoclast Press
ILLOGICAL MUSE
IMAGE: ART, FAITH, MYSTERY
INDEFINITE SPACE
INDUSTRY MINNE-ZINE
INTERNATIONAL ART POST
JOURNAL OF REGIONAL CRITICISM
Kenyette Productions
KESTREL: A Journal of Literature and Art
Allen A. Knoll Publishers
La Familia Publishing
Laguna Wilderness Press
LAKE SUPERIOR MAGAZINE
Leaf Garden Press
The Leaping Frog Press
LEFT CURVE
Lessiter Publications
LIGHTWORKS MAGAZINE
Lilly Press
Lincoln Springs Press
LINES + STARS
THE LISTENING EYE
LITTLE BALKANS REVIEW
LOST GENERATION JOURNAL
Lost Prophet Press
THE LUMMOX JOURNAL
Lunar Offensive Publications
THE MAD HATTER
MANDORLA: New Writing from the Americas / Nueva
    escritura de las Americas
Meridien PressWorks
Midmarch Arts Press
MINESHAFT
Missing Man Press
MISSISSIPPI CROW
Motom
N: NUDE & NATURAL
NATURALLY
NEW ORLEANS REVIEW
NIGHTJAR REVIEW
NORTH CAROLINA LITERARY REVIEW
North Country Books, Inc.
Obie Joe Media
Olympic Mountain School Press
One Less Press
Panther Books
Paradiso-Parthas Press
PIG IRON
POESY
PRAIRIE WINDS
PRETEXT
Peter E. Randall Publisher
Rapacious Press

Red Alder Books
Red Tiger Press
REDIVIDER
Re-invention UK Ltd
RIVER POETS JOURNAL
RIVER STYX
RIVET MAGAZINE
Ronsdale Press
Rural Messengers Press
SAGE OF CONSCIOUSNESS E-ZINE
Scars Publications
SCULPTURAL PURSUIT MAGAZINE
SeaCrab Publishing
SIDE OF GRITS
SKIDROW PENTHOUSE
SLIPSTREAM
SO TO SPEAK: A Feminist Journal of Language & Art
SOJOURN: A Journal of the Arts
THE SOUTHERN QUARTERLY: A Journal of the Arts in
   the South
SOUTHWEST COLORADO ARTS PERSPECTIVE
SP Turner Group
SPILLWAY
The Spirit That Moves Us Press, Inc.
Stormline Press, Inc.
STUDIO ONE
STYLUS
THE SUN, A Magazine of Ideas
SWINK
1097 MAGAZINE
TEXAS POETRY JOURNAL
Texas Tech University Press
THIN COYOTE
Three Bean Press
Titan Press
TURNROW
Twinteum Artist, Inc.
Two-Handed Engine Press
The Urbana Free Library
VALLUM: CONTEMPORARY POETRY
Visual Arts Press
Visual Studies Workshop
VLQ (Verse Libre Quarterly)
VOICE(S)
WAR, LITERATURE & THE ARTS: An International
   Journal of the Humanities
WAV MAGAZINE: Progressive Music Art Politics Culture
Whalesback Books
WHEELHOUSE MAGAZINE
THE WILDWOOD READER
WILLIAM AND MARY REVIEW
THE WORCESTER REVIEW
Word Forge Books
X-Ray Book Co.
Zon International Publishing Co.

PHYSICS

Adams-Blake Publishing
Al-Galaxy Publishing Corporation
THE ART OF ABUNDANCE
Clearwater Publishing Co.
JOURNAL OF PYROTECHNICS
JOURNAL OF REGIONAL CRITICISM
JOURNAL OF SCIENTIFIC EXPLORATION
UnKnownTruths.com Publishing Company
WILD DUCK REVIEW
Zagier & Urruty Publications

PICTURE BOOKS

A Cappela Publishing
Absey & Co.
Accendo Publishing
Ammons Communications; Imprint: Catch the Spirit of
   Appalachia
Authentic Publishing LLC
Barefoot Press
Birdsong Books
BlackBerry Fields Press

Book Garden Publishing,LLC
Book Marketing Solutions
Callawind Publications / Custom Cookbooks / Children's
   Books
Command Performance Press
Cornell Maritime Press/Tidewater Publishers
Cotton Tree Press
Crazy Woman Creek Press
Creative Writing and Publishing Company
Cypress Creek Publishing
Dawn Publications
Dervla Publishing, LLC
Dharma Publishing
Dream Catcher Publishing
Dream Publishing Co.
Dreams Due Media Group, Inc.
E & E Publishing
FOTOTEQUE
Fruitbearer Publishing, LLC
GEM Literary Foundation Press
Harobed Publishing Creations
His Work Christian Publishing
Ika, LLC
Images Unlimited and Snaptail Press, a Division of Images
   Unlimited Publishing
Jigsaw Press
Laguna Wilderness Press
LEAF GARDEN
Llumina Press
New Day Publishing, Inc.
New Voices Publishing
NIS America, Inc.
Oolichan Books
Papillon Presse
Parenting Press, Inc.
Peachtree Publishers, Ltd.
Perrin Press
Playdate Kids Publishing
Portal Press
Peter E. Randall Publisher
Rapacious Press
Raven Tree Press, A Division of Delta Systems Inc
RTMC Organization, LLC
Savor Publishing House, Inc.
Soto Publishing Company
Stonehenge Publishing, LLC
Stunt Publishing
Successful Kids Publishing
Three Bean Press
Titus Home Publishing
Tortuga Books
Trellis Publishing, Inc.
UmbraProjects Publishing
Waters Edge Press
Whispering Pine Press
William Joseph K Publications
WindRiver Publishing
Windward Publishing, An Imprint of Finney Company
Word Forge Books

POETRY

A Midsummer Night's Press
ABBEY
Abbey Press, Northern Ireland
Abecedarian books, Inc.
ABRAMELIN: a Journal of Poetry and Magick
ABRAXAS
ABZ A Magazine of Poetry
ABZ Poetry Press
Adastra Press
THE ADIRONDACK REVIEW
Adventure Books Inc.
AERIAL
AFRICAN AMERICAN REVIEW
Agathon Books
AGNI
THE AGUILAR EXPRESSION
Ahsahta Press

AIS Publications
ALABAMA LITERARY REVIEW
ALASKA QUARTERLY REVIEW
Alice James Books
All Nations Press
All That Productions,Inc.
Allbook Books
THE ALLEGHENY REVIEW
Ally Press
Alms House Press
AMBIT
THE AMERICAN DISSIDENT
THE AMERICAN DRIVEL REVIEW
AMERICAN INDIAN CULTURE AND RESEARCH
   JOURNAL
American Indian Studies Center
AMERICAN JONES BUILDING & MAINTENANCE
AMERICAN LETTERS & COMMENTARY
American Literary Press
AMERICAN LITERARY REVIEW
THE AMERICAN POETRY JOURNAL
AMERICAN POETRY REVIEW
AMERICAN TANKA
Ammons Communications; Imprint: Catch the Spirit of
   Appalachia
ANCIENT PATHS
Anderson Publishing; also RC Anderson Books
Androgyne Books
Anhinga Press
ANOTHER CHICAGO MAGAZINE(ACM)
Anti-Aging Press
THE ANTIGONISH REVIEW
THE ANTIOCH REVIEW
APOSTROPHE: USCB Journal of the Arts
APPLE VALLEY REVIEW: A Journal of Contemporary
   Literature
AQUARIUS
Aquarius Press
ARC
Arctos Press
Arjuna Library Press
The Ark
ARSENIC LOBSTER MAGAZINE
ART:MAG
Artamo Press
Arte Publico Press
ARTELLA: the waltz of words and art
ARTFUL DODGE
ARTISTIC RAMBLINGS
ARTS & LETTERS: Journal of Contemporary Culture
Arts End Books
The Ashland Poetry Press
Athanata Arts, Ltd.
ATLANTA REVIEW
ATLANTIC PACIFIC PRESS
AURA LITERARY ARTS REVIEW
Authentic Publishing LLC
Autumn House Press
Avocet Press Inc.
AXE FACTORY REVIEW
The B & R Samizdat Express
BABYSUE
The Bacchae Press
Back House Books
The Backwaters Press
Bad Noise Productions
BAGAZINE
THE BALTIMORE REVIEW
Banta & Pool Literary Properties
Bard Press
BARNWOOD
The Barnwood Press
BARROW STREET
Barrow Street Press
Barrytown/Station Hill Press
BASALT
BATHTUB GIN
Bauhan Publishing, LLC

Bay Area Poets Coalition
BAYOU
THE BEAR DELUXE MAGAZINE
Bear House Publishing
Bear Star Press
BEAUTY/TRUTH: A Journal of Ekphrastic Poetry
BEGGARS & CHEESEBURGERS
BEGINNING MAGAZINE
BEGINNINGS - A Magazine for the Novice Writer
Bel Canto Press
BELIEVERS EXCHANGE NEWSLETTER
BELLEVUE LITERARY REVIEW
BELLINGHAM REVIEW
BELLOWING ARK
Bellowing Ark Press
BELOIT POETRY JOURNAL
BELTWAY POETRY QUARTERLY
BIG MUDDY: Journal of the Mississippi River Valley
BIG SCREAM
Bilingual Review Press
Biographical Publishing Company
Birch Brook Press
BIRMINGHAM POETRY REVIEW
BITTER OLEANDER
BkMk Press
Black Bear Publications
BLACK BEAR REVIEW
BLACK BOOK PRESS: The Poetry Zine id
Black Buzzard Press
Black Dress Press
Black Forest Press and The Tennessee Publishing House
Black Lawrence Press
BLACK MAGNOLIAS LITERARY JOURNAL
Black Oak Press
Black Radish Books
Black Thistle Press
BLACK WARRIOR REVIEW
BlackBerry Fields Press
BLADES
BLOODJET LITERARY MAGAZINE
BLUE MESA REVIEW
Blue Scarab Press
Blue Tiger Press
BLUE UNICORN
Blue Unicorn Press, Inc.
BLUELINE
BOA Editions, Ltd.
Bogg Publications
BOGG: A Journal of Contemporary Writing
Bombshelter Press
Book Marketing Solutions
BOOKS FROM FINLAND: Online literature journal of
   writing from and about Finland
BORDERLANDS: Texas Poetry Review
Borealis Press Limited
BOTTLE
Bottle of Smoke Press
Bottom Dog Press / Bird Dog Publishing
BOULEVARD
Brentwood Christian Press
THE BRIAR CLIFF REVIEW
BrickHouse Books, Inc.
Bright Hill Press
BRILLIANT CORNERS: A Journal of Jazz & Literature
THE BROADKILL REVIEW: A Journal of Literature
THE BROADSIDER: An Annual Magazine of Rescued
   Poems
Broken Jaw Press
Broken Shadow Publications
Bronze Girl Productions, Inc.
Brooding Heron Press
Brookline Books
Brooks Books
BRYANT LITERARY REVIEW
BUCKLE &
The Bunny & The Crocodile Press/Forest Woods Media
   Productions, Inc
Burning Deck Press

BURNSIDE REVIEW
BUTTON
BYLINE
C & M Online Media Inc.
C&R Press
Cadmus Editions
Caernarvon Press
CAIRN: The New St. Andrews Review
CAKETRAIN
Caketrain Journal and Press
Calaca Press
CALIFORNIA QUARTERLY (CQ)
Calyx Books
CALYX: A Journal of Art and Literature by Women
CANADIAN LITERATURE
CANADIAN POETRY
CANDELABRUM POETRY MAGAZINE
THE CANNON'S MOUTH
Canvas Press
THE CAPE ROCK
THE CAPILANO REVIEW
THE CAROLINA QUARTERLY
Carolina Wren Press
CAUSE & EFFECT MAGAZINE
CC. Marimbo
CELEBRATION
CELLAR
Celo Valley Books
Center for Japanese Studies
Center for Literary Publishing
Center for Thanatology Research & Education, Inc.
CENTER: A Journal of the Literary Arts
Central Avenue Press
CERISE PRESS
Cervena Barva Press
CHANTEH, the Iranian Cross-Cultural Quarterly
CHAPMAN
CHARITON REVIEW
Chase Publishing
Chatoyant
Chax Press
Cherry Valley Editions
Chicago Spectrum Press
Chicory Blue Press, Inc.
CHILDREN, CHURCHES AND DADDIES, A Non Religious, Non Familial Literary Magazine
CHIRON REVIEW
CHRYSANTHEMUM
CIMARRON REVIEW
City Life Books, LLC
City Lights Books
Clamp Down Press
Clamshell Press
CLARK STREET REVIEW
CLEMSON POETRY REVIEW
Cleveland State Univ. Poetry Center
Cloud 9 Publishing
Cloudkeeper Press
Clover Valley Press, LLC
CMP Publishing Group LLC
COCONUT
Coconut Books
Coffee House Press
COLD-DRILL
COLLECTION
COLORADO REVIEW
COMPASS ROSE
Comrades Press
THE COMSTOCK REVIEW
CONCEIT MAGAZINE
CONCRETE JUNGLE JOURNAL
Concrete Jungle Press
Concrete Wolf Press
CONDUIT
CONJUNCTIONS
THE CONNECTICUT POET
CONNECTICUT REVIEW
CONTEMPORARY GHAZALS

CONTRARY
Copper Beech Press
Cornerstone Press
THE CORTLAND REVIEW
COSMOPSIS QUARTERLY
Coteau Books
Cotton Tree Press
COTTONWOOD
Cottonwood Press
Cottonwood Press, Inc.
CRAB CREEK REVIEW
CRAB ORCHARD REVIEW
CRANNOG
CRAZYHORSE
THE CREAM CITY REVIEW
Creative With Words Publications (CWW)
Creative Writing and Publishing Company
Cross-Cultural Communications
R.L. Crow Publications
CRUCIBLE
CUTBANK
CUTTHROAT, A JOURNAL OF THE ARTS
Cyberwit.net
Cynic Press
Cypress Creek Publishing
THE DALHOUSIE REVIEW
DARK ANIMUS
DARK GOTHIC RESURRECTED
deep cleveland press
Deep Well Publishing Company
Deerbrook Editions
DELAWARE POETRY REVIEW
DENVER QUARTERLY
DESCANT
DESCANT
DESIRE STREET
Devenish Press
Dignified Designs
Paul Dilsaver, Publisher
THE DMQ REVIEW
Doctor Jazz Press
DOWN IN THE DIRT LITERARY MAGAZINE, the prose & poetry magazine revealing all your dirty little secrets
Dream Catcher Publishing
DREAM FANTASY INTERNATIONAL
Dream Horse Press
DREAM NETWORK
Dreams Due Media Group, Inc.
Drinian Press
Paul Dry Books
Dufour Editions Inc.
DWANG: Outsider poetry and prose
EARTH'S DAUGHTERS: Feminist Arts Periodical
THE EAST HAWAII OBSERVER
Eastern Washington University Press
EbonyEnergy Publishing, Inc.
ECOTONE: Reimagining Place
Edgewise Press
EDGZ
The Edwin Mellen Press
The Eighth Mountain Press
88: A Journal of Contemporary American Poetry
EKPHRASIS
ELIXIR
Elixir Press
Ellechor Publishing House
ELT Press
The Emergency Response Unit
EMRYS JOURNAL
Emrys Press
EPICENTER: A LITERARY MAGAZINE
EPOCH MAGAZINE
Equine Graphics Publishing Group: New Concord Press, SmallHorse Press, SunDrop
Erespin Press
EROSHA
Etched Press
EVANSVILLE REVIEW

Evening Street Press
EVENING STREET REVIEW
EVENT
Everflowing Publications
EXIT 13 MAGAZINE
Expanded Media Editions
FAT TUESDAY
FEMINIST STUDIES
THE FIDDLEHEAD
FIELD: Contemporary Poetry and Poetics
Finishing Line Press
First Books
FIRST CLASS
FISH DRUM MAGAZINE
Fithian Press
5 AM
580 SPLIT
Five Fingers Press
FIVE FINGERS REVIEW
FIVE POINTS
FIVE WILLOWS MAGAZINE
Flapjack Press
Floating Bridge Press
THE FLORIDA REVIEW
FLUENT ASCENSION
Flume Press
FLYWAY: A Journal of Writing and Environment
FOLIO: A Literary Journal of American University
Four Way Books
4 Your Spirit Productions
4AM POETRY REVIEW
Four-Sep Publications
FOURTEEN HILLS: The SFSU Review
FRANK: AN INTERNATIONAL JOURNAL OF CON-
    TEMPORARY WRITING AND ART
Free Books Inc.
FREEDOM AND STRENGTH PRESS FORUM
French Bread Publications
FRESHWATER
Frith Press
From Here Press
FROZEN WAFFLES
Frozen Waffles Press/Shattered Sidewalks Press; 45th
    Century Chapbooks
Fruitbearer Publishing, LLC
FUGUE
FUTURECYCLE POETRY
FutureCycle Press
Galaxy Press
The Galileo Press Ltd.
GARGOYLE
Geekspeak Unique Press
GEM Literary Foundation Press
GENRE: WRITER AND WRITINGS
THE GEORGIA REVIEW
GERTRUDE
Gertrude Press
Gesture Press
THE GETTYSBURG REVIEW
Ghost Pony Press
GHOTI MAGAZINE
GIN BENDER POETRY REVIEW
Gingerbread House
Gival Press
GLB Publishers
GOLD DUST
Goldfish Press
GoodSAMARitan Press
Goose River Press
Goss Press
GRAMMAR CRISIS
GRASSLANDS REVIEW
GRASSLIMB
Gray Dog Press
Grayson Books
Graywolf Press
GREAT RIVER REVIEW
THE GREEN HILLS LITERARY LANTERN

Green Hut Press
GREEN MOUNTAINS REVIEW
Green River Press
Green River Writers, Inc./Grex Press
Greenhouse Review Press
THE GREENSBORO REVIEW
Grey Sparrow Press
The Groundwater Press
GUD MAGAZINE (Greatest Uncommon Denominator)
GULF COAST
HAIGHT ASHBURY LITERARY JOURNAL
Halo Publishing International
HANGING LOOSE
Hanging Loose Press
H-NGM-N
Hannacroix Creek Books, Inc
HAPA NUI
HAPPENINGNOW!EVERYWHERE
HARP-STRINGS
HARVARD REVIEW
HAWAI'I REVIEW
HAWAI'I PACIFIC REVIEW
HAYDEN'S FERRY REVIEW
Heat Press
HEAVEN BONE MAGAZINE
Heaven Bone Press
Heidelberg Graphics
Helicon Nine Editions
HELIOTROPE, A JOURNAL OF POETRY
Hermes House Press
The Heyeck Press
Hidden Valley Farm, Publisher
Higganum Hill Books
High Plains Press
Highest Hurdle Press
Hippopotamus Press
HIRAM POETRY REVIEW
His Work Christian Publishing
Hobblebush Books
Hole Books
Holmes House
Holy Cow! Press
HOLY ROLLERS
HOME PLANET NEWS
Home Planet Publications
The Hosanna Press
HOT FLASHES: Not a Menopause Thang
HUBBUB
IAMBS & TROCHEES
IBBETSON ST.
Ibbetson St. Press
Ibex Publishers, Inc.
Icarus Press
ICON
ICONOCLAST
Iconoclast Press
THE IDAHO REVIEW
Idylls Press
Igneus Press
ILLOGICAL MUSE
ILLUMINATIONS
ILLUMINATIONS LITERARY JOURNAL
IMAGE: ART, FAITH, MYSTERY
Imago Press
Immediate Direction Publications
In Between Books
IN OUR OWN WORDS
INDEFINITE SPACE
INDIANA REVIEW
Indigo Ink Press, Inc.
INDUSTRY MINNE-ZINE
The Infinity Group
Iniquity Press/Vendetta Books
THE INK SLINGER REVIEW
Inkwater Press
INKWELL
INSURANCE
INTERNATIONAL POETRY REVIEW

732

INTO THE TEETH WIND
IODINE POETRY JOURNAL
IOTA
THE IOWA REVIEW
Iris Publishing Group, Inc (Iris Press / Tellico Books)
IRISH LITERARY SUPPLEMENT
IRON HORSE LITERARY REVIEW
ISSUES
ISTANBUL LITERARY REVIEW
Ithuriel's Spear
J & J Consultants, Inc.
J. Mark Press
Jackson Harbor Press
Jako Books
JAVELINA BI-MONTHLY
JONES AV
THE JOURNAL
JOURNAL OF CANADIAN POETRY
JOURNAL OF NEW JERSEY POETS
JUBILAT
Judah Magnes Museum Publications
Junction Press
Just Sisters Publications
KALDRON, An International Journal Of Visual Poetry
KALEIDOSCOPE: Exploring the Experience of Disability
    through Literature & the Fine Arts
Kamini Press
KARAMU
Keiki O Ka Aina Press
THE KELSEY REVIEW
Kelsey St. Press
Kenyette Productions
THE KENYON REVIEW
THE KERF
KESTREL: A Journal of Literature and Art
Kilmog Press
Kings Estate Press
KNUCKLE MERCHANT - The Journal of Naked Literary
    Aggression
KOKAKO
KotaPress
KRAX
KUMQUAT MERINGUE
KUUMBA
La Alameda Press
La Familia Publishing
LAKE EFFECT
Lamp Light Press
LANGUAGEANDCULTURE.NET
THE LAUGHING DOG
THE LAUREL REVIEW
LDP, an occasional journal of aesthetics & language
LEAF GARDEN
Leaf Garden Press
Leapfrog Press
Leaping Dog Press
Leave No Sister Behind Publications
THE LEDGE
THE LEDGE POETRY & FICTION MAGAZINE
LEFT CURVE
Les Figues Press
Level 4 Press, Inc.
Libellum
LIFTOUTS
LIGHT: The Quarterly of Light Verse
LILLIPUT REVIEW
Lilly Press
Limberlost Press
Lincoln Springs Press
LINES + STARS
LINQ
Liquid Paper Press
THE LISTENING EYE
LITERALLY HORSES/REMUDA
LITERARY HOUSE REVIEW
LITERARY IMAGINATION: The Review of the Associa-
    tion of Literary Scholars and Critics
LITTLE BALKANS REVIEW

THE LITTLE MAGAZINE
Little Pear Press
Little Poem Press
LIVE MAG!
Lockhart Press
LONE STARS MAGAZINE
Lone Willow Press
Longhouse
Loom Press
Loonfeather Press
Lost Horse Press
Lost Prophet Press
Lotus Press, Inc.
Lotus Press, Inc.
THE LOUISIANA REVIEW
THE LOUISVILLE REVIEW
LULLABY HEARSE
LULLWATER REVIEW
THE LUMMOX JOURNAL
Lummox Press
Luna Bisonte Prods
Lunar Offensive Publications
LUNGFULL! MAGAZINE
Lynx House Press
THE LYRIC
THE MACGUFFIN
THE MAD HATTER
Mad River Press
THE MADISON REVIEW
Magic Circle Press
MAIN CHANNEL VOICES: A Dam Fine Literary
    Magazines
MAIN STREET RAG
THE MAINE EVENT
MANDORLA: New Writing from the Americas / Nueva
    escritura de las Americas
THE MANHATTAN REVIEW
Manifold Press
MANOA: A Pacific Journal of International Writing
MANY MOUNTAINS MOVING
Marathon International Book Company
March Street Press
THE MARLBORO REVIEW
Marsh Hawk Press
Marymark Press
MATCHBOOK
Maui arThoughts Co.
Maverick Duck Press
Mayapple Press
Mayhaven Publishing, Inc.
ME MAGAZINE
THE MEADOW
MELEE
A Melody from an Immigrant's Soul
Menard Press
Meridien PressWorks
Merrimack Books
Merwood Books
Metacom Press
Miami University Press
Mica Press - Paying Our Dues Productions
MID-AMERICAN REVIEW
Mid-List Press
Midmarch Arts Press
MIDWEST POETRY REVIEW
THE MIDWEST QUARTERLY
Midwest Villages & Voices
Milkweed Editions
Mille Grazie Press
Millennium Vision Press
The Kenneth G. Mills Foundation
MindGlow Media
MINESHAFT
MIP Company
Missing Spoke Press
MISSISSIPPI CROW
MISSISSIPPI REVIEW
Montemayor Press

Moon Pie Press
Moonrise Press
THE MORNING DEW REVIEW
MOTHER EARTH JOURNAL: An International Quarterly
Motom
Moving Parts Press
MUDFISH
MUDLARK
MURDER CROWS
The Muse Media
MUSE: A Quarterly Journal of The Lit
MYSTERY ISLAND MAGAZINE
Mystery Island Publications
Nada Press
THE NATIONAL POETRY REVIEW
NATURAL BRIDGE
NEBO
THE NEBRASKA REVIEW
NEO: Literary Magazine
NERVE COWBOY
NEW ALTERNATIVES
NEW AMERICAN IMAGIST
NEW AMERICAN WRITING
NEW DELTA REVIEW
NEW ENGLAND REVIEW
THE NEW FORMALIST
NEW HOPE INTERNATIONAL REVIEW
New Issues Poetry & Prose
THE NEW LAUREL REVIEW
NEW LETTERS
NEW MADRID
NEW MEXICO POETRY REVIEW
NEW MIRAGE QUARTERLY
New Native Press
NEW ORLEANS REVIEW
New Orphic Publishers
THE NEW ORPHIC REVIEW
THE NEW RENAISSANCE, an international magazine of
    ideas & opinions, emphasizing literature & the arts
New Rivers Press, Inc.
NEW STONE CIRCLE
NEW VERSE NEWS, THE
NEW VOICES REVISITED: Poetry, Contests and Short
    Stories.
New World Press
THE NEW WRITER
THE NEW YORK QUARTERLY
Night Bomb Press
THE NIGHT BOMB REVIEW
Night Horn Books
NIGHTJAR REVIEW
Nightsun Books
NIMROD INTERNATIONAL JOURNAL
nine muses books
Ninety-Six Press
Noemi Press
NORTH AMERICAN REVIEW
NORTH CAROLINA LITERARY REVIEW
North Stone Editions
NORTHWEST REVIEW
Northwestern University Press
NOSTOC MAGAZINE
NOTRE DAME REVIEW
NOUN VS. VERB
Nova House Press
NOW AND THEN
O!!Zone
O!!ZONE, A LITERARY-ART ZINE
Oberlin College Press
Obie Joe Media
OBSIDIAN III: Literature in the African Diaspora
OFF THE COAST
Ohio University Press/Swallow Press
THE OLD RED KIMONO
ON EARTH
One Eyed Press
One Less Press
Oolichan Books

OPEN MINDS QUARTERLY
Open University of America Press
Open Wide Books
ORACLE POETRY
Oracle Press
ORBIS
Orchises Press
OREGON EAST
THE ORPHAN LEAF REVIEW
OSIRIS
Osric Publishing
THE OTHER HERALD
Otoliths
OTOLITHS
OUT OF LINE
OUTPOSTS POETRY QUARTERLY
Outrider Press
Owl Creek Press
The Owl Press
THE OXFORD AMERICAN
OYEZ REVIEW
OYSTER BOY REVIEW
Oyster River Press
P.R.A. Publishing
PACIFIC COAST JOURNAL
THE PACIFIC REVIEW
PADDLEFISH
Padishah Press
PAGAN AMERICA
PAJ NTAUB VOICE
PALO ALTO REVIEW
Pancake Press
Pangaea
Panther Creek Press
PAPERPLATES
Paradiso-Parthas Press
Paris Press
PARNASSUS: Poetry in Review
PASSAGER
PASSAGES NORTH
PASSAIC REVIEW
Passeggiata Press, Inc.
Passion Power Press, Inc
The Passion Profit Company
THE PATERSON LITERARY REVIEW
Pathwise Press
PAVEMENT SAW
Pavement Saw Press
Paycock Press
PEARL
Pearl Editions
Pearl-Win Publishing Co.
Pecan Grove Press
THE PEDESTAL MAGAZINE.COM
PEGASUS
THE PEGASUS REVIEW
PEMBROKE MAGAZINE
PEMMICAN
Pemmican Press
Pendragonian Publications
PENNINE INK MAGAZINE
PENNINE PLATFORM
PENNY DREADFUL: Tales and Poems of Fantastic Terror
The People's Press
Persephone Press
Perugia Press
Petroglyph Press, Ltd.
Philos Press
PHOEBE: A Journal of Literature and Art
Phrygian Press
Piano Press
PIG IRON
Pig Iron Press
THE PINCH
PINE ISLAND JOURNAL OF NEW ENGLAND POETRY
PINYON
The Place In The Woods
Plain View Press

Plan B Press
THE PLASTIC TOWER
PLEASANT LIVING
Pleasure Boat Studio: A Literary Press (including imprints Caravel Books and Aequitas Books, and the division Empty Bowl Press)
PLOUGHSHARES
Pluma Productions
PMS POEMMEMOIRSTORY
Pocol Press
POEM
POEMELEON: A Journal of Poetry
POEMS & PLAYS
POESY
POET LORE
Poet Tree Press
POETALK
Poetic Matrix Press
POETICA MAGAZINE, Reflections of Jewish Thought
POETRY
The Poetry Center
The Poetry Center Press/Shoestring Press
Poetry Direct
POETRY EAST
THE POETRY EXPLOSION NEWSLETTER (THE PEN)
POETRY FLASH
Poetry Harbor
POETRY KANTO
THE POETRY MISCELLANY
POETRY NOW, Sacramento's Literary Review and Calendar
The Poetry Project
THE POETRY PROJECT NEWSLETTER
POETRY REVIEW
POETRYREPAIRS: Contemporary International Poetry
POETS & WRITERS MAGAZINE
Poets & Writers, Inc.
POETS AT WORK
POETS ON THE LINE
POETS' ROUNDTABLE
Poets Wear Prada
POETSWEST ONLINE
POGO STICK
POIESIS
Polar Bear & Company
Poltroon Press
Poor Souls Press/Scaramouche Books
Poptritus Press
Portals Press
PORTLAND REVIEW
The Post-Apollo Press
THE PRAIRIE JOURNAL OF CANADIAN LITERATURE
Prairie Journal Press
PRAIRIE SCHOONER
PRAIRIE WINDS
Prakalpana Literature
PRAKALPANA SAHITYA/PRAKALPANA LITERATURE
Preludium Publishers
PREMONITIONS
PRESA
Press Here
PRETEXT
Printed Matter Press (Tokyo)
PRISM INTERNATIONAL
Prospect Press
Protean Press
PROVINCETOWN ARTS
Psychedelic Literature
PTOLEMY/BROWNS MILLS REVIEW
PublishAmerica, LLLP.
Pudding House Publications
PUDDING MAGAZINE: The International Journal of Applied Poetry
PUERTO DEL SOL
PULSAR POETRY WEBZINE
Puna Press
PUNKIN HOUSE DIGEST

Punkin House Press
PURPLE PATCH
Pygmy Forest Press
Pyncheon House
QRL POETRY SERIES
Quale Press
Quarterly Review of Literature Press
QUARTERLY WEST
QUERCUS REVIEW
THE QUIET FEATHER
Rabeth Publishing Company
Ragged Raven Press
RAINBOW CURVE
RALPH'S REVIEW
RAMBUNCTIOUS REVIEW
Rarach Press
RATTAPALLAX
RATTLE
RATTLESNAKE REVIEW
THE RAVEN CHRONICLES
Raw Dog Press
REACTIONS
Red Alder Books
Red Candle Press
Red Dragon Press
Red Dust
RED FEZ ENTERTAINMENT
RED HAWK
Red Hen Press
RED LAMP
RED ROCK REVIEW
Red Tiger Press
RED WHEELBARROW
Redgreene Press
REDIVIDER
REFLECTIONS LITERARY JOURNAL
Re-invention UK Ltd
A RESOURCE FOR EMBEDDED HAIKU
REVERIE: MIDWEST AFRICAN AMERICAN LITERATURE
RFD
Rhiannon Press
RHINO: THE POETRY FORUM
Ridgeway Press of Michigan
RIVER KING POETRY SUPPLEMENT
RIVER POETS JOURNAL
RIVER STYX
RIVERBED HAIKU
RIVERSEDGE
Riverstone, A Press for Poetry
RIVET MAGAZINE
Roaring Lion Publishing
THE ROCKFORD REVIEW
ROGER, an art & literary magazine
Ronsdale Press
ROOM
Rose Alley Press
ROSEBUD
Rowan Mountain Press
RUBIES IN THE DARKNESS
THE RUE BELLA
The Runaway Spoon Press
Rural Messengers Press
S4N Books
Sabellapress
The Sacred Beverage Press
Sadorian Publications
Sage Hill Press
SAGE OF CONSCIOUSNESS E-ZINE
St. Andrews College Press
SALAMANDER
SALMAGUNDI
Salmon Poetry Ltd.
Salt Publishing
Saqi Books Publisher
Sarabande Books
Sassy Sunflower Books
Saturday Press

Saturnalia Books
Savant Garde Workshop
Scarlet Tanager Books
Scars Publications
SCHUYLKILL VALLEY JOURNAL
Scienter Press
Scots Plaid Press
THE SCRIBIA
Scripta Humanistica
SCRIVENER
SCULPTURAL PURSUIT MAGAZINE
Second Aeon Publications
Second Coming Press
SEEMS
The Seer Press
SENECA REVIEW
SENSATIONS MAGAZINE
Serpent & Eagle Press
Seven Buffaloes Press
SEWANEE REVIEW
Shared Roads Press
SHATTERED WIG REVIEW
SHENANDOAH: The Washington and Lee University
    Review
Sherman Asher Publishing
SHIRIM
SIDE OF GRITS
Signpost Press Inc.
Silenced Press
Silverfish Review Press
Six Ft. Swells Press
Sixteen Rivers Press
SKIDROW PENTHOUSE
Skullvines Press
SKYLINE LITERARY MAGAZINE
Skyline Publications
SLANT: A Journal of Poetry
Slapering Hol Press
SLIPSTREAM
Small Dogma Publishing, Inc.
SMARTISH PACE
The Smith (subsidiary of The Generalist Assn., Inc.)
SMOKE
Smyrna Press
Snapshot Press
SNOW MONKEY
SNOWY EGRET
SNREVIEW
SO TO SPEAK: A Feminist Journal of Language & Art
SO YOUNG!
SOJOURN: A Journal of the Arts
SOLO CAFE
SOLO FLYER
SONG OF THE SAN JOAQUIN
SONGS OF INNOCENCE
SOUNDINGS EAST
SOUTH CAROLINA REVIEW
SOUTH DAKOTA REVIEW
Southeast Missouri State University Press
SOUTHERN CALIFORNIA REVIEW
SOUTHERN HUMANITIES REVIEW
SOUTHERN POETRY REVIEW
THE SOUTHERN REVIEW
SOUTHWEST COLORADO ARTS PERSPECTIVE
SOUTHWEST REVIEW
SOU'WESTER
THE SOW'S EAR POETRY REVIEW
The Sow's Ear Press
SP QUILL MAGAZINE
SP Turner Group
SPILLWAY
Spinifex Press
SPINNING JENNY
SPINNINGS...INTENSE TALES OF LIFE MAGAZINE
The Spirit That Moves Us Press, Inc.
SPITBALL: The Literary Baseball Magazine
Split Oak Press
SPOON RIVER POETRY REVIEW

SPORE
SPOUT
Spout Press
Spring Grass
SRLR Press
Starlight Press
Steel Toe Books
Stellaberry Press
SterlingHouse Publisher
THE STINGING FLY
STRINGTOWN
STRUGGLE: A Magazine of Proletarian Revolutionary
    Literature
STUDIO - A Journal of Christians Writing
STUDIO ONE
Suburban Wilderness Press
Summer Stream Press
Summerset Press
Sun Dog Press
THE SUN, A Magazine of Ideas
Sunlight Publishers
SunShine Press Publications, Inc.
SUPERIOR CHRISTIAN NEWS
Superior Christian Press
Swamp Press
SWILL
SWINK
SYCAMORE REVIEW
synaesthesia press
Synergetic Press
Syukhtun Editions
Talisman House, Publishers
Tamal Vista Publications
Tameme
Tangerine Press
TAPROOT LITERARY REVIEW
Taproot Press Publishing Co.
TAPROOT, a journal of older writers
TAR RIVER POETRY
THE TARPEIAN ROCK
Taurean Horn Press
TEACHERS & WRITERS
Tears in the Fence
TEARS IN THE FENCE
Tebot Bach
TEEN VOICES MAGAZINE
The Teitan Press, Inc.
Telephone Books
Temple Inc.
1097 MAGAZINE
Ten Penny Players, Inc.
Tesseract Publications
TEXAS POETRY JOURNAL
THEECLECTICS
Theytus Books Ltd.
THIN COYOTE
THIRD COAST
THIRDEYE MAGAZINE
Thirdeye Publications
13TH MOON
The Thirty First Bird Press
THIS IS IMPORTANT
Thorp Springs Press
THE THREEPENNY REVIEW
Thunder Rain Publishing Corp.
Tia Chucha Press
TIGHTROPE
Timberline Press
Time Barn Books
TIME FOR RHYME
Titan Press
Titus Home Publishing
Toad Press International Chapbook Series
Toadlily Press
Tombouctou Books
TOUCHSTONE LITERARY JOURNAL
TREATING YOURSELF: The Alternative Medicine Jour-
    nal

POLAND

POLITICAL SCIENCE

Mercer University Press
MEXICAN STUDIES/ESTUDIOS MEXICANOS
Nautilus Publishing Company
New Falcon Publications
Northern Illinois University Press
Open Hand Publishing LLC
OUT OF LINE
Paragon House Publishers
Pathfinder Press
Poplar Leaf Press
THE PUBLIC EYE
QED Press
Rada Press, Inc.
Razor7 Publishing
RFF Press / Resources for the Future
Saqi Books Publisher
SCIENCE AND TECHNOLOGY
STATE AND LOCAL GOVERNMENT REVIEW
Strata Publishing, Inc.
TELOS
Temple Inc.
UBC Press
United Nations University Press
Univelt, Inc.
University of Arkansas Press
University of Calgary Press
University Press of Colorado
Van Cleave Publishing
West Virginia University Press
Whitston Publishing Co.
WindRiver Publishing
Writers House Press

POLITICS

A2Z Publications LLC
Aardvark Enterprises (Sole Proprietorship of J. Alvin
    Speers)
Glen Allen Press
ALTERNATIVE PRESS INDEX
America West Publishers
ANOTHER CHICAGO MAGAZINE(ACM)
Archer Books
Arden Press, Inc.
BALLOT ACCESS NEWS
Banta & Pool Literary Properties
Bay Press
Bay Tree Publishing
Benchmark Publications Inc.
BLACK BOOK PRESS: The Poetry Zine id
Blackwater Publications
THE BOOMERPHILE
BORDERLANDS: Texas Poetry Review
BOTH SIDES NOW
BOULDER HERETIC
Brave Ulysses Books
Caribbean Books-Panama
Cassandra Press, Inc.
CESUM MAGAZINE
Chandler & Sharp Publishers, Inc.
Chelsea Green Publishing Company
Chicago Review Press
Children Of Mary
CINEASTE MAGAZINE
City Lights Books
Comstock Bonanza Press
CONSCIENCE: The Newsjournal of Catholic Opinion
CRITICAL REVIEW
CUTTHROAT, A JOURNAL OF THE ARTS
Dervla Publishing, LLC
dreamslaughter
Dufour Editions Inc.
Elderberry Press, Inc.
Encore Publishing
Encounter Books
EPICENTER: A LITERARY MAGAZINE
FEMINIST REVIEW
FEMINIST STUDIES
FIDELIS ET VERUS

FIFTH ESTATE
The Film Instruction Company of America
FOURTH WORLD REVIEW
Free People Press
Frontline Publications
THE FUNNY TIMES
Gain Publications
Glenbridge Publishing Ltd.
Good Hope Enterprises, Inc.
GREEN ANARCHY
Guernica Editions, Inc.
HARMONY: Voices for a Just Future
Heyday Books
History Compass, LLC
Ho Logos Press
Hoover Institution Press
HUMOR TIMES
INDUSTRY MINNE-ZINE
Insight Press
International Publishers Co. Inc.
JEWISH CURRENTS
Kettering Foundation Press
KETTERING REVIEW
Kumarian Press
LATIN AMERICAN PERSPECTIVES
LEFT CURVE
THE (LIBERTARIAN) CONNECTION
Library Juice Press
LO STRANIERO: The Stranger, Der Fremde, L'Etranger
THE LONG TERM VIEW: A Journal of Informed Opinion
Lunar Offensive Publications
MAIN STREET RAG
MEAT: A Journal of Writing and Materiality
Mehring Books, Inc.
MELEE
Menard Press
Mercer University Press
Missing Spoke Press
Mountain Media
MOUTH: Voice of the Dis-Labeled Nation
Moving Parts Press
NAMBLA BULLETIN
THE NEO-COMINTERN
THE NEW ENGLAND QUARTERLY
THE NEW RENAISSANCE, an international magazine of
    ideas & opinions, emphasizing literature & the arts
NEW VERSE NEWS, THE
NEWS FROM NATIVE CALIFORNIA
nine muses books
OFF OUR BACKS
Open Wide Books
OUT OF LINE
Path Press, Inc.
Pathfinder Press
PEMMICAN
Pig Iron Press
Poplar Leaf Press
Progressive Press; Tree of Life Publications
THE PUBLIC EYE
Quarterly Committee of Queen's University
QUEEN'S QUARTERLY: A Canadian Review
THE QUIET FEATHER
RED LAMP
Red Letter Press
RFD
Ridenbaugh Press
Saint Bob Press
Saqi Books Publisher
See Sharp Press
SHARE INTERNATIONAL
Sound Enterprises Publishing
South End Press
SOUTHWEST COLORADO ARTS PERSPECTIVE
SterlingHouse Publisher
STORMWARNING!
SYMPLOKE: A Journal for the Intermingling of Literary,
    Cultural and Theoretical Scholarship
Syracuse Cultural Workers/Tools for Change

738

TELOS
Telos Press
UBC Press
United Nations University Press
University of Akron Press
Upper Access Inc. Book Publishers
Van Cleave Publishing
THE VIRGINIA QUARTERLY REVIEW
Wellington House Publishing Company
West End Press
WEST GOES SOUTH
West Virginia University Press
WHAT IS ENLIGHTENMENT?
Wheatmark Book Publishing
WHEELHOUSE MAGAZINE
WILD DUCK REVIEW
WindRiver Publishing
WORDKNOT AUDIO: A Literary Podcast Magazine

PORTUGAL

INTERNATIONAL POETRY REVIEW
NEO: Literary Magazine
TORRE DE PAPEL
WORLD POETRY SHOWCASE

POST MODERN

AD/VANCE
All Nations Press
Artamo Press
Asylum Arts
Bad Noise Productions
Black Radish Books
BOGG: A Journal of Contemporary Writing
C & M Online Media Inc.
THE CAPILANO REVIEW
Casperian Books LLC
CESUM MAGAZINE
Chax Press
Church Leadership Library (Canadian Office)
Church Leadership Library (US Office)
COLLEGE LITERATURE
COMPASS ROSE
CONJUNCTIONS
COSMOPSIS QUARTERLY
Dnar Kaker Basa
ELIXIR
Enigmatic Ink
Eros Books
FIRST CLASS
Four-Sep Publications
GHOTI MAGAZINE
GRAMMAR CRISIS
Highest Hurdle Press
LAKE EFFECT
LDP, an occasional journal of aesthetics & language
LEFT CURVE
McPherson & Company Publishers
MEAT FOR TEA: THE VALLEY REVIEW
MEAT: A Journal of Writing and Materiality
Midmarch Arts Press
THE NEO-COMINTERN
New Native Press
OUTER-ART
Phrygian Press
Poptritus Press
PSYCHE
RAINBOW CURVE
RED MARE
RED ROCK REVIEW
SIDE OF GRITS
SKIDROW PENTHOUSE
SOUNDINGS REVIEW
Starcherone Books
Telos Press
Thirdeye Publications
VOX Press
THE WALLACE STEVENS JOURNAL
WEST COAST LINE: A Journal of Contemporary Writing

and Criticism
WHAT IS ENLIGHTENMENT?
WHITE FUNGUS
ZYX

POSTCARDS

BAGAZINE
BANANA RAG
Barefoot Press
Fotofolio, Inc.
Gesture Press
Harobed Publishing Creations
INKY TRAIL NEWS
POSTCARD CLASSICS (formerly DELTIOLOGY)
Raw Dog Press
Rural Messengers Press
Waters Edge Press
Westgate Press

PRESIDENTS

A2Z Publications LLC
Academy Press of America
Blackwater Publications
CESUM MAGAZINE
Truman State University Press

ELVIS PRESLEY

The Bess Press
THE BOOMERPHILE

PRINTING

ART BUREAU
BOOK ARTS CLASSIFIED
BOOK MARKETING UPDATE
Bottle of Smoke Press
Chax Press
Chicago Spectrum Press
Communication Creativity
FEMINIST COLLECTIONS: A QUARTERLY OF WO-
    MEN'S STUDIES RESOURCES
Harobed Publishing Creations
J'ECRIS
JLA Publications, A Division Of Jeffrey Lant Associates,
    Inc.
LOST GENERATION JOURNAL
Oak Knoll Press
The Poetry Center Press/Shoestring Press
Poltroon Press
PUBLISHING POYNTERS
QED Press
Rural Messengers Press
SPEX (SMALL PRESS EXCHANGE)
Stewart Publishing & Printing
Success Publishing
Three Bean Press
Univelt, Inc.
University of Tampa Press
VOICE(S)
Winslow Publishing
Women's Studies Librarian, University of Wisconsin
    System

PRISON

Aaron Communications III
AIS Publications
BlackBerry Fields Press
Burns Park Publishers
COALITION FOR PRISONERS' RIGHTS NEWSLETTER
CORRECTION(S): A Literary Journal for Inmate Writing
CORRECTIONS TODAY
Global Options
Gorilla Convict Publications
GREEN ANARCHY
Maisonneuve Press
MindGlow Media
Mystery Island Publications
Nish Publishing Company
PRISON LEGAL NEWS

PRISONERS' SPEAK!
Pygmy Forest Press
Raven Publishing, Inc.
RFD
SOCIAL JUSTICE: A JOURNAL OF CRIME, CONFLICT, & WORLD ORDER
TURNING THE TIDE: Journal of Anti-Racist Action, Research & Education
WeWrite LLC
Writers House Press

PROSE

ALASKA QUARTERLY REVIEW
THE AMERICAN DRIVEL REVIEW
AMERICAN LETTERS & COMMENTARY
ANCIENT PATHS
Androgyne Books
ARC
Artamo Press
ARTELLA: the waltz of words and art
ARTISTIC RAMBLINGS
Asylum Arts
Atelier Press
Bad Noise Productions
THE BALTIMORE REVIEW
Bandanna Books
Bear House Publishing
BEGINNING MAGAZINE
BELLEVUE LITERARY REVIEW
BkMk Press
BLACK BOOK PRESS: The Poetry Zine id
BlackBerry Fields Press
Blue Cubicle Press, LLC
BOGG: A Journal of Contemporary Writing
BOOKS FROM FINLAND: Online literature journal of writing from and about Finland
THE BRIAR CLIFF REVIEW
BRILLIANT CORNERS: A Journal of Jazz & Literature
THE BROADKILL REVIEW: A Journal of Literature
Bronx River Press
BUST DOWN THE DOOR AND EAT ALL THE CHICKENS: A Journal of Absurd and Surreal Fiction
C&R Press
CAKETRAIN
Carolina Wren Press
Casperian Books LLC
Cervena Barva Press
CESUM MAGAZINE
CIMARRON REVIEW
CLARK STREET REVIEW
Cloud 9 Publishing
COMPASS ROSE
CONCEIT MAGAZINE
CONJUNCTIONS
Cornerstone Press
Coteau Books
CRAZYHORSE
CUTBANK
DREAM FANTASY INTERNATIONAL
DWANG: Outsider poetry and prose
THE EAST HAWAII OBSERVER
Eastern Washington University Press
ECOTONE: Reimagining Place
The Eighth Mountain Press
EPICENTER: A LITERARY MAGAZINE
EROSHA
EVANSVILLE REVIEW
EVENT
THE FLORIDA REVIEW
FLUENT ASCENSION
FOLIO: A Literary Journal of American University
4 Your Spirit Productions
FOURTEEN HILLS: The SFSU Review
Galaxy Press
GERTRUDE
GHOTI MAGAZINE
GIN BENDER POETRY REVIEW
GOLD DUST

GRAMMAR CRISIS
GRASSLIMB
Gray Dog Press
Graywolf Press
GUD MAGAZINE (Greatest Uncommon Denominator)
HAPPENINGNOW!EVERYWHERE
Harobed Publishing Creations
HARVARD REVIEW
HAWAI'I REVIEW
ICONOCLAST
Impassio Press
INDIANA REVIEW
Indigo Ink Press, Inc.
THE INK SLINGER REVIEW
Inkwater Press
INKWELL
INSURANCE
THE IOWA REVIEW
Iris Publishing Group, Inc (Iris Press / Tellico Books)
ISTANBUL LITERARY REVIEW
JAMES DICKEY REVIEW
KALEIDOSCOPE: Exploring the Experience of Disability through Literature & the Fine Arts
LEAF GARDEN
Les Figues Press
LIGHT: The Quarterly of Light Verse
Lilly Press
Lincoln Springs Press
LINES + STARS
LITERALLY HORSES/REMUDA
LITERARY HOUSE REVIEW
THE LOUISIANA REVIEW
LULLABY HEARSE
LULLWATER REVIEW
MANDORLA: New Writing from the Americas / Nueva escritura de las Americas
MID-AMERICAN REVIEW
Milkweed Editions
The Kenneth G. Mills Foundation
MINESHAFT
MURDER CROWS
Murder Slim Press
NATURAL BRIDGE
New Rivers Press, Inc.
Night Bomb Press
THE NIGHT BOMB REVIEW
NIGHTJAR REVIEW
NORTHWEST REVIEW
One Less Press
ORBIS
THE ORPHAN LEAF REVIEW
THE OTHER HERALD
OTOLITHS
The Owl Press
PAGAN AMERICA
Paris Press
PASSAGES NORTH
Passing Through Publications
Pathwise Press
PAVEMENT SAW
Pavement Saw Press
PENNINE INK MAGAZINE
Philos Press
PINYON
POETICA MAGAZINE, Reflections of Jewish Thought
PORTLAND REVIEW
PRETEXT
PUNKIN HOUSE DIGEST
Punkin House Press
QUARTER AFTER EIGHT
THE QUIET FEATHER
THE RAGING FACE: Goofball Prose
RAINBOW CURVE
RATTAPALLAX
RED FEZ ENTERTAINMENT
RED ROCK REVIEW
Red Tiger Press
RIVER POETS JOURNAL

THE ROCKFORD REVIEW
ROGER, an art & literary magazine
ROSEBUD
Sabellapress
SAGE OF CONSCIOUSNESS E-ZINE
Santa Fe Writers Project
74th Street Productions, L.L.C.
Shared Roads Press
SIDE OF GRITS
Silenced Press
SKYLINE LITERARY MAGAZINE
The Smith (subsidiary of The Generalist Assn., Inc.)
SNOW MONKEY
SOUNDINGS REVIEW
SOUTHWEST COLORADO ARTS PERSPECTIVE
SPECS
Starcherone Books
THE STINGING FLY
SUB-TERRAIN
SunShine Press Publications, Inc.
SWILL
Syukhtun Editions
Tangerine Press
Tears in the Fence
TEARS IN THE FENCE
1097 MAGAZINE
THIRDEYE MAGAZINE
The Thirty First Bird Press
Thunder Rain Publishing Corp.
Toad Press International Chapbook Series
TSAR Publications
Tupelo Press
twentythreebooks
Twisted Spoon Press
U.S.1 WORKSHEETS
University of Tampa Press
UPSTAIRS AT DUROC
Vanilla Heart Publishing
VERSAL
Vintage Romance Publishing, LLC
Wellington House Publishing Company
Westgate Press
Whelks Walk Press
Zelda Wilde Publishing
WILLIAM AND MARY REVIEW
WILLOW SPRINGS
Wintertree Press
Women and Men Books
WORKERS WRITE!
Writers House Press
Xenos Books
Zerx Press

PSYCHIATRY

Brookline Books
Compact Clinicals
Consumer Press
Holbrook Street Press
Hole Books
JOURNAL OF PSYCHOACTIVE DRUGS
Loving Healing Press, Inc.
OPEN MINDS QUARTERLY
Playdate Kids Publishing
Total Cardboard Publishing
Vanguard Press

PSYCHOLOGY

Act on Wisdom
Alamo Square Press
Alpine Guild, Inc.
Altair Publications
America West Publishers
Anthony Publishing Company
THE ART OF ABUNDANCE
Ash Lad Press
The B & R Samizdat Express
Barrytown/Station Hill Press
Bauu Press

Bay Tree Publishing
Bayhampton Publications
BEGINNING MAGAZINE
Behavioral Sciences Research Press, Inc.
Best Life Media
Beynch Press Publishing Company
Beyond Words Publishing, Inc.
Birth Day Publishing Company
BOULDER HERETIC
Brason-Sargar Publications
Brookline Books
Burns Park Publishers
Celo Valley Books
Center for Thanatology Research & Education, Inc.
The Center Press
Common Boundaries
Compact Clinicals
Consumer Press
CORRECTIONS TODAY
Creative Roots, Inc.
CRITICAL REVIEW
Dharma Publishing
Down There Press
DREAM FANTASY INTERNATIONAL
DREAM NETWORK
Energy Psychology Press
ETC Publications
Fisher King Press
Friendly Oaks Publications
Gateways Books And Tapes
GLB Publishers
Glenbridge Publishing Ltd.
Green Hut Press
Gurze Books
Health Press NA Inc.
Holbrook Street Press
Howln Moon Press
Hunter House Inc., Publishers
Ice Cube Press
ILLUMINATIONS LITERARY JOURNAL
Impact Publishers, Inc.
INKY TRAIL NEWS
Inner City Books
InsideOut Press
International University Line (IUL)
Intuitive Moon Media
Islewest Publishing
ITALIAN AMERICANA
J & J Consultants, Inc.
Joelle Publishing
JOURNAL OF PSYCHOACTIVE DRUGS
THE JOURNAL OF PSYCHOHISTORY
Kallisti Publishing
Lake Street Press
Lemon Grove Press
Life Energy Media
LifeSkill Institute, Inc.
Lockhart Press
The Love and Logic Press, Inc.
Loving Healing Press, Inc.
March Books
Markowski International Publishers
MUSIC PERCEPTION
Mystery Island Publications
NEW AMERICAN IMAGIST
New Falcon Publications
New Knowledge Press
New World Library
Nightsun Books
Open Court Publishing Company
Origin Press
Papoose Publishing
Practically Shameless Press
PSYCHE
Psychohistory Press
Pudding House Publications
PUDDING MAGAZINE: The International Journal of
    Applied Poetry

Quarterly Committee of Queen's University
QUEEN'S QUARTERLY: A Canadian Review
Rainbow Books, Inc.
Raven Rocks Press
Red Alder Books
River Press
RTMC Organization, LLC
The Runaway Spoon Press
Sagamore Publishing
See Sharp Press
Sentient Publications, LLC
Sibyl Publications, Inc
Sidran Institute
SKEPTICAL INQUIRER
THE SOCIOLOGICAL QUARTERLY
STARNOTES
State University of New York Press
Tuvela Press
VanderWyk & Burnham
Vestibular Disorders Association
Volcano Press, Inc
WHAT IS ENLIGHTENMENT?
Whole Person Associates Inc.
Wilshire Books Inc.
Wisdom Publications, Inc.
Women of Diversity Productions, Inc.
Yes International Publishers
Zoilita Grant MS CCHt.

PUBLIC AFFAIRS

A2Z Publications LLC
THE ANTIOCH REVIEW
Archer Books
Bay Tree Publishing
Bellevue Literary Press
Blackwater Publications
Borealis Press Limited
Camel Press
CANADIAN JOURNAL OF PROGRAM EVALUATION
Chandler & Sharp Publishers, Inc.
CKO UPDATE
CONSCIENCE: The Newsjournal of Catholic Opinion
Continuing Education Press
Crandall, Dostie & Douglass Books, Inc.
The Denali Press
DUST (From the Ego Trip)
FOURTH WORLD REVIEW
Fulcrum, Inc.
Gain Publications
Grace House Publishing
Hoover Institution Press
International Publishers Co. Inc.
KETTERING REVIEW
THE LONG TERM VIEW: A Journal of Informed Opinion
Maisonneuve Press
Missing Spoke Press
Noontide Press
THE OTHER ISRAEL
Pendant Publishing Inc.
RFF Press / Resources for the Future
Small Helm Press
Starry Night Publishing
TAPROOT, a journal of older writers
Thorp Springs Press
UBC Press
Volcano Press, Inc
Wellington House Publishing Company

PUBLIC RELATIONS/PUBLICITY

Best Books Plus
CKO UPDATE
D.B.A. Books
EQUAL CONSTRUCTION RECORD
Info Net Publishing
Kobalt Books
MOBILE BEAT: The Mobile Entertainer's Magazine
The Passion Profit Company
Penworth Publishing

SAPONIFIER
SEDUCTIVE SELLING
Sources
THE SOURCES HOTLINK
Trellis Publishing, Inc.
Visual Arts Press
Zelda Wilde Publishing
World Gumbo Publishing

PUBLISHING

Alpine Guild, Inc.
ART BUREAU
Assilem 9 Publications
Atelier Press
BLACK BOOK PRESS: The Poetry Zine id
BlackBerry Fields Press
BOOK MARKETING UPDATE
C&R Press
THE CAROUSEL
Communication Creativity
COOK PARTNERS
Cornerstone Publishing, Inc.
COUNTERPOISE: For Social Responsibilities, Liberty and Dissent
Creative Writing and Publishing Company
Dumouriez Publishing
Dustbooks
EEI Press
Ellechor Publishing House
ERDC Publishing
Gemstone House Publishing
Happy About
Helm Publishing
A HUDSON VIEW POETRY DIGEST
ILLOGICAL MUSE
INDEPENDENT PUBLISHER ONLINE
Juel House Publishers and Literary Services
Kobalt Books
Lamp Light Press
LAUGHING BEAR NEWSLETTER
Lilly Press
Litwin Books
LONE STARS MAGAZINE
Myriad Press
Open Horizons Publishing Company
Para Publishing
The Passion Profit Company
Penworth Publishing
Platinum Dreams Publishing
Playdate Kids Publishing
PUBLISHING POYNTERS
READ, AMERICA!
ROCKY MOUNTAIN KC NEWS
Rocky Mountain KC Publishing Co.
Salmon Poetry Ltd.
SEDUCTIVE SELLING
SENSATIONS MAGAZINE
Sentient Publications, LLC
SKYLINE LITERARY MAGAZINE
THE SMALL PRESS REVIEW/SMALL MAGAZINE REVIEW
SPINNINGS...INTENSE TALES OF LIFE MAGAZINE
Storm Publishing Group
TRUE POET MAGAZINE
TSAR Publications
Twilight Tales, Inc.
WHEELHOUSE MAGAZINE
Wilshire Books Inc.
WindRiver Publishing
WRITERS' JOURNAL
ZINE WORLD: A Reader's Guide to the Underground Press
ZYX

PUERTO RICO

Inner City Press
Iris Publishing Group, Inc (Iris Press / Tellico Books)
Pangaea
POINT OF CONTACT, The Journal of Verbal & Visual

742

Arts
TORRE DE PAPEL
Tortuga Books
TURNING THE TIDE: Journal of Anti-Racist Action, Research & Education

QUILTING, SEWING

C & T Publishing
Cooperative Press
DOLLS UNITED INTERACTIVE MAGAZINE
Eagle's View Publishing
Fruitbearer Publishing, LLC
MIDWEST ART FAIRS
Naturegraph Publishers
Storm Publishing Group
Success Publishing

QUOTATIONS

AIS Publications
ARTISTIC RAMBLINGS
Brason-Sargar Publications
CKO UPDATE
dreamslaughter
Nicolin Fields Publishing, Inc.
Happy About
The Intrepid Traveler
Library Juice Press
LrnIT Publishing Div. LRNIT CORPORATION
Music City Publishing
Open Horizons Publishing Company
THE OTHER HERALD
PULSAR POETRY WEBZINE
Red Eye Press
Set Sail Productions, LLC
Titlewaves Publishing; Writers Direct

RACE

A2Z Publications LLC
Authentic Publishing LLC
Back House Books
BLK
BLUE COLLAR REVIEW
THE CAPILANO REVIEW
COLLEGE LITERATURE
COLORLINES
Comstock Bonanza Press
Crandall, Dostie & Douglass Books, Inc.
DLite Press
Ecrivez!
Forest Dale Publishing Company
MacDonald/Sward Publishing Company
Margaret Media, Inc.
McQuinn Publishing
New Sins Press
Partisan Press
THE PUBLIC EYE
SOCIAL JUSTICE: A JOURNAL OF CRIME, CONFLICT, & WORLD ORDER
South End Press
State University of New York Press
SYMPLOKE: A Journal for the Intermingling of Literary, Cultural and Theoretical Scholarship
TEEN VOICES MAGAZINE
TURNING THE TIDE: Journal of Anti-Racist Action, Research & Education
The Wessex Collective
WEST COAST LINE: A Journal of Contemporary Writing and Criticism
West Virginia University Press
WORDKNOT AUDIO: A Literary Podcast Magazine

RADIO

BearManor Media
BOOK MARKETING UPDATE
IT'S JUST THIS LITTLE CHROMIUM SWITCH HERE
THE NOISE
Sonoran Publishing
Wind River Institute Press/Wind River Broadcasting

READING

Abernathy House Publishing
Academy Press of America
THE ART OF ABUNDANCE
Brick Road Poetry Press
COLLEGE LITERATURE
EEI Press
THE FLORIDA REVIEW
Graywolf Press
THE LEDGE
Lightning Bug Learning Press
Maupin House Publishing, Inc.
Moo-Cow Fan Club
New Day Publishing, Inc.
NEW VOICES REVISITED: Poetry, Contests and Short Stories.
OTHER INVESTIGATIONS
PARENTEACHER MAGAZINE
Perrin Press
Punkin House Press
READ, AMERICA!
Reading Connections
SYMPLOKE: A Journal for the Intermingling of Literary, Cultural and Theoretical Scholarship

REAL ESTATE

Adams-Blake Publishing
Atlantic Publishing Group, Inc.
CANADIAN MONEYSAVER
Communication Creativity
Consumer Press
EQUAL CONSTRUCTION RECORD
First Books
Fountain Publisher Limited
Gemstone House Publishing
GLOBAL ONE MAGAZINE
Happy About
The Heather Foundation
Long & Silverman Publishing, Inc.
Noved Audio
Rolling Hills Publishing
Sourcebooks, Inc.
Storm Publishing Group
Tax Property Investor, Inc.
Tres Picos Press
Upper Access Inc. Book Publishers
Wheatmark Book Publishing

REFERENCE

Affinity Publishers Services
Alan Wofsy Fine Arts
Appalachian Consortium Press
Arden Press, Inc.
Ariko Publications
The Bess Press
Black Forest Press and The Tennessee Publishing House
Blowtorch Press
Brenner Information Group
Center for Japanese Studies
Center For Self-Sufficiency
CONNEXIONS DIGEST
Connexions Information Services, Inc.
Cooper Hill Press
COUNTERPOISE: For Social Responsibilities, Liberty and Dissent
Dash-Hill, LLC
Dawn Sign Press
The Denali Press
dreamslaughter
Dustbooks
The Edwin Mellen Press
Falk Art Reference
The Fiction Works
Galen Press, Ltd.
Global Sports Productions, Ltd.
Good Book Publishing Company
Ho Logos Press

Hollywood Creative Directory
Howln Moon Press
INVENTED LANGUAGES
Irish Genealogical Foundation
Kali Press
Lake Claremont Press
Library Juice Press
Litwin Books
Maledicta Press
Peter Marcan Publications
Menasha Ridge Press
Muse World Media Group
NEW VOICES REVISITED: Poetry, Contests and Short
    Stories.
Next Decade, Inc.
Nolo Press Occidental
Oak Knoll Press
Panther Creek Press
Papoose Publishing
Pineapple Press, Inc.
Poets & Writers, Inc.
Rayve Productions Inc.
Red Eye Press
Reference Service Press
Sagamore Publishing
Santa Monica Press
Scentouri, Publishing Division
Selah Publishing Co. Inc.
SILVER WINGS
THE SMALL PRESS REVIEW/SMALL MAGAZINE
    REVIEW
Sources
Univelt, Inc.
Upper Access Inc. Book Publishers
Velazquez Press
Volcano Press, Inc

RELATIONSHIPS

Abernathy House Publishing
Accendo Publishing
Allwrite Advertising and Publishing
APPLE VALLEY REVIEW: A Journal of Contemporary
    Literature
THE ART OF ABUNDANCE
Aspicomm Media
Atlantic Publishing Group, Inc.
Blue Lupin Press
Brick Road Poetry Press
Bronze Girl Productions, Inc.
Burns Park Publishers
Cantarabooks LLC
Church Leadership Library (US Office)
City Life Books, LLC
Cladach Publishing
Cornerstone Publishing, Inc.
Defiant Times Press
Down There Press
DRAMA GARDEN
Dreams Due Media Group, Inc.
Ecrivez!
Forest Dale Publishing Company
4 Your Spirit Productions
Grace Creek Press
HEAL Foundation Press
Hunter House Inc., Publishers
Impact Publishers, Inc.
In Between Books
InsideOut Press
Intuitive Moon Media
Islewest Publishing
KABBALAH
Lake Street Press
Legacy Audio Books, Inc.
Looking Beyond Publishing
LOVING MORE: New Models for Relationships
Luminous Epinoia Press
March Books
Meek Publishing

Mo'omana'o Press
Moon Pie Press
Muse World Media Group
Music City Publishing
New Creature Press
Nilgiri Press
Nolo Press Occidental
Nushape Publication
P.R.A. Publishing
PhoeniX in Print
Platinum Dreams Publishing
Poetry
Practically Shameless Press
PSYCHE
Rainbow Books, Inc.
RED FEZ ENTERTAINMENT
River Press
Roaring Lion Publishing
Rodnik Publishing Co.
Search Institute
Sentient Publications, LLC
Signalman Publishing
SONG OF THE SAN JOAQUIN
SPINNINGS...INTENSE TALES OF LIFE MAGAZINE
Starry Night Publishing
Sweet People Publishing
Synergy Press
Third Dimension Publishing
Top 20 Press
Total Package Publications, LLC
Tuvela Press
2L Publishing, LLC
Vanilla Heart Publishing
Whole Person Associates Inc.
Willfam Publishing Co.

RELIGION

AAIMS Publishers
Aardvark Enterprises (Sole Proprietorship of J. Alvin
    Speers)
Act on Wisdom
ADVENTURES
Al-Galaxy Publishing Corporation
Allwrite Advertising and Publishing
America West Publishers
ANCIENT PATHS
The Apostolic Press
ASCENT
Axios Newletter, Inc.
The B & R Samizdat Express
Banks Channel Books
Bel Canto Press
BELIEVERS EXCHANGE NEWSLETTER
Birth Day Publishing Company
BlackBerry Fields Press
BLUE MOUNTAIN
BOTH SIDES NOW
BOULDER HERETIC
Branden Books
Brentwood Christian Press
BRIDGES: An Interdisciplinary Journal of Theology,
    Philosophy, History, and Science
Bronze Girl Productions, Inc.
Caribbean Books-Panama
Celo Valley Books
Celtic Heritage Books
Center for Japanese Studies
CESUM MAGAZINE
CHANTEH, the Iranian Cross-Cultural Quarterly
Children Of Mary
CHRISTIAN*NEW AGE QUARTERLY
Church Leadership Library (Canadian Office)
Church Leadership Library (US Office)
The Colbert House LLC
CONSCIENCE: The Newsjournal of Catholic Opinion
CONTEMPORARY GHAZALS
CORNERSTONE
CROSS CURRENTS

744

Cynic Press
DAILY WORD
Demarche Publishing LLC
Dervla Publishing, LLC
Dharma Publishing
DRAMA GARDEN
Dumouriez Publishing
Dunamis House
Dwarf Lion Press
Eborn Books
The Edwin Mellen Press
Wm.B. Eerdmans Publishing Co.
Elderberry Press, Inc.
Ellechor Publishing House
Encounter Books
EnlightenNext
Ephemera Bound Publishing
Famaco Publishers (Qalam Books)
FIDELIS ET VERUS
FISH DRUM MAGAZINE
THE FIT CHRISTIAN A Christian Health & Fitness
    Magazine
4 Your Spirit Productions
Free People Press
FREETHOUGHT HISTORY
Fruitbearer Publishing, LLC
Galaxy Press
Galde Press, Inc.
GLOBAL VEDANTA
Gloger Family Books
Good Book Publishing Company
Grace Acres Press
Grace Creek Press
Gray Dog Press
Harbor House
The Haworth Press
Heidelberg Graphics
Heritage Global Publishing
Himalayan Institute Press
Ho Logos Press
Hohm Press
HOLY ROLLERS
Hope Publishing House
Horned Owl Publishing
Iconoclast Press
IMAGE: ART, FAITH, MYSTERY
In Print Publishing
INTERCULTURE
ISSUES
Jewish Publication Society
Kar-Ben Publishing, Inc.
Kenyette Productions
KEREM: Creative Explorations in Judaism
Kobalt Books
Lake Street Press
A.P. Lee & Co., Ltd.
Legacy Audio Books, Inc.
Lion's Den Publishing
Lone Willow Press
Looking Beyond Publishing
LPD Press
Lycanthrope Press
MacDonald/Sward Publishing Company
Malki-Ballena Press
Peter Marcan Publications
Maryland Historical Press (also MHPress)
Massey-Reyner Publishing
Mercer University Press
THE MONIST: An International Quarterly Journal of
    General Philosophical Inquiry
Mo'omana'o Press
Mountain Automation Corporation
Multnomah Publishers, Inc.
My Heart Yours Publishing
Mystery Island Publications
NEW AMERICAN IMAGIST
New Concept Press
New Creature Press
New Day Publishing, Inc.
New Falcon Publications
NEW VOICES REVISITED: Poetry, Contests and Short
    Stories.
New World Library
NEWWITCH
Nilgiri Press
NOLA-MAGICK Press
Northern Illinois University Press
NOVA RELIGIO
OFFICE NUMBER ONE
Open Court Publishing Company
Origin Press
OUT OF LINE
PAGAN AMERICA
Parallax Press
Penthe Publishing
Pilgrims Book House
Plain Philosophy Center
Pocol Press
Practically Shameless Press
PREP Publishing
The Press at Foggy Bottom
QUARTZ HILL JOURNAL OF THEOLOGY:A Journal of
    Bible and Contemporary Theological Thought
Quartz Hill Publishing House
QUEEN OF ALL HEARTS
Rabeth Publishing Company
Ragged Edge Press
RELIGION & AMERICAN CULTURE
REPORTS OF THE NATIONAL CENTER FOR SCIENCE
    EDUCATION
S4N Books
Saint Mary's Press
Saqi Books Publisher
SCP JOURNAL
SeaCrab Publishing
SECRETUM MEUM MIHI
Secretum Meum Mihi Press
SelectiveHouse Publishers, Inc.
SHAMAN'S DRUM: A Journal of Experiential Shamanism
Signalman Publishing
SPECS
Spring Grass
Square One Publishers, Inc.
Starik Publishing
State University of New York Press
SterlingHouse Publisher
STUDIO - A Journal of Christians Writing
Sherwood Sugden & Company, Publishers
Superior Christian Press
Swedenborg Foundation
Sweet People Publishing
TELOS
Third Dimension Publishing
Thirteen Colonies Press
The Thirty First Bird Press
THRESHOLDS JOURNAL
Timeless Books
Truman State University Press
TRUTH SEEKER
Tuvela Press
Tyr Publishing
Unity House
UNITY MAGAZINE
University of South Carolina Press
UnKnownTruths.com Publishing Company
Vedanta Press
VOICES ISRAEL
Volcano Press, Inc
Wayside Publications
WEST GOES SOUTH
WHAT IS ENLIGHTENMENT?
Wheatmark Book Publishing
White Buck Publishing
Wilderness Ministries
WindRiver Publishing
WinePress Publishing

Wisdom Publications, Inc.
Wytherngate Press
Yaldah Publishing
Zygote Publishing

RENAISSANCE

Avari Press
Blue Moose Press
Chatterley Press International
Italica Press, Inc.
Lake Street Press
Magnifico Publications
SCULPTURAL PURSUIT MAGAZINE
Truman State University Press

REPRINTS

Alan Wofsy Fine Arts
ALTERNATIVE PRESS REVIEW
Avery Color Studios
Bloated Toe Publishing
Blue Cubicle Press, LLC
BOTH SIDES NOW
Carousel Press
Center for Japanese Studies
Creative Creations Consulting Publishing Company
Dixon-Price Publishing
Dumouriez Publishing
Eagle's View Publishing
Eastern Washington University Press
Ecrivez!
The Feminist Press at the City University of New York
Free People Press
GUD MAGAZINE (Greatest Uncommon Denominator)
Heidelberg Graphics
Heritage Books, Inc.
Irish Genealogical Foundation
JUBILAT
Allen A. Knoll Publishers
Libertarian Press, Inc./American Book Distributors
Loonfeather Press
McPherson & Company Publishers
Mid-List Press
Mountain Press Publishing Co.
NEW AMERICAN IMAGIST
Oregon State University Press
OUT YOUR BACKDOOR: The Magazine of Do-It-Yourself Adventure and Homegrown Culture
Paladin Enterprises, Inc.
Paladin Media Group
Saint Bob Press
Saqi Books Publisher
Slipdown Mountain Publications LLC
Sherwood Sugden & Company, Publishers
UNITED LUMBEE NATION TIMES
Village Lane Press
THE VIRGINIA QUARTERLY REVIEW
Wordcraft of Oregon, LLC
WORDKNOT AUDIO: A Literary Podcast Magazine
Zumaya Publications LLC

RESEARCH

ATLANTIS: A Women's Studies Journal/Revue d'etudes sur les femmes
Aura Productions, LLC
Benecton Press
Brenner Information Group
Buenos Books
CANADIAN POETRY
Church Leadership Library (Canadian Office)
Church Leadership Library (US Office)
COGNITIO: A Graduate Humanities Journal
Creative Creations Consulting Publishing Company
The Edwin Mellen Press
EEI Press
Eros Books
Frontline Publications
Green Square Publishing
GUD MAGAZINE (Greatest Uncommon Denominator)

Happy About
HEARING HEALTH
Journal of Pyrotechnics
JOURNAL OF PYROTECHNICS
Library Juice Press
PALO ALTO REVIEW
Platte Purchase Publishers
Scientia Publishing, LLC
THE SOCIOLOGICAL QUARTERLY
STATE OF CALIFORNIA LABOR
Vestibular Disorders Association
Wheatmark Book Publishing

RESISTANCE

Iniquity Press/Vendetta Books
MOUTH: Voice of the Dis-Labeled Nation
RED LAMP
XCP: CROSS-CULTURAL POETICS

REVIEWS

ALTERNATIVE PRESS REVIEW
THE AMERICAN DRIVEL REVIEW
Androgyne Books
ANOTHER CHICAGO MAGAZINE(ACM)
Aquarius Press
AzurAlive
THE BALTIMORE REVIEW
BELOIT POETRY JOURNAL
THE BELTANE PAPERS: A Journal of Women's Mysteries
BOGG: A Journal of Contemporary Writing
BOOK MARKETING UPDATE
BOOK/MARK QUARTERLY REVIEW
BORDERLANDS: Texas Poetry Review
CAUSE & EFFECT MAGAZINE
CERISE PRESS
CESUM MAGAZINE
CHIRON REVIEW
CIMARRON REVIEW
COGNITIO: A Graduate Humanities Journal
COLLEGE LITERATURE
CONCRETE JUNGLE JOURNAL
CORRECTIONS TODAY
THE CORTLAND REVIEW
COUNTERPOISE: For Social Responsibilities, Liberty and Dissent
THE CREAM CITY REVIEW
Cyberwit.net
CYNIC BOOK REVIEW
DREAM NETWORK
EEI Press
88: A Journal of Contemporary American Poetry
ENGLISH LITERATURE IN TRANSITION, 1880-1920
EPICENTER: A LITERARY MAGAZINE
EVENT
THE FLORIDA REVIEW
FUTURECYCLE POETRY
FutureCycle Press
THE GEORGIA REVIEW
GHOTI MAGAZINE
GRAY AREAS
GREEN ANARCHY
THE GREEN HILLS LITERARY LANTERN
HAPPENINGNOW!EVERYWHERE
IAMBS & TROCHEES
ILLOGICAL MUSE
ILLUMINATIONS
Immediate Direction Publications
INDEPENDENT PUBLISHER ONLINE
INDIANA REVIEW
IOTA
IT'S JUST THIS LITTLE CHROMIUM SWITCH HERE
JAMES JOYCE BROADSHEET
THE JOURNAL
THE JOURNAL OF AFRICAN TRAVEL-WRITING
Juel House Publishers and Literary Services
KABBALAH
KALEIDOSCOPE: Exploring the Experience of Disability

through Literature & the Fine Arts
THE KENYON REVIEW
KOKAKO
LAUGHING BEAR NEWSLETTER
LIGHT: The Quarterly of Light Verse
LITERARY MAGAZINE REVIEW
THE LUMMOX JOURNAL
Lummox Press
Lunar Offensive Publications
MAIN STREET RAG
THE MARLBORO REVIEW
MATCHBOOK
MEAT: A Journal of Writing and Materiality
Mica Press - Paying Our Dues Productions
MID-AMERICAN REVIEW
MIDNIGHT STREET
MINESHAFT
THE MYSTERY REVIEW
NEW DELTA REVIEW
THE NEW ENGLAND QUARTERLY
NEW HOPE INTERNATIONAL REVIEW
THE NEW RENAISSANCE, an international magazine of
ideas & opinions, emphasizing literature & the arts
NEW VOICES REVISITED: Poetry, Contests and Short
Stories.
North Stone Editions
NOTRE DAME REVIEW
OPEN WIDE MAGAZINE
OYSTER BOY REVIEW
PACIFIC COAST JOURNAL
Partisan Press
Pendragonian Publications
PENNINE PLATFORM
PENNY DREADFUL: Tales and Poems of Fantastic Terror
Phoenix Illusion
PLEASANT LIVING
POEMELEON: A Journal of Poetry
POET LORE
POETICA MAGAZINE, Reflections of Jewish Thought
POETRY NOW, Sacramento's Literary Review and Calen-
dar
PORTLAND REVIEW
PRAIRIE SCHOONER
PRAKALPANA   SAHITYA/PRAKALPANA   LITERA-
TURE
PRESA
QUARTERLY WEST
RAIN TAXI REVIEW OF BOOKS
THE RAVEN CHRONICLES
READ, AMERICA!
RED LAMP
RED ROCK REVIEW
REVERIE: MIDWEST AFRICAN AMERICAN LITERA-
TURE
RUMINATIONS: The Nigerian Dwarf & Mini Dairy Goat
Magazine
SAPONIFIER
SEWANEE REVIEW
SIDE OF GRITS
THE SMALL PRESS REVIEW/SMALL MAGAZINE
REVIEW
SMARTISH PACE
SONGS OF INNOCENCE
THE SOURCES HOTLINK
Southeast Missouri State University Press
SPOON RIVER POETRY REVIEW
THE STINGING FLY
SYCAMORE REVIEW
13TH MOON
Thunder Rain Publishing Corp.
TOUCHSTONE LITERARY JOURNAL
TREATING YOURSELF: The Alternative Medicine Jour-
nal
TRUTH SEEKER
UNDERSTANDING MAGAZINE
URBAN REFLECTIONS MAGAZINE
VALLUM: CONTEMPORARY POETRY
WORLD POETRY SHOWCASE

WSQ (formerly WOMEN'S STUDIES QUARTERLY)
XCP: CROSS-CULTURAL POETICS
ZINE WORLD: A Reader's Guide to the Underground Press

ROBOTICS

firefall editions

ROMANCE

Affluent Publishing Corp.
BeachSide Press
BEGINNINGS - A Magazine for the Novice Writer
Blue Planet Books Inc.
C & M Online Media Inc.
Casperian Books LLC
CONCEIT MAGAZINE
Cotton Tree Press
Crystal Dreams Publishing
Demarche Publishing LLC
DLite Press
Ephemera Bound Publishing
Equine Graphics Publishing Group: New Concord Press,
SmallHorse Press, SunDrop
Eros Books
The Fiction Works
First Chance Publishing
Foremost Press
4AllSeasons Publishing
Gemstone House Publishing
Gray Dog Press
Homa & Sekey Books
A HUDSON VIEW POETRY DIGEST
Ika, LLC
In Between Books
J. Mark Press
Kobalt Books
L&L Dreamspell
LITERARY HOUSE REVIEW
Llumina Press
Lyons Publishing Limited
Maverick Books
MCM Entertainment, Inc. Publishing Division
Mills Custom Services Publishing
Mondial
Multi-Media Publications Inc.
Oak Tree Press
Outrider Press
P.R.A. Publishing
Papillon Presse
Premium Press America
PREP Publishing
PublishAmerica, LLLP.
PUNKIN HOUSE DIGEST
Pussywillow
Raular Publishing
Roaring Lion Publishing
RTMC Organization, LLC
Skyline Publications
Smirk Books
SPINNINGS...INTENSE TALES OF LIFE MAGAZINE
Star Publish LLC
Starik Publishing
Steel Balls Press
Triskelion Publishing
Tuvela Press
Twin Souls Publications
Two Thousand Three Associates
UmbraProjects Publishing
URBAN REFLECTIONS MAGAZINE
Vanilla Heart Publishing
Vintage Romance Publishing, LLC
The WhaleInn Publishing House (1998)
Whiskey Creek Press
WindRiver Publishing
The Wolf Pirate Project Inc.
Wytherngate Press

ROMANIAN STUDIES

BIBLIOPHILOS

RUSSIA

ABSINTHE: New European Writing
All Nations Press
Mehring Books, Inc.
MIP Company
Rodnik Publishing Co.
Russian Information Services
RUSSIAN LIFE

SAFETY

AB
Dash-Hill, LLC
Future Horizons, Inc.
GLOBAL ONE MAGAZINE
HAMPTON ROADS HEALTH JOURNAL
HEALMB Publishing
Saber Press
SO YOUNG!
Chuck Stewart
Varro Press

SAN FRANCISCO

Alamo Square Press
Androgyne Books
Carousel Press
Deep Well Publishing Company
Devil Mountain Books
firefall editions
Heritage House Publishers
Ithuriel's Spear
The Live Oak Press, LLC
Pocol Press
Scottwall Associates, Publishers

SATIRE

ABRAXAS
ACME Press
ART:MAG
AXE FACTORY REVIEW
BABYSUE
Black Oak Press
Bronx River Press
BUST DOWN THE DOOR AND EAT ALL THE
    CHICKENS: A Journal of Absurd and Surreal Fiction
C & M Online Media Inc.
Casperian Books LLC
The Center Press
CONCRETE JUNGLE JOURNAL
CONJUNCTIONS
DREAM FANTASY INTERNATIONAL
EPICENTER: A LITERARY MAGAZINE
Erespin Press
EVANSVILLE REVIEW
FAT TUESDAY
FLUENT ASCENSION
GIUSEPPE: A Magazine of Literature and Impersonation
HAPA NUI
HAWAI'I PACIFIC REVIEW
HUMOR TIMES
Juel House Publishers and Literary Services
The Leaping Frog Press
McPherson & Company Publishers
THE MINDERBINDER REVIEW OF BOOKS
Paladin Media Group
Pleasure Boat Studio: A Literary Press (including imprints
    Caravel Books and Aequitas Books, and the division
    Empty Bowl Press)
Poor Souls Press/Scaramouche Books
Punkin House Press
THE RAGING FACE: Goofball Prose
RAINBOW CURVE
THE ROCKFORD REVIEW
Santa Fe Writers Project
SIDE OF GRITS
Smirk Books
SPOTops Books
Starcherone Books

STRUGGLE: A Magazine of Proletarian Revolutionary
    Literature
SUB-TERRAIN
SWILL
Syukhtun Editions
Transcending Mundane, Inc.
twentythreebooks
UNDERSTANDING MAGAZINE
VOICE(S)
Vulgar Marsala Press
THE WILDWOOD READER
Wintertree Press
The Wolf Pirate Project Inc.
Wordcraft of Oregon, LLC
Zirlinson Publishing

SCANDINAVIA

ABSINTHE: New European Writing
Cross-Cultural Communications
Horned Owl Publishing
Southern Illinois University Press
World Gumbo Publishing

SCIENCE

A2Z Publications LLC
AAS HISTORY SERIES
AB
ADVANCES IN THE ASTRONAUTICAL SCIENCES
Anderson Publishing; also RC Anderson Books
ATLANTIS: A Women's Studies Journal/Revue d'etudes
    sur les femmes
Bauu Press
Bellevue Literary Press
Benecton Press
BIOLOGY DIGEST
BRIDGES: An Interdisciplinary Journal of Theology,
    Philosophy, History, and Science
Buenos Books
Central Avenue Press
Chicago Review Press
Clearwater Publishing Co.
Clover Park Press
CONDUIT
Continuing Education Press
CROSSCURRENTS
Dawn Publications
The Denali Press
Dog's Eye View Media
firefall editions
Flowerfield Enterprises, LLC
Frontline Publications
The Heather Foundation
History Compass, LLC
Immunizations for Public Health
Insight Press
International University Line (IUL)
Ion Imagination Publishing, Ion Imagination Entertainment,
    Inc.
Island Press
Journal of Pyrotechnics
JOURNAL OF PYROTECHNICS
JOURNAL OF SCIENTIFIC EXPLORATION
Jupiter Scientific Publishing
Logos Press
Medi-Ed Press
Micron Press
Moo-Cow Fan Club
Mo'omana'o Press
Muse World Media Group
Orchises Press
Plexus Publishing, Inc.
Pocahontas Press, Inc.
Quale Press
Quarterly Committee of Queen's University
QUEEN'S QUARTERLY: A Canadian Review
Rainbow Books, Inc.
REPORTS OF THE NATIONAL CENTER FOR SCIENCE
    EDUCATION

Savant Garde Workshop
SB&F (SCIENCE BOOKS & FILMS)
School for Advanced Research Press
SCIENCE AND TECHNOLOGY
Scientia Publishing, LLC
SKEPTICAL INQUIRER
SPOTops Books
Titan Press
Trickle Creek Books
Tyr Publishing
Univelt, Inc.
UnKnownTruths.com Publishing Company
Vanguard Press
WHAT IS ENLIGHTENMENT?
Wintertree Press

SCIENCE FICTION

AAS HISTORY SERIES
Abecedarian books, Inc.
Adamantine Publishing House
Affluent Publishing Corp.
ALMOST NORMAL COMICS and Other Oddities
Apex Book Company
APEX Magazine
Aquila Ink Publishing
Argo Press
ARTISTIC RAMBLINGS
Arx Publishing LLC
AXE FACTORY REVIEW
Bereshith Publishing
Bladestar Publishing
Blue Planet Books Inc.
BOMB MAGAZINE
BUST DOWN THE DOOR AND EAT ALL THE
    CHICKENS: A Journal of Absurd and Surreal Fiction
C & M Online Media Inc.
Caribbean Books-Panama
Casperian Books LLC
Central Avenue Press
Citiria Publishing
A COMPANION IN ZEOR
Crystal Dreams Publishing
Demarche Publishing LLC
DIET SOAP
DLite Press
DREAM FANTASY INTERNATIONAL
Earth Star Publications
EASTGATE QUARTERLY REVIEW OF HYPERTEXT
Ecrivez!
EDGE Science Fiction and Fantasy Publishing
Elderberry Press, Inc.
Ellechor Publishing House
The Fiction Works
FISH DRUM MAGAZINE
Flapjack Press
Foremost Press
Free Books Inc.
Gateways Books And Tapes
Glass Tower Press
GRASSLIMB
Gray Dog Press
Gryphon Books
GUD MAGAZINE (Greatest Uncommon Denominator)
Helm Publishing
Idylls Press
THE ILLUMINATA
Imago Press
Immediate Direction Publications
IMPress
Inkwater Press
INVENTED LANGUAGES
IT GOES ON THE SHELF
Journey Books Publishing
LOW BUDGET SCIENCE FICTION
Manuscript Press
Mayapple Press
Micron Press
MIDNIGHT STREET

Mountain Media
Multi-Media Publications Inc.
Munsey Music
MYSTERY ISLAND MAGAZINE
Mystery Island Publications
New Falcon Publications
New Victoria Publishers
NOVA EXPRESS
OmegaRoom Press
ON SPEC
Orchard House Press
PAPERBACK PARADE
Penthe Publishing
Pig Iron Press
Pixiu Press
POGO STICK
Portals Press
PREMONITIONS
PublishAmerica, LLLP.
PUNKIN HOUSE DIGEST
Punkin House Press
Purple Mouth Press
RALPH'S REVIEW
Razor7 Publishing
RedJack
Santa Fe Writers Project
Sassy Sunflower Books
Savant Garde Workshop
SelectiveHouse Publishers, Inc.
Skullvines Press
Skyline Publications
Slipdown Mountain Publications LLC
SOM Publishing, division of School of Metaphysics
Soto Publishing Company
SOUNDINGS REVIEW
SPACE AND TIME
Space and Time Press
SPECTACULAR SPECULATIONS
SPINNINGS...INTENSE TALES OF LIFE MAGAZINE
SPOTops Books
Star Publish LLC
SterlingHouse Publisher
Subsynchronuos Press
SWILL
THE TARPEIAN ROCK
THRESHOLDS JOURNAL
Triskelion Publishing
Triumvirate Publications
Tuvela Press
Twilight Tales, Inc.
Twilight Times Books
Tyrannosaurus Press
Ultramarine Publishing Co., Inc.
Univelt, Inc.
Van Cleave Publishing
Vanilla Heart Publishing
VEIL: Journal of Darker Musings
Virginia City Publishing Co. LLC
The WhaleInn Publishing House (1998)
Whiskey Creek Press
Willfam Publishing Co.
WindRiver Publishing
Wintertree Press
The Wolf Pirate Project Inc.
Wordcraft of Oregon, LLC
Youthful Wisdom Press
ZAHIR: A Journal of Speculative Fiction
Zirlinson Publishing
Zumaya Publications LLC

SCOTLAND

ABSINTHE: New European Writing
Celtic Heritage Books
Dufour Editions Inc.
Rowan Mountain Press
Stewart Publishing & Printing

SCOUTING

dbS Productions

SELF-HELP

Act on Wisdom
Al-Galaxy Publishing Corporation
Allwrite Advertising and Publishing
Anti-Aging Press
Arden Press, Inc.
THE AUROREAN
Balanced Books Publishing
Bayhampton Publications
Beagle Bay Books / Creative Minds Press
Behavioral Sciences Research Press, Inc.
Best Life Media
Beyond Words Publishing, Inc.
Black Forest Press and The Tennessee Publishing House
Blue Lupin Press
Book Marketing Solutions
Brain Injury Success Books
Brason-Sargar Publications
Brenner Information Group
Broken Jaw Press
Bronze Girl Productions, Inc.
CANADIAN MONEYSAVER
Capalo Press
Center for Thanatology Research & Education, Inc.
Chicago Spectrum Press
Citiria Publishing
Common Boundaries
Communication Creativity
Crane Press
Creative Creations Consulting Publishing Company
Crystal Dreams Publishing
Cypress House
D.B.A. Books
DAILY WORD
Dancing Lemur Press, L.L.C.
Dash-Hill, LLC
Dawn Sign Press
Delaney Day Press
DLite Press
Dominion Global Publishing
Down There Press
dreamslaughter
DTS Group, Inc.
EbonyEnergy Publishing, Inc.
Ecrivez!
Edenscape Publishing Company
Elite Books
Equine Graphics Publishing Group: New Concord Press, SmallHorse Press, SunDrop
Falcon Publishing, LTD
Nicolin Fields Publishing, Inc.
FMA Publishing
Foremost Press
Fulcrum, Inc.
Future Horizons, Inc.
Goblin Fern Press
GoldenHouse Publishing Group
Green Square Publishing
Hannacroix Creek Books, Inc
Harbor House Law Press, Inc.
HEAL Foundation Press
Health Press NA Inc.
Himalayan Institute Press
Holbrook Street Press
Hunter House Inc., Publishers
IMOCO Publishing
Impact Publishers, Inc.
Inkwater Press
InsideOut Press
Intuitive Moon Media
Islewest Publishing
JOURNAL OF PSYCHOACTIVE DRUGS
JPS Publishing Company
KABBALAH

Kallisti Publishing
Knowledge Concepts Publishing
Lake Street Press
Leave No Sister Behind Publications
A.P. Lee & Co., Ltd.
Legacy Audio Books, Inc.
Lemon Grove Press
LifeSkill Institute, Inc.
LightLines Publishing
LIVING CHEAP NEWS
Long & Silverman Publishing, Inc.
The Love and Logic Press, Inc.
Loving Healing Press, Inc.
Luminous Epinoia Press
Markowski International Publishers
Meek Publishing
Mendham Publishing
Middleway Press
Millennium Vision Press
Mind Power Publishing
Music City Publishing
New Paradigm Books
New Win Publishing
New World Library
New World Library
Nolo Press Occidental
North Star Books
Noved Audio
Nunciata
Oak Tree Press
Origin Press
Paladin Media Group
Papoose Publishing
Peachtree Publishers, Ltd.
Penworth Publishing
Perpetual Press
Plain Philosophy Center
Platinum Dreams Publishing
The Poetry Center Press/Shoestring Press
Practically Shameless Press
Princess Publishing
QED Press
Quill Driver Books
Rainbow Books, Inc.
Ravenhawk Books
RedJack
River Press
Ronin Publishing, Inc.
Sagamore Publishing
Sassy Sunflower Books
See Sharp Press
Sidran Institute
SO YOUNG!
Socratic Consulting Group
Soto Publishing Company
Sound View Publishing, Inc.
Star Publish LLC
STARNOTES
Starry Night Publishing
Steel Balls Press
Stewart Publishing & Printing
Studio 4 Productions An imprint of Quick Publishing, LC
Successful Kids Publishing
Summerland Publishing
Sunrise Health Coach Publications
Swedenborg Foundation
Sweet People Publishing
Third Dimension Publishing
Timeless Books
Top 20 Press
Twilight Times Books
Unity House
UNITY MAGAZINE
Upheaval Media
Upper Access Inc. Book Publishers
VanderWyk & Burnham
Virginia City Publishing Co. LLC
Vision Works Publishing

Wheatmark Book Publishing
Whiskey Creek Press
Whole Person Associates Inc.
Willfam Publishing Co.
Wilshire Books Inc.
WindRiver Publishing
Wisdom Publications, Inc.
Women of Diversity Productions, Inc.
Women of Diversity Productions, Inc.
World Gumbo Publishing
Write Now Publishing Company
Yes International Publishers
Zoilita Grant MS CCHt.
Zumaya Publications LLC

SENIOR CITIZENS

Creative With Words Publications (CWW)
Down There Press
Dunamis House
Equine Graphics Publishing Group: New Concord Press, SmallHorse Press, SunDrop
Fitness Press
Grace House Publishing
Guarionex Press Ltd.
HEALMB Publishing
LifeCircle Press
Pineapple Press, Inc.
The Poetry Center Press/Shoestring Press
Quill Driver Books
Rayve Productions Inc.
Sagamore Publishing
SO YOUNG!
Sound Enterprises Publishing
Starry Night Publishing
Studio 4 Productions An imprint of Quick Publishing, LC
TAPROOT, a journal of older writers
Wise Press

SEX, SEXUALITY

A Midsummer Night's Press
AK Press
Al-Galaxy Publishing Corporation
ANHEDONIA
Assilem 9 Publications
BLACK LACE
BLACKFIRE
CAUSE & EFFECT MAGAZINE
CESUM MAGAZINE
CONSCIENCE: The Newsjournal of Catholic Opinion
Crystal Dreams Publishing
Cynic Press
EbonyEnergy Publishing, Inc.
Enlightened Living Publishing, LLC
Ephemera Bound Publishing
FEMINIST STUDIES
FLUENT ASCENSION
GEM Literary Foundation Press
GLB Publishers
GRAY AREAS
HARVARD JOURNAL OF LAW AND GENDER
The Haworth Press
HOT FLASHES: Not a Menopause Thang
Hunter House Inc., Publishers
HYPATIA: A Journal of Feminist Philosophy
Impact Publishers, Inc.
Knowledge Concepts Publishing
KUMQUAT MERINGUE
LOVING MORE: New Models for Relationships
Luminous Epinoia Press
Lunar Offensive Publications
MALEDICTA: The International Journal of Verbal Aggression
March Books
MEAT FOR TEA: THE VALLEY REVIEW
MEAT: A Journal of Writing and Materiality
A Melody from an Immigrant's Soul
MGW (Mom Guess What) Newsmagazine
MIP Company

Muse World Media Group
NAMBLA BULLETIN
One Spirit Press
PAGAN AMERICA
Passion Power Press, Inc
Pussywillow
Red Alder Books
RED FEZ ENTERTAINMENT
Red Rock Press
Rodnik Publishing Co.
Sentient Publications, LLC
SHORTRUNS
Six Ft. Swells Press
Skullvines Press
Speck Press
Squire Press
Steel Balls Press
SterlingHouse Publisher
Synergy Press
Titan Press
Transcending Mundane, Inc.
The True Bill Press
2L Publishing, LLC
Willfam Publishing Co.
Wilshire Books Inc.
Zygote Publishing

SEXUAL ABUSE

Assilem 9 Publications
Colerith Press
CURRENTS: New Scholarship in the Human Services
GEM Literary Foundation Press
Islewest Publishing
Jalmar Press/Innerchoice Publishing
JOURNAL OF CHILD AND YOUTH CARE
Kodiak Media Group
Loving Healing Press, Inc.
Metallo House Publishers
Parenting Press, Inc.
Practically Shameless Press
Sidran Institute
Synergy Press
TEEN VOICES MAGAZINE

SHAKER

Blue Moose Press
TRUTH SEEKER

SHAKESPEARE

APOSTROPHE: USCB Journal of the Arts
Bandanna Books
Blue Moose Press
Empire Publishing Service
THE ENGLISH CLARION
Five Star Publications, Inc.
Idylls Press
Players Press, Inc.
74th Street Productions, L.L.C.
THE SHAKESPEARE NEWSLETTER

SHIPWRECKS

Caribbean Books-Panama
The Glencannon Press
LAKE SUPERIOR MAGAZINE
WEST GOES SOUTH
Wilderness Adventure Books
WORLD POETRY SHOWCASE

G.B. SHAW

ENGLISH LITERATURE IN TRANSITION, 1880-1920
THE INDEPENDENT SHAVIAN
IRISH LITERARY SUPPLEMENT
Limelight Editions
Pennsylvania State University Press
SHAW: THE ANNUAL OF BERNARD SHAW STUDIES

SHORT STORIES

Abecedarian books, Inc.

THE ADIRONDACK REVIEW
Ageless Press
ALASKA QUARTERLY REVIEW
THE AMERICAN DRIVEL REVIEW
AMERICAN JONES BUILDING & MAINTENANCE
AMERICAN LETTERS & COMMENTARY
AMERICAN LITERARY REVIEW
ANCIENT PATHS
Androgyne Books
APPLE VALLEY REVIEW: A Journal of Contemporary
  Literature
ART:MAG
ARTISTIC RAMBLINGS
Assilem 9 Publications
Asylum Arts
THE BALTIMORE REVIEW
Bandanna Books
THE BEAR DELUXE MAGAZINE
Bear Star Press
BEATLICK NEWS
BEGINNING MAGAZINE
Bel Canto Press
BIG MUDDY: Journal of the Mississippi River Valley
Biographical Publishing Company
BITTER OLEANDER
BkMk Press
Black Forest Press and The Tennessee Publishing House
Black Heron Press
Black Lawrence Press
BLACK MAGNOLIAS LITERARY JOURNAL
Blue Cubicle Press, LLC
Blue Lupin Press
BLUELINE
Brave Ulysses Books
Broken Jaw Press
Broken Shadow Publications
BUFFALO SPREE
Burning Books
CAIRN: The New St. Andrews Review
Cantarabooks LLC
CAPCAT
CAUSE & EFFECT MAGAZINE
Central Avenue Press
Cervena Barva Press
CHIRON REVIEW
CIMARRON REVIEW
Clark-Nova Books
Cloud 9 Publishing
Coffee House Press
COLD-DRILL
COMPASS ROSE
CONCEIT MAGAZINE
CONJUNCTIONS
COSMOPSIS QUARTERLY
Cotton Tree Press
CRAB CREEK REVIEW
CRAB ORCHARD REVIEW
THE CREAM CITY REVIEW
Culturelink Press
CUTTHROAT, A JOURNAL OF THE ARTS
Cyberwit.net
Deerbrook Editions
Devil Mountain Books
DLite Press
DOWNSTATE STORY
DREAM FANTASY INTERNATIONAL
ECOTONE: Reimagining Place
Ecrivez!
Edenscape Publishing Company
Eros Books
EVANSVILLE REVIEW
Evening Street Press
First Journey Publishing Company
Fithian Press
Five Fingers Press
FIVE FINGERS REVIEW
Flapjack Press
THE FLORIDA REVIEW

FLUENT ASCENSION
Flume Press
FOLIO: A Literary Journal of American University
Four Way Books
4 Your Spirit Productions
FOURTEEN HILLS: The SFSU Review
THE FUNNY TIMES
The Galileo Press Ltd.
THE GEORGIA REVIEW
GERTRUDE
Gertrude Press
GHOTI MAGAZINE
GIN BENDER POETRY REVIEW
Glass Tower Press
GOLD DUST
GoodSAMARitan Press
Goose River Press
Gorilla Convict Publications
Goss Press
GRASSLANDS REVIEW
GRASSLIMB
Graywolf Press
GUD MAGAZINE (Greatest Uncommon Denominator)
GULF COAST
HAPA NUI
HARDBOILED
HAWAI'I PACIFIC REVIEW
Helicon Nine Editions
Hidden Valley Farm, Publisher
Homa & Sekey Books
Hood Press
A HUDSON VIEW POETRY DIGEST
ICONOCLAST
ILLOGICAL MUSE
Imago Press
Immediate Direction Publications
IMPress
In Between Books
Indigo Ink Press, Inc.
THE INK SLINGER REVIEW
INKY TRAIL NEWS
ISTANBUL LITERARY REVIEW
ITALIAN AMERICANA
Jako Books
THE JOURNAL OF AFRICAN TRAVEL-WRITING
Juel House Publishers and Literary Services
THE KENYON REVIEW
KESTREL: A Journal of Literature and Art
Kings Estate Press
Allen A. Knoll Publishers
LAKE EFFECT
THE LEDGE
LEFT CURVE
LEO Productions LLC.
Liberty Publishing Company, Inc.
Light of New Orleans Publishing
Lilly Press
LINES + STARS
THE LISTENING EYE
LITERARY HOUSE REVIEW
LITTLE BALKANS REVIEW
Loonfeather Press
LULLWATER REVIEW
THE LUMMOX JOURNAL
Lummox Press
THE MACGUFFIN
MAIN STREET RAG
MANOA: A Pacific Journal of International Writing
MANY MOUNTAINS MOVING
McPherson & Company Publishers
THE MEADOW
MEAT FOR TEA: THE VALLEY REVIEW
A Melody from an Immigrant's Soul
MID-AMERICAN REVIEW
Mid-List Press
MIDNIGHT STREET
MINESHAFT
MIP Company

MISSISSIPPI CROW
Mountain State Press
Murder Slim Press
MUSE: A Quarterly Journal of The Lit
MYSTERY ISLAND MAGAZINE
NATURAL BRIDGE
NEO: Literary Magazine
NEW ENGLAND BY RAIL
NEW MADRID
THE NEW RENAISSANCE, an international magazine of
   ideas & opinions, emphasizing literature & the arts
New Rivers Press, Inc.
NORTH CAROLINA LITERARY REVIEW
NORTHWEST REVIEW
NOUN VS. VERB
One Less Press
OPEN MINDS QUARTERLY
Open Wide Books
ORACLE STORY
THE ORPHAN LEAF REVIEW
Oyster River Press
PACIFIC COAST JOURNAL
Paladin Media Group
PAPERPLATES
Papillon Presse
Paris Press
Partisan Press
PASSAGES NORTH
Passing Through Publications
PAVEMENT SAW
PEARL
Pendragonian Publications
PENNY DREADFUL: Tales and Poems of Fantastic Terror
Phoenix Illusion
THE PINCH
PLEASANT LIVING
Pocol Press
POETICA MAGAZINE, Reflections of Jewish Thought
The Poetry Center
POGO STICK
Polar Bear & Company
PORTLAND REVIEW
PRAIRIE SCHOONER
PREMONITIONS
The Press at Foggy Bottom
PublishAmerica, LLLP.
Punkin House Press
Pussywillow
Pygmy Forest Press
Pyncheon House
THE QUIET FEATHER
RAINBOW CURVE
RATTAPALLAX
Raular Publishing
THE RAVEN CHRONICLES
Red Coyote Press
Red Dragon Press
RED FEZ ENTERTAINMENT
RED ROCK REVIEW
Red Tiger Press
RED WHEELBARROW
The Reed Edwards Company
REFLECTIONS LITERARY JOURNAL
RIVER POETS JOURNAL
Rowan Mountain Press
THE RUE BELLA
Rural Messengers Press
SAGE OF CONSCIOUSNESS E-ZINE
SALAMANDER
Salt Publishing
THE SAVAGE KICK LITERARY MAGAZINE
SEWANEE REVIEW
Shared Roads Press
SHORT STORY
SIDE OF GRITS
Silenced Press
Skullvines Press
SKYLINE LITERARY MAGAZINE

Skyline Publications
Slipdown Mountain Publications LLC
The Smith (subsidiary of The Generalist Assn., Inc.)
Gibbs Smith, Publisher
SOJOURN: A Journal of the Arts
SONGS OF INNOCENCE
Soto Publishing Company
SOUNDINGS REVIEW
SOUTH DAKOTA REVIEW
Southeast Missouri State University Press
Southern Methodist University Press
SP QUILL MAGAZINE
SPINNINGS...INTENSE TALES OF LIFE MAGAZINE
The Spirit That Moves Us Press, Inc.
THE STINGING FLY
Stormline Press, Inc.
STRUGGLE: A Magazine of Proletarian Revolutionary
   Literature
STUDIO ONE
SUB-TERRAIN
SunShine Press Publications, Inc.
SWILL
SWINK
SYCAMORE REVIEW
Synergy Press
TAPROOT LITERARY REVIEW
Taproot Press Publishing Co.
THE TARPEIAN ROCK
The Teitan Press, Inc.
1097 MAGAZINE
THIRD COAST
THIRDEYE MAGAZINE
Thirdeye Publications
13TH MOON
Three Bean Press
Thunder Rain Publishing Corp.
Tupelo Press
Turnstone Press
Twilight Tales, Inc.
2L Publishing, LLC
Underwhich Editions
UPSTAIRS AT DUROC
Vehicule Press
VERSAL
THE VIRGINIA QUARTERLY REVIEW
VOICE(S)
WEBER: The Contemporary West
The WhaleInn Publishing House (1998)
White Pine Press
Wise Press
Wordcraft of Oregon, LLC
Wordsonthestreet
Wordwrights Canada
WORKERS WRITE!
Write Now Publishing Company
Writers House Press
XAVIER REVIEW
X-Ray Book Co.
Zerx Press

SINGLES

Aspicomm Media
Down There Press
Fruitbearer Publishing, LLC
JPS Publishing Company
Nunciata
Papillon Presse
Penthe Publishing
Pussywillow
SHORTRUNS
SO YOUNG!
Steel Balls Press

SOCIAL MOVEMENTS

Allbook Books
ALTERNATIVE PRESS INDEX
ATLANTIS: A Women's Studies Journal/Revue d'etudes
   sur les femmes

Banks Channel Books
Calaca Press
Deep Well Publishing Company
Hood Press
Insight Press
MOUTH: Voice of the Dis-Labeled Nation
Obie Joe Media
Partisan Press
POETRYREPAIRS: Contemporary International Poetry
Poplar Leaf Press
South End Press
THIRDEYE MAGAZINE
WHEELHOUSE MAGAZINE

SOCIAL SECURITY

CURRENTS: New Scholarship in the Human Services
Vestibular Disorders Association

SOCIAL WORK

Authentic Publishing LLC
CURRENTS: New Scholarship in the Human Services
Dreams Due Media Group, Inc.
The Haworth Press
INTERCULTURE
Islewest Publishing
JOURNAL OF CHILD AND YOUTH CARE
JOURNAL OF PSYCHOACTIVE DRUGS
Loving Healing Press, Inc.
Lyceum Books, Inc.
MGW (Mom Guess What) Newsmagazine
OPEN MINDS QUARTERLY
Passion Power Press, Inc
The Press at Foggy Bottom
Raven Publishing, Inc.
THE SOCIOLOGICAL QUARTERLY
Studio 4 Productions An imprint of Quick Publishing, LC
SYMBOLIC INTERACTION
VanderWyk & Burnham

SOCIALIST

AIM MAGAZINE
ALTERNATIVE PRESS INDEX
BLUE COLLAR REVIEW
Children Of Mary
Clarity Press, Inc.
Dufour Editions Inc.
FIDELIS ET VERUS
Global Options
International Publishers Co. Inc.
JEWISH CURRENTS
LEFT CURVE
Library Juice Press
Litwin Books
Maisonneuve Press
Mehring Books, Inc.
THE NEO-COMINTERN
NEW UNIONIST
Open Wide Books
Partisan Press
Pathfinder Press
PEMMICAN
Quale Press
RED LAMP
Red Letter Press
Smyrna Press
SOCIAL JUSTICE: A JOURNAL OF CRIME, CONFLICT, & WORLD ORDER
STRUGGLE: A Magazine of Proletarian Revolutionary Literature
SUB-TERRAIN
West End Press

SOCIETY

Assilem 9 Publications
Authentic Publishing LLC
AZTLAN: A Journal of Chicano Studies
Back House Books
BLUE COLLAR REVIEW

BORDERLANDS: Texas Poetry Review
Borealis Press Limited
Chelsea Green Publishing Company
Community Service, Inc.
COSMOPSIS QUARTERLY
Crandall, Dostie & Douglass Books, Inc.
CRITICAL REVIEW
Dog's Eye View Media
DRAMA GARDEN
The Edwin Mellen Press
ETC Publications
FOURTH WORLD REVIEW
Frontline Publications
GLB Publishers
Global Options
The Heather Foundation
INTERCULTURE
Kettering Foundation Press
KETTERING REVIEW
LIBERTY
Life Media
THE LONG TERM VIEW: A Journal of Informed Opinion
March Books
MEDICAL HISTORY
Midnight Whistler Publishers
THE MIDWEST QUARTERLY
New Creature Press
NEW SOLUTIONS
NIGHTLIFE MAGAZINE
Nish Publishing Company
OTHER INVESTIGATIONS
Partisan Press
The People's Press
POETRYREPAIRS: Contemporary International Poetry
Ragged Edge Press
Red Alder Books
Saint Bob Press
Savant Garde Workshop
SHARE INTERNATIONAL
SOCIAL JUSTICE: A JOURNAL OF CRIME, CONFLICT, & WORLD ORDER
SOCIAL PROBLEMS
Southwest Research and Information Center
THOUGHTS FOR ALL SEASONS: The Magazine of Epigrams
Thundercloud Books
UBC Press
UCLA Chicano Studies Research Center Press
UTNE READER
Volcano Press, Inc
Wellcome Trust Centre for the History of Medicine at UCL
The Wessex Collective

SOCIOLOGY

African American Images
AIM MAGAZINE
ALTERNATIVE PRESS INDEX
Appalachian Consortium Press
THE ART OF ABUNDANCE
Bauu Press
Black Rose Books Ltd.
Broken Rifle Press
Canadian Educators' Press
Chandler & Sharp Publishers, Inc.
CINEASTE MAGAZINE
Community Service, Inc.
CONTEXTS: UNDERSTANDING PEOPLE IN THEIR SOCIAL WORLDS
dreamslaughter
The Edwin Mellen Press
ESPERANTIC STUDIES
FEMINIST STUDIES
Frontline Publications
Gain Publications
Gallaudet University Press
Global Options
GRAY AREAS
Haight-Ashbury Publications

The Heather Foundation
INTERCULTURE
Interlink Publishing Group, Inc.
ITALIAN AMERICANA
JOURNAL OF PSYCHOACTIVE DRUGS
KAIROS, A Journal of Contemporary Thought and
   Criticism
KETTERING REVIEW
Kumarian Press
Libertas Press, LLC.
Library Juice Press
Litwin Books
LO STRANIERO: The Stranger, Der Fremde, L'Etranger
The Love and Logic Press, Inc.
MOUTH: Voice of the Dis-Labeled Nation
THE NEW ENGLAND QUARTERLY
NEW SOLUTIONS
NOVA RELIGIO
Open Court Publishing Company
OPEN MINDS QUARTERLY
Papoose Publishing
Pleasure Boat Studio: A Literary Press (including imprints
   Caravel Books and Aequitas Books, and the division
   Empty Bowl Press)
Poor Richard's Press
RED LAMP
RELIGION & AMERICAN CULTURE
School for Advanced Research Press
SCIENCE AND TECHNOLOGY
SOCIAL JUSTICE: A JOURNAL OF CRIME, CONFLICT,
   & WORLD ORDER
SOCIAL PROBLEMS
SOCIOLOGICAL PERSPECTIVES
THE SOCIOLOGICAL QUARTERLY
Superior Christian Press
SYMBOLIC INTERACTION
Univelt, Inc.
Unlimited Publishing LLC
WSQ (formerly WOMEN'S STUDIES QUARTERLY)

SOLAR

Brenner Information Group
The Film Instruction Company of America
Life Media
NATURAL LIFE

SOUTH

Anvil Publishers, Inc.
Appalachian Consortium Press
APPLE VALLEY REVIEW: A Journal of Contemporary
   Literature
BIG MUDDY: Journal of the Mississippi River Valley
John F. Blair, Publisher
Bright Mountain Books
Harbor House
JAMES DICKEY REVIEW
Margaret Media, Inc.
Midmarch Arts Press
NEW MADRID
Ninety-Six Press
Old Sport Publishing Company
REFLECTIONS LITERARY JOURNAL
Saint Bob Press
THE SOUTHERN QUARTERLY: A Journal of the Arts in
   the South
Sherwood Sugden & Company, Publishers
University of Arkansas Press
XAVIER REVIEW

SOUTH AMERICA

Hope Publishing House
Inner City Press
Montemayor Press
University Press of Colorado

SOUTH CAROLINA

Iris Publishing Group, Inc (Iris Press / Tellico Books)
Premium Press America

Rock Spring Press Inc.
University of South Carolina Press

SOUTHWEST

APPLE VALLEY REVIEW: A Journal of Contemporary
   Literature
Balcony Media, Inc.
BOOKS OF THE SOUTHWEST
BORDERLANDS: Texas Poetry Review
CONCHO RIVER REVIEW
FISH DRUM MAGAZINE
Hill Country Books
JAVELINA BI-MONTHLY
KUMQUAT MERINGUE
La Alameda Press
LPD Press
Malki-Ballena Press
THE MEADOW
Mountain Media
Naturegraph Publishers
Pruett Publishing Company
RED ROCK REVIEW
Santa Fe Writers Project
School for Advanced Research Press
Gibbs Smith, Publisher
SOUTH DAKOTA REVIEW
Southern Methodist University Press
Southwest Research and Information Center
Sunstone Press
TRADICION REVISTA
Two Eagles Press International
University of Utah Press
Utah State University Press
VOICES FROM THE EARTH
WEBER: The Contemporary West
WESTERN AMERICAN LITERATURE

SPACE

AAS HISTORY SERIES
ADVANCES IN THE ASTRONAUTICAL SCIENCES
EcceNova Editions
JAMES DICKEY REVIEW
JOURNAL OF SCIENTIFIC EXPLORATION
ODYSSEY: Adventures in Science
RedJack
SCIENCE AND TECHNOLOGY
THE STAR BEACON
Windward Publishing, An Imprint of Finney Company

SPAIN

ABSINTHE: New European Writing
INTERNATIONAL POETRY REVIEW
Latin American Literary Review Press
New Win Publishing
SYMPOSIUM
TORRE DE PAPEL

SPEAKING

Book Marketing Solutions
Crane Press
Finney Company, Inc.
Goblin Fern Press
Multi-Media Publications Inc.
Music City Publishing
74th Street Productions, L.L.C.
Strata Publishing, Inc.
Unlimited Publishing LLC
Wheatmark Book Publishing
WOMEN AND LANGUAGE
World Gumbo Publishing

SPIRITUAL

ABRAMELIN: a Journal of Poetry and Magick
Act on Wisdom
Alamo Square Press
Allwrite Advertising and Publishing
Altair Publications
America West Publishers

Aquila Ink Publishing
THE ART OF ABUNDANCE
ASCENT
Ash Tree Publishing
Athanor Books
Aura Productions, LLC
Auromere Books and Imports
Balanced Books Publishing
Barney Press
Barrytown/Station Hill Press
BEGINNINGS - A Magazine for the Novice Writer
THE BELTANE PAPERS: A Journal of Women's
  Mysteries
Best Life Media
Beyond Words Publishing, Inc.
Birth Day Publishing Company
BLUE MOUNTAIN
BOTH SIDES NOW
Brason-Sargar Publications
Brick Road Poetry Press
Burns Park Publishers
C&R Press
Cassandra Press, Inc.
Children Of Mary
CHRISTIAN*NEW AGE QUARTERLY
Church Leadership Library (Canadian Office)
Church Leadership Library (US Office)
CIRCLE INC., THE MAGAZINE
Circle of Friends Books
Clearwater Publishing Co.
Common Boundaries
CONCEIT MAGAZINE
DAILY WORD
Delaney Day Press
Dervla Publishing, LLC
Devi Press, Inc.
Dharma Publishing
Dominion Global Publishing
DREAM FANTASY INTERNATIONAL
dreamslaughter
Dumouriez Publishing
Earth Star Publications
EMERGING
EnlightenNext
Flapjack Press
4 Your Spirit Productions
FRIENDS OF PEACE PILGRIM
Galde Press, Inc.
Gateways Books And Tapes
Gloger Family Books
Goblin Fern Press
Good Book Publishing Company
Grateful Press
Guarionex Press Ltd.
Halo Publishing International
Harbor House
HEAL Foundation Press
Heartsong Books
HEAVEN BONE MAGAZINE
Heaven Bone Press
Himalayan Institute Press
Ho Logos Press
Holmes House
HOLY ROLLERS
Hope Publishing House
A HUDSON VIEW POETRY DIGEST
Iconoclast Press
ILLUMINATIONS LITERARY JOURNAL
IMAGE: ART, FAITH, MYSTERY
In Print Publishing
InsideOut Press
J. Mark Press
Jigsaw Press
Just Sisters Publications
KABBALAH
KEREM: Creative Explorations in Judaism
Lake Street Press
Lamp Light Press

The Leaping Frog Press
A.P. Lee & Co., Ltd.
Lemieux International Ltd.
LEO Productions LLC.
Life Energy Media
LightLines Publishing
LP Publications (Teleos Institute)
A Melody from an Immigrant's Soul
The Kenneth G. Mills Foundation
Missing Man Press
Morgen Publishing Incorporated
Munsey Music
My Heart Yours Publishing
Nautilus Publishing Company
New Atlantean Press
New Knowledge Press
New Native Press
New Paradigm Books
New World Library
NEWWITCH
Nilgiri Press
NOLA-MAGICK Press
One Spirit Press
Origin Press
OUT OF LINE
Paragon House Publishers
Pellingham Casper Communications
PhoeniX in Print
Platinum Dreams Publishing
Practically Shameless Press
PREP Publishing
PublishAmerica, LLLP.
THE QUILLDRIVER
Raular Publishing
RFD
Roaring Lion Publishing
Ronin Publishing, Inc.
S4N Books
SAGEWOMAN
Saint Mary's Press
SCP JOURNAL
SECRETUM MEUM MIHI
Secretum Meum Mihi Press
SelectiveHouse Publishers, Inc.
Sentient Publications, LLC
SHAMAN'S DRUM: A Journal of Experiential Shamanism
SHARE INTERNATIONAL
Sibyl Publications, Inc
SO YOUNG!
Socratic Consulting Group
SOM Publishing, division of School of Metaphysics
SPIRITCHASER
THE STAR BEACON
STARNOTES
State University of New York Press
Stewart Publishing & Printing
Summerland Publishing
SunShine Press Publications, Inc.
Swedenborg Foundation
Synergy Press
T'AI CHI
Three Pyramids Publishing
THRESHOLDS JOURNAL
Timeless Books
Titan Press
Titlewaves Publishing; Writers Direct
TURNING WHEEL
Twinteum Artist, Inc.
Tyr Publishing
Unity House
UNITY MAGAZINE
UnKnownTruths.com Publishing Company
VOICES ISRAEL
Wayfarer Publications
The Wessex Collective
WHAT IS ENLIGHTENMENT?
White Buck Publishing
White Thread Press

756

Wilderness Ministries
Willowood Press
Wind Eagle Press
Wisdom Publications, Inc.
THE WISE WOMAN
Write Now Publishing Company
Yes International Publishers
YMAA Publication Center
Zumaya Publications LLC

SPORTS, OUTDOORS

ADIRONDAC
Adirondack Mountain Club, Inc.
AMERICAN FORESTS
AMERICAN HIKER
American Hiking Society
Anchor Cove Publishing, Inc.
Appalachian House
Authentic Publishing LLC
Avery Color Studios
Avery Color Studios
AzurAlive
Backcountry Publishing
Birch Brook Press
Black Dome Press Corp.
John F. Blair, Publisher
Bonus Books, Inc.
CATAMARAN SAILOR
The Center Press
Chicago Review Press
Clearwater Publishing Co.
Coastal 181
Cornell Maritime Press/Tidewater Publishers
dbS Productions
DISCGOLFER
Dixon-Price Publishing
Dunamis House
DWELLING PORTABLY
Ecopress, An Imprint of Finney Company
ETC Publications
Nicolin Fields Publishing, Inc.
Flying Pencil Publications
Front Row Experience
Fulcrum, Inc.
The Glencannon Press
Global Sports Productions, Ltd.
The Great Rift Press
HANG GLIDING & PARAGLIDING
Heyday Books
Hill Country Books
Iconoclast Press
Info Net Publishing
Kakibubu Media Limited
Keokee Co. Publishing, Inc.
Laureate Press
Liberty Publishing Company, Inc.
THE LISTENING EYE
McBooks Press, Inc.
Menasha Ridge Press
MGW (Mom Guess What) Newsmagazine
Mountain Press Publishing Co.
NATIONAL MASTERS NEWS
New England Cartographics, Inc.
New Win Publishing
Nish Publishing Company
Northern Publishing
Old Sport Publishing Company
OUT YOUR BACKDOOR: The Magazine of Do-It-Yourself Adventure and Homegrown Culture
Paladin Enterprises, Inc.
Para Publishing
Pavement Saw Press
Peartree Books & Music
Penthe Publishing
Perpetual Press
Pocol Press
Premium Press America
Price World Publishing

Pruett Publishing Company
Ram Press
Redwood Creek Publishing
Sagamore Publishing
SANDPOINT MAGAZINE
SEA KAYAKER
Set Sail Productions, LLC
Genny Smith Books
Southern Methodist University Press
SPECIALTY TRAVEL INDEX
SPITBALL: The Literary Baseball Magazine
Summerset Press
Sunbelt Publications
Synergistic Press
Tamal Vista Publications
Tortuga Books
Tres Picos Press
Two Thousand Three Associates
Two Thousand Three Associates
University of Virginia Press
John Wade, Publisher
WASHINGTON TRAILS
Whitston Publishing Co.
Wilderness Adventure Books
Wilderness Press
WISCONSIN TRAILS
Wish Publishing
Wood Thrush Books
YMAA Publication Center
Zagier & Urruty Publications

STOICISM

SIDE OF GRITS

STORYTELLING

Aardvark Enterprises (Sole Proprietorship of J. Alvin Speers)
Alaska Native Language Center
Ammons Communications; Imprint: Catch the Spirit of Appalachia
ARTELLA: the waltz of words and art
Caribbean Books-Panama
COSMOPSIS QUARTERLY
Empire Publishing Service
Faith Builders Resource Group
Falcon Publishing, LTD
Grey Sparrow Press
Halo Publishing International
HOT FLASHES: Not a Menopause Thang
A HUDSON VIEW POETRY DIGEST
JUNIOR STORYTELLER
THE KIDS' STORYTELLING CLUB WEBSITE
Lilly Press
LITERARY HOUSE REVIEW
Malki Museum Press
March Books
MISSISSIPPI CROW
Music City Publishing
New Day Publishing, Inc.
THE NEW FORMALIST
Nish Publishing Company
Panther Books
PAPERPLATES
Perrin Press
THE PINCH
The Press at Foggy Bottom
RAINBOW CURVE
THE RAVEN CHRONICLES
RED ROCK REVIEW
RIVER TEETH: A Journal of Nonfiction Narrative
Roaring Lion Publishing
ROCTOBER COMICS AND MUSIC
Sagamore Publishing
Sassy Sunflower Books
Savor Publishing House, Inc.
SKYLINE LITERARY MAGAZINE
Starcherone Books
Stormline Press, Inc.

Storycraft Publishing
TAPROOT LITERARY REVIEW
THE2NDHAND
Titus Home Publishing
Ultra Media Publications
VOICE(S)
The Wessex Collective
Willowood Press
Yellow Moon Press

SUFISM

CONTEMPORARY GHAZALS
Hohm Press
Ibex Publishers, Inc.
New Paradigm Books
One Spirit Press
Progressive Press; Tree of Life Publications
S4N Books
White Thread Press

SUPERNATURAL

BEGINNINGS - A Magazine for the Novice Writer
Cheops Books
EcceNova Editions
Enigmatic Ink
The Fiction Works
Flapjack Press
Galde Press, Inc.
Glass Tower Press
Harbor House
Harvest Shadows Publications
Immediate Direction Publications
Intuitive Moon Media
Jigsaw Press
L&L Dreamspell
Lake Claremont Press
LOW BUDGET SCIENCE FICTION
LULLABY HEARSE
March Books
MIDNIGHT STREET
MYSTERY ISLAND MAGAZINE
NEWWITCH
North Country Books, Inc.
RED MARE
ROCKY MOUNTAIN KC NEWS
Rocky Mountain KC Publishing Co.
Skullvines Press
SPINNINGS...INTENSE TALES OF LIFE MAGAZINE
STARNOTES
Three Pyramids Publishing
Triskelion Publishing
UnKnownTruths.com Publishing Company
Vanilla Heart Publishing
Westgate Press
Whiskey Creek Press
Willfam Publishing Co.
The Wolf Pirate Project Inc.
Youthful Wisdom Press
ZAHIR: A Journal of Speculative Fiction

SURREALISM

AK Press
Androgyne Books
APPLE VALLEY REVIEW: A Journal of Contemporary
  Literature
Arjuna Library Press
Asylum Arts
Biographical Publishing Company
BITTER OLEANDER
BUST DOWN THE DOOR AND EAT ALL THE
  CHICKENS: A Journal of Absurd and Surreal Fiction
Citiria Publishing
COMPASS ROSE
DIET SOAP
Enigmatic Ink
GRASSLIMB
Highest Hurdle Press
JOURNAL OF REGIONAL CRITICISM

Leaf Garden Press
Leaping Dog Press
Lunar Offensive Publications
Marymark Press
MISSISSIPPI CROW
New Native Press
O!!Zone
O!!ZONE, A LITERARY-ART ZINE
Otoliths
Panther Books
PAVEMENT SAW
Pavement Saw Press
PEMMICAN
Phrygian Press
PLOPLOP
PRESA
Quale Press
Ridgeway Press of Michigan
Sage Hill Press
Silenced Press
SOUNDINGS REVIEW
Starcherone Books
Subsynchronuos Press
SWILL
Toad Press International Chapbook Series
Transcending Mundane, Inc.
Twisted Spoon Press
UNDERSTANDING MAGAZINE
VEIL: Journal of Darker Musings
VOX
VOX Press
Vulgar Marsala Press
The Wessex Collective
Westgate Press
Xenos Books
ZAHIR: A Journal of Speculative Fiction
ZYX

T'AI CHI

Abecedarian books, Inc.
Best Life Media
Syukhtun Editions
THE2NDHAND
YMAA Publication Center

TAPES & RECORDS

Affinity Publishers Services
ALMOST NORMAL COMICS and Other Oddities
Barrytown/Station Hill Press
Black Forest Press and The Tennessee Publishing House
Center For Self-Sufficiency
Cynic Press
DIRTY LINEN
EbonyEnergy Publishing, Inc.
FISH DRUM MAGAZINE
Free Books Inc.
Global Options
GRAY AREAS
Impact Publishers, Inc.
In Print Publishing
Ion Imagination Publishing, Ion Imagination Entertainment,
  Inc.
IT'S JUST THIS LITTLE CHROMIUM SWITCH HERE
MOBILE BEAT: The Mobile Entertainer's Magazine
NEW HOPE INTERNATIONAL REVIEW
New World Library
nine muses books
North Country Books, Inc.
Norton Coker Press
Open Wide Books
Piano Press
PLANTAGENET PRODUCTIONS, Libraries of Spoken
  Word Recordings and of Stagescripts
PULSAR POETRY WEBZINE
Pygmy Forest Press
Quiet Tymes, Inc.
SHORTRUNS
SO YOUNG!

Timeless Books
Underwhich Editions
Volcano Press, Inc
X-Ray Book Co.
Yellow Moon Press

TAROT

Aquila Ink Publishing
Best Life Media
Intuitive Moon Media
A Melody from an Immigrant's Soul
NEWWITCH
SAGEWOMAN
STARNOTES
Three Pyramids Publishing
White Crosslet Publishing Co
Zumaya Publications LLC

TAXES

CANADIAN MONEYSAVER
Claitor's Law Books & Publishing Division, Inc.
Long & Silverman Publishing, Inc.
Set Sail Productions, LLC
Tax Property Investor, Inc.
THE2NDHAND
TRUTH SEEKER
Upper Access Inc. Book Publishers

TECHNOLOGY

AB
Adams-Blake Publishing
Aegean Publishing Company
Brenner Information Group
EQUAL CONSTRUCTION RECORD
Frontline Publications
GREEN ANARCHY
Hobar Publications, A Division of Finney Company
IROL Press, LLC
Library Juice Press
MOBILE BEAT: The Mobile Entertainer's Magazine
New Knowledge Press
Open University of America Press
Piano Press
Rada Press, Inc.
Signalman Publishing
University of Akron Press
UnKnownTruths.com Publishing Company

TELEVISION

BOOK MARKETING UPDATE
Creative Writing and Publishing Company
Explorer Press
THE FREEDONIA GAZETTE: The Magazine Devoted to the Marx Brothers
Hollywood Creative Directory
Playdate Kids Publishing
RedJack
ROCTOBER COMICS AND MUSIC
Whelks Walk Press

TENNESSEE

Crane Press
Inner City Press
Iris Publishing Group, Inc (Iris Press / Tellico Books)
Premium Press America
UNDERSTANDING MAGAZINE

TEXAS

BORDERLANDS: Texas Poetry Review
Arthur H. Clark Co.
CONCHO RIVER REVIEW
HILL COUNTRY SUN
Historical Resources Press
IRON HORSE LITERARY REVIEW
JAVELINA BI-MONTHLY
Lazywood Press
LPD Press
Midmarch Arts Press

Nolo Press Occidental
Panther Creek Press
Premium Press America
Shearer Publishing
Southern Methodist University Press
Texas Tech University Press
TRADICION REVISTA
Two Eagles Press International
Van Cleave Publishing
WESTERN AMERICAN LITERATURE
Wings Press

TEXTBOOKS

Adams-Blake Publishing
Allwrite Advertising and Publishing
Aquarius Press
Ariko Publications
Bandanna Books
Black Forest Press and The Tennessee Publishing House
Bonus Books, Inc.
Book Marketing Solutions
Brookline Books
Canadian Educators' Press
Canadian Educators' Press
Chandler & Sharp Publishers, Inc.
Chicago Spectrum Press
Children Of Mary
Church Leadership Library (Canadian Office)
Church Leadership Library (US Office)
Citiria Publishing
Claitor's Law Books & Publishing Division, Inc.
Clearwater Publishing Co.
Cornell Maritime Press/Tidewater Publishers
Creative Creations Consulting Publishing Company
Crystal Publishers, Inc.
Ellechor Publishing House
Fathom Publishing Co.
The Fiction Works
FIDELIS ET VERUS
Focus Publishing/R. Pullins Co.
Fountain Publisher Limited
Front Row Experience
Galen Press, Ltd.
Gallaudet University Press
Gival Press
Green Hut Press
The Haworth Press
Hunter Publishing Corporation
Jamenair Ltd.
Journal of Pyrotechnics
Lamp Light Press
Lawells Publishing
Lightning Bug Learning Press
Loving Healing Press, Inc.
LrnIT Publishing Div. LRNIT CORPORATION
Nunciata
THE ORPHAN LEAF REVIEW
Paragon House Publishers
RFF Press / Resources for the Future
Saber Press
Saint Mary's Press
Scentouri, Publishing Division
Gibbs Smith, Publisher
Stewart Publishing & Printing
Sherwood Sugden & Company, Publishers
Wordsonthestreet

TEXTILES

Cooperative Press
DOLLS UNITED INTERACTIVE MAGAZINE
Mount Ida Press
NEW HOPE INTERNATIONAL REVIEW
ORNAMENT
Texas Tech University Press
TRADICION REVISTA
WORN FASHION JOURNAL

THEATRE

A & U AMERICA'S AIDS MAGAZINE
AFRICAN AMERICAN REVIEW
ANQ: A Quarterly Journal of Short Articles, Notes, and Reviews
BOMB MAGAZINE
Bordighera, Inc.
THE BROADKILL REVIEW: A Journal of Literature
Cantarabooks LLC
CAPCAT
Center for Japanese Studies
Cervena Barva Press
Creative Writing and Publishing Company
THE DALHOUSIE REVIEW
THE DRAMATIST
Empire Publishing Service
THE EUGENE O'NEILL REVIEW
4 Your Spirit Productions
THE FREEDONIA GAZETTE: The Magazine Devoted to the Marx Brothers
HAWAI'I REVIEW
Hollywood Creative Directory
HOME PLANET NEWS
ILLUMINATIONS LITERARY JOURNAL
IMAGE: ART, FAITH, MYSTERY
IRISH LITERARY SUPPLEMENT
LEO Productions LLC.
Limelight Editions
Magic Circle Press
MARQUEE
Nautilus Publishing Company
New Concept Press
THE NEW RENAISSANCE, an international magazine of ideas & opinions, emphasizing literature & the arts
Northwestern University Press
Open Hand Publishing LLC
Paris Press
Passeggiata Press, Inc.
Players Press, Inc.
Pogo Press, Incorporated
THE PRAIRIE JOURNAL OF CANADIAN LITERATURE
Preludium Publishers
The Press at Foggy Bottom
Roaring Lion Publishing
Santa Monica Press
Sentient Publications, LLC
74th Street Productions, L.L.C.
74th Street Productions, L.L.C.
THE SHAKESPEARE NEWSLETTER
Skullvines Press
THE SOUTHERN QUARTERLY: A Journal of the Arts in the South
SOUTHWEST COLORADO ARTS PERSPECTIVE
Spinifex Press
SUB-TERRAIN
THE THREEPENNY REVIEW
Tomart Publications
University of Tampa Press

THEOSOPHICAL

Altair Publications
Dwarf Lion Press
Ho Logos Press
A.P. Lee & Co., Ltd.
Luminous Epinoia Press
Lycanthrope Press
New Paradigm Books
NOLA-MAGICK Press
One Spirit Press
The Teitan Press, Inc.
Vulgar Marsala Press
WHAT IS ENLIGHTENMENT?
White Buck Publishing

THIRD WORLD, MINORITIES

ALTERNATIVE PRESS INDEX
Aunt Lute Books

Back House Books
BORDERLANDS: Texas Poetry Review
Bordighera, Inc.
Broken Rifle Press
Clarity Press, Inc.
COLLEGE LITERATURE
COLORLINES
THE COMSTOCK REVIEW
COOK PARTNERS
Disparate Voices
EbonyEnergy Publishing, Inc.
The Feminist Press at the City University of New York
First Journey Publishing Company
Florida Academic Press
FOURTH WORLD REVIEW
FROZEN WAFFLES
Frozen Waffles Press/Shattered Sidewalks Press; 45th Century Chapbooks
Global Options
Goldfish Press
Heyday Books
INDIA CURRENTS
INTERCULTURE
Kumarian Press
LEFT CURVE
Lotus Press, Inc.
Mehring Books, Inc.
OBSIDIAN III: Literature in the African Diaspora
OFF OUR BACKS
THE OTHER ISRAEL
Panther Creek Press
Path Press, Inc.
Pathfinder Press
Pilgrims Book House
The Place In The Woods
POETRYREPAIRS: Contemporary International Poetry
Red Letter Press
RHINO: THE POETRY FORUM
Sagamore Publishing
Saqi Books Publisher
SHARE INTERNATIONAL
SHENANDOAH NEWSLETTER
Smyrna Press
SOCIAL JUSTICE: A JOURNAL OF CRIME, CONFLICT, & WORLD ORDER
STRUGGLE: A Magazine of Proletarian Revolutionary Literature
TURNING THE TIDE: Journal of Anti-Racist Action, Research & Education
White Cliffs Media, Inc.
WSQ (formerly WOMEN'S STUDIES QUARTERLY)

DYLAN THOMAS

Cross-Cultural Communications
THE NEW FORMALIST
Six Ft. Swells Press

H.D. THOREAU

THE AMERICAN DISSIDENT
CONCRETE JUNGLE JOURNAL

J.R.R. TOLKIEN

Avari Press
Tyr Publishing
W.W. Publications

TRADE

A Cappela Publishing
Clark-Nova Books
Gallaudet University Press
SAPONIFIER
Search Institute
Signalman Publishing
University of Arkansas Press
University of Utah Press
Zelda Wilde Publishing
Windward Publishing, An Imprint of Finney Company

760

Fantail
The Glencannon Press
Golden West Books
Heritage House Publishers
History Compass, LLC
Hot Box Press / Southern Roots Publishing
Italica Press, Inc.
THE JOURNAL OF AFRICAN TRAVEL-WRITING
Keokee Co. Publishing, Inc.
Lion Press
Mock Turtle Press
Mountain Automation Corporation
Mountain Press Publishing Co.
NEW ENGLAND BY RAIL
Passing Through Publications
Passport Press
Perpetual Press
Pilgrims Book House
Rayve Productions Inc.
Sasquatch Books
SPECIALTY TRAVEL INDEX
Synergistic Press
The Urbana Free Library

TRAVEL

AB
Adirondack Mountain Club, Inc.
All Nations Press
AMERICAN ROAD
Anacus Press, An Imprint of Finney Company
Anagnosis
Arbutus Press
Art of Living, PrimaMedia,Inc
Ash Lad Press
AzurAlive
Beagle Bay Books / Creative Minds Press
BEATLICK NEWS
The Bess Press
Bright Mountain Books
Callawind Publications / Custom Cookbooks / Children's
    Books
The Center Press
Central Avenue Press
Channel Lake, Inc.
Cladach Publishing
Clover Park Press
Cotton Tree Press
Culturelink Press
Dixon-Price Publishing
Dog's Eye View Media
Dreams Due Media Group, Inc.
Dumouriez Publishing
THE EAST HAWAII OBSERVER
ECOTONE: Reimagining Place
The Eighth Mountain Press
EXIT 13 MAGAZINE
Farcountry Press
Floreant Press
GERMAN LIFE
HILL COUNTRY SUN
Huntington Press
INKY TRAIL NEWS
Intercultural Press, Inc.
Interlink Publishing Group, Inc.
The Intrepid Traveler
JAMES DICKEY REVIEW
THE JOURNAL OF AFRICAN TRAVEL-WRITING
Kakibubu Media Limited
Laguna Wilderness Press
Lake Claremont Press
LAKE SUPERIOR MAGAZINE
Lemieux International Ltd.
Lexicus Press
Liberty Publishing Company, Inc.
The Live Oak Press, LLC
Menasha Ridge Press
Mills Custom Services Publishing
MINESHAFT

Mock Turtle Press
Moo-Cow Fan Club
Moon Pie Press
Mountain Automation Corporation
Museon Publishing
N: NUDE & NATURAL
The Narrative Press
NATURALLY
NEO: Literary Magazine
NEW ENGLAND BY RAIL
NOLA-MAGICK Press
North Star Books
Northern Publishing
Outrider Press
THE OXFORD AMERICAN
PALO ALTO REVIEW
Pangaea
Park Place Publications
Pendant Publishing Inc.
Pineapple Press, Inc.
PLEASANT LIVING
Pogo Press, Incorporated
THE QUIET FEATHER
Russian Information Services
SANDPOINT MAGAZINE
Santa Monica Press
Sasquatch Books
SEA KAYAKER
Six Ft. Swells Press
SPECIALTY TRAVEL INDEX
Speck Press
Standish Press
Storm Publishing Group
Studio 4 Productions An imprint of Quick Publishing, LC
Summerset Press
Sunbelt Publications
Thirsty Turtle Press
Thundercloud Books
Titlewaves Publishing; Writers Direct
Tortuga Books
Turnstone Press
Two Thousand Three Associates
Upheaval Media
Wide World Publishing
Windward Publishing, An Imprint of Finney Company
WISCONSIN TRAILS
WORLD POETRY SHOWCASE
Zante Publishing

TREASURE

UnKnownTruths.com Publishing Company

TRIVIA

C & M Online Media Inc.
East West Discovery Press
The Intrepid Traveler
Mills Custom Services Publishing
World Gumbo Publishing

MARK TWAIN

BOULDER HERETIC
Mercer University Press
Genny Smith Books
Tres Picos Press

U.S. HISPANIC

Aaron Communications III
Archer Books
Banta & Pool Literary Properties
BILINGUAL REVIEW/Revista Bilingue
Buenos Books
Calaca Press
Carolina Wren Press
COLORLINES
Disparate Voices
FEMINIST STUDIES
LPD Press
MANDORLA: New Writing from the Americas / Nueva

762

escritura de las Americas
POINT OF CONTACT, The Journal of Verbal & Visual
    Arts
RHINO: THE POETRY FORUM
Sunbelt Publications
Two Eagles Press International
Wings Press

U.S.S.R.

ABSINTHE: New European Writing
firefall editions
Hoover Institution Press
Mehring Books, Inc.
A Melody from an Immigrant's Soul
MIP Company
Pathfinder Press
Russian Information Services
Xenos Books

UNIVERSITY PRESS

Duke University Press
The Edwin Mellen Press
Litwin Books
NORTHWEST REVIEW
University of Akron Press
University of Alabama Press
University of Arkansas Press
University of Calgary Press
University of California Press
University of Iowa Press
University of Massachusetts Press
University of Michigan Press
University of Nebraska Press
University of Nevada Press
University of Pittsburgh Press
University of Scranton Press
University of South Carolina Press
University of Tampa Press
The University of TX-Pan American Press
University of Utah Press
University of Virginia Press
University of Wisconsin Press
University Press of Colorado

UTAH

American Legacy Media
Arthur H. Clark Co.
Farcountry Press
Jon's Adventure Productions
Gibbs Smith, Publisher
Thundercloud Books
University of Utah Press
Utah State University Press
WEBER: The Contemporary West

VEGETARIANISM

Abecedarian books, Inc.
Affinity Publishers Services
Art of Living, PrimaMedia,Inc
ASCENT
Blue Moose Press
Center For Self-Sufficiency
Cookbook Resources, LLC
Cooperative Press
Himalayan Institute Press
INDIA CURRENTS
JPS Publishing Company
Life Media
McBooks Press, Inc.
Micah Publications Inc.
Portal Press
Princess Publishing
Square One Publishers, Inc.
VEGETARIAN JOURNAL
The Vegetarian Resource Group
White Crosslet Publishing Co

VIETNAM

ATLANTIC PACIFIC PRESS
Caernarvon Press
Galen Press, Ltd.
Insight Press
Islewest Publishing
Plank Road Publishing
Pocol Press
Rodnik Publishing Co.
Rowan Mountain Press
The Sektor Co.
STORMWARNING!
Texas Tech University Press
University of Massachusetts Press
Vintage Romance Publishing, LLC
WAR, LITERATURE & THE ARTS: An International
    Journal of the Humanities

VIRGINIA

Farcountry Press
HAMPTON ROADS HEALTH JOURNAL
JAMES DICKEY REVIEW
PLEASANT LIVING
Pocahontas Press, Inc.
Premium Press America
University of Virginia Press

VISUAL ARTS

A & U AMERICA'S AIDS MAGAZINE
AFTERIMAGE
Allworth Press
ART BUREAU
ARTELLA: the waltz of words and art
ASCENT
BLACKBIRD
BLADES
Blue Lupin Press
BOMB MAGAZINE
Burning Books
THE CAPILANO REVIEW
Center for Thanatology Research & Education, Inc.
DOLLS UNITED INTERACTIVE MAGAZINE
Down There Press
THE EAST HAWAII OBSERVER
EbonyEnergy Publishing, Inc.
ECOTONE: Reimagining Place
Edgewise Press
FISH DRUM MAGAZINE
THE FLORIDA REVIEW
FLUENT ASCENSION
FOLIO: A Literary Journal of American University
FOLK ART MESSENGER
Free Books Inc.
Gesture Press
Green Hut Press
Grey Sparrow Press
GUD MAGAZINE (Greatest Uncommon Denominator)
GULF COAST
HAND PAPERMAKING
HAPA NUI
Harobed Publishing Creations
Helicon Nine Editions
Highest Hurdle Press
Hollywood Creative Directory
HOME PLANET NEWS
The Hosanna Press
Hotel des Bains Editions
IMAGE: ART, FAITH, MYSTERY
Indigo Ink Press, Inc.
Interalia/Design Books
INTERNATIONAL ART POST
JAMES JOYCE BROADSHEET
JUBILAT
KALDRON, An International Journal Of Visual Poetry
KESTREL: A Journal of Literature and Art
Allen A. Knoll Publishers
KNUCKLE MERCHANT - The Journal of Naked Literary

Aggression
Leaf Garden Press
LEFT CURVE
LIGHTWORKS MAGAZINE
LO STRANIERO: The Stranger, Der Fremde, L'Etranger
Luna Bisonte Prods
THE MAD HATTER
MANDORLA: New Writing from the Americas / Nueva escritura de las Americas
MANOA: A Pacific Journal of International Writing
Midmarch Arts Press
MISSISSIPPI CROW
MOBILE BEAT: The Mobile Entertainer's Magazine
NATURALLY
NEW ENGLAND REVIEW
THE NEW RENAISSANCE, an international magazine of ideas & opinions, emphasizing literature & the arts
NIGHTLIFE MAGAZINE
Nightsun Books
Norton Coker Press
O!!ZONE, A LITERARY-ART ZINE
One Less Press
OUTER-ART
THE PEDESTAL MAGAZINE.COM
Phelps Publishing Company
Philos Press
THE PINCH
POGO STICK
The Post-Apollo Press
PRISM INTERNATIONAL
PROVINCETOWN ARTS
Puna Press
RATTAPALLAX
THE RAVEN CHRONICLES
RUBBERSTAMPMADNESS
The Runaway Spoon Press
SAGE OF CONSCIOUSNESS E-ZINE
Santa Monica Press
SCULPTURAL PURSUIT MAGAZINE
SO TO SPEAK: A Feminist Journal of Language & Art
THE SOUTHERN QUARTERLY: A Journal of the Arts in the South
THE SOW'S EAR POETRY REVIEW
SPOUT
Spring Grass
STYLUS
Synergetic Press
Syracuse Cultural Workers/Tools for Change
Syukhtun Editions
13TH MOON
Twinteum Artist, Inc.
VALLUM: CONTEMPORARY POETRY
VERSAL
WAR, LITERATURE & THE ARTS: An International Journal of the Humanities
Water Mark of Lyons PPP: papers press and permaculture
WESTERN AMERICAN LITERATURE
Westgate Press
WHITE FUNGUS
Willowood Press

WALES

ABSINTHE: New European Writing
Cross-Cultural Communications
VARIOUS ARTISTS

WAR

American Legacy Media
ATLANTIC PACIFIC PRESS
Burd Street Press
Elderberry Press, Inc.
The Glencannon Press
GREEN ANARCHY
Ho Logos Press
JAMES DICKEY REVIEW
Lunar Offensive Publications
MacDonald/Sward Publishing Company
Mercer University Press

Murder Slim Press
Open Hand Publishing LLC
Paladin Enterprises, Inc.
PEACEWORK
Progressive Press; Tree of Life Publications
Rowan Mountain Press
THE SAVAGE KICK LITERARY MAGAZINE
STORMWARNING!
TURNING THE TIDE: Journal of Anti-Racist Action, Research & Education
VOICES ISRAEL
WAR, LITERATURE & THE ARTS: An International Journal of the Humanities
White Mane Publishing Company, Inc.

WASHINGTON (STATE)

AMERICAN JONES BUILDING & MAINTENANCE
Arthur H. Clark Co.
CMP Publishing Group LLC
Dunamis House
Eastern Washington University Press
Farcountry Press
La Familia Publishing
Raven Publishing, Inc.
Ridenbaugh Press
SNOW MONKEY
Whispering Pine Press

WASHINGTON, D.C.

BELTWAY POETRY QUARTERLY
FOLIO: A Literary Journal of American University
Inner City Press

WATER

Accendo Publishing
AQUATERRA, METAECOLOGY & CULTURE
Cornell Maritime Press/Tidewater Publishers
Goblin Fern Press
Island Press
Kali Press
LAKE SUPERIOR MAGAZINE
New England Cartographics, Inc.
Oregon State University Press
Ram Press
Ridenbaugh Press
SEA KAYAKER
Genny Smith Books
Southwest Research and Information Center
VOICES FROM THE EARTH
Water Mark of Lyons PPP: papers press and permaculture

WEAPONS

Hole In The Head Press
Lunar Offensive Publications
Paladin Enterprises, Inc.
Varro Press
WAR, LITERATURE & THE ARTS: An International Journal of the Humanities
Zygote Publishing

WEATHER

Elderberry Press, Inc.
Goblin Fern Press
Pocahontas Press, Inc.
Word Forge Books

WEAVING

THE JOURNAL OF CALIFORNIA AND GREAT BASIN ANTHROPOLOGY
Open Hand Publishing LLC
ORNAMENT
TRADICION REVISTA

WEDDINGS

Art of Living, PrimaMedia,Inc
Biographical Publishing Company
First Books

THE WEST

The Bear Wallow Publishing Company
Arthur H. Clark Co.
Clover Park Press
Comstock Bonanza Press
Cornell Maritime Press/Tidewater Publishers
Crazy Woman Creek Press
Deep Well Publishing Company
Dervla Publishing, LLC
Devil Mountain Books
Dignified Designs
Eagle's View Publishing
Farcountry Press
Floreant Press
Flying Pencil Publications
The Glencannon Press
HIGH COUNTRY NEWS
High Plains Press
In Between Books
JAVELINA BI-MONTHLY
Lahontan Images
LITERALLY HORSES/REMUDA
Malki-Ballena Press
THE MEADOW
Mountain Automation Corporation
Mountain Media
Mountain Press Publishing Co.
Native West Press
Nip and Tuck Publishing
Oregon State University Press
OVERLAND JOURNAL
PACIFIC COAST JOURNAL
PACIFIC HISTORICAL REVIEW
Platte Purchase Publishers
RED ROCK REVIEW
Ridenbaugh Press
Sand River Press
Skyline West Press/Wyoming Almanac
Genny Smith Books
SOUTH DAKOTA REVIEW
Sunbelt Publications
Texas Tech University Press
Tres Picos Press
University of Calgary Press
University of Utah Press
University Press of Colorado
Utah State University Press
WEBER: The Contemporary West
WESTERN AMERICAN LITERATURE
Wexford & Barrow, Publishers
World Love Press Publishing
Zon International Publishing Co.

WHALING

NewSage Press
Ocean Publishing
Windward Publishing, An Imprint of Finney Company

WALT WHITMAN

S4N Books
SCHUYLKILL VALLEY JOURNAL
WALT WHITMAN QUARTERLY REVIEW

WICCA

Harvest Shadows Publications
Horned Owl Publishing
NEWWITCH
NOLA-MAGICK Press
Zumaya Publications LLC

WILDLIFE

Birdsong Books
Cornell Maritime Press/Tidewater Publishers
Corvus Publishing Company
Dog's Eye View Media
Farcountry Press
Greatland Graphics

Kakibubu Media Limited
Laguna Wilderness Press
Ocean Publishing
Outrider Press
PLEASANT LIVING
Sherman Asher Publishing
SONG OF THE SAN JOAQUIN
Utah State University Press

WINE, WINERIES

Atlantic Publishing Group, Inc.
Cuore Libre Publishing
Ika, LLC
MY TABLE: Houston's Dining Magazine
Passion Power Press, Inc
Premium Press America
Pruett Publishing Company
Rayve Productions Inc.
Stonemark Publishing
Trafton Publishing
Yellowstone Publishing, LLC

WISCONSIN

AT THE LAKE MAGAZINE
Clover Valley Press, LLC
Faded Banner Publications
FEMINIST COLLECTIONS: A QUARTERLY OF WO-
    MEN'S STUDIES RESOURCES
Jackson Harbor Press
MIDWEST ART FAIRS
Poetry Harbor
Zelda Wilde Publishing
WISCONSIN ACADEMY REVIEW
WISCONSIN TRAILS
Women's Studies Librarian, University of Wisconsin
    System

WOMEN

AAIMS Publishers
Abecedarian books, Inc.
ABRAMELIN: a Journal of Poetry and Magick
Accendo Publishing
AFRICAN AMERICAN REVIEW
Alaska Native Language Center
Alice James Books
All That Productions,Inc.
American Literary Press
Anderson Publishing; also RC Anderson Books
Andros Books
Anomaly Press
APPLE VALLEY REVIEW: A Journal of Contemporary
    Literature
Arden Press, Inc.
Ash Tree Publishing
ATLANTIS: A Women's Studies Journal/Revue d'etudes
    sur les femmes
Aunt Lute Books
Back House Books
Banks Channel Books
THE BELTANE PAPERS: A Journal of Women's
    Mysteries
Biographical Publishing Company
Blanket Fort Publishing
BLK
BOOKS TO WATCH OUT FOR
Bordighera, Inc.
Calyx Books
CALYX: A Journal of Art and Literature by Women
CANADIAN WOMAN STUDIES/les cahiers de la femme
Carolina Wren Press
Chandler & Sharp Publishers, Inc.
Chatterley Press International
Chicory Blue Press, Inc.
CHILDREN, CHURCHES AND DADDIES, A Non
    Religious, Non Familial Literary Magazine
City Life Books, LLC
Clover Park Press
Clover Valley Press, LLC

CMP Publishing Group LLC
Common Boundaries
Communication Creativity
Comstock Bonanza Press
THE COMSTOCK REVIEW
CONSCIENCE: The Newsjournal of Catholic Opinion
Consumer Press
Cypress House
Deep Well Publishing Company
Dervla Publishing, LLC
Dignified Designs   .
Disparate Voices
DLite Press
DOWN IN THE DIRT LITERARY MAGAZINE, the prose
    & poetry magazine revealing all your dirty little secrets
Down There Press
Dumouriez Publishing
EARTH'S DAUGHTERS: Feminist Arts Periodical
The Edwin Mellen Press
The Eighth Mountain Press
FEMINIST COLLECTIONS: A QUARTERLY OF WO-
    MEN'S STUDIES RESOURCES
FEMINIST PERIODICALS: A CURRENT LISTING OF
    CONTENTS
The Feminist Press at the City University of New York
FEMINIST REVIEW
FEMINIST STUDIES
Floreant Press
FMA Publishing
4AllSeasons Publishing
FREEDOM AND STRENGTH PRESS FORUM
Fulcrum, Inc.
GAYELLOW PAGES
Gemini Publishing Company
GLB Publishers
Goblin Fern Press
Grace House Publishing
Gurze Books
HAMPTON ROADS HEALTH JOURNAL
HARVARD JOURNAL OF LAW AND GENDER
HEALMB Publishing
HECATE
Helicon Nine Editions
Heyday Books
Hidden Valley Farm, Publisher
History Compass, LLC
Hunter House Inc., Publishers
HYPATIA: A Journal of Feminist Philosophy
Iconoclast Press
Ika, LLC
ILLUMINATIONS LITERARY JOURNAL
Impact Publishers, Inc.
IN OUR OWN WORDS
Info Net Publishing
Inkwater Press
INKY TRAIL NEWS
International Publishers Co. Inc.
Juel House Publishers and Literary Services
KABBALAH
KALLIOPE, A Journal of Women's Literature and Art
Kelsey St. Press
Kenyette Productions
Knowledge Concepts Publishing
Lawells Publishing
LILITH
LINQ
Lion Press
Lotus Press, Inc.
Luminous Epinoia Press
Lunar Offensive Publications
Magic Circle Press
Maisonneuve Press
Malafemmina Press
Margaret Media, Inc.
Maverick Books
Mayapple Press
McGavick Field Publishing
Midmarch Arts Press

Minnesota Historical Society Press
Montemayor Press
Mo'omana'o Press
Moon Pie Press
Moondance Press
MOTHERVERSE: A Journal of Contemporary Motherhood
NEW BOOKS ON WOMEN, GENDER, & FEMINISM
New Victoria Publishers
New World Library
NewSage Press
NEWWITCH
Nip and Tuck Publishing
Nushape Publication
OFF OUR BACKS
Open Hand Publishing LLC
ORBIS
Outrider Press
PAGAN AMERICA
Paris Press
PASSAGER
Passing Through Publications
Passion Power Press, Inc
Pathfinder Press
Penthe Publishing
Perugia Press
The Place In The Woods
Plain View Press
THE PRAIRIE JOURNAL OF CANADIAN LITERATURE
Prairie Journal Press
Premium Press America
Pussywillow
QED Press
Rapacious Press
Red Alder Books
Reference Service Press
RESOURCES FOR FEMINIST RESEARCH/DOCUMEN-
    TATION SUR LA RECHERCHE FEMINISTE
Rhiannon Press
RHINO: THE POETRY FORUM
ROOM MAGAZINE
SAGEWOMAN
Salt Publishing
Scars Publications
SECRETUM MEUM MIHI
Secretum Meum Mihi Press
SENSATIONS MAGAZINE
Sibyl Publications, Inc
SINISTER WISDOM
Genny Smith Books
Smyrna Press
SO TO SPEAK: A Feminist Journal of Language & Art
SO YOUNG!
Soto Publishing Company
Spinifex Press
Spring Grass
Squire Press
Starry Night Publishing
STRUGGLE: A Magazine of Proletarian Revolutionary
    Literature
TEEN VOICES MAGAZINE
Third Dimension Publishing
13TH MOON
TORRE DE PAPEL
TRUTH SEEKER
TSAR Publications
TULSA STUDIES IN WOMEN'S LITERATURE
Twilight Times Books
2L Publishing, LLC
University of Calgary Press
University of Utah Press
URBAN REFLECTIONS MAGAZINE
VanderWyk & Burnham
VARIOUS ARTISTS
West End Press
White Mane Publishing Company, Inc.
Whole Person Associates Inc.
WIN NEWS
Wish Publishing

WOMEN AND LANGUAGE
Women and Men Books
WOMEN IN THE ARTS BULLETIN/NEWSLETTER
Women of Diversity Productions, Inc.
Women's Studies Librarian, University of Wisconsin System
Write Now Publishing Company
WRITER'S CHRONICLE
WSQ (formerly WOMEN'S STUDIES QUARTERLY)
Yaldah Publishing
Yellow Moon Press
Yes International Publishers

WOOD ENGRAVING/WOODWORKING

Bauhan Publishing, LLC
Clamp Down Press
Cornell Maritime Press/Tidewater Publishers
Hobar Publications, A Division of Finney Company
Rolling Hills Publishing
Storm Publishing Group
WOODWORKER'S JOURNAL

WORKER

AMERICAN JONES BUILDING & MAINTENANCE
Back House Books
Black Forest Press and The Tennessee Publishing House
BLUE COLLAR REVIEW
Blue Cubicle Press, LLC
Finney Company, Inc.
International Publishers Co. Inc.
Mehring Books, Inc.
Missing Spoke Press
Partisan Press
West End Press
WHEELHOUSE MAGAZINE
WORKERS WRITE!
WORKERS WRITE!

WORLD WAR II

American Legacy Media
ATLANTIC PACIFIC PRESS
Bauhan Publishing, LLC
R.J. Bender Publishing
Black Forest Press and The Tennessee Publishing House
Bluestocking Press
A. Borough Books
Burd Street Press
Cable Publishing
Cypress House
THE ENGLISH CLARION
The Glencannon Press
Heidelberg Graphics
Historical Resources Press
Ho Logos Press
Magnifico Publications
McBooks Press, Inc.
MCM Entertainment, Inc. Publishing Division
A Melody from an Immigrant's Soul
Noontide Press
Path Press, Inc.
Pocol Press
SeaCrab Publishing
The Sektor Co.
Slipdown Mountain Publications LLC
Stardate Publishing Company
University of Nebraska Press
University of Utah Press
Vintage Romance Publishing, LLC
Virginia City Publishing Co. LLC
The WhaleInn Publishing House (1998)
White Mane Publishing Company, Inc.
Wilde Publishing

WRITERS/WRITING

Academy Press of America
ALASKA QUARTERLY REVIEW
Allworth Press
Aquarius Press

Arden Press, Inc.
Artamo Press
ARTELLA: the waltz of words and art
Bandanna Books
BOOK MARKETING UPDATE
BOOK/MARK QUARTERLY REVIEW
Bordighera, Inc.
BRADY MAGAZINE
THE BROADKILL REVIEW: A Journal of Literature
BYLINE
C&R Press
CANADIAN POETRY
THE CANNON'S MOUTH
THE CAPILANO REVIEW
The Center Press
Central Avenue Press
Chax Press
CIMARRON REVIEW
City Life Books, LLC
Clearwater Publishing Co.
Cleveland State Univ. Poetry Center
Communication Creativity
THE COMSTOCK REVIEW
COOK PARTNERS
Disparate Voices
THE DRAMATIST
Dumouriez Publishing
E & E Publishing
EEI Press
ELEMENTS
Ellechor Publishing House
Encore Publishing
Gingerbread House
Global Learning
GOLD DUST
Graywolf Press
Gryphon Books
Helm Publishing
Hidden Valley Farm, Publisher
His Work Christian Publishing
Idylls Press
ILLOGICAL MUSE
ILLUMINATIONS LITERARY JOURNAL
IMAGE: ART, FAITH, MYSTERY
Immediate Direction Publications
Impassio Press
In Between Books
INKY TRAIL NEWS
J'ECRIS
Leaf Garden Press
Lilly Press
LULLWATER REVIEW
THE LUMMOX JOURNAL
Maui arThoughts Co.
A Melody from an Immigrant's Soul
Mills Custom Services Publishing
Moon Pie Press
Muse World Media Group
MUSE: A Quarterly Journal of The Lit
Myriad Press
NEW ENGLAND REVIEW
NEW HOPE INTERNATIONAL REVIEW
NEW VERSE NEWS, THE
NEW VOICES REVISITED: Poetry, Contests and Short Stories.
THE NEW WRITER
North Stone Editions
NORTHWEST REVIEW
NOUN VS. VERB
OPEN WIDE MAGAZINE
THE OTHER HERALD
OYEZ REVIEW
PAPERBACK PARADE
Para Publishing
Parthian
THE PINCH
Platinum Dreams Publishing
The Poetry Center

PRETEXT
PULSAR POETRY WEBZINE
Quill Driver Books
Rapacious Press
RED LAMP
Red Tiger Press
Redgreene Press
Riverwinds Publishing
Rose Alley Press
ROSEBUD
Sage Hill Press
SAGE OF CONSCIOUSNESS E-ZINE
Salt Publishing
SCULPTURAL PURSUIT MAGAZINE
SENSATIONS MAGAZINE
74th Street Productions, L.L.C.
SEWANEE REVIEW
Sherman Asher Publishing
SKYLINE LITERARY MAGAZINE
SMARTISH PACE
SO TO SPEAK: A Feminist Journal of Language & Art
SPECS
Square One Publishers, Inc.
Standish Press
Star Publish LLC
THE STINGING FLY
Stormline Press, Inc.
Strata Publishing, Inc.
SUB-TERRAIN
SYCAMORE REVIEW
TEACHERS & WRITERS
Three Dog Press
TORRE DE PAPEL
TRUE POET MAGAZINE
twentythreebooks
Twilight Tales, Inc.
Twilight Times Books
Twinteum Artist, Inc.
UmbraProjects Publishing
UNDERSTANDING MAGAZINE
VALLUM: CONTEMPORARY POETRY
VARIOUS ARTISTS
Verve Press
Vox Humana Books
WILD DUCK REVIEW
Wordcraft of Oregon, LLC
Wordwrights Canada
WORKING WRITER
WRITER'S CHRONICLE
WRITERS' JOURNAL
ZINE WORLD: A Reader's Guide to the Underground Press
ZYX

WYOMING

The Bear Wallow Publishing Company
Dignified Designs
Farcountry Press
firefall editions
The Great Rift Press
High Plains Press
Laguna Wilderness Press
THE MEADOW
Pruett Publishing Company
Skyline West Press/Wyoming Almanac

YOGA

Best Life Media
Dharma Publishing
HAMPTON ROADS HEALTH JOURNAL
THE HEALTH JOURNALS
Himalayan Institute Press
ILLUMINATIONS LITERARY JOURNAL
INDIA CURRENTS
Rapacious Press
Swing-Hi Press
Timeless Books
The Wessex Collective
Wexford & Barrow, Publishers

Whole Person Associates Inc.
Yes International Publishers
YogaVidya.com

YOSEMITE

Clover Park Press
The Live Oak Press, LLC
Poetic Matrix Press
Tres Picos Press

YOUNG ADULT

Abecedarian books, Inc.
Abernathy House Publishing
Absey & Co.
Annick Press Ltd.
Aquila Ink Publishing
Atelier Press
Authentic Publishing LLC
Avari Press
Avisson Press, Inc.
Bandanna Books
Banks Channel Books
Bel Canto Press
The Bess Press
Birdsong Books
Blue Moose Press
Book Marketing Solutions
Cave Hollow Press
Central Avenue Press
Cheops Books
Chicken Soup Press, Inc.
Citiria Publishing
Clark-Nova Books
CMP Publishing Group LLC
Concrete Jungle Press
Cornerstone Publishing, Inc.
Dancing Lemur Press, L.L.C.
Delaney Day Press
Dervla Publishing, LLC
Desert Bloom Press
DLite Press
Earthshaker Books
East West Discovery Press
Empyrean Hill Books, Inc.
Faith Builders Resource Group
Falls Media
The Fiction Works
Finney Company, Inc.
First Books
Flowerfield Enterprises, LLC
Gallaudet University Press
Gingerbread House
Glass Tower Press
Grace House Publishing
Gray Dog Press
Great West Publishing
Halo Publishing International
Inkwater Press
Jalmar Press/Innerchoice Publishing
Juel House Publishers and Literary Services
JUNIOR STORYTELLER
Keiki O Ka Aina Press
THE KIDS' STORYTELLING CLUB WEBSITE
Lawells Publishing
LEO Productions LLC.
Lily Ruth Publishing
LJW Publishing
Lucky Press, LLC
Luminous Epinoia Press
THE MAD HATTER
March Books
Mayhaven Publishing, Inc.
Micron Press
Montemayor Press
Mo'omana'o Press
Munsey Music
NAMBLA BULLETIN
Neshui Publishing

768

NEW VOICES REVISITED: Poetry, Contests and Short Stories.
NIGHTLIFE MAGAZINE
NSR Publications
ORBIS
Paladin Media Group
Papillon Presse
PARENTEACHER MAGAZINE
Paris Press
Peachtree Publishers, Ltd.
Pineapple Press, Inc.
Platinum Dreams Publishing
POGO STICK
Practically Shameless Press
PUNKIN HOUSE DIGEST
THE QUILLDRIVER
RTMC Organization, LLC
Sabellapress
Saint Mary's Press
Sassy Sunflower Books
Signalman Publishing
Small Dogma Publishing, Inc.
Soto Publishing Company
SPEAK UP
Speak Up Press
SPECTACULAR SPECULATIONS
Star Publish LLC
Starik Publishing
STORMWARNING!
Storycraft Publishing
TEEN VOICES MAGAZINE
Top 20 Press
Total Package Publications, LLC
Twilight Times Books
UmbraProjects Publishing
Upheaval Media
Vision Works Publishing
VISIONHOPE NEWSLETTER
The WhaleInn Publishing House (1998)
Whiskey Creek Press
Wings Press
Wordsonthestreet
Yaldah Publishing
Youthful Wisdom Press

ZEN

Abecedarian books, Inc.
Alamo Square Press
Allbook Books
ASCENT
Best Life Media
Bottom Dog Press / Bird Dog Publishing
Brooks Books
Enigmatic Ink
EPIPHANY, A Literary Journal
FAT TUESDAY
FISH DRUM MAGAZINE
Fisher King Press
FROZEN WAFFLES
Frozen Waffles Press/Shattered Sidewalks Press; 45th Century Chapbooks
HERE AND NOW
Iconoclast Press
Ika, LLC
Ithuriel's Spear
La Alameda Press
Motom
One Spirit Press
Parallax Press
Poetic Matrix Press
Press Here
Shared Roads Press
Socratic Consulting Group
SPOTops Books
Squire Press
Total Cardboard Publishing
TURNING WHEEL
Turtle Press, division of S.K. Productions Inc.

Water Mark of Lyons PPP: papers press and permaculture
WHAT IS ENLIGHTENMENT?
White Pine Press
Zelda Wilde Publishing
World Love Press Publishing
Zygote Publishing

ZINES

ALMOST NORMAL COMICS and Other Oddities
ART BUREAU
ARTELLA: the waltz of words and art
BAGAZINE
BEATLICK NEWS
BEGGARS & CHEESEBURGERS
Blue Cubicle Press, LLC
Cooperative Press
DIET SOAP
Dnar Kaker Basa
Flapjack Press
GIN BENDER POETRY REVIEW
GREEN ANARCHY
Grey Sparrow Press
Gryphon Books
Hidden Valley Farm, Publisher
A HUDSON VIEW POETRY DIGEST
Iniquity Press/Vendetta Books
IT'S JUST THIS LITTLE CHROMIUM SWITCH HERE
THE LEDGE
Lilly Press
THE LUMMOX JOURNAL
Missing Spoke Press
NOUN VS. VERB
OTHER INVESTIGATIONS
Poptritus Press
PRAKALPANA SAHITYA/PRAKALPANA LITERATURE
THE RAGING FACE: Goofball Prose
RIVER POETS JOURNAL
Rural Messengers Press
SAGE OF CONSCIOUSNESS E-ZINE
SECRETUM MEUM MIHI
SIGNALS
Soft Skull Press
Thunder Rain Publishing Corp.
UmbraProjects Publishing
X-Ray Book Co.
ZINE WORLD: A Reader's Guide to the Underground Press